BOLLINGEN SERIES LXXI

THE
COLLECTED DIALOGUES OF
PLATO

INCLUDING THE LETTERS

Edited by

EDITH HAMILTON

and

HUNTINGTON CAIRNS

With Introduction and Prefatory Notes

BOLLINGEN SERIES LXXI

PRINCETON UNIVERSITY PRESS

Published by PRINCETON UNIVERSITY PRESS *at Princeton, New Jersey*

THIS IS THE SEVENTY-FIRST
IN A SERIES OF BOOKS
SPONSORED BY
BOLLINGEN FOUNDATION
Second printing, with corrections, March 1963
Third printing, October 1964
Fourth printing, October 1966
Fifth printing, March 1969
Sixth printing, May 1971
Seventh printing, August 1973

ISBN 0-691-09718-6
Library of Congress Catalogue Card No. 61–11758
Manufactured in the United States of America
DESIGNED BY ANDOR BRAUN

Translators

Lane Cooper · F. M. Cornford · W. K. C. Guthrie

R. Hackforth · Michael Joyce · Benjamin Jowett

L. A. Post · W. H. D. Rouse · Paul Shorey

J. B. Skemp · A. E. Taylor · Hugh Tredennick

W. D. Woodhead · J. Wright

CONTENTS

EDITORIAL NOTE

The notes which preface each of the dialogues were written by Miss Edith Hamilton.

The translations comprising this edition have been subject to only slight editing. The following general revisions may be noted. All commentaries, summaries, and footnotes of the original texts have been omitted. (In Theaetetus and Sophist, the translator's summaries have been replaced by the text of Jowett's translation, third edition.) Spelling and, to some degree, punctuation and capitalization have been standardized, in accordance with American preferences. For measurements, money, etc., the Greek terms have been substituted for modern equivalents (such as furlong and shilling). Occasionally, where clarity would be served, Greek words and phrases have been inserted in brackets. Quotation marks are not used to set off speeches, but the use or nonuse of speakers' names has been left as it was. In addition, footnotes have usually been added to identify quotations.

The index is based on the Abbott-Knight index to the third edition of Jowett's translation, though it has been entirely remade to answer the requirements of the present edition. An attempt has been made, by means of cross-references, to assist the reader with the philosophical vocabulary of the different translators. The index is the work of Edward J. Foye. The chief work of preparing the contents of this volume for the press has been done by Mrs. Donna Bishop under the supervision of the editors of Bollingen Series. The editors also are indebted to Mrs. Mabel A. Barry for special editorial assistance and other help.

*

Acknowledgment is gratefully made to the following publishers and persons for the use of the contents of this volume:

R. Hackforth's translations of Philebus (1945) and Phaedrus (1952), by permission of the Cambridge University Press, Cambridge and New York, publishers.

Benjamin Jowett's translations of Charmides, Laches, Timaeus, and Greater Hippias, in the fourth edition, revised by order of the Jowett Copyright Trustees (1953), by permission of the Clarendon Press, Oxford. Jowett's translations of Menexenus, Lesser Hippias, and Cratylus, and excerpts of his translations of Theaetetus and

Sophist *are from the third edition* (*1892*), *also published by the Clarendon Press.*

Lane Cooper's translations of Ion *and* Euthyphro (*copyright respectively 1938 and 1941 by him*), *by permission of Professor Cooper and of the Cornell University Press, Ithaca, New York, publishers.*

A. E. Taylor's translation of Laws (*1934*), *J. Wright's translation of* Lysis (*1910*), *and Michael Joyce's translation of* Symposium (*1935*), *by permission of J. M. Dent and Sons, London, and E. P. Dutton and Co., New York, publishers of these works in Everyman's Library.*

Paul Shorey's translation of Republic (*1930*), *by permission of the Harvard University Press, Cambridge, Mass., publishers, and the Trustees of the Loeb Classical Library.*

A. E. Taylor's translation of Critias (*1929*), *by permission of Methuen and Co., London, publishers.*

W. D. Woodhead's translation of Gorgias (*1953*) *and A. E. Taylor's translation of* Epinomis, *edited by Raymond Klibansky* (*1956*), *by permission of Thomas Nelson and Sons, Edinburgh and New York, publishers.*

Hugh Tredennick's translations of Apology, Crito, *and* Phaedo (*1954*) *and W. K. C. Guthrie's translations of* Protagoras *and* Meno (*1956*), *by arrangement with Penguin Books, Harmondsworth, England, publishers.*

L. A. Post's translation of the Epistles (*1925*), *by permission of Professor Post.*

W. H. D. Rouse's translation of Euthydemus, *here first published, by permission of Mr. Philip G. Rouse and Mr. J. C. G. Rouse. Acknowledgment is gratefully made to the New American Library of World Literature, New York, for assistance in this connection.*

F. M. Cornford's translations of Theaetetus *and* Sophist (*1935*) *and* Parmenides (*1939*), *by permission of Routledge and Kegan Paul, London, publishers.*

J. B. Skemp's translation of Statesman (*1952*), *by permission of Professor Skemp, the Yale University Press, New Haven, and Routledge and Kegan Paul, London, publishers.*

INTRODUCTION

THESE DIALOGUES were written twenty-three hundred years ago, and the thought of the ancient world, the Middle Ages, the Renaissance, and that of contemporary times, have all come under their influence. They have been praised as the substance of Western thought, as the corrective for the excesses to which the human mind is subject, and as setting forth the chief lines of the Western view of the world as they have never been delineated before or since in philosophy, politics, logic, and psychology. It has been held that a return to the insights of the dialogues is a return to our roots. But the dialogues have also had their enemies. They have been attacked as politically aristocratic and as philosophically mystical. However, few serious and fair students of the dialogues have ever denied their suggestiveness and the extent to which they stimulate thought. Many strands are interwoven in the dialogues but always at the center as their meaning is the Greek insight that Reason, the *logos,* is nature steering all things from within. In this approach nature is neither supernatural nor material; it is an organic whole, and man is not outside nature but within it. By concentration on this point of view and its implications Greek thought and art achieved a clarity never equaled elsewhere and Plato became its supreme spokesman.

Plato has been presented to us as a man of the study, a weaver of idealistic dreams; he has also been held up as a man with great experience of the world. There is no denying that he was learned, fully aware of the intellectual currents of his day. The variety of the quotations and allusions which appear in the dialogues show that he had read the extant literature. His life covered the period from the Peloponnesian War and the death of Pericles to Philip's capture of Olynthus. He was born about 428 B.C. and died at the age of eighty or eighty-one about 348 B.C. His family was an ancient one with political connections in high places and it is reasonable to assume that he saw military service in his youth. He had a wide acquaintance with the prominent men of his time, traveled extensively abroad, and at the age of forty founded the Academy and directed its affairs until his death. Thereafter the Academy had a continuous life of nine hundred years, a longer life span than that of any other educational institution in the West. This is scarcely the portrait of an armchair philosopher spinning theories in a study lined with books from floor to ceiling. It still leaves open, however, the question of the extent of

Plato's actual grasp of worldly affairs. Not infrequently scholars with experiences in life comparable to those of Plato confess themselves helpless in the planning of concrete undertakings, although plainly Plato himself would not have made that admission. Plato's abilities must here be judged by the merits of the specific proposals he outlines in the dialogues. It is not necessary to read them closely to be impressed with his intense interest in the correction of social and political abuses. That many of his suggestions had intrinsic value is adequately attested by their subsequent adoption in educational and political practice and the persistence of their influence even to the present.

Plato nowhere offers an explanation of why he cast his writings in the dialogue form rather than in that of the reasoned treatise. In the *Phaedrus* he argues that writing is like painting; it has the appearance of life but if you ask it a question it preserves a solemn silence. The written word cannot explain itself if it is misunderstood. Writing, he concludes, is a pastime, a game, but a noble one in which a man may discourse seriously and merrily about justice and the like. He wrote mimes in his youth, and with the example before him of the Socratic method of leading men to knowledge by question and answer it was perhaps natural that he should adopt the form he did. At any rate it gave his poetic powers great latitude. He was a stylist of the first order and as a poet he was able to present philosophy dramatically. He believed as a philosopher that the world is pervaded by Reason, and that its beauty is an outward manifestation of its ultimate nature. The dialogue form permitted him to lead men to this insight, it permitted the playfulness and the bitterness, the irony and the fairness, for which the dialogues are also famous. It allowed him almost the freedom of the contemporary novelist. As a form it imposed no limitations on his poetic imagery, and it allowed him also the utmost philosophical seriousness. But notwithstanding his unrivaled mastery of the dialogue he never subordinated meaning to form. Contentless art, he held, is not art.

All this is not separate from but intertwined with his task as a philosopher. In the physical sciences hypotheses are tested by experimental means, but the philosopher's resource is thought in the form of a conversation with himself or others. The dialogue form therefore is not arbitrarily chosen, not a report of how Greeks conversed on street corners, in the bath and the gymnasium, and certainly not an inquiry of the kind conducted in the assembly where many minds are assumed, somehow, to be the source of wisdom. On the contrary Plato held that inquiry, when not directed by one who knows, is futile. The dialogue therefore is the dialectic, a skillfully directed technique of questioning. For this reason he described the dialectician as the midwife tending us in the act, in the "labor," of knowing. To change the metaphor, the dialectician is like the gardener who aids his plants but is unable to do for them what they must do themselves.

This is the content, and the instrument which leads us to knowledge is the form. For Plato it is the one certain way to knowledge. Its effectiveness lies in the effort it demands on the part of the participants, and its achievement, as in the case of the plant, is fulfillment. In fact, the essence of Platonism may be said to be the realization that we can and must know, not by trial and error, which teaches too late, if indeed it teaches much at all, but by coming to see what is possible, and what is not possible, in the world in which we live. In Aristotle's view Plato's form was halfway between poetry and prose.

Plato was a philosopher and poet, but not a mystic. He was a poet in the sense that he wrote formal verse and is the author of one of the most notable of the Greek epigrams. Beyond that, as the author of the dialogues, he was a philosopher-poet exercising consummate artistry in his presentation of ideas. In this respect he differs from Lucretius, Dante, Pope, and others who have attempted to set forth in verse systems of thought not their own. If we put aside the requirement that poetry must be written in meter Plato is one of the supreme poets of the world as well as of Greece; he has a place with Homer, Aeschylus, and Dante, although no one of these men is also a philosopher. But his poetic insight has often been confused with mysticism, even with mysticism's most obscurantist manifestations. His discussion of the one and the many, the doctrine of love and eternal beauty, the Demiurgos, and similar matters, have all been mistakenly used, by mystics and occultists, as grounds for their own doctrines. He has been a source of inspiration to many types of mysticism but his writings have been repeatedly misread. This misunderstanding has been greatly promoted and popularized by the writings of Philo and Plotinus. Philo claimed that Plato's Ideas and the Biblical angels are one and the same, and Plotinus' mysticism is actually called Neoplatonism. But Plato saw the world to be intelligible, that is, he held that system pervades all things. In order to indicate the nature of that reality he resorted to story, metaphor, and playfulness which have given comfort from time to time to esoteric writers. But the difference between Plato and the mysticism that has attached itself to his philosophy is essential. Plato's aim is to take the reader by steps, with as severe a logic as the conversational method permits, to an insight into the ultimate necessity of Reason. And he never hesitates to submit his own ideas to the harshest critical scrutiny; he carried this procedure so far in the *Parmenides* that some commentators have held that his own doubts in this dialogue prevail over his affirmations. But the beliefs of mystics are not products of critical examination and logical clarification; they are, on the contrary, a series of apprehensions, flashes, based on feeling, denying the rational order. The mystic's reports of his experiences are beyond discussion inasmuch as they are subjective and emotional; they must be accepted, by one who wishes to believe them, as a matter of faith, not knowledge. Plato's view of the world is that of an intelligible system that man can know by disciplined intellect alone. He was, in fact, the founder of logic, a logician and a poet, but he was not a mystic, he never exalted feeling above reason.

In several senses Plato was an aristocrat, but not in the opprobrious sense of some of his critics. His family on both his father's and his mother's side was a distinguished one and had produced men sufficiently able to assume the obligations of leadership. Plato accepted the responsibility of his inherited position. His dominant aim was to prevent the further disintegration of Greece. Two courses were open to him, either the assumption of public office or the re-establishment of the clarity of the Greek intellect which had become corrupted by many influences. The fate of Socrates perhaps suggested to him that his special strength lay in the restoration of the Greek view of life. His position in the *Republic* is that good government can be conserved only by statesmen with knowledge in proportion to their task. In the *Laws* he attempted a more direct approach through the formulation of a specific legislative program. He was also aristocratic in the lifelong discipline with which he held himself to this task. His view that the final stage of the statesman's education should not be undertaken before the age of fifty would have little support today in conjunction with our desperate efforts at mass education. In Plato's hands aristocracy meant the rule of the best, from whatever class they came. The able were to receive special training for the responsibilities requiring great ability; the less able were to perform the tasks suitable to their ability. Plato's political theory is an implication of the system of nature, and to call this philosophy aristocratic is meaningful only in the sense that nature is itself aristocratic. But to call any philosophy aristocratic in the sense of class interest is meaningless; preoccupation with the interests of one class to the detriment of others is not philosophy. Philosophy is disinterested or it is not philosophy. When ideas are manipulated for personal ends, for class or group interests, the name for this in Plato's day was sophistry. It was against this that his dialogues were directed. To accuse Plato of being in league with the sophistic forces that undermined the classical world is an instance of the more subtle misrepresentation of his position. Plato's disinterested pursuit of knowledge has not only made the word *Platonism* synonymous with the word *philosophy*, it has marked him as the aristocrat of aristocrats, the paragon of excellence emulated by high-minded men for over two thousand years.

In the dialogues Plato appears to address himself to particular topics and in no one place in the conventional sense does he set forth a complete system of philosophy. This circumstance has prompted the view, especially during the nineteenth century, that the dialogues display an evolutionary development, that Plato gradually felt or thought his way to a final position which is displayed in the later writings. It has also led to the belief that as a philosopher he must have put forth a formal system and that it is now lost to us. We know that he lectured at the Academy and we have the authority of Aristotle that these lectures constituted "the philosophy of Plato." It is therefore argued that Platonism as a formal system was expounded in the lecture room very much in the manner of Aristotle. It may be so, but the notion is conjectural. The evolutionary view of the dialogues is also difficult to maintain. In them the same thoughts appear again and again, expressed in different words, in different contexts, and with varying emphasis. Plato was the culmination of several centuries of Greek speculation and he took full advantage of the insight which his predecessors had developed. But speculation assumes intelligibility. The insight that the world is system, is organic, therefore both orderly and alive, is the Greek view as far back as we have records. Because of this previous work in philosophy he was able relatively early in life to see the world as an entirety and to grapple with its implications. The Greek organic view stressed a living entirety made up of members. Plato's dialogues dealt with increasingly difficult problems but there is no shift in his convictions. His method throughout is one of exploration, of clarification, but the same insight dominates and the same principles recur. The world view they display is clear when the dialogues are seen as a whole. It is not stated all at once, or in any one place; it is unfolded gradually and its implications are explored. The important point is that the dialogues as a whole are alone a statement of his position. Plato was fully aware of the value of system in the search for knowledge, of the desirability of stating as clearly as possible the principles on which the inquiry turns. He chose a method quite distinct both from that of the positivist science of the present day which purports to start with the "facts," and from that of the deductive method of the system builders of the seventeenth century. But his approach on that account is no less rigorous and valid. His system unfolds as a flower unfolds, and halfway in its development we see its center, the *Republic*, holding the many petals firmly. Later, when the system has fully flowered, its periphery may well be said to be the *Laws*. He does not treat the various topics of his discourse, such as ethics, psychology, epistemology, as meaningful in themselves, but as organic, interrelated subjects meaningful only as variations upon a single theme. In this respect he differs from scientists who see the different departments of inquiry as having their own special components.

At the heart of Plato's philosophy is the doctrine of Ideas. It is the great discovery in the history of philosophy, and although it is the subject of extensive discussion in accounts of Plato's thought, the actual amount of space devoted to it by this name in the dialogues is scanty. Nevertheless it is the basic assumption behind everything he wrote. Thus Plato's technique combined example with exposition; to grasp fully what he intended to say about the theory of Ideas the dialogues must be understood as acts of knowing, examples of how knowledge is acquired. Expositions of Plato's position in treatise form can therefore be misleading. According to Aristotle, Plato accepted Heraclitus' doctrine that things, as we are aware of them through our organs of touch, taste, sight, and hearing, are all in constant flux and therefore our sense organs cannot give us knowledge. If the dominant color of a painting is one thing under the northern light of the sky and a different thing under artificial illumination it is apparent that the information we derive from our senses varies with conditions. Aristotle says that Plato was thus led to the view that if we are to have knowledge it must be of permanent entities distinct from those we know through the senses. Plato generally called these entities *Forms* or *Ideas*, terms which are misleading in English but which are now standard usage in Platonic studies. Today the word "idea" carries a subjective connotation, and the word "form" may be taken to mean form itself whereas Plato was talking about the principle of form. There has been a vast discussion of the nature of these entities, and Plato himself, as one dialogue followed another, touched on the question from many points of view. At one time they have been regarded by his critics as reified concepts and at another as ideas in the mind of God. Actually, however, they appear to be the ordering principle of which the world is constituted, the order in nature that all investigation seeks whether in physical science or in speculative philosophy. They are the meaning of the world of flux. The main point of Plato's argument is that the realm of Ideas is the reality of the objects which are ordered. What our senses report about objects is not wholly responsible and must be corrected by intelligence. All the sciences attempt to discover the laws which are the order of the phenomena in their particular fields. In physics, for example, the order is expressed by the laws of the conservation of energy, mass, momentum, gravitation, electric charge, and others, and in physiology by the laws of the general metabolism of the organism. In Platonism order is not the sum of the laws that science discovers but the principle of all laws, the *logos* or Intelligence itself. Plato approached this problem on the assumption that when we classify things under a general name we do so because permanence and order are there. Thus in the *Euthyphro, Charmides, Laches,* and the *Greater Hippias* the inquiry concerns the class, the Idea. The questions asked are, What is piety? What is temperance? What is courage? What is beauty? In the *Euthyphro* Socrates observes that there are many instances of piety but that he is searching for the Idea, the permanent, that which makes pious acts pious. From this elementary beginning in an exploration of the meaning of class names Plato passed on in the later dialogues to more sophisticated statements of his doctrine and its applicability to all aspects of the world. He saw it as the refutation of the view that all is flux and that man is the measure of things. These latter notions have recurred calling themselves naturalism, pragmatism, positivism, analysis, and existentialism. Plato's theory of Ideas is difficult to grasp in its full implications and while it can be stated its meaning is not obvious and will be understood only upon reflection. He has no doubt that the Ideas exist outside the human mind, and shows that by turning our attention to ultimate problems we attain knowledge, for our intelligence, like the eye, beholds that toward which it is turned; if we do not look we do not see.

Plato's artistry and philosophical power are nowhere shown to better advantage than in his discussion of friendship and love. Here he was venturing into a domain which poets have thought to be their special province but he took the subject further than it had been taken by any predecessor. More, he placed it on a basis from which the poetry of the West has derived sustenance to the present. In the *Lysis* Socrates and his companions endeavor to determine whether friendship or love is the attraction of likes or opposites, a theme of the novelist from *Daphnis and Chloë* to Proust and Joyce. Plato leaves the question unresolved in the *Lysis* but argues that friendship must have a purpose, and he identifies this purpose with the highest purpose—individual wholeness—the good. In the *Phaedrus* he discusses the madness of the lover, his struggle with appetite, and his desire to mold his beloved into the image of the Idea. At the end of this dialogue, when the discussion is over, Socrates addresses Pan praying for the beauty toward which the discussion has led.

Beloved Pan, and all ye other gods who haunt this place, give me beauty in the inward soul; and may the outward and the inward man be at one. May I reckon the wise to be the wealthy, and may I have such a quantity of gold as a temperate man and he only can bear and carry.

In the *Symposium* Plato carries the phenomenon of love from physical desire through the artistic impulse manifested in the way we do things (this includes the organization of States), to the love of the beautiful or Good which is the Idea that molds the world. It is this aspect of Plato's thought which received great attention in the sixteenth and seventeenth centuries and which passed into romantic literature as the vulgar notion of "Platonic love." The utilitarianism of today is more occupied with the proposals in the *Republic* and the *Laws* for the regulation of marriage and the enforcement of monogamy, but in the classical tradition Plato's doctrine of Eros or Love is seen for what it is, namely, as an integral part of his philosophy binding all things, making each a distinct whole.

Plato's doctrine of the soul, which has been associated with the Pythagoreans and the Orphic Mysteries in one direction, and was extended by Neoplatonism and Christianity in another, remains one of the perplexing puzzles in his philosophy. In his cosmology he allots to the soul forms of existence, sameness, and difference intermediate between the real being of the Ideas and physical objects. Since the soul is akin to the Ideas it is immortal; it is the chief author of change in physical bodies. Plato thus clearly believed in the imperishability of the soul (*psyche*) as the activating principle of change. Physical objects come and go but the activating power of Being is constant. In one of the greatest of all the dialogues, the *Phaedo*, Plato discussed the question of the immortality of the human soul in the sense of the survival of human consciousness after death. There are also references and arguments with respect to the same issue in other dialogues. None of the arguments is conclusive as Plato himself must have been aware, and as numerous commentators since his day have pointed out. It cannot be shown that Plato believed in immortality in this sense, and the precise meaning of his doctrine of the soul has been endlessly debated from ancient times to the present both on the basis of the text and from the implications of his philosophy as a whole. The problem has never been resolved and it appears unlikely that it ever will be. At the heart, however, of the doctrine was the insistence upon the supreme duty of "tending the soul" and making it as perfect as possible. By this Plato meant that it is man's obligation to know, to grasp the meaning of the world rationally, and to manage his conduct in accordance with that insight. In the myths he assumes the immortality of the individual soul but this may be understood, not as the affirmation of a truth, but as a necessary regulative principle in the State. At the end of the *Laws* he touches on the problem for the final time. The great lesson about death, he says, is that the soul is superior to the body, and that it is the soul which makes us what we are. In death man departs to render his account to the gods. Not much help can be given him now. While he was alive he should have been aided to live the good life by all connected with him so that after death he would have nothing to fear.

But the problem of individual immortality is only one aspect of Plato's treatment of the soul. To begin with, the word "soul," with its accretions of meanings during the centuries, is an unfortunate translation of the Greek word *psyche*. It is more properly translated, according to the various contexts, as Reason, Mind, Intelligence, Life, the vital principle in things as well as in man; it is the constant that causes change but itself does not change. In fact, Plato's use of many different words for the rational order has caused much confusion. One explanation of his use of different words suggests that he hoped to make us realize that meaning lies not in words but only in that for which words stand. Another likely explanation is that no one word is adequate to account for the ideational nature of reality. In any event, the soul, because it is Intelligence, is tripartite; it is one and also many and the proportion that fuses them.

Plato therefore associated his theory of the State with the tripartite nature of the soul. He remarks that the State does not spring from oaks or rocks but from the characters of its citizens. Nevertheless the connections that exist between the elements that comprise human nature and those that make up the structure of the State are, he warns us, to be taken only analogically; it is not a proof but a method that will be helpful in disclosing the essential nature of the State. Plato's theory of human nature is a complicated one and his tripartite division of it into human intelligence, courage, and appetite is not an instance of a primitive psychology. The division was made for the purpose in hand and was not intended to be exhaustive. Plato works out in considerable detail the connections between the appetitive aspect of human nature, its desires and wants on the one side, and the economic class on the other. Similarly he associates the courageous element with the military class. This division of human nature is represented by the fighting instinct in man, his competitiveness, and his sense of injustice. Finally, the rational or philosophical element is connected with the governing class. In a famous image Plato compares man's intelligence to a charioteer driving two horses, one spirited and one sluggish, but the three forming a unit. The just man, Plato therefore says, is governed by intelligence even as the just State is governed by its most intelligent members.

Plato's theory of art, like everything he wrote, is an implication of the doctrine of Ideas. To him the world was a living system of Ideas and, true to this view, he never treats aspects of knowledge in isolation. We, as part of this system, know potentially; he therefore tries to lead us to see for ourselves. This has prompted some scholars to imagine that he leaves, not only philosophy itself but the theory of art, unanchored and unsystematic. But each dialogue, although exploring a different aspect of knowledge, has within it, by implication, the whole of knowledge as he envisaged it. In the *Timaeus*— Plato's poetic account of the universe—God is the Demiurgos, the craftsman, and the world is his product. He is the artist working toward fully understood ends, he is Intelligence forming all things from within. Thus when man understands the world he too can be an artist in all that he does. This is man's distinctive function, and the essential artist is the Statesman. Art is imitation, not of things, but of the nature of things, and man is an imitator, not a creator. Dante carried on this tradition when he wrote, "Art is the grandchild of God."

Much has been made of Plato's criticism of the poets, particularly of Homer, Hesiod, and the tragic drama. He criticized them for what he considered their excesses. Zeus should not have been pictured as subject to love potions administered by the scheming Hera, and Achilles' grief over the death of Patroclus Plato thought excessive; in tragic drama too he found excesses of emotion. Excess, he held, violates proportion and makes bad art and bad ethics. He concluded that the arts, so effective for good or evil, should be guided by the more intelligent members of the State, the philosophers, whose concern, training, and innate ability best equip them for that function. He was not hostile to art or poetry as such but only to unintelligent art, for he would not admit that imagination had a claim to the allegiance of men superior to the claim of intellect. "Let our artists," he wrote, "rather be those who are gifted to discern the true nature of the beautiful and graceful; then will our youth dwell in a land of health, amid fair sights and sounds, and receive the good in everything; and beauty, the effluence of fair works, shall flow into the eye and ear, like a health-giving breeze from a purer region, and insensibly draw the soul from earliest years into likeness and sympathy with the beauty of reason." No one has seen more deeply than Plato the beneficent effects of great art, but he argues that unfettered imagination and formless intuitionalism lead to error. Emotion like all things is beneficial when in balance, but art out of balance is not art. The great poet is one who does not misrepresent the world, but who discloses its real nature.

When Plato turned his attention to moral and political problems he did so from the point of view of his theory of Ideas. His purpose is to show that ethics and politics can be studied rationally if approached from the vantage ground which his philosophy gives us. In his view ethics and politics are indivisible implications of the natural order. He was not interested in describing existing states inasmuch as he thought they were all bad. He wanted to discover the real nature of the State, what it necessarily is if its full purpose is realized. This has always been the practice of even the most advanced sciences which proceed on the basis of ideal entities such as frictionless engines, perfect levers, perfectly rigid bodies, and similar constructions. Plato believed that a state, like all other things, possesses certain characteristics or it does not function properly and it was his intention to examine them. His standard, the rational order, conditions the structure and practices of the State. Evidence for this lies in the need men have for the different abilities of different individuals. The State is therefore a system of reciprocal services. This implies Plato's second great principle, the division of labor or specialization of function. Each man will perform the task for which he is best suited and the surplus of his product will be exchanged for the surplus of other specialists. In this way political life conserves its natural unity. Too often, political groups lose their unity by becoming divided into camps, rich and poor; but if each man cultivates his own abilities, such as they are, he will be happy and healthy, and the State will be healthy and whole. It is important to recognize that the political standard is the opposite of uniformity since different capacities are needed and each member has the greatest possible latitude to develop his own different abilities.

Owing to the necessity of difference Plato recognized three classes of men: the workers, merchants, traders, and businessmen who make up the bulk of the population, whose interest and therefore function is economic, supplying the material needs of the State; and the guardians, consisting of two classes, the statesmen who manage the public affairs and the soldiers and educators who protect the State against its internal and external enemies. The members of the three classes are born with differentiated interests which should be trained for their own individual fulfillment and happiness, and they will find their way to their proper occupation through their natural inclinations and abilities helped by educational facilities. Plato recognizes that this is a class, not a caste system, since the individual's position is not founded on heredity but on demonstrated qualities. At the peak of the system is the statesman, the man who has a grasp of the scheme of things. In the course of his argument Plato develops elaborate views on the conservation of this order by control of wealth, the regulation and equality of the sexes, education, and the place of art in political life. His analysis of the political order has found proponents and antagonists in succeeding ages, and it is clear that the problems he discussed are the problems that do not change. In the *Republic*, which he wrote in middle age, he found that with intelligent leadership and with the educational advantages of a healthy political life there would be little need for positive law. But in the *Laws* written at the end of his life, he is concerned with the alternative to intelligent leadership—the need for a few necessary laws clearly stated and firmly enforced.

His argument reaches one of its peaks in his defense of the natural order as justice. He means no more than what he has already said. Justice is realized in political life when the members of the State discharge their proper functions excellently and do not assume tasks beyond their competence. Justice is the principle which makes the State a whole and maintains its parts in due proportion. Through the observance of this principle both the State and the individual can achieve a satisfactory life. This alone gives the State its meaning, its proportion, what, in its absence, would cause it to perish. The principle of justice is the principle of the State, for the State has no other end than the conservation of its natural order.

It is evident that Plato's explorations were conducted on the basis of a firm grasp of logical principles. Unlike Aristotle he did not put forward a systematic account of logical rules, and in that sense he did not see logic as a discipline possessing a distinct subject mat-ter. But the revival of interest in logical studies, which has been a feature of contemporary thought, has brought about a corresponding concern with its development in the hands of ancient Greek thinkers. There have been efforts to show that on important points, such as the logic of the syllogism, the concept, and judgments, Plato was the first to work out the general theory. When he touches on logical mat-ters Plato's vocabulary, as in his mathematical discussions, can on occasion be technical in the extreme. It is the writing of a man who is a master of his subject matter.

It is also evident that Plato saw logic as more than an instru-ment. It was the essence of philosophy because it sought to discover the invariant laws of being, those necessities grounded in nature against which, as he says, not even the gods contend. Those logical truths, such as the relation of incompatibility or the principle of identity, are expressions of something that obtains in the external world; they are more objectively true than the circumstance that physical science affirms. They are the invariants that constitute the order of the world. They are not comparable, as is sometimes alleged, to the rules of chess where we do not ask if a particular game is "true," but rather "was the game played in accordance with the rules?" In Plato's logic we do ask if it is true that a relation of incompatibility exists. We put that question because the absence of incompatibility in nature is evidence of its intelligibility. For this reason Plato's logic implies that logical truth is itself a principle of the order of nature.

After the "logical" dialogues Plato gave an account in the *Timaeus* of his views on cosmology. It is a myth and, as Plato says, no more than a "likely story." It is presented as a continuation of the *Republic*, and in ancient times, and even today, it is held to embody Plato's last thoughts on the ultimate nature of things. In part it is a reflection of the science and mathematics of his time, but it too is dominated by the idea that the universe is the product of Reason seeking to realize itself. In a key sentence Plato says that the world is a composite result generated by Reason and Necessity. Reason overruled Necessity by persuading her to conduct to the best end the greater part of things. By this he seems to mean that the intelligi-bility of the world is due to the imposition on certain necessities of nature, its "errant causes," of a directing or teleological principle. This distinction between Reason and Necessity is one of the peculi-arities of the *Timaeus* which perhaps caused Hegel to deny that it could have been written by Plato; it was, he argued, an old Py-thagorean manuscript. Plato's own philosophy rests on the doctrine that at the heart of things there is Intelligence at work endeavoring everywhere to fulfill itself. The *Timaeus* must be read as a poem, more profound in its insight than the *De rerum natura* of Lucretius since it allowed for all that Lucretius described and made it plain that the materialist view is insufficient to account for the world.

Although the *Timaeus* takes the form of a myth, a vision of the physical world, it should not be supposed that it is less profound than the other dialogues. In the *Timaeus* Plato's aim is to reveal order in terms of the world of things. But notwithstanding its mythical form, or perhaps because of it, the *Timaeus* has been one of Plato's most influential dialogues. However, it is a dangerous undertaking to make the *Timaeus* or other writings of Plato say more than Plato intended or to interpret his remarks as anticipations of later developments. The Christian Fathers and the Middle Ages found in the first sentence of the *Timaeus* a foreknowledge of the Trinity. We are told in our own sophisticated age by a responsible historian of science that Plato himself formulated the idea of negative numbers and that he advanced the germ of the Newtonian-Leibnizian calculus. We are also told that the theory of Ideas is a counterpart of contemporary mathematical logic. Today the Copenhagen quantum physicists argue that the views of Plato in the *Timaeus* more closely approximate the fundamental law of nature than those of his opponents in the classical world. The *Timaeus* is a poem on the inauguration of the world, penetrating, compact, and great in conception. Whatever anticipations of contemporary knowledge it may disclose neither add to nor subtract from its importance as Plato's effort at a comprehensive vision of nature. His own insight is elaborated in other dialogues and it is by the truth or falsity of that insight that he must stand or fall.

Plato's philosophy is unique in the history of thought since what he said has been stated only once. His great commentators from Aristotle to Hegel have all attempted to improve upon him. He was poet, thinker, scientist all in one and there has been no such combination of powers displayed by anyone before or since. To understand Plato is to be educated; it is to see the nature of the world in which we live. The vitality of what he has to say is due to one factor. He took his point of departure from what is and not from what man wants. One by one he took up the great problems and if he did not solve them he left them at least in a framework in which subsequent ages could see them in their essential nature. He has been misunderstood, and adapted to points of view completely antithetical to his own; but these aberrations have always run their course, and it is by a return to Plato's insights that the thought of the West has continually renewed itself.

H. C.

THE COLLECTED DIALOGUES
OF PLATO

SOCRATES' DEFENSE

(APOLOGY)

The first three dialogues given here are an account of the last days and the death of Socrates. In what order Plato wrote the dialogues we do not know, but in reading them there is a good reason for beginning with those that center in the death of the chief personage. Only in them is Socrates himself the subject. In the others, although almost always the main speaker, he rarely speaks of himself. Indeed, in two of the three latest dialogues he is only a listener, and in the last he does not even appear. But in these first three he talks at length about his life and his beliefs.

In his Defense, Socrates explains himself to his fellow citizens when he is brought before an Athenian court on a most serious charge. "Socrates is guilty of corrupting the minds of the young, and of believing in deities of his own invention instead of the gods recognized by the state." In the Apology, as it is generally known, he gives a detailed account of the way he has lived and the convictions he has reached.

At the end, when he is condemned to death, the few words in which he accepts the sentence are in themselves a vivid picture of the man he was, unlike any other there has ever been. Great spiritual leaders and great saints adorn the pages of history, but Socrates is not like any of them. He is, indeed, the servant of the divine power, living in complete obedience to God; yet he always views the world of men with a bit of humor, a touch of irony. He spends his life in the effort to kindle into a flame the spark of good in every man, but when he fails, when he comes up against blind obstinacy or stupid conceit or the indifference of egotism, or when he draws down on himself bitter enmity, then along with his regret—because he cares for everyone— is mingled a little amusement, a feeling, as it were, of rueful sympathy, as if he said to himself, "What silly children we are." Socrates never condemned.

This significant clue to what he was is given most clearly in Socrates' Defense.

17 I do not know what effect my accusers have had upon you, gentlemen, but for my own part I was almost carried away by them—their arguments were so convincing. On the other hand, scarcely a word of what they said was true. I was especially astonished at one of their many misrepresentations; I mean when they told you that you must be careful not to let me deceive you—the implication being that I am
b a skillful speaker. I thought that it was peculiarly brazen of them to tell you this without a blush, since they must know that they will soon be effectively confuted, when it becomes obvious that I have not the slightest skill as a speaker—unless, of course, by a skillful speaker they mean one who speaks the truth. If that is what they mean, I would agree that I am an orator, though not after their pattern.

My accusers, then, as I maintain, have said little or nothing that is true, but from me you shall hear the whole truth—not, I can assure you, gentlemen, in flowery language like theirs, decked out with fine
c words and phrases. No, what you will hear will be a straightforward speech in the first words that occur to me, confident as I am in the justice of my cause, and I do not want any of you to expect anything different. It would hardly be suitable, gentlemen, for a man of my age to address you in the artificial language of a schoolboy orator. One thing, however, I do most earnestly beg and entreat of you. If you hear me defending myself in the same language which it has been my habit to use, both in the open spaces of this city—where many of you have heard me—and elsewhere, do not be surprised, and do not inter-
d rupt. Let me remind you of my position. This is my first appearance in a court of law, at the age of seventy, and so I am a complete stranger to the language of this place. Now if I were really from another country, you would naturally excuse me if I spoke in the manner and
18 dialect in which I had been brought up, and so in the present case I make this request of you, which I think is only reasonable, to disregard the manner of my speech—it may be better or it may be worse —and to consider and concentrate your attention upon this one question, whether my claims are fair or not. That is the first duty of the juryman, just as it is the pleader's duty to speak the truth.

The proper course for me, gentlemen of the jury, is to deal first with the earliest charges that have been falsely brought against me, and with my earliest accusers, and then with the later ones. I make
b this distinction because I have already been accused in your hearing by a great many people for a great many years, though without a word of truth, and I am more afraid of those people than I am of Anytus and his colleagues, although they are formidable enough. But the others are still more formidable. I mean the people who took hold of so many of you when you were children and tried to fill your minds with

From *The Last Days of Socrates*, translated and with an introduction by Hugh Tredennick (Penguin Classics, Harmondsworth, Middlesex, 1954).

untrue accusations against me, saying, There is a wise man called Socrates who has theories about the heavens and has investigated everything below the earth, and can make the weaker argument defeat the stronger.

It is these people, gentlemen, the disseminators of these rumors, c who are my dangerous accusers, because those who hear them suppose that anyone who inquires into such matters must be an atheist. Besides, there are a great many of these accusers, and they have been accusing me now for a great many years. And what is more, they approached you at the most impressionable age, when some of you were children or adolescents, and they literally won their case by default, because there was no one to defend me. And the most fantastic thing of all is that it is impossible for me even to know and tell you their names, unless one of them happens to be a playwright. All these d people, who have tried to set you against me out of envy and love of slander—and some too merely passing on what they have been told by others—all these are very difficult to deal with. It is impossible to bring them here for cross-examination; one simply has to conduct one's defense and argue one's case against an invisible opponent, because there is no one to answer. So I ask you to accept my statement that my critics fall into two classes, on the one hand my immediate accusers, and on the other those earlier ones whom I have mentioned, e and you must suppose that I have first to defend myself against the latter. After all, you heard them abusing me longer ago and much more violently than these more recent accusers.

Very well, then, I must begin my defense, gentlemen, and I must try, in the short time that I have, to rid your minds of a false impres- 19 sion which is the work of many years. I should like this to be the result, gentlemen, assuming it to be for your advantage and my own; and I should like to be successful in my defense, but I think that it will be difficult, and I am quite aware of the nature of my task. However, let that turn out as God wills. I must obey the law and make my defense.

Let us go back to the beginning and consider what the charge is that has made me so unpopular, and has encouraged Meletus to draw b up this indictment. Very well, what did my critics say in attacking my character? I must read out their affidavit, so to speak, as though they were my legal accusers: Socrates is guilty of criminal meddling, in that he inquires into things below the earth and in the sky, and makes the weaker argument defeat the stronger, and teaches others to follow his example. It runs something like that. You have seen it c for yourselves in the play by Aristophanes, where Socrates goes whirling round, proclaiming that he is walking on air, and uttering a great deal of other nonsense about things of which I know nothing whatsoever. I mean no disrespect for such knowledge, if anyone really is versed in it—I do not want any more lawsuits brought against me by

Meletus—but the fact is, gentlemen, that I take no interest in it.
d What is more, I call upon the greater part of you as witnesses to my
statement, and I appeal to all of you who have ever listened to me
talking—and there are a great many to whom this applies—to clear
your neighbors' minds on this point. Tell one another whether any
one of you has ever heard me discuss such questions briefly or at
length, and then you will realize that the other popular reports about
me are equally unreliable.

The fact is that there is nothing in any of these charges, and if
you have heard anyone say that I try to educate people and charge a
e fee, there is no truth in that either. I wish that there were, because I
think that it is a fine thing if a man is qualified to teach, as in the
case of Gorgias of Leontini and Prodicus of Ceos and Hippias of
Elis. Each one of these is perfectly capable of going into any city and
actually persuading the young men to leave the company of their fel-
20 low citizens, with any of whom they can associate for nothing, and
attach themselves to him, and pay money for the privilege, and be
grateful into the bargain.

There is another expert too from Paros who I discovered was here
on a visit; I happened to meet a man who has paid more in Sophists'
fees than all the rest put together—I mean Callias, the son of Hipponicus. So I asked him—he has two sons, you see—Callias, I said, if
your sons had been colts or calves, we should have had no difficulty
b in finding and engaging a trainer to perfect their natural qualities,
and this trainer would have been some sort of horse dealer or agri-
culturalist. But seeing that they are human beings, whom do you intend to get as their instructor? Who is the expert in perfecting the
human and social qualities? I assume from the fact of your having
sons that you must have considered the question. Is there such a person or not?

Certainly, said he.

Who is he, and where does he come from? said I. And what
does he charge?

Evenus of Paros, Socrates, said he, and his fee is five minas.

c   I felt that Evenus was to be congratulated if he really was a master of this art and taught it at such a moderate fee. I should certainly
plume myself and give myself airs if I understood these things, but
in fact, gentlemen, I do not.

Here perhaps one of you might interrupt me and say, But
what is it that you do, Socrates? How is it that you have been misrepresented like this? Surely all this talk and gossip about you would
never have arisen if you had confined yourself to ordinary activities,
but only if your behavior was abnormal. Tell us the explanation, if
d you do not want us to invent it for ourselves.

This seems to me to be a reasonable request, and I will try to explain to you what it is that has given me this false notoriety. So

please give me your attention. Perhaps some of you will think that I am not being serious, but I assure you that I am going to tell you the whole truth.

I have gained this reputation, gentlemen, from nothing more or less than a kind of wisdom. What kind of wisdom do I mean? Human wisdom, I suppose. It seems that I really am wise in this limited sense. Presumably the geniuses whom I mentioned just now are wise in a e wisdom that is more than human. I do not know how else to account for it. I certainly have no knowledge of such wisdom, and anyone who says that I have is a liar and willful slanderer. Now, gentlemen, please do not interrupt me if I seem to make an extravagant claim, for what I am going to tell you is not my own opinion. I am going to refer you to an unimpeachable authority. I shall call as witness to my wisdom, such as it is, the god at Delphi.

You know Chaerephon, of course. He was a friend of mine from 21 boyhood, and a good democrat who played his part with the rest of you in the recent expulsion and restoration. And you know what he was like, how enthusiastic he was over anything that he had once undertaken. Well, one day he actually went to Delphi and asked this question of the god—as I said before, gentlemen, please do not interrupt—he asked whether there was anyone wiser than myself. The priestess replied that there was no one. As Chaerephon is dead, the evidence for my statement will be supplied by his brother, who is here in court.

Please consider my object in telling you this. I want to explain to b you how the attack upon my reputation first started. When I heard about the oracle's answer, I said to myself, What does the god mean? Why does he not use plain language? I am only too conscious that I have no claim to wisdom, great or small. So what can he mean by asserting that I am the wisest man in the world? He cannot be telling a lie; that would not be right for him.

After puzzling about it for some time, I set myself at last with considerable reluctance to check the truth of it in the following way. I went to interview a man with a high reputation for wisdom, because I felt that here if anywhere I should succeed in disproving the c oracle and pointing out to my divine authority, You said that I was the wisest of men, but here is a man who is wiser than I am.

Well, I gave a thorough examination to this person—I need not mention his name, but it was one of our politicians that I was studying when I had this experience—and in conversation with him I formed the impression that although in many people's opinion, and especially in his own, he appeared to be wise, in fact he was not. Then when I began to try to show him that he only thought he was wise and was not really so, my efforts were resented both by him and by d many of the other people present. However, I reflected as I walked away, Well, I am certainly wiser than this man. It is only too likely that neither of us has any knowledge to boast of, but he thinks that he knows something which he does not know, whereas I am quite conscious of my ignorance. At any rate it seems that I am wiser than he is to this small extent, that I do not think that I know what I do not know.

e   After this I went on to interview a man with an even greater reputation for wisdom, and I formed the same impression again, and here too I incurred the resentment of the man himself and a number of others.

From that time on I interviewed one person after another. I realized with distress and alarm that I was making myself unpopular, but I felt compelled to put my religious duty first. Since I was trying to find out the meaning of the oracle, I was bound to interview everyone who had a reputation for knowledge. And by dog, gentlemen, for I

22 must be frank with you, my honest impression was this. It seemed to me, as I pursued my investigation at the god's command, that the people with the greatest reputations were almost entirely deficient, while others who were supposed to be their inferiors were much better qualified in practical intelligence.

I want you to think of my adventures as a sort of pilgrimage undertaken to establish the truth of the oracle once for all. After I had finished with the politicians I turned to the poets, dramatic, lyric, and

b   all the rest, in the belief that here I should expose myself as a comparative ignoramus. I used to pick up what I thought were some of their most perfect works and question them closely about the meaning of what they had written, in the hope of incidentally enlarging my own knowledge. Well, gentlemen, I hesitate to tell you the truth, but it must be told. It is hardly an exaggeration to say that any of the bystanders could have explained those poems better than their actual authors. So I soon made up my mind about the poets too. I decided

c   that it was not wisdom that enabled them to write their poetry, but a kind of instinct or inspiration, such as you find in seers and prophets who deliver all their sublime messages without knowing in the least what they mean. It seemed clear to me that the poets were in much the same case, and I also observed that the very fact that they were poets made them think that they had a perfect understanding of all other subjects, of which they were totally ignorant. So I left that line of inquiry too with the same sense of advantage that I had felt in the case of the politicians.

Last of all I turned to the skilled craftsmen. I knew quite well

d   that I had practically no technical qualifications myself, and I was sure that I should find them full of impressive knowledge. In this I was not disappointed. They understood things which I did not, and to that extent they were wiser than I was. But, gentlemen, these professional experts seemed to share the same failing which I had noticed in the poets. I mean that on the strength of their technical proficiency they claimed a perfect understanding of every other subject, however important, and I felt that this error more than outweighed their positive wisdom. So I made myself spokesman for the oracle, and asked myself whether I would rather be as I was—neither wise with e their wisdom nor stupid with their stupidity—or possess both qualities as they did. I replied through myself to the oracle that it was best for me to be as I was.

The effect of these investigations of mine, gentlemen, has been to arouse against me a great deal of hostility, and hostility of a 23 particularly bitter and persistent kind, which has resulted in various malicious suggestions, including the description of me as a professor of wisdom. This is due to the fact that whenever I succeed in disproving another person's claim to wisdom in a given subject, the bystanders assume that I know everything about that subject myself. But the truth of the matter, gentlemen, is pretty certainly this, that real wisdom is the property of God, and this oracle is his way of telling us that human wisdom has little or no value. It seems to me that he is not referring literally to Socrates, but has merely taken my name as b an example, as if he would say to us, The wisest of you men is he who has realized, like Socrates, that in respect of wisdom he is really worthless.

That is why I still go about seeking and searching in obedience to the divine command, if I think that anyone is wise, whether citizen or stranger, and when I think that any person is not wise, I try to help the cause of God by proving that he is not. This occupation has kept me too busy to do much either in politics or in my own affairs. In fact, my service to God has reduced me to extreme poverty. c

There is another reason for my being unpopular. A number of young men with wealthy fathers and plenty of leisure have deliberately attached themselves to me because they enjoy hearing other people cross-questioned. These often take me as their model, and go on to try to question other persons. Whereupon, I suppose, they find an unlimited number of people who think that they know something, but really know little or nothing. Consequently their victims become annoyed, not with themselves but with me, and they complain that there is a pestilential busybody called Socrates who fills young people's heads with wrong ideas. If you ask them what he does, and what he d teaches that has this effect, they have no answer, not knowing what to say. But as they do not want to admit their confusion, they fall back on the stock charges against any philosopher, that he teaches his pupils about things in the heavens and below the earth, and to disbelieve in gods, and to make the weaker argument defeat the stronger. They would be very loath, I fancy, to admit the truth—which is that they are being convicted of pretending to knowledge when they are entirely ignorant. So, jealous, I suppose, for their own reputation, and e also energetic and numerically strong, and provided with a plausible and carefully worked-out case against me, these people have been dinning into your ears for a long time past their violent denunciations of myself.

There you have the causes which led to the attack upon me by Meletus and Anytus and Lycon, Meletus being aggrieved on behalf of the poets, Anytus on behalf of the professional men and politicians, 24 and Lycon on behalf of the orators. So, as I said at the beginning, I should be surprised if I were able, in the short time that I have, to rid your minds of a misconception so deeply implanted.

There, gentlemen, you have the true facts, which I present to you without any concealment or suppression, great or small. I am fairly certain that this plain speaking of mine is the cause of my unpopularity, and this really goes to prove that my statements are true, and that I have described correctly the nature and the grounds of the calumny which has been brought against me. Whether you in-
b quire into them now or later, you will find the facts as I have just described them.

So much for my defense against the charges brought by the first group of my accusers. I shall now try to defend myself against Meletus—high-principled and patriotic as he claims to be—and after that against the rest.

Let us first consider their deposition again, as though it represented a fresh prosecution. It runs something like this: Socrates is guilty of corrupting the minds of the young, and of believing in deities of his own invention instead of the gods recognized by the state.
c Such is the charge. Let us examine its points one by one.

First it says that I am guilty of corrupting the young. But I say, gentlemen, that Meletus is guilty of treating a serious matter with levity, since he summons people to stand their trial on frivolous grounds, and professes concern and keen anxiety in matters about which he has never had the slightest interest. I will try to prove this to your satisfaction.

d   Come now, Meletus, tell me this. You regard it as supremely important, do you not, that our young people should be exposed to the best possible influence?
I do.
Very well, then, tell these gentlemen who it is that influences the young for the better. Obviously you must know, if you are so much interested. You have discovered the vicious influence, as you say, in myself, and you are now prosecuting me before these gentlemen. Speak up and inform them who it is that has a good influence upon the young. . . . You see, Meletus, that you are tongue-tied and cannot answer. Do you not feel that this is discreditable, and a sufficient proof in itself of what I said, that you have no interest in the subject? Tell me, my friend, who is it that makes the young good?
The laws.

That is not what I mean, my dear sir. I am asking you to name e
the *person* whose first business it is to know the laws.

These gentlemen here, Socrates, the members of the jury.

Do you mean, Meletus, that they have the ability to educate
the young, and to make them better?

Certainly.

Does this apply to all jurymen, or only to some?

To all of them.

Excellent! A generous supply of benefactors. Well, then, do these
spectators who are present in court have an improving influence, or
not?

Yes, they do.   25

And what about the members of the Council?

Yes, the councilors too.

But surely, Meletus, the members of the Assembly do not corrupt
the young? Or do all of them too exert an improving influence?

Yes, they do.

Then it would seem that the whole population of Athens has a refining effect upon the young, except myself, and I alone demoralize
them. Is that your meaning?

Most emphatically, yes.

This is certainly a most unfortunate quality that you have detected in me. Well, let me put another question to you. Take the case
of horses. Do you believe that those who improve them make up the
whole of mankind, and that there is only one person who has a bad b
effect on them? Or is the truth just the opposite, that the ability to improve them belongs to one person or to very few persons, who are
horse trainers, whereas most people, if they have to do with horses
and make use of them, do them harm? Is not this the case, Meletus,
both with horses and with all other animals? Of course it is, whether
you and Anytus deny it or not. It would be a singular dispensation of
fortune for our young people if there is only one person who corrupts
them, while all the rest have a beneficial effect. But I need say no
more. There is ample proof, Meletus, that you have never bothered c
your head about the young, and you make it perfectly clear that you
have never taken the slightest interest in the cause for the sake of
which you are now indicting me.

Here is another point. Tell me seriously, Meletus, is it better to
live in a good or in a bad community? Answer my question, like a good
fellow; there is nothing difficult about it. Is it not true that wicked
people have a bad effect upon those with whom they are in the closest
contact, and that good people have a good effect?

Quite true.

Is there anyone who prefers to be harmed rather than benefited d
by his associates? Answer me, my good man; the law commands you
to answer. Is there anyone who prefers to be harmed?

Of course not.

Well, then, when you summon me before this court for corrupting the young and making their characters worse, do you mean that I do so intentionally or unintentionally?

I mean intentionally.

Why, Meletus, are you at your age so much wiser than I at mine? You have discovered that bad people always have a bad effect,
e and good people a good effect, upon their nearest neighbors. Am I so hopelessly ignorant as not even to realize that by spoiling the character of one of my companions I shall run the risk of getting some harm from him? Because nothing else would make me commit this grave offense intentionally. No, I do not believe it, Meletus, and I do
26 not suppose that anyone else does. Either I have not a bad influence, or it is unintentional, so that in either case your accusation is false. And if I unintentionally have a bad influence, the correct procedure in cases of such involuntary misdemeanors is not to summon the culprit before this court, but to take him aside privately for instruction and reproof, because obviously if my eyes are opened, I shall stop doing what I do not intend to do. But you deliberately avoided my company in the past and refused to enlighten me, and now you bring me before this court, which is the place appointed for those who need punishment, not for those who need enlightenment.

It is quite clear by now, gentlemen, that Meletus, as I said before,
b has never shown any degree of interest in this subject. However, I invite you to tell us, Meletus, in what sense you make out that I corrupt the minds of the young. Surely the terms of your indictment make it clear that you accuse me of teaching them to believe in new deities instead of the gods recognized by the state. Is not that the teaching of mine which you say has this demoralizing effect?

That is precisely what I maintain.

c   Then I appeal to you, Meletus, in the name of these same gods about whom we are speaking, to explain yourself a little more clearly to myself and to the jury, because I cannot make out what your point is. Is it that I teach people to believe in some gods—which implies that I myself believe in gods, and am not a complete atheist, so that I am not guilty on that score—but in different gods from those recognized by the state, so that your accusation rests upon the fact that they are different? Or do you assert that I believe in no gods at all, and teach others to do the same?

Yes, I say that you disbelieve in gods altogether.

You surprise me, Meletus. What is your object in saying that? Do
d you suggest that I do not believe that the sun and moon are gods, as is the general belief of all mankind?

He certainly does not, gentlemen of the jury, since he says that the sun is a stone and the moon a mass of earth.

Do you imagine that you are prosecuting Anaxagoras, my dear

Meletus? Have you so poor an opinion of these gentlemen, and do you assume them to be so illiterate as not to know that the writings of Anaxagoras of Clazomenae are full of theories like these? And do you seriously suggest that it is from me that the young get these ideas, when they can buy them on occasion in the market place for a drachma at most, and so have the laugh on Socrates if he claims e them for his own, to say nothing of their being so silly? Tell me honestly, Meletus, is that your opinion of me? Do I believe in no god?

No, none at all, not in the slightest degree.

You are not at all convincing, Meletus—not even to yourself, I suspect. In my opinion, gentlemen, this man is a thoroughly selfish bully, and has brought this action against me out of sheer wanton aggressiveness and self-assertion. He seems to be devising a sort of in- 27 telligence test for me, saying to himself, Will the infallible Socrates realize that I am contradicting myself for my own amusement, or shall I succeed in deceiving him and the rest of my audience?

It certainly seems to me that he is contradicting himself in this indictment, which might just as well run: Socrates is guilty of not believing in the gods, but believing in the gods. And this is pure flippancy.

I ask you to examine with me, gentlemen, the line of reasoning which leads me to this conclusion. You, Meletus, will oblige us by answering my questions. Will you all kindly remember, as I requested b at the beginning, not to interrupt if I conduct the discussion in my customary way?

Is there anyone in the world, Meletus, who believes in human activities, and not in human beings? Make him answer, gentlemen, and don't let him keep on making these continual objections. Is there anyone who does not believe in horses, but believes in horses' activities? Or who does not believe in musicians, but believes in musical activities? No, there is not, my worthy friend. If you do not want to answer, I will supply it for you and for these gentlemen too. But the next question you must answer. Is there anyone who believes in c supernatural activities and not in supernatural beings?

No.

How good of you to give a bare answer under compulsion by the court! Well, do you assert that I believe and teach others to believe in supernatural activities? It does not matter whether they are new or old. The fact remains that I believe in them according to your statement; indeed you solemnly swore as much in your affidavit. But if I believe in supernatural activities, it follows inevitably that I also believe in supernatural beings. Is not that so? It is. I assume your assent, since you do not answer. Do we not hold that supernatural beings are either gods or the children of gods? Do you agree or not?   d

Certainly.

Then if I believe in supernatural beings, as you assert, if these supernatural beings are gods in any sense, we shall reach the conclusion which I mentioned just now when I said that you were testing my intelligence for your own amusement, by stating first that I do not believe in gods, and then again that I do, since I believe in supernatural beings. If on the other hand these supernatural beings are bastard children of the gods by nymphs or other mothers, as they are reputed to be, who in the world would believe in the children of gods and not in the gods themselves? It would be as ridiculous as to believe in the e young of horses or donkeys and not in horses and donkeys themselves. No, Meletus, there is no avoiding the conclusion that you brought this charge against me as a test of my wisdom, or else in despair of finding a genuine offense of which to accuse me. As for your prospect of convincing any living person with even a smattering of intelligence that belief in supernatural and divine activities does not imply belief in supernatural and divine beings, and vice versa, it is outside all the 28 bounds of possibility.

As a matter of fact, gentlemen, I do not feel that it requires much defense to clear myself of Meletus' accusation. What I have said already is enough. But you know very well the truth of what I said in an earlier part of my speech, that I have incurred a great deal of bitter hostility, and this is what will bring about my destruction, if anything does—not Meletus nor Anytus, but the slander and jealousy of a very large section of the people. They have been fatal to a great many b other innocent men, and I suppose will continue to be so; there is no likelihood that they will stop at me. But perhaps someone will say, Do you feel no compunction, Socrates, at having followed a line of action which puts you in danger of the death penalty?

I might fairly reply to him, You are mistaken, my friend, if you think that a man who is worth anything ought to spend his time weighing up the prospects of life and death. He has only one thing to consider in performing any action—that is, whether he is acting rightly or wrongly, like a good man or a bad one. On your view the he- c roes who died at Troy would be poor creatures, especially the son of Thetis. He, if you remember, made light of danger in comparison with incurring dishonor when his goddess mother warned him, eager as he was to kill Hector, in some such words as these, I fancy: My son, if you avenge your comrade Patroclus' death and kill Hector, you will die yourself—'Next after Hector is thy fate prepared.' When he heard this warning, he made light of his death and danger, being much more d afraid of an ignoble life and of failing to avenge his friends. 'Let me die forthwith,' said he, 'when I have requited the villain, rather than remain here by the beaked ships to be mocked, a burden on the ground.' [1] Do you suppose that he gave a thought to death and danger?

[1] *Iliad* 18.96 sq.

The truth of the matter is this, gentlemen. Where a man has once taken up his stand, either because it seems best to him or in obedience to his orders, there I believe he is bound to remain and face the danger, taking no account of death or anything else before dishonor.

This being so, it would be shocking inconsistency on my part, gentlemen, if, when the officers whom you chose to command me assigned me my position at Potidaea and Amphipolis and Delium, I remained at my post like anyone else and faced death, and yet afterward, when God appointed me, as I supposed and believed, to the duty of leading the philosophical life, examining myself and others, I were then through fear of death or of any other danger to desert my post. That would indeed be shocking, and then I might really with justice be summoned into court for not believing in the gods, and disobeying the oracle, and being afraid of death, and thinking that I am wise when I am not. For let me tell you, gentlemen, that to be afraid of death is only another form of thinking that one is wise when one is not; it is to think that one knows what one does not know. No one knows with regard to death whether it is not really the greatest blessing that can happen to a man, but people dread it as though they were certain that it is the greatest evil, and this ignorance, which thinks that it knows what it does not, must surely be ignorance most culpable. This, I take it, gentlemen, is the degree, and this the nature of my advantage over the rest of mankind, and if I were to claim to be wiser than my neighbor in any respect, it would be in this—that not possessing any real knowledge of what comes after death, I am also conscious that I do not possess it. But I do know that to do wrong and to disobey my superior, whether God or man, is wicked and dishonorable, and so I shall never feel more fear or aversion for something which, for all I know, may really be a blessing, than for those evils which I know to be evils.

Suppose, then, that you acquit me, and pay no attention to Anytus, who has said that either I should not have appeared before this court at all, or, since I have appeared here, I must be put to death, because if I once escaped your sons would all immediately become utterly demoralized by putting the teaching of Socrates into practice. Suppose that, in view of this, you said to me, Socrates, on this occasion we shall disregard Anytus and acquit you, but only on one condition, that you give up spending your time on this quest and stop philosophizing. If we catch you going on in the same way, you shall be put to death.

Well, supposing, as I said, that you should offer to acquit me on these terms, I should reply, Gentlemen, I am your very grateful and devoted servant, but I owe a greater obedience to God than to you, and so long as I draw breath and have my faculties, I shall never stop practicing philosophy and exhorting you and elucidating the truth for everyone that I meet. I shall go on saying, in my usual way, My very

good friend, you are an Athenian and belong to a city which is the greatest and most famous in the world for its wisdom and strength. Are you not ashamed that you give your attention to acquiring as
e much money as possible, and similarly with reputation and honor, and give no attention or thought to truth and understanding and the perfection of your soul?

And if any of you disputes this and professes to care about these things, I shall not at once let him go or leave him. No, I shall question him and examine him and test him; and if it appears that in spite of his profession he has made no real progress toward goodness, I shall
30 reprove him for neglecting what is of supreme importance, and giving his attention to trivialities. I shall do this to everyone that I meet, young or old, foreigner or fellow citizen, but especially to you, my fellow citizens, inasmuch as you are closer to me in kinship. This, I do assure you, is what my God commands, and it is my belief that no greater good has ever befallen you in this city than my service to my God. For I spend all my time going about trying to persuade you, young and old, to make your first and chief concern not for your bod-
b ies nor for your possessions, but for the highest welfare of your souls, proclaiming as I go, Wealth does not bring goodness, but goodness brings wealth and every other blessing, both to the individual and to the state.

Now if I corrupt the young by this message, the message would seem to be harmful, but if anyone says that my message is different from this, he is talking nonsense. And so, gentlemen, I would say, You can please yourselves whether you listen to Anytus or not, and whether you acquit me or not. You know that I am not going to alter
c my conduct, not even if I have to die a hundred deaths.

Order, please, gentlemen! Remember my request to give me a hearing without interruption. Besides, I believe that it will be to your advantage to listen. I am going to tell you something else, which may provoke a storm of protest, but please restrain yourselves. I assure you that if I am what I claim to be, and you put me to death, you will harm yourselves more than me. Neither Meletus nor Anytus can do me any
d harm at all; they would not have the power, because I do not believe that the law of God permits a better man to be harmed by a worse. No doubt my accuser might put me to death or have me banished or deprived of civic rights, but even if he thinks—as he probably does, and others too, I dare say—that these are great calamities, I do not think so. I believe that it is far worse to do what he is doing now, trying to put an innocent man to death. For this reason, gentlemen, so far from pleading on my own behalf, as might be supposed, I am really pleading on yours, to save you from misusing the gift of God by condemning
e me. If you put me to death, you will not easily find anyone to take my place. It is literally true, even if it sounds rather comical, that God has specially appointed me to this city, as though it were a large thorough-

bred horse which because of its great size is inclined to be lazy and needs the stimulation of some stinging fly. It seems to me that God has attached me to this city to perform the office of such a fly, and all day long I never cease to settle here, there, and everywhere, rousing, persuading, reproving every one of you. You will not easily find an- 31 other like me, gentlemen, and if you take my advice you will spare my life. I suspect, however, that before long you will awake from your drowsing, and in your annoyance you will take Anytus' advice and finish me off with a single slap, and then you will go on sleeping till the end of your days, unless God in his care for you sends someone to take my place.

If you doubt whether I am really the sort of person who would have been sent to this city as a gift from God, you can convince your- b selves by looking at it in this way. Does it seem natural that I should have neglected my own affairs and endured the humiliation of allowing my family to be neglected for all these years, while I busied myself all the time on your behalf, going like a father or an elder brother to see each one of you privately, and urging you to set your thoughts on goodness? If I had got any enjoyment from it, or if I had been paid for my good advice, there would have been some explanation for my conduct, but as it is you can see for yourselves that although my accusers unblushingly charge me with all sorts of other crimes, there is one thing that they have not had the impudence to pretend on any tes- c timony, and that is that I have ever exacted or asked a fee from anyone. The witness that I can offer to prove the truth of my statement is, I think, a convincing one—my poverty.

It may seem curious that I should go round giving advice like this and busying myself in people's private affairs, and yet never venture publicly to address you as a whole and advise on matters of state. The reason for this is what you have often heard me say before on many other occasions—that I am subject to a divine or supernatural experi- d ence, which Meletus saw fit to travesty in his indictment. It began in my early childhood—a sort of voice which comes to me, and when it comes it always dissuades me from what I am proposing to do, and never urges me on. It is this that debars me from entering public life, and a very good thing too, in my opinion, because you may be quite sure, gentlemen, that if I had tried long ago to engage in politics, I should long ago have lost my life, without doing any good either to you or to myself. Please do not be offended if I tell you the truth. No man e on earth who conscientiously opposes either you or any other organized democracy, and flatly prevents a great many wrongs and illegalities from taking place in the state to which he belongs, can possibly escape with his life. The true champion of justice, if he intends to sur- 32 vive even for a short time, must necessarily confine himself to private life and leave politics alone.

I will offer you substantial proofs of what I have said—not

theories, but what you can appreciate better, facts. Listen while I describe my actual experiences, so that you may know that I would never
submit wrongly to any authority through fear of death, but would refuse even at the cost of my life. It will be a commonplace story, such
as you often hear in the courts, but it is true.

b   The only office which I have ever held in our city, gentlemen, was
when I was elected to the Council. It so happened that our group was
acting as the executive when you decided that the ten commanders
who had failed to rescue the men who were lost in the naval engagement should be tried en bloc, which was illegal, as you all recognized
later. On this occasion I was the only member of the executive who insisted that you should not act unconstitutionally, and voted against
the proposal; and although your leaders were all ready to denounce
and arrest me, and you were all urging them on at the top of your
c   voices, I thought that it was my duty to face it out on the side of law
and justice rather than support you, through fear of prison or death,
in your wrong decision.

      This happened while we were still under a democracy. When the
oligarchy came into power, the Thirty Commissioners in their turn
summoned me and four others to the Round Chamber and instructed
us to go and fetch Leon of Salamis from his home for execution. This
was of course only one of many instances in which they issued such
instructions, their object being to implicate as many people as possible
in their wickedness. On this occasion, however, I again made it clear
d   not by my words but by my actions that death did not matter to me at
all—if that is not too strong an expression—but that it mattered all
the world to me that I should do nothing wrong or wicked. Powerful
as it was, that government did not terrify me into doing a wrong action. When we came out of the Round Chamber, the other four went
off to Salamis and arrested Leon, and I went home. I should probably
have been put to death for this, if the government had not fallen soon
e   afterward. There are plenty of people who will testify to these statements.

      Do you suppose that I should have lived as long as I have if I had
moved in the sphere of public life, and conducting myself in that
sphere like an honorable man, had always upheld the cause of right,
and conscientiously set this end above all other things? Not by a very
33   long way, gentlemen; neither would any other man. You will find that
throughout my life I have been consistent in any public duties that I
have performed, and the same also in my personal dealings. I have
never countenanced any action that was incompatible with justice on
the part of any person, including those whom some people maliciously
call my pupils. I have never set up as any man's teacher, but if anyone,
young or old, is eager to hear me conversing and carrying out my private mission, I never grudge him the opportunity; nor do I charge a
b   fee for talking to him, and refuse to talk without one. I am ready to

answer questions for rich and poor alike, and I am equally ready if anyone prefers to listen to me and answer my questions. If any given one of these people becomes a good citizen or a bad one, I cannot fairly be held responsible, since I have never promised or imparted any teaching to anybody, and if anyone asserts that he has ever learned or heard from me privately anything which was not open to everyone else, you may be quite sure that he is not telling the truth.

But how is it that some people enjoy spending a great deal of time in my company? You have heard the reason, gentlemen; I told you c quite frankly. It is because they enjoy hearing me examine those who think that they are wise when they are not—an experience which has its amusing side. This duty I have accepted, as I said, in obedience to God's commands given in oracles and dreams and in every other way that any other divine dispensation has ever impressed a duty upon man. This is a true statement, gentlemen, and easy to verify. If it is a fact that I am in process of corrupting some of the young, and have d succeeded already in corrupting others, and if it were a fact that some of the latter, being now grown up, had discovered that I had ever given them bad advice when they were young, surely they ought now to be coming forward to denounce and punish me. And if they did not like to do it themselves, you would expect some of their families— their fathers and brothers and other near relations—to remember it now, if their own flesh and blood had suffered any harm from me. Certainly a great many of them have found their way into this court, as I can see for myself—first Crito over there, my contemporary and near e neighbor, the father of this young man Critobulus, and then Lysanias of Sphettus, the father of Aeschines here, and next Antiphon of Cephisus, over there, the father of Epigenes. Then besides there are all those whose brothers have been members of our circle—Nicostratus, the son of Theozotides, the brother of Theodotus, but Theodotus is dead, so he cannot appeal to his brother, and Paralus here, the son of Demodocus, whose brother was Theages. And here is Adimantus, 34 the son of Ariston, whose brother Plato is over there, and Aeantodorus, whose brother Apollodorus is here on this side. I can name many more besides, some of whom Meletus most certainly ought to have produced as witnesses in the course of his speech. If he forgot to do so then, let him do it now—I am willing to make way for him. Let him state whether he has any such evidence to offer. On the contrary, gentlemen, you will find that they are all prepared to help me—the corrupter and evil genius of their nearest and dearest relatives, as Meletus and Anytus say. The actual victims of my corrupting in- b fluence might perhaps be excused for helping me; but as for the uncorrupted, their relations of mature age, what other reason can they have for helping me except the right and proper one, that they know Meletus is lying and I am telling the truth?

There, gentlemen, that, and perhaps a little more to the same

effect, is the substance of what I can say in my defense. It may be that
c some one of you, remembering his own case, will be annoyed that
whereas he, in standing his trial upon a less serious charge than this,
made pitiful appeals to the jury with floods of tears, and had his infant children produced in court to excite the maximum of sympathy,
and many of his relatives and friends as well, I on the contrary intend to do nothing of the sort, and that, although I am facing, as it
might appear, the utmost danger. It may be that one of you, reflecting
on these facts, will be prejudiced against me, and being irritated by his
reflections, will give his vote in anger. If one of you is so disposed—I
d do not expect it, but there is the possibility—I think that I should be
quite justified in saying to him, My dear sir, of course I have some relatives. To quote the very words of Homer, even I am not sprung 'from
an oak or from a rock,' [2] but from human parents, and consequently I
have relatives—yes, and sons too, gentlemen, three of them, one almost grown up and the other two only children—but all the same I
am not going to produce them here and beseech you to acquit me.

Why do I not intend to do anything of this kind? Not out of per-
e versity, gentlemen, nor out of contempt for you; whether I am brave
or not in the face of death has nothing to do with it. The point is that
for my own credit and yours and for the credit of the state as a whole,
I do not think that it is right for me to use any of these methods at my
age and with my reputation—which may be true or it may be false,
35 but at any rate the view is held that Socrates is different from the
common run of mankind. Now if those of you who are supposed to be
distinguished for wisdom or courage or any other virtue are to behave
in this way, it would be a disgrace. I have often noticed that some people of this type, for all their high standing, go to extraordinary lengths
when they come up for trial, which shows that they think it will be a
dreadful thing to lose their lives—as though they would be immortal
if you did not put them to death! In my opinion these people bring disgrace upon our city. Any of our visitors might be excused for thinking
b that the finest specimens of Athenian manhood, whom their fellow
citizens select on their merits to rule over them and hold other high
positions, are no better than women. If you have even the smallest
reputation, gentlemen, you ought not to descend to these methods;
and if we do so, you must not give us license. On the contrary, you
must make it clear that anyone who stages these pathetic scenes and
so brings ridicule upon our city is far more likely to be condemned
than if he kept perfectly quiet.

But apart from all question of appearances, gentlemen, I do not
c think that it is right for a man to appeal to the jury or to get himself
acquitted by doing so; he ought to inform them of the facts and convince them by argument. The jury does not sit to dispense justice as

[2] *Odyssey* 19.163.

a favor, but to decide where justice lies, and the oath which they have sworn is not to show favor at their own discretion, but to return a just and lawful verdict. It follows that we must not develop in you, nor you allow to grow in yourselves, the habit of perjury; that would be sinful for us both. Therefore you must not expect me, gentlemen, to behave toward you in a way which I consider neither reputable nor moral nor consistent with my religious duty, and above all you must not expect d it when I stand charged with impiety by Meletus here. Surely it is obvious that if I tried to persuade you and prevail upon you by my entreaties to go against your solemn oath, I should be teaching you contempt for religion, and by my very defense I should be accusing myself of having no religious belief. But that is very far from the truth. I have a more sincere belief, gentlemen, than any of my accusers, and I leave it to you and to God to judge me as it shall be best for me and for yourselves.

There are a great many reasons, gentlemen, why I am not dis- e tressed by this result—I mean your condemnation of me—but the 36 chief reason is that the result was not unexpected. What does surprise me is the number of votes cast on the two sides. I should never have believed that it would be such a close thing, but now it seems that if a mere thirty votes had gone the other way, I should have been acquitted. Even as it is, I feel that so far as Meletus' part is concerned I have been acquitted, and not only that, but anyone can see that if Anytus and Lycon had not come forward to accuse me, Meletus would actually have forfeited his one thousand drachmas for not having ob- b tained one fifth of the votes.

However, we must face the fact that he demands the death penalty. Very good. What alternative penalty shall I propose to you, gentlemen? Obviously it must be adequate. Well, what penalty do I deserve to pay or suffer, in view of what I have done?

I have never lived an ordinary quiet life. I did not care for the things that most people care about—making money, having a comfortable home, high military or civil rank, and all the other activities, political appointments, secret societies, party organizations, which go on in our city. I thought that I was really too strict in my principles c to survive if I went in for this sort of thing. So instead of taking a course which would have done no good either to you or to me, I set myself to do you individually in private what I hold to be the greatest possible service. I tried to persuade each one of you not to think more of practical advantages than of his mental and moral well-being, or in general to think more of advantage than of well-being in the case of the state or of anything else. What do I deserve for behaving in this way? Some reward, gentlemen, if I am bound to suggest what I d really deserve, and what is more, a reward which would be appropriate for myself. Well, what is appropriate for a poor man who is a

public benefactor and who requires leisure for giving you moral encouragement? Nothing could be more appropriate for such a person than free maintenance at the state's expense. He deserves it much more than any victor in the races at Olympia, whether he wins with a single horse or a pair or a team of four. These people give you the
e semblance of success, but I give you the reality; they do not need maintenance, but I do. So if I am to suggest an appropriate penalty
37 which is strictly in accordance with justice, I suggest free maintenance by the state.

   Perhaps when I say this I may give you the impression, as I did in my remarks about exciting sympathy and making passionate appeals, that I am showing a deliberate perversity. That is not so, gentlemen. The real position is this. I am convinced that I never wrong anyone intentionally, but I cannot convince you of this, because we have had so little time for discussion. If it was your practice, as it is with other
b nations, to give not one day but several to the hearing of capital trials, I believe that you might have been convinced, but under present conditions it is not easy to dispose of grave allegations in a short space of time. So, being convinced that I do no wrong to anybody, I can hardly be expected to wrong myself by asserting that I deserve something bad, or by proposing a corresponding penalty. Why should I? For fear of suffering this penalty proposed by Meletus, when, as I said, I do not know whether it is a good thing or a bad? Do you expect me to choose something which I know very well is bad by making my
c counterproposal? Imprisonment? Why should I spend my days in prison, in subjection to the periodically appointed officers of the law? A fine, with imprisonment until it is paid? In my case the effect would be just the same, because I have no money to pay a fine. Or shall I suggest banishment? You would very likely accept the suggestion.

   I should have to be desperately in love with life to do that, gentlemen. I am not so blind that I cannot see that you, my fellow citizens,
d have come to the end of your patience with my discussions and conversations. You have found them too irksome and irritating, and now you are trying to get rid of them. Will any other people find them easy to put up with? That is most unlikely, gentlemen. A fine life I should have if I left this country at my age and spent the rest of my days trying one city after another and being turned out every time! I know very well that wherever I go the young people will listen to my conversation just as they do here, and if I try to keep them off, they will make their elders drive me out, while if I do not, the fathers and
e other relatives will drive me out of their own accord for the sake of the young.

   Perhaps someone may say, But surely, Socrates, after you have left us you can spend the rest of your life in quietly minding your own business.

   This is the hardest thing of all to make some of you understand.

If I say that this would be disobedience to God, and that is why I cannot 'mind my own business,' you will not believe that I am serious. If on the other hand I tell you that to let no day pass without discussing 38 goodness and all the other subjects about which you hear me talking and examining both myself and others is really the very best thing that a man can do, and that life without this sort of examination is not worth living, you will be even less inclined to believe me. Nevertheless that is how it is, gentlemen, as I maintain, though it is not easy to convince you of it. Besides, I am not accustomed to think of myself as deserving punishment. If I had money, I would have suggested a fine that I could afford, because that would not have done me any b harm. As it is, I cannot, because I have none, unless of course you like to fix the penalty at what I could pay. I suppose I could probably afford a mina. I suggest a fine of that amount.

One moment, gentlemen. Plato here, and Crito and Critobulus and Apollodorus, want me to propose thirty minas, on their security. Very well, I agree to this sum, and you can rely upon these gentlemen for its payment. c

Well, gentlemen, for the sake of a very small gain in time you are going to earn the reputation—and the blame from those who wish to disparage our city—of having put Socrates to death, 'that wise man' —because they will say I am wise even if I am not, these people who want to find fault with you. If you had waited just a little while, you would have had your way in the course of nature. You can see that I am well on in life and near to death. I am saying this not to all of you but to those who voted for my execution, and I have something else to d say to them as well.

No doubt you think, gentlemen, that I have been condemned for lack of the arguments which I could have used if I had thought it right to leave nothing unsaid or undone to secure my acquittal. But that is very far from the truth. It is not a lack of arguments that has caused my condemnation, but a lack of effrontery and impudence, and the fact that I have refused to address you in the way which would give you most pleasure. You would have liked to hear me weep and wail, doing and saying all sorts of things which I regard as unworthy of e myself, but which you are used to hearing from other people. But I did not think then that I ought to stoop to servility because I was in danger, and I do not regret now the way in which I pleaded my case. I would much rather die as the result of this defense than live as the result of the other sort. In a court of law, just as in warfare, neither I nor any other ought to use his wits to escape death by any means. In battle 39 it is often obvious that you could escape being killed by giving up your arms and throwing yourself upon the mercy of your pursuers, and in every kind of danger there are plenty of devices for avoiding death if you are unscrupulous enough to stick at nothing. But I

suggest, gentlemen, that the difficulty is not so much to escape death;
the real difficulty is to escape from doing wrong, which is far more
b fleet of foot. In this present instance I, the slow old man, have been
overtaken by the slower of the two, but my accusers, who are clever
and quick, have been overtaken by the faster—by iniquity. When I
leave this court I shall go away condemned by you to death, but they
will go away convicted by truth herself of depravity and wickedness.
And they accept their sentence even as I accept mine. No doubt it was
bound to be so, and I think that the result is fair enough.

c   Having said so much, I feel moved to prophesy to you who have
given your vote against me, for I am now at that point where the gift
of prophecy comes most readily to men—at the point of death. I tell
you, my executioners, that as soon as I am dead, vengeance shall fall
upon you with a punishment far more painful than your killing of me.
You have brought about my death in the belief that through it you
will be delivered from submitting your conduct to criticism, but I say
that the result will be just the opposite. You will have more critics,
d whom up till now I have restrained without your knowing it, and being younger they will be harsher to you and will cause you more annoyance. If you expect to stop denunciation of your wrong way of life
by putting people to death, there is something amiss with your reasoning. This way of escape is neither possible nor creditable. The best
and easiest way is not to stop the mouths of others, but to make yourselves as good men as you can. This is my last message to you who
e voted for my condemnation.

As for you who voted for my acquittal, I should very much like to
say a few words to reconcile you to the result, while the officials are
busy and I am not yet on my way to the place where I must die. I ask
you, gentlemen, to spare me these few moments. There is no reason
why we should not exchange fancies while the law permits. I look
40 upon you as my friends, and I want you to understand the right way
of regarding my present position.

Gentlemen of the jury—for *you* deserve to be so called—I have
had a remarkable experience. In the past the prophetic voice to which
I have become accustomed has always been my constant companion,
opposing me even in quite trivial things if I was going to take the
wrong course. Now something has happened to me, as you can see,
which might be thought and is commonly considered to be a supreme
b calamity; yet neither when I left home this morning, nor when I was
taking my place here in the court, nor at any point in any part of my
speech did the divine sign oppose me. In other discussions it has often
checked me in the middle of a sentence, but this time it has never
opposed me in any part of this business in anything that I have said or
done. What do I suppose to be the explanation? I will tell you. I suspect that this thing that has happened to me is a blessing, and we
c are quite mistaken in supposing death to be an evil. I have good

grounds for thinking this, because my accustomed sign could not have failed to oppose me if what I was doing had not been sure to bring some good result.

We should reflect that there is much reason to hope for a good result on other grounds as well. Death is one of two things. Either it is annihilation, and the dead have no consciousness of anything, or, as we are told, it is really a change—a migration of the soul from this place to another. Now if there is no consciousness but only a dream- d less sleep, death must be a marvelous gain. I suppose that if anyone were told to pick out the night on which he slept so soundly as not even to dream, and then to compare it with all the other nights and days of his life, and then were told to say, after due consideration, how many better and happier days and nights than this he had spent in the course of his life—well, I think that the Great King himself, to e say nothing of any private person, would find these days and nights easy to count in comparison with the rest. If death is like this, then, I call it gain, because the whole of time, if you look at it in this way, can be regarded as no more than one single night. If on the other hand death is a removal from here to some other place, and if what we are told is true, that all the dead are there, what greater blessing could there be than this, gentlemen? If on arrival in the other world, beyond 41 the reach of our so-called justice, one will find there the true judges who are said to preside in those courts, Minos and Rhadamanthus and Aeacus and Triptolemus and all those other half-divinities who were upright in their earthly life, would that be an unrewarding journey? Put it in this way. How much would one of you give to meet Orpheus and Musaeus, Hesiod and Homer? I am willing to die ten times over if this account is true. It would be a specially interesting experience for me to join them there, to meet Palamedes and Ajax, the son of Tel- b amon, and any other heroes of the old days who met their death through an unfair trial, and to compare my fortunes with theirs— it would be rather amusing, I think. And above all I should like to spend my time there, as here, in examining and searching people's minds, to find out who is really wise among them, and who only thinks that he is. What would one not give, gentlemen, to be able to question the leader of that great host against Troy, or Odysseus, or c Sisyphus, or the thousands of other men and women whom one could mention, to talk and mix and argue with whom would be unimaginable happiness? At any rate I presume that they do not put one to death there for such conduct, because apart from the other happiness in which their world surpasses ours, they are now immortal for the rest of time, if what we are told is true.

You too, gentlemen of the jury, must look forward to death with confidence, and fix your minds on this one belief, which is certain —that nothing can harm a good man either in life or after death, and d his fortunes are not a matter of indifference to the gods. This present experience of mine has not come about mechanically. I am quite clear that the time had come when it was better for me to die and be released from my distractions. That is why my sign never turned me back. For my own part I bear no grudge at all against those who condemned me and accused me, although it was not with this kind intention that they did so, but because they thought that they were hurting

e me; and that is culpable of them. However, I ask them to grant me one favor. When my sons grow up, gentlemen, if you think that they are putting money or anything else before goodness, take your revenge by plaguing them as I plagued you; and if they fancy themselves for no reason, you must scold them just as I scolded you, for neglecting the important things and thinking that they are good for something

42 when they are good for nothing. If you do this, I shall have had justice at your hands, both I myself and my children.

Now it is time that we were going, I to die and you to live, but which of us has the happier prospect is unknown to anyone but God.

CRITO

Nearly a month elapsed between Socrates' condemnation and execution, a delay not at all in accordance with Athenian custom. The day before the trial, however, a state galley had been sent on a sacred annual mission and until it returned no one could be put to death. For various reasons the mission took much longer than usual, and Socrates' friends used the time to make a plan for getting him out of prison and away from Athens.

The evening before the Crito opens the galley had been sighted, and very early on the following morning Socrates' old and devoted friend, Crito, comes to the prison to lay the plan before him and beseech him to let his friends save him. It will be easy to bribe his jailers. He himself has far more money than will be needed, and there are many others who are eager to contribute. Athens is not the only place where Socrates can live happily. He will find friends wherever he goes.

To this Socrates answers by asking him if it can ever be right to defend oneself against evil by doing evil. Granted that it was unjust to condemn him to death, can it be right for him to escape by breaking the law? What will happen to a state if individual men are able to set aside the laws? A man must always do what his country orders him unless he can change her view of what the law should be.

" 'If you leave the city, Socrates,' the laws argue, 'you shall return wrong for wrong and evil for evil, breaking your agreements and covenants with us, and injuring those whom you least ought to injure —yourself, your friends, your country, and us.'

"That, my dear friend Crito, I do assure you, is what I seem to hear them saying . . . and the sound of their arguments rings so loudly in my head that I cannot hear the other side. However, if you think that you will do any good by it, say what you like."

"Socrates, I have nothing to say."

"Then, Crito, let us follow this course, since God points out the way."

43   SOCRATES: Here already, Crito? Surely it is still early?
CRITO: Indeed it is.
SOCRATES: About what time?
CRITO: Just before dawn.
SOCRATES: I wonder that the warder paid any attention to you.

CRITO: He is used to me now, Socrates, because I come here so often. Besides, he is under some small obligation to me.

SOCRATES: Have you only just come, or have you been here for long?

CRITO: Fairly long.

b   SOCRATES: Then why didn't you wake me at once, instead of sitting by my bed so quietly?

CRITO: I wouldn't dream of such a thing, Socrates. I only wish I were not so sleepless and depressed myself. I have been wondering at you, because I saw how comfortably you were sleeping, and I deliberately didn't wake you because I wanted you to go on being as comfortable as you could. I have often felt before in the course of my life how fortunate you are in your disposition, but I feel it more than ever now in your present misfortune when I see how easily and placidly you put up with it.

SOCRATES: Well, really, Crito, it would be hardly suitable for a
c man of my age to resent having to die.

CRITO: Other people just as old as you are get involved in these misfortunes, Socrates, but their age doesn't keep them from resenting it when they find themselves in your position.

SOCRATES: Quite true. But tell me, why have you come so early?

CRITO: Because I bring bad news, Socrates—not so bad from your point of view, I suppose, but it will be very hard to bear for me and your other friends, and I think that I shall find it hardest of all.

SOCRATES: Why, what is this news? Has the boat come in
d from Delos—the boat which ends my reprieve when it arrives?

CRITO: It hasn't actually come in yet, but I expect that it will be here today, judging from the report of some people who have just arrived from Sunium and left it there. It's quite clear from their account that it will be here today, and so by tomorrow, Socrates, you will have to . . . to end your life.

SOCRATES: Well, Crito, I hope that it may be for the best. If the
44 gods will it so, so be it. All the same, I don't think it will arrive today.

CRITO: What makes you think that?

SOCRATES: I will try to explain. I think I am right in saying that I have to die on the day after the boat arrives?

From *The Last Days of Socrates*, translated and with an introduction by Hugh Tredennick (Penguin Classics, Harmondsworth, Middlesex, 1954).

CRITO: That's what the authorities say, at any rate.

SOCRATES: Then I don't think it will arrive on this day that is just beginning, but on the day after. I am going by a dream that I had in the night, only a little while ago. It looks as though you were right not to wake me up.

CRITO: Why, what was the dream about?

SOCRATES: I thought I saw a gloriously beautiful woman dressed in white robes, who came up to me and addressed me in these words: Socrates, 'To the pleasant land of Phthia on the third day thou b shalt come.'[1]

CRITO: Your dream makes no sense, Socrates.

SOCRATES: To my mind, Crito, it is perfectly clear.

CRITO: Too clear, apparently. But look here, Socrates, it is still not too late to take my advice and escape. Your death means a double calamity for me. I shall not only lose a friend whom I can never possibly replace, but besides a great many people who don't know you and me very well will be sure to think that I let you down, because I could have saved you if I had been willing to spend the money. And what c could be more contemptible than to get a name for thinking more of money than of your friends? Most people will never believe that it was you who refused to leave this place although we tried our hardest to persuade you.

SOCRATES: But my dear Crito, why should we pay so much attention to what 'most people' think? The really reasonable people, who have more claim to be considered, will believe that the facts are exactly as they are.

CRITO: You can see for yourself, Socrates, that one has to think d of popular opinion as well. Your present position is quite enough to show that the capacity of ordinary people for causing trouble is not confined to petty annoyances, but has hardly any limits if you once get a bad name with them.

SOCRATES: I only wish that ordinary people had an unlimited capacity for doing harm; then they might have an unlimited power for doing good, which would be a splendid thing, if it were so. Actually they have neither. They cannot make a man wise or stupid; they simply act at random.

CRITO: Have it that way if you like, but tell me this, Socrates. I e hope that you aren't worrying about the possible effects on me and the rest of your friends, and thinking that if you escape we shall have trouble with informers for having helped you to get away, and have to forfeit all our property or pay an enormous fine, or even incur some further punishment? If any idea like that is troubling you, you can 45 dismiss it altogether. We are quite entitled to run that risk in saving you, and even worse, if necessary. Take my advice, and be reasonable.

[1] *Iliad* 9.363.

SOCRATES : All that you say is very much in my mind, Crito, and a great deal more besides.

CRITO : Very well, then, don't let it distress you. I know some people who are willing to rescue you from here and get you out of the country for quite a moderate sum. And then surely you realize how cheap these informers are to buy off; we shan't need much money to
b settle them, and I think you've got enough of my money for yourself already. And then even supposing that in your anxiety for my safety you feel that you oughtn't to spend my money, there are these foreign gentlemen staying in Athens who are quite willing to spend theirs. One of them, Simmias of Thebes, has actually brought the money with him for this very purpose, and Cebes and a number of others are quite ready to do the same. So, as I say, you mustn't let any fears on these grounds make you slacken your efforts to escape, and you mustn't feel any misgivings about what you said at your trial—that you wouldn't know what to do with yourself if you left this country. Wherever you go, there are plenty of places where you will find a wel-
c come, and if you choose to go to Thessaly, I have friends there who will make much of you and give you complete protection, so that no one in Thessaly can interfere with you.

Besides, Socrates, I don't even feel that it is right for you to try to do what you are doing, throwing away your life when you might save it. You are doing your best to treat yourself in exactly the same way as your enemies would, or rather did, when they wanted to ruin you. What is more, it seems to me that you are letting your sons down too. You have it in your power to finish their bringing-up and education,
d and instead of that you are proposing to go off and desert them, and so far as you are concerned they will have to take their chance. And what sort of chance are they likely to get? The sort of thing that usually happens to orphans when they lose their parents. Either one ought not to have children at all, or one ought to see their upbringing and education through to the end. It strikes me that you are taking the line of least resistance, whereas you ought to make the choice of a good man and a brave one, considering that you profess to have made goodness your object all through life. Really, I am ashamed, both on
e your account and on ours, your friends'. It will look as though we had played something like a coward's part all through this affair of yours. First there was the way you came into court when it was quite unnecessary—that was the first act. Then there was the conduct of the defense—that was the second. And finally, to complete the farce, we get this situation, which makes it appear that we have let you slip out of our hands through some lack of courage and enterprise on our
46 part, because we didn't save you, and you didn't save yourself, when it would have been quite possible and practicable, if we had been any use at all.

There, Socrates, if you aren't careful, besides the suffering there will be all this disgrace for you and us to bear. Come, make up your mind. Really it's too late for that now; you ought to have it made up already. There is no alternative; the whole thing must be carried through during this coming night. If we lose any more time, it can't be done; it will be too late. I appeal to you, Socrates, on every ground; take my advice and please don't be unreasonable!

SOCRATES: My dear Crito, I appreciate your warm feelings b very much—that is, assuming that they have some justification. If not, the stronger they are, the harder they will be to deal with. Very well, then, we must consider whether we ought to follow your advice or not. You know that this is not a new idea of mine; it has always been my nature never to accept advice from any of my friends unless reflection shows that it is the best course that reason offers. I cannot abandon the principles which I used to hold in the past simply because this accident has happened to me; they seem to me to be much as they were, and I respect and regard the same principles now as be- c fore. So unless we can find better principles on this occasion, you can be quite sure that I shall not agree with you—not even if the power of the people conjures up fresh hordes of bogies to terrify our childish minds, by subjecting us to chains and executions and confiscations of our property.

Well, then, how can we consider the question most reasonably? Suppose that we begin by reverting to this view which you hold about people's opinions. Was it always right to argue that some opinions should be taken seriously but not others? Or was it always wrong? d Perhaps it was right before the question of my death arose, but now we can see clearly that it was a mistaken persistence in a point of view which was really irresponsible nonsense. I should like very much to inquire into this problem, Crito, with your help, and to see whether the argument will appear in any different light to me now that I am in this position, or whether it will remain the same, and whether we shall dismiss it or accept it.

Serious thinkers, I believe, have always held some such view as the one which I mentioned just now, that some of the opinions which people entertain should be respected, and others should not. e Now I ask you, Crito, don't you think that this is a sound principle? You are safe from the prospect of dying tomorrow, in all human probability, and you are not likely to have your judgment upset by this 47 impending calamity. Consider, then, don't you think that this is a sound enough principle, that one should not regard all the opinions that people hold, but only some and not others? What do you say? Isn't that a fair statement?

CRITO: Yes, it is.

SOCRATES: In other words, one should regard the good ones and not the bad?

CRITO: Yes.

SOCRATES : The opinions of the wise being good, and the opinions of the foolish bad?

CRITO : Naturally.

SOCRATES : To pass on, then, what do you think of the sort of
b illustration that I used to employ? When a man is in training, and taking it seriously, does he pay attention to all praise and criticism and opinion indiscriminately, or only when it comes from the one qualified person, the actual doctor or trainer?

CRITO : Only when it comes from the one qualified person.

SOCRATES : Then he should be afraid of the criticism and welcome the praise of the one qualified person, but not those of the general public.

CRITO : Obviously.

SOCRATES : So he ought to regulate his actions and exercises and eating and drinking by the judgment of his instructor, who has expert knowledge, rather than by the opinions of the rest of the public.

CRITO : Yes, that is so.

c   SOCRATES : Very well. Now if he disobeys the one man and disregards his opinion and commendations, and pays attention to the advice of the many who have no expert knowledge, surely he will suffer some bad effect?

CRITO : Certainly.

SOCRATES : And what is this bad effect? Where is it produced? I mean, in what part of the disobedient person?

CRITO : His body, obviously; that is what suffers.

SOCRATES : Very good. Well now, tell me, Crito—we don't want to go through all the examples one by one—does this apply as a general rule, and above all to the sort of actions which we are trying to decide about, just and unjust, honorable and dishonorable, good and bad? Ought we to be guided and intimidated by the opinion of the
d many or by that of the one—assuming that there is someone with expert knowledge? Is it true that we ought to respect and fear this person more than all the rest put together, and that if we do not follow his guidance we shall spoil and mutilate that part of us which, as we used to say, is improved by right conduct and destroyed by wrong? Or is this all nonsense?

CRITO : No, I think it is true, Socrates.

SOCRATES : Then consider the next step. There is a part of us which is improved by healthy actions and ruined by unhealthy ones.
e If we spoil it by taking the advice of nonexperts, will life be worth living when this part is once ruined? The part I mean is the body. Do you accept this?

CRITO : Yes.

SOCRATES : Well, is life worth living with a body which is worn out and ruined in health?

CRITO : Certainly not.

SOCRATES: What about the part of us which is mutilated by wrong actions and benefited by right ones? Is life worth living with this part ruined? Or do we believe that this part of us, whatever it may be, in which right and wrong operate, is of less importance than 48 the body?

CRITO: Certainly not.

SOCRATES: It is really more precious?

CRITO: Much more.

SOCRATES: In that case, my dear fellow, what we ought to consider is not so much what people in general will say about us but how we stand with the expert in right and wrong, the one authority, who represents the actual truth. So in the first place your proposition is not correct when you say that we should consider popular opinion in questions of what is right and honorable and good, or the opposite. Of course one might object, All the same, the people have the power to put us to death.

CRITO: No doubt about that! Quite true, Socrates. It is a possi- b ble objection.

SOCRATES: But so far as I can see, my dear fellow, the argument which we have just been through is quite unaffected by it. At the same time I should like you to consider whether we are still satisfied on this point, that the really important thing is not to live, but to live well.

CRITO: Why, yes.

SOCRATES: And that to live well means the same thing as to live honorably or rightly?

CRITO: Yes.

SOCRATES: Then in the light of this agreement we must consider whether or not it is right for me to try to get away without an official discharge. If it turns out to be right, we must make the attempt; c if not, we must let it drop. As for the considerations you raise about expense and reputation and bringing up children, I am afraid, Crito, that they represent the reflections of the ordinary public, who put people to death, and would bring them back to life if they could, with equal indifference to reason. Our real duty, I fancy, since the argument leads that way, is to consider one question only, the one which we raised just now. Shall we be acting rightly in paying money and showing gratitude to these people who are going to rescue me, and in escaping or arranging the escape ourselves, or shall we really be act- d ing wrongly in doing all this? If it becomes clear that such conduct is wrong, I cannot help thinking that the question whether we are sure to die, or to suffer any other ill effect for that matter, if we stand our ground and take no action, ought not to weigh with us at all in comparison with the risk of doing what is wrong.

CRITO: I agree with what you say, Socrates, but I wish you would consider what we ought to do.

SOCRATES: Let us look at it together, my dear fellow; and if e you can challenge any of my arguments, do so and I will listen to you; but if you can't, be a good fellow and stop telling me over and over again that I ought to leave this place without official permission. I am very anxious to obtain your approval before I adopt the course which I have in mind. I don't want to act against your convictions. Now give your attention to the starting point of this inquiry—I hope that you will be satisfied with my way of stating it—and try to answer my 49 questions to the best of your judgment.

CRITO: Well, I will try.

SOCRATES: Do we say that one must never willingly do wrong, or does it depend upon circumstances? Is it true, as we have often agreed before, that there is no sense in which wrongdoing is good or honorable? Or have we jettisoned all our former convictions in these last few days? Can you and I at our age, Crito, have spent all these years in serious discussions without realizing that we were no b better than a pair of children? Surely the truth is just what we have always said. Whatever the popular view is, and whether the alternative is pleasanter than the present one or even harder to bear, the fact remains that to do wrong is in every sense bad and dishonorable for the person who does it. Is that our view, or not?

CRITO: Yes, it is.

SOCRATES: Then in no circumstances must one do wrong.

CRITO: No.

SOCRATES: In that case one must not even do wrong when one is wronged, which most people regard as the natural course.

c CRITO: Apparently not.

SOCRATES: Tell me another thing, Crito. Ought one to do injuries or not?

CRITO: Surely not, Socrates.

SOCRATES: And tell me, is it right to do an injury in retaliation, as most people believe, or not?

CRITO: No, never.

SOCRATES: Because, I suppose, there is no difference between injuring people and wronging them.

CRITO: Exactly.

SOCRATES: So one ought not to return a wrong or an injury to d any person, whatever the provocation is. Now be careful, Crito, that in making these single admissions you do not end by admitting something contrary to your real beliefs. I know that there are and always will be few people who think like this, and consequently between those who do think so and those who do not there can be no agreement on principle; they must always feel contempt when they observe one another's decisions. I want even you to consider very carefully whether you share my views and agree with me, and whether we can proceed with our discussion from the established hypothesis that it is never right to do a wrong or return a wrong or defend oneself against injury by retaliation, or whether you dissociate yourself from any share in this view as a basis for discussion. I have held it for a long e time, and still hold it, but if you have formed any other opinion, say so and tell me what it is. If, on the other hand, you stand by what we have said, listen to my next point.

CRITO: Yes, I stand by it and agree with you. Go on.

SOCRATES: Well, here is my next point, or rather question. Ought one to fulfill all one's agreements, provided that they are right, or break them?

CRITO: One ought to fulfill them.

SOCRATES: Then consider the logical consequence. If we leave this place without first persuading the state to let us go, are we or are 50 we not doing an injury, and doing it in a quarter where it is least justifiable? Are we or are we not abiding by our just agreements?

CRITO: I can't answer your question, Socrates. I am not clear in my mind.

SOCRATES: Look at it in this way. Suppose that while we were preparing to run away from here—or however one should describe it —the laws and constitution of Athens were to come and confront us and ask this question, Now, Socrates, what are you proposing to do? Can you deny that by this act which you are contemplating you intend, so far as you have the power, to destroy us, the laws, and the b whole state as well? Do you imagine that a city can continue to exist and not be turned upside down, if the legal judgments which are pronounced in it have no force but are nullified and destroyed by private persons?

How shall we answer this question, Crito, and others of the same kind? There is much that could be said, especially by a professional advocate, to protest against the invalidation of this law which enacts that judgments once pronounced shall be binding. Shall we say, Yes, I do intend to destroy the laws, because the state wronged me by pass- c ing a faulty judgment at my trial? Is this to be our answer, or what?

CRITO: What you have just said, by all means, Socrates.

SOCRATES: Then what supposing the laws say, Was there provision for this in the agreement between you and us, Socrates? Or did you undertake to abide by whatever judgments the state pronounced?

If we expressed surprise at such language, they would probably say, Never mind our language, Socrates, but answer our questions; after all, you are accustomed to the method of question and answer. Come now, what charge do you bring against us and the state, that d you are trying to destroy us? Did we not give you life in the first place? Was it not through us that your father married your mother and begot you? Tell us, have you any complaint against those of us laws that deal with marriage?

No, none, I should say.

Well, have you any against the laws which deal with children's upbringing and education, such as you had yourself? Are you not grateful to those of us laws which were instituted for this end, for requiring your father to give you a cultural and physical education?

e   Yes, I should say.

Very good. Then since you have been born and brought up and educated, can you deny, in the first place, that you were our child and servant, both you and your ancestors? And if this is so, do you imagine that what is right for us is equally right for you, and that whatever we try to do to you, you are justified in retaliating? You did not have equality of rights with your father, or your employer—supposing that you had had one—to enable you to retaliate. You were not allowed

51   to answer back when you were scolded or to hit back when you were beaten, or to do a great many other things of the same kind. Do you expect to have such license against your country and its laws that if we try to put you to death in the belief that it is right to do so, you on your part will try your hardest to destroy your country and us its laws in return? And will you, the true devotee of goodness, claim that you are justified in doing so? Are you so wise as to have forgotten that compared with your mother and father and all the rest of your ances-

b   tors your country is something far more precious, more venerable, more sacred, and held in greater honor both among gods and among all reasonable men? Do you not realize that you are even more bound to respect and placate the anger of your country than your father's anger? That if you cannot persuade your country you must do whatever it orders, and patiently submit to any punishment that it imposes, whether it be flogging or imprisonment? And if it leads you out to war, to be wounded or killed, you must comply, and it is right that you should do so. You must not give way or retreat or abandon your position. Both in war and in the law courts and everywhere else you

c   must do whatever your city and your country command, or else persuade them in accordance with universal justice, but violence is a sin even against your parents, and it is a far greater sin against your country.

What shall we say to this, Crito—that what the laws say is true, or not?

CRITO: Yes, I think so.

SOCRATES: Consider, then, Socrates, the laws would probably continue, whether it is also true for us to say that what you are now trying to do to us is not right. Although we have brought you into the world and reared you and educated you, and given you and all your

d   fellow citizens a share in all the good things at our disposal, nevertheless by the very fact of granting our permission we openly proclaim this principle, that any Athenian, on attaining to manhood and seeing for himself the political organization of the state and us its laws, is permitted, if he is not satisfied with us, to take his property and go

away wherever he likes. If any of you chooses to go to one of our colonies, supposing that he should not be satisfied with us and the state,
or to emigrate to any other country, not one of us laws hinders or
prevents him from going away wherever he likes, without any loss of
property. On the other hand, if any one of you stands his ground when e
he can see how we administer justice and the rest of our public organization, we hold that by so doing he has in fact undertaken to do
anything that we tell him. And we maintain that anyone who disobeys is guilty of doing wrong on three separate counts: first because
we are his parents, and secondly because we are his guardians, and
thirdly because, after promising obedience, he is neither obeying us
nor persuading us to change our decision if we are at fault in any way.
And although all our orders are in the form of proposals, not of savage 52
commands, and we give him the choice of either persuading us or doing what we say, he is actually doing neither. These are the charges,
Socrates, to which we say that you will be liable if you do what you
are contemplating, and you will not be the least culpable of your fellow countrymen, but one of the most guilty.

    If I asked why, they would no doubt pounce upon me with perfect
justice and point out that there are very few people in Athens who
have entered into this agreement with them as explicitly as I have.
They would say, Socrates, we have substantial evidence that you are b
satisfied with us and with the state. You would not have been so exceptionally reluctant to cross the borders of your country if you had
not been exceptionally attached to it. You have never left the city to
attend a festival or for any other purpose, except on some military expedition. You have never traveled abroad as other people do, and you
have never felt the impulse to acquaint yourself with another country
or constitution. You have been content with us and with our city. You c
have definitely chosen us, and undertaken to observe us in all your activities as a citizen, and as the crowning proof that you are satisfied
with our city, you have begotten children in it. Furthermore, even at
the time of your trial you could have proposed the penalty of banishment, if you had chosen to do so—that is, you could have done then
with the sanction of the state what you are now trying to do without
it. But whereas at that time you made a noble show of indifference if
you had to die, and in fact preferred death, as you said, to banishment, now you show no respect for your earlier professions, and no
regard for us, the laws, whom you are trying to destroy. You are behaving like the lowest type of menial, trying to run away in spite of d
the contracts and undertakings by which you agreed to live as a member of our state. Now first answer this question. Are we or are we not
speaking the truth when we say that you have undertaken, in deed if
not in word, to live your life as a citizen in obedience to us?

    What are we to say to that, Crito? Are we not bound to admit it?
    CRITO: We cannot help it, Socrates.

SOCRATES: It is a fact, then, they would say, that you are
e breaking covenants and undertakings made with us, although you
made them under no compulsion or misunderstanding, and were not
compelled to decide in a limited time. You had seventy years in which
you could have left the country, if you were not satisfied with us or
felt that the agreements were unfair. You did not choose Sparta or
Crete—your favorite models of good government—or any other Greek
53 or foreign state. You could not have absented yourself from the city
less if you had been lame or blind or decrepit in some other way. It is
quite obvious that you stand by yourself above all other Athenians in
your affection for this city and for us its laws. Who would care for a
city without laws? And now, after all this, are you not going to stand
by your agreement? Yes, you are, Socrates, if you will take our advice,
and then you will at least escape being laughed at for leaving the
city.

We invite you to consider what good you will do to yourself or
your friends if you commit this breach of faith and stain your con-
b science. It is fairly obvious that the risk of being banished and either
losing their citizenship or having their property confiscated will extend to your friends as well. As for yourself, if you go to one of the
neighboring states, such as Thebes or Megara, which are both well governed, you will enter them as an enemy to their constitution, and all
good patriots will eye you with suspicion as a destroyer of law and order. Incidentally you will confirm the opinion of the jurors who tried
c you that they gave a correct verdict; a destroyer of laws might very
well be supposed to have a destructive influence upon young and foolish human beings. Do you intend, then, to avoid well-governed states
and the higher forms of human society? And if you do, will life be
worth living? Or will you approach these people and have the impudence to converse with them? What arguments will you use, Socrates?
The same which you used here, that goodness and integrity, institutions and laws, are the most precious possessions of mankind? Do you
not think that Socrates and everything about him will appear in a dis-
d reputable light? You certainly ought to think so.

But perhaps you will retire from this part of the world and go to
Crito's friends in Thessaly? That is the home of indiscipline and laxity, and no doubt they would enjoy hearing the amusing story of how
you managed to run away from prison by arraying yourself in some
costume or putting on a shepherd's smock or some other conventional
runaway's disguise, and altering your personal appearance. And will
no one comment on the fact that an old man of your age, probably
with only a short time left to live, should dare to cling so greedily to
e life, at the price of violating the most stringent laws? Perhaps not, if
you avoid irritating anyone. Otherwise, Socrates, you will hear a good
many humiliating comments. So you will live as the toady and slave
of all the populace, literally 'roistering in Thessaly,' as though you had

left this country for Thessaly to attend a banquet there. And where will your discussions about goodness and uprightness be then, we should like to know? But of course you want to live for your chil- 54 dren's sake, so that you may be able to bring them up and educate them. Indeed! By first taking them off to Thessaly and making foreigners of them, so that they may have that additional enjoyment? Or if that is not your intention, supposing that they are brought up here with you still alive, will they be better cared for and educated without you, because of course your friends will look after them? Will they look after your children if you go away to Thessaly, and not if you go away to the next world? Surely if those who profess to be your friends b are worth anything, you must believe that they would care for them.

No, Socrates, be advised by us your guardians, and do not think more of your children or of your life or of anything else than you think of what is right, so that when you enter the next world you may have all this to plead in your defense before the authorities there. It seems clear that if you do this thing, neither you nor any of your friends will be the better for it or be more upright or have a cleaner conscience here in this world, nor will it be better for you when you reach the next. As it is, you will leave this place, when you do, as the victim of a wrong done not by us, the laws, but by your fellow men. c But if you leave in that dishonorable way, returning wrong for wrong and evil for evil, breaking your agreements and covenants with us, and injuring those whom you least ought to injure—yourself, your friends, your country, and us—then you will have to face our anger in your lifetime, and in that place beyond when the laws of the other world know that you have tried, so far as you could, to destroy even us their brothers, they will not receive you with a kindly welcome. Do not take Crito's advice, but follow ours.   d

That, my dear friend Crito, I do assure you, is what I seem to hear them saying, just as a mystic seems to hear the strains of music, and the sound of their arguments rings so loudly in my head that I cannot hear the other side. I warn you that, as my opinion stands at present, it will be useless to urge a different view. However, if you think that you will do any good by it, say what you like.

CRITO: No, Socrates, I have nothing to say.

SOCRATES: Then give it up, Crito, and let us follow this course, e since God points out the way.

PHAEDO

Some time after Socrates' death Phaedo, a devoted pupil who had been with him to the end, gives an account of his last hours to a number of his friends.

It was not until evening, he tells them, that Socrates drank the poison. The day had been passed in conversation, as was his way in prison or out, and the talk had turned on the immortality of the soul. Various so-called proofs were discussed, the chief one being that "our birth is but a sleep and a forgetting," that to learn is in part to re-member knowledge which must have been gained in another life. In the end, however, this argument is discarded with all the others. Then Socrates brings up a new idea. The soul is immortal because it can perceive, have a share in, truth, goodness, beauty, which are eter-nal. Man can know God because he has in him something akin to the eternal which cannot die. This is accepted by all present, and Soc-rates goes on to declare that only in another life can God's justice be shown and to give a lively picture of heaven and hell. But most char-acteristically he bids his hearers not to accept this description as the truth, and yet "something of the kind must be true."

So the long talk ends. The poison is drunk—one that caused no pain—and does its work. The last words Socrates speaks show better than all the arguments what he believed. As he felt the poison creeping up to his heart he said, "Crito, we ought to offer a cock to Asclepius." It was the Greek custom after recovery from an illness to make an of-fering to the divine healer, Asclepius. To himself Socrates was recover-ing, not dying. He was entering not into death, but into life, "life more abundantly."

ECHECRATES: Were you there with Socrates yourself, Phaedo, 57 when he was executed, or did you hear about it from somebody else?

PHAEDO: No, I was there myself, Echecrates.

ECHECRATES: Then what did the master say before he died, and how did he meet his end? I should very much like to know. None of the people in Phlius go to Athens much in these days, and it is a long time since we had any visitor from there who could give us any b definite information, except that he was executed by drinking hemlock. Nobody could tell us anything more than that.

PHAEDO: Then haven't you even heard how his trial went? 58

ECHECRATES: Yes, someone told us about that, and we were surprised because there was obviously a long interval between it and the execution. How was that, Phaedo?

PHAEDO: A fortunate coincidence, Echecrates. It so happened that on the day before the trial they had just finished garlanding the stern of the ship which Athens sends to Delos.

ECHECRATES: What ship is that?

PHAEDO: The Athenians say that it is the one in which Theseus sailed away to Crete with the seven youths and seven maidens, and saved their lives and his own as well. The story says that the Atheni- b ans made a vow to Apollo that if these young people's lives were saved they would send a solemn mission to Delos every year, and ever since then they have kept their vow to the god, right down to the present day. They have a law that as soon as this mission begins the city must be kept pure, and no public executions may take place until the ship has reached Delos and returned again, which sometimes takes a long time, if the winds happen to hold it back. The mission is con- c sidered to begin as soon as the priest of Apollo has garlanded the stern of the ship, and this happened, as I say, on the day before the trial. That is why Socrates spent such a long time in prison between his trial and execution.

ECHECRATES: But what about the actual circumstances of his death, Phaedo? What was said and done, and which of the master's companions were with him? Or did the authorities refuse them admission, so that he passed away without a friend at his side?

PHAEDO: Oh no, some of them were there—quite a number, d in fact.

ECHECRATES: I wish you would be kind enough to give us a really detailed account—unless you are pressed for time.

PHAEDO: No, not at all. I will try to describe it for you. Nothing gives me more pleasure than recalling the memory of Socrates, either by talking myself or by listening to someone else.

ECHECRATES: Well, Phaedo, you will find that your audience

From *The Last Days of Socrates*, translated and with an introduction by Hugh Tredennick (Penguin Classics, Harmondsworth, Middlesex, 1954).

feels just the same about it. Now try to describe every detail as carefully as you can.

e   PHAEDO: In the first place, my own feelings at the time were quite extraordinary. It never occurred to me to feel sorry for him, as you might have expected me to feel at the deathbed of a very dear friend. The master seemed quite happy, Echecrates, both in his manner and in what he said; he met his death so fearlessly and nobly. I could not help feeling that even on his way to the other world he would be under the providence of God, and that when he arrived there 59 all would be well with him, if it ever has been so with anybody. So I felt no sorrow at all, as you might have expected on such a solemn occasion, and at the same time I felt no pleasure at being occupied in our usual philosophical discussions—that was the form that our conversation took. I felt an absolutely incomprehensible emotion, a sort of curious blend of pleasure and pain combined, as my mind took it in that in a little while my friend was going to die. All of us who were there were affected in much the same way, between laughing and crying; one of us in particular, Apollodorus—you know what b he is like, don't you?

ECHECRATES: Of course I do.

PHAEDO: Well, he quite lost control of himself, and I and the others were very much upset.

ECHECRATES: Who were actually there, Phaedo?

PHAEDO: Why, of the local people there were this man Apollodorus, and Critobulus and his father, and then there were Hermogenes and Epigenes and Aeschines and Antisthenes. Oh yes, and Ctesippus of Paeania, and Menexenus, and some other local people. I believe that Plato was ill.

ECHECRATES: Were there any visitors from outside?

c   PHAEDO: Yes, Simmias of Thebes, with Cebes and Phaedondas, and Euclides and Terpsion from Megara.

ECHECRATES: Why, weren't Aristippus and Cleombrotus there?

PHAEDO: No, they were in Aegina, apparently.

ECHECRATES: Was there anybody else?

PHAEDO: I think that's about all.

ECHECRATES: Well, what form did the discussion take?

PHAEDO: I will try to tell you all about it from the very be- d ginning. We had all made it our regular practice, even in the period before, to visit Socrates every day. We used to meet at daybreak by the courthouse where the trial was held, because it was close to the prison. We always spent some time in conversation while we waited for the door to open, which was never very early, and when it did open, we used to go in to see Socrates, and generally spent the day with him. On this particular day we met earlier than usual, because e when we left the prison on the evening before, we heard that the boat had just arrived back from Delos; so we urged one another to meet at the same place as early as possible. When we arrived, the porter, instead of letting us in as usual, told us to wait and not to come in until he gave us the word. The commissioners are taking off Socrates' chains, he said, and warning him that he is to die today.

After a short interval he came back and told us to go in. When we went inside we found Socrates just released from his chains, and 60 Xanthippe—you know her!—sitting by him with the little boy on her knee. As soon as Xanthippe saw us she broke out into the sort of remark you would expect from a woman, Oh, Socrates, this is the last time that you and your friends will be able to talk together!

Socrates looked at Crito. Crito, he said, someone had better take her home.

Some of Crito's servants led her away crying hysterically. Socrates sat up on the bed and drew up his leg and massaged it, saying as b he did so, What a queer thing it is, my friends, this sensation which is popularly called pleasure! It is remarkable how closely it is connected with its conventional opposite, pain. They will never come to a man both at once, but if you pursue one of them and catch it, you are nearly always compelled to have the other as well; they are like two bodies attached to the same head. I am sure that if Aesop had thought c of it he would have made up a fable about them, something like this— God wanted to stop their continual quarreling, and when he found that it was impossible, he fastened their heads together; so wherever one of them appears, the other is sure to follow after. That is exactly what seems to be happening to me. I had a pain in my leg from the fetter, and now I feel the pleasure coming that follows it.

Here Cebes broke in and said, Oh yes, Socrates, I am glad you reminded me. Evenus asked me a day or two ago, as others have done before, about the lyrics which you have been composing lately by d adapting Aesop's fables and 'The Prelude' to Apollo. He wanted to know what induced you to write them now after you had gone to prison, when you had never done anything of the kind before. If you would like me to be able to answer Evenus when he asks me again— as I am sure he will—tell me what I am to say.

Tell him the truth, said Socrates, that I did not compose them to rival either him or his poetry—which I knew would not be easy. I did e it in the attempt to discover the meaning of certain dreams, and to clear my conscience, in case this was the art which I had been told to practice. It is like this, you see. In the course of my life I have often had the same dream, appearing in different forms at different times, but always saying the same thing, 'Socrates, practice and cultivate the arts.' In the past I used to think that it was impelling and exhorting me to do what I was actually doing; I mean that the dream, like a spectator encouraging a runner in a race, was urging me on to do what I was doing already, that is, practicing the arts, because phi- 61 losophy is the greatest of the arts, and I was practicing it. But ever since my trial, while the festival of the god has been delaying my execution, I have felt that perhaps it might be this popular form of art that the dream intended me to practice, in which case I ought to practice it and not disobey. I thought it would be safer not to take my departure before I had cleared my conscience by writing poetry and so obeying the dream. I began with some verses in honor of the god whose festival it was. When I had finished my hymn, I reflected that a poet, if he is to be worthy of the name, ought to work on imaginative themes, not descriptive ones, and I was not good at inventing stories. So I availed myself of some of Aesop's fables which were ready to hand and familiar to me, and I versified the first of them that suggested themselves. You can tell Evenus this, Cebes, and bid him farewell from me, and tell him, if he is wise, to follow me as quickly as he can. I shall be going today, it seems; those are my country's orders.

What a piece of advice for Evenus, Socrates! said Simmias. I have had a good deal to do with him before now, and from what I know of him he will not be at all ready to obey you.

Why? he asked. Isn't Evenus a philosopher?

So I believe, said Simmias.

Well then, he will be quite willing, just like anyone else who is properly grounded in philosophy. However, he will hardly do himself violence, because they say that it is not legitimate.

As he spoke he lowered his feet to the ground, and sat like this for the rest of the discussion.

Cebes now asked him, Socrates, what do you mean by saying that it is not legitimate to do oneself violence, although a philosopher will be willing to follow a friend who dies?

Why, Cebes, have you and Simmias never heard about these things while you have been with Philolaus?

Nothing definite, Socrates.

Well, even my information is only based on hearsay, but I don't mind at all telling you what I have heard. I suppose that for one who is soon to leave this world there is no more suitable occupation than inquiring into our views about the future life, and trying to imagine what it is like. What else can one do in the time before sunset?

Tell me then, Socrates, what are the grounds for saying that suicide is not legitimate? I have heard it described as wrong before now, as you suggested, both by Philolaus, when he was staying with us, and by others as well, but I have never yet heard any definite explanation for it.

Well, you must not lose heart, he said. Perhaps you will hear one someday. However, no doubt you will feel it strange that this should be the one question that has an unqualified answer—I mean, if it never happens in the case of life and death, as it does in all other connections, that sometimes and for some people death is better than life. And it probably seems strange to you that it should not be right for those to whom death would be an advantage to benefit themselves, but that they should have to await the services of someone else.

Cebes laughed gently and, dropping into his own dialect, said, Aye, that it does.

Yes, went on Socrates, put in that way it certainly might seem b unreasonable, though perhaps it has some justification. The allegory which the mystics tell us—that we men are put in a sort of guard post, from which one must not release oneself or run away—seems to me to be a high doctrine with difficult implications. All the same, Cebes, I believe that this much is true, that the gods are our keepers, and we men are one of their possessions. Don't you think so?

Yes, I do, said Cebes.

Then take your own case. If one of your possessions were to de- c stroy itself without intimation from you that you wanted it to die, wouldn't you be angry with it and punish it, if you had any means of doing so?

Certainly.

So if you look at it in this way I suppose it is not unreasonable to say that we must not put an end to ourselves until God sends some compulsion like the one which we are facing now.

That seems likely, I admit, said Cebes. But what you were saying just now, that philosophers would be readily willing to die—that seems illogical, Socrates, assuming that we were right in saying a moment ago that God is our keeper and we are his possessions. If this d service is directed by the gods, who are the very best of masters, it is inexplicable that the very wisest of men should not be grieved at quitting it, because he surely cannot expect to provide for himself any better when he is free. On the other hand a stupid person might get the idea that it would be to his advantage to escape from his master. He might not reason it out that one should not escape from a good e master, but remain with him as long as possible, and so he might run away unreflectingly. A sensible man would wish to remain always with his superior. If you look at it in this way, Socrates, the probable thing is just the opposite of what we said just now. It is natural for the wise to be grieved when they die, and for fools to be happy.

When Socrates had listened to this he seemed to me to be amused 63 at Cebes' persistence, and looking round at us he said, You know, Cebes is always investigating arguments, and he is not at all willing to accept every statement at its face value.

Simmias said, Well, but, Socrates, I think that this time there is something in what he says. Why should a really wise man want to desert masters who are better than himself, and to get rid of them so lightly? I think Cebes is aiming his criticism at you, because you are making so light of leaving us, and the gods too, who as you admit are good masters.

What you and Cebes say is perfectly fair, said Socrates. You b mean, I suppose, that I must make a formal defense against this charge.

Exactly, said Simmias.

Very well then, let me try to make a more convincing defense to you than I made at my trial. If I did not expect to enter the company, first, of other wise and good gods, and secondly of men now dead who are better than those who are in this world now, it is true that I should be wrong in not grieving at death. As it is, you can be assured that I

c expect to find myself among good men. I would not insist particularly on this point, but on the other I assure you that I shall insist most strongly—that I shall find there divine masters who are supremely good. That is why I am not so much distressed as I might be, and why I have a firm hope that there is something in store for those who have died, and, as we have been told for many years, something much better for the good than for the wicked.

Well, what is your idea, Socrates? asked Simmias. Do you mean to keep this knowledge to yourself now that you are leaving us, or will you communicate it to us too? I think that we ought to have a share in

d this comfort; besides, it will serve as your defense, if we are satisfied with what you say.

Very well, I will try, he replied. But before I begin, Crito here seems to have been wanting to say something for some time. Let us find out what it is.

Only this, Socrates, said Crito, that the man who is to give you the poison has been asking me for a long time to tell you to talk as little as possible. He says that talking makes you heated, and that you ought not to do anything to affect the action of the poison. Otherwise

e it is sometimes necessary to take a second dose, or even a third.

That is his affair, said Socrates. Let him make his own preparations for administering it twice or three times if necessary.

I was pretty sure you would say that, said Crito, but he's been bothering me for a long time.

Never mind him, said Socrates. Now for you, my jury. I want to explain to you how it seems to me natural that a man who has really devoted his life to philosophy should be cheerful in the face of death,

64 and confident of finding the greatest blessing in the next world when his life is finished. I will try to make clear to you, Simmias and Cebes, how this can be so.

Ordinary people seem not to realize that those who really apply themselves in the right way to philosophy are directly and of their own accord preparing themselves for dying and death. If this is true, and they have actually been looking forward to death all their lives, it would of course be absurd to be troubled when the thing comes for which they have so long been preparing and looking forward.

Simmias laughed and said, Upon my word, Socrates, you have

b made me laugh, though I was not at all in the mood for it. I am

sure that if they heard what you said, most people would think—and
our fellow countrymen would heartily agree—that it was a very good
hit at the philosophers to say that they are half dead already, and that
they, the normal people, are quite aware that death would serve the
philosophers right.

And they would be quite correct, Simmias—except in thinking
that they are 'quite aware.' They are not at all aware in what sense
true philosophers are half dead, or in what sense they deserve death,
or what sort of death they deserve. But let us dismiss them and talk c
among ourselves. Do we believe that there is such a thing as death?

Most certainly, said Simmias, taking up the role of answering.

Is it simply the release of the soul from the body? Is death nothing more or less than this, the separate condition of the body by itself
when it is released from the soul, and the separate condition by itself of the soul when released from the body? Is death anything else
than this?

No, just that.

Well then, my boy, see whether you agree with me. I fancy that
this will help us to find out the answer to our problem. Do you think d
that it is right for a philosopher to concern himself with the so-called
pleasures connected with food and drink?

Certainly not, Socrates, said Simmias.

What about sexual pleasures?

No, not at all.

And what about the other attentions that we pay to our bodies?
Do you think that a philosopher attaches any importance to them? I
mean things like providing himself with smart clothes and shoes and
other bodily ornaments; do you think that he values them or despises
them—in so far as there is no real necessity for him to go in for that
sort of thing? e

I think the true philosopher despises them, he said.

Then it is your opinion in general that a man of this kind is not
concerned with the body, but keeps his attention directed as much
as he can away from it and toward the soul?

Yes, it is.

So it is clear first of all in the case of physical pleasures that the
philosopher frees his soul from association with the body, so far as is 65
possible, to a greater extent than other men?

It seems so.

And most people think, do they not, Simmias, that a man who
finds no pleasure and takes no part in these things does not deserve to
live, and that anyone who thinks nothing of physical pleasures has
one foot in the grave?

That is perfectly true.

Now take the acquisition of knowledge. Is the body a hindrance
or not, if one takes it into partnership to share an investigation?

What I mean is this. Is there any certainty in human sight and
b hearing, or is it true, as the poets are always dinning into our ears,
that we neither hear nor see anything accurately? Yet if these senses
are not clear and accurate, the rest can hardly be so, because they are
all inferior to the first two. Don't you agree?

Certainly.

Then when is it that the soul attains to truth? When it tries to investigate anything with the help of the body, it is obviously led astray.

c   Quite so.

Is it not in the course of reflection, if at all, that the soul gets a
clear view of facts?

Yes.

Surely the soul can best reflect when it is free of all distractions such as hearing or sight or pain or pleasure of any kind—that
is, when it ignores the body and becomes as far as possible independent, avoiding all physical contacts and associations as much as it
can, in its search for reality.

That is so.

Then here too—in despising the body and avoiding it, and en-
d deavoring to become independent—the philosopher's soul is ahead of
all the rest.

It seems so.

Here are some more questions, Simmias. Do we recognize such a
thing as absolute uprightness?

Indeed we do.

And absolute beauty and goodness too?

Of course.

Have you ever seen any of these things with your eyes?

Certainly not, said he.

Well, have you ever apprehended them with any other bodily
sense? By 'them' I mean not only absolute tallness or health or
strength, but the real nature of any given thing—what it actually is.
e Is it through the body that we get the truest perception of them?
Isn't it true that in any inquiry you are likely to attain more nearly to
knowledge of your object in proportion to the care and accuracy
with which you have prepared yourself to understand that object in itself?

Certainly.

Don't you think that the person who is likely to succeed in this
attempt most perfectly is the one who approaches each object, as far
as possible, with the unaided intellect, without taking account of any
66 sense of sight in his thinking, or dragging any other sense into his
reckoning—the man who pursues the truth by applying his pure and
unadulterated thought to the pure and unadulterated object, cutting
himself off as much as possible from his eyes and ears and virtually all
the rest of his body, as an impediment which by its presence prevents

the soul from attaining to truth and clear thinking? Is not this the person, Simmias, who will reach the goal of reality, if anybody can?

What you say is absolutely true, Socrates, said Simmias.

All these considerations, said Socrates, must surely prompt b serious philosophers to review the position in some such way as this. It looks as though this were a bypath leading to the right track. So long as we keep to the body and our soul is contaminated with this imperfection, there is no chance of our ever attaining satisfactorily to our object, which we assert to be truth. In the first place, the body provides us with innumerable distractions in the pursuit of our necessary sustenance, and any diseases which attack us hinder our quest c for reality. Besides, the body fills us with loves and desires and fears and all sorts of fancies and a great deal of nonsense, with the result that we literally never get an opportunity to think at all about anything. Wars and revolutions and battles are due simply and solely to the body and its desires. All wars are undertaken for the acquisition of wealth, and the reason why we have to acquire wealth is the body, because we are slaves in its service. That is why, on all these ac- d counts, we have so little time for philosophy. Worst of all, if we do obtain any leisure from the body's claims and turn to some line of inquiry, the body intrudes once more into our investigations, interrupting, disturbing, distracting, and preventing us from getting a glimpse of the truth. We are in fact convinced that if we are ever to have pure knowledge of anything, we must get rid of the body and contemplate things by themselves with the soul by itself. It seems, to e judge from the argument, that the wisdom which we desire and upon which we profess to have set our hearts will be attainable only when we are dead, and not in our lifetime. If no pure knowledge is possible in the company of the body, then either it is totally impossible to acquire knowledge, or it is only possible after death, be- cause it is only then that the soul will be separate and independent of 67 the body. It seems that so long as we are alive, we shall continue closest to knowledge if we avoid as much as we can all contact and association with the body, except when they are absolutely necessary, and instead of allowing ourselves to become infected with its nature, purify ourselves from it until God himself gives us deliverance. In this way, by keeping ourselves uncontaminated by the follies of the body, we shall probably reach the company of others like ourselves and gain direct knowledge of all that is pure and uncontaminated b —that is, presumably, of truth. For one who is not pure himself to attain to the realm of purity would no doubt be a breach of universal justice.

Something to this effect, Simmias, is what I imagine all real lovers of learning must think themselves and say to one another. Don't you agree with me?

Most emphatically, Socrates.

Very well, then, said Socrates, if this is true, there is good reason for anyone who reaches the end of this journey which lies before me to hope that there, if anywhere, he will attain the object to which all our efforts have been directed during my past life. So this journey
c which is now ordained for me carries a happy prospect for any other man also who believes that his mind has been prepared by purification.

It does indeed, said Simmias.

And purification, as we saw some time ago in our discussion, consists in separating the soul as much as possible from the body, and accustoming it to withdraw from all contact with the body and con-
d centrate itself by itself, and to have its dwelling, so far as it can, both now and in the future, alone by itself, freed from the shackles of the body. Does not that follow?

Yes, it does, said Simmias.

Is not what we call death a freeing and separation of soul from body?

Certainly, he said.

And the desire to free the soul is found chiefly, or rather only, in the true philosopher. In fact the philosopher's occupation consists precisely in the freeing and separation of soul from body. Isn't that so?

Apparently.

Well then, as I said at the beginning, if a man has trained him-
e self throughout his life to live in a state as close as possible to death, would it not be ridiculous for him to be distressed when death comes to him?

It would, of course.

Then it is a fact, Simmias, that true philosophers make dying their profession, and that to them of all men death is least alarming. Look at it in this way. If they are thoroughly dissatisfied with the body, and long to have their souls independent of it, when this happens would it not be entirely unreasonable to be frightened and distressed? Would they not naturally be glad to set out for the place where there is a prospect of attaining the object of their lifelong desire
68 —which is wisdom—and of escaping from an unwelcome association? Surely there are many who have chosen of their own free will to follow dead lovers and wives and sons to the next world, in the hope of seeing and meeting there the persons whom they loved. If this is so, will a true lover of wisdom who has firmly grasped this same conviction—that he will never attain to wisdom worthy of the name else-
b where than in the next world—will he be grieved at dying? Will he not be glad to make that journey? We must suppose so, my dear boy, that is, if he is a real philosopher, because then he will be of the firm belief that he will never find wisdom in all its purity in any other place. If this is so, would it not be quite unreasonable, as I said just now, for such a man to be afraid of death?

It would, indeed.

So if you see anyone distressed at the prospect of dying, said Socrates, it will be proof enough that he is a lover not of wisdom but of the body. As a matter of fact, I suppose he is also a lover of wealth c and reputation—one or the other, or both.

Yes, you are quite right.

Doesn't it follow, Simmias, he went on, that the virtue which we call courage belongs primarily to the philosophical disposition?

Yes, no doubt it does, he said.

Self-control, too, as it is understood even in the popular sense— not being carried away by the desires, but preserving a decent indifference toward them—is not this appropriate only to those who regard the body with the greatest indifference and spend their lives in philosophy?

Certainly, he said. d

If you care to consider courage and self-control as practiced by other people, said Socrates, you will find them illogical.

How so, Socrates?

You know, don't you, that everyone except the philosopher regards death as a great evil?

Yes, indeed.

Isn't it true that when a brave man faces death he does so through fear of something worse?

Yes, it is true.

So in everyone except the philosopher courage is due to fear and dread, although it is illogical that fear and cowardice should make a man brave.

Quite so. e

What about temperate people? Is it not, in just the same way, a sort of self-indulgence that makes them self-controlled? We may say that this is impossible, but all the same those who practice this simple form of self-control are in much the same case as that which I have just described. They are afraid of losing other pleasures which they desire, so they refrain from one kind because they cannot resist the other. Although they define self-indulgence as the condition of being ruled by pleasure, it is really because they cannot resist some 69 pleasures that they succeed in resisting others, which amounts to what I said just now—that they control themselves, in a sense, by self-indulgence.

Yes, that seems to be true.

I congratulate you on your perception, Simmias. No, I am afraid that, from the moral standpoint, it is not the right method to exchange one degree of pleasure or pain or fear for another, like coins of different values. There is only one currency for which all these tokens of ours should be exchanged, and that is wisdom. In fact, it is wisdom that makes possible courage and self-control and integrity or, b in a word, true goodness, and the presence or absence of pleasures and fears and other such feelings makes no difference at all, whereas a system of morality which is based on relative emotional values is a mere illusion, a thoroughly vulgar conception which has nothing sound in it and nothing true. The true moral ideal, whether self-control or integrity or courage, is really a kind of purgation from all these c emotions, and wisdom itself is a sort of purification. Perhaps these people who direct the religious initiations are not so far from the mark, and all the time there has been an allegorical meaning beneath their doctrine that he who enters the next world uninitiated and unenlightened shall lie in the mire, but he who arrives there purified and enlightened shall dwell among the gods. You know how the initid ation practitioners say, 'Many bear the emblems, but the devotees are few'? Well, in my opinion these devotees are simply those who have lived the philosophical life in the right way—a company which, all through my life, I have done my best in every way to join, leaving nothing undone which I could do to attain this end. Whether I was right in this ambition, and whether we have achieved anything, we shall know for certain, if God wills, when we reach the other world, and that, I imagine, will be fairly soon.

This is the defense which I offer you, Simmias and Cebes, to show that it is natural for me to leave you and my earthly rulers e without any feeling of grief or bitterness, since I believe that I shall find there, no less than here, good rulers and good friends. If I am any more convincing in my defense to you than I was to my Athenian jury, I shall be satisfied.

When Socrates had finished, Cebes made his reply. The rest of 70 your statement, Socrates, he said, seems excellent to me, but what you said about the soul leaves the average person with grave misgivings that when it is released from the body it may no longer exist anywhere, but may be dispersed and destroyed on the very day that the man himself dies, as soon as it is freed from the body, that as it emerges it may be dissipated like breath or smoke, and vanish away, so that nothing is left of it anywhere. Of course if it still existed as an independent unity, released from all the evils which you have just described, there would be a strong and glorious hope, Socrates, that b what you say is true. But I fancy that it requires no little faith and assurance to believe that the soul exists after death and retains some active force and intelligence.

Quite true, Cebes, said Socrates. But what are we to do about it? Is it your wish that we should go on speculating about the subject, to see whether this view is likely to be true or not?

For my part, said Cebes, I should be very glad to hear what you think about it.

At any rate, said Socrates, I hardly think that anyone who heard c us now—even a comic poet—would say that I am wasting time and discoursing on subjects which do not concern me. So if that is how you feel, we had better continue our inquiry. Let us approach it from this point of view. Do the souls of the departed exist in another world or not?

There is an old legend, which we still remember, to the effect that they *do* exist there, after leaving here, and that they return again to this world and come into being from the dead. If this is so—that the living come into being again from the dead—does it not follow that d our souls exist in the other world? They could not come into being again if they did not exist, and it will be sufficient proof that my contention is true if it really becomes apparent that the living come from the dead, and from nowhere else. But if this is not so, we shall need some other argument.

Quite so, said Cebes.

If you want to understand the question more readily, said Socrates, consider it with reference not only to human beings but to all animals and plants. Let us see whether in general everything that admits of generation is generated in this way and no other—opposites e from opposites, wherever there is an opposite—as for instance beauty is opposite to ugliness and right to wrong, and there are countless other examples. Let us consider whether it is a necessary law that everything which has an opposite is generated from that opposite and from no other source. For example, when a thing becomes bigger, it must, I suppose, have been smaller first before it became bigger?

Yes.

And similarly if it becomes smaller, it must be bigger first, and become smaller afterward? 71

That is so, said Cebes.

And the weaker comes from the stronger, and the faster from the slower?

Certainly.

One more instance. If a thing becomes worse, is it not from being better? And if more just, from being more unjust?

Of course.

Are we satisfied, then, said Socrates, that everything is generated in this way—opposites from opposites?

Perfectly.

Here is another question. Do not these examples present another feature, that between each pair of opposites there are two processes of generation, one from the first to the second, and another from the b second to the first? Between a larger and a smaller object are there not the processes of increase and decrease, and do we not describe them in this way as increasing and decreasing?

Yes, said Cebes.

Is it not the same with separating and combining, cooling and heating, and all the rest of them? Even if we sometimes do not use

the actual terms, must it not in fact hold good universally that they
come one from the other, and that there is a process of generation
from each to the other?

Certainly, said Cebes.

c   Well then, said Socrates, is there an opposite to living, as sleeping is opposite to waking?

Certainly.

What?

Being dead.

So if they are opposites, they come from one another, and have
their two processes of generation between the two of them?

Of course.

Very well, then, said Socrates, I will state one pair of opposites
which I mentioned just now—the opposites themselves and the processes between them—and you shall state the other. My opposites are
sleeping and waking, and I say that waking comes from sleeping and

d   sleeping from waking, and that the processes between them are going
to sleep and waking up. Does that satisfy you, he asked, or not?

Perfectly.

Now you tell me in the same way, he went on, about life and
death. Do you not admit that death is the opposite of life?

I do.

And that they come from one another?

Yes.

Then what comes from the living?

The dead.

And what, asked Socrates, comes from the dead?

I must admit, he said, that it is the living.

So it is from the dead, Cebes, that living things and people come?

e   Evidently.

Then our souls do exist in the next world.

So it seems.

And one of the two processes in this case is really quite certain—
dying is certain enough, isn't it?

Yes, it is, said Cebes.

What shall we do, then? Shall we omit the complementary process, and leave a defect here in the law of nature? Or must we supply
an opposite process to that of dying?

Surely we must supply it, he said.

And what is it?

Coming to life again.

Then if there is such a thing as coming to life again, said Soc-

72 rates, it must be a process from death to life?

Quite so.

So we agree upon this too—that the living have come from the
dead no less than the dead from the living. But I think we decided

that if this was so, it was a sufficient proof that the souls of the dead must exist in some place from which they are reborn.

It seems to me, Socrates, he said, that this follows necessarily from our agreement.

I think there is another way too, Cebes, in which you can see that we were not wrong in our agreement. If there were not a constant correspondence in the process of generation between the two sets of opposites, going round in a sort of cycle, if generation were a straight b path to the opposite extreme without any return to the starting point or any deflection, do you realize that in the end everything would have the same quality and reach the same state, and change would cease altogether?

What do you mean?

Nothing difficult to understand, replied Socrates. For example, if 'falling asleep' existed, and 'waking up' did not balance it by making something come out of sleep, you must realize that in the end everything would make Endymion look foolish. He would be nowhere, because the whole world would be in the same state—asleep. And if c everything were combined and nothing separated, we should soon have Anaxagoras' 'all things together.' In just the same way, my dear Cebes, if everything that has some share of life were to die, and if after death the dead remained in that form and did not come to life again, would it not be quite inevitable that in the end everything should be dead and nothing alive? If living things came from other living things, and the living things died, what possible means could d prevent their number from being exhausted by death?

None that I can see, Socrates, said Cebes. What you say seems to be perfectly true.

Yes, Cebes, he said, if anything is true, I believe that this is, and we were not mistaken in our agreement upon it. Coming to life again is a fact, and it is a fact that the living come from the dead, and a fact that the souls of the dead exist. e

Besides, Socrates, rejoined Cebes, there is that theory which you have often described to us—that what we call learning is really just recollection. If that is true, then surely what we recollect now we must have learned at some time before, which is impossible unless our souls existed somewhere before they entered this human shape. So in that way too it seems likely that the soul is immortal. 73

How did the proofs of that theory go, Cebes? broke in Simmias. Remind me, because at the moment I can't quite remember.

One very good argument, said Cebes, is that when people are asked questions, if the question is put in the right way they can give a perfectly correct answer, which they could not possibly do unless they had some knowledge and a proper grasp of the subject. And then if you confront people with a diagram or anything like that, the way b in which they react is an unmistakable proof that the theory is correct.

And if you don't find that convincing, Simmias, said Socrates, see whether this appeals to you. I suppose that you find it hard to understand how what we call learning can be recollection?

Not at all, said Simmias. All that I want is to be helped to do what we are talking about—to recollect. I can practically remember enough to satisfy me already, from Cebes' approach to the subject, but I should be nonetheless glad to hear how you meant to approach it.

c   I look at it in this way, said Socrates. We are agreed, I suppose, that if a person is to be reminded of anything, he must first know it at some time or other?

Quite so.

Are we also agreed in calling it recollection when knowledge comes in a particular way? I will explain what I mean. Suppose that a person on seeing or hearing or otherwise noticing one thing not only becomes conscious of that thing but also thinks of a something else which is an object of a different sort of knowledge. Are we not justified

d   in saying that he was reminded of the object which he thought of?

What do you mean?

Let me give you an example. A human being and a musical instrument, I suppose you will agree, are different objects of knowledge.

Yes, certainly.

Well, you know what happens to lovers when they see a musical instrument or a piece of clothing or any other private property of the person whom they love. When they recognize the thing, their minds conjure up a picture of its owner. That is recollection. In the same way the sight of Simmias often reminds one of Cebes, and of course there are thousands of other examples.

Yes, of course there are, said Simmias.

e   So by recollection we mean the sort of experience which I have just described, especially when it happens with reference to things which we had not seen for such a long time that we had forgotten them.

Quite so.

Well, then, is it possible for a person who sees a picture of a horse or a musical instrument to be reminded of a person, or for someone who sees a picture of Simmias to be reminded of Cebes?

Perfectly.

And is it possible for someone who sees a portrait of Simmias to be reminded of Simmias himself?

74   Yes, it is.

Does it not follow from all this that recollection may be caused either by similar or by dissimilar objects?

Yes, it does.

When you are reminded by similarity, surely you must also be conscious whether the similarity is perfect or only partial.

Yes, you must.

Here is a further step, said Socrates. We admit, I suppose, that there is such a thing as equality—not the equality of stick to stick and stone to stone, and so on, but something beyond all that and distinct from it—absolute equality. Are we to admit this or not?

Yes indeed, said Simmias, most emphatically.   b

And do we know what it is?

Certainly.

Where did we get our knowledge? Was it not from the particular examples that we mentioned just now? Was it not from seeing equal sticks or stones or other equal objects that we got the notion of equality, although it is something quite distinct from them? Look at it in this way. Is it not true that equal stones and sticks sometimes, without changing in themselves, appear equal to one person and unequal to another?

Certainly.

Well, now, have you ever thought that things which were abso- c lutely equal were unequal, or that equality was inequality?

No, never, Socrates.

Then these equal things are not the same as absolute equality.

Not in the least, as I see it, Socrates.

And yet it is these equal things that have suggested and conveyed to you your knowledge of absolute equality, although they are distinct from it?

Perfectly true.

Whether it is similar to them or dissimilar?

Certainly.

It makes no difference, said Socrates. So long as the sight of one thing suggests another to you, it must be a cause of recollection, d whether the two things are alike or not.

Quite so.

Well, now, he said, what do we find in the case of the equal sticks and other things of which we were speaking just now? Do they seem to us to be equal in the sense of absolute equality, or do they fall short of it in so far as they only approximate to equality? Or don't they fall short at all?

They do, said Simmias, a long way.

Suppose that when you see something you say to yourself, This thing which I can see has a tendency to be like something else, but it falls short and cannot be really like it, only a poor imitation. Don't e you agree with me that anyone who receives that impression must in fact have previous knowledge of that thing which he says that the other resembles, but inadequately?

Certainly he must.

Very well, then, is that our position with regard to equal things and absolute equality?

Exactly.

75 Then we must have had some previous knowledge of equality before the time when we first saw equal things and realized that they were striving after equality, but fell short of it.

That is so.

And at the same time we are agreed also upon this point, that we have not and could not have acquired this notion of equality except by sight or touch or one of the other senses. I am treating them as being all the same.

They are the same, Socrates, for the purpose of our argument.

So it must be through the senses that we obtained the notion that all sensible equals are striving after absolute equality but fall-
b ing short of it. Is that correct?

Yes, it is.

So before we began to see and hear and use our other senses we must somewhere have acquired the knowledge that there is such a thing as absolute equality. Otherwise we could never have realized, by using it as a standard for comparison, that all equal objects of sense are desirous of being like it, but are only imperfect copies.

That is the logical conclusion, Socrates.

Did we not begin to see and hear and possess our other senses from the moment of birth?

Certainly.

c But we admitted that we must have obtained our knowledge of equality before we obtained them.

Yes.

So we must have obtained it before birth.

So it seems.

Then if we obtained it before our birth, and possessed it when we were born, we had knowledge, both before and at the moment of birth, not only of equality and relative magnitudes, but of all absolute standards. Our present argument applies no more to equality than it
d does to absolute beauty, goodness, uprightness, holiness, and, as I maintain, all those characteristics which we designate in our discussions by the term 'absolute.' So we must have obtained knowledge of all these characteristics before our birth.

That is so.

And unless we invariably forget it after obtaining it we must always be born *knowing* and continue to *know* all through our lives, because 'to know' means simply to retain the knowledge which one has acquired, and not to lose it. Is not what we call 'forgetting' simply the loss of knowledge, Simmias?
e Most certainly, Socrates.

And if it is true that we acquired our knowledge before our birth, and lost it at the moment of birth, but afterward, by the exercise of our senses upon sensible objects, recover the knowledge which we had once before, I suppose that what we call learning will be the recovery of our own knowledge, and surely we should be right in calling this recollection.

Quite so.

Yes, because we saw that it is possible for the perception of an 76 object by sight or hearing or any of the other senses to suggest to the percipient, through association, whether there is any similarity or not, another object which he has forgotten. So, as I maintain, there are two alternatives. Either we are all born with knowledge of these standards, and retain it throughout our lives, or else, when we speak of people learning, they are simply recollecting what they knew before. In other words, learning is recollection.

Yes, that must be so, Socrates.

Which do you choose, then, Simmias? That we are born with knowledge, or that we recollect after we are born the things of which b we possessed knowledge before we were born?

I don't know which to choose on the spur of the moment, Socrates.

Well, here is another choice for you to make. What do you think about this? Can a person who knows a subject thoroughly explain what he knows?

Most certainly he can.

Do you think that everyone can explain these questions about which we have just been talking?

I should like to think so, said Simmias, but I am very much afraid that by this time tomorrow there will be no one on this earth who can do it properly.

So you don't think, Simmias, that everyone has knowledge about c them?

Far from it.

Then they just recollect what they once learned.

That must be the right answer.

When do our souls acquire this knowledge? It cannot be after the beginning of our mortal life.

No, of course not.

Then it must be before.

Yes.

Then our souls had a previous existence, Simmias, before they took on this human shape. They were independent of our bodies, and they were possessed of intelligence.

Unless perhaps it is at the moment of birth that we acquire knowledge of these things, Socrates. There is still that time available.

No doubt, my dear fellow, but just tell me, what other time is d there to lose it in? We have just agreed that we do not possess it when we are born. Do we lose it at the same moment that we acquire it? Or can you suggest any other time?

No, of course not, Socrates. I didn't realize what nonsense I was talking.

Well, how do we stand now, Simmias? If all these absolute realities, such as beauty and goodness, which we are always talking about, really exist, if it is to them, as we rediscover our own former knowledge of them, that we refer, as copies to their patterns, all the objects
e of our physical perception—if these realities exist, does it not follow that our souls must exist too even before our birth, whereas if they do not exist, our discussion would seem to be a waste of time? Is this the position, that it is logically just as certain that our souls exist before our birth as it is that these realities exist, and that if the one is impossible, so is the other?

It is perfectly obvious to me, Socrates, said Simmias, that the same logical necessity applies to both. It suits me very well that your
77 argument should rely upon the point that our soul's existence before our birth stands or falls with the existence of your grade of reality. I cannot imagine anything more self-evident than the fact that absolute beauty and goodness and all the rest that you mentioned just now exist in the fullest possible sense. In my opinion the proof is quite satisfactory.

What about Cebes? said Socrates. We must convince Cebes too.

To the best of my belief he is satisfied, replied Simmias. It is true that he is the most obstinate person in the world at resisting an
b argument, but I should think that he needs nothing more to convince him that our souls existed before our birth. As for their existing after we are dead as well, even I don't feel that that has been proved, Socrates. Cebes' objection still holds—the common fear that a man's soul may be disintegrated at the very moment of his death, and that this may be the end of its existence. Supposing that it *is* born and constituted from some source or other, and exists before it enters a human body. After it has entered one, is there any reason why, at the moment of release, it should not come to an end and be destroyed itself?
c Quite right, Simmias, said Cebes. It seems that we have got the proof of one half of what we wanted—that the soul existed before birth—but now we need also to prove that it will exist after death no less than before birth, if our proof is to be complete.

As a matter of fact, my dear Simmias and Cebes, said Socrates, it is proved already, if you will combine this last argument with the one about which we agreed before, that every living thing comes from the dead. If the soul exists before birth, and if when it proceeds
d toward life and is born it must be born from death or the dead state, surely it must also exist after death, if it must be born again. So the

point which you mention has been proved already. But in spite of
this I believe that you and Simmias would like to spin out the discussion still more. You are afraid, as children are, that when the soul
emerges from the body the wind may really puff it away and scatter
it, especially when a person does not die on a calm day but with a   e
gale blowing.

Cebes laughed. Suppose that we are afraid, Socrates, he said, and
try to convince us. Or rather don't suppose that it is we that are
afraid. Probably even in us there is a little boy who has these childish
terrors. Try to persuade him not to be afraid of death as though it
were a bogy.

What you should do, said Socrates, is to say a magic spell over
him every day until you have charmed his fears away.

But, Socrates, said Simmias, where shall we find a magician who   78
understands these spells now that you . . . are leaving us?

Greece is a large country, Cebes, he replied, which must have
good men in it, and there are many foreign races too. You must ran-
sack all of them in your search for this magician, without sparing
money or trouble, because you could not spend your money more op-
portunely on any other object. And you must search also by your own
united efforts, because it is probable that you would not easily find
anyone better fitted for the task.

We will see to that, said Cebes. But let us return to the point
where we left off, if you have no objection.   b

Of course not. Why should I?

Thank you, said Cebes.

We ought, I think, said Socrates, to ask ourselves this. What sort
of thing is it that would naturally suffer the fate of being dispersed?
For what sort of thing should we fear this fate, and for what should
we not? When we have answered this, we should next consider to
which class the soul belongs, and then we shall know whether to
feel confidence or fear about the fate of our souls.

Quite true.

Would you not expect a composite object or a natural compound   c
to be liable to break up where it was put together? And ought not
anything which is really incomposite to be the one thing of all others
which is not affected in this way?

That seems to be the case, said Cebes.

Is it not extremely probable that what is always constant and
invariable is incomposite, and what is inconstant and variable is composite?

That is how it seems to me.

Then let us return to the same examples which we were discussing before. Does that absolute reality which we define in our discus- d
sions remain always constant and invariable, or not? Does absolute
equality or beauty or any other independent entity which really exists

ever admit change of any kind? Or does each one of these uniform
and independent entities remain always constant and invariable,
never admitting any alteration in any respect or in any sense?

They must be constant and invariable, Socrates, said Cebes.

Well, what about the concrete instances of beauty—such as men,
e horses, clothes, and so on—or of equality, or any other members of
a class corresponding to an absolute entity? Are they constant, or are
they, on the contrary, scarcely ever in the same relation in any sense
either to themselves or to one another?

With them, Socrates, it is just the opposite; they are never free
from variation.

79   And these concrete objects you can touch and see and perceive
by your other senses, but those constant entities you cannot possibly
apprehend except by thinking; they are invisible to our sight.

That is perfectly true, said Cebes.

So you think that we should assume two classes of things, one
visible and the other invisible?

Yes, we should.

The invisible being invariable, and the visible never being the
same?

Yes, we should assume that too.

b   Well, now, said Socrates, are we not part body, part soul?

Certainly.

Then to which class do we say that the body would have the
closer resemblance and relation?

Quite obviously to the visible.

And the soul, is it visible or invisible?

Invisible to men, at any rate, Socrates, he said.

But surely we have been speaking of things visible or invisible to
our human nature. Do you think that we had some other nature in
view?

No, human nature.

What do we say about the soul, then? Is it visible or invisible?

Not visible.

Invisible, then?

Yes.

So soul is more like the invisible, and body more like the visible?

c   That follows inevitably, Socrates.

Did we not say some time ago that when the soul uses the instrumentality of the body for any inquiry, whether through sight or
hearing or any other sense—because using the body implies using
the senses—it is drawn away by the body into the realm of the variable, and loses its way and becomes confused and dizzy, as though it
were fuddled, through contact with things of a similar nature?

Certainly.

d   But when it investigates by itself, it passes into the realm of the pure and everlasting and immortal and changeless, and being of a kindred nature, when it is once independent and free from interference, consorts with it always and strays no longer, but remains, in that realm of the absolute, constant and invariable, through contact with beings of a similar nature. And this condition of the soul we call wisdom.

An excellent description, and perfectly true, Socrates.

Very well, then, in the light of all that we have said, both now and before, to which class do you think that the soul bears the closer e resemblance and relation?

I think, Socrates, said Cebes, that even the dullest person would agree, from this line of reasoning, that the soul is in every possible way more like the invariable than the variable.

And the body?

To the other.

Look at it in this way too. When soul and body are both in the same place, nature teaches the one to serve and be subject, the other 80 to rule and govern. In this relation which do you think resembles the divine and which the mortal part? Don't you think that it is the nature of the divine to rule and direct, and that of the mortal to be subject and serve?

I do.

Then which does the soul resemble?

Obviously, Socrates, soul resembles the divine, and body the mortal.

Now, Cebes, he said, see whether this is our conclusion from all that we have said. The soul is most like that which is divine, im- b mortal, intelligible, uniform, indissoluble, and ever self-consistent and invariable, whereas body is most like that which is human, mortal, multiform, unintelligible, dissoluble, and never self-consistent. Can we adduce any conflicting argument, my dear Cebes, to show that this is not so?

No, we cannot.

Very well, then, in that case is it not natural for body to disintegrate rapidly, but for soul to be quite or very nearly indissoluble?

Certainly. c

Of course you know that when a person dies, although it is natural for the visible and physical part of him, which lies here in the visible world and which we call his corpse, to decay and fall to pieces and be dissipated, none of this happens to it immediately. It remains as it was for quite a long time, even if death takes place when the body is well nourished and in the warm season. Indeed, when the body is dried and embalmed, as in Egypt, it remains almost intact for an incredible time, and even if the rest of the body decays, some parts of it—the bones and sinews and anything else like them—are prac- d tically everlasting. That is so, is it not?

Yes.

But the soul, the invisible part, which goes away to a place that is, like itself, glorious, pure, and invisible—the true Hades or unseen world—into the presence of the good and wise God, where, if God so wills, my soul must shortly go—will it, if its very nature is such as I have described, be dispersed and destroyed at the moment of its re-
e lease from the body, as is the popular view? Far from it, my dear Simmias and Cebes. The truth is much more like this. If at its release the soul is pure and carries with it no contamination of the body, be-cause it has never willingly associated with it in life, but has shunned it and kept itself separate as its regular practice—in other words, if it has pursued philosophy in the right way and really practiced how
81 to face death easily—this is what 'practicing death' means, isn't it?

Most decidedly.

Very well, if this is its condition, then it departs to that place which is, like itself, invisible, divine, immortal, and wise, where, on its arrival, happiness awaits it, and release from uncertainty and folly, from fears and uncontrolled desires, and all other human evils, and where, as they say of the initiates in the Mysteries, it really spends the rest of time with God. Shall we adopt this view, Cebes, or some other?

This one, by all means, said Cebes.

b But, I suppose, if at the time of its release the soul is tainted and impure, because it has always associated with the body and cared for it and loved it, and has been so beguiled by the body and its passions and pleasures that nothing seems real to it but those physical things which can be touched and seen and eaten and drunk and used for sexual enjoyment, and if it is accustomed to hate and fear and avoid what is invisible and hidden from our eyes, but intelligible and com-prehensible by philosophy—if the soul is in this state, do you think
c that it will escape independent and uncontaminated?

That would be quite impossible, he said.

On the contrary, it will, I imagine, be permeated by the corporeal, which fellowship and intercourse with the body will have ingrained in its very nature through constant association and long practice.

Certainly.

And we must suppose, my dear fellow, that the corporeal is heavy, oppressive, earthly, and visible. So the soul which is tainted by its presence is weighed down and dragged back into the visible world, through fear, as they say, of Hades or the invisible, and hovers
d about tombs and graveyards. The shadowy apparitions which have actually been seen there are the ghosts of those souls which have not got clear away, but still retain some portion of the visible, which is why they can be seen.

That seems likely enough, Socrates.

Yes, it does, Cebes. Of course these are not the souls of the good, but of the wicked, and they are compelled to wander about these places as a punishment for their bad conduct in the past. They continue wandering until at last, through craving for the corporeal, which unceasingly pursues them, they are imprisoned once more in a e body. And as you might expect, they are attached to the same sort of character or nature which they have developed during life.

What sort do you mean, Socrates?

Well, those who have cultivated gluttony or selfishness or drunkenness, instead of taking pains to avoid them, are likely to assume the form of donkeys and other perverse animals. Don't you think so? 82

Yes, that is very likely.

And those who have deliberately preferred a life of irresponsible lawlessness and violence become wolves and hawks and kites, unless we can suggest any other more likely animals.

No, the ones which you mention are exactly right.

So it is easy to imagine into what sort of animals all the other kinds of soul will go, in accordance with their conduct during life.

Yes, certainly.

I suppose that the happiest people, and those who reach the best destination, are the ones who have cultivated the goodness of an ordinary citizen—what is called self-control and integrity—which is acquired by habit and practice, without the help of philosophy and b reason.

How are these the happiest?

Because they will probably pass into some other kind of social and disciplined creature like bees, wasps, and ants, or even back into the human race again, becoming decent citizens.

Very likely.

But no soul which has not practiced philosophy, and is not absolutely pure when it leaves the body, may attain to the divine nature; c that is only for the lover of wisdom. This is the reason, my dear Simmias and Cebes, why true philosophers abstain from all bodily desires and withstand them and do not yield to them. It is not because they are afraid of financial loss or poverty, like the average man who thinks of money first, nor because they shrink from dishonor and a bad reputation, like those who are ambitious for distinction and authority.

No, those would be unworthy motives, Socrates, said Cebes.

They would indeed, he agreed. And so, Cebes, those who care d about their souls and do not subordinate them to the body dissociate themselves firmly from these others and refuse to accompany them on their haphazard journey, and, believing that it is wrong to oppose philosophy with her offer of liberation and purification, they turn and follow her wherever she leads.

What do you mean, Socrates?

I will explain, he said. Every seeker after wisdom knows that up
e to the time when philosophy takes it over his soul is a helpless
prisoner, chained hand and foot in the body, compelled to view
reality not directly but only through its prison bars, and wallowing
in utter ignorance. And philosophy can see that the imprisonment is
83 ingeniously effected by the prisoner's own active desire, which makes
him first accessory to his own confinement. Well, philosophy takes
over the soul in this condition and by gentle persuasion tries to set it
free. She points out that observation by means of the eyes and ears
and all the other senses is entirely deceptive, and she urges the soul to
refrain from using them unless it is necessary to do so, and encourages it to collect and concentrate itself by itself, trusting noth-
b ing but its own independent judgment upon objects considered in
themselves, and attributing no truth to anything which it views
indirectly as being subject to variation, because such objects are sensible and visible but what the soul itself sees is intelligible and invisible. Now the soul of the true philosopher feels that it must not reject
this opportunity for release, and so it abstains as far as possible from
pleasures and desires and griefs, because it reflects that the result
of giving way to pleasure or fear or desire is not as might be supposed
the trivial misfortune of becoming ill or wasting money through
c self-indulgence, but the last and worst calamity of all, which the
sufferer does not recognize.

What is that, Socrates? asked Cebes.

When anyone's soul feels a keen pleasure or pain it cannot help
supposing that whatever causes the most violent emotion is the plain-
est and truest reality, which it is not. It is chiefly visible things that
have this effect, isn't it?

Quite so.

d   Is it not on this sort of occasion that soul passes most completely into the bondage of body?

How do you make that out?

Because every pleasure or pain has a sort of rivet with which it
fastens the soul to the body and pins it down and makes it corporeal,
accepting as true whatever the body certifies. The result of agreeing
with the body and finding pleasure in the same things is, I imagine,
that it cannot help becoming like it in character and training, so that
it can never get entirely away to the unseen world, but is always saturated with the body when it sets out, and so soon falls back again into
e another body, where it takes root and grows. Consequently it is excluded from all fellowship with the pure and uniform and divine.

Yes, that is perfectly true, Socrates, said Cebes.

It is for these reasons, Cebes, that true philosophers exhibit self-
control and courage—not for the reasons which are generally supposed. Or do you think that the popular view is right?
84   No, certainly not.

No, indeed. A philosopher's soul will take the view which I have described. It will not first expect to be set free by philosophy, and then allow pleasure and pain to reduce it once more to bondage, thus taking upon itself an endless task, like Penelope when she undid her own weaving. No, this soul secures immunity from its desires by following reason and abiding always in her company, and by contemplating the true and divine and unconjecturable, and drawing inspiration from it, because such a soul believes that this is the right way to live while life endures, and that after death it reaches a place b which is kindred and similar to its own nature, and there is rid forever of human ills. After such a training, my dear Simmias and Cebes, the soul can have no grounds for fearing that on its separation from the body it will be blown away and scattered by the winds, and so disappear into thin air, and cease to exist altogether.

There was silence for some time after Socrates had said this. He c himself, to judge from his appearance, was still occupied with the argument which he had just been stating, and so were most of us, but Simmias and Cebes went on talking in a low voice.

When Socrates noticed them he said, Why, do you feel that my account is inadequate? Of course it is still open to a number of doubts and objections, if you want to examine it in detail. If it is something else that you two are considering, never mind, but if you feel any difficulty about our discussion, don't hesitate to put forward your own views, and point out any way in which you think that my account could be improved. And by all means make use of my services d too, if you think I can help at all to solve the difficulty.

Very well, Socrates, said Simmias, I will be quite open with you. We have both been feeling difficulties for some time, and each of us has been urging the other to ask questions. We are anxious to have your answers, but we did not like to bother you, for fear of annoying you in your present misfortune.

When Socrates heard this he laughed gently and said, I am surprised at you, Simmias. I shall certainly find it difficult to convince the outside world that I do not regard my present lot as a misfortune if I cannot even convince you, and you are afraid that I am more e irritable now than I used to be. Evidently you think that I have less insight into the future than a swan; because when these birds feel that the time has come for them to die, they sing more loudly and sweetly than they have sung in all their lives before, for joy that they are going away into the presence of the god whose servants they are. It is 85 quite wrong for human beings to make out that the swans sing their last song as an expression of grief at their approaching end. People who say this are misled by their own fear of death, and fail to reflect that no bird sings when it is hungry or cold or distressed in any other way—not even the nightingale or swallow or hoopoe, whose song is supposed to be a lament. In my opinion neither they nor the swans

sing because they are sad. I believe that the swans, belonging as they
b do to Apollo, have prophetic powers and sing because they know the
good things that await them in the unseen world, and they are happier on that day than they have ever been before. Now I consider that
I am in the same service as the swans, and dedicated to the same god,
and that I am no worse endowed with prophetic powers by my master
than they are, and no more disconsolate at leaving this life. So far as
that fear of yours is concerned, you may say and ask whatever you
like, so long as the Athenian officers of justice permit.

Thank you, said Simmias. I will tell you my difficulty first and
c then Cebes shall tell you where he finds your theory unacceptable. I
think, just as you do, Socrates, that although it is very difficult if not
impossible in this life to achieve certainty about these questions, at
the same time it is utterly feeble not to use every effort in testing the
available theories, or to leave off before we have considered them
in every way, and come to the end of our resources. It is our duty to do
one of two things, either to ascertain the facts, whether by seeking
instruction or by personal discovery, or, if this is impossible, to select
the best and most dependable theory which human intelligence can
d supply, and use it as a raft to ride the seas of life—that is, assuming
that we cannot make our journey with greater confidence and security by the surer means of a divine revelation. And so now, after what
you have said, I shall not let any diffidence prevent me from asking
my question, and so make me blame myself afterward for not having
spoken my mind now. The fact is, Socrates, that on thinking it over,
and discussing it with Cebes here, I feel that your theory has serious flaws in it.

e   Your feeling is very likely right, my dear boy, said Socrates, but
tell me where you think the flaws are.

What I mean is this, said Simmias. You might say the same
thing about tuning the strings of a musical instrument, that the attunement is something invisible and incorporeal and splendid and
divine, and located in the tuned instrument, while the instrument
86 itself and its strings are material and corporeal and composite and
earthly and closely related to what is mortal. Now suppose that the
instrument is broken, or its strings cut or snapped. According to your
theory the attunement must still exist—it cannot have been destroyed,
because it would be inconceivable that when the strings are broken
the instrument and the strings themselves, which have a mortal
nature, should still exist, and the attunement, which shares the nature
and characteristics of the divine and immortal, should exist no
b longer, having predeceased its mortal counterpart. You would say
that the attunement must still exist somewhere just as it was, and
that the wood and strings will rot away before anything happens to it.
I say this, Socrates, because, as I think you yourself are aware, we
Pythagoreans have a theory of the soul which is roughly like this.

The body is held together at a certain tension between the extremes of hot and cold, and dry and wet, and so on, and our soul is a temperament or adjustment of these same extremes, when they are combined in just the right proportion. Well, if the soul is really an adjustment, c obviously as soon as the tension of our body is lowered or increased beyond the proper point, the soul must be destroyed, divine though it is—just like any other adjustment, either in music or in any product of the arts and crafts, although in each case the physical remains last considerably longer until they are burned up or rot away. Find us an answer to this argument, if someone insists that the soul, being a d temperament of physical constituents, is the first thing to be destroyed by what we call death.

Socrates opened his eyes very wide—a favorite trick of his—and smiled. Really, he said, Simmias' criticism is quite justified, so if any of you are readier-witted than I am, you had better answer him. It seems to me that he is not handling the argument at all badly. However, before we have the answer, I think we should hear what criticisms Cebes has to make in his turn, so that we may have time e to decide what we shall say. When we have heard him, we must either agree with them if they seem to be at all on the right note, or if not, we must then proceed to champion our theory.

Come on, Cebes, he said, tell us what has been troubling you.

Very well, said Cebes. It seems to me that the argument is just where it was. I mean that it is open to the same criticism that we made before. The proof that our soul existed before it took on this 87 present shape is perfectly satisfying—I might even say convincing. I am not changing my position about that. But as for its still existing somewhere after we are dead, I think that the proof fails in this way. Mind you, I don't agree with Simmias' objection that soul is not stronger and more durable than body; it seems to me to be far superior in every way like that. Then why, your theory might inquire, are you still skeptical, when you can see that after a man dies even the weaker part of him continues to exist? Don't you think the more durable part of him must logically survive as long?

Well, here is my answer. I want you to consider whether there is b anything in what I say—because like Simmias I must have recourse to an illustration. Suppose that an elderly tailor has just died. Your theory would be just like saying that the man is not dead, but still exists somewhere safe and sound, and offering as proof the fact that the coat which he had made for himself and was wearing has not perished but is still intact. If anyone was skeptical, I suppose you would ask him which is likely to last longer, a man or a coat which is c being regularly used and worn, and when he replied that the former was far more likely, you would imagine that you had proved conclusively that the man is safe and sound, since the less-enduring object has not perished. But surely this is not so, Simmias—because I

want your opinion too. Anyone would dismiss such a view as absurd.
The tailor makes and wears out any number of coats, but although he
d outlives all the others, presumably he perishes before the last one,
and this does not mean that a man is inferior to a coat, or has a
weaker hold upon life. I believe that this analogy might apply to the
relation of soul to body, and I think that it would be reasonable to say
of them in the same way that soul is a long-lived thing, whereas body
is relatively feeble and short-lived. But while we may admit that each
soul wears out a number of bodies, especially if it lives a great many
years—because although the body is continually changing and disin-
tegrating all through life, the soul never stops replacing what is worn
e away—still we must suppose that when the soul dies it is still in possession of its latest covering, and perishes before it in this case only,
although when the soul has perished the body at last reveals its natural frailty and quickly rots away. If you accept this view there is no
justification yet for any confidence that after death our souls still exist
somewhere.

88   Suppose that one conceded to the exponent of immortality even
more than you claim, granting not only that our souls existed before
our birth, but also that some of them may continue to exist or come
into existence after death, and be born and die again several times—
soul having such natural vitality that it persists through successive
incarnations—unless in granting this he made the further concession
that the soul suffers no ill effects in its various rebirths, and so does
not, at one of its 'deaths,' perish altogether. If he had to admit that
nobody knows which of these 'deaths' or separations from the body
b may prove fatal to the soul, because such insight is impossible for any
of us—on these terms, Socrates, no one but a fool is entitled to face
death with confidence, unless he can prove that the soul is absolutely
immortal and indestructible. Otherwise everyone must always feel
apprehension at the approach of death, for fear that in this particular separation from the body his soul may be finally and utterly destroyed.

c   Well, when we had heard them state their objections, we all felt
very much depressed, as we told one another later. We had been quite
convinced by the earlier part of the discussion, and now we felt
that they had upset our convictions and destroyed our confidence not
only in what had been said already, but also in anything that was to
follow later. Perhaps we were incompetent to judge, or the facts themselves might prove to be unreliable.

      ECHECRATES : You certainly have my full sympathy, Phaedo.
After hearing your account I find myself faced with the same mis-
d giving. How can we believe in anything after this? Socrates' argument
was absolutely convincing, and now it is completely discredited. That
theory that our soul is a sort of attunement has always had an extraordinary attraction for me, and when I heard it stated it reminded

me that I myself had formed the same opinion. What I really need now is another proof, right from the beginning, to convince me that when a man dies his soul does not die with him. Tell me, how did Socrates pick up the trail again? And did he show any sign of being e upset, like the rest of you, or did he quietly come to the rescue of the argument? And did he rescue it effectively or not? Tell us every detail as accurately as you can.

PHAEDO: I can assure you, Echecrates, that Socrates often astonished me, but I never admired him more than on this particu- 89 lar occasion. That he should have been ready with an answer was, I suppose, nothing unusual, but what impressed me was, first, the pleasant, kindly, appreciative way in which he received the two boys' objections, then his quick recognition of how the turn of the discussion had affected us, and lastly the skill with which he healed our wounds, rallied our scattered forces, and encouraged us to join him in pursuing the inquiry.

ECHECRATES: How did he do that?

PHAEDO: I will tell you. I happened to be sitting to the right of his bed, on a footstool, and he was much higher than I was. So he b laid his hand on my head and gathered up the curls on my neck—he never missed a chance of teasing me about my curls—and said, To-morrow, I suppose, Phaedo, you will cut off this beautiful hair.

I expect so, Socrates, I said.

Not if you take my advice.

Why not? I asked.

Because I shall cut off mine today, and you ought to do the same, said Socrates, that is, if we let our argument die and fail to bring it to life again. What is more, if I were you, and let the truth escape me, I should make a vow like the Argives' never to let my hair grow c again until I had defeated the argument of Simmias and Cebes in a return battle.

But, I objected, not even Heracles can take on two at once.

You had better call upon me to be your Iolaus, he said, while the daylight lasts.

Very well, I said, but I am Iolaus appealing to Heracles, not Her-acles to Iolaus.

The effect will be just the same, he said. But first there is one danger that we must guard against.

What sort of danger? I asked.

Of becoming misologic, he said, in the sense that people become d misanthropic. No greater misfortune could happen to anyone than that of developing a dislike for argument. Misology and misanthropy arise in just the same way. Misanthropy is induced by believing in somebody quite uncritically. You assume that a person is absolutely truthful and sincere and reliable, and a little later you find that he is shoddy and unreliable. Then the same thing happens again. After

repeated disappointments at the hands of the very people who might
e be supposed to be your nearest and most intimate friends, constant
irritation ends by making you dislike everybody and suppose that
there is no sincerity to be found anywhere. Have you never noticed
this happening?

Indeed, I have.

Don't you feel that it is reprehensible? Isn't it obvious that such
a person is trying to form human relationships without any critical
understanding of human nature? Otherwise he would surely recognize the truth—that there are not many very good or very bad people,
90 but the great majority are something between the two.

How do you make that out? I asked.

On the analogy of very large or small objects, he said. Can you
think of anything more unusual than coming across a very large or
small man, or dog, or any other creature? Or one which is very swift
or slow, ugly or beautiful, white or black? Have you never realized
that extreme instances are few and rare, while intermediate ones are
many and plentiful?

Certainly.

b So you think that if there were a competition in wickedness,
very few would distinguish themselves even there?

Probably.

Yes, it is probable, said Socrates. However, you have led me
into a digression. The resemblance between arguments and human
beings lies not in what I said just now, but in what I said before, that
when one believes that an argument is true without reference to the
art of logic, and then a little later decides rightly or wrongly that it is
false, and the same thing happens again and again—you know how
c it is, especially with those who spend their time in arguing both sides
—they end by believing that they are wiser than anyone else, because
they alone have discovered that there is nothing stable or dependable
either in facts or in arguments, and that everything fluctuates just like
the water in a tidal channel, and never stays at any point for any
time.

That is perfectly true, I said.

Well, then, Phaedo, he said, supposing that there is an argument
which is true and valid and capable of being discovered, if anyone
d nevertheless, through his experience of these arguments which seem
to the same people to be sometimes true and sometimes false, attached no responsibility to himself and his lack of technical ability,
but was finally content, in exasperation, to shift the blame from himself to the arguments, and spend the rest of his life loathing and
decrying them, and so missed the chance of knowing the truth about
reality—would it not be a deplorable thing?

It would indeed, I said.

Very well, he said, that is the first thing that we must guard

against. We must not let it enter our minds that there may be no e
validity in argument. On the contrary we should recognize that we
ourselves are still intellectual invalids, but that we must brace ourselves and do our best to become healthy—you and the others partly
with a view to the rest of your lives, but I directly in view of my
death, because at the moment I am in danger of regarding it not phil- 91
osophically but self-assertively. You know how, in an argument, people who have no real education care nothing for the facts of the case,
and are only anxious to get their point of view accepted by the audience? Well, I feel that at this present moment I am as bad as they are,
only with this difference, that my anxiety will be not to convince my
audience, except incidentally, but to produce the strongest possible
conviction in myself. This is how I weigh the position, my dear fellow—see how selfish I am! If my theory is really true, it is right to be- b
lieve it, while, even if death is extinction, at any rate during this time
before my death I shall be less likely to distress my companions by
giving way to self-pity, and this folly of mine will not live on with me
—which would be a calamity—but will shortly come to an end.

That, my dear Simmias and Cebes, is the spirit in which I am
prepared to approach the discussion. As for you, if you will take my
advice, you will think very little of Socrates, and much more of the
truth. If you think that anything I say is true, you must agree with c
me; if not, oppose it with every argument that you have. You must
not allow me, in my enthusiasm, to deceive both myself and you, and
leave my sting behind when I fly away.

Well, we must go ahead, he continued. First remind me of what
you said, if you find my memory inaccurate. Simmias, I believe, is
troubled with doubts. He is afraid that, even if the soul is more divine
and a higher thing than the body, it may nevertheless be destroyed
first, as being a kind of attunement. Cebes on the other hand appeared d
to agree with me that soul is more enduring than body, but to maintain that no one can be sure that, after repeatedly wearing out a great
many bodies, it does not at last perish itself, leaving the last body behind; and he thinks that death may be precisely this, the destruction
of the soul, because the body never stops perishing all the time. Am I
right, Simmias and Cebes, in thinking that these are the objections
which we have to investigate?

They agreed that this was so.   e

Well, then, he said, do you reject all our previous arguments,
or only some of them?

Only some of them, they said.

What is your opinion of the reasoning by which we asserted that
learning is recollection, and that, if this is so, our souls must have
existed somewhere else before they were confined in the body?   92

Speaking for myself, said Cebes, I found it remarkably convincing at the time, and I stick to it still as I do to no other theory.

Yes, indeed, said Simmias, it is just the same with me. I should be very much surprised if I ever changed my opinion about that.

But you will have to change it, my Theban friend, said Socrates, if the conception stands that an attunement is a composite thing, and that the soul is an attunement composed of our physical elements at a given tension. I imagine that you would not accept even from yourself the assertion that a composite attunement existed before the elements of which it was to be composed. Or would you?

b

Not for a moment, Socrates.

Don't you see that that is just what it amounts to when you say that the soul exists before it enters the human form or body, and also that it is composed of elements which do not yet exist? Surely an attunement is not at all like the object of your comparison. The instrument and the strings and their untuned notes come first. The attunement is the last of all to be constituted and the first to be destroyed. How will this account harmonize with the other?

c

Not at all, said Simmias.

And yet, said Socrates, if any account ought to be harmonious, it should be an account of attunement.

Yes, it should, said Simmias.

Well, said Socrates, this one does not harmonize with your view. Make up your mind which theory you prefer—that learning is recollection, or that soul is an attunement.

The former, without any hesitation, Socrates, he said. The other appealed to me, without any proof to support it, as being based on plausible analogy, which is why most people find it attractive. But I realize that theories which rest their proof upon plausibility are impostors, and unless you are on your guard, they deceive you properly, both in geometry and everywhere else. On the other hand, the theory of recollection and learning derives from a hypothesis which is worthy of acceptance. The theory that our soul exists even before it enters the body surely stands or falls with the soul's possession of the ultimate standard of reality—a view which I have, to the best of my belief, fully and rightly accepted. It seems therefore that I must not accept, either from myself or from anyone else, the assertion that soul is an attunement.

d

e

There is this way of looking at it too, Simmias, said Socrates. Do you think that an attunement, or any other composite thing, should be in a condition different from that of its component elements?

93

No, I do not.

And it should not act, or be acted upon, I presume, differently from them?

He agreed.

So an attunement should not control its elements, but should follow their lead?

He assented.

There is no question of its conflicting with them, either in movement or in sound or in any other way.

None at all.

Very well, then, is it not the nature of every attunement to be an
attunement in so far as it is tuned?

I don't understand.

Surely, said Socrates, if it is tuned more, that is, in a greater degree—supposing this to be possible—it must be more of an attune- b
ment, and if it is tuned less, that is, in a lesser degree, it must be less
of an attunement.

Quite so.

And is this the case with the soul—that one soul is, even minutely, more or less of a soul than another?

Not in the least.

Now please give me your closest attention, said Socrates. Do we
say that one kind of soul possesses intelligence and goodness, and is
good, and that another possesses stupidity and wickedness, and is
evil? And is this true?   c

Yes, it is true.

Then how will a person who holds that the soul is an attunement account for the presence in it of goodness and badness?
Will he describe them as yet another attunement or lack of it? Will
he say that the good soul is in tune, and not only is an attunement
itself, but contains another, whereas the bad soul is out of tune and
does not contain another attunement?

I really could not say, replied Simmias, but obviously anyone
who held that view would have to say something of the sort.

But we have already agreed, said Socrates, that no soul can be d
more or less of a soul than another, and this is the same as agreeing
that no attunement can be more of an attunement and in a greater degree, or less of an attunement and in a lesser degree, than another. Is
that not so?

Certainly.

And that what is neither more nor less of an attunement is
neither more nor less in tune. Is that so?

Yes.

Does that which is neither more nor less in tune contain a
greater or smaller proportion of attunement, or an equal one? e

An equal one.

Then since no soul is any more or less than just a soul, it is neither more nor less in tune.

That is so.

Under this condition it cannot contain a greater proportion of
discord or attunement.

Certainly not.

And again under this condition can one soul contain a greater

proportion of badness or goodness than another, assuming that badness is discord and goodness attunement?

No, it cannot.

94   Or rather, I suppose, Simmias, by strict reasoning no soul will
contain any share of badness, if it is an attunement, because surely
since attunement is absolutely attunement and nothing else, it can
never contain any share of discord.

No, indeed.

Nor can the soul, since it is absolutely soul, contain a share of
badness.

Not in the light of what we have said.

So on this theory every soul of every living creature will be
equally good—assuming that it is the nature of all souls to be equally
souls and nothing else.

I think that follows, Socrates.

Do you also think that this view is right? Would the argument
b ever have come to this if our hypothesis, that the soul is an attunement, had been correct?

Not the least chance of it.

Well, said Socrates, do you hold that it is any other part of a man
than the soul that governs him, especially if it is a wise one?

No, I do not.

Does it yield to the feelings of the body, or oppose them? I mean,
for instance, that when a person is feverish and thirsty it impels him
the other way, not to drink, and when he is hungry, not to eat, and
c there are thousands of other ways in which we see the soul opposing
the physical instincts. Is that not so?

Certainly.

Did we not also agree a little while ago that if it is an attunement
it can never sound a note that conflicts with the tension or relaxation
or vibration or any other condition of its constituents, but must always follow them and never direct them?

Yes, we did, of course.

Well, surely we can see now that the soul works in just the opposite way. It directs all the elements of which it is said to consist, opposing them in almost everything all through life, and exercising
d every form of control—sometimes by severe and unpleasant methods
like those of physical training and medicine, and sometimes by milder
ones, sometimes scolding, sometimes encouraging—and conversing
with the desires and passions and fears as though it were quite separate and distinct from them. It is just like Homer's description in the
Odyssey where he says that Odysseus

> Then beat his breast, and thus reproved his heart,
e > Endure, my heart; still worse hast thou endured.[1]

---

[1] *Odyssey* 20.17 sq.

Do you suppose that when he wrote that he thought that the soul was an attunement, liable to be swayed by physical feelings? Surely he regarded it as capable of swaying and controlling them, as something much too divine to rank as an attunement.

That is certainly how it seems to me, Socrates.

Good. In that case there is no justification for our saying that soul is a kind of attunement. We should neither agree with Homer nor 95 be consistent ourselves.

That is so.

Well now, said Socrates, we seem to have placated the Theban lady Harmonia with moderate success. But what about Cadmus, Cebes? How shall we placate him, and what argument shall we use?

I think that you will find a way, said Cebes. This argument which you brought forward against the attunement theory far surpassed all my expectations. When Simmias was explaining his difficulties I wondered very much whether anyone would be able to do b anything with his argument; so I was quite astonished that it could not stand up against your very first attack. I should not be surprised if Cadmus' argument met the same fate.

My dear fellow, said Socrates, don't boast, or some misfortune will upset the forthcoming argument. However, we will leave that to God; it is our task to come to close quarters in the Homeric manner and test the validity of your contention.

What you require, in a nutshell, is this. You consider that unless the confidence of a philosopher who at the point of dying believes c that after death he will be better off for having lived and ended his life in philosophy than in any other way of living is to be a blind and foolish confidence, the soul must be proved to be indestructible and immortal. To show that it has great vitality and a godlike nature, and even that it existed before we were born—all this, you say, may very well indicate not that the soul is immortal, but merely that it is long-lived, and pre-existed somewhere for a prodigious period of time, enjoying a great measure of knowledge and activity. But all this did not make it any the more immortal. Indeed its very entrance into the d human body was, like a disease, the beginning of its destruction; it lives this life in increasing weariness, and finally perishes in what we call death. You also say that, to our individual fears, it makes no difference whether it enters the body once or often. Anyone who does not know and cannot prove that the soul is immortal must be afraid, unless he is a fool.

That, I believe, is the substance of your objection, Cebes. I am deliberately reviewing it more than once, in order that nothing may es- e cape us, and that you may add to it or subtract from it anything that you wish.

Cebes said, But at the present moment there is no need for me to add or subtract anything; that is precisely my point of view.

After spending some time in reflection Socrates said, What you require is no light undertaking, Cebes. It involves a full treatment of the causes of generation and destruction. If you like, I will describe

96 my own experiences in this connection, and then, if you find anything helpful in my account, you can use it to reassure yourself about your own objections.

Yes, indeed, said Cebes, I should like that very much.

Then listen, and I will tell you. When I was young, Cebes, I had an extraordinary passion for that branch of learning which is called natural science. I thought it would be marvelous to know the causes for which each thing comes and ceases and continues to be. I was

b constantly veering to and fro, puzzling primarily over this sort of question. Is it when heat and cold produce fermentation, as some have said, that living creatures are bred? Is it with the blood that we think, or with the air or the fire that is in us? Or is it none of these, but the brain that supplies our senses of hearing and sight and smell, and from these that memory and opinion arise, and from memory and opinion, when established, that knowledge comes? Then again I

c would consider how these faculties are lost, and study celestial and terrestrial phenomena, until at last I came to the conclusion that I was uniquely unfitted for this form of inquiry. I will give you a sufficient indication of what I mean. I had understood some things plainly before, in my own and other people's estimation, but now I was so befogged by these speculations that I unlearned even what I had thought I knew, especially about the cause of growth in human beings. Previously I had thought that it was quite obviously due to eating and

d drinking—that when, from the food which we consume, flesh is added to flesh and bone to bone, and when in the same way the other parts of the body are augmented by their appropriate particles, the bulk which was small is now large, and in this way the small man becomes a big one. That is what I used to believe—reasonably, don't you think?

Yes, I do, said Cebes.

Consider a little further. I had been content to think, when I saw a tall man standing beside a short one, that he was taller by a head, and similarly in the case of horses. And it seemed to me even more

e obvious that ten is more than eight because it contains two more, and that two feet is bigger than one because it exceeds it by half its own length.

And what do you believe about them now? asked Cebes.

Why, upon my word, that I am very far from supposing that I know the explanation of any of these things. I cannot even convince myself that when you add one to one either the first or the second

97 one becomes two, or they both become two by the addition of the one to the other. I find it hard to believe that, although when they were separate each of them was one and they were not two, now that they

have come together the cause of their becoming two is simply the union caused by their juxtaposition. Nor can I believe now, when you divide one, that this time the cause of its becoming two is the division, because this cause of its becoming two is the opposite of the former one; then it was because they were brought close together and added one to the other, but now it is because they are taken apart and separated one from the other. Nor can I now persuade myself that I understand how it is that things become one, nor, in short, why anything else comes or ceases or continues to be, according to this method of inquiry. So I reject it altogether, and muddle out a haphazard method of my own.

However, I once heard someone reading from a book, as he said, by Anaxagoras, and asserting that it is mind that produces order and is the cause of everything. This explanation pleased me. Somehow it seemed right that mind should be the cause of everything, and I reflected that if this is so, mind in producing order sets everything in order and arranges each individual thing in the way that is best for it. Therefore if anyone wished to discover the reason why any given thing came or ceased or continued to be, he must find out how it was best for that thing to be, or to act or be acted upon in any other way. On this view there was only one thing for a man to consider, with regard both to himself and to anything else, namely the best and highest good, although this would necessarily imply knowing what is less good, since both were covered by the same knowledge.

These reflections made me suppose, to my delight, that in Anaxagoras I had found an authority on causation who was after my own heart. I assumed that he would begin by informing us whether the earth is flat or round, and would then proceed to explain in detail the reason and logical necessity for this by stating how and why it was better that it should be so. I thought that if he asserted that the earth was in the center, he would explain in detail that it was better for it to be there; and if he made this clear, I was prepared to give up hankering after any other kind of cause. I was prepared also in the same way to receive instruction about the sun and moon and the other heavenly bodies, about their relative velocities and their orbits and all the other phenomena connected with them—in what way it is better for each one of them to act or be acted upon as it is. It never entered my head that a man who asserted that the ordering of things is due to mind would offer any other explanation for them than that it is best for them to be as they are. I thought that by assigning a cause to each phenomenon separately and to the universe as a whole he would make perfectly clear what is best for each and what is the universal good. I would not have parted with my hopes for a great sum of money. I lost no time in procuring the books, and began to read them as quickly as I possibly could, so that I might know as soon as possible about the best and the less good.

It was a wonderful hope, my friend, but it was quickly dashed. As I read on I discovered that the fellow made no use of mind and assigned to it no causality for the order of the world, but adduced

c causes like air and æther and water and many other absurdities. It seemed to me that he was just about as inconsistent as if someone were to say, The cause of everything that Socrates does is mind— and then, in trying to account for my several actions, said first that the reason why I am lying here now is that my body is composed of bones and sinews, and that the bones are rigid and separated at the

d joints, but the sinews are capable of contraction and relaxation, and form an envelope for the bones with the help of the flesh and skin, the latter holding all together, and since the bones move freely in their joints the sinews by relaxing and contracting enable me somehow to bend my limbs, and that is the cause of my sitting here in a bent position. Or again, if he tried to account in the same way for my conversing with you, adducing causes such as sound and air and hearing and a thousand others, and never troubled to mention the real

e reasons, which are that since Athens has thought it better to condemn me, therefore I for my part have thought it better to sit here, and more right to stay and submit to whatever penalty she orders. Because,

99 by dog, I fancy that these sinews and bones would have been in the neighborhood of Megara or Boeotia long ago—impelled by a conviction of what is best!—if I did not think that it was more right and honorable to submit to whatever penalty my country orders rather than take to my heels and run away. But to call things like that causes is too absurd. If it were said that without such bones and sinews and all the rest of them I should not be able to do what I think is right, it would be true. But to say that it is because of them that I

b do what I am doing, and not through choice of what is best—although my actions are controlled by mind—would be a very lax and inaccurate form of expression. Fancy being unable to distinguish between the cause of a thing and the condition without which it could not be a cause! It is this latter, as it seems to me, that most people, groping in the dark, call a cause—attaching to it a name to which it has no right. That is why one person surrounds the earth with a vortex, and so keeps it in place by means of the heavens, and another props it up on a pedestal of air, as though it were a wide platter. As for a power which keeps things disposed at any given moment in

c the best possible way, they neither look for it nor believe that it has any supernatural force. They imagine that they will someday find a more mighty and immortal and all-sustaining Atlas, and they do not think that anything is really bound and held together by goodness or moral obligation. For my part, I should be delighted to learn about the workings of such a cause from anyone, but since I have been denied knowledge of it, and have been unable either to discover it myself or to learn about it from another, I have worked out my own

makeshift approach to the problem of causation. Would you like me
to give you a demonstration of it, Cebes?   d
    I should like it very much indeed.
    Well, after this, said Socrates, when I was worn_out with my
physical investigations, it occurred to me that I must guard against
the same sort of risk which people run when they watch and study
an eclipse of the sun; they really do sometimes injure their eyes, unless they study its reflection in water or some other medium. I conceived of something like this happening to myself, and I was afraid
that by observing objects with my eyes and trying to comprehend them
with each of my other senses I might blind my soul altogether. So I e
decided that I must have recourse to theories, and use them in trying
to discover the truth about things. Perhaps my illustration is not
quite apt, because I do not at all admit that an inquiry by means of 100
theory employs 'images' any more than one which confines itself to
facts. But however that may be, I started off in this way, and in every
case I first lay down the theory which I judge to be soundest, and
then whatever seems to agree with it—with regard either to causes or
to anything else—I assume to be true, and whatever does not I assume
not to be true. But I should like to express my meaning more clearly,
because at present I don't think that you understand.
    No, indeed I don't, said Cebes, not a bit.
    Well, said Socrates, what I mean is this, and there is nothing new b
about it. I have always said it; in fact I have never stopped saying it,
especially in the earlier part of this discussion. As I am going to try
to explain to you the theory of causation which I have worked out
myself, I propose to make a fresh start from those principles of mine
which you know so well—that is, I am assuming the existence of absolute beauty and goodness and magnitude and all the rest of
them. If you grant my assumption and admit that they exist, I hope
with their help to explain causation to you, and to find a proof that
soul is immortal.
    Certainly I grant it, said Cebes. You need lose no time in draw- c
ing your conclusion.
    Then consider the next step, and see whether you share my opin-
ion. It seems to me that whatever else is beautiful apart from absolute
beauty is beautiful because it partakes of that absolute beauty, and for
no other reason. Do you accept this kind of causality?
    Yes, I do.
    Well, now, that is as far as my mind goes; I cannot understand
these other ingenious theories of causation. If someone tells me that
the reason why a given object is beautiful is that it has a gorgeous d
color or shape or any other such attribute, I disregard all these other
explanations—I find them all confusing—and I cling simply and
straightforwardly and no doubt foolishly to the explanation that the
one thing that makes that object beautiful is the presence in it or

association with it, in whatever way the relation comes about, of absolute beauty. I do not go so far as to insist upon the precise details —only upon the fact that it is by beauty that beautiful things are beautiful. This, I feel, is the safest answer for me or for anyone else to give, and I believe that while I hold fast to this I cannot fall; it is safe
e for me or for anyone else to answer that it is by beauty that beautiful things are beautiful. Don't you agree?

Yes, I do.

Then is it also by largeness that large things are large and larger things larger, and by smallness that smaller things are smaller?

Yes.

So you too, like myself, would refuse to accept the statement that one man is taller than another 'by a head,' and that the shorter man is shorter by the same. You would protest that the only view
101 which you yourself can hold is that whatever is taller than something else is so simply by tallness—that is, because of tallness— and that what is shorter is so simply by shortness, that is, because of shortness. You would be afraid, I suppose, that if you said that one man is taller than another by a head, you would be faced by a logical objection—first that the taller should be taller and the shorter shorter by the same thing, and secondly that the taller person should be taller by a head, which is a short thing, and that it is unnatural that
b a man should be made tall by something short. Isn't that so?

Cebes laughed and said, Yes, it is.

Then you would be afraid to say that ten is more than eight 'by two,' or that two is the cause of its excess over eight, instead of saying that it is more than eight by, or because of, being a larger number, and you would be afraid to say that a length of two feet is greater than one foot by a half, instead of saying that it is greater by its larger size—because there is the same danger here too?

Quite so.

Suppose next that we add one to one. You would surely avoid say-
c ing that the cause of our getting two is the addition, or in the case of a divided unit, the division. You would loudly proclaim that you know of no other way in which any given object can come into being except by participation in the reality peculiar to its appropriate universal, and that in the cases which I have mentioned you recognize no other cause for the coming into being of two than participation in duality, and that whatever is to become two must participate in this, and whatever is to become one must participate in unity. You would dismiss these divisions and additions and other such niceties, leaving them for persons wiser than yourself to use in their explanations,
d while you, being nervous of your own shadow, as the saying is, and of your inexperience, would hold fast to the security of your hypothesis and make your answers accordingly. If anyone should fasten upon the hypothesis itself, you would disregard him and refuse to answer until you could consider whether its consequences were mutually con-

sistent or not. And when you had to substantiate the hypothesis itself, you would proceed in the same way, assuming whatever more ultimate hypothesis commended itself most to you, until you reached one which was satisfactory. You would not mix the two things together e by discussing both the principle and its consequences, like one of these destructive critics—that is, if you wanted to discover any part of the truth. They presumably have no concern or care whatever for such an object, because their cleverness enables them to muddle everything up without disturbing their own self-complacence, but you, I imagine, if you are a philosopher, will follow the course which I describe.   102

You are perfectly right, said Simmias and Cebes together.

ECHECRATES: I can assure you, Phaedo, I am not surprised. It seems to me that Socrates made his meaning extraordinarily clear to even a limited intelligence.

PHAEDO: That was certainly the feeling of all of us who were present, Echecrates.

ECHECRATES: No doubt, because it is just the same with us who were not present and are hearing it now for the first time. But how did the discussion go on?

PHAEDO: I think that when Socrates had got this accepted, and it was agreed that the various forms exist, and that the reason why b other things are called after the forms is that they participate in the forms, he next went on to ask, If you hold this view, I suppose that when you say that Simmias is taller than Socrates but shorter than Phaedo, you mean that at that moment there are in Simmias both tallness and shortness?

Yes, I do.

But do you agree that the statement 'Simmias is bigger than Socrates' is not true in the form in which it is expressed? Surely the real reason why Simmias is bigger is not because he is Simmias but because of the height which he incidentally possesses, and conversely c the reason why he is bigger than Socrates is not because Socrates is Socrates, but because Socrates has the attribute of shortness in comparison with Simmias' height.

True.

And again Simmias' being smaller than Phaedo is due not to the fact that Phaedo is Phaedo, but to the fact that Phaedo has the attribute of tallness in comparison with Simmias' shortness.

Quite so.

So that is how Simmias comes to be described as both short and tall, because he is intermediate between the two of them, and allows his shortness to be surpassed by the tallness of the one while he as- d serts his superior tallness over the shortness of the other.

He added with a smile, I seem to be developing an artificial style, but the facts are surely as I say.

Simmias agreed.

I am saying all this because I want you to share my point of view. It seems to me not only that the form of tallness itself absolutely declines to be short as well as tall, but also that the tallness which is in us never admits smallness and declines to be surpassed. It does one of two things. Either it gives way and withdraws as its opposite shortness
e approaches, or it has already ceased to exist by the time that the other arrives. It cannot stand its ground and receive the quality of shortness in the same way as I myself have done. If it did, it would become different from what it was before, whereas I have not lost my identity by acquiring the quality of shortness—I am the same man, only short —but my tallness could not endure to be short instead of tall. In the same way the shortness that is in us declines ever to become or be tall, nor will any other quality, while still remaining what it was, at
103 the same time become or be the opposite quality; in such a situation it either withdraws or ceases to exist.

I agree with you entirely, said Cebes.

At this point one of the company—I can't remember distinctly who it was—said, Look here! Didn't we agree, earlier in the discussion, on the exact opposite of what you are saying now—that the bigger comes from the smaller and the smaller from the bigger, and that it is precisely from their opposites that opposites come? Now the view seems to be that this is impossible.

Socrates had listened with his head turned toward the speaker. It was brave of you to refresh my memory, he said, but you don't realize
b the difference between what we are saying now and what we said then. Then we were saying that opposite *things* come from opposite *things;* now we are saying that the opposite *itself* can never become opposite to *itself*—neither the opposite which is in us nor that which is in the real world. Then, my friend, we were speaking about objects which possess opposite qualities, and calling them by the names of the latter, but now we are speaking about the qualities themselves, from whose presence in them the objects which are called after them
c derive their names. We maintain that the opposites themselves would absolutely refuse to tolerate coming into being from one another.

As he spoke he looked at Cebes. I suppose that nothing in what he said worried you too, Cebes?

No, not this time, said Cebes, though I don't deny that a good many other things do.

So we are agreed upon this as a general principle, that an opposite can never be opposite to itself.

Absolutely.

Then consider this point too, and see whether you agree about it too. Do you admit that there are such things as heat and cold?

Yes, I do.

Do you think they are the same as snow and fire?
d   Certainly not.

Heat is quite distinct from fire, and cold from snow?

Yes.

But I suppose you agree, in the light of what we said before, that snow, being what it is, can never admit heat and still remain snow, just as it was before, only with the addition of heat. It must either withdraw at the approach of heat, or cease to exist.

Quite so.

Again, fire must either retire or cease to exist at the approach of cold. It will never have the courage to admit cold and still remain fire, just as it was, only with the addition of cold.

That is true.   e

So we find, in certain cases like these, that the name of the form is eternally applicable not only to the form itself, but also to something else, which is not the form but invariably possesses its distinguishing characteristic. But perhaps another example will make my meaning clearer. Oddness must always be entitled to this name by which I am now calling it, isn't that so?

Certainly.

This is the question. Is it unique in this respect, or is there something else, not identical with oddness, to which we are bound always 104 to apply not only its own name but that of odd as well, because by its very nature it never loses its oddness? What I mean is illustrated by the case of the number three; there are plenty of other examples, but take the case of three. Don't you think that it must always be described not only by its own name but by that of odd, although odd and three are not the same thing? It is the very nature of three and five and all the alternate integers that every one of them is invariably odd, although it is not identical with oddness. Similarly two and four and all the rest of the other series are not identical with even, but b each one of them always *is* even. Do you admit this, or not?

Of course I do.

Well, then, pay careful attention to the point which I want to make, which is this. It seems clear that the opposites themselves do not admit one another, but it also looks as though any things which, though not themselves opposites, always have opposites in them, similarly do not admit the opposite form to that which is in them, but on its approach either cease to exist or retire before it. Surely we must assert that three will sooner cease to exist or suffer any c other fate than submit to become even while it is still three?

Certainly, said Cebes.

And yet two and three are not opposites.

No, they are not.

So it is not only the opposite forms that cannot face one another's approach; there are other things too which cannot face the approach of opposites.

That is quite true.

Shall we try, if we can, to define what sort of things these are?

By all means.

d   Well, then, Cebes, would this describe them—that they are things which are compelled by some form which takes possession of them to assume not only its own form but invariably also that of some other form which is an opposite?

What do you mean?

Just what we were saying a minute ago. You realize, I suppose, that when the form of three takes possession of any group of objects, it compels them to be odd as well as three.

Certainly.

Then I maintain that into such a group the opposite form to the one which has this effect can never enter.

No, it cannot.

And it was the form of odd that had this effect?

Yes.

And the opposite of this is the form of even?

Yes.

e   So the form of even will never enter into three.

No, never.

In other words, three is incompatible with evenness.

Quite.

So the number three is uneven.

Yes.

I proposed just now to define what sort of things they are which, although they are not themselves directly opposed to a given opposite, nevertheless do not admit it, as in the present example, three, although not the opposite of even, nevertheless does not admit it, because three is always accompanied by the opposite of even—and similarly with two and odd, or fire and cold, and hosts of others. Well, see
105   whether you accept this definition. Not only does an opposite not admit its opposite, but if anything is accompanied by a form which has an opposite, and meets that opposite, then the thing which is accompanied never admits the opposite of the form by which it is accompanied. Let me refresh your memory; there is no harm in hearing a thing several times. Five will not admit the form of even, nor will ten, which is double five, admit the form of odd. Double has an opposite of its own, but at the same time it will not admit the form of
b   odd. Nor will one and a half, or other fractions such as one half or three quarters and so on, admit the form of whole. I assume that you follow me and agree.

I follow and agree perfectly, said Cebes.

Then run over the same ground with me from the beginning, and don't answer in the exact terms of the question, but follow my example. I say this because besides the 'safe answer' that I described at first, as the result of this discussion I now see another means of safety.

Suppose, for instance, that you ask me what must be present in body to make it hot. I shall not return the safe but ingenuous answer that it c is heat, but a more sophisticated one, based on the results of our discussion—namely that it is fire. And if you ask what must be present in a body to make it diseased, I shall say not disease but fever. Similarly if you ask what must be present in a number to make it odd, I shall say not oddness but unity, and so on. See whether you have a sufficient grasp now of what I want from you.

Quite sufficient.

Then tell me, what must be present in a body to make it alive?

Soul.

Is this always so? d

Of course.

So whenever soul takes possession of a body, it always brings life with it?

Yes, it does.

Is there an opposite to life, or not?

Yes, there is.

What?

Death.

Does it follow, then, from our earlier agreement, that soul will never admit the opposite of that which accompanies it?

Most definitely, said Cebes.

Well, now, what name did we apply just now to that which does not admit the form of even?

Uneven.

And what do we call that which does not admit justice, or culture?

Uncultured, and the other unjust. e

Very good. And what do we call that which does not admit death?

Immortal.

And soul does not admit death?

No.

So soul is immortal.

Yes, it is immortal.

Well, said Socrates, can we say that that has been proved? What do you think?

Most completely, Socrates.

Here is another question for you, Cebes. If the uneven were necessarily imperishable, would not three be imperishable? 106

Of course.

Then again, if what is not hot were necessarily imperishable, when you applied heat to snow, would not the snow withdraw still intact and unmelted? It could not cease to exist, nor on the other hand could it remain where it was and admit the heat.

That is true.

In the same way I assume that if what is not cold were imperishable, when anything cold approached fire, it could never go out or cease to exist; it would depart and be gone unharmed.

That must be so.

b   Are we not bound to say the same of the immortal? If what is immortal is also imperishable, it is impossible that at the approach of death soul should cease to be. It follows from what we have already said that it cannot admit death, or be dead—just as we said that three cannot be even, nor can odd; nor can fire be cold, nor can the heat which is in the fire. But, it may be objected, granting, as has been agreed, that odd does not become even at the approach of even, why should it not cease to exist, and something even take its place? In

c   reply to this we could not insist that the odd does not cease to exist—because what is not even is not imperishable—but if this were conceded, we could easily insist that, at the approach of even, odd and three retire and depart. And we could be equally insistent about fire and heat and all the rest of them, could we not?

Certainly.

So now in the case of the immortal, if it is conceded that this is also imperishable, soul will be imperishable as well as immortal.

d   Otherwise we shall need another argument.

There is no need on that account, said Cebes. If what is immortal and eternal cannot avoid destruction, it is hard to see how anything else can.

And I imagine that it would be admitted by everyone, said Socrates, that God at any rate, and the form of life, and anything else that is immortal, can never cease to exist.

Yes indeed, by all men certainly, and even more, I suppose, by the gods.

e   Then since what is immortal is also indestructible, if soul is really immortal, surely it must be imperishable too.

Quite inevitably.

So it appears that when death comes to a man, the mortal part of him dies, but the immortal part retires at the approach of death and escapes unharmed and indestructible.

Evidently.

Then it is as certain as anything can be, Cebes, that soul is im-
107 mortal and imperishable, and that our souls will really exist in the next world.

Well, Socrates, said Cebes, for my part I have no criticisms, and no doubt about the truth of your argument. But if Simmias here or anyone else has any criticism to make, he had better not keep it to himself, because if anyone wants to say or hear any more about this subject, I don't see to what other occasion he is to defer it.

As a matter of fact, said Simmias, I have no doubts myself either now, in view of what you have just been saying. All the same, the

subject is so vast, and I have such a poor opinion of our weak human b
nature, that I can't help still feeling some misgivings.

Quite right, Simmias, said Socrates, and what is more, even if
you find our original assumptions convincing, they still need more accurate consideration. If you and your friends examine them closely
enough, I believe that you will arrive at the truth of the matter, in so
far as it is possible for the human mind to attain it, and if you are sure
that you have done this, you will not need to inquire further.

That is true, said Simmias.

But there is a further point, gentlemen, said Socrates, which de- c
serves your attention. If the soul is immortal, it demands our care not
only for that part of time which we call life, but for all time. And indeed it would seem now that it will be extremely dangerous to neglect
it. If death were a release from everything, it would be a boon for the
wicked, because by dying they would be released not only from the
body but also from their own wickedness together with the soul, but
as it is, since the soul is clearly immortal, it can have no escape or security from evil except by becoming as good and wise as it possibly d
can. For it takes nothing with it to the next world except its education
and training, and these, we are told, are of supreme importance in
helping or harming the newly dead at the very beginning of his journey there.

This is how the story goes. When any man dies, his own guardian
spirit, which was given charge over him in his life, tries to bring him
to a certain place where all must assemble, and from which, after submitting their several cases to judgment, they must set out for the
next world, under the guidance of one who has the office of escorting e
souls from this world to the other. When they have there undergone
the necessary experiences and remained as long as is required, another guide brings them back again after many vast periods of time.

Of course this journey is not as Aeschylus makes Telephus describe it. He says that the path to Hades is straightforward, but it 108
seems clear to me that it is neither straightforward nor single. If it
were, there would be no need for a guide, because surely nobody could
lose his way anywhere if there were only one road. In fact, it seems
likely that it contains many forkings and crossroads, to judge from
the ceremonies and observances of this world.

Well, the wise and disciplined soul follows its guide and is not ignorant of its surroundings, but the soul which is deeply attached to
the body, as I said before, hovers round it and the visible world for a b
long time, and it is only after much resistance and suffering that it is
at last forcibly led away by its appointed guardian spirit. And when
it reaches the same place as the rest, the soul which is impure through
having done some impure deed, either by setting its hand to lawless
bloodshed or by committing other kindred crimes which are the work
of kindred souls, this soul is shunned and avoided by all. None will

c company with it or guide it, and it wanders alone in utter desolation until certain times have passed, whereupon it is borne away of necessity to its proper habitation. But every soul that has lived throughout its life in purity and soberness enjoys divine company and guidance, and each inhabits the place which is proper to it. There are many wonderful regions in the earth, and the earth itself is neither in nature nor in size such as geographers suppose it to be—so someone has assured me.

d   How can you say that, Socrates? said Simmias. I myself have heard a great many theories about the earth, but not this belief of yours. I should very much like to hear it.

Why, really, Simmias, I don't think that it calls for the skill of a Glaucus to explain what my belief is, but to prove that it is true seems to me to be too difficult even for a Glaucus. In the first place I should probably be unable to do it, and in the second, even if I knew how, it seems to me, Simmias, that my life is too short for a long explanation. However, there is no reason why I should not tell you what I believe e about the appearance of the earth and regions in it.

Well, said Simmias, even that will do.

This is what I believe, then, said Socrates. In the first place, if the earth is spherical and in the middle of the heavens, it needs neither 109 air nor any other such force to keep it from falling; the uniformity of the heavens and the equilibrium of the earth itself are sufficient to support it. Any body in equilibrium, if it is set in the middle of a uniform medium, will have no tendency to sink or rise in any direction more than another, and having equal impulses will remain suspended. This is the first article of my belief.

And quite right too, said Simmias.

Next, said Socrates, I believe that it is vast in size, and that we b who dwell between the river Phasis and the Pillars of Hercules inhabit only a minute portion of it—we live round the sea like ants or frogs round a pond—and there are many other peoples inhabiting similar regions. There are many hollow places all round the earth, places of every shape and size, into which the water and mist and air have collected. But the earth itself is as pure as the starry heaven in which it c lies, and which is called aether by most of our authorities. The water, mist, and air are the dregs of this aether, and they are continually draining into the hollow places in the earth. We do not realize that we are living in its hollows, but assume that we are living on the earth's surface. Imagine someone living in the depths of the sea. He might think that he was living on the surface, and seeing the sun and the other heavenly bodies through the water; he might think that the sea was the sky. He might be so sluggish and feeble that he had never d reached the top of the sea, never emerged and raised his head from the sea into this world of ours, and seen for himself—or even heard from someone who had seen it—how much purer and more beautiful it really is than the one in which his people lives. Now we are in just the same position. Although we live in a hollow of the earth, we assume that we are living on the surface, and we call the air heaven, as though it were the heaven through which the stars move. And this point too is the same, that we are too feeble and sluggish to make our e way out to the upper limit of the air. If someone could reach to the summit, or put on wings and fly aloft, when he put up his head he would see the world above, just as fishes see our world when they put up their heads out of the sea. And if his nature were able to bear the sight, he would recognize that that is the true heaven and the true light and the true earth. For this earth and its stones and all the re- 110 gions in which we live are marred and corroded, just as in the sea everything is corroded by the brine, and there is no vegetation worth mentioning, and scarcely any degree of perfect formation, but only caverns and sand and measureless mud, and tracts of slime wherever there is earth as well, and nothing is in the least worthy to be judged beautiful by our standards. But the things above excel those of our world to a degree far greater still. If this is the right moment for an b imaginative description, Simmias, it will be worth your while to hear what it is really like upon the earth which lies beneath the heavens.

Yes, indeed, Socrates, said Simmias, it would be a great pleasure to us, at any rate, to hear this description.

Well, my dear boy, said Socrates, the real earth, viewed from above, is supposed to look like one of these balls made of twelve pieces of skin, variegated and marked out in different colors, of which the colors which we know are only limited samples, like the paints which artists use, but there the whole earth is made up of such colors, and c others far brighter and purer still. One section is a marvelously beautiful purple, and another is golden. All that is white of it is whiter than chalk or snow, and the rest is similarly made up of the other colors, still more and lovelier than those which we have seen. Even these very hollows in the earth, full of water and air, assume a kind of color as they gleam amid the different hues around them, so that there ap- d pears to be one continuous surface of varied colors. The trees and flowers and fruits which grow upon this earth are proportionately beautiful. The mountains too and the stones have a proportionate smoothness and transparency, and their colors are lovelier. The pebbles which are so highly prized in our world—the jaspers and rubies and emeralds and the rest—are fragments of these stones, but there e everything is as beautiful as they are, or better still. This is because the stones there are in their natural state, not damaged by decay and corroded by salt water as ours are by the sediment which has collected here, and which causes disfigurement and disease to stones and earth, and animals and plants as well. The earth itself is adorned not only

111 with all these stones but also with gold and silver and the other metals, for many rich veins of them occur in plain view in all parts of the
earth, so that to see them is a sight for the eyes of the blessed.

There are many kinds of animals upon it, and also human beings, some of whom live inland, others round the air, as we live round
the sea, and others in islands surrounded by air but close to the mainland. In a word, as water and the sea are to us for our purposes, so is
b air to them, and as air is to us, so the æther is to them. Their climate is
so temperate that they are free from disease and live much longer
than people do here, and in sight and hearing and understanding and
all other faculties they are as far superior to us as air is to water or
æther to air in clarity.

They also have sanctuaries and temples which are truly inhabited by gods, and oracles and prophecies and visions and all other
c kinds of communion with the gods occur there face to face. They see
the sun and moon and stars as they really are, and the rest of their
happiness is after the same manner.

Such is the nature of the earth as a whole and of the things that
are upon it. In the earth itself, all over its surface, there are many hollow regions, some deeper and more widely spread than that in which
we live, others deeper than our region but with a smaller expanse,
d some both shallower than ours and broader. All these are joined together underground by many connecting channels, some narrower,
some wider, through which, from one basin to another, there flows a
great volume of water—monstrous unceasing subterranean rivers of
waters both hot and cold—and of fire too, great rivers of fire, and many
of liquid mud, some clearer, some more turbid, like the rivers in Sicily
e that flow mud before the lava comes, and the lava stream itself. By
these the several regions are filled in turn as the flood reaches them.

All this movement to and fro is caused by an oscillation inside
the earth, and this oscillation is brought about by natural means, as
follows.

One of the cavities in the earth is not only larger than the rest,
but pierces right through from one side to the other. It is of this that
112 Homer speaks when he says, 'Far, far away, where lies earth's deep-
est chasm,'[2] while elsewhere both he and many other poets refer to it
as Tartarus. Into this gulf all the rivers flow together, and from it
they flow forth again, and each acquires the nature of that part of the
b earth through which it flows. The cause of the flowing in and out of
all these streams is that the mass of liquid has no bottom or foundation; so it oscillates and surges to and fro, and the air or breath that
belongs to it does the same, for it accompanies the liquid both as it
rushes to the further side of the earth and as it returns to this. And
just as when we breathe we exhale and inhale the breath in a continu-

[2] *Iliad* 8.14.

ous stream, so in this case too the breath, oscillating with the liquid, causes terrible and monstrous winds as it passes in and out. So when the water retires to the so-called lower region the streams in the earth c flow into those parts and irrigate them fully, and when in turn it ebbs from there and rushes back this way, it fills our streams again, and when they are filled they flow through their channels and through the earth; and arriving in those regions to which their ways have been severally prepared, they make seas and lakes and rivers and springs. Then sinking again beneath the ground, some by way of more and d further regions, others by fewer and nearer, they empty themselves once more into Tartarus, some much lower, some only a little lower than the point at which they were emitted, but they all flow in at a level deeper than their rise. Some flow in on the opposite side to that on which they came out, and others on the same side, while some make a complete circle and, winding like a snake one or even more times round the earth, descend as far as possible before they again discharge their waters. It is possible to descend in either direction as e far as the center, but no further, for either direction from the center is uphill, whichever way the streams are flowing.

Among these many various mighty streams there are four in particular. The greatest of these, and the one which describes the outermost circle, is that which is called Oceanus. Directly opposite to this and with a contrary course is Acheron, which not only flows through other desolate regions but passes underground and arrives at the 113 Acherusian Lake, where the souls of the dead for the most part come, and after staying there for certain fixed periods, longer or shorter, are sent forth again to the births of living creatures. Halfway between these two a third river has its rise, and near its source issues into a great place burning with sheets of fire, where it forms a boiling lake of muddy water greater than our sea. From there it follows a circular course, flowing turbid and muddy, and as it winds round in- b side the earth it comes at last to the margin of the Acherusian Lake, but does not mingle with the waters, and after many windings underground, it plunges into Tartarus at a lower point. This is the river called Pyriphlegethon, whose fiery stream belches forth jets of lava here and there in all parts of the world. Directly opposite to this in its turn the fourth river breaks out, first, they say, into a wild and dreadful place, all leaden gray, which is called the Stygian region, and the c lake which the river forms on its entry is called Styx. After falling into this, and acquiring mysterious powers in its waters, the river passes underground and follows a spiral course contrary to that of Pyriphlegethon, which it meets from the opposite direction in the Acherusian Lake. This river too mingles its stream with no other waters, but circling round falls into Tartarus opposite Pyriphlegethon, and its name, the poets say, is Cocytus.

Such is the conformation of the earth and its rivers. And when d the newly dead reach the place to which each is conducted by his guardian spirit, first they submit to judgment, both those who have lived well and holily, and those who have not. Those who are judged to have lived a neutral life set out for Acheron, and embarking in those vessels which await them, are conveyed in them to the lake, and there they dwell, and undergoing purification are both absolved by punishment from any sins that they have committed, and rewarded

e for their good deeds, according to each man's deserts. Those who on account of the greatness of their sins are judged to be incurable, as having committed many gross acts of sacrilege or many wicked and lawless murders or any other such crimes—these are hurled by their appropriate destiny into Tartarus, from whence they emerge no more.

Others are judged to have been guilty of sins which, though great, are curable—if, for example, they have offered violence to fa-

114 ther or mother in a fit of passion, but spent the rest of their lives in penitence, or if they have committed manslaughter after the same fashion. These too must be cast into Tartarus, but when this has been done and they have remained there for a year, the surge casts them out—the manslayers down Cocytus and the offenders against their parents down Pyriphlegethon. And when, as they are swept along, they come past the Acherusian Lake, there they cry aloud and call upon those whom they have killed or misused, and calling, beg and entreat for leave to pass from the stream into the lake, and be re-

b ceived by them. If they prevail, they come out and there is an end of their distress, but if not, they are swept away once more into Tartarus and from there back into the rivers, and find no release from their sufferings until they prevail upon those whom they have wronged, for this is the punishment which their judge has appointed for them.

But those who are judged to have lived a life of surpassing holiness—these are they who are released and set free from confinement in these regions of the earth, and passing upward to their pure abode,

c make their dwelling upon the earth's surface. And of these such as have purified themselves sufficiently by philosophy live thereafter altogether without bodies, and reach habitations even more beautiful, which it is not easy to portray—nor is there time to do so now. But the reasons which we have already described provide ground enough, as you can see, Simmias, for leaving nothing undone to attain during life some measure of goodness and wisdom, for the prize is glorious and the hope great.

d   Of course, no reasonable man ought to insist that the facts are exactly as I have described them. But that either this or something very like it is a true account of our souls and their future habitations —since we have clear evidence that the soul is immortal—this, I think, is both a reasonable contention and a belief worth risking, for the risk is a noble one. We should use such accounts to inspire ourselves with confidence, and that is why I have already drawn out my tale so long.

There is one way, then, in which a man can be free from all anxiety about the fate of his soul—if in life he has abandoned bodily e pleasures and adornments, as foreign to his purpose and likely to do more harm than good, and has devoted himself to the pleasures of acquiring knowledge, and so by decking his soul not with a borrowed beauty but with its own—with self-control, and goodness, and courage, and liberality, and truth—has fitted himself to await his journey 115 to the next world. You, Simmias and Cebes and the rest, will each make this journey someday in the future, but for me the fated hour, as a tragic character might say, calls even now. In other words, it is about time that I took my bath. I prefer to have a bath before drinking the poison, rather than give the women the trouble of washing me when I am dead.

When he had finished speaking, Crito said, Very well, Socrates. b But have you no directions for the others or myself about your children or anything else? What can we do to please you best?

Nothing new, Crito, said Socrates, just what I am always telling you. If you look after yourselves, whatever you do will please me and mine and you too, even if you don't agree with me now. On the other hand, if you neglect yourselves and fail to follow the line of life as I have laid it down both now and in the past, however fervently you agree with me now, it will do no good at all.   c

We shall try our best to do as you say, said Crito. But how shall we bury you?

Any way you like, replied Socrates, that is, if you can catch me and I don't slip through your fingers.

He laughed gently as he spoke, and turning to us went on, I can't persuade Crito that I am this Socrates here who is talking to you now and marshaling all the arguments. He thinks that I am the one whom he will see presently lying dead, and he asks how he is to bury d me! As for my long and elaborate explanation that when I have drunk the poison I shall remain with you no longer, but depart to a state of heavenly happiness, this attempt to console both you and myself seems to be wasted on him. You must give an assurance to Crito for me—the opposite of the one which he gave to the court which tried me. He undertook that I should stay, but you must assure him that when I am dead I shall not stay, but depart and be gone. That will help Crito to bear it more easily, and keep him from being distressed e on my account when he sees my body being burned or buried, as if something dreadful were happening to me, or from saying at the funeral that it is Socrates whom he is laying out or carrying to the grave or burying. Believe me, my dear friend Crito, misstatements are not merely jarring in their immediate context; they also have a bad effect upon the soul. No, you must keep up your spirits and say that it is only my body that you are burying, and you can bury it as you please, in 116 whatever way you think is most proper.

With these words he got up and went into another room to bathe, and Crito went after him, but told us to wait. So we waited, discussing and reviewing what had been said, or else dwelling upon the greatness of the calamity which had befallen us, for we felt just as though we were losing a father and should be orphans for the rest of our lives. Meanwhile, when Socrates had taken his bath, his children were b brought to see him—he had two little sons and one big boy—and the women of his household, you know, arrived. He talked to them in Crito's presence and gave them directions about carrying out his wishes. Then he told the women and children to go away, and came back himself to join us.

It was now nearly sunset, because he had spent a long time inside. He came and sat down, fresh from the bath, and he had only been talking for a few minutes when the prison officer came in, and walked up to him.

c Socrates, he said, at any rate I shall not have to find fault with you, as I do with others, for getting angry with me and cursing when I tell them to drink the poison—carrying out government orders. I have come to know during this time that you are the noblest and the gentlest and the bravest of all the men that have ever come here, and now especially I am sure that you are not angry with me, but with them, because you know who are responsible. So now—you know what I have come to say—good-by, and try to bear what must be as easily as you can.

d As he spoke he burst into tears, and turning round, went away.

Socrates looked up at him and said, Good-by to you, too. We will do as you say.

Then addressing us he went on, What a charming person! All the time I have been here he has visited me, and sometimes had discussions with me, and shown me the greatest kindness—and how generous of him now to shed tears for me at parting! But come, Crito, let us do as he says. Someone had better bring in the poison, if it is ready-prepared; if not, tell the man to prepare it.

e But surely, Socrates, said Crito, the sun is still upon the mountains; it has not gone down yet. Besides, I know that in other cases people have dinner and enjoy their wine, and sometimes the company of those whom they love, long after they receive the warning, and only drink the poison quite late at night. No need to hurry. There is still plenty of time.

It is natural that these people whom you speak of should act in that way, Crito, said Socrates, because they think that they gain by it. And it is also natural that I should not, because I believe that I should 117 gain nothing by drinking the poison a little later—I should only make myself ridiculous in my own eyes if I clung to life and hugged it when it has no more to offer. Come, do as I say and don't make difficulties.

At this Crito made a sign to his servant, who was standing near by. The servant went out and after spending a considerable time returned with the man who was to administer the poison. He was carrying it ready-prepared in a cup.

When Socrates saw him he said, Well, my good fellow, you understand these things. What ought I to do?

Just drink it, he said, and then walk about until you feel a weight in your legs, and then lie down. Then it will act of its own accord.   b

As he spoke he handed the cup to Socrates, who received it quite cheerfully, Echecrates, without a tremor, without any change of color or expression, and said, looking up under his brows with his usual steady gaze, What do you say about pouring a libation from this drink? Is it permitted, or not?

We only prepare what we regard as the normal dose, Socrates, he replied.

I see, said Socrates. But I suppose I am allowed, or rather bound, c to pray the gods that my removal from this world to the other may be prosperous. This is my prayer, then, and I hope that it may be granted.

With these words, quite calmly and with no sign of distaste, he drained the cup in one breath.

Up till this time most of us had been fairly successful in keeping back our tears, but when we saw that he was drinking, that he had actually drunk it, we could do so no longer. In spite of myself the tears came pouring out, so that I covered my face and wept brokenheartedly—not for him, but for my own calamity in losing such a friend. d Crito had given up even before me, and had gone out when he could not restrain his tears. But Apollodorus, who had never stopped crying even before, now broke out into such a storm of passionate weeping that he made everyone in the room break down, except Socrates himself, who said, Really, my friends, what a way to behave! Why, that was my main reason for sending away the women, to prevent this sort of disturbance, because I am told that one should make one's end in a e tranquil frame of mind. Calm yourselves and try to be brave.

This made us feel ashamed, and we controlled our tears. Socrates walked about, and presently, saying that his legs were heavy, lay down on his back—that was what the man recommended. The man— he was the same one who had administered the poison—kept his hand upon Socrates, and after a little while examined his feet and legs, then pinched his foot hard and asked if he felt it. Socrates said no. Then he did the same to his legs, and moving gradually upward in this 118 way let us see that he was getting cold and numb. Presently he felt him again and said that when it reached the heart, Socrates would be gone.

The coldness was spreading about as far as his waist when Socrates uncovered his face, for he had covered it up, and said—they were his last words—Crito, we ought to offer a cock to Asclepius. See to it, and don't forget.

No, it shall be done, said Crito. Are you sure that there is nothing else?

Socrates made no reply to this question, but after a little while he stirred, and when the man uncovered him, his eyes were fixed. When Crito saw this, he closed the mouth and eyes.

Such, Echecrates, was the end of our comrade, who was, we may fairly say, of all those whom we knew in our time, the bravest and also the wisest and most upright man.

CHARMIDES

In the Charmides, as in the Lysis and the Laches, Socrates' aim is not to convert his hearers to what he believes, but to arouse each one to think for himself. There is no other dialogue in which he so quickly convicts the company of that—to the Greek—dark and dismal failure, ignorance, or in which he so completely disarms them by putting himself in the same sad case with them.

But the Charmides presents a difficulty absent from the other two. We can translate the Greek word for courage used in the Laches and the word for friendship in the Lysis, as the two dialogues prove, but the subject of the Charmides is, What is sophrosyne?—and that word cannot be translated by any one English word. The truth is that this quality, this sophrosyne, which to the Greeks was an ideal second to none in importance, is not among our ideals. We have lost the conception of it. Enough is said about it in Greek literature for us to be able to describe it in some fashion, but we cannot give it a name. It was the spirit behind the two great Delphic sayings, "Know thyself" and "Nothing in excess." Arrogance, insolent self-assertion, was the quality most detested by the Greeks. Sophrosyne was the exact opposite. It meant accepting the bounds which excellence lays down for human nature, restraining impulses to unrestricted freedom, to all excess, obeying the inner laws of harmony and proportion.

Considered as an argument, the dialogue is inferior to both the Lysis and the Laches. Socrates shows himself a master of quibbling often enough to keep up a sense of irritation in the reader, and to leave him after pages of hairsplitting definitions with very little idea of what all the talk has been about. He will almost certainly echo Socrates' conclusion, "I have failed utterly to discover what sophrosyne is."

153 Yesterday evening we returned from the army at Potidaea, and having been a good while away, I thought that I should like to go and look at my old haunts. So I went into the palaestra of Taureas, which is over against the temple of Basile, and there I found a number of persons, most of whom I knew, but not all. My visit was unexpected, and no sooner did they see me entering than they saluted me from afar on
b all sides, and Chaerephon, who always behaves like a madman, started up from among them and ran to me, seizing my hand and saying, How did you escape from the battle, Socrates? An engagement had taken place at Potidaea not long before we came away, of which the news had only just reached Athens.

Just as you see me now, I replied.

There was a report, he said, that the engagement was very severe,
c and that many of our acquaintance had fallen.

That, I replied, was not far from the truth.

I suppose, he said, that you were present.

I was.

Then sit down here, and tell us the whole story, which as yet we have only heard imperfectly.

So saying he led me to a place by the side of Critias, the son of Callaeschrus, and when I had sat down and saluted him and the rest
d of the company, I told them the news from the army, and answered their several inquiries.

Then, when there had been enough of this, I, in my turn, began to make inquiries about matters at home—about the present state of philosophy, and about the youth. I asked whether any of them were remarkable for wisdom or beauty, or both.

154   Critias glanced at the door and saw some youths coming in, and disputing noisily with one another, followed by a crowd. Of the beauties, Socrates, he said, I fancy that you will soon be able to form a judgment. For those who are just entering are the advance guard and lovers of the great beauty of the day, as he is thought to be, and he is likely to be not far off himself.

Who is he, I said, and who is his father?

Charmides, he replied, is his name. He is my cousin, and the son
b of my uncle Glaucon. I rather think that you know him too, although he was not grown up at the time of your departure.

Certainly, I know him, I said, for he was remarkable even then when he was still a child, and I should imagine that by this time he must be almost a young man.

You will see, he said, in a moment what age he has reached and

From *The Dialogues of Plato*, translated with analyses and introductions by B. Jowett (4th edn., revised by order of the Jowett Copyright Trustees, Oxford, 1953; 1st edn., 1871).

what he is like. He had scarcely said the word, when Charmides entered.

Now you know, my friend, that I am not good at measuring, and in the presence of the beautiful I am like a measuring line without marks, for almost all young persons appear to be beautiful in my eyes. But at that moment, when I saw him, I confess that I was quite c astonished at his beauty and stature. All the company seemed to be enamored of him. Amazement and confusion reigned when he entered, and a second troop of lovers followed behind him. That grown-up men like ourselves should have been affected in this way was not surprising, but I observed the boys and saw that all of them, down to the very smallest, turned and looked at him, as if he had been a statue.

Chaerephon called me and said, What do you think of the young d man, Socrates? Has he not a beautiful face?

Most beautiful, I said.

But you would think nothing of his face, he replied, if you could see his naked form; he is absolutely perfect.

And to this they all agreed.

Ye gods, I said, what a paragon, if he has only one other slight addition!

What is that? said Critias.

If he has a noble soul. And being of your house, Critias, he may e be expected to have this.

He is as fair and good within, as he is without, replied Critias.

Then, before we see his body, should we not ask him to strip and show us his soul? He is surely just of an age at which he will like to talk.

That he will, said Critias, and I can tell you that he is indeed a 155 philosopher already, and also a considerable poet, not in his own opinion only, but in that of others.

That, my dear Critias, I replied, is a distinction which has long been in your family, and is inherited by you from Solon. But why do you not call him, and show him to me? For even if he were younger than he is, there could be no impropriety in his talking to us before you, his guardian and cousin.

Very well, he said, then I will call him. And turning to the attendant, he said, Call Charmides, and tell him that I want him to come b and see a physician about the illness of which he spoke to me the day before yesterday.

Then again addressing me, he added, He has been complaining lately of having a headache when he rises in the morning. Now why should you not make him believe that you know a cure for the headache?

Why not, I said, if only he will come.

He will be sure to come, he replied.

So he came as he was bidden. Great amusement was occasioned
c by everyone making room and pushing with might and main at his
neighbor in order to sit next to him, until at the two ends of the row
one had to get up and the other was rolled over sideways. And he
came and sat down between Critias and me. But I, my friend, was beginning to feel awkward. My former bold belief in my powers of
conversing naturally with him had vanished. And when Critias told
him that I was the person who had the cure, he looked at me in an in-
d describable manner, and made as though to ask me a question. And
all the people in the palaestra crowded about us, and at that moment,
my good friend, I caught a sight of the inwards of his garment, and
took the flame. Then I could no longer contain myself. I thought how
well Cydias understood the nature of love, when, in speaking of a fair
youth, he warns someone 'not to bring the fawn in the sight of the
e lion to be devoured by him,' for I felt that I had been overcome by a
sort of wild-beast appetite. But still when he asked me if I knew the
cure for the headache, I answered, though with an effort, that I did
know.

And what is it? he said.

I replied that it was a kind of leaf, which required to be accompanied by a charm, and if a person would repeat the charm at the
same time that he used the cure, he would be made whole, but that
without the charm the leaf would be of no avail.

156   Then I will write out the charm from your dictation, he said.

With my consent? I said. Or without my consent?

With your consent, Socrates, he said, laughing.

Very good, I said. So you know my name, do you?

I ought to know you, he replied, for there is a great deal said
about you among my companions, and I remember when I was a child
seeing you in company with Critias here.

I am glad to find that you remember me, I said, for I shall now
b be more at home with you and shall be better able to explain the nature of the charm, about which I felt a difficulty before. For the charm
will do more, Charmides, than only cure the headache. I dare say that
you have heard eminent physicians say to a patient who comes to
them with bad eyes, that they cannot undertake to cure his eyes by
c themselves, but that if his eyes are to be cured, his head must be
treated too. And then again they say that to think of curing the head
alone, and not the rest of the body also, is the height of folly. And arguing in this way they apply their regime to the whole body, and try to
treat and heal the whole and the part together. Did you ever observe
that this is what they say?

Yes, he said.

And they are right, and you would agree with them?

Yes, he said, certainly I should.

d   His approving answers reassured me, and I began by degrees to regain confidence, and my natural heat returned to me. Such, Charmides, I said, is the nature of the charm, which I learned when serving with the army from one of the physicians of the Thracian king Zalmoxis who are said to be able even to give immortality. This Thracian told me that in these notions of theirs, which I was just now mentioning, the Greek physicians are quite right as far as they go, but Zalmoxis, he added, our king, who is also a god, says further, 'that as e you ought not to attempt to cure the eyes without the head, or the head without the body, so neither ought you to attempt to cure the body without the soul. And this,' he said, 'is the reason why the cure of many diseases is unknown to the physicians of Hellas, because they disregard the whole, which ought to be studied also, for the part can never be well unless the whole is well.' For all good and evil, whether in the body or in the whole man, originates, as he declared, in the soul, and overflows from thence, as if from the head into the eyes. And therefore if the head and body are to be well, you must begin by 157 curing the soul—that is the first and essential thing. And the cure of the soul, my dear youth, has to be effected by the use of certain charms, and these charms are fair words, and by them temperance is implanted in the soul, and where temperance comes and stays, there health is speedily imparted, not only to the head, but to the whole b body. And when he taught me the cure and the charm he added, 'Let no one persuade you to cure his head, until he has first given you his soul to be cured by the charm. For this,' he said, 'is the great error of our day in the treatment of human beings, that men try to be physicians of health and temperance separately.' And he strictly enjoined me not to let anyone, however rich or noble or fair, persuade me to give him the cure, without the charm. Now I have sworn, and I must c keep my oath, and therefore if you will allow me to apply the Thracian charm first to your soul, as the stranger directed, I will afterward proceed to apply the cure to your head. But if not, I do not know what I am to do with you, my dear Charmides.

Critias, when he heard this, said, The headache will be a blessing to my young cousin, if the pain in his head compels him to improve his mind. Yet I can tell you, Socrates, that Charmides is not only pre- d eminent in beauty among his equals, but also in that quality for which you say you have the charm—temperance, is it not?

Yes, I said.

Then let me tell you that he is the most temperate of the young men of today, and for his age inferior to none in any quality.

Indeed, Charmides, I said, I think that you ought to excel others in all good qualities, for if I am not mistaken there is no one present e who could easily point out two Athenian houses, whose union would be likely to produce a better or nobler scion than the two from which you are sprung. There is your father's house, which is descended from Critias, the son of Dropides, whose family has been commemorated

158 in the panegyrics of Anacreon, Solon, and many other poets, as famous for beauty and virtue and all other high fortune. And your
mother's house is equally distinguished, for your maternal uncle, Pyrilampes, is reputed never to have found his superior for stature and
beauty in Persia at the court of the Great King, or anywhere on the
continent of Asia in all the places to which he went as ambassador;
that whole family is not a whit inferior to the other. Having such an-
b cestors you ought to be first in all things, and, sweet son of Glaucon,
your outward form is no dishonor to any of them. If to beauty you
add temperance, and if in other respects you are what Critias declares
you to be, then, dear Charmides, blessed is the son your mother bore.
And here lies the point. For if, as he declares, you have this gift of
temperance already, and are temperate enough, in that case you have
no need of any charms, whether of Zalmoxis or of Abaris the Hyperborean, and I may as well let you have the cure of the head at once.
c But if you have not yet acquired this quality, I must use the charm before I give you the medicine. Please, therefore, to inform me whether
you admit the truth of what Critias has been saying. Have you or
have you not this quality of temperance?

Charmides blushed, and the blush heightened his beauty, for
modesty is becoming in youth. He then made the graceful reply that
he really could not at once answer, either yes or no, to the question
d which I had asked. For, said he, if I affirm that I am not temperate,
that would be a strange thing for me to say against myself, and also I
should give the lie to Critias, and to many others who, according to
him, think that I am temperate. But, on the other hand, if I say that I
am, I shall have to praise myself, which would be ill manners, and
therefore I do not know how to answer you.

I said to him, That is a natural reply, Charmides, and I think
that you and I ought together to inquire whether you have this quality
about which I am asking or not, and then you will not be compelled
e to say what you do not like; neither shall I rashly have recourse to
medicine. Therefore, if you please, I will share the inquiry with you,
but I will not press you if you would rather not.

There is nothing which I should like better, he said, and as far
as I am concerned you may proceed in the way which you think best.

I think, I said, that it would be best to approach the question in
this way. If temperance abides in you, you must have an opinion about
her. She must give some intimation of her nature and qualities, which
159 may enable you to form a notion of her. Is not that true?

Yes, he said, that I think is true.

You know your native language, I said, and therefore you must be
able also to express your opinion.

Perhaps, he said.

In order, then, that we may form a conjecture whether you have

temperance abiding in you or not, tell me, I said, what, in your opinion, is temperance?

At first he hesitated, and was not very willing to answer. Then he b
said that he thought temperance was doing all things orderly and
quietly—for example, walking in the streets, and talking, and indeed
doing everything in that way. In a word, he said, I should answer that,
in my opinion, temperance is a kind of quietness.

Are you right, Charmides? I said. No doubt some would affirm
that the quiet are temperate, but let us see whether there is anything
in this view. And first tell me whether you would not acknowledge
temperance to be of the class of the noble and good?   c

Yes.

But which is better when you are at the writing master's, to write
the same letters quickly or quietly?

Quickly.

And to read quickly or slowly?

Quickly again.

And in playing the lyre, or wrestling, quickness and sharpness
are far better than quietness and slowness?

Yes.

And the same holds in boxing and in the pancratium?

Certainly.

And in leaping and running and in bodily exercises generally, actions done quickly and with agility are good and noble; those done d
slowly and quietly are bad and unsightly?

It seems so.

Then, I said, in all bodily actions, not quietness, but the greatest
agility and quickness, is noblest and best?

Yes, certainly.

And is temperance a good?

Yes.

Then, in reference to the body, not quietness, but quickness will
be the more temperate, if temperance is a good?

Apparently, he said.

Again, I said, which is better—facility in learning, or difficulty in e
learning?

Facility.

Yes, I said, and facility in learning is learning quickly, and difficulty in learning is learning quietly and slowly?

True.

And is it not better to teach another quickly and energetically,
rather than quietly and slowly?

Yes.

Once more, which is better, to call to mind and to remember
quickly and readily, or quietly and slowly?

The former.

160   And is not cleverness a quickness of the soul, and not a quietness?

True.

Is it not then better to understand what is said, whether at the writing master's or the music master's or anywhere else, not as quietly as possible, but as quickly as possible?

Yes.

And further, in the searchings or deliberations of the soul, not the quietest, as I imagine, and he who with difficulty deliberates and discovers, is thought worthy of praise, but he who does so most b easily and quickly?

Quite true, he said.

Well then, in all that concerns either body or soul, swiftness and activity are clearly better than slowness and quietness?

Probably.

Then temperance is not quietness, nor is the temperate life quiet —certainly not upon this view, for the life which is temperate is admitted to be the good. And of two things one is true—either never, or c very seldom, do the quiet actions in life appear to be better than the quick and energetic ones, or supposing at the best that of the nobler actions there are as many quiet as quick and vehement; still, even if we grant this, temperance will not be acting quietly any more than acting quickly and energetically, either in walking or talking or in d anything else. Nor will the quiet life be more temperate than the unquiet, seeing that temperance was placed by us among the good and noble things, and the quick have been shown to be as good as the quiet.

I think that you are right, Socrates, he said.

Then once more, Charmides, I said, fix your attention more closely and look within you. Consider the effect which temperance has upon yourself, and the nature of that which should have this ef- e fect. Think over all this, and tell me truly and courageously—what is temperance?

After a moment's pause, in which he made a real manly effort to think, he said, My opinion is, Socrates, that temperance makes a man ashamed or modest, and that temperance is the same as modesty.

Very good, I said, and did not you admit, just now, that temperance is noble?

Yes, certainly, he said.

And therefore that temperate men are good men?

Yes.

And can that be good which does not make men good?

Certainly not.

And you would infer that temperance is not only noble, but also good?

That is my opinion.

Well, I said, but surely you would agree with Homer when he 161
says, 'Modesty is not good for a needy man'? [1]

Yes, he said, I agree.

Then I suppose that modesty is and is not good?

Apparently.

But temperance, whose presence makes men only good, and not
bad, is always good?

That appears to me to be as you say.

And the inference is that temperance cannot be modesty—if
temperance is good, and if modesty is as much an evil as a good?   b

All that, Socrates, appears to me to be true, but I should like to
know what you think about another definition of temperance, which
I have just remembered that I heard from someone, 'Temperance is
doing our own business.' Please consider whether he was right who
affirmed that.

You wicked boy! I said. This is what Critias, or some other philosopher has told you.   c

Someone else then, said Critias, for certainly I have not.

But what matter, said Charmides, from whom I heard this?

No matter at all, I replied, for the point is not who said the words,
but whether they are true or not.

There you are in the right, Socrates, he replied.

To be sure, I said. Yet I should be surprised if we are able to discover their truth or falsehood, for they are a kind of riddle.

What makes you think so? he said.

Because, I said, he who uttered them seems to me to have meant d
one thing, and said another. Is the schoolmaster, for example, to be
regarded as doing nothing when he reads or writes?

I should rather think that he was doing something.

And does the schoolmaster write or read, or teach you boys to
write or read, his own name only, or did you write your enemies'
names as well as your own and your friends'?

As much one as the other.

And was there anything meddling or intemperate in this?   e

Certainly not.

And yet you were doing what was not your own business if reading and writing are a form of doing.

But they certainly are.

And the healing art, my friend, and building, and weaving, and
doing anything whatever which is done by art—these all clearly come
under the head of doing?

Certainly.

And do you think that a state would be well ordered by a law

[1] *Odyssey* 17.347.

which compelled every man to weave and wash his own coat, and
make his own shoes, and his own flask and strigil, and other imple-
162 ments, on this principle of everyone doing and performing his own,
and abstaining from what is not his own?

I think not, he said.

But, I said, a temperate state will be a well-ordered state.

Of course, he replied.

Then temperance, I said, will not be doing one's own business—
not at least in this way, or doing things of this sort?

It seems not.

Then, as I was just now saying, he who declared that temperance
is a man doing his own business had a hidden meaning, for I do not
think that he could have been such a fool as to mean this. Was he a
b fool who told you, Charmides?

Nay, he replied, I certainly thought him a very wise man.

Then I am quite certain that he put forth his definition as a riddle,
thinking that no one would easily discover the meaning of the words,
'doing his own business.'

I dare say, he replied.

And what is the meaning of a man doing his own business? Can
you tell me?

Indeed, I cannot, and I should not wonder if the man himself
who used this phrase did not understand what he meant.

Whereupon he laughed slyly, and looked at Critias. Critias had
c long been showing uneasiness, for he felt that he had a reputation to
maintain with Charmides and the rest of the company. He had, however, hitherto managed to restrain himself, but now he could no longer
forbear, and I am convinced of the truth of the suspicion which I
entertained at the time, that it was from Critias that Charmides had
heard this answer about temperance. And Charmides, who did not
want to defend it himself, but to make Critias defend it, tried to stir
d him up. He went on pointing out that he had been refuted, at which
Critias grew angry, and appeared, as I thought, inclined to quarrel
with him—just as a poet might quarrel with an actor who spoiled his
poems in reciting them. So he looked hard at him and said, Do you
imagine, Charmides, because you do not understand the meaning of
this definition of temperance that its author likewise did not understand the meaning of his own words?

Why, at his age, I said, most excellent Critias, he can hardly be
e expected to understand, but you, who are older, and have studied, may
well be assumed to know the meaning of them. And therefore, if you
agree, and accept his definition of temperance, I would much rather
argue with you than with him about the truth or falsehood of the definition.

I entirely agree, said Critias, and accept the definition.

Very good, I said, and now let me repeat my question. Do you admit, as I was just now saying, that all craftsmen make or do something?

I do.

And do they make or do their own business only, or that of others 163 also?

That of others also.

And are they temperate, seeing that they do not make or do their own business only?

Why not? he said.

No objection on my part, I said, but there may be a difficulty on his who proposes as a definition of temperance, 'doing one's own business,' and then says that there is no reason why those who do the business of others should not be temperate.

Nay, said he, did I ever acknowledge that those who do the business of others are temperate? I said those who make, not those who do.

What! I asked. Do you mean to say that doing and making are b not the same?

No more, he replied, than making and working are the same. Thus much I have learned from Hesiod, who says that 'work is no disgrace.' [2] Now do you imagine that if he had meant by working and doing such things as you were describing, he would have said that there was no disgrace in them—for example, in the manufacture of shoes, or in selling dried fish, or sitting for hire in a house of ill fame? That, Socrates, is not to be supposed, but I conceive him to have distinguished making from doing and work, and, while admitting that c making anything might sometimes become a disgrace, when the employment was not honorable, to have thought that work was never any disgrace at all. For things nobly and usefully made he called works, and such makings he called workings, and doings. And he must be supposed to have deemed only such things to be man's proper business, and all that is hurtful, not to be his business, and in that sense Hesiod, and any other wise man, may be reasonably supposed to call him wise who does his own work.

O Critias, I said, no sooner had you opened your mouth than I d pretty well knew that you would call that which is proper to a man, and that which is his own, good, and that the makings of the good you would call doings, for I am no stranger to the endless distinctions which Prodicus draws about names. Now I have no objection to your giving names any signification which you please, if you will only tell me to what you apply them. Please then to begin again, and be a little plainer. Do you mean that this doing or making, or whatever is the e word which you would use, of good things, is temperance?

I do, he said.

Then not he who does evil, but he who does good, is temperate?

[2] *Works and Days* 309.

Yes, he said, and you, friend, would agree.

No matter whether I should or not. Just now, not what I think, but what you are saying, is the point at issue.

Well, he answered, I mean to say that he who does evil, and not good, is not temperate, and that he is temperate who does good, and not evil. For temperance I define in plain words to be the doing of good actions.

164   And you may be very likely right in what you are saying, but I am surprised that you think temperate men to be ignorant of their own temperance?

I do not think so, he said.

And yet were you not saying, just now, that craftsmen might be temperate in doing another's work, as well as in doing their own?

I was, he replied, but what is your drift?

I have no particular drift, but I wish that you would tell me
b   whether a physician who cures a patient may do good to himself and good to his patient also.

I think that he may.

And he who does so does his duty?

Yes.

And does not he who does his duty act temperately or wisely?

Yes, he acts wisely.

But must the physician necessarily know when his treatment is likely to prove beneficial, and when not? And must every worker necessarily know when he is likely to be benefited, and when not to be benefited, by the work which he is doing?

I suppose not.

Then, I said, the physician may sometimes do good or harm,
c   without knowing which he has done, and yet in doing good, as you say, he has done temperately or wisely. Was not that your statement?

Yes.

Then, as would seem, in doing good he may act wisely or temperately, and be wise or temperate, but not know his own wisdom or temperance?

But that, Socrates, he said, is impossible, and therefore if this is, as you imply, the necessary consequence of any of my previous
d   admissions, I will withdraw them and will not be ashamed to acknowledge that I made a mistake, rather than admit that a man can be temperate or wise who does not know himself. For I would almost say that self-knowledge is the very essence of temperance, and in this I agree with him who dedicated the inscription 'Know thyself!' at Delphi. That inscription, if I am not mistaken, is put there as a sort of salutation which the god addresses to those who enter the temple—as
e   much as to say that the ordinary salutation of 'Hail!' is not right, and that the exhortation 'Be temperate!' is far better. If I rightly understand the meaning of the inscription, the god speaks to those who en-

ter his temple, not as men speak, but whenever a worshiper enters, the first word which he hears is 'Be temperate!' This, however, like a prophet he expresses in a sort of riddle, for 'Know thyself!' and 'Be temperate!' are the same, as I maintain, and as the words imply, and yet they may be thought to be different. And succeeding sages who 165 added 'Never too much,' or 'Give a pledge, and evil is nigh at hand,' would appear to have so distinguished them, for they imagined that 'Know thyself!' was a piece of advice which the god gave, and not his salutation of the worshipers at their first coming in, and they dedicated their own inscriptions under the idea that they too would give equally useful pieces of advice. Shall I tell you, Socrates, why I say all this? My object is to leave the previous discussion—in which I know not whether you or I are more right, but, at any rate, no clear result b was attained—and to raise a new one in which I will attempt to prove, if you deny it, that temperance is self-knowledge.

Yes, I said, Critias, but you come to me as though I professed to know about the questions which I ask, and as though I could, if I only would, agree with you. Whereas the fact is that I am inquiring with you into the truth of that which is advanced from time to time, just because I do not know, and when I have inquired, I will say whether I agree with you or not. Please then to allow me time to reflect. c

Reflect, he said.

I am reflecting, I replied, and discover that temperance or wisdom, if it is a species of knowledge, must be a science, and a science of something.

Yes, he said, the science of a man's self.

Is not medicine the science of health?

True.

And suppose that I were asked by you what is the use or effect of medicine, which is this science of health. I should answer that medicine is of very great use in producing health, which, as you will ad- d mit, is an excellent effect.

Granted.

And if you were to ask me what is the result or effect of architecture, which is the science of building, I should say houses, and so of other arts, which all have their different results. Now I want you, Critias, to answer a similar question about temperance or wisdom, which, according to you, is the science of a man's self. Admitting this view, I ask of you, what good work, worthy of the name wise, does temperance or wisdom, which is the science of a man's self, effect? An- e swer me.

That is not the true way of pursuing the inquiry, Socrates, he said, for wisdom is not like the other sciences, any more than they are like one another, but you proceed as if they were alike. For tell me, he said, what result is there of computation or geometry, in the same sense as a house is the result of building, or a garment of weaving, or

166 any other work of any of the many other arts? Can you show me any such result of them? You cannot.

That is true, I said, but still I can show you that each of these sciences has a subject which is different from the science. The art of computation, for instance, has to do with odd and even numbers in their numerical relations to themselves and to each other. Is not that true?

Yes.

And the odd and even numbers are not the same with the art of computation?

They are not.

b   The art of weighing, again, has to do with lighter and heavier, but the art of weighing is one thing, and the heavy and the light are another. Do you admit that?

Yes.

Now, I want to know, what is that which is not wisdom, and of which wisdom is the science?

You are just falling into the old error, Socrates, he said. You come asking wherein wisdom or temperance differs from the other sciences, and then you try to discover some respect in which it is like

c   them. But it is not, for all the other sciences are of something else, and not of themselves. Wisdom alone is a science of other sciences and of itself. And of this, as I believe, you are very well aware, and you are only doing what you denied that you were doing just now, trying to refute me, instead of pursuing the argument.

And what if I am? How can you think that I have any other motive in refuting you but what I should have in examining into myself? This motive would be just a fear of my unconsciously fancying

d   that I knew something of which I was ignorant. And at this moment, I assure you, I pursue the argument chiefly for my own sake, and perhaps in some degree also for the sake of my other friends. For would you not say that the discovery of things as they truly are is a good common to all mankind?

Yes, certainly, Socrates, he said.

Then, I said, be cheerful, sweet sir, and give your opinion in answer to the question which I asked, never minding whether Critias

e   or Socrates is the person refuted. Attend only to the argument, and see what will come of the refutation.

I think that is reasonable, he replied, and I will do as you say.

Tell me, then, I said, what you mean to affirm about wisdom.

I mean to say that wisdom is the only science which is the science of itself as well as of the other sciences.

But the science of science, I said, will also be the science of the absence of science.

Very true, he said.

167   Then the wise or temperate man, and he only, will know himself,

and be able to examine what he knows or does not know, and to see what others know and think that they know and do really know, and what they do not know and fancy that they know when they do not. No other person will be able to do this. And this is wisdom and temperance and self-knowledge—for a man to know what he knows, and what he does not know. That is your meaning?

Yes, he said.

Now then, I said, since the third time brings luck, let us begin again, and ask, in the first place, whether it is or is not possible for a b person to know that he knows what he knows and that he does not know what he does not know, and in the second place, whether, if perfectly possible, such knowledge is of any use.

That is what we have to consider, he said.

Well then, Critias, I said, see if you are in a better position than I am. I am in a difficulty. Shall I tell you the nature of the difficulty?

By all means.

Does not what you have been saying, if true, amount to this, that there must be a single science which is wholly a science of itself and of other sciences, and that the same is also the science of the absence c of science?

Yes.

But consider how monstrous this proposition is, my friend. In any parallel case, the impossibility will be obvious to you.

How is that? And in what cases do you mean?

In such cases as this. Suppose that there is a kind of vision which is not like the ordinary vision, but a vision of itself and of other sorts of vision, and of the defect of them, which in seeing sees no color, but only itself and other sorts of vision. Do you think that there is such a d kind of vision?

Certainly not.

Or is there a kind of hearing which hears no sound at all, but only itself and other sorts of hearing, or the defects of them?

There is not.

Or take all the senses together. Can you imagine that there is any sense which is a sense of itself and of other senses, but is incapable of perceiving the objects of the senses?

I think not.

Could there be any desire which is not the desire of any pleasure, e but of itself and of all other desires?

Certainly not.

Or can you imagine a wish which wishes for no good, but only for itself and all other wishes?

I should answer no.

Or would you say that there is a love which is not the love of beauty, but of itself and of other loves?

I should not.

168   Or did you ever know of a fear which fears itself or other fears,
but none of the objects of fear?

I never did, he said.

Or of an opinion which is an opinion of itself and of other opinions, and which has no opinion on the subjects of opinion in general?

Certainly not.

But, it seems, we are assuming a science of this kind, which, having no subject matter, is a science of itself and of the other sciences?

Yes, that is what is affirmed.

It is certainly a curiosity if it really exists. We must not however
as yet absolutely deny the possibility of such a science, but continue
to inquire whether it exists.

b   You are quite right.

Well then, this science of which we are speaking is a science of
something, and is of a nature to be a science of something?

Yes.

Just as that which is greater is of a nature to be greater than
something else?

Yes.

And this something else is less, if the other is conceived to be
greater?

To be sure.

And if we could find something which is at once greater than itself and greater than other great things, but not greater than those
things in comparison of which the others are greater, then that thing
c   would have the property of being greater and also less than itself?

That, Socrates, he said, is the inevitable inference.

Or if there be a double which is double of itself and of other doubles, both they and itself will be halves, for the double is relative to
the half?

That is true.

And that which is more than itself will also be less, and that
which is heavier will also be lighter, and that which is older will also
d   be younger—and the same of other things. That which has a nature
relative to self will retain also the nature of its object; I mean to say,
for example, that hearing is, as we say, of sound or voice. Is that
true?

Yes.

Then if hearing hears itself, it must hear a voice, for there is no
other way of hearing.

Certainly.

And sight also, my excellent friend, if it sees itself must have a
e   color, for sight cannot see that which has no color.

No.

Do you remark, Critias, that in several of the examples which have been recited the notion of a relation to self is altogether inadmissible, and in other cases hardly credible—inadmissible, for example, in the case of magnitudes, numbers, and the like?

Very true.

But in the case of hearing and sight, or in the power of self-motion, and the power of heat to burn, and so on, this relation to self will be regarded as incredible by some, but perhaps not by others. 169 And some great man, my friend, is wanted, who will satisfactorily determine for us whether there is nothing which has an inherent property of relation to self rather than to something else, or some things only and not others, and whether in this class of self-related things, if there be such a class, that science which is called wisdom or temperance is included. I altogether distrust my own power of determining these matters. I am not certain whether such a science of science b can possibly exist, and even if it does undoubtedly exist, I should not acknowledge it to be wisdom or temperance, until I can also see whether such a science would or would not do us any good, for I have an impression that temperance is a benefit and a good. And therefore, O son of Callaeschrus, as you maintain that temperance or wisdom is a science of science, and also of the absence of science, I will request you to show in the first place, as I was saying before, the possibility, and in the second place, the advantage, of such a science. And then perhaps you may satisfy me that you are right in your view of tem- c perance.

Critias heard me say this, and saw that I was in a difficulty, and as one person when another yawns in his presence catches the infection of yawning from him, so did he seem to be driven into a difficulty by my difficulty. But as he had a reputation to maintain, he was ashamed to admit before the company that he could not answer my challenge or determine the question at issue, and he made an unintelligible attempt to hide his perplexity. d

In order that the argument might proceed, I said to him, Well then, Critias, if you like, let us assume that this science of science is possible—whether the assumption is right or wrong may hereafter be investigated. Admitting its complete possibility, will you tell me how such a science enables us to distinguish what we know or do not know, which, as we were saying, is self-knowledge or wisdom? Was not that it?

Yes, Socrates, he said, and the rest I think follows. For he who has this science or knowledge which knows itself will become like the knowledge which he has, in the same way that he who has swift- e ness will be swift, and he who has beauty will be beautiful, and he who has knowledge will know. In the same way he who has that knowledge which is self-knowing, will know himself.

I do not doubt, I said, that a man will know himself, when he possesses that which has self-knowledge, but what necessity is there that, having this, he should know what he knows and what he does not know?

170   Because, Socrates, they are the same.

Very likely, I said, but I fear I remain as stupid as ever, for still I fail to comprehend how this knowing what you know and do not know is the same as the knowledge of self.

What do you mean? he said.

This is what I mean, I replied. I will admit that there is a science of science. Can this do more than determine that of two things one is and the other is not science or knowledge?

No, just that.

b   Is it then the same thing as knowledge or want of knowledge of health, or the same as knowledge or want of knowledge of justice?

Certainly not.

The one is medicine, and the other is politics, whereas that of which we are speaking is knowledge pure and simple.

Very true.

And if a man has only knowledge of knowledge, without any further knowledge of health and justice, the probability is that he will only know that he knows something, and has a certain knowledge, both in his own case and in that of others.

True.

Then how will this knowledge or science teach him to know what
c he knows? For he knows health not through wisdom or temperance but through the art of medicine, and he has learned harmony from the art of music and building from the art of building, but in neither case from wisdom or temperance—and the same of other things.

It seems so.

How will wisdom, regarded only as a knowledge of knowledge or science of science, ever teach him that he knows health, or that he knows building?

It is impossible.

Then he who is ignorant of these things will only know that he knows, but not what he knows?

True.

d   Then wisdom or being wise appears to be not the knowledge of the things which we do or do not know, but only the knowledge that we know or do not know?

That is the inference.

Then he who has this knowledge will not be able to establish whether a claimant knows or does not know that which he says that he knows; he will only know that he has a knowledge of some kind, but wisdom will not show him of what the knowledge is?

It seems not.

e   Neither will he be able to distinguish the pretender in medicine

from the true physician, nor between any other true and false professor of knowledge. Let us consider the matter in this way. If the
wise man or any other man wants to distinguish the true physician
from the false, how will he proceed? He will not talk to him about the
science of medicine, for as we were saying, the physician understands
nothing but health and disease.

True.

But the physician knows nothing about science, for this has been
assumed to be the province of wisdom alone.

True.

And further, since medicine is science, we must infer that he   171
does not know anything about medicine.

Exactly.

Then the wise man may indeed know that the physician has
some kind of science or knowledge, but when he wants to discover the
nature of this he will ask, What is the subject matter? For the several
sciences are distinguished not by the mere fact that they are sciences,
but by the nature of their subjects. Is not that true?

Quite true.

And medicine is distinguished from other sciences as having the
subject matter of health and disease?

Yes.

And he who would inquire into the nature of medicine must test
it in health and disease, which are the sphere of medicine, and not in   b
what is extraneous and is not its sphere?

True.

And he who wishes to make a fair test of the physician as a physician will test him in what relates to these?

He will.

He will consider whether what he says is true, and whether what
he does is right, in relation to health and disease?

He will.

But can anyone pursue the inquiry into either unless he have a
knowledge of medicine?

He cannot.

No one at all, it would seem, except the physician can have this   c
knowledge—and therefore not the wise man. He would have to be a
physician as well as a wise man.

Very true.

Then, assuredly, wisdom or temperance, if it is no more than a
science of science and of the absence of science or knowledge, will not
be able to distinguish the physician who knows what concerns his profession from one who does not know but pretends or thinks that he
knows, or any other professor of anything at all. Like any other artist,
the wise or temperate man will only know the man of his own trade,
and no one else.

That is evident, he said.

d   But then what profit, Critias, I said, is there any longer in wisdom or temperance which yet remains, if this is wisdom? If, indeed, as we were supposing at first, the wise man were able to distinguish what he knew and did not know, and that he knew the one and did not know the other, and to recognize a similar faculty of discernment in others, there would certainly be a great advantage in being wise, for then we should never make a mistake, but should pass through life the unerring guides of ourselves and of those who are under us. We

e   should not attempt to do what we did not know, but we should find out those who know, and hand the business over to them and trust in them. Nor should we allow those who were under us to do anything which they were not likely to do well, and they would be likely to do well just that of which they had knowledge. And the house or state which was ordered or administered under the guidance of wisdom, and everything else of which wisdom was the lord, would be sure to be

172   well ordered, for with truth guiding and error eliminated, in all their doings men must do nobly and well, and doing well means happiness. Was not this, Critias, what we spoke of as the great advantage of wisdom—to know what is known and what is unknown to us?

Very true, he said.

And now you perceive, I said, that no such science is to be found anywhere.

I perceive, he said.

b   May we assume then, I said, that wisdom, viewed in this new light as a knowledge of knowledge and ignorance, has this advantage —that he who possesses such knowledge will more easily learn anything which he learns, and that everything will be clearer to him, because, in addition to the several objects of knowledge, he sees the science, and this also will better enable him to test the knowledge which others have of what he knows himself, whereas the inquirer who is without this knowledge may be supposed to have a feebler and less effective insight? Are not these, my friend, the real advan-

c   tages which are to be gained from wisdom? And are not we looking and seeking after something more than is to be found in her?

It may be, he said.

Perhaps it may, I said, or perhaps again we have been inquiring to no purpose—as I am led to infer, because I observe that if this is wisdom, some strange consequences would follow. Let us, if you please, assume the possibility of this science of sciences, and not refuse to allow that, as was originally suggested, wisdom is the knowl-

d   edge of what we know and do not know. Assuming all this, let us consider more closely, Critias, whether wisdom, such as this, would do us much good. For we were wrong, I think, in supposing, as we were saying just now, that such wisdom ordering the government of house or state would be a great benefit.

How so? he said.

Why, I said, we were far too ready to admit the great benefits which mankind would obtain from their severally doing the things which they knew, and committing the things of which they are ignorant to those who were better acquainted with them.

Were we not right in making that admission?   e

I think not.

How very strange, Socrates!

There, I said, I most emphatically agree with you, and I was thinking as much just now when I said that strange consequences would follow, and that I was afraid we were on the wrong track. For however sure we may be that this is wisdom, I certainly cannot make out what good this sort of thing does to us.   173

What do you mean? he said. I wish that you could make me understand what you mean.

I dare say that what I am saying is nonsense, I replied, and yet if a man has any feeling of what is due to himself, he cannot let the thought which comes into his mind pass away unheeded and unexamined.

I like that, he said.

Hear, then, I said, my own dream—whether coming through the horn or the ivory gate, I cannot tell. The dream is this. Let us suppose that wisdom is such as we are now defining, and that she has absolute sway over us. Then, each action will be done according to the arts   b or sciences, and no one professing to be a pilot when he is not, no physician or general or anyone else pretending to know matters of which he is ignorant, will deceive or elude us. Our health will be improved; our safety at sea, and also in battle, will be assured; our coats and shoes, and all other instruments and implements will be skillfully   c made, because the workmen will be good and true. Aye, and if you please, you may suppose that prophecy will be a real knowledge of the future, and will be under the control of wisdom, who will deter deceivers and set up the true prophets in their place as the revealers of the future. Now I quite agree that mankind, thus provided, would live and act according to knowledge, for wisdom would watch and pre-   d vent ignorance from intruding on us in our work. But whether by acting according to knowledge we shall act well and be happy, my dear Critias—this is a point which we have not yet been able to determine.

Yet I think, he replied, that if you discard knowledge, you will hardly find the crown of happiness in anything else.

Well, just answer me one small question, I said. Of what is this knowledge? Do you mean a knowledge of shoemaking?

God forbid.   e

Or of working in brass?

Certainly not.

Or in wool, or wood, or anything of that sort?

No, I do not.

Then, I said, we are giving up the doctrine that he who lives according to knowledge is happy, for these live according to knowledge, and yet they are not allowed by you to be happy. But I think that you mean to confine happiness to those who live according to knowledge of some particular thing, such for example as the prophet, who, as I
174 was saying, knows the future. Is it of him you are speaking or of someone else?

Yes, I mean him, but there are others as well.

Who? I said. Evidently someone who knows the past and present as well as the future, and is ignorant of nothing. Let us suppose that there is such a person, and if there is, you will allow that he is the most knowing of all living men.

Certainly he is.

Yet I should like to know one thing more. Which of the different kinds of knowledge makes him happy? Or do all equally make him happy?

Not all equally, he replied.

b   But which most tends to make him happy? The knowledge of what past, present, or future thing? Is it, for example, the knowledge of the game of draughts?

Nonsense, draughts indeed!

Or of computation?

No.

Or of health?

That is nearer the truth, he said.

And that knowledge which is nearest of all, I said, is the knowledge of what?

The knowledge with which he discerns good and evil.

You villain! I said. You have been carrying me round in a circle, and all this time hiding from me the fact that it is not the life accord-
c ing to knowledge which makes men act rightly and be happy, not even if it be knowledge of all the sciences, but one science only, that of good and evil. For, let me ask you, Critias, whether, if you take away this science from the others, medicine will not equally give health, and shoemaking equally produce shoes, and the art of the weaver clothes—whether the art of the pilot will not equally save our lives at sea, and the art of the general in war?

Equally.

And yet, my dear Critias, none of these things will be well or ben-
d eficially done, if the science of the good be wanting.

True.

But this science, it seems, is not wisdom or temperance, but a science of human advantage—not a science of other sciences, or of ignorance, but of good and evil. And if this be of advantage, then wisdom or temperance must be something else.

And why, he replied, will not wisdom be of advantage? For, however much we assume that wisdom is a science of sciences, and has a sway over other sciences, surely she will have this particular science of the good under her control, and in this way will benefit us. e

And will wisdom give health? I said. Is not this rather the effect of medicine? Or does wisdom do the work of any of the other arts—do they not each of them do their own work? Have we not long ago asseverated that wisdom is only the knowledge of knowledge and of ignorance, and of nothing else?

It seems so.

Then wisdom will not be the producer of health?

Certainly not.

We found that health belonged to a different art? 175

Yes.

Nor does wisdom give advantage, my good friend, for that again we have just now been attributing to another art.

Very true.

How then can wisdom be advantageous, when it produces no advantage?

Apparently it cannot, Socrates.

You see, then, Critias, that I was not far wrong in fearing that I was making no sound inquiry into wisdom—I was quite right in depreciating myself, for that which is admitted to be the best of all things would never have seemed to us useless, if I had been good for b anything at an inquiry. But now I have been utterly defeated, and have failed to discover what that is to which the lawgiver gave this name of temperance or wisdom. And yet many more admissions were made by us than could be fairly granted, for we admitted that there was a science of science, although the argument said no, and protested against us. And we admitted further that this science knew the works of the other sciences—although this too was denied by the c argument—because we wanted to show that the wise man had knowledge of what he knew and of what he did not know. We generously made the concession, and never even considered the impossibility of a man knowing in a sort of way that which he does not know at all. According to our admission, he knows that which he does not know—than which nothing, as I think, can be more irrational. And yet, after finding us so easy and good-natured, the inquiry is still unable to d discover the truth, but mocks us to a degree, and has insolently proved the inutility of temperance or wisdom if truly described by a definition such as we have spent all this time in discussing and fashioning together—which result, as far as I am concerned, is not so much to be lamented.

But for your sake, Charmides, I am very sorry—that you, having such beauty and such wisdom and temperance of soul, should have e no profit nor good in life from your wisdom and temperance. And still more am I grieved about the charm which I learned with so much pain, and to so little profit, from the Thracian, in order to produce a thing which is nothing worth. I think indeed that there is a mistake, and that I must be a bad inquirer, for wisdom or temperance I believe to be really a great good. And happy are you, Charmides, if you possess 176 it. Wherefore examine yourself, and see whether you have this gift and can do without the charm, for if you can, I would rather advise you to regard me simply as a fool who is never able to reason out anything, and to rest assured that the more wise and temperate you are, the happier you will be.

Charmides said, I am sure that I do not know, Socrates, whether I have or have not this gift of wisdom and temperance, for how can I know whether I have a thing, of which even you and Critias are, as you say, unable to discover the nature? Yet I do not quite believe you, b and I am sure, Socrates, that I do need the charm, and as far as I am concerned, I shall be willing to be charmed by you daily, until you say that I have had enough.

Very good, Charmides, said Critias. If you do this I shall have a proof of your temperance—that is, if you allow yourself to be charmed by Socrates, and never desert him in things great or small.

You may depend on my following and not deserting him, said c Charmides. If you who are my guardian command me, I should be very wrong not to obey you.

And I do command you, he said.

Then I will do as you say, and begin this very day.

You, sirs, I said, what are you conspiring about?

We are not conspiring, said Charmides. We have conspired already.

And you are about to use violence, without even giving me a hearing in court?

Yes, I shall use violence, he replied, since he orders me, and therefore you had better consider what you will do.

d But the time for consideration has passed, I said. When you are determined on anything, and in the mood of violence, you are irresistible.

Do not you resist me then, he said.

I shall not resist you then, I replied.

LACHES

When this dialogue is added to the Lysis Socrates' method as a teacher is clear. In both he discusses a quality that is perfectly familiar to everyone present, with the same result. They finally realize that although they have always taken it for granted, they cannot state what it is because they do not really know it. In the Laches this quality is courage, and the conclusion is the more striking because two of the speakers are distinguished generals, Laches and Nicias, and because the former describes the great courage he had seen Socrates show on the field. All three are conspicuous examples of what they are discussing, but this does not affect Socrates' demonstration that since none of them, himself included, can define it, they have no real knowledge of it. Merely to act bravely without knowing what bravery is belongs only to the ignorant and inferior. To be virtuous without any clear idea of virtue itself is of small importance—"The unexamined life is not worth living." He tells them that the whole company had best go to school again and try to get educated. He will do so himself.

Of all the dialogues this is perhaps the easiest to read. The argument is clear, the characters come vividly to life, and nowhere is Socrates more delightfully presented.

178 LYSIMACHUS: You have seen the exhibition of the man fighting in armor, Nicias and Laches, but we did not tell you at the time the reason why my friend Melesias and I asked you to go with us and see him. I think that we may as well confess what this was, for we certainly ought not to have any reserve with you. Some laugh at the very notion of consulting others, and when they are asked will not say b what they think. They guess at the wishes of the person who asks them, and answer according to his, and not according to their own, opinion. But as we know that you are good judges, and will say exactly what you think, we have taken you into our counsels. The matter about which I am making all this preface is as follows. Melesias and I have each a son. That is his son, and he is named Thucydides, after 179 his grandfather, and this is mine, who is also called after his grandfather, my father, Aristides. Now, we are resolved to take the greatest care of the youths, and not, like most fathers, to let them do as they please when they are no longer children, but we mean to begin at once and do the utmost that we can for them. And knowing you to have b sons of your own, we thought that you of all men were most likely to have attended to their training and improvement, and, if perchance you have seldom given any thought to the subject, we may remind you that you ought to have done so, and would invite you to assist us in the fulfillment of a common duty. I will tell you, Nicias and Laches, even at the risk of being tedious, how we came to think of this.

Melesias and I live together, and our sons live with us. And now, c as I was saying at first, we are going to be open with you. Both of us often talk to the lads about the many noble deeds which our own fathers did in war and peace—in managing the affairs of the allies, and those of the city—but neither of us has any deeds of his own which he can show. The truth is that we are ashamed of this contrast being seen by them, and we blame our fathers for letting us be d spoiled in the days of our youth, while they were occupied with the concerns of others. And we urge all this upon the lads, pointing out to them that they will not grow up to honor if they are rebellious and take no pains about themselves, but that if they take pains they may, perhaps, become worthy of the names which they bear. They, on their part, promise to comply with our wishes, and our care is to discover what studies or pursuits are likely to be most improving to them. e Someone commended to us the art of fighting in armor, which he thought an excellent accomplishment for a young man to learn, and he praised the man whose exhibition you have seen, and told us to go and see him. And we determined that we would go, and get you to accompany us to see the sight—intending at the same time to ask you to

From *The Dialogues of Plato*, translated with analyses and introductions by B. Jowett (4th edn., revised by order of the Jowett Copyright Trustees, Oxford, 1953; 1st edn., 1871).

advise us, and, if you wish, to share in our project for the education
of our sons. That is the matter which we wanted to talk over with you,
and we hope that you will give us your opinion about this art of fight- 180
ing in armor, and about any other studies or pursuits which you would
or would not recommend for a young man, and will tell us whether
you would like to join in our proposal.

  NICIAS : As far as I am concerned, Lysimachus and Melesias, I
applaud your purpose and will gladly join with you, and I believe that
you, Laches, will be equally glad.

  LACHES : Certainly, Nicias, and I quite approve of the remark b
which Lysimachus made about his own father and the father of Melesias, and which is applicable, not only to them, but to us, and to everyone who is occupied with public affairs. As he says, such persons are
too apt to be negligent and careless of their own children and their
private concerns. There is much truth in that remark of yours, Lysimachus. But why, besides consulting us, do you not consult our friend c
Socrates about the education of the youths? He is of the same deme
with you, and is always passing his time in places where the youth
have any noble study or pursuit, such as you are inquiring after.

  LYSIMACHUS : Why, Laches, has Socrates ever attended to
matters of this sort?

  LACHES : Certainly, Lysimachus.

  NICIAS : That I have the means of knowing as well as Laches,
for quite lately he supplied me with a teacher of music for my son—
Damon, the pupil of Agathocles, who is a most accomplished man in d
every way, as well as a musician, and a companion of inestimable
value for young men at their age.

  LYSIMACHUS : Those who have reached my time of life, Socrates and Nicias and Laches, fall out of acquaintance with the young,
because they are generally detained at home by old age, but you, O son
of Sophroniscus, should let your fellow demesman have the benefit of
any advice which you are able to give. Moreover, I have a claim upon e
you as an old friend of your father, for he and I were always companions and friends, and to the hour of his death there never was a
difference between us. And now it comes back to me, at the mention of
your name, that I have heard these lads talking to one another at
home, and often speaking of Socrates in terms of the highest praise,
but I have never thought to ask them whether the son of Sophroniscus
was the person whom they meant. Tell me, my boys, whether this is 181
the Socrates of whom you have often spoken?

  SON : Certainly, father, this is he.

  LYSIMACHUS : I am delighted to hear, Socrates, that you maintain the name of your father, who was a most excellent man, and I
further rejoice at the prospect of our family ties being renewed.

  LACHES : Indeed, Lysimachus, you ought not to give him up, for
I can assure you that I have seen him maintaining, not only his

b father's, but also his country's name. He was my companion in the retreat from Delium, and I can tell you that if others had only been
like him, the honor of our country would have been upheld, and the
great defeat would never have occurred.

LYSIMACHUS : That praise is truly honorable to you, Socrates,
given as it is by witnesses entitled to all credit and for such qualities
as those which they ascribe to you. Let me tell you the pleasure which
I feel in hearing of your fame, and I hope that you will regard me as
one of your warmest friends. You ought to have visited us long ago,
c and made yourself at home with us, but now, from this day forward,
as we have at last found one another out, do as I say—come and
make acquaintance with me, and with these young men, that you
and yours may continue as my friends. I shall expect you to do so, and
shall venture at some future time to remind you of your duty. But
what say you all of the matter of which we were beginning to speak—
the art of fighting in armor? Is that a practice in which the lads may
be advantageously instructed?

d   SOCRATES : I will endeavor to advise you, Lysimachus, as far
as I can in this matter, and also in every way will comply with your
wishes; but as I am younger and not so experienced, I think that I
ought certainly to hear first what my elders have to say, and to learn
of them, and if I have anything to add, then I may venture to give my
opinion and advice to them as well as to you. Suppose, Nicias, that
one or other of you begin.

NICIAS : I have no objection, Socrates, and my opinion is that
e the acquirement of this art is in many ways useful to young men. It
is an advantage to them that instead of the favorite amusements of
their leisure hours they should have one which tends to improve their
bodily health. No gymnastics could be better or harder exercise, and
182 this, and the art of riding, are of all arts most befitting to a free man,
for they who are thus exercised in the use of arms are the only persons
being trained for the contest in which we are engaged, and in the accomplishments which it requires. Moreover in actual battle, when
you have to fight in a line with a number of others, such an acquirement will be of some use, and will be of the greatest service whenever
the ranks are broken and you have to fight singly, either in pursuit,
b when you are attacking someone who is defending himself, or in
flight, when you have to defend yourself against an assailant. Certainly he who possessed the art could not meet with any harm at the
hands of a single person, or perhaps of several, and in every case he
would have a great advantage. Further, this sort of skill inclines a
man to the love of other noble lessons, for every man who has learned
how to fight in armor will desire to learn the proper arrangement of an
army, which is the sequel of the lesson. And when he has learned
c this, and his ambition is once fired, he will go on to learn the complete art of the general. There is no difficulty in seeing that the knowl-

edge and practice of other military arts will be honorable and valuable to a man, and this lesson may be the beginning of them.

Let me add a further advantage, which is by no means a slight one—that this science will make any man a great deal more daring and resolute in the field. And I will not disdain to mention, what by some may be thought to be a small matter—he will have a more impressive appearance at the right time, that is to say, at the time when his appearance will strike terror into his enemies. My opinion then, d Lysimachus, is, as I say, that the youths should be instructed in this art, and for the reasons which I have given. But Laches may take a different view, and I shall be very glad to hear what he has to say.

LACHES : I should not like to maintain, Nicias, that any kind of knowledge is not to be learned, for all knowledge appears to be a good. And if, as the teachers of the art affirm, this use of arms is e really a species of knowledge, and if it is such as Nicias describes, then it ought to be learned, but if not, and if those who profess to teach it are deceivers only, or if it be knowledge, but not of a valuable sort, then what is the use of learning it? I say this, because I think that if it had been really valuable, the Lacedaemonians, whose whole life is passed in finding out and practicing the arts which give them an ad- 183 vantage over other nations in war, would have discovered this one. And even if they have not, still these professors of the art cannot have failed to discover that of all the Hellenes the Lacedaemonians have the greatest interest in such matters, and that a master of the art who was honored among them would be sure to make his fortune among other nations, just as a tragic poet would who is honored among ourselves—which is the reason why he who fancies that he can write a tragedy does not go about exhibiting in the states outside Attica, but b rushes hither straight, and exhibits at Athens, and this is natural. Whereas I perceive that these fighters in armor regard Lacedaemon as a sacred inviolable territory, which they do not touch with the point of their foot, but they make a circuit of the neighboring states, and would rather exhibit to any others than to the Spartans—and particularly to those who would themselves acknowledge that they are by no means first-rate in the arts of war.

Further, Lysimachus, I have encountered a good many of these c gentlemen in actual service, and have taken their measure, which I can give you at once, for none of these masters of fence have ever been distinguished in war—there has been a sort of fatality about them; while in all other arts the men of note have been always those who have practiced the art, these appear to be a most unfortunate exception. For example, this very Stesilaus, whom you and I have just witnessed exhibiting in all that crowd and making such great pro- d fessions of his powers, I had a better opportunity of seeing at another time making in actual battle a real exhibition of himself involuntarily. He was a marine on board a ship which charged a transport

vessel, and was armed with a weapon, half spear, half scythe; the weapon was as singular as its owner. To make a long story short, I will only tell you what happened to this notable invention of the scythe-
e spear. He was fighting, and the scythe was caught in the rigging of the other ship, and stuck fast, and he tugged, but was unable to get his weapon free. The two ships were passing one another. He first ran along his own ship holding on to the spear, but as the other ship passed by and drew him after as he was holding on to the spear, he let it slip through his hand until he retained only the end of the han-
184 dle. The people in the transport clapped their hands, and laughed at his ridiculous figure, and when someone threw a stone, which fell on the deck at his feet, and he quitted his hold of the scythe-spear, the crew of his own trireme also burst out laughing; they could not refrain when they beheld the weapon waving in the air, suspended from the transport.

Now I do not deny that there may be something in such an art, as Nicias asserts, but I tell you my experience, and, as I said at first,
b whether this be an art of which the advantage is so slight, or not an art at all but only an imposition, in either case such an acquirement is not worth having. For my opinion is that if the professor of this art be a coward, he will be likely to become rash, and his character will be only more clearly revealed, or if he be brave, and fail ever so little, other men will be on the watch, and he will be greatly traduced. For
c there is a jealousy of such pretenders, and unless a man be pre-eminent in valor, he cannot help being ridiculous, if he says that he has this sort of skill. Such is my judgment, Lysimachus, on the study of this art, but, as I said at first, ask Socrates, and do not let him go until he has given you his opinion of the matter.

LYSIMACHUS : I am going to ask this favor of you, Socrates, as
d is the more necessary because the two counselors disagree, and someone is in a manner still needed who will decide between them. Had they agreed, no arbiter would have been required. But as Laches has voted one way and Nicias another, I should like to hear with which of our two friends you agree.

SOCRATES : What, Lysimachus, are you going to accept the opinion of the majority?

LYSIMACHUS : Why, yes, Socrates. What else am I to do?

SOCRATES : And would you do so too, Melesias? If you were de-
e liberating about the gymnastic training of your son, would you follow the advice of the majority of us, or the opinion of the one who had been trained and exercised under a skillful master?

MELESIAS : The latter, Socrates, as would surely be reasonable.

SOCRATES : His one vote would be worth more than the vote of all us four?

MELESIAS : Presumably.

SOCRATES: And for this reason, as I imagine—because a good decision is based on knowledge and not on numbers?

MELESIAS: To be sure.

SOCRATES: Now too, then, must we not first of all ask whether there is any one of us who is an expert in that about which we are de- 185 liberating? If there is, let us take his advice, though he be one only, and not mind the rest; if there is not, let us seek further counsel. Is this a trifle which you and Lysimachus have at stake? Are you not risking the greatest of your possessions? For children are your riches, and upon their turning out well or ill depends the whole order of their father's house.

MELESIAS: That is true.

SOCRATES: Great care, then, is required in this matter?

MELESIAS: Certainly.

SOCRATES: Suppose, as I was just now saying, that we were b considering, or wanting to consider, which of us had the best knowledge of gymnastics. Should we not select him who had learned and practiced the art, and had good teachers?

MELESIAS: I think that we should.

SOCRATES: But would there not arise a prior question about the nature of the art of which we want to find the teachers?

MELESIAS: I do not understand.

SOCRATES: Let me try to make my meaning plainer then. I do not think that we have as yet decided what that is about which we are consulting, when we ask which of us is or is not skilled in the art, and has or has not had teachers of the art.   c

NICIAS: Why, Socrates, is not the question whether young men ought or ought not to learn the art of fighting in armor?

SOCRATES: Yes, Nicias, but there is also a prior question, which I may illustrate in this way. When a person considers about applying a medicine to the eyes, would you say that he is consulting about the medicine or about the eyes?

NICIAS: About the eyes.

SOCRATES: And when he considers whether he shall set a bri- d dle on a horse and at what time, he is thinking of the horse and not of the bridle?

NICIAS: True.

SOCRATES: And in a word, when he considers anything for the sake of another thing, he thinks of the end and not of the means?

NICIAS: Certainly.

SOCRATES: And when you call in an adviser, you should see whether he too is skillful in the accomplishment of the end which you have in view?

NICIAS: Most true.

SOCRATES: And at present we have in view some knowledge, of e which the end is the soul of youth?

NICIAS: Yes.

SOCRATES: And we must inquire whether any of us is skillful or successful in the treatment of the soul, and which of us has had good teachers?

LACHES: Well but, Socrates, did you never observe that some persons who have had no teachers are more skillful than those who have, in some things?

SOCRATES: Yes, Laches, I have observed that, but you would not be very willing to trust them if they professed to be masters of their art, unless they could show some proof of their skill or excel-
186 lence in one or more works.

LACHES: That is true.

SOCRATES: And therefore, Laches and Nicias, as Lysimachus and Melesias, in their anxiety to improve the minds of their sons, have asked our advice about them, we likewise should tell them, if we can, what teachers we know of who were in the first place men of merit and experienced trainers of the minds of youth, and then taught also
b ourselves. Or if any of us says that he has had no teacher but that he has works of his own to show, then he should point out to them what Athenians or strangers, bond or free, he is generally acknowledged to have improved. But if we can show neither teachers nor works, then we should tell them to look out for other advisers; we should not run the risk of spoiling the children of friends, and thereby incurring the most formidable accusation which can be brought against anyone by those nearest to him.

As for myself, Lysimachus and Melesias, I am the first to confess
c that I have never had a teacher of the art of virtue, although I have always from my earliest youth desired to have one. But I am too poor to give money to the Sophists, who are the only professors of moral improvement, and to this day I have never been able to discover the art myself, though I should not be surprised if Nicias or Laches has discovered or learned it; for they are far wealthier than I am, and may therefore have learned of others, and they are older too, so that they
d have had more time to make the discovery. And I really believe that they are able to educate a man, for unless they had been confident in their own knowledge, they would never have spoken thus unhesitatingly of the pursuits which are advantageous or hurtful to a young man. I repose confidence in both of them, but I am surprised to find that they differ from one another. And therefore, Lysimachus, as Laches suggested that you should detain me, and not let me go until I answered, I in turn earnestly beseech and advise you to detain Laches
e and Nicias, and question them. I would have you say to them, Socrates avers that he has no knowledge of the matter—he is unable to decide which of you speaks truly—neither discoverer nor student is he of anything of the kind. But you, Laches and Nicias, should each of you tell us who is the most skillful educator whom you have ever known,

and whether you invented the art yourselves, or learned of another, and if you learned, who were your respective teachers, and who were 187 their brothers in the art. And then, if you are too much occupied in politics to teach us yourselves, let us go to them, and present them with gifts, or make interest with them, or both, in the hope that they may be induced to take charge of our children and of yours, and then they will not grow up to be worthless, and disgrace their ancestors. But if you are yourselves original discoverers in that field, give us some proof of your skill. Who are they who, having been worthless persons, have become under your care good and noble? For if this is your first attempt at education, there is a danger that you may be trying the experiment, not on the *vile corpus* of a Carian slave, but on b your own sons or the sons of your friends, and, as the proverb says, 'break the large vessel in learning to make pots.' Tell us then, what qualifications you claim or do not claim.

Make them tell you that, Lysimachus, and do not let them off.

LYSIMACHUS : I very much approve of the words of Socrates, my friends, but you, Nicias and Laches, must determine whether you will be questioned, and give an explanation about matters of this sort. c Assuredly, Melesias and I would be greatly pleased to hear you answer the questions which Socrates asks, if you will, for I began by saying that we took you into our counsels because we thought that no doubt you had attended to the subject, especially as you have children who, like our own, are nearly of an age to be educated. Well then, if you have no objection, suppose that you take Socrates into partner- d ship, and do you and he ask and answer one another's questions, for, as he has well said, we are deliberating about the most important of our concerns. I hope that you will see fit to comply with our request.

NICIAS : I see very clearly, Lysimachus, that you have only known Socrates' father, and have no acquaintance with Socrates himself—at least, you can only have known him when he was a child, and may have met him among his fellow demesmen, in company with e his father, at a sacrifice or at some other gathering. You clearly show that you have never known him since he arrived at manhood.

LYSIMACHUS : Why do you say that, Nicias?

NICIAS : Because you seem not to be aware that anyone who is close to Socrates and enters into conversation with him is liable to be drawn into an argument, and whatever subject he may start, he will be continually carried round and round by him, until at last he finds that he has to give an account both of his present and past life, and when he is once entangled, Socrates will not let him go until he 188 has completely and thoroughly sifted him. Now I am used to his ways, and I know that he will certainly do as I say, and also that I myself shall be the sufferer, for I am fond of his conversation, Lysimachus. And I think that there is no harm in being reminded of any wrong thing which we are, or have been, doing; he who does not fly from b

reproof will be sure to take more heed of his afterlife. As Solon says,
he will wish and desire to be learning so long as he lives, and will not
think that old age of itself brings wisdom.[1] To me, to be cross-ex-
amined by Socrates is neither unusual nor unpleasant. Indeed, I was
fairly certain all along that where Socrates was, the subject of discussion would soon be ourselves, not our sons, and therefore, I say for
c   my part, I am quite willing to discourse with Socrates in his own manner. But you had better ask our friend Laches what his feeling may be.

LACHES : I have but one feeling, Nicias, or shall I say two feelings, about discussions? Some would think that I am a lover, and to
others I may seem to be a hater, of discourse. For when I hear a man
discoursing of virtue, or of any sort of wisdom, who is a true man
d   and worthy of his theme, I am delighted beyond measure, and I compare the man and his words, and note the harmony and correspondence of them. And such a one I deem to be the true musician, attuned
to a fairer harmony than that of the lyre, or any pleasant instrument
of music, for he truly has in his own life a harmony of words and
deeds arranged—not in the Ionian, or in the Phrygian mode, nor yet
in the Lydian, but in the true Hellenic mode, which is the Dorian, and
no other. Such a one makes me merry with the sound of his voice, and
e   when I hear him I am thought to be a lover of discourse; so eager am I
in drinking in his words. But a man whose actions do not agree with
his words is an annoyance to me, and the better he speaks the more
I hate him, and then I seem to be a hater of discourse.

As to Socrates, I have no knowledge of his words, but of old, as
appears, I have had experience of his deeds, and his deeds show that
189   he is entitled to noble sentiments and complete freedom of speech.
And if his words accord, then I am of one mind with him, and shall be
delighted to be interrogated by a man such as he is, and shall not be
annoyed at having to learn of him, for I too agree with Solon, 'that I
would fain grow old, learning many things.' [2] But I must be allowed to
add 'from the good only.' Socrates must be willing to allow that the
teacher himself is a good man, or I shall be a dull and reluctant pupil, but that the teacher is rather young, or not as yet in repute—any-
b   thing of that sort is of no account with me. And therefore, Socrates, I
invite you to teach and confute me as much as ever you like, and also
learn of me anything which I know. So high is the opinion which I
have entertained of you ever since the day on which you were my
companion in danger, and gave a proof of your valor such as only
the man of merit can give. Therefore, say whatever you like, and do
not mind about the difference of our ages.

c   SOCRATES : I cannot say that either of you shows any reluctance to take counsel and advise with me.

LYSIMACHUS : But this is our proper business, and yours as

----

[1] Solon, fr. 10.   [2] Ibid.

well as ours, for I reckon you as one of us. Please then to take my
place, and find out from Nicias and Laches what we want to know, for
the sake of the youths, and talk and consult with them, for I am old,
and my memory is bad, and I do not remember the questions which I
intend to ask, or the answers to them, and if there is any digression I
lose the thread. I will therefore beg of you to carry on the proposed d
discussion by yourselves, and I will listen, and Melesias and I will
act upon your conclusions.

SOCRATES: Let us, Nicias and Laches, comply with the request
of Lysimachus and Melesias. There will be no harm in asking ourselves the question which was proposed to us just now. Who have
been our own instructors in this sort of training, or whom have we
ourselves made better? But another mode of carrying on the inquiry e
will bring us equally to the same point, and perhaps starts nearer to
first principles. For if we know that the addition of something would
improve some other thing, and are able to make the addition, then,
clearly, we must know how that about which we are advising may be
best and most easily attained. Perhaps you do not understand what I
mean. Then let me make my meaning plainer in this way. Suppose we 190
know that the addition of sight makes better the eyes which possess
this gift, and also are able to impart sight to the eyes; then, clearly, we
know the nature of sight, and should be able to advise how this gift
of sight may be best and most easily attained. But if we knew neither
what sight is, nor what hearing is, we should not be very good medical
advisers about the eyes or the ears, or about the best mode of giving
sight and hearing to them.   b

LACHES: That is true, Socrates.

SOCRATES: And are not our two friends, Laches, at this very
moment inviting us to consider in what way the gift of virtue may be
imparted to their sons for the improvement of their minds?

LACHES: Very true.

SOCRATES: Then must we not first know the nature of virtue?
For how can we advise anyone about the best mode of attaining something of whose nature we are wholly ignorant?   c

LACHES: I do not think that we can, Socrates.

SOCRATES: We say then, Laches, that we know the nature of
virtue.

LACHES: Yes.

SOCRATES: And that which we know we must surely be able to
tell?

LACHES: Certainly.

SOCRATES: I would not have us begin, my friend, with inquiring about the whole of virtue, for that may be more than we can accomplish. Let us first consider whether we have a sufficient knowledge
of a part; the inquiry will thus probably be made easier to us.   d

LACHES: Let us do as you wish, Socrates.

SOCRATES : Then which of the parts of virtue shall we select? Must we not select that to which the art of fighting in armor is supposed to conduce? And is not that generally thought to be courage?

LACHES : Yes, certainly.

SOCRATES : Then, Laches, suppose that we first set about determining the nature of courage, and in the second place proceed to in-
e quire how the young men may attain this quality by the help of studies and pursuits. Tell me, if you can, what is courage.

LACHES : Indeed, Socrates, I see no difficulty in answering. He is a man of courage who does not run away, but remains at his post and fights against the enemy. There can be no mistake about that.

SOCRATES : Very good, Laches, and yet I fear that I did not express myself clearly, and therefore you have answered not the question which I intended to ask, but another.

LACHES : What do you mean, Socrates?

191   SOCRATES : I will endeavor to explain. You would call a man courageous who remains at his post, and fights with the enemy?

LACHES : Certainly I should.

SOCRATES : And so should I, but what would you say of another man, who fights flying, instead of remaining?

LACHES : How flying?

SOCRATES : Why, as the Scythians are said to fight, flying as well as pursuing, and as Homer says in praise of the horses of Aeneas, that they knew 'how to pursue, and fly quickly hither and
b thither,' and he passes an encomium on Aeneas himself, as having a knowledge of fear or flight, and calls him 'a deviser of fear or flight.' [3]

LACHES : Yes, Socrates, and there Homer is right, for he was speaking of chariots, as you were speaking of the Scythian cavalry. Now cavalry have that way of fighting, but the heavy-armed soldier fights, as I say, remaining in his rank.

SOCRATES : And yet, Laches, you must except the Lacedaemo-
c nians at Plataea, who, when they came upon the light shields of the Persians, are said not to have been willing to stand and fight, and to have fled. But when the ranks of the Persians were broken, they turned upon them like cavalry, and won the Battle of Plataea.

LACHES : That is true.

SOCRATES : That was my meaning when I said that I was to blame in having put my question badly, and that this was the reason of your answering badly. For I meant to ask you not only about the
d courage of the heavy-armed soldiers, but about the courage of cavalry and every other style of soldier—and not only who are courageous in war, but who are courageous in perils by sea, and who in disease, or in poverty, or again in politics, are courageous, and not only who are courageous against pain or fear, but mighty to contend against de-

[3] *Iliad* 5.223, 8.108.

sires and pleasures, either fixed in their rank or turning upon their e
enemy. There is this sort of courage—is there not, Laches?

LACHES: Certainly, Socrates.

SOCRATES: Now all these are courageous, but some have courage in pleasures and some in pains, some in desires and some in
fears. And some are cowards under the same conditions, as I should
imagine.

LACHES: Very true.

SOCRATES: I was asking about courage and cowardice in general. And I will begin with courage, and once more ask what is that
common quality, which is the same in all these cases, and which is
called courage? Do you now understand what I mean?

LACHES: Not overwell.

SOCRATES: I mean this. As I might ask what is that quality 192
which is called quickness, and which is found in running, in playing the lyre, in speaking, in learning, and in many other similar actions, or rather which we possess in nearly every action that is
worth mentioning of arms, legs, mouth, voice, mind—would you not
apply the term quickness to all of them?

LACHES: Quite true.

SOCRATES: And suppose I were to be asked by someone, What
is that common quality, Socrates, which, in all these activities, you
call quickness? I should say the quality which accomplishes much in b
a little time—whether in running, speaking, or in any other sort of
action.

LACHES: You would be quite correct.

SOCRATES: And now, Laches, do you try and tell me in like
manner, What is that common quality which is called courage,
and which includes all the various uses of the term when applied both
to pleasure and pain, and in all the cases to which I was just now
referring?

LACHES: I should say that courage is a sort of endurance of the
soul, if I am to speak of the universal nature which pervades them all. c

SOCRATES: But that is what we must do if we are to answer our
own question. And yet I cannot say that every kind of endurance is,
in my opinion, to be deemed courage. Hear my reason. I am sure,
Laches, that you would consider courage to be a very noble quality.

LACHES: Most noble, certainly.

SOCRATES: And you would say that a wise endurance is also
good and noble?

LACHES: Very noble.

SOCRATES: But what would you say of a foolish endurance? d
Is not that, on the other hand, to be regarded as evil and hurtful?

LACHES: True.

SOCRATES: And is anything noble which is evil and hurtful?

LACHES: I ought not to say that, Socrates.

SOCRATES : Then you would not admit that sort of endurance to be courage—for it is not noble, but courage is noble?

LACHES : You are right.

SOCRATES : Then, according to you, only the wise endurance is courage?

LACHES : It seems so.

e SOCRATES : But as to the epithet 'wise'—wise in what? In all things small as well as great? For example, if a man shows the quality of endurance in spending his money wisely, knowing that by spending he will acquire more in the end, do you call him courageous?

LACHES : Assuredly not.

SOCRATES : Or, for example, if a man is a physician, and his son, or some patient of his, has inflammation of the lungs, and begs that he may be allowed to eat or drink something, and the other is inflexible and refuses, is that courage?

193 LACHES : No, that is not courage at all, any more than the last.

SOCRATES : Again, take the case of one who endures in war, and is willing to fight, and wisely calculates and knows that others will help him, and that there will be fewer and inferior men against him than there are with him, and suppose that he has also advantages in position—would you say of such a one who endures with all this wisdom and preparation that he or some man in the opposing army who is in the opposite circumstances to these and yet endures and remains at his post is the braver?

b LACHES : I should say that the latter, Socrates, was the braver.

SOCRATES : But, surely, this is a foolish endurance in comparison with the other?

LACHES : That is true.

SOCRATES : Then you would say that he who in an engagement of cavalry endures, having a knowledge of horsemanship, is not so courageous as he who endures, having no such knowledge?

LACHES : So I should say.

SOCRATES : And he who endures, having a knowledge of the use of the sling, or the bow, or of any other art, is not so courageous as he who endures, not having such a knowledge?

c LACHES : True.

SOCRATES : And he who descends into a well, and dives, and holds out in this or any similar action, having no skill in diving or the like, is, as you would say, more courageous than those who have this skill?

LACHES : Why, Socrates, what else can a man say?

SOCRATES : Nothing, if that be what he thinks.

LACHES : But that is what I do think.

SOCRATES : And yet men who thus run risks and endure are foolish, Laches, in comparison with those who do the same things, having the skill to do them.

LACHES: That is true.

SOCRATES: But foolish boldness and endurance appeared be- d
fore to be base and hurtful to us?

LACHES: Quite true.

SOCRATES: Whereas courage was acknowledged to be a noble
quality.

LACHES: True.

SOCRATES: And now on the contrary we are saying that the
foolish endurance, which was before held in dishonor, is courage.

LACHES: So we are.

SOCRATES: And are we right in saying so?

LACHES: Indeed, Socrates, I am sure that we are not right.

SOCRATES: Then according to your statement, you and I,
Laches, are not attuned to the Dorian mode, which is a harmony of e
words and deeds, for our deeds are not in accordance with our words.
Anyone would say that we had courage who saw us in action, but not,
I imagine, he who heard us talking about courage just now.

LACHES: That is most true.

SOCRATES: And is this condition of ours satisfactory?

LACHES: Quite the reverse.

SOCRATES: Suppose, however, that we admit the principle of
which we are speaking to a certain extent?

LACHES: To what extent and what principle do you mean? 194

SOCRATES: The principle of endurance. If you agree, we too
must endure and persevere in the inquiry, and then courage will not
laugh at our faintheartedness in searching for courage, which after
all may frequently be endurance.

LACHES: I am ready to go on, Socrates, and yet I am unused to
investigations of this sort. But the spirit of controversy has been
aroused in me by what has been said, and I am really grieved at being
thus unable to express my meaning. For I fancy that I do know the b
nature of courage, but, somehow or other, she has slipped away from
me, and I cannot get hold of her and tell her nature.

SOCRATES: But, my dear friend, should not the good sportsman
follow the track, and not give up?

LACHES: Certainly, he should.

SOCRATES: Shall we then invite Nicias to join us? He may be
better at the sport than we are. What do you say?

LACHES: I should like that. c

SOCRATES: Come then, Nicias, and do what you can to help
your friends, who are tossing on the waves of argument, and at the
last gasp. You see our extremity, and may save us and also settle your
own opinion, if you tell us what you think about courage.

NICIAS: I have been thinking, Socrates, that you and Laches
are not defining courage in the right way, for you have forgotten an
excellent saying which I have heard from your own lips.

SOCRATES : What is it, Nicias?

d   NICIAS : I have often heard you say that 'Every man is good in that in which he is wise, and bad in that in which he is unwise.'

SOCRATES : That is certainly true, Nicias.

NICIAS : And therefore if the brave man is good, he is also wise.

SOCRATES : Do you hear him, Laches?

LACHES : Yes, I hear him, but I do not very well understand him.

SOCRATES : I think that I understand him, and he appears to me to mean that courage is a sort of wisdom.

LACHES : What sort of wisdom, Socrates?

e   SOCRATES : That is a question which you must ask of him.

LACHES : Yes.

SOCRATES : Tell him then, Nicias, what sort of wisdom you think courage to be, for you surely do not mean the wisdom which plays the flute?

NICIAS : Certainly not.

SOCRATES : Nor the wisdom which plays the lyre?

NICIAS : No.

SOCRATES : But what is this knowledge then, and of what?

LACHES : I think that you put the question to him very well, Socrates, and I would like him to say what is the nature of this knowledge or wisdom.

195   NICIAS : I mean to say, Laches, that courage is the knowledge of that which inspires fear or confidence in war, or in anything.

LACHES : How strangely he is talking, Socrates.

SOCRATES : Why do you say so, Laches?

LACHES : Why, surely courage is one thing, and wisdom another.

SOCRATES : That is just what Nicias denies.

LACHES : Yes, that is what he denies; that is where he is so silly.

SOCRATES : Suppose that we instruct instead of abusing him?

NICIAS : Certainly, Socrates, but having been proved to be
b talking nonsense himself, Laches wants to prove that I have been doing the same.

LACHES : Very true, Nicias, and you are talking nonsense, as I shall endeavor to show. Let me ask you a question. Do not physicians know the dangers of disease? Or do the courageous know them? Or are the physicians the same as the courageous?

NICIAS : Not at all.

LACHES : No more than the husbandmen who know the dangers of husbandry, or than other craftsmen, who have a knowledge of that which inspires them with fear or confidence in their own arts, and yet
c they are not courageous a whit the more for that.

SOCRATES : What do you think of Laches' argument, Nicias? He appears to be saying something of importance.

NICIAS : Yes, he is saying something, but it is not true.

SOCRATES : How so?

NICIAS : Why, because he thinks that the physician's knowledge of illness extends beyond the nature of health and disease. But in fact the physician knows no more than this. Do you imagine, Laches, that he knows whether health or illness is the more terrible to a man? Had not many a man better never get up from a sickbed? I should like to know whether you think that life is always better than death. May not death often be the better of the two?   d

LACHES : Yes, certainly so in my opinion.

NICIAS : And do you think that the same things are terrible to those who had better die, and to those who had better live?

LACHES : Certainly not.

NICIAS : And do you suppose that the physician knows this, or indeed any other specialist, except the man who is skilled in the grounds of fear and hope? And him I call the courageous.

SOCRATES : Do you understand his meaning, Laches?

LACHES : Yes, I suppose that, in his way of speaking, the sooth- e
sayers are the courageous men. For who but one of them can know to whom to die or to live is better? And yet, Nicias, would you allow that you are yourself a soothsayer, or are you neither a soothsayer nor courageous?

NICIAS : What! Do you mean to say that the soothsayer ought to know the grounds of hope or fear?

LACHES : Indeed I do. Who but he?

NICIAS : Much rather I should say he of whom I speak, for the soothsayer ought to know only the signs of things that are about to come to pass, whether it be death or disease, or loss of property, or victory, or defeat in war or in any sort of contest. But whether the 196
suffering or not-suffering of these things will be best for a man is a question which is no more for a soothsayer to decide than for anyone else.

LACHES : I cannot understand what Nicias would be at, Socrates, for he represents the courageous as neither a soothsayer, nor a physician, nor in any other character—unless he means to say that he is a god. My opinion is that he does not like honestly to confess that he is talking nonsense, but that he shuffles up and down in order b
to conceal the difficulty into which he has got himself. You and I, Socrates, might have practiced a similar shuffle just now, if we had only wanted to avoid the appearance of inconsistency. And if we had been arguing in a court of law there might have been reason in so doing, but why should a man deck himself out with vain words at a meeting of friends such as this?

SOCRATES : I quite agree with you, Laches, that he should not. c
But perhaps Nicias is serious, and not merely talking for the sake of talking. Let us ask him just to explain what he means, and if he has

reason on his side we will agree with him; if not, we will instruct him.

LACHES : Do you ask him, Socrates, if you will. I think that I have asked enough.

SOCRATES : I do not see why I should not, and my questioning will do for both of us.

LACHES : Very good.

SOCRATES : Then tell me, Nicias, or rather tell us, for Laches
d and I are partners in the argument, do you mean to affirm that courage is the knowledge of the grounds of hope and fear?

NICIAS : I do.

SOCRATES : And not every man has this knowledge; the physician and the soothsayer have it not, and they will not be courageous unless they acquire it—that is what you were saying?

NICIAS : I was.

SOCRATES : Then this is certainly not a thing which every sow would know, as the proverb says, and therefore she could not be courageous.

NICIAS : I think not.

e SOCRATES : Clearly not, Nicias, not even the sow of Crommyon would be called by you courageous. And this I say not as a joke, but because I think that he who assents to your doctrine cannot allow that any wild beast is courageous, unless he admits that a lion, or a leopard, or perhaps a boar, has such a degree of wisdom that he knows things which but a few human beings ever know by reason of their difficulty. He who takes your view of courage must affirm that a lion is not naturally more disposed to courage than a stag, nor a bull than a monkey.

197   LACHES : Capital, Socrates. Upon my word, that is truly good. And I hope, Nicias, that you will tell us whether you really mean that those animals which we all admit to be courageous are in fact wiser than mankind, or whether you will have the boldness, in the face of universal opinion, to deny their courage.

NICIAS : Why, Laches, I do not describe as courageous animals or any other creatures which have no fear of dangers because they are devoid of understanding, but only as fearless and senseless. Do you imagine that I should call all little children courageous, who fear no
b dangers because they have no understanding? There is a difference, to my way of thinking, between fearlessness and courage. I am of opinion that thoughtful courage is a quality possessed by very few, but that rashness and boldness, and fearlessness which has no forethought, are very common qualities possessed by many men, many women, many children, many animals. And you, and men in general, call by the term 'courageous' actions which I call rash—my coura-
c geous actions are wise actions.

LACHES : Behold, Socrates, how admirably, as he thinks, he

dresses himself out in words, while seeking to deprive of the honor of courage those whom all the world acknowledges to be courageous.

NICIAS: Not you, Laches, so do not be alarmed. I am quite willing to say of you, and also of Lamachus and of many other Athenians, that you are wise, being courageous.

LACHES: I could answer that, but I would not have you cast in my teeth that I am a haughty Aexonian.

SOCRATES: Do not answer him, Laches. I rather fancy that you d are not aware of the source from which his wisdom is derived. He has got all this from my friend Damon, and Damon is always with Prodicus, who, of all the Sophists, is considered to be the best at analyzing the meaning of words of this sort.

LACHES: Yes, Socrates, and the examination of such niceties is a much more proper employment for a Sophist than for a great statesman whom the city chooses to preside over her affairs.

SOCRATES: Yes, my sweet friend, but great affairs and great e minds properly go together. And I think that Nicias deserves that we should see what he has in view when he so defines courage.

LACHES: Then see for yourself, Socrates.

SOCRATES: That is what I am going to do, my dear friend. Do not, however, suppose I shall let you out of the partnership, for I shall expect you to apply your mind, and join with me in the consideration of the question.

LACHES: I will if you think that I ought.

SOCRATES: Yes, I do, but I must beg of you, Nicias, to begin 198 again. You remember that we originally considered courage to be a part of virtue.

NICIAS: Very true.

SOCRATES: And you yourself said that it was a part, and there were many other parts, all of which taken together are called virtue.

NICIAS: Certainly.

SOCRATES: Do you agree with me about the parts? For I say that justice, temperance, and the like, are all of them parts of virtue as well as courage. Would you not say the same?   b

NICIAS: Certainly.

SOCRATES: Well then, so far we are agreed. And now let us proceed a step, and try to arrive at a similar agreement about the fearful and the hopeful. I do not want you to be thinking one thing and us another. Let me then tell you our opinion, and if I am wrong you shall set us right. In our opinion the terrible and the hopeful are the things which do and do not create fear, and fear is not of the present nor of the past, but is of future and expected evil. Do you not agree to that, Laches?   c

LACHES: Yes, Socrates, entirely.

SOCRATES: That is our view, Nicias. The terrible things, as I should say, are the evils which are future, and the hopeful are the good or not-evil things which are future. Do you or do you not agree with me?

NICIAS : I agree.

SOCRATES : And the knowledge of these things you call courage?

NICIAS : Precisely.

SOCRATES : And now let me see whether you agree with Laches and myself as to a third point.

NICIAS : What is that?

d   SOCRATES : I will tell you. He and I have a notion that there is not one knowledge or science of the past, another of the present, a third of what may and will be best in the future, but that of all three there is one science only. For example, there is one science of medicine which is concerned with the superintendence of health equally e in all times, present, past, and future, and one science of husbandry in like manner, which is concerned with the productions of the earth in all times. As to the military art, you yourselves will be my witnesses that it makes excellent provision for the future as well as the present, and that the general claims to be the master and not the servant 199 of the soothsayer, because he knows better what is happening or is likely to happen in war, and accordingly the law places the soothsayer under the general, and not the general under the soothsayer. Am I not correct in saying so, Laches?

LACHES : Quite correct.

SOCRATES : And do you, Nicias, also acknowledge that the same science has understanding of the same things, whether future, present, or past?

NICIAS : Yes, indeed, Socrates, that is my opinion.

SOCRATES : And courage, my friend, is, as you say, a knowledge b of the fearful and of the hopeful?

NICIAS : Yes.

SOCRATES : And the fearful, and the hopeful, are admitted to be future goods and future evils?

NICIAS : True.

SOCRATES : And the same science has to do with the same things in the future or at any time?

NICIAS : That is true.

SOCRATES : Then courage is a science which is concerned not only with the fearful and hopeful, for they are future only. Courage, like the other sciences, is concerned not only with good and evil c of the future, but of the present and past, and of any time.

NICIAS : That, as I suppose, is true.

SOCRATES : Then the answer which you have given, Nicias, includes only a third part of courage, but our question extended to the whole nature of courage. And according to your view—that is, according to your present view—courage is not only the knowledge of the hopeful and the fearful, but seems to include nearly every good and evil without reference to time. What do you say to that altera- d tion in your statement?

NICIAS: I agree, Socrates.

SOCRATES: But then, my dear friend, if a man knew all good and evil, and how they are and have been and will be produced, would he not be perfect, and wanting in no virtue, whether justice or temperance or holiness? He alone would be competent to distinguish between what is to be feared and what is not, whether it be super- natural or natural, and would take the proper precautions to secure that all shall be well, for he would know how to deal aright both e with gods and with men.

NICIAS: I think, Socrates, that there is a great deal of truth in what you say.

SOCRATES: But then, Nicias, courage, according to this new definition of yours, instead of being only a part of virtue, will be all virtue?

NICIAS: It would seem so.

SOCRATES: But we were saying that courage is one of the parts of virtue?

NICIAS: Yes, that was what we were saying.

SOCRATES: And that is in contradiction with our present view?

NICIAS: That appears to be the case.

SOCRATES: Then, Nicias, we have not discovered what cour- age is.

NICIAS: It seems not.

LACHES: And yet, friend Nicias, I imagined that you would 200 have made the discovery, when you were so contemptuous of the an- swers which I made to Socrates. I had very great hopes that you would have been led to it by the wisdom of Damon.

NICIAS: I perceive, Laches, that you think nothing of having displayed your ignorance of the nature of courage, but you look only to see whether I have not made a similar display. And if we are both equally ignorant of the things which a man with any self-respect should know, that, I suppose, will be of no consequence. You cer- tainly appear to me very like the rest of the world, looking at your b neighbor and not at yourself. I am of opinion that enough has been said on the subject which we have been discussing, and if the treat- ment has been in any way inadequate, that may be hereafter corrected with the help of Damon, whom you think to laugh down although you have never seen him, and of others. And when I am satisfied my- self, I will freely impart my satisfaction to you, for I think that you are very much in want of knowledge. c

LACHES: You are a philosopher, Nicias; of that I am aware. Nevertheless I would recommend Lysimachus and Melesias not to take you and me as advisers about the education of their children, but, as I said at first, they should ask Socrates and not let him off; if my own sons were old enough, I should do the same.

NICIAS : To that I quite agree, if Socrates is willing to take them under his charge. I should not wish for anyone else to be the tutor of
d Niceratus. But I observe that whenever I mention the matter to him he recommends to me some other tutor and refuses himself. Perhaps he may be more ready to listen to you, Lysimachus.

LYSIMACHUS : He ought, Nicias, for certainly I would do things for him which I would not do for many others. What do you say, Socrates—will you comply? And are you ready to give assistance in the improvement of the youths?

e SOCRATES : Indeed, Lysimachus, I should be very wrong in refusing to aid in the improvement of anybody. And if I had shown in this conversation that I had a knowledge which Nicias and Laches have not, then I admit that you would be right in inviting me to perform this duty, but as we are all in the same perplexity, why should one of us be preferred to another? I certainly think that no one should,
201 and under these circumstances, let me offer you a piece of advice— and this need not go farther than ourselves. I maintain, my friends, that every one of us should seek out the best teacher whom he can find, first for ourselves who are greatly in need of one, and then for the youths, regardless of expense or anything. But I cannot advise that we remain as we are. And if anyone laughs at us for going to school at
b our age, I would quote to them the authority of Homer, who says, 'Modesty is not good for a needy man.' ⁴ Let us then, regardless of what may be said of us, concern ourselves both with our own education and that of the youths, together.

LYSIMACHUS : I like your proposal, Socrates, and as I am the oldest, I am also the most eager to go to school with the boys. Let me
c beg a favor of you. Come to my house tomorrow at dawn, and we will advise about these matters. For the present, let us make an end of the conversation.

SOCRATES : I will come to you tomorrow, Lysimachus, as you propose, God willing.

⁴ *Odyssey* 17.347.

LYSIS

The interest of the Lysis does not lie in the matter of the discussion but in the manner. Socrates questions two boys, close friends, on what friendship is. They are sure that they know, but the more they try to explain the less they feel that they really know. They come to see under Socrates' guiding hand that every statement they make is unsatisfactory. But his object is by no means to resolve their difficulties for them. He declares that he knows as little as they do. How ridiculous it is, he tells them at the end, that he and they who are friends should not know what friendship is.

This method of teaching is Socrates' own among the great teachers of mankind. All of the others would have been concerned to give Lysis and his friend a higher ideal of friendship, to point them on to a loftier idea, to form in their young minds a mold of nobility which might persist. That Socrates would have been pleased to do all this is a matter of course; the reason he made no attempt is that he did not believe it could be done. It was his conviction that truth cannot be taught, it must be sought. His only desire in talking to the boys was to make them use their minds. To him the best that could be done for them was to arouse them to think. In that way they might finally turn the process to their own inner world and examine themselves —"The unexamined life is not worth living"—and learn to know themselves. So and only so could they discover the spark of good within, which they alone could kindle into a flame. Among the dialogues the Lysis has no superior as an illustration of Socrates' method.

203 I was walking straight from the Academy to the Lyceum, by the road which skirts the outside of the walls, and had reached the little gate where is the source of the Panops, when I fell in with Hippothales, the son of Hieronymus, Ctesippus the Paeanian, and some more young men, standing together in a group.

Hippothales, seeing me approach, called out, Ha, Socrates, whither
b and whence?

From the Academy, I replied, and I am going straight to the Lyceum.

Straight to us, I hope, cried he. Won't you turn in? It will be worth your while.

Turn in where? said I. And whom do you mean by us?

There, he replied, pointing out to me an enclosure facing the wall, with a door open. There we are passing our time, he added, we whom you see, and a great many other fine fellows too.

And what's all this, pray? And how are you passing your time?
204 This is a palaestra that has been lately erected, and we are passing our time principally in conversations, of which we should be very glad to give you a share.

You are very kind, I answered. And who is your teacher there?

A friend and admirer of yours, Miccus.

And no ordinary man either, I rejoined, a most competent Sophist.

Won't you come with us, then, he said, to see both him and all our party there too?
b Here, where I am, was my reply, I should like first to be informed, what I am to enter for, and who is your prime beauty?

Some think one, and some another, Socrates.

But whom do you think, Hippothales? Tell me this.

He answered only with a blush. So I added, Hippothales, son of Hieronymus, there is no longer any need for you to tell me whether you are in love or not, since I am sure you are not only in love, but pretty far gone in it too by this time. For though in most matters I am
c a poor useless creature, yet by some means or other I have received from heaven the gift of being able to detect at a glance both a lover and a beloved.

On hearing this, he blushed still more deeply than before. Whereupon Ctesippus broke in, It is very fine of you, Hippothales, turning red in this way, and making such a fuss about telling Socrates the name, when he is quite sure, if he stays ever so short a time in your company, to be bored to death by hearing it always repeated. At any rate, Socrates, he has deafened *our* ears for us, and filled them
d full of Lysis. Nay, if he be but a little tipsy when he talks of him,

From *Socratic Discourses by Plato and Xenophon*, translated by J. Wright (Everyman's Library, London and New York, first pub. 1910).

we can easily fancy, on waking, even the next morning, that we are
still hearing the name of Lysis. But his constant talk about him, bad
as it is, is not the worst—nothing like so bad as when he begins to
deluge us with his poems and speeches, and, worse and worse, to sing
a song on his darling in a portentous voice, which we are compelled
to listen to with patience.

Your Lysis must be quite a juvenile, I rejoined. I conjecture this e
from my not knowing the name when you mentioned it.

Why, they don't often call him by his own name, Socrates; he
still goes by his father's, the latter being so well known. Still, I am
sure, you cannot be a stranger to the boy's appearance; that's quite
enough to know him by.

Say, then, whose son he is.

Democrates' of Aexone, his eldest.

Well done, Hippothales, said I. A noble, and in every way a brilliant choice is this which you have made. But come now, go on 205
about him with me, just as you do with your friends here, that I
may know what language a lover ought to hold with regard to his favorite, either to his face or before others.

And do you really, Socrates, set any value on what this fellow
says?

Do you mean, I asked, absolutely to deny being in love with the
person he mentions?

No, not that, he answered, but I do the making verses or speeches
on him.

He is out of his senses, doting, mad, cried Ctesippus.

But, I replied, I don't want to hear any of your verses, Hippothales, nor any song either that you may have composed upon your b
darling, but I should like to have an idea of their sense, that I may
know how you behave toward your favorite.

Ctesippus will tell you all about it, Socrates, I don't doubt. He
must remember it well enough, if it be true, as he says, that I dinned
it into his ears till he was deaf.

Oh, I know it, cried Ctesippus, right thoroughly too. It is such a
joke, Socrates. The idea of a lover devoting himself exclusively to the
object of his love, and yet having nothing of a personal interest to
say to him that any child might not say—isn't it absurd? But stories c
that all the city rings with, about Democrates, and Lysis, the boy's
grandfather, and all his ancestors—their wealth, their breeds of
horses, their victories at the Pythian, Isthmian, Nemean with four
steeds and single—all these he works into poem and speech, aye, and
stories too, still further out-of-date than these. For in a sort of poem
the other day, he gave us the whole account of Heracles' entertainment, telling us how their ancestor received that hero into his house d
on the strength of his relationship, being himself son of Zeus, by the
daughter of the founder of Aexone. Yes, Socrates, such, among others,

are the old wives' tales that our lover here is ever singing and reciting, and condemning us moreover to listen to.

On hearing this, I said to the lover, You ridiculous Hippothales, before you have gained the victory, you compose and sing a hymn of praise on yourself.

It isn't on myself, Socrates, that I either make or sing it.

You fancy not, said I.

How is it so? said he.

e   In every way, I replied, these songs have reference to you. If you succeed in winning such a youth as you describe, all that you have said and sung will redound to your honor, and be in fact your hymn of triumph, as if you had gained a victory in obtaining such a favorite. But if he escape your grasp, then the higher the eulogium you have passed on him, the greater will be the blessings which you will seem to have missed, and the greater consequently the ridicule you will
206 incur. All connoisseurs, therefore, in matters of love, are careful of praising their favorites before they have won them, from their doubts as to the result of the affair. Moreover, your beauties, when lauded and made much of, become gorged with pride and arrogance. Don't you think so?

I do, he replied.

And the more arrogant they are, the harder they become to be caught?

It is to be expected, at any rate.

Well, what should you say to a huntsman that frightened the prey he was in chase of, and rendered it harder to be caught?

b   That he was a very sorry one, certainly.

And if by speech and song he renders it wild instead of luring it, he can be no favorite of the Muses, can he?

I think not.

Have a care then, Hippothales, that you do not lay yourself open with your poetry to all these reproaches. And yet I am sure, that to a man who injured himself by his poetry, you would not be willing to accord the title of a good poet, so long as he did himself harm.

No, indeed, that would be too unreasonable, he replied. But it is
c on this very account, Socrates, that I put myself in your hands, and beg you to give me any advice you may have to bestow, as to the course of conduct or conversation that a lover ought to adopt in order to render himself agreeable to the object of his affection.

That were no such easy matter, I replied. But if you would bring me to speak with Lysis, perhaps I could give you a specimen of what you ought to say to him, in place of the speeches and songs which you are in the habit of treating him with, according to your friends here.

Well, there is no difficulty in that, he rejoined. If you will only go into the palaestra with Ctesippus, and sit down and begin to talk, I

have little doubt that he will come to you of his own accord, for he is
singularly fond of listening. And, moreover, as they are keeping the
Hermaea, boys and men are all mixed up together today. So he is d
pretty certain to join you. But if he does not, Ctesippus knows him,
through his cousin Menexenus, who is Lysis' particular friend. You
can get Ctesippus, therefore, to summon him, in case he does not come
of himself.

This be our plan, I cried. And taking Ctesippus with me, I walked
toward the palaestra, the rest following.   e

On entering we found that the boys had finished their sacrifices,
and, the ceremony being now pretty well over, were playing together
at knucklebones, all in their holiday dress. The greater part were
carrying on their game in the court outside, but some of them were in
a corner of the dressing room, playing at odd and even with a number
of bones which they drew out of small baskets. Round these were stationed others looking on, among whom was Lysis, and he stood in the
midst of boys and youths with a chaplet on his head, unmatched in
face or form. You would say he was not beautiful merely, but even 207
of a noble mien. For ourselves, we withdrew to the opposite part of
the room, and sitting down, as nothing was going on there, began to
talk. While thus engaged, Lysis kept turning round and eyeing us, evidently wishing to join us. For some time though he remained in doubt,
not liking to walk up alone. But when Menexenus looked in from his
game in the court and on seeing Ctesippus and me came to sit down b
with us, Lysis also followed at sight of his friend, and took a seat by
his side.

There came up, moreover, the rest of our party, among them
Hippothales, who, seeing them form into a good-sized group, screened
himself behind them in a position where he did not think he could be
seen by Lysis—so fearful was he of giving him offense. And thus
placed near him, he listened to our conversation.

I began it by turning my eyes on Menexenus, and saying, Son of
Demophon, which of you two is the elder?   c

It is a disputed point, he replied.

And do you dispute, too, which is the better fellow?

Right heartily, was his answer.

And so too, I suppose, which is the more beautiful?

At this they both laughed.

I will not ask you, I added, which is the wealthier, for you are
friends, are you not?

Oh dear, yes! they both cried.

And friends, they tell us, share and share alike; so in this respect, at any rate, there will be no difference between you, if only you
give me a true account of your friendship.

To this they both assented.

I was then proceeding to inquire which of the two excelled in d

justice, and which in wisdom, when someone came up and carried off
Menexenus, telling him that the master of the palaestra wanted him
—I presume, on business connected with the sacrifice. Accordingly he
left us, and I went on questioning Lysis.

Lysis, said I, I suppose your father and mother love you very
dearly?

Very dearly, he answered.

They would wish you then to be as happy as possible.

Of course.

e   Do you think a man happy if he is a slave, and may not do anything he wants?

No, that indeed I don't.

Well, if your father and mother love you, and wish you to become happy, it is clear that they try in every way to make you happy.

To be sure they do.

They allow you then, I suppose, to do what you wish, and never
scold you, or hinder you from doing what you want to do?

Yes, but they do though, Socrates, and pretty frequently too.

208   How? said I. They wish you to be happy, and yet hinder you from
doing what you want. But tell me this. If you wanted to ride on one of
your father's chariots, and take the reins during a race, would they
not allow you?

No, most assuredly they would not.

Whom would they then? I asked.

There is a charioteer paid by my father.

Paid! cried I. Do they allow a paid servant in preference to you
to do what he pleases with the horses, and, what is more, give him
money for so doing?

b   Not a doubt about it, Socrates, he replied.

Well, but your pair of mules I am sure they let you drive, and
even if you wished to take the whip and whip them, they would allow you.

Allow me, would they? said he.

Would they not? said I. Is there no one allowed to whip them?

Of course there is—the mule driver.

Is he a slave or free?

A slave, he answered.

A slave then, it appears, they think of more account than you,
their son; they entrust their property to him rather than to you, and
they allow him to do what he pleases, while you they hinder. But an-
c   swer me further. Do they let you rule yourself, or not even allow you
this?

Rule myself! I should think not, said he.

You have someone to rule you, then?

Yes, my governor here.

Not a slave?

Yes, but he is, though, ours.

Shocking! I exclaimed. A free man to be ruled by a slave. But how, pray, does this governor exercise his authority?

He takes me to school, of course.

And do you mean to say that they rule you there, too—the schoolmasters?

Most certainly they do.

Very many then, it appears, are the masters and rulers whom d your father sets over you on purpose. But come now, when you go home to your mother, she, I am sure, lets you do what you please— that you may be as happy as she can make you—either with her wool or her loom, when she is spinning. It cannot possibly be that she hinders you from touching her comb or her shuttle, or any other of her spinning implements.

He burst out laughing. I can assure you, Socrates, he said, she not only hinders me, but would get me a good beating if I did touch e them.

Beating! cried I. You haven't done your father or mother any wrong, have you?

Not I, he answered.

Whatever is the reason, then, that they hinder you, in this shock-ing manner, from being happy, and acting as you please, and keep you, all the day long, in a state of bondage to someone or other—and, in a word, of doing hardly anything at all you want to do? So that it seems you get no good whatever from your fortune, large as it is, but all have control over it, rather than you, nor, again, from that beauti- 209 ful person of yours, for it, too, is under the care and charge of other people, while you, poor Lysis, have control over nothing at all, nor do a single thing you wish.

Because I'm not old enough yet, Socrates.

That should be no hindrance, son of Democrates, since there are things, I fancy, which both your father and mother allow you to do, without waiting for you to be old enough. When they wish, for exam-ple, to have anything written or read, it is you, I conceive, whom they appoint to the office, before anyone else in the house. Isn't it? b

Beyond a question, he replied.

In these matters, then, you are allowed to do as you please; you may write whichever letter you like first, and whichever you like sec-ond. And in reading you enjoy the same liberty. And when you take up your lyre, neither father nor mother, I imagine, hinders you from tightening or loosening such strings as you choose, or from playing with your fingers or stick, as you may think proper. Or do they hinder you in such matters?

Oh dear, no! he exclaimed.

What in the world, then, can be the reason, Lysis, that in these matters they don't hinder you, while in the former they do? c

I suppose it is, Socrates, because I understand the one, and don't understand the other.

Oh! That's it, is it, my fine fellow? It is not, then, for you to be old enough that your father is waiting in all cases, but on the very day that he thinks you are wiser than he is, he will hand over to you himself and his property.

I shouldn't wonder, said he.

Nor I, said I. But again. Does your neighbor follow the same rule that your father does with regard to you? Do you expect he will
d hand over to you his house to manage, as soon as he thinks you have a better idea of the management of a house than he has himself, or will he keep it in his own hands?

Hand it over to me, I should think.

And the Athenians? Will they, do you imagine, hand over to you their matters directly they perceive that you are wise enough to manage them?

Yes, I expect so.

But come now, I asked, what will the Great King do? When his meat is cooking, will he allow his eldest son, heir to the throne of Asia,
e to throw into the gravy whatever he chooses, or us, rather, if we come before him, and prove that we have a better idea than his son has of dressing a dish?

Us, to be sure, said he.

And the prince he won't allow to put in the least morsel even, while with us he would make no difficulty, though we wished to throw in salt by handfuls?

Exactly.

Once more. If his son had something the matter with his eyes, would he allow him to touch them himself, if he thought him ignorant
210 of the healing art, or rather hinder him?

Hinder him.

But against us, on the other hand, if he conceived us to be skilled in the art, he would, I imagine, make no objection, even though we wished to force open the eyes, and sprinkle in ashes, as he would suppose us to be rightly advised.

True, he would not.

And so, with everything else whatsoever, he would entrust it to us rather than to himself or his son, if he believed that we knew more about it than either of them did.

Necessarily he would, Socrates.

You see then, said I, how the case stands, dear Lysis. All matters of which we have a good idea will be put into our hands by all
b people, whether Greeks or barbarians, men or women. We shall act, with regard to them, exactly as we please; no one will intentionally stand in our way. And not only shall we be free ourselves in these matters, but we shall be lords over others, and they will be in fact our

property, as we shall have the enjoyment of them. With regard to matters, on the other hand, into which we have acquired no insight, no one will ever allow us to act as we think proper, but all persons, to the best of their power, will hinder us from meddling with them— not only strangers, but even our own father and mother, and if we c possess any nearer relation. And we ourselves, in these matters, shall be subject to others, and they will be, in fact, the property of others, as we shall derive no advantage from them. Do you allow this to be the case?

I do.

Will anyone, then, count us his friends, will anyone love us in those matters in which we are of no use?

Indeed no.

According to this, then, not even you are loved by your own father, nor is anyone else by anyone else in the world, in so far as you or he is useless?

So it would appear, he said.

If, therefore, you acquire knowledge, my son, all men will be d friendly to you, all men will be attached to you, for you will be useful and good. If not, you will have no friend in anyone, not even in your father or mother, or any of your own family. Now is it possible, Lysis, for a man to have a great idea of himself in those matters of which he has yet no idea?

How can he possibly? he replied.

And if you still require, as you do, an instructor, you are still without ideas.

True, he answered.

It cannot be, then, that you have a great idea of yourself, if as yet you have no idea.

No, really, Socrates, I don't see how I can.

On receiving this reply from Lysis, I turned my eyes on Hip- e pothales, and was on the point of making a great blunder. For it came into my head to say, This is the way, Hippothales, that you should talk to your favorite, humbling and checking, instead of puffing him up and pampering him, as you now do. However, on seeing him writhing with agitation at the turn the conversation was taking, I recollected that though standing so near, he didn't wish to be seen by Lysis. So I recovered myself in time, and forbore to address him.

At this moment, too, Menexenus returned and took the seat by 211 Lysis, from which he had previously arisen.

Whereupon Lysis, in a boyish fondling way, said to me in a low voice, so that Menexenus couldn't hear, I say, Socrates, say over again to Menexenus what you have been saying to me.

No, Lysis, I replied, *you* must tell him that; you were certainly attending.

I should think I was too, he rejoined.

Try to remember it then, as well as you can, that you may give
b him a clear account of the whole, and if there's anything you forget,
ask me about it some other day—the first time you meet me.

Well, I'll do as you tell me, Socrates, with all my heart; you may
rely upon that. But say something else to him now, will you, that I,
too, may hear it, till it's time for me to go home.

Well, I must do so, I replied, since it's you who bid me. But
mind you come to my aid, if Menexenus tries to baffle me. You know,
don't you, that he's fond of a dispute?

Oh yes, desperately, I know. And that's the very reason I want
c you to talk with him.

That I may make myself ridiculous, eh?

Oh dear, no, Socrates, but that you may put him down.

Put him down, indeed, cried I. That's no such easy matter. He's
a redoubtable man, this, a scholar of Ctesippus'. And here's his master
too, himself, to help him—don't you see?—Ctesippus.

Trouble yourself about no one, Socrates, he said, but begin, attack him.

As you will, said I.

At this point of our byplay Ctesippus cried out, What's that you
d two there are feasting on by yourselves, without giving us a share?

Never fear, said I, you shall have a share. There's something I've
said that Lysis here doesn't understand. He says, though, he thinks
Menexenus knows, and bids me ask him.

Why don't you ask him then? he rejoined.

Just what I mean to do, I replied. Answer, Menexenus, the questions I ask. From my earliest childhood I have had a particular
e fancy; everyone has. One longs for horses, another for dogs, a third
for money, a fourth for office. For my part, I look on these matters
with equanimity, but on the acquisition of friends, with all a lover's
passion, and I would choose to obtain a good friend rather than the
best quail or cock in the world; I should prefer one to both horse and
dog—nay, I fully believe, that I would far sooner acquire a friend
and companion, than all the gold of Darius, aye, or than Darius him-
212 self. So fond am I of friendship. On seeing, therefore, you and Lysis, I
am lost in wonder, while I count you most happy, at your being able,
at your years, to acquire this treasure with such readiness and ease—
in that you, Menexenus, have gained so early and true a friend in
Lysis, and he the same in you—while I, on the contrary, am so far
from making the acquisition, that I do not even know how one man
becomes the friend of another, but wish on this very point to appeal
to you as a connoisseur. Answer me this. As soon as one man loves
another, which of the two becomes the friend—the lover of the loved,
b or the loved of the lover? Or does it make no difference?

None in the world, that I can see, he replied.

How? said I. Are both friends, if only one loves?

I think so, he answered.

Indeed! Is it not possible for one who loves, not to be loved in return by the object of his love?

It is.

Nay, is it not possible for him even to be hated—treatment, if I mistake not, which lovers frequently fancy they receive at the hands of their favorites? Though they love their darlings as dearly as possible, they often imagine that they are not loved in return, often that they are even hated. Don't you believe this to be true? c

Quite true, he replied.

Well, in such a case as this, the one loves, the other is loved.

Just so.

Which of the two, then, is the friend of the other—the lover of the loved, whether or no he be loved in return, and even if he be hated, or the loved of the lover? Or is neither the friend of the other, unless both love each other?

The latter certainly seems to be the case, Socrates.

If so, I continued, we think differently now from what we did be- d fore. Then it appeared that if one loved, both were friends, but now, that unless both love, neither are friends.

Yes, I'm afraid we have contradicted ourselves.

This being the case then, the lover is not a friend to anything that does not love him in return.

Apparently not.

People, then, are not friends to horses, unless their horses love them in return, nor friends to quails or to dogs, nor again, to wine or to gymnastics, unless their love be returned—nor friends to wisdom, unless wisdom loves them in return. But in each of these cases, the individual loves the object, but is not a friend to it, and the poet is wrong who says, e

Happy the man who, to whom he's a friend, has children, and horses
Mettlesome, dogs of the chase, guest in a faraway land.[1]

I don't think he is wrong, Socrates.

But do you think he's right?

Yes, I do.

The lover then, it appears, Menexenus, is a friend to the object of his love, whether the object love, or even hate him. Just as to quite young children, who are either not yet old enough to love, or who are 213 old enough to feel hatred when punished by father or mother, their parents, all the time even that they are being hated, are friends in the very highest degree.

Yes, such appears to be the case.

---

[1] Solon 21.2.

By this reasoning, then, it is not the object of love that is the friend, but the lover.

Apparently.

And so, not the object of hatred that is the enemy, but the hater.

Clearly.

It frequently happens, then, that people are enemies to those b who love them, and friends to those who hate them—that is, are enemies to their friends, and friends to their enemies—if it be true that the lover is the friend, but not the loved. But surely, my dear friend, it were grossly unreasonable, nay, rather, I think altogether impossible, for a man to be a friend to his enemy, and an enemy to his friend.

Yes, Socrates, it does seem impossible.

Well, then, if this be impossible, it must be the object of the love that is the friend to the lover.

Clearly.

And so again, the object of the hatred that is the enemy to the hater.

Necessarily.

But if this be true, we cannot help arriving at the same conclu- c sion as we did in the former case—namely, that it often happens that a man is not a friend, but even an enemy to a friend, as often, that is, as he is not loved, but even hated by the man whom he loves—and often again, that he is not an enemy, but even a friend to an enemy, as often, in fact, as he is not hated, but even loved by the man whom he hates.

No, I'm afraid we can't.

What are we to do then, said I, if neither those who love are to be friends, nor those who are loved, nor, again, those who both love and are loved? Are there any other people besides these that we can say become friends to each other?

To tell you the truth, Socrates, said he, I don't see my way at all.

d   Is it possible, Menexenus, said I, that from first to last we have been conducting our search improperly?

I am sure I think it is, Socrates, cried Lysis. And he blushed as he said so. For the words seemed to burst from him against his will in the intensity of the interest he was paying to the conversation—an interest which his countenance had evinced all the time we were talking.

I then, wishing to relieve Menexenus, and charmed with the other's intelligence, turned to Lysis, and directing my discourse to him, e observed, Yes, Lysis, you are quite right, I think, in saying that if we had conducted our search properly, we should never have lost ourselves in this manner. Let us proceed, however, on this line of inquiry no longer—for I look upon it as a very difficult sort of road—but let us go back again to that point at which we turned aside, and fol- 214 low in the steps of the poets. For poets, I conceive, are as good as fa-

thers and guides to us in matters of wisdom. Well, the poets, if I mistake not, put forward no slight claims for those who happen to be
friends, but tell us that it is God himself who makes them friends, by
leading them one to another. They express, if I remember right, their
opinion thus: 'Like men, I trow, to like, God ever leads,'[2] and makes
them known. You have met with the verse, have you not?   b
      Oh, yes.
      And also with the writings of those learned sages which tell
the same story—namely, that like must of necessity be ever friendly
with like. And these are they, if I mistake not, who talk and write on
nature and the universe.
      True, they are.
      Well, do you think they are right in what they say? I asked.
      Perhaps, said he.
      Perhaps, I answered, in half—perhaps, too, even in all—only we
don't understand. For, as it appears to us, the nearer wicked men   c
come to each other, and the more they see of each other, the greater
enemies they become. For they injure each other. And it is impossible,
I take it, for men to be friends, if they injure and are injured in turn.
      So it is, he replied.
      By this, then, it would appear, that half of their assertion can-
not be true, if we suppose them to mean that wicked men are like one
another.
      So it would.
      But they mean to say, I imagine, that the good are like and
friendly with the good, but that the bad, as is remarked of them in
another place, are not ever even like themselves, but are variable and
not to be reckoned upon. And if a thing be unlike and at variance with   d
itself, it will be long, I take it, before it becomes like to or friendly
with anything else. Don't you think so too?
      I do, he answered.
      When, therefore, my friend, our authors assert that like is
friendly with like, they mean, I imagine, to intimate, though obscurely
enough, that the good man is a friend to the good man only, but that
the bad man never engages in a true friendship either with a good or a
bad man. Do you agree?
      He nodded assent.
      We know then now, I continued, who it is that are friends, for
our argument shows us that it must be those who are good.
      Quite clearly too, I think, said he.   e
      And so do I, I rejoined. Still there is a something in the way that
troubles me; so let us, with the help of heaven, see what it is that I
suspect. Like men are friendly with like men, in so far as they are
like, and such a man is useful to such a man. Or rather, let us put it in

[2] *Odyssey* 17.218.

this way. Is there any good or harm that a like thing can do to a like
215 thing, which it cannot also do to itself? Is there any that can be done
to it, which cannot also be done to it by itself? And if not, how can
such things be held in regard by each other, when they have no means
of assisting one another? Can this possibly be?

No, not possibly.

And if a thing be not held in regard, can it be a friend?

Certainly not.

But, you will say, the like man is not a friend to the like man, but
the good will be a friend to the good, in so far as he is good, not in
so far as he is like.

Perhaps I may.

And I should rejoin, Will not the good man, in so far as he is
good, be found to be sufficient for himself?

Yes.

b   And if sufficient, he will want nothing so far as his sufficiency
goes.

Of course not.

And if he does not want anything he won't feel regard for anything either.

To be sure not.

And what he does not feel regard for, he cannot love.

Not he.

And if he does not love, he won't be a friend.

Clearly not.

How then, I wonder, will the good be ever friends at all with the
good, when neither in absence do they feel regret for each other, being
sufficient for themselves apart, nor when present together have they
any need of one another? Is there any possible way by which such
people can be brought to care for each other?

None whatever.

c   And if they do not care for each other, they cannot possibly be
friends.

True, they cannot.

Look and see then, Lysis, how we have been led into error. If I
mistake not, we are deceived in the whole, and not only in the half.

How so? he asked.

Once upon a time, I replied, I heard a statement made which
has just this moment flashed across my mind. It was that nothing is
so hostile to like as like, none so hostile to the good as the good. And
among other arguments, my informant adduced the authority of
d Hesiod, telling me that, according to him, 'Potter ever jars with potter, bard with bard, and poor with poor.'[3] And so, he added, by a
universal and infallible law the nearer any two things resemble one

---

[3] *Works and Days* 25.

another, the fuller do they become of envy, strife, and hatred—and the greater the dissimilarity, the greater the friendship. For the poor are obliged to make themselves friends of the rich, and the weak of the strong, for the sake of their assistance; the sick man also must be friendly with the physician, and, in short, everyone who is without knowledge must feel regard and affection for those who possess it. Nay, he proceeded with increased magnificence of position to assert e that the like was so far from being friendly with the like, that the exact opposite was the case; the more any two things were contrary, the more were they friendly to each other. For everything, he says, craves for its contrary, and not for its like—the dry craves for moisture, the cold for heat, the bitter for sweetness, the sharp for bluntness, the empty to be filled, the full to be emptied. And everything else follows the same rule. For the contrary, he added, is food to the contrary; the like can derive no advantage from the like. And I can assure you I thought him extremely clever as he said all this. He stated 216 his case so well. But you, my friends, what do you think of it?

Oh, it seems very fair at first hearing, said Menexenus.

Shall we admit then that nothing is so friendly to a thing as its contrary?

By all means.

But if we do, Menexenus, will there not spring upon us suddenly and uncouthly and exultingly those universal-knowledge men, the masters of dispute, and ask us, whether there is anything in the world so contrary to enmity as friendship? And if they do, what must be our answer? Can we possibly help admitting that they are right? b

No, we cannot.

Well then, they will say, is friendship a friend to enmity, or enmity to friendship?

Neither one nor the other, he replied.

But justice, I suppose, is a friend to injustice, temperance to intemperance, good to evil.

No, I don't think this can be the case.

Well but, I rejoined, if one thing is friend to another thing in virtue of being its contrary, these things must of necessity be friendly.

So they must, he allowed.

It follows then, I think, that neither like is friendly with like, nor contrary with contrary.

Apparently it does.

Well, then, said I, let us look again, and see whether we be not c still as far as ever from finding friendship, since it is clearly none of these things I have mentioned, but whether that which is neither good nor evil may not possibly turn out, however late, to be friendly with the good.

How do you mean? he asked.

Why, to tell you the truth, said I, I don't know myself, being quite

dizzied by the entanglement of the subject. I am inclined though to think that, in the words of the old proverb, the beautiful is friendly. Certainly the friendly has the appearance of being something soft and
d smooth and slippery, and probably it is from being of this character that it slides and slips through our fingers so easily. Now I am of this opinion, because the good, I assert, is beautiful. Don't you think so?

I do, said he.

I further assert, with a diviner's foresight, that to the beautiful and good that which is neither good nor evil is friendly. And my reasons for divining this I will tell you. I conceive I recognize three distinct classes, good, evil, and, thirdly, that which is neither good nor evil. Do you allow this distinction?

I do.

Now that good is friendly with good, or evil with evil, or good with evil, we are hindered by our previous arguments from believing. It re-
e mains then that, if there be anything friendly with anything, that which is neither good nor evil must be friendly either with the good or with that which resembles itself. For nothing, I am sure, can be friendly with evil.

True.

But neither can like be friendly with like; this we also said, did we not?

We did.

That then which is neither good nor evil will not be friendly with that which resembles itself.

Clearly not.

217 It follows then, I conceive, that friendship can only exist between good and that which is neither evil nor good.

Necessarily, as it appears.

What think you then, my children? I proceeded to say. Is our present position guiding us in a right direction? If we look attentively, we perceive that a body which is in health has no need whatever of the medical art or of any assistance, for it is sufficient in itself. And therefore no one in health is friendly with a physician on account of his health.

Just so, he replied.

But the sick man is, I imagine, on account of his sickness.

Undoubtedly.
b Sickness, you will allow, is an evil, the art of medicine, both useful and good.

Yes.

But a body, if I mistake not, in so far as it is a body, is neither good nor evil.

Exactly.

A body though is compelled, on account of sickness, to embrace and love the medical art.

I think so.

That, then, which is neither evil nor good becomes friendly with good, on account of the presence of evil.

Apparently.

But evidently it becomes so before it is itself made evil by the evil which it contains. For, once become evil, it can no longer, you will allow, be desirous of or friendly with good, for evil, we said, cannot c possibly be friendly with good.

No, it cannot possibly.

Now mark what I say. I say that some things are themselves such as that which is present with them, some things are not such. For example, if you dye a substance with any color, the color which is dyed in is present, I imagine, with the substance which is dyed.

To be sure it is.

After the process then, is the dyed substance such, in point of color, as that which is applied?

I don't understand, he said.

But you will thus, said I. If anyone were to dye your locks of d gold with white lead, would they, after the dyeing, be, or appear, white?

Appear.

And yet whiteness would, at any rate, be present with them.

True.

But still they would not, as yet, be at all the more white on that account, but though whiteness is present with them, they are neither white nor black.

Precisely.

But when, my dear Lysis, old age has brought upon them this same color, then they become really such as that which is present with them, white by the presence of white.

Yes, indeed they do.

This, then, is the question I want to ask. If a thing be present e in a substance, will the substance be such as that which is present with it, or will it be such, if the thing is present under certain conditions, under certain conditions not?

The latter rather, said he.

That then which is neither evil nor good is, in some cases, when evil is present with it, not evil as yet; in other cases it has already become such.

Exactly.

Well then, said I, when it is not evil as yet, though evil be present with it, this very presence of evil makes it desirous of good, but the presence which makes it evil deprives it, at the same time, of its desire and friendship for good. For it is no longer a thing neither evil 218 nor good, but already evil, and evil, we said, cannot be friendly with good.

True, it cannot be.

On the same ground then we may further assert that those who are already wise are no longer friends to wisdom, be they gods, or be they men, nor, again, are those friends to wisdom who are so possessed of foolishness as to be evil, for no evil and ignorant man is a friend to wisdom. There remain then those who possess indeed this evil, the evil of foolishness, but who are not, as yet, in consequence of it, foolish or ignorant, but still understand that they do not know the things they do not know. And thus, you see, it is those who are neither good nor evil, as yet, that are friends to wisdom [philosophers], but those who are evil are not friends, nor again are the good. For that contrary is not friendly with contrary, nor like with like, was made apparent in the former part of our discourse. Do you remember?

Oh perfectly, they both cried.

Now then, Lysis and Menexenus, I continued, we have, as it appears, discovered, beyond a dispute, what it is that is friendly, and not friendly. Whether in respect of the soul, or of the body, or of anything else whatsoever, that, we pronounce, which is neither evil nor good is friendly with good on account of the presence of evil.

To this conclusion they both yielded a hearty and entire assent.

For myself, I was rejoicing, with all a hunter's delight, at just grasping the prey I had been so long in chase of, when presently there came into my mind, from what quarter I cannot tell, the strangest sort of suspicion. It was that the conclusions to which we had arrived were not true, and, sorely discomfited, I cried, Alackaday, Lysis, alack, Menexenus, we have, I fear me, but dreamed our treasure.

Why so? said Menexenus.

I am afraid, I answered, that, just as if with lying men, we have fallen in with some such false reasonings in our search after friendship.

How do you mean? he asked.

Look here, said I. If a man be a friend, is he a friend to someone, or not?

To someone, of course.

For the sake of nothing, and on account of nothing, or for the sake and on account of something?

For the sake of and on account of something.

Is he a friend to that thing, for the sake of which he is a friend to his friend, or is he to it neither friend nor foe?

I don't quite follow, he said.

No wonder, said I, but perhaps you will if we take this course, and I too, I think, shall better understand what I am saying. The sick man, as we just now said, is a friend to the physician. Is he not?

He is.

On account of sickness, for the sake of health?

Yes.

Sickness is an evil?

Beyond a doubt.

But what is health? I asked. A good, an evil, or neither one nor the other?

A good, he replied.   219

We further stated, I think, that the body, a thing neither good nor evil, is, on account of sickness—that is to say, on account of an evil—a friend to the medical art. And the medical art is a good, and it is for the sake of health that the medical art has received the friendship, and health is a good, is it not?

It is.

Is the body a friend, or not a friend, to health?

A friend.

And a foe to sickness?

Most decidedly.

That, then, it appears, which is neither good nor evil is a friend b to good on account of an evil to which it is a foe, for the sake of a good to which it is a friend?

So it seems.

The friendly, then, is a friend for the sake of that to which it is a friend, on account of that to which it is a foe?

Apparently.

Very well, said I. But arrived as we are, I added, at this point, let us pay all heed, my children, that we be not misled. That friend is become friend to friend—that is to say, that like is become friend to like, which we declared to be impossible—is a matter I will allow to pass, but there is another point which we must attentively consider, in order that we may not be deceived by our present position. A man is a friend, we said, to the medical art for the sake of health.   c

We did.

Is he a friend to health too?

To be sure he is.

For the sake of something?

Yes.

For the sake of something, then, to which he is friendly, if this, too, is to follow our previous admission?

Certainly.

But is he not again a friend to that thing for the sake of some other thing to which he is a friend?

Yes.

Can we possibly help, then, being weary of going on in this manner, and is it not necessary that we advance at once to a beginning, which will not again refer us to friend upon friend, but arrive at that to which we are in the first instance friends, and for the sake of which we say we are friends to all the rest?   d

It is necessary, he answered.

This, then, is what I say we must consider, in order that all those other things, to which we said we were friendly, for the sake of that one thing, may not, like so many shadows of it, lead us into error, but that we may establish that thing as the first, to which we are really and truly friends. For let us view the matter thus. If a man sets a high value upon a thing—for instance, if, as is frequently the case, a father prizes a son above everything else he has in the world—may such a
e father be led by the extreme regard he has for his son to set a high value upon other things also? Suppose, for example, he were to hear of his having drunk some hemlock; would he set a high value on wine, if he believed that wine would cure his son?

Of course he would.

And on the vessel also which contained the wine?

Certainly.

Do you mean to say, then, that he sets an equal value on both, on a cup of earthenware and his own son, on his own son and a quart of wine? Or is the truth rather thus? All such value as this is set not on those things which are procured for the sake of another thing, but on that for the sake of which all such things are procured. We often talk,
220 I do not deny, about setting a high value on gold and silver, but is the truth on this account at all the more so? No, what we value supremely is that, whatever it may be found to be, for the sake of which gold, and all other subsidiaries, are procured. Shall we not say so?

Unquestionably.

And does not the same reasoning hold with regard to friendship? When we say we are friendly to things for the sake of a thing to which we are friendly, do we not clearly use a term with regard to them which belongs to another? And do we not appear to be in reality
b friendly only with that in which all these so-called friendships terminate?

Yes, he said, this would appear to be the truth.

With that, then, to which we are truly friendly, we are not friendly for the sake of any other thing to which we are friendly.

True, we are not.

This point, then, we dismiss, as sufficiently proved. But, to proceed, are we friends to good?

I imagine so.

And good is loved on account of evil, and the case stands thus. If,
c of the three classes that we just now distinguished, good, evil, and that which is neither evil nor good, two only were to be left to us, but evil were to be removed out of our path, and were never again to come in contact either with body or soul, or any other of these things, which in themselves we say are neither good nor evil, would it not come to pass that good would no longer be useful to us, but have become useless? For if there were nothing any more to hurt us, we

should have no need whatever of any assistance. And thus you see it d
would then be made apparent that it was only on account of evil that
we felt regard and affection for good, as we considered good to be a
medicine for evil, and evil to be a disease. But where there is no disease, there is, we are aware, no need of medicine. This, then, it appears, is the nature of good. It is loved on account of evil by us who
are intermediate between evil and good, but in itself, and for itself, it
is of no use.

Yes, he said, such would seem to be the case.

It follows, then, I think, that the original thing to which we are
friendly, that wherein all those other things terminate to which we
said we were friendly for the sake of another thing, bears to these
things no resemblance at all. For to these things we called ourselves
friendly for the sake of another thing to which we were friendly, but e
that to which we are really friendly appears to be of a nature exactly
the reverse of this, since we found that we were friendly to it for the
sake of a thing to which we were unfriendly, and, if this latter be removed, we are, it seems, friendly to it no longer.

Apparently not, said he, according at least to our present position.

But tell me this, said I. If evil be extinguished, will it no longer be
possible to feel hunger or thirst, or any similar desire? Or will hunger
exist, as long as man and the whole animal creation exist, but exist 221
without being hurtful? And will thirst, too, and all other desires exist,
but not be evil, inasmuch as evil is extinct? It is ridiculous though, to
ask what will exist or not exist, in such a case, for who can know? But
this, at any rate, we do know, that even at present it is possible for a
man to be injured by the sensation of hunger, and possible for him
also to be profited. Is it not?

Certainly it is.

And so, too, a man who feels thirst, or any similar desire, may
feel it in some cases with profit to himself, in other cases with hurt, b
and in other cases again, with neither one nor the other.

Assuredly he may.

Well, if evil is being extinguished, is there any reason in the
world for things that are not evil to be extinguished with it?

None whatever.

There will exist, then, those desires which are neither evil nor
good, even if evil be extinct.

Clearly.

Is it possible for a man who is desirous and enamored not to love
that of which he is desirous and enamored?

I think not.

There will exist then, it appears, even if evil be extinct, certain
things to which we are friendly. c

Yes, there will.

But if evil were the cause of our being friendly to anything, it would not be possible, when evil was extinct, for any man to be friendly to anything. For if a cause be extinct, surely it is no longer possible for that to exist of which it was the cause.

True, it is not.

But earlier we agreed that the friendly loved something, and on account of something, and at the same time we were of opinion that it was on account of evil that that which is neither good nor evil loved the good.

So we were.

d   But now, it appears, we have discovered some other cause of loving and being loved.

So it does.

Is it true, then, as we were just now saying, that desire is the cause of friendship, and that whatever desires is friendly to that which it desires, and friendly at the time of its feeling the desire? And was all that, which we previously said about being friendly, mere idle talk, put together after the fashion of a lengthy poem?

I am afraid it was, he replied.

But that, I continued, which feels desire, feels desire for that of which it is in want. Does it not?

Yes.

e   And that which is in want is friendly with that of which it is in want.

I imagine so.

And becomes in want of that which is taken from it?

Of course.

That then which belongs to a man, is found, it seems, Lysis and Menexenus, to be the object of his love, and friendship, and desire.

They both assented.

If, then, you two are friendly to each other, by some tie of nature you belong to each other?

To be sure we do, they cried together.

And so, in general, said I, if one man, my children, is desirous and enamored of another, he can never have conceived his desire, or love,

222   or friendship, without in some way belonging to the object of his love, either in his soul, or in some quality of his soul, or in disposition, or in form.

I quite believe you, cried Menexenus—but Lysis said not a word.

Well, then, I continued, that which by nature belongs to us, it has been found necessary for us to love.

So it appears, said Menexenus.

It cannot possibly be then, but that a true and genuine lover is loved in return by the object of his love.

b   To this conclusion Lysis and Menexenus nodded a sort of reluctant assent, while Hippothales in his rapture kept changing from color to color.

I, however, with a view of reconsidering the subject, proceeded to say, Well, if there is a difference between that which belongs to us and that which is like, we are now, I conceive, in a condition to say what is meant by a friend. But if they happen to be the same, it's no such easy matter to get rid of our former assertion, that like was useless to like, in so far as it was like, for to admit ourselves friendly with that which is useless were outrageous. What say you then, said I, since we are, as it were, intoxicated by our talk, to our allowing that c there is a difference between that which belongs and that which is like?

Let us do so by all means, he replied.

Shall we further say that good belongs to everyone and that to everyone evil is a stranger, or rather, that good belongs to good, evil to evil, and that which is neither evil nor good, to that which is of the same nature?

They both agreed that the latter was their opinion in each particular.

It appears then, said I, that we have fallen again into positions, d with regard to friendship, which we previously rejected. For, according to our present admission, the unjust will be no less friendly to the unjust, and the evil no less friendly to the evil, than the good to the good.

So it would appear, said he.

And again, said I, if we assert that what is good and what belongs to us are one and the same, will it not result that none are friendly with the good but the good? And this, too, I think, is a position in which we imagined that we proved ourselves wrong. Don't you remember?

Oh, yes, they both cried.

What other way then is left us of treating the subject? Clearly e none. I therefore, like our clever pleaders at the bar, request you to reckon up all that I have said. If neither those who love or are loved, neither the like nor the unlike, nor the good, nor those who belong to us, nor any other of all the suppositions which we passed in review —they are so numerous that I can remember no more—if, I say, not one of them is the object of friendship, I no longer know what I am to say.

With this confession, I was just on the point of rousing to my aid 223 one of the elders of our party, when all of a sudden, like beings of another world, there came down upon us the attendants of Menexenus and Lysis, holding their brothers by the hand, and calling out to the young gentlemen to come home, as it was already late. At first, both we and the bystanders were for driving them off, but finding that they did not mind us at all, but grumbled at us in sad Greek, and persisted in calling the boys—fancying, moreover, that from having tippled at b the feast, they would prove awkward people to deal with—we owned ourselves vanquished, and broke up the party.

However, just as they were leaving, I managed to call out, Well, Lysis and Menexenus, we have made ourselves rather ridiculous today, I, an old man, and you children. For our hearers here will carry away the report that though we conceive ourselves to be friends with each other—you see I class myself with you—we have not as yet been able to discover what we mean by a friend.

EUTHYPHRO

Socrates and Euthyphro meet at the entrance to the law courts, and to
Euthyphro's surprised question—"What has taken you from your
haunts in the Lyceum?"—Socrates answers that a charge has been
brought against him which is rather a grand one, that of corrupting the
youth of Athens, and that the prosecutor knows just how it is done and
how Socrates is doing it. But why, he asks in turn, is Euthyphro here?
The reason, the latter answers, is that he is prosecuting his own father
on a charge of murder. Socrates' astonishment at this does not disturb
him. He is by profession an interpreter of religion, a theologian, and
he tells Socrates that with his special insight into what is right and
wrong he knows that he is acting in the spirit of true piety. When
Socrates asks what then is piety, he gives the answer characteristic of
the orthodox everywhere—in effect, "Piety is thinking as I do." His sincerity is as patent as his conceit. He really believes that he ought to
prosecute his father who though certainly not a murderer is not free
from blame.

The conversation that follows is chiefly an attempt to define
piety, and comes to nothing, but in the course of it Socrates makes a
distinction fundamental in reasoning and often disregarded, that the
good is not good because the gods approve it, but the gods approve it
because it is good.

The real interest of the dialogue, however, is the picture of Socrates just before his trial. There is no question that he realized the
danger he was in, but Plato, who knew him best of all, shows him engaging humorously and ironically and keenly in a discussion completely removed from his own situation. Just at the end he says that if
only Euthyphro will instruct him in what true piety is he will tell his
accuser that he has become the pupil of a great theologian and is going to lead a better life. But Euthyphro, by this time in no mood to
define anything, gives up. "Another time, then, Socrates," he says and
hurries away.

2 EUTHYPHRO: This, Socrates, is something new? What has taken you from your haunts in the Lyceum, and makes you spend your time at the royal porch? You surely cannot have a case at law, as I have, before the Archon-King.

SOCRATES: My business, Euthyphro, is not what is known at Athens as a case at law; it is a criminal prosecution.

b EUTHYPHRO: How is that? You mean that somebody is prosecuting you? I never would believe that you were prosecuting anybody else.

SOCRATES: No indeed.

EUTHYPHRO: Then somebody is prosecuting you?

SOCRATES: Most certainly.

EUTHYPHRO: Who is it?

SOCRATES: I am not too clear about the man myself, Euthyphro. He appears to me to be a young man, and unknown. I think, however, that they call him Meletus, and his deme is Pitthos, if you happen to know anyone named Meletus of that deme—a hook-nosed man with long straight hair, and not much beard.

EUTHYPHRO: I don't recall him, Socrates. But tell me, of what
c does he accuse you?

SOCRATES: His accusation? It is no mean charge. For a man of his age it is no small thing to have settled a question of so much importance. He says, in fact, that he knows the method by which young people are corrupted, and knows who the persons are that do it. He is, quite possibly, a wise man, and, observing that my ignorance has led me to corrupt his generation, comes like a child to his mother to accuse me to the city. And to me he appears to be the only one who be-
d gins his political activity aright, for the right way to begin is to pay attention to the young, and make them just as good as possible—precisely as the able farmer will give his attention to the young plants
3 first, and afterward care for the rest. And so Meletus no doubt begins by clearing us away, the ones who ruin, as he says, the tender shoots of the young. That done, he obviously will care for the older generation, and will thus become the cause, in the highest and widest measure, of benefit to the state. With such a notable beginning, his chances of success look good.

EUTHYPHRO: I hope so, Socrates, but I'm very much afraid it will go the other way. When he starts to injure you, it simply looks to me like beginning at the hearth to hurt the state. But tell me what he says you do to corrupt the young.

b SOCRATES: It sounds very queer, my friend, when first you hear it. He says I am a maker of gods; he charges me with making new

---

From *On the Trial and Death of Socrates*, translated with introduction by Lane Cooper (Ithaca, New York, 1941; copyright 1941 by Lane Cooper).

gods, and not believing in the old ones. These are his grounds for prosecuting me, he says.

EUTHYPHRO: I see it, Socrates. It is because you say that ever and anon you have the spiritual sign! So he charges you in this indictment with introducing novelties in religion, and that is the reason why he comes to court with this slanderous complaint, well knowing how easily such matters can be misrepresented to the crowd. For my own part, when I speak in the Assembly about matters of religion, and c tell them in advance what will occur, they laugh at me as if I were a madman, and yet I never have made a prediction that did not come true. But the truth is, they are jealous of all such people as ourselves. No, we must not worry over them, but go to meet them.

SOCRATES: Dear Euthyphro, if we were only laughed at, it would be no serious matter. The Athenians, as it seems to me, are not very much disturbed if they think that so-and-so is clever, so long as he does not impart his knowledge to anybody else. But the moment they suspect that he is giving his ability to others, they get angry, whether out of jealousy, as you say, or, it may be, for some other d reason.

EUTHYPHRO: With regard to that, I am not very eager to test their attitude to me.

SOCRATES: Quite possibly you strike them as a man who is chary of himself, and is unwilling to impart his wisdom; as for me, I fear I am so kindly they will think that I pour out all I have to everyone, and not merely without pay—nay, rather, glad to offer something if it would induce someone to hear me. Well then, as I said just now, if they were going to laugh at me, as you say they do at you, it wouldn't be at all unpleasant to spend the time laughing and joking in court. But if they take the matter seriously, then there is no knowing e how it will turn out. Only you prophets can tell!

EUTHYPHRO: Well, Socrates, perhaps no harm will come of it at all, but you will carry your case as you desire, and I think that I shall carry mine.

SOCRATES: Your case, Euthyphro? What is it? Are you prosecuting, or defending?

EUTHYPHRO: Prosecuting.

SOCRATES: Whom?

EUTHYPHRO: One whom I am thought a maniac to be at- 4 tacking.

SOCRATES: How so? Is it someone who has wings to fly away with?

EUTHYPHRO: He is far from being able to do that; he happens to be old, a very old man.

SOCRATES: Who is it, then?

EUTHYPHRO: It is my father.

SOCRATES: Your father, my good friend?

EUTHYPHRO: Just so.

SOCRATES: What is the complaint? Of what do you accuse him?

EUTHYPHRO: Of murder, Socrates.

SOCRATES: Good heavens, Euthyphro! Surely the crowd is ignorant of the way things ought to go. I fancy it is not correct for any ordinary person to do that [to prosecute his father on this charge],
b but only for a man already far advanced in point of wisdom.

EUTHYPHRO: Yes, Socrates, by heaven! Far advanced!

SOCRATES: And the man your father killed, was he a relative of yours? Of course he was? You never would prosecute your father, would you, for the death of anybody who was not related to you?

EUTHYPHRO: You amuse me, Socrates. You think it makes a difference whether the victim was a member of the family, or not related, when the only thing to watch is whether it was right or not for the man who did the deed to kill him. If he was justified, then let him go; if not, you have to prosecute him, no matter if the man who killed
c him shares your hearth, and sits at table with you. The pollution is the same if, knowingly, you associate with such a man, and do not cleanse yourself, and him as well, by bringing him to justice. The victim in this case was a laborer of mine, and when we were cultivating land in Naxos, we employed him on our farm. One day he had been drinking, and became enraged at one of our domestics, and cut his throat; whereupon my father bound him hand and foot, and threw him into a ditch. Then he sent a man to Athens to find out from the seer what ought to be done—meanwhile paying no attention to the
d man who had been bound, neglecting him because he was a murderer and it would be no great matter even if he died. And that was just what happened. Hunger, cold, and the shackles finished him before the messenger got back from visiting the seer. That is why my father and my other kin are bitter at me when I prosecute my father as a murderer. They say he did not kill the man, and had he actually done it, the victim was himself a murderer, and for such a man one need have no consideration. They say that for a son to prosecute his
e father as a murderer is unholy. How ill they know divinity in its relation, Socrates, to what is holy or unholy!

SOCRATES: But you, by heaven! Euthyphro, you think that you have such an accurate knowledge of things divine, and what is holy and unholy, that, in circumstances such as you describe, you can accuse your father? You are not afraid that you yourself are doing an unholy deed?

EUTHYPHRO: Why, Socrates, if I did not have an accurate
5 knowledge of all that, I should be good for nothing, and Euthyphro would be no different from the general run of men.

SOCRATES: Well then, admirable Euthyphro, the best thing I can do is to become your pupil, and challenge Meletus before the trial comes on. Let me tell him that in the past I have considered it of great importance to know about things divine, and that now, when he asserts that I erroneously put forward my own notions and inventions on this head, I have become your pupil. I could say, Come, Meletus, if you agree that Euthyphro has wisdom in such matters, you must admit as well that I hold the true belief, and must not prosecute. If you do not, you must lodge your complaint, not against me, but against my aforesaid master; accuse him of corrupting the elder generation, me and his own father—me by his instruction, his father by correcting and chastising him.

And if he would not yield, would neither quit the suit nor yet indict you rather than myself, then I would say the same in court as when I challenged him!

EUTHYPHRO: Yes, Socrates, by heaven! If he undertook to bring me into court, I guess I would find out his rotten spot, and our talk there would concern him sooner by a long shot than ever it would me!

SOCRATES: Yes, my dear friend, that I know, and so I wish to be your pupil. This Meletus, I perceive, along presumably with everybody else, appears to overlook you, but sees into me so easily and keenly that he has attacked me for impiety. So, in the name of heaven, tell me now about the matter you just felt sure you knew quite thoroughly. State what you take piety and impiety to be with reference to murder and all other cases. Is not the holy always one and the same thing in every action, and, again, is not the unholy always opposite to the holy, and like itself? And as unholiness does it not always have its one essential form, which will be found in everything that is unholy?

EUTHYPHRO: Yes, surely, Socrates.

SOCRATES: Then tell me. How do you define the holy and the unholy?

EUTHYPHRO: Well then, I say that the holy is what I am now doing, prosecuting the wrongdoer who commits a murder or a sacrilegious robbery, or sins in any point like that, whether it be your father, or your mother, or whoever it may be. And not to prosecute would be unholy. And, Socrates, observe what a decisive proof I will give you that such is the law. It is one I have already given to others; I tell them that the right procedure must be not to tolerate the impious man, no matter who. Does not mankind believe that Zeus is the most excellent and just among the gods? And these same men admit that Zeus shackled his own father [Cronus] for swallowing his [other] sons unjustly, and that Cronus in turn had gelded his father [Uranus] for like reasons. But now they are enraged at me when I proceed against my father for wrongdoing, and so they contradict themselves in what they say about the gods and what they say of me.

SOCRATES: There, Euthyphro, you have the reason why the

charge is brought against me. It is because, whenever people tell such stories about the gods, I am prone to take it ill, and, so it seems, that is why they will maintain that I am sinful. Well, now, if you who are
b so well versed in matters of the sort entertain the same beliefs, then necessarily, it would seem, I must give in, for what could we urge who admit that, for our own part, we are quite ignorant about these matters? But, in the name of friendship, tell me! Do you actually believe that these things happened so?

EUTHYPHRO: Yes, Socrates, and things even more amazing, of which the multitude does not know.

SOCRATES: And you actually believe that war occurred among the gods, and there were dreadful hatreds, battles, and all sorts of fearful things like that? Such things as the poets tell of, and good
c artists represent in sacred places; yes, and at the great Panathenaic festival the robe that is carried up to the Acropolis is all inwrought with such embellishments? What is our position, Euthyphro? Do we say that these things are true?

EUTHYPHRO: Not these things only, Socrates, but, as I just now said, I will, if you wish, relate to you many other stories about the gods, which I am certain will astonish you when you hear them.

SOCRATES: I shouldn't wonder. You shall tell me all about them when we have the leisure at some other time. At present try to tell me more clearly what I asked you a little while ago, for, my friend,
d you were not explicit enough before when I put the question. What is holiness? You merely said that what you are now doing is a holy deed —namely, prosecuting your father on a charge of murder.

EUTHYPHRO: And, Socrates, I told the truth.

SOCRATES: Possibly. But, Euthyphro, there are many other things that you will say are holy.

EUTHYPHRO: Because they are.

SOCRATES: Well, bear in mind that what I asked of you was not to tell me one or two out of all the numerous actions that are holy; I wanted you to tell me what is the essential form of holiness which makes all holy actions holy. I believe you held that there is one ideal form by which unholy things are all unholy, and by which all holy
e things are holy. Do you remember that?

EUTHYPHRO: I do.

SOCRATES: Well then, show me what, precisely, this ideal is, so that, with my eye on it, and using it as a standard, I can say that any action done by you or anybody else is holy if it resembles this ideal, or, if it does not, can deny that it is holy.

EUTHYPHRO: Well, Socrates, if that is what you want, I certainly can tell you.

SOCRATES: It is precisely what I want.

EUTHYPHRO: Well then, what is pleasing to the gods is holy,
7 and what is not pleasing to them is unholy.

SOCRATES: Perfect, Euthyphro! Now you give me just the answer that I asked for. Meanwhile, whether it is right I do not know, but obviously you will go on to prove your statement true.

EUTHYPHRO: Indeed I will.

SOCRATES: Come now, let us scrutinize what we are saying. What is pleasing to the gods, and the man that pleases them, are holy; what is hateful to the gods, and the man they hate, unholy. But the holy and unholy are not the same; the holy is directly opposite to the unholy. Isn't it so?

EUTHYPHRO: It is.

SOCRATES: And the matter clearly was well stated.

EUTHYPHRO: I accept it, Socrates; that was stated.   b

SOCRATES: Was it not also stated, Euthyphro, that the gods revolt and differ with each other, and that hatreds come between them?

EUTHYPHRO: That was stated.

SOCRATES: Hatred and wrath, my friend—what kind of disagreement will produce them? Look at the matter thus. If you and I were to differ about numbers, on the question which of two was the greater, would a disagreement about that make us angry at each other, and make enemies of us? Should we not settle things by calculation, c and so come to an agreement quickly on any point like that?

EUTHYPHRO: Yes, certainly.

SOCRATES: And similarly if we differed on a question of greater length or less, we would take a measurement, and quickly put an end to the dispute?

EUTHYPHRO: Just that.

SOCRATES: And so, I fancy, we should have recourse to scales, and settle any question about a heavier or lighter weight?

EUTHYPHRO: Of course.

SOCRATES: What sort of thing, then, is it about which we differ, till, unable to arrive at a decision, we might get angry and be enemies to one another? Perhaps you have no answer ready, but listen to d me. See if it is not the following—right and wrong, the noble and the base, and good and bad. Are not these the things about which we differ, till, unable to arrive at a decision, we grow hostile, when we do grow hostile, to each other, you and I and everybody else?

EUTHYPHRO: Yes, Socrates, that is where we differ, on these subjects.

SOCRATES: What about the gods, then, Euthyphro? If, indeed, they have dissensions, must it not be on these subjects?

EUTHYPHRO: Quite necessarily.

SOCRATES: Accordingly, my noble Euthyphro, by your ac- e count some gods take one thing to be right, and others take another, and similarly with the honorable and the base, and good and bad. They would hardly be at variance with each other, if they did not differ on these questions. Would they?

EUTHYPHRO: You are right.

SOCRATES: And what each one of them thinks noble, good, and just, is what he loves, and the opposite is what he hates?

EUTHYPHRO: Yes, certainly.

SOCRATES: But it is the same things, so you say, that some of
8 them think right, and others wrong, and through disputing about these they are at variance, and make war on one another. Isn't it so?

EUTHYPHRO: It is.

SOCRATES: Accordingly, so it would seem, the same things will be hated by the gods and loved by them; the same things would alike displease and please them.

EUTHYPHRO: It would seem so.

SOCRATES: And so, according to this argument, the same things, Euthyphro, will be holy and unholy.

EUTHYPHRO: That may be.

SOCRATES: In that case, admirable friend, you have not answered what I asked you. I did not ask you to tell me what at once is holy and unholy, but it seems that what is pleasing to the gods is also
b hateful to them. Thus, Euthyphro, it would not be strange at all if what you now are doing in punishing your father were pleasing to Zeus, but hateful to Cronus and Uranus, and welcome to Hephaestus, but odious to Hera, and if any other of the gods disagree about the matter, satisfactory to some of them, and odious to others.

EUTHYPHRO: But, Socrates, my notion is that, on this point, there is no difference of opinion among the gods—not one of them but thinks that if a person kills another wrongfully, he ought to pay for it.

SOCRATES: And what of men? Have you never heard a man
c contending that someone who has killed a person wrongfully, or done some other unjust deed, ought not to pay the penalty?

EUTHYPHRO: Why! There is never any end to their disputes about these matters; it goes on everywhere, above all in the courts. People do all kinds of wrong, and then there is nothing they will not do or say in order to escape the penalty.

SOCRATES: Do they admit wrongdoing, Euthyphro, and, while admitting it, deny that they ought to pay the penalty?

EUTHYPHRO: No, not that, by any means.

SOCRATES: Then they will not do and say quite everything. Unless I am mistaken, they dare not say or argue that if they do wrong they should not pay the penalty. No, I think that they deny
d wrongdoing. How about it?

EUTHYPHRO: It is true.

SOCRATES: Therefore they do not dispute that anybody who does wrong should pay the penalty. No, the thing that they dispute about is likely to be who is the wrongdoer, what he did, and when.

EUTHYPHRO: That is true.

SOCRATES: Well then, isn't that precisely what goes on among the gods, if they really do have quarrels about right and wrong, as you say they do? One set will hold that some others do wrong, and the other set deny it? For that other thing, my friend, I take it no one, whether god or man, will dare to say—that the wrongdoer should not e pay the penalty!

EUTHYPHRO: Yes, Socrates, what you say is true—in the main.

SOCRATES: It is the individual act, I fancy, Euthyphro, that the disputants dispute about, both men and gods, if gods ever do dispute. They differ on a certain act; some hold that it was rightly done, the others that it was wrong. Isn't it so?

EUTHYPHRO: Yes, certainly.

SOCRATES: Then come, dear Euthyphro, teach me as well, and 9 let me grow more wise. What proof have you that all the gods think that your servant died unjustly, your hireling, who, when he had killed a man, was shackled by the master of the victim, and perished, dying because of his shackles before the man who shackled him could learn from the seers what ought to be done with him? What proof have you that for a man like him it is right for a son to prosecute his father, and indict him on a charge of murder? Come on. Try to make it clear to me beyond all doubt that under these conditions the gods must all consider this action to be right. If you can adequately b prove it to me, I will never cease from praising you for your wisdom.

EUTHYPHRO: But, Socrates, that, very likely, would be no small task, although I could indeed make it very clear to you.

SOCRATES: I understand. You think that I am duller than the judges; obviously you will demonstrate to them that what your father did was wrong, and that the gods all hate such deeds.

EUTHYPHRO: I shall prove it absolutely, Socrates, if they will listen to me.

SOCRATES: They are sure to listen if they think that you speak c well. But while you were talking, a notion came into my head, and I asked myself, Suppose that Euthyphro proved to me quite clearly that all the gods consider such a death unjust; would I have come one whit the nearer for him to knowing what the holy is, and what is the unholy? The act in question, seemingly, might be displeasing to the gods, but then we have just seen that you cannot define the holy and unholy in that way, for we have seen that a given thing may be displeasing, and also pleasing, to gods. So on this point, Euthyphro, I will let you off; if you like, the gods shall all consider the act unjust, and they all shall hate it. But suppose that we now correct our definition, and d say what the gods all hate is unholy, and what they love is holy, whereas what some of them love, and others hate, is either both or neither. Are you willing that we now define the holy and unholy in this way?

EUTHYPHRO: What is there to prevent us, Socrates?

SOCRATES: Nothing to prevent me, Euthyphro. As for you, see whether when you take this definition you can quite readily instruct me, as you promised.

e   EUTHYPHRO: Yes, I would indeed affirm that holiness is what the gods all love, and its opposite is what the gods all hate, unholiness.

SOCRATES: Are we to examine this position also, Euthyphro, to see if it is sound? Or shall we let it through, and thus accept our own and others' statement, and agree to an assertion simply when somebody says that a thing is so? Must we not look into what the speaker says?

EUTHYPHRO: We must. And yet, for my part, I regard the present statement as correct.

10   SOCRATES: We shall soon know better about that, my friend. Now think of this. Is what is holy holy because the gods approve it, or do they approve it because it is holy?

EUTHYPHRO: I do not get your meaning.

SOCRATES: Well, I will try to make it clearer. We speak of what is carried and the carrier, do we not, of led and leader, of the seen and that which sees? And you understand that in all such cases the things are different, and how they differ?

EUTHYPHRO: Yes, I think I understand.

SOCRATES: In the same way what is loved is one thing, and what loves is another?

EUTHYPHRO: Of course.

b   SOCRATES: Tell me now, is what is carried 'carried' because something carries it, or is it for some other reason?

EUTHYPHRO: No, but for that reason.

SOCRATES: And what is led, because something leads it? And what is seen, because something sees it?

EUTHYPHRO: Yes, certainly.

SOCRATES: Then it is not because a thing is seen that something sees it, but just the opposite—because something sees it, therefore it is seen. Nor because it is led, that something leads it, but because something leads it, therefore it is led. Nor because it is carried, that something carries it, but because something carries it, therefore c it is carried. Do you see what I wish to say, Euthyphro? It is this. Whenever an effect occurs, or something is effected, it is not the thing effected that gives rise to the effect; no, there is a cause, and then comes this effect. Nor is it because a thing is acted on that there is this effect; no, there is a cause for what it undergoes, and then comes this effect. Don't you agree?

EUTHYPHRO: I do.

SOCRATES: Well then, when a thing is loved, is it not in process of becoming something, or of undergoing something, by some other thing?

EUTHYPHRO: Yes, certainly.

SOCRATES: Then the same is true here as in the previous cases. It is not because a thing is loved that they who love it love it, but it is loved because they love it.

EUTHYPHRO: Necessarily.

SOCRATES: Then what are we to say about the holy, Euthy- d phro? According to your argument, is it not loved by all the gods?

EUTHYPHRO: Yes.

SOCRATES: Because it is holy, or for some other reason?

EUTHYPHRO: No, it is for that reason.

SOCRATES: And so it is because it is holy that it is loved; it is not holy because it is loved.

EUTHYPHRO: So it seems.

SOCRATES: On the other hand, it is beloved and pleasing to the gods just because they love it?

EUTHYPHRO: No doubt of that.

SOCRATES: So what is pleasing to the gods is not the same as what is holy, Euthyphro, nor, according to your statement, is the holy the same as what is pleasing to the gods. They are two different things.

EUTHYPHRO: How may that be, Socrates?   e

SOCRATES: Because we are agreed that the holy is loved because it is holy, and is not holy because it is loved. Isn't it so?

EUTHYPHRO: Yes.

SOCRATES: Whereas what is pleasing to the gods is pleasing to them just because they love it, such being its nature and its cause. Its being loved of the gods is not the reason of its being loved.

EUTHYPHRO: You are right.

SOCRATES: But suppose, dear Euthyphro, that what is pleasing to the gods and what is holy were not two separate things. In that case if holiness were loved because it was holy, then also what 11 was pleasing to the gods would be loved because it pleased them. And, on the other hand, if what was pleasing to them pleased because they loved it, then also the holy would be holy because they loved it. But now you see that it is just the opposite, because the two are absolutely different from each other, for the one [what is pleasing to the gods] is of a sort to be loved because it is loved, whereas the other [what is holy] is loved because it is of a sort to be loved. Consequently, Euthyphro, it looks as if you had not given me my answer—as if when you were asked to tell the nature of the holy, you did not wish to explain the essence of it. You merely tell an attribute of it, namely, that it appertains to holiness to be loved by all the gods. What it *is*, as yet you have not said. So, if you please, do not conceal this from me. b No, begin again. Say what the holy is, and never mind if gods do love it, nor if it has some other attribute; on that we shall not split. Come, speak out. Explain the nature of the holy and unholy.

EUTHYPHRO: Now, Socrates, I simply don't know how to tell you what I think. Somehow everything that we put forward keeps moving about us in a circle, and nothing will stay where we put it.

SOCRATES: Your statements, Euthyphro, look like the work of
c Daedalus, founder of my line. If I had made them, and they were my positions, no doubt you would poke fun at me, and say that, being in his line, the figures I construct in words run off, as did his statues, and will not stay where they are put. Meanwhile, since they are your definitions, we need some other jest, for in fact, as you see yourself, they will not stand still.

EUTHYPHRO: But, Socrates, it seems to me that the jest is quite to the point. This tendency in our statements to go in a circle, and
d not to stay in one place, it is not I who put it there. To my mind, it is you who are the Daedalus; so far as I am concerned, they would have held their place.

SOCRATES: If so, my friend, I must be more expert in his art than he, in that he merely made his own works capable of moving, whereas I give this power not merely to my own, but, seemingly, to the works of other men as well. And the rarest thing about my talent is that I am an unwilling artist, since I would rather see our arguments
e stand fast and hold their ground than have the art of Daedalus plus all the wealth of Tantalus to boot. But enough of this. And since, to my mind, you are languid, I will myself make bold with you to show how you might teach me about holiness. Do not weaken. See if you do not think that of necessity all that is holy is just.

EUTHYPHRO: Yes, I do.

SOCRATES: Well then, is all justice holy too? Or, granted that
12 all holiness is just, is justice not all holy, but some part of it is holy, and some part of it is not?

EUTHYPHRO: I do not follow, Socrates.

SOCRATES: And yet you surpass me in your wisdom not less than by your youth. I repeat, you are languid through your affluence in wisdom. Come, lucky friend, exert yourself! What I have to say is not so hard to grasp. I mean the very opposite of what the poet wrote.

> Zeus, who brought that all to pass, and made it all to grow,
b > You will not name, for where fear is, there too is reverence.[1]

On that I differ from the poet. Shall I tell you why?

EUTHYPHRO: By all means.

SOCRATES: I do not think that 'where fear is, there too is reverence.' For it seems to me that there are many who fear sickness, poverty, and all the like, and so are afraid, but have no reverence whatever for the things they are afraid of. Does it not seem so to you?

EUTHYPHRO: Yes, certainly.

[1] Stasinus, fr. 20.

SOCRATES: Where, however, you have reverence, there you have fear as well. Is there anybody who has reverence and a sense of shame about an act, and does not at the same time dread and fear an evil reputation?   c

EUTHYPHRO: Yes, he will be afraid of it.

SOCRATES: So it is not right to say that 'where fear is, there too is reverence.' No, you may say that where reverence is, there too is fear—not, however, that where fear is, there always you have reverence. Fear, I think, is wider in extent than reverence. Reverence is a part of fear, as the uneven is a part of number; thus you do not have the odd wherever you have number, but where you have the odd you must have number. I take it you are following me now?

EUTHYPHRO: Yes, indeed.

SOCRATES: Well then, what I asked you was like that. I asked you if wherever justice is, there is holiness as well; or, granted that d wherever there is holiness, there is justice too, if where justice is, the holy is not always to be found. Thus holiness would be a part of justice. Shall we say so, or have you a different view?

EUTHYPHRO: No, that is my opinion. I think that you are clearly right.

SOCRATES: Then see what follows. If holiness is a part of justice, it seems to me that we must find out what part of justice it is. Suppose, for instance, in our case just now, you had asked me what part of number is the even, and which the even number is. I would have said it is the one that corresponds to the isosceles, and not to the scalene. Does it not seem so to you?

EUTHYPHRO: It does.

SOCRATES: Then try to show me in this way what part of the e just is holiness, so that we may tell Meletus to cease from wronging me, and to give up prosecuting me for irreligion, because we have adequately learned from you of piety and holiness, and the reverse.

EUTHYPHRO: Well then, Socrates, I think that the part of justice which is religious and is holy is the part that has to do with the service of the gods; the remainder is the part of justice that has to do with the service of mankind.

SOCRATES: And what you say there, Euthyphro, to me seems 13 excellent. There is one little point, however, on which I need more light. I am not yet quite clear about the thing which you call 'service.' I suppose you do not mean the sort of care we give to other things. The 'service' of the gods is not like that—the sort of thing we have in mind when we assert that it is not everybody who knows how to care for horses. It is the horseman that knows, is it not?

EUTHYPHRO: Yes, certainly.

SOCRATES: I suppose it is the special care that appertains to horses?

EUTHYPHRO: Yes.

SOCRATES: In the same way, it is not everyone who knows about the care of dogs; it is the huntsman.

EUTHYPHRO: True.

b   SOCRATES: The art of the huntsman is the care of dogs.

EUTHYPHRO: Yes.

SOCRATES: And that of the herdsman is the care of cattle.

EUTHYPHRO: Yes, certainly.

SOCRATES: And in the same way, Euthyphro, holiness and piety mean caring for the gods? Do you say so?

EUTHYPHRO: I do.

SOCRATES: And so the aim of all this care and service is the same? I mean it thus. The care is given for the good and welfare of the object that is served. You see, for instance, how the horses that are cared for by the horseman's art are benefited and made better. Don't you think so?

EUTHYPHRO: Yes, I do.

SOCRATES: And so no doubt the dogs by the art of the hunts-
c man, the cattle by that of the herdsman, and in like manner all the rest. Unless, perhaps, you think that the care may tend to injure the object that is cared for?

EUTHYPHRO: By heaven, not I!

SOCRATES: The care aims at its benefit?

EUTHYPHRO: Most certainly.

SOCRATES: Then holiness, which is the service of the gods, must likewise aim to benefit the gods and make them better? Are you prepared to say that when you do a holy thing you make some deity better?

EUTHYPHRO: By heaven, not I!

SOCRATES: Nor do I fancy, Euthyphro, that you mean it so—
d far from it. No, it was on this account that I asked just what you meant by service of the gods, supposing that, in fact, you did not mean that sort of care.

EUTHYPHRO: And, Socrates, you were right. I do not mean it so.

SOCRATES: Good. And now what kind of service of the gods will holiness be?

EUTHYPHRO: Socrates, it is the kind that slaves give to their masters.

SOCRATES: I understand. It seems to be a kind of waiting on the gods.

EUTHYPHRO: Just that.

SOCRATES: See if you can tell me this. The art which serves physicians, what result does it serve to produce? Don't you think that it is health?

EUTHYPHRO: I do.

SOCRATES: Further, what about the art that serves the ship- e
wrights? What result does it serve to produce?

EUTHYPHRO: Obviously, Socrates, the making of a ship.

SOCRATES: And that which serves the builders serves the building of a house?

EUTHYPHRO: Yes.

SOCRATES: Now tell me, best of friends, about the service of
the gods. What result will this art serve to produce? You obviously
know, since you profess to be the best informed among mankind on
things divine!

EUTHYPHRO: Yes, Socrates, I say so, and I tell the truth.

SOCRATES: Then tell me, I adjure you, what is that supreme
result which the gods produce when they employ our services?

EUTHYPHRO: They do many things and noble, Socrates.

SOCRATES: Just as the generals do, my friend. All the same 14
you would have no trouble in summing up what they produce, by saying it is victory in war. Isn't it so?

EUTHYPHRO: Of course.

SOCRATES: And the farmers too, I take it, produce many fine
results, but the net result of their production is the food they get
from the earth.

EUTHYPHRO: Yes, surely.

SOCRATES: Well now, of the many fine and noble things
which the gods produce, what is the sum of their production?

EUTHYPHRO: Just a little while ago I told you, Socrates, that
the task is not a light one to learn precisely how all these matters b
stand. I will, however, simply tell you this. If anyone knows how to
say and do things pleasing to the gods in prayer and sacrifice, that is
holiness, and such behavior saves the family in private life together
with the common interests of the state. To do the opposite of things
pleasing to the gods is impious, and this it is that upsets all and ruins
everything.

SOCRATES: Surely, Euthyphro, if you had wished, you could
have summed up what I asked for much more briefly. But the fact is
that you are not eager to instruct me. That is clear. But a moment
since, you were on the very point of telling me—and you slipped c
away. Had you given the answer, I would now have learned from you
what holiness is, and would be content. As it is—for perforce the
lover must follow the loved one wherever he leads the way—once
more, how do you define the holy, and what is holiness? Don't you
say that it is a science of sacrifice and prayer?

EUTHYPHRO: I do.

SOCRATES: Well, and is not sacrifice a giving to the gods, and
prayer an asking them to give?

EUTHYPHRO: Precisely, Socrates.

d   SOCRATES : By this reasoning, holiness would be the science of asking from the gods and giving to them.

EUTHYPHRO : Quite right, Socrates; you have caught my meaning perfectly.

SOCRATES : Yes, my friend, for I have my heart set on your wisdom, and give my mind to it, so that nothing you say shall be lost. No, tell me, what is this service to the gods? You say it is to ask of them and give to them?

EUTHYPHRO : I do.

SOCRATES : And hence to ask aright will be to ask them for those things of which we stand in need from them?

EUTHYPHRO : What else?

e   SOCRATES : And, on the other hand, to give aright will be to give them in return those things which they may need to receive from us? I take it there would be no art in offering anyone a gift of something that he did not need.

EUTHYPHRO : True, Socrates.

SOCRATES : And therefore, Euthyphro, holiness will be a mutual art of commerce between gods and men.

EUTHYPHRO : An art of commerce, if you like to call it so.

SOCRATES : Well, I do not like it if it is not so. But tell me, what advantage could come to the gods from the gifts which they receive
15 from us? Everybody sees what they give us. No good that we possess but is given by them. What advantage can they gain by what they get from us? Have we so much the better of them in this commerce that we get all good things from them, and they get nothing from us?

EUTHYPHRO : What! Socrates. Do you suppose that the gods gain anything by what they get from us?

SOCRATES : If not, then what would be the meaning, Euthyphro, of these gifts to the gods from us?

EUTHYPHRO : What do you think they ought to mean but worship, honor, and, as I just now said, good will?

b   SOCRATES : So, Euthyphro, the holy is what pleases them, not what is useful to them, nor yet what the gods love?

EUTHYPHRO : I believe that what gives them pleasure is precisely what they love.

SOCRATES : And so once more, apparently the holy is that which the gods love.

EUTHYPHRO : Most certainly.

SOCRATES : After that, will you be amazed to find your statements walking off, and not staying where you put them? And will you accuse me as the Daedalus who makes them move, when you are yourself far more expert than Daedalus, and make them go round in a circle? Don't you see that our argument has come full circle to the point where it began? Surely you have not forgotten how in what was

said before we found that holiness and what is pleasing to the gods c
were not the same, but different from each other. Do you not remember?

EUTHYPHRO: I do.

SOCRATES: And are you not aware now that you say that what
the gods love is holy? But is not what the gods love just the same as
what is pleasing to the gods?

EUTHYPHRO: Yes, certainly.

SOCRATES: Well then, either we were wrong in our recent conclusion, or if that was right, our position now is wrong.

EUTHYPHRO: So it seems.

SOCRATES: And so we must go back again, and start from the
beginning to find out what the holy is. As for me, I never will give up
until I know. Ah! Do not spurn me, but give your mind with all your d
might now at length to tell me the absolute truth, for if anybody
knows, of all mankind, it is you, and one must not let go of you, you
Proteus, until you tell. If you did not know precisely what is holy and
unholy, it is unthinkable that for a simple hireling you ever would
have moved to prosecute your aged sire on a charge of murder. No,
you would have feared to risk the wrath of the gods on the chance
that you were not doing right, and would have been afraid of the
talk of men. But now I am sure that you think you know exactly what
is holy and what is not. So tell me, peerless Euthyphro, and do not e
hide from me what you judge it to be.

EUTHYPHRO: Another time, then, Socrates, for I am in a hurry,
and must be off this minute.

SOCRATES: What are you doing, my friend? Will you leave,
and dash me down from the mighty expectation I had of learning
from you what is holy and what is not, and so escaping from Meletus'
indictment? I counted upon showing him that now I had gained
wisdom about things divine from Euthyphro, and no longer out of 16
ignorance made rash assertions and forged innovations with regard
to them, but would lead a better life in future.

MENEXENUS

This dialogue stands apart from all the others. It is not a dialogue—
it is a speech of Socrates that professes to review the history of Athens, especially from the days of Marathon on. Its authorship has
been questioned, but less today than formerly. If it is by Plato then
the question shifts to why he wrote it, and no ready answer presents
itself. Certainly not because he was interested in its subject, the
unqualified praise of Athens. Socrates declares that she has an unbroken record of glorious deeds. She has never been conquered by others. The Peloponnesian War is described at some length without so
much as a hint that the Spartans were the victors.

Still, if the speech—oration, rather—had some claim to be read,
except that Plato wrote it, if it were wise or amusing or at all like Socrates, that sort of thing would matter little, but it is as full of copy-
book maxims as of bad history. The beginning is entertaining when
Socrates talks about Aspasia who, he declared, has been teaching
him a speech, a funeral oration, but all the rest is dullness unre-
lieved, not a characteristic of Plato.

Those who uphold his authorship say it is a satire on Fourth-of-
July orations in general and in particular on Pericles' famous funeral oration in which Athens is praised to the skies. If that is the
case, the satire is so far in the background as to be out of sight, except just at the beginning and a few sentences at the end where we
might be listening to Socrates.

SOCRATES: Whence come you, Menexenus? Are you from the 234
Agora?

MENEXENUS: Yes, Socrates, I have been at the Council.

SOCRATES: And what might you be doing at the Council? And yet I need hardly ask, for I see that you, believing yourself to have arrived at the end of education and of philosophy, and to have had enough of them, are mounting upward to things higher still, and, though rather young for the post, are intending to govern us elder men, like the rest of your family, which has always provided someone b who kindly took care of us.

MENEXENUS: Yes, Socrates, I shall be ready to hold office, if you allow and advise that I should, but not if you think otherwise. I went to the Council Chamber because I heard that the Council was about to choose someone who was to speak over the dead. For you know that there is to be a public funeral?

SOCRATES: Yes, I know. And whom did they choose?

MENEXENUS: No one. They delayed the election until tomorrow, but I believe that either Archinus or Dion will be chosen.

SOCRATES: O Menexenus! Death in battle is certainly in many respects a noble thing. The dead man gets a fine and costly funeral, al- c though he may have been poor, and an elaborate speech is made over him by a wise man who has long ago prepared what he has to say, although he who is praised may not have been good for much. The speakers praise him for what he has done and for what he has not 235 done—that is the beauty of them—and they steal away our souls with their embellished words. In every conceivable form they praise the city, and they praise those who died in war, and all our ancestors who went before us, and they praise ourselves also who are still alive, until I feel quite elevated by their laudations, and I stand listening to their words, Menexenus, and become enchanted by them, and all in a moment I imagine myself to have become a greater and nobler and b finer man than I was before. And if, as often happens, there are any foreigners who accompany me to the speech, I become suddenly conscious of having a sort of triumph over them, and they seem to experience a corresponding feeling of admiration at me, and at the greatness of the city, which appears to them, when they are under the influence of the speaker, more wonderful than ever. This consciousness of dignity lasts me more than three days, and not until the fourth or fifth day do I come to my senses and know where I am—in the c meantime I have been living in the Islands of the Blessed. Such is the art of our rhetoricians, and in such manner does the sound of their words keep ringing in my ears.

MENEXENUS: You are always making fun of the rhetoricians,

From *The Dialogues of Plato*, translated with analyses and introductions by B. Jowett (3rd edn., Oxford, 1892; 1st edn., 1871).

Socrates. This time, however, I am inclined to think that the speaker who is chosen will not have much to say, for he has been called upon to speak at a moment's notice, and he will be compelled almost to improvise.

d   SOCRATES : But why, my friend, should he not have plenty to say? Every rhetorician has speeches ready-made, nor is there any difficulty in improvising that sort of stuff. Had the orator to praise Athenians among Peloponnesians, or Peloponnesians among Athenians, he must be a good rhetorician who could succeed and gain credit. But there is no difficulty in a man's winning applause when he is contending for fame among the persons whom he is praising.

MENEXENUS : Do you think not, Socrates?

SOCRATES : Certainly not.

e   MENEXENUS : Do you think that you could speak yourself if there should be a necessity, and if the Council were to choose you?

SOCRATES : That I should be able to speak is no great wonder, Menexenus, considering that I have an excellent mistress in the art of rhetoric—she who has made so many good speakers, and one who was the best among all the Hellenes, Pericles, the son of Xanthippus.

MENEXENUS : And who is she? I suppose that you mean Aspasia.

SOCRATES : Yes, I do, and besides her I had Connus, the son of
236 Metrobius, as a master, and he was my master in music, as she was in rhetoric. No wonder that a man who has received such an education should be a finished speaker. Even the pupil of very inferior masters—say, for example, one who had learned music of Lamprus and rhetoric of Antiphon the Rhamnusian—might make a figure if he were to praise the Athenians among the Athenians.

MENEXENUS : And what would you be able to say if you had to speak?

SOCRATES : Of my own wit, most likely nothing, but yesterday
b I heard Aspasia composing a funeral oration about these very dead. For she had been told, as you were saying, that the Athenians were going to choose a speaker, and she repeated to me the sort of speech which he should deliver—partly improvising and partly from previous thought, putting together fragments of the funeral oration which Pericles spoke, but which, as I believe, she composed.

MENEXENUS : And can you remember what Aspasia said?

SOCRATES : I ought to be able, for she taught me, and she was
c ready to strike me because I was always forgetting.

MENEXENUS : Then why will you not rehearse what she said?

SOCRATES : Because I am afraid that my mistress may be angry with me if I publish her speech.

MENEXENUS : Nay, Socrates, let us have the speech, whether Aspasia's or anyone else's, no matter. I hope that you will oblige me.

SOCRATES: But I am afraid that you will laugh at me if I continue the games of youth in old age.

MENEXENUS: Far otherwise, Socrates. Let us by all means have the speech.

SOCRATES: Truly I have such a disposition to oblige you that if you bid me dance naked I should not like to refuse, since we are alone. d Listen then. If I remember rightly, she began as follows, with the mention of the dead.

There is a tribute of deeds and of words. The departed have already had the first, when going forth on their destined journey they were attended on their way by the state and by their friends; the tribute of words remains to be given to them, as is meet and by law ordained. For noble words are a memorial and a crown of noble ac- e tions, which are given to the doers of them by the hearers. A word is needed which will duly praise the dead and gently admonish the living, exhorting the brethren and descendants of the departed to imitate their virtue, and consoling their fathers and mothers and the survivors, if any, who may chance to be alive of the previous generation. 237 What sort of a word will this be, and how shall we rightly begin the praises of these brave men? In their life they rejoiced their own friends with their valor, and their death they gave in exchange for the salvation of the living. And I think that we should praise them in the order in which nature made them good, for they were good because they were sprung from good fathers. Wherefore let us first of all praise the goodness of their birth, secondly, their nurture and educa- tion, and then let us set forth how noble their actions were, and how b worthy of the education which they had received.

And first as to their birth. Their ancestors were not strangers, nor are these their descendants sojourners only, whose fathers have come from another country, but they are the children of the soil, dwelling and living in their own land. And the country which brought them up is not like other countries, a stepmother to her children, but their own true mother; she bore them and nourished them and received them, and in her bosom they now repose. It is meet and right, c therefore, that we should begin by praising the land which is their mother, and that will be a way of praising their noble birth.

The country is worthy to be praised, not only by us, but by all mankind—first, and above all, as being dear to the gods. This is proved by the strife and contention of the gods respecting her. And ought not the country which the gods praise to be praised by all man- d kind? The second praise which may be fairly claimed by her is that at the time when the whole earth was sending forth and creating diverse animals, tame and wild, she our mother was free and pure from savage monsters, and out of all animals selected and brought forth man, who is superior to the rest in understanding, and alone has justice

e and religion. And a great proof that she brought forth the common ancestors of us and of the departed is that she provided the means of
support for her offspring. For as a woman proves her motherhood by
giving milk to her young ones—and she who has no fountain of milk
is not a mother—so did this our land prove that she was the mother
of men, for in those days she alone and first of all brought forth
wheat and barley for human food, which is the best and noblest sus-
238 tenance for man, whom she regarded as her true offspring. And these
are truer proofs of motherhood in a country than in a woman, for the
woman in her conception and generation is but the imitation of the
earth, and not the earth of the woman. And of the fruit of the earth
she gave a plenteous supply, not only to her own, but to others also,
and afterward she made the olive to spring up to be a boon to her
children, and to help them in their toils. And when she had herself
b nursed them and brought them up to manhood, she gave them gods
to be their rulers and teachers, whose names are well known, and
need not now be repeated. They are the gods who ordered our lives,
and instructed us, first of all men, in the arts for the supply of our
daily needs, and taught us the acquisition and use of arms for the
defense of the country.

Thus born into the world and thus educated, the ancestors of
the departed lived and made themselves a government, which I ought
c briefly to commemorate. For government is the nurture of man,
and the government of good men is good, and of bad men bad. And I
must show that our ancestors were trained under a good government,
and for this reason they were good, and our contemporaries are also
good, among whom our departed friends are to be reckoned. Then as
now, and indeed always, from that time to this, speaking generally,
our government was an aristocracy—a form of government which
receives various names, according to the fancies of men, and is some-
d times called democracy, but is really an aristocracy or government of
the best which has the approval of the many. For kings we have always had, first hereditary and then elected, and authority is mostly in
the hands of the people, who dispense offices and power to those
who appear to be most deserving of them. Neither is a man rejected
from weakness or poverty or obscurity of origin, nor honored by reason
of the opposite, as in other states, but there is one principle—he who
appears to be wise and good is a governor and ruler. The basis of
e this our government is equality of birth, for other states are made up of
all sorts and unequal conditions of men, and therefore their governments are unequal—there are tyrannies and there are oligarchies, in
which the one party are slaves and the others masters. But we and our
239 citizens are brethren, the children all of one mother, and we do not
think it right to be one another's masters or servants, but the natural equality of birth compels us to seek for legal equality, and to recognize no superiority except in the reputation of virtue and wisdom.

And so their and our fathers, and these, too, our brethren, being nobly born and having been brought up in all freedom, did both in their public and private capacity many noble deeds famous over the whole world. They were the deeds of men who thought that they ought to fight both against Hellenes for the sake of Hellenes on behalf b of freedom, and against barbarians in the common interest of Hellas. Time would fail me to tell of their defense of their country against the invasion of Eumolpus and the Amazons, or of their defense of the Argives against the Cadmeans, or of the Heraclidae against the Argives. Besides, the poets have already declared in song to all mankind their glory, and therefore any commemoration of their deeds in prose c which we might attempt would hold a second place. They already have their reward, and I say no more of them, but there are other worthy deeds of which no poet has worthily sung, and which are still wooing the poet's Muse. Of these I am bound to make honorable mention, and shall invoke others to sing of them also in lyric and other strains, in a manner becoming the actors.

And first I will tell how the Persians, lords of Asia, were en- d slaving Europe, and how the children of this land, who were our fathers, held them back. Of these I will speak first, and praise their valor, as is meet and fitting. He who would rightly estimate them should place himself in thought at that time, when the whole of Asia was subject to the third king of Persia. The first king, Cyrus, by his valor freed the Persians, who were his countrymen, and subjected the Medes, who were their lords, and he ruled over the rest of Asia, as far e as Egypt. And after him came his son, who ruled all the accessible part of Egypt and Libya. The third king was Darius, who extended the land boundaries of the empire to Scythia, and with his fleet held the sea and the islands. None presumed to be his equal; the minds of 240 all men were enthralled by him—so many and mighty and warlike nations had the power of Persia subdued.

Now Darius had a quarrel against us and the Eretrians, because, as he said, we had conspired against Sardis, and he sent half a million men in transports and vessels of war, and three hundred ships, and Datis as commander, telling him to bring the Eretrians and Athenians to the king, if he wished to keep his head on his shoulders. He sailed against the Eretrians, who were reputed to be among the noblest and b most warlike of the Hellenes of that day, and they were numerous, but he conquered them all in three days. And when he had conquered them, in order that no one might escape, he searched the whole country after this manner. His soldiers, coming to the borders of Eretria and spreading from sea to sea, joined hands and passed through the whole country, in order that they might be able to tell the king that c no one had escaped them. And from Eretria they went to Marathon with a like intention, expecting to bind the Athenians in the same yoke of necessity in which they had bound the Eretrians.

Having effected one half of their purpose, they were in the act of attempting the other, and none of the Hellenes dared to assist either the Eretrians or the Athenians, except the Lacedaemonians, and they arrived a day too late for the battle, but the rest were panic-stricken

d and kept quiet, too happy in having escaped for a time. He who has present to his mind that conflict will know what manner of men they were who received the onset of the barbarians at Marathon, and chastened the pride of the whole of Asia, and by the victory which they gained over the barbarians first taught other men that the power of the Persians was not invincible, but that hosts of men and the multitude of riches alike yield to valor. And I assert that those men are

e the fathers not only of ourselves, but of our liberties and of the liberties of all who are on the continent, for that was the action to which the Hellenes looked back when they ventured to fight for their own safety in the battles which ensued—they became disciples of the men of Marathon.

241   To them, therefore, I assign in my speech the first place, and the second to those who fought and conquered in the sea fights at Salamis and Artemisium, for of them, too, one might have many things to say—of the assaults which they endured by sea and land, and how they repelled them. I will mention only that act of theirs which appears to me to be the noblest, and which followed that of Marathon and came nearest to it. For the men of Marathon only showed the

b Hellenes that it was possible to ward off the barbarians by land, the many by the few, but there was no proof that they could be defeated by ships, and at sea the Persians retained the reputation of being invincible in numbers and wealth and skill and strength. This is the glory of the men who fought at sea, that they dispelled the second terror which had hitherto possessed the Hellenes, and so made the fear of numbers, whether of ships or men, to cease among them. And so the soldiers of Marathon and the sailors of Salamis became the

c schoolmasters of Hellas—the one teaching and habituating the Hellenes not to fear the barbarians at sea, and the others not to fear them by land.

Third in order, for the number and valor of the combatants, and third in the salvation of Hellas, I place the Battle of Plataea. And now the Lacedaemonians as well as the Athenians took part in the struggle. They were all united in this greatest and most terrible conflict of all, wherefore their virtues will be celebrated in times to come,

d as they are now celebrated by us. But at a later period many Hellenic tribes were still on the side of the barbarians, and there was a report that the Great King was going to make a new attempt upon the Hellenes, and therefore justice requires that we should also make mention of those who crowned the previous work of our salvation, and drove and purged away all barbarians from the sea. These were the

e men who fought by sea at the river Eurymedon, and who went on the expedition to Cyprus, and who sailed to Egypt and diverse other places, and they should be gratefully remembered by us, because they compelled the king in fear for himself to look to his own safety instead of plotting the destruction of Hellas.

And so the war against the barbarians was fought out to the end 242 by the whole city on their own behalf, and on behalf of their countrymen. There was peace, and our city was held in honor. And then, as prosperity makes men jealous, there succeeded a jealousy of her, and jealousy begot envy, and so she became engaged against her will in a war with the Hellenes. On the breaking out of war, our citizens met the Lacedaemonians at Tanagra, and fought for the freedom of the Boeotians; the issue was doubtful, and was decided by b the engagement which followed. For when the Lacedaemonians had gone on their way, leaving the Boeotians, whom they were aiding, on the third day after the Battle of Tanagra, our countrymen conquered at Oenophyta, and righteously restored those who had been unrighteously exiled. And they were the first after the Persian War who fought on behalf of liberty in aid of Hellenes against Hellenes. They were brave men, and freed those whom they aided, and were the first too who were honorably interred in this sepulcher by the state. c

Afterward there was a mighty war, in which all the Hellenes joined, and devastated our country, which was very ungrateful of them. And our countrymen, after defeating them in a naval engagement and taking their leaders, the Spartans, at Sphagia, when they might have destroyed them, spared their lives, and gave them back, d and made peace, considering that they should war with their fellow countrymen only until they gained a victory over them, and not because of the private anger of the state destroy the common interest of Hellas—but that with barbarians they should war to the death. Worthy of praise are they also who waged this war, and are here interred, for they proved, if anyone doubted the superior prowess of the Athenians in the former war with the barbarians, that their doubts had no foundation—showing by their victory in the civil war with Hellas, in which they subdued the other chief state of the Hellenes, e that they could conquer singlehanded those with whom they had been allied in the war against the barbarians.

After the peace there followed a third war, which was of a terrible and desperate nature, and in this many brave men who are here interred lost their lives—many of them had won victories in Sicily, whither they had gone over the seas to fight for the liberties of the 243 Leontines, to whom they were bound by oaths, but owing to the distance the city was unable to help them, and they lost heart and came to misfortune, their very enemies and opponents winning more renown for valor and temperance than the friends of others. Many also fell in naval engagements at the Hellespont, after having in one day taken all the ships of the enemy, and defeated them in other naval b engagements. And what I call the terrible and desperate nature of the war is that the other Hellenes, in their extreme animosity toward the city, should have entered into negotiations with their bitterest enemy, the king of Persia, whom they, together with us, had expelled—him, without us, they again brought back, barbarian against Hellenes, and all the hosts, both of Hellenes and barbarians, were united against c Athens. And then shone forth the power and valor of our city. Her enemies had supposed that she was exhausted by the war, and our ships were blockaded at Mytilene. But the citizens themselves embarked, and came to the rescue with sixty other ships, and their valor was confessed of all men, for they conquered their enemies and delivered their friends. And yet by some evil fortune they were left to perish at sea, and therefore are not interred here. Ever to be re- d membered and honored are they, for by their valor not only that sea fight was won for us, but the entire war was decided by them, and through them the city gained the reputation of being invincible, even though attacked by all mankind. And that reputation was a true one, for the defeat which came upon us was our own doing. We were never conquered by others, and to this day we are still unconquered by them, but we were our own conquerors, and received defeat at our own hands.

e　　Afterward there was quiet and peace abroad, but there sprang up war at home, and if men are destined to have civil war, no one could have desired that his city should take the disorder in a milder form. How joyful and natural was the reconciliation of those who came from the Piraeus and those who came from the city. With what moderation did they order the war against the tyrants in Eleusis, and 244 in a manner how unlike what the other Hellenes expected! And the reason of this gentleness was the veritable tie of blood, which created among them a friendship as of kinsmen, faithful not in word only, but in deed. And we ought also to remember those who then fell by one another's hands, and on such occasions as these to reconcile them with sacrifices and prayers, praying to those who have power over them, that they may be reconciled even as we are reconciled. For they did not attack one another out of malice or enmity, but they b were unfortunate. And that such was the fact we ourselves are witnesses, who are of the same race with them, and have mutually received and granted forgiveness of what we have done and suffered.

After this there was perfect peace, and the city had rest. And her feeling was that she forgave the barbarians, who had severely suffered at her hands and severely retaliated, but that she was indignant at the ingratitude of the Hellenes, when she remembered how they had received good from her and returned evil, having made common cause c with the barbarians, depriving her of the ships which had once been their salvation, and dismantling our walls, which had preserved their own from falling. She thought that she would no longer defend the

Hellenes, when enslaved either by one another or by the barbarians, and did accordingly. This was our feeling, while the Lacedaemonians were thinking that we who were the champions of liberty had fallen, and that their business was to subject the remaining Hellenes. And why should I say more? For the events of which I am speaking hap- d pened not long ago and we can all of us remember how the chief peoples of Hellas, Argives and Boeotians and Corinthians, came to feel the need of us, and, what is the greatest miracle of all, the Persian king himself was driven to such extremity as to come round to the opinion, that from this city, of which he was the destroyer, and from no other, his salvation would proceed.

And if a person desired to bring a deserved accusation against e our city, he would find only one charge which he could justly urge— that she was too compassionate and too favorable to the weaker side. And in this instance she was not able to hold out or keep her resolution of refusing aid to her injurers when they were being enslaved, but she was softened, and did in fact send out aid, and delivered the Hel- 245 lenes from slavery, and they were free until they afterward enslaved themselves, whereas to the Great King she refused to give the assistance of the state, for she could not forget the trophies of Marathon and Salamis and Plataea, but she allowed exiles and volunteers to assist him, and they were his salvation. And she herself, when she was compelled, entered into the war, and built walls and ships, and b fought with the Lacedaemonians on behalf of the Parians. Now the king fearing this city and wanting to stand aloof, when he saw the Lacedaemonians growing weary of the war at sea, asked of us, as the price of his alliance with us and the other allies, to give up the Hellenes in Asia, whom the Lacedaemonians had previously handed over to him—he thinking that we should refuse, and that then he might have a pretense for withdrawing from us. About the other al- c lies he was mistaken, for the Corinthians and Argives and Boeotians, and the other states, were quite willing to let them go, and swore and covenanted that, if he would pay them money, they would make over to him the Hellenes of the continent, and we alone refused to give them up and swear. Such was the natural nobility of this city, so sound and healthy was the spirit of freedom among us, and the instinctive dislike of the barbarian, because we are pure Hellenes, hav- d ing no admixture of barbarism in us. For we are not like many others, descendants of Pelops or Cadmus or Aegyptus or Danaus, who are by nature barbarians, and yet pass for Hellenes, and dwell in the midst of us, but we are pure Hellenes, uncontaminated by any foreign element, and therefore the hatred of the foreigner has passed unadulterated into the lifeblood of the city. And so, notwithstanding our noble sentiments, we were again isolated, because we were unwilling e to be guilty of the base and unholy act of giving up Hellenes to barbarians. And we were in the same case as when we were subdued

before, but, by the favor of heaven, we managed better, for we ended
the war without the loss of our ships or walls or colonies; the enemy
was only too glad to be quit of us. Yet in this war we lost many brave
men, such as were those who fell owing to the ruggedness of the
ground at the Battle of Corinth, or by treason at Lechaeum. Brave
246 men, too, were those who delivered the Persian king, and drove the
Lacedaemonians from the sea. I remind you of them, and you must
celebrate them together with me, and do honor to their memories.

Such were the actions of the men who are here interred, and
of others who have died on behalf of their country; many and glorious things I have spoken of them, and there are yet many more, and
more glorious, things remaining to be told—many days and nights
b would not suffice to tell of them. Let them not be forgotten, and let
every man remind their descendants that they also are soldiers who
must not desert the ranks of their ancestors, or from cowardice fall
behind. Even so I exhort you this day, and in all future time, whenever
I meet with any of you, shall continue to remind and exhort you, O ye
c sons of heroes, that you strive to be the bravest of men. And I think
that I ought now to repeat what your fathers desired to have said to
you who are their survivors, when they went out to battle, in case
anything happened to them. I will tell you what I heard them say,
and what, if they had only speech, they would fain be saying, judging
from what they then said. And you must imagine that you hear them
saying what I now repeat to you.

d   Sons, the event proves that your fathers were brave men, for we
might have lived dishonorably, but have preferred to die honorably
rather than bring you and your children into disgrace, and rather than
dishonor our own fathers and forefathers—considering that life is
not life to one who is a dishonor to his race, and that to such a one
neither men nor gods are friendly, either while he is on the earth or
after death in the world below. Remember our words, then, and what-
e ever is your aim let virtue be the condition of the attainment of your
aim, and know that without this all possessions and pursuits are dishonorable and evil. For neither does wealth bring honor to the owner,
if he be a coward; of such a one the wealth belongs to another, and
not to himself. Nor do beauty and strength of body, when dwelling
in a base and cowardly man, appear comely, but the reverse of
comely, making the possessor more conspicuous, and manifesting
forth his cowardice. And all knowledge, when separated from justice
247 and virtue, is seen to be cunning and not wisdom; wherefore make this
your first and last and constant and all-absorbing aim—to exceed, if
possible, not only us but all your ancestors in virtue, and know that
to excel you in virtue only brings us shame, but that to be excelled
by you is a source of happiness to us. And we shall most likely be
defeated, and you will most likely be victors in the contest, if you
b learn so to order your lives as not to abuse or waste the reputation

of your ancestors, knowing that to a man who has any self-respect, nothing is more dishonorable than to be honored, not for his own sake, but on account of the reputation of his ancestors. The honor of parents is a fair and noble treasure to their posterity, but to have the use of a treasure of wealth and honor, and to leave none to your successors, because you have neither money nor reputation of your own, is alike base and dishonorable. And if you follow our precepts you will be received by us as friends, when the hour of destiny brings c you hither, but if you neglect our words and are disgraced in your lives, no one will welcome or receive you. This is the message which is to be delivered to our children.

Some of us have fathers and mothers still living, and we would urge them, if, as is likely, we shall die, to bear the calamity as lightly as possible, and not to condole with one another, for they have sor- d rows enough, and will not need anyone to stir them up. While we gently heal their wounds, let us remind them that the gods have heard the chief part of their prayers, for they prayed, not that their children might live forever, but that they might be brave and renowned. And this, which is the greatest good, they have attained. A mortal man cannot expect to have everything in his own life turning out accord- ing to his will, and they, if they bear their misfortunes bravely, will be truly deemed brave fathers of the brave. But if they give way to their e sorrows, either they will be suspected of not being our parents, or we of not being such as our panegyrists declare. Let not either of the two alternatives happen, but rather let them be our chief and true panegyrists, who show in their lives that they are true men, and had men for their sons. Of old the saying, 'Nothing too much,' appeared to be, and really was, well said. For he whose happiness rests with him- 248 self, if possible, wholly, and if not, as far as possible, who is not hang- ing in suspense on other men, or changing with the vicissitude of their fortune, has his life ordered for the best. He is the temperate and valiant and wise, and when his riches come and go, when his children are given and taken away, he will remember the proverb, 'Neither rejoicing overmuch nor grieving overmuch,' for he relies upon him- self. And such we would have our parents to be—that is our word and wish, and as such we now offer ourselves, neither lamenting over- b much, nor fearing overmuch, if we are to die at this time. And we entreat our fathers and mothers to retain these feelings throughout their future life, and to be assured that they will not please us by sorrowing and lamenting over us. But, if the dead have any knowledge of the living, they will displease us most by making themselves miser- able and by taking their misfortunes too much to heart, and they c will please us best if they bear their loss lightly and temperately. For our life will have the noblest end which is vouchsafed to man, and should be glorified rather than lamented. And if they will direct their minds to the care and nurture of our wives and children, they will

soonest forget their misfortunes, and live in a better and nobler way,
d and be dearer to us.

This is all that we have to say to our families, and to the state
we would say, Take care of our parents and of our sons—let her
worthily cherish the old age of our parents, and bring up our sons in
the right way. But we know that she will of her own accord take care
of them, and does not need any exhortation of ours.

This, O ye children and parents of the dead, is the message
e which they bid us deliver to you, and which I do deliver with the utmost seriousness. And in their name I beseech you, the children, to
imitate your fathers, and you, parents, to be of good cheer about
yourselves, for we will nourish your age, and take care of you both
publicly and privately in any place in which one of us may meet one
of you who are the parents of the dead. And the care of you which the
city shows, you know yourselves, for she has made provision by law
concerning the parents and children of those who die in war; the
249 highest authority is specially entrusted with the duty of watching
over them above all other citizens, and they will see that the fathers
and mothers have no wrong done to them. The city herself shares in
the education of the children, desiring as far as it is possible that
their orphanhood may not be felt by them. While they are children
she is a parent to them, and when they have arrived at man's estate
she sends them to their several duties, in full armor clad; and bringing freshly to their minds the ways of their fathers, she places in
b their hands the instruments of their fathers' virtues. For the sake of
the omen, she would have them from the first begin to rule over their
own houses arrayed in the strength and arms of their fathers. And
as for the dead, she never ceases honoring them, celebrating, in common for all, rites which become the property of each, and in addition
to this, holding gymnastic and equestrian contests, and musical
festivals of every sort. She is to the dead in the place of a son and heir,
c and to their sons in the place of a father, and to their parents and
elder kindred in the place of a guardian—ever and always caring for
them. Considering this, you ought to bear your calamity the more
gently, for thus you will be most endeared to the dead and to the living,
and your sorrows will heal and be healed. And now do you and all,
having lamented the dead in common according to the law, go your
d ways.

You have heard, Menexenus, the oration of Aspasia the Milesian.

MENEXENUS : Truly, Socrates, I marvel that Aspasia, who is
only a woman, should be able to compose such a speech—she must be
a rare one.

SOCRATES : Well, if you are incredulous, you may come with
me and hear her.

MENEXENUS : I have often met Aspasia, Socrates, and know
what she is like.

SOCRATES: Well, and do you not admire her, and are you not grateful for her speech?

MENEXENUS: Yes, Socrates, I am very grateful to her or to him who told you, and still more to you who have told me.   e

SOCRATES: Very good. But you must take care not to tell of me, and then at some future time I will repeat to you many other excellent political speeches of hers.

MENEXENUS: Fear not. Only let me hear them, and I will keep the secret.

SOCRATES: Then I will keep my promise.

LESSER HIPPIAS

This dialogue can be ascribed to Plato only because it always has been, from Aristotle's day on. It is inferior to all the others. The argument is between Socrates and a Sophist, Hippias, who says that he has never found anyone superior to him in anything. It turns upon voluntary and involuntary wrongdoing, Hippias maintaining that it is better to do wrong unintentionally than intentionally and Socrates taking the opposite side. He starts with the assertion that a wrestler is better who falls purposely than one who falls because he cannot help it, and that to sing out of tune because one has a bad ear is worse than to do so deliberately, and thus that to make mistakes voluntarily is better than to err involuntarily, and so on, to the inevitable conclusion that the good man is he who knowingly does wrong.

At this point Hippias demurs and Socrates says that he sympathizes with him, but then he is just an ordinary man, ignorant and in a very bad way if the wisest Sophist cannot show him the truth.

EUDICUS: Why are you silent, Socrates, after the magnificent dis- 363
play which Hippias has been making? Why do you not either refute
his words, if he seems to you to have been wrong in any point, or join
with us in commending him? There is the more reason why you
should speak, because we are now alone, and the audience is confined
to those who may fairly claim to take part in a philosophical discussion.

SOCRATES: I should greatly like, Eudicus, to ask Hippias the
meaning of what he was saying just now about Homer. I have heard b
your father, Apemantus, declare that the *Iliad* of Homer is a finer
poem than the *Odyssey* in the same degree that Achilles was a better man than Odysseus; Odysseus, he would say, is the central figure
of the one poem and Achilles of the other. Now, I should like to know,
if Hippias has no objection to tell me, what he thinks about these two
heroes, and which of them he maintains to be the better. He has already told us in the course of his exhibition many things of various c
kinds about Homer and diverse other poets.

EUDICUS: I am sure that Hippias will be delighted to answer
anything which you would like to ask. Tell me, Hippias, if Socrates
asks you a question, will you answer him?

HIPPIAS: Indeed, Eudicus, I should be strangely inconsistent
if I refused to answer Socrates, when at each Olympic festival, as I
went up from my house at Elis to the temple of Olympia, where all d
the Hellenes were assembled, I continually professed my willingness
to perform any of the exhibitions which I had prepared, and to answer
any questions which anyone had to ask.

SOCRATES: Truly, Hippias, you are to be congratulated, if at 364
every Olympic festival you have such an encouraging opinion of your
own wisdom when you go up to the temple. I doubt whether any mus-
cular hero would be so fearless and confident in offering his body to
the combat at Olympia, as you are in offering your mind.

HIPPIAS: And with good reason, Socrates, for since the day
when I first entered the lists at Olympia I have never found any man
who was my superior in anything.

SOCRATES: What an ornament, Hippias, will the reputation of b
your wisdom be to the city of Elis and to your parents! But to return,
what say you of Odysseus and Achilles? Which is the better of the
two? And in what particular does either surpass the other? For when
you were exhibiting and there was company in the room, though I
could not follow you, I did not like to ask what you meant, because a
crowd of people were present, and I was afraid that the question
might interrupt your exhibition. But now that there are not so many
of us, and my friend Eudicus bids me ask, I wish you would tell me

From *The Dialogues of Plato*, translated with analyses and introductions
by B. Jowett (3rd edn. Oxford, 1892; 1st edn., 1871).

c what you were saying about these two heroes, so that I may clearly understand. How did you distinguish them?

HIPPIAS: I shall have much pleasure, Socrates, in explaining to you more clearly than I could in public my views about these and also about other heroes. I say that Homer intended Achilles to be the bravest of the men who went to Troy, Nestor the wisest, and Odysseus the wiliest.

SOCRATES: O rare Hippias, will you be so good as not to laugh, if I find a difficulty in following you, and repeat my questions several
d times over? Please to answer me kindly and gently.

HIPPIAS: I should be greatly ashamed of myself, Socrates, if I, who teach others and take money of them, could not, when I was asked by you, answer in a civil and agreeable manner.

SOCRATES: Thank you. The fact is that I seemed to understand what you meant when you said that the poet intended Achilles to be
e the bravest of men, and also that he intended Nestor to be the wisest, but when you said that he meant Odysseus to be the wiliest, I must confess that I could not understand what you were saying. Will you tell me, and then I shall perhaps understand you better, has not Homer made Achilles wily?

HIPPIAS: Certainly not, Socrates. He is the most straightforward of mankind, and when Homer introduces them talking with one another in the passage called 'The Prayers,' Achilles is supposed by the poet to say to Odysseus,

365   Son of Laertes, sprung from heaven, crafty Odysseus, I will speak out plainly the word which I intend to carry out in act, and which will, I be-
b lieve, be accomplished. For I hate him like the gates of death who thinks one thing and says another. But I will speak that which shall be accomplished.[1]

Now, in these verses he clearly indicates the character of the two men. He shows Achilles to be true and simple, and Odysseus to be wily and false, for he supposes Achilles to be addressing Odysseus in these lines.

SOCRATES: Now, Hippias, I think that I understand your meaning. When you say that Odysseus is wily, you clearly mean that he is false?
c   HIPPIAS: Exactly so, Socrates. It is the character of Odysseus, as he is represented by Homer in many passages of both the *Iliad* and the *Odyssey*.

SOCRATES: And Homer must be presumed to have meant that the true man is not the same as the false?

HIPPIAS: Of course, Socrates.

SOCRATES: And is that your own opinion, Hippias?

---

[1] *Iliad* 9.308 sq.

HIPPIAS: Certainly. How can I have any other?

SOCRATES: Well, then, as there is no possibility of asking Homer what he meant in these verses of his, let us leave him, but as d you show a willingness to take up his cause, and your opinion agrees with what you declare to be his, will you answer on behalf of yourself and him?

HIPPIAS: I will. Ask shortly anything which you like.

SOCRATES: Do you say that the false, like the sick, have no power to do things, or that they have the power to do things?

HIPPIAS: I should say that they have power to do many e things, and in particular to deceive mankind.

SOCRATES: Then, according to you, they are both powerful and wily, are they not?

HIPPIAS: Yes.

SOCRATES: And are they wily, and do they deceive by reason of their simplicity and folly, or by reason of their cunning and a certain sort of prudence?

HIPPIAS: By reason of their cunning and prudence, most certainly.

SOCRATES: Then they are prudent, I suppose?

HIPPIAS: So they are—very.

SOCRATES: And if they are prudent, do they know or do they not know what they do?

HIPPIAS: Of course, they know very well, and that is why they do mischief to others.

SOCRATES: And having this knowledge, are they ignorant, or are they wise?   366

HIPPIAS: Wise, certainly, at least in so far as they can deceive.

SOCRATES: Stop, and let us recall to mind what you are saying. Are you not saying that the false are powerful and prudent and knowing and wise in those things about which they are false?

HIPPIAS: To be sure.

SOCRATES: And the true differ from the false—the true and the false are the very opposite of each other?

HIPPIAS: That is my view.

SOCRATES: Then, according to your view, it would seem that the false are to be ranked in the class of the powerful and wise?

HIPPIAS: Assuredly.

SOCRATES: And when you say that the false are powerful and b wise in so far as they are false, do you mean that they have or have not the power of uttering their falsehoods if they like?

HIPPIAS: I mean to say that they have the power.

SOCRATES: In a word, then, the false are they who are wise and have the power to speak falsely?

HIPPIAS: Yes.

SOCRATES: Then a man who has not the power of speaking falsely and is ignorant cannot be false?

HIPPIAS: You are right.

SOCRATES: And every man has power who does that which he wishes at the time when he wishes. I am not speaking of any special

c case in which he is prevented by disease or something of that sort, but I am speaking generally, as I might say of you that you are able to write my name when you like. Would you not call a man able who could do that?

HIPPIAS: Yes.

SOCRATES: And tell me, Hippias, are you not a skillful calculator and arithmetician?

HIPPIAS: Yes, Socrates, assuredly I am.

SOCRATES: And if someone were to ask you what is the sum of 3 multiplied by 700, you would tell him the true answer in a moment, if you pleased?

d HIPPIAS: Certainly I should.

SOCRATES: Is not that because you are the wisest and ablest of men in these matters?

HIPPIAS: Yes.

SOCRATES: And being as you are the wisest and ablest of men in these matters of calculation, are you not also the best?

HIPPIAS: To be sure, Socrates, I am the best.

SOCRATES: And, therefore, you would be the most able to tell the truth about these matters, would you not?

e HIPPIAS: Yes, I should.

SOCRATES: And could you speak falsehoods about them equally well? I must beg, Hippias, that you will answer me with the same frankness and magnanimity which has hitherto characterized you. If a person were to ask you what is the sum of 3 multiplied by 700, would not you be the best and most consistent teller of a falsehood, having always the power of speaking falsely as you have of speaking truly, about these same matters, if you wanted to tell a falsehood, and

367 not to answer truly? Would the ignorant man be better able to tell a falsehood in matters of calculation than you would be, if you chose? Might he not sometimes stumble upon the truth, when he wanted to tell a lie, because he did not know, whereas you who are the wise man, if you wanted to tell a lie would always and consistently lie?

HIPPIAS: Yes, there you are quite right.

SOCRATES: Does the false man tell lies about other things, but not about number, or when he is making a calculation?

HIPPIAS: To be sure, he would tell as many lies about number as about other things.

SOCRATES: Then may we further assume, Hippias, that there are men who are false about calculation and number?

b HIPPIAS: Yes.

SOCRATES: Who can they be? For you have already admitted that he who is false must have the ability to be false. You said, as you will remember, that he who is unable to be false will not be false.

HIPPIAS: Yes, I remember, it was so said.

SOCRATES: And were you not yourself just now shown to be best able to speak falsely about calculation?

HIPPIAS: Yes, that was another thing which was said.

SOCRATES: And are not you likewise said to speak truly c about calculation?

HIPPIAS: Certainly.

SOCRATES: Then the same person is able to speak both falsely and truly about calculation? And that person is he who is good at calculation—the arithmetician?

HIPPIAS: Yes.

SOCRATES: Who, then, Hippias, is discovered to be false at calculation? Is he not the good man? For the good man is the able man, and he is the true man.

HIPPIAS: That is evident.

SOCRATES: Do you not see, then, that the same man is false and also true about these same matters? And the true man is not a whit better than the false, for indeed he is the same with him and d not the very opposite, as you were just now imagining.

HIPPIAS: Not in that instance, clearly.

SOCRATES: Shall we examine other instances?

HIPPIAS: Certainly, if you are disposed.

SOCRATES: Are you not also skilled in geometry?

HIPPIAS: I am.

SOCRATES: Well, and does not the same hold in that science also? Is not the same person best able to speak falsely or to speak truly about diagrams, and he is—the geometrician?

HIPPIAS: Yes.

SOCRATES: He and no one else is good at it?

HIPPIAS: Yes, he and no one else.   e

SOCRATES: Then the good and wise geometer has this double power in the highest degree, and if there be a man who is false about diagrams the good man will be he, for he is able to be false, whereas the bad is unable, and for this reason is not false, as has been admitted.

HIPPIAS: True.

SOCRATES: Once more—let us examine a third case, that of the astronomer, in whose art, again, you, Hippias, profess to be a still greater proficient than in the preceding, do you not?

HIPPIAS: Yes, I am.   368

SOCRATES: And does not the same hold of astronomy?

HIPPIAS: True, Socrates.

SOCRATES: And in astronomy, too, if any man be able to speak

falsely it will be the good astronomer, but he who is not able will not
speak falsely, for he has no knowledge.

HIPPIAS : Clearly not.

SOCRATES : Then in astronomy also, the same man will be
true and false?

HIPPIAS : It would seem so.

SOCRATES : And now, Hippias, consider the question at large
b about all the sciences, and see whether the same principle does not
always hold. I know that in most arts you are the wisest of men, as I
have heard you boasting in the Agora at the tables of the money-
changers, when you were setting forth the great and enviable stores
of your wisdom, and you said that upon one occasion, when you went
to the Olympic games, all that you had on your person was made by
yourself. You began with your ring, which was of your own workmanship, and you said that you could engrave rings, and you had an-
c other seal which was also of your own workmanship, and a strigil and
an oil flask, which you had made yourself. You said also that you
had made the shoes which you had on your feet, and the cloak and
the short tunic, but what appeared to us all most extraordinary, and
a proof of singular art, was the girdle of your tunic, which, you said,
was as fine as the most costly Persian fabric, and of your own weaving. Moreover, you told us that you had brought with you poems,
epic, tragic, and dithyrambic, as well as prose writings of the most
d various kinds, and you said that your skill was also pre-eminent in the
arts which I was just now mentioning, and in the true principles of
rhythm and harmony and of orthography. And, if I remember rightly,
there were a great many other accomplishments in which you excelled. I have forgotten to mention your art of memory, which you regard as your special glory, and I dare say that I have forgotten many
e other things, but, as I was saying, only look to your own arts—and
there are plenty of them—and to those of others, and tell me, having
regard to the admissions which you and I have made, whether you
discover any department of art or any description of wisdom or cunning, whichever name you use, in which the true and false are differ-
369 ent and not the same. Tell me, if you can, of any. But you cannot.

HIPPIAS : Not without consideration, Socrates.

SOCRATES : Nor will consideration help you, Hippias, as I believe, but then if I am right, remember what the consequence will be.

HIPPIAS : I do not know what you mean, Socrates.

SOCRATES : I suppose that you are not using your art of memory, doubtless because you think that such an accomplishment is not
needed on the present occasion. I will therefore remind you of what
you were saying. Were you not saying that Achilles was a true man,
b and Odysseus false and wily?

HIPPIAS : I was.

SOCRATES : And now do you perceive that the same person has

turned out to be false as well as true? If Odysseus is false he is also true, and if Achilles is true he is also false, and so the two men are not opposed to one another, but they are alike.

HIPPIAS : O Socrates, you are always weaving the meshes of an argument, selecting the most difficult point, and fastening upon details instead of grappling with the matter in hand as a whole. Come c now, and I will demonstrate to you, if you will allow me, by many satisfactory proofs, that Homer has made Achilles a better man than Odysseus, and a truthful man too, and that he has made the other crafty, and a teller of many untruths, and inferior to Achilles. And then, if you please, you shall make a speech on the other side, in order to prove that Odysseus is the better man, and this may be compared to mine, and then the company will know which of us is the better speaker.

SOCRATES : O Hippias, I do not doubt that you are wiser than d I am. But I have a way, when anybody else says anything, of giving close attention to him, especially if the speaker appears to me to be a wise man. Having a desire to understand, I question him, and I examine and analyze and put together what he says, in order that I may understand, but if the speaker appears to me to be a poor hand, I do not interrogate him, or trouble myself about him. And you may know by this who they are whom I deem to be wise men, for you will see that when I am talking with a wise man, I am very attentive to what he says and ask questions of him, in order that I may learn and be im- e proved by him. And I could not help remarking while you were speaking, when you recited the verses in which Achilles, as you argued, attacks Odysseus as a deceiver, that you must be strangely mistaken, because Odysseus, the man of wiles, is never found to tell a lie, but Achilles is found to be wily on your own showing. At any rate he 370 speaks falsely, for first he utters these words, which you just now repeated,

He is hateful to me even as the gates of death who thinks one thing and says another.[2]

And then he says, a little while afterward, he will not be persuaded by b Odysseus and Agamemnon; neither will he remain at Troy, but, says he,

Tomorrow, when I have offered sacrifices to Zeus and all the gods, having loaded my ships well, I will drag them down into the deep. And then you shall see, if you have a mind, and if such things are a care to you, early in the morning my ships sailing over the fishy Hellespont, and my men eagerly plying the oar, and, if the illustrious shaker of the c earth gives me a good voyage, on the third day I shall reach the fertile Phthia.[3]

[2] *Iliad* 9.308 sq.   [3] *Iliad* 9.357 sq.

And before that, when he was reviling Agamemnon, he said,

> And now to Phthia I will go, since to return home in the beaked
> ships is far better, nor am I inclined to stay here in dishonor and amass
> d wealth and riches for you.[4]

But although on that occasion, in the presence of the whole army, he
spoke after this fashion, and on the other occasion to his companions, he appears never to have made any preparation or attempt to
draw down the ships, as if he had the least intention of sailing home
—so nobly regardless was he of the truth. Now I, Hippias, originally
asked you the question, because I was in doubt as to which of the two
heroes was intended by the poet to be the better, and because I
e thought that both of them were pre-eminent, and that it would be
difficult to decide which was the better of them, not only in respect of
truth and falsehood, but of virtue generally, for even in this matter of
speaking the truth they are much upon a par.

HIPPIAS : There you are wrong, Socrates, for in so far as Achilles speaks falsely, the falsehood is obviously unintentional. He is
compelled against his will to remain and rescue the army in their
misfortune. But when Odysseus speaks falsely he is voluntarily and
intentionally false.

SOCRATES : You, sweet Hippias, like Odysseus, are a deceiver
yourself.

371   HIPPIAS : Certainly not, Socrates. What makes you say so?

SOCRATES : Because you say that Achilles does not speak
falsely from design, when he is not only a deceiver, but besides being
a braggart, in Homer's description of him is so cunning, and so far
superior to Odysseus in lying and pretending, that he dares to contradict himself, and Odysseus does not find him out; at any rate he
does not appear to say anything to him which would imply that he
b perceived his falsehood.

HIPPIAS : What do you mean, Socrates?

SOCRATES : Did you not observe that afterward, when he is
speaking to Odysseus, he says that he will sail away with the early
dawn, but to Ajax he tells quite a different story?

HIPPIAS : Where is that?

SOCRATES : Where he says,

> I will not think about bloody war until the son of warlike Priam, illus-
> c trious Hector, comes to the tents and ships of the Myrmidons, slaughtering
> the Argives and burning the ships with fire. And about my tent and dark
> ship, I suspect that Hector, although eager for the battle, will nevertheless
> stay his hand.[5]

Now, do you really think, Hippias, that the son of Thetis, who had

---

[4] *Iliad* 1.169 sq.   [5] *Iliad* 9.650.

been the pupil of the sage Chiron, had such a bad memory, or would d
have carried the art of lying to such an extent—when he had been
assailing liars in the most violent terms only the instant before—as to
say to Odysseus that he would sail away, and to Ajax that he would
remain, and that he was not rather practicing upon the simplicity of
Odysseus, whom he regarded as an ancient, and thinking that he
would get the better of him by his own cunning and falsehood?

HIPPIAS: No, I do not agree with you, Socrates, but I believe
that Achilles is induced to say one thing to Ajax, and another to e
Odysseus, in the innocence of his heart, whereas Odysseus, whether he
speaks falsely or truly, speaks always with a purpose.

SOCRATES: Then Odysseus would appear after all to be better
than Achilles?

HIPPIAS: Certainly not, Socrates.

SOCRATES: Why, were not the voluntary liars only just now
shown to be better than the involuntary?

HIPPIAS: And how, Socrates, can those who intentionally err,
and voluntarily and designedly commit iniquities, be better than those
who err and do wrong involuntarily? Surely there is a great excuse to 372
be made for a man telling a falsehood or doing an injury or any sort
of harm to another, in ignorance. And the laws are obviously far
more severe on those who lie or do evil, voluntarily, than on those
who do evil involuntarily.

SOCRATES: You see, Hippias, as I have already told you, how
pertinacious I am in questioning wise men. And I think that this is the b
only good point about me, for I am full of defects, and always getting things wrong in some way or other. My deficiency is proved to
me by the fact that when I meet one of you who are famous for wisdom, and to whose wisdom all the Hellenes are witnesses, I am found
out to know nothing. For speaking generally, I hardly ever have the
same opinion about anything which you have, and what proof of ignorance can be greater than to differ from wise men? But I have c
one singular good quality, which is my salvation. I am not ashamed to
learn, and I ask and inquire, and am very grateful to those who answer me, and never fail to give them my grateful thanks. And when I
learn a thing I never deny my teacher, or pretend that the lesson
is a discovery of my own, but I praise his wisdom, and proclaim what
I have learned from him. And now I cannot agree in what you are saying, but I strongly disagree. Well, I know that this is my own fault, and d
is a defect in my character, but I will not pretend to be more than I
am, and my opinion, Hippias, is the very contrary of what you are saying, for I maintain that those who hurt or injure mankind, and speak
falsely and deceive, and err voluntarily, are better far than those
who do wrong involuntarily. Sometimes, however, I am of the opposite opinion, for I am all abroad in my ideas about this matter, a condition obviously occasioned by ignorance. And just now I happen to

e be in a crisis of my disorder at which those who err voluntarily appear to me better than those who err involuntarily. My present state
of mind is due to our previous argument, which inclines me to believe
that in general those who do wrong involuntarily are worse than those
who do wrong voluntarily, and therefore I hope that you will be good
to me, and not refuse to heal me, for you will do me a much greater

373 benefit if you cure my soul of ignorance than you would if you were to
cure my body of disease. I must, however, tell you beforehand, that if
you make a long oration to me you will not cure me, for I shall not be
able to follow you; but if you will answer me, as you did just now, you
will do me a great deal of good, and I do not think that you will be any
the worse yourself. And I have some claim upon you also, O son of
Apemantus, for you incited me to converse with Hippias, and now, if
Hippias will not answer me, you must entreat him on my behalf.

EUDICUS: But I do not think, Socrates, that Hippias will re-
b quire any entreaty of mine, for he has already said that he will
refuse no man. Did you not say so, Hippias?

HIPPIAS: Yes, I did, but then, Eudicus, Socrates is always troublesome in an argument, and appears to be dishonest.

SOCRATES: Excellent Hippias, I do not do so intentionally—if
I did, it would show me to be a wise man and a master of wiles, as
you would argue—but unintentionally, and therefore you must pardon me, for, as you say, he who is unintentionally dishonest should
be pardoned.

c EUDICUS: Yes, Hippias, do as he says, and for our sake, and
also that you may not belie your profession, answer whatever Socrates asks you.

HIPPIAS: I will answer, as you request me, and do you ask whatever you like.

SOCRATES: I am very desirous, Hippias, of examining this
question, as to which are the better—those who err voluntarily or involuntarily? And if you will answer me, I think that I can put you
in the way of approaching the subject. You would admit, would you
not, that there are good runners?

d HIPPIAS: Yes.

SOCRATES: And there are bad runners?

HIPPIAS: Yes.

SOCRATES: And he who runs well is a good runner, and he who
runs ill is a bad runner?

HIPPIAS: Very true.

SOCRATES: And he who runs slowly runs ill, and he who runs
quickly runs well?

HIPPIAS: Yes.

SOCRATES: Then in a race, and in running, swiftness is a good,
and slowness is an evil quality?

HIPPIAS: To be sure.

SOCRATES: Which of the two then is a better runner? He who

runs slowly voluntarily, or he who runs slowly involuntarily?

HIPPIAS: He who runs slowly voluntarily.

SOCRATES: And is not running a species of doing?

HIPPIAS: Certainly.

SOCRATES: And if a species of doing, a species of action?

HIPPIAS: Yes.

SOCRATES: Then he who runs badly does a bad and dishonor- e
able action in a race?

HIPPIAS: Yes, a bad action, certainly.

SOCRATES: And he who runs slowly runs badly?

HIPPIAS: Yes.

SOCRATES: Then the good runner does this bad and disgrace-ful action voluntarily, and the bad involuntarily?

HIPPIAS: That is to be inferred.

SOCRATES: Then he who involuntarily does evil actions is worse in a race than he who does them voluntarily?

HIPPIAS: Yes, in a race.

SOCRATES: Well, but at a wrestling match—which is the better 374
wrestler, he who falls voluntarily or involuntarily?

HIPPIAS: He who falls voluntarily, doubtless.

SOCRATES: And is it worse and more dishonorable at a wres-tling match, to fall, or to throw another?

HIPPIAS: To fall.

SOCRATES: Then, at a wrestling match, he who voluntarily does base and dishonorable actions is a better wrestler than he who does them involuntarily?

HIPPIAS: That appears to be the truth.

SOCRATES: And what would you say of any other bodily exercise—is not he who is better made able to do both that which is strong and that which is weak, that which is fair and that which is foul, so that when he does bad actions with the body, he b who is better made does them voluntarily, and he who is worse made does them involuntarily?

HIPPIAS: Yes, that appears to be true about strength.

SOCRATES: And what do you say about grace, Hippias? Is not he who is better made able to assume evil and disgraceful figures and postures voluntarily, as he who is worse made assumes them in-voluntarily?

HIPPIAS: True.

SOCRATES: Then voluntary ungracefulness comes from ex-cellence of the bodily frame, and involuntary from the defect of the bodily frame? c

HIPPIAS: True.

SOCRATES: And what would you say of an unmusical voice? Would you prefer the voice which is voluntarily or involuntarily out of tune?

HIPPIAS: That which is voluntarily out of tune.

SOCRATES : The involuntary is the worse of the two?

HIPPIAS : Yes.

SOCRATES : And would you choose to possess goods or evils?

HIPPIAS : Goods.

SOCRATES : And would you rather have feet which are voluntarily or involuntarily lame?

d   HIPPIAS : Feet which are voluntarily lame.

SOCRATES : But is not lameness a defect or deformity?

HIPPIAS : Yes.

SOCRATES : And is not blinking a defect of the eyes?

HIPPIAS : Yes.

SOCRATES : And would you rather always have eyes with which you might voluntarily blink and not see, or with which you might involuntarily blink?

HIPPIAS : I would rather have eyes which voluntarily blink.

SOCRATES : Then in your own case you deem that which voluntarily acts ill better than that which involuntarily acts ill?

HIPPIAS : Yes, certainly, in cases such as you mention.

SOCRATES : And does not the same hold of ears, nostrils, mouth, and of all the senses—those which involuntarily act ill are not
e to be desired, as being defective, and those which voluntarily act ill are to be desired as being good?

HIPPIAS : I agree.

SOCRATES : And what would you say of instruments—which are the better sort of instruments to have to do with, those with which a man acts ill voluntarily or involuntarily? For example, had a man better have a rudder with which he will steer ill, voluntarily or involuntarily?

HIPPIAS : He had better have a rudder with which he will steer ill voluntarily.

SOCRATES : And does not the same hold of the bow and the lyre, the flute and all other things?

HIPPIAS : Very true.

375   SOCRATES : And would you rather have a horse of such a temper that you may ride him ill voluntarily or involuntarily?

HIPPIAS : I would rather have a horse which I could ride ill voluntarily.

SOCRATES : That would be the better horse?

HIPPIAS : Yes.

SOCRATES : Then with a horse of better temper, vicious actions would be produced voluntarily, and with a horse of bad temper involuntarily?

HIPPIAS : Certainly.

SOCRATES : And that would be true of a dog, or of any other animal?

HIPPIAS : Yes.

SOCRATES: And is it better to possess the mind of an archer who voluntarily or involuntarily misses the mark?

HIPPIAS: Of him who voluntarily misses.   b

SOCRATES: This would be the better mind for the purposes of archery?

HIPPIAS: Yes.

SOCRATES: Then the mind which involuntarily errs is worse than the mind which errs voluntarily?

HIPPIAS: Yes, certainly, in the use of the bow.

SOCRATES: And what would you say of the art of medicine—has not the mind which voluntarily works harm to the body more of the healing art?

HIPPIAS: Yes.

SOCRATES: Then in the art of medicine the voluntary is better than the involuntary?

HIPPIAS: Yes.

SOCRATES: Well, and in lute playing and in flute playing, and in all arts and sciences, is not that mind the better which voluntarily c does what is evil and dishonorable, and goes wrong, and is not the worse that which does so involuntarily?

HIPPIAS: That is evident.

SOCRATES: And what would you say of the characters of slaves? Should we not prefer to have those who voluntarily do wrong and make mistakes, and are they not better in their mistakes than those who commit them involuntarily?

HIPPIAS: Yes.

SOCRATES: And should we not desire to have our own minds in the best state possible?

HIPPIAS: Yes.

SOCRATES: And will our minds be better if they do wrong and d make mistakes voluntarily, or involuntarily?

HIPPIAS: Oh, Socrates, it would be a monstrous thing to say that those who do wrong voluntarily are better than those who do wrong involuntarily!

SOCRATES: And yet that appears to be the only inference.

HIPPIAS: I do not think so.

SOCRATES: But I imagined, Hippias, that you did. Please to answer once more. Is not justice a power, or knowledge, or both? Must not justice, at all events, be one of these?

HIPPIAS: Yes.   e

SOCRATES: But if justice is a power of the soul, then the soul which has the greater power is also the more just, for that which has the greater power, my good friend, has been proved by us to be the better.

HIPPIAS: Yes, that has been proved.

SOCRATES: And if justice is knowledge, then the wiser will be the juster soul, and the more ignorant the more unjust?

HIPPIAS : Yes.

SOCRATES : But if justice be power as well as knowledge—then will not the soul which has both knowledge and power be the more just, and that which is the more ignorant be the more unjust? Must it not be so?

HIPPIAS : Clearly.

SOCRATES : And is not the soul which has the greater power and wisdom also better, and better able to do both good and evil in every action?

376 HIPPIAS : Certainly.

SOCRATES : The soul, then, which acts ill, acts voluntarily by power and art—and these, either one or both of them, are elements of justice?

HIPPIAS : That seems to be true.

SOCRATES : And to do injustice is to do ill, and not to do injustice is to do well?

HIPPIAS : Yes.

SOCRATES : And will not the better and abler soul, when it does wrong, do wrong voluntarily, and the bad soul involuntarily?

HIPPIAS : Clearly.

b   SOCRATES : And the good man is he who has the good soul, and the bad man is he who has the bad?

HIPPIAS : Yes.

SOCRATES : Then the good man will do wrong voluntarily, and the bad man involuntarily, if the good man is he who has the good soul?

HIPPIAS : Which he certainly has.

SOCRATES : Then, Hippias, he who voluntarily does wrong and disgraceful things, if there be such a man, will be the good man?

HIPPIAS : There I cannot agree with you.

SOCRATES : Nor can I agree with myself, Hippias, and yet that
c seems to be the conclusion which, as far as we can see at present, must follow from our argument. As I was saying before, I am all abroad, and being in perplexity am always changing my opinion. Now, that I or any ordinary man should wander in perplexity is not surprising, but if you wise men also wander, and we cannot come to you and rest from our wandering, the matter begins to be serious both to us and to you.

ION

In this little dialogue Plato is amusing himself. Socrates talks with Ion whose profession is to give recitals of Homer on special occasions and who is convinced that he is the greatest artist in that line throughout Greece. His naïve and complete self-satisfaction is amusingly contrasted with Socrates' very gentle irony. Ion is no antagonist to draw down upon him anything more drastic. Socrates treats him most gently and he feels as self-satisfied at the end as he did at the beginning.

The real interest in the conversation—it cannot be called a discussion—is what Socrates says about art. Heretofore in all the arts in Athens the emotions and the intellect had worked together. There was a balance of power. That is the uniqueness of Greek art; it is an intellectual art. In the Ion Socrates disputes the possibility of such a balance. Art, he says, is not dependent upon the emotions; it belongs to the realm of knowledge. "Each separate art has had assigned to it by the deity the power of knowing a particular occupation," as the art of the physician or the sculptor, but poetry is not art; it is not guided by rules as art is. It is inspiration, not knowledge. Poets and their interpreters like Ion are "not in their senses," but "a poet is a light and winged thing, and holy, and never able to compose until he has become inspired, and is beside himself, and reason is no longer in him."

The dialogue by itself is proof that the balance between opposites which had made the Periclean Age possible was passing away and had already passed to such a degree that the greatest of the Athenians had to put his effort into counteracting the rapidly growing disorder in a state ruled more and more not by the mind, but by the emotions.

530   SOCRATES: Welcome, Ion! And whence come you now to pay us a visit? From your home in Ephesus?

ION: No, Socrates, I come from Epidaurus and the festival of Asclepius.

SOCRATES: What! Do the citizens of Epidaurus, in honoring the god, have a contest between rhapsodes too?

ION: Indeed they do. They have every sort of musical competition.

SOCRATES: So? And did you compete? And how did you succeed?

b   ION: We carried off first prize, Socrates.

SOCRATES: Well done! See to it, now, that we win the Panathenaea also.

ION: It shall be so, God willing.

SOCRATES: I must say, Ion, I am often envious of you rhapsodists in your profession. Your art requires of you always to go in fine array, and look as beautiful as you can, and meanwhile you must be conversant with many excellent poets, and especially with Homer, the best and most divine of all. You have to understand his thought, and c not merely learn his lines. It is an enviable lot! In fact, one never could be a rhapsode if one did not comprehend the utterances of the poet, for the rhapsode must become an interpreter of the poet's thought to those who listen, and to do this well is quite impossible unless one knows just what the poet is saying. All that, of course, will excite one's envy.

ION: What you say is true, Socrates; to me, at all events, this aspect of the art has given the most concern. And I judge that I, of all men, have the finest things to say on Homer, that neither Metrodorus d of Lampsacus, nor Stesimbrotus of Thasos, nor Glaucon, nor anyone else who ever lived, had so many reflections, or such fine ones, to present on Homer as have I.

SOCRATES: That is pleasant news, Ion, for obviously you will not begrudge me a display of your talent.

ION: Not at all. And, Socrates, it really is worth while to hear how well I have embellished Homer. In my opinion I deserve to be crowned with a wreath of gold by the Homeridae.

SOCRATES: Another time I shall find leisure to hear your reci-
531 tation. At the moment do but answer me so far. Are you skilled in Homer only, or in Hesiod and Archilochus as well?

ION: No, only in regard to Homer; to me that seems enough.

SOCRATES: Is there any point on which both Homer and Hesiod say the same thing?

ION: Indeed, I think so; there are many cases of it.

From *Phaedrus, Ion, Gorgias, and Symposium*, translated with introduction by Lane Cooper (Ithaca, New York, 1955; copyright 1938 by Lane Cooper).

SOCRATES: In those cases, then, would you interpret what Homer says better than what Hesiod says?

ION: In the cases where they say the same, Socrates, I should do b equally well with both.

SOCRATES: But what about the cases where they do not say the same? For example, take the art of divination; Homer and Hesiod both speak of it.

ION: Quite so.

SOCRATES: Well then, where they say the same on the art of divination, and where they differ on it, would you interpret better what these two poets say, or would one of the diviners, one of the good ones, do so?

ION: One of the diviners.

SOCRATES: But suppose you were a diviner. If you were competent to explain the passages where they agree, would you not be competent to explain as well the passages where they differ?

ION: Manifestly, yes.

SOCRATES: How is it, then, that you are skilled in Homer, but c not in Hesiod or the other poets? Does Homer treat of matters different from those that all the other poets treat of? Wasn't his subject mainly war, and hasn't he discussed the mutual relations of men good and bad, or the general run as well as special craftsmen, the relations of the gods to one another and to men, as they forgather, the phenomena of the heavens and occurrences in the underworld, and the birth of gods and heroes? Are not these the subjects Homer dealt with in his d poetry?

ION: What you say is true, Socrates.

SOCRATES: And what about the other poets? Haven't they dealt with these same themes?

ION: Yes, but, Socrates, not in the same way.

SOCRATES: How so? In a worse way than he?

ION: Far worse.

SOCRATES: He in a better way?

ION: Better indeed, I warrant you.

SOCRATES: Well now, Ion darling, tell me. When several persons are discussing number, and one of them talks better than the rest, there will be someone who distinguishes the good speaker?

ION: I agree.

SOCRATES: It will be the same one who distinguishes those who e are speaking badly, or will it be another?

ION: No doubt the same.

SOCRATES: And this will be the one who knows the art of numbers?

ION: Yes.

SOCRATES: Tell me. When several are discussing diet, and what foods are wholesome, and one of them speaks better than the rest, will a given person see the excellence of the best speaker, and another the inferiority of the worse, or will the same man distinguish both?

ION : Obviously, I think, the same.

SOCRATES : Who is he? What is he called?

ION : The doctor.

SOCRATES : We may therefore generalize, and say: When several persons are discussing a given subject, the man who can distinguish the one who is talking well on it, and the one who is
532 talking badly, will always be the same. Or, if he does not recognize the one who is talking badly, then, clearly, neither will he recognize the one who is talking well, granted that the subject is the same.

ION : That is so.

SOCRATES : Then the same man will be skilled with respect to both?

ION : Yes.

SOCRATES : Now you assert that Homer and the other poets, among them Hesiod and Archilochus, all treat of the same subjects, yet not all in the same fashion, but the one speaks well, and the rest of them speak worse.

ION : And what I say is true.

b   SOCRATES : Then you, if you can recognize the poet who speaks well, could also recognize the poets who speak worse, and see that they speak worse.

ION : So it seems.

SOCRATES : Well then, my best of friends, when we say that Ion has equal skill in Homer and all other poets, we shall not be mistaken. It must be so, since you yourself admit that the same man will be competent to judge of all who speak of the same matters, and that the poets virtually all deal with the same subjects.

ION : Then what can be the reason, Socrates, for my behavior?
c When anyone discusses any other poet, I pay no attention, and can offer no remark of any value. I frankly doze. But whenever anyone mentions Homer, immediately I am awake, attentive, and full of things to say.

SOCRATES : The riddle is not hard to solve, my friend. No, it is plain to everyone that not from art and knowledge comes your power to speak concerning Homer. If it were art that gave you power, then you could speak about all the other poets as well. There is an art of poetry as a whole? Am I not right?

ION : Yes.

d   SOCRATES : And is not the case the same with any other art you please, when you take it as a whole? The same method of inquiry holds for all the arts? Do you want some explanation, Ion, of what I mean by that?

ION : Yes, Socrates, upon my word I do. It gives me joy to listen to you wise men.

SOCRATES : I only wish you were right in saying that, Ion. But 'wise men'! That means you, the rhapsodists and actors, and the men whose poems you chant, while I have nothing else to tell besides the truth, after the fashion of the ordinary man. For example, take the e question I just now asked you. Observe what a trivial and common-place remark it was that I uttered, something anyone might know, when I said that the inquiry is the same whenever one takes an art in its entirety. Let us reason the matter out. There is an art of painting taken as a whole?

ION : Yes.

SOCRATES : And there are and have been many painters, good and bad?

ION : Yes indeed.

SOCRATES : Now, take Polygnotus, son of Aglaophon. Have you ever seen a man with the skill to point out what is good and what is not in the works of Polygnotus, but without the power to do so in the 533 works of other painters? A man who, when anybody shows the works of other painters, dozes off, is at a loss, has nothing to suggest, but when he has to express a judgment on one particular painter, say Polygnotus or anyone else you choose, wakes up, and is attentive, and is full of things to say?

ION : No, on my oath, I never saw the like.

SOCRATES : Or, again, take sculpture. Have you ever seen a man with the skill to judge the finer works of Daedalus, son of Metion, or of Epeus, son of Panopeus, or of Theodorus of Samos, or b the works of any other single sculptor, but, confronted by the works of other sculptors, is at a loss, and dozes off, without a thing to say?

ION : No, on my oath, I never saw one.

SOCRATES : Yet further, as I think, the same is true of playing on the flute, and on the harp, and singing to the harp, and rhapsody. You never saw a man with the skill to judge of Olympus, of Thamyras, or of Orpheus, or of Phemius, the rhapsodist at Ithaca, but is at a c loss, has no remark to make concerning Ion the Ephesian, and his success or failure in reciting.

ION : On that I cannot contradict you, Socrates. But of this thing I am conscious, that I excel all men in speaking about Homer, and on him have much to say, and that everybody else avers I do it well, but on the other poets I do not. Well then, see what that means.

SOCRATES : I do see, Ion, and in fact will proceed to show you what to my mind it betokens. As I just now said, this gift you have of d speaking well on Homer is not an art; it is a power divine, impelling you like the power in the stone Euripides called the magnet, which most call 'stone of Heraclea.' This stone does not simply attract the

iron rings, just by themselves; it also imparts to the rings a force enabling them to do the same thing as the stone itself, that is, to attract
e another ring, so that sometimes a chain is formed, quite a long one, of
iron rings, suspended from one another. For all of them, however,
their power depends upon that loadstone. Just so the Muse. She first
makes men inspired, and then through these inspired ones others share
in the enthusiasm, and a chain is formed, for the epic poets, all the
good ones, have their excellence, not from art, but are inspired, possessed, and thus they utter all these admirable poems. So is it also
534 with the good lyric poets; as the worshiping Corybantes are not in
their senses when they dance, so the lyric poets are not in their senses
when they make these lovely lyric poems. No, when once they launch
into harmony and rhythm, they are seized with the Bacchic transport,
and are possessed—as the bacchants, when possessed, draw milk and
honey from the rivers, but not when in their senses. So the spirit of
the lyric poet works, according to their own report. For the poets tell
us, don't they, that the melodies they bring us are gathered from rills
b that run with honey, out of glens and gardens of the Muses, and they
bring them as the bees do honey, flying like the bees? And what they
say is true, for a poet is a light and winged thing, and holy, and never
able to compose until he has become inspired, and is beside himself,
and reason is no longer in him. So long as he has this in his possession, no man is able to make poetry or to chant in prophecy. There-
c fore, since their making is not by art, when they utter many things
and fine about the deeds of men, just as you do about Homer, but is by
lot divine—therefore each is able to do well only that to which the
Muse has impelled him—one to make dithyrambs, another panegyric
odes, another choral songs, another epic poems, another iambs. In all
the rest, each one of them is poor, for not by art do they utter these,
but by power divine, since if it were by art that they knew how to treat
one subject finely, they would know how to deal with all the others too.
Herein lies the reason why the deity has bereft them of their senses,
d and uses them as ministers, along with soothsayers and godly seers; it
is in order that we listeners may know that it is not they who utter
these precious revelations while their mind is not within them, but
that it is the god himself who speaks, and through them becomes articulate to us. The most convincing evidence of this statement is offered by Tynnichus of Chalcis. He never composed a single poem
worth recalling, save the song of praise which everyone repeats, well-
nigh the finest of all lyrical poems, and absolutely what he called it,
e an 'Invention of the Muses.' By this example above all, it seems to
me, the god would show us, lest we doubt, that these lovely poems
are not of man or human workmanship, but are divine and from the
gods, and that the poets are nothing but interpreters of the gods, each
one possessed by the divinity to whom he is in bondage. And to prove

this, the deity on purpose sang the loveliest of all lyrics through the most miserable poet. Isn't it so, Ion? Don't you think that I am right? 535

ION: You are indeed, I vow! Socrates, your words in some way touch my very soul, and it does seem to me that by dispensation from above good poets convey to us these utterances of the gods.

SOCRATES: Well, and you rhapsodists, again, interpret the utterances of the poets?

ION: There also you are right.

SOCRATES: Accordingly, you are interpreters of interpreters?

ION: Undeniably.

SOCRATES: Wait now, Ion; tell me this. And answer frankly b what I ask you. Suppose you are reciting epic poetry well, and thrill the spectators most deeply. You are chanting, say, the story of Odysseus as he leaped up to the dais, unmasked himself to the suitors, and poured the arrows out before his feet, or of Achilles rushing upon Hector, or one of the pitiful passages, about Andromache, or Hecuba, or Priam. When you chant these, are you in your senses? Or are you carried out of yourself, and does not your soul in an ecstasy conceive c herself to be engaged in the actions you relate, whether they are in Ithaca, or Troy, or wherever the story puts them?

ION: How vivid, Socrates, you make your proof for me! I will tell you frankly that whenever I recite a tale of pity, my eyes are filled with tears, and when it is one of horror or dismay, my hair stands up on end with fear, and my heart goes leaping.

SOCRATES: Well now, Ion, what are we to say of a man like d that? There he is, at a sacrifice or festival, got up in holiday attire, adorned with golden chaplets, and he weeps, though he has lost nothing of his finery. Or he recoils with fear, standing in the presence of more than twenty thousand friendly people, though nobody is stripping him or doing him damage. Shall we say that the man is in his senses?

ION: Never, Socrates, upon my word. That is strictly true.

SOCRATES: Now then, are you aware that you produce the same effects in most of the spectators too?

ION: Yes, indeed, I know it very well. As I look down at them e from the stage above, I see them, every time, weeping, casting terrible glances, stricken with amazement at the deeds recounted. In fact, I have to give them very close attention, for if I set them weeping, I myself shall laugh when I get my money, but if they laugh, it is I who have to weep at losing it.

SOCRATES: Well, do you see that the spectator is the last of the rings I spoke of, which receive their force from one another by virtue of the loadstone? You, the rhapsodist and actor, are the middle ring, 536 and the first one is the poet himself. But it is the deity who, through all the series, draws the spirit of men wherever he desires, transmitting

the attractive force from one into another. And so, as from the load-stone, a mighty chain hangs down, of choric dancers, masters of the chorus, undermasters, obliquely fastened to the rings which are suspended from the Muse. One poet is suspended from one Muse, another
b from another; we call it being 'possessed,' but the fact is much the same, since he is *held*. And from these primary rings, the poets, others are in turn suspended, some attached to this one, some to that, and are filled with inspiration, some by Orpheus, others by Musaeus. But the majority are possessed and held by Homer, and, Ion, you are one of these, and are possessed by Homer. And whenever anyone chants the work of any other poet, you fall asleep, and haven't a thing to say, but when anybody gives tongue to a strain of this one, you are
c awake at once, your spirit dances, and you have much to say, for not by art or science do you say of Homer what you say, but by dispensation from above and by divine possession. So the worshiping Corybantes have a lively feeling for that strain alone which is of the deity by whom they are possessed, and for that melody are well supplied with attitudes and utterances, and heed no others. And so it is with you, Ion. When anyone mentions Homer, you are ready, but about the
d other poets you are at a loss. You ask me why you are ready about Homer and not about the rest. Because it is not by art but by lot divine that you are eloquent in praise of Homer.

ION : Well put, I grant you, Socrates. And yet I should be much surprised if by your argument you succeeded in convincing me that I am possessed or mad when I praise Homer. Nor do I think that you yourself would find me so if you heard me speaking upon Homer.

SOCRATES : And indeed I wish to hear you, but not until you
e have answered me as follows. On what point in Homer do you speak well? Not on all points, I take it.

ION : I assure you, Socrates, I do it on every point, without exception.

SOCRATES : Yet not, I fancy, on those matters of which you happen to be ignorant, but Homer tells of?

ION : And the matters Homer tells of, and I do not know, what are they?

537   SOCRATES : Why, does not Homer in many passages speak of arts, and have much to say about them? About driving a chariot, for instance; if I can recollect the lines, I'll repeat them to you.

ION : No, let me do it, for I know them.

SOCRATES : Then recite for me what Nestor says to Antilochus, his son, where he warns him to be careful at the turning post, in the lay of the horse race in honor of Patroclus.

ION :

Thyself lean slightly in the burnished car
b   To the left of them, then call upon the off horse
With goad and voice; with hand give him free rein.

And at the post let the near horse come so close
That the nave of the well-wrought wheel shall seem
To graze the stone. Which yet beware to strike! [1]

SOCRATES: That will do. Now, Ion, in these lines, which will c
be more capable of judging whether Homer speaks aright or not, a
doctor or a charioteer?

ION: The charioteer, no doubt.

SOCRATES: Because that is his art, or for some other reason?

ION: No, because it is his art.

SOCRATES: Each separate art, then, has had assigned to it by
the deity the power of knowing a particular occupation? I take it that
what we know by the pilot's art we do not know by the art of medicine
as well.

ION: No indeed.   d

SOCRATES: And what we know by medical art we do not know
by the builder's art as well.

ION: No indeed.

SOCRATES: Well, and so it is with all the arts? What we know
by one of them, we do not know by another? But before you answer
that, just tell me this. Do you allow a distinction between arts? One
differs from another?

ION: Yes.

SOCRATES: Now with me the mark of differentiation is that
one art means the knowledge of one kind of thing, another art the
knowledge of another, and so I give them their respective names. Do
you do that?

ION: Yes.

SOCRATES: If they meant simply knowledge of the same e
things, why should we distinguish one art from another? Why call
them different, when both would give us the same knowledge? For
example, take these fingers. I know that there are five of them, and
you know the same as I about them. Suppose I asked you if we
knew this same matter, you and I, by the same art, that of arithmetic,
or by different arts. I fancy you would hold that we knew it by the
same?

ION: Yes.

SOCRATES: Then tell me now what just a little while ago I was 538
on the point of asking you. Does that seem true to you of all the arts
—that, necessarily, the same art makes us know the same, another art
not the same, but, if it really is another art, it must make us know
something else?

ION: That is my opinion Socrates.

SOCRATES: Well then, if one does not possess a given art, one

[1] *Iliad* 23.335.

will not be capable of rightly knowing what belongs to it in word or action?

b   ION : That is true.

SOCRATES : Then, in the lines which you recited, which will have the better knowledge whether Homer speaks aright or not, you or a charioteer?

ION : The charioteer.

SOCRATES : Doubtless because you are a rhapsode, and not a charioteer?

ION : Yes.

SOCRATES : The rhapsode's art is different from the charioteer's?

ION : Yes.

SOCRATES : If it is another art, then, it is a knowledge also about other matters.

ION : Yes.

SOCRATES : Now what about the passage in which Homer tells
c how Hecamede, Nestor's concubine, gave the wounded Machaon the broth to drink? The passage runs something like this :

> She grated goat's-milk cheese in Pramnian wine,
> With brazen grater, adding onion as a relish to the brew.[2]

On the question whether Homer here speaks properly or not, is it for the art of the physician, or the rhapsode's art, to discriminate aright?

ION : The art of the physician.

SOCRATES : What of this? The passage in which Homer says :

d   She plunged to the bottom like a leaden sinker
Which, mounted on the horntip from a field ox,
Speeds its way bringing mischief to voracious fish.[3]

What shall we say? Is it rather for the art of fishing, or the rhapsode's art, to decide on what the verses mean, and whether they are good or not?

ION : Obviously, Socrates, it is for the art of fishing.

SOCRATES : Reflect now. Suppose that you were questioning,
e and asked me, 'Now, Socrates, you find it is for these several arts to judge in Homer, severally, what appertains to each of them. Come then, pick me out the passages concerning the diviner, and the diviner's art, the kind of things that appertain to him, regarding which he must be able to discern whether the poetry is good or bad?' Observe how easily and truly I can answer you. The poet does, in fact, treat of this matter in the *Odyssey* too—for example, when a scion of Melampus, the diviner Theoclymenus, says to the wooers :

539   Ah, wretched men, what bane is this ye suffer? Shrouded in night

---

[2] *Iliad* 11:639–40.   [3] *Iliad* 24.80 sq.

Are your heads and your faces and your limbs below,
And kindled is the voice of wailing, and cheeks are wet with tears.
And the porch is full of ghosts; the hall is full of them,
Hastening hellward beneath the gloom, and the sun
Has perished out of heaven, and an evil mist infolds the world.[4]   b

And he treats of it in many places in the *Iliad*—for instance, in the
lay of the battle at the wall. There he says:

For, as they were eager to pass over, a bird approached them,
An eagle of lofty flight, skirting the host on the left,
And in its talons bearing a monstrous blood-red serpent,   c
Still alive and struggling; nor had it yet forgot the joy of battle.
Writhing back, it smote the bird that held it, upon the breast
Beside the neck, and the bird did cast it from him,
In the agony of pain, to the earth,
And dropped it in the middle of the throng.
And, with a cry, himself went flying on the gusty wind.[5]   d

These passages, I contend, and others like them, appertain to the diviner to examine and to judge.

ION: And, Socrates, you are right.

SOCRATES: And you are right too, Ion, when you say so. Come
now, you do for me what I have done for you. From both the *Odyssey*
and *Iliad* I picked out for you the passages belonging to the doctor, the
diviner, and the fisherman; now you likewise, since you are better e
versed than I in Homer, pick out for me the sort of passages, Ion, that
concern the rhapsode and the rhapsode's art, the passages it befits the
rhapsode, above all other men, to examine and to judge.

ION: *All* passages, Socrates, is what I say.

SOCRATES: Surely, Ion, you don't mean *all!* Are you really so
forgetful? Indeed, it would ill become a man who is a rhapsode to
forget.

ION: Why? What am I forgetting?   540

SOCRATES: Don't you remember how you stated that the art
of the rhapsode was different from the charioteer's?

ION: I remember.

SOCRATES: Well, and you admitted also that, being different, it
had another field of knowledge?

ION: Yes.

SOCRATES: Well then, by your own account the art of rhapsody
will not know everything, nor the rhapsode either.

ION: The exceptions, Socrates, are doubtless only such matters
as that.

SOCRATES: In 'such matters' you must include approximately b
all the other arts. Well, as the rhapsode does not know the subject

[4] *Odyssey* 20.351 sq.   [5] *Iliad* 12.200 sq.

matter of them all, what sort of matters *will* he know?

ION : The kind of thing, I judge, that a man would say, and a woman would say, and a slave and a free man, a subject and a ruler— the suitable thing for each.

SOCRATES : You mean, the rhapsode will know better what the ruler of a ship in a storm at sea should say than will the pilot?

ION : No, in that case the pilot will know better.

c SOCRATES : But suppose it is the ruler of a sick man. Will the rhapsode know better what the ruler should say than will the doctor?

ION : No, not in that case, either.

SOCRATES : But you say, 'the kind of speech that suits a slave.'

ION : Yes.

SOCRATES : You mean, for instance, if the slave is a cowherd, it is not he who will know what one should say to quiet angry cattle, but the rhapsode?

ION : Surely not.

SOCRATES : Well, 'the kind of speech that suits a woman'—one who spins—about the working up of wool?

d ION : No.

SOCRATES : Well, the rhapsodist will know 'the kind of speech that suits a man'—a general exhorting his soldiers?

ION : Yes! That is the sort of thing the rhapsodist will know.

SOCRATES : What! Is the rhapsode's art the general's?

ION : At all events I ought to know the kind of speech a general should make.

SOCRATES : Indeed, you doubtless have the talents of a general, Ion! And suppose you happened to have skill in horsemanship, along with skill in playing on the lyre, you would know when horses were well or badly ridden, but if I asked you, 'By which art, Ion, do you know that horses are well managed—is it because you are a horseman, or because you play the lyre?' What answer would you give me?

ION : I should say, 'It is by my skill as horseman.'

SOCRATES : Then, too, if you were picking out good players on the lyre, you would admit that you discerned them by your art in playing the lyre, and not by your art as horseman?

ION : Yes.

SOCRATES : But when you know of military matters, do you know them because you are competent as a general, or as a rhapsode?

ION : I cannot see a bit of difference.

541 SOCRATES : What, no difference, you say? You mean to call the art of the rhapsode and the art of the general a single art, or two?

ION : To me, there is a single art.

SOCRATES : And so, whoever is an able rhapsode is going to be an able general as well?

ION : Unquestionably, Socrates.

SOCRATES: And then, whoever happens to be an able general is
an able rhapsode too.

ION: No, I do not think that holds.

SOCRATES: But you think the other does? That whoever is an b
able rhapsode is an able general too?

ION: Absolutely!

SOCRATES: Well, and you are the ablest rhapsodist in Greece?

ION: Yes, Socrates, by far.

SOCRATES: And the ablest general, Ion? The ablest one in
Greece?

ION: You may be sure of it, for, Socrates, I learned this also out
of Homer.

SOCRATES: Then, Ion, how in heaven's name is this? You are
at once the ablest general and ablest rhapsodist among the Greeks,
and yet you go about Greece performing as a rhapsode, but not as c
general. What think you? The Greeks are in great need of a rhapsode
adorned with a wreath of gold, and do not need a general at all?

ION: It is because my native city, Socrates, is under your dominion, and your military rule, and has no need whatever of a general. As for yours and Lacedaemon, neither would choose me for
general; you think yourselves sufficient to yourselves.

SOCRATES: Excellent Ion, you know who Apollodorus is, of
Cyzicus, don't you?

ION: What might he be?

SOCRATES: The man whom the Athenians at various times
have chosen for their general, although he is an alien. The same is d
true of Phanosthenes of Andros, and Heraclides of Clazomenae, also
aliens, who nevertheless, when they had shown their competence,
were raised to the generalship by the city, and put in other high positions. And Ion of Ephesus, will she not elect him general, and accord
him honors, if his worth becomes apparent? Why, you inhabitants of
Ephesus are originally Athenians, are you not, and Ephesus is a city e
inferior to none? But the fact is, Ion, that if you are right, if it really is
by art and knowledge that you are able to praise Homer, then you do
me wrong. You assure me that you have much fine knowledge about
Homer, and you keep offering to display it, but you are deceiving me.
Far from giving the display, you will not even tell me what subject it
is on which you are so able, though all this while I have been entreat-
ing you to tell. No, you are just like Proteus; you twist and turn, this
way and that, assuming every shape, until finally you elude my grasp
and reveal yourself as a general. And all in order not to show how 542
skilled you are in the lore concerning Homer! So if you are an artist,
and, as I said just now, if you only promised me a display on Homer in
order to deceive me, then you are at fault. But if you are not an artist,
if by lot divine you are possessed by Homer, and so, knowing nothing,

speak many things and fine about the poet, just as I said you did, then you do no wrong. Choose, therefore, how you will be called by us, whether we shall take you for a man unjust, or for a man divine.

b   ION: The difference, Socrates, is great. It is far lovelier to be deemed divine.

SOCRATES: This lovelier title, Ion, shall be yours, to be in our minds divine, and not an artist, in praising Homer.

GORGIAS

In this dialogue Socrates is different. Except for two passing allusions his usual profession of ignorance has been dropped. He never says that he cannot teach because he does not know. In the Gorgias he does know, he is eager to teach—at times he talks with the fervor of an evangelist. This is not the case in the first half, where the aged Gorgias, a famous teacher of rhetoric, is refuted by Socrates when he tries to state what is the greatest good for mankind, and a pupil, Polus, eagerly takes up the argument on his behalf. Polus starts with the assertion that the greatest good is power—the all-powerful tyrant is the happy man. Slowly he is driven by Socrates to the conclusion that far from being happy the tyrant is more miserable than those he injures because to do wrong is misery; to suffer wrong is as nothing in comparison. Furthermore, the wrongdoer who is not punished, as is the case of the powerful, is more miserable than the one who is. These statements astonish Polus and dismay him even while Socrates makes them, but he sees that they result inevitably from the argument.

At this point a third man, Callicles, steps in. Is Socrates just making fun? he asks. If not, he is turning human life upside down. He pretends to be seeking for the truth, but really he is just talking religion. (Callicles calls it philosophy, but he means by it what we mean by religion.) A little religion, he says, is all very well, even good for the young, but if a man keeps on with it he is ruined. He will never gain wealth and honor that way. On the contrary, anybody can injure him and he won't defend himself. He will let himself be boxed on the ears with impunity. This is when Socrates begins to talk with fervor. He is speaking now not only to Callicles—he is thinking of all men. "For you see the subject of our discussion—and on what subject should even a man of slight intelligence be more serious?—namely, what kind of life one should live."

Callicles states his position briefly and clearly. The happy man is he who has let his passions and desires grow to the uttermost and has the power to satisfy them. This is acting according to nature and not mere convention. Men praise self-control and the like only out of weakness and cowardice, because they have not the power to take what they want. Socrates in answer repeats what he had said to

Polus. To do wrong is the worst that can befall a man. To suffer wrong is little in comparison.

What follows can hardly be called an argument. The two men cannot agree enough to be able to argue. They are too far apart. Finally Callicles is silenced, but nothing more, though Socrates' intense desire to convince him, to convert him, grows clearer and clearer. In the end he is not reasoning with him, he is exhorting him, preaching to him. He must induce him to see that the good is altogether different from the safe. He begs him not to mind if someone insults and strikes him. "For heaven's sake, let him and be of good cheer." (Turn to him the other cheek.) You can suffer by doing right, but you can never suffer harm.

The reader remembers what Phaedo said before Socrates drank the poison, "It never occurred to me to feel sorry for him. He seemed quite happy."

---

447   CALLICLES: This is how they say you should take part in warfare and battle, Socrates.

SOCRATES: What, have we arrived at the latter end of a feast, as the saying goes?

CALLICLES: Yes, and a very charming feast, for Gorgias has just given us a fine and varied display.

SOCRATES: Well, Chaerephon here is to blame, Callicles, for he compelled us to loiter in the market place.

b   CHAEREPHON: 'Tis no matter, Socrates, for I can supply the remedy too. Gorgias is a friend of mine, and will treat us to another display, now, if you want, or if not, later.

CALLICLES: What, Chaerephon? Is Socrates anxious to hear Gorgias?

CHAEREPHON: That is the very reason why we are here.

CALLICLES: Any time you like to come home with me, then, for Gorgias is staying with me and will give you an exhibition.

SOCRATES: Most kind of you, Callicles, but would he also be

c willing to converse with us? I want to learn from him what is the scope of his art and just what he professes and teaches. As for the exhibition, let him give us that, as you suggest, on some other occasion.

From *Socratic Dialogues,* translated and edited by W. D. Woodhead with an introduction by G. C. Field (Edinburgh and New York, 1953).

CALLICLES: There's nothing like asking him, Socrates, for that was one feature of his display. He bade any one of the company present just now ask any questions he pleased, and said he would answer all such questions.

SOCRATES: Splendid! Chaerephon, ask him.

CHAEREPHON: Ask him what?

SOCRATES: Who he is.   d

CHAEREPHON: What do you mean?

SOCRATES: Well, supposing he were a maker of shoes, he would surely answer you that he was a cobbler. You see what I mean, do you not?

CHAEREPHON: I see, and I will ask him. Tell me, Gorgias, is Callicles right in saying that you profess to answer any question you are asked?

GORGIAS: He is right, Chaerephon; that is the very statement I 448 made just now, and I assure you that nobody has asked me a new question these many years.

CHAEREPHON: You must indeed be ready with your answers, Gorgias.

GORGIAS: You are at liberty to make the experiment, Chaerephon.

POLUS: Yes indeed, and upon me, if you wish, Chaerephon, for Gorgias, I think, is played out; he has already spoken at great length.

CHAEREPHON: Why, Polus, do you think you could answer better than Gorgias?

POLUS: What does that matter, if it is well enough for you?   b

CHAEREPHON: Not at all, but since you want to, you may answer.

POLUS: Proceed.

CHAEREPHON: I will. If Gorgias were an expert in the same art as his brother Herodicus, what should we rightly call him? By the same professional name as his brother?

POLUS: Assuredly.

CHAEREPHON: Then we should be correct in calling him a doctor?

POLUS: Yes.

CHAEREPHON: And if he were skilled in the same art as Aristophon, son of Aglaophon, or Aristophon's brother, what should we rightly call him?

POLUS: Obviously a painter.   c

CHAEREPHON: But, as it is, in what craft is he expert, and by what name should we correctly call him?

POLUS: There are many arts, Chaerephon, among mankind experimentally devised by experience, for experience guides our life along the path of art, inexperience along the path of chance. And in each of these different arts different men partake in different ways, the best men following the best arts. And Gorgias here is one of the best and partakes in the noblest of arts.

d   SOCRATES : It is plain, Gorgias, that Polus is well equipped to make speeches, but he fails to accomplish what he promised to Chaerephon.

GORGIAS : Pray, how is that, Socrates?

SOCRATES : It seems that he does not quite answer the question asked.

GORGIAS : Well, if you prefer it, you may ask him yourself.

SOCRATES : No, not if you are ready to answer instead; I would much rather question you. For it is obvious from what Polus has said that he is much better versed in what is called rhetoric than in dialogue.

e   POLUS : How is that, Socrates?

SOCRATES : Why, Polus, because when Chaerephon asks in what art Gorgias is proficient, you praise his art as though someone were attacking it, but neglect to answer what it is.

POLUS : Did I not answer that it was the noblest of arts?

SOCRATES : Certainly. But no one is asking in what kind of art Gorgias is engaged but what it actually is and what we should call Gorgias. On the lines laid down before by Chaerephon, when you an-
449 swered correctly and briefly, tell us now in similar manner what this art is and what name we must give to Gorgias. Or rather, Gorgias, tell us yourself in what art you are expert and what we should call you.

GORGIAS : The art of rhetoric, Socrates.

SOCRATES : Then we must call you a rhetorician?

GORGIAS : Yes, and a good one, Socrates, if you really want to call me what, in Homer's expression, I boast myself to be.

SOCRATES : That is what I want.

GORGIAS : Then call me so.

b   SOCRATES : Are we to say that you can make rhetoricians of others also?

GORGIAS : That is the profession I make both here and elsewhere.

SOCRATES : Would you be willing, Gorgias, to continue our present method of conversing by question and answer, postponing to some other occasion lengthy discourses of the type begun by Polus? You must not, however, disappoint us in your promise but show yourself ready to answer the question briefly.

GORGIAS : There are certain answers, Socrates, that must neces-
c sarily be given at length; however, I will attempt to answer as briefly as possible. For that too is one of the claims I make, that nobody could give the same answers more briefly than I.

SOCRATES : That is what I want, Gorgias; give me an exhibition of this brevity of yours, and reserve a lengthy discourse for another time.

GORGIAS : I will do so, and you will admit you have never heard a speaker more concise.

SOCRATES : Well then, you claim that you are an expert in the art of rhetoric and that you can make rhetoricians of others. Now just d what is the scope of rhetoric? Weaving, for example, has to do with the making of garments. You agree?

GORGIAS : Yes.

SOCRATES : And music with composing melodies?

GORGIAS : Yes.

SOCRATES : By Hera, Gorgias, I marvel at your answers; they could not be briefer.

GORGIAS : Yes, I think I succeed pretty well, Socrates.

SOCRATES : Good, and now answer in the same way about rhetoric. What is the field of this science?

GORGIAS : Words.

SOCRATES : Of what kind, Gorgias? Those that reveal to the sick what treatment will restore their health?   e

GORGIAS : No.

SOCRATES : Then rhetoric is not concerned with every kind of words.

GORGIAS : Certainly not.

SOCRATES : Yet it makes men able to speak.

GORGIAS : Yes.

SOCRATES : And able to think also about the matter of their discourse?

GORGIAS : Of course.

SOCRATES : Now does not the science of medicine, which we 450 have just mentioned, make men able to think and to speak about their patients?

GORGIAS : Assuredly.

SOCRATES : Then medicine also, it seems, is concerned with words.

GORGIAS : Yes.

SOCRATES : Words about diseases?

GORGIAS : Certainly.

SOCRATES : And is not gymnastics concerned with words that relate to good or bad bodily condition?

GORGIAS : Undoubtedly.

SOCRATES : And so it is with the other arts also, Gorgias. Each b of them is concerned with words that have to do with its own subject matter.

GORGIAS : Evidently.

SOCRATES : Then, as the other arts have to do with words, why do you not call them by the name of 'rhetoric,' since you call rhetoric any art that is concerned with words?

GORGIAS : Because all the knowledge of the other arts is in

general, Socrates, concerned with manual crafts and similar activities, whereas rhetoric deals with no such manual product but all its
c activity and all that it accomplishes is through the medium of words. Therefore I claim that the art of rhetoric has to do with words, and maintain that my claim is correct.

SOCRATES : I wonder whether I understand the kind of thing you wish to call it. But I shall soon know more clearly. Answer me this. We admit, do we not, the existence of arts?

GORGIAS : Yes.

SOCRATES : Among the various arts there are, I think, some that consist for the most part of action and have little need of words, and some in fact have no need, but their function can be achieved in silence, as for instance painting and sculpture and many others. I fancy it is with such arts that you say rhetoric has no concern, is it
d not?

GORGIAS : You are entirely right in your opinion, Socrates.

SOCRATES : But there are other arts that secure their result entirely through words and have practically no need, or very little need, of action—arithmetic, for instance, and calculation and geometry and the game of draughts and many other arts, some of which involve almost as many words as actions, and many of them far more, their
e whole achievement and effect in general being due to words. It is to this kind of art, I believe, that you assign rhetoric.

GORGIAS : You are right.

SOCRATES : But I do not imagine that you intend to call any of these aforementioned arts rhetoric, though your actual expression was that 'the art which secures its effect through words is rhetoric.' And anyone who wished to make trouble in our debate might object: Then you call arithmetic rhetoric, Gorgias? But I do not think you mean by rhetoric either arithmetic or geometry.

451 GORGIAS : You are right, Socrates, and your supposition is quite correct.

SOCRATES : Come then, and complete for yourself the answer for which I asked. Since rhetoric is one of those arts that for the most part employ words, and since there are other such arts also, try to tell me what is the field of that particular art securing its effect through words which is called rhetoric. Suppose that somebody should ask me about any of the arts recently mentioned: Socrates, what is the art of
b arithmetic? I should reply, as you did just now, that it is one of the arts which secure their effect through speech. And if he should further inquire in what field, I should reply that of the odd and the even, however great their respective numbers might be. And if he should next inquire, What art do you call calculation? I should say that this art too is one of those that secure their entire effect through words. And if he should further demand in what field, I should reply, like the mover of an amendment in the Assembly, that in details 'hereinbe-

fore mentioned' the art of calculation resembles arithmetic—for its c
field is the same, the even and the odd—but that calculation differs in
this respect, that it investigates how the odd and the even are related both to themselves and to each other in regard to number. And
if anyone should ask about astronomy and, when I said that this science too secures its effect entirely through words, should demand,
What is the field of discourses relating to astronomy, Socrates? I
should reply, the movement of the stars, the sun, and the moon, and
their relative speed.

GORGIAS : Your statement, Socrates, is quite correct.

SOCRATES : And now let us have your reply, Gorgias. Rhetoric d
is one of the arts that achieve and fulfill their function entirely
through words, is it not?

GORGIAS : That is so.

SOCRATES : Tell me then in what field. What is the subject matter of the words employed by rhetoric?

GORGIAS : The greatest and noblest of human affairs, Socrates.

SOCRATES : But, Gorgias, what you are now saying is dis-
putable and not yet clear. I think you must have heard men singing at e
drinking parties the familiar song in which they enumerate our blessings, health being the first, beauty the second, and third, as the composer of the song claims, wealth obtained without dishonesty.

GORGIAS : I have heard it. But what is the point of your remark?

SOCRATES : Suppose the men who produce the blessings 452
praised by the author of that song should suddenly appear, the doctor, the trainer, and the businessman, and the doctor should speak
first and say, Socrates, Gorgias is deceiving you. It is not his craft, but
mine, that is concerned with the greatest blessing to mankind.

If I were to ask him, Who are you that make such a claim? he
would, I suppose, answer that he was a physician.

Then what do you mean? Is the product of your art the greatest
blessing of all?

Of course, he would doubtless reply. Health, Socrates! What
greater blessing has man than health?

And then suppose that after him the physical trainer should say, b
I too should be surprised if Gorgias could display to you a blessing
greater than mine.

I should say to him in turn, And who are you, my good fellow,
and what is your function?

A trainer, he would answer, and my task is to make men strong
and beautiful of body.

And after the trainer the businessman would speak, in utter contempt, I imagine, of all others, Pray consider, Socrates, whether you
believe there is any greater blessing than wealth, whether in the c
pocket of Gorgias or of any other man.

What? we should say to him. Is that what you make?

236 PLATO: COLLECTED DIALOGUES

Yes, he would reply.

And who are you?

A businessman.

Then, we shall say, do you judge wealth to be the greatest blessing for man?

Of course, he will answer.

And yet Gorgias here insists that his art produces greater benefits than yours, we shall say.

It is obvious then that he will next inquire, And what is this benefit? Let Gorgias tell us.

d   And so come, Gorgias, imagine you are questioned by these men and by myself as well, and answer what it is you claim to be the greatest blessing to man, and claim also to produce.

GORGIAS: Something, Socrates, that is in very truth the greatest boon, for it brings freedom to mankind in general and to each man dominion over others in his own country.

SOCRATES: And what exactly do you mean by that?

e   GORGIAS: I mean the power to convince by your words the judges in court, the senators in Council, the people in the Assembly, or in any other gathering of a citizen body. And yet possessed of such power you will make the doctor, you will make the trainer your slave, and your businessman will prove to be making money, not for himself, but for another, for you who can speak and persuade multitudes.

SOCRATES: Now at last, Gorgias, you have revealed most precisely, it seems to me, what art you consider rhetoric to be, and if I 453 understand you aright, you assert that rhetoric is a creator of persuasion, and that all its activity is concerned with this, and this is its sum and substance. Can you state any wider scope for rhetoric than to produce persuasion in the soul of the hearer?

GORGIAS: By no means, Socrates; I think you define it adequately, for that is its sum and substance.

SOCRATES: Then listen, Gorgias. I am convinced, you may be b sure, that if there is any man who in a discussion with another is anxious to know just what is the real subject under discussion, I am such a man, and I am confident that you are too.

GORGIAS: What then, Socrates?

SOCRATES: I will tell you. Just what that persuasion is which you claim is produced by rhetoric, and with what subjects it deals, I assure you, I do not know, but I have a suspicion as to what persuasion you mean, and its field. Yet I shall ask you nonetheless what you mean by the conviction produced by rhetoric and what is its province.

c And why shall I ask you instead of speaking myself, when I have this suspicion? Not for your sake, but because I am anxious that the argument should so proceed as to clarify to the utmost the matter under discussion. Consider whether I am right in asking you that further question. If I had asked you what kind of painter Zeuxis was and you had answered, a painter of living creatures, might I not with justice ask you what kind of living creatures, and where they may be found?

GORGIAS: Certainly.

SOCRATES: And the reason is that there are other painters with d many other living subjects?

GORGIAS: Yes.

SOCRATES: Whereas, if Zeuxis had been the only painter, yours would have been a good answer?

GORGIAS: Certainly.

SOCRATES: Then come, tell me about rhetoric. Do you think that rhetoric alone produces persuasion, or do other arts as well? What I mean is this. When a man teaches a subject, does he persuade where he teaches, or not?

GORGIAS: One cannot deny that, Socrates; certainly he persuades.

SOCRATES: Let us take once more the same arts as we discussed e just now. Arithmetic and the arithmetician teach us, do they not, the properties of a number?

GORGIAS: Certainly.

SOCRATES: And consequently persuade us?

GORGIAS: Yes.

SOCRATES: Then arithmetic is also a creator of persuasion?

GORGIAS: Evidently.

SOCRATES: Now, if anyone should ask us what kind of persuasion and in what field, we shall answer him, I suppose, that which teaches about the odd and the even in all their quantities, and we 454 shall be able to prove that all the other arts just mentioned are creators of persuasion and name the type and the field, shall we not?

GORGIAS: Yes.

SOCRATES: Then rhetoric is not the only creator of persuasion.

GORGIAS: That is true.

SOCRATES: Then since other arts besides rhetoric produce this result, we should be justified in asking next, as in the case of the painter, Of what kind of persuasion is rhetoric the art, and what is its province? Do you not think that is a fair question to ask next?   b

GORGIAS: I do.

SOCRATES: Then answer, Gorgias, since you share my opinion.

GORGIAS: The kind of persuasion employed in the law courts and other gatherings, Socrates, as I said just now, and concerned with right and wrong.

SOCRATES: I suspected too, Gorgias, that you meant this kind of persuasion, with such a province; it is merely that you may not be surprised if a little later I ask you the same kind of question, though the answer seems clear to me. Yet I may repeat it—for, as I said, I am c questioning you, not for your own sake, but in order that the argument may be carried forward consecutively, and that we may not form the habit of suspecting and anticipating each other's views, but that you may complete your own statements as you please, in accordance with your initial plan.

GORGIAS : I think your method is right, Socrates.

SOCRATES : Then let us consider the next point. Is there a state which you call 'having learned'?

GORGIAS : There is.

SOCRATES : And such a thing as 'having believed'?

GORGIAS : There is.

d   SOCRATES : Now do you think that to have learned and to have believed, or knowledge and belief, are one and the same or different?

GORGIAS : I consider them different, Socrates.

SOCRATES : You are right, and you can prove it thus. If anybody were to say to you, Can there be both a false belief and a true, Gorgias? you would, I think, say that there is.

GORGIAS : Yes.

SOCRATES : But can there be both a false and a true knowledge?

GORGIAS : By no means.

SOCRATES : Then it is obvious that knowledge and belief are not the same.

GORGIAS : You are right.

e   SOCRATES : But both those who have learned and those who believe have been persuaded.

GORGIAS : That is so.

SOCRATES : Shall we lay it down then that there are two forms of persuasion, the one producing belief without knowledge, the other knowledge?

GORGIAS : Certainly.

SOCRATES : Now which kind of conviction about right and wrong is produced in the law courts and other gatherings by rhetoric? That which issues in belief without knowledge, or that which issues in knowledge?

GORGIAS : Evidently, Socrates, that which issues in belief.

455   SOCRATES : Then rhetoric apparently is a creator of a conviction that is persuasive but not instructive about right and wrong.

GORGIAS : Yes.

SOCRATES : Then the rhetorician too does not instruct courts and other assemblies about right and wrong, but is able only to persuade them, for surely he could not instruct so large a gathering in a short time about matters so important.

GORGIAS : No indeed.

SOCRATES : Well then, let us see just exactly what we are saying about rhetoric, for I cannot myself yet understand what I mean.

Whenever there is a gathering in the city to choose doctors or ship- b
wrights or any other professional group, surely the rhetorician will
not then give his advice, for it is obvious that in each such choice it is
the real expert who must be selected. And when it is a question about
the building of walls or equipment of harbors or dockyards, we
consult, not the rhetoricians, but the master builders, and again
when we need advice about a choice of generals or some tactical
formation against the enemy or the occupation of positions, military experts will advise us, not rhetoricians. Or what do you say,
Gorgias, about such matters? Since you claim yourself to be a rheto- c
rician and to make rhetoricians of others, it is right to examine
you on the qualities of your art. And so, imagine that my interest is
on your behalf, for perhaps some of those present are anxious to
become your disciples—there are some, I know, quite a number, in
fact—who would be bashful perhaps about questioning you. And so,
just imagine that when I inquire, they too are asking, What shall we d
gain, Gorgias, if we associate with you? On what subjects shall we be
able to advise the city, about right and wrong alone, or the subjects
just mentioned by Socrates?

Try to answer them, then.

GORGIAS : Well, Socrates, I will try to reveal to you clearly the
full scope of rhetoric, for you have shown me the path excellently.
You know, of course, that your dockyards and the walls of Athens and
her harbor equipment are due to the advice, partly of Themistocles, e
partly of Pericles, not to that of architects.

SOCRATES : That is what they say, Gorgias, about Themistocles,
and Pericles I myself heard when he recommended the building of
the middle wall.

GORGIAS : And when any of the choices you mentioned just now 456
is in question, Socrates, you see that it is the orators who give advice
and carry their motions.

SOCRATES : That is what surprises me, Gorgias, and that is why
I asked you long since what is the scope of rhetoric. When so looked
at, it seems to me to possess almost superhuman importance.

GORGIAS : Ah, if only you knew all, Socrates, and realized that
rhetoric includes practically all other faculties under her control.
And I will give you good proof of this. I have often, along with my b
brother and with other physicians, visited one of their patients who
refused to drink his medicine or submit to the surgeon's knife or
cautery, and when the doctor was unable to persuade them, I did so,
by no other art but rhetoric. And I claim too that, if a rhetorician and
a doctor visited any city you like to name and they had to contend
in argument before the Assembly or any other gathering as to which
of the two should be chosen as doctor, the doctor would be nowhere,
but the man who could speak would be chosen, if he so wished. And c
if he should compete against any other craftsman whatever, the

rhetorician rather than any other would persuade the people to choose him, for there is no subject on which a rhetorician would not speak more persuasively than any other craftsman, before a crowd. Such then is the scope and character of rhetoric, but it should be used, Socrates, like every other competitive art. We must not employ other
d competitive arts against one and all merely because we have learned boxing or mixed fighting or weapon combat, so that we are stronger than our friends and foes; we must not, I say, for this reason strike our friends or wound or kill them. No indeed, and if a man who is physically sound has attended the wrestling school and has become a good boxer, and then strikes his father or mother or any others of his kinsmen or friends, we must not for this reason detest or banish
e from our cities the physical trainers or drill instructors. For they imparted this instruction for just employment against enemies or wrongdoers, in self-defense not aggression, but such people per-
457 versely employ their strength and skill in the wrong way. And so the teachers are not guilty, and the craft is not for this reason evil or to blame, but rather, in my opinion, those who make improper use of it. And the same argument applies also to rhetoric. The rhetorician is competent to speak against anybody on any subject, and to prove
b himself more convincing before a crowd on practically every topic he wishes, but he should not any the more rob the doctors—or any other craftsmen either—of their reputation, merely because he has this power. One should make proper use of rhetoric as of athletic gifts. And if a man becomes a rhetorician and makes a wrongful use of this faculty and craft, you must not, in my opinion, detest and
c banish his teacher from the city. For he imparted it for a good use, but the pupil abuses it. And therefore it is the man who abuses it whom we should rightly detest and banish and put to death, not his instructor.

SOCRATES: I think, Gorgias, that, like myself, you have had much experience in discussions and must have observed that speakers can seldom define the topic of debate and after mutual instruc-
d tion and enlightenment bring the meeting to a close, but if they are in dispute and one insists that the other's statements are incorrect or obscure, they grow angry and imagine their opponent speaks with malice toward them, being more anxious for verbal victory than to investigate the subject under discussion. And finally some of them part in the most disgraceful fashion, after uttering and listening to such abusive language that their audience are disgusted with them-
e selves for having deigned to give ear to such fellows. Now why do I say this? Because, it seems to me, what you are now saying is not quite consistent or in tune with what you said at first about rhetoric. But I am afraid to cross-examine you, for fear you might think my pertinacity is directed against you, and not to the clarification of the

matter in question. Now, if you are the same kind of man as I am, I 458
should be glad to question you; if not, I will let you alone. And what
kind of man am I? One of those who would gladly be refuted if anything I say is not true, and would gladly refute another who says
what is not true, but would be no less happy to be refuted myself than
to refute, for I consider that a greater benefit, inasmuch as it is a
greater boon to be delivered from the worst of evils oneself than to deliver another. And I believe there is no worse evil for man than a false
opinion about the subject of our present discussion. If you then are the b
same kind of man as I am, let us continue, but if you feel that we
should drop the matter, then let us say good-by to the argument and
dismiss it.

GORGIAS: No, I claim to be myself the type of man you indicate, but perhaps we ought to have been thinking of our audience. For
quite a time ago before your arrival I gave a long display to the company present, and now, perhaps, if we continue our debate, it will be
a prolonged affair. So we should consider the convenience of our
audience, in case we are detaining here some who are anxious to be c
doing something else.

CHAEREPHON: You can hear for yourselves, Gorgias and Socrates, the protests of the company, who are eager to hear whatever
you have to say; as for me, heaven forbid I should have any engagement so pressing as to desert a conversation of such a character and
between such interlocutors for however profitable an occupation.

CALLICLES: Indeed, Chaerephon, I too have listened to many d
a debate, but I think I have never enjoyed one so much as this. I shall
be delighted in fact if you are ready to talk all day long.

SOCRATES: Well, I have no objections to offer, if Gorgias is
willing.

GORGIAS: After all this, Socrates, it would be disgraceful of me
to refuse, when I personally volunteered to meet any question that
might be put. But if those present agree, carry on the conversation and
ask what you will. e

SOCRATES: Then listen, Gorgias, to what surprises me in your
statement, for perhaps you were right and I misunderstood you. You
claim you can make a rhetorician of any man who wishes to learn
from you?

GORGIAS: Yes.

SOCRATES: With the result that he would be convincing about
any subject before a crowd, not through instruction but by persuasion?

GORGIAS: Certainly. 459

SOCRATES: Well, you said just now that a rhetorician will be
more persuasive than a doctor regarding health.

GORGIAS: Yes, I said so, before a crowd.

SOCRATES: And before a crowd means among the ignorant, for surely, among those who know, he will not be more convincing than the doctor.

GORGIAS: That is quite true.

SOCRATES: Then if he is more persuasive than the doctor, he is more persuasive than the man who knows?

GORGIAS: Certainly.

b   SOCRATES: Though not himself a doctor.

GORGIAS: Yes.

SOCRATES: And he who is not a doctor is surely ignorant of what a doctor knows.

GORGIAS: Obviously.

SOCRATES: Therefore when the rhetorician is more convincing than the doctor, the ignorant is more convincing among the ignorant than the expert. Is that our conclusion, or is something else?

GORGIAS: That is the conclusion, in this instance.

SOCRATES: Is not the position of the rhetorician and of rhetoric the same with respect to other arts also? It has no need to know the truth about things but merely to discover a technique of persuasion, c so as to appear among the ignorant to have more knowledge than the expert?

GORGIAS: But is not this a great comfort, Socrates, to be able without learning any other arts but this one to prove in no way inferior to the specialists?

SOCRATES: Whether or not the rhetorician is inferior to other craftsmen for this reason, we will consider later, if the question should prove relevant. But now let us first investigate whether the re- d lation of the rhetorician to right and wrong, the noble and the base, the just and the unjust is the same as it is to health and the objects of the other arts—whether he does not know what is right or wrong, noble or base, just or unjust, but has contrived a technique of persuasion in these matters, so that, though ignorant, he appears among the ignorant to know better than the expert. Or must your prospective e pupil in rhetoric have such knowledge and bring it with him when he comes to you? And if he is ignorant, will you, his teacher of rhetoric, teach your pupil none of these things—for that is not your concern— but make him appear before the crowd to have such knowledge, when he has it not, and appear to be a good man, when he is not? Or will you be utterly unable to teach him rhetoric if he does not beforehand know the truth about these matters? How do we stand here, Gorgias? In heaven's name, reveal, as you promised just now, the true 460 power of rhetoric.

GORGIAS: Well, Socrates, I suppose that if he does not possess this knowledge, he can learn these things also from me.

SOCRATES: Stop one moment! What you say is right. If you make a rhetorician of any man, he must already have knowledge of right and wrong either by previous acquaintance or by learning it from you.

GORGIAS : Certainly.

SOCRATES : Now is not the man who has learned the art of car- b pentry a carpenter?

GORGIAS : Yes.

SOCRATES : And he who has learned the art of music a musician?

GORGIAS : Yes.

SOCRATES : And he who has learned medicine a physician? And so too on the same principle, the man who has learned anything becomes in each case such as his knowledge makes him?

GORGIAS : Certainly.

SOCRATES : Then according to this principle he who has learned justice is just.

GORGIAS : Most assuredly.

SOCRATES : And the just man, I suppose, does just acts?

GORGIAS : Yes.

SOCRATES : Now the rhetorician must necessarily be just, and c the man must wish to do just actions?

GORGIAS : Evidently.

SOCRATES : Then the just man will never wish to do injustice?

GORGIAS : Necessarily.

SOCRATES : And our argument demands that the rhetorician be just?

GORGIAS : Yes.

SOCRATES : Then the rhetorician will never wish to do wrong?

GORGIAS : Evidently not.

SOCRATES : Now do you remember saying a short while ago that we should not blame our trainers or expel them from our cities, d if a boxer practices his art in a wrongful manner and does injury, and so too if a rhetorician makes wrongful use of his rhetoric, we should not censure or banish his instructor but rather the guilty man who wrongly employs rhetoric? Was this said or not?

GORGIAS : It was said.

SOCRATES : But now it is clear that this same rhetorician e would never do wrong, is it not?

GORGIAS : It is clear.

SOCRATES : And in our earlier discussion, Gorgias, it was stated that rhetoric is concerned with words that deal, not with the odd and even, but with right and wrong. Is that so?

GORGIAS : Yes.

SOCRATES : Now at the time when you stated this, I considered that rhetoric could never be a thing of evil, since its discourse is always concerned with justice. But when a little later you said that the rhetorician might actually make an evil use of rhetoric, I was 461 surprised, and considering that what was said was inconsistent, I spoke as I did, saying that if, like myself, you thought it of value to be refuted, it was worth while pursuing the conversation, but if not, we should let it drop. And as a result of our subsequent review you can see for yourself it is admitted that the rhetorician is incapable of making a wrong use of rhetoric and unwilling to do wrong. Now, by

b the dog, Gorgias, it will need no short discussion to settle satisfactorily where the truth lies.

POLUS : What, Socrates? Is what you are saying your true opinion about rhetoric? Or do you imagine just because Gorgias was ashamed not to admit that the rhetorician will know the just also and the honorable and the good, and that, if any man came to him without this knowledge, he himself would instruct him, and then, as result, I suppose, of this admission a contradiction arose in the argu-

c ment—which is just what you love and you yourself steer the argument in that direction—why, who do you think will deny that he himself knows the right and will teach it to others? But it is the height of bad taste to lead discussions into such channels.

SOCRATES : My noble friend Polus, the very reason why we acquire friends and children is that when we ourselves grow old and make slips, you younger people present may set us right both in ac-

d tions and in words. And now if Gorgias and I are tripping anywhere in our argument, here you are to lend a helping hand—it is only right that you should do so—and if you think that any of our admissions are at fault, I am willing to retract whatever you desire, provided that you observe one condition.

POLUS : What is that?

SOCRATES : That you restrain that exuberance, Polus, which you set out to use at first.

POLUS : What? May I not speak at what length I please?

e SOCRATES : It would indeed be hard on you, my good friend, if, on coming to Athens, the one spot in Greece where there is the utmost freedom of speech, you alone should be denied it. But look at my side. Would it not be hard on me also, if I may not go away and refuse to listen, when you speak at length and will not answer the question? But

462 if you have any interest in what has been said and wish to set it right, then, as I said just now, retract whatever you please, question and answer in turn, as Gorgias and I did, and refute me and be refuted. For you say, to be sure, that you know what Gorgias knows, do you not?

POLUS : I do.

SOCRATES : And do you not also bid anyone at any time to ask you what he will, since you know how to answer?

POLUS : Certainly.

b SOCRATES : Then do whichever of the two you choose now, question or answer.

POLUS: Well then, I will do so. Answer me, Socrates. Since Gorgias seems to you at a loss regarding the nature of rhetoric, what do you say it is?

SOCRATES: Are you asking what art I hold it to be?

POLUS: I am.

SOCRATES: To tell you the truth, Polus, no art at all.

POLUS: But what do you think rhetoric is?

SOCRATES: Something of which you claim to have made an art in your treatise which I recently read.   c

POLUS: What do you mean?

SOCRATES: I call it a kind of routine.

POLUS: Then you think rhetoric is a routine?

SOCRATES: Subject to your approval, I do.

POLUS: What kind of routine?

SOCRATES: One that produces gratification and pleasure.

POLUS: Then you do not think rhetoric a fine thing, if it can produce gratification among men?

SOCRATES: What, Polus? Have you already learned from me what I consider rhetoric to be, that you proceed to ask if I do not d think it a fine thing?

POLUS: Have I not learned that you call it a kind of routine?

SOCRATES: Well, since you prize gratification so highly, will you gratify me to a small extent?

POLUS: I will.

SOCRATES: Then ask me what kind of art I consider cookery.

POLUS: I will. What art is cookery?

SOCRATES: No art, Polus.

POLUS: Then what is it? Tell me.

SOCRATES: In my opinion, a kind of routine.

POLUS: Tell me, what routine?

SOCRATES: One that produces gratification and pleasure, I e claim, Polus.

POLUS: Then cookery and rhetoric are identical?

SOCRATES: By no means, but each is a part of the same activity.

POLUS: And what is that?

SOCRATES: I am afraid it may sound unmannerly to tell the truth, and I hesitate for fear that Gorgias may think I am caricaturing his profession. For my part, I do not know whether this is the rhetoric that Gorgias practices—for we reached no definite conclusion 463 in our recent argument as to his opinion—but what I mean by rhetoric is part of an activity that is not very reputable.

GORGIAS: What is it, Socrates? Tell us and feel no scruples about me.

SOCRATES: Well then, Gorgias, the activity as a whole, it seems to me, is not an art, but the occupation of a shrewd and

enterprising spirit, and of one naturally skilled in its dealings with
b men, and in sum and substance I call it 'flattery.' Now it seems to me
that there are many other parts of this activity, one of which is cookery. This is considered an art, but in my judgment is no art, only a
routine and a knack. And rhetoric I call another part of this general
activity, and beautification, and sophistic—four parts with four distinct objects. Now if Polus wishes to question me, let him do so, for he
has not yet ascertained what part of flattery I call rhetoric. He does not
c realize that I have not yet answered him, but proceeds to ask if I do
not think it something fine. But I shall not answer whether I consider
rhetoric a fine thing or a bad until I have first answered what it is.
For that is not right, Polus. Then if you wish to question me, ask me
what part of flattery I claim rhetoric to be.

POLUS : I will then; answer, what part?

d   SOCRATES : I wonder whether you will understand my answer. Rhetoric in my opinion is the semblance of a part of politics.

POLUS : Well then, do you call it good or bad?

SOCRATES : Bad—for evil things I call bad—if I must answer
you as though you already understood what I mean.

GORGIAS : Why, Socrates, even I myself do not grasp your
meaning.

e   SOCRATES : Naturally enough, Gorgias, for I have not yet clari-
fied my statement. But Polus here, like a foal, is young and flighty.

GORGIAS : Well, let him alone, and tell me what you mean by
saying that rhetoric is the semblance of a part of politics.

SOCRATES : I will try to explain to you my conception of rhetoric, and if it is wrong, Polus will refute me. You admit the existence
of bodies and souls?

464   GORGIAS : Of course.

SOCRATES : And do you not consider that there is a healthy condition for each?

GORGIAS : I do.

SOCRATES : And a condition of apparent, but not real health?
For example, many people appear to be healthy of body, and no one
could perceive they are not so, except a doctor or some physical
trainer.

GORGIAS : That is true.

SOCRATES : There exists, I maintain, both in body and in soul, a
condition which creates an impression of good health in each
case, although it is false.

b   GORGIAS : That is so.

SOCRATES : Let me see now if I can explain more clearly what
I mean. To the pair, body and soul, there correspond two arts—that
concerned with the soul I call the political art; to the single art that relates to the body I cannot give a name offhand. But this single art

that cares for the body comprises two parts, gymnastics and medicine, and in the political art what corresponds to gymnastics is legislation, while the counterpart of medicine is justice. Now in each case c
the two arts encroach upon each other, since their fields are the same,
medicine upon gymnastics, and justice upon legislation; nevertheless
there is a difference between them. There are then these four arts
which always minister to what is best, one pair for the body, the other
for the soul. But flattery perceiving this—I do not say by knowledge
but by conjecture—has divided herself also into four branches, and
insinuating herself into the guise of each of these parts, pretends to be d
that which she impersonates. And having no thought for what is
best, she regularly uses pleasure as a bait to catch folly and deceives
it into believing that she is of supreme worth. Thus it is that cookery
has impersonated medicine and pretends to know the best foods for
the body, so that, if a cook and a doctor had to contend in the presence of children or of men as senseless as children, which of the
two, doctor or cook, was an expert in wholesome and bad food, the
doctor would starve to death. This then I call a form of flattery, and e
I claim that this kind of thing is bad—I am now addressing you, 465
Polus—because it aims at what is pleasant, ignoring the good, and I
insist that it is not an art but a routine, because it can produce no
principle in virtue of which it offers what it does, nor explain the
nature thereof, and consequently is unable to point to the cause of
each thing it offers. And I refuse the name of art to anything irrational.
But if you have any objections to lodge, I am willing to submit to further examination.

Cookery then, as I say, is a form of flattery that corresponds to b
medicine, and in the same way gymnastics is personated by beautification, a mischievous, deceitful, mean, and ignoble activity, which
cheats us by shapes and colors, by smoothing and draping, thereby
causing people to take on an alien charm to the neglect of the natural
beauty produced by exercise.

To be brief, then, I will express myself in the language of
geometricians—for by now perhaps you may follow me. Sophistic is c
to legislation what beautification is to gymnastics, and rhetoric to
justice what cookery is to medicine. But, as I say, while there is this
natural distinction between them, yet because they are closely related, Sophist and rhetorician, working in the same sphere and upon
the same subject matter, tend to be confused with each other, and
they know not what to make of each other, nor do others know what
to make of them. For if the body was under the control, not of the d
soul, but of itself, and if cookery and medicine were not investigated
and distinguished by the soul, but the body instead gave the verdict,
weighing them by the bodily pleasures they offered, then the principle
of Anaxagoras would everywhere hold good—that is something you

know about, my dear Polus—and all things would be mingled in indiscriminate confusion, and medicine and health and cookery would be indistinguishable.

e Well, now you have heard my conception of rhetoric. It is the counterpart in the soul of what cookery is to the body. And perhaps I have acted strangely in speaking at such great length after forbidding you a lengthy discourse. But it is only fair that you should excuse me, for when I spoke briefly you did not understand and you were unable to make anything of the answer I gave you but needed an explanation.

466 If then I cannot follow any answer of yours, you too may speak at length; but if I can, then indulge me by being brief, for that is fair. And now, make what you can of my answer.

POLUS : What is it you say then? Do you hold that rhetoric is flattery?

SOCRATES : No, I said 'a part of flattery.' Can you not remember at your age, Polus? What will you do when you are older?

POLUS : Do you think then that good rhetoricians are considered but poor creatures in the cities because they are flatterers?

b SOCRATES : Is that a question, or the beginning of a speech?

POLUS : It is a question I am asking.

SOCRATES : In my opinion they are not considered at all.

POLUS : How are they not considered? Are they not most powerful in their cities?

SOCRATES : No, if by power you mean something good for its possessor.

POLUS : I do indeed mean that.

SOCRATES : Then in my opinion rhetoricians have the least power of any in the state.

POLUS : What? Do they not, like tyrants, put to death any man c they will, and deprive of their fortunes and banish whomsoever it seems best?

SOCRATES : By the dog, at every word you utter, Polus, I am puzzled as to whether you are speaking for yourself and expressing your own views, or questioning me.

POLUS : I am questioning you.

SOCRATES : Well, my friend, then you ask me two questions at once.

POLUS : What two questions?

SOCRATES : Did you not say just now, Do not the orators put to death whomsoever they will, and deprive of their fortunes and banish d from the state whomsoever it seems best?

POLUS : I did.

SOCRATES : Then I claim that there are two questions here, and I will answer both. I say, Polus, that orators and tyrants have the very least power of any in our cities, as I stated just now, for they do

practically nothing that they will, but do only what seems best to
them.   e

POLUS: Well, is not that to possess great power?

SOCRATES: No indeed, according to Polus.

POLUS: According to me? Indeed I affirm that it is.

SOCRATES: By the ——, you do not, since you said that great
power was a good for its possessor.

POLUS: So I do say.

SOCRATES: Do you call it good, then, if a man without intelligence does what seems best to him? And do you call this great power?

POLUS: Not I.

SOCRATES: Then refute me and prove that orators have intelligence and that rhetoric is an art, not a form of flattery. But if you   467
leave me unrefuted, then the orators who do what seems good to
them in our cities and the tyrants will possess no benefit herein, for
power, as you say, is a good, but you too admit that to do what seems
good to you without intelligence is an evil, do you not?

POLUS: I do.

SOCRATES: Then how can rhetoricians or tyrants possess great
power in our cities, unless Polus proves against Socrates that they
do what they will?

POLUS: This fellow . . .   b

SOCRATES: I deny that they do what they will; now refute me.

POLUS: Did you not just now admit that they do what seems
best to them?

SOCRATES: Yes, and I still admit it.

POLUS: Then are they not doing what they will?

SOCRATES: That I deny.

POLUS: When they do what seems good to them?

SOCRATES: Yes.

POLUS: What you say is shocking and fantastic, Socrates.

SOCRATES: No need to offend, Polus, my friend—to address
you in your own style. But if you have any questions to ask me, prove c
that my view is false; if not, answer for yourself.

POLUS: Well, I am willing to answer, if only to learn what
you mean.

SOCRATES: Do you consider, then, that men will what on any
occasion they are doing, or rather that for the sake of which they act
as they do? For example, do you consider that those who drink medicine at the doctor's orders will what they are doing, namely the drinking of medicine with all its unpleasantness, or the health for the sake
of which they drink?

POLUS: Obviously, the health.

SOCRATES: So too with those who sail the seas and engage in d
money-making in general—they do not will what they do on each

occasion. For who desires to sail and suffer dangers and troubles? But they will, in my opinion, that for the sake of which they sail, namely wealth, for it is for wealth's sake that they sail.

POLUS : Certainly.

SOCRATES : And is not this a general truth? If a man acts with some purpose, he does not will the act, but the purpose of the act.

e   POLUS : Yes.

SOCRATES : Now is there anything in the world that is not either good or bad or intermediate between the two, neither good nor bad?

POLUS : Things must inevitably be so, Socrates.

SOCRATES : And by good you mean wisdom and health and wealth and other such things, and by evils their opposites?

POLUS : I do.

SOCRATES : And by neither good nor bad you mean such things
468   as partake now of the one, now of the other, and sometimes of neither, as for example, sitting, walking, running, and sailing, or again such objects as stones and timbers and the like? Is not that what you mean? Or do you mean some other class of objects by what is neither good nor bad?

POLUS : No, I mean these.

SOCRATES : Now do men, when they act, perform these indifferent actions for the sake of good, or the good for the sake of the indifferent?

POLUS : Surely the indifferent for the sake of the good.

b   SOCRATES : It is in pursuit of the good, then, that we walk when we walk, thinking this the better course, and when on the contrary we stand, we stand for the same reason, for the sake of the good. Is it not so?

POLUS : Yes.

SOCRATES : And do we not kill a man, when we do so, or banish him or confiscate his property, because we think it better so to act than not?

POLUS : Certainly.

SOCRATES : Then those who act thus always act for the sake of the good.

POLUS : I agree.

SOCRATES : Now did we not admit that when we act with some
c   purpose in view, we do not will the act but the purpose of the act?

POLUS : Certainly.

SOCRATES : Then when we slaughter or banish from the city or deprive of property, we do not thus simply will these acts. But if they are advantageous to us, we will them; if harmful, we do not. For as you say, we will the good, not what is neither good nor evil, nor what is evil. Do you think my statement is true or not, Polus? Why do you not answer?

POLUS: It is true.

SOCRATES: If we admit this, then if a man, whether tyrant d or rhetorician, kills another or banishes him or confiscates his property, because he thinks it to his advantage, and it proves to be to his harm, the man surely does what seems good to him, does he not?

POLUS: Yes.

SOCRATES: But is he doing what he wills, if his conduct proves harmful? Why do you not answer?

POLUS: No, it seems to me he is not doing what he wills.

SOCRATES: Can such a man possibly possess great power then e in his city, if, as you yourself admit, great power is a good thing?

POLUS: It is impossible.

SOCRATES: Then I was right in saying it is possible that a man who does what seems good to him in the state has no great power and does not do what he wills.

POLUS: Just as if you, Socrates, would not like to be at liberty to do whatever seemed good to you in the state rather than not, and are not jealous when you see a man killing or imprisoning or depriving of property as seems good to him!

SOCRATES: Do you mean justly or unjustly?

POLUS: Whichever way, is he not to be envied in either case?   469

SOCRATES: Hush, Polus!

POLUS: Why?

SOCRATES: Because we should not envy the unenviable and miserable, but pity them.

POLUS: What? Is that your impression of the men of whom I am speaking?

SOCRATES: Of course.

POLUS: Then you consider miserable and pitiable him who puts to death any man he pleases, and does so justly?

SOCRATES: No, not that, but he is not to be envied either.

POLUS: Did you not call him miserable just now?

SOCRATES: The man who puts to death unjustly, my friend, b and he is pitiable too, but he who does so justly is not to be envied.

POLUS: Surely it is the man unjustly put to death who is pitiable and wretched.

SOCRATES: Less so than his slayer, Polus, and less than he who is put to death justly.

POLUS: How is that Socrates?

SOCRATES: In view of the fact that to do wrong is the greatest of evils.

POLUS: Is that the greatest? Is it not a greater to suffer wrong?

SOCRATES: Most certainly not.

POLUS : Then you would wish rather to suffer than to do wrong?

c   SOCRATES : I would not wish either, but if I had either to do or to suffer wrong, I would choose rather to suffer than to do it.

POLUS : Then you would not be ready to become a tyrant?

SOCRATES : No, if by tyrant you mean what I do.

POLUS : I mean what I said just now, to be at liberty to do what I please in the state—to kill, to exile, and to follow my own pleasure in every act.

SOCRATES : Heavens, man! Let me have my say and then attack me with your argument. Supposing I should meet you in the d crowded market place with a dagger up my sleeve and say to you, Polus, I have just recently acquired a wondrous power, a tyranny. If I resolve that any of these people you see now should die, he will be dead in an instant. And if I decide that anyone should have his head broken, it will be broken at once, or that his cloak shall be torn, it will be torn. So great is my power in the city.

e   If then you disbelieve me and I showed you the dagger, you would, I imagine, say on seeing it, Socrates, in this sense anybody might have great power, for in this way one might burn any house he pleased, yes, and the Athenian dockyards too and all the warships and any vessel public or private.

But after all merely to do what one pleases is not to possess great power, do you think so?

POLUS : Not in the circumstances mentioned.

470   SOCRATES : Can you tell me then what fault you find with such power?

POLUS : I can.

SOCRATES : What is it? Tell me.

POLUS : It is that a man who thus behaves must surely be punished.

SOCRATES : And is not punishment an evil?

POLUS : Certainly.

SOCRATES : Does it not seem to you on the contrary, my strange friend, that when a man does what he pleases, if his action is accompanied by advantage, it is a good thing and this apparently is the meaning of great power, but otherwise, it is an evil thing and implies b small power? Let us examine this point too. Do we not admit that sometimes it is better to do the things we have just mentioned, to kill men and banish and confiscate their property, and sometimes not?

POLUS : Certainly.

SOCRATES : On this point, then, it seems, both you and I are in agreement.

POLUS : Yes.

SOCRATES : Now when do you say it is better to do these things? Tell me what is your criterion?

POLUS : No, you answer that, Socrates.

SOCRATES: Then if you prefer to hear the answer from me, c
I say it is better so to act, Polus, when it is a just action, worse when
it is unjust.

POLUS: It is difficult indeed to refute you, Socrates! Why, even
a child could prove you are wrong.

SOCRATES: Then I shall be very grateful to that child, and
equally so to you, if you refute me and rid me of my nonsense. Be
not weary of doing a kindness to a friend, but refute me.

POLUS: Well, there is no need to consult ancient history to
refute you, for events that took place yesterday or the day before are
sufficient to refute you and prove that many men who do wrong are d
happy.

SOCRATES: What events are these?

POLUS: You see that Archelaus, son of Perdiccas, is ruler of
Macedonia.

SOCRATES: If I do not see it, I at least hear it.

POLUS: Now do you consider him happy or wretched?

SOCRATES: I do not know, Polus. I have never met the man.

POLUS: What, must you have met him to know? Can you not e
judge offhand that he is happy?

SOCRATES: No indeed, I cannot.

POLUS: Obviously then you will say that you do not know
whether the Great King himself is happy.

SOCRATES: And I shall be telling the truth, for I do not know
how he stands in education and justice.

POLUS: What? Does happiness rest entirely upon this?

SOCRATES: Yes, in my opinion, Polus, for the man and woman
who are noble and good I call happy, but the evil and base I call
wretched.

POLUS: Then according to you Archelaus is wretched.   471

SOCRATES: If, my friend, he is wicked.

POLUS: Wicked? Of course he is! He had no claim to the power
he now enjoys, being the son of a woman who was a slave to Alcetas,
the brother of Perdiccas, and by rights he was the slave of Alcetas. And
if he had chosen to act justly, he would still have been his slave and,
according to you, would have been happy, but now he has become
monstrous unhappy, since he has done the greatest of wrongs. In the b
first place he sent for this master and uncle of his, ostensibly to restore to him the power of which Perdiccas had deprived him, and
then entertained the man and his son, Alexander, who was his own
cousin and about his own age, and after making them drunk he flung
them into a wagon, took them away by night, and made away with
them by murder. And these crimes he committed without realizing
that he was the most wretched of men, and felt no regrets. But a little
later, so far from wishing to become happy by justly bringing up the c
rightful heir to the throne, his own brother, the legitimate son of

Perdiccas, a child of about seven years, and restoring the throne to him, he threw him into a well and drowned him, and then told the child's mother, Cleopatra, that the boy had fallen in and killed himself while chasing a goose. And so now, after committing greater crimes than any in Macedonia, he is the most wretched, not the happiest, of all Macedonians, and I suppose there are other Athe-

d nians besides yourself who would prefer to be any Macedonian rather than Archelaus.

SOCRATES : At the very beginning of our discussion, Polus, I praised you for being in my opinion well trained in rhetoric, though you had neglected dialectic. And now is this the argument whereby even a child might refute me, and have I now, as you imagine, been refuted by it when I claim that the wrongdoer is not happy? How so, my good fellow? Indeed I do not admit a word of what you say.

e   POLUS : You refuse to, though you really think as I do.

SOCRATES : My dear sir, you are trying to refute me orator-fashion, like those who fancy they are refuting in the law courts. For there one group imagines it is refuting the other when it produces many reputable witnesses to support its statements whereas the opposing party produces but one or none. But this method of proof is

472 worthless toward discovering the truth, for at times a man may be the victim of false witness on the part of many people of repute. And now practically all men, Athenians and strangers alike, will support your statements, if you wish to produce them as witnesses that my view is false. If you choose, you may cite as witnesses Nicias, son of Niceratus, and his brothers, who dedicated the long line of tripods in the precinct of Dionysus; or, if you choose, Aristocrates, son of Scellias,

b who made that splendid offering at the shrine of Apollo; or, if you choose, the whole household of Pericles or any other family you like to select in Athens. Yet I, who am but one, do not agree with you, for you cannot compel me to; you are merely producing many false witnesses against me in your endeavor to drive me out of my property, the truth. But if I cannot produce in you yourself a single witness in agreement with my views, I consider that I have accomplished noth-

c ing worth speaking of in the matter under debate; and the same, I think, is true for you also, if I, one solitary witness, do not testify for you and if you do not leave all these others out of account. Now here is one form of refutation accepted by you and by many others, but there is also another, according to my opinion. Let us compare them, then, and consider whether there is any difference between them. For the questions in dispute are by no means trivial, but are, one might say, matters wherein knowledge is noblest and ignorance most shameful—the sum and substance of them being knowledge or ignorance of who is happy and who is not. For example, to take first

d the subject of our present discussion, you think it possible for a man to be happy though he is evil and acts wickedly, since you judge Archelaus wicked and yet happy. Are we to consider this is your opinion?

POLUS: Certainly.

SOCRATES: But I say it is impossible. That is one point in dispute. Well, the evildoer will be happy, will he not, if he meets with justice and punishment?

POLUS: Decidedly not. Under those conditions he would be most unhappy.

SOCRATES: Then according to you, if the evildoer is not pun- e ished, he will be happy.

POLUS: That is what I say.

SOCRATES: But according to my opinion, Polus, the wicked man and the doer of evil is in any case unhappy, but more unhappy if he does not meet with justice and suffer punishment, less unhappy if he pays the penalty and suffers punishment from gods and men.

POLUS: That is a preposterous theory you are attempting to up- 473 hold, Socrates.

SOCRATES: I shall try to make you share it with me, my friend, for I account you a friend. For the moment then, these are our points of difference—just consider for yourself. I said a short while ago that it was worse to do than to suffer wrong.

POLUS: Certainly.

SOCRATES: But you said it was worse to suffer it.

POLUS: Yes.

SOCRATES: And I said that evildoers are unhappy and was confuted by you.

POLUS: Yes, unquestionably.

SOCRATES: According to your opinion.   b

POLUS: And my opinion is right.

SOCRATES: Possibly so. And you maintain evildoers are happy, if they escape punishment.

POLUS: Certainly.

SOCRATES: But I claim they are the unhappiest of all, and that those who are punished are less so. Do you want to refute that?

POLUS: That of course is more difficult to refute than your first point, Socrates.

SOCRATES: Not difficult, Polus, but impossible, for the truth is never refuted.

POLUS: What do you mean? If a man is caught in a criminal plot to make himself tyrant, and when caught is put to the rack and c mutilated and has his eyes burned out and after himself suffering and seeing his wife and children suffer many other signal outrages of various kinds is finally impaled or burned in a coat of pitch, will he be happier than if he escaped arrest, established himself as a tyrant,

and lived the rest of his life a sovereign in his state, doing what he
pleased, an object of envy and felicitation among citizens and stran-
d gers alike? Is this what you say is impossible to refute?

SOCRATES: Now you are trying to make my flesh creep, my
noble friend, instead of refuting me, and just now you were appealing
to witnesses. However, refresh my memory a trifle. Did you say
'criminally plotting to make himself a tyrant'?

POLUS: I did.

SOCRATES: In that case neither one will be happier than the
other, neither he who by evil means achieves a tyranny nor he who
is punished—for of two miserable creatures one cannot be the happier—but he who escapes detection and becomes a tyrant is the more
e wretched. What is this, Polus? Do you laugh? Is this another form of
rebutting, to laugh at a man when he speaks, instead of refuting
him?

POLUS: Do you not consider yourself already refuted, Socrates,
when you put forward views that nobody would accept? Why, ask
anyone present!

SOCRATES: I am no politician, Polus, and last year when I became a member of the Council and my tribe was presiding and it was
my duty to put the question to the vote, I raised a laugh because I
474 did not know how to. And so do not on this occasion either bid me put
the question to those present, but if you can contrive no better refutation than this, then leave it to me in my turn, as I suggested just now,
and try out what I consider the proper form of refutation. For I know
how to produce one witness to the truth of what I say, the man
with whom I am debating, but the others I ignore. I know how to secure one man's vote, but with the many I will not even enter into
b discussion. Consider then whether you are willing in your turn to
submit to the test by answering my questions. For I think that you and
all other men as well as myself hold it worse to do than to suffer
wrong and worse to escape than to suffer punishment.

POLUS: And I maintain that neither I nor any other man so believes. Why, would you rather suffer than do wrong?

SOCRATES: Yes, and so would you and everyone else.

POLUS: Far from it! Neither I nor you nor anyone.

c   SOCRATES: Will you answer then?

POLUS: Certainly, for I am anxious to know what you will say.

SOCRATES: If you wish to know then, answer me, as if I were
beginning my questions to you. Which do you consider the worse,
Polus, to do or to suffer wrong?

POLUS: I? To suffer wrong.

SOCRATES: Well, and is it more shameful to do or to suffer
wrong?

POLUS: To do wrong.

SOCRATES: Is it not worse also, if more shameful?

POLUS: By no means.

SOCRATES: I see. Apparently you do not consider the good and d the fair to be the same, nor the evil and the shameful.

POLUS: I do not.

SOCRATES: And the next point. When you call things fair, such as bodies and colors and figures and sounds and institutions, you must do so surely with reference to some standard. For instance, in the first place do you not call bodies fair either in virtue of the service for which each one is useful, or the pleasure which the sight of them produces in the beholder? Is there any reason outside these which you can give for calling a body fair?

POLUS: I can give none.

SOCRATES: Do you not in the same way name all other things e also—figures perhaps or colors—fair either because of some pleasure or use they render or for both reasons together?

POLUS: I do.

SOCRATES: And similarly with sounds and all that is concerned with music?

POLUS: Yes.

SOCRATES: And further, with regard to laws and institutions— the fine ones, I mean—their beauty does not lie outside these limits of the pleasurable, the useful, or both?

POLUS: No, I do not think so.

SOCRATES: And it is the same with the beauty of forms of 475 learning.

POLUS: Certainly, and now you are offering a fine definition of the beautiful, Socrates, in defining it by pleasure and the good.

SOCRATES: Then you define the base by the opposites, pain and evil?

POLUS: Necessarily.

SOCRATES: Therefore when of two things that are fine one excels the other in beauty, that superior excellence is due to superior pleasure or usefulness or both?

POLUS: Certainly.

SOCRATES: And when of two things shameful one exceeds the other in baseness, this excess will be due to an excess either of pain or b of evil. Must it not be so?

POLUS: Yes.

SOCRATES: Well then, what was said just now about doing and suffering wrong? Did you not say it is worse to suffer wrong, but more shameful to inflict it?

POLUS: I said so.

SOCRATES: Then if it is more shameful to do than to suffer wrong, it is either more painful, and more shameful through excess of pain, or of evil, or of both. Must this not be so?

POLUS: Of course.

c   SOCRATES : Now let us first consider whether the infliction of wrong exceeds the suffering of it in pain, and whether wrongdoers suffer more pain than their victims.

POLUS : That can never be, Socrates.

SOCRATES : Then the excess is not in pain?

POLUS : Surely not.

SOCRATES : And if not in pain, the excess could not be in both?

POLUS : Evidently not.

SOCRATES : Then only the other alternative is left?

POLUS : Yes.

SOCRATES : Namely, evil.

POLUS : So it appears.

SOCRATES : Then to inflict wrong is worse than to suffer it through an excess of evil.

POLUS : That is obvious.

d   SOCRATES : Now were not you and the majority of men in agreement before that it is more shameful to do than to suffer wrong?

POLUS : Yes.

SOCRATES : And now it has been shown to be more evil.

POLUS : So it appears.

SOCRATES : And would you choose the more evil and shameful in preference to the less? Do not hesitate to answer, Polus, for it will do you no hurt, but submit nobly to the argument as you would to a doctor, and say either yes or no to my question.

e   POLUS : No, I would not prefer it, Socrates.

SOCRATES : And would anyone else?

POLUS : Not according to this argument, I think.

SOCRATES : Then I spoke truth when I said that neither I nor you nor any man whatever would rather do than suffer wrong, for to do it is worse.

POLUS : Evidently.

SOCRATES : You see then, Polus, that when our proofs are set side by side there is no resemblance. And though all other men except 476 me agree with you, I require no witness to testify for me to save you alone, and putting you alone to the vote I ignore the rest. Well, so much for that. And now let us investigate the second point at issue between us, whether, as you thought, to be punished when guilty is the greatest of evils or, as I thought, it is a greater evil to escape punishment.

Let us consider it in the following way. Would you say that to suffer punishment is the same thing as to be justly chastised when guilty?

POLUS : I would.

b   SOCRATES : Now can you deny that all just things are fine in so far as they are just? Think well before you answer.

POLUS : In my opinion they are, Socrates.

SOCRATES : Now consider this further point. When a man acts, must there not always be something acted upon by the agent?

POLUS : I think so.

SOCRATES : And does it not experience what the agent does, and is not the quality of the experience and the action the same? I mean, for example, if a man strikes, there must be something stricken.

POLUS : There must.

SOCRATES : And if the striker strikes hard or fast, the blow received by the stricken must be of like quality.   c

POLUS : Yes.

SOCRATES : Then the experience of the stricken is of the same quality as the action of the striker?

POLUS : Certainly.

SOCRATES : And if a man burns, there must be a thing burned?

POLUS : Of course.

SOCRATES : And if he burns severely or painfully, the thing burned must be burned in the same way?

POLUS : Certainly.

SOCRATES : And the same reasoning applies if a man cuts; there is a thing cut.

POLUS : Yes.

SOCRATES : And if the cut be big or deep or painful, the ob- d ject cut must be cut in the same way?

POLUS : Evidently.

SOCRATES : Then consider whether you agree to what I said just now as a general rule in every case, namely, that the quality of the patient's experience corresponds to that of the agent's action.

POLUS : I agree.

SOCRATES : This being admitted, tell me whether to be punished is to suffer or to act.

POLUS : Necessarily, it is to suffer, Socrates.

SOCRATES : At the hands of some agent?

POLUS : Of course, the inflicter of the punishment.

SOCRATES : And he who rightly inflicts it punishes justly?

POLUS : Yes.   e

SOCRATES : Acting justly or not?

POLUS : Justly.

SOCRATES : And so he who is punished suffers justly when he pays the just penalty?

POLUS : Evidently.

SOCRATES : And we have agreed that things just are fine or honorable.

POLUS : Certainly.

SOCRATES : Then of the two one does, the other, the punished, suffers, what is honorable?

POLUS: Yes.

477   SOCRATES: And if honorable, good, for the honorable is either pleasant or profitable.

POLUS: Assuredly.

SOCRATES: So he who is punished justly suffers what is good?

POLUS: Apparently.

SOCRATES: And is therefore benefited?

POLUS: Yes.

SOCRATES: Is it the kind of benefit that I imagine? Is his soul bettered if he is justly punished?

POLUS: It seems probable.

SOCRATES: Then he who is punished is rid of evil in the soul?

POLUS: Yes.

b   SOCRATES: Is he not then freed from the greatest of evils? Look at it in this way. In the fabric of a man's material estate do you see any other evil than poverty?

POLUS: No, only poverty.

SOCRATES: And what about his bodily constitution? Would you say its evil is weakness and sickness and ugliness and such things?

POLUS: I would.

SOCRATES: And do you consider there is an evil condition of the soul?

POLUS: Certainly.

SOCRATES: And do you call this injustice and ignorance and cowardice and the like?

POLUS: Certainly.

c   SOCRATES: Then for these three, material fortune, body, and soul, you have named three evils, poverty, disease, and injustice?

POLUS: Yes.

SOCRATES: Now which of these evils is the most shameful? Is it not injustice and the evil of the soul in general?

POLUS: Yes, by far.

SOCRATES: And if the most shameful, then also the worst?

POLUS: How do you mean, Socrates?

SOCRATES: I mean that what is most shameful is so, as we have already admitted, because it produces the greatest pain or harm or both.

POLUS: Certainly.

SOCRATES: And we have just now agreed that injustice and all evil of the soul is most shameful?

d   POLUS: We have agreed.

SOCRATES: Then it is either most painful, and most shameful through an excess of pain, or else of harm, or of both?

POLUS: That is necessary.

SOCRATES: Now are injustice and intemperance and coward-ice and ignorance more painful than poverty and sickness?

POLUS: That does not seem to result from our discussion, Socrates.

SOCRATES: Then if evil of the soul, by your verdict, does not exceed other evils in painfulness, its superlative shamefulness must be due to a harm and a viciousness immeasurably and surpassingly great.   e

POLUS: Evidently.

SOCRATES: But that which exceeds most in harm must be the greatest of all possible evils.

POLUS: Yes.

SOCRATES: Then injustice and intemperance and other vices of the soul are the greatest of all evils.

POLUS: Clearly.

SOCRATES: Now what art rids us of poverty? Is it not the art of making money?

POLUS: Yes.

SOCRATES: And what art frees us from sickness? Is it not medicine?

POLUS: It must be.   478

SOCRATES: And what art from vice and injustice? If this is not so clear to you, look at it like this. Where and to whom do we take the sick in body?

POLUS: To the doctors, Socrates.

SOCRATES: And the unjust and intemperate?

POLUS: To the judges, do you mean?

SOCRATES: To suffer punishment?

POLUS: Yes.

SOCRATES: And do not those who punish rightly do so with the aid of a certain justice?

POLUS: Obviously.

SOCRATES: Then money-making rids us of poverty, medicine of sickness, and justice of intemperance and injustice.   b

POLUS: Evidently.

SOCRATES: Then of these which is the finest?

POLUS: Of which do you mean?

SOCRATES: Of money-making, medicine, and justice?

POLUS: Justice is far superior, Socrates.

SOCRATES: Then if finest, must it not produce either the greatest pleasure or the greatest profit, or both?

POLUS: Yes.

SOCRATES: Is medical regimen a pleasant thing, and do pa-tients enjoy it?

POLUS: Not in my opinion.

SOCRATES: But it is beneficial, is it not?

c   POLUS: Yes.

SOCRATES: For the patient is freed from a great evil, so that it is profitable to submit to the pain and recover health.

POLUS: Of course.

SOCRATES: And would a man be happiest about his bodily state if he submitted to healing or if he were never sick at all?

POLUS: Obviously if he were never sick at all.

SOCRATES: For happiness, after all, it seems, consists not in a release from evil but in never having contracted it.

POLUS: That is so.

d   SOCRATES: Again, of two who suffer evil either in body or in soul, which is the more wretched, the man who submits to treatment and gets rid of the evil, or he who is not treated but still retains it?

POLUS: Evidently the man who is not treated.

SOCRATES: And was not punishment admitted to be a release from the greatest of evils, namely wickedness?

POLUS: It was.

SOCRATES: Yes, because a just penalty disciplines us and makes us more just and cures us of evil.

POLUS: I agree.

SOCRATES: Then the happiest of men is he who has no evil in his soul, since this was shown to be the greatest of evils?

e   POLUS: That is plain.

SOCRATES: And second in order surely is he who is delivered from it.

POLUS: Apparently.

SOCRATES: And we found this was the man who is admonished and rebuked and punished.

POLUS: Yes.

SOCRATES: Then his life is most unhappy who is afflicted with evil and does not get rid of it.

POLUS: Evidently.

SOCRATES: And is not this just the man who does the greatest wrong and indulges in the greatest injustice and yet contrives to es-
479 cape admonition, correction, or punishment—the very condition you describe as achieved by Archelaus and other tyrants, orators, and potentates?

POLUS: It seems so.

SOCRATES: For what these have contrived, my good friend, is pretty much as if a man afflicted with the most grievous ailments should contrive not to pay to the doctors the penalty of his sins against his body by submitting to treatment, because he is afraid, like a
b child, of the pain of cautery or surgery. Do you not agree?

POLUS: I do.

SOCRATES: He is evidently ignorant of the meaning of health and physical fitness. For apparently, as our recent admissions prove, those who escape punishment also act much in the same way, Polus. They see its painfulness but are blind to its benefit and know not how much more miserable than a union with an unhealthy body is a union with a soul that is not healthy but corrupt and impious and evil, and so they leave nothing undone to avoid being punished and c liberated from the greatest of ills, providing themselves with money and friends and the highest attainable powers of persuasive rhetoric. But if we have been right in our admissions, Polus, do you see the results of our argument, or shall we sum them up together?

POLUS: Yes, if you wish.

SOCRATES: Is not our conclusion then that injustice and the doing of wrong is the greatest of evils?

POLUS: Evidently.

SOCRATES: And it was shown that punishment rids us of this d evil?

POLUS: Apparently.

SOCRATES: And when punishment is evaded, the evil abides?

POLUS: Yes.

SOCRATES: Then wrongdoing itself holds the second place among evils, but first and greatest of all evils is to do wrong and escape punishment.

POLUS: So it seems.

SOCRATES: Now did we not differ, my friend, about this very point, when you maintained that Archelaus was happy because he remained unpunished despite the enormity of his crimes, whereas I e was of the contrary opinion—that Archelaus or any other man who escapes punishment for his misdeeds must be miserable far beyond all other men, and that invariably the doer of wrong is more wretched than his victim, and he who escapes punishment than he who is punished? Was not that what I was saying?

POLUS: Yes.

SOCRATES: And has it not been proved that it is true?

POLUS: Clearly.

SOCRATES: Well then, if this is true, Polus, what great use is 480 there in rhetoric? Our recent admissions show, do they not, that a man must take every precaution not to do wrong, since he would thereby suffer great harm?

POLUS: Certainly.

SOCRATES: But if he or anyone of those for whom he cares has done wrong, he ought to go of his own accord where he will most speedily be punished, to the judge as though to a doctor, in his eager- b ness to prevent the distemper of evil from becoming ingrained and producing a festering and incurable ulcer in his soul. Or what else can we say, Polus, if our previous admissions hold good? Must it not be true that only in this, and in no other way, can our present views be in harmony with what we said before?

POLUS : What else indeed can we say, Socrates?

SOCRATES : Then for the purpose of defending one's own guilt or that of his parents or friends or children, or his country when c guilty, Polus, rhetoric is of no use whatever—unless we should on the contrary assume that a man ought to accuse himself first and foremost, and then his kinsfolk and any friend who at any time is guilty of wrongdoing, and that he ought not to hide the evil away but bring it to light in order that the culprit may be punished and regain his health. And he should prevail upon himself and the others not to play the coward but to submit as a patient submits bravely with closed eyes to the knife or cautery of the surgeon, ever pursuing what is good and honorable and heeding not the pain, but if his guilty deeds be d worthy of flogging, submitting to the lash; if of imprisonment, to bonds; if of a fine, to the payment thereof; if of exile, to exile; if of death, to death. He should be the first to accuse himself and his kinsmen, and should use rhetoric for the sole purpose of exposing his own misdeeds and ridding himself of the greatest of all evils, wickedness. Are we to accept this or not, Polus?

e   POLUS : To me it seems fantastic, Socrates, but I suppose it is consistent with what was said before.

SOCRATES : Then surely we must disprove that, or else this view must follow.

POLUS : Yes, that is so.

SOCRATES : Then conversely again, if after all it is right to injure anybody, whether it be an enemy or whoever it be—always provided that you have not been yourself the victim of injury by him, for this you must guard against—but if your enemy injures another, you should contrive by every possible means, both by word and by deed, 481 that he escape punishment and come not before the judge. But if he does appear, you must see to it that your enemy be not sentenced and punished, but that, if he has robbed others of a large sum of money, he shall not pay it back but shall keep it and squander it, in defiance of god and man, upon himself and his friends; and, if his crimes are worthy of death, that, if possible, he shall never die but live forever in his wickedness, or, if not this, shall at any rate live as long as possible in this character. Rhetoric is of service for such purposes b in my opinion, Polus, but does not seem to be of much use for a man who does not intend to do wrong, if indeed it is of any use at all— and our previous discussion has revealed none.

CALLICLES : Tell me, Chaerephon, is Socrates in earnest or joking?

CHAEREPHON : In my opinion, Callicles, he is in deadly earnest, but there is nothing like asking him.

CALLICLES: By heaven, that is just what I am anxious to do. Tell me, Socrates, are we to consider you serious now or jesting? For if you are serious and what you say is true, then surely the life of us c mortals must be turned upside down and apparently we are everywhere doing the opposite of what we should.

SOCRATES: Callicles, if mankind did not share one common emotion which was the same though varying in its different manifestations, but some of us experienced peculiar feelings unshared by the rest, it would not be easy for one of us to reveal his feelings to another. This I say because I have observed that you and I have now d undergone much the same experience, for each one of us is in love with two objects—I with Alcibiades, son of Clinias, and philosophy, and you also with two, the Athenian demos and Demos, son of Pyrilampes. Now I notice on every occasion that, clever though you be, whatever your favorite says and however he describes things to be, you cannot contradict him, but constantly shift to and fro. In the Assembly, if any statement of yours is contradicted by the Athenian e demos, you change about and say what it wishes, and you behave much the same toward the handsome young son of Pyrilampes. For you are incapable of resisting the words and designs of your favorite, with the result that if anyone should be astonished at the absurdities you utter again and again under their spell, you would probably say, if you were willing to tell the truth, that unless somebody stops your favorites from saying what they do, you yourself too will never stop 482 speaking thus. You must think yourself bound then to hear much the same things from me, and do not be astonished at my speaking thus, but stop my favorite, philosophy, from saying what she does. It is she, my friend, who says what you now hear from me, and she is far less unstable than my other favorite, for the son of Clinias is at the mercy now of one argument, now of another, but philosophy holds always to the same, and she says what now astonishes you, and you were here b when the words were spoken. You must either then prove against her, as I said just now, that to do wrong and evade punishment for wrongdoing is not the worst of all evils; or if you leave this unrefuted, then, by the dog that is god in Egypt, Callicles himself will not agree with you, Callicles, but will be at variance with you throughout your life. And yet I think it better, my good friend, that my lyre should be discordant and out of tune, and any chorus I might train, and that the c majority of mankind should disagree with and oppose me, rather than that I, who am but one man, should be out of tune with and contradict myself.

CALLICLES: Socrates, it seems to me that you run wild in your talk like a true mob orator, and now you are haranguing us in this way because Polus fell into the very error which he blamed Gorgias for being drawn into by you. Gorgias, he said, was asked by you whether, in case a prospective pupil of rhetoric came to him without a

d knowledge of justice, he himself would teach him, and he was shamed
into saying he would do so, because the general conventional view demanded it and men would be vexed if one refused. It was through this
admission that he was forced to contradict himself, and that is just
what you like. And Polus, in my opinion, was quite right in laughing
at you at the time, but now he himself in turn has been caught in the
same way. And I do not think much of Polus for the very reason that
he agreed with you that it is more disgraceful to do than to suffer in-
e justice, for it was as a result of this admission that he was caught in
the toils of your argument and silenced, because he was ashamed to
say what he thought. For, Socrates, though you claim to pursue the
truth, you actually drag us into these tiresome popular fallacies, looking to what is fine and noble, not by nature, but by convention. Now,
for the most part, these two, nature and convention, are antagonistic
to each other. And so, if a man is ashamed and dares not say what he
483 thinks, he is compelled to contradict himself. And you have discovered this clever trick and do not play fair in your arguments, for if a
man speaks on the basis of convention, you slyly question him on the
basis of nature, but if he follows nature, you follow convention. For
example, in our present discussion of doing and suffering wrong,
when Polus spoke of what was conventionally the more shameful, you
followed it up by appealing to nature. For by nature everything that is
worse is more shameful, suffering wrong for instance, but by convention it is more shameful to do it. For to suffer wrong is not even fit for
b a man but only for a slave, for whom it is better to be dead than alive,
since when wronged and outraged he is unable to help himself or any
other for whom he cares. But in my opinion those who framed the
laws are the weaker folk, the majority. And accordingly they frame
the laws for themselves and their own advantage, and so too with
c their approval and censure, and to prevent the stronger who are able
to overreach them from gaining the advantage over them, they
frighten them by saying that to overreach others is shameful and
evil, and injustice consists in seeking the advantage over others. For
they are satisfied, I suppose, if being inferior they enjoy equality of
status. That is the reason why seeking an advantage over the many is
by convention said to be wrong and shameful, and they call it injustice. But in my view nature herself makes it plain that it is right for
d the better to have the advantage over the worse, the more able over the
less. And both among all animals and in entire states and races of
mankind it is plain that this is the case—that right is recognized to
be the sovereignty and advantage of the stronger over the weaker. For
what justification had Xerxes in invading Greece or his father in invading Scythia? And there are countless other similar instances one
e might mention. But I imagine that these men act in accordance with
the true nature of right, yes and, by heaven, according to nature's own
law, though not perhaps by the law we frame. We mold the best and

strongest among ourselves, catching them young like lion cubs, and by spells and incantations we make slaves of them, saying that they must be content with equality and that this is what is right and fair. But if a man arises endowed with a nature sufficiently strong, he will, I believe, shake off all these controls, burst his fetters, and break loose. 484 And trampling upon our scraps of paper, our spells and incantations, and all our unnatural conventions, he rises up and reveals himself our master who was once our slave, and there shines forth nature's true justice. And it seems to me that Pindar expresses what I am saying in b that ode in which he writes,

> Law is the sovereign of all,
>> Of mortals and immortals alike,

and it is law, he says, that

> Carries all, justifying the most violent deed
> With victorious hand; this I prove
> By the deeds of Heracles, for without paying the price— [1]

it runs something like that—for I do not know the poem by heart—but it says that he drove off the oxen of Geryon which were neither given to him nor paid for, because this is natural justice, that the cattle and c all other possessions of the inferior and weaker belong to the superior and stronger.

    This is the truth then, and you will realize it if you will now abandon philosophy and rise to greater things. For philosophy, you know, Socrates, is a pretty thing if you engage in it moderately in your youth; but if you continue in it longer than you should, it is the ruin of any man. For if a man is exceptionally gifted and yet pursues philosophy far on in life, he must prove entirely unacquainted with all d the accomplishments requisite for a gentleman and a man of distinction. Such men know nothing of the laws in their cities, or of the language they should use in their business associations both public and private with other men, or of human pleasures and appetites, and in a word they are completely without experience of men's characters. And so when they enter upon any activity public or private they appear ridiculous, just as public men, I suppose, appear ridiculous when they e take part in your discussions and arguments. For what Euripides says is true:

> All shine in that and eagerly pursue it—
> Giving the better part of the day thereto—
> In which they find themselves most excellent,[2]

but that in which they are inferior they shun and abuse, praising the 485 other out of partiality to themselves, with the idea that they are thus praising themselves. But to my mind the right course is to partake of

---

[1] Pindar, fr. 169.   [2] *Antiope*, fr. 20.

both. It is a good thing to engage in philosophy just so far as it is an aid to education, and it is no disgrace for a youth to study it, but when a man who is now growing older still studies philosophy, the situation

b becomes ridiculous, Socrates, and I feel toward philosophers very much as I do toward those who lisp and play the child. When I see a little child, for whom it is still proper enough to speak in this way, lisping and playing, I like it and it seems to me pretty and ingenuous and appropriate to the child's age, and when I hear it talking with precision, it seems to me disagreeable and it vexes my ears and appears to me more fitting for a slave, but when one hears a grown man

c lisping or sees him playing the child, it look ridiculous and unmanly and worthy of a beating. I feel exactly the same too about students of philosophy. When I see a youth engaged in it, I admire it and it seems to me natural and I consider such a man ingenuous, and the man who does not pursue it I regard as illiberal and one who will never aspire

d to any fine or noble deed, but when I see an older man still studying philosophy and not deserting it, that man, Socrates, is actually asking for a whipping. For as I said just now, such a man, even if exceptionally gifted, is doomed to prove less than a man, shunning the city center and market place, in which the poet said that men win distinction, and living the rest of his life sunk in a corner and whispering with three or four boys, and incapable of any utterance that is free and

e lofty and brilliant. Now I am quite friendly disposed toward you, Socrates, and I suppose I feel much as Zethus, whom I mentioned, felt toward Amphion in Euripides. For I am moved to say to you the same kind of thing as he said to his brother, 'You neglect, Socrates, what you most ought to care for, and pervert a naturally noble spirit

486 by putting on a childlike semblance, and you could neither contribute a useful word in the councils of justice nor seize upon what is plausible and convincing, nor offer any brilliant advice on another's behalf.' [3] And yet, my dear Socrates—and do not be angry with me, for I am saying this out of good will toward you—do you not consider it a disgrace to be in the condition I think you are in, you and the others who advance ever farther into philosophy? For now if anyone should seize you or any others like you and drag you off to prison, claiming you are guilty when you are not, you realize that you would not know

b what to do, but you would reel to and fro and gape openmouthed, without a word to say, and when you came before the court, even with an utterly mean and rascally accuser, you would be put to death, if he chose to demand the death penalty. And yet what wisdom is there in this, Socrates, in 'an art which finds a man well-gifted and leaves him worse' [4]—able neither to help himself nor to save from the extremes of danger either himself or anybody else, but fated to be robbed by his

c enemies of all his property and to live literally like one disfranchised

[3] *Antiope*, fr. 21.   [4] *Antiope*, fr. 25.

in his own city? And such a man, if I may put it somewhat crudely, one may even box on the ears with impunity. But, my good fellow, 'cease your questioning, and practice the fairer music of affairs' and try something that will win you a name for good sense, and leave to others 'these dainty devices,' whether we should call them babblings or follies, 'which will set you to dwell in empty mansions.' You should not emulate those who investigate these trifling matters but those who enjoy a livelihood and a reputation and many other blessings. d

SOCRATES: If my soul were wrought of gold, Callicles, do you not think I should be delighted to find one of those stones wherewith they test gold—the best of them—which I could apply to it, and if it established that my soul had been well nurtured, I should be assured that I was in good condition and in need of no further test?

CALLICLES: What is your point in asking me this, Socrates? e

SOCRATES: I will tell you. I consider that in meeting you I have encountered such a godsend.

CALLICLES: Why?

SOCRATES: I am convinced that if you agree with the opinions held by my soul, then at last we have attained the actual truth. For I observe that anyone who is to test adequately a human soul for good 487 or evil living must possess three qualifications, all of which you possess, namely knowledge, good will, and frankness. Now I encounter many who cannot test me because they are not wise like you, and others are wise but are unwilling to tell the truth because they do not care for me as you do, and our two guests here, Gorgias and Polus, while they are wise men and friends of mine, are more deficient than they ought to be in outspokenness and somewhat too bashful. How b could it be otherwise, when their bashfulness is so great that out of sheer timidity each of them ventures to contradict himself in the presence of many people, and that too about matters of supreme importance? But you possess all the qualifications lacking in the others. You have received a good education, as many Athenians would agree, and you are well disposed toward me. What evidence have I of this? I will c tell you. I know that you, Callicles, and three others are partners in wisdom—you, and Tisander of Aphidnae, Andron, the son of Androtion, and Nausicydes of Cholargeis—and I once overheard you discussing up to what point one should study philosophy. And I know that some such opinion as this prevailed among you, that we should not be zealous to pursue it in the nicest detail, but you advised each other to beware of becoming wiser than you should, for fear of un- d knowingly becoming corrupted by it. And so when I hear you giving me the same advice as you gave your closest companions, that to me is sufficient proof that you really are well disposed toward me. Moreover, that you are inclined to be frank and not bashful is borne out by your own statement and confirmed by the speech you made a short

time ago. Evidently, then, the case at the moment is this. If at any point in our discussion you agree with me, that matter will already
e have been adequately tested both by you and by me, and there will no longer be any need to refer it to any other touchstone. For you would never have agreed with me through lack of wisdom or excess of modesty, nor again would you agree with me with intent to deceive, for you are my friend, as you yourself claim. In fact, then, any agreement between you and me will have attained the consummation of the truth. And of all inquiries, Callicles, the noblest is that which concerns the very matter with which you have reproached me—namely, what a man should be, and what he should practice and to what ex-
488 tent, both when older and when young. As for me, if I act wrongly at all in the conduct of my life, you may be assured that my error is not voluntary but due to my ignorance. Now that you have begun to admonish me, therefore, do not give it up, but reveal to me clearly what course I must follow and how I may achieve it; and if you catch me agreeing with you now but later not doing what I agreed to, you may consider me an utter dolt and refuse to admonish me any more as a
b worthless creature. But please take up the question again from the beginning and tell me what 'natural justice' is according to you and Pindar—that the more powerful carries off by force the property of the weaker, the better rules over the worse, and the nobler takes more than the meaner? Have you any other conception of justice than this, or is my memory right?

CALLICLES : No, that is what I said then and still hold to.

SOCRATES : And is it the same man whom you call better and more powerful? I could not grasp at the time, you know, just what you
c meant. Is it the physically stronger that you call more powerful, and must the weaker obey the stronger—as, for example, you seemed to indicate at the time by saying that great cities assail small ones in accordance with natural justice, because they are more powerful and stronger, the more powerful and stronger and better being one and the same thing—or is it possible to be better but weaker and less powerful, or more powerful but more evil? Or have you the same defini-
d tion for the better and the more powerful? Please make your distinction clear, whether you consider the more powerful, the better, and the stronger as the same thing or different.

CALLICLES : Well, I can plainly assure you that they are the same.

SOCRATES : Are not the many more powerful by nature than the one? And it is these who, as you yourself said just now, frame their laws to restrain the one.

CALLICLES : Of course.

SOCRATES : Then the ordinances of the many are those of the more powerful?

CALLICLES: Certainly.

SOCRATES: And of the better also? For the more powerful are e far better, according to you.

CALLICLES: Yes.

SOCRATES: Then their ordinances are naturally noble, since they are those of the more powerful.

CALLICLES: I agree.

SOCRATES: Now do the many hold the opinion, as you just now stated, that justice means equal shares and that it is more shameful to do than to suffer wrong? Is this true or not? And mind that you 489 yourself are not caught this time a victim of modesty. Is it the view of the many, or not, that justice means equal shares, not excess, and that it is more shameful to do than to suffer wrong? Do not grudge me my answer, Callicles; then, if you agree with me, I may now confirm the truth by the admission of one fully competent to decide.

CALLICLES: Well, that is the view of the majority.

SOCRATES: Then it is not by convention only, but also by nature that it is more shameful to do than to suffer wrong and true jus- b tice to share equally; so apparently what you said previously was not true and you were mistaken in attacking me when you said that convention and nature are opposed and that I have recognized this and do not play fairly in debate, but invoke convention if a man refers to nature, or nature, when he refers to convention.

CALLICLES: Will this fellow never stop driveling? Tell me, Socrates, are you not ashamed to be captious about words at your age, considering it a godsend if one makes a slip in an expression? Do you c imagine that by the more powerful I mean anything else but the better? Did I not tell you long ago that I identify the better and the more powerful? Do you think I mean that, if a rabble of slaves and nondescripts who are of no earthly use except for their bodily strength are gathered together and make some pronouncement, this is law?

SOCRATES: Well, most sage Callicles, is this what you have to say?

CALLICLES: Most certainly.

SOCRATES: Well, my strange friend, I myself guessed long d since that you meant something like this by 'the more powerful,' and I repeat my questions only because I am eager to understand clearly what you mean. For surely you do not consider that two are better than one or that your slaves are better than you because they are stronger. But start once again and tell me what you mean by 'the better,' since you do not mean the stronger, and, my admirable friend, lead me on the path of knowledge more gently, that I may not run away from your school.

CALLICLES: You are ironical, Socrates.   e

SOCRATES: No indeed, Callicles, by that very Zethus of whom you made use just now to heap your irony upon me, but come, tell me, whom do you mean by 'the better'?

CALLICLES: I mean the nobler.

SOCRATES: You see then that you yourself are playing with words but revealing nothing. Will you not tell me whether by 'the better' and 'the more powerful' you mean the wiser or some other class?

CALLICLES: By heaven, I do mean those, and most emphatically.

490   SOCRATES: Then according to your account one sensible man is often more powerful than ten thousand fools and it is right that he should rule and they be subjects and that the ruler should have more than his subjects; that, I think, is what you mean to say—and I am not trapping you with words—if the one is more powerful than ten thousand.

CALLICLES: That is what I mean, for natural justice I consider to be this, that the better and wiser man should rule over and have more than the inferior.

b   SOCRATES: Hold there a moment! What is it you mean this time? If many of us are gathered together, as now, in the same place, with plenty of food and drink in common, and if we are of various kinds, some strong, some weak, and one of us, being a doctor, is wiser in these matters and, as is likely, is stronger than some, weaker than others, then surely, being wiser than we are, he will be better and more powerful in this field.

CALLICLES: Certainly.

c   SOCRATES: Then must he have a larger portion of the food than we do, because he is better, or in virtue of his authority should he do all the distributing, but in the use and expenditure of it ought he to seek no excessive portion for his own body, if he is not to suffer for it, but to receive more than some and less than others? And if he happens to be the weakest of all, then must not the best man get the smallest share of all, Callicles? Is it not so, my good friend?

CALLICLES: You keep talking about food and drink and doctors d and nonsense. I am not speaking of these things.

SOCRATES: Do you not say the wiser man is the better? Yes or no?

CALLICLES: I do.

SOCRATES: But should not the better have a larger share?

CALLICLES: Not of food or drink.

SOCRATES: I see. Of clothes perhaps, and the most expert weaver should have the largest cloak and should go around clad in the most numerous and handsome garments?

CALLICLES: Garments indeed!

SOCRATES: Well then, the best and wisest expert in shoes

should obviously have the advantage in them. The cobbler, I suppose, e
should have the largest and most numerous shoes in which to walk
around.

CALLICLES: Shoes! You keep talking nonsense.

SOCRATES: Well, if that is not what you mean, here it is perhaps. A farmer for instance who is an expert with good sound knowledge about the soil should have a larger share of seed and use the most
seed possible on his own land.

CALLICLES: How you keep saying the same things, Socrates!

SOCRATES: Not only that, Callicles, but about the same
matters.

CALLICLES: By heaven, you literally never stop talking about 491
cobblers and fullers and cooks and doctors, as if we were discussing
them.

SOCRATES: Then will you not yourself say in what matters a
superiority in wisdom and power justly entitles a man to a larger
share? Or will you neither put up with my suggestions nor tell me
yourself?

CALLICLES: But I have been telling you for a long time. First
of all I mean by the more powerful, not cobblers or cooks, but those
who are wise in affairs of the state and the best methods of adminis- b
tering it, and not only wise but courageous, being competent to accomplish their intentions and not flagging through weakness of soul.

SOCRATES: You see, my good Callicles, that you do not find the
same fault with me as I with you. For you claim that I keep saying
the same things, and reproach me with it, but I make the opposite
statement of you, that you never say the same things about the same
subjects. Previously you defined the better and more powerful as the
stronger, and next as the wiser, and now you come forward with some- c
thing else; the better and the more powerful are now described by
you as the more courageous. But, my good sir, tell me and have done
with it, whom you mean by the better and more powerful, and what is
their sphere of action.

CALLICLES: But I told you—those who are wise in the affairs
of the state and courageous. It is proper that these should govern
states, and this is the meaning of justice, that these should have more d
than the others, the rulers than the subjects.

SOCRATES: Tell me, my friend, what is their relation to themselves? Are they rulers or subjects?

CALLICLES: What do you mean?

SOCRATES: I mean that every man is his own master, or is there
no need for him to govern himself but only to govern others?

CALLICLES: What do you mean by governing himself?

SOCRATES: Nothing very subtle, but merely the popular notion
of being temperate and in control of oneself, and mastering one's own
pleasures and appetites.   e

CALLICLES: What charming innocence! By temperate you mean simpletons.

SOCRATES: How could I? Everybody must realize that that is not my meaning.

CALLICLES: Most certainly it is, Socrates. Why, how could a man be happy when a slave to anybody at all? No, but the naturally noble and just is what I now describe to you with all frankness—namely that anyone who is to live aright should suffer his appetites to grow to the greatest extent and not check them, and through courage
492 and intelligence should be competent to minister to them at their greatest and to satisfy every appetite with what it craves. But this, I imagine, is impossible for the many; hence they blame such men through a sense of shame to conceal their own impotence, and, as I remarked before, they claim that intemperance is shameful and they make slaves of those who are naturally better. And because they themselves are unable to procure satisfaction for their pleasures, they
b are led by their own cowardice to praise temperance and justice. For to those whose lot it has been from the beginning to be the sons of kings or whose natural gifts enable them to acquire some office or tyranny or supreme power, what in truth could be worse and more shameful than temperance and justice? For though at liberty without any hindrance to enjoy their blessings, they would themselves invite the laws, the talk, and the censure of the many to be masters over
c them. And surely this noble justice and temperance of theirs would make miserable wretches of them, if they could bestow no more upon their friends than on their enemies, and that too when they were rulers in their own states. But the truth, Socrates, which you profess to follow, is this. Luxury and intemperance and license, when they have sufficient backing, are virtue and happiness, and all the rest is tinsel, the unnatural catchwords of mankind, mere nonsense and of no account.

d   SOCRATES: You make a brave attack, Callicles, with so frank an outburst, for clearly you are now saying what others may think but are reluctant to express. I entreat you therefore on no account to weaken, in order that it may really be made plain how life should be lived. And tell me. You say we should not curb our appetites, if we are to be what we should be, but should allow them the fullest possible
e growth and procure satisfaction for them from whatever source, and this, you say, is virtue.

CALLICLES: That is what I say.

SOCRATES: Then those who are in need of nothing are not rightly called happy.

CALLICLES: No, in that case stones and corpses would be supremely happy.

SOCRATES: Well, life as you describe it is a strange affair. I

should not be surprised, you know, if Euripides was right when he
said, 'Who knows, if life be death, and death be life?' [5] And perhaps we   493
are actually dead, for I once heard one of our wise men say that we are
now dead, and that our body is a tomb, and that that part of the soul
in which dwell the desires is of a nature to be swayed and to shift to
and fro. And so some clever fellow, a Sicilian perhaps or Italian,
writing in allegory, by a slight perversion of language named this part
of the soul a jar, because it can be swayed and easily persuaded, and   b
the foolish he called the uninitiate, and that part of the soul in foolish
people where the desires reside—the uncontrolled and nonretentive
part—he likened to a leaky jar, because it can never be filled. And in
opposition to you, Callicles, he shows that of those in Hades—the unseen world he means—these uninitiate must be the most unhappy, for
they will carry water to pour into a perforated jar in a similarly perforated sieve. And by the sieve, my informant told me, he means the   c
soul, and the soul of the foolish he compared to a sieve, because it is
perforated and through lack of belief and forgetfulness unable to hold
anything. These ideas may naturally seem somewhat absurd, but they
reveal what I want to put before you, to persuade you, if I can, to retract your view and to choose in place of an insatiable and uncontrolled life the life of order that is satisfied with what at any time it
possesses. But do I persuade you to change and admit that orderly folk
are happier than the undisciplined, or even if I offer many other such   d
allegories, will you not withdraw an inch?

CALLICLES : That is more like the truth.

SOCRATES : Come then, let me offer you another image from
the same school as the last. Consider whether you would say this of
each type of life, the temperate and the undisciplined. Imagine that
each of the two men has several jars, in the one case in sound condi-   e
tion and filled, one with wine, another with honey, another with milk,
and many others with a variety of liquids, but that the sources of
these liquids are scanty and hard to come by, procured only with much
hard labor. Imagine then that the one after filling his vessels does not
trouble himself to draw in further supplies but as far as the jars are
concerned is free from worry; in the case of the other man the sources,
as in the first instance are procurable but difficult to come by, but his
vessels are perforated and unsound and he is ever compelled to spend
day and night in replenishing them, if he is not to suffer the greatest   494
agony. If this is the character of each of the lives, do you still insist
that the life of the uncontrolled man is happier than that of the orderly? Do I or do I not persuade you with this image that the disciplined life is better than the intemperate?

CALLICLES : You do not, Socrates. The man who has filled his
vessels can no longer find any pleasure, but this is what I just now

[5] *Polyidus*, fr. 7.

described as living the life of a stone. Once the vessels are filled, there is neither pleasure nor pain any more. But a life of pleasure demands b the largest possible influx.

SOCRATES: Then if there is a big influx, must there not also be a great outflow, and must not the holes for the outflow be large?

CALLICLES: Certainly.

SOCRATES: It is the life of a plover you mean, not that of a corpse or a stone. And now tell me. You are thinking of some such thing as being hungry and, when hungry, eating?

CALLICLES: I am.

c SOCRATES: And being thirsty and, when thirsty, drinking?

CALLICLES: Yes, and experiencing all the other appetites and being able to satisfy them and living happily in the enjoyment of them.

SOCRATES: Good, my worthy friend, just continue as you began, and mind you do not falter through shame. And I too, it seems, must throw all shame aside. First of all then, tell me whether one who suffers from the itch and longs to scratch himself, if he can scratch himself to his heart's content and continue scratching all his life, can be said to live happily.

d CALLICLES: How absurd you are, Socrates, a regular mob orator!

SOCRATES: That, Callicles, is why I frightened Polus and Gorgias and put them to shame, but you surely will not be dismayed or abashed, for you have courage. Only give me your answer.

CALLICLES: Well then, I say that even one who scratches himself would live pleasantly.

SOCRATES: And if pleasantly, happily?

CALLICLES: Certainly.

e SOCRATES: If it was only his head that he wanted to scratch— or can I push the question further? Think what you will answer, Callicles, if anyone should ask all the questions that naturally follow. And as a climax of all such cases, the life of a catamite—is not that shocking and shameful and miserable? Will you dare to say that such people are happy, if they have what they desire in abundance?

CALLICLES: Are you not ashamed, Socrates, to drag our discussion into such topics?

SOCRATES: Is it I who do this, my noble friend, or the man who says so unequivocally that pleasure, whatever its nature, is the key to happiness, and does not distinguish between pleasures good and evil? 495 But enlighten me further as to whether you say that the pleasant and the good are identical, or that there are some pleasures which are not good.

CALLICLES: To avoid inconsistency if I say they are different, I assert they are the same.

SOCRATES: Then you ruin your earlier statement, Callicles,

and you can no longer properly investigate the truth with me, if you
speak contrary to your opinions.

CALLICLES : You are doing just the same, Socrates.   b

SOCRATES : Then I am not acting rightly, if I am so doing, nor
are you. But my good sir, consider whether pleasures so indiscriminate
can after all be the good. For if it is so, then the many shocking things
we just now hinted at must evidently result, and many others too.

CALLICLES : So *you* think, Socrates.

SOCRATES : But do you really maintain this, Callicles?

CALLICLES : I do.

SOCRATES : Then we are to take up the argument in the belief c
that you are serious?

CALLICLES : Most assuredly.

SOCRATES : Well then, since that is agreed, resolve this point
for me. Does something exist that you call knowledge?

CALLICLES : Yes.

SOCRATES : Did you not speak just now of a certain courage
which accompanies knowledge.

CALLICLES : I did.

SOCRATES : And you spoke of them as two things because courage is different from knowledge?

CALLICLES : Certainly.

SOCRATES : Again, are pleasure and knowledge the same thing,
or different?

CALLICLES : Different, I suppose, O paragon of wisdom.   d

SOCRATES : And courage is also different from pleasure?

CALLICLES : Of course.

SOCRATES : Let us remember this then, that Callicles of Acharnae says pleasure and the good are the same, but that knowledge and
courage are different from each other and from the good.

CALLICLES : But Socrates of Alopece does not agree with this.
Or does he?

SOCRATES : He does not, and I think Callicles will not either e
when he comes to know himself aright. Tell me, do you not think that
those who fare well experience the opposite of those who fare ill?

CALLICLES : I do.

SOCRATES : Then if these things are opposites, the same must
hold true of them as of health and sickness. A man cannot be both in
health and sick at the same time, nor be rid of both conditions at the
same time.

CALLICLES : How do you mean?

SOCRATES : Take, for example, any part of the body separately
and consider it. A man perhaps has trouble with his eyes, which is 496
called ophthalmia.

CALLICLES : Of course.

SOCRATES : Then his eyes are not at the same time sound.

CALLICLES: By no means.

SOCRATES: And what of when he is rid of ophthalmia? Does he then get rid of the health of his eyes, and is he finally quit of both conditions?

CALLICLES: Certainly not.

b   SOCRATES: For that would be miraculous and irrational, would it not?

CALLICLES: Very much so.

SOCRATES: But, I suppose, he acquires and gets rid of each in turn.

CALLICLES: I agree.

SOCRATES: And is it not the same with strength and weakness?

CALLICLES: Yes.

SOCRATES: And swiftness and slowness?

CALLICLES: Certainly.

SOCRATES: And good things and happiness, and their opposites, evils and wretchedness—does he possess and get rid of each of these in turn?

CALLICLES: Assuredly, I think.

c   SOCRATES: Then if we discover certain things which a man possesses and gets rid of simultaneously, it is obvious that these cannot be the good and the evil. Do we agree on this? Do not answer until you have considered it carefully.

CALLICLES: I am in the most complete possible accord.

SOCRATES: Back then to our previous admissions. Did you say hunger was pleasant or painful? Actual hunger, I mean.

CALLICLES: Painful, but to satisfy hunger by eating is pleasant.

d   SOCRATES: I understand. But hunger itself at least is painful, is it not?

CALLICLES: I agree.

SOCRATES: And thirst too?

CALLICLES: Most certainly.

SOCRATES: Am I to ask any further then, or do you admit that every deficiency and desire is painful?

CALLICLES: I admit it; you need not ask.

SOCRATES: Very well then, but to drink when thirsty you say is pleasant?

CALLICLES: I do.

SOCRATES: Now in this statement the word 'thirsty' implies pain, I presume.

e   CALLICLES: Yes.

SOCRATES: And drinking is a satisfaction of the deficiency and a pleasure?

CALLICLES: Yes.

SOCRATES: Then you say that in drinking there is pleasure?

CALLICLES : Certainly.

SOCRATES : When one is thirsty?

CALLICLES : I agree.

SOCRATES : That is, when in pain?

CALLICLES : Yes.

SOCRATES : Then do you realize the result—that you say a man enjoys pleasure simultaneously with pain, when you say that he drinks when thirsty? Does not this happen at the same time and the same place, whether in body or soul? For I fancy it makes no difference. Is this so or not?

CALLICLES : It is.

SOCRATES : Yes, but you say also that when one is faring well it is impossible for him at the same time to fare ill.

CALLICLES : I do.   497

SOCRATES : But you have agreed it is possible to experience pleasure at the same time as pain.

CALLICLES : Apparently.

SOCRATES : Then pleasure is not the same as faring well, nor pain as faring ill, and so the pleasant is different from the good.

CALLICLES : I do not understand what your quibbles mean, Socrates.

SOCRATES : You understand, Callicles, but you are playing coy. But push on a little further, that you may realize how cunning you b are, you who admonish me. Does not each one of us cease at the same time from thirsting and from his pleasure in drinking?

CALLICLES : I do not know what you mean.

GORGIAS : Do not behave so, Callicles, but answer for our sakes too, that the arguments may be concluded.

CALLICLES : But Socrates is always the same, Gorgias. He asks these trivial and useless questions and then refutes.

GORGIAS : What difference does that make to you? In any case you do not have to pay the price, Callicles, but suffer Socrates to cross-examine you as he will.

CALLICLES : Well then, ask these petty little questions, since c Gorgias so wishes.

SOCRATES : You are lucky, Callicles, in having been initiated in the Great Mysteries before the Little; I did not think it was permitted. Answer then from where you left off, whether thirst and the pleasure of drinking do not cease for each of us at the same time.

CALLICLES : I agree.

SOCRATES : And does not one cease from hunger and other desires, and from pleasures at the same time?

CALLICLES : That is so.

SOCRATES : Does he not then cease from pains and pleasures at d the same time?

CALLICLES : Yes.

SOCRATES: Yes, but he does not cease from experiencing the good and the ill simultaneously, as you yourself agreed. Do you not agree now?

CALLICLES: I do. What of it?

SOCRATES: Only this, that the good is not the same as the pleasant, my friend, nor the evil as the painful. For we cease from the one pair at the same time, but not from the other, because they are distinct. How then could the pleasant be the same as the good, or the painful as the evil? Let us look at it in a different way, if you like, for
e I think that even here you do not agree. But just consider. Do you not call good people by that name because of the presence in them of things good, just as you call beautiful those in whom beauty is present.

CALLICLES: I do.

SOCRATES: Again, do you call fools or cowards good men? You did not just now, but it was the brave and the wise, or do you not call these good?

CALLICLES: Certainly I do.

SOCRATES: And have you ever seen a silly child enjoying pleasure?

CALLICLES: I have.

SOCRATES: And never seen a silly man enjoying pleasure?

CALLICLES: Yes, I suppose so, but what of it?

498   SOCRATES: Nothing, just answer.

CALLICLES: I have seen.

SOCRATES: And a sensible man experiencing pain or pleasure?

CALLICLES: I have.

SOCRATES: And which feels more pain or pleasure, the sensible or the fool?

CALLICLES: I do not think there is much difference.

SOCRATES: That is quite enough. And have you ever seen a coward in battle?

CALLICLES: Of course.

SOCRATES: Well, which of the two seemed more to rejoice, when the enemy retreated, the cowards or the brave?

b   CALLICLES: Both equally, I think, or if not, pretty much so.

SOCRATES: It makes no difference. At least cowards too feel pleasure?

CALLICLES: Most certainly.

SOCRATES: And fools too, it appears.

CALLICLES: Yes.

SOCRATES: And is it cowards only or the brave too that feel pain at the enemy's approach?

CALLICLES: Both.

SOCRATES: To a like degree?

CALLICLES: Cowards, perhaps, more.

SOCRATES: And they rejoice more at the enemy's retreat?

CALLICLES: Perhaps.

SOCRATES: Then fools and wise, cowards and brave feel pain and pleasure to a like degree, as you say, but the coward more so than c the brave?

CALLICLES: I agree.

SOCRATES: But the wise and the brave are good, cowards and fools bad.

CALLICLES: Yes.

SOCRATES: Then the good and the bad feel pleasure and pain to a like degree.

CALLICLES: I agree.

SOCRATES: Now are the good and the bad good and evil to a similar degree? Or are the bad even better than the good?

CALLICLES: Good heavens, I do not understand what you d mean.

SOCRATES: Do you not understand that according to you the good are good through the presence of good things, and the bad, of evil things, and that—according to you—pleasures are good things, and pains evil?

CALLICLES: I do.

SOCRATES: Then good things, that is, pleasures, are present to those who rejoice, if they rejoice.

CALLICLES: Of course.

SOCRATES: And is it not through the presence of good things that those who rejoice are good?

CALLICLES: Yes.

SOCRATES: Again, evil things, namely pains, are present for those who suffer pain.

CALLICLES: They are present.

SOCRATES: And it is through the presence of evil things that e you claim the evil are evil. Or do you no longer hold to that?

CALLICLES: I do.

SOCRATES: Then those who feel pleasure are good, those who feel pain, bad.

CALLICLES: Certainly.

SOCRATES: More, less, or equally good or bad, according as they feel these things more, less, or equally?

CALLICLES: Yes.

SOCRATES: Now do you not say that the wise and the fool, the brave and the coward feel pleasure and pain to a like degree, or the coward even to a greater degree?

CALLICLES: I do.

SOCRATES: Then reckon up along with me what is the result of our admissions, for they say that it is good to repeat and examine twice and once again what is good. We say the wise and the brave man 499 is good, do we not?

CALLICLES: Yes.

SOCRATES : And the fool and coward is bad?

CALLICLES : Certainly.

SOCRATES : And he who enjoys pleasure is good?

CALLICLES : Yes.

SOCRATES : And he who suffers pain is bad?

CALLICLES : Necessarily so.

SOCRATES : And the good and the bad experience pain and pleasure to a like degree, though perhaps the bad even more so.

CALLICLES : Yes.

SOCRATES : Then the evil man becomes just as bad and good as b the good man, or even more good. Is not this the result, along with what we said before, if anyone identifies the pleasant and the good? Must not this be so, Callicles?

CALLICLES : I have been listening to you for a long time, Socrates, and agreeing with you, as I reflected that, if one concedes something to you even in play, you gladly seize hold of it like a child. Just as if you really think that I or anyone else does not hold some pleasures to be better and others worse!

SOCRATES : Ho, ho, Callicles! What a rascal you are, treating c me like a child and deceiving me by saying the same things are now thus, now different. And yet I did not think at the beginning that you would willingly deceive me, since you are my friend. But now I have been misled, and apparently, as the old proverb goes, I must make the best of the circumstances and take just what you give me. What you now say, it seems, is that some pleasures are good, and some bad. Is it not so?

d   CALLICLES : Yes.

SOCRATES : And are the good ones the profitable, the bad ones the harmful?

CALLICLES : Certainly.

SOCRATES : And the profitable are those that do some good, the harmful some evil?

CALLICLES : I agree.

SOCRATES : Now is this what you mean? Of the bodily pleasures of eating and drinking, for instance, that we mentioned just now, are those that produce health in the body or strength or any other bodily excellence, good pleasures, and those that produce the opposite effects bad?

e   CALLICLES : Certainly.

SOCRATES : And similarly with pains, some are good, some bad?

CALLICLES : Of course.

SOCRATES : Now should we not choose and practice good pleasures and pains?

CALLICLES : Certainly.

SOCRATES : And not the bad?

CALLICLES : Obviously.

SOCRATES: Yes, because Polus and I agreed, if you remember, that all our actions should be for the sake of the good. Do you too share our opinion, that the good is the end of all actions and that everything else should be done for its sake, not the good for the sake of everything else? Do you of the third part add your vote to ours?   500

CALLICLES: I do.

SOCRATES: Then the pleasant as well as everything else should be done for the sake of the good, not the good for the sake of the pleasant.

CALLICLES: Certainly.

SOCRATES: Now can any and every man choose which pleasures are good and which bad, or do we need an expert in each case?

CALLICLES: We need an expert.

SOCRATES: Let us recapitulate then what I was saying to Polus and Gorgias. I said, if you remember, that there are certain processes aiming at pleasure which secure pleasure alone but know nothing of b the better and the worse, and others that know what is good and evil. And among those concerned with pleasures I named cookery, which is a routine, not an art, and among those concerned with the good the medical art. And, by the god of friendship, Callicles, do not fancy that you should play with me, and give me no haphazard answers contrary to your opinion. And do not either take what I say as if I were merely playing, for you see the subject of our discussion—and on c what subject should even a man of slight intelligence be more serious? —namely, what kind of life one should live, the life to which you invite me, that of a 'real man,' speaking in the Assembly and practicing rhetoric and playing the politician according to your present fashion, or the life spent in philosophy, and how the one differs from the other. Perhaps then it is best for us, as I endeavored to do just now, to distin- d guish between them, and after distinguishing and coming to an agreement together, then, if there are two such lives distinct, to consider in what way they differ from one another and which one should be lived. Now perhaps you do not yet understand what I mean.

CALLICLES: Indeed I do not.

SOCRATES: Well, I will tell you more clearly. Since you and I have agreed that there is a good and there is a pleasant, and that the pleasant is different from the good, and that there is a method of studying and contriving to acquire each of them, one method for pursuing pleasure, another for pursuing the good—but first of all you must either agree with or reject this statement. Do you agree?   e

CALLICLES: It is as you state.

SOCRATES: Then come, tell me that you agree also with what I said to Gorgias and Polus, if you think that after all I spoke the truth then. I said, I believe, that in my opinion cookery differed from medicine in being, not an art, but a routine, pointing out that the other, that is, medicine, has investigated the nature of the subject it treats 50:

and the cause of its actions and can give a rational account of each of them, whereas its counterpart, which is exclusively devoted to cultivating pleasure, approaches it in a thoroughly unscientific way, without once having investigated the nature of pleasure or its cause; and without any pretense whatever to reason and practically no effort to classify, it preserves by mere experience and routine a memory of
b what usually happens, thereby securing its pleasures. Consider then first of all whether you are satisfied with this statement and whether you believe that there are certain other occupations relating to the soul also—some of them in the nature of arts, exercising forethought for what is best for the soul, others neglecting this but, as in the case of the body, preoccupied entirely with the soul's pleasure, and how it may be achieved—but as to which pleasures are better or worse, this they have never considered, their sole concern being to gratify these
c pleasures, whether for better or for worse. For I believe, Callicles, that there are such processes, and behavior of this kind I call flattery, whether it concerns the body or the soul or whatever the object to whose pleasure it ministers without paying any heed to what is better or worse. Do you subscribe to the same opinion with me, or oppose it?

CALLICLES: Oh, not I. I agree, in order that the argument may be finished, and to gratify Gorgias here.

d   SOCRATES: And is this true about one soul, but not about two or many?

CALLICLES: No, it is true also of two or many.

SOCRATES: Is it not possible to gratify large numbers collectively without any consideration for what is best?

CALLICLES: I suppose it is.

SOCRATES: Can you tell me then which are the occupations that do this? Or rather, if you prefer it, I will ask and wherever an occupation seems to you to belong to this type, say so, wherever it does
e not, say no. And first let us look at flute playing. Do you not think, Callicles, that it conforms to this type, pursuing our pleasure only, with no thought for anything else?

CALLICLES: I think so.

SOCRATES: And is it not the same with all such occupations, as for example playing the lyre at contests?

CALLICLES: Yes.

SOCRATES: And what about the training of choruses and dithyrambic poetry? Do you not think it similar in character? Do you imagine that Cinesias, son of Meles, is in the slightest concerned with saying anything likely to improve his hearers, or merely what will
502 gratify the mob of spectators?

CALLICLES: That is quite obvious, Socrates, at least in the case of Cinesias.

SOCRATES: And what about his father, Meles? Do you think he looked to what is for the best, when he sang to his lyre? He did not even look to what is most pleasant, for his audience found his songs most tiresome. But think it over. Do you not consider that all music for the lyre and dithyrambic poetry were invented to give pleasure?

CALLICLES: I do.

SOCRATES: And what is the aim of that stately and marvelous b creature, tragic drama? Is it her endeavor and ambition, in your opinion, merely to gratify the spectators; or, if there be anything pleasant and charming, but evil, to struggle against uttering it, but to declaim and sing anything that is unwelcome but beneficial, whether they like it or not? For which of these two aims do you think tragic poetry is equipped?

CALLICLES: It is indeed quite evident, Socrates, that her impulse is rather toward pleasure and the gratification of the spectators. c

SOCRATES: And did we not just now describe such an activity as flattery?

CALLICLES: Certainly.

SOCRATES: Well now, if you should strip from all poetry its music, rhythm, and meter, the residue would be nothing else but speech?

CALLICLES: That must be so.

SOCRATES: And these speeches are addressed to a huge mob of people?

CALLICLES: I agree.

SOCRATES: Then poetry is a kind of public address?

CALLICLES: Evidently.   d

SOCRATES: Must it not be a rhetorical public address? Do you not consider that the poets engage in rhetoric in the theaters?

CALLICLES: I do.

SOCRATES: Then we have now discovered a form of rhetoric addressed to a people composed alike of children and women and men, slaves and free—a form which we cannot much admire, for we describe it as a kind of flattery.

CALLICLES: Certainly.

SOCRATES: Well, but what of the rhetoric addressed to the Athenian people and other free peoples in various cities—what does that mean to us? Do the orators seem to you always to speak with an e eye to what is best, their sole aim being to render the citizens as perfect as possible by their speeches, or is their impulse also to gratify the citizens, and do they neglect the common good for their personal interest and treat the people like children, attempting only to please them, with no concern whatever whether such conduct makes them better or worse?   503

CALLICLES: This is not a single question you are asking, for some say what they say in the interest of the citizens, but there are others such as you describe.

SOCRATES: That is sufficient for me, for even if there are two sides to this, yet one part of it, I suppose, would be flattery and shameful mob appeal, while the other is something fine—the effort to perfect as far as possible the souls of the citizens and the struggle to say always what is best, whether it be welcome or unwelcome to the hearers. But you yourself have never seen rhetoric of this kind, or if you

b can mention any such orator, why do you not tell me his name at once?

CALLICLES : Well, by heaven, I cannot give you the names of any such orators living today.

SOCRATES : Why then, can you name any one of the orators of old, from the time of whose first appearance to address the public, the citizens, who had previously been worse, are said to have been improved? I do not know of any such man.

c CALLICLES : What, have you never been told that Themistocles was a good man, and Cimon and Miltiades, and Pericles who died recently, and whom you have heard speak yourself?

SOCRATES : Yes, if what you previously spoke of as virtue is truly so, namely to satisfy to the full your own appetites and those of others, but if this is not so, but, as in our later argument we were compelled to admit, only those desires, the satisfaction of which

d makes man better, should be indulged, not those which make us worse, and if for this there is a special art—I cannot admit that any of those mentioned satisfied these demands.

CALLICLES : Well, if you make good search, you will find one.

SOCRATES : Then let us just quietly consider whether any of them had this quality. Well now, the good man who speaks for the best surely will not say what he says at random but with some pur-

e pose in view, just as all other craftsmen do not each choose and apply materials to their work at random, but with the view that each of their productions should have a certain form. Look, for example, if you will, at painters, builders, shipwrights, and all other craftsmen—any of them you choose—and see how each one disposes each element he contributes in a fixed order, and compels one to fit and harmonize

504 with the other until he has combined the whole into something well ordered and regulated. Other craftsmen in general and those we were speaking of just now, who have to do with the body, physical trainers and doctors, give order, I think, and discipline to the body. Do we admit the truth of this or not?

CALLICLES : Let it be granted.

SOCRATES : Then harmony and order will make a building good, but disorder bad.

CALLICLES : I agree.

SOCRATES : Is it not the same too with a ship?

b CALLICLES : Yes.

SOCRATES : And with our bodies also, we say?

CALLICLES : Certainly.

SOCRATES: And what about the soul? Will it be good if disordered, or rather if it achieves a certain order and discipline?

CALLICLES: Here too our previous argument demands that we agree.

SOCRATES: Now what is the name of that bodily quality resulting from order and discipline?

CALLICLES: Health and strength, I suppose you mean.

SOCRATES: I do. And the effect of order and discipline in the c soul? Try to discover and name it, as in the other case.

CALLICLES: Why do you not name it yourself, Socrates?

SOCRATES: Well, if you prefer that, I will do so, and do you, if you think I am right, agree; if not, refute me and do not let me escape. It seems to me that the word healthy is applied to all regularity in the body, and from this come health and general bodily excellence. Is it so or not?

CALLICLES: It is.

SOCRATES: And the words lawfulness and law are applied to d all order and regularity of the soul, whence men become orderly and law-abiding, and this means justice and temperance. Yes or no?

CALLICLES: So be it.

SOCRATES: And is it not with his eye on these things that our orator, the good and true artist, will bring to bear upon our souls the words he utters and all his actions too, and give any gift he gives, or take away what he takes—his mind always occupied with one thought, how justice may be implanted in the souls of the citizens and injustice banished, and how temperance may be implanted and e indiscipline banished, and how goodness in general may be engendered and wickedness depart? Do you agree or not?

CALLICLES: I agree.

SOCRATES: For what benefit is there, Callicles, when a body is sick and distempered, in giving it abundant food and the most delicious drinks or other such things, which, so far from profiting it, will on the contrary, if the truth be told, do it more harm? Is this true?

CALLICLES: So be it. 505

SOCRATES: For it is not worth while in my opinion for a man to live with a diseased body; in that case he must live a diseased life. Is it not so?

CALLICLES: Yes.

SOCRATES: Now when a man is well, do not the doctors generally allow him to satisfy his appetites, eating as much as he wishes when hungry or drinking when thirsty, but when he is sick, practically never allow him to take his fill of what he craves? Do you and I agree upon this?

CALLICLES: I agree.

SOCRATES: And is it not the same, my good friend, with the b soul? So long as it is evil, senseless and undisciplined and unjust and impious, it should be restrained from its desires and suffered to do nothing but what will improve it. Do you agree or not?

CALLICLES: I agree.

SOCRATES: For thus, I suppose, it will be better for the soul itself.

CALLICLES: Certainly.

SOCRATES: And to restrain it from its desires is to discipline it?

CALLICLES: Yes.

SOCRATES: Then to be disciplined is better for the soul than indiscipline, which you preferred just now.

c   CALLICLES: I do not know what you are talking about, Socrates; ask someone else.

SOCRATES: This fellow will not put up with being improved and experiencing the very treatment now under discussion, the process of discipline.

CALLICLES: No, for I have not the slightest interest in what you are saying. I answered you only to gratify Gorgias.

SOCRATES: Well, what shall we do then? Break off our discussion in the middle?

CALLICLES: You may decide for yourself.

SOCRATES: Well, they say it is not right to leave even tales un-
d finished, but we should fit a head on them, that they may not go about headless. Give us the rest of the answers then, that our discussion may acquire a head.

CALLICLES: How importunate you are, Socrates; if you will listen to me, you will bid good-by to this argument, or else debate with somebody else.

SOCRATES: Then who else is willing? You know, we must not leave the discussion incomplete.

CALLICLES: Could you not carry it through alone, either speaking on your own or answering your own questions?

e   SOCRATES: Just to fulfill the saying of Epicharmus—and prove competent alone for what 'ere now two men said'? But it seems as if it must be done that way. However, if we are to do this, I think we should all be contentiously eager to know what is true and what false in the subject under discussion, for it is a common benefit that
506 this be revealed to all alike. I will then carry the argument through in accordance with my own ideas, and if any of you believe that what I admit to myself is not the truth, you must break in upon it and refute me. For I do not speak with any pretense to knowledge, but am searching along with you, and so if there appears to be anything in what my opponent says, I shall be the first to yield to him. But I say this only if you think the debate should be carried through to the end. If you do not wish it, let us drop it now and take our departure.

GORGIAS: Well, I do not think, Socrates, that we ought yet to depart, but you should carry through the discussion, and I think the b others too agree with me. I myself am anxious to hear you go through what remains.

SOCRATES : I myself too, Gorgias, would have liked to continue the argument with Callicles here, until I had paid him back with the speech of Amphion in reply to that of Zethus. But since you are unwilling, Callicles, to help me finish the argument, you can at least listen and interrupt if at any point you think I am wrong. And if you c refute me, I shall not be vexed with you as you are with me, but you shall be enrolled as the greatest of my benefactors.

CALLICLES : Go on alone, my dear sir, and finish the argument.

SOCRATES : Then listen, but first let me recapitulate the argument from the beginning.

Are the pleasant and the good identical? They are not, as Callicles and I agreed. Should the pleasant be done for the sake of the good, or the good for the sake of the pleasant? The pleasant for the sake of the good. And is the pleasant that at whose presence we are d pleased, the good that whose presence makes us good? Certainly. But the goodness of ourselves and of all other good things is due to the presence of some excellence? That seems necessarily true, Callicles. But surely the goodness of anything, whether implement or body or soul or any living thing, does not best come to it merely by haphazard, but through a certain rightness and order and through the art that is assigned to each of them. Is this so? I certainly agree. Then the e goodness of anything is due to order and arrangement? I should agree. It is then the presence in each thing of the order appropriate to it that makes everything good? So it appears to me. The soul then that has its own appropriate order is better than that which has none? Necessarily. But further, the soul possessed of order is orderly? Of course. And the orderly is the temperate? Most necessarily. Then the temperate soul is the good. I myself can offer no objection to this, my 507 dear Callicles, but if you can, please instruct me.

CALLICLES : Go on, my good sir.

SOCRATES : I assert then that, if the temperate soul is good, then the soul in the opposite condition to the temperate is evil, and this, we saw, was the foolish and undisciplined. Certainly. Moreover the sound-minded man would do his duty by gods and men, for he would not be sound of mind if he did what was unfitting. That must b necessarily be so. And doing his duty by men, he would be acting justly, and doing it by the gods, piously, and the doer of just and pious deeds must be just and pious. That is so. And further, he must be brave, for it is not the part of a man of sound mind to pursue or avoid what he should not, but to pursue or avoid what he should, whether it be things, or people, or pleasures, or pains, and to stand his ground, where duty bids, and remain steadfast. So there is every necessity, Callicles, that the sound-minded and temperate man, being, as we c have demonstrated, just and brave and pious, must be completely good, and the good man must do well and finely whatever he does, and he who does well must be happy and blessed, while the evil man who does ill must be wretched, and he would be the opposite of the temperate man, the undisciplined creature of whom you approve.

This then is the position I take, and I affirm it to be true, and if it is true, then the man who wishes to be happy must, it seems, pursue
d and practice temperance, and each of us must flee from indiscipline with all the speed in his power and contrive, preferably to have no need of being disciplined, but if he or any of his friends, whether individual or city, has need of it, then he must suffer punishment and be disciplined, if he is to be happy. This I consider to be the mark to which a man should look throughout his life, and all his own endeavors and those of his city he should devote to the single purpose of
e so acting that justice and temperance shall dwell in him who is to be truly blessed. He should not suffer his appetites to be undisciplined and endeavor to satisfy them by leading the life of a brigand—a mischief without end. For such a man could be dear neither to any other man nor to God, since he is incapable of fellowship, and where there is no fellowship, friendship cannot be. Wise men, Callicles, say that
508 the heavens and the earth, gods and men, are bound together by fellowship and friendship, and order and temperance and justice, and for this reason they call the sum of things the 'ordered' universe, my friend, not the world of disorder or riot. But it seems to me that you pay no attention to these things in spite of your wisdom, but you are unaware that geometric equality is of great importance among gods and men alike, and you think we should practice overreaching others, for you neglect geometry. Well, either we must refute this argument and prove that happiness does not come to the happy through the pos-
b session of justice and temperance, nor does misery come through the possession of wickedness, or, if my argument is true, we must consider the consequences. And the consequences are all those previously mentioned, about which you asked me, Callicles, if I was speaking seriously when I said that a man should accuse himself and his son and his friend, if guilty of any wrong deed, and should employ rhetoric for this purpose, and what you thought Polus admitted through a sense of shame is true after all—that it is as much more evil
c as it is more shameful to do than to suffer wrong, and he who is to become a rhetorician in the right way must after all be a just man with a knowledge of what is just—an admission which Gorgias in turn made, according to Polus, through a sense of shame.

This being so, let us consider whether or not you spoke aright in your reproaches to me, when you said that I am not able to help myself or any of my friends and relations, or to save them from the
d gravest perils, but like outlawed men am at the mercy of anyone, whether he wishes to box my ears, as you so forcefully expressed it,

or rob me of my money, or drive me out of the city, or, worst of all, put me to death, and, according to your view, to be in this plight is of all things the most shameful. But as to my own view, though it has often been expressed already, there is no harm in my expressing it once more. I maintain, Callicles, that it is not the most shameful of things to be wrongfully boxed on the ears, nor again to have either my purse or my person cut, but it is both more disgraceful and more e wicked to strike or to cut me or what is mine wrongfully, and, further, theft and kidnaping and burglary and in a word any wrong done to me and mine is at once more shameful and worse for the wrongdoer than for me the sufferer. These facts, which were shown to be as I state them some time earlier in our previous discussion, are buckled fast and clamped together—to put it somewhat crudely—by arguments of steel and adamant—at least so it would appear as matters 509 stand. And unless you or one still more enterprising than yourself can undo them, it is impossible to speak aright except as I am now speaking. For what I say is always the same—that I know not the truth in these affairs, but I do know that of all whom I have ever met either before or now no one who put forward another view has failed to appear ridiculous. And so once more I hold these things to be so, and if they are, and if injustice is the greatest of evils to the wrong- b doer and, greatest though it be, it is an even greater evil, if that be possible, to escape punishment when one does wrong, what is that help, the failure to avail himself of which makes a man in very truth ridiculous? Is it not that which will avert from us the greatest harm? This must surely be the help which it is most shameful to be unable to render to oneself and one's friends and relations, and next to this the second most shameful, and after that the third and so with the rest; as is the magnitude of the evil in each case, so too will be the c beauty of being able to help oneself to meet such evil and the shame of being unable. Am I right or wrong, Callicles?

CALLICLES : You are right.

SOCRATES : Of these two then, inflicting and suffering wrong, we say it is a greater evil to inflict it, a lesser to suffer it. Now what provision should a man make for helping himself, so as to achieve d both these benefits, that of doing and that of suffering no wrong? Is it a matter of power or of will? What I mean is this. Can a man avoid being wronged if it be his will to avoid it, or only if he acquire power to avoid it?

CALLICLES : That is quite evident; he must acquire the power.

SOCRATES : And what about doing wrong? Is it quite enough if he does not choose to do wrong—for then he will not do it—or must he equip himself here also with a certain power and an art on the e ground that, if he does not learn and practice this, he will do wrong? Why will you not answer me this very question, Callicles—whether you think that Polus and I were or were not rightly compelled in our previous argument to agree in admitting that no one voluntarily does wrong, but that all who do wrong do so against their own will?

510   CALLICLES: Let it be so, Socrates, that you may conclude the argument.

SOCRATES: Then it is also for the purpose of avoiding wrong-doing that we must equip ourselves with a certain power and art.

CALLICLES: Certainly.

SOCRATES: Now what is the art of contriving to suffer no wrong or as little as possible? See whether you agree with my opinion, which is this. You must either be yourself the ruling power or even a tyrant in your city, or else a partisan of the government in power.

CALLICLES: You see, Socrates, that I am ready to applaud you,
b if you speak aright, and now I think you have said something really excellent.

SOCRATES: Well, consider whether you think I am right in this point too. The closest friendships, I believe, exist, as the sages of old tell us, between like and like. Do you not agree?

CALLICLES: I do.

SOCRATES: Now where a tyrant is in power who is savage and illiterate, if there should be anyone in his city far better than himself, the tyrant, I presume, would be afraid of him, and the man could
c never in his heart of hearts be the tyrant's true friend.

CALLICLES: That is so.

SOCRATES: Nor could one who was much the tyrant's in-ferior, for the tyrant would despise him and would never feel for him the warmth of a friend.

CALLICLES: That also is true.

SOCRATES: There remains then only one person as a friend worth reckoning to such a man, namely one of the same character, who agrees with his tastes and dislikes, and is willing to be subject and subservient to the ruler. And he will have great power in the
d state, and no one will wrong him with impunity. Is it not so?

CALLICLES: Yes.

SOCRATES: Then if any of the young men in this city should ponder how he might win great power and none could wrong him, this, it seems, is the path for him, to accustom himself from childhood to feel pleasure and annoyance at the same things as his master, and to contrive to be as like him as possible. Is it not so?

CALLICLES: Yes.

SOCRATES: Now according to your theory he will thus have
e contrived to suffer no wrong and to possess great power in the state.

CALLICLES: Certainly.

SOCRATES: And to do no wrong as well? Or is this far from be-ing the case, if he is to resemble a master who is evil and to possess great influence with him? No, I think that, quite the contrary, he will thus prepare himself to be able to do the greatest possible wrong and to escape punishment for doing it. Will he not?

CALLICLES: Evidently.

SOCRATES: Then the greatest possible evil will dwell in him, for 511 he will be depraved of soul and ruined through his imitation of his master, and through his power.

CALLICLES: Somehow or other you keep twisting our arguments this way and that, Socrates. Do you not realize that this imitator of the tyrant will, if he so wishes, put to death the man who refuses to imitate him, or will deprive him of his property?

SOCRATES: I know, my good sir, if I am not deaf, for I have b heard it often enough from you and Polus recently, and from practically everyone else in the city. But I tell you in turn that though he may kill the other, if he wishes, it will be a villain murdering a good and worthy man.

CALLICLES: Is not this the very feature that fills one with indignation?

SOCRATES: Not if you are a sensible person, as the argument proves. Or do you imagine that one should bend his efforts to living as long as possible and practice those arts that constantly save us from dangers, such as the rhetoric you bid me practice, which preserves one's life in the law courts? c

CALLICLES: Yes, by heaven, and it was good advice too.

SOCRATES: What now, my good friend? Do you consider the art of swimming to be something particularly wonderful?

CALLICLES: No indeed, not I.

SOCRATES: And yet even that art saves men from death whenever they fall into some situation where such knowledge is needed. But if this seems to you insignificant, I can tell you of one greater than d this, the pilot's art which, like rhetoric, saves not only our lives but also our bodies and our goods from the gravest dangers. And this art is unpretentious and orderly, and does not put on airs or make believe that its accomplishments are astonishing. But, in return for the same results as those achieved by the advocate, if it brings you here safely from Aegina, it asks but two obols, and if from Egypt or the Black Sea, for this mighty service of bringing home safely all that I men- e tioned just now, oneself and children and goods and womenfolk and disembarking them in the harbor, it asks two drachmas at the most, and the man who possesses this art and achieves these results goes ashore and walks alongside his ship with modest bearing. For I suppose he is capable of reflecting that it is uncertain which of his passengers he has benefited and which he has harmed by not suffering them to be drowned, knowing as he does that those he has landed 512 are in no way better than when they embarked, either in body or in soul. He knows that if anyone afflicted in the body with serious and incurable diseases has escaped drowning the man is wretched for not having died and has received no benefit from him; he therefore reckons that if any man suffers many incurable diseases in the soul, which is so much more precious than the body, for such a man life is not worth while and it will be no benefit to him if he, the pilot, saves

b him from the sea or from the law court or from any other risk. For he knows it is not better for an evil man to live, for he must needs live ill.

   This is why the pilot is not accustomed to give himself airs, even though he saves us; no, my strange friend, nor the engineer either, who at times has no less power to save life than the general or anyone else, not to mention the pilot, for at times he preserves entire cities. Do you place him in the same class as the advocate? And yet if he were inclined to speak as you people do, Callicles, making much of his services, he would bury us under the weight of his arguments, urging

c and exhorting us on the necessity of becoming engineers, since all other professions are valueless, for he can make a good case for himself. But you disdain him and his craft nonetheless, and would call him 'engineer' as a term of reproach, and you would never be willing to give your daughter to his son or to take his daughter yourself. And yet if we look at the reasons for which you praise your own accomplishments, what just cause have you for disdaining the engineer and

d the others I mentioned just now? I know you would say you are a better man and of better family. But if by 'better' you do not mean what I do, but goodness consists merely in saving oneself and one's property, whatever one's character, it is ridiculous to find fault with the engineer and the doctor and the other crafts devised for the purpose of giving safety. But, my good sir, just reflect whether what is good and noble is not something more than saving and being

e saved. Perhaps the true man should ignore this question of living for a certain span of years and should not be so enamored of life, but should leave these things to God and, trusting the womenfolk who say that no man whatever could escape his destiny, should consider the ensuing question—in what way one can best live the life that is to be his, whether by assimilating himself to the type of government under which he lives—so that now, after all, you must become as like

513 as possible to the Athenian people, if you are to be dear to them and wield great power in the city. Consider, my good friend, whether this is of benefit to you and to me, so that we may not suffer what they say is the fate of the Thessalian witches who draw down the moon from heaven, and find that our choice of such power in the city means the sacrifice of what is dearest to us. But if you imagine that anyone in the world will deliver to you an art which will win you great power in

b the city, unless either for better or for worse you resemble its government, then in my opinion you are mistaken, Callicles. You must not be a mere imitator, but must bear a natural resemblance, if you are to effect a genuine friendship with the Athenian demos, yes, and, by heaven, the Demos of Pyrilampes as well. So whoever makes you most resemble these, will make of you the kind of statesman and rhetorician you desire to be, for each takes pleasure in the words that ap- c peal to his own character, but dislikes those that appeal to another's —unless you have any objections to offer, dear heart. What do you say in answer to this, Callicles?

CALLICLES : It seems to me, I know not how, that you are right, Socrates, but I feel as the many do. I am not quite convinced by you.

SOCRATES : That is because the love of demos dwells in your soul, Callicles, and resists me, but if perchance we investigate these same problems better, you will be persuaded. Remember at least that d we said there were two processes that aim in each case at tending body and soul, one that makes pleasure the end of its association, the other, what is best, this latter not indulging in pleasure but battling against it. Are not these the distinctions we made at the time?

CALLICLES : Certainly.

SOCRATES : Now the one of these, that aims at pleasure, is ignoble and just nothing but flattery, is it not so?

CALLICLES : So be it, if you wish.   e

SOCRATES : But the aim of the other is that what we tend, whether it happen to be body or soul, shall be as perfect as possible.

CALLICLES : Certainly.

SOCRATES : Should we not then take in hand the tending of the city and its citizens with the aim of making the citizens themselves as good as possible? For, as we discovered previously, without this there is no use in rendering any other kindly service, unless, that is to say, the thoughts of those who are to obtain much money and sovereignty or any other power whatever are good and noble. Are we to say 514 my view is right?

CALLICLES : Certainly, if it pleases you.

SOCRATES : If then when we contemplated some public undertaking for the state, we were to enlist each other's aid in a task of building, the construction perhaps of important buildings such as walls or dockyards or temples, ought we not to look to ourselves and examine ourselves, to discover first of all whether or not we are experts in the art of building, and from whom we learned it? Ought we b to or not?

CALLICLES : Certainly.

SOCRATES : And then again, secondly, whether we have ever erected a building previously for one of our friends or for ourselves, and whether this building is beautiful or ugly, and if on review we discovered that we had had good and distinguished teachers and that c with these teachers we had erected many fine buildings, and then also many on our own account when we had finished with our teachers— if this were our position, we might, as sensible men, aspire to public works, but if we had no master to point to, and either no buildings

whatever or many worthless ones, then it would surely be folly to undertake public works and to invite each other thereto. Shall we admit
d that this is true or not?

CALLICLES : Certainly.

SOCRATES : So too in every other case. If, for example, we had
aspired to public practice and encouraged each other thereto as competent physicians, we would surely have made mutual investigation of
each other, and you would have asked, Let me see, in heaven's name,
how about Socrates himself in the matter of bodily health? Or has
anybody else, slave or free, ever been cured of sickness by Socrates?

And I, too, I fancy, should have made the same inquiries about
you, and if we could find no one, whether citizen or stranger, man or
e woman, whose bodily health has been improved by our means, then
surely, Callicles, it would be ridiculous for anyone, before practicing
in private often with indifferent results, and often with success, and
achieving sufficient experience in the profession, to begin, as the
saying goes, his apprenticeship in pottery upon a large vessel, to aspire himself to public practice, and encourage others to do the same.
Do you not consider such behavior folly?

CALLICLES : I do.

515   SOCRATES : And now, my best of friends, since you are just beginning to enter public life and invite me also and reproach me for
not doing so, shall we not examine each other and ask, Come now,
has Callicles ever yet improved any of the citizens? Is there any man
who previously was evil, unjust, undisciplined, and senseless, and
through Callicles has become an upright and worthy man, be he stranger or citizen, slave or free?

Tell me, if anyone should examine you on these points, Callicles,
b what will you say? What man will you claim to have improved by your
company? Do not hesitate, before you aspire to a public career, to
answer if you can point to any such achievement of yours as a private
citizen.

CALLICLES : You are contentious, Socrates.

SOCRATES : It is not contentiousness that makes me ask, but a
true desire to know what you consider the right standard of public
life in our city. Or when you embark upon a public career, pray will
c you concern yourself with anything else than how we citizens can
be made as good as possible? Have we not many times already
agreed that this should be the task of a statesman? Have we acknowledged it or not? Answer me. We have; I shall answer on your behalf.
If then the good man ought to contrive this for his own city, carry your
mind back to those men of whom you spoke a little earlier, and tell
me whether you still think they proved themselves good citizens—
d Pericles and Cimon and Miltiades and Themistocles.

CALLICLES : I do.

SOCRATES : Then if they were good, obviously each of them

made better citizens of those who were worse before. Did he do this or not?

CALLICLES : Yes.

SOCRATES : So when Pericles began to speak before the people, the Athenians were worse than when he spoke for the last time?

CALLICLES : Perhaps.

SOCRATES : There can be no 'perhaps' about it, my good friend; it must be so from what we have admitted, if he was really a good citizen.

CALLICLES : Well, what then?   e

SOCRATES : Nothing, but tell me next whether the Athenians are said to have been improved by means of Pericles or, quite the contrary, to have been corrupted by him. For I am told that Pericles made the Athenians idle and cowardly and talkative and covetous, because he was the first to establish pay for service among them.

CALLICLES : You hear this, Socrates, from the gentlemen with battered ears.

SOCRATES : Well, this at least is not a matter of hearsay, but you know it as well as I do, that Pericles enjoyed a good reputation at first and was never convicted on any disgraceful charge by the Athenians, when they were worse. But when he had made good and worthy citizens of them, at the end of his life, he was convicted of theft by them and narrowly escaped a death sentence, obviously because they 516 held him an evil man.

CALLICLES : Well, what about it? Does that make Pericles a villain?

SOCRATES : At any rate one who tended asses or horses or cattle would be considered bad if he showed a similar character—if when he assumed charge they did not kick or butt or bite him, but he made them wild enough to do all these things. Or do you not consider any man a poor trainer of any animal whatever, if they are tame when he b takes them over, but he makes them wilder than when he assumed charge? Do you agree or not?

CALLICLES : Certainly, to please you.

SOCRATES : Then please me still further by answering this. Is a man a member of the animal kingdom or not?

CALLICLES : Of course he is.

SOCRATES : And was it not men of whom Pericles assumed charge?

CALLICLES : Yes.

SOCRATES : Then ought he not, as we agreed just now, to have made them more just rather than more unjust, if indeed he was a good statesman when he was in charge of them?   c

CALLICLES : Certainly.

SOCRATES : Now just men are gentle according to Homer. But what do you say? Is it not so?

298 PLATO : COLLECTED DIALOGUES

CALLICLES : Yes.

SOCRATES : But Pericles made them wilder than when he assumed charge of them, and toward himself too, the last person he would have wished to suffer.

CALLICLES : Do you want me to agree with you?

SOCRATES : If you think I am telling the truth.

CALLICLES : Then let it be granted.

SOCRATES : And if wilder, more unjust and worse?

d   CALLICLES : Granted.

SOCRATES : Then Pericles was no good statesman by this account.

CALLICLES : So *you* say.

SOCRATES : Yes, and by what you yourself admit. Tell me about Cimon too in turn. Did not those whom he served ostracize him, that they might not hear his voice for ten years? And Themistocles they treated in the same way and in addition punished him by banishment. And Miltiades, the victor of Marathon, they voted to throw into the pit, and he would have suffered this fate but for the president of the e Council. And yet if, as you say, these had been good men, they would never have been so treated. It is not true at any rate that, while good charioteers are not thrown from their chariots in their first contests, they are thrown later, when they have trained their horses and have themselves become better drivers. This is not the case in chariot racing or in any other activity, or do you think it is?

CALLICLES : No, not I.

SOCRATES : Then, after all, it seems, our previous statement was true, that we do not know of any man who has proved a good 517 statesman in this city. You admitted that there are none of the present day, but claimed some of days gone by, and chose the men just now mentioned, but they have proved to be on a level with those of our time, and so, if they were orators, they did not employ the true rhetoric—else they would not have been driven out—nor the rhetoric of flattery either.

CALLICLES : But, Socrates, men of our day are far indeed from b having achieved what was accomplished by any you like to name among those others.

SOCRATES : My good friend, I too find no fault with them, at least as servants of the city; in fact I consider they were more successful servants than those of today and better able to provide the city with what she desired. But as to giving those desires a different direction instead of allowing them free scope, by persuading and compelling citizens to adopt courses that would improve them—why, c therein they were practically in no way superior to the statesmen of today, though this is the only true office of a good citizen. I too agree with you that they were more clever than their successors in providing ships and walls and dockyards and many other such things.

Now you and I are behaving absurdly in this discussion, for throughout the time of our argument we have never ceased returning in circles
to the same point in a constant failure to understand each other's
meaning. I at least consider you have admitted time and again and
realize that we are concerned with a twofold activity related to both d
body and soul, and that one of these is menial and by it can be provided food, if our bodies are hungry; drink, if they are thirsty; and if
they are cold, clothing, bedding, shoes, or anything else that our bodies come to desire—I purposely use the same images, that you may
the more quickly understand. For it is no wonder that a purveyor of
these things, whether huckster, merchant, or manufacturer of any of e
them—baker or cook or weaver or cobbler or tanner—should because of his character appear both to himself and to others a true
minister to the body—to everyone, that is, who does not know that
there is above and beyond all these an art of gymnastics and of medicine, which is the genuine ministry to the body and should properly
control all these crafts and employ their products, because it alone
knows, while all the others know not, what food or drink is good or
bad for the health of the body. And for this reason, while these other 518
crafts are servile and menial and illiberal in their concern with the
body, gymnastics and medicine are by rights their masters. Now when
I tell you that the same holds good of the soul, at one time you appear to understand, and you agree as though you grasped my meaning,
but a little later you proceed to say that there have been upright and
worthy citizens in our state. And when I ask you their names, you b
seem to put forward the same types in the field of politics as if, when
I asked you who in the realm of gymnastics had been or now were
good trainers of the body, you should answer with the utmost seriousness, Thearion, the baker, and Mithaecus, who wrote the Sicilian
cookery book, and Sarambus, the tavern keeper—for these have
proved of wonderful service to the body, the one providing bread, the
second dainties, the third wine of marvelous quality. Now perhaps you c
would be annoyed if I said to you, Fellow, you know nothing about
gymnastics. You talk to me of servants who cater to our desires but
have no fine or sound views about them, men who, if it so chances,
will gorge and fatten men's bodies and win their praises for it, but will
finally rob them of what flesh they had before. And their victims in
turn, in their ignorance, will not blame for their maladies and for the d
loss of their original flesh those who feasted them, but any who may
happen at the time to be present and give them any advice when the
surfeit of the past has some time later brought sickness upon them,
because it disregarded the rules of health—these they will blame
and abuse and injure, if they can, while they praise the others who
were responsible for their troubles.   e
   And you are now doing much the same thing as this, Callicles.
You praise those who have banqueted our citizens with all the dainties

they desire. And men say it is these who have made our city great, never realizing that it is swollen and festering through these statesmen of old. For they have paid no heed to discipline and justice, but
519   have filled our city with harbors and dockyards and walls and revenues and similar rubbish, and so, when the crisis of her infirmity comes, they will hold their present advisers responsible and will sing the praises of Themistocles and Cimon and Pericles, who caused their misfortunes. And if you are not on your guard, they may perhaps lay hands on you and on my friend Alcibiades, when they have lost what
b   they once owned in addition to what they have since acquired, though you are not the authors, but perhaps the collaborators, in their troubles. And yet there is a ridiculous thing that I see taking place today and hear took place with regard to their statesmen of old. I notice that, whenever the city treats any of its statesmen as wrongdoers, they are indignant and violently protest that they are shockingly treated; so, after doing the city many services, they are now being unjustly ruined by her, according to their story. But all this is a fabri-
c   cation. For there is never a ruler of a city who would unjustly be ruined by the very city he ruled. Conditions, it seems, are much the same for those who pretend to be statesmen and for Sophists. Your Sophists, wise as they are in other matters, are in one point guilty of absurd behavior, for they claim to be teachers of goodness, yet they often accuse their pupils of wronging them by withholding their fees and showing no gratitude either for benefits received from them.
d   And what could be more illogical than this claim that men who have become good and just, men who have been stripped of injustice by their teacher and have acquired righteousness, should act unjustly by means of an injustice which does not dwell in them? Does not this seem absurd to you, my friend? You really have compelled me to play the orator, Callicles, by refusing to answer.

    CALLICLES : You could not speak, I suppose, if there were not somebody to answer you.
e   SOCRATES : Apparently I can; at least I am making quite lengthy speeches, since you will not reply to me. But, my good sir, in friendship's name, tell me, does it not seem ridiculous, when you claim to have made a man good, to find fault with him because, though you have made him good and he still is, yet he remains wicked?

    CALLICLES : It seems so to me.

    SOCRATES : But do you not hear such language from those who claim to educate men in goodness?

520   CALLICLES : I do, but why speak about worthless people?

    SOCRATES : But what would you say about those who pretend to govern the city and see to it that she be as good as possible, and then, when occasion serves, accuse her of being most evil? Do you think they are in any way different from those others? Sophist and orator, my good sir, are the same thing, or pretty nearly so, as I said to

Polus. But you through ignorance consider the one thing, rhetoric, to be something very fine, and despise the other. In actual fact sophistic b is better than rhetoric to the extent that legislation is finer than the administration of justice or gymnastics than medicine. But I always thought myself that political orators and Sophists alone were not entitled to find fault with what received their training for wicked behavior toward them; otherwise the very words they utter are at the same time a condemnation of themselves for having done no good to those whom they claim to benefit. Is it not so?

CALLICLES: Certainly.   c

SOCRATES: And further, if their claims were true, they alone, it seems, were at liberty to give their good services freely without pay. For a man who received any other benefit—swiftness of foot, for instance, through a trainer—might perhaps deny the trainer his due recompense, if he had given him instruction freely without any agreement that he should receive his fee as nearly as possible at the time when he had taught his pupil to be swift-footed. For acts of injustice are due, I suppose, not to slowness of foot, but to injustice. Is it not so?   d

CALLICLES: Yes.

SOCRATES: Then if an instructor eliminates this one quality of injustice, there is no danger of his suffering from it, but for him alone is it safe to bestow this kind of service, if in reality a man could make others good. Is this not true?

CALLICLES: I agree.

SOCRATES: For this reason then, there is no disgrace in taking money for giving other advice, about building, for instance, and the other arts.

CALLICLES: So it seems, at least.   e

SOCRATES: But when it is a question of how one may become as good as possible and best administer his own home or his city, it is considered disgraceful to refuse advice unless one is paid for it. Is it not so?

CALLICLES: Yes.

SOCRATES: The reason obviously is that this is the only kind of service which makes its recipient eager to make a like return, so that it is thought to be a good sign when one who has rendered such a kindness receives a like return; but if he does not, it is not so. Is this the truth of the matter?

CALLICLES: It is.   521

SOCRATES: Then distinguish for me what kind of care for the city you recommend to me, that of doing battle with the Athenians, like a doctor, to make them as good as possible, or to serve and minister to their pleasures? Tell me the truth, Callicles, for it is only fair that, as you spoke your mind frankly to me at first, you should continue to say what you think. And so speak up truly and bravely now.

CALLICLES: I say then, to serve and minister.

b   SOCRATES: Then you invite me, my noble friend, to play the flatterer?

CALLICLES: Yes, if you prefer the most offensive term, for if you do not . . .

SOCRATES: Please do not say what you have said so often — that anyone who wishes will slay me, only for me to repeat in turn that then a villain will slay a good man, nor that anyone will rob me of anything I possess, only for me to repeat that, once he has robbed me, he will not know what to do with his spoil, but even as he robbed me unjustly, so too he will make an unjust use of it, and if unjust,
c   shameful, and if shameful, wicked.

CALLICLES: How confident you seem, Socrates, that you can never experience any of these troubles whatever, as if you dwelt apart and could never be haled into court by, it may be, some utterly mean and vile creature.

SOCRATES: Then I must indeed be a senseless person, Callicles, if I do not think that in this city anything whatever may happen to anybody. But this at least I know well, that if I am brought into court
d   to face any such danger as you mention, it will be an evil man who prosecutes me—for no good man would drag a guiltless person into court—and it would not be surprising if I were put to death. Would you like me to tell you why I expect this?

CALLICLES: Certainly.

SOCRATES: I think that I am one of very few Athenians, not to say the only one, engaged in the true political art, and that of the men of today I alone practice statesmanship. Since therefore when I speak on any occasion it is not with a view to winning favor, but I aim at what is best, not what is most pleasant, and since I am unwilling to en-
e   gage in those 'dainty devices' that you recommend, I shall have nothing to say for myself when in court. And the same figure occurs to me that I used to Polus. My trial will be like that of a doctor prosecuted by a cook before a jury of children. Just consider what kind of defense such a man could offer in such a predicament, if the plaintiff should accuse him in these terms: Children of the jury, this fellow has done all of you abundant harm, and the youngest among you he is ruining
522 by surgery and cautery, and he bewilders you by starving and choking you, giving you bitter draughts and compelling you to hunger and thirst, whereas I used to feast you with plenty of sweetmeats of every kind.

What do you think a doctor could find to say in such a desperate situation? If he spoke the truth and said, All this I did, children, in the interests of health, what a shout do you think such a jury would utter? Would it not be a loud one?

CALLICLES: Perhaps; one must suppose so.

SOCRATES: Do you not think he would be utterly baffled as to b what to say?

CALLICLES: Certainly.

SOCRATES: Well, I too know that my experience would be similar, if I were brought into court. For I shall not be able to tell them of pleasures that I have purveyed—pleasures which *they* hold to be benefits and services, but I can envy neither those who purvey them nor those for whom they are provided. And if anyone claims either that I corrupt the young by bewildering them or that I abuse the older in bitter terms either in private or public, I shall neither be able to tell the truth and claim that I am right in saying all that I do and that it is your interests I am serving in this, gentlemen of the jury, nor shall c I be able to say anything else, and so perhaps anything whatever may happen to me.

CALLICLES: Do you think then, Socrates, that all is well with a man who is in this plight and is unable to help himself in his own country?

SOCRATES: Yes, if he should possess that one means of help which you have so often acknowledged; if he has helped himself by doing no wrong in word or deed either to gods or to men, for this we have often admitted to be the best of all aids to oneself. Now if any- d one should convict me of being unable to render this aid to myself or another, I should feel ashamed, whether I was convicted before many or few or man to man, and I should be vexed if I had to die through lack of such power as this. But if I should meet my death owing to a deficiency of flattering rhetoric, I am confident you would find me taking my death calmly. For no one who is not utterly irrational and cowardly is afraid of the mere act of dying; it is evil-doing that he e fears. For to arrive in the other world with a soul surcharged with many wicked deeds is the worst of all evils. And if you like, I am ready to tell you a tale which will prove that this is so.

CALLICLES: Well, since you have finished all else, you may finish this too.

SOCRATES: Give ear then, as they say, to a very fine story, 523 which you, I suppose, will consider fiction, but I consider fact, for what I am going to tell you I shall recount as the actual truth. As Homer says, Zeus and Poseidon and Pluto divided their kingdom among themselves after inheriting it from their father. Now in the days of Cronus there was this law about mankind, which from then till now has prevailed among the gods, that the man who has led a godly and righteous life departs after death to the Isles of the b Blessed and there lives in all happiness exempt from ill, but the godless and unrighteous man departs to the prison of vengeance and punishment which they call Tartarus. And in the days of Cronus and even when Zeus was but lately come to power, living men rendered

judgment on the living, pronouncing sentence on the very day on which these were to die, and so the verdicts were not well given. Accordingly, Pluto and the stewards from the Isles of the Blessed came
c and told Zeus that the wrong people were going to both places. Then Zeus said, 'Well, I will put a stop to that. Cases are judged badly now,' said he, 'because those who are tried come to judgment with their clothes on, for they are still alive when judged. And therefore many,' said he, 'who possessed evil souls are invested with fine bodies and lineage and wealth, and when the trial takes place, many witnesses come forward to testify that they have lived righteous lives. So the
d judges are dazzled by these, and at the same time they are clothed themselves when they give sentence, their eyes, their ears, and their whole bodies acting as a screen before their souls. They have all these hindrances before them, both their own clothing and that of those on trial. First of all then,' said he, 'men must be stopped from foreknowing their deaths, for now they have knowledge beforehand. Pro-
e metheus has already been told to stop this foreknowledge. Next they must be stripped naked of all these things before trial, for they must be judged after death. And the judge must be naked too and dead, scanning with his soul itself the souls of all immediately after death, deprived of all his kinsmen and with all that fine attire of his left on earth, that his verdict may be just. Now I had realized all this before you, and I have appointed sons of mine as judges, two from Asia, Minos and Rhadamanthus, and one, Aeacus, from Europe. And when
524 these are dead, they will hold court in the meadow, at the crossroads from which two paths lead, one to the Isles of the Blessed, the other to Tartarus. And Rhadamanthus will judge those who come from Asia, Aeacus those from Europe, and to Minos I will grant the privileges of court of appeal, if the other two are in doubt, so that the judgment about which path men take may be as just as possible.'

This is what I have heard, Callicles, and I believe it to be true,
b and from this story I infer the following conclusion. Death, in my opinion, is nothing else but the separation from each other of two things, soul and body, and when therefore they are separated from one another, each of them retains pretty much the same condition as when the man was alive, the body retaining its own nature, with all
c the marks of treatment or experience plainly visible. For instance if a man's body was large either by nature or through diet or through both causes while he was alive, after death too his corpse will be large, and if fat when living then fat too after death, and so on, and if again he habitually wore his hair long, his corpse too will be long-haired. And further if a man was a jailbird and bore traces of the blows he received when living, in the form of scars on his body inflicted by the lash or from other wounds, you may see the same marks on his body after death too, or if any of his limbs were broken or distorted in his life-
d time, the same things are evident in death. And, in a word, of the

physical characteristics acquired in life all or the greater part are visible for some time after death. And so I believe that the same thing is true of the soul, Callicles; once it has been stripped of the body, everything in the soul is manifest—its natural characteristics and the experiences which a man's soul has encountered through occupations of various kinds. When therefore they arrive before their judge— those from Asia before Rhadamanthus—he halts them and scans the e soul of each, quite unaware whose it is, but he will often lay hold of the Great King or any other king or potentate and see that there is no sign of health in his soul but that it is torn to ribbons by the scourge and full of scars due to perjuries and crime—the marks branded on 525 the soul by every evil deed—and that everything is crooked through falsehood and imposture, and nothing straight because it has been reared a stranger to truth. And he sees that owing to the license and luxury and presumption and incontinence of its actions the soul is surcharged with disproportion and ugliness, and seeing this he sends it away in ignominy straight to the prison house, where it is doomed on its arrival to endure the sufferings proper to it. And it is proper for everyone who suffers a punishment rightly inflicted by another that b he should either be improved and benefited thereby or become a warn- ing to the rest, in order that they may be afraid when they see him suffering what he does and may become better men. Now, those who are benefited through suffering punishment by gods and men are beings whose evil deeds are curable; nevertheless it is from pain and agony that they derive their benefit both here and in the other world, for it is impossible to be rid of evil otherwise. But those who have been c guilty of the most heinous crimes and whose misdeeds are past cure —of these warnings are made, and they are no longer capable them- selves of receiving any benefit, because they are incurable—but oth- ers are benefited who behold them suffering throughout eternity the greatest and most excruciating and terrifying tortures because of their misdeeds, literally suspended as examples there in the prison house in Hades, a spectacle and a warning to any evildoers who from time to time arrive. And one of these, I maintain, is Archelaus, if Polus tells d us the truth, and any other tyrant too of like character, and I think that most of these warning examples are chosen from tyrants and kings and potentates and politicians, for these, owing to the license they enjoy, are guilty of the greatest and most impious crimes.

Now Homer bears me out in this, for he has represented as those who suffer eternal punishment in Hades kings and princes, Tantalus e and Sisyphus and Tityus, but Thersites or any other private person who did wrong has by no one been represented as afflicted with cruel punishment because incurable, for I suppose he had not the power, and therefore was happier than those who had. But, Callicles, it is among the most powerful that you find the superlatively wicked. Still there is nothing to prevent good men from finding a place even among 526 the powerful, and those who do so are deserving of special admiration, for it is difficult, Callicles, and most praiseworthy to pass through life in righteousness when you have every license to do wrong. But men of this kind are few, though both in Athens and elsewhere there have been and, I fancy, will yet be honorable men and true, who possess the

b virtue of managing justly whatever is entrusted to them, and one of these won great renown even among the rest of the Greeks, Aristides, son of Lysimachus, but most of those in power, my good friend, prove evil.

As I said then, whenever Rhadamanthus receives one of these, he knows nothing else about him, his name or origin, only that he is evil, and when he perceives this, he dispatches him straight to Tartarus after first setting a seal upon him to show whether he appears to him curable or incurable, and on arrival there he undergoes the ap-

c propriate punishment. But sometimes he sees another soul, that has lived in piety and truth, that of a private citizen or any other—but in especial, I maintain, Callicles, the soul of a philosopher who has applied himself to his own business and not played the busybody in his life—and he is filled with admiration and sends him forthwith to the Isles of the Blessed. And Aeacus behaves in exactly the same way—each of the two gives sentence staff in hand—and Minos sits as judge of appeal, and he alone bears a scepter of gold, even as Odysseus

d in Homer says he saw him, 'holding a scepter of gold, rendering laws to the dead.' [6]

Now I have been convinced by these stories, Callicles, and I am considering how I may present to my judge the healthiest possible soul, and so I renounce the honors sought by most men, and pursuing the truth I shall really endeavor both to live and, when death comes,

e to die, as good a man as I possibly can be. And I exhort all other men thereto to the best of my power, and you above all I invite in return to share this life and to enlist in this contest which I maintain excels all other contests, and I reproach you in your turn because you will not be able to help yourself when the trial and judgment takes place of which I spoke just now. But when you come before your judge, the

527 son of Aegina, and he seizes hold of you, you will gape and reel to and fro there, no less than I do here, and perhaps someone will humiliate you by boxing your ears and will do you every kind of outrage.

Now perhaps all this seems to you like an old wife's tale and you despise it, and there would be nothing strange in despising it if our searches could discover anywhere a better and truer account, but as it is you see that you three, who are the wisest Greeks of the day, you and Polus and Gorgias, cannot demonstrate that we should live

b any other life than this, which is plainly of benefit also in the other world. But amid all these arguments, while others were refuted, this

---

[6] *Odyssey* 11.569.

alone stands steadfast, that we should be more on our guard against doing than suffering wrong, and that before all things a man should study not to seem but to be good, whether in private or in public life, and that if anyone proves evil in any way, he should be chastised, and next to being good the second-best thing is to become good and to make amends by punishment, and that we should avoid every form of c flattery, whether to ourselves or to others, whether to few or to many, and that rhetoric and every other activity should ever so be employed, to attain justice. If you will listen to me then, you will follow me where on your arrival you will win happiness both in life and after death, as our account reveals. And you may let anyone despise you as a fool and do you outrage, if he wishes, yes, and you may cheerfully let him strike you with that humiliating blow, for you will suffer no harm thereby if you really are a good man and an honorable, and pur- d sue virtue. And after such training in common together, then at last, if we think fit, we may enter public life, or we may take counsel together on whatever course suggests itself, when we are better able to take counsel than now. For it seems to me shameful that, being what apparently at this moment we are, we should consider ourselves to be fine fellows, when we can never hold to the same views about the same questions—and those too the most vital of all—so deplorably uneducated are we! Then let us follow the guidance of the argument e now made manifest, which reveals to us that this is the best way of life—to live and die in the pursuit of righteousness and all other virtues. Let us follow this, I say, inviting others to join us, not that which you believe in and commend to me, for it is worthless, dear Callicles.

PROTAGORAS

The reader who is interested only in Plato's philosophy would do well to pass over the first part of the Protagoras, the first three-quarters of it, in fact, up to the discussion about pleasure and pain when Socrates begins to speak in earnest. In this the familiar Platonic doctrine is brought out that no man does evil voluntarily, that is, thinking it to be evil, and the conclusion is reached—not only Platonic, but essentially and peculiarly Greek—that virtue is one with wisdom and that wickedness has its roots in ignorance.

To the general reader, however, the dialogue is second to none in giving a picture of Greek life, above all, of the intensity of interest the Athenians took in the purely intellectual. The eager lad who wakes Socrates before daybreak begging to be introduced to the great teacher Protagoras, just arrived in Athens, has many counterparts in the large company he and Socrates find when they enter the house where the man of wisdom is staying. All want to learn from him and they finally persuade him to take on an argument with Socrates which, most understandably, he is reluctant to do. The result, however, is not what one would expect, Protagoras' complete defeat. Far from that, he is shown to have the better reason a number of times and Socrates not only appears as occasionally advocating the worse, but even now and then splitting hairs and being tiresome.

The dialogue is a little comedy. Plato is amusing himself, laughing at everyone, including his beloved master, showing up, but very pleasantly, good old Protagoras' amiable vanity, taking a sly dig at a distinguished teacher's passion for finicky verbal distinctions, and giving gravely another's advice to Socrates to pay some attention to talking elegantly, not merely briefly and accurately. A final delightful picture of the Athenians emerges, their charming manners, never affected by the hottest argument, their love of fair play, and, when it is settled that there shall be a discussion, how all of them felt great delight "at the prospect of listening to wise men."

FRIEND: Where have you come from, Socrates? No doubt from pur- suit of the captivating Alcibiades. Certainly when I saw him only a day or two ago, he seemed to be still a handsome man, but between ourselves, Socrates, 'man' is the word. He's actually growing a beard.

SOCRATES: What of it? Aren't you an enthusiast for Homer, who says that the most charming age is that of the youth with his first b beard, just the age of Alcibiades now?

FRIEND: Well what's the news? Have you just left the young man, and how is he disposed toward you?

SOCRATES: Very well, I think, particularly today, since he came to my assistance and spoke up for me at some length. For as you guessed, I have only just left him. But I will tell you a surprising thing. Although he was present, I had no thought for him, and often forgot him altogether.

FRIEND: Why, what can have happened between you and him c to make such a difference? You surely can't have met someone more handsome—not in Athens at least?

SOCRATES: Yes, much more.

FRIEND: Really? An Athenian or a foreigner?

SOCRATES: A foreigner.

FRIEND: Where from?

SOCRATES: Abdera.

FRIEND: And this stranger struck you as such a handsome person that you put him above the son of Clinias in that respect?

SOCRATES: Yes. Must not perfect wisdom take the palm for handsomeness?

FRIEND: You mean you have just been meeting some wise man?

SOCRATES: Say rather the wisest man now living, if you agree d that that description fits Protagoras.

FRIEND: What? Protagoras is in Athens?

SOCRATES: And has been for two days.

FRIEND: And you have just now come from seeing him?

SOCRATES: Yes, we had a long talk together. 310

FRIEND: Then lose no time in telling me about your conversation, if you are free. Sit down here; the slave will make room for you.

SOCRATES: Certainly I shall, and be grateful to you for listening.

FRIEND: And I to you for your story.

SOCRATES: That means a favor on both sides. Listen then.

Last night, a little before daybreak, Hippocrates, son of Apollodorus, Phason's brother, knocked violently on my door with his stick, and when it was opened, came straight in in a great hurry and shouted b out, Socrates, are you awake or asleep?

From *Protagoras and Meno*, translated and with an introduction by W. K. C. Guthrie (Penguin Classics, Harmondsworth, Middlesex, 1956).

I recognized his voice and said, That will be Hippocrates. No bad news I hope?

Nothing but good, he replied.

I'm glad to hear it, said I. What is it then, and what brings you here at such an hour?

Protagoras has arrived, he said, taking his stand beside me.

The day before yesterday. Have you only just found out?

Only last evening.

c   As he said this he felt for the bed and sat by my feet, adding, Yes, yesterday evening, when I got back late from Oenoe. My slave Satyrus had run away from me. I meant to let you know that I was going after him, but something put it out of my head. When I got back and we had had dinner and were just going to bed, my brother mentioned to me that Protagoras had come. Late as it was, I nearly
d   came to see you straightaway; then I decided it was really too far into the night, but as soon as I had slept off my tiredness, I got up at once and came here as you see.

I recognized his determination and the state of excitement he was in, and asked him, What is your concern in this? Has Protagoras done you any harm?

Of course he has, Socrates, replied Hippocrates laughing. He keeps his wisdom to himself instead of sharing it with me.

Not at all, said I. If you pay him sufficient to persuade him, he will make you wise too.

e   If it were only a question of that! he said despairingly. I shouldn't keep back a penny of my own money, or my friends' money either. But this is just the reason why I have come to you, to persuade you to speak to him on my behalf. For one thing I am too young, and for another I have never seen nor heard Protagoras. Last time he came to Athens I was still a child. But you know, Socrates, everyone is singing his praises and saying that he is the cleverest of speakers. Do let's
311 pay him a visit at once, to make sure of finding him in. He's staying, so I'm told, with Callias, son of Hipponicus. Come on.

My dear Hippocrates, I said, we can't go there at this early hour. Let's come out here into the courtyard and walk around it to pass the time until it gets light. Then we can go. Protagoras spends most of his time indoors, so don't worry; we are pretty sure to catch him there.

So then we got up and walked about in the courtyard, and to try
b   Hippocrates' mettle I began to examine and question him. Tell me this, Hippocrates, I said. It is your present intention to go to Protagoras and pay him money as a fee on your behalf. Now whom do you think you are going to, and what will he make of you? Suppose for instance you had it in mind to go to your namesake Hippocrates of Cos, the doctor, and pay him a fee on your own behalf, and someone
c   asked you in what capacity you thought of Hippocrates with the intention of paying him, what would you answer?

I should say, in his capacity as a doctor.

And what would you hope to become?

A doctor.

And suppose your idea was to go to Polyclitus of Argos or Phidias of Athens and pay them fees for your own benefit, and someone asked you in what capacity you thought of paying this money to them, what would you answer?

I should say, in their capacity as sculptors.

To make you what?

A sculptor, obviously.

Right, said I. Now here are you and I going to Protagoras prepared d to pay him money as a fee for you—our own if it is enough to satisfy him, or if not, our friends' resources thrown in as well. If then, seeing us so full of enthusiasm, someone should ask, Tell me, Socrates and Hippocrates, what do you suppose Protagoras is, that you intend to pay him money? what should we answer him? What particular name do we hear attached to Protagoras in the sort of way that Phidias is e called a sculptor and Homer a poet?

Well, Sophist, I suppose, Socrates, is the name generally given to him.

Then it is as a Sophist that we will go to him and pay him?

Yes.

And if you had to face the further question, What do you yourself hope to become by your association with Protagoras?   312

He blushed at this—there was already a streak of daylight to betray him—and replied, If this is like the other cases, I must say 'to become a Sophist.'

But wouldn't a man like you be ashamed, said I, to face your fellow countrymen as a Sophist?

If I am to speak my real mind, I certainly should.

Perhaps then this is not the kind of instruction you expect to get from Protagoras, but rather the kind you got from the school- b masters who taught you letters and music and gymnastics. You didn't learn these for professional purposes, to become a practitioner, but in the way of liberal education, as a layman and a gentleman should.

That exactly describes, said he, the sort of instruction I expect from Protagoras.

Well then, I went on, do you understand what you are now going to do, or not?

In what respect?

I mean that you are going to entrust the care of your soul to a c man who is, in your own words, a Sophist, though I should be surprised if you know just what a Sophist is. And yet if you don't know that, you don't know to whom you are entrusting your soul, nor whether he represents something good or bad.

I think I know, said he.

Tell me then, what do you think a Sophist is?

I suppose, as the name implies, one who has knowledge of wise things.

One could say the same, said I, of painters and builders, that they are those who have knowledge of wise things. But if we were
d asked what *sort* of wisdom painters understand, we should reply, wisdom concerned with the making of likenesses, and so on with the others. If then we were asked what sort of wise things the Sophist has knowledge of, what should we answer? Of what is he the master?

The only answer we could give is that he is master of the art of making clever speakers.

Well, our answer might be true, but would hardly be sufficient. It invites the further question, On what matter does the Sophist make
e one a clever speaker? For example, the teacher of lyre playing I suppose makes people clever at speaking on his own subject, namely lyre playing, doesn't he?

Yes.

Well, on what subject does the Sophist make clever speakers?

Obviously on the subject of which he imparts knowledge.

Very probably. And what is this subject on which the Sophist is both an expert himself and can make his pupil expert?

313   I give up, he said. I can't tell you.

Well then, I continued, do you realize the sort of danger to which you are going to expose your soul? If it were a case of putting your body into the hands of someone and risking the treatment's turning out beneficial or the reverse, you would ponder deeply whether to entrust it to him or not, and would spend many days over the question, calling on the counsel of your friends and relations. But when it comes to something which you value more highly than your body, namely your soul—something on whose beneficial or harmful treat-
b ment your whole welfare depends—you have not consulted either your father or your brother or any of us who are your friends on the question whether or not to entrust your soul to this stranger who has arrived among us. On the contrary, having heard the news in the evening, so you tell me, here you come at dawn, not to discuss or consult me on this question of whether or not to entrust yourself to Protagoras, but ready to spend both your own money and that of your friends as if you had already made up your mind that you must at all costs associate with this man—whom you say you do not know and
c have never spoken to, but call a Sophist, and then turn out not to know what a Sophist is though you intend to put yourself into his hands.

When he heard this he said, It looks like it, Socrates, from what you say.

Can we say then, Hippocrates, that a Sophist is really a merchant or peddler of the goods by which a soul is nourished? To me he appears to be something like that.

But what is it that nourishes a soul?

What it learns, presumably, I said. And we must see that the Sophist in commending his wares does not deceive us, like the wholesaler and the retailer who deal in food for the body. These people do not know themselves which of the wares they offer is good or bad for d the body, but in selling them praise all alike, and those who buy from them don't know either, unless one of them happens to be a trainer or a doctor. So too those who take the various subjects of knowledge from city to city, and offer them for sale retail to whoever wants them, commend everything that they have for sale, but it may be, my dear Hippocrates, that some of these men also are ignorant of the beneficial or harmful effects on the soul of what they have for sale, and e so too are those who buy from them, unless one of them happens to be a physician of the soul. If then you chance to be an expert in discerning which of them is good or bad, it is safe for you to buy knowledge from Protagoras or anyone else, but if not, take care you don't find yourself gambling dangerously with all of you that is dearest to 314 you. Indeed the risk you run in purchasing knowledge is much greater than that in buying provisions. When you buy food and drink, you can carry it away from the shop or warehouse in a receptacle, and before you receive it into your body by eating or drinking you can store it away at home and take the advice of an expert as to what you should eat and drink and what not, and how much you should consume and when; so there is not much risk in the actual purchase. But knowledge cannot be taken away in a parcel. When you have paid for it b you must receive it straight into the soul. You go away having learned it and are benefited or harmed accordingly. So I suggest we give this matter some thought, not only by ourselves, but also with those who are older than we, for we are still rather young to examine such a large problem. However, now let us carry out our plan to go and hear the man, and when we have heard him we can bring others into our consultations also, for Protagoras is not here by himself. There is Hippias of Elis, and I think Prodicus of Ceos too, and many other wise c men.

Having agreed on this we started out. When we found ourselves in the doorway, we stood there and continued a discussion which had arisen between us on the way. So that we might not leave it unfinished, but have it out before we went in, we were standing in the doorway talking until we should reach agreement. I believe the porter, a eunuch, overheard us, and it seems likely that the crowd of Sophists d had put him in a bad temper with visitors. At any rate when we knocked at the door he opened it, saw us and said, Ha, Sophists! He's busy. And thereupon he slammed the door as hard as he could with both hands. We knocked again, and he answered through the closed door, Didn't you hear me say he's busy?

My good man, I said, we have not come to see Callias and we are
e   not Sophists. Cheer up. It is Protagoras we want to see, so announce us. So at last the fellow reluctantly opened the door to us.

When we were inside, we came upon Protagoras walking in the portico, and walking with him in a long line were, on one side Callias, son of Hipponicus; his stepbrother Paralus, the son of Pericles; and
315 Charmides, son of Glaucon; and on the other side Pericles' other son, Xanthippus; Philippides, son of Philomelus; and Antimoerus of Mende, the most eminent of Protagoras' pupils, who is studying professionally, to become a Sophist. Those who followed behind listening to their conversation seemed to be for the most part foreigners— Protagoras draws them from every city that he passes through, charming them with his voice like Orpheus, and they follow spellbound
b   —but there were some Athenians in the band as well. As I looked at the party I was delighted to notice what special care they took never to get in front or to be in Protagoras' way. When he and those with him turned round, the listeners divided this way and that in perfect order, and executing a circular movement took their places each time in the rear. It was beautiful.

'After that I recognized,' [1] as Homer says, Hippias of Elis, sitting
c   on a seat of honor in the opposite portico, and around him were seated on benches Eryximachus, son of Acumenus, and Phaedrus of Myrrhinus and Andron, son of Androtion, with some fellow citizens of his and other foreigners. They appeared to be asking him questions on natural science, particularly astronomy, while he gave each his explanation ex cathedra and held forth on their problems.
d   'And there too spied I Tantalus' [2]—for Prodicus of Ceos was also in town, and was occupying a room which Hipponicus used to use for storage, but now owing to the number of people staying in the house Callias had cleared it out and made it into a guest room. Prodicus was still in bed, wrapped up in rugs and blankets, and plenty of them, as far as one could see, and beside him on the neighboring couches sat Pausanias from Cerameis and with him someone who was still a young boy—a lad of fine character I think, and certainly very good-looking.
e   I think I heard that his name is Agathon, and I shouldn't be surprised if Pausanias is particularly attached to him. Well there was this boy and the two Adimantuses—the son of Cepis and the son of Leucolophides—and a few others. But what they were talking about I couldn't discover from outside, although I was very keen to hear
316 Prodicus, whom I regard as a man of inspired genius. You see, he has such a deep voice that there was a kind of booming noise in the room which drowned the words. Just after we had come in, there entered

---

[1] *Odyssey* 11.601.   [2] *Odyssey* 11.582.

close on our heels the handsome Alcibiades as you call him—and I quite agree—and Critias, son of Callaeschrus.

When we entered, then, we paused for a few moments to drink b in the scene and then approached Protagoras, and I said, Protagoras, this is Hippocrates, and it is you that we have come to see.

Do you wish to speak to me alone, he asked, or with the others?

It is all the same to us, I replied. Hear what we have come for and then decide for yourself.

And what have you come for?

Hippocrates here is one of our citizens, son of Apollodorus. He comes of a great and prosperous family, and is considered the equal of any of his contemporaries in natural gifts. I think he is anxious to c make a name for himself in the city, and he believes that the most likely way to success is to become a pupil of yours. So now it is for you to decide whether you think this calls for a conversation between ourselves or with others.

I appreciate your forethought on my behalf, Socrates. A man has to be careful when he visits powerful cities as a foreigner, and induces their most promising young men to forsake the company of others, relatives or acquaintances, older or younger, and consort with him on the grounds that his conversation will improve them. Such conduct d arouses no small resentment and various forms of hostility and intrigue. Personally I hold that the Sophist's art is an ancient one, but that those who put their hand to it in former times, fearing the odium which it brings, adopted a disguise and worked under cover. Some used poetry as a screen, for instance Homer and Hesiod and Simonides; others religious rites and prophecy, like Orpheus and Musaeus and their school; some even—so I have noticed—physical training, like Iccus of Tarentum and in our own day Herodicus of Selymbria, the former Megarian, as great a Sophist as any. Music was e used as cover by your own Agathocles, a great Sophist, and Pythoclides of Ceos and many others. All of them, as I say, used these arts as a screen to escape malice. I myself, however, am not of their mind in 317 this. I don't believe they accomplished their purpose, for they did not pass unobserved by the men who held the reins of power in their cities, though it is on their account that these disguises are adopted; the mass of people notice nothing, but simply echo what the leaders tell them. Now to run away and fail to escape, but be discovered instead, turns the attempt into sheer folly, and cannot fail to arouse even greater hostility, for people think that the man who behaves like this b is in addition to his other faults an unprincipled rogue. I therefore have always gone the opposite way to my predecessors'. I admit to being a Sophist and an educator, and I consider this a better precaution than the other—admission rather than denial. I have devised other precautions as well, so that, if heaven will forgive the boast, I come to no harm through being a confessed Sophist, though I have c

been many years in the profession. Indeed I am getting on in life now
—so far as age goes I might be the father of any one of you—so if
there is anything you want of me, I should much prefer to say my say
in front of the whole company.

Thereupon, suspecting that he wanted to display his skill to
Prodicus and Hippias and get some glory from the fact that we had
come as his professed admirers, I remarked, Then why should we not
d call Prodicus and Hippias, and the people who are with them, to
listen to us?

By all means, said Protagoras.

Would you like to make a regular circle, said Callias, so that you
can talk sitting down?

Everyone agreed that this was the thing to do, and at the prospect
of listening to wise men we all eagerly took hold of the benches and
couches with our own hands and arranged them beside Hippias,
e where the benches were. Meanwhile Callias and Alcibiades got
Prodicus out of bed and fetched him along with his companions.

When we were all seated, Protagoras began, Now that these gentlemen are present, Socrates, perhaps you will say something about
the matter you mentioned to me just now on this young man's
318 behalf.

I can only begin as I did before, by telling you of our purpose in
coming. Hippocrates has a feeling that he would like to become one
of your followers. He says therefore that he would be glad to be told
what effect it will have on him. That is all we have to say.

Then Protagoras replied, Young man, if you come to me, your
gain will be this. The very day you join me, you will go home a better
man, and the same the next day. Each day you will make progress
toward a better state.

b   On hearing this I said, Protagoras, what you say is not at all surprising, but very natural. Even you, for all your years and wisdom,
would become better, if someone were to teach you something that
you didn't happen to know. Please don't answer like this, but give us
the kind of reply that Hippocrates would get if he suddenly changed
his mind and took a fancy to study with that young man who has just
lately come to live at Athens, Zeuxippus of Heraclea. Suppose he went
to him, just as he has come to you, and heard him say the same thing,
c that each day he spent with him he would get better and make progress, and asked him the further question, 'What shall I get better at,
and where shall I make progress?' Zeuxippus would say, 'In painting.'
Or if he were with Orthagoras of Thebes, and having heard the same
reply as he got from you, went on to ask in what respect he would get
daily better by being with him, Orthagoras would say, 'In playing the
flute.' Now give a similar answer to the lad and to me who am putting
d the question for him. Hippocrates, by becoming a pupil of Protagoras,
will, on the very day he joins him, go home a better man, and on each

successive day will make similar progress—toward what, Protagoras, and better at what?

Protagoras heard me out and said, You put your questions well, and I enjoy answering good questioners. When he comes to me, Hippocrates will not be put through the same things that another Sophist would inflict on him. The others treat their pupils badly; these young men, who have deliberately turned their backs on specialization, e they take and plunge into special studies again, teaching them arithmetic and astronomy and geometry and music—here he glanced at Hippias—but from me he will learn only what he has come to learn. What is that subject? The proper care of his personal affairs, so that he may best manage his own household, and also of the state's affairs, so as to become a real power in the city, both as speaker and man of 319 action.

Do I follow you? said I. I take you to be describing the art of politics, and promising to make men good citizens.

That, said he, is exactly what I profess to do.

Then it is a truly splendid accomplishment that you have mastered, said I, if indeed you have mastered it. I warn you that you will hear nothing from me but my real mind. The fact is, I did not think b this was something that could be taught, though when you say otherwise I cannot doubt your word. But it is up to me to say why I believe it cannot be taught nor furnished by one man to another. I hold that the Athenians, like the rest of the Hellenes, are sensible people. Now when we meet in the Assembly, then if the state is faced with some building project, I observe that the architects are sent for and consulted about the proposed structures, and when it is a matter of shipbuilding, the naval designers, and so on with everything which the Assembly regards as a subject for learning and teaching. If anyone c else tries to give advice, whom they do not consider an expert, however handsome or wealthy or nobly born he may be, it makes no difference; the members reject him noisily and with contempt, until either he is shouted down and desists, or else he is dragged off or ejected by the police on the orders of the presiding magistrates. That is how they behave over subjects they consider technical. But when it is something to do with the government of the country that is to be debated, d the man who gets up to advise them may be a builder or equally well a blacksmith or a shoemaker, merchant or shipowner, rich or poor, of good family or none. No one brings it up against any of these, as against those I have just mentioned, that here is a man who without any technical qualifications, unable to point to anybody as his teacher, is yet trying to give advice. The reason must be that they do not think this is a subject that can be taught.

And you must not suppose that this is true only of the community at large. Individually also the wisest and best of our countrymen are e unable to hand on to others the virtue which they possess. Pericles, for

instance, the father of these two boys, gave them the very best education in everything that depends on teaching, but in his own special
320   kind of wisdom he neither trains them himself nor hands them over
to any other instructor; they simply browse around on their own like
sacred cattle, on the chance of picking up virtue automatically. To take
a different example, Clinias, the younger brother of Alcibiades here,
is a ward of that same Pericles, who for fear that Alcibiades would
corrupt him, took him away and tried to give him a better upbringing by placing him in the household of Ariphron. Before six
months were out, Ariphron gave him back; he could make nothing of
b   him. I could mention plenty of others too, excellent men themselves,
who never made anyone else better, either their own relatives or
others.

With these facts in mind, Protagoras, I do not believe that virtue
can be taught. But when I hear you speaking as I do, my skepticism
is shaken and I suppose there is truth in what you say, for I regard you as a man of wide experience, deep learning, and original
thought. If then you can demonstrate more plainly to us that virtue
c   is something that can be taught, please don't hoard your wisdom but
explain.

I shall not be a miser, Socrates, he replied. Now shall I, as an old
man speaking to his juniors, put my explanation in the form of a
story, or give it as a reasoned argument?

Many of the audience answered that he should relate it in
whichever form he pleased.

Then I think, he said, it will be pleasanter to tell you a story.

Once upon a time, there existed gods but no mortal creatures.
d   When the appointed time came for these also to be born, the gods
formed them within the earth out of a mixture of earth and fire and
the substances which are compounded from earth and fire. And when
they were ready to bring them to the light, they charged Prometheus
and Epimetheus with the task of equipping them and allotting suitable powers to each kind. Now Epimetheus begged Prometheus to allow him to do the distribution himself—'and when I have done it,' he
said, 'you can review it.' So he persuaded him and set to work. In his
allotment he gave to some creatures strength without speed, and
e   equipped the weaker kinds with speed. Some he armed with weapons,
while to the unarmed he gave some other faculty and so contrived
means for their preservation. To those that he endowed with smallness, he granted winged flight or a dwelling underground; to those
which he increased in stature, their size itself was a protection. Thus
321   he made his whole distribution on a principle of compensation, being
careful by these devices that no species should be destroyed.

When he had sufficiently provided means of escape from mutual
slaughter, he contrived their comfort against the seasons sent from
Zeus, clothing them with thick hair or hard skins sufficient to ward

off the winter's cold, and effective also against heat, and he b
planned that when they went to bed, the same coverings should
serve as proper and natural bedclothes for each species. He shod them
also, some with hoofs, others with hard and bloodless skin.

Next he appointed different sorts of food for them—to some
the grass of the earth, to others the fruit of trees, to others roots. Some
he allowed to gain their nourishment by devouring other animals, and
these he made less prolific, while he bestowed fertility on their victims, and so preserved the species.

Now Epimetheus was not a particularly clever person, and before
he realized it he had used up all the available powers on the brute c
beasts, and being left with the human race on his hands unprovided
for, did not know what to do with them. While he was puzzling about
this, Prometheus came to inspect the work, and found the other animals well off for everything, but man naked, unshod, unbedded, and
unarmed, and already the appointed day had come, when man too
was to emerge from within the earth into the daylight. Prometheus therefore, being at a loss to provide any means of salvation
for man, stole from Hephaestus and Athena the gift of skill in the arts, d
together with fire—for without fire it was impossible for anyone to
possess or use this skill—and bestowed it on man. In this way man acquired sufficient resources to keep himself alive, but had no political
wisdom. This was in the keeping of Zeus, and Prometheus no longer
had the right of entry to the citadel where Zeus dwelt; moreover the
sentinels of Zeus were terrible. But into the dwelling shared by Athena
and Hephaestus, in which they practiced their art, he penetrated by e
stealth, and carrying off Hephaestus' art of working with fire, and
the art of Athena as well, he gave them to man. Through this gift man
had the means of life, but Prometheus, so the story says, thanks to 322
Epimetheus, had later on to stand his trial for theft.

Since, then, man had a share in the portion of the gods, in the
first place because of his divine kinship he alone among living creatures believed in gods, and set to work to erect altars and images of
them. Secondly, by the art which they possessed, men soon discovered
articulate speech and names, and invented houses and clothes and
shoes and bedding and got food from the earth.

Thus provided for, they lived at first in scattered groups; there
were no cities. Consequently they were devoured by wild beasts, since b
they were in every respect the weaker, and their technical skill,
though a sufficient aid to their nurture, did not extend to making war
on the beasts, for they had not the art of politics, of which the art of
war is a part. They sought therefore to save themselves by coming together and founding fortified cities, but when they gathered in communities they injured one another for want of political skill, and so
scattered again and continued to be devoured. Zeus therefore, fearing c
the total destruction of our race, sent Hermes to impart to men the

qualities of respect for others and a sense of justice, so as to bring order into our cities and create a bond of friendship and union.

Hermes asked Zeus in what manner he was to bestow these gifts on men. 'Shall I distribute them as the arts were distributed—that is, on the principle that one trained doctor suffices for many laymen, and so with the other experts? Shall I distribute justice and respect for their fellows in this way, or to all alike?'

d 'To all,' said Zeus. 'Let all have their share. There could never be cities if only a few shared in these virtues, as in the arts. Moreover, you must lay it down as my law that if anyone is incapable of acquiring his share of these two virtues he shall be put to death as a plague to the city.'

Thus it is, Socrates, and from this cause, that in a debate involving skill in building, or in any other craft, the Athenians, like other e men, believe that few are capable of giving advice, and if someone outside those few volunteers to advise them, then as you say, they do 323 not tolerate it—rightly so, in my submission. But when the subject of their counsel involves political wisdom, which must always follow the path of justice and moderation, they listen to every man's opinion, for they think that everyone must share in this kind of virtue; otherwise the state could not exist. That, Socrates, is the reason for this.

Here is another proof that I am not deceiving you in saying that all men do in fact believe that everyone shares a sense of justice and civic virtue. In specialized skills, as you say, if a man claims to be good at the flute or at some other art when he is not, people either b laugh at him or are annoyed, and his family restrain him as if he were crazy. But when it comes to justice and civic virtue as a whole, even if someone is known to be wicked, yet if he publicly tells the truth about himself, his truthfulness, which in the other case was counted a virtue, is here considered madness. Everyone, it is said, ought to say he is good, whether he is or not, and whoever does not make such a claim is out of his mind, for a man cannot be without some share in c justice, or he would not be human.

So much then for the point that men rightly take all alike into their counsels concerning virtue of this sort, because they believe that all have a share in it. I shall next try to demonstrate to you that they do not regard it as innate or automatic, but as acquired by instruction and taking thought. No one is angered by the faults which d are believed to be due to nature or chance, nor do people rebuke or teach or punish those who exhibit them, in the hope of curing them; they simply pity them. Who would be so foolish as to treat in that way the ugly or dwarfish or weak? Everyone knows that it is nature or chance which gives this kind of characteristics to a man, both the good and the bad. But it is otherwise with the good qualities which are thought to be acquired through care and practice and instruction. It e is the absence of these, surely, and the presence of the corresponding vices, that call forth indignation and punishment and admonition. Among these faults are to be put injustice and irreligion and in general everything that is contrary to civic virtue. In this field indigna- 324 tion and admonition are universal, evidently because of a belief that such virtue can be acquired by taking thought or by instruction. Just consider the function of punishment, Socrates, in relation to the wrongdoer. That will be enough to show you that men believe it possible to impart goodness. In punishing wrongdoers, no one concentrates on the fact that a man has done wrong in the past, or punishes him on that account, unless taking blind vengeance like a beast. No, b punishment is not inflicted by a rational man for the sake of the crime that has been committed—after all one cannot undo what is past—but for the sake of the future, to prevent either the same man or, by the spectacle of his punishment, someone else, from doing wrong again. But to hold such a view amounts to holding that virtue can be instilled by education; at all events the punishment is inflicted as a deterrent. This then is the view held by all who inflict it c whether privately or publicly. And your fellow countrymen, the Athenians, certainly do inflict punishment and correction on supposed wrongdoers, as do others also. This argument therefore shows that they too think it possible to impart and teach goodness.   d

I think that I have now sufficiently demonstrated to you, first that your countrymen act reasonably in accepting the advice of smith and shoemaker on political matters, and secondly, that they do believe goodness to be something imparted by teaching. There remains the question which troubles you about good men—why it is that whereas they teach their sons the subjects that depend on instruction, and make them expert in these things, yet in their own brand of goodness they do not make them any better than others. On this, Socrates, I will offer you a plain argument rather than a parable as I did before. Think of it like this. Is there or is there not some one thing in which all citizens must share, if a state is to exist at all? In the answer e to this question, if anywhere, lies the solution of your difficulty. If there is, and this one essential is not the art of building or forging or pottery but justice and moderation and holiness of life, or to concen- 325 trate it into a single whole, manly virtue—if, I say, it is this in which all must share and which must enter into every man's actions whatever other occupation he chooses to learn and practice; if the one who lacks it, man, woman, or child, must be instructed and corrected until by punishment he is reformed, and whoever does not respond to punishment and instruction must be expelled from the state or put b to death as incurable—if all this is true, and in these circumstances our good men teach their sons other accomplishments but not this one thing, then think what extraordinary people good men must be! We have already shown that they believe it can be taught, both publicly and privately. But although virtue can be taught and cultivated, yet it

seems they have their sons instructed in other arts, ignorance of which is no matter for capital punishment, but although if they are left ignorant of virtue and morally uncultivated they may be punished
c by death or exile—and not only death but alienation of property and in a word the ruin of their estates—are we to suppose that they neglect this side of their education? Don't they rather bestow every care and attention upon it? Of course they do, Socrates. They teach and admonish them from earliest childhood and throughout their lives. As soon as a child can understand what is said to him, nurse, mother,
d tutor, and the father himself vie with each other to make him as good as possible, instructing him through everything he does or says, pointing out, 'This is right and that is wrong, this honorable and that disgraceful, this holy, that impious; do this, don't do that.' If he is obedient, well and good. If not, they straighten him with threats and beatings, like a warped and twisted plank.

Later on when they send the children to school, their instructions to the masters lay much more emphasis on good behavior than
e on letters or music. The teachers take good care of this, and when boys have learned their letters and are ready to understand the written
326 word as formerly the spoken, they set the works of good poets before them on their desks to read and make them learn them by heart, poems containing much admonition and many stories, eulogies, and panegyrics of the good men of old, so that the child may be inspired to imitate them and long to be like them.

The music masters by analogous methods instill self-control and deter the young from evil-doing. And when they have learned to play the lyre, they teach them the works of good poets of another sort,
b namely the lyrical, which they accompany on the lyre, familiarizing the minds of the children with the rhythms and melodies. By this means they become more civilized, more balanced, and better adjusted in themselves and so more capable in whatever they say or do, for rhythm and harmonious adjustment are essential to the whole of human life.

Over and above this, they are sent to a trainer, so that a good mind may have a good body to serve it, and no one be forced by physi-
c cal weakness to play the coward in war and other ordeals.

All this is done by those best able to do it—that is, by the wealthy—and it is their sons who start their education at the earliest age and continue it the longest. When they have finished with teachers, the state compels them to learn the laws and use them as a pattern for their life, lest left to themselves they should drift aimlessly. You know how, when children are not yet good at writing, the writing
d master traces outlines with the pencil before giving them the slate, and makes them follow the lines as a guide in their own writing; well, similarly the state sets up the laws, which are inventions of good lawgivers of ancient times, and compels the citizens to rule and be ruled

in accordance with them. Whoever strays outside the lines, it punishes, and the name given to this punishment both among yourselves e
and in many other places is correction, intimating that the penalty
corrects or guides.

Seeing then that all this care is taken over virtue, both individually and by the state, are you surprised that virtue should be teachable, and puzzled to know whether it is? There is nothing to be
surprised at. The wonder would be if it were not teachable.

Why then, you ask, do many sons of good men turn out worthless? I will tell you this too. It is nothing surprising, if what I said
earlier was true, that this faculty, virtue, is something in which no one 327
may be a layman if a state is to exist at all. If it is as I say—and
most assuredly it is—consider the matter with the substitution of
any art you like. Suppose a state could not exist unless we were all
flute players to the best of our ability, and everyone taught everyone
else that art both privately and publicly, and scolded the bad flute
player, and no one held back on this subject any more than anyone b
now begrudges information on what is right and lawful or makes a
secret of it as of certain other techniques. After all, it is to our advantage that our neighbor should be just and virtuous, and therefore
everyone gladly talks about it to everyone else and instructs him in
justice and the law. If then, as I say, it were so with flute playing, and
we all showed equal eagerness and willingness to teach one another,
do you think, Socrates, that the sons of good players would become
good players in their turn any more than the sons of bad ones? Not so,
I think, but whoever had a son with the greatest natural talent for the
flute, his son would rise to fame, and a son without this talent would c
remain in obscurity. The son of a good performer would often be a
poor one, and vice versa, but at any rate all would be good enough in
comparison with someone who knew nothing of flute playing at all.

Now apply this analogy to our present condition. The man who
in a civilized and humane society appears to you the most wicked
must be thought just—a practitioner, as one might say, of justice—if
one has to judge him in comparison with men who have neither edu- d
cation nor courts of justice nor laws nor any constraint compelling
them to be continually heedful of virtue—savages in fact like those
whom the playwright Pherecrates brought onto the stage at last year's
Lenaea. If you found yourself among such people—people like the
man-haters of his chorus—you would be only too glad to meet a
Eurybatus and a Phrynondas, and would bitterly regret the very
depravity of our own society. But as it is you are spoiled, Socrates, e
in that all are teachers of virtue to the best of their ability, and so you
think that no one is. In the same way if you asked who teaches the 328
Greek language you would not find anyone, and again if you looked for
a teacher of the sons of our artisans in the craft which they have in
fact learned from their father to the best of their ability, and from his

friends in the same trade, there again I don't think it would be easy to point to a master, though in the case of a complete tyro it would be easy enough. Thus it is with virtue and everything else, so that if we can find someone only a little better than the others at advancing us on the road to virtue, we must be content.

b   My claim is that I am one of these, rather better than anyone else at helping a man to acquire a good and noble character, worthy indeed of the fee which I charge and even more, as my pupils themselves agree. On this account I have adopted the following method of assessing my payment. Anyone who comes to learn from me may either

c pay the fee I ask for or, if he prefers, go to a temple, state on oath what he believes to be the worth of my instruction, and deposit that amount.

There, Socrates, you have both the parable and the argument by which I have sought to show that virtue is teachable and that the Athenians believe it to be so, and that at the same time it is quite natural for the sons of good fathers to turn out good for nothing, and vice versa. Why, even the sons of Polyclitus, who are contemporaries of Paralus and Xanthippus here, cannot hold a candle to their father, nor can the sons of many other craftsmen. But it is too early to bring

d such a charge against these two; they are young, and there is still promise in them.

Here Protagoras brought to an end his long and magnificent display of eloquence. For a long time I gazed at him spellbound, eager to catch any further word that he might utter. When I saw that he had really finished, I collected myself with an effort and said, turning to Hippocrates: Son of Apollodorus, how grateful I am to you for induc-

e ing me to come here. To have heard what Protagoras has just said is something I value very highly. I used to think that it was by no human diligence that good men acquired their goodness, but now I am convinced. There is just one small thing holding me back, which Protagoras I know will easily explain, now that he has instructed us on

329 so many points. It is true that if a man talked on these matters with any of our popular orators, he might possibly hear similar discourses from Pericles or some other proficient speaker, but if one asks any of them an additional question, like books they cannot either answer or ask a question on their own account. Ask them the smallest thing supplementary to what they have said, and like a gong which booms out when you strike it and goes on until you lay a hand on it, so

b our orators at a tiny question spin out a regular Marathon of speech. Protagoras on the other hand, though he is perfectly capable of long and splendid speeches as we have seen, has also the faculty of answering a question briefly, and when he asks one himself, of waiting and listening to the answer—a rare accomplishment.

Now then, Protagoras, there is just one small question left, your answer to which will give me all I want. You say that virtue is teachable, and there is no one I would believe sooner than you. But there is one thing which took me by surprise in your speech, and I should like c you to fill this gap in my mind. You said that Zeus bestowed on men justice and respect for their fellows, and again at several points in your discourse justice and self-control and holiness and the rest were mentioned as if together they made up one thing, virtue. This is the point I want you to state for me with more precision. Is virtue a single whole, and are justice and self-control and holiness parts of it, or are these latter all names for one and the same thing? That is d what I still want to know.

Well, that is easy to answer, said he. Virtue is one, and the qualities you ask about are parts of it.

Do you mean, said I, as the parts of a face are parts—mouth, nose, eyes, and ears—or like the parts of a piece of gold, which do not differ from one another or from the whole except in size?

In the first way, I should say—that is, they are in the relation of the parts of a face to the whole.   e

Then do men so share in these parts of virtue that some have one and some another, or must a man who possesses one of them possess them all?

By no means. Many men are brave but unjust, and others are just but not wise.

Are these also parts of virtue? said I. Wisdom, I mean, and courage?

Most emphatically. Wisdom indeed is the greatest of the parts. 330
And each of them is different from the others?
Yes.

Has each also its own function? In a face, the eye is not like the ear nor has it the same function. Nor do the other parts resemble one another in function any more than in other respects. Is this how the parts of virtue differ, both in themselves and in their function? It b must be so, I suppose, if the parallel holds good.

Yes it is so, Socrates.

Then no other part of virtue resembles knowledge or justice or courage or temperance or holiness.

He agreed.

Now let us consider together what sort of thing each is. First of all, is there such a thing as justice or not? I think there is.   c

So do I, he said.

Well, if someone asked you and me, 'Tell me, you two, this thing that you mentioned a moment ago—justice—is it itself just or unjust?' I myself should answer that it was just. Which way would you vote?

The same as you, he said.

Then we would both answer that justice is of such a nature as to be just?

d   He agreed.

If he next asked, 'You say that there is also such a thing as holiness?' we should agree I suppose?

Yes.

'Meaning that holiness too is a thing?' We should still assent?

He agreed again.

'Do you then say that this thing is of a nature to be holy or unholy?' Personally I should be annoyed at this, and say, 'What a blasphemous question! Nothing else could well be holy if we won't allow
e   holiness itself to be so.' What about you? Wouldn't that be your answer?

Certainly, he said.

Suppose now he went on to ask us, 'But what did you say a few minutes ago? Didn't I hear you rightly? I thought you said that the
331   parts of virtue are so related that one does not resemble the other.' For my part I should reply, 'You have got most of it right, but your ears deceived you if you think I said that myself. It was Protagoras' answer to a question I put.' Now if he asks you, 'Is this true, Protagoras? Is it you who say that one part of virtue does not resemble another? Is this your statement?'—what would you answer?

I should have to admit it, he said.

Then having agreed about this, what shall we say if he goes on to ask, 'Then it is not the nature of holiness to be something just, nor of justice to be holy; it will be not-holy, and holiness will be not-just—
b   that is, unjust, and justice unholy?' What shall we answer? I should say on my own behalf that justice is holy and holiness just, and on your behalf, if you would allow me, I should make the same reply, that justice is either the same thing as holiness or very like it, and that justice unquestionably resembles holiness and holiness justice. Are you going to prevent me from making this answer, or do you agree with me?

I don't think it is quite so simple, Socrates. I can't really admit
c   that justice is holy and holiness just; I think there is some difference there. However, he said, what does it matter? If you like, let us assume that justice is holy and holiness just.

Excuse me, I said. It isn't this 'if you like' and 'if that's what you think' that I want us to examine, but you and me ourselves. What I mean is, I think the argument will be most fairly tested, if we take the 'if' out of it.

d   Well of course, he replied, justice does have some resemblance to holiness. After all, everything resembles everything else up to a point. There is a sense in which white resembles black, and hard soft, and so on with all other things that present the most contrary appearances. Even the parts of the face, which we described earlier as having different functions and not being like each other, have a certain resemblance and are like each other in some way. So by your method you can prove, if you want to, that they too all resemble one another. But it is not right to call things similar because they have e some one point of similarity, even when the resemblance is very slight, any more than to call things dissimilar that have some point of dissimilarity.

At this I said in some surprise, And is this how you suppose justice to be related to holiness, that there is only a slight resemblance between them?

Not quite that, but not on the other hand in the way that you seem to believe.

Well, said I, this line of argument doesn't seem to be agreeable to 332 you, so let us drop it and look at something else that you said. You recognize the existence of folly?

Yes.

Is not wisdom altogether contrary to it?

Yes.

And when men act rightly and advantageously, do you regard them as acting temperately or not?

Temperately.

That is to say with temperance?

Of course.   b

And those who act wrongly act foolishly, and in doing so do not behave temperately?

He agreed.

Then foolish behavior is the opposite of temperate?

Yes.

And foolish behavior is the outcome of folly, and temperate of temperance?

Yes.

If something is done with strength, it is done strongly, and if with weakness weakly, if with speed quickly, and if with slowness slowly?

Yes.

What is done in the same manner is done by the same agency, c and if contrariwise, by the contrary?

He agreed.

Again, said I, you recognize the existence of the fair?

He did.

Has it any contrary except the foul?

No.

And the good too you recognize?

Yes.

Has it any contrary except the bad?

No.

And also high pitch in sound? And has it any other contrary but low?

No.

In short, said I, to everything that admits of a contrary there is one contrary and no more.

He conceded the point.

d Now, said I, let us recapitulate our points of agreement. We agreed that each thing has one contrary and no more, that what is done in a contrary manner is done by a contrary agency, that a foolish action is contrary to a temperate one, and that a temperate action is performed with temperance and a foolish one with folly.

e He admitted all this.

If then what is done in a contrary manner is done by a contrary agency, and one action is performed with temperance and the other with folly—in a contrary manner and so by contrary agencies—then folly is the contrary of temperance.

It seems so.

Now you remember our earlier agreement that folly was the contrary of wisdom?

Yes.

And that one thing has one contrary?

Certainly.

333 Then which statement are we to give up? The dictum 'one thing one contrary' or the statement that wisdom is a distinct thing from temperance, both being parts of virtue, and that in addition to each being distinct they are dissimilar both in themselves and in their functions, like the parts of a face? Which shall we renounce? The two statements are not very harmonious. They don't chime well together or fit in with each other. How could they, if one thing can have only

b one opposite, and yet though folly is only one thing, temperance as well as wisdom appears to be contrary to it? Isn't that the way of it, Protagoras?

He agreed, though most reluctantly.

Then must not temperance and wisdom be the same, just as earlier justice and holiness turned out to be much the same? Come now, Protagoras, we must not falter, but complete our inquiry. Do you think that a man who commits an injustice acts temperately in

c committing it?

For my part I should be ashamed to agree to that, he replied. Of course many people do.

Well, shall I direct my argument against them or against you?

If you wish, he said, argue first against the proposition of the many.

It is all the same to me, said I, provided you make the replies, whether it is your own opinion or not. It is the argument itself that I wish to probe, though it may turn out that both I who question and you who answer are equally under scrutiny.

d At first Protagoras began to make difficulties, alleging that it would be hard to conduct a discussion on these terms, but in the end he agreed to answer.

Good, said I. Now let us start from the beginning. You believe that some people show temperance in doing wrong?

We will suppose so, he said.

And to show temperance is to show good sense?

Yes.

Which means that in doing wrong they have planned well?

So be it.

If their wrongdoing is successful or unsuccessful?

If it is successful.

You agree that some things are good?

Yes.

And do you mean by good those things which are beneficial to men?

Not only those, he said. Even if they are not beneficial to me, I e still call them good.

At this point I thought Protagoras was beginning to bristle, ready for a quarrel and preparing to do battle with his answers. Seeing this I became more cautious and proceeded gently with my questioning: Do you mean things which are beneficial to no human being, or things 334 that are not beneficial at all? Do you call them good also?

Of course not, he said. But I know plenty of things—foods, drinks, drugs, and many others—which are harmful to men, and others which are beneficial, and others again which, so far as men are concerned, are neither, but are harmful or beneficial to horses, and others only to cattle or dogs. Some have no effect on animals, but only on trees, and some again are good for the roots of trees but injurious to the young growths. Manure, for instance, is good for all plants b when applied to their roots, but utterly destructive if put on the shoots or young branches. Or take olive oil. It is very bad for plants, and most inimical to the hair of all animals except man, whereas men find it of service both to the hair and to the rest of the body. So diverse and multiform is goodness that even with us the same thing is good when applied externally but deadly when taken internally. Thus all c doctors forbid the sick to use oil in preparing their food, except in the very smallest quantities, just enough to counteract the disagreeable smell which food and sauces may have for them.

The audience vigorously applauded this speech. Then said I, I'm a forgetful sort of man, Protagoras, and if someone speaks at length, I lose the thread of the argument. If I were a little deaf, you would d recognize the necessity of raising your voice if you wanted to talk to me; so now since you find me forgetful, cut down your answers and make them shorter if I am to follow you.

What do you mean by 'make my answers short'? Am I to make them shorter than the subject demands?

Of course not.

As long as is necessary then?

e   Yes.

As long a reply as *I* think necessary, or *you*?

What they told me, I answered, is that you have the gift both of speaking yourself and of teaching others to speak, just as you prefer— either at length, so that you never run dry, or so shortly that no one

335 could beat you for brevity. If then you are going to talk to me, please use the second method and be brief.

Frankly, Socrates, said he, I have fought many a contest of words, and if I had done as you bid me, that is, adopted the method chosen by my opponent, I should have proved no better than any- one else, nor would the name of Protagoras have been heard of in Greece.

I saw that he was dissatisfied with his own performance in the answers he had given, and would not of his own free will continue in

b the role of answerer, and it seemed to me that it was not my business to remain any longer in the discussions. Well, I said, I have no wish myself to insist on continuing our conversation in a way that you don't approve. I will talk with you another time, when you are willing to converse so that I can follow. You for your part, as others say and you say for yourself, can carry on a discussion both in long and short

c speeches, for you are a gifted man. I on the other hand cannot man- age these long speeches—I wish I could. It was for you, who can do both, to indulge me and so make our discussion possible. But since you would rather not, and I have something to do and could not stay while you spin out your long speeches, I will leave you. I really ought to be going. Otherwise I should probably be glad to hear them.

With these words I got up to leave. As I did so Callias caught my

d hand with his right hand, and with his left took hold of this old coat of mine and said, We shan't let you go, Socrates. Our talk won't be the same without you. Please stay with us. There is nothing that I would rather listen to than a conversation between you and Protagoras. You will be doing us all a kindness.

I was already standing up to go, and answered, Son of Hip- ponicus, I have always admired your enthusiasm for wisdom. Believe

e me, I praise and love you for it now, and would gladly do what you wish, if your request were within my power to fulfill. But it's as if you were to ask me to keep up with Crison, the runner from Himera, when he was in his prime, or to run a race against some three-miler or

336 Marathon champion. I would say that to run with them would please me even more than it would please you, but I can't do it. If you want to see me and Crison running together, you must ask him to lower his standards, for I can't run fast, but he can run slowly. So if you want to hear Protagoras and me, ask him to go on answering me as he did at first, briefly and keeping to the point of my questions. How can

we have a discussion otherwise? Personally I thought that compan- b
ionable talk was one thing, and public speaking another.

But don't you see, Socrates? he said. Protagoras is surely right
in thinking that he is entitled to talk in the way that suits him, just as
much as you are.

Here Alcibiades broke in. No, no, Callias, he said. Socrates admits frankly that long speeches are beyond him and that Protagoras
has the better of him there, but in discussion and the intelligent give- c
and-take of arguments I doubt if he would give any man best. If Protagoras in his turn admits that Socrates beats him in discussion,
Socrates will be satisfied. But if he maintains his claim, let him continue the discussion with question and answer, not meeting every
question with a long oration, eluding the arguments and refusing to
meet them properly, spinning it out until most of his hearers have for- d
gotten what the question was about—not that Socrates will be the
one to forget it. I'll guarantee that, in spite of his little joke about
being forgetful. I hold then that what Socrates proposes is the more
reasonable, and I suppose it's right for each of us to say what he
thinks.

After Alcibiades, so far as I remember, it was Critias who spoke,
addressing his remarks to Prodicus and Hippias. Callias, he said,
seems to me to be very much on the side of Protagoras, and Al- e
cibiades is always out to win when he takes up a cause. But it is not
for us to be partisans either of Socrates or of Protagoras. Let us implore them both alike not to break up the discussion in mid-career.

Hearing this, Prodicus began, You are quite right, Critias. Those 337
who are present at discussions of this kind must divide their attention between the speakers impartially, but not equally. The two things
are not the same. They must hear both alike, but not give equal
weight to each. More should be given to the wiser, and less to the
other. I add my plea, Protagoras and Socrates, that you should be
reconciled. Let your conversation be a discussion, not a dispute. A b
discussion is carried on among friends with good will, but a dispute
is between rivals and enemies. In this way our meeting will be best
conducted. You, the speakers, will be esteemed by us—esteemed, I say,
not praised, for esteem is a genuine feeling in the hearts of the audience, whereas praise is often on the lips of men belying their true
conviction—and we who listen will experience enjoyment rather than c
pleasure. Enjoyment can result from learning and partaking in the intellectual activity of the mind alone, but pleasure arises rather
from eating or other forms of physical indulgence.

So said Prodicus, and a large number of those present expressed
agreement. After him the wise Hippias spoke up. Gentlemen, he
said, I count you all my kinsmen and family and fellow citizens—by
nature, not by convention. By nature like is kin to like, but custom, d
the tyrant of mankind, does much violence to nature. For us then who

understand the nature of things, who are the intellectual leaders of
Greece and in virtue of that very fact are now assembled in Athens,
the center and shrine of Greek wisdom, and in this the finest house of
e that city, it would be a disgrace if we produced nothing worthy of our
fame but fell to bickering like the lowest of mankind.

And so my request and my advice to you, Protagoras and Socrates,
is to be reconciled, allowing us to act as mediators and bring you
338 together in a compromise. Socrates should not insist on the strict
forms of discussion, carried on through the briefest of exchanges, if
it is unwelcome to Protagoras, but should give way and slacken the
reins of his discourse, so that it may wear for us a more dignified and
elegant air, and Protagoras should refrain from shaking out every reef
and running before the wind, launching out on a sea of words till he
is out of sight of land. Let both take a middle course. Do this, take my
advice, and appoint an arbitrator, referee, or president to preserve a
b moderate length in the speeches of both of you.

This counsel won general consent and a round of applause. Callias refused to let me go and they told us to choose an overseer. But
I said that it would be unfitting to choose an arbitrator over our
words. If he were a man of lesser attainments, it would be wrong to
set him over his betters, and if he were someone like ourselves it
would still not be proper, for in resembling us he would act like us,
c and his appointment would be superfluous.

Well then, you will say, we will choose someone superior. But the
fact is, in my opinion, that it would be impossible for you to choose
anyone wiser than Protagoras, and if you choose some lesser man and
pretend he is better, this again would be to insult him, appointing
someone over him as if he were a nobody. For myself I am indifferent.

I have another proposal to enable our discussion to proceed as
d you wish it to. If Protagoras is unwilling to give replies, let him be the
questioner and I will answer, and at the same time try to show him
how, in my submission, the respondent should speak. When I have answered as many questions as he likes to put, let him in return render
similar account to me. Then if he does not seem to wish to answer a
question as put, you and I will appeal to him jointly, as you did to
me, not to spoil the discussion. For this purpose we have no need of a
e single arbitrator; you will all keep watch on us together.

Everyone thought this was the right way to proceed. Protagoras
was most unwilling, but he had to agree to be the questioner, and
then when he had questioned me sufficiently, to submit himself to me
in turn and make brief replies.

He began his questions something like this. In my view, Soc-
339 rates, the most important part of a man's education is to become an
authority on poetry. This means being able to criticize the good and
bad points of a poem with understanding, to know how to distinguish
them, and give one's reasons when asked. My question to you therefore

will concern the subject of our present discussion, namely virtue, but transferred to the realm of poetry. That will be the only difference. Simonides in one of his poems says to Scopas, son of Creon of Thessaly,

> Hard is it on the one hand to become   b
> A good man truly, hands and feet and mind
> Foursquare, wrought without blame.

Do you know the piece, or should I recite it all to you?

There is no need, I said. I know it and have given it quite a lot of study.

Good. Now do you think it a beautiful and well-written poem?

Yes, both beautiful and well written.

And do you think a poem beautifully written if the poet contradicts himself?

No.

Then look at it more closely.

But really I have given it enough thought.   c

Then you must know that as the poem proceeds he says:

> Nor do I count as sure the oft-quoted word
> Of Pittacus, though wise indeed he was
> Who spoke it. To be noble, said the sage,
> Is hard.

You understand that this is the same poet as wrote the previous lines?

Yes.

Then you think the two passages are consistent?

For my part I do, said I, though not without a fear that he might be right. Don't you?

How can a man be thought consistent when he says both these d things? First he lays it down himself that it is hard for a man to become truly good; then when he is a little further on in the poem he forgets. He finds fault with Pittacus, who said the same thing as he did himself, that it is hard to be noble, and refuses to accept it from him; but in censuring the man who said the same as he does, he obviously censures himself. Either his first or his second statement is wrong.

This sally evoked praise and applause from many of the audience, and at first I was like a man who has been hit by a good boxer; at e his words and the applause things went dark and I felt giddy. Then I turned to Prodicus—and to tell you the truth, this was a move to gain time to consider what the poet meant—and appealed to him by name. Prodicus, I said, Simonides is of course your fellow citizen; you ought to come to his aid. I think I will call on you as the river 340 Scamander in Homer called on the Simois when hard pressed by Achilles, with the words:

334 P L A T O : C O L L E C T E D D I A L O G U E S

Dear brother, let us both together stem the hero's might.[3]

So I appeal to you lest our Simonides be sacked by Protagoras like another Troy, since truly to justify Simonides calls for that art of yours
b whereby you discern the difference between 'wish' and 'desire' and
make all those other elegant distinctions which we heard just now. So
see whether you agree with me. I don't believe Simonides contradicts
himself. Now let us have your opinion first. Do you think 'to become'
and 'to be' are the same, or different?

Different, most certainly, said Prodicus.

Well, at the beginning Simonides gave his own view, that it is
c difficult to become a good man, didn't he?

True, said Prodicus.

But as for Pittacus, he censures him not, as Protagoras thinks,
for saying the same thing, but something different. According to Pittacus, the difficulty is not to *become* noble, as Simonides said it was,
but to *be*. As Prodicus says, Protagoras, to be and to become are not the
same; and if to be is not the same as to become, Simonides is not contradicting himself. I shouldn't be surprised if Prodicus and many oth-
d ers would agree with Hesiod that it is difficult to *become* good—he
says, you remember,

> The gods have put sweat on the path to virtue,

but when

> The summit's reached,
> Hard though it was, thenceforth the task is light
> To keep it.[4]

Prodicus commended my explanation, but Protagoras said, Your
justification, Socrates, involves a greater error than the one it sets out
to defend.

It seems then, said I, that I have done harm, and am a contempti-
e ble physician, whose cure inflames the disease.

Well, it is so.

Explain, said I.

The poet must be very stupid, if he says that it is such a light matter to hold on to virtue, when everyone agrees that there is nothing
more difficult.

To this I rejoined, It's a remarkably lucky thing that our friend
Prodicus happens to be present at this discussion. I have a notion that
his branch of wisdom is an old and god-given one, beginning perhaps
341 with Simonides or going even further back. Your learning covers
many things but not, it appears, this. You are not acquainted with it
as I have become through being a pupil of Prodicus. So now I don't
think you understand that Simonides may not have taken this word

[3] *Iliad* 21.308.   [4] *Works and Days* 289.

'hard' as you do. It may be like the word 'terrible' which Prodicus is always scolding me about, when in praising you or someone else I say, 'Protagoras is a terribly clever person.' He asks me if I'm not ashamed b to call good things terrible. What is terrible, he says, is bad. No one speaks of 'terrible wealth' or 'terrible peace,' but rather of 'a terrible disease,' 'a terrible war,' 'terrible poverty.' Perhaps then the Ceans and Simonides understand 'hard' as connoting something bad, or something else which you don't know. Let's ask Prodicus, for he is the right man to ask about the dialect of Simonides. Prodicus, what does c Simonides mean by 'hard'?

Bad, he replied.

Then that is why he blames Pittacus for saying, 'It is hard to be noble,' just as if he had heard him saying that it was bad to be noble.

What else do you suppose Simonides means? said Prodicus. He is reproaching Pittacus with not knowing how to distinguish meanings properly, being a Lesbian and brought up in a barbarous dialect.

Do you hear that, Protagoras? said I. Have you anything to say d to it?

It is not at all like that, said Protagoras. I know very well that by 'hard' Simonides meant what the rest of us mean—not 'bad,' but what is not easy, only accomplished with much effort.

I believe myself that that is what Simonides meant, said I, and I am sure Prodicus knew it. He is joking, and wants to test your ability to stand up for your own opinion. Actually the very next e words provide ample proof that Simonides did not equate 'hard' with 'bad.' He goes on,

A god alone can have this privilege,

and presumably he does not first say 'it is bad to be noble' and then add that only a god could achieve it, and allot it as a privilege entirely divine. That would mean that Prodicus is calling Simonides quite unprincipled and no true Cean. However, I am ready to tell you my own opinion of Simonides' meaning in this song, if you wish to test my 342 skill in poetry, as you call it, but if you prefer it I will listen to you.

Please speak if you will, said Protagoras when he heard this, and Prodicus, Hippias, and the others urged me strongly.

Well then, said I, I will try to expound to you the view that I take. The most ancient and fertile homes of philosophy among the Greeks are Crete and Sparta, where are to be found more Sophists than anywhere on earth. But they conceal their wisdom like the b Sophists Protagoras spoke of, and pretend to be fools, so that their superiority over the rest of Greece may not be known to lie in wisdom, but seem to consist in fighting and courage. Their idea is that if their real excellence became known, everyone would set to work to become wise. By this disguise they have taken in the pro-Spartans in other

cities, who to emulate them go about with bruised ears, bind their
c hands with thongs, take to physical training, and wear short cloaks,
under the impression that these are the practices which have made
the Spartans a great power in Greece; whereas the Spartans, when
they want to resort freely to their wise men and are tired of meeting
them in secret, expel all resident aliens, whether they be sympathizers
with the Spartan way of life or not, and converse with the Sophists
d unbeknown to any foreigners. Conversely they don't allow any of
their youths to go abroad, for fear they should forget what they have
learned at home. No more do the Cretans. And in these states there
are not only men but also women who are proud of their intellectual culture.

Now this is how you may know that I am telling the truth and
that the Spartans are the best educated in philosophy and speaking. If you talk to the most ordinary Spartan, you will find that for
e most of the time he shows himself a quite unimpressive speaker. But
then, at some chance point in the conversation, like a brilliant marks-
man he shoots in a telling phrase, brief and taut, showing up whoever is talking to him to be as helpless as a child.

Now there are some, both at the present day and in the past, who
have tumbled to this fact, namely that to be Spartan implies a taste
for intellectual rather than physical exercise, for they realize that to
343 frame such utterances is a mark of the highest culture. Of these were
Thales of Miletus, Pittacus of Mytilene, Bias of Priene, our own Solon,
Cleobulus of Lindus, and Myson of Chen, and the seventh of their
company, we are told, was a Spartan, Chilon. All these were emulators,
admirers, and disciples of Spartan culture, and their wisdom may be
recognized as belonging to the same category, consisting of pithy and
b memorable dicta uttered by each. Moreover they met together and
dedicated the first fruits of their wisdom to Apollo in his temple at
Delphi, inscribing those words which are on everyone's lips, 'Know
thyself' and 'Nothing too much.'

I mention these facts to make the point that, among the ancients,
this Laconic brevity was the characteristic expression of philosophy.
In particular this saying of Pittacus, 'Hard is it to be noble,' got into
circulation privately and earned the approval of the wise. It occurred
c therefore to Simonides, with his philosophical ambitions, that if he
could floor this favorite maxim with a triumphant knockout, he would
become the favorite of his own day. In my judgment he wrote the
whole poem against the saying of Pittacus and on its account, in a deliberate effort to damage its fame.

Now let us all examine it together, to see whether I am right. At
the very beginning of the poem, it seems crazy, if he wished to say
d that it is hard to become a good man, that he should then insert 'on the
one hand.' The insertion seems to make no sense, except on the supposition that Simonides is speaking polemically against the saying of

Pittacus. Pittacus said, 'Hard is it to be noble,' and Simonides replied, disputing the point, 'No, to *become* a good man is hard truly'—not, by the way, 'to become truly good'—he does not refer the 'truly' to that, as e if some men were truly good and others good but not truly so. That would strike people as silly and unlike Simonides. We must transpose the word 'truly' in the poem, thus as it were implying the saying of Pittacus before it, as if he spoke first and Simonides were answering his words. Thus, 'O men, hard is it to be noble,' and Simonides replies, 344 'That is not true, Pittacus; not to *be* but to *become* a good man, four-square in hands and feet and mind, wrought without blame, that is hard truly.'

On this view we find that 'on the one hand' comes in reasonably, and that 'truly' finds its proper place at the end. Everything that follows bears out my opinion that this is the sense. Much could be said about each phrase in the poem to testify to the excellence of its com- b position—it is indeed an elegant and well-thought-out production—but to go through it in such detail would take too long. Nevertheless let us review its general character and intention, which is undoubtedly to constitute, throughout its length, a refutation of the saying of Pittacus.

A little further on Simonides says, as if he were developing an argument, that although to become a good man is truly difficult, yet it is possible, for a while at least, 'but having become good, to remain in c this state and *be* a good man—which is what you were speaking of, Pittacus—is impossible and superhuman. This is the privilege of a god alone, whereas

> He cannot but be bad, whom once
> Misfortune irredeemable casts down.'

Now who is cast down by irredeemable misfortune in the management of a ship? Clearly not the passenger, for he has *been* down all the time. You cannot knock down a man who is lying on the ground; you can only knock him down if he is standing, and put him on the ground. In the same way irredeemable misfortune may cast down the re- d sourceful, but not the man who is helpless all the time. The steersman may be reduced to helplessness by the onset of a great storm, the farmer by a bad season, and the doctor from some analogous misfortune. For the good may become bad, as another poet has testified in the line,

> The good are sometimes bad and sometimes noble,

but the bad man cannot become bad, but *is* so of necessity. So it is that e the resourceful and wise and good, when irredeemable disaster brings him to nought, cannot but be bad.

You say, Pittacus, 'Hard is it to be noble,' whereas to *become* noble is hard, though possible, but to *be* so is impossible,

> For when he fares well every man is good,
> But in ill faring, evil.

345 Now what is faring well in letters, and what makes a man good at
them? Clearly the learning of them. And what is the faring well that
makes a good doctor? Clearly it is learning how to heal the sick. 'But in
ill faring, evil.' Who is it who becomes a bad doctor? Clearly a man
who is both a doctor and a good doctor; he might become a bad doctor
also. But we who are laymen in medicine could never by faring ill become doctors or builders or any other kind of technician, and he who
b cannot by faring badly become a doctor cannot, obviously, become a
bad doctor. Even so the good man may as easily be made bad, by lapse
of time or fatigue or illness or some other accident, seeing that this is
the only real ill faring, to be deprived of knowledge. But the bad man
cannot be made bad, for he is so all the time. If he is to *become* bad, he
c must first become good. Thus this part of the poem also teaches the
same lesson, that to be a good man—continuing good—is not possible,
but a man may *become* good, and the same man bad, and those are
best for the longest time whom the gods love.

All this, then, is aimed at Pittacus, and the next bit even more
plainly so, for he goes on,

> Then never shall I vainly cast away
> In hopeless search my little share of life,
> Seeking a thing impossible to be,
> A man all blameless, among those who reap
> The fruit of the broad earth. But should I find him
> I'll send you word.

d See how violently, throughout the poem, he attacks the saying of
Pittacus—

> But all who do no baseness willingly
> I praise and love. The gods themselves strive not
> Against necessity.

This is all to the same purpose. Simonides was not so ignorant as to
say that he praised all who did no evil voluntarily, as if there were any
e who did evil voluntarily. For myself I am fairly certain that no wise
man believes anyone sins willingly or willingly perpetrates any evil or
base act. They know very well that all evil or base action is involuntary. So here Simonides is not saying that he praises whoever does no
evil willingly. The word 'willingly' applies to himself. His view was
346 that a good man often forces himself into love and praise, as when
someone's mother or father or native land is unsympathetic to him.
The less worthy, when they find themselves in such a position, seem
to accept it happily and expose the unworthiness of parents or country with reproaches and denunciations, so that they may neglect their
duty toward them without thereby incurring the blame or reproaches of

others. They even exaggerate their censure and add gratuitous hostil- b
ity to that which cannot be helped. Good men on the other hand conceal such faults and are constrained to praise, and if they feel anger at
some wrong done to them by parents or country, they calm themselves and seek reconciliation, compelling themselves to love and
praise their own kin. No doubt Simonides had in mind that he himself had often eulogized a tyrant or someone of that stamp not of his
own free will but under compulsion.

This then is addressed to Pittacus in particular, as if to say, My
reason for blaming you, Pittacus, is not that I am a faultfinder, for c

> to me that man suffices
> Who is not bad nor overweak, but sound
> In heart and knowing righteousness, the weal
> Of nations. I shall find no fault with him—

I am not, he says, a censorious man—

> For beyond number is the tribe of fools.

So, he implies, if anyone takes pleasure in faultfinding, he may have
his fill in censuring them.

> All is fair that is unmixed with foul.

He does not say this in the sense in which he might say, 'all is white d
that is unmixed with black'—that would be ridiculous on many counts
—but meaning that for his part he accepts without censure the middle
state. I do not seek, he has said,

> A man all blameless, among those who reap
> The fruit of the broad earth. But should I find him
> I'll send you word.

If I wait for perfection I shall praise no one. For me it is enough if he
reach the mean and do no evil, since

> I praise and love all—

note that he uses the Lesbian dialect here because he is addressing
Pittacus—   e

> I praise and love all willingly

—this is where the pause is to be made in speaking it, at 'willingly'—

> Who do no baseness,

though there are those whom I praise and love against my will. If then
you spoke with an even moderate degree of reasonableness and truth,
Pittacus, I should never blame you. But as it is you have made an ut- 347
terly false statement about something of the highest import, and it
passes for true. For that I do blame you.

That, gentlemen, I concluded, is my interpretation of the mind of Simonides in writing this poem.

This exposition of yours, said Hippias, seems to me highly meri-
b torious. However, I also have an interesting thesis on the poem, which I will expound to you if you wish.

Yes, another time, Hippias, said Alcibiades. But at present Socrates and Protagoras must carry out their agreement. Let Socrates reply if Protagoras wants to ask further questions, or if he prefers to answer Socrates, then let Socrates do the questioning.

Then, said I, I leave it to Protagoras to do whichever pleases him.
c But if he is agreeable, I suggest we leave the subject of songs and poems, for I should be glad to reach a conclusion, Protagoras, in a joint investigation with you, on the matters about which I asked you at the beginning. Conversation about poetry reminds me too much of the wine parties of second-rate and commonplace people. Such men, be-ing too uneducated to entertain themselves as they drink by using
d their own voices and conversational resources, put up the price of fe-male musicians, paying well for the hire of an extraneous voice—that of the pipe—and find their entertainment in its warblings. But where the drinkers are men of worth and culture, you will find no girls pip-ing or dancing or harping. They are quite capable of enjoying their own company without such frivolous nonsense, using their own voices in sober discussion and each taking his turn to speak or listen—even
e if the drinking is really heavy. In the same way gatherings like our own, if they consist of men such as most of us claim to be, call for no extraneous voices—not even of poets. No one can interrogate poets about what they say, and most often when they are introduced into the discussion some say the poet's meaning is one thing and some an-other, for the topic is one on which nobody can produce a conclusive argument. The best people avoid such discussions, and entertain each
348 other from their own resources, testing one another's mettle in what they have to say themselves. These are the people, in my opinion, whom you and I should follow, setting the poets aside and conducting the conversation on the basis of our own ideas. It is the truth, and our own minds, that we should be testing. If you want to go on with your questions, I am ready to offer myself as an answerer, or, if you prefer, be my respondent, to bring to its conclusion the discussion which we broke off in the middle.

b   When I said this, and more to the same effect, Protagoras gave no clear indication of which he would do. Alcibiades then glanced at Callias and said, Do you still approve of what Protagoras is doing, re-fusing to say whether or not he will be the answerer? I don't. Let him either continue the discussion or tell us that he is unwilling, so that we may know where we are with him, and Socrates can talk to some-one else, or any of the rest of us start a conversation.

These words of Alcibiades, and requests from Callias and almost c
all those present, made Protagoras feel ashamed, or so I thought, and
induced him to return reluctantly to the discussion. He said therefore
that he would answer and told me to put my questions.

Protagoras, I began, please don't think that I have any other purpose in this discussion than to investigate questions which continually baffle me. I believe Homer hit a nail on the head when he said, 'If
two go together, one perceives before the other.' [5] Somehow we all feel d
better fortified in this way for any action or speech or thought. But to
continue the quotation, 'If one alone perceive'—why he goes off at
once looking for someone to whom he can show his idea and with
whom he can confirm it, and will not rest till he finds him. That is
why I would rather talk to you than to anyone else, because I think you
are the most capable of elucidating the kind of questions that a good
man gives his mind to, and in particular the question of virtue. After e
all, whom else should I look for? Not only are you, as you believe, an
excellent member of society yourself—there are some men very good
in themselves who cannot pass on their good qualities to others—but
you have also the ability to make others good, and with such confidence that although some have made a secret of their art you openly 349
announce yourself to the Greeks by the name of Sophist and set up as
a teacher of culture and virtue, the first to claim payment for this service. Naturally I must call on you for assistance in pondering these
subjects and enlist you with me by asking you questions. It could not
be otherwise.

I want then to go back to the beginning, to my first questions to
you on this subject. Some things I want you to remind me of, and others I want to investigate with your help. The question, if I am not mistaken, was this. Wisdom, temperance, courage, justice, and holiness b
are five terms. Do they stand for a single reality, or has each term
a particular entity underlying it, a reality with its own separate function, each different from the other? Your answer was that they are not
names for the same thing, but that each of these terms applies to its c
own separate reality, and that all these things are parts of virtue, not
like the parts of a lump of gold all homogeneous with each other and
with the whole of which they are parts, but like the parts of a face,
resembling neither the whole nor each other and each having a separate function. If you are still of the same mind, say so, but if not, then
declare yourself. I certainly shall not hold you to your words if you
now express yourself differently. Very likely you spoke as you did to
test me.

No, he said. My view is that all these are parts of virtue, and that d
four of them resemble each other fairly closely, but courage is very

[5] *Iliad* 10.224.

different from all the rest. The proof of what I say is that you can find many men who are quite unjust, unholy, intemperate, and ignorant, yet outstandingly courageous.

e   Stop, said I. What you say merits investigation. Do you qualify the courageous as confident, or in any other way?

As confident, yes, and keen to meet dangers from which most men shrink in fear.

Then again, you consider virtue an honorable thing, and it is on the assumption that it is honorable that you offer to teach it?

Unless I am quite mad, it is the most honorable of all things.

Part base and part honorable, I asked, or all honorable?

All honorable, as honorable as can be.

350   Now do you know which men plunge fearlessly into tanks?

Yes, divers.

Is that because they know their job or for some other reason?

Because they know their job.

And what men feel confidence in a cavalry engagement—trained or untrained riders?

Trained.

And in fighting with the light shield—peltasts or nonpeltasts?

Peltasts. And this holds good generally, if that is what you are after. Those with the relevant knowledge have more confidence than

b   those without it, and more when they have learned the job than they themselves had before.

But, said I, have you ever seen men with no understanding of any of these dangerous occupations who yet plunge into them with confidence?

Indeed yes, with only too much confidence.

Then does not their confidence involve courage too?

No, for if so, courage would be something to be ashamed of. Such men are mad.

How then do you define the courageous? Did you not say they were the confident?

Yes, I still maintain it.

c   Well, those who are thus ignorantly confident show themselves not courageous but mad, and conversely, in the other case it is the wisest that are also most confident, and therefore most courageous? On this argument it is their knowledge that must be courage.

No, Socrates, he said. You have not remembered rightly what I said in my reply. When you asked me whether the courageous are confident, I agreed, but I was not asked whether the confident are also courageous—if you had asked me that at the time, I should have said

d   'not all of them'—and you have nowhere disproved my admission by showing that the courageous are not confident. Further, when you argue that those who have knowledge are more confident than they were before, and also than others who are ignorant, and thereupon conclude that courage and wisdom are the same thing, you might as well go on and conclude that physical strength is knowledge. First of all you would proceed to ask me whether the strong are powerful, and I should agree. Next, whether those who know how to wrestle are more e powerful than those who do not, and more powerful after they have learned than before; again I should agree, and it would then be open to you to say, adducing the same proofs, that on my own admission wisdom is physical strength. But here again I nowhere admit that the powerful are strong, only that the strong are powerful. Power and 351 strength are not the same. Power can result from knowledge, and also from madness or passion, whereas strength is a matter of natural constitution and bodily nurture. Similarly in our present discussion, I deny that confidence and courage are the same, and it follows that the courageous are confident but not all the confident are courageous. Confidence, like power, may be born of skill, or equally of madness or passion, but courage is a matter of nature and the proper nurture of b the soul.

Well, said I, you speak of some men living well, and others badly?

He agreed.

Do you think then that a man would be living well who passed his life in pain and vexation?

No.

But if he lived it out to the end with enjoyment, you would count him as having lived well?

Yes.

Then to live pleasurably is good, to live painfully bad? c

Yes, if one's pleasure is in what is honorable.

What's this, Protagoras? Surely you don't follow the common opinion that some pleasures are bad and some pains good? I mean to say, in so far as they are pleasant, are they not also good, leaving aside any consequence that they may entail? And in the same way pains, in so far as they are painful, are bad?

I'm not sure Socrates, he said, whether I ought to give an answer as unqualified as your question suggests, and say that everything d pleasant is good, and everything painful evil. But with a view not only to my present answer but to the whole of the rest of my life, I believe it is safest to reply that there are some pleasures which are not good, and some pains which are not evil, others on the other hand which are, and a third class which are neither evil nor good.

Meaning by pleasures, said I, what partakes of pleasure or gives it?

Certainly.

My question then is, whether they are not, qua pleasant, good. I am asking in fact whether pleasure itself is not a good thing. e

Let us, he replied, as you are so fond of saying yourself, investigate the question; then if the proposition we are examining seems reasonable, and pleasant and good appear identical, we shall agree on it. If not, that will be the time to differ.

Good, said I. Will you lead the inquiry or should I?

It is for you to take the lead, since you introduced the subject.

352   I wonder then, said I, if we can make it clear to ourselves like this. If a man were trying to judge, by external appearance, of another's health or some particular physical function, he might look at his face and hands and then say, 'Let me see your chest and back too, so that I may make a more satisfactory examination.' Something like this is what I want for our present inquiry. Observing that your attitude to the good and the pleasant is what you say, I want to go on something like this. Now uncover another part of your mind, Protag-

b oras. What is your attitude to knowledge? Do you share the common view about that also? Most people think, in general terms, that it is nothing strong, no leading or ruling element. They don't see it like that. They hold that it is not the knowledge that a man possesses which governs him, but something else—now passion, now pleasure, now pain, sometimes love, and frequently fear. They just think of

c knowledge as a slave, pushed around by all the other affections. Is this your view too, or would you rather say that knowledge is a fine thing quite capable of ruling a man, and that if he can distinguish good from evil, nothing will force him to act otherwise than as knowledge dictates, since wisdom is all the reinforcement he needs?

Not only is this my view, replied Protagoras, but I above all men

d should think it shame to speak of wisdom and knowledge as anything but the most powerful elements in human life.

Well and truly answered, said I. But I expect you know that most men don't believe us. They maintain that there are many who recognize the best but are unwilling to act on it. It may be open to them, but they do otherwise. Whenever I ask what can be the reason for this,

e they answer that those who act in this way are overcome by pleasure or pain or some other of the things I mentioned just now.

Well, Socrates, it's by no means uncommon for people to say what is not correct.

Then come with me and try to convince them, and show what really happens when they speak of being overcome by pleasure and

353 therefore, though recognizing what is best, failing to do it. If we simply declare, 'You are wrong, and what you say is false,' they will ask us, 'If it is not being overcome by pleasure, what can it be? What do you two say it is? Tell us.'

But why must we look into the opinions of the common man, who says whatever comes into his head?

b   I believe, I replied, that it will help us to find out how courage is related to the other parts of virtue. So if you are content to keep to our decision, that I should lead the way in whatever direction I think we shall best see the light, then follow me. Otherwise, if you wish, I shall give it up.

No, you are right, he said. Carry on as you have begun.

To return then, If they should ask us, 'What is your name for c what we called being worsted by pleasure?' I should reply, 'Listen. Protagoras and I will try to explain it to you. We take it that you say this happens to you when, for example, you are overcome by the desire of food or drink or sex—which are pleasant things—and though you recognize them as evil, nevertheless indulge in them.' They would agree. Then we should ask them, 'In what respect do you call them evil? Is it because for the moment each of them provides its pleasure and is pleasant, or because they lay up for the future disease or pov- d erty or suchlike? If they led to none of these things, but produced pure enjoyment, would they nevertheless be evils—no matter why or how they give enjoyment?' Can we expect any other answer than this, that they are not evil on account of the actual momentary pleasure which they produce, but on account of their consequences, disease and the e rest?

I believe that would be their answer, said Protagoras.

'Well, to cause disease and poverty is to cause pain.' They would agree, I think?

He nodded.

'So the only reason why these pleasures seem to you to be evil is, we suggest, that they result in pains and deprive us of future pleasures.' Would they agree?

We both thought they would.   354

Now suppose we asked them the converse question. 'You say also that pains may be good. You mean, I take it, such things as physical training, military campaigns, doctors' treatment involving cautery or the knife or drugs or starvation diet? These, you say, are good but painful?' Would they agree?

They would.

'Do you then call them good in virtue of the fact that at the time b they cause extreme pain and agony, or because in the future there result from them health, bodily well-being, the safety of one's country, dominion over others, wealth?' The latter, I think they would agree.

Protagoras thought so too.

'And are they good for any other reason than that their outcome is pleasure and the cessation or prevention of pain? Can you say that you have any other end in mind, when you call them good, than pleas- c ures or pains?' I think they would say no.

I too, said he.

'So you pursue pleasure as being good, and shun pain as evil?'

He agreed.

'Then your idea of evil is pain, and of good is pleasure. Even

enjoying yourself you call evil whenever it leads to the loss of a pleasure greater than its own, or lays up pains that outweigh its pleasures.
d If it is in any other sense, or without anything else in mind, that you call enjoyment evil, no doubt you could tell us what it is, but you cannot.'

I agree that they cannot, said Protagoras.

'Isn't it the same when we turn back to pain? To suffer pain you call good when it either rids us of greater pains than its own or leads to pleasures that outweigh them. If you have anything else in mind
e when you call the actual suffering of pain a good thing, you could tell us what it is, but you cannot.'

True, said Protagoras.

'Now my good people,' I went on, 'if you ask me what is the point of all this rigmarole, I beg your indulgence. It isn't easy to explain the real meaning of what you call being overcome by pleasure, and any explanation is bound up with this point. You may still change your
355 minds, if you can say that the good is anything other than pleasure, or evil other than pain. Is it sufficient for you to live life through with pleasure and without pain? If so, and you can mention no good or evil which cannot in the last resort be reduced to these, then listen to my next point.

'This position makes your argument ridiculous. You say that a man often recognizes evil actions as evil, yet commits them, under no
b compulsion, because he is led on and distracted by pleasure, and on the other hand that, recognizing the good, he refrains from following it because he is overcome by the pleasures of the moment. The absurdity of this will become evident if we stop using all these names together—pleasant, painful, good, and evil—and since they have turned out to be only two, call them by only two names—first of all good and evil, and only at a different stage pleasure and pain. Having
c agreed on this, suppose we now say that a man does evil though he recognizes it as evil. Why? Because he is overcome. By what? We can no longer say by pleasure, because it has changed its name to good. Overcome, we say. By what, we are asked. By the good, I suppose we shall say. I fear that if our questioner is ill-mannered, he will laugh
d and retort, What ridiculous nonsense, for a man to do evil, knowing it is evil and that he ought not to do it, because he is overcome by good. Am I to suppose that the good in you is or is not a match for the evil? Clearly we shall reply that the good is not a match; otherwise the man whom we speak of as being overcome by pleasure would not have done wrong. And in what way, he may say, does good fail to be a match for evil, or evil for good? Is it not by being greater or smaller, more or
e less than the other? We shall have to agree. Then by being overcome you must mean taking greater evil in exchange for lesser good.

'Having noted this result, suppose we reinstate the names pleasant and painful for the same phenomena, thus: A man does—*evil* we said before, but now we shall say *painful* actions, knowing them to be painful, because overcome by pleasures—pleasures, obviously, which were not a match for the pains. And what meaning can we attach to the phrase *not a match for*, when used of pleasure in relation to pain, 356 except the excess or deficiency of one as compared with the other? It depends on whether one is greater or smaller, more or less intense than the other. If anyone objects that there is a great difference between present pleasure and pleasure or pain in the future, I shall reply that the difference cannot be one of anything else but pleasure and pain. So like an expert in weighing, put the pleasures and the pains to- b gether, set both the near and distant in the balance, and say which is the greater quantity. In weighing pleasures against pleasures, one must always choose the greater and the more; in weighing pains against pains, the smaller and the less; whereas in weighing pleasures against pains, if the pleasures exceed the pains, whether the distant, the near, or vice versa, one must take the course which brings those pleasures; but if the pains outweigh the pleasures, avoid it. Is this not c so, good people?' I should say, and I am sure they could not deny it.

Protagoras agreed.

'That being so then, answer me this,' I shall go on. 'The same magnitudes seem greater to the eye from near at hand than they do from a distance. This is true of thickness and also of number, and sounds of equal loudness seem greater near at hand than at a distance. If now our happiness consisted in doing, I mean in choosing, greater d lengths and avoiding smaller, where would lie salvation? In the art of measurement or in the impression made by appearances? Haven't we seen that the appearance leads us astray and throws us into confusion so that in our actions and our choices between great and small we are constantly accepting and rejecting the same things, whereas the metric art would have canceled the effect of the impression, and by re- e vealing the true state of affairs would have caused the soul to live in peace and quiet and abide in the truth, thus saving our life?' Faced with these considerations, would people agree that our salvation would lie in the art of measurement?

He agreed that they would.

'Again, what if our welfare lay in the choice of odd and even numbers, in knowing when the greater number must rightly be chosen and when the less, whether each sort in relation to itself or one in relation to the other, and whether they were near or distant? What would assure us a good life then? Surely knowledge, and specifically 357 a science of measurement, since the required skill lies in the estimation of excess and defect—or to be more precise, arithmetic, since it deals with odd and even numbers.' Would people agree with us?

Protagoras thought they would.

'Well then,' I shall say, 'since our salvation in life has turned out to lie in the correct choice of pleasure and pain—more or less, greater

b or smaller, nearer or more distant—is it not in the first place a
question of measurement, consisting as it does in a consideration of
relative excess, defect, or equality?'
      It must be.
      'And if so, it must be a special skill or branch of knowledge.'
      Yes, they will agree.
      'What skill, or what branch of knowledge it is, we shall leave till
later; the fact itself is enough for the purposes of the explanation
c which you have asked for from Protagoras and me. To remind you of
your question, it arose because we two agreed that there was nothing
more powerful than knowledge, but that wherever it is found it always
has the mastery over pleasure and everything else. You on the other
hand, who maintain that pleasure often masters even the man who
knows, asked us to say what this experience really is, if it is not being
d mastered by pleasure. If we had answered you straight off that it is ignorance, you would have laughed at us, but if you laugh at us now,
you will be laughing at yourselves as well, for you have agreed that
when people make a wrong choice of pleasures and pains—that is, of
good and evil—the cause of their mistake is lack of knowledge. We
can go further, and call it, as you have already agreed, a science of
e measurement, and you know yourselves that a wrong action which is
done without knowledge is done in ignorance. So that is what being
mastered by pleasure really is—ignorance, and most serious ignorance, the fault which Protagoras, Prodicus, and Hippias profess to
cure. You on the other hand, because you believe it to be something
else, neither go nor send your children to these Sophists, who are the
experts in such matters. Holding that it is nothing that can be taught,
you are careful with your money and withhold it from them—a bad
policy both for yourselves and for the community.'
      That then is the answer we should make to the ordinary run of
358 people, and I ask you—Hippias and Prodicus as well as Protagoras, for
I want you to share our discussion—whether you think what I say is
true.
      They all agreed most emphatically that it was true.
      You agree then, said I, that the pleasant is good and the painful
bad. I ask exemption from Prodicus' precise verbal distinctions.
Whether you call it pleasant, agreeable, or enjoyable, my dear Prodi-
b cus, or whatever name you like to apply to it, please answer in the
sense of my request.
      Prodicus laughed and assented, and so did the others.
      Well, here is another point, I continued. All actions aimed at this
end, namely a pleasant and painless life, must be fine actions, that
is, good and beneficial.
      They agreed.
      Then if the pleasant is the good, no one who either knows or be-

lieves that there is another possible course of action, better than the
one he is following, will ever continue on his present course when he c
might choose the better. To 'act beneath yourself' is the result of pure
ignorance; to 'be your own master' is wisdom.

All agreed.

And may we define ignorance as having a false opinion and being
mistaken on matters of great moment?

They approved this too.

Then it must follow that no one willingly goes to meet evil or
what he thinks to be evil. To make for what one believes to be evil, instead of making for the good, is not, it seems, in human nature, and
when faced with the choice of two evils no one will choose the greater d
when he might choose the less.

General agreement again.

Now you recognize the emotion of fear or terror. I wonder if you
conceive it as I do? I say this to you, Prodicus. Whether you call it fear
or terror, I define it as expectation of evil.

Protagoras and Hippias thought this covered both fear and terror, but Prodicus said it applied to fear but not to terror.

Well, Prodicus, said I, it makes no difference. This is the point. If e
what I have said is true, will anyone be willing to go to meet what he
fears, when it is open to him to go in the opposite direction? Do not
our agreed conclusions make this impossible? It is admitted that what
he fears he regards as evil, and that no one willingly meets or accepts
what he thinks evil.

They all assented.   359

On this agreed basis, I went on, let Protagoras make his defense
and show us how his original answer can be right. I don't mean what
he said at the very beginning, when he maintained that there were
five parts of virtue none of which resembled any other, and that each
had its separate function, but what he said later, that four of them are
fairly similar, but one, namely courage, is quite different from the b
rest. This, he said, the following evidence would show me: 'You will
find, Socrates, men who are utterly impious, unjust, licentious, and
ignorant, yet very brave, which will show you that courage is quite different from the other parts of virtue.' I was much surprised by this answer at the time, and now that we have had this discussion it surprises
me even more. Anyway, I asked him if he described the brave as confident, and he replied, 'Yes, and eager.' Do you remember saying this, c
Protagoras?

He admitted it.

Tell me then, said I, in what direction are the brave eager to go?
Toward the same things as cowards?

No.

Toward something else then?

Yes.

Is it that cowards go to meet what inspires confidence, and brave men to what is terrible?

So men say, Socrates.

I know they do, but that was not my question. What do *you* say
d brave men go eagerly to meet? Is it what is terrible, knowing it to be terrible?

Your own argument has shown that to be impossible.

True again, so that if my argument was sound, no one goes to meet what he believes to be terrible, since not being one's own master was shown to be due to ignorance.

He admitted this.

But as for what inspires confidence, everyone makes for that, cowards and brave men alike, and thus cowards and brave men make
e for the same things.

Whatever you say, he replied. What the coward makes for is precisely the opposite of what the brave man makes for. For instance, the brave are willing to enter battle; the others are not.

Is this willingness an honorable thing, or disgraceful?

Honorable, said he.

Then if honorable, we agreed earlier that it is good, for we agreed that all honorable actions are good.

That is true, and I still think so.

360 Quite rightly too, said I. But which class did you say were unwilling to enter battle although that is a fine and good thing to do?

The cowards, he replied.

Well, if it is honorable and good, it is also pleasant.

We certainly agreed to that.

Then do the cowards act with knowledge when they refuse to approach what is the more honorable and better and pleasanter thing?

If we say so, he replied, we shall confound our former conclusions.

Now take the brave man. He makes for what is more honorable, better, and pleasanter?

I cannot deny it.

b And in general when the brave feel fear, there is no disgrace in their fears, nor in their confidence when they are confident?

True.

So both are honorable, and if honorable then good?

Yes.

Cowards on the other hand, and likewise the rash and the mad, feel fears or confidence which are discreditable, and can they exhibit discreditable fear or confidence from any other cause than ignorance?

No.

c Well then, is it cowardice or courage that makes a man a coward?

Cowardice.

Yet we have seen that it is ignorance of what is to be feared that makes them cowards; and if this ignorance makes them cowards, and you agree that what makes them cowards is cowardice, ignorance of what is and is not to be feared must be cowardice.

He nodded.   d

Well, courage is the opposite of cowardice.

He agreed.

And knowledge of what is and is not to be feared is the opposite of ignorance of these things.

He nodded again.

Which is cowardice.

Here he assented with great reluctance.

Therefore knowledge of what is and is not to be feared is courage.

At this point he could no longer bring himself to assent, but was silent; so I said, What, Protagoras, won't you say either yes or no to my questions?

Finish it yourself, said he.

Just one more question first, I replied. Do you still believe, as you   e
did at first, that men can be utterly ignorant yet very brave?

You seem to be bent on having your own way, Socrates, and getting me to give the answers; so to humor you, I will say that on our agreed assumptions it seems to be impossible.

I assure you, said I, that in asking all these questions I have nothing else in view but my desire to learn the truth about virtue and what it is in itself. I know that if we could be clear about that, it would 361 throw the fullest light on the question over which you and I have spun such a coil of argument, I maintaining that virtue was not teachable and you that it was. It seems to me that the present outcome of our talk is pointing at us, like a human adversary, the finger of accusation and scorn. If it had a voice it would say, 'What an absurd pair you are, Socrates and Protagoras. One of you, having said at the beginning that virtue is not teachable, now is bent upon contradicting b himself by trying to demonstrate that everything is knowledge—justice, temperance, and courage alike—which is the best way to prove that virtue *is* teachable. If virtue were something other than knowledge, as Protagoras tried to prove, obviously it could not be taught. But if it turns out to be, as a single whole, knowledge—which is what you are urging, Socrates—then it will be most surprising if it cannot be taught. Protagoras on the other hand, who at the beginning supposed it to be teachable, now on the contrary seems to be bent on showing that it is almost anything rather than knowledge, and this would c make it least likely to be teachable.'

For my part, Protagoras, when I see the subject in such utter confusion I feel the liveliest desire to clear it up. I should like to follow up our present talk with a determined attack on virtue itself and its essential nature. Then we could return to the question whether or

not it can be taught, thus guarding against the possibility that your
d Epimetheus might trip us up and cheat us in our inquiry, just as according to the story he overlooked us in the distribution. I liked
Prometheus in the myth better than Epimetheus; so I follow his lead
and spend my time on all these matters as a means of taking forethought for my whole life. If you should be willing, then as I said at
the beginning, you are the one with whom I would most gladly share
the inquiry.

I congratulate you on your keenness, Socrates, responded Protagoras, and your skill in exposition. I hope I am not too bad a charac-
e ter, and I am the last man to be jealous. I have told a great many
people that I never met anyone I admire nearly as much as you, certainly not among your contemporaries, and I say now that I should not
be surprised if you became one of our leading philosophers. Well, we
will talk of these matters at some future meeting, whenever you like,
but now it is time to turn to other things.

362   So be it, said I, if that is your wish. Indeed I ought long ago to
have kept the appointment I mentioned. I only stayed as a concession
to the blandishments of Callias.

That was the end of the conversation, and we went away.

MENO

Can virtue be taught? asks Meno. Socrates replies that he certainly cannot do it for he does not know what virtue is. Meno does and can tell him and gives him forthwith a list of various virtuous qualities, only to be caught up by Socrates, who points out that, as people say in jest when a person breaks something, he has merely made a singular into a plural. Can Meno state what virtue is while leaving it whole and not broken into such pieces as justice, temperance, and so on? Meno finally comes out with the statement that it is the desire of the good. But, Socrates says, everyone desires the good, no one ever desires evil. "For what else is unhappiness but desiring evil things and getting them?"

The two agree to try seriously to find out what virtue is in its essential nature. Socrates thinks this can be done because people who are inspired like poets and priests believe that we are born not in entire forgetfulness nor yet in utter nakedness, but that "the soul of man is immortal. At one time it comes to an end and at another is born again, but is never finally exterminated." We can recollect if we try hard enough what our souls knew in former lives. He gives a proof of this by making one of Meno's slaves, a completely uneducated lad, reason out facts about squares and triangles all by himself without the slightest help from anyone. He was able to do so, Socrates says, because truths his soul knew before birth still existed in it and could with a great effort be recalled. Meno and he can try like the slave to recollect the knowledge they once had in another existence.

The last part of the dialogue is taken up with Socrates' demonstration and Meno's reluctant agreement that virtue is not taught anywhere so that it is not knowledge which can be and is taught. No further definition is attempted, but Socrates' conclusion, characteristically Greek, is that if ever there could be a man who in addition to being virtuous knew what virtue was and could teach it, he would be among other men like a reality among flitting shades.

The third speaker, Anytus, who comes in toward the end, is generally considered to be the Anytus who proposed at Socrates' trial that he should be put to death, and his contribution to the argument here is at all points consistent with this view.

70   MENO: Can you tell me, Socrates—is virtue something that can be taught? Or does it come by practice? Or is it neither teaching nor practice that gives it to a man but natural aptitude or something else?

SOCRATES: Well, Meno, in the old days the Thessalians had a great reputation among the Greeks for their wealth and their horse-

b manship. Now it seems they are philosophers as well—especially the men of Larissa, where your friend Aristippus comes from. It is Gorgias who has done it. He went to that city and captured the hearts of the foremost of the Aleuadae for his wisdom—among them your own ad-mirer Aristippus—not to speak of other leading Thessalians. In par-

c ticular he got you into the habit of answering any question you might be asked, with the confidence and dignity appropriate to those who know the answers, just as he himself invites questions of every kind from anyone in the Greek world who wishes to ask, and never fails to answer them. But here at Athens, my dear Meno, it is just the reverse. There is a dearth of wisdom, and it looks as if it had migrated from

71 our part of the country to yours. At any rate if you put your question to any of our people, they will all alike laugh and say, You must think I am singularly fortunate, to know whether virtue can be taught or how it is acquired. The fact is that far from knowing whether it can be taught, I have no idea what virtue itself is.

b   That is my own case. I share the poverty of my fellow country-men in this respect, and confess to my shame that I have no knowl-edge about virtue at all. And how can I know a property of something when I don't even know what it is? Do you suppose that somebody en-tirely ignorant who Meno is could say whether he is handsome and rich and wellborn or the reverse? Is that possible, do you think?

MENO: No. But is this true about yourself, Socrates, that you

c don't even know what virtue is? Is this the report that we are to take home about you?

SOCRATES: Not only that, you may say also that, to the best of my belief, I have never yet met anyone who did know.

MENO: What! Didn't you meet Gorgias when he was here?

SOCRATES: Yes.

MENO: And you still didn't think he knew?

SOCRATES: I'm a forgetful sort of person, and I can't say just now what I thought at the time. Probably he did know, and I expect

d you know what he used to say about it. So remind me what it was, or tell me yourself if you will. No doubt you agree with him.

MENO: Yes, I do.

SOCRATES: Then let's leave him out of it, since after all he isn't here. What do you yourself say virtue is? I do ask you in all earnest-ness not to refuse me, but to speak out. I shall be only too happy to be

From *Protagoras and Meno*, translated with an introduction by W. K. C. Guthrie (Penguin Classics, Harmondsworth, Middlesex, 1956).

proved wrong if you and Gorgias turn out to know this, although I said I had never met anyone who did.

MENO: But there is no difficulty about it. First of all, if it is e manly virtue you are after, it is easy to see that the virtue of a man consists in managing the city's affairs capably, and so that he will help his friends and injure his foes while taking care to come to no harm himself. Or if you want a woman's virtue, that is easily described. She must be a good housewife, careful with her stores and obedient to her husband. Then there is another virtue for a child, male or female, and another for an old man, free or slave as you like, and a great many more kinds of virtue, so that no one need be at a loss to say what it is. 72 For every act and every time of life, with reference to each separate function, there is a virtue for each one of us, and similarly, I should say, a vice.

SOCRATES: I seem to be in luck. I wanted one virtue and I find that you have a whole swarm of virtues to offer. But seriously, to carry on this metaphor of the swarm, suppose I asked you what a bee is, b what is its essential nature, and you replied that bees were of many different kinds. What would you say if I went on to ask, And is it in being bees that they are many and various and different from one another? Or would you agree that it is not in this respect that they differ, but in something else, some other quality like size or beauty?

MENO: I should say that in so far as they are bees, they don't differ from one another at all.

SOCRATES: Suppose I then continued, Well, this is just what I c want you to tell me. What is that character in respect of which they don't differ at all, but are all the same? I presume you would have something to say?

MENO: I should.

SOCRATES: Then do the same with the virtues. Even if they are many and various, yet at least they all have some common character which makes them virtues. That is what ought to be kept in view by anyone who answers the question, What is virtue? Do you follow me? d

MENO: I think I do, but I don't yet really grasp the question as I should wish.

SOCRATES: Well, does this apply in your mind only to virtue, that there is a different one for a man and a woman and the rest? Is it the same with health and size and strength, or has health the same character everywhere, if it is health, whether it be in a man or any other creature? e

MENO: I agree that health is the same in a man or in a woman.

SOCRATES: And what about size and strength? If a woman is strong, will it be the same thing, the same strength, that makes her strong? My meaning is that in its character as strength, it is no different, whether it be in a man or in a woman. Or do you think it is?

MENO: No.

73   SOCRATES: And will virtue differ, in its character as virtue, whether it be in a child or an old man, a woman or a man?

MENO: I somehow feel that this is not on the same level as the other cases.

SOCRATES: Well then, didn't you say that a man's virtue lay in directing the city well, and a woman's in directing her household well?

MENO: Yes.

b   SOCRATES: And is it possible to direct anything well—city or household or anything else—if not temperately and justly?

MENO: Certainly not.

SOCRATES: And that means with temperance and justice?

MENO: Of course.

SOCRATES: Then both man and woman need the same qualities, justice and temperance, if they are going to be good.

MENO: It looks like it.

SOCRATES: And what about your child and old man? Could they be good if they were incontinent and unjust?

MENO: Of course not.

SOCRATES: They must be temperate and just?

MENO: Yes.

c   SOCRATES: So everyone is good in the same way, since they become good by possessing the same qualities.

MENO: So it seems.

SOCRATES: And if they did not share the same virtue, they would not be good in the same way.

MENO: No.

SOCRATES: Seeing then that they all have the same virtue, try to remember and tell me what Gorgias and you, who share his opinion, say it is.

MENO: It must be simply the capacity to govern men, if you are
d looking for one quality to cover all the instances.

SOCRATES: Indeed I am. But does this virtue apply to a child or a slave? Should a slave be capable of governing his master, and if he does, is he still a slave?

MENO: I hardly think so.

SOCRATES: It certainly doesn't sound likely. And here is another point. You speak of 'capacity to govern.' Shall we not add, 'justly but not otherwise'?

MENO: I think we should, for justice is virtue.

e   SOCRATES: Virtue, do you say, or *a* virtue?

MENO: What do you mean?

SOCRATES: Something quite general. Take roundness, for instance. I should say that it is a shape, not simply that it is shape, my reason being that there are other shapes as well.

MENO: I see your point, and I agree that there are other virtues besides justice.

SOCRATES: Tell me what they are. Just as I could name other 74 shapes if you told me to, in the same way mention some other virtues.

MENO: In my opinion then courage is a virtue and temperance and wisdom and dignity and many other things.

SOCRATES: This puts us back where we were. In a different way we have discovered a number of virtues when we were looking for one only. This single virtue, which permeates each of them, we cannot find.

MENO: No, I cannot yet grasp it as you want, a single virtue covering them all, as I do in other instances.　　　　　　　　　　b

SOCRATES: I'm not surprised, but I shall do my best to get us a bit further if I can. You understand, I expect, that the question applies to everything. If someone took the example I mentioned just now, and asked you, 'What is shape?' and you replied that roundness is shape, and he then asked you as I did, 'Do you mean it is shape or *a* shape?' you would reply of course that it is *a* shape.

MENO: Certainly.

SOCRATES: Your reason being that there are other shapes as c well.

MENO: Yes.

SOCRATES: And if he went on to ask you what they were, you would tell him.

MENO: Yes.

SOCRATES: And the same with color—if he asked you what it is, and on your replying, 'White,' took you up with, 'Is white color or *a* color?' you would say that it is *a* color, because there are other colors as well.

MENO: I should.

SOCRATES: And if he asked you to, you would mention other colors which are just as much colors as white is.　　　　　　　d

MENO: Yes.

SOCRATES: Suppose then he pursued the question as I did, and objected, 'We always arrive at a plurality, but that is not the kind of answer I want. Seeing that you call these many particulars by one and the same name, and say that every one of them is a shape, even though they are the contrary of each other, tell me what this is which embraces round as well as straight, and what you mean by shape when you say that straightness is a shape as much as roundness. You e do say that?'

MENO: Yes.

SOCRATES: 'And in saying it, do you mean that roundness is no more round than straight, and straightness no more straight than round?'

MENO: Of course not.

SOCRATES: 'Yet you do say that roundness is no more a shape than straightness, and the other way about.'

MENO: Quite true.

SOCRATES: Then what is this thing which is called "shape"? 75 Try to tell me.' If when asked this question either about shape or color you said, 'But I don't understand what you want, or what you mean,' your questioner would perhaps be surprised and say, 'Don't you see that I am looking for what is the same in all of them?' Would you even so be unable to reply, if the question was, 'What is it that is common to roundness and straightness and the other things which you call shapes?' Do your best to answer, as practice for the question about virtue.

b   MENO: No, you do it, Socrates.

SOCRATES: Do you want me to give in to you?

MENO: Yes.

SOCRATES: And will you in your turn give me an answer about virtue?

MENO: I will.

SOCRATES: In that case I must do my best. It's in a good cause.

MENO: Certainly.

SOCRATES: Well now, let's try to tell you what shape is. See if you accept this definition. Let us define it as the only thing which always accompanies color. Does that satisfy you, or do you want it in some other way? I should be content if your definition of virtue were c on similar lines.

MENO: But that's a naïve sort of definition, Socrates.

SOCRATES: How?

MENO: Shape, if I understand what you say, is what always accompanies color. Well and good—but if somebody says that he doesn't know what color is, but is no better off with it than he is with shape, what sort of answer have you given him, do you think?

SOCRATES: A true one, and if my questioner were one of the clever, disputatious, and quarrelsome kind, I should say to him, 'You d have heard my answer. If it is wrong, it is for you to take up the argument and refute it.' However, when friendly people, like you and me, want to converse with each other, one's reply must be milder and more conducive to discussion. By that I mean that it must not only be true, but must employ terms with which the questioner admits he is familiar. So I will try to answer you like that. Tell me, therefore, e whether you recognize the term 'end'; I mean limit or boundary—all these words I use in the same sense. Prodicus might perhaps quarrel with us, but I assume you speak of something being bounded or coming to an end. That is all I mean, nothing subtle.

MENO: I admit the notion, and believe I understand your meaning.

SOCRATES: And again, you recognize 'surface' and 'solid,' as 76 they are used in geometry?

MENO: Yes.

SOCRATES: Then with these you should by this time understand my definition of shape. To cover all its instances, I say that shape is that in which a solid terminates, or more briefly, it is the limit of a solid.

MENO: And how do you define color?

SOCRATES: What a shameless fellow you are, Meno. You keep bothering an old man to answer, but refuse to exercise your memory and tell me what was Gorgias' definition of virtue.   b

MENO: I will, Socrates, as soon as you tell me this.

SOCRATES: Anyone talking to you could tell blindfold that you are a handsome man and still have your admirers.

MENO: Why so?

SOCRATES: Because you are forever laying down the law as spoiled boys do, who act the tyrant as long as their youth lasts. No doubt you have discovered that I can never resist good looks. Well, I c will give in and let you have your answer.

MENO: Do by all means.

SOCRATES: Would you like an answer à la Gorgias, such as you would most readily follow?

MENO: Of course I should.

SOCRATES: You and he believe in Empedocles' theory of effluences, do you not?

MENO: Wholeheartedly.

SOCRATES: And passages to which and through which the effluences make their way?

MENO: Yes.

SOCRATES: Some of the effluences fit into some of the passages, whereas others are too coarse or too fine.   d

MENO: That is right.

SOCRATES: Now you recognize the term 'sight'?

MENO: Yes.

SOCRATES: From these notions, then, 'grasp what I would tell,' [1] as Pindar says. Color is an effluence from shapes commensurate with sight and perceptible by it.

MENO: That seems to me an excellent answer.

SOCRATES: No doubt it is the sort you are used to. And you probably see that it provides a way to define sound and smell and many similar things.   e

MENO: So it does.

SOCRATES: Yes, it's a high-sounding answer, so you like it better than the one on shape.

[1] Pindar, fr. 82.

MENO: I do.

SOCRATES: Nevertheless, son of Alexidemus, I am convinced that the other is better, and I believe you would agree with me if you had not, as you told me yesterday, to leave before the Mysteries, but could stay and be initiated.

77   MENO: I would stay, Socrates, if you gave me more answers like this.

SOCRATES: You may be sure I shan't be lacking in keenness to do so, both for your sake and mine, but I'm afraid I may not be able to do it often. However, now it is your turn to do as you promised, and try to tell me the general nature of virtue. Stop making many out of one, as the humorists say when somebody breaks a plate. Just leave virtue whole and sound and tell me what it is, as in the examples I have b given you.

MENO: It seems to me then, Socrates, that virtue is, in the words of the poet, 'to rejoice in the fine and have power,' and I define it as desiring fine things and being able to acquire them.

SOCRATES: When you speak of a man desiring fine things, do you mean it is good things he desires?

MENO: Certainly.

SOCRATES: Then do you think some men desire evil and others c good? Doesn't everyone, in your opinion, desire good things?

MENO: No.

SOCRATES: And would you say that the others suppose evils to be good, or do they still desire them although they recognize them as evil?

MENO: Both, I should say.

SOCRATES: What? Do you really think that anyone who recognizes evils for what they are, nevertheless desires them?

MENO: Yes.

SOCRATES: Desires in what way? To possess them?

MENO: Of course.

d   SOCRATES: In the belief that evil things bring advantage to their possessor, or harm?

MENO: Some in the first belief, but some also in the second.

SOCRATES: And do you believe that those who suppose evil things bring advantage understand that they are evil?

MENO: No, that I can't really believe.

SOCRATES: Isn't it clear then that this class, who don't recog- e nize evils for what they are, don't desire evil but what they think is good, though in fact it is evil; those who through ignorance mistake bad things for good obviously desire the good?

MENO: For them I suppose that is true.

SOCRATES: Now as for those whom you speak of as desiring evils in the belief that they do harm to their possessor, these presumably know that they will be injured by them?

MENO: They must.

SOCRATES: And don't they believe that whoever is injured is, in so far as he is injured, unhappy?

MENO: That too they must believe.

SOCRATES: And unfortunate?   78

MENO: Yes.

SOCRATES: Well, does anybody want to be unhappy and unfortunate?

MENO: I suppose not.

SOCRATES: Then if not, nobody desires what is evil, for what else is unhappiness but desiring evil things and getting them?

MENO: It looks as if you are right, Socrates, and nobody desires b what is evil.

SOCRATES: Now you have just said that virtue consists in a wish for good things plus the power to acquire them. In this definition the wish is common to everyone, and in that respect no one is better than his neighbor.

MENO: So it appears.

SOCRATES: So if one man is better than another, it must evidently be in respect of the power, and virtue, according to your account, is the power of acquiring good things.

MENO: Yes, my opinion is exactly as you now express it.   c

SOCRATES: Let us see whether you have hit the truth this time. You may well be right. The power of acquiring good things, you say, is virtue?

MENO: Yes.

SOCRATES: And by good do you mean such things as health and wealth?

MENO: I include the gaining both of gold and silver and of high and honorable office in the state.

SOCRATES: Are these the only classes of goods that you recognize?

MENO: Yes, I mean everything of that sort.   d

SOCRATES: Right. In the definition of Meno, hereditary guest-friend of the Great King, the acquisition of gold and silver is virtue. Do you add 'just and righteous' to the word 'acquisition,' or doesn't it make any difference to you? Do you call it virtue all the same even if they are unjustly acquired?

MENO: Certainly not.

SOCRATES: Vice then?

MENO: Most certainly.

SOCRATES: So it seems that justice or temperance or piety, or some other part of virtue, must attach to the acquisition. Other- e wise, although it is a means to good things, it will not be virtue.

MENO: No, how could you have virtue without these?

SOCRATES: In fact lack of gold and silver, if it results from failure to acquire it—either for oneself or another—in circumstances which would have made its acquisition unjust, is itself virtue.

MENO: It would seem so.

SOCRATES: Then to have such goods is no more virtue than to lack them. Rather we may say that whatever is accompanied by jus-
79 tice is virtue, whatever is without qualities of that sort is vice.

MENO: I agree that your conclusion seems inescapable.

SOCRATES: But a few minutes ago we called each of these —justice, temperance, and the rest—a part of virtue?

MENO: Yes, we did.

SOCRATES: So it seems you are making a fool of me.

MENO: How so, Socrates?

SOCRATES: I have just asked you not to break virtue up into fragments, and given you models of the type of answer I wanted, but taking no notice of this you tell me that virtue consists in the acqui-
b sition of good things with justice, and justice, you agree, is a part of virtue.

MENO: True.

SOCRATES: So it follows from your own statements that to act with a part of virtue is virtue, if you call justice and all the rest parts of virtue. The point I want to make is that whereas I asked you to give me an account of virtue as a whole, far from telling me what it is it-self you say that every action is virtue which exhibits a part of virtue,
c as if you had already told me what the whole is, so that I should recognize it even if you chop it up into bits. It seems to me that we must put the same old question to you, my dear Meno—the question, What is virtue?—if every act becomes virtue when combined with a part of virtue. That is, after all, what it means to say that every act performed with justice is virtue. Don't you agree that the same ques-tion needs to be put? Does anyone know what a part of virtue is, with-out knowing the whole?

MENO: I suppose not.

d   SOCRATES: No, and if you remember, when I replied to you about shape just now, I believe we rejected the type of answer that employs terms which are still in question and not yet agreed upon.

MENO: We did, and rightly.

SOCRATES: Then please do the same. While the nature of virtue as a whole is still under question, don't suppose that you can explain it to anyone in terms of its parts, or by any similar type of explanation. Understand rather that the same question remains to be answered;
e you say this and that about virtue, but what *is* it? Does this seem non-sense to you?

MENO: No, to me it seems right enough.

SOCRATES: Then go back to the beginning and answer my ques-tion. What do you and your friend say that virtue is?

MENO: Socrates, even before I met you they told me that in plain truth you are a perplexed man yourself and reduce others to 80 perplexity. At this moment I feel you are exercising magic and witchcraft upon me and positively laying me under your spell until I am just a mass of helplessness. If I may be flippant, I think that not only in outward appearance but in other respects as well you are exactly like the flat sting ray that one meets in the sea. Whenever anyone comes into contact with it, it numbs him, and that is the sort of thing that you seem to be doing to me now. My mind and my lips are literally numb, and I have nothing to reply to you. Yet I have spoken b about virtue hundreds of times, held forth often on the subject in front of large audiences, and very well too, or so I thought. Now I can't even say what it is. In my opinion you are well advised not to leave Athens and live abroad. If you behaved like this as a foreigner in another country, you would most likely be arrested as a wizard.

SOCRATES: You're a real rascal, Meno. You nearly took me in.

MENO: Just what do you mean?

SOCRATES: I see why you used a simile about me.   c

MENO: Why do you think?

SOCRATES: To be compared to something in return. All good-looking people, I know perfectly well, enjoy a game of comparisons. They get the best of it, for naturally handsome folk provoke handsome similes. But I'm not going to oblige you. As for myself, if the sting ray paralyzes others only through being paralyzed itself, then the comparison is just, but not otherwise. It isn't that, knowing the answers myself, I perplex other people. The truth is rather that I infect them also with the perplexity I feel myself. So with virtue now. I don't know what it is. You may have known before you came into contact with d me, but now you look as if you don't. Nevertheless I am ready to carry out, together with you, a joint investigation and inquiry into what it is.

MENO: But how will you look for something when you don't in the least know what it is? How on earth are you going to set up something you don't know as the object of your search? To put it another way, even if you come right up against it, how will you know that what you have found is the thing you didn't know?

SOCRATES: I know what you mean. Do you realize that what e you are bringing up is the trick argument that a man cannot try to discover either what he knows or what he does not know? He would not seek what he knows, for since he knows it there is no need of the inquiry, nor what he does not know, for in that case he does not even know what he is to look for.

MENO: Well, do you think it a good argument?   81

SOCRATES: No.

MENO: Can you explain how it fails?

SOCRATES: I can. I have heard from men and women who understand the truths of religion . . .

MENO: What did they say?

SOCRATES: Something true, I thought, and fine.

MENO: What was it, and who were they?

SOCRATES: Those who tell it are priests and priestesses of the sort who make it their business to be able to account for the functions b which they perform. Pindar speaks of it too, and many another of the poets who are divinely inspired. What they say is this—see whether you think they are speaking the truth. They say that the soul of man is immortal. At one time it comes to an end—that which is called death—and at another is born again, but is never finally exterminated. On these grounds a man must live all his days as righteously as possible. For those from whom

> Persephone receives requital for ancient doom,
> In the ninth year she restores again
> Their souls to the sun above.
> From whom rise noble kings
c > And the swift in strength and greatest in wisdom,
> And for the rest of time
> They are called heroes and sanctified by men.[2]

Thus the soul, since it is immortal and has been born many times, and has seen all things both here and in the other world, has learned everything that is. So we need not be surprised if it can recall the knowledge of virtue or anything else which, as we see, it once pos-d sessed. All nature is akin, and the soul has learned everything, so that when a man has recalled a single piece of knowledge—*learned* it, in ordinary language—there is no reason why he should not find out all the rest, if he keeps a stout heart and does not grow weary of the search, for seeking and learning are in fact nothing but recollection.

We ought not then to be led astray by the contentious argument you quoted. It would make us lazy, and is music in the ears of e weaklings. The other doctrine produces energetic seekers after knowledge, and being convinced of its truth, I am ready, with your help, to inquire into the nature of virtue.

MENO: I see, Socrates. But what do you mean when you say that we don't learn anything, but that what we call learning is recollection? Can you teach me that it is so?

SOCRATES: I have just said that you're a rascal, and now you 82 ask me if I can teach you, when I say there is no such thing as teaching, only recollection. Evidently you want to catch me contradicting myself straightaway.

MENO: No, honestly, Socrates, I wasn't thinking of that. It was just habit. If you can in any way make clear to me that what you say is true, please do.

SOCRATES: It isn't an easy thing, but still I should like to do

[2] Pindar, fr. 133.

what I can since you ask me. I see you have a large number of retainers b
here. Call one of them, anyone you like, and I will use him to demonstrate it to you.

MENO: Certainly. [*To a slave boy.*] Come here.

SOCRATES: He is a Greek and speaks our language?

MENO: Indeed yes—born and bred in the house.

SOCRATES: Listen carefully then, and see whether it seems to
you that he is learning from me or simply being reminded.

MENO: I will.

SOCRATES: Now boy, you know that a square is a figure like
this?

(*Socrates begins to draw figures in the sand at his feet. He points
to the square* ABCD.)

BOY: Yes.

SOCRATES: It has all these four sides equal?   c

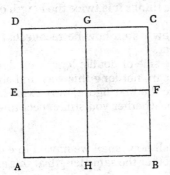

BOY: Yes.

SOCRATES: And these lines which go through the middle of it
are also equal? [EF, GH.]

BOY: Yes.

SOCRATES: Such a figure could be either larger or smaller,
could it not?

BOY: Yes.

SOCRATES: Now if this side is two feet long, and this side the
same, how many feet will the whole be? Put it this way. If it were
two feet in this direction and only one in that, must not the area be
two feet taken once?

BOY: Yes.

SOCRATES: But since it is two feet this way also, does it not be- d
come twice two feet?

BOY: Yes.

SOCRATES: And how many feet is twice two? Work it out and
tell me.

BOY: Four.

SOCRATES: Now could one draw another figure double the size of this, but similar, that is, with all its sides equal like this one?

BOY: Yes.

SOCRATES: How many feet will its area be?

BOY: Eight.

SOCRATES: Now then, try to tell me how long each of its sides
e will be. The present figure has a side of two feet. What will be the side of the double-sized one?

BOY: It will be double, Socrates, obviously.

SOCRATES: You see, Meno, that I am not teaching him anything, only asking. Now he thinks he knows the length of the side of the eight-foot square.

MENO: Yes.

SOCRATES: But does he?

MENO: Certainly not.

SOCRATES: He thinks it is twice the length of the other.

MENO: Yes.

SOCRATES: Now watch how he recollects things in order—the proper way to recollect.

83   You say that the side of double length produces the double-sized figure? Like this I mean, not long this way and short that. It must be equal on all sides like the first figure, only twice its size, that is, eight feet. Think a moment whether you still expect to get it from doubling the side.

BOY: Yes, I do.

SOCRATES: Well now, shall we have a line double the length of this [A B] if we add another the same length at this end [B J]?

BOY: Yes.

SOCRATES: It is on this line then, according to you, that we shall make the eight-foot square, by taking four of the same length?
b   BOY: Yes.

SOCRATES: Let us draw in four equal lines [i.e., counting A J and adding J K, K L, and L A made complete by drawing in its second half L D], using the first as a base. Does this not give us what you call the eight-foot figure?

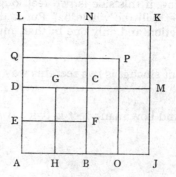

BOY: Certainly.

SOCRATES: But does it contain these four squares, each equal to the original four-foot one?

(*Socrates has drawn in the lines* CM, CN *to complete the squares that he wishes to point out.*)

BOY: Yes.

SOCRATES: How big is it then? Won't it be four times as big?

BOY: Of course.

SOCRATES: And is four times the same as twice?

BOY: Of course not.

SOCRATES: So doubling the side has given us not a double but c a fourfold figure?

BOY: True.

SOCRATES: And four times four are sixteen, are they not?

BOY: Yes.

SOCRATES: Then how big is the side of the eight-foot figure? This one has given us four times the original area, hasn't it?

BOY: Yes.

SOCRATES: And a side half the length gave us a square of four feet?

BOY: Yes.

SOCRATES: Good. And isn't a square of eight feet double this one and half that?

BOY: Yes.

SOCRATES: Will it not have a side greater than this one but less than that?

BOY: I think it will.   d

SOCRATES: Right. Always answer what you think. Now tell me. Was not this side two feet long, and this one four?

BOY: Yes.

SOCRATES: Then the side of the eight-foot figure must be longer than two feet but shorter than four?

BOY: It must.

SOCRATES: Try to say how long you think it is.   e

BOY: Three feet.

SOCRATES: If so, shall we add half of this bit [BO, *half of* BJ] and make it three feet? Here are two, and this is one, and on this side similarly we have two plus one, and here is the figure you want.

(*Socrates completes the square* AOPQ.)

BOY: Yes.

SOCRATES: If it is three feet this way and three that, will the whole area be three times three feet?

BOY: It looks like it.

SOCRATES: And that is how many?

BOY: Nine.

SOCRATES: Whereas the square double our first square had to be how many?

BOY: Eight.

SOCRATES: But we haven't yet got the square of eight feet even from a three-foot side?

BOY: No.

SOCRATES: Then what length will give it? Try to tell us exactly.
84 If you don't want to count it up, just show us on the diagram.

BOY: It's no use, Socrates, I just don't know.

SOCRATES: Observe, Meno, the stage he has reached on the path of recollection. At the beginning he did not know the side of the square of eight feet. Nor indeed does he know it now, but then he thought he knew it and answered boldly, as was appropriate—he felt no perplexity. Now however he does feel perplexed. Not only does he
b not know the answer; he doesn't even think he knows.

MENO: Quite true.

SOCRATES: Isn't he in a better position now in relation to what he didn't know?

MENO: I admit that too.

SOCRATES: So in perplexing him and numbing him like the sting ray, have we done him any harm?

MENO: I think not.

SOCRATES: In fact we have helped him to some extent toward finding out the right answer, for now not only is he ignorant of it but he will be quite glad to look for it. Up to now, he thought he could speak well and fluently, on many occasions and before large audi-
c ences, on the subject of a square double the size of a given square, maintaining that it must have a side of double the length.

MENO: No doubt.

SOCRATES: Do you suppose then that he would have attempted to look for, or learn, what he thought he knew, though he did not, before he was thrown into perplexity, became aware of his ignorance, and felt a desire to know?

MENO: No.

SOCRATES: Then the numbing process was good for him?

MENO: I agree.

SOCRATES: Now notice what, starting from this state of per-plexity, he will discover by seeking the truth in company with me,
d though I simply ask him questions without teaching him. Be ready to catch me if I give him any instruction or explanation instead of simply interrogating him on his own opinions.

(*Socrates here rubs out the previous figures and starts again.*)

Tell me, boy, is not this our square of four feet? [ABCD.] You understand?

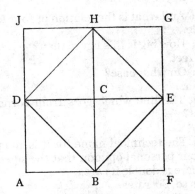

BOY: Yes.

SOCRATES: Now we can add another equal to it like this?
[BCEF.]

BOY: Yes.

SOCRATES: And a third here, equal to each of the others?
[CEGH.]

BOY: Yes.

SOCRATES: And then we can fill in this one in the corner?
[DCHJ.]

BOY: Yes.

SOCRATES: Then here we have four equal squares?

BOY: Yes.

SOCRATES: And how many times the size of the first square is
the whole?

BOY: Four times.

SOCRATES: And we want one double the size. You remember?

BOY: Yes.

SOCRATES: Now does this line going from corner to corner cut
each of these squares in half?

BOY: Yes.

SOCRATES: And these are four equal lines enclosing this area?
[BEHD.]

BOY: They are.

SOCRATES: Now think. How big is this area?

BOY: I don't understand.

SOCRATES: Here are four squares. Has not each line cut off the
inner half of each of them?

BOY: Yes.

SOCRATES: And how many such halves are there in this figure?
[BEHD.]

BOY: Four.

SOCRATES: And how many in this one? [ABCD.]

BOY: Two.

SOCRATES : And what is the relation of four to two?

BOY : Double.

SOCRATES : How big is this figure then?

b   BOY : Eight feet.

SOCRATES : On what base?

BOY : This one.

SOCRATES : The line which goes from corner to corner of the square of four feet?

BOY : Yes.

SOCRATES : The technical name for it is 'diagonal'; so if we use that name, it is your personal opinion that the square on the diagonal of the original square is double its area.

BOY : That is so, Socrates.

SOCRATES : What do you think, Meno? Has he answered with any opinions that were not his own?

c   MENO : No, they were all his.

SOCRATES : Yet he did not know, as we agreed a few minutes ago.

MENO : True.

SOCRATES : But these opinions were somewhere in him, were they not?

MENO : Yes.

SOCRATES : So a man who does not know has in himself true opinions on a subject without having knowledge.

MENO : It would appear so.

SOCRATES : At present these opinions, being newly aroused, have a dreamlike quality. But if the same questions are put to him on many occasions and in different ways, you can see that in the end he
d   will have a knowledge on the subject as accurate as anybody's.

MENO : Probably.

SOCRATES : This knowledge will not come from teaching but from questioning. He will recover it for himself.

MENO : Yes.

SOCRATES : And the spontaneous recovery of knowledge that is in him is recollection, isn't it?

MENO : Yes.

SOCRATES : Either then he has at some time acquired the knowledge which he now has, or he has always possessed it. If he always possessed it, he must always have known; if on the other hand he
e   acquired it at some previous time, it cannot have been in this life, unless somebody has taught him geometry. He will behave in the same way with all geometric knowledge, and every other subject. Has anyone taught him all these? You ought to know, especially as he has been brought up in your household.

MENO : Yes, I know that no one ever taught him.

SOCRATES : And has he these opinions, or hasn't he?

MENO: It seems we can't deny it.

SOCRATES: Then if he did not acquire them in this life, isn't it immediately clear that he possessed and had learned them during 86 some other period?

MENO: It seems so.

SOCRATES: When he was not in human shape?

MENO: Yes.

SOCRATES: If then there are going to exist in him, both while he is and while he is not a man, true opinions which can be aroused by questioning and turned into knowledge, may we say that his soul has been forever in a state of knowledge? Clearly he always either is or is not a man.

MENO: Clearly.

SOCRATES: And if the truth about reality is always in our soul, b the soul must be immortal, and one must take courage and try to discover—that is, to recollect—what one doesn't happen to know, or, more correctly, remember, at the moment.

MENO: Somehow or other I believe you are right.

SOCRATES: I think I am. I shouldn't like to take my oath on the whole story, but one thing I am ready to fight for as long as I can, in word and act—that is, that we shall be better, braver, and more active men if we believe it right to look for what we don't know than if we believe there is no point in looking because what we don't know we c can never discover.

MENO: There too I am sure you are right.

SOCRATES: Then since we are agreed that it is right to inquire into something that one does not know, are you ready to face with me the question, 'What is virtue?'

MENO: Quite ready. All the same, I would rather consider the question as I put it at the beginning, and hear your views on it—that is, are we to pursue virtue as something that can be taught, or do men d have it as a gift of nature or how?

SOCRATES: If I were your master as well as my own, Meno, we should not have inquired whether or not virtue can be taught until we had first asked the main question—what it is. But not only do you make no attempt to govern your own actions—you prize your freedom, I suppose—but you attempt to govern mine. And you succeed too, so I shall let you have your way. There's nothing else for it, and it seems we must inquire into a single property of something about whose es- e sential nature we are still in the dark. Just grant me one small relaxation of your sway, and allow me, in considering whether or not it can be taught, to make use of a hypothesis—the sort of thing, I mean, that geometers often use in their inquiries. When they are asked, for example, about a given area, whether it is possible for this area to be inscribed as a triangle in a given circle, they will probably reply, 'I don't 87 know yet whether it fulfills the conditions, but I think I have a hypothesis which will help us in the matter. It is this. If the area is such that, when one has applied it [sc. as a rectangle] to the given line [i.e., the diameter] of the circle, it is deficient by another rectangle similar to the one which is applied, then, I should say, one result follows; if not, the result is different. If you ask me, then, about b the inscription of the figure in the circle—whether it is possible or not—I am ready to answer you in this hypothetical way.'

Let us do the same about virtue. Since we don't know what it is or what it resembles, let us use a hypothesis in investigating whether it is teachable or not. We shall say, 'What attribute of the soul must virtue be, if it is to be teachable or otherwise?' Well, in the first place, if it is anything else but knowledge, is there a possibility of anyone teaching c it—or, in the language we used just now, reminding someone of it? We needn't worry about which name we are to give to the process, but simply ask, Will it be teachable? Isn't it plain to everyone that a man is not taught anything except knowledge?

MENO: That would be my view.

SOCRATES: If on the other hand virtue is some sort of knowledge, clearly it could be taught.

MENO: Certainly.

SOCRATES: So that question is easily settled—I mean, on what condition virtue would be teachable.

MENO: Yes.

SOCRATES: The next point then, I suppose, is to find out whether virtue is knowledge or something different.

d   MENO: That is the next question, I agree.

SOCRATES: Well then, do we assert that virtue is something good? Is that assumption a firm one for us?

MENO: Undoubtedly.

SOCRATES: That being so, if there exists any good thing different from, and not associated with, knowledge, virtue will not necessarily be any form of knowledge. If on the other hand knowledge embraces everything that is good, we shall be right to suspect that virtue is knowledge.

MENO: Agreed.

e   SOCRATES: First then, is it virtue which makes us good?

MENO: Yes.

SOCRATES: And if good, then advantageous. All good things are advantageous, are they not?

MENO: Yes.

SOCRATES: So virtue itself must be something advantageous?

MENO: That follows also.

SOCRATES: Now suppose we consider what are the sorts of things that profit us. Take them in a list. Health, we may say, and strength and good looks, and wealth—these and their like we call advantageous, you agree?

MENO: Yes.

SOCRATES: Yet we also speak of these things as sometimes do- 88
ing harm. Would you object to that statement?

MENO: No, it is so.

SOCRATES: Now look here. What is the controlling factor
which determines whether each of these is advantageous or harmful?
Isn't it right use which makes them advantageous, and lack of it,
harmful?

MENO: Certainly.

SOCRATES: We must also take spiritual qualities into consideration. You recognize such things as temperance, justice, courage,
quickness of mind, memory, nobility of character, and others?

MENO: Yes, of course I do.   b

SOCRATES: Then take any such qualities which in your view
are not knowledge but something different. Don't you think they may
be harmful as well as advantageous? Courage, for instance, if it is
something thoughtless, just a sort of confidence. Isn't it true that to be
confident without reason does a man harm, whereas a reasoned confidence profits him?

MENO: Yes.

SOCRATES: Temperance and quickness of mind are no different. Learning and discipline are profitable in conjunction with wisdom, but without it harmful.

MENO: That is emphatically true.

SOCRATES: In short, everything that the human spirit under- c
takes or suffers will lead to happiness when it is guided by wisdom,
but to the opposite, when guided by folly.

MENO: A reasonable conclusion.

SOCRATES: If then virtue is an attribute of the spirit, and one
which cannot fail to be beneficial, it must be wisdom, for all spiritual
qualities in and by themselves are neither advantageous nor harmful, but become advantageous or harmful by the presence with them d
of wisdom or folly. If we accept this argument, then virtue, to be something advantageous, must be a sort of wisdom.

MENO: I agree.

SOCRATES: To go back to the other class of things, wealth and
the like, of which we said just now that they are sometimes good and
sometimes harmful, isn't it the same with them? Just as wisdom
when it governs our other psychological impulses turns them to advantage, and folly turns them to harm, so the mind by its right use and
control of these material assets makes them profitable, and by wrong e
use renders them harmful.

MENO: Certainly.

SOCRATES: And the right user is the mind of the wise man, the
wrong user the mind of the foolish.

MENO: That is so.

SOCRATES : So we may say in general that the goodness of non-spiritual assets depends on our spiritual character, and the goodness
89 of that on wisdom. This argument shows that the advantageous element must be wisdom, and virtue, we agree, is advantageous; so that amounts to saying that virtue, either in whole or in part, is wisdom.

MENO : The argument seems to me fair enough.

SOCRATES : If so, good men cannot be good by nature.

MENO : I suppose not.

b   SOCRATES : There is another point. If they were, there would probably be experts among us who could recognize the naturally good at an early stage. They would point them out to us and we should take them and shut them away safely in the Acropolis, sealing them up more carefully than bullion to protect them from corruption and ensure that when they came to maturity they would be of use to the state.

MENO : It would be likely enough.

SOCRATES : Since then goodness does not come by nature, is
c it got by learning?

MENO : I don't see how we can escape the conclusion. Indeed it is obvious on our assumption that, if virtue is knowledge, it is teachable.

SOCRATES : I suppose so. But I wonder if we were right to bind ourselves to that.

MENO : Well, it seemed all right just now.

SOCRATES : Yes, but to be sound it has got to seem all right not only 'just now' but at this moment and in the future.

d   MENO : Of course. But what has occurred to you to make you turn against it and suspect that virtue may not be knowledge?

SOCRATES : I'll tell you. I don't withdraw from the position that if it is knowledge, it must be teachable, but as for its being knowledge, see whether you think my doubts on this point are well founded. If anything—not virtue only—is a possible subject of instruction, must there not be teachers and students of it?

MENO : Surely.

e   SOCRATES : And what of the converse, that if there are neither teachers nor students of a subject, we may safely infer that it cannot be taught?

MENO : That is true. But don't you think there are teachers of virtue?

SOCRATES : All I can say is that I have often looked to see if there are any, and in spite of all my efforts I cannot find them, though I have had plenty of fellow searchers, the kind of men especially whom I believe to have most experience in such matters. But look, Meno,
90 here's a piece of luck. Anytus has just sat down beside us. We couldn't do better than make him a partner in our inquiry. In the first place he

is the son of Anthemion, a man of property and good sense, who didn't get his money out of the blue or as a gift—like Ismenias of Thebes who has just come into the fortune of a Croesus—but earned it by his own brains and hard work. Besides this he shows himself a decent, modest citizen with no arrogance or bombast or offensiveness about him. Also he brought up his son well and had him properly educated, as the Athenian people appreciate. Look how they elect him b into the highest offices in the state. This is certainly the right sort of man with whom to inquire whether there are any teachers of virtue, and if so who they are.

Please help us, Anytus—Meno, who is a friend of your family, and myself—to find out who may be the teachers of this subject. Look at it like this. If we wanted Meno to become a good doctor, shouldn't we send him to the doctors to be taught? c

ANYTUS: Of course.

SOCRATES: And if we wanted him to become a shoemaker, to the shoemakers?

ANYTUS: Yes.

SOCRATES: And so on with other trades?

ANYTUS: Yes.

SOCRATES: Now another relevant question. When we say that to make Meno a doctor we should be right in sending him to the doctors, have we in mind that the sensible thing is to send him to those d who profess the subject rather than to those who don't, men who charge a fee as professionals, having announced that they are prepared to teach whoever likes to come and learn?

ANYTUS: Yes.

SOCRATES: The same is surely true of flute playing and other accomplishments. If you want to make someone a performer e on the flute it would be very foolish to refuse to send him to those who undertake to teach the art and are paid for it, but to go and bother other people instead and have him try to learn from them—people who don t set up to be teachers or take any pupils in the subject which we want our young man to learn. Doesn't that sound very unreasonable?

ANYTUS: Sheer stupidity, I should say.

SOCRATES: I agree. And now we can both consult together 91 about our visitor Meno. He has been telling me all this while that he longs to acquire the kind of wisdom and virtue which fits men to manage an estate or govern a city, to look after their parents, and to entertain and send off guests in proper style, both their own countrymen and foreigners. With this in mind, to whom would it be right to send b him? What we have just said seems to show that the right people are those who profess to be teachers of virtue and offer their services freely to any Greek who wishes to learn, charging a fixed fee for their instruction.

ANYTUS : Whom do you mean by that, Socrates?

SOCRATES : Surely you know yourself that they are the men called Sophists.

c   ANYTUS : Good heavens, what a thing to say! I hope no relative of mine or any of my friends, Athenian or foreign, would be so mad as to go and let himself be ruined by those people. That's what they are, the manifest ruin and corruption of anyone who comes into contact with them.

SOCRATES : What, Anytus? Can they be so different from other claimants to useful knowledge that they not only don't do good, like the rest, to the material that one puts in their charge, but on the contrary spoil it—and have the effrontery to take money for doing

d so? I for one find it difficult to believe you. I know that one of them alone, Protagoras, earned more money from being a Sophist than an outstandingly fine craftsman like Phidias and ten other sculptors put together. A man who mends old shoes or restores coats couldn't get

e away with it for a month if he gave them back in worse condition than he received them; he would soon find himself starving. Surely it is incredible that Protagoras took in the whole of Greece, corrupting his pupils and sending them away worse than when they came to him, for more than forty years. I believe he was nearly seventy when he died, and had been practicing for forty years, and all that time—indeed to this very day—his reputation has been consistently high, and there are plenty of others besides Protagoras, some before his time

92 and others still alive. Are we to suppose from your remark that they consciously deceive and ruin young men, or are they unaware of it themselves? Can these remarkably clever men—as some regard them—be mad enough for that?

ANYTUS : Far from it, Socrates. It isn't they who are mad, but rather the young men who hand over their money, and those re-

b sponsible for them, who let them get into the Sophists' hands, are even worse. Worst of all are the cities who allow them in, or don't expel them, whether it be a foreigner or one of themselves who tries that sort of game.

SOCRATES : Has one of the Sophists done you a personal injury, or why are you so hard on them?

ANYTUS : Heavens, no! I've never in my life had anything to do with a single one of them, nor would I hear of any of my family doing so.

SOCRATES : So you've had no experience of them at all?

ANYTUS : And don't want any either.

c   SOCRATES : You surprise me. How can you know what is good or bad in something when you have no experience of it?

ANYTUS : Quite easily. At any rate I know *their* kind, whether I've had experience or not.

SOCRATES : It must be second sight, I suppose, for how else you know about them, judging from what you tell me yourself, I can't imagine. However, we are not asking whose instruction it is that would ruin Meno's character. Let us say that those are the Sophists, if you **d** like, and tell us instead about the ones we want. You can do a good turn to a friend of your father's house if you will let him know to whom in our great city he should apply for proficiency in the kind of virtue I have just described.

ANYTUS: Why not tell him yourself?

SOCRATES: Well, I did mention the men who in my opinion teach these things, but apparently I was talking nonsense. So you say, and you may well be right. Now it is your turn to direct him; men- **e** tion the name of any Athenian you like.

ANYTUS: But why mention a particular individual? Any decent Athenian gentleman whom he happens to meet, if he follows his advice, will make him a better man than the Sophists would.

SOCRATES: And did these gentlemen get their fine qualities spontaneously—self-taught, as it were, and yet able to teach this untaught virtue to others?   **93**

ANYTUS: I suppose they in their turn learned it from forebears who were gentlemen like themselves. Would you deny that there have been many good men in our city?

SOCRATES: On the contrary, there are plenty of good statesmen here in Athens and have been as good in the past. The question is, have they also been good teachers of their own virtue? That is the point we are discussing now—not whether or not there are good men in Athens or whether there have been in past times, but whether virtue **b** can be taught. It amounts to the question whether the good men of this and former times have known how to hand on to someone else the goodness that was in themselves, or whether on the contrary it is not something that can be handed over, or that one man can receive from another. That is what Meno and I have long been puzzling over. Look at it from your own point of view. You would say that Themistocles was a good man?   **c**

ANYTUS: Yes, none better.

SOCRATES: And that he, if anyone, must have been a good teacher of his own virtue?

ANYTUS: I suppose so, if he wanted to be.

SOCRATES: But don't you think he must have wanted others to become worthy men—above all, surely, his own son? Do you suppose he grudged him this and purposely didn't pass on his own virtue to him? You must have heard that he had his son Cleophantus so well **d** trained in horsemanship that he could stand upright on horseback and throw a javelin from that position, and many other wonderful accomplishments the young man had, for his father had him taught and made expert in every skill that a good instructor could impart. You must have heard this from older people?

ANYTUS : Yes.

SOCRATES : No one, then, could say that there was anything wrong with the boy's natural powers?

e   ANYTUS : Perhaps not.

SOCRATES : But have you ever heard anyone, young or old, say that Cleophantus, the son of Themistocles, was a good and wise man in the way that his father was?

ANYTUS : Certainly not.

SOCRATES : Must we conclude then that Themistocles' aim was to educate his son in other accomplishments, but not to make him any better than his neighbors in his own type of wisdom—that is, supposing that virtue could be taught?

ANYTUS : I hardly think we can.

SOCRATES : So much then for Themistocles as a teacher of virtue, whom you yourself agree to have been one of the best men of
94 former times. Take another example, Aristides, son of Lysimachus. You accept him as a good man?

ANYTUS : Surely.

SOCRATES : He too gave his son Lysimachus the best education in Athens, in all subjects where a teacher could help, but did he make him a better man than his neighbor? You know him, I think, and can say what he is like. Or again there is Pericles, that great and
b wise man. He brought up two sons, Paralus and Xanthippus, and had them taught riding, music, athletics, and all the other skilled pursuits till they were as good as any in Athens. Did he then not want to make them good men? Yes, he wanted that, no doubt, but I am afraid it is something that cannot be done by teaching. And in case you should think that only very few, and those the most insignificant,
c lacked this power, consider that Thucydides also had two sons, Melesias and Stephanus, to whom he gave an excellent education. Among other things they were the best wrestlers in Athens, for he gave one to Xanthias to train and the other to Eudoxus—the two who, I understand, were considered the finest wrestlers of their time. You remember?

ANYTUS : I have heard of them.

SOCRATES : Surely then he would never have had his children
d taught these expensive pursuits and yet refused to teach them to be good men—which would have cost nothing at all—if virtue could have been taught? You are not going to tell me that Thucydides was a man of no account, or that he had not plenty of friends both at Athens and among the allies? He came of an influential family and was a great power both here and in the rest of Greece. If virtue could have been taught, he would have found the man to make his sons good,
e either among our own citizens or abroad, supposing his political duties left him no time to do it himself. No, my dear Anytus, it looks as if it cannot be taught.

ANYTUS: You seem to me, Socrates, to be too ready to run people down. My advice to you, if you will listen to it, is to be careful. I dare say that in all cities it is easier to do a man harm than good, and it is certainly so here, as I expect you know yourself. 95

SOCRATES: Anytus seems angry, Meno, and I am not surprised. He thinks I am slandering our statesmen, and moreover he believes himself to be one of them. He doesn't know what slander really is; if he ever finds out he will forgive me.

However, tell me this yourself. Are there not similar fine characters in your country?

MENO: Yes, certainly.

SOCRATES: Do they come forward of their own accord to teach b the young? Do they agree that they are teachers and that virtue can be taught?

MENO: No indeed, they don't agree on it at all. Sometimes you will hear them say that it can be taught, sometimes that it cannot.

SOCRATES: Ought we then to class as teachers of it men who are not even agreed that it can be taught?

MENO: Hardly, I think.

SOCRATES: And what about the Sophists, the only people who profess to teach it? Do you think they do?

MENO: The thing I particularly admire about Gorgias, Socrates, c is that you will never hear him make this claim; indeed he laughs at the others when he hears them do so. In his view his job is to make clever speakers.

SOCRATES: So you too don't think the Sophists are teachers?

MENO: I really can't say. Like most people I waver—sometimes I think they are and sometimes I think they are not.

SOCRATES: Has it ever occurred to you that you and our statesmen are not alone in this? The poet Theognis likewise says in one place that virtue is teachable and in another that it is not. d

MENO: Really? Where?

SOCRATES: In the elegiacs in which he writes:

> Eat, drink, and sit with men of power and weight,
> Nor scorn to gain the favor of the great.
> For fine men's teaching to fine ways will win thee;
> Low company destroys what wit is in thee.[3] e

There he speaks as if virtue can be taught, doesn't he?

MENO: Clearly.

SOCRATES: But elsewhere he changes his ground a little.

> Were mind by art created and instilled
> Immense rewards had soon the pockets filled

of the people who could do this. Moreover,

---

[3] Theognis 33 sq.

96
>   No good man's son would ever worthless be,
>   Taught by wise counsel. But no teacher's skill
>   Can turn to good what is created ill.[4]

Do you see how he contradicts himself?

MENO: Plainly.

SOCRATES: Can you name any other subject, in which the professed teachers are not only not recognized as teachers of others, but are thought to have no understanding of it themselves, and to be no
b good at the very subject they profess to teach, whereas those who are acknowledged to be the best at it are in two minds whether it can be taught or not? When people are so confused about a subject, can you say that they are in a true sense teachers?

MENO: Certainly not.

SOCRATES: Well, if neither the Sophists nor those who display fine qualities themselves are teachers of virtue, I am sure no one else can be, and if there are no teachers, there can be no students either.

MENO: I quite agree.

c SOCRATES: And we have also agreed that a subject of which there were neither teachers nor students was not one which could be taught.

MENO: That is so.

SOCRATES: Now there turn out to be neither teachers nor students of virtue, so it would appear that virtue cannot be taught.

d MENO: So it seems, if we have made no mistake, and it makes me wonder, Socrates, whether there are in fact no good men at all, or how they are produced when they do appear.

SOCRATES: I have a suspicion, Meno, that you and I are not much good. Our masters Gorgias and Prodicus have not trained us properly. We must certainly take ourselves in hand, and try to find
e someone who will improve us by hook or by crook. I say this with our recent discussion in mind, for absurdly enough we failed to perceive that it is not only under the guidance of knowledge that human action is well and rightly conducted. I believe that may be what prevents us from seeing how it is that men are made good.

MENO: What do you mean?

97 SOCRATES: This. We were correct, were we not, in agreeing that good men must be profitable or useful? It cannot be otherwise, can it?

MENO: No.

SOCRATES: And again that they will be of some use if they conduct our affairs aright—that also was correct?

MENO: Yes.

SOCRATES: But in insisting that knowledge was a *sine qua non* for right leadership, we look like being mistaken.

---

[4] Theognis 435 sq.

MENO: How so?

SOCRATES: Let me explain. If someone knows the way to Larissa, or anywhere else you like, then when he goes there and takes others with him he will be a good and capable guide, you would agree?

MENO: Of course.

SOCRATES: But if a man judges correctly which is the road, b though he has never been there and doesn't know it, will he not also guide others aright?

MENO: Yes, he will.

SOCRATES: And as long as he has a correct opinion on the points about which the other has knowledge, he will be just as good a guide, believing the truth but not knowing it.

MENO: Just as good.

SOCRATES: Therefore true opinion is as good a guide as knowledge for the purpose of acting rightly. That is what we left out just now in our discussion of the nature of virtue, when we said that knowledge is the only guide to right action. There was also, it seems, c true opinion.

MENO: It seems so.

SOCRATES: So right opinion is something no less useful than knowledge.

MENO: Except that the man with knowledge will always be successful, and the man with right opinion only sometimes.

SOCRATES: What? Will he not always be successful so long as he has the right opinion?

MENO: That must be so, I suppose. In that case, I wonder why knowledge should be so much more prized than right opinion, and in- d deed how there is any difference between them.

SOCRATES: Shall I tell you the reason for your surprise, or do you know it?

MENO: No, tell me.

SOCRATES: It is because you have not observed the statues of Daedalus. Perhaps you don't have them in your country.

MENO: What makes you say that?

SOCRATES: They too, if no one ties them down, run away and escape. If tied, they stay where they are put.

MENO: What of it? e

SOCRATES: If you have one of his works untethered, it is not worth much; it gives you the slip like a runaway slave. But a tethered specimen is very valuable, for they are magnificent creations. And that, I may say, has a bearing on the matter of true opinions. True opinions are a fine thing and do all sorts of good so long as they stay in their place, but they will not stay long. They run away from a 98 man's mind; so they are not worth much until you tether them by working out the reason. That process, my dear Meno, is recollection, as we agreed earlier. Once they are tied down, they become knowledge, and are stable. That is why knowledge is something more valuable than right opinion. What distinguishes one from the other is the tether.

MENO: It does seem something like that, certainly.

b   SOCRATES: Well of course, I have only been using an analogy myself, not knowledge. But it is not, I am sure, a mere guess to say that right opinion and knowledge are different. There are few things that I should claim to know, but that at least is among them, whatever else is.

MENO: You are quite right.

SOCRATES: And is this right too, that true opinion when it governs any course of action produces as good a result as knowledge?

MENO: Yes, that too is right, I think.

c   SOCRATES: So that for practical purposes right opinion is no less useful than knowledge, and the man who has it is no less useful than the one who knows.

MENO: That is so.

SOCRATES: Now we have agreed that the good man is useful.

MENO: Yes.

SOCRATES: To recapitulate then, assuming that there are men good and useful to the community, it is not only knowledge that makes
d   them so, but also right opinion, and neither of these comes by nature but both are acquired—or do you think either of them *is* natural?

MENO: No.

SOCRATES: So if both are acquired, good men themselves are not good by nature.

MENO: No.

SOCRATES: That being so, the next thing we inquired was whether their goodness was a matter of teaching, and we decided that it would be, if virtue were knowledge, and conversely, that if it could be taught, it would be knowledge.

MENO: Yes.

e   SOCRATES: Next, that if there were teachers of it, it could be taught, but not if there were none.

MENO: That was so.

SOCRATES: But we have agreed that there are no teachers of it, and so that it cannot be taught and is not knowledge.

MENO: We did.

SOCRATES: At the same time we agreed that it is something good, and that to be useful and good consists in giving right guidance.

MENO: Yes.

99   SOCRATES: And that these two, true opinion and knowledge, are the only things which direct us aright and the possession of which makes a man a true guide. We may except chance, because what turns out right by chance is not due to human direction, and say that where human control leads to right ends, these two principles are directive, true opinion and knowledge.

MENO: Yes, I agree.

SOCRATES: Now since virtue cannot be taught, we can no b longer believe it to be knowledge, so that one of our two good and useful principles is excluded, and knowledge is not the guide in public life.

MENO: No.

SOCRATES: It is not then by the possession of any wisdom that such men as Themistocles, and the others whom Anytus mentioned just now, became leaders in their cities. This fact, that they do not owe their eminence to knowledge, will explain why they are unable to make others like themselves.

MENO: No doubt it is as you say.

SOCRATES: That leaves us with the other alternative, that it is well-aimed conjecture which statesmen employ in upholding their c countries' welfare. Their position in relation to knowledge is no different from that of prophets and tellers of oracles, who under divine inspiration utter many truths, but have no knowledge of what they are saying.

MENO: It must be something like that.

SOCRATES: And ought we not to reckon those men divine who with no conscious thought are repeatedly and outstandingly successful in what they do or say?

MENO: Certainly.

SOCRATES: We are right therefore to give this title to the oracular priests and the prophets that I mentioned, and to poets of d every description. Statesmen too, when by their speeches they get great things done yet know nothing of what they are saying, are to be considered as acting no less under divine influence, inspired and possessed by the divinity.

MENO: Certainly.

SOCRATES: Women, you know, Meno, do call good men 'divine,' and the Spartans too, when they are singing a good man's praises, say, 'He is divine.'

MENO: And it looks as if they are right—though our friend e Anytus may be annoyed with you for saying so.

SOCRATES: I can't help that. We will talk to him some other time. If all we have said in this discussion, and the questions we have asked, have been right, virtue will be acquired neither by nature nor by teaching. Whoever has it gets it by divine dispensation without tak- 100 ing thought, unless he be the kind of statesman who can create another like himself. Should there be such a man, he would be among the living practically what Homer said Tiresias was among the dead, when he described him as the only one in the underworld who kept his wits—'the others are mere flitting shades.' [5] Where virtue is concerned such a man would be just like that, a solid reality among shadows.

[5] *Odyssey* 10.494.

b   MENO: That is finely put, Socrates.

SOCRATES: On our present reasoning then, whoever has virtue gets it by divine dispensation. But we shall not understand the truth of the matter until, before asking how men get virtue, we try to discover what virtue is in and by itself. Now it is time for me to go, and my request to you is that you will allay the anger of your friend Anytus

c by convincing him that what you now believe is true. If you succeed, the Athenians may have cause to thank you.

EUTHYDEMUS

This is perhaps of all the dialogues the one that makes the Athens of Socrates and Plato seem farthest removed from us. We are taken back to a time when language had begun to be of great importance in itself and reasoning was largely verbal. A pun or a double meaning might decide a serious discussion. Here Socrates confronts Euthydemus and his brother who are both so-called eristics, or fighters with words, and in their fight with Socrates, who professes to be only their pupil, this sort of verbal trickery occurs constantly and becomes extremely tiresome. For instance, when Socrates asks the sense of a phrase used by Dionysodorus, he is in turn asked, "Is there soul in things which have sense, when they have sense? Or have also the soul-less things sense?" Socrates answers, "Only the things with soul." He is then triumphantly refuted, "Then do you know any phrase which has soul?" And to Socrates' answer he replies, "Then why did you ask me just now what sense my phrase had?" This is acknowledged by the large audience gathered around them to be a knockout blow.

Plato, of course, is holding up to ridicule all that sort of talk, but he is also concerned to point out how hard it is to put an idea into words. A Russian poet with all the resources of modern dictionaries at his disposal has said, "A thought when spoken is a lie." Something like that must often have been in Plato's mind as he sought not only to know the truth, but to discover a way to express it. He had to devise his own language, the language all philosophy would henceforth use, at a time when it was becoming the fashion to use words without regard to sense. The Euthydemus shows vividly what Plato had to contend with.

271 CRITO: Who was it, Socrates, you were talking to yesterday in the Lyceum? There was such a great crowd about you people that I myself, wanting to hear, could not get any nearer or hear anything clearly; however I stretched up and had a look over, and I thought it was a stranger you were talking to. Who was it?

SOCRATES: Which do you mean, Crito? There were two of them, not one.

CRITO: The one I mean was sitting third from you on your
b right, and between you was Axiochus' boy. I thought he had grown quite a lot, Socrates, almost as big as our own Critobulus; but Critobulus is thinnish, and this boy is well-grown and handsome and good-looking.

SOCRATES: Euthydemus is the man you ask about, Crito, and the one sitting on my left next to me was his brother Dionysodorus. This man is a partner in the talks.

CRITO: I don't know either of them, Socrates. These are new men again, I suppose Sophists. Where do they come from? And what
c is their line?

SOCRATES: They come from somewhere in these parts, I think, from Chios, and went away and joined the colony at Thurii, but they were turned out and they have spent a good many years since then in this part of the world. You ask their line—it will surprise you, Crito—they simply take every line, they are regular knowalls. I never knew till now what all-round athletes were! These two are quite all-champions! They surpass the two Acarnanian brothers, those all-round athletes, for those could do nothing but fight with
d their bodies. But these! First of all they are first-rate in fighting with their bodies and battling with all comers—they are themselves masters at fighting in armor, and can make anyone else expert who
272 would pay their fee. Next, in the battle of the law courts they are champions; they can compete themselves and teach others to speak, and they can compose speeches suitable to deliver in court. Well, hitherto this was all they were clever at, but now they have put the finishing touch on their all-round virtuosity, for they have now mastered the only battle left to them, so that no one will dare so much as to put up his hands against them—they have become so skillful in wordy warfare that they can confute with equal success anything
b which anyone says, whether false or true! So now, my dear Crito, I have it in mind to become their pupil, for they say that in quite a short time they would make anyone else as skillful as they are.

CRITO: I say, Socrates! Aren't you afraid, at your time of life, that you are too old?

Translated by W. H. D. Rouse and edited by Philip G. Rouse. Copyright ©
1961 by John Clive Graves Rouse. Published here for the first time. See
p. 420.

SOCRATES: Not the least, my dear Crito, I have proof and encouragement enough to make me quite fearless. The two men themselves were what you might call old men before they started at this science, disputation, which I want to acquire; last year or the year before they had not yet got it. The only thing I really do fear is that I c may bring discredit on the two strangers, as on poor Connus, Metrobius' son the harpist, who is now still trying to teach me to play the harp; the boys, my schoolfellows, look on and laugh at me and call Connus 'old Gaffer-Teacher'! Someone may taunt the two strangers with the same nickname, and quite likely they might refuse me as a pupil for fear of it. But anyhow, my dear Crito, I have persuaded a few other ancients to come with me to learn at Connus', and I will d try to do the same here. What about you—will you be my schoolfellow? We will bring your sons with us as a bait. I am sure they will teach us too, because they will want the boys.

CRITO: I'm willing, Socrates, if you wish it. But tell me first what their science is, and then I shall know what we are to learn.

SOCRATES: I can do that at once. I can't pretend that I did not pay attention for I certainly did, and I remember it well and will try to tell you the whole story from the beginning.

I happened providentially to be sitting in the place where you saw me, alone in the undressing room, and had just thought it was time to e get up; but as I was getting up, I had my usual divine presentiment. So I sat down again, and soon after in came these two, Euthydemus 273 and Dionysodorus, and others with them—a number of pupils I think. The two men came in, and walked round in the cloisters. They had hardly gone round two or three times when Clinias also came in, the one you say has grown so much, and you are quite right; behind him were a great many of his admirers, and among them Ctesippus, from Paeania, a fine handsome young man but rather wild as young men are. Clinias saw me from the entrance, sitting alone, so he came b straight to me and sat beside me on my right, just as you say. When Dionysodorus and Euthydemus caught sight of him, first they stood and talked to each other for a time, throwing glance after glance at us—for I watched them carefully—then they came up, and one, Euthydemus, sat down beside the boy, the other by me on my left, and the rest as each happened.

I said good day to the two, as it was some time since I had seen c them; after that I said to Clinias, These two men, Clinias, Euthydemus and Dionysodorus, are men of wisdom, and no small wisdom indeed. They know everything about war, as much as is needed for becoming a general, all about tactics, and how to lead an army, and how to fight in full armor, and moreover they can make a man able to defend himself in the law courts if he is wronged.

They turned up their noses at this; they looked at each other and d laughed, and Euthydemus said, We don't trouble about those things now, Socrates, we treat them just as side shows.

That surprised me, and I replied, Your main show must be a fine one, if such great subjects as those have come to be side shows. Tell me what this fine show is, in heaven's name!

Virtue, Socrates! We believe we can impart it—no one in the world so well or so quickly!

e   O God! said I. What an achievement! Where did you find this godsend? As I said just now, I thought of you two especially as skillful at fighting in full armor, and that is what I said of you; for when you first stayed in this town, I remember this was what you professed. Well, if you now truly have this knowledge, O be gracious!—for I humbly address you as gods, and I pray your pardon for what I said
274 before. But do think, Euthydemus and Dionysodorus—are you quite sure this is the truth? One cannot help feeling doubtful at such a portentous announcement.

Be assured, Socrates, they said, that this is true.

Then I felicitate you on your possession, much more than I would congratulate the Great King on his empire! Let me ask you if you have it in mind to demonstrate this wisdom? Or what do you mean to do?

That's the very reason why we are here, Socrates, to demonstrate
b and to teach, if anyone is willing to learn.

I will go bail that all those who have not got it will be willing! First myself, then Clinias here, and no doubt Ctesippus and these others, I said, pointing at the admirers of Clinias—they were all standing around us by this time. For Ctesippus was sitting, so I thought, a good way off from Clinias, but what happened was that
c Euthydemus as he talked to me, leaning forward, hid Clinias, who was between us, from Ctesippus; so Ctesippus wishing to watch his dear boy and also greedy to hear, had jumped up and came and stood right in front of us; the others seeing him did the same and gathered round us, both the admirers of Clinias and the companions of Euthydemus and Dionysodorus. These I pointed to when I said all
d were ready to learn, and Ctesippus eagerly said yes and so did the others, and they all asked the two brothers to demonstrate the power of their wisdom to all the company.

So I said, My friends Euthydemus and Dionysodorus, I beg you, do all you can to oblige these people, and for my sake also do demonstrate. A great task, if you take it as a complete whole. But please tell me one thing—can you make a man a good man only if he is already
e convinced that he must learn from you, or can you do it also to one who is not yet convinced, through doubting that the thing, virtue, can be learned at all or that you two can teach it? If you please, for a man in that condition, is it the work of the same art to convince him both that virtue is teachable and that you here are the people from whom one could best learn it? Or are these two different arts?

No, said Dionysodorus, no, Socrates, it is the same art—our art.

So you, Dionysodorus, I said, would be the best people in the world to incline a man toward philosophy and the practice of virtue? 275

Yes, Socrates, we think so.

Very well, said I, leave the rest of the demonstration for another time, and just demonstrate this one thing. Persuade this young man that he must love wisdom and practice virtue, and you will oblige me and all these. For the truth about this boy is that both I myself and all these anxiously desire that he should become as good as a man can be. This is the son of Axiochus and the grandson of the famous Alcibiades, and cousin of the present Alcibiades; his name is Clinias. b He is young, and we are afraid for him, as for other young men, that someone may get in first and turn his mind in some other direction, and ruin him. You have come, then, most fortunately. If you do not mind, please make trial of the lad, and talk with him before us.

When I had spoken, almost in these very words, Euthydemus answered bravely and boldly, Oh, we don't mind, Socrates, if the young man is only willing to answer. c

Why, he is quite used to that, I said. These people here are always coming and talking with him and asking all sorts of questions, so he is not at all shy in answering.

What followed, Crito, how could I describe properly? It is not a small business to recall and repeat wisdom ineffably great! So I must begin my description as the poets do, by invoking the Muses and Memory herself!

Well, Euthydemus began something like this, I think. d

Now Clinias, which of mankind are the learners, the wise or the ignorant?

This was a large question; so the boy blushed, and looked at me in doubt. Seeing that he was troubled I said, My dear Clinias, cheer up and answer like a man, whichever you think, for perhaps it will do e you a deal of good.

Just then, Dionysodorus leaned over me, and whispered in my ear, smiling all over his face, Now look here, Socrates, I prophesy that whichever the lad answers, he will be refuted!

While he spoke, Clinias made his answer, so I had no chance to warn the boy to take care, and he answered that the wise were the 276 learners.

And Euthydemus said, There are people you call teachers, aren't there?

He agreed.

The teachers are teachers of the learners; for example, the music master and the grammar master were teachers of you and the other boys, and you were learners?

He said yes.

Of course at the time when you were learning, you did not yet know the things you were learning?

No, he said.

b   Then you were wise when you did not know these things?
Certainly not, said he.
If not wise, then ignorant?
Yes.
So you boys, while learning what you did not know, were ignorant and were learning?
The boy nodded.
So the ignorant learn, my dear Clinias, not the wise as you suppose.
When he said this, it was like conductor and chorus—he sig-
c naled, and they all cheered and laughed, I mean Dionysodorus and Euthydemus and their followers. Then before the boy could take one good breath, Dionysodorus took over and said, What happened, my dear Clinias, when the grammar man dictated to you? Which of the boys learned the things dictated, wise or ignorant?
The wise ones, said Clinias.
Then the wise ones learn and not the ignorant, and you answered wrong just now to my brother.
d   Then indeed the two men's admirers laughed loud and long, applauding their wisdom, but all the rest of us were dumb-struck and had nothing to say. Euthydemus noticed that we were dumb-struck and wanted us to admire him more; so he would not let the boy alone, but went on asking, doubling and twisting around the same question like a clever dancer. He said, Do the learners learn what they know, or what they don't know?
And Dionysodorus whispered softly to me again, Here's another,
e Socrates, just like the first.
Good heavens, I said, really I thought that first one of yours a fine question!
All our questions are like that, Socrates—no escape!
Now, I said, I can see why you have such a reputation among your pupils!
Meanwhile Clinias answered Euthydemus that the learners learned what they did not know, and he went on in the same way as
277 before: Very well; do you not know your letters?
Yes, said Clinias.
All of them, eh?
He agreed.
And when a teacher dictates anything, does he not dictate letters?
He agreed.
Then he dictates a bit of what you know, if you know them all?
He agreed to this too.
Very well, said he, *you* do not learn what someone dictates, but only the one who does not know letters learns them? Eh?
No, no, he said, I do learn them.

Then you learn what you know, since you know all the letters.
He agreed.   b
Then you did not answer right, said Euthydemus.

The word had scarcely come out of his mouth, when Dionysodorus caught it like a ball and aimed it again at the boy, saying,
Euthydemus is cheating you, my dear Clinias. Just tell me, is not
learning getting knowledge of whatever one learns?

Clinias agreed.

But to know, he went on, is surely to have knowledge of something already?

He said yes.

Then not to know is not yet to have knowledge?

He agreed with this.   c

Well, are those who get anything, those who have it already, or
those who have not?

Those who have not.

Have you not agreed that those who do not know belong also to
this class, those who have not?

He nodded.

And the learners are of the class who get, not those who have?

He said yes.

Then those who do not know, learn, not those who do.

Now Euthydemus was getting ready to give the young man the d
third fall in this wrestling match, but I saw the boy was out of his
depth, and hoped to give him time to rest that he might not let us
down; so I said, to encourage him, My dear Clinias, do not be surprised if the arguments appear strange to you. Perhaps you do not
understand what our visitors are doing with you. They are doing the
same as the Corybantes do in their initiations, when the one to be
initiated is being enthroned. There is dancing and play there also,
as you know if you have been initiated; and now these are only dancing round you in play, meaning to initiate you afterward. So consider e
now that you are hearing the beginnings of the sophistic ritual. For
you must learn first of all, as Prodicus says, the right use of words;
and this is just what the two visitors are showing to you, because
you did not know that people use the word *learn* in two senses—first,
when one has no knowledge at the beginning about something, and 278
then afterward gets the knowledge, and second, when one already
having the knowledge uses this knowledge to examine this same thing
done or spoken. The second is called understanding rather than
learning, but sometimes it is also called learning. But you missed
this, as these show it; they hold the same word as applying to people
in opposite senses, to one who knows and one who does not. It was
much the same in the second question, in which they asked you b
whether people learn what they know or what they don't. Well, all
this is just a little game of learning, and so I say they are playing

with you; I call it a game, because if one learned many such things or even all of them, one would be no nearer knowing what the things really are, but would be able to play with people because of the different sense of the words, tripping them up and turning them upside down, just as someone pulls a stool away when someone else is going to sit down, and then people roar with joy when they see him
c lying on his back. So you must consider that all this was a game on the part of these gentlemen, but I feel sure, Clinias, that from now on this distinguished pair will show you serious things, and I will give them a lead as to what they promised me to provide. You remember they said they would demonstrate their skill in drawing you on, but so far I suppose they thought it better to begin by playing with you.

Then, my dear Euthydemus and Dionysodorus, let your play end
d here—perhaps we have had enough—but now please demonstrate by attracting the boy and showing him how he must practice wisdom and virtue.

But first I will show to you what my notion of it is, and the sort of thing I should like to hear. If you think I am clumsy and ridiculous in doing this, don't laugh at me; I am only eager to listen to your wis-
e dom, and so I will be daring enough to make a rough sketch before you. Put up with me then, and listen without laughing, both you and your pupils. And as for you, Master Clinias, answer.

Do we all wish to do well in the world? Or perhaps this is one of the questions which I feared you might laugh at, for it is foolish, no doubt, even to ask such things. Who in the world does not wish to do well?

Not a single one, said Clinias.

279   Very well, said I. Next then, since we all wish to do well, how could we do well? If we had plenty of good things, eh? Perhaps that is a sillier question than the other. For it is clear, I suppose, that that is true?

He agreed.

Very well, which shall we say are good for us, of all the things there are? This is an easy question, I think; it needs no solemn person to supply an answer, for everyone would tell us that to be rich is good. What do you say?

Yes indeed, he said.

b   Also to be healthy, and to be handsome, and to have enough of all the other bodily blessings.

He thought so too.

Again, good birth and power and honor in your own country, these are clearly good?

He agreed.

Then what good things are left to us? What is it to be temperate and upright and brave? What do you think, in heaven's name, Clinias

—if we put these among the good things, shall we be right, or not? For perhaps someone might quarrel with this. What do *you* think?

They are good, said Clinias.

Very well, said I, where shall we put wisdom in our parade? c Among the good things, or where do you say?

Among the good things.

Take care now that we leave out none of the good things worth mentioning.

Oh no, said Clinias, I think there is nothing left out.

Suddenly I remembered one, and said, Upon my word, we are nearly leaving out the greatest good of all!

What is that? he asked.

Good fortune, Clinias, which everyone says is the greatest good of all; even the commonest fools say that.

Quite true, said he.

Then I thought again for a moment, and said, We have almost d made ourselves ridiculous before these visitors, you and I, my dear young gentleman!

What's the matter now? he asked.

Because we put good fortune among the first lot, and now here we are talking about the same again!

Well, what is the matter then?

It is ridiculous, I suppose, when something has been lying before us all this time, to lay it before us again and to say the same things twice!

How do you mean? he asked.

I said, Wisdom, I suppose, is good fortune; even a child would know that.

He was astonished, so young and simple he still is. Seeing him wondering I said, Why, Clinias, consider for example doing well with e pipe music, don't you think the pipers have the best fortune?

He said yes.

And in the writing and reading of letters, I said, the grammar men?

Certainly.

Consider the dangers of the sea. Surely you don't think that anyone has better fortune than wise pilots, as a general rule?

Of course not.

Well then, on a campaign, which would you like better to share danger and fortune with, a wise captain or an ignorant one?

A wise one.

And if you were ill, which would you prefer to run risks with, a wise physician or an ignorant one?

A wise one.

Don't you think, then, I said, that it would be better fortune to do 280 anything along with a wise man, than with an ignorant one?

He agreed.

Then wisdom everywhere makes men to have good fortune. For wisdom, I suppose, could never make a mistake, but must always do right and have right fortune, or else it would not be wisdom any longer.

b   We came to an agreement in the end somehow or other, to sum up thus: when wisdom is present, whoever has it needs no more good fortune than that. And when we had come to this agreement, I asked him how our former admissions would stand now. We agreed, I said, that if we had plenty of good things, we should be happy and do well.

He said yes.

Then should we be happy because of the good things we had, if they gave us benefit, or if they did not?

c   If they gave us benefit, he said.

And would a thing give benefit, if we only had it but did not use it? For example, if we had plenty of food, but ate nothing, and plenty of drink, but drank nothing, should we get any benefit?

No, none, he said.

And all the craftsmen, now, if each of them had everything ready that was necessary for his work, but used nothing, would these do well just because of having, because they had all the things which the craftsman must have? A carpenter, for instance, if he had provided all his tools and wood enough but did no carpentering, would he get any benefit from just having?

d   None at all, said he.

Again, if a man were possessed of wealth and all the good things we named lately, but if he did not use them, would he be happy just because he possessed the good things?

Not at all.

Then it is necessary, I said, as it seems, that the one who is to be happy must not only get possession of such good things, but also must use them, or else there is no benefit from having them.

Quite true.

e   Very well then, Clinias, is that enough now to make a man happy, both to possess the good things and to use them?

I think so.

Is that if he uses them aright, or is it the same if he uses them wrongly?

If he uses them right.

Quite so, said I. It is more harmful, I should think, if one uses anything wrongly than if one leaves it alone—the first is bad; the second is neither bad nor good. Don't you agree?

He did.

281   Very well, in the working and the use of woodwork, that which produces the right use is just simply knowledge of carpentry, don't you think so?

It is just that.

Moreover knowledge, I suppose, is what produces right use of equipment?

He agreed.

Well then, I said, what about the use of the good things which we mentioned at first—wealth and health and good looks—for using all such things right, was knowledge the guide which directed the action, or was it something else?   b

Knowledge, he said.

Then not only good fortune but good doing, as it seems, is provided by knowledge for mankind in every getting and doing.

He agreed.

Then in God's name, said I, does any benefit come from the other possessions, without intelligence and wisdom? Could a man get benefit, possessing plenty and doing much, if he had no sense—would he not benefit more by doing little with sense? Just consider. If he did less he would make fewer mistakes, if he made fewer mistakes he   c would do less badly, if he did less badly he would be less miserable?

Certainly, he said.

Which would be more likely to do less, a poor man or a rich man?

A poor man, he said.

A weak man or a strong man?

A weak man.

A man in high place or in low place?

Low place.

Would a brave and temperate man do less, or a coward?

A coward.

So also an idle rather than an active man?

He agreed.

And a slow man rather than a quick one, shortsighted and hard of hearing rather than sharp?

In all such comparisons we agreed.   d

Then to sum up, my dear Clinias, I said, the truth is that in all those things which we said at first were good, the question is not how they are in themselves naturally good, but this is the point, it seems. If ignorance leads them, they are greater evils than their opposites, inasmuch as they are more able to serve the leader which is evil; but if intelligence leads, and wisdom, they are greater goods, while in themselves neither kind is worth anything at all.

It seems to be so, as you say, he said.   e

Then what follows from what has been said? That none of the things is either good or bad, except these two, and of these wisdom is good, and ignorance bad.

He agreed.

Then let us consider what remains, I said. Since we all desire to   282 be happy, and we have been shown to be happy by using things and using them aright, and rightness and good fortune were provided by knowledge, what seems to be necessary, you see, is that every man in every way shall try to become as wise as possible. Is not that correct?

Yes, he said.

b   And I suppose we think that he should get this from his father much rather than wealth, and from guardians and friends and especially from those who profess to be lovers, native or foreign; he should beg and beseech them to give him some wisdom. For wisdom's sake, Clinias, there is no disgrace, no reproach, in being servant and slave to a lover and to anyone, for a man willing to give honorable service in the passion to become wise. Don't you think so? I said.

I think you are quite right, he replied.

c   Yes, Clinias, I said, if only wisdom can be taught, if only it is not something that comes to men of itself—for that is a point we have not considered, that has not yet been agreed between me and you.

Well, Socrates, he said, I think wisdom can be taught.

I was delighted, and replied, Well said, admirable boy! I am much obliged to you for sparing me from a long inquiry on just that question, whether wisdom can or cannot be taught. Now, then, since you think it can, and that wisdom alone in the wide world makes a
d   man happy and fortunate, don't you say it is necessary to love wisdom, and don't you mean to do it yourself?

That I do, Socrates, he said, as hard as ever I can!

I was glad to hear it. And I said, There's my specimen, my dear Dionysodorus and Euthydemus, of the sort of thing I wish words of attraction to be; it is clumsy perhaps, and too long, and tedious. Now then let either of you who wishes demonstrate the same thing for us,
e   doing it neatly like an artist. Or if you do not care to do that, then begin where I left off, and show the boy in due order whether he must get every knowledge, or if there is one single knowledge which he must get to be happy and a good man, and what this is. For as I said at the beginning, it would really mean a great deal to us that this young man should become wise and good.

283   That is what I said, Crito, and I paid particular attention to what should follow, and I watched how they would tackle the argument, and where they would begin, in trying to encourage the young man to practice wisdom and virtue. So Dionysodorus, the elder brother, began first, and we all watched him expecting to hear something won-
b   derful there and then. As indeed we did, Crito, for it was a wonderful argument which the man was beginning, and it is worth your while to hear what sort of encouragement to virtue it was.

Tell me, Socrates, he said, and all you gentlemen here who say you desire that this young man should become wise, whether you are jesting in saying this, or do you truly and seriously desire it?

This made me suppose that they thought we were jesting before, when we asked them to converse with the young man, and that this

was the reason why they jested and did not take it seriously. So I told c
them still more earnestly that we were really serious about it.

Then Dionysodorus said, Take care, Socrates; you may have to
deny what you say now.

I have taken care, I replied. I shall never deny it.

Very well, he said. You say you want him to become wise.

Most certainly.

But now, said he, is Clinias wise or not?

He says, not yet, said I. He's no boaster, you know.

And you people, said Dionysodorus, want him to become wise,
and not to be a dunce?

We agreed.

Then you wish him to become one that he is not, and no longer d
to be one that he is.

I was troubled when I heard this, and he, seeing me troubled, took
me up: One further word. Since you want him no longer to be one that
he is now, you want him to be destroyed, it seems! Indeed, precious
friends and lovers they must be who would give a great deal to have
their darlings done away with!

Ctesippus flew into a rage for his pet when he heard this, and e
said, Mr. Thurian Visitor, if it weren't too rude I would say, Same
be done to you! How could you let yourself tell such a lie about me and
the rest of us, something to my mind not decent to repeat, that I would
wish this young gentleman to be done away with!

My dear Ctesippus, said Euthydemus, do you really think it is
possible to tell a lie?

Yes, by heaven, or else I am out of my senses.

In making the statement objected to, or not in making it?

In making it, he replied.   284

In that case, *if* he states it, is he not telling another of the *facts*,
differing from what he actually says?

How could he? said Ctesippus.

Clearly what he tells is an extra one of the facts, distinct from his
other facts.

Quite so!

Therefore in stating *that*, he said, he is stating the extra fact?

Yes.

Now then, he who states this fact and the other facts is telling
the truth; so Dionysodorus, since he states the facts, tells the truth
and tells no lie about you.

Yes, said Ctesippus, but he that makes *these* statements, Euthy- b
demus, is not stating the facts—is not saying the things that are.

Then Euthydemus went on, Surely the things that are not, are
not?

They are not.

Surely the things that are not can only be nowhere?

Nowhere.

Is it possible then that anyone, I don't care who he is, could *do* something about these things that are not, so as to *make* them *to be* the things that are nowhere?

I don't think so, said Ctesippus.

Very well. When the orators speak in public, do they do nothing?

Oh yes, they do something.

Then if they do, they also make?

Yes.

c Then to speak is both to do and to make?

He agreed.

Then, said he, no one ever says the things that are not—for he would at once make them something, and you have admitted that no one can make that which is not—so according to what you say, no one tells lies, but since Dionysodorus says it, he says the truth and the things that are.

Right, on my word, said Ctesippus, only he says the things that are in a certain way, but not as they really are.

d What, Ctesippus! broke in Dionysodorus. Are there indeed people who say things as they are?

Certainly there are, he replied, all gentlemen and those who *speak the truth*.

Very well, said Dionysodorus, are not good things well, and bad things ill?

He agreed.

You agree that gentlemen speak as things are?

I do.

Then, Ctesippus, gentlemen speak ill of things ill, since they speak as things are.

Yes, upon my word, said he, very much so at least of rude men;

e you will take care not to be one yourself, if you will listen to me, or the good men may speak ill of *you*. You can be sure that the good speak ill of the ill!

And do they speak bigly of the big, said Euthydemus, and hotly of the hot?

That they do, said Ctesippus, at least they speak flatly of the flat, like your discussion.

Vulgar abuse, Ctesippus, said Dionysodorus, vulgar abuse.

Not a bit of it, Dionysodorus, said he, since I am fond of you, but I am warning you as a friend, and I am trying to persuade you never

285 to say, so rudely to my face, that I want these to be done away with, whom I value most!

As I saw they were getting rather wild with each other, I began to make game of Ctesippus and said, My dear Ctesippus, I think we ought to accept from our visitors what they tell us, if they are kind enough to do us this favor, and we should not quarrel over a word. If they understand how to destroy men so as to make good and sensible ones out of bad and foolish ones, whether this be their own invention, or they learned from someone else a kind of death or de- b struction, such that they can destroy a bad one and produce a good one instead: if they understand this—and it is clear they do understand it; at least they said that their art newly discovered was to make good men out of bad—let us give them leave; let them destroy the lad and make him sensible, and all the rest of us too! But if you young ones are afraid, make the experiment on me, as your Carian slave; I c am only an old man, so I am ready to run the risk, and I deliver myself to Dionysodorus here as if he were Medea of Colchis. Let him destroy me, boil me too if he likes, only let him turn me out good.

Then Ctesippus said, I'm quite ready, myself, Socrates, to let our visitors take me on, and if they like they may flay me even worse than they do now, so long as my skin shall not end as a leather bottle, like that of Marsyas, but in virtue. You see Dionysodorus here d thinks I am angry with him; but I'm not angry, I am only speaking against what I think he is not speaking nicely to me. Look here, Dionysodorus, be generous, don't say that to speak against you is vulgar abuse; that is something quite different, vulgar abuse!

Dionysodorus answered, Do you think there is such a thing as 'speaking against' one, Ctesippus, when you say that?

Why yes, of course, he said, very much so; do you think there is e not, my dear Dionysodorus?

Anyway, he replied, you could not show that you had ever heard anyone 'speaking against' anyone else.

Indeed? said Ctesippus, On the contrary, let us hear now whether I can show you Ctesippus speaking against Dionysodorus.

And would you undertake to prove that?

Certainly, he said.

Well then, said Dionysodorus, are there words describing each of the things that are?

Certainly.

As each thing is, then, or as it is not?

As it is.

Yes, for if you remember, Ctesippus, he said, we showed just now 286 that no one speaks of anything as it is not, for it was made clear that no one speaks what is not.

Well, what then? said Ctesippus. Are you and I speaking against each other any the less?

Then should we be speaking against each other when we both spoke describing the same thing, or should we not in that case be saying the same things?

He admitted it.

b   But when neither of us speaks the word describing the thing, he
said, should we then be speaking against each other? Surely in this
case neither of us would be thinking of the thing at all?

He admitted this too.

On the other hand, he said, when I speak the word describing the
thing, and you describing something else, are we speaking against
each other then? Or am I describing the thing, and you saying nothing about it at all? And how could he that says nothing be speaking
against him that is speaking?

Ctesippus was silent, but I was astonished at the whole argu-
c ment, and said, What do you mean, Dionysodorus? I confess that I
have heard this argument from many, and however often I hear it
I am always astonished; even Protagoras and his people used it with
vigor, and others before them. It was always a wonder to me how it
confounded everyone else, and indeed confounded itself—however, I
think I shall hear the truth of it best from you. Is it really impossible to
tell a lie? For this is what the argument means. Is it? Come, must one
tell the truth or say nothing?

He agreed.

d   Then is it impossible to tell a lie, but possible to have a false
opinion?

Not even that, he said.

Then there is no such thing at all as a false opinion, I said.

No, he said.

And no ignorance, or ignorant people? Would not ignorance, if
it did exist, be this—being deceived about things?

Certainly, he said.

But that is not possible, I said.

No, said he.

Are you speaking just for the sake of speaking, Dionysodorus, I
said, only to say something odd and strange, or do you really think
that no one in the world is ignorant?

e   Just you refute me, said he.

Is there such a thing as refute, to use your own argument, if no
one speaks falsely?

There is not, said Euthydemus.

And so, it seems Dionysodorus did not this moment bid me refute? I said.

No, for how could anyone bid what is not? he replied. Do you?

My dear Euthydemus, I said, I fear I do not quite understand
these clever things and admirable things but my mind is somewhat
dense about them, so perhaps I am going to speak like a common or
vulgar man, but please forgive me. Look here, if it is impossible to
287 be false, or to think falsely, or to be ignorant, then is it not impossible
to make a mistake when one does anything? For in doing, one cannot
make a mistake in what one does—is not that what you say?

Certainly, he answered.

Then here is my common or vulgar question, I said. For if we make no mistake either in doing or in speaking or in thinking, then what in God's name do you come here to teach, if that is so? Did you not say just now that you could impart virtue better than all the world to one who wanted to learn? b

Here Dionysodorus broke in, Are you such an old dotard, Socrates, that you remind us now what we said at first, and if I said something last year you will remember that now, but you don't know what to do with what is being said at the present moment?

Because what is being said now is very difficult—naturally, since it is said by very wise men—indeed this last thing is wholly difficult to deal with, as you say. For what do you mean, Dionysodorus, when you say I don't know what to do with it? Isn't it clear you mean that I can't refute it? Just tell me, what else is the sense of the phrase, 'I c don't know what to do' with what is said?

But as to what *you* say, that is not very difficult to do with, he said. Just answer me.

Before *you* answer *me*? I said.

Won't you answer? he said.

Is that fair?

Quite fair, he said.

On what reasoning? said I. Is not this your reasoning—that you visit us as one all-wise about words, and you know when you are bound to answer and when not, and now you will not answer anything d since you perceive that you are not bound?

You just chatter, he said, without troubling to answer. Come, my good man, do as I say and answer, since you yourself admit that I am wise.

Then I must do as you say, said I, and I can't help it, as it seems, for you are master. Ask away.

Is there soul in things which have sense, when they have sense? Or have also the soulless things sense?

Only the things with soul.

Then do you know any phrase which has soul?

No indeed.

Then why did you ask me just now what sense my phrase had? e

Oh, I said, it was simply a mistake I made through my stupidity —or perhaps it was not a mistake, and I was right in saying that phrases have sense. Do you say it was a mistake or not? For if it was not a mistake, then you will not refute me although you are wise, and you do not know what to do with my saying; and if it was a mistake, then you do not say right when you declare it is impossible to make 288 a mistake. I am not now speaking of things you said last year. It seems really, I said, my dear Dionysodorus and Euthydemus, that our present talk is getting us no further, and is still so to speak the old 'knockdown and tumble down,' and even your skill has not yet found out how to keep it from that, wonderful though it is for exactitude in speaking.

Then Ctesippus said, Truly amazing things you do say, honorable gentlemen of Thurii or Chios, or whence or however you like to get
b your names—you don't seem to mind what nonsense you babble!

I was afraid of another bout of rudeness and tried again to calm Ctesippus by saying, My dear Ctesippus, what I said to Clinias a moment ago I say now to you, that you do not know how astonishing is the depth of our visitors' wisdom, only they are not willing to demonstrate it in earnest; they are doing conjuring tricks with us like Proteus, the Egyptian Sophist. So let us follow the example of
c Menelaus, and not let go of the men until they make clear to us their real serious shape, for I believe that something very fine will appear when they begin to be in earnest. Come, let us pray and beseech them to show themselves. I really think the best thing is for me once more to give them a lead myself, and show them in what shape I beg them to reveal themselves. I will proceed from where I formerly left off, and I will try to follow up what comes next as well as I can, in the
d hope that I may bring them out, and they may pity my earnest attempt and be themselves in earnest.

Now then, Clinias, I said, it is your turn. Remind me where we left off. I think it was hereabout. We agreed in the end, didn't we, that one must love wisdom? What do you say?

Yes, he said.

And to love wisdom is to get knowledge? Is that right?

Yes, he said.

What knowledge then should we do right to get? Is not the answer simply the knowledge that shall benefit us?
e Certainly, he said.

Would it benefit us at all, if we knew how to go about the country and recognize where in the earth the greatest quantity of gold is buried?

Perhaps, he said.

But before that, I said, we had proved that we should gain nothing, even if we got all the gold offhand without digging; so that even if
289 we knew how to turn all the stones into gold, the knowledge would be worth nothing to us; for unless we know also how to use the gold, we saw there was no benefit in it. Don't you remember? said I.

Oh yes, I remember, he said.

In the same way, it seems, there is no benefit in any other knowledge, of business or of physic for example, or anything else which knows how to make something but not how to use what it makes. Is not that so?

He said yes.
b Even if there is a knowledge how to make men immortal, with-

out the knowledge how to use immortality even this seems to bring no benefit, if we are to judge from our former admissions.

We both agreed about that.

Then, my charming boy, I said, we need such a knowledge as combines both how to make something and how to use what is made.

It appears so, he said.

Then we must be nothing at all like those who make harps, for instance; we do not want to become masters of knowledge like that; for there the making art is one thing, the using art quite another, c and each art deals separately with the harp. For the arts of harp making and harp playing are very different. Is not that so?

He said yes.

Nor do we want pipe making, clearly; this is another like that.

He agreed.

Well, said I, if we should learn the art of speechmaking, tell me in heaven's name, is this the art which when got will make us happy?

No, I don't think so, answered Clinias.

What's your evidence? I asked.   d

He replied, I see certain speechmakers who do not know how to use the speeches which they make themselves, like harp makers with their harps; but here also there are others able to use the speeches which the others have made, some who are themselves unable to make the speeches. It is clear then that, in speeches also, making is one art and using another.

I think you give proof enough, I said, that the art of the speechmakers is not that which if anyone gets he would be happy. However, I did think that somewhere about here would appear the knowledge e which we have been seeking so long. For indeed the men who make the speeches, when I meet them, do seem to me to be superwise, Clinias, and their very art seems to be something divine and lofty. However, that is nothing to wonder at, for it is a portion of the art of enchanters, but falls short a little. For the enchanter's art is the 290 charming of adders and tarantulas and scorpions and other vermin and pests, but this is really the charming and persuasion of juries and parliaments and any sort of crowds. Don't you think it is like that?

Yes, clearly that is just what it is like, he said.

Then where are we to turn to now? I said. What art is there?

I'm sure I can't say, he replied.

Why! said I. I think I have found it myself!

What art? said Clinias.

The general's art! I said. That seems to be most certainly the art, b which he who gets will be happy!

I do not think so.

Why not? I said.

This art seems to me a sort of hunting men.

What then? said I.

No art of hunting, he said, goes further than to hunt and to capture; but when they have captured what they hunted, they cannot use it; huntsmen and fishermen hand over to the cooks. Geometers and astronomers and calculators—for these are a sort of hunters too, since they are not mere makers of diagrams, but they try to find out the real meanings—so because they do not know how to use them, but only how to hunt, they hand over their discoveries, I take it, to the dialecticians to use up, at least all of them hand over who are not quite without sense.

Good, good, I said. O Clinias, most beautiful boy, most wise reasoner! Is that really so?

Certainly it is so! he replied. And the same with the generals. As soon as they have hunted a city or an army, they hand it over to the politicians—for they do not know themselves how to use their captures—just as quail hunters hand over to the quail keepers. If, therefore, went on Clinias, we need that art, which will itself know how to use what it got by making or hunting, and will be such as to make us blessed, then we must seek some other art, instead of the general's.

CRITO: What do you say, Socrates? That young boy said all that?

SOCRATES: Don't you think so, Crito?

CRITO: Not a bit of it! I think that if he said it, he did not need Euthydemus or anyone else to educate him!

SOCRATES: Heaven preserve us, my dear man, I wonder if Ctesippus was the one who said it! That memory of mine!

CRITO: Ctesippus? Surely not!

SOCRATES: Well, I am sure of one thing, it was neither Euthydemus nor Dionysodorus who said that. Good God, Crito! Can it be that some higher power was there and uttered the words! I heard them, I am sure of it.

CRITO: Oh yes, oh yes, Socrates, it was some higher power. That's what I think, no doubt about it. But after this, did you go on looking for the art? Did you find what you wanted, or didn't you?

SOCRATES: Find it, good heavens! No, you would have laughed at us—we were like children after larks, always thought we were going to catch each knowledge by the tail, and the knowledge always got away. Why make a long story of it? We came to the art of kings, and examined that to see if that provided and manufactured happiness. Then it seemed like falling into a labyrinth; we thought we were at the finish, but our way bent round and we found ourselves as it were back at the beginning, and just as far from that which we were seeking at first.

CRITO: How did this happen to you, Socrates?

SOCRATES: I will tell you. We thought the art of politics and the art of kings were the same.

CRITO: And what next?

SOCRATES: To this art the generals and the rest gave over the control of the works of their own trades, as being the only art knowing how to use them. Thus it seemed clear to us that this was the art we sought, and the cause of doing right in the state, exactly as the verse d of Aeschylus describes it, sitting alone at the helm of state, steering all and ruling all, and making all useful.

CRITO: And you thought this a good notion, Socrates?

SOCRATES: You shall judge of that, Crito, if you will hear what happened to us next. You see we went on looking at it like this. Pray does this royal art, ruling all, make anything for us, or not? Certainly it does, we said to each other. Wouldn't you say the same, Crito?   e

CRITO: Yes, I should.

SOCRATES: Then what would you say it makes? Put it in this way. If I should ask you whether the physician's art, ruling all that it rules, makes anything for us, would you not say it makes health?

CRITO: Yes, I should.

SOCRATES: And what of your art of agriculture? Ruling all which it rules, what does it make? Wouldn't you say it produces for 292 us the food from the earth?

CRITO: Yes.

SOCRATES: Then what of the art of kings, ruling all which it rules? What does it make? Perhaps you cannot say exactly.

CRITO: No indeed, I cannot.

SOCRATES: Nor could we, my dear Crito. But I know one thing, that if it is the art we seek, it must be helpful.

CRITO: Certainly.

SOCRATES: Then surely it must provide something good for us?

CRITO: Obviously, Socrates.

SOCRATES: But good, as Clinias and I agreed together, is noth- b ing but some kind of knowledge.

CRITO: Yes, you said so.

SOCRATES: Again, all the other 'works of politics' as one might call them—and there are many, for example, to make the people rich and free and without party spirit—all these things turned out to be neither good nor bad, but the necessary thing was to make them wise and to give them a share of knowledge, since knowledge was to be that which profited them and made them happy.   c

CRITO: That is true, that is what you agreed, according to your report of what was said.

SOCRATES: Then does the art of kings make the people wise and good?

CRITO: Why not, Socrates?

SOCRATES: But does it make all of them good, and good in all respects? Does it impart every knowledge, shoemaking and carpentry and all the others?

CRITO: I do not think so, Socrates.

d   SOCRATES: But what knowledge does it teach? And what are
we to do with it? For it must not be a contriver of any of those products which are neither good nor bad; it must impart no knowledge but
itself alone. Can we say then what it is, and what we are to do with
it? Would you like us to say it is the one by which we shall make other
men good?

CRITO: Yes, certainly.

SOCRATES: And what shall these be good for, and how useful to
us? Shall we say, to make others the same, and they to make others,
e   and so on and on? And good at what? We cannot see, since we have
despised what are generally said to be the works of statecraft, and as
the proverb goes, it is always 'Corinthus, son of Zeus.' We are just as
far from knowing, or farther, what is that knowledge which will make
us happy.

CRITO: Yes, indeed, Socrates, it seems you got yourselves into
a nice mess.

SOCRATES: Well all I could do, my dear man, since I found my-
293 self in this mess, was to cry and clamor, praying to the two visitors
like a second pair of savior gods [Castor and Polydeuces], to save us,
me and the boy, from this tempest of logic, and to play no more but to
be serious, and show to us which is the knowledge which once gained
would bring us well through the rest of our life.

CRITO: What then? Was Euthydemus willing to show you?

SOCRATES: Why, of course! And he began, my good friend, in
this magnificent fashion.

b   Which do you prefer, then, my dear Socrates? Shall I teach you
this knowledge which has been puzzling you for so long, or shall I
show that you have it?

Heaven bless us, my dear man! said I. Can you do that?

That I can, said he.

Then show that I have it, I do beseech you, said I, for that is
much easier than learning for an old man like me.

Very well, he said, just answer. Is there anything you do know?

Oh yes, I said, plenty of things, but only small ones.

Quite enough, said he. Then do you think it is possible for anything whatever of the things which are, not to be what it is?

c   Why no, I don't, said I.

You know something then? said he.

I do.

Then you are knowing, since you know?

Certainly, in that same something.

That makes no difference, he said. Isn't it necessary that you
know everything since you are knowing?

Why, no indeed, I said. There are many other things I do not
know.

Then if you do not know something, you are not knowing.

Not knowing that, my friend, said I.

Are you any the less not knowing? But just now you said you were knowing, and so you are really this very same you, and again not the same, in relation to the same things at the same time!   d

All right, Euthydemus! I said. As the proverb goes, 'You never say a word amiss, it's always either that or this!' And what then is my understanding of that knowledge we were looking for? I suppose it is this. It is impossible for the same thing both to be and not to be. If I know one thing I know all things, for I could not be knowing and not knowing at the same time. And so since I know everything, I have *that* knowledge too! There you are—isn't that what you tell us, isn't that your word of wisdom?

Look here, said he, you are refuting *yourself*, Socrates!   e

Well, but what about you, Euthydemus? I said. Weren't *you* in this same difficulty? Anyway, so long as I keep with you and with dear old Dionysodorus, I shall not feel at all vexed at any difficulty we get into! Tell me, don't you two know some of the things which are, and not know others of them?

By no means, said Dionysodorus.

What's that! said I. Don't you know anything?

Oh yes, we do, he said.

Then you know everything, I asked, since you know something?   294

Everything, he answered, and so do you. If you know one thing, you know all things.

O God! I said. Here's a wonder and a manifest miracle! Can it be that all the other men in the world know everything, or nothing?

Surely, he said, they cannot know some things and not others, or they would be at once knowing and not knowing.

Knowing what? I said.

Everyone, said he, knows everything, if he knows one thing.

Good heavens! I said. Good heavens, Dionysodorus! I see now b you are both in earnest, and what a job I had to persuade you to take us in earnest! Do you both really and truly know everything? Carpentry and shoemaking, for instance?

Certainly, he said.

So you are able to stitch leather?

Yes, and to do cobbling too, he said.

And do you know things like these, the number of the stars, and the sand?

Certainly, he said. Do you think we would not admit that too?

Then Ctesippus broke in. Show me a proof, Dionysodorus, for God's sake, by which I may know that you two are telling the truth.   c

What shall I show you? he said.

Do you know how many teeth Euthydemus has, and does he know how many you have?

Is it not enough for you, he said, to be told that we know everything?

Not that, please, said Ctesippus. Just tell us this one thing more and show you are speaking the truth; if you each say how many teeth the other has, and if we count them and prove that you know, we will at once believe all the rest.

d   They thought he was making fun, so they were unwilling, but they kept on saying they knew everything, as Ctesippus asked them one question after another without the smallest restraint. And he left out nothing, not even the ugliest, but asked them if they knew that. They faced up boldly against every question maintaining that they did know, like wild boars charging against the spear thrust, so that I also became quite incredulous, Crito, and at last I myself was driven to ask if Dionysodorus knew how to dance.

e   He said, Oh yes!

Well, I said, I suppose you can't do a sword dance, and roll about on a wheel, at your age? Have you got that far in skill?

There's nothing I can't do, he said.

And do you know everything only now, I asked, or have you known it always?

Always, he said.

Even when you were children, and as soon as you were born, did you know everything?

Yes, they said, both together.

295   This seemed incredible to us, and Euthydemus asked, Do you not believe it, Socrates?

I can only say, I replied, that you must be a wise pair.

But if you will answer me, he said, I will prove that you also admit these surprising things.

Oh, well, I said, I shall be very glad to be shown up like that. For if I have been wise without knowing it myself, and if you will show that I know everything and always did, what greater piece of luck could I have in all my life!

Answer then, he said.

b   All right, ask away. I will answer.

Tell me then, Socrates, he said, are you knowing in something or not?

I am.

Then do you know by that by which you are knowing, or by something else?

By that by which I am knowing. I suppose you mean the soul, or do you not mean this?

Aren't you ashamed, Socrates? he said. When you are asked one question, do you ask another?

Oh dear, I said, what am I to do? I will do just as you tell me. When I am not clear what you are asking, do you tell me to answer all the same, and not to ask anything myself?

c   I suppose you conceive some notion in what I say?

Yes, I do, was my reply.

Then answer according to the notion which you conceive.

Well, I said, what if you mean it in one way when you ask, and I conceive my notion in another way, and then I answer according to my notion—is it enough for you if I answer not at all to the point?

Enough for me, he said, but however, not enough for you, as I take it.

Then, Euthydemus, I won't answer, I tell you that, said I, before I find out.

You will not answer, he said, according to your notion in each case, because you are more of an old fool than you need be, and *will* go on talking drivel.

Now I saw he was angry with me for picking holes in the phrases d used, because he was trying to catch me in his net of words. So I remembered that Connus also is angry whenever I will not give way to him, and now he takes less trouble about me because he thinks me ignorant. And since I had the notion to be a pupil of this other one, I thought I ought to give way to him, or he might think me stupid and refuse to accept me. So I said, Well, Euthydemus, if you think it e proper to do like this, so be it. For anyway you know dialectic far better than I do, who have only the skill of an outsider. Then ask again from the beginning.

Very well then, he said, answer again. Do you know what you know by something or not?

Yes, I said, by the soul.

There he goes again, said he, answering more than he is asked! I 296 did not ask by what, but whether by something.

Oh well, I answered too much, I said, from want of education. Do forgive me; I will from now on answer simply—I know what I know by something.

Is it by this same thing always, he asked, or by this thing one time, and by another thing another time?

Always, I said, when I do know, it is by this thing.

Oh, do stop putting things in! he said.

But I don't want this 'always' to trip us up!

It will not trip *us* up, he said, but *you*, if anybody. But answer. Do b you know always by this?

Always, I said, since I must take out the when.

Then you know always by this. But knowing always, do you know some things by this and other things by something else, or everything by this?

By this all things—all which I know, I replied.

Here we are again! he said. The old addition!

Well, I said, I take away that 'which I know.'

Oh, don't take away a single thing, he said. I don't ask of you any favors. But answer me. Could you know all things, if you did not c know everything?

That would be a miracle! I said.

He said then, Go on, add what you like, you admit that you know all things.

It seems like it, I said, since the words 'which I know' have been made powerless, and it seems I know everything.

Then also you have admitted that you know always by this thing by which you know, whether 'when you do know' or however you like, for you have admitted that you know always, and at the same time everything. It is clear therefore that you knew as a child, and when d you were born, and when you were begotten, and that before you came into being, and before heaven and earth came into being, you knew all things, since you always know. And by God, he said, you yourself always will know, and all things, if I choose.

Oh, do choose! I said. O my precious friend Euthydemus, if you are really and truly telling the truth. Only I don't quite believe you can, unless your brother Dionysodorus here would choose too; if so, it may be all right. But tell me, both of you, I said, I would not dare to e dispute with men of such miraculous genius and say that I do not know everything when you both say I do, but there are some things which, how can I say that I know, Euthydemus, such as that good men are unjust? If you please, do I know that or not?

You know it sure enough, said he.

What? I said.

That good men are not unjust.

Oh yes, I said, I knew that long ago, but that is not my question. 297 But where did I learn that good men *are* unjust?

Nowhere, said Dionysodorus.

Then I don't know this, I said.

Euthydemus said to his brother, You are spoiling the argument, and it will be shown up that this man does not know, and he will be at the same time knowing and not knowing.

Dionysodorus flushed red, and I said, But you, what do you mean, b Euthydemus? Do you think your brother who knows everything was not right?

Dionysodorus quickly broke in with, Am I brother to Euthydemus?

I said, Let me be, my good man, until Euthydemus has taught me that I know that good men are unjust. Don't grudge me the lesson.

You are running away, Socrates, said Dionysodorus, and don't want to answer.

Naturally, I replied. I am not a match for either of you, so it is c very likely I should run from the two! I am much weaker of course than Heracles, and he was not able to fight it out with the Hydra, a high-brow clever enough to produce many heads of argument instead of one if somebody cut one off, because another high-brow, just arrived from foreign parts I should think, came ashore out of the sea in

the shape of a crab, and kept causing much pain to the hero by talking and biting at him on his left. So Heracles called in his nephew
Iolaus to his help, and Iolaus helped him effectively. But if my Iolaus
were to come, he would do more harm than good.   d

Answer now, said Dionysodorus, when you have done this incan-
tation. Was Iolaus any more the nephew of Heracles than he was
yours?

Well, the best thing for me is to answer you, Dionysodorus, I
said. For you will never have done with your questions, I am pretty
well sure of that, envious and interfering, to keep Euthydemus from
teaching me that bit of wisdom.

Answer now, said he.

I answer now, said I, that Iolaus was the nephew of Heracles,
but mine, I think, not one little bit. For my brother Patrocles was not   e
his father, but one with a name something like that, Iphicles, was the
brother of Heracles.

And Patrocles was yours? said he.

Yes, I said, we had one mother but not one father.

Then he is your brother and not your brother.

Not on the father's side, my dear man, I said, for his father was
Chaeredemus, and mine Sophroniscus.

But Sophroniscus was father and Chaeredemus father?

Certainly, I said, one mine, and one his.

Then, said he, Chaeredemus was other than the father?   298

Than mine, I said.

Then was a father being other than a father? Are you the same
as the stone?

I'm afraid you may prove me so, I said, but I don't think I am.

Then you are other than the stone? said he.

Other to be sure, said I.

Then being other than a stone, said he, you are not a stone?
And being other than gold, you are not gold?

That is all true.

So then Chaeredemus, he said, being other than a father, would
not be a father.

It seems, I said, that he is not a father.

Euthydemus now chimed in: I suppose if Chaeredemus is a   b
father, Sophroniscus again being other than a father is not a father,
so that you, Socrates, are fatherless.

Ctesippus took it on now, and said, But is not the father of you
two in the same case? He is other than my father.

Not at all, said Euthydemus.

What! said he. Is he the same?

The same to be sure.

I hope not. But, Euthydemus, is he only my father or the father   c
of everyone in the world?

Father of the others too, he said. Or do you think the same man being a father is not a father?

I did not think so, said Ctesippus.

Eh, and that being gold a thing is not gold, or being a man one is not a man?

The two threads don't match, as the proverb goes, Euthydemus, said Ctesippus. You tell a strange thing, if your father is father of all.

But he is.

Of men and horses and all the other animals?

All, replied Euthydemus.

d   And is your mother mother of all?

My mother too.

Of the sea urchins then, he said, since your mother is mother of the sea animals!

So is yours, he said.

Then you are brother of gudgeons and puppy dogs and little pigs! said Ctesippus.

So are you, said Euthydemus.

And a boar is your papa, and a dog!

Your papa too, he said.

Yes, and in a moment, if you would answer me, said Dionysodorus, you will admit these things yourself, Ctesippus. Just tell me, have you a dog?

Yes, and a very bad one, said Ctesippus.

Has he got puppies?

e   Very much so, he said, as bad as he is.

Then the dog is their father?

I have seen him myself, he said, on the job with the bitch.

Very well, isn't the dog yours?

Certainly, he said.

Then being a father he is yours, so the dog becomes your father and you the puppies' brother.

Dionysodorus quickly broke in again, that Ctesippus might not get in his retort first. One more little question. Do you beat this dog?

Ctesippus said with a laugh, No mistake, I do, for I can't beat you!

299   Well then, you beat your own father, the other said.

Well certainly, said Ctesippus, there would be much better reason for me to beat *your* father. What can have induced him to beget two such clever sons, Euthydemus? I wonder if much good has come from that cleverness of yours, for your father—and the puppy dogs' father —to enjoy!

But he does not want a lot of good, Ctesippus, neither he nor you.

Nor you yourself, Euthydemus?

Nor anyone else in the world. Tell me, Ctesippus, do you think it
b good for a sick man to drink medicine, or not good, when he needs it? Or that when he goes to war, he had better be armed than unarmed?

I certainly do, he replied, but I think a bit of your pretty wit is coming!

You will soon find out, said he. Just answer. You admitted that medicine is good for a man to drink, when necessary; then surely he needs to drink this good thing as much as he can, and it will have an excellent effect if someone will grind up and mix him a cartload of hellebore!

Ctesippus said, Very good indeed, Euthydemus, provided your drinker is as big as the statue in Delphi!   c

And then again in war, it's good to carry arms; so you must carry as many spears and shields as you can, since it is a good thing!

I suppose it is, he said, but I doubt if you think so, Euthydemus. Don't you prefer one shield and one spear?

Yes, I do.

Then what about Geryon, said Ctesippus, and old hundred-hand Briareus—would you arm them with only one each? I thought you knew more about it than that, you the heavy-armed fighter, and your comrade too!

Euthydemus fell silent, but Dionysodorus went back to the earlier answer of Ctesippus, and asked him, Gold too—don't you think it good d to have gold?

Yes indeed, he replied, and a lot of it!

Very well then, don't you think we ought to have good things always and everywhere?

As much as possible! he said.

And you admit gold also to be good?

Oh yes, he said, I have admitted that.

Then one ought always to have it everywhere, especially in one-self! And wouldn't a man be happiest if he had three talents of gold in e his belly, and a talent in his skull, and a golden stater in each eye?

Well, they do say, Euthydemus, said Ctesippus, that those are happiest among the Scythians, and the best men, who have a whole lot of gold in their 'own' skulls—as you spoke of 'own-ing' that father dog —and more astonishing still, that they even drink out of their own gilded skulls, holding each his own head in his hands, and can see the gold inside!

They see, yes, said Euthydemus, and do they see, whether Scyth- 300 ians or anybody else, things possible to see, or things impossible?

Possible, I suppose.

Then do you too? said he.

Yes, I do too.

You see our clothes then?

Yes.

Then these clothes are able to see!

Marvelous! said Ctesippus.

And what do they see? he asked.

They see nothing, replied Ctesippus. But perhaps you don't think they do see? You sweet simple soul! Well then, Euthydemus, I think you are sleeping wide awake, and if it is possible to speak saying nothing, you are doing that!

b   Isn't a speaking of the silent possible? said Dionysodorus.

Quite impossible, said Ctesippus.

Or a silence of the speaking?

Still less, he said.

Well, when you speak of pieces of stone and wood and iron, do you not speak of the silent?

I don't if I walk through a smithy; on the contrary the irons there talk with great clangs and booms if anyone handles them; so for this question your wisdom stopped you from noticing that you were saying nothing. Still, go on and demonstrate to me the other thing, how there is a silence of the speaking.

c   I thought Ctesippus was showing off because of his favorite.

When you are silent, said Euthydemus, are you not silent in everything?

Yes, he said.

Then you are silent in the speaking things also, for those are part of all things.

What? said Ctesippus. Is not everything silent?

I suppose not, said Euthydemus.

Then, my dear sir, is everything speaking?

The speaking things, I suppose.

But I do not ask that, he said. I ask whether everything is silent or speaking.

d   Dionysodorus now rushed in. Neither, and both! he said. I am sure you will not know what to do with that answer!

Ctesippus burst into a great guffaw, as usual, and said, My dear Euthydemus, your brother has 'bebothed' away your argument; it is beaten and done for!

And Clinias was delighted and laughed; so Ctesippus swelled bigger than ten Ctesippuses. But I think that rogue Ctesippus had picked up his skill from these men themselves, for such cleverness could not come nowadays from anyone else in the world.

e   Then I said, Why do you laugh, Clinias, at things so serious and beautiful?

What about you, Socrates, said Dionysodorus, have you ever seen a beautiful thing?

Yes, I have, said I, and many of them, Dionysodorus.

Were they different from the beautiful, he asked, or the same as 301 the beautiful?

Here I was really in a fix, and I thought I deserved it for my grumbling; however, I said they were different from the beautiful itself, but each of them had some beauty with it.

Then, he said, if you have an ox with you, you are an ox, and because I am with you now, you are Dionysodorus?

Oh stop, don't say that! I said.

But how can it be, he said, that when a different thing is with a different thing, the different thing should be different?

Does that worry you? I asked—I was already trying to imitate the b two men's wisdom, which I longed to have.

How can I help being worried, he said, both I and everybody else on earth, about that which is not?

What do you mean, Dionysodorus? I said. Is not the beautiful beautiful, and the ugly ugly?

If I think so, said he.

And don't you think so?

Certainly, he said.

Then is not the same the same, and the different different? For I suppose the different is not the same, and I should think even a child c would not be worried about this and think the different is not different. But, my dear Dionysodorus, you passed over that on purpose, for I think you two work out your dialectic perfectly, as good craftsmen do with their jobs proper to each.

Then do you know, he said, what job is proper to each kind of craftsmen? First, who is it whose proper job is to work metal, do you know?

Yes, the smith.

And to make pottery?

The potter.

Well, to slaughter and skin and cut up meat small and then boil and roast it?

The cook, said I.

And if anyone does his proper job, he will do right?　　　　　　　　　d

Especially so.

You say that cutting up and skinning is proper for the cook? Did you admit that or not?

I did, said I, but spare me please.

It is clear, then, he said, that if someone butchers the cook and cuts him up and boils and roasts him, he will be doing his proper job, and anyone who forges the smith and pots the potter, he does the proper job too.

O Poseidon! I said. Now you put the finishing touch to your wis- e dom! Ah, will this never be with me for my very own!

Could you recognize it as your very own, Socrates, he said, if it became yours?

Clearly I could, I said, if *you* choose.

Well, said he, do you believe that you can recognize your own things?

Unless you tell me that I can't, for I must begin from you, and finish up at Euthydemus here.

Very well, then, said he, do you think those things are yours, which you are master of and you can use as you will—an ox and a 302 sheep, for example, you would think are yours, if you are free to sell and give and sacrifice them to any god you like? But things are not yours, if you cannot use them so?

I knew that something beautiful was going to emerge out of their questions, and besides I wanted to hear it as soon as possible; so I said, Certainly that is right; only such things are mine.

Well, he said, you call animals those which have life?

Yes, I said.

b   You admit, then, that of the animals those only are yours which you have liberty to deal with as I said just now?

I admit that.

He made a mysterious pause with the air of pondering some mighty problem, and said, Socrates, have you a family Zeus?

Suspecting that the speech was going to lead to the end which it came to finally, I made a desperate twist to escape, and at once I was like a fish caught wriggling in a net. I said, No, Dionysodorus, I have not.

You must be some wretched outcast then and no Athenian at all,
c a man without family gods and sacrifices or anything else good and beautiful.

That will do Dionysodorus, I said. Hush now, and don't preach me an unkind sermon. I have my own altars and my own religion and family prayers and all that sort of thing, as much as any other Athenian.

Then the other Athenians have no family Zeus? he asked.

I said, None of the Ionians give him that title, neither ourselves nor any of the colonials from the city; ours is family Apollo because
d of Ion's parentage. Our Zeus is not called family god, but courtyard god and clan god, and Athena is our clan goddess.

Oh, that's quite enough, said Dionysodorus. For it seems you have both Apollo and Zeus, and Athena.

Yes, I said.

Then these would be your gods? he said.

Ancestors, I said, and masters.

Yours, anyway, he said. Did you not admit they were yours?

I did, said I, for how could I help it?

e   Then, said he, are not these gods also animals? For you admitted that whatever has life is an animal. Have not these gods life?

They have, said I.

Then they are also animals?

Yes, animals, I said.

But you have admitted that of the animals those are yours which you are free to give and sell, and sacrifice to any god you will.

I have admitted that, I said, for there is no way out for me, Euthydemus.

Tell me then straight, said Euthydemus, since you admit that

Zeus is yours, and those other gods, are you free to sell them or give
them or do what you will with them just as with the other animals?   303

Well, Crito, I was, so to speak, knocked out now by the argument,
and lying speechless. But Ctesippus came to my help, and shouted,
Bravo! O Heracles! What a fine speech!

And Dionysodorus said, Is Heracles a bravo or is the bravo
Heracles?

Then Ctesippus said, O Poseidon, terribly clever speeches! I give
in, the two men are invincible.

Then indeed, my dear Crito, all those present without exception   b
praised them to the skies, the two men and their speech, laughing and
clapping and cheering till they nearly wore themselves out. Hitherto
there had been a real good noise at each point they made, but only from
the admirers of Euthydemus, but now almost the very pillars in the
Lyceum resounded with pleasure at the two men. I was ready myself
to admit that I had never before in my life seen people so clever; I was
altogether enslaved by their skill, and I began to praise and congratu-   c
late them myself, saying, O happy pair, blessed are you for your wonderful genius, to have perfected so great a work so quickly and so soon!
Your speeches are full of fine things, Euthydemus and Dionysodorus;
but most magnificent of all is this, that you do not concern yourselves
with the multitude of men, nor men of solemn looks or great reputation, but only with those like yourselves. For I am quite sure that there   d
are very few men like you who would appreciate these arguments, and
all the rest know so little of them that they would feel more ashamed
to refute others by such ways of speech than to be refuted themselves.
Here is another thing in your way of speaking that shows public spirit
and kindness. When you say that nothing is beautiful and good, or
white or so forth, and there are no differences at all, really and truly   e
you sew up the mouths of people, just as you profess to do; since however you not only sew up other people's mouths, but seem to sew up
your own also, you do a most graceful thing which takes all offense
from your words. Chief of all, you have everything so neat and thought
out with such art, that in a very short time any man alive can learn
it; I myself carefully watched Ctesippus, and I noticed that he too was
quickly able to copy you on the spot. One thing about your system—
it is excellent for putting over quickly, but it is not suitable to exhibit in 304
public. If I dare advise you, take care not to speak before a crowd, or
they may learn it quickly and forget to thank you. The best thing would
be for you two to argue against each other in private; or if there must
be another then let it be one who will give you a fee. Give the same advice to your pupils, if you are prudent, never to argue with anybody else   b
but with you or themselves. What is rare, is dear, Euthydemus; but
water, which is best, as Pindar said, is cheapest. If you please, I said,
accept me and Clinias here as your pupils.

After this talk, Crito, and a little more, we parted. You must be

sure to come with us to be schooled by the two men; they declared, you
c know, that they were able to teach anyone who would pay the fee, no
age and no brains barred—all welcome, all would easily learn their
clever system—and it is proper to add, for your benefit especially, they
said it did not in any way hinder a man from making money.

CRITO : Oh well, Socrates, I am curious to hear, and always glad
to learn something. But the truth is I am one of those not like Euthy-
d demus, one of the others you mentioned yourself, who would prefer to
be refuted by such talk rather than to refute. Now it is ridiculous for
me to advise you, but I do however wish to report something I heard
just now. I must tell you that someone came away from your crowd
and met me walking about; he thinks himself to be a man of ability,
one of those who are clever at making speeches for the law courts,
and he said, Hullo, Crito, don't you sit at the feet of these wise men?

My word, no, said I. I tried to stand close but I could not hear for
the crowd.

Well, it was worth hearing, he said.

What was it? I asked
e You might have heard men using dialectic who are the cleverest
men alive of those engaged in such speaking.

Then I said, What did you think of them?

Think of them? What anyone would think who heard such people
talking nonsense and making an unworthy fuss about matters worth
nothing at all.

That is how he put it, word for word. I said then, However, philosophy is a charming thing.

Pooh, pooh, he said, charming, bless you! Worth nothing, I tell
305 you! But if you had been there just now, I feel sure you would have
been ashamed of your own familiar friend; he was such a fool as to
want to put himself in the hands of men who just grapple with every
phrase and don't care what they say. And these, as I said, are among
the most powerful men of the day. Indeed, Crito, the whole system
and the men engaged in the system are contemptible and ridiculous.
b   In my opinion, Socrates, he was not right in blaming the system
nor would anyone else be right, but as to being willing to argue with
such men before a whole crowd of people, I thought he was right to disapprove of that.

SOCRATES : My dear Crito, such men are amazing. But I do not
know as yet what I am to say. Which class did the man belong to who
came to you and found fault with philosophy? Was he one of those
skilled in contesting cases in court, an orator, or one of those who send
such people in, who compose the speeches which the orators deliver?
c   CRITO : Not an orator, no indeed; I don't think he ever went up
into a court of law. But I assure you they say he understands the business—a clever man, composes clever speeches.

SOCRATES : Ah, now I know. Those were the ones I was just going to speak of. Those are the men, my dear Crito, whom Prodicus

called the frontiersmen between philosophy and politics. They think they themselves are the wisest of men, and that they not only are, but also are thought such by very many, so that the only rivals in the way of their universal fame are the students of philosophy, none else. They d believe therefore that if they can reduce the reputation of these, and make them of no account, they will at once win the prize of undisputed victory in public opinion as men of wisdom; they believe they are truly the most wise, but that in informal conversation, whenever they lag behind, they are being cut short by the Euthydemus group. It is quite reasonable if they think themselves wise; they know they are moderately well up in philosophy, and moderately well up in politics, quite e reasonably, for they have as much as was wanted in both, and they keep clear of both danger and conflict, while they enjoy the fruits of wisdom.

CRITO: What do you think, then, Socrates? Is there something in what they say? There is no doubt that their account of themselves looks well.

SOCRATES: Yes, that's exactly it, Crito, looks well rather than truly is well. For it is not easy to persuade them what is the truth about 306 these borderlands. Both men and things, if they stand between two and have a share of both, when these two are bad and good, are better than the one and worse than the other; when they stand between two good things which do not aim at the same object, they are worse than both the two components for that for which each is useful; when these two things are bad, but not directed to the same thing, and they are composed of both and stand between them, these alone are better than either of those things of which they have a part. Then if both philoso- b phy and political action are good, but each aims at a different thing, and if these persons are between them and have a part of both, there is nothing in what they say, for they are worse than both; if the things are one good and one bad, they are worse than the one and better than the other; if both are bad, then these people would be speaking some truth, but otherwise not at all. Now I do not think they would admit that the c two are both bad, nor that one is good and one bad; but in reality these persons who partake of both are worse than both for each thing which politics and philosophy are important for, and although they are really third, they try to be thought first. We must then not be hard on them, because of their ambition; we must not be angry, but we must believe them to be such as they are. For we ought to be content with every man who says anything which comes near to wisdom, when he bravely follows it up and works it out. d

CRITO: Well, you know, Socrates, as I always tell you, I am in perplexity about my sons and what I am to do with them. The younger is quite small still, but Critobulus is already growing up and needs someone to help him on. The fact is, whenever I meet you, I think of all the trouble I have taken, for the sake of the children, about many other things, as about marrying a woman of the best family to be their

e mother, and about money that they may be as rich as we can manage. And after all that it seems to me to be simple madness to neglect their education. But when I glance at any one of those who profess to educate people, I am horrified; each one I look at seems to me to be quite
307 unsuitable, to tell you the truth, so I don't see how I am to direct the boy to philosophy.

SOCRATES: My dear Crito, don't you know that in every line of life the stupid are many and worthless, the serious are few and worth everything? What about gymnastics? Doesn't that seem a good line to you, and business and oratory, and leadership in war?

CRITO: Most certainly they do.

SOCRATES: Very well, don't you see that in each of these pro-
b fessions the many are just laughable at their professional work?

CRITO: Yes, I do. What you say is perfectly true.

SOCRATES: Will that be a reason for yourself avoiding all the professions and not giving one to your son?

CRITO: That would not be fair, Socrates.

SOCRATES: Then, Crito, don't do what you ought not. Do not trouble about those who practice philosophy, whether they are good or bad; but examine the thing itself well and carefully. And if philos-
c ophy appears a bad thing to you, turn every man from it, not only your sons; but if it appears to you such as I think it to be, take courage, pursue it, and practice it, as the saying is, 'both you and your house.'

NOTE

My cousin, Dr. W. H. D. Rouse, was unfortunately prevented, by the volume of other work which he undertook, from giving his translation of *Euthydemus* a final revision in detail before his death in February 1950.

In doing this revision I have tried to clear up the few inconsistencies and obscurities which he had not removed, and at the same time to interrupt as little as possible the distinctive character of his translation.

By far the greater part of his work remains unaltered, but at 283e–284b, in order to make the sense more intelligible to the reader, I have revised the whole short passage containing the quibble 'Is it possible to tell a lie?' and have there introduced 'the facts' as a rendering of τῶν ὄντων instead of the usual rendering 'things that are.'

I am grateful to Professor Eric H. Warmington, my co-editor of *Great Dialogues of Plato* translated by W. H. D. Rouse (the *Republic* and six other dialogues), for finally reading through this revision for me and making some very helpful comments.

PHILIP G. ROUSE

CRATYLUS

This dialogue has to do with the origin of language, then essentially a new subject. Socrates' discourse on it contains many fantastic guesses, but occasionally an insight, even a deep insight, into the truth. He will have nothing to do with the suggestion that the first words came to men from God. That, he says, is not a reason, but merely an excuse for having no reason. It is to act as a tragic poet does when he has a difficulty and brings in a deus ex machina to solve it.

The main part of the dialogue is given over to guesses about the derivation of Greek words, comprehensible, of course, only to those who can read Greek and finally, like all guessing, tiresome to them, too. The dialogue will be passed over by most readers and that is a pity, for the portrait of Socrates that emerges after much wearisome reading is delightful. He is often at his best in making fun of the endless power of the human mind to spin intricate arguments about nothing at all and "evermore come out by the same door wherein it went." "After much study," he remarks, "I found myself more puzzled than I was before I began to learn."

Just at the end, the jesting and the irony are put away. All these verbal niceties and changes are no help, he says, in finding the truth. Goodness and beauty exist and are permanent, but the words by which we try to express them will never be adequate. "Reflect well," he bids Cratylus. "And when you have found the truth, come and tell me."

383   HERMOGENES : Suppose that we make Socrates a party to the argument.

CRATYLUS : If you please.

HERMOGENES : I should explain to you, Socrates, that our friend Cratylus has been arguing about names. He says that they are natural and not conventional—not a portion of the human voice which men agree to use—but that there is a truth or correctness in
b them, which is the same for Hellenes as for barbarians. Whereupon I ask him whether his own name of Cratylus is a true name or not, and he answers yes. And Socrates? Yes. Then every man's name, as I tell him, is that which he is called. To this he replies, If all the world were to call you Hermogenes, that would not be your name. And when I am anxious to have a further explanation he is ironical and mys-
384 terious, and seems to imply that he has a notion of his own about the matter if he would only tell, and could entirely convince me if he chose to be intelligible. Tell me, Socrates, what this oracle means, or rather tell me, if you will be so good, what is your own view of the truth or correctness of names, which I would far sooner hear.

SOCRATES : Son of Hipponicus, there is an ancient saying that
b 'hard is the knowledge of the good.' And the knowledge of names is a great part of knowledge. If I had not been poor, I might have heard the fifty-drachma course of the great Prodicus, which is a complete education in grammar and language—these are his own words—and then I should have been at once able to answer your question about the correctness of names. But, indeed, I have only heard the single-
c drachma course, and therefore I do not know the truth about such matters. I will, however, gladly assist you and Cratylus in the investigation of them. When he declares that your name is not really Hermogenes, I suspect that he is only making fun of you; he means to say that you are no true son of Hermes, because you are always looking after a fortune and never in luck. But, as I was saying, there is a good deal of difficulty in this sort of knowledge, and therefore we had better leave the question open until we have heard both sides.

HERMOGENES : I have often talked over this matter, both with Cratylus and others, and cannot convince myself that there is any
d principle of correctness in names other than convention and agreement. Any name which you give, in my opinion, is the right one, and if you change that and give another, the new name is as correct as the old—we frequently change the names of our slaves, and the newly imposed name is as good as the old. For there is no name given to anything by nature; all is convention and habit of the users.

From *The Dialogues of Plato*, translated with analyses and introductions by B. Jowett (3rd edn., Oxford, 1892; 1st edn., 1871).

Such is my view. But if I am mistaken I shall be happy to hear and learn of Cratylus, or of anyone else.

SOCRATES: I dare say that you may be right, Hermogenes. Let 385 us see—your meaning is that the name of each thing is only that which anybody agrees to call it?

HERMOGENES: That is my notion.

SOCRATES: Whether the giver of the name be an individual or a city?

HERMOGENES: Yes.

SOCRATES: Well, now, let me take an instance. Suppose that I call a man a horse or a horse a man. You mean to say that a man will be rightly called a horse by me individually, and rightly called a man by the rest of the world, and a horse again would be rightly called a man by me and a horse by the world—that is your meaning?

HERMOGENES: He would, according to my view.   b

SOCRATES: But how about truth, then? You would acknowledge that there is in words a true and a false?

HERMOGENES: Certainly.

SOCRATES: And there are true and false propositions?

HERMOGENES: To be sure.

SOCRATES: And a true proposition says that which is, and a false proposition says that which is not?

HERMOGENES: Yes, what other answer is possible?

SOCRATES: Then in a proposition there is a true and false?

HERMOGENES: Certainly.

SOCRATES: But is a proposition true as a whole only, and are c the parts untrue?

HERMOGENES: No, the parts are true as well as the whole.

SOCRATES: Would you say the large parts and not the smaller ones, or every part?

HERMOGENES: I should say that every part is true.

SOCRATES: Is a proposition resolvable into any part smaller than a name?

HERMOGENES: No, that is the smallest.

SOCRATES: Then the name is a part of the true proposition?

HERMOGENES: Yes.

SOCRATES: Yes, and a true part, as you say.

HERMOGENES: Yes.

SOCRATES: And is not the part of a falsehood also a falsehood?

HERMOGENES: Yes.

SOCRATES: Then, if propositions may be true and false, names may be true and false?

HERMOGENES: So we must infer.

SOCRATES: And the name of anything is that which anyone d affirms to be the name?

HERMOGENES : Yes.

SOCRATES : And will there be so many names of each thing as everybody says that there are? And will they be true names at the time of uttering them?

HERMOGENES : Yes, Socrates, I can conceive no correctness of names other than this. You give one name, and I another, and in dif-
e ferent cities and countries there are different names for the same things. Hellenes differ from barbarians in their use of names, and the several Hellenic tribes from one another.

SOCRATES : But would you say, Hermogenes, that the things
386 differ as the names differ? And are they relative to individuals, as Protagoras tells us? For he says that man is the measure of all things, and that things are to me as they appear to me, and that they are to you as they appear to you. Do you agree with him, or would you say that things have a permanent essence of their own?

HERMOGENES : There have been times, Socrates, when I have been driven in my perplexity to take refuge with Protagoras, not that I agree with him at all.

SOCRATES : What! Have you ever been driven to admit that
b there was no such thing as a bad man?

HERMOGENES : No, indeed, but I have often had reason to think that there are very bad men, and a good many of them.

SOCRATES : Well, and have you ever found any very good ones?

HERMOGENES : Not many.

SOCRATES : Still you have found them?

HERMOGENES : Yes.

SOCRATES : And would·you hold that the very good were the very wise, and the very evil very foolish? Would that be your view?

HERMOGENES : It would.

c SOCRATES : But if Protagoras is right, and the truth is that things are as they appear to anyone, how can some of us be wise and some of us foolish?

HERMOGENES : Impossible.

SOCRATES : And if, on the other hand, wisdom and folly are really distinguishable you will allow, I think, that the assertion of Protagoras can hardly be correct. For if what appears to each man is true to him, one man cannot in reality be wiser than another.

d HERMOGENES : He cannot.

SOCRATES : Nor will you be disposed to say with Euthydemus that all things equally belong to all men at the same moment and always, for neither on his view can there be some good and others bad, if virtue and vice are always equally to be attributed to all.

HERMOGENES : There cannot.

SOCRATES : But if neither is right, and things are not relative to individuals, and all things do not equally belong to all at the same moment and always, they must be supposed to have their own proper

and permanent essence; they are not in relation to us, or influenced e
by us, fluctuating according to our fancy, but they are independent,
and maintain to their own essence the relation prescribed by nature.

HERMOGENES : I think, Socrates, that you have said the truth.

SOCRATES : Does what I am saying apply only to the things
themselves, or equally to the actions which proceed from them? Are
not actions also a class of being?

HERMOGENES : Yes, the actions are real as well as the things.

SOCRATES : Then the actions also are done according to their 387
proper nature, and not according to our opinion of them? In cutting,
for example, we do not cut as we please, and with any chance instrument, but we cut with the proper instrument only, and according to
the natural process of cutting, and the natural process is right and will
succeed, but any other will fail and be of no use at all.

HERMOGENES : I should say that the natural way is the right
way.

SOCRATES : Again, in burning, not every way is the right way,
but the right way is the natural way, and the right instrument the
natural instrument.   b

HERMOGENES : True.

SOCRATES : And this holds good of all actions?

HERMOGENES : Yes.

SOCRATES : And speech is a kind of action?

HERMOGENES : True.

SOCRATES : And will a man speak correctly who speaks as he
pleases? Will not the successful speaker rather be he who speaks in c
the natural way of speaking, and as things ought to be spoken, and
with the natural instrument? Any other mode of speaking will result
in error and failure.

HERMOGENES : I quite agree with you.

SOCRATES : And is not naming a part of speaking? For in giving names men speak.

HERMOGENES : That is true.

SOCRATES : And if speaking is a sort of action and has a relation to acts, is not naming also a sort of action?

HERMOGENES : True.

SOCRATES : And we saw that actions were not relative to our- d
selves, but had a special nature of their own?

HERMOGENES : Precisely.

SOCRATES : Then the argument would lead us to infer that
names ought to be given according to a natural process, and with a
proper instrument, and not at our pleasure; in this and no other way
shall we name with success.

HERMOGENES : I agree.

SOCRATES : But again, that which has to be cut has to be cut
with something?

HERMOGENES : Yes.

e   SOCRATES : And that which has to be woven or pierced has to be woven or pierced with something?

HERMOGENES : Certainly.

SOCRATES : And that which has to be named has to be named with something?

HERMOGENES : True.

SOCRATES : What is that with which we pierce?

HERMOGENES : An awl.

388   SOCRATES : And with which we weave?

HERMOGENES : A shuttle.

SOCRATES : And with which we name?

HERMOGENES : A name.

SOCRATES : Very good. Then a name is an instrument?

HERMOGENES : Certainly.

SOCRATES : Suppose that I ask, What sort of instrument is a shuttle? And you answer, A weaving instrument.

HERMOGENES : Well.

b   SOCRATES : And I ask again, What do we do when we weave? The answer is that we separate or disengage the warp from the woof.

HERMOGENES : Very true.

SOCRATES : And may not a similar description be given of an awl, and of instruments in general?

HERMOGENES : To be sure.

SOCRATES : And now suppose that I ask a similar question about names. Will you answer me? Regarding the name as an instrument, what do we do when we name?

HERMOGENES : I cannot say.

SOCRATES : Do we not give information to one another, and distinguish things according to their natures?

HERMOGENES : Certainly we do.

c   SOCRATES : Then a name is an instrument of teaching and of distinguishing natures, as the shuttle is of distinguishing the threads of the web.

HERMOGENES : Yes.

SOCRATES : And the shuttle is the instrument of the weaver?

HERMOGENES : Assuredly.

SOCRATES : Then the weaver will use the shuttle well—and well means like a weaver? And the teacher will use the name well—and well means like a teacher?

HERMOGENES : Yes.

SOCRATES : And when the weaver uses the shuttle, whose work will he be using well?

HERMOGENES : That of the carpenter.

SOCRATES : And is every man a carpenter, or the skilled only?

HERMOGENES : Only the skilled.

SOCRATES: And when the piercer uses the awl, whose work will d he be using well?

HERMOGENES: That of the smith.

SOCRATES: And is every man a smith, or only the skilled?

HERMOGENES: The skilled only.

SOCRATES: And when the teacher uses the name, whose work will he be using?

HERMOGENES: There again I am puzzled.

SOCRATES: Cannot you at least say who gives us the names which we use?

HERMOGENES: Indeed I cannot.

SOCRATES: Does not the law seem to you to give us them?

HERMOGENES: Yes, I suppose so.

SOCRATES: Then the teacher, when he gives us a name, uses e the work of the legislator?

HERMOGENES: I agree.

SOCRATES: And is every man a legislator, or the skilled only?

HERMOGENES: The skilled only.

SOCRATES: Then, Hermogenes, not every man is able to give a name, but only a maker of names, and this is the legislator, who of all 389 skilled artisans in the world is the rarest.

HERMOGENES: True.

SOCRATES: And how does the legislator make names? And to what does he look? Consider this in the light of the previous instances. To what does the carpenter look in making the shuttle? Does he not look to that which is naturally fitted to act as a shuttle?

HERMOGENES: Certainly.

SOCRATES: And suppose the shuttle to be broken in making. b Will he make another, looking to the broken one? Or will he look to the form according to which he made the other?

HERMOGENES: To the latter, I should imagine.

SOCRATES: Might not that be justly called the true or ideal shuttle?

HERMOGENES: I think so.

SOCRATES: And whatever shuttles are wanted, for the manufacture of garments, thin or thick, of flaxen, woolen, or other material, ought all of them to have the true form of the shuttle, and whatever is the shuttle best adapted to each kind of work, that ought to be the c form which the maker produces in each case?

HERMOGENES: Yes.

SOCRATES: And the same holds of other instruments. When a man has discovered the instrument which is naturally adapted to each work, he must express this natural form, and not others which he fancies, in the material, whatever it may be, which he employs. For example, he ought to know how to put into iron the forms of awls adapted by nature to their several uses?

HERMOGENES: Certainly.

SOCRATES: And how to put into wood forms of shuttles adapted by nature to their uses?

HERMOGENES: True.

d   SOCRATES: For the several forms of shuttles naturally answer to the several kinds of webs, and this is true of instruments in general.

HERMOGENES: Yes.

SOCRATES: Then, as to names, ought not our legislator also to know how to put the true natural name of each thing into sounds and syllables, and to make and give all names with a view to the ideal name, if he is to be a namer in any true sense? And we must remem-

e ber that different legislators will not use the same syllables. For neither does every smith, although he may be making the same instrument for the same purpose, make them all of the same iron. The form must be the same, but the material may vary, and still the instrument

390 may be equally good of whatever iron made, whether in Hellas or in a foreign country—there is no difference.

HERMOGENES: Very true.

SOCRATES: And the legislator, whether he be Hellene or barbarian, is not therefore to be deemed by you a worse legislator, provided he gives the true and proper form of the name in whatever syllables—this or that country makes no matter.

HERMOGENES: Quite true.

b   SOCRATES: But who then is to determine whether the proper form is given to the shuttle, whatever sort of wood may be used? The carpenter who makes, or the weaver who is to use them?

HERMOGENES: I should say, he who is to use them, Socrates.

SOCRATES: And who uses the work of the lyre maker? Will not he be the man who knows how to direct what is being done, and who will know also whether the work is being well done or not?

HERMOGENES: Certainly.

SOCRATES: And who is he?

HERMOGENES: The player of the lyre.

SOCRATES: And who will direct the shipwright?

c   HERMOGENES: The pilot.

SOCRATES: And who will be best able to direct the legislator in his work, and will know whether the work is well done, in this or any other country? Will not the user be the man?

HERMOGENES: Yes.

SOCRATES: And this is he who knows how to ask questions?

HERMOGENES: Yes.

SOCRATES: And how to answer them?

HERMOGENES: Yes.

SOCRATES: And him who knows how to ask and answer you would call a dialectician?

HERMOGENES: Yes, that would be his name.

SOCRATES: Then the work of the carpenter is to make a rudder, d
and the pilot has to direct him, if the rudder is to be well made.

HERMOGENES: True.

SOCRATES: And the work of the legislator is to give names, and
the dialectician must be his director if the names are to be rightly
given?

HERMOGENES: That is true.

SOCRATES: Then, Hermogenes, I should say that this giving of
names can be no such light matter as you fancy, or the work of light
or chance persons. And Cratylus is right in saying that things have
names by nature, and that not every man is an artificer of names, but e
he only who looks to the name which each thing by nature has, and
is able to express the true forms of things in letters and syllables.

HERMOGENES: I cannot answer you, Socrates, but I find a difficulty in changing my opinion all in a moment, and I think that I 391
should be more readily persuaded, if you would show me what this is
which you term the natural fitness of names.

SOCRATES: My good Hermogenes, I have none to show. Was I
not telling you just now—but you have forgotten—that I knew
nothing, and was I not proposing to share the inquiry with you? But
now that you and I have talked over the matter, a step has been
gained, for we have discovered that names have by nature a truth, b
and that not every man knows how to give a thing a name.

HERMOGENES: Very good.

SOCRATES: And what is the nature of this truth or correctness
of names? That, if you care to know, is the next question.

HERMOGENES: Certainly, I care to know.

SOCRATES: Then reflect.

HERMOGENES: How shall I reflect?

SOCRATES: The true way is to have the assistance of those
who know, and you must pay them well both in money and in thanks
—these are the Sophists, of whom your brother, Callias, has, rather c
dearly, bought the reputation of wisdom. But you have not yet come
into your inheritance, and therefore you had better go to him, and
beg and entreat him to tell you what he has learned from Protagoras
about the fitness of names.

HERMOGENES: But how inconsistent should I be, if, while
repudiating Protagoras and his truth, I were to attach any value to
what he and his book affirm!

SOCRATES: Then if you despise him, you must learn of d
Homer and the poets.

HERMOGENES: And where does Homer say anything about
names, and what does he say?

SOCRATES: He often speaks of them—notably and nobly in the
places where he distinguishes the different names which gods and
men give to the same things. Does he not in these passages make a

e remarkable statement about the correctness of names? For the gods must clearly be supposed to call things by their right and natural names, do you not think so?

HERMOGENES : Why, of course they call them rightly, if they call them at all. But to what are you referring?

SOCRATES : Do you not know what he says about the river in Troy who had a single combat with Hephaestus—'whom,' as he says, 'the gods call Xanthus, and men call Scamander'? [1]

HERMOGENES : I remember.

392 SOCRATES : Well, and about this river—to know that he ought to be called Xanthus and not Scamander—is not that a solemn lesson? Or about the bird which, as he says, 'the gods call *chalcis,* and men *cymindis'*? [2] To be taught how much more correct the name *chalcis* is than the name *cymindis*—do you deem that a light matter? Or about Batiea and Myrina? And there are many other observa-
b tions of the same kind in Homer and other poets. Now, I think that this is beyond the understanding of you and me, but the names of Scamandrius and Astyanax, which he affirms to have been the names of Hector's son, are more within the range of human faculties, as I am disposed to think, and what the poet means by correctness may be more readily apprehended in that instance. You will remember, I dare say, the lines to which I refer.

HERMOGENES : I do.

SOCRATES : Let me ask you, then, which did Homer think the more correct of the names given to Hector's son—Astyanax or Scamandrius?

c HERMOGENES : I do not know.

SOCRATES : How would you answer, if you were asked whether the wise or the unwise are more likely to give correct names?

HERMOGENES : I should say the wise, of course.

SOCRATES : And are the men or the women of a city, taken as a class, the wiser?

HERMOGENES : I should say, the men.

SOCRATES : And Homer, as you know, says that the Trojan
d men called him Astyanax (king of the city), but if the men called him Astyanax, the other name of Scamandrius could only have been given to him by the women.

HERMOGENES : That may be inferred.

SOCRATES : And must not Homer have imagined the Trojans to be wiser than their wives?

HERMOGENES : To be sure.

SOCRATES : Then he must have thought Astyanax to be a more correct name for the boy than Scamandrius?

HERMOGENES : Clearly.

SOCRATES : And what is the reason of this? Let us consider.

[1] *Iliad* 20.74.   [2] *Iliad* 14.291.

Does he not himself suggest a very good reason, when he says, 'For
he alone defended their city and long walls'? [3] This appears to be a e
good reason for calling the son of the savior king of the city which his
father was saving, as Homer observes.

HERMOGENES : I see.

SOCRATES : Why, Hermogenes, I do not as yet see myself, and
do you?

HERMOGENES : No, indeed, not I.

SOCRATES : But tell me, friend, did not Homer himself also 393
give Hector his name?

HERMOGENES : What of that?

SOCRATES : The name appears to me to be very nearly the same
as the name of Astyanax—both are Hellenic. And a king (ἄναξ) and
a holder (ἕκτωρ) have nearly the same meaning, and are both descriptive of a king, for a man is clearly the holder of that of which he
is king—he rules, and owns, and holds it. But, perhaps, you may think b
that I am talking nonsense, and indeed I believe that I myself did not
know what I meant when I imagined that I had found some indication of the opinion of Homer about the correctness of names.

HERMOGENES : I assure you that I think otherwise, and I believe you to be on the right track.

SOCRATES : There is reason, I think, in calling the lion's whelp
a lion, and the foal of a horse a horse; I am speaking only of the
ordinary course of nature, when an animal produces after his kind,
and not of extraordinary births. If contrary to nature a horse have a c
calf, then I should not call that a foal but a calf; nor do I call any
inhuman birth a man, but only a natural birth. And the same may be
said of trees and other things. Do you agree with me?

HERMOGENES : Yes, I agree.

SOCRATES : Very good. But you had better watch me and see
that I do not play tricks with you. For on the same principle the son
of a king is to be called a king. And whether the syllables of the name d
are the same or not the same makes no difference, provided the meaning is retained; nor does the addition or subtraction of a letter make
any difference so long as the essence of the thing remains in possession of the name and appears in it.

HERMOGENES : What do you mean?

SOCRATES : A very simple matter. I may illustrate my meaning
by the names of letters, which you know are not the same as the letters themselves with the exception of the four, ε, υ, ο, ω. The names of
the rest, whether vowels or consonants, are made up of other letters
which we add to them, but so long as we introduce the meaning, and e
there can be no mistake, the name of the letter is quite correct. Take,
for example, the letter beta—the addition of η, τ, α gives no offense,

---

[3] *Iliad* 22.507.

and does not prevent the whole name from having the value which the legislator intended—so well did he know how to give the letters names.

HERMOGENES : I believe you are right.

394   SOCRATES : And may not the same be said of a king? A king will often be the son of a king, the good son or the noble son of a good or noble sire, and similarly the offspring of every kind, in the regular course of nature, is like the parent, and therefore has the same name. Yet the syllables may be disguised until they appear different to the ignorant person, and he may not recognize them, although they are the same, just as any one of us would not recognize the same drugs under different disguises of color and smell, although to the physician,

b who regards the power of them, they are the same, and he is not put out by the addition. And in like manner the etymologist is not put out by the addition or transposition or subtraction of a letter or two, or indeed by the change of all the letters, for this need not interfere with the meaning. As was just now said, the names of Hector and Astyanax have only one letter alike, which is the τ, and yet they have the same meaning. And how little in common with the letters of

c their names has Archepolis (ruler of the city)—and yet the meaning is the same. And there are many other names which just mean *king*. Again, there are several names for a general, as, for example, Agis (leader) and Polemarchus (chief in war) and Eupolemus (good warrior), and others which denote a physician, as Iatrocles (famous healer) and Acesimbrotus (curer of mortals), and there are many others which might be cited, differing in their syllables and letters, but having the same meaning. Would you not say so?

d   HERMOGENES : Yes.

SOCRATES : The same names, then, ought to be assigned to those who follow in the course of nature?

HERMOGENES : Yes.

SOCRATES : And what of those who follow out of the course of nature, and are prodigies? For example, when a good and religious man has an irreligious son, he ought to bear the name not of his father, but of the class to which he belongs, just as in the case which was before supposed of a horse foaling a calf.

HERMOGENES : Quite true.

SOCRATES : Then the irreligious son of a religious father should

e be called irreligious?

HERMOGENES : Certainly.

SOCRATES : He should not be called Theophilus (beloved of God) or Mnesitheus (mindful of God), or any of these names—if names are correctly given, his should have an opposite meaning.

HERMOGENES : Certainly, Socrates.

SOCRATES : Again, Hermogenes, there is Orestes (the man of the mountains), who appears to be rightly called, whether chance gave the name, or perhaps some poet who meant to express the brutality and fierceness and mountain wilderness of his hero's nature.

HERMOGENES: That is very likely, Socrates.

SOCRATES: And his father's name is also according to nature.

HERMOGENES: Clearly.

SOCRATES: Yes, for as his name, so also is his nature. Agamemnon (admirable for remaining) is one who is patient and persevering in the accomplishment of his resolves, and by his virtue crowns them, and his continuance at Troy with all the vast army is a proof of that admirable endurance in him which is signified by the name b Agamemnon. I also think that Atreus is rightly called, for his murder of Chrysippus and his exceeding cruelty to Thyestes are damaging and destructive to his reputation. The name is a little altered and disguised so as not to be intelligible to everyone, but to the etymologist there is no difficulty in seeing the meaning, for whether you think of him as ἀτειρής the stubborn, or as ἄτρεστος the fearless, or as ἀτηρός c the destructive one, the name is perfectly correct in every point of view. And I think that Pelops is also named appropriately, for, as the name implies, he is rightly called Pelops who sees what is near only (ὁ τὰ πέλας ὁρῶν).

HERMOGENES: How so?

SOCRATES: Because, according to the tradition, he had no forethought or foresight of all the evil which the murder of Myrtilus would entail upon his whole race in remote ages; he saw only what d was at hand and immediate, or in other words, πέλας (near), in his eagerness to win Hippodamia by all means for his bride. Everyone would agree that the name of Tantalus is rightly given and in accordance with nature, if the traditions about him are true.

HERMOGENES: And what are the traditions?

SOCRATES: Many terrible misfortunes are said to have happened to him in his life—last of all, came the utter ruin of his country—and after his death he had the stone suspended (ταλαντεία) e over his head in the world below. All this agrees wonderfully well with his name. You might imagine that some person who wanted to call him ταλάντατος (most weighed down by misfortune) disguised the name by altering it into Tantalus, and into this form, by some accident of tradition, it has actually been transmuted. The name of Zeus, who is his alleged father, has also an excellent meaning, although hard to be understood, because really like a sentence, which is 396 divided into two parts, for some call him Zena (Ζῆνα), and use the one half, and others who use the other half call him Dia (Δία); the two together signify the nature of the god, and the business of a name, as we were saying, is to express the nature. For there is none who is more the author of life to us and to all than the lord and king of all. Wherefore we are right in calling him Zena and Dia, which are one b name, although divided, meaning the god through whom all creatures always have life (δι' ὃν ζῆν ἀεὶ πᾶσι τοῖς ζῶσιν ὑπάρχει). There is an irreverence, at first sight, in calling him son of Cronus, who is a proverb for stupidity, and we might rather expect Zeus to be the child of a mighty intellect, which is the fact, for this is the meaning of his father's name—Κρόνος quasi Κόρος (κορέω, to sweep), not in the sense of a youth, but signifying τὸ καθαρὸν καὶ ἀκήρατον τοῦ νοῦ, the pure and garnished mind (sc. ἀπὸ τοῦ κορεῖν). He, as we are informed by c tradition, was begotten of Uranus, rightly so called (ἀπὸ τοῦ ὁρᾶν τὰ ἄνω) from looking upward, which, as philosophers tell us, is the way to have a pure mind, and the name Uranus is therefore correct. If I could remember the genealogy of Hesiod, I would have gone on and tried more conclusions of the same sort on the remoter ancestors of the gods—then I might have seen whether this wisdom, which has come to me all in an instant, I know not whence, will or will not hold d good to the end.

HERMOGENES : You seem to me, Socrates, to be quite like a prophet newly inspired, and to be uttering oracles.

SOCRATES : Yes, Hermogenes, and I believe that I caught the inspiration from the great Euthyphro of the Prospaltian deme, who gave me a long lecture which commenced at dawn. He talked and I listened, and his wisdom and enchanting ravishment have not only e filled my ears but taken possession of my soul, and today I shall let his superhuman power work and finish the investigation of names—that will be the way—but tomorrow, if you are so disposed, we will conjure him away, and make a purgation of him, if we can only find some 397 priest or Sophist who is skilled in purifications of this sort.

HERMOGENES : With all my heart, for I am very curious to hear the rest of the inquiry about names.

SOCRATES : Then let us proceed, and where would you have us begin, now that we have got a sort of outline of the inquiry? Are there any names which witness of themselves that they are not given arbitrarily, but have a natural fitness? The names of heroes and of men in b general are apt to be deceptive because they are often called after ancestors with whose names, as we were saying, they may have no business, or they are the expression of a wish, like Eutychides (the son of good fortune), or Sosias (the Savior), or Theophilus (the beloved of God), and others. But I think that we had better leave these, for there will be more chance of finding correctness in the names of immutable essences—there ought to have been more care taken about them when they were named, and perhaps there may have been some c more-than-human power at work occasionally in giving them names.

HERMOGENES : I think so, Socrates.

SOCRATES : Ought we not to begin with the consideration of the gods, and show that they are rightly named gods?

HERMOGENES : Yes, that will be well.

SOCRATES: My notion would be something of this sort. I suspect that the sun, moon, earth, stars, and heaven, which are still the gods of many barbarians, were the only gods known to the aboriginal d Hellenes. Seeing that they were always moving and running, from their running nature they were called gods or runners (θεούς, θέοντας), and when men became acquainted with the other gods, they proceeded to apply the same name to them all. Do you think that likely?

HERMOGENES: I think it very likely indeed.

SOCRATES: What shall follow the gods?

HERMOGENES: Must not daemons and heroes and men come e next?

SOCRATES: Daemons! And what do you consider to be the meaning of this word? Tell me if my view is right.

HERMOGENES: Let me hear.

SOCRATES: You know how Hesiod uses the word?

HERMOGENES: I do not.

SOCRATES: Do you not remember that he speaks of a golden race of men who came first?

HERMOGENES: Yes, I do.

SOCRATES: He says of them,

> But now that Fate has closed over this race,
> They are holy daemons upon the earth,
> Beneficent, averters of ills, guardians of mortal men.[4]

HERMOGENES: What is the inference? 398

SOCRATES: What is the inference! Why, I suppose that he means by the golden men, not men literally made of gold, but good and noble, and I am convinced of this, because he further says that we are the iron race.

HERMOGENES: That is true.

SOCRATES: And do you not suppose that good men of our own day would by him be said to be of golden race? b

HERMOGENES: Very likely.

SOCRATES: And are not the good wise?

HERMOGENES: Yes, they are wise.

SOCRATES: And therefore I have the most entire conviction that he called them daemons, because they were δαήμονες (knowing or wise), and in our older Attic dialect the word itself occurs. Now he and other poets say truly that when a good man dies he has honor and a mighty portion among the dead, and becomes a daemon, which is a c name given to him signifying wisdom. And I say too, that every wise man who happens to be a good man is more than human (δαιμόνιον) both in life and death, and is rightly called a daemon.

HERMOGENES: Then I rather think that I am of one mind

---

[4] *Works and Days* 121.

with you, but what is the meaning of the word *hero* (ἥρως, in the old writing ἔρως)?

SOCRATES : I think that there is no difficulty in explaining, for the name is not much altered, and signifies that they were born of love.

HERMOGENES : What do you mean?

SOCRATES : Do you not know that the heroes are demigods?

HERMOGENES : What then?

d   SOCRATES : All of them sprang either from the love of a god for a mortal woman, or of a mortal man for a goddess. Think of the word in the old Attic, and you will see better that the name *heros* is only a slight alteration of Eros, from whom the heroes sprang. Either this is the meaning, or, if not this, then they must have been skillful as rhetoricians and dialecticians, and able to put the question (ἐρωτᾶν), for εἴρειν is equivalent to λέγειν. And therefore, as I was saying, in e the Attic dialect the heroes turn out to be rhetoricians and questioners. All this is easy enough; the noble breed of heroes are a tribe of Sophists and rhetors. But can you tell me why men are called ἄνθρωποι? That is more difficult.

HERMOGENES : No, I cannot, and I would not try even if I could, because I think that you are the more likely to succeed.

399   SOCRATES : That is to say, you trust to the inspiration of Euthyphro.

HERMOGENES : Of course.

SOCRATES : Your faith is not vain, for at this very moment a new and ingenious thought strikes me, and, if I am not careful, before tomorrow's dawn I shall be wiser than I ought to be. Now, attend to me, and first, remember that we often put in and pull out letters in words, and give names as we please and change the accents. Take, for b example, the word Διὶ φίλος; in order to convert this from a sentence into a noun, we omit one *iota* and sound the middle syllable grave instead of acute, as, on the other hand, letters are sometimes inserted in words instead of being omitted, and the acute takes the place of the grave.

HERMOGENES : That is true.

SOCRATES : The name ἄνθρωπος, which was once a sentence, and is now a noun, appears to be a case just of this sort, for one letter, which is the α, has been omitted, and the acute on the last syllable has been changed to a grave.

HERMOGENES : What do you mean?

c   SOCRATES : I mean to say that the word *man* implies that other animals never examine, or consider, or look up at (ἀναθρεῖ) what they see, but that man not only sees (ὄπωπε) but considers and looks up at that which he sees, and hence he alone of all animals is rightly called ἄνθρωπος, meaning ἀναθρῶν ἃ ὄπωπεν.

HERMOGENES: May I ask you to examine another word about which I am curious?

SOCRATES: Certainly.

HERMOGENES: I will take that which appears to me to follow d next in order. You know the distinction of soul and body?

SOCRATES: Of course.

HERMOGENES: Let us endeavor to analyze them like the previous words.

SOCRATES: You want me first of all to examine the natural fitness of the word ψυχή (soul) and then of the word σῶμα (body)?

HERMOGENES: Yes.

SOCRATES: If I am to say what occurs to me at the moment, I should imagine that those who first used the name ψυχή meant to express that the soul when in the body is the source of life, and gives the power of breath and revival (ἀναψῦχον), and when this reviving e power fails then the body perishes and dies, and this, if I am not mistaken, they called *psyche*. But please stay a moment. I fancy that I can discover something which will be more acceptable to the disciples of Euthyphro, for I am afraid that they will scorn this ex- 400 planation. What do you say to another?

HERMOGENES: Let me hear.

SOCRATES: What is that which holds and carries and gives life and motion to the entire nature of the body? What else but the soul?

HERMOGENES: Just that.

SOCRATES: And do you not believe with Anaxagoras that mind or soul is the ordering and containing principle of all things?

HERMOGENES: Yes, I do.

SOCRATES: Then you may well call that power φυσέχη which b carries and holds nature (ἡ φύσιν ὀχεῖ καὶ ἔχει), and this may be refined away into ψυχή.

HERMOGENES: Certainly, and this derivation is, I think, more scientific than the other.

SOCRATES: It is so, but I cannot help laughing, if I am to suppose that this was the true meaning of the name.

HERMOGENES: But what shall we say of the next word?

SOCRATES: You mean σῶμα (body).

HERMOGENES: Yes.

SOCRATES: That may be variously interpreted, and yet more variously if a little permutation is allowed. For some say that the body is the grave (σῆμα) of the soul which may be thought to be buried in c our present life, or again the index of the soul, because the soul gives indications to (σημαίνει) the body. Probably the Orphic poets were the inventors of the name, and they were under the impression that the soul is suffering the punishment of sin, and that the body is an enclosure or prison in which the soul is incarcerated, kept safe (σῶμα, σώζηται), as the name σῶμα implies, until the penalty is paid. According to this view, not even a letter of the word need be changed.

d   HERMOGENES : I think, Socrates, that we have said enough of this class of words. But have we any more explanations of the names of the gods, like that which you were giving of Zeus? I should like to know whether any similar principle of correctness is to be applied to them.

SOCRATES : Yes, indeed, Hermogenes, and there is one excellent principle which, as men of sense, we must acknowledge—that of the gods we know nothing, either of their natures or of the names which they give themselves, but we are sure that the names by which they call themselves, whatever they may be, are true. And this is the

e   best of all principles, and the next best is to say, as in prayers, that we will call them by any sort or kind of names or patronymics which

401 they like, because we do not know of any other. That also, I think, is a very good custom, and one which I should much wish to observe. Let us, then, if you please, in the first place announce to them that we are not inquiring about them—we do not presume that we are able to do so. But we are inquiring about the meaning of men in giving them these names—in this there can be small blame.

HERMOGENES : I think, Socrates, that you are quite right, and I should like to do as you say.

b   SOCRATES : Shall we begin, then, with Hestia, according to custom?

HERMOGENES : Yes, that will be very proper.

SOCRATES : What may we suppose him to have meant who gave the name Hestia?

HERMOGENES : That is another and certainly a most difficult question.

SOCRATES : My dear Hermogenes, the first imposers of names must surely have been considerable persons; they were philosophers, and had a good deal to say.

HERMOGENES : Well, and what of them?

SOCRATES : They are the men to whom I should attribute the

c   imposition of names. Even in foreign names, if you analyze them, a meaning is still discernible. For example, that which we term οὐσία is by some called ἐσσία, and by others again ὠσία. Now that the essence of things should be called ἑστία, which is akin to the first of these (ἐσσία = ἑστία), is rational enough. And there is reason in the Athenians' calling that ἑστία which participates in οὐσία. For in ancient times we too seem to have said ἐσσία for οὐσία, and this you may note

d   to have been the idea of those who appointed that sacrifices should be first offered to ἑστία, which was natural enough if they meant that ἑστία was the essence of things. Those again who said ὠσία seem to have inclined to the opinion of Heraclitus, that all things flow and nothing stands; with them the pushing principle (ὠθοῦν) was the

cause and ruling power of all things, and was therefore rightly called
ὡσία. Enough of this, which is all that we who know nothing can affirm. Next in order after Hestia we ought to consider Rhea and Cronus, e
although the name of Cronus has been already discussed. But I dare
say that I am talking great nonsense.

HERMOGENES : Why, Socrates?

SOCRATES : My good friend, I have discovered a hive of wisdom.

HERMOGENES : Of what nature?

SOCRATES : Well, rather ridiculous, and yet plausible.   402

HERMOGENES : How plausible?

SOCRATES : I fancy to myself Heraclitus repeating wise traditions of antiquity as old as the days of Cronus and Rhea, and of which
Homer also spoke.

HERMOGENES : How do you mean?

SOCRATES : Heraclitus is supposed to say that all things are in
motion and nothing at rest; he compares them to the stream of a
river, and says that you cannot go into the same water twice.

HERMOGENES : That is true.

SOCRATES : Well, then, how can we avoid inferring that he who b
gave the names of Cronus and Rhea to the ancestors of the gods
agreed pretty much in the doctrine of Heraclitus? Is the giving of the
names of streams to both of them purely accidental? Compare the line
in which Homer, and, as I believe, Hesiod also, tells of 'Oceanus, the
origin of gods, and mother Tethys.' [5] And again, Orpheus says that
'The fair river of Oceanus was the first to marry, and he espoused his
sister Tethys, who was his mother's daughter.' [6] You see that this is a
remarkable coincidence, and all in the direction of Heraclitus.   c

HERMOGENES : I think that there is something in what you
say, Socrates, but I do not understand the meaning of the name
Tethys.

SOCRATES : Well, that is almost self-explained, being only the
name of a spring, a little disguised, for that which is strained and
filtered (διαττώμενον, ἠθούμενον) may be likened to a spring, and the d
name Tethys is made up of these two words.

HERMOGENES : The idea is ingenious, Socrates.

SOCRATES : To be sure. But what comes next? Of Zeus we have
spoken.

HERMOGENES : Yes.

SOCRATES : Then let us next take his two brothers, Poseidon
and Pluto, whether the latter is called by that or by his other name.

HERMOGENES : By all means.

SOCRATES : Poseidon is ποσίδεσμος, the chain of the feet. The e
original inventor of the name had been stopped by the watery element

[5] *Iliad* 14.201.   [6] *Iliad* 14.302.

in his walks, and not allowed to go on, and therefore he called the ruler of this element Poseidon; the ε was probably inserted as an ornament. Yet, perhaps, not so, but the name may have been originally
403 written with a double λ and not with a σ, meaning that the god knew many things (πολλὰ εἰδώς). And perhaps also he, being the shaker of the earth, has been named from shaking (σείειν), and then π and δ have been added. Pluto gives wealth (πλοῦτος), and his name means the giver of wealth, which comes out of the earth beneath. People in general appear to imagine that the term Hades is connected with the invisible (ἀειδές), and so they are led by their fears to call the god Pluto instead.

b   HERMOGENES : And what is the true derivation?

SOCRATES : In spite of the mistakes which are made about the power of this deity, and the foolish fears which people have of him, such as the fear of always being with him after death, and of the soul denuded of the body going to him, my belief is that all is quite consistent, and that the office and name of the god really correspond.

HERMOGENES : Why, how is that?

c   SOCRATES : I will tell you my own opinion. But first I should like to ask you which chain does any animal feel to be the stronger, and which confines him more to the same spot—desire or necessity?

HERMOGENES : Desire, Socrates, is stronger far.

SOCRATES : And do you not think that many a one would escape from Hades, if he did not bind those who depart to him by the strongest of chains?

HERMOGENES : Assuredly they would.

SOCRATES : And if by the greatest of chains, then by some desire, as I should certainly infer, and not by necessity?

HERMOGENES : That is clear.

SOCRATES : And there are many desires?

HERMOGENES : Yes.

d   SOCRATES : And therefore by the greatest desire, if the chain is to be the greatest?

HERMOGENES : Yes.

SOCRATES : And is any desire stronger than the thought that you will be made better by associating with another?

HERMOGENES : Certainly not.

SOCRATES : And is not that the reason, Hermogenes, why no one, who has been to him, is willing to come back to us? Even the Sirens, like all the rest of the world, have been laid under his spells.
e Such a charm, as I imagine, is the god able to infuse into his words. And, according to this view, he is the perfect and accomplished Sophist, and the great benefactor of the inhabitants of the other world, and even to us who are upon earth he sends from below exceeding blessings. For he has much more than he wants down there; wherefore he is called Pluto (the rich). Note also that he will have

nothing to do with men while they are in the body, but only when the
soul is liberated from the desires and evils of the body. Now there is 404
a great deal of philosophy and reflection in that, for in their liberated
state he can bind them with the desire of virtue, but while they are
flustered and maddened by the body, not even father Cronus himself
would suffice to keep them with him in his own far-famed chains.

HERMOGENES : There is a deal of truth in what you say.

SOCRATES : Yes, Hermogenes, and the legislator called him b
Hades, not from the unseen (ἀειδές)—far otherwise—but from his
knowledge (εἰδέναι) of all noble things.

HERMOGENES : Very good. And what do we say of Demeter,
and Hera, and Apollo, and Athena, and Hephaestus, and Ares, and the
other deities?

SOCRATES : Demeter is ἡ διδοῦσα μήτηρ, who gives food like a
mother. Hera is the lovely one (ἐρατή), for Zeus, according to tradition, loved and married her; possibly also the name may have been c
given when the legislator was thinking of the heavens, and may be
only a disguise of the air (ἀήρ), putting the end in the place of the beginning. You will recognize the truth of this if you repeat the letters
of Hera several times over. People dread the name of Pherephatta as
they dread the name of Apollo—and with as little reason. The fear, if
I am not mistaken, only arises from their ignorance of the nature of
names, but they go changing the name into Phersephone, and they
are terrified at this, whereas the new name means only that the god- d
dess is wise (σοφή). For seeing that all things in the world are in motion (φερομένων), that principle which embraces and touches and is
able to follow them is wisdom. And therefore the goddess may be
truly called Pherepapha (Φερεπάφα), or some name like it, because
she touches that which is in motion (τοῦ φερομένου ἐφαπτομένη),
herein showing her wisdom. And Hades, who is wise, consorts with
her, because she is wise. They alter her name into Pherephatta nowadays, because the present generation care for euphony more than
truth. There is the other name, Apollo, which, as I was saying, is gener- e
ally supposed to have some terrible signification. Have you remarked
this fact?

HERMOGENES : To be sure, I have, and what you say is true.

SOCRATES : But the name, in my opinion, is really most expressive of the power of the god.

HERMOGENES : How so?

SOCRATES : I will endeavor to explain, for I do not believe that
any single name could have been better adapted to express the at- 405
tributes of the god, embracing and in a manner signifying all four of
them—music, and prophecy, and medicine, and archery.

HERMOGENES : That must be a strange name, and I should like
to hear the explanation.

SOCRATES : Say rather a harmonious name, as beseems the

god of harmony. In the first place, the purgations and purifications which doctors and diviners use, and their fumigations with drugs
b magical or medicinal, as well as their washings and lustral sprinklings, have all one and the same object, which is to make a man pure both in body and soul.

HERMOGENES: Very true.

SOCRATES: And is not Apollo the purifier, and the washer, and the absolver from all impurities?

HERMOGENES: Very true.

SOCRATES: Then in reference to his ablutions and absolutions,
c as being the physician who orders them, he may be rightly called Ἀπολούων (purifier), or in respect of his powers of divination, and his truth and sincerity, which is the same as truth, he may be most fitly called Ἁπλῶς, from ἁπλοῦς (sincere), as in the Thessalian dialect, for all the Thessalians call him Ἁπλός. Also, he is ἀεὶ βάλλων (always shooting), because he is a master archer who never misses. Or again, the name may refer to his musical attributes, and then, as in ἀκόλουθος and ἄκοιτις, and in many other words, the α is supposed to mean 'together'; so the meaning of the name Apollo will be 'moving together,' whether in the poles of heaven as they are called, or in the
d harmony of song, which is termed concord, because he moves all together by a harmonious power, as astronomers and musicians ingeniously declare. And he is the god who presides over harmony, and makes all things move together, both among gods and among men. And as in the words ἀκόλουθος and ἄκοιτις the α is substituted for ὁμο; so the name Ἀπόλλων is equivalent to ὁμοπολῶν; only the second λ is
e added in order to avoid the ill-omened sound of destruction (ἀπολῶν). Now the suspicion of this destructive power still haunts the minds of some who do not consider the true value of the name, which, as I was
406 saying just now, has reference to all the powers of the god, who is the single one, the ever-darting, the purifier, the mover-together (ἁπλοῦς, ἀεὶ βάλλων, ἀπολούων, ὁμοπολῶν).

The name of the Muses and of music would seem to be derived from their making philosophical inquiries (μῶσθαι). And Leto is called by this name, because she is such a gentle goddess, and so willing (ἐθελήμων) to grant our requests, or her name may be Letho, as she is often called by strangers—they seem to imply by it her amiability,
b and her smooth and easy-going way of behaving. Artemis is named from her healthy (ἀρτεμής), well-ordered nature, and because of her love of virginity, perhaps because she is a proficient in virtue (ἀρετή), and perhaps also as hating intercourse of the sexes (τὸν ἄροτον μισήσασα). He who gave the goddess her name may have had any or all of these reasons.

HERMOGENES: What is the meaning of Dionysus and Aphrodite?

SOCRATES: Son of Hipponicus. you ask a solemn question.

There is a serious and also a facetious explanation of both these names; the serious explanation is not to be had from me, but there is c no objection to your hearing the facetious one, for the gods too love a joke. Διόνυσος is simply διδοὺς οἶνον (giver of wine)—Διδοίνυσος, as he might be called in fun—and οἶνος is properly οἰόνους, because wine makes those who drink think (οἴεσθαι) that they have a mind (νοῦν) when they have none. The derivation of Aphrodite, born of the foam (ἀφρός), may be fairly accepted on the authority of Hesiod.   d

HERMOGENES : Still there remains Athena, whom you, Socrates, as an Athenian, will surely not forget; there are also Hephaestus and Ares.

SOCRATES : I am not likely to forget them.

HERMOGENES : No, indeed.

SOCRATES : There is no difficulty in explaining the other appellation of Athena.

HERMOGENES : What other appellation?

SOCRATES : We call her Pallas.

HERMOGENES : To be sure.

SOCRATES : And we cannot be wrong in supposing that this is derived from armed dances. For the elevation of oneself or anything e else above the earth, or by the use of the hands, we call shaking (πάλλειν), or dancing.   407

HERMOGENES : That is quite true.

SOCRATES : Then that is the explanation of the name Pallas?

HERMOGENES : Yes, but what do you say of the other name?

SOCRATES : Athena?

HERMOGENES : Yes.

SOCRATES : That is a graver matter, and there, my friend, the modern interpreters of Homer may, I think, assist in explaining the view of the ancients. For most of these, in their explanations of the b poet, assert that he meant by Athena mind (νοῦς) and intelligence (διάνοια). And the maker of names appears to have had a singular notion about her, and indeed calls her by a still higher title, divine intelligence (θεοῦ νόησις), as though he would say, This is she who has the mind of God (θεονόα)—using α as a dialectic variety for η, and taking away ι and σ. Perhaps, however, the name Θεονόη may mean she who knows divine things (θεῖα νοοῦσα) better than others. Nor shall we be far wrong in supposing that the author of it wished to identify this goddess with moral intelligence (ἐν ἤθει νόησιν), and therefore gave her the name 'Ηθονόη, which, however, either he or his c successors have altered into what they thought a nicer form, and called her Athena.

HERMOGENES : But what do you say of Hephaestus?

SOCRATES : Speak you of the princely lord of light (φάεος ἵστορα)?

HERMOGENES : Surely.

SOCRATES : Ἥφαιστος is Φαῖστος, and has added the η by attraction; that is obvious to anybody.

HERMOGENES : That is very probable, until some more probable notion gets into your head.

SOCRATES : To prevent that, you had better ask what is the derivation of Ares.

HERMOGENES : What is Ares?

d   SOCRATES : Ares may be called, if you will, from his manhood (ἄρρεν) and manliness, or if you please, from his hard and unchangeable nature, which is the meaning of ἄρρατος; the latter is a derivation in every way appropriate to the god of war.

HERMOGENES : Very true.

SOCRATES : And now, by the gods, let us have no more of the gods, for I am afraid of them. Ask about anything but them, and thou shalt see how the steeds of Euthyphro can prance.

e   HERMOGENES : Only one more god! I should like to know about Hermes, of whom I am said not to be a true son. Let us make him out, and then I shall know whether there is any meaning in what Cratylus says.

SOCRATES : I should imagine that the name Hermes has to do

408 with speech, and signifies that he is the interpreter (ἑρμηνεύς), or messenger, or thief; or liar, or bargainer; all that sort of thing has a great deal to do with language. As I was telling you, the word εἴρειν is expressive of the use of speech, and there is an often-recurring Homeric word ἐμήσατο, which means he contrived. Out of these two words, εἴρειν and μήσασθαι, the legislator formed the name of the god who invented language and speech, and we may imagine him dictat-

b   ing to us the use of this name. O my friends, says he to us, seeing that he is the contriver of tales or speeches, you may rightly call him Εἰρέμης. And this has been improved by us, as we think, into Hermes. Iris also appears to have been called from the verb to tell (εἴρειν), because she was a messenger.

HERMOGENES : Then I am very sure that Cratylus was quite right in saying that I was no true son of Hermes (Ἑρμογένης), for I am not a good hand at speeches.

SOCRATES : There is also reason, my friend, in Pan's being the double-formed son of Hermes.

c   HERMOGENES : How do you make that out?

SOCRATES : You are aware that speech signifies all things (πᾶν), and is always turning them round and round, and has two forms, true and false?

HERMOGENES : Certainly.

SOCRATES : Is not the truth that is in him the smooth or sacred form which dwells above among the gods, whereas falsehood dwells among men below, and is rough like the goat of tragedy, for tales and falsehoods have generally to do with the tragic or goatish life, and tragedy is the place of them?

HERMOGENES : Very true.

SOCRATES : Then surely Pan, who is the declarer of all things (πᾶν) and the perpetual mover (ἀεὶ πολῶν) of all things, is rightly d called αἰπόλος (goatherd), he being the two-formed son of Hermes, smooth in his upper part, and rough and goatlike in his lower regions. And, as the son of Hermes, he is speech or the brother of speech, and that brother should be like brother is no marvel. But, as I was saying, my dear Hermogenes, let us get away from the gods.

HERMOGENES : From this sort of gods, by all means, Socrates. But why should we not discuss another kind of gods—the sun, moon, stars, earth, aether, air, fire, water, the seasons, and the year?   e

SOCRATES : You impose a great many tasks upon me. Still, if you wish, I will not refuse.

HERMOGENES : You will oblige me.

SOCRATES : How would you have me begin? Shall I take first of all him whom you mentioned first—the sun?

HERMOGENES : Very good.

SOCRATES : The origin of the sun will probably be clearer in the Doric form, for the Dorians call him ἅλιος, and this name is given to 409 him because when he rises he gathers (ἁλίζοι) men together or because he is always rolling in his course (ἀεὶ εἰλεῖν ἰών) about the earth, or from αἰολεῖν, of which the meaning is the same as ποικίλλειν (to variegate), because he variegates the productions of the earth.

HERMOGENES : But what is σελήνη (the moon)?

SOCRATES : That name is rather unfortunate for Anaxagoras.

HERMOGENES : How so?

SOCRATES : The word seems to forestall his recent discovery, b that the moon receives her light from the sun.

HERMOGENES : Why do you say so?

SOCRATES : The two words σέλας (brightness) and φῶς (light) have much the same meaning?

HERMOGENES : Yes.

SOCRATES : This light about the moon is always new (νέον) and always old (ἕνον), if the disciples of Anaxagoras say truly. For the sun in his revolution always adds new light, and there is the old light of the previous month.

HERMOGENES : Very true.

SOCRATES : The moon is not infrequently called σελαναία.

HERMOGENES : True.

SOCRATES : And as she has a light which is always old and always new (ἕνον νέον ἀεί), she may very properly have the name c σελαενονεοάεια, and this when hammered into shape becomes σελαναία.

HERMOGENES : A real dithyrambic sort of name that, Socrates. But what do you say of the month and the stars?

SOCRATES : Μείς (month) is called from μειοῦσθαι (to lessen), because suffering diminution; the name of ἄστρα (stars) seems to be derived from ἀστραπή (blinding light), which is an improvement on ἀναστρωπή, signifying the upsetting of the eyes (ἀναστρέφειν ὦπα).

HERMOGENES: What do you say of πῦρ (fire) and ὕδωρ (water)?

d   SOCRATES: I am at a loss how to explain πῦρ; either the Muse of Euthyphro has deserted me, or there is some very great difficulty in the word. Please, however, to note the contrivance which I adopt whenever I am in a difficulty of this sort.

HERMOGENES: What is it?

SOCRATES: I will tell you, but I should like to know first whether you can tell me what is the meaning of the word πῦρ.

HERMOGENES: Indeed I cannot.

SOCRATES: Shall I tell you what I suspect to be the true explanation of this and several other words? My belief is that they are of
e   foreign origin. For the Hellenes, especially those who were under the dominion of the barbarians, often borrowed from them.

HERMOGENES: What is the inference?

SOCRATES: Why, you know that anyone who seeks to demonstrate the fitness of these names according to the Hellenic language, and not according to the language from which the words are derived, is rather likely to be at fault.

HERMOGENES: Yes, certainly.

410   SOCRATES: Well then, consider whether this πῦρ is not foreign, for the word is not easily brought into relation with the Hellenic tongue, and the Phrygians may be observed to have the same word slightly changed, just as they have ὕδωρ (water) and κύνες (dogs), and many other words.

HERMOGENES: That is true.

SOCRATES: Any violent interpretations of the words should be avoided, for something to say about them may easily be found. And
b   thus I get rid of πῦρ and ὕδωρ. 'Αήρ (air), Hermogenes, may be explained as the element which raises (αἴρει) things from the earth, or as ever flowing (ἀεὶ ῥεῖ), or because the flux of the air is wind, and the poets call the winds air blasts, (ἀῆται); he who uses the term may mean, so to speak, air flux (ἀητόρρουν), in the sense of wind flux (πνευματόρρουν), and because this moving wind may be expressed by either term he employs the word air (ἀήρ = ἀήτης ῥέω). Αἰθήρ (aether) I should interpret as ἀειθεήρ; this may be correctly said, because this element is always running in a flux about the air (ἀεὶ θεῖ περὶ τὸν ἀέρα ῥέων). The meaning of the word γῆ (earth) comes out
c   better when in the form of γαῖα, for the earth may be truly called mother (γαῖα, γεννήτειρα), as in the language of Homer γεγάασι means γεγεννῆσθαι.

HERMOGENES: Good.

SOCRATES: What shall we take next?

HERMOGENES: There are ὧραι (the seasons), and the two names of the year, ἐνιαυτός and ἔτος.

SOCRATES: The ὧραι should be spelled in the old Attic way, if you desire to know the probable truth about them; they are rightly called the ὅραι because they divide (ὁρίζουσιν) the summers and winters and winds and the fruits of the earth. The words ἐνιαυτός and ἔτος appear to be the same—that which brings to light the plants and d growths of the earth in their turn, and passes them in review within itself (ἐν ἑαυτῷ ἐξετάζει)—this is broken up into two words, ἐνιαυτός from ἐν ἑαυτῷ, and ἔτος from ἐτάζει, just as the original name of Ζεύς was divided into Ζῆνα and Δία, and the whole proposition means that this power of reviewing from within is one, but has two names, two words ἔτος and ἐνιαυτός being thus formed out of a single proposition.

HERMOGENES: Indeed, Socrates, you make surprising e progress.

SOCRATES: I am run away with.

HERMOGENES: Very true.

SOCRATES: But am not yet at my utmost speed.

HERMOGENES: I should like very much to know, in the next 411 place, how you would explain the virtues. What principle of correctness is there in those charming words—wisdom, understanding, justice, and the rest of them?

SOCRATES: That is a tremendous class of names which you are disinterring; still, as I have put on the lion's skin, I must not be faint of heart. And I suppose that I must consider the meaning of wisdom (φρόνησις) and understanding (σύνεσις), and judgment (γνώμη) and knowledge (ἐπιστήμη), and all those other charming words, as b you call them.

HERMOGENES: Surely, we must not leave off until we find out their meaning.

SOCRATES: By the dog of Egypt I have not a bad notion which came into my head only this moment. I believe that the primeval givers of names were undoubtedly like too many of our modern philosophers, who, in their search after the nature of things, are always getting dizzy from constantly going round and round, and then they imagine that the world is going round and round and moving in all directions. And this appearance, which arises out of their own internal c condition, they suppose to be a reality of nature; they think that there is nothing stable or permanent, but only flux and motion, and that the world is always full of every sort of motion and change. The consideration of the names which I mentioned has led me into making this reflection.

HERMOGENES: How is that, Socrates?

SOCRATES: Perhaps you did not observe that in the names which have just been cited the motion or flux or generation of things is most surely indicated.

HERMOGENES: No, indeed, I never thought of it.

SOCRATES: Take the first of those which you mentioned; d clearly that is a name indicative of motion.

HERMOGENES: What was the name?

SOCRATES: Φρόνησις (wisdom), which may signify φορᾶς καὶ ῥοῦ νόησις (perception of motion and flux), or perhaps φορᾶς ὄνησις (the blessing of motion), but is at any rate connected with φέρεσθαι (motion); γνώμη (judgment), again, certainly implies the ponderation or consideration (νώμησις) of generation (γονή), for to ponder is the same as to consider. Or, if you would rather, here is νόησις, the very word just now mentioned, which is νέου ἕσις (the desire of the new); the word νέος implies that the world is always in process of creation.

e The giver of the name wanted to express his longing of the soul, for the original name was νεόεσις, and not νόησις, but η took the place of a double ε. The word σωφροσύνη is the salvation (σωτηρία) of that wisdom

412 (φρόνησις) which we were just now considering. Ἐπιστήμη (knowledge) is akin to this, and indicates that the soul which is good for anything follows (ἕπεται) the motion of things, neither anticipating them nor falling behind them; wherefore the word should rather be read as ἐπειστήμη, inserting ε. Σύνεσις (understanding) may be regarded in like manner as a kind of conclusion; the word is derived from συνιέναι (to go along with), and, like ἐπίστασθαι (to know), implies the progression

b of the soul in company with the nature of things. Σοφία (wisdom) is very dark, and appears not to be of native growth; the meaning is *touching the motion or stream of things.* You must remember that the poets, when they speak of the commencement of any rapid motion, often use the word ἐσύθη (he rushed), and there was a famous Lacedaemonian who was named Σοῦς (Rush), for by this word the Lacedaemonians signify rapid motion, and the touching (ἐπαφή) of motion is expressed by σοφία, for all things are supposed to be in mo-

c tion. Good (ἀγαθόν) is the name which is given to the admirable (ἀγαστῷ) in nature, for, although all things move, still there are degrees of motion—some are swifter, some slower—but there are some things which are admirable for their swiftness, and this admirable part of nature is called ἀγαθόν.

Δικαιοσύνη (justice) is clearly δικαίου σύνεσις (understanding of the just), but the actual word δίκαιον is more difficult. Men are only agreed to a certain extent about justice, and then they begin to dis-

d agree. For those who suppose all things to be in motion conceive the greater part of nature to be a mere receptacle, and they say that there is a penetrating power which passes through all this, and is the instrument of creation in all, and is the subtlest and swiftest element, for if it were not the subtlest, and a power which none can keep out, and also the swiftest, passing by other things as if they were standing still, it could not penetrate through the moving universe. And this

e element, which superintends all things and pierces (διαϊόν) all, is rightly called δίκαιον; the letter κ is only added for the sake of euphony. Thus far, as I was saying, there is a general agreement about

413 the nature of justice, but I, Hermogenes, being an enthusiastic disciple, have been told in a mystery that the justice of which I am speak-

ing is also the cause of the world. Now a cause is that because of which anything is created, and someone comes and whispers in my ear that justice is rightly so called because partaking of the nature of the cause. And I begin, after hearing what he has said, to interrogate him gently. Well, my excellent friend, say I, but if all this be true, I still want to know what is justice. Thereupon they think that I ask tiresome questions, and am leaping over the barriers, and have been already sufficiently answered, and they try to satisfy me with one deri- b vation after another, and at length they quarrel. For one of them says that justice is the sun, and that he only is the piercing (διαϊόντα) and burning (κάοντα) element which is the guardian of nature. And when I joyfully repeat this beautiful notion, I am answered by the satirical remark, What, is there no justice in the world when the sun is down? And when I earnestly beg my questioner to tell me his own honest opinion, he says, Fire in the abstract. But this is not very in- c telligible. Another says, No, not fire in the abstract, but the abstraction of heat in the fire. Another man professes to laugh at all this, and says, as Anaxagoras says, that justice is mind, for mind, as they say, has absolute power, and mixes with nothing, and orders all things, and passes through all things. At last, my friend, I find myself in far greater perplexity about the nature of justice than I was before I began to learn. But still I am of the opinion that the name, which has led me into this digression, was given to justice for the reasons which d I have mentioned.

HERMOGENES : I think, Socrates, that you are not improvising now. You must have heard this from someone else.

SOCRATES : And not the rest?

HERMOGENES : Hardly.

SOCRATES : Well, then, let me go on in the hope of making you believe in the originality of the rest. What remains after justice? I do not think that we have as yet discussed courage (ἀνδρεία). Injustice (ἀδικία), which is obviously nothing more than a hindrance to the e penetrating principle (διαϊόντος), need not be considered. Well, then, the name of ἀνδρεία seems to imply a battle—this battle is in the world of existence, and according to the doctrine of flux is only the counterflux (ἐναντία ῥοή). If you extract the δ from ἀνδρεία, the name at once signifies the thing, and you may clearly understand that ἀνδρεία is not the stream opposed to every stream, but only to that which is contrary to justice, for otherwise courage would not have 414 been praised. The words ἄρρην (male) and ἀνήρ (man) also contain a similar allusion to the same principle of the upward flux (τῇ ἄνω ῥοῇ). Γυνή (woman) I suspect to be the same word as γονή (birth); θῆλυ (female) appears to be partly derived from θηλή (the teat), because the teat is like rain, and makes things flourish (τεθηλέναι).

HERMOGENES : That is surely probable.

SOCRATES : Yes, and the very word θάλλειν (to flourish) seems

to figure the growth of youth, which is swift and sudden ever. And
b this is expressed by the legislator in the name, which is a compound of
θεῖν (running) and ἅλλεσθαι (leaping). Pray observe how I gallop
away when I get on smooth ground. There are a good many names
generally thought to be of importance, which have still to be explained.

HERMOGENES : True.

SOCRATES : There is the meaning of the word τέχνη (art), for
example.

HERMOGENES : Very true.

SOCRATES : That may be identified with ἐχονόη, and expresses
c the possession of mind—you have only to take away the τ and insert
o, between the χ and ν, and between the ν and η.

HERMOGENES : That is a very shabby etymology.

SOCRATES : Yes, my dear friend, but then you know that the
original names have been long ago buried and disguised by people
sticking on and stripping off letters for the sake of euphony, and twisting and bedizening them in all sorts of ways, and time too may have
had a share in the change. Take, for example, the word κάτοπτρον
(mirror). Why is the letter ρ inserted? This must surely be the addi-
d tion of someone who cares nothing about the truth, but thinks only of
putting the mouth into shape. And the additions are often such that
at last no human being can possibly make out the original meaning of
the word. Another example is the word σφίγξ, σφιγγός, which ought
properly to be φίγξ, φιγγός, and there are other examples.

HERMOGENES : That is quite true, Socrates.

SOCRATES : And yet, if you are permitted to put in and pull out
any letters which you please, names will be too easily made, and any
name may be adapted to any object.
e   HERMOGENES : True.

SOCRATES : Yes, that is true. And therefore a wise dictator, like
yourself, should observe the laws of moderation and probability.

HERMOGENES : Such is my desire.

SOCRATES : And mine, too, Hermogenes. But do not be too
415 much of a precisian, or 'you will unnerve me of my strength.' [7] When
you have allowed me to add μηχανή (contrivance) to τέχνη (art) I shall
be at the top of my bent, for I conceive μηχανή to be a sign of great accomplishment (ἄνειν), for μῆκος has the meaning of greatness, and
these two, μῆκος and ἄνειν, make up the word μηχανή. But, as I was
saying, being now at the top of my bent, I should like to consider the
b meaning of the two words ἀρετή (virtue) and κακία (vice); ἀρετή I do
not as yet understand, but κακία is transparent, and agrees with the
principles which preceded, for all things being in a flux (ἰόντων),
κακία is κακῶς ἰόν (going badly), and this evil motion when existing in

[7] *Iliad* 6.265.

the soul has the general name of κακία, or vice, specially appropriated to it. The meaning of κακῶς ἰέναι may be further illustrated by the use of δειλία (cowardice), which ought to have come after ἀνδρεία, but was c forgotten, and, as I fear, is not the only word which has been passed over. Δειλία signifies that the soul is bound with a strong chain (δεσμός), for λίαν means strength, and therefore δειλία expresses the greatest and strongest bond of the soul. And ἀπορία (difficulty) is an evil of the same nature (from α *not* and πορεύεσθαι *to go*), like anything else which is an impediment to motion and movement. Then the word κακία appears to mean κακῶς ἰέναι, or going badly, or limping and halting, of which the consequence is that the soul becomes filled with vice. And if κακία is the name of this sort of thing, ἀρετή will be the opposite of it, signifying in the first place ease of motion, then that the d stream of the good soul is unimpeded, and has therefore the attribute of ever flowing without let or hindrance, and is therefore called ἀρετή, or, more correctly, ἀειρειτή (ever flowing), and may perhaps have had another form, αἱρετή (eligible), indicating that nothing is more eligible than virtue, and this has been hammered into ἀρετή. I dare say that e you will deem this to be another invention of mine, but I think that if the previous word κακία was right, then ἀρετή is also right.

HERMOGENES: But what is the meaning of κακόν (bad), which 416 has played so great a part in your previous discourse?

SOCRATES: That is a very singular word about which I can hardly form an opinion, and therefore I must have recourse to my ingenious device.

HERMOGENES: What device?

SOCRATES: The device of a foreign origin, which I shall give to this word also.

HERMOGENES: Very likely you are right, but suppose that we leave these words, and endeavor to see the rationale of καλόν (beautiful) and αἰσχρόν (ugly).

SOCRATES: The meaning of αἰσχρόν is evident, being only ἀεὶ ἴσχον ῥοῆς (always preventing from flowing), and this is in accord- b ance with our former derivations. For the name giver was a great enemy to stagnation of all sorts, and hence he gave the name ἀεισχοροῦν to that which hindered the flux (ἀεὶ ἴσχον ῥοῦν), and this is now beaten together into αἰσχρόν.

HERMOGENES: But what do you say of καλόν?

SOCRATES: That is more obscure; yet the form is only due to the quantity, and has been changed by altering ου into ο.

HERMOGENES: What do you mean?

SOCRATES: This name appears to denote mind.

HERMOGENES: How so?

SOCRATES: Let me ask you what is the cause why anything c has a name. Is not the principle which imposes the name the cause?

HERMOGENES: Certainly.

SOCRATES : And must not this be the mind of gods, or of men, or of both?

HERMOGENES : Yes.

SOCRATES : Is not mind that which called (καλέσαν) things by their names, and is not mind the beautiful (καλόν)?

HERMOGENES : That is evident.

SOCRATES : And are not the works of intelligence and mind worthy of praise, and are not other works worthy of blame?

HERMOGENES : Certainly.

d   SOCRATES : Physic does the work of a physician, and carpentering does the works of a carpenter?

HERMOGENES : Exactly.

SOCRATES : And the principle of beauty does the works of beauty?

HERMOGENES : Of course.

SOCRATES : And that principle we affirm to be mind?

HERMOGENES : Very true.

SOCRATES : Then mind is rightly called beauty because she does the works which we recognize and speak of as the beautiful?

HERMOGENES : That is evident.

e   SOCRATES : What more names remain to us?

HERMOGENES : There are the words which are connected with
417 ἀγαθόν and καλόν, such as συμφέρον and λυσιτελοῦν, ὠφέλιμον, κερδαλέον, and their opposites.

SOCRATES : The meaning of συμφέρον (expedient) I think that you may discover for yourself by the light of the previous examples, for it is a sister word to ἐπιστήμη, meaning just the motion (φορά) of the soul accompanying the world, and things which are done upon this principle are called σύμφορα or συμφέροντα, because they are carried round with the world.

HERMOGENES : That is probable.

SOCRATES : Again, κερδαλέον (gainful) is called from κέρδος
b (gain), but you must alter the ν into δ if you want to get at the meaning, for this word also signifies good, but in another way; he who gave the name intended to express the power of admixture (κεραννύμενον) and universal penetration in the good; in forming the word, however, he inserted a δ instead of a ν, and so made κέρδος.

HERMOGENES : Well, but what is λυσιτελοῦν (profitable)?

SOCRATES : I suppose, Hermogenes, that people do not mean by the profitable the gainful or that which pays (λύει) the retailer, but they use the word in the sense of swift. You regard the profitable
c (λυσιτελοῦν) as that which, being the swiftest thing in existence, allows of no stay in things and no pause or end of motion, but always, if there begins to be any end, lets things go again (λύει), and makes motion immortal and unceasing. And from this point of view, as appears to me, the good was happily denominated λυσιτελοῦν—being

that which looses (λύον) the end (τέλος) of motion. Ὠφέλιμον (the advantageous) is derived from ὀφέλλειν, meaning that which creates and increases; this latter is a common Homeric word, and has a foreign character.

HERMOGENES: And what do you say of their opposites? d

SOCRATES: Of such as mere negatives I hardly think that I need speak.

HERMOGENES: Which are they?

SOCRATES: The words ἀξύμφορον (inexpedient), ἀνωφελές (unprofitable), ἀλυσιτελές (unadvantageous), ἀκερδές (ungainful).

HERMOGENES: True.

SOCRATES: I would rather take the words βλαβερόν (harmful), ζημιῶδες (hurtful).

HERMOGENES: Good.

SOCRATES: The word βλαβερόν is that which is said to hinder or harm (βλάπτειν) the stream (ῥοῦν); βλάπτον is βουλόμενον ἅπτειν e (seeking to hold or bind), for ἅπτειν is the same as δεῖν, and δεῖν is always a term of censure; βουλόμενον ἅπτειν ῥοῦν (wanting to bind the stream) would properly be βουλαπτεροῦν, and this, as I imagine, is improved into βλαβερόν.

HERMOGENES: You bring out curious results, Socrates, in the use of names, and when I hear the word βουλαπτεροῦν I cannot help imagining that you are making your mouth into a flute, and puffing away at some prelude to Athena. 418

SOCRATES: That is the fault of the makers of the name, Hermogenes—not mine.

HERMOGENES: Very true, but what is the derivation of ζημιῶδες?

SOCRATES: What is the meaning of ζημιῶδες? Let me remark, Hermogenes, how right I was in saying that great changes are made in the meaning of words by putting in and pulling out letters; even a very slight permutation will sometimes give an entirely opposite sense. I may instance the word δέον, which occurs to me at the moment, and b reminds me of what I was going to say to you, that the fine fashionable language of modern times has twisted and disguised and entirely altered the original meaning both of δέον and of ζημιῶδες, which in the old language is clearly indicated.

HERMOGENES: What do you mean?

SOCRATES: I will try to explain. You are aware that our forefathers loved the sounds ι and δ, especially the women, who are most conservative of the ancient language, but now they change ι into η or c ε, and δ into ζ—this is supposed to increase the grandeur of the sound.

HERMOGENES: How do you mean?

SOCRATES: For example, in very ancient times they called the day either ἱμέρα or ἐμέρα, which is called by us ἡμέρα.

HERMOGENES: That is true.

SOCRATES: Do you observe that only the ancient form shows the intention of the giver of the name? The reason is that men long d for (ἱμείρουσι) and love the light which comes after the darkness, and is therefore called ἱμέρα, from ἵμερος (desire).

HERMOGENES: Clearly.

SOCRATES: But now the name is so travestied that you cannot tell the meaning, although there are some who imagine the day to be called ἡμέρα because it makes things gentle (ἥμερα).

HERMOGENES: Such is my view.

SOCRATES: And do you know that the ancients said δυογόν and not ζυγόν?

HERMOGENES: They did so.

SOCRATES: And ζυγόν (yoke) has no meaning—it ought to be e δυογόν, which word expresses the binding of two together (δυεῖν ἀγωγή) for the purpose of drawing—this has been changed into ζυγόν. And there are many other examples of similar changes.

HERMOGENES: There are.

SOCRATES: Proceeding in the same train of thought I may remark that the word δέον (obligation) has a meaning which is the opposite of all the other appellations of good, for δέον is here a species of good, and is, nevertheless, the chain (δεσμός) or hinderer of motion, and therefore own brother of βλαβερόν.

HERMOGENES: Yes, Socrates, that is quite plain.

SOCRATES: Not if you restore the ancient form, which is more 419 likely to be the correct one, and read διόν instead of δέον. If you convert the ε into an ι after the old fashion, this word will then agree with other words meaning good, for διόν, not δέον, signifies the good, and is a term of praise. And the author of names has not contradicted himself, but in all these various appellations, δέον (obligatory), ὠφέλιμον (advantageous), λυσιτελοῦν (profitable), κερδαλέον (gainful), ἀγαθόν (good), συμφέρον (expedient), εὔπορον (plenteous), the same conception is implied of the ordering or all-pervading principle which is praised, and the restraining and binding principle which is censured. b And this is further illustrated by the word ζημιῶδης (hurtful), which if the ζ is only changed into δ, as in the ancient language, becomes δημιῶδης, and this name, as you will perceive, is given to that which binds motion (δοῦντι ἰόν).

HERMOGENES: What do you say of ἡδονή (pleasure), λύπη (pain), ἐπιθυμία (desire), and the like, Socrates?

SOCRATES: I do not think, Hermogenes, that there is any great difficulty about them—ἡδονή is ἡ ὄνησις, the action which tends to advantage, and the original form may be supposed to have been ἡονή, c but this has been altered by the insertion of the δ. Λύπη appears to be derived from the relaxation (λύειν) which the body feels when in sorrow; ἀνία (trouble) is the hindrance of motion (α and ἰέναι); ἀλγηδών (distress), if I am not mistaken, is a foreign word, which is derived from ἀλγεινός (grievous); ὀδύνη (grief) is called from the putting on (ἔνδυσις) of sorrow; in ἀχθηδών (vexation) 'the word too labors,' as anyone may see; χαρά (joy) is the very expression of the fluency and diffusion of the soul (χέω); τέρψις (delight) is so called from the pleasure creeping (ἕρπον) through the soul, which may be likened to a d breath (πνοή) and is properly ἑρπνοῦν, but has been altered by time into τερπνόν. Εὐφροσύνη (cheerfulness) and ἐπιθυμία explain themselves; the former, which ought to be εὐφεροσύνη and has been changed into εὐφροσύνη, is named, as everyone may see, from the soul moving (φέρεσθαι) in harmony with nature; ἐπιθυμία is really ἡ ἐπὶ τὸν θυμὸν ἰοῦσα δύναμις, the power which enters into the soul. Θυμός (passion) is called from the rushing (θύσεως) and boiling of the soul ἵμερος e (desire) denotes the stream (ῥοῦς) which most draws the soul διὰ τὴν ἕσιν τῆς ῥοῆς, because flowing with desire (ἱέμενος), and expresses a longing after things and violent attraction of the soul to 420 them, and is termed ἵμερος from possessing this power; πόθος (longing) is expressive of the desire of that which is not present but absent, and in another place (που); this is the reason why the name πόθος is applied to things absent, as ἵμερος is to things present. Ἔρως (love) is so called because flowing in (ἐσρῶν) from without; the stream is not inherent, but is an influence introduced through the eyes, and from flowing in was called ἔσρος (influx) in the old time when they used ο for ω, b and is called ἔρως, now that ω is substituted for ο. But why do you not give me another word?

HERMOGENES: What do you think of δόξα (opinion), and that class of words?

SOCRATES: Δόξα is either derived from δίωξις (pursuit), and expresses the march of the soul in the pursuit of knowledge, or from the shooting of a bow (τόξον). The latter is more likely, and is confirmed by οἴησις (thinking), which is only οἶσις (moving), and implies c the movement of the soul to the essential nature of each thing, just as βουλή (counsel) has to do with shooting (βολή), and βούλεσθαι (to wish) combines the notion of aiming and deliberating—all these words seem to follow δόξα, and all involve the idea of shooting, just as ἀβουλία, absence of counsel, on the other hand, is a mishap, or missing, or mistaking of the mark, or aim, or proposal, or object.

HERMOGENES: You are quickening your pace now, Socrates. d

SOCRATES: Why yes, the end I now dedicate to God, not, however, until I have explained ἀνάγκη (necessity), which ought to come next, and ἑκούσιον (the voluntary). Ἑκούσιον is certainly the yielding (εἶκον) and unresisting—the notion implied is yielding and not opposing, yielding, as I was just now saying, to that motion which is in accordance with our will. But the necessary and resistant, being contrary to our will, implies error and ignorance; the idea is taken from walking through a ravine which is impassable, and rugged, and overgrown, and impedes motion—and this is the derivation of the word e ἀναγκαῖον (necessary), ἀν' ἄγκη ἰόν, going through a ravine. But while my strength lasts let us persevere, and I hope that you will persevere with your questions.

421   HERMOGENES : Well, then, let me ask about the greatest and noblest, such as ἀλήθεια (truth) and ψεῦδος (falsehood) and ὄν (being), not forgetting to inquire why the word ὄνομα (name), which is the theme of our discussion, has this name of ὄνομα.

SOCRATES : You know the word μαίεσθαι (to seek)?

HERMOGENES : Yes—meaning the same as ζητεῖν (to inquire).

SOCRATES : The word ὄνομα seems to be a compressed sentence, signifying ὄν οὗ ζήτημα (being for which there is a search), as is still more obvious in ὀνομαστόν (notable), which states in so many words that real existence is that for which there is a seeking (ὄν οὗ μάσμα);
b ἀλήθεια is also an agglomeration of θεία ἄλη (divine wandering), implying the divine motion of existence. Ψεῦδος (falsehood) is the opposite of motion; here is another ill name given by the legislator to stagnation and forced inaction, which he compares to sleep (εὕδειν), but the original meaning of the word is disguised by the addition of ψ. Ὄν and οὐσία are ἰόν with an ι broken off; this agrees with the true principle, for being (ὄν) is also moving (ἰόν), and the same may be
c said of not-being, which is likewise called not-going (οὐκίον or οὐκὶ ὄν = οὐκ ἰόν).

HERMOGENES : You have hammered away at them manfully, but suppose that someone were to say to you, What is the word ἰόν, and what are ῥέον and δοῦν? Show me their fitness.

SOCRATES : You mean to say, how should I answer him?

HERMOGENES : Yes.

SOCRATES : One way of giving the appearance of an answer has been already suggested.

HERMOGENES : What way?

SOCRATES : To say that names which we do not understand are
d of foreign origin, and this is very likely the right answer, and something of this kind may be true of them, but also the original forms of words may have been lost in the lapse of ages; names have been so twisted in all manner of ways that I should not be surprised if the old language when compared with that now in use would appear to us to be a barbarous tongue.

HERMOGENES : Very likely.

SOCRATES : Yes, very likely. But still the inquiry demands our earnest attention and we must not flinch. For we should remember that if a person goes on analyzing names into words, and inquiring
e also into the elements out of which the words are formed, and keeps on always repeating this process, he who has to answer him must at last give up the inquiry in despair.

HERMOGENES : Very true.

SOCRATES: And at what point ought he to lose heart and give 422
up the inquiry? Must he not stop when he comes to the names which
are the elements of all other names and sentences? For these cannot
be supposed to be made up of other names. The word ἀγαθόν (good),
for example, is, as we were saying, a compound of ἀγαστός (admirable) and θοός (swift). And probably θοός is made up of other elements, and these again of others. But if we take a word which is b
incapable of further resolution, then we shall be right in saying that
we have at last reached a primary element, which need not be resolved
any further.

HERMOGENES: I believe you to be in the right.

SOCRATES: And suppose the names about which you are now
asking should turn out to be primary elements. Must not their truth or
law be examined according to some new method?

HERMOGENES: Very likely.

SOCRATES: Quite so, Hermogenes. All that has preceded
would lead to this conclusion. And if, as I think, the conclusion is c
true, then I shall again say to you, come and help me, that I may not
fall into some absurdity in stating the principle of primary names.

HERMOGENES: Let me hear, and I will do my best to assist you.

SOCRATES: I think that you will acknowledge with me that one
principle is applicable to all names, primary as well as secondary—
when they are regarded simply as names, there is no difference in
them.

HERMOGENES: Certainly not.

SOCRATES: All the names that we have been explaining were d
intended to indicate the nature of things.

HERMOGENES: Of course.

SOCRATES: And that this is true of the primary quite as much
as of the secondary names is implied in their being names.

HERMOGENES: Surely.

SOCRATES: But the secondary, as I conceive, derive their significance from the primary.

HERMOGENES: That is evident.

SOCRATES: Very good, but then how do the primary names
which precede analysis show the natures of things, as far as they can
be shown, which they must do, if they are to be real names? And here e
I will ask you a question. Suppose that we had no voice or tongue, and
wanted to communicate with one another. Should we not, like the
deaf and dumb, make signs with the hands and head and the rest of
the body?

HERMOGENES: There would be no choice, Socrates.

SOCRATES: We should imitate the nature of the thing; the ele- 423
vation of our hands to heaven would mean lightness and upwardness;
heaviness and downwardness would be expressed by letting them

drop to the ground; if we were describing the running of a horse, or any other animal, we should make our bodies and their gestures as like as we could to them.

HERMOGENES : I do not see that we could do anything else.

SOCRATES : We could not, for by bodily imitation only can the
b body ever express anything.

HERMOGENES : Very true.

SOCRATES : And when we want to express ourselves, either with the voice, or tongue, or mouth, the expression is simply their imitation of that which we want to express?

HERMOGENES : It must be so, I think.

SOCRATES : Then a name is a vocal imitation of that which the vocal imitator names or imitates?

HERMOGENES : I think so.

c SOCRATES : Nay, my friend, I am disposed to think that we have not reached the truth as yet.

HERMOGENES : Why not?

SOCRATES : Because if we have we shall be obliged to admit that the people who imitate sheep, or cocks, or other animals, name that which they imitate.

HERMOGENES : Quite true.

SOCRATES : Then could I have been right in what I was saying?

HERMOGENES : In my opinion, no. But I wish that you would tell me, Socrates, what sort of an imitation is a name?

SOCRATES : In the first place, I should reply, not a musical imi-
d tation, although that is also vocal, nor, again, an imitation of what music imitates; these, in my judgment, would not be naming. Let me put the matter as follows. All objects have sound and figure, and many have color?

HERMOGENES : Certainly.

SOCRATES : But the art of naming appears not to be concerned with imitations of this kind. The arts which have to do with them are music and drawing?

HERMOGENES : True.

e SOCRATES : Again, is there not an essence of each thing, just as there is a color, or sound? And is there not an essence of color and sound as well as of anything else which may be said to have an essence?

HERMOGENES : I should think so.

SOCRATES : Well, and if anyone could express the essence of each thing in letters and syllables, would he not express the nature of each thing?

424 HERMOGENES : Quite so.

SOCRATES : The musician and the painter were the two names which you gave to the two other imitators. What will this imitator be called?

HERMOGENES : I imagine, Socrates, that he must be the namer, or name giver, of whom we are in search.

SOCRATES : If this is true, then I think that we are in a condition to consider the names ῥοή (stream), ἰέναι (to go), σχέσις (retention), about which you were asking, and we may see whether the namer has grasped the nature of them in letters and syllables in such b a manner as to imitate the essence or not.

HERMOGENES : Very good.

SOCRATES : But are these the only primary names, or are there others?

HERMOGENES : There must be others.

SOCRATES : So I should expect. But how shall we further analyze them, and where does the imitator begin? Imitation of the essence is made by syllables and letters. Ought we not, therefore, first to separate the letters, just as those who are beginning rhythm c first distinguish the powers of elementary and then of compound sounds, and when they have done so, but not before, proceed to the consideration of rhythms?

HERMOGENES : Yes.

SOCRATES : Must we not begin in the same way with letters— first separating the vowels, and then the consonants and mutes, into classes, according to the received distinctions of the learned, also the semivowels, which are neither vowels nor yet mutes, and distinguishing into classes the vowels themselves? And when we have perfected d the classification of things, we shall give their names, and see whether, as in the case of letters, there are any classes to which they may be all referred, and hence we shall see their natures, and see, too, whether they have in them classes as there are in the letters. And when we have well considered all this, we shall know how to apply them to what they resemble, whether one letter is used to denote one thing, or whether there is to be an admixture of several of them, just as, in painting, the painter who wants to depict anything sometimes uses purple only, or any other color, and sometimes mixes up several e colors, as his method is when he has to paint flesh color or anything of that kind—he uses his colors as his figures appear to require them. And so, too, we shall apply letters to the expression of objects, either single letters when required, or several letters, and so we shall form syllables, as they are called, and from syllables make nouns and verbs, and thus, at last, from the combinations of nouns and verbs arrive at 425 language, large and fair and whole. And as the painter made a figure, even so shall we make speech by the art of the namer or the rhetorician, or by some other art. Not that I am literally speaking of ourselves, but I was carried away—meaning to say that this was the way in which not we, but the ancients formed language, and what they put together we must take to pieces in like manner, if we are to attain a scientific view of the whole subject. And we must see whether the b primary, and also whether the secondary elements are rightly given or not, for if they are not, the composition of them, my dear Hermogenes, will be a sorry piece of work, and in the wrong direction.

HERMOGENES : That, Socrates, I can quite believe.

SOCRATES : Well, but do you suppose that you will be able to analyze them in this way? For I am certain that I should not.

HERMOGENES : Much less am I likely to be able.

SOCRATES : Shall we leave them, then? Or shall we seek to discover, if we can, something about them, according to the measure of

c our ability, saying by way of preface, as I said before of the gods, that of the truth about them we know nothing, and do but entertain human notions of them. And in this present inquiry, let us say to ourselves, before we proceed, that the higher method is the one which we or others who would analyze language to any good purpose must follow, but under the circumstances, as men say, we must do as well as we can. What do you think?

HERMOGENES : I very much approve.

d SOCRATES : That objects should be imitated in letters and syllables, and so find expression, may appear ridiculous, Hermogenes, but it cannot be avoided—there is no better principle to which we can look for the truth of first names. Deprived of this, we must have recourse to divine help, like the tragic poets, who in any perplexity have their gods waiting in the air, and must get out of our difficulty in like fashion, by saying that 'the gods gave the first names, and therefore

e they are right.' This will be the best contrivance, or perhaps that other notion may be even better still, of deriving them from some barbarous people, for the barbarians are older than we are, or we may say that antiquity has cast a veil over them, which is the same sort of excuse

426 as the last, for all these are not reasons but only ingenious excuses for having no reasons concerning the truth of words. And yet any sort of ignorance of first or primitive names involves an ignorance of secondary words, for they can only be explained by the primary. Clearly then the professor of languages should be able to give a very lucid explanation of first names, or let him be assured he will only talk non-

b sense about the rest. Do you not suppose this to be true?

HERMOGENES : Certainly, Socrates.

SOCRATES : My first notions of original names are truly wild and ridiculous, though I have no objection to imparting them to you if you desire, and I hope that you will communicate to me in return anything better which you may have.

HERMOGENES : Fear not. I will do my best.

c SOCRATES : In the first place, the letter ρ appears to me to be the general instrument expressing all motion (κίνησις). But I have not yet explained the meaning of this latter word, which is just ἴεσις (going), for the letter η was not in use among the ancients, who only employed ε, and the root is κίειν, which is a foreign form, the same as ἰέναι. And the old word κίνησις will be correctly given as ἵεσις in corresponding modern letters. Assuming this foreign root κίειν, and allowing for the change of the η and the insertion of the ν, we have κίνησις, which should have been κιείνησις or εἶσις, and στᾶσις is the d negative of ἰέναι (or εἶσις), and has been improved into στάσις. Now the letter ρ, as I was saying, appeared to the imposer of names an excellent instrument for the expression of motion, and he frequently uses the letter for this purpose. For example, in the actual words ῥεῖν and ῥοή he represents motion by ρ—also in the words τρόμος (trembling), τραχύς (rugged), and again, in words such as κρούειν (strike), θραύειν (crush), ἐρείκειν (bruise), θρύπτειν (break), κερματίζειν (crumble), ῥυμβεῖν (whirl). Of all these sorts of movements he generally finds an expression in the letter ρ, because, as I imagine, he had observed that the tongue was most agitated and least at rest in the pronunciation of this letter, which he therefore used in order to express motion, just as by the letter ι he expresses the subtle elements which pass through all things. This is why he uses the letter ι as imitative of motion, ἰέναι, ἵεσθαι. And there is another class of letters, φ, ψ, σ, and ζ, of which 427 the pronunciation is accompanied by great expenditure of breath; these are used in the imitation of such notions as ψυχρόν (shivering), ζέον (seething), σείεσθαι (to be shaken), σεισμός (shock), and are always introduced by the giver of names when he wants to imitate what is φυσῶδες (windy). He seems to have thought that the closing and pressure of the tongue in the utterance of δ and τ were ex- b pressive of binding and rest in a place. He further observed the liquid movement of λ, in the pronunciation of which the tongue slips, and in this he found the expression of smoothness, as in λεῖος (level), and in the word ὀλισθάνειν (to slip) itself, λιπαρόν (sleek), in the word κολλῶδες (gluey), and the like; the heavier sound of γ detained the slipping tongue, and the union of the two gave the notion of a glutinous clammy nature, as in γλίσχρος, γλυκύς, γλοιῶδες. The ν he observed to be sounded from within, and therefore to have a notion of c inwardness; hence he introduced the sound in ἔνδον and ἐντός; α he assigned to the expression of size, and η of length, because they are great letters; o was the sign of roundness, and therefore there is plenty of o mixed up in the word γογγύλον (round). Thus did the legislator, reducing all things into letters and syllables, and impressing on them names and signs, and out of them by imitation compounding other signs. That is my view, Hermogenes, of the truth of names, but I d should like to hear what Cratylus has more to say.

HERMOGENES: But, Socrates, as I was telling you before, Cratylus mystifies me; he says that there is a fitness of names, but he never explains what is this fitness, so that I cannot tell whether his obscurity is intended or not. Tell me now, Cratylus, here in the pres- e ence of Socrates, do you agree in what Socrates has been saying about names, or have you something better of your own? And if you have,

462 PLATO: COLLECTED DIALOGUES

tell me what your view is, and then you will either learn of Socrates, or Socrates and I will learn of you.

CRATYLUS: Well, but surely, Hermogenes, you do not suppose that you can learn, or I explain, any subject of importance all in a moment—at any rate, not such a subject as language, which is, perhaps, the very greatest of all.

HERMOGENES: No, indeed, but, as Hesiod says, and I agree with him, 'to add little to little'[8] is worth while. And, therefore, if you think that you can add anything at all, however small, to our knowledge, take a little trouble and oblige Socrates, and me too, who certainly have a claim upon you.

SOCRATES: I am by no means positive, Cratylus, in the view which Hermogenes and myself have worked out, and therefore do not hesitate to say what you think, which if it be better than my own view I shall gladly accept. And I should not be at all surprised to find that you have found some better notion. For you have evidently reflected on these matters and have had teachers, and if you have really a better theory of the truth of names, you may count me in the number of your disciples.

CRATYLUS: You are right, Socrates, in saying that I have made a study of these matters, and I might possibly convert you into a disciple. But I fear that the opposite is more probable, and I already find myself moved to say to you what Achilles in the 'Prayers' says to Ajax,

Illustrious Ajax, son of Telamon, lord of the people,
You appear to have spoken in all things much to my mind.[9]

And you, Socrates, appear to me to be an oracle, and to give answers much to my mind, whether you are inspired by Euthyphro, or whether some Muse may have long been an inhabitant of your breast, unconsciously to yourself.

SOCRATES: Excellent Cratylus, I have long been wondering at my own wisdom. I cannot trust myself. And I think that I ought to stop and ask myself, What am I saying? For there is nothing worse than self-deception—when the deceiver is always at home and always with you—it is quite terrible, and therefore I ought often to retrace my steps and endeavor to 'look fore and aft,'[10] in the words of the aforesaid Homer. And now let me see, where are we? Have we not been saying that the correct name indicates the nature of the thing? Has this proposition been sufficiently proved?

CRATYLUS: Yes, Socrates, what you say, as I am disposed to think, is quite true.

SOCRATES: Names, then, are given in order to instruct?

[8] *Works and Days* 9.359.   [9] *Iliad* 9.644 sq.
[10] *Iliad* 1.343, 3.109.

CRATYLUS: Certainly.

SOCRATES: And naming is an art, and has artificers?

CRATYLUS: Yes.

SOCRATES: And who are they?

CRATYLUS: The legislators, of whom you spoke at first.   429

SOCRATES: And does this art grow up among men like other arts? Let me explain what I mean. Of painters, some are better and some worse?

CRATYLUS: Yes.

SOCRATES: The better painters execute their works, I mean their figures, better, and the worse execute them worse. And of builders also, the better sort build fairer houses, and the worse build them worse.

CRATYLUS: True.

SOCRATES: And among legislators, there are some who do their b work better and some worse?

CRATYLUS: No, there I do not agree with you.

SOCRATES: Then you do not think that some laws are better and others worse?

CRATYLUS: No, indeed.

SOCRATES: Or that one name is better than another?

CRATYLUS: Certainly not.

SOCRATES: Then all names are rightly imposed?

CRATYLUS: Yes, if they are names at all.

SOCRATES: Well, what do you say to the name of our friend Hermogenes, which was mentioned before—assuming that he has c nothing of the nature of Hermes in him, shall we say that this is a wrong name, or not his name at all?

CRATYLUS: I should reply that Hermogenes is not his name at all, but only appears to be his, and is really the name of somebody else, who has the nature which corresponds to it.

SOCRATES: And if a man were to call him Hermogenes, would he not be even speaking falsely? For there may be a doubt whether you can call him Hermogenes, if he is not.

CRATYLUS: What do you mean?

SOCRATES: Are you maintaining that falsehood is impossible? d For if this is your meaning I should answer that there have been plenty of liars in all ages.

CRATYLUS: Why, Socrates, how can a man say that which is not—say something and yet say nothing? For is not falsehood saying the thing which is not?

SOCRATES: Your argument, friend, is too subtle for a man of my age. But I should like to know whether you are one of those philosophers who think that falsehood may be spoken but not said? e

CRATYLUS: Neither spoken nor said.

SOCRATES: Nor uttered nor addressed? For example, if a person, saluting you in a foreign country, were to take your hand and say, Hail, Athenian stranger, Hermogenes, son of Smicrion—these words, whether spoken, said, uttered, or addressed, would have no application to you but only to our friend Hermogenes, or perhaps to nobody at all?

CRATYLUS : In my opinion, Socrates, the speaker would only be talking nonsense.

430   SOCRATES : Well, but that will be quite enough for me, if you will tell me whether the nonsense would be true or false, or partly true and partly false, which is all that I want to know.

CRATYLUS : I should say that he would be putting himself in motion to no purpose, and that his words would be an unmeaning sound like the noise of hammering at a brazen pot.

SOCRATES : But let us see, Cratylus, whether we cannot find a meeting point, for you would admit that the name is not the same with the thing named?

CRATYLUS : I should.

b   SOCRATES : And would you further acknowledge that the name is an imitation of the thing?

CRATYLUS : Certainly.

SOCRATES : And you would say that pictures are also imitations of things, but in another way?

CRATYLUS : Yes.

SOCRATES : I believe you may be right, but I do not rightly understand you. Please to say, then, whether both sorts of imitation— I mean both pictures or words—are not equally attributable and applicable to the things of which they are the imitation.

c   CRATYLUS : They are.

SOCRATES : First look at the matter thus. You may attribute the likeness of the man to the man, and of the woman to the woman, and so on?

CRATYLUS : Certainly.

SOCRATES : And conversely you may attribute the likeness of the man to the woman, and of the woman to the man?

CRATYLUS : Very true.

SOCRATES : And are both modes of assigning them right, or only the first?

CRATYLUS : Only the first.

SOCRATES : That is to say, the mode of assignment which attributes to each that which belongs to it and is like it?

CRATYLUS : That is my view.

d   SOCRATES : Now then, as I am desirous that we being friends should have a good understanding about the argument, let me state my view to you. The first mode of assignment, whether applied to figures or to names, I call right, and when applied to names only, true as well as right, and the other mode of giving and assigning the name which is unlike, I call wrong, and in the case of names, false as well as wrong.

CRATYLUS: That may be true, Socrates, in the case of pictures; they may be wrongly assigned. But not in the case of names —they must be always right. e

SOCRATES: Why, what is the difference? May I not go to a man and say to him, This is your picture, showing him his own likeness, or perhaps the likeness of a woman, and when I say show, I mean bring before the sense of sight.

CRATYLUS: Certainly.

SOCRATES: And may I not go to him again, and say, This is your name? For the name, like the picture, is an imitation. May I not 431 say to him, This is your name? And may I not then bring to his sense of hearing the imitation of himself, when I say, This is a man, or of a female of the human species, when I say, This is a woman, as the case may be? Is not all that quite possible?

CRATYLUS: I would fain agree with you, Socrates, and therefore I say, granted.

SOCRATES: That is very good of you, if I am right, which need hardly be disputed at present. But if I can assign names as well as pictures to objects, the right assignment of them we may call truth, and b the wrong assignment of them falsehood. Now if there be such a wrong assignment of names, there may also be a wrong or inappropriate assignment of verbs, and if of names and verbs then of the sentences, which are made up of them. What do you say, Craty- c lus?

CRATYLUS: I agree, and think that what you say is very true.

SOCRATES: And further, primitive nouns may be compared to pictures, and in pictures you may either give all the appropriate colors and figures, or you may not give them all—some may be wanting— or there may be too many or too much of them—may there not?

CRATYLUS: Very true.

SOCRATES: And he who gives all gives a perfect picture or figure, and he who takes away or adds also gives a picture or figure, but not a good one. d

CRATYLUS: Yes.

SOCRATES: In like manner, he who by syllables and letters imitates the nature of things, if he gives all that is appropriate will produce a good image, or in other words a name, but if he subtracts or perhaps adds a little, he will make an image but not a good one; whence I infer that some names are well and others ill made.

CRATYLUS: That is true.

SOCRATES: Then the artist of names may be sometimes good, e or he may be bad?

CRATYLUS: Yes.

SOCRATES: And this artist of names is called the legislator?

CRATYLUS: Yes.

SOCRATES: Then like other artists the legislator may be good or he may be bad; it must surely be so if our former admissions hold good.

CRATYLUS: Very true, Socrates, but the case of language, you see, is different. For when by the help of grammar we assign the letters
432 α or β, or any other letters, to a certain name, then, if we add, or subtract, or misplace a letter, the name which is written is not only written wrongly, but not written at all, and in any of these cases becomes other than a name.

SOCRATES: But I doubt whether your view is altogether correct, Cratylus.

CRATYLUS: How so?

SOCRATES: I believe that what you say may be true about numbers, which must be just what they are, or not be at all. For example, the number ten at once becomes other than ten if a unit be added or
b subtracted, and so of any other number, but this does not apply to that which is qualitative or to anything which is represented under an image. I should say rather that the image, if expressing in every point the entire reality, would no longer be an image. Let us suppose the existence of two objects. One of them shall be Cratylus, and the other the image of Cratylus, and we will suppose, further, that some god makes not only a representation such as a painter would make of your outward form and color, but also creates an inward organization like yours, having the same warmth and softness, and into this infuses
c motion, and soul, and mind, such as you have, and in a word copies all your qualities, and places them by you in another form. Would you say that this was Cratylus and the image of Cratylus, or that there were two Cratyluses?

CRATYLUS: I should say that there were two Cratyluses.

SOCRATES: Then you see, my friend, that we must find some other principle of truth in images, and also in names, and not insist that an image is no longer an image when something is added or sub-
d tracted. Do you not perceive that images are very far from having qualities which are the exact counterpart of the realities which they represent?

CRATYLUS: Yes, I see.

SOCRATES: But then how ridiculous would be the effect of names on things, if they were exactly the same with them! For they would be the doubles of them, and no one would be able to determine which were the names and which were the realities.

CRATYLUS: Quite true.

SOCRATES: Then fear not, but have the courage to admit that
e one name may be correctly and another incorrectly given, and do not insist that the name shall be exactly the same with the thing, but allow the occasional substitution of a wrong letter, and if of a letter also

of a noun in a sentence, and if of a noun in a sentence also of a sentence which is not appropriate to the matter, and acknowledge that the thing may be named, and described, so long as the general character of the thing which you are describing is retained. And this, as you will remember, was remarked by Hermogenes and myself in the particular instance of the names of the letters.   433

CRATYLUS: Yes, I remember.

SOCRATES: Good, and when the general character is preserved, even if some of the proper letters are wanting, still the thing is signified—well, if all the letters are given, not well, when only a few of them are given. I think that we had better admit this, lest we be punished like travelers in Aegina who wander about the street late at night, and be likewise told by truth herself that we have arrived too b late. Or if not, you must find out some new notion of correctness of names, and no longer maintain that a name is the expression of a thing in letters or syllables, for if you say both, you will be inconsistent with yourself.

CRATYLUS: I quite acknowledge, Socrates, what you say to be very reasonable.

SOCRATES: Then as we are agreed thus far, let us ask ourselves whether a name rightly imposed ought not to have the proper letters.

CRATYLUS: Yes.

SOCRATES: And the proper letters are those which are like the c things?

CRATYLUS: Yes.

SOCRATES: Enough then of names which are rightly given. And in names which are incorrectly given, the greater part may be supposed to be made up of proper and similar letters, or there would be no likeness, but there will be likewise a part which is improper and spoils the beauty and formation of the word. You would admit that?

CRATYLUS: There would be no use, Socrates, in my quarreling with you, since I cannot be satisfied that a name which is incorrectly given is a name at all.

SOCRATES: Do you admit a name to be the representation of a d thing?

CRATYLUS: Yes, I do.

SOCRATES: But do you not allow that some nouns are primitive, and some derived?

CRATYLUS: Yes, I do.

SOCRATES: Then if you admit that primitive or first nouns are representations of things, is there any better way of framing representations than by assimilating them to the objects as much as you can? Or do you prefer the notion of Hermogenes and of many others, e who say that names are conventional, and have a meaning to those who have agreed about them, and who have previous knowledge of the things intended by them, and that convention is the only principle? And whether you abide by our present convention, or make a new and opposite one, according to which you call small great and great small—that, they would say, makes no difference, if you are only agreed. Which of these two notions do you prefer?

434   CRATYLUS : Representation by likeness, Socrates, is infinitely better than representation by any chance sign.

SOCRATES : Very good, but if the name is to be like the thing, the letters out of which the first names are composed must also be like things. Returning to the image of the picture, I would ask how anyone could ever compose a picture which would be like anything at all, if there were not pigments in nature which resembled the things
b imitated, and out of which the picture is composed.

CRATYLUS : Impossible.

SOCRATES : No more could names ever resemble any actually existing thing, unless the original elements of which they are compounded bore some degree of resemblance to the objects of which the names are the imitation. And the original elements are letters?

CRATYLUS : Yes.

SOCRATES : Let me now invite you to consider what Her-
c mogenes and I were saying about sounds. Do you agree with me that the letter ρ is expressive of rapidity, motion, and hardness? Were we right or wrong in saying so?

CRATYLUS : I should say that you were right.

SOCRATES : And that λ was expressive of smoothness, and softness, and the like?

CRATYLUS : There again you were right.

SOCRATES : And yet, as you are aware, that which is called by us σκληρότης, is by the Eretrians called σκληρότηρ.

CRATYLUS : Very true.

SOCRATES : But are the letters ρ and σ equivalents, and is there the same significance to them in the termination ρ, which there is to us in σ, or is there no significance to one of us?
d   CRATYLUS : Nay, surely there is a significance to both of us.

SOCRATES : In so far as they are like, or in so far as they are unlike?

CRATYLUS : In so far as they are like.

SOCRATES : Are they altogether alike?

CRATYLUS : Yes, for the purpose of expressing motion.

SOCRATES : And what do you say of the insertion of the λ? For that is expressive not of hardness but of softness.

CRATYLUS : Why, perhaps the letter λ is wrongly inserted, Socrates, and should be altered into ρ, as you were saying to Hermogenes, and in my opinion rightly, when you spoke of adding and subtracting letters upon occasion.

SOCRATES: Good, but still the word is intelligible to both of us. e
When I say σκληρός (hard), you know what I mean.

CRATYLUS: Yes, my dear friend, and the explanation of that is custom.

SOCRATES: And what is custom but convention? When I utter a sound which I understand, and you know that I understand the meaning of the sound—this is what you are saying?

CRATYLUS: Yes.

SOCRATES: And if when I speak you know my meaning, there is an indication given by me to you?

CRATYLUS: Yes.

SOCRATES: This indication of my meaning may proceed from unlike as well as from like, for example, in the λ of σκληρότης. But if this is true, then you have made a convention with yourself, and the correctness of a name turns out to be convention, since letters which are unlike are indicative equally with those which are like, if they are sanctioned by custom and convention. And even supposing that you distinguish custom from convention ever so much, still you b must say that the signification of words is given by custom and not by likeness, for custom may indicate by the unlike as well as by the like. But as we are agreed thus far, Cratylus, for I shall assume that your silence gives consent, then custom and convention must be supposed to contribute to the indication of our thoughts. For suppose we take the instance of number. How can you ever imagine, my good friend, that you will find names resembling every individual number, unless you allow that which you term convention and agreement to have authority in determining the correctness of names? I quite c agree with you that words should as far as possible resemble things, but I fear that this dragging in of resemblance, as Hermogenes says, is a shabby thing, which has to be supplemented by the mechanical aid of convention with a view to correctness. For I believe that if we could always, or almost always, use likenesses, which are perfectly appropriate, this would be the most perfect state of language, as the opposite is the most imperfect. But let me ask you, what is the d force of names, and what is the use of them?

CRATYLUS: The use of names, Socrates, as I should imagine, is to inform. The simple truth is that he who knows names knows also the things which are expressed by them.

SOCRATES: I suppose you mean to say, Cratylus, that as the name is, so also is the thing, and that he who knows the one will also know the other, because they are similars, and all similars fall under e the same art or science, and therefore you would say that he who knows names will also know things.

CRATYLUS: That is precisely what I mean.

SOCRATES: But let us consider what is the nature of this

information about things which, according to you, is given us by
names. Is it the best sort of information? Or is there any other? What
do you say?

436   CRATYLUS : I believe that to be both the only and the best sort
of information about them—there can be no other.

SOCRATES : But do you believe that in the discovery of them
he who discovers the names discovers also the things, or is this only
the method of instruction, and is there some other method of inquiry
and discovery?

CRATYLUS : I certainly believe that the methods of inquiry and
discovery are of the same nature as instruction.

SOCRATES : Well, but do you not see, Cratylus, that he who fol-
b lows names in the search after things, and analyzes their meaning, is
in great danger of being deceived?

CRATYLUS : How so?

SOCRATES : Why clearly he who first gave names gave them according to his conception of the things which they signified—did
he not?

CRATYLUS : True.

SOCRATES : And if his conception was erroneous, and he gave
names according to his conception, in what position shall we who are
his followers find ourselves? Shall we not be deceived by him?

CRATYLUS : But, Socrates, am I not right in thinking that he
c must surely have known, or else, as I was saying, his names would not
be names at all? And you have a clear proof that he has not missed
the truth, and the proof is—that he is perfectly consistent. Did you
ever observe in speaking that all the words which you utter have a
common character and purpose?

SOCRATES : But that, friend Cratylus, is no answer. For if he
did begin in error, he may have forced the remainder into agreement
d with the original error and with himself; there would be nothing
strange in this, any more than in geometric diagrams, which have
often a slight and invisible flaw in the first part of the process, and are
consistently mistaken in the long deductions which follow. And
this is the reason why every man should expend his chief thought and
attention on the consideration of his first principles—are they or are
they not rightly laid down? And when he has duly sifted them, all the
e rest will follow. Now I should be astonished to find that names are
really consistent. And here let us revert to our former discussion. Were
we not saying that all things are in motion and progress and flux,
and that this idea of motion is expressed by names? Do you not conceive that to be the meaning of them?

CRATYLUS : Yes, that is assuredly their meaning, and the true
meaning.

437   SOCRATES : Let us revert to ἐπιστήμη (knowledge), and observe

how ambiguous this word is, seeming rather to signify stopping the soul at things than going round with them, and therefore we should leave the beginning as at present, and not reject the ε, but make an insertion of an ι instead of an ε (not πιστήμη, but ἐπιστήμη). Take another example. Βέβαιον (sure) is clearly the expression of station and position, and not of motion. Again, the word ἱστορία (inquiry) bears b upon the face of it the stopping (ἱστάναι) of the stream, and the word πιστόν (faithful) certainly indicates cessation of motion; then, again, μνήμη (memory), as anyone may see, expresses rest in the soul, and not motion. Moreover, words such as ἁμαρτία and συμφορά, which have a bad sense, viewed in the light of their etymologies will be the same as σύνεσις and ἐπιστήμη and other words which have a good sense (cf. ὁμαρτεῖν, συνιέναι, ἔπεσθαι, συμφέρεσθαι). And much the same may be said of ἀμαθία and ἀκολασία, for ἀμαθία (ignorance) may be explained as ἡ ἅμα θεῷ ἰόντος πορεία (the progress of one who goes with God), c and ἀκολασία (unrestraint) as ἡ ἀκολουθία τοῖς πράγμασιν (movement in company with things). Thus the names which in these instances we find to have the worst sense will turn out to be framed on the same principle as those which have the best. And anyone I believe who would take the trouble might find many other examples in which the giver of names indicates, not that things are in motion or progress, but that they are at rest, which is the opposite of motion.

CRATYLUS: Yes, Socrates, but observe, the greater number ex- d press motion.

SOCRATES: What of that, Cratylus? Are we to count them like votes? And is correctness of names the voice of the majority? Are we to say of whichever sort there are most, those are the true ones?

CRATYLUS: No, that is not reasonable.

SOCRATES: Certainly not. But let us have done with this question and proceed to another, about which I should like to know whether you think with me. Were we not lately acknowledging that e the first givers of names in states, both Hellenic and barbarous, were the legislators, and that the art which gave names was the art of the legislator?

CRATYLUS: Quite true.

SOCRATES: Tell me, then, did the first legislators, who were the givers of the first names, know or not know the things which they named?

CRATYLUS: They must have known, Socrates.

SOCRATES: Why, yes, friend Cratylus, they could hardly have 438 been ignorant.

CRATYLUS: I should say not.

SOCRATES: Let us return to the point from which we digressed. You were saying, if you remember, that he who gave names must have known the things which he named. Are you still of that opinion?

CRATYLUS: I am.

SOCRATES: And would you say that the giver of the first names had also a knowledge of the things which he named?

CRATYLUS: I should.

SOCRATES: But how could he have learned or discovered things b from names if the primitive names were not yet given? For, if we are correct in our view, the only way of learning and discovering things is either to discover names for ourselves or to learn them from others.

CRATYLUS: I think that there is a good deal in what you say, Socrates.

SOCRATES: But if things are only to be known through names, how can we suppose that the givers of names had knowledge, or were legislators, before there were names at all, and therefore before they could have known them?

c   CRATYLUS: I believe, Socrates, the true account of the matter to be that a power more than human gave things their first names, and that the names which are thus given are necessarily their true names.

SOCRATES: Then how came the giver of the names, if he was an inspired being or god, to contradict himself? For were we not saying just now that he made some names expressive of rest and others of motion? Were we mistaken?

CRATYLUS: But I suppose one of the two not to be names at all.

SOCRATES: And which, then, did he make, my good friend— those which are expressive of rest, or those which are expressive of motion? This is a point which, as I said before, cannot be determined by counting them.

d   CRATYLUS: No, not in that way, Socrates.

SOCRATES: But if this is a battle of names, some of them asserting that they are like the truth, others contending that *they* are, how or by what criterion are we to decide between them? For there are no other names to which appeal can be made, but obviously recourse must be had to another standard which, without employing names, will make clear which of the two are right, and this must be a standard which shows the truth of things.

e   CRATYLUS: I agree.

SOCRATES: But if that is true, Cratylus, then I suppose that things may be known without names?

CRATYLUS: Clearly.

SOCRATES: But how would you expect to know them? What other way can there be of knowing them, except the true and natural way, through their affinities, when they are akin to each other, and through themselves? For that which is other and different from them must signify something other and different from them.

CRATYLUS: What you are saying is, I think, true.

439   SOCRATES: Well, but reflect. Have we not several times ac-

knowledged that names rightly given are the likenesses and images of the things which they name?

CRATYLUS: Yes.

SOCRATES: Let us suppose that to any extent you please you can learn things through the medium of names, and suppose also that you can learn them from the things themselves. Which is likely to be the nobler and clearer way—to learn of the image, whether the image and the truth of which the image is the expression have been rightly conceived, or to learn of the truth whether the truth and the b image of it have been duly executed?

CRATYLUS: I should say that we must learn of the truth.

SOCRATES: How real existence is to be studied or discovered is, I suspect, beyond you and me. But we may admit so much, that the knowledge of things is not to be derived from names. No, they must be studied and investigated in themselves.

CRATYLUS: Clearly, Socrates.

SOCRATES: There is another point. I should not like us to be imposed upon by the appearance of such a multitude of names, all c tending in the same direction. I myself do not deny that the givers of names did really give them under the idea that all things were in motion and flux, which was their sincere but, I think, mistaken opinion. And having fallen into a kind of whirlpool themselves, they are carried round, and want to drag us in after them. There is a matter, master Cratylus, about which I often dream, and should like to ask your opinion. Tell me whether there is or is not any absolute beauty or good, or any other absolute existence.   d

CRATYLUS: Certainly, Socrates, I think so.

SOCRATES: Then let us seek the true beauty, not asking whether a face is fair, or anything of that sort, for all such things appear to be in a flux, but let us ask whether the true beauty is not always beautiful.

CRATYLUS: Certainly.

SOCRATES: And can we rightly speak of a beauty which is al- e ways passing away, and is first this and then that? Must not the same thing be born and retire and vanish while the word is in our mouths?

CRATYLUS: Undoubtedly.

SOCRATES: Then how can that be a real thing which is never in the same state? For obviously things which are the same cannot change while they remain the same, and if they are always the same and in the same state, and never depart from their original form, they can never change or be moved.

CRATYLUS: Certainly they cannot.

SOCRATES: Nor yet can they be known by anyone, for at the 440 moment that the observer approaches, then they become other and of another nature, so that you cannot get any further in knowing their nature or state, for you cannot know that which has no state.

CRATYLUS : True.

SOCRATES : Nor can we reasonably say, Cratylus, that there is knowledge at all, if everything is in a state of transition and there is nothing abiding. For knowledge too cannot continue to be knowledge b unless continuing always to abide and exist. But if the very nature of knowledge changes, at the time when the change occurs there will be no knowledge, and if the transition is always going on, there will always be no knowledge, and, according to this view, there will be no one to know and nothing to be known. But if that which knows and that which is known exist ever, and the beautiful and the good and every other thing also exist, then I do not think that they can resemble a process or flux, as we were just now supposing. Whether c there is this eternal nature in things, or whether the truth is what Heraclitus and his followers and many others say, is a question hard to determine, and no man of sense will like to put himself or the education of his mind in the power of names. Neither will he so far trust names or the givers of names as to be confident in any knowledge which condemns himself and other existences to an unhealthy state of unreality; he will not believe that all things leak like a pot, or imagine that the world is a man who has a running at the nose. This may d be true, Cratylus, but is also very likely to be untrue, and therefore I would not have you be too easily persuaded of it. Reflect well and like a man, and do not easily accept such a doctrine, for you are young and of an age to learn. And when you have found the truth, come and tell me.

CRATYLUS : I will do as you say, though I can assure you, Socrates, that I have been considering the matter already, and the result e of a great deal of trouble and consideration is that I incline to Heraclitus.

SOCRATES : Then, another day, my friend, when you come back, you shall give me a lesson, but at present, go into the country, as you are intending, and Hermogenes shall set you on your way.

CRATYLUS : Very good, Socrates. I hope, however, that you will continue to think about these things yourself.

PHAEDRUS

This is one of the greatest of the dialogues. It should be read with the Symposium. The two together give Plato's idea of love. The Phaedrus is a conversation, not a discourse or a succession of questions and answers directed to a single subject. Socrates and Phaedrus take a walk into the country and talk about whatever occurs to them, but they are Athenians and one of them is Socrates and their notion—and Plato's—of how to pass the time pleasantly while walking is something quite different from our own.

Love is the first matter they take up. Phaedrus has with him a piece of writing about it which he greatly admires and reads to Socrates who objects to it as making love chiefly a physical desire. To him it is an impulse full of beauty and goodness, a kind of divine madness which lifts the soul up and can enable it to enter the path which leads to the truth. The first movement to philosophy, the impulse to seek what is higher—in Plato's phrase, "the beyond"—comes from falling in love with visible, physical beauty.

It is really impossible for us to grasp what beauty meant to the Greeks. It was a mighty power exercising a profound influence upon their daily lives. The greatest leader Thebes produced was said to have told his countrymen that they would never conquer Athens until they had brought the Parthenon to Thebes. Any Greek would understand that. Of course the Thebans would be better men, more courageous, wiser, too, with that beauty always before them. In the Republic, Plato's philosopher-rulers must be graceful as well as wise. Socrates gives Phaedrus a description of what a lover feels which leaves our love poetry far behind. To fall truly in love starts a man on the path upward to where love is satisfied in the perfect beauty of the truth.

The stress in the Phaedrus is on visible beauty, but the reader of Plato must always remember that Socrates, the most beloved and the most lovely of all, was completely without it. Again and again his snub nose is mentioned, his protruding eyes, and so on. He had "no form nor comeliness that we should desire him." His wonderful beauty was within.

The last part of the dialogue is about the inferiority of books and writing in general to pure thought and to discussion concerned only with seeking for knowledge, not with putting it into a shape accept-

*able to others, the inferiority of reading to reasoning and of rhet-
oric to dialectic. The best books do no more than remind us of what
we know. The only truly valuable way to write is to inscribe justice
and beauty and goodness upon a soul.*

---

227   SOCRATES: Where do you come from, Phaedrus my friend, and
where are you going?

PHAEDRUS: I've been with Lysias, Socrates, the son of Cephalus, and I'm off for a walk outside the wall, after a long morning's
sitting there. On the instructions of our common friend Acumenus
I take my walks on the open roads; he tells me that is more invigorat-
ing than walking in the colonnades.

b   SOCRATES: Yes, he's right in saying so. But Lysias, I take it, was
in town.

PHAEDRUS: Yes, staying with Epicrates, in that house where
Morychus used to live, close to the temple of Olympian Zeus.

SOCRATES: Well, how were you occupied? No doubt Lysias was
giving the company a feast of eloquence.

PHAEDRUS: I'll tell you, if you can spare time to come along
with me and listen.

SOCRATES: What? Don't you realize that I should account it,
in Pindar's words, 'above all business' [1] to hear how you and Lysias
passed your time?

c   PHAEDRUS: Lead on then.

SOCRATES: Please tell me.

PHAEDRUS: As a matter of fact the topic is appropriate for your
ears, Socrates, for the discussion that engaged us may be said to have
concerned love. Lysias, you must know, has described how a handsome boy was tempted, but not by a lover—that's the clever part of it.
He maintains that surrender should be to one who is not in love
rather than to one who is.

SOCRATES: Splendid! I wish he would add that it should be
to a poor man rather than a rich one, an elderly man rather than a
d   young one, and, in general, to ordinary folk like myself. What an attractive democratic theory that would be! However, I'm so eager to
hear about it that I vow I won't leave you even if you extend your

---

[1] *Isthmionikai* i.i.

From *Plato's Phaedrus*, translated with introduction and commentary by
R. Hackforth (Cambridge and New York, 1952).

walk as far as Megara, up to the walls and back again as recommended by Herodicus.

PHAEDRUS: What do you mean, my good man? Do you expect 228 an amateur like me to repeat by heart, without disgracing its author, the work of the ablest writer of our day, which it took him weeks to compose at his leisure? That is far beyond me, though I'd rather have had the ability than come into a fortune.

SOCRATES: I know my Phaedrus. Yes indeed, I'm as sure of him as of my own identity. I'm certain that the said Phaedrus didn't listen just once to Lysias' speech; time after time he asked him to repeat it to him, and Lysias was very ready to comply. Even that would b not content him. In the end he secured the script and began poring over the parts that specially attracted him, and thus engaged he sat there the whole morning, until he grew weary and went for a walk. Upon my word, I believe he had learned the whole speech by heart, unless it was a very long one, and he was going into the country to practice declaiming it. Then he fell in with one who has a passion for listening to discourses, and when he saw him he was delighted to think he would have someone to share his frenzied enthusiasm; so he asked him to join him on his way. But when the lover of discourses c begged him to discourse, he became difficult, pretending he didn't want to, though he meant to do so ultimately, even if he had to force himself on a reluctant listener. So beg him, Phaedrus, to do straightway what he will soon do in any case.

PHAEDRUS: Doubtless it will be much my best course to deliver myself to the best of my ability, for I fancy you will never let me go until I have given you some sort of a speech.

SOCRATES: You are quite right about my intention.

PHAEDRUS: Then here's what I will do. It really is perfectly d true, Socrates, that I have not got the words by heart, but I will sketch the general purport of the several points in which the lover and the nonlover were contrasted, taking them in order one by one, and beginning at the beginning.

SOCRATES: Very well, my dear fellow, but you must first show me what it is that you have in your left hand under your cloak, for I surmise that it is the actual discourse. If that is so, let me assure you of this, that much as I love you I am not altogether inclined to let e you practice your oratory on me when Lysias himself is here present. Come now, show it me.

PHAEDRUS: Say no more, Socrates; you have dashed my hope of trying out my powers on you. Well, where would you like us to sit for our reading?

SOCRATES: Let us turn off here and walk along the Ilissus; 229 then we can sit down in any quiet spot you choose.

PHAEDRUS: It's convenient, isn't it, that I chance to be barefoot; you of course always are so. There will be no trouble in wading

in the stream, which is especially delightful at this hour of a summer's day.

SOCRATES: Lead on then, and look out for a place to sit down.

PHAEDRUS: You see that tall plane tree over there?

SOCRATES: To be sure.

b   PHAEDRUS: There's some shade, and a little breeze, and grass
to sit down on, or lie down if we like.

SOCRATES: Then make for it.

PHAEDRUS: Tell me, Socrates, isn't it somewhere about here
that they say Boreas seized Orithyia from the river?

SOCRATES: Yes, that is the story.

PHAEDRUS: Was this the actual spot? Certainly the water
looks charmingly pure and clear; it's just the place for girls to be playing beside the stream.

c   SOCRATES: No, it was about a quarter of a mile lower down,
where you cross to the sanctuary of Agra; there is, I believe, an altar
dedicated to Boreas close by.

PHAEDRUS: I have never really noticed it, but pray tell me,
Socrates, do you believe that story to be true?

SOCRATES: I should be quite in the fashion if I disbelieved it,
as the men of science do. I might proceed to give a scientific account
of how the maiden, while at play with Pharmacia, was blown by a
gust of Boreas down from the rocks hard by, and having thus met her
d death was said to have been seized by Boreas, though it may have
happened on the Areopagus, according to another version of the occurrence. For my part, Phaedrus, I regard such theories as no doubt
attractive, but as the invention of clever, industrious people who are
not exactly to be envied, for the simple reason that they must then go
on and tell us the real truth about the appearance of centaurs and the
Chimera, not to mention a whole host of such creatures, Gorgons and
e Pegasuses and countless other remarkable monsters of legend flock-
ing in on them. If our skeptic, with his somewhat crude science, means
to reduce every one of them to the standard of probability, he'll need
a deal of time for it. I myself have certainly no time for the business,
230 and I'll tell you why, my friend. I can't as yet 'know myself,' as the
inscription at Delphi enjoins, and so long as that ignorance remains
it seems to me ridiculous to inquire into extraneous matters. Consequently I don't bother about such things, but accept the current beliefs
about them, and direct my inquiries, as I have just said, rather to myself, to discover whether I really am a more complex creature and
more puffed up with pride than Typhon, or a simpler, gentler being
whom heaven has blessed with a quiet, un-Typhonic nature. By the
b way, isn't this the tree we were making for?

PHAEDRUS: Yes, that's the one.

SOCRATES: Upon my word, a delightful resting place, with this
tall, spreading plane, and a lovely shade from the high branches of

the *agnos*. Now that it's in full flower, it will make the place ever so fragrant. And what a lovely stream under the plane tree, and how cool to the feet! Judging by the statuettes and images I should say it's consecrated to Achelous and some of the nymphs. And then too, c isn't the freshness of the air most welcome and pleasant, and the shrill summery music of the cicada choir! And as crowning delight the grass, thick enough on a gentle slope to rest your head on most comfortably. In fact, my dear Phaedrus, you have been the stranger's perfect guide.

PHAEDRUS: Whereas you, my excellent friend, strike me as the oddest of men. Anyone would take you, as you say, for a stranger being shown the country by a guide instead of a native—never leav- d ing town to cross the frontier nor even, I believe, so much as setting foot outside the walls.

SOCRATES: You must forgive me, dear friend; I'm a lover of learning, and trees and open country won't teach me anything, whereas men in the town do. Yet you seem to have discovered a recipe for getting me out. A hungry animal can be driven by dangling a carrot or a bit of greenstuff in front of it; similarly if you proffer me volumes of speeches I don't doubt you can cart me all round Attica, and anywhere else you please. Anyhow, now that we've got here I pro- e pose for the time being to lie down, and you can choose whatever posture you think most convenient for reading, and proceed.

PHAEDRUS: Here you are then.

You know how I am situated, and I have told you that I think it to our advantage that this should happen. Now I claim that I should not be refused what I ask simply because I am not your lover. Lovers, 231 when their craving is at an end, repent of such benefits as they have conferred, but for the other sort no occasion arises for regretting what has passed. For being free agents under no constraint, they regulate their services by the scale of their means, with an eye to their own personal interest. Again, lovers weigh up profit and loss accruing to their account by reason of their passion, and with the extra item of labor expended decide that they have long since made full payment for b favors received, whereas the nonlovers cannot allege any consequential neglect of their personal affairs, nor record any past exertions on the debit side, nor yet complain of having quarreled with their relatives; hence, with all these troubles removed, all they have left to do is to devote their energies to such conduct as they conceive likely to gratify the other party.

Again, it is argued that a lover ought to be highly valued because c he professes to be especially kind toward the loved one, and ready to gratify him in words and deeds while arousing the dislike of everyone else. If this is true, however, it is obvious that he will set greater store by the loved one of tomorrow than by that of today, and will doubtless do an injury to the old love if required by the new.

And really, what sense is there in lavishing what is so precious
d upon one laboring under an affliction which nobody who knew anything of it would even attempt to remove? Why, the man himself
admits that he is not sound, but sick, that he is aware of his folly,
but cannot control himself. How then, when he comes to his senses, is
he likely to approve of the intentions that he formed in his aberration?

And observe this. If you are to choose the best of a number of
lovers, your choice will be only among a few, whereas a general choice
of the person who most commends himself to you gives you a wide
e field, so that in that wide field you have a much better prospect of
finding someone worthy of your friendship.

Now maybe you respect established conventions, and anticipate
odium if people get to hear about you; if so, it may be expected that a
232 lover, conceiving that everyone will admire him as he admires himself,
will be proud to talk about it and flatter his vanity by declaring to all
and sundry that his enterprise has been successful, whereas the other
type, who can control themselves, will prefer to do what is best rather
than shine in the eyes of their neighbors.

Again, a lover is bound to be heard about and seen by many people, consorting with his beloved and caring about little else, so that
b when they are observed talking to one another, the meeting is taken
to imply the satisfaction, actual or prospective, of their desires,
whereas, with the other sort, no one ever thinks of putting a bad construction on their association, realizing that a man must have someone to talk to by way of friendship or gratification of one sort or
another.

And observe this. Perhaps you feel troubled by the reflection that
it is hard for friendship to be preserved, and that whereas a quarrel
arising from other sources will be a calamity shared by both parties,
c one that follows the sacrifice of your all will involve a grievous hurt
to yourself; in that case it is doubtless the lover who should cause you
the more alarm, for he is very ready to take offense, and thinks the
whole affair is to his own hurt. Hence he discourages his beloved
from consorting with anyone else, fearing that a wealthy rival may
overreach him with his money, or a cultured one outdo him with his
intelligence, and he is perpetually on guard against the influence of
d those who possess other advantages. So by persuading you to become
estranged from such rivals he leaves you without a friend in the
world; alternatively, if you look to your own interest and show more
good sense than your lover, you will find yourself quarreling with him.
On the other hand, one who is not a lover, but has achieved what he
asked of you by reason of his merit, will not be jealous of others who
seek your society, but will rather detest those who avoid it, in the
belief that the latter look down on him, whereas the former are serv-

ing his turn. Consequently the object of his attentions is far more e
likely to make friends than enemies out of the affair.

And observe this. A lover more often than not wants to possess
you before he has come to know your character or become familiar
with your general personality, and that makes it uncertain whether he
will still want to be your friend when his desires have waned, whereas 233
in the other case, the fact that the pair were already friends before
the affair took place makes it probable that instead of friendship diminishing as the result of favors received, these favors will abide as
a memory and promise of more to come.

And observe this. It ought to be for your betterment to listen to
me rather than to a lover, for a lover commends anything you say or
do even when it is amiss, partly from fear that he may offend you,
partly because his passion impairs his own judgment. For the record b
of Love's achievement is, first, that when things go badly, he makes
a man count that an affliction which normally causes no distress; secondly, that when things go well, he compels his subjects to extol
things that ought not to gratify them, which makes it fitting that
they should be pitied far more than admired by the objects of their
passion. On the other hand, if you listen to me, my intercourse with
you will be a matter of ministering not to your immediate pleasure but
to your future advantage, for I am the master of myself, rather than c
the victim of love; I do not bring bitter enmity upon myself by resenting trifling offenses. On the contrary, it is only on account of serious
wrongs that I am moved, and that but slowly, to mild indignation,
pardoning what is done unintentionally, and endeavoring to hinder
what is done of intent, for these are the tokens of lasting friendship.
If however you are disposed to think that there can be no firm friendship save with a lover, you should reflect that in that case we should d
not set store by sons, or fathers, or mothers, nor should we possess
any trustworthy friends. No, it is not to erotic passion that we owe
these, but to conduct of a different order.

Again, if we ought to favor those who press us most strongly, then
in other matters too we should give our good offices not to the worthiest people but to the most destitute, for since their distress is the
greatest, they will be the most thankful to us for relieving them.
And observe this further consequence. When we give private banquets, e
the right people to invite will be not our friends but beggars and those
in need of a good meal, for it is they that will be fond of us and attend
upon us and flock to our doors; it is they that will be most delighted
and most grateful and call down blessings on our heads. No, the
proper course, surely, is to show favor not to the most importunate
but to those most able to make us a return—not to mere beggars, but
to the deserving; not to those who will regale themselves with your 234
youthful beauty, but to those who will let you share their prosperity

when you are older; not to those who, when they have had their will of you, will flatter their vanity by telling the world, but to those who will keep a strict and modest silence; not to those who are devoted to you for a brief period, but to those who will continue to be your friends as long as you live; not to those who, when their passion is spent, will look for an excuse to turn against you, but to those who, when your beauty is past, will make that the time for displaying their own goodness.

b   Do you therefore be mindful of what I have said and reflect that, while lovers are admonished by their friends and relatives for the wrongness of their conduct, the other sort have never been reproached by one of their family on the score of behaving to the detriment of their own interest.

Perhaps you will ask me whether I recommend you to accord your favors to all and sundry of this sort. Well, I do not suppose that even a lover would bid you to be favorable toward all and sundry lovers; in

c the first place a recipient would not regard it as meriting so much gratitude, and in the second you would find it more difficult if you wished to keep your affairs concealed, and what is wanted is that the business should involve no harm, but mutual advantage.

And now I think I have said all that is needed; if you think I have neglected anything, and want more, let me know.

What do you think of the speech, Socrates? Isn't it extraordinarily fine, especially in point of language?

d   SOCRATES : Amazingly fine indeed, my friend. I was thrilled by it. And it was you, Phaedrus, that made me feel as I did. I watched your apparent delight in the words as you read. And as I'm sure that you understand such matters better than I do, I took my cue from you, and therefore joined in the ecstasy of my right worshipful companion.

PHAEDRUS : Come, come! Do you mean to make a joke of it?

SOCRATES : Do you think I am joking, and don't mean it seriously?

e   PHAEDRUS : No more of that, Socrates. Tell me truly, as one friend to another, do you think there is anyone in Greece who could make a finer and more exhaustive speech on the same subject?

SOCRATES : What? Are you and I required to extol the speech not merely on the score of its author's lucidity and terseness of expression, and his consistently precise and well-polished vocabulary, but also for his having said what he ought? If we are, we shall have to allow it only on your account, for my feeble intelligence failed

235 to appreciate it; I was only attending to it as a piece of rhetoric, and as such I couldn't think that even Lysias himself would deem it adequate. Perhaps you won't agree with me, Phaedrus, but really it seemed to me that he said the same things several times over. Maybe he's not very clever at expatiating at length on a single theme, or pos-

sibly he has no interest in such topics. In fact it struck me as an extravagant performance, to demonstrate his ability to say the same thing twice, in different words but with equal success.

PHAEDRUS: Not a bit of it, Socrates. The outstanding feature b of the discourse is just this, that it has not overlooked any important aspect of the subject, so making it impossible for anyone else to outdo what he has said with a fuller or more satisfactory oration.

SOCRATES: If you go as far as that I shall find it impossible to agree with you; if I were to assent out of politeness, I should be confuted by the wise men and women who in past ages have spoken and written on this theme.

PHAEDRUS: To whom do you refer? Where have you heard any- c thing better than this?

SOCRATES: I can't tell you offhand, but I'm sure I have heard something better, from the fair Sappho maybe, or the wise Anacreon, or perhaps some prose writer. What ground, you may ask, have I for saying so? Good sir, there is something welling up within my breast, which makes me feel that I could find something different, and something better, to say. I am of course well aware it can't be anything originating in my own mind, for I know my own ignorance; so I suppose it can only be that it has been poured into me, through my ears, as into a vessel, from some external source, though in my stupid d fashion I have actually forgotten how, and from whom, I heard it.

PHAEDRUS: Well said! You move me to admiration. I don't mind your not telling me, even though I should press you, from whom and how you heard it, provided you do just what you say. You have undertaken to make a better speech than that in the book here and one of not less length which shall owe nothing to it; I in my turn undertake like the nine Archons to set up at Delphi a golden life-sized e statue, not only of myself but of you also.

SOCRATES: How kind you are, Phaedrus, and what a pattern of golden-age simplicity, in supposing me to mean that Lysias has wholly missed the mark and that another speech could avoid all his points! Surely that couldn't be so even with the most worthless of writers. Thus, as regards the subject of the speech, do you imagine that anybody could argue that the nonlover should be favored, rather than the lover, without praising the wisdom of the one and censuring the folly of the other? That he could dispense with these essential points, and 236 then bring up something different? No, no, surely we must allow such arguments, and forgive the orator for using them, and in that sort of field what merits praise is not invention, but arrangement; but when it comes to nonessential points, that are difficult to invent, we should praise arrangement and invention too.

PHAEDRUS: I agree. What you say seems fair enough. For my part, this is what I will do. I will allow you to take it for granted that b the lover is less sane than the nonlover, and for the rest, if you can replace what we have here by a fuller speech of superior merit, up with your statue in wrought gold beside the offering of the Cypselids at Olympia.

SOCRATES: Have you taken me seriously, Phaedrus, for teasing you with an attack on your darling Lysias? Can you possibly suppose that I shall make a real attempt to rival his cleverness with something more ornate?

PHAEDRUS: As to that, my friend, I've got you where I can re-
c turn your fire. Assuredly you must do what you can in the way of a speech, or else we shall be driven, like vulgar comedians, to capping each other's remarks. Beware. Do not deliberately compel me to utter the words, 'Don't I know my Socrates? If not, I've forgotten my own identity,' or 'He wanted to speak, but made difficulties about it.' No, make up your mind that we're not going to leave this spot until you have delivered yourself of what you told me you had within your breast. We are by ourselves in a lonely place, and I am stronger and
d younger than you, for all which reasons 'mistake not thou my bidding' and please don't make me use force to open your lips.

SOCRATES: But, my dear good Phaedrus, it will be courting ridicule for an amateur like me to improvise on the same theme as an accomplished writer.

PHAEDRUS: Look here, I'll have no more of this affectation, for I'm pretty sure I have something to say which will compel you to speak.

SOCRATES: Then please don't say it.

PHAEDRUS: Oh, but I shall, here and now, and what I say will
e be on oath. I swear to you by—but by whom, by what god? Or shall it be by this plane tree? I swear that unless you deliver your speech here in its very presence, I will assuredly never again declaim nor report any other speech by any author whatsoever.

SOCRATES: Aha, you rogue! How clever of you to discover the means of compelling a lover of discourse to do your bidding!

PHAEDRUS: Then why all this twisting?

SOCRATES: I give it up, in view of what you've sworn. For how could I possibly do without such entertainment?

237   PHAEDRUS: Then proceed.

SOCRATES: Well, do you know what I'm going to do?

PHAEDRUS: Do about what?

SOCRATES: I shall cover my head before I begin; then I can rush through my speech at top speed without looking at you and breaking down for shame.

PHAEDRUS: You can do anything else you like, provided you make your speech.

SOCRATES: Come then, ye clear-voiced Muses, whether it be from the nature of your song, or from the musical people of Liguria that ye came to be so styled, 'assist the tale I tell' under compulsion

by my good friend here, to the end that he may think yet more highly
of one dear to him, whom he already accounts a man of wisdom.   b

Well then, once upon a time there was a very handsome boy, or
rather young man, who had a host of lovers, and one of them was
wily, and had persuaded the boy that he was not in love with him,
though really he was, quite as much as the others. And on one occasion, in pressing his suit he actually sought to convince him that he
ought to favor a nonlover rather than a lover. And this is the purport
of what he said.

My boy, if anyone means to deliberate successfully about anything, there is one thing he must do at the outset. He must know what c
it is he is deliberating about; otherwise he is bound to go utterly astray.
Now most people fail to realize that they don't know what this or that
really is; consequently when they start discussing something, they
dispense with any agreed definition, assuming that they know the
thing; then later on they naturally find, to their cost, that they agree
neither with each other nor with themselves. That being so, you and I
would do well to avoid what we charge against other people, and
as the question before us is whether one should preferably consort
with a lover or a nonlover, we ought to agree upon a definition of love
which shows its nature and its effects, so that we may have it before
our minds as something to refer to while we discuss whether love is d
beneficial or injurious.

Well now, it is plain to everyone that love is some sort of desire,
and further we know that men desire that which is fair without being
lovers. How then are we to distinguish one who loves from one who
does not? We must go on to observe that within each one of us there
are two sorts of ruling or guiding principle that we follow. One is an
innate desire for pleasure, the other an acquired judgment that aims
at what is best. Sometimes these internal guides are in accord, sometimes at variance; now one gains the mastery, now the other. And e
when judgment guides us rationally toward what is best, and has the
mastery, that mastery is called temperance, but when desire drags us 238
irrationally toward pleasure, and has come to rule within us, the name
given to that rule is wantonness. But in truth wantonness itself has
many names, as it has many branches or forms, and when one
of these forms is conspicuously present in a man it makes that man
bear its name, a name that it is no credit or distinction to possess. If it
be in the matter of food that desire has the mastery over judgment of
what is for the best, and over all other desires, it is called gluttony,
and the person in question will be called a glutton, or again if desire b
has achieved domination in the matter of drink, it is plain what term
we shall apply to its subject who is led down that path, and no less
plain what are the appropriate names in the case of other such persons
and of other such desires, according as this one or that holds sway.

Now the reason for saying all this can hardly remain in doubt;

yet even so a statement of it will be illuminating. When irrational desire, pursuing the enjoyment of beauty, has gained the mastery c over judgment that prompts to right conduct, and has acquired from other desires, akin to it, fresh strength to strain toward bodily beauty, that very strength provides it with its name—it is the strong passion called love.

Well, Phaedrus my friend, do you think, as I do, that I am divinely inspired?

PHAEDRUS : Undoubtedly, Socrates, you have been vouchsafed a quite unusual eloquence.

SOCRATES : Then listen to me in silence. For truly there seems d to be a divine presence in this spot, so that you must not be surprised if, as my speech proceeds, I become as one possessed; already my style is not far from dithyrambic.

PHAEDRUS : Very true.

SOCRATES : But for that you are responsible. Still, let me continue; possibly the menace may be averted. However, that must be as God wills; our business is to resume our address to the boy.

Very well then, my good friend, the true nature of that on which we have to deliberate has been stated and defined, and so, with that e definition in mind, we may go on to say what advantage or detriment may be expected to result to one who accords his favor to a lover and a nonlover, respectively.

Now a man who is dominated by desire and enslaved to pleasure is of course bound to aim at getting the greatest possible pleasure out of his beloved, and what pleases a sick man is anything that does not thwart him, whereas anything that is as strong as, or stronger than, himself gives him offense. Hence he will not, if he can avoid it, 239 put up with a favorite that matches or outdoes him in strength, but will always seek to make him weaker and feebler, and weakness is found in the ignorant, the cowardly, the poor speaker, the slow thinker, as against the wise, the brave, the eloquent, the quick-minded. All these defects of mind and more in the beloved are bound to be a source of pleasure to the lover; if they do not exist already as innate qualities, he will cultivate them, for not to do so means depriving himself of immediate pleasure. And of course he is bound to be jealous, b constantly debarring the boy not only, to his great injury, from the advantages of consorting with others, which would make a real man of him, but, greatest injury of all, from consorting with that which would most increase his wisdom—by which I mean divine philosophy. No access to that can possibly be permitted by the lover, for he dreads becoming thereby an object of contempt. And in general he must aim at making the boy totally ignorant and totally dependent on his lover, by way of securing the maximum of pleasure for himself, and the maximum of damage to the other.

c   Hence in respect of the boy's mind it is anything but a profitable investment to have as guardian or partner a man in love.

After the mind, the body; we must see what sort of physical condition will be fostered, and how it will be fostered, in the boy that has become the possession of one who is under compulsion to pursue pleasure instead of goodness. We shall find him, of course, pursuing a weakling rather than a sturdy boy, one who has had a cozy, sheltered upbringing instead of being exposed to the open air, who has given himself up to a soft unmanly life instead of the toil and sweat of manly exercise, who for lack of natural charm tricks himself out d with artificial cosmetics, and resorts to all sorts of other similar practices which are too obvious to need further enumeration. Yet before leaving the topic we may sum it up in a sentence. The boy will be of that physical type which in wartime, and other times that try a man's mettle, inspires confidence in his enemies and alarm in his friends, aye and in his very lovers too.

And now let us pass from these obvious considerations and raise e the next question. What advantage or detriment in respect of property and possessions shall we find resulting from the society and guardianship of a lover? Well, one thing is plain enough to anyone, and especially to the lover, namely that his foremost wish will be for the boy to be bereft of his dearest possessions, his treasury of kindness and ideal affection—father and mother, kinsmen and friends—he will want him to be robbed of them all, as likely to make difficulties 240 and raise objections to the intercourse which he finds so pleasant. If however the boy possesses property, in money or whatever it may be, he will reckon that he will not be so easy to capture, or if captured to manage; hence a lover is bound to nurse a grudge against one who possesses property, and to rejoice when he loses it. Furthermore he will want his beloved to remain as long as possible without wife or child or home, so as to enjoy for as long as may be his own delights.

There are, to be sure, other evils in life, but with most of them heaven has mixed some momentary pleasure. Thus in the parasite, a b fearsome and most pernicious creature, nature has mingled a dash of pleasing wit or charm; a courtesan may well be branded as pernicious, not to mention many other similar creatures with their respective callings; yet in everyday life they can be very agreeable, but a lover, besides being pernicious, is the most disagreeable of all men for a boy to spend his days with. There's an old saying about 'not match- c ing May with December,' based, I suppose, on the idea that similarity of age tends to similarity of pleasures and consequently makes a couple good friends; still even with such a couple the association is apt to pall. Then again, in addition to the dissimilarity of age, there is that compulsion which is burdensome for anybody in any circumstances, but especially so in the relations of such a pair.

The elderly lover will not, if he can help it, suffer any desertion by his beloved by day or by night; he is driven on by a compelling, d goading power, lured by the continual promise of pleasure in the sight, hearing, touching, or other physical experience of the beloved; to

minister unfailingly to the boy's needs is his delight. But what pleasure or what solace will he have to offer to the beloved? How will he save him from experiencing the extremity of discomfort in those long hours at his lover's side, as he looks upon a face which years have
e robbed of its beauty, together with other consequences which it is unpleasant even to hear mentioned, let alone to have continually to cope with in stark reality. And what of the suspicious precautions with which he is incessantly guarded, with whomsoever he associates, the unseasonable fulsome compliments to which he has to listen, alternating with reproaches which when uttered in soberness are hard to endure, but coming from one in his cups, in language of unlimited, undisguised coarseness, are both intolerable and disgusting?

To continue, if while his love lasts he is harmful and offensive, in later days, when it is spent, he will show his bad faith. He was lavish with promises, interspersed among his vows and entreaties, regarding those later days, contriving with some difficulty to secure
241 his partner's endurance of an intercourse which even then was burdensome, by holding out hopes of benefits to come. But when the time comes for fulfilling the promises, a new authority takes the place within him of the former ruler; love and passion are replaced by wisdom and temperance; he has become a different person. But the boy does not realize it, and demands a return for what he gave in the past, reminding him of what had been done and said, as though he were talking to the same person, while the erstwhile lover, who has now acquired wisdom and temperance, cannot for very shame bring him-
b self to declare that he has become a new man, nor yet see his way to redeeming the solemn assurances and promises made under the old regime of folly; he fears that if he were to go on acting as before he would revert to his old character, his former self. So he runs away from his obligations as one compelled to default; it's 'tails' this time instead of 'heads,' and he has to turn tail and rush away. But the boy must needs run after him, crying indignantly to high heaven, though from start to finish he has never understood that he ought not to have yielded to a lover inevitably devoid of reason, but far rather
c to one possessed of reason and not in love. He should have known that the wrong choice must mean surrendering himself to a faithless, peevish, jealous, and offensive captor, to one who would ruin his property, ruin his physique, and above all ruin his spiritual development, which is assuredly and ever will be of supreme value in the sight of gods and men alike.

Let that then, my boy, be your lesson. Be sure that the attentions of a lover carry no good will; they are no more than a glutting of his
d appetite, for 'As wolf to lamb, so lover to his lad.'

There, I knew I should [break out into verse], Phaedrus. Not a word more shall you have from me; let that be the end of my discourse.

PHAEDRUS : Why, I thought you were only halfway through

and would have an equal amount to say about the nonlover, enumerating his good points and showing that he should be the favored suitor. Why is it, Socrates, that instead of that you break off?

SOCRATES : My dear good man, haven't you noticed that I've got e beyond dithyramb, and am breaking out into epic verse, despite my faultfinding? What do you suppose I shall do if I start extolling the other type? Don't you see that I shall clearly be possessed by those nymphs into whose clutches you deliberately threw me? I therefore tell you, in one short sentence, that to each evil for which I have abused the one party there is a corresponding good belonging to the other. So why waste words? All has been said that needs saying about them both. And that being so, my story can be left to the fate appropriate to it, and I will take myself off across the river here before you 242 drive me to greater lengths.

PHAEDRUS : Oh, but you must wait until it gets cooler, Socrates. Don't you realize that it's just about the hour of 'scorching noonday,' as the phrase goes? Let us wait and discuss what we've heard; when it has got cool perhaps we will go.

SOCRATES : Phaedrus, your enthusiasm for discourse is sublime, and really moves me to admiration. Of the discourses pronounced during your lifetime no one, I fancy, has been responsible b for more than you, whether by delivering them yourself or by compelling others to do so by one means or another—with one exception, Simmias of Thebes; you are well ahead of all the rest. And now it seems that once more you are the cause of my having to deliver myself.

PHAEDRUS : It might be a lot worse! But how so? To what do you refer?

SOCRATES : At the moment when I was about to cross the river, dear friend, there came to me my familiar divine sign—which always checks me when on the point of doing something or other— c and all at once I seemed to hear a voice, forbidding me to leave the spot until I had made atonement for some offense to heaven. Now, you must know, I am a seer—not a very good one, it's true, but, like a poor scholar, good enough for my own purposes—hence I understand already well enough what my offense was. The fact is, you know, Phaedrus, the mind itself has a kind of divining power, for I felt disturbed some while ago as I was delivering that speech, and had a misgiving lest I might, in the words of Ibycus, 'By sinning in the d sight of God win high renown from man.' [2] But now I realize my sin.

PHAEDRUS : And what is it?

SOCRATES : That was a terrible theory, Phaedrus, a terrible theory that you introduced and compelled me to expound.

PHAEDRUS : How so?

[2] *Ibycus*, fr. 24.

SOCRATES: It was foolish, and somewhat blasphemous, and what could be more terrible than that?

PHAEDRUS: I agree, if it merits your description.

SOCRATES: Well, do you not hold Love to be a god, the child of Aphrodite?

PHAEDRUS: He is certainly said to be.

SOCRATES: But not according to Lysias, and not according to e that discourse of yours which you caused my lips to utter by putting a spell on them. If Love is, as he is indeed, a god or a divine being, he cannot be an evil thing; yet this pair of speeches treated him as evil. That then was their offense toward Love, to which was added the most exquisite folly of parading their pernicious rubbish as though it were good sense because it might deceive a few miserable people and win 243 their applause.

And so, my friend, I have to purify myself. Now for such as offend in speaking of gods and heroes there is an ancient mode of purification, which was known to Stesichorus, though not to Homer. When Stesichorus lost the sight of his eyes because of his defamation of Helen, he was not, like Homer, at a loss to know why. As a true artist he understood the reason, and promptly wrote the lines:

> False, false the tale.
> Thou never didst sail in the well-decked ships
b > Nor come to the towers of Troy.[3]

And after finishing the composition of his so-called palinode he straightway recovered his sight. Now it's here that I shall show greater wisdom than these poets. I shall attempt to make my due palinode to Love before any harm comes to me for my defamation of him, and no longer veiling my head for shame, but uncovered.

PHAEDRUS: Nothing you could say, Socrates, would please me more.

c   SOCRATES: Yes, dear Phaedrus, you understand how irreverent the two speeches were, the one in the book and that which followed. Suppose we were being listened to by a man of generous and humane character, who loved or had once loved another such as himself. Suppose he heard us saying that for some trifling cause lovers conceive bitter hatred and a spirit of malice and injury toward their loved ones. Wouldn't he be sure to think that we had been brought up among the scum of the people and had never seen a case of noble d love? Wouldn't he utterly refuse to accept our vilification of Love?

PHAEDRUS: Indeed, Socrates, he well might.

SOCRATES: Then out of respect for him, and in awe of Love himself, I should like to wash the bitter taste out of my mouth with a

---

[3] Stesichorus, fr. 32.

draught of wholesome discourse, and my advice to Lysias is that he should lose no time in telling us that, other things being equal, favor should be accorded to the lover rather than to the nonlover.

PHAEDRUS : Rest assured; that will be done. When you have delivered your encomium of the lover, I shall most certainly make e Lysias compose a new speech to the same purport.

SOCRATES : I'm sure of that, so long as you continue to be the man you are.

PHAEDRUS : Then you may confidently proceed.

SOCRATES : Where is that boy I was talking to? He must listen to me once more, and not rush off to yield to his nonlover before he hears what I have to say.

PHAEDRUS : Here he is, quite close beside you, whenever you want him.

SOCRATES : Now you must understand, fair boy, that whereas the preceding discourse was by Phaedrus, son of Pythocles, of Myr- 244 rhinus, that which I shall now pronounce is by Stesichorus, son of Euphemus, of Himera. This then is how it must run.

'False is the tale' that when a lover is at hand favor ought rather to be accorded to one who does not love, on the ground that the former is mad, and the latter sound of mind. That would be right if it were an invariable truth that madness is an evil, but in reality, the greatest blessings come by way of madness, indeed of madness that is heaven-sent. It was when they were mad that the prophetess at Delphi b and the priestesses at Dodona achieved so much for which both states and individuals in Greece are thankful; when sane they did little or nothing. As for the Sibyl and others who by the power of inspired prophecy have so often foretold the future to so many, and guided them aright, I need not dwell on what is obvious to everyone. Yet it is in place to appeal to the fact that madness was accounted no shame nor disgrace by the men of old who gave things their names; otherwise they would not have connected that greatest of arts, whereby the future is discerned, with this very word 'madness,' and c named it accordingly. No, it was because they held madness to be a valuable gift, when due to divine dispensation, that they named that art as they did, though the men of today, having no sense of values, have put in an extra letter, making it not *manic* but *mantic*. That is borne out by the name they gave to the art of those sane prophets who inquire into the future by means of birds and other signs; the name was '*oionoistic*,' which by its components indicated that the prophet attained understanding and information by a purely human activity of thought belonging to his own intelligence, though a younger generation has come to call it '*oionistic*,' lengthening the quantity of the *o* to make it sound impressive. You see then what this ancient evi- d dence attests. Corresponding to the superior perfection and value of the prophecy of inspiration over that of omen reading, both in name and in fact, is the superiority of heaven-sent madness over man-made sanity.

　　And in the second place, when grievous maladies and afflictions have beset certain families by reason of some ancient sin, madness
e has appeared among them, and breaking out into prophecy has secured relief by finding the means thereto, namely by recourse to prayer and worship, and in consequence thereof rites and means of purification were established, and the sufferer was brought out of danger, alike for the present and for the future. Thus did madness secure, for him that was maddened aright and possessed, deliverance from his troubles.

245　　There is a third form of possession or madness, of which the Muses are the source. This seizes a tender, virgin soul and stimulates it to rapt passionate expression, especially in lyric poetry, glorifying the countless mighty deeds of ancient times for the instruction of posterity. But if any man come to the gates of poetry without the madness of the Muses, persuaded that skill alone will make him a good poet, then shall he and his works of sanity with him be brought to nought by the poetry of madness, and behold, their place is nowhere to be found.

b　　Such then is the tale, though I have not told it fully, of the achievements wrought by madness that comes from the gods. So let us have no fears simply on that score; let us not be disturbed by an argument that seeks to scare us into preferring the friendship of the sane to that of the passionate. For there is something more that it must prove if it is to carry the day, namely that love is not a thing sent from heaven for the advantage both of lover and beloved. What we
c have to prove is the opposite, namely that this sort of madness is a gift of the gods, fraught with the highest bliss. And our proof assuredly will prevail with the wise, though not with the learned.

　　Now our first step toward attaining the truth of the matter is to discern the nature of soul, divine and human, its experiences, and its activities. Here then our proof begins.

　　All soul is immortal, for that which is ever in motion is immortal. But that which while imparting motion is itself moved by something else can cease to be in motion, and therefore can cease to live; it is only that which moves itself that never intermits its motion, inasmuch as it cannot abandon its own nature; moreover this self-mover is the source and first principle of motion for all other things that are
d moved. Now a first principle cannot come into being, for while anything that comes to be must come to be from a first principle, the latter itself cannot come to be from anything whatsoever; if it did, it would cease any longer to be a first principle. Furthermore, since it does not come into being, it must be imperishable, for assuredly if a first principle were to be destroyed, nothing could come to be out of it, nor could anything bring the principle itself back into existence, see-

ing that a first principle is needed for anything to come into being.

The self-mover, then, is the first principle of motion, and it is as impossible that it should be destroyed as that it should come into being; were it otherwise, the whole universe, the whole of that which comes to be, would collapse into immobility, and never find another e source of motion to bring it back into being.

And now that we have seen that that which is moved by itself is immortal, we shall feel no scruple in affirming that precisely that is the essence and definition of soul, to wit, self-motion. Any body that has an external source of motion is soulless, but a body deriving its motion from a source within itself is animate or *besouled*, which implies that the nature of soul is what has been said.

And if this last assertion is correct, namely that 'that which moves itself' is precisely identifiable with soul, it must follow that soul 246 is not born and does not die.

As to soul's immortality then we have said enough, but as to its nature there is this that must be said. What manner of thing it is would be a long tale to tell, and most assuredly a god alone could tell it, but what it resembles, that a man might tell in briefer compass. Let this therefore be our manner of discourse. Let it be likened to the union of powers in a team of winged steeds and their winged charioteer. Now all the gods' steeds and all their charioteers are good, and of good stock, but with other beings it is not wholly so. With us men, in b the first place, it is a pair of steeds that the charioteer controls; moreover one of them is noble and good, and of good stock, while the other has the opposite character, and his stock is opposite. Hence the task of our charioteer is difficult and troublesome.

And now we must essay to tell how it is that living beings are called mortal and immortal. All soul has the care of all that is inanimate, and traverses the whole universe, though in ever-changing forms. Thus when it is perfect and winged it journeys on high and c controls the whole world, but one that has shed its wings sinks down until it can fasten on something solid, and settling there it takes to itself an earthy body which seems by reason of the soul's power to move itself. This composite structure of soul and body is called a living being, and is further termed 'mortal'; 'immortal' is a term applied on no basis of reasoned argument at all, but our fancy pictures the god whom we have never seen, nor fully conceived, as an immortal liv- d ing being, possessed of a soul and a body united for all time. Howbeit, let these matters, and our account thereof, be as God pleases; what we must understand is the reason why the soul's wings fall from it, and are lost. It is on this wise.

The natural property of a wing is to raise that which is heavy and carry it aloft to the region where the gods dwell, and more than any other bodily part it shares in the divine nature, which is fair, wise, e and good, and possessed of all other such excellences. Now by these excellences especially is the soul's plumage nourished and fostered, while by their opposites, even by ugliness and evil, it is wasted and destroyed. And behold, there in the heaven Zeus, mighty leader, drives his winged team. First of the host of gods and daemons he proceeds, ordering all things and caring therefor, and the host follows 247 after him, marshaled in eleven companies. For Hestia abides alone in the gods' dwelling place, but for the rest, all such as are ranked in the number of the twelve as ruler gods lead their several companies, each according to his rank.

Now within the heavens are many spectacles of bliss upon the highways whereon the blessed gods pass to and fro, each doing his own work, and with them are all such as will and can follow them, for jealousy has no place in the choir divine. But at such times as they go to their feasting and banquet, behold they climb the steep ascent b even unto the summit of the arch that supports the heavens, and easy is that ascent for the chariots of the gods, for they are well balanced and readily guided. But for the others it is hard, by reason of the heaviness of the steed of wickedness, which pulls down his driver with his weight, except that driver have schooled him well.

And now there awaits the soul the extreme of her toil and struggling. For the souls that are called immortal, so soon as they are at the summit, come forth and stand upon the back of the world, and c straightway the revolving heaven carries them round, and they look upon the regions without.

Of that place beyond the heavens none of our earthly poets has yet sung, and none shall sing worthily. But this is the manner of it, for assuredly we must be bold to speak what is true, above all when our discourse is upon truth. It is there that true being dwells, without color or shape, that cannot be touched; reason alone, the soul's pilot, can behold it, and all true knowledge is knowledge thereof. Now even d as the mind of a god is nourished by reason and knowledge, so also is it with every soul that has a care to receive her proper food; wherefore when at last she has beheld being she is well content, and contemplating truth she is nourished and prospers, until the heaven's revolution brings her back full circle. And while she is borne round she discerns justice, its very self, and likewise temperance, and knowledge, not the knowledge that is neighbor to becoming and varies e with the various objects to which we commonly ascribe being, but the veritable knowledge of being that veritably is. And when she has contemplated likewise and feasted upon all else that has true being, she descends again within the heavens and comes back home. And having so come, her charioteer sets his steeds at their manger, and puts ambrosia before them and draught of nectar to drink withal.

248 　　Such is the life of gods. Of the other souls that which best follows a god and becomes most like thereunto raises her charioteer's head into the outer region, and is carried round with the gods in the

revolution, but being confounded by her steeds she has much ado to
discern the things that are; another now rises, and now sinks, and
by reason of her unruly steeds sees in part, but in part sees not. As for
the rest, though all are eager to reach the heights and seek to follow,
they are not able; sucked down as they travel they trample and tread
upon one another, this one striving to outstrip that. Thus confusion b
ensues, and conflict and grievous sweat. Whereupon, with their charioteers powerless, many are lamed, and many have their wings all
broken, and for all their toiling they are balked, every one, of the full
vision of being, and departing therefrom, they feed upon the food of
semblance.

Now the reason wherefore the souls are fain and eager to behold
the plain of Truth, and discover it, lies herein—to wit, that the pasturage that is proper to their noblest part comes from that meadow, c
and the plumage by which they are borne aloft is nourished thereby.

Hear now the ordinance of Necessity. Whatsoever soul has followed in the train of a god, and discerned something of truth, shall be
kept from sorrow until a new revolution shall begin, and if she can do
this always, she shall remain always free from hurt. But when she is
not able so to follow, and sees none of it, but meeting with some mischance comes to be burdened with a load of forgetfulness and
wrongdoing, and because of that burden sheds her wings and falls to
the earth, then thus runs the law. In her first birth she shall not be d
planted in any brute beast, but the soul that hath seen the most of
being shall enter into the human babe that shall grow into a seeker
after wisdom or beauty, a follower of the Muses and a lover; the next,
having seen less, shall dwell in a king that abides by law, or a warrior
and ruler; the third in a statesman, a man of business, or a trader; the
fourth in an athlete, or physical trainer, or physician; the fifth shall e
have the life of a prophet or a Mystery priest; to the sixth that of a
poet or other imitative artist shall be fittingly given; the seventh shall
live in an artisan or farmer; the eighth in a Sophist or demagogue;
the ninth in a tyrant.

Now in all these incarnations he who lives righteously has a better lot for his portion, and he who lives unrighteously a worse. For a
soul does not return to the place whence she came for ten thousand
years, since in no lesser time can she regain her wings, save only his 249
soul who has sought after wisdom unfeignedly, or has conjoined his
passion for a loved one with that seeking. Such a soul, if with three
revolutions of a thousand years she has thrice chosen this philosophical life, regains thereby her wings, and speeds away after three thousand years; but the rest, when they have accomplished their first life,
are brought to judgment, and after the judgment some are taken to be
punished in places of chastisement beneath the earth, while others are
borne aloft by Justice to a certain region of the heavens, there to live
in such manner as is merited by their past life in the flesh. And after b

a thousand years these and those alike come to the allotment and choice of their second life, each choosing according to her will; then does the soul of a man enter into the life of a beast, and the beast's soul that was aforetime in a man goes back to a man again. For only the soul that has beheld truth may enter into this our human form— seeing that man must needs understand the language of forms, pass-
c ing from a plurality of perceptions to a unity gathered together by reasoning—and such understanding is a recollection of those things which our souls beheld aforetime as they journeyed with their god, looking down upon the things which now we suppose to be, and gazing up to that which truly is.

Therefore is it meet and right that the soul of the philosopher alone should recover her wings, for she, so far as may be, is ever near in memory to those things a god's nearness whereunto makes him truly god. Wherefore if a man makes right use of such means of remembrance, and ever approaches to the full vision of the perfect mysteries, he and he alone becomes truly perfect. Standing aside
d from the busy doings of mankind, and drawing nigh to the divine, he is rebuked by the multitude as being out of his wits, for they know not that he is possessed by a deity.

Mark therefore the sum and substance of all our discourse touching the fourth sort of madness—to wit, that this is the best of all forms of divine possession, both in itself and in its sources, both for him that has it and for him that shares therein—and when he that
e loves beauty is touched by such madness he is called a lover. Such a one, as soon as he beholds the beauty of this world, is reminded of true beauty, and his wings begin to grow; then is he fain to lift his wings and fly upward; yet he has not the power, but inasmuch as he gazes upward like a bird, and cares nothing for the world beneath, men charge it upon him that he is demented.

Now, as we have said, every human soul has, by reason of her nature, had contemplation of true being; else would she never have
250 entered into this human creature; but to be put in mind thereof by things here is not easy for every soul. Some, when they had the vision, had it but for a moment; some when they had fallen to earth consorted unhappily with such as led them to deeds of unrighteousness, wherefore they forgot the holy objects of their vision. Few indeed are left that can still remember much, but when these discern some likeness of the things yonder, they are amazed, and no longer masters of themselves, and know not what is come upon them by reason of
b their perception being dim.

Now in the earthly likenesses of justice and temperance and all other prized possessions of the soul there dwells no luster; nay, so dull are the organs wherewith men approach their images that hardly can a few behold that which is imaged, but with beauty it is otherwise. Beauty it was ours to see in all its brightness in those days when, amidst that happy company, we beheld with our eyes that blessed vision, ourselves in the train of Zeus, others following some other god; then were we all initiated into that mystery which is rightly accounted blessed beyond all others; whole and unblemished were we that did c celebrate it, untouched by the evils that awaited us in days to come; whole and unblemished likewise, free from all alloy, steadfast and blissful were the spectacles on which we gazed in the moment of final revelation; pure was the light that shone around us, and pure were we, without taint of that prison house which now we are encompassed withal, and call a body, fast bound therein as an oyster in its shell.

There let it rest then, our tribute to a memory that has stirred us to linger awhile on those former joys for which we yearn. Now beauty, d as we said, shone bright amidst these visions, and in this world below we apprehend it through the clearest of our senses, clear and resplendent. For sight is the keenest mode of perception vouchsafed us through the body; wisdom, indeed, we cannot see thereby—how passionate had been our desire for her, if she had granted us so clear an image of herself to gaze upon—nor yet any other of those beloved objects, save only beauty; for beauty alone this has been ordained, to be most manifest to sense and most lovely of them all.

Now he whose vision of the mystery is long past, or whose purity e has been sullied, cannot pass swiftly hence to see beauty's self yonder, when he beholds that which is called beautiful here; wherefore he looks upon it with no reverence, and surrendering to pleasure he essays to go after the fashion of a four-footed beast, and to beget offspring of the flesh, or consorting with wantonness he has no fear nor shame in running after unnatural pleasure. But when one who is 251 fresh from the mystery, and saw much of the vision, beholds a godlike face or bodily form that truly expresses beauty, first there come upon him a shuddering and a measure of that awe which the vision inspired, and then reverence as at the sight of a god, and but for fear of being deemed a very madman he would offer sacrifice to his beloved, as to a holy image of deity. Next, with the passing of the shudder, a strange sweating and fever seizes him. For by reason of the stream of b beauty entering in through his eyes there comes a warmth, whereby his soul's plumage is fostered, and with that warmth the roots of the wings are melted, which for long had been so hardened and closed up that nothing could grow; then as the nourishment is poured in, the stump of the wing swells and hastens to grow from the root over the whole substance of the soul, for aforetime the whole soul was furnished with wings. Meanwhile she throbs with ferment in every c part, and even as a teething child feels an aching and pain in its gums when a tooth has just come through, so does the soul of him who is beginning to grow his wings feel a ferment and painful irritation. Wherefore as she gazes upon the boy's beauty, she admits a flood of

particles streaming therefrom—that is why we speak of a 'flood of
passion'—whereby she is warmed and fostered; then has she respite
d from her anguish, and is filled with joy. But when she has been parted
from him and become parched, the openings of those outlets at
which the wings are sprouting dry up likewise and are closed, so that
the wing's germ is barred off. And behind its bars, together with the
flood aforesaid, it throbs like a fevered pulse, and pricks at its proper
outlet, and thereat the whole soul round about is stung and goaded
into anguish; howbeit she remembers the beauty of her beloved, and
rejoices again. So between joy and anguish she is distraught at being
e in such strange case, perplexed and frenzied; with madness upon her
she can neither sleep by night nor keep still by day, but runs hither
and thither, yearning for him in whom beauty dwells, if haply she
may behold him. At last she does behold him, and lets the flood
pour in upon her, releasing the imprisoned waters; then has she refreshment and respite from her stings and sufferings, and at that moment tastes a pleasure that is sweet beyond compare. Nor will she
252 willingly give it up. Above all others does she esteem her beloved in
his beauty; mother, brother, friends, she forgets them all. Nought
does she reck of losing worldly possessions through neglect. All the
rules of conduct, all the graces of life, of which aforetime she was
proud, she now disdains, welcoming a slave's estate and any couch
where she may be suffered to lie down close beside her darling, for besides her reverence for the possessor of beauty she has found in him
b the only physician for her grievous suffering.

Hearken, fair boy to whom I speak. This is the experience that
men term love (ἔρως), but when you hear what the gods call it, you
will probably smile at its strangeness. There are a couple of verses on
love quoted by certain Homeric scholars from the unpublished works,
the second of which is remarkably bold and a trifle astray in its quantities. They run as follows:

> Eros, cleaver of air, in mortals' speech is he named,
> But, since he must grow wings, Pteros the celestials call him.

c You may believe that or not, as you please; at all events the cause and
the nature of the lover's experience are in fact what I have said.

Now if he whom Love has caught be among the followers of Zeus,
he is able to bear the burden of the winged one with some constancy,
but they that attend upon Ares, and did range the heavens in his train,
when they are caught by Love and fancy that their beloved is doing
them some injury, will shed blood and not scruple to offer both
themselves and their loved ones in sacrifice. And so does each lover
d live, after the manner of the god in whose company he once was,
honoring him and copying him so far as may be, so long as he remains
uncorrupt and is still living in his first earthly period, and in like manner does he comport himself toward his beloved and all his other as-

sociates. And so each selects a fair one for his love after his disposition, and even as if the beloved himself were a god he fashions for himself as it were an image, and adorns it to be the object of his veneration and worship.

Thus the followers of Zeus seek a beloved who is Zeuslike in e soul; wherefore they look for one who is by nature disposed to the love of wisdom and the leading of men, and when they have found him and come to love him they do all in their power to foster that disposition. And if they have not aforetime trodden this path, they now set out upon it, learning the way from any source that may offer or finding it for themselves, and as they follow up the trace within themselves of the nature of their own god their task is made easier, inasmuch 253 as they are constrained to fix their gaze upon him, and reaching out after him in memory they are possessed by him, and from him they take their ways and manners of life, in so far as a man can partake of a god. But all this, mark you, they attribute to the beloved, and the draughts which they draw from Zeus they pour out, like bacchants, into the soul of the beloved, thus creating in him the closest possible likeness to the god they worship.   b

Those who were in the train of Hera look for a royal nature, and when they have found him they do unto him all things in like fashion. And so it is with the followers of Apollo and each other god. Every lover is fain that his beloved should be of a nature like to his own god, and when he has won him, he leads him on to walk in the ways of their god, and after his likeness, patterning himself thereupon and giving counsel and discipline to the boy. There is no jealousy nor petty spitefulness in his dealings, but his every act is aimed at bringing the beloved to be every whit like unto himself and unto the c god of their worship.

So therefore glorious and blissful is the endeavor of true lovers in that mystery rite, if they accomplish that which they endeavor after the fashion of which I speak, when mutual affection arises through the madness inspired by love. But the beloved must needs be captured, and the manner of that capture I will now tell.

In the beginning of our story we divided each soul into three parts, two being like steeds and the third like a charioteer. Well and good. Now of the steeds, so we declare, one is good and the other is d not, but we have not described the excellence of the one nor the badness of the other, and that is what must now be done. He that is on the more honorable side is upright and clean-limbed, carrying his neck high, with something of a hooked nose; in color he is white, with black eyes; a lover of glory, but with temperance and modesty; one that consorts with genuine renown, and needs no whip, being driven by the word of command alone. The other is crooked of frame, e a massive jumble of a creature, with thick short neck, snub nose, black skin, and gray eyes; hot-blooded, consorting with wantonness and vainglory; shaggy of ear, deaf, and hard to control with whip and goad.

254 Now when the driver beholds the person of the beloved, and causes a sensation of warmth to suffuse the whole soul, he begins to experience a tickling or pricking of desire, and the obedient steed, constrained now as always by modesty, refrains from leaping upon the beloved. But his fellow, heeding no more the driver's goad or whip, leaps and dashes on, sorely troubling his companion and his driver, and forcing them to approach the loved one and remind him of the b delights of love's commerce. For a while they struggle, indignant that he should force them to a monstrous and forbidden act, but at last, finding no end to their evil plight, they yield and agree to do his bidding. And so he draws them on, and now they are quite close and behold the spectacle of the beloved flashing upon them. At that sight the driver's memory goes back to that form of beauty, and he sees her once again enthroned by the side of temperance upon her holy seat; then in awe and reverence he falls upon his back, and therewith is c compelled to pull the reins so violently that he brings both steeds down on their haunches, the good one willing and unresistant, but the wanton sore against his will. Now that they are a little way off, the good horse in shame and horror drenches the whole soul with sweat, while the other, contriving to recover his wind after the pain of the bit and his fall, bursts into angry abuse, railing at the charioteer d and his yokefellow as cowardly treacherous deserters. Once again he tries to force them to advance, and when they beg him to delay awhile he grudgingly consents. But when the time appointed is come, and they feign to have forgotten, he reminds them of it—struggling and neighing and pulling until he compels them a second time to approach the beloved and renew their offer—and when they have come close, with head down and tail stretched out he takes the bit between e his teeth and shamelessly plunges on. But the driver, with resentment even stronger than before, like a racer recoiling from the starting rope, jerks back the bit in the mouth of the wanton horse with an even stronger pull, bespatters his railing tongue and his jaws with blood, and forcing him down on legs and haunches delivers him over to anguish.

And so it happens time and again, until the evil steed casts off his wantonness; humbled in the end, he obeys the counsel of his driver, and when he sees the fair beloved is like to die of fear. Wherefore at long last the soul of the lover follows after the beloved with reverence and awe.

255 Thus the loved one receives all manner of service, as peer of the gods, from a lover that is no pretender but loves in all sincerity; of his own nature, too, he is kindly disposed to him who pays such service. Now it may be that in time past he has been misled, by his schoolfellows or others, who told him that it is shameful to have commerce

with a lover, and by reason of this he may repel his advances. Nevertheless as time goes on ripening age and the ordinance of destiny together lead him to welcome the other's society, for assuredly fate b does not suffer one evil man to be friend to another, nor yet one good man to lack the friendship of another.

And now that he has come to welcome his lover and to take pleasure in his company and converse, it comes home to him what a depth of kindliness he has found, and he is filled with amazement, for he perceives that all his other friends and kinsmen have nothing to offer in comparison with this friend in whom there dwells a god. So as he continues in this converse and society, and comes close to his lover in the gymnasium and elsewhere, that flowing stream which c Zeus, as the lover of Ganymede, called the 'flood of passion,' pours in upon the lover. And part of it is absorbed within him, but when he can contain no more the rest flows away outside him, and as a breath of wind or an echo, rebounding from a smooth hard surface, goes back to its place of origin, even so the stream of beauty turns back and re-enters the eyes of the fair beloved. And so by the natural channel it reaches his soul and gives it fresh vigor, watering the roots of the wings and quickening them to growth, whereby the soul of the beloved, d in its turn, is filled with love. So he loves, yet knows not what he loves; he does not understand, he cannot tell what has come upon him; like one that has caught a disease of the eye from another, he cannot account for it, not realizing that his lover is as it were a mirror in which he beholds himself. And when the other is beside him, he shares his respite from anguish; when he is absent, he likewise shares his longing and being longed for, since he possesses that counterlove which is the image of love, though he supposes it to be friend- e ship rather than love, and calls it by that name. He feels a desire—like the lover's, yet not so strong—to behold, to touch, to kiss him, to share his couch, and now ere long the desire, as one might guess, leads to the act.

So when they lie side by side, the wanton horse of the lover's soul would have a word with the charioteer, claiming a little guerdon for all his trouble. The like steed in the soul of the beloved has no 256 word to say, but, swelling with desire for he knows not what, embraces and kisses the lover, in grateful acknowledgment of all his kindness. And when they lie by one another, he is minded not to refuse to do his part in gratifying his lover's entreaties; yet his yokefellow in turn, being moved by reverence and heedfulness, joins with the driver in resisting. And so, if the victory be won by the higher elements of mind guiding them into the ordered rule of the philosophical life, their days on earth will be blessed with happiness and concord, for b the power of evil in the soul has been subjected, and the power of goodness liberated; they have won self-mastery and inward peace. And when life is over, with burden shed and wings recovered they stand

victorious in the first of the three rounds in that truly Olympic struggle; nor can any nobler prize be secured whether by the wisdom that is
of man or by the madness that is of god.

c   But if they turn to a way of life more ignoble and unphilosophical, yet covetous of honor, then mayhap in a careless hour, or when
the wine is flowing, the wanton horses in their two souls will catch
them off their guard, bring the pair together, and choosing that part
which the multitude account blissful achieve their full desire. And this
once done, they continue therein, albeit but rarely, seeing that their
minds are not wholly set thereupon. Such a pair as this also are dear
friends, but not so dear as that other pair, one to another, both in the
d time of their love and when love is past, for they feel that they have
exchanged the most binding pledges, which it were a sin to break by
becoming enemies. When death comes they quit the body wingless indeed, yet eager to be winged, and therefore they carry off no mean reward for their lovers' madness, for it is ordained that all such as have
taken the first steps on the celestial highway shall no more return to
the dark pathways beneath the earth, but shall walk together in a life
e of shining bliss, and be furnished in due time with like plumage the
one to the other, because of their love.

These then, my boy, are the blessings great and glorious which
will come to you from the friendship of a lover. He who is not a lover
can offer a mere acquaintance flavored with worldly wisdom, dis-
pensing a niggardly measure of worldly goods; in the soul to which
he is attached he will engender an ignoble quality extolled by the
multitude as virtue, and condemn it to float for nine thousand years
257 hither and thither, around the earth and beneath it, bereft of understanding.

Thus then, dear god of love, I have offered the fairest recantation
and fullest atonement that my powers could compass; some of its language, in particular, was perforce poetical, to please Phaedrus.
Grant me thy pardon for what went before, and thy favor for what
ensued; be merciful and gracious, and take not from me the lover's
talent wherewith thou hast blessed me; neither let it wither by reason
of thy displeasure, but grant me still to increase in the esteem of the
b fair. And if anything that Phaedrus and I said earlier sounded discordant to thy ear, set it down to Lysias, the only begetter of that discourse, and staying him from discourses after this fashion turn him
toward the love of wisdom, even as his brother Polemarchus has
been turned. Then will his loving disciple here present no longer halt
between two opinions, as now he does, but live for Love in singleness
of purpose with the aid of philosophical discourse.

PHAEDRUS: If that be for our good, Socrates, I join in your
c prayer for it. And I have this long while been filled with admiration
for your speech as a far finer achievement than the one you made before. It makes me afraid that I shall find Lysias cutting a poor figure,

if he proves to be willing to compete with another speech of his own. The fact is that only the other day, my dear good sir, one of our politicians was railing at him and reproaching him on this very score, constantly dubbing him a 'speech writer'; so possibly we shall find him desisting from further composition to preserve his reputation.

SOCRATES: What a ridiculous line to take, young man! And how utterly you misjudge our friend, if you suppose him to be such a d timid creature! Am I to believe you really do think that the person you speak of meant his raillery as a reproach?

PHAEDRUS: He gave me that impression, Socrates, and of course you know as well as I do that the men of greatest influence and dignity in political life are reluctant to write speeches and bequeath to posterity compositions of their own, for fear of the verdict of later ages, which might pronounce them Sophists.

SOCRATES: Phaedrus, you are unaware that the expression 'Pleasant Bend' comes from the long bend in the Nile, and besides e the matter of the Bend you are unaware that the proudest of politicians have the strongest desire to write speeches and bequeath compositions; why, whenever they write a speech, they are so pleased to have admirers that they put in a special clause at the beginning with the names of the persons who admire the speech in question.

PHAEDRUS: What do you mean? I don't understand.

SOCRATES: You don't understand that when a politician be- 258 gins a composition the first thing he writes is the name of his admirer.

PHAEDRUS: Is it?

SOCRATES: Yes, he says maybe, 'Resolved by the Council' or 'by the people' or by both, and then 'Proposed by so-and-so'—a pompous piece of self-advertisement on the part of the author—after which he proceeds with what he has to say, showing off his own wisdom to his admirers, sometimes in a very lengthy composition. This sort of thing amounts, don't you think, to composing a speech?

PHAEDRUS: Yes, I think it does. b

SOCRATES: Then if the speech holds its ground, the author quits the scene rejoicing, but if it is blotted out, and he loses his status as a recognized speech writer, he goes into mourning, and his friends with him.

PHAEDRUS: Quite so.

SOCRATES: Which clearly implies that their attitude to the profession is not one of disdain, but of admiration.

PHAEDRUS: To be sure.

SOCRATES: Tell me then, when an orator, or a king, succeeds in acquiring the power of a Lycurgus, a Solon, or a Darius, and so c winning immortality among his people as a speech writer, doesn't he deem himself a peer of the gods while still living, and do not people of later ages hold the same opinion of him when they contemplate his writings?

PHAEDRUS : Yes, indeed.

SOCRATES : Then do you suppose that anyone of that type, whoever he might be, and whatever his animosity toward Lysias, could reproach him simply on the ground that he writes?

PHAEDRUS : What you say certainly makes that improbable, for apparently he would be reproaching what he wanted to do himself.

d   SOCRATES : Then the conclusion is obvious, that there is nothing shameful in the mere writing of speeches.

PHAEDRUS : Of course.

SOCRATES : But in speaking and writing shamefully and badly, instead of as one should, that is where the shame comes in, I take it.

PHAEDRUS : Clearly.

SOCRATES : Then what is the nature of good writing and bad? Is it incumbent on us, Phaedrus, to examine Lysias on this point, and all such as have written or mean to write anything at all, whether in the field of public affairs or private, whether in the verse of the poet or the plain speech of prose?

e   PHAEDRUS : Is it incumbent! Why, life itself would hardly be worth living save for pleasures like this—certainly not for those pleasures that involve previous pain, as do almost all concerned with the body, which for that reason are rightly called slavish.

SOCRATES : Well, I suppose we can spare the time, and I think too that the cicadas overhead, singing after their wont in the hot sun and conversing with one another, don't fail to observe us as well. So

259 if they were to see us two behaving like ordinary folk at midday, not conversing but dozing lazy-minded under their spell, they would very properly have the laugh of us, taking us for a pair of slaves that had invaded their retreat like sheep, to have their midday sleep beside the spring. If however they see us conversing and steering clear of their bewitching Siren song, they might feel respect for us and grant us

b that boon which heaven permits them to confer upon mortals.

PHAEDRUS : Oh, what is that? I don't think I have heard of it.

SOCRATES : Surely it is unbecoming in a devotee of the Muses not to have heard of a thing like that! The story is that once upon a time these creatures were men—men of an age before there were any Muses—and that when the latter came into the world, and music made its appearance, some of the people of those days were so thrilled

c with pleasure that they went on singing, and quite forgot to eat and drink until they actually died without noticing it. From them in due course sprang the race of cicadas, to which the Muses have granted the boon of needing no sustenance right from their birth, but of singing from the very first, without food or drink, until the day of their death, after which they go and report to the Muses how they severally are paid honor among mankind, and by whom. So for those whom they report as having honored Terpsichore in the dance they win that

d Muse's favor, for those that have worshiped in the rites of love the

favor of Erato, and so with all the others, according to the nature of
the worship paid to each. To the eldest, Calliope, and to her next
sister, Urania, they tell of those who live a life of philosophy and so
do honor to the music of those twain whose theme is the heavens and
all the story of gods and men, and whose song is the noblest of
them all.

Thus there is every reason for us not to yield to slumber in the
noontide, but to pursue our talk.

PHAEDRUS : Of course we must pursue it.

SOCRATES : Well, the subject we proposed for inquiry just now e
was the nature of good and bad speaking and writing; so we are to
inquire into that.

PHAEDRUS : Plainly.

SOCRATES : Then does not a good and successful discourse presuppose a knowledge in the mind of the speaker of the truth about his
subject?

PHAEDRUS : As to that, dear Socrates, what I have heard is that
the intending orator is under no necessity of understanding what is 260
truly just, but only what is likely to be thought just by the body of
men who are to give judgment; nor need he know what is truly
good or noble, but what will be thought so, since it is on the latter, not
the former, that persuasion depends.

SOCRATES : 'Not to be lightly rejected,'[4] Phaedrus, is any word
of the wise. Perhaps they are right; one has to see. And in particular this present assertion must not be dismissed.

PHAEDRUS : I agree.

SOCRATES : Well, here is my suggestion for discussion.

PHAEDRUS : Yes?

SOCRATES : Suppose I tried to persuade you to acquire a horse to b
use in battle against the enemy, and suppose that neither of us knew
what a horse was, but I knew this much about you, that Phaedrus believes a horse to be that tame animal which possesses the largest ears.

PHAEDRUS : A ridiculous thing to suppose, Socrates.

SOCRATES : Wait a moment. Suppose I continued to urge upon
you in all seriousness, with a studied encomium of a donkey, that it
was what I called it, a horse, that it was highly important for you to
possess the creature, both at home and in the field, that it was just
the animal to ride on into battle, and that it was handy, into the bar- c
gain, for carrying your equipment and so forth.

PHAEDRUS : To go to that length would be utterly ridiculous.

SOCRATES : Well, isn't it better to be a ridiculous friend than
a clever enemy?

PHAEDRUS : I suppose it is.

SOCRATES : Then when a master of oratory, who is ignorant of
good and evil, employs his power of persuasion on a community as

[4] *Iliad* 2.361.

ignorant as himself, not by extolling a miserable donkey as being
really a horse, but by extolling evil as being really good, and when by
studying the beliefs of the masses he persuades them to do evil in-
d stead of good, what kind of crop do you think his oratory is likely to
reap from the seed thus sown?

PHAEDRUS : A pretty poor one.

SOCRATES : Well now, my good friend, have we been too scurrilous in our abuse of the art of speech? Might it not retort, 'Why do
you extraordinary people talk such nonsense? I never insist on ignorance of the truth on the part of one who would learn to speak; on the
contrary, if my advice goes for anything, it is that he should only resort to me after he has come into possession of truth; what I do however pride myself on is that without my aid knowledge of what is true
will get a man no nearer to mastering the art of persuasion.'

e PHAEDRUS : And will not such a retort be just?

SOCRATES : Yes, if the arguments advanced against oratory
sustain its claim to be an art. In point of fact, I fancy I can hear certain arguments advancing, and protesting that the claim is false, that
it is no art, but a knack that has nothing to do with art, inasmuch as
there is, as the Spartans put it, no 'soothfast' art of speech, nor assuredly will there ever be one, without a grasp of truth.

261 PHAEDRUS : We must have these arguments, Socrates. Come,
bring them up before us, and examine their purport.

SOCRATES : Come hither then, you worthy creatures, and impress upon Phaedrus, who is so blessed in his offspring, that unless he
gets on with his philosophy he will never get on as a speaker on any
subject, and let Phaedrus be your respondent.

PHAEDRUS : I await their questions.

SOCRATES : Must not the art of rhetoric, taken as a whole, be a
kind of influencing of the mind by means of words, not only in courts
of law and other public gatherings, but in private places also? And
must it not be the same art that is concerned with great issues and
b small, its right employment commanding no more respect when dealing with important matters than with unimportant? Is that what you
have been told about it?

PHAEDRUS : No indeed, not exactly that. It is principally, I
should say, to lawsuits that an art of speaking and writing is applied
—and of course to public harangues also. I know of no wider application.

SOCRATES : What? Are you acquainted only with the 'Arts' or
manuals of oratory by Nestor and Odysseus, which they composed in
their leisure hours at Troy? Have you never heard of the work of Palamedes?

c PHAEDRUS : No, upon my word, nor of Nestor either, unless you
are casting Gorgias for the role of Nestor, with Odysseus played by
Thrasymachus, or maybe Theodorus.

SOCRATES: Perhaps I am. But anyway we may let them be, and do you tell me, what is it that the contending parties in law courts do? Do they not in fact contend with words, or how else should we put it?

PHAEDRUS: That is just what they do.

SOCRATES: About what is just and unjust?

PHAEDRUS: Yes.

SOCRATES: And he who possesses the art of doing this can make the same thing appear to the same people now just, now unjust, d at will?

PHAEDRUS: To be sure.

SOCRATES: And in public harangues, no doubt, he can make the same things seem to the community now good, and now the reverse of good?

PHAEDRUS: Just so.

SOCRATES: Then can we fail to see that the Palamedes of Elea has an art of speaking, such that he can make the same things appear to his audience like and unlike, or one and many, or again at rest and in motion?

PHAEDRUS: Indeed he can.

SOCRATES: So contending with words is a practice found not only in lawsuits and public harangues but, it seems, wherever men e speak we find this single art, if indeed it is an art, which enables people to make out everything to be like everything else, within the limits of possible comparison, and to expose the corresponding attempts of others who disguise what they are doing.

PHAEDRUS: How so, pray?

SOCRATES: I think that will become clear if we put the following question. Are we misled when the difference between two things is wide, or narrow?

PHAEDRUS: When it is narrow. 262

SOCRATES: Well then, if you shift your ground little by little, you are more likely to pass undetected from so-and-so to its opposite than if you do so at one bound.

PHAEDRUS: Of course.

SOCRATES: It follows that anyone who intends to mislead another, without being misled himself, must discern precisely the degree of resemblance and dissimilarity between this and that.

PHAEDRUS: Yes, that is essential.

SOCRATES: Then if he does not know the truth about a given thing, how is he going to discern the degree of resemblance between that unknown thing and other things?

PHAEDRUS: It will be impossible. b

SOCRATES: Well now, when people hold beliefs contrary to fact, and are misled, it is plain that the error has crept into their minds through the suggestion of some similarity or other.

PHAEDRUS: That certainly does happen.

SOCRATES : But can anyone possibly master the art of using similarities for the purpose of bringing people round, and leading them away from the truth about this or that to the opposite of the truth, or again can anyone possibly avoid this happening to himself, unless he has knowledge of what the thing in question really is?

PHAEDRUS : No, never.

c SOCRATES : It would seem to follow, my friend, that the art of speech displayed by one who has gone chasing after beliefs, instead of knowing the truth, will be a comical sort of art, in fact no art at all.

PHAEDRUS : I dare say.

SOCRATES : Then would you like to observe some instances of what I call the presence and absence of art in that speech of Lysias which you are carrying, and in those which I have delivered?

PHAEDRUS : Yes, by all means. At present our discussion is somewhat abstract, for want of adequate illustrations.

SOCRATES : Why, as to that it seems a stroke of luck that in the
d two speeches we have a sort of illustration of the way in which one who knows the truth can mislead his audience by playing an oratorical joke on them. I myself, Phaedrus, put that down to the local deities, or perhaps those mouthpieces of the Muses that are chirping over our heads have vouchsafed us their inspiration, for of course I don't lay claim to any oratorical skill myself.

PHAEDRUS : I dare say that is so, but please explain your point.

SOCRATES : Well, come along, read the beginning of Lysias' speech.

e PHAEDRUS : 'You know how I am situated, and I have told you that I think it to our advantage that the thing should be done. Now I claim that I should not be refused what I ask simply because I am not your lover. Lovers repent when . . .'

SOCRATES : Stop. Our business is to indicate where the speaker is at fault, and shows absence of art, isn't it?

263 PHAEDRUS : Yes.

SOCRATES : Well now, is not the following assertion obviously true—that there are some words about which we all agree, and others about which we are at variance?

PHAEDRUS : I think I grasp your meaning, but you might make it still plainer.

SOCRATES : When someone utters the word 'iron' or 'silver,' we all have the same object before our minds, haven't we?

PHAEDRUS : Certainly.

SOCRATES : But what about the words 'just' and 'good'? Don't we diverge, and dispute not only with one another but with our own selves?

PHAEDRUS : Yes indeed.

b SOCRATES : So in some cases we agree, and in others we don't.

PHAEDRUS : Quite so.

SOCRATES: Now in which of the cases are we more apt to be misled, and in which is rhetoric more effective?

PHAEDRUS: Plainly in the case where we fluctuate.

SOCRATES: Then the intending student of the art of rhetoric ought, in the first place, to make a systematic division of words, and get hold of some mark distinguishing the two kinds of words, those namely in the use of which the multitude are bound to fluctuate, and those in which they are not.

PHAEDRUS: To grasp that, Socrates, would certainly be an ex- c cellent piece of discernment.

SOCRATES: And secondly, I take it, when he comes across a particular word he must realize what it is, and be swift to perceive which of the two kinds the thing he proposes to discuss really belongs to.

PHAEDRUS: To be sure.

SOCRATES: Well then, shall we reckon love as one of the disputed terms, or as one of the other sort?

PHAEDRUS: As a disputed term, surely. Otherwise can you suppose it would have been possible for you to say of it what you said just now, namely that it is harmful both to the beloved and the lover, and then to turn round and say that it is really the greatest of goods?

SOCRATES: An excellent point. But now tell me this, for thanks d to my inspired condition I can't quite remember. Did I define love at the beginning of my speech?

PHAEDRUS: Yes indeed, and immensely thorough you were about it.

SOCRATES: Upon my word, you rate the nymphs of Achelous and Pan, son of Hermes, much higher as artists in oratory than Lysias, son of Cephalus. Or am I quite wrong? Did Lysias at the beginning of his discourse on love compel us to conceive of it as a certain definite entity, with a meaning he had himself decided upon? And did he pro- e ceed to bring all his subsequent remarks, from first to last, into line with that meaning? Shall we read his first words once again?

PHAEDRUS: If you like, but what you are looking for isn't there.

SOCRATES: Read it out, so that I can listen to the author himself.

PHAEDRUS: 'You know how I am situated, and I have told you that I think it to our advantage that the thing should be done. Now I claim that I should not be refused what I ask simply because I am not 264 your lover. Lovers, when their craving is at an end, repent of such benefits as they have conferred.'

SOCRATES: No, he doesn't seem to get anywhere near what we are looking for; he goes about it like a man swimming on his back, in reverse, and starts from the end instead of the beginning; his opening words are what the lover would naturally say to his boy only when he had finished. Or am I quite wrong, dear Phaedrus?

b   PHAEDRUS : I grant you, Socrates, that the substance of his address is really a peroration.

SOCRATES : And to pass to other points, doesn't his matter strike
you as thrown out at haphazard? Do you find any cogent reason for
his next remark, or indeed any of his remarks, occupying the place it
does? I myself, in my ignorance, thought that the writer, with a fine
abandon, put down just what came into his head. Can you find any
cogent principle of composition which he observed in setting down
his observations in this particular order?

PHAEDRUS : You flatter me in supposing that I am competent to
c see into his mind with all that accuracy.

SOCRATES : Well, there is one point at least which I think you
will admit, namely that any discourse ought to be constructed like a
living creature, with its own body, as it were; it must not lack either
head or feet; it must have a middle and extremities so composed as to
suit each other and the whole work.

PHAEDRUS : Of course.

SOCRATES : Then ask yourself whether that is or is not the case
with your friend's speech. You will find that it is just like the epitaph
said to have been carved on the tomb of Midas the Phrygian.
d   PHAEDRUS : What is that, and what's wrong with it?

SOCRATES : It runs like this:

> A maid of bronze I stand on Midas' tomb,
> So long as waters flow and trees grow tall,
> Abiding here on his lamented grave,
> I tell the traveler Midas here is laid.

e I expect you notice that it makes no difference what order the lines
come in.

PHAEDRUS : Socrates, you are making a joke of our speech!

SOCRATES : Well, to avoid distressing you, let us say no more of
that—though indeed I think it provides many examples which it
would be profitable to notice, provided one were chary of imitating
them—and let us pass to the other speeches, for they, I think, presented a certain feature which everyone desirous of examining oratory
would do well to observe.
265   PHAEDRUS : To what do you refer?

SOCRATES : They were of opposite purport, one maintaining
that the lover should be favored, the other the nonlover.

PHAEDRUS : Yes, they did so very manfully.

SOCRATES : I thought you were going to say—and with truth—
madly, but that reminds me of what I was about to ask. We said, did
we not, that love is a sort of madness?

PHAEDRUS : Yes.

SOCRATES : And that there are two kinds of madness, one resulting from human ailments, the other from a divine disturbance of
our conventions of conduct.

PHAEDRUS: Quite so.   b

SOCRATES: And in the divine kind we distinguished four types,
ascribing them to four gods: the inspiration of the prophet to Apollo,
that of the mystic to Dionysus, that of the poet to the Muses, and a
fourth type which we declared to be the highest, the madness of the
lover, to Aphrodite and Eros. Moreover we painted, after a fashion, a
picture of the lover's experience, in which perhaps we attained some
degree of truth, though we may well have sometimes gone astray—
the blend resulting in a discourse which had some claim to plausibility, or shall we say a mythical hymn of praise, in due religious c
language, a festal celebration of my master and yours too, Phaedrus,
that god of love who watches over the young and fair.

PHAEDRUS: It certainly gave me great pleasure to listen to it.

SOCRATES: Then let us take one feature of it, the way in which
the discourse contrived to pass from censure to encomium.

PHAEDRUS: Well now, what do you make of that?

SOCRATES: For the most part I think our festal hymn has
really been just a festive entertainment, but we did casually allude to
a certain pair of procedures, and it would be very agreeable if we could d
seize their significance in a scientific fashion.

PHAEDRUS: What procedures do you mean?

SOCRATES: The first is that in which we bring a dispersed plurality under a single form, seeing it all together—the purpose being to
define so-and-so, and thus to make plain whatever may be chosen as
the topic for exposition. For example, take the definition given just
now of love. Whether it was right or wrong, at all events it was that
which enabled our discourse to achieve lucidity and consistency.

PHAEDRUS: And what is the second procedure you speak of,
Socrates?

SOCRATES: The reverse of the other, whereby we are enabled to e
divide into forms, following the objective articulation; we are not to
attempt to hack off parts like a clumsy butcher, but to take example
from our two recent speeches. The single general form which they
postulated was irrationality; next, on the analogy of a single natural 266
body with its pairs of like-named members, right arm or leg, as we say,
and left, they conceived of madness as a single objective form existing
in human beings. Wherefore the first speech divided off a part on the
left, and continued to make divisions, never desisting until it discovered one particular part bearing the name of 'sinister' love, on which
it very properly poured abuse. The other speech conducted us to the
forms of madness which lay on the right-hand side, and upon discovering a type of love that shared its name with the other but was
divine, displayed it to our view and extolled it as the source of the b
greatest goods that can befall us.

PHAEDRUS: That is perfectly true.

SOCRATES: Believe me, Phaedrus, I am myself a lover of these
divisions and collections, that I may gain the power to speak and to

think, and whenever I deem another man able to discern an objective unity and plurality, I follow 'in his footsteps where he leadeth as a god.' [5] Furthermore—whether I am right or wrong in doing so, God alone knows—it is those that have this ability whom for the present I call dialecticians.

c   But now tell me what we ought to call them if we take instruction from Lysias and yourself. Or is what I have been describing precisely that art of oratory thanks to which Thrasymachus and the rest of them have not only made themselves masterly orators, but can do the same for anyone else who cares to bring offerings to these princes among men?

PHAEDRUS: Doubtless they behave like princes, but assuredly they do not possess the kind of knowledge to which you refer. No, I think you are right in calling the procedure that you have described dialectic, but we still seem to be in the dark about rhetoric.

d   SOCRATES: What? Can there really be anything of value that admits of scientific acquisition despite the lack of that procedure? If so, you and I should certainly not disdain it, but should explain what this residuum of rhetoric actually consists in.

PHAEDRUS: Well, Socrates, of course there is plenty of matter in the rhetorical manuals.

SOCRATES: Thank you for the reminder. The first point, I suppose, is that a speech must begin with a preamble. You are referring, are you not, to such niceties of the art?

e   PHAEDRUS: Yes.

SOCRATES: And next comes exposition accompanied by direct evidence; thirdly, indirect evidence; fourthly, probabilities; besides which there are the proof and supplementary proof mentioned by the Byzantine master of rhetorical artifice.

PHAEDRUS: You mean the worthy Theodorus?

267   SOCRATES: Of course. And we are to have a refutation and supplementary refutation both for prosecution and defense. And can we leave the admirable Evenus of Paros out of the picture, the inventor of covert allusion and indirect compliment and, according to some accounts, of the indirect censure in mnemonic verse? A real master, that. But we won't disturb the rest of Tisias and Gorgias, who realized that probability deserves more respect than truth, who could make trifles seem important and important points trifles by the force of their

b   language, who dressed up novelties as antiques and vice versa, and found out how to argue concisely or at interminable length about anything and everything. This last accomplishment provoked Prodicus once to mirth when he heard me mention it; he remarked that he and he alone had discovered what sort of speeches the art demands—to wit, neither long ones nor short, but of fitting length.

---

[5] *Odyssey* 5.193.

PHAEDRUS: Masterly, Prodicus!

SOCRATES: Are we forgetting Hippias? I think Prodicus' view would be supported by the man of Elis.

PHAEDRUS: No doubt.

SOCRATES: And then Polus. What are we to say of his *Muses' Treasury of Phrases* with its reduplications and maxims and similes, c and of words à la Licymnius which that master made him a present of as a contribution to his fine writing?

PHAEDRUS: But didn't Protagoras in point of fact produce some such works, Socrates?

SOCRATES: Yes, my young friend, there is his *Correct Diction*, and many other excellent works. But to pass now to the application of pathetic language to the poor and aged, the master in that style seems to me to be the mighty man of Chalcedon, who was also expert at rousing a crowd to anger and then soothing them down again with d his spells, to quote his own saying, while at casting aspersions and dissipating them, whatever their source, he was unbeatable.

But to resume, on the way to conclude a speech there seems to be general agreement, though some call it recapitulation and others by some other name.

PHAEDRUS: You mean the practice of reminding the audience e toward the end of a speech of its main points?

SOCRATES: Yes. And now if you have anything further to add about the art of rhetoric . . .

PHAEDRUS: Only a few unimportant points.

SOCRATES: If they are unimportant, we may pass them over. 268 But let us look at what we have got in a clearer light, to see what power the art possesses, and when.

PHAEDRUS: A very substantial power, Socrates, at all events in large assemblies.

SOCRATES: Yes indeed. But have a look at it, my good sir, and see whether you discern some holes in the fabric, as I do.

PHAEDRUS: Do show them me.

SOCRATES: Well, look here. Suppose someone went up to your friend Eryximachus, or his father Acumenus, and said, 'I know how to apply such treatment to a patient's body as will induce warmth or coolness, as I choose; I can make him vomit, if I see fit, or go to stool, b and so on and so forth. And on the strength of this knowledge I claim to be a competent physician, and to make a competent physician of anyone to whom I communicate this knowledge.' What do you imagine they would have to say to that?

PHAEDRUS: They would ask him, of course, whether he also knew which patients ought to be given the various treatments, and when, and for how long.

SOCRATES: Then what if he said, 'Oh, no, but I expect my pupils to manage what you refer to by themselves'?   c

PHAEDRUS : I expect they would say, 'The man is mad; he thinks he has made himself a doctor by picking up something out of a book, or coming across some common drug or other, without any real knowledge of medicine.'

SOCRATES : Now suppose someone went up to Sophocles or Euripides and said he knew how to compose lengthy dramatic speeches about a trifling matter, and quite short ones about a matter of moment, that he could write pathetic passages when he chose, or again
d passages of intimidation and menace, and so forth, and that he considered that by teaching these accomplishments he could turn a pupil into a tragic poet.

PHAEDRUS : I imagine that they too would laugh at anyone who supposed that you could make a tragedy otherwise than by so arranging such passages as to exhibit a proper relation to one another and to the whole of which they are parts.

SOCRATES : Still I don't think they would abuse him rudely, but rather treat him as a musician would treat a man who fancied himself to be a master of harmony simply because he knew how to produce the highest possible note and the lowest possible on his strings.
e The musician would not be so rude as to say, 'You miserable fellow, you're off your head,' but rather, in the gentler language befitting his profession, 'My good sir, it is true that one who proposes to become a master of harmony must know the things you speak of, but it is perfectly possible for one who has got as far as yourself to have not the slightest real knowledge of harmony. You are acquainted with what has to be learned before studying harmony, but of harmony itself you know nothing.'

PHAEDRUS : Perfectly true.

269   SOCRATES : Similarly then Sophocles would tell the man who sought to show off to himself and Euripides that what he knew was not tragic composition but its antecedents, and Acumenus would make the same distinction between medicine and the antecedents of medicine.

PHAEDRUS : I entirely agree.

SOCRATES : And if 'mellifluous' [6] Adrastus, or shall we say Pericles, were to hear of those admirable artifices that we were referring to just now—the brachylogies and imageries and all the rest of them, which we enumerated and deemed it necessary to examine in a clear light—are we to suppose that they would address those who practice and teach this sort of thing, under the name of the art of rhetoric, with
b the severity you and I displayed, and in rude, coarse language? Or would they, in their ampler wisdom, actually reproach us and say, 'Phaedrus and Socrates, you ought not to get angry, but to make allowances for such people; it is because they are ignorant of dialectic that they are incapable of properly defining rhetoric, and that in turn

[6] Tyrtaeus, fr. 9, 7.

leads them to imagine that by possessing themselves of the requisite antecedent learning they have discovered the art itself. And so they c teach these antecedents to their pupils, and believe that that constitutes a complete instruction in rhetoric; they don't bother about employing the various artifices in such a way that they will be effective, or about organizing a work as a whole; that is for the pupils to see to for themselves when they come to make speeches.'

PHAEDRUS : Well yes, Socrates, I dare say that does more or less describe what the teachers and writers in question regard as the art of rhetoric; personally I think what you say is true. But now by what means and from what source can one attain the art of the true rheto- d rician, the real master of persuasion?

SOCRATES : If you mean how can one become a finished performer, then probably—indeed I might say undoubtedly—it is the same as with anything else. If you have an innate capacity for rhetoric, you will become a famous rhetorician, provided you also acquire knowledge and practice, but if you lack any of these three you will be correspondingly unfinished. As regards the art itself, as distinct from the artist, I fancy that the line of approach adopted by Lysias and Thrasymachus is not the one I have in view.

PHAEDRUS : Then what is?

SOCRATES : I am inclined to think, my good friend, that it was e not surprising that Pericles became the most finished exponent of rhetoric there has ever been.

PHAEDRUS : Why so?

SOCRATES : All the great arts need supplementing by a study of nature; your artist must cultivate garrulity and high-flown specula- 270 tion; from that source alone can come the mental elevation and thoroughly finished execution of which you are thinking, and that is what Pericles acquired to supplement his inborn capacity. He came across the right sort of man, I fancy, in Anaxagoras, and by enriching himself with high speculation and coming to recognize the nature of wisdom and folly—on which topics of course Anaxagoras was always discoursing—he drew from that source and applied to the art of rhetoric what was suitable thereto.

PHAEDRUS : How do you mean?

SOCRATES : Rhetoric is in the same case as medicine, don't you b think?

PHAEDRUS : How so?

SOCRATES : In both cases there is a nature that we have to determine, the nature of body in the one, and of soul in the other, if we mean to be scientific and not content with mere empirical routine when we apply medicine and diet to induce health and strength, or words and rules of conduct to implant such convictions and virtues as we desire.

PHAEDRUS : You are probably right, Socrates.

c   SOCRATES : Then do you think it possible to understand the nature of the soul satisfactorily without taking it as a whole?
       PHAEDRUS : If we are to believe Hippocrates, the Asclepiad, we
can't understand even the body without such a procedure.
       SOCRATES : No, my friend, and he is right. But we must not just
rely on Hippocrates; we must examine the assertion and see whether
it accords with the truth.
       PHAEDRUS : Yes.
       SOCRATES : Then what is it that Hippocrates and the truth have
d   to say on this matter of nature? I suggest that the way to reflect about
the nature of anything is as follows: first, to decide whether the object
in respect of which we desire to have scientific knowledge, and to be
able to impart it to others, is simple or complex; secondly, if it is simple, to inquire what natural capacity it has of acting upon another
thing, and through what means; or by what other thing, and through
what means, it can be acted upon; or, if it is complex, to enumerate its
parts and observe in respect of each what we observe in the case of the
simple object, to wit what its natural capacity, active or passive, consists in.
       PHAEDRUS : Perhaps so, Socrates.
       SOCRATES : Well, at all events, to pursue an inquiry without do-
e ing so would be like a blind man's progress. Surely we mustn't make
out that any sort of scientific inquirer resembles a blind or deaf person. No, it is plain that if we are to address people scientifically, we
shall show them precisely what is the real and true nature of that object on which our discourse is brought to bear. And that object, I take
it, is the soul.
       PHAEDRUS : To be sure.
271   SOCRATES : Hence the speaker's whole effort is concentrated on
that, for it is there that he is attempting to implant conviction. Isn't
that so?
       PHAEDRUS : Yes.
       SOCRATES : Then it is plain that Thrasymachus, or anyone else
who seriously proffers a scientific rhetoric, will, in the first place, describe the soul very precisely, and let us see whether it is single and
uniform in nature or, analogously to the body, complex. For to do that
is, we maintain, to show a thing's nature.
       PHAEDRUS : Yes, undoubtedly.
       SOCRATES : And secondly he will describe what natural capacity
it has to act upon what, and through what means, or by what it can be
acted upon.
       PHAEDRUS : Quite so.
b   SOCRATES : Thirdly, he will classify the types of discourse and
the types of soul, and the various ways in which souls are affected, explaining the reasons in each case, suggesting the type of speech appropriate to each type of soul, and showing what kind of speech can be

relied on to create belief in one soul and disbelief in another, and why.

PHAEDRUS: I certainly think that would be an excellent procedure.

SOCRATES: Yes, in fact I can assure you, my friend, that no other scientific method of treating either our present subject or any c other will ever be found, whether in the models of the schools or in speeches actually delivered. But the present-day authors of manuals of rhetoric, of whom you have heard, are cunning folk who know all about the soul but keep their knowledge out of sight. So don't let us admit their claim to write scientifically until they compose their speeches and writings in the way we have indicated.

PHAEDRUS: And what way is that?

SOCRATES: To give the actual words would be troublesome, but I am quite ready to say how one ought to compose if he means to be as scientific as possible.

PHAEDRUS: Then please do.

SOCRATES: Since the function of oratory is in fact to influence men's souls, the intending orator must know what types of soul there d are. Now these are of a determinate number, and their variety results in a variety of individuals. To the types of soul thus discriminated there corresponds a determinate number of types of discourse. Hence a certain type of hearer will be easy to persuade by a certain type of speech to take such and such action for such and such reason, while another type will be hard to persuade. All this the orator must fully understand, and next he must watch it actually occurring, exemplified in men's conduct, and must cultivate a keenness of perception in e following it, if he is going to get any advantage out of the previous instruction that he was given in the school. And when he is competent to say what type of man is susceptible to what kind of discourse; when, further, he can, on catching sight of so-and-so, tell himself, 'That is 272 the man, that character now actually before me is the one I heard about in school, and in order to persuade him of so-and-so I have to apply *these* arguments in *this* fashion'; and when, on top of all this, he has further grasped the right occasions for speaking and for keeping quiet, and has come to recognize the right and the wrong time for the brachylogy, the pathetic passage, the exacerbation, and all the rest of his accomplishments—then and not till then has he well and truly achieved the art. But if in his speaking or teaching or writing he fails in any of these requirements, he may tell you that he has the art of b speech, but one mustn't believe all one is told.

And now maybe our author will say, 'Well, what of it, Phaedrus and Socrates? Do you agree with me, or should we accept some other account of the art of speech?'

PHAEDRUS: Surely we can't accept any other, Socrates; still it does seem a considerable business.

SOCRATES: You are right, and that makes it necessary

thoroughly to overhaul all our arguments, and see whether there is
c some easier and shorter way of arriving at the art; we don't want to
waste effort in going off on a long rough road, when we might take a
short smooth one. But if you can help us at all through what you have
heard from Lysias or anyone else, do try to recall it.

PHAEDRUS : As far as trying goes, I might, but I can suggest
nothing on the spur of the moment.

SOCRATES : Then would you like me to tell you something I have
heard from those concerned with these matters?

PHAEDRUS : Why, yes.

SOCRATES : Anyhow, Phaedrus, we are told that even the devil's
advocate ought to be heard.

d   PHAEDRUS : Then you can put his case.

SOCRATES : Well, they tell us that there is no need to make such
a solemn business of it, or fetch such a long compass on an uphill
road. As we remarked at the beginning of this discussion, there is, they
maintain, absolutely no need for the budding orator to concern himself with the truth about what is just or good conduct, nor indeed
about who are just and good men whether by nature or education. In
the law courts nobody cares a rap for the truth about these matters,
e but only about what is plausible. And that is the same as what is probable, and is what must occupy the attention of the would-be master
of the art of speech. Even actual facts ought sometimes not be stated,
if they don't tally with probability; they should be replaced by what is
probable, whether in prosecution or defense; whatever you say, you
simply must pursue this probability they talk of, and can say good-by
273 to the truth forever. Stick to that all through your speech, and you are
equipped with the art complete.

PHAEDRUS : Your account, Socrates, precisely reproduces what
is said by those who claim to be experts in the art of speech. I remember that we did touch briefly on this sort of contention a while ago,
and the professionals regard it as a highly important point.

SOCRATES : Very well then, take Tisias himself; you have
thumbed him carefully, so let Tisias tell us this. Does he maintain that
b the probable is anything other than that which commends itself to the
multitude?

PHAEDRUS : How could it be anything else?

SOCRATES : Then in consequence, it would seem, of that profound scientific discovery he laid down that if a weak but brave man is
arrested for assaulting a strong but cowardly one, whom he has
robbed of his cloak or some other garment, neither of them ought to
state the true facts; the coward should say that the brave man didn't
assault him singlehanded, and the brave man should contend that
there were only the two of them, and then have recourse to the famous
c plea, 'How could a little fellow like me have attacked a big fellow
like him?' Upon which the big fellow will not avow his own poltroon-

ery but will try to invent some fresh lie which will probably supply his opponent with a means of refuting him. And similar 'scientific' rules are given for other cases of the kind. Isn't that so, Phaedrus?

PHAEDRUS: To be sure.

SOCRATES: Bless my soul! It appears that he made a brilliant discovery of a buried art, your Tisias, or whoever it really was and whatever he is pleased to be called after. But, my friend, shall we or shall we not say to him . . .

PHAEDRUS: Say what?   d

SOCRATES: This. 'In point of fact, Tisias, we have for some time before you came on the scene been saying that the multitude get their notion of probability as the result of a likeness to truth, and we explained just now that these likenesses can always be best discovered by one who knows the truth. Therefore if you have anything else to say about the art of speech, we should be glad to hear it, but if not we shall adhere to the point we made just now, namely that unless the aspirant to oratory can on the one hand list the various natures among his prospective audiences, and on the other divide things into their e kinds and embrace each individual thing under a single form, he will never attain such success as is within the grasp of mankind. Yet he will assuredly never acquire such competence without considerable diligence, which the wise man should exert not for the sake of speaking to and dealing with his fellow men, but that he may be able to speak what is pleasing to the gods, and in all his dealings to do their pleasure to the best of his ability. For you see, Tisias, what we are told by those wiser than ourselves is true, that a man of sense ought never 274 to study the gratification of his fellow slaves, save as a minor consideration, but that of his most excellent masters. So don't be surprised that we have to make a long detour; it is because the goal is glorious, though not the goal you think of.' Not but what those lesser objects also, if you would have them, can best be attained, so our argument assures us, as a consequence of the greater.

PHAEDRUS: Your project seems to be excellent, Socrates, if only one could carry it out.

SOCRATES: Well, when a man sets his hand to something good, it is good that he should take what comes to him.   b

PHAEDRUS: Yes, of course.

SOCRATES: Then we may feel that we have said enough about the art of speech, both the true art and the false?

PHAEDRUS: Certainly.

SOCRATES: But there remains the question of propriety and impropriety in writing, that is to say the conditions which make it proper or improper. Isn't that so?

PHAEDRUS: Yes.

SOCRATES: Now do you know how we may best please God, in practice and in theory, in this matter of words?

PHAEDRUS : No indeed. Do you?

c   SOCRATES : I can tell you the tradition that has come down from our forefathers, but they alone know the truth of it. However, if we could discover that for ourselves, should we still be concerned with the fancies of mankind?

PHAEDRUS : What a ridiculous question! But tell me the tradition you speak of.

SOCRATES : Very well. The story is that in the region of Naucratis in Egypt there dwelt one of the old gods of the country, the god to whom the bird called Ibis is sacred, his own name being Theuth. He

d it was that invented number and calculation, geometry and astronomy, not to speak of draughts and dice, and above all writing. Now the king of the whole country at that time was Thamus, who dwelt in the great city of Upper Egypt which the Greeks call Egyptian Thebes, while Thamus they call Ammon. To him came Theuth, and revealed his arts, saying that they ought to be passed on to the Egyptians in general. Thamus asked what was the use of them all, and when

e Theuth explained, he condemned what he thought the bad points and praised what he thought the good. On each art, we are told, Thamus had plenty of views both for and against; it would take too long to give them in detail. But when it came to writing Theuth said, 'Here, O king, is a branch of learning that will make the people of Egypt wiser and improve their memories; my discovery provides a recipe for memory and wisdom.' But the king answered and said, 'O man full of arts, to one it is given to create the things of art, and to another to judge what measure of harm and of profit they have for those that shall employ

275 them. And so it is that you, by reason of your tender regard for the writing that is your offspring, have declared the very opposite of its true effect. If men learn this, it will implant forgetfulness in their souls; they will cease to exercise memory because they rely on that which is written, calling things to remembrance no longer from within themselves, but by means of external marks. What you have discovered is a recipe not for memory, but for reminder. And it is no true wisdom that you offer your disciples, but only its semblance, for by telling them of many things without teaching them you will make them

b seem to know much, while for the most part they know nothing, and as men filled, not with wisdom, but with the conceit of wisdom, they will be a burden to their fellows.'

PHAEDRUS : It is easy for you, Socrates, to make up tales from Egypt or anywhere else you fancy.

SOCRATES : Oh, but the authorities of the temple of Zeus at Dodona, my friend, said that the first prophetic utterances came from an oak tree. In fact the people of those days, lacking the wisdom of you young people, were content in their simplicity to listen to trees

c or rocks, provided these told the truth. For you apparently it makes a difference who the speaker is, and what country he comes from; you don't merely ask whether what he says is true or false.

PHAEDRUS : I deserve your rebuke, and I agree that the man of Thebes is right in what he said about writing.

SOCRATES : Then anyone who leaves behind him a written manual, and likewise anyone who takes it over from him, on the supposition that such writing will provide something reliable and permanent, must be exceedingly simple-minded; he must really be ignorant of Ammon's utterance, if he imagines that written words can do anything more than remind one who knows that which the writing is con- d cerned with.

PHAEDRUS : Very true.

SOCRATES : You know, Phaedrus, that's the strange thing about writing, which makes it truly analogous to painting. The painter's products stand before us as though they were alive, but if you question them, they maintain a most majestic silence. It is the same with written words; they seem to talk to you as though they were intelligent, but if you ask them anything about what they say, from a desire to be instructed, they go on telling you just the same thing forever. And once a thing is put in writing, the composition, whatever it may e be, drifts all over the place, getting into the hands not only of those who understand it, but equally of those who have no business with it; it doesn't know how to address the right people, and not address the wrong. And when it is ill-treated and unfairly abused it always needs its parent to come to its help, being unable to defend or help itself.

PHAEDRUS : Once again you are perfectly right.

SOCRATES : But now tell me, is there another sort of discourse, 276 that is brother to the written speech, but of unquestioned legitimacy? Can we see how it originates, and how much better and more effective it is than the other?

PHAEDRUS : What sort of discourse have you now in mind, and what is its origin?

SOCRATES : The sort that goes together with knowledge, and is written in the soul of the learner, that can defend itself, and knows to whom it should speak and to whom it should say nothing.

PHAEDRUS : You mean no dead discourse, but the living speech, the original of which the written discourse may fairly be called a kind of image.

SOCRATES : Precisely. And now tell me this. If a sensible farmer b had some seeds to look after and wanted them to bear fruit, would he with serious intent plant them during the summer in a garden of Adonis, and enjoy watching it producing fine fruit within eight days? If he did so at all, wouldn't it be in a holiday spirit, just by way of pastime? For serious purposes wouldn't he behave like a scientific farmer, sow his seeds in suitable soil, and be well content if they came to maturity within eight months?

PHAEDRUS : I think we may distinguish as you say, Socrates, be- c tween what the farmer would do seriously and what he would do in a different spirit.

SOCRATES : And are we to maintain that he who has knowledge of what is just, honorable, and good has less sense than the farmer in dealing with his seeds?

PHAEDRUS : Of course not.

SOCRATES : Then it won't be with serious intent that he writes them in water' or that black fluid we call ink, using his pen to sow words that can't either speak in their own defense or present the truth adequately.

PHAEDRUS : It certainly isn't likely.

d   SOCRATES : No, it is not. He will sow his seed in literary gardens, I take it, and write when he does write by way of pastime, collecting a store of refreshment both for his own memory, against the day 'when age oblivious comes,' and for all such as tread in his footsteps, and he will take pleasure in watching the tender plants grow up. And when other men resort to other pastimes, regaling themselves with drinking parties and suchlike, he will doubtless prefer to indulge in the recreation I refer to.

e   PHAEDRUS : And what an excellent one it is, Socrates! How far superior to the other sort is the recreation that a man finds in words, when he discourses about justice and the other topics you speak of.

SOCRATES : Yes indeed, dear Phaedrus. But far more excellent, I think, is the serious treatment of them, which employs the art of dialectic. The dialectician selects a soul of the right type, and in it he plants and sows his words founded on knowledge, words which can

277   defend both themselves and him who planted them, words which instead of remaining barren contain a seed whence new words grow up in new characters, whereby the seed is vouchsafed immortality, and its possessor the fullest measure of blessedness that man can attain unto.

PHAEDRUS : Yes, that is a far more excellent way.

SOCRATES : Then now that that has been settled, Phaedrus, we can proceed to the other point.

PHAEDRUS : What is that?

SOCRATES : The point that we wanted to look into before we arrived at our present conclusion. Our intention was to examine the reproach leveled against Lysias on the score of speech writing, and

b   therewith the general question of speech writing and what does and does not make it an art. Now I think we have pretty well cleared up the question of art.

PHAEDRUS : Yes, we did think so, but please remind me how we did it.

SOCRATES : The conditions to be fulfilled are these. First, you must know the truth about the subject that you speak or write about; that is to say, you must be able to isolate it in definition, and having so defined it you must next understand how to divide it into kinds, until you reach the limit of division; secondly, you must have a correspond-

ing discernment of the nature of the soul, discover the type of speech c
appropriate to each nature, and order and arrange your discourse accordingly, addressing a variegated soul in a variegated style that
ranges over the whole gamut of tones, and a simple soul in a simple
style. All this must be done if you are to become competent, within human limits, as a scientific practitioner of speech, whether you propose
to expound or to persuade. Such is the clear purport of all our foregoing discussion.

PHAEDRUS: Yes, that was undoubtedly how we came to see the
matter.

SOCRATES: And now to revert to our other question, whether d
the delivery and composition of speeches is honorable or base, and in
what circumstances they may properly become a matter of reproach,
our earlier conclusions have, I think, shown . . .

PHAEDRUS: Which conclusions?

SOCRATES: They have shown that any work, in the past or in
the future, whether by Lysias or anyone else, whether composed in a
private capacity or in the role of a public man who by proposing a law
becomes the author of a political composition, is a matter of reproach
to its author—whether or no the reproach is actually voiced—if he regards it as containing important truth of permanent validity. For ignorance of what is a waking vision and what is a mere dream image
of justice and injustice, good and evil, cannot truly be acquitted of e
involving reproach, even if the mass of men extol it.

PHAEDRUS: No indeed.

SOCRATES: On the other hand, if a man believes that a written
discourse on any subject is bound to contain much that is fanciful,
that nothing that has ever been written whether in verse or prose merits much serious attention—and for that matter nothing that has ever
been spoken in the declamatory fashion which aims at mere persuasion without any questioning or exposition—that in reality such compositions are, at the best, a means of reminding those who know the 278
truth, that lucidity and completeness and serious importance belong
only to those lessons on justice and honor and goodness that are expounded and set forth for the sake of instruction, and are veritably
written in the soul of the listener, and that such discourses as these
ought to be accounted a man's own legitimate children—a title to be
applied primarily to such as originate within the man himself, and
secondarily to such of their sons and brothers as have grown up aright b
in the souls of other men—the man, I say, who believes this, and disdains all manner of discourse other than this, is, I would venture to
affirm, the man whose example you and I would pray that we might
follow.

PHAEDRUS: My own wishes and prayers are most certainly to
that effect.

SOCRATES: Then we may regard our literary pastime as having

reached a satisfactory conclusion. Do you now go and tell Lysias that we two went down to the stream where is the holy place of the nymphs, and there listened to words which charged us to deliver a
c message, first to Lysias and all other composers of discourses, secondly to Homer and all others who have written poetry whether to be read or sung, and thirdly to Solon and all such as are authors of political compositions under the name of laws—to wit, that if any of them has done his work with a knowledge of the truth, can defend his statements when challenged, and can demonstrate the inferiority of his writings out of his own mouth, he ought not to be designated by a name drawn from those writings, but by one that indicates his seri-
d ous pursuit.

PHAEDRUS : Then what names would you assign him?

SOCRATES : To call him wise, Phaedrus, would, I think be going too far; the epithet is proper only to a god. A name that would fit him better, and have more seemliness, would be 'lover of wisdom,' or something similar.

PHAEDRUS : Yes, that would be quite in keeping.

SOCRATES : On the other hand, one who has nothing to show of more value than the literary works on whose phrases he spends hours,
e twisting them this way and that, pasting them together and pulling them apart, will rightly, I suggest, be called a poet or speech writer or law writer.

PHAEDRUS : Of course.

SOCRATES : Then that is what you must tell your friend.

PHAEDRUS : But what about yourself? What are you going to do? You too have a friend who should not be passed over.

SOCRATES : Who is that?

PHAEDRUS : The fair Isocrates. What will be your message to him, Socrates, and what shall we call him?

SOCRATES : Isocrates is still young, Phaedrus, but I don't mind
279 telling you the future I prophesy for him.

PHAEDRUS : Oh, what is that?

SOCRATES : It seems to me that his natural powers give him a superiority over anything that Lysias has achieved in literature, and also that in point of character he is of a nobler composition; hence it would not surprise me if with advancing years he made all his literary predecessors look like very small-fry—that is, supposing him to persist in the actual type of writing in which he engages at present—still more so, if he should become dissatisfied with such work, and a sublimer impulse lead him to do greater things. For that mind of his, Phaedrus, contains an innate tincture of philosophy.
b   Well then, there's the report I convey from the gods of this place to Isocrates my beloved, and there's yours for your beloved Lysias.

PHAEDRUS : So be it. But let us be going, now that it has become less oppressively hot.

SOCRATES: Oughtn't we first to offer a prayer to the divinities here?

PHAEDRUS: To be sure.

SOCRATES: Dear Pan, and all ye other gods that dwell in this place, grant that I may become fair within, and that such outward things as I have may not war against the spirit within me. May I count c him rich who is wise, and as for gold, may I possess so much of it as only a temperate man might bear and carry with him.

Is there anything more we can ask for, Phaedrus? The prayer contents me.

PHAEDRUS: Make it a prayer for me too, since friends have all things in common.

SOCRATES: Let us be going.

SYMPOSIUM

It is agreed that the Symposium is one of Plato's two greatest dialogues, either greater than the Republic or next to it. Of all of them it tells the most vivid story and it gives the most arresting and the most detailed portrait of Socrates. Also it contains the loftiest expression of Plato's inmost conviction that it is the things not seen which are eternal and eternally important.

There is little need for any introduction to it and no need for any explanation. It presents no difficulties. It is not an argument to be followed, but a series of speeches made at a supper party, a symposium. These speeches are not connected with each other except that they all have the same subject, love, all love in all its degrees of low, higher, highest. The culminating speech is, of course, spoken by Socrates. It follows that of the host, Agathon, a poet, whose words make the reader recall the thirteenth chapter of First Corinthians written some four hundred years later, Paul's unapproachable praise of love.

Like Paul in First Corinthians, Agathon speaks of human love. Socrates in his speech passes from the human to the divine, much as does John. (If we love one another God dwelleth in us.) We begin, Socrates says, by loving beauty in people and go on to loving not the beauty we see, but that which is unseen, the beautiful soul. From there we go on to love beautiful thoughts and ideas, ever ascending under the influence of true love. So we draw nearer to the vast sea of beauty until at last we perceive beauty itself, not existing in any being, but beauty alone, absolute, simple, and everlasting. Thither looking we become the friends of God. To that consummation we are led by love.

From this height Plato leads us down rapidly by way of Alcibiades, who never occupied any height whatsoever and who, moreover, when he breaks in upon the supper party declares that he is very drunk. And yet he pays a hardly to be surpassed tribute to Socrates, who alone, he says, has made him ashamed of the poor, trivial life he is living, so ashamed that he has sometimes felt it unendurable. For

*greatness and goodness, he concludes, Socrates stands alone among
all the men there have ever been. To all of this the reader sees Socrates
listening with a smile, kindly and amused.*

APOLLODORUS: Oh, if that's what you want to know, it isn't long 172
since I had occasion to refresh my memory. Only the day before yesterday, as I was coming up to the city from my place at Phalerum, a
friend of mine caught sight of me from behind, and while I was still a
long way ahead he shouted after me, Here, I say, Apollodorus! Can't
you wait for me?

So I stopped and waited for him.

Apollodorus, he said as he came up, you're the very man I'm looking for. I want to ask you about this party at Agathon's, when Socrates and Alcibiades and the rest of them were at dinner there. What
were all these speeches they were making about Love? I've heard b
something about them from a man who'd been talking to Phoenix, but
his information was rather sketchy and he said I'd better come to you.
So you'll have to tell me the whole story, for you know we always
count on you, Apollodorus, to report your beloved Socrates. But before you begin, tell me, were you there yourself?

Well, said I, whoever was your informant I can well believe he
wasn't very clear about it if you gathered it was such a recent party
that I could have been there!   c

That was my impression, said he.

My dear Glaucon, I protested, how could it have been? Have you
forgotten how long Agathon's been away from Athens? And don't you
know it's only two or three years since I started spending so much of
my time with Socrates, and making it my business to follow every- 173
thing he says and does from day to day? Because, you know, before
that I used to go dashing about all over the place, firmly convinced
that I was leading a full and interesting life, when I was really as
wretched as could be—much the same as you, for instance, for I
know philosophy's the last thing *you'd* spend your time on.

Now don't start girding at me, said Glaucon, but tell me, when
was this party, then?

It was given, I told him, when you and I were in the nursery, the
day after Agathon's celebrations with the players when he'd won the
prize with his first tragedy.

Plato's Symposium, or The Drinking Party, translated by Michael Joyce
(Everyman's Library, London and New York, 1935).

Yes, he admitted, that must have been a good many years ago. But who told you about it—Socrates himself?

b   No, no, I said. I had it from the same source as Phoenix—Aristodemus of Cydathenaeum, a little fellow who used to go about barefoot. He was there himself; indeed I fancy he was one of Socrates' most impassioned admirers at the time. As a matter of fact I did ask Socrates about one or two points later on, and he confirmed what Aristodemus had told me.

Very well, said Glaucon, then you must tell me all about it before we reach the city. I'm sure it'll pass the time most agreeably.

Well, I told him all about it as we went along, and so, as I was c saying, I've got the story pretty pat, and if you want to hear it too I suppose I may as well begin. For that matter I don't know anything that gives me greater pleasure, or profit either, than talking or listening to philosophy. But when it comes to ordinary conversation, such as the stuff you talk about financiers and the money market, well, I find it pretty tiresome personally, and I feel sorry that my friends should think they're being very busy when they're really doing ab- d solutely nothing. Of course, I know your idea of me; you think I'm just a poor unfortunate, and I shouldn't wonder if you're right. But then, I don't *think* that *you're* unfortunate—I know you are.

FRIEND: There you go again, Apollodorus! Always running down yourself and everybody else! You seem to have some extrava- e gant idea that the whole world, with the sole exception of Socrates, is in a state of utter misery—beginning with yourself. You're always the same—perhaps that's why people think you're mad—always girding at yourself and all the rest of us, except Socrates of course.

APOLLODORUS: My dear man, of course I am! And of course I shouldn't *dream* of thinking such things about myself or about my friends if I weren't completely crazy.

FRIEND: Oh, come now, Apollodorus! We needn't go into that. For heaven's sake, man, don't fly off at a tangent, but simply answer our question. What were these speeches about Love?

APOLLODORUS: Well then, they were something like this—but 174 perhaps I'd better begin at the beginning and tell you in Aristodemus' own words.

I met Socrates, he told me, looking very spruce after his bath, with a nice pair of shoes on although, as you know, he generally goes about barefoot. So I asked him where he was going, cutting such a dash.

I'm going to dinner with Agathon, he said. I kept away from the public celebrations yesterday because I was afraid there'd be a crush, but I promised I'd go along this evening. And I've got myself up like this because I don't want to disgrace such a distinguished host. b But what about you? he went on. How would you like to join the party uninvited?

Just as you think, I replied.

Then come along with me, he said, and we'll adapt the proverb, 'Unbidden do the good frequent the tables of the good.' Though, if it comes to that, Homer himself has not so much adapted that very proverb as exploded it, for after making Agamemnon extremely stout and warlike, and Menelaus a most indifferent spearman, he c shows Agamemnon making merry after the sacrifice and Menelaus coming to his table uninvited—that is, the lesser man coming to supper with the greater.

I'm afraid, said I, that Homer's version is the apter so far as I'm concerned—an uninvited ignoramus going to dinner with a man of letters. So you'd better be preparing your excuses on the way, for you needn't think I'll apologize for coming without an invitation—I shall plead that you invited me.   d

Two heads are better than one, he said, when it comes to excuses. Well, anyway, let's be off.

Having settled this point, continued Aristodemus, we started out, and as we went along Socrates fell into a fit of abstraction and began to lag behind, but when I was going to wait for him he told me to go on ahead. So when I arrived at Agathon's, where the door was stand- e ing wide-open, I found myself in rather a curious position, for a servant immediately showed me in and announced me to the assembled company, who were already at table and just about to begin.

However, the moment Agathon saw me he cried, Ah! Here's Aristodemus—just in time for dinner, and if you've come on business it'll have to wait, that's flat. I was going to invite you yesterday, only I couldn't get hold of you. But I say, where's Socrates? Haven't you brought him with you?

I looked round, supposing that Socrates was bringing up the rear, but he was nowhere to be seen; so I explained that we'd been coming along together, and that I'd come at his invitation.

Very nice of you, said Agathon, but what on earth can have happened to the man?

He was just coming in behind me; I can't think where he can be. 175

Here, said Agathon to one of the servants, run along and see if you can find Socrates, and show him in. And now, my dear Aristodemus, may I put you next to Eryximachus?

And so, Aristodemus went on, I made my toilet and sat down, the servant meanwhile returning with the news that our friend Socrates had retreated into the next-door neighbor's porch.

And there he stood, said the man. And when I asked him in he wouldn't come.

This is very odd, said Agathon. You must speak to him again, and insist.

But here I broke in. I shouldn't do that, I said. You'd much b better leave him to himself. It's quite a habit of his, you know; off he

goes and there he stands, no matter where it is. I've no doubt he'll be
with us before long, so I really don't think you'd better worry him.

Oh, very well, said Agathon. I expect you know best. We won't
wait then, he said, turning to the servants. Now you understand, you
fellows are to serve whatever kind of dinner you think fit; I'm leaving
it entirely to you. I know it's a new idea, but you'll simply have to
imagine that we've all come here as your guests. Now go ahead and
show us what you can do.

c   Well, we started dinner, and still there was no sign of Socrates;
Agathon still wanted to send for him, but I wouldn't let him. And
when at last he did turn up, we weren't more than halfway through
dinner, which was pretty good for him.

As he came in, Agathon, who was sitting by himself at the far
end of the table, called out, Here you are, Socrates. Come and sit next
to me; I want to share this great thought that's just struck you in the
porch next door. I'm sure you must have mastered it, or you'd still
d   be standing there.

My dear Agathon, Socrates replied as he took his seat beside
him, I only wish that wisdom *were* the kind of thing one could share
by sitting next to someone—if it flowed, for instance, from the one
that was full to the one that was empty, like the water in two cups
finding its level through a piece of worsted. If that were how it
e   worked, I'm sure I'd congratulate myself on sitting next to you, for
you'd soon have me brimming over with the most exquisite kind of
wisdom. My own understanding is a shadowy thing at best, as equivo-
cal as a dream, but yours, Agathon, glitters and dilates—as which of
us can forget that saw you the other day, resplendent in your youth,
visibly kindled before the eyes of more than thirty thousand of your
fellow Greeks.

Now, Socrates, said Agathon, I know you're making fun of me;
however, I shall take up this question of wisdom with you later on,
and let Bacchus judge between us. In the meantime you must really
show a little interest in your food.

So Socrates drew up and had his dinner with the rest of them, and
176   then, after the libation and the usual hymn and so forth, they began
to turn their attention to the wine. It was Pausanias, so far as Aristodemus could remember, who opened the conversation.

Well, gentlemen, he began, what do you say? What sort of a
night shall we make of it? Speaking for myself, I'm not quite up to
form. I'm still a bit the worse for what I had last night, and I don't
suppose you're most of you much better—we were all in the same
boat. Anyhow, what do you say? How does everybody feel about the
b   drink?

That's a most sensible question of yours, Pausanias, said Aristophanes. We don't want to make a burden of it—I speak as one who
was pretty well soaked last night.

I quite agree, observed Eryximachus, and there is just one question I should like to add. What about Agathon? Has he sufficiently recovered to feel like drinking?

Not I, said Agathon. You can count me out.

So much the better for me, then, said Eryximachus, and so much c the better for Aristodemus and Phaedrus and one or two more I could mention. We never could keep up with heavy drinkers like the rest of you. I say nothing of Socrates, for we know he's equal to any occasion, drunk or sober. And now, gentlemen, since nobody seems very anxious to get drunk tonight, I may perhaps be pardoned if I take this opportunity of saying a few words on the true nature of inebriation. My own experience in medicine has entirely satisfied me d that vinous excess is detrimental to the human frame. And therefore I can never be a willing party to heavy drinking, as regards either myself or my friends—especially when one is only partially recovered from the excesses of the previous night.

But here Phaedrus broke in. My dear Eryximachus, he said, I always do what you tell me to, specially when it really is a case of 'doctor's orders,' and I think the others would be well advised to do the same.

Whereupon it was unanimously agreed that this was not to be a e drunken party, and that the wine was to be served merely by way of refreshment.

Very well, then, said Eryximachus, since it is agreed that we need none of us drink more than we think is good for us, I also propose that we dispense with the services of the flute girl who has just come in, and let her go and play to herself or to the women inside there, whichever she prefers, while we spend our evening in discussion of a subject which, if you think fit, I am prepared to name.

It was generally agreed that he should go on with his proposal. 177 So he continued, If I may preface my remarks by a tag from Euripides, 'The tale is not my own,'[1] as Melanippe says, that I am going to tell, but properly belongs to my friend Phaedrus here, who is continually coming to me with the following complaint. Is it not, he asks me, an extraordinary thing that, for all the hymns and anthems that have been addressed to the other deities, not one single poet has ever sung a song in praise of so ancient and so powerful a god as Love?   b

Take such distinguished men of letters as Prodicus, for instance, with their eulogies in prose of Heracles and all the rest of them—not that *they're* so much out of the way either, but do you know, I once came across a book which enumerated the uses of common salt and sang its praises in the most extravagant terms, and not only salt but all kinds of everyday commodities. Now isn't it, as I say, an extraor- c dinary thing, Eryximachus, that while all these screeds have

---

[1] *Melanippe*, fr. 488.

been written on such trivial subjects, the god of love has found no man bold enough to sing his praises as they should be sung—is it not, in short, amazing that there should be so little reverence shown to such a god!

This, gentlemen, is Phaedrus' complaint, and I must say I think it is justified. And, moreover, not only am I willing to oblige him with a contribution on my own account, but also I suggest that this is a most suitable occasion for each one of us to pay homage to the god.
d If therefore, gentlemen, this meets with your approval, I venture to think we may spend a very pleasant evening in discussion. I suppose the best way would be for each in turn from left to right to address the company and speak to the best of his ability in praise of Love. Phaedrus, I think, should open the debate, for besides being head of the table he is the real author of our discussion.

The motion is carried, Eryximachus, said Socrates, unanimously, I should think. Speaking for myself, I couldn't very well dissent when I claim that love is the one thing in the world I under-
e stand—nor could Agathon and Pausanias; neither could Aristophanes, whose whole life is devoted to Dionysus and Aphrodite; no more could any of our friends who are here with us tonight. Of course, your procedure will come very hard on us who are sitting at the bottom of the table, but if the earlier speeches are fine enough, I promise you we shan't complain. So let Phaedrus go ahead with his eulogy of Love—and good luck to him.

178   Then all the rest of them agreed, and told Phaedrus to begin—but before I go on I must make it quite clear that Aristodemus did not pretend to reproduce the various speeches verbatim, any more than I could repeat them word for word as I had them from him. I shall simply recount such passages as the speaker or the thought itself made, so far as I could judge, especially memorable.

As I was saying, then, Phaedrus opened with some such arguments as these—that Love was a great god, wonderful alike to the gods and to mankind, and that of all the proofs of this the greatest was his birth.

The worship of this god, he said, is of the oldest, for Love is un-
b begotten, nor is there mention of his parentage to be found anywhere in either prose or verse, while Hesiod tells us expressly that Chaos first appeared, and then

> From Chaos rose broad-bosomed Earth, the sure
> And everlasting seat of all that is,
> And after, Love . . .[2]

Acusilaus agrees with Hesiod, for he holds that after Chaos were brought forth these twain, Earth and Love, and Parmenides writes of the creative principle.

[2] *Theogony* 116 sq.

And Love she framed the first of all the gods.[3]

Thus we find that the antiquity of Love is universally admitted, c and in very truth he is the ancient source of all our highest good. For I, at any rate, could hardly name a greater blessing to the man that is to be than a generous lover, or, to the lover, than the beloved youth. For neither family, nor privilege, nor wealth, nor anything but Love can light that beacon which a man must steer by when he sets out to live the better life. How shall I describe it—as that contempt for the d vile, and emulation of the good, without which neither cities nor citizens are capable of any great or noble work. And I will say this of the lover, that, should he be discovered in some inglorious act, or in abject submission to ill-usage, he could better bear that anyone—father, friends, or who you will—should witness it than his beloved. And the same holds good of the beloved—that his confusion would be e more than ever painful if he were seen by his lovers in an unworthy light.

If only, then, a city or an army could be composed of none but lover and beloved, how could they deserve better of their country than by shunning all that is base, in mutual emulation? And men like these fighting shoulder to shoulder, few as they were, might conquer 179 —I had almost said—the whole world in arms. For the lover would rather anyone than his beloved should see him leave the ranks or throw away his arms in flight—nay, he would sooner die a thousand deaths. Nor is there any lover so faint of heart that he could desert his beloved or fail to help him in the hour of peril, for the very presence of Love kindles the same flame of valor in the faintest heart that burns in those whose courage is innate. And so, when Homer b writes that some god 'breathed might'[4] into one of the heroes, we may take it that this is what the power of Love effects in the heart of the lover.

And again, nothing but Love will make a man offer his life for another's—and not only man but woman, of which last we Greeks can ask no better witness than Alcestis, for she alone was ready to lay down her life for her husband—for all he had a father and a mother, whose love fell so far short of hers in charity that they seemed to be c alien to their own son, and bound to him by nothing but a name. But hers was accounted so great a sacrifice, not only by mankind but by the gods, that in recognition of her magnanimity it was granted— and among the many doers of many noble deeds there is only the merest handful to whom such grace has been given—that her soul should rise again from the Stygian depths.

Thus heaven itself has a peculiar regard for ardor and resolution d in the cause of Love. And yet the gods sent Orpheus away from Hades empty-handed, and showed him the mere shadow of the woman he

[3] Parmenides, fr. 132.   [4] Iliad 10.482, 15.262.

had come to seek. Eurydice herself they would not let him take, because he seemed, like the mere minstrel that he was, to be a lukewarm lover, lacking the courage to die as Alcestis died for love, and choosing rather to scheme his way, living, into Hades. And it was for this that the gods doomed him, and doomed him justly, to meet his death at the hands of women.

e   How different was the fate of Achilles, Thetis' son, whom they sent with honors to the Islands of the Blessed, because, after learning from his mother that if he slew Hector he should die, while if he spared him he should end his days at home in the fullness of his years, he made the braver choice and went to rescue his lover Patroclus, avenged his death, and so died, not only *for* his friend, but to be with his friend in death. And it was because his lover had been so precious to him that he was honored so signally by the gods.

180   I may say that Aeschylus has reversed the relation between them by referring to Patroclus as Achilles' darling, whereas Achilles, we know, was much handsomer than Patroclus or any of the heroes, and was besides still beardless and, as Homer says, by far the younger of the two. I make a point of this because, while in any case the gods display especial admiration for the valor that springs from Love, they are even more amazed, delighted, and beneficent when the beloved shows such devotion to his lover, than when the lover does the same for his beloved. For the lover, by virtue of Love's inspiration, is

b always nearer than his beloved to the gods. And this, I say, is why they paid more honor to Achilles than to Alcestis, and sent him to the Islands of the Blessed.

In short, this, gentlemen, is my theme, that Love is the oldest and most glorious of the gods, the great giver of all goodness and happiness to men, alike to the living and to the dead.

c   This, to the best of Aristodemus' recollection, was Phaedrus' speech. It was followed by several more which had almost, if not quite, escaped him; so he went straight on to Pausanias, who spoke as follows.

I am afraid, my dear Phaedrus, that our arrangement won't work very well if it means that we are simply to pronounce a eulogy of Love. It would be all very well if there were only one kind of Love, but unfortunately this is not the case, and we should therefore have begun by stipulating which kind in particular was to receive our homage. In

d the circumstances I will try to set the matter right by first defining the Love whom we are to honor, and then singing his praises in terms not unworthy, I hope, of his divinity.

Now you will all agree, gentlemen, that without Love there could be no such goddess as Aphrodite. If, then, there were only one goddess of that name, we might suppose that there was only one kind of Love, but since in fact there are two such goddesses there must also be two kinds of Love. No one, I think, will deny that there are two goddesses of that name—one, the elder, sprung from no mother's womb but from the heavens themselves, we call the Uranian, the heavenly Aphrodite, while the younger, daughter of Zeus and Dione, we call Pandemus, the earthly Aphrodite. It follows, then, that e Love should be known as earthly or as heavenly according to the goddess in whose company his work is done. And our business, gentlemen —I need hardly say that every god must command our homage— our business at the moment is to define the attributes peculiar to each of these two.

Now it may be said of any kind of action that the action itself, as such, is neither good nor bad. Take, for example, what we are doing 181 now. Neither drinking nor singing nor talking has any virtue in itself, for the outcome of each action depends upon how it is performed. If it is done rightly and finely, the action will be good; if it is done basely, bad. And this holds good of loving, for Love is not of himself either admirable or noble, but only when he moves us to love nobly.

Well then, gentlemen, the earthly Aphrodite's Love is a very b earthly Love indeed, and does his work entirely at random. It is he that governs the passions of the vulgar. For, first, they are as much attracted by women as by boys; next, whoever they may love, their desires are of the body rather than of the soul; and, finally, they make a point of courting the shallowest people they can find, looking forward to the mere act of fruition and careless whether it be a worthy or unworthy consummation. And hence they take their pleasures where they find them, good and bad alike. For this is the Love of the younger Aphrodite, whose nature partakes of both male and female.   c

But the heavenly Love springs from a goddess whose attributes have nothing of the female, but are altogether male, and who is also the elder of the two, and innocent of any hint of lewdness. And so those who are inspired by this other Love turn rather to the male, preferring the more vigorous and intellectual bent. One can always tell— d even among the lovers of boys—the man who is wholly governed by this elder Love, for no boy can please him until he has shown the first signs of dawning intelligence, signs which generally appear with the first growth of beard. And it seems to me that the man who falls in love with a youth of such an age will be prepared to spend all his time with him, to share his whole life with him, in fact; nor will he be likely to take advantage of the lad's youth and credulity by seducing him and then turning with a laugh to some newer love.

But I cannot help thinking, gentlemen, that there should be a e law to forbid the loving of mere boys, a law to prevent so much time and trouble being wasted upon an unknown quantity—for what else, after all, is the future of any boy, and who knows whether he will follow the paths of virtue or of vice, in body and in soul? Of course, your man of principle is a law unto himself, but these followers of the earthly Love should be legally compelled to observe a similar

restraint—just as we prevent them, as far as possible, from making
182 love to our own wives and daughters—for it is their behavior that has
brought the name of Love into such disrepute that one has even
heard it held to be degrading to yield to a lover's solicitation. Anyone
who can hold such a view must surely have in mind these earthly
lovers, with their offensive importunities, for there can be nothing
derogatory in any conduct which is sanctioned both by decency and
custom.

Then again, gentlemen, may I point out that, while in all the
other states of Hellas the laws that deal with Love are so simple and
well defined that they are easy enough to master, our own code is most
b involved. In Elis and Boeotia, for instance, and wherever else the
people are naturally inarticulate, it has been definitely ruled that it
is right for the lover to have his way. Nor does anyone, old or young,
presume to say that it is wrong—the idea being, I suppose, to save
themselves from having to plead with the young men for their favors,
which is rather difficult for lovers who are practically dumb.

On the other hand, in Ionia and many other countries under oriental rule, the very same thing is held to be disgraceful. Indeed, the
c oriental thinks ill not only of Love but also of both philosophy and
sport, on account of the despotism under which he lives. For I suppose it does not suit the rulers for their subjects to indulge in high
thinking, or in staunch friendship and fellowship, which Love more
than anything is likely to beget. And those who seized the power here
in Athens learned the same lesson from bitter experience, for it was
the might of Aristogiton's love and Harmodius' friendship that
brought their reign to an end. Thus, wherever the law enacts that it is
d wrong to yield to the lover, you may be sure that the fault lies with the
legislators—that is to say, it is due to the oppression of the rulers
and the servility of their subjects. On the other hand, wherever you
find the same thing expressly sanctioned, you may blame the legislators' mental inertia.

But in Athens, gentlemen, we have a far more admirable code—
a code which, as I was saying, is not nearly so easy to understand.
Take for instance our maxim that it is better to love openly than in
secret, especially when the object of one's passion is eminent in nobility and virtue, and even if his personal appearance should lack
the same distinction. And think how we all love to cheer the lover on,
without the least idea that he is doing anything unworthy, and how
e we see honor in his success and shame in his defeat. And remember,
gentlemen, what latitude the law offers to the lover in the prosecution
of his suit, and how he may be actually applauded for conduct which,
in any other circumstances or in any other cause, would call down
upon him the severest censure.
183   Imagine what would happen to a man who wanted to get money
out of someone, or a post, or powers of some kind, and who therefore

thought fit to behave as the lover behaves to his beloved—urging his need with prayers and entreaties, and vowing vows, and sleeping upon doorsteps, subjecting himself, in short, to a slavery which no slave would ever endure—why, gentlemen, not only his friends, but his very enemies, would do their best to stop him, for his enemies would accuse him of the most abject servility, while his friends would take him to task because they felt ashamed of him.

But when it is a lover who does this kind of thing people only b think the more of him, and the law expressly sanctions his conduct as the means to an honorable end. And, what is the most extraordinary thing of all, it is popularly supposed that the lover is the one man whom the gods will pardon for breaking his vows, for lovers' promises, they say, are made to be forsworn. And so, gentlemen, we see what complete indulgence, not only human but divine, is ac- c corded to the lover by our Athenian code.

In view of this, one would have thought that, here if anywhere, loving and being kind to one's lover would have been positively applauded. Yet we find in practice that if a father discovers that someone has fallen in love with his son, he puts the boy in charge of an attendant, with strict injunctions not to let him have anything to do with his lover. And if the boy's little friends and playmates see anything of that kind going on, you may be sure they'll call him names, while their elders will neither stop their being rude nor tell them they d are talking nonsense. So if there were no more to it than that, anyone would think that we Athenians were really shocked at the idea of yielding to a lover.

But I fancy we can account for the apparent contradiction if we remember that the moral value of the act is not what one might call a constant. We agreed that love itself, as such, was neither good nor bad, but only in so far as it led to good or bad behavior. It is base to indulge a vicious lover viciously, but noble to gratify a virtuous lover e virtuously. Now the vicious lover is the follower of the earthly Love who desires the body rather than the soul; his heart is set on what is mutable and must therefore be inconstant. And as soon as the body he loves begins to pass the first flower of its beauty, he 'spreads his wings and flies away,' giving the lie to all his pretty speeches and dishonoring his vows, whereas the lover whose heart is touched by moral beauties is constant all his life, for he has become one with what will never fade.

Now it is the object of the Athenian law to make a firm dis- 184 tinction between the lover who should be encouraged and the lover who should be shunned. And so it enjoins pursuit in certain cases, and flight in others, and applies various touchstones and criteria to discriminate between the two classes of lover and beloved. And this is why it is immoral, according to our code, to yield too promptly to solicitation; there should first be a certain lapse of time, which is b generally considered to be the most effective test. Secondly, it is immoral when the surrender is due to financial or political considerations, or to unmanly fear of ill-treatment; it is immoral, in short, if the youth fails to show the contempt he should for any advantage he may gain in pocket or position. For in motives such as these we can find nothing fixed or permanent, except, perhaps, the certainty that they have never been the cause of any noble friendship.

c   There remains, therefore, only one course open to the beloved if he is to yield to his lover without offending our ideas of decency. It is held that, just as the lover's willing and complete subjection to his beloved is neither abject nor culpable, so there is one other form of voluntary submission that shall be blameless—a submission which is made for the sake of virtue. And so, gentlemen, if anyone is prepared to devote himself to the service of another in the belief that through him he will find increase of wisdom or of any other virtue, we hold that such willing servitude is neither base nor abject.

d   We must therefore combine these two laws—the one that deals with the love of boys and the one that deals with the pursuit of wisdom and the other virtues—before we can agree that the youth is justified in yielding to his lover. For it is only when lover and beloved come together, each governed by his own especial law—the former lawfully enslaving himself to the youth he loves, in return for his compliance, the latter lawfully devoting his services to the friend who is helping him to become wise and good—the one sharing his

e wealth of wisdom and virtue, and the other drawing, in his poverty, upon his friend for a liberal education—it is then, I say, and only then, when the observance of the two laws coincides, that it is right for the lover to have his way.

There is no shame in being disappointed of such hopes as these, but any other kind of hope, whether it comes true or not, is shame-
185 ful in itself. Take the case of a youth who gratifies his lover in the belief that he is wealthy and in the hope of making money. Such hopes will be nonetheless discreditable if he finds in the event that he has been the prey of a penniless seducer, for he will have shown himself for what he is, the kind of person, namely, who will do anything for money—which is nothing to be proud of. But suppose that he had yielded because he believed in his lover's virtue, and hoped to be improved by such an association; then, even if he discovered in the end
b that he had been duped by an unholy blackguard, there would still have been something noble in his mistake, for he, too, would have shown himself for what he was—the kind of person who will do anything for anybody for the sake of progress in the ways of virtue. And what, gentlemen, could be more admirable than that? I conclude, therefore, that it is right to let the lover have his way in the interests of virtue.

Such, then, is the Love of the heavenly Aphrodite, heavenly in

himself and precious alike to cities and to men, for he constrains both
lover and beloved to pay the most earnest heed to their moral wel- c
fare, but all the rest are followers of the other, the earthly Aphrodite.
And this, Phaedrus, is all I have to say, extempore, on the subject of
Love.

When Pausanias had paused—you see the kind of tricks we catch
from our philologists, with their punning derivations—the next
speaker, so Aristodemus went on to tell me, should have been Aristophanes; only as it happened, whether he'd been overeating I don't
know, but he had got the hiccups so badly that he really wasn't fit to
make a speech. So he said to the doctor, Eryximachus, who was d
sitting next below him, Eryximachus, you'll either have to cure my
hiccups or take my turn and go on speaking till they've stopped.

I'm prepared to do both, said Eryximachus. I'll take your turn to
speak, and then when you've recovered you can take mine. Meanwhile, you'd better try holding your breath, or if that won't stop your
hiccup try gargling with a little water, or if it's particularly stubborn e
you'll have to get something that you can tickle your nostrils with,
and sneeze, and by the time you've done that two or three times you'll
find that it will stop, however bad it is.

Go ahead, then, said Aristophanes. You make your speech, and
I'll be doing as you say.

Whereupon Eryximachus spoke as follows.

Well, gentlemen, since Pausanias broke off, after an excellent
beginning, without having really finished, I must try to wind up his 186
argument myself. I admit that in defining the two kinds of Love he has
drawn a very useful distinction, but the science of medicine seems to
me to prove that, besides attracting the souls of men to human
beauty, Love has many other objects and many other subjects, and
that his influence may be traced both in the brute and the vegetable creations, and I think I may say in every form of existence—
so great, so wonderful, and so all-embracing is the power of Love in b
every activity, whether sacred or profane.

I propose, in deference to my own profession, to begin with the
medical aspect. I would have you know that the body comprehends
in its very nature the dichotomy of Love, for, as we all agree, bodily
health and sickness are both distinct and dissimilar, and unlike clings
to unlike. And so the desires of health are one thing, while the desires
of sickness are quite another. I confirm what Pausanias has observed,
that it is right to yield to the virtuous and wrong to yield to the vicious c
lover, and similarly, in the case of the body, it is both right and necessary to gratify such desires as are sound and healthy in each particular
case, and this is what we call the art of medicine. But it is utterly
wrong to indulge such desires as are bad and morbid, nor must anyone
who hopes to become expert in this profession lend his countenance
to such indulgence. For medicine may be described as the science of

what the body loves, or desires, as regards repletion and evacuation, d and the man who can distinguish between what is harmful and what is beneficial in these desires may claim to be a physician in the fullest sense of the word. And if he can replace one desire with another, and produce the requisite desire when it is absent, or, if necessary, remove it when it is present, then we shall regard him as an expert practitioner.

Yes, gentlemen, he must be able to reconcile the jarring elements of the body, and force them, as it were, to fall in love with one another. Now, we know that the most hostile elements are the opposites —hot and cold, sweet and sour, wet and dry, and so on—and if, as I do myself, we are to believe these poets of ours, it was his skill in imposing love and concord upon these opposites that enabled our illus- e trious progenitor Asclepius to found the science of medicine.

And so, gentlemen, I maintain that medicine is under the sole direction of the god of love, as are also the gymnastic and the agro- 187 nomic arts. And it must be obvious to the most casual observer that the same holds good of music—which is, perhaps, what Heraclitus meant us to understand by that rather cryptic pronouncement, 'The one in conflict with itself is held together, like the harmony of the bow and of the lyre.' [5] Of course it is absurd to speak of harmony as being in conflict, or as arising out of elements which are still conflicting, but perhaps he meant that the art of music was to create har- b mony by resolving the discord between the treble and the bass. There can certainly be no harmony of treble and bass while they are still in conflict, for harmony is concord, and concord is a kind of sympathy, and sympathy between things which are in conflict is impossible so long as that conflict lasts. There is, on the other hand, a kind of discord which it is not impossible to resolve, and here we may effect a harmony—as, for instance, we produce rhythm by re- c solving the difference between fast and slow. And just as we saw that the concord of the body was brought about by the art of medicine, so this other harmony is due to the art of music, as the creator of mutual love and sympathy. And so we may describe music, too, as a science of love, or of desire—in this case in relation to harmony and rhythm.

It is easy enough to distinguish the principle of Love in this rhythmic and harmonic union, nor is there so far any question of Love's dichotomy. But when we come to the application of rhythm and harmony to human activities—as for instance the composition of a d song, or the instruction of others in the correct performance of airs and measures which have already been composed—then, gentlemen, we meet with difficulties which call for expert handling. And this brings us back to our previous conclusion, that we are justified in

[5] Heraclitus, fr. 45.

yielding to the desires of the temperate—and of the intemperate in so far as such compliance will tend to sober them, and to this Love, gentlemen, we must hold fast, for he is the fair and heavenly one, born of Urania, the Muse of heaven. But as for that other, the earthly Love, he is sprung from Polyhymnia, the Muse of many songs, and e whatever we have to do with him we must be very careful not to add the evils of excess to the enjoyment of the pleasures he affords— just as, in my own profession, it is an important part of our duties to regulate the pleasures of the table so that we may enjoy our meals without being the worse for them. And so in music, in medicine, and in every activity, whether sacred or profane, we must do our utmost to distinguish the two kinds of Love, for you may be sure that they will both be there. 188

And again, we find these two elements in the seasons of the year, for when the regulating principle of Love brings together those opposites of which I spoke—hot and cold, wet and dry—and compounds them in an ordered harmony, the result is health and plenty for mankind, and for the animal and vegetable kingdoms, and all goes as it should. But when the seasons are under the influence of that other Love, all is mischief and destruction, for now plague and disease of b every kind attack both herds and crops, and not only these, but frost and hail and blight—and all of them are due to the uncontrolled and the acquisitive in that great system of Love which the astronomer observes when he investigates the movements of the stars and the seasons of the year.

And further, the sole concern of every rite of sacrifice and divination—that is to say, the means of communion between god and man—is either the preservation or the repair of Love. For most of our c impiety springs from our refusal to gratify the more temperate Love, and to respect and defer to him in everything we do, and from our following that other Love in our attitude toward our parents, whether alive or dead, and toward the gods. It is the diviner's office to be the guide and healer of these Loves, and his art of divination, with its power to distinguish those principles of human love that tend to decency and reverence, is, in fact, the source of concord between d god and man.

And so, gentlemen, the power of Love in its entirety is various and mighty, nay, all-embracing, but the mightiest power of all is wielded by that Love whose just and temperate consummation, whether in heaven or on earth, tends toward the good. It is he that bestows our every joy upon us, and it is through him that we are capable of the pleasures of society, aye, and friendship even, with the gods our masters.

And now, gentlemen, if, as is not unlikely, there are many points I have omitted in my praise of Love, let me assure you that such omis- e sions have been unintentional. It is for you, Aristophanes, to make

542 PLATO: COLLECTED DIALOGUES

good my deficiencies, that is unless you're thinking of some other kind of eulogy. But in any case, let us hear what you have to say—now you've recovered from your hiccups.

189 To which, Aristodemus went on to tell me, Aristophanes replied, Yes, I'm better now, thank you, but not before I'd had recourse to sneezing—which made me wonder, Eryximachus, how your orderly principle of the body could possibly have called for such an appalling union of noise and irritation; yet there's no denying that the hiccups stopped immediately I sneezed.

Now, Aristophanes, take care, retorted Eryximachus, and don't try to raise a laugh before you've even started. You'll only have your-
b self to thank if I'm waiting to pounce on your silly jokes, instead of giving your speech a proper hearing.

Aristophanes laughed. You're quite right, Eryximachus, he said. I take it all back. But don't be too hard on me. Not that I mind if what I'm going to say is funny—all the better if it is; besides, a comic poet is supposed to be amusing. I'm only afraid of being utterly absurd.

Now, Aristophanes, said Eryximachus, I know the way you loose your shafts of ridicule and run away. But don't forget that anything
c you say may be used against you—and yet, who knows? Perhaps I shall decide to let you go with a caution.

Well then, Eryximachus, Aristophanes began, I propose, as you suggested, to take quite a different line from you and Pausanias. I am convinced that mankind has never had any conception of the power of Love, for if we had known him as he really is, surely we should have raised the mightiest temples and altars, and offered the most splendid sacrifices, in his honor, and not—as in fact we do—have utterly neglected him. Yet he of all the gods has the best title to
d our service, for he, more than all the rest, is the friend of man; he is our great ally, and it is he that cures us of those ills whose relief opens the way to man's highest happiness. And so, gentlemen, I will do my best to acquaint you with the power of Love, and you in your turn shall pass the lesson on.

First of all I must explain the real nature of man, and the change which it has undergone—for in the beginning we were nothing like we are now. For one thing, the race was divided into three; that is to say, besides the two sexes, male and female, which we have at pres-
e ent, there was a third which partook of the nature of both, and for which we still have a name, though the creature itself is forgotten. For though 'hermaphrodite' is only used nowadays as a term of contempt, there really was a man-woman in those days, a being which was half male and half female.

And secondly, gentlemen, each of these beings was globular in shape, with rounded back and sides, four arms and four legs, and two
190 faces, both the same, on a cylindrical neck, and one head, with one face one side and one the other, and four ears, and two lots of privates,

and all the other parts to match. They walked erect, as we do ourselves, backward or forward, whichever they pleased, but when they
broke into a run they simply stuck their legs straight out and went
whirling round and round like a clown turning cartwheels. And
since they had eight legs, if you count their arms as well, you can
imagine that they went bowling along at a pretty good speed.

The three sexes, I may say, arose as follows. The males were
descended from the Sun, the females from the Earth, and the her- b
maphrodites from the Moon, which partakes of either sex, and they
were round and they *went* round, because they took after their parents. And such, gentlemen, were their strength and energy, and such
their arrogance, that they actually tried—like Ephialtes and Otus in
Homer—to scale the heights of heaven and set upon the gods.

At this Zeus took counsel with the other gods as to what was to c
be done. They found themselves in rather an awkward position; they
didn't want to blast them out of existence with thunderbolts as they
did the giants, because that would be saying good-by to all their offerings and devotions, but at the same time they couldn't let them get altogether out of hand. At last, however, after racking his brains, Zeus
offered a solution.

I think I can see my way, he said, to put an end to this disturbance by weakening these people without destroying them. What I
propose to do is to cut them all in half, thus killing two birds with d
one stone, for each one will be only half as strong, and there'll be
twice as many of them, which will suit us very nicely. They can
walk about, upright, on their two legs, and if, said Zeus, I have any
more trouble with them, I shall split them up again, and they'll have
to hop about on one.

So saying, he cut them all in half just as you or I might chop up
sorb apples for pickling, or slice an egg with a hair. And as each half e
was ready he told Apollo to turn its face, with the half-neck that was
left, toward the side that was cut away—thinking that the sight of
such a gash might frighten it into keeping quiet—and then to heal
the whole thing up. So Apollo turned their faces back to front, and,
pulling in the skin all the way round, he stretched it over what we
now call the belly—like those bags you pull together with a string—
and tied up the one remaining opening so as to form what we call the
navel. As for the creases that were left, he smoothed most of them
away, finishing off the chest with the sort of tool a cobbler uses to 191
smooth down the leather on the last, but he left a few puckers round
about the belly and the navel, to remind us of what we suffered long
ago.

Now, when the work of bisection was complete it left each half
with a desperate yearning for the other, and they ran together and
flung their arms around each other's necks, and asked for nothing
better than to be rolled into one. So much so, that they began to die

b of hunger and general inertia, for neither would do anything without the other. And whenever one half was left alone by the death of its mate, it wandered about questing and clasping in the hope of finding a spare half-woman—or a whole woman, as we should call her nowadays—or half a man. And so the race was dying out.

Fortunately, however, Zeus felt so sorry for them that he devised another scheme. He moved their privates round to the front, for of course they had originally been on the outside—which was now the back—and they had begotten and conceived not upon each other, but,
c like the grasshoppers, upon the earth. So now, as I say, he moved their members round to the front and made them propagate among themselves, the male begetting upon the female—the idea being that if, in all these clippings and claspings, a man should chance upon a woman, conception would take place and the race would be continued, while if man should conjugate with man, he might at least obtain such satisfaction as would allow him to turn his attention and his energies to the everyday affairs of life. So you see, gentlemen,
d how far back we can trace our innate love for one another, and how this love is always trying to redintegrate our former nature, to make two into one, and to bridge the gulf between one human being and another.

And so, gentlemen, we are all like pieces of the coins that children break in half for keepsakes—making two out of one, like the flatfish—and each of us is forever seeking the half that will tally with himself. The man who is a slice of the hermaphrodite sex, as it was called, will naturally be attracted by women—the adulterer, for instance—and women who run after men are of similar descent—as,
e for instance, the unfaithful wife. But the woman who is a slice of the original female is attracted by women rather than by men—in fact she is a Lesbian—while men who are slices of the male are followers of the male, and show their masculinity throughout their boyhood by the way they make friends with men, and the delight they take in lying beside them and being taken in their arms. And these are the
192 most hopeful of the nation's youth, for theirs is the most virile constitution.

I know there are some people who call them shameless, but they are wrong. It is not immodesty that leads them to such pleasures, but daring, fortitude, and masculinity—the very virtues that they recognize and welcome in their lovers—which is proved by the fact that in after years they are the only men who show any real manliness in public life. And so, when they themselves have come to manhood, their love in turn is lavished upon boys. They have no natu-
b ral inclination to marry and beget children. Indeed, they only do so in deference to the usage of society, for they would just as soon renounce marriage altogether and spend their lives with one another.

Such a man, then, gentlemen, is of an amorous disposition,

and gives his love to boys, always clinging to his like. And so, when this boy lover—or any lover, for that matter—is fortunate enough to meet his other half, they are both so intoxicated with affection, with friendship, and with love, that they cannot bear to let each other out of sight for a single instant. It is such reunions as these that impel men c to spend their lives together, although they may be hard put to it to say what they really want with one another, and indeed, the purely sexual pleasures of their friendship could hardly account for the huge delight they take in one another's company. The fact is that both their souls are longing for a something else—a something to which they can neither of them put a name, and which they can only give an inkling of in cryptic sayings and prophetic riddles.   d

Now, supposing Hephaestus were to come and stand over them with his tool bag as they lay there side by side, and suppose he were to ask, Tell me, my dear creatures, what do you really want with one another?

And suppose they didn't know what to say, and he went on, How would you like to be rolled into one, so that you could always be together, day and night, and never be parted again? Because if that's e what you want, I can easily weld you together, and then you can live your two lives in one, and, when the time comes, you can die a common death and still be two-in-one in the lower world. Now, what do you say? Is that what you'd like me to do? And would you be happy if I did?

We may be sure, gentlemen, that no lover on earth would dream of refusing such an offer, for not one of them could imagine a happier fate. Indeed, they would be convinced that this was just what they'd been waiting for—to be merged, that is, into an utter oneness with the beloved.

And so all this to-do is a relic of that original state of ours, when 193 we were whole, and now, when we are longing for and following after that primeval wholeness, we say we are in love. For there was a time, I repeat, when we were one, but now, for our sins, God has scattered us abroad, as the Spartans scattered the Arcadians. Moreover, gentlemen, there is every reason to fear that, if we neglect the worship of the gods, they will split us up again, and then we shall have to go about with our noses sawed asunder, part and counterpart, like the basso-relievos on the tombstones. And therefore it is our duty one and all to inspire our friends with reverence and piety, for so we may ensure our safety and attain that blessed union by enlisting in the army b of Love and marching beneath his banners.

For Love must never be withstood—as we do, if we incur the displeasure of the gods. But if we cling to him in friendship and reconciliation, we shall be among the happy few to whom it is given in these latter days to meet their other halves. Now, I don't want any coarse remarks from Eryximachus. I don't mean Pausanias and c Agathon, though for all I know they may be among the lucky ones, and both be sections of the male. But what I am trying to say is this —that the happiness of the whole human race, women no less than men, is to be found in the consummation of our love, and in the healing of our dissevered nature by finding each his proper mate. And if this be a counsel of perfection, then we must do what, in our present circumstances, is next best, and bestow our love upon the natures most congenial to our own.

d And so I say that Love, the god who brings all this to pass, is worthy of our hymns, for his is the inestimable and present service of conducting us to our true affinities, and it is he that offers this great hope for the future—that, if we do not fail in reverence to the gods, he will one day heal us and restore us to our old estate, and establish us in joy and blessedness.

Such, Eryximachus, is my discourse on Love—as different as could be from yours. And now I must ask you again. Will you please refrain from making fun of it, and let us hear what all the others have to say—or rather, the other two, for I see there's no one left but e Agathon and Socrates.

Well, you shall have your way, said Eryximachus, and, joking apart, I enjoyed your speech immensely. Indeed, if I were not aware that Socrates and Agathon were both authorities on Love, I should be wondering what they could find to say after being treated to such a wealth and variety of eloquence. But, knowing what they are, I've no doubt we'll find them equal to the occasion.

194 To which Socrates retorted, It's all very well for you to talk, Eryximachus, after your own magnificent display, but if you were in my shoes now—or rather when Agathon has finished speaking— you'd be just as nervous as I am.

Now, Socrates, said Agathon, I suppose you're trying to upset me by insisting on the great things my public is expecting of me.

My dear Agathon, said Socrates, do you think I don't remember b your ease and dignity as you took the stage with the actors the other day, and how you looked that vast audience in the face, as cool as you please, and obviously prepared to show them what you were made of? And am I to suppose that the sight of two or three friends will put you out of countenance?

Ah, but, Socrates, protested Agathon, you mustn't think I'm so infatuated with the theater as to forget that a man of any judgment cares more for a handful of brains than an army of blockheads.

c Oh, I should never make such a mistake, Socrates assured him, as to credit *you*, my dear Agathon, with ideas that smacked of the illiterate. I've no doubt that if you found yourself in what you really considered intellectual company, you'd be more impressed by their opinion than by the mob's. But we, alas, can't claim to be your intelligent minority, for we were there too, you know, helping to swell that very crowd. But tell me, if you were with some other set of people, whose judgment you respected, I suppose you'd feel uncomfortable if they saw you doing anything you thought beneath you. Am I right?

Perfectly, said Agathon.

And yet, Socrates went on, you wouldn't feel uncomfortable if the *mob* saw you doing something equally unworthy?

But here Phaedrus stepped in. My dear Agathon, he said, if you d go on answering his questions he won't care twopence what becomes of our debate, so long as there's someone he can argue with—especially if it's somebody good-looking. Now, much as I enjoy listening to Socrates' arguments, it's my duty as chairman to insist that each man makes his speech. So I must ask you both to pay your tribute to the god, and then you can argue as much as you please.

Phaedrus is right, said Agathon. I'm quite prepared to speak. e After all, I can argue with Socrates any day.

Now, before I begin my speech I want to explain what sort of a speech I think it ought to be. For to my way of thinking the speakers we have heard so far have been at such pains to congratulate mankind upon the blessings of Love that they have quite forgotten to extol 195 the god himself, and have thrown no light at all upon the nature of our divine benefactor. Yet surely, if we are to praise anyone, no matter whom, no matter how, there is only one way to go about it, and that is to indicate the nature of him whose praises we are to sing, and of the blessings he is the author of. And so, gentlemen, with Love. Our duty is first to praise him for what he is, and secondly, for what he gives.

And so I shall begin by maintaining that, while all the gods are blessed, Love—be it said in all reverence—is the blessedest of all, for he is the loveliest and the best. The loveliest, I say, because first of all, Phaedrus, he is the youngest of the gods, which is proved by his flight, aye, and his escape, from the ravages of time, who travels b fast enough—too fast, at any rate, for us poor mortals. But Love was born to be the enemy of age, and shuns the very sight of senility, clinging always to his like in the company of youth, because he is young himself.

I agreed with most of Phaedrus' speech, but not with his suggestion that Love was older than even Cronus or Iapetus. No, gentlemen, Love, in his imperishable youth, is, I repeat, the youngest of c them all. And as for those old stories of the gods we have read in Hesiod and Parmenides, we may be sure that any such proceedings were the work not of Love but of Necessity—if, indeed, such tales are credible at all. For if Love had been among them then, they would neither have fettered nor gelded one another; they would have used no violence at all, but lived together in peace and concord as they do today, and as they have done since Love became their heavenly overlord.

It is clear, then, that he is young, and not only young but

dainty, with a daintiness that only a Homer could describe. For it is
d Homer, is it not, who writes of Ate as being both divine and dainty
—dainty of foot, that is. 'How delicate,' he says—

> How delicate her feet who shuns the ground,
> Stepping a-tiptoe on the heads of men.[6]

Now, you will agree that to prefer what is soft to what is hard is
proof enough of being dainty, and the same argument will demon-
e strate the daintiness of Love, for he never treads upon the ground,
nor even on our heads—which, after all, are not so very soft—but lives
and moves in the softest thing in the whole of nature. He makes the
dispositions and the hearts of gods and men his dwelling place—not,
however, without discrimination, for if the heart he lights upon be
hard he flies away to settle in a softer. And so, not only treading on
but altogether clinging to the softest of the soft, he must indeed be
exquisitely dainty.

196   We see, then, that Love is for one thing the youngest, and for
another the most delicate, thing in the world, and thirdly, gentlemen,
we find that he is tender and supple. For if he were hampered by the
least inflexibility, how could he wind us in such endless convolutions,
and steal into all our hearts so secretly—aye, and leave them, too,
when he pleases? And that elegance of his, which all the world confesses, bears witness to his suppleness and symmetry, for Love and
unsightliness will never be at peace. Moreover, his life among the
flowers argues in himself a loveliness of hue, for Love will never settle
upon bodies, or souls, or anything at all where there is no bud to
b blossom, or where the bloom is faded. But where the ground is thick
with flowers and the air with scent, there he will settle, gentlemen,
and there he loves to linger.

I shall say no more about Love's loveliness—though much remains to say—because we must now consider his moral excellence,
and in particular the fact that he is never injured by, nor ever injures,
either god or man. For, whatever Love may suffer, it cannot be by
violence—which, indeed, cannot so much as touch him—nor does he
c need to go to work by force, for the world asks no compulsion,
but is glad to serve him, and, as we know, a compact made in mutual
good will is held to be just and binding by the sovereign power of the
law.

Added to his righteousness is his entire temperance. I may take it,
I suppose, for granted that temperance is defined as the power to control our pleasures and our lusts, and that none of these is more powerful than Love. If, therefore, they are weaker, they will be overcome
by Love, and he will be their master, so that Love, controlling, as I
said, our lusts and pleasures, may be regarded as temperance itself.

[6] *Iliad* 19.92 sq.

Then, as to valor, as the poet sings, 'But him not even Ares can d withstand.'[7] For, as the story goes, it was not Ares that captured Love, but Love that captured Ares—love, that is, of Aphrodite. Now, the captor is stronger than the captive, and therefore Love, by overcoming one who is mightier than all the rest, has shown himself the mightiest of all.

So much, gentlemen, for the righteousness of Love, his temperance, and his valor; there remains his genius, to which I must do such scanty justice as I can. First of all, then—if, like Eryximachus, I may e give pride of place to my own vocation—Love is himself so divine a poet that he can kindle in the souls of others the poetic fire, for no matter what dull clay we seemed to be before, we are every one of us a poet when we are in love. We need ask no further proof than this that Love is a poet deeply versed in every branch of what I may define succinctly as creative art, for, just as no one can give away what he has not got, so no one can teach what he does not know.

And who will deny that the creative power by which all living 197 things are begotten and brought forth is the very genius of Love? Do we not, moreover, recognize that in every art and craft the artist and the craftsman who work under the direction of this same god achieve the brightest fame, while those that lack his influence grow old in the shadow of oblivion? It was longing and desire that led Apollo to found the arts of archery, healing, and divination—so he, too, was a scholar in the school of Love. It was thus that the fine arts were founded by the b Muses, the smithy by Hephaestus, and the loom by Pallas, and thus it was that Zeus himself attained the 'governance of gods and men.' And hence the actions of the gods were governed by the birth of Love— love, that is, of beauty, for, as we know, he will have none of ugliness. We are told, as I have already said, that in the beginning there were many strange and terrible happenings among them, because Necessity was king, but ever since the birth of the younger god, Love—the love of what is lovely—has showered every kind of blessing upon gods and men.

And so I say, Phaedrus, that Love, besides being in himself the c loveliest and the best, is the author of those very virtues in all around him. And now I am stirred to speak in numbers, and to tell how it is he that brings

> Peace upon earth, the breathless calm
> That lulls the long-tormented deep,
> Rest to the winds, and that sweet balm
> And solace of our nature, sleep.

And it is he that banishes estrangement and ushers friendship in; d it is he that unites us in such friendly gatherings as this—presiding at

---

[7] Sophocles, *Thyestes*, fr. 235.

the table, at the dance, and at the altar, cultivating courtesy and weeding out brutality, lavish of kindliness and sparing of malevolence, affable and gracious, the wonder of the wise, the admiration of the gods, the despair of him that lacks, and the happiness of him that has, the father of delicacy, daintiness, elegance, and grace, of longing and desire, heedful of the good and heedless of the bad, in toil or terror,
e in drink or dialectic, our helmsman and helper, our pilot and preserver, the richest ornament of heaven and earth alike, and, to conclude, the noblest and the loveliest of leaders, whom every one of us must follow, raising our voices in harmony with the heavenly song of Love that charms both mortal and immortal hearts.

And there, my dear Phaedrus, he said, you have my speech. Such is my offering to the god of love. I have done my best to be at once amusing and instructive.

198 Agathon took his seat, continued Aristodemus, amid a burst of applause, for we all felt that his youthful eloquence did honor to himself as well as to the god.

Then Socrates turned to Eryximachus and said, Well, Eryximachus, you laughed at my misgivings, but you see—they've been justified by the event. There's not much left for *me* to say after the wonderful speech we've just had from Agathon.

I admit, Eryximachus replied, that your prognosis was correct so far as Agathon's eloquence was concerned, but as to your own embarrassment, I'm not so sure.

b My dear sir, protested Socrates, what chance have I or anyone of knowing what to say, after listening to such a flood of eloquence as that? The opening, I admit, was nothing out of the way, but when he came to his peroration, why, he held us all spellbound with the sheer beauty of his diction, while I, personally, was so mortified when I compared it with the best that I could ever hope to do, that for two pins I'd have tried to sneak away. Besides, his speech reminded me so
c strongly of that master of rhetoric, Gorgias, that I couldn't help thinking of Odysseus, and his fear that Medusa would rise from the lower world among the ghosts, and I was afraid that when Agathon got near the end he would arm his speech against mine with the Gorgon's head of Gorgias' eloquence, and strike me as dumb as a stone.

d And then I saw what a fool I'd been to agree to take part in this eulogy of yours, and, what was worse, to claim a special knowledge of the subject, when, as it turned out, I had not the least idea how this or any other eulogy should be conducted. I had imagined in my innocence that one began by stating the facts about the matter in hand, and then proceeded to pick out the most attractive points and display them to the best advantage. And I flattered myself that my speech would be a great success, because I knew the facts. But the truth, it seems, is the last thing the successful eulogist cares about; on the contrary, what he does is simply to run through all the attributes of

power and virtue, however irrelevant they may be, and the whole
thing may be a pack of lies, for all it seems to matter.   e

I take it then that what we undertook was to flatter, rather than
to praise, the god of love, and that's why you're all prepared to say the
first thing about him that comes into your heads, and to claim that he
either is, or is the cause of, everything that is loveliest and best. And
of course the uninitiated are impressed by the beauty and grandeur
of your encomiums; yet those who know will not be taken in so easily.   199
Well then, I repeat, the whole thing was a misunderstanding, and it
was only in my ignorance that I agreed to take part at all. I protest,
with Euripides' Hippolytus, it was my lips that promised, not my soul,
and that, gentlemen, is that. I won't have anything to do with your
eulogy, and what is more, I couldn't if I tried. But I don't mind telling
you the truth about Love, if you're interested; only, if I do, I must tell b
it in my own way, for I'm not going to make a fool of myself, at my age,
trying to imitate the grand manner that sits so well on the rest of
you. Now, Phaedrus, it's for you to say. Have you any use for a
speaker who only cares whether his matter is correct and leaves his
manner to take care of itself?

Whereupon Phaedrus and the others told him to go ahead and   c
make whatever kind of speech he liked.

Very well, said he, but there's just one other thing. Has our chairman any objection to my asking Agathon a few simple questions? I
want to make certain we're not at cross-purposes before I begin my
speech.

Ask what you like, said Phaedrus. I don't mind.

Whereupon Socrates began, so far as Aristodemus could trust
his memory, as follows.

I must say, my dear Agathon, that the remarks with which you
prefaced your speech were very much to the point. You were quite
right in saying that the first thing you had to do was to acquaint us
with the nature of the god, and the second to tell us what he did. Yes,
your introduction was admirable. But now that we've had the pleasure of hearing your magnificent description of Love, there's just one
little point I'm not quite clear about. Tell me. Do you think it is the
nature of Love to be the love of somebody, or of nobody? I don't   d
mean, is he a mother's or a father's love? That would be a silly sort of
question, but suppose I were to ask you whether a father, *as* a father,
must be *somebody's* father, or not; surely the only reasonable answer would be that a father must be the father of a son or a daughter.
Am I right?

Why, yes, said Agathon.

And could we say the same thing about a mother?

Yes.

Good. And now, if you don't mind answering just one or two more e
questions, I think you'll see what I'm driving at. Suppose I were to ask,

what about a brother, *as* a brother? Must he be *somebody's* brother, or not?

Of course he must.

You mean, he must be the brother of a brother or a sister.

Precisely, said Agathon.

Well, then, Socrates went on, I want you to look at Love from the same point of view. Is he the love of something, or of nothing?

200   Of something, naturally.

And now, said Socrates, bearing in mind what Love is the love of, tell me this. Does he long for what he is in love with, or not?

Of course he longs for it.

And does he long for whatever it is he longs for, and is he in love with it, when he's got it, or when he hasn't?

When he hasn't got it, probably.

Then isn't it probable, said Socrates, or rather isn't it certain that everything longs for what it lacks, and that nothing longs for
b what it doesn't lack? I can't help thinking, Agathon, that that's about as certain as anything could be. Don't you think so?

Yes, I suppose it is.

Good. Now, tell me. Is it likely that a big man will want to be big, or a strong man to be strong?

Not if we were right just now.

Quite, for the simple reason that neither of them would be lacking in that particular respect.

Exactly.

For if, Socrates continued, the strong were to long for strength, and the swift for swiftness, and the healthy for health—for I suppose it *might* be suggested that in such cases as these people long for the very things they have, or are, already, and so I'm trying to imagine
c such a case, to make quite sure we're on the right track—people in their position, Agathon, if you stop to think about them, are bound here and now to have those very qualities, whether they want them or not; so why should they trouble to want them? And so, if we heard someone saying, 'I'm healthy, and I want to be healthy; I'm rich, and I want to be rich; and in fact I want just what I've got,' I think we should be justified in saying, 'But, my dear sir, you've *got* wealth and
d health and strength already, and what you want is to go on having them, for at the moment you've got them whether you want them or not. Doesn't it look as if, when you say you want these things here and now, you really mean, what you've got now, you want to go on keeping?' Don't you think, my dear Agathon, that he'd be bound to agree?

Why, of course he would, said Agathon.

Well, then, continued Socrates, desiring to secure something to oneself forever may be described as loving something which is not
e yet to hand.

Certainly.

And therefore, whoever feels a want is wanting something which is not yet to hand, and the object of his love and of his desire is whatever he isn't, or whatever he hasn't got—that is to say, whatever he is lacking in.

Absolutely.

And now, said Socrates, are we agreed upon the following conclusions? One, that Love is always the love of something, and two, that that something is what he lacks.

Agreed, said Agathon.   201

So far, so good, said Socrates. And now, do you remember what you said were the objects of Love, in your speech just now? Perhaps I'd better jog your memory. I fancy it was something like this—that the actions of the gods were governed by the love of beauty—for of course there was no such thing as the love of ugliness. Wasn't that pretty much what you said?

It was, said Agathon.

No doubt you were right, too, said Socrates. And if that's so, doesn't it follow that Love is the love of beauty, and not of ugliness?

It does.

And haven't we agreed that Love is the love of something which b he hasn't got, and consequently lacks?

Yes.

Then Love has no beauty, but is lacking in it?

Yes, that must follow.

Well then, would you suggest that something which lacked beauty and had no part in it was beautiful itself?

Certainly not.

And, that being so, can you still maintain that Love is beautiful? c

To which Agathon could only reply, I begin to be afraid, my dear Socrates, that I didn't know what I was talking about.

Never mind, said Socrates, it was a lovely speech, but there's just one more point. I suppose you hold that the good is also beautiful?

I do.

Then, if Love is lacking in what is beautiful, and if the good and the beautiful are the same, he must also be lacking in what is good.

Just as you say, Socrates, he replied. I'm afraid you're quite unanswerable.

No, no, dear Agathon. It's the truth you find unanswerable, not Socrates. And now I'm going to leave you in peace, because I want to talk about some lessons I was given, once upon a time, by a Mantinean d woman called Diotima—a woman who was deeply versed in this and many other fields of knowledge. It was she who brought about a ten years' postponement of the great plague of Athens on the occasion of a certain sacrifice, and it was she who taught me the philosophy of Love. And now I am going to try to connect her teaching—as well

as I can without her help—with the conclusions that Agathon and I have just arrived at. Like him, I shall begin by stating who and what
e Love is, and go on to describe his functions, and I think the easiest way will be to adopt Diotima's own method of inquiry by question and answer. I'd been telling her pretty much what Agathon has just been telling me—how Love was a great god, and how he was the love of what is beautiful, and she used the same arguments on me that I've just brought to bear on Agathon to prove that, on my own showing, Love was neither beautiful nor good.

Whereupon, My dear Diotima, I asked, are you trying to make me believe that Love is bad and ugly?
202   Heaven forbid, she said. But do you really think that if a thing isn't beautiful it's therefore bound to be ugly?

Why, naturally.

And that what isn't learned must be ignorant? Have you never heard of something which comes between the two?

And what's that?

Don't you know, she asked, that holding an opinion which is in fact correct, without being able to give a reason for it, is neither true knowledge—how can it be knowledge without a reason?—nor ignorance—for how can we call it ignorance when it happens to be true? So may we not say that a correct opinion comes midway between knowledge and ignorance?
b   Yes, I admitted, that's perfectly true.

Very well, then, she went on, why must you insist that what isn't beautiful is ugly, and that what isn't good is bad? Now, coming back to Love, you've been forced to agree that he is neither good nor beautiful, but that's no reason for thinking that he must be bad and ugly. The fact is that he's between the two.

And yet, I said, it's generally agreed that he's a great god.

It all depends, she said, on what you mean by 'generally.' Do you mean simply people that don't know anything about it, or do you include the people that do?

I meant everybody.
c   At which she laughed, and said, Then can you tell me, my dear Socrates, how people can agree that he's a great god when they deny that he's a god at all?

What people do you mean? I asked her.

You for one, and I for another.

What on earth do you mean by that?

Oh, it's simple enough, she answered. Tell me, wouldn't you say that all the gods were happy and beautiful? Or would you suggest that any of them were neither?

Good heavens, no! said I.

And don't you call people happy when they possess the beautiful and the good?

Why, of course.

And yet you agreed just now that Love lacks, and consequently d
longs for, those very qualities?

Yes, so I did.

Then, if he has no part in either goodness or beauty, how can he
be a god?

I suppose he can't be, I admitted.

And now, she said, haven't I proved that you're one of the people
who don't believe in the divinity of Love?

Yes, but what can he be, then? I asked her. A mortal?

Not by any means.

Well, what then?

What I told you before—halfway between mortal and immortal.

And what do you mean by that, Diotima?

A very powerful spirit, Socrates, and spirits, you know, are half- e
way between god and man.

What powers have they, then? I asked.

They are the envoys and interpreters that ply between heaven
and earth, flying upward with our worship and our prayers, and de-
scending with the heavenly answers and commandments, and since
they are between the two estates they weld both sides together and
merge them into one great whole. They form the medium of the
prophetic arts, of the priestly rites of sacrifice, initiation, and incanta- 203
tion, of divination and of sorcery, for the divine will not mingle directly with the human, and it is only through the mediation of the
spirit world that man can have any intercourse, whether waking or
sleeping, with the gods. And the man who is versed in such matters is
said to have spiritual powers, as opposed to the mechanical powers of
the man who is expert in the more mundane arts. There are many
spirits, and many kinds of spirits, too, and Love is one of them.

Then who were his parents? I asked.

I'll tell you, she said, though it's rather a long story. On the day b
of Aphrodite's birth the gods were making merry, and among them
was Resource, the son of Craft. And when they had supped, Need
came begging at the door because there was good cheer inside. Now,
it happened that Resource, having drunk deeply of the heavenly
nectar—for this was before the days of wine—wandered out into the
garden of Zeus and sank into a heavy sleep, and Need, thinking that
to get a child by Resource would mitigate her penury, lay down beside
him and in time was brought to bed of Love. So Love became the c
follower and servant of Aphrodite because he was begotten on
the same day that she was born, and further, he was born to love the
beautiful since Aphrodite is beautiful herself.

Then again, as the son of Resource and Need, it has been his
fate to be always needy; nor is he delicate and lovely as most of us believe, but harsh and arid, barefoot and homeless, sleeping on the

d naked earth, in doorways, or in the very streets beneath the stars of heaven, and always partaking of his mother's poverty. But, secondly, he brings his father's resourcefulness to his designs upon the beautiful and the good, for he is gallant, impetuous, and energetic, a mighty hunter, and a master of device and artifice—at once desirous and full of wisdom, a lifelong seeker after truth, an adept in sorcery, enchantment, and seduction.

e He is neither mortal nor immortal, for in the space of a day he will be now, when all goes well with him, alive and blooming, and now dying, to be born again by virtue of his father's nature, while what he gains will always ebb away as fast. So Love is never altogether in or out of need, and stands, moreover, midway between igno-
204 rance and wisdom. You must understand that none of the gods are seekers after truth. They do not long for wisdom, because they are wise—and why should the wise be seeking the wisdom that is already theirs? Nor, for that matter, do the ignorant seek the truth or crave to be made wise. And indeed, what makes their case so hopeless is that, having neither beauty, nor goodness, nor intelligence, they are satisfied with what they are, and do not long for the virtues they have never missed.

Then tell me, Diotima, I said, who are these seekers after truth, if they are neither the wise nor the ignorant?

b Why, a schoolboy, she replied, could have told you that, after what I've just been saying. They are those that come between the two, and one of them is Love. For wisdom is concerned with the loveliest of things, and Love is the love of what is lovely. And so it follows that Love is a lover of wisdom, and, being such, he is placed between wisdom and ignorance—for which his parentage also is responsible, in that his father is full of wisdom and resource, while his mother is devoid of either.

Such, my dear Socrates, is the spirit of Love, and yet I'm not alto-
c gether surprised at your idea of him, which was, judging by what you said, that Love was the beloved rather than the lover. So naturally you thought of Love as utterly beautiful, for the beloved is, in fact beautiful, perfect, delicate, and prosperous—very different from the lover, as I have described him.

Very well, dear lady, I replied, no doubt you're right. But in that case, what good can Love be to humanity?

d That's just what I'm coming to, Socrates, she said. So much, then, for the nature and the origin of Love. You were right in thinking that he was the love of what is beautiful. But suppose someone were to say, Yes, my dear Socrates. Quite so, my dear Diotima. But what do you mean by the love of what is beautiful? Or, to put the question more precisely, what is it that the lover of the beautiful is longing for?

He is longing to make the beautiful his own, I said.

Very well, she replied, but your answer leads to another question. What will he gain by making the beautiful his own?

This, as I had to admit, was more than I could answer on the spur of the moment.

Well then, she went on, suppose that, instead of the beautiful, you were being asked about the good. I put it to you, Socrates. What is it that the lover of the good is longing for?

To make the good his own.

Then what will he gain by making it his own?

I can make a better shot at answering that, I said. He'll gain happiness.

Right, said she, for the happy are happy inasmuch as they possess the good, and since there's no need for us to ask why men should want to be happy, I think your answer is conclusive.

Absolutely, I agreed.

This longing, then, she went on, this love—is it common to all mankind? What do you think, do we all long to make the good our own?

Yes, I said, as far as that goes we're all alike.

Well then, Socrates, if we say that everybody always loves the same thing, does that mean that everybody is in love? Or do we mean that some of us are in love, while some of us are not?

I was a little worried about that myself, I confessed.

Oh, it's nothing to worry about, she assured me. You see, what we've been doing is to give the name of Love to what is only one single aspect of it; we make just the same mistake, you know, with a lot of other names.

For instance . . . ?

For instance, poetry. You'll agree that there is more than one kind of poetry in the true sense of the word—that is to say, calling something into existence that was not there before, so that every kind of artistic creation is poetry, and every artist is a poet.

True.

But all the same, she said, we don't call them all poets, do we? We give various names to the various arts, and only call the one particular art that deals with music and meter by the name that should be given to them all. And that's the only art that we call poetry, while those who practice it are known as poets.

Quite.

And that's how it is with Love. For 'Love, that renowned and all-beguiling power,' includes every kind of longing for happiness and for the good. Yet those of us who are subject to this longing in the various fields of business, athletics, philosophy, and so on, are never said to be in love, and are never known as lovers, while the man who devotes himself to what is only one of Love's many activities is given the name that should apply to all the rest as well.

Yes, I said, I suppose you must be right.

I know it has been suggested, she continued, that lovers are people who are looking for their other halves, but as I see it, Socrates,

e Love never longs for either the half or the whole of anything except the good. For men will even have their hands and feet cut off if they are once convinced that those members are bad for them. Indeed I think we only prize our own belongings in so far as we say that the
206 good belongs to us, and the bad to someone else, for what we love is the good and nothing but the good. Or do you disagree?

Good heavens, no! I said.

Then may we state categorically that men are lovers of the good?

Yes, I said, we may.

And shouldn't we add that they long for the good to be their own?

We should.

And not merely to be their own but to be their own forever?

Yes, that must follow.

In short, that Love longs for the good to be his own forever?

Yes, I said, that's absolutely true.

b Very well, then. And that being so, what course will Love's followers pursue, and in what particular field will eagerness and exertion be known as Love? In fact, what *is* this activity? Can you tell me that, Socrates?

If I could, my dear Diotima, I retorted, I shouldn't be so much amazed at *your* grasp of the subject, and I shouldn't be coming to you to learn the answer to that very question.

Well, I'll tell you, then, she said. To love is to bring forth upon the beautiful, both in body and in soul.

c I'm afraid that's too deep, I said, for my poor wits to fathom.

I'll try to speak more plainly, then. We are all of us prolific, Socrates, in body and in soul, and when we reach a certain age our nature urges us to procreation. Nor can we be quickened by ugliness, but only by the beautiful. Conception, we know, takes place when man and woman come together, but there's a divinity in human propagation, an immortal something in the midst of man's mortality which is incompatible with any kind of discord. And ugliness is at
d odds with the divine, while beauty is in perfect harmony. In propagation, then, Beauty is the goddess of both fate and travail, and so when procreancy draws near the beautiful it grows genial and blithe, and birth follows swiftly on conception. But when it meets with ugliness it is overcome with heaviness and gloom, and turning away it shrinks into itself and is not brought to bed, but still labors under its painful burden. And so, when the procreant is big with child, he is strangely stirred by the beautiful, because he knows that beauty's
e tenant will bring his travail to an end. So you see, Socrates, that Love is not exactly a longing for the beautiful, as you suggested.

Well, what is it, then?

A longing not for the beautiful itself, but for the conception and generation that the beautiful effects.

Yes. No doubt you're right.

Of course I'm right, she said. And why all this longing for propagation? Because this is the one deathless and eternal element in our
mortality. And since we have agreed that the lover longs for the good
to be his own forever, it follows that we are bound to long for im- 207
mortality as well as for the good—which is to say that Love is a longing for immortality.

So much I gathered, gentlemen, at one time and another from
Diotima's dissertations upon Love.

And then one day she asked me, Well, Socrates, and what do
you suppose is the cause of all this longing and all this love?
Haven't you noticed what an extraordinary effect the breeding instinct has upon both animals and birds, and how obsessed they are
with the desire, first to mate, and then to rear their litters and their b
broods, and how the weakest of them are ready to stand up to the
strongest in defense of their young, and even die for them, and how
they are content to bear the pinch of hunger and every kind of hardship, so long as they can rear their offspring?

With men, she went on, you might put it down to the power of
reason, but how can you account for Love's having such remarkable c
effects upon the brutes? What do you say to that, Socrates?

Again I had to confess my ignorance.

Well, she said, I don't know how you can hope to master the philosophy of Love, if *that's* too much for you to understand.

But, my dear Diotima, I protested, as I said before, that's just
why I'm asking you to teach me—because I realize how ignorant I am.
And I'd be more than grateful if you'd enlighten me as to the cause not
only of this, but of all the various effects of Love.

Well, she said, it's simple enough, so long as you bear in mind
what we agreed was the object of Love. For here, too, the principle
holds good that the mortal does all it can to put on immortality. And d
how can it do that except by breeding, and thus ensuring that there
will always be a younger generation to take the place of the old?

Now, although we speak of an individual as being the same so
long as he continues to exist in the same form, and therefore assume
that a man is the same person in his dotage as in his infancy, yet, for
all we call him the same, every bit of him is different, and every day
he is becoming a new man, while the old man is ceasing to exist, as
you can see from his hair, his flesh, his bones, his blood, and all the
rest of his body. And not only his body, for the same thing happens e
to his soul. And neither his manners, nor his disposition, nor his
thoughts, nor his desires, nor his pleasures, nor his sufferings, nor
his fears are the same throughout his life, for some of them grow,
while others disappear.

And the application of this principle to human knowledge is even
more remarkable, for not only do some of the things we know increase, while some of them are lost, so that even in our knowledge

we are not always the same, but the principle applies as well to every single branch of knowledge. When we say we are studying, we really mean that our knowledge is ebbing away. We forget, because our knowledge disappears, and we have to study so as to replace what we

208 are losing, so that the state of our knowledge may seem, at any rate, to be the same as it was before.

This is how every mortal creature perpetuates itself. It cannot, like the divine, be still the same throughout eternity; it can only leave behind new life to fill the vacancy that is left in its species by obso-

b lescence. This, my dear Socrates, is how the body and all else that is temporal partakes of the eternal; there is no other way. And so it is no wonder that every creature prizes its own issue, since the whole creation is inspired by this love, this passion for immortality.

Well, Diotima, I said, when she had done, that's a most impres-

c sive argument. I wonder if you're right.

Of course I am, she said with an air of authority that was almost professorial. Think of the ambitions of your fellow men, and though at first they may strike you as upsetting my argument, you'll see how right I am if you only bear in mind that men's great incentive is the love of glory, and that their one idea is 'To win eternal mention in the deathless roll of fame.'

For the sake of fame they will dare greater dangers, even, than for their children; they are ready to spend their money like water and to wear their fingers to the bone, and, if it comes to that, to die.

d   Do you think, she went on, that Alcestis would have laid down her life to save Admetus, or that Achilles would have died for the love he bore Patroclus, or that Codrus, the Athenian king, would have sacrificed himself for the seed of his royal consort, if they had not hoped to win 'the deathless name for valor,' which, in fact, posterity has granted them? No, Socrates, no. Every one of us, no matter what he does, is longing for the endless fame, the incomparable glory that is theirs, and the nobler he is, the greater his ambition, because he

e is in love with the eternal.

Well then, she went on, those whose procreancy is of the body turn to woman as the object of their love, and raise a family, in the blessed hope that by doing so they will keep their memory green,

209 'through time and through eternity.' But those whose procreancy is of the spirit rather than of the flesh—and they are not unknown, Socrates—conceive and bear the things of the spirit. And what are they? you ask. Wisdom and all her sister virtues; it is the office of every poet to beget them, and of every artist whom we may call creative.

Now, by far the most important kind of wisdom, she went on, is that which governs the ordering of society, and which goes by the

b names of justice and moderation. And if any man is so closely allied to the divine as to be teeming with these virtues even in his youth, and if, when he comes to manhood, his first ambition is to be begetting, he too, you may be sure, will go about in search of the loveliness— and never of the ugliness—on which he may beget. And hence his procreant nature is attracted by a comely body rather than an ill-favored one, and if, besides, he happens on a soul which is at once beautiful, distinguished, and agreeable, he is charmed to find so welcome an alliance. It will be easy for him to talk of virtue to such a listener, and to discuss what human goodness is and how the virtu- c ous should live—in short, to undertake the other's education.

And, as I believe, by constant association with so much beauty, and by thinking of his friend when he is present and when he is away, he will be delivered of the burden he has labored under all these years. And what is more, he and his friend will help each other rear the issue of their friendship—and so the bond between them will be more binding, and their communion even more complete, than that which comes of bringing children up, because they have created something lovelier and less mortal than human seed.

And I ask you, who would not prefer such fatherhood to merely human propagation, if he stopped to think of Homer, and Hesiod, and d all the greatest of our poets? Who would not envy them their im-mortal progeny, their claim upon the admiration of posterity?

Or think of Lycurgus, she went on, and what offspring he left behind him in his laws, which proved to be the saviors of Sparta and, perhaps, the whole of Hellas. Or think of the fame of Solon, the father of Athenian law, and think of all the other names that are remembered in Grecian cities and in lands beyond the sea for the noble deeds they did before the eyes of all the world, and for all the di- e verse virtues that they fathered. And think of all the shrines that have been dedicated to them in memory of their immortal issue, and tell me if you can of *anyone* whose mortal children have brought him so much fame.

Well now, my dear Socrates, I have no doubt that even you might be initiated into these, the more elementary mysteries of Love. But I 210 don't know whether you could apprehend the final revelation, for so far, you know, we are only at the bottom of the true scale of perfection.

Never mind, she went on, I will do all I can to help you under-stand, and you must strain every nerve to follow what I'm saying.

Well then, she began, the candidate for this initiation cannot, if his efforts are to be rewarded, begin too early to devote himself to the beauties of the body. First of all, if his preceptor instructs him as he should, he will fall in love with the beauty of one individual body, so that his passion may give life to noble discourse. Next he must consider how nearly related the beauty of any one body is to the b beauty of any other, when he will see that if he is to devote himself to loveliness of form it will be absurd to deny that the beauty of each and every body is the same. Having reached this point, he must set himself to be the lover of every lovely body, and bring his passion for the one into due proportion by deeming it of little or of no importance.

Next he must grasp that the beauties of the body are as nothing to the beauties of the soul, so that wherever he meets with spiritual loveliness, even in the husk of an unlovely body, he will find it beautiful enough to fall in love with and to cherish—and beautiful enough to quicken in his heart a longing for such discourse as tends toward the building of a noble nature. And from this he will be led to contemplate the beauty of laws and institutions. And when he discovers how nearly every kind of beauty is akin to every other he will conclude that the beauty of the body is not, after all, of so great moment.

And next, his attention should be diverted from institutions to the sciences, so that he may know the beauty of every kind of knowledge. And thus, by scanning beauty's wide horizon, he will be saved from a slavish and illiberal devotion to the individual loveliness of a single boy, a single man, or a single institution. And, turning his eyes toward the open sea of beauty, he will find in such contemplation the seed of the most fruitful discourse and the loftiest thought, and reap a golden harvest of philosophy, until, confirmed and strengthened, he will come upon one single form of knowledge, the knowledge of the beauty I am about to speak of.

And here, she said, you must follow me as closely as you can. Whoever has been initiated so far in the mysteries of Love and has viewed all these aspects of the beautiful in due succession, is at last drawing near the final revelation. And now, Socrates, there bursts upon him that wondrous vision which is the very soul of the beauty he has toiled so long for. It is an everlasting loveliness which neither comes nor goes, which neither flowers nor fades, for such beauty is the same on every hand, the same then as now, here as there, this way as that way, the same to every worshiper as it is to every other.

Nor will his vision of the beautiful take the form of a face, or of hands, or of anything that is of the flesh. It will be neither words, nor knowledge, nor a something that exists in something else, such as a living creature, or the earth, or the heavens, or anything that is—but subsisting of itself and by itself in an eternal oneness, while every lovely thing partakes of it in such sort that, however much the parts may wax and wane, it will be neither more nor less, but still the same inviolable whole.

And so, when his prescribed devotion to boyish beauties has carried our candidate so far that the universal beauty dawns upon his inward sight, he is almost within reach of the final revelation. And this is the way, the only way, he must approach, or be led toward, the sanctuary of Love. Starting from individual beauties, the quest for the universal beauty must find him ever mounting the heavenly ladder, stepping from rung to rung—that is, from one to two, and from two to *every* lovely body, from bodily beauty to the beauty of institutions, from institutions to learning, and from learning in general to the special lore that pertains to nothing but the beautiful itself—until at last he comes to know what beauty is.

And if, my dear Socrates, Diotima went on, man's life is ever d worth the living, it is when he has attained this vision of the very soul of beauty. And once you have seen it, you will never be seduced again by the charm of gold, of dress, of comely boys, or lads just ripening to manhood; you will care nothing for the beauties that used to take your breath away and kindle such a longing in you, and many others like you, Socrates, to be always at the side of the beloved and feasting your eyes upon him, so that you would be content, if it were possible, to deny yourself the grosser necessities of meat and drink, so long as you were with him.

But if it were given to man to gaze on beauty's very self—un- e sullied, unalloyed, and freed from the mortal taint that haunts the frailer loveliness of flesh and blood—if, I say, it were given to man to see the heavenly beauty face to face, would you call *his*, she asked me, an unenviable life, whose eyes had been opened to the vision, and who had gazed upon it in true contemplation until it had become his own forever?

And remember, she said, that it is only when he discerns beauty 212 itself through what makes it visible that a man will be quickened with the true, and not the seeming, virtue—for it is virtue's self that quickens him, not virtue's semblance. And when he has brought forth and reared this perfect virtue, he shall be called the friend of god, and if ever it is given to man to put on immortality, it shall be given to him.

This, Phaedrus—this, gentlemen—was the doctrine of Dio- b tima. I was convinced, and in that conviction I try to bring others to the same creed, and to convince them that, if we are to make this gift our own, Love will help our mortal nature more than all the world. And this is why I say that every man of us should worship the god of love, and this is why I cultivate and worship all the elements of Love myself, and bid others do the same. And all my life I shall pay the power and the might of Love such homage as I can. So you may call this my eulogy of Love, Phaedrus, if you choose; if not, well, call it c what you like.

Socrates took his seat amid applause from everyone but Aristophanes, who was just going to take up the reference Socrates had made to his own theories, when suddenly there came a knocking at the outer door, followed by the notes of a flute and the sound of festive brawling in the street.

d   Go and see who it is, said Agathon to the servants. If it's one of
our particular friends you can ask him in, but if not, you'd better say
the party's over and there's nothing left to drink.

Well, it wasn't long before they could hear Alcibiades shouting in
the courtyard, evidently very drunk, and demanding where Agathon
was, because he *must* see Agathon at once. So the flute girl and some
of his other followers helped him stagger in, and there he stood in the
doorway, with a mass of ribbons and an enormous wreath of ivy and
e violets sprouting on his head, and addressed the company.

Good evening, gentlemen, he said. I'm pretty well bottled already,
so if you'd rather I didn't join the party, only say the word and I'll go
away, as soon as I've hung this wreath on Agathon's head—which is
what I really came for. I couldn't get along yesterday, so here I am
tonight, with a bunch of ribbons on my head, all ready to take them
off and put them on the head of the cleverest, the most attractive,
and, I may say—well, anyway, I'm going to crown him. And now I
suppose you're laughing at me, just because I'm drunk. Go on, have
213 your laugh out, don't mind me. I'm not so drunk that I don't know
what I'm saying, and you can't deny it's true. Well, what do you say,
gentlemen? Can I come in on that footing? And shall we all have a
drink together, or shan't we?

At that they all cheered and told him to come in and make himself at home, while Agathon gave him a more formal invitation. And
while his people helped him in he started pulling off the ribbons, so
that he could transfer them to Agathon's head as soon as he was near
enough. As it happened, the wreath slipped over his eyes and he didn't
notice Socrates, although he sat down on the same couch, between
him and Agathon—for Socrates had made room for him as soon as he
b came in. So down he sat, with a 'How d' you do!' to Agathon, and began to tie the ribbons round his head.

Then Agathon said to the servants, Here, take off Alcibiades'
shoes, so that we can all three make ourselves comfortable.

Yes, do, said Alcibiades. But just a minute, who's the third?

And when he turned round and saw who it was, he leaped out of
his seat and cried, Well I'll be damned! You again, Socrates! So that's
what you're up to, is it?—The same old game of lying in wait and
c popping out at me when I least expect you. Well, what's in the wind
tonight? And what do you mean by sitting *here*, and not by Aristophanes or one of these other humorists? Why make such a point of
sitting next to the handsomest man in the room?

I say, Agathon, said Socrates, I'll have to ask you to protect me.
You know, it's a dreadful thing to be in love with Alcibiades. It's been
d the same ever since I fell in love with him; I've only got to look at
anyone who's in the least attractive, or say a single word to him,
and he flies into a fit of jealous fury, and calls me the most dreadful
names, and behaves as if it was all he could do to keep his hands off

me. So I hope you'll keep an eye on him, in case he tries to do me an injury. If you can get him to be friends, so much the better, but if you can't, and if he gets violent, you'll really have to protect me—for I shudder to think what lengths he might go to in his amorous transports.

Friends with *you*? said Alcibiades. Not on your life! I'll be getting my own back on you one of these days, but at the moment— Agathon, give me back some of those ribbons, will you? I want to crown e Socrates' head as well—and a most extraordinary head it is. I don't want him to say I wreathed a garland for Agathon and none for him, when *his* words have been too much for all the world—and all his life too, Agathon, not just the other day, like yours.

So saying, he crowned Socrates' head with a bunch of ribbons, and took his seat again.

And now, gentlemen, he said, as he settled himself on the couch, can I be right in thinking that you're sober? I say, you know, we can't have this! Come on, drink up! You promised to have a drink with me. Now, I'll tell you, there's no one fit to take the chair at this meeting—until you've all got reasonably drunk—but me. Come on, Agathon, tell them to bring out something that's worth drinking out of.

No, never mind, he went on. Here, you, just bring me that wine cooler, will you?

He saw it would hold a couple of quarts or so. He made them fill it up, and took the first drink himself, after which he told them to fill 214 it again for Socrates, and remarked to the others, But I shan't get any change out of *him*. It doesn't matter *how* much you make him drink, it never makes him drunk.

Meanwhile the servant had filled the wine cooler up for Socrates and he had his drink.

But here Eryximachus broke in, Is this the way to do things, Alcibiades? he asked. Is there to be no grace before we drink? Are b we to pour the wine down our throats like a lot of thirsty savages?

Why, there's Eryximachus, said Alcibiades, the noblest, soberest father's soberest, noblest son, what? Hallo, Eryximachus!

Hallo yourself, said Eryximachus. Well, what do you say?

What do *you* say? retorted Alcibiades. We have to take *your* orders, you know. What's the tag?—'A good physician's more than all the world.' [8] So let's have your prescription.

Here it is, then, said Eryximachus. Before you came in we had arranged for each of us in turn, going round from left to right, to c make the best speech he could in praise of Love. Well, we've all had our turn; so since you've had your drink without having made a speech I think it's only right that you should make it now. And then, when you've finished, you can tell Socrates to do whatever you like and he

---

[8] *Iliad* 11.514.

can do the same to the next man on his right, and so on all the way round.

That's a very good idea, Eryximachus, said Alcibiades. Only you know it's hardly fair to ask a man that's more than half cut already to compete with a lot of fellows who are practically sober. And another thing, my dear Eryximachus. You mustn't believe a word of what Soc-
d rates has just been telling you. Don't you see that it's just the other way round? It's him that can't keep his hands off *me* if he hears me say a good word for anyone—god or man—but him.

Oh, do be quiet, said Socrates.

You can't deny it, retorted Alcibiades. God knows I've never been able to praise anyone else in front of you.

Now there's a good idea, said Eryximachus. Why don't you give us a eulogy of Socrates?

e   Do you really mean that? asked Alcibiades. Do you think I ought to, Eryximachus? Shall I go for him, and let you all hear me get my own back?

Here, I say, protested Socrates. What are you up to now? Do you want to make me look a fool with this eulogy, or what?

I'm simply going to tell the truth—you won't mind that, will you?

Oh, of course, said Socrates, you may tell the truth; in fact I'll go so far as to say you must.

Then here goes, said Alcibiades. There's one thing, though. If I say a word that's not the solemn truth I want you to stop me right away and tell me I'm a liar—but I promise you it won't be my fault
215 if I do. On the other hand, you mustn't be surprised if I tell them about you just as it comes into my head, and jump from one thing to another. You can't expect anyone that's as drunk as I am to give a clear and systematic account of all *your* eccentricities.

Well, gentlemen, I propose to begin my eulogy of Socrates with a simile. I expect he'll think I'm making fun of him, but, as it happens, I'm using this particular simile not because it's funny, but because it's true. What he reminds me of more than anything is one of
b those little sileni that you see on the statuaries' stalls; you know the ones I mean—they're modeled with pipes or flutes in their hands, and when you open them down the middle there are little figures of the gods inside. And then again, he reminds me of Marsyas the satyr.

Now I don't think even you, Socrates, will have the face to deny that you *look* like them, but the resemblance goes deeper than that, as I'm going to show. You're quite as impudent as a satyr, aren't you? If you plead not guilty I can call witnesses to prove it. And aren't you a piper as well? I should think you were—and a far more wonderful piper than Marsyas, who had only to put his flute to his lips to
c bewitch mankind. It can still be done, too, by anyone who can play the tunes he used to play. Why, there wasn't a note of Olympus'

melodies that he hadn't learned from Marsyas. And whoever plays them, from an absolute virtuoso to a twopenny-halfpenny flute girl, the tunes will still have a magic power, and by virtue of their own divinity they will show which of us are fit subjects for divine initiation.

Now the only difference, Socrates, between you and Marsyas is that you can get just the same effect without any instrument at all— with nothing but a few simple words, not even poetry. Besides, when we listen to anyone else talking, however eloquent he is, we don't d really care a damn what he says. But when we listen to you, or to someone else repeating what you've said, even if he puts it ever so badly, and never mind whether the person who's listening is man, woman, or child, we're absolutely staggered and bewitched. And speaking for myself, gentlemen, if I wasn't afraid you'd tell me I was completely bottled, I'd swear on oath what an extraordinary effect his words have had on me—and still do, if it comes to that. For the moment I hear him speak I am smitten with a kind of sacred rage, worse than any Corybant, and my heart jumps into my mouth and the tears start e into my eyes—oh, and not only me, but lots of other men.

Yes, I've heard Pericles and all the other great orators, and very eloquent I thought they were, but they never affected me like that; they never turned my whole soul upside down and left me feeling as if I were the lowest of the low. But this latter-day Marsyas, here, has often left me in such a state of mind that I've felt I simply couldn't 216 go on living the way I did—now, Socrates, you can't say that isn't true —and I'm convinced that if I were to listen to him at this very moment I'd feel just the same again. I simply couldn't help it. He makes me admit that while I'm spending my time on politics I am neglecting all the things that are crying for attention in myself. So I just refuse to listen to him—as if he were one of those Sirens, you know— and get out of earshot as quick as I can, for fear he keep me sitting listening till I'm positively senile.

And there's one thing I've never felt with anybody else—not b the kind of thing you'd expect to find in me, either—and that is a sense of shame. Socrates is the only man in the world that can make me feel ashamed. Because there's no getting away from it, I know I ought to do the things he tells me to, and yet the moment I'm out of his sight I don't care what I do to keep in with the mob. So I dash off like a runaway slave, and keep out of his way as long as I can, and then next time I meet him I remember all that I had to admit the time before, and naturally I feel ashamed. There are times when I'd c honestly be glad to hear that he was dead, and yet I know that if he did die I'd be more upset than ever—so I ask you, what is a man to do?

Well, that's what this satyr does for me, and plenty like me, with his pipings. And now let me show you how apt my comparison was in other ways, and what extraordinary powers he has got. Take my word for it, there's not one of you that really knows him. But now I've started on him, I'll show him up. Notice, for instance, how Socrates is attracted by good-looking people, and how he hangs around them, positively gaping with admiration. Then again, he loves to appear utterly uninformed and ignorant—isn't that like Silenus? Of course it is. Don't you see that it's just his outer casing, like those little figures I was telling you about? But believe me, friends and fellow drunks, you've only got to open him up and you'll find him so full of temperance and sobriety that you'll hardly believe your eyes. Because, you know, he doesn't really care a row of pins about good looks —on the contrary, you can't think how much he looks down on them—or money, or any of the honors that most people care about. He doesn't care a curse for anything of that kind, or for any of us either—yes, I'm telling you—and he spends his whole life playing his little game of irony, and laughing up his sleeve at all the world.

I don't know whether anybody else has ever opened him up when he's been being serious, and seen the little images inside, but I saw them once, and they looked so godlike, so golden, so beautiful, and so utterly amazing that there was nothing for it but to do exactly what he told me. I used to flatter myself that he was smitten with my youthful charms, and I thought this was an extraordinary piece of luck because I'd only got to be a bit accommodating and I'd hear everything he had to say—I tell you, I'd a pretty high opinion of my own attractions. Well, I thought it over, and then, instead of taking a servant with me as I always used to, I got rid of the man, and went to meet Socrates by myself. Remember, I'm bound to tell you the whole truth and nothing but the truth; so you'd all better listen very carefully, and Socrates must pull me up if I begin telling lies.

Well, gentlemen, as I was saying, I used to go and meet him, and then, when we were by ourselves, I quite expected to hear some of those sweet nothings that lovers whisper to their darlings when they get them alone—and I liked the idea of that. But not a bit of it! He'd go on talking just the same as usual till it was time for him to go, and then he said good-by and went.

So then I suggested we should go along to the gymnasium and take a bit of exercise together, thinking that something was bound to happen there. And, would you believe it, we did our exercises together and wrestled with each other time and again, with not a soul in sight, and still I got no further. Well, I realized that there was nothing to be gained in *that* direction, but having put my hand to the plow I wasn't going to look back till I was absolutely certain how I stood; so I decided to make a frontal attack. I asked him to dinner, just as if I were the lover trying to seduce his beloved, instead of the other way round. It wasn't easy, either, to get him to accept, but in the end I managed to.

Well, the first time he came he thought he ought to go as soon as we'd finished dinner, and I was too shy to stop him. But next time, I contrived to keep him talking after dinner, and went on far into the night, and then, when he said he must be going, I told him it was much too late and pressed him to stay the night with me. So he turned in on the couch beside me—where he'd sat at dinner—and the two of us had the room to ourselves.

So far I've said nothing I need blush to repeat in any company, e but you'd never have heard what I'm going to tell you now if there wasn't something in the proverb, 'Drunkards and children tell the truth'—drunkards anyway. Besides, having once embarked on my eulogy of Socrates it wouldn't be fair not to tell you about the arrogant way he treated me. People say, you know, that when a man's been bitten by a snake he won't tell anybody what it feels like except a fellow sufferer, because no one else would sympathize with him if the pain 218 drove him into making a fool of himself. Well, that's just how I feel, only I've been bitten by something much more poisonous than a snake; in fact, mine is the most painful kind of bite there is. I've been bitten in the heart, or the mind, or whatever you like to call it, by Socrates' philosophy, which clings like an adder to any young and gifted mind it can get hold of, and does exactly what it likes with it. And looking round me, gentlemen, I see Phaedrus, and Agathon, and Eryximachus, and Pausanias, and Aristodemus, and Aristophanes, b and all the rest of them—to say nothing of Socrates himself—and every one of you has had his taste of this philosophical frenzy, this sacred rage; so I don't mind telling *you* about it because I know you'll make allowances for me—both for the way I behaved with Socrates and for what I'm saying now. But the servants must put their fingers in their ears, and so must anybody else who's liable to be at all profane or beastly.

Well then, gentlemen, when the lights were out and the servants had all gone, I made up my mind to stop beating about the bush and c tell him what I thought point-blank.

So I nudged him and said, Are you asleep, Socrates?

No, I'm not, he said.

Then do you know what I think? I asked.

Well, what?

I think, I said, you're the only lover I've ever had who's been really worthy of me. Only you're too shy to talk about it. Well, this is how I look at it. I think it'd be just as absurd to refuse you *this* as anything else you wanted that belonged to me or any of my friends. If d there's one thing I'm keen on it's to make the best of myself, and I think you're more likely to help me there than anybody else, and I'm sure I'd find it harder to justify myself to men of sense for refusing to accommodate a friend of that sort than to defend myself to the vulgar if I *had* been kind to him.

He heard me out, and then said with that ironical simplicity of his, My dear Alcibiades, I've no doubt there's a lot in what you say, if
e you're right in thinking that I have some kind of power that would make a better man of you, because in that case you must find me so extraordinarily beautiful that your own attractions must be quite eclipsed. And if you're trying to barter your own beauty for the beauty you have found in me, you're driving a very hard bargain, let me tell you. You're trying to exchange the semblance of beauty for the thing itself—like Diomede and Glaucus swapping bronze for gold. But you know, my dear fellow, you really must be careful. Suppose you're mak-
219 ing a mistake, and I'm not worth anything at all. The mind's eye begins to see clearly when the outer eyes grow dim—and I fancy yours are still pretty keen.

To which I replied, Well, I've told you exactly how I feel about it, and now it's for you to settle what's best for us both.

That sounds reasonable enough, he said. We must think it over
b one of these days, and do whatever seems best for the two of us—about this and everything else.

Well, by this time I felt that I had shot my bolt, and I'd a pretty shrewd idea that I'd registered a hit. So I got up, and, without giving him a chance to say a word, I wrapped my own cloak round him—for this was in the winter—and, creeping under his shabby old mantle, I took him in my arms and lay there all night with this godlike and ex-
c traordinary man—you can't deny that, either, Socrates. And after *that* he had the insolence, the infernal arrogance, to laugh at my youthful beauty and jeer at the one thing I was really proud of, gentlemen of the jury—I say 'jury' because that's what you're here for, to try the man Socrates on the charge of arrogance—and believe it, gentlemen, or believe it not, when I got up next morning I had no more *slept* with Socrates, within the meaning of the act, than if he'd been
d my father or an elder brother.

You can guess what I felt like after *that*. I was torn between my natural humiliation and my admiration for his manliness and self-control, for this was strength of mind such as I had never hoped to meet. And so I couldn't take offense and cut myself off from his society, but neither was there any way I could think of to attract him. I
e knew very well that I'd no more chance of getting at him with money than I had of getting at Ajax with a spear, and the one thing I'd made sure would catch him had already failed. So I was at my wits' end, and went about in a state of such utter subjection to the man as was never seen before.

It was after all this, you must understand, that we were both sent on active service to Potidaea, where we messed together. Well, to begin with, he stood the hardships of the campaign far better than I
220 did, or anyone else, for that matter. And if—and it's always liable to happen when there's fighting going on—we were cut off from our sup-

plies, there was no one who put such a good face on it as he. But on the other hand, when there was plenty to eat he was the one man who really seemed to enjoy it, and though he didn't drink for choice, if we ever pressed him to he'd beat the lot of us. And, what's the most extraordinary thing of all, there's not a man living that's ever seen Socrates drunk. And I dare say he'll have a chance to show what he's made of before *this* party's over.

Then again, the way he got through that winter was most impressive, and the winters over there are pretty shocking. There was one time when the frost was harder than ever, and all the rest of us b stayed inside, or if we did go out we wrapped ourselves up to the eyes and tied bits of felt and sheepskins over our shoes, but Socrates went out in the same old coat he'd always worn, and made less fuss about walking on the ice in his bare feet than we did in our shoes. So much so, that the men began to look at him with some suspicion and actually took his toughness as a personal insult to themselves.

Well, so much for that. And now I must tell you about another c thing 'our valiant hero dared and did'[9] in the course of the same campaign. He started wrestling with some problem or other about sunrise one morning, and stood there lost in thought, and when the answer wouldn't come he still stood there thinking and refused to give it up. Time went on, and by about midday the troops noticed what was happening, and naturally they were rather surprised and began telling each other how Socrates had been standing there thinking ever since daybreak. And at last, toward nightfall, some of the Ionians brought out their bedding after supper—this was in the summer, of course— d partly because it was cooler in the open air, and partly to see whether he was going to stay there all night. Well, there he stood till morning, and then at sunrise he said his prayers to the sun and went away.

And now I expect you'd like to hear what kind of a show he made when we went into action, and I certainly think you ought to know. They gave me a decoration after one engagement, and do you know, e Socrates had saved my life, absolutely singlehanded. I'd been wounded and he refused to leave me, and he got me out of it, too, armor and all. And as you know, Socrates, I went straight to the general staff and told them *you* ought to have the decoration, and you can neither deny that nor blame me for doing it. But the authorities thought they'd rather give it to me, because of my family connections and so forth, and you were even keener than they were that I should have it instead of you.

And then, gentlemen, you should have seen him when we were in 221 retreat from Delium. I happened to be in the cavalry, while he was serving with the line. Our people were falling back in great disorder and he was retreating with Laches when I happened to catch sight of

---

[9] *Odyssey* 4.252.

them. I shouted to them not to be downhearted and promised to stand by them. And this time I'd a better chance of watching Socrates than I'd had at Potidaea—you see, being mounted, I wasn't quite so frightened. And I noticed for one thing how much cooler he was than Laches, and for another how—to borrow from a line of yours, Aris-

b tophanes—he was walking with the same 'lofty strut and sideways glance' [10] that he goes about with here in Athens. His 'sideways glance' was just as unconcerned whether he was looking at his own friends or at the enemy, and you could see from half a mile away that if you tackled *him* you'd get as good as you gave—with the result that he and Laches both got clean away. For you're generally pretty safe if that's the way you look when you're in action; it's the man whose one idea it is to get away that the other fellow goes for.

c   Well, there's a lot more to be said about Socrates, all very peculiar and all very much to his credit. No doubt there's just as much to be said about any of his little ways, but personally I think the most amazing thing about him is the fact that he is absolutely unique; there's no one like him, and I don't believe there ever was. You could point to some likeness to Achilles in Brasidas and the rest of them; you might compare Nestor and Antenor, and so on, with Pericles. There are plenty of such parallels in history, but you'll never find anyone like

d Socrates, or any ideas like his ideas, in our own times or in the past— unless, of course, you take a leaf out of my book and compare him, not with human beings, but with sileni and satyrs—and the same with his ideas.

Which reminds me of a point I missed at the beginning; I should have explained how his arguments, too, were exactly like those sileni

e that open down the middle. Anyone listening to Socrates for the first time would find his arguments simply laughable; he wraps them up in just the kind of expressions you'd expect of such an insufferable satyr. He talks about pack asses and blacksmiths and shoemakers and tanners, and he always seems to be saying the same old thing in just the same old way, so that anyone who wasn't used to his style and wasn't very quick on the uptake would naturally take it for the most

222 utter nonsense. But if you open up his arguments, and really get into the skin of them, you'll find that they're the only arguments in the world that have any sense at all, and that nobody else's are so godlike, so rich in images of virtue, or so peculiarly, so entirely pertinent to those inquiries that help the seeker on his way to the goal of true nobility.

And there, gentlemen, you have my eulogy of Socrates, with a few complaints thrown in about the unspeakable way he's treated me.

b I'm not the only one, either; there's Charmides, and Euthydemus, and ever so many more. He's made fools of them all, just as if he were the

[10] Aristophanes, *Clouds* 362.

beloved, not the lover. Now, Agathon, I'm telling you this for your own good, so that you'll know what to look out for, and I hope you'll learn from our misfortunes, and not wait for your own to bring it home to you, like the poor fool in the adage.

As Alcibiades took his seat there was a good deal of laughter at c his frankness—especially as he seemed to be still in love with Socrates. But the latter said, I don't believe you're as drunk as you make out, Alcibiades, or you'd never have given the argument such a subtle twist and obscured the real issue. What you were really after—though you only slipped it in casually toward the end—was to make trouble between me and Agathon, so that I as your lover, and he as your beloved, d should both belong to you and nobody else. But you can't humbug me; I can see what you're getting at with all this satyr and silenus business. I only hope, Agathon, my dear, that he won't succeed, and I hope you'll be very careful not to let anybody come between us.

I'm inclined to think you're right, Socrates, said Agathon. Remember how he sat down in the middle so as to keep us apart. But I'll e come round and sit next to you, so that won't help him very much.

Yes, do, said Socrates. Come round the other side.

Oh, God! cried Alcibiades. Look what I have to put up with! He's determined to drive me off the field. All the same, Socrates, I think you might let Agathon sit in the middle.

Oh, no, said Socrates, that would never do. Now you've finished singing my praises, I've got to do the same by the next man on my right. So you see, if he sat next to you, he'd have to start eulogizing me before he'd had my eulogy of him. So be a good chap and let the boy alone; you mustn't grudge him the praise I'm going to give him, because I'm dying to start my eulogy. 223

Aha! cried Agathon. You don't catch me staying *here* much longer, Alcibiades. I shall certainly change places if it means a tribute from Socrates.

Oh, it's always the same, said Alcibiades bitterly. No one else gets a look in with the beauties when Socrates is there. Look how easily he trumped up an excuse for Agathon to sit beside him.

And then, all of a sudden, just as Agathon was getting up to go b and sit by Socrates, a whole crowd of revelers came to the door, and finding it open, as someone was just going out, they marched straight in and joined the party. No sooner had they sat down than the whole place was in an uproar; decency and order went by the board, and everybody had to drink the most enormous quantities of wine. By this time Eryximachus and Phaedrus and some of the others were beginning to leave, so Aristodemus told me, while he himself fell c off to sleep.

He slept on for some time, for this was in the winter and the nights were long, and when at last he woke it was near daybreak and the cocks were crowing. He noticed that all the others had either gone home or fallen asleep, except Agathon and Aristophanes and Socrates, who were still awake and drinking out of an enormous bowl which they kept passing round from left to right. Socrates was arguing with the others—not that Aristodemus could remember very much of

d what he said, for, besides having missed the beginning, he was still more than half asleep. But the gist of it was that Socrates was forcing them to admit that the same man might be capable of writing both comedy and tragedy—that the tragic poet might be a comedian as well.

But as he clinched the argument, which the other two were scarcely in a state to follow, they began to nod, and first Aristophanes fell off to sleep and then Agathon, as day was breaking. Whereupon Socrates tucked them up comfortably and went away, followed, of course, by Aristodemus. And after calling at the Lyceum for a bath, he spent the rest of the day as usual, and then, toward evening, made his way home to rest.

REPUBLIC

The Republic *is the best known and generally considered the greatest of the dialogues. It is in chief part a construction of the ideal state undertaken by Socrates at the insistence of two young men who have been listening to a discussion in which Socrates has stated that the just man, not the unjust, is the happy man. At this point the two, Glaucon and Adimantus, break in, declaring that they have never heard the superiority of the just asserted convincingly by anyone, and they challenge Socrates to do so.*

What follows is a summary of the way they see the argument.

Let Socrates describe what happens to a perfectly just and a perfectly unjust man and prove if he can that the advantage rests with the former. He must allow to the unjust the ability to conceal his injustice—anyone who is found out is a mere nobody. He will also be able to paint black white by his determination and command of money and supporters.

Then put beside him the just man, noble, single-minded, wanting not to seem, but to be good. He will be unpopular and misunderstood because he is so superior. He will always act with perfect justice and constantly be misjudged. Certainly he will suffer many hardships, be thrown into prison very likely, scourged, racked, even put to death, when at last he will see that he ought to have seemed, but never to have been, just. Whereas a man who is, but never seems, unjust will be honored everywhere. He can act in business and in politics always to his own advantage because he has no misgiving about injustice.

Are you going to say, But what about the world to come? Suppose there isn't any. Even if there is, we can repent for our sins and pray and be forgiven and so on, and in the end, after death, perhaps not be punished at all. What we are saying is realistic. Don't answer it by telling us that justice is noble and injustice base. Tell us what effect they have on a man which makes the one a pure good and the other a pure evil.

Socrates declares that he is delighted at the opportunity, but in taking up so serious a subject he will suggest that they begin with something easier than two individual men, something bigger where the just and the unjust can be seen more clearly. "Perhaps there would be more justice in the larger object," he says. "Let us first look for its quality in states, and then only examine it in the individual." They agree and the first and by far the greatest of all utopias ever imagined is the result. It is, of course, not ruled by laws under which injustice inevitably occurs, but by men and women who have been carefully selected in youth and become wise and good by a long training. The world will never be justly ruled until rulers are philosophers, that is, until they are themselves ruled by the idea of the good, which is divine perfection and brings about justice, which is human perfection.

But the Republic is more than the construction of the best possible state as a standard for all states and for all officials who toil at politics for the public good, not as though it was something fine, but only something necessary to be done. The Republic also lays down a standard for human life. To order a state rightly men's souls must be raised to behold the universal light. There is truth beyond this shifting, changing world and men can seek and find it. The just state may never come into being, but a man can always be just, and only the just can know what justice is. Of this Socrates himself was the proof. He showed the truth by living it and dying for it.

At the end of Book IX of the Republic when the perfect state has finally been constructed, Adimantus says, "I think that it can be found nowhere on earth."

"Perhaps," answers Socrates, "there is a pattern of it laid up in heaven for him who wishes to contemplate it. But it makes no difference whether it exists now or ever will come into being." A man can order his life by its laws.

BOOK I

327   I went down yesterday to the Piraeus with Glaucon, the son of Ariston, to pay my devotions to the goddess, and also because I wished to see how they would conduct the festival, since this was its inauguration.

I thought the procession of the citizens very fine, but it was no better than the show made by the marching of the Thracian contingent.

b   After we had said our prayers and seen the spectacle we were starting for town when Polemarchus, the son of Cephalus, caught sight of us from a distance as we were hastening homeward and or-

---

From *Plato: The Republic*, with an English translation by Paul Shorey (Loeb Classical Library, Cambridge, Mass., and London, 1953, 1956; first printed, 1930), 2 vols.

dered his boy run and bid us to wait for him, and the boy caught hold
of my himation from behind and said, Polemarchus wants you to wait.

And I turned around and asked where his master was.

There he is, he said, behind you, coming this way. Wait for him.

So we will, said Glaucon. And shortly after Polemarchus came c
up and Adimantus, the brother of Glaucon, and Niceratus, the son of
Nicias, and a few others apparently from the procession.

Whereupon Polemarchus said, Socrates, you appear to have
turned your faces townward and to be going to leave us.

Not a bad guess, said I.

But you see how many we are? he said.

Surely.

You must either then prove yourselves the better men or stay here.

Why, is there not left, said I, the alternative of our persuading
you that you ought to let us go?

But *could* you persuade us, said he, if we refused to listen?

Nohow, said Glaucon.

Well, we won't listen, and you might as well make up your minds
to it.

Do you mean to say, interposed Adimantus, that you haven't 328
heard that there is to be a torchlight race this evening on horseback in
honor of the goddess?

On horseback? said I. That is a new idea. Will they carry torches
and pass them along to one another as they race with the horses, or
how do you mean?

That's the way of it, said Polemarchus, and, besides, there is to be
a night festival which will be worth seeing. For after dinner we will get
up and go out and see the sights and meet a lot of the lads there and
have good talk. So stay and do as we ask.

It looks as if we should have to stay, said Glaucon.   b

Well, said I, if it so be, so be it.

So we went with them to Polemarchus' house, and there we found
Lysias and Euthydemus, the brothers of Polemarchus, yes, and
Thrasymachus, too, of Chalcedon, and Charmantides of the deme of
Paeania, and Clitophon, the son of Aristonymus. And the father of
Polemarchus, Cephalus, was also at home.

And I thought him much aged, for it was a long time since I
had seen him. He was sitting on a sort of chair with cushions and he
had a chaplet on his head, for he had just finished sacrificing in the c
court. So we went and sat down beside him, for there were seats there
disposed in a circle.

As soon as he saw me Cephalus greeted me and said, You are not
a very frequent visitor, Socrates. You don't often come down to the
Piraeus to see us. That is not right. For if I were still able to make the d
journey up to town easily there would be no need of your resorting
hither, but we would go to visit you. But as it is you should not space

too widely your visits here. For I would have you know that, for my part, as the satisfactions of the body decay, in the same measure my desire for the pleasures of good talk and my delight in them increase. Don't refuse then, but be yourself a companion to these lads and make our house your resort and regard us as your very good friends and intimates.

e   Why, yes, Cephalus, said I, and I enjoy talking with the very aged. For to my thinking we have to learn of them as it were from wayfarers who have preceded us on a road on which we too, it may be, must sometime fare—what it is like. Is it rough and hard-going or easy and pleasant to travel? And so now I would fain learn of you what you think of this thing, now that your time has come to it, the thing that the poets call 'the threshold of old age.' Is it a hard part of life to bear or what report have you to make of it?

329   Yes, indeed, Socrates, he said, I will tell you my own feeling about it. For it often happens that some of us elders of about the same age come together and verify the old saw of like to like. At these reunions most of us make lament, longing for the lost joys of youth and recalling to mind the pleasures of wine, women, and feasts, and other things thereto appertaining, and they repine in the belief that the greatest things have been taken from them and that then they lived well and now it is no life at all. And some of them complain of the indignities that friends and kinsmen put upon old age and thereto

b recite a doleful litany of all the miseries for which they blame old age. But in my opinion, Socrates, they do not put the blame on the real cause. For if it were the cause I too should have had the same experience so far as old age is concerned, and so would all others who have come to this time of life. But in fact I have ere now met with others who do not feel in this way, and in particular I remember hearing Sophocles the poet greeted by a fellow who asked, How about your

c service of Aphrodite, Sophocles—is your natural force still unabated? And he replied, Hush, man, most gladly have I escaped this thing you talk of, as if I had run away from a raging and savage beast of a master. I thought it a good answer then and now I think so still more. For in very truth there comes to old age a great tranquillity in such matters and a blessed release. When the fierce tensions of the passions and desires relax, then is the word of Sophocles approved, and we are

d rid of many and mad masters. But indeed, in respect of these complaints and in the matter of our relations with kinsmen and friends there is just one cause, Socrates—not old age, but the character of the man. For if men are temperate and cheerful even old age is only moderately burdensome. But if the reverse, old age, Socrates, and youth are hard for such dispositions.

And I was filled with admiration for the man by these words, and

e desirous of hearing more I tried to draw him out and said, I fancy, Cephalus, that most people, when they hear you talk in this way, are

not convinced but think that you bear old age lightly not because of
your character but because of your wealth, for the rich, they say, have
many consolations.

You are right, he said. They don't accept my view and there is
something in their objection, though not so much as they suppose. But
the retort of Themistocles comes in pat here, who, when a man from
the little island of Seriphus grew abusive and told him that he owed
his fame not to himself but to the city from which he came, replied 330
that neither would he himself ever have made a name if he had been
born in Seriphus nor the other if he had been an Athenian. And the
same principle applies excellently to those who not being rich take old
age hard, for neither would the reasonable man find it altogether easy
to endure old age conjoined with poverty, nor would the unreasonable
man by the attainment of riches ever attain to self-contentment and a
cheerful temper.

May I ask, Cephalus, said I, whether you inherited most of your
possessions or acquired them yourself?

Acquired, quotha? he said. As a money-maker, I hold a place b
somewhere halfway between my grandfather and my father. For my
grandfather and namesake inherited about as much property as I now
possess and multiplied it many times, my father Lysanias reduced it
below the present amount, and I am content if I shall leave the estate
to these boys not less but by some slight measure more than my inheritance.

The reason I asked, I said, is that you appear to me not to be over-
fond of money. And that is generally the case with those who have not c
earned it themselves. But those who have themselves acquired it have
a double reason in comparison with other men for loving it. For just
as poets feel complacency about their own poems and fathers about
their own sons, so men who have made money take this money seriously as their own creation and they also value it for its uses as other
people do. So they are hard to talk to since they are unwilling to commend anything except wealth.

You are right, he replied.

I assuredly am, said I. But tell me further this. What do you re- d
gard as the greatest benefit you have enjoyed from the possession of
property?

Something, he said, which I might not easily bring many to believe if I told them. For let me tell you, Socrates, he said, that when a
man begins to realize that he is going to die, he is filled with apprehensions and concern about matters that before did not occur to him. The
tales that are told of the world below and how the men who have done
wrong here must pay the penalty there, though he may have laughed
them down hitherto, then begin to torture his soul with the doubt that e
there may be some truth in them. And apart from that the man himself either from the weakness of old age or possibly as being now

nearer to the things beyond has a somewhat clearer view of them. Be that as it may, he is filled with doubt, surmises, and alarms and begins to reckon up and consider whether he has ever wronged anyone. Now he to whom the ledger of his life shows an account of many evil deeds starts up even from his dreams like a child again and again in

331 affright and his days are haunted by anticipations of worse to come. But on him who is conscious of no wrong that he has done a sweet hope ever attends and a goodly, to be nurse of his old age, as Pindar too says. For a beautiful saying it is, Socrates, of the poet that when a man lives out his days in justice and piety, 'sweet companion with him, to cheer his heart and nurse his old age, accompanieth hope, who chiefly ruleth the changeful mind of mortals.' [1] That is a fine saying and an admirable. It is for this, then, that I affirm that the posses-

b sion of wealth is of most value, not it may be to every man but to the good man. Not to cheat any man even unintentionally or play him false, not remaining in debt to a god for some sacrifice or to a man for money, so to depart in fear to that other world—to this result the possession of property contributes not a little. It has also many other uses. But, setting one thing against another, I would lay it down, Socrates, that for a man of sense this is the chief service of wealth.

c   An admirable sentiment, Cephalus, said I. But speaking of this very thing, justice, are we to affirm thus without qualification that it is truthtelling and paying back what one has received from anyone, or may these very actions sometimes be just and sometimes unjust? I mean, for example, as everyone I presume would admit, if one took over weapons from a friend who was in his right mind and then the lender should go mad and demand them back, that we ought not to return them in that case and that he who did so return them would not be acting justly—nor yet would he who chose to speak nothing but the truth to one who was in that state.

d   You are right, he replied.
      Then this is not the definition of justice—to tell the truth and return what one has received.
      Nay, but it is, Socrates, said Polemarchus breaking in, if indeed we are to put any faith in Simonides.
      Very well, said Cephalus, indeed I make over the whole argument to you. For it is time for me to attend the sacrifices.
      Well, said I, is not Polemarchus the heir of everything that is yours?
      Certainly, said he with a laugh, and at the same time went out to the sacred rites.

e   Tell me, then, you the inheritor of the argument, what it is that you affirm that Simonides says and rightly says about justice.
      That it is just, he replied, to render to each his due. In saying this I think he speaks well.

[1] Pindar, fr. 214.

I must admit, said I, that it is not easy to disbelieve Simonides. For he is a wise and inspired man. But just what he may mean by this you, Polemarchus, doubtless know, but I do not. Obviously he does not mean what we were just speaking of, this return of a deposit to anyone whatsoever even if he asks it back when not in his right mind. And yet what the man deposited is due to him in a sense, is it not?   332

Yes.

But rendered to him it ought not to be by any manner of means when he demands it not being in his right mind.

True, said he.

It is then something other than this that Simonides must, as it seems, mean by the saying that it is just to render back what is due.

Something else in very deed, he replied, for he believes that friends owe it to friends to do them some good and no evil.

I see, said I. You mean that he does not render what is due or owing who returns a deposit of gold if this return and the acceptance prove harmful and the returner and the recipient are friends. Isn't b that what you say Simonides means?

Quite so.

But how about this—should one not render to enemies what is their due?

By all means, he said, what is due and owing to them, and there is due and owing from an enemy to an enemy what also is proper for him, some evil.

It was a riddling definition of justice, then, that Simonides gave after the manner of poets, for while his meaning, it seems, was that c justice is rendering to each what befits him, the name that he gave to this was 'the due.'

What else do you suppose? said he.

In heaven's name! said I. Suppose someone had questioned him thus. Tell me, Simonides, the art that renders what that is due and befitting to what is called the art of medicine? What do you take it would have been his answer?

Obviously, he said, the art that renders to bodies drugs, foods, and drinks.

And the art that renders to what things what that is due and befitting is called the culinary art?

Seasoning to meats.

Good. In the same way tell me the art that renders what to whom d would be denominated justice.

If we are to follow the previous examples, Socrates, it is that which renders benefits and harms to friends and enemies.

To do good to friends and evil to enemies, then, is justice in his meaning?

I think so.

Who then is the most able when they are ill to benefit friends and harm enemies in respect to disease and health?

    The physician.

e   And who navigators in respect of the perils of the sea?

    The pilot.

    Well then, the just man, in what action and for what work is he the most competent to benefit friends and harm enemies?

    In making war and as an ally, I should say.

    Very well. But now if they are not sick, friend Polemarchus, the physician is useless to them.

    True.

    And so to those who are not at sea the pilot.

    Yes.

    Shall we also say this, that for those who are not at war the just man is useless?

    By no means.

333   There is a use then even in peace for justice?

    Yes, it is useful.

    But so is agriculture, isn't it?

    Yes.

    Namely, for the getting of a harvest?

    Yes.

    But likewise the cobbler's art?

    Yes.

    Namely, I presume you would say, for the getting of shoes.

    Certainly.

    Then tell me, for the service and getting of what would you say that justice is useful in time of peace?

    In engagements and dealings, Socrates.

    And by dealings do you mean associations, partnerships, or something else?

    Associations, of course.

b   Is it the just man, then, who is a good and useful associate and partner in the placing of draughts or the draughts player?

    The player.

    And in the placing of bricks and stones is the just man a more useful and better associate than the builder?

    By no means.

    Then what is the association in which the just man is a better partner than the harpist as a harpist is better than the just man for striking the chords?

    For money dealings, I think.

    Except, I presume, Polemarchus, for the use of money when there

c is occasion to buy in common or sell a horse. Then, I take it, the man who knows horses, isn't it so?

    Apparently.

    And again, if it is a vessel, the shipwright or the pilot.

    It would seem so.

What then is the use of money in common for which a just man
is the better partner?

When it is to be deposited and kept safe, Socrates.

You mean when it is to be put to no use but is to lie idle?

Quite so.

Then it is when money is useless that justice is useful in relation d
to it?

It looks that way.

And similarly when a scythe is to be kept safe, then justice is useful both in public and private. But when it is to be used, the vine-
dresser's art is useful?

Apparently.

And so you will have to say that when a shield and a lyre are to be
kept and put to no use, justice is useful, but when they are to be made
use of, the military art and music.

Necessarily.

And so in all other cases, in the use of each thing, justice is useless but in its uselessness useful?

It looks that way.

Then, my friend, justice cannot be a thing of much worth if it is e
useful only for things out of use and useless. But let us consider this
point. Is not the man who is most skillful to strike or inflict a blow in
a fight, whether as a boxer or elsewhere, also the most wary to guard
against a blow?

Assuredly.

Is it not also true that he who best knows how to guard against
disease is also most cunning to communicate it and escape detection?

I think so.

But again, the very same man is a good guardian of an army who 334
is good at stealing a march upon the enemy in respect of their designs
and proceedings generally.

Certainly.

Of whatsoever, then, anyone is a skillful guardian, of that he is
also a skillful thief?

It seems so.

If then the just man is an expert in guarding money he is an expert in stealing it.

The argument certainly points that way.

A kind of thief then the just man it seems has turned out to be,
and it is likely that you acquired this idea from Homer. For he regards
with complacency Autolycus, the maternal uncle of Odysseus, and b
says, 'he was gifted beyond all men in thievery and perjury.' [2] So justice, according to you and Homer and Simonides, seems to be a kind

[2] *Odyssey* 19.395.

of stealing, with the qualification that it is for the benefit of friends and the harm of enemies. Isn't that what you meant?

No, by Zeus, he replied. I no longer know what I did mean. Yet this I still believe, that justice benefits friends and harms enemies.

c May I ask whether by friends you mean those who seem to a man to be worthy or those who really are so, even if they do not seem, and similarly of enemies?

It is likely, he said, that men will love those whom they suppose to be good and dislike those whom they deem bad.

Do not men make mistakes in this matter so that many seem good to them who are not and the reverse?

They do.

For those, then, who thus err the good are their enemies and the bad their friends?

Certainly.

d But all the same it is then just for them to benefit the bad and injure the good?

It would seem so.

But again, the good are just and incapable of injustice.

True.

On your reasoning then it is just to wrong those who do no injustice.

Nay, nay, Socrates, he said, the reasoning can't be right.

Then, said I, it is just to harm the unjust and benefit the just.

That seems a better conclusion than the other.

It will work out, then, for many, Polemarchus, who have mis-
e judged men that it is just to harm their friends, for they have got bad ones, and to benefit their enemies, for they are good. And so we shall find ourselves saying the very opposite of what we affirmed Simonides to mean.

Most certainly, he said, it does work out so. But let us change our ground, for it looks as if we were wrong in the notion we took up about the friend and the enemy.

What notion, Polemarchus?

That the man who seems to us good is the friend.

And to what shall we change it now? said I.

335 That the man who both seems and is good is the friend, but that he who seems but is not really so seems but is not really the friend. And there will be the same assumption about the enemy.

Then on this view it appears the friend will be the good man and the bad the enemy.

Yes.

So you would have us qualify our former notion of the just man by an addition. We then said it was just to do good to a friend and evil to an enemy, but now we are to add that it is just to benefit the friend if he is good and harm the enemy if he is bad?

By all means, he said, that, I think, would be the right way to b put it.

Is it then, said I, the part of a good man to harm anybody whatsoever?

Certainly it is, he replied. A man ought to harm those who are both bad and his enemies.

When horses are harmed does it make them better or worse?

Worse.

In respect of the excellence or virtue of dogs or that of horses?

Of horses.

And do not also dogs when harmed become worse in respect of canine and not of equine virtue?

Necessarily.

And men, my dear fellow, must we not say that when they are c harmed it is in respect of the distinctive excellence or virtue of man that they become worse?

Assuredly.

And is not justice the specific virtue of man?

That too must be granted.

Then it must also be admitted, my friend, that men who are harmed become more unjust.

It seems so.

Do musicians then make men unmusical by the art of music?

Impossible.

Well, do horsemen by horsemanship unfit men for dealing with horses?

No.

By justice then do the just make men unjust, or in sum do the good by virtue make men bad?   d

Nay, it is impossible.

It is not, I take it, the function of heat to chill but of its opposite.

Yes.

Nor of dryness to moisten but of its opposite.

Assuredly.

Nor yet of the good to harm but of its opposite.

So it appears.

But the just man is good?

Certainly.

It is not then the function of the just man, Polemarchus, to harm either friend or anyone else, but of his opposite, the unjust.

I think you are altogether right, Socrates.

If, then, anyone affirms that it is just to render to each his due e and he means by this that injury and harm is what is due to his enemies from the just man and benefits to his friends, he was no truly wise man who said it. For what he meant was not true. For it has been made clear to us that in no case is it just to harm anyone.

I concede it, he said.

We will take up arms against him, then, said I, you and I to-gether, if anyone affirms that either Simonides or Bias or Pittacus or any other of the wise and blessed said such a thing.

I, for my part, he said, am ready to join in the battle with you.

336   Do you know, said I, to whom I think the saying belongs—this statement that it is just to benefit friends and harm enemies?

To whom? he said.

I think it was the saying of Periander or Perdiccas or Xerxes or Ismenias the Theban or some other rich man who had great power in his own conceit.

That is most true, he replied.

Very well, said I, since it has been made clear that this too is not justice and the just, what else is there that we might say justice to be?

b   Now Thrasymachus, even while we were conversing, had been trying several times to break in and lay hold of the discussion but he was restrained by those who sat by him who wished to hear the argu-ment out. But when we came to a pause after I had said this, he couldn't any longer hold his peace. But gathering himself up like a wild beast he hurled himself upon us as if he would tear us to pieces. And Polemarchus and I were frightened and fluttered apart.

He bawled out into our midst, What balderdash is this that you
c have been talking, and why do you Simple Simons truckle and give way to one another? But if you really wish, Socrates, to know what the just is, don't merely ask questions or plume yourself upon contro-verting any answer that anyone gives—since your acumen has per-ceived that it is easier to ask questions than to answer them—but do you yourself answer and tell what you say the just is. And don't you
d be telling me that it is that which ought to be, or the beneficial or the profitable or the gainful or the advantageous, but express clearly and precisely whatever you say. For I won't take from you any such drivel as that!

And I, when I heard him, was dismayed, and looking upon him was filled with fear, and I believe that if I had not looked at him be-fore he did at me I should have lost my voice. But as it is, at the very moment when he began to be exasperated by the course of the argu-ment I glanced at him first, so that I became capable of answering
e him, and said with a slight tremor, Thrasymachus, don't be harsh with us. If I, and my friend, have made mistakes in the consideration of the question, rest assured that it is unwillingly that we err. For you surely must not suppose that while, if our quest were for gold, we would never willingly truckle to one another and make concessions in the search and so spoil our chances of finding it, yet that when we are searching for justice, a thing more precious than much fine gold, we should then be so foolish as to give way to one another and not rather do our serious best to have it discovered. You surely must not sup-

pose that, my friend. But you see it is our lack of ability that is at fault.
It is pity then that we should far more reasonably receive from clever 337
fellows like you than severity.

And he, on hearing this, gave a great guffaw and laughed sardoni-
cally and said, Ye gods! Here we have the well-known irony of Socrates, and I knew it and predicted that when it came to replying you
would refuse and dissemble and do anything rather than answer any
question that anyone asked you.

That's because you are wise, Thrasymachus, and so you knew
very well that if you asked a man how many are twelve, and in put- b
ting the question warned him, Don't you be telling me, fellow, that
twelve is twice six or three times four or six times two or four times
three, for I won't accept any such drivel as that from you as an answer
—it was obvious, I fancy, to you that no one could give an answer to a
question framed in that fashion. Suppose he had said to you, Thrasymachus, what do you mean? Am I not to give any of the prohibited answers, not even, do you mean to say, if the thing really is one of these,
but must I say something different from the truth, or what do you
mean?—What would have been your answer to him?   c

Humph! said he. How very like the two cases are!

There is nothing to prevent it, said I. Yet even granted that they
are not alike, yet if it appears to the person asked the question that
they are alike, do you suppose that he will any the less answer what
appears to him, whether we forbid him or whether we don't?

Is that, then, said he, what you are going to do? Are you going to
give one of the forbidden answers?

I shouldn't be surprised, I said, if on reflection that would be my
view.

What then, he said, if I show you another answer about justice d
differing from all these, a better one—what penalty do you think you
deserve?

Why, what else, said I, than that which it befits anyone who is ignorant to suffer? It befits him, I presume, to learn from the one who
does know. That then is what I propose that I should suffer.

I like your simplicity, said he. But in addition to 'learning' you
must pay a fine of money.

Well, I will when I have got it, I said.

It is there, said Glaucon. If money is all that stands in the way,
Thrasymachus, go on with your speech. We will all contribute for
Socrates.

Oh yes, of course, said he, so that Socrates may contrive, as he e
always does, to evade answering himself but may cross-examine the
other man and refute his replies.

Why, how, I said, my dear fellow, could anybody answer if in the
first place he did not know and did not even profess to know, and secondly, even if he had some notion of the matter, he had been told by a

man of weight that he mustn't give any of his suppositions as an answer? Nay, it is more reasonable that you should be the speaker. For you do affirm that you know and are able to tell. Don't be obstinate,
338 but do me the favor to reply and don't be chary of your wisdom, and instruct Glaucon here and the rest of us.

When I had spoken thus Glaucon and the others urged him not to be obstinate. It was quite plain that Thrasymachus was eager to speak in order that he might do himself credit, since he believed that he had a most excellent answer to our question. But he demurred and pretended to make a point of my being the respondent. Finally he
b gave way and then said, Here you have the wisdom of Socrates, to refuse himself to teach, but go about and learn from others and not even pay thanks therefor.

That I learn from others, I said, you said truly, Thrasymachus. But in saying that I do not pay thanks you are mistaken. I pay as much as I am able. And I am able only to bestow praise. For money I lack. But that I praise right willingly those who appear to speak well you will well know forthwith as soon as you have given your answer. For I think that you will speak well.

c   Hearken and hear then, said he. I affirm that the just is nothing else than the advantage of the stronger. Well, why don't you applaud? Nay, you'll do anything but that.

Provided only I first understand your meaning, said I, for I don't yet apprehend it. The advantage of the stronger is what you affirm the just to be. But what in the world do you mean by this? I presume you don't intend to affirm this, that if Polydamas, the pancratiast, is stronger than we are and the flesh of beef is advantageous for him,
d for his body, this viand is also for us who are weaker than he both advantageous and just.

You are a buffoon, Socrates, and take my statement in the most detrimental sense.

Not at all, my dear fellow, said I. I only want you to make your meaning plainer.

Don't you know then, said he, that some cities are governed by tyrants, in others democracy rules, in others aristocracy?

Assuredly.

And is not this the thing that is strong and has the mastery in each—the ruling party?

Certainly.

e   And each form of government enacts the laws with a view to its own advantage, a democracy democratic laws and tyranny autocratic and the others likewise, and by so legislating they proclaim that the just for their subjects is that which is for their—the rulers'—advantage and the man who deviates from this law they chastise as a lawbreaker and a wrongdoer. This, then, my good sir, is what I understand as the identical principle of justice that obtains in all states—

the advantage of the established government. This I presume you 339
will admit holds power and is strong, so that, if one reasons rightly, it
works out that the just is the same thing everywhere, the advantage of
the stronger.

Now, said I, I have learned your meaning, but whether it is true
or not I have to try to learn. The advantageous, then, is also your reply, Thrasymachus, to the question, what is the just—though you forbade me to give that answer. But you add thereto that of the stronger.

A trifling addition perhaps you think it, he said.

It is not yet clear whether it is a big one either, but that we must b
inquire whether what you say is true is clear. For since I too admit
that the just is something that is of advantage—but you are for making an addition and affirm it to be the advantage of the stronger, while
I don't profess to know—we must pursue the inquiry.

Inquire away, he said.

I will do so, said I. Tell me, then, you affirm also, do you not, that
obedience to rulers is just?

I do.

May I ask whether the rulers in the various states are infallible
or capable sometimes of error?   c

Surely, he said, they are liable to err.

Then in their attempts at legislation they enact some laws rightly
and some not rightly, do they not?

So I suppose.

And by rightly we are to understand for their advantage, and by
wrongly to their disadvantage? Do you mean that or not?

That.

But whatever they enact must be performed by their subjects and
is justice?

Of course.

Then on your theory it is just not only to do what is the advantage of the stronger but also the opposite, what is not to his advantage. d

What's that you're saying? he replied.

What you yourself are saying, I think. Let us consider it more
closely. Have we not agreed that the rulers in giving orders to the ruled
sometimes mistake their own advantage, and that whatever the rulers
enjoin it is just for the subjects to perform? Was not that admitted?

I think it was, he replied.

Then you will have to think, I said, that to do what is disadvan- e
tageous to the rulers and the stronger has been admitted by you to be
just in the case when the rulers unwittingly enjoin what is bad for
themselves, while you affirm that it is just for the others to do what
they enjoined. In that way does not this conclusion inevitably follow,
my most sapient Thrasymachus, that it is just to do the very opposite of what you say? For it is in that case surely the disadvantage of
the stronger or superior that the inferior are commanded to perform.

Yes, by Zeus, Socrates, said Polemarchus, nothing could be more conclusive.

340   Of course, said Clitophon, breaking in, if you are his witness.

What need is there of a witness? Polemarchus said. Thrasymachus himself admits that the rulers sometimes enjoin what is evil for themselves and yet says that it is just for the subjects to do this.

That, Polemarchus, is because Thrasymachus laid it down that it is just to obey the orders of the rulers.

Yes, Clitophon, but he also took the position that the advantage
b of the stronger is just. And after these two assumptions he again admitted that the stronger sometimes bid the inferior and their subjects do what is to the disadvantage of the rulers. And from these admissions the just would no more be the advantage of the stronger than the contrary.

Oh well, said Clitophon, by the advantage of the superior he meant what the superior supposed to be for his advantage. This was what the inferior had to do, and that this is the just was his position.

That isn't what he said, replied Polemarchus.

c   Never mind, Polemarchus, said I. But if that is Thrasymachus' present meaning, let us take it from him in that sense. So tell me, Thrasymachus, was this what you intended to say, that the just is the advantage of the superior as it appears to the superior whether it really is or not? Are we to say this was your meaning?

Not in the least, he said. Do you suppose that I call one who is in error a superior when he errs?

I certainly did suppose that you meant that, I replied, when you agreed that rulers are not infallible but sometimes make mistakes.

d   That is because you argue like a pettifogger, Socrates. Why, to take the nearest example, do you call one who is mistaken about the sick a physician in respect of his mistake or one who goes wrong in a calculation a calculator when he goes wrong and in respect of this error? Yet that is what we say literally—we say that the physician erred, and the calculator and the schoolmaster. But the truth, I take it,
e is, that each of these in so far as he is that which we entitle him never errs, so that, speaking precisely, since you are such a stickler for precision, no craftsman errs. For it is when his knowledge abandons him that he who goes wrong goes wrong—when he is not a craftsman. So that no craftsman, wise man, or ruler makes a mistake then when he is a ruler, though everybody would use the expression that the physician made a mistake and the ruler erred. It is in this loose way of speaking, then, that you must take the answer I gave you a little while ago. But the most precise statement is that other, that the ruler in so far forth as ruler does not err, and not erring he enacts what is best
341 for himself, and this the subject must do, so that, even as I meant from the start, I say the just is to do what is for the advantage of the stronger.

So then, Thrasymachus, said I, my manner of argument seems to you pettifogging?

It does, he said.

You think, do you, that it was with malice aforethought and trying to get the better of you unfairly that I asked that question?

I don't think it, I know it, he said, and you won't make anything by it, for you won't get the better of me by stealth and, failing stealth, b you are not of the force to beat me in debate.

Bless your soul, said I, I wouldn't even attempt such a thing. But that nothing of the sort may spring up between us again, define in which sense you take the ruler and stronger. Do you mean the so-called ruler or that ruler in the precise sense of whom you were just now telling us, and for whose advantage as being the superior it will be just for the inferior to act?

I mean the ruler in the very most precise sense of the word, he said. Now bring on against this your cavils and your shyster's tricks if you are able. I ask no quarter. But you'll find yourself unable.

Why, do you suppose, I said, that I am so mad as to try to beard a c lion and try the pettifogger on Thrasymachus?

You did try it just now, he said, paltry fellow though you be.

Something too much of this sort of thing, said I. But tell me, your physician in the precise sense, of whom you were just now speaking, is he a money-maker, an earner of fees, or a healer of the sick? And remember to speak of the physician who is really such.

A healer of the sick, he replied.

And what of the pilot—the pilot rightly so called—is he a ruler of sailors or a sailor?

A ruler of sailors.

We don't, I fancy, have to take into account the fact that he ac- d tually sails in the ship, nor is he to be denominated a sailor. For it is not in respect of his sailing that he is called a pilot but in respect of his art and his ruling of the sailors.

True, he said.

Then for each of them is there not a something that is for his advantage?

Quite so.

And is it not also true, said I, that the art naturally exists for this, to discover and provide for each his advantage?

Yes, for this.

Is there, then, for each of the arts any other advantage than to be as perfect as possible?

What do you mean by that question? e

Just as if, I said, you should ask me whether it is enough for the body to be the body or whether it stands in need of something else, I would reply, By all means it stands in need. That is the reason why the art of medicine has now been invented, because the body is defective and such defect is unsatisfactory. To provide for this, then, what is advantageous, that is the end for which the art was devised. Do you think that would be a correct answer, or not?

342   Correct, he said.

But how about this? Is the medical art itself defective or faulty, or has any other art any need of some virtue, quality, or excellence —as the eyes of vision, the ears of hearing—and for this reason is there need of some art over them that will consider and provide what is advantageous for these very ends? Does there exist in the art itself some defect and does each art require another art to consider its advantage and is there need of still another for the considering art and so on ad infinitum, or will the art look out for its own advantage? Or

b is it a fact that it needs neither itself nor another art to consider its advantage and provide against its deficiency? For there is no defect or error at all that dwells in any art. Nor does it befit an art to seek the advantage of anything else than that of its object. But the art itself is free from all harm and admixture of evil, and is right so long as each art is precisely and entirely that which it is. And consider the matter in that 'precise' way of speaking. Is it so or not?

It appears to be so, he said.

c   Then medicine, said I, does not consider the advantage of medicine but of the body?

Yes.

Nor horsemanship of horsemanship but of horses, nor does any other art look out for itself—for it has no need—but for that of which it is the art.

So it seems, he replied.

But surely, Thrasymachus, the arts do hold rule and are stronger than that of which they are the arts.

He conceded this but it went very hard.

Then no art considers or enjoins the advantage of the stronger

d but every art that of the weaker which is ruled by it.

This too he was finally brought to admit though he tried to contest it.

Can we deny, then, said I, that neither does any physician in so far as he is a physician seek or enjoin the advantage of the physician but that of the patient? For we have agreed that the physician, 'precisely' speaking, is a ruler and governor of bodies and not a money-maker. Did we agree on that?

He assented.

And so the 'precise' pilot is a ruler of sailors, not a sailor?

e   That was admitted.

Then that sort of a pilot and ruler will not consider and enjoin the advantage of the pilot but that of the sailor whose ruler he is.

He assented reluctantly.

Then, said I, Thrasymachus, neither does anyone in any office of

rule in so far as he is a ruler consider and enjoin his own advantage
but that of the one whom he rules and for whom he exercises his
craft, and he keeps his eyes fixed on that and on what is advantageous
and suitable to that in all that he says and does.

When we had come to this point in the discussion and it was ap- 343
parent to everybody that his formula of justice had suffered a reversal
of form, Thrasymachus, instead of replying, said, Tell me, Socrates,
have you got a nurse?

What do you mean? said I. Why didn't you answer me instead of
asking such a question?

Because, he said, she lets her little snotty run about driveling
and doesn't wipe your face clean, though you need it badly, if she can't
get you to know the difference between the shepherd and the sheep.

And what, pray, makes you think that? said I.

Because you think that the shepherds and the neatherds are con- b
sidering the good of the sheep and the cattle and fatten and tend them
with anything else in view than the good of their masters and themselves. And by the same token you seem to suppose that the rulers in
our cities, I mean the real rulers, differ at all in their thoughts of the
governed from a man's attitude toward his sheep or that they think of
anything else night and day than the sources of their own profit. And
you are so far out concerning the just and justice and the unjust and c
injustice that you don't know that justice and the just are literally the
other fellow's good—the advantage of the stronger and the ruler, but
a detriment that is all his own of the subject who obeys and serves—
while injustice is the contrary and rules those who are simple in every
sense of the word and just, and they being thus ruled do what is for
his advantage who is the stronger and make him happy by serving
him, but themselves by no manner of means. And you must look at the
matter, my simple-minded Socrates, in this way, that the just man al- d
ways comes out at a disadvantage in his relation with the unjust. To
begin with, in their business dealings in any joint undertaking of the
two you will never find that the just man has the advantage over the
unjust at the dissolution of the partnership but that he always has
the worst of it. Then again, in their relations with the state, if there are
direct taxes or contributions to be paid, the just man contributes more
from an equal estate and the other less, and when there is a distribution the one gains much and the other nothing. And so when each e
holds office, apart from any other loss the just man must count on his
own affairs' falling into disorder through neglect, while because of
his justice he makes no profit from the state, and thereto he will displease his friends and his acquaintances by his unwillingness to serve
them unjustly. But to the unjust man all the opposite advantages accrue. I mean, of course, the one I was just speaking of, the man who
has the ability to overreach on a large scale. Consider this type of 344
man, then, if you wish to judge how much more profitable it is to him

personally to be unjust than to be just. And the easiest way of all to understand this matter will be to turn to the most consummate form of injustice which makes the man who has done the wrong most happy and those who are wronged and who would not themselves willingly do wrong most miserable. And this is tyranny, which both by stealth and by force takes away what belongs to others, both sacred and profane, both private and public, not little by little but at one swoop. For each several part of such wrongdoing the malefactor who fails to escape detection is fined and incurs the extreme of contumely, for temple robbers, kidnapers, burglars, swindlers, and thieves are the
b appellations of those who commit these several forms of injustice. But when in addition to the property of the citizens men kidnap and enslave the citizens themselves, instead of these opprobrious names
c they are pronounced happy and blessed not only by their fellow citizens but by all who hear the story of the man who has committed complete and entire injustice. For it is not the fear of doing but of suffering wrong that calls forth the reproaches of those who revile injustice. Thus, Socrates, injustice on a sufficiently large scale is a stronger, freer, and more masterful thing than justice, and, as I said in the beginning, it is the advantage of the stronger that is the just, while the unjust is what profits a man's self and is for his advantage.

d   After this Thrasymachus was minded to depart when like a bathman he had poured his speech in a sudden flood over our ears. But the company would not suffer him and were insistent that he should remain and render an account of what he had said. And I was particularly urgent and said, I am surprised at you, Thrasymachus. After hurling such a doctrine at us, can it be that you propose to depart without staying to teach us properly or learn yourself whether this
e thing is so or not? Do you think it a small matter that you are attempting to determine and not the entire conduct of life that for each of us would make living most worth while?

Well, do I deny it? said Thrasymachus.

You seem to, said I, or else to care nothing for us and so feel no concern whether we are going to live worse or better lives in our ignorance of what you affirm that you know. Nay, my good fellow, do your best to make the matter clear to us also—it will be no bad invest-
345 ment for you, any benefit that you bestow on such a company as this. For I tell you for my part that I am not convinced; neither do I think that injustice is more profitable than justice, not even if one gives it free scope and does not hinder it of its will. But, suppose, sir, a man to be unjust and to be able to act unjustly either because he is not detected or can maintain it by violence. All the same he does not convince me that it is more profitable than justice. Now it may be that there is someone else among us who feels in this way and that I am
b not the only one. Persuade us, then, my dear fellow, convince us satisfactorily that we are ill advised in preferring justice to injustice.

And how am I to persuade you? he said. If you are not convinced by what I just now was saying, what more can I do for you? Shall I take the argument and ram it into your head?

Heaven forbid! I said. Don't do that. But in the first place when you have said a thing stand by it, or if you shift your ground change openly and don't try to deceive us. But, as it is, you see, Thrasymachus —let us return to the previous examples—you see that while you be- c gan by taking the physician in the true sense of the word, you did not think fit afterward to be consistent and maintain with precision the notion of the true shepherd, but you apparently think that he herds his sheep in his quality of shepherd, not with regard to what is best for the sheep, but as if he were a banqueter about to be feasted with regard to the good cheer, or again with a view to the sale of them, as if he were a money-maker and not a shepherd. But the art of the shepherd surely is d concerned with nothing else than how to provide what is best for that over which it is set, since its own affairs, its own best estate, are surely sufficiently provided for so long as it in nowise fails of being the shepherd's art. And in like manner I supposed that we just now were constrained to acknowledge that every form of rule in so far as it is rule considers what is best for nothing else than that which is governed and cared for by it, alike in political and private rule. Why, do e you think that the rulers and holders of office in our cities—the true rulers—willingly hold office and rule?

I don't think, he said, I know right well they do.

But what of other forms of rule, Thrasymachus? Do you not perceive that no one chooses of his own will to hold the office of rule? Men demand pay, which implies that not to them will benefit accrue 346 from their holding office but to those whom they rule. Tell me this. We ordinarily say, do we not, that each of the arts is different from others because its power or function is different? And, my dear fellow, in order that we may reach some result, don't answer counter to your real belief.

Well, yes, he said, that is what renders it different.

And does not each art also yield us benefit that is peculiar to itself and not general, as for example medicine health, the pilot's art safety at sea, and the other arts similarly?

Assuredly.   b

And does not the wage earner's art yield wages? For that is its function. Would you identify medicine and the pilot's art? Or if you please to discriminate 'precisely' as you proposed, none the more if a pilot regains his health because a sea voyage is good for him, no whit the more, I say, for this reason do you call his art medicine, do you?

Of course not, he said.

Neither, I take it, do you call wage earning medicine if a man earning wages is in health.

Surely not.

PLATO: COLLECTED DIALOGUES

But what of this? Do you call medicine wage earning, if a man
c when giving treatment earns wages?

No, he said.

And did we not agree that the benefit derived from each art is
peculiar to it?

So be it, he said.

Any common or general benefit that all craftsmen receive, then,
they obviously derive from their common use of some further identical thing.

It seems so, he said.

And we say that the benefit of earning wages accrues to the
craftsmen from their further exercise of the wage-earning art.

d   He assented reluctantly.

Then the benefit, the receiving of wages, does not accrue to each
from his own art. But if we are to consider it 'precisely,' medicine produces health but the fee-earning art the pay, and architecture a house
but the fee-earning art accompanying it the fee, and so with all the
others—each performs its own task and benefits that over which it is
set. But unless pay is added to it, is there any benefit which the craftsman receives from the craft?

Apparently not, he said.

e   Does he then bestow no benefit either when he works for
nothing?

I'll say he does.

Then, Thrasymachus, is not this immediately apparent, that no
art or office provides what is beneficial for itself—but as we said long
ago it provides and enjoins what is beneficial to its subject, considering the advantage of that, the weaker, and not the advantage of the
stronger? That was why, friend Thrasymachus, I was just now saying
that no one of his own will chooses to hold rule and office and take
other people's troubles in hand to straighten them out, but everybody
347 expects pay for that, because he who is to exercise the art rightly never
does what is best for himself or enjoins it when he gives commands
according to the art, but what is best for the subject. That is the reason, it seems, why pay must be provided for those who are to consent
to rule, either in the form of money or honor or a penalty if they
refuse.

What do you mean by that, Socrates? said Glaucon. The two
wages I recognize, but the penalty you speak of and described as a
form of wage I don't understand.

Then, said I, you don't understand the wages of the best men for
the sake of which the finest spirits hold office and rule when they
b consent to do so. Don't you know that to be covetous of honor and
covetous of money is said to be and is a reproach?

I do, he said.

Well, then, said I, that is why the good are not willing to rule ei-

ther for the sake of money or of honor. They do not wish to collect pay
openly for their service of rule and be styled hirelings, nor to take it by
stealth from their office and be called thieves, nor yet for the sake of
honor, for they are not covetous of honor. So there must be imposed
some compulsion and penalty to constrain them to rule if they are to c
consent to hold office. That is perhaps why to seek office oneself and
not await compulsion is thought disgraceful. But the chief penalty is
to be governed by someone worse if a man will not himself hold office
and rule. It is from fear of this, as it appears to me, that the better
sort hold office when they do, and then they go to it not in the expectation of enjoyment nor as to a good thing, but as to a necessary evil d
and because they are unable to turn it over to better men than themselves or to their like. For we may venture to say that, if there
should be a city of good men only, immunity from office holding
would be as eagerly contended for as office is now, and there it would
be made plain that in very truth the true ruler does not naturally seek
his own advantage but that of the ruled, so that every man of understanding would rather choose to be benefited by another than to
be bothered with benefiting him. This point then I by no means con- e
cede to Thrasymachus, that justice is the advantage of the superior.
But that we will reserve for another occasion. A far weightier matter seems to me Thrasymachus' present statement, his assertion that
the life of the unjust man is better than that of the just. Which now
do you choose, Glaucon? And which seems to you to be the truer
statement?

That the life of the just man is more profitable, I say, he replied.

Did you hear, said I, all the goods that Thrasymachus just now 348
enumerated for the life of the unjust man?

I heard, he said, but I am not convinced.

Do you wish us then to try to persuade him, supposing we can
find a way, that what he says is not true?

Of course I wish it, he said.

If then we oppose him in a set speech enumerating in turn the
advantages of being just and he replies and we rejoin, we shall have to
count up and measure the goods listed in the respective speeches and b
we shall forthwith be in need of judges to decide between us. But if, as
in the preceding discussion, we come to terms with one another as to
what we admit in the inquiry, we shall be ourselves both judges and
pleaders.

Quite so, he said.

Which method do you like better? said I.

This one, he said.

Come then, Thrasymachus, I said, go back to the beginning and
answer us. You affirm that perfect and complete injustice is more
profitable than justice that is complete.

I affirm it, he said, and have told you my reasons.   c

Tell me then how you would express yourself on this point about
them. You call one of them, I presume, a virtue and the other a vice?

Of course.

Justice the virtue and injustice the vice?

It is likely, you innocent, when I say that injustice pays and justice doesn't pay.

But what then, pray?

The opposite, he replied.

What! Justice vice?

No, but a most noble simplicity or goodness of heart.

d   Then do you call injustice badness of heart?

No, but goodness of judgment.

Do you also, Thrasymachus, regard the unjust as intelligent and
good?

Yes, if they are capable of complete injustice, he said, and are
able to subject to themselves cities and tribes of men. But you probably suppose that I mean those who take purses. There is profit to be
sure even in that sort of thing, he said, if it goes undetected. But
such things are not worth taking into the account, but only what I just
described.

e   I am not unaware of your meaning in that, I said, but this is what
surprised me, that you should range injustice under the head of virtue
and wisdom, and justice in the opposite class.

Well, I do so class them, he said.

That, said I, is a stiffer proposition, my friend, and if you are going as far as that it is hard to know what to answer. For if your position were that injustice is profitable yet you conceded it to be vicious
and disgraceful as some other disputants do, there would be a chance
for an argument on conventional principles. But, as it is, you obviously
349   are going to affirm that it is honorable and strong and you will attach to it all the other qualities that we were assigning to the just,
since you don't shrink from putting it in the category of virtue and
wisdom.

You are a most veritable prophet, he replied.

Well, said I, I mustn't flinch from following out the logic of the
inquiry, so long as I conceive you to be saying what you think. For
now, Thrasymachus, I absolutely believe that you are not 'mocking' us
but telling us your real opinions about the truth.

What difference does it make to you, he said, whether I believe
it or not? Why don't you test the argument?

b   No difference, said I, but here is something I want you to tell me
in addition to what you have said. Do you think the just man would
want to overreach or exceed another just man?

By no means, he said. Otherwise he would not be the delightful
simpleton that he is.

And would he exceed or overreach or go beyond the just action?

Not that either, he replied.

But how would he treat the unjust man—would he deem it proper and just to outdo, overreach, or go beyond him or would he not?

He would, he said, but he wouldn't be able to.

That is not my question, I said, but whether it is not the fact that the just man does not claim or wish to outdo the just man but only the c unjust?

That is the case, he replied.

How about the unjust then? Does he claim to overreach and outdo the just man and the just action?

Of course, he said, since he claims to overreach and get the better of everything.

Then the unjust man will overreach and outdo also both the unjust man and the unjust action, and all his endeavor will be to get the most in everything for himself.

That is so.

Let us put it in this way, I said. The just man does not seek to take advantage of his like but of his unlike, but the unjust man of both.   d

Admirably put, he said.

But the unjust man is intelligent and good and the just man neither.

That, too, is right, he said.

Is it not also true, I said, that the unjust man is like the intelligent and good and the just man is not?

Of course, he said, being such he will be like to such and the other not.

Excellent. Then each is such as that to which he is like.

What else do you suppose? he said.

Very well, Thrasymachus, but do you recognize that one man is a musician and another unmusical?   e

I do.

Which is the intelligent and which the unintelligent?

The musician, I presume, is the intelligent and the unmusical the unintelligent.

And is he not good in the things in which he is intelligent and bad in the things in which he is unintelligent?

Yes.

And the same of the physician?

The same.

Do you think then, my friend, that any musician in the tuning of a lyre would want to overreach another musician in the tightening and relaxing of the strings or would claim and think fit to exceed or outdo him?

I do not.

But would he the unmusical man?

Of necessity, he said.

350   And how about the medical man? In prescribing food and drink would he want to outdo the medical man or the medical procedure?

Surely not.

But he would the unmedical man?

Yes.

Consider then with regard to all forms of knowledge and ignorance whether you think that anyone who knows would choose to do or say other or more than what another who knows would do or say, and not rather exactly what his like would do in the same action.

Why, perhaps it must be so, he said, in such cases.

But what of the ignorant man—of him who does not know?

b   Would he not overreach or outdo equally the knower and the ignorant?

It may be.

But the one who knows is wise?

I'll say so.

And the wise is good?

I'll say so.

Then he who is good and wise will not wish to overreach his like but his unlike and opposite.

It seems so, he said.

But the bad man and the ignoramus will overreach both like and unlike?

So it appears.

And does not our unjust man, Thrasymachus, overreach both unlike and like? Did you not say that?

I did, he replied.

c   But the just man will not overreach his like but only his unlike?

Yes.

Then the just man is like the wise and good, and the unjust is like the bad and the ignoramus.

It seems likely.

But furthermore we agreed that each is such as that to which he is like.

Yes, we did.

Then the just man has turned out on our hands to be good and wise and the unjust man bad and ignorant.

Thrasymachus made all these admissions not as I now lightly

d   narrate them, but with much balking and reluctance and prodigious sweating, it being summer, and it was then I beheld what I had never seen before—Thrasymachus blushing. But when we did reach our conclusion that justice is virtue and wisdom and injustice vice and ignorance, Good, said I, let this be taken as established. But we were also affirming that injustice is a strong and potent thing. Don't you remember, Thrasymachus?

I remember, he said, but I don't agree with what you are now

saying either and I have an answer to it, but if I were to attempt to
state it, I know very well that you would say that I was delivering a
harangue. Either then allow me to speak at such length as I desire, or, e
if you prefer to ask questions, go on questioning and I, as we do for
old wives telling their tales, will say, 'Very good,' and will nod assent
and dissent.

No, no, said I, not counter to your own belief.

Yes, to please you, he said, since you don't allow me freedom of
speech. And yet what more do you want?

Nothing, indeed, said I, but if this is what you propose to do, do it,
and I will ask the questions.

Ask on, then.

This, then, is the question I ask, the same as before, so that our
inquiry may proceed in sequence. What is the nature of injustice as 351
compared with justice? For the statement made, I believe, was that
injustice is a more potent and stronger thing than justice. But now, I
said, if justice is wisdom and virtue, it will easily, I take it, be shown
to be also a stronger thing than injustice, since injustice is ignorance
—no one could now fail to recognize that—but what I want is not
quite so simple as that. I wish, Thrasymachus, to consider it in some
such fashion as this. A city, you would say, may be unjust and try to b
enslave other cities unjustly, have them enslaved and hold many of
them in subjection.

Certainly, he said, and this is what the best state will chiefly do,
the state whose injustice is most complete.

I understand, I said, that this was your view. But the point that I
am considering is this, whether the city that thus shows itself superior
to another will have this power without justice or whether she must
of necessity combine it with justice.

If, he replied, what you were just now saying holds good, that jus- c
tice is wisdom, with justice; if it is as I said, with injustice.

Admirable, Thrasymachus, I said. You not only nod assent and
dissent, but give excellent answers.

I am trying to please you, he replied.

Very kind of you. But please me in one thing more and tell me
this. Do you think that a city, an army, or bandits, or thieves, or any
other group that attempted any action in common, could accomplish
anything if they wronged one another?

Certainly not, said he.   d

But if they didn't, wouldn't they be more likely to?

Assuredly.

For factions, Thrasymachus, are the outcome of injustice, and hatreds and internecine conflicts, but justice brings oneness of mind and
love. Is it not so?

So be it, he replied, not to differ from you.

That is good of you, my friend, but tell me this. If it is the

business of injustice to engender hatred wherever it is found, will it
not, when it springs up either among free men or slaves, cause them
to hate and be at strife with one another, and make them incapable
e of effective action in common?

By all means.

Suppose, then, it springs up between two, will they not be at outs
with and hate each other and be enemies both to one another and to
the just?

They will, he said.

And then will you tell me that if injustice arises in one it will lose
its force and function or will it nonetheless keep it?

Have it that it keeps it, he said.

And is it not apparent that its force is such that wherever it is
found in city, family, camp, or in anything else, it first renders the
352 thing incapable of co-operation with itself owing to faction and difference, and secondly an enemy to itself and to its opposite in every
case, the just? Isn't that so?

By all means.

Then in the individual too, I presume, its presence will operate
all these effects which it is its nature to produce. It will in the first
place make him incapable of accomplishing anything because of inner faction and lack of self-agreement, and then an enemy to himself
and to the just. Is it not so?

Yes.

But, my friend, the gods too are just.

Have it that they are, he said.

b   So to the gods also, it seems, the unjust man will be hateful, but
the just man dear.

Revel in your discourse, he said, without fear, for I shall not oppose you, so as not to offend your partisans here.

Fill up the measure of my feast, then, and complete it for me, I
said, by continuing to answer as you have been doing. Now that the
just appear to be wiser and better and more capable of action and the
unjust incapable of any common action, and that if we ever say that
c any men who are unjust have vigorously combined to put something
over, our statement is not altogether true, for they would not have kept
their hands from one another if they had been thoroughly unjust, but
it is obvious that there was in them some justice which prevented
them from wronging at the same time one another too as well as those
whom they attacked. And by dint of this they accomplished whatever
they did and set out to do injustice only half corrupted by injustice,
since utter rascals completely unjust are completely incapable of effective action—all this I understand to be the truth, and not what you
d originally laid down. But whether it is also true that the just have a
better life than the unjust and are happier, which is the question we

afterward proposed for examination, is what we now have to consider. It appears even now that they are, I think, from what has already been said. But all the same we must examine it more carefully. For it is no ordinary matter that we are discussing, but the right conduct of life.

Proceed with your inquiry, he said.

I proceed, said I. Tell me then—would you say that a horse has a e specific work or function?

I would.

Would you be willing to define the work of a horse or of anything else to be that which one can do only with it or best with it?

I don't understand, he replied.

Well, take it this way. Is there anything else with which you can see except the eyes?

Certainly not.

Again, could you hear with anything but ears?

By no means.

Would you not rightly say that these are the functions of these organs?

By all means.

Once more, you could use a dirk to trim vine branches and a knife 353 and many other instruments.

Certainly.

But nothing so well, I take it, as a pruning knife fashioned for this purpose.

That is true.

Must we not then assume this to be the work or function of that?

We must.

You will now, then, I fancy, better apprehend the meaning of my question when I asked whether that is not the work of a thing which it only or it better than anything else can perform.

Well, he said, I do understand, and agree that the work of any- b thing is that.

Very good, said I. Do you not also think that there is a specific virtue or excellence of everything for which a specific work or function is appointed? Let us return to the same examples. The eyes we say have a function?

They have.

Is there also a virtue of the eyes?

There is.

And was there not a function of the ears?

Yes.

And so also a virtue?

Also a virtue.

And what of all other things? Is the case not the same?

The same.

c   Take note now. Could the eyes possibly fulfill their function
well if they lacked their own proper excellence and had in its stead
the defect?

How could they? he said. For I presume you meant blindness instead of vision.

Whatever, said I, the excellence may be. For I have not yet come
to that question, but am only asking whether whatever operates will
not do its own work well by its own virtue and badly by its own defect.

That much, he said, you may safely affirm to be true.

Then the ears, too, if deprived of their own virtue will do their
work ill?

Assuredly.

d   And do we then apply the same principle to all things?

I think so.

Then next consider this. The soul, has it a work which you
couldn't accomplish with anything else in the world, as for example,
management, rule, deliberation, and the like? Is there anything else
than soul to which you could rightly assign these and say that they
were its peculiar work?

Nothing else.

And again life? Shall we say that too is the function of the soul?

Most certainly, he said.

And do we not also say that there is an excellence or virtue of the
soul?

We do.

e   Will the soul ever accomplish its own work well if deprived of its
own virtue, or is this impossible?

It is impossible.

Of necessity, then, a bad soul will govern and manage things
badly while the good soul will in all these things do well.

Of necessity.

And did we not agree that the excellence or virtue of soul is justice and its defect injustice?

Yes, we did.

The just soul and the just man then will live well and the unjust
ill?

So it appears, he said, by your reasoning.

354   But furthermore, he who lives well is blessed and happy, and he
who does not the contrary.

Of course.

Then the just is happy and the unjust miserable.

So be it, he said.

But it surely does not pay to be miserable, but to be happy.

Of course not.

Never, then, most worshipful Thrasymachus, can injustice be
more profitable than justice.

Let this complete your entertainment, Socrates, at the festival of Bendis.

A feast furnished by you, Thrasymachus, I said, now that you have become gentle with me and are no longer angry. I have not dined well, however—by my own fault, not yours. But just as gluttons b snatch at every dish that is handed along and taste it before they have properly enjoyed the preceding, so I, methinks, before finding the first object of our inquiry—what justice is—let go of that and set out to consider something about it, namely whether it is vice and ignorance or wisdom and virtue. And again, when later the view was sprung upon us that injustice is more profitable than justice I could not refrain from turning to that from the other topic. So that for me the present outcome of the discussion is that I know nothing. For if I don't know what the just is, I shall hardly know whether it is a virtue or not, and whether its possessor is or is not happy.

BOOK II

When I had said this I supposed that I was done with the subject, but 357 it all turned out to be only a prelude. For Glaucon, who is always an intrepid, enterprising spirit in everything, would not on this occasion acquiesce in Thrasymachus' abandonment of his case, but said, Socrates, is it your desire to seem to have persuaded us or really to per- b suade us that it is without exception better to be just than unjust?

Really, I said, if the choice rested with me.

Well, then, you are not doing what you wish. For tell me, do you agree that there is a kind of good which we would choose to possess, not from desire for its aftereffects, but welcoming it for its own sake? As, for example, joy and such pleasures as are harmless and nothing results from them afterward save to have and to hold the enjoyment.

I recognize that kind, said I.

And again a kind that we love both for its own sake and for its c consequences, such as understanding, sight, and health? For these I presume we welcome for both reasons.

Yes, I said.

And can you discern a third form of good under which fall exercise and being healed when sick and the art of healing and the making of money generally? For of them we would say that they are laborious and painful yet beneficial, and for their own sake we would not accept them, but only for the rewards and other benefits that accrue from d them.

Why yes, I said, I must admit this third class also. But what of it?

In which of these classes do you place justice? he said.

In my opinion, I said, it belongs in the fairest class, that which a 358 man who is to be happy must love both for its own sake and for the results.

Yet the multitude, he said, do not think so, but that it belongs to the toilsome class of things that must be practiced for the sake of rewards and repute due to opinion but that in itself is to be shunned as an affliction.

I am aware, said I, that that is the general opinion and Thrasymachus has for some time been disparaging it as such and praising injustice. But I, it seems, am somewhat slow to learn.

b   Come now, he said, hear what I too have to say and see if you agree with me. For Thrasymachus seems to me to have given up to you too soon, as if he were a serpent that you had charmed, but I am not yet satisfied with the proof that has been offered about justice and injustice. For what I desire is to hear what each of them is and what potency and effect each has in and of itself dwelling in the soul, but to dismiss their rewards and consequences. This, then, is what I propose
c   to do, with your concurrence. I will renew the argument of Thrasymachus and will first state what men say is the nature and origin of justice, secondly, that all who practice it do so reluctantly, regarding it as something necessary and not as a good, and thirdly, that they have plausible grounds for thus acting, since forsooth the life of the unjust man is far better than that of the just man—as they say, though I, Socrates, don't believe it. Yet I am disconcerted when my ears are dinned by the arguments of Thrasymachus and innumerable
d   others. But the case for justice, to prove that it is better than injustice, I have never yet heard stated by any as I desire to hear it. What I desire is to hear an encomium on justice in and by itself. And I think I am most likely to get that from you. For which reason I will lay myself out in praise of the life of injustice, and in so speaking will give you an example of the manner in which I desire to hear from you in turn the dispraise of injustice and the praise of justice. Consider whether my proposal pleases you.

Nothing could please me more, said I, for on what subject would a man of sense rather delight to hold and hear discourse again and again?

e   That is excellent, he said, and now listen to what I said would be the first topic—the nature and origin of justice.

By nature, they say, to commit injustice is a good and to suffer it is an evil, but that the excess of evil in being wronged is greater than the excess of good in doing wrong, so that when men do wrong and are
359 wronged by one another and taste of both, those who lack the power to avoid the one and take the other determine that it is for their profit to make a compact with one another neither to commit nor to suffer injustice, and that this is the beginning of legislation and of covenants between men, and that they name the commandment of the law the lawful and the just, and that this is the genesis and essential nature of justice—a compromise between the best, which is to do wrong with impunity, and the worst, which is to be wronged and be impotent

to get one's revenge. Justice, they tell us, being midway between the
two, is accepted and approved, not as a real good, but as a thing hon- b
ored in the lack of vigor to do injustice, since anyone who had the
power to do it and was in reality 'a man' would never make a compact
with anybody neither to wrong nor to be wronged, for he would be
mad. The nature, then, of justice is this and such as this, Socrates,
and such are the conditions in which it originates, according to the
theory.

But as for the second point, that those who practice it do so unwillingly and from want of power to commit injustice, we shall be
most likely to apprehend that if we entertain some such supposition
as this in thought—if we grant to both the just and the unjust license c
and power to do whatever they please, and then accompany them in
imagination and see whither desire will conduct them. We should
then catch the just man in the very act of resorting to the same conduct as the unjust man because of the self-advantage which every
creature by its nature pursues as a good, while by the convention of
law it is forcibly diverted to paying honor to 'equality.' The license
that I mean would be most nearly such as would result from supposing them to have the power which men say once came to the ancestor d
of Gyges the Lydian. They relate that he was a shepherd in the service
of the ruler at that time of Lydia, and that after a great deluge of rain
and an earthquake the ground opened and a chasm appeared in the
place where he was pasturing, and they say that he saw and wondered
and went down into the chasm. And the story goes that he beheld
other marvels there and a hollow bronze horse with little doors, and
that he peeped in and saw a corpse within, as it seemed, of more
than mortal stature, and that there was nothing else but a gold ring on
its hand, which he took off, and so went forth. And when the shep- e
herds held their customary assembly to make their monthly report to
the king about the flocks, he also attended, wearing the ring. So as he
sat there it chanced that he turned the collet of the ring toward himself, toward the inner part of his hand, and when this took place they
say that he became invisible to those who sat by him and they spoke of
him as absent, and that he was amazed, and again fumbling with the 360
ring turned the collet outward and so became visible. On noting this
he experimented with the ring to see if it possessed this virtue, and he
found the result to be that when he turned the collet inward he became invisible, and when outward visible, and becoming aware of
this, he immediately managed things so that he became one of the
messengers who went up to the king, and on coming there he seduced b
the king's wife and with her aid set upon the king and slew him and
possessed his kingdom.

If now there should be two such rings, and the just man should
put on one and the unjust the other, no one could be found, it would
seem, of such adamantine temper as to persevere in justice and

endure to refrain his hands from the possessions of others and not touch them, though he might with impunity take what he wished even
c from the market place, and enter into houses and lie with whom he pleased, and slay and loose from bonds whomsoever he would, and in all other things conduct himself among mankind as the equal of a god. And in so acting he would do no differently from the other man, but both would pursue the same course. And yet this is a great proof, one might argue, that no one is just of his own will but only from constraint, in the belief that justice is not his personal good, inasmuch as every man, when he supposes himself to have the power to do wrong, does wrong. For that there is far more profit for him personally
d in injustice than in justice is what every man believes, and believes truly, as the proponent of this theory will maintain. For if anyone who had got such a license within his grasp should refuse to do any wrong or lay his hands on others' possessions, he would be regarded as most pitiable and a great fool by all who took note of it, though they would praise him before one another's faces, deceiving one another because of their fear of suffering injustice. So much for this point.
e   But to come now to the decision between our two kinds of life, if we separate the most completely just and the most completely unjust man, we shall be able to decide rightly, but if not, not. How, then, is this separation to be made? Thus. We must subtract nothing of his injustice from the unjust man or of his justice from the just, but assume the perfection of each in his own mode of conduct. In the first place, the unjust man must act as clever craftsmen do. A first-rate pilot or physician, for example, feels the difference between impossi-
361 bilities and possibilities in his art and attempts the one and lets the others go, and then, too, if he does happen to trip, he is equal to correcting his error. Similarly, the unjust man who attempts injustice rightly must be supposed to escape detection if he is to be altogether unjust, and we must regard the man who is caught as a bungler. For the height of injustice is to seem just without being so. To the perfectly unjust man, then, we must assign perfect injustice and withhold nothing of it, but we must allow him, while committing the
b greatest wrongs, to have secured for himself the greatest reputation for justice, and if he does happen to trip, we must concede to him the power to correct his mistakes by his ability to speak persuasively if any of his misdeeds come to light, and when force is needed, to employ force by reason of his manly spirit and vigor and his provision of friends and money. And when we have set up an unjust man of this character, our theory must set the just man at his side—a simple and noble man, who, in the phrase of Aeschylus, does not wish to seem but to be good. Then we must deprive him of the seeming. For if he is going
c to be thought just he will have honors and gifts because of that esteem. We cannot be sure in that case whether he is just for justice' sake or for the sake of the gifts and the honors. So we must strip him

bare of everything but justice and make his state the opposite of his imagined counterpart. Though doing no wrong he must have the repute of the greatest injustice, so that he may be put to the test as regards justice through not softening because of ill repute and the consequences thereof. But let him hold on his course unchangeable even unto death, seeming all his life to be unjust though being just, so that, both men attaining to the limit, the one of injustice, the other of justice, we may pass judgment which of the two is the happier. d

Bless me, my dear Glaucon, said I. How strenuously you polish off each of your two men for the competition for the prize as if it were a statue!

To the best of my ability, he replied, and if such is the nature of the two, it becomes an easy matter, I fancy, to unfold the tale of the sort of life that awaits each. We must tell it, then, and even if my language is somewhat rude and brutal, you must not suppose, Socrates, that it is I who speak thus, but those who commend injustice above justice. What they will say is this, that such being his disposition the just man will have to endure the lash, the rack, chains, the branding iron in his eyes, and finally, after every extremity of suffering, he will be crucified, and so will learn his lesson that not to be but to seem just is what we ought to desire. And the saying of Aeschylus was, it seems, far more correctly applicable to the unjust man. For it is literally true, they will say, that the unjust man, as pursuing what clings closely to reality, to truth, and not regulating his life by opinion, desires not to seem but to be unjust, e

362

> Exploiting the deep furrows of his wit
> From which there grows the fruit of counsels shrewd,[3]   b

first office and rule in the state because of his reputation for justice, then a wife from any family he chooses, and the giving of his children in marriage to whomsoever he pleases, dealings and partnerships with whom he will, and in all these transactions advantage and profit for himself because he has no squeamishness about committing injustice. And so they say that if he enters into lawsuits, public or private, he wins and gets the better of his opponents, and, getting the better, is rich and benefits his friends and harms his enemies, and he performs sacrifices and dedicates votive offerings to the gods adequately and magnificently, and he serves and pays court to men whom he favors and to the gods far better than the just man, so that he may reasonably expect the favor of heaven also to fall rather to him than to the just. So much better they say, Socrates, is the life that is prepared for the unjust man from gods and men than that which awaits the just. c

When Glaucon had thus spoken, I had a mind to make some d

reply thereto, but his brother Adimantus said, You surely don't suppose, Socrates, that the statement of the case is complete?

Why, what else? I said.

The very most essential point, said he, has not been mentioned.

Then, said I, the proverb has it, 'Let a brother help a man'—and
so, if Glaucon omits any word or deed, do you come to his aid. Though
for my part what he has already said is quite enough to overthrow
me and incapacitate me for coming to the rescue of justice.

e   Nonsense, he said, but listen to this further point. We must set
forth the reasoning and the language of the opposite party, of those
who commend justice and dispraise injustice, if what I conceive to be
Glaucon's meaning is to be made more clear. Fathers, when they address exhortations to their sons, and all those who have others in
363 their charge, urge the necessity of being just, not by praising justice
itself, but the good repute with mankind that accrues from it, the object that they hold before us being that by seeming to be just the man
may get from the reputation office and alliances and all the good
things that Glaucon just now enumerated as coming to the unjust
man from his good name. But those people draw out still further this
topic of reputation. For, throwing in good standing with the gods, they
have no lack of blessings to describe, which they affirm the gods give
b to pious men, even as the worthy Hesiod and Homer declare—the one
that the gods make the oaks bear for the just

> Acorns on topmost branches and swarms of bees on their mid-
> trunks,

and he tells how the

> Flocks of the fleece-bearing sheep are laden and weighted with
> soft wool,[4]

and of many other blessings akin to these, and similarly the other
poet,

> Even as when a good king, who rules in the fear of the high gods,
> Upholds justice and right, and the black earth yields him her
> foison,
c> Barley and wheat, and his trees are laden and weighted with fair
> fruits,
> Increase comes to his flocks and the ocean is teeming with fishes.[5]

And Musaeus and his son have a more excellent song than these of the
blessings that the gods bestow on the righteous. For they conduct
them to the house of Hades in their tale and arrange a symposium of
the saints, where, reclined on couches and crowned with wreaths,
d they entertain the time henceforth with wine, as if the fairest meed
of virtue were an everlasting drunk. And others extend still further

----
[4] *Works and Days* 232 sq.   [5] *Odyssey* 19.109 sq.

the rewards of virtue from the gods. For they say that the children's children of the pious and oath-keeping man and his race thereafter never fail. Such and suchlike are their praises of justice. But the impious and the unjust they bury in mud in the house of Hades and compel them to fetch water in a sieve, and, while they still live, they bring them into evil repute, and all the sufferings that Glaucon enumerated e as befalling just men who are thought to be unjust, these they recite about the unjust, but they have nothing else to say. Such is the praise and the censure of the just and of the unjust.

Consider further, Socrates, another kind of language about justice and injustice employed by both laymen and poets. All with one 364 accord reiterate that soberness and righteousness are fair and honorable, to be sure, but unpleasant and laborious, while licentiousness and injustice are pleasant and easy to win and are only in opinion and by convention disgraceful. They say that injustice pays better than justice, for the most part, and they do not scruple to felicitate bad men who are rich or have other kinds of power and to do them honor in public and private, and to dishonor and disregard those who are in any way weak or poor, even while admitting that they are better men b than the others. But the strangest of all these speeches are the things they say about the gods and virtue—how it is that the gods themselves assign to many good men misfortunes and an evil life, but to their opposites a contrary lot, and begging priests and soothsayers go to rich men's doors and make them believe that they by means of sacrifices and incantations have accumulated a treasure of power from the gods that can expiate and cure with pleasurable festivals any misdeed of a man or his ancestors, and that if a man wishes to harm an c enemy, at slight cost he will be enabled to injure just and unjust alike, since they are masters of spells and enchantments that constrain the gods to serve their end. And for all these sayings they cite the poets as witnesses, with regard to the ease and plentifulness of vice, quoting,

> Evildoing in plenty a man shall find for the seeking.
> Smooth is the way, and it lies near at hand and is easy to enter,
> But on the pathway of virtue the gods put sweat from the first   d
> step,[6]

and a certain long and uphill road. And others cite Homer as a witness to the beguiling of gods by men, since he too said,

> The gods themselves are moved by prayers,
> And men by sacrifice and soothing vows,   e
> And incense and libation turn their wills
> Praying, whene'er they have sinned and made transgression.[7]

And they produce a bushel of books of Musaeus and Orpheus, the offspring of the Moon and of the Muses, as they affirm, and these books

[6] Hesiod, *Works and Days* 287 sq.   [7] *Iliad* 9.497 sq.

they use in their ritual, and make not only ordinary men but states believe that there really are remissions of sins and purifications for deeds of injustice, by means of sacrifice and pleasant sport for the living, and that there are also special rites for the defunct, which
365 they call functions, that deliver us from evils in that other world, while terrible things await those who have neglected to sacrifice.

What, Socrates, do we suppose is the effect of all such sayings about the esteem in which men and gods hold virtue and vice upon the souls that hear them, the souls of young men who are quick-witted and capable of flitting, as it were, from one expression of opinion to another and inferring from them all the character and the path
b whereby a man would lead the best life? Such a youth would most likely put to himself the question Pindar asks, 'Is it by justice or by crooked deceit that I the higher tower shall scale and so live my life out in fenced and guarded security?' The consequences of my being just are, unless I likewise seem so, not assets, they say, but liabilities, labor, and total loss, but if I am unjust and have procured myself a reputation for justice, a godlike life is promised. Then since it is 'the
c seeming,' as the wise men show me, that 'masters the reality' and is lord of happiness, to this I must devote myself without reserve. For a front and a show I must draw about myself a shadow outline of virtue, but trail behind me the fox of the most sage Archilochus,
d shifty and bent on gain. Nay, 'tis objected, it is not easy for a wrongdoer always to lie hid. Neither is any other big thing facile, we shall reply. But all the same if we expect to be happy, we must pursue the path to which the footprints of our arguments point. For with a view to lying hid we will organize societies and political clubs, and there are teachers of cajolery who impart the arts of the popular assembly and the courtroom, so that, partly by persuasion, partly by force, we shall contrive to overreach with impunity. But against the gods, it may be said, neither secrecy nor force can avail. Well, if there are no gods, or they do not concern themselves with the doings of men, neither need we concern ourselves with eluding their observation. If
e they do exist and pay heed, we know and hear of them only from such discourses and from the poets who have described their pedigrees. But these same authorities tell us that the gods are capable of being persuaded and swerved from their course by 'sacrifice and soothing vows' and dedications. We must believe them in both or neither. And if we are to believe them, the thing to do is to commit injustice and offer sacrifice from the fruits of our wrongdoing. For if we
366 are just, we shall, it is true, be unscathed by the gods, but we shall be putting away from us the profits of injustice, but if we are unjust, we shall win those profits, and, by the importunity of our prayers, when we transgress and sin we shall persuade them and escape scot free. Yes, it will be objected, but we shall be brought to judgment in the world below for our unjust deeds here, we or our children's children.

Nay, my dear sir, our calculating friend will say, here again the rites
for the dead have much efficacy, and the absolving divinities, as the
greatest cities declare, and the sons of gods, who became the poets b
and prophets of the gods, and who reveal that this is the truth.

On what further ground, then, could we prefer justice to supreme
injustice? If we combine this with a counterfeit decorum, we shall
prosper to our heart's desire, with gods and men, in life and death, as
the words of the multitude and of men of the highest authority declare. In consequence, then, of all that has been said, what possibility
is there, Socrates, that any man who has the power of any resources of c
mind, money, body, or family should consent to honor justice and
not rather laugh when he hears her praised? In sooth, if anyone is able
to show the falsity of these arguments, and has come to know with
sufficient assurance that justice is best, he feels much indulgence for
the unjust, and is not angry with them, but is aware that except a
man by inborn divinity of his nature disdains injustice, or, having d
won to knowledge, refrains from it, no one else is willingly just, but
that it is from lack of manly spirit or from old age or some other
weakness that men dispraise injustice, lacking the power to practice
it. The fact is patent. For no sooner does such a one come into the
power than he works injustice to the extent of his ability.

And the sole cause of all this is the fact that was the starting
point of this entire plea of my friend here and of myself to you, Socrates, pointing out how strange it is that of all you self-styled advocates of justice, from the heroes of old whose discourses survive to the e
men of the present day, not one has ever censured injustice or commended justice otherwise than in respect of the repute, the honors,
and the gifts that accrue from each. But what each one of them is in
itself, by its own inherent force, when it is within the soul of the possessor and escapes the eyes of both gods and men, no one has ever
adequately set forth in poetry or prose—the proof that the one is the
greatest of all evils that the soul contains within itself, while justice is 367
the greatest good. For if you had all spoken in this way from the beginning and from our youth up had sought to convince us, we should
not now be guarding against one another's injustice, but each would
be his own best guardian, for fear lest by working injustice he should
dwell in communion with the greatest of evils.

This, Socrates, and perhaps even more than this, Thrasymachus
and haply another might say in pleas for and against justice and injustice, inverting their true potencies, as I believe, grossly. But I—for
I have no reason to hide anything from you—am laying myself out to
the utmost on the theory, because I wish to hear its refutation from b
you. Do not merely show us by argument that justice is superior to injustice, but make clear to us what each in and of itself does to its possessor, whereby the one is evil and the other good. But do away with
the repute of both, as Glaucon urged. For, unless you take away from

either the true repute and attach to each the false, we shall say that it is not justice that you are praising but the semblance, nor injustice that you censure, but the seeming, and that you really are exhorting
c us to be unjust but conceal it, and that you are at one with Thrasymachus in the opinion that justice is the other man's good, the advantage of the stronger, and that injustice is advantageous and profitable to oneself but disadvantageous to the inferior. Since, then, you have admitted that justice belongs to the class of those highest goods which are desirable both for their consequences and still more
d for their own sake, as sight, hearing, intelligence, yes and health too, and all other goods that are productive by their very nature and not by opinion, this is what I would have you praise about justice—the benefit which it and the harm which injustice inherently works upon its possessor. But the rewards and the honors that depend on opinion, leave to others to praise. For while I would listen to others who thus commended justice and disparaged injustice, bestowing their praise and their blame on the reputation and the rewards of either, I could
e not accept that sort of thing from you unless you say I must, because you have passed your entire life in the consideration of this very matter. Do not, then, I repeat, merely prove to us in argument the superiority of justice to injustice, but show us what it is that each inherently does to its possessor—whether he does or does not escape the eyes of gods and men—whereby the one is good and the other evil.

While I had always admired the genius of Glaucon and Adimantus, I was especially pleased by their words on this occasion, and
368 said, It was excellently spoken of you, sons of the man we know, in the beginning of the elegy which the admirer of Glaucon wrote when you distinguished yourselves in the battle of Megara—'Sons of Ariston, whose race from a glorious sire is godlike.' This, my friends, I think, was well said. For there must indeed be a touch of the godlike in your disposition if you are not convinced that injustice is preferable to justice though you can plead its case in such fashion. And I believe
b that you are really not convinced. I infer this from your general character, since from your words alone I should have distrusted you. But the more I trust you the more I am at a loss what to make of the matter. I do not know how I can come to the rescue. For I doubt my ability for the reason that you have not accepted the arguments whereby I thought I proved against Thrasymachus that justice is better than injustice. Nor yet again do I know how I can refuse to come to the rescue. For I fear lest it be actually impious to stand
c idly by when justice is reviled and be fainthearted and not defend her so long as one has breath and can utter his voice. The best thing, then, is to aid her as best I can.

Glaucon, then, and the rest besought me by all means to come to the rescue and not to drop the argument but to pursue to the end the investigation as to the nature of each and the truth about their respective advantages. I said then as I thought, The inquiry we are undertaking is no easy one but calls for keen vision, as it seems to me. So, d since we are not clever persons, I think we should employ the method of search that we should use if we, with not very keen vision, were bidden to read small letters from a distance, and then someone had observed that these same letters exist elsewhere larger and on a larger surface. We should have accounted it a godsend, I fancy, to be allowed to read those letters first, and then examine the smaller, if they are the same.

Quite so, said Adimantus, but what analogy to this do you detect in the inquiry about justice?   e

I will tell you, I said. There is a justice of one man, we say, and, I suppose, also of an entire city?

Assuredly, said he.

Is not the city larger than the man?

It is larger, he said.

Then, perhaps, there would be more justice in the larger object, and more easy to apprehend. If it please you, then, let us first look for its quality in states, and then only examine it also in the individual, 369 looking for the likeness of the greater in the form of the less.

I think that is a good suggestion, he said.

If, then, said I, our argument should observe the origin of a state, we should see also the origin of justice and injustice in it?

It may be, said he.

And if this is done, we may expect to find more easily what we are seeking?

Much more.   b

Shall we try it, then, and go through with it? I fancy it is no slight task. Reflect, then.

We have reflected, said Adimantus. Proceed and don't refuse.

The origin of the city, then, said I, in my opinion, is to be found in the fact that we do not severally suffice for our own needs, but each of us lacks many things. Do you think any other principle establishes the state?

No other, said he.

As a result of this, then, one man calling in another for one serv- c ice and another for another, we, being in need of many things, gather many into one place of abode as associates and helpers, and to this dwelling together we give the name city or state, do we not?

By all means.

And between one man and another there is an interchange of giving, if it so happens, and taking, because each supposes this to be better for himself.

Certainly.

Come, then, let us create a city from the beginning, in our theory. Its real creator, as it appears, will be our needs.

Obviously.

d   Now the first and chief of our needs is the provision of food for existence and life.

Assuredly.

The second is housing and the third is raiment and that sort of thing.

That is so.

Tell me, then, said I, how our city will suffice for the provision of all these things. Will there not be a farmer for one, and a builder, and then again a weaver? And shall we add thereto a cobbler and some other purveyor for the needs of the body?

Certainly.

The indispensable minimum of a city, then, would consist of four or five men.

e   Apparently.

What of this, then? Shall each of these contribute his work for the common use of all? I mean, shall the farmer, who is one, provide food for four and spend fourfold time and toil on the production of food and share it with the others, or shall he take no thought for them

370 and provide a fourth portion of the food for himself alone in a quarter of the time and employ the other three-quarters, the one in the provision of a house, the other of a garment, the other of shoes, and not have the bother of associating with other people, but, himself for himself, mind his own affairs?

And Adimantus said, But, perhaps, Socrates, the former way is easier.

It would not, by Zeus, be at all strange, said I, for now that you have mentioned it, it occurs to me myself that, to begin with, our sev-

b eral natures are not all alike but different. One man is naturally fitted for one task, and another for another. Don't you think so?

I do.

Again, would one man do better working at many tasks or one at one?

One at one, he said.

And, furthermore, this, I fancy, is obvious—that if one lets slip the right season, the favorable moment in any task, the work is spoiled.

Obvious.

That, I take it, is because the business will not wait upon the leisure of the workman, but the workman must attend to it as his

c main affair, and not as a bywork.

He must indeed.

The result, then, is that more things are produced, and better and more easily when one man performs one task according to his nature, at the right moment, and at leisure from other occupations.

By all means.

Then, Adimantus, we need more than four citizens for the provision of the things we have mentioned. For the farmer, it appears, will not make his own plow if it is to be a good one, nor his hoe, nor his other agricultural implements, nor will the builder, who also needs d many, and similarly the weaver and cobbler.

True.

Carpenters, then, and smiths and many similar craftsmen, associating themselves with our hamlet, will enlarge it considerably.

Certainly.

Yet it still wouldn't be very large even if we should add to them neatherds and shepherds and other herders, so that the farmers might have cattle for plowing, and the builders oxen to use with the farm- e ers for transportation, and the weavers and cobblers hides and fleeces for their use.

It wouldn't be a small city, either, if it had all these.

But further, said I, it is practically impossible to establish the city in a region where it will not need imports.

It is.

There will be a further need, then, of those who will bring in from some other city what it requires.

There will.

And again, if our servitor goes forth empty-handed, not taking 371 with him any of the things needed by those from whom they procure what they themselves require, he will come back with empty hands, will he not?

I think so.

Then their home production must not merely suffice for themselves but in quality and quantity meet the needs of those of whom they have need.

It must.

So our city will require more farmers and other craftsmen.

Yes, more.

And also of other ministrants who are to export and import the merchandise. These are traders, are they not?

Yes.

We shall also need traders, then.

Assuredly.

And if the trading is carried on by sea, we shall need quite a num- b ber of others who are expert in maritime business.

Quite a number.

But again, within the city itself how will they share with one another the products of their labor? This was the very purpose of our association and establishment of a state.

Obviously, he said, by buying and selling.

A market place, then, and money as a token for the purpose of exchange will be the result of this.

By all means.

c   If, then, the farmer or any other craftsman taking his products to the market place does not arrive at the same time with those who desire to exchange with him, is he to sit idle in the market place and lose time from his own work?

By no means, he said, but there are men who see this need and appoint themselves for this service—in well-conducted cities they are generally those who are weakest in body and those who are useless

d for any other task. They must wait there in the agora and exchange money for goods with those who wish to sell, and goods for money with as many as desire to buy.

This need, then, said I, creates the class of shopkeepers in our city. Or is not 'shopkeepers' the name we give to those who, planted in the agora, serve us in buying and selling, while we call those who roam from city to city merchants?

Certainly.

e   And there are, furthermore, I believe, other servitors who in the things of the mind are not altogether worthy of our fellowship, but whose strength of body is sufficient for toil; so they, selling the use of this strength and calling the price wages, are designated, I believe, 'wage earners,' are they not?

Certainly.

Wage earners, then, it seems, are the complement that helps to fill up the state.

I think so.

Has our city, then, Adimantus, reached its full growth, and is it complete?

Perhaps.

Where, then, can justice and injustice be found in it? And along with which of the constituents that we have considered do they come into the state?

I cannot conceive, Socrates, he said, unless it be in some need

372 that those very constituents have of one another.

Perhaps that is a good suggestion, said I. We must examine it and not hold back.

First of all, then, let us consider what will be the manner of life of men thus provided. Will they not make bread and wine and garments and shoes? And they will build themselves houses and carry on their work in summer for the most part unclad and unshod and in

b winter clothed and shod sufficiently. And for their nourishment they will provide meal from their barley and flour from their wheat, and kneading and cooking these they will serve noble cakes and loaves on some arrangement of reeds or clean leaves. And, reclined on rustic beds strewed with bryony and myrtle, they will feast with their children, drinking of their wine thereto, garlanded and singing hymns to

c the gods in pleasant fellowship, not begetting offspring beyond their means lest they fall into poverty or war.

Here Glaucon broke in, No relishes apparently, he said, for the men you describe as feasting.

True, said I, I forgot that they will also have relishes—salt, of course, and olives and cheese, and onions and greens, the sort of things they boil in the country, they will boil up together. But for dessert we will serve them figs and chick-peas and beans, and they will toast myrtle berries and acorns before the fire, washing them down with moderate potations. And so, living in peace and health, they will probably die in old age and hand on a like life to their off- d spring.

And he said, If you were founding a city of pigs, Socrates, what other fodder than this would you provide?

Why, what would you have, Glaucon? said I.

What is customary, he replied. They must recline on couches, I presume, if they are not to be uncomfortable, and dine from tables and have dishes and sweetmeats such as are now in use.   e

Good, said I. I understand. It is not merely the origin of a city, it seems, that we are considering but the origin of a luxurious city. Perhaps that isn't such a bad suggestion, either. For by observation of such a city it may be we could discern the origin of justice and injustice in states. The true state I believe to be the one we have described—the healthy state, as it were. But if it is your pleasure that we contemplate also a fevered state, there is nothing to hinder. For there are some, it appears, who will not be contented with this sort of fare or with this way of life, but couches will have to be added thereto 373 and tables and other furniture, yes, and relishes and myrrh and incense and girls and cakes—all sorts of all of them. And the requirements we first mentioned, houses and garments and shoes, will no longer be confined to necessities, but we must set painting to work and embroidery, and procure gold and ivory and similar adornments, must we not?

Yes, he said.   b

Then shall we not have to enlarge the city again? For that healthy state is no longer sufficient, but we must proceed to swell out its bulk and fill it up with a multitude of things that exceed the requirements of necessity in states, as, for example, the entire class of huntsmen, and the imitators, many of them occupied with figures and colors and many with music—the poets and their assistants, rhapsodists, actors, chorus dancers, contractors—and the manufacturers of all kinds of articles, especially those that have to do with women's adornment. And so we shall also want more servitors. Don't c you think that we shall need tutors, nurses wet and dry, beauty-shop ladies, barbers, and yet again cooks and chefs? And we shall have need, further, of swineherds; there were none of these creatures in our former city, for we had no need of them, but in this city there will be this further need. And we shall also require other cattle in great numbers if they are to be eaten, shall we not?

Yes.

Doctors, too, are something whose services we shall be much
d more likely to require if we live thus than as before?

Much.

And the territory, I presume, that was then sufficient to feed the
then population, from being adequate will become too small. Is that so
or not?

It is.

Then we shall have to cut out a cantle of our neighbor's land if
we are to have enough for pasture and plowing, and they in turn of
ours if they too abandon themselves to the unlimited acquisition of
wealth, disregarding the limit set by our necessary wants.

e   Inevitably, Socrates.

We shall go to war as the next step, Glaucon—or what will
happen?

What you say, he said.

And we are not yet to speak, said I, of any evil or good effect of
war, but only to affirm that we have further discovered the origin of
war, namely, from those things from which the greatest disasters,
public and private, come to states when they come.

Certainly.

Then, my friend, we must still further enlarge our city by no
374 small increment, but by a whole army, that will march forth and fight
it out with assailants in defense of all our wealth and the luxuries we
have just described.

How so? he said. Are the citizens themselves not sufficient for
that?

Not if you, said I, and we all were right in the admission we
made when we were molding our city. We surely agreed, if you remember, that it is impossible for one man to do the work of many
arts well.

True, he said.

b   Well, then, said I, don't you think that the business of fighting is
an art and a profession?

It is indeed, he said.

Should our concern be greater, then, for the cobbler's art than for
the art of war?

By no means.

Can we suppose, then, that while we were at pains to prevent the
cobbler from attempting to be at the same time a farmer, a weaver, or
a builder instead of just a cobbler, to the end that we might have the
cobbler's business well done, and similarly assigned to each and
every one man one occupation, for which he was fit and naturally
c adapted and at which he was to work all his days, at leisure from
other pursuits and not letting slip the right moments for doing the
work well, and that yet we are in doubt whether the right accomplishment of the business of war is not of supreme moment? Is it so easy

that a man who is cultivating the soil will be at the same time a soldier
and one who is practicing cobbling or any other trade, though no man
in the world could make himself a competent expert at draughts or
the dice who did not practice that and nothing else from childhood but
treated it as an occasional business? And are we to believe that a man
who takes in hand a shield or any other instrument of war springs d
up on that very day a competent combatant in heavy armor or in any
other form of warfare—though no other tool will make a man be an
artist or an athlete by his taking it in hand, nor will it be of any service to those who have neither acquired the science of it nor sufficiently
practiced themselves in its use?

Great indeed, he said, would be the value of tools in that case!

Then, said I, in the same degree that the task of our guardians is
the greatest of all, it would require more leisure than any other business and the greatest science and training.   e

I think so, said he.

Does it not also require a nature adapted to that very pursuit?

Of course.

It becomes our task, then, it seems, if we are able, to select which
and what kind of natures are suited for the guardianship of a state.

Yes, ours.

Upon my word, said I, it is no light task that we have taken upon
ourselves. But we must not faint so far as our strength allows.

No, we mustn't.

Do you think, said I, that there is any difference between the
nature of a well-bred hound for this watchdog's work and that of a 375
wellborn lad?

What point have you in mind?

I mean that each of them must be keen of perception, quick in
pursuit of what it has apprehended, and strong too if it has to fight it
out with its captive.

Why, yes, said he, there is need of all these qualities.

And it must, further, be brave if it is to fight well.

Of course.

And will a creature be ready to be brave that is not high-spirited,
whether horse or dog or anything else? Have you never observed what
an irresistible and invincible thing is spirit, the presence of which b
makes every soul in the face of everything fearless and unconquer-
able?

I have.

The physical qualities of the guardian, then, are obvious.

Yes.

And also those of his soul, namely that he must be of high spirit.

Yes, this too.

How then, Glaucon, said I, will they escape being savage to one
another and to the other citizens if this is to be their nature?

Not easily, by Zeus, said he.

c   And yet we must have them gentle to their friends and harsh to
their enemies; otherwise they will not await their destruction at the
hands of others, but will be first themselves in bringing it about.

True, he said.

What, then, are we to do? said I. Where shall we discover a
disposition that is at once gentle and great-spirited? For there appears to be an opposition between the spirited type and the gentle
nature.

There does.

d   But yet if one lacks either of these qualities, a good guardian he
never can be. But these requirements resemble impossibilities, and so
the result is that a good guardian is impossible.

It seems likely, he said.

And I was at a standstill, and after reconsidering what we had
been saying, I said, We deserve to be at a loss, my friend, for we have
lost sight of the comparison that we set before ourselves.

What do you mean?

We failed to note that there are after all such natures as we
thought impossible, endowed with these opposite qualities.

Where?

It may be observed in other animals, but especially in that which
e we likened to the guardian. You surely have observed in well-bred
hounds that their natural disposition is to be most gentle to their familiars and those whom they recognize, but the contrary to those
whom they do not know.

I am aware of that.

The thing is possible, then, said I, and it is not an unnatural requirement that we are looking for in our guardian.

It seems not.

And does it seem to you that our guardian-to-be will also need, in
addition to the being high-spirited, the further quality of having the
love of wisdom in his nature?

How so? he said. I don't apprehend your meaning.

376   This too, said I, is something that you will discover in dogs and
which is worth our wonder in the creature.

What?

That the sight of an unknown person angers him before he has
suffered any injury, but an acquaintance he will fawn upon though he
has never received any kindness from him. Have you never marveled
at that?

I never paid any attention to the matter before now, but that he
acts in some such way is obvious.

b   But surely that is an exquisite trait of his nature and one that
shows a true love of wisdom.

In what respect, pray?

In respect, said I, that he distinguishes a friendly from a hostile aspect by nothing save his apprehension of the one and his failure to recognize the other. How, I ask you, can the love of learning be denied to a creature whose criterion of the friendly and the alien is intelligence and ignorance?

It certainly cannot, he said.

But you will admit, said I, that the love of learning and the love of wisdom are the same?

The same, he said.

Then may we not confidently lay it down, in the case of man too, that if he is to be in some sort gentle to friends and familiars he must c be by nature a lover of wisdom and of learning?

Let us so assume, he replied.

The love of wisdom, then, and high spirit and quickness and strength will be combined for us in the nature of him who is to be a good and true guardian of the state.

By all means, he said.

Such, then, I said, would be the basis of his character. But the rearing of these men and their education, how shall we manage that? And will the consideration of this topic advance us in any way toward discerning what is the object of our entire inquiry—the origin of justice and injustice in a state—our aim must be to omit nothing of a d sufficient discussion, and yet not to draw it out to tiresome length?

And Glaucon's brother replied, Certainly, I expect that this inquiry will bring us nearer to that end.

Certainly, then, my dear Adimantus, said I, we must not abandon it even if it prove to be rather long.

No, we must not.

Come, then, just as if we were telling stories or fables and had ample leisure, let us educate these men in our discourse.

So we must.   e

What, then, is our education? Or is it hard to find a better than that which long time has discovered—which is, I suppose, gymnastics for the body, and for the soul, music?

It is.

And shall we not begin education in music earlier than in gymnastics?

Of course.

And under music you include tales, do you not?

I do.

And tales are of two species, the one true and the other false?

Yes.

And education must make use of both, but first of the false?   377

I don't understand your meaning.

Don't you understand, I said, that we begin by telling children fables, and the fable is, taken as a whole, false, but there is truth in it also? And we make use of fable with children before gymnastics.

That is so.

That, then, is what I meant by saying that we must take up music before gymnastics.

You were right, he said.

b Do you not know, then, that the beginning in every task is the chief thing, especially for any creature that is young and tender? For it is then that it is best molded and takes the impression that one wishes to stamp upon it.

Quite so.

Shall we, then, thus lightly suffer our children to listen to any chance stories fashioned by any chance teachers and so to take into their minds opinions for the most part contrary to those that we shall think it desirable for them to hold when they are grown up?

By no manner of means will we allow it.

c We must begin, then, it seems, by a censorship over our story-makers, and what they do well we must pass and what not, reject. And the stories on the accepted list we will induce nurses and mothers to tell to the children and so shape their souls by these stories far rather than their bodies by their hands. But most of the stories they now tell we must reject.

What sort of stories? he said.

The example of the greater stories, I said, will show us the lesser also. For surely the pattern must be the same, and the greater and the less must have a like tendency. Don't you think so?

d I do, he said, but I don't apprehend which you mean by the greater, either.

Those, I said, that Hesiod and Homer and the other poets related to us. These, methinks, composed false stories which they told and still tell to mankind.

Of what sort? he said. And with what in them do you find fault?

With that, I said, which one ought first and chiefly to blame, especially if the lie is not a pretty one.

What is that?

e When anyone images badly in his speech the true nature of gods and heroes, like a painter whose portraits bear no resemblance to his models.

It is certainly right to condemn things like that, he said, but just what do we mean and what particular things?

There is, first of all, I said, the greatest lie about the things of greatest concernment, which was no pretty invention of him who told how Uranus did what Hesiod says he did to Cronus, and how Cronus 378 in turn took his revenge, and then there are the doings and sufferings of Cronus at the hands of his son. Even if they were true I should not think that they ought to be thus lightly told to thoughtless young persons. But the best way would be to bury them in silence, and if there were some necessity for relating them, only a very small audience should be admitted under pledge of secrecy and after sacrificing, not a pig, but some huge and unprocurable victim, to the end that as few as possible should have heard these tales.

Why, yes, said he, such stories are hard sayings.

Yes, and they are not to be told, Adimantus, in our city, nor is it b to be said in the hearing of a young man that in doing the utmost wrong he would do nothing to surprise anybody, nor again in punishing his father's wrongdoings to the limit, but would only be following the example of the first and greatest of the gods.

No, by heaven, said he, I do not myself think that they are fit to be told.

Neither must we admit at all, said I, that gods war with gods and plot against one another and contend—for it is not true either—if we wish our future guardians to deem nothing more shameful than lightly to fall out with one another. Still less must we make battles of c gods and giants the subject for them of stories and embroideries, and other enmities many and manifold of gods and heroes toward their kith and kin. But if there is any likelihood of our persuading them that no citizen ever quarreled with his fellow citizen and that the very idea of it is an impiety, that is the sort of thing that ought rather to be said by their elders, men and women, to children from the be- d ginning and as they grow older, and we must compel the poets to keep close to this in their compositions. But Hera's fetterings by her son and the hurling out of heaven of Hephaestus by his father when he was trying to save his mother from a beating, and the battles of the gods in Homer's verse are things that we must not admit into our city either wrought in allegory or without allegory. For the young are not able to distinguish what is and what is not allegory, but whatever opinions are taken into the mind at that age are wont to prove indelible and unalterable. For which reason, maybe, we should do our e utmost that the first stories that they hear should be so composed as to bring the fairest lessons of virtue to their ears.

Yes, that is reasonable, he said, but if again someone should ask us to be specific and say what these compositions may be and what are the tales, what could we name?

And I replied, Adimantus, we are not poets, you and I at present, 379 but founders of a state. And to founders it pertains to know the patterns on which poets must compose their fables and from which their poems must not be allowed to deviate, but the founders are not required themselves to compose fables.

Right, he said, but this very thing—the patterns or norms of right speech about the gods—what would they be?

Something like this, I said. The true quality of God we must always surely attribute to him whether we compose in epic, melic, or tragic verse.

We must.

b   And is not God of course good in reality and always to be spoken of as such?

Certainly.

But further, no good thing is harmful, is it?

I think not.

Can what is not harmful harm?

By no means.

Can that which does not harm do any evil?

Not that either.

But that which does no evil would not be cause of any evil either?

How could it?

Once more, is the good beneficent?

Yes.

It is the cause, then, of welfare?

Yes.

Then the good is not the cause of all things, but of things that are well it is the cause—of things that are ill it is blameless.

c   Entirely so, he said.

Neither, then, could God, said I, since he is good, be, as the multitude say, the cause of all things, but for mankind he is the cause of few things, but of many things not the cause. For good things are far fewer with us than evil, and for the good we must assume no other cause than God, but the cause of evil we must look for in other things and not in God.

What you say seems to me most true, he replied.

Then, said I, we must not accept from Homer or any other poet
d the folly of such error as this about the gods, when he says,

Two urns stand on the floor of the palace of Zeus and are filled with
Dooms he allots, one of blessings, the other of gifts that are evil.[8]

And to whomsoever Zeus gives of both commingled

Now upon evil he chances and now again good is his portion.

But the man for whom he does not blend the lots, but to whom he gives unmixed evil—

Hunger devouring drives him, a wanderer over the wide world.

Nor will we tolerate the saying that

e   Zeus is dispenser alike of good and of evil to mortals.

But as to the violation of the oaths and the truce by Pandarus, if anyone affirms it to have been brought about by the action of Athena and Zeus, we will not approve, nor that the strife and contention of

[8] *Iliad* 24.527 sq.

the gods were the doing of Themis and Zeus, nor again must we permit
our youth to hear what Aeschylus says.

> A god implants the guilty cause in men   380
> When he would utterly destroy a house.

But if any poets compose a 'Sorrows of Niobe,' the poem that contains
these iambics, or a tale of the Pelopidae or of Troy, or anything else
of the kind, we must either forbid them to say that these woes are the
work of God, or they must devise some such interpretation as we now
require, and must declare that what God did was righteous and good, b
and they were benefited by their chastisement. But that they were
miserable who paid the penalty, and that the doer of this was God,
is a thing that the poet must not be suffered to say. If on the other
hand he should say that for needing chastisement the wicked were
miserable and that in paying the penalty they were benefited by God,
that we must allow. But as to saying that God, who is good, becomes
the cause of evil to anyone, we must contend in every way that neither
should anyone assert this in his own city if it is to be well governed,
nor anyone hear it, neither younger nor older, neither telling a story
in meter or without meter, for neither would the saying of such
things, if they are said, be holy, nor would they be profitable to us or c
concordant with themselves.

I cast my vote with yours for this law, he said, and am well
pleased with it.

This, then, said I, will be one of the laws and patterns concerning
the gods to which speakers and poets will be required to conform, that
God is not the cause of all things, but only of the good.

And an entirely satisfactory one, he said.

And what of this, the second? Do you think that God is a wizard d
and capable of manifesting himself by design, now in one aspect, now
in another, at one time himself changing and altering his shape in
many transformations and at another deceiving us and causing us to
believe such things about him, or that he is simple and less likely
than anything else to depart from his own form?

I cannot say offhand, he replied.

But what of this? If anything went out from its own form, would
it not be displaced and changed, either by itself or by something else? e

Necessarily.

Is it not true that to be altered and moved by something else
happens least to things that are in the best condition, as, for example,
a body by food and drink and toil, and plants by the heat of the sun
and winds and similar influences—is it not true that the healthiest
and strongest is least altered?

Certainly.

And is it not the soul that is bravest and most intelligent that 381
would be least disturbed and altered by any external affection?

Yes.

And, again, it is surely true of all composite implements, edifices, and habiliments, by parity of reasoning, that those which are well made and in good condition are least liable to be changed by time and other influences.

That is so.

b It is universally true, then, that that which is in the best state by nature or art or both admits least alteration by something else.

So it seems.

But God, surely, and everything that belongs to God, is in every way in the best possible state.

Of course.

From this point of view, then, it would be least of all likely that there would be many forms in God.

Least indeed.

But would he transform and alter himself?

Obviously, he said, if he is altered.

Then does he change himself for the better and to something fairer, or for the worse and to something uglier than himself?

c It must necessarily, said he, be for the worse if he is changed. For we surely will not say that God is deficient in either beauty or excellence.

Most rightly spoken, said I. And if that were his condition, do you think, Adimantus, that any one god or man would of his own will worsen himself in any way?

Impossible, he replied.

It is impossible then, said I, even for a god to wish to alter himself, but, as it appears, each of them, being the fairest and best possible, abides forever simply in his own form.

An absolutely necessary conclusion to my thinking.

d No poet then, I said, my good friend, must be allowed to tell us that 'The gods, in the likeness of strangers, many disguises assume as they visit the cities of mortals.' [9] Nor must anyone tell falsehoods about Proteus and Thetis, nor in any tragedy or in other poems bring in Hera disguised as a priestess collecting alms 'for the life-giving sons of

e Inachus, the Argive stream.' [10] And many similar falsehoods they must not tell. Nor again must mothers under the influence of such poets terrify their children with harmful tales, how there are certain gods whose apparitions haunt the night in the likeness of many strangers from all manner of lands, lest while they speak evil of the gods they at the same time make cowards of the children.

They must not, he said.

But, said I, may we suppose that while the gods themselves are

---

[9] *Odyssey* 17.485 sq.   [10] Aeschylus, *Xanthians*, fr. 159.

incapable of change they cause us to fancy that they appear in many shapes deceiving and practicing magic upon us?

Perhaps, said he.

Consider, said I. Would a god wish to deceive, or lie, by presenting in either word or action what is only appearance?

I don't know, said he.

Don't you know, said I, that the veritable lie, if the expression is permissible, is a thing that all gods and men abhor?

What do you mean? he said.

This, said I, that falsehood in the most vital part of themselves, and about their most vital concerns, is something that no one willingly accepts, but it is there above all that everyone fears it.

I don't understand yet either.

That is because you suspect me of some grand meaning, I said, but what I mean is, that deception in the soul about realities, to have been deceived and to be blindly ignorant and to have and hold the falsehood there, is what all men would least of all accept, and it is in that case that they loathe it most of all.

Quite so, he said.

But surely it would be most wholly right, as I was just now saying, to describe this as in very truth falsehood—ignorance namely in the *soul* of the man deceived. For the falsehood in *words* is a copy of the affection in the soul, an afterrising image of it and not an altogether unmixed falsehood. Is not that so?

By all means.

Essential falsehood, then, is hated not only by gods but by men.

I agree.

But what of the falsehood in words—when and for whom is it serviceable so as not to merit abhorrence? Will it not be against enemies? And when any of those whom we call friends owing to madness or folly attempts to do some wrong, does it not then become useful to avert the evil —as a medicine? And also in the fables of which we were just now speaking, owing to our ignorance of the truth about antiquity. we liken the false to the true as far as we may and so make it edifying.

We most certainly do, he said.

Tell me, then, on which of these grounds falsehood would be serviceable to God. Would he because of his ignorance of antiquity make false likenesses of it?

An absurd supposition, that, he said.

Then there is no lying poet in God.

I think not.

Well then, would it be through fear of his enemies that he would lie?

Far from it.

Would it be because of the folly or madness of his friends?

Nay, no fool or madman is a friend of God.

Then there is no motive for God to deceive.

None.

So from every point of view the divine and the divinity are free from falsehood.

By all means.

Then God is altogether simple and true in deed and word, and neither changes himself nor deceives others by visions or words or the sending of signs in waking or in dreams.

383   I myself think so, he said, when I hear you say it.

You concur then, I said, in this as our second norm or canon for speech and poetry about the gods—that neither are they wizards in shape shifting nor do they mislead us by falsehoods in words or deed?

I concur.

Then, though there are many other things that we praise in Homer, this we will not applaud, the sending of the dream by Zeus to Agamemnon, nor shall we approve of Aeschylus when his Thetis avers

b   that Apollo, singing at her wedding, 'foretold the happy fortunes of her issue,'

> Their days prolonged, from pain and sickness free,
> And rounding out the tale of heaven's blessings,
> Raised the proud paean, making glad my heart.
> And I believed that Phoebus' mouth divine,
> Filled with the breath of prophecy, could not lie.
> But he himself, the singer, himself who sat
> At meat with us, himself who promised all,
> Is now himself the slayer of my son.

c   When anyone says that sort of thing about the gods, we shall be wroth with him, we will refuse him a chorus. Neither will we allow teachers to use him for the education of the young if our guardians are to be god-fearing men and godlike in so far as that is possible for humanity.

By all means, he said, I accept these norms and would use them as canons and laws.

BOOK III

386   Concerning the gods then, said I, this is the sort of thing that we must allow or not allow them to hear from childhood up, if they are to honor the gods and their fathers and mothers, and not to hold their friendship with one another in light esteem.

That was our view and I believe it right.

What then of this? If they are to be brave, must we not extend our prescription to include also the sayings that will make them least

likely to fear death? Or do you suppose that anyone could ever become b
brave who had that dread in his heart?

No indeed, I do not, he replied.

And again, if he believes in the reality of the underworld and its
terrors, do you think that any man will be fearless of death and in
battle will prefer death to defeat and slavery?

By no means.

Then it seems we must exercise supervision also, in the matter of
such tales as these, over those who undertake to supply them and request them not to dispraise in this undiscriminating fashion the life
in Hades but rather praise it, since what they now tell us is neither
true nor edifying to men who are destined to be warriors.   c

Yes, we must, he said.

Then, said I, beginning with this verse we will expunge everything of the same kind,

> Liefer were I in the fields up above to be serf to another
> Tiller of some poor plot which yields him a scanty subsistence,
> Than to be ruler and king over all the dead who have perished,[11]

and this,

> Lest unto men and immortals the homes of the dead be uncovered
> Horrible, noisome, dank, that the gods too hold in abhorrence,[12]   d

and,

> Ah me! So it is true that e'en in the dwellings of Hades
> Spirit there is and wraith, but within there is no understanding,[13]

and this [of Tiresias],

> Sole to have wisdom and wit, but the others are shadowy phantoms,[14]

and,

> Forth from his limbs unwilling his spirit flitted to Hades,
> Wailing its doom and its lustihood lost and the May of its manhood,[15]

and,

> Under the earth like a vapor vanished the gibbering soul,[16]   387

and,

> Even as bats in the hollow of some mysterious grotto
> Fly with a flittermouse shriek·when one of them falls from the
>   cluster,
> Whereby they hold to the rock and are clinging the one to the other,
> Flitted their gibbering ghosts.[17]

[11] *Odyssey* 11.489 sq.   [13] *Iliad* 23.103.   [15] *Iliad* 16.856.
[12] *Iliad* 20.64.   [14] *Odyssey* 10.495.   [16] *Iliad* 23.100.
                         [17] *Odyssey* 24.6 sq.

b We will beg Homer and the other poets not to be angry if we cancel those and all similar passages, not that they are not poetic and pleasing to most hearers, but because the more poetic they are the less are they suited to the ears of boys and men who are destined to be free and to be more afraid of slavery than of death.

By all means.

Then we must further taboo in these matters the entire vocabulary of terror and fear, Cocytus named of lamentation loud, abhorred
c Styx, the flood of deadly hate, the people of the infernal pit and of the charnel house, and all other terms of this type, whose very names send a shudder through all the hearers every year. And they may be excellent for other purposes, but we are in fear for our guardians lest the habit of such thrills make them more sensitive and soft than we would have them.

And we are right in so fearing.

We must remove those things then?

Yes.

And the opposite type to them is what we must require in speech and in verse?

Obviously.

d And shall we also do away with the wailings and lamentations of men of repute?

That necessarily follows, he said, from the other.

Consider, said I, whether we shall be right in thus getting rid of them or not. What we affirm is that a good man will not think that for a good man, whose friend he also is, death is a terrible thing.

Yes, we say that.

Then it would not be for his friend's sake as if he had suffered something dreadful that he would make lament.

Certainly not.

But we also say this, that such a one is most of all men sufficient unto himself for a good life and is distinguished from other men in
e having least need of anybody else.

True, he replied.

Least of all then to him is it a terrible thing to lose son or brother or his wealth or anything of the sort.

Least of all.

Then he makes the least lament and bears it most moderately when any such misfortune overtakes him.

Certainly.

Then we should be right in doing away with the lamentations of men of note and in attributing them to women, and not to the most
388 worthy of them either, and to inferior men, in order that those whom we say we are breeding for the guardianship of the land may disdain to act like these.

We should be right, said he.

Again then we shall request Homer and the other poets not to portray Achilles, the son of a goddess, as, 'lying now on his side, and then again on his back, and again on his face,' [18] and then rising up and 'drifting distraught on the shore of the waste unharvested ocean,' [19] nor as clutching with both hands the sooty dust and strewing it over b his head, nor as weeping and lamenting in the measure and manner attributed to him by the poet, nor yet Priam, near kinsman of the gods, making supplication and rolling in the dung, 'calling aloud unto each, by name to each man appealing.' [20] And yet more than this shall we beg of them at least not to describe the gods as lamenting and crying, 'Ah, woe is me, woeful mother who bore to my sorrow the c bravest,' [21] and if they will so picture the gods, at least not to have the effrontery to present so unlikely a likeness of the supreme god as to make him say,

> Out on it, dear to my heart is the man whose pursuit around Troy
>   town
> I must behold with my eyes while my spirit is grieving within me,[22]

and,

> Ah, woe is me! Of all men to me is Sarpedon the dearest,
> Fated to fall by the hands of Patroclus, Menoetius' offspring.[23]   d

For if, dear Adimantus, our young men should seriously incline to listen to such tales and not laugh at them as unworthy utterances, still less likely would any man be to think such conduct unworthy of himself and to rebuke himself if it occurred to him to do or say anything of that kind, but without shame or restraint full many a dirge for trifles would he chant and many a lament.

You say most truly, he replied.   e

But that must not be, as our reasoning but now showed us, in which we must put our trust until someone convinces us with a better reason.

No, it must not be.

Again, they must not be prone to laughter. For ordinarily when one abandons himself to violent laughter his condition provokes a violent reaction.

I think so, he said.

Then if anyone represents men of worth as overpowered by laughter we must not accept it, much less if gods.

Much indeed, he replied.   389

Then we must not accept from Homer such sayings as these either about the gods.

[18] *Iliad* 24.10 sq.   [20] *Iliad* 22.414 sq.   [22] *Iliad* 22.168.
[19] *Iliad* 24.12 sq.   [21] *Iliad* 18.54.   [23] *Iliad* 16.433 sq.

> Quenchless then was the laughter that rose from the blessed immortals
> When they beheld Hephaestus officiously puffing and panting.[24]

We must not accept them on your view.

If it pleases you to call it mine, he said. At any rate we must not
b accept them.

But further we must surely prize truth most highly. For if we were right in what we were just saying and falsehood is in very deed useless to gods, but to men useful as a remedy or form of medicine, it is obvious that such a thing must be assigned to physicians, and laymen should have nothing to do with it.

Obviously, he replied.

The rulers then of the city may, if anybody, fitly lie on account of enemies or citizens for the benefit of the state; no others may have
c anything to do with it. But for a layman to lie to rulers of that kind we shall affirm to be as great a sin, nay a greater, than it is for a patient not to tell his physician or an athlete his trainer the truth about his bodily condition, or for a man to deceive the pilot about the ship and the sailors as to the real condition of himself or a fellow sailor, and how they fare.

Most true, he replied.

d   If then the ruler catches anybody else in the city lying, any of the craftsmen, 'whether a prophet or healer of sickness or joiner of timbers,' [25] he will chastise him for introducing a practice as subversive and destructive of a state as it is of a ship.

He will, he said, if deed follows upon word.

Again, will our lads not need the virtue of self-control?

Of course.

And for the multitude are not the main points of self-control
e these—to be obedient to their rulers and themselves to be rulers over the bodily appetites and pleasures of food, drink, and the rest?

I think so.

Then, I take it, we will think well said such sayings as that of Homer's Diomedes,

> Friend, sit down and be silent and hark to the word of my bidding,[26]

and what follows,

> Breathing high spirit the Greeks marched silently fearing their captains,[27]

and all similar passages.

Yes, well said.

But what of this sort of thing,

---

[24] *Iliad* 1.599.
[25] *Odyssey* 17.383 sq.

[26] *Iliad* 4.412.
[27] *Iliad* 3.8 and 4.431.

Heavy with wine, with the eyes of a dog and the heart of a fleet deer,[28]

and the lines that follow? Are these well—and other impertinences in 390 prose or verse of private citizens to their rulers?

They are not well.

They certainly are not suitable for youth to hear for the inculcation of self-control. But if from another point of view they yield some pleasure we must not be surprised, or what is your view of it?

This, he said.

Again, to represent the wisest man as saying that this seems to him the fairest thing in the world,

> When the bounteous tables are standing b
> Laden with bread and with meat and the cupbearer ladles the sweet wine
> Out of the mixer and bears it and empties it into the beakers,[29]

do you think the hearing of that sort of thing will conduce to a young man's temperance or self-control? Or this?

> Hunger is the most piteous death that a mortal may suffer.[30]

Or to hear how Zeus lightly forgot all the designs which he devised, awake while the other gods and men slept, because of the excitement of his passions, and was so overcome by the sight of Hera that he is not c even willing to go to their chamber, but wants to lie with her there on the ground and says that he is possessed by a fiercer desire than when they first consorted with one another, 'deceiving their dear parents'? [31] Nor will it profit them to hear of Hephaestus' fettering of Ares and Aphrodite for a like motive.

No, by Zeus, he said, I don't think it will.

But any words or deeds of endurance in the face of all odds attributed to famous men are suitable for our youth to see represented and to hear, such as, d

> He smote his breast and chided thus his heart,
> Endure, my heart, for worse hast thou endured.[32]

By all means, he said. e

It is certain that we cannot allow our men to be accepters of bribes or greedy for gain.

By no means.

Then they must not chant, 'Gifts move the gods and gifts persuade dread kings.' Nor should we approve Achilles' attendant Phoenix as speaking fairly when he counseled him if he received gifts for it to defend the Achaeans, but without gifts not to lay aside his

---

[28] *Iliad* 1.225.   [30] *Odyssey* 12.342.
[29] *Odyssey* 9.8 sq.   [31] *Iliad* 14.294 sq.
                  [32] *Odyssey* 20.17 sq.

wrath. Nor shall we think it proper nor admit that Achilles himself was so greedy as to accept gifts from Agamemnon and again to give up a dead body after receiving payment but otherwise to refuse.

391   It is not right, he said, to commend such conduct.

But, for Homer's sake, said I, I hesitate to say that it is positively impious to affirm such things of Achilles and to believe them when told by others, or again to believe that he said to Apollo,

> Me thou hast balked, far-darter, the most pernicious of all gods,
> Mightily would I requite thee if only my hands had the power,[33]

b and how he was disobedient to the river, who was a god, and was ready to fight with him, and again that he said of the locks of his hair, consecrated to the other river, Spercheus,

> This let me give to take with him my hair to the hero, Patroclus,[34]

who was a dead body. And that he did so we must not believe. And again the trailings of Hector's body round the grave of Patroclus and the slaughter of the living captives upon his pyre, all these we will c affirm to be lies, nor will we suffer our youth to believe that Achilles, the son of a goddess and of Peleus, the most chaste of men, grandson of Zeus, and himself bred under the care of the most sage Chiron, was of so perturbed a spirit as to be affected with two contradictory maladies, the greed that becomes no free man and at the same time overweening arrogance toward gods and men.

You are right, he said.

Neither, then, said I, must we believe this, or suffer it to be said, that Theseus, the son of Poseidon, and Pirithous, the son of Zeus, at- d tempted such dreadful rapes, nor that any other child of a god or hero would have brought himself to accomplish the terrible and impious deeds that they now falsely relate of them. But we must constrain the poets either to deny that these are their deeds or that they are the children of gods, but not to make both statements or attempt to persuade our youth that the gods are the begetters of evil, and that heroes are no better than men. For, as we were saying, such utter- e ances are both impious and false. For we proved, I take it, that for evil to arise from gods is an impossibility.

Certainly.

And they are furthermore harmful to those that hear them. For every man will be very lenient with his own misdeeds if he is convinced that such are and were the actions of

> The near-sown seed of gods,
> Close kin to Zeus, for whom on Ida's top
> Ancestral altars flame to highest heaven,
> Nor in their lifeblood fails the fire divine.[35]

[33] *Iliad* 22.15.   [34] *Iliad* 23.151.   [35] Aeschylus, *Niobe*, fr. 146.

For which cause we must put down such fables, lest they breed in our
youth great laxity in turpitude.   392

Most assuredly.

What type of discourse remains for our definition of our prescriptions and proscriptions? We have declared the right way of speaking about gods and daemons and heroes and that other world?

We have.

Speech, then, about men would be the remainder.

Obviously.

It is impossible for us, my friend, to place this here.

Why?

Because I presume we are going to say that so it is that both
poets and writers of prose speak wrongly about men in matters of b
greatest moment, saying that there are many examples of men who,
though unjust, are happy, and of just men who are wretched, and
that there is profit in injustice if it be concealed, and that justice is
the other man's good and your own loss, and I presume that we shall
forbid them to say this sort of thing and command them to sing and
fable the opposite. Don't you think so?

Nay, I well know it, he said.

Then, if you admit that I am right, I will say that you have
conceded the original point of our inquiry?

Rightly apprehended, he said.

Then, as regards men, that speech must be of this kind, that is a c
point that we will agree upon when we have discovered the nature of
justice and the proof that it is profitable to its possessor whether he
does or does not appear to be just.

Most true, he replied.

So this concludes the topic of tales. That of diction, I take it, is
to be considered next. So we shall have completely examined both
the matter and the manner of speech.

And Adimantus said, I don't understand what you mean by this.

Well, said I, we must have you understand. Perhaps you will be d
more likely to apprehend it thus. Is not everything that is said by
fabulists or poets a narration of past, present, or future things?

What else could it be? he said.

Do not they proceed either by pure narration or by a narrative
that is effected through imitation, or by both?

This too, he said, I still need to have made plainer.

I seem to be a ridiculous and obscure teacher, I said. So, like men
who are unable to express themselves I won't try to speak in wholes
and universals but will separate off a particular part and by the example of that try to show you my meaning. Tell me, do you know the e
first lines of the *Iliad* in which the poet says that Chryses implored
Agamemnon to release his daughter, and that the king was angry

393 and that Chryses, failing of his request, imprecated curses on the
Achaeans in his prayers to the god?
     You know then that as far as these verses,

> And prayed unto all the Achaeans,
> Chiefly to Atreus's sons, twin leaders who marshaled the people.[36]

the poet himself is the speaker and does not even attempt to suggest
to us that anyone but himself is speaking. But what follows he de-
b livers as if he were himself Chryses and tries as far as may be to
make us feel that not Homer is the speaker, but the priest, an old
man. And in this manner he has carried on nearly all the rest of his
narration about affairs in Ilium, all that happened in Ithaca, and the
entire *Odyssey*.
     Quite so, he said.
     Now, it is narration, is it not, both when he presents the several
speeches and the matter between the speeches?
     Of course.
c   But when he delivers a speech as if he were someone else, shall
we not say that he then assimilates thereby his own diction as far as
possible to that of the person whom he announces as about to speak?
     We shall, obviously.
     And is not likening oneself to another in speech or bodily bearing
an imitation of him to whom one likens oneself?
     Surely.
     In such case then, it appears, he and the other poets effect their
narration through imitation.
     Certainly.
     But if the poet should conceal himself nowhere, then his entire
poetizing and narration would have been accomplished without imita-
d tion. And lest you may say again that you don't understand, I will explain to you how this would be done. If Homer, after telling us that
Chryses came with the ransom of his daughter and as a suppliant of
the Achaeans but chiefly of the kings, had gone on speaking not as
if made or being Chryses but still as Homer, you are aware that it
would not be imitation but narration, pure and simple. It would have
been somewhat in this wise. I will state it without meter for I am not
a poet. The priest came and prayed that to them the gods should
e grant to take Troy and come safely home, but that they should accept
the ransom and release his daughter, out of reverence for the god,
and when he had thus spoken the others were of reverent mind and
approved, but Agamemnon was angry and bade him depart and
not come again lest the scepter and the fillets of the god should not
avail him. And ere his daughter should be released, he said, she would
grow old in Argos with himself, and he ordered him to be off and not

[36] *Iliad* 1.15 sq.

vex him if he wished to get home safe. And the old man on hearing 394
this was frightened and departed in silence, and having gone apart
from the camp he prayed at length to Apollo, invoking the appellations
of the god, and reminding him of and asking requital for any of his
gifts that had found favor whether in the building of temples or the
sacrifice of victims. In return for these things he prayed that the
Achaeans should suffer for his tears by the god's shafts.

It is in this way, my dear fellow, I said, that without imitation b
simple narration results.

I understand, he said.

Understand then, said I, that the opposite of this arises when one
removes the words of the poet between and leaves the alternation of
speeches.

This too I understand, he said. It is what happens in tragedy.

You have conceived me most rightly, I said, and now I think I
can make plain to you what I was unable to before, that there is one
kind of poetry and taletelling which works wholly through imitation, c
as you remarked, tragedy and comedy, and another which employs the
recital of the poet himself, best exemplified, I presume, in the
dithyramb, and there is again that which employs both, in epic poetry
and in many other places, if you apprehend me.

I understand now, he said, what you then meant.

Recall then also the preceding statement that we were done with
the 'what' of speech and still had to consider the 'how.'

I remember.

What I meant then was just this, that we must reach a decision d
whether we are to suffer our poets to narrate as imitators or in part as
imitators and in part not, and what sort of things in each case, or not
allow them to imitate at all.

I divine, he said, that you are considering whether we shall admit
tragedy and comedy into our city or not.

Perhaps, said I, and perhaps even more than that. For I certainly
do not yet know myself, but whithersoever the wind, as it were, of the
argument blows, there lies our course.

Well said, he replied.

This then, Adimantus, is the point we must keep in view. Do we e
wish our guardians to be good mimics or not? Or is this also a consequence of what we said before, that each one could practice well only
one pursuit and not many, but if he attempted the latter, dabbling in
many things, he would fail of distinction in all?

Of course it is.

And does not the same rule hold for imitation, that the same
man is not able to imitate many things well as he can one?

No, he is not.

Still less, then, will he be able to combine the practice of any 395
worthy pursuit with the imitation of many things and the quality of

a mimic, since, unless I mistake, the same men cannot practice well at once even the two forms of imitation that appear most nearly akin, as the writing of tragedy and comedy. Did you not just now call these two imitations?

I did, and you are right in saying that the same men are not able to succeed in both.

Nor yet to be at once good rhapsodists and actors?

True.

But neither can the same men be actors for tragedies and come-
b dies—and all these are imitations, are they not?

Yes, imitations.

And to still smaller coinage than this, in my opinion, Adimantus, proceeds the fractioning of human faculty, so as to be incapable of imitating many things or of doing the things themselves of which the imitations are likenesses.

Most true, he replied.

If, then, we are to maintain our original principle, that our guardians, released from all other crafts, are to be expert craftsmen
c of civic liberty, and pursue nothing else that does not conduce to this, it would not be fitting for these to do nor yet to imitate anything else. But if they imitate they should from childhood up imitate what is appropriate to them—men, that is, who are brave, sober, pious, free, and all things of that kind—but things unbecoming the free man they should neither do nor be clever at imitating, nor yet any other shameful thing, lest from the imitation they imbibe the reality. Or
d have you not observed that imitations, if continued from youth far into life, settle down into habits and second nature in the body, the speech, and the thought?

Yes, indeed, said he.

We will not then allow our charges, whom we expect to prove good men, being men, to play the parts of women and imitate a woman young or old wrangling with her husband, defying heaven, loudly boasting, fortunate in her own conceit, or involved in mis-
e fortune and possessed by grief and lamentation—still less a woman that is sick, in love, or in labor.

Most certainly not, he replied.

Nor may they imitate slaves, female and male, doing the offices of slaves.

No, not that either.

Nor yet, as it seems, bad men who are cowards and who do the opposite of the things we just now spoke of, reviling and lampooning one another, speaking foul words in their cups or when sober and in
396 other ways sinning against themselves and others in word and deed after the fashion of such men. And I take it they must not form the habit of likening themselves to madmen either in words nor yet in

deeds. For while knowledge they must have both of mad and bad
men and women, they must do and imitate nothing of this kind.

Most true, he said.

What of this? I said. Are they to imitate smiths and other craftsmen or the rowers of triremes and those who call the time to them b
or other things connected therewith?

How could they, he said, since it will be forbidden them even to
pay any attention to such things?

Well, then, neighing horses and lowing bulls, and the noise of
rivers and the roar of the sea and the thunder and everything of that
kind—will they imitate these?

Nay, they have been forbidden, he said, to be mad or liken themselves to madmen.

If, then, I understand your meaning, said I, there is a form of
diction and narrative in which the really good and true man would c
narrate anything that he had to say, and another form unlike this to
which the man of the opposite birth and breeding would cleave and
in which he would tell his story.

What are these forms? he said.

A man of the right sort, I think, when he comes in the course
of his narrative to some word or act of a good man will be willing to impersonate the other in reporting it, and will feel no shame
at that kind of mimicry, by preference imitating the good man when d
he acts steadfastly and sensibly, and less and more reluctantly when
he is upset by sickness or love or drunkenness or any other mishap.
But when he comes to someone unworthy of himself, he will not wish
to liken himself in earnest to one who is inferior, except in the few
cases where he is doing something good, but will be embarrassed
both because he is unpracticed in the mimicry of such characters,
and also because he shrinks in distaste from molding and fitting him- e
self to the types of baser things. His mind disdains them, unless it be
for jest.

Naturally, he said.

Then the narrative that he will employ will be of the kind that
we just now illustrated by the verses of Homer, and his diction will
be one that partakes of both, of imitation and simple narration, but
there will be a small portion of imitation in a long discourse—or is
there nothing in what I say?

Yes, indeed, he said, that *is* the type and pattern of such a 397
speaker.

Then, said I, the other kind of speaker, the more debased he is the
less will he shrink from imitating anything and everything. He will
think nothing unworthy of himself, so that he will attempt, seriously
and in the presence of many, to imitate all things, including those we
just now mentioned—claps of thunder, and the noise of wind and

hail and axles and pulleys, and the notes of trumpets and flutes and
b Panpipes, and the sounds of all instruments, and the cries of dogs,
sheep, and birds—and so his style will depend wholly on imitation in
voice and gesture, or will contain but a little of pure narration.

That too follows of necessity, he said.

These, then, said I, were the two types of diction of which I was
speaking.

There are those two, he replied.

Now does not one of the two involve slight variations, and if we
assign a suitable pitch and rhythm to the diction, is not the result that
the right speaker speaks almost on the same note and in one cadence
c —for the changes are slight—and similarly in a rhythm of nearly the
same kind?

Quite so.

But what of the other type? Does it not require the opposite, every
kind of pitch and all rhythms, if it too is to have appropriate expression, since it involves manifold forms of variation?

Emphatically so.

And do all poets and speakers hit upon one type or the other of
diction or some blend which they combine of both?

They must, he said.

d   What, then, said I, are we to do? Shall we admit all of these into
the city, or one of the unmixed types, or the mixed type?

If my vote prevails, he said, the unmixed imitator of the good.

Nay, but the mixed type also is pleasing, Adimantus, and far most
pleasing to boys and their tutors and the great mob is the opposite of
your choice.

Most pleasing it is.

But perhaps, said I, you would affirm it to be ill suited to our
e polity, because there is no twofold or manifold man among us, since
every man does one thing.

It is not suited.

And is this not the reason why such a city is the only one in
which we shall find the cobbler a cobbler and not a pilot in addition to
his cobbling, and the farmer a farmer and not a judge added to his
farming, and the soldier a soldier and not a money-maker in addition
to his soldiery, and so of all the rest?

True, he said.

398   If a man, then, it seems, who was capable by his cunning of assuming every kind of shape and imitating all things should arrive in
our city, bringing with himself the poems which he wished to exhibit,
we should fall down and worship him as a holy and wondrous and delightful creature, but should say to him that there is no man of that
kind among us in our city, nor is it lawful for such a man to arise
among us, and we should send him away to another city, after pouring

myrrh down over his head and crowning him with fillets of wool, but we ourselves, for our souls' good, should continue to employ the more austere and less delightful poet and taleteller, who would imitate the b diction of the good man and would tell his tale in the patterns which we prescribed in the beginning, when we set out to educate our soldiers.

We certainly should do that if it rested with us.

And now, my friend, said I, we may say that we have completely finished the part of music that concerns speeches and tales. For we have set forth what is to be said and how it is to be said.

I think so too, he replied.

After this, then, said I, comes the manner of song and tunes?   c
Obviously.

And having gone thus far, could not everybody discover what we must say of their character in order to conform to what has already been said?

I am afraid that 'everybody' does not include me, laughed Glaucon. I cannot sufficiently divine offhand what we ought to say, though I have a suspicion.

You certainly, I presume, said I, have a sufficient understanding of this—that the song is composed of three things, the words, the tune, and the rhythm?   d

Yes, said he, that much.

And so far as it is words, it surely in no manner differs from words not sung in the requirement of conformity to the patterns and manner that we have prescribed?

True, he said.

And again, the music and the rhythm must follow the speech.

Of course.

But we said we did not require dirges and lamentations in words.

We do not.

What, then, are the dirgelike modes of music? Tell me, for you e are a musician.

The mixed Lydian, he said, and the tense or higher Lydian, and similar modes.

These, then, said I, we must do away with. For they are useless even to women who are to make the best of themselves, let alone to men.

Assuredly.

But again, drunkenness is a thing most unbefitting guardians, and so is softness and sloth.

Yes.

What, then, are the soft and convivial modes?

There are certain Ionian and also Lydian modes that are called lax.

399   Will you make any use of them for warriors?

None at all, he said, but it would seem that you have left the Dorian and the Phrygian.

I don't know the musical modes, I said, but leave us that mode that would fittingly imitate the utterances and the accents of a brave man who is engaged in warfare or in any enforced business, and who,
b when he has failed, either meeting wounds or death or having fallen into some other mishap, in all these conditions confronts fortune with steadfast endurance and repels her strokes. And another for such a man engaged in works of peace, not enforced but voluntary, either trying to persuade somebody of something and imploring him— whether it be a god, through prayer, or a man, by teaching and admonition—or contrariwise yielding himself to another who is petitioning or teaching him or trying to change his opinions, and in consequence faring according to his wish, and not bearing himself arrogantly, but in all this acting modestly and moderately and acquiescing in the
c outcome. Leave us these two modes—the enforced and the voluntary—that will best imitate the utterances of men failing or succeeding, the temperate, the brave—leave us these.

Well, said he, you are asking me to leave none other than those I just spoke of.

Then, said I, we shall not need in our songs and airs instruments of many strings or whose compass includes all the harmonies.

Not in my opinion, said he.

Then we shall not maintain makers of triangles and harps and all
d other many-stringed and polyharmonic instruments.

Apparently not.

Well, will you admit to the city flute makers and flute players? Or is not the flute the most 'many-stringed' of instruments and do not the panharmonics themselves imitate it?

Clearly, he said.

You have left, said I, the lyre and the cithara. These are useful in the city, and in the fields the shepherds would have a little piccolo to pipe on.

So our argument indicates, he said.
e   We are not innovating, my friend, in preferring Apollo and the instruments of Apollo to Marsyas and his instruments.

No, by heaven! he said. I think not.

And by the dog, said I, we have all unawares purged the city which a little while ago we said was luxurious.

In that we show our good sense, he said.

Come then, let us complete the purification. For upon harmonies would follow the consideration of rhythms; we must not pursue complexity nor great variety in the basic movements, but must ob-
400 serve what are the rhythms of a life that is orderly and brave, and after observing them require the foot and the air to conform to that

kind of man's speech and not the speech to the foot and the tune.
What those rhythms would be, it is for you to tell us as you did the
musical modes.

Nay, in faith, he said, I cannot tell. For that there are some three
forms from which the feet are combined, just as there are four in the
notes of the voice whence come all harmonies, is a thing that I have
observed and could tell. But which are imitations of which sort of
life, I am unable to say.

Well, said I, on this point we will take counsel with Damon, too, b
as to which are the feet appropriate to illiberality, and insolence or
madness or other evils, and what rhythms we must leave for their
opposites. And I believe I have heard him obscurely speaking of a foot
that he called the *enoplios*, a composite foot, and a dactyl and a heroic
foot, which he arranged, I know not how, to be equal up and down in
the interchange of long and short, and unless I am mistaken he used
the term iambic, and there was another foot that he called the
trochaic, and he added the quantities long and short. And in some of c
these, I believe, he censured and commended the tempo of the foot no
less than the rhythm itself, or else some combination of the two, I
can't say. But, as I said, let this matter be postponed for Damon's consideration. For to determine the truth of these would require no
little discourse. Do you think otherwise?

No, by heaven, I do not.

But this you are able to determine—that seemliness and unseem-
liness are attendant upon the good rhythm and the bad.

Of course.

And, further, that good rhythm and bad rhythm accompany, the d
one fair diction, assimilating itself thereto, and the other the opposite,
and so of the apt and the unapt, if, as we were just now saying, the
rhythm and harmony follow the words and not the words these.

They certainly must follow the speech, he said.

And what of the manner of the diction, and the speech? said I. Do
they not follow and conform to the disposition of the soul?

Of course.

And all the rest to the diction?

Yes.

Good speech, then, good accord, and good grace, and good rhythm
wait upon a good disposition, not that weakness of head which we e
euphemistically style goodness of heart, but the truly good and fair
disposition of the character and the mind.

By all means, he said.

And must not our youth pursue these everywhere if they are to
do what it is truly theirs to do?

They must indeed.

And there is surely much of these qualities in painting and in 401
all similar craftsmanship—weaving is full of them and embroidery

and architecture and likewise the manufacture of household furnish-
ings and thereto the natural bodies of animals and plants as well. For
in all these there is grace or gracelessness. And gracelessness and evil
rhythm and disharmony are akin to evil speaking and the evil temper,
but the opposites are the symbols and the kin of the opposites, the
sober and good disposition.

Entirely so, he said.

b   Is it, then, only the poets that we must supervise and compel to
embody in their poems the semblance of the good character or else not
write poetry among us, or must we keep watch over the other craftsmen, and forbid them to represent the evil disposition, the licentious,
the illiberal, the graceless, either in the likeness of living creatures or
in buildings or in any other product of their art, on penalty, if unable
to obey, of being forbidden to practice their art among us, that our
guardians may not be bred among symbols of evil, as it were in a pas-
c turage of poisonous herbs, lest grazing freely and cropping from
many such day by day they little by little and all unawares accumulate
and build up a huge mass of evil in their own souls. But we must look
for those craftsmen who by the happy gift of nature are capable of
following the trail of true beauty and grace, that our young men,
dwelling as it were in a salubrious region, may receive benefit from all
things about them, whence the influence that emanates from works
of beauty may waft itself to eye or ear like a breeze that brings from
d wholesome places health, and so from earliest childhood insensibly
guide them to likeness, to friendship, to harmony with beautiful
reason.

Yes, he said, that would be far the best education for them.

And is it not for this reason, Glaucon, said I, that education in
music is most sovereign, because more than anything else rhythm and
harmony find their way to the inmost soul and take strongest hold
e upon it, bringing with them and imparting grace, if one is rightly
trained, and otherwise the contrary? And further, because omissions
and the failure of beauty in things badly made or grown would be
most quickly perceived by one who was properly educated in music,
402 and so, feeling distaste rightly, he would praise beautiful things and
take delight in them and receive them into his soul to foster its growth
and become himself beautiful and good. The ugly he would rightly disapprove of and hate while still young and yet unable to apprehend
the reason, but when reason came the man thus nurtured would be the
first to give her welcome, for by this affinity he would know her.

I certainly think, he said, that such is the cause of education in
music.

It is, then, said I, as it was when we learned our letters and
felt that we knew them sufficiently only when the separate letters did
not elude us, appearing as few elements in all the combinations that

convey them, and when we did not disregard them in small things or b
great and think it unnecessary to recognize them, but were eager to
distinguish them everywhere, in the belief that we should never be
literate and letter-perfect till we could do this.

True.

And is it not also true that if there are any likenesses of letters
reflected in water or mirrors, we shall never know them until we know
the originals, but such knowledge belongs to the same art and discipline?

By all means.

Then, by heaven, am I not right in saying that by the same token
we shall never be true musicians, either—neither we nor the guard- c
ians that we have undertaken to educate—until we are able to recognize the forms of soberness, courage, liberality, and high-mindedness,
and all their kindred and their opposites, too, in all the combinations that contain and convey them, and to apprehend them and their
images wherever found, disregarding them neither in trifles nor in
great things, but believing the knowledge of them to belong to the
same art and discipline?

The conclusion is inevitable, he said.

Then, said I, when there is a coincidence of a beautiful disposi- d
tion in the soul and corresponding and harmonious beauties of the
same type in the bodily form—is not this the fairest spectacle for one
who is capable of its contemplation?

Far the fairest.

And surely the fairest is the most lovable.

Of course.

The true musician, then, would love by preference persons of this
sort, but if there were disharmony he would not love this.

No, he said, not if there was a defect in the soul, but if it were in
the body he would bear with it and still be willing to bestow his love. e

I understand, I said, that you have or have had favorites of this
sort and I grant your distinction. But tell me this—can there be any
communion between soberness and extravagant pleasure?

How could there be, he said, since such pleasure puts a man beside himself no less than pain?

Or between it and virtue generally?

By no means.

    403

But is there between pleasure and insolence and license?

Most assuredly.

Do you know of greater or keener pleasure than that associated
with Aphrodite?

I don't, he said, nor yet of any more insane.

But is not the right love a sober and harmonious love of the orderly and the beautiful?

It is indeed, said he.

Then nothing of madness, nothing akin to license, must be allowed to come nigh the right love?

No.

b Then this kind of pleasure may not come nigh, nor may lover and beloved who rightly love and are loved have anything to do with it?

No, by heaven, Socrates, he said, it must not come nigh them.

Thus, then, as it seems, you will lay down the law in the city that we are founding, that the lover may kiss and pass the time with and touch the beloved as a father would a son, for honorable ends, if he persuade him. But otherwise he must so associate with the objects of his care that there should never be any suspicion of anything fur-
c ther, on penalty of being stigmatized for want of taste and true musical culture.

Even so, he said.

Do you not agree, then, that our discourse on music has come to an end? It has certainly made a fitting end, for surely the end and consummation of culture is the love of the beautiful.

I concur, he said.

After music our youth are to be educated by gymnastics?

Certainly.

d In this too they must be carefully trained from boyhood through life, and the way of it is this, I believe, but consider it yourself too. For I, for my part, do not believe that a sound body by its excellence makes the soul good, but on the contrary that a good soul by its virtue renders the body the best that is possible. What is your opinion?

I think so too.

Then if we should sufficiently train the mind and turn over to it the minutiae of the care of the body, and content ourselves with
e merely indicating the norms or patterns, not to make a long story of it, we should be acting rightly?

By all means.

From intoxication we said that they must abstain. For a guardian is surely the last person in the world to whom it is allowable to get drunk and not know where on earth he is.

Yes, he said, it would be absurd that a guardian should need a guard.

What next about their food? These men are athletes in the greatest of contests, are they not?

Yes.

404 Is, then, the bodily habit of the athletes we see about us suitable for such?

Perhaps.

Nay, said I, that is a drowsy habit and precarious for health. Don't you observe that they sleep away their lives, and that if they depart ever so little from their prescribed regimen these athletes are liable to great and violent diseases?

I do.

Then, said I, we need some more ingenious form of training for our athletes of war, since these must be as it were sleepless hounds, and have the keenest possible perceptions of sight and hearing, and in their campaigns undergo many changes in their drinking water, b their food, and in exposure to the heat of the sun and to storms, without disturbance of their health.

I think so.

Would not, then, the best gymnastics be akin to the music that we were just now describing?

What do you mean?

It would be a simple and flexible gymnastic training, and especially so in the training for war.

In what way?

One could learn that, said I, even from Homer. For you are aware that in the banqueting of the heroes on campaign he does not feast them on fish, though they are at the seaside on the Hellespont, nor on c boiled meat, but only on roast, which is what soldiers could most easily procure. For everywhere, one may say, it is of easier provision to use the bare fire than to convey pots and pans along.

Indeed it is.

Neither, as I believe, does Homer ever make mention of sweet-meats. Is not that something which all men in training understand— that if one is to keep his body in good condition he must abstain from such things altogether?

They are right, he said, in that they know it and do abstain.

Then, my friend, if you think this is the right way, you apparently do not approve of a Syracusan table and the Sicilian variety of dishes. d

I think not.

You would frown, then, on a little Corinthian maid as the *chère amie* of men who were to keep themselves fit?

Most certainly.

And also on the seeming delights of Attic pastry?

Inevitably.

In general, I take it, if we likened that kind of food and regimen to music and song expressed in the panharmonic mode and in every e variety of rhythm it would be a fair comparison.

Quite so.

And there variety engendered licentiousness, did it not, but here disease, while simplicity in music begets sobriety in the souls, and in gymnastic training it begets health in bodies?

Most true, he said.

And when licentiousness and disease multiply in a city, are not 405 many courts of law and dispensaries opened? And the arts of chicane

and medicine give themselves airs when even free men in great numbers take them very seriously.

How can they help it? he said.

Will you be able to find a surer proof of an evil and shameful
state of education in a city than the necessity of first-rate physicians
and judges, not only for the base and mechanical, but for those who
claim to have been bred in the fashion of free men? Do you not think
b it disgraceful and a notable mark of bad breeding to have to make use
of a justice imported from others, who thus become your masters and
judges, from lack of such qualities in yourself?

The most shameful thing in the world.

Is it? said I. Or is this still more shameful—when a man not only
wears out the better part of his days in the courts of law as defendant
or accuser, but from the lack of all true sense of values is led to plume
himself on this very thing, as being a smart fellow to 'put over' an un-
c just act and cunningly to try every dodge and practice, every evasion,
and wriggle out of every hold in defeating justice, and that too for
trifles and worthless things, because he does not know how much
nobler and better it is to arrange his life so as to have no need of a
nodding juryman?

That is, said he, still more shameful than the other.

And to require medicine, said I, not merely for wounds or the in-
d cidence of some seasonal maladies, but, because of sloth and such a
regimen as we described, to fill one's body up with winds and humors
like a marsh and compel the ingenious sons of Asclepius to invent
for diseases such names as fluxes and flatulences—don't you think
that disgraceful?

Those surely are, he said, newfangled and monstrous strange
names of diseases.

There was nothing of the kind, I fancy, said I, in the days of
Asclepius. I infer this from the fact that at Troy his sons did not
e find fault with the damsel who gave to the wounded Eurypylus to
drink a posset of Pramnian wine plentifully sprinkled with barley and
406 gratings of cheese, inflammatory ingredients of a surety, nor did they
censure Patroclus, who was in charge of the case.

It was indeed, said he, a strange potion for a man in that condition.

Not so strange, said I, if you reflect that the former Asclepiads
made no use of our modern coddling medication of diseases before
the time of Herodicus. But Herodicus was a trainer and became a
b valetudinarian, and blended gymnastics and medicine, for the tor-
ment first and chiefly of himself and then of many successors.

How so? he said.

By lingering out his death, said I. For living in perpetual observance of his malady, which was incurable, he was not able to effect a

cure, but lived through his days unfit for the business of life, suffering
the tortures of the damned if he departed a whit from his fixed regimen. And struggling against death, by reason of his science he won
the prize of a doting old age.

A noble prize indeed for his science, he said.

The appropriate one, said I, for a man who did not know that it c
was not from ignorance or inacquaintance with this type of medicine
that Asclepius did not discover it to his descendants, but because he
knew that for all well-governed peoples there is a work assigned to
each man in the city which he must perform, and no one has leisure
to be sick and doctor himself all his days. And this we absurdly enough
perceive in the case of a craftsman, but don't see in the case of the
rich and so-called fortunate.

How so? he said.

A carpenter, said I, when he is sick expects his physician to give d
him a drug which will operate as an emetic on the disease, or to get
rid of it by purging or the use of cautery or the knife. But if anyone
prescribes for him a long course of treatment with swathings about
the head and their accompaniments, he hastily says that he has no
leisure to be sick, and that such a life of preoccupation with his illness
and neglect of the work that lies before him isn't worth living. And
thereupon he bids farewell to that kind of physician, enters upon his e
customary way of life, regains his health, and lives attending to his
affairs—or, if his body is not equal to the strain, he dies and is freed
from all his troubles.

For such a man, he said, that appears to be the right use of medicine.

And is not the reason, I said, that he had a task and that life 407
wasn't worth acceptance on condition of not doing his work?

Obviously, he said.

But the rich man, we say, has no such appointed task, the necessity of abstaining from which renders life intolerable.

I haven't heard of any.

Why, haven't you heard that saying of Phocylides, that after a
man has 'made his pile' he ought to practice virtue?

Before, too, I fancy, he said.

Let us not quarrel with him on that point, I said, but inform ourselves whether this virtue is something for the rich man to practice,
and life is intolerable if he does not, or whether we are to suppose b
that while valetudinarianism is a hindrance to single-minded attention to carpentry and the other arts, it is no obstacle to the fulfillment
of Phocylides' exhortation.

Yes, indeed, he said, this excessive care for the body that goes beyond simple gymnastics is about the greatest of all obstacles.

For it is troublesome in household affairs and military service and sedentary offices in the city. And, chief of all, it puts difficulties in the way of any kind of instruction, thinking, or private meditation—

c   forever imagining headaches and dizziness and attributing their origin to philosophy. So that wherever this kind of virtue is practiced and tested it is in every way a hindrance. For it makes the man always fancy himself sick and never cease from anguishing about his body.

Naturally, he said.

Then shall we not say that it was because Asclepius knew this, that for those who were by nature and course of life sound of body but had some localized disease, that for such, I say, and for this habit he

d   revealed the art of medicine, and, driving out their disease by drugs and surgery, prescribed for them their customary regimen in order not to interfere with their civic duties, but that, when bodies were diseased inwardly and throughout, he did not attempt by diet and by gradual evacuations and infusions to prolong a wretched existence for the man and have him beget in all likelihood similar wretched offspring? But if a man was incapable of living in the established round and or-

e   der of life, he did not think it worth while to treat him, since such a fellow is of no use either to himself or to the state.

A most politic Asclepius you're telling us of, he said.

Obviously, said I, that was his character. And his sons too, don't

408 you see that at Troy they proved themselves good fighting men and practiced medicine as I described it? Don't you remember that in the case of Menelaus too, from the wound that Pandarus inflicted 'they sucked the blood, and soothing simples sprinkled'? [37] But what he was to eat or drink thereafter they no more prescribed than for Eurypylus, taking it for granted that the remedies sufficed to heal men who before their wounds were healthy and temperate in diet even if they did hap-

b   pen for the nonce to drink a posset. But they thought that the life of a man constitutionally sickly and intemperate was of no use to himself or others, and that the art of medicine should not be for such nor should they be given treatment even if they were richer than Midas.

Very ingenious fellows, he said, you make out these sons of Asclepius to be.

'Tis fitting, said I, and yet in disregard of our principles the trage-dians and Pindar affirm that Asclepius, though he was the son of Apollo, was bribed by gold to heal a man already at the point of death,

c   and that for this cause he was struck by the lightning. But we in ac-cordance with the aforesaid principles refuse to believe both state-ments. If he was the son of a god he was not avaricious, we will insist, and if he was greedy of gain he was not the son of a god.

That much, said he, is most certainly true. But what have you to say to this, Socrates? Must we not have good physicians in our city? And they would be the most likely to be good who had treated the

[37] *Iliad* 4.218.

greatest number of healthy and diseased men, and so good judges **d** would be those who had associated with all sorts and conditions of men.

Most assuredly I want them good, I said, but do you know whom I regard as such?

I'll know if you tell, he said.

Well, I will try, said I. You, however, have put unlike cases in one question.

How so? said he.

Physicians, it is true, I said, would prove most skilled if, from childhood up, in addition to learning the principles of the art they had familiarized themselves with the greatest possible number of the most sickly bodies, and if they themselves had suffered all diseases and were not of very healthy constitution. For you see they do not treat the **e** body by the body. If they did, it would not be allowable for their bodies to be or to have been in evil condition. But they treat the body with the mind—and it is not competent for a mind that is or has been evil to treat anything well.

Right, he said.

But a judge, mark you, my friend, rules soul with soul and it is **409** not allowable for a soul to have been bred from youth up among evil souls and to have grown familiar with them, and itself to have run the gauntlet of every kind of wrongdoing and injustice so as quickly to infer from itself the misdeeds of others as it might diseases in the body, but it must have been inexperienced in evil natures and uncontaminated by them while young, if it is to be truly fair and good and judge soundly of justice. For which cause the better sort seem to be simpleminded in youth and are easily deceived by the wicked, since they do **b** not have within themselves patterns answering to the affections of the bad.

That is indeed their experience, he said.

Therefore it is, said I, that the good judge must not be a youth but an old man, a late learner of the nature of injustice, one who has not become aware of it as a property in his own soul, but one who has through the long years trained himself to understand it as an alien thing in alien souls, and to discern how great an evil it is by the instrument of mere knowledge and not by experience of his own. **c**

That at any rate, he said, appears to be the noblest kind of judge.

And what is more, a good one, I said, which was the gist of your question. For he who has a good soul is good. But that cunning fellow quick to suspect evil, and who has himself done many unjust acts and who thinks himself a smart trickster, when he associates with his like does appear to be clever, being on his guard and fixing his eyes on the patterns within himself. But when the time comes for him to mingle with the good and his elders, then on the contrary he appears stupid. He is unseasonably distrustful and he cannot recognize **d** a sound character because he has no such pattern in himself. But since he more often meets with the bad than the good, he seems to himself and to others to be rather wise than foolish.

That is quite true, he said.

Well then, said I, such a one must not be our ideal of the good and wise judge but the former. For while badness could never come to know both virtue and itself, native virtue through education will at last acquire the science of both itself and badness. This one, then, e as I think, is the man who proves to be wise and not the bad man.

And I concur, he said.

Then will you not establish by law in your city such an art of medicine as we have described in conjunction with this kind of justice? And these arts will care for the bodies and souls of such of your 410 citizens as are truly wellborn, but those who are not, such as are defective in body, they will suffer to die, and those who are evil-natured and incurable in soul they will themselves put to death.

This certainly, he said, has been shown to be the best thing for the sufferers themselves and for the state.

And so your youths, said I, employing that simple music which we said engendered sobriety will, it is clear, guard themselves against falling into the need of the justice of the courtroom.

Yes, he said.

b   And will not our musician, pursuing the same trail in his use of gymnastics, if he please, get to have no need of medicine save when indispensable?

I think so.

And even the exercises and toils of gymnastics he will undertake with a view to the spirited part of his nature to arouse that rather than for mere strength, unlike ordinary athletes, who treat diet and exercise only as a means to muscle.

Nothing could be truer, he said.

Then may we not say, Glaucon, said I, that those who established c an education in music and gymnastics had not the purpose in view that some attribute to them in so instituting, namely to treat the body by one and the soul by the other?

But what? he said.

It seems likely, I said, that they ordained both chiefly for the soul's sake.

How so?

Have you not observed, said I, the effect on the disposition of the mind itself of lifelong devotion to gymnastics with total neglect of music? Or the disposition of those of the opposite habit?

In what respect do you mean? he said.

d   In respect of savagery and hardness or, on the other hand, of softness and gentleness?

I have observed, he said, that the devotees of unmitigated gymnastics turn out more brutal than they should be and those of music softer than is good for them.

And surely, said I, this savagery is a quality derived from the high-spirited element in our nature, which, if rightly trained, becomes brave, but if overstrained, would naturally become hard and harsh.

I think so, he said.

And again, is not the gentleness a quality which the philosophical e nature would yield? This if relaxed too far would be softer than is desirable but if rightly trained gentle and orderly?

That is so.

But our requirement, we say, is that the guardians should possess both natures.

It is.

And must they not be harmoniously adjusted to one another?

Of course.

And the soul of the man thus attuned is sober and brave?   411

Certainly.

And that of the ill-adjusted is cowardly and rude?

It surely is.

Now when a man abandons himself to music, to play upon him and pour into his soul as it were through the funnel of his ears those sweet, soft, and dirgelike airs of which we were just now speaking, and gives his entire time to the warblings and blandishments of song, the first result is that the principle of high spirit, if he had it, is softened like iron and is made useful instead of useless and brittle. But when he continues the practice without remission and is spellbound, b the effect begins to be that he melts and liquefies till he completely dissolves away his spirit, cuts out as it were the very sinews of his soul and makes of himself a 'feeble warrior.' [38]

Assuredly, he said.

And if, said I, he has to begin with a spiritless nature he reaches this result quickly, but if a high-spirited, by weakening the spirit he makes it unstable, quickly irritated by slight stimuli, and as quickly quelled. The outcome is that such men are choleric and irascible instead of high-spirited, and are peevish and discontented.   c

Precisely so.

On the other hand, if a man toils hard at gymnastics and eats right lustily and holds no truck with music and philosophy, does he not at first get very fit and full of pride and high spirit and become more brave and bold than he was?

He does indeed.

But what if he does nothing but this and has no contact with the Muse in any way? Is not the result that even if there was some prin- d ciple of the love of knowledge in his soul, since it tastes of no instruc-

[38] *Iliad* 17.588.

tion nor of any inquiry and does not participate in any discussion or any other form of culture, it becomes feeble, deaf, and blind, because it is not aroused or fed nor are its perceptions purified and quickened?

That is so, he said.

And so such a man, I take it, becomes a misologist and a stranger to the Muses. He no longer makes any use of persuasion by speech but e achieves all his ends like a beast by violence and savagery, and in his brute ignorance and ineptitude lives a life of disharmony and gracelessness.

That is entirely true, he said.

For these two, then, it seems there are two arts which I would say some god gave to mankind, music and gymnastics for the service of the high-spirited principle and the love of knowledge in them—not for the soul and the body except incidentally, but for the harmonious 412 adjustment of these two principles by the proper degree of tension and relaxation of each.

Yes, so it appears, he said.

Then he who best blends gymnastics with music and applies them most suitably to the soul is the man whom we should most rightly pronounce to be the most perfect and harmonious musician, far rather than the one who brings the strings into unison with one another.

That seems likely, Socrates, he said.

And shall we not also need in our city, Glaucon, a permanent overseer of this kind if its constitution is to be preserved?

b   We most certainly shall.

Such would be the outlines of their education and breeding. For why should one recite the list of the dances of such citizens, their hunts and chases with hounds, their athletic contests and races? It is pretty plain that they must conform to these principles and there is no longer any difficulty in discovering them.

There is, it may be, no difficulty, he said.

Very well, said I. What, then, have we next to determine? Is it not which ones among them shall be the rulers and the ruled?

c   Certainly.

That the rulers must be the elder and the ruled the younger is obvious.

It is.

And that the rulers must be their best?

This too.

And do not the best of the farmers prove the best farmers?

Yes.

And in this case, since we want them to be the best of the guardians, must they not be the best guardians, the most regardful of the state?

Yes.

They must then to begin with be intelligent in such matters and capable, and furthermore careful of the interests of the state?

That is so.   d

But one would be most likely to be careful of that which he loved.

Necessarily.

And again, one would be most likely to love that whose interests he supposed to coincide with his own, and thought that when it prospered he too would prosper and if not, the contrary.

So it is, he said.

Then we must pick out from the other guardians such men as to our observation appear most inclined through the entire course of their lives to be zealous to do what they think for the interest of the e
state, and who would be least likely to consent to do the opposite.

That would be a suitable choice, he said.

I think, then, we shall have to observe them at every period of life, to see if they are conservators and guardians of this conviction in their minds and never by sorcery nor by force can be brought to expel from their souls unawares this conviction that they must do what is best for the state.

What do you mean by the 'expelling'? he said.

I will tell you, said I. It seems to me that the exit of a belief from the mind is either voluntary or involuntary. Voluntary is the departure of the false belief from one who learns better, involuntary that 413
of every true belief.

The voluntary, he said, I understand, but I need instruction about the involuntary.

How now, said I, don't you agree with me in thinking that men are unwillingly deprived of good things but willingly of evil? Or is it not an evil to be deceived in respect of the truth and a good to possess truth? And don't you think that to opine the things that are is to possess the truth?

Why, yes, said he, you are right, and I agree that men are unwillingly deprived of true opinions.

And doesn't this happen to them by theft, by the spells of sorcery, b
or by force?

I don't understand now either, he said.

I must be talking in high tragic style, I said. By those who have their opinions stolen from them I mean those who are overpersuaded and those who forget, because in the one case time, in the other argument strips them unawares of their beliefs. Now I presume you understand, do you not?

Yes.

Well then, by those who are constrained or forced I mean those whom some pain or suffering compels to change their minds.

That too I understand and you are right.

c   And the victims of sorcery I am sure you too would say are they who alter their opinions under the spell of pleasure or terrified by some fear.

Yes, he said, everything that deceives appears to cast a spell upon the mind.

Well then, as I was just saying, we must look for those who are the best guardians of the indwelling conviction that what they have to do is what they at any time believe to be best for the state. Then we must observe them from childhood up and propose for them tasks in which one would be most likely to forget this principle or be deceived, and he whose memory is sure and who cannot be beguiled we must

d accept and the other kind we must cross off from our list. Is not that so?

Yes.

And again we must subject them to toils and pains and competitions in which we have to watch for the same traits.

Right, he said.

Then, said I, must we not institute a third kind of competitive test with regard to sorcery and observe them in that? Just as men conduct colts to noises and uproar to see if they are liable to take fright,

e so we must bring these lads while young into fears and again pass them into pleasures, testing them much more carefully than men do gold in the fire, to see if the man remains immune to such witchcraft and preserves his composure throughout, a good guardian of himself and the culture which he has received, maintaining the true rhythm and harmony of his being in all those conditions, and the character that would make him most useful to himself and to the state. And he who as boy, lad, and man endures the test and issues from it un-

414 spoiled we must establish as ruler over our city and its guardian, and bestow rewards upon him in life, and in death the allotment of the supreme honors of burial rites and other memorials. But the man of the other type we must reject. Such, said I, appears to me, Glaucon, the general notion of our selection and appointment of rulers and guardians as sketched in outline, but not drawn out in detail.

I too, he said, think much the same.

Then would it not truly be most proper to designate these as

b guardians in the full sense of the word, watchers against foemen without and friends within, so that the latter shall not wish and the former shall not be able to work harm, but to name those youths whom we were calling guardians just now helpers and aids for the decrees of the rulers?

I think so, he replied.

How, then, said I, might we contrive one of those opportune falsehoods of which we were just now speaking, so as by one noble lie to

c persuade if possible the rulers themselves, but failing that the rest of the city?

What kind of a fiction do you mean? said he.

Nothing unprecedented, said I, but a sort of Phoenician tale, something that has happened ere now in many parts of the world, as the poets aver and have induced men to believe, but that has not happened and perhaps would not be likely to happen in our day and demanding no little persuasion to make it believable.

You act like one who shrinks from telling his thought, he said.

You will think that I have right good reason for shrinking when I have told, I said.

Say on, said he, and don't be afraid.

Very well, I will. And yet I hardly know how to find the audacity d or the words to speak and undertake to persuade first the rulers themselves and the soldiers and then the rest of the city that in good sooth all our training and educating of them were things that they imagined and that happened to them as it were in a dream, but that in reality at that time they were down within the earth being molded and fostered themselves while their weapons and the rest of their equipment were being fashioned. And when they were quite finished the earth as e being their mother delivered them, and now as if their land were their mother and their nurse they ought to take thought for her and defend her against any attack and regard the other citizens as their brothers and children of the selfsame earth.

It is not for nothing, he said, that you were so bashful about coming out with your lie.

It was quite natural that I should be, I said, but all the same hear 415 the rest of the story. While all of you in the city are brothers, we will say in our tale, yet God in fashioning those of you who are fitted to hold rule mingled gold in their generation, for which reason they are the most precious—but in the helpers silver, and iron and brass in the farmers and other craftsmen. And as you are all akin, though for the b most part you will breed after your kinds, it may sometimes happen that a golden father would beget a silver son and that a golden offspring would come from a silver sire and that the rest would in like manner be born of one another. So that the first and chief injunction that the god lays upon the rulers is that of nothing else are they to be such careful guardians and so intently observant as of the intermixture of these metals in the souls of their offspring, and if sons are born to them with an infusion of brass or iron they shall by no means c give way to pity in their treatment of them, but shall assign to each the status due to his nature and thrust them out among the artisans or the farmers. And again, if from these there are born sons with unexpected gold or silver in their composition they shall honor such and bid them go up higher, some to the office of guardian, some to the assistantship, alleging that there is an oracle that the state shall then be overthrown when the man of iron or brass is its guardian. Do you see any way of getting them to believe this tale?

d　　No, not these themselves, he said, but I do their sons and successors and the rest of mankind who come after.

Well, said I, even that would have a good effect in making them more inclined to care for the state and one another. For I think I apprehend your meaning. And this shall fall out as tradition guides. But let us arm these sons of earth and conduct them under the leadership of their rulers. And when they have arrived they must look out for the fairest site in the city for their encampment, a position from which
e they could best hold down rebellion against the laws from within and repel aggression from without as of a wolf against the fold. And after they have encamped and sacrificed to the proper gods they must make their lairs, must they not?

Yes, he said.

And these must be of a character to keep out the cold in winter and be sufficient in summer?

Of course. For I presume you are speaking of their houses.

Yes, said I, the houses of soldiers, not of money-makers.

416　　What distinction do you intend by that? he said.

I will try to tell you, I said. It is surely the most monstrous and shameful thing in the world for shepherds to breed the dogs who are to help them with their flocks in such wise and of such a nature that from indiscipline or hunger or some other evil condition the dogs themselves shall attack the sheep and injure them and be likened to wolves instead of dogs.

A terrible thing, indeed, he said.

b　　Must we not then guard by every means in our power against our helpers' treating the citizens in any such way and, because they are the stronger, converting themselves from benign assistants into savage masters?

We must, he said.

And would they not have been provided with the chief safeguard if their education has really been a good one?

But it surely has, he said.

That, said I, dear Glaucon, we may not properly affirm, but what
c we were just now saying we may, that they must have the right education, whatever it is, if they are to have what will do most to make them gentle to one another and to their charges.

That is right, he said.

In addition, moreover, to such an education a thoughtful man would affirm that their houses and the possessions provided for them ought to be such as not to interfere with the best performance of their
d own work as guardians and not to incite them to wrong the other citizens.

He will rightly affirm that.

Consider then, said I, whether, if that is to be their character, their habitations and ways of life must not be something after this fashion. In the first place, none must possess any private property save the indispensable. Secondly, none must have any habitation or treasure house which is not open for all to enter at will. Their food, in such quantities as are needful for athletes of war sober and brave, they e must receive as an agreed stipend from the other citizens as the wages of their guardianship, so measured that there shall be neither superfluity at the end of the year nor any lack. And resorting to a common mess like soldiers on campaign they will live together. Gold and silver, we will tell them, they have of the divine quality from the gods always in their souls, and they have no need of the metal of men nor does holiness suffer them to mingle and contaminate that heavenly possession with the acquisition of mortal gold, since 417 many impious deeds have been done about the coin of the multitude, while that which dwells within them is unsullied. But for these only of all the dwellers in the city it is not lawful to handle gold and silver and to touch them nor yet to come under the same roof with them, nor to hang them as ornaments on their limbs nor to drink from silver and gold. So living they would save themselves and save their city. But whenever they shall acquire for themselves land of their own and houses and coin, they will be householders and farmers instead b of guardians, and will be transformed from the helpers of their fellow citizens to their enemies and masters, and so in hating and being hated, plotting and being plotted against, they will pass their days fearing far more and rather the townsmen within than the foemen without—and then even then laying the course of near shipwreck for themselves and the state. For all these reasons, said I, let us declare that such must be the provision for our guardians in lodging and other respects and so legislate. Shall we not?

By all means, said Glaucon.

BOOK IV

And Adimantus broke in and said, What will be your defense, Socra- 419 tes, if anyone objects that you are not making these men very happy, and that through their own fault? For the city really belongs to them and yet they get no enjoyment out of it as ordinary men do by owning lands and building fine big houses and providing them with suitable furniture and winning the favor of the gods by private sacrifices and entertaining guests and enjoying too those possessions which you just now spoke of, gold and silver and all that is customary for those who are expecting to be happy. But they seem, one might say, to be established in idleness in the city, exactly like hired mercenaries, with nothing to do but keep guard.

Yes, said I, and what is more, they serve for board wages and do 420 not even receive pay in addition to their food as others do, so that they will not even be able to take a journey on their own account, if they wish to, or make presents to their mistresses, or spend money in other directions according to their desires like the men who are thought to be happy. These and many similar counts of the indictment you are omitting.

Well, said he, assume these counts too.

b   What then will be our apology you ask?

Yes.

By following the same path I think we shall find what to reply. For we shall say that while it would not surprise us if these men thus living prove to be the most happy, yet the object on which we fixed our eyes in the establishment of our state was not the exceptional happiness of any one class but the greatest possible happiness of the city as a whole. For we thought that in a state so constituted we should be most likely to discover justice as we should injustice in the worst-governed state, and that when we had made these out we could pass

c   judgment on the issue of our long inquiry. Our first task then, we take it, is to mold the model of a happy state—we are not isolating a small class in it and postulating their happiness, but that of the city as a whole. But the opposite type of state we will consider presently. It is as if we were coloring a statue and someone approached and censured us, saying that we did not apply the most beautiful pigments to the most beautiful parts of the image, since the eyes, which are the most beautiful part, have not been painted with purple but with black. We

d   should think it a reasonable justification to reply, Don't expect us, quaint friend, to paint the eyes so fine that they will not be like eyes at all, nor the other parts, but observe whether by assigning what is proper to each we render the whole beautiful. And so in the present case you must not require us to attach to the guardians a happiness that will make them anything but guardians. For in like manner we

e   could clothe the farmers in robes of state and deck them with gold and bid them cultivate the soil at their pleasure, and we could make the potters recline on couches from left to right before the fire drinking toasts and feasting with their wheel alongside to potter with when they are so disposed, and we can make all the others happy in the same fashion, so that thus the entire city may be happy. But urge us

421   not to this, since, if we yield, the farmer will not be a farmer nor the potter a potter, nor will any other of the types that constitute a state keep its form. However, for the others it matters less. For cobblers who deteriorate and are spoiled and pretend to be the workmen that they are not are no great danger to a state. But guardians of laws and of the city who are not what they pretend to be, but only seem, destroy utterly, I would have you note, the entire state, and on the other hand, they alone are decisive of its good government and happiness. If then we are forming true guardians and keepers of our liberties, men least

b   likely to harm the commonwealth, but the proponent of the other ideal is thinking of farmers and 'happy' feasters as it were in a festival and not in a civic community, he would have something else in mind than a state. Consider, then, whether our aim in establishing the guardians is the greatest possible happiness among them or whether that is something we must look to see develop in the city as a whole, but these helpers and guardians are to be constrained and persuaded c to do what will make them the best craftsmen in their own work, and similarly all the rest. And so, as the entire city develops and is ordered well, each class is to be left to the share of happiness that its nature comports.

Well, he said, I think you are right.

And will you then, I said, also think me reasonable in another point akin to this?

What pray?

Consider whether these are the causes that corrupt other crafts- d men too so as positively to spoil them.

What causes?

Wealth and poverty, said I.

How so?

Thus! Do you think a potter who grew rich would any longer be willing to give his mind to his craft?

By no means, said he.

But will he become more idle and negligent than he was?

Far more.

Then he becomes a worse potter?

Far worse too.

And yet again, if from poverty he is unable to provide himself with tools and other requirements of his art, the work that he turns out will be worse, and he will also make inferior workmen of his sons e or any others whom he teaches.

Of course.

From both causes, then, poverty and wealth, the products of the arts deteriorate, and so do the artisans?

So it appears.

Here, then, is a second group of things, it seems, that our guardians must guard against and do all in their power to keep from slipping into the city without their knowledge.

What are they?

Wealth and poverty, said I, since the one brings luxury, idleness, 422 and innovation, and the other illiberality and the evil of bad workmanship in addition to innovation.

Assuredly, he said. Yet here is a point for your consideration, Socrates—how our city, possessing no wealth, will be able to wage war, especially if compelled to fight a large and wealthy state.

Obviously, said I, it would be rather difficult to fight one such, but easier to fight two.   b

What did you mean by that? he said.

Tell me first, I said, whether, if they have to fight, they will not be fighting as athletes of war against men of wealth?

Yes, that is true, he said.

Answer me then, Adimantus. Do you not think that one boxer perfectly trained in the art could easily fight two fat rich men who knew nothing of it?

Not at the same time perhaps, said he.

c Not even, said I, if he were allowed to retreat and then turn and strike the one who came up first, and if he repeated the procedure many times under a burning and stifling sun? Would not such a fighter down even a number of such opponents?

Doubtless, he said, it wouldn't be surprising if he did.

Well, don't you think that the rich have more of the skill and practice of boxing than of the art of war?

I do, he said.

It will be easy, then, for our athletes in all probability to fight with double and triple their number.

I shall have to concede the point, he said, for I believe you are right.

Well then, if they send an embassy to the other city and say d what is in fact true, 'We make no use of gold and silver nor is it lawful for us, but it is for you; do then join us in the war and keep the spoils of the enemy'—do you suppose any who heard such a proposal would choose to fight against hard and wiry hounds rather than with the aid of the hounds against fat and tender sheep?

I think not. Yet consider whether the accumulation of all the e wealth of other cities in one does not involve danger for the state that has no wealth.

What happy innocence, said I, to suppose that you can properly use the name city of any other than the one we are constructing.

Why, what should we say? he said.

A greater predication, said I, must be applied to the others. For they are each one of them many cities, not a city, as it goes in the game. There are two at the least at enmity with one another, the 423 city of the rich and the city of the poor, and in each of these there are many. If you deal with them as one you will altogether miss the mark, but if you treat them as a multiplicity by offering to the one faction the property, the power, the very persons of the other, you will continue always to have few enemies and many allies. And so long as your city is governed soberly in the order just laid down, it will be the greatest of cities. I do not mean greatest in repute, but in reality, even though it have only a thousand defenders. For a city of this size that is really b one you will not easily discover either among Greeks or barbarians— but of those that seem so you will find many and many times the size of this. Or do you think otherwise?

No, indeed I don't, said he.

Would not this, then, be the best rule and measure for our governors of the proper size of the city and of the territory that they should mark off for a city of that size and seek no more?

What is the measure?

I think, said I, that they should let it grow so long as in its growth it consents to remain a unity, but no further.   c

Excellent, he said.

Then is not this still another injunction that we should lay upon our guardians, to keep guard in every way that the city shall not be too small, nor great only in seeming, but that it shall be a sufficient city and one?

That behest will perhaps be an easy one for them, he said.

And still easier, haply, I said, is this that we mentioned before when we said that if a degenerate offspring was born to the guardians d he must be sent away to the other classes, and likewise if a superior to the others he must be enrolled among the guardians, and the purport of all this was that the other citizens too must be sent to the task for which their natures were fitted, one man to one work, in order that each of them fulfilling his own function may be not many men, but one, and so the entire city may come to be not a multiplicity but a unity.

Why yes, he said, this is even more trifling than that.

These are not, my good Adimantus, as one might suppose, numerous and difficult injunctions that we are imposing upon them, but they are all easy, provided they guard, as the saying is, the one great e thing—or instead of great let us call it sufficient.

What is that? he said.

Their education and nurture, I replied. For if a right education makes of them reasonable men they will easily discover everything of this kind—and other principles that we now pass over, as that the possession of wives and marriage, and the procreation of children and 424 all that sort of thing should be made as far as possible the proverbial goods of friends that are common.

Yes, that would be the best way, he said.

And, moreover, said I, the state, if it once starts well, proceeds as it were in a cycle of growth. I mean that a sound nurture and education if kept up create good natures in the state, and sound natures in turn receiving an education of this sort develop into better men than their predecessors both for other purposes and for the production of b offspring, as among animals also.

It is probable, he said.

To put it briefly, then, said I, it is to this that the overseers of our state must cleave and be watchful against its insensible corruption. They must throughout be watchful against innovations in music and gymnastics counter to the established order, and to the best of their power guard against them, fearing when anyone says that that song is

most regarded among men 'which hovers newest on the singer's lips,' [39]
c lest haply it be supposed that the poet means not new songs but a new
way of song and is commending this. But we must not praise that sort
of thing nor conceive it to be the poet's meaning. For a change to a
new type of music is something to beware of as a hazard of all our fortunes. For the modes of music are never disturbed without unsettling
of the most fundamental political and social conventions, as Damon
affirms and as I am convinced.

Set me too down in the number of the convinced, said Adimantus.

d It is here, then, I said, in music, as it seems, that our guardians
must build their guardhouse and post of watch.

It is certain, he said, that this is the kind of lawlessness that easily insinuates itself unobserved.

Yes, said I, because it is supposed to be only a form of play and to
work no harm.

Nor does it work any, he said, except that by gradual infiltration
it softly overflows upon the characters and pursuits of men and from
these issues forth grown greater to attack their business dealings, and
from these relations it proceeds against the laws and the constitution
e with wanton license, Socrates, till finally it overthrows all things
public and private.

Well, said I, are these things so?

I think so, he said.

Then, as we were saying in the beginning, our youth must join in
a more law-abiding play, since, if play grows lawless and the children
425 likewise, it is impossible that they should grow up to be men of serious temper and lawful spirit.

Of course, he said.

And so we may reason that when children in their earliest play
are imbued with the spirit of law and order through their music, the
opposite of the former supposition happens—this spirit waits upon
them in all things and fosters their growth, and restores and sets up
again whatever was overthrown in the other type of state.

True indeed, he said.

Then such men rediscover for themselves those seemingly trifling
conventions which their predecessors abolished altogether.

Of what sort?

b Such things as the becoming silence of the young in the presence
of their elders, the giving place to them and rising up before them,
and dutiful service of parents, and the cut of the hair and the garments and the fashion of the footgear, and in general the deportment
of the body and everything of the kind. Don't you think so?

I do.

[39] *Odyssey* I.351.

Yet to enact them into laws would, I think, be silly. For such laws are not obeyed nor would they last, being enacted only in words and on paper.

How could they?

At any rate, Adimantus, I said, the direction of the education from whence one starts is likely to determine the quality of what fol- c lows. Does not like ever summon like?

Surely.

And the final outcome, I presume, we would say is one complete and vigorous product of good or the reverse.

Of course, said he.

For my part, then, I said, for these reasons I would not go on to try to legislate on such matters.

With good reason, said he.

But what, in heaven's name, said I, about business matters, the deals that men make with one another in the agora—and, if you please, contracts with workmen and actions for foul language and as- d sault, the filing of declarations, the impaneling of juries, the payment and exaction of any dues that may be needful in markets or harbors and in general market, police, or harbor regulations and the like— can we bring ourselves to legislate about these?

Nay, 'twould not be fitting, he said, to dictate to good and honorable men. For most of the enactments that are needed about these e things they will easily, I presume, discover.

Yes, my friend, provided God grants them the preservation of the principles of law that we have already discussed.

Failing that, said he, they will pass their lives multiplying such petty laws and amending them in the expectation of attaining what is best.

You mean, said I, that the life of such citizens will resemble that of men who are sick, yet from intemperance are unwilling to abandon their unwholesome regimen.

By all means.

And truly, said I, these latter go on in a most charming fashion. 426 For with all their doctoring they accomplish nothing except to complicate and augment their maladies. And they are always hoping that someone will recommend a panacea that will restore their health.

A perfect description, he said, of the state of such invalids.

And isn't this a charming trait in them, that they hate most in all the world him who tells them the truth, that until a man stops drinking and gorging and wenching and idling, neither drugs nor cautery b nor the knife, no, nor spells nor periapts nor anything of that kind will be of any avail?

Not altogether charming, he said, for there is no grace or charm in being angry with him who speaks well.

You do not seem to be an admirer of such people, said I.

No, by heaven, I am not.

Neither then, if an entire city, as we were just now saying, acts in this way, will it have your approval, or don't you think that the way of such invalids is precisely that of those cities which being badly governed forewarn their citizens not to meddle with the general constitu-

c tion of the state, denouncing death to whosoever attempts that—while whoever most agreeably serves them governed as they are and who curries favor with them by fawning upon them and anticipating their desires and by his cleverness in gratifying them, him they will account the good man, the man wise in worthwhile things, the man they will delight to honor?

Yes, he said, I think their conduct is identical, and I don't approve it in the very least.

d   And what again of those who are willing and eager to serve such states? Don't you admire their valiance and lighthearted irresponsibility?

I do, he said, except those who are actually deluded and suppose themselves to be in truth statesmen because they are praised by the many.

What do you mean? Can't you make allowances for the men? Do you think it possible for a man who does not know how to measure when a multitude of others equally ignorant assure him that he is

e four cubits tall not to suppose this to be the fact about himself?

Why no, he said, I don't think that.

Then don't be harsh with them. For surely such fellows are the most charming spectacle in the world when they enact and amend such laws as we just now described and are perpetually expecting to find a way of putting an end to frauds in business and in the other matters of which I was speaking because they can't see that they are in very truth trying to cut off a Hydra's head.

427   Indeed, he said, that is exactly what they are doing.

I, then, said I, should not have supposed that the true lawgiver ought to work out matters of that kind in the laws and the constitution of either an ill-governed or a well-governed state—in the one because they are useless and accomplish nothing, in the other because some of them anybody could discover and others will result spontaneously from the pursuits already described.

b   What part of legislation, then, he said, is still left for us?

And I replied, For us nothing, but for the Apollo of Delphi, the chief, the fairest, and the first of enactments.

What are they? he said.

The founding of temples, and sacrifices, and other forms of worship of gods, daemons, and heroes, and likewise the burial of the dead and the services we must render to the dwellers in the world beyond to keep them gracious. For of such matters we neither know anything

c nor in the founding of our city if we are wise shall we entrust them to any other or make use of any other interpreter than the god of our fathers. For this god surely is in such matters for all mankind the interpreter of the religion of their fathers who from his seat in the middle and at the very navel of the earth delivers his interpretation.

Excellently said, he replied, and that is what we must do.

At last, then, son of Ariston, said I, your city may be considered as established. The next thing is to procure a sufficient light somewhere and to look yourself, and call in the aid of your brother and of Polemarchus and the rest, if we may in any wise discover where justice and injustice should be in it, wherein they differ from one another, and which of the two he must have who is to be happy, alike whether his condition is known or not known to all gods and men.

Nonsense, said Glaucon, you promised that you would carry on the search yourself, admitting that it would be impious for you not to come to the aid of justice by every means in your power.

A true reminder, I said, and I must do so, but you also must lend a hand.

Well, he said, we will.

I expect then, said I, that we shall find it in this way. I think our city, if it has been rightly founded, is good in the full sense of the word.

Necessarily, he said.

Clearly, then, it will be wise, brave, sober, and just.

Clearly.

Then if we find any of these qualities in it, the remainder will be that which we have not found?

Surely.

Take the case of any four other things. If we were looking for any one of them in anything and recognized the object of our search first, that would have been enough for us, but if we had recognized the other three first, that in itself would have made known to us the thing we were seeking. For plainly there was nothing left for it to be but the remainder.

Right, he said.

And so, since these are four, we must conduct the search in the same way.

Clearly.

And, moreover, the first thing that I think I clearly see therein is the wisdom, and there is something odd about that, it appears.

What? said he.

Wise in very deed I think the city that we have described is, for it is well counseled, is it not?

Yes.

And surely this very thing, good counsel, is a form of wisdom. For it is not by ignorance but by knowledge that men counsel well.

Obviously.

But there are many and manifold knowledges or sciences in
c the city.

Of course.

Is it then owing to the science of her carpenters that a city is to be
called wise and well advised?

By no means for that, but rather mistress of the arts of building.

Then a city is not to be styled wise because of the deliberations of
the science of wooden utensils for their best production?

No, I grant you.

Is it, then, because of that of brass implements or any other of
that kind?

None whatsoever, he said.

Nor yet because of the science of the production of crops from the
soil, but the name it takes from that is agricultural.

I think so.

Then, said I, is there any science in the city just founded by us
residing in any of its citizens which does not take counsel about
d some particular thing in the city but about the city as a whole and the
betterment of its relations with itself and other states?

Why, yes, there is.

What is it, said I, and in whom is it found?

It is the science of guardianship or government and it is to be
found in those rulers to whom we just now gave the name of guardians in the full sense of the word.

And what term then do you apply to the city because of this
knowledge?

Well-advised, he said, and truly wise.

e Which class, then, said I, do you suppose will be the more numerous in our city, the smiths or these true guardians?

The smiths, by far, he said.

And would not these rulers be the smallest of all the groups of
those who possess special knowledge and receive distinctive appellations?

By far.

Then it is by virtue of its smallest class and minutest part of itself, and the wisdom that resides therein, in the part which takes the
lead and rules, that a city established on principles of nature would be
429 wise as a whole. And as it appears these are by nature the fewest, the
class to which it pertains to partake of the knowledge which alone of
all forms of knowledge deserves the name of wisdom.

Most true, he said.

This one of our four, then, we have, I know not how, discovered,
the thing itself and its place in the state.

I certainly think, said he, that it has been discovered sufficiently.

But again there is no difficulty in seeing bravery itself and the
part of the city in which it resides for which the city is called brave.

How so?

Who, said I, in calling a city cowardly or brave would fix his eyes b on any other part of it than that which defends it and wages war in its behalf?

No one at all, he said.

For the reason, I take it, said I, that the cowardice or the bravery of the other inhabitants does not determine for it the one quality or the other.

It does not.

Bravery too, then, belongs to a city by virtue of a part of itself owing to its possession in that part of a quality that under all conditions will preserve the conviction that things to be feared are precisely those c which and such as the lawgiver inculcated in their education. Is not that what you call bravery?

I don't altogether understand what you said, he replied, but say it again.

A kind of conservation, I said, is what I mean by bravery.

What sort of a conservation?

The conservation of the conviction which the law has created by education about fearful things—what and what sort of things are to be feared. And by the phrase 'under all conditions' I mean that the brave man preserves it both in pain and pleasures and in desires and fears and does not expel it from his soul. And I may illustrate it by a d similitude if you please.

I do.

You are aware that dyers when they wish to dye wool so as to hold the purple hue begin by selecting from the many colors there be the one nature of the white and then give it a careful preparatory treatment so that it will take the hue in the best way, and after the treatment, then and then only, dip it in the dye. And things that are dyed by this process become fast-colored and washing either with or e without lyes cannot take away the sheen of their hues. But otherwise you know what happens to them, whether anyone dips other colors or even these without the preparatory treatment.

I know, he said, that they present a ridiculous and washed-out appearance.

By this analogy, then, said I, you must conceive what we too to the best of our ability were doing when we selected our soldiers and educated them in music and exercises of the body. The sole aim of our 430 contrivance was that they should be convinced and receive our laws like a dye as it were, so that their belief and faith might be fastcolored about both the things that are to be feared and all other things because of the fitness of their nature and nurture, and that so their dyes might not be washed out by those lyes that have such dread power to scour our faiths away, pleasure more potent than any detergent or abstergent to accomplish this, and pain and fear, and desire b more sure than any lye. This power in the soul, then, this unfailing conservation of right and lawful belief about things to be and not to be feared is what I call and would assume to be courage, unless you have something different to say.

No, nothing, said he, for I presume that you consider mere right opinion about the same matters not produced by education, that which may manifest itself in a beast or a slave, to have little or nothing to do with law and that you would call it by another name than courage.

c   That is most true, said I.

Well then, he said, I accept this as bravery.

Do so, said I, and you will be right, with the reservation that it is the courage of a citizen. Some other time, if it please you, we will discuss it more fully. At present we were not seeking this but justice, and for the purpose of that inquiry I believe we have done enough.

You are quite right, he said.

d   Two things still remain, said I, to make out in our city, soberness and the object of the whole inquiry, justice.

Quite so.

If there were only some way to discover justice so that we need not further concern ourselves about soberness.

Well, I, for my part, he said, neither know of any such way nor would I wish justice to be discovered first if that means that we are not to go on to the consideration of soberness. But if you desire to please me, consider this before that.

e   It would certainly be very wrong of me not to desire it, said I.

Go on with the inquiry then, he said.

I must go on, I replied, and viewed from here it bears more likeness to a kind of concord and harmony than the other virtues did.

How so?

Soberness is a kind of beautiful order and a continence of certain pleasures and appetites, as they say, using the phrase 'master of himself' I know not how, and there are other similar expressions that as it were point us to the same trail. Is that not so?

Most certainly.

Now the phrase 'master of himself' is an absurdity, is it not? For
431 he who is master of himself would also be subject to himself, and he who is subject to himself would be master. For the same person is spoken of in all these expressions.

Of course.

But, said I, the intended meaning of this way of speaking appears to me to be that the soul of a man within him has a better part and a worse part, and the expression self-mastery means the control of the worse by the naturally better part. It is, at any rate, a term of praise. But when, because of bad breeding or some association, the better part, which is the smaller, is dominated by the multitude of the worse,

I think that our speech censures this as a reproach, and calls the man b
in this plight unself-controlled and licentious.

That seems likely, he said.

Turn your eyes now upon our new city, said I, and you will find
one of these conditions existent in it. For you will say that it is justly
spoken of as master of itself if that in which the superior rules the inferior is to be called sober and self-mastered.

I do turn my eyes upon it, he said, and it is as you say.

And again, the mob of motley appetites and pleasures and pains
one would find chiefly in children and women and slaves and in the c
base rabble of those who are free men in name.

By all means.

But the simple and moderate appetites which with the aid of reason and right opinion are guided by consideration you will find in few
and those the best born and best educated.

True, he said.

And do you not find this too in your city and a domination there
of the desires in the multitude and the rabble by the desires and the
wisdom that dwell in the minority of the better sort?   d

I do, he said.

If, then, there is any city that deserves to be described as master
of its pleasures and desires and self-mastered, this one merits that
designation.

Most assuredly, he said.

And is it not also to be called sober in all these respects?

Indeed it is, he said.

And yet again, if there is any city in which the rulers and the
ruled are of one mind as to who ought to rule, that condition will be e
found in this. Don't you think so?

I most emphatically do, he said.

In which class of the citizens, then, will you say that the virtue of
soberness has its seat when this is their condition? In the rulers or in
the ruled?

In both, I suppose, he said.

Do you see then, said I, that our intuition was not a bad one just
now that discerned a likeness between soberness and a kind of harmony?

Why so?

Because its operation is unlike that of courage and wisdom, which
residing in separate parts respectively made the city, the one wise and
the other brave. That is not the way of soberness, but it extends liter- 432
ally through the entire gamut throughout, bringing about the unison
in the same chant of the strongest, the weakest, and the intermediate,
whether in wisdom or, if you please, in strength, or for that matter in
numbers, wealth, or any similar criterion. So that we should be quite
right in affirming this unanimity to be soberness, the concord of the

naturally superior and inferior as to which ought to rule in both the state and the individual.

b   I entirely concur, he said.

Very well, said I, we have made out these three forms in our city to the best of our present judgment. What can be the remaining form that would give the city still another virtue? For it is obvious that the remainder is justice.

Obvious.

Now then, Glaucon, is the time for us like huntsmen to surround the covert and keep close watch that justice may not slip through and get away from us and vanish from our sight. It plainly must be some-

c   where hereabout. Keep your eyes open then and do your best to descry it. You may see it before I do and point it out to me.

Would that I could, he said, but I think rather that if you find in me one who can follow you and discern what you point out to him you will be making a very fair use of me.

Pray for success then, said I, and follow along with me.

That I will do, only lead on, he said.

And truly, said I, it appears to be an inaccessible place, lying in deep shadows.

It certainly is a dark covert, not easy to beat up.

d   But all the same, on we must go.

Yes, on.

And I caught view and gave a halloo and said, Glaucon, I think we have found its trail and I don't believe it will get away from us.

I am glad to hear that, said he.

Truly, said I, we were slackers indeed.

How so?

Why, all the time, bless your heart, the thing apparently was tum-bling about our feet from the start and yet we couldn't see it, but were

e   most ludicrous, like people who sometimes hunt for what they hold in their hands. So we did not turn our eyes upon it, but looked off into the distance, which was perhaps the reason it escaped us.

What do you mean? he said.

This, I replied, that it seems to me that though we were speaking of it and hearing about it all the time we did not understand our-selves or realize that we were speaking of it in a sense.

That is a tedious prologue, he said, for an eager listener.

433   Listen then, said I, and learn if there is anything in what I say. For what we laid down in the beginning as a universal requirement when we were founding our city, this I think, or some form of this, is justice. And what we did lay down, and often said, if you recall, was that each one man must perform one social service in the state for which his nature was best adapted.

Yes, we said that.

And again, that to do one's own business and not to be a busybody is justice is a saying that we have heard from many and have very often repeated ourselves.   b

We have.

This, then, I said, my friend, if taken in a certain sense appears to be justice, this principle of doing one's own business. Do you know whence I infer this?

No, but tell me, he said.

I think that this is the remaining virtue in the state after our consideration of soberness, courage, and intelligence, a quality which made it possible for them all to grow up in the body politic and which when they have sprung up preserves them as long as it is present. And I hardly need to remind you that we said that justice would c be the residue after we had found the other three.

That is an unavoidable conclusion, he said.

But moreover, said I, if we were required to decide what it is whose indwelling presence will contribute most to making our city good, it would be a difficult decision whether it was the unanimity of rulers and ruled or the conservation in the minds of the soldiers of the convictions produced by law as to what things are or are not to be feared, or the watchful intelligence that resides in the guardians, or whether this is the chief cause of its goodness, the principle embodied in child, woman, slave, free, artisan, ruler, and ruled, that each per- d formed his one task as one man and was not a versatile busybody.

Hard to decide indeed, he said.

A thing, then, that in its contribution to the excellence of a state vies with and rivals its wisdom, its soberness, its bravery, is this principle of everyone in it doing his own task.

It is indeed, he said.

And is not justice the name you would have to give to the principle that rivals these as conducting to the virtue of a state?   e

By all means.

Consider it in this wise too, if so you will be convinced. Will you not assign the conduct of lawsuits in your state to the rulers?

Of course.

Will not this be the chief aim of their decisions, that no one shall have what belongs to others or be deprived of his own?

Nothing else but this.

On the assumption that this is just?

Yes.

From this point of view too, then, the having and doing of one's 434 own and what belongs to oneself would admittedly be justice.

That is so.

Consider now whether you agree with me. A carpenter undertaking to do the work of a cobbler or a cobbler of a carpenter or their interchange of one another's tools or honors or even the attempt of the same man to do both—the confounding of all other functions would not, think you, greatly injure a state, would it?

Not much, he said.

b But when, I fancy, one who is by nature an artisan or some kind of money-maker tempted and incited by wealth or command of votes or bodily strength or some similar advantage tries to enter into the class of the soldiers or one of the soldiers into the class of counselors and guardians, for which he is not fitted, and these interchange their tools and their honors or when the same man undertakes all these functions at once, then, I take it, you too believe that this kind of substitution and meddlesomeness is the ruin of a state.

By all means.

The interference with one another's business, then, of three existent classes, and the substitution of the one for the other, is the c greatest injury to a state and would most rightly be designated as the thing which chiefly works it harm.

Precisely so.

And the thing that works the greatest harm to one's own state, will you not pronounce to be injustice?

Of course.

This, then, is injustice. Again, let us put it in this way. The proper functioning of the money-makers, the helpers, and the guardians, each doing his own work in the state, being the reverse of that just described, would be justice and would render the city just.

d I think the case is thus and no otherwise, said he.

Let us not yet affirm it quite fixedly, I said, but if this form, when applied to the individual man, is accepted there also as a definition of justice, we will then concede the point—for what else will there be to say? But if not, then we will look for something else. But now let us work out the inquiry in which we supposed that, if we found some e larger thing that contained justice and viewed it there, we should more easily discover its nature in the individual man. And we agreed that this larger thing is the city, and so we constructed the best city in our power, well knowing that in the good city it would of course be found. What, then, we thought we saw there we must refer back to the individual and, if it is confirmed, all will be well. But if something different manifests itself in the individual, we will return again 435 to the state and test it there and it may be that, by examining them side by side and rubbing them against one another, as it were from the fire sticks we may cause the spark of justice to flash forth, and when it is thus revealed confirm it in our own minds.

Well, he said, that seems a sound method and that is what we must do.

Then, said I, if you call a thing by the same name whether it is

big or little, is it unlike in the way in which it is called the same or
like?

  Like, he said.

  Then a just man too will not differ at all from a just city in respect b
of the very form of justice, but will be like it.

  Yes, like.

  But now the city was thought to be just because three natural
kinds existing in it performed each its own function, and again it was
sober, brave, and wise because of certain other affections and habits
of these three kinds.

  True, he said.

  Then, my friend, we shall thus expect the individual also to have
these same forms in his soul, and by reason of identical affections of c
these with those in the city to receive properly the same appellations.

  Inevitable, he said.

  Goodness gracious, said I, here is another trifling inquiry into
which we have plunged, the question whether the soul really contains
these three forms in itself or not.

  It does not seem to me at all trifling, he said, for perhaps, Socrates, the saying is true that 'fine things are difficult.'

  Apparently, said I, and let me tell you, Glaucon, that in my
opinion we shall never apprehend this matter accurately from such d
methods as we are now employing in discussion. For there is another
longer and harder way that conducts to this. Yet we may perhaps discuss it on the level of our previous statements and inquiries.

  May we not acquiesce in that? he said. I for my part should be
quite satisfied with that for the present.

  And I surely should be more than satisfied, I replied.

  Don't you weary then, he said, but go on with the inquiry.

  Is it not, then, said I, impossible for us to avoid admitting this e
much, that the same forms and qualities are to be found in each one
of us that are in the state? They could not get there from any other
source. It would be absurd to suppose that the element of high spirit
was not derived in states from the private citizens who are reputed to
have this quality, as the populations of the Thracian and Scythian
lands and generally of northern regions, or the quality of love of
knowledge, which would chiefly be attributed to the region where
we dwell, or the love of money which we might say is not least 436
likely to be found in Phoenicians and the population of Egypt.

  One certainly might, he replied.

  This is the fact then, said I, and there is no difficulty in recognizing it.

  Certainly not.

  But the matter begins to be difficult when you ask whether we do
all these things with the same thing or whether there are three things

and we do one thing with one and one with another—learn with one part of ourselves, feel anger with another, and with yet a third desire the pleasures of nutrition and generation and their kind, or whether
b it is with the entire soul that we function in each case when we once begin. That is what is really hard to determine properly.

I think so too, he said.

Let us then attempt to define the boundary and decide whether they are identical with one another in this way.

How?

It is obvious that the same thing will never do or suffer opposites in the same respect in relation to the same thing and at the same time. So that if ever we find these contradictions in the functions of the
c mind we shall know that it was not the same thing functioning but a plurality.

Very well.

Consider, then, what I am saying.

Say on, he replied.

Is it possible for the same thing at the same time in the same respect to be at rest and in motion?

By no means.

Let us have our understanding still more precise, lest as we proceed we become involved in dispute. If anyone should say of a man standing still but moving his hands and head that the same man is at the same time at rest and in motion we should not, I take it, regard
d that as the right way of expressing it, but rather that a part of him is at rest and a part in motion. Is not that so?

It is.

Then if the disputant should carry the jest still further with the subtlety that tops at any rate stand still as a whole at the same time that they are in motion when with the peg fixed in one point they revolve, and that the same is true of any other case of circular motion about the same spot—we should reject the statement on the ground
e that the repose and the movement in such cases were not in relation to the same parts of the objects. But we would say that there was a straight line and a circumference in them and that in respect of the straight line they are standing still since they do not incline to either side, but in respect of the circumference they move in a circle, but that when as they revolve they incline the perpendicular to right or left or forward or back, then they are in no wise at rest.

And that would be right, he said.

No such remarks then will disconcert us or any whit the more make us believe that it is ever possible for the same thing at the same
437 time in the same respect and the same relation to suffer, be, or do opposites.

They will not me, I am sure, said he.

All the same, said I, that we may not be forced to examine at tedious length the entire list of such contentions and convince ourselves that they are false, let us proceed on the hypothesis that this is so, with the understanding that, if it ever appear otherwise, everything that results from the assumption shall be invalidated.

That is what we must do, he said.

Will you not then, said I, set down as opposed to one another as- b sent and dissent, and the endeavor after a thing to the rejection of it, and embracing to repelling—do not these and all things like these belong to the class of opposite actions or passions, it will make no difference which?

None, said he, but they are opposites.

What then, said I, of thirst and hunger and the appetites generally, and again consenting and willing—would you not put them all somewhere in the classes just described? Will you not say, for ex- c ample, that the soul of one who desires either strives for that which he desires or draws toward its embrace what it wishes to accrue to it, or again, in so far as it wills that anything be presented to it, nods assent to itself thereon as if someone put the question, striving toward its attainment?

I would say so, he said.

But what of not-willing and not-consenting nor yet desiring? Shall we not put these under the soul's rejection and repulsion from itself and generally into the opposite class from all the former?

Of course.   d

This being so, shall we say that the desires constitute a class and that the most conspicuous members of that class are what we call thirst and hunger?

We shall, said he.

Is not the one desire of drink, the other of food?

Yes.

Then in so far as it is thirst, would it be of anything more than that of which we say it is a desire in the soul? I mean is thirst thirst for hot drink or cold or much or little or in a word for a draught of any particular quality, or is it the fact that if heat is attached to the thirst it would further render the desire—a desire of cold, and if cold of e hot? But if owing to the presence of muchness the thirst is much it would render it a thirst for much and if little for little. But mere thirst will never be desire of anything else than that of which it is its nature to be, mere drink, and so hunger of food.

That is so, he said. Each desire in itself is of that thing only of which it is its nature to be. The epithets belong to the quality—such or such.

Let no one then, said I, disconcert us when off our guard with the 438 objection that everybody desires not drink but good drink and not food but good food, because, the argument will run, all men desire good, and so, if thirst is desire, it would be of good drink or of good whatsoever it is, and so similarly of other desires.

Why, he said, there perhaps would seem to be something in that objection.

But I need hardly remind you, said I, that of relative terms those b that are somehow qualified are related to a qualified correlate, those that are severally just themselves to a correlate that is just itself.

I don't understand, he said.

Don't you understand, said I, that the greater is such as to be greater than something?

Certainly.

Is it not than the less?

Yes.

But the much greater than the much less. Is that not so?

Yes.

And may we add the onetime greater than the onetime less and that which will be greater than that which will be less?

Surely.

c And similarly of the more toward the fewer, and the double toward the half and of all like cases, and again of the heavier toward the lighter, the swifter toward the slower, and yet again of the hot toward the cold and all cases of that kind—does not the same hold?

By all means.

But what of the sciences? Is not the way of it the same? Science, which is just that, is of knowledge which is just that, or is of whatsoever we must assume the correlate of science to be. But a particular science of a particular kind is of some particular thing of a particular d kind. I mean something like this. As there was a science of making a house it differed from other sciences so as to be named architecture.

Certainly.

Was not this by reason of its being of a certain kind such as no other of all the rest?

Yes.

And was it not because it was of something of a certain kind that it itself became a certain kind of science? And similarly of the other arts and sciences?

That is so.

This then, said I, if haply you now understand, is what you must say I then meant, by the statement that of all things that are such as to be of something, those that are just themselves only are of things just themselves only, but things of a certain kind are of things of a e kind. And I don't at all mean that they are of the same kind as the things of which they are, so that we are to suppose that the science of health and disease is a healthy and diseased science and that of evil and good, evil and good. I only mean that as science became the science not of just the thing of which science is but of some particular kind of thing, namely, of health and disease, the result was that it it- self became some kind of science and this caused it to be no longer called simply science but, with the addition of the particular kind, medical science.

'I understand, he said, and agree that it is so.

To return to thirst, then, said I, will you not class it with the 439 things that are of something and say that it is what it is in relation to something—and it is, I presume, thirst?

I will, said he, namely of drink.

Then if the drink is of a certain kind, so is the thirst, but thirst that is just thirst is neither of much nor little nor good nor bad, nor in a word of any kind, but just thirst is naturally of just drink only.

By all means.

The soul of the thirsty then, in so far as it thirsts, wishes nothing else than to drink, and yearns for this and its impulse is toward this. b

Obviously.

Then if anything draws it back when thirsty it must be something different in it from that which thirsts and drives it like a beast to drink. For it cannot be, we say, that the same thing with the same part of itself at the same time acts in opposite ways about the same thing.

We must admit that it does not.

So I fancy it is not well said of the archer that his hands at the same time thrust away the bow and draw it nigh, but we should rather say that there is one hand that puts it away and another that draws it to.

By all means, he said. c

Are we to say, then, that some men sometimes though thirsty re- fuse to drink?

We are indeed, he said, many and often.

What then, said I, should one affirm about them? Is it not that there is a something in the soul that bids them drink and a something that forbids, a different something that masters that which bids?

I think so.

And is it not the fact that that which inhibits such actions arises when it arises from the calculations of reason, but the impulses which d draw and drag come through affections and diseases?

Apparently.

Not unreasonably, said I, shall we claim that they are two and different from one another, naming that in the soul whereby it reckons and reasons the rational, and that with which it loves, hun- gers, thirsts, and feels the flutter and titillation of other desires, the irrational and appetitive—companion of various repletions and pleasures.

It would not be unreasonable but quite natural, he said, for us to e think this.

These two forms, then, let us assume to have been marked off as actually existing in the soul. But now the *thumos*, or principle of high spirit, that with which we feel anger, is it a third, or would it be identical in nature with one of these?

Perhaps, he said, with one of these, the appetitive.

But, I said, I once heard a story which I believe, that Leontius the son of Aglaion, on his way up from the Piraeus under the outer side of the northern wall, becoming aware of dead bodies that lay at the place of public execution at the same time felt a desire to see them and a repugnance and aversion, and that for a time he resisted and veiled 440 his head, but overpowered in despite of all by his desire, with wide staring eyes he rushed up to the corpses and cried, There, ye wretches, take your fill of the fine spectacle!

I too, he said, have heard the story.

Yet, surely, this anecdote, I said, signifies that the principle of anger sometimes fights against desires as an alien thing against an alien.

Yes, it does, he said.

And do we not, said I, on many other occasions observe when his b desires constrain a man contrary to his reason that he reviles himself and is angry with that within which masters him, and that as it were in a faction of two parties the high spirit of such a man becomes the ally of his reason? But its making common cause with the desires against the reason when reason whispers low, Thou must not—that, I think, is a kind of thing you would not affirm ever to have perceived in yourself, nor, I fancy, in anybody else either.

No, by heaven, he said.

c   Again, when a man thinks himself to be in the wrong, is it not true that the nobler he is the less is he capable of anger though suffering hunger and cold and whatsoever else at the hands of him whom he believes to be acting justly therein, and as I say his spirit refuses to be aroused against such a one?

True, he said.

But what when a man believes himself to be wronged? Does not his spirit in that case seethe and grow fierce—and also because of his suffering hunger, cold, and the like—and make itself the ally of what d he judges just? And in noble souls it endures and wins the victory and will not let go until either it achieves its purpose, or death ends all, or, as a dog is called back by a shepherd, it is called back by the reason within and calmed.

Your similitude is perfect, he said, and it confirms our former statements that the helpers are as it were dogs subject to the rulers who are as it were the shepherds of the city.

You apprehend my meaning excellently, said I. But do you also take note of this?

e   Of what?

That what we now think about the spirited element is just the opposite of our recent surmise. For then we supposed it to be a part of the appetitive, but now, far from that, we say that, in the factions of the soul, it much rather marshals itself on the side of the reason.

By all means, he said.

Is it then distinct from this too, or is it a form of the rational, so that there are not three but two kinds in the soul, the rational and the appetitive? Or just as in the city there were three existing kinds that   441 composed its structure, the money-makers, the helpers, the counselors, so also in the soul does there exist a third kind, this principle of high spirit, which is the helper of reason by nature unless it is corrupted by evil nurture?

We have to assume it as a third, he said.

Yes, said I, provided it shall have been shown to be something different from the rational, as it has been shown to be other than the appetitive.

That is not hard to be shown, he said, for that much one can see in children, that they are from their very birth chock-full of rage and high spirit, but as for reason, some of them, to my thinking, never   b participate in it, and the majority quite late.

Yes, by heaven, excellently said, I replied, and further, one could see in animals that what you say is true. And to these instances we may add the testimony of Homer quoted above, 'He smote his breast and chided thus his heart.' [40] For there Homer has clearly represented that in us which has reflected about the better and the worse as re-   c buking that which feels unreasoning anger as if it were a distinct and different thing.

You are entirely right, he said.

Through these waters, then, said I, we have with difficulty made our way and we are fairly agreed that the same kinds equal in number are to be found in the state and in the soul of each one of us.

That is so.

Then does not the necessity of our former postulate immediately follow, that as and whereby the state was wise, so and thereby is the individual wise?

Surely.

And so whereby and as the individual is brave, thereby and so is   d the state brave, and that both should have all the other constituents of virtue in the same way?

Necessarily.

Just too, then, Glaucon, I presume we shall say a man is in the same way in which a city was just.

That too is quite inevitable.

But we surely cannot have forgotten this, that the state was just

[40] *Odyssey* 20.17.

by reason of each of the three classes found in it fulfilling its own function.

I don't think we have forgotten, he said.

We must remember, then, that each of us also in whom the
e several parts within him perform each their own task—he will be a just man and one who minds his own affair.

We must indeed remember, he said.

Does it not belong to the rational part to rule, being wise and exercising forethought in behalf of the entire soul, and to the principle of high spirit to be subject to this and its ally?

Assuredly.

Then is it not, as we said, the blending of music and gymnastics that will render them concordant, intensifying and fostering the one
442 with fair words and teachings and relaxing and soothing and making gentle the other by harmony and rhythm?

Quite so, said he.

And these two, thus reared and having learned and been educated to do their own work in the true sense of the phrase, will preside over the appetitive part which is the mass of the soul in each of us and the most insatiate by nature of wealth. They will keep watch upon it, lest, by being filled and infected with the so-called pleasures associated with the body and so waxing big and strong, it may not
b keep to its own work but may undertake to enslave and rule over the classes which it is not fitting that it should, and so overturn the entire life of all.

By all means, he said.

Would not these two, then, best keep guard against enemies from without also in behalf of the entire soul and body, the one taking counsel, the other giving battle, attending upon the ruler, and by its courage executing the ruler's designs?

That is so.

c   Brave, too, then, I take it, we call each individual by virtue of this part in him, when, namely, his high spirit preserves in the midst of pains and pleasures the rule handed down by the reason as to what is or is not to be feared.

Right, he said.

But wise by that small part that ruled in him and handed down these commands, by its possession in turn within it of the knowledge of what is beneficial for each and for the whole, the community composed of the three.

By all means.

And again, was he not sober by reason of the friendship and concord of these same parts, when, namely, the ruling principle and its
d two subjects are at one in the belief that the reason ought to rule, and do not raise faction against it?

The virtue of soberness certainly, said he, is nothing else than this, whether in a city or an individual.

But surely, now, a man is just by that which and in the way we have so often described.

That is altogether necessary.

Well then, said I, has our idea of justice in any way lost the edge of its contour so as to look like anything else than precisely what it showed itself to be in the state?

I think not, he said.

We might, I said, completely confirm your reply and our own conviction thus, if anything in our minds still disputes our definition —by applying commonplace and vulgar tests to it.   e

What are these?

For example, if an answer were demanded to the question concerning that city and the man whose birth and breeding was in harmony with it, whether we believe that such a man, entrusted with a deposit of gold or silver, would withhold it and embezzle it, who do 443 you suppose would think that he would be more likely so to act than men of a different kind?

No one would, he said.

And would not he be far removed from sacrilege and theft and betrayal of comrades in private life or of the state in public?

He would.

And, moreover, he would not be in any way faithless either in the keeping of his oaths or in other agreements.

How could he?

Adultery, surely, and neglect of parents and of the due service of the gods would pertain to anyone rather than to such a man.

To anyone indeed, he said.

And is not the cause of this to be found in the fact that each of b the principles within him does its own work in the matter of ruling and being ruled?

Yes, that and nothing else.

Do you still, then, look for justice to be anything else than this potency which provides men and cities of this sort?

No, by heaven, he said, I do not.

Finished, then, is our dream and perfected—the surmise we spoke of, that, by some providence, at the very beginning of our foun- c dation of the state, we chanced to hit upon the original principle and a sort of type of justice.

Most assuredly.

It really was, it seems, Glaucon, which is why it helps, a sort of adumbration of justice, this principle that it is right for the cobbler by nature to cobble and occupy himself with nothing else, and the carpenter to practice carpentry, and similarly all others.

Clearly.

But the truth of the matter was, as it seems, that justice is indeed something of this kind, yet not in regard to the doing of one's d own business externally, but with regard to that which is within and in the true sense concerns one's self, and the things of one's self. It means that a man must not suffer the principles in his soul to do each the work of some other and interfere and meddle with one another, but that he should dispose well of what in the true sense of the word is properly his own, and having first attained to self-mastery and beautiful order within himself, and having harmonized these three principles, the notes or intervals of three terms quite literally the lowest, the highest, and the mean, and all others there may be be- e tween them, and having linked and bound all three together and made of himself a unit, one man instead of many, self-controlled and in unison, he should then and then only turn to practice if he find aught to do either in the getting of wealth or the tendance of the body or it may be in political action or private business—in all such doings believing and naming the just and honorable action to be that which preserves and helps to produce this condition of soul, and wisdom the science that presides over such conduct, and believing and naming 444 the unjust action to be that which ever tends to overthrow this spiritual constitution, and brutish ignorance to be the opinion that in turn presides over this.

What you say is entirely true, Socrates.

Well, said I, if we should affirm that we had found the just man and state and what justice really is in them, I think we should not be much mistaken.

No indeed, we should not, he said.

Shall we affirm it, then?

Let us so affirm.

So be it, then, said I. Next after this, I take it, we must consider injustice.

Obviously.

b   Must not this be a kind of civil war of these three principles, their meddlesomeness and interference with one another's functions, and the revolt of one part against the whole of the soul that it may hold therein a rule which does not belong to it, since its nature is such that it befits it to serve as a slave to the ruling principle? Something of this sort, I fancy, is what we shall say, and that the confusion of these principles and their straying from their proper course is injustice and licentiousness and cowardice and brutish ignorance and, in general, all turpitude.

Precisely this, he replied.

c   Then, said I, to act unjustly and be unjust and in turn to act justly—the meaning of all these terms becomes at once plain and clear, since injustice and justice are so.

How so?

Because, said I, these are in the soul what the healthful and the diseaseful are in the body; there is no difference.

In what respect? he said.

Healthful things surely engender health and diseaseful disease.

Yes.

Then does not doing just acts engender justice and unjust in- d justice?

Of necessity.

But to produce health is to establish the elements in a body in the natural relation of dominating and being dominated by one another, while to cause disease is to bring it about that one rules or is ruled by the other contrary to nature.

Yes, that is so.

And is it not likewise the production of justice in the soul to establish its principles in the natural relation of controlling and being controlled by one another, while injustice is to cause the one to rule or be ruled by the other contrary to nature?

Exactly so, he said.

Virtue, then, as it seems, would be a kind of health and beauty e and good condition of the soul, and vice would be disease, ugliness, and weakness.

It is so.

Then is it not also true that beautiful and honorable pursuits tend to the winning of virtue and the ugly to vice?

Of necessity.

And now at last, it seems, it remains for us to consider whether it 445 is profitable to do justice and practice honorable pursuits and be just, whether one is known to be such or not, or whether injustice profits, and to be unjust, if only a man escape punishment and is not bettered by chastisement.

Nay, Socrates, he said, I think that from this point on our inquiry becomes an absurdity—if, while life is admittedly intolerable with a ruined constitution of body even though accompanied by all the food and drink and wealth and power in the world, we are yet to be asked to suppose that, when the very nature and constitution of that whereby we live is disordered and corrupted, life is going to be worth b living, if a man can only do as he pleases, and pleases to do anything save that which will rid him of evil and injustice and make him possessed of justice and virtue—now that the two have been shown to be as we have described them.

Yes, it is absurd, said I, but nevertheless, now that we have won to this height, we must not grow weary in endeavoring to discover with the utmost possible clearness that these things are so.

That is the last thing in the world we must do, he said.

Come up here then, said I, that you may see how many are the c kinds of evil, I mean those that it is worth while to observe and distinguish.

I am with you, he said. Only do you say on.

And truly, said I, now that we have come to this height of argument I seem to see as from a point of outlook that there is one form of excellence, and that the forms of evil are infinite, yet that there are some four among them that it is worth while to take note of.

What do you mean? he said.

As many as are the varieties of political constitutions that constitute specific types, so many, it seems likely, are the characters of soul.

How many, pray?

d   There are five kinds of constitutions, said I, and five kinds of soul.

Tell me what they are, he said.

I tell you, said I, that one way of government would be the constitution that we have just expounded, but the names that might be applied to it are two. If one man of surpassing merit rose among the rulers, it would be denominated royalty; if more than one, aristocracy.

True, he said.

Well, then, I said, this is one of the forms I have in mind. For e neither would a number of such men, nor one if he arose among them, alter to any extent worth mentioning the laws of our city—if he preserved the breeding and the education that we have described.

It is not likely, he said.

BOOK V

449 To such a city, then, or constitution I apply the terms good and right —and to the corresponding kind of man—but the others I describe as bad and mistaken, if this one is right, in respect both to the administration of states and to the formation of the character of the individual soul, they falling under four forms of badness.

What are these? he said.

And I was going on to enumerate them in what seemed to me b the order of their evolution from one another, when Polemarchus—he sat at some little distance from Adimantus—stretched forth his hand, and, taking hold of his garment from above by the shoulder, drew the other toward him and, leaning forward himself, spoke a few words in his ear, of which we overheard nothing else save only this. Shall we let him off, then, he said, or what shall we do?

By no means, said Adimantus, now raising his voice.

What, pray, said I, is it that you are not letting off?

You, said he.

c   And for what special reason, pray? said I.

We think you are a slacker, he said, and are trying to cheat us out of a whole division, and that not the least, of the argument to avoid the trouble of expounding it, and expect to 'get away with it' by observing thus lightly that, of course, in respect to women and children it is obvious to everybody that the possessions of friends will be in common.

Well, isn't that right, Adimantus? I said.

Yes, said he, but this word 'right,' like other things, requires defining as to the way and manner of such a community. There might be many ways. Don't, then, pass over the one that you have in mind. d For we have long been lying in wait for you, expecting that you would say something both of the procreation of children and their bringing-up, and would explain the whole matter of the community of women and children of which you speak. We think that the right or wrong management of this makes a great difference, all the difference in the world, in the constitution of a state; so now, since you are beginning on another constitution before sufficiently defining this, we are firmly resolved, as you overheard, not to let you go till you have 450 expounded all this as fully as you did the rest.

Set me down, too, said Glaucon, as voting this ticket.

Surely, said Thrasymachus, you may consider it a joint resolution of us all, Socrates.

What a thing you have done, said I, in thus challenging me! What a huge debate you have started afresh, as it were, about this polity, in the supposed completion of which I was rejoicing, being only too glad to have it accepted as I then set it forth! You don't realize b what a swarm of arguments you are stirring up by this demand, which I foresaw and evaded to save us no end of trouble.

Well, said Thrasymachus, do you suppose this company has come here to prospect for gold and not to listen to discussions?

Yes, I said, in measure.

Nay, Socrates, said Glaucon, the measure of listening to such discussions is the whole of life for reasonable men. So don't consider us, and do not you yourself grow weary in explaining to us what we ask for, your views as to how this communion of wives and children c among our guardians will be managed, and also about the rearing of the children while still young in the interval between birth and formal schooling which is thought to be the most difficult part of education. Try, then, to tell us what must be the manner of it.

It is not an easy thing to expound, my dear fellow, said I, for even more than the provisions that precede it, it raises many doubts. For one might doubt whether what is proposed is possible and, even conceding the possibility, one might still be skeptical whether it is best. For which reason one, as it were, shrinks from touching on the matter d lest the theory be regarded as nothing but a 'wish-thought,' my dear friend.

Do not shrink, he said, for your hearers will not be inconsiderate nor distrustful nor hostile.

And I said, My good fellow, is that remark intended to encourage me?

It is, he said.

Well then, said I, it has just the contrary effect. For, if I were confident that I was speaking with knowledge, it would be an excellent
e encouragement. For there are both safety and boldness in speaking the truth with knowledge about our greatest and dearest concerns to those who are both wise and dear. But to speak when one doubts him-
451 self and is seeking while he talks, as I am doing, is a fearful and slippery venture. The fear is not of being laughed at, for that is childish, but, lest, missing the truth, I fall down and drag my friends with me in matters where it most imports not to stumble. So I salute Nemesis, Glaucon, in what I am about to say. For, indeed, I believe that involuntary homicide is a lesser fault than to mislead opinion about the honorable, the good, and the just. This is a risk that it is better
b to run with enemies than with friends, so that your encouragement is none.

And Glaucon, with a laugh, said, Nay, Socrates, if any false note in the argument does us any harm, we release you as in a homicide case, and warrant you pure of hand and no deceiver of us. So speak on with confidence.

Well, said I, he who is released in that case is counted pure as the law bids, and, presumably, if there, here too.

Speak on, then, he said, for all this objection.

We must return then, said I, and say now what perhaps ought to
c have been said in due sequence there. But maybe this way is right, that after the completion of the male drama we should in turn go through with the female, especially since you are so urgent.

For men, then, born and bred as we described, there is in my opinion no other right possession and use of children and women than that which accords with the start we gave them. Our endeavor, I believe, was to establish these men in our discourse as the guardians of a flock?

Yes.

d Let us preserve the analogy, then, and assign them a generation and breeding answering to it, and see if it suits us or not.

In what way? he said.

In this. Do we expect the females of watchdogs to join in guarding what the males guard and to hunt with them and share all their pursuits or do we expect the females to stay indoors as being incapacitated by the bearing and the breeding of the whelps while the males toil and have all the care of the flock?

e They have all things in common, he replied, except that we treat the females as weaker and the males as stronger.

Is it possible, then, said I, to employ any creature for the same ends as another if you do not assign it the same nurture and education?

It is not possible.

If, then, we are to use the women for the same things as the men, we must also teach them the same things. 452

Yes.

Now music together with gymnastics was the training we gave the men.

Yes.

Then we must assign these two arts to the women also and the offices of war and employ them in the same way.

It would seem likely from what you say, he replied.

Perhaps, then, said I, the contrast with present custom would make much in our proposals look ridiculous if our words are to be realized in fact.

Yes, indeed, he said.

What then, said I, is the funniest thing you note in them? Is it not obviously the women exercising unclad in the palaestra together with the men, not only the young, but even the older, like old men b in gymnasiums, when, though wrinkled and unpleasant to look at, they still persist in exercising?

Yes, on my word, he replied, it would seem ridiculous under present conditions.

Then, said I, since we have set out to speak our minds, we must not fear all the gibes with which the wits would greet so great a revolution, and the sort of things they would say about gymnastics and c culture, and most of all about the bearing of arms and the bestriding of horses.

You're right, he said.

But since we have begun we must go forward to the rough part of our law, after begging these fellows not to mind their own business but to be serious, and reminding them that it is not long since the Greeks thought it disgraceful and ridiculous, as most of the barbarians do now, for men to be seen naked. And when the practice of athletics began, first with the Cretans and then with the Lacedaemonians, it was open to the wits of that time to make fun of these d practices, don't you think so?

I do.

But when, I take it, experience showed that it is better to strip than to veil all things of this sort, then the laughter of the eyes faded away before that which reason revealed to be best, and this made it plain that he talks idly who deems anything else ridiculous but evil, and who tries to raise a laugh by looking to any other pattern of absurdity than that of folly and wrong or sets up any other standard of e the beautiful as a mark for his seriousness than the good.

Most assuredly, said he.

453 Then is not the first thing that we have to agree upon with regard to these proposals whether they are possible or not? And we must throw open the debate to anyone who wishes either in jest or in earnest to raise the question whether female human nature is capable of sharing with the male all tasks or none at all, or some but not others, and under which of these heads this business of war falls. Would not this be that best beginning which would naturally and proverbially lead to the best end?

Far the best, he said.

Shall we then conduct the debate with ourselves in behalf of those others so that the case of the other side may not be taken defenseless and go by default?

b Nothing hinders, he said.

Shall we say then in their behalf, There is no need, Socrates and Glaucon, of others disputing against you, for you yourselves at the beginning of the foundation of your city agreed that each one ought to mind as his own business the one thing for which he was fitted by nature? We did so agree, I think, certainly! Can it be denied then that there is by nature a great difference between men and women?

c Surely there is. Is it not fitting, then, that a different function should be appointed for each corresponding to this difference of nature? Certainly. How, then, can you deny that you are mistaken and in contradiction with yourselves when you turn around and affirm that the men and the women ought to do the same thing, though their natures are so far apart? Can you surprise me with an answer to that question?

Not easily on this sudden challenge, he replied, but I will and do beg you to lend your voice to the plea in our behalf, whatever it may be.

d These and many similar difficulties, Glaucon, said I, I foresaw and feared, and so shrank from touching on the law concerning the getting and breeding of women and children.

It does not seem an easy thing, by heaven, he said, no, by heaven.

No, it is not, said I, but the fact is that whether one tumbles into a little diving pool or plump into the great sea he swims all the same.

By all means.

Then we, too, must swim and try to escape out of the sea of argument in the hope that either some dolphin will take us on its back or some other desperate rescue.

e So it seems, he said.

Come then, consider, said I, if we can find a way out. We did agree that different natures should have differing pursuits and that the natures of men and women differ. And yet now we affirm that these differing natures should have the same pursuits. That is the indictment?

It is.

What a grand thing, Glaucon, said I, is the power of the art of 454
contradiction!

Why so?

Because, said I, many appear to me to fall into it even against
their wills, and to suppose that they are not wrangling but arguing,
owing to their inability to apply the proper divisions and distinctions
to the subject under consideration. They pursue purely verbal oppo-
sitions, practicing eristic, not dialectic on one another.

Yes, this does happen to many, he said, but does this observation
apply to us too at present?

Absolutely, said I. At any rate I am afraid that we are unawares b
slipping into contentiousness.

In what way?

The principle that natures not the same ought not to share in the
same pursuits we are following up most manfully and eristically in
the literal and verbal sense, but we did not delay to consider at all
what particular kind of diversity and identity of nature we had in
mind and with reference to what we were trying to define it when
we assigned different pursuits to different natures and the same to
the same.

No, we didn't consider that, he said.

Wherefore, by the same token, I said, we might ask ourselves c
whether the natures of bald and long-haired men are the same and
not, rather, the contrary. And, after agreeing that they were opposed,
we might, if the bald cobbled, forbid the long-haired to do so, or vice
versa.

That would be ridiculous, he said.

Would it be so, said I, for any other reason than that we did not
then posit likeness and difference of nature in any and every sense,
but were paying heed solely to the kind of diversity and homogeneity
that was pertinent to the pursuits themselves? We meant, for example, that a man and a woman who have a physician's mind have d
the same nature. Don't you think so?

I do.

But that a man physician and a man carpenter have different
natures?

Certainly, I suppose.

Similarly, then, said I, if it appears that the male and the female
sex have distinct qualifications for any arts or pursuits, we shall affirm that they ought to be assigned respectively to each. But if it appears that they differ only in just this respect that the female bears e
and the male begets, we shall say that no proof has yet been produced
that the woman differs from the man for our purposes, but we shall
continue to think that our guardians and their wives ought to follow
the same pursuits.

And rightly, said he.

Then, is it not the next thing to bid our opponent tell us precisely
455 for what art or pursuit concerned with the conduct of a state the
woman's nature differs from the man's?

That would be at any rate fair.

Perhaps, then, someone else, too, might say what you were saying
a while ago, that it is not easy to find a satisfactory answer on a sudden, but that with time for reflection there is no difficulty.

He might say that.

Shall we, then, beg the raiser of such objections to follow us, if
b we may perhaps prove able to make it plain to him that there is no
pursuit connected with the administration of a state that is peculiar to
woman?

By all means.

Come then, we shall say to him, answer our question. Was this
the basis of your distinction between the man naturally gifted for
anything and the one not so gifted—that the one learned easily, the
other with difficulty, that the one with slight instruction could discover much for himself in the matter studied, but the other, after
much instruction and drill, could not even remember what he had
learned, and that the bodily faculties of the one adequately served
his mind, while, for the other, the body was a hindrance? Were there
c any other points than these by which you distinguish the well-en-
dowed man in every subject and the poorly endowed?

No one, said he, will be able to name any others.

Do you know, then, of anything practiced by mankind in which
the masculine sex does not surpass the female on all these points?
Must we make a long story of it by alleging weaving and the watching of pancakes and the boiling pot, whereon the sex plumes itself
d and wherein its defeat will expose it to most laughter?

You are right, he said, that the one sex is far surpassed by the
other in everything, one may say. Many women, it is true, are better
than many men in many things, but broadly speaking, it is as you say.

Then there is no pursuit of the administrators of a state that belongs to a woman because she is a woman or to a man because he is a
man. But the natural capacities are distributed alike among both crea-
e tures, and women naturally share in all pursuits and men in all—yet
for all the woman is weaker than the man.

Assuredly.

Shall we, then, assign them all to men and nothing to women?

How could we?

We shall rather, I take it, say that one woman has the nature of
a physician and another not, and one is by nature musical, and another unmusical?

Surely.

Can we, then, deny that one woman is naturally athletic and 456
warlike and another unwarlike and averse to gymnastics?

I think not.

And again, one a lover, another a hater, of wisdom? And one
high-spirited, and the other lacking spirit?

That also is true.

Then it is likewise true that one woman has the qualities of a
guardian and another not. Were not these the natural qualities of the
men also whom we selected for guardians?

They were.

The women and the men, then, have the same nature in respect
to the guardianship of the state, save in so far as the one is weaker, the
other stronger.

Apparently.

Women of this kind, then, must be selected to cohabit with men b
of this kind and to serve with them as guardians since they are capable of it and akin by nature.

By all means.

And to the same natures must we not assign the same pursuits?

The same.

We come round, then, to our previous statement, and agree that it
does not run counter to nature to assign music and gymnastics to the
wives of the guardians.

By all means.

Our legislation, then, was not impracticable or utopian, since the c
law we proposed accorded with nature. Rather, the other way of doing
things, prevalent today, proves, as it seems, unnatural.

Apparently.

The object of our inquiry was the possibility and the desirability
of what we were proposing?

It was.

That it is possible has been admitted.

Yes.

The next point to be agreed upon is that it is the best way.

Obviously.

For the production of a female guardian, then, our education
will not be one thing for men and another for women, especially since
the nature which we hand over to it is the same.   d

There will be no difference.

How are you minded, now, in this matter?

In what?

In the matter of supposing some men to be better and some
worse, or do you think them all alike?

By no means.

In the city, then, that we are founding, which do you think will prove the better men, the guardians receiving the education which we have described or the cobblers educated by the art of cobbling?

An absurd question, he said.

e   I understand, said I, and are not these the best of all the citizens?

By far.

And will not these women be the best of all the women?

They, too, by far.

Is there anything better for a state than the generation in it of the best possible women and men?

There is not.

457   And this, music and gymnastics applied as we described will effect.

Surely.

Then the institution we proposed is not only possible but the best for the state.

That is so.

The women of the guardians, then, must strip, since they will be clothed with virtue as a garment, and must take their part with the men in war and the other duties of civic guardianship and have no other occupation. But in these very duties lighter tasks must be assigned to the women than to the men because of their weakness as a

b   class. But the man who ridicules unclad women, exercising because it is best that they should, 'plucks the unripe fruit' of laughter and does not know, it appears, the end of his laughter nor what he would be at. For the fairest thing that is said or ever will be said is this, that the helpful is fair and the harmful foul.

Assuredly.

In this matter, then, of the regulation of women, we may say

c   that we have surmounted one of the waves of our paradox and have not been quite swept away by it in ordaining that our guardians and female guardians must have all pursuits in common, but that in some sort the argument concurs with itself in the assurance that what it proposes is both possible and beneficial.

It is no slight wave that you are thus escaping.

You will not think it a great one, I said, when you have seen the one that follows.

Say on then and show me, said he.

This, said I, and all that precedes has for its sequel, in my opinion, the following law.

What?

d   That these women shall all be common to all these men, and that none shall cohabit with any privately, and that the children shall be common, and that no parent shall know its own offspring nor any child its parent.

This is a far bigger paradox than the other, and provokes more distrust as to its possibility and its utility.

I presume, said I, that there would be no debate about its utility, no denial that the community of women and children would be the greatest good, supposing it possible. But I take it that its possibility or the contrary would be the chief topic of contention.

Both, he said, would be right sharply debated.   e

You mean, said I, that I have to meet a coalition of arguments. But I expected to escape from one of them, and that if you agreed that the thing was beneficial, it would remain for me to speak only of its feasibility.

You have not escaped detection, he said, in your attempted flight, but you must render an account of both.

I must pay the penalty, I said, yet do me this much grace. Permit me to take a holiday, just as men of lazy minds are wont to feast 458 themselves on their own thoughts when they walk alone. Such persons, without waiting to discover how their desires may be realized, dismiss that topic to save themselves the labor of deliberating about possibilities and impossibilities, assume their wish fulfilled, and proceed to work out the details in imagination, and take pleasure in portraying what they will do when it is realized, thus making still more idle a mind that is idle without that. I too now succumb to this b weakness and desire to postpone and examine later the question of feasibility, but will at present assume that, and will, with your permission, inquire how the rulers will work out the details in practice, and try to show that nothing could be more beneficial to the state and its guardians than the effective operation of our plan. This is what I would try to consider first together with you, and thereafter the other topic, if you allow it.

I do allow it, he said. Proceed with the inquiry.

I think, then, said I, that the rulers, if they are to deserve that name, and their helpers likewise, will, the one, be willing to accept c orders, and the other, to give them, in some things obeying our laws, and imitating them in others which we leave to their discretion.

Presumably.

You, then, the lawgiver, I said, have picked these men and similarly will select to give over to them women as nearly as possible of the same nature. And they, having houses and meals in common, and no private possessions of that kind, will dwell together, and d being commingled in gymnastics and in all their life and education, will be conducted by innate necessity to sexual union. Is not what I say a necessary consequence?

Not by the necessities of geometry, he said, but by those of love, which are perhaps keener and more potent than the other to persuade and constrain the multitude.

They are, indeed, I said. But next, Glaucon, disorder and promiscuity in these unions or in anything else they do would be an unhallowed thing in a happy state and the rulers will not suffer it.   e

It would not be right, he said.

Obviously, then, we must arrange marriages, sacramental so far as may be. And the most sacred marriages would be those that were most beneficial.

By all means.

459   How, then, would the greatest benefit result? Tell me this, Glaucon. I see that you have in your house hunting dogs and a number of pedigreed cocks. Have you ever considered something about their unions and procreations?

What? he said.

In the first place, I said, among these themselves, although they are a select breed, do not some prove better than the rest?

They do.

Do you then breed from all indiscriminately, or are you careful to breed from the best?

From the best.

b   And, again, do you breed from the youngest or the oldest, or, so far as may be, from those in their prime?

From those in their prime.

And if they are not thus bred, you expect, do you not, that your birds' breed and hounds will greatly degenerate?

I do, he said.

And what of horses and other animals? I said. Is it otherwise with them?

It would be strange if it were, said he.

Gracious, said I, dear friend, how imperative, then, is our need of the highest skill in our rulers, if the principle holds also for mankind.

c   Well, it does, he said, but what of it?

This, said I, that they will have to employ many of those drugs of which we were speaking. We thought that an inferior physician sufficed for bodies that do not need drugs but yield to diet and regimen. But when it is necessary to prescribe drugs we know that a more enterprising and venturesome physician is required.

True, but what is the pertinency?

This, said I. It seems likely that our rulers will have to make considerable use of falsehood and deception for the benefit of their sub-
d   jects. We said, I believe, that the use of that sort of thing was in the category of medicine.

And that was right, he said.

In our marriages, then, and the procreation of children, it seems there will be no slight need of this kind of 'right.'

How so?

It follows from our former admissions, I said, that the best men must cohabit with the best women in as many cases as possible and the worst with the worst in the fewest, and that the offspring of the

one must be reared and that of the other not, if the flock is to be as per- e
fect as possible. And the way in which all this is brought to pass
must be unknown to any but the rulers, if, again, the herd of guardians is to be as free as possible from dissension.

Most true, he said.

We shall, then, have to ordain certain festivals and sacrifices, in
which we shall bring together the brides and the bridegrooms, and
our poets must compose hymns suitable to the marriages that then 460
take place. But the number of the marriages we will leave to the discretion of the rulers, that they may keep the number of the citizens
as nearly as may be the same, taking into account wars and diseases
and all such considerations, and that, so far as possible, our city may
not grow too great or too small.

Right, he said.

Certain ingenious lots, then, I suppose, must be devised so that
the inferior man at each conjugation may blame chance and not the
rulers.

Yes, indeed, he said.

And on the young men, surely, who excel in war and other pur- b
suits we must bestow honors and prizes, and, in particular, the opportunity of more frequent intercourse with the women, which will at
the same time be a plausible pretext for having them beget as many of
the children as possible.

Right.

And the children thus born will be taken over by the officials appointed for this, men or women or both, since, I take it, the official
posts too are common to women and men.

Yes.

The offspring of the good, I suppose, they will take to the pen or c
crèche, to certain nurses who live apart in a quarter of the city, but
the offspring of the inferior, and any of those of the other sort who are
born defective, they will properly dispose of in secret, so that no one
will know what has become of them.

That is the condition, he said, of preserving the purity of the
guardians' breed.

They will also supervise the nursing of the children, conducting
the mothers to the pen when their breasts are full, but employing
every device to prevent anyone from recognizing her own infant. And
they will provide others who have milk if the mothers are insufficient. d
But they will take care that the mothers themselves shall not suckle
too long, and the trouble of wakeful nights and similar burdens
they will devolve upon the nurses, wet and dry.

You are making maternity a soft job for the women of the
guardians.

It ought to be, said I, but let us pursue our design. We said that
the offspring should come from parents in their prime.

True.

e   Do you agree that the period of the prime may be fairly estimated at twenty years for a woman and thirty for a man?

How do you reckon it? he said.

The women, I said, beginning at the age of twenty, shall bear for the state to the age of forty, and the man shall beget for the state from the time he passes his prime in swiftness in running to the age of fifty-five.

461   That is, he said, the maturity and prime for both of body and mind.

Then, if anyone older or younger than the prescribed age meddles with procreation for the state, we shall say that his error is an impiety and an injustice, since he is begetting for the city a child whose birth, if it escapes discovery, will not be attended by the sacrifices and the prayers which the priests and priestesses and the entire city prefer at the ceremonial marriages, that ever better offspring may spring from good sires and from fathers helpful to the state sons more
b   helpful still. But this child will be born in darkness and conceived in foul incontinence.

Right, he said.

And the same rule will apply, I said, if any of those still within the age of procreation goes in to a woman of that age with whom the ruler has not paired him. We shall say that he is imposing on the state a baseborn, uncertified, and unhallowed child.

Most rightly, he said.

But when, I take it, the men and the women have passed the age of lawful procreation, we shall leave the men free to form such rela-
c   tions with whomsoever they please, except daughter and mother and their direct descendants and ascendants, and likewise the women, save with son and father, and so on, first admonishing them prefera- bly not even to bring to light anything whatever thus conceived, but if they are unable to prevent a birth to dispose of it on the understand- ing that we cannot rear such an offspring.

All that sounds reasonable, he said, but how are they to dis-
d   tinguish one another's fathers and daughters, and the other degrees of kin that you have just mentioned?

They won't, said I, except that a man will call all male offspring born in the tenth and in the seventh month after he became a bride- groom his sons, and all female, daughters, and they will call him fa- ther. And, similarly, he will call their offspring his grandchildren and they will call his group grandfathers and grandmothers. And all children born in the period in which their fathers and mothers were procreating will regard one another as brothers and sisters. This
e   will suffice for the prohibitions of intercourse of which we just now spoke. But the law will allow brothers and sisters to cohabit if the lot so falls out and the Delphic oracle approves.

Quite right, said he.

This, then, Glaucon, is the manner of the community of wives and children among the guardians. That it is consistent with the rest of our polity and by far the best way is the next point that we must get confirmed by the argument. Is not that so?

It is, indeed, he said.   462

Is not the logical first step toward such an agreement to ask ourselves what we could name as the greatest good for the constitution of a state and the proper aim of a lawgiver in his legislation, and what would be the greatest evil, and then to consider whether the proposals we have just set forth fit into the footprints of the good and do not suit those of the evil?

By all means, he said.

Do we know of any greater evil for a state than the thing that distracts it and makes it many instead of one, or a greater good than b that which binds it together and makes it one?

We do not.

Is not, then, the community of pleasure and pain the tie that binds, when, so far as may be, all the citizens rejoice and grieve alike at the same births and deaths?

By all means, he said.

But the individualization of these feelings is a dissolvent, when some grieve exceedingly and others rejoice at the same happenings to the city and its inhabitants?   c

Of course.

And the chief cause of this is when the citizens do not utter in unison such words as 'mine' and 'not mine,' and similarly with regard to the word 'alien'?

Precisely so.

That city, then, is best ordered in which the greatest number use the expression 'mine' and 'not mine' of the same things in the same way.

Much the best.

And the city whose state is most like that of an individual man. For example, if the finger of one of us is wounded, the entire community of bodily connections stretching to the soul for 'integra- d tion' with the dominant part is made aware, and all of it feels the pain as a whole, though it is a part that suffers, and that is how we come to say that the man has a pain in his finger. And for any other member of the man the same statement holds, alike for a part that labors in pain or is eased by pleasure.

The same, he said, and, to return to your question, the best-governed state most nearly resembles such an organism.

That is the kind of a state, then, I presume, that, when anyone of the citizens suffers aught of good or evil, will be most likely to speak e of the part that suffers as its own and will share the pleasure or the pain as a whole.

Inevitably, he said, if it is well governed.

It is time, I said, to return to our city and observe whether it, rather than any other, embodies the qualities agreed upon in our argument.

We must, he said.

463   Well, then, there are to be found in other cities rulers and the people as in our city, are there not?

There are.

Will not all these address one another as fellow citizens?

Of course.

But in addition to citizens, what do the people in other states call their rulers?

In most cities, masters, in democratic cities, just this—rulers.

But what of the people in our city. In addition to citizens, what do they call their rulers?

b   Saviors and helpers, he said.

And what term do these apply to the people?

Payers of their wage and supporters.

And how do the rulers in other states denominate the populace?

Slaves, he said.

And how do the rulers describe one another?

Corulers, he said.

And ours?

Coguardians.

Can you tell me whether any of the rulers in other states would speak of some of their corulers as 'belonging' and others as outsiders?

Yes, many would.

And such a one thinks and speaks of the one that 'belongs' as his
c own, doesn't he, and of the outsider as not his own?

That is so.

But what of your guardians? Could any of them think or speak of his coguardian as an outsider?

By no means, he said, for no matter whom he meets, he will feel that he is meeting a brother, a sister, a father, a mother, a son, a daughter, or the offspring or forebears of these.

Excellent, said I, but tell me this further. Will it be merely the names of this kinship that you have prescribed for them or must all
d their actions conform to the names in all customary observance toward fathers and in awe and care and obedience for parents, if they look for the favor of either gods or men, since any other behavior would be neither just nor pious? Shall these be the unanimous oracular voices that they hear from all the people, or shall some other kind of teaching beset the ears of your children from their birth, both concerning what is due to those who are pointed out as their fathers and to their other kin?

e   These, he said, for it would be absurd for them merely to pronounce with their lips the names of kinship without the deeds.

Then, in this city more than in any other, when one citizen fares well or ill, men will pronounce in unison the word of which we spoke, It is *mine* that does well, or, It is *mine* that does ill.

That is most true, he said.

And did we not say that this conviction and way of speech brings 464 with it a community in pleasures and pains?

And rightly, too.

Then these citizens, above all others, will have one and the same thing in common which they will name *mine,* and by virtue of this communion they will have their pleasures and pains in common.

Quite so.

And is not the cause of this, besides the general constitution of the state, the community of wives and children among the guardians?

It will certainly be the chief cause, he said.

But we further agreed that this unity is the greatest blessing for b a state, and we compared a well-governed state to the human body in its relation to the pleasure and pain of its parts.

And we were right in so agreeing.

Then it is the greatest blessing for a state of which the community of women and children among the helpers has been shown to be the cause.

Quite so, he said.

And this is consistent with what we said before. For we said, I believe, that these helpers must not possess houses of their own or land or any other property, but that they should receive from the c other citizens for their support the wage of their guardianship and all spend it in common. That was the condition of their being true guardians.

Right, he said.

Is it not true, then, as I am trying to say, that those former and these present prescriptions tend to make them still more truly guardians and prevent them from distracting the city by referring *mine* not to the same but to different things, one man dragging off to his own house anything he is able to acquire apart from the rest, and another doing the same to his own separate house, and having women and d children apart, thus introducing into the state the pleasures and pains of individuals? They should all rather, we said, share one conviction about their own, tend to one goal, and so far as practicable have one experience of pleasure and pain.

By all means, he said.

Then will not lawsuits and accusations against one another vanish, one may say, from among them, because they have nothing in private possession but their bodies, but all else in common? So that we can count on their being free from the dissensions that arise among men from the possession of property, children, and kin.   e

They will necessarily be quit of these, he said.

And again, there could not rightly arise among them any lawsuit for assault or bodily injury. For as between agefellows we shall say that self-defense is honorable and just, thereby compelling them to keep their bodies in condition.

Right, he said.

465 And there will be the further advantage in such a law that an angry man, satisfying his anger in such wise, would be less likely to carry the quarrel to further extremes.

Assuredly.

As for an older man, he will always have the charge of ruling and chastising the younger.

Obviously.

Again, it is plain that the young man, except by command of the rulers, will probably not do violence to an elder or strike him, or, I take it, dishonor him in any other way. There being the two competent guardians to prevent that, fear and awe, awe restraining him from b laying hands on one who may be his parent, and fear in that the others will rush to the aid of the sufferer, some as sons, some as brothers, some as fathers.

That is the way it works out, he said.

Then in all cases the laws will leave these men to dwell in peace together.

Great peace.

And if these are free from dissensions among themselves, there is no fear that the rest of the city will ever start faction against them or with one another.

No, there is not.

But I hesitate, so unseemly are they, even to mention the pettiest c troubles of which they would be rid, the flatterings of the rich, the embarrassments and pains of the poor in the bringing-up of their children and the procuring of money for the necessities of life for their households, the borrowings, the repudiations, all the devices with which they acquire what they deposit with wives and servitors to husband, and all the indignities that they endure in such matters, which are obvious and ignoble and not deserving of mention.

d Even a blind man can see these, he said.

From all these, then, they will be finally free, and they will live a happier life than that men count most happy, the life of the victors at Olympia.

How so?

The things for which those are felicitated are a small part of what is secured for these. Their victory is fairer and their public support more complete. For the prize of victory that they win is the salvation of the entire state, the fillet that binds their brows is the public e support of themselves and their children—they receive honor from the city while they live and when they die a worthy burial.

A fair guerdon, indeed, he said.

Do you recall, said I, that in the preceding argument the objection of somebody or other rebuked us for not making our guardians 466 happy, since, though it was in their power to have everything of the citizens, they had nothing, and we, I believe, replied that this was a consideration to which we would return if occasion offered, but that at present we were making our guardians guardians and the city as a whole as happy as possible, and that we were not modeling our ideal of happiness with reference to any one class?

I do remember, he said.

Well then, since now the life of our helpers has been shown to be far fairer and better than that of the victors at Olympia, need we compare it with the life of cobblers and other craftsmen and farmers? b

I think not, he said.

But further, we may fairly repeat what I was saying then also, that if the guardian shall strive for a kind of happiness that will unmake him as a guardian and shall not be content with the way of life that is so moderate and secure and, as we affirm, the best, but if some senseless and childish opinion about happiness shall beset him and impel him to use his power to appropriate everything in the city for himself, then he will find out that Hesiod was indeed wise, who said c that the half was in some sort more than the whole.

If he accepts my counsel, he said, he will abide in this way of life.

You accept, then, as we have described it, this partnership of the women with our men in the matter of education and children and the guardianship of the other citizens, and you admit that both within the city and when they go forth to war they ought to keep guard together and hunt together as it were like hounds, and have all things in d every way, so far as possible, in common, and that so doing they will do what is for the best and nothing that is contrary to female human nature in comparison with male or to their natural fellowship with one another.

I do admit it, he said.

Then, I said, is not the thing that it remains to determine this, whether, namely, it is possible for such a community to be brought about among men as it is in the other animals, and in what way it is possible?

You have anticipated, he said, the point I was about to raise.

For as for their wars, I said, the manner in which they will con- e duct them is too obvious for discussion.

How so? said he.

It is obvious that they will march out together, and, what is more, will conduct their children to war when they are sturdy, in order that, like the children of other craftsmen, they may observe the processes of which they must be masters in their maturity, and in addition to looking on they must assist and minister in all the business

467 of war and serve their fathers and mothers. Or have you never noticed the practice in the arts, how for example the sons of potters look on as helpers a long time before they put their hands to the clay?

They do, indeed.

Should these then be more concerned than our guardians to train the children by observation and experience of what is to be their proper business?

That would be ridiculous, he said.

But, further, when it comes to fighting, every creature will do bet-
b ter in the presence of its offspring?

That is so, but the risk, Socrates, is not slight, in the event of disasters such as may happen in war, that, losing their children as well as themselves, they make it impossible for the remnant of the state to recover.

What you say is true, I replied, but, in the first place, is it your idea that the one thing for which we must provide is the avoidance of all danger?

By no means.

c   And, if they must incur danger, should it not be for something in which success will make them better?

Clearly.

Do you think it makes a slight difference and not worth some risk whether men who are to be warriors do or do not observe war as boys?

No, it makes a great difference for the purpose of which you speak.

Starting, then, from this assumption that we are to make the boys spectators of war, we must further contrive security for them and all will be well, will it not?

Yes.

To begin with, then, said I, will not the fathers be, humanly speaking, not ignorant of war and shrewd judges of which campaigns
d are hazardous and which not?

Presumably, he said.

They will take the boys with them to the one and avoid the others?
Rightly.

And for officers, I presume, said I, they will put in charge of them not those who are good for nothing else but men who by age and experience are qualified to serve at once as leaders and as caretakers of children.

Yes, that would be the proper way.

Still, we may object, it is the unexpected that happens to many in many cases.

Yes, indeed.

To provide against such chances, then, we must wing the chil-

dren from the start so that if need arises they may fly away and
escape.

What do you mean? he said.   e

We must mount them when very young, said I, and first have
them taught to ride, and then conduct them to the scene of war, not
on mettlesome war steeds, but on the swiftest and gentlest horses
possible, for thus they will have the best view of their own future business and also, if need arises, will most securely escape to safety in the
train of elder guides.

I think you are right, he said.

But now what of the conduct of war? What should be the atti-   468
tude of the soldiers to one another and the enemy? Am I right in my
notions or not?

Tell me what notions, he said.

Any one of them who deserts his post, or flings away his weapons,
or is guilty of any similar act of cowardice, should be reduced to
the artisan or farmer class, should he not?

By all means.

And anyone who is taken alive by the enemy we will make a present of to his captors, shall we not, to deal with their catch as they
please?

Quite so.   .   b

And don't you agree that the one who wins the prize of valor and
distinguishes himself shall first be crowned by his fellows in the campaign, by the lads and boys each in turn?

I do.

And be greeted with the right hand?

That, too.

But I presume you wouldn't go as far as this?

What?

That he should kiss and be kissed by everyone?   c

By all means, he said, and I add to the law the provision that during that campaign none whom he wishes to kiss be allowed to refuse,
so that if one is in love with anyone, male or female, he may be the
more eager to win the prize.

Excellent, said I, and we have already said that the opportunity of
marriage will be more readily provided for the good man, and that he
will be more frequently selected than the others for participation in
that sort of thing, in order that as many children as possible may be
born from such stock.

We have, he replied.

But, furthermore, we may cite Homer too for the justice of honoring in such ways the valiant among our youth. For Homer says that d
Ajax, who had distinguished himself in the war, was honored with the
long chine, assuming that the most fitting meed for a brave man in

the prime of his youth is that from which both honor and strength will accrue to him.

Most rightly, he said.

We will then, said I, take Homer as our guide in this at least. We, too, at sacrifices and on other like occasions, will reward the good so far as they have proved themselves good with hymns and the other
e privileges of which we have just spoken, and also with 'seats of honor and meat and full cups,'[41] so as to combine physical training with honor for the good, both men and women.

Nothing could be better, he said.

Very well, and of those who die on campaign, if anyone's death has been especially glorious, shall we not, to begin with, affirm that he belongs to the golden race?

By all means.

And shall we not believe Hesiod who tells us that when men of this race die, so it is that they become

469   Hallowed spirits dwelling on earth, averters of evil,
        Guardians watchful and good of articulate-speaking mortals?[42]

We certainly shall believe him.

We will inquire of Apollo, then, how and with what distinction we are to bury men of more than human, of divine, qualities, and deal with them according to his response.

How can we do otherwise?

And ever after we will bestow on their graves the tendance and
b worship paid to spirits divine. And we will practice the same observance when any who have been adjudged exceptionally good in the ordinary course of life die of old age or otherwise?

That will surely be right, he said.

But again, how will our soldiers conduct themselves toward enemies?

In what respect?

First, in the matter of making slaves of the defeated, do you think it right for Greeks to reduce Greek cities to slavery, or rather that, so far as they are able, they should not suffer any other city to
c do so, but should accustom Greeks to spare Greeks, foreseeing the danger of enslavement by the barbarians?

Sparing them is wholly and altogether the better, said he.

They are not, then, themselves to own Greek slaves, either, and they should advise the other Greeks not to?

By all means, he said. At any rate in that way they would be more likely to turn against the barbarians and keep their hands from one another.

And how about stripping the dead after victory of anything except

---

[41] *Iliad* 8.162.   [42] *Works and Days* 121 sq.

their weapons—is that well? Does it not furnish a pretext to cowards not to advance on the living foe, as if they were doing something d needful when poking about the dead? Has not this snatching at the spoils ere now destroyed many an army?

Yes, indeed.

And don't you think it illiberal and greedy to plunder a corpse, and is it not the mark of a womanish and petty spirit to deem the body of the dead an enemy when the real foeman has flown away and left behind only the instrument with which he fought? Do you see any difference between such conduct and that of the dogs who snarl at the e stones that hit them but don't touch the thrower?

Not the slightest.

We must abandon, then, the plundering of corpses and the refusal to permit their burial.

By heaven, we certainly must, he said.

And again, we will not take weapons to the temples for dedicatory offerings, especially the weapons of Greeks, if we are at all concerned 470 to preserve friendly relations with the other Greeks. Rather we shall fear that there is pollution in bringing such offerings to the temples from our kind unless in a case where the god bids otherwise.

Most rightly, he said.

And in the matter of devastating the land of Greeks and burning their houses, how will your soldiers deal with their enemies? I would gladly hear your opinion of that.

In my view, said I, they ought to do neither, but confine them- b selves to taking away the annual harvest. Shall I tell you why?

Do.

In my opinion, just as we have the two terms, war and faction, so there are also two things, distinguished by two differentiae. The two things I mean are the friendly and kindred on the one hand and the alien and foreign on the other. Now the term employed for the hostility of the friendly is faction, and for that of the alien is war.

What you say is in nothing beside the mark, he replied.

Consider, then, if this goes to the mark. I affirm that the Hellenic c race is friendly to itself and akin, and foreign and alien to the barbarian.

Rightly, he said.

We shall then say that Greeks fight and wage war with barbarians, and barbarians with Greeks, and are enemies by nature, and that war is the fit name for this enmity and hatred. Greeks, however, we shall say, are still by nature the friends of Greeks when they act in this way, but that Greece is sick in that case and divided by faction, and faction is the name we must give to that enmity.   d

I will allow you that habit of speech, he said.

Then observe, said I, that when anything of this sort occurs in faction, as the word is now used, and a state is divided against itself,

if either party devastates the land and burns the houses of the other such factional strife is thought to be an accursed thing and neither party to be true patriots. Otherwise, they would never have endured thus to outrage their nurse and mother. But the moderate and reasonable thing is thought to be that the victors shall take away the crops of the vanquished, but that their temper shall be that of men who ex-
e pect to be reconciled and not always to wage war.

That way of feeling, he said, is far less savage than the other.

Well, then, said I, is not the city that you are founding to be a Greek city?

It must be, he said.

Will they then not be good and gentle?

Indeed they will.

And won't they be philhellenes, lovers of Greeks, and will they not regard all Greece as their own and not renounce their part in the holy places common to all Greeks?

Most certainly.

Will they not then regard any difference with Greeks who are their own people as a form of faction and refuse even to speak of it as war?

Most certainly.

471   And they will conduct their quarrels always looking forward to a reconciliation?

By all means.

They will correct them, then, for their own good, not chastising them with a view to their enslavement or their destruction, but acting as correctors, not as enemies.

They will, he said.

They will not, being Greeks, ravage Greek territory nor burn habitations, and they will not admit that in any city all the population are their enemies, men, women, and children, but will say that only a few at any time are their foes, those, namely, who are to blame for
b the quarrel. And on all these considerations they will not be willing to lay waste the soil, since the majority are their friends, nor to destroy the houses, but will carry the conflict only to the point of compelling the guilty to do justice by the pressure of the suffering of the innocent.

I, he said, agree that our citizens ought to deal with their Greek opponents on this wise, while treating barbarians as Greeks now treat Greeks.

Shall we lay down this law also, then, for our guardians, that
c they are not to lay waste the land or burn the houses?

Let us so decree, he said, and assume that this and our preceding prescriptions are right. But I fear, Socrates, that, if you are allowed to go on in this fashion, you will never get to speak of the matter you put aside in order to say all this, namely, the possibility of such a polity coming into existence, and the way in which it could be brought to pass. I too am ready to admit that if it could be realized everything would be lovely for the state that had it, and I will add what you passed by, that they would also be most successful in war because they would be least likely to desert one another, knowing and address- d ing each other by the names of brothers, fathers, sons. And if the females should also join in their campaigns, whether in the ranks or marshaled behind to intimidate the enemy, or as reserves in case of need, I recognize that all this too would make them irresistible. And at home, also, I observe all the benefits that you omit to mention. But, taking it for granted that I concede these and countless other advantages, consequent on the realization of this polity, don't labor that e point further, but let us at once proceed to try to convince ourselves of just this, that it is possible and how it is possible, dismissing everything else.

This is a sudden assault, indeed, said I, that you have made on 472 my theory, without any regard for my natural hesitation. Perhaps you don't realize that when I have hardly escaped the first two waves, you are now rolling up against me the 'great third wave' of paradox, the worst of all. When you have seen and heard that, you will be very ready to be lenient, recognizing that I had good reason after all for shrinking and fearing to enter upon the discussion of so paradoxical a notion.

The more such excuses you offer, he said, the less you will be released by us from telling in what way the realization of this polity is b possible. Speak on, then, and do not put us off.

The first thing to recall, then, I said, is that it was the inquiry into the nature of justice and injustice that brought us to this pass.

Yes, but what of it? he said.

Oh, nothing, I replied, only this. If we do discover what justice is, are we to demand that the just man shall differ from it in no respect, but shall conform in every way to the ideal? Or will it suffice us if he approximate to it as nearly as possible and partake of it more than others? c

That will content us, he said.

A pattern, then, said I, was what we wanted when we were inquiring into the nature of ideal justice and asking what would be the character of the perfectly just man, supposing him to exist, and, likewise, in regard to injustice and the completely unjust man. We wished to fix our eyes upon them as types and models, so that whatever we discerned in them of happiness or the reverse would necessarily apply to ourselves in the sense that whosoever is likest them will have the allotment most like to theirs. Our purpose was not to demonstrate the possibility of the realization of these ideals. d

In that, he said, you speak truly.

Do you think, then, that he would be any the less a good painter, who, after portraying a pattern of the ideally beautiful man and omitting no touch required for the perfection of the picture, should not be able to prove that it is actually possible for such a man to exist?

Not I, by Zeus, he said.

Then were not we, as we say, trying to create in words the pattern of a good state?

e   Certainly.

Do you think, then, that our words are any the less well spoken if we find ourselves unable to prove that it is possible for a state to be governed in accordance with our words?

Of course not, he said.

That, then, said I, is the truth of the matter. But if, to please you, we must do our best to show how most probably and in what respect these things would be most nearly realized, again, with a view to such a demonstration, grant me the same point.

What?

473   Is it possible for anything to be realized in deed as it is spoken in word, or is it the nature of things that action should partake of exact truth less than speech, even if some deny it? Do you admit it or not?

I do, he said.

Then don't insist, said I, that I must exhibit as realized in action precisely what we expounded in words. But if we can discover how a state might be constituted most nearly answering to our description, you must say that we have discovered that possibility of

b   realization which you demanded. Will you not be content if you get this? I for my part would.

And I too, he said.

Next, it seems, we must try to discover and point out what it is that is now badly managed in our cities, and that prevents them from being so governed, and what is the smallest change that would bring a state to this manner of government, preferably a change in one thing, if not, then in two, and, failing that, the fewest possible in number and the slightest in potency.

c   By all means, he said.

There is one change, then, said I, which I think that we can show would bring about the desired transformation. It is not a slight or an easy thing but it is possible.

What is that? said he.

I am on the very verge, said I, of what we likened to the greatest wave of paradox. But say it I will, even if, to keep the figure, it is likely to wash us away on billows of laughter and scorn. Listen.

I am all attention, he said.

Unless, said I, either philosophers become kings in our states or

d   those whom we now call our kings and rulers take to the pursuit of philosophy seriously and adequately, and there is a conjunction of these two things, political power and philosophical intelligence, while

the motley horde of the natures who at present pursue either apart
from the other are compulsorily excluded, there can be no cessation of
troubles, dear Glaucon, for our states, nor, I fancy, for the human race e
either. Nor, until this happens, will this constitution which we have
been expounding in theory ever be put into practice within the
limits of possibility and see the light of the sun. But this is the thing
that has made me so long shrink from speaking out, because I saw that
it would be a very paradoxical saying. For it is not easy to see that
there is no other way of happiness either for private or public life.

Whereupon he said, Socrates, after hurling at us such an utterance and statement as that, you must expect to be attacked by a great
multitude of our men of light and leading, who forthwith will, so to
speak, cast off their garments and strip and, snatching the first 474
weapon that comes to hand, rush at you with might and main, prepared to do dreadful deeds. And if you don't find words to defend yourself against them, and escape their assault, then to be scorned
and flouted will in very truth be the penalty you will have to pay.

And isn't it you, said I, that have brought this upon me and are to
blame?

And a good thing, too, said he, but I won't let you down, and will
defend you with what I can. I can do so with my good will and my
encouragement, and perhaps I might answer your questions more
suitably than another. So, with such an aid to back you, try to make it b
plain to the doubters that the truth is as you say.

I must try, I replied, since you proffer so strong an alliance. I
think it requisite, then, if we are to escape the assailants you speak
of, that we should define for them whom we mean by the philosophers,
who we dare to say ought to be our rulers. When these are clearly
discriminated it will be possible to defend ourselves by showing that to c
them by their very nature belong the study of philosophy and political
leadership, while it befits the other sort to let philosophy alone and to
follow their leader.

It is high time, he said, to produce your definition.

Come, then, follow me on this line, if we may in some fashion or
other explain our meaning.

Proceed, he said.

Must I remind you, then, said I, or do you remember, that when
we affirm that a man is a lover of something, it must be apparent that
he is fond of all of it? It will not do to say that some of it he likes and
some does not.

I think you will have to remind me, he said, for I don't appre- d
hend at all.

That reply, Glaucon, said I, befitted another rather than you. It
does not become a lover to forget that all adolescents in some sort
sting and stir the amorous lover of youth and appear to him deserving
of his attention and desirable. Is not that your 'reaction' to the

fair? One, because his nose is tiptilted, you will praise as piquant, the beak of another you pronounce right royal, the intermediate type you
e say strikes the harmonious mean, the swarthy are of manly aspect, the white are children of the gods divinely fair, and as for honey-hued, do you suppose the very word is anything but the euphemistic invention of some lover who can feel no distaste for sallowness when it accompanies the blooming time of youth? And, in short, there is
475 no pretext you do not allege and there is nothing you shrink from saying to justify you in not rejecting any who are in the bloom of their prime.

If it is your pleasure, he said, to take me as your example of this trait in lovers, I admit it for the sake of the argument.

Again, said I, do you not observe the same thing in the lovers of wine? They welcome every wine on any pretext.

They do, indeed.

And so I take it you have observed that men who are covetous of honor, if they can't get themselves elected generals, are captains of
b a company. And if they can't be honored by great men and dignitaries, are satisfied with honor from little men and nobodies. But honor they desire and must have.

Yes, indeed.

Admit, then, or reject my proposition. When we say a man is keen about something, shall we say that he has an appetite for the whole class or that he desires only a part and a part not?

The whole, he said.

Then the lover of wisdom, too, we shall affirm, desires all wisdom, not a part and a part not.

Certainly.

The student, then, who is finical about his studies, especially
c when he is young and cannot yet know by reason what is useful and what is not, we shall say is not a lover of learning or a lover of wisdom, just as we say that one who is dainty about his food is not really hungry, has not an appetite for food, and is not a lover of food, but a poor feeder.

We shall rightly say so.

But the one who feels no distaste in sampling every study, and who attacks his task of learning gladly and cannot get enough of it, him we shall justly pronounce the lover of wisdom, the philosopher, shall we not?
d   To which Glaucon replied, You will then be giving the name to a numerous and strange band, for all the lovers of spectacles are what they are, I fancy, by virtue of their delight in learning something. And those who always want to hear some new thing are a very queer lot to be reckoned among philosophers. You couldn't induce them to attend a serious debate or any such entertainment, but as if they had farmed out their ears to listen to every chorus in the land, they

run about to all the Dionysiac festivals, never missing one, either in the towns or in the country villages. Are we to designate all these, then, and similar folk and all the practitioners of the minor arts as e philosophers?

Not at all, I said, but they do bear a certain likeness to philosophers.

Whom do you mean, then, by the true philosophers?

Those for whom the truth is the spectacle of which they are enamored, said I.

Right again, said he, but in what sense do you mean it?

It would be by no means easy to explain it to another, I said, but I think that you will grant me this.

What?

That since the fair and honorable is the opposite of the base and ugly, they are two.

Of course.   476

And since they are two, each is one.

That also.

And in respect of the just and the unjust, the good and the bad, and all the ideas or forms, the same statement holds, that in itself each is one, but that by virtue of their communion with actions and bodies and with one another they present themselves everywhere, each as a multiplicity of aspects.

Right, he said.

This, then, said I, is my division. I set apart and distinguish those of whom you were just speaking, the lovers of spectacles and the arts, and men of action, and separate from them again those with whom our argument is concerned and who alone deserve the appellation of b philosophers or lovers of wisdom.

What do you mean? he said.

The lovers of sounds and sights, I said, delight in beautiful tones and colors and shapes and in everything that art fashions out of these, but their thought is incapable of apprehending and taking delight in the nature of the beautiful in itself.

Why, yes, he said, that is so.

And on the other hand, will not those be few who would be able to approach beauty itself and contemplate it in and by itself?

They would, indeed.   c

He, then, who believes in beautiful things, but neither believes in beauty itself nor is able to follow when someone tries to guide him to the knowledge of it—do you think that his life is a dream or a waking? Just consider. Is not the dream state, whether the man is asleep or awake, just this—the mistaking of resemblance for identity?

I should certainly call that dreaming, he said.

Well, then, take the opposite case, the man whose thought recognizes a beauty in itself, and is able to distinguish that self-beautiful d and the things that participate in it, and neither supposes the participants to be it nor it the participants—is his life, in your opinion, a waking or a dream state?

He is very much awake, he replied.

Could we not rightly, then, call the mental state of the one as knowing, knowledge, and that of the other as opining, opinion?

Assuredly.

Suppose, now, he who we say opines but does not know should be angry and challenge our statement as not true—can we find any
e way of soothing him and gently winning him over, without telling him too plainly that he is not in his right mind?

We must try, he said.

Come, then, consider what we are to say to him, or would you have us question him in this fashion—premising that if he knows anything, nobody grudges it him, but we should be very glad to see him knowing something—but tell us this, Does he who knows know something or nothing? Do you reply in his behalf.

I will reply, he said, that he knows something.

Is it something that is or is not?
477 That is. How could that which is not be known?

We are sufficiently assured of this, then, even if we should examine it from every point of view, that that which entirely *is* is entirely knowable, and that which in no way *is* is in every way unknowable?

Most sufficiently.

Good. If a thing, then, is so conditioned as both to be and not to be, would it not lie between that which absolutely and unqualifiedly is and that which in no way is?

Between.

Then since knowledge pertains to that which is and ignorance of necessity to that which is not, for that which lies between we must
b seek for something between nescience and science, if such a thing there be.

By all means.

Is there a thing which we call opinion?

Surely.

Is it a different faculty from science or the same?

A different.

Then opinion is set over one thing and science over another, each by virtue of its own distinctive power or faculty.

That is so.

May we say, then, that science is naturally related to that which is, to know that and how that which is is? But rather, before we proceed, I think we must draw the following distinctions.

What ones?
c Shall we say that faculties, powers, abilities are a class of entities

by virtue of which we and all other things are able to do what we or they are able to do? I mean that sight and hearing, for example, are faculties, if so be that you understand the class or type that I am trying to describe.

I understand, he said.

Hear, then, my notion about them. In a faculty I cannot see any color or shape or similar mark such as those on which in many other cases I fix my eyes in discriminating in my thought one thing from another. But in the case of a faculty I look to one thing only—that to which it is related and what it effects, and it is in this way that I come to call each one of them a faculty, and that which is related to the same thing and accomplishes the same thing I call the same faculty, d and that to another I call other. How about you, what is your practice?

The same, he said.

To return, then, my friend, said I, to science or true knowledge, do you say that it is a faculty and a power, or in what class do you put it?

Into this, he said, the most potent of all faculties.

And opinion—shall we assign it to some other class than faculty? e

By no means, he said, for that by which we are able to opine is nothing else than the faculty of opinion.

But not long ago you agreed that science and opinion are not identical.

How could any rational man affirm the identity of the infallible with the fallible?

Excellent, said I, and we are plainly agreed that opinion is a dif- 478 ferent thing from scientific knowledge.

Yes, different.

Each of them, then, since it has a different power, is related to a different object.

Of necessity.

Science, I presume, to that which is, to know the condition of that which is?

Yes.

But opinion, we say, opines.

Yes.

Does it opine the same thing that science knows, and will the knowable and the opinable be identical, or is that impossible?

Impossible by our admissions, he said. If different faculties are naturally related to different objects and both opinion and science b are faculties, but each different from the other, as we say—these admissions do not leave place for the identity of the knowable and the opinable.

Then, if that which is a knowable, something other than that which is would be the opinable.

Something else.

Does it opine that which is not, or is it impossible even to opine that which is not? Reflect. Does not he who opines bring his opinion to bear upon something or shall we reverse ourselves and say that it is possible to opine, yet opine nothing?

That is impossible.

Then he who opines opines some one thing?

Yes.

c   But surely that which is not could not be designated as some one thing, but most rightly as nothing at all.

Yes.

To that which is not we of necessity assigned nescience, and to that which is, knowledge.

Rightly, he said.

Then neither that which is nor that which is not is the object of opinion.

It seems not.

Then opinion would be neither nescience nor knowledge.

So it seems.

Is it then a faculty outside of these, exceeding either knowledge in lucidity or ignorance in obscurity?

It is neither.

But do you deem opinion something darker than knowledge but brighter than ignorance?

Much so, he said.

d   And does it lie within the boundaries of the two?

Yes.

Then opinion would be between the two.

Most assuredly.

Were we not saying a little while ago that if anything should turn up such that it both is and is not, that sort of thing would lie between that which purely and absolutely is and that which wholly is not, and that the faculty correlated with it would be neither science nor nescience, but that which should appear to hold a place correspondingly between nescience and science.

Right.

And now there has turned up between these two the thing that we call opinion.

There has.

e   It would remain, then, as it seems, for us to discover that which partakes of both, of *to be* and *not to be*, and that could not be rightly designated either in its exclusive purity, so that, if it shall be discovered, we may justly pronounce it to be the opinable, thus assigning extremes to extremes and the intermediate to the intermediate. Is not that so?

It is.

This much premised, let him tell me, I will say, let him answer 479
me, that good fellow who does not think there is a beautiful in itself
or any idea of beauty in itself always remaining the same and unchanged, but who does believe in many beautiful things—the lover of
spectacles, I mean, who cannot endure to hear anybody say that
the beautiful is one and the just one, and so of other things—and this
will be our question. My good fellow, is there any one of these many
fair and honorable things that will not sometimes appear ugly and
base? And of the just things, that will not seem unjust? And of the
pious things, that will not seem impious?

No, it is inevitable, he said, that they would appear to be both b
beautiful in a way and ugly, and so with all the other things you asked
about.

And again, do the many double things appear any the less halves
than doubles?

None the less.

And likewise of the great and the small things, the light and the
heavy things—will they admit these predicates any more than their opposites?

No, he said, each of them will always hold of, partake of, both.

Then is each of these multiples rather than it is not that which
one affirms it to be?

They are like those jesters who palter with us in a double sense
at banquets, he replied, and resemble the children's riddle about the c
eunuch and his hitting of the bat—with what and as it sat on what
they signify that he struck it. For these things too equivocate, and it
is impossible to conceive firmly any one of them to be or not to be or
both or neither.

Do you know what to do with them, then? said I. And can you find
a better place to put them than that midway between existence or
essence and the not to be? For we shall surely not discover a darker
region than not-being that they should still more not be, nor a
brighter than being that they should still more be.   d

Most true, he said.

We would seem to have found, then, that the many conventions
of the many about the fair and honorable and other things are tumbled about in the mid-region between that which is not and that
which is in the true and absolute sense.

We have so found it.

But we agreed in advance that if anything of that sort should be
discovered, it must be denominated opinable, not knowable, the wanderer between being caught by the faculty that is betwixt and between.

We did.

We shall affirm, then, that those who view many beautiful things e
but do not see the beautiful itself and are unable to follow another's

guidance to it, and many just things, but not justice itself, and so in all cases—we shall say that such men have opinions about all things, but know nothing of the things they opine.

Of necessity.

And, on the other hand, what of those who contemplate the very things themselves in each case, ever remaining the same and unchanged—shall we not say that they know and do not merely opine?

That, too, necessarily follows.

Shall we not also say that the one welcomes to his thought and loves the things subject to knowledge and the other those to opinion?

480   Do we not remember that we said that those loved and regarded tones and beautiful colors and the like, but they could not endure the notion of the reality of the beautiful itself?

We do remember.

Shall we then offend their ears if we call them *doxophilists* rather than philosophers and will they be very angry if we so speak?

Not if they heed my counsel, he said, for to be angry with truth is not lawful.

Then to those who in each and every kind welcome the true being, lovers of wisdom and not lovers of opinion is the name we must give.

By all means.

BOOK VI

484   So now, Glaucon, I said, our argument after winding a long and weary way has at last made clear to us who are the philosophers or lovers of wisdom and who are not.

Yes, he said, a shorter way is perhaps not feasible.

Apparently not, I said. I, at any rate, think that the matter would have been made still plainer if we had had nothing but this to speak of, and if there were not so many things left which our purpose

b   of discerning the difference between the just and the unjust life requires us to discuss.

What, then, he said, comes next?

What else, said I, but the next in order? Since the philosophers are those who are capable of apprehending that which is eternal and unchanging, while those who are incapable of this, but lose themselves and wander amid the multiplicities of multifarious things, are not philosophers, which of the two kinds ought to be the leaders in a state?

What, then, he said, would be a fair statement of the matter?

Whichever, I said, appear competent to guard the laws and pur-

c   suits of society, these we should establish as guardians.

Right, he said.

Is this, then, said I, clear, whether the guardian who is to keep watch over anything ought to be blind or keen of sight?

Of course it is clear, he said.

Do you think, then, that there is any appreciable difference between the blind and those who are veritably deprived of the knowledge of the veritable being of things, those who have no vivid pattern in their souls and so cannot, as painters look to their models, fix their eyes on the absolute truth, and always with reference to that ideal and d in the exactest possible contemplation of it establish in this world also the laws of the beautiful, the just, and the good, when that is needful, or guard and preserve those that are established?

No, by heaven, he said, there is not much difference.

Shall we, then, appoint these blind souls as our guardians, rather than those who have learned to know the ideal reality of things and who do not fall short of the others in experience and are not second to them in any part of virtue?

It would be strange indeed, he said, to choose others than the philosophers, provided they were not deficient in those other respects, for this very knowledge of the ideal would perhaps be the greatest of superiorities.

Then what we have to say is how it would be possible for the 485 same persons to have both qualifications, is it not?

Quite so.

Then, as we were saying at the beginning of this discussion, the first thing to understand is the nature that they must have from birth, and I think that if we sufficiently agree on this we shall also agree that the combination of qualities that we seek belongs to the same persons, and that we need no others for guardians of states than these.

How so?

We must accept as agreed this trait of the philosophical nature, that it is ever enamored of the kind of knowledge which reveals to them something of that essence which is eternal, and is not wandering b between the two poles of generation and decay.

Let us take that as agreed.

And, further, said I, that their desire is for the whole of it and that they do not willingly renounce a small or a great, a more precious or a less honored, part of it. That was the point of our former illustration drawn from lovers and men covetous of honor.

You are right, he said.

Consider, then, next whether the men who are to meet our requirements must not have this further quality in their natures.   c

What quality?

The spirit of truthfulness, reluctance to admit falsehood in any form, the hatred of it and the love of truth.

It is likely, he said.

It is not only likely, my friend, but there is every necessity that he who is by nature enamored of anything should cherish all that is akin and pertaining to the object of his love.

Right, he said.

Could you find anything more akin to wisdom than truth?

Impossible, he said.

d   Then can the same nature be a lover of wisdom and of falsehood?

By no means.

Then the true lover of knowledge must, from childhood up, be most of all a striver after truth in every form.

By all means.

But, again, we surely are aware that when in a man the desires incline strongly to any one thing, they are weakened for other things. It is as if the stream had been diverted into another channel.

Surely.

So, when a man's desires have been taught to flow in the channel of learning and all that sort of thing, they will be concerned, I presume, with the pleasures of the soul in itself, and will be indifferent

e to those of which the body is the instrument, if the man is a true and not a sham philosopher.

That is quite necessary.

Such a man will be temperate and by no means greedy for wealth, for the things for the sake of which money and great expenditure are eagerly sought others may take seriously, but not he.

It is so.

486   And there is this further point to be considered in distinguishing the philosophical from the unphilosophical nature.

What point?

You must not overlook any touch of illiberality. For nothing can be more contrary than such pettiness to the quality of a soul that is ever to seek integrity and wholeness in all things human and divine.

Most true, he said.

Do you think that a mind habituated to thoughts of grandeur and the contemplation of all time and all existence can deem this life of man a thing of great concern?

Impossible, said he.

b   Hence such a man will not suppose death to be terrible?

Least of all.

Then a cowardly and illiberal spirit, it seems, could have no part in genuine philosophy.

I think not.

What then? Could a man of orderly spirit, not a lover of money, not illiberal, nor a braggart nor a coward, ever prove unjust, or a driver of hard bargains?

Impossible.

This too, then, is a point that in your discrimination of the philosophical and unphilosophical soul you will observe—whether the man is from youth up just and gentle or unsocial and savage.

Assuredly.   c

Nor will you overlook this, I fancy.

What?

Whether he is quick or slow to learn. Or do you suppose that anyone could properly love a task which he performed painfully and with little result from much toil?

That could not be.

And if he could not keep what he learned, being steeped in oblivion, could he fail to be void of knowledge?

How could he?

And so, having all his labor for nought, will he not finally be constrained to loathe himself and that occupation?

Of course.

The forgetful soul, then, we must not list in the roll of com- d petent lovers of wisdom, but we require a good memory.

By all means.

But assuredly we should not say that the want of harmony and seemliness in a nature conduces to anything else than the want of measure and proportion.

Certainly.

And do you think that truth is akin to measure and proportion or to disproportion?

To proportion.

Then in addition to our other requirements we look for a mind endowed with measure and grace, whose native disposition will make it easily guided to the aspect of the ideal reality in all things.

Assuredly.

Tell me, then, is there any flaw in the argument? Have we not e proved the qualities enumerated to be necessary and compatible with one another for the soul that is to have a sufficient and perfect apprehension of reality?

Nay, most necessary, he said.

Is there any fault, then, that you can find with a pursuit which a 487 man could not properly practice unless he were by nature of good memory, quick apprehension, magnificent, gracious, friendly, and akin to truth, justice, bravery, and sobriety?

Momus himself, he said, could not find fault with such a combination.

Well, then, said I, when men of this sort are perfected by education and maturity of age, would you not entrust the state solely to them?

And Adimantus said, No one, Socrates, would be able to contro- b vert these statements of yours. But, all the same, those who

occasionally hear you argue thus feel in this way. They think that owing to their inexperience in the game of question and answer they are at every question led astray a little bit by the argument, and when these bits are accumulated at the conclusion of the discussion mighty is their fall, and the apparent contradiction of what they at
c first said, and that just as by expert draughts players the unskilled are finally shut in and cannot make a move, so they are finally blocked and have their mouths stopped by this other game of draughts played not with counters but with words; yet the truth is not affected by that outcome. I say this with reference to the present case, for in this instance one might say that he is unable in words to contend against you at each question, but that when it comes to facts he sees that of those who turn to philosophy, not merely touching upon
d it to complete their education and dropping it while still young, but lingering too long in the study of it, the majority become cranks, not to say rascals, and those accounted the finest spirits among them are still rendered useless to society by the pursuit which you commend.

And I, on hearing this, said, Do you think that they are mistaken in saying so?

I don't know, said he, but I would gladly hear your opinion.

You may hear, then, that I think that what they say is true.
e   How, then, he replied, can it be right to say that our cities will never be freed from their evils until the philosophers, whom we admit to be useless to them, become their rulers?

Your question, I said, requires an answer expressed in a comparison or parable.

And you, he said, of course, are not accustomed to speak in comparisons!

So, said I, you are making fun of me after driving me into such an impasse of argument. But, all the same, hear my comparison so
488 that you may still better see how I strain after imagery. For so cruel is the condition of the better sort in relation to the state that there is no single thing like it in nature. But to find a likeness for it and a defense for them one must bring together many things in such a combination as painters mix when they portray goat stags and similar creatures. Conceive this sort of thing happening either on many ships or on one. Picture a shipmaster in height and strength surpassing all
b others on the ship, but who is slightly deaf and of similarly impaired vision, and whose knowledge of navigation is on a par with his sight and hearing. Conceive the sailors to be wrangling with one another for control of the helm, each claiming that it is his right to steer though he has never learned the art and cannot point out his teacher or any time when he studied it. And what is more, they affirm that it cannot be taught at all, but they are ready to make mincemeat of anyone who says that it can be taught, and meanwhile they are al-
c ways clustered about the shipmaster importuning him and sticking

at nothing to induce him to turn over the helm to them. And sometimes, if they fail and others get his ear, they put the others to death
or cast them out from the ship, and then, after binding and stupefying
the worthy shipmaster with mandragora or intoxication or otherwise,
they take command of the ship, consume its stores and, drinking and
feasting, make such a voyage of it as is to be expected from such,
and as if that were not enough, they praise and celebrate as a navi- d
gator, a pilot, a master of shipcraft, the man who is most cunning to
lend a hand in persuading or constraining the shipmaster to let them
rule, while the man who lacks this craft they censure as useless. They
have no suspicion that the true pilot must give his attention to the time
of the year, the seasons, the sky, the winds, the stars, and all that
pertains to his art if he is to be a true ruler of a ship, and that he does
not believe that there is any art or science of seizing the helm with or
without the consent of others, or any possibility of mastering this e
alleged art and the practice of it at the same time with the science of
navigation. With such goings on aboard ship do you not think that 489
the real pilot would in very deed be called a stargazer, an idle babbler,
a useless fellow, by the sailors in ships managed after this fashion?

Quite so, said Adimantus.

You take my meaning, I presume, and do not require us to put the
comparison to the proof and show that the condition we have described is the exact counterpart of the relation of the state to the true
philosophers.

It is indeed, he said.

To begin with, then, teach this parable to the man who is surprised that philosophers are not honored in our cities, and try to con- b
vince him that it would be far more surprising if they were honored.

I will teach him, he said.

And say to him further, You are right in affirming that the finest
spirits among the philosophers are of no service to the multitude. But
bid him blame for this uselessness, not the finer spirits, but those who
do not know how to make use of them. For it is not the natural course
of things that the pilot should beg the sailors to be ruled by him or
that wise men should go to the doors of the rich. The author of
that epigram was a liar. But the true nature of things is that whether c
the sick man be rich or poor he must needs go to the door of the physician, and everyone who needs to be governed to the door of the man
who knows how to govern, not that the ruler should implore his natural subjects to let themselves be ruled, if he is really good for anything. But you will make no mistake in likening our present political
rulers to the sort of sailors we were just describing, and those whom
these call useless and stargazing ideologists to the true pilots.

Just so, he said.

Hence, and under these conditions, we cannot expect that the
noblest pursuit should be highly esteemed by those whose way of life

d is quite the contrary. But far the greatest and chief disparagement of philosophy is brought upon it by the pretenders to that way of life, those whom you had in mind when you affirmed that the accuser of philosophy says that the majority of her followers are rascals and the better sort useless, while I admitted that what you said was true. Is not that so?

Yes.

Have we not, then, explained the cause of the uselessness of the better sort?

We have.

Shall we next set forth the inevitableness of the degeneracy of
e the majority, and try to show if we can that philosophy is not to be blamed for this either?

By all means.

Let us begin, then, what we have to say and hear by recalling the starting point of our description of the nature which he who is to
490 be a scholar and gentleman must have from birth. The leader of the choir for him, if you recollect, was truth. *That* he was to seek always and altogether, on pain of being an impostor without part or lot in true philosophy.

Yes, that was said.

Is not this one point quite contrary to the prevailing opinion about him?

It is indeed, he said.

Will it not be a fair plea in his defense to say that it was the nature of the real lover of knowledge to strive emulously for true
b being and that he would not linger over the many particulars that are opined to be real, but would hold on his way, and the edge of his passion would not be blunted nor would his desire fail till he came into touch with the nature of each thing in itself by that part of his soul to which it belongs to lay hold on that kind of reality—the part akin to it, namely—and through that approaching it, and consorting with reality really, he would beget intelligence and truth, attain to knowledge, and truly live and grow, and so find surcease from his travail of soul, but not before?

No plea could be fairer.

Well, then, will such a man love falsehood, or, quite the contrary, hate it?
c Hate it, he said.

When truth led the way, no choir of evils, we, I fancy, would say, could ever follow in its train.

How could it?

But rather a sound and just character, which is accompanied by temperance.

Right, he said.

What need, then, of repeating from the beginning our proof of the necessary order of the choir that attends on the philosophical nature? You surely remember that we found pertaining to such a nature courage, grandeur of soul, aptness to learn, memory. And when you interposed the objection that though everybody will be compelled to admit our statements, yet, if we abandoned mere words and fixed our eyes on the persons to whom the words referred, everyone would say that he actually saw some of them to be useless and most of them base d with all baseness—it was in our search for the cause of this ill repute that we came to the present question. Why is it that the majority are bad? And, for the sake of this, we took up again the nature of the true philosophers and defined what it must necessarily be?

That is so, he said.   e

We have, then, I said, to contemplate the causes of the corruption of this nature in the majority, while a small part escapes, even those whom men call not bad but useless. And after that in turn we are to 491 observe those who imitate this nature and usurp its pursuits, and see what types of souls they are that thus entering upon a way of life which is too high for them and exceeds their powers, by the many discords and disharmonies of their conduct everywhere and among all men, bring upon philosophy the repute of which you speak.

Of what corruptions are you speaking?

I will try, I said, to explain them to you if I can. I think everyone will grant us this point, that a nature such as we just now postulated for the perfect philosopher is a rare growth among men and is found b in only a few. Don't you think so?

Most emphatically.

Observe, then, the number and magnitude of the things that operate to destroy these few.

What are they?

The most surprising fact of all is that each of the gifts of nature which we praise tends to corrupt the soul of its possessor and divert it from philosophy. I am speaking of bravery, sobriety, and the entire list.

That does sound like a paradox, said he.

Furthermore, said I, all the so-called goods corrupt and divert, c beauty and wealth and strength of body and powerful family connections in the city and all things akin to them—you get my general meaning?

I do, he said, and I would gladly hear a more precise statement of it.

Well, said I, grasp it rightly as a general proposition and the matter will be clear and the preceding statement will not seem to you so strange.

How do you bid me proceed? he said.

We know it to be universally true of every seed and growth, d whether vegetable or animal, that the more vigorous it is the more it falls short of its proper perfection when deprived of the food, the season, the place that suits it. For evil is more opposed to the good than to the not-good.

Of course.

So it is, I take it, natural that the best nature should fare worse than the inferior under conditions of nurture unsuited to it.

It is.

e   Then, said I, Adimantus, shall we not similarly affirm that the best endowed souls become worse than the others under a bad education? Or do you suppose that great crimes and unmixed wickedness spring from a slight nature and not from a vigorous one corrupted by its nurture, while a weak nature will never be the cause of anything great, either for good or evil?

No, he said, that is the case.

492   Then the nature which we assumed in the philosopher, if it receives the proper teaching, must needs grow and attain to consummate excellence, but, if it be sown and planted and grown in the wrong environment, the outcome will be quite the contrary unless some god comes to the rescue. Or are you too one of the multitude who believe that there are young men who are corrupted by the Sophists, and that there are Sophists in private life who corrupt to any extent worth mentioning, and that it is not rather the very men who

b   talk in this strain who are the chief Sophists and educate most effectively and mold to their own heart's desire young and old, men and women?

When? said he.

Why, when, I said, the multitude are seated together in assemblies or in courtrooms or theaters or camps or any other public gathering of a crowd, and with loud uproar censure some of the things that are said and done and approve others, both in excess, with full-

c   throated clamor and clapping of hands, and thereto the rocks and the region round about re-echoing redouble the din of the censure and the praise. In such case how do you think the young man's heart, as the saying is, is moved within him? What private teaching do you think will hold out and not rather be swept away by the torrent of censure and applause, and borne off on its current, so that he will affirm the same things that they do to be honorable and base, and will do as they do, and be even such as they?

d   That is quite inevitable, Socrates, he said.

And, moreover, I said, we have not yet mentioned the chief necessity and compulsion.

What is it? said he.

That which these 'educators' and Sophists impose by action when their words fail to convince. Don't you know that they chastise the recalcitrant with loss of civic rights and fines and death?

They most emphatically do, he said.

What other Sophist, then, or what private teaching do you think
will prevail in opposition to these?

None, I fancy, said he.   e

No, said I, the very attempt is the height of folly. For there is not,
never has been, and never will be a divergent type of character and
virtue created by an education running counter to theirs—humanly
speaking, I mean, my friend. For the divine, as the proverb says, all
rules fail. And you may be sure that, if anything is saved and turns out
well in the present condition of society and government, in saying
that the providence of God preserves it you will not be speaking ill.   493

Neither do I think otherwise, he said.

Then, said I, think this also in addition.

What?

Each of these private teachers who work for pay, whom the politicians call Sophists and regard as their rivals, inculcates nothing
else than these opinions of the multitude which they opine when they
are assembled and calls this knowledge wisdom. It is as if a man were
acquiring the knowledge of the humors and desires of a great strong   b
beast which he had in his keeping, how it is to be approached and
touched, and when and by what things it is made most savage or gentle, yes, and the several sounds it is wont to utter on the occasion of
each, and again what sounds uttered by another make it tame or fierce,
and after mastering this knowledge by living with the creature and by
lapse of time should call it wisdom, and should construct thereof a
system and art and turn to the teaching of it, knowing nothing in reality about which of these opinions and desires is honorable or base,   c
good or evil, just or unjust, but should apply all these terms to the
judgments of the great beast, calling the things that pleased it good,
and the things that vexed it bad, having no other account to render of
them, but should call what is necessary just and honorable, never having observed how great is the real difference between the necessary
and the good, and being incapable of explaining it to another. Do
you not think, by heaven, that such a one would be a strange educator?

I do, he said.

Do you suppose that there is any difference between such a one
and the man who thinks that it is wisdom to have learned to know the   d
moods and the pleasures of the motley multitude in their assembly,
whether about painting or music or, for that matter, politics? For if a
man associates with these and offers and exhibits to them his poetry
or any other product of his craft or any political service, and grants
the mob authority over himself more than is unavoidable, the proverbial necessity of Diomedes will compel him to give the public what it
likes, but that what it likes is really good and honorable, have you ever
heard an attempted proof of this that is not simply ridiculous?

No, he said, and I fancy I never shall hear it either.   e

Bearing all this in mind, recall our former question. Can the multitude possibly tolerate or believe in the reality of the beautiful in itself as opposed to the multiplicity of beautiful things, or can they
494 believe in anything conceived in its essence as opposed to the many particulars?

Not in the least, he said.

Philosophy, then, the love of wisdom, is impossible for the multitude.

Impossible.

It is inevitable, then, that those who philosophize should be censured by them.

Inevitable.

And so likewise by those laymen who, associating with the mob, desire to curry favor with it.

Obviously.

From this point of view do you see any salvation that will suffer
b the born philosopher to abide in the pursuit and persevere to the end? Consider it in the light of what we said before. We agreed that quickness in learning, memory, courage, and magnificence were the traits of this nature.

Yes.

Then even as a boy among boys such a one will take the lead in all things, especially if the nature of his body matches the soul.

How could he fail to do so? he said.

His kinsmen and fellow citizens, then, will desire, I presume, to make use of him when he is older for their own affairs.

Of course.
c   Then they will fawn upon him with petitions and honors, anticipating and flattering the power that will be his.

That certainly is the usual way.

How, then, do you think such a youth will behave in such conditions, especially if it happen that he belongs to a great city and is rich and wellborn therein, and thereto handsome and tall? Will his soul not be filled with unbounded ambitious hopes, and will he not think himself capable of managing the affairs of both Greeks and barbari-
d ans, and thereupon exalt himself, haughty of mien and stuffed with empty pride and void of sense?

He surely will, he said.

And if to a man in this state of mind someone gently comes and tells him what is the truth, that he has no sense and sorely needs it, and that the only way to get it is to work like a slave to win it, do you think it will be easy for him to lend an ear to the quiet voice in the midst of and in spite of these evil surroundings?

Far from it, said he.

And even supposing, said I, that owing to a fortunate disposition
e and his affinity for the words of admonition one such youth appre-

hends something and is moved and drawn toward philosophy, what do
we suppose will be the conduct of those who think that they are losing
his service and fellowship? Is there any word or deed that they will
stick at to keep him from being persuaded and to incapacitate anyone
who attempts it, both by private intrigue and public prosecution in the
court?

That is inevitable, he said.   495

Is there any possibility of such a one continuing to philosophize?
None at all, he said.

Do you see, then, said I, that we were not wrong in saying that
the very qualities that make up the philosophical nature do, in fact,
become, when the environment and nurture are bad, in some sort the
cause of its backsliding, and so do the so-called goods—riches and
all such instrumentalities?

No, he replied, it was rightly said.

Such, my good friend, and so great as regards the noblest pursuit, b
is the destruction and corruption of the most excellent nature, which
is rare enough in any case, as we affirm. And it is from men of this
type that those spring who do the greatest harm to communities and
individuals, and the greatest good when the stream chances to be
turned into that channel, but a small nature never does anything
great to a man or a city.

Most true, said he.

Those, then, to whom she properly belongs, thus falling away and
leaving philosophy forlorn and unwed, themselves live an unreal and c
alien life, while other unworthy wooers rush in and defile her as an
orphan bereft of her kin, and attach to her such reproaches as you say
her revilers taunt her with, declaring that some of her consorts are of
no account and the many accountable for many evils.

Why, yes, he replied, that is what they do say.

And plausibly, said I, for other manikins, observing that the place
is unoccupied and full of fine terms and pretensions, just as men es- d
cape from prison to take sanctuary in temples, so these gentlemen joy-
ously bound away from the mechanical arts to philosophy, those that
are most cunning in their little craft. For in comparison with the other
arts the prestige of philosophy even in her present low estate retains a
superior dignity, and this is the ambition and aspiration of that multitude of pretenders unfit by nature, whose souls are bowed and muti- e
lated by their vulgar occupations even as their bodies are marred by
their arts and crafts. Is not that inevitable?

Quite so, he said.

Is not the picture which they present, I said, precisely that of a
little bald-headed tinker who has made money and just been freed
from bonds and had a bath and is wearing a new garment and has got
himself up like a bridegroom and is about to marry his master's
daughter who has fallen into poverty and abandonment?

496   There is no difference at all, he said.

Of what sort will probably be the offspring of such parents? Will they not be bastard and base?

Inevitably.

And so when men unfit for culture approach philosophy and consort with her unworthily, what sort of ideas and opinions shall we say they beget? Will they not produce what may in very deed be fairly called sophisms, and nothing that is genuine or that partakes of true intelligence?

Quite so, he said.

There is a very small remnant, then, Adimantus, I said, of those
b who consort worthily with philosophy, some wellborn and well-bred nature, it may be, held in check by exile, and so in the absence of corrupters remaining true to philosophy, as its quality bids, or it may happen that a great soul born in a little town scorns and disregards its parochial affairs, and a small group perhaps might by natural affinity be drawn to it from other arts which they justly disdain, and the bridle of our companion Theages also might operate as a restraint. For in
c the case of Theages all other conditions were at hand for his backsliding from philosophy, but his sickly habit of body keeping him out of politics holds him back. My own case, the divine sign, is hardly worth mentioning—for I suppose it has happened to few or none before me. And those who have been of this little company and have tasted the sweetness and blessedness of this possession and who have also come to understand the madness of the multitude sufficiently and have seen that there is nothing, if I may say so, sound or right in any present politics, and that there is no ally with whose aid the champion
d of justice could escape destruction, but that he would be as a man who has fallen among wild beasts, unwilling to share their misdeeds and unable to hold out singly against the savagery of all, and that he would thus, before he could in any way benefit his friends or the state, come to an untimely end without doing any good to himself or others —for all these reasons I say the philosopher remains quiet, minds his own affair, and, as it were, standing aside under shelter of a wall in a storm and blast of dust and sleet and seeing others filled full of lawlessness, is content if in any way he may keep himself free from iniq-
e uity and unholy deeds through this life and take his departure with fair hope, serene and well content when the end comes.

Well, he said, that is no very slight thing to have achieved before taking his departure.

497   He would not have accomplished any very great thing either, I replied, if it were not his fortune to live in a state adapted to his nature. In such a state only will he himself rather attain his full stature and together with his own preserve the commonweal. The causes and the injustice of the calumniation of philosophy, I think, have been fairly set forth, unless you have something to add.

No, he said, I have nothing further to offer on that point. But

which of our present governments do you think is suitable for philoso- b
phy?

None whatever, I said, but the very ground of my complaint is
that no polity of today is worthy of the philosophical nature. This is
just the cause of its perversion and alteration; as a foreign seed sown
in an alien soil is wont to be overcome and die out into the native
growth, so this kind does not preserve its own quality but falls away
and degenerates into an alien type. But if ever it finds the best polity c
as it itself is the best, then will it be apparent that this was in truth
divine and all the others human in their natures and practices. Obviously then you are next going to ask what is this best form of government.

Wrong, he said. I was going to ask not that but whether it is this
one that we have described in our establishment of a state or another.

In other respects it is this one, said I, but there is one special further point that we mentioned even then, namely, that there would always have to be resident in such a state an element having the same d
conception of its constitution that you the lawgiver had in framing its
laws.

That was said, he replied.

But it was not sufficiently explained, I said, from fear of those
objections on your part which have shown that the demonstration of
it is long and difficult. And apart from that the remainder of the exposition is by no means easy.

Just what do you mean?

The manner in which a state that occupies itself with philosophy
can escape destruction. For all great things are precarious and, as the
proverb truly says, 'fine things are hard.'

All the same, he said, our exposition must be completed by mak- e
ing this plain.

It will be no lack of will, I said, but if anything, a lack of ability,
that would prevent that. But you shall observe for yourself my zeal.
And note again how zealously and recklessly I am prepared to say that
the state ought to take up this pursuit in just the reverse of our present
fashion.

In what way?

At present, said I, those who do take it up are youths, just out of 498
boyhood, who in the interval before they engage in business and
money-making approach the most difficult part of it, and then drop it
—and these are regarded forsooth as the best exemplars of philosophy. By the most difficult part I mean discussion. In later life they
think they have done much if, when invited, they deign to listen to the
philosophical discussions of others. That sort of thing they think
should be bywork. And toward old age, with few exceptions, their
light is quenched more completely than the sun of Heraclitus, inas- b
much as it is never rekindled.

And what should they do? he said.

Just the reverse. While they are lads and boys they should occupy themselves with an education and a culture suitable to youth, and while their bodies are growing to manhood take right good care of them, thus securing a basis and a support for the intellectual life. But with the advance of age, when the soul begins to attain its maturity, c they should make its exercises more severe, and when the bodily strength declines and they are past the age of political and military service, then at last they should be given free range of the pasture and do nothing but philosophize, except incidentally, if they are to live happily, and, when the end has come, crown the life they have lived with a consonant destiny in that other world.

You really seem to be very much in earnest, Socrates, he said. Yet I think most of your hearers are even more earnest in their opposition and will not be in the least convinced, beginning with Thrasymachus.

Do not try to breed a quarrel between me and Thrasymachus, who d have just become friends and were not enemies before either. For we will spare no effort until we either convince him and the rest or achieve something that will profit them when they come to that life in which they will be born again and meet with such discussions as these.

A brief time your forecast contemplates, he said.

Nay, nothing at all, I replied, as compared with eternity. However, the unwillingness of the multitude to believe what you say is nothing surprising. For of the thing here spoken they have never beheld a token, but only the forced and artificial chiming of word and e phrase, not spontaneous and accidental as has happened here. But the figure of a man 'equilibrated' and 'assimilated' to virtue's self perfectly, so far as may be, in word and deed, and holding rule in a city of like 499 quality, that is a thing they have never seen in one case or in many. Do you think they have?

By no means.

Neither, my dear fellow, have they ever seriously inclined to hearken to fair and free discussions whose sole endeavor was to search out the truth at any cost for knowledge's sake, and which dwell apart and salute from afar all the subtleties and cavils that lead to nought but opinion and strife in courtroom and in private talk.

They have not, he said.

b   For this cause and foreseeing this, we then despite our fears declared under compulsion of the truth that neither city nor polity nor man either will ever be perfected until some chance compels this uncorrupted remnant of philosophers, who now bear the stigma of uselessness, to take charge of the state whether they wish it or not, and constrains the citizens to obey them, or else until by some divine inc spiration a genuine passion for true philosophy takes possession either of the sons of the men now in power and sovereignty or of themselves. To affirm that either or both of these things cannot possibly come to pass is, I say, quite unreasonable. Only in that case could we be justly ridiculed as uttering things as futile as daydreams are. Is not that so?

It is.

If, then, the best philosophical natures have ever been constrained to take charge of the state in infinite time past, or now are in some barbaric region far beyond our ken, or shall hereafter be, we are prepared to maintain our contention that the constitution we have described has been, is, or will be realized when this philosophical Muse has taken control of the state. It is not a thing impossible to happen, nor are we speaking of impossibilities. That it is difficult we too admit.

I also think so, he said.

But the multitude—are you going to say?—does not think so, said I.

That may be, he said.

My dear fellow, said I, do not thus absolutely condemn the multitude. They will surely be of another mind if in no spirit of contention but soothingly and endeavoring to do away with the dispraise of learning you point out to them whom you mean by philosophers, and define as we recently did their nature and their pursuits so that the people may not suppose you to mean those of whom they are thinking. Or even if they do look at them in that way, are you still going to deny that they will change their opinion and answer differently? Or do you think that anyone is ungentle to the gentle or grudging to the ungrudging if he himself is ungrudging and mild? I will anticipate you and reply that I think that only in some few and not in the mass of mankind is so ungentle or harsh a temper to be found.

And I, you may be assured, he said, concur.

And do you not also concur in this very point that the blame for this harsh attitude of the many toward philosophy falls on that riotous crew who have burst in where they do not belong, wrangling with one another, filled with spite, and always talking about persons, a thing least befitting philosophy?

Least of all, indeed, he said.

For surely, Adimantus, the man whose mind is truly fixed on eternal realities has no leisure to turn his eyes downward upon the petty affairs of men, and so engaging in strife with them to be filled with envy and hate, but he fixes his gaze upon the things of the eternal and unchanging order, and seeing that they neither wrong nor are wronged by one another, but all abide in harmony as reason bids, he will endeavor to imitate them and, as far as may be, to fashion himself in their likeness and assimilate himself to them. Or do you think it possible not to imitate the things to which anyone attaches himself with admiration?

Impossible, he said.

d   Then the lover of wisdom associating with the divine order will himself become orderly and divine in the measure permitted to man. But calumny is plentiful everywhere.

Yes, truly.

If, then, I said, some compulsion is laid upon him to practice stamping on the plastic matter of human nature in public and private the patterns that he visions there, and not merely to mold and fashion himself, do you think he will prove a poor craftsman of sobriety and justice and all forms of ordinary civic virtue?

By no means, he said.

But if the multitude become aware that what we are saying of
e the philosopher is true, will they still be harsh with philosophers, and will they distrust our statement that no city could ever be blessed unless its lineaments were traced by artists who used the heavenly model?

501   They will not be harsh, he said, if they perceive that. But tell me, what is the manner of that sketch you have in mind?

They will take the city and the characters of men, as they might a tablet, and first wipe it clean—no easy task. But at any rate you know that this would be their first point of difference from ordinary reformers, that they would refuse to take in hand either individual or state or to legislate before they either received a clean slate or themselves made it clean.

And they would be right, he said.

And thereafter, do you not think that they would sketch the figure of the constitution?

b   Surely.

And then, I take it, in the course of the work they would glance frequently in either direction, at justice, beauty, sobriety and the like as they are in the nature of things, and alternately at that which they were trying to reproduce in mankind, mingling and blending from various pursuits that hue of the flesh, so to speak, deriving their judgment from that likeness of humanity which Homer too called, when it appeared in men, the image and likeness of God.

Right, he said.

c   And they would erase one touch or stroke and paint it another until in the measure of the possible they had made the characters of men pleasing and dear to God as may be.

That at any rate would be the fairest painting

Are we then making any impression on those who you said were advancing to attack us with might and main? Can we convince them that such a political artist of character and such a painter exists as the one we then were praising when our proposal to entrust the state to him angered them, and are they now in a gentler mood when they hear what we are now saying?

Much gentler, he said, if they are reasonable.

How *can* they controvert it? Will they deny that the lovers of wis- d
dom are lovers of reality and truth?

That would be monstrous, he said.

Or that their nature as we have portrayed it is akin to the highest
and best?

Not that either.

Well, then, can they deny that such a nature bred in the pursuits
that befit it will be perfectly good and philosophical so far as that can
be said of anyone? Or will they rather say it of those whom we have
excluded?

Surely not.   e

Will they, then, any longer be fierce with us when we declare that,
until the philosophical class wins control, there will be no surcease
of trouble for city or citizens nor will the polity which we fable in
words be brought to pass in deed?

They will perhaps be less so, he said.

Instead of less so, may we not say that they have been altogether tamed and convinced, so that for very shame, if for no other 502
reason, they may assent?

Certainly, said he.

Let us assume, then, said I, that they are won over to this view.
Will anyone contend that there is no chance that the offspring of kings
and rulers should be born with the philosophical nature?

Not one, he said.

And can anyone prove that if so born they must necessarily be
corrupted? The difficulty of their salvation we too concede, but that in
all the course of time not one of all could be saved, will anyone main- b
tain that?

How could he?

But surely, said I, the occurrence of one such is enough, if he has
a state which obeys him, to realize all that now seems so incredible.

Yes, one is enough, he said.

For if such a ruler, I said, ordains the laws and institutions that
we have described it is surely not impossible that the citizens should
be content to carry them out.

By no means.

Would it, then, be at all strange or impossible for others to come
to the opinion to which we have come?

I think not, said he.   c

And further that these things are best, if possible, has already, I
take it, been sufficiently shown.

Yes, sufficiently.

Our present opinion, then, about this legislation is that our plan
would be best if it could be realized and that this realization is difficult
yet not impossible.

That is the conclusion, he said.

This difficulty disposed of, we have next to speak of what re-
d mains, in what way, namely, and as a result of what studies and pursuits, these preservers of the constitution will form a part of our
state, and at what ages they will severally take up each study.

Yes, we have to speak of that, he said.

I gained nothing, I said, by my cunning in omitting heretofore
the distasteful topic of the possession of women and procreation of
children and the appointment of rulers—because I knew that the absolutely true and right way would provoke censure and is difficult of
e realization—for now I am nonetheless compelled to discuss them. The
matter of the women and children has been disposed of, but the education of the rulers has to be examined again, I may say, from the
503 starting point. We were saying, if you recollect, that they must approve themselves lovers of the state when tested in pleasures and
pains, and make it apparent that they do not abandon this fixed faith
under stress of labors or fears or any other vicissitude, and that anyone who could not keep that faith must be rejected, while he who always issued from the test pure and intact, like gold tried in the fire, is
to be established as ruler and to receive honors in life and after death
and prizes as well. Something of this sort we said while the argument
b slipped by with veiled face in fear of starting our present debate.

Most true, he said. I remember.

We shrank, my friend, I said, from uttering the audacities which
have now been hazarded. But now let us find courage for the definitive
pronouncement that as the most perfect guardians we must establish
philosophers.

Yes, assume it to have been said, said he.

Note, then, that they will naturally be few, for the different components of the nature which we said their education presupposed
rarely consent to grow in one, but for the most part these qualities are
found apart.

c What do you mean? he said.

Facility in learning, memory, sagacity, quickness of apprehension, and their accompaniments, and youthful spirit and magnificence in soul are qualities, you know, that are rarely combined in
human nature with a disposition to live orderly, quiet, and stable
lives, but such men, by reason of their quickness, are driven about
just as chance directs, and all steadfastness is gone out of them.

You speak truly, he said.

And on the other hand, the steadfast and stable temperaments,
d whom one could rather trust in use, and who in war are not easily
moved and aroused to fear, are apt to act in the same way when confronted with studies. They are not easily aroused, learn with difficulty, as if benumbed, and are filled with sleep and yawning when an
intellectual task is set them.

It is so, he said.

But we affirmed that a man must partake of both temperaments in due and fair combination or else participate in neither the highest education nor in honors nor in rule.

And rightly, he said.

Do you not think, then, that such a blend will be a rare thing?

Of course.

They must, then, be tested in the toils and fears and pleasures of e which we then spoke, and we have also now to speak of a point we then passed by, that we must exercise them in many studies, watching them to see whether their nature is capable of enduring the great- 504 est and most difficult studies or whether it will faint and flinch as men flinch in the trials and contests of the body.

That is certainly the right way of looking at it, he said. But what do you understand by the greatest studies?

You remember, I presume, said I, that after distinguishing three kinds in the soul, we established definitions of justice, sobriety, bravery, and wisdom severally.

If I did not remember, he said, I should not deserve to hear the rest.

Do you also remember what was said before this?   b

What?

We were saying, I believe, that for the most perfect discernment of these things another longer way was requisite which would make them plain to one who took it, but that it was possible to add proofs on a par with the preceding discussion. And you said that that was sufficient, and it was on this understanding that what we then said was said, falling short of ultimate precision as it appeared to me, but if it contented you it is for you to say.

Well, he said, it was measurably satisfactory to me, and apparently to the rest of the company.

Nay, my friend, said I, a measure of such things that in the least c degree falls short of reality proves no measure at all. For nothing that is imperfect is the measure of anything, though some people sometimes think that they have already done enough and that there is no need of further inquiry.

Yes, indeed, he said, many experience this because of their sloth.

An experience, said I, that least of all befits the guardians of a state and of its laws.

That seems likely, he said.

Then, said I, such a one must go around the longer way and must labor no less in studies than in the exercises of the body, or else, as we d were just saying, he will never come to the end of the greatest study and that which most properly belongs to him.

Why, are not these things the greatest? said he. But is there still something greater than justice and the other virtues we described?

There is not only something greater, I said, but of these very things we need not merely to contemplate an outline as now, but we must omit nothing of their most exact elaboration. Or would it not be absurd to strain every nerve to attain to the utmost precision and clar-
e ity of knowledge about other things of trifling moment and not to de-mand the greatest precision for the greatest matters?

It would indeed, he said, but do you suppose that anyone will let you go without asking what is the greatest study and with what you think it is concerned?

By no means, said I, but do you ask the question. You certainly have heard it often, but now you either do not apprehend or again you are minded to make trouble for me by attacking the argument. I sus-
505 pect it is rather the latter. For you have often heard that the greatest thing to learn is the idea of good by reference to which just things and all the rest become useful and beneficial. And now I am almost sure you know that this is what I am going to speak of and to say further that we have no adequate knowledge of it. And if we do not know it, then, even if without the knowledge of this we should know all other things never so well, you are aware that it would avail us nothing, just as no possession either is of any avail without the possession of the
b good. Or do you think there is any profit in possessing everything ex-cept that which is good, or in understanding all things else apart from the good while understanding and knowing nothing that is fair and good?

No, by Zeus, I do not, he said.

But, furthermore, you know this too, that the multitude believe pleasure to be the good, and the finer spirits intelligence or knowledge.

Certainly.

And you are also aware, my friend, that those who hold this latter view are not able to point out what knowledge it is but are finally com-pelled to say that it is the knowledge of the good.

c   Most absurdly, he said.

Is it *not* absurd, said I, if while taunting us with our ignorance of good they turn about and talk to us as if we knew it? For they say it is the knowledge of the good, as if we understood their meaning when they utter the word 'good.'

Most true, he said.

Well, are those who define the good as pleasure infected with any less confusion of thought than the others? Or are not they in like manner compelled to admit that there are bad pleasures?

Most assuredly.

The outcome is, I take it, that they are admitting the same things to be both good and bad, are they not?

Certainly.

d   Then is it not apparent that there are many and violent disputes about it?

Of course.

And again, is it not apparent that while in the case of the just and the honorable many would prefer the semblance without the reality in action, possession, and opinion, yet when it comes to the good nobody is content with the possession of the appearance but all men e seek the reality, and the semblance satisfies nobody here?

Quite so, he said.

That, then, which every soul pursues and for its sake does all that it does, with an intuition of its reality, but yet baffled and unable to apprehend its nature adequately, or to attain to any stable belief about it as about other things, and for that reason failing of any possible 506 benefit from other things—in a matter of this quality and moment, can we, I ask you, allow a like blindness and obscurity in those best citizens to whose hands we are to entrust all things?

Least of all, he said.

I fancy, at any rate, said I, that the just and the honorable, if their relation and reference to the good is not known, will not have secured a guardian of much worth in the man thus ignorant, and my surmise is that no one will understand them adequately before he knows this.

You surmise well, he said.

Then our constitution will have its perfect and definitive organization only when such a guardian, who knows these things, over- b sees it.

Necessarily, he said. But you yourself, Socrates, do you think that knowledge is the good or pleasure or something else and different?

What a man it is, said I. You made it very plain long ago that you would not be satisfied with what others think about it.

Why, it does not seem right to me either, Socrates, he said, to be ready to state the opinions of others but not one's own when one has occupied himself with the matter so long.

But then, said I, do you think it right to speak as having knowl- c edge about things one does not know?

By no means, he said, as having knowledge, but one ought to be willing to tell as his opinion what he opines.

Nay, said I, have you not observed that opinions divorced from knowledge are ugly things? The best of them are blind. Or do you think that those who hold some true opinion without intelligence differ appreciably from blind men who go the right way?

They do not differ at all, he said.

Is it, then, ugly things that you prefer to contemplate, things d blind and crooked, when you might hear from others what is luminous and fair?

Nay, in heaven's name, Socrates, said Glaucon, do not draw back, as it were, at the very goal. For it will content us if you explain the good even as you set forth the nature of justice, sobriety, and the other virtues.

It will right well content me, my dear fellow, I said, but I fear that my powers may fail and that in my eagerness I may cut a sorry figure and become a laughingstock. Nay, my beloved, let us dismiss e for the time being the nature of the good in itself, for to attain to my present surmise of that seems a pitch above the impulse that wings my flight today. But of what seems to be the offspring of the good and most nearly made in its likeness I am willing to speak if you too wish it, and otherwise to let the matter drop.

Well, speak on, he said, for you will duly pay me the tale of the parent another time.

507   I could wish, I said, that I were able to make and you to receive the payment and not merely as now the interest. But at any rate receive this interest and the offspring of the good. Have a care, however, lest I deceive you unintentionally with a false reckoning of the interest.

We will do our best, he said, to be on our guard. Only speak on.

Yes, I said, after first coming to an understanding with you and b reminding you of what has been said here before and often on other occasions.

What? said he.

We predicate 'to be' of many beautiful things and many good things, saying of them severally that they *are,* and so define them in our speech.

We do.

And again, we speak of a self-beautiful and of a good that is only and merely good, and so, in the case of all the things that we then posited as many, we turn about and posit each as a single idea or aspect, assuming it to be a unity and call it that which each really is.

It is so.

And the one class of things we say can be seen but not thought, while the ideas can be thought but not seen.

c   By all means.

With which of the parts of ourselves, with which of our faculties, then, do we see visible things?

With sight, he said.

And do we not, I said, hear audibles with hearing, and perceive all sensibles with the other senses?

Surely.

Have you ever observed, said I, how much the greatest expenditure the creator of the senses has lavished on the faculty of seeing and being seen?

Why, no, I have not, he said.

Well, look at it thus. Do hearing and voice stand in need of another medium so that the one may hear and the other be heard, in the absence of which third element the one will not hear and the other not be heard?

They need nothing, he said.

Neither, I fancy, said I, do many others, not to say that none require anything of the sort. Or do you know of any?

Not I, he said.

But do you not observe that vision and the visible do have this further need?

How?

Though vision may be in the eyes and its possessor may try to use it, and though color be present, yet without the presence of a third thing specifically and naturally adapted to this purpose, you are aware that vision will see nothing and the colors will remain invisible.   e

What is this thing of which you speak? he said.

The thing, I said, that you call light.

You say truly, he replied.

The bond, then, that yokes together visibility and the faculty of   508 sight is more precious by no slight form than that which unites the other pairs, if light is not without honor.

It surely is far from being so, he said.

Which one can you name of the divinities in heaven as the author and cause of this, whose light makes our vision see best and visible things to be seen?

Why, the one that you too and other people mean, he said, for your question evidently refers to the sun.

Is not this, then, the relation of vision to that divinity?

What?

Neither vision itself nor its vehicle, which we call the eye, is identical with the sun.

Why, no.   b

But it is, I think, the most sunlike of all the instruments of sense.

By far the most.

And does it not receive the power which it possesses as an influx, as it were, dispensed from the sun?

Certainly.

Is it not also true that the sun is not vision, yet as being the cause thereof is beheld by vision itself?

That is so, he said.

This, then, you must understand that I meant by the offspring of the good which the good begot to stand in a proportion with itself. As the good is in the intelligible region to reason and the objects of reason, so is this in the visible world to vision and the objects of vision.   c

How is that? he said. Explain further.

You are aware, I said, that when the eyes are no longer turned upon objects upon whose colors the light of day falls but that of the dim luminaries of night, their edge is blunted and they appear almost blind, as if pure vision did not dwell in them.   d

Yes, indeed, he said.

But when, I take it, they are directed upon objects illumined by the sun, they see clearly, and vision appears to reside in these same eyes.

Certainly.

Apply this comparison to the soul also in this way. When it is firmly fixed on the domain where truth and reality shine resplendent it apprehends and knows them and appears to possess reason, but when it inclines to that region which is mingled with darkness, the world of becoming and passing away, it opines only and its edge is blunted, and it shifts its opinions hither and thither, and again seems as if it lacked reason.

Yes, it does.

e   This reality, then, that gives their truth to the objects of knowledge and the power of knowing to the knower, you must say is the idea of good, and you must conceive it as being the cause of knowledge, and of truth in so far as known. Yet fair as they both are, knowledge and truth, in supposing it to be something fairer still than these 509   you will think rightly of it. But as for knowledge and truth, even as in our illustration it is right to deem light and vision sunlike, but never to think that they are the sun, so here it is right to consider these two their counterparts, as being like the good or boniform, but to think that either of them is the good is not right. Still higher honor belongs to the possession and habit of the good.

An inconceivable beauty you speak of, he said, if it is the source of knowledge and truth, and yet itself surpasses them in beauty. For you surely cannot mean that it is pleasure.

Hush, said I, but examine the similitude of it still further in this way.

b   How?

The sun, I presume you will say, not only furnishes to visibles the power of visibility but it also provides for their generation and growth and nurture though it is not itself generation.

Of course not.

In like manner, then, you are to say that the objects of knowledge not only receive from the presence of the good their being known, but their very existence and essence is derived to them from it, though the good itself is not essence but still transcends essence in dignity and surpassing power.

c   And Glaucon very ludicrously said, Heaven save us, hyperbole can no further go.

The fault is yours, I said, for compelling me to utter my thoughts about it.

And don't desist, he said, but at least expound the similitude of the sun, if there is anything that you are omitting.

Why, certainly, I said, I am omitting a great deal.

Well, don't omit the least bit, he said.

I fancy, I said, that I shall have to pass over much, but nevertheless so far as it is at present practicable I shall not willingly leave anything out.

Do not, he said.

Conceive then, said I, as we were saying, that there are these two d entities, and that one of them is sovereign over the intelligible order and region and the other over the world of the eyeball, not to say the sky-ball, but let that pass. You surely apprehend the two types, the visible and the intelligible.

I do.

Represent them then, as it were, by a line divided into two unequal sections and cut each section again in the same ratio—the section, that is, of the visible and that of the intelligible order—and then as an expression of the ratio of their comparative clearness and e obscurity you will have, as one of the sections of the visible world, images. By images I mean, first, shadows, and then reflections in wa- 510 ter and on surfaces of dense, smooth, and bright texture, and everything of that kind, if you apprehend.

I do.

As the second section assume that of which this is a likeness or an image, that is, the animals about us and all plants and the whole class of objects made by man.

I so assume it, he said.

Would you be willing to say, said I, that the division in respect of reality and truth or the opposite is expressed by the proportion—as is the opinable to the knowable so is the likeness to that of which it is a likeness?

I certainly would.   b

Consider then again the way in which we are to make the division of the intelligible section.

In what way?

By the distinction that there is one section of it which the soul is compelled to investigate by treating as images the things imitated in the former division, and by means of assumptions from which it proceeds not up to a first principle but down to a conclusion, while there is another section in which it advances from its assumption to a beginning or principle that transcends assumption, and in which it makes no use of the images employed by the other section, relying on ideas only and progressing systematically through ideas.

I don't fully understand what you mean by this, he said.

Well, I will try again, said I, for you will better understand after c this preamble. For I think you are aware that students of geometry and reckoning and such subjects first postulate the odd and the even and the various figures and three kinds of angles and other things akin to these in each branch of science, regard them as known, and, treating them as absolute assumptions, do not deign to render any further account of them to themselves or others, taking it for granted that

they are obvious to everybody. They take their start from these, and
d pursuing the inquiry from this point on consistently, conclude with
that for the investigation of which they set out.

Certainly, he said, I know that.

And do you not also know that they further make use of the visible forms and talk about them, though they are not thinking of them
but of those things of which they are a likeness, pursuing their inquiry for the sake of the square as such and the diagonal as such, and
not for the sake of the image of it which they draw? And so in all
cases. The very things which they mold and draw, which have shad-
e ows and images of themselves in water, these things they treat in their
turn as only images, but what they really seek is to get sight of those
realities which can be seen only by the mind.

511   True, he said.

This then is the class that I described as intelligible, it is true,
but with the reservation first that the soul is compelled to employ assumptions in the investigation of it, not proceeding to a first principle
because of its inability to extricate itself from and rise above its assumptions, and second, that it uses as images or likenesses the very
objects that are themselves copied and adumbrated by the class below
them, and that in comparison with these latter are esteemed as clear
and held in honor.

b   I understand, said he, that you are speaking of what falls under
geometry and the kindred arts.

Understand then, said I, that by the other section of the intelligible I mean that which the reason itself lays hold of by the power of
dialectic, treating its assumptions not as absolute beginnings but literally as hypotheses, underpinnings, footings, and springboards so to
speak, to enable it to rise to that which requires no assumption and
is the starting point of all, and after attaining to that again taking
hold of the first dependencies from it, so to proceed downward to the
c conclusion, making no use whatever of any object of sense but only of
pure ideas moving on through ideas to ideas and ending with ideas.

I understand, he said, not fully, for it is no slight task that you appear to have in mind, but I do understand that you mean to distinguish the aspect of reality and the intelligible, which is contemplated
by the power of dialectic, as something truer and more exact than the
object of the so-called arts and sciences whose assumptions are arbitrary starting points. And though it is true that those who contemplate
d them are compelled to use their understanding and not their senses,
yet because they do not go back to the beginning in the study of them
but start from assumptions you do not think they possess true intelligence about them although the things themselves are intelligibles
when apprehended in conjunction with a first principle. And I think
you call the mental habit of geometers and their like mind or under-

standing and not reason because you regard understanding as something intermediate between opinion and reason.

Your interpretation is quite sufficient, I said. And now, answering to these four sections, assume these four affections occurring
in the soul—intellection or reason for the highest, understanding for
the second, belief for the third, and for the last, picture thinking or e
conjecture—and arrange them in a proportion, considering that they
participate in clearness and precision in the same degree as their objects partake of truth and reality.

I understand, he said. I concur and arrange them as you bid.

BOOK VII

Next, said I, compare our nature in respect of education and its lack 514
to such an experience as this. Picture men dwelling in a sort of subterranean cavern with a long entrance open to the light on its entire
width. Conceive them as having their legs and necks fettered from
childhood, so that they remain in the same spot, able to look forward
only, and prevented by the fetters from turning their heads. Picture b
further the light from a fire burning higher up and at a distance behind them, and between the fire and the prisoners and above them a
road along which a low wall has been built, as the exhibitors of puppet shows have partitions before the men themselves, above which
they show the puppets.

All that I see, he said.

See also, then, men carrying past the wall implements of all
kinds that rise above the wall, and human images and shapes of ani- c
mals as well, wrought in stone and wood and every material, some of 515
these bearers presumably speaking and others silent.

A strange image you speak of, he said, and strange prisoners.

Like to us, I said. For, to begin with, tell me do you think that
these men would have seen anything of themselves or of one another
except the shadows cast from the fire on the wall of the cave that
fronted them?

How could they, he said, if they were compelled to hold their b
heads unmoved through life?

And again, would not the same be true of the objects carried past
them?

Surely.

If then they were able to talk to one another, do you not think
that they would suppose that in naming the things that they saw they
were naming the passing objects?

Necessarily.

And if their prison had an echo from the wall opposite them,
when one of the passers-by uttered a sound, do you think that they

would suppose anything else than the passing shadow to be the speaker?

By Zeus, I do not, said he.

c   Then in every way such prisoners would deem reality to be nothing else than the shadows of the artificial objects.

Quite inevitably, he said.

Consider, then, what would be the manner of the release and healing from these bonds and this folly if in the course of nature something of this sort should happen to them. When one was freed from his fetters and compelled to stand up suddenly and turn his head around and walk and to lift up his eyes to the light, and in doing all this felt pain and, because of the dazzle and glitter of the light, was unable to discern the objects whose shadows he formerly saw, what do you suppose would be his answer if someone told him that what he

d   had seen before was all a cheat and an illusion, but that now, being nearer to reality and turned toward more real things, he saw more truly? And if also one should point out to him each of the passing objects and constrain him by questions to say what it is, do you not think that he would be at a loss and that he would regard what he formerly saw as more real than the things now pointed out to him?

Far more real, he said.

e   And if he were compelled to look at the light itself, would not that pain his eyes, and would he not turn away and flee to those things which he is able to discern and regard them as in very deed more clear and exact than the objects pointed out?

It is so, he said.

And if, said I, someone should drag him thence by force up the ascent which is rough and steep, and not let him go before he had drawn him out into the light of the sun, do you not think that he would find it painful to be so haled along, and would chafe at it, and

516   when he came out into the light, that his eyes would be filled with its beams so that he would not be able to see even one of the things that we call real?

Why, no, not immediately, he said.

Then there would be need of habituation, I take it, to enable him to see the things higher up. And at first he would most easily discern the shadows and, after that, the likenesses or reflections in water of men and other things, and later, the things themselves, and from these he would go on to contemplate the appearances in the heavens

b   and heaven itself, more easily by night, looking at the light of the stars and the moon, than by day the sun and the sun's light.

Of course.

And so, finally, I suppose, he would be able to look upon the sun itself and see its true nature, not by reflections in water or phantasms of it in an alien setting, but in and by itself in its own place.

Necessarily, he said.

And at this point he would infer and conclude that this it is that provides the seasons and the courses of the year and presides over all things in the visible region, and is in some sort the cause of all these c things that they had seen.

Obviously, he said, that would be the next step.

Well then, if he recalled to mind his first habitation and what passed for wisdom there, and his fellow bondsmen, do you not think that he would count himself happy in the change and pity them?

He would indeed.

And if there had been honors and commendations among them which they bestowed on one another and prizes for the man who is quickest to make out the shadows as they pass and best able to remember their customary precedences, sequences, and coexistences, and so d most successful in guessing at what was to come, do you think he would be very keen about such rewards, and that he would envy and emulate those who were honored by these prisoners and lorded it among them, or that he would feel with Homer and greatly prefer while living on earth to be serf of another, a landless man, and endure anything rather than opine with them and live that life?

Yes, he said, I think that he would choose to endure anything e rather than such a life.

And consider this also, said I. If such a one should go down again and take his old place would he not get his eyes full of darkness, thus suddenly coming out of the sunlight?

He would indeed.

Now if he should be required to contend with these perpetual 517 prisoners in 'evaluating' these shadows while his vision was still dim and before his eyes were accustomed to the dark—and this time required for habituation would not be very short—would he not provoke laughter, and would it not be said of him that he had returned from his journey aloft with his eyes ruined and that it was not worth while even to attempt the ascent? And if it were possible to lay hands on and to kill the man who tried to release them and lead them up, would they not kill him?

They certainly would, he said.

This image then, dear Glaucon, we must apply as a whole to all that has been said, likening the region revealed through sight to the b habitation of the prison, and the light of the fire in it to the power of the sun. And if you assume that the ascent and the contemplation of the things above is the soul's ascension to the intelligible region, you will not miss my surmise, since that is what you desire to hear. But Gods knows whether it is true. But, at any rate, my dream as it appears to me is that in the region of the known the last thing to be seen and hardly seen is the idea of good, and that when seen it must needs point us to the conclusion that this is indeed the cause for all things c of all that is right and beautiful, giving birth in the visible world to light, and the author of light and itself in the intelligible world being the authentic source of truth and reason, and that anyone who is to act wisely in private or public must have caught sight of this.

I concur, he said, so far as I am able.

Come then, I said, and join me in this further thought, and do not be surprised that those who have attained to this height are not willing to occupy themselves with the affairs of men, but their souls ever

d feel the upward urge and the yearning for that sojourn above. For this, I take it, is likely if in this point too the likeness of our image holds.

Yes, it is likely.

And again, do you think it at all strange, said I, if a man returning from divine contemplations to the petty miseries of men cuts a sorry figure and appears most ridiculous, if, while still blinking through the gloom, and before he has become sufficiently accustomed to the environing darkness, he is compelled in courtrooms or elsewhere to contend about the shadows of justice or the images that cast the shad-

e ows and to wrangle in debate about the notions of these things in the minds of those who have never seen justice itself?

It would be by no means strange, he said.

518   But a sensible man, I said, would remember that there are two distinct disturbances of the eyes arising from two causes, according as the shift is from light to darkness or from darkness to light, and, believing that the same thing happens to the soul too, whenever he saw a soul perturbed and unable to discern something, he would not laugh unthinkingly, but would observe whether coming from a brighter life its vision was obscured by the unfamiliar darkness, or whether the passage from the deeper dark of ignorance into a more luminous world and the greater brightness had dazzled its vision. And so he

b would deem the one happy in its experience and way of life and pity the other, and if it pleased him to laugh at it, his laughter would be less laughable than that at the expense of the soul that had come down from the light above.

That is a very fair statement, he said.

Then, if this is true, our view of these matters must be this, that education is not in reality what some people proclaim it to be in their professions. What they aver is that they can put true knowledge into a

c soul that does not possess it, as if they were inserting vision into blind eyes.

They do indeed, he said.

But our present argument indicates, said I, that the true analogy for this indwelling power in the soul and the instrument whereby each of us apprehends is that of an eye that could not be converted to the light from the darkness except by turning the whole body. Even so this organ of knowledge must be turned around from the world of be-

coming together with the entire soul, like the scene-shifting periactus
in the theater, until the soul is able to endure the contemplation of
essence and the brightest region of being. And this, we say, is the
good, do we not?   d
    Yes.
    Of this very thing, then, I said, there might be an art, an art of
the speediest and most effective shifting or conversion of the soul, not
an art of producing vision in it, but on the assumption that it possesses
vision but does not rightly direct it and does not look where it should,
an art of bringing this about.
    Yes, that seems likely, he said.
    Then the other so-called virtues of the soul do seem akin to those
of the body. For it is true that where they do not pre-exist, they are
afterward created by habit and practice. But the excellence of thought, e
it seems, is certainly of a more divine quality, a thing that never loses
its potency, but, according to the direction of its conversion, becomes
useful and beneficent, or, again, useless and harmful. Have you never 519
observed in those who are popularly spoken of as bad, but smart men
how keen is the vision of the little soul, how quick it is to discern the
things that interest it, a proof that it is not a poor vision which it has,
but one forcibly enlisted in the service of evil, so that the sharper its
sight the more mischief it accomplishes?
    I certainly have, he said.
    Observe then, said I, that this part of such a soul, if it had been
hammered from childhood, and had thus been struck free of the
leaden weights, so to speak, of our birth and becoming, which attaching themselves to it by food and similar pleasures and gluttonies turn b
downward the vision of the soul—if, I say, freed from these, it had
suffered a conversion toward the things that are real and true, that
same faculty of the same men would have been most keen in its vision
of the higher things, just as it is for the things toward which it is now
turned.
    It is likely, he said.
    Well, then, said I, is not this also likely and a necessary conse-
quence of what has been said, that neither could men who are uneducated and inexperienced in truth ever adequately preside over a
state, nor could those who had been permitted to linger on to the end c
in the pursuit of culture—the one because they have no single aim and
purpose in life to which all their actions, public and private, must
be directed, and the others, because they will not voluntarily engage
in action, believing that while still living they have been transported
to the Islands of the Blessed?
    True, he said.
    It is the duty of us, the founders, then, said I, to compel the best
natures to attain the knowledge which we pronounced the greatest,

d and to win to the vision of the good, to scale that ascent, and when they have reached the heights and taken an adequate view, we must not allow what is now permitted.

What is that?

That they should linger there, I said, and refuse to go down again among those bondsmen and share their labors and honors, whether they are of less or of greater worth.

Do you mean to say that we must do them this wrong, and compel them to live an inferior life when the better is in their power?

e You have again forgotten, my friend, said I, that the law is not concerned with the special happiness of any class in the state, but is trying to produce this condition in the city as a whole, harmonizing and adapting the citizens to one another by persuasion and compulsion, and requiring them to impart to one another any benefit which 520 they are severally able to bestow upon the community, and that it itself creates such men in the state, not that it may allow each to take what course pleases him, but with a view to using them for the binding together of the commonwealth.

True, he said, I did forget it.

Observe, then, Glaucon, said I, that we shall not be wronging, either, the philosophers who arise among us, but that we can justify our action when we constrain them to take charge of the other citizens and be their guardians. For we will say to them that it is natural that men of similar quality who spring up in other cities should not b share in the labors there. For they grow up spontaneously from no volition of the government in the several states, and it is justice that the self-grown, indebted to none for its breeding, should not be zealous either to pay to anyone the price of its nurture. But you we have engendered for yourselves and the rest of the city to be, as it were, king bees and leaders in the hive. You have received a better and more complete education than the others, and you are more capable c of sharing both ways of life. Down you must go then, each in his turn, to the habitation of the others and accustom yourselves to the observation of the obscure things there. For once habituated you will discern them infinitely better than the dwellers there, and you will know what each of the 'idols' is and whereof it is a semblance, because you have seen the reality of the beautiful, the just and the good. So our city will be governed by us and you with waking minds, and not, as most cities now which are inhabited and ruled darkly as in a dream d by men who fight one another for shadows and wrangle for office as if that were a great good, when the truth is that the city in which those who are to rule are least eager to hold office must needs be best administered and most free from dissension, and the state that gets the contrary type of ruler will be the opposite of this.

By all means, he said.

Will our alumni, then, disobey us when we tell them this, and will they refuse to share in the labors of state each in his turn while permitted to dwell most of the time with one another in that purer world?

Impossible, he said, for we shall be imposing just commands on e men who are just. Yet they will assuredly approach office as an unavoidable necessity, and in the opposite temper from that of the present rulers in our cities.

For the fact is, dear friend, said I, if you can discover a better way of life than office holding for your future rulers, a well-governed 521 city becomes a possibility. For only in such a state will those rule who are really rich, not in gold, but in the wealth that makes happiness— a good and wise life. But if, being beggars and starvelings from lack of goods of their own, they turn to affairs of state thinking that it is thence that they should grasp their own good, then it is impossible. For when office and rule become the prizes of contention, such a civil and internecine strife destroys the office seekers themselves and the city as well.

Most true, he said.

Can you name any other type or ideal of life that looks with scorn b on political office except the life of true philosophers? I asked.

No, by Zeus, he said.

But what we require, I said, is that those who take office should not be lovers of rule. Otherwise there will be a contest with rival lovers.

Surely.

What others, then, will you compel to undertake the guardianship of the city than those who have most intelligence of the principles that are the means of good government and who possess distinctions of another kind and a life that is preferable to the political life?

No others, he said.

Would you, then, have us proceed to consider how such men may c be produced in a state and how they may be led upward to the light even as some are fabled to have ascended from Hades to the gods?

Of course I would.

So this, it seems, would not be the whirling of the shell in the children's game, but a conversion and turning about of the soul from a day whose light is darkness to the veritable day—that ascension to reality of our parable which we will affirm to be true philosophy.

By all means.

Must we not, then, consider what studies have the power to effect d this?

Of course.

What, then, Glaucon, would be the study that would draw the soul away from the world of becoming to the world of being? A thought strikes me while I speak. Did we not say that these men in youth must be athletes of war?

We did.

Then the study for which we are seeking must have this additional qualification.

What one?

That it be not useless to soldiers.

Why, yes, it must, he said, if that is possible.

e   But in our previous account they were educated in gymnastics and music.

They were, he said.

And gymnastics, I take it, is devoted to that which grows and perishes, for it presides over the growth and decay of the body.

Obviously.

522   Then this cannot be the study that we seek.

No.

Is it, then, music, so far as we have already described it?

Nay, that, he said, was the counterpart of gymnastics, if you remember. It educated the guardians through habits, imparting by the melody a certain harmony of spirit that is not science, and by the rhythm measure and grace, and also qualities akin to these in the words of tales that are fables and those that are more nearly true.

b   But it included no study that tended to any such good as you are now seeking.

Your recollection is most exact, I said, for in fact it had nothing of the kind. But in heaven's name, Glaucon, what study could there be of that kind? For all the arts were in our opinion base and mechanical.

Surely, and yet what other study is left apart from music, gymnastics, and the arts?

Come, said I, if we are unable to discover anything outside of these, let us take something that applies to all alike.

What?

c   Why, for example, this common thing that all arts and forms of thought and all sciences employ, and which is among the first things that everybody must learn.

What? he said.

This trifling matter, I said, of distinguishing one and two and three. I mean, in sum, number and calculation. Is it not true of them that every art and science must necessarily partake of them?

Indeed it is, he said.

The art of war too? said I.

Most necessarily, he said.

d   Certainly, then, said I, Palamedes in the play is always making Agamemnon appear a most ridiculous general. Have you not noticed that he affirms that by the invention of number he marshaled the troops in the army at Troy in ranks and companies and enumerated

the ships and everything else as if before that they had not been
counted, and Agamemnon apparently did not know how many feet
he had if he couldn't count? And yet what sort of a general do you
think he would be in that case?

A very queer one in my opinion, he said, if that was true.

Shall we not, then, I said, set down as a study requisite for a e
soldier the ability to reckon and number?

Most certainly, if he is to know anything whatever of the ordering of his troops—or rather if he is to be a man at all.

Do you observe then, said I, in this study what I do?

What?

It seems likely that it is one of those studies which we are seeking 523
that naturally conduce to the awakening of thought, but that no one
makes the right use of it, though it really does tend to draw the mind
to essence and reality.

What do you mean? he said.

I will try, I said, to show you at least my opinion. Do you keep
watch and observe the things I distinguish in my mind as being or not
being conducive to our purpose, and either concur or dissent, in order
that here too we may see more clearly whether my surmise is right.

Point them out, he said.

I do point them out, I said, if you can discern that some reports b
of our perceptions do not provoke thought to reconsideration because
the judgment of them by sensation seems adequate, while others
always invite the intellect to reflection because the sensation yields
nothing that can be trusted.

You obviously mean distant appearances, he said, and shadow
painting.

You have quite missed my meaning, said I.

What do you mean? he said.

The experiences that do not provoke thought are those that do
not at the same time issue in a contradictory perception. Those that c
do have that effect I set down as provocatives, when the perception no
more manifests one thing than its contrary, alike whether its impact
comes from nearby or afar. An illustration will make my meaning
plain. Here, we say, are three fingers, the little finger, the second,
and the middle.

Quite so, he said.

Assume that I speak of them as seen near at hand. But this is the
point that you are to consider.

What?

Each one of them appears to be equally a finger, and in this respect it makes no difference whether it is observed as intermediate or d
at either extreme, whether it is white or black, thick or thin, or of
any other quality of this kind. For in none of these cases is the soul

of most men impelled to question the reason and to ask what in the world is a finger, since the faculty of sight never signifies to it at the same time that the finger is the opposite of a finger.

Why, no, it does not, he said.

Then, said I, it is to be expected that such a perception will not provoke or awaken reflection and thought.

e   It is.

But now, what about the bigness and the smallness of these objects? Is our vision's view of them adequate, and does it make no difference to it whether one of them is situated outside or in the middle, and similarly of the relation of touch, to thickness and thinness, softness and hardness? And are not the other senses also defective in
524 their reports of such things? Or is the operation of each of them as follows? In the first place, the sensation that is set over the hard is of necessity related also to the soft, and it reports to the soul that the same thing is both hard and soft to its perception.

It is so, he said.

Then, said I, is not this again a case where the soul must be at a loss as to what significance for it the sensation of hardness has, if the sense reports the same thing as also soft? And, similarly, as to what the sensation of light and heavy means by light and heavy, if it reports the heavy as light, and the light as heavy?

b   Yes, indeed, he said, these communications to the soul are strange and invite reconsideration.

Naturally, then, said I, it is in such cases as these that the soul first summons to its aid the calculating reason and tries to consider whether each of the things reported to it is one or two.

Of course.

And if it appears to be two, each of the two is a distinct unit.

Yes.

If, then, each is one and both two, the very meaning of 'two' is that the soul will conceive them as distinct. For if they were not separable, it would not have been thinking of two, but of one.

Right.

c   Sight too saw the great and the small, we say, not separated but confounded. Is not that so?

Yes.

And for the clarification of this, the intelligence is compelled to contemplate the great and small, not thus confounded but as distinct entities, in the opposite way from sensation.

True.

And is it not in some such experience as this that the question first occurs to us, What in the world, then, is the great and the small?

By all means.

And this is the origin of the designation *intelligible* for the one, and *visible* for the other.

Just so, he said.   d

This, then, is just what I was trying to explain a little while ago
when I said that some things are provocative of thought and some
are not, defining as provocative things that impinge upon the senses
together with their opposites, while those that do not I said do not
tend to awaken reflection.

Well, now I understand, he said, and agree.

To which class, then, do you think number and the one belong?

I cannot conceive, he said.

Well, reason it out from what has already been said. For, if unity
is adequately seen by itself or apprehended by some other sensation,
it would not tend to draw the mind to the apprehension of essence, as
we were explaining in the case of the finger. But if some contra-   e
diction is always seen coincidentally with it, so that it no more appears to be one than the opposite, there would forthwith be need of
something to judge between them, and it would compel the soul to be
at a loss and to inquire, by arousing thought in itself, and to ask,
whatever then is the one as such, and thus the study of unity will be
one of the studies that guide and convert the soul to the contemplation 525
of true being.

But surely, he said, the visual perception of it does especially involve this. For we see the same thing at once as one and as an indefinite plurality.

Then if this is true of the one, I said, the same holds of all number, does it not?

Of course.

But, further, reckoning and the science of arithmetic are wholly
concerned with number.

They are, indeed.

And the qualities of number appear to lead to the apprehension   b
of truth.

Beyond anything, he said.

Then, as it seems, these would be among the studies that we are
seeking. For a soldier must learn them in order to marshal his troops,
and a philosopher because he must rise out of the region of generation
and lay hold on essence or he can never become a true reckoner.

It is so, he said.

And our guardian is soldier and philosopher in one.

Of course.

It is befitting, then, Glaucon, that this branch of learning should
be prescribed by our law and that we should induce those who are to
share the highest functions of state to enter upon that study of calcu- c
lation and take hold of it, not as amateurs, but to follow it up until
they attain to the contemplation of the nature of number, by pure
thought, not for the purpose of buying and selling, as if they were preparing to be merchants or hucksters, but for the uses of war and for

facilitating the conversion of the soul itself from the world of generation to essence and truth.

Excellently said, he replied.

And, further, I said, it occurs to me, now that the study of reckon-
d ing has been mentioned, that there is something fine in it, and that it
is useful for our purpose in many ways, provided it is pursued for the
sake of knowledge and not for huckstering.

In what respect? he said.

Why, in respect of the very point of which we were speaking, that
it strongly directs the soul upward and compels it to discourse about
pure numbers, never acquiescing if anyone proffers to it in the discussion numbers attached to visible and tangible bodies. For you are
e doubtless aware that experts in this study, if anyone attempts to cut
up the 'one' in argument, laugh at him and refuse to allow it, but if
you mince it up, *they* multiply, always on guard lest the one should
appear to be not one but a multiplicity of parts.

Most true, he replied.

526 Suppose now, Glaucon, someone were to ask them, My good
friends, what numbers are these you are talking about, in which the
one is such as you postulate, each unity equal to every other without
the slightest difference and admitting no division into parts? What do
you think would be their answer?

This, I think—that they are speaking of units which can only
be conceived by thought, and which it is not possible to deal with in
any other way.

You see, then, my friend, said I, that this branch of study really
b seems to be indispensable for us, since it plainly compels the soul to
employ pure thought with a view to truth itself.

It most emphatically does.

Again, have you ever noticed this, that natural reckoners are by
nature quick in virtually all their studies? And the slow, if they are
trained and drilled in this, even if no other benefit results, all improve
and become quicker than they were?

It is so, he said.

c And, further, as I believe, studies that demand more toil in the
learning and practice than this we shall not discover easily nor find
many of them.

You will not, in fact.

Then, for all these reasons, we must not neglect this study, but
must use it in the education of the best-endowed natures.

I agree, he said.

Assuming this one point to be established, I said, let us in the
second place consider whether the study that comes next is suited to
our purpose.

What is that? Do you mean geometry? he said.

Precisely that, said I.

So much of it, he said, as applies to the conduct of war is ob- d
viously suitable. For in dealing with encampments and the occupation of strong places and the bringing of troops into column and
line and all the other formations of an army in actual battle and on
the march, an officer who had studied geometry would be a very different person from what he would be if he had not.

But still, I said, for such purposes a slight modicum of geometry
and calculation would suffice. What we have to consider is whether
the greater and more advanced part of it tends to facilitate the ap- e
prehension of the idea of good. That tendency, we affirm, is to be
found in all studies that force the soul to turn its vision round to the
region where dwells the most blessed part of reality, which it is imperative that it should behold.

You are right, he said.

Then if it compels the soul to contemplate essence, it is suitable;
if genesis, it is not.

So we affirm.   527

This at least, said I, will not be disputed by those who have even
a slight acquaintance with geometry, that this science is in direct contradiction with the language employed in it by its adepts.

How so? he said.

Their language is most ludicrous, though they cannot help it,
for they speak as if they were doing something and as if all their
words were directed toward action. For all their talk is of squaring
and applying and adding and the like, whereas in fact the real object
of the entire study is pure knowledge.

That is absolutely true, he said.   b

And must we not agree on a further point?

What?

That it is the knowledge of that which always is, and not of a
something which at some time comes into being and passes away.

That is readily admitted, he said, for geometry is the knowledge
of the eternally existent.

Then, my good friend, it would tend to draw the soul to truth,
and would be productive of a philosophical attitude of mind, directing
upward the faculties that now wrongly are turned earthward.

Nothing is surer, he said.

Then nothing is surer, said I, than that we must require that the c
men of your fair city shall never neglect geometry, for even the by-
products of such study are not slight.

What are they? said he.

What you mentioned, said I, its uses in war, and also we are
aware that for the better reception of all studies there will be an im-
measurable difference between the student who has been imbued with
geometry and the one who has not.

Immense indeed, by Zeus, he said.

Shall we, then, lay this down as a second branch of study for our lads?

Let us do so, he said.

d   Shall we set down astronomy as a third, or do you dissent?

I certainly agree, he said, for quickness of perception about the seasons and the courses of the months and the years is serviceable, not only to agriculture and navigation, but still more to the military art.

I am amused, said I, at your apparent fear lest the multitude may suppose you to be recommending useless studies. It is indeed no trifling task, but very difficult to realize that there is in every soul an
e   organ or instrument of knowledge that is purified and kindled afresh by such studies when it has been destroyed and blinded by our ordinary pursuits, a faculty whose preservation outweighs ten thousand eyes, for by it only is reality beheld. Those who share this faith will think your words superlatively true. But those who have and have had no inkling of it will naturally think them all moonshine. For they can
528 see no other benefit from such pursuits worth mentioning. Decide, then, on the spot, to which party you address yourself. Or are you speaking to neither, but chiefly carrying on the discussion for your own sake, without however grudging any other who may be able to profit by it?

This is the alternative I choose, he said, that it is for my own sake chiefly that I speak and ask questions and reply.

Fall back a little, then, said I, for we just now did not rightly select the study that comes next after geometry.

What was our mistake? he said.

b   After plane surfaces, said I, we went on to solids in revolution before studying them in themselves. The right way is next in order after the second dimension to take the third. This, I suppose, is the dimension of cubes and of everything that has depth.

Why, yes, it is, he said, but this subject, Socrates, does not appear to have been investigated yet.

There are two causes of that, said I. First, inasmuch as no city holds them in honor, these inquiries are languidly pursued owing to their difficulty. And secondly, the investigators need a director, who is indispensable for success and who, to begin with, is not easy to find, and then, if he could be found, as things are now, seekers in this field
c   would be too arrogant to submit to his guidance. But if the state as a whole should join in superintending these studies and honor them, these specialists would accept advice, and continuous and strenuous investigation would bring out the truth. Since even now, lightly esteemed as they are by the multitude and hampered by the ignorance of their students as to the true reasons for pursuing them, they nevertheless in the face of all these obstacles force their way by

their inherent charm and it would not surprise us if the truth about d
them were made apparent.

It is true, he said, that they do possess an extraordinary attractiveness and charm. But explain more clearly what you were just
speaking of. The investigation of plane surfaces, I presume, you took
to be geometry?

Yes, said I.

And then, he said, at first you took astronomy next and then you
drew back.

Yes, I said, for in my haste to be done I was making less speed.
For, while the next thing in order is the study of the third dimension
or solids, I passed it over because of our absurd neglect to investigate
it, and mentioned next after geometry astronomy, which deals with
the movements of solids.

That is right, he said.   e

Then, as our fourth study, said I, let us set down astronomy, assuming that this science, the discussion of which has been passed
over, is available, provided, that is, that the state pursues it.

That is likely, said he, and instead of the vulgar utilitarian
commendation of astronomy, for which you just now rebuked me,
Socrates, I now will praise it on your principles. For it is obvious to 529
everybody, I think that this study certainly compels the soul to look
upward and leads it away from things here to those higher things.

It may be obvious to everybody except me, said I, for I do not
think so.

What do you think? he said.

As it is now handled by those who are trying to lead us up to
philosophy, I think that it turns the soul's gaze very much downward.

What do you mean? he said.

You seem to me in your thought to put a most liberal interpretation on the 'study of higher things,' I said, for apparently if anyone
with back-thrown head should learn something by staring at deco- b
rations on a ceiling, you would regard him as contemplating them
with the higher reason and not with the eyes. Perhaps you are right
and I am a simpleton. For I, for my part, am unable to suppose that
any other study turns the soul's gaze upward than that which deals
with being and the invisible. But if anyone tries to learn about the
things of sense, whether gaping up or blinking down, I would never
say that he really learns—for nothing of the kind admits of true
knowledge—nor would I say that his soul looks up, but down, even c
though he study floating on his back on sea or land.

A fair retort, he said. Your rebuke is deserved. But how, then,
did you mean that astronomy ought to be taught contrary to the
present fashion if it is to be learned in a way to conduce to our purpose?

Thus, said I. These sparks that paint the sky, since they are decorations on a visible surface, we must regard, to be sure, as the fairest
d and most exact of material things, but we must recognize that they fall far short of the truth, the movements, namely, of real speed and real slowness in true number and in all true figures both in relation to one another and as vehicles of the things they carry and contain. These can be apprehended only by reason and thought, but not by sight, or do you think otherwise?

By no means, he said.

Then, said I, we must use the blazonry of the heavens as patterns to aid in the study of those realities, just as one would do who
e chanced upon diagrams drawn with special care and elaboration by Daedalus or some other craftsman or painter. For anyone acquainted with geometry who saw such designs would admit the beauty of the workmanship, but would think it absurd to examine them seriously in the expectation of finding in them the absolute truth with regard to
530 equals or doubles or any other ratio.

How could it be otherwise than absurd? he said.

Do you not think, said I, that one who was an astronomer in very truth would feel in the same way when he turned his eyes upon the movements of the stars? He will be willing to concede that the artisan of heaven fashioned it and all that it contains in the best possible manner for such a fabric. But when it comes to the proportions of day and night, and of their relation to the month, and that of the month
b to the year, and of the other stars to these and one another, do you not suppose that he will regard as a very strange fellow the man who believes that these things go on forever without change or the least deviation—though they possess bodies and are visible objects—and that his unremitting quest is the realities of these things?

I at least do think so, he said, now that I hear it from you.

It is by means of problems, then, said I, as in the study of
c geometry, that we will pursue astronomy too, and we will let be the things in the heavens, if we are to have a part in the true science of astronomy and so convert to right use from uselessness that natural indwelling intelligence of the soul.

You enjoin a task, he said, that will multiply the labor of our present study of astronomy many times.

And I fancy, I said, that our other injunctions will be of the same kind if we are of any use as lawgivers. However, what suitable studies have you to suggest?

Nothing, he said, thus offhand.

Yet, surely, said I, motion in general provides not one but many forms or species, according to my opinion. To enumerate them all
d will perhaps be the task of a wise man, but even to us two of them are apparent.

What are they?

In addition to astronomy, its counterpart, I replied.

What is that?

We may venture to suppose, I said, that as the eyes are framed for astronomy so the ears are framed for the movements of harmony, and these are in some sort kindred sciences, as the Pythagoreans affirm and we admit, do we not, Glaucon?

We do, he said.

Then, said I, since the task is so great, shall we not inquire of e them what their opinion is and whether they have anything to add? And we in all this will be on the watch for what concerns us.

What is that?

To prevent our fosterlings from attempting to learn anything that does not conduce to the end we have in view, and does not always come out at what we said ought to be the goal of everything, as we were just now saying about astronomy. Or do you not know that they repeat the same procedure in the case of harmonies? They transfer it 531 to hearing and measure audible concords and sounds against one another, expending much useless labor just as the astronomers do.

Yes, by heaven, he said, and most absurdly too. They talk of something they call minims and, laying their ears alongside, as if trying to catch a voice from next door, some affirm that they can hear a note between and that this is the least interval and the unit of measurement, while others insist that the strings now render identical sounds, both preferring their ears to their minds. b

You, said I, are speaking of the worthies who vex and torture the strings and rack them on the pegs, but—not to draw out the comparison with strokes of the plectrum and the musician's complaints of too responsive and too reluctant strings—I drop the figure, and tell you that I do not mean these people, but those others whom we just now said we would interrogate about harmony. Their method exactly corresponds to that of the astronomer, for the numbers they seek are c those found in these heard concords, but they do not ascend to generalized problems and the consideration which numbers are inherently concordant and which not and why in each case.

A superhuman task, he said.

Say, rather, useful, said I, for the investigation of the beautiful and the good, but if otherwise pursued, useless.

That is likely, he said.

And what is more, I said, I take it that if the investigation of all these studies goes far enough to bring out their community and kin- d ship with one another, and to infer their affinities, then to busy ourselves with them contributes to our desired end, and the labor taken is not lost, but otherwise it is vain.

I too so surmise, said he, but it is a huge task of which you speak, Socrates.

Are you talking about the prelude, I said, or what? Or do we not know that all this is but the preamble of the law itself, the prelude of the strain that we have to apprehend? For you surely do not suppose that experts in these matters are reasoners and dialecticians?

e   No, by Zeus, he said, except a very few whom I have met.

But have you ever supposed, I said, that men who could not render and exact an account of opinions in discussion would ever 532 know anything of the things we say must be known?

No is surely the answer to that too.

This, then, at last, Glaucon, I said, is the very law which dialectic recites, the strain which it executes, of which, though it belongs to the intelligible, we may see an imitation in the progress of the faculty of vision, as we described its endeavor to look at living things themselves and the stars themselves and finally at the very sun. In like manner, when anyone by dialectic attempts through discourse of reason and apart from all perceptions of sense to find his way to the very essence of each thing and does not desist till he apprehends by b thought itself the nature of the good in itself, he arrives at the limit of the intelligible, as the other in our parable came to the goal of the visible.

By all means, he said.

What, then, will you not call this progress of thought dialectic? Surely.

And the release from bonds, I said, and the conversion from the shadows to the images that cast them and to the light and the ascent from the subterranean cavern to the world above, and there the persisting inability to look directly at animals and plants and the light c of the sun, but the ability to see the phantasms created by God in water and shadows of objects that are real and not merely, as before, the shadows of images cast through a light which, compared with the sun, is as unreal as they—all this procedure of the arts and sciences that we have described indicates their power to lead the best part of the soul up to the contemplation of what is best among realities, as in our parable the clearest organ in the body was turned to the contem- d plation of what is brightest in the corporeal and visible region.

I accept this, he said, as the truth, and yet it appears to me very hard to accept, and again, from another point of view, hard to reject. Nevertheless, since we have not to hear it at this time only, but are to repeat it often hereafter, let us assume that these things are as now has been said, and proceed to the melody itself, and go through with it as we have gone through the prelude. Tell me, then, what is the nature e of this faculty of dialectic? Into what divisions does it fall? And what are its ways? For it is these, it seems, that would bring us to the place where we may, so to speak, rest on the road and then come to the end of our journeying.

533   You will not be able, dear Glaucon, to follow me further, though on my part there will be no lack of good will. And, if I could, I would

show you, no longer an image and symbol of my meaning, but the very truth, as it appears to me—though whether rightly or not I may not properly affirm. But that something like this is what we have to see, I must affirm. Is not that so?

Surely.

And may we not also declare that nothing less than the power of dialectic could reveal this, and that only to one experienced in the studies we have described, and that the thing is in no other wise possible?

That, too, he said, we may properly affirm.

This, at any rate, said I, no one will maintain in dispute against b us, that there is any other way of inquiry that attempts systematically and in all cases to determine what each thing really is. But all the other arts have for their object the opinions and desires of men or are wholly concerned with generation and composition or with the service and tendance of the things that grow and are put together, while the remnant which we said did in some sort lay hold on reality— geometry and the studies that accompany it—are, as we see, dreaming c about being, but the clear waking vision of it is impossible for them as long as they leave the assumptions which they employ undisturbed and cannot give any account of them. For where the starting point is something that the reasoner does not know, and the conclusion and all that intervenes is a tissue of things not really known, what possibility is there that assent in such cases can ever be converted into true knowledge or science?

None, said he.

Then, said I, is not dialectic the only process of inquiry that advances in this manner, doing away with hypotheses, up to the first principle itself in order to find confirmation there? And it is literally d true that when the eye of the soul is sunk in the barbaric slough of the Orphic myth, dialectic gently draws it forth and leads it up, employing as helpers and co-operators in this conversion the studies and sciences which we enumerated, which we called sciences often from habit, though they really need some other designation, connoting more clearness than opinion and more obscurity than science. 'Understanding,' I believe, was the term we employed. But I presume we shall not dispute about the name when things of such moment lie before us for consideration.

No, indeed, he said.

Are you satisfied, then, said I, as before, to call the first division e science, the second understanding, the third belief, and the fourth conjecture or picture thought—and the last two collectively opinion, and the first two intellection, opinion dealing with generation, and intellection with essence, and this relation being expressed in the pro- 534 portion: as essence is to generation, so is intellection to opinion, and as intellection is to opinion, so is science to belief, and understanding

to image thinking or surmise? But the relation between their objective correlates and the division into two parts of each of these, the opinable, namely, and the intelligible, let us dismiss, Glaucon, lest it
b involve us in discussion many times as long as the preceding.

Well, he said, I agree with you about the rest of it, so far as I am able to follow.

And do you not also give the name dialectician to the man who is able to exact an account of the essence of each thing? And will you not say that the one who is unable to do this, in so far as he is incapable of rendering an account to himself and others, does not possess full reason and intelligence about the matter?

How could I say that he does? he replied.

And is not this true of the good likewise—that the man who is unable to define in his discourse and distinguish and abstract from
c all other things the aspect or idea of the good, and who cannot, as it were in battle, running the gauntlet of all tests, and striving to examine everything by essential reality and not by opinion, hold on his way through all this without tripping in his reasoning—the man who lacks this power, you will say, does not really know the good itself or any particular good, but if he apprehends any adumbration of it, his contact with it is by opinion, not by knowledge, and dreaming and
d dozing through his present life, before he awakens here he will arrive at the house of Hades and fall asleep forever?

Yes, by Zeus, said he, all this I will stoutly affirm.

But, surely, said I, if you should ever nurture in fact your children whom you are now nurturing and educating in word, you would not suffer them, I presume, to hold rule in the state, and determine the greatest matters, being themselves as irrational as the lines so called in geometry.

Why, no, he said.

Then you will provide by law that they shall give special heed to the discipline that will enable them to ask and answer questions in the most scientific manner?
e I will so legislate, he said, in conjunction with you.

Do you agree, then, said I, that we have set dialectic above all other studies to be as it were the coping stone—and that no other higher kind of study could rightly be placed above it, but that our discussion of studies is now complete?

I do, he said.
535 The distribution, then, remains, said I, to whom we are to assign these studies and in what way.

Clearly, he said.

Do you remember, then, the kind of man we chose in our former selection of rulers?

Of course, he said.

In most respects, then, said I, you must suppose that we have to

choose those same natures. The most stable, the most brave and enterprising are to be preferred, and, so far as practicable, the most
comely. But in addition we must now require that they not only be b
virile and vigorous in temper, but that they possess also the gifts of
nature suitable to this type of education.

What qualities are you distinguishing?

They must have, my friend, to begin with, a certain keenness for
study, and must not learn with difficulty. For souls are much more
likely to flinch and faint in severe studies than in gymnastics, because the toil touches them more nearly, being peculiar to them and
not shared with the body.

True, he said.

And we must demand a good memory and doggedness and in- c
dustry in every sense of the word. Otherwise how do you suppose
anyone will consent both to undergo all the toils of the body and to
complete so great a course of study and discipline?

No one could, he said, unless most happily endowed.

Our present mistake, said I, and the disesteem that has in consequence fallen upon philosophy are, as I said before, caused by the
unfitness of her associates and wooers. They should not have been
bastards but true scions.

What do you mean? he said.

In the first place, I said, the aspirant to philosophy must not limp d
in his industry, in the one half of him loving, in the other shunning,
toil. This happens when anyone is a lover of gymnastics and hunting
and all the labors of the body, yet is not fond of learning or of listening
or inquiring, but in all such matters hates work. And he too is lame
whose industry is one-sided in the reverse way.

Most true, he said.

Likewise in respect of truth, I said, we shall regard as maimed in
precisely the same way the soul that hates the voluntary lie and is e
troubled by it in its own self and greatly angered by it in others, but
cheerfully accepts the involuntary falsehood and is not distressed
when convicted of lack of knowledge, but wallows in the mud of ignorance as insensitively as a pig.

By all means, he said.

And with reference to sobriety, said I, and bravery and loftiness 536
of soul and all the parts of virtue, we must especially be on our
guard to distinguish the baseborn from the trueborn. For when the
knowledge necessary to make such discriminations is lacking in individual or state, they unawares employ at random for any of these purposes the crippled and baseborn natures, as their friends or rulers.

It is so indeed, he said.

But we, I said, must be on our guard in all such cases, since, if
we bring men sound of limb and mind to so great a study and so severe b
a training, justice herself will have no fault to find with us, and we

shall preserve the state and our polity. But, if we introduce into it the other sort, the outcome will be just the opposite, and we shall pour a still greater flood of ridicule upon philosophy.

That would indeed be shameful, he said.

Most certainly, said I, but here again I am making myself a little ridiculous.

In what way?

c   I forgot, said I, that we were jesting, and I spoke with too great intensity. For, while speaking, I turned my eyes upon philosophy, and when I saw how she is undeservedly reviled, I was revolted, and, as if in anger, spoke too earnestly to those who are in fault.

No, by Zeus, not too earnestly for me as a hearer.

But too much so for me as a speaker, I said. But this we must not forget, that in our former selection we chose old men, but in this one d   that will not do. For we must not take Solon's word for it that growing old a man is able to learn many things. He is less able to do that than to run a race. To the young belong all heavy and frequent labors.

Necessarily, he said.

Now, all this study of reckoning and geometry and all the preliminary studies that are indispensable preparation for dialectic must be presented to them while still young, not in the form of compulsory instruction.

Why so?

e   Because, said I, a free soul ought not to pursue any study slavishly, for while bodily labors performed under constraint do not harm the body, nothing that is learned under compulsion stays with the mind.

True, he said.

Do not, then, my friend, keep children to their studies by compulsion but by play. That will also better enable you to discern the 537 natural capacities of each.

There is reason in that, he said.

And do you not remember, I said, that we also declared that we must conduct the children to war on horseback to be spectators, and wherever it may be safe, bring them to the front and give them a taste of blood as we do with whelps?

I do remember.

And those who as time goes on show the most facility in all these toils and studies and alarms are to be selected and enrolled on a list.

At what age? he said.

b   When they are released from their prescribed gymnastics. For that period, whether it be two or three years, incapacitates them for other occupations. For great fatigue and much sleep are the foes of study, and moreover one of our tests of them, and not the least, will be their behavior in their physical exercises.

Surely it is, he said.

After this period, I said, those who are given preference from the twenty-year class will receive greater honors than the others, and they will be required to gather the studies which they disconnectedly c pursued as children in their former education into a comprehensive survey of their affinities with one another and with the nature of things.

That, at any rate, he said, is the only instruction that abides with those who receive it.

And it is also, said I, the chief test of the dialectic nature and its opposite. For he who can view things in their connection is a dialectician; he who cannot, is not.

I concur, he said.

With these qualities in mind, I said, it will be your task to make a d selection of those who manifest them best from the group who are steadfast in their studies and in war and in all lawful requirements, and when they have passed the thirtieth year to promote them, by a second selection from those preferred in the first, to still greater honors, and to prove and test them by the power of dialectic to see which of them is able to disregard the eyes and other senses and go on to being itself in company with truth. And at this point, my friend, the greatest care is requisite.

How so? he said.

Do you not note, said I, how great is the harm caused by our e present treatment of dialectic?

What is that? he said.

Its practitioners are infected with lawlessness.

They are indeed.

Do you suppose, I said, that there is anything surprising in this state of mind, and do you not think it pardonable?

In what way, pray? he said.

Their case, said I, resembles that of a supposititious son reared in abundant wealth and a great and numerous family amid many flat- 538 terers, who on arriving at manhood should become aware that he is not the child of those who call themselves his parents, and should not be able to find his true father and mother. Can you divine what would be his feelings toward the flatterers and his supposed parents in the time when he did not know the truth about his adoption, and, again, when he knew it? Or would you like to hear my surmise?

I would.

Well, then, my surmise is, I said, that he would be more likely to honor his reputed father and mother and other kin than the flatterers, b and that there would be less likelihood of his allowing them to lack for anything, and that he would be less inclined to do or say to them anything unlawful, and less liable to disobey them in great matters than to disobey the flatterers—during the time when he did not know the truth.

It is probable, he said.

But when he found out the truth, I surmise that he would grow more remiss in honor and devotion to them and pay more regard to the flatterers, whom he would heed more than before and would c henceforth live by their rule, associating with them openly, while for that former father and his adoptive kin he would not care at all, unless he was naturally of a very good disposition.

All that you say, he replied, would be likely to happen. But what is the pertinency of this comparison to the novices of dialectic?

It is this. We have, I take it, certain convictions from childhood about the just and the honorable, in which, in obedience and honor to them, we have been bred as children under their parents.

Yes, we have.

d   And are there not other practices going counter to these, that have pleasures attached to them and that flatter and solicit our souls, but do not win over men of any decency; but they continue to hold in honor the teachings of their fathers and obey them?

It is so.

Well, then, said I, when a man of this kind is met by the question, What is the honorable? and on his giving the answer which he learned from the lawgiver, the argument confutes him, and by many and various refutations upsets his faith and makes him believe that this e thing is no more honorable than it is base, and when he has had the same experience about the just and the good and everything that he chiefly held in esteem, how do you suppose that he will conduct himself thereafter in the matter of respect and obedience to this traditional morality?

It is inevitable, he said, that he will not continue to honor and obey as before.

And then, said I, when he ceases to honor these principles and 539 to think that they are binding on him, and cannot discover the true principles, will he be likely to adopt any other way of life than that which flatters his desires?

He will not, he said.

He will, then, seem to have become a rebel to law and convention instead of the conformer that he was.

Necessarily.

And is not this experience of those who take up dialectic in this fashion to be expected and, as I just now said, deserving of much leniency?

Yes, and of pity too, he said.

Then that we may not have to pity thus your thirty-year-old disciples, must you not take every precaution when you introduce them to the study of dialectic?

Yes, indeed, he said.

b   And is it not one chief safeguard not to suffer them to taste of it while young? For I fancy you have not failed to observe that lads, when they first get a taste of disputation, misuse it as a form of sport, always employing it contentiously, and, imitating confuters, they themselves confute others. They delight like puppies in pulling about and tearing with words all who approach them.

Exceedingly so, he said.

And when they have themselves confuted many and been con- c futed by many, they quickly fall into a violent distrust of all that they formerly held true, and the outcome is that they themselves and the whole business of philosophy are discredited with other men.

Most true, he said.

But an older man will not share this craze, said I, but will rather choose to imitate the one who consents to examine truth dialec- d tically than the one who makes a jest and a sport of mere contra- diction, and so he will himself be more reasonable and moderate, and bring credit rather than discredit upon his pursuit.

Right, he said.

And were not all our preceding statements made with a view to this precaution—our requirement that those permitted to take part in such discussions must have orderly and stable natures, instead of the present practice of admitting to it any chance and unsuitable applicant?

By all means, he said.

Is it enough, then, to devote to the continuous and strenuous study of dialectic undisturbed by anything else, as in the correspond- ing discipline in bodily exercises, twice as many years as were allotted to that?

Do you mean six or four? he said.   e

Well, I said, set it down as five. For after that you will have to send them down into the cave again, and compel them to hold com- mands in war and the other offices suitable to youth, so that they may not fall short of the other type in experience either. And in these offices, too, they are to be tested to see whether they will remain steadfast under diverse solicitations or whether they will flinch and swerve.

How much time do you allow for that? he said.   540

Fifteen years, said I, and at the age of fifty those who have sur- vived the tests and approved themselves altogether the best in every task and form of knowledge must be brought at last to the goal. We shall require them to turn upward the vision of their souls and fix their gaze on that which sheds light on all, and when they have thus beheld the good itself they shall use it as a pattern for the right ordering of the state and the citizens and themselves throughout the remainder of their lives, each in his turn, devoting the greater part of b their time to the study of philosophy, but when the turn comes for each, toiling in the service of the state and holding office for the city's sake, regarding the task not as a fine thing but a necessity. And so, when each generation has educated others like themselves to take their place as guardians of the state, they shall depart to the Islands of the Blessed and there dwell. And the state shall establish public me-

c morials and sacrifices for them as to divinities if the Pythian oracle approves or, if not, as to divine and godlike men.

A most beautiful finish, Socrates, you have put upon your rulers, as if you were a statuary.

And on the women too, Glaucon, said I, for you must not suppose that my words apply to the men more than to all women who arise among them endowed with the requisite qualities.

That is right, he said, if they are to share equally in all things with the men as we laid it down.

d Well, then, said I, do you admit that our notion of the state and its polity is not altogether a daydream, but that though it is difficult, it is in a way possible and in no other way than that described— when genuine philosophers, many or one, becoming masters of the state scorn the present honors, regarding them as illiberal and worth-less, but prize the right and the honors that come from that above all

e things, and regarding justice as the chief and the one indispen-sable thing, in the service and maintenance of that reorganize and administer their city?

In what way? he said.

541 All inhabitants above the age of ten, I said, they will send out into the fields, and they will take over the children, remove them from the manners and habits of their parents, and bring them up in their own customs and laws which will be such as we have described. This is the speediest and easiest way in which such a city and consti-tution as we have portrayed could be established and prosper and bring most benefit to the people among whom it arises.

b Much the easiest, he said, and I think you have well explained the manner of its realization if it should ever be realized.

Then, said I, have we not now said enough about this state and the corresponding type of man—for it is evident what our conception of him will be?

It is evident, he said, and, to answer your question, I think we have finished.

BOOK VIII

543 Very good. We are agreed then, Glaucon, that the state which is to achieve the height of good government must have community of wives and children and all education, and also that the pursuits of men and women must be the same in peace and war, and that the rulers or kings over them are to be those who have approved themselves the best in both war and philosophy.

We are agreed, he said.

And we further granted this, that when the rulers are established b in office they shall conduct these soldiers and settle them in habitations such as we described, that have nothing private for anybody but are common for all, and in addition to such habitations we agreed, if you remember, what should be the nature of their possessions.

Why, yes, I remember, he said, that we thought it right that none of them should have anything that ordinary men now possess, but that, being as it were athletes of war and guardians, they should receive from the others as pay for their guardianship each year their c yearly sustenance, and devote their entire attention to the care of themselves and the state.

That is right, I said. But now that we have finished this topic let us recall the point at which we entered on the digression that has brought us here, so that we may proceed on our way again by the same path.

That is easy, he said, for at that time, almost exactly as now, on the supposition that you had finished the description of the city, you were going on to say that you assumed such a city as you then de- d scribed and the corresponding type of man to be good, and that too though, as it appears, you had a still finer city and type of man to tell 544 of, but at any rate you were saying that the others are aberrations, if this city is right. But regarding the other constitutions, my recollection is that you said there were four species worth speaking of and observing their defects and the corresponding types of men, in order that when we had seen them all and come to an agreement about the best and the worst man, we might determine whether the best is the happiest and the worst most wretched or whether it is otherwise. And when I was asking what were the four constitutions you had in mind, b Polemarchus and Adimantus thereupon broke in, and that was how you took up the discussion again and brought it to this point.

Your memory is most exact, I said.

A second time then, as in a wrestling match, offer me the same hold, and when I repeat my question try to tell me what you were then about to say.

I will if I can, said I.

And indeed, said he, I am eager myself to hear what four forms c of government you meant.

There will be no difficulty about that, said I. For those I mean are precisely those that have names in common usage—that which the many praise, your Cretan and Spartan constitution, and the second in place and in honor, that which is called oligarchy, a constitution teeming with many ills, and its sequent counterpart and opponent, democracy, and then the noble tyranny surpassing them all, the fourth and final malady of a state. Can you mention any other type of gov- d ernment, I mean any other that constitutes a distinct species? For, no doubt, there are hereditary principalities and purchased kingships, and similar intermediate constitutions which one could find in even greater numbers among the barbarians than among the Greeks.

Certainly many strange ones are reported, he said.

Are you aware, then, said I, that there must be as many types of character among men as there are forms of government? Or do you suppose that constitutions spring from the proverbial oak or rock and not from the characters of the citizens, which, as it were, by their
e momentum and weight in the scales draw other things after them?

They could not possibly come from any other source, he said.

Then if the forms of government are five, the patterns of individual souls must be five also.

Surely.

Now we have already described the man corresponding to aristocracy or the government of the best, whom we aver to be the truly
545 good and just man.

We have.

Must we not, then, next after this, survey the inferior types, the man who is contentious and covetous of honor, corresponding to the Laconian constitution, and the oligarchic man in turn, and the democratic and the tyrannical, in order that, after observing the most unjust of all, we may oppose him to the most just, and complete our inquiry as to the relation of pure justice and pure injustice in respect of the happiness and unhappiness of the possessor, so that we may
b either follow the counsel of Thrasymachus and pursue injustice or the present argument and pursue justice?

Assuredly, he said, that is what we have to do.

Shall we, then, as we began by examining moral qualities in states before individuals, as being more manifest there, so now consider first the constitution based on the love of honor? I do not know of any special name for it in use. We must call it either timocracy or timarchy. And then in connection with this we will consider the man
c of that type, and thereafter oligarchy and the oligarch, and again, fixing our eyes on democracy, we will contemplate the democratic man, and fourthly, after coming to the city ruled by a tyrant and observing it, we will in turn take a look into the tyrannical soul, and so try to make ourselves competent judges of the question before us.

That would be at least a systematic and consistent way of conducting the observation and the decision, he said.

Come, then, said I, let us try to tell in what way a timocracy would arise out of an aristocracy. Or is this the simple and unvarying rule,
d that in every form of government revolution takes its start from the ruling class itself, when dissension arises in that, but so long as it is at one with itself, however small it be, innovation is impossible?

Yes, that is so.

How, then, Glaucon, I said, will disturbance arise in our city, and how will our helpers and rulers fall out and be at odds with one another and themselves? Shall we, like Homer, invoke the Muses to tell 'how faction first fell upon them,' and say that these goddesses e playing with us and teasing us as if we were children address us in lofty, mock-serious tragic style?

How?

Somewhat in this fashion. Hard in truth it is for a state thus 546 constituted to be shaken and disturbed, but since for everything that has come into being destruction is appointed, not even such a fabric as this will abide for all time, but it shall surely be dissolved, and this is the manner of its dissolution. Not only for plants that grow from the earth but also for animals that live upon it there is a cycle of bearing and barrenness for soul and body as often as the revolutions of their orbs come full circle, in brief courses for the short-lived and oppositely for the opposite. But the laws of prosperous birth or infer- b tility for your race, the men you have bred to be your rulers will not for all their wisdom ascertain by reasoning combined with sensation, but they will escape them, and there will be a time when they will beget children out of season. Now for divine begettings there is a period comprehended by a perfect number, and for mortal by the first in which augmentations dominating and dominated when they have attained to three distances and four limits of the assimilating and the dissimilating, the waxing and the waning, render all things conversa- c ble and commensurable with one another, whereof a basal four thirds wedded to the pempad yields two harmonies at the third augmentation, the one the product of equal factors taken one hundred times, the other of equal length one way but oblong—one dimension of a hundred numbers determined by the rational diameters of the pempad lacking one in each case, or of the irrational lacking two; the other dimension of a hundred cubes of the triad. And this entire geometric number is determinative of this thing, of better and inferior d births. And when your guardians, missing this, bring together brides and bridegrooms unseasonably, the offspring will not be wellborn or fortunate. Of such offspring the previous generation will establish the best, to be sure, in office, but still these, being unworthy, and having entered in turn into the powers of their fathers, will first as guardians begin to neglect us, paying too little heed to music and then to gymnastics, so that our young men will deteriorate in their culture, and the rulers selected from them will not approve themselves very e efficient guardians for testing Hesiod's and our races of gold, silver, 547 bronze, and iron. And this intermixture of the iron with the silver and the bronze with the gold will engender unlikeness and an unharmonious unevenness, things that always beget war and enmity wherever they arise. 'Of this lineage, look you,' we must aver the dissension to be, wherever it occurs and always.

'And rightly too,' he said, we shall affirm that the Muses answer.

They must needs, I said, since they are Muses.

b   Well, then, said he, what do the Muses say next?

When strife arose, said I, the two groups were pulling against each other, the iron and bronze toward money-making and the acquisition of land and houses and gold and silver, and the other two, the golden and silver, not being poor, but by nature rich in their souls, were trying to draw them back to virtue and their original constitution, and thus, striving and contending against one another, they compromised on the plan of distributing and taking for themselves the land and the houses, enslaving and subjecting as *perioeci* and serfs

c   their former friends and supporters, of whose freedom they had been the guardians, and occupying themselves with war and keeping watch over these subjects.

I think, he said, that this is the starting point of the transformation.

Would not this polity, then, said I, be in some sort intermediate between aristocracy and oligarchy?

By all means.

By this change, then, it would arise. But after the change what

d   will be its way of life? Is it not obvious that in some things it will imitate the preceding polity, in some the oligarchy, since it is intermediate, and that it will also have some qualities peculiar to itself?

That is so, he said.

Then in honoring its rulers and in the abstention of its warrior class from farming and handicraft and money-making in general, and in the provision of common public tables and the devotion to physical training and expertness in the game and contest of war—in all these traits it will copy the preceding state?

Yes.

e   But in its fear to admit clever men to office, since the men it has of this kind are no longer simple and strenuous but of mixed strain, and in its inclining rather to the more high-spirited and simple-minded

548   type, who are better suited for war than for peace, and in honoring the stratagems and contrivances of war and occupying itself with war most of the time—in these respects for the most part its qualities will be peculiar to itself?

Yes.

Such men, said I, will be avid of wealth, like those in an oligarchy, and will cherish a fierce secret lust for gold and silver, owning storehouses and private treasuries where they may hide them away,

b   and also the enclosures of their homes, literal private love nests in which they can lavish their wealth on their women and any others they please with great expenditure.

Most true, he said.

And will they not be stingy about money, since they prize it and are not allowed to possess it openly, prodigal of others' wealth because of their appetites, enjoying their pleasures stealthily, and running away from the law as boys from a father, since they have not been educated by persuasion but by force because of their neglect of the true Muse, the companion of discussion and philosophy, and because of their preference of gymnastics to music?   c

You perfectly describe, he said, a polity that is a mixture of good and evil.

Why, yes, the elements have been mixed, I said, but the most conspicuous feature in it is one thing only, due to the predominance of the high-spirited element, namely contentiousness and covetousness of honor.

Very much so, said he.

Such, then, would be the origin and nature of this polity if we may merely outline the figure of a constitution in words and not elaborate it precisely, since even the sketch will suffice to show us the most d just and the most unjust type of man, and it would be an impracticable task to set forth all forms of government without omitting any, and all customs and qualities of men.

Quite right, he said.

What, then, is the man that corresponds to this constitution? What is his origin and what his nature?

I fancy, Adimantus said, that he comes rather close to Glaucon here in point of contentiousness.

Perhaps, said I, in that, but I do not think their natures are alike e in the following respects.

In what?

He will have to be somewhat self-willed and lacking in culture, yet a lover of music and fond of listening to talk and speeches, though by no means himself a rhetorician. And to slaves such a one would 549 be harsh, not scorning them as the really educated do, but he would be gentle with the freeborn and very submissive to officials, a lover of office and of honor, not basing his claim to office on ability to speak or anything of that sort but on his exploits in war or preparation for war, and he would be a devotee of gymnastics and hunting.

Why, yes, he said, that is the spirit of that polity.

And would not such a man be disdainful of wealth too in his youth, but the older he grew the more he would love it because of his b participation in the covetous nature and because his virtue is not sincere and pure since it lacks the best guardian?

What guardian? said Adimantus.

Reason, said I, blended with culture, which is the only indwelling preserver of virtue throughout life in the soul that possesses it.

Well said, he replied.

This is the character, I said, of the timocratic youth, resembling the city that bears his name.

By all means.

c   His origin is somewhat on this wise. Sometimes he is the young son of a good father who lives in a badly governed state and avoids honors and office and lawsuits and all such meddlesomeness and is willing to forbear something of his rights in order to escape trouble.

How does he originate? he said.

Why, when, to begin with, I said, he hears his mother complain-
d ing that her husband is not one of the rulers and for that reason she is slighted among the other women, and when she sees that her husband is not much concerned about money and does not fight and brawl in private lawsuits and in the public assembly, but takes all such matters lightly, and when she observes that he is self-absorbed in his thoughts and neither regards nor disregards her overmuch, and in consequence of all this laments and tells the boy that his father is too
e slack and no kind of a man, with all the other complaints with which women nag in such cases.

Many indeed, said Adimantus, and after their kind.

You are aware, then, said I, that the very house slaves of such men, if they are loyal and friendly, privately say the same sort of things to the sons, and if they observe a debtor or any other wrong-doer whom the father does not prosecute, they urge the boy to pun-
550 ish all such when he grows to manhood and prove himself more of a man than his father, and when the lad goes out he hears and sees the same sort of thing. Men who mind their own affairs in the city are spoken of as simpletons and are held in slight esteem, while meddlers who mind other people's affairs are honored and praised. Then it is that the youth, hearing and seeing such things, and on the other hand listening to the words of his father, and with a near view of his pursuits contrasted with those of other men, is solicited by both, his fa-
b ther watering and fostering the growth of the rational principle in his soul and the others the appetitive and the passionate; and as he is not by nature of a bad disposition but has fallen into evil communications, under these two solicitations he comes to a compromise and turns over the government in his soul to the intermediate principle of ambition and high spirit and becomes a man haughty of soul and covetous of honor.

You have, I think, most exactly described his origin.

c   Then, said I, we have our second polity and second type of man.

We have, he said.

Shall we then, as Aeschylus would say, tell of another champion before another gate, or rather, in accordance with our plan, the city first?

That, by all means, he said.

The next polity, I believe, would be oligarchy.

And what kind of a regime, said he, do you understand by oligarchy?

That based on a property qualification, said I, wherein the rich
hold office and the poor man is excluded.   d

I understand, said he.

Then, is not the first thing to speak of how timocracy passes
over into this?

Yes.

And truly, said I, the manner of the change is plain even to the
proverbial blind man.

How so?

That treasure house which each possesses filled with gold destroys that polity, for first they invent ways of expenditure for them- e
selves and pervert the laws to this end, and neither they nor their
wives obey them.

That is likely, he said.

And then, I take it, by observing and emulating one another they
bring the majority of them to this way of thinking.

That is likely, he said.

And so, as time goes on, and they advance in the pursuit of
wealth, the more they hold that in honor the less they honor virtue.
May not the opposition of wealth and virtue be conceived as if each
lay in the scale of a balance inclining opposite ways?

Yes, indeed, he said.

So, when wealth is honored in a state, and the wealthy, virtue and 551
the good are less honored.

Obviously.

And that which men at any time honor they practice, and what
is not honored is neglected.

It is so.

Thus, finally, from being lovers of victory and lovers of honor
they become lovers of gain getting and of money, and they commend
and admire the rich man and put him in office but despise the man
who is poor.

Quite so.

And is it not then that they pass a law defining the limits of an b
oligarchic polity, prescribing a sum of money, a larger sum where it is
more of an oligarchy, where it is less a smaller, and proclaiming that
no man shall hold office whose property does not come up to the required valuation? And this law they either put through by force of
arms, or without resorting to that they establish their government
by terrorization. Is not that the way of it?

It is.

The establishment then, one may say, is in this wise.

Yes, he said, but what is the character of this constitution, and
what are the defects that we said it had?   c

To begin with, said I, consider the nature of its constitutive and defining principle. Suppose men should appoint the pilots of ships in this way, by property qualification, and not allow a poor man to navigate, even if he were a better pilot.

A sorry voyage they would make of it, he said.

And is not the same true of any other form of rule?

I think so.

Except of a city, said I, or does it hold for a city too?

d   Most of all, he said, by as much as that is the greatest and most difficult rule of all.

Here, then, is one very great defect in oligarchy.

So it appears.

Well, and is this a smaller one?

What?

That such a city should of necessity be not one, but two, a city of the rich and a city of the poor, dwelling together, and always plotting against one another.

No, by Zeus, said he, it is not a bit smaller.

Nor, further, can we approve of this—the likelihood that they will not be able to wage war, because of the necessity of either arm-

e ing and employing the multitude, and fearing them more than the enemy, or else, if they do not make use of them, of finding themselves on the field of battle, oligarchs indeed, and rulers over a few. And to this must be added their reluctance to contribute money, because they are lovers of money.

No, indeed, that is not admirable.

And what of the trait we found fault with long ago—the fact

552 that in such a state the citizens are busybodies and Jacks-of-all-trades, farmers, financiers, and soldiers all in one? Do you think that is right?

By no manner of means.

Consider now whether this polity is not the first that admits that which is the greatest of all such evils.

What?

The allowing a man to sell all his possessions, which another is permitted to acquire, and after selling them to go on living in the city, but as no part of it, neither a money-maker, nor a craftsman, nor a knight, nor a foot soldier, but classified only as a pauper and a dependent.

b   This is the first, he said.

There certainly is no prohibition of that sort of thing in oligarchic states. Otherwise some of their citizens would not be excessively rich, and others out-and-out paupers.

Right.

But observe this. When such a fellow was spending his wealth, was he then of any more use to the state in the matters of which we

were speaking, or did he merely seem to belong to the ruling class,
while in reality he was neither ruler nor helper in the state, but only
a consumer of goods?

It is so, he said. He only seemed, but was just a spendthrift.   c

Shall we, then, say of him that as the drone springs up in the cell,
a pest of the hive, so such a man grows up in his home, a pest of the
state?

By all means, Socrates, he said.

And has not God, Adimantus, left the drones which have
wings and fly stingless one and all, while of the drones here who travel
afoot he has made some stingless but has armed others with terrible
stings? And from the stingless finally issue beggars in old age, but d
from those furnished with stings all that are denominated malefac-
tors?

Most true, he said.

It is plain, then, said I, that wherever you see beggars in a city,
there are somewhere in the neighborhood concealed thieves and cut-
purses and temple robbers and similar artists in crime.

Clearly, he said.

Well, then, in oligarchic cities do you not see beggars?

Nearly all are such, he said, except the ruling class.

Are we not to suppose, then, that there are also many criminals e
in them furnished with stings, whom the rulers by their surveillance
forcibly restrain?

We must think so, he said.

And shall we not say that the presence of such citizens is the
result of a defective culture and bad breeding and a wrong constitution of the state?

We shall.

Well, at any rate such would be the character of the oligarchic
state, and these, or perhaps even more than these, would be the evils
that afflict it.

Pretty nearly these, he said.

Then, I said, let us regard as disposed of the constitution called 553
oligarchy, whose rulers are determined by a property qualification.
And next we are to consider the man who resembles it—how he arises
and what after that his character is.

Quite so, he said.

Is not the transition from that timocratic youth to the oligarchic
type mostly on this wise?

How?

When a son born to the timocratic man at first emulates his
father, and follows in his footsteps, and then sees him suddenly
dashed, as a ship on a reef, against the state, and making complete b
wreckage of both his possessions and himself—perhaps he has been

a general, or has held some other important office, and has then been dragged into court by mischievous sycophants and put to death or banished or outlawed and has lost all his property . . .

It is likely, he said.

And the son, my friend, after seeing and suffering these things, and losing his property, grows timid, I fancy, and forthwith thrusts c headlong from his bosom's throne that principle of love of honor and that high spirit, and being humbled by poverty turns to the getting of money, and greedily and stingily and little by little by thrift and hard work collects property. Do you not suppose that such a one will then establish on that throne the principle of appetite and avarice, and set it up as the great king in his soul, adorned with tiaras and collars of gold, and girt with the Persian sword?

I do, he said.

And under this domination he will force the rational and high-d spirited principles to crouch lowly to right and left as slaves, and will allow the one to calculate and consider nothing but the ways of making more money from a little, and the other to admire and honor nothing but riches and rich men, and to take pride in nothing but the possession of wealth and whatever contributes to that?

There is no other transformation so swift and sure of the ambitious youth into the avaricious type.

e   Is this, then, our oligarchic man? said I.

He is developed, at any rate, out of a man resembling the constitution from which the oligarchy sprang.

Let us see, then, whether he will have a like character.

554   Let us see.

Would he not, in the first place, resemble it in prizing wealth above everything?

Inevitably.

And also by being thrifty and laborious, satisfying only his own necessary appetites and desires and not providing for expenditure on other things, but subduing his other appetites as vain and unprofitable?

By all means.

He would be a squalid fellow, said I, looking for a surplus of profit b in everything, and a hoarder, the type the multitude approves. Would not this be the character of the man who corresponds to such a polity?

I certainly think so, he said. Property, at any rate, is the thing most esteemed by that state and that kind of man.

That, I take it, said I, is because he has never turned his thoughts to true culture.

I think not, he said, else he would not have made the blind one leader of his choir and first in honor.

Well said, I replied. But consider this. Shall we not say that owing to this lack of culture the appetites of the drone spring up in him, some the beggarly, others the rascally, but that they are forcibly re- c strained by his general self-surveillance and self-control?

We shall indeed, he said.

Do you know, then, said I, to what you must look to discern the rascalities of such men?

To what? he said.

To guardianships of orphans, and any such opportunities of doing injustice with impunity.

True.

And is it not apparent by this that in other dealings, where he enjoys the repute of a seeming just man, he by some better element in d himself forcibly keeps down other evil desires dwelling within, not persuading them that it 'is better not' nor taming them by reason, but by compulsion and fear, trembling for his possessions generally.

Quite so, he said.

Yes, by Zeus, said I, my friend. In most of them, when there is occasion to spend the money of others, you will discover the existence of dronelike appetites.

Most emphatically.

Such a man, then, would not be free from internal dissension. He would not be really one, but in some sort a double man. Yet for the e most part, his better desires would have the upper hand over the worse.

It is so.

And for this reason, I presume, such a man would be more seemly, more respectable, than many others, but the true virtue of a soul in unison and harmony with itself would escape him and dwell afar.

I think so.

And again, the thrifty stingy man would be a feeble competitor 555 personally in the city for any prize of victory or in any other honorable emulation. He is unwilling to spend money for fame and rivalries of that sort, and, fearing to awaken his prodigal desires and call them into alliance for the winning of the victory, he fights in true oligarchic fashion with a small part of his resources and is defeated for the most part and—finds himself rich!

Yes indeed, he said.

Have we any further doubt, then, I said, as to the correspondence and resemblance between the thrifty and money-making man b and the oligarchic state?

None, he said.

We have next to consider, it seems, the origin and nature of democracy, that we may next learn the character of that type of man and range him beside the others for our judgment.

That would at least be a consistent procedure.

Then, said I, is not the transition from oligarchy to democracy effected in some such way as this—by the insatiate greed for that which it set before itself as the good, the attainment of the greatest possible wealth?

In what way?

c Why, since its rulers owe their offices to their wealth, they are not willing to prohibit by law the prodigals who arise among the youth from spending and wasting their substance. Their object is, by lending money on the property of such men, and buying it in, to become still richer and more esteemed.

By all means.

And is it not at once apparent in a state that this honoring of wealth is incompatible with a sober and temperate citizenship, but that one or the other of these two ideals is inevitably neglected.

d That is pretty clear, he said.

And such negligence and encouragement of licentiousness in oligarchies not infrequently has reduced to poverty men of no ignoble quality.

It surely has.

And there they sit, I fancy, within the city, furnished with stings, that is, arms, some burdened with debt, others disfranchised, others both, hating and conspiring against the acquirers of their estates and the rest of the citizens, and eager for revolution.

'Tis so.

e But these money-makers with down-bent heads, pretending not even to see them, but inserting the sting of their money into any of the remainder who do not resist, and harvesting from them in interest 556 as it were a manifold progeny of the parent sum, foster the drone and pauper element in the state.

They do indeed multiply it, he said.

And they are not willing to quench the evil as it bursts into flame either by way of a law prohibiting a man from doing as he likes with his own, or in this way, by a second law that does away with such abuses.

What law?

The law that is next best, and compels the citizens to pay heed b to virtue. For if a law commanded that most voluntary contracts should be at the contractor's risk, the pursuit of wealth would be less shameless in the state and fewer of the evils of which we spoke just now would grow up there.

Much fewer, he said.

But as it is, and for all these reasons, this is the plight to which the rulers in the state reduce their subjects, and as for themselves and their offspring, do they not make the young spoiled wantons averse to c toil of body and mind, and too soft to stand up against pleasure and pain, and mere idlers?

Surely.

And do they not fasten upon themselves the habit of neglect of everything except the making of money, and as complete an indifference to virtue as the paupers exhibit?

Little they care.

And when, thus conditioned, the rulers and the ruled are brought together on the march, in wayfaring, or in some other common undertaking, either a religious festival, or a campaign, or as shipmates or fellow soldiers or, for that matter, in actual battle, and observe one another, then the poor are not in the least scorned by the rich, but on d the contrary, do you not suppose it often happens that when a lean, sinewy, sunburned pauper is stationed in battle beside a rich man bred in the shade, and burdened with superfluous flesh, and sees him panting and helpless—do you not suppose he will think that such fellows keep their wealth by the cowardice of the poor, and that when the latter are together in private, one will pass the word to another, 'our e men are good for nothing'?

Nay, I know very well that they do, said he.

And just as an unhealthy body requires but a slight impulse from outside to fall into sickness, and sometimes, even without that, all the man is one internal war, in like manner does not the corresponding type of state need only a slight occasion, the one party bringing in allies from an oligarchic state, or the other from a democratic, to become diseased and wage war with itself, and sometimes even apart from any external impulse faction arises?   557

Most emphatically.

And a democracy, I suppose, comes into being when the poor, winning the victory, put to death some of the other party, drive out others, and grant the rest of the citizens an equal share in both citizenship and offices—and for the most part these offices are assigned by lot.

Why, yes, he said, that is the constitution of democracy alike whether it is established by force of arms or by terrorism resulting in the withdrawal of one of the parties.

What, then, said I, is the manner of their life and what is the quality of such a constitution? For it is plain that the man of this b quality will turn out to be a democratic sort of man.

It is plain, he said.

To begin with, are they not free? And is not the city chock-full of liberty and freedom of speech? And has not every man license to do as he likes?

So it is said, he replied.

And where there is such license, it is obvious that everyone would arrange a plan for leading his own life in the way that pleases him.

Obvious.

All sorts and conditions of men, then, would arise in this polity c more than in any other?

Of course.

Possibly, said I, this is the most beautiful of polities; as a garment of many colors, embroidered with all kinds of hues, so this, decked and diversified with every type of character, would appear the most beautiful. And perhaps many would judge it to be the most beautiful, like boys and women when they see bright-colored things.

Yes indeed, he said.

d   Yes, said I, and it is the fit place, my good friend, in which to look for a constitution.

Why so?

Because, owing to this license, it includes all kinds, and it seems likely that anyone who wishes to organize a state, as we were just now doing, must find his way to a democratic city and select the model that pleases him, as if in a bazaar of constitutions, and after making his choice, establish his own.

e   Perhaps at any rate, he said, he would not be at a loss for patterns.

And the freedom from all compulsion to hold office in such a city, even if you are qualified, or again, to submit to rule, unless you please, or to make war when the rest are at war, or to keep the peace when the others do so, unless you desire peace, and again, the liberty, in defiance of any law that forbids you, to hold office and sit on juries nonetheless, if it occurs to you to do so, is not all that a heavenly and delicious entertainment for the time being?

558   Perhaps, he said, for so long.

And is not the placability of some convicted criminals exquisite? Or have you never seen in such a state men condemned to death or exile who nonetheless stay on, and go to and fro among the people, and as if no one saw or heeded him, the man slips in and out like a revenant?

Yes, many, he said.

And the tolerance of democracy, its superiority to all our meticu-
b lous requirements, its disdain for our solemn pronouncements made when we were founding our city, that except in the case of transcendent natural gifts no one could ever become a good man unless from childhood his play and all his pursuits were concerned with things fair and good—how superbly it tramples underfoot all such ideals, caring nothing from what practices and way of life a man turns to politics, but honoring him if only he says that he loves the people!

c   It is a noble polity, indeed! he said.

These and qualities akin to these democracy would exhibit, and it would, it seems, be a delightful form of government, anarchic and motley, assigning a kind of equality indiscriminately to equals and unequals alike!

Yes, he said, everybody knows that.

Observe, then, the corresponding private character. Or must we first, as in the case of the polity, consider the origin of the type?

Yes, he said.

Is not this, then, the way of it? Our thrifty oligarchic man would   d have a son bred in his father's ways.

Why not?

And he, too, would control by force all his appetites for pleasure that are wasters and not winners of wealth, those which are denominated unnecessary.

Obviously.

And in order not to argue in the dark, shall we first define our distinction between necessary and unnecessary appetites?

Let us do so.

Well, then, desires that we cannot divert or suppress may be properly called necessary, and likewise those whose satisfaction is   e beneficial to us, may they not? For our nature compels us to seek their satisfaction. Is not that so?

Most assuredly.   559

Then we shall rightly use the word 'necessary' of them?

Rightly.

And what of the desires from which a man could free himself by discipline from youth up, and whose presence in the soul does no good and in some cases harm? Should we not fairly call all such unnecessary?

Fairly indeed.

Let us select an example of either kind, so that we may apprehend the type.

Let us do so.

Would not the desire of eating to keep in health and condition and the appetite for mere bread and relishes be necessary?

I think so.   b

The appetite for bread is necessary in both respects, in that it is beneficial and in that if it fails we die.

Yes.

And the desire for relishes, so far as it conduces to fitness?

By all means.

And should we not rightly pronounce unnecessary the appetite   c that exceeds these and seeks other varieties of food, and that by correction and training from youth up can be got rid of in most cases and is harmful to the body and a hindrance to the soul's attainment of intelligence and sobriety?

Nay, most rightly.

And may we not call the one group the spendthrift desires and the other the profitable, because they help production?

Surely.

And we shall say the same of sexual and other appetites?

The same.

And were we not saying that the man whom we nicknamed the

drone is the man who teems with such pleasures and appetites, and
who is governed by his unnecessary desires, while the one who is ruled
d by his necessary appetites is the thrifty oligarchic man?

Why, surely.

To return, then, said I, we have to tell how the democratic man
develops from the oligarchic type. I think it is usually in this way.

How?

When a youth, bred in the illiberal and niggardly fashion that
we were describing, gets a taste of the honey of the drones and associates with fierce and cunning creatures who know how to purvey
pleasures of every kind and variety and condition, there you must
e doubtless conceive is the beginning of the transformation of the oligarchy in his soul into democracy.

Quite inevitably, he said.

May we not say that just as the revolution in the city was brought
about by the aid of an alliance from outside, coming to the support of
the similar and corresponding party in the state, so the youth is revolutionized when a like and kindred group of appetites from outside
comes to the aid of one of the parties in his soul?

By all means, he said.

And if, I take it, a counteralliance comes to the rescue of the oli-
560 garchic part of his soul, either it may be from his father or from his
other kin, who admonish and reproach him, then there arise faction
and counterfaction and internal strife in the man with himself.

Surely.

And sometimes, I suppose, the democratic element retires before
the oligarchic, some of its appetites having been destroyed and others
expelled, and a sense of awe and reverence grows up in the young
man's soul and order is restored.

That sometimes happens, he said.

b   And sometimes, again, another brood of desires akin to those expelled are stealthily nurtured to take their place, owing to the father's ignorance of true education, and wax numerous and strong.

Yes, that is wont to be the way of it.

And they tug and pull back to the same associations and in secret
intercourse engender a multitude.

Yes indeed.

And in the end, I suppose, they seize the citadel of the young
man's soul, finding it empty and unoccupied by studies and honorable
pursuits and true discourses, which are the best watchmen and guard-
c ians in the minds of men who are dear to the gods.

Much the best, he said.

And then false and braggart words and opinions charge up the
height and take their place and occupy that part of such a youth.

They do indeed.

And then he returns, does he not, to those lotus-eaters and with-

out disguise lives openly with them. And if any support comes from
his kin to the thrifty element in his soul, those braggart discourses
close the gates of the royal fortress within him and refuse admission
to the auxiliary force itself, and will not grant audience as to envoys
to the words of older friends in private life. And they themselves pre- d
vail in the conflict, and naming reverence and awe 'folly' thrust it
forth, a dishonored fugitive. And temperance they call 'want of manhood' and banish it with contumely, and they teach that moderation
and orderly expenditure are 'rusticity' and 'illiberality,' and they combine with a gang of unprofitable and harmful appetites to drive them
over the border.

They do indeed.

And when they have emptied and purged of all these the soul of e
the youth that they have thus possessed and occupied, and whom they
are initiating with these magnificent and costly rites, they proceed
to lead home from exile insolence and anarchy and prodigality and
shamelessness, resplendent in a great attendant choir and crowned
with garlands, and in celebration of their praises they euphemistically
denominate insolence 'good breeding,' license 'liberty,' prodigality
'magnificence,' and shamelessness 'manly spirit.' And is it not in some 561
such way as this that in his youth the transformation takes place
from the restriction to necessary desires in his education to the liberation and release of his unnecessary and harmful desires?

Yes, your description is most vivid, said he.

Then, in his subsequent life, I take it, such a one expends money
and toil and time no more on his necessary than on his unnecessary
pleasures. But if it is his good fortune that the period of storm and
stress does not last too long, and as he grows older the fiercest tumult b
within him passes, and he receives back a part of the banished elements and does not abandon himself altogether to the invasion of the
others, then he establishes and maintains all his pleasures on a footing of equality, forsooth, and so lives turning over the guardhouse of
his soul to each as it happens along until it is sated, as if it had drawn
the lot for that office, and then in turn to another, disdaining none
but fostering them all equally.

Quite so.

And he does not accept or admit into the guardhouse the
words of truth when anyone tells him that some pleasures arise from c
honorable and good desires, and others from those that are base, and
that we ought to practice and esteem the one and control and subdue
the others, but he shakes his head at all such admonitions and avers
that they are all alike and to be equally esteemed.

Such is indeed his state of mind and his conduct.

And does he not, said I, also live out his life in this fashion, day
by day indulging the appetite of the day, now winebibbing and abandoning himself to the lascivious pleasing of the flute and again d

drinking only water and dieting, and at one time exercising his body, and sometimes idling and neglecting all things, and at another time seeming to occupy himself with philosophy. And frequently he goes in for politics and bounces up and says and does whatever enters his head. And if military men excite his emulation, thither he rushes, and if moneyed men, to that he turns, and there is no order or compulsion in his existence, but he calls this life of his the life of pleasure and freedom and happiness and cleaves to it to the end.

e   That is a perfect description, he said, of a devotee of equality.

I certainly think, said I, that he is a manifold man stuffed with most excellent differences, and that like that city he is the fair and many-colored one whom many a man and woman would count fortunate in his life, as containing within himself the greatest number of patterns of constitutions and qualities.

Yes, that is so, he said.

562   Shall we definitely assert, then, that such a man is to be ranged with democracy and would properly be designated as democratic?

Let that be his place, he said.

And now, said I, the fairest polity and the fairest man remain for us to describe, the tyranny and the tyrant.

Certainly, he said.

Come then, tell me, dear friend, how tyranny arises. That it is an outgrowth of democracy is fairly plain.

Yes, plain.

Is it, then, in a sense, in the same way in which democracy arises out of oligarchy that tyranny arises from democracy?

b   How is that?

The good that they proposed to themselves and that was the cause of the establishment of oligarchy—it was wealth, was it not?

Yes.

Well, then, the insatiate lust for wealth and the neglect of everything else for the sake of money-making were the cause of its undoing.

True, he said.

c   And is not the avidity of democracy for that which is its definition and criterion of good the thing which dissolves it too?

What do you say its criterion to be?

Liberty, I replied, for you may hear it said that this is best managed in a democratic city, and for this reason that is the only city in which a man of free spirit will care to live.

Why, yes, he replied, you hear that saying everywhere.

Then, as I was about to observe, is it not the excess and greed of this and the neglect of all other things that revolutionizes this constitution too and prepares the way for the necessity of a dictatorship?

How? he said.

Why, when a democratic city athirst for liberty gets bad cup-
d bearers for its leaders and is intoxicated by drinking too deep of that

unmixed wine, and then, if its so-called governors are not extremely
mild and gentle with it and do not dispense the liberty unstintedly,
it chastises them and accuses them of being accursed oligarchs.

Yes, that is what they do, he replied.

But those who obey the rulers, I said, it reviles as willing slaves
and men of nought, but it commends and honors in public and private rulers who resemble subjects and subjects who are like rulers. Is
it not inevitable that in such a state the spirit of liberty should go e
to all lengths?

Of course.

And this anarchic temper, said I, my friend, must penetrate into
private homes and finally enter into the very animals.

Just what do we mean by that? he said.

Why, I said, the father habitually tries to resemble the child and
is afraid of his sons, and the son likens himself to the father and
feels no awe or fear of his parents, so that he may be forsooth a free
man. And the resident alien feels himself equal to the citizen and the
citizen to him, and the foreigner likewise.   563

Yes, these things do happen, he said.

They do, said I, and such other trifles as these. The teacher in
such case fears and fawns upon the pupils, and the pupils pay no
heed to the teacher or to their overseers either. And in general the
young ape their elders and vie with them in speech and action,
while the old, accommodating themselves to the young, are full of
pleasantry and graciousness, imitating the young for fear they may b
be thought disagreeable and authoritative.

By all means, he said.

And the climax of popular liberty, my friend, I said, is attained
in such a city when the purchased slaves, male and female, are no
less free than the owners who paid for them. And I almost forgot to
mention the spirit of freedom and equal rights in the relation of men
to women and women to men.

Shall we not, then, said he, in Aeschylean phrase, say 'whatever c
rises to our lips'?

Certainly, I said, so I will. Without experience of it no one would
believe how much freer the very beasts subject to men are in such
a city than elsewhere. The dogs literally verify the adage and 'like their
mistresses become.' And likewise the horses and asses are wont to
hold on their way with the utmost freedom and dignity, bumping
into everyone who meets them and who does not step aside. And so all
things everywhere are just bursting with the spirit of liberty.   d

It is my own dream you are telling me, he said, for it often happens to me when I go to the country.

And do you note that the sum total of all these items when footed
up is that they render the souls of the citizens so sensitive that they
chafe at the slightest suggestion of servitude and will not endure it?

For you are aware that they finally pay no heed even to the laws written or unwritten, so that forsooth they may have no master anywhere
e over them.

I know it very well, said he.

This, then, my friend, said I, is the fine and vigorous root from
which tyranny grows, in my opinion.

Vigorous indeed, he said, but what next?

The same malady, I said, that, arising in oligarchy, destroyed it,
this more widely diffused and more violent as a result of this license,
enslaves democracy. And in truth, any excess is wont to bring about
564 a corresponding reaction to the opposite in the seasons, in plants, in
animal bodies, and most especially in political societies.

Probably, he said.

And so the probable outcome of too much freedom is only too
much slavery in the individual and the state.

Yes, that is probable.

Probably, then, tyranny develops out of no other constitution
than democracy—from the height of liberty, I take it, the fiercest extreme of servitude.

That is reasonable, he said.

b   That, however, I believe, was not your question, but what identical malady arising in democracy as well as in oligarchy enslaves it?

You say truly, he replied.

That then, I said, was what I had in mind, the class of idle and
spendthrift men, the most enterprising and vigorous portion being
leaders and the less manly spirits followers. We were likening them to
drones, some equipped with stings and others stingless.

And rightly too, he said.

These two kinds, then, I said, when they arise in any state, create
a disturbance like that produced in the body by phlegm and gall. And
c so a good physician and lawgiver must be on his guard from afar
against the two kinds, like a prudent apiarist, first and chiefly to prevent their springing up, but if they do arise to have them as quickly as
may be cut out, cells and all.

Yes, by Zeus, he said, by all means.

Then let us take it in this way, I said, so that we may contemplate our purpose more distinctly.

How?

Let us in our theory make a tripartite division of the democratic
state, which is in fact its structure. One such class, as we have de-
d scribed, grows up in it because of the license, no less than in the
oligarchic state.

That is so.

But it is far fiercer in this state than in that.

How so?

There, because it is not held in honor, but is kept out of office, it is not exercised and does not grow vigorous. But in a democracy this is the dominating class, with rare exceptions, and the fiercest part of it makes speeches and transacts business, and the remainder swarms and settles about the speaker's stand and keeps up a buzzing and tolerates no dissent, so that everything with slight exceptions is adminis- e tered by that class in such a state.

Quite so, he said.

And so from time to time there emerges or is secreted from the multitude another group of this sort.

What sort? he said.

When all are pursuing wealth the most orderly and thrifty natures for the most part become the richest.

It is likely.

Then they are the most abundant supply of honey for the drones, and it is the easiest to extract.

Why, yes, he said, how could one squeeze it out of those who have little?

The capitalistic class is, I take it, the name by which they are designated—the pasture of the drones.

Pretty much so, he said.   565

And the third class, composing the 'people,' would comprise all quiet cultivators of their own farms who possess little property. This is the largest and most potent group in a democracy when it meets in assembly.

Yes, it is, he said, but it will not often do that, unless it gets a share of the honey.

Well, does it not always share, I said, to the extent that the men at the head find it possible, in distributing to the people what they take from the well-to-do, to keep the lion's share for themselves?

Why, yes, he said, it shares in that sense.   b

And so, I suppose, those who are thus plundered are compelled to defend themselves by speeches in the assembly and any action in their power.

Of course.

And thereupon the charge is brought against them by the other party, though they may have no revolutionary designs, that they are plotting against the people, and it is said that they are oligarchs.

Surely.

And then finally, when they see the people, not of its own will but through misapprehension, and being misled by the calumniators, attempting to wrong them, why then, whether they wish it or not, they become in very deed oligarchs, not willingly, but this evil too is en- c gendered by those drones which sting them.

Precisely.

And then there ensue impeachments and judgments and lawsuits on either side.

Yes, indeed.

And is it not always the way of a demos to put forward one man as its special champion and protector and cherish and magnify him?

Yes, it is.

d   This, then, is plain, said I, that when a tyrant arises he sprouts from a protectorate root and from nothing else.

Very plain.

What, then, is the starting point of the transformation of a protector into a tyrant? Is it not obviously when the protector's acts begin to reproduce the legend that is told of the shrine of Lycaean Zeus in Arcadia?

What is that? he said.

The story goes that he who tastes of the one bit of human entrails minced up with those of other victims is inevitably transformed into a
e wolf. Have you not heard the tale?

I have.

And is it not true that in like manner a leader of the people who, getting control of a docile mob, does not withhold his hand from the shedding of tribal blood, but by the customary unjust accusations brings a citizen into court and assassinates him, blotting out a human life, and with unhallowed tongue and lips that have tasted kin-
566 dred blood, banishes and slays and hints at the abolition of debts and the partition of lands—is it not the inevitable consequence and a decree of fate that such a one be either slain by his enemies or become a tyrant and be transformed from a man into a wolf?

It is quite inevitable, he said.

He it is, I said, who becomes the leader of faction against the possessors of property.

Yes, he.

May it not happen that he is driven into exile and, being restored in defiance of his enemies, returns a finished tyrant?

Obviously.

And if they are unable to expel him or bring about his death by
b calumniating him to the people, they plot to assassinate him by stealth.

That is certainly wont to happen, said he.

And thereupon those who have reached this stage devise that famous petition of the tyrant—to ask from the people a bodyguard to make their city safe for the friend of democracy.

They do indeed, he said.

And the people grant it, I suppose, fearing for him but unconcerned for themselves.

c   Yes, indeed.

And when he sees this, the man who has wealth and with his wealth the repute of hostility to democracy, then in the words of the oracle delivered to Croesus, 'By the pebble-strewn strand of the

Hermus, swift is his flight; he stays not nor blushes to show the white feather.'

No, for he would never get a second chance to blush.

And he who is caught, methinks, is delivered to his death.

Inevitably.

And then obviously that protector does not lie prostrate, 'mighty with far-flung limbs,' in Homeric overthrow, but overthrowing many others towers in the car of state transformed from a protector into a d perfect and finished tyrant.

What else is likely? he said.

Shall we, then, portray the happiness, said I, of the man and the state in which such a creature arises?

By all means let us describe it, he said.

Then at the start and in the first days does he not smile upon all men and greet everybody he meets and deny that he is a tyrant, e and promise many things in private and public, and having freed men from debts, and distributed lands to the people and his own associates, he affects a gracious and gentle manner to all?

Necessarily, he said.

But when, I suppose, he has come to terms with some of his exiled enemies and has got others destroyed and is no longer disturbed by them, in the first place he is always stirring up some war so that the people may be in need of a leader.

That is likely.

And also that being impoverished by war taxes they may have to 567 devote themselves to their daily business and be less likely to plot against him?

Obviously.

And if, I presume, he suspects that there are free spirits who will not suffer his domination, his further object is to find pretexts for destroying them by exposing them to the enemy? From all these motives a tyrant is compelled to be always provoking wars?

Yes, he is compelled to do so.

And by such conduct will he not the more readily incur the hos- b tility of the citizens?

Of course.

And is it not likely that some of those who helped to establish and now share in his power, voicing their disapproval of the course of events, will speak out frankly to him and to one another—such of them as happen to be the bravest?

Yes, it is likely.

Then the tyrant must do away with all such if he is to maintain his rule, until he has left no one of any worth, friend or foe.

Obviously.

He must look sharp to see, then, who is brave, who is great-souled, c who is wise, who is rich, and such is his good fortune that, whether he wishes it or not, he must be their enemy and plot against them all until he purge the city.

A fine purgation, he said.

Yes, said I, just the opposite of that which physicians practice on our bodies. For while they remove the worst and leave the best, he does the reverse.

Yes, for apparently he must, he said, if he is to keep his power.

Blessed, then, is the necessity that binds him, said I, which bids
d him dwell for the most part with base companions who hate him, or else forfeit his life.

Such it is, he said.

And would he not, the more he offends the citizens by such conduct, have the greater need of more and more trustworthy bodyguards?

Of course.

Whom, then, may he trust, and whence shall he fetch them?

Unbidden, he said, they will wing their way to him in great numbers if he furnish their wage.

e Drones, by the dog, I said, I think you are talking of again, an alien and motley crew.

You think rightly, he said.

But what of the home supply, would he not choose to employ that?

How?

By taking their slaves from the citizens, emancipating them and enlisting them in his bodyguard.

Assuredly, he said, since these are those whom he can most trust.

Truly, said I, this tyrant business is a blessed thing on your show-
568 ing, if such are the friends and 'trusties' he must employ after destroying his former associates.

But such are indeed those he does make use of, he said.

And these companions admire him, I said, and these new citizens are his associates, while the better sort hate and avoid him.

Why should they not?

Not for nothing, said I, is tragedy in general esteemed wise, and Euripides beyond other tragedians.

Why, pray?

Because among other utterances of pregnant thought he said,
b 'Tyrants are wise by converse with the wise.' He meant evidently that these associates of the tyrant are the wise.

Yes, he and the other poets, he said, call the tyrant's power 'likest God's' and praise it in many other ways.

Wherefore, said I, being wise as they are, the poets of tragedy will pardon us and those whose politics resemble ours for not admitting them into our polity, since they hymn the praises of tyranny.

I think, he said, that the subtle minds among them will pardon us.   c

But going about to other cities, I fancy, collecting crowds and hiring fine, loud, persuasive voices, they draw the polities toward tyrannies or democracies.

Yes, indeed.

And, further, they are paid and honored for this, chiefly, as is to be expected, by tyrants, and secondly by democracy. But the higher they go, breasting constitution hill, the more their honor fails, as it   d were from lack of breath unable to proceed.

Quite so.

But this, said I, is a digression. Let us return to that fair, multitudinous, diversified, and ever-changing bodyguard of the tyrant and tell how it will be supported.

Obviously, he said, if there are sacred treasures in the city he will spend these as long as they last and the property of those he has destroyed, thus requiring smaller contributions from the populace.

But what when these resources fail?

Clearly, he said, his father's estate will have to support him and   e his wassailers, his fellows and his she-fellows.

I understand, I said, that the people which begot the tyrant will have to feed him and his companions.

It cannot escape from that, he said.

And what have you to say, I said, in case the people protests and says that it is not right that a grown-up son should be supported by his father, but the reverse, and that it did not beget and establish him   569 in order that, when he had grown great, it, in servitude to its own slaves, should feed him and the slaves together with a nondescript rabble of aliens, but in order that, with him for protector, it might be liberated from the rule of the rich and the so-called 'better classes,' and that it now bids him and his crew depart from the city as a father expels from his house a son together with troublesome revelers?

The demos, by Zeus, he said, will then learn to its cost what it   b is and what a creature it begot and cherished and bred to greatness, and that in its weakness it tries to expel the stronger.

What do you mean? said I. Will the tyrant dare to use force against his father, and, if he does not yield, to strike him?

Yes, he said, after he has once taken from him his arms.

A very parricide, said I, you make the tyrant out to be, and a cruel nurse of old age, and, as it seems, this is at last tyranny open and avowed, and, as the saying goes, the demos trying to escape the smoke of submission to the free would have plunged into the fire of enslavement to slaves, and in exchange for that excessive and un-   c seasonable liberty has clothed itself in the garb of the most cruel and bitter servile servitude.

Yes indeed, he said, that is just what happens.

Well, then, said I, shall we not be fairly justified in saying that we have sufficiently described the transformation of a democracy into a tyranny and the nature of the tyranny itself?

Quite sufficiently, he said.

BOOK IX

571 There remains for consideration, said I, the tyrannical man himself— the manner of his development out of the democratic type and his character and the quality of his life, whether wretched or happy.

Why, yes, he still remains, he said.

Do you know, then, what it is that I still miss?

What?

In the matter of our desires I do not think we sufficiently distinguished their nature and number. And so long as this is lacking our b inquiry will lack clearness.

Well, said he, will our consideration of them not still be opportune?

By all means. And observe what it is about them that I wish to consider. It is this. Of our unnecessary pleasures and appetites there are some lawless ones, I think, which probably are to be found in us all, but which, when controlled by the laws and the better desires in alliance with reason, can in some men be altogether got rid of, or so nearly so that only a few weak ones remain, while in others the remnant is stronger and more numerous.

c   What desires do you mean? he said.

Those, said I, that are awakened in sleep when the rest of the soul, the rational, gentle and dominant part, slumbers, but the beastly and savage part, replete with food and wine, gambols and, repelling sleep, endeavors to sally forth and satisfy its own instincts. You are aware that in such case there is nothing it will not venture to undertake as being released from all sense of shame and all reason.

d It does not shrink from attempting to lie with a mother in fancy or with anyone else, man, god, or brute. It is ready for any foul deed of blood; it abstains from no food, and, in a word, falls short of no extreme of folly and shamelessness.

Most true, he said.

But when, I suppose, a man's condition is healthy and sober, and he goes to sleep after arousing his rational part and entertaining it with fair words and thoughts, and attaining to clear self-consciousness, while he has neither starved nor indulged to repletion his ap-

e petitive part, so that it may be lulled to sleep and not disturb the

572 better part by its pleasure or pain, but may suffer that in isolated purity to examine and reach out toward and apprehend some of the things unknown to it, past, present, or future, and when he has in like manner tamed his passionate part, and does not after a quarrel fall

asleep with anger still awake within him, but if he has thus quieted the two elements in his soul and quickened the third, in which reason resides, and so goes to his rest, you are aware that in such case he is most likely to apprehend truth, and the visions of his dreams are b least likely to be lawless.

I certainly think so, he said.

This description has carried us too far, but the point that we have to notice is this, that in fact there exists in every one of us, even in some reputed most respectable, a terrible, fierce, and lawless brood of desires, which it seems are revealed in our sleep. Consider, then, whether there is anything in what I say, and whether you admit it.

Well, I do.

Now recall our characterization of the democratic man. His de- c velopment was determined by his education from youth under a thrifty father who approved only the acquisitive appetites and disapproved the unnecessary ones whose object is entertainment and display. Is not that so?

Yes.

And by association with more sophisticated men, teeming with the appetites we have just described, he is impelled toward every form of insolence and outrage, and to the adoption of their way of life by his hatred of his father's niggardliness. But since his nature is better than that of his corrupters, being drawn both ways he settles down d in a compromise between the two tendencies, and indulging and enjoying each in moderation, forsooth, as he supposes, he lives what he deems a life that is neither illiberal nor lawless, now transformed from an oligarch to a democrat.

That was and is our belief about this type.

Assume, then, again, said I, that such a man when he is older has a son bred in turn in his ways of life.

I so assume.

And suppose the experience of his father to be repeated in his case. He is drawn toward utter lawlessness, which is called by his se- e ducers complete freedom. His father and his other kin lend support to these compromise appetites while the others lend theirs to the opposite group. And when these dread magi and kingmakers come to realize that they have no hope of controlling the youth in any other way, 573 they contrive to engender in his soul a ruling passion to be the protector of his idle and prodigal appetites, a monstrous winged drone. Or do you think the spirit of desire in such men is aught else?

Nothing but that, he said.

And when the other appetites, buzzing about it, replete with incense and myrrh and chaplets and wine, and the pleasures that are released in such revelries, magnifying and fostering it to the utmost, b awaken in the drone the sting of unsatisfied yearnings, why then this protector of the soul has madness for his bodyguard and runs amuck,

and if it finds in the man any opinions or appetites accounted worthy
and still capable of shame, it slays them and thrusts them forth until
it purges him of sobriety and fills and infects him with frenzy
brought in from outside.

A perfect description, he said, of the generation of the tyrannical
man.

And is not this analogy, said I, the reason why Love has long
since been called a tyrant?

That may well be, he said.

c And does not a drunken man, my friend, I said, have something
of this tyrannical temper?

Yes, he has.

And again the madman, the deranged man, attempts and expects
to rule over not only men but gods.

Yes indeed, he does, he said.

Then a man becomes tyrannical in the full sense of the word, my
friend, I said, when either by nature or by habits or by both he has
become even as the drunken, the erotic, the maniacal.

Assuredly.

d Such, it seems, is his origin and character, but what is his manner
of life?

As the wits say, you shall tell *me*.

I do, I said, for, I take it, next there are among them feasts and
carousals and revelings and courtesans and all the doings of those
whose souls are entirely swayed by the indwelling tyrant Eros.

Inevitably, he said.

And do not many and dread appetites shoot up beside this master
passion every day and night in need of many things?

Many indeed.

And so any revenues there may be are quickly expended.

e Of course.

And after this there are borrowings and levyings upon the estate?

Of course.

And when all these resources fail, must there not come a cry from
the frequent and fierce nestlings of desire hatched in his soul, and
must not such men, urged, as it were by goads, by the other desires,
and especially by the ruling passion itself as captain of their body-
574 guard—to keep up the figure—must they not run wild and look to see
who has aught that can be taken from him by deceit or violence?

Most certainly.

And so he is compelled to sweep it in from every source or else be
afflicted with great travail and pain.

He is.

And just as the new, upspringing pleasures in him got the better of the original passions of his soul and robbed them, so he himself, though younger, will claim the right to get the better of his father

and mother, and, after spending his own share, to seize and convert to his own use a portion of his father's estate.

Of course, he said, what else?

And if they resist him, would he not at first attempt to rob and b steal from his parents and deceive them?

Certainly.

And if he failed in that, would he not next seize it by force?

I think so, he said.

And then, good sir, if the old man and the old woman clung to it and resisted him, would he be careful to refrain from the acts of a tyrant?

I am not without my fears, he said, for the parents of such a one.

Nay, Adimantus, in heaven's name, do you suppose that, for the sake of a newly found *belle amie* bound to him by no necessary tie, c such a one would strike the dear mother, his by necessity and from his birth? Or for the sake of a blooming new-found *bel ami*, not necessary to his life, he would rain blows upon the aged father past his prime, closest of his kin and oldest of his friends? And would he subject them to those new favorites if he brought them under the same roof?

Yes, by Zeus, he said.

A most blessed lot it seems to be, said I, to be the parent of a tyrant son.

It does indeed, he said.

And again, when the resources of his father and mother are ex- d hausted and fail such a one, and the swarm of pleasures collected in his soul is grown great, will he not first lay hands on the wall of someone's house or the cloak of someone who walks late at night, and thereafter he will make a clean sweep of some temple, and in all these actions the beliefs which he held from boyhood about the honorable and the base, the opinions accounted just, will be overmastered by the opinions newly emancipated and released, which, serving as bodyguards of the ruling passion, will prevail in alliance with it—I mean the opinions that formerly were freed from restraint in sleep, when, being still under the control of his father and the laws, he maintained the democratic constitution in his soul. But now, when under the tyranny of his ruling passion, he is continuously and in waking hours what he rarely became in sleep, and he will refrain e from no atrocity of murder nor from any food or deed, but the passion that dwells in him as a tyrant will live in utmost anarchy and lawless- 575 ness, and, since it is itself sole autocrat, will urge the polity, so to speak, of him in whom it dwells to dare anything and everything in order to find support for himself and the hubbub of his henchmen, in part introduced from outside by evil associations, and in part released and liberated within by the same habits of life as his. Is not this the life of such a one?

It is this, he said.

b   And if, I said, there are only a few of this kind in a city, and the others, the multitude as a whole, are sober-minded, the few go forth into exile and serve some tyrant elsewhere as bodyguard or become mercenaries in any war there may be. But if they spring up in time of peace and tranquillity they stay right there in the city and effect many small evils.

What kind of evils do you mean?

Oh, they just steal, break into houses, cut purses, strip men of their garments, plunder temples, and kidnap, and if they are fluent speakers they become sycophants and bear false witness and take bribes.

c   Yes, small evils indeed, he said, if the men of this sort are few.

Why, yes, I said, for small evils are relatively small compared with great, and in respect of the corruption and misery of a state all of them together, as the saying goes, don't come within hail of the mischief done by a tyrant. For when men of this sort and their followers become numerous in a state and realize their numbers, then it is they who, in conjunction with the folly of the people, create a tyrant out of that one of them who has the greatest and mightiest tyrant in his own soul.

d   Naturally, he said, for he would be the most tyrannical.

Then if the people yield willingly—'tis well, but if the city resists him, then, just as in the previous case the man chastised his mother and his father, so now in turn will he chastise his fatherland if he can, bringing in new boon companions beneath whose sway he will hold and keep enslaved his once dear motherland—as the Cretans name her—and fatherland. And this would be the end of such a man's desire.

e   Yes, he said, this, just this.

Then, said I, is not this the character of such men in private life and before they rule the state—to begin with they associate with flatterers, who are ready to do anything to serve them, or, if they themselves want something, they themselves fawn and shrink from no contortion or abasement in protest of their friendship, though, once
576 the object gained, they sing another tune.

Yes indeed, he said.

Throughout their lives, then, they never know what it is to be the friends of anybody. They are always either masters or slaves, but the tyrannical nature never tastes freedom or true friendship.

Quite so.

May we not rightly call such men faithless?

Of course.

Yes, and unjust to the last degree, if we were right in our previous
b agreement about the nature of justice.

But surely, he said, we were right.

Let us sum up, then, said I, the most evil type of man. He is, I presume, the man who, in his waking hours, has the qualities we found in his dream state.

Quite so.

And he is developed from the man who, being by nature most of a tyrant, achieves sole power, and the longer he lives as an actual tyrant the stronger this quality becomes.

Inevitably, said Glaucon, taking up the argument.

And shall we find, said I, that the man who is shown to be the most evil will also be the most miserable, and the man who is most of c a tyrant for the longest time is most and longest miserable in sober truth? Yet the many have many opinions.

That much, certainly, he said, must needs be true.

Does not the tyrannical man, said I, correspond to the tyrannical state in similitude, the democratic to the democratic and the others likewise?

Surely.

And may we not infer that the relation of state to state in respect of virtue and happiness is the same as that of the man to the man?

Of course. d

What is, then, in respect of virtue, the relation of a city ruled by a tyrant to a royal city as we first described it?

They are direct contraries, he said. The one is the best, the other the worst.

I'll not ask which is which, I said, because that is obvious. But again in respect of happiness and wretchedness, is your estimate the same or different? And let us not be dazzled by fixing our eyes on that one man, the tyrant, or a few of his court, but let us enter into and survey the entire city, as is right, and declare our opinion only after we have so dived to its uttermost recesses and contemplated e its life as a whole.

That is a fair challenge, he said, and it is clear to everybody that there is no city more wretched than that in which a tyrant rules, and none more happy than that governed by a true king.

And would it not also be a fair challenge, said I, to ask you to ac- cept as the only proper judge of the two men the one who is able in 577 thought to enter with understanding into the very soul and temper of a man, and who is not like a child viewing him from outside, over- awed by the tyrants' great attendance, and the pomp and circumstance which they assume in the eyes of the world, but is able to see through it all? And what if I should assume, then, that the man to whom we ought all to listen is he who has this capacity of judgment and who has lived under the same roof with a tyrant and has wit- nessed his conduct in his own home and observed in person his deal- b ings with his intimates in each instance where he would best be seen stripped of his vesture of tragedy, and who had likewise observed his behavior in the hazards of his public life—and if we should ask the man who has seen all this to be the messenger to report on the happiness or misery of the tyrant as compared with other men?

That also would be a most just challenge, he said.

Shall we, then, make believe, said I, that we are of those who are thus able to judge and who have ere now lived with tyrants, so that we may have someone to answer our questions?

By all means.

c   Come, then, said I, examine it thus. Recall the general likeness between the city and the man, and then observe in turn what happens to each of them.

What things? he said.

In the first place, said I, will you call the state governed by a tyrant free or enslaved, speaking of it as a state?

Utterly enslaved, he said.

And yet you see in it masters and free men.

I see, he said, a small portion of such, but the entirety, so to speak, and the best part of it, is shamefully and wretchedly enslaved.

d   If, then, I said, the man resembles the state, must not the same proportion obtain in him, and his soul teem with boundless servility and illiberality, the best and most reasonable parts of it being enslaved, while a small part, the worst and the most frenzied, plays the despot?

Inevitably, he said.

Then will you say that such a soul is enslaved or free?

Enslaved, I should suppose.

Again, does not the enslaved and tyrannized city least of all do what it really wishes?

Decidedly so.

e   Then the tyrannized soul—to speak of the soul as a whole—also will least of all do what it wishes, but being always perforce driven and drawn by the gadfly of desire it will be full of confusion and repentance.

Of course.

And must the tyrannized city be rich or poor?

Poor.

578   Then the tyrant soul also must of necessity always be needy and suffer from unfulfilled desire.

So it is, he said.

And again, must not such a city, as well as such a man, be full of terrors and alarms?

It must indeed.

And do you think you will find more lamentations and groans and wailing and anguish in any other city?

By no means.

And so of man, do you think these things will more abound in any other than in this tyrant type, that is maddened by its desires and passions?

How could it be so? he said.

In view of all these and other like considerations, then, I take it, b you judged that this city is the most miserable of cities.

And was I not right? he said.

Yes, indeed, said I. But of the tyrant man, what have you to say in view of these same things?

That he is far and away the most miserable of all, he said.

I cannot admit, said I, that you are right in that too.

How so? said he.

This one, said I, I take it, has not yet attained the acme of misery.

Then who has?

Perhaps you will regard the one I am about to name as still more wretched.

What one?   c

The one, said I, who, being of tyrannical temper, does not live out his life in private station but is so unfortunate that by some unhappy chance he is enabled to become an actual tyrant.

I infer from what has already been said, he replied, that you speak truly.

Yes, said I, but it is not enough to suppose such things. We must examine them thoroughly by reason and an argument such as this. For our inquiry concerns the greatest of all things, the good life or the bad life.

Quite right, he replied.

Consider, then, if there is anything in what I say. For I think we d must get a notion of the matter from these examples.

From which?

From individual wealthy private citizens in our states who possess many slaves. For these resemble the tyrant in being rulers over many, only the tyrant's numbers are greater.

Yes, they are.

You are aware, then, that they are unafraid and do not fear their slaves?

What should they fear?

Nothing, I said, but do you perceive the reason why?

Yes, because the entire state is ready to defend each citizen.

You are right, I said. But now suppose some god should catch up e a man who has fifty or more slaves and waft him with his wife and children away from the city and set him down with his other possessions and his slaves in a solitude where no free man could come to his rescue. What and how great would be his fear, do you suppose, lest he and his wife and children be destroyed by the slaves?

The greatest in the world, he said, if you ask me.   579

And would he not forthwith find it necessary to fawn upon some of the slaves and make them many promises and emancipate them, though nothing would be further from his wish? And so he would turn out to be the flatterer of his own servants.

He would certainly have to, he said, or else perish.

But now suppose, said I, that god established round about him numerous neighbors who would not tolerate the claim of one man to be master of another, but would inflict the utmost penalties on any such person on whom they could lay their hands.

b   I think, he said, that his plight would be still more desperate, encompassed by nothing but enemies.

And is not that the sort of prison house in which the tyrant is pent, being of a nature such as we have described and filled with multitudinous and manifold terrors and appetites? Yet greedy and avid of spirit as he is, he only of the citizens may not travel abroad or view any of the sacred festivals that other free men yearn to see, but he

c must live for the most part cowering in the recesses of his house like a woman, envying among the other citizens anyone who goes abroad and sees any good thing.

Most certainly, he said.

And does not such a harvest of ills measure the difference between the man who is merely ill governed in his own soul, the man of tyrannical temper, whom you just now judged to be most miserable, and the man who, having this disposition, does not live out his life in private station but is constrained by some ill-hap to become an actual tyrant, and while unable to control himself attempts to rule over others, as if a man with a sick and incontinent body should not live

d the private life but should be compelled to pass his days in contention and strife with other persons?

Your analogy is most apt and true, Socrates, he said.

Is not that then, dear Glaucon, said I, a most unhappy experience in every way? And is not the tyrant's life still worse than that which was judged by you to be the worst?

Precisely so, he said.

Then it is the truth, though some may deny it, that the real tyrant is really enslaved to cringings and servitudes beyond compare, a flat-

e terer of the basest men, and that, so far from finding even the least satisfaction for his desires, he is in need of most things, and is a poor man in very truth, as is apparent if one knows how to observe a soul in its entirety. And throughout his life he teems with terrors and is full of convulsions and pains, if in fact he resembles the condition of the city which he rules, and he is like it, is he not?

Yes, indeed, he said.

580   And in addition, shall we not further attribute to him all that we spoke of before, and say that he must needs be, and, by reason of his rule, come to be still more than he was, envious, faithless, unjust, friendless, impious, a vessel and nurse of all iniquity, and so in consequence be himself most unhappy and make all about him so?

No man of sense will gainsay that, he said.

Come then, said I, now at last, even as the judge of last instance pronounces, so do you declare who in your opinion is first in happi- b ness and who second, and similarly judge the others, all five in succession, the royal, the timocratic, the oligarchic, the democratic, and the tyrannical man.

Nay, he said, the decision is easy. For as if they were choruses I judge them in the order of their entrance, and so rank them in respect of virtue and vice, happiness and its contrary.

Shall we hire a herald, then, said I, or shall I myself make proclamation that the son of Ariston pronounced the best man and the most c righteous to be the happiest, and that he is the one who is the most kingly and a king over himself, and declared that the most evil and most unjust is the most unhappy, who again is the man who, having the most of the tyrannical temper in himself, becomes most of a tyrant over himself and over the state?

Let it have been so proclaimed by you, he said.

Shall I add the clause 'alike whether their character is known to all men and gods or is not known'?

Add that to the proclamation, he said.

Very good, said I. This, then, would be one of our proofs, but examine this second one and see if there is anything in it.   d

What is it?

Since, said I, corresponding to the three types in the city, the soul also is tripartite, it will admit, I think, of another demonstration also.

What is that?

The following. The three parts have also, it appears to me, three kinds of pleasure, one peculiar to each, and similarly three appetites and controls.

What do you mean? he said.

One part, we say, is that with which a man learns, one is that with which he feels anger. But the third part, owing to its manifold forms, we could not easily designate by any one distinctive name, but e gave it the name of its chief and strongest element, for we called it the appetitive part because of the intensity of its appetites concerned with food and drink and love and their accompaniments, and likewise the money-loving part, because money is the chief instrument for the 581 gratification of such desires.

And rightly, he said.

And if we should also say that its pleasure and its love were for gain or profit, should we not thus best bring it together under one head in our discourse so as to understand each other when we speak of this part of the soul, and justify our calling it the money-loving and gain-loving part?

I, at any rate, think so, he said.

And, again, of the high-spirited element, do we not say that it is wholly set on predominance and victory and good repute?

Yes, indeed.

b   And might we not appropriately designate it as the ambitious part and that which is covetous of honor?

Most appropriately.

But surely it is obvious to everyone that all the endeavor of the part by which we learn is ever toward knowledge of the truth of things, and that it least of the three is concerned for wealth and reputation.

Much the least.

Lover of learning and lover of wisdom would be suitable designations for that.

Quite so, he said.

c   Is it not also true, I said, that the ruling principle of men's souls is in some cases this faculty and in others one of the other two, as it may happen?

That is so, he said.

And that is why we say that the primary classes of men also are three, the philosopher or lover of wisdom, the lover of victory, and the lover of gain.

Precisely so.

And also that there are three forms of pleasure, corresponding respectively to each?

By all means.

Are you aware, then, said I, that if you should choose to ask men of these three classes, each in turn, which is the most pleasurable of

d these lives, each will chiefly commend his own? The financier will affirm that in comparison with profit the pleasures of honor or of learning are of no value except in so far as they produce money.

True, he said.

And what of the lover of honor? said I. Does he not regard the pleasure that comes from money as vulgar and low, and again that of learning, save in so far as the knowledge confers honor, mere fume and moonshine.

It is so, he said.

And what, said I, are we to suppose the philosopher thinks of the

e other pleasures compared with the delight of knowing the truth and the reality, and being always occupied with that while he learns? Will he not think them far removed from true pleasure, and call them literally the pleasures of necessity, since he would have no use for them if necessity were not laid upon him?

We may be sure of that, he said.

Since, then, there is contention between the several types of pleasure and the lives themselves, not merely as to which is the more

582 honorable or the more base, or the worse or the better, but which is actually the more pleasurable or free from pain, how could we determine which of them speaks most truly?

In faith, I cannot tell, he said.

Well, consider it thus. By what are things to be judged, if they are to be judged rightly? Is it not by experience, intelligence, and discussion? Or could anyone name a better criterion than these?

How could he? he said.

Observe, then. Of our three types of men, which has had the most experience of all the pleasures we mentioned? Do you think that the lover of gain by study of the very nature of truth has more experience of the pleasure that knowledge yields than the philosopher has b of that which results from gain?

There is a vast difference, he said, for the one, the philosopher, must needs taste of the other two kinds of pleasure from childhood, but the lover of gain is not only under no necessity of tasting or experiencing the sweetness of the pleasure of learning the true natures of things, but he cannot easily do so even if he desires and is eager for it.

The lover of wisdom, then, said I, far surpasses the lover of gain in experience of both kinds of pleasure.

Yes, far.   c

And how does he compare with the lover of honor? Is he more unacquainted with the pleasure of being honored than that other with that which comes from knowledge?

Nay, honor, he said, if they achieve their several objects, attends them all, for the rich man is honored by many and the brave man and the wise, so that all are acquainted with the kind of pleasure that honor brings, but it is impossible for anyone except the lover of wisdom to have savored the delight that the contemplation of true being and reality brings.

Then, said I, so far as experience goes, he is the best judge of the d three.

By far.

And again, he is the only one whose experience will have been accompanied by intelligence.

Surely.

And yet again, that which is the instrument, or ὄργανον, of judgment is the instrument, not of the lover of gain or of the lover of honor, but of the lover of wisdom.

What is that?

It was by means of words and discussion that we said the judgment must be reached, was it not?

Yes.

And they are the instrument mainly of the philosopher.

Of course.

Now if wealth and profit were the best criteria by which things e are judged, the things praised and censured by the lover of gain would necessarily be truest and most real.

Quite necessarily.

And if honor, victory, and courage, would it not be the things praised by the lover of honor and victory?

Obviously.

But since the tests are experience and wisdom and discussion, what follows?

Of necessity, he said, that the things approved by the lover of wisdom and discussion are most valid and true.

583 There being, then, three kinds of pleasure, the pleasure of that part of the soul whereby we learn is the sweetest, and the life of the man in whom that part dominates is the most pleasurable.

How could it be otherwise? he said.

At any rate the man of intelligence speaks with authority when he commends his own life.

And to what life and to what pleasure, I said, does the judge assign the second place?

Obviously to that of the warrior and honor-loving type, for it is nearer to the first than is the life of the money-maker.

And so the last place belongs to the lover of gain, as it seems.

Surely, said he.

That, then, would be two points in succession and two victories b for the just man over the unjust. And now for the third in the Olympian fashion to the savior and to Olympian Zeus—observe that other pleasure than that of the intelligence is not altogether even real or pure, but is a kind of scene painting, as I seem to have heard from some wise man, and yet this would be the greatest and most decisive overthrow.

Much the greatest. But what do you mean?

c   I shall discover it, I said, if you will answer my questions while I seek.

Ask, then, he said.

Tell me, then, said I, do we not say that pain is the opposite of pleasure?

We certainly do.

And is there not such a thing as a neutral state?

There is.

Is it not intermediate between them, and in the mean, being a kind of quietude of the soul in these respects? Or is not that your notion of it?

It is that, said he.

Do you not recall the things men say in sickness?

What sort of things?

d   Why, that after all there is nothing sweeter than to be well, though they were not aware that it is the highest pleasure before they were ill.

I remember, he said.

And do you not hear men afflicted with severe pain saying that there is no greater pleasure than the cessation of this suffering?

I do.

And you perceive, I presume, many similar conditions in which men while suffering pain praise freedom from pain and relief from that as the highest pleasure, and not positive delight.

Yes, he said, for this in such cases is perhaps what is felt as pleasurable and acceptable—peace.

And so, I said, when a man's delight comes to an end, the cessa- e tion of pleasure will be painful.

It may be so, he said.

What, then, we just now described as the intermediate state between the two—this quietude—will sometimes be both pain and pleasure.

It seems so.

Is it really possible for that which is neither to become both?

I think not.

And further, both pleasure and pain arising in the soul are a kind of motion, are they not?

Yes.

And did we not just now see that to feel neither pain nor pleasure 584 is a quietude of the soul and an intermediate state between the two?

Yes, we did.

How, then, can it be right to think the absence of pain pleasure, or the absence of joy painful?

In no way.

This is not a reality, then, but an illusion, said I. In such case the quietude in juxtaposition with the pain appears pleasure, and in juxtaposition with the pleasure pain. And these illusions have no real bearing on the truth of pleasure, but are a kind of jugglery.

So at any rate our argument signifies, he said. b

Take a look, then, said I, at pleasures which do not follow on pain, so that you may not haply suppose for the present that it is the nature of pleasure to be a cessation from pain and pain from pleasure.

Where shall I look, he said, and what pleasures do you mean?

There are many others, I said, and especially, if you please to note them, the pleasures connected with smell. For these with no antecedent pain suddenly attain an indescribable intensity, and their cessation leaves no pain after them.

Most true, he said.

Let us not believe, then, that the riddance of pain is pure pleasure c or that of pleasure pain.

No, we must not.

Yet, surely, said I, the affections that find their way through the body to the soul and are called pleasures are, we may say, the most and the greatest of them, of this type, in some sort releases from pain.

Yes, they are.

And is not this also the character of the anticipatory pleasures and pains that precede them and arise from the expectation of them?

It is.

d   Do you know, then, what their quality is and what they most resemble?

What? he said.

Do you think that there is such a thing in nature as up and down and in the middle?

I do.

Do you suppose, then, that anyone who is transported from below to the center would have any other opinion than that he was moving upward? And if he took his stand at the center and looked in the direction from which he had been transported, do you think he would suppose himself to be anywhere but above, never having seen that which is really above?

No, by Zeus, he said, I do not think that such a person would have any other notion.

e   And if he were borne back, I said, he would both think himself to be moving downward and would think truly.

Of course.

And would not all this happen to him because of his nonacquaintance with the true and real up and down and middle?

Obviously.

Would it surprise you, then, said I, if similarly men without experience of truth and reality hold unsound opinions about many other matters, and are so disposed toward pleasure and pain and the intermediate neutral condition that, when they are moved in the direction 585 of the painful, they truly think themselves to be, and really are, in a state of pain, but, when they move from pain to the middle and neutral state, they intensely believe that they are approaching fulfillment and pleasure, and just as if, in ignorance of white, they were comparing gray with black, so, being inexperienced in true pleasure, they are deceived by viewing painlessness in its relation to pain?

No, by Zeus, he said, it would not surprise me, but far rather if it were not so.

In *this* way, then, consider it. Are not hunger and thirst and simi-
b lar states inanitions or emptinesses of the bodily habit?

Surely.

And is not ignorance and folly in turn a kind of emptiness of the habit of the soul?

It is indeed.

And he who partakes of nourishment and he who gets wisdom fills the void and is filled?

Of course.

And which is the truer filling and fulfillment, that of the less or of the more real being?

Evidently that of the more real.

And which of the two groups or kinds do you think has a greater

part in pure essence, the class of foods, drinks, and relishes and nour- c
ishment generally, or the kind of true opinion, knowledge and reason,
and, in sum, all the things that are more excellent? Form your judgment thus. Which do you think more truly *is*, that which clings to
what is ever like itself and immortal and to the truth, and that which
is itself of such a nature and is born in a thing of that nature, or that
which clings to what is mortal and never the same and is itself such
and is born in such a thing?

That which cleaves to what is ever the same far surpasses,
he said.

Does the essence of that which never abides the same partake of
real essence any more than of knowledge?

By no means.

Or of truth and reality?

Not of that, either.

And if a thing has less of truth has it not also less of real essence
or existence?

Necessarily.   d

And is it not generally true that the kinds concerned with the
service of the body partake less of truth and reality than those that
serve the soul?

Much less.

And do you not think that the same holds of the body itself in
comparison with the soul?

I do.

Then is not that which is fulfilled of what more truly is, and
which itself more truly is, more truly filled and satisfied than that
which being itself less real is filled with more unreal things?

Of course.

If, then, to be filled with what befits nature is pleasure, then that
which is more really filled with real things would more really and e
truly cause us to enjoy a true pleasure, while that which partakes of
the less truly existent would be less truly and surely filled and would
partake of a less trustworthy and less true pleasure.

Most inevitably, he said.

Then those who have no experience of wisdom and virtue but are 586
ever devoted to feastings and that sort of thing are swept downward, it
seems, and back again to the center, and so sway and roam to and fro
throughout their lives, but they have never transcended all this and
turned their eyes to the true upper region nor been wafted there, nor
ever been really filled with real things, nor ever tasted stable and pure
pleasure, but with eyes ever bent upon the earth and heads bowed
down over their tables they feast like cattle, grazing and copulating, b
ever greedy for more of these delights, and in their greed kicking and
butting one another with horns and hoofs of iron they slay one another in sateless avidity, because they are vainly striving to satisfy

with things that are not real the unreal and incontinent part of their souls.

You describe in quite oracular style, Socrates, said Glaucon, the life of the multitude.

And are not the pleasures with which they dwell inevitably commingled with pains, phantoms of true pleasure, illusions of scene painting, so colored by contrary juxtaposition as to seem intense in
c either kind, and to beget mad loves of themselves in senseless souls, and to be fought for, as Stesichorus says the wraith of Helen was fought for at Troy through ignorance of the truth?

It is quite inevitable, he said, that it should be so.

So, again, must not the like hold of the high-spirited element, whenever a man succeeds in satisfying that part of his nature—his
d covetousness of honor by envy, his love of victory by violence, his ill temper by indulgence in anger, pursuing these ends without regard to consideration and reason?

The same sort of thing, he said, must necessarily happen in this case too.

Then, said I, may we not confidently declare that in both the gain-loving and the contentious part of our nature all the desires that wait upon knowledge and reason, and, pursuing their pleasures in conjunction with them, take only those pleasures which reason approves, will, since they follow truth, enjoy the truest pleasures, so far as that is possible for them, and also the pleasures that are proper to
e them and their own, if for everything that which is best may be said to be most its 'own'?

But indeed, he said, it is most truly its very own.

Then when the entire soul accepts the guidance of the wisdom-loving part and is not filled with inner dissension, the result for each part is that it in all other respects keeps to its own task and is just,
587 and likewise that each enjoys its own proper pleasures and the best pleasures and, so far as such a thing is possible, the truest.

Precisely so.

And so when one of the other two gets the mastery the result for it is that it does not find its own proper pleasure and constrains the others to pursue an alien pleasure and not the true.

That is so, he said.

And would not that which is furthest removed from philosophy and reason be most likely to produce this effect?

Quite so, he said.

And is not that furthest removed from reason which is furthest from law and order?

Obviously.

And was it not made plain that the furthest removed are the
b erotic and tyrannical appetites?

Quite so.

And least so the royal and orderly?

Yes.

Then the tyrant's place, I think, will be fixed at the furthest remove from true and proper pleasure, and the king's at the least.

Necessarily.

Then the tyrant's life will be least pleasurable and the king's most.

There is every necessity of that.

Do you know, then, said I, how much less pleasurably the tyrant lives than the king?

I'll know if you tell me, he said.

There being as it appears three pleasures, one genuine and two spurious, the tyrant in his flight from law and reason crosses the bor- c der beyond the spurious, cohabits with certain slavish, mercenary pleasures, and the measure of his inferiority is not easy to express except perhaps thus.

How? he said.

The tyrant, I believe, we found at the third remove from the oligarch, for the democrat came between.

Yes.

And would he not also dwell with a phantom of pleasure in respect of reality three stages removed from that other, if all that we have said is true?

That is so.

And the oligarch in turn is at the third remove from the royal man d if we assume the identity of the aristocrat and the king.

Yes, the third.

Three times three, then, by numerical measure is the interval that separates the tyrant from true pleasure.

Apparently.

The phantom of the tyrant's pleasure is then by longitudinal mensuration a plane number.

Quite so.

But by squaring and cubing it is clear what the interval of this separation becomes.

It is clear, he said, to a reckoner.

Then taking it the other way about, if one tries to express the ex- e tent of the interval between the king and the tyrant in respect of true pleasure he will find on completion of the multiplication that he lives seven hundred and twenty-nine times as happily and that the tyrant's life is more painful by the same distance.

An overwhelming and baffling calculation, he said, of the difference between the just and the unjust man in respect of pleasure and 588 pain!

And what is more, it is a true number and pertinent to the lives of men if days and nights and months and years pertain to them.

They certainly do, he said.

Then if in point of pleasure the victory of the good and just man over the bad and unjust is so great as this, he will surpass him inconceivably in decency and beauty of life and virtue.

Inconceivably indeed, by Zeus, he said.

b   Very good, said I. And now that we have come to this point in the argument, let us take up again the statement with which we began and that has brought us to this pass. It was, I believe, averred that injustice is profitable to the completely unjust man who is reputed just. Was not that the proposition?

Yes, that.

Let us, then, reason with its proponent now that we have agreed on the essential nature of injustice and just conduct.

How? he said.

By fashioning in our discourse a symbolic image of the soul, that the maintainer of that proposition may see precisely what it is that he was saying.

What sort of an image? he said.

c   One of those natures that the ancient fables tell of, said I, as that of the Chimera or Scylla or Cerberus, and the numerous other examples that are told of many forms grown together in one.

Yes, they do tell of them.

Mold, then, a single shape of a manifold and many-headed beast that has a ring of heads of tame and wild beasts and can change them and cause to spring forth from itself all such growths.

It is the task of a cunning artist, he said, but nevertheless, since d speech is more plastic than wax and other such media, assume that it has been so fashioned.

Then fashion one other form of a lion and one of a man and let the first be far the largest and the second second in size.

That is easier, he said, and is done.

Join the three in one, then, so as in some sort to grow together.

They are so united, he said.

Then mold about them outside the likeness of one, that of the e man, so that to anyone who is unable to look within but who can see only the external sheath it appears to be one living creature, the man.

The sheath is made fast about him, he said.

Let us then say to the speaker who avers that it pays this man to be unjust, and that to do justice is not for his advantage, that he is affirming nothing else than that it profits him to feast and make strong 589 the multifarious beast and the lion and all that pertains to the lion, but to starve the man and so enfeeble him that he can be pulled about whithersoever either of the others drag him, and not to familiarize or reconcile with one another the two creatures but suffer them to bite and fight and devour one another.

Yes, he said, that is precisely what the panegyrist of injustice will be found to say.

And on the other hand, he who says that justice is the more profitable affirms that all our actions and words should tend to give the man within us complete domination over the entire man and make b him take charge of the many-headed beast—like a farmer who cherishes and trains the cultivated plants but checks the growth of the wild—and he will make an ally of the lion's nature, and caring for all the beasts alike will first make them friendly to one another and to himself, and so foster their growth.

Yes, that in turn is precisely the meaning of the man who commends justice.

From every point of view, then, the panegyrist of justice speaks truly and the panegyrist of injustice falsely. For whether we consider pleasure, reputation, or profit, he who commends justice speaks the c truth, while there is no soundness or real knowledge of what he censures in him who disparages it.

None whatever, I think, said he.

Shall we, then, try to persuade him gently, for he does not willingly err, by questioning him thus. Dear friend, should we not also say that the things which law and custom deem fair or foul have been accounted so for a like reason—the fair and honorable things being those that subject the brutish part of our nature to that which is human in us, or rather, it may be, to that which is divine, while the foul d and base are the things that enslave the gentle nature to the wild? Will he assent or not?

He will if he is counseled by me.

Can it profit any man in the light of this thought to accept gold unjustly if the result is to be that by the acceptance he enslaves the best part of himself to the worst? Or is it conceivable that, while, if the taking of the gold enslaved his son or daughter and that too to e fierce and evil men, it would not profit him, no matter how large the sum, yet that, if the result is to be the ruthless enslavement of the divinest part of himself to the most despicable and godless part, he is 590 not to be deemed wretched and is not taking the golden bribe much more disastrously than Eriphyle did when she received the necklace as the price of her husband's life?

Far more, said Glaucon, for I will answer you in his behalf.

And do you not think that the reason for the old objection to licentiousness is similarly because that sort of thing emancipates that dread, that huge and manifold beast overmuch?

Obviously, he said.

And do we not censure self-will and irascibility when they foster and intensify disproportionately the element of the lion and the snake b in us?

By all means.

And do we not reprobate luxury and effeminacy for their loosening and relaxation of this same element when they engender cowardice in it?

Surely.

And flattery and illiberality when they reduce this same high-spirited element under the rule of the moblike beast and habituate it for the sake of wealth and the unbridled lusts of the beast to endure all manner of contumely from youth up and become an ape instead of a lion?

c   Yes, indeed, he said.

And why do you suppose that 'base mechanic' handicraft is a term of reproach? Shall we not say that it is solely when the best part is naturally weak in a man so that it cannot govern and control the brood of beasts within him but can only serve them and can learn nothing but the ways of flattering them?

So it seems, he said.

Then is it not in order that such a one may have a like government with the best man that we say he ought to be the slave of that
d   best man who has within himself the divine governing principle, not because we suppose, as Thrasymachus did in the case of subjects, that the slave should be governed for his own harm, but on the ground that it is better for everyone to be governed by the divine and the intelligent, preferably indwelling and his own, but in default of that imposed from without, in order that we all so far as possible may be akin and friendly because our governance and guidance are the same?

e   Yes, and rightly so, he said.

And it is plain, I said, that this is the purpose of the law, which is the ally of all classes in the state, and this is the aim of our control of children, our not leaving them free before we have established, so to
591 speak, a constitutional government within them and, by fostering the best element in them with the aid of the like in ourselves, have set up in its place a similar guardian and ruler in the child, and then, and then only, we leave it free.

Yes, that is plain, he said.

In what way, then, Glaucon, and on what principle, shall we say that it profits a man to be unjust or licentious or do any shameful thing that will make him a worse man, but otherwise will bring him more wealth or power?

In no way, he said.

b   And how that it pays him to escape detection in wrongdoing and not pay the penalty? Or is it not true that he who evades detection becomes a still worse man, while in the one who is discovered and chastened the brutish part is lulled and tamed and the gentle part liberated, and the entire soul, returning to its nature at the best, attains to a much more precious condition in acquiring sobriety and righteousness together with wisdom, than the body does when it gains strength and beauty conjoined with health, even as the soul is more precious than the body?

Most assuredly, he said.

Then the wise man will bend all his endeavors to this end c throughout his life; he will, to begin with, prize the studies that will give this quality to his soul and disprize the others.

Clearly, he said.

And then, I said, he not only will not abandon the habit and nurture of his body to the brutish and irrational pleasure and live with his face set in that direction, but he will not even make health his chief aim, nor give the first place to the ways of becoming strong or healthy or beautiful unless these things are likely to bring with them soberness of spirit, but he will always be found attuning the harmonies of his body for the sake of the concord in his soul.   d

By all means, he replied, if he is to be a true musician.

And will he not deal likewise with the ordering and harmonizing of his possessions? He will not let himself be dazzled by the felicitations of the multitude and pile up the mass of his wealth without measure, involving himself in measureless ills.

No, I think not, he said.

He will rather, I said, keep his eyes fixed on the constitution in e his soul, and taking care and watching lest he disturb anything there either by excess or deficiency of wealth, will so steer his course and add to or detract from his wealth on this principle, so far as may be.

Precisely so, he said.

And in the matter of honors and office too this will be his guiding principle. He will gladly take part in and enjoy those which he thinks 592 will make him a better man, but in public and private life he will shun those that may overthrow the established habit of his soul.

Then, if that is his chief concern, he said, he will not willingly take part in politics.

Yes, by the dog, said I, in his own city he certainly will, yet perhaps not in the city of his birth, except in some providential conjuncture.

I understand, he said. You mean the city whose establishment we have described, the city whose home is in the ideal, for I think that it can be found nowhere on earth.   b

Well, said I, perhaps there is a pattern of it laid up in heaven for him who wishes to contemplate it and so beholding to constitute himself its citizen. But it makes no difference whether it exists now or ever will come into being. The politics of this city only will be his and of none other.

That seems probable, he said.

BOOK X

And truly, I said, many other considerations assure me that we were 595 entirely right in our organization of the state, and especially, I think, in the matter of poetry.

What about it? he said.

In refusing to admit at all so much of it as is imitative, for that it is certainly not to be received is, I think, still more plainly apparent b now that we have distinguished the several parts of the soul.

What do you mean?

Why, between ourselves—for you will not betray me to the tragic poets and all other imitators—that kind of art seems to be a corruption of the mind of all listeners who do not possess as an antidote a knowledge of its real nature.

What is your idea in saying this? he said.

I must speak out, I said, though a certain love and reverence for Homer that has possessed me from a boy would stay me from speak-c ing. For he appears to have been the first teacher and beginner of all these beauties of tragedy. Yet all the same we must not honor a man above truth, but, as I say, speak our minds.

By all means, he said.

Listen, then, or rather, answer my question.

Ask it, he said.

Could you tell me in general what imitation is? For neither do I myself quite apprehend what it would be at.

It is likely, then, he said, that *I* should apprehend!

596   It would be nothing strange, said I, since it often happens that the dimmer vision sees things in advance of the keener.

That is so, he said, but in your presence I could not even be eager to try to state anything that appears to me, but do you yourself consider it.

Shall we, then, start the inquiry at this point by our customary procedure? We are in the habit, I take it, of positing a single idea or form in the case of the various multiplicities to which we give the same name. Do you not understand?

I do.

In the present case, then, let us take any multiplicity you please; b for example, there are many couches and tables.

Of course.

But these utensils imply, I suppose, only two ideas or forms, one of a couch and one of a table.

Yes.

And are we not also in the habit of saying that the craftsman who produces either of them fixes his eyes on the idea or form, and so makes in the one case the couches and in the other the tables that we use, and similarly of other things? For surely no craftsman makes the idea itself. How could he?

By no means.

c   But now consider what name you would give to this craftsman.

What one?

Him who makes all the things that all handicraftsmen severally produce.

A truly clever and wondrous man you tell of.

Ah, but wait, and you will say so indeed, for this same handi-craftsman is not only able to make all implements, but he produces all plants and animals, including himself, and thereto earth and heaven and the gods and all things in heaven and in Hades under the earth.

A most marvelous Sophist, he said.   d

Are you incredulous? said I. Tell me, do you deny altogether the possibility of such a craftsman, or do you admit that in a sense there could be such a creator of all these things, and in another sense not? Or do you not perceive that you yourself would be able to make all these things in a way?

And in what way, I ask you, he said.

There is no difficulty, said I, but it is something that the crafts-man can make everywhere and quickly. You could do it most quickly if you should choose to take a mirror and carry it about everywhere. You will speedily produce the sun and all the things in the sky, and e speedily the earth and yourself and the other animals and implements and plants and all the objects of which we just now spoke.

Yes, he said, the appearance of them, but not the reality and the truth.

Excellent, said I, and you come to the aid of the argument oppor-tunely. For I take it that the painter too belongs to this class of pro-ducers, does he not?

Of course.

But you will say, I suppose, that his creations are not real and true. And yet, after a fashion, the painter too makes a couch, does he not?

Yes, he said, the appearance of one, he too.

What of the cabinetmaker? Were you not just now saying that he 597 does not make the idea or form which we say is the real couch, the couch in itself, but only some particular couch?

Yes, I was.

Then if he does not make that which really is, he could not be said to make real being but something that resembles real being but is not that. But if anyone should say that being in the complete sense belongs to the work of the cabinetmaker or to that of any other handi-craftsman, it seems that he would say what is not true.

That would be the view, he said, of those who are versed in this kind of reasoning.

We must not be surprised, then, if this too is only a dim adumbra- b tion in comparison with reality.

No, we must not.

Shall we, then, use these very examples in our quest for the true nature of this imitator?

If you please, he said.

We get, then, these three couches, one, that in nature, which, I take it, we would say that God produces, or who else?

No one, I think.

And then there was one which the carpenter made.

Yes, he said.

And one which the painter. Is not that so?

So be it.

The painter, then, the cabinetmaker, and God, there are these three presiding over three kinds of couches.

Yes, three.

c   Now God, whether because he so willed or because some compulsion was laid upon him not to make more than one couch in nature, so wrought and created one only, the couch which really and in itself is. But two or more such were never created by God and never will come into being.

How so? he said.

Because, said I, if he should make only two, there would again appear one of which they both would possess the form or idea, and that would be the couch that really is in and of itself, and not the other two.

Right, he said.

d   God, then, I take it, knowing this and wishing to be the real author of the couch that has real being and not of some particular couch, nor yet a particular cabinetmaker, produced it in nature unique.

So it seems.

Shall we, then, call him its true and natural begetter, or something of the kind?

That would certainly be right, he said, since it is by and in nature that he has made this and all other things.

And what of the carpenter? Shall we not call him the creator of a couch?

Yes.

Shall we also say that the painter is the creator and maker of that sort of thing?

By no means.

What will you say he is in relation to the couch.

e   This, said he, seems to me the most reasonable designation for him, that he is the imitator of the thing which those others produce.

Very good, said I. The producer of the product three removes from nature you call the imitator?

By all means, he said.

This, then, will apply to the maker of tragedies also, if he is an imitator and is in his nature three removes from the king and the truth, as are all other imitators.

It would seem so.

We are in agreement, then, about the imitator. But tell me now this about the painter. Do you think that what he tries to imitate is in 598 each case that thing itself in nature or the works of the craftsmen?

The works of the craftsmen, he said.

Is it the reality of them or the appearance? Define that further point.

What do you mean? he said.

This. Does a couch differ from itself according as you view it from the side or the front or in any other way? Or does it differ not at all in fact though it appears different, and so of other things?

That is the way of it, he said. It appears other but differs not b at all.

Consider, then, this very point. To which is painting directed in every case, to the imitation of reality as it is or of appearance as it appears? Is it an imitation of a phantasm or of the truth?

Of a phantasm, he said.

Then the mimetic art is far removed from truth, and this, it seems, is the reason why it can produce everything, because it touches or lays hold of only a small part of the object and that a phantom, as, for example, a painter, we say, will paint us a cobbler, a carpenter, and other craftsmen, though he himself has no expertness in any of these arts, but nevertheless if he were a good painter, by exhibiting at c a distance his picture of a carpenter he would deceive children and foolish men, and make them believe it to be a real carpenter.

Why not?

But for all that, my friend, this, I take it, is what we ought to bear in mind in all such cases. When anyone reports to us of someone, that he has met a man who knows all the crafts and everything else that men severally know, and that there is nothing that he does not know more exactly than anybody else, our tacit rejoinder must be d that he is a simple fellow, who apparently has met some magician or sleight-of-hand man and imitator and has been deceived by him into the belief that he is all-wise, because of his own inability to put to the proof and distinguish knowledge, ignorance, and imitation.

Most true, he said.

Then, said I, have we not next to scrutinize tragedy and its leader Homer, since some people tell us that these poets know all the arts e and all things human pertaining to virtue and vice, and all things divine? For the good poet, if he is to poetize things rightly, must, they argue, create with knowledge or else be unable to create. So we must consider whether these critics have not fallen in with such imitators and been deceived by them, so that looking upon their works they 599 cannot perceive that these are three removes from reality, and easy to produce without knowledge of the truth. For it is phantoms, not realities, that they produce. Or is there something in their claim, and do good poets really know the things about which the multitude fancy they speak well?

We certainly must examine the matter, he said.

Do you suppose, then, that if a man were able to produce both the exemplar and the semblance, he would be eager to abandon himself to the fashioning of phantoms and set this in the forefront of his life as the best thing he had?

b   I do not.

But, I take it, if he had genuine knowledge of the things he imitates he would far rather devote himself to real things than to the imitation of them, and would endeavor to leave after him many noble deeds and works as memorials of himself, and would be more eager to be the theme of praise than the praiser.

I think so, he said, for there is no parity in the honor and the gain.

Let us not, then, demand a reckoning from Homer or any other of the poets on other matters by asking them, if any one of them was a c physician and not merely an imitator of a physician's talk, what men any poet, old or new, is reported to have restored to health as Asclepius did, or what disciples of the medical art he left after him as Asclepius did his descendants, and let us dismiss the other arts and d not question them about them. But concerning the greatest and finest things of which Homer undertakes to speak, wars and generalship and the administration of cities and the education of men, it surely is fair to question him and ask, 'Friend Homer, if you are not at the third remove from truth and reality in human excellence, being merely that creator of phantoms whom we defined as the imitator, but if you are even in the second place and were capable of knowing what pursuits make men better or worse in private or public life, tell us what city was better governed owing to you, even as Lacedaemon e was because of Lycurgus, and many other cities great and small because of other legislators. But what city credits you with having been a good legislator and having benefited them? Italy and Sicily say this of Charondas and we of Solon. But who says it of you?' Will he be able to name any?

I think not, said Glaucon. At any rate none is mentioned even by the Homeridae themselves.

600   Well, then, is there any tradition of a war in Homer's time that was well conducted by his command or counsel?

None.

Well, then, as might be expected of a man wise in practical affairs, are many and ingenious inventions for the arts and business of life reported of Homer as they are of Thales the Milesian and Anacharsis the Scythian?

Nothing whatever of the sort.

Well, then, if no public service is credited to him, is Homer reported while he lived to have been a guide in education to men who took pleasure in associating with him and transmitted to posterity a b certain Homeric way of life just as Pythagoras was himself especially honored for this, and his successors, even to this day, denominating a certain way of life the Pythagorean, are distinguished among their contemporaries?

No, nothing of this sort either is reported, for Creophylus, Socrates, the friend of Homer, would perhaps be even more ridiculous than his name as a representative of Homeric culture and education, if what is said about Homer is true. For the tradition is that Homer was completely neglected in his own lifetime by that friend of the c flesh.

Why, yes, that is the tradition, said I, but do you suppose, Glaucon, that, if Homer had really been able to educate men and make them better and had possessed not the art of imitation but real knowledge, he would not have acquired many companions and been honored and loved by them? But are we to believe that while Protagoras of Abdera and Prodicus of Ceos and many others are able by private teaching to impress upon their contemporaries the conviction that they will not be capable of governing their homes or the city unless d they put them in charge of their education, and make themselves so beloved for this wisdom that their companions all but carry them about on their shoulders, yet, forsooth, that Homer's contemporaries, if he had been able to help men to achieve excellence, would have suffered him or Hesiod to roam about rhapsodizing and would not have clung to them far rather than to their gold, and constrained them to dwell with them in their homes, or failing to persuade them, would e themselves have escorted them wheresoever they went until they should have sufficiently imbibed their culture?

What you say seems to me to be altogether true, Socrates, he said.

Shall we, then, lay it down that all the poetic tribe, beginning with Homer, are imitators of images of excellence and of the other things that they 'create,' and do not lay hold on truth, but, as we were just now saying, the painter will fashion, himself knowing nothing of the cobbler's art, what appears to be a cobbler to him and likewise 601 to those who know nothing but judge only by forms and colors?

Certainly.

And similarly, I suppose, we shall say that the poet himself, knowing nothing but how to imitate, lays on with words and phrases the colors of the several arts in such fashion that others equally ignorant, who see things only through words, will deem his words most excellent, whether he speak in rhythm, meter, and harmony about cobbling or generalship or anything whatever. So mighty is the spell b that these adornments naturally exercise, though when they are stripped bare of their musical coloring and taken by themselves, I think you know what sort of a showing these sayings of the poets make. For you, I believe, have observed them.

I have, he said.

Do they not, said I, resemble the faces of adolescents, young but not really beautiful, when the bloom of youth abandons them?

By all means, he said.

Come, then, said I, consider this point. The creator of the phan-
c tom, the imitator, we say, knows nothing of the reality but only the appearance. Is not that so?

Yes.

Let us not, then, leave it half said but consider it fully.

Speak on, he said.

The painter, we say, will paint both reins and a bit.

Yes.

But the maker will be the cobbler and the smith.

Certainly.

Does the painter, then, know the proper quality of reins and bit? Or does not even the maker, the cobbler, and the smith know that, but only the man who understands the use of these things, the horseman?

Most true.

And shall we not say that the same holds true of everything?
d What do you mean?

That there are some three arts concerned with everything, the user's art, the maker's, and the imitator's.

Yes.

Now do not the excellence, the beauty, the rightness of every implement, living thing, and action refer solely to the use for which each is made or by nature adapted?

That is so.
e It quite necessarily follows, then, that the user of anything is the one who knows most of it by experience, and that he reports to the maker the good or bad effects in use of the thing he uses. As, for example, the flute player reports to the flute maker which flutes respond and serve rightly in flute playing, and will order the kind that must be made, and the other will obey and serve him.

Of course.

The one, then, possessing knowledge, reports about the goodness or the badness of the flutes, and the other, believing, will make them.

Yes.

Then in respect of the same implement the maker will have right belief about its excellence and defects from association with the
602 man who knows and being compelled to listen to him, but the user will have true knowledge.

Certainly.

And will the imitator from experience or use have knowledge

whether the things he portrays are or are not beautiful and right, or will he, from compulsory association with the man who knows and taking orders from him for the right making of them, have right opinion?

Neither.

Then the imitator will neither know nor opine rightly concerning the beauty or the badness of his imitations.

It seems not.

Most charming, then, would be the state of mind of the poetical imitator in respect of true wisdom about his creations.

Not at all.

Yet still he will nonetheless imitate, though in every case he does b not know in what way the thing is bad or good. But, as it seems, the thing he will imitate will be the thing that appears beautiful to the ignorant multitude.

Why, what else?

On this, then, as it seems, we are fairly agreed, that the imitator knows nothing worth mentioning of the things he imitates, but that imitation is a form of play, not to be taken seriously, and that those who attempt tragic poetry, whether in iambics or heroic verse, are all altogether imitators.

By all means.

In heaven's name, then, this business of imitation is concerned c with the third remove from truth, is it not?

Yes.

And now again, to what element in man is its function and potency related?

Of what are you speaking?

Of this. The same magnitude, I presume, viewed from near and from far does not appear equal.

Why, no.

And the same things appear bent and straight to those who view them in water and out, or concave and convex, owing to similar errors of vision about colors, and there is obviously every confusion of this d sort in our souls. And so scene painting in its exploitation of this weakness of our nature falls nothing short of witchcraft, and so do jugglery and many other such contrivances.

True.

And have not measuring and numbering and weighing proved to be most gracious aids to prevent the domination in our soul of the apparently greater or less or more or heavier, and to give the control to that which has reckoned and numbered or even weighed?

Certainly.   e

But this surely would be the function of the part of the soul that reasons and calculates.

Why, yes, of that.

And often when this has measured and declares that certain things are larger or that some are smaller than the others or equal, there is at the same time an appearance of the contrary.

Yes.

And did we not say that it is impossible for the same thing at one time to hold contradictory opinions about the same thing?

And we were right in affirming that.

603   The part of the soul, then, that opines in contradiction of measurement could not be the same with that which conforms to it.

Why, no.

But, further, that which puts its trust in measurement and reckoning must be the best part of the soul.

Surely.

Then that which opposes it must belong to the inferior elements of the soul.

Necessarily.

This, then, was what I wished to have agreed upon when I said
b that poetry, and in general the mimetic art, produces a product that is far removed from truth in the accomplishment of its task, and associates with the part in us that is remote from intelligence, and is its companion and friend for no sound and true purpose.

By all means, said he.

Mimetic art, then, is an inferior thing cohabiting with an inferior and engendering inferior offspring.

It seems so.

Does that, said I, hold only for vision or does it apply also to hearing and to what we call poetry?

Presumably, he said, to that also.

Let us not, then, trust solely to the plausible analogy from paint-
c ing, but let us approach in turn that part of the mind to which mimetic poetry appeals and see whether it is the inferior or the nobly serious part.

So we must.

Let us, then, put the question thus. Mimetic poetry, we say, imitates human beings acting under compulsion or voluntarily, and as a result of their actions supposing themselves to have fared well or ill and in all this feeling either grief or joy. Did we find anything else but this?

Nothing.

Is a man, then, in all this of one mind with himself, or just as in the domain of sight there was faction and strife and he held within
d himself contrary opinions at the same time about the same things, so also in our actions there is division and strife of the man with himself? But I recall that there is no need now of our seeking agreement on this point, for in our former discussion we were sufficiently agreed

that our soul at any one moment teems with countless such self-contradictions.

Rightly, he said.

Yes, rightly, said I, but what we then omitted must now, I think, be set forth.   e

What is that? he said.

When a good and reasonable man, said I, experiences such a stroke of fortune as the loss of a son or anything else that he holds most dear, we said, I believe, then too, that he will bear it more easily than the other sort.

Assuredly.

But now let us consider this. Will he feel no pain, or, since that is impossible, shall we say that he will in some sort be moderate in his grief?

That, he said, is rather the truth.

Tell me now this about him. Do you think he will be more likely 604 to resist and fight against his grief when he is observed by his equals or when he is in solitude alone by himself?

He will be much more restrained, he said, when he is on view.

But when left alone, I fancy, he will permit himself many utterances which, if heard by another, would put him to shame, and will do many things which he would not consent to have another see him doing.

So it is, he said.

Now is it not reason and law that exhorts him to resist, while that which urges him to give way to his grief is the bare feeling itself? b

True.

And where there are two opposite impulses in a man at the same time about the same thing we say that there must needs be two things in him.

Of course.

And is not the one prepared to follow the guidance of the law as the law leads and directs?

How so?

The law, I suppose, declares that it is best to keep quiet as far as possible in calamity and not to chafe and repine, because we cannot know what is really good and evil in such things and it advantages us nothing to take them hard, and nothing in mortal life is worthy of c great concern, and our grieving checks the very thing we need to come to our aid as quickly as possible in such case.

What thing, he said, do you mean?

To deliberate, I said, about what has happened to us, and, as it were in the fall of the dice, to determine the movements of our affairs with reference to the numbers that turn up, in the way that reason indicates would be the best, and, instead of stumbling like children,

clapping one's hands to the stricken spot and wasting the time in wail-
d ing, ever to accustom the soul to devote itself at once to the curing of
the hurt and the raising up of what has fallen, banishing threnody by
therapy.

That certainly, he said, would be the best way to face misfortune
and deal with it.

Then, we say, the best part of us is willing to conform to these
precepts of reason.

Obviously.

And shall we not say that the part of us that leads us to dwell in
memory on our suffering and impels us to lamentation, and cannot
get enough of that sort of thing, is the irrational and idle part of us,
the associate of cowardice?

Yes, we will say that.

e   And does not the fretful part of us present many and varied occasions for imitation, while the intelligent and temperate disposition,
always remaining approximately the same, is neither easy to imitate
nor to be understood when imitated, especially by a nondescript mob
assembled in the theater? For the representation imitates a type that
is alien to them.

By all means.

605   And is it not obvious that the nature of the mimetic poet is not
related to this better part of the soul and his cunning is not framed to
please it, if he is to win favor with the multitude, but is devoted to
the fretful and complicated type of character because it is easy to imitate?

It is obvious.

This consideration, then, makes it right for us to proceed to lay
hold of him and set him down as the counterpart of the painter, for he
resembles him in that his creations are inferior in respect of reality,
b and the fact that his appeal is to the inferior part of the soul and not
to the best part is another point of resemblance. And so we may at last
say that we should be justified in not admitting him into a well-
ordered state, because he stimulates and fosters this element in the
soul, and by strengthening it tends to destroy the rational part, just as
when in a state one puts bad men in power and turns the city over to
them and ruins the better sort. Precisely in the same manner we shall
say that the mimetic poet sets up in each individual soul a vicious
constitution by fashioning phantoms far removed from reality, and by
currying favor with the senseless element that cannot distinguish the
c greater from the less, but calls the same thing now one, now the
other.

By all means.

But we have not yet brought our chief accusation against it. Its
power to corrupt, with rare exceptions, even the better sort is surely
the chief cause for alarm.

How could it be otherwise, if it really does that?

Listen and reflect. I think you know that the very best of us, when we hear Homer or some other of the makers of tragedy imitating one of the heroes who is in grief, and is delivering a long tirade in d his lamentations or chanting and beating his breast, feel pleasure, and abandon ourselves and accompany the representation with sympathy and eagerness, and we praise as an excellent poet the one who most strongly affects us in this way.

I do know it, of course.

But when in our own lives some affliction comes to us, you are also aware that we plume ourselves upon the opposite, on our ability to remain calm and endure, in the belief that this is the conduct of a man, and what we were praising in the theater that of a woman. e

I do note that.

Do you think, then, said I, that this praise is rightfully bestowed when, contemplating a character that we would not accept but would be ashamed of in ourselves, we do not abominate it but take pleasure and approve?

No, by Zeus, he said, it does not seem reasonable.

Oh yes, said I, if you would consider it in this way. 606

In what way?

If you would reflect that the part of the soul that in the former case, in our own misfortunes, was forcibly restrained, and that has hungered for tears and a good cry and satisfaction, because it is its nature to desire these things, is the element in us that the poets satisfy and delight, and that the best element in our nature, since it has never been properly educated by reason or even by habit, then relaxes its guard over the plaintive part, inasmuch as this is contemplating the b woes of others and it is no shame to it to praise and pity another who, claiming to be a good man, abandons himself to excess in his grief, but it thinks this vicarious pleasure is so much clear gain, and would not consent to forfeit it by disdaining the poem altogether. That is, I think, because few are capable of reflecting that what we enjoy in others will inevitably react upon ourselves. For after feeding fat the emotion of pity there, it is not easy to restrain it in our own sufferings.

Most true, he said. c

Does not the same principle apply to the laughable, namely, that if in comic representations, or for that matter in private talk, you take intense pleasure in buffooneries that you would blush to practice yourself, and do not detest them as base, you are doing the same thing as in the case of the pathetic? For here again what your reason, for fear of the reputation of buffoonery, restrained in yourself when it fain would play the clown, you release in turn, and so, fostering its youthful impudence, let yourself go so far that often ere you are aware you become yourself a comedian in private.

d   Yes, indeed, he said.

And so in regard to the emotions of sex and anger, and all the appetites and pains and pleasures of the soul which we say accompany all our actions, the effect of poetic imitation is the same. For it waters and fosters these feelings when what we ought to do is to dry them up, and it establishes them as our rulers when they ought to be ruled, to the end that we may be better and happier men instead of worse and more miserable.

I cannot deny it, said he.

e   Then, Glaucon, said I, when you meet encomiasts of Homer who tell us that this poet has been the educator of Hellas, and that for the conduct and refinement of human life he is worthy of our study and devotion, and that we should order our entire lives by the guidance of

607 this poet, we must love and salute them as doing the best they can, and concede to them that Homer is the most poetic of poets and the first of tragedians, but we must know the truth, that we can admit no poetry into our city save only hymns to the gods and the praises of good men. For if you grant admission to the honeyed Muse in lyric or epic, pleasure and pain will be lords of your city instead of law and that which shall from time to time have approved itself to the general reason as the best.

Most true, he said.

b   Let us, then, conclude our return to the topic of poetry and our apology, and affirm that we really had good grounds then for dismissing her from our city, since such was her character. For reason constrained us. And let us further say to her, lest she condemn us for harshness and rusticity, that there is from of old a quarrel between philosophy and poetry. For such expressions as 'the yelping hound barking at her master and mighty in the idle babble of fools,' and 'the mob that masters those who are too wise for their own good,' and the

c   subtle thinkers who reason that after all they are poor, and countless others are tokens of this ancient enmity. But nevertheless let it be declared that, if the mimetic and dulcet poetry can show any reason for her existence in a well-governed state, we would gladly admit her, since we ourselves are very conscious of her spell. But all the same it would be impious to betray what we believe to be the truth. Is not that so, friend? Do not you yourself feel her magic and especially when

d   Homer is her interpreter?

Greatly.

Then may she not justly return from this exile after she has pleaded her defense, whether in lyric or other measure?

By all means.

And we would allow her advocates who are not poets but lovers of poetry to plead her cause in prose without meter, and show that she is not only delightful but beneficial to orderly government and all the life of man. And we shall listen benevolently, for it will be clear

gain for us if it can be shown that she bestows not only pleasure but e
benefit.

How could we help being the gainers? said he.

But if not, my friend, even as men who have fallen in love, if they
think that the love is not good for them, hard though it be, nevertheless refrain, so we, owing to the love of this kind of poetry inbred in us
by our education in these fine polities of ours, will gladly have the best
possible case made out for her goodness and truth, but so long as she 608
is unable to make good her defense we shall chant over to ourselves as
we listen the reasons that we have given as a countercharm to her
spell, to preserve us from slipping back into the childish loves of the
multitude, for we have come to see that we must not take such poetry
seriously as a serious thing that lays hold on truth, but that he who
lends an ear to it must be on his guard fearing for the polity in his b
soul and must believe what we have said about poetry.

By all means, he said, I concur.

Yes, for great is the struggle, I said, dear Glaucon, a far greater
contest than we think it, that determines whether a man prove good
or bad, so that not the lure of honor or wealth or any office, no, nor of
poetry either, should incite us to be careless of righteousness and all
excellence.

I agree with you, he replied, in view of what we have set forth,
and I think that anyone else would do so too.

And yet, said I, the greatest rewards of virtue and the prizes pro- c
posed for her we have not set forth.

You must have in mind an inconceivable magnitude, he replied,
if there are other things greater than those of which we have spoken.

What great thing, said I, could there be in a little time? For
surely the whole time from the boy to the old man would be small
compared with all time.

Nay, it is nothing, he said.

What then? Do you think that an immortal thing ought to be
seriously concerned for such a little time, and not rather for all time? d

I think so, he said, but what is this that you have in mind?

Have you never perceived, said I, that our soul is immortal and
never perishes?

And he, looking me full in the face in amazement, said, No, by
Zeus, not I, but are *you* able to declare this?

I certainly ought to be, said I, and I think you too can, for it is
nothing hard.

It is for me, he said, and I would gladly hear from you this thing
that is not hard.

Listen, said I.

Just speak on, he replied.

You speak of good and evil, do you not?

I do.

e   Is your notion of them the same as mine?

What is it?

That which destroys and corrupts in every case is the evil; that which preserves and benefits is the good.

Yes, I think so, he said.

How about this? Do you say that there is for everything its special
609   good and evil, as for example for the eyes ophthalmia, for the entire body disease, for grain mildew, rotting for wood, rust for bronze and iron, and, as I say, for practically everything its congenital evil and disease?

I do, he said.

Then when one of these evils comes to anything does it not make the thing to which it attaches itself bad, and finally disintegrate and destroy it?

Of course.

Then the congenital evil of each thing and its own vice destroys it, or if that is not going to destroy it, nothing else remains that could, for
b   obviously the good will never destroy anything, nor yet again will that which is neutral and neither good nor evil.

How could it? he said.

If, then, we discover anything that has an evil which vitiates it, yet is not able to dissolve and destroy it, shall we not thereupon know that of a thing so constituted there can be no destruction?

That seems likely, he said.

Well, then, said I, has not the soul something that makes it evil?

Indeed it has, he said, all the things that we were just now
c   enumerating, injustice and licentiousness and cowardice and ignorance.

Does any one of these things dissolve and destroy it? And reflect, lest we be misled by supposing that when an unjust and foolish man is taken in his injustice he is then destroyed by the injustice, which is the vice of soul. But conceive it thus. Just as the vice of body which is disease wastes and destroys it so that it no longer is a body at all, in like manner in all the examples of which we spoke it is the
d   specific evil which, by attaching itself to the thing and dwelling in it with power to corrupt, reduces it to nonentity. Is not that so?

Yes.

Come, then, and consider the soul in the same way. Do injustice and other wickedness dwelling in it, by their indwelling and attachment to it, corrupt and wither it till they bring it to death and separate it from the body?

They certainly do not do that, he said.

But surely, said I, it is unreasonable to suppose that the vice of something else destroys a thing while its own does not.

Yes, unreasonable.

e   For observe, Glaucon, said I, that we do not think it proper to say

of the body either that it is destroyed by the badness of foods themselves, whether it be staleness or rottenness or whatever it is, but
when the badness of the foods themselves engenders in the body the
defect of body, then we shall say that it is destroyed *owing to* these
foods, but *by* its own vice, which is disease. But the body being one
thing and the foods something else, we shall never expect the body to
be destroyed by their badness, that is by an alien evil that has not pro- 610
duced in it the evil that belongs to it by nature.

You are entirely right, he replied.

On the same principle, said I, if the badness of the body does not
produce in the soul the soul's badness we shall never expect the soul
to be destroyed by an alien evil apart from its own defect—one thing,
that is, by the evil of another.

That is reasonable, he said.

Either, then, we must refute this and show that we are mistaken,
or, so long as it remains unrefuted, we must never say that by fever or b
any other disease, or yet by the knife at the throat or the chopping to
bits of the entire body, there is any more likelihood of the soul perishing because of these things, until it is proved that owing to these affections of the body the soul itself becomes more unjust and unholy.
But when an evil of something else occurs in a different thing and the
evil that belongs to the thing is not engendered in it, we must not suf- c
fer it to be said that the soul or anything else is in this way destroyed.

But you may be sure, he said, that nobody will ever prove this,
that the souls of the dying are made more unjust by death.

But if anyone, said I, dares to come to grips with the argument
and say, in order to avoid being forced to admit the soul's immortality,
that a dying man does become more wicked and unjust, we will postulate that, if what he says is true, injustice must be fatal to its possessor as if it were a disease, and that those who catch it die because it d
kills them by its own inherent nature, those who have most of it quickest, and those who have less more slowly, and not, as now in fact happens, that the unjust die owing to this but by the action of others who
inflict the penalty.

Nay, by Zeus, he said, injustice will not appear a very terrible
thing after all if it is going to be fatal to its possessor, for that would
be a release from all troubles. But I rather think it will prove to be
quite the contrary, something that kills others when it can, but ren- e
ders its possessor very lively indeed, and not only lively but wakeful,
so far, I ween, does it dwell from deadliness.

You say well, I replied, for when the natural vice and the evil
proper to it cannot kill and destroy the soul, still less will the evil appointed for the destruction of another thing destroy the soul or anything else, except that for which it is appointed.

Still less indeed, he said, in all probability.

Then since it is not destroyed by any evil whatever, either its own

611 or alien, it is evident that it must necessarily exist always, and that if
it always exists it is immortal.

Necessarily, he said.

Let this, then, I said, be assumed to be so. But if it is so, you will
observe that these souls must always be the same. For if none perishes
they could not, I suppose, become fewer nor yet more numerous. For
if any class of immortal things increased you are aware that its increase would come from the mortal and all things would end by becoming immortal.

You say truly.

But, said I, we must not suppose this, for reason will not suffer
b it, nor yet must we think that in its truest nature the soul is the kind of
thing that teems with infinite diversity and unlikeness and contradiction in and with itself.

How am I to understand that? he said.

It is not easy, said I, for a thing to be immortal that is composed
of many elements not put together in the best way, as now appeared
to us to be the case with the soul.

It is not likely.

Well, then, that the soul is immortal our recent argument and
our other proofs would constrain us to admit. But to know its true na-
c ture we must view it not marred by communion with the body and
other miseries as we now contemplate it, but consider adequately in
the light of reason what it is when it is purified, and then you will
find it to be a far more beautiful thing and will more clearly distinguish justice and injustice and all the matters that we have now discussed. But though we have stated the truth of its present appearance,
its condition as we have now contemplated it resembles that of the
d sea god Glaucus whose first nature can hardly be made out by those
who catch glimpses of him, because the original members of his body
are broken off and mutilated and crushed and in every way marred
by the waves, and other parts have attached themselves to him, accretions of shells and seaweed and rocks, so that he is more like any
wild creature than what he was by nature—even such, I say, is our vision of the soul marred by countless evils. But we must look elsewhere,
Glaucon.

Where? said he.

e   To its love of wisdom. And we must note the things of which it
has apprehensions, and the associations for which it yearns, as being
itself akin to the divine and the immortal and to eternal being, and
so consider what it might be if it followed the gleam unreservedly and
were raised by this impulse out of the depths of this sea in which it is
now sunk, and were cleansed and scraped free of the rocks and barna-
612 cles which, because it now feasts on earth, cling to it in wild profusion of earthy and stony accretion by reason of these feastings that
are accounted happy. And then one might see whether in its real na-

ture it is manifold or single in its simplicity, or what is the truth about it and how. But for the present we have, I think, fairly well described its sufferings and the forms it assumes in this human life of ours.

We certainly have, he said.

Then, said I, we have met all the other demands of the argument, and we have not invoked the rewards and reputes of justice as you b said Homer and Hesiod do, but we have proved that justice in itself is the best thing for the soul itself, and that the soul ought to do justice whether it possess the ring of Gyges or not, or the helmet of Hades to boot.

Most true, he said.

Then, said I, Glaucon, there can no longer be any objection, can there, to our assigning to justice and virtue generally, in addition, all c the various rewards and wages that they bring to the soul from men and gods, both while the man still lives and after his death?

There certainly can be none, he said.

Will you, then, return to me what you borrowed in the argument? What, pray?

I granted to you that the just man should seem and be thought to be unjust and the unjust just, for you thought that, even if the concealment of these things from gods and men was an impossibility in fact, nevertheless it ought to be conceded for the sake of the argument, in order that the decision might be made between absolute justice and absolute injustice. Or do you not remember? d

It would be unjust of me, he said, if I did not.

Well, then, now that they have been compared and judged, I demand back from you in behalf of justice the repute that she in fact enjoys from gods and men, and I ask that we admit that she is thus esteemed in order that she may gather in the prizes which she wins from the seeming and bestows on her possessors, since she has been proved to bestow the blessings that come from the reality and not to deceive those who truly seek and win her.

That is a just demand, he said. e

Then, said I, will not the first of these restorations be that the gods certainly are not unaware of the true character of each of the two, the just and the unjust?

We will restore that, he said.

And if they are not concealed, the one will be dear to the gods and the other hateful to them, as we agreed in the beginning.

That is so.

And shall we not agree that all things that come from the gods work together for the best for him that is dear to the gods, apart from 613 the inevitable evil caused by sin in a former life?

By all means.

This, then, must be our conviction about the just man, that whether he fall into poverty or disease or any other supposed evil, for him all these things will finally prove good, both in life and in death. For by the gods assuredly that man will never be neglected who is will-

b ing and eager to be righteous, and by the practice of virtue to be likened unto God so far as that is possible for man.

It is reasonable, he said, that such a one should not be neglected by his like.

And must we not think the opposite of the unjust man?

Most emphatically.

Such then are the prizes of victory which the gods bestow upon the just.

So I think, at any rate, he said.

But what, said I, does he receive from men? Is not this the case, if we are now to present the reality? Do not your smart but wicked men fare as those racers do who run well from the scratch but not back from the turn? They bound nimbly away at the start, but in the end

c are laughed to scorn and run off the field uncrowned and with their ears on their shoulders. But the true runners when they have come to the goal receive the prizes and bear away the crown. Is not this the usual outcome for the just also, that toward the end of every action and association and of life as a whole they have honor and bear away the prizes from men?

So it is indeed.

Will you, then, bear with me if I say of them all that you said of

d the unjust? For I am going to say that the just, when they become older, hold the offices in their own city if they choose, marry from what families they will, and give their children in marriage to what families they please, and everything that you said of the one I now repeat of the other, and in turn I will say of the unjust that the most of them, even if they escape detection in youth, at the end of their course are caught and derided, and their old age is made miserable by the contumelies of strangers and townsfolk. They are lashed and suffer

e all things which you truly said are unfit for ears polite. Suppose yourself to have heard from me a repetition of all that they suffer. But, as I say, consider whether you will bear with me.

Assuredly, he said, for what you say is just.

614 Such then while he lives are the prizes, the wages, and the gifts that the just man receives from gods and men in addition to those blessings which justice herself bestowed.

And right fair and abiding rewards, he said.

Well, these, I said, are nothing in number and magnitude compared with those that await both after death. And we must listen to the tale of them, said I, in order that each may have received in full what is due to be said of him by our argument.

b Tell me, he said, since there are not many things to which I would more gladly listen.

It is not, let me tell you, said I, the tale to Alcinous told that I shall unfold, but the tale of a warrior bold, Er, the son of Armenius, by race a Pamphylian. He once upon a time was slain in battle, and when the corpses were taken up on the tenth day already decayed, was found intact, and having been brought home, at the moment of his funeral, on the twelfth day as he lay upon the pyre, revived, and after coming to life related what, he said, he had seen in the world beyond. He said that when his soul went forth from his body he journeyed with a great company and that they came to a mysterious c region where there were two openings side by side in the earth, and above and over against them in the heaven two others, and that judges were sitting between these, and that after every judgment they bade the righteous journey to the right and upward through the heaven with tokens attached to them in front of the judgment passed d upon them, and the unjust to take the road to the left and downward, they too wearing behind signs of all that had befallen them, and that when he himself drew near they told him that he must be the messenger to mankind to tell them of that other world, and they charged him to give ear and to observe everything in the place. And so he said that here he saw, by each opening of heaven and earth, the souls departing after judgment had been passed upon them, while, by the other pair of openings, there came up from the one in the earth souls full of squalor and dust, and from the second there came down from heaven a second procession of souls clean and pure, and that those which arrived from time to time appeared to have come as it were e from a long journey and gladly departed to the meadow and encamped there as at a festival, and acquaintances greeted one another, and those which came from the earth questioned the others about conditions up yonder, and those from heaven asked how it fared with those others. And they told their stories to one another, the one lamenting and wailing as they recalled how many and how dreadful things they had suffered and seen in their journey beneath the earth 615 —it lasted a thousand years—while those from heaven related their delights and visions of a beauty beyond words. To tell it all, Glaucon, would take all our time, but the sum, he said, was this. For all the wrongs they had ever done to anyone and all whom they had severally wronged they had paid the penalty in turn tenfold for each, and b the measure of this was by periods of a hundred years each, so that on the assumption that this was the length of human life the punishment might be ten times the crime—as for example that if anyone had been the cause of many deaths or had betrayed cities and armies and reduced them to slavery, or had been participant in any other iniquity, they might receive in requital pains tenfold for each of these wrongs, and again if any had done deeds of kindness and been just and holy men they might receive their due reward in the same measure. And other things not worthy of record he said of those who had just been born and lived but a short time, and he had still greater c

requitals to tell of piety and impiety toward the gods and parents and of self-slaughter. For he said that he stood by when one was questioned by another, 'Where is Ardiaeus the Great?' Now this Ardiaeus had been tyrant in a certain city of Pamphylia just a thousand years before that time and had put to death his old father and his elder
d brother, and had done many other unholy deeds, as was the report. So he said that the one questioned replied, 'He has not come,' said he, 'nor will he be likely to come here. For indeed this was one of the dreadful sights we beheld; when we were near the mouth and about to issue forth and all our other sufferings were ended, we suddenly
e caught sight of him and of others, the most of them, I may say, tyrants. But there were some of private station, of those who had committed great crimes. And when these supposed that at last they were about to go up and out, the mouth would not receive them, but it bellowed when any one of the incurably wicked or of those who had not completed their punishment tried to come up. And thereupon,' he said, 'savage men of fiery aspect who stood by and took note of the
616 voice laid hold on them and bore them away. But Ardiaeus and others they bound hand and foot and head and flung down and flayed them and dragged them by the wayside, carding them on thorns and signifying to those who from time to time passed by for what cause they were borne away, and that they were to be hurled into Tartarus.'

And then, though many and manifold dread things had befallen them, this fear exceeded all—lest each one should hear the voice when he tried to go up, and each went up most gladly when it had kept silence. And the judgments and penalties were somewhat after
b this manner, and the blessings were their counterparts.

But when seven days had elapsed for each group in the meadow, they were required to rise up on the eighth and journey on, and they came in four days to a spot whence they discerned, extended from above throughout the heaven and the earth, a straight light like a pillar, most nearly resembling the rainbow, but brighter and purer. To this they came after going forward a day's journey, and they saw there at the middle of the light the extremities of its fastenings
c stretched from heaven, for this light was the girdle of the heavens like the undergirders of triremes, holding together in like manner the entire revolving vault. And from the extremities was stretched the spindle of Necessity, through which all the orbits turned. Its staff and its hook were made of adamant, and the whorl of these and other
d kinds was commingled. And the nature of the whorl was this. Its shape was that of those in our world, but from his description we must conceive it to be as if in one great whorl, hollow and scooped out, there lay enclosed, right through, another like it but smaller, fitting into it as boxes that fit into one another, and in like manner another, a third, and a fourth, and four others, for there were eight of the whorls in all, lying within one another, showing their rims as

circles from above and forming the continuous back of a single whorl e
about the shaft, which was driven home through the middle of the
eighth. Now the first and outmost whorl had the broadest circular
rim, that of the sixth was second, and third was that of the fourth,
and fourth was that of the eighth, fifth that of the seventh, sixth that
of the fifth, seventh that of the third, eighth that of the second. And
that of the greatest was spangled, that of the seventh brightest, that 617
of the eighth took its color from the seventh, which shone upon it. The
colors of the second and fifth were like one another and more yellow
than the two former. The third had the whitest color, and the fourth
was of a slightly ruddy hue; the sixth was second in whiteness. The
staff turned as a whole in a circle with the same movement, but
within the whole as it revolved the seven inner circles revolved gently
in the opposite direction to the whole, and of these seven the eighth
moved most swiftly, and next and together with one another the b
seventh, sixth, and fifth, and third in swiftness, as it appeared to
them, moved the fourth with returns upon itself, and fourth the third
and fifth the second. And the spindle turned on the knees of Necessity, and up above on each of the rims of the circles a Siren stood,
borne around in its revolution and uttering one sound, one note, and
from all the eight there was the concord of a single harmony. And
there were three others who sat round about at equal intervals, each c
one on her throne, the Fates, daughters of Necessity, clad in white
vestments with filleted heads, Lachesis, and Clotho, and Atropos,
who sang in unison with the music of the Sirens, Lachesis singing the
things that were, Clotho the things that are, and Atropos the things
that are to be. And Clotho with the touch of her right hand helped to
turn the outer circumference of the spindle, pausing from time to
time. Atropos with her left hand in like manner helped to turn the
inner circles, and Lachesis alternately with either hand lent a hand to d
each.

Now when they arrived they were straightway bidden to go before
Lachesis, and then a certain prophet first marshaled them in orderly
intervals, and thereupon took from the lap of Lachesis lots and patterns of lives and went up to a lofty platform and spoke, 'This is the
word of Lachesis, the maiden daughter of Necessity, "Souls that live
for a day, now is the beginning of another cycle of mortal generation
where birth is the beacon of death. No divinity shall cast lots for you, e
but you shall choose your own deity. Let him to whom falls the first
lot first select a life to which he shall cleave of necessity. But virtue
has no master over her, and each shall have more or less of her as he
honors her or does her despite. The blame is his who chooses. God is
blameless." ' So saying, the prophet flung the lots out among them all,
and each took up the lot that fell by his side, except himself; him 618
they did not permit. And whoever took up a lot saw plainly what number he had drawn. And after this again the prophet placed the

patterns of lives before them on the ground, far more numerous than the assembly. They were of every variety, for there were lives of all kinds of animals and all sorts of human lives, for there were tyrannies among them, some uninterrupted till the end and others destroyed midway and issuing in penuries and exiles and beggaries, and there were lives of men of repute for their forms and beauty and bodily

b strength otherwise and prowess and the high birth and the virtues of their ancestors, and others of ill repute in the same things, and similarly of women. But there was no determination of the quality of soul, because the choice of a different life inevitably determined a different character. But all other things were commingled with one another and with wealth and poverty and sickness and health and the intermediate conditions.

And there, dear Glaucon, it appears, is the supreme hazard for a
c man. And this is the chief reason why it should be our main concern that each of us, neglecting all other studies, should seek after and study this thing—if in any way he may be able to learn of and discover the man who will give him the ability and the knowledge to distinguish the life that is good from that which is bad, and always and everywhere to choose the best that the conditions allow, and, taking into account all the things of which we have spoken and estimating the effect on the goodness of his life of their conjunction or their severance, to know how beauty commingled with poverty or
d wealth and combined with what habit of soul operates for good or for evil, and what are the effects of high and low birth and private station and office and strength and weakness and quickness of apprehension and dullness and all similar natural and acquired habits of the soul, when blended and combined with one another, so that with consideration of all these things he will be able to make a reasoned choice between the better and the worse life, with his eyes fixed on the
e nature of his soul, naming the worse life that which will tend to make it more unjust and the better that which will make it more just. But all other considerations he will dismiss, for we have seen that this is the best choice, both for life and death. And a man must take with
619 him to the house of death an adamantine faith in this, that even there he may be undazzled by riches and similar trumpery, and may not precipitate himself into tyrannies and similar doings and so work many evils past cure and suffer still greater himself, but may know how always to choose in such things the life that is seated in the mean and shun the excess in either direction, both in this world so far as
b may be and in all the life to come, for this is the greatest happiness for man.

And at that time also the messenger from that other world reported that the prophet spoke thus. 'Even for him who comes forward last, if he make his choice wisely and live strenuously, there is reserved an acceptable life, no evil one. Let not the foremost in the

choice be heedless nor the last be discouraged.' When the prophet had
thus spoken he said that the drawer of the first lot at once sprang to
seize the greatest tyranny, and that in his folly and greed he chose it
without sufficient examination, and failed to observe that it involved c
the fate of eating his own children, and other horrors, and that when
he inspected it at leisure he beat his breast and bewailed his choice,
not abiding by the forewarning of the prophet. For he did not blame
himself for his woes, but fortune and the gods and anything except
himself. He was one of those who had come down from heaven, a
man who had lived in a well-ordered polity in his former existence,
participating in virtue by habit and not by philosophy, and one may
perhaps say that a majority of those who were thus caught were of the d
company that had come from heaven, inasmuch as they were un-
exercised in suffering. But the most of those who came up from the
earth, since they had themselves suffered and seen the sufferings of
others, did not make their choice precipitately. For which reason also
there was an interchange of good and evil for most of the souls, as
well as because of the chances of the lot. Yet if at each return to the
life of this world a man loved wisdom sanely, and the lot of his choice e
did not fall out among the last, we may venture to affirm, from what
was reported thence, that not only will he be happy here but that the
path of his journey thither and the return to this world will not be
underground and rough but smooth and through the heavens. For he
said that it was a sight worth seeing to observe how the several souls
selected their lives. He said it was a strange, pitiful, and ridiculous
spectacle, as the choice was determined for the most part by the
habits of their former lives. He saw the soul that had been Orpheus', 620
he said, selecting the life of a swan, because from hatred of the tribe
of women, owing to his death at their hands, it was unwilling to be
conceived and born of a woman. He saw the soul of Thamyras choosing the life of a nightingale, and he saw a swan changing to the choice
of the life of man, and similarly other musical animals. The soul
that drew the twentieth lot chose the life of a lion; it was the soul b
of Ajax, the son of Telamon, which, because it remembered the adjudication of the arms of Achilles, was unwilling to become a man.
The next, the soul of Agamemnon, likewise from hatred of the human
race because of its sufferings, substituted the life of an eagle. Drawing
one of the middle lots the soul of Atalanta caught sight of the great
honors attached to an athlete's life and could not pass them by but
snatched at them. After her, he said, he saw the soul of Epeus, the son c
of Panopeus, entering into the nature of an arts and crafts woman.
Far off in the rear he saw the soul of the buffoon Thersites clothing
itself in the body of an ape. And it fell out that the soul of Odysseus
drew the last lot of all and came to make its choice, and, from memory of its former toils having flung away ambition, went about for a
long time in quest of the life of an ordinary citizen who minded his

own business, and with difficulty found it lying in some corner dis-
d regarded by the others, and upon seeing it said that it would have done
the same had it drawn the first lot, and chose it gladly. And in like
manner, of the other beasts some entered into men and into one another, the unjust into wild creatures, the just transformed to tame,
and there was every kind of mixture and combination.

But when, to conclude, all the souls had chosen their lives in the
order of their lots, they were marshaled and went before Lachesis.
e And she sent with each, as the guardian of his life and the fulfiller of
his choice, the genius that he had chosen, and this divinity led the
soul first to Clotho, under her hand and her turning of the spindle
to ratify the destiny of his lot and choice, and after contact with her
the genius again led the soul to the spinning of Atropos to make the
621 web of its destiny irreversible, and then without a backward look it
passed beneath the throne of Necessity. And after it had passed
through that, when the others also had passed, they all journeyed to
the Plain of Oblivion, through a terrible and stifling heat, for it was
bare of trees and all plants, and there they camped at eventide by the
River of Forgetfulness, whose waters no vessel can contain. They
were all required to drink a measure of the water, and those who were
b not saved by their good sense drank more than the measure, and each
one as he drank forgot all things. And after they had fallen asleep
and it was the middle of the night, there was a sound of thunder and
a quaking of the earth, and they were suddenly wafted thence, one
this way, one that, upward to their birth like shooting stars. Er himself, he said, was not allowed to drink of the water, yet how and in
what way he returned to the body he said he did not know, but
suddenly recovering his sight he saw himself at dawn lying on the
funeral pyre.

And so, Glaucon, the tale was saved, as the saying is, and was not
c lost. And it will save us if we believe it, and we shall safely cross
the River of Lethe, and keep our soul unspotted from the world. But if
we are guided by me we shall believe that the soul is immortal and
capable of enduring all extremes of good and evil, and so we shall
hold ever to the upward way and pursue righteousness with wisdom always and ever, that we may be dear to ourselves and to the
gods both during our sojourn here and when we receive our reward,
d as the victors in the games go about to gather in theirs. And thus both
here and in that journey of a thousand years, whereof I have told
you, we shall fare well.

THEAETETUS

In this dialogue three persons discuss what knowledge is: Socrates, Theodorus, an old man and a distinguished mathematician, and his pupil, the young Theaetetus, who is a charming lad, modest, well-mannered, and quick of apprehension. When Socrates says he suspects him of being very intelligent, he answers that that is by no means true; he only wants to know. "But," Socrates says, "you then are truly philosophical, for philosophy begins in wonder." With that they are launched upon the argument. What is wisdom? What is it to know anything?

This search into the nature of knowledge can be seen in its profound seriousness only when the reader keeps before him that to Socrates virtue was knowledge. To be wise was to be good. The text of the dialogue might well be Christ's saying, "He that willeth to do the will of God shall know the doctrine." To Plato always Socrates' life and death were the final proof of his truth.

In the dialogue, however, no definition of knowledge is reached. We are told only what it is not. It is neither sense perception nor true opinion, nor true opinion with a rational explanation. Even so, a light is thrown upon the question in the digressions from the argument, which are allowed by Socrates because, as he says, they are all three free men and therefore able to take their time and never be in a hurry, and which are warmly welcomed by Theodorus and Theaetetus. "For my part, I rather prefer listening to your digressions," says Theodorus—quite understandably when Socrates is engaged in arguing, "Take things you know. You can suppose them to be other things which you both know and perceive, or to be things you do not know, but do perceive, or you can confuse two things which you both know and perceive."

At this Theaetetus gives up in despair: "Now I am more in the dark than ever."

But they, and the reader, feel different when Socrates stops arguing and sets the peace of the man of wisdom against the restlessness of the busy man who is always in a hurry because to him life is a race for success. He becomes keen and shrewd, but his soul is small and mean. Fears of risks and dangers have proved too much for his honesty and growth and independence. Yet he is sure that he knows *what life is and can deal with it. Beside him the man of wisdom, who really knows, appears often very poor. He is not good even in ordinary talk because he knows no scandals to amuse people—they do not interest him. He cannot help laughing when somebody speaks proudly of a long line of rich and cultivated ancestors. He says to himself, "Doesn't the fellow stop to think that if he goes back far enough, when"—to translate the Greek into familiar English—"Adam delved and Eve span, who was then the gentleman?" But if the roles are changed and the man of wisdom draws the man of business into the upper air to contemplate justice and injustice and what happiness and misery are and the like, then the narrow keen little mind is dismayed and lost. He believes only in what he can hold in his hands; the invisible is nonexistent to him. He does not know what life is, that truly to live is to strive to become like God as far as that is possible. He does not know what the certain penalty is of living as he has done—not prison or death or anything of that sort, but that he will surely grow more and more like himself.*

In the end Socrates tells Theaetetus that the argument has served them even though they reached no conclusion, because they have learned through it not to think they know when they do not.

EUCLIDES: Have you only just come to town, Terpsion?

TERPSION: No, some time ago. What is more, I was looking for you in the market place and surprised that I could not find you.

EUCLIDES: I was not in the city.

TERPSION: Where were you, then?

EUCLIDES: On my way down to the harbor I met them carrying Theaetetus to Athens from the camp at Corinth.

TERPSION: Alive or dead?

EUCLIDES: Only just alive. He is suffering from severe wounds, b and still more from having caught the sickness that has broken out in the army.

TERPSION: The dysentery?

EUCLIDES: Yes.

TERPSION: How sad that such a man should be so near death!

EUCLIDES: An admirable man, Terpsion, and a brave one. Indeed, only just now I was hearing warm praise of his conduct in the battle.

TERPSION: There is nothing strange in that; it would have been much more surprising if he had behaved otherwise. But why did he c not stay here at Megara?

EUCLIDES: He was eager to get home. I begged him to stay, but he would not listen to my advice. I went some way with him, and then, as I was coming back, I recalled what Socrates had said about him, and was filled with wonder at this signal instance of his prophetic insight. Socrates must have met him shortly before his own death, when Theaetetus was little more than a boy. They had some talk together, and Socrates was delighted with the promise he showed. When I visited Athens he repeated to me their conversation, which d was well worth the hearing, and he added that Theaetetus could not fail to become a remarkable man if he lived.

TERPSION: And apparently he was right. But what was this conversation? Could you repeat it?

EUCLIDES: Certainly not, just from memory. But I made 143 some notes at the time, as soon as I got home, and later on I wrote out what I could recall at my leisure. Then, every time I went to Athens, I questioned Socrates upon any point where my memory had failed and made corrections on my return. In this way I have pretty well the whole conversation written down.

TERPSION: True. I have heard you mention it before, and indeed I have always meant to ask you to show it to me; only I have let

---

From *Plato's Theory of Knowledge: the Theaetetus and the Sophist*, translated with a running commentary by Francis Macdonald Cornford (London, 1935); with an interpolation from the translation by B. Jowett in *The Dialogues of Plato*, 3rd edn. (Oxford, 1892; 1st edn., 1871).

the matter slip till this moment. Why should we not go through it now? In any case I am in need of a rest after my walk to town.

b   EUCLIDES : For that matter, I should be glad of a rest myself, for I went as far as Erineum with Theaetetus. Let us go indoors, and, while we are resting, my servant shall read to us.

TERPSION : Very well.

EUCLIDES : This is the book, Terpsion. You see how I wrote the conversation—not in narrative form, as I heard it from Socrates, but as a dialogue between him and the other persons he told me had taken part. These were Theodorus the geometer and Theaetetus. I wanted to

c avoid in the written account the tiresome effect of bits of narrative interrupting the dialogue, such as 'and I said' or 'and I remarked' wherever Socrates was speaking of himself, and 'he assented' or 'he did not agree,' where he reported the answer. So I left out everything of that sort, and wrote it as a direct conversation between the actual speakers.

TERPSION : That was quite a good notion, Euclides.

EUCLIDES : Well, boy, take the book and read.

d   SOCRATES : If I took more interest in the affairs of Cyrene, Theodorus, I should ask you for the news from those parts and whether any of the young men there are devoting themselves to geometry or to any other sort of liberal study. But really I care more for our young men here and I am anxious rather to know which of them are thought likely to distinguish themselves. That is what I am always on the lookout for myself, to the best of my powers, and I make inquiries of anyone whose society I see the young men ready to seek. Now you attract a large following, as you deserve for your skill in

e geometry, not to mention your other merits. So, if you have met with anyone worthy of mention, I should be glad to hear of it.

THEODORUS : Yes, Socrates, I have met with a youth of this city who certainly deserves mention, and you will find it worth while to hear me describe him. If he were handsome, I should be afraid to use strong terms, lest I should be suspected of being in love with him. However, he is not handsome, but—forgive my saying so—he resembles you in being snub-nosed and having prominent eyes, though

144 these features are less marked in him. So I can speak without fear. I assure you that, among all the young men I have met with—and I have had to do with a good many—I have never found such admirable gifts. The combination of a rare quickness of intelligence with exceptional gentleness and of an incomparably virile spirit with both, is a thing that I should hardly have believed could exist, and I have never seen it before. In general, people who have such keen

b and ready wits and such good memories as he are also quick-tempered and passionate; they dart about like ships without ballast, and their temperament is rather enthusiastic than strong, whereas the steadier sort are somewhat dull when they come to face study, and they forget everything. But his approach to learning and inquiry, with the perfect quietness of its smooth and sure progress, is like the noiseless flow of a stream of oil. It is wonderful how he achieves all this at his age.

SOCRATES: That is good news. Who is his father?

THEODORUS: I have heard the name, but I do not remember it. However, there he is, the middle one of those three who are coming c toward us. He and these friends of his have been rubbing themselves with oil in the portico outside, and, now they have finished, they seem to be coming this way. See if you recognize him.

SOCRATES: Yes, I do; his father was Euphronius of Sunium, just such another as his son is by your account. He was a man of good standing, and I believe he left a considerable fortune. But I don't know the lad's name.

THEODORUS: His name is Theaetetus, Socrates, but I fancy the d property has been squandered by trustees. Nonetheless, liberality with his money is another of his admirable traits.

SOCRATES: You give him a noble character. Please ask him to come and sit down with us.

THEODORUS: I will. Theaetetus, come this way and sit by Socrates.

SOCRATES: Yes, do, Theaetetus, so that I may study the character of my own countenance, for Theodorus tells me it is like yours. Now, suppose we each had a lyre, and Theodorus said they were both e tuned to the same pitch, should we take his word at once, or should we try to find out whether he was a musician?

THEAETETUS: We should try to find that out.

SOCRATES: And believe him, if we discovered that he was musical, but not otherwise?

THEAETETUS: True.

SOCRATES: And now, if this alleged likeness of our faces is a matter of any interest to us, we must ask whether it is a skilled draftsman who informs us of it.

THEAETETUS: I agree.   145

SOCRATES: Well, is Theodorus a painter?

THEAETETUS: Not so far as I know.

SOCRATES: Nor an expert in geometry either?

THEAETETUS: Of course he is, Socrates, very much so.

SOCRATES: And also in astronomy and calculation and music and in all the liberal arts?

THEAETETUS: I am sure he is.

SOCRATES: Then, if, in the way of compliment or otherwise, he tells us of some physical likeness between us, there is no special reason why we should attend to him.

THEAETETUS: Possibly not.

SOCRATES: But suppose he should praise the mind of either of b us for its virtue and intelligence. Would there not be good reason why the one who heard the other praised should be eager to examine him, and he should be equally eager to show his quality?

THEAETETUS : Certainly, Socrates.

SOCRATES : Now is the time, then, my dear Theaetetus, for you to show your qualities and for me to examine them. I can assure you that, often as Theodorus has spoken to me in praise of citizen or stranger, he has never praised anyone as he was praising you just now.

c   THEAETETUS : That is good hearing, Socrates. But perhaps he was not speaking seriously.

SOCRATES : No, that would not be like Theodorus. Do not try to slip out of your bargain on the pretext that he was not serious. We don't want him to have to give evidence on oath. In any case no one is going to indict him for perjury; so do not be afraid to abide by your agreement.

THEAETETUS : Well, so it shall be, if you wish it.

SOCRATES : Tell me, then, you are learning some geometry from Theodorus?

THEAETETUS : Yes.

d   SOCRATES : And astronomy and harmonics and arithmetic?

THEAETETUS : I certainly do my best to learn.

SOCRATES : So do I, from him and from anyone else who seems to understand these things. I do moderately well in general, but all the same I am puzzled about one small matter which you and our friends must help me to think out. Tell me, is it not true that learning about something means becoming wiser in that matter?

THEAETETUS : Of course.

SOCRATES : And what makes people wise is wisdom, I suppose.

THEAETETUS : Yes.

e   SOCRATES : And is that in any way different from knowledge?

THEAETETUS : Is what different?

SOCRATES : Wisdom. Are not people wise in the things of which they have knowledge?

THEAETETUS : Certainly.

SOCRATES : Then knowledge and wisdom are the same thing?

THEAETETUS : Yes.

146   SOCRATES : Well, that is precisely what I am puzzled about. I cannot make out to my own satisfaction what knowledge is. Can we answer that question? What do you all say? Which of us will speak first? Everyone who misses shall 'sit down and be donkey,' as children say when they are playing at ball; anyone who gets through without missing shall be king and have the right to make us answer any question he likes. Why are you all silent? I hope, Theodorus, that my passion for argument is not making me ill-mannered, in my eager-

ness to start a conversation and set us all at ease with one another like friends?

THEODORUS: Not at all, Socrates; there is nothing ill-mannered b in that. But please ask one of these young people to answer your questions; I am not at home in an abstract discussion of this sort, nor likely to become so at my age. But it is just the thing for them, and they have a far better prospect of improvement; youth, indeed, is capable of improving at anything. So do not let Theaetetus off; go on putting your questions to him.

SOCRATES: You hear what Theodorus says, Theaetetus. I do not think you will want to disobey him, and it would be wrong for you c not to do what an older and wiser man bids you. So tell me, in a generous spirit, what you think knowledge is.

THEAETETUS: Well, Socrates, I cannot refuse, since you and Theodorus ask me. Anyhow, if I do make a mistake, you will set me right.

SOCRATES: By all means, if we can.

THEAETETUS: Then I think the things one can learn from Theodorus are knowledge—geometry and all the sciences you men- d tioned just now, and then there are the crafts of the cobbler and other workmen. Each and all of these are knowledge and nothing else.

SOCRATES: You are generous indeed, my dear Theaetetus—so openhanded that, when you are asked for one simple thing, you offer a whole variety.

THEAETETUS: What do you mean, Socrates?

SOCRATES: There may be nothing in it, but I will explain what my notion is. When you speak of cobbling, you mean by that word precisely a knowledge of shoemaking?

THEAETETUS: Precisely.

SOCRATES: And when you speak of carpentry, you mean just a e knowledge of how to make wooden furniture?

THEAETETUS: Yes.

SOCRATES: In both cases, then, you are defining what the craft is a knowledge of?

THEAETETUS: Yes.

SOCRATES: But the question you were asked, Theaetetus, was not, what are the objects of knowledge, nor yet how many sorts of knowledge there are. We did not want to count them, but to find out what the thing itself—knowledge—is. Is there nothing in that?

THEAETETUS: No, you are quite right.

SOCRATES: Take another example. Suppose we were asked 147 about some obvious common thing, for instance, what clay is; it would be absurd to answer: potter's clay, and ovenmaker's clay, and brickmaker's clay.

THEAETETUS: No doubt.

SOCRATES : To begin with, it is absurd to imagine that our answer conveys any meaning to the questioner, when we use the word 'clay,' no matter whose clay we call it—the dollmaker's or any other
b craftsman's. You do not suppose a man can understand the name of a thing, when he does not know what the thing is?

THEAETETUS : Certainly not.

SOCRATES : Then, if he has no idea of knowledge, 'knowledge about shoes' conveys nothing to him?

THEAETETUS : No.

SOCRATES : 'Cobblery,' in fact, or the name of any other art has no meaning for anyone who has no conception of knowledge.

THEAETETUS : That is so.

SOCRATES : Then, when we are asked what knowledge is, it is
c absurd to reply by giving the name of some art. The answer is 'knowledge of so-and-so,' but that was not what the question called for.

THEAETETUS : So it seems.

SOCRATES : And besides, we are going an interminable way round, when our answer might be quite short and simple. In this question about clay, for instance, the simple and ordinary thing to say is that clay is earth mixed with moisture, never mind whose clay it may be.

THEAETETUS : It appears easy now, Socrates, when you put it like that. The meaning of your question seems to be the same sort of
d thing as a point that came up when your namesake, Socrates here, and I were talking not long ago.

SOCRATES : What was that, Theaetetus?

THEAETETUS : Theodorus here was proving to us something about square roots, namely, that the sides [or roots] of squares representing three square feet and five square feet are not commensurable in length with the line representing one foot, and he went on in this way, taking all the separate cases up to the root of seventeen square feet. There for some reason he stopped. The idea occurred to us, seeing that these square roots were evidently infinite in number, to try to arrive at a single collective term by which we could designate all these roots.

e   SOCRATES : And did you find one?

THEAETETUS : I think so, but I should like your opinion.

SOCRATES : Go on.

THEAETETUS : We divided number in general into two classes. Any number which is the product of a number multiplied by itself we likened to the square figure, and we called such a number 'square' or 'equilateral.'

SOCRATES : Well done!

THEAETETUS : Any intermediate number, such as three or five
148 or any number that cannot be obtained by multiplying a number by itself, but has one factor either greater or less than the other, so that

the sides containing the corresponding figure are always unequal, we likened to the oblong figure, and we called it an oblong number.

SOCRATES: Excellent. And what next?

THEAETETUS: All the lines which form the four equal sides of the plane figure representing the equilateral number we defined as b *length*, while those which form the sides of squares equal in area to the oblongs we called *roots* [surds], as not being commensurable with the others in length, but only in the plane areas to which their squares are equal. And there is another distinction of the same sort in the case of solids.

SOCRATES: Nothing could be better, my young friends; I am sure there will be no prosecuting Theodorus for false witness.

THEAETETUS: But, Socrates, I cannot answer your question about knowledge as we answered the question about the length and the root. And yet you seem to want something of that kind; so, on the contrary, it does appear that Theodorus was not speaking the truth.

SOCRATES: Why, if he had praised your powers of running and declared that he had never met with a young man who was so good a c runner, and then you had been beaten in a race by the greatest of runners at the height of his powers, do you think that his praise would have been any the less truthful?

THEAETETUS: No, I don't.

SOCRATES: Well, as I said just now, do you fancy it is a small matter to discover the nature of knowledge? Is it not one of the hardest questions?

THEAETETUS: One of the very hardest, I should say.

SOCRATES: You may be reassured, then, about Theodorus' account of you, and set your mind on finding a definition of knowledge, d as of anything else, with all the zeal at your command.

THEAETETUS: If it depends on my zeal, Socrates, the truth will come to light.

SOCRATES: Forward, then, on the way you have just shown so well. Take as a model your answer about the roots. Just as you found a single character to embrace all that multitude, so now try to find a single formula that applies to the many kinds of knowledge.

THEAETETUS: But I assure you, Socrates, I have often set my- e self to study that problem, when I heard reports of the questions you ask. But I cannot persuade myself that I can give any satisfactory solution or that anyone has ever stated in my hearing the sort of answer you require. And yet I cannot get the question out of my mind.

SOCRATES: My dear Theaetetus, that is because your mind is not empty or barren. You are suffering the pains of travail.

THEAETETUS: I don't know about that, Socrates. I am only telling you how I feel.

SOCRATES: How absurd of you, never to have heard that I am 149 the son of a midwife, a fine buxom woman called Phaenarete!

THEAETETUS: I have heard that.

SOCRATES: Have you also been told that I practice the same art?

THEAETETUS: No, never.

SOCRATES: It is true, though; only don't give away my secret. It is not known that I possess this skill; so the ignorant world describes me in other terms as an eccentric person who reduces people to hope-
b less perplexity. Have you been told that too?

THEAETETUS: I have.

SOCRATES: Shall I tell you the reason?

THEAETETUS: Please do.

SOCRATES: Consider, then, how it is with all midwives; that will help you to understand what I mean. I dare say you know that they never attend other women in childbirth so long as they themselves can conceive and bear children, but only when they are too old for that.

THEAETETUS: Of course.

SOCRATES: They say that is because Artemis, the patroness of childbirth, is herself childless, and so, while she did not allow barren
c women to be midwives, because it is beyond the power of human nature to achieve skill without any experience, she assigned the privilege to women who were past childbearing, out of respect to their likeness to herself.

THEAETETUS: That sounds likely.

SOCRATES: And it is more than likely, is it not, that no one can tell so well as a midwife whether women are pregnant or not?

THEAETETUS: Assuredly.

SOCRATES: Moreover, with the drugs and incantations they
d administer, midwives can either bring on the pains of travail or allay them at their will, make a difficult labor easy, and at an early stage cause a miscarriage if they so decide.

THEAETETUS: True.

SOCRATES: Have you also observed that they are the cleverest matchmakers, having an unerring skill in selecting a pair whose marriage will produce the best children?

THEAETETUS: I was not aware of that.

SOCRATES: Well, you may be sure they pride themselves on
e that more than on cutting the umbilical cord. Consider the knowledge of the sort of plant or seed that should be sown in any given soil. Does not that go together with skill in tending and harvesting the fruits of the earth? They are not two different arts?

THEAETETUS: No, the same.

SOCRATES: And so with a woman; skill in the sowing is not to be separated from skill in the harvesting?

150 THEAETETUS: Probably not.

SOCRATES: No. Only, because there is that wrong and ignorant way of bringing together man and woman which they call pandering, midwives, out of self-respect, are shy even of matchmaking, for fear of falling under the accusation of pandering. Yet the genuine midwife is the only successful matchmaker.

THEAETETUS: That is clear.

SOCRATES: All this, then, lies within the midwife's province, but her performance falls short of mine. It is not the way of women sometimes to bring forth real children, sometimes mere phantoms, such that it is hard to tell the one from the other. If it were so, the b highest and noblest task of the midwife would be to discern the real from the unreal, would it not?

THEAETETUS: I agree.

SOCRATES: My art of midwifery is in general like theirs; the only difference is that my patients are men, not women, and my concern is not with the body but with the soul that is in travail of birth. And the highest point of my art is the power to prove by every test c whether the offspring of a young man's thought is a false phantom or instinct with life and truth. I am so far like the midwife that I cannot myself give birth to wisdom, and the common reproach is true, that, though I question others, I can myself bring nothing to light because there is no wisdom in me. The reason is this. Heaven constrains me to serve as a midwife, but has debarred me from giving birth. So of my- d self I have no sort of wisdom, nor has any discovery ever been born to me as the child of my soul. Those who frequent my company at first appear, some of them, quite unintelligent, but, as we go further with our discussions, all who are favored by heaven make progress at a rate that seems surprising to others as well as to themselves, although it is clear that they have never learned anything from me. The many admirable truths they bring to birth have been discovered by themselves from within. But the delivery is heaven's work and mine.

The proof of this is that many who have not been conscious of my assistance but have made light of me, thinking it was all their own e doing, have left me sooner than they should, whether under others' influence or of their own motion, and thenceforward suffered miscarriage of their thoughts through falling into bad company, and they have lost the children of whom I had delivered them by bringing them up badly, caring more for false phantoms than for the true. And so at last their lack of understanding has become apparent to themselves and to everyone else. Such a one was Aristides, son of Lysimachus, 151 and there have been many more. When they come back and beg for a renewal of our intercourse with extravagant protestations, sometimes the divine warning that comes to me forbids it; with others it is permitted, and these begin again to make progress. In yet another way those who seek my company have the same experience as a woman with child; they suffer the pains of labor and, by night and day, are

full of distress far greater than a woman's, and my art has power to
b bring on these pangs or to allay them. So it fares with these, but there
are some, Theaetetus, whose minds, as I judge, have never conceived
at all. I see that they have no need of me and with all good will I seek
a match for them. Without boasting unduly, I can guess pretty well
whose society will profit them. I have arranged many of these
matches with Prodicus, and with other men of inspired sagacity.

And now for the upshot of this long discourse of mine. I suspect
that, as you yourself believe, your mind is in labor with some thought
it has conceived. Accept, then, the ministration of a midwife's son
c who himself practices his mother's art, and do the best you can to answer the questions I ask. Perhaps when I examine your statements I
may judge one or another of them to be an unreal phantom. If I then
take the abortion from you and cast it away, do not be savage with me
like a woman robbed of her first child. People have often felt like that
toward me and been positively ready to bite me for taking away some
foolish notion they have conceived. They do not see that I am doing
d them a kindness. They have not learned that no divinity is ever ill-
disposed toward man, nor is such action on my part due to unkind-
ness; it is only that I am not permitted to acquiesce in falsehood and
suppress the truth.

So, Theaetetus, start again and try to explain what knowledge is.
Never say it is beyond your power; it will not be so, if heaven wills and
you take courage.

THEAETETUS : Well, Socrates, with such encouragement from
e a person like you, it would be a shame not to do one's best to say what
one can. It seems to me that one who knows something is perceiving
the thing he knows, and, so far as I can see at present, knowledge is
nothing but perception.

SOCRATES : Good. That is the right spirit in which to express
one's opinion. But now suppose we examine your offspring together,
and see whether it is a mere wind egg or has some life in it. Perception,
you say, is knowledge?

THEAETETUS : Yes.

SOCRATES : The account you give of the nature of knowledge is
152 not, by any means, to be despised. It is the same that was given by
Protagoras, though he stated it in a somewhat different way. He says,
you will remember, that 'man is the measure of all things—alike of
the being of things that are and of the not-being of things that are
not.' No doubt you have read that.

THEAETETUS : Yes, often.

SOCRATES : He puts it in this sort of way, doesn't he, that any
given thing 'is to me such as it appears to me, and is to you such as it
appears to you,' you and I being men?

THEAETETUS : Yes, that is how he puts it.

b SOCRATES : Well, what a wise man says is not likely to be nonsense. So let us follow up his meaning. Sometimes, when the same wind is blowing, one of us feels chilly, the other does not, or one may feel slightly chilly, the other quite cold.

THEAETETUS: Certainly.

SOCRATES: Well, in that case are we to say that the wind in itself is cold or not cold? Or shall we agree with Protagoras that it is cold to the one who feels chilly, and not to the other?

THEAETETUS: That seems reasonable.

SOCRATES: And further that it so 'appears' to each of us?

THEAETETUS: Yes.

SOCRATES: And 'appears' means that he 'perceives' it so?

THEAETETUS: True.

SOCRATES: 'Appearing,' then, is the same thing as 'perceiving,' c in the case of what is hot or anything of that kind. They *are* to each man such as he *perceives* them.

THEAETETUS: So it seems.

SOCRATES: Perception, then, is always of something that *is*, and, as being knowledge, it is infallible.

THEAETETUS: That is clear.

SOCRATES: Can it be, then, that Protagoras was a very ingenious person who threw out this dark saying for the benefit of the common herd like ourselves, and reserved the truth as a secret doctrine to be revealed to his disciples?

THEAETETUS: What do you mean by that, Socrates?   d

SOCRATES: I will tell you, and indeed the doctrine is a remarkable one. It declares that nothing is *one* thing just by itself, nor can you rightly call it by some definite name, nor even say it is of any definite sort. On the contrary, if you call it 'large,' it will be found to be also small, if 'heavy,' to be also light, and so on all through, because nothing is *one* thing or *some* thing or of any definite sort. All the things we are pleased to say 'are,' really are in process of becoming, as a result of movement and change and of blending one with another. We are wrong to speak of them as 'being,' for none of them ever is; they are always becoming. In this matter let us take it that, with the e exception of Parmenides, the whole series of philosophers agree— Protagoras, Heraclitus, Empedocles—and among the poets the greatest masters in both kinds, Epicharmus in comedy, Homer in tragedy. When Homer speaks of 'Oceanus, source of the gods, and mother Tethys,' [1] he means that all things are the offspring of a flowing stream of change. Don't you understand him so?

THEAETETUS: Certainly.

SOCRATES: Who, then, could challenge so great an array, with 153 Homer for its captain, and not make himself a laughingstock?

THEAETETUS: That would be no light undertaking, Socrates.

---

[1] *Iliad* 14.201, 302.

SOCRATES : It would not, Theaetetus. Their doctrine that 'being,' so called, and 'becoming' are produced by motion, 'not-being' and perishing by rest, is well supported by such proofs as these. The hot or fire, which generates and controls all other things, is itself generated by movement and friction—both forms of change. These are ways of producing fire, aren't they?

b   THEAETETUS : Yes.

SOCRATES : And further, all living things are born by the same processes?

THEAETETUS : Assuredly.

SOCRATES : Again, the healthy condition of the body is undermined by inactivity and indolence, and to a great extent preserved by exercise and motion, isn't it?

THEAETETUS : Yes.

SOCRATES : And so with the condition of the soul. The soul acquires knowledge and is kept going and improved by learning and practice, which are of the nature of movements. By inactivity, dull-
c ness, and neglect of exercise, it learns nothing and forgets what it has learned.

THEAETETUS : True.

SOCRATES : So, of the two, motion is a good thing for both soul and body, and immobility is bad.

THEAETETUS : So it appears.

SOCRATES : Need I speak further of such things as stagnation in air or water, where stillness causes corruption and decay, when motion would keep things fresh, or, to complete the argument, press into its service that 'golden rope' [2] in Homer, proving that he means by
d it nothing more nor less than the sun, and signifies that so long as the heavens and the sun continue to move round, all things in heaven and earth are kept going, whereas if they were bound down and brought to a stand, all things would be destroyed and the world, as they say, turned upside down?

THEAETETUS : I agree with your interpretation, Socrates.

SOCRATES : Think of it, then, in this way. First, to take the case of the eyes, you must conceive that what you call white color has no being as a distinct thing outside your eyes nor yet inside them, nor
e must you assign it any fixed place. Otherwise, of course, it would have its being in an assigned place and abide there, instead of arising in a process of becoming.

THEAETETUS : Well, but how am I to think of it?

SOCRATES : Let us follow out our recent statement and lay it down that there is no single thing that is in and by itself. On that showing we shall see that black or white or any color you choose is a thing that has arisen out of the meeting of our eyes with the appro-
154 priate motion. What we say 'is' this or that color will be neither the

[2] *Iliad* 8.18 sq.

eye which encounters the motion nor the motion which is encountered, but something which has arisen between the two and is peculiar to each several percipient. Or would you be prepared to maintain that every color appears to a dog or any other creature just such as it appears to you?

THEAETETUS: Certainly not.

SOCRATES: Or to another man? Does anything you please appear to him such as it appears to you? Are you quite sure of that? Are you not much rather sure that it does not even appear the same to yourself, because you never remain in the same condition?

THEAETETUS: I think that is much nearer the mark.

SOCRATES: So then, if the thing that we measure ourselves b against or the thing we touch really were large or white or hot, it would never become different the moment it encountered a different person, supposing it to undergo no change in itself. And again, if the thing which measures itself against the object or touches it were any one of these things [large, white, etc.], then, when a different thing came into contact with it or were somehow modified, it, on its side, if it were not affected in itself, would not become different. For as things are, we are too easily led into making statements which Protagoras and anyone who maintains the same position would call strange and absurd.

THEAETETUS: How so? What statements do you mean?

SOCRATES: Take a simple example, which will make my mean- c ing quite clear. When you compare six dice with four, we say that the six are more than the four or half as many again, while if you compare them with twelve, the six are fewer—only half as many—and one cannot say anything else. Or do you think one can?

THEAETETUS: Certainly not.

SOCRATES: Well then, suppose Protagoras or somebody else asks you, Can anything become larger or more otherwise than by being increased? What will you answer?

THEAETETUS: I should answer no, if I were to speak my mind with reference to this last question, but having regard to your previous d one, I might reply yes, to guard against contradicting myself.

SOCRATES: An excellent answer; really, you might be inspired. But apparently, if you say yes, it will be like the situation in Euripides; the tongue will be incontrovertible, but not the heart.

THEAETETUS: True.

SOCRATES: Now, if you and I were like those clever persons who have canvassed all the thoughts of the heart, we might allow ourselves the luxury of trying one another's strength in a regular sophisti- e cal set-to, with a great clashing of arguments. But being only ordinary people, we shall prefer first to study the notions we have in our own minds and find out what they are and whether, when we compare them, they agree or are altogether inconsistent.

THEAETETUS: I should certainly prefer that.

SOCRATES: So do I, and, that being so, suppose we look at the question again in a quiet and leisurely spirit, not with any impatience but genuinely examining ourselves to see what we can make of these apparitions that present themselves to our minds. Looking at the first of them, I suppose we shall assert that nothing can become greater or less, either in size or in number, so long as it remains equal to itself. Is it not so?

THEAETETUS: Yes.

SOCRATES: And secondly, that a thing to which nothing is added and from which nothing is taken away is neither increased nor diminished, but always remains the same in amount.

THEAETETUS: Undoubtedly.

SOCRATES: And must we not say, thirdly, that a thing which was not at an earlier moment cannot be at a later moment without becoming and being in process of becoming?

THEAETETUS: It certainly seems so.

SOCRATES: Now these three admissions, I fancy, fight among themselves in our minds when we make those statements about the dice, or when we say that I, being of the height you see, without gaining or losing in size, may within a year be taller, as I am now, than a youth like you, and later on be shorter, not because I have lost anything in bulk, but because you have grown. For apparently I am later what I was not before, and yet have not become so, for without the process of becoming the result is impossible, and I could not be in process of becoming shorter without losing some of my bulk. I could give you countless other examples, if we are to accept these. For I think you follow me, Theaetetus; I fancy, at any rate, such puzzles are not altogether strange to you.

THEAETETUS: No, indeed it is extraordinary how they set me wondering whatever they can mean. Sometimes I get quite dizzy with thinking of them.

SOCRATES: That shows that Theodorus was not wrong in his estimate of your nature. This sense of wonder is the mark of the philosopher. Philosophy indeed has no other origin, and he was a good genealogist who made Iris the daughter of Thaumas.

Do you now begin to see the explanation of all this which follows from the theory we are attributing to Protagoras? Or is it not yet clear?

THEAETETUS: I can't say it is yet.

SOCRATES: Then perhaps you will be grateful if I help you to penetrate to the truth concealed in the thoughts of a man—or, I should say, of men—of such distinction.

THEAETETUS: Of course I shall be very grateful.

SOCRATES: Then just take a look round and make sure that none of the uninitiate overhears us. I mean by the uninitiate the people who believe that nothing is real save what they can grasp with their hands and do not admit that actions or processes or anything invisible can count as real.

THEAETETUS: They sound like a very hard and repellent sort of people.

SOCRATES: It is true, they are remarkably crude. The others, 156 into whose secrets I am going to initiate you, are much more refined and subtle. Their first principle, on which all that we said just now depends, is that the universe really is motion and nothing else. And there are two kinds of motion. Of each kind there are any number of instances, but they differ in that the one kind has the power of acting, the other of being acted upon. From the intercourse and friction of these with one another arise offspring, endless in number, but in pairs of twins. One of each pair is something perceived, the other a perception, whose birth always coincides with that of the thing perceived. b Now, for the perceptions we have names like 'seeing,' 'hearing,' 'smelling,' 'feeling cold,' 'feeling hot,' and again pleasures and pains and desires and fears, as they are called, and so on. There are any number that are nameless, though names have been found for a whole multitude. On the other side, the brood of things perceived always comes to birth at the same moment with one or another of these—with instances of seeing, colors of corresponding variety, with instances of c hearing, sounds in the same way, and with all the other perceptions, the other things perceived that are akin to them. Now, what light does this story throw on what has gone before, Theaetetus? Do you see?

THEAETETUS: Not very clearly, Socrates.

SOCRATES: Well, consider whether we can round it off. The point is that all these things are, as we were saying, in motion, but there is a quickness or slowness in their motion. The slow sort has its motion without change of place and with respect to what comes within range of it, and that is how it generates offspring, but the offspring d generated are quicker, inasmuch as they move from place to place and their motion consists in change of place. As soon, then, as an eye and something else whose structure is adjusted to the eye come within range and give birth to the whiteness together with its cognate perception—things that would never have come into existence if either of the two had approached anything else—then it is that, as the vision from the eyes and the whiteness from the thing that joins in giving birth to the color pass in the space between, the eye becomes filled with vision and now sees, and becomes, not vision, but a seeing eye, while the other parent of the color is saturated with whiteness e and becomes, on its side, not whiteness, but a white thing, be it stock or stone or whatever else may chance to be so colored.

And so, too, we must think in the same way of the rest—'hard,' 'hot,' and all of them—that no one of them has any being just by itself, as indeed we said before, but that it is in their intercourse with

one another that all arise in all their variety as a result of their motion, since it is impossible to have any 'firm notion,' as they say, of either what is active or what is passive in them, in any single case, as having
157 any being. For there is no such thing as an agent until it meets with a patient, nor any patient until it meets with its agent. Also what meets with something and behaves as agent, if it encounters something different at another time, shows itself as patient.

The conclusion from all this is, as we said at the outset, that nothing *is* one thing just by itself, but is always in process of becoming for someone, and being is to be ruled out altogether, though, needless
b to say, we have been betrayed by habit and inobservance into using the word more than once only just now. But that was wrong, these wise men tell us, and we must not admit the expressions 'something' or 'somebody's' or 'mine' or 'this' or 'that' or any other word that brings things to a standstill, but rather speak, in accordance with nature, of what is 'becoming,' 'being produced,' 'perishing,' 'changing.' For anyone who talks so as to bring things to a standstill is easily refuted. So we must express ourselves in each individual case and in speaking of an assemblage of many—to which assemblage people give the name
c of 'man' or 'stone' or of any living creature or kind.

Does all this please you, Theaetetus? Will you accept it as palatable to your taste?

THEAETETUS : Really, I am not sure, Socrates. I cannot even make out about you, whether you are stating this as something you believe or merely putting me to the test.

SOCRATES : You forget, my friend, that I know nothing of such matters and cannot claim to be producing any offspring of my own. I am only trying to deliver yours, and to that end uttering charms over you and tempting your appetite with a variety of delicacies from the table of wisdom, until by my aid your own belief shall be brought to
d light. Once that is done, I shall see whether it proves to have some life in it or not. Meanwhile, have courage and patience, and answer my questions bravely in accordance with your convictions.

THEAETETUS : Go on with your questioning.

SOCRATES : Once more, then, tell me whether you like this notion that nothing is, but is always becoming, good or beautiful or any of the other things we mentioned?

THEAETETUS : Well, when I hear you explaining it as you have, it strikes me as extraordinarily reasonable, and to be accepted as you have stated it.

e SOCRATES : Then let us not leave it incomplete. There remains the question of dreams and disorders, especially madness and all the mistakes madness is said to make in seeing or hearing or otherwise misperceiving. You know, of course, that in all these cases the theory
158 we have just stated is supposed to be admittedly disproved, on the ground that in these conditions we certainly have false perceptions,

and that so far from its being true that what appears to any man also is, on the contrary none of these appearances is real.

THEAETETUS: That is quite true, Socrates.

SOCRATES: What argument, then, is left for one who maintains that perception is knowledge, and that what appears to each man also 'is' for him to whom it appears?

THEAETETUS: I hesitate to say that I have no reply, Socrates, because just now you rebuked me for saying that. Really, I cannot undertake to deny that madmen and dreamers believe what is false, b when madmen imagine they are gods or dreamers think they have wings and are flying in their sleep.

SOCRATES: Have you not taken note of another doubt that is raised in these cases, especially about sleeping and waking?

THEAETETUS: What is that?

SOCRATES: The question I imagine you have often heard asked —what evidence could be appealed to, supposing we were asked at this very moment whether we are asleep or awake, dreaming all that passes through our minds or talking to one another in the waking c state?

THEAETETUS: Indeed, Socrates, I do not see by what evidence it is to be proved, for the two conditions correspond in every circumstance like exact counterparts. The conversation we have just had might equally well be one that we merely think we are carrying on in our sleep, and when it comes to thinking in a dream that we are telling other dreams, the two states are extraordinarily alike.

SOCRATES: You see, then, that there is plenty of room for doubt, when we even doubt whether we are asleep or awake. And in d fact, our time being equally divided between waking and sleeping, in each condition our mind strenuously contends that the convictions of the moment are certainly true, so that for equal times we affirm the reality of the one world and of the other, and are just as confident of both.

THEAETETUS: Certainly.

SOCRATES: And the same holds true of disorders and madness, except that the times are not equal.

THEAETETUS: That is so.

SOCRATES: Well, is the truth to be decided by length or shortness of time?

THEAETETUS: No, that would be absurd in many ways. e

SOCRATES: Have you any other certain test to show which of these beliefs is true?

THEAETETUS: I don't think I have.

SOCRATES: Then let me tell you what sort of account would be given of these cases by those who lay it down that whatever at any time seems to anyone is true to him. I imagine they would ask this question, 'Tell us, Theaetetus, when one thing is entirely different from another, it cannot be in any respect capable of behaving in the same way as that other, can it? We are not to understand that the thing we speak of is in some respects the same though different in others, but that it is entirely different.'

159   THEAETETUS : If so, it can have nothing in common, either in its capabilities of behavior or in any other respect, when it is altogether different.

SOCRATES : Must we not admit, then, that such a thing is unlike the other?

THEAETETUS : I agree.

SOCRATES : So if it happens that something comes to be like or unlike either itself or something else, we shall say that when it is made like it becomes the *same*, when unlike, *different*.

THEAETETUS : Necessarily.

SOCRATES : And we said earlier that there was no limit to the number of things that are active or of things that are acted upon by them.

THEAETETUS : Yes.

SOCRATES : And further, that when one of these is married to a succession of different partners, the offspring produced will be not the same but different.

b   THEAETETUS : Certainly.

SOCRATES : Now let us take you or me or any other instance to which the principle applies—Socrates in health and Socrates ill. Are we to call one of these *like* the other or unlike?

THEAETETUS : You mean, is the ill Socrates taken as a whole like Socrates in health taken as a whole?

SOCRATES : You understand me perfectly; that is just what I mean.

THEAETETUS : Then of course he is unlike.

SOCRATES : And consequently, inasmuch as he is unlike, a different thing?

THEAETETUS : Necessarily.

c   SOCRATES : And you would say the same of Socrates asleep or in any other of the conditions we mentioned?

THEAETETUS : Yes.

SOCRATES : Then any one of the objects whose nature it is to act upon something will, according as it finds Socrates well or ill, treat me as a different thing?

THEAETETUS : Of course it will.

SOCRATES : And consequently the pair of us—I who am acted upon and the thing that acts on me—will have different offspring in the two cases?

THEAETETUS : Naturally.

SOCRATES : Now when I am in health and drink wine, it seems pleasant to me and sweet.

THEAETETUS : Yes.

SOCRATES: Because, in accordance with the account we accepted earlier, agent and patient give birth to sweetness and a sensa- d tion, both movements that pass simultaneously. The sensation, on the patient's side, makes the tongue percipient, while, on the side of the wine, the sweetness, moving in the region of the wine, causes it both to be and to appear sweet to the healthy tongue.

THEAETETUS: Certainly that was what we agreed upon.

SOCRATES: But when it finds me in ill-health, to begin with, the person it finds is not really the same, for the one it now meets with is unlike the other.

THEAETETUS: Yes.

SOCRATES: And so this pair—Socrates in this condition and the e drinking of the wine—produce a different offspring, in the region of the tongue a sensation of sourness, and in the region of the wine a sourness that arises as a movement there. The wine becomes, not sourness, but sour, while I become, not a sensation, but sentient.

THEAETETUS: Undoubtedly.

SOCRATES: It follows, then, that (a) that, on my side, I shall never become percipient in just this way of any other thing, for to a differ- 160 ent object belongs a different perception, and in acting on its percipient it is acting on a person who is in a different condition and so a different person. Also (b) on its side, the thing which acts on me can never meet with someone else and generate the same offspring and come to be of just this quality, for when it brings to birth another thing from another person, it will itself come to be of another quality.

THEAETETUS: That is so.

SOCRATES: Further, (c) I shall not come to have this sensation *for myself*, nor will the object come to be of such a quality *for itself*.

THEAETETUS: No.

SOCRATES: Rather, when I become percipient, I must become percipient *of something*, for I cannot have a perception and have it of nothing, and equally the object, when it becomes sweet or sour and b so on, must become so *to someone*—it cannot become sweet and yet sweet to nobody.

THEAETETUS: Quite so.

SOCRATES: Nothing remains, then, I suppose, but that it and I should be or become—whichever expression we are to use—*for each other*. Necessity binds together our existence, but binds neither of us to anything else, nor each of us to himself; so we can only be bound to one another. Accordingly, whether we speak of something 'being' or of its 'becoming,' we must speak of it as being or becoming *for someone*, or *of something*, or *toward something*, but we must not speak, or allow others to speak, of a thing as either being or becoming any- c thing just in and by itself. That is the conclusion to which our argument points.

THEAETETUS: Certainly, Socrates.

SOCRATES : And so, since what acts upon me is for me and for no one else, I, and no one else, am actually perceiving it.

THEAETETUS : Of course.

SOCRATES : Then my perception is true for me, for its object at any moment is my reality, and I am, as Protagoras says, a judge of what is for me, that it is, and of what is not, that it is not.

THEAETETUS : So it appears.

d   SOCRATES : If, then, I am infallible and make no mistake in my state of mind about what is or becomes, how can I fail to have knowledge of the things of which I have perception?

THEAETETUS : You cannot possibly fail.

SOCRATES : So you were perfectly right in saying that knowledge is nothing but perception. And it has turned out that these three doctrines coincide—the doctrine of Homer and Heraclitus and all their tribe that all things move like flowing streams, the doctrine of Protagoras, wisest of men, that man is the measure of all things, and

e   Theaetetus' conclusion that, on these grounds, it results that perception is knowledge.

Is it not so, Theaetetus? May we say that this is your newborn child which I have brought to birth? What do you say?

THEAETETUS : I can only agree, Socrates.

SOCRATES : Here at last, then, after our somewhat painful labor, is the child we have brought to birth, whatever sort of creature it may be. His birth should be followed by the ceremony of carrying him round the hearth; we must look at our offspring from every angle

161   to make sure we are not taken in by a lifeless phantom not worth the rearing. Or do you think an infant of yours must be reared in any case and not exposed? Will you bear to see him put to the proof, and not be in a passion if your first-born should be taken away?

THEODORUS : Theaetetus will bear it, Socrates; he is thoroughly good-tempered. But do explain what is wrong with the conclusion.

SOCRATES : You have an absolute passion for discussion, Theodorus. I like the way you take me for a sort of bag full of arguments, and imagine I can easily pull out a proof to show that our con-

b   clusion is wrong. You don't see what is happening. The arguments never come out of me; they always come from the person I am talking with. I am only at a slight advantage in having the skill to get some account of the matter from another's wisdom and entertain it with fair treatment. So now, I shall not give any explanation myself, but try to get it out of our friend.

THEODORUS : That is better, Socrates; do as you say.

SOCRATES : Well then, Theodorus, shall I tell you a thing that surprises me in your friend Protagoras?

c   THEODORUS : What is that?

SOCRATES : The opening words of his treatise. In general, I am delighted with his statement that what seems to anyone also is, but I am surprised that he did not begin his *Truth* with the words, The measure of all things is the pig, or the baboon, or some sentient creature still more uncouth. There would have been something magnificent in so disdainful an opening, telling us that all the time, while we were admiring him for a wisdom more than mortal, he was in fact no wiser than a tadpole, to say nothing of any other human being. d What else can we say, Theodorus? If what every man believes as a result of perception is indeed to be true for him; if, just as no one is to be a better judge of what another experiences, so no one is better entitled to consider whether what another thinks is true or false, and, as we have said more than once, every man is to have his own beliefs for himself alone and they are all right and true—then, my friend, where is the wisdom of Protagoras, to justify his setting up to teach others and to be handsomely paid for it, and where is our comparative e ignorance or the need for us to go and sit at his feet, when each of us is himself the measure of his own wisdom? Must we not suppose that Protagoras speaks in this way to flatter the ears of the public? I say nothing of my own case or of the ludicrous predicament to which my art of midwifery is brought, and, for that matter, this whole business of philosophical conversation, for to set about overhauling and testing one another's notions and opinions when those of each and every one are right, is a tedious and monstrous display of folly, if the Truth 162 of Protagoras is really truthful and not amusing herself with oracles delivered from the unapproachable shrine of his book.

THEODORUS: Protagoras was my friend, Socrates, as you were saying, and I would rather he were not refuted by means of any admissions of mine. On the other hand, I cannot resist you against my convictions; so you had better go back to Theaetetus, whose answers have shown, in any case, how well he can follow your meaning.

SOCRATES: If you went to a wrestling school at Sparta, Theo- b dorus, would you expect to look on at the naked wrestlers, some of them making a poor show, and not strip so as to let them compare your own figure?

THEODORUS: Why not, if they were likely to listen to me and not insist, just as I believe I shall persuade you to let me look on now? The limbs are stiff at my age, and instead of dragging me into your exercises, you will try a fall with a more supple youth.

SOCRATES: Well, Theodorus, as the proverb says, 'What likes you mislikes not me.' So I will have recourse to the wisdom of The- c aetetus.

Tell me, then, first, Theaetetus, about the point we have just made. Are not *you* surprised that you should turn out, all of a sudden, to be every bit as wise as any other man and even as any god? Or would you say that Protagoras' maxim about the measure does not apply to gods just as much as to men?

THEAETETUS : Certainly I think it does, and, to answer your question, I am very much surprised. When we were discussing what they mean by saying that what seems to anyone really is to him who d thinks it so, that appeared to me quite satisfactory, but now, all in a moment, it has taken on a very different complexion.

SOCRATES : That, my friend, is because you are young; so you lend a ready ear to claptrap and it convinces you. Protagoras or his representative will have an answer to this. He will say, 'You good people sitting there, boys and old men together, this is all claptrap. You drag in the gods, whose existence or nonexistence I expressly refuse to e discuss in my speeches and writings, and you count upon appeals to the vulgar such as this. How strange that any human individual is to be no wiser than the lowest of the brutes! You go entirely by what looks probable, without a word of argument or proof. If a mathematician like Theodorus elected to argue from probability in geometry, he wouldn't be worth an ace. So you and Theodorus might consider whether you are going to allow questions of this importance to be 163 settled by plausible appeals to mere likelihood.'

THEAETETUS : Well, you would not think that right, Socrates, any more than we should.

SOCRATES : It seems, then, we must attack the question in another way. That is what you and Theodorus think?

THEAETETUS : Certainly we must.

SOCRATES : Let us look at it in this way, then—this question whether knowledge and perception are, after all, the same thing or not. For that, you remember, was the point to which our whole discussion was directed, and it was for its sake that we stirred up all this swarm of queer doctrines, wasn't it?

b   THEAETETUS : Quite true.

SOCRATES : Well, are we going to agree that, whenever we perceive something by sight or hearing, we also at the same time know it? Take the case of a foreign language we have not learned. Are we to say that we do not hear the sounds that foreigners utter, or that we both hear and know what they are saying? Or again, when we don't know our letters, are we to maintain that we don't see them when we look at them, or that, since we see them, we do know them?

THEAETETUS : We shall say, Socrates, that we know just so much of them as we do see or hear. The shape and color of the letters c we both see and know; we hear and at the same time know the rising and falling accents of the voice. But we neither perceive by sight and hearing nor yet know what a schoolmaster or an interpreter could tell us about them.

SOCRATES : Well done, Theaetetus. I had better not raise objections to that, for fear of checking your growth. But look, here is another objection threatening. How are we going to parry it?

THEAETETUS : What is that?

SOCRATES : It is this. Suppose someone to ask, 'Is it possible d for a man who has once come to know something and still preserves a memory of it, not to know just that thing that he remembers at the moment when he remembers it?' This is, perhaps, rather a long-winded way of putting the question. I mean, can a man who has become acquainted with something and remembers it, not know it?

THEAETETUS : Of course not, Socrates, the supposition is monstrous.

SOCRATES : Perhaps I am talking nonsense, then. But consider, you call seeing 'perceiving,' and sight 'perception,' don't you?

THEAETETUS : I do.

SOCRATES : Then, according to our earlier statement, a man e who sees something acquires from that moment knowledge of the thing he sees?

THEAETETUS : Yes.

SOCRATES : Again, you recognize such a thing as memory?

THEAETETUS : Yes.

SOCRATES : Memory of nothing, or of something?

THEAETETUS : Of something, surely.

SOCRATES : Of what one has become acquainted with and perceived—that sort of thing?

THEAETETUS : Of course.

SOCRATES : So a man sometimes remembers what he has seen?

THEAETETUS : He does.

SOCRATES : Even when he shuts his eyes? Or does he forget when he shuts them?

THEAETETUS : No, Socrates, that would be a monstrous thing 164 to say.

SOCRATES : All the same, we shall have to say it, if we are to save our former statement. Otherwise, it goes by the board.

THEAETETUS : I certainly have a suspicion that you are right, but I don't quite see how. You must tell me.

SOCRATES : In this way. One who sees, we say, acquires knowledge of what he sees, because it is agreed that sight or perception and knowledge are the same thing.

THEAETETUS : Certainly.

SOCRATES : But suppose this man who sees and acquires knowledge of what he has seen, shuts his eyes; then he remembers the thing, but does not see it. Isn't that so?

THEAETETUS : Yes.

SOCRATES : But 'does not see it' means 'does not know it,' since b 'sees' and 'knows' mean the same.

THEAETETUS : True.

SOCRATES: Then the conclusion is that a man who has come to know a thing and still remembers it does not know it, since he does not see it, and we said that would be a monstrous conclusion.

THEAETETUS: Quite true.

SOCRATES: Apparently, then, if you say that knowledge and perception are the same thing, it leads to an impossibility.

THEAETETUS: So it seems.

SOCRATES: Then we shall have to say they are different.

THEAETETUS: I suppose so.

SOCRATES: What, then, can knowledge be? Apparently we c must begin all over again. But wait a moment, Theaetetus. What are we doing?

THEAETETUS: Doing about what?

SOCRATES: It seems to me we are behaving toward our theory like an ill-bred gamecock who springs away from his adversary and starts crowing over him before he is beaten.

THEAETETUS: How so?

SOCRATES: It looks as if we were content to have reached an agreement resting on mere verbal consistency and to have got the better of the theory by the methods of a professional controversialist. We profess to be seeking wisdom, not competing for victory, but we d are unconsciously behaving just like one of those redoubtable disputants.

THEAETETUS: I still don't understand what you mean.

SOCRATES: Well, I will try to make the point clear, so far as I can see it. We were asking whether one who had become acquainted with something and remembered it could fail to know it. Then we pointed out that a man who shuts his eyes after seeing something, remembers but does not see, and so concluded that at the same moment he both remembers the thing and does not know it. That, we said, was impossible. And so no one was left to tell Protagoras' tale, or e yours either, about knowledge and perception being the same thing.

THEAETETUS: So it appears.

SOCRATES: I fancy it would be very different if the author of the first story were still alive. He would have put up a good fight for his offspring. But he is dead, and here are we trampling on the orphan. Even its appointed guardians, like Theodorus here, will not come to the rescue. However, we will step into the breach ourselves and see that it has fair play.

165 THEODORUS: In point of fact, Socrates, it is rather Callias, son of Hipponicus, who is Protagoras' trustee. My own inclinations diverted me at rather an early age from abstract discussions to geometry. All the same, I shall be grateful for any succor you can give him.

SOCRATES: Very good, Theodorus. You shall see what my help will amount to. For one might commit oneself to even stranger conclusions, if one were as careless in the use of language as we commonly are in our assertions and denials. Am I to enlarge upon this to you or to Theaetetus?

THEODORUS: To the company in general, but let the younger man answer your questions. It will not be such a disgrace to him to b be caught tripping.

SOCRATES: Let me put, then, the most formidable poser of all, which I take to be this. Can the same person know something and also not know that which he knows?

THEODORUS: Well, Theaetetus, what are we to answer?

THEAETETUS: That it is impossible, I suppose.

SOCRATES: Not if you say that seeing is knowing. How are you going to deal with a question that leaves no loophole, when you are trapped like a beast in a pit and an imperturbable gentleman puts his hand over one of your eyes and asks if you can see his coat with c the eye that is covered?

THEAETETUS: I suppose I should say, No, not with that one, but I can with the other.

SOCRATES: So you both see and do not see the same thing at the same time?

THEAETETUS: Yes, in a sort of way.

SOCRATES: Never mind about the sort of way, he will reply. That was not the question I set you, but whether, when you know a thing, you also do not know it. In this instance you are obviously seeing something you don't see, and you have agreed that seeing is knowing and not-seeing is not-knowing. Now draw your conclusion. What is the consequence?

THEAETETUS: Well, I conclude that the consequence contra- d dicts my thesis.

SOCRATES: Yes, and you might have been reduced to the same condition by a number of further questions—whether knowing can be keen or dim, whether you can know from close at hand what you cannot know from a distance, or know the same thing with more or less intensity. A mercenary skirmisher in the war of words might lie in wait for you armed with a thousand such questions, once you have identified knowledge and perception. He would make his assaults upon hearing and smelling and suchlike senses and put you to confusion, sustaining his attack until your admiration of his in- e estimable skill betrayed you into his toils, and thereupon, leading you captive and bound, he would hold you to ransom for such a sum as you and he might agree upon.

And now, perhaps, you may wonder what argument Protagoras will find to defend his position. Shall we try to put it into words?

THEAETETUS: By all means.

SOCRATES: No doubt, then, Protagoras will make all the points we have put forward in our attempt to defend him, and at the same 166 time will come to close quarters with the assailant, dismissing us with contempt. Your admirable Socrates, he will say, finds a little boy who is scared at being asked whether one and the same person can remember and at the same time not know one and the same thing. When the child is frightened into saying no, because he cannot foresee the consequence, Socrates turns the conversation so as to make a figure of fun of my unfortunate self. You take things much too easily,

b Socrates. The truth of the matter is this. When you ask someone questions in order to canvass some opinion of mine and he is found tripping, then I am refuted only if his answers are such as I should have given; if they are different, it is he who is refuted, not I. For instance, do you think you will find anyone to admit that one's present memory of a past impression is an impression of the same character as one had during the original experience, which is now over? It is nothing of the sort. Or again, will anyone shrink from admitting that it is possible for the same person to know and not to know the same thing? Or, if he is frightened of saying that, will he ever allow that a person who is changed is the *same* as he was before the change occurred, or rather, that he is *one* person at all, and not several, indeed an infinite succession of persons, provided change goes on happening—if we are

c really to be on the watch against one another's attempts to catch at words?

No, he will say, show a more generous spirit by attacking what I actually say, and prove, if you can, that we have not, each one of us, his peculiar perceptions, or that, granting them to be peculiar, it would not follow that what appears to each becomes—or is, if we may use the word 'is'—for him alone to whom it appears. With this talk of pigs and baboons, you are behaving like a pig yourself, and, what is more, you tempt your hearers to treat my writings in the same way,

d which is not fair. For I do indeed assert that the truth is as I have written. Each one of us is a measure of what is and of what is not, but there is all the difference in the world between one man and another just in the very fact that what is and appears to one is different from what is and appears to the other. And as for wisdom and the wise man, I am very far from saying they do not exist. By a wise man I mean precisely a man who can change any one of us, when what is bad appears and is to him, and make what is good appear and be to him. In this statement, again, don't set off in chase of words, but let

e me explain still more clearly what I mean. Remember how it was put earlier in the conversation. To the sick man his food appears sour and is so; to the healthy man it is and appears the opposite. Now there is no call to represent either of the two as wiser—that cannot be—nor is

167 the sick man to be pronounced unwise because he thinks as he does, or the healthy man wise because he thinks differently. What is wanted is a change to the opposite condition, because the other state is better.

And so too in education a change has to be effected from the worse condition to the better; only, whereas the physician produces a change by means of drugs, the Sophist does it by discourse. It is not that a man makes someone who previously thought what is false think what is true, for it is not possible either to think the thing that is not or to think anything but what one experiences, and all experiences are true. Rather, I should say, when someone by reason of a b depraved condition of mind has thoughts of a like character, one makes him, by reason of a sound condition, think other and sound thoughts, which some people ignorantly call true, whereas I should say that one set of thoughts is better than the other, but not in any way truer. And as for the wise, my dear Socrates, so far from calling them frogs, I call them, when they have to do with the body, physicians, and when they have to do with plants, husbandmen. For I assert that husbandmen too, when plants are sickly and have depraved c sensations, substitute for these sensations that are sound and healthy, and moreover that wise and honest public speakers substitute in the community sound for unsound views of what is right. For I hold that whatever practices seem right and laudable to any particular state are so, for that state, so long as it holds by them. Only, when the practices are, in any particular case, unsound for them, the wise man substitutes others that are and appear sound. On the same principle the Sophist, since he can in the same manner guide his pupils in the way they should go, is wise and worth a considerable fee to them d when their education is completed. In this way it is true both that some men are wiser than others and that no one thinks falsely, and you, whether you like it or not, must put up with being a measure, since by these considerations my doctrine is saved from shipwreck.

Now if you can dispute this doctrine in principle, do so by argument stating the case on the other side, or by asking questions, if you prefer that method, which has no terrors for a man of sense; on the contrary it ought to be specially agreeable to him. Only there is this rule to be observed. Do not conduct your questioning unfairly. It is e very unreasonable that one who professes a concern for virtue should be constantly guilty of unfairness in argument. Unfairness here consists in not observing the distinction between a debate and a conversation. A debate need not be taken seriously and one may trip up an opponent to the best of one's power, but a conversation should be taken in earnest; one should help out the other party and bring home to him only those slips and fallacies that are due to himself or to his earlier instructors. If you follow this rule, your associates will lay 168 the blame for their confusions and perplexities on themselves and not on you; they will like you and court your society, and disgusted with themselves, will turn to philosophy, hoping to escape from their former selves and become different men. But if, like so many, you take the opposite course, you will reach the opposite result; instead of turning your companions to philosophy, you will make them hate b

the whole business when they get older. So, if you will take my advice, you will meet us in the candid spirit I spoke of, without hostility or contentiousness, and honestly consider what we mean when we say that all things are in motion and that what seems also is, to any individual or community. The further question whether knowledge is, or is not, the same thing as perception, you will consider as a consequence of these principles, not, as you did just now, basing your
c argument on the common use of words and phrases, which the vulgar twist into any sense they please and so perplex one another in all sorts of ways.

Such, Theodorus, is my contribution to the defense of your friend —the best I can make from my small means. Were he alive to speak for himself, it would be a much more impressive affair.

THEODORUS : You are not serious, Socrates; your defense was most spirited.

SOCRATES : Thank you, my friend. And now, did you notice how Protagoras was reproaching us for taking a child to argue with
d and using the boy's timidity to get the better of his own position in what he called a mere play of wit, in contrast to the solemnity of his measure of all things, and how he exhorted us to be serious about his doctrine?

THEODORUS : Of course I did, Socrates.

SOCRATES : What then? Do you think we should do as he says?

THEODORUS : Most certainly.

SOCRATES : Well, the company, as you see, are all children, ex-
e cept yourself. If we are to treat his doctrine seriously, as he enjoins, you and I must question one another. So we shall at any rate escape the charge of making light of it by discussing it with boys.

THEODORUS : Why, surely Theaetetus can follow up such an investigation better than a great many men with long beards.

SOCRATES : But not better than you, Theodorus. So don't im-
169 agine that you have no duty to your departed friend, but can leave it to me to make the best defense for him. Please come with us a little of the way at any rate—just until we know whether, in the matter of mathematical demonstrations, you cannot help being a measure, or everybody is just as competent as you in geometry and astronomy and all the other subjects you are supposed to excel in.

THEODORUS : It is no easy matter to escape questioning in your company, Socrates. I was deluded when I said you would leave me in peace and not force me into the ring like the Spartans; you seem to be
b as unrelenting as Sciron. The Spartans tell you to go away if you will not wrestle, but Antaeus is more in your line; you will let no one who comes near you go until you have stripped him by force for a trial of strength.

SOCRATES : Your comparisons exactly fit what is wrong with me, Theodorus, but my capacity for endurance is even greater. I have

encountered many heroes in debate, and times without number a
Hercules or a Theseus has broken my head, but I have so deep a passion for exercise of this sort that I stick to it all the same. So don't c
deny me the pleasure of a trial, for your own benefit as well as mine.

THEODORUS: I have no more to say; lead me where you will.
You are like Fate. No one can elude the toils of argument you spin for
him. But I shall not be able to oblige you beyond the point you have
proposed.

SOCRATES: Enough, if you will go so far. And please be on the
watch for fear we should be betrayed into arguing frivolously and be d
blamed for that again.

THEODORUS: I will try as well as I can.

SOCRATES: Let us begin, then, by coming to grips with the
doctrine at the same point as before. Let us see whether or not our dis-
content was justified, when we criticized it as making every individual
self-sufficient in wisdom. Protagoras then conceded that some people
were superior in the matter of what is better or worse, and these, he
said, were wise. Didn't he?

THEODORUS: Yes.

SOCRATES: If he were here himself to make that admission, instead of our conceding it for him in our defense, there would be no e
need to reopen the question and make sure of our ground, but, as
things are, we might be said to have no authority to make the admission on his behalf. So it will be more satisfactory to come to a more
complete and clear agreement on this particular point, for it makes a
considerable difference, whether this is so or not.

THEODORUS: That is true.

SOCRATES: Let us, then, as briefly as possible, obtain his agree- 170
ment, not through any third person, but from his own statement.

THEODORUS: How?

SOCRATES: In this way. He says, doesn't he, that what seems
true to anyone is true for him to whom it seems so?

THEODORUS: He does.

SOCRATES: Well now, Protagoras, we are expressing what
seems true to a man, or rather to all men, when we say that everyone
without exception holds that in some respects he is wiser than his
neighbors and in others they are wiser than he. For instance, in moments of great danger and distress, whether in war or in sickness
or at sea, men regard as a god anyone who can take control of the b
situation and look to him as a savior, when his only point of superiority is his knowledge. Indeed, the world is full of people looking for
those who can instruct and govern men and animals and direct their
doings, and on the other hand of people who think themselves quite
competent to undertake the teaching and governing. In all these
cases what can we say, if not that men do hold that wisdom and ignorance exist among them?

THEODORUS : We must say that.

SOCRATES : And they hold that wisdom lies in thinking truly, and ignorance in false belief?

c   THEODORUS : Of course.

SOCRATES : In that case, Protagoras, what are we to make of your doctrine? Are we to say that what men think is always true, or that it is sometimes true and sometimes false? From either supposition it results that their thoughts are not always true, but both true and false. For consider, Theodorus. Are you, or is any Protagorean, prepared to maintain that no one regards anyone else as ignorant or as making false judgments?

THEODORUS : That is incredible, Socrates.

d   SOCRATES : That, however, is the inevitable consequence of the doctrine which makes man the measure of all things.

THEODORUS : How so?

SOCRATES : When you have formed a judgment on some matter in your own mind and express an opinion about it to me, let us grant that, as Protagoras' theory says, it is true for you, but are we to understand that it is impossible for us, the rest of the company, to pronounce any judgment upon your judgment, or, if we can, that we always pronounce your opinion to be true? Do you not rather find thousands of opponents who set their opinion against yours on every occasion and hold that your judgment and belief are false?

e   THEODORUS : I should just think so, Socrates—thousands and tens of thousands, as Homer says, and they give me all the trouble in the world.

SOCRATES : And what then? Would you have us say that in such a case the opinion you hold is true for yourself and false for these tens of thousands?

THEODORUS : The doctrine certainly seems to imply that.

SOCRATES : And what is the consequence for Protagoras himself? Is it not this? Supposing that not even he believed in man being the measure and the world in general did not believe it either—as in 171 fact it doesn't—then this *Truth* which he wrote would not be true for anyone. If, on the other hand, he did believe it, but the mass of mankind does not agree with him, then, you see, it is more false than true by just so much as the unbelievers outnumber the believers.

THEODORUS : That follows, if its truth or falsity varies with each individual opinion.

SOCRATES : Yes, and besides that it involves a really exquisite conclusion. Protagoras, for his part, admitting as he does that everybody's opinion is true, must acknowledge the truth of his opponents' belief about his own belief, where they think he is wrong.

THEODORUS : Certainly.

b   SOCRATES : That is to say, he would acknowledge his own belief to be false, if he admits that the belief of those who think him wrong is true?

THEODORUS: Necessarily.

SOCRATES: But the others, on their side, do not admit to themselves that they are wrong.

THEODORUS: No.

SOCRATES: Whereas Protagoras, once more, according to what he has written, admits that this opinion of theirs is as true as any other.

THEODORUS: Evidently.

SOCRATES: On all hands, then, Protagoras included, his opinion will be disputed, or rather Protagoras will join in the general consent —when he admits to an opponent the truth of his contrary opinion, from that moment Protagoras himself will be admitting that a dog or c the man in the street is not a measure of anything whatever that he does not understand. Isn't that so?

THEODORUS: Yes.

SOCRATES: Then, since it is disputed by everyone, the *Truth* of Protagoras is true to nobody—to himself no more than to anyone else.

THEODORUS: We are running my old friend too hard, Socrates.

SOCRATES: But it is not clear that we are outrunning the truth, my friend. Of course it is likely that, as an older man, he was d wiser than we are, and if at this moment he could pop his head up through the ground there as far as to the neck, very probably he would expose me thoroughly for talking such nonsense and you for agreeing to it, before he sank out of sight and took to his heels. However, we must do our best with such lights as we have and continue to say what we think. Now, for instance, must we not say that everyone would agree at least to this, that one man can be wiser or more ignorant than another?

THEODORUS: I certainly think so.

SOCRATES: And further, shall we say that the doctrine would find its firmest footing in the position we traced out in our defense of e Protagoras, that most things—hot, dry, sweet, everything of that sort —are to each person as they appear to him? Whereas, if there is any case in which the theory would concede that one man is superior to another, it might consent to admit that, in the matter of good or bad health, not any woman or child—or animal, for that matter—knows what is wholesome for it and is capable of curing itself, but that here, if anywhere, one person is superior to another.

THEODORUS: I should certainly say so.

SOCRATES: And again in social matters, the theory will say 172 that, so far as good and bad customs or rights and wrongs or matters of religion are concerned, whatever any state makes up its mind to enact as lawful for itself, really is lawful for it, and in this field no individual or state is wiser than another. But where it is a question of laying down what is for its advantage or disadvantage, once more there, if anywhere, the theory will admit a difference between two advisers or between the decisions of two different states in respect of b truth, and would hardly venture to assert that any enactment which a state supposes to be for its advantage will quite certainly be so.

But, in that field I am speaking of—in right and wrong and matters of religion—people are ready to affirm that none of these things is natural, with a reality of its own, but rather that the public decision becomes true at the moment when it is made and remains true so long as the decision stands, and those who do not argue altogether as c Protagoras does carry on their philosophy on these lines.

But one theory after another is coming upon us, Theodorus, and the last is more important than the one before.

THEODORUS : Well, Socrates, we have time at our disposal.

SOCRATES : Evidently. And it strikes me now, as often before, how natural it is that men who have spent much time in philosophical studies should look ridiculous when they appear as speakers in a court of law.

THEODORUS : How do you mean?

SOCRATES : When you compare men who have knocked about from their youth up in law courts and such places with others d bred in philosophical pursuits, the one set seem to have been trained as slaves, the others as free men.

THEODORUS : In what way?

SOCRATES : In the way you spoke of. The free man always has time at his disposal to converse in peace at his leisure. He will pass, as we are doing now, from one argument to another—we have just reached the third. Like us, he will leave the old for a fresh one which takes his fancy more, and he does not care how long or short the discussion may be, if only it attains the truth. The orator is always talk- e ing against time, hurried on by the clock; there is no space to enlarge upon any subject he chooses, but the adversary stands over him ready to recite a schedule of the points to which he must confine himself. He is a slave disputing about a fellow slave before a master sitting in judgment with some definite plea in his hand, and the issue is never indifferent, but his personal concerns are always at stake, sometimes 173 even his life. Hence he acquires a tense and bitter shrewdness; he knows how to flatter his master and earn his good graces, but his mind is narrow and crooked. An apprenticeship in slavery has dwarfed and twisted his growth and robbed him of his free spirit, driving him into devious ways, threatening him with fears and dangers which the tenderness of youth could not face with truth and honesty; so, turning from the first to lies and the requital of wrong with wrong, b warped and stunted, he passes from youth to manhood with no soundness in him and turns out, in the end, a man of formidable intellect— as he imagines.

So much for the orator, Theodorus. Shall I now describe the philosophical choir to which we belong, or would you rather leave that and go back to our discussion? We must not abuse that freedom we claimed of ranging from one subject to another.

THEODORUS: No, Socrates, let us have your description first. As you said quite rightly, we are not the servants of the argument, c which must stand and wait for the moment when we choose to pursue this or that topic to a conclusion. We are not in a court under the judge's eye, nor in the theater with an audience to criticize our philosophical evolutions.

SOCRATES: Then, if that is your wish, let us speak of the leaders in philosophy, for the weaker members may be neglected. From their youth up they have never known the way to market place or law d court or Council Chamber or any other place of public assembly; they never hear a decree read out or look at the text of a law. To take any interest in the rivalries of political cliques, in meetings, dinners, and merrymakings with flute girls, never occurs to them even in dreams. Whether any fellow citizen is well- or ill-born or has inherited some defect from his ancestors on either side, the philosopher knows no more than how many pints of water there are in the sea. He is not even aware that he knows nothing of all this, for if he holds aloof, it is not for reputation's sake, but because it is really only his body that so- e journs in his city, while his thought, disdaining all such things as worthless, takes wings, as Pindar says, 'beyond the sky, beneath the earth,' searching the heavens and measuring the plains, everywhere seeking the true nature of everything as a whole, never sinking to what 174 lies close at hand.

THEODORUS: What do you mean, Socrates?

SOCRATES: The same thing as the story about the Thracian maidservant who exercised her wit at the expense of Thales, when he was looking up to study the stars and tumbled down a well. She scoffed at him for being so eager to know what was happening in the sky that he could not see what lay at his feet. Anyone who gives his life to philosophy is open to such mockery. It is true that he is un- b aware what his next-door neighbor is doing, hardly knows, indeed, whether the creature is a man at all; he spends all his pains on the question, what man is, and what powers and properties distinguish such a nature from any other. You see what I mean, Theodorus?

THEODORUS: Yes, and it is true.

SOCRATES: And so, my friend, as I said at first, on a public occasion or in private company, in a law court or anywhere else, when c he is forced to talk about what lies at his feet or is before his eyes, the whole rabble will join the maidservants in laughing at him, as from inexperience he walks blindly and stumbles into every pitfall. His terrible clumsiness makes him seem so stupid. He cannot engage in an exchange of abuse, for, never having made a study of anyone's peculiar weaknesses, he has no personal scandals to bring up; so in his helplessness he looks a fool. When people vaunt their own or other d men's merits, his unaffected laughter makes him conspicuous and they think he is frivolous. When a despot or king is eulogized, he fancies he is hearing some keeper of swine or sheep or cows being

congratulated on the quantity of milk he has squeezed out of his flock; only he reflects that the animal that princes tend and milk is more given than sheep or cows to nurse a sullen grievance, and that a herds-
e man of this sort, penned up in his castle, is doomed by sheer press of work to be as rude and uncultivated as the shepherd in his mountain fold. He hears of the marvelous wealth of some landlord who owns ten thousand acres or more, but that seems a small matter to one accus- tomed to think of the earth as a whole. When they harp upon birth— some gentleman who can point to seven generations of wealthy an- cestors—he thinks that such commendation must come from men of
175 purblind vision, too uneducated to keep their eyes fixed on the whole or to reflect that any man has had countless myriads of ancestors and among them any number of rich men and beggars, kings and slaves, Greeks and barbarians. To pride oneself on a catalogue of twenty-five progenitors going back to Heracles, son of Amphitryon, strikes him as showing a strange pettiness of outlook. He laughs at a man who can-
b not rid his mind of foolish vanity by reckoning that before Amphit- ryon there was a twenty-fifth ancestor, and before him a fiftieth, whose fortunes were as luck would have it. But in all these matters the world has the laugh of the philosopher, partly because he seems arro- gant, partly because of his helpless ignorance in matters of daily life.

THEODORUS: Yes, Socrates, that is exactly what happens.

SOCRATES: On the other hand, my friend, when the philoso-
c pher drags the other upward to a height at which he may consent to drop the question, 'What injustice have I done to you or you to me?' and to think about justice and injustice in themselves, what each is, and how they differ from one another and from anything else, or to stop quoting poetry about the happiness of kings or of men with gold in store and think about the meaning of kingship and the whole ques- tion of human happiness and misery, what their nature is, and how
d humanity can gain the one and escape the other—in all this field, when that small, shrewd, legal mind has to render an account, then the situation is reversed. Now it is he who is dizzy from hanging at such an unaccustomed height and looking down from mid-air. Lost and dismayed and stammering, he will be laughed at, not by maid- servants or the uneducated—they will not see what is happening— but by everyone whose breeding has been the antithesis of a slave's.
e Such are the two characters, Theodorus. The one is nursed in freedom and leisure, the philosopher, as you call him. He may be ex- cused if he looks foolish or useless when faced with some menial task, if he cannot tie up bedclothes into a neat bundle or flavor a dish with spices and a speech with flattery. The other is smart in the dis-
176 patch of all such services, but has not learned to wear his cloak like a gentleman, or caught the accent of discourse that will rightly cele- brate the true life of happiness for gods and men.

THEODORUS: If you could convince everyone, Socrates, as you

convince me, there would be more peace and fewer evils in the world.

SOCRATES: Evils, Theodorus, can never be done away with, for the good must always have its contrary; nor have they any place in the divine world, but they must needs haunt this region of our mortal nature. That is why we should make all speed to take flight from this b world to the other, and that means becoming like the divine so far as we can, and that again is to become righteous with the help of wisdom. But it is no such easy matter to convince men that the reasons for avoiding wickedness and seeking after goodness are not those which the world gives. The right motive is not that one should seem innocent and good—that is no better, to my thinking, than an old wives' tale—but let us state the truth in this way. In the divine there is no shadow of unrighteousness, only the perfection of righteousness, c and nothing is more like the divine than any one of us who becomes as righteous as possible. It is here that a man shows his true spirit and power or lack of spirit and nothingness. For to know this is wisdom and excellence of the genuine sort; not to know it is to be manifestly blind and base. All other forms of seeming power and intelligence in the rulers of society are as mean and vulgar as the mechanic's skill in handicraft. If a man's words and deeds are unrighteous and profane, d he had best not persuade himself that he is a great man because he sticks at nothing, glorying in his shame as such men do when they fancy that others say of them, They are no fools, no useless burdens to the earth, but men of the right sort to weather the storms of public life.

Let the truth be told. They are what they fancy they are not, all the more for deceiving themselves, for they are ignorant of the very thing it most concerns them to know—the penalty of injustice. This is not, as they imagine, stripes and death, which do not always fall on the wrongdoer, but a penalty that cannot be escaped.   e

THEODORUS: What penalty is that?

SOCRATES: There are two patterns, my friend, in the unchangeable nature of things, one of divine happiness, the other of godless misery—a truth to which their folly makes them utterly blind, unaware that in doing injustice they are growing less like one of these patterns and more like the other. The penalty they pay is the life they 177 lead, answering to the pattern they resemble. But if we tell them that, unless they rid themselves of their superior cunning, that other region which is free from all evil will not receive them after death, but here on earth they will dwell for all time in some form of life resembling their own and in the society of things as evil as themselves, all this will sound like foolishness to such strong and unscrupulous minds.

THEODORUS: So it will, Socrates.

SOCRATES: I have good reason to know it, my friend. But there b is one thing about them; when you get them alone and make them explain their objections to philosophy, then, if they are men enough to face a long examination without running away, it is odd how they end by finding their own arguments unsatisfying. Somehow their flow of eloquence runs dry, and they become as speechless as an infant.

All this, however, is a digression. We must stop now, and dam the flood of topics that threatens to break in and drown our original
c argument. With your leave, let us go back to where we were before.

THEODORUS : For my part, I rather prefer listening to your digressions, Socrates; they are easier to follow at my time of life. However, let us go back, if you like.

SOCRATES : Very well. I think the point we had reached was this. We were saying that the believers in a perpetually changing reality and in the doctrine that what seems to an individual at any time also is for him would, in most matters, strongly insist upon their principle, and not least in the case of what is right they would maintain that any enactments a state may decide on certainly are right for that state so long as they remain in force. But when it comes to what is good, we said that the boldest would not go to the length of contend-
d ing that whatever a state may believe and declare to be advantageous for itself is in fact advantageous for so long as it is declared to be so— unless he meant that the name 'advantageous' would continue to be so applied, but that would be turning our subject into a joke.

THEODORUS : Certainly.
e SOCRATES : We will suppose, then, that he does not mean the name, but has in view the thing that bears it.

THEODORUS : We will.

SOCRATES : Whatever name the state may give it, advantage is surely the aim of its legislation, and all its laws, to the full extent of its belief and power, are laid down as being for its own best profit. Or has it any other object in view when it makes laws?
178 THEODORUS : None.

SOCRATES : Then does it also hit the mark every time? Or does every state often miss its aim completely?

THEODORUS : I should say that mistakes are often made.

SOCRATES : We may have a still better chance of getting everyone to assent to that, if we start from a question covering the whole class of things which includes the advantageous. It is, I suggest, a thing that has to do with future time. When we legislate, we make our laws with the idea that they *will be* advantageous in time to come. We may call this class 'what is going to be.'
b THEODORUS : Certainly.

SOCRATES : Here, then, is a question for Protagoras or anyone else who agrees with him. According to you and your friends, Protagoras, man is the measure of all things—of white and heavy and light and everything of that sort. He possesses in himself the test of these things, and believing them to be such as he experiences them, he believes what is true and real for him. Is that right?

THEODORUS: Yes.

SOCRATES: Is it also true, Protagoras, we shall continue, that he possesses within himself the test of what is going to be in the future, and that whatever a man believes will be, actually comes to pass for him who believes it? Take heat, for example. When some layman believes that he is going to catch a fever and that this hotness is going to exist, and another, who is a physician, believes the contrary, are we to suppose that the future event will turn out in accordance with one of the two opinions, or in accordance with both opinions, so that to the physician the patient will not be hot or in a fever, while he will be both these things to himself?

THEODORUS: That would be absurd.

SOCRATES: And on the question whether a wine is going to be sweet or dry, I imagine the vinegrower's judgment is authoritative, not a flute player's.

THEODORUS: Of course.

SOCRATES: Or again, on the question whether a piece of music is going to be in tune or not, a gymnastic trainer would not have a better opinion than a musician as to what the trainer himself will later judge to be in good tune.

THEODORUS: By no means.

SOCRATES: And when a feast is being prepared, the guest who is to be invited, supposing him not to be an expert in cookery, will have a less authoritative opinion than the confectioner upon the pleasure that will result. We will not dispute yet about what already is or has been pleasant to any individual, but about what will in the future seem and be to anyone, is every man the best judge for himself, or would you, Protagoras—at least in the matter of the arguments that any one of us would find convincing for a court of law—have a better opinion beforehand than any untrained person?

THEODORUS: Certainly, Socrates, in that matter he did emphatically profess to be superior to everybody.

SOCRATES: Bless your soul, I should think he did. No one would have paid huge sums to talk with him, if he had not convinced the people who came to him that no one whatever, not even a prophet, could judge better than he what was going to be and appear in the future.

THEODORUS: Quite true.

SOCRATES: And legislation, too, and the question of advantageousness are matters concerned with the future, and everyone would agree that a state, when it makes its laws, must often fail to hit upon its own greatest advantage?

THEODORUS: Assuredly.

SOCRATES : Then we may quite reasonably put it to your master
b that he must admit that one man is wiser than another and that the
wiser man is the measure, whereas an ignorant person like myself is
not in any way bound to be a measure, as our defense of Protagoras
tried to make me, whether I liked it or not.

THEODORUS : I think that is the weakest point in the theory,
Socrates, though it is also assailable in that it makes other people's
opinions valid when, as it turns out, they hold Protagoras' assertions
to be quite untrue.

c   SOCRATES : There are many other ways, Theodorus, of assailing such a position and proving that not every opinion of every person
is true. But with regard to what the individual experiences at the moment—the source of his sensations and the judgments in accordance
with them—it is harder to assail the truth of these. Perhaps it is
wrong to say 'harder'; maybe they are unassailable, and those who
assert that they are transparently clear and are instances of knowledge may be in the right, and Theaetetus was not beside the mark
d when he said that perception and knowledge were the same thing.

We must, then, look more closely into the matter, as our defense
of Protagoras enjoined, and study this moving reality, ringing its
metal to hear if it sounds true or cracked. However that may be,
there has been no inconsiderable battle over it, and not a few combatants.

THEODORUS : Anything but inconsiderable; in Ionia, indeed, it
is actually growing in violence. The followers of Heraclitus lead the
choir of this persuasion with the greatest vigor.

SOCRATES : All the more reason, my dear Theodorus, to look
e into it carefully and to follow their lead by tracing it to its source.

THEODORUS : By all means. For there is no discussing these
principles of Heraclitus—or, as you say, of Homer or still more ancient sages—with the Ephesians themselves, who profess to be familiar with them; you might as well talk to a maniac. Faithful to their
own treatises they are literally in perpetual motion; their capacity
for staying still to attend to an argument or a question or for a quiet
180 interchange of question and answer amounts to less than nothing, or
rather even a minus quantity is too strong an expression for the absence of the least modicum of repose in these gentry. When you put a
question, they pluck from their quiver little oracular aphorisms to let
fly at you, and if you try to obtain some account of their meaning, you
will be instantly transfixed by another, barbed with some newly forged
metaphor. You will never get anywhere with any of them; for that
matter they cannot get anywhere with one another, but they take very
good care to leave nothing settled either in discourse or in their own
b minds. I suppose they think that would be something stationary—a
thing they will fight against to the last and do their utmost to banish
from the universe.

SOCRATES: Perhaps, Theodorus, you have seen these gentlemen in the fray and never met them in their peaceable moments; indeed they are no friends of yours. I dare say they keep such matters to be explained at leisure to their pupils whom they want to make like themselves.

THEODORUS: Pupils indeed! My good friend, there is no such thing as a master or pupil among them; they spring up like mush- c rooms. Each one gets his inspiration wherever he can, and not one of them thinks that another understands anything. So, as I was going to say, you can never bring them to book, either with or without their consent. We must take over the question ourselves and try to solve it like a problem.

SOCRATES: That is a reasonable proposal. As to this problem, then, have we not here a tradition from the ancients, who hid their meaning from the common herd in poetical figures, that Oceanus and d Tethys, the source of all things, are flowing streams and nothing is at rest? And do not the moderns, in their superior wisdom, declare the same quite openly, in order that the very cobblers may hear and understand their wisdom and, abandoning their simple faith that some things stand still while others move, may reverence those who teach them that everything is in motion?

But I had almost forgotten, Theodorus, another school which teaches just the opposite—that reality 'is one, immovable, being is the e name of the all,' [3] and much else that men like Melissus and Parmenides maintain in opposition to all those people, telling us that all things are a unity which stays still within itself, having no room to move in. How are we to deal with all these combatants? For, little by little, our 181 advance has brought us, without our knowing it, between the two lines, and, unless we can somehow fend them off and slip through, we shall suffer for it, as in that game they play in the wrestling schools, where the players are caught by both sides and dragged both ways at once across the line. The best plan, I think, will be to begin by taking a look at the party whom we first approached, the men of flux, and if there seems to be anything in what they say, we will help them to pull us over to their side and try to elude the others. But if we find more truth in the partisans of the immovable whole, we will desert to them from these revolutionaries who leave no landmark unremoved. If both sides turn out to be quite unreasonable, we shall merely look foolish if b we suppose that nobodies like ourselves can make any contribution after rejecting such paragons of ancient wisdom. Do you think it worth while to go further in the teeth of such danger, Theodorus?

THEODORUS: Certainly, Socrates. I could not bear to stop before we have found out what each of the two parties means.

SOCRATES: Well, if you feel so strongly about it, we must look

[3] Parmenides, line 98 (ed. Mullach).

into the matter. I think our study of change should begin with the
c question, What after all do they mean when they say all things are in
change? What I mean is this. Do they recognize one kind of change
or two? I think there are two, but I must not be alone in my opinion;
you must take your share in the risk, so that we may meet together
whatever fate shall befall us. Tell me, do you call it change when
something removes from place to place or revolves in the same place?

THEODORUS : Yes.

SOCRATES : Let that be one kind, then. Now suppose a thing
stays in the same place but grows old or turns black instead of white or
d hard instead of soft or alters in some other way, isn't it proper to call
that a different kind of change?

THEODORUS : Yes, it must be.

SOCRATES : So I should recognize these as two kinds of change
—alteration and local movement.

THEODORUS : And you are right.

SOCRATES : Having made that distinction, then, let us now begin our talk with these people who say that everything is in change
and ask them, Do you say everything is in both sorts of change—both
e moving in place and altering—or that part changes in both ways, part
in only one of the two?

THEODORUS : I really cannot tell, but I think they would say 'in
both ways.'

SOCRATES : Yes, my friend; otherwise they will find things at
rest as well as things in change, and it will be no more correct to say
that everything is changing than to say that everything is at rest.

THEODORUS : Quite true.

SOCRATES : So, since they are to be in change and unchanging-
182 ness must be impossible anywhere, all things are always in every kind
of change.

THEODORUS : That follows.

SOCRATES : Now consider this point in their theory. The account they gave of the genesis of hotness or whiteness or whatever it
may be, we stated, didn't we, in this sort of way—that any one of these
things is something that moves in place, simultaneously with a perception, between agent and patient, and that the patient becomes per-
ceptive, not a perception, while the agent comes to have a quality,
rather than to be a quality? Perhaps this word 'quality' strikes you as
queer and uncouth and you don't understand it as a general expres-
b sion; so let me give particular instances. The agent does not become
hotness or whiteness, but hot or white, and so on with all the rest. No
doubt you remember how we put this earlier—that nothing has any
being as one thing just by itself, no more has the agent or patient, but,
as a consequence of their intercourse with one another, in giving birth
to the perceptions and the things perceived, the agents come to be of
such and such a quality, and the patients come to be percipient.

THEODORUS: I remember, of course.

SOCRATES: Very well, then, we will not inquire into other parts c of their theory, whether they mean this or that, but keep to the point we have in view and ask them this. All things, by your account, are in a perpetual stream of change. Is that so?

THEODORUS: Yes.

SOCRATES: With both the kinds of change we distinguished—both moving in place and altering?

THEODORUS: Certainly, if they are to be completely in change.

SOCRATES: Well now, if they only moved in place without altering in quality, we should be able to say what qualities they have as they move in this stream, shouldn't we?

THEODORUS: Yes.

SOCRATES: Since, however, there is nothing constant here ei- d ther—the flowing thing does not flow white but changes, so that the very whiteness itself flows and shifts into another color, in order that the thing may escape the charge of constancy in that respect—can we ever give it the name of any color and be sure that we are naming it rightly?

THEODORUS: How can that be done, Socrates? Or how can anything else of the kind you mean be called by its right name, if, while we are speaking, it is all the time slipping away from us in this stream?

SOCRATES: And again, what are we to say of a perception of any sort—for instance, the perception of seeing or hearing? Are we to say that it ever abides in its own nature as seeing or hearing?   e

THEODORUS: It certainly ought not, if all things are in change.

SOCRATES: Then it has no right to be called seeing, any more than not-seeing, nor is any other perception entitled to be called perception rather than not-perception, if everything is changing in every kind of way.

THEODORUS: No, it hasn't.

SOCRATES: And moreover perception is knowledge, according to Theaetetus and me.

THEODORUS: Yes, you did say so.

SOCRATES: In that case, our answer to the question, what knowledge is, did not mean knowledge any more than not-knowledge.

THEODORUS: So it appears.

SOCRATES: That would be a pretty result of the improvement 183 we made upon that first answer, when we were so eager to prove it right by showing that everything is in change. Now it seems that what has in fact come to light is that, if all things are in change, any answer that can be given to any question is equally right; you may say it is so and it is not so—or 'becomes,' if you prefer to avoid any term that would bring these people to a standstill.

THEODORUS: You are right.

SOCRATES: Except, Theodorus, that I used the words 'so' and 'not so,' whereas we have no right to use this word 'so'—what is 'so' b would cease to be in change—nor yet 'not so'; there is no change in that either. Some new dialect will have to be instituted for the exponents of this theory, since, as it is, they have no phrases to fit their fundamental proposition—unless indeed it were 'not even nohow.' That might be an expression indefinite enough to suit them.

THEODORUS: A most appropriate idiom.

SOCRATES: So, Theodorus, we are quit of your old friend, and not yet ready to concede to him that every man is the measure of all c things, if he is not a wise man. Also, we shall not admit that knowledge is perception, at least on the basis of the theory that all things are in change, unless Theaetetus has some objection.

THEODORUS: That is excellent, Socrates. For now these questions are disposed of, it was agreed that I should be quit of answering your questions, as soon as the discussion of Protagoras' theory should come to an end.

THEAETETUS: No, Theodorus, you must not be released until you and Socrates, as you proposed just now, have discussed those oth-d ers who assert that the whole of things is at rest.

THEODORUS: Would you teach your elders, Theaetetus, to dishonor their agreements? No, for what remains you must prepare yourself to carry on the argument with Socrates.

THEAETETUS: Yes, if he wishes, though I would much rather have been a listener while this subject is discussed.

THEODORUS: To invite Socrates to an argument is like inviting cavalry to fight on level ground. You will have something to listen to, if you question him.

SOCRATES: Well, but, Theodorus, I think I shall not comply e with Theaetetus' request.

THEODORUS: Not comply? What do you mean?

SOCRATES: A feeling of respect keeps me from treating in an unworthy spirit Melissus and the others who say the universe is one and at rest, but there is one being whom I respect above all. Parmenides himself is in my eyes, as Homer says, a 'reverend and awful' [4] figure. I met him when I was quite young and he quite elderly, and I 184 thought there was a sort of depth in him that was altogether noble. I am afraid we might not understand his words and still less follow the thought they express. Above all, the original purpose of our discussion—the nature of knowledge—might be thrust out of sight, if we attend to these importunate topics that keep breaking in upon us. In particular, this subject we are raising now is of vast extent. It cannot be fairly treated as a side issue, and an adequate handling would take so long that we should lose sight of our question about knowledge.

---

[4] *Iliad* 3.172; *Odyssey* 8.22; 14.234.

Either course would be wrong. My business is rather to try, by means of my midwife's art, to deliver Theaetetus of his conceptions about b knowledge.

THEODORUS: Well, do so, if you think that best.

SOCRATES: Well then, Theaetetus, here is a point for you to consider. The answer you gave was that knowledge is perception, wasn't it?

THEAETETUS: Yes.

SOCRATES: Now suppose you were asked, When a man sees white or black things or hears high or low tones, what does he see or hear with? I suppose you would say with eyes and ears.

THEAETETUS: Yes, I should.

SOCRATES: To use words and phrases in an easygoing way c without scrutinizing them too curiously is not, in general, a mark of ill breeding; on the contrary there is something lowbred in being too precise. But sometimes there is no help for it, and this is a case in which I must take exception to the form of your answer. Consider. Is it more correct to say that we see and hear *with* our eyes and ears or *through* them?

THEAETETUS: I should say we always perceive through them, rather than with them.

SOCRATES: Yes, it would surely be strange that there should be d a number of senses ensconced inside us, like the warriors in the Trojan horse, and all these things should not converge and meet in some single nature—a mind, or whatever it is to be called—*with* which we perceive all the objects of perception *through* the senses as instruments.

THEAETETUS: Yes, I think that is a better description.

SOCRATES: My object in being so precise is to know whether there is some part of ourselves, the same in all cases, with which we apprehend black or white through the eyes, and objects of other kinds e through the other senses. Can you, if the question is put to you, refer all such acts of apprehension to the body? Perhaps, however, it would be better you should speak for yourself in reply to questions, instead of my taking the words out of your mouth. Tell me, all these instruments through which you perceive what is warm or hard or light or sweet are parts of the body, aren't they, not of anything else?

THEAETETUS: Of nothing else.

SOCRATES: Now will you also agree that the objects you per- 185 ceive through one faculty cannot be perceived through another—objects of hearing, for instance, through sight, or objects of sight through hearing?

THEAETETUS: Of course I will.

SOCRATES: Then, if you have some thought about both objects at once, you cannot be having a perception including both at once through either the one or the other organ.

THEAETETUS: No.

SOCRATES: Now take sound and color. Have you not, to begin with, this thought which includes both at once—that they both *exist*?

THEAETETUS: I have.

SOCRATES: And, further, that each of the two is *different* from the other and the *same* as itself?

b   THEAETETUS: Naturally.

SOCRATES: And again, that both together are *two,* and each of them is *one*?

THEAETETUS: Yes.

SOCRATES: And also you can ask yourself whether they are *unlike* each other or *alike*?

THEAETETUS: No doubt.

SOCRATES: Then through what organ do you think all this about them both? What is common to them both cannot be apprehended either through hearing or through sight. Besides, here is further evidence for my point. Suppose it were possible to inquire whether sound and color were both brackish or not; no doubt you c   could tell me what faculty you would use—obviously not sight or hearing, but some other.

THEAETETUS: Of course, the faculty that works through the tongue.

SOCRATES: Very good. But now, through what organ does that faculty work, which tells you what is common not only to these objects but to all things—what you mean by the words 'exists' and 'does not exist' and the other terms applied to them in the questions I put a moment ago? What sort of organs can you mention, corresponding to all these terms, through which the perceiving part of us perceives each one of them?

THEAETETUS: You mean existence and nonexistence, likeness and unlikeness, sameness and difference, and also unity and numbers d   in general as applied to them, and clearly your question covers 'even' and 'odd' and all that kind of notions. You are asking through what part of the body our mind perceives these?

SOCRATES: You follow me most admirably, Theaetetus; that is exactly my question.

THEAETETUS: Really, Socrates, I could not say, except that I think there is no special organ at all for these things, as there is for the e   others. It is clear to me that the mind in itself is its own instrument for contemplating the common terms that apply to everything.

SOCRATES: In fact, Theaetetus, you are handsome, not ugly as Theodorus said you were, for in a discussion handsome is that handsome does. And you have treated me more than handsomely in saving me the trouble of a very long argument, if it is clear to you that the mind contemplates some things through its own instrumentality, oth-

ers through the bodily faculties. That was indeed what I thought myself, but I wanted you to agree.

THEAETETUS: Well, it is clear to me.

SOCRATES: Under which head, then, do you place existence? 186
For that is, above all, a thing that belongs to everything.

THEAETETUS: I should put it among the things that the mind
apprehends by itself.

SOCRATES: And also likeness and unlikeness and sameness and
difference?

THEAETETUS: Yes.

SOCRATES: And how about 'honorable' and 'dishonorable' and
'good' and 'bad'?

THEAETETUS: Those again seem to me, above all, to be things
whose being is considered, one in comparison with another, by the b
mind, when it reflects within itself upon the past and the present with
an eye to the future.

SOCRATES: Wait a moment. The hardness of something hard
and the softness of something soft will be perceived by the mind
through touch, will they not?

THEAETETUS: Yes.

SOCRATES: But their existence and the fact that they both exist, and their contrariety to one another and again the existence of this
contrariety are things which the mind itself undertakes to judge for
us, when it reflects upon them and compares one with another.

THEAETETUS: Certainly.

SOCRATES: Is it not true, then, that whereas all the impressions which penetrate to the mind through the body are things which
men and animals alike are naturally constituted to perceive from the c
moment of birth, reflections about them with respect to their existence and usefulness only come, if they come at all, with difficulty
through a long and troublesome process of education?

THEAETETUS: Assuredly.

SOCRATES: Is it possible, then, to reach truth when one cannot reach existence?

THEAETETUS: It is impossible.

SOCRATES: But if a man cannot reach the truth of a thing, can
he possibly know that thing?

THEAETETUS: No, Socrates, how could he?   d

SOCRATES: If that is so, knowledge does not reside in the impressions, but in our reflection upon them. It is there, seemingly, and
not in the impressions, that it is possible to grasp existence and truth.

THEAETETUS: Evidently.

SOCRATES: Then are you going to give the same name to two
things which differ so widely?

THEAETETUS: Surely that would not be right.

892 PLATO : COLLECTED DIALOGUES

SOCRATES : Well then, what name do you give to the first one—to seeing, hearing, smelling, feeling cold and feeling warm?

e   THEAETETUS : Perceiving. What other name is there for it?

SOCRATES : Taking it all together, then, you call this perception?

THEAETETUS : Necessarily.

SOCRATES : A thing which, we agree, has no part in apprehending truth, since it has none in apprehending existence.

THEAETETUS : No, it has none.

SOCRATES : Nor, consequently, in knowledge either.

THEAETETUS : No.

SOCRATES : Then, Theaetetus, perception and knowledge cannot possibly be the same thing.

THEAETETUS : Evidently not, Socrates. Indeed, it is now perfectly plain that knowledge is something different from perception.

187   SOCRATES : But when we began our talk it was certainly not our object to find out what knowledge is not, but what it is. Still, we have advanced so far as to see that we must not look for it in sense perception at all, but in what goes on when the mind is occupied with things by itself, whatever name you give to that.

THEAETETUS : Well, Socrates, the name for that, I imagine, is 'making judgments.'

b   SOCRATES : You are right, my friend. Now begin all over again. Blot out all we have been saying, and see if you can get a clearer view from the position you have now reached. Tell us once more what knowledge is.

THEAETETUS : I cannot say it is judgment as a whole, because there is false judgment, but perhaps true judgment is knowledge. You may take that as my answer. If, as we go further, it turns out to be less convincing than it seems now, I will try to find another.

SOCRATES : Good, Theaetetus. This promptness is much better c than hanging back as you did at first. If we go on like this, either we shall find what we are after, or we shall be less inclined to imagine we know something of which we know nothing whatever, and that surely is a reward not to be despised. And now, what is this you say— that there are two sorts of judgment, one true, the other false, and you define knowledge as judgment that is true?

THEAETETUS : Yes, that is the view I have come to now.

SOCRATES : Then, had we better go back to a point that came up about judgment?

THEAETETUS : What point do you mean?

d   SOCRATES : A question that worries me now, as often before, and has much perplexed me in my own mind and also in talking to others. I cannot explain the nature of this experience we have, or how it can arise in our minds.

THEAETETUS: What experience?

SOCRATES: Making a false judgment. At this moment I am still in doubt and wondering whether to let that question alone or to follow it further, not as we did a while ago, but in a new way.

THEAETETUS: Why not, Socrates, if it seems to be in the least necessary? Only just now, when you and Theodorus were speaking of leisure, you said very rightly that there is no pressing hurry in a discussion of this sort.

SOCRATES: A good reminder, for this may be the right moment e to go back upon our track. It is better to carry through a small task well than make a bad job of a big one.

THEAETETUS: Certainly it is.

SOCRATES: How shall we set about it, then? What is it that we do mean? Do we assert that there is in every case a false judgment, and that one of us thinks what is false, another what is true, such being the nature of things?

THEAETETUS: Certainly we do.

SOCRATES: And, in each and all cases, it is possible for us ei- 188 ther to know a thing or not to know it? I leave out of account for the moment becoming acquainted with things and forgetting, considered as falling between the two. Our argument is not concerned with them just now.

THEAETETUS: Well then, Socrates, there is no third alternative left in any case, besides knowing and not-knowing.

SOCRATES: And it follows at once that when one is thinking he must be thinking either of something he knows or of something he does not know?

THEAETETUS: Necessarily.

SOCRATES: And further, if you know a thing, you cannot also b not know it, and if you do not know it, you cannot also know it?

THEAETETUS: Of course.

SOCRATES: Then is the man who thinks what is false supposing that things he knows are not those things but other things he knows, so that, while he knows both, he fails to recognize either?

THEAETETUS: No, that is impossible, Socrates.

SOCRATES: Well then, is he supposing that things he does not know are other things he does not know? Is this possible—that a man who knows neither Theaetetus nor Socrates should take it into his head that Socrates is Theaetetus or Theaetetus Socrates?

THEAETETUS: No. How could he?   c

SOCRATES: But surely a man does not imagine that things he does know are things he does not know, or that things he does not know are things he knows?

THEAETETUS: No, that would be a miracle.

SOCRATES: What other way is there, then, of judging falsely?

There is, presumably, no possibility of judging outside these alternatives, granted that everything is either known by us or not known, and inside them there seems to be no room for a false judgment.

THEAETETUS : Quite true.

SOCRATES : Perhaps, then, we had better approach what we are looking for by way of another alternative. Instead of 'knowing or d not-knowing,' let us take 'being or not-being.'

THEAETETUS : How do you mean?

SOCRATES : May it not simply be that one who thinks *what is not* about anything cannot but be thinking what is false, whatever his state of mind may be in other respects?

THEAETETUS : There is some likelihood in that, Socrates.

SOCRATES : Then what shall we say, Theaetetus, if we are asked, 'But is what you describe possible for anyone? Can any man think what is not, either about something that is or absolutely?' I suppose we must answer to that, 'Yes, when he believes something and e what he believes is not true.' Or what are we to say?

THEAETETUS : We must say that.

SOCRATES : Then is the same sort of thing possible in any other case?

THEAETETUS : What sort of thing?

SOCRATES : That a man should see something, and yet what he sees should be nothing.

THEAETETUS : No. How could that be?

SOCRATES : Yet surely if what he sees is something, it must be a thing that is. Or do you suppose that 'something' can be reckoned among things that have no being at all?

THEAETETUS : No, I don't.

SOCRATES : Then, if he sees something, he sees a thing that is.

THEAETETUS : Evidently.

189 SOCRATES : And if he hears a thing, he hears something and hears a thing that is.

THEAETETUS : Yes.

SOCRATES : And if he touches a thing, he touches something, and if something, then a thing that is.

THEAETETUS : That also is true.

SOCRATES : And if he thinks, he thinks something, doesn't he?

THEAETETUS : Necessarily.

SOCRATES : And when he thinks something, he thinks a thing that is?

THEAETETUS : I agree.

SOCRATES : So to think what is not is to think nothing.

THEAETETUS : Clearly.

SOCRATES : But surely to think nothing is the same as not to think at all.

THEAETETUS : That seems plain.

SOCRATES: If so, it is impossible to think what is not, either b about anything that is, or absolutely.

THEAETETUS: Evidently.

SOCRATES: Then thinking falsely must be something different from thinking what is not.

THEAETETUS: So it seems.

SOCRATES: False judgment, then, is no more possible for us on these lines than on those we were following just now.

THEAETETUS: No, it certainly is not.

SOCRATES: Well, does the thing we call false judgment arise in this way?

THEAETETUS: How?

SOCRATES: We do recognize the existence of false judgment as a sort of misjudgment that occurs when a person interchanges in his c mind two things, both of which are, and asserts that the one is the other. In this way he is always thinking of something which is, but of one thing in place of another, and since he misses the mark he may fairly be said to be judging falsely.

THEAETETUS: I believe you have got it quite right now. When a person thinks 'ugly' in place of 'beautiful' or 'beautiful' in place of 'ugly,' he is really and truly thinking what is false.

SOCRATES: I can see that you are no longer in awe of me, Theaetetus, but beginning to despise me.

THEAETETUS: Why, precisely?

SOCRATES: I believe you think I shall miss the opening you give me by speaking of '*truly* thinking what is *false*,' and not ask you d whether a thing can be slowly quick or heavily light or whether any contrary can desert its own nature and behave like its opposite. However, I will justify your boldness by letting that pass. So you like this notion that false judgment is mistaking.

THEAETETUS: I do.

SOCRATES: According to you, then, it is possible for the mind to take one thing for another, and not for itself.

THEAETETUS: Yes, it is.

SOCRATES: And when the mind does that, must it not be think- e ing either of both things or of one of the two?

THEAETETUS: Certainly it must, either at the same time or one after the other.

SOCRATES: Excellent. And do you accept my description of the process of thinking?

THEAETETUS: How do you describe it?

SOCRATES: As a discourse that the mind carries on with itself about any subject it is considering. You must take this explanation as coming from an ignoramus, but I have a notion that, when the mind is thinking, it is simply talking to itself, asking questions and answer- 190 ing them, and saying yes or no. When it reaches a decision—which may come slowly or in a sudden rush—when doubt is over and the two voices affirm the same thing, then we call that its 'judgment.' So I should describe thinking as discourse, and judgment as a statement pronounced, not aloud to someone else, but silently to oneself.

THEAETETUS: I agree.

SOCRATES: It seems, then, that when a person thinks of one thing as another, he is affirming to himself that the one is the other.

b THEAETETUS: Of course.

SOCRATES: Now search your memory and see if you have ever said to yourself, 'Certainly, what is beautiful is ugly,' or 'What is unjust is just.' To put it generally, consider if you have ever set about convincing yourself that any one thing is certainly another thing, or whether, on the contrary, you have never, even in a dream, gone so far as to say to yourself that odd numbers must be even, or anything of that sort.

THEAETETUS: That is true.

c SOCRATES: Do you suppose anyone else, mad or sane, ever goes so far as to talk himself over, in his own mind, into stating seriously that an ox must be a horse or that two must be one?

THEAETETUS: Certainly not.

SOCRATES: So, if making a statement to oneself is the same as judging, then, so long as a man is making a statement or judgment about both things at once and his mind has hold of both, he cannot say or judge that one of them is the other. You, in your turn, must not cavil at my language; I mean it in the sense that no one thinks 'the ugly is beautiful' or anything of that kind.

d THEAETETUS: I will not cavil, Socrates. I agree with you.

SOCRATES: So long, then, as a person is thinking of both, he cannot think of the one as the other.

THEAETETUS: So it appears.

SOCRATES: On the other hand, if he is thinking of one only and not of the other at all, he will never think that the one is the other.

THEAETETUS: True, for then he would have to have before his mind the thing he was not thinking of.

SOCRATES: It follows, then, that 'mistaking' is impossible, whether he thinks of both things or of one only. So there will be no sense in defining false judgment as 'misjudgment.' It does not appear that false judgment exists in us in this form any more than in those we dismissed earlier.

THEAETETUS: So it seems.

SOCRATES: And yet, Theaetetus, if we cannot show that false judgment does exist, we shall be driven into admitting all sorts of absurdities.

THEAETETUS: For instance?

SOCRATES: I will not mention them until I have tried to look at the question from every quarter. So long as we cannot see our way, I should feel some shame at our being forced into such admissions.

But if we find the way out, then, as soon as we are clear, it will be time to speak of others as caught in the ludicrous position we shall have ourselves escaped; though, if we are completely baffled, then, I suppose, we must be humble and let the argument do with us what it will, like a sailor trampling over seasick passengers. So let me tell you where I still see an avenue open for us to follow.

THEAETETUS: Do tell me.

SOCRATES: I shall say we were wrong to agree that a man can- b not think that things he knows are things he does not know and so be deceived. In a way it is possible.

THEAETETUS: Do you mean something that crossed my mind at the moment when we said that was impossible? It occurred to me that sometimes I, who am acquainted with Socrates, imagine that a stranger whom I see at a distance is the Socrates whom I know. In a case like that a mistake of the kind you describe does occur.

SOCRATES: And we were shy of saying that, because it would have made us out as both knowing and not knowing what we know?

THEAETETUS: Exactly.

SOCRATES: We must, in fact, put the case in a different way. Perhaps the barrier will yield somewhere, though it may defy our ef- c forts. Anyhow, we are in such straits that we must turn every argument over and put it to the test. Now, is there anything in this? Is it possible to become acquainted with something one did not know before?

THEAETETUS: Surely.

SOCRATES: And the process can be repeated with one thing after another?

THEAETETUS: Of course.

SOCRATES: Imagine, then, for the sake of argument, that our minds contain a block of wax, which in this or that individual may be larger or smaller, and composed of wax that is comparatively pure or muddy, and harder in some, softer in others, and sometimes of just the right consistency.   d

THEAETETUS: Very well.

SOCRATES: Let us call it the gift of the Muses' mother, Memory, and say that whenever we wish to remember something we see or hear or conceive in our own minds, we hold this wax under the perceptions or ideas and imprint them on it as we might stamp the impression of a seal ring. Whatever is so imprinted we remember and know so long as the image remains; whatever is rubbed out or has not succeeded in leaving an impression we have forgotten and do not e know.

THEAETETUS: So be it.

SOCRATES: Now take a man who knows things in this way, and is attending to something that he sees or hears. Is there not here a possibility of his making a false judgment?

THEAETETUS: How?

SOCRATES: By thinking that things he knows are other things he knows, or sometimes things he does not know. We were wrong when we agreed earlier that this was impossible.

THEAETETUS: What do you think about it now?

192   SOCRATES: Mistake is impossible in the following cases.

* (1) No one can think one thing to be another when he does not perceive either of them, but has the memorial or seal of both of them in his mind; nor can any mistaking of one thing for another occur, when he only knows one, and does not know, and has no impression of the other; nor can he think that one thing which he does not know is another thing which he does not know, or that what he does not know is what he knows; nor (2) that one thing which he perceives is

b another thing which he perceives, or that something which he perceives is something which he does not perceive; or that something which he does not perceive is something else which he does not perceive; or that something which he does not perceive is something which he perceives; nor again (3) can he think that something which he knows and perceives, and of which he has the impression coinciding with sense, is something else which he knows and perceives, and of which he has the impression coinciding with sense; — this last case, if possible, is still more inconceivable than the others; nor (4) can he think that something which he knows and perceives, and of which he has the memorial coinciding with sense, is something else which he knows; nor so long as these agree, can he think that a

c thing which he knows and perceives is another thing which he perceives; or that a thing which he does not know and does not perceive, is the same as another thing which he does not know and does not perceive; — nor again, can he suppose that a thing which he does not know and does not perceive is the same as another thing which he does not know; or that a thing which he does not know and does not perceive is another thing which he does not perceive: — All these utterly and absolutely exclude the possibility of false opinion.*

* The passage beginning and ending with an asterisk is interpolated from the Jowett translation. In Cornford's translation, the following summary is given at this point:

"(a) If neither object is now perceived, I cannot mistake an acquaintance for another acquaintance, or confuse him with a stranger, or confuse two strangers.

"(b) If perception only is involved, I cannot confuse two things which I see, or an object seen with an object not seen, or two objects neither of which is seen.

"(c) Where both knowledge and perception are involved, I cannot confuse two acquaintances both now seen and recognized, or confuse an acquaintance now seen and recognized with an absent acquaintance or with a stranger who is present. And there can be no confusion of two total strangers, whether I now see one of them or not."

There remain, then, the following cases in which, if anywhere, false judgment can occur.

THEAETETUS: What are they? Perhaps they may help me to understand better. At present I cannot follow.

SOCRATES: Take things you know. You can suppose them to be other things which you both know and perceive, or to be things you do not know, but do perceive, or you can confuse two things which you d both know and perceive.

THEAETETUS: Now I am more in the dark than ever.

SOCRATES: Let me start again, then, and put it in this way. I know Theodorus and have a memory in my mind of what he is like, and the same with Theaetetus. At certain moments I see or touch or hear or otherwise perceive them; at other times, though I have no perception of you and Theodorus, I nevertheless remember you both and have you before my mind. Isn't that so?

THEAETETUS: Certainly.   e

SOCRATES: That, then, is the first point I want to make clear— that it is possible either to perceive or not to perceive something one is acquainted with.

THEAETETUS: True.

SOCRATES: And it is also possible, when one is not acquainted with a thing, sometimes not to perceive it either, sometimes merely to perceive it and nothing more.

THEAETETUS: That is possible too.

SOCRATES: Then see if you can follow me better now. If Socra- 193 tes knows Theodorus and Theaetetus, but sees neither and has no sort of present perception of them, he can never think in his own mind that Theaetetus is Theodorus. Is that good sense?

THEAETETUS: Yes, that is true.

SOCRATES: Well, that was the first of the cases I mentioned.

THEAETETUS: Yes.

SOCRATES: And the second was this. If I know one of you but not the other and perceive neither, once more I could never think that the one I know is the other whom I do not know.

THEAETETUS: True.   b

SOCRATES: And thirdly, if I neither know nor perceive either of you, I cannot think that one unknown person is another unknown person. And now take it as if I had gone over the whole list of cases again, in which I shall never judge falsely about you and Theodorus, whether I know both or neither or only one of you. And the same applies to perceiving, if you follow me.

THEAETETUS: I follow now.

SOCRATES: It remains, then, that false judgment should occur in a case like this—when I, who know you and Theodorus and possess imprints of you both like seal impressions in the waxen block, see you c both at a distance indistinctly and am in a hurry to assign the proper

imprint of each to the proper visual perception, like fitting a foot into
its own footmark to effect a recognition, and then make the mistake
of interchanging them, like a man who thrusts his feet into the wrong
shoes, and apply the perception of each to the imprint of the other.
Or my mistake might be illustrated by the sort of thing that happens
d in a mirror when the visual current transposes right to left. In that
case mistaking or false judgment does result.

THEAETETUS: I think it does, Socrates. That is an admirable
description of what happens to judgment.

SOCRATES: Then there is also the case where I know both and
perceive only one, and do not get the knowledge I have of that one to
correspond with my perception. That is the expression I used before,
which you did not understand.

THEAETETUS: No, I did not.

SOCRATES: Well, that is what I was saying. If you know one of
e two people and also perceive him and if you get the knowledge you
have to correspond with the perception of him, you will never think he
is another person whom you both know and perceive, if your knowledge of him likewise is got to correspond with the perception. That was
so, wasn't it?

THEAETETUS: Yes.

SOCRATES: But there was leftover the case I have been describ-
194 ing now, in which we say false judgment does occur—the possibility
that you may know both and see or otherwise perceive both, but not
get the two imprints to correspond each with its proper perception.
Like a bad archer, you may shoot to one side and miss the mark—
which is indeed another phrase we use for error.

THEAETETUS: With good reason.

SOCRATES: Also, when a perception is present which belongs to
one of the imprints, but none which belongs to the other, and the
mind fits to the present perception the imprint belonging to the absent
one, in all such cases it is in error. To sum up, in the case of objects
one does not know and has never perceived, there is, it seems, no pos-
b sibility of error or false judgment, if our present account is sound,
but it is precisely in the field of objects both known and perceived
that judgment turns and twists about and proves false or true—true
when it brings impressions straight to their proper imprints, false
when it misdirects them crosswise to the wrong imprint.

THEAETETUS: Surely that is a satisfactory account, isn't it,
Socrates?

c   SOCRATES: You will think still better of it when you hear the
rest. To judge truly is a fine thing and there is something discreditable
in error.

THEAETETUS: Of course.

SOCRATES: Well, they say the differences arise in this way.
When a man has in his mind a good thick slab of wax, smooth and

kneaded to the right consistency, and the impressions that come through the senses are stamped on these tables of the 'heart' [5]—Homer's word hints at the mind's likeness to wax—then the imprints are clear and deep enough to last a long time. Such people are quick d to learn and also have good memories, and besides they do not interchange the imprints of their perceptions but think truly. These imprints being distinct and well spaced are quickly assigned to their several stamps—the 'real things' as they are called—and such men are said to be clever. Do you agree?

THEAETETUS : Most emphatically.

SOCRATES : When a person has what the poet's wisdom com- e mends as a 'shaggy heart,' or when the block is muddy or made of impure wax, or oversoft or hard, the people with soft wax are quick to learn, but forgetful, those with hard wax the reverse. Where it is shaggy or rough, a gritty kind of stuff containing a lot of earth or dirt, the impressions obtained are indistinct; so are they too when the 195 stuff is hard, for they have no depth. Impressions in soft wax also are indistinct, because they melt together and soon become blurred. And if, besides this, they overlap through being crowded together into some wretched little narrow mind, they are still more indistinct. All these types, then, are likely to judge falsely. When they see or hear or think of something, they cannot quickly assign things to their several imprints. Because they are so slow and sort things into the wrong places, they constantly see and hear and think amiss, and we say they are mistaken about things and stupid.

THEAETETUS : Your description could not be better, Socrates. b

SOCRATES : We are to conclude, then, that false judgments do exist in us?

THEAETETUS : Most certainly.

SOCRATES : And true ones also, I suppose?

THEAETETUS : True ones also.

SOCRATES : At last, then, we believe we have reached a satisfactory agreement that both these kinds of judgments certainly exist?

THEAETETUS : Most emphatically.

SOCRATES : It really does seem to be true, Theaetetus, that a garrulous person is a strange and disagreeable creature.

THEAETETUS : Why, what makes you say that?

SOCRATES : Disgust at my own stupidity. I am indeed garrulous c —what else can you call a man who goes on bandying arguments to and fro because he is such a dolt that he cannot make up his mind and is loath to surrender any one of them?

THEAETETUS : But why are you disgusted with yourself?

SOCRATES : I am not merely disgusted but anxious about the answer I shall make if someone asks, So, Socrates, you have made a

[5] *Iliad* 2.851; 16.554.

discovery—that false judgment resides, not in our perceptions among
d themselves nor yet in our thoughts, but in the fitting together of perception and thought? I suppose I shall say yes, and plume myself on
this brilliant discovery of ours.

THEAETETUS: I don't see anything to be ashamed of in what
you have just pointed out, Socrates.

SOCRATES: On the other hand, he will continue, you also say
that we can never imagine that a man whom we merely think of and
do not see is a horse which again we do not see or touch but merely
think of without perceiving it in any way? I suppose I shall say yes
to that.

THEAETETUS: And rightly.

e SOCRATES: On that showing, he will say, a man could never
imagine that eleven, which he merely thinks of, is twelve, which
again he merely thinks of.

Come, you must find the answer now.

THEAETETUS: Well, I shall answer that, if he saw or handled
eleven things, he might suppose they were twelve, but he will never
make that judgment about the eleven and the twelve he has in his
thoughts.

SOCRATES: Well now, does a man ever consider in his own
196 mind five and seven—I don't mean five men and seven men or anything of that sort, but just five and seven themselves, which we describe as records in that waxen block of ours, among which there
can be no false judgment—does anyone ever take these into consideration and ask himself in his inward conversation how much they
amount to, and does one man believe and state that they make eleven,
another that they make twelve, or does everybody agree they make
twelve?

b THEAETETUS: Far from it. Many people say eleven, and if
larger numbers are involved, the more room there is for mistakes, for
you are speaking generally of any numbers, I suppose.

SOCRATES: Yes, that is right. Now consider what happens in
this case. Is it not thinking that the twelve itself that is stamped on
the waxen block is eleven?

THEAETETUS: It seems so.

SOCRATES: Then haven't we come round again to our first argument? For when this happens to someone, he is thinking that one
thing he knows is another thing he knows, and that, we said, was im-
c possible. That was the very ground on which we were led to make out
that there could be no such thing as false judgment; it was in order to
avoid the conclusion that the same man must at the same time know
and not know the same thing.

THEAETETUS: Quite true.

SOCRATES: If so, we must account for false judgment in some
other way than as the misfitting of thought to perception. If it were

that, we should never make mistakes among our thoughts themselves. As the case stands now, either there is no such thing as false judgment, or it is possible not to know what one does know. Which alternative do you choose?

THEAETETUS: I see no possible choice, Socrates.

SOCRATES: But the argument is not going to allow both alterna- d tives. However, we must stick at nothing; suppose we try being quite shameless.

THEAETETUS: In what way?

SOCRATES: By making up our minds to describe what knowing is like.

THEAETETUS: How is that shameless?

SOCRATES: You seem to be unaware that our whole conversation from the outset has been an inquiry after the nature of knowledge on the supposition that we did not know what it was.

THEAETETUS: No, I am quite aware of that.

SOCRATES: Then, doesn't it strike you as shameless to explain what knowing is like, when we don't know what knowledge is? The truth is, Theaetetus, that for some time past there has been a vicious e taint in our discussion. Times out of number we have said, 'we know,' 'we do not know,' 'we have knowledge,' 'we have no knowledge,' as if we could understand each other while we still know nothing about knowledge. At this very moment, if you please, we have once more used the words 'know nothing' and 'understand,' as if we had a right to use them while we are still destitute of knowledge.

THEAETETUS: Well, but how are you going to carry on a discussion, Socrates, if you keep clear of those words?

SOCRATES: I cannot, being the man I am, though I might if I 197 were an expert in debate. If such a person were here now, he would profess to keep clear of them and rebuke us severely for my use of language. As we are such bunglers, then, shall I be so bold as to describe what knowing is like? I think it might help us.

THEAETETUS: Do so, then, by all means. And if you cannot avoid those words, you shall not be blamed.

SOCRATES: Well, you have heard what 'knowing' is commonly said to be?

THEAETETUS: Possibly, but I don't remember at the moment.

SOCRATES: They say it is 'having knowledge.' b

THEAETETUS: True.

SOCRATES: Let us make a slight amendment and say, 'possessing knowledge.'

THEAETETUS: What difference would you say that makes?

SOCRATES: None, perhaps, but let me tell you my idea and you shall help me test it.

THEAETETUS: I will if I can.

SOCRATES: 'Having' seems to me different from 'possessing.' If c a man has bought a coat and owns it, but is not wearing it, we should say he possesses it without having it about him.

THEAETETUS : True.

SOCRATES : Now consider whether knowledge is a thing you can possess in that way without having it about you, like a man who has caught some wild birds—pigeons or what not—and keeps them in an aviary he has made for them at home. In a sense, of course,

d we might say he 'has' them all the time inasmuch as he possesses them, mightn't we?

THEAETETUS : Yes.

SOCRATES : But in another sense he 'has' none of them, though he has got control of them, now that he has made them captive in an enclosure of his own; he can take and have hold of them whenever he likes by catching any bird he chooses, and let them go again, and it is open to him to do that as often as he pleases.

e   THEAETETUS : That is so.

SOCRATES : Once more then, just as a while ago we imagined a sort of waxen block in our minds, so now let us suppose that every mind contains a kind of aviary stocked with birds of every sort, some in flocks apart from the rest, some in small groups, and some solitary, flying in any direction among them all.

THEAETETUS : Be it so. What follows?

SOCRATES : When we are babies we must suppose this receptacle empty, and take the birds to stand for pieces of knowledge. Whenever a person acquires any piece of knowledge and shuts it up in his enclosure, we must say he has learned or discovered the thing of which this is the knowledge, and that is what 'knowing' means.

THEAETETUS : Be it so.

198   SOCRATES : Now think of him hunting once more for any piece of knowledge that he wants, catching and holding it, and letting it go again. In what terms are we to describe that—the same that we used of the original process of acquisition, or different ones? An illustration may help you to see what I mean. There is a science you call 'arithmetic.'

THEAETETUS : Yes.

SOCRATES : Conceive that, then, as a chase after pieces of knowledge about all the numbers, odd or even.

THEAETETUS : I will.

SOCRATES : That, I take it, is the science in virtue of which a

b man has in his control pieces of knowledge about numbers and can hand them over to someone else.

THEAETETUS : Yes.

SOCRATES : And when he hands them over, we call it 'teaching,' and when the other takes them from him, that is 'learning,' and when he has them in the sense of possessing them in that aviary of his, that is 'knowing.'

THEAETETUS: Certainly.

SOCRATES: Now observe what follows. The finished arithmetician knows all numbers, doesn't he? There is no number the knowledge of which is not in his mind.

THEAETETUS: Naturally.

SOCRATES: And such a person may sometimes count either the c numbers themselves in his own head or some set of external things that have a number.

THEAETETUS: Of course.

SOCRATES: And by counting we shall mean simply trying to find out what some particular number amounts to?

THEAETETUS: Yes.

SOCRATES: It appears, then, that the man who, as we admitted, knows every number, is trying to find out what he knows as if he had no knowledge of it. No doubt you sometimes hear puzzles of that sort debated.

THEAETETUS: Indeed I do.

SOCRATES: Well, our illustration from hunting pigeons and d getting possession of them will enable us to explain that the hunting occurs in two ways—first, before you possess your pigeon in order to have possession of it; secondly, after getting possession of it, in order to catch and hold in your hand what you have already possessed for some time. In the same way, if you have long possessed pieces of knowledge about things you have learned and know, it is still possible to get to know the same things again, by the process of recovering the knowledge of some particular thing and getting hold of it. It is knowledge you have possessed for some time, but you had not got it handy in your mind.

THEAETETUS: True.

SOCRATES: That, then, was the drift of my question—what e terms should be used to describe the arithmetician who sets about counting or the literate person who sets about reading—because it seemed as if, in such a case, the man was setting about learning again from himself what he already knew.

THEAETETUS: That sounds odd, Socrates.

SOCRATES: Well, but can we say he is going to read or count something he does *not* know, when we have already granted that he 199 knows all the letters or all the numbers?

THEAETETUS: No, that is absurd too.

SOCRATES: Shall we say, then, that we care nothing about words, if it amuses anyone to turn and twist the expressions 'knowing' and 'learning'? Having drawn a distinction between possessing knowledge and having it about one, we agree that it is impossible not to possess what one does possess, and so we avoid the result that a man should not know what he does know, but we say that it is possible for him to get hold of a false judgment about it. For he may not have b about him the knowledge of that thing, but a different piece of knowledge instead, if it so happens that, in hunting for some particular piece of knowledge, among those that are fluttering about, he misses it and catches hold of a different one. In that case, you see, he mistakes eleven for twelve, because he has caught hold of the knowledge of eleven that is inside him, instead of his knowledge of twelve, as he might catch a dove in place of a pigeon.

THEAETETUS : That seems reasonable.

SOCRATES : Whereas, when he catches the piece of knowledge he is trying to catch, he is not mistaken but thinks what is true. In
c this way both true and false judgments can exist, and the obstacles that were troubling us are removed. You will agree to this, perhaps? Or will you not?

THEAETETUS : I will.

SOCRATES : Yes, for now we are rid of the contradiction about people not knowing what they do know. That no longer implies our not possessing what we do possess, whether we are mistaken about something or not. But it strikes me that a still stranger consequence is coming in sight.

THEAETETUS : What is that?

SOCRATES : That the interchange of pieces of knowledge should ever result in a judgment that is false.

THEAETETUS : How do you mean?

d SOCRATES : In the first place, that a man should have knowledge of something and at the same time fail to recognize that very thing, not for want of knowing it but by reason of his own knowledge, and next that he should judge that thing to be something else and vice versa—isn't that very unreasonable, that when a piece of knowledge presents itself, the mind should fail to recognize anything and know nothing? On this showing, the presence of ignorance might just as well make us know something, or the presence of blindness make us see—if knowledge can ever make us fail to know.

e THEAETETUS : Perhaps, Socrates, we were wrong in making the birds stand for pieces of knowledge only, and we ought to have imagined pieces of ignorance flying about with them in the mind. Then, in chasing them, our man would lay hold sometimes of a piece of knowledge, sometimes of a piece of ignorance, and the ignorance would make him judge falsely, the knowledge truly, about the same thing.

SOCRATES : It is not easy to disapprove of anything you say,
200 Theaetetus, but think again about your suggestion. Suppose it is as you say; then the man who lays hold of the piece of ignorance will judge falsely. Is that right?

THEAETETUS : Yes.

SOCRATES : But of course he will not think he is judging falsely.

THEAETETUS : Of course not.

SOCRATES: No, he will think he is judging truly, and his attitude of mind will be the same as if he knew the thing he is mistaken about.

THEAETETUS: Naturally.

SOCRATES: So he will imagine that, as a result of his chase, he has got hold of a piece of knowledge, not a piece of ignorance.

THEAETETUS: Clearly.

SOCRATES: Then we have gone a long way round only to find ourselves confronted once more with our original difficulty. Our de- b structive critic will laugh at us. You wonderful people, he will say, are we to understand that a man knows both a piece of knowledge and a piece of ignorance, and then supposes that one of these things he knows is the other which he also knows? Or does he know neither, and then judge that one of these unknown things is the other? Or does he know only one, and identify this known thing with the unknown one, or the unknown one with the known? Or are you going to tell me that there are yet further pieces of knowledge *about* your pieces of knowledge and ignorance, and that their owner keeps these shut up in yet another of your ridiculous aviaries or waxen blocks, knowing them c so long as he possesses them, although he may not have them at hand in his mind? On that showing you will find yourselves perpetually driven round in a circle and never getting any further.

What are we to reply to that, Theaetetus?

THEAETETUS: Really, Socrates, I don't know what we are to say.

SOCRATES: Maybe, my young friend, we have deserved this rebuke, and the argument shows that we were wrong to leave knowledge d on one side and look first for an explanation of false judgment. That cannot be understood until we have a satisfactory account of the nature of knowledge.

THEAETETUS: As things now stand, Socrates, one cannot avoid that conclusion.

SOCRATES: To start all over again, then, what is one to say that knowledge is? For surely we are not going to give up yet.

THEAETETUS: Not unless you do so.

SOCRATES: Then tell me, what definition can we give with the least risk of contradicting ourselves?   e

THEAETETUS: The one we tried before, Socrates. I have nothing else to suggest.

SOCRATES: What was that?

THEAETETUS: That true belief is knowledge. Surely there can at least be no mistake in believing what is true and the consequences are always satisfactory.

SOCRATES: Try, and you will see, Theaetetus, as the man said 201 when he was asked if the river was too deep to ford. So here, if we go forward on our search, we may stumble upon something that will reveal the thing we are looking for. We shall make nothing out, if we stay where we are.

THEAETETUS : True. Let us go forward and see.

SOCRATES : Well, we need not go far to see this much. You will find a whole profession to prove that true belief is not knowledge.

THEAETETUS : How so? What profession?

SOCRATES : The profession of those paragons of intellect known as orators and lawyers. There you have men who use their skill to produce conviction, not by instruction, but by making people believe whatever they want them to believe. You can hardly imagine
b teachers so clever as to be able, in the short time allowed by the clock, to instruct their hearers thoroughly in the true facts of a case of robbery or other violence which those hearers had not witnessed.

THEAETETUS : No, I cannot imagine that, but they can convince them.

SOCRATES : And by convincing you mean making them believe something.

THEAETETUS : Of course.

SOCRATES : And when a jury is rightly convinced of facts which can be known only by an eyewitness, then, judging by hearsay and accepting a true belief, they are judging without knowledge, although,
c if they find the right verdict, their conviction is correct?

THEAETETUS : Certainly.

SOCRATES : But if true belief and knowledge were the same thing, the best of jurymen could never have a correct belief without knowledge. It now appears that they must be different things.

THEAETETUS : Yes, Socrates, I have heard someone make the distinction. I had forgotten, but now it comes back to me. He said that
d true belief with the addition of an account (λόγος) was knowledge, while belief without an account was outside its range. Where no account could be given of a thing, it was not 'knowable'—that was the word he used—where it could, it was knowable.

SOCRATES : A good suggestion. But tell me how he distinguished these knowable things from the unknowable. It may turn out that what you were told tallies with something I have heard said.

THEAETETUS : I am not sure if I can recall that, but I think I should recognize it if I heard it stated.

SOCRATES : If you have had a dream, let me tell you mine in
e return. I seem to have heard some people say that what might be called the first elements of which we and all other things consist are such that no account can be given of them. Each of them just by
202 itself can only be named; we cannot attribute to it anything further or say that it exists or does not exist, for we should at once be attaching to it existence or nonexistence, whereas we ought to add nothing if we are to express just it alone. We ought not even to add 'just' or 'it'

or 'each' or 'alone' or 'this,' or any other of a host of such terms. These terms, running loose about the place, are attached to everything, and they are distinct from the things to which they are applied. If it were possible for an element to be expressed in any formula exclusively belonging to it, no other terms ought to enter into that expression. But in fact there is no formula in which any element can b be expressed; it can only be named, for a name is all there is that belongs to it. But when we come to things composed of these elements, then, just as these things are complex, so the names are combined to make a description (λόγος), a description being precisely a combination of names. Accordingly, elements are inexplicable and unknowable, but they can be perceived, while complexes ('syllables') are knowable and explicable, and you can have a true notion of them. So when a man gets hold of the true notion of something without an account, his mind does think truly of it, but he does not know it, for if c one cannot give and receive an account of a thing, one has no knowledge of that thing. But when he has also got hold of an account, all this becomes possible to him and he is fully equipped with knowledge.

Does that version represent the dream as you heard it, or not?

THEAETETUS: Perfectly.

SOCRATES: So this dream finds favor and you hold that a true notion with the addition of an account is knowledge?

THEAETETUS: Precisely.

SOCRATES: Can it be, Theaetetus, that, all in a moment, we d have found out today what so many wise men have grown old in seeking and have not found?

THEAETETUS: I, at any rate, am satisfied with our present statement, Socrates.

SOCRATES: Yes, the statement just in itself may well be satisfactory, for how can there ever be knowledge without an account and right belief? But there is one point in the theory as stated that does not find favor with me.

THEAETETUS: What is that?

SOCRATES: What might be considered its most ingenious feature. It says that the elements are unknowable, but whatever is complex ('syllables') can be known.   e

THEAETETUS: Is not that right?

SOCRATES: We must find out. We hold as a sort of hostage for the theory the illustration in terms of which it was stated.

THEAETETUS: Namely?

SOCRATES: Letters—the elements of writing—and syllables. That and nothing else was the prototype the author of this theory had in mind, don't you think?

THEAETETUS: Yes, it was.   203

SOCRATES: Let us take up that illustration, then, and put it to the question, or rather put the question to ourselves. Did we learn our letters on that principle or not? To begin with, is it true that an account can be given of syllables, but not of letters?

THEAETETUS: It may be so.

SOCRATES: I agree, decidedly. Suppose you are asked about the first syllable of 'Socrates.' Explain, Theaetetus, what is SO? How will you answer?

THEAETETUS: S and O.

SOCRATES: And you have there an account of the syllable?

THEAETETUS: Yes.

b SOCRATES: Go on, then, give me a similar account of S.

THEAETETUS: But how can one state the elements of an element? The fact is, of course, Socrates, that S is one of the consonants, nothing but a noise, like a hissing of the tongue, while B not only has no articulate sound but is not even a noise, and the same is true of most of the letters. So they may well be said to be inexplicable, when the clearest of them, the seven vowels themselves, have only a sound, and no sort of account can be given of them.

SOCRATES: So far, then, we have reached a right conclusion about knowledge.

THEAETETUS: Apparently.

c SOCRATES: But now, have we been right in declaring that the letter cannot be known, though the syllable can?

THEAETETUS: That seems all right.

SOCRATES: Take the syllable then. Do we mean by that both the two letters or, if there are more than two, all the letters? Or do we mean a single entity that comes into existence from the moment when they are put together?

THEAETETUS: I should say we mean all the letters.

SOCRATES: Then take the case of the two letters S and O. The two together are the first syllable of my name. Anyone who knows
d that syllable knows both the letters, doesn't he?

THEAETETUS: Naturally.

SOCRATES: So he knows the S and the O.

THEAETETUS: Yes.

SOCRATES: But has he, then, no knowledge of *each* letter, so that he knows both without knowing either?

THEAETETUS: That is a monstrous absurdity, Socrates.

SOCRATES: And yet, if it is necessary to know each of two things before one can know both, he simply must know the letters first, if he is ever to know the syllable, and so our fine theory will vanish and leave us in the lurch.

e THEAETETUS: With a startling suddenness.

SOCRATES: Yes, because we are not keeping a good watch upon it. Perhaps we ought to have assumed that the syllable was not the letters but a single entity that arises out of them with a unitary character of its own and different from the letters.

THEAETETUS: By all means. Indeed, it may well be so rather than the other way.

SOCRATES: Let us consider that. We ought not to abandon an imposing theory in this poor-spirited manner.

THEAETETUS: Certainly not.   204

SOCRATES: Suppose, then, it is as we say now. The syllable arises as a single entity from any set of letters which can be combined, and that holds of every complex, not only in the case of letters.

THEAETETUS: By all means.

SOCRATES: In that case, it must have no parts.

THEAETETUS: Why?

SOCRATES: Because, if a thing has parts, the whole thing must be the same as all the parts. Or do you say that a whole likewise is a single entity that arises out of the parts and is different from the aggregate of the parts?

THEAETETUS: Yes, I do.

SOCRATES: Then do you regard the sum (τὸ πᾶν) as the same thing as the whole, or are they different?   b

THEAETETUS: I am not at all clear, but you tell me to answer boldly, so I will take the risk of saying they are different.

SOCRATES: Your boldness, Theaetetus, is right; whether your answer is so, we shall have to consider.

THEAETETUS: Yes, certainly.

SOCRATES: Well, then, the whole will be different from the sum, according to our present view.

THEAETETUS: Yes.

SOCRATES: Well but now, is there any difference between the sum and all the things it includes? For instance, when we say, 'one, two, three, four, five, six,' or 'twice three' or 'three times two' or 'four   c and two' or 'three and two and one,' are we in all these cases express- ing the same thing or different things?

THEAETETUS: The same.

SOCRATES: Just six, and nothing else?

THEAETETUS: Yes.

SOCRATES: In fact, in each form of expression we have ex- pressed all the six.

THEAETETUS: Yes.

SOCRATES: But when we express them all, is there no sum that we express?

THEAETETUS: There must be.

SOCRATES: And is that sum anything else than 'six'?

THEAETETUS: No.

SOCRATES: Then, at any rate in the case of things that consist   d of a number, the words 'sum' and 'all the things' denote the same thing.

THEAETETUS : So it seems.

SOCRATES : Let us put our argument, then, in this way. The number of [square feet in] an acre, and the acre are the same thing, aren't they?

THEAETETUS : Yes.

SOCRATES : And so too with the number of [feet in] a mile?

THEAETETUS : Yes.

SOCRATES : And again with the number of [soldiers in] an army and the army, and so on, in all cases. The total number is the same as the total thing in each case.

THEAETETUS : Yes.

e   SOCRATES : But the number of [units in] any collection of things cannot be anything but *parts* of that collection?

THEAETETUS : No.

SOCRATES : Now, anything that has parts consists of parts.

THEAETETUS : Evidently.

SOCRATES : But all the parts, we have agreed, are the same as the sum, if the total number is to be the same as the total thing.

THEAETETUS : Yes.

SOCRATES : The whole, then, does not consist of parts, for if it were all the parts it would be a sum.

THEAETETUS : Apparently not.

SOCRATES : But can a part be a part of anything but its whole?

THEAETETUS : Yes, of the sum.

205   SOCRATES : You make a gallant fight of it, Theaetetus. But does not 'the sum' mean precisely something from which nothing is missing?

THEAETETUS : Necessarily.

SOCRATES : And is not a whole exactly the same thing—that from which nothing whatever is missing? Whereas, when something is removed, the thing becomes neither a whole nor a sum; it changes at the same moment from being both to being neither.

THEAETETUS : I think now that there is no difference between a sum and a whole.

SOCRATES : Well, we were saying, were we not, that when a thing has parts, the whole or sum will be the same thing as all the parts?

THEAETETUS : Certainly.

SOCRATES : To go back, then, to the point I was trying to make just now, if the syllable is not the same thing as the letters, does it b not follow that it cannot have the letters as parts of itself; other-wise, being the same thing as the letters, it would be neither more nor less knowable than they are?

THEAETETUS : Yes.

SOCRATES: And it was to avoid that consequence that we supposed the syllable to be different from the letters.

THEAETETUS: Yes.

SOCRATES: Well, if the letters are not parts of the syllable, can you name any things, other than its letters, that are parts of a syllable?

THEAETETUS: Certainly not, Socrates. If I admitted that it had any parts, it would surely be absurd to set aside the letters and look for parts of any other kind.

SOCRATES: Then, on the present showing, a syllable will be a c thing that is absolutely one and cannot be divided into parts of any sort?

THEAETETUS: Apparently.

SOCRATES: Do you remember then, my dear Theaetetus, our accepting a short while ago a statement that we thought satisfactory —that no account could be given of the primary things of which other things are composed, because each of them, taken just by itself, was incomposite, and that it was not correct to attribute even 'existence' to it, or to call it 'this,' on the ground that these words expressed different things that were extraneous to it, and this was the ground for making the primary thing inexplicable and unknowable?

THEAETETUS: I remember.

SOCRATES: Then is not exactly this, and nothing else, the d ground of its being simple in nature and indivisible into parts? I can see no other.

THEAETETUS: Evidently there is no other.

SOCRATES: Then has not the syllable now turned out to be a thing of the same sort, if it has no parts and is a unitary thing?

THEAETETUS: Certainly.

SOCRATES: To conclude, then, if, on the one hand, the syllable is the same thing as a number of letters and is a whole with the letters as its parts, then the letters must be neither more nor less knowable and explicable than syllables, since we made out that all the parts are the same thing as the whole.

THEAETETUS: True. e

SOCRATES: But if, on the other hand, the syllable is a unity without parts, syllable and letter likewise are equally incapable of explanation and unknowable. The same reason will make them so.

THEAETETUS: I see no way out of that.

SOCRATES: If so, we must not accept this statement—that the syllable can be known and explained, the letter cannot.

THEAETETUS: No, not if we hold by our argument.

SOCRATES: And again, would not your own experience in learning your letters rather incline you to accept the opposite view? 206

THEAETETUS: What view do you mean?

SOCRATES: This—that all the time you were learning you were

doing nothing else but trying to distinguish by sight or hearing each letter by itself, so as not to be confused by any arrangement of them in spoken or written words.

THEAETETUS: That is quite true.

SOCRATES: And in the music school the height of accomplishment lay precisely in being able to follow each several note and tell
b which string it belonged to, and notes, as everyone would agree, are the elements of music.

THEAETETUS: Precisely.

SOCRATES: Then, if we are to argue from our own experience of elements and complexes to other cases, we shall conclude that elements in general yield knowledge that is much clearer than knowledge of the complex and more effective for a complete grasp of anything we seek to know. If anyone tells us that the complex is by its nature knowable, while the element is unknowable, we shall suppose that, whether he intends it or not, he is playing with us.

THEAETETUS: Certainly.

c SOCRATES: Indeed we might, I think, find other arguments to prove that point. But we must not allow them to distract our attention from the question before us, namely, what can really be meant by saying that an account added to true belief yields knowledge in its most perfect form.

THEAETETUS: Yes, we must see what that means.

SOCRATES: Well then, what is this term 'account' intended to convey to us? I think it must mean one of three things.

THEAETETUS: What are they?

d SOCRATES: The first will be giving overt expression to one's thought by means of vocal sound with names and verbs, casting an image of one's notion on the stream that flows through the lips, like a reflection in a mirror or in water. Do you agree that expression of that sort is an 'account'?

THEAETETUS: I do. We certainly call that expressing ourselves in speech (λέγειν).

SOCRATES: On the other hand, that is a thing that anyone can do more or less readily. If a man is not born deaf or dumb, he can signify what he thinks on any subject. So in this sense anyone whatever who has a correct notion evidently will have it 'with an account,'
e and there will be no place left anywhere for a correct notion apart from knowledge.

THEAETETUS: True.

SOCRATES: Then we must not be too ready to charge the author of the definition of knowledge now before us with talking nonsense. Perhaps that is not what he meant. He may have meant being able to
207 reply to the question, what any given thing is, by enumerating its elements.

THEAETETUS: For example, Socrates?

SOCRATES: For example, Hesiod says about a wagon, 'In a wagon are a hundred pieces of wood.'[6] I could not name them all; no more, I imagine, could you. If we were asked what a wagon is, we should be content if we could mention wheels, axle, body, rails, yoke.

THEAETETUS: Certainly.

SOCRATES: But I dare say he would think us just as ridiculous as if we replied to the question about your own name by telling the syllables. We might think and express ourselves correctly, but we should be absurd if we fancied ourselves to be grammarians and able to give such an account of the name Theaetetus as a grammarian would offer. He would say it is impossible to give a scientific account of anything, short of adding to your true notion a complete catalogue of the elements, as, I think, was said earlier.

THEAETETUS: Yes, it was.

SOCRATES: In the same way, he would say, we may have a correct notion of the wagon, but the man who can give a complete statement of its nature by going through those hundred parts has thereby added an account to his correct notion and, in place of mere belief, has arrived at a technical knowledge of the wagon's nature, by going through all the elements in the whole.

THEAETETUS: Don't you approve, Socrates?

SOCRATES: Tell me if you approve, my friend, and whether you accept the view that the complete enumeration of elements is an account of any given thing, whereas description in terms of syllables or of any larger unit still leaves it unaccounted for. Then we can look into the matter further.

THEAETETUS: Well, I do accept that.

SOCRATES: Do you think, then, that anyone has knowledge of whatever it may be, when he thinks that one and the same thing is a part sometimes of one thing, sometimes of a different thing, or again when he believes now one and now another thing to be part of one and the same thing?

THEAETETUS: Certainly not.

SOCRATES: Have you forgotten, then, that when you first began learning to read and write, that was what you and your schoolfellows did?

THEAETETUS: Do you mean, when we thought that now one letter and now another was part of the same syllable, and when we put the same letter sometimes into the proper syllable, sometimes into another?

SOCRATES: That is what I mean.

THEAETETUS: Then I have certainly not forgotten, and I do not think that one has reached knowledge so long as one is in that condition.

b

c

d

e

---

[6] *Works and Days* 456 (454).

SOCRATES: Well then, if at that stage you are writing 'Theaetetus' and you think you ought to write T and H and E and do so,
208 and again when you are trying to write 'Theodorus,' you think you
ought to write T and E and do so, can we say that you know the first
syllable of your two names?

THEAETETUS: No, we have just agreed that one has not knowledge so long as one is in that condition.

SOCRATES: And there is no reason why a person should not
be in the same condition with respect to the second, third, and fourth
syllables as well?

THEAETETUS: None whatever.

SOCRATES: Can we, then, say that whenever in writing 'Theaetetus' he puts down all the letters in order, then he is in possession of
the complete catalogue of elements together with correct belief?

THEAETETUS: Obviously.

b   SOCRATES: Being still, as we agree, without knowledge, though
his beliefs are correct?

THEAETETUS: Yes.

SOCRATES: Although he possesses the 'account' in addition to
right belief. For when he wrote he was in possession of the catalogue
of the elements, which we agreed was the 'account.'

THEAETETUS: True.

SOCRATES: So, my friend, there is such a thing as right belief
together with an account, which is not yet entitled to be called knowledge.

THEAETETUS: I am afraid so.

SOCRATES: Then, apparently, our idea that we had found the
perfectly true definition of knowledge was no better than a golden
dream. Or shall we not condemn the theory yet? Perhaps the mean-
c   ing to be given to 'account' is not this, but the remaining one of the
three, one of which we said must be intended by anyone who defines
knowledge as correct belief together with an account.

THEAETETUS: A good reminder. There is still one meaning left.
The first was what might be called the image of thought in spoken
sound, and the one we have just discussed was going all through the
elements to arrive at the whole. What is the third?

SOCRATES: The meaning most people would give—being able
to name some mark by which the thing one is asked about differs from
everything else.

THEAETETUS: Could you give me an example of such an account of a thing?

d   SOCRATES: Take the sun as an example. I dare say you will be
satisfied with the account of it as the brightest of the heavenly bodies
that go round the earth.

THEAETETUS: Certainly.

SOCRATES: Let me explain the point of this example. It is to illustrate what we were just saying—that if you get hold of the difference distinguishing any given thing from all others, then, so some people say, you will have an 'account' of it, whereas, so long as you fix upon something common to other things, your account will embrace all the things that share it.

THEAETETUS: I understand. I agree that what you describe e may fairly be called an 'account.'

SOCRATES: And if, besides a right notion about a thing, whatever it may be, you also grasp its difference from all other things, you will have arrived at knowledge of what, till then, you had only a notion of.

THEAETETUS: We do say that, certainly.

SOCRATES: Really, Theaetetus, now I come to look at this statement at close quarters, it is like a scene painting. I cannot make it out at all, though, so long as I kept at a distance, there seemed to be some sense in it.

THEAETETUS: What do you mean? Why so?

SOCRATES: I will explain, if I can. Suppose I have a correct 209 notion about you; if I add to that the account of you, then, we are to understand, I know you. Otherwise I have only a notion.

THEAETETUS: Yes.

SOCRATES: And 'account' means putting your differentness into words.

THEAETETUS: Yes.

SOCRATES: So, at the time when I had only a notion, my mind did not grasp any of the points in which you differ from others?

THEAETETUS: Apparently not.

SOCRATES: Then I must have had before my mind one of those common things which belong to another person as much as to you.   b

THEAETETUS: That follows.

SOCRATES: But look here! If that was so, how could I possibly be having a notion of you rather than of anyone else? Suppose I was thinking, Theaetetus is one who is a man and has a nose and eyes and a mouth and so forth, enumerating every part of the body. Will thinking in that way result in my thinking of Theaetetus rather than of Theodorus or, as they say, of the man in the street?

THEAETETUS: How should it?

SOCRATES: Well, now suppose I think not merely of a man with a nose and eyes, but of one with a snub nose and prominent c eyes. Once more shall I be having a notion of you any more than of myself or anyone else of that description?

THEAETETUS: No.

SOCRATES: In fact, there will be no notion of Theaetetus in my mind, I suppose, until this particular snubness has stamped and registered within me a record distinct from all the other cases of snubness that I have seen, and so with every other part of you. Then, if I meet you tomorrow, that trait will revive my memory and give me a correct notion about you.

THEAETETUS: Quite true.

d   SOCRATES: If that is so, the correct notion of anything must itself include the differentness of that thing.

THEAETETUS: Evidently.

SOCRATES: Then what meaning is left for getting hold of an 'account' in addition to the correct notion? If, on the one hand, it means adding the notion of how a thing differs from other things, such an injunction is simply absurd.

THEAETETUS: How so?

SOCRATES: When we have a correct notion of the way in which certain things differ from other things, it tells us to add a correct notion of the way in which they differ from other things. On
e   this showing, the most vicious of circles would be nothing to this injunction. It might better deserve to be called the sort of direction a blind man might give. To tell us to get hold of something we already have, in order to get to know something we are already thinking of, suggests a state of the most absolute darkness.

THEAETETUS: Whereas, if . . . ? The supposition you made just now implied that you would state some alternative. What was it?

SOCRATES: If the direction to add an 'account' means that we are to get to *know* the differentness, as opposed to merely having a notion of it, this most admirable of all definitions of knowledge will be a pretty business, because 'getting to know' means acquiring knowledge, doesn't it?

210   THEAETETUS: Yes.

SOCRATES: So, apparently, to the question, 'What is knowledge?' our definition will reply, 'Correct belief together with knowledge of a differentness,' for, according to it, 'adding an account' will come to that.

THEAETETUS: So it seems.

SOCRATES: Yes, and when we are inquiring after the nature of knowledge, nothing could be sillier than to say that it is correct belief together with a *knowledge* of differentness or of anything whatever.

So, Theaetetus, neither perception, nor true belief, nor the ad-
b dition of an 'account' to true belief can be knowledge.

THEAETETUS: Apparently not.

SOCRATES: Are we in labor, then, with any further child, my friend, or have we brought to birth all we have to say about knowledge?

THEAETETUS: Indeed we have, and for my part I have already, thanks to you, given utterance to more than I had in me.

SOCRATES: All of which our midwife's skill pronounces to be mere wind eggs and not worth the rearing?

THEAETETUS : Undoubtedly.

SOCRATES : Then supposing you should ever henceforth try to conceive afresh, Theaetetus, if you succeed, your embryo thoughts will be the better as a consequence of today's scrutiny, and if you re- c main barren, you will be gentler and more agreeable to your companions, having the good sense not to fancy you know what you do not know. For that, and no more, is all that my art can effect; nor have I any of that knowledge possessed by all the great and admirable men of our own day or of the past. But this midwife's art is a gift from heaven; my mother had it for women, and I for young men of a generous spirit and for all in whom beauty dwells. d

Now I must go to the portico of the King-Archon to meet the indictment which Meletus has drawn up against me. But tomorrow morning, Theodorus, let us meet here again.

PARMENIDES

The Parmenides presents a great difficulty to the reader. The best Platonists differ about its meaning. The ordinary person will be hard put to it to discover any meaning at all. The argument runs on and on in words that appear to make sense and yet convey nothing to the mind. Examples are on every page, as, for instance, "The one is also younger than itself at the time when, in becoming older, it coincides with the present. But the present is with the one always throughout its existence. Therefore, at all times the one both is and is becoming older and younger than itself."

Socrates is represented as a young man awed to be in the presence of Parmenides, one of the greatest thinkers in the generation just before his. In later years he called him "venerable and awful" and said, "I met him when he was old and I a mere youth and he seemed to me to have a glorious depth of mind."

In the dialogue he turns that mind on what we call the Platonic Ideas and attacks them, certainly a curious procedure since in the end he apparently neither demolishes them nor establishes them—we are left in doubt. Why Plato did this has been a subject of discussion ever since and seems likely to remain so. To some people, however, it is only what is to be expected from Plato, never out to defend his own views, always with one object alone, to know the truth, and always on his guard against his desires and preconceptions. It would be natural for him to do his best to find out if what he had built up could be torn down.

The Parmenides seems to disclaim any achievement at all. Finally, the great man says to his audience, "It seems that, whether there is or is not a one, both that one and the others alike are and are not, and appear and do not appear to be."

"Most true," says Socrates, and the dialogue ends. Whether this "truth" is for or against the theory of Ideas is left undecided.

After leaving our home at Clazomenae we arrived at Athens and met Adimantus and Glaucon in the market place. Adimantus took my hand. Welcome, Cephalus, he said. If there is anything we can do for you here, you must let us know.

Well, I replied, I have come for that very purpose. There is something you and your brother can do for me.

Please tell us what it is.

What, I asked, was the name of your half brother on the mother's b side? I cannot remember. He was only a child, you know, when I was here before, and that is a long while ago now. His father's name was Pyrilampes, I think.

Yes, and his own is Antiphon. But why do you ask?

My companions here, I answered, are fellow citizens of mine, deeply interested in philosophy. They have been told that Antiphon has been much in the company of someone called Pythodorus, who was a friend of Zeno's, and that Pythodorus has related to him that conversation which Socrates once had with Zeno and Parmenides. c Antiphon is said to have heard it so often that he can repeat it by heart.

That is true.

Well, said I, that is what we want—to hear that conversation.

There is no difficulty about that, he replied. Before he was grown up, Antiphon worked hard at getting that conversation by heart, though nowadays he takes after his grandfather of the same name and devotes most of his time to horses. If you like, let us go and see him. He has just gone home from here. His house is close by, in Melite.

So we set out to walk there. We found Antiphon at home, giving 127 instructions to a smith about making a bit or something of the sort. When he had done with the man, and his brothers began to tell him what we had come for, he recognized me from his memory of my earlier visit and said he was glad to see me. We then asked him to repeat the conversation. At first he was reluctant. It was no easy matter, he said. However, he ended by telling us the whole story.

According to Antiphon, then, this was Pythodorus' account. Zeno and Parmenides once came to Athens for the Great Pan- b athenaea. Parmenides was a man of distinguished appearance. By that time he was well advanced in years, with hair almost white; he may have been sixty-five. Zeno was nearing forty, a tall and attractive figure. It was said that he had been Parmenides' favorite. They were staying with Pythodorus outside the walls in the Ceramicus. Socrates c and a few others came there, anxious to hear a reading of Zeno's treatise, which the two visitors had brought for the first time to

From *Plato and Parmenides: Parmenides' "Way of Truth" and Plato's "Parmenides,"* translated with an introduction and a running commentary by Francis Macdonald Cornford (London, 1939).

Athens. Socrates was then quite young. Zeno himself read it to them;
Parmenides at the moment had gone out. The reading of the argu-
d ments was very nearly over when Pythodorus himself came in,
accompanied by Parmenides and Aristoteles, the man who was afterward one of the Thirty; so they heard only a small part of the treatise.
Pythodorus himself, however, had heard it read by Zeno before.

When Zeno had finished, Socrates asked him to read once more
the first hypothesis of the first argument. He did so, and Socrates
e asked, What does this statement mean, Zeno? 'If things are many,'
you say, 'they must be both like and unlike. But that is impossible;
unlike things cannot be like, nor like things unlike.' That is what you
say, isn't it?

Yes, replied Zeno.

And so, if unlike things cannot be like or like things unlike, it is
also impossible that things should be a plurality; if many things did
exist, they would have impossible attributes. Is this the precise purpose of your arguments—to maintain, against everything that is commonly said, that things are not a plurality? Do you regard every one of
your arguments as evidence of exactly that conclusion, and so hold
that, in each argument in your treatise, you are giving just one more
proof that a plurality does not exist? Is that what you mean, or am I
understanding you wrongly?

128   No, said Zeno, you have quite rightly understood the purpose of
the whole treatise.

I see, Parmenides, said Socrates, that Zeno's intention is to associate himself with you by means of his treatise no less intimately
than by his personal attachment. In a way, his book states the same
position as your own; only by varying the form he tries to delude us
into thinking that his thesis is a different one. You assert, in your
b poem, that the all is one, and for this you advance admirable proofs.
Zeno, for his part, asserts that it is not a plurality, and he too has
many weighty proofs to bring forward. You assert unity; he asserts
no plurality; each expresses himself in such a way that your arguments seem to have nothing in common, though really they come to
very much the same thing. That is why your exposition and his seem
to be rather over the heads of outsiders like ourselves.

Yes, Socrates, Zeno replied, but you have not quite seen the real
c character of my book. True, you are as quick as a Spartan hound to
pick up the scent and follow the trail of the argument, but there is a
point you have missed at the outset. The book makes no pretense
of disguising from the public the fact that it was written with the purpose you describe, as if such deception were something to be proud of.
What you have pointed out is only incidental; the book is in fact a sort
d of defense of Parmenides' argument against those who try to make
fun of it by showing that his supposition, that there is a one, leads to
many absurdities and contradictions. This book, then, is a retort

against those who assert a plurality. It pays them back in the same coin with something to spare, and aims at showing that, on a thorough examination, their own supposition that there is a plurality leads to even more absurd consequences than the hypothesis of the one. It was written in that controversial spirit in my young days, and someone copied it surreptitiously, so that I had not even the chance to consider whether it should see the light or not. That is where you e are mistaken, Socrates; you imagine it was inspired, not by a youthful eagerness for controversy, but by the more dispassionate aims of an older man, though, as I said, your description of it was not far wrong.

I accept that, said Socrates, and I have no doubt it is as you say. But tell me this. Do you not recognize that there exists, just by itself, a form of likeness and again another contrary form, unlikeness 129 itself, and that of these two forms you and I and all the things we speak of as 'many' come to partake? Also, that things which come to partake of likeness come to be alike in that respect and just in so far as they do come to partake of it, and those that come to partake of unlikeness come to be unlike, while those which come to partake of both come to be both? Even if all things come to partake of both, contrary as they are, and by having a share in both are at once like and unlike one another, what is there surprising in that? If one could point to b things which are simply 'alike' or 'unlike' proving to be unlike or alike, that no doubt would be a portent, but when things which have a share in both are shown to have both characters, I see nothing strange in that, Zeno, nor yet in a proof that all things are one by having a share in unity and at the same time many by sharing in plurality. c But if anyone can prove that what is simply unity itself is many or that plurality itself is one, then I shall begin to be surprised.

And so in all other cases, if the kinds or forms themselves were shown to have these contrary characters among themselves, there would be good ground for astonishment, but what is there surprising in someone pointing out that I am one thing and also many? When he wants to show that I am many things, he can say that my right side is a different thing from my left, my front from my back, my upper parts from my lower, since no doubt I do partake of plurality. When he wants to prove that I am one thing, he will say that I am one person d among the seven of us, since I partake also of unity. So both statements are true. Accordingly, if anyone sets out to show about things of this kind—sticks and stones, and so on—that the same thing is many and one, we shall say that what he is proving is that *something* is many and one, not that unity is many or that plurality is one; he is not telling us anything wonderful, but only what we should all admit. But, as I said just now, if he begins by distinguishing the forms apart just by themselves—likeness, for instance, and unlikeness, plurality and unity, rest and motion, and all the rest—and then shows that e

these forms among themselves can be combined with, or separated from, one another, then, Zeno, I should be filled with admiration. I am sure you have dealt with this subject very forcibly, but, as I say, my
130 admiration would be much greater if anyone could show that these same perplexities are everywhere involved in the forms themselves— among the objects we apprehend in reflection, just as you and Parmenides have shown them to be involved in the things we see.

While Socrates was speaking, Pythodorus said he was expecting every moment that Parmenides and Zeno would be annoyed, but they listened very attentively and kept on exchanging glances and smiles in admiration of Socrates. When he ended, Parmenides expressed this feeling.

b   Socrates, he said, your eagerness for discussion is admirable. And now tell me. Have you yourself drawn this distinction you speak of and separated apart on the one side forms themselves and on the other the things that share in them? Do you believe that there is such a thing as likeness itself apart from the likeness that we possess, and so on with unity and plurality and all the terms in Zeno's argument that you have just been listening to?

Certainly I do, said Socrates.

And also in cases like these, asked Parmenides, is there, for example, a form of rightness or of beauty or of goodness, and of all such things?

Yes.

c   And again, a form of man, apart from ourselves and all other men like us—a form of man as something by itself? Or a form of fire or of water?

I have often been puzzled about those things, Parmenides, whether one should say that the same thing is true in their case or not.

Are you also puzzled, Socrates, about cases that might be thought absurd, such as hair or mud or dirt or any other trivial and undignified objects? Are you doubtful whether or not to assert that each
d of these has a separate form distinct from things like those we handle?

Not at all, said Socrates. In these cases, the things are just the things we see; it would surely be too absurd to suppose that they have a form. All the same, I have sometimes been troubled by a doubt whether what is true in one case may not be true in all. Then, when I have reached that point, I am driven to retreat, for fear of tumbling into a bottomless pit of nonsense. Anyhow, I get back to the things which we were just now speaking of as having forms, and occupy my time with thinking about them.

e   That, replied Parmenides, is because you are still young, Socrates, and philosophy has not yet taken hold of you so firmly as I believe it will someday. You will not despise any of these objects then, but at present your youth makes you still pay attention to what the

world will think. However that may be, tell me this. You say you hold
that there exist certain forms, of which these other things come to
partake and so to be called after their names; by coming to partake of 131
likeness or largeness or beauty or justice, they become like or large or
beautiful or just?

Certainly, said Socrates.

Then each thing that partakes receives as its share either the
form as a whole or a part of it? Or can there be any other way of partaking besides this?

No, how could there be?

Do you hold, then, that the form as a whole, a single thing, is in
each of the many, or how?

Why should it not be in each, Parmenides?

If so, a form which is one and the same will be at the same time, b
as a whole, in a number of things which are separate, and consequently will be separate from itself.

No, it would not, replied Socrates, if it were like one and the same
day, which is in many places at the same time and nevertheless is not
separate from itself. Suppose any given form is in them all at the
same time as one and the same thing in that way.

I like the way you make out that one and the same thing is in
many places at once, Socrates. You might as well spread a sail over a
number of people and then say that the one sail as a whole was over
them all. Don't you think that is a fair analogy?

Perhaps it is.

Then would the sail as a whole be over each man, or only a part c
over one, another part over another?

Only a part.

In that case, Socrates, the forms themselves must be divisible
into parts, and the things which have a share in them will have a part
for their share. Only a part of any given form, and no longer the whole
of it, will be in each thing.

Evidently, on that showing.

Are you, then, prepared to assert that we shall find the single
form actually being divided? Will it still be one?

Certainly not.

No, for consider this. Suppose it is largeness itself that you are
going to divide into parts, and that each of the many large things is d
to be large by virtue of a part of largeness which is smaller than largeness itself. Will not that seem unreasonable?

It will indeed.

And again, if it is equality that a thing receives some small part
of, will that part, which is less than equality itself, make its possessor
equal to something else?

No, that is impossible.

Well, take smallness. Is one of us to have a portion of smallness,

and is smallness to be larger than that portion, which is a part of it? On this supposition again smallness itself will be larger, and anything
e to which the portion taken is added will be smaller, and not larger, than it was before.

That cannot be so.

Well then, Socrates, how are the other things going to partake of your forms, if they can partake of them neither in part nor as wholes?

Really, said Socrates, it seems no easy matter to determine in any way.

Again, there is another question.

What is that?

How do you feel about this? I imagine your ground for believing
132 in a single form in each case is this. When it seems to you that a number of things are large, there seems, I suppose, to be a certain single character which is the same when you look at them all; hence you think that largeness is a single thing.

True, he replied.

But now take largeness itself and the other things which are large. Suppose you look at all these in the same way in your mind's eye, will not yet another unity make its appearance—a largeness by virtue of which they all appear large?

So it would seem.

If so, a second form of largeness will present itself, over and above
b largeness itself and the things that share in it, and again, covering all these, yet another, which will make all of them large. So each of your forms will no longer be one, but an indefinite number.

But, Parmenides, said Socrates, may it not be that each of these forms is a thought, which cannot properly exist anywhere but in a mind. In that way each of them can be one and the statements that have just been made would no longer be true of it.

Then, is each form one of these thoughts and yet a thought of nothing?

No, that is impossible.

So it is a thought of something?

Yes.
c Of something that is, or of something that is not?

Of something that is.

In fact, of some *one* thing which that thought observes to cover all the cases, as being a certain single character?

Yes.

Then will not this thing that is thought of as being one and always the same in all cases be a form?

That again seems to follow.

And besides, said Parmenides, according to the way in which you assert that the other things have a share in the forms, must you not hold either that each of those things consists of thoughts, so that all things think, or else that they are thoughts which nevertheless do not think?

That too is unreasonable, replied Socrates. But, Parmenides, the best I can make of the matter is this—that these forms are as it were d patterns fixed in the nature of things. The other things are made in their image and are likenesses, and this participation they come to have in the forms is nothing but their being made in their image.

Well, if a thing is made in the image of the form, can that form fail to be like the image of it, in so far as the image was made in its likeness? If a thing is like, must it not be like something that is like it?

It must.

And must not the thing which is like share with the thing that is e like it in one and the same thing [character]?

Yes.

And will not that in which the like things share, so as to be alike, be just the form itself that you spoke of?

Certainly.

If so, nothing can be like the form, nor can the form be like anything. Otherwise a second form will always make its appearance over and above the first form, and if that second form is like anything, 133 yet a third. And there will be no end to this emergence of fresh forms, if the form is to be like the thing that partakes of it.

Quite true.

It follows that the other things do not partake of forms by being like them; we must look for some other means by which they partake.

So it seems.

You see then, Socrates, said Parmenides, what great difficulties there are in asserting their existence as forms just by themselves?

I do indeed.

I assure you, then, you have as yet hardly a notion of how great they will be, if you are going to set up a single form for every distinc- b tion you make among things.

How so?

The worst difficulty will be this, though there are plenty more. Suppose someone should say that the forms, if they are such as we are saying they must be, cannot even be known. One could not convince him that he was mistaken in that objection, unless he chanced to be a man of wide experience and natural ability, and were willing to follow one through a long and remote train of argument. Otherwise there would be no way of convincing a man who maintained that the forms were unknowable.   c

Why so, Parmenides?

Because, Socrates, I imagine that you or anyone else who asserts that each of them has a real being 'just by itself,' would admit, to begin with, that no such real being exists in our world.

True, for how could it then be just by itself?

Very good, said Parmenides. And further, those forms which are what they are with reference to one another have their being in such references among themselves, not with reference to those likenesses,
d or whatever we are to call them, in our world, which we possess and so come to be called by their several names. And, on the other hand, these things in our world which bear the same names as the forms are related among themselves, not to the forms, and all the names of that sort that they bear have reference to one another, not to the forms.

How do you mean? asked Socrates.

Suppose, for instance, one of us is master or slave of another; he
e is not, of course, the slave of master itself, the essential master, nor, if he is a master, is he master of slave itself, the essential slave, but, being a man, is master or slave of another man, whereas mastership itself is what it is [mastership] of slavery itself, and slavery itself is slavery to mastership itself. The significance of things in our world is not with reference to things in that other world, nor have these their
134 significance with reference to us, but, as I say, the things in that world are what they are with reference to one another and toward one another, and so likewise are the things in our world. You see what I mean?

Certainly I do.

And similarly knowledge itself, the essence of knowledge, will be knowledge of that reality itself, the essentially real.

Certainly.

And again, any given branch of knowledge in itself will be knowledge of some department of real things as it is in itself, will it not?

Yes.

Whereas the knowledge in our world will be knowledge of the reality in our world, and it will follow again that each branch of knowl-
b edge in our world must be knowledge of some department of things that exist in our world.

Necessarily.

But, as you admit, we do not possess the forms themselves, nor can they exist in our world.

No.

And presumably the forms, just as they are in themselves, are known by the form of knowledge itself?

Yes.

The form which we do not possess.

True.

Then, none of the forms is known by us, since we have no part in knowledge itself.

Apparently not.
c   So beauty itself or goodness itself and all the things we take as forms in themselves are unknowable to us.

I am afraid that is so.

Then here is a still more formidable consequence for you to consider.

What is that?

You will grant, I suppose, that if there is such a thing as a form, knowledge itself, it is much more perfect than the knowledge in our world, and so with beauty and all the rest.

Yes.

And if anything has part in this knowledge itself, you would agree that a god has a better title than anyone else to possess the most perfect knowledge?

Undoubtedly.

Then will the god, who possesses knowledge itself, be able to d know the things in our world?

Why not?

Because we have agreed that those forms have no significance with reference to things in our world, nor have things in our world any significance with reference to them. Each set has it only among themselves.

Yes, we did.

Then if this most perfect mastership and most perfect knowledge are in the god's world, the gods' mastership can never be exercised over us, nor their knowledge know us or anything in our world. Just as we do not rule over them by virtue of rule as it exists in our world and e we know nothing that is divine by our knowledge, so they, on the same principle, being gods, are not our masters nor do they know anything of human concerns.

But surely, said Socrates, an argument which would deprive the gods of knowledge would be too strange.

And yet, Socrates, Parmenides went on, these difficulties and 135 many more besides are inevitably involved in the forms, if these characters of things really exist and one is going to distinguish each form as a thing just by itself. The result is that the hearer is perplexed and inclined either to question their existence, or to contend that, if they do exist, they must certainly be unknowable by our human nature. Moreover, there seems to be some weight in these objections, and, as we were saying, it is extraordinarily difficult to convert the objector. Only a man of exceptional gifts will be able to see that a form, or essence just by itself, does exist in each case, and it will require some- b one still more remarkable to discover it and to instruct another who has thoroughly examined all these difficulties.

I admit that, Parmenides. I quite agree with what you are saying.

But on the other hand, Parmenides continued, if, in view of all these difficulties and others like them, a man refuses to admit that forms of things exist or to distinguish a definite form in every case, he c will have nothing on which to fix his thought, so long as he will not allow that each thing has a character which is always the same, and in so doing he will completely destroy the significance of all discourse. But of that consequence I think you are only too well aware.

True.

What are you going to do about philosophy, then? Where will you turn while the answers to these questions remain unknown?

I can see no way out at the present moment.

d That is because you are undertaking to define 'beautiful,' 'just,' 'good,' and other particular forms, too soon, before you have had a preliminary training. I noticed that the other day when I heard you talking here with Aristoteles. Believe me, there is something noble and inspired in your passion for argument, but you must make an effort and submit yourself, while you are still young, to a severer training in what the world calls idle talk and condemns as useless. Otherwise, the truth will escape you.

What form, then, should this exercise take, Parmenides?

e The form that Zeno used in the treatise you have been listening to. With this exception—there was one thing you said to him which impressed me very much—you would not allow the survey to be confined to visible things or to range only over that field; it was to extend to those objects which are specially apprehended by discourse and can be regarded as forms.

Yes, because in that other field there seems to be no difficulty about showing that things are both like and unlike and have any other character you please.

You are right. But there is one thing more you must do. If you want to be thoroughly exercised, you must not merely make the sup-

136 position that such and such a thing *is* and then consider the consequences; you must also take the supposition that that same thing *is not*.

How do you mean?

Take, if you like, the supposition that Zeno made—'*If there is a plurality of things.*' You must consider what consequences must follow both for those many things with reference to one another and to the one, and also for the one with reference to itself and to the many. Then again, on the supposition that *there is not a plurality*, you must consider what will follow both for the one and for the many,

b with reference to themselves and to each other. Or, once more, if you suppose that 'likeness exists,' or 'does not exist,' what will follow on either supposition both for the terms supposed and for other things, with reference to themselves and to each other. And so again with unlikeness, motion, and rest, coming-to-be and perishing, and being and not-being themselves. In a word, whenever you suppose that anything whatsoever exists or does not exist or has any other character, you ought to consider the consequences with reference to itself and to any one of the other things that you may select, or several of them, or all of

them together, and again you must study these others with reference
both to one another and to any one thing you may select, whether c
you have assumed the thing to exist or not to exist, if you are really
going to make out the truth after a complete course of discipline.

There would be no end to such an undertaking, Parmenides, and
I don't altogether understand. Why not enlighten me by illustrating
the method on some supposition of your own choice?

That is a heavy task, Socrates, to lay on a man of my age. d

But you, Zeno, said Socrates, why don't you give us the illustration?

Zeno laughed and replied, Let us beg Parmenides himself to do
it, Socrates. What he means is no light matter, I am afraid. You must
see what a task you are setting. If we were a larger company, it would
not be fair to ask him. Such a discourse would be unsuitable before a
large audience, particularly in a man of his age, because most people
are unaware that you cannot hit upon truth and gain understanding
without ranging in this way over the whole field. So, Parmenides, I join e
with Socrates in his request, in the hope of sitting at your feet again
myself after all these years.

After these words from Zeno, Pythodorus joined with Aristoteles
and the rest in begging Parmenides not to disappoint them, but to
demonstrate the method he had in mind.

Parmenides replied, I cannot refuse, although I feel like the old 137
race horse in Ibycus, who trembles at the start of the chariot race,
knowing from long experience what is in store for him. The poet compares his own reluctance on finding himself, so late in life, forced into
the lists of love, and my memories too make me frightened of setting
out, at my age, to traverse so vast and hazardous a sea. However, I b
must do as you wish, for after all, as Zeno says, we are all friends here.
Where shall we begin, then? What supposition shall we start with?
Would you like me, since we are committed to play out this laborious game, to begin with myself and my own original supposition?
Shall I take the one itself and consider the consequences of assuming
that there is, or is not, a one?

By all means, said Zeno.

Then who will answer the questions I shall put? Shall it be the
youngest? He will be likely to give the least trouble and to be the
most ready to say what he thinks, and I shall get a moment's rest
while he is answering.

The youngest means me, Parmenides, said Aristoteles, and I am c
ready. Put your questions and I will answer them.

Well then, said Parmenides, if there is a *one*, of course the one
will not be many. Consequently it cannot have any parts or be a
whole. For a part is a part of a whole, and a whole means that from
which no part is missing; so, whether you speak of it as 'a whole' or as
'having parts,' in either case the one would consist of parts and in that

d way be many and not one. But it is to be one and not many. Therefore, if the one is to be one, it will not be a whole nor have parts.

And, if it has no parts, it cannot have a beginning or an end or a middle, for such things would be parts of it. Further, the beginning and end of a thing are its limits. Therefore, if the one has neither beginning nor end, it is without limits.

e Consequently the one has no shape; it is not either round or straight. Round is that whose extremity is everywhere equidistant from its center, and straight is that of which the middle is in front of both extremities. So if the one had either straight or round shape, it 138 would have parts and so be many. Therefore, since it has no parts, it is neither straight nor round.

Further, being such as we have described, it cannot be anywhere, for it cannot be either (a) in another, or (b) in itself.

(a) If it were in another, it would be encompassed all round by that in which it was contained, and would have many contacts with it at many points, but there cannot be contact at many points all round with a thing which is one and has no parts and is not round.

(b) On the other hand, if it were in itself, it would have, to encompass it, none other than itself, since it would actually be within b itself, and nothing can be within something without being encompassed by that thing. Thus the encompassing thing would be one thing, the encompassed another, for the same thing cannot as a whole both encompass and be encompassed at the same time, and so, in that case, the one would no longer be one, but two.

Therefore, the one is not anywhere, being neither in itself nor in another.

Next consider whether, such being its condition, it can be (a) in motion or (b) at rest.

(a) If it were in motion, it would have to be either moving in c place or undergoing alteration, for there are no other kinds of motion.

Now, if the one alters, so as to become different from itself, it surely cannot still be one. Therefore, it does not move in the sense of suffering alteration.

Does it, then, move in place? If it does, then it must either turn round in the same place or shift from one place to another. If it turns round, it must rest on a center and have those parts which revolve round the center as different parts of itself. But a thing which d cannot have a center or parts cannot possibly be carried round on its center. If it moves at all, then, it must move by changing its place and coming to be in different places at different times. Now we saw that it could not *be* anywhere in anything. It is still more impossible that it should *come to be* in anything. If a thing is coming to be in something, it cannot be in that thing so long as it is still coming to be in it, nor yet can it be altogether outside it, since it is already coming to be e in it. Accordingly this can happen only to a thing which has parts,

for part of it will be already in the other thing and part of it outside
at the same time, and a thing which has no parts surely cannot possibly
be, at the same time, neither wholly inside nor wholly outside something. It is still more impossible that a thing which has no parts and is
not a whole should *come to be* in anything, since it cannot do so either
part by part or as a whole. Hence it does not change its place either
by traveling anywhere and coming to be in something, or by re- 139
volving in the same place, or by changing.

Therefore the one is immovable in respect of every kind of motion.

(*b*) On the other hand, we also assert that it cannot actually *be*
in anything. Consequently it can never be in *the same* [place or con-
dition], because then it would *be* in that selfsame [place or condition],
and we saw that it could not be either in itself or in anything else. The
one, then, is never in the same [place or condition]. But what is never
in the same [place or condition] is not at rest or stationary.　　　　b

It appears, then, that the one is neither at rest nor in motion.

Further the one cannot be either the same as another or the same
as itself, nor yet other than itself or other than another.

(*a*) Were it other than itself, it would be other than one and so
would not be one. (*b*) And if it were the same as another, it would
be that other and not be itself, so that, in this case again, it would not c
be just what it is, one, but other than one.

Therefore the one will not be the same as another or other than
itself.

(*c*) Nor can it be other than another, so long as it is one. To be
other than something properly belongs, not to 'one,' but only to an
'other-than-another.' Consequently it will not be other in virtue of its
being one, and so not in virtue of being itself, and so not *as* itself,
and if as itself it is not in any sense other, it cannot be other than anything.

(*d*) Nor yet can it be the same as itself. For the character (φύσις) d
of unity is one thing, the character of sameness another. This is evident because when a thing becomes 'the same' as something, it does
not become 'one.' For instance, if it becomes the same as the many, it
must become many, not one, whereas if there were no difference whatever between unity and sameness, whenever a thing became 'the
same,' it would always become one, and whenever one, the same.
So if the one is to be the same as itself, it will not be one with itself, e
and thus will be one and not one, and that is impossible. Consequently
it is equally impossible for the one to be either other than another or
the same as itself.

Thus the one cannot be other than, or the same as, either itself or
another.

Nor can the one be (*a*) like or (*b*) unlike anything, whether itself or another.

(*a*) A like thing is a thing which has an identical character. But we have seen that the character 'same' is distinct from the character 'one.' Now if the one has any character distinct from being one, 140 it must have the character of being more things than one, and that is impossible. So it is quite impossible that the one should be a thing 'having the same character' as either another or itself.

Therefore the one cannot be like another or like itself.

(*b*) But neither is it true of the one that it is different, for, in that case again, it would be true of it that it was more things than one. But if 'like' means that of which the same thing is true, a thing that b is unlike itself or another will be that which can be truly said to be different from itself or another. And the one, it appears, cannot be said to be different in any way. Consequently, the one is in no way unlike either itself or anything else.

Therefore the one cannot be like or unlike either another or itself.

Further, the one, being such as we have described, will not be either (*a*) equal or (*b*) unequal either to itself or to another.

If it is equal, it will have the same number of measures as any- c thing to which it is equal. If greater or less, it will have more or fewer measures than things, less or greater than itself, which are commensurable with it. Or, if they are incommensurable with it, it will have smaller measures in the one case, greater in the other.

(*a*) Now a thing which has no sameness cannot have the same number of measures or of anything else. Therefore the one, not having the same number of measures, cannot be equal to itself or to another.

(*b*) On the other hand, if it had more or fewer measures, it d would have as many parts as measures, and thus, once more, it would be no longer one, but as many as its measures. And if it were of one measure, it would be equal to that measure, whereas we saw that it could not be equal to anything.

Therefore, since it has neither one measure, nor many, nor few, and has no sameness at all, it appears that it can never be equal to itself or to another, nor yet greater or less than itself or another.

e   Again, can it be held that the one can be older or younger than anything or of the same age with anything?

If it is of the same age with itself or another, it will have equality of duration and likeness, and we have said that the one has neither likeness nor equality. We also said that it has no unlikeness or in-141 equality. Such a thing cannot, then, be either older or younger than, or of the same age with, anything.

Therefore the one cannot be younger or older than, or of the same age with, either itself or another.

We may infer that the one, if it is such as we have described, cannot even occupy time at all. Whatever occupies time must always be becoming older than itself, and 'older' always means older than

something younger. Consequently, whatever is becoming older than it- b
self, if it is to have something *than* which it is becoming older, must
also be at the same time becoming younger than itself. What I mean
is this. If one thing is already different from another, there is no question of its becoming different; either they both are now, or they both
have been, or they both will be, different. But if one is in process of
becoming different, you cannot say that the other has been, or will
be, or as yet is, different; it can only be in process of becoming different. Now the difference signified by 'older' is always a difference c
from something younger. Consequently, what is becoming older than
itself must also at the same time be becoming younger than itself.
Now, in the process of becoming it cannot take a longer or shorter
time than itself; it must take the same time with itself, whether it is
becoming, or is, or has been, or will be. So, it seems, any one of the
things that occupy time and have a temporal character must be of the
same age as itself and also be becoming at once both older and d
younger than itself. But we saw that none of these characters can attach to the one.

Therefore the one has nothing to do with time and does not occupy any stretch of time.

Again, the words 'was,' 'has become,' 'was becoming' are understood to mean connection with past time; 'will be,' 'will be becoming,' e
'will become,' with future time; 'is' and 'is becoming,' with time now
present. Consequently, if the one has nothing to do with any time, it
never has become or was becoming or was, nor can you say it has become now or is becoming or is, or that it will be becoming or will become or will be in the future. Now a thing can have being only in one
of these ways. There is, accordingly, no way in which the one has
being.

Therefore the one in no sense *is*.

It cannot, then, 'be' even to the extent of 'being' one, for then it
would be a thing that is and has being. Rather, if we can trust such an
argument as this, it appears that the one neither is one nor is at all. 142

And if a thing is not, you cannot say that it 'has' anything or
that there is anything 'of' it. Consequently, it cannot *have* a name or be
spoken of, nor can there be any knowledge or perception or opinion *of*
it. It is not named or spoken of, not an object of opinion or of knowledge, not perceived by any creature.

Now can this possibly be the case with the one?

I do not think so, said Aristoteles.

Shall we, then, go back to our hypothesis and reconsider it from b
the beginning, in the hope of bringing to light some different result?

'If a one is,' we say, we have to agree what sort of consequences
follow concerning it. Start afresh, then, and consider. If a one *is*, it
cannot be, and yet not *have* being. So there will also be the being which
the one has, and this is not the same thing as the one; otherwise

c that being would not be *its* being, nor would it, the one, *have* that being, but to say 'a one *is*' would be tantamount to saying 'a one [is] *one.*' But in fact the supposition whose consequences we are to consider is not 'if a one [is] *one*,' but 'if a one *is*.' This implies that 'is' and 'one' stand for different things. Thus the short statement 'a one is' simply means that the one has being.

Let us, then, once more state what will follow, if a one is. Consider whether this supposition does not necessarily imply that the d one is such as to have parts. That follows in this way. Since 'is' is asserted to belong to this *one* which is, and 'one' is asserted to belong to this *being* which is one, and since '*being*' and '*one*' are not the same thing, but both belong to the same thing, namely that 'one which is' that we are supposing, it follows that it is 'one being' as a whole, and 'one' and 'being' will be its parts. So we must speak of each of these parts, not merely as a part, but as part of a whole.

Therefore, any 'one that is' is a whole and also has parts.

e Again, take each of these two parts of the one being—its unity and its being. Unity can never be lacking to the part 'being,' nor being to the part 'unity.' Thus each of the two parts, in its turn, will possess both unity and being; any part proves to consist of at least two parts, and so on forever by the same reasoning. Whatever part we arrive at always possesses these two parts, for a 'one' always has being, and a 'being' always has unity. Hence any part always proves to be 143 two and can never be one.

In this way, then, what is 'one being' must be unlimited in multitude.

We may also proceed in another way, as follows. We are saying that the one has being. That is why it *is*, and it was for that reason that a 'one which is' was seen to be a plurality. Now take just this 'one' which we are saying has being and conceive it just by itself alone apart from the being which we say it has. Will this 'one' itself be found to be merely one or also a plurality? Consider. The 'one' it-b self and its being must be *different* things since the one is not being, but, as one, *has* being. If, then, the one and its being are each different from the other, it is not in virtue of being one that the one is different from the being, nor is it in virtue of being 'being' that the being is other than the one; they differ from one another in virtue of being *different* or *other*. Thus [the term] 'different' is not identical with either 'one' or 'being.'

c Now suppose we take a selection of these terms, [say] 'being' and 'different,' or 'being' and 'one,' or 'one' and 'different.' In each case we are selecting a pair which may be spoken of as 'both.' I mean, we can speak of 'being,' and again of 'one.' We have thus named each member of a pair. And when I say 'being and one' or 'being and different,' or 'different and one,' and so on in every possible combination, I am in d each case speaking of 'both.' And a pair that can properly be called 'both' must be *two*. And if a pair of things are two, each of them must be *one*. This applies to our terms. Since each set forms a couple, each term must be one. And if so, then, when any one is added to any pair, the sum will be *three*. And three is odd, two even. Now if there are two, there must also be *twice times*, if three, *three times*, since two is e twice times one and three is three times one. And if there are two and twice times, three and three times, there must be *twice times two* and *three times three*. And, if there are three which occur twice and two which occur three times, there must be *twice times three* and *three times two*. Thus there will be even multiples of even sets, odd multi- 144 ples of odd sets, odd multiples of even sets, and even multiples of odd sets. That being so, there is no number left, which must not necessarily be.

Therefore, if a one is, there must also be number.

Now, if number is, there must be many things, and indeed an unlimited plurality of things, that *are*, for we must admit that number, unlimited in plurality, also proves to have being. And if all number has being, each part of number must have being also. Thus being is distributed throughout all the members of a plurality of beings, and b is lacking to none of these beings from the smallest to the greatest; indeed it is nonsense to suggest that anything that *is* should lack being. Thus being is parceled out among beings of every possible order from smallest to greatest; it is subdivided to the furthest possible point and has an illimitable number of parts. So its parts form the greatest of multitudes.   c

Again, among all these parts there cannot be any which *is* part of being and yet not *a* [one] part. If it *is*, then, so long as it is, it must always be some *one* part; it cannot be *no* [not one] part. Consequently, unity must belong to every part of being, and be lacking to none, smaller or greater. And unity, being one, cannot be in many places d at once as a whole. And if not as a whole, it must be as divided into parts; only so can it be present to all the parts of being at the same time. Further, that which is divided into parts must be as many as its parts. So we were wrong to say just now that being was distributed into the 'greatest' multitude of parts. Its parts are not more numerous than those into which unity is distributed, but equal in num- e ber, for nothing that *is* lacks unity, and nothing that is *one* lacks being; the two maintain their equality all through. It appears, then, that unity itself is parceled out by being, and is not only many but indefinitely numerous.

Thus not only is a 'one which is' a plurality, but unity itself is distributed by being and is necessarily many.

Further, since its parts are parts of a whole, the one, in respect of its wholeness, will be limited. For the parts are contained by the 145 whole, and a container must be a limit.

Therefore, a 'one which is' is both one and many, whole and parts, limited as well as indefinitely numerous.

Since it is limited, then, it will have extremities, and if a whole,

it will have beginning, middle, and end. A thing cannot be a whole without all these three; if any one of them is lacking it will no longer
b be a whole. Thus the one will have beginning and end and middle. But the middle can only be what is equidistant from the extremities.

So a one, such as we have described, will have some shape, straight or round or a mixture of both.

Then, if it has these properties, it will be both (a) in itself and (b) in another.

(a) Each part is, of course, in the whole; none is outside the
c whole. And all the parts are contained by the whole. Now, the one is all its own parts, and neither more nor less than all. And the one is also the whole. Accordingly, since all the parts are in a whole, and the one is both all the parts and the whole, and all the parts are contained in the whole, the one must be contained by the one. In this sense it follows that one must be in itself.

(b) On the other hand, the whole is not in the parts, neither in
d all the parts nor in any part.

If it were in all, it would have to be also in one part, for if there were some one in which it was not, it could not be in all. But if this one part is one among all the parts, and the whole is not in this one, we can no longer say it is in all the parts.

But neither is it in some of the parts. If the whole were in some of the parts, the greater would be contained in the less, which is impossible.

If, then, the whole is not in several of its parts, nor in one, nor yet in all, it must be either in something else or nowhere at all. But if
e nowhere at all, it would be nothing, whereas it is a whole and so, since [as a whole] it is not in itself, it must be in something else.

Thus as a whole the one is in something else; as all the parts it is in itself, and thus the one must be both in itself and in another.

Now, if the one is of this character, it must be both (a) at rest and (b) in motion.
146   (a) It is at rest, since it is in itself. For if it is in one thing, and does not shift out of that thing, it will be in the same [place], namely itself, and that which is always in the same [place] must of course always be at rest.

(b) On the other hand, what is always in another must never be in the same, and therefore never at rest, and not being at rest, it must be in motion.

Therefore the one, being always both in itself and in another, must always be both in motion and at rest.

Further, if the one has the foregoing attributes, it must be (a)
b the same with itself and (b) different from itself, and similarly both (c) different from and (d) the same with the others.

(a) Anything is related to anything in one of the following ways. Either it is the same or different, or, if neither the same nor different, it must stand as part to whole, or as whole to part. Now the one cannot be part of itself, nor can it stand as whole to itself as part. Again the one is not different from one, and so not different c from itself.

Therefore, since it is not different and does not stand to itself either as whole to part or as part to whole, it follows that it must be the same with itself.

(*b*) Again, if a thing is in a place the same with itself and also in a place other than that self, it must be different from itself; otherwise it could not be in a different place. But we saw that this was true of the one. It was at once in itself and in another.

In this respect, therefore, the one must be different from itself.

(*c*) Again, if something is different from something else, that something else must be different. Now, all the things which are 'not one' must be different from the one, and the one also must be different from them.

Therefore, the one is different from the others.   d

(*d*) Now consider. Sameness itself and difference are contrary to one another. So sameness will never be in what is different, nor difference in what is the same. And if difference will never be in what is the same, there is nothing that is in which difference is present for any length of time, for if it were in something for any length of time e whatsoever, during that time difference would be in what is the same. And since it is never in what is the same, difference can never be in anything that is, and consequently neither in the 'not-ones' nor in the one. Therefore it is not difference that could make the one different from the 'not-ones,' or the 'not-ones' different from the one. Nor yet will they be different from one another by virtue of being themselves, if they do not possess difference.   147

Therefore, if neither their own character nor difference can make them different, every possibility of their being different escapes us.

Further, things which are 'not one' do not possess unity either; if they did, they would not be 'not one,' but in a sense one. So things which are 'not one' cannot be a number; if they had number, once more they would not be 'not one' in every sense. Again, the things which are 'not one,' cannot be parts of the one, because once more they would then possess unity. Consequently, if the one is one in b every sense, and the things that are 'not one' are not one in every sense, the one cannot stand to the things that are 'not one' either as whole to parts or as part to whole, nor again can the things which are 'not one' be parts of the one or wholes of which the one is part. But we said that things which do not stand to one another either as parts or as wholes, and are not different from one another, must be the same with one another. Therefore, we must say that, since the one stands in this way to the things that are 'not one,' it is the same as they.

It appears, then, that the one is different both from the others and from itself, and also the same both with them and with itself.

The argument certainly seems to lead to that conclusion, said Aristoteles.

c   Is the one also both like and unlike itself and the others?

(a) Since, as we have seen, the one is different from the others, the others also of course must be different from it. And it differs from them neither more nor less than they differ from it, but just as they do, and if neither more nor less, then in a like manner. Accordingly, in so far as it has the character of 'being different' from the others, and the others in just the same way have the character of 'being different' from it, in so far the one and the others will have the same character.

d   What I mean is this. When you use any word, you use it to stand for something. You can use it once or many times, but in either case you are speaking of the thing whose name it is. However many times you utter the same word, you must always mean the same thing. Now

e   'different' is a word that stands for something; so when you utter it, whether once or many times, you are using it to stand for, or naming, just that thing whose name it is. Hence when we say 'the others are different from the one' and 'the one is different from the others,' we use the word 'different' twice, but nevertheless we always use it to stand for just that character whose name it is. Consequently in so far as the one is different from the others and the others are different

148   from the one, just in respect of having the character 'different' the one and the others have precisely the same character, and to have the same character is to be alike.

Thus, in so far as the one has the character of being different from the others, just in that respect it and they must be entirely alike, because they are entirely different.

(b) On the other hand, 'like' and 'unlike' are contraries, and so also are 'different' and 'same.' Now we have also seen that the one is the same as the others. And 'being the same as the others' is the contrary character to 'being different from the others.' And it has been

b   shown that, in so far as the one is different, it is like them. Consequently, in so far as it is the same, it will be unlike them, in respect of the character contrary to that which made it like them, namely difference. Sameness, then, will make it unlike; otherwise sameness will not be the contrary of difference.

c   Therefore the one will be like and unlike the others—like in so far as different, unlike in so far as the same.

Aristoteles interposed, Yes, it seems possible to argue the case in that way.

Yes, and it can also be argued as follows. We may say that in so far as the one has the character of being 'the same' [as the others], it has not a diverse character, and so is not unlike, and so is like. And in so far as it has the character of being 'other' [than the others], it has a diverse character, and so is unlike.

Therefore, because the one is the same as the others and because it is different, on both grounds together or on either singly it will be both like and unlike the others.   d

Similarly, in relation to itself. Since, as we have seen, it is both different from itself and the same with itself, on both grounds together and on either singly it will be both like itself and unlike itself.

Again, there is the question of the one having, or not having, contact with itself and with the others.

We have seen that the one is in itself as a whole. It is also in the others. Accordingly, (a) as being in the others, it will have contact e with the others, and (b) as being in itself, while it will be precluded from contact with the others, it will have contact with itself.

In this way, then, the one will have contact both with itself and with the others.

From another point of view, if anything is to touch something it must be situated next to that thing, occupying the position adjacent to the position of the thing it touches.

(c) Accordingly, if the one is to touch itself, it must be situated next to itself, occupying the place adjacent to the place in which itself is. If the one were two, it might do this and be in two places at once, 149 but not so long as it remains one.

Therefore the same necessity which forbids the one to be two forbids it to touch itself.

(d) On the other hand, the one will not touch the others either for this reason. We are asserting that, in order to have contact, a thing must be distinct from, but next to, the thing it is to touch, and there must be no third thing between them. So, if there is to be contact, there must be at least two things. And if to the two terms a third b be added next to them, the number of terms will be three, the number of contacts two. And so the addition of every fresh term will mean the addition of one fresh contact, with the result that the contacts are always fewer by one than the amount of the numbers. For every subsequent total of terms exceeds the total of contacts by the same amount as the original pair of terms exceeded the contacts, since at c every step one term and one contact are added. Thus, however many things there are, their contacts are always fewer by one. And if there is only a one, not a pair of things, there will be no contact.

Now things that are other than one, we say, are not one and have not unity, since they are other. Consequently they do not possess number, because there is no one among them. Thus they are neither one nor two nor any other number you could name. The one, d then, is the only thing that is one, and there will be no pair, and consequently no contact. Therefore, contact being nonexistent, the one does not touch the others, nor the others the one.

Thus the total result of these considerations is that the one both touches, and does not touch, both itself and the others.

We may next inquire whether the one is both equal and unequal, alike to itself and to the others.

If the one is to be greater or less than the others or they are to
e be greater or less than it, neither will be greater or less than the other merely in virtue of being what they are—the one being one, and the others being other than the one—but if, besides each being such as it is, they should each possess equality, then they would be equal to one another, or if the others possess greatness, the one smallness, or the one possesses greatness, the others smallness, then whichever possesses greatness will be greater, whichever possesses smallness, less.

This pair of characters, then, greatness and smallness, must exist, for surely, if they did not exist, they could not be contrary to one another and come to be in things.

150   If, then, smallness comes to be in the one, it must be either (a) in the one as a whole or (b) in a part of it.

(a) Suppose it comes to be in the one as a whole. Then it must either stretch throughout the whole extent of the one or contain the one. If it is coextensive with the one, the smallness will be equal to the one; if containing it, greater. But smallness cannot be equal to, or greater than, anything and so discharge, not its own function, but that of greatness or equality. Therefore, smallness cannot be in the one as a whole.

b   (b) Hence, if it is in the one at all, it must be in a part. But not in all that part; otherwise the effect would be the same as in the case of the whole. It would be either equal to, or larger than, any part in which it might be. Therefore smallness will never be in anything, if it cannot come to be in either a part or the whole, and there will be nothing small except smallness itself.

It follows that greatness will not be in the one either, for then there would be something else, besides greatness itself, that would be
c 'greater,' namely the thing in which greatness was—and that in spite of the thing's having no smallness, which is required for greatness to surpass, if it is to be great. And there can be no such smallness, since smallness is not in anything anywhere.

Further, the only thing than which greatness itself is greater is smallness itself, and the only thing than which smallness is smaller is greatness itself. Hence, the others, not possessing greatness or smallness, are not greater or smaller than the one; also this pair themselves
d [greatness and smallness] possess their power of exceeding or being exceeded only with reference to each other, not with reference to the one, and the one in its turn, not possessing either greatness or smallness, cannot be greater or smaller than they or than the others.

It follows that the one, if it is neither greater nor smaller than the others, cannot either exceed them or be exceeded by them, and that which neither exceeds nor is exceeded must be of equal extent, and so equal.

Moreover, the one will also stand in this relation to itself. If it has e in itself neither largeness nor smallness, it cannot either exceed or be exceeded by itself, but must be coextensive and so equal to itself.

Therefore the one will be equal both to itself and to the others.

(c) Further, if it is in itself, it must also encompass itself on the outside, and as container it will be greater than itself, and as contained, less. In this way the one will be greater and less than itself. 151

(d) Also, there can be nothing besides the one and the others. Further, anything that is must always be somewhere. And that which is in something will be in it as a less in a greater; only so can one thing be in another.

Now, since there is nothing else besides the others and the one, and they must be in something, it follows at once that they must be in each other—the others in the one and the one in the others—or be nowhere at all. Consequently, since the one is in the others, the others, b as containing the one, must be greater than it, and the one, as contained by them, less than they. And since the others are in the one, by the same reasoning the one must be greater than the others, and they less than the one.

Therefore, the one is alike equal to, greater than, and less than, both itself and the others.

Further, the one, if greater, less, and equal, must be of equal measures with itself and with the others, and also of more and fewer, and if of measures, then of parts. And, being of equal, more, and c fewer measures, it will also be correspondingly fewer than, more than, and equal to, both itself and the others in number. For if it is greater than anything, it will contain a greater number of measures and so of parts; if less, a smaller number; if equal, the same number.

Hence, the one, being greater and less than itself and also equal, will contain more and fewer and the same number of measures, and d hence of parts. So, as having the same number of parts, it will be equal to itself in number, and as having more or fewer, more or less than itself in number.

The one will also stand in the same way to the others. Since it is seen to be greater and smaller and of the same magnitude as the others, it must also be more, fewer, and equal to them in number.

Thus, once more, it appears that the one will be alike, equal to, e and more and fewer than both itself and the others in number.

Next is the question whether the one exists in time, and, as so existing, both is and becomes younger and older than itself and the others, and also neither is nor becomes younger or older than itself or the others.

Since the one *is* one, of course it has being, and to 'be' means precisely having existence in conjunction with time present, as 'was'

152   or 'will be' means having existence in conjunction with past or future time. So if the one is, it is in time.

(a) Time, moreover, is advancing. Hence since the one moves forward temporally, it is always becoming older than itself. And we remember that what is becoming older becomes older than something that is becoming younger. So, since the one is becoming older than itself, that self must be becoming younger.

b   Therefore, in this sense, it is becoming both younger and older than itself.

(b) Also it *is* older when, in this process of becoming, it is *at* the present time which lies between 'was' and 'will be,' for of course, as it travels from past to future, it will never overstep the present. So, when it coincides with the present, it stops becoming older; at that

c   time it is not becoming, but already *is*, older. For if it were getting ahead, it could never be caught up by the present, since to get ahead would mean to be in touch with both the present and the future, leaving the present behind and reaching out to the future, and so passing between the two. Whereas, if it is true of anything which is becoming that it can never pass beyond the present, it constantly stops becoming when it is at the present, and it then *is* whatever it may be that it was becoming.

This applies to the one. When, in becoming older, it coincides

d   with the present, it stops becoming and *is* then older. Moreover, it is older than the thing it was becoming older than, namely itself. And older means older than a younger. Hence the one is also younger than itself at the time when, in becoming older, it coincides with the pres-

e   ent. But the present is with the one always throughout all its existence, for at whatever time it is existing, it is existing 'now.'

Therefore, at all times the one both is and is becoming older and younger than itself.

(c) Also in thus being or becoming it cannot take a longer time than itself; it must take the same time. But if it is, or is becoming, for the same length of time, it is of the same age, and so neither older nor younger.

Therefore, the one, which is and is becoming for the same length of time as itself, neither is nor becomes older or younger than itself.

Next, is the one similarly related to the others?

153   (a) Things other than the one, being different things and not *a* different thing, are more than one; *a* different thing would be one, but different things must be more than one and have plurality. Hence they have a number greater than that of the one. And of a number the lesser part comes, or has come, into being before the greater part, and first of all the least, namely the one. Thus in all things that have

b   number the one comes first, and the others, being others and not an other, are always things that have number. And what comes first comes earlier, while the others, coming later, are younger.

In this way the others will be younger than the one, the one older than the others.

Again, the one can have come to be only in a way consistent with its own nature. Now we saw that the one has parts, and hence a begin- c ning, an end, and a middle. And the beginning of anything, whether it be the one itself or any one of the others, always comes into being first, and after the beginning, all the rest up to the end. Moreover, by 'all the rest' we shall mean parts of the whole or one, and this itself comes to be, as a one or whole, at the same moment as the end. But the end is the last part to come into being, and it is the nature of the one to come into being simultaneously with the last. Hence, if the one d must come to be in a way consistent with its nature, we must say it is the nature of the one, as having come into being at the same time with the end, to come later than all the others.

Therefore, the one is younger than the others, the others older than the one.

(b) But again, a beginning or any part whatsoever of the one or of anything else, if it is *a* part and not parts, must be one. So 'one' must come to be along with the first part that comes to be, and again e along with the second part, and cannot be lacking to every subsequent part that is added, until, on reaching the last part, a one whole is formed; it cannot be missing at the formation of any part, first, middle, or last. Therefore the one is of the same age as all the others, so that, if the one is not to contradict its own nature, it will have come to be neither before nor after the others, but at the same time.

Thus, according to this argument, the one will be neither 154 older nor younger than the others, nor they than it, whereas by our former argument it was both older and younger, and so were the others.

So much for what it *is* and *has* become.

Next there is the question whether the one is becoming both older and younger than the others, and they than it, and also not becoming younger or older. Does the case stand with becoming as with being, or not?

(c) If one thing actually is older than another, it cannot be be- b coming older still, nor the younger younger still, by any more than their original difference in age, for if equals be added to unequals, the difference that results, in time or any other magnitude, will always be the same as the original difference. Consequently what *is* older or younger can never be becoming older or younger than what *is* younger or older, the difference in age being constant at all times. The c one is or has become older, the other younger, but neither is becoming so.

Therefore, the one, if it *is* so, is not becoming, either older or younger than the others which *are* so.

(d) From another point of view, both are becoming older and

younger. We have seen that (α) the one is older than the others, and (β) they are older than it. (α) When the one is older than the others, it has, of course, been in existence for a longer time than they.
d Now, if an equal time is added to a greater time and to a less, the greater will exceed the less by a smaller fraction. Hence, the difference in age between the one and the others will not remain into the future what it originally was; the addition of the same time to each will make the difference in age constantly less. And if a thing differs
e less in age from something than it formerly did, it must be becoming younger than it was relatively to those things in relation to which it was formerly older. And if it is becoming younger, those other things in their turn must be becoming older than they were in relation to it. Hence what has come to be [later and is] younger is becoming older in relation to what has come to be earlier and is older. It never *is* older than the other, but it is always becoming so, since that other is progressing toward being younger, while it is progressing toward being
155 older. And the older thing, in its turn, is becoming younger than the younger in the same way. As the two move in contrary directions, they are becoming each other's contrary—the younger becoming older than the older, the older becoming younger than the younger— but they can never finally become so; if they did, they would no longer be becoming, but would be so. As it is, each is becoming older and younger than the other. The one is becoming younger than the others, because, as we saw, it is older and came into existence earlier; the
b others are becoming older than the one, because they came into existence later. By the same reasoning, (β) the others stand in the same way to the one, since, as we saw, they are older and came into existence earlier.

Thus, from the point of view (c) in which there is no question of one thing becoming either older or younger than another, since their distance in age remains always the same, the one will not be becoming older or younger than the others, nor they than it. But from another
c point of view (d) in which the difference between things which come into existence earlier and later must be a constantly diminishing fraction, the one and the others must be becoming both older and younger than each other.

So the conclusion of all these arguments is that the one both is, and is becoming, older and younger than itself and than the others, and also neither is, nor is becoming, either older or younger than itself or than the others.

Now, since the one is in time and has the property of becoming
d older and younger, it has a past, a future, and a present. Consequently the one was and is and will be, and it was becoming, is becoming, and will become.

Also, it can be said to *have* something, and there can be something *of* it, alike in past, present, and future. So there can be knowl-

edge and opinion and perception *of* it; in fact we are now exercising
all these activities with respect to it. Further, it will *have* a name and
can be spoken of; indeed it actually is being named and spoken of.
And all the other characters which belong to any other things of e
which the above statements are true belong equally to the one.

To take up the argument yet a third time, if there is a one such
as we have described—a one which is both one and many and neither
one nor many and is in time—it follows that since it *is* one, it has
existence at some time, and again since it *is not* one, at some time it
has not existence. And since it cannot both have and not have existence at the same time, it can only have existence at one time and not
have existence at another. And there must also be a time when it 156
comes to possess existence and a time when it ceases to possess it; it
can possess a thing at one time and not at another only if there are
times when it acquires that thing and loses it. Now acquiring existence
is called 'coming into existence,' and losing existence is called 'ceasing
to exist.'

It appears, then, that the one, when it acquires or loses existence, comes into existence and ceases to exist.   b

Also, since it is one and many and a thing that comes to be and
ceases to be, when it comes to be one, its being many ceases to be,
and when it comes to be many, its being one ceases to be. And as
coming to be one it must be combined, as coming to be many, separated.

Further, when it becomes like or unlike, it is subject to assimilation or dissimilation.

Also, when it becomes greater or less or equal, it must be increased or diminished or equalized.

But when, being in motion, it comes to a stand, or, being at rest, c
it changes to being in motion, it cannot itself occupy any time at all
for this reason. Suppose it is first at rest and later in motion, or first
in motion and later at rest; that cannot happen to it without its changing. But there is no time during which a thing can be at once neither
in motion nor at rest. On the other hand it does not change without
making a transition. When does it make the transition, then? Not
while it is at rest or while it is in motion, or while it is occupying d
time. Consequently, the time at which it will be when it makes the
transition must be that queer thing, the instant. The word 'instant'
appears to mean something such that *from it* a thing passes to one
or other of the two conditions. There is no transition *from* a state
of rest so long as the thing is still at rest, nor *from* motion so long as it
is still in motion, but this queer thing, the instant, is situated between
the motion and the rest; it occupies no time at all, and the transition
of the moving thing to the state of rest, or of the stationary thing to
being in motion, takes place *to* and *from* the instant. Accordingly, the e
one, since it both is at rest and is in motion, must pass from the one

condition to the other—only so can it do both things—and when it passes, it makes the transition instantaneously; it occupies no time in making it and at that moment it cannot be either in motion or at rest.

157   The same holds good of its other transitions. When it passes from being in existence to ceasing to exist or from being nonexistent to coming into existence, it is then between certain motions and states; it is then neither existent nor nonexistent, and it is neither coming into existence nor ceasing to exist. By the same reasoning when it passes from one to many or from many to one, it is not either one or many, and it is not being separated or being combined. Similarly when it passes from like to unlike or from unlike to like, it is neither b like nor unlike, and it is neither becoming like nor becoming unlike. And when it passes from small to great or equal or in the opposite direction, it is not small or great or equal, nor is it being increased or being diminished or being equalized.

All these changes, then, may happen to the one, if it exists.

We have next to consider what will be true of the others, if there is a one. Supposing, then, that there is a one, what must be said of the things other than the one?

Since they are other than the one, they are not the one; if they c were, they could not be other than it. Yet the others are not wholly destitute of the one [unity], but partake of it in a way. For things other than the one are others as having parts; if they had no parts they would be absolutely one. And parts, we say, are parts of a whole, while a whole must be a one consisting of many, and the parts will be parts of this one whole.

For each part must be part, not of a many, but of a whole, for this d reason. If a thing were to be part of a many, among which itself were included, then it would be a part of itself—which is absurd—and also a part of every one of the rest, since it is supposed to be a part of them all. For if there is one of them of which it is not a part, it will be a part of the remainder exclusive of that one, and, if we proceed in that way, it will prove not to be a part of each successive one that we take, and so, not being a part of each one, it will not be a part of any one of the many. But if a thing is a part, or whatever else you please, of no one of a number of things, it cannot be a part of all those things, of no one of which it is a part. Therefore a part is part not of many or of all, but of a single entity or 'one' which we call a whole, a com- e plete 'one' composed of all. Hence if the others have parts, they must also possess wholeness and unity.

Therefore, the things other than the one must be one complete whole having parts.

Further, the same reasoning holds of each part. It is also true of 158 each part that it must have unity. For if each of them is a part, 'each' means that it *is one* thing, distinct from the rest and having its independent being, if we are to call it 'each.' As having unity, it will plainly be other than unity; otherwise it would not have unity, but simply be unity itself, whereas nothing but unity itself can be unity. But both the whole and the part must *have* unity, for the whole is *one* whole, of which the parts are parts, while every part that is part of a whole is *one* part of that whole.

Now things that have a share in the one [possess unity] will be different from the one that they share in [the unity they possess]. And b things different from the one will naturally be many, for if the things other than the one were neither one nor more than one, they would be nothing.

Moreover, since both things that *have* the unity of a part and things that have the unity of a whole are more than one, it follows that those things which come to *acquire* unity, must, just in themselves, be without limit of multitude. We may see that in this way. Evidently, at the time when they come to acquire unity they are not one and do not possess unity. So they are multitudes which do not con- c tain unity. Now if we choose to take in thought from such multitudes the least portion we can conceive, that portion also, if it does not possess unity, must be not one but a multitude. And if we go on in that way considering, just by itself, the nature other than the form, any portion of it that comes into view will be without limit of multitude.

Further, when each single part becomes a part, they now have a limit in relation both to one another and to the whole, and so has the d whole in relation to the parts. Thus the consequence for the things other than the one appears to be that from the combination of unity and themselves there comes to be in them something fresh, which gives them a limit with reference to one another, whereas their own nature gives them, in themselves, unlimitedness.

Thus the things other than the one, both as wholes and part by part, are unlimited and also have limit.

Moreover they are also both like and unlike one another and e themselves.

In so far as they are all unlimited in respect of their own nature, they have the same character, and also in so far as they all have limit. But in so far as they have both characters, limited and unlimited, they have characters which are contrary to one another, and contraries are as unlike as possible. Thus in respect of either character 159 singly they are like themselves and one another, but in respect of both characters taken together they are quite contrary and unlike both themselves and one another.

Thus the others will be both like and unlike themselves and one another.

Also, since we have found this to be true of them, there will be no further difficulty in showing that the things other than the one are the same as, and different from, one another, and both in motion and at rest, and have all the contrary characters. b

Suppose, then, we pass over those further consequences as obvious and consider once more whether, if there is a one, it will not also be true that things other than the one have none of these characters. Let us start again from the beginning and ask, If there is a one, what must be true of the things other than the one?

The one, then, must be separate from the others and they from it. For there is no further thing distinct from both the one and the others; when we have named the one and the others, we have named c all things. So there is no further thing besides them, in which the one and the others alike might be. Hence they are never in the same thing, and therefore must be separate.

Also we cannot admit that what is really and truly one has parts. Therefore the one cannot be in the others as a whole, nor can parts of it be so, if it is separate from the others and also has no parts.

Consequently, the things other than the one, not possessing unity d either in part or as a whole, can have no unity in any way. The others, then, are not one in any sense, and there is no 'one thing' to be found among them.

It follows that the others are not many either. For if they were many, each of them would be *one* part of the whole, whereas, in fact, not having unity in any sense, they are neither one nor many, neither a whole nor parts.

Nor yet, consequently, are the others two or three, and no two things or three things can be in them, since they are altogether destitute of unity.

e   It follows that the others are not like the one, nor yet unlike it; there is no likeness and unlikeness in them. If they were like and unlike or had likeness and unlikeness in them, they would then have in them two characters contrary to one another. But, as we saw, it is impossible for things which do not even possess unity to possess any 160 *two* things. Therefore the others are neither like nor unlike nor both at once, for, if like or unlike, they would have *one* of two characters; if both, *two* contrary characters, and that we have seen to be impossible.

Nor yet, accordingly, are they the same, or different, or in motion, or at rest, or coming to be, or ceasing to be, or greater, or less, or equal, nor have they any other characters of that kind. If the others admit any such character, they will also admit of being one, two, b three, odd and even, and we have seen that they cannot have those characters, being altogether destitute of unity.

Thus, if there is a one, the one is both all things and nothing whatsoever, alike with reference to itself and to the others.

We have next to consider what follows, if the one is not.

What, then, is the meaning of this supposition, 'if a one [one thing] does not exist'? It differs from the supposition, 'if a not-one c [no-thing] does not exist,' and not only differs from it, but is the direct contrary.

Now suppose one says, 'if largeness does not exist,' or 'if smallness does not exist,' or any other statement of that type. Obviously in each case it is a different thing that is spoken of as nonexistent. And so in the present case, if a man says 'if a one [one thing] does not exist,' it is plain that the thing he is saying does not exist is something different from other things, and we know what he is speaking of. So in speaking of a 'one' [one thing] he is speaking, in the first place, of something knowable, and in the second of something different from other things, no matter whether he attributes existence to it or non-existence; even if he says it is nonexistent, we nevertheless know what   d is said not to exist, and that it is distinguishable from other things.

Starting afresh, then, from this supposition, 'if a one [one thing] does not exist,' we are to consider what consequences follow.

First, it seems, this must be true of it, that there is knowledge of it; otherwise the very meaning of the supposition that 'a one does not exist' would be unknown.

Also, it must be true that other things are different from it; other-wise it could not be spoken of as different from them. So, besides being knowable, it must have difference in character, for when you speak of the one as different from the others, you are speaking of its   e difference in character, not of theirs.

And further this nonexistent one has the characters of being 'that' and 'something,' and of being related 'to this' or 'to these,' and all other such characters. If it were not 'something' and had not all those other characters, we could not have spoken of 'the one' or of things different from the one, or of anything as belonging to it or as being of it, nor could we have spoken of it as 'something.' Thus although the one cannot have existence, if it does not exist, there is nothing against its having many characters; indeed it must, if it is this one, and not another that does not exist. If what is not to exist is neither the one nor this and the statement is about something else, we ought not so much as to open our lips, but granted that we are supposing the non-existence of this one and not of something else, it must have the character of being this and many other characters as well.   161

It follows that the one possesses unlikeness with respect to the others. For the others, being different, will actually be of different char-acter—that is, of other character—that is, unlike. And if they are un-like the one, unlikes must be unlike an unlike. Therefore the one also   b will possess unlikeness, with respect to which the others are unlike it.

Moreover, if it has unlikeness to the others, it must have likeness to itself. For if the one has unlikeness to the one, what we are speaking of will not be such as the one in character, and our supposition will not be about a one, but about something other than a one. But that is inadmissible.

The one, therefore, must have likeness to itself.   c

Further, the one is not equal to the others. If it were equal, that would at once imply that it exists and also is like them in respect of

this equality. But both implications are impossible, if a one does not exist. And since it is not equal to the others, the others must be not equal to it. And things that are not equal are unequal, and unequal
d things are unequal to an unequal. So the one has inequality, with reference to which the others are unequal to it.

On the other hand, inequality implies greatness and smallness, and accordingly these must belong to such a one as we are describing. Now greatness and smallness are always kept apart from one another. So there is always something between them, and this can only be equality. Accordingly, anything that has greatness and smallness has also equality between the two.
e   So a one which does not exist will, it appears, have equality, greatness, and smallness.

Further, it must in some sense even possess being. For it must be in the state we are ascribing to it; otherwise we should not be speaking the truth in saying that the one does not exist. If we are speaking the truth, evidently the things we are speaking of must *be*. So, since we do claim to be speaking the truth, we must also assert that we are
162 speaking of things that are. So it appears that the one *is* nonexistent. If it *is not* nonexistent, if it somehow slips away from being so to not being so, it will at once follow that it *is* existent. Accordingly, if it is not to exist, it must have the fact of *being* nonexistent to secure its nonexistence, just as the existent must have the fact of *not being* nonexistent, in order that it may be possible for it completely to exist. The only way to secure that the existent shall exist, and that the nonexistent shall not exist, is this. The existent must have the 'being' implied in 'being existent' and the 'not-being' implied in 'not being nonexistent,' if it is to have complete existence, and the nonexistent, if it is to
b have complete nonexistence, must have the 'not-being' implied in 'not being existent' and the 'being' implied in 'being nonexistent.' Thus, since the existent has not-being and the nonexistent has being, the one also, since it does not exist, must have being in order to be nonexistent.

Thus it appears that the one has being, if it *is* nonexistent, and also, since it *is not* existent, has not-being.

Now a thing which is in a certain condition can not-be in that
c condition only by passing out of it. So anything that both is, and is not, in such and such a condition implies transition, and transition is motion. Now we have seen that the one is existent and also is non-existent, and accordingly is, and is not, in a certain condition. Therefore the nonexistent one has been shown to be a thing that moves, since it admits transition from being to not-being.

On the other hand, if the one is not anywhere in the world of existence—and it is not, if it does not exist—it cannot shift from one
d place to another. Therefore it cannot move by shifting its position. Nor yet can it revolve in the same [place], since it has no point of

contact with what is the same, for what is the same is existent, and the nonexistent cannot be *in* anything that exists. Therefore the one, if nonexistent, cannot revolve in that in which it is not.

Nor can the one, either when existent or when nonexistent, alter from itself in character; if it did, we should no longer be speaking of the one, but of something other than it.

If, then, it does not alter in character and neither revolves in the same place nor shifts from one place to another, there is no other motion it can have. And the motionless must be at rest, and, if at rest, e stationary.

It appears, then, that the nonexistent one is both at rest and in motion.

Further, if it does move, it must become unlike, since in whatever respect a thing moves, to that extent it is no longer in the same 163 condition as before, but in a different condition. So, as moving, the one does become unlike. Also in so far as it is not moving in any respect, it will not be becoming unlike in any way. Consequently, the nonexistent one, in so far as it moves, becomes unlike, and in those respects in which it has no motion, it does not become unlike.

Therefore, the nonexistent one both becomes, and does not become, unlike.

And a thing that becomes unlike must *come to be* different from what it was, and must *cease to be* in its former condition; while what does not become unlike does not come to be or cease to be. And b so the nonexistent one, as becoming unlike, comes to be and ceases to be, and as not becoming unlike, it does neither.

Thus the nonexistent one both comes to be and ceases to be, and also does not come to be or cease to be.

Once more, then, let us go back to our starting point to see whether we shall reach results different from these. Our question is, If a one is not, what will follow concerning it? c

The words 'is not' mean simply the absence of being from anything that we say is not. We do not mean that the thing in a sense is not, though in another sense it is. The words mean without any qualification that the thing which is not in no sense or manner is, and does not possess being in any way. So what is not cannot exist or have being in any sense or manner.

And 'coming to be' and 'ceasing to be' mean, as we said, nothing d else than acquiring being and losing it. But a thing which has nothing at all to do with being cannot acquire or lose it. So the one, since it 'is' in no sense whatever, must not possess being or lose or acquire it in any way. Therefore the one which is not, not possessing being in any sense, neither ceases to be nor comes to be.

Consequently, neither does it change in character in any way, e for if it suffered such change it would be coming to be or ceasing to be.

And if it does not change in character, it cannot be in motion. On the other hand, we cannot speak of what is nowhere at all as being at rest either, for what is at rest must always be in something [some place or condition] that is the same. Thus that which is not must not be said ever to be in motion or at rest.

Further, nothing that is can belong to it; to have a character that 164 *is* would imply that it had being. Therefore it has not greatness or smallness or equality. Nor can it have likeness to, or difference of character from, either itself or the others.

And if nothing can stand in relation to it, the others cannot be anything *to* it. They cannot be either like it or unlike, the same or different.

Again, we cannot attribute to 'what is not' anything that is; we cannot say it is 'something' or 'this thing,' or that it is so-and-so 'of this' or 'of another' or 'to another,' or that it is at any time, past, present, or future, or that there is anything '*of* it'—any knowledge or opinion, or perception *of* it—or that it *has* anything, even a name, so as to be the subject of discourse.

Thus a one which is not cannot have any character whatsoever.

Let us go on, then, to the question, If there is no one, what must be true of the others?

Obviously it must be true that they are others; if it were not, we could not be talking about 'the others.' And if we are talking about the others, things that are others must be different; 'other' and 'different' are two names for the same thing. Moreover, we speak of a thing as different from, or other than, something that is different from, or other than, it. So the others must have something to be 'other than.' What can this something be? Not the one, for there is no one. They must, then, be other than each other; that is the only possibility left, if they are not to be other than nothing.

Accordingly they must differ from each other as multitudes from multitudes; they cannot differ as one thing from another one, since there is no one [one thing]. Rather, it seems, each mass of them must be without limit of multitude; if you take what seems to be a minimum, suddenly, as might happen in a dream, what you took to be one appears many, and what had seemed to be least appears enormous in comparison with the small change for it. It is, then, as masses of this sort that the others are other than each other, if they are other without there being any one.

And there will be many such masses, each appearing to be one, but not really being so, if there is to be no one. So they will seem to have number, since each seems to be one, and they are many. And some among them will appear even, some odd, but falsely, if there is to be no one.

Further, they will seem, as we are saying, to have a smallest in 165 them, but this smallest appears as a 'many,' which is great in comparison with the smallness of each of that many. Also each mass will be imagined equal to the many smalls, for it could not pass in appearance from larger to smaller without seeming to reach the intermediate stage, which will be a semblance of equality.

Also each mass will appear as having a limit in relation to another mass. With respect to itself, it has neither beginning nor end nor middle, since whenever you fix your thought on any part of them and take that as beginning or middle or end, another beginning always b appears before the beginning, another end leftover after the end, and within the middle others that are more in the middle and smaller, because you cannot apprehend any of them as a 'one,' since there is no one. So anything there is, upon which you may fix your thought, must be frittered away in subdivision; anything we may take will always be a mass without a one. To a dim and distant view such a thing must appear one, but to closer and keener inspection each must ap- c pear without limit of multitude, being destitute of that one which does not exist.

Thus, if there is no one, but only things other than the one, each of these others must appear both unlimited in multitude and limited, both one and many.

Also, they will appear both like and unlike. As with scene paintings, to the distant spectator all will appear as one thing, and seem to have the same character and so to be alike, but if you approach nearer, they seem many and different and this semblance of difference will d make them seem different in character and unlike one another. Thus these masses must appear both like and unlike themselves and each other.

Moreover, they must appear both the same and different from one another, both in contact and apart from one another, both in every sort of motion and at rest in every respect, both coming to be and ceasing to be and doing neither, and so on with all characters of that sort, which could easily be enumerated. All this follows, if there are many, but no one. e

Now let us go back to the beginning for the last time and ask, If there is no one, but only things other than one, what must follow?

The others will not be one, but neither will they be many. For if they are to be many, there must be a one among them, since, if none of them is one thing (ἕν), they will all be no-thing (οὐδέν), and so not many either. But there is no one among them; so the others are neither one nor many. 166

Nor do they appear one or many. For the others cannot in any sense or manner have any connection with a nonentity, nor can any element of a nonentity be present to any of them, since a nonentity has no elements. Consequently neither can any appearance or seeming (δόξα) of that which has no being be found in the others, nor can any notion whatsoever of what has no being be entertained as applied

to the others. So if there is no one, none of the others can be so much
b as imagined to be one, nor yet to be many, for you cannot imagine
many without a one.

Therefore, if there is no one, the others neither are, nor can be
imagined to be, one or many.

Nor yet, if there is no one, can the others be or appear like or unlike, or the same or different, or in contact or apart, and so on with all
the other characters which we have just been saying they appear to
have.

Thus, in sum, we may conclude, If there is no one, there is nothing at all.

To this we may add the conclusion. It seems that, whether there
is or is not a one, both that one and the others alike are and are not,
and appear and do not appear to be, all manner of things in all manner
of ways, with respect to themselves and to one another.

Most true.

SOPHIST

The Parmenides, Philebus, Sophist, *and* Statesman *are a group of dialogues which resemble each other and are different from all the rest. They are the last writing Plato did, with the exception of the* Laws, *which stands in a class by itself. In the* Philebus, *as has been pointed out, Plato announces that he is entering upon a new path, he is "forging weapons of another make," changing his method of arguing. The dialogues cease to be conversations. They are close arguments rarely relieved by illustration, and only in the* Philebus *is the chief part given to Socrates. In the* Sophist *and the* Statesman *he is present, but takes no share in the discussion. He is not mentioned in the* Laws.

In the Statesman, *which follows the* Sophist, *there is a striking passage about "an impression of tediousness experienced in the discussion regarding the Sophist and the being of not-being." Plato follows this up with—to paraphrase somewhat—"I know that it was felt to be too long and I reproached myself with this, fearing it was not only tedious, but irrelevant." Here we are introduced to Plato's audience, clearly a critical one. It charged Plato with being dull, the most intolerable of all accusations because the only one nobody can defend himself against. Plato was stung too sharply by it to bear this fact in mind. His attempt at defense is made with calm superiority. "We shall not look for such length in an argument as is 'suitable' for giving pleasure. If either a full-length statement of an argument or an unusually brief one leaves the hearer more able to find real forms, there must be no expression of annoyance at its length or its brevity as the case may be. A man who criticizes the length of an argument must be required to support his grumble with a proof that a briefer statement would have left him more able to demonstrate real truth by reasoned argument. Blame and praise on other grounds we must simply ignore and act as though we had not heard them at all." For a moment Plato stands on the ordinary human level.*

A very little reading in the Sophist *shows how justified the critics were. It abounds in such statements as, "What is different is always so called with reference to another thing. It would not be so, if existence and difference were not very different things. If difference partook of both characters as existence does, there would sometimes be, within the class of different things, something that was different not*

957

with reference to another thing." Or, "Motion really is a thing that is not and a thing that is. It must, then, be possible for 'that which is not' to be, not only in the case of motion but of all the other kinds. For in the case of them all the nature of difference makes each one of them different from existence, and hence we shall be right to speak of them all as things that 'are not,' and again, because they partake of existence, to say that they 'are.' " To this the young Theaetetus, who has already shown his brilliant mind in the dialogue of that name, answers, "No doubt."

Through this mist of words it finally emerges that Plato is demolishing a widespread notion which was threatening the very basis of reasoning, that a false statement is impossible. "No one," the argument ran, "could either think or say 'what is not,' because what is not never has any sort of being." It seems incredible to us that this sort of verbal trickery could have stood in the way of real thought, but so it was, and this dialogue marked a genuine advance in the use of the tools of the mind when Plato showed that if you say A is not B you do not say that A is not something, i.e., that it is nothing, but merely that it is "other," different from B.

The argument is hung on the figure of the Sophist apparently quite arbitrarily. No real picture is given of the men who were the professional instructors of Greece for many years. All Plato does is to ascribe to them every notion he disapproves. He detested the whole band of Sophists. To him they were shallow-minded, pretentious, superficial, mercenary—they were really doing what Socrates was charged with, corrupting the minds of the young.

---

216   THEODORUS : Here we are, Socrates, faithful to our appointment of yesterday, and, what is more, we have brought a guest with us. Our friend here is a native of Elea; he belongs to the school of Parmenides and Zeno, and is devoted to philosophy.

SOCRATES : Perhaps, Theodorus, it is no ordinary guest but some god that you have brought us unawares. Homer tells us that gods attend upon the goings of men of mercy and justice, and not least

b   among them the god of strangers comes to mark the orderly or lawless doings of mankind. Your companion may be one of those higher powers, who intends to observe and expose our weakness in philosophical discourse, like a very spirit of refutation.

From *Plato's Theory of Knowledge: the Theaetetus and the Sophist*, translated with a running commentary by Francis Macdonald Cornford (London, 1935); with a passage from the translation by B. Jowett in *The Dialogues of Plato*, 3rd edn. (Oxford, 1931; first printed, 1892).

THEODORUS: That is not our friend's way, Socrates; he is more reasonable than the devotees of verbal dispute. I should not call him a god by any means, but there is something divine about him. I would say that of any philosopher.   c

SOCRATES: And rightly, my friend, but one might almost say that the type you mention is hardly easier to discern than the god. Such men—the genuine, not the sham philosophers—as they go from city to city surveying from a height the life beneath them, appear, owing to the world's blindness, to wear all sorts of shapes. To some they seem of no account, to others above all worth; now they wear the guise of statesmen, now of Sophists, and sometimes they may give the d impression of simply being mad. But if our guest will allow me, I should like to ask him what his countrymen thought and how they 217 used these names.

THEODORUS: What names?

SOCRATES: Sophist, statesman, philosopher.

THEODORUS: What is your question exactly? What sort of difficulty about these names have you in mind?

SOCRATES: This. Did they think of all these as a single type, or as two, or did they distinguish three types and attach one of the three corresponding names to each?

THEODORUS: I imagine you are quite welcome to the information. Is not that so, sir?

STRANGER: Yes, Theodorus, perfectly welcome, and the answer b is not difficult. They thought of them as three different types, but it is not so short and easy a task to define each one of them clearly.

THEODORUS: As luck would have it, Socrates, you have hit upon a subject closely allied to one on which we were pressing him with questions before we came here. He tried to put us off with the same excuse he has just made to you, though he admits he has been thoroughly instructed and has not forgotten what he heard.

SOCRATES: Do not deny us, then, the first favor we ask. Tell us c this much. Which do you commonly prefer—to discourse at length by yourself on any matter you wish to make clear, or to use the method of asking questions, as Parmenides himself did on one occasion in developing some magnificent arguments in my presence, when I was young and he quite an elderly man?

STRANGER: When the other party to the conversation is tract- d able and gives no trouble, to address him is the easier course; otherwise, to speak by oneself.

SOCRATES: Then you may choose any of the company you will; they will all follow you and respond amenably. But if you take my advice, you will choose one of the younger men—Theaetetus here or any other you may prefer.

STRANGER: I feel some shyness, Socrates, at the notion that, at my first meeting with you and your friends, instead of exchanging our

ideas in the give-and-take of ordinary conversation, I should spin out
e a long discourse by myself or even address it to another, as if I were
giving a display of eloquence. For indeed the question you have just
raised is not so easy a matter as one might suppose, on hearing it so
simply put, but it calls for a very long discussion. On the other hand,
to refuse you and your friends a request, especially one put to me in
218 such terms as you have used, strikes me as a breach of civility in a
guest. That Theaetetus should be the other party to our conversation is
a proposal which my earlier talk with him, as well as your recommendation, makes exceedingly welcome.

THEAETETUS: Then do as you say, sir; you will, as Socrates
said, be conferring a favor on us all.

STRANGER: On that point, Theaetetus, no more need be said;
the discussion from now onward must, it seems, be carried on with
you. But if the long task should after all weigh heavy on you, your
friends here, not I, must bear the blame.

b   THEAETETUS: I do not feel at this moment as if I should sink
under it, but should something of that sort happen, we will call in Socrates' namesake here, who is of my own age and shares my pursuits.
He is quite used to working out most questions with me.

STRANGER: A good suggestion. That shall be for you to consider
as our conversation goes forward. What now concerns us both is our
joint inquiry. We had better, I think, begin by studying the Sophist
c and try to bring his nature to light in a clear formula. At present, you
see, all that you and I possess in common is the name. The thing to
which each of us gives that name we may perhaps have privately before our minds, but it is always desirable to have reached an agreement about the thing itself by means of explicit statements, rather
than be content to use the same word without formulating what it
means. It is not so easy to comprehend this group we intend to examine or to say what it means to be a Sophist. However, when some great
d task is to be properly carried through, everyone has long since found
it a good rule to take something comparatively small and easy and
practice on that, before attempting the big thing itself. That is the
course I recommend for us now, Theaetetus. Judging the Sophist to
be a very troublesome sort of creature to hunt down, let us first practice the method of tracking him on some easier quarry—unless you
have some readier means to suggest?

THEAETETUS: No, I have none.

* STRANGER: Then suppose that we work out some lesser example, which will be a pattern of the greater?

---

* [The translator here omits the long passage (218d–230e) in which
the Stranger illustrates the method to be used in defining the Sophist. The
editors prefer to avoid this break in the Platonic text. The translation of
this passage is that of B. Jowett.]

THEAETETUS: Good.   e

STRANGER: What is there which is well known and not great, and is yet as susceptible of definition as any larger thing? Shall I say an angler? He is familiar to all of us, and not a very interesting or important person.

THEAETETUS: He is not.

STRANGER: Yet I suspect that he will furnish us with the sort   219 of definition and line of inquiry which we want.

THEAETETUS: Very good.

STRANGER: Let us begin by asking whether he is a man having art or not having art, but some other power.

THEAETETUS: He is clearly a man of art.

STRANGER: And of arts there are two kinds?

THEAETETUS: What are they?

STRANGER: There is agriculture, and the tending of mortal creatures, and the art of constructing or molding vessels, and there is the art of imitation—all these may be appropriately called by a single   b name.

THEAETETUS: What do you mean? And what is the name?

STRANGER: He who brings into existence something that did not exist before is said to be a producer, and that which is brought into existence is said to be produced.

THEAETETUS: True.

STRANGER: And all the arts which were just now mentioned are characterized by this power of producing?

THEAETETUS: They are.

STRANGER: Then let us sum them up under the name of productive or creative art.

THEAETETUS: Very good.   c

STRANGER: Next follows the whole class of learning and cognition; then comes trade, fighting, hunting. And since none of these produces anything, but is only engaged in conquering by word or deed, or in preventing others from conquering, things which exist and have been already produced—in each and all of these branches there appears to be an art which may be called acquisitive.

THEAETETUS: Yes, that is the proper name.

STRANGER: Seeing, then, that all arts are either acquisitive or   d creative, in which class shall we place the art of the angler?

THEAETETUS: Clearly in the acquisitive class.

STRANGER: And the acquisitive may be subdivided into two parts. There is exchange, which is voluntary and is effected by gifts, hire, purchase, and the other part of acquisitive, which takes by force of word or deed, may be termed conquest?

THEAETETUS: That is implied in what has been said.

STRANGER: And may not conquest be again subdivided?

THEAETETUS: How?

e   STRANGER: Open force may be called fighting, and secret force may have the general name of hunting?

THEAETETUS: Yes.

STRANGER: And there is no reason why the art of hunting should not be further divided.

THEAETETUS: How would you make the division?

STRANGER: Into the hunting of living and of lifeless prey.

THEAETETUS: Yes, if both kinds exist.

220   STRANGER: Of course they exist, but the hunting after lifeless things having no special name, except some sorts of diving, and other small matters, may be omitted; the hunting after living things may be called animal hunting.

THEAETETUS: Yes.

STRANGER: And animal hunting may be truly said to have two divisions, land animal hunting, which has many kinds and names, and water animal hunting, or the hunting after animals who swim?

THEAETETUS: True.

b   STRANGER: And of swimming animals, one class lives on the wing and the other in the water?

THEAETETUS: Certainly.

STRANGER: Fowling is the general term under which the hunting of all birds is included.

THEAETETUS: True.

STRANGER: The hunting of animals who live in the water has the general name of fishing.

THEAETETUS: Yes.

STRANGER: And this sort of hunting may be further divided also into two principal kinds?

THEAETETUS: What are they?

STRANGER: There is one kind which takes them in nets, another which takes them by a blow.

THEAETETUS: What do you mean, and how do you distinguish them?

c   STRANGER: As to the first kind—all that surrounds and encloses anything to prevent egress, may be rightly called an enclosure.

THEAETETUS: Very true.

STRANGER: For which reason twig baskets, casting nets, nooses, creels, and the like may all be termed 'enclosures'?

THEAETETUS: True.

STRANGER: And therefore this first kind of capture may be called by us capture with enclosures, or something of that sort?

THEAETETUS: Yes.

STRANGER: The other kind, which is practiced by a blow with
d hooks and three-pronged spears, when summed up under one name, may be called striking, unless you, Theaetetus, can find some better name?

THEAETETUS: Never mind the name—what you suggest will do very well.

STRANGER: There is one mode of striking, which is done at night, and by the light of a fire, and is by the hunters themselves called firing, or spearing by firelight.

THEAETETUS: True.

STRANGER: And the fishing by day is called by the general name of barbing, because the spears, too, are barbed at the point.

THEAETETUS: Yes, that is the term.   e

STRANGER: Of this barb fishing, that which strikes the fish who is below from above is called spearing, because this is the way in which the three-pronged spears are mostly used.

THEAETETUS: Yes, it is often called so.

STRANGER: Then now there is only one kind remaining.

THEAETETUS: What is that?

STRANGER: When a hook is used, and the fish is not struck in any chance part of his body, as he is with the spear, but only about the head and mouth, and is then drawn out from below upward with reeds and rods—what is the right name of that mode of fishing, The-   221
aetetus?

THEAETETUS: I suspect that we have now discovered the object of our search.

STRANGER: Then now you and I have come to an understanding not only about the name of the angler's art, but about the definition of the thing itself. One half of all art was acquisitive—half of the   b
acquisitive art was conquest or taking by force, half of this was hunting, and half of hunting was hunting animals; half of this was hunting water animals; of this again, the under half was fishing; half of fishing was striking; a part of striking was fishing with a barb, and one half of this again, being the kind which strikes with a hook and draws   c
the fish from below upward, is the art which we have been seeking, and which from the nature of the operation is denoted angling or drawing up (ἀσπαλιευτική, ἀνασπᾶσθαι).

THEAETETUS: The result has been quite satisfactorily brought out.

STRANGER: And now, following this pattern, let us endeavor to find out what a Sophist is.

THEAETETUS: By all means.

STRANGER: The first question about the angler was, whether he was a skilled artist or unskilled?

THEAETETUS: True.

STRANGER: And shall we call our new friend unskilled, or a   d
thorough master of his craft?

THEAETETUS: Certainly not unskilled, for his name, as, indeed, you imply, must surely express his nature.

STRANGER: Then he must be supposed to have some art.

THEAETETUS: What art?

STRANGER: By heaven, they are cousins! It never occurred to us.

THEAETETUS: Who are cousins?

STRANGER: The angler and the Sophist.

THEAETETUS: In what way are they related?

STRANGER: They both appear to me to be hunters.

e   THEAETETUS: How the Sophist? Of the other we have spoken.

STRANGER: You remember our division of hunting, into hunting after swimming animals and land animals?

THEAETETUS: Yes.

STRANGER: And you remember that we subdivided the swimming and left the land animals, saying that there were many kinds of them?

222   THEAETETUS: Certainly.

STRANGER: Thus far, then, the Sophist and the angler, starting from the art of acquiring, take the same road?

THEAETETUS: So it would appear.

STRANGER: Their paths diverge when they reach the art of animal hunting—the one going to the seashore, and to the rivers, and to the lakes, and angling for the animals which are in them.

THEAETETUS: Very true.

STRANGER: While the other goes to land and water of another sort—rivers of wealth and broad meadowlands of generous youth, and he also is intending to take the animals which are in them.

b   THEAETETUS: What do you mean?

STRANGER: Of hunting on land there are two principal divisions.

THEAETETUS: What are they?

STRANGER: One is the hunting of tame, and the other of wild animals.

THEAETETUS: But are tame animals ever hunted?

STRANGER: Yes, if you include man under tame animals. But if you like you may say that there are no tame animals, or that, if there are, man is not among them, or you may say that man is a tame animal but is not hunted—you shall decide which of these alternatives you prefer.

c   THEAETETUS: I should say, Stranger, that man is a tame animal, and I admit that he is hunted.

STRANGER: Then let us divide the hunting of tame animals into two parts.

THEAETETUS: How shall we make the division?

STRANGER: Let us define piracy, manstealing, tyranny, the whole military art, by one name, as hunting with violence.

THEAETETUS: Very good.

STRANGER: But the art of the lawyer, of the popular orator,

and the art of conversation may be called in one word the art of per- d
suasion.

THEAETETUS: True.

STRANGER: And of persuasion, there may be said to be two kinds?

THEAETETUS: What are they?

STRANGER: One is private, and the other public.

THEAETETUS: Yes, each of them forms a class.

STRANGER: And of private hunting, one sort receives hire, and the other brings gifts.

THEAETETUS: I do not understand you.

STRANGER: You seem never to have observed the manner in which lovers hunt.

THEAETETUS: To what do you refer?

STRANGER: I mean that they lavish gifts on those whom they e hunt in addition to other inducements.

THEAETETUS: Most true.

STRANGER: Let us admit this, then, to be the amatory art.

THEAETETUS: Certainly.

STRANGER: But that sort of hireling whose conversation is pleasing and who baits his hook only with pleasure and exacts nothing but his maintenance in return, we should all, if I am not mistaken, describe as possessing flattery or an art of making things pleasant.   223

THEAETETUS: Certainly.

STRANGER: And that sort, which professes to form acquaintances only for the sake of virtue, and demands a reward in the shape of money, may be fairly called by another name?

THEAETETUS: To be sure.

STRANGER: And what is the name? Will you tell me?

THEAETETUS: It is obvious enough, for I believe that we have discovered the Sophist—which is, as I conceive, the proper name for the class described.

STRANGER: Then now, Theaetetus, his art may be traced as a b branch of the appropriative, acquisitive family—which hunts animals, living, land, tame animals—which hunts man, privately, for hire, taking money in exchange, having the semblance of education— and this is termed Sophistry, and is a hunt after young men of wealth and rank—such is the conclusion.

THEAETETUS: Just so.

STRANGER: Let us take another branch of his genealogy, for he c is a professor of a great and many-sided art. And if we look back at what has preceded we see that he presents another aspect, besides that of which we are speaking.

THEAETETUS: In what respect?

STRANGER: There were two sorts of acquisitive art—the one concerned with hunting, the other with exchange.

THEAETETUS: There were.

STRANGER: And of the art of exchange there are two divisions, the one of giving, and the other of selling.

THEAETETUS: Let us assume that.

STRANGER: Next, we will suppose the art of selling to be divided into two parts.

d   THEAETETUS: How?

STRANGER: There is one part which is distinguished as the sale of a man's own productions; another, which is the exchange of the works of others.

THEAETETUS: Certainly.

STRANGER: And is not that part of exchange which takes place in the city, being about half of the whole, termed retailing?

THEAETETUS: Yes.

STRANGER: And that which exchanges the goods of one city for those of another by selling and buying is the exchange of the merchant?

THEAETETUS: To be sure.

e   STRANGER: And you are aware that this exchange of the merchant is of two kinds; it is partly concerned with food for the use of the body, and partly with the food of the soul which is bartered and received in exchange for money.

THEAETETUS: What do you mean?

STRANGER: You want to know what is the meaning of food for the soul; the other kind you surely understand.

THEAETETUS: Yes.

STRANGER: Take music in general, and painting and mario-
224 nette playing, and many other things, which are purchased in one city, and carried away and sold in another—wares of the soul which are hawked about either for the sake of instruction or amusement. May not he who takes them about and sells them be quite as truly called a merchant as he who sells meats and drinks?

THEAETETUS: To be sure he may.

b   STRANGER: And would you not call by the same name him who buys up knowledge and goes about from city to city exchanging his wares for money?

THEAETETUS: Certainly I should.

STRANGER: Of this merchandise of the soul, may not one part be fairly termed the art of display? And there is another part which is certainly not less ridiculous, but being a trade in learning must be called by some name germane to the matter?

THEAETETUS: Certainly.

c   STRANGER: The latter should have two names—one descriptive of the sale of the knowledge of virtue, and the other of the sale of other kinds of knowledge.

THEAETETUS: Of course.

STRANGER: The name of art seller corresponds well enough to the latter, but you must try and tell me the name of the other.

THEAETETUS: He must be the Sophist, whom we are seeking; no other name can possibly be right.

STRANGER: No other, and so this trader in virtue again turns out to be our friend the Sophist, whose art may now be traced from the art of acquisition through exchange, trade, merchandise, to a merchandise of the soul which is concerned with speech and the knowl- d edge of virtue.

THEAETETUS: Quite true.

STRANGER: And there may be a third reappearance of him— for he may have settled down in a city, and may fabricate as well as buy these same wares, intending to live by selling them, and he would still be called a Sophist?

THEAETETUS: Certainly.

STRANGER: Then that part of acquisitive art which exchanges, e and of exchange which either sells a man's own productions or retails those of others, as the case may be, and in either way sells the knowledge of virtue, you would again term Sophistry?

THEAETETUS: I must, if I am to keep pace with the argument.

STRANGER: Let us consider once more whether there may not be yet another aspect of Sophistry.

THEAETETUS: What is it?

STRANGER: In the acquisitive there was a subdivision of the 225 combative or fighting art.

THEAETETUS: There was.

STRANGER: Perhaps we had better divide it.

THEAETETUS: What shall be the divisions?

STRANGER: There shall be one division of the competitive, and another of the pugnacious.

THEAETETUS: Very good.

STRANGER: That part of the pugnacious which is a contest of bodily strength may be properly called by some such name as violent.

THEAETETUS: True.

STRANGER: And when the war is one of words, it may be b termed controversy?

THEAETETUS: Yes.

STRANGER: And controversy may be of two kinds?

THEAETETUS: What are they?

STRANGER: When long speeches are answered by long speeches, and there is public discussion about the just and unjust, that is forensic controversy.

THEAETETUS: Yes.

STRANGER: And there is a private sort of controversy, which is cut up into questions and answers, and this is commonly called disputation?

THEAETETUS : Yes, that is the name.

c   STRANGER : And of disputation, that sort which is only a discussion about contracts, and is carried on at random, and without rules of art, is recognized by the reasoning faculty to be a distinct class, but has hitherto had no distinctive name, and does not deserve to receive one from us.

THEAETETUS : No, for the different sorts of it are too minute and heterogeneous.

STRANGER : But that which proceeds by rules of art to dispute about justice and injustice in their own nature, and about things in general, we have been accustomed to call argumentation [eristic]?

THEAETETUS : Certainly.

d   STRANGER : And of argumentation, one sort wastes money, and the other makes money.

THEAETETUS : Very true.

STRANGER : Suppose we try and give to each of these two classes a name.

THEAETETUS : Let us do so.

STRANGER : I should say that the habit which leads a man to neglect his own affairs for the pleasure of conversation, of which the style is far from being agreeable to the majority of his hearers, may be fairly termed loquacity. Such is my opinion.

THEAETETUS : That is the common name for it.

e   STRANGER : But now who the other is, who makes money out of private disputation, it is your turn to say.

THEAETETUS : There is only one true answer. He is the wonderful Sophist, of whom we are in pursuit, and who reappears again for the fourth time.

226   STRANGER : Yes, and with a fresh pedigree, for he is the money-making species of the eristic, disputatious, controversial, pugnacious, combative, acquisitive family, the argument has already proved.

THEAETETUS : Certainly.

STRANGER : How true was the observation that he was a many-sided animal, and not to be caught with one hand, as they say!

THEAETETUS : Then you must catch him with two.

b   STRANGER : Yes, we must, if we can. And therefore let us try another track in our pursuit of him. You are aware that there are certain menial occupations which have names among servants?

THEAETETUS : Yes, there are many such. Which of them do you mean?

STRANGER : I mean such as sifting, straining, winnowing, threshing.

THEAETETUS : Certainly.

STRANGER : And besides these there are a great many more, such as carding, spinning, adjusting the warp and the woof, and thousands of similar expressions are used in the arts.

THEAETETUS: Of what are they to be patterns, and what are c we going to do with them all?

STRANGER: I think that in all of these there is implied a notion of division.

THEAETETUS: Yes.

STRANGER: Then if, as I was saying, there is one art which includes all of them, ought not that art to have one name?

THEAETETUS: And what is the name of the art?

STRANGER: The art of discerning or discriminating.

THEAETETUS: Very good.

STRANGER: Think whether you cannot divide this.

THEAETETUS: I should have to think a long while.

STRANGER: In all the previously named processes either like d has been separated from like or the better from the worse.

THEAETETUS: I see now what you mean.

STRANGER: There is no name for the first kind of separation; of the second, which throws away the worse and preserves the better, I do know a name.

THEAETETUS: What is it?

STRANGER: Every discernment or discrimination of that kind, as I have observed, is called a purification.

THEAETETUS: Yes, that is the usual expression.

STRANGER: And anyone may see that purification is of two e kinds.

THEAETETUS: Perhaps so, if he were allowed time to think, but I do not see at this moment.

STRANGER: There are many purifications of bodies which may with propriety be comprehended under a single name.

THEAETETUS: What are they, and what is their name?

STRANGER: There is the purification of living bodies in their 227 inward and in their outward parts, of which the former is duly effected by medicine and gymnastics, the latter by the not very dignified art of the bathman, and there is the purification of inanimate substances—to this the arts of fulling and furbishing in general attend in a number of minute particulars, having a variety of names which are thought ridiculous.

THEAETETUS: Very true.

STRANGER: There can be no doubt that they are thought ridiculous, Theaetetus, but then the dialectic art never considers whether the benefit to be derived from the purge is greater or less than that to be derived from the sponge, and has not more interest in the one than b in the other. Her endeavor is to know what is and is not kindred in all arts, with a view to the acquisition of intelligence, and having this in view, she honors them all alike. And when she makes comparisons, she counts one of them not a whit more ridiculous than another, nor does she esteem him who adduces as his example of hunting, the

general's art, at all more decorous than another who cites that of the
vermin destroyer, but only as the greater pretender of the two. And as
to your question concerning the name which was to comprehend all
these arts of purification, whether of animate or inanimate bodies,
c the art of dialectic is in no wise particular about fine words, if she may
be only allowed to have a general name for all other purifications,
binding them up together and separating them off from the purification of the soul or intellect. For this is the purification at which she
wants to arrive, and this we should understand to be her aim.

THEAETETUS : Yes, I understand, and I agree that there are two
sorts of purification, and that one of them is concerned with the soul,
and that there is another which is concerned with the body.

STRANGER : Excellent, and now listen to what I am going to
d say, and try to divide further the first of the two.

THEAETETUS : Whatever line of division you suggest, I will endeavor to assist you.

STRANGER : Do we admit that virtue is distinct from vice in the
soul?

THEAETETUS : Certainly.

STRANGER : And purification was to leave the good and to cast
out whatever is bad?

THEAETETUS : True.

STRANGER : Then any taking away of evil from the soul may be
properly called purification?

THEAETETUS : Yes.

STRANGER : And in the soul there are two kinds of evil.

THEAETETUS : What are they?

228   STRANGER : The one may be compared to disease in the body,
the other to deformity.

THEAETETUS : I do not understand.

STRANGER : Perhaps you have never reflected that disease and
discord are the same.

THEAETETUS : To this, again, I know not what I should reply.

STRANGER : Do you not conceive discord to be a dissolution of
kindred elements, originating in some disagreement?

THEAETETUS : Just that.

STRANGER : And is deformity anything but the want of measure, which is always unsightly?

b   THEAETETUS : Exactly.

STRANGER : And do we not see that opinion is opposed to desire, pleasure to anger, reason to pain, and that all these elements are
opposed to one another in the souls of bad men?

THEAETETUS : Certainly.

STRANGER : And yet they must all be akin?

THEAETETUS : Of course.

STRANGER : Then we shall be right in calling vice a discord and
disease of the soul?

THEAETETUS: Most true.

STRANGER: And when things having motion, and aiming at an c appointed mark, continually miss their aim and glance aside, shall we say that this is the effect of symmetry among them, or of the want of symmetry?

THEAETETUS: Clearly of the want of symmetry.

STRANGER: But surely we know that no soul is voluntarily ignorant of anything?

THEAETETUS: Certainly not.

STRANGER: And what is ignorance but the aberration of a mind which is bent on truth, and in which the process of understanding is d perverted?

THEAETETUS: True.

STRANGER: Then we are to regard an unintelligent soul as deformed and devoid of symmetry?

THEAETETUS: Very true.

STRANGER: Then there are these two kinds of evil in the soul—the one which is generally called vice, and is obviously a disease of the soul . . .

THEAETETUS: Yes.

STRANGER: And there is the other, which they call ignorance, and which, because existing only in the soul, they will not allow to be vice.

THEAETETUS: I certainly admit what I at first disputed—that e there are two kinds of vice in the soul, and that we ought to consider cowardice, intemperance, and injustice to be all alike forms of disease in the soul, and ignorance, of which there are all sorts of varieties, to be deformity.

STRANGER: And in the case of the body are there not two arts which have to do with the two bodily states?

THEAETETUS: What are they?

STRANGER: There is gymnastics, which has to do with deform- 229 ity, and medicine, which has to do with disease.

THEAETETUS: True.

STRANGER: And where there are insolence and injustice and cowardice, is not the chastisement the art that is most required?

THEAETETUS: That certainly appears to be the opinion of mankind.

STRANGER: Again, of the various kinds of ignorance, may not instruction be rightly said to be the remedy?

THEAETETUS: True.

STRANGER: And of the art of instruction, shall we say that b there is one or many kinds? At any rate there are two principal ones. Think.

THEAETETUS: I will.

STRANGER: I believe that I can see how we shall soonest arrive at the answer to this question.

THEAETETUS: How?

STRANGER: If we can discover a line which divides ignorance into two halves. For a division of ignorance into two parts will certainly imply that the art of instruction is also twofold, answering to the two divisions of ignorance.

THEAETETUS: Well, and do you see what you are looking for?

c   STRANGER: I do seem to myself to see one very large and bad sort of ignorance which is quite separate, and may be weighed in the scale against all other sorts of ignorance put together.

THEAETETUS: What is it?

STRANGER: When a person supposes that he knows, and does not know; this appears to be the great source of all the errors of the intellect.

THEAETETUS: True.

STRANGER: And this, if I am not mistaken, is the kind of ignorance which specially earns the title of stupidity.

THEAETETUS: True.

STRANGER: What name, then, shall be given to the sort of instruction which gets rid of this?

d   THEAETETUS: The instruction which you mean, Stranger, is, I should imagine, not the teaching of handicraft arts, but what, thanks to us, has been termed education in this part of the world.

STRANGER: Yes, Theaetetus, and by nearly all Hellenes. But we have still to consider whether education admits of any further division deserving a name.

THEAETETUS: We have.

STRANGER: I think that there is a point at which such a division is possible.

THEAETETUS: Where?

e   STRANGER: Of education, one method appears to be rougher, and another smoother.

THEAETETUS: How are we to distinguish the two?

STRANGER: There is the time-honored mode which our fathers commonly practiced toward their sons, and which is still adopted by
230   many—either of roughly reproving their errors, or of gently advising them—which varieties may be correctly included under the general term of admonition.

THEAETETUS: True.

STRANGER: But whereas some appear to have arrived at the conclusion that all ignorance is involuntary, and that no one who thinks himself wise is willing to learn any of those things in which he is conscious of his own cleverness, and that the admonitory sort of education gives much trouble and does little good . . .

THEAETETUS: There they are quite right.

b   STRANGER: Accordingly, they set to work to eradicate the spirit of conceit in another way.

THEAETETUS: In what way?

STRANGER: They cross-examine a man's words, when he thinks that he is saying something and is really saying nothing, and easily convict him of inconsistencies in his opinions; these they then collect by the dialectic process, and placing them side by side, show that they contradict one another about the same things, in relation to the same things, and in the same respect. He, seeing this, is angry with himself, and grows gentle toward others, and thus is entirely delivered from c great prejudices and harsh notions, in a way which is most amusing to the hearer, and produces the most lasting good effect on the person who is the subject of the operation. For as the physician considers that the body will receive no benefit from taking food until the internal obstacles have been removed, so the purifier of the soul is conscious that his patient will receive no benefit from the application of knowledge until he is refuted, and from refutation learns modesty; he must d be purged of his prejudices first and made to think that he knows only what he knows, and no more.

THEAETETUS: That is certainly the best and wisest state of mind.

STRANGER: For all these reasons, Theaetetus, we must admit that refutation is the greatest and chiefest of purifications, and he who has not been refuted, though he be the Great King himself, is in an awful state of impurity; he is uninstructed and deformed in those e things in which he who would be truly blessed ought to be fairest and purest.

THEAETETUS: Very true.

* STRANGER: Well, what name shall we give to the practitioners of this art? For my part I shrink from calling them Sophists. 231

THEAETETUS: Why so?

STRANGER: For fear of ascribing to them too high a function.

THEAETETUS: And yet your description has some resemblance to that type [the Sophist].

STRANGER: So has the dog to the wolf—the fiercest of animals to the tamest. But a cautious man should above all be on his guard against resemblances; they are a very slippery sort of thing. However, be it so [i.e., let them pass for Sophists], for should they ever set up an adequate defense of their confines, the boundary in dispute will be b of no small importance.

THEAETETUS: That is likely enough.

STRANGER: Let us take it, then, that under the art of separation there is a method of purification, that we have distinguished that kind of purification which is concerned with the soul, and under that, instruction, and under that again, education. Within the art of education, the examination which confutes the vain conceit of wisdom we

* [With this speech of the Stranger, the Cornford translation resumes.]

will allow to pass, in the argument which has now come in by a side wind, by no other name than the sophistry that is of noble lineage (ἡ γένει γενναία σοφιστική).

THEAETETUS: Let it pass by that name. But by this time the
c Sophist has appeared in so many guises that for my part I am puzzled to see what description one is to maintain as truly expressing his real nature.

STRANGER: You may well be puzzled. But we may suppose that by now the Sophist too is very much puzzled to see how he is once more to slip through the meshes of our argument, for it is a true saying that you cannot easily evade all the wrestler's grips. So now is the moment of all others to set upon him.

THEAETETUS: Well and good.

STRANGER: First, then, let us stand and take breath, and while
d we are resting let us reckon up between ourselves in how many guises the Sophist has appeared. First, I think, he was found as the hired hunter of rich young men.

THEAETETUS: Yes.

STRANGER: And secondly as a sort of merchant of learning as nourishment for the soul.

THEAETETUS: Certainly.

STRANGER: Thirdly, he showed himself as a retail dealer in the same wares, did he not?

THEAETETUS: Yes, and fourthly as selling the products of his own manufacture.

STRANGER: Your memory serves you well. His fifth appearance
e I will myself try to recall. He was an athlete in debate, appropriating that subdivision of contention which consists in the art of eristic.

THEAETETUS: He was.

STRANGER: His sixth appearance was open to doubt; however, we conceded his claim to be described as a purifier of the soul from conceits that block the way to understanding.

THEAETETUS: Quite so.

232 STRANGER: Now does it strike you that when one who is known by the name of a single art appears to be master of many, there is something wrong with this appearance? If one has that impression of any art, plainly it is because one cannot see clearly that feature of it in which all these forms of skill converge, and so one calls their possessor by many names instead of one.

THEAETETUS: I dare say that is the gist of the situation.

b STRANGER: If so, we must not be so lazy as to let that happen to us in our inquiry. Let us begin by going back to one among the characteristics we attributed to the Sophist. There was one that struck me particularly as revealing his character.

THEAETETUS: What was that?

STRANGER: We said, I believe, that he was a controversialist.

THEAETETUS: Yes.

STRANGER: And further that he figures as an instructor of others in controversy.

THEAETETUS: Certainly.

STRANGER: Let us consider, then, in what field these people profess to turn out controversialists. Let us go to the root of the matter and set about it in this way. Tell me, does their pupils' competence extend to divine things that are hidden from common eyes?　　　c

THEAETETUS: So it is said of them, at any rate.

STRANGER: And also to all that is visible in sky and earth and everything of that sort.

THEAETETUS: Surely.

STRANGER: And in private circles, whenever any general statement is made about becoming or reality, we are aware how cleverly they can controvert it and make others able to do the same.

THEAETETUS: Certainly.

STRANGER: And then again where laws are in question or any political matter, do they not promise to produce debaters?　　　d

THEAETETUS: If they did not hold out that promise, hardly anyone would take part in their discussions.

STRANGER: And about the crafts in general and each particular craft, the arguments to be used in controversy with any actual craftsman have been published broadcast for all who choose to learn.

THEAETETUS: I take it you mean what Protagoras wrote on　e wrestling and the other arts.

STRANGER: Yes, and on many other things. In fact, the pretensions of this art of controversy amount, it seems, to a capacity for disputation on any subject whatsoever.

THEAETETUS: It certainly seems that nothing worth speaking of is beyond its scope.

STRANGER: Do you, then, my young friend, really think that possible? You young people may perhaps see more clearly; my eyes are too dim.

THEAETETUS: Is what possible? What am I meant to see? I　233 don't clearly understand what you are asking me.

STRANGER: Whether it is possible for any human being to know everything.

THEAETETUS: Mankind would indeed be happy, if it were so.

STRANGER: Then if a man who has no knowledge controverts one who does know, how can there be any sound sense in what he says?

THEAETETUS: There cannot be.

STRANGER: Then what can be the secret of this magical power of sophistry?

THEAETETUS: In what respect?

STRANGER: I mean, how they can ever create a belief in the　b minds of young men that they are the wisest of men on all subjects? For clearly if they were not in the right in their controversies or did not appear to be so in the young men's eyes, and if that appearance did not enhance the belief that they are wise because they can dispute, then, to quote your own remark, it is hard to see why anyone should want to pay their fees and be taught this art of disputation.

THEAETETUS: Hard indeed.

STRANGER: But in actual fact there is a demand.

THEAETETUS: Quite a brisk one.

c STRANGER: No doubt because the Sophists are believed to possess a knowledge of their own in the subjects they dispute about.

THEAETETUS: No doubt.

STRANGER: And, we say, there is no subject they do not dispute about.

THEAETETUS: Yes.

STRANGER: So they appear to their pupils to be wise on all subjects.

THEAETETUS: Certainly.

STRANGER: Although they are not really wise, for that, we saw, is impossible.

THEAETETUS: It must be impossible.

STRANGER: The upshot is, then, that the Sophist possesses a sort of reputed and apparent knowledge on all subjects, but not the reality.

d THEAETETUS: I quite agree, and perhaps this is the truest thing that has yet been said about them.

STRANGER: Let us, then, take an analogy that will throw more light on their position.

THEAETETUS: What is that?

STRANGER: It is this. Try to give me your closest attention in answering.

THEAETETUS: What is your question?

STRANGER: Suppose a man professed to know, not how to speak or dispute about everything, but how to produce all things in actual fact by a single form of skill.

e THEAETETUS: What do you mean by 'all things'?

STRANGER: My meaning is beyond your comprehension at the very outset. It seems you do not understand what is meant by 'all things.'

THEAETETUS: No.

STRANGER: Well, 'all things' is meant to include you and me and, besides ourselves, all other animals and plants.

THEAETETUS: How do you mean?

STRANGER: Suppose a man should undertake to produce you and me and all creatures.

THEAETETUS: What sort of production do you mean? You can- 234
not mean some sort of farmer, for you spoke of him as producing animals as well.

STRANGER: Yes, and besides that, sea and sky and earth and
gods and everything else there is. What is more, after producing any
one of them with a turn of the hand he sells them for quite a moderate sum.

THEAETETUS: You mean in some kind of play?

STRANGER: Well, a man who says he knows everything and
could teach it to another for a small fee in a short time can hardly be
taken in earnest.

THEAETETUS: Assuredly not.

STRANGER: And of all forms of play, could you think of any
more skillful and amusing than imitation?   b

THEAETETUS: No. When you take that one form with all that
it embraces, it covers a very large variety.

STRANGER: Well, we know this about the man who professes to
be able, by a single form of skill, to produce all things, that when he
creates with his pencil representations bearing the same name as real
things, he will be able to deceive the innocent minds of children, if he
shows them his drawings at a distance, into thinking that he is capable of creating, in full reality, anything he chooses to make.

THEAETETUS: Of course.   c

STRANGER: Then must we not expect to find a corresponding
form of skill in the region of discourse, making it possible to impose
upon the young who are still far removed from the reality of things, by
means of words that cheat the ear, exhibiting images of all things in a
shadow play of discourse, so as to make them believe that they are
hearing the truth and that the speaker is in all matters the wisest of
men?

THEAETETUS: There may well be such an art as you describe.   d

STRANGER: And is it not inevitable that, after a long enough
time, as these young hearers advance in age and, coming into closer
touch with realities, are forced by experience to apprehend things
clearly as they are, most of them should abandon those former beliefs,
so that what seemed important will now appear trifling and what
seemed easy, difficult, and all the illusions created in discourse will
be completely overturned by the realities which encounter them in the
actual conduct of life?   e

THEAETETUS: Yes, so far as I can judge at my age, but I suppose I am one of those who are still at a distance.

STRANGER: That is why all of us here must try, as we are in
fact trying, to bring you as close as possible to the realities and spare
you the experience.

But about the Sophist, tell me, is it now clear that he is a sort of

235 wizard, an imitator of real things—or are we still uncertain whether he may not possess genuine knowledge of all the things he seems capable of disputing about?

THEAETETUS : He cannot, sir. It is clear enough from what has been said that he is one of those whose province is play.

STRANGER : Then we may class him as a wizard and an imitator of some sort.

THEAETETUS : Certainly.

STRANGER : Come then, it is now for us to see that we do not b again relax the pursuit of our quarry. We may say that we have him enveloped in such a net as argument provides for hunting of this sort. He cannot shuffle out of this.

THEAETETUS : Out of what?

STRANGER : Out of being somewhere within the class of illusionists.

THEAETETUS : So far I quite agree with you.

STRANGER : Agreed then that we should at once quarter the ground by dividing the art of image making, and if, as soon as we descend into that enclosure, we meet with the Sophist at bay, we should c arrest him on the royal warrant of reason, report the capture, and hand him over to the sovereign. But if he should find some lurking place among the subdivisions of this art of imitation, we must follow hard upon him, constantly dividing the part that gives him shelter, until he is caught. In any event there is no fear that he or any other kind shall ever boast of having eluded a process of investigation so minute and so comprehensive.

THEAETETUS : Good, that is the way to go to work.

STRANGER : Following, then, the same method of division as d before, I seem once more to make out two forms of imitation, but as yet I do not feel able to discover in which of the two the type we are seeking is to be found.

THEAETETUS : Make your division first, at any rate, and tell us what two forms you mean.

STRANGER : One art that I see contained in it is the making of likenesses (εἰκαστική). The perfect example of this consists in creating a copy that conforms to the proportions of the original in all three e dimensions and giving moreover the proper color to every part.

THEAETETUS : Why, is not that what all imitators try to do?

STRANGER : Not those sculptors or painters whose works are of 236 colossal size. If they were to reproduce the true proportions of a well-made figure, as you know, the upper parts would look too small, and the lower too large, because we see the one at a distance, the other close at hand.

THEAETETUS : That is true.

STRANGER : So artists, leaving the truth to take care of itself, do in fact put into the images they make, not the real proportions, but those that will appear beautiful.

THEAETETUS : Quite so.

STRANGER : The first kind of image, then, being like the original, may fairly be called a likeness (εἰκόν).

THEAETETUS : Yes.

STRANGER : And the corresponding subdivision of the art of imitation may be called by the name we used just now—likeness b making.

THEAETETUS : It may.

STRANGER : Now, what are we to call the kind which only appears to be a likeness of a well-made figure because it is not seen from a satisfactory point of view, but to a spectator with eyes that could fully take in so large an object would not be even like the original it professes to resemble? Since it seems to be a likeness, but is not really so, may we not call it a semblance (φάντασμα)?

THEAETETUS : By all means.

STRANGER : And this is a very extensive class, in painting and c in imitation of all sorts.

THEAETETUS : True.

STRANGER : So the best name for the art which creates, not a likeness, but a semblance will be semblance making (φανταστική).

THEAETETUS : Quite so.

STRANGER : These, then, are the two forms of image making I meant—the making of likenesses and the making of semblances.

THEAETETUS : Good.

STRANGER : Yes, but even now I cannot see clearly how to settle the doubt I then expressed—under which of the two arts [likeness making and semblance making] we must place the Sophist. It is really surprising how hard it is to get a clear view of the man. At this d very moment he has, with admirable cleverness, taken refuge in a class which baffles investigation.

THEAETETUS : So it seems.

STRANGER : You assent, but do you recognize the class I mean, or has the current of the argument carried you along to agree so readily from force of habit?

THEAETETUS : How? What are you referring to?

STRANGER : The truth is, my friend, that we are faced with an extremely difficult question. This 'appearing' or 'seeming' without e really 'being,' and the saying of something which yet is not true—all these expressions have always been and still are deeply involved in perplexity. It is extremely hard, Theaetetus, to find correct terms in 237 which one may say or think that falsehoods have a real existence, without being caught in a contradiction by the mere utterance of such words.

THEAETETUS: Why?

STRANGER: The audacity of the statement lies in its implication that 'what is not' has being, for in no other way could a falsehood come to have being. But, my young friend, when we were of your age the great Parmenides from beginning to end testified against this, constantly telling us what he also says in his poem, 'Never shall this be proved—that things that are not are, but do thou, in thy inquiry, hold back thy thought from this way.'

b   So we have the great man's testimony, and the best way to obtain a confession of the truth may be to put the statement itself to a mild degree of torture. So, if it makes no difference to you, let us begin by studying it on its own merits.

THEAETETUS: I am at your disposal. As for the argument, you must consider the way that will best lead to a conclusion, and take me with you along it.

STRANGER: It shall be done. Now tell me, we do not hesitate to utter the phrase 'that which has no sort of being'?

THEAETETUS: Surely not.

STRANGER: Then setting aside disputation for its own sake c and playing with words, suppose one of this company were seriously required to concentrate his mind and tell us to what this name can be applied—'that which is not.' Of what thing or of what sort of thing should we expect him to use it himself, and what would he indicate by it to the inquirer?

THEAETETUS: That is a hard question. It is scarcely for a person like me to find an answer at all.

STRANGER: Well, this much is clear at any rate, that the term 'what is not' must not be applied to anything that exists.

THEAETETUS: Certainly not.

STRANGER: And since it cannot be applied to what exists, neither can it properly be applied to 'something.'

THEAETETUS: How so?

d   STRANGER: Surely we can see that this expression 'something' is always used of a thing that exists. We cannot use it just by itself in naked isolation from everything that exists, can we?

THEAETETUS: No.

STRANGER: Is your assent due to the reflection that to speak of 'something' is to speak of 'some *one* thing'?

THEAETETUS: Yes.

STRANGER: Because you will admit that 'something' stands for one thing, as 'some things' stands for two or more.

THEAETETUS: Certainly.

e   STRANGER: So it seems to follow necessarily that to speak of what is not 'something' is to speak of no thing at all.

THEAETETUS: Necessarily.

STRANGER: Must we not even refuse to allow that in such a

case a person is *saying* something, though he may be speaking of nothing? Must we not assert that he is not even saying anything when he sets about uttering the sounds 'a thing that is not'?

THEAETETUS: That would certainly end our bewilderment.

STRANGER: 'No time for boasting yet.' There is more to come, 238 in fact the chief of all the difficulties and the first, for it goes to the very root of the matter.

THEAETETUS: How do you mean? Do not hesitate to state it.

STRANGER: When a thing exists, I suppose something else that exists may be attributed to it.

THEAETETUS: Certainly.

STRANGER: But can we say it is possible for something that exists to be attributed to what has no existence?

THEAETETUS: How could it be?

STRANGER: Well, among things that exist we include number in general.

THEAETETUS: Yes, number must exist, if anything does. b

STRANGER: We must not, then, so much as attempt to attach either plurality or unity in number to the nonexistent.

THEAETETUS: That would certainly seem to be wrong, according to our argument.

STRANGER: How then can anyone utter the words 'things which are not,' or 'that which is not,' or even conceive such things in his mind at all, apart from number?

THEAETETUS: How do you mean?

STRANGER: When we speak of '*things* that are not,' are we not undertaking to attribute plurality to them? c

THEAETETUS: Yes.

STRANGER: And unity, when we speak of '*that* which is not'?

THEAETETUS: Clearly.

STRANGER: And yet we admit that it is not justifiable or correct to set about attaching something that exists to the nonexistent.

THEAETETUS: Quite true.

STRANGER: You see the inference then. One cannot legitimately utter the words, or speak or think of that which just simply is not; it is unthinkable, not to be spoken of or uttered or expressed.

THEAETETUS: Quite true.

STRANGER: Perhaps then I was mistaken in saying just now d that I was going to state the greatest difficulty it presents, whereas there is a worse one still that we can formulate.

THEAETETUS: What is that?

STRANGER: I am surprised you do not see from the very phrases I have just used that the nonexistent reduces even one who is refuting its claims to such straits that, as soon as he sets about doing so, he is forced to contradict himself.

THEAETETUS: How? Explain more clearly.

STRANGER: You must not look to me for illumination. I who
e laid it down that the nonexistent could have neither unity nor plurality, have not only just now but at this very moment spoken of it as one
thing, for I am saying '*the* nonexistent.' You see what I mean?

THEAETETUS: Yes.

STRANGER: And again a little while ago I was speaking of its
being a thing not to be uttered or spoken of or expressed. Do you follow?

THEAETETUS: Yes, of course.

STRANGER: Well, then, in trying to apply that term 'being' to it,
was I not contradicting what I said before?

239   THEAETETUS: Evidently.

STRANGER: And again in applying the term 'the,' was I not addressing it as singular?

THEAETETUS: Yes.

STRANGER: And again in speaking of it as 'a thing not to be expressed or spoken of or uttered,' I was using language as if referring
to a single thing.

THEAETETUS: Certainly.

STRANGER: Whereas we are admitting that, if we are to speak
strictly, we ought not to specify it as either one thing or many or even
to call it 'it' at all, for even that appellation means ascribing to it the
character of singleness.

THEAETETUS: Quite so.

b   STRANGER: In that case there is nothing to be said for me. I
shall be found to have had the worst of it, now and all along, in my
criticism of the nonexistent. Accordingly, as I said, we must not look
to anything I have to say for the correct way of describing the nonexistent; we must turn to you for that. Come along now.

THEAETETUS: What do you mean?

STRANGER: Come, you are young; show your spirit and make
the best effort you can. Try, without attributing being or unity or plurality to the nonexistent, to find some form of words describing it
correctly.

c   THEAETETUS: I should need an extraordinary zeal for such an
enterprise in face of what has happened to you.

STRANGER: Well, if you agree, we will leave ourselves out of
account, and until we meet with someone who can perform this feat,
let us say that the Sophist with extreme cunning has found an impenetrable lurking place.

THEAETETUS: It certainly seems so.

STRANGER: Accordingly, if we are going to say he possesses an
d art of creating 'semblances,' he will readily take advantage of our handling our arguments in this way to grapple with us and turn them
against ourselves. When we call him a maker of images, he will ask
what on earth we mean in speaking of an 'image' at all. So we must

consider, Theaetetus, how this truculent person's question is to be answered.

THEAETETUS: Clearly we shall say we mean images in water or in mirrors, and again images made by the draftsman or the sculptor, and any other things of that sort.

STRANGER: It is plain, Theaetetus, that you have never seen a e Sophist.

THEAETETUS: Why?

STRANGER: He will make as though his eyes were shut or he had no eyes at all.

THEAETETUS: How so?

STRANGER: When you offer him your answer in such terms, if you speak of something to be found in mirrors or in sculpture, he will 240 laugh at your words, as implying that he can see. He will profess to know nothing about mirrors or water or even eyesight, and will confine his question to what can be gathered from discourse.

THEAETETUS: Namely?

STRANGER: The common character in all these things you mentioned and thought fit to call by a single name when you used the expression 'image' as one term covering them all. State it, then, and hold your ground against the man without yielding an inch.

THEAETETUS: Well, sir, what could we say an image was, if not another thing of the same sort, copied from the real thing?

STRANGER: 'Of the same sort'? Do you mean another real thing, b or what does 'of the same sort' signify?

THEAETETUS: Certainly not real, but like it.

STRANGER: Meaning by 'real' a thing that really exists.

THEAETETUS: Yes.

STRANGER: And by 'not real' the opposite of real?

THEAETETUS: Of course.

STRANGER: Then by what is 'like' you mean what has not real existence, if you are going to call it 'not real.'

THEAETETUS: But it has some sort of existence.

STRANGER: Only not real existence, according to you.

THEAETETUS: No, except that it is really a likeness.

STRANGER: So, not having real existence, it really is what we call a likeness?

THEAETETUS: Real and unreal do seem to be combined in that c perplexing way, and very queer it is.

STRANGER: Queer indeed. You see that now again by dovetailing them together in this way our Hydra-headed Sophist has forced us against our will to admit that 'what is not' has some sort of being.

THEATETUS: Yes, I do.

STRANGER: And what now? How can we define his art without contradicting ourselves?

THEAETETUS: How do you mean? What sort of contradiction do you fear?

d STRANGER: When we say that he deceives with that semblance we spoke of and that his art is a practice of deception, shall we be saying that, as the effect of his art, our mind thinks what is false, or what shall we mean?

THEAETETUS: Just that. What else could we mean?

STRANGER: And false thinking, again, will be thinking things contrary to the things that are?

THEAETETUS: Yes.

STRANGER: You mean, then, by false thinking, thinking things that are not?

THEAETETUS: Necessarily.

e STRANGER: Does that mean thinking that things that are not, are not, or that things that are not in any way, in some way are?

THEAETETUS: It must at least mean thinking that things that are not, are in some way, if anyone is ever to be in error even to the smallest extent.

STRANGER: And also surely thinking that things which certainly are, are not in any way at all?

THEAETETUS: Yes.

STRANGER: That also is error?

THEAETETUS: Yes, that also.

STRANGER: And a false statement, I suppose, is to be regarded in the same light, as stating that things that are, are not, and that things that are not, are.

THEAETETUS: Yes. How else could it be false?

241 STRANGER: Hardly in any other way. But the Sophist will deny that. How could a sensible man agree, when the admissions we made earlier are set beside this one? We understand, Theaetetus, what he is referring to?

THEAETETUS: Of course we understand. He will say that we b are contradicting what was said just now, when we have the face to say that falsehoods exist in thoughts and in statements, for we are constantly being obliged to attribute what has being to what is not, after agreeing just now that this was altogether impossible.

STRANGER: Your recollection is correct. But you must now consider what we are to do about the Sophist, for if we pursue our search for him by ranking him under the art of the illusionists and creators of error, you see what an easy opening we offer to many perplexities and counterattacks.

THEAETETUS: I do.

STRANGER: They are almost without number and we have c stated only a small fraction of them.

THEAETETUS: If that is so, it looks as if it were impossible to catch the Sophist.

STRANGER: What then? Are we to lose heart and give up now?

THEAETETUS: I don't think we ought to, if we have the least chance of being able to lay hands on him somehow.

STRANGER: Then I may count on your indulgence, and, as you now say, you will be content if we can by some twist free ourselves, even to the least extent, from the grip of so powerful an argument?

THEAETETUS: By all means.

STRANGER: Then I have another still more pressing request.   d

THEAETETUS: What is that?

STRANGER: That you will not think I am turning into a sort of parricide.

THEAETETUS: In what way?

STRANGER: We shall find it necessary in self-defense to put to the question that pronouncement of father Parmenides, and establish by main force that what is not, in some respect has being, and conversely that what is, in a way is not.

THEAETETUS: It is plain that the course of the argument requires us to maintain that at all costs.

STRANGER: Plain enough for the blind to see, as they say. Unless these propositions are either refuted or accepted, anyone who talks of false statements or false judgment as being images or likenesses or copies or semblances, or of any of the arts concerned with e such things, can hardly escape becoming a laughingstock by being forced to contradict himself.

THEAETETUS: Quite true.

STRANGER: That is why we must now dare to lay unfilial hands 242 on that pronouncement, or else, if some scruple holds us back, drop the matter entirely.

THEAETETUS: As for that, we must let no scruple hinder us.

STRANGER: In that case, for the third time, I have a small favor to ask.

THEAETETUS: You have only to mention it.

STRANGER: I believe I confessed just now that on this point the task of refutation has always proved too much for my powers, and still does so.

THEAETETUS: You did say that.

STRANGER: Well, that confession, I am afraid, may make you think me scatterbrained when at every turn I shift my position to and fro. It is for your satisfaction that we shall attempt to refute the pro- b nouncement, if we can refute it.

THEAETETUS: Then you may take it that I shall never think you are overstepping the limits by entering on your refutation and proof. So far as that goes, you may proceed with an easy mind.

STRANGER: Come then, where is one to make a start on so hazardous a theme? I think I see the path we must inevitably follow.

THEAETETUS: And that is?

STRANGER: To take first things that are now supposed to be
c quite clear and see whether we are not in some confusion about them
and too easily reaching conclusions on the assumption that we understand them well enough.

THEAETETUS: Tell me more plainly what you mean.

STRANGER: It strikes me that Parmenides and everyone else
who has set out to determine how many real things there are and
what they are like, have discoursed to us in rather an offhand
fashion.

THEAETETUS: How so?

STRANGER: They each and all seem to treat us as children to
whom they are telling a story. According to one there are three real
things, some of which now carry on a sort of warfare with one another,
and then make friends and set about marrying and begetting and
bringing up their children. Another tells us that there are two—moist
and dry, or hot and cold—whom he marries off, and makes them set
d up house together. In our part of the world the Eleatic set, who hark
back to Xenophanes or even earlier, unfold their tale on the assumption that what we call 'all things' are only one thing. Later, certain
muses in Ionia and Sicily perceived that safety lay rather in com-
e bining both accounts and saying that the real is both many and one
and is held together by enmity and friendship. 'In parting asunder it is
always being drawn together' say the stricter of these muses. The
243 milder relax the rule that this should always be so and tell us of alternate states, in which the universe is now one and at peace through
the power of love, and now many and at war with itself owing to
some sort of strife.

In all this, whether any one of them has told the truth or not is a
hard question, and it is in bad taste to find fault so grossly with men
of long-established fame. But one observation may be made without
offense.

THEAETETUS: And that is?

STRANGER: That they have shown too little consideration for
b ordinary people like ourselves in talking over our heads. Each school
pursues its own argument to the conclusion without caring whether
we follow what they say or get left behind.

THEAETETUS: How do you mean?

STRANGER: When one or another of them in his discourse uses
these expressions 'there really are' or 'have come to be' or 'are
coming to be' 'many things' or 'one thing' or 'two,' or again another
speaks of 'hot being mixed with cold,' assuming 'combinations' and
'separations,' do you, Theaetetus, understand a single word he says?
Speaking for myself, when I was younger I thought I understood
quite clearly when someone spoke of this thing that is now puzzling
us—'the unreal.' But now you see how completely perplexed we are
about that.

THEAETETUS: I do.   c

STRANGER: Possibly, then, our minds are in the same state of confusion about reality. We profess to be quite at our ease about the real and to understand the word when it is spoken, though we may not understand the unreal, when perhaps we are equally in the dark about both.

THEAETETUS: Perhaps.

STRANGER: And we may take it that the same is true of the other expressions I have just mentioned.

THEAETETUS: Certainly.

STRANGER: The general run of these expressions we will consider later, if we so decide. We must begin now with the chief and d most important of them all.

THEAETETUS: Which is that? Of course you mean we ought to begin by studying 'reality' and finding out what those who use the word think it stands for.

STRANGER: You have hit my meaning precisely, Theaetetus; I do mean that we must take this line. Imagine them here before us, and let us put this question, 'You who say that hot and cold or some such pair *really are* all things, what exactly does this expression convey e that you apply to both when you say that they both are "real" or each of them is "real"? How are we to understand this "reality" you speak of? Are we to suppose it is a third thing alongside the other two and that the all is no longer, as you say, two things, but three? For surely you do not give the name "reality" to one of the two and then say that both alike are real, for then there will be only one thing, whichever of the two it may be, and not two.'

THEAETETUS: True.

STRANGER: 'Well then, do you intend to give the name "reality" to the pair of them?'

THEAETETUS: Perhaps.

STRANGER: 'But that again,' we shall object, 'will clearly be 244 speaking of your two things as one.'

THEAETETUS: You are quite right.

STRANGER: 'We are completely puzzled, then, and you must clear up the question for us, what you do intend to signify when you use the word "real." Obviously you must be quite familiar with what you mean, whereas we, who formerly imagined we knew, are now at a loss. First, then, enlighten us on just this point, so that we may not fancy we understand what you have to tell us, when in fact we are as far as possible from understanding.'   b

If we put our case in that way to these people and to any others who say that the all is more than one thing, will there be anything unwarrantable in our request?

THEAETETUS: Not at all.

STRANGER: Again, there are those who say that the all is one thing. Must we not do our best to find out what they mean by 'reality'?

THEAETETUS: Surely.

STRANGER: Let them answer this question, then, 'You say, we understand, that there is only one thing?' 'We do,' they will reply, won't they?

THEAETETUS: Yes.

STRANGER: 'And there is something to which you give the name *real*?'

THEAETETUS: Yes.

c   STRANGER: 'Is it the same thing as that to which you give the name *one*? Are you applying two names to the same thing, or what do you mean?'

THEAETETUS: What will their next answer be?

STRANGER: Obviously, Theaetetus, it is not so very easy for one who has laid down their fundamental assertion to answer this question or any other.

THEAETETUS: How so?

STRANGER: In the first place, it is surely absurd for him to admit the existence of *two* names, when he has laid down that there is no more than one thing.

THEAETETUS: Of course.

d   STRANGER: And further, it is equally absurd to allow anyone to assert that a name can have any existence, when that would be inexplicable.

THEAETETUS: How is it inexplicable?

STRANGER: If, on the one hand, he assumes that the name is different from the thing, he is surely speaking of *two* things.

THEAETETUS: Yes.

STRANGER: Whereas, if he assumes that the name is the same as the thing, either he will have to say it is not the name of anything, or if he says it is the name of something, it will follow that the name is merely a name of a name and of nothing else whatsoever.

THEAETETUS: That is so.

STRANGER: . . .*

THEAETETUS: Necessarily.

STRANGER: And what of 'the whole'? Will they say that this is other than their 'one real thing' or the same?

e   THEAETETUS: Certainly that it is the same. In fact they do say so.

STRANGER: Then if it is a whole—as indeed Parmenides says, 'Every way like the mass of a well-rounded sphere, evenly balanced

---

* [Cornford omitted this speech as corrupt and without point. As translated by Jowett: "And 'the one' can refer only to one thing—that is to say, to a name." (*The Dialogues of Plato*, 4th edn., Oxford, 1953.)]

from the midst in every direction, for there must not be something more nor something less here than there'—if the real is like that, it has a middle and extremities, and consequently it must have parts, must it not?

THEAETETUS: It must.

STRANGER: Well, if a thing is divided into parts, there is noth- 245 ing against its having the property of unity as applied to the aggregate of all the parts and being in that way one, as being a sum or whole.

THEAETETUS: Of course.

STRANGER: On the other hand, the thing which has these properties cannot be just unity itself, can it?

THEAETETUS: Why not?

STRANGER: Surely unity in the true sense and rightly defined must be altogether without parts.

THEAETETUS: Yes, it must.

STRANGER: Whereas a thing such as we described, consisting b of several parts, will not answer to that definition.

THEAETETUS: I see.

STRANGER: Then, (a) is the real one and a whole in the sense that it has the property of unity, or (b) are we to say that the real is not a whole at all?

THEAETETUS: That is a hard choice.

STRANGER: Quite true. For if (a) the real has the property of being in a sense one, it will evidently not be the same thing as unity, and so all things will be more than one.

THEAETETUS: Yes.

STRANGER: And again (b) if the real is not a whole by virtue c of having this property of unity, while (α) at the same time whole-ness itself is real, it follows that the real falls short of itself.

THEAETETUS: Certainly.

STRANGER: So, on this line of argument too, the real will be deprived of reality and will not be a thing that is.

THEAETETUS: Yes.

STRANGER: And further, once more all things will be more than one, since reality on the one side and wholeness on the other have now each a distinct nature.

THEAETETUS: Yes.

STRANGER: But if, (β) on the other hand, there is no such thing as wholeness at all, not only are the same things true of the real, but also that, besides not being a thing that really is, it could never d even become such.

THEAETETUS: Why not?

STRANGER: Whenever a thing comes into being, at that mo-ment it has come to be as a whole; accordingly, if you do not reckon unity or wholeness among real things, you have no right to speak of either being or coming-into-being as having any existence.

THEAETETUS : That seems perfectly true.

STRANGER : And further, what is not a whole cannot have any definite number either, for if a thing has a definite number, it must amount to that number, whatever it may be, as a whole.

THEAETETUS : Assuredly.

STRANGER : And countless other difficulties, each involved in
e measureless perplexity, will arise, if you say that the real is either two things or only one.

THEAETETUS : That is plain enough from those we have had a glimpse of now. One leads to another, and each carries us further into a wilderness of doubt about every theory as it is mentioned.

STRANGER : So much, then, for those who give an exact account of what is real or unreal. We have not gone through them all, but
246 let this suffice. Now we must turn to look at those who put the matter in a different way, so that, from a complete review of all, we may see that reality is just as hard to define as unreality.

THEAETETUS : We had better go on, then, to their position.

STRANGER : What we shall see is something like a battle of gods and giants going on between them over their quarrel about reality.

THEAETETUS : How so?

STRANGER : One party is trying to drag everything down to earth out of heaven and the unseen, literally grasping rocks and trees in their hands, for they lay hold upon every stock and stone and strenuously affirm that real existence belongs only to that which can be handled and offers resistance to the touch. They define reality as
b the same thing as body, and as soon as one of the opposite party asserts that anything without a body is real, they are utterly contemptuous and will not listen to another word.

THEAETETUS : The people you describe are certainly a formidable crew. I have met quite a number of them before now.

STRANGER : Yes, and accordingly their adversaries are very wary in defending their position somewhere in the heights of the unseen, maintaining with all their force that true reality consists in certain intelligible and bodiless forms. In the clash of argument they shatter and pulverize those bodies which their opponents wield, and
c what those others allege to be true reality they call, not real being, but a sort of moving process of becoming. On this issue an interminable battle is always going on between the two camps.

THEAETETUS : True.

STRANGER : Suppose, then, we challenge each party in turn to render an account of the reality they assert.

THEAETETUS : How shall we do so?

STRANGER : It will be easier to obtain from those who place reality in forms, because they are more civilized—harder, from those whose violence would drag everything down to the level of body—

perhaps, all but impossible. However, I think I see the right way to d
deal with them.

THEAETETUS: What is that?

STRANGER: Best of all, if it were anyhow possible, would be to
bring about a real change of heart, but if that is beyond our power,
to imagine them reformed and assume them willing to moderate their
present lawlessness in answering our questions. The better a man's
character is, the more force there will be in any agreement you make
with him. However, we are not concerned with them so much as
with our search for the truth.

THEAETETUS: You are quite right.   e

STRANGER: Well then, call upon these reformed characters to
oblige you with an answer, and you shall act as their spokesman.

THEAETETUS: I will.

STRANGER: Let them tell us, then, whether they admit that
there is such a thing as a mortal living creature.

THEAETETUS: Of course they do.

STRANGER: And they will agree that it is a body animated by a
soul?

THEAETETUS: Certainly.

STRANGER: Taking a soul to be something real?

THEAETETUS: Yes.   247

STRANGER: Again, they allow that one soul may be just, another unjust, or one wise, another foolish?

THEAETETUS: Naturally.

STRANGER: And that any soul comes to be just or the reverse
by possessing justice or the reverse, which is present in it?

THEAETETUS: Yes, they agree to that too.

STRANGER: But surely they will admit that whatever can come
to be present in a thing or absent from it is certainly a real thing.

THEAETETUS: Yes.

STRANGER: Granted, then, that justice or wisdom or any other b
sort of goodness or badness is real, and moreover that a soul in which
they come to exist is real, do they maintain that any one of these
things is visible and tangible, or are they all invisible?

THEAETETUS: They can hardly say that any one of them is
visible.

STRANGER: And do they really assert that something that is not
visible has a body?

THEAETETUS: That question they do not answer as a whole
without a distinction. The soul itself, they think, does possess a sort of
body, but when it comes to wisdom or any of the other things you
asked about, they have not the face either to accept the inference that
they have no place among real things or to persist in maintaining that c
they are all bodies.

STRANGER: That shows, Theaetetus, that they are genuinely reformed characters. The giants among them, of the true earthborn breed, would not stick at any point; they would hold out to the end, that whatever they cannot squeeze between their hands is just nothing at all.

THEAETETUS: I dare say that describes their state of mind.

d STRANGER: Let us question them further, then, for it is quite enough for our purpose if they consent to admit that even a small part of reality is bodiless. They must now tell us this. When they say that these bodiless things and the other things which have body are alike 'real,' what common character that emerges as covering both sets of things have they in view? It is possible they may be at a loss for an answer. If that is their state of mind, you must consider whether they would accept at our suggestion a description of the real and agree to it.

THEAETETUS: What description? Perhaps we can tell, if you will state it.

e STRANGER: I suggest that anything has real being that is so constituted as to possess any sort of power either to affect anything else or to be affected, in however small a degree, by the most insignificant agent, though it be only once. I am proposing as a mark to distinguish real things that they are nothing but power.

THEAETETUS: Well, they accept that, having for the moment no better suggestion of their own to offer.

STRANGER: That will do, for later on both they and we perhaps
248 may change our minds. For the present, then, let us take it that this agreement stands between us and the one party.

THEAETETUS: It does.

STRANGER: Let us turn, then, to the opposite party, the friends of forms. Once more you shall act as their spokesman.

THEAETETUS: I will.

STRANGER: We understand that you make a distinction between 'becoming' and 'real being' and speak of them as separate. Is that so?

THEAETETUS: Yes.

STRANGER: And you say that we have intercourse with becoming by means of the body through sense, whereas we have intercourse with real being by means of the soul through reflection. And real being, you say, is always in the same unchanging state, whereas becoming is variable.

b THEAETETUS: We do.

STRANGER: Admirable. But now what are we to take you as meaning by this expression 'intercourse' which you apply to both? Don't you mean what we described a moment ago?

THEAETETUS: What was that?

STRANGER: The experiencing an effect or the production of

one, arising, as the result of some power, from things that encounter one another. Perhaps, Theaetetus, you may not be able to catch their answer to this, but I, who am familiar with them, may be more successful.

THEAETETUS: What have they to say, then?

STRANGER: They do not agree to the proposition we put just c now to the earthborn giants about reality.

THEAETETUS: You mean . . . ?

STRANGER: We proposed as a sufficient mark of real things the presence in a thing of the power of being acted upon or of acting in relation to however insignificant a thing.

THEAETETUS: Yes.

STRANGER: Well, to that they reply that a power of acting and being acted upon belongs to becoming, but neither of these powers is compatible with real being.

THEAETETUS: And there is something in that answer?

STRANGER: Something to which we must reply by a request for more enlightenment. Do they acknowledge further that the soul d knows and real being is known?

THEAETETUS: Certainly they agree to that.

STRANGER: Well, do you agree that knowing or being known is an action, or is it experiencing an effect, or both? Or is one of them experiencing an effect, the other an action? Or does neither of them come under either of these heads at all?

THEAETETUS: Evidently neither; otherwise our friends would be contradicting what they said earlier.

STRANGER: I see what you mean. They would have to say this. If knowing is to be acting on something, it follows that what is known must be acted upon by it, and so, on this showing, reality when it is e being known by the act of knowledge must, in so far as it is known, be changed owing to being so acted upon—and that, we say, cannot happen to the changeless.

THEAETETUS: Exactly.

STRANGER: But tell me, in heaven's name, are we really to be so 249 easily convinced that change, life, soul, understanding have no place in that which is perfectly real—that it has neither life nor thought, but stands immutable in solemn aloofness, devoid of intelligence?

THEAETETUS: That, sir, would be a strange doctrine to accept.

STRANGER: But can we say it has intelligence without having life?

THEAETETUS: Surely not.

STRANGER: But if we say it contains both, can we deny that it has soul in which they reside?

THEAETETUS: How else could it possess them?

STRANGER: But then, if it has intelligence, life, and soul, can

we say that a living thing remains at rest in complete changeless-
ness?

b   THEAETETUS: All that seems to me unreasonable.

STRANGER: In that case we must admit that what changes and
change itself are real things.

THEAETETUS: Certainly.

STRANGER: From this, however, it follows, Theaetetus, first,
that if all things are unchangeable, no intelligence can really exist
anywhere in anything with regard to any object.

THEAETETUS: Quite so.

STRANGER: And, on the other hand, if we allow that all things
are moving and changing, on that view equally we shall be excluding
intelligence from the class of real things.

THEAETETUS: How so?

STRANGER: Do you think that, without rest, there could ever
c be anything that abides constant in the same condition and in the
same respects?

THEAETETUS: Certainly not.

STRANGER: And without such objects can you make out that
intelligence exists or could ever exist anywhere?

THEAETETUS: It would be quite impossible.

STRANGER: Well then, all the force of reasoning must be enlisted to oppose anyone who tries to maintain any assertion about
anything at the same time that he suppresses knowledge or understanding or intelligence.

THEAETETUS: Most certainly.

STRANGER: On these grounds, then, it seems that only one
course is open to the philosopher who values knowledge and the
rest above all else. He must refuse to accept from the champions
d either of the one or of the many forms the doctrine that all reality is
changeless, and he must turn a deaf ear to the other party who
represent reality as everywhere changing. Like a child begging for
'both,' he must declare that reality or the sum of things is both at once
—all that is unchangeable and all that is in change.

THEAETETUS: Perfectly true.

STRANGER: Well then, does it not look now as if we had fairly
caught reality within the compass of our description?

THEAETETUS: Certainly it does.

STRANGER: And yet—oh dear, Theaetetus, what if I say after
all that I think it is just at this point that we shall come to see how
baffling this question of reality is?

e   THEAETETUS: How so? Why do you say that?

STRANGER: My good friend, don't you see that now we are
wholly in the dark about it, though we fancy we are talking good
sense?

THEAETETUS: I certainly thought so, and I don't at all understand how we can be deceived about our condition.

STRANGER: Then consider these last conclusions of ours more 250
carefully, and whether, when we agree to them, we might not fairly
be posed with the same question we put earlier to those who said that
the sum of things 'really is' hot and cold.

THEAETETUS: You must remind me what that question was.

STRANGER: By all means, and I will try to do it by questioning
you in the same way as I questioned them, so that we may get a little
further at the same time.

THEAETETUS: Very good.

STRANGER: Come along then. When you speak of movement
and rest, these are things completely opposed to one another, aren't
they?

THEAETETUS: Of course.

STRANGER: At the same time you say of both and of each
severally, that they are real?

THEAETETUS: I do.

STRANGER: And when you admit that they are real, do you
mean that either or both are in movement?

THEAETETUS: Certainly not.

STRANGER: Then, perhaps, by saying both are real you mean
they are both at rest?

THEAETETUS: No, how could I?

STRANGER: So, then, you conceive of reality [realness] as a
third thing over and above these two, and when you speak of both as
being real, you mean that you are taking both movement and rest together as embraced by reality and fixing your attention on their
common association with reality?

THEAETETUS: It does seem as if we discerned reality as a third c
thing, when we say that movement and rest are real.

STRANGER: So reality is not motion and rest 'both at once,' but
something distinct from them.

THEAETETUS: Apparently.

STRANGER: In virtue of its own nature, then, reality is neither
at rest nor in movement.

THEAETETUS: I suppose so.

STRANGER: If so, where is the mind to turn for help if one
wants to reach any clear and certain conclusion about reality?

THEAETETUS: Where indeed?

STRANGER: It seems hard to find help in any quarter. If a
thing is not in movement, how can it not be at rest? Or how can what d
is not in any way at rest fail to be in movement? Yet reality is now
revealed to us as outside both alternatives. Is that possible?

THEAETETUS: As impossible as anything could be.

STRANGER: Then there is one thing that ought to be remembered at this point.

THEAETETUS: And that is?

STRANGER: That we were completely puzzled when we were

asked to what the name 'unreal' should be applied. You remember?

THEAETETUS: Of course.

e   STRANGER: And now we are in no less perplexity about reality?

THEAETETUS: In even greater, I should say, sir, if that be possible.

STRANGER: Let us take it, then, that our difficulty is now completely stated. But since reality and unreality are equally puzzling, there is henceforward some hope that any light, whether dim or 251 bright, thrown upon the one will illuminate the other to an equal degree, and if, on the other hand, we cannot get sight of either, at any rate we will make the best we can of it under these conditions and force a passage through the argument with both elbows at once.

THEAETETUS: Very good.

STRANGER: Let us explain, then, how it is that we call the same thing—whatever is in question at the moment—by several names.

THEAETETUS: For instance? Give me an example.

STRANGER: Well, when we speak of a man we give him many additional names—we attribute to him colors and shapes and sizes and defects and good qualities, and in all these and countless other b statements we say he is not merely a 'man' but also 'good' and any number of other things. And so with everything else. We take any given thing as one and yet speak of it as many and by many names.

THEAETETUS: True.

STRANGER: And thereby, I fancy, we have provided a magnificent entertainment for the young and for some of their elders who have taken to learning late in life. Anyone can take a hand in the game and at once object that many things cannot be one, nor one thing many; indeed, they delight in forbidding us to speak of a man as 'good'—we must only speak of a good as good, and of the man as man. c I imagine, Theaetetus, you often meet with these enthusiasts, sometimes elderly men who, being poorly endowed with intelligence, gape with wonder at these discoveries and fancy they have lighted here on the very treasure of complete wisdom.

THEAETETUS: I have indeed.

STRANGER: Well then, we want our argument to be addressed to all alike who have ever had anything to say about existence; so let us take it that the questions we shall put now are intended not only for these people but for all those others whom we have been conversing with earlier.

THEAETETUS: And what are the questions?

STRANGER: Are we not to attach existence to motion and rest, d nor anything else to anything else, but rather to treat them in our discourse as incapable of any blending or participation in one another? Or are we to lump them all together as capable of association with one another? Or shall we say that this is true of some and not of

others? Which of these possibilities shall we say they prefer, Theae- e
tetus?

THEAETETUS: I am not prepared to answer that on their behalf.

STRANGER: Then why not answer the questions one at a time
and see what are the consequences in each case?

THEAETETUS: Very good.

STRANGER: And first, if you like, let us suppose them to say
that nothing has any capacity for combination with anything else for 252
any purpose. Then movement and rest will have no part in existence.

THEAETETUS: No.

STRANGER: Well then, will either of them exist, if it has no
association with existence?

THEAETETUS: No, it will not exist.

STRANGER: That admission seems to make short work of all
theories; it upsets at one blow those who have a universe in motion,
and those who make it a motionless unity, and all who say their
realities exist in forms that are always the same in all respects, for
they all attribute existence to things, some saying they really *are* in
movement, some that they really *are* at rest.

THEAETETUS: Quite so.

STRANGER: And further, those who make all things come to- b
gether at one time and separate at another, whether they bring innumerable things into a unity and out of a unity, or divide things into
and combine them out of a limited set of elements—no matter
whether they suppose this to happen in alternation or to be going
on all the time—however it may be, all this would be meaningless if
there is no blending at all.

THEAETETUS: True.

STRANGER: Moreover, the greatest absurdity of all results from
pursuing the theory of those very people who will not allow one thing
to share in the quality of another and so be called by its name.

THEAETETUS: How so? c

STRANGER: Why, in referring to anything they cannot help
using the words 'being' and 'apart' and 'from the others' and 'by itself' and any number more. They cannot refrain from these expressions or from connecting them in their statements, and so need
not wait for others to refute them; the foe is in their own household,
as the saying goes, and, like that queer fellow Eurycles, they carry
about with them wherever they go a voice in their own bellies to contradict them.

THEAETETUS: True, your comparison is very much to the pur- d
pose.

STRANGER: Well, suppose we allow that all are capable of
combining with one another.

THEAETETUS: Even I can dispose of that suggestion.

STRANGER: How?

THEAETETUS: Because then movement itself would come to a complete standstill, and again rest itself would be in movement, if each were to supervene upon the other.

STRANGER: And that is to the last degree impossible—that movement should come to be at rest and rest be in motion?

THEAETETUS: Surely.

STRANGER: Then only the third choice is left.

THEAETETUS: Yes.

STRANGER: And observe that one of these alternatives must be
e true—either all will blend, or none, or some will and some will not.

THEAETETUS: Certainly.

STRANGER: And two of the three have been found impossible.

THEAETETUS: Yes.

STRANGER: Whoever, then, wishes to give a right answer will assert the remaining one.

THEAETETUS: Quite so.

STRANGER: Then since some will blend, some not, they
253 might be said to be in the same case with the letters of the alphabet. Some of these cannot be conjoined; others will fit together.

THEAETETUS: Of course.

STRANGER: And the vowels are specially good at combination —a sort of bond pervading them all, so that without a vowel the others cannot be fitted together.

THEAETETUS: That is so.

STRANGER: And does everyone know which can combine with which, or does one need an art to do it rightly?

THEAETETUS: It needs art.

STRANGER: And that art is?

THEAETETUS: Grammar.

b STRANGER: Again, is it not the same with sounds of high or low pitch? To possess the art of recognizing the sounds that can or cannot be blended is to be a musician; if one doesn't understand that, one is unmusical.

THEAETETUS: True.

STRANGER: And we shall find differences of the same sort between competence and incompetence in any other art.

THEAETETUS: Of course.

STRANGER: Well, now that we have agreed that the kinds stand toward one another in the same way as regards blending, is not some science needed as a guide on the voyage of discourse, if one is to succeed in pointing out which kinds are consonant, and which are incompatible with one another—also, whether there are certain kinds
c that pervade them all and connect them so that they can blend, and again, where there are divisions [separations], whether there are certain others that traverse wholes and are responsible for the division?

THEAETETUS: Surely some science is needed—perhaps the most important of all.

STRANGER: And what name shall we give to this science? Or—good gracious, Theaetetus, have we stumbled unawares upon the free man's knowledge and, in seeking for the Sophist, chanced to find the philosopher first?

THEAETETUS: How do you mean?

STRANGER: Dividing according to kinds, not taking the same d form for a different one or a different one for the same—is not that the business of the science of dialectic?

THEAETETUS: Yes.

STRANGER: And the man who can do that discerns clearly *one* form everywhere extended throughout many, where each one lies apart, and *many* forms, different from one another, embraced from without by one form, and again *one* form connected in a unity through many wholes, and *many* forms, entirely marked off apart. That means knowing how to distinguish, kind by kind, in what ways the several kinds can or cannot combine. e

THEAETETUS: Most certainly.

STRANGER: And the only person, I imagine, to whom you would allow this mastery of dialectic is the pure and rightful lover of wisdom.

THEAETETUS: To whom else could it be allowed?

STRANGER: It is, then, in some such region as this that we shall find the philosopher now or later, if we should look for him. He too may be difficult to see clearly, but the difficulty in his case is not the same as in the Sophist's. 254

THEAETETUS: What is the difference?

STRANGER: The Sophist takes refuge in the darkness of not-being, where he is at home and has the knack of feeling his way, and it is the darkness of the place that makes him so hard to perceive.

THEAETETUS: That may well be.

STRANGER: Whereas the philosopher, whose thoughts constantly dwell upon the nature of reality, is difficult to see because his region is so bright, for the eye of the vulgar soul cannot endure to b keep its gaze fixed on the divine.

THEAETETUS: That may well be no less true.

STRANGER: Then we will look more closely at the philosopher presently, if we are still in the mind to do so; meanwhile clearly we must not loosen our grip on the Sophist until we have studied him thoroughly.

THEAETETUS: I entirely agree.

STRANGER: Now that we are agreed, then, that some of the kinds will combine with one another and some will not, and that some combine to a small extent, others with a large number, while some pervade all and there is nothing against their being combined c

with everything, let us next follow up the argument in this way. We will not take all the forms, for fear of getting confused in such a multitude, but choose out some of those that are recognized as most [*or* very] important, and consider first their several natures and then how they stand in respect of being capable of combination with one another. In this way, though we may not be able to conceive being and not-being with perfect clearness, we may at least give as satisfactory an account of them as we can under the conditions of our present inquiry, and see if there is any opening allowing us to assert
d that what is not, *really is* what is not, and to escape unscathed.

THEAETETUS : Yes, we had better do that.

STRANGER : Now, among the kinds, those we were just now discussing—existence itself and rest and motion—*are* very important.

THEAETETUS : Quite so.

STRANGER : And observe, we say that two of the three will not blend with one another.

THEAETETUS : Certainly.

STRANGER : Whereas existence can be blended with both, for surely they both exist.

THEAETETUS : Of course.

STRANGER : So they make three in all. And each one of them [existence, motion, rest] is *different* from the other two, and the *same* as itself.

e   THEAETETUS : That is so.

STRANGER : But what do we mean by these words we have just used—'same' and 'different'? Are they a pair of kinds distinct from those three, though always necessarily blending with them, so that we must consider the forms as five in all, not three? Or, when we say 'same' or 'different,' are we unconsciously using a name that belongs
255 to one or another of those three kinds?

THEAETETUS : Possibly.

STRANGER : Well, motion and rest at any rate cannot be [identical with] difference or sameness.

THEAETETUS : Why not?

STRANGER : Neither motion nor rest can be [identical with] anything that we say of both of them in common.

THEAETETUS : Why?

STRANGER : Because motion would then be at rest, and rest in motion, for whichever of the two [motion or rest] becomes applicable to both [by being identified with either sameness or difference, which *are* applicable to both] will force the other [rest or motion] to change to the contrary of its own nature, as thus coming to partake of its
b contrary.

THEAETETUS : Quite so.

STRANGER : But both do partake of sameness and difference.

THEAETETUS : Yes.

STRANGER : Then we must not say that sameness or difference is [identical with] motion, nor yet with rest.

THEAETETUS : No.

STRANGER : Are we, however, to think of existence and sameness as a single thing?

THEAETETUS : Perhaps.

STRANGER : But if 'existence' and 'sameness' have no difference in meaning, once more, when we say that motion and rest both c 'exist,' we shall thereby be speaking of them as being 'the same.'

THEAETETUS : But that is impossible.

STRANGER : Then sameness and existence cannot be one thing.

THEAETETUS : Hardly.

STRANGER : We may, then, set down sameness as a fourth form, additional to our three.

THEAETETUS : Certainly.

STRANGER : And are we to call difference a fifth? Or must we think of difference and existence as two names for a single kind?

THEAETETUS : Perhaps.

STRANGER : But I suppose you admit that, among things that exist, some are always spoken of as being what they are just in themselves, others as being what they are with reference to other things.

THEAETETUS : Of course.

STRANGER : And what is different is always so called with refer- d ence to another thing, isn't it?

THEAETETUS : That is so.

STRANGER : It would not be so, if existence and difference were not very different things. If difference partook of both characters as existence does, there would sometimes be, within the class of different things, something that was different not with reference to another thing. But in fact we undoubtedly find that whatever is different, as a necessary consequence, is what it is with reference to another.

THEAETETUS : It is as you say.

STRANGER : Then we must call the nature of difference a fifth among the forms we are singling out. e

THEAETETUS : Yes.

STRANGER : And moreover we shall say that this nature pervades all the forms, for each one is different from the rest, not by virtue of its own nature, but because it partakes of the character of difference.

THEAETETUS : Quite so.

STRANGER : Now, then, taking our five kinds one by one, let us make some statements about them.

THEAETETUS : What statements?

STRANGER : First about motion, let us say that motion is altogether different from rest. Or is that not so?

THEAETETUS : It is so.

STRANGER : So motion is not rest.

THEAETETUS : Not in any sense.

STRANGER : But motion *is* [exists], by virtue of partaking of existence.

256   THEAETETUS : Yes.

STRANGER : And once more motion is different from the same [sameness].

THEAETETUS : No doubt.

STRANGER : So motion is not the same [sameness].

THEAETETUS : No.

STRANGER : But on the other hand, motion, we said, is the same as itself, because everything partakes of the same [sameness].

THEAETETUS : Certainly.

STRANGER : Motion, then, is both the same and not the same; we must admit that without boggling at it. For when we say it is 'the same' and 'not the same' we are not using the expression in the same

b   sense; we call it 'the same' on account of its participation in the same with reference to itself, but we call it 'not the same' because of its combination with difference, a combination that separates it off from the same [sameness] and makes it not the same but different, so that we have the right to say this time that it is 'not the same.'

THEAETETUS : Certainly.

STRANGER : So too, supposing motion itself did in any way participate in rest, there would be nothing outrageous in speaking of it as stationary. But it does not in fact participate in rest at all.

THEAETETUS : No, it does not.

c   STRANGER : Whereas it does participate both in sameness and in difference, so that it is correct to speak of it as both the same and not the same.

THEAETETUS : Perfectly correct, provided that we are to agree that some of the kinds will blend with one another, some will not.

STRANGER : Well, that is a conclusion we proved at an earlier stage, when we showed that such was indeed their nature.

THEAETETUS : Of course.

STRANGER : To go back to our statements, then, is motion different from different [difference], just as it was other than the same [sameness] and other than rest?

THEAETETUS : Necessarily.

STRANGER : Motion, then, in a sense is not different, and also is different, in accordance with the argument we stated just now.

THEAETETUS : True.

STRANGER : What, then, of the next point? Are we to say that motion is different from three of the four, but not from the fourth,

when we have agreed that there were five kinds in the field we set be- d
fore us for examination?

THEAETETUS: How can we? We cannot allow that their number is less than it was shown to be.

STRANGER: So we may fearlessly contend that motion is different from existence.

THEAETETUS: Without the smallest fear.

STRANGER: In fact, it is clear that motion really is a thing that is not [existence] and a thing that is, since it partakes of existence.

THEAETETUS: Perfectly clear.

STRANGER: It must, then, be possible for 'that which is not' [i.e., is different from existence] to be [to exist], not only in the case of motion but of all the other kinds. For in the case of them all the nature of difference makes each one of them different from existence e and so makes it a thing that 'is not,' and hence we shall be right to speak of them all on the same principle as things that in this sense 'are not,' and again, because they partake of existence, to say that they 'are' [exist] and call them things that have being [existence].

THEAETETUS: No doubt.

STRANGER: So, in the case of every one of the forms there is much that it *is* and an indefinite number of things that it *is not*.

THEAETETUS: So it appears.   257

STRANGER: And, moreover, existence itself must be called different from the rest.

THEAETETUS: Necessarily.

STRANGER: We find, then, that existence likewise 'is not' in as many respects as there are other things, for, not being those others, while it *is* its single self, it *is not* all that indefinite number of other things.

THEAETETUS: That is so.

STRANGER: Then we must not boggle even at that conclusion, granted that kinds are of a nature to admit combination with one another. If anyone denies that, he must win over our earlier arguments to his side before he tries to win over their consequences.

THEAETETUS: That is a fair demand.

STRANGER: Now let us mark this.

THEAETETUS: Yes?   b

STRANGER: When we speak of 'that which is not,' it seems that we do not mean something contrary to what exists but only something that is different.

THEAETETUS: How?

STRANGER: In the same way that when, for example, we speak of something as 'not tall,' we may just as well mean by that phrase 'what is equal' as 'what is short,' mayn't we?

THEAETETUS: Certainly.

STRANGER: So, when it is asserted that a negative signifies a contrary, we shall not agree, but admit no more than this—that the prefix 'not' indicates something different from the words that follow, c or rather from the things designated by the words pronounced after the negative.

THEAETETUS: Exactly.

STRANGER: And here, if you agree, is a point for us to consider.

THEAETETUS: Namely?

STRANGER: The nature of the different [difference] appears to be parceled out, in the same way as knowledge.

THEAETETUS: How so?

STRANGER: Knowledge also is surely one, but each part of it that commands a certain field is marked off and given a special name d proper to itself. Hence language recognizes many arts and forms of knowledge.

THEAETETUS: Certainly.

STRANGER: And the same thing is true of the parts of the single nature of the different.

THEAETETUS: Perhaps, but shall we explain how?

STRANGER: There exists a part of the different that is set in contrast to the beautiful?

THEAETETUS: Yes.

STRANGER: Are we to say it is nameless, or has it a special name?

THEAETETUS: It has. Whenever we use the expression 'not beautiful,' the thing we mean is precisely that which is different from the nature of the beautiful.

STRANGER: Then tell me this.

e   THEAETETUS: What?

STRANGER: May we not say that the *existence* of the not-beautiful is constituted by its being marked off from a single definite kind among existing things and again set in contrast with something that exists?

THEAETETUS: Yes.

STRANGER: So it appears that the not-beautiful is an instance of something that exists being set in contrast to something that exists.

THEAETETUS: Perfectly.

STRANGER: What then? On this showing has the not-beautiful any less claim than the beautiful to be a thing that exists?

THEAETETUS: None whatever.

258   STRANGER: And so the not-tall must be said to exist just as much as the tall itself.

THEAETETUS: Just as much.

STRANGER: And we must also put the not-just on the same footing as the just with respect to the fact that the one exists no less than the other.

THEAETETUS: Certainly.

STRANGER: And we shall say the same of all the rest, since we have seen that the nature of the different is to be ranked among things that exist, and, once it exists, its parts also must be considered as existing just as much as anything else.

THEAETETUS: Of course.

STRANGER: So, it seems, when a part of the nature of the different and a part of the nature of the existent [existence] are set in contrast to one another, the contrast is, if it be permissible to say so, as much a reality as existence itself; it does not mean what is contrary to 'existent,' but only what is different from that existent. b

THEAETETUS: That is quite clear.

STRANGER: What name are we to give it, then?

THEAETETUS: Obviously this is just that 'what-is-not' which we were seeking for the sake of the Sophist.

STRANGER: Has it then, as you say, an existence inferior to none of the rest in reality? May we now be bold to say that 'that which is not' unquestionably *is* a thing that has a nature of its own—just as the tall was tall and the beautiful was beautiful, so too with the not-tall and the not-beautiful—and in that sense 'that which is not' also, on the same principle, both was and *is* 'what is not,' a single form to be reckoned among the many realities? Or have we any further doubts with regard to it, Theaetetus? c

THEAETETUS: None at all.

STRANGER: You see, then, that in our disobedience to Parmenides we have trespassed far beyond the limits of his prohibition.

THEAETETUS: In what way?

STRANGER: In pushing forward on our quest, we have shown him results in a field which he forbade us even to explore.

THEAETETUS: How?

STRANGER: He says, you remember, 'Never shall this be proved, that things that are not, are, but keep back thy thought from this way of inquiry.'[1] d

THEAETETUS: Yes, he does say that.

STRANGER: Whereas we have not merely shown that things that are not, are, but we have brought to light the real character of 'not-being.' We have shown that the nature of the different has existence and is parceled out over the whole field of existent things with reference to one another, and of every part of it that is set in contrast to 'that which is' we have dared to say that precisely that *is* really 'that which is not.' e

THEAETETUS: Yes, sir, and I think what we have said is perfectly true.

STRANGER: Then let no one say that it is the contrary of the

[1] Parmenides, 52 sq. (ed. Mullach).

existent that we mean by 'what is not,' when we make bold to say that 'what is not' exists. So far as any contrary of the existent is concerned, we have long ago said good-by to the question whether there is such a thing or not and whether any account can be given of it or none whatsoever.

259   But with respect to the 'what-is-not' that we have now asserted to exist, an opponent must either convince us that our account is wrong by refuting it, or, so long as he proves unable to do that, he must accept our statements (*a*) that the kinds blend with one another, (*b*) that existence and difference pervade them all, and pervade one another, (*c*) that difference [or the different], by partaking of existence, *is* by virtue of that participation, but on the other hand *is not* that existence of which it partakes, but is different, and since it is different from existence [or an existent], quite clearly it must be possible that it should *be* a thing that *is not*, (*d*) and again, existence,
b having a part in difference, will be different from all the rest of the kinds, and, because it is different from them all, it *is not* any one of them nor yet all the others put together, but is only itself, with the consequence, again indisputable, that existence *is not* myriads upon myriads of things, and that all the other kinds in the same way, whether taken severally or all together, in many respects *are* and in many respects *are not*.

THEAETETUS: True.

STRANGER: And if anyone mistrusts these apparent contradictions, he should study the question and produce some better explanation than we have now given, whereas if he imagines he has
c discovered an embarrassing puzzle and takes delight in reducing argument to a tug of war, he is wasting his pains on a triviality, as our present argument declares. There is nothing clever in such a discovery, nor is it hard to make; what is hard and at the same time worth the pains is something different.

THEAETETUS: And that is?

STRANGER: What I said before—leaving such quibbling alone as leading nowhere, to be able to follow our statements step by step and, in criticizing the assertion that a different thing is the same or the same thing is different in a certain sense, to take account of the
d precise sense and the precise respect in which they are said to be one or the other. Merely to show that in some unspecified way the same is different or the different is the same, the tall short, the like unlike, and to take pleasure in perpetually parading such contradictions in argument—that is not genuine criticism, but may be recognized as the callow offspring of a too recent contact with reality.

THEAETETUS: I quite agree.

STRANGER: Yes, my friend, and the attempt to separate every
e thing from every other thing not only strikes a discordant note but amounts to a crude defiance of the philosophical Muse.

THEAETETUS: Why?

STRANGER: This isolation of everything from everything else means a complete abolition of all discourse, for any discourse we can 260 have owes its existence to the weaving together of forms.

THEAETETUS: True.

STRANGER: Observe, then, how opportune was our struggle with those separatists, when we forced them to allow one form to blend with another.

THEAETETUS: In what respect?

STRANGER: In respect of securing the position of discourse as one of the kinds of things that exist. To rob us of discourse would be to rob us of philosophy. That would be the most serious consequence, but, besides that, we need at the present moment to come to an agreement about the nature of discourse, and if its very existence had been taken from us, we should naturally not be able to discourse any further. And that would have happened, if we had yielded the b point that there is no blending of any one form with another.

THEAETETUS: That is certainly true. But I do not understand why we need an agreement about discourse at the present moment.

STRANGER: I may be able to suggest a line of thought that will help you to understand.

THEAETETUS: What is that?

STRANGER: We saw that 'not-being' is a single kind among the rest, dispersed over the whole field of realities.

THEAETETUS: Yes.

STRANGER: We have next to consider whether it blends with thinking and discourse.

THEAETETUS: Why that?

STRANGER: If it does not blend with them, everything must be c true, but if it does, we shall have false thinking and discourse, for thinking or saying 'what is not' comes, I suppose, to the same thing as falsity in thought and speech.

THEAETETUS: Yes.

STRANGER: And if falsity exists, deception is possible.

THEAETETUS: Yes.

STRANGER: And once deception exists, images and likenesses and appearance will be everywhere rampant.

THEAETETUS: Of course.

STRANGER: And the Sophist, we said, had taken refuge some- d where in that region, but then he had denied the very existence of falsity; no one could either think or say 'what is not,' because what is not never has any sort of being.

THEAETETUS: So he said.

STRANGER: But now that 'what is not' has been found to have its share in existence, perhaps he will not fight with us further on that point.

On the other hand, he may perhaps say that some things partake of not-being, some do not, and that speech and thinking are among those that do not, and so once more he might contend that the art of
e creating images and semblances, where we say he is to be found, has no existence at all, since thought and speech have no share in not-being, and without that combination there is no such thing as falsity.

That is why we must begin by investigating the nature of discourse and thinking and appearance, in order that we may then make
261 out their combination with not-being and so prove that falsity exists, and by that proof pin down the Sophist there, if he is amenable to capture, or else let him go and pursue our search in some other kind.

THEAETETUS : Certainly, sir, what we said at the outset about the Sophist seems true—that he is a hard sort of beast to hunt down. Evidently he possesses a whole armory of problems, and every time that he puts one forward to shield him, we have to fight our way through it before we can get at him. So now, hardly have we got the better of his defense that 'what is not' cannot exist, when another ob-
b stacle is raised in our path. We must, it seems, prove that falsity exists both in speech and thought, and after that perhaps something else, and so on. It looks as if the end would never be in sight.

STRANGER : A man should be of good courage, Theaetetus, if he can make only a little headway at each step. If he loses heart then, what will he do in another case where he cannot advance at all or even
c perhaps loses ground? No city, as they say, will surrender to so faint a summons. And now that we have surmounted the barrier you speak of, we may have already taken the highest wall and the rest may be easier to capture.

THEAETETUS : That is encouraging.

STRANGER : Then, as I said, let us take first statement and judgment, so as to establish clearly whether not-being has any point of contact with them, or both are altogether true and there is never falsity in either.

THEAETETUS : Very good.

d   STRANGER : Now, remembering what we said about forms and letters, let us consider words in the same way. The solution of our present problem promises to lie in that quarter.

THEAETETUS : What are you going to ask me about words?

STRANGER : Whether they all fit together, or none of them, or some will and some will not.

THEAETETUS : That is plain enough. Some will, some will not.

STRANGER : You mean perhaps something like this. Words which, when spoken in succession, signify something, do fit together,
e while those which mean nothing when they are strung together, do not.

THEAETETUS : What do you mean?

STRANGER : What I supposed you had in your mind when you

gave your assent. The signs we use in speech to signify being are surely of two kinds.

THEAETETUS: How?

STRANGER: One kind called 'names,' the other 'verbs.'

THEAETETUS: Give me a description of each.

STRANGER: By 'verb' we mean an expression which is applied to 262 actions.

THEAETETUS: Yes.

STRANGER: And by a 'name' the spoken sign applied to what performs these actions.

THEAETETUS: Quite so.

STRANGER: Now a statement never consists solely of names spoken in succession, nor yet of verbs apart from names.

THEAETETUS: I don't follow that.

STRANGER: Evidently you had something else in mind when b you agreed with me just now, because what I meant was just this— that these words spoken in a string in this way do not make a statement.

THEAETETUS: In what way?

STRANGER: For example, 'walks runs sleeps,' and so on with all the other verbs signifying actions—you may utter them all one after another, but that does not make a statement.

THEAETETUS: Naturally.

STRANGER: And again, if you say 'lion stag horse' and any other names given to things that perform actions, such a string never makes up a statement. Neither in this example nor in the other c do the sounds uttered signify any action performed or not performed or nature of anything that exists or does not exist, until you combine verbs with names. The moment you do that, they fit together and the simplest combination becomes a statement of what might be called the simplest and briefest kind.

THEAETETUS: Then how do you make a statement of that kind?

STRANGER: When one says, 'A man understands,' do you agree that this is a statement of the simplest and shortest possible kind?

THEAETETUS: Yes. d

STRANGER: Because now it gives information about facts or events in the present or past or future; it does not merely name something but gets you somewhere by weaving together verbs with names. Hence we say it 'states' something, not merely 'names' something, and in fact it is this complex that we mean by the word 'statement.'

THEAETETUS: True.

STRANGER: And so, just as some things fit together, some do not, so with the signs of speech; some do not fit, but those that do fit e make a statement.

THEAETETUS: Quite so.

STRANGER: Now another small point.

THEAETETUS: Yes?

STRANGER: Whenever there is a statement, it must be about something; it cannot be about nothing.

THEAETETUS: That is so.

STRANGER: And must it not have a certain character?

THEAETETUS: Of course.

STRANGER: Now let us fix our attention on ourselves.

THEAETETUS: We will.

STRANGER: I will make a statement to you, then, putting together a thing with an action by means of a name and a verb. You are to tell me what the statement is about.

THEAETETUS: I will do my best.

263   STRANGER: 'Theaetetus sits'—not a lengthy statement, is it?

THEAETETUS: No, of very modest length.

STRANGER: Now it is for you to say what it is about—to whom it belongs.

THEAETETUS: Clearly about me. It belongs to me.

STRANGER: Now take another.

THEAETETUS: Namely?

STRANGER: 'Theaetetus, whom I am talking to at this moment, flies.'

THEAETETUS: That too can only be described as belonging to me and about me.

b   STRANGER: And moreover we agree that any statement must have a certain character.

THEAETETUS: Yes.

STRANGER: Then what sort of character can we assign to each of these?

THEAETETUS: One is false, the other true.

STRANGER: And the true one states about you the things that are [*or* the facts] as they are.

THEAETETUS: Certainly.

STRANGER: Whereas the false statement states about you things *different* from the things that are.

THEAETETUS: Yes.

STRANGER: And accordingly states *things that are not* as being.

THEAETETUS: No doubt.

STRANGER: Yes, but things that *exist*, different from things that *exist* in your case. For we said that in the case of everything there are many things that are and also many that are not.

THEAETETUS: Quite so.

c   STRANGER: So the second statement I made about you, in the first place, according to our definition of the nature of a statement, must itself necessarily be one of the shortest possible.

THEAETETUS: So we agreed just now.

STRANGER: And secondly it must be about something.

THEAETETUS: Yes.

STRANGER: And if it is not about you, it is not about anything else.

THEAETETUS: Certainly.

STRANGER: And if it were about nothing, it would not be a statement at all, for we pointed out that there could not be a statement that was a statement about nothing.

THEAETETUS: Quite true.

STRANGER: So what is stated about you, but so that what is dif-   d
ferent is stated as the same or what is not as what is—a combination of verbs and names answering to that description finally seems to be really and truly a false statement.

THEAETETUS: Perfectly true.

STRANGER: And next, what of thinking and judgment and appearing? Is it not now clear that all these things occur in our minds both as false and as true?

THEAETETUS: How so?

STRANGER: You will see more easily if you begin by letting me give you an account of their nature and how each differs from the   e
others.

THEAETETUS: Let me have it.

STRANGER: Well, thinking and discourse are the same thing, except that what we call thinking is, precisely, the inward dialogue carried on by the mind with itself without spoken sound.

THEAETETUS: Certainly.

STRANGER: Whereas the stream which flows from the mind through the lips with sound is called discourse.

THEAETETUS: True.

STRANGER: And further there is a thing which we know occurs in discourse.

THEAETETUS: Namely?

STRANGER: Assertion and denial.

THEAETETUS: Yes.   264

STRANGER: Then when this occurs in the mind in the course of silent thinking, can you call it anything but judgment?

THEAETETUS: No.

STRANGER: And suppose judgment occurs, not independently, but by means of perception; the only right name for such a state of mind is 'appearing.'

THEAETETUS: Yes.

STRANGER: Well then, since we have seen that there is true and false statement, and of these mental processes we have found thinking to be a dialogue of the mind with itself, and judgment to be the conclusion of thinking, and what we mean by 'it appears' a blend   b
of perception and judgment, it follows that these also, being of the same nature as statement, must be, some of them and on some occasions, false.

THEAETETUS: Of course.

STRANGER: You see, then, that we have discovered the nature of false judgment and false statement sooner than we expected just now when we feared there would be no end to the task we were setting ourselves in the search for them.

THEAETETUS: I do.

STRANGER: Then let us not lose courage for what remains to be
c done. Now that these matters are cleared up, let us recall our earlier divisions by forms.

THEAETETUS: Which do you mean?

STRANGER: We distinguished two forms of image making—the making of likenesses and the making of semblances.

THEAETETUS: Yes.

STRANGER: And we said we were puzzled to tell under which of these two we should place the Sophist.

THEAETETUS: We did.

STRANGER: And to increase our perplexity we were plunged in a whirl of confusion by the apparition of an argument that called in question all these terms and disputed the very existence of any copy
d or image or semblance, on the ground that falsity never has any sort of existence anywhere.

THEAETETUS: True.

STRANGER: But now that we have brought to light the existence of false statement and of false judgment, it is possible that there should be imitations of real things and that this condition of mind [false judgment] should account for the existence of an art of deception.

THEAETETUS: Yes, it is.

STRANGER: And we agreed earlier that the Sophist does come under one or other of the two kinds mentioned.

THEAETETUS: Yes.

STRANGER: Now, then, let us set to work again and, as we
e divide the kind proposed in two, keep to the right-hand section at each stage. Holding fast to the characters of which the Sophist partakes until we have stripped off all that he has in common with others and left only the nature that is peculiar to him, let us so make that nature
265 plain, in the first place to ourselves, and secondly to others whose temperament finds a procedure of this sort congenial.

THEAETETUS: Very good.

STRANGER: Well, we began by dividing art into productive and acquisitive.

THEAETETUS: Yes.

STRANGER: And under the head of the acquisitive we had glimpses of the Sophist in the arts of hunting, contention, trafficking, and other kinds of that sort.

THEAETETUS: Certainly.

STRANGER: But now that he has been included under an art of imitation, clearly we must start by dividing into two the productive branch of art. For imitation is surely a kind of production, though it be only a production of images, as we say, not of originals of every sort. b Is that not so?

THEAETETUS: Assuredly.

STRANGER: Let us begin, then, by recognizing two kinds of production.

THEAETETUS: What are they?

STRANGER: The one divine, the other human.

THEAETETUS: I don't understand yet.

STRANGER: Production—to recall what we said at the outset— we defined as any power that can bring into existence what did not exist before.

THEAETETUS: I remember.

STRANGER: Now take all mortal animals and also all things c that grow—plants that grow above the earth from seeds and roots, and lifeless bodies compacted beneath the earth, whether fusible or not fusible. Must we not attribute the coming-into-being of these things out of not-being to divine craftsmanship and nothing else? Or are we to fall in with the belief that is commonly expressed?

THEAETETUS: What belief do you mean?

STRANGER: That nature gives birth to them as a result of some spontaneous cause that generates without intelligence. Or shall we say that they come from a cause which, working with reason and art, is divine and proceeds from divinity?

THEAETETUS: Perhaps because I am young, I often shift from d one belief to the other, but at this moment, looking at your face and believing you to hold that these things have a divine origin, I too am convinced.

STRANGER: Well said, Theaetetus. If I thought you were the sort of person that might believe otherwise in the future, I should now try by force of persuasion to make you accept that account. But I can see clearly that, without any arguments of mine, your nature will come of itself to the conclusion which you tell me attracts you at this e moment. So I will let that pass; I should be wasting time. I will only lay it down that the products of nature, as they are called, are works of divine art, as things made out of them by man are works of human art. Accordingly there will be two kinds of production, one human, the other divine.

THEAETETUS: Good.

STRANGER: Once more, then, divide each of these two into two parts.

THEAETETUS: How?

STRANGER: As you have just divided the whole extent of pro- 266 duction horizontally, now divide it vertically.

THEAETETUS : Be it so.

STRANGER : The result is four parts in all—two on our side, human, two on the side of the gods, divine.

THEAETETUS : Yes.

STRANGER : And taking the divisions made in the first way [horizontally, divine and human], one section of each part will be the production of originals, and the remaining two sections will be best described as production of images. So we have a second division of production on that principle [originals and images].

b   THEAETETUS : Explain once more how each of the two parts [divine and human] is divided.

STRANGER : Ourselves, I take it, and all other living creatures and the elements of natural things—fire, water, and their kindred— are all originals, the offspring, as we are well assured, of divine workmanship. Is it not so?

THEAETETUS : Yes.

STRANGER : And every one of these products is attended by images which are not the actual thing, and which also owe their existence to divine contrivance.

THEAETETUS : You mean . . . ?

STRANGER : Dream images, and in daylight all those naturally produced semblances which we call 'shadow' when dark patches interrupt the light, or a 'reflection' when the light belonging to the eye
c   meets and coalesces with light belonging to something else on a bright and smooth surface and produces a form yielding a perception that is the reverse of the ordinary direct view.

THEAETETUS : There are, indeed, these two products of divine workmanship—the original and the image that in every case accompanies it.

STRANGER : And what of our human art? Must we not say that in building it produces an actual house, and in painting a house of a different sort, as it were a man-made dream for waking eyes?
d   THEAETETUS : Certainly.

STRANGER : And so in all cases, we find once more twin products of our own productive activity in pairs—one an actual thing, the other an image.

THEAETETUS : I understand better now, and I recognize two forms of production, each of them twofold—divine and human according to one division, and according to the other a production of actual things and of some sort of likenesses.

STRANGER : Let us remind ourselves, then, that of this production of images there were to be two kinds, one producing likenesses, the other semblances, provided that falsity should be shown to
e   be a thing that really is false and of such a nature as to have a place among existing things.

THEAETETUS : Yes, it was to be so.

STRANGER: And that has now been shown; so on that ground shall we now reckon the distinction of these two forms as beyond dispute?

THEAETETUS: Yes.

STRANGER: Once more, then, let us divide in two the kind that 267 produces semblances.

THEAETETUS: How?

STRANGER: There is the semblance produced by means of tools, and another sort where the producer of the semblance takes his own person as an instrument.

THEAETETUS: How do you mean?

STRANGER: When someone uses his own person or voice to counterfeit your traits or speech, the proper name for creating such a semblance is, I take it, mimicry.

THEAETETUS: Yes.

STRANGER: Let us reserve that section, then, under the name of mimicry, and indulge ourselves so far as to leave all the rest for b someone else to collect into a unity and give it an appropriate name.

THEAETETUS: So be it.

STRANGER: But there is still ground for thinking that mimicry is of two sorts. Let me put it before you.

THEAETETUS: Do.

STRANGER: Some mimics know the thing they are impersonating; others do not. And could we find a more important distinction than that of knowing from not knowing?

THEAETETUS: No.

STRANGER: And the mimicry we have just mentioned goes with knowledge, for to impersonate you, one must be acquainted with you and your traits.

THEAETETUS: Of course.   c

STRANGER: And what of the traits of justice and of virtue generally? Are there not many who, having no knowledge of virtue but only some sort of opinion about it, zealously set about making it appear that they embody virtue as they conceive it, mimicking it as effectively as they can in their words and actions?

THEAETETUS: Only too many.

STRANGER: And are they always unsuccessful in appearing to be virtuous when they are not really virtuous at all? Do they not rather succeed perfectly?

THEAETETUS: They do.

STRANGER: We must, then, distinguish the ignorant mimic d from the other, who has knowledge.

THEAETETUS: Yes.

STRANGER: Where, then, must we look for a suitable name for each? No doubt it is hard to find one, because the ancients, it would seem, suffered from a certain laziness and lack of discrimination

with regard to the division of kinds by forms, and not one of them even tried to make such divisions, with the result that there is a serious shortage of names. However, though the expression may seem daring,
e for purposes of distinction let us call mimicry guided by opinion 'conceit mimicry,' and the sort that is guided by knowledge 'mimicry by acquaintance.'

THEAETETUS: So be it.

STRANGER: It is the former, then, that concerns us, for the Sophist was not among those who have knowledge, but he has a place among mimics.

THEAETETUS: Certainly.

STRANGER: Then let us take this conceit mimic and see if his metal rings sound or there is still a crack in it somewhere.

THEAETETUS: Let us do so.

STRANGER: Well, there is a gaping crack. There is the simple-
268 minded type who imagines that what he believes is knowledge, and an opposite type who is versed in discussion, so that his attitude betrays no little misgiving and suspicion that the knowledge he has the air of possessing in the eyes of the world is really ignorance.

THEAETETUS: Certainly both the types you describe exist.

STRANGER: We may, then, set down one of these mimics as sincere, the other as insincere.

THEAETETUS: So it appears.

STRANGER: And the insincere—is he of two kinds or only one?

THEAETETUS: That is for you to consider.
b STRANGER: I will, and I can clearly make out a pair of them. I see one who can keep up his dissimulation publicly in long speeches to a large assembly. The other uses short arguments in private and forces others to contradict themselves in conversation.

THEAETETUS: Very true.

STRANGER: And with whom shall we identify the more long-winded type—with the statesman or with the demagogue?

THEAETETUS: The demagogue.

STRANGER: And what shall we call the other—wise man or Sophist?

THEAETETUS: We cannot surely call him wise, because we set him down as ignorant, but as a mimic of the wise man he will clearly
c assume a title derived from his, and I now see that here at last is the man who must be truly described as the real and genuine Sophist.

STRANGER: Shall we, then, as before collect all the elements of his description, from the end to the beginning, and draw our threads together in a knot?

THEAETETUS: By all means.

STRANGER: The art of contradiction making, descended from an insincere kind of conceited mimicry, of the semblance-making

breed, derived from image making, distinguished as a portion, not di- d
vine but human, of production, that presents a shadow play of words
—such are the blood and lineage which can, with perfect truth, be
assigned to the authentic Sophist.

THEAETETUS : I entirely agree.

STATESMAN

The Statesman *is generally ranked among Plato's most important dialogues, but the first part of it presents difficulties to the reader, not because the thought is hard to understand, but because it is often long drawn out. Plato is by now in love with classification, as indeed he is also in the* Sophist, *but there only briefly. In the* Statesman *there are pages of division and subdivision in order to reach a definition of what the statesman is. Land dwellers are divided from sea dwellers, the horned from the hornless, the four-legged from the biped, and so on, until we get to man. Government is then divided into that over willing and that over unwilling subjects. But Plato cannot leave it at that. He must also illustrate what government is, first by a mythical story which shows that this world of imperfection has a close relation to the divine, and then by a practical example because, to paraphrase, "there is no outward and visible image of the greatest and noblest things"—the things that are seen are temporal— "and we must learn to give a rational account of them." Such illuminating ideas occur again and again throughout the dialogue.*

Weaving is chosen to illustrate the statesman's art of rightly dealing with "herds of free bipeds," and many pages are devoted to cutting off the weaver's art from the others and then describing the process of weaving which separates the wool into threads and combines them into cloth, thus exemplifying the many in the one and the one in the many. In the same way the separate activities of men, many as they are, combine under the guidance of the statesman into the firm and enduring union of the good state.

Of greater interest is the discussion in the last third of the dialogue about the various forms of government and the part law plays in them. The best government is lawless. It is guided by the true statesman whose rule is flexible and can be adapted to each individual case. The rule of law, on the contrary, is rigid and inflexible. The difference can be illustrated clearly if we imagine the two methods applied to any art, the art of medicine, for instance. If it were ruled by law, a majority in a general assembly would decide what methods should be used in doctoring people and that these should be invariably followed. Whoever was detected inquiring into its methods would be indicted in court on the charge of corrupting the young, persuading

*them to give medicine in an unlawful manner. If we were to do this
in everything, science, art, agriculture, carpentry, and so on, what
would be the result? They would all perish and could never spring up
again because inquiry would be forbidden. "The result would be that
life, which is hard enough as it is, would be quite impossible then and
not to be endured."*

*The best government then is independent of law. Statesmanship
is an art just as painting is. A good state can no more be produced
and maintained by laws than a good picture can be painted by formu-
las for mixing colors. When the true statesman rules he knows of himself how to deal justly with all, whereas the law can be the cause of
great injustice. But the state is not like a beehive; there is no single,
visible head. If no true statesman appears, the rule of law is the next
best. Experience has played a signal part in drawing up laws. Un-
adaptable though they are, they are better than the forms of government without them. But only the true statesman can rightly weave
the web of the state, bringing the many minds of men into firm and
enduring union.*

SOCRATES: Theodorus, I am really very much indebted to you for my   257
introduction to Theaetetus and to our guest from Elea.

THEODORUS: Good, but you are likely to be three times as much
in my debt, Socrates, when they have done their task and defined the
statesman and the philosopher as well as the Sophist for you.

SOCRATES: Three times as much? Really, my dear Theodorus,
must it go on record that we heard our greatest mathematician and
geometer say that?

THEODORUS: What do you mean, Socrates?   b

SOCRATES: Are we to say that we heard you reckoning all these
three as of equal value when their real values differ to an extent that
defies all your mathematical expressions of proportion?

THEODORUS: By Ammon, god of Libya, well said, Socrates, and
a fair hit! Your dropping on my blunder in calculation like this
shows that you have really remembered your mathematics! But I will
have my revenge for this some other time. Now, sir, we turn to you.

From *Plato's Statesman*, translated with introductory essays and footnotes
by J. B. Skemp (New Haven and London, 1952). Minor corrections have
been made, as suggested by G. E. L. Owen, in his review in *Mind*, LXII, No.
246 (April 1953). A few English colloquialisms have been changed to
standard English.

Pray do not tire of favoring us with your assistance but go on to define the statesman or the philosopher, whichever you prefer to seek.

c   STRANGER: Yes, we must do that, Theodorus. We have set ourselves to the task and now we must not withdraw from it till all our definitions are complete. But we must also consider Theaetetus here—what ought I to do about him?

THEODORUS: In what way?

STRANGER: Shall we give him a rest from philosophical wrestling and take on his fellow gymnast, the young Socrates, in his place—or have you any other suggestion?

THEODORUS: No, take on young Socrates this time, as you suggest. They are both young and will be better able to carry through stiff exercise by being rested in turn.

d   SOCRATES: Furthermore, sir, they might both be said to have some sort of kinship with me. Theaetetus, according to you, is like me
258 in looks and Socrates bears the same name. Sharing a name entails kinship in some sense, and, of course, we ought always to seize opportunities of discovering those who may be our kinsfolk by conversing with them. Yesterday I joined in discussion with Theaetetus; today I have listened to him answering you. I have not heard Socrates speak either in discussion or in reply. He too must be tested. So he shall reply to me another time, but this afternoon let him answer you.

STRANGER: Very good! Socrates, you hear what Socrates says?

YOUNG SOCRATES: Yes.

STRANGER: Do you agree to his proposal?

YOUNG SOCRATES: Yes, certainly.

b   STRANGER: Evidently you are putting no obstacles in the way of our advance, and I think I am still less entitled to do so. Well, then, after finding the Sophist, the task we now have to face together is to search out the statesman, or so it seems to me. Tell me, then, Socrates, whether he too must be classified as one of those who possess some kind of expert knowledge, or must we begin with some other kind of definition?

YOUNG SOCRATES: No, he is to be defined as a kind of expert.

STRANGER: Well then, must we distinguish the forms of knowledge as we did when looking for his predecessor?

YOUNG SOCRATES: It would seem so.

STRANGER: But the line of cleavage required now appears to differ from the previous one, Socrates.

YOUNG SOCRATES: What then?

c   STRANGER: It follows another division.

YOUNG SOCRATES: It may well be so.

STRANGER: Where shall a man find the way of the statesman then? For we must distinguish this path from all the rest by setting upon it the special sign of its distinctive form. All roads divergent from it we must mark out also as one common class. Thus we must bring our minds to conceive of all forms of knowledge as falling under one or the other of these two classes—statecraft and knowledge other than statecraft.

YOUNG SOCRATES: This must be your task, sir. It is not for me to attempt it.

STRANGER: Yes, but it will be your achievement as well, Soc- d rates, when all becomes clear to us both.

YOUNG SOCRATES: It is kind of you to say so.

STRANGER: Then consider the science of number and certain other sciences closely akin to it. Are they not unconcerned with any form of practical activity, yielding us pure knowledge only?

YOUNG SOCRATES: That is the case.

STRANGER: But it is quite otherwise with carpentry and manufacture in general. These possess science embodied as it were in a practical activity and inseparable from it. Their products do not e exist before the arts come into operation and their operation is an integral part of the emergence of the product from its unworked state.

YOUNG SOCRATES: True. What of it?

STRANGER: You must use this distinction to divide the totality of sciences into two classes. Name the one 'applied,' the other 'pure.'

YOUNG SOCRATES: I agree. Let your distinction be drawn, and let all science be divided into these two parts.

STRANGER: Are we then to regard the statesman, the king, the slavemaster, and the master of a household as essentially one though we use all these names for them, or shall we say that four distinct sciences exist, each of them corresponding to one of the four titles? But let me put this in another way easier to follow.

YOUNG SOCRATES: And what is that?   259

STRANGER: I will tell you. Suppose we find a medical man who is not himself practicing as a public medical officer but who nevertheless is competent to advise a doctor actually serving in that capacity? Must not the expert knowledge the adviser possesses be described by the same title as that of the functionary whom he is advising?

YOUNG SOCRATES: Yes.

STRANGER: Well then, consider a man who, though himself a private citizen, is capable of giving expert advice to the ruler of a country. Shall we not say that he possesses the same science as the ruler himself possesses—or, rather ought to have possessed?

YOUNG SOCRATES: We shall indeed say so.

STRANGER: But the science possessed by the true king is the sci- b ence of kingship?

YOUNG SOCRATES: Yes.

STRANGER: The possessor of this science then, whether he is

in fact in power or has only the status of a private citizen, will properly be called a 'statesman' since his knowledge of the art qualifies him for the title whatever his circumstances.

YOUNG SOCRATES : Yes, he is undoubtedly entitled to that name.

STRANGER : Then consider a further point. The slavemaster and the master of a household are identical.

YOUNG SOCRATES : Yes.

STRANGER : Furthermore, is there much difference between a large household organization and a small-sized city, so far as the exercise of authority over it is concerned?

YOUNG SOCRATES : None.

c   STRANGER : Well then, our point is clearly made. One science covers all these several spheres and we will not quarrel with a man who prefers any one of the particular names for it; he can call it royal science, political science, or science of household management.

YOUNG SOCRATES : It makes no difference.

STRANGER : Now comes another point that can hardly be controversial. What a king can do to maintain his rule by using his hands or his bodily faculties as a whole is very slight in comparison with what he can do by mental power and force of personality.

YOUNG SOCRATES : Manifestly.

STRANGER : So a king's art is closer to theoretical knowledge
d than to manual work or indeed to practical work in general?

YOUNG SOCRATES : Yes.

STRANGER : You agree then that we may speak either of statesmanship and the statesman or of kingship and the king, these terms being convertible, since they are identical in force?

YOUNG SOCRATES : Certainly.

STRANGER : Let us go on to the next stage and see if we can proceed to a division of the kinds of theoretical knowledge.

YOUNG SOCRATES : Good.

STRANGER : Look attentively then and see if we cannot discover a natural cleavage within such knowledge.

YOUNG SOCRATES : Tell me where it is.

e   STRANGER : See, it is here. There exists, we agree, an art of counting.

YOUNG SOCRATES : Yes.

STRANGER : That belongs quite definitely to the class of theoretical sciences, I presume.

YOUNG SOCRATES : Of course.

STRANGER : Now when the art of counting has ascertained a numerical difference we do not assign it any further task save that of pronouncing on what has been ascertained, do we?

YOUNG SOCRATES : No.

STRANGER: Now consider a master builder. No master builder is a manual worker—he directs the work of others.

YOUNG SOCRATES: Yes.

STRANGER: He provides the knowledge but not the manual labor.

YOUNG SOCRATES: True.

STRANGER: So he might fairly be said to possess one of the 260 theoretical forms of science.

YOUNG SOCRATES: He might indeed.

STRANGER: But it is characteristic of him that when he has delivered a verdict on the facts he has not ended his task in the way the calculator has. The master builder must give the appropriate directions to each of the workmen and see that they complete the work assigned.

YOUNG SOCRATES: That is so.

STRANGER: Therefore all this class of sciences are quite as 'theoretical' as calculation and its kindred sciences are, but the two groups differ from one another in that the latter are content to give a verdict, b but the former issue a command for performance of further actions.

YOUNG SOCRATES: This is clearly the difference between them.

STRANGER: Well then, may we claim that it is a sound division to split the whole of theoretical science into two parts and to call one critical and the other directive?

YOUNG SOCRATES: Yes—I would agree to it at any rate.

STRANGER: I hope so, for it is much to be desired that those sharing a task should be of one mind.

YOUNG SOCRATES: Indeed it is.

STRANGER: So long as we ourselves share this happy agreement we can let the judgments of the rest of the world look after themselves.

YOUNG SOCRATES: Yes.

STRANGER: Well then, in which of these groups of sciences do c we find a place for the king? In the critical class—as though he were a mere spectator of truth? Is he not rather in the other, directive class? Does not his position in control of men imply this?

YOUNG SOCRATES: Of course he is in the second group.

STRANGER: Good, but we must now look further at the directive class and see if we find a cleavage in it somewhere. I think I have lighted on one. There is a difference between kings and heralds d analogous to the difference between the art of the producer-salesman and of that of the retailer.

YOUNG SOCRATES: How so?

STRANGER: Retailers take over what someone else has made and then sell a second time what was first sold to them.

YOUNG SOCRATES: Quite so.

STRANGER: Similarly heralds receive commands which have been thought out and issued by someone else; then they issue them at second hand to others.

YOUNG SOCRATES: Very true.

SOCRATES: Well then, are we going to confound the science of
e kingship with the science of the interpreter, the coxswain, the prophet, or the herald, or with any of this large group of kindred sciences, simply because all of them are concerned, as admittedly they are, with issuing orders? We thought out an analogy just now. Cannot we think out a name as well, seeing that unfortunately there is no normal description of the general class of 'givers of firsthand orders'? We will make the cleavage at this point and name a 'predirective' class into which we will put the race of kings. The other class, now distinct, we can neglect, leaving it to someone else to invent a further common name for the tribes it covers. It is for the king we are searching—not for his opposite.

YOUNG SOCRATES: Exactly.

261   STRANGER: Well then, his group has been distinguished from the others, the decisive factor being that the kingly group issues its own commands while the other group merely passes commands on. Now we must subdivide the kingly group if we find it susceptible of a division.

YOUNG SOCRATES: We must look for one.

STRANGER: Yes, and I think I have found one. Keep close to me and share the work of dividing.

YOUNG SOCRATES: Where is the division?

STRANGER: Take any ruler we may observe at his work of is-
b suing orders. Is not the purpose of his action the production of something?

YOUNG SOCRATES: Of course.

STRANGER: Products in general need not detain us; they are easily divided into two classes.

YOUNG SOCRATES: How?

STRANGER: Considering them as a whole we find some lifeless, the rest alive.

YOUNG SOCRATES: Yes.

STRANGER: By this distinction we can divide, if we wish to do so, the directive group of theoretical sciences.

YOUNG SOCRATES: How?

STRANGER: We assign one section to superintendence of the production of lifeless things, the other to superintendence of the pro-
c duction of living things. This effects an exhaustive division of the group.

YOUNG SOCRATES: Yes, it does.

STRANGER: Let us put aside the one section and, taking the other as our unit, divide it into two.

YOUNG SOCRATES : Which of the two sections do you suggest that we take for subdivision?

STRANGER : Surely the section concerned with the issue of directives about living creatures. It goes without saying that the king is never concerned with directives concerning lifeless things in the way the master builder is. Kingship is a nobler thing; it works among living creatures and its functions have to do with these alone.   d

YOUNG SOCRATES : True.

STRANGER : Now the breeding and nurturing of living creatures can be seen to be of two kinds. They may either be reared singly or in flocks collectively.

YOUNG SOCRATES : They may.

STRANGER : But we shall certainly not find the statesman to be a man in charge of one creature like some cowman or groom. He is much more like the man in charge of a whole herd of cows or of a stud of horses.

YOUNG SOCRATES : That is quite clear, once it is put as you have put it now.

STRANGER : How shall we describe the section of the art of rear- e ing living things which has to do with rearing them collectively? Shall we call it 'herd nurture' or 'collective nurture'?

YOUNG SOCRATES : We can use whichever name better helps our argument.

STRANGER : Excellently said, Socrates. If you hold fast to this principle of avoiding contention over names you will be seen to be rich with an ever greater store of wisdom as you come to old age. We will apply this sound principle to the present case and do as you bid me. Do you see how we can divide the nurture of herds into twin 262 sections, so as to cordon off the object of our search in one of them and leave him an area only half the size of the one he is free to roam in at present?

YOUNG SOCRATES : I will try my hardest to cordon him off. I think the division is to be made between nurture of men and nurture of beasts.

STRANGER : You were keenness itself and you fenced the king off like a man, but I think we must not let this happen again if we can help it.

YOUNG SOCRATES : Why, what has happened? What have we done?

STRANGER : We must beware lest we break off one small fragment of a class and then contrast it with all the important sections b left behind. We must only divide where there is a real cleavage between specific forms. The section must always possess a specific form. It is splendid if one really can divide off the class sought for immediately from all the rest—that is, if the structure of reality authorizes such immediate division. You had such direct tactics in mind just now and hastened the argument to its conclusion. You saw that our search led us to men, and so you thought you had found the real division. But, it is dangerous, Socrates, to chop reality up into small portions. It is always safer to go down the middle to make our cuts. The real cleavages among the forms are more likely to be found thus, and c the whole art of these definitions consists in finding these cleavages.

YOUNG SOCRATES: What do you mean, sir?

STRANGER: I will try to be still clearer, Socrates, for you are the kind of person it is a pleasure to teach. A fully satisfactory demonstration is not possible now, circumstances being what they are, but we must try for the sake of clearness to push the explanation a stage further.

YOUNG SOCRATES: Thank you, but what kind of mistake do you say that we made in our division just now?

STRANGER: The kind of mistake a man would make who, seek-d ing to divide the class of human beings into two, divided them into Greeks and barbarians. This is a division most people in this part of the world make. They separate the Greeks from all other nations making them a class apart; thus they group all other nations together as a class, ignoring the fact that it is an indeterminate class made up of peoples who have no intercourse with each other and speak different languages. Lumping all this non-Greek residue together, they think it must constitute one real class because they have a common name 'barbarian' to attach to it. Take another example. A man might think that he was dividing number into its true classes if he cut off the number ten thousand from all others and set it apart as one class. He might go on to invent a single name for the whole of the rest of number, e and then claim that because it possessed the invented common name it was in fact the other true class of number—'number other than ten thousand.' Surely it would be better and closer to the real structure of the forms to make a central division of number into odd and even or of humankind into male and female. A division setting Lydians or Phrygians or any other peoples in contradistinction to all the rest can only be made when a man fails to arrive at a true division into two groups each of which after separation is not only a portion of the 263 whole class to be divided but also a real subdivision of it.

YOUNG SOCRATES: Quite so, sir, but this is just the difficulty. How can one learn to distinguish more clearly between a mere portion and a true subdivision and recognize them as being really different?

STRANGER: My dear Socrates, this is no light order. We have already strayed rather too far from the argument set as our task, and here you are asking that we stray still further! For the moment let us go back to the argument as is only right. We will get on the track of b your problem some other time when we are free to do so and then we will follow it out to the end. But there is one caution I will add here.

Do not suppose that in what I say now I have given you a full explanation of the principle.

YOUNG SOCRATES: What principle do you mean?

STRANGER: The principle that a portion and a subdivision of a class are not identical.

YOUNG SOCRATES: Can you be more explicit?

STRANGER: Where a true subdivision of a wider class is made, this subdivision must necessarily also be a portion of the total class of which it is declared a subdivision. But the converse is not true, since a portion is not necessarily a true subdivision. You can claim my authority, Socrates, for asserting this and for denying the contrary.

YOUNG SOCRATES: This ruling will be followed.

STRANGER: Good! Now help me to settle the next question.   c

YOUNG SOCRATES: What is that?

STRANGER: Consider the class which caused us to stray from the argument and brought us to this point. I think that the trouble began at the moment when you were asked how we were to divide the science of tending herds and you answered with alacrity that there are two classes of living creatures, one of them being mankind, and the other the rest of the animals lumped together.

YOUNG SOCRATES: True.

STRANGER: It became clear to me then that you were breaking off a mere portion, and that because you were able to give the common name 'animals' to what was left, namely to all creatures other than man, you thought that these creatures do in actual fact make up one class.

YOUNG SOCRATES: Yes, that was so.   d

STRANGER: But, my gallant young friend, pray consider this! This kind of classification might be undertaken by any other creature capable of rational thought—for instance cranes are reputed to be rational in this way and there may be others. They might invest themselves with a unique and proper dignity and classify the race of cranes as being distinct from all other creatures; the rest they might well lump together, men included, giving them the common appellation of 'the beasts.' So let us try to be on the watch against mistakes   e of that kind.

YOUNG SOCRATES: How can we avoid them?

STRANGER: By not attempting too general a division of the class of living creatures. We shall be less liable to such errors if we avoid this.

YOUNG SOCRATES: Indeed we must not do it.

STRANGER: No, for it was here our mistake was made just now.

YOUNG SOCRATES: What precisely was it?

STRANGER: The directive section of theoretical science, in so far as it directs the rearing of living creatures was our concern, but we added 'the rearing of them in *herds*.' That is so, is it not?

YOUNG SOCRATES: Yes.

264   STRANGER: This last element of the definition, 'rearing in herds,' implied a prior division of all living creatures according to wildness and tameness. Types amenable to training and control we call tame animals; those resisting control, wild animals.

YOUNG SOCRATES: True.

STRANGER: Now it will be conceded that the science we are hunting down has always been and still is one that works among tame creatures; furthermore, it is to be looked for among tame creatures which are gregarious.

YOUNG SOCRATES: Yes.

STRANGER: Let us avoid making divisions in the way we did just now, in a desperate hurry and with our attention fixed only on the whole class. Only thus shall we reach the statesman in good time.
b This statesman's art has already landed us in the situation the proverb warns us against!

YOUNG SOCRATES: Which proverb is this?

STRANGER: 'More haste' in our work of correct division has meant 'less speed' for us.

YOUNG SOCRATES: But it has been a happy mischance, sir.

STRANGER: That may be so, but now let us try again from the beginning to divide the science of collective rearing. It may well be that the argument itself as we proceed with it will show you more clearly the very thing you are in such eagerness to discover. Answer me this.

YOUNG SOCRATES: What?

STRANGER: I want to know if you happen to have heard people
c speak of something you can hardly have seen for yourself—herds of tame fishes. I know you have not been to see them in the aquariums in the Nile or in the Great King's ponds. But you might possibly have seen such fishes in ornamental fountains yourself.

YOUNG SOCRATES: Of course I have seen them, and I have heard many people speak of the others.

STRANGER: It is the same with the flocks of tame cranes and tame geese in Thessaly—you have never toured the Thessalian plains but you have at least heard of them and you believe that such flocks exist.

YOUNG SOCRATES: Yes, of course.

d   STRANGER: My reason for asking you all this is to show that creatures reared in herds may be of two kinds. Some live in water; others live on land.

YOUNG SOCRATES: Yes, I agree.

STRANGER: Have I your agreement, then, that we have to divide herd rearing on this principle into two sections? May we assign

one subdivision to each of these subsidiary sciences and call the one
'water herd rearing,' the other 'land herd rearing'?

YOUNG SOCRATES: Again, I agree.

STRANGER: One need hardly ask to which of these sciences the
kingly art belongs—the answer is obvious.   e

YOUNG SOCRATES: Of course.

STRANGER: The next subdivision of the land herd rearing section of herd rearing can be made by anyone.

YOUNG SOCRATES: How?

STRANGER: By dividing it between walkers and fliers.

YOUNG SOCRATES: Oh yes, of course.

STRANGER: Well then, is not the statesman's art to be sought
among the arts dealing with walking herds? Do you not think that
practically everyone, even the most witless, would judge this to be so?

YOUNG SOCRATES: Yes, I do.

STRANGER: Then we must effect a subdivision of land herd
tendance into two parts, just as we recently divided number into two.

YOUNG SOCRATES: Clearly.

STRANGER: But see what has happened. In the region into   265
which the argument has moved we see two paths lying before us
inviting us to our goal. One path reaches the goal more quickly but
divides off a small class from a large one. The other is a longer way
round but it observes the principle we enunciated before, that we
should always divide down the middle where possible. We can go on by
whichever of these paths we prefer.

YOUNG SOCRATES: Is it impossible to take them both?

STRANGER: To take both at once is impossible—that is an
amazing suggestion, Socrates! But obviously you can take first one,
then the other.

YOUNG SOCRATES: Then I vote for taking first one way, then   b
the other.

STRANGER: That is easy, for there is not much farther to go. At
the outset or halfway your command would have been difficult for
us to obey, but since we are nearly there and you desire it, let us take
the longer path first; we shall get to its end more easily now while we
are fresher. See this division then.

YOUNG SOCRATES: Tell me what it is.

STRANGER: We find a division of tame herded walking creatures ready-made in nature.

YOUNG SOCRATES: What is it?

STRANGER: Some have horns; the rest have none.

YOUNG SOCRATES: That is evident.   c

STRANGER: Divide then the science of rearing walking herds
into two sections, assigning each its sphere, but use a general description in doing so. For if you are anxious about naming each, the business will be complicated needlessly.

YOUNG SOCRATES: How shall we state the matter then?

STRANGER: We will say this. The science of rearing walking herds has been divided into two. The one section of it is assigned to rearing horned herds, and the other to rearing hornless herds.

d   YOUNG SOCRATES: The division shall stand in these terms. In any case there can be no further question about it.

STRANGER: See now, our king stands out clearly once more; he is shepherd of a hornless herd.

YOUNG SOCRATES: Unmistakably so!

STRANGER: Let us divide up this herd into its component parts then, and try to assign to the king the place really belonging to him.

YOUNG SOCRATES: By all means.

STRANGER: Where shall we divide it? By distinguishing whole-hoofed and cloven-hoofed, or interbreeding and noninterbreeding? Which do you prefer? You understand what I mean, I suppose?

YOUNG SOCRATES: About what?

e   STRANGER: You know that horses and asses are capable of interbreeding?

YOUNG SOCRATES: Yes.

STRANGER: But all other tame hornless herds are incapable of interbreeding.

YOUNG SOCRATES: Of course.

STRANGER: What of the statesman then? Is the herd he has in his charge capable of interbreeding with another or incapable?

YOUNG SOCRATES: Incapable, of course.

STRANGER: This group we must now divide again into two as before, it would seem.

YOUNG SOCRATES: Yes, we must.

266   STRANGER: But the class of tame, gregarious living creatures has already been reduced to its component elements save for the division of two of these from each other. For dogs cannot claim to be counted in the class of gregarious animals.

YOUNG SOCRATES: No they cannot, but by what means are we to separate the remaining pair?

STRANGER: By a method very appropriate for application by Theaetetus and yourself, seeing that both of you are geometers.

YOUNG SOCRATES: What is that?

STRANGER: I would say, 'by the diagonal and secondly by the diagonal of the diagonal.'

YOUNG SOCRATES: What do you mean?

b   STRANGER: What say you of our human constitution? How is this human race of ours endowed? So far as its peripatetic potential is concerned, is it not very like the diagonal? Has it not a potency of two feet?

YOUNG SOCRATES: So it has.

STRANGER: Moreover the character of the remaining component of the class is in turn of the potency possessed by the diagonal of our human diagonal, since its native peripatetic potential is one of two feet twice over.

YOUNG SOCRATES: Of course it is, and I think I see what you are meaning to say.

STRANGER: Good! Now here is another conclusion which we c have reached by our divisions which is not without its interest for the comedians. Do we see it, Socrates?

YOUNG SOCRATES: What is it?

STRANGER: For neighbor and competitor in the race this humanity of ours has the most portly and the most easygoing of all the creatures.

YOUNG SOCRATES: Yes, I see. What a funny coincidence!

STRANGER: Still, isn't it reasonable after all? The slowest shuffle in—or snuffle in—last.

YOUNG SOCRATES: Yes, of course you're right.

STRANGER: But there is another thing to notice. What a funny situation the king is in! He has kept pace with his herd and so he has been running a race with the man who is of all men best trained for d living an easy life!

YOUNG SOCRATES: Yes, just so.

STRANGER: This is a still clearer illustration of the principle we laid down in our inquiry concerning the Sophist.

YOUNG SOCRATES: What was that?

STRANGER: That in a philosophical search for a definition, like the present one, the presence or absence of dignity in the object under definition is an irrelevance. Lowly and exalted must receive equal consideration and the argument must proceed by proper stages in its own right to reach the truest conclusion obtainable.

YOUNG SOCRATES: That seems to be right.

STRANGER: Well now, am I to lead you, without waiting for you to ask me, along the shorter of the roads which we discovered as e leading to the definition of the king?

YOUNG SOCRATES: Do so, please.

STRANGER: In my opinion then, we must start from the point we reached by separating out herded creatures on land and this time divide these forthwith into two-footed and four-footed. We shall then see the human race sharing the occupation of the two-footed class with the winged tribes and none else; having observed this, we shall divide the two-footed herds into winged and wingless. Then the science of shepherding mankind will have been brought to light. Now we must bring our statesman and king and set him over this class like a charioteer, and hand over to him the reins of government of the state, for they belong to him and his alone is this art of government.

YOUNG SOCRATES: Your debt to me, sir, is nobly discharged by 267 the definition you have made—and you have more than paid the debt, for you have thrown in the digression by way of interest.

STRANGER: Come then, let us gather up the threads of our

argument and work out from start to finish our definition of what is called 'political science.'

YOUNG SOCRATES : Let us do so by all means.

STRANGER : We made a first division of theoretical science by taking the directive part of it. Of this we took the part which we described by analogy with the producer-salesman as 'predirective.' From b this predirective science we cut off that which directs the rearing of living things, a very important part of the whole. Animal rearing was divided and we chose out of it rearing in herds, and, next to this, rearing of herds of creatures that live on land. Dividing this again, we chose rearing of hornless herds. We then took a part of this, and if one must employ its name, it will be a name three words long—'non-c interbreeding herd tendance.' As for the further divisions, only the class 'man tendance' is left in the two-footed section of the last-named class—and so we reach the object of our search, namely, statesmanship or kingship, which is another name for statesmanship.

YOUNG SOCRATES : Yes, we really have reached our conclusion.

STRANGER : Do you really think so, Socrates? Do you think our task as complete as you make out?

YOUNG SOCRATES : Why do you ask?

STRANGER : Have we dealt fully with the problem we were given d to solve? Is there not a fault and a very grave one in our treatment of it, the fault of arriving at a definition of a king but failing to work through to a really complete and adequate definition?

YOUNG SOCRATES : What do you mean?

STRANGER : I will try to make my meaning clearer—to myself as well as to you.

YOUNG SOCRATES : Do so, please.

STRANGER : We found just now many arts of herd tendance of which statesmanship is one particular instance. Statesmanship is in charge of the rearing of a particular kind of herd.

YOUNG SOCRATES : Yes.

STRANGER : Our argument defined it as the science of the collective rearing of men—as distinct from the rearing of horses or other animals.

YOUNG SOCRATES : Quite so.

e STRANGER : But we have to notice one respect in which a king differs from all other herdsmen.

YOUNG SOCRATES : What is that?

STRANGER : Do we find any other herdsman challenged by a rival who practices another art and yet claims that he shares with the herdsman the duty of feeding the herd?

YOUNG SOCRATES : How do you mean?

STRANGER : You see how merchants, farmers, and all who prepare the grain for food—yes, and teachers of gymnastics and doctors as well—would all dispute the title 'feeders of mankind' with the herdsman we have called 'statesman.' These others would all contend that they are in charge of the feeding of mankind—and of feeding the 268 leaders themselves as well as the mass of the herd.

YOUNG SOCRATES : Would they not be quite right?

STRANGER : Maybe. We will examine this point further, but we can say at once with certainty that no one else disputes a cowherd's position in any of these matters. He feeds his herd himself, and he is also its doctor. He is its matchmaker too, one might say, and none but he understands the midwife's duties when confinements occur and b babies have to be brought into the world. Furthermore, in so far as his charges feel a need for games and music, who so good as he to cheer them, who so gifted to charm and soothe them? For he is master of the music best suited to his herd, be it rendered on the pipes or in song unaccompanied. And so it is in the case of every other herdsman, is it not?

YOUNG SOCRATES : Certainly it is.

STRANGER : How then can the definition of the king reached in our discussion show up as correct and flawless in the light of these new facts? We are claiming that he alone is herdsman and shepherd c of the human flock, but we are merely singling him out as such from a host of competitors.

YOUNG SOCRATES : Certainly this will not do.

STRANGER : Then we were quite right to feel anxious a little while ago when the suspicion came over us that though the figure we described was a kingly one we had not yet achieved a real portrait of the statesman. We might well hesitate, for we cannot reveal him finally in his proper quality till we have removed and put apart from him the throng of rivals that crowds around him and claims to share his herdsmanship.

YOUNG SOCRATES : Yes, we were quite right to hesitate.   d

STRANGER : So we must aim at a complete description, Socrates, unless we are to bring disgrace on our argument in the end.

YOUNG SOCRATES : Yes, for we must avoid that at all costs.

STRANGER : Then we must begin all over again from another starting point and travel by another road.

YOUNG SOCRATES : What kind of road must this be?

STRANGER : We have to bring in some pleasant stories to relieve the strain. There is a mass of ancient legend a large part of which we must now use for our purposes; after that we must go on as before, dividing always and choosing one part only, until we arrive at the e summit of our climb and the object of our journey. Shall we begin?

YOUNG SOCRATES : Yes, certainly.

STRANGER : Come then, listen closely to my story as a child would. After all, you are not so very many years too old for stories.

YOUNG SOCRATES : Do continue, please.

STRANGER: These old stories have been told before and will be told again. Among them is the one about the portent that settled the famous quarrel between Atreus and Thyestes. I expect you have heard the story and remember the details of it as they are described to us.

YOUNG SOCRATES: You refer, I suppose, to the strange sign of the golden lamb.

269   STRANGER: Oh no, not to that, but to the alteration in rising and setting of the sun and the other planets. The story tells us that on this famous occasion these all set where they now rise and rose where they now set. Afterward, however, when he had testified by this miracle to the justice of Atreus's claims, Zeus restored all these heavenly bodies to their present system of motion.

YOUNG SOCRATES: Yes, that comes into the story too.

STRANGER: Then again, we have heard of the reign of Cronus from many storytellers.

b   YOUNG SOCRATES: From most of them, I should say.

STRANGER: Yes, and what else? Are we not told that men of that former age were earthborn and not born of human parents?

YOUNG SOCRATES: That is also one of the old stories.

STRANGER: All these stories originate from the same event in cosmic history, and so do hosts of others yet more marvelous than these. However, as this great event took place so long ago, some of them have faded from man's memory; others survive but they have become scattered and have come to be told in a way which obscures their real connection with one another. No one has related the great event of history which gives the setting of all of them; it is this event which we must now recount. Once it has been related, its relevance to our present demonstration of the nature of a king will become apparent.

c

YOUNG SOCRATES: Excellent, sir. Please go on, and leave nothing unsaid.

STRANGER: Listen then, and you shall hear. There is an era in which God himself assists the universe on its way and guides it by imparting its rotation to it. There is also an era in which he releases his control. He does this when its circuits under his guidance have completed the due limit of the time thereto appointed. Thereafter it begins to revolve in the contrary sense under its own impulse—for it is a living creature and has been endowed with reason by him who framed it in the beginning. Now this capacity for rotation in reverse is of necessity native to it for a reason I must tell.

d

YOUNG SOCRATES: Of what nature is it?

STRANGER: Ever to be the same, steadfast and abiding, is the prerogative of the divinest of things only. The nature of the bodily does not entitle it to this rank. Now the heaven, or the universe as we have chosen to call it, has received many blessed gifts from him who brought it into being, but it has also been made to partake of bodily form. Hence it is impossible that it should abide forever free from e change, and yet, as far as may be, its movement is uniform, invariable, and in one place. Thus it is that it has received from God a rotation in reverse—the least possible variation of its proper motion. To revolve ever in the same sense belongs to none but the lord and leader of all things that move, and even he cannot move the universe now in the one sense now in the other—for this would flout eternal decrees. For all these reasons there are many doctrines we are forbidden to affirm concerning this universe. We must not say that it moves itself, perpetually revolving in one and the same sense. We may not say that it is God who turns it in its entirety throughout all time in two opposed alternating revolutions. We may not say that a pair of divinities make it revolve alternately in these opposed senses 270 because the mind of the one god is contrary to the mind of the other. We must therefore affirm the doctrine stated above, which is the one remaining possibility. In the one era it is assisted on its way by the transcendent divine cause, receiving a renewal of life from its creator, an immortality of his contriving. In the other era, when it has been released, it moves by its innate force and it has stored up so much momentum at the time of its release that it can revolve in the reverse sense for thousands of revolutions, because its size is so great, its balance so perfect, and the pivot on which it turns so very small.

YOUNG SOCRATES: Your whole account seems to me very b consistent and very probable.

STRANGER: Let us think about this together. Let us study this great cosmic fact underlying all these miraculous stories in the light of what we have just said. It is this great fact that I have been speaking about.

YOUNG SOCRATES: What is it?

STRANGER: The fact that the revolution of the heaven is sometimes in its present sense, sometimes in the reverse sense.

YOUNG SOCRATES: How would you state its significance?

STRANGER: This change of motion we must regard as the most c important and the most complete of all 'turnings-back' occurring in the celestial orbits.

YOUNG SOCRATES: It would seem so.

STRANGER: We must believe then, that at the time such changes take place in the universe we human beings living within that universe have to undergo the most drastic changes also.

YOUNG SOCRATES: That is to be expected.

STRANGER: Do we not know from experience that when great changes of any kind come upon them at once, all living beings feel the strain intensely and can hardly stand it?

YOUNG SOCRATES: We do indeed.

STRANGER: So it must needs be that in the cosmic crisis there is widespread destruction of living creatures other than man and d that only a remnant of the human race survives. Many strange new experiences befall this remnant, but there is one of deeper import than all. It follows on God's first taking over the rewinding of the universe, at the moment when the revolution counter to the one now prevalent begins to operate.

YOUNG SOCRATES : What is it?

STRANGER : First of all, every living creature, whatever the stage of life it had attained, ceased to grow any older. All mortal beings halted on their way to bent and hoary age, and each began to grow

e backward, as it were, toward youth and ever greater immaturity. The white hairs of the older men began to grow dark again; the cheeks of bearded men grew smooth once more and restored to each the long-lost bloom of his youth. The bodies of the young men lost the signs of manhood and, growing smaller every day and every night, they returned again to the condition of newborn children, being made like to them in mind as well as in body. Next they faded into non-existence and one by one they were gone. Moreover the bodies of those who died by violence in that time of crisis exhibited these same changes—and did so with such rapidity that in their case disappearance took place within a few days.

271   YOUNG SOCRATES : But how did living creatures come into being in that era, sir? How did they produce their offspring?

STRANGER : Clearly, Socrates, it was no part of man's natural endowment in that era to beget children by intercourse. Our legends tell us that once upon a time there was an earthborn race. Now it was this race which at that moment of crisis began to return to life out of the earth. The memory of it has lived on, for it was handed down to us by the earliest of our forebears. These earliest forebears were the children of earthborn parents; they lived in the period directly following

b the end of the era of the earthborn, at the close of the former period of cosmic rotation and the beginning of the present one. These ancestors of ours passed on to us these stories of the earthborn, and it is an unsound judgment to disbelieve them as so many do nowadays. For I think that we must consider what follows in the cosmic story. It is only to be expected that along with the reversal of the old men's course of life and their return to childhood, a new race of men should arise too—a new race formed from men dead and long laid in earth but now formed in her womb anew and thence returning to life once more. Such resurrection of the dead was in keeping with the cosmic change, all creation being now turned in the reverse direction. This race was, as it needs must be, 'born from the earth'; hence comes

c the name and hence the legend. Birth out of the ground was the law for all of them, save for some few whom God translated to another destiny.

YOUNG SOCRATES : Yes, this is fully in keeping with what went before, but tell me about the life of man in the reign of Cronus

of which you speak. Did this life obtain in the former world era or in
this one? For clearly a change of direction of sun and planets occurs
at both points in history at which the universe changes its sense of
rotation.

STRANGER: You have followed the story closely. As for your inquiry concerning the age when all good things come without man's d
labor, the answer is that this also most certainly belongs to the former
era, not to the present one. In that era God was supreme governor in
charge of the actual rotation of the universe as a whole, but divine
also, and in like manner was the government of its several regions,
for these were all portioned out to be provinces under the surveillance
of tutelary deities. Over every herd of living creatures throughout all
their tribes was set a heavenly daemon to be its shepherd. Each of
them was all in all to his flock—providing for the needs of all his e
charges. So it befell that savagery was nowhere to be found nor prey-
ing of creature on creature, nor did war rage nor any strife whatsoever. There were numberless consequences of this divine ordering of
the world, but we must leave them all aside save those concerning
man, for we must go on to explain the origin of our traditions concerning man's life in that paradise. A god was their shepherd and had
charge of them and fed them even as men now have charge of the
other creatures inferior to them—for men are closer to the divine
than they. When God was shepherd there were no political constitutions and no taking of wives and begetting of children. For all men 272
rose up anew into life out of the earth, having no memory of the former things. Instead they had fruits without stint from trees and
bushes; these needed no cultivation but sprang up of themselves out
of the ground without man's toil. For the most part they disported
themselves in the open needing neither clothing nor couch, for the
seasons were blended evenly so as to work them no hurt, and the grass
which sprang up out of the earth in abundance made a soft bed for
them. This is the story, Socrates, of the life of men under the govern- b
ment of Cronus. Our present life—said to be under the government
of Zeus—you are alive to experience for yourself. But which of these
two makes for greater happiness do you think? Can you give a verdict? And will you do so?

YOUNG SOCRATES: No, I cannot decide.

STRANGER: Do you want me to make a tentative decision for
you?

YOUNG SOCRATES: Yes, please do.

STRANGER: The crucial question is—did the nurslings of Cronus make a right use of their time? They had abundance of leisure
and were at an advantage in being able to converse with the animals
as well as with one another. Did they use all these advantages to promote philosophical inquiry? As they associated with one another and c
with the animals, did they seek to learn from each several tribe of

creatures whether its special faculties enabled it to apprehend some distinctive truth not available to the rest which it could bring as its contribution to swell the common treasure store of wisdom? If they really did all this, it is easy to decide that the happiness of the men of that era was a thousandfold greater than ours. But if, when they had taken their fill of eating and of drinking, the discussions they had with each other and with the animals were of the kind that the surviving stories make them out to have been, then, according to my

d judgment at any rate, it is equally clear what our verdict must be. But be that as it may, let us leave this question aside till we find someone who can inform us accurately whether or not their hearts were set on gaining knowledge and on the true commerce of minds. But this much must be stated here, so that we may be free to proceed to the rest of the story, for it was precisely to see the age of Cronus in its true setting that we brought the whole story to life again.

For when this whole order of things had come to its destined end, there must needs be universal change once more. For the earthborn seed had by now become quite exhausted—each soul had run through

e its appointed number of births and had returned as seed to the earth as many times as had been ordained for it. And now the pilot of the ship of the universe—for so we may speak of it—let go the handle of its rudder and retired to his conning tower in a place apart. Then destiny and its own inborn urge took control of the world again and reversed the revolution of it. Then the gods of the provinces, who had ruled under the greatest god, knew at once what was happening and

273 relinquished the oversight of their regions. A shudder passed through the world at the reversing of its rotation, checked as it was between the old control and the new impulse which had turned end into beginning for it and beginning into end. This shock set up a great quaking which caused—in this crisis of the world just as in the former one —destruction of living creatures of all kinds. Then, after the interval needed for its recovery, it gained relief at last from its clamors and confusion, and attaining quiet after great upheaval it returned to its ordered course and continued in it, having control and government of

b itself and of all within it and remembering, so far as it was able, the instruction it had received from God, its maker and its father. At first it remembered his instructions more clearly, but as time went on its recollection grew dim. The bodily element in its constitution was responsible for its failure. This bodily factor belonged to it in its most primeval condition, for before it came into its present order as a universe it was an utter chaos of disorder. It is from God's act when he set it in its order that it has received all the virtues it possesses, while

c it is from its primal chaotic condition that all the wrongs and evils arise in it—evils which it engenders in turn in the living creatures within it. When it is guided by the divine pilot, it produces much good and but little evil in the creatures it raises and sustains. When it must travel on without God, things go well enough in the years immediately after he abandons control, but as time goes on and forgetfulness of God arises in it, the ancient condition of chaos also begins to assert its sway. At last, as this cosmic era draws to its close, this disorder comes to a head. The few good things it produces it corrupts d with so gross a taint of evil that it hovers on the very brink of destruction, both of itself and of the creatures in it.

The God looks upon it again, he who first set it in order. Beholding it in its troubles, and anxious for it lest it sink racked by storms and confusion, and be dissolved again in the bottomless abyss of unlikeness, he takes control of the helm once more. Its former sickness he heals; what was disrupted in its former revolution under its e own impulse he brings back into the way of regularity, and, so ordering and correcting it, he achieves for it its agelessness and deathlessness.

This is the full tale told, but to meet our need—the delineation of the king—it is enough if we take up the earlier part of our tale. When the most recent cosmic crisis occurred and the cosmic order now existing was established, the course of man's life stood still once more and then began to manifest changes in the opposite sense to the changes accompanying the other cosmic crisis. Creatures which were well nigh disappearance because of their smallness began to grow again; those who were just born from the earth, stalwart in their prime of life, now grew snowy-haired and then died and returned to 274 the earth again. Following the change in the universe, all other things had to change, and, in particular, a new law governing conception, birth, and nurture was made binding on the whole universe—and therefore on all the creatures, for they must needs imitate its ways. For it was no longer possible for creatures to be brought to birth in the earth by the formative action of external agents. It has now been ordained that the universe must take sole responsibility and control of its course. And so by a like ruling, the same impulse bade its constituent elements achieve by their own power, so far as they might, conception, procreation, and rearing of young. We have now come to the point which the whole of this story of ours has been seeking to reach. b It would take long to tell of all the changes that befell the various creatures and show whence these arose and how they were effected, but man's story is shorter and more relevant for us now. Bereft of the guardian care of the daemon who had governed and reared us up, we had become weak and helpless, and we began to be ravaged by wild beasts—for the many evil-natured beasts had by now turned savage. Men lacked all tools and all crafts in the early years. The earth no c longer supplied their food spontaneously and they did not yet know how to win it for themselves; in the absence of necessity they had never been made to learn this. For all these reasons they were in direst straits. It was to meet this need that the gifts of the gods famous in ancient story were given, along with such teaching and instruction as was indispensable. Fire was the gift of Prometheus, the secrets of the d crafts were made known by Hephaestus and his partner in craftsmanship, and seeds and plants were made known by other gods. From these gifts everything has come which has furnished human life since the divine guardianship of men ceased—in the way our story has just described—and men had to manage their lives and fend for themselves in the same way as the whole universe was forced to do. Thus likened to the universe and following its destiny through all time, our life and our begetting are now on this wise now on that.

e Here let our work of storytelling come to its end, but now we must use the story to discern the extent of the mistake we made in our earlier argument in our delineation of the king or statesman.

YOUNG SOCRATES : How did we go wrong then? Do you think that we are seriously off the track?

STRANGER : One mistake was not so serious, but the other was a mistake on the grand scale. It is graver and more far-reaching than I thought it was.

YOUNG SOCRATES : In what way?

275 STRANGER : We were asked to define the king and statesman of this present era, and of humanity as we know it, but in fact we took from the contrary cosmic era the shepherd of the human flock as it then was, and described him as the statesman. He is a god, not a mortal. We went as far astray as that. Furthermore, we showed him as ruler of all the life of the state but did not specify the manner of his rule. Here too, what was said was true, but it cannot be regarded as the whole truth or as a clear and sufficient description. We have gone wrong in this also, though not as badly wrong as on the other issue.

YOUNG SOCRATES : True.

STRANGER : Obviously then we must try to define the way in which the statesman controls the state. We can be reasonably confident that in doing this we shall achieve the complete definition of the statesman.

YOUNG SOCRATES : Very good.

b STRANGER : But our aim when we actually introduced the story was to show two things at once concerning the 'nurture of the herd.' We were anxious to show the host of rivals with whose claims to be 'nurturers of the herd' the statesman whom we now seek has to compete, but we were still more anxious to follow out our analogy and to see the statesman himself in a clearer light as being alone entitled to be called 'shepherd of the people,' feeding humankind in the way shepherds feed their sheep and cowherds their cattle.

YOUNG SOCRATES : True.

STRANGER : It appears to me now, Socrates, that the divine c shepherd is so exalted a figure that no king can be said to attain to his eminence. Those who rule these states of ours in this present era are like their subjects, far closer to them in training and in nurture than ever shepherd could be to flock.

YOUNG SOCRATES: Yes, that is certainly so.

STRANGER: But whether they are human or superhuman creatures, we are still as committed as we were—neither more so nor less —to the task of seeking to reveal their true nature.

YOUNG SOCRATES: Of course.

STRANGER: We must go back again for reconsideration of one of our divisions. We said that there is a 'predirective' art concerned with living creatures, and with these in herds rather than as individuals. Without further division, we described this as 'the science of the *rearing* of herds.' You recall this, do you not? d

YOUNG SOCRATES: Yes, I do.

STRANGER: It was at a point in our tracking down of this art that we began to lose the scent. We did not catch the statesman at all in this definition or name him properly. He eluded us without our knowing it while we were intent on the process of naming.

YOUNG SOCRATES: How did he do it?

STRANGER: There is no other herdsman who is not charged with the bodily nurture of his herd. This characteristic is absent in the statesman and yet we called him a herdsman. We should have used a wider name, covering all guardians, whether nurturers or not. e

YOUNG SOCRATES: You are right if there is in fact such a name.

STRANGER: Surely 'concern' is available as such a class name; it implies no specific limitation to bodily nurture or to any other specific activity. If we had named the art 'concern for herds,' 'attention to herds,' or 'charge of herds'—all of them terms which cover all species—we could have included the statesman with the rest, for the run of the argument was indicating to us that we ought to do this.

YOUNG SOCRATES: True, but how would the subsequent division have proceeded? 276

STRANGER: On the same lines as before. We divided 'nurture of herds' into nurture of land animals, wingless, noninterbreeding, and hornless. We could have divided 'care of herds' in the same way and our definition would then have included both the shepherd king of the reign of Cronus and the ruler of our present era.

YOUNG SOCRATES: That seems clear, but I still want to know what follows.

STRANGER: It is clear that if we had used this correct term 'concern for herds' we should not have had to face the unreasonable objection that some make, that ruling is in *no* sense an art of tendance, b as well as the other reasonable objection we met that there is no specific art of nurture of *human beings* and that if there were, there would be many more directly involved in its exercise than any ruler is.

YOUNG SOCRATES: True.

STRANGER: But if it is a question of an art of 'responsible charge' of a whole community, what art has a better or prior claim than statesmanship to fulfill this function? What other art can claim c to be the art of bearing sovereign rule, the art which bears sovereign rule over all men?

YOUNG SOCRATES: None can.

STRANGER: Yes, Socrates, but do we realize that we fell into another considerable error at the very end of our definition?

YOUNG SOCRATES: What was that?

STRANGER: However clearly we had determined in our minds that there exists an art of nurture of two-footed herds, we were not entitled without further examination to name this art kingship or statesmanship, thereby implying that a full definition of it had been obtained.

YOUNG SOCRATES: What should we have done then?

STRANGER: First of all, as we have just been saying, the class d name has to be modified from 'nurture' to 'concern.' Secondly, this 'concern' must be subdivided, for several further divisions are possible.

YOUNG SOCRATES: Which are they?

STRANGER: By one division we should have set apart the divine shepherd and the human tender of men.

YOUNG SOCRATES: True.

STRANGER: By another division we should have divided into two the art assigned to this human tender of men.

YOUNG SOCRATES: By what division?

STRANGER: By distinguishing enforced tendance from tendance voluntarily accepted.

YOUNG SOCRATES: Surely.

e   STRANGER: I think we really went wrong at this point in our earlier definitions; we made a confusion—a needlessly stupid one—of the king and the tyrant, and these are entirely different people, differing in the manner of their rule.

YOUNG SOCRATES: Yes, they are.

STRANGER: Then let us be right this time, and, as I said, let us divide the art of concern for men into two—enforced tendance and tendance accepted voluntarily.

YOUNG SOCRATES: Certainly.

STRANGER: Tendance of human herds by violent control is the tyrant's art; tendance freely accepted by herds of free bipeds we call statesmanship. Shall we now declare that he who possesses this latter art and practices this tendance is the true king and the true statesman?

277   YOUNG SOCRATES: Yes, and I should think, sir, that at this point we have really completed our definition of the statesman.

STRANGER: That would be excellent, Socrates, but it is not

enough for you to think so; I must think so too. Now as a matter of fact I think that the likeness of the statesman has not been perfectly drawn yet. Sculptors sometimes rush at their work in ill-timed enthusiasm and then elaborate the details of the work to such an extent that they have to bring in extra material to complete it and this in the end slows down their progress. Something like this happened earlier in our discussion, when we wanted to make it immediately clear b where we were mistaken and to give a really impressive demonstration of the point. Supposing that where a king was concerned only large-scale illustrations could be suitable, we reared our massive myth and then had to use more myth material than the occasion warranted; thus our demonstration became too long and we did not give the myth a complete form after all. Our definition, too, seems to me like a portrait which is as yet an outline sketch and does not represent the original clearly because it has still to be painted in colors properly c balanced with one another. Remember, however, that a definition couched in words is a better description of a living creature than a drawing or any model of it can be—a better description, I mean, for those capable of following such a definition; for those who cannot do so the model or visible illustration is appropriate enough.

YOUNG SOCRATES: Yes, that is true, but pray make clear where you still find our description of the statesman inadequate.

STRANGER: It is difficult, my dear Socrates, to demonstrate d anything of real importance without the use of examples. Every one of us is like a man who sees things in a dream and thinks that he knows them perfectly and then wakes up, as it were, to find that he knows nothing.

YOUNG SOCRATES: What do you mean by this?

STRANGER: I have made a real fool of myself by choosing this moment to discuss our strange human plight where the winning of knowledge is concerned.

YOUNG SOCRATES: What do you mean?

STRANGER: Example, my good friend, has been found to require an example.

YOUNG SOCRATES: What is this? Say on and do not hesitate e for my sake.

STRANGER: I will—in fact, I must, since you are so ready to follow. When young children have only just learned their letters . . .

YOUNG SOCRATES: What is this?

STRANGER: We know that they distinguish particular letters only in the shortest and simplest syllables; in these, however, they do 278 distinguish them and can tell you correctly what each of them is.

YOUNG SOCRATES: Yes.

STRANGER: But if they see the same letters combined into other syllables, they fall into doubt once more, and judge them incorrectly by making wrong identifications.

YOUNG SOCRATES : True.

STRANGER : What then is the easiest and best method of leading them to the knowledge they have not yet reached? I think I know it.

YOUNG SOCRATES : What is it?

STRANGER : Take them to the syllables in which they have
b identified the letters correctly; then set them in front of the syllables they cannot decipher; then place known syllables and unknown syllables side by side and point out to them the similar nature of the letters occurring in both. In the end, by this method when the rightly identified letters have been shown to them and set alongside all the unknown letters—and by being shown thus the known letters have been used as *examples*—the teacher will achieve his aim, which is to have each letter rightly recognized and named in every syllable, for
c then the pupil will have identified each letter with itself and distinguished it from all the others.

YOUNG SOCRATES : Certainly.

STRANGER : Have we not gathered enough information now to show how the method of example proceeds? It operates, does it not, when a factor identical with a factor in a less-known object is rightly believed to exist in some other better-known object in quite another sphere of life? This common factor in each object, when it has been made the basis of a parallel examination of them both, makes it possible for us to achieve a single true judgment about each of them as forming one of a pair.

YOUNG SOCRATES : That appears to be how it works.

STRANGER : Would we be surprised, then, to find our own mind
d reacting in the same way to the letters with which the universe is spelled out? Truth sometimes guides the mind to a comprehension of every member of some groups of things and yet the same mind a moment later is hopelessly adrift in its attempt to cope with the members that make up another group. Somehow or other it makes a right judgment of a particular combination of elements but when it sees the same elements transferred to the long and very difficult syllables of everyday existence, it fails to recognize again the very elements it discerned a moment before.

YOUNG SOCRATES : One cannot wonder at it.

STRANGER : It is impossible, is it not, to achieve real under-
e standing in an approach to any part of the total area of true reality, however small, if one begins from a false opinion?

YOUNG SOCRATES : I should say that it is quite impossible.

STRANGER : Well then, if this is the true state of the case, you and I could claim to be sound in our former method and in what we plan to do now. We have tried to discover the nature of example in general by studying a small and particular example of example. What we intend now is to discover scientifically by means of the method of example the nature of 'tendance' as applied to the whole community, and we intend to do it by taking from lesser realms the quality identical with the kingly quality and to use its lesser manifestation there in order to discern its supreme manifestation in him.

YOUNG SOCRATES: We will hope so.

STRANGER: So we must take up once again an earlier stage of 279 our discussion. For seeing that there prove to be any number of competitors to dispute with the kingly class the duties of the tendance of states, we must surely set aside all competitors and leave only the king in possession. It was to help us to this end that we decided that we needed to employ an example.

YOUNG SOCRATES: True.

STRANGER: Well then, what example is there on a really small scale which we can take and set beside kingship, and which, because it comprises an activity common to it and to kingship can be of real help to us in finding what we are looking for? By heaven, Socrates, I believe I know one. Do you agree that, if there is no other example ready to hand, it would be quite in order for us to se- b lect the art of weaving for the purpose. Would you be prepared for us to choose out weaving—if there is nothing else obviously suitable? Moreover, if you agree, we will not take the whole of weaving, for I think that a part of it, the art of weaving woolens, will prove adequate for us. I suspect that just this section of the weaver's art, if it were chosen as our example, would give the evidence we require concerning the statesman.

YOUNG SOCRATES: It might well prove to be so.

STRANGER: No dallying, then! Why should we not divide weaving now just as we divided the other classes of things, dividing it into its true parts? We must run through each stage as briefly and c quickly as we can so as to come back to what is relevant to our present discussion.

YOUNG SOCRATES: What do you mean?

STRANGER: I can best explain by making the actual division for you.

YOUNG SOCRATES: Excellent!

STRANGER: All we make and all we get has one of two aims— the aim of doing something, or the aim of preventing something being done. Preventives may be divided into (a) charms, divine or human, against evils and (b) protections—protections into (a) warlike armaments or defenseworks and (b) other means of fending off— nonmilitary means of fending off into (a) screens and (b) protections from storm and heat—protections from storm and heat into d (a) housing and (b) shields for the person—shields for the person into (a) blankets spread below and (b) garments spread around. Garments that we put around us are of one piece or compounded of several. Those compounded of several are either stitched or combined by

a method other than stitching; of the unstitched some are made of
e vegetable fibers, others are made of hair; of those made of hair, some
are felted by water and earth, others are combined by their inherent
substance. To these manufactured means of warding off which are
coverings of the person and compacted in their own substance we
give the name 'clothes.' The art specifically concerned with producing
clothes we will describe from the name of its product as the 'clothes-
280 working' art, just as we called the art of controlling a state statesmanship. We may also say that the art of weaving—or at any rate that
very large section of it concerned with the production of clothes—is
distinct in nothing but name from this 'art of clothesworking,' just as
in the other case we regarded the arts of kingship and statesmanship
as synonymous.

YOUNG SOCRATES : Quite right.

STRANGER : Let us observe now that it might be supposed at
b this point that the definition of the art of weaving clothes, as drawn
up in these terms, had been complete and sufficient. But if one supposed this, one would have failed to see that the art has not yet been
distinguished from arts exercising a closely similar function to it,
and that in spite of this many other arts which are akin to it have been
severed from it.

YOUNG SOCRATES : What are these kindred arts of which you
are thinking?

STRANGER : Evidently you are not following what has been
said. We must go back then, and begin from the other end, for if you
really can apprehend affinities between arts you will find that some
kindred arts are detached from weaving in our recent division. For
instance, in the division of what is put under from what is put around
we divided off the art of blanketmaking from the art of clothes-
making.

YOUNG SOCRATES : Yes, I see.

c STRANGER : Furthermore, we disjoined from weaving all
fabrication of flax, of Spanish broom, and of all the natural products
we termed vegetable fibers. We also disjoined from it felting and the
art of fashioning by piercing and sewing—the art of which the shoemaker is the chief practitioner.

YOUNG SOCRATES : We did.

STRANGER : Then in excluding the art of making garments of
one piece we excluded the art of the skinner. Among arts of protective
housing we excluded the art of stemming inroads of water along
d with housebuilding, erection in wood, and similar arts. We also excluded all the arts of fencing off, but these include the arts of providing means of preventing theft and other violence, arts connected
with making lids and door fastenings normally assigned as sections
of the arts of joinery. We also cut off the whole art of armormaking,
which is an extensive and extremely various section of the art of

producing defenses. Finally we separated off, right at the beginning of
our definition, the magician's art and that of making spells to ward off e
evil. The remainder when all these had been excluded was, we might
fairly suppose, the art we had been seeking—the art concerned with
producing works of woolen protection designed to ward off violences
of climate, called by the name 'weaving.'

    YOUNG SOCRATES: Yes, that seems to be accurate.

    STRANGER: But we have not yet achieved a complete descrip-
tion of the matter under discussion. For it is evident that the man
responsible for the first stage in the production of clothes does just 281
the opposite of weaving.

    YOUNG SOCRATES: How do you mean?

    STRANGER: The process of weaving is, I take it, a form of plait-
ing together?

    YOUNG SOCRATES: Yes.

    STRANGER: But the art I spoke of is an art of dissociating
strands from a mass of material in which they are found close and
matted.

    YOUNG SOCRATES: What is that?

    STRANGER: The work done by the art of carding. Dare we call
carding weaving, or speak of the carder as a weaver?

    YOUNG SOCRATES: Certainly not.

    STRANGER: Now consider the art which produces warp and
woof. If one calls that art 'weaving' it sounds odd, but it is more than b
that—it is false in fact.

    YOUNG SOCRATES: Of course.

    STRANGER: Furthermore, consider the art of the fuller in all its
forms, and that of darning. Are we going to deny that these are, in a
sense, arts of tendance or care of clothes? But if we admit that they
are such, does it follow that we shall call them all arts of weaving?

    YOUNG SOCRATES: By no means.

    STRANGER: And yet, the claim to preside over the care and the
production of clothes is a claim which all of these arts dispute with
the weavers' mystery. They are ready to concede to weaving a very
considerable part of the whole province of clothesworking, but at the
same time they demand the assignment of no small part of it to themselves.

    YOUNG SOCRATES: That is very true.   c

    STRANGER: Then in addition to these arts we have to consider
the arts which produce the instruments by which the weaving process
is carried out. We must suppose that all have their claim to be at least
contributory to the making of every piece of fabric actually woven.

    YOUNG SOCRATES: That is so.

    STRANGER: Do we still suppose that weaving—or rather our
selected portion of it—will have been adequately defined if we declare it to be 'the highest and most dignified of all the arts concerned

d with woolen clothing'? Would not this definition, though true as far as it goes, lack clearness and finality until we have dissociated all these other arts from weaving?

YOUNG SOCRATES : It would.

STRANGER : Then our next duty is to make this separation, so that our definition may proceed by the right stages.

YOUNG SOCRATES : Yes.

STRANGER : To begin with, let us observe that two groups of arts are involved in active operations of all kinds.

YOUNG SOCRATES : What are they?

STRANGER : One class contributory to the production, the other actually producing.

YOUNG SOCRATES : In what way?

e STRANGER : I mean by 'contributory' arts those which do not fashion the product itself but prepare the tools for the arts which actually produce it—they are arts without whose previous assistance the specific task of the productive arts could never be performed. The arts which fashion the product itself are the 'productive' arts, strictly speaking.

YOUNG SOCRATES : That is at any rate a reasonable distinction.

STRANGER : Then may we take the further step of distinguishing arts which manufacture spindles, shuttles, and all the other instruments of clothes manufacture as 'contributory arts' from the directly 'productive' arts which actually treat and produce the clothes?

YOUNG SOCRATES : We certainly may.

282 STRANGER : Among these 'productive' arts those of washing, darning, and general servicing of clothes—the relevant section of the very extensive art of adornment—may fairly be grouped together and we may call the whole group 'the art of the fuller.'

YOUNG SOCRATES : We may.

STRANGER : Carding and spinning and all the other special processes involved in the manufacture of woolen garments together form part of the art of wool manufacture. This time we have an art with a name familiar to everyone.

YOUNG SOCRATES : Of course.

b STRANGER : Woolworking has two principal sections; each of them is comprised of arts which are parts of a pair of arts.

YOUNG SOCRATES : What do you mean?

STRANGER : Carding, half the operation of the shuttle and all the processes which pull strands of close material apart—let us class these together as one art and this art is manifestly part of woolworking. But we must remember too the pair of arts we found to be of universal scope, the art of combining and that of separating.

YOUNG SOCRATES : Yes.

STRANGER: Well, carding and the other arts just mentioned come under separation. Thus it is *separation* of the raw wool and c *separation* of the strands of warp—the former being done by hand, the latter by the shuttle—which have been given their respective names which we used a moment ago.

YOUNG SOCRATES: Very true.

STRANGER: Now let us consider in turn the art of combination and look for the part of it which coincides with part of the art of woolworking. We must now omit all sections of woolworking which come under separation. Then we shall have divided woolworking by distinguishing the part which combines and the part which separates.

YOUNG SOCRATES: Let us assume this division.

STRANGER: Then, Socrates, you will find that we have to subdivide the part of woolworking which combines, if we are to run our d quarry to earth by finding the art of weaving which we made our objective.

YOUNG SOCRATES: Then we must divide again.

STRANGER: We must. To name the divisions let us call one section of the art 'twisting' and the other 'plaiting.'

YOUNG SOCRATES: Do I understand you? I take you to mean by 'twisting' the art concerned with producing the threads of warp.

STRANGER: Yes, but not of the warp only—of the woof too. You surely do not imagine that we shall find it produced by some process other than twisting?

YOUNG SOCRATES: No.

STRANGER: Now divide each of these two arts, for you may e well find this division significant.

YOUNG SOCRATES: At what point must I divide?

STRANGER: I will tell you. The finished product of the carding processes, when it has achieved certain recognized dimensions, we describe as a 'flock' of wool.

YOUNG SOCRATES: Yes.

STRANGER: The thread twisted out of this by the spindle to form a firm yarn you will, no doubt, describe as 'warp' and the art directing its production as warp spinning.

YOUNG SOCRATES: Yes.

STRANGER: But there are other threads from the flock which are only loosely twisted so as to be soft enough for intertwining with the warp but strong enough to stand up to the dressing process after 283 being intertwined with it. These threads we call 'woof' and the art superintending their manufacture woof spinning.

YOUNG SOCRATES: Quite so.

STRANGER: Well then, the section of the art of weaving which b we selected is now clearly defined for all to see. When the section of the art of combination which is also a section of the art of woolworking produces a fabric by the due intertwining of warp and woof, we call the finished fabric a woolen garment and the art superintending its production the art of weaving.

YOUNG SOCRATES: That is perfectly correct.

STRANGER: Good. But why did we not distinguish weaving straightaway as the art of intertwining warp and woof? Why did we set about it in this roundabout fashion defining so pointlessly a host of arts we met on the way?

YOUNG SOCRATES: Oh no, sir! So far as I can see, there was nothing pointless in the whole course of our argument.

STRANGER: I am not surprised that you think so now, but someday you may think differently. I want to administer a prophylactic against this malady of doubt, should it one day come upon you as indeed from time to time it well may. There would be nothing surprising in its doing so! Listen, then, to a prophylactic argument
c applicable to all troublesome questions of this kind.

YOUNG SOCRATES: Pray explain it, sir.

STRANGER: First let us examine excess and deficiency in general. In this way we shall obtain a standard of length applicable to what is said on any occasion in this kind of discussion—a standard by which we can accord praise to what is said or censure it, either as excessive or as deficient.

YOUNG SOCRATES: Let us make the examination then.

STRANGER: We can only discuss the matter effectively by considering these qualities in their real nature.

YOUNG SOCRATES: Which qualities?

d   STRANGER: Length and brevity, and excess and defect in general. We are agreed, I presume, that the art of measurement is involved in all these.

YOUNG SOCRATES: Yes.

STRANGER: Let us divide it into two then. We must do so to get to the conclusion we are eager to reach.

YOUNG SOCRATES: Please tell us where the division comes.

STRANGER: I will. We divide the art of measurement into a section concerned with the relative greatness or smallness of objects and another section concerned with their size in relation to the fixed norm to which they must approximate if they are to exist at all.

YOUNG SOCRATES: What do you mean?

STRANGER: Do you not agree that in the nature of things 'the greater' can be so called only in relation to the less and to nothing else,
e and, conversely, that 'the less' can only be 'less' than a greater? It cannot be 'less' than anything else.

YOUNG SOCRATES: It cannot. I quite agree.

STRANGER: On the other hand, will we not also be ready to assert that we do in fact hear words spoken and see acts done which at one time exceed the essentially right measure and at another time fall short of it? Is it not just this matter of attaining the due measure which marks off good men from bad in human society?

YOUNG SOCRATES: It is evident.

STRANGER: Then we must posit two types and two standards of greatness and smallness. We must not assert as we did just now that the only standard possible is that of relative comparison. We have just seen how we must amend the statement. The standard of relative comparison will remain, but we must acknowledge a second standard, which is a standard of comparison with the due measure. Do we want to know why this must be admitted?

YOUNG SOCRATES: Why is it needed?

STRANGER: If a man refuses to admit the possibility of a 284 'greater' except in relation to a 'lesser' he will rule out all possibility of relating it to a due measure, will he not?

YOUNG SOCRATES: He will.

STRANGER: Are we really prepared for the consequences of this refusal? Are we going to abolish the arts and all their products? In particular, shall we deprive statecraft, which we are trying to define, and weaving, which we have just defined, of their very existence? For it seems clear to me that all such arts guard against exceeding the due measure or falling short of it. Certainly they do not treat such excess or defect as meaningless—on the contrary, they shun it as a very real peril. In fact it is precisely by this effort they make to maintain the due measure that they achieve effectiveness b and beauty in all that they produce.

YOUNG SOCRATES: That is very true.

STRANGER: But you must admit that if we dismiss statecraft as unreal, we shall have blocked all means of approach to any subsequent study of the science of kingly rule.

YOUNG SOCRATES: Obviously.

STRANGER: Must we not do now what we had to do when discussing the Sophist? We had to insist then on the admission of an additional postulate, that 'what is "not x" nevertheless exists.' We had to introduce this postulate because the only alternative to asserting it which our argument left us was to allow the Sophist to escape definition altogether. In our present discussion too there is an additional postulate on which we must insist, and it is this. 'Excess and deficiency are measurable not only in relative terms but also in respect of attainment of a norm or due measure.' For if we cannot first gain assent to this postulate, we are bound to fail if we advance the c claim that a man possesses statecraft, or indeed that a man possesses any other of the special forms of knowledge that function in human society.

YOUNG SOCRATES: In that case we must certainly follow the precedent and admit the additional postulate in our present discussion too.

STRANGER : Our present task is greater than the previous one, Socrates, and we can hardly have forgotten what a very long time that took us. However, while discussing these problems, there is one thing to be said at the outset that it is perfectly right and proper to say here.

YOUNG SOCRATES : What is this?

d STRANGER : That when one day we come to give a full exposition of true accuracy in dialectic method, we shall find the need of this postulate concerning the due measure which we have just enunciated. However, the statement in the form that we have made it and with the demonstration—adequate for present purposes—which we have given of it, is a very great help to us, or so it seems to me. For it shows that two propositions stand or fall together. The first is that the arts exist; the second is that excess and deficiency are measurable not only relatively but in terms of the realization of a norm or due measure. Thus if measure in this second sense exists, so do the arts, and, conversely, if there are arts, then there is this second kind of measurement. To deny either is to deny both.

e YOUNG SOCRATES : So much is fully established, but what follows?

STRANGER : Clearly we should divide the art of measurement into two on the principle enunciated by dividing it at this point. One section will comprise all arts of measuring number, length, depth, breadth, or velocity of objects by relative standards. The other section comprises arts concerned with due occasion, due time, due performance, and all such standards as have removed their abode from the extremes and are now settled about the mean.

YOUNG SOCRATES : Each of the subdivisions you have named is very extensive, and the one differs vastly from the other.

STRANGER : Does not the statement we have just made turn out
285 to be precisely what many of our 'erudite' friends say from time to time—and say with the air of men uttering a profound truth? We are saying like them that measurement is involved in all that is brought into being. For all activities directed by arts involve measurement in some form or other. But our friends, for all their erudition, have not been trained to study things by dividing them into real classes. As a result here we find them confusing these two types of measurement, which are in fact so different, just because they have judged them to be of like nature. There are other classes of things about which they commit the opposite error; they distinguish them but fail to distinguish according to the real distinctions. Now the following
b would be the right method. Whenever it is the essential *affinity* between a given group of forms which the philosopher perceives on first inspection, he ought not to forsake his task until he sees clearly as many true differences as exist within the whole complex unity— the differences which exist in reality and constitute the several species. Conversely, when he begins by contemplating all the *unlikenesses* of

one kind or another which are to be found in various groups of forms, the true philosopher must not pull a wry face and give up in disgust, until he has gathered together all the forms which are in fact cognate and has penned them safely in their common fold by comprehending them all in their real general group. But let this suffice on these topics and on excess and deficiency in general. Let us, however, be careful to maintain the ground we have won. We have discovered beyond dispute two distinct forms of the art of measurement concerned with excess and deficiency and we must remember what we have declared   c them to be.

YOUNG SOCRATES: We shall not forget.

STRANGER: So much for that theme. Now let us prepare to entertain another which has to do not only with our present inquiry but with all discussions of this kind as well.

YOUNG SOCRATES: What is it?

STRANGER: Suppose someone asked us this question about our class of elementary schoolchildren learning to read. 'When a child is asked what letters spell a word—it can be any word you please— are we to regard this exercise as undertaken to discover the correct   d spelling of the particular word the teacher set or as designed rather to make the child better able to deal with all words he may be asked to spell?'

YOUNG SOCRATES: Surely we reply that the purpose is to teach him to read them all.

STRANGER: How then does this principle apply to our present search for the statesman? Why did we set ourselves the problem? Is our chief purpose to find the statesman, or have we the larger aim of becoming better philosophers, more able to tackle all questions?

YOUNG SOCRATES: Here, too, the answer is clear; we aim to be able to solve all problems.

STRANGER: Exactly, for I cannot think that any reasonable person would want to trace down the definition of the art of weaving just for its own sake. But there is a paradox here which, it seems to   e me, most thinkers have failed to notice. Likenesses which the senses can grasp are available in nature to those real existents which are in themselves easy to understand, so that when someone asks for an account of these existents one has no trouble at all—one can simply indicate the sensible likeness and dispense with any account in words. But to the highest and most important class of existents there are no   286 corresponding visible resemblances, no work of nature clear for all to look upon. In these cases nothing visible can be pointed out to satisfy the inquiring mind; the instructor cannot cause the inquirer to perceive something with one or other of his senses and so make him really satisfied that he understands the thing under discussion. Therefore we must train ourselves to give and to understand a *rational* account of every existent thing. For the existents which have no visible embodiment, the existents which are of highest value and chief importance, are demonstrable only by reason and are not to be apprehended by any other means. All our present discussions have the aim of training us to apprehend this highest class of existents. For purposes of practice, however, it is easier in every case to work on lesser objects rather than on greater ones.

YOUNG SOCRATES : You are quite right.

STRANGER : Let us then recall what led us to this long digression on these matters.

YOUNG SOCRATES : What was it?

STRANGER : Was it not mainly due to the impatience we felt and expressed at the long-windedness, as we presumed to call it, of our definition of the art of weaving? We felt a like impatience with the long account of reversal of rotation in the universe and with our inquiry into the Sophist when we had to discuss the existence of not-being. We conceived the notion that these discussions had been too lengthy, and we blamed ourselves for this because we feared that they had been irrelevant too. Please realize, therefore, that the principles we have just worked out together apply to all discussions of this kind and not just to this one, and that they are intended to prevent any like apprehensions in future.

YOUNG SOCRATES : It shall be so, sir, but, pray, proceed.

STRANGER : I say then, that it is your duty and mine to observe the principles we have just laid down whenever we have to accord praise or blame to an argument on the score of its length or its brevity. The length of one discourse is not to be compared simply with the length of another. We said just now that we must never forget the second section of the art of measuring, and it is this standard we must always apply in judgments like these—the standard of suitability I mean.

YOUNG SOCRATES : Quite so.

STRANGER : Yes, but even 'suitability' is not in every case an adequate criterion. For instance, we shall not look for such length in an argument as is 'suitable' for giving pleasure, except as a very incidental consideration. Again, ease and speed in reaching the answer to the problem propounded are most commendable, but our principle requires that this be only a secondary, not a primary reason for commending an argument. What we must value first and foremost, above all else, is the philosophical method itself, and this consists in ability to divide according to real forms. If, therefore, either a full-length statement of an argument or an unusually brief one leaves the hearer more able to find real forms, it is this presentation of it which must be diligently carried through; there must be no expression of annoyance at its length or at its brevity as the case may be. Furthermore, if we find a man who criticizes the length of an argu-

ment while a discussion like the present one is in progress and refuses
to wait for the proper rounding-off of the process of reasoning, he is
not to be permitted to escape thus with a mere grumble that 'these 287
discussions are long drawn out'; he must be required to support his
grumble with a proof that a briefer statement of the case would have
left him and his fellow disputants better philosophers, more able to
demonstrate real truth by reasoned argument. Blame and praise on
other grounds, aimed at other merely incidental traits in our discourse, we must simply ignore and act as though we had not heard
them at all. Now we may leave this topic, if I carry you with me in
this judgment. Let us go back to the statesman, our real subject, and b
set beside him for comparison the art of weaving as we have just defined it.

YOUNG SOCRATES: Excellent. Let us do as you say.

STRANGER: Well then, the kingly art has been set apart from
most of those occupying the same region—from all, that is to say,
which have to do with control of herds. But in the actual community
of citizens there are other arts not yet distinguished from statesmanship. They comprise both contributory and directive productive arts,
and these must first be distinguished.

YOUNG SOCRATES: Very well.

STRANGER: Do you realize that in this case they resist division
into two? I think that the reason will become evident to us as we go c
on to enumerate them.

YOUNG SOCRATES: Let us do so then.

STRANGER: Seeing that we cannot bisect them, let us divide
them according to their natural divisions as we would carve a sacrificial victim. For we must in every case divide into the minimum number of divisions that the structure permits.

YOUNG SOCRATES: How shall we do it then, in the present
instance?

STRANGER: As we did before. All the arts which provide tools
for weaving we distinguished then as 'contributory.'

YOUNG SOCRATES: We did.

STRANGER: We must do the same now as then, but with even
greater care. Every art which fashions any object, large or small, d
which ministers to the needs of an organized human community
must be classed as 'contributory.' For without the things provided by
these arts there could be no community and so no art of rule, and yet
we can hardly regard it as the duty of the kingly art to produce any of
these things.

YOUNG SOCRATES: No.

STRANGER: We are attempting a difficult thing when we try to
distinguish this instrumental class of arts from the others. For
anything whatever can be shown with some plausibility to be an

e instrumental means to something or other. However, there is a class of things a community must acquire to which we must proceed to give a different name.

YOUNG SOCRATES: In what way different?

STRANGER: In that its function differs from that of instruments. It is not made, as an instrument is, with a view to the production of something but in order to preserve a thing once it has been produced.

YOUNG SOCRATES: What kind of thing do you mean?

STRANGER: A class of objects wrought in the greatest variety of shapes and used for holding liquids or solids, some made for standing on the fire, some not able to do so. As a general name we term such an object a 'container.' It is a ubiquitous class of objects, and again, I think, the arts manufacturing it have nothing whatever to do with

288 the art of the ruler which we are now seeking.

YOUNG SOCRATES: Nothing at all.

STRANGER: We must now recognize a third class of things to be acquired, also a very large one. Some things belonging to it are on land, others on water; some move from place to place, others do not; some are of high honor, others are not so distinguished. All share one name and form a class because each is made to support something or serve as a base for something.

YOUNG SOCRATES: What common name have they?

STRANGER: 'Carriage,' I should say—and the production of such things is the work of the carpenter, the potter, or the chariot builder, not of the statesman.

YOUNG SOCRATES: I understand.

b STRANGER: What is our fourth class? Must we not distinguish from all these three a further class to which most of the things mentioned in our definition of weaving belong—the whole class of clothing, most armor, all walls, all earth or stonework defenses erected around a city, and many other such things. All exist for defensive protection and so the whole class can best be called 'defenses.' To provide these is in most cases the work of the builder or weaver, and never that of the statesman.

YOUNG SOCRATES: Of course.

c STRANGER: Might we agree to name a fifth class including all arts concerned in decoration and portraiture and every art which produces artistic representations whether in these visual arts or for the ear in poetry and music? The works all these arts produce are wrought simply to give pleasure, and all may properly be included under one description.

YOUNG SOCRATES: What is that?

STRANGER: We use the expression 'diversion,' do we not?

YOUNG SOCRATES: Yes, what of it?

STRANGER: Then this is the name we can apply to the products of this whole group of arts. None of them has a serious purpose; all are performed for pure amusement.

YOUNG SOCRATES: I think I understand this too.   d

STRANGER: Consider now those arts which provide the stuffs which are wrought by the arts we have been talking about. This is a most various class of arts. Often such an art is itself working on the products of several yet more primitive arts. Shall we not name this the sixth kind?

YOUNG SOCRATES: Of what are you thinking?

STRANGER: Gold and silver and all mined metals, all the pioneer work done by the woodman and the sawmill to provide material for carpentry and wickerwork, the currier's art which removes the skins of animals, the art of stripping bark which has the same e function in the plant realm, and all arts kindred to these, the arts of making cork, papyrus, and rope. All these arts produce the main types of raw material for working up into the more complex kinds of objects which we use. Let us call this class of object by the general description, 'basic material at the stage of its first working when it is not yet wrought into particular objects,' and the production of this is obviously no concern of the kingly science.

YOUNG SOCRATES: True.

STRANGER: We come lastly to the getting of food and of all the substances the parts of which are capable of combining with the parts of the body to promote its health. This we will make a seventh 289 class and call it 'nourishment' unless we can find some better name for it. Provision of it is rightly to be assigned to the arts of farming, hunting, gymnastics, medicine, or butchering rather than to political science.

YOUNG SOCRATES: Of course.

STRANGER: I think that possessions of practically every kind that we find belonging to men have been enumerated in these seven classes, with the single exception of tame living creatures. Listen while I run through the list. First place in it should really have been taken by 'basic material at its first working'; after that come instruments, then vessels, carriages, defenses, diversions, and nourish- b ments. We may neglect any class of merely slight importance which may have escaped us, for it can be made to fit in one or other of these main classes. For example, consider the class consisting of coins, seals, and every other kind of engraved dies. These have not, as a class, one of the great classes with which all coincide. Some have to be subsumed under 'diversions,' some under 'instruments'; it is a forced classification, but they can be made to fit into one or other of these classes somehow or other. As for tame animals other than slaves, all these clearly come under the art of nourishing herds which c we have previously analyzed.

YOUNG SOCRATES: Yes, they do.

STRANGER : The class that remains, then, is that of slaves and personal servants of all kinds. It is just here that I strongly suspect that those will be discovered who really dispute the fashioning of the web of state with the king in the way that we found spinners, carders, and the rest disputing the fashioning of clothes with the weavers. All the others, since they pursue what we have described as 'contributory' arts, have been disposed of along with their occupations which we have enumerated just now, and thus they have all been severed d from any share in the kingly art of ruling the state.

YOUNG SOCRATES : So at any rate it would seem.

STRANGER : Come then, let us examine the rest and approach them more closely to scrutinize them more effectively.

YOUNG SOCRATES : Let us do so.

STRANGER : The most extensive class of servants, as seen from our new vantage point, we find to be engaged in pursuits and sunk in a condition of life quite contrary to those we had suspected we might discover.

YOUNG SOCRATES : To whom do you refer?

STRANGER : To those who are bought and sold and so become e their master's property. No one would think of challenging our description of these as slaves or our contention that they cannot possibly claim any share in the practice of the art of ruling.

YOUNG SOCRATES : That goes without saying.

STRANGER : But what of servants who are personally free? What of those among them who of their own volition place themselves and their services at the disposal of the various craftsmen we have named and effect a systematic distribution of agricultural and manufactured products maintaining an economic balance between them? Some of these do their work at home in the market square, but others are travelers from city to city, either overland or by sea routes. They exchange money for goods or one currency for another. Our 290 names for them are money-changers, merchants, venturers, retailers. They cannot be said to dispute the province of the ruler, can they?

YOUNG SOCRATES : I wonder if they might—in the realm of commerce, that is to say.

STRANGER : Certainly not. You can be sure that such men who can be hired for pay, who work for a daily wage and who are always ready to work for any employer, will never be found daring to claim any share in the art of ruling.

YOUNG SOCRATES : No, of course not.

STRANGER : But there are those who render other kinds of service.

YOUNG SOCRATES : What kinds of service? Whom do you mean?

b   STRANGER : Heralds and clerks, who often develop great facility from long performance of their form of service, and certain other very able minor civil servants who do all manner of administrative work for the elected officials. What shall we call these?

YOUNG SOCRATES: What you just called them—civil servants, but not rulers exercising an independent authority in the state.

STRANGER: I was not cheated by a mere dream, I think, when I said that it was here that the king's serious challengers in the art of rule would reveal themselves. But how strange to have to look for them in a servant class!   c

YOUNG SOCRATES: Very strange.

STRANGER: Now let us tackle those we have not yet put under examination. First come the soothsayers, practicing their particular form of expert ministration. For do we not recognize them as serving as interpreters of the gods to men?

YOUNG SOCRATES: Yes.

STRANGER: Next come the priestly tribe. According to the orthodox view they understand how to offer our gifts to the gods in sacrifices in a manner pleasing to them, and they know, too, the right d forms of prayer for petitioning the gods to bestow blessings on us. Both of these expert activities are parts of the art of ministration, are they not?

YOUNG SOCRATES: Well, it would seem that they are.

STRANGER: In that case I think that we are coming at last upon the tracks of our quarry, so to speak. For the priest and the diviner have great social standing and a keen sense of their own importance. They win veneration and respect because of the high tasks they undertake. This is shown in the fact that in Egypt none can be king unless he belongs to the priestly caste, and if a man of some other caste succeeds in forcing his way to the throne, he must then be e made a priest by special ordination. In many of the Greek cities also one finds that the duty of making the chief sacrifice on the state's behalf is laid upon the chief officers of state. You have a very striking example of it here in Athens, for I am led to understand that the most solemn ancestral sacrifices of this nation are the responsibility of the archon whom the lot designates as King-Archon.

YOUNG SOCRATES: That is so.

STRANGER: Very well, we must study these kings chosen by 291 lot and these priests with their ministerial assistants, very closely. But we must also look at another group—quite a large mob, in fact, which is coming clearly into view now that all these particular groups have been distinguished.

YOUNG SOCRATES: And who are these you speak of?

STRANGER: A very queer crowd.

YOUNG SOCRATES: What do you mean?

STRANGER: A race of many tribes—or so they seem to be at first sight. Some are like lions, some like centaurs, or similar mon- b sters. A great many are satyrs or chameleons, beasts that are masters of quick change in order to conceal their weakness. Indeed they take each other's shapes and characters with bewildering rapidity. Yes, Socrates, and I think I have now identified these gentlemen.

YOUNG SOCRATES: Tell me about them. You seem to look upon a strange sight.

STRANGER: Yes, strange until recognized! I was actually impressed by them myself at first sight. Coming suddenly on this strange

c cry of players acting their part in public life I did not know what to make of them.

YOUNG SOCRATES: What players can these be?

STRANGER: The chief wizards among all the Sophists, the chief pundits of the deceiver's art. Such impersonators are hard to distinguish from the real statesmen and kings; yet we must distinguish them and thrust them aside if we are to see clearly the king we are seeking.

YOUNG SOCRATES: Well, we must not abandon the search.

STRANGER: No, I agree. Tell me this now.

YOUNG SOCRATES: Well?

d STRANGER: Is not monarchy one of the possible forms of government as we know it?

YOUNG SOCRATES: Yes.

STRANGER: Next to monarchy one would naturally mention the constitution in which it is the few who wield power.

YOUNG SOCRATES: Yes.

STRANGER: Then the third type must be the rule of the many —democracy as it is called.

YOUNG SOCRATES: Of course.

STRANGER: These are the three main constitutions, but do not the three in a sense become five by evolving two further types out of themselves?

YOUNG SOCRATES: What are these?

e STRANGER: If we consider the violence or consent, the poverty or riches, the law-abidingness or disregard of law which they exhibit we shall find that two of the three forms of government are really twofold and can therefore be divided. Monarchy then yields us two forms, called tyranny and constitutional monarchy, respectively.

YOUNG SOCRATES: Yes.

STRANGER: Constitutions where the few wield power can always be similarly divided; the subdivisions are aristocracy and oligarchy.

YOUNG SOCRATES: Quite so.

292 STRANGER: In the case of democracy we do not usually alter the name. Democracy is always 'democracy' whether the masses control the wealthy by force or by consent and whether or not it abides strictly by the laws.

YOUNG SOCRATES: That is true.

STRANGER: What then? Do we imagine that any of these constitutions can be declared a 'true' constitution so long as the only criteria for judging it are whether one, few, or many rule, whether it be rich or poor, whether it rule by violence or consent, whether it have or lack a code of laws?

YOUNG SOCRATES: But what prevents our judging it to be a true constitution by such criteria?

STRANGER: Try to follow what I am going to say and you will b be bound to see more clearly.

YOUNG SOCRATES: What line are you going to take?

STRANGER: Shall we abide by our original argument or are we now going against it?

YOUNG SOCRATES: Which argument do you mean?

STRANGER: We decided, did we not, that the art of rule is one of the sciences?

YOUNG SOCRATES: Yes.

STRANGER: Furthermore we agreed that it is a particular kind of science. Out of the whole class of sciences we selected the judging class and more particularly the directive class.

YOUNG SOCRATES: We did.

STRANGER: We divided the directive into direction of lifeless things and direction of living beings, and by this process of subdi- c vision we arrived by regular stages where we are now, never losing sight of the fact that statesmanship is a form of knowledge but unable as yet to say precisely what form of knowledge it is.

YOUNG SOCRATES: You are quite right.

STRANGER: Do we realize, then, that the real criterion in judging constitutions must not be whether few or many rule, whether rule is by violence or consent, or whether the rulers are poor or rich? If we are going to abide by our previous conclusions, the criterion must be the presence or absence of an art directing the ruling.

YOUNG SOCRATES: Yes, for we simply must abide by those d conclusions.

STRANGER: Then we are forced to look at the issue in this light. In which, if any, of these constitutions do we find the art of ruling being practiced in the actual government of men? What art is more difficult to learn? But what art is more important to us? We must see it for what it is so as to be able to decide which are the other public figures we must remove from the true king's company, those personages who claim to be statesmen, who win over the mass of men to believe them to be statesmen, but are in actual fact nothing of the kind.

YOUNG SOCRATES: We must indeed, for this was the task set for our discussion.

STRANGER: Do you think that any considerable number of men e in a particular city will be capable of acquiring the art of statesmanship?

YOUNG SOCRATES: That is quite out of the question.

STRANGER: In a city with a population of a thousand, could a hundred, say, acquire it satisfactorily—or could fifty, perhaps?

YOUNG SOCRATES: Statesmanship would be the easiest of the arts if so many could acquire it. We know quite well that there would never be fifty first-class draughts players among a thousand inhabitants—that is, not if they were judged by proper inter-Hellenic standards. How much less can you expect to find fifty kings! For according to our former argument it is only the man possessed of the art of kingship who must be called a king, though he is just as much a king when he is not in power as when he is.

293   STRANGER: You have very rightly recalled that point. I think it follows that if the art of government is to be found in this world at all in its pure form, it will be found in the possession of one or two, or, at most, of a select few.

YOUNG SOCRATES: Yes.

b   STRANGER: On this principle it is the men who possess the art of ruling and these only, whom we are to regard as rulers, whatever constitutional form their rule may take. It makes no difference whether their subjects be willing or unwilling; they may rule with or without a code of laws; they may be poor or wealthy. It is the same with doctors. We do not assess the medical qualification of a doctor by the degree of willingness on our part to submit to his knife or cautery or other painful treatment. Doctors are still doctors whether they work according to fixed prescriptions or without them and whether they be poor or wealthy. So long as they control our health on a scientific basis, they may purge and reduce us or they may build us up, but they still remain doctors. The one essential condition is that they act for the good of our bodies to make them better instead of worse, and treat men's ailments in every case as healers act-
c   ing to preserve life. We must insist that in this disinterested scientific ability we see the distinguishing mark of true authority in medicine —and of true authority everywhere else as well.

YOUNG SOCRATES: Quite so.

STRANGER: Then the constitution par excellence, the only constitution worthy of the name, must be the one in which the rulers are not men making a show of political cleverness but men really possessed of scientific understanding of the art of government. Then we must not take into consideration on any sound principle of judgment whether their rule be by laws or without them over willing or
d unwilling subjects or whether they themselves be rich men or poor men.

YOUNG SOCRATES: No.

STRANGER: They may purge the city for its better health by putting some of the citizens to death or banishing others. They may lessen the citizen body by sending off colonies like bees swarming off from a hive, or they may bring people in from other cities and naturalize them so as to increase the number of citizens. So long as they work on a reasoned scientific principle following essential justice and act to preserve and improve the life of the state so far as may be, we must call them real statesmen according to our standards of judgment and say that the state they rule alone enjoys good government and has a real constitution. We must go on to say that all the other state e fabrics called constitutions are not genuine, but counterfeit; they imitate the true constitution. Those which we call law-abiding copy it fairly closely, but the rest are more or less shocking caricatures of it.

YOUNG SOCRATES: All the rest, sir, I believe to have been spoken in due measure—but the saying about ruling without laws is a hard saying for us to hear.

STRANGER: You are a little too quick for me, Socrates! I was 294 just going to cross-examine you to see if you really accepted all I have said or felt some objection. I realize, however, from what you say that the point we are anxious to discuss in detail is this question whether a good governor can govern without laws.

YOUNG SOCRATES: Yes, it is.

STRANGER: In one sense it is evident that the art of kingship does include the art of lawmaking. But the political ideal is not full authority for laws but rather full authority for a man who understands the art of kingship and has kingly ability. Do you understand why?

YOUNG SOCRATES: No, please tell me why.

STRANGER: Law can never issue an injunction binding on all which really embodies what is best for each; it cannot prescribe with b perfect accuracy what is good and right for each member of the community at any one time. The differences of human personality, the variety of men's activities, and the inevitable unsettlement attending all human experience make it impossible for any art whatsoever to issue unqualified rules holding good on all questions at all times. I suppose that so far we are agreed.

YOUNG SOCRATES: Most emphatically.

STRANGER: But we find practically always that the law tends to issue just this invariable kind of rule. It is like a self-willed, ig- c norant man who lets no one do anything but what he has ordered and forbids all subsequent questioning of his orders even if the situation has shown some marked improvement on the one for which he originally legislated.

YOUNG SOCRATES: Yes, that is just how the law treats us all.

STRANGER: It is impossible, then, for something invariable and unqualified to deal satisfactorily with what is never uniform and constant.

YOUNG SOCRATES: I am afraid it is impossible.

STRANGER: But why then must there be a system of laws,

d seeing that law is not the ideal form of control? We must find out why a legal system is necessary.

YOUNG SOCRATES: We must.

STRANGER: You have courses of training here in Athens, have you not, just as they have in other cities—courses in which pupils are trained in a group to fit themselves for athletic contests in running or in other sports?

YOUNG SOCRATES: Of course. We have quite a number of them.

STRANGER: Let us call to mind the commands which professional trainers give to the athletes under their regimen in these courses.

YOUNG SOCRATES: In what particular?

STRANGER: The view such trainers take is that they cannot do their work in detail and issue special commands adapted to the condition of each member of the group. When they lay down rules for
e physical welfare they find it necessary to give bulk instructions having regard to the general benefit of the average pupil.

YOUNG SOCRATES: Quite so.

STRANGER: That is why we find them giving the same exercises to whole groups of pupils, starting or stopping all of them at the same time in their running, wrestling, or whatever it may be.

YOUNG SOCRATES: Yes.

295 STRANGER: Similarly we must expect that the legislator who has to give orders to whole communities of human creatures in matters of right and of mutual contractual obligation will never be able in the laws he prescribes for the whole group to give every individual his due with absolute accuracy.

YOUNG SOCRATES: Very probably not.

STRANGER: But we shall find him making the law for the generality of his subjects under average circumstances. Thus he will legislate for all individual citizens, but it will be by what may be called a 'bulk' method rather than an individual treatment, and this method of 'bulk' prescription will be followed by him whether he makes a written code of law or refrains from issuing such a code, preferring to legislate by using unwritten ancestral customs.

YOUNG SOCRATES: Yes, and quite rightly so.

STRANGER: Of course he is right, Socrates. How could any law-
b giver be capable of prescribing every act of a particular individual and sit at his side, so to speak, all through his life and tell him just what to do? And if among the few who have really attained this true statesmanship there arose one who was free to give this detailed guidance to an individual, he would hardly put obstacles in his own way by deliberately framing legal codes of the kind we are criticizing.

YOUNG SOCRATES: That certainly follows, sir, from what has been said.

STRANGER: I would rather say, Socrates, that it follows from what is going to be said.

YOUNG SOCRATES: And what is that?

STRANGER: Let us put this case to ourselves. A doctor or trainer plans to travel abroad and expects to be away from his c charges for quite a long time. The doctor might well think that his patients would forget any verbal instructions he gave and the trainer might think likewise. In these circumstances each might want to leave written reminders of his orders—do you not think so yourself, Socrates?

YOUNG SOCRATES: Exactly so, sir.

STRANGER: Well now, suppose our doctor did not stay abroad as long as he had expected and so came back the sooner to his patients. Would he hesitate to substitute different prescriptions for the original ones if his patients' condition happened to be better than an- d ticipated because of a climatic improvement or some other unusual and unexpected development of that kind? Would the doctor feel it his duty to maintain stubbornly that there must be no transgression of the strict letter of those original prescriptions of his? Would he refuse to issue new prescriptions or conditions, or condemn a patient who was venturing to act contrary to the prescriptions he had written out for him? Would the doctor declare all such action must be wrong because those former prescriptions were the true canons of medicine and of health and therefore that all contravention of them must lead to disease and be contrary to medical science? Surely any such claims, in circumstances where a science is involved and a real art is at work, would only make the man who made the claim and his precious pre- e scriptions supremely ridiculous.

YOUNG SOCRATES: Yes, it would indeed.

STRANGER: Imagine then the case of a scientific legislator. Suppose that by a written code or by support given to unwritten customs he has laid down what is just and honorable and what is not, and what benefits society and what hurts it. Suppose him to do this service for the several communities of the human flock who live in their cities as their appointed pasture shepherded by the codes their legislators have provided. If this man, who drew up his code by the art of statesmanship, wishes to amend it, or if another scientific legislator of this kind appears on the scene, will these be forbidden to enact new laws differing from the earlier ones? Surely such a prohibition would ap- 296 pear as ridiculous in the case of the legislator as it was in the case of the doctor, would it not?

YOUNG SOCRATES: Of course.

STRANGER: But are you familiar with the argument one usually hears advanced when an issue like this is raised?

YOUNG SOCRATES: No, I cannot remember it at the moment, at any rate.

STRANGER: It is quite a plausible argument, I grant that. They contend that if a man discovers better laws than those already enacted he is entitled to get them brought into effect, but only if in every instance he has first persuaded his own city to accept them.

YOUNG SOCRATES: But what of this? Surely this is a sound contention.

b   STRANGER: It may be, but answer this question. Suppose a man fails to persuade his city and forces his better laws upon it, what name are we to apply to force so used? But no, do not answer me that question yet, for there are others to be answered first.

YOUNG SOCRATES: What can they be?

STRANGER: Consider once more the case of the patient under the doctor's treatment. Suppose that the doctor fails to persuade the patient but has a mastery of medical knowledge, and suppose that he forces a particular course of treatment which goes against written prescription but is actually more salutary on a child patient, maybe, or on a man or a woman. What are we to call force of this kind? Whatever we decide to call it, we shall not call it 'the sin against true medicine' or 'a breach of the laws of health.' Surely the very last

c   thing a patient who is so constrained is entitled to say is that the doctor's act in applying the constraint was contrary to good medicine and an aggravation of his disease.

YOUNG SOCRATES: You are quite right.

STRANGER: By what name, then, do we call the sin against the art of statesmanship? Would it not be called dishonor, vice, injustice?

YOUNG SOCRATES: Assuredly.

STRANGER: What, then, shall we say of citizens of a state who have been forced to do things which are contrary to written laws and ancestral customs but are nevertheless juster, more effective, and more noble than the directions of these traditional authorities? How shall we regard censure by these citizens of the force which has applied in these circumstances? Unless they wish to appear ridiculous in the

d   extreme there is one thing they must refrain from saying. They must not assert in any such instance that in being subjected to compulsion they have suffered disgrace, injustice, or evil at the hands of those who compelled them.

YOUNG SOCRATES: That is quite true.

STRANGER: Can it be the case that acts imposed under compulsion are right if the compeller is rich, but wrong if he is poor? Surely what matters is that with or without persuasion, rich or poor, ac-

e   cording to a code or against it, the ruler does what is really beneficial. These are the real issues and all is well if he passes this test, the only genuine test of good government in a community and the only principle by which the understanding and upright ruler will administer

297   the affairs of those whom he rules. The ship's captain fixes his attention on the real welfare at any given time of his ship and his crew. He lays down no written enactments but supplies a law in action by

practical application of his knowledge of seamanship to the needs of the voyage. It is in this way that he preserves the lives of all in his ship. Would not a true constitution be just like this and work in the same way if the rulers really understood what government is and employed their art as a stronger power for good than any written laws? By rulers with this sound attitude of mind no wrong can possibly be done so long as they keep firmly to the one great principle, that they must always administer impartial justice to their subjects under the guidance of intelligence and the art of government. Then they will not b only preserve the lives of their subjects but reform their characters too, so far as human nature permits of this.

YOUNG SOCRATES: There can be no objection to your last remarks at any rate.

STRANGER: No, nor can there be to my earlier ones either.

YOUNG SOCRATES: To which are you referring?

STRANGER: You remember that we said that in no community whatsoever could it happen that a large number of people received this gift of political wisdom and the power to govern by pure intelligence which would accompany it. Only in the hands of the select few or c of the enlightened individual can we look for that right exercise of political power which is itself the one true constitution. For we must call all other constitutions mere imitations of this. Some are more perfect copies of it; others are grosser and less adequate imitations.

YOUNG SOCRATES: What do you really mean by this? For I must admit that I did not really understand what you said before about these 'imitations.'

STRANGER: But I must make you understand. It would be a serious failing to start a discussion of this issue and then simply drop it without exposing the error which is rampant today in all that is said d about it.

YOUNG SOCRATES: And what is this error?

STRANGER: That is what we must now seek out, though it involves a search over unfamiliar ground and the error is hard to discover. We may say, then, that there is only one constitution in the true sense—the one we have described. For the rest of them owe their very preservation to their following a code of laws enacted for this true state and to a strict adherence to a rule which we admit to be desirable though it falls short of the ideal.

YOUNG SOCRATES: What rule is this?

STRANGER: The rule that none of the citizens may venture to e do any act contrary to the laws, and that if any of them ventures to do such act, the penalty is to be death or the utmost rigor of punishment. This is the justest and most desirable course as a second best when the ideal we have just described has been set aside. We must now go on to say how this state of affairs we have just called second best is achieved in practice, must we not?

YOUNG SOCRATES: Yes, we must.

STRANGER: Let us go back once again to the parallel cases with which we have constantly to compare the ruler who really is a statesman.

YOUNG SOCRATES: Who are they?

STRANGER: Our good friend the ship's captain and the doctor 'worth a dozen other men.' Let us picture to ourselves a situation in which they might find themselves and see how it all works out in their case.

YOUNG SOCRATES: What situation?

298   STRANGER: Suppose we all suddenly decided that we are the victims of the worst possible outrages at their hands. Every doctor, you see, can preserve the life of any he will among us, and can hurt any he will by knife or cautery or by demanding fees which are nothing but imposed taxes—for only the tiniest proportion of them is spent on medicaments for the patient and all the rest goes to keep the doctor and his household. Their final enormity is to accept bribes from b the patient's relations or from his enemies and put him to death. Ships' captains are guilty of a different set of crimes, but they are just as heinous. They will enter into a conspiracy to put out to sea with you and then leave you stranded, or else they will scuttle the ship and throw the passengers overboard—and these are not all their misdeeds. Suppose we formed this view of doctors and captains and then held a council at which the following decree was passed.

Neither medicine nor seamanship may be trusted in future with c absolute control in its particular sphere, either over slaves or over free citizens. We therefore resolve to gather together an assembly of *all,* or *of the wealthy among,* the people. It shall be lawful for men of no calling or men of any other calling to advise this assembly on seamanship and medicine—that is to say, on the drugs and surgical instruments appropriate to the treatment of the sick, on ships and their d tackle, on the handling of vessels, and on perils of the sea, including risks arising from wind and tide, risks arising from encountering pirates, and risks arising from maneuver of warships against enemy warships in the event of a naval engagement.

So much for the decree on these matters. The executive is to embody this decree of the assembly of the people—based, you remember, on the advice of a few doctors and sailors maybe, but certainly on the advice of many unqualified people too—in laws which they are to inscribe on tablets of wood and of stone, and in the case of some of the rules so resolved upon, they must see that they find their place e among the unwritten ancestral customs. Thereafter forever medicine and navigation may only be practiced according to these laws and customs.

YOUNG SOCRATES: A pretty state of affairs this!

STRANGER: But we have not done yet. Suppose that they resolve further to appoint magistrates chosen by lot annually from the citizen body, whether from the wealthy only or from all citizens. Some of these magistrates, once they are appointed, are to take command of ships and navigate them; others are to cure the sick according to the written code.

YOUNG SOCRATES: This is getting worse!

STRANGER: But we have not done—see what follows. When the year of office of each of these magistrates expires, a court must be established and a jury chosen by lot, perhaps from among wealthier 299 citizens whose names are on a list of previously selected jurors, perhaps from the people as a whole. The magistrates are to be summoned before this court and it is to subject them to audit. It is open to anyone to lay an accusation against them that during their year of office they failed to sail the ships according to the written laws or the ancient custom of our forebears. Similar charges may be brought concerning the healers of the sick. If the verdict goes against any of them, the court must assess the penalty or the fine the convicted parties must pay.

YOUNG SOCRATES: Well then, the man who took office voluntarily in such a society would deserve any punishment and any b fine that might be imposed.

STRANGER: Then there can be further misdemeanors, and we must enact a law to provide against them. It will be a law against independent research. If a man be found guilty of inquiry into seamanship or medicine in contravention of this law—of inquiry into nautical practice, for instance, or into climatic influences and bodily temperatures, and especially if he be guilty of airing theories of his own on such things, action must be taken to suppress him. First we must deny him the title of 'doctor' or 'captain.' Instead we must call him a man with his head in the clouds, one of these chattering Sophists. Furthermore it will be lawful for any citizen so desiring to indict him before a court of justice—or what passes for such a court—on the charge of corrupting the younger men and influencing them to go in for seamanship and medicine in an illegal manner by setting up as c doctors or captains on their own authority. If he is found guilty of influencing young or old against the laws and written enactments, he shall suffer the utmost penalties. For there can be no claim to possess wisdom greater than the wisdom of the laws. No one need be ignorant of seamanship or medicine, of sailing regulations or health regulations. The laws are there written out for our conning; the ancient cus- d toms are firmly established in our midst. Any who really desire to learn may learn.

Suppose, Socrates, that all the arts are treated like this. How do you imagine that generalship and hunting in all its forms would be affected? What would happen to painting and other representational arts, or to building and manufacture of all types of implements under such conditions, and how could farming or any cultivation whatever

be carried on? Imagine the rearing of horses and other animals tied down to legal prescription, or divination and similar ministerial functions so controlled. What would legally governed draughts be like or
e legal mathematics, whether simple arithmetic, plane geometry, stereometry, or kinematics? What would the world be like if everything worked on this principle, organized throughout according to written laws instead of according to the relevant arts?

YOUNG SOCRATES : It is quite clear that the arts as we know them would be annihilated and that they could never be resurrected because of this law which puts an embargo on all research. The result would be that life, which is hard enough as it is, would be quite impossible then and not to be endured.

STRANGER : Yes, but there is a further possible degradation to
300 consider. Suppose we compel each of these arts to function according to a legal code and place a magistrate in charge of this code either by election or by the fall of the lot, and make him rule according to it. Suppose then that he has no regard for the code and acts only from motives of ambition and favoritism. He embarks on a course of action contrary to law but does not act on any basis of scientific knowledge. Evil as the former state was, will not this latter one be still worse?

YOUNG SOCRATES : It will indeed.

b STRANGER : The laws which have been laid down represent the fruit of experience—one must admit that. Each of them has been put forward by some advocate who has been fortunate enough to hit on the right method of commending it and who has thus persuaded the public Assembly to enact it. Any man who dares by his action to infringe these laws is guilty of a wrong many times greater than the wrong done by strict laws, for such transgression, if tolerated, would do even more than a rigid code to pervert all ordered activity.

YOUNG SOCRATES : Yes, of course it would.

c STRANGER : Then so long as men enact laws and written codes governing any department of life, our second-best method of government is to forbid any individual or any group to perform any act in contravention of these laws.

YOUNG SOCRATES : True.

STRANGER : Then laws would seem to be written copies of scientific truth in the various departments of life they cover, copies based as far as possible on the instructions received from those who really possess the scientific truth on these matters.

YOUNG SOCRATES : Yes, of course.

STRANGER : And yet we must never lose sight of the truth we stated before. The man with the real knowledge, the true statesman, will in many instances allow his activities to be dictated by his art and pay no regard to written prescriptions. He will do this whenever he is convinced that there are measures which are better than the instructions he previously wrote and sent to people at a time when he could d not be there to control them personally.

YOUNG SOCRATES : Yes, that was what we said.

STRANGER : So an individual or a group who possess a code of laws but try to introduce some change in them because they consider it an improvement are doing the same thing according to their lights as the true statesman.

YOUNG SOCRATES : Yes.

STRANGER : But if they acted like this with minds unenlightened by knowledge, they would indeed try to copy the true original, but would copy it very badly. If on the other hand they possessed scientific knowledge, it would no longer be a case of copying at all; it would e be the real and original statesmanship we are talking about.

YOUNG SOCRATES : Yes—or so I should say.

STRANGER : Now it has been argued already and we have agreed that no large group of men is capable of acquiring any art, be it what you will.

YOUNG SOCRATES : That stands as our agreed conclusion.

STRANGER : Granted then that an art of kingly rule exists, the wealthy group or the whole citizen body would never be able to acquire this scientific art of statesmanship.

YOUNG SOCRATES : How could they?

STRANGER : It seems to follow that there is an invariable rule which these imitative constitutions must obey if they mean to reproduce as far as they can that one real constitution, which is gov- 301 ernment by a real statesman using real statecraft. They must all keep strictly to the laws once they have been laid down and never transgress written enactments or established national customs.

YOUNG SOCRATES : Quite right.

STRANGER : When the wealthy seek to copy the ideal constitution we call the constitution which results 'aristocracy,' but when they disregard the laws, the constitution produced is 'oligarchy.'

YOUNG SOCRATES : I suppose so.

STRANGER : But when one individual governs according to laws, imitating the truly wise ruler, we call him 'king.' We make no b difference in name between the individual ruler guided by political science and the individual ruler guided by a right opinion and acting according to the laws.

YOUNG SOCRATES : That seems to be so.

STRANGER : And so if there really were an example of a truly wise ruler in power his name would undoubtedly be the same—'the king'—it could not be anything else. So the total of the names of the constitutions now under consideration comes to five only.

YOUNG SOCRATES : So it seems.

STRANGER : But stay, what of the case where one man rules but does not govern his actions either by laws or by ancient customs, c but claims falsely what only the truly wise ruler has a right to claim, and says that the 'best' course must be taken in defiance of written codes? If in fact it is only his passion and his ignorance that lead him to attempt to copy the true statesman in this defiance of law, must we not call him and all like him by the name of tyrant?

YOUNG SOCRATES : Unquestionably.

STRANGER : So then we have the tyrant and the king, then oligarchy and aristocracy, then democracy, all of which arise when men turn down the idea of the one true and scientific ruler. Men doubt whether any man will ever be found fit to bear such perfect rule. They despair of finding any one man willing and able to rule with
d moral and intellectual insight and to render every man his due with strictest fairness. They feel sure that a man with such absolute power will be bound to employ it to the hurt and injury of his personal enemies and to put them out of the way. But it remains true that if the ideal ruler we have described were to appear on earth he would be acclaimed, and he would spend his days guiding in strictest justice and perfect felicity that one and only true commonwealth worthy of the name.

YOUNG SOCRATES : That is so of course.

STRANGER : We must take things as they are, however, and kings do not arise in cities in the natural course of things in the way
e the royal bee is born in a beehive—one individual obviously outstanding in body and mind and capable of taking charge of things at once. And therefore it seems men gather together and work out written codes, chasing as fast as they can the fading vision of the true constitution.

YOUNG SOCRATES : So it would seem.

STRANGER : Is it any wonder that under these makeshift constitutions of ours hosts of ills have arisen and more must be expected in the future? They all rest on the sandy foundation of action according to law and custom without real scientific insight. Another art that
302 worked on such a foundation would obviously ruin all that it sought to build up. But something even more remarkable than these besetting ills is the sheer native strength a city possesses nevertheless. For all our cities, as we know, have been subject to such ills for many generations now, and yet some of them have not come to ruin but still stand firm. However, we see many instances of cities going down like sinking ships to their destruction. There have been such wrecks in the past and there surely will be others in the future, caused by the wickedness of captains and crews alike. For these are guilty men, whose sin is supreme ignorance of what matters most. They are men
b who know little or nothing of real political truth and yet they consider themselves to know it from end to end and suppose that they are better instructed in this art than in any other.

YOUNG SOCRATES : Very true.

STRANGER: All these imperfect constitutions are difficult to live under, but we might ask ourselves which of them is hardest to bear and which is most tolerable. Ought we perhaps to examine this matter, though it is not directly relevant to our appointed theme? After all one must remember that, speaking quite generally, the aim of all the actions of men everywhere is to secure for themselves the most tolerable life they can.

YOUNG SOCRATES: Then we can hardly help considering the question.

STRANGER: There is one of three constitutions which you must c regard as being at once the hardest to live under and the easiest.

YOUNG SOCRATES: How do you mean?

STRANGER: I just want to remind you that at the beginning of this supplementary discussion we enumerated three constitutions— the rule of one, the rule of the few, and the rule of the many.

YOUNG SOCRATES: We did.

STRANGER: Dividing each of three into two let us make six, having first separated the true constitution from all, calling it the seventh.

YOUNG SOCRATES: How shall we divide the three others?

STRANGER: Under the rule of one we get kingly rule and d tyranny; under the rule of the few, as we said, come the auspicious form of it, aristocracy, and also oligarchy. As for the subdividing of democracy, though we gave both forms of it one name previously, we must now treat it as twofold.

YOUNG SOCRATES: How is this? How can it be divided?

STRANGER: By the same division as the others, even though the word 'democracy' proves to be doing double duty. Rule according to e law is as possible under democracy as under the other constitutions.

YOUNG SOCRATES: Yes, it is.

STRANGER: This division of democracy into two kinds was not serviceable previously as we indicated at the time, for we were seeking then to define a perfect constitution. Now, however, we have excluded the perfect constitution from our reckoning and have before us those that have to serve us as constitutions in default of it. In this group we find the principle of obedience to law or contravention of law dividing each type of ruler into two types.

YOUNG SOCRATES: So it seems from the argument that was put forward just now.

STRANGER: The rule of one man, if it has been kept within the traces, so to speak, by the written rules we call laws, is the best of all the six. But when it is lawless it is hard, and the most grievous to have to endure.

YOUNG SOCRATES: So it would seem.

STRANGER: As for the rule of a few, just as the few constitute a 303 middle term between the one and the many, so we must regard the rule of the few as of middle potency for good or ill. The rule of the many is weakest in every way; it is not capable of any real good or of any serious evil as compared with the other two. This is because in a democracy sovereignty has been divided out in small portions among a large number of rulers. If therefore all three constitutions are law-abiding, democracy is the worst of the three, but if all three flout the laws, democracy is the best of them. Thus if all constitutions are unprincipled the best thing to do is to live in a democracy. But when constitutions are lawful and ordered, democracy is the least desirable, and monarchy, the first of the six, is by far the best to live under—unless of course the seventh is possible, for that must always be exalted, like a god among mortals, above all other constitutions.

YOUNG SOCRATES: Things do seem to work out in this way, and so we must take your advice and act as you say.

STRANGER: Therefore all who take part in one of these governments—apart from the one based on real knowledge—are to be distinguished from the true statesman. They are not statesmen; they are party leaders, leaders of bogus governments and themselves as bogus as their systems. The supreme imitators and tricksters, they are of all Sophists the arch-Sophists.

YOUNG SOCRATES: It seems to me that the wheel has come full circle, now that the title of Sophist goes to those who most deserve it, to the men who get themselves called political leaders.

STRANGER: So this fantastic pageant that seemed like some strange masque of centaurs or some band of satyrs stands revealed for what it is. At much pains we have succeeded at last in distinguishing them and setting them apart, as we must, from all true practice of statesmanship.

YOUNG SOCRATES: So we see.

STRANGER: There remains another task, and it is even more difficult because the class to be set apart is closer akin to the kingly ruler and also in itself harder to discern clearly. It seems to me that we have reached a point where we have to act like gold refiners.

YOUNG SOCRATES: How so?

STRANGER: We are told that at the first stage of their work they separate off earth and stones and much else from the ore. When these are gone there still remain those precious substances akin to gold which are so combined with it as to be separable only in the furnace; I mean bronze and silver and sometimes adamant as well. These are removed only with difficulty as the metal is tried in the refining fire until at last the process yields the sight of unalloyed gold separated off by itself.

YOUNG SOCRATES: Yes, they do say that refining is done like that.

STRANGER: It looks as though we are in a like situation. We have separated off the elements which are quite different from statesmanship, the elements which are quite foreign and repugnant to it, but there still remain the precious elements which are akin to it. These include the art of generalship, the art of administering justice, and that department of the art of public speaking which is closely allied to the kingly art. This last persuades men to do what is right 304 and therefore takes its share in controlling what goes on in a true community. How can we best separate these arts also from statesmanship and so bring out the nature of the statesman as such, in his essential character? That, after all, is our present object.

YOUNG SOCRATES: Clearly we must make the attempt by one means or another.

STRANGER: If trying will do it, he shall be shown in his true character. Music will provide us with an example which will help us in our task. I will begin by putting a question to you.

YOUNG SOCRATES: What is it?

STRANGER: There is such a thing as learning the principles of b music or the principles of any of the crafts, is there not?

YOUNG SOCRATES: Yes.

STRANGER: But are we willing to admit that there exists an art of a higher order also concerned with this process of acquiring special skills? This second art is the one whose province is to decide whether or not we *ought* to learn any particular art.

YOUNG SOCRATES: Yes, we will attest the existence of an art of this higher order.

STRANGER: We must also agree then, that it is to be distinguished from all arts of the lower order.

YOUNG SOCRATES: Yes.

STRANGER: Ought there to be no priority at all as between these two orders of art? On the other hand, if there is to be priority, must c the lower order control the higher or the higher guide and control the lower?

YOUNG SOCRATES: The higher order should control the lower.

STRANGER: Your decision is then, that the art which decides whether we learn a skill or not ought to have control of the art which actually teaches us that skill.

YOUNG SOCRATES: Yes, certainly.

STRANGER: Then in the same way the art which decides whether persuasion should or should not be used ought to control the operation of the art of persuasion itself.

YOUNG SOCRATES: Undoubtedly.

STRANGER: Which is the art to which we must assign the task of persuading the general mass of the population by telling them suitable stories rather than by giving them formal instruction? d

YOUNG SOCRATES: I should say that it is obvious that this is the province to be assigned to rhetoric.

STRANGER: But to which art must we assign the function of

deciding whether in any particular situation we must proceed by persuasion, or by coercive measures against a group of men, or whether it is right to take no action at all?

YOUNG SOCRATES : The art which can teach us how to decide that will be the art which controls rhetoric and the art of public speaking.

STRANGER : This activity can be none other than the work of the statesman, I suggest.

YOUNG SOCRATES : Excellent! That is exactly what it is.

STRANGER : Oratory, it seems, has been quickly set apart from
e statesmanship. It is distinct from statesmanship, and yet its auxiliary.

YOUNG SOCRATES : Yes.

STRANGER : Now we must consider the working of another art.

YOUNG SOCRATES : Which is that?

STRANGER : Consider the taking of decisions on military strategy once war has been declared by the state on an enemy state. What shall we say about this? Is such decision governed by no art at all, or shall we say that there is most certainly an art involved here?

YOUNG SOCRATES : How could we dream of saying that no art is concerned? Surely generalship and the whole art of warfare operates precisely in this field.

STRANGER : But which is the art which possesses the knowledge and capacity to form a reasoned decision whether to fight or settle a dispute on friendly terms? Is this the work of generalship or does it belong to another art?

YOUNG SOCRATES : Consistency to our earlier argument requires us to say that it is a different one which is involved.

305 STRANGER : So if our views here are to be consistent with our earlier views on the place of rhetoric, we must decide that this second art controls generalship.

YOUNG SOCRATES : I agree.

STRANGER : What art can we attempt to enthrone as queen over that mighty and dreadful art, the art of war in all its range, except the art of truly royal rule?

YOUNG SOCRATES : None other.

STRANGER : Then we must not describe the art that generals practice as statesmanship, for it proves to be but a servant of statesmanship.

YOUNG SOCRATES : Apparently that is so.

b STRANGER : Now turn to another art and let us consider the activity of judges who make straight judgments.

YOUNG SOCRATES : By all means.

STRANGER : Does its province extend beyond the sphere of the mutual contractual obligations of the citizens? It has to act in this sphere by judging what is just or unjust according to the standards set up for it and embodied in the legal rules which it has received from the kingly lawgiver. It shows its peculiar virtue by coming to an impartial decision on the conflicting claims it examines, by refusing to pervert the lawgiver's ordinance through yielding to bribery or threats c or sentimental appeals, and by rising above all considerations of personal friendship or enmity.

YOUNG SOCRATES: Yes, that is so. You have given us, sir, a succinct account of the juryman's function and of his duty.

STRANGER: We find, then, that the power of the judges is a lesser thing than the power of the king. The judge guards the law and serves the king.

YOUNG SOCRATES: So it would seem.

STRANGER: If you will view the three arts we have spoken of as a group with a common character you will be bound to see that none of them has turned out to be itself the art of statesmanship. This is because it is not the province of the real kingly art to act for itself but d rather to control the work of the arts which instruct us in the methods of action. The kingly art controls them according to its power to perceive the right occasions for undertaking and setting in motion the great enterprises of state. The other arts must do what they are told to do by the kingly art.

YOUNG SOCRATES: Precisely so.

STRANGER: The three arts we have just treated in detail may not control one another. They may not even control themselves, in fact. Each has its special field of action and each is entitled to the name which designates its proper sphere.

YOUNG SOCRATES: So it would seem.   e

STRANGER: There is an art which controls all these arts. It is concerned with the laws and with all that belongs to the life of the community. It weaves all into its unified fabric with perfect skill. It is a universal art and so we call it by a name of universal scope. That name is one which I believe to belong to this art and to this alone, the name of 'statesmanship.'

YOUNG SOCRATES: Yes, I agree absolutely.

STRANGER: Now that all the classes of arts active in the government of the state have been distinguished, shall we go on to scrutinize statesmanship and base our scrutiny of it on the art of weaving which provides our example for it?

YOUNG SOCRATES: Most certainly.

STRANGER: Then we must describe the kingly weaving process. What is it like? How is it done? What is the fabric that results from its labors?

YOUNG SOCRATES: These are just the questions we must an- 306 swer.

STRANGER: The task of finding the answers is hard, but we cannot shirk it.

YOUNG SOCRATES: No, we must find them at all costs.

STRANGER: To say that 'one kind of goodness clashes with another kind of goodness' is to preach a doctrine which is an easy target for the disputatious who appeal to commonly accepted ideas.

b   YOUNG SOCRATES: I do not follow you.

STRANGER: Then let me put the matter in this way. You regard courage as one part of virtue I suppose.

YOUNG SOCRATES: Surely.

STRANGER: Moderation differs from courage but is a specific kind of goodness just as courage is.

YOUNG SOCRATES: Yes.

STRANGER: We have now to be daring and make a startling statement about these two virtues.

YOUNG SOCRATES: What is it?

STRANGER: This pair of virtues are in a certain sense enemies

c   from of old, ranged in opposition to each other in many realms of life.

YOUNG SOCRATES: What do you mean?

STRANGER: The doctrine is not a familiar one by any means. I suppose that the usual statement is that all the several parts of goodness are in mutual accord.

YOUNG SOCRATES: Yes.

STRANGER: Then we must give our very special attention to the matter. Is the position quite so simple as that? Is there not, on the contrary, something inherent in them which keeps alive a family quarrel among them?

YOUNG SOCRATES: Certainly we must consider this. Please tell us how we are to do so.

STRANGER: We must consider instances drawn from all levels of existence of things which we regard as excellent and yet classify as mutually opposed.

YOUNG SOCRATES: Please explain still more clearly.

STRANGER: Take swiftness and speed as an instance—swift-

d   ness of mind and body and rapid vibration of sound in a voice. Such swiftness may be seen in an actual living person or it may be represented in music or painting. Have you ever praised examples of such swiftness or listened with approval when one of your friends praised them?

YOUNG SOCRATES: Yes.

STRANGER: Do you happen to remember the way in which the approval is expressed in all these instances?

YOUNG SOCRATES: No, I can't say that I remember that in the least.

STRANGER: I wonder if I could really manage to put my thoughts on the subject into words and make them clear to you.

e   YOUNG SOCRATES: I am sure you could.

STRANGER: You seem to think it a light task! However, let us see the principle at work wherever those mutually opposite qualities are manifested. We admire speed and intensity and vivacity in many forms of action and under all kinds of circumstances. But whether the swiftness of mind or body or the vibrant power of the voice is being praised, we always find ourselves using one word to praise it—the word 'vigorous.'

YOUNG SOCRATES: How so?

STRANGER: 'That is alert and vigorous,' we say in the first instance, in another case, 'That is speedy and vigorous,' or, in yet another case, 'That is intense and vigorous.' In all the instances we use this epithet 'vigorous,' as applying in common to the people or things concerned, in order to express our approval of this quality in them.

YOUNG SOCRATES: True.   307

STRANGER: On the other hand, do we not quite often find ourselves approving gentleness and quietness when it is shown in many kinds of human behavior?

YOUNG SOCRATES: Yes, very decidedly.

STRANGER: Do we not describe this behavior by using an epithet which is the exact opposite of 'vigorous,' which was the term we applied to the other group of things?

YOUNG SOCRATES: How do you mean?

STRANGER: We constantly admire quietness and moderation, in processes of restrained thinking, in gentle deeds, in a smooth deep voice, in steady balance in movement, or in suitable restraint in ar- b tistic representation. Whenever we express such approval do we not use the expression 'controlled' to describe all these excellences rather than the word 'vigorous'?

YOUNG SOCRATES: Very true.

STRANGER: But when we find either of these kinds of behavior appearing out of its due time, we have different names for each of them and in that case we express our censure by attributing quite contrary qualities when we mention them.

YOUNG SOCRATES: How so?

STRANGER: If speed and swiftness are excessive and unseasonable and if the voice is harsh to the point of being violent we speak of all these as 'excessive' and even 'maniacal.' Unseasonable heaviness, slowness, or softness we call 'cowardly' or 'indolent.' One c can generalize further. The very classes 'energy' and 'moderation' are ranged in mutual exclusiveness and in opposition to each other; it is not simply a case of conflict between these particular manifestations of them. They never meet in the activities of life without causing conflicts, and if we pursue the matter further, by studying people whose characters come to be dominated by either of them, we shall find inevitable conflict between them and people of the opposite type.

YOUNG SOCRATES: In what sphere do these conflicts occur?

STRANGER: In all the things we have just considered, of course, d but in many others too, I think. Men react to situations in one way or another according to the affinities of their own dispositions. They favor some forms of action as being akin to their own character, and they recoil from acts arising from opposite tendencies as being foreign to themselves. Thus men come into violent conflict with one another on many issues.

YOUNG SOCRATES: Yes, they seem to do so.

STRANGER: Considered as a conflict of temperaments, this is a mere trifle, but when the conflict arises over matters of high public importance it becomes the most inimical of all the plagues which can threaten the life of a community.

YOUNG SOCRATES: What kind of evils do you mean?

e STRANGER: Of course I mean all which concern the organization of the community as a whole. Men who are notable for moderation are always ready to support 'peace and tranquillity.' They want to keep themselves to themselves and to mind their own business. They conduct all their dealings with their fellow citizens on this principle and are prone to take the same line in foreign policy and preserve peace at any price with foreign states. Because of their indulgence of this passion for peace at the wrong times, whenever they are able to carry their policy into effect they become unwarlike themselves without being aware of it and render their young men unwarlike as well. Thus they are at the mercy of the chance aggressor. He swoops down on them and the result is that within a very few years they and their children and all the community to which they belong wake up to find that their freedom is gone and that they are reduced to slavery.

308 YOUNG SOCRATES: You have described a hard and bitter experience.

STRANGER: What then is the history of the party whose bent is rather toward strong action? Do we not find them forever dragging their cities into war and bringing them up against powerful foes on all sides just because they love a military existence too fiercely? And what is the result? Either they destroy their country altogether, or else they bring it into subjection to its enemies just as surely as the peace party did.

b YOUNG SOCRATES: Yes, that is true too.

STRANGER: Can we deny, then, that in these high matters the two types of character concerned are bound to become hostile to one another and so take up opposing party lines?

YOUNG SOCRATES: We are bound to admit it.

STRANGER: We have discovered, then, the answer to the question into which we set out to inquire when we began this conversation. We find that important parts of goodness are at variance with one another and that they set at variance the men in whom they predominate.

YOUNG SOCRATES: So it seems.

STRANGER: There is a further point to consider.

YOUNG SOCRATES: What is it?

STRANGER: Does any art which works by combining materials c deliberately choose to make any of its products, even the least important of them, out of a combination of good material with bad? Does not every art, whatever material it works in, reject bad material as far as possible and use what is good and serviceable? The materials may be alike or dissimilar, but surely it is desirable that they should be sound, so that the art may combine them to form one product and fashion them to a structure proper to their specific function.

YOUNG SOCRATES: Yes.

STRANGER: Surely then the true and genuine statesmanship d we are concerned with could never choose deliberately to construct the life of any community out of a combination of good characters with bad characters? Obviously it will first put the young children to the test in games. After this first test it will go on to entrust the young to competent educators trained to render this particular service, but it will retain direction and oversight of them all the time. This is exactly like weaving. The art of weaving hands over the materials it intends to use for the fabric to the carders and others concerned with preparatory processes, and yet it watches their work at every stage, retaining the direction and oversight itself and indicating to each auxiliary art such duties as it deems that each can usefully perform to make e ready the threads for its own task of fashioning the web.

YOUNG SOCRATES: Precisely.

STRANGER: This is the way I see the true statesman dealing with those who rear and educate children according to the educational laws. He keeps the power of direction to himself. The only form of training he will permit is the one by which the educator produces the type of character fitted for his own task of weaving the web of state. He bids the educator encourage the young in these activities and in no others. Some pupils cannot be taught to be courageous and moderate and to acquire the other virtuous tendencies, but are impelled to godlessness and to vaunting pride and injustice by the drive of an evil nature. These the king expels from the community. He puts them to death or banishes them or else he chastises them by the severest public disgrace.

YOUNG SOCRATES: So one usually hears it stated.

STRANGER: Furthermore, he makes those who prove incapable of rising above ignorance and groveling subservience slaves to the rest 309 of the community.

YOUNG SOCRATES: Quite rightly.

STRANGER: The statesman will then take over all the rest—all those who, under the training process, do in fact achieve sufficient nobility of character to stand up to the royal weaving process and yet to b submit to it while it combines them all scientifically into a unity. Those in whom courage predominates will be treated by the statesman as having the firm warplike character as one might call it. The others will be used by him for what we may likewise call the supple, soft, wooflike strands of the web. He then sets about his task of combining and weaving together these two groups exhibiting their mutually opposed characters.

YOUNG SOCRATES: How does he do it?

c   STRANGER: He first unites that element in their souls which is supernatural by a divine bond, since this element in them is akin to the divine. After this supernatural link will come the natural bond, human ties to supplement the divine ones.

YOUNG SOCRATES: What do you mean by this? Once more I do not follow.

STRANGER: When there arises in the soul of men a right opinion concerning what is good, just, and profitable, and what is the opposite of these—an opinion based on absolute truth and settled as an unshakable conviction—I declare that such a conviction is a manifestation of the divine occurring in a race which is in truth of supernatural lineage.

YOUNG SOCRATES: It could not be more suitably described.

d   STRANGER: Do we realize that it is the true statesman, in that he is the good and true lawgiver, who alone is able—for who else should possess the power—to forge by the wondrous inspiration of the kingly art this bond of true conviction uniting the hearts of the young folk of whom we were speaking just now—the young folk who have profited as they should from their education?

YOUNG SOCRATES: That is certainly as one would expect.

STRANGER: The ruler who cannot weld that bond we will never honor with those glorious titles, 'statesman' and 'king.'

YOUNG SOCRATES: Most rightly not.

STRANGER: Well then, will it not work out like this? The soul
e   full of vigor and courage will be made gentle by its grasp of this truth and there is nothing as well calculated as this to make it a willing member of a community based on justice. If such a soul refused this gift, it will sink in the scale and become savage like a beast.

YOUNG SOCRATES: True.

STRANGER: What of the moderate soul? Sharing this firm conviction of truth, will it not be truly moderate and prudent, or at any rate prudent enough, to meet its public duties? But if it refuses to share this conviction, it deserves to be called foolish and our reproach of it is entirely proper.

YOUNG SOCRATES: It is indeed.

STRANGER: Do we agree then that this interweaving, this linking together, can never be lasting and permanent if vicious men are joined with other vicious men or good men with vicious? Surely no art would seriously try to forge such links where these faults of character exist?

YOUNG SOCRATES: How could it?

STRANGER: But in those of noble nature from their earliest 310 days whose nurture too has been all it should be, the laws can foster the growth of this common bond of conviction and only in these. This is the talisman appointed for them by the design of pure intelligence. This most godlike bond alone can unite the elements of goodness which are diverse in nature and would else be opposing in tendency.

YOUNG SOCRATES: Most true.

STRANGER: There remain the other bonds, the human ones. When one sets to work with the divine link already forged it is not very difficult to see what these are and then to set about the forging of them.

YOUNG SOCRATES: But what are these links and how can b they be forged?

STRANGER: They are forged by establishing intermarriage between the two types so that the children of the mixed marriages are so to speak shared between them and by restricting private arrangements for marrying off daughters. Most men make unsuitable matches from the point of view of the begetting of children of the best type of character.

YOUNG SOCRATES: What can you mean?

STRANGER: Would anyone think it worth while to censure in any respect the prevalent practice of pursuing wealth or influence when making such matches?

YOUNG SOCRATES: No, there is nothing very wrong in it.

STRANGER: But when we are specially concerned with the very people who make much of being 'well connected,' justice requires that we should be all the more outspoken if we find them acting un- c suitably.

YOUNG SOCRATES: That is reasonable.

STRANGER: They do not act on any sound or self-consistent principle. See how they pursue the immediate satisfaction of their desire by hailing with delight those who are like themselves and by disliking those who are different. Thus they assign far too great an importance to their own likes and dislikes.

YOUNG SOCRATES: In what way?

STRANGER: The moderate natures look for a partner like themselves, and so far as they can, they choose their wives from women of this quiet type. When they have daughters to bestow in marriage, once again they look for this type of character in the prospective husband. The courageous class does just the same thing and looks for others of d the same type. All this goes on, though both types should be doing exactly the opposite.

YOUNG SOCRATES: How can they, and why should they?

STRANGER : Because if a courageous character is reproduced for many generations without any admixture of the moderate type, the natural course of development is that at first it becomes superlatively powerful but in the end it breaks out into sheer fury and madness.

YOUNG SOCRATES : That is to be expected.

STRANGER : But the character which is too full of modest reti-
e cence and untinged by valor and audacity, if reproduced after its kind for many generations, becomes too dull to respond to the challenges of life and in the end becomes quite incapable of acting at all.

YOUNG SOCRATES : Yes, this is also the result one would expect.

STRANGER : I repeat what I was saying. There is no difficulty in forging these human bonds if the divine bond has been forged first. That bond is a conviction about values and standards shared by both types of character. There is one absorbing preoccupation for the kingly weaver as he makes the web of state. He must never permit the gentle characters to be separated from the brave ones; to avoid this he must make the fabric close and firm by working common con-
311 victions in the hearts of each type of citizen and making public honors and triumphs subserve this end, and finally, each must be involved with the other in the solemn pledges of matrimony. When he has woven his web smooth and 'close-woven,' as the phrase goes, out of men of these differing types, he must entrust the various offices of state to them to be shared in all cases between them.

YOUNG SOCRATES : How can he do this?

STRANGER : When a single magistrate happens to be needed, the statesman must choose a man possessing both characteristics and set him in authority. Where several magistrates are wanted he must bring together some representatives of each type to share the duties. Magistrates of the moderate type are exceedingly cautious, fair, and tenacious of precedent, but they lack pungency and the drive which makes for efficiency.

YOUNG SOCRATES : Yes, that certainly seems to be a fair summing up of the case.

b   STRANGER : The courageous type for their part have far less of the gifts of fairness and caution than their moderate brethren, but they have in a marked degree the drive that gets things done. A community can never function well either in the personal intercourse of its citizens or in its public activities unless both of these elements of character are present and active.

YOUNG SOCRATES : Of course that is so.

STRANGER : Now we have reached the appointed end of the weaving of the web of state. It is fashioned by the statesman's weaving; the strands run true, and these strands are the gentle and the brave. Here these strands are woven together into a unified character.
c For this unity is won where the kingly art draws the life of both types

into a true fellowship by mutual concord and by ties of friendship. It is the finest and best of all fabrics. It infolds all who dwell in the city, bond or free, in its firm contexture. Its kingly weaver maintains his control and oversight over it, and it lacks nothing that makes for happiness so far as happiness is obtainable in a human community.

SOCRATES : You have done what we requested of you, sir, and you have set beside your definition of the Sophist a picture drawn to perfection of the true king and statesman.

PHILEBUS

The characters in the dialogue are Socrates and a young man, Protarchus, who has come to see Socrates with some of his friends. One of these, Philebus, has been discussing with Socrates whether wisdom or pleasure is the greater good, Socrates maintaining the first and Philebus the second. When the dialogue opens the latter has stepped out of the argument and Protarchus has taken it on. Strictly speaking, however, there is no argument. Socrates does all the talking; Protarchus merely agrees or asks a question.

Little or nothing would be lost if Plato had dropped the dialogue form and made Socrates deliver a lecture, or left him entirely out and put the subject into an essay, for Socrates himself does not come through. There is never a touch of irony or gay self-depreciation or anything that recalls the vivid personality the earlier dialogues bring to us. Toward the end of his life Plato's writing changed. He has Socrates say to Philebus that he "must have weapons different from those of my previous arguments, though possibly some may be the same." But no idea of his amusing himself as he did in the Protagoras or the Symposium is now admitted, no laughing sketch of Very Important People, philosophers, mathematicians, statesmen, no pictures of delightful lads or of a grassy bank and a clear-flowing river. In the last dialogues there is an almost fierce concentration on the question to be solved. Plato is old and the end is too near to permit of digressions.

In the Philebus wisdom and pleasure are analyzed and contrasted again and again, always with the conclusion that the things of the mind are superior to all the enjoyments of the senses. Some pleasures are innocent and can have a part in the good life, but mind is a thousand times nearer and more akin to the excellent than any or all pleasures. Never, not even if every creature on earth proclaims that pleasure comes first, Socrates tells us, will we cease to seek the good —with the power and faculty which the soul has of loving the truth and of doing all things for the sake of the truth.

SOCRATES: Now, Protarchus, consider what the two theories are— 11
the one which you mean now to take over from Philebus, and the
other which I and my friends maintain, and which you are to dispute
if you don't find it to your liking. Would you like us to summarize b
them both?

PROTARCHUS: Yes, do.

SOCRATES: Well, Philebus says that the good for all animate
beings consists in enjoyment, pleasure, delight, and whatever can be
classed as consonant therewith, whereas our contention is that the
good is not that, but that thought, intelligence, memory, and things
akin to these, right opinion and true reasoning, prove better and
more valuable than pleasure for all such beings as can participate in c
them, and that for all these, whether now living or yet to be born,
nothing in the world is more profitable than so to participate. That, I
think, Philebus, is the substance of our respective theories, is it not?

PHILEBUS: Yes, Socrates, that is perfectly correct.

SOCRATES: Well, Protarchus, will you take over this argument
now offered to you?

PROTARCHUS: I must. Our fair friend Philebus has cried off.

SOCRATES: Then ought we to do everything we can to get at
the truth of the matter?

PROTARCHUS: Indeed we ought. d

SOCRATES: Well then, I want us to reach agreement on one
further point.

PROTARCHUS: What is that?

SOCRATES: What you and I are now to attempt is to put forward
a certain state or condition of the soul which can render the life of
every man a happy life. Am I right?

PROTARCHUS: Quite right.

SOCRATES: Then you people put forward the state of enjoyment, whereas we put forward that of intelligence?

PROTARCHUS: Yes.

SOCRATES: But suppose some other state better than these be
found; then, if it were found more akin to pleasure, I imagine that e
while we both of us yield to the life that securely possesses the features in question, the life of pleasure overcomes that of intelligence. 12

PROTARCHUS: Yes.

SOCRATES: But if it were found more akin to intelligence, then
intelligence is victorious over pleasure, and it is pleasure that is
worsted. What do you two say? Is that agreed?

PROTARCHUS: I think so, for my part.

SOCRATES: And you, Philebus? What do you say?

From *Plato's Examination of Pleasure: A Translation of the Philebus*, with
introduction and commentary by R. Hackforth (Cambridge and New York,
1945).

PHILEBUS: What I think, and shall continue to think, is that pleasure is victorious whatever happens. But you must decide for yourself, Protarchus.

PROTARCHUS: Now that you have handed over the argument to us, Philebus, you are no longer in a position to agree with Socrates or to disagree.

b   PHILEBUS: True, but no matter. I wash my hands of the affair, and hereby call the goddess herself to witness that I do so.

PROTARCHUS: You can have ourselves too as additional witnesses to one point, namely that you have said what you have. And now, Socrates, we must attempt—and Philebus may choose to help us or do as he likes—to come to a conclusion on what comes next.

SOCRATES: Yes, we must make the attempt, and plainly we shall begin with the goddess herself, who, according to our friend, is called Aphrodite, though her truest name, he tells us, is Pleasure.

PROTARCHUS: Excellent.

c   SOCRATES: For myself, Protarchus, in the matter of naming the gods I am always more fearful than you would think a man could be; nothing indeed makes me so afraid. So in this case I call Aphrodite by any name that is pleasing to her, but as for pleasure, I know that it is a thing of variety and, as I said, it is with pleasure that we must start, turning our thoughts to an examination of its nature. Of course the mere word 'pleasure' suggests a unity, but surely the forms it assumes are of all sorts and, in a sense, unlike each other. For example, we say that an immoral man feels pleasure, and that a moral man feels it too just in being moral; again, we say the same of a fool whose mind is a mass of foolish opinions and hopes; or once again an intelligent man, we say, is pleased just by being intelligent. Now if anyone asserts that these several kinds of pleasure are like each other, surely he will deserve to be thought foolish?

PROTARCHUS: They are unlike, because they arise from opposite sources, Socrates; nevertheless in themselves they are not opposites. How could pleasure be opposite to pleasure? Surely nothing in e   the world could be more completely similar than a thing to itself.

SOCRATES: As, of course, color to color. What a man you are! Certainly, in respect simply of its all being color there will be no difference, but for all that everyone recognizes that black is not merely different from white, but in fact its absolute opposite. Then again the same applies as between figure and figure; taken as a class all figure is one, but of its divisions some are absolutely opposite to each other, 13   while others have countless points of difference, and we can find many other instances of the same thing. So you mustn't put any faith in this argument that makes all sorts of absolutely opposite things into one thing. I am afraid we are going to find pleasures in some cases opposite to pleasures.

PROTARCHUS: Maybe, but what harm will that do to the argument of our side?

SOCRATES: This, that though the things in question are unlike you designate them by a name other than their own; that is what we shall reply. You say, I mean, that all pleasant things are good. Now of course nobody attempts to maintain the thesis that pleasant things are not pleasant, but though they are in some cases, indeed in most, b bad and in others good—so those who think with me maintain— nevertheless you designate them all as good, although you would agree that they are unlike if anyone were to press you in argument. What then is the identical element present alike in the bad pleasures and in the good that makes you use the term 'good' in reference to them all?

PROTARCHUS: What do you mean, Socrates? Do you imagine that anyone will agree, after maintaining that pleasure is the good— that having done that he will endure to be told by you that certain pleasures are good, and certain others bad?   c

SOCRATES: Well, at all events you will allow that they are unlike, and in some cases opposite to, each other.

PROTARCHUS: Not in so far as they are just pleasures.

SOCRATES: We are drifting back to the old position, Protarchus; it seems that we are not going to allow even that one pleasure differs from another, all being alike. The examples given just now cause us no compunction; our beliefs and assertions will be those of the most commonplace persons, and most puerile in discussion.   d

PROTARCHUS: What exactly are you referring to?

SOCRATES: I mean this. Supposing that I were to retort by copying your method and were brazen enough to maintain that a pair of completely dissimilar things are completely similar; then I could say just what you say, with the result that we should be shown up as extraordinarily puerile, and our discussion would 'stranded be and perish.' Let us get it back again, then, into the water; then I dare say we shall be able to get fairly to grips and possibly come to agreement with each other.

PROTARCHUS: Tell me how, will you?   e

SOCRATES: You must be the questioner this time, Protarchus, and I will answer.

PROTARCHUS: What question precisely?

SOCRATES: When I was asked originally what the good is, I suggested intelligence, knowledge, mind, and so on, as being good. Now won't they be in the same case with your own suggestion?

PROTARCHUS: Will they? Why?

SOCRATES: Knowledge taken in its entirety will seem to be a plurality in which this knowledge is unlike that—even, it may be, this knowledge opposite to that, but, if it were, should I be a fit person to 14 carry on this present discussion if I took alarm at the point in question and maintained that knowledge is never unlike knowledge, thereby bringing our discussion to an end like a tale that is told, while we ourselves escaped from the wreck on a quibble?

PROTARCHUS: Well, of course, we've got to escape, but it mustn't be like that. However, I am attracted by having your thesis on all fours with my own. Let us take it that there are this plurality and unlikeness, or difference, in pleasure as in knowledge.

b SOCRATES: Well then, Protarchus, don't let us shut our eyes to the variety that attaches to your good as to mine. Let us have the varieties fairly before us and make a bold venture in the hope that perhaps they may, on inspection, reveal whether we ought to give the title of the good to pleasure or to intelligence or to some third thing. For I imagine we are not striving merely to secure a victory for my suggestions or for yours; rather we ought both of us to fight in support of the truth and the whole truth.

PROTARCHUS: We ought indeed.

c SOCRATES: Then let us come to an agreement that will give us a still surer basis for this assertion.

PROTARCHUS: To what assertion do you refer?

SOCRATES: The one that causes everybody trouble, whether they want it to, as some people sometimes do, or not, as others sometimes do not.

PROTARCHUS: I wish you would be plainer.

SOCRATES: I am referring to the assertion which came our way just now, and which is of a truly remarkable character. For really it is a remarkable thing to say that many are one, and one is many; a person who suggests either of these things may well encounter opposition.

PROTARCHUS: Do you mean a person who says that I, Pro-
d tarchus, though I am one human being am nevertheless many Protarchuses of opposite kinds, making me out to be both tall and short, both heavy and light, and so on and so forth, though I am really always the same person?

SOCRATES: That isn't what I mean, Protarchus; the remarkable instances of one and many that you have mentioned are commonplace. Almost everyone agrees nowadays that there is no need to concern oneself with things like that, feeling that they are childish, obvious, and a great nuisance to argument; for that matter, the same applies to another class of instances, in which you discriminate a
e man's several limbs and members, get your opponent to admit that the individual in question is all those limbs and members, and then make him look ridiculous by showing that he has been compelled to make the incredible assertions that the one is many and indeed infinitely many, and that the many are only one.

15 PROTARCHUS: Then if these are commonplace instances, Soc-

rates, and everyone agrees about them, what are the other sort that you speak of involving this same assertion?

SOCRATES: The one that is taken, my dear boy, may be something that comes into being and perishes, as it was in the cases we have just been speaking of; with such cases, with a one like that, it is admitted, as we said a moment ago, that there is no need to thrash the matter out. But suppose you venture to take as your one such things as man, ox, the beautiful, the good; then you have the sort of unities that involve you in dispute if you give them your serious attention and subject them to division.

PROTARCHUS: What sort of dispute?

SOCRATES: First, whether we ought to believe in the real exist- b ence of monads of this sort; secondly, how we are to conceive that each of them, being always one and the same and subject neither to generation nor destruction, nevertheless is, to begin with, most assuredly this single unity and yet subsequently comes to be in the infinite number of things that come into being—an identical unity being thus found simultaneously in unity and in plurality. Is it torn in pieces, or does the whole of it, and this would seem the extreme of impossibility, get apart from itself? It is not your questions, Protarchus, but these questions, where the one and many are of another c kind, that cause all manner of dissatisfaction if they are not properly settled, and satisfaction if they are.

PROTARCHUS: Then there, Socrates, is the first task for us to achieve here and now.

SOCRATES: That is what I should say.

PROTARCHUS: Well then, you may regard all of us here as agreeing with you herein. As for Philebus, perhaps we had better not put him any more questions at present, but let the sleeping dog lie.

SOCRATES: Very well. Now what is to be our first move in the d great battle of all arms that rages on this issue? Here's a suggestion.

PROTARCHUS: Yes?

SOCRATES: We'll put the thing like this. We get this identity of the one and the many cropping up everywhere as the result of the sentences we utter; in every single sentence ever uttered, in the past and in the present, there it is. What we are dealing with is a problem that will assuredly never cease to exist; this is not its first appearance. Rather it is, in my view, something incidental to sentences themselves, never to pass, never to fade. As soon as a young man gets wind of it, he is as delighted as if he had discovered an intellectual gold mine; he is beside himself with delight, and loves to try every move in e the game. First he rolls the stuff to one side and jumbles it into one; then he undoes it again and takes it to pieces, to the confusion first and foremost of himself, next of his neighbors at the moment, whether they be younger or older or of his own age. He has no mercy on his

16 father or mother or anyone else listening to him—a little more, and he would victimize even animals, as well as human beings in general, including foreigners, to whom of course he would never show mercy provided he could get hold of an interpreter.

PROTARCHUS: Let me call your attention, Socrates, to the fact that there are plenty of us here, all young people. Aren't you afraid that we shall join with Philebus in an assault on you, if you keep abusing us? Well, well, we realize what you mean. Perhaps there is some way, some device for getting this bothersome business to oblige us by removing itself from our discussion, and we might discover some

b more attractive method of approach to the subject; if so, pray do your best about it, and we will keep you company—to the best of our power, that is, for we have a big subject in front of us, Socrates.

SOCRATES: Big indeed, my boys, if I may adopt Philebus' style of addressing you. Nevertheless there is not, and cannot be, a more attractive method than that to which I have always been devoted, though often in the past it has eluded me so that I was left desolate and helpless.

PROTARCHUS: Do tell us what it is.

c SOCRATES: It is a method quite easy to indicate, but very far from easy to employ. It is indeed the instrument through which every discovery ever made in the sphere of the arts and sciences has been brought to light. Let me describe it for your consideration.

PROTARCHUS: Please do.

SOCRATES: There is a gift of the gods—so at least it seems evident to me—which they let fall from their abode, and it was through Prometheus, or one like him, that it reached mankind, together with a fire exceeding bright. The men of old, who were better than ourselves and dwelt nearer the gods, passed on this gift in the form of a saying. All things, so it ran, that are ever said to be consist of a one and a

d many, and have in their nature a conjunction of limit and unlimitedness. This then being the ordering of things we ought, they said, whatever it be that we are dealing with, to assume a single form and search for it, for we shall find it there contained; then, if we have laid hold of that, we must go on from one form to look for two, if the case admits of there being two, otherwise for three or some other number of forms. And we must do the same again with each of the 'ones' thus reached, until we come to see not merely that the one that we started with is a one and an unlimited many, but also just how many it is. But we are not to apply the character of unlimitedness to our plurality until we have discerned the total number of forms the thing in question has intermediate between its one and its unlimited number. It is

e only then, when we have done that, that we may let each one of all these intermediate forms pass away into the unlimited and cease bothering about them. There then, that is how the gods, as I told you, have committed to us the task of inquiry, of learning, and of teaching

one another, but your clever modern man, while making his one—or 17
his many, as the case may be—more quickly or more slowly than is
proper, when he has got his one proceeds to his unlimited number
straightaway, allowing the intermediates to escape him, whereas it is
the recognition of those intermediates that makes all the difference
between a philosophical and a contentious discussion.

PROTARCHUS : I think I understand, more or less, part of what
you say, Socrates, but there are some points I want to get further
cleared up.

SOCRATES : My meaning, Protarchus, is surely clear in the
case of the alphabet; so take the letters of your school days as illustrat- b
ing it.

PROTARCHUS : How do you mean?

SOCRATES : The sound that proceeds through our mouths, yours
and mine and everybody's, is one, isn't it, and also an unlimited variety?

PROTARCHUS : To be sure.

SOCRATES : And we have no real understanding if we stop short
at knowing it either simply as an unlimited variety, or simply as one.
What makes a man 'lettered' is knowing the number and the kinds of
sounds.

PROTARCHUS : Very true.

SOCRATES : Then again, it is just the same sort of thing that
makes a man musical.

PROTARCHUS : How so?

SOCRATES : If you take the art of music, don't you get, as before,
a sound that is one?   c

PROTARCHUS : Of course.

SOCRATES : And may we put down a distinction between low,
high, and the level in pitch?

PROTARCHUS : That's right.

SOCRATES : But you wouldn't be a person of real understanding in music if you knew no more than these three terms, though indeed if you didn't know them you'd be of practically no account in
musical matters.

PROTARCHUS : I should indeed.

SOCRATES : But when you have grasped, my dear friend, the
number and nature of the intervals formed by high pitch and low pitch d
in sound, and the notes that bound those intervals, and all the systems of notes that result from them, the systems which we have
learned, conformably to the teaching of the men of old days who discerned them, to call 'scales,' and when, further, you have grasped
certain corresponding features of the performer's bodily movements,
features that must, so we are told, be numerically determined and be
called 'figures' and 'measures,' bearing in mind all the time that this
is always the right way to deal with the one-and-many problem—only

e then, when you have grasped all this, have you gained real understanding, and whatever be the 'one' that you have selected for investigating, that is the way to get insight about it. On the other hand, the
unlimited variety that belongs to and is inherent in the particulars
leaves one, in each particular case, an unlimited ignoramus, a person of no account, a veritable back number because he hasn't ever addressed himself to finding number in anything.

18   PROTARCHUS : Philebus, I think that what Socrates is now saying is excellent good sense.

PHILEBUS : What he's saying now, yes, so do I. But why,
may I ask, is it addressed to us, and what is its purpose?

SOCRATES : A very proper question that, Protarchus, which
Philebus has asked us.

PROTARCHUS : Indeed it is; so do you give him an answer.

SOCRATES : I will do so, but first a small additional point to
what I have been saying. When you have got your 'one,' you remember,
whatever it may be, you must not immediately turn your eyes to the
unlimited, but to a number; now the same applies when it is the unlimited that you are compelled to start with. You must not immediately
b turn your eyes to the one, but must discern this or that number embracing the multitude, whatever it may be; reaching the one must be
the last step of all. We might take our letters again to illustrate
what I mean now.

PROTARCHUS : How so?

SOCRATES : The unlimited variety of sound was once discerned
by some god, or perhaps some godlike man; you know the story that
there was some such person in Egypt called Theuth. He it was who
originally discerned the existence, in that unlimited variety, of the
vowels—not 'vowel' in the singular but 'vowels' in the plural—and
c then of other things which, though they could not be called articulate
sounds, yet were noises of a kind. There were a number of them too,
not just one, and as a third class he discriminated what we now call
the mutes. Having done that, he divided up the noiseless ones or
mutes until he got each one by itself, and did the same thing with the
vowels and the intermediate sounds; in the end he found a number of
the things, and affixed to the whole collection, as to each single member of it, the name 'letter.' It was because he realized that none of us
could ever get to know one of the collection all by itself, in isolation
from all the rest, that he conceived of 'letter' as a kind of bond of unity,
d uniting as it were all these sounds into one, and so he gave utterance
to the expression 'art of letters,' implying that there was one art that
dealt with the sounds.

PHILEBUS : Comparing the illustrations with one another, Protarchus, I understand the last one even more clearly than the others, but I still feel the same dissatisfaction about what has been said
as I did a while ago.

SOCRATES: You mean, Philebus, what is the relevance of it all?

PHILEBUS: Yes, that is what Protarchus and I have been trying to find out for a long time.

SOCRATES: Yet surely this that you tell me you have been long
trying to find out is already right in front of you.   e

PHILEBUS: How so?

SOCRATES: Our discussion started, didn't it, with the question
which of the two should be chosen, intelligence or pleasure?

PHILEBUS: Certainly.

SOCRATES: And of course we can say that each of them is one
thing.

PHILEBUS: Undoubtedly so.

SOCRATES: Then what the foregoing discourse requires of us is
just this, to show how each of them is both one and many, and how
—mind you, we are not to take the unlimited variety straightaway—
each possesses a certain number before the unlimited variety is
reached.

PROTARCHUS: Philebus, it's no easy problem that Socrates has   19
plunged us into with his curiously roundabout methods. Which of us,
do you think, should answer the present question? Perhaps it is a
trifle ridiculous that I, after giving a full undertaking to replace
you in the discussion, should require you to take the business on again
because of my inability to answer the question now put, but it would
be far more ridiculous, I think, if neither of us could do so. So what   b
shall we do, do you think? Socrates, I take it, is now raising the question of kinds of pleasure. Has it different kinds, or has it not, and if
it has, how many are there and what are they like? And exactly the
same question arises with regard to intelligence.

SOCRATES: Precisely, son of Callias. If we are incapable of
doing this in respect of everything that is one, like, identical, and is
also, as our foregoing account revealed, the opposite, then none of us
will ever be any good at anything.

PROTARCHUS: That's about how it stands, Socrates. Still,   c
though the ideal for a sensible person is to know everything, I fancy it's
not such a bad alternative to realize one's own position. Now why
do I say that at this moment? I'll tell you. You made all of us a free
offer of this discussion, in which you yourself, Socrates, were to
share, for the purpose of deciding what is the best of all things possessed by man. When Philebus said pleasure, delight, enjoyment, and
so forth, you rejoined that it was not those, but a different kind of
things, which we have been glad frequently to remind ourselves of, as   d
we were right to do, so as to have the two kinds of things side by side
in our memory while we subject them to examination. What you,
I gather, maintain is that there is something which may properly be
called a better good than pleasure at all events—namely, reason,
knowledge, understanding, skill, and all that is akin to these things

—and that it is these, not pleasure and so on, that we ought to acquire. Now when these two views had been put forward, one maintained against the other, we threatened you by way of a joke that we would
e not let you go home until the discussion had been worked out and brought to a satisfactory termination, upon which you agreed to the demand, and allowed us to keep you for that purpose. What we tell you now is, as children say, that you can't take back a present once you have duly given it. So stop your present method of dealing with the questions before us.

SOCRATES : What method do you mean?

20 PROTARCHUS : That of plunging us into difficulties, and putting questions that it is impossible for us to answer satisfactorily here and now. We ought not to imagine that the object of our present endeavors is to get ourselves all into difficulties; no, if we are incapable of doing the job, it's for you to do it, since you gave your promise. And that being so, please make up your mind for yourself whether you must classify the kinds of pleasure and of knowledge or may pass them over —supposing, that is, that you are able and willing to follow another method and clear up our points of dispute in some other way.

b SOCRATES : Well, as you put it like that, there's no need for your poor victim to expect any further terrors; that 'if you are willing' banishes all my fears on every score. And what's more, I fancy some god has recalled to my mind something that will help us.

PROTARCHUS : Really? What is it?

SOCRATES : I remember a theory that I heard long ago—I may have dreamed it—about pleasure and intelligence, to the effect that neither of them is the good, but that it is something else, different from either and better than both. Now, you know, if we could get a clear
c sight of this third thing now, then a victory for pleasure is out of the question; it couldn't continue to be identical with the good, could it?

PROTARCHUS : No.

SOCRATES : No, and as to methods for classifying the kinds of pleasure, we shan't need them any longer, I imagine. However, we shall see better as we go on.

PROTARCHUS : That's good, and may your conclusion be so too.

SOCRATES : Well, I should be glad if we could settle a few small points first.

PROTARCHUS : What are they?

d SOCRATES : Must that which ranks as the good be perfect or imperfect?

PROTARCHUS : The most perfect of all things, Socrates, of course.

SOCRATES : And must the good be adequate also?

PROTARCHUS : Yes indeed. In fact it must surpass everything in that respect.

SOCRATES : And surely there is one more feature of it that

needs stressing, namely that every creature that recognizes it goes in pursuit of it, and makes quest of it, desiring to capture it and secure it for its very own, and caring for nothing save such things as involve this or that good in the course of their realization.

PROTARCHUS: I cannot but agree with that.

SOCRATES: Now if we're going to have a critical inspection of the life of pleasure and the life of intelligence, let us see them sep- e arately.

PROTARCHUS: How do you mean?

SOCRATES: Let us have no intelligence in the life of pleasure, and no pleasure in the life of intelligence. For if either of them is the good it must have no need of anything else to be added to it, and if we find that either has such a need, presumably it ceases to be possible 21 for it to be our true good.

PROTARCHUS: Quite so.

SOCRATES: Then shall we take you as the subject on which to try our experiment?

PROTARCHUS: By all means.

SOCRATES: Then here's a question for you.

PROTARCHUS: Yes?

SOCRATES: Would you care, Protarchus, to live your whole life in the enjoyment of the greatest pleasures?

PROTARCHUS: Certainly.

SOCRATES: Then you wouldn't think you needed anything else, if you had that in the fullest measure?

PROTARCHUS: I'm sure I shouldn't.

SOCRATES: Now be careful, are you sure you wouldn't need any- thing in the way of thought, intelligence, calculating what is fitting, b and so on?

PROTARCHUS: Why should I? If I had my enjoyment what more could I want?

SOCRATES: Then if you lived your whole life long like that you would be enjoying the greatest pleasures, would you?

PROTARCHUS: Of course.

SOCRATES: But if you were without reason, memory, knowl- edge, and true judgment, you would necessarily, I imagine, in the first place be unaware even whether you were, or were not, enjoying yourself, as you would be destitute of all intelligence.

PROTARCHUS: Necessarily.

SOCRATES: And surely again, if you had no memory you would necessarily, I imagine, not even remember that you had been enjoy- ing yourself; of the pleasure you encountered at one moment not a c vestige of memory would be left at the next. Once more, if you had no true judgment you couldn't judge that you were enjoying yourself when you were; if you were bereft of the power of calculation you couldn't even calculate that you would enjoy yourself later on. You would be living the life not of a human being but of some sort of sea lung or one of those creatures of the ocean whose bodies are incased in shells. Am I right, or can we imagine the situation to be otherwise?

d   PROTARCHUS: We cannot.

SOCRATES: Then is a life like that one that we can desire?

PROTARCHUS: Your argument, Socrates, has reduced me for the moment to complete speechlessness.

SOCRATES: Well, don't let us lose heart yet; let us turn our attention to the life of reason, and have a look at that.

PROTARCHUS: What is the 'life of reason'?

SOCRATES: Imagine one of us choosing to live in the possession of intelligence, thought, knowledge, and a complete memory of every-

e   thing, but without an atom of pleasure, or indeed of pain, in a condition of utter insensibility to such things.

PROTARCHUS: Neither of these lives seems desirable to me, Socrates, and unless I'm very much mistaken, nobody else will think them so either.

22   SOCRATES: And what about the combined life, Protarchus, the joint life consisting in a mixture of the two?

PROTARCHUS: You mean of pleasure, on the one hand, and reason with intelligence on the other?

SOCRATES: Yes, those are the sorts of ingredients I mean.

PROTARCHUS: Anybody, I imagine, will prefer this mixed life to either of those others. Indeed I will go further—everybody will.

SOCRATES: Then do we realize what result now emerges in our discussion?

PROTARCHUS: Yes, to be sure. Three lives were offered us, and

b   of the first two neither is sufficient or desirable for any human being or any animal.

SOCRATES: Then surely it is obvious by this time that, if you take these two lives, neither of them proves to contain the good. If it did, it would be sufficient and complete and desirable for all plants and animals that had the capacity of living their lives under such conditions from start to finish, and if any of us preferred something else, he would be mistaking the nature of what is truly desirable, and taking what he never meant to take, as the result of ignorance or some sort of unhappy necessity.

PROTARCHUS: It certainly looks as if that were so.

c   SOCRATES: Well then, I think we've said all that needs saying to show that Philebus' goddess must not be conceived of as identical with the good.

PHILEBUS: No, and your 'reason' isn't the good either, Socrates; the case against it looks like being just the same.

SOCRATES: That may well apply to *my* reason, Philebus—not, however, to the true, divine reason which, I fancy, is in rather a different position. Still I am not arguing at present for the claim of reason to win the first prize, as against the combined life, but certainly we ought to look and see what we are going to do about the second prize. d For as to the cause that makes this combined life what it is, very likely one of us will say it is reason, and the other pleasure, so that while neither of the two would, on this showing, be the good, one of them might very possibly be that which makes the good what it is. This then is the point for which I will contend with Philebus even more warmly than before—that whatever it is which, by its inclusion in this mixed life, makes that life both desirable and good, it is something to which reason is nearer and more akin than pleasure. If that be so, pleasure cannot rightly be said to have any sort of claim either to the first prize or to the second; it misses even the third, if we may e put any faith in my reasoning at this moment.

PROTARCHUS: Well yes, Socrates, it does look to me now as if pleasure had been given a knockout blow by your last arguments; in 23 the fight for the victor's prize she has fallen. But I think we may say that it was prudent of reason not to put in for the first prize, as it would have meant a similar defeat. But if pleasure were to be disappointed of even second prize, she would undoubtedly find herself somewhat slighted by her own admirers; even they wouldn't think her as fair as they did.

SOCRATES: In that case hadn't we better leave her alone, and not cause her pain by subjecting her to the ordeal of a stringent examination?

PROTARCHUS: That's nonsense, Socrates.

SOCRATES: You mean it's impossible to talk of 'paining pleas- b ure'?

PROTARCHUS: Not so much that, as that you don't realize that none of us will let you go until you have argued this matter out to the end.

SOCRATES: Phew! A considerable business still in front of us, Protarchus, and not exactly an easy one, I should say, to deal with now. It really looks as though I need fresh tactics. If my objective is to secure the second prize for reason I must have weapons different from those of my previous arguments, though possibly some may be the same. Is it to be, then?

PROTARCHUS: Yes, of course.

SOCRATES: Let us try to be very careful what starting point we c take.

PROTARCHUS: Starting point?

SOCRATES: Of all that now exists in the universe let us make a twofold division, or rather, if you don't mind, a threefold.

PROTARCHUS: On what principle, may I ask?

SOCRATES: We might apply part of what we were saying a while ago.

PROTARCHUS : What part?

SOCRATES : We said, I fancy, that God had revealed two constituents of things, the unlimited and the limit.

PROTARCHUS : Certainly.

SOCRATES : Then let us take these as two of our classes, and, as
d the third, something arising out of the mixture of them both, though I
fear I'm a ridiculous sort of person with my sortings of things into
classes and my enumerations.

PROTARCHUS : What are you making out, my good sir?

SOCRATES : It appears to me that I now need a fourth kind as
well.

PROTARCHUS : Tell me what it is.

SOCRATES : Consider the cause of the mixing of these two
things with each other, and put down that, please, as number four
to be added to the other three.

PROTARCHUS : Are you sure you won't need a fifth to effect
separation?

SOCRATES : Possibly, but not, I think, at the moment. But should
e the need arise, I expect you will forgive me if I go chasing after a fifth.

PROTARCHUS : Yes, to be sure.

SOCRATES : Well then, let us confine our attention in the first
place to three out of our four, and let us take two of these three, observing how each of them is split into many and torn apart, and then
collecting each of them into one again, and so try to discern in what
possible way each of them is in fact both a one and a many.

24   PROTARCHUS : Could you make it all a little clearer still? If so,
I dare say I could follow you.

SOCRATES : Well, in putting forward 'two of the three' I mean
just what I mentioned a while ago, the unlimited, and that which has
limit. I will try to explain that in a sense the unlimited is a many;
the limited may await our later attention.

PROTARCHUS : It shall.

SOCRATES : Your attention now, please. The matter which I request you to attend to is difficult and controversial, but I request you
nonetheless. Take 'hotter' and 'colder' to begin with, and ask yourself
whether you can ever observe any sort of limit attaching to them, or
whether these kinds of thing have 'more' and 'less' actually resident
in them, so that for the period of that residence there can be no ques-
b tion of suffering any bounds to be set. Set a term, and it means the
term of their own existence.

PROTARCHUS : That is perfectly true.

SOCRATES : And in point of fact 'more' and 'less' are always,
we may assert, found in 'hotter' and 'colder.'

PROTARCHUS : To be sure.

SOCRATES : Our argument then demonstrates that this pair is

always without bounds, and being boundless means, I take it, that they must be absolutely unlimited.

PROTARCHUS: I feel that strongly, Socrates.

SOCRATES: Ah yes, a good answer, my dear Protarchus, which reminds me that this 'strongly' that you have just mentioned, and c 'slightly' too, have the same property as 'more' and 'less.' When they are present in a thing they never permit it to be of a definite quantity, but introduce into anything we do the character of being 'strongly' so-and-so as compared with 'mildly' so-and-so, or the other way round. They bring about a 'more' or a 'less,' and obliterate definite quantity. For, as we were saying just now, if they didn't obliterate definite quantity, but permitted definite and measured quantity to find a place where 'more and less' and 'strongly and slightly' reside, these lat- d ter would find themselves turned out of their own quarters. Once you give definite quantity to 'hotter' and 'colder' they cease to be; 'hotter' never stops where it is but is always going a point further, and the same applies to 'colder,' whereas definite quantity is something that has stopped going on and is fixed. It follows therefore from what I say that 'hotter,' and its opposite with it, must be unlimited.

PROTARCHUS: It certainly looks like it, Socrates, though, as you said, these matters are not easy to follow. Still, if things are said again and yet again, there is some prospect of the two parties to a e discussion being brought to a tolerable agreement.

SOCRATES: Quite right. That's what we must try to do. However, for the present, to avoid going over the whole long business, see whether we can accept what I shall say as a mark of the nature of the unlimited.

PROTARCHUS: What is it then?

SOCRATES: When we find things becoming 'more' or 'less' so-and-so, or admitting of terms like 'strongly,' 'slightly,' 'very,' and so forth, we ought to reckon them all as belonging to a single kind, namely 25 that of the unlimited; that will conform to our previous statement, which was, if you remember, that we ought to do our best to collect all such kinds as are torn and split apart, and stamp a single character on them.

PROTARCHUS: I remember.

SOCRATES: Then things that don't admit of these terms, but admit of all the opposite terms like 'equal' and 'equality' in the first place, and then 'double' and any term expressing a ratio of one number to another, or one unit of measurement to another, all these things b we may set apart and reckon—I think we may properly do so—as coming under the limit. What do you say to that?

PROTARCHUS: Excellent, Socrates.

SOCRATES: All right. Now what description are we going to give of number three, the mixture of these two?

PROTARCHUS: That, I think, will be for you to tell me.

SOCRATES: Or rather for a god to tell us, if one comes to listen to my prayers.

PROTARCHUS: Then offer your prayer, and look to see if he does.

SOCRATES: I am looking, and I fancy, Protarchus, that one of them has befriended us for some little time.

c PROTARCHUS: Really? What makes you believe that?

SOCRATES: I'll explain, of course. Please follow what I say.

PROTARCHUS: Pray go on.

SOCRATES: We spoke just now, I believe, of 'hotter' and 'colder,' did we not?

PROTARCHUS: Yes.

SOCRATES: Now add to these 'drier and wetter,' 'higher and lower,' 'quicker and slower,' 'greater and smaller,' and everything that we brought together a while ago as belonging to that kind of being which admits of 'the more' and 'the less.'

d PROTARCHUS: You mean the kind that is unlimited?

SOCRATES: Yes. And now, as the next step, combine with it the family of the limit.

PROTARCHUS: What is that?

SOCRATES: The one we omitted to collect just now; just as we collected the family of the unlimited together, so we ought to have collected that family which shows the character of limit, but we didn't.

e Still perhaps it will come to the same thing in spite of that, if in the process of collecting these two kinds the family we have spoken of is going to become plain to view.

PROTARCHUS: What family? Please explain.

SOCRATES: That of 'equal' and 'double,' and any other that puts an end to the conflict of opposites with one another, making them well proportioned and harmonious by the introduction of number.

PROTARCHUS: I see. By mixing in these you mean, apparently, that we find various products arising as they are respectively mixed.

SOCRATES: You take my meaning aright.

PROTARCHUS: Then continue.

SOCRATES: In cases of sickness does not the right association of these factors bring about health?

26 PROTARCHUS: Unquestionably.

SOCRATES: And in the case of high and low in pitch, or of swift and slow, which are unlimited, does not the introduction of these same elements at once produce limit and establish the whole art of music in full perfection?

PROTARCHUS: Admirably put.

SOCRATES: And then again, if they are introduced where there is severe cold and stifling heat they remove all that is excessive and unlimited, and create measure and balance.

PROTARCHUS: Certainly.

SOCRATES: Then it is here that we find the source of fair weather and all other beautiful things, namely in a mixture of the un- b limited with that which has limit?

PROTARCHUS: Of course.

SOCRATES: And indeed there are countless more things which I may omit to enumerate, such as beauty and strength along with health, besides a whole host of fair things found in our souls. For that goddess of ours, fair Philebus, must have observed the lawlessness and utter wickedness of mankind due to an absence of limit in men's pleasures and appetites, and therefore established among them a law and order that are marked by limit. You maintain that she thereby spoiled them. I assert that on the contrary she preserved them. What c do you think about it, Protarchus?

PROTARCHUS: I am thoroughly satisfied, Socrates.

SOCRATES: Well, there are the three things I have spoken of, if you follow me.

PROTARCHUS: Yes, I think I see what you mean. You are asserting, I gather, two factors in things—first the unlimited, second the limit. But I can't altogether grasp what you mean by the third thing that you mention.

SOCRATES: The reason for that, my dear good sir, is that you are confused by the multiplicity of that third kind. And yet a plurality of forms was presented by the unlimited too, and in spite of that we stamped on them the distinguishing mark of 'the more' and its op- d posite, and so saw them as a unity.

PROTARCHUS: True.

SOCRATES: Then again we did not complain about the limit, either that it exhibited a plurality, or that it was not a real unity.

PROTARCHUS: No, there was no reason to do so.

SOCRATES: None whatever. And now as to the third kind, I am reckoning all this progeny of our two factors as a unity, and you may take me to mean a coming-into-being, resulting from those measures that are achieved with the aid of the limit.

PROTARCHUS: I understand.

SOCRATES: And now to continue. We said that besides the three e kinds there is a fourth kind to be considered, and it is for our joint consideration. Now I expect you regard it as necessary that all things that come to be should come to be because of some cause.

PROTARCHUS: Yes, I do. Without that how could they come to be?

SOCRATES: Well, is there anything more than a verbal difference between a cause and a maker? Wouldn't it be proper to call that which makes things and that which causes them one and the same?

27   PROTARCHUS: Quite proper.

SOCRATES: And further, shall we find that between that which is made and that which comes to be there is, once again, a mere verbal difference?

PROTARCHUS: Yes.

SOCRATES: And isn't it natural that that which makes should have the leading position, while that which is made follows in its train when coming into being?

PROTARCHUS: Certainly.

SOCRATES: Hence a cause and that which, as a condition of coming to be, is subservient to a cause are not the same but different?

PROTARCHUS: Of course.

SOCRATES: Now our three kinds gave us all things that come to be, and the constituents from which they come to be, did they not?

PROTARCHUS: Quite so.

SOCRATES: And this fourth kind that we are speaking of, which
b fashions all these things, this cause, is pretty clearly different from them?

PROTARCHUS: Yes, different certainly.

SOCRATES: But now that the four kinds have been discriminated it will do no harm to enumerate them in order, so that we may remember each by itself.

PROTARCHUS: I agree.

SOCRATES: The first, then, I call the unlimited, the second the limit, and the third the being that has come to be by the mixture of these two; as to the fourth, I hope I shall not be at fault in calling it
c the cause of the mixture and of the coming-to-be?

PROTARCHUS: No indeed.

SOCRATES: Come along now, what is our next point, and what was our purpose in getting where we have got? Wasn't it that we were trying to find out whether the second prize would go to pleasure or to intelligence? Was not that it?

PROTARCHUS: Yes, it was.

SOCRATES: Then shall we perhaps be in a better position, now that we have discriminated these kinds as we have, to achieve our decision about the first place and the second? For that of course was what we started to dispute about.

PROTARCHUS: Perhaps.

SOCRATES: Come on then. We laid it down, I think, that vic-
d tory went to the mixed life of pleasure and intelligence. Was that so?

PROTARCHUS: It was.

SOCRATES: Then of course we can see what kind of life this is and to which kind it belongs?

PROTARCHUS: Undoubtedly.

SOCRATES: In fact we shall assert, I suppose, that it is a part of our third kind. For that kind does not consist of just two things, but of all unlimited things bound fast by the limit; hence it is correct to make our victorious life a part of it.

PROTARCHUS: Yes, perfectly correct.

SOCRATES: Very well. And what about your pleasant un- e mixed life, Philebus? Under which of the kinds that we have mentioned should we be correct in saying that that falls? But before you express your view let us have your answer to a question I will put.

PHILEBUS: Please put it.

SOCRATES: Do pleasure and pain contain a limit, or are they among the things that admit of 'the more' and 'the less'?

PHILEBUS: They are, Socrates; they admit of 'the more.' Pleasure would not be supremely good, if it were not of its very nature unlimited both in quantity and degree.

SOCRATES: And similarly, Philebus, pain would not be su- 28 premely bad; hence we must look for something other than the character of being unlimited to explain how an element of good attaches to pleasures. Well, we may leave that topic, if you please, as one of unlimited speculation. But I will ask both of you, in which of our above-mentioned kinds may we now reckon intelligence, knowledge, and reason, without sinning against the light? I fancy a great deal turns on our present inquiry, according as we give the right answer or the wrong.

PHILEBUS: You are glorifying your own god, Socrates. b

SOCRATES: And you your own goddess, my friend; still we ought to give an answer to our question.

PROTARCHUS: Socrates is right, you know, Philebus; we must do as he tells us.

PHILEBUS: Well, you have volunteered to speak on my behalf, have you not, Protarchus?

PROTARCHUS: Certainly, but at the moment I am rather at a loss, and beg you, Socrates, to state the case to us yourself; otherwise you may find us striking a false note and making mistakes about your candidate.

SOCRATES: I must do as you say, Protarchus; as a matter of fact c it is no difficult task you impose on me. But did I really cause you alarm by my playful glorification, as Philebus has called it, when I asked you to which kind reason and knowledge belong?

PROTARCHUS: Very much so, Socrates.

SOCRATES: But really it's an easy question. For all the wise agree, thereby glorifying themselves in earnest, that in reason we have the king of heaven and earth. And I fancy they are right. But I should like us, if you don't mind, to make a fuller investigation of the kind in question itself.

PROTARCHUS: Proceed as you like, Socrates, and please feel no d concern about being lengthy; we shan't quarrel with you.

SOCRATES: Thank you. Then let us begin, shall we, by putting the following question.

PROTARCHUS: What is it?

SOCRATES: Are we to say, Protarchus, that the sum of things or what we call this universe is controlled by a power that is irrational and blind, and by mere chance, or on the contrary to follow our predecessors in saying that it is governed by reason and a wondrous regulating intelligence?

e   PROTARCHUS: A very different matter, my dear good Socrates. What you are suggesting now seems to me sheer blasphemy. To maintain that reason orders it all does justice to the spectacle of the ordered universe, of the sun, the moon, the stars, and the revolution of the whole heaven, and for myself I should never express nor conceive any contrary view on the matter.

SOCRATES: Then are you willing that we should assent to what earlier thinkers agree upon, that this is the truth? And ought we not merely to think fit to record the opinions of other people without

29   any risk to ourselves, but to participate in the risk and take our share of censure when some clever person asserts that the world is not as we describe it, but devoid of order?

PROTARCHUS: I am certainly willing to do so.

SOCRATES: Come then, and direct your attention to the point that confronts us next.

PROTARCHUS: What is it, please?

SOCRATES: We can discern certain constituents of the corporeal nature of all animals, namely, fire, water, breath, and 'earth too like storm-tossed sailors we discern,' as the saying goes; these are all present in their composition.

b   PROTARCHUS: Quite so, and storm-tossed in truth we are by difficulty in our present discussion.

SOCRATES: Well now, let me point out to you something that applies to each of these elements in our make-up.

PROTARCHUS: What?

SOCRATES: In each case it is only an inconsiderable fragment that is in us, and that too very far from being pure in quality or possessing a power befitting its real nature. Let me explain to you in one instance, which you must regard as applying to them all. There is fire, is there not, belonging to ourselves, and again fire in the universe?

PROTARCHUS: Of course.

c   SOCRATES: And isn't the fire that belongs to ourselves small in quantity and weak and inconsiderable, whereas the fire in the universe is wonderful in respect of its mass, its beauty, and all the powers that belong to fire?

PROTARCHUS: What you say is perfectly true.

SOCRATES: And to continue, is the universal fire sustained and produced and increased by the fire that belongs to us, or is the opposite true, that my fire and yours and that of all other creatures owe all this to that other?

PROTARCHUS : That question doesn't even merit an answer.

SOCRATES : You are right; indeed I imagine you will say the d same about the earth that we have here in creatures and the earth in the universe, and in fact about all the elements that I mentioned in my question a moment ago. Will your answer be as I suppose?

PROTARCHUS : Could anyone giving a different answer be deemed right in his head?

SOCRATES : I hardly think so, whoever he were. But come with me now to the next point. If we regard all these elements that I have been speaking of as a collective unity we give them, do we not, the name of body?

PROTARCHUS : Of course.

SOCRATES : Well, let me point out that the same holds good of e what we call the ordered universe; on the same showing it will be a body, will it not, since it is composed of the same elements?

PROTARCHUS : You are quite right.

SOCRATES : Then, to put it generally, is the body that belongs to us sustained by this body of the universe, has it derived and obtained therefrom all that I referred to just now, or is the converse true?

PROTARCHUS : That is another question, Socrates, that doesn't deserve to be put.

SOCRATES : Well, does this one then? I wonder what you will 30 say.

PROTARCHUS : Tell me what it is.

SOCRATES : Shall we not admit that the body belonging to us has a soul?

PROTARCHUS : Plainly we shall.

SOCRATES : And where, Protarchus my friend, could it have got it from, if the body of the universe, which has elements the same as our own though still fairer in every respect, were not in fact possessed of a soul?

PROTARCHUS : Plainly there can be no other source, Socrates.

SOCRATES : No, for surely we cannot suppose, Protarchus, that those four kinds, limit, unlimited, combined, and cause, which is b present in all things as a fourth kind—we cannot suppose that this last-named, while on the one hand it furnishes the elements that belong to our bodies with soul, maintains our physique and cures a body when it has come to harm, and provides all sorts of arrangements and remedial measures, in virtue of all which we recognize it as wisdom in all her diverse applications, has nevertheless failed in the case of the elements of the universe—although they are these same elements that pervade the whole heaven on a great scale, fair moreover and untainted—failed, I say, there to contrive that which is fairest and most precious.

c   PROTARCHUS : No, to suppose that would be utterly unreasonable.

SOCRATES : Discarding that, then, we should do better to follow the other view and say, as we have said many times already, that there exist in the universe much 'unlimited' and abundance of 'limit,' and a presiding cause of no mean power, which orders and regulates the years, the seasons, and the months, and has every claim to the names of wisdom and reason.

PROTARCHUS : Every claim indeed.

SOCRATES : But wisdom and reason cannot come into existence without soul.

PROTARCHUS : They cannot.

d   SOCRATES : Hence you will say that in the nature of Zeus a royal soul and a royal reason come to dwell by virtue of the power of the cause, while in other gods other perfections dwell, according to the names by which they are pleased to be called.

PROTARCHUS : Quite so.

SOCRATES : Now don't suppose, Protarchus, that we have spoken of this matter purposelessly; on the contrary it supports those ancient thinkers that we mentioned, who declared that reason always rules all things.

PROTARCHUS : Yes indeed it does.

SOCRATES : And, what's more, it has provided an answer to my
e   inquiry, to the effect that mind belongs to the family of what we called the cause of all things. By this time, I imagine, you grasp what our answer is.

PROTARCHUS : Yes, I grasp it completely, though indeed I hadn't realized you had given it.

SOCRATES : Well, Protarchus, playfulness is sometimes a relief from seriousness.

31   PROTARCHUS : You are right.

SOCRATES : I think, my friend, that we have now arrived at a fairly satisfactory demonstration of what kind reason belongs to, and what function it possesses.

PROTARCHUS : I am sure of it.

SOCRATES : And as for pleasure's kind, that we found some time ago.

PROTARCHUS : Exactly.

SOCRATES : Then let us have these points in mind about the pair of them, namely that reason was found akin to cause and belonging, we may say, to that kind, whereas pleasure is itself unlimited and belongs to the kind that does not and never will contain within itself and derived from itself either beginning, or middle, or end.

b   PROTARCHUS : We shall bear that in mind, naturally.

SOCRATES : And now what we must do next is to see in what each of them is found, and what happens to bring it about that they occur whenever they do. Take pleasure first; we took it first when examining its kind, and we will do the same in the present case. However, we shall never be able properly to examine pleasure apart from pain.

PROTARCHUS: Well, if that ought to be our line of approach, let us take it.

SOCRATES: Now I wonder if you share my view as regards their occurrence?

PROTARCHUS: What is your view?   c

SOCRATES: That both pleasure and pain are natural experiences that occur in the 'combined' class.

PROTARCHUS: Will you remind us, my dear Socrates, which of our previously mentioned classes you allude to by the term 'combined'?

SOCRATES: Really, Protarchus! Well, I'll do my best.

PROTARCHUS: Thank you.

SOCRATES: Let us understand 'combined' as the third of our four classes.

PROTARCHUS: The one you spoke of after the unlimited and the limit, and in which you put health and harmony, I think, also.

SOCRATES: Perfectly right. Now please give me your most care- d
ful attention.

PROTARCHUS: Continue, please.

SOCRATES: I maintain that, when we find a disturbance of the harmony in a living creature, that is the time at which its natural condition is disturbed and distress therewith occurs.

PROTARCHUS: That sounds very probable.

SOCRATES: Conversely, when the harmony is being restored and a return is made to its natural condition, we may say that pleasure occurs. I am permitting myself a very brief and rapid statement of a most important fact.

PROTARCHUS: I think you are right, Socrates, but let us try to e
express this same truth even more clearly.

SOCRATES: Well, I suppose commonplace, obvious instances will be the easiest to understand.

PROTARCHUS: Such as?

SOCRATES: Hunger, say, is a form of disturbance, of pain, isn't it?

PROTARCHUS: Yes.

SOCRATES: And eating, as the corresponding restoration, is a form of pleasure?

PROTARCHUS: Yes.   32

SOCRATES: Then again, thirst is a form of destruction, of pain, whereas the restoration effected by a liquid acting on that which has become dried up is a form of pleasure. Or once again, the unnatural disruption or dissolution brought about by stifling heat is a pain, whereas the coolness which restores us to our natural state is a pleasure.

PROTARCHUS: Certainly.

SOCRATES: And the disturbance of a creature's natural state consequent on the freezing of its liquids by cold is a pain, while the reverse process, which restores that state when that which is frozen breaks up and returns to its former condition, is a pleasure. Now consider whether this statement is satisfactory, which puts the thing in a general formula. When the natural state of a living organism, con-
b stituted, as I have maintained, of the unlimited and the limit, is destroyed, that destruction is pain; conversely, when such organisms return to their own true nature, this reversion is invariably pleasure.

PROTARCHUS: So be it; I think that gives us at least an outline.

SOCRATES: Well then, may we take it that one kind of pleasure and pain consists in this pair of experiences?

PROTARCHUS: We may.

SOCRATES: Now take what the soul itself feels when expecting
c these experiences, the pleasant, confident feeling of anticipation that precedes a pleasure, and the apprehensive, distressful feeling that precedes a pain.

PROTARCHUS: Yes, of course, that is a different kind of pleasure and pain, which belongs to the soul itself, apart from the body, and arises through expectation.

SOCRATES: You grasp what I mean. I think, if I may put my own view, that by taking these two experiences pure and without any
d admixture of pain in the one case and pleasure in the other—I think that we shall get a clear answer to the question about pleasure, the question whether everything classed as pleasure is to be welcomed, or whether we ought to grant that to some other of those classes that we previously distinguished, while with pleasure and pain the case stands as with hot and cold and all things like that, namely that sometimes they are to be welcomed and sometimes are not—the reason being that they are not in themselves good, though some of them sometimes and somehow acquire the character of good things.

PROTARCHUS: You are quite right; that is the proper sort of way to thrash out the subject of our present quest.

SOCRATES: First, then, let us look together into the following point. If what we are maintaining is really true, if there is distress at
e the time of deterioration and pleasure at the time of restoration, then let us consider any such creatures as are experiencing neither deterioration nor restoration, and ask what their condition must be at the time in question. Please pay careful attention to what I ask, and tell me, is it not beyond all doubt that at such a time a creature feels neither pleasure nor pain in any degree whatever?

PROTARCHUS: Yes, it is beyond doubt.

SOCRATES: So this is a third sort of condition that we have, distinct alike from the condition of one who feels pleasure and from 33 that of one who feels pain?

PROTARCHUS: Certainly.

SOCRATES: Come along then, and do your best to bear it in mind; it will make a big difference as regards our judgment of pleasure whether you do bear it in mind or do not. Now there is a small point in this connection that we had better settle, if you please.

PROTARCHUS: Tell me what it is.

SOCRATES: You know that for one who has chosen the life of intelligence there is nothing to prevent him living in this fashion.

PROTARCHUS: A life, you mean, of neither pleasure nor pain? b

SOCRATES: Yes, for when we were comparing the lives just now we said, I believe, that for one who had chosen the life of reason and intelligence there must be no experiencing of any pleasure, great or small.

PROTARCHUS: That was certainly what we said.

SOCRATES: Then he at all events has it in his power to live after this fashion, and perhaps it is not a wild surmise that this is of all lives the most godlike.

PROTARCHUS: Certainly it is not to be supposed that the gods feel either pleasure or its opposite.

SOCRATES: No, of course it is not; it would be unseemly for either feeling to arise in them. But to that question we will give further consideration later on, if it should be relevant, and we will set c down the point to the score of intelligence in the competition for second prize, if we cannot do so in the competition for the first.

PROTARCHUS: Quite right.

SOCRATES: Now to continue, pleasure of this second kind, which belongs, as we said, to the soul alone, always involves memory.

PROTARCHUS: How so?

SOCRATES: I fancy that we must first take up the inquiry what memory is, or perhaps even, before memory, what sensation is, if we mean to get properly clear about these matters.

PROTARCHUS: What do you mean? d

SOCRATES: You must take it that among the experiences that are constantly affecting our bodies some are exhausted in the body before passing through to the soul, thus leaving the latter unaffected, while others penetrate both body and soul and set up a sort of disturbance which is both peculiar to each and common to both.

PROTARCHUS: Let us take it to be so.

SOCRATES: Now shall we be right if we say that those which do not penetrate both are undetected by the soul, while those which do penetrate both are not undetected thereby?

PROTARCHUS: Of course. e

SOCRATES: You must not suppose that by 'being undetected' I

mean that a process of forgetting is involved; forgetting is the passing away of memory, whereas in the case we are discussing memory has not as yet come to be, and it would be absurd to talk of the loss of what does not exist and never has existed, would it not?

PROTARCHUS: Of course.

SOCRATES: Then just alter the names.

PROTARCHUS: How?

34   SOCRATES: Instead of speaking, as you now do, of 'forgetting' what is undetected by the soul when it is unaffected by the disturbances of the body, you must substitute the term 'nonsensation.'

PROTARCHUS: I understand.

SOCRATES: And if you apply to that movement, which occurs when soul and body come together in a single affection and are moved both together, the term 'sensation,' you will be expressing yourself properly.

PROTARCHUS: Very true.

SOCRATES: Then we understand already what we mean by sensation.

PROTARCHUS: Certainly.

SOCRATES: Memory it would, in my opinion, be right to call the preservation of sensation.

b   PROTARCHUS: Quite so.

SOCRATES: Then by 'recollection' we mean, do we not, something different from memory?

PROTARCHUS: I suppose so.

SOCRATES: I will suggest the point of difference.

PROTARCHUS: What is it?

SOCRATES: When that which has been experienced by the soul in common with the body is recaptured, so far as may be, by and in the soul itself apart from the body, then we speak of 'recollecting' some-
c thing. Is that not so?

PROTARCHUS: Undoubtedly.

SOCRATES: And further, when the soul that has lost the memory of a sensation or what it has learned resumes that memory within itself and goes over the old ground, we regularly speak of these processes as 'recollections.'

PROTARCHUS: I agree.

SOCRATES: And now I will tell you the point of all we have been saying.

PROTARCHUS: What is it?

SOCRATES: To get the clearest notion that we possibly can of the pleasure of soul apart from body, and of desire as well. I think that the procedure we are adopting promises to explain them both.

PROTARCHUS: Let us proceed then, Socrates.

SOCRATES: Our examination will necessarily, I think, involve
d saying a good deal about the origin of pleasure and the various shapes

it takes. And in point of fact it seems necessary to preface that with an understanding of the nature of desire and the seat of its occurrence.

PROTARCHUS: Then let us examine that; we shan't be the losers.

SOCRATES: Oh yes we shall, Protarchus, and I'll tell you of what; if we find what we are now looking for, we shall be the losers of the very perplexity that now besets us.

PROTARCHUS: A good retort! Then let us try to deal with our next point.

SOCRATES: Were we not saying just now that hunger, thirst, e and so on and so forth, are desires of some sort?

PROTARCHUS: Unquestionably.

SOCRATES: What was the identical feature, then, that we had in view that makes us call such widely different things by one name?

PROTARCHUS: Upon my word, Socrates, I'm afraid it is not easy to answer that; still, answer it we must.

SOCRATES: Then let us go back to where we were and start afresh.

PROTARCHUS: Go back where?

SOCRATES: We talk commonly, do we not, of a man 'having a thirst'?

PROTARCHUS: Certainly.

SOCRATES: Meaning that he is becoming empty?

PROTARCHUS: Of course.

SOCRATES: Then is his thirst a desire?

PROTARCHUS: Yes, a desire for drink.

SOCRATES: For drink, or for a replenishment by drink?   35

PROTARCHUS: For a replenishment, I should think.

SOCRATES: When one becomes empty then, apparently he desires the opposite of what he is experiencing; being emptied, he longs to be filled.

PROTARCHUS: Obviously.

SOCRATES: Well now, is it possible that one who is emptied for the first time could apprehend replenishment whether by means of a perception or a memory, replenishment being something that he is neither experiencing in the present nor has ever experienced in the past?

PROTARCHUS: Of course not.

SOCRATES: Nevertheless we must admit that one who desires, b desires something.

PROTARCHUS: Yes, of course.

SOCRATES: Then it is not what he is experiencing that he desires, for he is thirsty, and thirst is an emptying, whereas what he desires is replenishment.

PROTARCHUS: Yes.

SOCRATES: Then there must be something in the make-up of a thirsty man which apprehends replenishment.

PROTARCHUS: Necessarily.

SOCRATES: And it cannot be the body, for that of course is being emptied.

PROTARCHUS: No.

SOCRATES: Hence the only alternative is that the soul apprehends the replenishment, and does so obviously through memory. For c through what else could it do so?

PROTARCHUS: It's hard to point to anything else.

SOCRATES: Then do we realize what has emerged from this discussion?

PROTARCHUS: What?

SOCRATES: It has told us that desire does not belong to the body.

PROTARCHUS: How so?

SOCRATES: Because it has revealed that the effort of every creature is opposed to that which its body is experiencing.

PROTARCHUS: Quite so.

SOCRATES: Moreover, the fact that impulse leads the creature in a direction opposite to its experience proves, I fancy, the existence of a memory of something opposite to that experience.

PROTARCHUS: Undoubtedly.

d   SOCRATES: Our discussion then, inasmuch as it has proved that memory is what leads us on to the objects of our desire, has made it plain that it is to the soul that all impulse and desire, and indeed the determining principle of the whole creature, belong.

PROTARCHUS: You are perfectly right.

SOCRATES: Then there can be no gainsaying that our bodies cannot possibly feel thirst or hunger or anything of that sort?

PROTARCHUS: Very true.

SOCRATES: Now here is a further point that calls for our remark in this same connection. It seems to me that our argument aims at revealing a certain sort of life amidst these very things we have been speaking of.

e   PROTARCHUS: What things? What kind of life are you speaking of?

SOCRATES: The processes of replenishment and being emptied, in fact all processes concerned with the preservation or decay of living beings, and our alternating feelings of distress and pleasure, according as we pass from one of these processes to the other.

PROTARCHUS: Quite so.

SOCRATES: And what about such times as we are in an intermediate state?

PROTARCHUS: Intermediate?

SOCRATES: When we feel distress by reason of what we are ex-

periencing, and at the same time remember the pleasures whose occurrence would relieve our distress, though the replenishment in
question is still in the future. How do we stand then? May we say that
we are in an intermediate state, or may we not?   36

PROTARCHUS: By all means.

SOCRATES: And is the state as a whole one of distress or of
pleasure?

PROTARCHUS: Pleasure! No, indeed, rather a state of twofold
pain, pain of the body in respect of its actual experience, and pain of
the soul in respect of an unsatisfied expectation.

SOCRATES: What makes you call it twofold pain, Protarchus?
Is it not the case that sometimes the emptying process is associated
with a distinct hope of coming replenishment, while at other times
there is no such hope?   b

PROTARCHUS: Yes, of course.

SOCRATES: Then don't you think that when hoping for replenishment we feel pleasure through what we remember, though
nevertheless we feel pain simultaneously because of the emptying
process going on at the times in question?

PROTARCHUS: Yes, no doubt.

SOCRATES: At such a time then men, and animals too, feel both
pain and pleasure at once.

PROTARCHUS: It looks like it.

SOCRATES: Now take the case when we are being emptied and
have no hope of attaining replenishment. Is it not then that there occurs that twofold feeling of pain which you descried just now, though
you thought the pain to be 'simply double,' drawing no distinctions? c

PROTARCHUS: Very true, Socrates.

SOCRATES: Now let me suggest a use to which we may put our
examination of these experiences.

PROTARCHUS: What is it?

SOCRATES: Shall we say that these pains and pleasures are true
or false? Or that some are true, and others not?

PROTARCHUS: But how, Socrates, can pleasures or pains be
false?

SOCRATES: How can fears be true or false, Protarchus? Or expectations, or opinions?

PROTARCHUS: For myself, I should be inclined to allow it in d
the case of opinions, but not in the other cases.

SOCRATES: What's that? It really looks as if we were raising a
question of no small magnitude.

PROTARCHUS: That is true.

SOCRATES: But is it relevant to what has preceded? Philebus
the younger should ask himself that question.

PROTARCHUS: That question perhaps, yes.

SOCRATES: Anyhow, we ought to have nothing to do with extraneous disquisitions, or with anything in the way of irrelevant discussion.

PROTARCHUS: You are right.

e   SOCRATES: Now tell me this. I have felt curious ever so long about these same problems that we raised just now. What do you maintain? Are there not false, as opposed to true, pleasures?

PROTARCHUS: How could that be?

SOCRATES: Then, according to you, no one, be he dreaming or waking, or insane or deranged, ever thinks that he feels pleasure but does not really feel it, or thinks he feels pain, but does not really feel it.

PROTARCHUS: All of us, Socrates, regard all that as holding good.

37   SOCRATES: Well, are you right? Ought we not to consider whether what you say is right or wrong?

PROTARCHUS: I think we ought.

SOCRATES: Then let us state in even plainer terms what you were just now saying about pleasure and opinion. There is such a thing, I imagine, as holding an opinion?

PROTARCHUS: Yes.

SOCRATES: And as feeling a pleasure?

PROTARCHUS: Yes.

SOCRATES: Is there also that about which the opinion is held?

PROTARCHUS: Of course.

SOCRATES: And that in which the pleasure is felt?

PROTARCHUS: Undoubtedly.

SOCRATES: Then the subject holding an opinion, whether it be rightly or wrongly held, is always in the position of really holding an opinion?

b   PROTARCHUS: Of course.

SOCRATES: And similarly the subject feeling pleasure, whether it be rightly or wrongly felt, will obviously be always in the position of really feeling a pleasure?

PROTARCHUS: Yes, that is so too.

SOCRATES: The question then must be faced, how it is that whereas we commonly find opinion both true and false, pleasure is true only, and that though in respect of reality holding an opinion and feeling a pleasure are on the same footing.

PROTARCHUS: Yes, that question must be faced.

SOCRATES: Is the point this, do you think, that in the case of opinion falsehood and truth supervene, with the result that it becomes c not merely an opinion but a certain sort of opinion, true or false, respectively?

PROTARCHUS: Yes.

SOCRATES: But then we have got a further question on which

we must come to an agreement, namely whether it is at all possible that, as against other things that have quality, pleasure and pain never have qualities but are simply what they are.

PROTARCHUS: Clearly so.

SOCRATES: But in point of fact it is easy to see that actually they do have qualities; we spoke a while ago of their being great, small, and intense, pains and pleasures alike.

PROTARCHUS: To be sure we did.   d

SOCRATES: And what's more, Protarchus, if badness is added to any of the things in question, shall we not say that it thereby becomes a bad opinion, and similarly a bad pleasure?

PROTARCHUS: Why, of course, Socrates.

SOCRATES: Once again, if rightness or its opposite is added to any of them, presumably we shall say that an opinion, if it has rightness, is right, and the same with a pleasure?

PROTARCHUS: Necessarily.

SOCRATES: But if the content of an opinion that is held be mis- e taken, then must we not agree that the opinion, inasmuch as it is making a mistake, is not right, not opining rightly?

PROTARCHUS: No, it cannot be.

SOCRATES: Well then, if we observe a pain or a pleasure making a mistake in regard to the object arousing the respective feelings, shall we attach to it any term of commendation such as 'right' or 'sound'?

PROTARCHUS: Impossible, if the pleasure is ex hypothesi mistaken.

SOCRATES: Now look here, I fancy we often experience pleasure in association with an opinion that is not right, but false.

PROTARCHUS: Of course, and then, that being so, Socrates, we 38 call the opinion false, but the pleasure itself nobody could ever term false.

SOCRATES: Well, Protarchus, you are putting up a gallant defense of the cause of pleasure by what you say now.

PROTARCHUS: Oh no, I am merely repeating what I have heard.

SOCRATES: But do we find no difference, my friend, between a pleasure associated with right opinion and knowledge and one associated, as is constantly happening to every one of us, with false opinion and ignorance?

PROTARCHUS: I should say they differ considerably.   b

SOCRATES: Then let us proceed to contemplate the difference.

PROTARCHUS: Pray take the road on which you descry it.

SOCRATES: Very well, I will take you along this one.

PROTARCHUS: Yes?

SOCRATES: Opinion, we agree, is sometimes false, sometimes true?

PROTARCHUS: That is so.

SOCRATES: And, as we said just now, pleasure and pain frequently accompany these true and false opinions.

PROTARCHUS: Quite so.

SOCRATES: Now is it not always memory and perception that give rise to opinion and to the attempts we make to reach a judgment?

c   PROTARCHUS: Certainly.

SOCRATES: Let me suggest what we must believe to occur in this connection.

PROTARCHUS: Well?

SOCRATES: If a man sees objects that come into his view from a distance and indistinctly, would you agree that he commonly wants to decide about what he sees?

PROTARCHUS: I should.

SOCRATES: Then the next step will be that he puts a question to himself.

PROTARCHUS: What question?

SOCRATES: 'What is that object which catches my eye there beside the rock under a tree?' Don't you think that is what he would say to himself, if he had caught sight of some appearance of the sort?

PROTARCHUS: Of course.

SOCRATES: And then he would answer his own question and say, if he got it right, 'It is a man.'

PROTARCHUS: Certainly.

SOCRATES: Or again, if he went astray and thought what he was looking at was something made by shepherds, he might very likely call it an image.

PROTARCHUS: He might quite well.

e   SOCRATES: And if he had someone with him, he would put what he said to himself into actual speech addressed to his companion, audibly uttering those same thoughts, so that what before we called opinion has now become assertion.

PROTARCHUS: Of course.

SOCRATES: Whereas if he is alone he continues thinking the same thing by himself, going on his way maybe for a considerable time with the thought in his mind.

PROTARCHUS: Undoubtedly.

SOCRATES: Well now, I wonder whether you share my view on these matters.

PROTARCHUS: What is it?

SOCRATES: It seems to me that at such times our soul is like a book.

PROTARCHUS: How so?

39   SOCRATES: It appears to me that the conjunction of memory with sensations, together with the feelings consequent upon memory

and sensation, may be said as it were to write words in our souls. And when this experience writes what is true, the result is that true opinion and true assertions spring up in us, while when the internal scribe that I have suggested writes what is false we get the opposite sort of opinions and assertions.

PROTARCHUS: That certainly seems to me right, and I approve of the way you put it.

SOCRATES: Then please give your approval to the presence of a b second artist in our souls at such a time.

PROTARCHUS: Who is that?

SOCRATES: A painter, who comes after the writer and paints in the soul pictures of these assertions that we make.

PROTARCHUS: How do we make out that he in his turn acts, and when?

SOCRATES: When we have got those opinions and assertions clear of the act of sight, or other sense, and as it were see in ourselves pictures or images of what we previously opined or asserted. That does happen with us, doesn't it? c

PROTARCHUS: Indeed it does.

SOCRATES: Then are the pictures of true opinions and assertions true, and the pictures of false ones false?

PROTARCHUS: Unquestionably.

SOCRATES: Well, if we are right so far, here is one more point in this connection for us to consider.

PROTARCHUS: What is that?

SOCRATES: Does all this necessarily befall us in respect of the present and the past, but not in respect of the future?

PROTARCHUS: On the contrary, it applies equally to them all.

SOCRATES: We said previously, did we not, that pleasures and d pains felt in the soul alone might precede those that come through the body? That must mean that we have anticipatory pleasures and anticipatory pains in regard to the future.

PROTARCHUS: Very true.

SOCRATES: Now do those writings and paintings, which a while ago we assumed to occur within ourselves, apply to past and present only, and not to the future? e

PROTARCHUS: Indeed they do.

SOCRATES: When you say 'indeed they do," do you mean that the last sort are all expectations concerned with what is to come, and that we are full of expectations all our life long?

PROTARCHUS: Undoubtedly.

SOCRATES: Well now, here is a further question for you to answer.

PROTARCHUS: Yes?

SOCRATES: Isn't a man who is just, pious, and in every way good dear to the gods?

PROTARCHUS : To be sure.

SOCRATES : And may not the opposite be said of one who is unjust and altogether bad?

40   PROTARCHUS : Of course.

SOCRATES : But every human being, as we said just now, is full of expectations?

PROTARCHUS : Certainly.

SOCRATES : But what we call expectations are in fact assertions that each of us makes to himself.

PROTARCHUS : Yes.

SOCRATES : To which must be added the representations produced by our painter. People often have visions of securing great quantites of gold, and pleasure upon pleasure in consequence; indeed they behold themselves in the picture immensely delighted with themselves.

b   PROTARCHUS : I know.

SOCRATES : Now may we say that what is written in the minds of the good is as a rule a true communication, since they are dear to the gods, while with the evil the opposite as a rule is the case? What do you think?

PROTARCHUS : Certainly we should say so.

c   SOCRATES : So the evil, no less than the good, have pleasures painted in their minds, but these pleasures, I imagine, are false.

PROTARCHUS : Of course.

SOCRATES : Bad men, then, delight for the most part in false pleasures, good men in true ones.

PROTARCHUS : Inevitably so.

SOCRATES : Hence we reach the result that false pleasures do exist in men's souls, being really a rather ridiculous imitation of true pleasures, and the same applies to pains.

PROTARCHUS : Yes, they do exist.

SOCRATES : Now we found that, though a person holding any opinion at all must hold it in fact, yet it might sometimes have reference to what was not a fact, either of the present, the past, or the future.

PROTARCHUS : Quite so.

d   SOCRATES : And there, I think, lay the source of our false opinion, of our holding opinions falsely. Did it not?

PROTARCHUS : Yes.

SOCRATES : Well then, should we not ascribe a corresponding condition, as regards these references, to pains and pleasures?

PROTARCHUS : How do you mean?

SOCRATES : I mean that though anyone who feels pleasure at all, no matter how groundless it be, always really feels that pleasure; yet sometimes it has no reference to any present or past fact, while in many cases, perhaps in most, it has reference to what never will be a fact.

PROTARCHUS: That too must be so, Socrates.   e

SOCRATES: Now will not the same principle hold good in respect of fear, anger, and all such feelings, namely that all of them are sometimes false?

PROTARCHUS: Assuredly.

SOCRATES: Tell me now, can we distinguish bad opinions from good in any other respect than their falsity?

PROTARCHUS: No.

SOCRATES: Then neither can we detect any other sense in which 41 pleasures are bad, save in that they are false.

PROTARCHUS: No, Socrates, what you say is just the opposite of the truth. Surely it is not at all because they are false that we set down pains and pleasures as bad, but because they involve some serious and considerable badness of another sort.

SOCRATES: Well, these bad pleasures whose character is due to badness we will speak of a little later on, if we still think fit to do so. We must, however, discuss those false pleasures—and they are numer- b ous and frequent—which exist or come to exist in us in another way. Maybe we shall find this useful for the decisions we have to make.

PROTARCHUS: Yes, of course, if there are any.

SOCRATES: Well, Protarchus, as I see it, there are. But of course we must not allow this belief to go unexamined until we have got it established.

PROTARCHUS: Very good.

SOCRATES: Then let us take up our positions for this next round in the argument.

PROTARCHUS: On we go.

SOCRATES: Well now, we said a while back, if our memory is correct, that when we have within us what we call 'desires,' the body c stands aloof from the soul and parts company with it in respect of its affections.

PROTARCHUS: Our memory is correct; we did say so.

SOCRATES: It was the soul, was it not, that desired a condition opposite to that of the body, and it was the body that caused our distress, or our pleasure, because of the way it was affected?

PROTARCHUS: It was.

SOCRATES: Then draw the inference in regard to what is happening.

PROTARCHUS: Tell me.

SOCRATES: Well, what happens at such a time is this. Pains and pleasures exist side by side; opposite as they are, we experience d them simultaneously, one beside the other, as appeared just now.

PROTARCHUS: It appears so, certainly.

SOCRATES: There is a further point that we have mentioned and agreed upon already as established, is there not?

PROTARCHUS: What is that?

SOCRATES: That pain and pleasure, both of them, admit of the more and the less, that is they belong to what is unlimited.

PROTARCHUS: We did say so. What then?

SOCRATES: What means have we of getting a right decision about these things?

e   PROTARCHUS: Decision? In what sense do you mean?

SOCRATES: I mean that our resolve to get a decision in these matters regularly takes some such form as seeking to determine the comparative magnitude, or degree, or intensity, of a pain and a pleasure, or of one pain or pleasure as against another.

PROTARCHUS: Yes, those are the kind of questions; that is what we want to decide.

42   SOCRATES: Well now, if it is true that, in the case of vision, to observe magnitudes from a distance and from close at hand obscures the truth and engenders false judgment, does not the same hold good in the case of pains and pleasures?

PROTARCHUS: Yes, Socrates, and to a much greater degree.

SOCRATES: So here we have the reverse of what we spoke of a little while ago.

PROTARCHUS: Have we? How?

SOCRATES: Just now it was the falsity or truth of those opin-
b ions that infected the pains and pleasures with what they had caught themselves.

PROTARCHUS: Very true.

SOCRATES: But now the reason why pleasures appear greater and more intense when compared with something painful, or again, in the reverse case, pains appear so by being compared with pleasures, is found in the pleasures and pains per se, according as we pass from a distant to a close observation of them, and set them beside one another.

PROTARCHUS: The reason for what you describe must necessarily be as you say.

SOCRATES: Then if you subtract from each that unreal and only apparent excess which makes them look respectively greater or
c smaller than they really are, you will acknowledge the subtracted portion to be an incorrect appearance, and you will refrain from asserting that such pleasure or pain as is felt in respect of that portion is correct and true.

PROTARCHUS: Yes indeed.

SOCRATES: And next, if we take the road ahead of us, we shall discern pleasures and pains in living beings that appear false and are false, even more so than this last kind.

PROTARCHUS: What do you mean? What are they?

SOCRATES: It has often been said, I think, that when the natural state of an organism is impaired by processes of combination
d and separation, of filling and emptying, and by certain kinds of growth

and decay, the result is pain, distress, suffering—in fact everything that we denote by names like these.

PROTARCHUS: Yes, that has often been said.

SOCRATES: And when the organisms are being established in their natural state, we satisfied ourselves that that establishment is a pleasure.

PROTARCHUS: And rightly so.

SOCRATES: But suppose none of these processes is going on in our body.

PROTARCHUS: When could that be so, Socrates?

SOCRATES: There, Protarchus, you have put a question that is e not to the point.

PROTARCHUS: Why not?

SOCRATES: Because you don't prevent me from repeating my own inquiry.

PROTARCHUS: What inquiry?

SOCRATES: What I shall say is, supposing, Protarchus, that nothing of the kind were to be going on, what inference should we have to draw?

PROTARCHUS: You mean, if the body is not experiencing movement in either direction?

SOCRATES: Yes.

PROTARCHUS: Then one thing at all events is plain, Socrates; in such a case there can be no pleasure and no pain.

SOCRATES: You are perfectly right. But I expect you are going 43 to tell me that we are assured by the wise that one of these processes must always be going on in us, since all things are always flowing up and down.

PROTARCHUS: Yes, they do assert that, and it is thought to carry some weight.

SOCRATES: Naturally. They are weighty persons. But as a matter of fact I should like to dodge this argument that is advancing upon us. Here is my intended line of retreat, on which I hope you will accompany me.

PROTARCHUS: Please explain the direction.

SOCRATES: Let us reply to them 'so be it,' but here is a question for yourself. Is a living being always conscious of everything that b happens to it? Do we invariably notice that we are growing, and so on, or is that quite the reverse of the truth?

PROTARCHUS: Surely it is absolutely the reverse; almost all such processes pass unnoticed by us.

SOCRATES: Then we are not right in what was said just now, to the effect that changes up and down produce pains and pleasures.

PROTARCHUS: Of course not.

SOCRATES: I will suggest a better formula, and one less open to c attack.

PROTARCHUS: Yes?

SOCRATES: Great changes cause us pains and pleasures, but moderate and small ones cause no pain or pleasure whatsoever.

PROTARCHUS: You are nearer the truth than you were, Socrates.

SOCRATES: Then, if that be so, here we are back again at the life we mentioned a while ago.

PROTARCHUS: What life?

SOCRATES: The one we described as painless, and devoid of joys.

PROTARCHUS: Very true.

SOCRATES: In view of this, let us recognize three sorts of life, d the pleasant, the painful, and that which is neither one nor the other. Or how do you see the matter?

PROTARCHUS: I see it precisely as you put it; the lives are three in number.

SOCRATES: Then to be without pain will not be the same as to feel pleasure?

PROTARCHUS: Certainly not.

SOCRATES: So when you hear someone say that the pleasantest of all things is to live one's whole life long without pain, what do you take his meaning to be?

PROTARCHUS: He appears to me to mean that being without pain is pleasant.

e   SOCRATES: Well now, let us take any three things you like, and, to give them more attractive names, call the first gold, the second silver, and the third neither gold nor silver.

PROTARCHUS: I accept that.

SOCRATES: Now can we possibly identify the third with either of the others, with gold or silver?

PROTARCHUS: No, of course not.

SOCRATES: Similarly then, it cannot be right either to hold the intermediate life to be pleasant or painful, if it is a question of holding an opinion, or, to speak of it so, if it is a question of speaking, unless indeed we desert right reasoning.

PROTARCHUS: It cannot.

44   SOCRATES: Still, my friend, we do observe people saying and thinking so.

PROTARCHUS: We do, certainly.

SOCRATES: Do they then think that at such times as they are not feeling pain they are feeling pleasure?

PROTARCHUS: They say so at all events.

SOCRATES: Then they do think so; otherwise they would not say so, I imagine.

PROTARCHUS: Maybe.

SOCRATES: Nevertheless their opinion about their feeling of

pleasure is false, if not being pained and feeling pleasure are really two different things.

PROTARCHUS: And different they have certainly proved.

SOCRATES: Then are we to take the line that these things are three in number, as we said just now, or that they are only two, pain being an evil for mankind, and release from pain being called pleasant b as in itself a good?

PROTARCHUS: How can we put that question to ourselves, Socrates, at this stage? I don't understand.

SOCRATES: The fact is, Protarchus, you don't understand what enemies Philebus here has.

PROTARCHUS: What enemies do you mean?

SOCRATES: People with a great reputation for natural science, who maintain that pleasures do not exist at all.

PROTARCHUS: Oh, how so?

SOCRATES: What Philebus and his friends call pleasures are, c according to them, never anything but escapes from pains.

PROTARCHUS: And do you recommend that we should believe them, Socrates, or what do you think?

SOCRATES: Not believe them, but avail ourselves of their gift of divination, which rests not on science but on the dourness, if I may call it so, of a nature far from ignoble. They are men who have come to hate pleasure bitterly, to regard it as thoroughly unsound; its very attractiveness they regard, not as real pleasure, but as trickery. Well, d you may avail yourself of their doctrine on this point, having regard at the same time to their other dour characteristics, and next you shall learn what pleasures I regard as true, so that when we have examined the nature of pleasure from both points of view we may have a comparative basis for our decision.

PROTARCHUS: Very good.

SOCRATES: Then let us follow up the track of these allies of ours, and see where their dour footsteps lead us. I fancy that their basic position is stated something like this. If we want to see the true nature of any form, whatever it may be, for example that of hardness, should we understand it best by fixing our attention on the hardest e things there are or on those that have a minimum of hardness? Now, Protarchus, you must answer our dour friends just as you would answer me.

PROTARCHUS: Quite so, and I tell them that our attention must be fixed on what has the maximum amount.

SOCRATES: Then if the form or kind whose true nature we wanted to see were pleasure, we should have to fix our attention not on minimum pleasures but on such as are said to be the highest and 45 intensest.

PROTARCHUS: Everyone would agree with what you say now.

SOCRATES: Now are not our obvious pleasures, which are in

fact by common admission the greatest, the pleasures of the body?

PROTARCHUS : Of course.

SOCRATES : And are they, or do they become, greater with those who are suffering from sickness or with healthy people? Now let us be careful not to take a false step by answering hastily. I dare say we
b shall be inclined to say, with healthy people.

PROTARCHUS : Probably.

SOCRATES : But tell me, are not the outstanding pleasures those which are preceded by the greatest desires?

PROTARCHUS : That is true.

SOCRATES : And isn't it the man suffering from a fever or some similar complaint who feels thirst and cold and all the common bodily troubles more than others, who is more than others acquainted with want, and who when the want comes to be satisfied has greater pleasures? Shall we not admit that to be true?

PROTARCHUS : Yes, it certainly seems true, now you put it so.

c SOCRATES : Well then, should we be plainly right if we said that anyone wishing to see the greatest pleasures should direct his attention not to health, but to sickness? You must be careful not to take me as intending to ask you whether the extremely sick have *more* pleasures than the healthy; you must realize that it is the magnitude of pleasure that I am concerned with. I am asking where instances of the extreme in point of magnitude are to be found. We must, as we said, understand the true nature of pleasure, and what account they give who maintain that there is no such thing at all.

d PROTARCHUS : I follow your meaning pretty well.

SOCRATES : I dare say, Protarchus, you will do just as well as my guide. Tell me this. In a profligate existence do you find greater pleasures—not *more* pleasures, mind you, but pleasures that stand out as extreme or in point of degree—than in a life of temperance? Give your mind to it, and tell me.

PROTARCHUS : I understand your point, and I find a wide difference. The temperate man, surely, is regularly restrained by the prover-
e bial warning, 'Never too much,' and heeds it, whereas the senseless profligate is mastered by his extreme pleasure, which ultimately drives him insane and makes him the talk of the town.

SOCRATES : Right. Then if that is so, clearly the greatest pleasures, and the greatest pains too, occur not when soul and body are good, but when they are bad.

46 PROTARCHUS : Certainly.

SOCRATES : And now we ought to select some of these and consider what characteristic made us call them the greatest.

PROTARCHUS : Yes, we must.

SOCRATES : Well, here is a type of malady, with pleasures whose characteristics I should like you to examine.

PROTARCHUS: What type is it?

SOCRATES: The offensive type, with its pleasures which are so thoroughly distasteful to the dour people we were speaking of.

PROTARCHUS: What pleasures are they?

SOCRATES: Relieving an itch, for example, by rubbing, and anything that calls for that sort of remedy. When we find ourselves experiencing that kind of thing, what, in heaven's name, are we to call it? Pleasure or pain?

PROTARCHUS: Well that, Socrates, I really think might be described as a mixed experience.

SOCRATES: Of course I did not introduce the subject with any b reference to Philebus, but without a look at these pleasures and others associated with them I hardly think we shall be able to settle the question before us.

PROTARCHUS: Then we must proceed to attack the kindred pleasures.

SOCRATES: You mean those that share that characteristic of mixture?

PROTARCHUS: Exactly.

SOCRATES: Well, some of the mixtures concern the body and are found in the body alone, while others are found in the soul and belong to the soul alone, and thirdly we shall discover cases of pains being mixed with pleasures that involve both soul and body, where the total experience is sometimes called pleasure, sometimes pain.

PROTARCHUS: What do you mean?

SOCRATES: When the natural state of an organism is being established or impaired, it may be subject to two opposite experiences at once. It may be warmed while shivering, or again cooled while burning. It is seeking, I imagine, to attain one thing and get rid of the other, and the 'bittersweet' mixture, if I may use the current phrase, when it is hard to get rid of the thing, causes an uneasiness which develops d into fierce excitement.

PROTARCHUS: What you are now saying is very true.

SOCRATES: Now in mixtures like these are not the pains and pleasures sometimes equal, while sometimes one or the other predominates?

PROTARCHUS: Of course.

SOCRATES: In the class in which the pains predominate over the pleasures you must count those pleasures of itching that we were speaking of, and of tickling. When the irritation or inflammation is internal, and by rubbing and scratching you fail to reach it and merely tear the surface skin, then, by bringing the parts affected near a fire e and seeking to reverse your condition by means of the heat it gives out, you procure at one moment immense pleasure, at another a contrast between interior and exterior, a combination of pains with pleasures,

the balance tilting now this way now that, this being due to the forci-
47 ble tearing apart of what was compact or the compressing of what
was diffused.

PROTARCHUS: Very true.

SOCRATES: On the other hand when anything of this kind is
happening and pleasure preponderates in the mixture, although the
slight element of pain causes a tickling and a mild uneasiness, yet the
inflowing stream of pleasure, which is much stronger, excites you and
sometimes makes you jump for joy; it produces all manner of varieties
in your complexion, in your attitude, in the very breath you draw, and
drives you clean out of your wits, shouting aloud like a lunatic.

b   PROTARCHUS: Yes indeed.

SOCRATES: And what's more, my friend, it makes people say of
themselves, and makes others say of them, that they are almost dying
of delight in these pleasures, and I would add that the more of a fool
and profligate a man is, the more wholeheartedly is he sure to pursue
them, calling them the greatest pleasures and accounting such as have
the greatest amount thereof in their lives the happiest of beings.

PROTARCHUS: Everything, Socrates, that most people agree in
thinking, is covered by your exposition.

c   SOCRATES: Yes, Protarchus, as far as concerns those pleasures
in which it is merely the body's superficial and internal parts that are
interconnected in mutual affections. But there are cases in which the
soul's contribution is opposed to that of the body, whether it be pain
as against the body's pleasure or pleasure as against the body's pain,
so that the two unite to form a single compound. These we discussed
previously, showing that at such times as we are emptied we desire
replenishment, and that we delight in the expectation of replenishment but are distressed by the process of emptying, but there is one
thing that we did not declare then but assert now, namely that in all
d these innumerable instances in which soul is at variance with body,
we find a single type of the mixture of pain and pleasure.

PROTARCHUS: I am inclined to think you are quite right.

SOCRATES: And now we have still left one more mixture of
pain and pleasure.

PROTARCHUS: Which is that?

SOCRATES: That mingling which, as we mentioned, the soul
alone takes to itself.

PROTARCHUS: In what sense do we maintain that?

e   SOCRATES: Anger, fear, longing, lamenting, love, emulation,
malice, and so forth—don't you class these as pains of the soul itself?

PROTARCHUS: I do.

SOCRATES: And shall we not find them replete with immense
pleasures? Or need we remind ourselves of that feature of passion
and anger—of the lines:

Wrath that spurs on the wisest mind to rage,
Sweeter by far than stream of flowing honey,[1]

or of the pleasures mixed up with the pains in lamentation and long-ing?

PROTARCHUS: No, what you say is precisely what must happen.

SOCRATES: Then again do you remember how spectators of a   48
tragedy sometimes feel pleasure and weep at once?

PROTARCHUS: Yes indeed.

SOCRATES: And if you take the state of our minds when we see
a comedy, do you realize that here again we have a mixture of pain
and pleasure?

PROTARCHUS: I don't quite take your meaning.

SOCRATES: No, Protarchus, for it is by no means easy to under-   b
stand that we are regularly affected in this way on such an occasion.

PROTARCHUS: It certainly does not seem easy to me.

SOCRATES: Still, the obscurity of the matter ought to make us
all the more eager to grasp it; we may make it easier for people to realize the mixture of pain and pleasure in other cases.

PROTARCHUS: Pray go on.

SOCRATES: We mentioned malice just now. Would you call
that a pain of the soul, or what?

PROTARCHUS: Yes.

SOCRATES: Nevertheless one will find the malicious man
pleased at his neighbors' ills.

PROTARCHUS: Undoubtedly.   c

SOCRATES: Now ignorance, or the condition we call stupidity,
is an ill thing.

PROTARCHUS: Well?

SOCRATES: That being so, observe the nature of the ridiculous.

PROTARCHUS: Be kind enough to tell me.

SOCRATES: Taking it generally it is a certain kind of badness,
and it gets its name from a certain state of mind. I may add that it is
that species of the genus 'badness' which is differentiated by the opposite of the inscription at Delphi.

PROTARCHUS: You mean, 'Know thyself,' Socrates?

SOCRATES: I do. Plainly the opposite of that would be for the
inscription to read, 'By no means know thyself.'   d

PROTARCHUS: Of course.

SOCRATES: Now, Protarchus, that is what you must split up
into three parts; see if you can.

PROTARCHUS: How do you mean? I am quite sure I can't.

---

[1] *Iliad* 18.109 sq.

SOCRATES: Do you then mean that I must make this division, here and now?

PROTARCHUS: That is what I mean, and indeed I beg you to do so.

SOCRATES: If anyone does not know himself, must it not be in one of three ways?

PROTARCHUS: How so?

e   SOCRATES: First, in respect of wealth, he may think himself richer than his property makes him.

PROTARCHUS: Plenty of people are affected that way, certainly.

SOCRATES: But there are even more who think themselves taller and more handsome and physically finer in general than they really and truly are.

PROTARCHUS: Quite so.

SOCRATES: But far the greatest number are mistaken as regards the third class of things, namely possessions of the soul. They
49 think themselves superior in virtue, when they are not.

PROTARCHUS: Yes indeed.

SOCRATES: And is it not the virtue of wisdom that the mass of men insist on claiming, interminably disputing, and lying about how wise they are?

PROTARCHUS: Of course.

SOCRATES: And certainly we should be justified in calling all such behavior as this evil.

PROTARCHUS: Undoubtedly.

SOCRATES: Well now, Protarchus, it is this that we must once more divide, by bisection, if we mean to see that curious mixture of pleasure and pain that lies in the malice that goes with entertainment.
b   How then, you will ask, do we make our bisection? All persons who are foolish enough to hold this false opinion about themselves fall, I think, like mankind in general, into two classes, those who are strong and powerful and those who are the reverse.

PROTARCHUS: Indubitably.

SOCRATES: Then make that your principle of division. Those whose delusion is accompanied by weakness, who are unable to retaliate when laughed at, you will be right in describing by the epithet 'ridiculous'; to those that have the ability and strength to retaliate you will most appropriately accord the epithets 'formidable' and 'hateful.'
c   For ignorance in the strong is hateful and ugly; it is fraught with mischief to all around, and so are its copies on the stage, but weak ignorance ranks as the ridiculous, which in fact it is.

PROTARCHUS: You are perfectly right. All the same, I am not yet clear about the mixture of pleasures and pains here.

SOCRATES: Well, take first the nature of malice.

PROTARCHUS: Pray continue.
d   SOCRATES: Both pain and pleasure can be wrongful, I imagine?

PROTARCHUS: Unquestionably.

SOCRATES: And to delight in our enemies' misfortunes is neither wrongful nor malicious?

PROTARCHUS: Of course not.

SOCRATES: Whereas to feel delight, as we sometimes do, instead of pain, when we see friends in misfortune, is wrongful, is it not?

PROTARCHUS: Of course.

SOCRATES: Now we said that ignorance is always an evil?

PROTARCHUS: That is so.

SOCRATES: Then if we find in our friends that imaginary wisdom and imaginary beauty, and the other delusions which we enumerated in our threefold classification just now, delusions that are ridiculous in the weak and hateful in the strong—if we find this disposition in its harmless form in our friends, shall we adhere, or shall we not, to my statement of a moment ago, namely that it is ridiculous?

PROTARCHUS: Certainly we shall.

SOCRATES: And do we not agree that, being ignorance, it is evil?

PROTARCHUS: Undoubtedly.

SOCRATES: And when we laugh at it, are we pleased or pained?

PROTARCHUS: Plainly we are pleased.   50

SOCRATES: And did we not say that it is malice that makes us feel pleasure in our friends' misfortunes?

PROTARCHUS: It must be.

SOCRATES: The upshot of our argument then is that when we laugh at what is ridiculous in our friends, we are mixing pleasure this time with malice, mixing, that is, our pleasure with pain, for we have been for some time agreed that malice is a pain in the soul, and that laughter is a pleasure, and both occur simultaneously on the occasions in question.

PROTARCHUS: True.

SOCRATES: Hence our argument now makes it plain that in laments and tragedies and comedies—and not only in those of the stage but in the whole tragicomedy of life—as well as on countless other occasions, pains are mixed with pleasures.

PROTARCHUS: The most determined of opponents could not but agree with what you say, Socrates.

SOCRATES: Moreover we made a list including anger, longing, lamentation, fear, love, malice, and so on, in all of which we said that we should find our oft-repeated mixture, did we not?

PROTARCHUS: Yes.

SOCRATES: Then do we realize that what we have just discussed was all concerned with lamentation, malice, and anger?

PROTARCHUS: I am sure we do.

SOCRATES: That being so, is there still much left to discuss?

PROTARCHUS: Yes indeed.

SOCRATES: Now what exactly do you suppose was my purpose in pointing out the mixture in comedy? Was it not to give you a ground
d for believing that it would be easy enough to demonstrate the same mingling in the case of fear, love, and the rest? I hoped that, having grasped the first example, you would relieve me of the necessity of entering upon a long argument about the others, and would grasp the general principle, that whether the body be affected apart from the soul, or the soul apart from the body, or both of them together, we constantly come upon the mixture of pleasure with pain. So tell me now, are you going to relieve me or will you keep me up till midnight? I fancy I shall secure your consent to release me if I just add this, that I shall be willing to go into the whole question with you tomorrow, but
e for the present I want to address myself to the matters which are still outstanding if we are to settle the problem set us by Philebus.

PROTARCHUS: Very good, Socrates, deal with the outstanding points as you fancy.

SOCRATES: Well, after the mixed pleasures we shall naturally go on in turn—indeed we can hardly avoid it—to the unmixed.

51   PROTARCHUS: Excellent.

SOCRATES: Then I will start afresh and try to indicate, to you and to myself, which they are. With those who maintain that all pleasures are a cessation of pains I am not altogether inclined to agree, but, as I said, I avail myself of their evidence that some pleasures are apparent and quite unreal, while others present themselves to us as being great and numerous, but are in fact jumbled up with pains and processes of relief from such severe suffering as besets both body and soul.

b   PROTARCHUS: But which, Socrates, should we be justified in regarding as true?

SOCRATES: Those that attach to colors that we call beautiful, to figures, to most odors, to sounds, and to all experiences in which the want is imperceptible and painless, but its fulfillment is perceptible and pleasant.

PROTARCHUS: In what sense, Socrates, does what you say hold good of these?

SOCRATES: Well, what I mean is not quite obvious immedi-
c ately; however, I must try to explain it. The beauty of figures which I am now trying to indicate is not what most people would understand as such, not the beauty of a living creature or a picture; what I mean, what the argument points to, is something straight, or round, and the surfaces and solids which a lathe, or a carpenter's rule and square, produces from the straight and the round. I wonder if you understand. Things like that, I maintain, are beautiful not, like most things, in a relative sense; they are always beautiful in their very nature, and they carry pleasures peculiar to themselves which are quite unlike the

pleasures of scratching. And there are colors too which have this d
characteristic. Do we grasp this? What do you say?

PROTARCHUS: I am trying to do so, Socrates. Perhaps you too
would try to put it still more plainly.

SOCRATES: Very well. Audible sounds which are smooth and
clear, and deliver a single series of pure notes, are beautiful not relatively to something else, but in themselves, and they are attended by
pleasures implicit in themselves.

PROTARCHUS: Yes, certainly that is so.

SOCRATES: Odors provide pleasures of a less sublime type, but e
the fact that no necessary pains are mixed with them, as well as the
general character and source of the experience, induces me to class
them as cognate with those just mentioned. Here then, if you follow
me, are two of the types of pleasure we are now concerned with.

PROTARCHUS: I follow you.

SOCRATES: Now let us proceed to add to them the pleasures of 52
learning, if we do in fact think that they involve no hunger, that no
initial distress is felt owing to a hunger for learning.

PROTARCHUS: I share that view.

SOCRATES: But suppose one who has been filled with learning
loses it afterward by forgetting it, do you find that such loss involves
distress?

PROTARCHUS: No, at least not to a man's natural self, but by
way of his reflection upon what has happened, when he feels pain because of the usefulness of what he has lost.   b

SOCRATES: But you know, my dear fellow, we are concerned at
present only with the actual experiences of the natural self, apart
from any reflections about them.

PROTARCHUS: Then you are right in saying that in cases of forgetting what we have learned we feel no pain.

SOCRATES: So we must assert that these pleasures of learning
are unmixed with pains, and that they belong not to the general run of
men but only to the very few.

PROTARCHUS: Certainly.

SOCRATES: Well, we have reached the point of drawing a satis- c
factory line between pure pleasures and those that may with fair justification be called impure, and now let us add to our statement that
those pleasures that are intense are marked by immoderateness, those
that are not by moderation. Pleasures that can go to great lengths or to
an intense degree, whether they actually do so often or seldom, let
us class as belonging to that 'unlimited' kind of which we spoke, which
penetrates body and soul alike in greater or in less degree, but the
other sort let us class among things moderate.   d

PROTARCHUS: You are quite right, Socrates.

SOCRATES: And now there is yet another feature of them which
we must look into.

PROTARCHUS : What is that?

SOCRATES : What are we to reckon as making for truth? That which is pure, perfectly clear, and sufficient, or that which is extreme, vast, and huge?

PROTARCHUS : What is the object of your question, Socrates?

SOCRATES : My object, Protarchus, is to do all I can to determine whether some sorts of pleasure, and some sorts of knowledge also, are pure and others not pure, for if, in deciding about them, we can get each in its pure form, that will facilitate the decision which you and I and all of us here have to make.

PROTARCHUS : Quite right.

SOCRATES : Well then, I will suggest a general method for the consideration of anything we call pure—namely, that we should begin by examining one selected example.

PROTARCHUS : And what are we to select?

53   SOCRATES : First and foremost, if you like, let us contemplate whiteness.

PROTARCHUS : By all means.

SOCRATES : How shall we get a pure white? What will it be? The greatest possible quantity or bulk of it, or the white with the least possible admixture, with no portion of any other color in its composition?

PROTARCHUS : Plainly it will be the most perfectly clear color.

SOCRATES : You are right. Then shall we not reckon that, Pro-
b tarchus, as the truest of all white things, and the fairest too, rather than a great quantity or bulk of the color?

PROTARCHUS : Quite right.

SOCRATES : Then we shall be absolutely right in saying that a small quantity of pure white is not only whiter, but also fairer and truer, than a large quantity of mixed white.

PROTARCHUS : Yes, perfectly.

SOCRATES : What then? I imagine we shall not need numerous examples of the same sort to make a pronouncement about pleasure, but are now in a position to realize that any and every sort of pleasure
c that is pure of pain will be pleasanter, truer, and fairer than one that is not, whatever be their comparative bulk or quantity.

PROTARCHUS : Unquestionably so. The example before us is sufficient.

SOCRATES : And now to pass to another point. Are we not told that pleasure is always something that comes to be, that there is no such thing as a pleasure that is? There again you have a theory which certain subtle thinkers endeavor to expound to us, and we should be grateful to them.

PROTARCHUS : Why so?

d   SOCRATES : That is precisely the point which I shall treat at some length in my questions to you, my dear Protarchus.

PROTARCHUS: Pray continue, and put them.

SOCRATES: There are, as you know, two kinds of thing—that which exists independently, and that which is always aiming at something else.

PROTARCHUS: How do you mean? What are they?

SOCRATES: The one has always pride of place, and the other is its inferior.

PROTARCHUS: Will you put it still more plainly?

SOCRATES: We have observed before now, I imagine, manly lovers together with the fair and excellent recipients of their admiration?

PROTARCHUS: To be sure.

SOCRATES: Then see if you can find counterparts to such pairs e throughout the world of existence, as we call it.

PROTARCHUS: May I say yet a third time, 'Please make your meaning plainer, Socrates'?

SOCRATES: It's nothing abstruse, Protarchus; our discussion has been taking a playful turn, but its meaning is that things are always of two kinds, namely those which are with a view to something else, and those for the sake of which the first sort come to be, whenever they do come to be.

PROTARCHUS: I understand more or less, thanks to your repetitions.

SOCRATES: I dare say we shall understand better before long, my boy, when the argument has made more progress.   54

PROTARCHUS: No doubt.

SOCRATES: Now let us take another pair.

PROTARCHUS: Yes?

SOCRATES: All becoming on the one hand, and all being on the other.

PROTARCHUS: I accept your pair, being and becoming.

SOCRATES: Very good. Now which of these shall we say is for the sake of which? Becoming for the sake of being, or being for the sake of becoming?

PROTARCHUS: Are you now inquiring whether what you call being is what it is for the sake of becoming?

SOCRATES: Clearly I am.

PROTARCHUS: Good heavens! Are you asking me something of b this sort—'Tell me, Protarchus, do you maintain that shipbuilding goes on for the sake of ships, rather than that ships are for the sake of shipbuilding?'—and so on and so forth?

SOCRATES: That is precisely what I mean, Protarchus.

PROTARCHUS: Then why haven't you answered your own question, Socrates?

SOCRATES: I might well do so, but you must take your share in the discussion.

PROTARCHUS : Yes, certainly.

c   SOCRATES : Now I hold that while it is with a view to something coming into being that anyone provides himself with medicine, or tools of any kind, or any sort of material, the becoming always takes place with a view to the being of this or that, so that becoming in general takes place with a view to being in general.

PROTARCHUS : Yes, clearly.

SOCRATES : Then there must be some being with a view to which pleasure comes to be, if it is true that pleasure is becoming.

PROTARCHUS : Of course.

SOCRATES : But where there is this regular relation of means to end, the end falls under the heading of good, while the means, my excellent friend, must find a place under another heading.

PROTARCHUS : Most decidedly.

d   SOCRATES : Hence if pleasure is becoming, we shall be right in setting it under some other heading than that of good?

PROTARCHUS : Yes, perfectly right.

SOCRATES : And so, as I said at the beginning of our present argument, we ought to be grateful to the author of the doctrine that pleasure is something that comes to be, but in no case ever is, for plainly he laughs to scorn those who assert that pleasure is good.

PROTARCHUS : Quite so.

SOCRATES : And what's more, this same thinker will not fail to e include in his scorn those who find their satisfaction in these becomings.

PROTARCHUS : How do you mean? To whom are you referring?

SOCRATES : To people who, when they find relief for their hunger or thirst or such other troubles as becoming relieves, are delighted on account of the becoming, which they regard as a pleasure, saying that they would not care to live without hungering and thirsting and having all the rest of the experiences that might be enumerated as going with hunger and thirst.

55   PROTARCHUS : Your description fits them, certainly.

SOCRATES : Well now, we should all admit that the opposite of becoming is passing away.

PROTARCHUS : Necessarily.

SOCRATES : Hence it is an alternation of passing away and becoming that will be chosen by those who choose a life like that in preference to the third life we spoke of, the life which included neither pleasure nor pain, but the purest possible activity of thought.

PROTARCHUS : It appears, Socrates, that a number of untenable consequences follow from the proposal to make pleasure our good.

SOCRATES : Yes, and for that matter we might reinforce the argument.

PROTARCHUS : How?

SOCRATES: Surely it is untenable that there should be nothing b good nor admirable in our bodies, nor yet in anything else whatever except in our souls, and that there it should be pleasure alone that is good, not courage nor temperance nor reason nor any of the goods proper to soul—these being no good at all—and, what is more, that one who feels not pleasure, but distress, should be forced to admit that every time he feels distress he is evil, though he be in fact the best of men, and conversely that one who feels pleasure should gain an additional excellence proportionate to his pleasure, every time he feels c that pleasure.

PROTARCHUS: The whole idea, Socrates, is as untenable as it well could be.

SOCRATES: Well now, we have been trying every possible method of reviewing pleasure, but don't let us show ourselves over-tender toward reason and knowledge. Rather let us test their metal with a good honest ring, to see if it contains any base alloy, for by so doing we shall detect what is really the purest element in them, and so use, for the purpose of our joint decision, their truest parts together with the truest parts of pleasure.

PROTARCHUS: Right.

SOCRATES: Now we may, I think, divide the knowledge in- d volved in our studies into technical knowledge, and that concerned with education and culture, may we not?

PROTARCHUS: Yes.

SOCRATES: Then taking the technical knowledge employed in handicraft, let us first consider whether one division is more closely concerned with knowledge, and the other less so, so that we are justified in regarding the first kind as the purest, and the second as relatively impure.

PROTARCHUS: Yes, we ought so to regard them.

SOCRATES: Should we then mark off the superior types of knowledge in the several crafts?

PROTARCHUS: How so? Which do you mean?

SOCRATES: If, for instance, from any craft you subtract the ele- e ment of numbering, measuring, and weighing, the remainder will be almost negligible.

PROTARCHUS: Negligible indeed.

SOCRATES: For after doing so, what you would have left would be guesswork and the exercise of your senses on a basis of experience and rule of thumb, involving the use of that ability to make lucky shots which is commonly accorded the title of art or craft, when it has consolidated its position by dint of industrious practice. 56

PROTARCHUS: I have not the least doubt you are right.

SOCRATES: Well now, we find plenty of it, to take one instance, in music when it adjusts its concords not by measurement but by lucky shots of a practiced finger—in the whole of music, flute playing and lyre playing alike, for this latter hunts for the proper length of each string as it gives its note, making a shot for the note, and attaining a most unreliable result with a large element of uncertainty.

PROTARCHUS : Very true.

b   SOCRATES : Then again we shall find the same sort of thing in medicine and agriculture and navigation and military science.

PROTARCHUS : Quite so.

SOCRATES : Building, however, makes a considerable use of measures and instruments, and the remarkable exactness thus attained makes it more scientific than most sorts of knowledge.

PROTARCHUS : In what respect?

SOCRATES : I am thinking of the building of ships and houses, and various other uses to which timber is put. It employs straightedge and peg-and-cord, I believe, and compasses and plummet, and an c ingenious kind of set-square.

PROTARCHUS : You are perfectly right, Socrates.

SOCRATES : Let us then divide the arts and crafts so called into two classes, those akin to music in their activities and those akin to carpentry, the two classes being marked by a lesser and a greater degree of exactness, respectively.

PROTARCHUS : So be it.

SOCRATES : And let us take those arts, which just now we spoke of as primary, to be the most exact of all.

PROTARCHUS : I take it you mean the art of numbering, and the others which you mentioned in association with it just now.

d   SOCRATES : To be sure. But ought we not, Protarchus, to recognize these themselves to be of two kinds? What do you think?

PROTARCHUS : What two kinds do you mean?

SOCRATES : To take first numbering or arithmetic, ought we not to distinguish between that of the ordinary man and that of the philosopher?

PROTARCHUS : On what principle, may I ask, is this discrimination of two arithmetics to be based?

SOCRATES : There is an important mark of difference, Protarchus. The ordinary arithmetician, surely, operates with unequal units; his 'two' may be two armies or two cows or two anythings from the smallest thing in the world to the biggest, while the philosopher e will have nothing to do with him, unless he consents to make every single instance of his unit precisely equal to every other of its infinite number of instances.

PROTARCHUS : Certainly you are right in speaking of an important distinction among those who concern themselves with number, which justifies the belief that there are two arithmetics.

SOCRATES : Then as between the calculating and measurement 57 employed in building or commerce and the geometry and calculation practiced in philosophy—well, should we say there is one sort of each, or should we recognize two sorts?

PROTARCHUS : On the strength of what has been said I should give my vote for there being two.

SOCRATES : Right. Now do you realize our purpose in bringing these matters onto the board?

PROTARCHUS : Possibly, but I should like you to pronounce on the point.

SOCRATES : Well, it seems to me that our discussion, now no less than when we embarked upon it, has propounded a question here analogous to the question about pleasures. It is inquiring whether one kind of knowledge is purer than another, just as one pleasure is b purer than another.

PROTARCHUS : Yes, it is quite clear that that has been its reason for attacking this matter.

SOCRATES : Well now, in what preceded had it not discovered that different arts, dealing with different things, possessed different degrees of precision?

PROTARCHUS : Certainly.

SOCRATES : And in what followed did it not first mention a certain art under one single name, making us think it really was one art, and then treat it as two, putting questions about the precision and purity of those two to find out whether the art as practiced by the phi- c losopher or by the nonphilosopher was the more exact?

PROTARCHUS : I certainly think that is the question which it puts.

SOCRATES : Then, Protarchus, what answer do we give it?

PROTARCHUS : We have got far enough, Socrates, to discern an astonishingly big difference between one kind of knowledge and another in respect of precision.

SOCRATES : Well, will that make it easier for us to answer?

PROTARCHUS : Of course, and let our statement be that the arts which we have had before us are superior to all others, and that those among them which involve the effort of the true philosopher d are, in their use of measure and number, immensely superior in point of exactness and truth.

SOCRATES : Let it be as you put it; then relying on you we shall confidently answer the clever twisters of argument . . .

PROTARCHUS : Answer what?

SOCRATES : That there are two arts of numbering and two arts of measuring, and plenty of other kindred arts which are similarly pairs of twins, though they share a single name.

PROTARCHUS : Let us give that answer, Socrates, with our e blessing to those clever folk, as you style them.

SOCRATES : Then these are the kinds of knowledge which we maintain to be pre-eminently exact?

PROTARCHUS : Certainly.

SOCRATES : But we, Protarchus, are likely to be repudiated by the art of dialectic, if we prefer any other to her.

58   PROTARCHUS: Then how ought we to describe her, in her turn?

SOCRATES: Plainly everyone will recognize her whom we now speak of. The cognition of that which is, that which exists in reality, ever unchanged, is held, I cannot doubt, by all people who have the smallest endowment of reason to be far and away truer than any other. What is your view? How would you, Protarchus, decide about this question?

PROTARCHUS: On the many occasions when I used to listen to Gorgias, he regularly said, Socrates, that the art of persuasion was b greatly superior to all others, for it subjugated all things not by violence but by willing submission, and was far and away the best of all arts, but on this occasion I should not care to take up a position against either you or him.

SOCRATES: 'Take up arms,' I fancy you meant to say, but you dropped them out of modesty.

PROTARCHUS: Well, have it as you choose.

SOCRATES: I wonder if I am to blame for your misconception.

PROTARCHUS: What is it?

SOCRATES: What I wanted to discover at present, my dear Protarchus, was not which art or which form of knowledge is superior to all others in respect of being the greatest or the best or the most serv- c iceable, but which devotes its attention to precision, exactness, and the fullest truth, though it may be small and of small profit—that is what we are looking for at this moment. What you must consider— and you won't give offense to Gorgias, if you allow his art the property of doing paramount service to mankind, while assigning to the procedure to which I have just referred just that property of possessing paramount truth which I illustrated by showing that a small quantity of d pure white color was superior to a large quantity of impure in that respect—what you must consider is, whether the art we have in mind may reasonably be said to possess in fullest measure reason and intelligence in their purity, or whether we ought to look for some other art with a better claim. The question calls for great thought and ample reflection, and we must have no regard for any benefits a science may confer or any repute it may enjoy. But if there is a certain faculty in our souls naturally directed to loving truth and doing all for the sake of truth, let us make diligent search and say what it is, and when we have done so you must consider the question I have put to you.

e   PROTARCHUS: Well, I have been thinking it over, and in my opinion it would be difficult to concede that any other science or art has more of a hold on truth than this one.

59   SOCRATES: Now does it occur to you, in saying what you have just said, that the majority of arts, as also those who are busied therewith, are in the first place concerned with opinions and pursue their energetic studies in the realm of opinion? And are you aware that those of them who do consider themselves students of reality spend a

whole lifetime in studying the universe around us, how it came to be, how it does things, and how things happen to it? May we say that is so? What do you think?

PROTARCHUS: We may.

SOCRATES: Then the task which such students among us have taken upon themselves has nothing to do with that which always is, but only with what is coming into being, or will come, or has come.

PROTARCHUS: Very true.

SOCRATES: And can we say that any precise and exact truth attaches to things, none of which are at this present, or ever were, or b ever will be free from change?

PROTARCHUS: Of course not.

SOCRATES: And how can we ever get a permanent grasp on anything that is entirely devoid of permanence?

PROTARCHUS: Nohow, I imagine.

SOCRATES: It follows then that reason too, and knowledge that gives perfect truth, are foreign to them.

PROTARCHUS: So it would seem.

SOCRATES: Then we should have done for good and all with your illustrious self, and mine, and with Gorgias and Philebus, and make the following reasoned declaration.

PROTARCHUS: Let us have it.   c

SOCRATES: That we find fixity, purity, truth, and what we have called perfect clarity, either in those things that are always, unchanged, unaltered, and free of all admixture, or in what is most akin to them; everything else must be called inferior and of secondary importance.

PROTARCHUS: What you say is very true.

SOCRATES: Then as regards names for what we have been discussing, will it not be fittest to assign the fairest names to the fairest things?

PROTARCHUS: I suppose so.

SOCRATES: And are not reason and intelligence the names that d command the greatest respect?

PROTARCHUS: Yes.

SOCRATES: Then these names can be properly established in usage as precisely appropriate to thought whose object is true being.

PROTARCHUS: Certainly.

SOCRATES: But I may point out that it was just these names about which I originally suggested that we had to make our decision.

PROTARCHUS: To be sure, Socrates.

SOCRATES: Very well. Then here, one may say, we have at hand the ingredients, intelligence and pleasure, ready to be mixed, the ma- e terials in which, or out of which, we as builders are to build our structure—that would not be a bad metaphor.

PROTARCHUS: Quite a good one.

SOCRATES: Next then, I suppose, we must set to work to mix them.

PROTARCHUS: Of course.

SOCRATES: I suggest that there are points which we might do well to remind ourselves of first.

PROTARCHUS: What are they?

SOCRATES: Points we mentioned before, but I think there is a
60 lot in the proverb about the need for repeating a good thing 'once and twice and once again.'

PROTARCHUS: To be sure.

SOCRATES: Come along, then, I beg and beseech you. I think I can give you the gist of what we said.

PROTARCHUS: Yes?

SOCRATES: Philebus maintains that pleasure is the proper quest of all living creatures, and that all ought to aim at it; in fact he says that the good for all is pleasure and nothing else, these two terms, pleasure and good, being properly applied to one thing, one sin-
b gle existent. Socrates on the other hand maintains that they are not one thing, but two, in fact as in name; 'good' and 'pleasant' are different from one another, and intelligence has more claim to be ranked as good than pleasure. Are not those the assertions, Protarchus, now as before?

PROTARCHUS: Exactly.

SOCRATES: And is there not a further point on which we should agree, now as then?

PROTARCHUS: What is that?

SOCRATES: That the good differs from everything else in a certain respect.

c   PROTARCHUS: In what respect?

SOCRATES: A creature that possesses it permanently, completely, and absolutely, has never any need of anything else; its satisfaction is perfect. Is that right?

PROTARCHUS: Yes, that is right.

SOCRATES: And we went on, by way of experiment, to imagine the individual lives corresponding to them when each was isolated from the other—that of pleasure unmixed with intelligence, and that of intelligence similarly devoid of any particle of pleasure.

PROTARCHUS: We did.

d   SOCRATES: And did we find that either of them was satisfactory to anybody?

PROTARCHUS: No indeed.

SOCRATES: But if we made any slip before, now is the time for anyone who likes to take the matter up and restate it more correctly. Let him class together memory, intelligence, knowledge, and true opinion, and ask himself whether there is anything whatever that he

would choose to have, or to get, without these—anything, let alone a
pleasure which, for all its magnitude or extreme intensity, he felt
without any true opinion that he felt it, without any recognition whatever of the character of his experience, without even a momentary
memory of it. And then let him put the same question about intel- e
ligence, whether anyone would choose to have intelligence unaccompanied by any pleasure, even of the most fleeting character, in
preference to its accompaniment by some, [or to have every pleasure
without any intelligence in preference to its accompaniment by
some].

PROTARCHUS: Impossible, Socrates. There is no need to put
that question more than once.

SOCRATES: Then neither of the two can be the perfect thing 61
that everyone desires, the absolute good.

PROTARCHUS: No.

SOCRATES: Then we shall have to grasp the good, either precisely or at least in rough outline, if we are to know to what we must
give, as we put it, the second prize.

PROTARCHUS: You are quite right.

SOCRATES: And haven't we in a sense found a way toward the
good?

PROTARCHUS: How?

SOCRATES: If you were looking for somebody and began by as-
certaining correctly where he lived, I imagine that would be a big b
step toward discovering the man you looked for.

PROTARCHUS: Of course.

SOCRATES: Well, so it is here. Our discussion has made it plain
to us, now as at the outset, that we must not look for the good in the
unmixed life, but in the mixed.

PROTARCHUS: Quite so.

SOCRATES: But there is more hope of what we are looking for
coming to light in what is well mixed than in what is badly mixed?

PROTARCHUS: Much more.

SOCRATES: Then let us mingle our ingredients, Protarchus,
with a prayer to the gods, to Dionysus or Hephaestus or whichever god c
has been assigned this function of mingling.

PROTARCHUS: By all means.

SOCRATES: Why, it's just as if we were supplying drinks, with
two fountains at our disposal; one would be of honey, standing for
pleasure, the other standing for intelligence, a sobering, unintoxicat-
ing fountain of plain, salubrious water. We must get to work and
make a really good mixture.

PROTARCHUS: Of course.

SOCRATES: Come then. To begin with, are we most likely to at- d
tain a good result by mixing all pleasure with all intelligence?

PROTARCHUS: Possibly.

SOCRATES: No, it's not safe. I think I can show you what seems a less dangerous method of mixture.

PROTARCHUS: Tell me, please.

SOCRATES: One pleasure, so we thought, had a truer being than another, and again this art was more exact than that?

PROTARCHUS: Of course.

SOCRATES: And knowledge differed from knowledge—one hav-
e ing regard to the things that come into being and perish, the other to those that do not come into being nor perish, but are always, unchanged and unaltered. Reviewing them on the score of truth, we concluded that the latter was truer than the former.

PROTARCHUS: Perfectly right.

SOCRATES: Then if we were to see which were the truest portions of each before we made our mixture, would the fusion of these portions suffice to constitute and provide us with the fully acceptable life, or should we still need something different?

62　PROTARCHUS: My own opinion is that we should act as you say.

SOCRATES: Now let us imagine a man who understands what justice itself is, and can give an account of it conformable to his knowledge, and who moreover has a like understanding of all else that is.

PROTARCHUS: Very well.

SOCRATES: Will such a man be adequately possessed of knowledge, if he can give his account of the divine circle and the divine sphere themselves, but knows nothing of these human spheres and
b circles of ours, so that, when he is building a house, the rules that he uses, no less than the circles, are of the other sort?

PROTARCHUS: I am moved to mirth, Socrates, by this description we are giving of ourselves confined to divine knowledge.

SOCRATES: What's that? Are we to throw in alongside of our other ingredients the art of the false rule and false circle, with all the lack of fixity and purity it involves?

PROTARCHUS: We must, if we are going to find the way home when we want it.

c　SOCRATES: And music too, which we said a while ago was so completely dependent on lucky shots and imitation, and so deficient in purity?

PROTARCHUS: I think we are bound to do so, if our life is ever to be a life at all.

SOCRATES: Do you want me, may I ask, to give way like a porter jostled and knocked about by the crowd, to fling open the doors and allow every sort of knowledge to stream in, the inferior mingling with the pure?

d　PROTARCHUS: I don't really see, Socrates, what harm one

would suffer by taking all those other sorts of knowledge, providing one had the first sort.

SOCRATES: Then I am to allow the whole company to stream in and be gathered together in a splendid Homeric mingling of the waters?

PROTARCHUS: Certainly.

SOCRATES: It is done. And now we must return to our fount of pleasures. The method of mixing our ingredients which we intended, namely taking parts of the true sorts first, has broken down; our acquiescence in every sort of knowledge has made us admit the whole of it at one swoop before admitting any pleasure.

PROTARCHUS: That is quite true.   e

SOCRATES: Hence it is time for us to raise the same question about pleasures, whether we are to let them all loose at once or should allow passage first to such of them as are true.

PROTARCHUS: It is most important in the interest of safety to let loose the true ones first.

SOCRATES: Then let that be taken as done. And what next? Ought we not to do as we did in the other case, and include in our mixture any necessary pleasures there may be?

PROTARCHUS: Oh yes, the necessary ones of course.

SOCRATES: Yes, but we found it harmless and useful to spend our lives in the knowledge of all the arts, and if we say the same about 63 pleasures, if, that is, it is advantageous and harmless to us all to spend our lives in the enjoyment of all pleasures, then we must mix in all of them.

PROTARCHUS: Then what are we to say on this particular point? How are we to act?

SOCRATES: The question ought to be addressed not to us, Protarchus, but to the pleasures themselves and the intelligences, and here is the sort of inquiry we should make about their mutual relations.

PROTARCHUS: Yes?   b

SOCRATES: 'Dear Pleasures—if that is the name by which I should call you, or whatever it ought to be—would you not choose to live in company with all intelligence rather than apart from any?' I imagine there can be no doubt about the reply they would make to that.

PROTARCHUS: What would it be?

SOCRATES: Conformably to what was previously said, it would be as follows: 'It is disadvantageous and hardly possible that one family should be kept in solitude and isolation, perfectly clear of all others, but our view is that, family for family, we cannot do better than c have the family of knowledge to live with us, knowledge of all things in general and of each of ourselves in particular to the fullest extent possible.'

PROTARCHUS : 'An excellent answer that,' we shall tell them.

SOCRATES : So we should. Then next we must put a question to intelligence and reason. 'Do you require any pleasures to be added to the mixture?' And when we ask that of reason and intelligence, they may possibly rejoin, 'What sort of pleasures?'

PROTARCHUS : I dare say.

d   SOCRATES : To which our rejoinder is this. 'Over and above the true pleasures that you know of, do you further require the greatest and intensest pleasures for your associates?' And they may well reply, 'Is that likely, Socrates, seeing that they put countless obstacles in our way, disturbing with frenzy the souls in which we dwell, and prevent us from ever coming into existence, while as to our offspring,

e   they utterly ruin them in most cases, so careless and forgetful do they make us. No, the pleasures you have spoken of as true and pure you may regard as more or less related to us, and besides them you may add to the mixture those that consort with health and temperance, and in fact all that attend upon virtue in general, following her every-

64   where as their divinity. But to mix with reason the pleasures that always go with folly and all other manner of evil would surely be the most senseless act for one who desired to see a mixture and fusion as fair and peaceable as might be, so that he might try to learn from it what the good is, in man and in the universe, and what form he should divine it to possess.'

Shall we not say that in the words that reason has here used it has answered wisely and 'reason-ably' on behalf of itself and memory and right opinion?

PROTARCHUS : Completely so.

SOCRATES : But there is still a certain thing we must have, and nothing in the world could come into being without it.

b   PROTARCHUS : What is that?

SOCRATES : Reality, for a thing with which we don't mean to mix reality will never really come into being, and if it ever did it wouldn't continue in being.

PROTARCHUS : No, of course not.

SOCRATES : No indeed. And now do you and Philebus tell me if there are any additional ingredients required. To me it appears that in our present discussion we have created what might be called an incorporeal ordered system for the rightful control of a corporeal subject in which dwells a soul.

PROTARCHUS : You may assure yourself, Socrates, that my own conclusion is the same.

c   SOCRATES : Then perhaps we should be more or less right in saying that we now stand upon the threshold of the good and of that habitation where all that is like thereto resides?

PROTARCHUS : I at least think so.

SOCRATES : And what, may I ask, shall we regard as the most

valuable thing in our mixture, that which makes an arrangement of this sort commend itself to us all? If we discover that, we can go on to consider whether this factor in the whole scheme of things is closer and more akin to pleasure, or to reason.

PROTARCHUS: Very good, what you propose will do much to d help us toward our decision.

SOCRATES: As a matter of fact, it is easy enough to see the cause that makes any mixture, be it what it may, possess high value or no value whatever.

PROTARCHUS: How so?

SOCRATES: Surely anyone in the world can recognize that.

PROTARCHUS: Recognize what?

SOCRATES: That any compound, whatever it be, that does not by some means or other exhibit measure and proportion, is the ruin both of its ingredients and, first and foremost, of itself; what you are bound to get in such cases is no real mixture, but literally a miserable e mass of unmixed messiness.

PROTARCHUS: Very true.

SOCRATES: So now we find that the good has taken refuge in the character of the beautiful, for the qualities of measure and proportion invariably, I imagine, constitute beauty and excellence.

PROTARCHUS: Yes indeed.

SOCRATES: And of course we said that truth was included along with these qualities in the mixture.

PROTARCHUS: Quite so.

SOCRATES: Then if we cannot hunt down the good under a 65 single form, let us secure it by the conjunction of three, beauty, proportion, and truth, and then, regarding these three as one, let us assert that *that* may most properly be held to determine the qualities of the mixture, and that because *that* is good the mixture itself has become so.

PROTARCHUS: Yes, that is quite proper.

SOCRATES: Well, Protarchus, by this time anyone would be competent to decide whether it is pleasure or intelligence that is more akin to the highest good, and more valuable with men and gods alike. b

PROTARCHUS: The answer is clear, but for all that it would be as well to formulate it explicitly.

SOCRATES: Then let us examine each of our three forms separately in relation to pleasure and reason, for we must see to which of the two we shall assign each of them on the ground of closer kinship.

PROTARCHUS: By 'each of them' you mean beauty, truth, and measuredness?

SOCRATES: Yes, and in the first place, Protarchus, take hold of truth, and having done so, have a look at the three things, reason, c truth, and pleasure, and then, taking your time, answer your own question whether pleasure or reason is the more akin to truth.

PROTARCHUS: What need for time? I think they differ widely. Pleasure is the worst of all impostors, and according to the accounts, when it is a question of the pleasures of love, which are commonly

d reckoned as the greatest, even perjury is forgiven by the gods—pleasures being presumably, like children, completely destitute of reason. Reason, on the other hand, if not identical with truth, is of all things the most like it, the truest thing in the world.

SOCRATES: Next then give a similar consideration to measuredness. Has pleasure more of it than intelligence, or is the reverse the case?

PROTARCHUS: There you set me another easy problem to consider. I don't think you could discover anything whatsoever more unmeasured in its character than pleasure and intense enjoyment, nor anything more measured than reason and knowledge.

e SOCRATES: Well said. However, there is still a third thing I want you to tell me. Has reason more part in beauty than pleasure, that is to say is reason more beautiful than pleasure, or is the opposite the case?

PROTARCHUS: Well, of course, Socrates, no one whether in his waking hours or in his dreams has had a vision of intelligence and reason as ugly; no one can ever possibly have conceived them as being or becoming ugly, or ever going to be so.

SOCRATES: Right.

PROTARCHUS: But I fancy that when we see someone, no matter whom, experiencing pleasures—and I think this is true especially

66 of the greatest pleasures—we detect in them an element either of the ridiculous or of extreme ugliness, so that we ourselves feel ashamed, and do our best to cover it up and hide it away, and we leave that sort of thing to the hours of darkness, feeling that it should not be exposed to the light of day.

SOCRATES: Then your message, Protarchus, to be sent out to the world at large and announced to your immediate listeners, will be this. Pleasure is not the first of all possessions, nor yet the second; rather, the first has been secured for everlasting tenure somewhere in the region of measure—of what is measured or appropriate, or whatever term may be deemed to denote the quality in question.

PROTARCHUS: So at least it appears on our present showing.

b SOCRATES: And the second lies in the region of what is proportioned and beautiful, and what is perfect and satisfying and so forth—whatever terms denote that kind of quality.

PROTARCHUS: That seems right.

SOCRATES: And if you accept what I divine, and put reason and intelligence third, you won't be very wide of the truth.

PROTARCHUS: Perhaps not.

SOCRATES: Nor again, if beside these three you put as fourth what we recognized as belonging to the soul itself, sciences and arts and what we called right opinions, inasmuch as these are more akin c than pleasure to the good.

PROTARCHUS: You may be right.

SOCRATES: And as fifth, the pleasures which we recognized and discriminated as painless, calling them pure pleasures of the soul itself—some of them attaching to knowledge, others to sensation.

PROTARCHUS: Perhaps so.

SOCRATES: 'But cease at sixth descent,' as Orpheus puts it, 'your ordered song'; really it looks as though our discussion, like the song, has ceased at the sixth choice. And now the only thing left for us to do is to crown our story with a capital. d

PROTARCHUS: That is what we must do.

SOCRATES: Come along then, let us have the 'third libation to the deliverer,' and repeat for the third time the same pronouncement that we made before.

PROTARCHUS: What is that?

SOCRATES: Philebus maintained that we find the good in the sum total and entirety of pleasure.

PROTARCHUS: I understand you, Socrates, to have meant by your 'third libation' just now that we were to recapitulate our original statement.

SOCRATES: Yes, and let us listen to what came next. I, having e in view the considerations which I have now detailed, and feeling distaste for the assertion which is not only that of Philebus but also frequently made by countless other people, maintained that reason is far better and more valuable than pleasure for human life.

PROTARCHUS: So you did.

SOCRATES: Moreover, while suspecting that many other things are so too, I said that if anything were to come to light that was better than both of these I should fight to the end on the side of reason against pleasure for the second prize, and that pleasure would be disappointed even of that.

PROTARCHUS: Yes, you did say so.

SOCRATES: And subsequently we were completely satisfied that 67 neither of them was satisfying.

PROTARCHUS: Very true.

SOCRATES: Then in that part of our argument had reason and pleasure alike been dismissed as being, neither of them, the good itself, inasmuch as they came short of self-sufficiency and the quality of being satisfying and perfect?

PROTARCHUS: Quite right.

SOCRATES: But now that we have found a third thing better than either of them, reason has been found ever so much nearer and more akin than pleasure to the character of the victor.

PROTARCHUS : Certainly.

SOCRATES : Then according to the decision now pronounced by our argument, pleasure will take fifth place.

PROTARCHUS : Apparently.

b   SOCRATES : And not first place, no, not even if all the oxen and horses and every other animal that exists tell us so by their pursuit of pleasure. It is the animals on which the multitude rely, just as diviners rely on birds, when they decide that pleasures are of the first importance to our living a good life, and suppose that animals' desires are authoritative evidence, rather than those desires that are known to reasoned argument, divining the truth of this and that by the power of the Muse of philosophy.

PROTARCHUS : The point has been reached, Socrates, at which we all agree that your conclusions are completely true.

SOCRATES : Then will you let me go?

PROTARCHUS : There is only a little still left to be done, Socrates. I am sure you won't give up sooner than we do; so I will remind you of the tasks that remain.

TIMAEUS

The Timaeus for many hundreds of years exercised a wide and profound influence over men's minds. It is Plato's account of the creation of the universe, but it is more than an account, it is an explanation. To Plato the universe was intelligible and therefore how it came to be could be discovered by the searching intellect. In the first chapter of Genesis, "God said, Let there be light, and there was light." That is not Plato's way of dealing with the matter. He thinks out what light is and how it must have come about. The chapter in Genesis is poetry; the Timaeus has a great deal of poetry in it, but its aim is science.

Plato sets himself to think out physics and astronomy and biology. His temper of mind nowhere even approaches the dogmatic, but in this dialogue it does so least of all. He hesitates and questions as he does in none of the ethical discussions in his earlier work. The statements he makes are possible, so he declares, even perhaps probable, but the only way to certainty about such matters would be to ask God and that is denied us. But at the very least it is better to use one's mind on these questions than to pass them by indolently without trying to think about them. Moreover, to do that kind of thinking, he says, is so diverting and refreshing—his prescription for resting a tired mind. "A man may sometimes set aside meditations about eternal things, and for recreation turn to consider the truths of generation, which are probable only; he will thus gain a pleasure not to be repented of, and secure for himself a wise and moderate pastime."

But when Plato's mind, never equaled for keenness and profundity, could not find a probable explanation to rest in, then he turned to the other realm where he was also at home, the realm of poetry. In the Timaeus he says that truth is an eternal now, unchangeable, forever inexpressible. Time ever is, never has been, nor will be; it can be described as past or future only figuratively. It is "a moving image of eternity." What Plato said has been repeated by poets through the ages. Two thousand years later Vaughan wrote,

> I saw Eternity the other night,
> Like a great Ring of pure and endless light,
>   All calm, as it was bright;

And round beneath it, Time in hours, days, years,
Driven by the spheres
Like a vast shadow moved . . .

That came straight out of the Timaeus.

We must read the dialogue with such thoughts in mind because most of it is no longer to us what it was to Plato and through him to the men for centuries after, up to and into the Middle Ages, a statement of scientific truth combined with mythical truth in which great spiritual truths could be found. Inevitably we read it, at least to begin with, as an account of the incredibilities antiquity believed. God creates the universe from innumerable triangles, described and compared with careful accuracy. When man is created the way breath is put into him is of an astounding complexity, also described in accurate and bewildering detail. No doubt, as Plato said, he had relaxed just then and was amusing himself by this kind of writing, but he was also feeling, as we no longer can, how reasonable it all was and quite possibly the very truth itself.

It is certain, however, that Plato would have taken with complete tranquillity our modern skepticism. He would have pointed out that science cannot be accurately true since it deals with the temporal, the finite, the forever changing, never with the eternal. But yet the visible world is a copy, an image, of what is eternal and true. It is a changing reflection of that which is changeless and therefore, imperfect though it is, in it can be found the truth, God the Creator, the all-good. That is the matter of importance, not scientific accuracy, but to catch a glimpse of "the beyond, which ever thereafter the soul will strive to reach."

Toward the close of the Timaeus *Plato says that death when it comes in old age is accompanied with pleasure, not pain. He was very old when he wrote that; he was near the end. The innumerable host of those who have learned from him and have loved him, who through the ages have found in him inspiration and guidance for life, vision to see "the beyond" and that the ultimate truth is God, our Creator and Father—all those whom he has taught so greatly have rejoiced that as death approached him he declared that he felt his soul "loosened from bonds and able to fly away with joy." Aristotle, who was best able to understand him, wrote that he had proved that the good man was the happy man. That is an aspect of Platonism which has been too little emphasized.*

SOCRATES: One, two, three, but where, my dear Timaeus, is the 17
fourth of those who were yesterday my guests and are to be my enter-
tainers today?

TIMAEUS: He has been taken ill, Socrates, for he would not
willingly have been absent from this gathering.

SOCRATES: Then, if he is not coming, you and the two others
must supply his place.

TIMAEUS: Certainly, and we will do our utmost not to disap- b
point you. Having been handsomely entertained by you yesterday,
those of us who remain should be only too glad to return your hospitality.

SOCRATES: Do you remember what were the points of which I
required you to speak?

TIMAEUS: We remember some of them, and you will be here to
remind us of anything which we have forgotten, or rather, if we are
not troubling you, will you briefly recapitulate the whole, and then the
particulars will be more firmly fixed in our memories?

SOCRATES: To be sure I will. The chief theme of my yesterday's c
discourse was the state—how constituted and of what citizens composed it would seem likely to be most perfect.

TIMAEUS: Yes, Socrates, and what you said of it was very much
to our mind.

SOCRATES: Did we not begin by separating the husbandmen
and the artisans from the class of defenders of the state?

TIMAEUS: Yes.

SOCRATES: And when we had given to each one that single employment and particular art which was suited to his nature, we spoke d
of those who were intended to be our warriors, and said that they were
to be guardians of the city against attacks from within as well as from
without, and to have no other employment; they were to be merciful 18
in judging their subjects, of whom they were by nature friends, but
fierce to their enemies, when they came across them in battle.

TIMAEUS: Exactly.

SOCRATES: We said, if I am not mistaken, that the guardians
should be gifted with a temperament in a high degree both passionate
and philosophical, and that then they would be as they ought to be—
gentle to their friends and fierce with their enemies.

TIMAEUS: Certainly.

SOCRATES: And what did we say of their education? Were they
not to be trained in gymnastics and music and all other sorts of knowledge which were proper for them?

TIMAEUS: Very true.

From *The Dialogues of Plato*, translated with analyses and introductions by
B. Jowett (4th edn., revised by order of the Jowett Copyright Trustees, Oxford, 1953; 1st edn., 1871).

b   SOCRATES: And being thus trained they were not to consider gold or silver or anything else to be their own private property. They were to be like hired troops, receiving pay for keeping guard from those who were protected by them—the pay was to be no more than would suffice for men of simple life—and they were to spend in common, and to live together in the continual practice of virtue, which was to be their sole pursuit.

TIMAEUS: That was also said.

c   SOCRATES: Neither did we forget the women, of whom we declared that their natures should be harmoniously developed by training, equally with those of the men, and that common pursuits should be assigned to them all both in time of war and in their ordinary life.

TIMAEUS: That, again, was as you say.

SOCRATES: And what about the procreation of children? Or rather was not the proposal too singular to be forgotten? For all wives and children were to be in common, to the intent that no one should ever know his own child, but they were to imagine that they were all
d one family; those who were within a suitable limit of age were to be brothers and sisters, those who were of an elder generation parents and grandparents, and those of a younger, children and grandchildren.

TIMAEUS: Yes, and the proposal is easy to remember, as you say.

SOCRATES: And do you also remember how, with a view of securing as far as we could the best breed, we said that the chief
e magistrates, male and female, should contrive secretly, by the use of certain lots, so to arrange the nuptial meeting that the bad of either sex and the good of either sex might pair with their like, and there was to be no quarreling on this account, for they would imagine that the union was a mere accident and was to be attributed to the lot?

TIMAEUS: I remember.

SOCRATES: And you remember how we said that the children
19 of the good parents were to be educated, and the children of the bad secretly dispersed among the inferior citizens, and while they were all growing up the rulers were to be on the lookout, and to bring up from below in their turn those who were worthy, and those among themselves who were unworthy were to take the places of those who came up?

TIMAEUS: True.

SOCRATES: Then have I now given you all the heads of our yesterday's discussion? Or is there anything more, my dear Timaeus, which has been omitted?

b   TIMAEUS: Nothing, Socrates. The discussion was just as you have said.

SOCRATES: I should like, before proceeding further, to tell you how I feel about the state which we have described. I might compare myself to a person who, on beholding beautiful animals either created by the painter's art, or, better still, alive but at rest, is seized with a desire of seeing them in motion or engaged in some struggle or conflict to which their forms appear suited—this is my feeling about the state c which we have been describing. There are conflicts which all cities undergo, and I should like to hear someone tell of our own city carrying on a struggle against her neighbors, and how she went out to war in a becoming manner, and when at war showed by the greatness of her actions and the magnanimity of her words in dealing with other cities a result worthy of her training and education. Now I, Critias and Hermocrates, am conscious that I myself should never be able to d celebrate the city and her citizens in a befitting manner, and I am not surprised at my own incapacity; to me the wonder is rather that the poets present as well as past are no better—not that I mean to depreciate them, but everyone can see that they are a tribe of imitators, and will imitate best and most easily the life in which they have been brought up, while that which is beyond the range of a man's education he finds hard to carry out in action, and still harder adequately to e represent in language. I am aware that the Sophists have plenty of brave words and fair conceits, but I am afraid that being only wanderers from one city to another, and having never had habitations of their own, they may fail in their conception of philosophers and statesmen and may not know what they do and say in time of war, when they are fighting or holding parley with their enemies. And thus people of your class are the only ones remaining who are fitted by nature and education to take part at once both in politics and philosophy. Here is Timaeus, of Locri in Italy, a city which has admira- 20 ble laws, who is himself in wealth and rank the equal of any of his fellow citizens; he has held the most important and honorable offices in his own state, and, as I believe, has scaled the heights of all philosophy. And here is Critias, whom every Athenian knows to be no novice in the matters of which we are speaking, and as to Hermocrates, I am assured by many witnesses that his genius and education qualify him to take part in any speculation of the kind. And therefore yesterday when I saw that you wanted me to describe the formation of the state, I readily assented, being very well aware that, b if you only would, none was better qualified to carry the discussion further, and that when you had engaged our city in a suitable war, you of all men living could best exhibit her playing a fitting part. When I had completed my task, I in return imposed this other task upon you. You conferred together and agreed to entertain me today, as I had entertained you, with a feast of discourse. Here am I in festive array, and c no man can be more ready for the promised banquet.

HERMOCRATES: And we too, Socrates, as Timaeus says, will not be wanting in enthusiasm, and there is no excuse for not complying with your request. As soon as we arrived yesterday at the guest-chamber of Critias, with whom we are staying, or rather on our way thither, we talked the matter over, and he told us an ancient tradition d which I wish, Critias, that you would repeat to Socrates, so that he may help us to judge whether it will satisfy his requirements or not.

CRITIAS : I will, if Timaeus, who is our other partner, approves.

TIMAEUS : I quite approve.

CRITIAS : Then listen, Socrates, to a tale which, though strange, is certainly true, having been attested by Solon, who was the e wisest of the seven sages. He was a relative and a dear friend of my great-grandfather, Dropides, as he himself says in many passages of his poems, and he told the story to Critias, my grandfather, who remembered and repeated it to us. There were of old, he said, great and 21 marvelous actions of the Athenian city, which have passed into oblivion through lapse of time and the destruction of mankind, and one in particular, greater than all the rest. This we will now rehearse. It will be a fitting monument of our gratitude to you, and a hymn of praise true and worthy of the goddess, on this her day of festival.

SOCRATES : Very good. And what is this ancient famous action of the Athenians, which Critias declared, on the authority of Solon, to be not a mere legend but an actual fact?

CRITIAS : I will tell an old-world story which I heard from an aged man, for Critias, at the time of telling it, was, as he said, nearly b ninety years of age, and I was about ten. Now the day was that day of the Apaturia which is called the Registration of Youth, at which, according to custom, our parents gave prizes for recitations, and the poems of several poets were recited by us boys, and many of us sang the poems of Solon, which at that time had not gone out of fashion. One of our tribe, either because he thought so or to please Critias, said c that in his judgment Solon was not only the wisest of men, but also the noblest of poets.

The old man, as I very well remember, brightened up at hearing this and said, smiling, Yes, Amynander, if Solon had only, like other poets, made poetry the business of his life and had completed the tale which he brought with him from Egypt, and had not been compelled, by reason of the factions and troubles which he found stirring in his own country when he came home, to attend to other matters, in my d opinion he would have been as famous as Homer or Hesiod, or any poet.

And what was the tale about, Critias? said Amynander.

About the greatest action which the Athenians ever did, and which ought to have been the most famous, but, through the lapse of time and the destruction of the actors, it has not come down to us.

Tell us, said the other, the whole story, and how and from whom Solon heard this veritable tradition.

e   He replied, In the Egyptian Delta, at the head of which the river Nile divides, there is a certain district which is called the district of

Sais, and the great city of the district is also called Sais, and is the city
from which King Amasis came. The citizens have a deity for their
foundress; she is called in the Egyptian tongue Neith, and is asserted
by them to be the same whom the Hellenes call Athena. They are great
lovers of the Athenians and say that they are in some way related to
them. To this city came Solon and was received there with great   22
honor; he asked the priests, who were most skillful in such matters,
about antiquity, and made the discovery that neither he nor any
other Hellene knew anything worth mentioning about the times of old.
On one occasion, wishing to draw them on to speak of antiquity, he
began to tell about the most ancient things in our part of the world—
about Phoroneus, who is called 'the first man,' and about Niobe, and
after the Deluge, of the survival of Deucalion and Pyrrha, and he
traced the genealogy of their descendants and, reckoning up the dates, b
tried to compute how many years ago the events of which he was
speaking happened.

Thereupon one of the priests, who was of a very great age, said,
O Solon, Solon, you Hellenes are never anything but children, and
there is not an old man among you.

Solon in return asked him what he meant.

I mean to say, he replied, that in mind you are all young; there is
no old opinion handed down among you by ancient tradition, nor any
science which is hoary with age. And I will tell you why. There have c
been, and will be again, many destructions of mankind arising out of
many causes; the greatest have been brought about by the agencies of
fire and water, and other lesser ones by innumerable other causes.
There is a story which even you have preserved, that once upon a time
Phaethon, the son of Helios, having yoked the steeds in his father's
chariot, because he was not able to drive them in the path of his father, burned up all that was upon the earth, and was himself destroyed
by a thunderbolt. Now this has the form of a myth, but really signifies a declination of the bodies moving in the heavens around the d
earth, and a great conflagration of things upon the earth which recurs
after long intervals; at such times those who live upon the mountains
and in dry and lofty places are more liable to destruction than those
who dwell by rivers or on the seashore. And from this calamity we are
preserved by the liberation of the Nile, who is our never-failing savior.
When, on the other hand, the gods purge the earth with a deluge
of water, the survivors in your country are herdsmen and shepherds
who dwell on the mountains, but those who, like you, live in cities
are carried by the rivers into the sea. Whereas in this land, neither e
then nor at any other time, does the water come down from above
on the fields, having always a tendency to come up from below, for
which reason the traditions preserved here are the most ancient. The
fact is that wherever the extremity of winter frost or of summer sun
does not prevent, mankind exist, sometimes in greater, sometimes in

23 lesser numbers. And whatever happened either in your country or in ours, or in any other region of which we are informed—if there were any actions noble or great or in any other way remarkable, they have all been written down by us of old and are preserved in our temples. Whereas just when you and other nations are beginning to be provided with letters and the other requisites of civilized life, after the usual interval, the stream from heaven, like a pestilence, comes pouring

b down and leaves only those of you who are destitute of letters and education, and so you have to begin all over again like children, and know nothing of what happened in ancient times, either among us or among yourselves.

As for those genealogies of yours which you just now recounted to us, Solon, they are no better than the tales of children. In the first place you remember a single deluge only, but there were many previous ones; in the next place, you do not know that there formerly dwelt in your land the fairest and noblest race of men which ever

c lived, and that you and your whole city are descended from a small seed or remnant of them which survived. And this was unknown to you, because, for many generations, the survivors of that destruction died, leaving no written word. For there was a time, Solon, before the great deluge of all, when the city which now is Athens was first in war and in every way the best-governed of all cities, and is said to have performed the noblest deeds and to have had the fairest constitution of

d any of which tradition tells, under the face of heaven.

Solon marveled at his words, and earnestly requested the priests to inform him exactly and in order about these former citizens.

You are welcome to hear about them, Solon, said the priest, both for your own sake and for that of your city, and above all, for the sake of the goddess who is the common patron and parent and educator of both our cities. She founded your city a thousand years before ours, re-

e ceiving from the Earth and Hephaestus the seed of your race, and afterward she founded ours, of which the constitution is recorded in our sacred registers to be eight thousand years old. As touching your citizens of nine thousand years ago, I will briefly inform you of their

24 laws and of their most famous action; the exact particulars of the whole we will hereafter go through at our leisure in the sacred registers themselves. If you compare these very laws with ours you will find that many of ours are the counterpart of yours as they were in the olden time. In the first place, there is the caste of priests, which is separated from all the others; next, there are the artificers, who ply their several crafts by themselves and do not intermix, and also there

b is the class of shepherds and of hunters, as well as that of husbandmen. And you will observe, too, that the warriors in Egypt are distinct from all the other classes, and are commanded by the law to devote themselves solely to military pursuits; moreover, the weapons which they carry are shields and spears—a style of equipment which the goddess taught of Asiatics first to us, as in your part of the world first to you.

Then as to wisdom, do you observe how our law from the very first made a study of the whole order of things, extending even to prophecy and medicine which gives health, out of these divine ele- c ments deriving what was needful for human life, and adding every sort of knowledge which was akin to them. All this order and arrangement the goddess first imparted to you when establishing your city, and she chose the spot of earth in which you were born, because she saw that the happy temperament of the seasons in that land would produce the wisest of men. Wherefore the goddess, who was a lover d both of war and of wisdom, selected and first of all settled that spot which was the most likely to produce men likest herself. And there you dwelt, having such laws as these and still better ones, and excelled all mankind in all virtue, as became the children and disciples of the gods.

Many great and wonderful deeds are recorded of your state in our histories. But one of them exceeds all the rest in greatness and valor. For these histories tell of a mighty power which unprovoked e made an expedition against the whole of Europe and Asia, and to which your city put an end. This power came forth out of the Atlantic Ocean, for in those days the Atlantic was navigable, and there was an island situated in front of the straits which are by you called the Pillars of Heracles. The island was larger than Libya and Asia put to- 25 gether, and was the way to other islands, and from these you might pass to the whole of the opposite continent which surrounded the true ocean, for this sea which is within the Straits of Heracles is only a harbor, having a narrow entrance, but that other is a real sea, and the land surrounding it on every side may be most truly called a boundless continent. Now in this island of Atlantis there was a great and wonderful empire which had rule over the whole island and several others, and over parts of the continent, and, furthermore, the men of b Atlantis had subjected the parts of Libya within the columns of Heracles as far as Egypt, and of Europe as far as Tyrrhenia. This vast power, gathered into one, endeavored to subdue at a blow our country and yours and the whole of the region within the straits, and then, Solon, your country shone forth, in the excellence of her virtue and strength, among all mankind. She was pre-eminent in courage and military skill, and was the leader of the Hellenes. And when the rest c fell off from her, being compelled to stand alone, after having undergone the very extremity of danger, she defeated and triumphed over the invaders, and preserved from slavery those who were not yet subjugated, and generously liberated all the rest of us who dwell within the Pillars. But afterward there occurred violent earthquakes and floods, and in a single day and night of misfortune all your warlike d men in a body sank into the earth, and the island of Atlantis in like manner disappeared in the depths of the sea. For which reason the sea in those parts is impassable and impenetrable, because there is a shoal of mud in the way, and this was caused by the subsidence of the island.

e   I have told you briefly, Socrates, what the aged Critias heard from Solon and related to us. And when you were speaking yesterday about your city and citizens, the tale which I have just been repeating to you came into my mind, and I remarked with astonishment how, by some mysterious coincidence, you agreed in almost every particular

26 with the narrative of Solon, but I did not like to speak at the moment. For a long time had elapsed, and I had forgotten too much; I thought that I must first of all run over the narrative in my own mind, and then I would speak. And so I readily assented to your request yesterday, considering that in all such cases the chief difficulty is to find a tale suitable to our purpose, and that with such a tale we should be fairly well provided.

And therefore, as Hermocrates has told you, on my way home

b yesterday I at once communicated the tale to my companions as I remembered it, and after I left them, during the night by thinking I recovered nearly the whole of it. Truly, as is often said, the lessons of our childhood make a wonderful impression on our memories, for I am not sure that I could remember all the discourse of yesterday, but I should be much surprised if I forgot any of these things which I have

c heard very long ago. I listened at the time with childlike interest to the old man's narrative; he was very ready to teach me, and I asked him again and again to repeat his words, so that, like an indelible picture, they were branded into my mind. As soon as the day broke, I rehearsed them as he spoke them to my companions, that they, as well as myself, might have something to say. And now, Socrates, to make an end of my preface, I am ready to tell you the whole tale. I will give you not only the general heads, but the particulars, as they were told to me. The city and citizens, which you yesterday described to us in fiction, we will now transfer to the world of reality. It shall be the

d ancient city of Athens, and we will suppose that the citizens whom you imagined were our veritable ancestors of whom the priest spoke; they will perfectly harmonize, and there will be no inconsistency in saying that the citizens of your republic are these ancient Athenians. Let us divide the subject among us, and all endeavor according to our ability gracefully to execute the task which you have imposed upon us. Consider then, Socrates, if this narrative is suited to the purpose, or

e whether we should seek for some other instead.

SOCRATES: And what other, Critias, can we find that will be better than this which is natural and suitable to the festival of the goddess, and has the very great advantage of being a fact and not a fiction? How or where shall we find another if we abandon this? We cannot, and therefore you must tell the tale, and good luck to you, and

27 I in return for my yesterday's discourse will now rest and be a listener.

CRITIAS: Let me proceed to explain to you, Socrates, the order in which we have arranged our entertainment. Our intention is that Timaeus, who is the most of an astronomer among us, and has made the nature of the universe his special study, should speak first, beginning with the generation of the world and going down to the creation of man; next, I am to receive the men whom he has created, and of whom some will have profited by the excellent education which you have given them; and then, in accordance with the tale of Solon, and b equally with his law, we will bring them into court and make them citizens, as if they were those very Athenians whom the sacred Egyptian record has recovered from oblivion, and thenceforward we will speak of them as Athenians and fellow citizens.

SOCRATES: I see that I shall receive in my turn a perfect and splendid feast of reason. And now, Timaeus, you, I suppose, should speak next, after duly calling upon the gods.

TIMAEUS: All men, Socrates, who have any degree of right feel- c ing, at the beginning of every enterprise, whether small or great, always call upon God. And we, too, who are going to discourse of the nature of the universe, how created or how existing without creation, if we be not altogether out of our wits, must invoke the aid of gods and goddesses and pray that our words may be above all acceptable to them and in consequence to ourselves. Let this, then, be our invocation of the gods, to which I add an exhortation of myself to speak in d such manner as will be most intelligible to you, and will most accord with my own intent.

First then, in my judgment, we must make a distinction and ask, What is that which always is and has no becoming, and what is that which is always becoming and never is? That which is apprehended by intelligence and reason is always in the same state, but that which is conceived by opinion with the help of sensation and without 28 reason is always in a process of becoming and perishing and never really is. Now everything that becomes or is created must of necessity be created by some cause, for without a cause nothing can be created. The work of the creator, whenever he looks to the unchangeable and fashions the form and nature of his work after an unchangeable pattern, must necessarily be made fair and perfect, but when he looks b to the created only and uses a created pattern, it is not fair or perfect. Was the heaven then or the world, whether called by this or by any other more appropriate name—assuming the name, I am asking a question which has to be asked at the beginning of an inquiry about anything—was the world, I say, always in existence and without beginning, or created, and had it a beginning? Created, I reply, being visible and tangible and having a body, and therefore sensible, and all sensible things are apprehended by opinion and sense, and are in a c process of creation and created. Now that which is created must, as we affirm, of necessity be created by a cause. But the father and

maker of all this universe is past finding out, and even if we found him, to tell of him to all men would be impossible. This question, however, we must ask about the world. Which of the patterns had the artificer in view when he made it—the pattern of the unchangeable or
29 of that which is created? If the world be indeed fair and the artificer good, it is manifest that he must have looked to that which is eternal, but if what cannot be said without blasphemy is true, then to the created pattern. Everyone will see that he must have looked to the eternal, for the world is the fairest of creations and he is the best of causes. And having been created in this way, the world has been framed in the likeness of that which is apprehended by reason and mind and is unchangeable, and must therefore of necessity, if this is
b admitted, be a copy of something. Now it is all-important that the beginning of everything should be according to nature. And in speaking of the copy and the original we may assume that words are akin to the matter which they describe; when they relate to the lasting and permanent and intelligible, they ought to be lasting and unalterable, and, as far as their nature allows, irrefutable and invincible—noth-
c ing less. But when they express only the copy or likeness and not the eternal things themselves, they need only be likely and analogous to the former words. As being is to becoming, so is truth to belief. If then, Socrates, amidst the many opinions about the gods and the generation of the universe, we are not able to give notions which are altogether and in every respect exact and consistent with one another, do not be surprised. Enough if we adduce probabilities as likely as
d any others, for we must remember that I who am the speaker and you who are the judges are only mortal men, and we ought to accept the tale which is probable and inquire no further.

SOCRATES: Excellent, Timaeus, and we will do precisely as you bid us. The prelude is charming and is already accepted by us—may we beg of you to proceed to the strain?

TIMAEUS: Let me tell you then why the creator made this
e world of generation. He was good, and the good can never have any jealousy of anything. And being free from jealousy, he desired that all
30 things should be as like himself as they could be. This is in the truest sense the origin of creation and of the world, as we shall do well in believing on the testimony of wise men. God desired that all things should be good and nothing bad, so far as this was attainable. Wherefore also finding the whole visible sphere not at rest, but moving in an irregular and disorderly fashion, out of disorder he brought order, considering that this was in every way better than the other. Now the deeds of the best could never be or have been other than the fairest,
b and the creator, reflecting on the things which are by nature visible, found that no unintelligent creature taken as a whole could ever be fairer than the intelligent taken as a whole, and again that intelligence could not be present in anything which was devoid of soul. For which

reason, when he was framing the universe, he put intelligence in soul, and soul in body, that he might be the creator of a work which was by nature fairest and best. On this wise, using the language of probability, we may say that the world came into being—a living creature truly endowed with soul and intelligence by the providence of God.   c

This being supposed, let us proceed to the next stage. In the likeness of what animal did the creator make the world? It would be an unworthy thing to liken it to any nature which exists as a part only, for nothing can be beautiful which is like any imperfect thing. But let us suppose the world to be the very image of that whole of which all other animals both individually and in their tribes are portions. For the original of the universe contains in itself all intelligible beings, d just as this world comprehends us and all other visible creatures. For the deity, intending to make this world like the fairest and most perfect of intelligible beings, framed one visible animal comprehending within itself all other animals of a kindred nature. Are we right in 31 saying that there is one world, or that they are many and infinite? There must be one only if the created copy is to accord with the original. For that which includes all other intelligible creatures cannot have a second or companion; in that case there would be need of another living being which would include both, and of which they would be parts, and the likeness would be more truly said to resemble not them, but that other which included them. In order then that the world might be solitary, like the perfect animal, the creator made not b two worlds or an infinite number of them, but there is and ever will be one only-begotten and created heaven.

Now that which is created is of necessity corporeal, and also visible and tangible. And nothing is visible where there is no fire, or tangible which has no solidity, and nothing is solid without earth. Wherefore also God in the beginning of creation made the body of the universe to consist of fire and earth. But two things cannot be rightly put together without a third; there must be some bond of union be- c tween them. And the fairest bond is that which makes the most complete fusion of itself and the things which it combines, and proportion is best adapted to effect such a union. For whenever in any three numbers, whether cube or square, there is a mean, which is to the last term what the first term is to it, and again, when the mean is to the 32 first term as the last term is to the mean—then the mean becoming first and last, and the first and last both becoming means, they will all of them of necessity come to be the same, and having become the same with one another will be all one. If the universal frame had been created a surface only and having no depth, a single mean would have sufficed to bind together itself and the other terms, but now, as the b world must be solid, and solid bodies are always compacted not by one mean but by two, God placed water and air in the mean between fire and earth, and made them to have the same proportion so far as was

possible—as fire is to air so is air to water, and as air is to water so is water to earth—and thus he bound and put together a visible and
c tangible heaven. And for these reasons, and out of such elements which are in number four, the body of the world was created, and it was harmonized by proportion, and therefore has the spirit of friendship, and having been reconciled to itself, it was indissoluble by the hand of any other than the framer.

Now the creation took up the whole of each of the four elements, for the creator compounded the world out of all the fire and all the water and all the air and all the earth, leaving no part of any of them nor any power of them outside. His intention was, in the first
d place, that the animal should be as far as possible a perfect whole
33 and of perfect parts, secondly, that it should be one, leaving no remnants out of which another such world might be created, and also that it should be free from old age and unaffected by disease. Considering that if heat and cold and other powerful forces surround composite bodies and attack them from without, they decompose them before their time, and by bringing diseases and old age upon them make them waste away—for this cause and on these grounds he made the world one whole, having every part entire, and being therefore perfect and
b not liable to old age and disease. And he gave to the world the figure which was suitable and also natural. Now to the animal which was to comprehend all animals, that figure would be suitable which comprehends within itself all other figures. Wherefore he made the world in the form of a globe, round as from a lathe, having its extremes in every direction equidistant from the center, the most perfect and the most like itself of all figures, for he considered that the like is infinitely fairer than the unlike. This he finished off, making the
c surface smooth all around for many reasons—in the first place, because the living being had no need of eyes when there was nothing remaining outside him to be seen, nor of ears when there was nothing to be heard, and there was no surrounding atmosphere to be breathed, nor would there have been any use of organs by the help of which he might receive his food or get rid of what he had already digested, since there was nothing which went from him or came into him, for there was nothing besides him. Of design he was created thus—his own waste providing his own food, and all that he did or suffered taking
d place in and by himself. For the creator conceived that a being which was self-sufficient would be far more excellent than one which lacked anything, and, as he had no need to take anything or defend himself against anyone, the creator did not think it necessary to bestow upon
34 him hands, nor had he any need of feet, nor of the whole apparatus of walking. But the movement suited to his spherical form was assigned to him, being of all the seven that which is most appropriate to mind and intelligence, and he was made to move in the same manner and on the same spot, within his own limits revolving in a circle. All the

other six motions were taken away from him, and he was made not to partake of their deviations. And as this circular movement required no feet, the universe was created without legs and without feet.

Such was the whole plan of the eternal God about the god that was to be; he made it smooth and even, having a surface in every b direction equidistant from the center, a body entire and perfect, and formed out of perfect bodies. And in the center he put the soul, which he diffused throughout the body, making it also to be the exterior environment of it, and he made the universe a circle moving in a circle, one and solitary, yet by reason of its excellence able to converse with itself, and needing no other friendship or acquaintance. Having these purposes in view he created the world a blessed god.

Now God did not make the soul after the body, although we are speaking of them in this order, for when he put them together he c would never have allowed that the elder should be ruled by the younger, but this is a random manner of speaking which we have, because somehow we ourselves too are very much under the dominion of chance. Whereas he made the soul in origin and excellence prior to and older than the body, to be the ruler and mistress, of whom the body was to be the subject. And he made her out of the following elements and on this wise. From the being which is indivisible and un- 35 changeable, and from that kind of being which is distributed among bodies, he compounded a third and intermediate kind of being. He did likewise with the same and the different, blending together the indivisible kind of each with that which is portioned out in bodies. Then, taking the three new elements, he mingled them all into one form, compressing by force the reluctant and unsociable nature of the different into the same. When he had mingled them with the inter- b mediate kind of being and out of three made one, he again divided this whole into as many portions as was fitting, each portion being a compound of the same, the different, and being. And he proceeded to divide after this manner. First of all, he took away one part of the whole [1], and then he separated a second part which was double the first [2], and then he took away a third part which was half as much again as the second and three times as much as the first [3], and then he took a fourth part which was twice as much as the second [4], and a fifth part which was three times the third [9], and a sixth part which was eight times the first [8], and a seventh part which was twenty- c seven times the first [27]. After this he filled up the double intervals [that is, between 1, 2, 4, 8] and the triple [that is, between 1, 3, 9, 27], 36 cutting off yet other portions from the mixture and placing them in the intervals, so that in each interval there were two kinds of means, the one exceeding and exceeded by equal parts of its extremes [as for example, 1, $\frac{4}{3}$, 2, in which the mean $\frac{4}{3}$ is one third of 1 more than 1, and one third of 2 less than 2], the other being that kind of mean which exceeds and is exceeded by an equal number. Where

there were intervals of ¾ and of 4⁄3 and of 9⁄8, made by the connecting
b terms in the former intervals, he filled up all the intervals of 4⁄3 with
the interval of 9⁄8, leaving a fraction over, and the interval which this
fraction expressed was in the ratio of 256 to 243. And thus the whole
mixture out of which he cut these portions was all exhausted by him.
This entire compound he divided lengthwise into two parts which he
joined to one another at the center like the letter X, and bent them
c into a circular form, connecting them with themselves and each other
at the point opposite to their original meeting point, and, comprehending them in a uniform revolution upon the same axis, he made
the one the outer and the other the inner circle. Now the motion of the
outer circle he called the motion of the same, and the motion of the
inner circle the motion of the other or diverse. The motion of the same
he carried round by the side to the right, and the motion of the diverse diagonally to the left. And he gave dominion to the motion of
d the same and like, for that he left single and undivided, but the inner
motion he divided in six places and made seven unequal circles having
their intervals in ratios of two and three, three of each, and bade the
orbits proceed in a direction opposite to one another. And three [sun,
Mercury, Venus] he made to move with equal swiftness, and the remaining four [moon, Saturn, Mars, Jupiter] to move with unequal
swiftness to the three and to one another, but in due proportion.

Now when the creator had framed the soul according to his will,
he formed within her the corporeal universe, and brought the two to-
e gether and united them center to center. The soul, interfused everywhere from the center to the circumference of heaven, of which also
she is the external envelopment, herself turning in herself, began a
divine beginning of never-ceasing and rational life enduring
37 throughout all time. The body of heaven is visible, but the soul is invisible and partakes of reason and harmony, and, being made by the
best of intellectual and everlasting natures, is the best of things created. And because she is composed of the same and of the different
and of being these three, and is divided and united in due proportion,
and in her revolutions returns upon herself, the soul, when touching
anything which has being, whether dispersed in parts or undivided, is
stirred through all her powers to declare the sameness or difference
of that thing and some other, and to what individuals are related,
b and by what affected, and in what way and how and when, both in the
world of generation and in the world of immutable being. And when
reason, which works with equal truth, whether she be in the circle of
the diverse or of the same—in voiceless silence holding her onward
course in the sphere of the self-moved—when reason, I say, is hover-
ing around the sensible world and when the circle of the diverse also
moving truly imparts the intimations of sense to the whole soul, then
c arise opinions and beliefs sure and certain. But when reason is concerned with the rational, and the circle of the same moving smoothly

declares it, then intelligence and knowledge are necessarily achieved. And if anyone affirms that in which these two are found to be other than the soul, he will say the very opposite of the truth.

When the father and creator saw the creature which he had made moving and living, the created image of the eternal gods, he rejoiced, and in his joy determined to make the copy still more like the original, and as this was an eternal living being, he sought to make the universe eternal, so far as might be. Now the nature of the ideal be- d ing was everlasting, but to bestow this attribute in its fullness upon a creature was impossible. Wherefore he resolved to have a moving image of eternity, and when he set in order the heaven, he made this image eternal but moving according to number, while eternity itself rests in unity, and this image we call time. For there were no days e and nights and months and years before the heaven was created, but when he constructed the heaven he created them also. They are all parts of time, and the past and future are created species of time, which we unconsciously but wrongly transfer to eternal being, for we say that it 'was,' or 'is,' or 'will be,' but the truth is that 'is' alone is 38 properly attributed to it, and that 'was' and 'will be' are only to be spoken of becoming in time, for they are motions, but that which is immovably the same forever cannot become older or younger by time, nor can it be said that it came into being in the past, or has come into being now, or will come into being in the future, nor is it subject at all to any of those states which affect moving and sensible things and of which generation is the cause. These are the forms of time, which imitates eternity and revolves according to a law of number. Moreover, when we say that what has become *is* become and what becomes *is* b becoming, and that what will become *is* about to become and that the nonexistent *is* nonexistent—all these are inaccurate modes of expression. But perhaps this whole subject will be more suitably discussed on some other occasion.

Time, then, and the heaven came into being at the same instant in order that, having been created together, if ever there was to be a dissolution of them, they might be dissolved together. It was framed after the pattern of the eternal nature—that it might resemble this as far as was possible, for the pattern exists from eternity, and the created heaven has been and is and will be in all time. Such was the c mind and thought of God in the creation of time. The sun and moon and five other stars, which are called the planets, were created by him in order to distinguish and preserve the numbers of time, and when he had made their several bodies, he placed them in the orbits in which the circle of the other was revolving—in seven orbits seven stars. First, d there was the moon in the orbit nearest the earth, and the next the sun, in the second orbit above the earth; then came the morning star and the star said to be sacred to Hermes, moving in orbits which have an equal swiftness with the sun, but in an opposite direction, and this

is the reason why the sun and Hermes and Lucifer regularly overtake
and are overtaken by each other. To enumerate the places which he
assigned to the other stars and to give all the reasons why he assigned
e them, although a secondary matter, would give more trouble than the
primary. These things at some future time, when we are at leisure,
may have the consideration which they deserve, but not at present.

Now, when each of the stars which were necessary to the creation of time had come to its proper orbit, and they had become living
creatures having bodies fastened by vital chains, and learned their appointed task—moving in the motion of the diverse, which is diagonal
39 and passes through and is governed by the motion of the same—they
revolved, some in a larger and some in a lesser orbit, those which
had the lesser orbit revolving faster, and those which had the larger
more slowly. Now by reason of the motion of the same, those which
revolved fastest appeared to be overtaken by those which moved
slower although they really overtook them, for the motion of the same
b made them all turn in a spiral, and, because some went one way and
some another, that which receded most slowly from the sphere of the
same, which was the swiftest, appeared to follow it most nearly. That
there might be some visible measure of their relative swiftness and
slowness as they proceeded in their eight courses, God lighted a fire,
which we now call the sun, in the second from the earth of these orbits,
that it might give light to the whole of heaven, and that the animals,
as many as nature intended, might participate in number, learning
c arithmetic from the revolution of the same and the like. Thus, then,
and for this reason the night and the day were created, being the
period of the one most intelligent revolution. And the month is accomplished when the moon has completed her orbit and overtaken the
sun, and the year when the sun has completed his own orbit. Mankind,
with hardly an exception, have not remarked the periods of the other
stars, and they have no name for them, and do not measure them
against one another by the help of number, and hence they can
d scarcely be said to know that their wanderings, being of vast number
and admirable for their variety, make up time. And yet there is no
difficulty in seeing that the perfect number of time fulfills the perfect
year when all the eight revolutions, having their relative degrees of swiftness, are accomplished together and attain their
completion at the same time, measured by the rotation of the same
and equally moving. After this manner, and for these reasons, came
into being such of the stars as in their heavenly progress received
reversals of motion, to the end that the created heaven might be
e as like as possible to the perfect and intelligible animal, by imitation
of its eternal nature.

Thus far and until the birth of time the created universe was made
in the likeness of the original, but inasmuch as all animals were not

yet comprehended therein, it was still unlike. Therefore, the creator proceeded to fashion it after the nature of the pattern in this remaining point. Now as in the ideal animal the mind perceives ideas or species of a certain nature and number, he thought that this created animal ought to have species of a like nature and number. There are four such. One of them is the heavenly race of the gods; 40 another, the race of birds whose way is in the air; the third, the watery species; and the fourth, the pedestrian and land creatures. Of the heavenly and divine, he created the greater part out of fire, that they might be the brightest of all things and fairest to behold, and he fashioned them after the likeness of the universe in the figure of a circle, and made them follow the intelligent motion of the supreme, distributing them over the whole circumference of heaven, which was to be a true cosmos or glorious world spangled with them all over. And he gave to each of them two movements—the first, a movement on the same spot after the same manner, whereby they ever b continue to think consistently the same thoughts about the same things, in the same respect; the second, a forward movement, in which they are controlled by the revolution of the same and the like—but by the other five motions they were unaffected, in order that each of them might attain the highest perfection. And for this reason the fixed stars were created, to be divine and eternal animals, ever abiding and revolving after the same manner and on the same spot, and the other stars which reverse their motion and are subject to deviations of this kind were created in the manner already described. The earth, which is our nurse, clinging around the pole which is extended through the universe, he framed to be the guardian and artificer of night and day, first and eldest of gods that are in the interior of c heaven. Vain would be the attempt to tell all the figures of them circling as in dance, and their juxtapositions, and the return of them in their revolutions upon themselves, and their approximations, and to say which of these deities in their conjunctions meet, and which of them are in opposition, and in what order they get behind and before one another, and when they are severally eclipsed to our sight and again reappear, sending terrors and intimations of the future to those d who cannot calculate their movements—to attempt to tell of all this without a visible representation of the heavenly system would be labor in vain. Enough on this head, and now let what we have said about the nature of the created and visible gods have an end.

To know or tell the origin of the other divinities is beyond us, and we must accept the traditions of the men of old time who affirm themselves to be the offspring of the gods—that is what they say— and they must surely have known their own ancestors. How can we e doubt the word of the children of the gods? Although they give no probable or certain proofs, still, as they declare that they are speaking of what took place in their own family, we must conform to custom and believe them. In this manner, then, according to them, the genealogy of these gods is to be received and set forth.

Oceanus and Tethys were the children of Earth and Heaven, and from these sprang Phorcys and Cronus and Rhea, and all that generation, and from Cronus and Rhea sprang Zeus and Hera, and all those
41 who are said to be their brethren, and others who were the children of these.

Now, when all of them, both those who visibly appear in their revolutions as well as those other gods who are of a more retiring nature, had come into being, the creator of the universe addressed them in these words. Gods, children of gods, who are my works and of whom I am the artificer and father, my creations are indissoluble, if
b so I will. All that is bound may be undone, but only an evil being would wish to undo that which is harmonious and happy. Wherefore, since ye are but creatures, ye are not altogether immortal and indissoluble, but ye shall certainly not be dissolved, nor be liable to the fate of death, having in my will a greater and mightier bond than those with which ye were bound at the time of your birth. And now listen to my instructions. Three tribes of mortal beings remain to be created— without them the universe will be incomplete, for it will not contain
c every kind of animal which it ought to contain, if it is to be perfect. On the other hand, if they were created by me and received life at my hands, they would be on an equality with the gods. In order then that they may be mortal, and that this universe may be truly universal, do ye, according to your natures, betake yourselves to the formation of animals, imitating the power which was shown by me in creating you. The part of them worthy of the name immortal, which is called divine and is the guiding principle of those who are willing to follow justice and you—of that divine part I will myself sow the seed, and having made a beginning, I will hand the work over to you. And do ye then
d interweave the mortal with the immortal and make and beget living creatures, and give them food and make them to grow, and receive them again in death.

Thus he spoke, and once more into the cup in which he had previously mingled the soul of the universe he poured the remains of the elements, and mingled them in much the same manner; they were not, however, pure as before, but diluted to the second and third degree. And having made it he divided the whole mixture into souls equal in number to the stars and assigned each soul to a star, and having there
e placed them as in a chariot he showed them the nature of the universe and declared to them the laws of destiny, according to which their first birth would be one and the same for all—no one should suffer a disadvantage at his hands. They were to be sown in the instruments of time severally adapted to them, and to come forth the most religious
42 of animals, and as human nature was of two kinds, the superior race

was of such and such a character, and would hereafter be called man.
Now, when they should be implanted in bodies by necessity and be
always gaining or losing some part of their bodily substance, then, in
the first place, it would be necessary that they should all have in them
one and the same faculty of sensation, arising out of irresistible impressions; in the second place, they must have love, in which pleasure
and pain mingle—also fear and anger, and the feelings which are b
akin or opposite to them. If they conquered these they would live
righteously, and if they were conquered by them, unrighteously. He
who lived well during his appointed time was to return and dwell in
his native star, and there he would have a blessed and congenial existence. But if he failed in attaining this, at the second birth he would
pass into a woman, and if, when in that state of being, he did not desist from evil, he would continually be changed into some brute who c
resembled him in the evil nature which he had acquired, and would
not cease from his toils and transformations until he helped the revolution of the same and the like within him to draw in its train the
turbulent mob of later accretions made up of fire and air and water
and earth, and by this victory of reason over the irrational returned to
the form of his first and better state. Having given all these laws to his d
creatures, that he might be guiltless of future evil in any of them, the
creator sowed some of them in the earth, and some in the moon, and
some in the other instruments of time. And when he had sown them
he committed to the younger gods the fashioning of their mortal bodies, and desired them to furnish what was still lacking to the human
soul, and having made all the suitable additions, to rule over them, e
and to pilot the mortal animal in the best and wisest manner which
they could and avert from him all but self-inflicted evils.

When the creator had made all these ordinances he remained in
his own accustomed nature, and his children heard and were obedient
to their father's word, and receiving from him the immortal principle
of a mortal creature, in imitation of their own creator they borrowed
portions of fire and earth and water and air from the world, which
were hereafter to be restored—these they took and welded them to- 43
gether, not with the indissoluble chains by which they were themselves bound, but with little pegs too small to be visible, making up
out of all the four elements each separate body, and fastening the
courses of the immortal soul in a body which was in a state of perpetual influx and efflux. Now these courses, detained as in a vast river, b
neither overcame nor were overcome, but were hurrying and hurried
to and fro, so that the whole animal was moved and progressed, irreg-
ularly however and irrationally and anyhow, in all the six directions
of motion, wandering backward and forward, and right and left, and
up and down, and in all the six directions. For great as was the advancing and retiring flood which provided nourishment, the affections
produced by external contact caused still greater tumult—when the

c body of anyone met and came into collision with some external fire or with the solid earth or the gliding waters, or was caught in the tempest borne on the air—and the motions produced by any of these impulses were carried through the body to the soul. All such motions have consequently received the general name of 'sensations,' which they still retain. And they did in fact at that time create a very great and mighty

d movement; uniting with the ever-flowing stream in stirring up and violently shaking the courses of the soul, they completely stopped the revolution of the same by their opposing current and hindered it from predominating and advancing, and they so disturbed the nature of the other or diverse that the three double intervals [that is, between 1, 2, 4, 8] and the three triple intervals [that is, between 1, 3, 9, 27], together with the mean terms and connecting links which are expressed by the ratios of 3:2 and 4:3 and of 9:8—these, although they cannot be wholly undone except by him who united them, were twisted

e by them in all sorts of ways, and the circles were broken and disordered in every possible manner, so that when they moved they were tumbling to pieces and moved irrationally, at one time in a reverse direction, and then again obliquely, and then upside down, as you might imagine a person who is upside down and has his head leaning upon the ground and his feet up against something in the air, and when he is in such a position, both he and the spectator fancy that the right of either is his left, and the left right. If, when powerfully experiencing these and similar effects, the revolutions of the soul come in contact

44 with some external thing, either of the class of the same or of the other, they speak of the same or of the other in a manner the very opposite of the truth, and they become false and foolish, and there is no course or revolution in them which has a guiding or directing power. And if again any sensations enter in violently from without and drag after them the whole vessel of the soul, then the courses of the soul, though they seem to conquer, are really conquered.

And by reason of all these affections, the soul, when incased in a

b mortal body, now, as in the beginning, is at first without intelligence, but when the flood of growth and nutriment abates and the courses of the soul, calming down, go their own way and become steadier as time goes on, then the several circles return to their natural form and their revolutions are corrected, and they call the same and the other by their right names and make the possessor of them to become a rational being. And if these combine in him with any true nurture or

c education, he attains the fullness and health of the perfect man, and escapes the worst disease of all, but if he neglects education he walks lame to the end of his life and returns imperfect and good for nothing to the world below. This, however, is a later stage; at present we must treat more exactly the subject before us, which involves a preliminary inquiry into the generation of the body and its members, and how the

soul was created—for what reason and by what providence of the
gods—and holding fast to probability we must pursue our way.   d

First, then, the gods, imitating the spherical shape of the universe, enclosed the two divine courses in a spherical body, that,
namely, which we now term the head, being the most divine part of
us and the lord of all that is in us; to this the gods, when they put together the body, gave all the other members to be servants, considering that it must partake of every sort of motion. In order then that it
might not tumble about among the high and deep places of the earth,   e
but might be able to get over the one and out of the other, they provided the body to be its vehicle and means of locomotion, which consequently had length and was furnished with four limbs extended and
flexible. These God contrived to be instruments of locomotion with
which it might take hold and find support, and so be able to pass   45
through all places, carrying on high the dwelling place of the most
sacred and divine part of us. Such was the origin of legs and hands,
which for this reason were attached to every man, and the gods, deeming the front part of man to be more honorable and more fit to command than the hinder part, made us to move mostly in a forward
direction. Wherefore man must needs have his front part unlike and
distinguished from the rest of his body. And so in the vessel of the
head, they first of all put a face in which they inserted organs to minister in all things to the providence of the soul, and they appointed
this part, which has authority, to be the natural front. And of the or- b
gans they first contrived the eyes to give light, and the principle according to which they were inserted was as follows. So much of fire as
would not burn, but gave a gentle light, they formed into a substance
akin to the light of everyday life, and the pure fire which is within us
and related thereto they made to flow through the eyes in a stream
smooth and dense, compressing the whole eye and especially the
center part, so that it kept out everything of a coarser nature and al- c
lowed to pass only this pure element. When the light of day surrounds
the stream of vision, then like falls upon like, and they coalesce, and
one body is formed by natural affinity in the line of vision, wherever
the light that falls from within meets with an external object. And the
whole stream of vision, being similarly affected in virtue of similarity, d
diffuses the motions of what it touches or what touches it over the
whole body, until they reach the soul, causing that perception which
we call sight. But when night comes on and the external and kindred
fire departs, then the stream of vision is cut off, for going forth to an
unlike element it is changed and extinguished, being no longer of one
nature with the surrounding atmosphere which is now deprived of
fire, and so the eye no longer sees, and we feel disposed to sleep. For e
when the eyelids, which the gods invented for the preservation of
sight, are closed, they keep in the internal fire, and the power of the

fire diffuses and equalizes the inward motions; when they are equalized, there is rest, and when the rest is profound, sleep comes over us
46 scarce disturbed by dreams, but where any greater motions still remain, according to their nature and locality, they engender within us corresponding visions in dreams, which are remembered by us when we awaken to the external world. And now there is no longer any difficulty in understanding the creation of images in mirrors and all smooth and bright surfaces. For from the communion of the internal and external fires, and again from the union of them and their numerous transformations when they meet in the mirror, all these ap-
b pearances of necessity arise when the fire from the face coalesces with the fire from the eye on the bright and smooth surface. And right appears left and left right, because the visual rays come into contact with the rays emitted by the object in a manner contrary to the usual mode of meeting. But the right appears right, and the left left, when the position of one of the two concurring lights is reversed, and this happens when the mirror is concave and its smooth surface repels
c the right stream of vision to the left side, and the left to the right. Or if the mirror be turned vertically, then the concavity makes the countenance appear to be all upside down, and the lower rays are driven upward and the upper downward.

All these are to be reckoned among the second and co-operative
d causes which God, carrying into execution the idea of the best as far as possible, uses as his ministers. They are thought by most men not to be the second, but the prime causes of all things, because they freeze and heat, and contract and dilate, and the like. But they are not so, for they are incapable of reason or intellect; the only being which can properly have mind is the invisible soul, whereas fire and water, and earth and air, are all of them visible bodies. The lover of
e intellect and knowledge ought to explore causes of intelligent nature first of all, and, secondly, of those things which, being moved by others, are compelled to move others. And this is what we too must do. Both kinds of causes should be acknowledged by us, but a distinction should be made between those which are endowed with mind and are the workers of things fair and good, and those which are deprived of intelligence and always produce chance effects without order or design. Of the second or co-operative causes of sight, which help to give to the eyes the power which they now possess, enough has been said. I will therefore now proceed to speak of the higher use and purpose
47 for which God has given them to us. The sight in my opinion is the source of the greatest benefit to us, for had we never seen the stars and the sun and the heaven, none of the words which we have spoken about the universe would ever have been uttered. But now the sight of day and night, and the months and the revolutions of the years have created number and have given us a conception of time, and the power of inquiring about the nature of the universe. And from this

source we have derived philosophy, than which no greater good ever b
was or will be given by the gods to mortal man. This is the greatest
boon of sight, and of the lesser benefits why should I speak? Even
the ordinary man if he were deprived of them would bewail his loss,
but in vain. Thus much let me say however. God invented and gave us
sight to the end that we might behold the courses of intelligence in the
heaven, and apply them to the courses of our own intelligence which
are akin to them, the unperturbed to the perturbed, and that we, learn- c
ing them and partaking of the natural truth of reason, might imitate
the absolutely unerring courses of God and regulate our own vagaries.
The same may be affirmed of speech and hearing. They have been
given by the gods to the same end and for a like reason. For this is the
principal end of speech, whereto it most contributes. Moreover, so
much of music as is adapted to the sound of the voice and to the sense
of hearing is granted to us for the sake of harmony. And harmony, d
which has motions akin to the revolutions of our souls, is not regarded by the intelligent votary of the Muses as given by them with a
view to irrational pleasure, which is deemed to be the purpose of it in
our day, but as meant to correct any discord which may have arisen
in the courses of the soul, and to be our ally in bringing her into harmony and agreement with herself, and rhythm too was given by them
for the same reason, on account of the irregular and graceless ways e
which prevail among mankind generally, and to help us against them.

Thus far in what we have been saying, with small exceptions, the
works of intelligence have been set forth, and now we must place by
the side of them in our discourse the things which come into being
through necessity—for the creation of this world is the combined work
of necessity and mind. Mind, the ruling power, persuaded necessity 48
to bring the greater part of created things to perfection, and thus and
after this manner in the beginning, through necessity made subject to
reason, this universe was created. But if a person will truly tell of the
way in which the work was accomplished, he must include the variable cause as well, and explain its influence. Wherefore, we must return again and find another suitable beginning—as about the former b
matters, so also about these. To which end we must consider the nature of fire and water and air and earth, such as they were prior to the
creation of the heaven, and what was happening to them in this previous state, for no one has as yet explained the manner of their generation, but we speak of fire and the rest of them, as though men knew
their natures, and we maintain them to be the first principles and letters or elements of the whole, when they cannot reasonably be compared by a man of any sense even to syllables or first compounds. And c
let me say thus much. I will not now speak of the first principle or
principles of all things, or by whatever name they are to be called, for
this reason—because it is difficult to set forth my opinion according
to the method of discussion which we are at present employing. Do not

imagine, any more than I can bring myself to imagine, that I should be right in undertaking so great and difficult a task. Remembering
d what I said at first about probability, I will do my best to give as probable an explanation as any other—or rather, more probable—and I will first go back to the beginning and try to speak of each thing and of all. Once more, then, at the commencement of my discourse, I call upon God and beg him to be our savior out of a strange and unwonted
e inquiry, and to bring us to the haven of probability. So now let us begin again.

This new beginning of our discussion of the universe requires a fuller division than the former, for then we made two classes; now a third must be revealed. The two sufficed for the former discussion. One, which we assumed, was a pattern intelligible and always the same, and the second was only the imitation of the pattern, generated
49 and visible. There is also a third kind which we did not distinguish at the time, conceiving that the two would be enough. But now the argument seems to require that we should set forth in words another kind, which is difficult of explanation and dimly seen. What nature are we to attribute to this new kind of being? We reply that it is the recepta-
b cle, and in a manner the nurse, of all generation. I have spoken the truth, but I must express myself in clearer language, and this will be an arduous task for many reasons, and in particular because I must first raise questions concerning fire and the other elements, and determine what each of them is, for to say, with any probability or certitude, which of them should be called water rather than fire, and which should be called any of them rather than all or some one of them, is a difficult matter. How, then, shall we settle this point, and what questions about the elements may be fairly raised?

In the first place, we see that what we just now called water, by
c condensation, I suppose, becomes stone and earth, and this same element, when melted and dispersed, passes into vapor and air. Air, again, when inflamed, becomes fire, and, again, fire, when condensed and extinguished, passes once more into the form of air, and once more, air, when collected and condensed, produces cloud and mist—and from these, when still more compressed, comes flowing water, and from water comes earth and stones once more—and thus genera-
d tion appears to be transmitted from one to the other in a circle. Thus, then, as the several elements never present themselves in the same form, how can anyone have the assurance to assert positively that any of them, whatever it may be, is one thing rather than another? No one can. But much the safest plan is to speak of them as follows. Anything which we see to be continually changing, as, for example, fire, we must not call 'this' or 'that,' but rather say that it is 'of such a nature,' nor let us speak of water as 'this,' but always as 'such,' nor must we imply that there is any stability in any of those things which we
e indicate by the use of the words 'this' and 'that,' supposing ourselves

to signify something thereby, for they are too volatile to be detained
in any such expressions as 'this,' or 'that,' or 'relative to this,' or any
other mode of speaking which represents them as permanent. We
ought not to apply 'this' to any of them, but rather the word 'such,'
which expresses the similar principle circulating in each and all of
them; for example, that should be called 'fire' which is of such a nature always, and so of everything that has generation. That in which
the elements severally grow up, and appear, and decay, is alone to be
called by the name 'this' or 'that,' but that which is of a certain nature, 50
hot or white, or anything which admits of opposite qualities, and all
things that are compounded of them, ought not to be so denominated.
Let me make another attempt to explain my meaning more clearly.
Suppose a person to make all kinds of figures of gold and to be always
remodeling each form into all the rest; somebody points to one of
them and asks what it is. By far the safest and truest answer is, 'That b
is gold,' and not to call the triangle or any other figures which are
formed in the gold 'these,' as though they had existence, since they
are in process of change while he is making the assertion, but if the
questioner be willing to take the safe and indefinite expression, 'such,'
we should be satisfied. And the same argument applies to the universal
nature which receives all bodies—that must be always called the
same, for, inasmuch as she always receives all things, she never departs at all from her own nature and never, in any way or at any time,
assumes a form like that of any of the things which enter into her; she
is the natural recipient of all impressions, and is stirred and informed c
by them, and appears different from time to time by reason of them.
But the forms which enter into and go out of her are the likenesses of
eternal realities modeled after their patterns in a wonderful and
mysterious manner, which we will hereafter investigate. For the present we have only to conceive of three natures: first, that which is in
process of generation; secondly, that in which the generation takes
place; and thirdly, that of which the thing generated is a resemblance d
naturally produced. And we may liken the receiving principle to a
mother, and the source or spring to a father, and the intermediate nature to a child, and may remark further that if the model is to take
every variety of form, then the matter in which the model is fashioned will not be duly prepared unless it is formless and free from the
impress of any of those shapes which it is hereafter to receive from
without. For if the matter were like any of the supervening forms, e
then whenever any opposite or entirely different nature was stamped
upon its surface, it would take the impression badly, because it would
intrude its own shape. Wherefore that which is to receive all forms
should have no form, as in making perfumes they first contrive that
the liquid substance which is to receive the scent shall be as inodorous
as possible, or as those who wish to impress figures on soft substances
do not allow any previous impression to remain, but begin by making

51 the surface as even and smooth as possible. In the same way that which is to receive perpetually and through its whole extent the resemblances of all eternal beings ought to be devoid of any particular form. Wherefore the mother and receptacle of all created and visible and in any way sensible things is not to be termed earth or air or fire or water, or any of their compounds, or any of the elements from which these are derived, but is an invisible and formless being which
b receives all things and in some mysterious way partakes of the intelligible, and is most incomprehensible. In saying this we shall not be far wrong; as far, however, as we can attain to a knowledge of her from the previous considerations, we may truly say that fire is that part of her nature which from time to time is inflamed, and water that which is moistened, and that the mother substance becomes earth and air, in so far as she receives the impressions of them.

c   Let us consider this question more precisely. Is there any self-existent fire, and do all those things which we call self-existent exist, or are only those things which we see or in some way perceive through the bodily organs truly existent, and nothing whatever besides them? And are those intelligible forms, of which we are accustomed to speak, nothing at all, and only a name? Here is a question which we must not leave unexamined or undetermined, nor must we affirm too confidently that there can be no decision; neither must we interpolate in
d our present long discourse a digression equally long, but if it is possible to set forth a great principle in a few words, that is just what we want.

Thus I state my view. If mind and true opinion are two distinct classes, then I say that there certainly are these self-existent ideas unperceived by sense, and apprehended only by the mind; if, however, as some say, true opinion differs in no respect from mind, then ev-
e erything that we perceive through the body is to be regarded as most real and certain. But we must affirm them to be distinct, for they have a distinct origin and are of a different nature; the one is implanted in us by instruction, the other by persuasion; the one is always accompanied by true reason, the other is without reason; the one cannot be overcome by persuasion, but the other can; and lastly, every man may be said to share in true opinion, but mind is the attribute of the gods and of very few men. Wherefore also we must acknowledge that one kind of being is the form which is always the same, uncreated
52 and indestructible, never receiving anything into itself from without, nor itself going out to any other, but invisible and imperceptible by any sense, and of which the contemplation is granted to intelligence only. And there is another nature of the same name with it, and like to it, perceived by sense, created, always in motion, becoming in place and again vanishing out of place, which is apprehended by opinion
b jointly with sense. And there is a third nature, which is space and is eternal, and admits not of destruction and provides a home for all

created things, and is apprehended, when all sense is absent, by a
kind of spurious reason, and is hardly real—which we, beholding as
in a dream, say of all existence that it must of necessity be in some
place and occupy a space, but that what is neither in heaven nor in
earth has no existence. Of these and other things of the same kind,
relating to the true and waking reality of nature, we have only this
dreamlike sense, and we are unable to cast off sleep and determine c
the truth about them. For an image, since the reality after which it is
modeled does not belong to it, and it exists ever as the fleeting shadow
of some other, must be inferred to be in another [that is, in space],
grasping existence in some way or other, or it could not be at all. But
true and exact reason, vindicating the nature of true being, maintains
that while two things [that is, the image and space] are different they
cannot exist one of them in the other and so be one and also two at
the same time.

Thus have I concisely given the result of my thoughts, and my d
verdict is that being and space and generation, these three, existed in
their three ways before the heaven, and that the nurse of generation,
moistened by water and inflamed by fire, and receiving the forms of
earth and air, and experiencing all the affections which accompany
these, presented a strange variety of appearances, and being full of
powers which were neither similar nor equally balanced, was never e
in any part in a state of equipoise, but swaying unevenly hither and
thither, was shaken by them, and by its motion again shook them, and
the elements when moved were separated and carried continually,
some one way, some another. As, when grain is shaken and winnowed
by fans and other instruments used in the threshing of corn, the close
and heavy particles are borne away and settle in one direction, and 53
the loose and light particles in another. In this manner, the four kinds
or elements were then shaken by the receiving vessel, which, moving
like a winnowing machine, scattered far away from one another the
elements most unlike, and forced the most similar elements into close
contact. Wherefore the various elements had distinct places also before they were arranged so as to form the universe. At first, however,
they were all without reason and measure. But when the world began b
to get into order, fire and water and earth and air did indeed show
faint traces of themselves, but were altogether in such a condition as
one may expect to find wherever God is absent. Such, I say, being their
nature, God now fashioned them by form and number. Let it be consistently maintained by us in all that we say that God made them as
far as possible the fairest and best, out of things which were not fair
and good. And now I will endeavor to show you the disposition and
generation of them by an unaccustomed argument which I am com- c
pelled to use. But I believe that you will be able to follow me, for your
education has made you familiar with the methods of science.

In the first place, then, as is evident to all, fire and earth and water

and air are bodies. And every sort of body possesses volume, and every volume must necessarily be bounded by surfaces, and every rectilinear surface is composed of triangles, and all triangles are originally of
d   two kinds, both of which are made up of one right and two acute angles; one of them has at either end of the base the half of a divided right angle, having equal sides, while in the other the right angle is divided into unequal parts, having unequal sides. These, then, proceeding by a combination of probability with demonstration, we assume to be the original elements of fire and the other bodies, but the principles which are prior to these God only knows, and he of men
e   who is the friend of God. And next we have to determine what are the four most beautiful bodies which could be formed, unlike one another, yet in some instances capable of resolution into one another, for having discovered thus much, we shall know the true origin of earth and fire and of the proportionate and intermediate elements. For we shall not be willing to allow that there are any distinct kinds of visible bodies fairer than these. Wherefore we must endeavor to construct the four forms of bodies which excel in beauty, and secure the
54   right to say that we have sufficiently apprehended their nature. Now of the two triangles, the isosceles has one form only; the scalene or unequal-sided has an infinite number. Of the infinite forms we must again select the most beautiful, if we are to proceed in due order, and anyone who can point out a more beautiful form than ours for the construction of these bodies, shall carry off the palm, not as an enemy, but as a friend. Now, the one which we maintain to be the most beautiful of all the many triangles—and we need not speak of the others— is that of which the double forms a third triangle which is equilateral.
b   The reason of this would be long to tell; he who disproves what we are saying, and shows that we are mistaken, may claim a friendly victory. Then let us choose two triangles, out of which fire and the other elements have been constructed, one isosceles, the other having the square of the longer side equal to three times the square of the lesser side.

Now is the time to explain what was before obscurely said. There was an error in imagining that all the four elements might be gen-
c   erated by and into one another; this, I say, was an erroneous supposition, for there are generated from the triangles which we have selected four kinds—three from the one which has the sides unequal, the fourth alone framed out of the isosceles triangle. Hence they cannot all be resolved into one another, a great number of small bodies being combined into a few large ones, or the converse. But three of them can be thus resolved and compounded, for they all spring from one, and when the greater bodies are broken up, many small bodies will
d   spring up out of them and take their own proper figures. Or, again, when many small bodies are dissolved into their triangles, by their total number, they can form one large mass of another kind. So much

for their passage into one another. I have now to speak of their several kinds, and show out of what combinations of numbers each of them was formed. The first will be the simplest and smallest construction, and its element is that triangle which has its hypotenuse twice the lesser side. When two such triangles are joined at the diagonal, and e this is repeated three times, and the triangles rest their diagonals and shorter sides on the same point as a center, a single equilateral triangle is formed out of six triangles, and four equilateral triangles, if put together, make out of every three plane angles one solid angle, being that which is nearest to the most obtuse of plane angles. And out of 55 the combination of these four angles arises the first solid form which distributes into equal and similar parts the whole circle in which it is inscribed. The second species of solid is formed out of the same triangles, which unite as eight equilateral triangles and form one solid angle out of four plane angles, and out of six such angles the second body is completed. And the third body is made up of one hundred and twenty triangular elements, forming twelve solid angles, each of them b included in five plane equilateral triangles, having altogether twenty bases, each of which is an equilateral triangle. The one element [that is, the triangle which has its hypotenuse twice the lesser side], having generated these figures, generated no more, but the isosceles triangle produced the fourth elementary figure, which is compounded of four such triangles, joining their right angles in a center, and forming one equilateral quadrangle. Six of these united form eight solid angles, each of which is made by the combination of three plane right angles; c the figure of the body thus composed is a cube, having six plane quadrangular equilateral bases. There was yet a fifth combination which God used in the delineation of the universe with figures of animals.

Now he who, duly reflecting on all this, inquires whether the worlds are to be regarded as indefinite or definite in number will be of opinion that the notion of their indefiniteness is characteristic of a sadly indefinite and ignorant mind. He, however, who raises the question whether they are to be truly regarded as one or five, takes up a d more reasonable position. Arguing from probabilities, I am of opinion that they are one; another, regarding the question from another point of view, will be of another mind. But, leaving this inquiry, let us proceed to distribute the elementary forms, which have now been created in idea, among the four elements.

To earth, then, let us assign the cubic form, for earth is the most immovable of the four and the most plastic of all bodies, and that e which has the most stable bases must of necessity be of such a nature. Now, of the triangles which we assumed at first, that which has two equal sides is by nature more firmly based than that which has unequal sides, and of the compound figures which are formed out of either, the plane equilateral quadrangle has necessarily a more stable

basis than the equilateral triangle, both in the whole and in the parts.
56 Wherefore, in assigning this figure to earth, we adhere to probability,
and to water we assign that one of the remaining forms which is the
least movable, and the most movable of them to fire, and to air that
which is intermediate. Also we assign the smallest body to fire, and
the greatest to water, and the intermediate in size to air, and, again,
the acutest body to fire, and the next in acuteness to air, and the third
to water. Of all these elements, that which has the fewest bases must
b necessarily be the most movable, for it must be the acutest and most
penetrating in every way, and also the lightest as being composed of
the smallest number of similar particles, and the second body has
similar properties in a second degree, and the third body, in the third
degree. Let it be agreed, then, both according to strict reason and according to probability, that the pyramid is the solid which is the original element and seed of fire, and let us assign the element which was
next in the order of generation to air, and the third to water. We must
c imagine all these to be so small that no single particle of any of the
four kinds is seen by us on account of their smallness, but when many
of them are collected together, their aggregates are seen. And the
ratios of their numbers, motions, and other properties, everywhere
God, as far as necessity allowed or gave consent, has exactly perfected
and harmonized in due proportion.

From all that we have just been saying about the elements or
d kinds, the most probable conclusion is as follows. Earth, when meeting with fire and dissolved by its sharpness, whether the dissolution
take place in the fire itself or perhaps in some mass of air or water, is
borne hither and thither until its parts, meeting together and mutually harmonizing, again become earth, for they can never take any
other form. But water, when divided by fire or by air, on re-forming,
e may become one part fire and two parts air, and a single volume of air
divided becomes two of fire. Again, when a small body of fire is contained in a larger body of air or water or earth, and both are moving,
and the fire struggling is overcome and broken up, then two volumes
of fire form one volume of air, and when air is overcome and cut up
into small pieces, two and a half parts of air are condensed into one
part of water. Let us consider the matter in another way. When one
57 of the other elements is fastened upon by fire and is cut by the sharpness of its angles and sides, it coalesces with the fire, and then ceases
to be cut by them any longer. For no element which is one and the
same with itself can be changed by or change another of the same
kind and in the same state. But so long as in the process of transition
the weaker is fighting against the stronger, the dissolution continues.
Again, when a few small particles, enclosed in many larger ones, are
b in process of decomposition and extinction, they only cease from their
tendency to extinction when they consent to pass into the conquering
nature, and fire becomes air and air water. But if bodies of another

kind go and attack them [that is, the small particles], the latter continue to be dissolved until, being completely forced back and dispersed, they make their escape to their own kindred, or else, being overcome and assimilated to the conquering power, they remain c where they are and dwell with their victors, and from being many become one. And owing to these affections, all things are changing their place, for by the motion of the receiving vessel the bulk of each class is distributed into its proper place, but those things which become unlike themselves and like other things are hurried by the shaking into the place of the things to which they grow like.

Now all unmixed and primary bodies are produced by such causes as these. As to the subordinate species which are included in the greater kinds, they are to be attributed to the varieties in the structure of the two original triangles. For either structure did not originally produce the triangle of one size only, but some larger and some d smaller, and there are as many sizes as there are species of the four elements. Hence when they are mingled with themselves and with one another there is an endless variety of them, which those who would arrive at the probable truth of nature ought duly to consider.

Unless a person comes to an understanding about the nature and conditions of rest and motion, he will meet with many difficulties in the discussion which follows. Something has been said of this matter e already, and something more remains to be said—which is that motion never exists in what is uniform. For to conceive that anything can be moved without a mover is hard or indeed impossible, and equally impossible to conceive that there can be a mover unless there be something which can be moved—motion cannot exist where either of these is wanting, and for these to be uniform is impossible; wherefore we must assign rest to uniformity and motion to the want of uni- 58 formity. Now inequality is the cause of the nature which is wanting in uniformity, and of this we have already described the origin. But there still remains the further point—why things when divided after their kinds do not cease to pass through one another and to change their place—which we will now proceed to explain. In the revolution of the universe are comprehended all the four elements, and this being circular and having a tendency to come together, compresses everything and will not allow any place to be left void. Wherefore also b fire, above all things, penetrates everywhere, and air next, as being next in rarity of the elements, and the two other elements in like manner penetrate according to their degrees of rarity. For those things which are composed of the largest particles have the largest void left in their compositions, and those which are composed of the smallest particles have the least. And the contraction caused by the compression thrusts the smaller particles into the interstices of the larger. And thus, when the small parts are placed side by side with the larger, and the lesser divide the greater and the greater unite the lesser, all c the elements are borne up and down and hither and thither toward their own places, for the change in the size of each changes its position in space. And these causes generate an inequality which is always maintained, and is continually creating a perpetual motion of the elements in all time.

In the next place we have to consider, first, that there are diverse kinds of fire. There are, for example, first, flame, secondly, those emanations of flame which do not burn but only give light to the eyes, and thirdly, the remains of fire, which are seen in red-hot embers

d after the flame has been extinguished. There are similar differences in the air, of which the brightest part is called the aether, and the most turbid sort mist and darkness, and there are various other nameless kinds which arise from the inequality of the triangles. Water, again, admits in the first place of a division into two kinds, the one liquid and the other fusile. The liquid kind is composed of the small and unequal particles of water, and moves itself and is moved by other bodies owing to the want of uniformity and the shape of its particles,

e whereas the fusile kind, being formed of large and uniform particles, is more stable than the other and is heavy and compact by reason of its uniformity. But when fire gets in and dissolves the particles and destroys the uniformity, it has greater mobility, and becoming fluid is thrust forth by the neighboring air and spreads upon the earth, and this dissolution of the solid masses is called melting, and their spread-

59 ing out upon the earth flowing. Again, when the fire goes out of the fusile substance, it does not pass into a vacuum, but into the neighboring air, and the air which is displaced forces together the liquid and still movable mass into the place which was occupied by the fire, and unites it with itself. Thus compressed the mass resumes its equability, and is again at unity with itself, because the fire which was the author of the inequality has retreated, and this departure of the fire is called cooling, and the coming together which follows upon it is termed

b congealment. Of all the kinds termed fusile, that which is the densest and is formed out of the finest and most uniform parts is that most precious possession called gold, which is hardened by filtration through rock; this is unique in kind, and has both a glittering and a yellow color. A shoot of gold, which is so dense as to be very hard, and takes a black color, is termed adamant. There is also another kind which has parts nearly like gold, and of which there are several spe-

c cies; it is denser than gold, and it contains a small and fine portion of earth and is therefore harder, yet also lighter because of the great interstices which it has within itself, and this substance, which is one of the bright and denser kinds of water, when solidified is called copper. There is an alloy of earth mingled with it which, when the two parts grow old and are disunited, shows itself separately and is called rust. The remaining phenomena of the same kind there will be no difficulty in reasoning out by the method of probabilities. A man

may sometimes set aside meditations about eternal things, and for
recreation turn to consider the truths of generation, which are prob- d
able only; he will thus gain a pleasure not to be repented of, and secure for himself, while he lives, a wise and moderate pastime. Let us
grant ourselves this indulgence and go through the probabilities relating to the same subjects which follow next in order.

Water which is mingled with fire, so much as is fine and liquid—
being so called by reason of its motion and the way in which it rolls
along the ground—and soft, because its bases give way and are less
stable than those of earth, when separated from fire and air and isolated, becomes more uniform, and by their retirement is compressed
into itself. And if the condensation be very great, the water above the e
earth becomes hail, but on the earth, ice, and that which is congealed
in a less degree and is only half solid, when above the earth is called
snow, and when upon the earth and condensed from dew, hoarfrost.
Then, again, there are the numerous kinds of water which have been
mingled with one another and are distilled through plants which grow
in the earth, and this whole class is called by the names of juices or
saps. The unequal admixture of these fluids creates a variety of spe- 60
cies—most of them are nameless, but four which are of a fiery nature
are clearly distinguished and have names. First, there is wine, which
warms the soul as well as the body; secondly, there is the oily nature,
which is smooth and divides the visual ray, and for this reason is
bright and shining and of a glistening appearance, including pitch,
the juice of the castorberry, oil itself, and other things of a like kind;
thirdly, there is the class of substances which expand the contracted b
parts of the mouth, until they return to their natural state, and by
reason of this property create sweetness—these are included under
the general name of honey; and, lastly, there is a frothy nature which
differs from all juices, having a burning quality which dissolves the
flesh and is called *opos* [a vegetable acid].

As to the kinds of earth, that which is filtered through water
passes into stone in the following manner. The water which mixes
with the earth and is broken up in the process changes into air, and
taking this form mounts into its own place. But as there is no sur- c
rounding vacuum it thrusts away the neighboring air, and this being
rendered heavy, and, when it is displaced, having been poured
around the mass of earth, forcibly compresses it and drives it into the
vacant space whence the new air had come up, and the earth when
compressed by the air into an indissoluble union with water becomes
rock. The fairer sort is that which is made up of equal and similar
parts and is transparent; that which has the opposite qualities is inferior. But when all the watery part is suddenly drawn out by fire, a
more brittle substance is formed to which we give the name of pottery. Sometimes also moisture may remain, and the earth which has d
been fused by fire becomes, when cool, a certain stone of a black color.

A like separation of the water which had been copiously mingled with them may occur in two substances composed of finer particles of earth and of a briny nature; out of either of them a half-solid body is then formed, soluble in water—the one, soda, which is used for purging away oil and earth, the other, salt, which harmonizes so well in com-binations pleasing to the palate, and is, as the law testifies, a sub-

e stance dear to the gods. The compounds of earth and water are not soluble by water, but by fire only, and for this reason. Neither fire nor air melts masses of earth, for their particles, being smaller than the interstices in its structure, have plenty of room to move without forc-ing their way, and so they leave the earth unmelted and undissolved, but particles of water, which are larger, force a passage and dissolve

61 and melt the earth. Wherefore earth when not consolidated by force is dissolved by water only; when consolidated, by nothing but fire, for this is the only body which can find an entrance. The cohesion of wa-ter again, when very strong, is dissolved by fire only; when weaker, then either by air or fire—the former entering the interstices, and the latter penetrating even the triangles. But nothing can dissolve air, when strongly condensed, which does not reach the elements or tri-angles, or if not strongly condensed, then only fire can dissolve it. As to bodies composed of earth and water, while the water occupies the

b vacant interstices of the earth in them which are compressed by force, the particles of water which approach them from without, finding no entrance, flow around the entire mass and leave it undissolved, but the particles of fire enter into the interstices of the water and fire does to water what water does to earth. Such particles are the sole causes of the compound body of earth and water liquefying and becoming fluid. Now these bodies are of two kinds. Some of them, such as glass

c and the fusible sort of stones, have less water than they have earth; on the other hand, substances of the nature of wax and incense have more of water entering into their composition.

   I have thus shown the various classes of bodies as they are diver-sified by their forms and combinations and changes into one another, and now I must endeavor to set forth their affections and the causes of them. In the first place, the bodies which I have been describing are necessarily objects of sense. But we have not yet considered the origin of flesh, or what belongs to flesh, or of that part of the soul which is

d mortal. And these things cannot be adequately explained without also explaining the affections which are concerned with sensation, nor the latter without the former, and yet to explain them together is hardly possible, for which reason we must assume first one or the other and afterward examine the nature of our hypothesis. In order, then, that the affections may follow regularly after the elements, let us presup-pose the existence of body and soul.

   First, let us inquire what we mean by saying that fire is hot, and about this we may reason from the dividing or cutting power which it

exercises on our bodies. We all of us feel that fire is sharp, and we may
further consider the fineness of the sides, and the sharpness of the e
angles, and the smallness of the particles, and the swiftness of the motion—all this makes the action of fire violent and sharp, so that it cuts 62
whatever it meets. And we must not forget that the original figure of
fire [that is, the pyramid], more than any other form, has a dividing
power which cuts our bodies into small pieces (κερματίζει), and thus
naturally produces that affection which we call heat, and hence the
origin of the name (θερμός, κέρμα). Now, the opposite of this is sufficiently manifest; nevertheless we will not fail to describe it. For the
larger particles of moisture which surround the body, entering in and
driving out the lesser, but not being able to take their places, compress b
the moist principle in us, and this, from being unequal and disturbed,
is forced by them into a state of rest which is due to equability and
compression. But things which are contracted contrary to nature are
by nature at war and force themselves apart, and to this war and con-
vulsion the name of shivering and trembling is given, and the whole
affection and the cause of the affection are both termed cold. That is
called hard to which our flesh yields, and soft which yields to our
flesh, and things are also termed hard and soft relatively to one another. That which yields has a small base, but that which rests on
quadrangular bases is firmly posed and belongs to the class which of- c
fers the greatest resistance; so, too, does that which is the most compact and therefore most repellent. The nature of the light and the
heavy will be best understood when examined in connection with our
notions of above and below, for it is quite a mistake to suppose that
the universe is parted into two regions, separate from and opposite to
each other—the one a lower to which all things tend which have any
bulk, and an upper to which things only ascend against their will. For
as the universe is in the form of a sphere, all the extremities, being d
equidistant from the center, are equally extremities, and the center,
which is equidistant from them, is equally to be regarded as the opposite of them all. Such being the nature of the world, when a person
says that any of these points is above or below, may he not be justly
charged with using an improper expression? For the center of the
world cannot be rightly called either above or below, but is the center
and nothing else, and the circumference is not the center, and has in
no one part of itself a different relation to the center from what it has
in any of the opposite parts. Indeed, when it is in every direction simi- e
lar, how can one rightly give to it names which imply opposition? For
if there were any solid body in equipoise at the center of the universe, 63
there would be nothing to draw it to this extreme rather than to that,
for they are all perfectly similar, and if a person were to go round the
world in a circle, he would often, when standing at the antipodes of
his former position, speak of the same point as above and below. For,
as I was saying just now, to speak of the whole which is in the form of

a globe as having one part above and another below is not like a sensible man. The reason why these names are used, and the circumstances under which they are ordinarily applied by us to the division
of the heavens, may be elucidated by the following supposition. If a
b person were to stand in that part of the universe which is the appointed place of fire, and where there is the great mass of fire to
which fiery bodies gather—if, I say, he were to ascend thither, and,
having the power to do this, were to abstract particles of fire and put
them in scales and weigh them, and then, raising the balance, were to
draw the fire by force toward the uncongenial element of the air, it
c would be very evident that he could compel the smaller mass more
readily than the larger, for when two things are simultaneously raised
by one and the same power, the smaller body must necessarily yield
to the superior power with less reluctance than the larger, and the
larger body is called heavy and said to tend downward, and the smaller
body is called light and said to tend upward. And we may detect ourselves who are upon the earth doing precisely the same thing. For we
often separate earthy natures, and sometimes earth itself, and draw
them into the uncongenial element of air by force and contrary to
nature, both clinging to their kindred elements. But that which is
d smaller yields to the impulse given by us toward the dissimilar element more easily than the larger, and so we call the former light, and
the place toward which it is impelled we call above, and the contrary
state and place we call heavy and below, respectively. Now the relations of these must necessarily vary because the principal masses of
the different elements hold opposite positions, for that which is light,
heavy, below, or above in one place will be found to be and become
e contrary and transverse and every way diverse in relation to that
which is light, heavy, below, or above in an opposite place. And about
all of them this has to be considered—that in some cases the tendency
of each toward its kindred element makes the body which is moved
heavy, and the place toward which the motion tends below, but things
which have an opposite tendency we call by an opposite name. Such
are the causes which we assign to these phenomena. As to the smooth
and the rough, anyone who sees them can explain the reason of them
64 to another. For roughness is hardness mingled with irregularity, and
smoothness is produced by the joint effect of uniformity and density.
    The most important of the affections which concern the whole
body remains to be considered—that is, the cause of pleasure and pain
in the perceptions of which I have been speaking, and in all other
things which are perceived by sense through the parts of the body, and
have both pains and pleasures attendant on them. Let us imagine the
causes of every affection, whether of sense or not, to be of the following nature, remembering that we have already distinguished between
b the nature which is easy and which is hard to move, for this is the direction in which we must hunt the prey which we mean to take. A

body which is of a nature to be easily moved, on receiving an impression however slight, spreads abroad the motion in a circle, the parts
communicating with each other, until at last, reaching the principle
of mind, they announce the quality of the agent. But a body of the
opposite kind, being immobile and not extending to the surrounding
region, merely receives the impression and does not stir any of the
neighboring parts, and since the parts do not distribute the original c
impression to other parts, it has no effect of motion on the whole animal, and therefore produces no effect on the patient. This is true of
the bones and hair and other more earthy parts of the human body,
whereas what was said above relates mainly to sight and hearing because they have in them the greatest amount of fire and air. Now we
must conceive of pleasure and pain in this way. An impression produced in us contrary to nature and violent, if sudden, is painful, and, d
again, the sudden return to nature is pleasant, but a gentle and gradual return is imperceptible and vice versa. On the other hand, the impression of sense which is easily produced is most readily felt, but is
not accompanied by pleasure or pain; such, for example, are the affections of the sight, which, as we said above, is a body naturally uniting with our body in the daytime, for cuttings and burnings and other
affections which happen to the sight do not give pain, nor is there
pleasure when the sight returns to its natural state; yet very clear and e
strong sensations arise for every affection of sight, whether the eye is
passive or is deliberately turned upon an object. The reason is that no
violence at all is involved in the separation and reunion of the visual
ray. But bodies formed of larger particles yield to the agent only with
a struggle, and then they impart their motions to the whole and cause
pleasure and pain—pain when alienated from their natural conditions, and pleasure when restored to them. Things which experience 65
gradual withdrawings and emptyings of their nature, and great and
sudden replenishments, fail to perceive the emptying, but are sensible
of the replenishment, and so they occasion no pain, but the greatest
pleasure, to the mortal part of the soul, as is manifest in the case of
perfumes. But things which are changed all of a sudden, and only
gradually and with difficulty return to their own nature, have effects
in every way opposite to the former, as is evident in the case of burn- b
ings and cuttings of the body.

Thus have we discussed the general affections of the whole body,
and the names of the agents which produce them. And now I will endeavor to speak of the affections of particular parts, and the causes
and agents of them, as far as I am able. In the first place, let us set
forth what was omitted when we were speaking of juices, concerning c
the affections peculiar to the tongue. These too, like most of the other
affections, appear to be caused by certain contractions and dilations,
but they have besides more of roughness and smoothness than is
found in other affections, for whenever earthy particles enter into

d the small veins which are the testing instruments of the tongue, reaching to the heart, and fall upon the moist, delicate portions of flesh—when, as they are dissolved, they contract and dry up the little veins, they are astringent if they are rougher, but if not so rough, then only harsh. Those particles which act upon these veins as an abstergent, and purge the whole surface of the tongue, if they do it in excess and so encroach as to consume some part of the flesh itself, like

e potash and soda, are all termed bitter. But the particles which are deficient in the alkaline quality, and which cleanse only moderately, are called salt, and having no bitterness or roughness are regarded as rather agreeable than otherwise. Bodies which share in and are made smooth by the heat of the mouth, and which are inflamed and again in turn inflame that which heats them, and which are so light that they are carried upward to the sensations of the head and cut all that

66 comes in their way, by reason of these qualities in them, are all termed pungent. There are other particles which, previously refined by putrefaction, enter into the narrow veins, and being duly proportioned to the particles of earth and air which are there, set them whirling about one another, and while they are in a whirl cause them to dash against and enter into one another, and so form hollows sur-

b rounding the particles that enter. These watery vessels of air—for a film of moisture, sometimes earthy, sometimes pure, is spread around the air—are hollow spheres of water, and those of them which are pure are transparent and are called bubbles, while those composed of the earthy liquid, which is in a state of general agitation and effervescence, are said to boil or ferment. Of all these affections the cause is termed acid. And there is the opposite affection arising from an op-

c posite cause, when the mass of entering particles, immersed in the moisture of the mouth, is congenial to the tongue, and smooths and oils over the roughness, and relaxes the parts which are unnaturally contracted, and contracts the parts which are relaxed, and disposes them all according to their nature—that sort of remedy of violent affections is pleasant and agreeable to every man, and has the name sweet. But enough of this.

d   The faculty of smell does not admit of differences of kind, for all smells are of a half-formed nature, and no element is so proportioned as to have any smell. The veins about the nose are too narrow to admit earth and water, and too wide to detain fire and air, and for this reason no one ever perceives the smell of any of them. But smells always proceed from bodies that are damp, or putrefying, or liquefying,

e or evaporating, and are perceptible only in the intermediate state, when water is changing into air and air into water, and all of them are either vapor or mist. That which is passing out of air into water is mist, and that which is passing from water into air is vapor, and hence all smells are thinner than water and thicker than air. The proof of this is that when there is any obstruction to the respiration and a man draws in his breath by force, then no smell filters through, but the air without the smell alone penetrates. Wherefore the varieties 67 of smell have no name, and they have not many or definite and simple kinds, but they are distinguished only as painful and pleasant, the one sort irritating and disturbing the whole cavity which is situated between the head and the navel, the other having a soothing influence and restoring this same region to an agreeable and natural condition.

In considering the third kind of sense, hearing, we must speak of the causes in which it originates. We may in general assume sound b to be a blow which passes through the ears, and is transmitted by means of the air, the brain, and the blood, to the soul, and that hearing is the vibration of this blow which begins in the head and ends in the region of the liver. The sound which moves swiftly is acute, and the sound which moves slowly is grave, and that which is regular is equable and smooth, and the reverse is harsh. A great body of sound is c loud, and a small body of sound the reverse. Respecting the harmonies of sound I must hereafter speak.

There is a fourth class of sensible things, having many intricate varieties, which must now be distinguished. They are called by the general name of colors and are a flame which emanates from every sort of body, and has particles corresponding to the sense of sight. I have spoken already, in what has preceded, of the causes which generate sight, and in this place it will be natural and suitable to give a d rational theory of colors.

Of the particles coming from other bodies which fall upon the sight, some are smaller and some are larger, and some are equal to the parts of the sight itself. Those which are equal are imperceptible, and we call them transparent. The larger produce contraction, the e smaller dilation, in the sight, exercising a power akin to that of hot and cold bodies on the flesh, or of astringent bodies on the tongue, or of those heating bodies which we termed pungent. White and black are similar effects of contraction and dilation in another sphere, and for this reason have a different appearance. Wherefore we ought to term white that which dilates the visual ray, and the opposite of this black. There is also a swifter motion of a different sort of fire which strikes and dilates the ray of sight until it reaches the eyes, forcing a way through their passages and melting them, and eliciting from them a 68 union of fire and water which we call tears, being itself an opposite fire which comes to them from an opposite direction—the inner fire flashes forth like lightning, and the outer finds a way in and is extinguished in the moisture, and all sorts of colors are generated by the mixture. This affection is termed dazzling, and the object which produces it is called bright and flashing. There is another sort of fire which is intermediate and which reaches and mingles with the mois- b ture of the eye without flashing, and in this the fire, mingling with the ray of the moisture, produces a color like blood, to which we give the name of red. A bright hue mingled with red and white gives the color called auburn (ξανθόν). The law of proportion, however, according to which the several colors are formed, even if a man knew he would be foolish in telling, for he could not give any necessary reason, nor in-

c deed any tolerable or probable explanation of them. Again, red, when mingled with black and white, becomes purple, but it becomes umber (ὄρφνινον) when the colors are burned as well as mingled and the black is more thoroughly mixed with them. Flame color (πυρρόν) is produced by a union of auburn and dun (φαιόν), dun by an admixture of black and white, and pale yellow (ὠχρόν) by an admixture of white and auburn. White and bright meeting, and falling upon a full black, become dark blue (κυανοῦν), and when dark blue mingles with white, a light blue (γλαυκόν) color is formed, as flame color with black

d makes leek-green (πράσιον). There will be no difficulty in seeing how and by what mixtures the colors derived from these are made according to the rules of probability. He, however, who should attempt to verify all this by experiment would forget the difference of the human and divine nature. For God only has the knowledge and also the power which are able to combine many things into one and again resolve the one into many. But no man either is or ever will be able to accomplish either the one or the other operation.

e   These are the elements, thus of necessity then subsisting, which the creator of the fairest and best of created things associated with himself when he made the self-sufficing and most perfect god, using the necessary causes as his ministers in the accomplishment of his work, but himself contriving the good in all his creations. Wherefore we may distinguish two sorts of causes, the one divine and the other necessary, and may seek for the divine in all things, as far as our na-

69 ture admits, with a view to the blessed life, but the necessary kind only for the sake of the divine, considering that without them and when isolated from them, these higher things for which we look cannot be apprehended or received or in any way shared by us.

    Seeing, then, that we have now prepared for our use the various classes of causes which are the material out of which the remainder of our discourse must be woven, just as wood is the material of the carpenter, let us revert in a few words to our beginning, and hasten back to the point from which we set out on our road hither. We may then

b endeavor to crown our tale with a suitable conclusion.

    As I said at first, when all things were in disorder, God created in each thing in relation to itself, and in all things in relation to each other, all the measures and harmonies which they could possibly receive. For in those days nothing had any proportion except by accident, nor was there anything deserving to be called by the names which we now use—as, for example, fire, water, and the rest of the

elements. All these the creator first set in order, and out of them he c
constructed the universe, which was a single animal comprehending
in itself all other animals, mortal and immortal. Now of the divine,
he himself was the creator, but the creation of the mortal he committed to his offspring. And they, imitating him, received from him
the immortal principle of the soul, and around this they proceeded to
fashion a mortal body, and made it to be the vehicle of the soul, and
constructed within the body a soul of another nature which was mortal, subject to terrible and irresistible affections—first of all, pleasure, d
the greatest incitement to evil; then, pain, which deters from good;
also rashness and fear, two foolish counselors, anger hard to be appeased, and hope easily led astray—these they mingled with irrational sense and with all-daring love according to necessary laws,
and so framed man. Wherefore, fearing to pollute the divine any more
than was absolutely unavoidable, they gave to the mortal nature a
separate habitation in another part of the body, placing the neck e
between them to be the isthmus and boundary, which they constructed between the head and breast, to keep them apart. And in the
breast, and in what is termed the thorax, they incased the mortal soul,
and as the one part of this was superior and the other inferior they
divided the cavity of the thorax into two parts, as the women's and 70
men's apartments are divided in houses, and placed the midriff to be a
wall of partition between them. That part of the inferior soul which is
endowed with courage and passion and loves contention, they
settled nearer the head, midway between the midriff and the neck,
in order that being obedient to the rule of reason it might join with it
in controlling and restraining the desires when they are no longer willing of their own accord to obey the word of command issuing from the
citadel.

The heart, the knot of the veins and the fountain of the blood b
which races through all the limbs, was set in the place of guard, that,
when the might of passion was roused by reason making proclamation
of any wrong assailing them from without or being perpetrated by
the desires within, quickly the whole power of feeling in the body, perceiving these commands and threats, might obey and follow through
every turn and alley, and thus allow the principle of the best to have
the command in all of them. But the gods, foreknowing that the palpi- c
tation of the heart in the expectation of danger and excitement of
passion must cause it to swell and become inflamed, formed and implanted as a supporter to the heart the lung, which was, in the first
place, soft and bloodless, and also had within hollows like the pores
of a sponge, in order that by receiving the breath and the drink, it
might give coolness and the power of respiration and alleviate the d
heat. Wherefore they cut the air channels leading to the lung, and
placed the lung about the heart as a soft spring, that, when passion

was rife within, the heart, beating against a yielding body, might be cooled and suffer less, and might thus become more ready to join with passion in the service of reason.

The part of the soul which desires meats and drinks and the other things of which it has need by reason of the bodily nature, they e placed between the midriff and the boundary of the navel, contriving in all this region a sort of manger for the food of the body, and there they bound it down like a wild animal which was chained up with man, and must be nourished if man was to exist. They appointed this lower creation his place here in order that he might be always feeding at the manger, and have his dwelling as far as might be from the 71 council chamber, making as little noise and disturbance as possible, and permitting the best part to advise quietly for the good of the whole and the individual. And knowing that this lower principle in man would not comprehend reason, and even if attaining to some degree of perception would never naturally care for rational notions, but that it would be especially led by phantoms and visions night and day— planning to make this very weakness serve a purpose, God combined b with it the liver and placed it in the house of the lower nature, con- triving that it should be solid and smooth, and bright and sweet, and should also have a bitter quality in order that the power of thought, which proceeds from the mind, might be reflected as in a mirror which receives likenesses of objects and gives back images of them to the sight, and so might strike terror into the desires when, making use of the bitter part of the liver, to which it is akin, it comes threatening and invading, and diffusing this bitter element swiftly through the whole liver produces colors like bile, and contracting every part c makes it wrinkled and rough, and twisting out of its right place and contorting the lobe and closing and shutting up the vessels and gates causes pain and loathing. And the converse happens when some gentle inspiration of the understanding pictures images of an opposite character, and allays the bile and bitterness by refusing to stir or touch the nature opposed to itself, but by making use of the natural sweetness of the liver corrects all things and makes them to be right d and smooth and free, and renders the portion of the soul which re- sides about the liver happy and joyful, enabling it to pass the night in peace, and to practice divination in sleep, inasmuch as it has no share in mind and reason. For the authors of our being, remembering the command of their father when he bade them create the human race as good as they could, that they might correct our inferior parts and e make them to attain a measure of truth, placed in the liver the seat of divination. And herein is a proof that God has given the art of divi- nation not to the wisdom, but to the foolishness of man. No man, when in his wits, attains prophetic truth and inspiration, but when he re- ceives the inspired word, either his intelligence is enthralled in sleep or he is demented by some distemper or possession. And he who would

understand what he remembers to have been said, whether in a dream
or when he was awake, by the prophetic and inspired nature, or would 72
determine by reason the meaning of the apparitions which he has
seen, and what indications they afford to this man or that, of past,
present, or future good and evil, must first recover his wits. But, while
he continues demented, he cannot judge of the visions which he sees
or the words which he utters; the ancient saying is very true—that
'only a man who has his wits can act or judge about himself and
his own affairs.' And for this reason it is customary to appoint interpreters to be judges of the true inspiration. Some persons call them b
prophets, being blind to the fact that they are only the expositors of
dark sayings and visions, and are not to be called prophets at all, but
only interpreters of prophecy.

Such is the nature of the liver, which is placed as we have described in order that it may give prophetic intimations. During the life
of each individual these intimations are plainer, but after his death
the liver becomes blind and delivers oracles too obscure to be intelligible. The neighboring organ [the spleen] is situated on the left-hand c
side and is constructed with a view of keeping the liver bright and
pure—like a napkin, always ready-prepared and at hand to clean the
mirror. And hence, when any impurities arise in the region of the
liver by reason of disorders of the body, the loose nature of the spleen,
which is composed of a hollow and bloodless tissue, receives them all
and clears them away, and when filled with the unclean matter, it d
swells and festers, but, again, when the body is purged, shrinks and
settles down into the same place as before.

Concerning the soul, as to which part is mortal and which divine,
and how and why they are separated, and in what company they are
placed, if God acknowledges that we have spoken the truth, then, and
then only, can we be confident; still, we may venture to assert that
what has been said by us is probable, and will be rendered more probable by investigation. Let us assume thus much.

The creation of the rest of the body follows next in order, and this e
we may investigate in a similar manner. And it appears to be very
meet that the body should be framed on the following principles.

The authors of our race were aware that we should be intemperate in eating and drinking and take a good deal more than was
necessary or proper, by reason of gluttony. In order then that disease
might not quickly destroy us, and lest our mortal race should perish
without fulfilling its end—intending to provide against this, the gods 73
made what is called the lower belly, to be a receptacle for the superfluous meat and drink, and formed the convolution of the bowels, so
that the food might be prevented from passing quickly through and
compelling the body to require more food, thus producing insatiable
gluttony and making the whole race an enemy to philosophy and culture, and rebellious against the divinest element within us.

b   The bones and flesh, and other similar parts of us, were made as
follows. The first principle of all of them was the generation of the
marrow. For the bonds of life which unite the soul with the body are
made fast there, and they are the root and foundation of the human
race. The marrow itself is created out of other materials. God took
such of the primary triangles as were straight and smooth and were
adapted to produce fire and water, and air and earth in the highest
c perfection—these, I say, he separated from their kinds, and mingling
them in due proportions with one another, made the marrow out of
them to be a universal seed of every mortal kind, and in this seed he
then planted and enclosed the souls, and in the original distribution
gave to the marrow as many and various forms as the different kinds
of souls were hereafter to receive. That which, like a field, was to receive the divine seed, he made round every way, and called that portion of the marrow 'brain,' intending that, when an animal was
d perfected, the vessel containing this substance should be the head, but
that which was intended to contain the remaining and mortal part of
the soul he distributed into figures at once round and elongated, and
he called them all by the name 'marrow.' And to these, as to anchors,
fastening the bonds of the whole soul, he proceeded to fashion around
them the entire framework of our body, constructing for the marrow,
first of all, a complete covering of bone.
      Bone was composed by him in the following manner. Having
e sifted pure and smooth earth he kneaded it and wetted it with marrow,
and after that he put it into fire and then into water, and once more
into fire and again into water—in this way, by frequent transfers
from one to the other, he made it insoluble by either. Out of this he
fashioned, as in a lathe, a globe made of bone, which he placed around
74 the brain, and in this he left a narrow opening, and around the marrow of the neck and back he formed vertebrae which he placed under
one another like pivots, beginning at the head and extending through
the whole of the trunk. Thus wishing to preserve the entire seed, he
enclosed it in a stonelike casing, inserting joints, and using in the
formation of them the power of the other or diverse as an intermediate nature, that they might have motion and flexure. Then again, con-
b sidering that the bone would be too brittle and inflexible, and when
heated and again cooled would soon mortify and destroy the seed
within—having this in view, he contrived the sinews and the flesh,
that so binding all the members together by the sinews, which admitted of being stretched and relaxed about the vertebrae, he might
thus make the body capable of flection and extension, while the
flesh would serve as a protection against the summer heat and against
the winter cold, and also against falls, softly and easily yielding to
c external bodies, like articles made of felt, and containing in itself a
warm moisture which in summer exudes and makes the surface
damp, would impart a natural coolness to the whole body, and again

in winter by the help of this internal warmth would form a very tolerable defense against the frost which surrounds it and attacks it from without. He who modeled us, considering these things, mixed earth with fire and water and blended them, and making a ferment of acid and salt, he mingled it with them and formed soft and succulent d flesh. As for the sinews, he made them of a mixture of bone and unfermented flesh, attempered so as to be in a mean, and gave them a yellow color; wherefore the sinews have a firmer and more glutinous nature than flesh, but a softer and moister nature than the bones. With these God covered the bones and marrow, binding them together by sinews, and then enshrouded them all in an upper covering of flesh. The more living and sensitive of the bones he enclosed in the thinnest e film of flesh, and those which had the least life within them in the thickest and most solid flesh. So again on the joints of the bones, where reason indicated that no more was required, he placed only a thin covering of flesh, that it might not interfere with the flection of our bodies and make them unwieldy because difficult to move, and also that it might not, by being crowded and pressed and matted together, destroy sensation by reason of its hardness, and impair the memory and dull the edge of intelligence. Wherefore also the thighs 75 and the shanks and the hips, and the bones of the arms and the forearms, and other parts which have no joints, and the inner bones, which on account of the rarity of the soul in their marrow are destitute of reason—all these are abundantly provided with flesh, but such as have mind in them are in general less fleshy, except where the creator has made some part solely of flesh in order to give sensation—as, for example, the tongue. But commonly this is not the case. For the nature which comes into being and grows up in us by a law of neces- b sity does not admit of the combination of solid bone and much flesh with acute perceptions. More than any other part, the framework of the head would have had them if they could have coexisted, and the human race, having a strong and fleshy and sinewy head, would have had a life twice or many times as long as it now has, and also more healthy and free from pain. But our creators, considering whether they should make a longer-lived race which was worse, or a shorter- c lived race which was better, came to the conclusion that everyone ought to prefer a shorter span of life, which was better, to a longer one, which was worse, and therefore they covered the head with thin bone, but not with flesh and sinews, since it had no joints, and thus the head was added, having more wisdom and sensation than the rest of the body, but also being in every man far weaker. For these rea- d sons and after this manner God placed the sinews at the extremity of the head, in a circle round the neck, and glued them together by the principle of likeness and fastened the extremities of the jawbones to them below the face, and the other sinews he dispersed throughout the body, fastening limb to limb. The framers of us

framed the mouth, as now arranged, having teeth and tongue and lips,
e with a view to the necessary and the good, contriving the way in for
necessary purposes, the way out for the best purposes. For that is
necessary which enters in and gives food to the body, but the river of
speech, which flows out of a man and ministers to the intelligence, is
the fairest and noblest of all streams. Still the head could neither be
left a bare frame of bones, on account of the extremes of heat and
cold in the different seasons, nor yet be allowed to be wholly covered
and so become dull and senseless by reason of an overgrowth of flesh.
The fleshy nature was not therefore wholly dried up, but a large sort of
76 peel was parted off and remained over, which is now called the skin.
This met and grew by the help of the cerebral moisture, and became
the circular envelopment of the head. And the moisture, rising up
under the sutures, watered and closed in the skin upon the crown,
forming a sort of knot. The diversity of the sutures was caused by
the power of the courses within the soul and of the food; the sutures
were more numerous where these were strongly opposed to one an-
b other, fewer if the struggle were less violent. This skin the divine
power pierced all round with fire, and out of the punctures which
were thus made the moisture issued forth, and the liquid and heat
which was pure came away, and a mixed part which was composed of
the same material as the skin, and had a fineness equal to the punctures, was borne up by its own impulse and extended far outside the
head, but, being too slow to escape, was thrust back by the external
c air and rolled up underneath the skin, where it took root. Thus the
hair sprang up in the skin, being akin to it because it is like threads of
leather, but rendered harder and closer through the pressure of
the cold, by which each hair, while in process of separation from the
skin, is compressed and cooled. Wherefore the creator formed the
head hairy, making use of the causes which I have mentioned, and re-
d flecting also that instead of flesh the brain needed the hair to be a
light covering or guard which would give shade in summer and shelter in winter, and at the same time would not impede our quickness of
perception. From the combination of sinew, skin, and bone, in the
structure of the finger, there arises a triple compound which, when
dried up, takes the form of one hard skin partaking of all three natures, and was fabricated by these second causes, but designed by
mind which is the principal cause with an eye to the future. For
e our creators well knew that women and other animals would someday
be framed out of men, and they further knew that many animals
would require the use of nails for many purposes; wherefore they
fashioned in men at their first creation the rudiments of nails. For
this purpose and for these reasons they caused skin, hair, and nails to
grow at the extremities of the limbs.

And now that all the parts and members of the mortal animal
77 had come together, since its life of necessity consisted of fire and

breath, and it therefore wasted away by dissolution and depletion, the gods contrived the following remedy. They mingled a nature akin to that of man with other forms and perceptions and thus created another kind of animal. These are the trees and plants and seeds which have been improved by cultivation and are now domesticated among us; anciently there were only the wild kinds, which are older than the cultivated. For everything that partakes of life may be truly b called a living being, and the animal of which we are now speaking partakes of the third kind of soul, which is said to be seated between the midriff and the navel, having no part in opinion or reason or mind, but only in feelings of pleasure and pain and the desires which accompany them. For this nature is always in a passive state, and is not endowed by nature with the power of revolving in and about itself, repelling the motion from without and using its own, in such a way as to observe and reflect upon any of its own concerns. Wherefore it c lives and does not differ from a living being, but is fixed and rooted in the same spot, having no power of self-motion.

Now after the superior powers had created all these natures to be food for us who are of the inferior nature, they cut various channels through the body as through a garden, that it might be watered as from a running stream. In the first place, they cut two hidden channels or veins down the back where the skin and the flesh join, which d answered severally to the right and left side of the body. These they let down along the backbone, so as to have the marrow of generation between them, where it was most likely to flourish, and in order that the stream coming down from above might flow freely to the other parts, and equalize the irrigation. In the next place, they divided the veins about the head, and interlacing them, they sent them in op- e posite directions; those coming from the right side they sent to the left of the body, and those from the left they diverted toward the right, so that they and the skin might together form a bond which should fasten the head to the body, since the crown of the head was not encircled by sinews, and also in order that the sensations from both sides might be distributed over the whole body. And next, they ordered the watercourses of the body in a manner which I will describe, and which will be more easily understood if we begin by admitting that 78 all things composed of lesser parts retain the greater, but those composed of greater parts cannot retain the lesser. Now of all natures fire has the smallest parts, and therefore penetrates through earth and water and air and their compounds, nor can anything hold it. And a similar principle applies to the human belly, for when meats and drinks enter it, it holds them, but it cannot hold air and fire because b the particles of which they consist are smaller than its own structure.

These elements, therefore, God employed for the sake of distributing moisture from the belly into the veins, weaving together a network of fire and air like a creel, having at the entrance two lesser

creels; further he constructed one of these with two openings, and from the lesser creels he extended cords reaching all round to the
c extremities of the network. All the interior of the net he made of fire, but the lesser creels and their cavity, of air. The network he took and spread over the newly formed animal in the following manner. He let the lesser creels pass into the mouth; there were two of them, and one he let down by the air pipes into the lungs, the other by the side of the air pipes into the belly. The former he divided into two branches, both of which he made to pass out at the channels of the nose, so that when the way through the mouth was not open, the streams of
d the mouth as well were replenished through the nose. With the other cavity [that is, of the greater creel] he enveloped the hollow parts of the body, and at one time he made all this to flow into the lesser creels, quite gently, for they are composed of air, and at another time he caused the lesser creels to flow back again. And the net he made to find a way in and out through the pores of the body, and the rays of fire which are bound fast within followed the pas-
e sage of the air either way, never at any time ceasing so long as the mortal being holds together. This process, as we affirm, the namegiver named inspiration and expiration. And all this movement, active as well as passive, takes place in order that the body, being watered and cooled, may receive nourishment and life. For when the respiration is going in and out, and the fire, which is fast bound within, follows it, and ever and anon moving to and fro, enters through the belly and
79 reaches the meat and drink, it dissolves them, and dividing them into small portions and guiding them through the passages where it goes, pumps them as from a fountain into the channels of the veins, and makes the stream of the veins flow through the body as through a conduit.

Let us once more consider the phenomena of respiration, and inquire into the causes which have made it what it is. They are as
b follows. Seeing that there is no such thing as a vacuum into which any of those things which are moved can enter, and the breath is carried from us into the external air, the next point is, as will be clear to everyone, that it does not go into a vacant space, but pushes its neighbor out of its place, and that which is thrust out in turn drives out its neighbor. And in this way everything of necessity at last comes round to that place from whence the breath came forth, and enters in there
c and following the breath fills up the vacant space, and this goes on like the rotation of a wheel, because there can be no such thing as a vacuum. Wherefore also the breast and the lungs, when they emit the breath, are replenished by the air which surrounds the body and which enters in through the pores of the flesh and is driven round in a circle, and again, the air which is sent away and passes out through the body forces the breath inward through the passage of the mouth and the nostrils. Now the origin of this movement may be supposed to be as

follows. In the interior of every animal the hottest part is that which is around the blood and veins; it is in a manner an internal fountain d of fire, which we compare to the network of a creel, being woven all of fire and extended through the center of the body, while the outer parts are composed of air. Now we must admit that heat naturally proceeds outward to its own place and to its kindred element, and as there are two exits for the heat, the one out through the body, and the other through the mouth and nostrils, when it moves toward the e one, it drives round the air at the other, and that which is driven round falls into the fire and becomes warm, and that which goes forth is cooled. But when the heat changes its place, and the particles at the other exit grow warmer, the hotter air inclining in that direction and carried toward its native element, fire, pushes round the air at the other, and this being affected in the same way and communicating the same impulse, a circular motion swaying to and fro is produced by the double process, which we call inspiration and expiration.

The phenomena of medical cupping glasses and of the swallowing of drink and of the projection of bodies, whether discharged in 80 the air or bowled along the ground, are to be investigated on a similar principle, and swift and slow sounds, which appear to be high and low, and are sometimes discordant on account of their inequality, and then again harmonic on account of the equality of the motion which they excite in us. For when the motions of the antecedent swifter sounds begin to pause and the two are equalized, the slower sounds overtake the swifter and then propel them. When they overtake them b they do not intrude a new and discordant motion, but introduce the beginnings of a slower which answers to the swifter as it dies away, thus producing a single mixed expression out of high and low, whence arises a pleasure which even the unwise feel, and which to the wise becomes a higher sort of delight, being an imitation of divine harmony in mortal motions. Moreover, as to the flowing of water, the fall of the thunderbolt, and the marvels that are observed about the at- c traction of amber and the Heraclean stones—in none of these cases is there any attraction, but he who investigates rightly will find that such wonderful phenomena are attributable to the combination of certain conditions—the nonexistence of a vacuum, the fact that objects push one another round, and that they change places, passing severally into their proper positions as they are divided or combined.

Such, as we have seen, is the nature and such are the causes of d respiration—the subject in which this discussion originated. For the fire cuts the food and following the breath surges up within, fire and breath rising together and filling the veins by drawing up out of the belly and pouring into them the cut portions of the food, and so the streams of food are kept flowing through the whole body in all animals. And fresh cuttings from kindred substances, whether the

e fruits of the earth or herb of the field, which God planted to be our daily food, acquire all sorts of colors by their intermixture, but red is the most pervading of them, a quality created by the cutting action of fire and by the impression which it makes on a moist substance, and hence the liquid which circulates in the body has a color such as we have described. The liquid itself we call blood, which nourishes the
81 flesh and the whole body, whence all parts are watered and empty places filled.

Now the process of repletion and evacuation is effected after the manner of the universal motion by which all kindred substances are drawn toward one another. For the external elements which surround us are always causing us to consume away and distributing and sending off like to like; the particles of blood, too, which are divided and contained within the frame of the animal as in a sort of heaven, are
b compelled to imitate the motion of the universe. Each, therefore, of the divided parts within us, being carried to its kindred nature, replenishes the void. When more is taken away than flows in, then we decay, and when less, we grow and increase.

The frame of the entire creature when young has the triangles of each kind new, and may be compared to the keel of a vessel which is just off the stocks; they are locked firmly together and yet the whole mass is soft and delicate, being freshly formed of marrow and nurtured
c on milk. Now when the triangles out of which meats and drinks are composed come in from without, and are comprehended in the body, being older and weaker than the triangles already there, the frame of the body gets the better of them and its newer triangles cut them up, and so the animal grows great, being nourished by a multitude of similar particles. But when the roots of the triangles are loosened by having undergone many conflicts with many things in the
d course of time, they are no longer able to cut or assimilate the food which enters, but are themselves easily divided by the bodies which come in from without. In this way every animal is overcome and decays, and this affection is called old age. And at last, when the bonds by which the triangles of the marrow are united no longer hold and are parted by the strain of existence, they in turn loosen the bonds of the soul, and she, obtaining a natural release, flies away with joy. For
e that which takes place according to nature is pleasant, but that which is contrary to nature is painful. And thus death, if caused by disease or produced by wounds, is painful and violent, but that sort of death which comes with old age and fulfills the debt of nature is the easiest of deaths, and is accompanied with pleasure rather than with pain.

Now everyone can see whence diseases arise. There are four
82 natures out of which the body is compacted—earth and fire and water and air—and the unnatural excess or defect of these, or the change of any of them from its own natural place into another, or, since there

are more kinds than one of fire and of the other elements, the assumption by any of these of a wrong kind, or any similar irregularity, produces disorders and diseases. For when any of them is produced or changed in a manner contrary to nature, the parts which were previously cool grow warm, and those which were dry become moist, b and the light become heavy, and the heavy light; all sorts of changes occur. For, as we affirm, a thing can only remain the same with itself, whole and sound, when the same is added to it, or subtracted from it, in the same respect and in the same manner and in due proportion, and whatever comes or goes away in violation of these laws causes all manner of changes and infinite diseases and corruptions. Now there is a second class of structures which are also natural, and this affords a second opportunity of observing diseases to him who would under- c stand them. For whereas marrow and bone and flesh and sinews are composed of the four elements, and the blood, though after another manner, is likewise formed out of them, most diseases originate in the way which I have described, but the worst of all owe their severity to the fact that the generation of these substances proceeds in a wrong order; they are then destroyed. For the natural order is that the flesh and sinews should be made of blood, the sinews out of the fibers to which they are akin, and the flesh out of the clots which are formed d when the fibers are separated. And the glutinous and rich matter which comes away from the sinews and the flesh, not only glues the flesh to the bones, but nourishes and imparts growth to the bone which surrounds the marrow, and there remains a part, consisting of the purest and smoothest and oiliest sort of triangles, which filters through the solid texture of the bones, from which it drops like dew and waters the marrow. Now when each process takes place in this e order, health commonly results; when in the opposite order, disease. For when the flesh becomes decomposed and sends back the wasting substance into the veins, then an oversupply of blood of diverse kinds, mingling with air in the veins, having variegated colors and bitter properties as well as acid and saline qualities, contains all sorts of bile and serum and phlegm. For all things go the wrong way, and having become corrupted, first, they taint the blood itself, and then 83 ceasing to give nourishment to the body they are carried along the veins in all directions, no longer preserving the order of their natural courses, but at war with themselves, because they receive no good from one another, and are hostile to the abiding constitution of the body, which they corrupt and dissolve. The oldest part of the flesh which is corrupted, being hard to decompose, from long burning grows black, and from being everywhere corroded becomes bitter, and is injurious to every part of the body which is still uncorrupted. b Sometimes, when the bitter element is refined away, the black part assumes an acidity which takes the place of the bitterness; at other times the bitterness being tinged with blood has a redder color, and

this, when mixed with black, takes the hue of grass, and again, an auburn color mingles with the bitter matter when new flesh is de-
c composed by the fire which surrounds the internal flame—to all which symptoms some physician, perhaps, or rather some philosopher who had the power of seeing in many dissimilar things one nature deserving of a name has assigned the common name of bile. But the other kinds of bile are variously distinguished by their colors. As for serum, that sort which is the watery part of blood is innocent, but that which is a secretion of black and acid bile is malignant when mingled by the power of heat with any salt substance, and is then called acid phlegm. Again, the substance which is formed by the liquefaction of new and tender flesh when air is present, if inflated and incased in
d liquid so as to form bubbles which separately are invisible owing to their small size, but when collected are of a bulk which is visible and have a white color arising out of the generation of foam—all this de-composition of tender flesh when intermingled with air is termed by us white phlegm. And the whey or sediment of newly formed
e phlegm is sweat and tears, and includes the various daily discharges by which the body is purified. Now all these become causes of disease when the blood is not replenished in a natural manner by food and drink, but gains bulk from opposite sources in violation of the laws
84 of nature. When the several parts of the flesh are separated by disease, if the foundation remains, the power of the disorder is only half as great, and there is still a prospect of an easy recovery, but when that which binds the flesh to the bones is diseased, and no longer being separated off from the muscles and sinews, ceases to give nourishment to the bone and to unite flesh and bone, and from being oily and smooth and glutinous becomes rough and salty and dry, owing to bad regimen, then all the substance thus corrupted crum-bles away under the flesh and the sinews and separates from the
b bone, and the fleshy parts fall away from their foundation and leave the sinews bare and full of brine, and the flesh again gets into the circulation of the blood and makes the previously mentioned dis-orders still greater. And if these bodily affections be severe, still worse are the prior disorders, as when the bone itself, by reason of the density of the flesh, does not obtain sufficient air, but becomes
c moldy and hot and gangrened and receives no nutriment, and the nat-ural process is inverted, and the bone crumbling passes into the food, and the food into the flesh, and the flesh again falling into the blood makes all maladies that may occur more virulent than those already mentioned. But the worst case of all is when the marrow is diseased, either from excess or defect, and this is the cause of the very greatest and most fatal disorders, in which the whole course of the body is reversed.

There is a third class of diseases which may be conceived of as arising in three ways, for they are produced sometimes by wind, and sometimes by phlegm, and sometimes by bile. When the lung, which d is the dispenser of the air to the body, is obstructed by rheums and its passages are not free, some of them not acting, while through others too much air enters, then the parts which are unrefreshed by air corrode, while in other parts the excess of air forcing its way through the veins distorts them and decomposing the body is enclosed in the midst of it and occupies the midriff; thus numberless painful diseases are produced, accompanied by copious sweats. And oftentimes when the e flesh is dissolved in the body, wind, generated within and unable to escape, is the source of quite as much pain as the air coming in from without, but the greatest pain is felt when the wind gets about the sinews and the veins of the shoulders and swells them up, and so twists back the great tendons and the sinews which are connected with them. These disorders are called tetanus and opisthotonos, by reason of the tension which accompanies them. The cure of them is difficult; relief is in most cases given by fever supervening. The white phlegm, though dangerous when detained within by reason of the air 85 bubbles, yet if it can communicate with the outside air, is less severe, and only discolors the body, generating leprous eruptions and similar diseases. When it is mingled with black bile and dispersed about the courses of the head, which are the divinest part of us, the attack, b if coming on in sleep, is not so severe, but when assailing those who are awake it is hard to be got rid of, and being an affection of a sacred part, is most justly called sacred. An acid and salt phlegm, again, is the source of all those diseases which take the form of catarrh, but they have many names because the places into which they flow are manifold.

Inflammations of the body come from burnings and inflamings, and all of them originate in bile. When bile finds a means of discharge, it boils up and sends forth all sorts of tumors, but when imprisoned c within, it generates many inflammatory diseases, above all when mingled with pure blood, since it then displaces the fibers which are scattered about in the blood and are designed to maintain the balance of rare and dense, in order that the blood may not be so liquefied by heat as to exude from the pores of the body, nor again become too dense and thus find a difficulty in circulating through the veins. The d fibers are so constituted as to maintain this balance, and if anyone brings them all together when the blood is dead and in process of cooling, then the blood which remains becomes fluid, but if they are left alone, they soon congeal by reason of the surrounding cold. The fibers having this power over the blood, bile, which is only stale blood, and which from being flesh is dissolved again into blood, at the first influx coming in little by little, hot and liquid, is congealed by the power of the fibers, and so congealing and made to cool, it pro- e duces internal cold and shuddering. When it enters with more of a flood and overcomes the fibers by its heat, and boiling up throws them into disorder, if it have power enough to maintain its supremacy, it penetrates the marrow and burns up what may be termed the cables of the soul, and sets her free, but when there is not so much of it, and the body though wasted still holds out, the bile is itself mastered and is either exuded from the whole body, or is thrust through the veins into the lower or upper belly, and is driven out of the body like

86 an exile from a state in which there has been civil war, whence arise diarrheas and dysenteries, and all such disorders. When the constitution is disordered by excess of fire, continuous heat and fever are the result; when excess of air is the cause, then the fever is quotidian; when of water, which is a more sluggish element than either fire or air, then the fever is a tertian; when of earth, which is the most sluggish of the four, and is only purged away in a fourfold period, the result is a quartan fever, which can with difficulty be shaken off.

b   Such is the manner in which diseases of the body arise; the disorders of the soul, which depend upon the body, originate as follows. We must acknowledge disease of the mind to be a want of intelligence, and of this there are two kinds—to wit, madness and ignorance. In whatever state a man experiences either of them, that state may be called disease, and excessive pains and pleasures are justly to be regarded as the greatest diseases to which the soul is liable. For a man

c who is in great joy or in great pain, in his unseasonable eagerness to attain the one and to avoid the other, is not able to see or to hear anything rightly, but he is mad and is at the time utterly incapable of any participation in reason. He who has the seed about the spinal marrow too plentiful and overflowing, like a tree overladen with fruit, has many throes, and also obtains many pleasures in his desires and their offspring, and is for the most part of his life deranged because his

d pleasures and pains are so very great; his soul is rendered foolish and disordered by his body; yet he is regarded not as one diseased, but as one who is voluntarily bad, which is a mistake. The truth is that sexual intemperance is a disease of the soul due chiefly to the moisture and fluidity which is produced in one of the elements by the loose consistency of the bones. And in general, all that which is termed the incontinence of pleasure and is deemed a reproach under the idea that the wicked voluntarily do wrong is not justly a

e matter for reproach. For no man is voluntarily bad, but the bad become bad by reason of an ill disposition of the body and bad education—things which are hateful to every man and happen to him against his will. And in the case of pain, too, in like manner the soul suffers much evil from the body. For where the acid and briny phlegm and other bitter and bilious humors wander about in the body and find no exit or escape, but are pent up within and mingle their

87 own vapors with the motions of the soul, and are blended with them, they produce all sorts of diseases, more or fewer, and in every degree of intensity, and being carried to the three places of the

soul, whichever they may severally assail, they create infinite varieties of ill temper and melancholy, of rashness and cowardice, and also of forgetfulness and stupidity. Further, when to this evil constitution of body evil forms of government are added and evil dis- b courses are uttered in private as well as in public, and no sort of instruction is given in youth to cure these evils, then all of us who are bad become bad from two causes which are entirely beyond our control. In such cases the planters are to blame rather than the plants, the educators rather than the educated. But however that may be, we should endeavor as far as we can, by education and pursuits and learning, to avoid vice and attain virtue; this, however, is part of another subject.

There is a corresponding inquiry concerning the mode of treat- c ment by which the mind and the body are to be preserved, about which it is meet and right that I should say a word in turn, for it is more our duty to speak of the good than of the evil. Everything that is good is fair, and the fair is not without proportion, and the animal which is to be fair must have due proportion. Now we perceive lesser symmetries or proportions and reason about them, but of the highest and greatest we take no heed, for there is no proportion or dispro- d portion more productive of health and disease, and virtue and vice, than that between soul and body themselves. This however we do not perceive, nor do we reflect that when a weak or small frame is the vehicle of a great and mighty soul, or conversely, when a little soul is incased in a large body, then the whole animal is not fair, for it lacks the most important of all symmetries, but the due proportion of mind and body is the fairest and loveliest of all sights to him who has the seeing eye. Just as a body which has a leg too long, or which is unsym- e metrical in some other respect, is an unpleasant sight, and also, when doing its share of work, is much distressed and makes convulsive efforts, and often stumbles through awkwardness, and is the cause of infinite evil to its own self—in like manner we should conceive of the double nature which we call the living being. And when in this compound there is an impassioned soul more powerful than the body, that 88 soul, I say, convulses and fills with disorders the whole inner nature of man, and when eager in the pursuit of some sort of learning or study, causes wasting. Or again, when teaching or disputing in private or in public, and strifes and controversies arise, inflames and dissolves the composite frame of man and introduces rheums, and the nature of this phenomenon is not understood by most professors of medicine, who ascribe it to the opposite of the real cause. And once more, when a body large and too strong for the soul is united to a small and weak intelligence, then inasmuch as there are two desires natural to b man—one of food for the sake of the body, and one of wisdom for the sake of the diviner part of us—then, I say, the motions of the stronger, getting the better and increasing their own power, but making the

soul dull and stupid and forgetful, engender ignorance, which is the
greatest of diseases. There is one protection against both kinds of disproportion—that we should not move the body without the soul or
the soul without the body, and thus they will be on their guard
c against each other and be healthy and well balanced. And therefore
the mathematician or anyone else whose thoughts are much absorbed
in some intellectual pursuit, must allow his body also to have due exercise, and practice gymnastics, and he who is careful to fashion the
body should in turn impart to the soul its proper motions and should
cultivate the arts and all philosophy if he would deserve to be called
truly fair and truly good. And the separate parts should be treated in
d the same manner, in imitation of the pattern of the universe, for as
the body is heated and also cooled within by the elements which enter
into it, and is again dried up and moistened by external things, and
experiences these and the like affections from both kinds of motions,
the result is that the body if given up to motion when in a state of
quiescence is overmastered and perishes. But if anyone, in imitation
of that which we call the foster mother and nurse of the universe, will
not allow the body ever to be inactive, but is always producing mo-
e tions and agitations through its whole extent, which form the
natural defense against other motions both internal and external, and
by moderate exercise reduces to order according to their affinities the
particles and affections which are wandering about the body, as we
have already said when speaking of the universe, he will not allow
enemy placed by the side of enemy to stir up wars and disorders in the
body, but he will place friend by the side of friend, so as to create
health. Now of all motions that is the best which is produced in a
89 thing by itself, for it is most akin to the motion of thought and of the
universe, but that motion which is caused by others is not so good,
and worst of all is that which moves the body, when at rest, in parts
only and by some external agency. Wherefore of all modes of purifying and reuniting the body the best is gymnastics; the next best is a
surging motion, as in sailing or any other mode of conveyance which
b is not fatiguing; the third sort of motion may be of use in a case of
extreme necessity, but in any other will be adopted by no man of sense
—I mean the purgative treatment of physicians, for diseases unless
they are very dangerous should not be irritated by medicines, since
every form of disease is in a manner akin to the living being, whose
complex frame has an appointed term of life. For not the whole race
c only, but each individual—barring inevitable accidents—comes into
the world having a fixed span, and the triangles in us are originally
framed with power to last for a certain time beyond which no man
can prolong his life. And this holds also of the constitution of
diseases; if anyone regardless of the appointed time tries to subdue
them by medicine, he only aggravates and multiplies them. Wherefore
we ought always to manage them by regimen, as far as a man can

spare the time, and not provoke a disagreeable enemy by medicines. d

Enough of the composite animal and of the body which is a part of him, and of the manner in which a man may train and be trained by himself so as to live most according to reason, and we must above and before all provide that the element which is to train him shall be the fairest and best-adapted to that purpose. A minute discussion of this subject would be a serious task, but if, as before, I am to give only e an outline, the subject may not unfitly be summed up as follows.

I have often remarked that there are three kinds of soul located within us, having each of them motions, and I must now repeat, in the fewest words possible, that one part, if remaining inactive and ceasing from its natural motion, must necessarily become very weak, but that which is trained and exercised, very strong. Wherefore we should take care that the movements of the different parts of the 90 soul should be in due proportion.

And we should consider that God gave the sovereign part of the human soul to be the divinity of each one, being that part which, as we say, dwells at the top of the body, and inasmuch as we are a plant not of an earthly but of a heavenly growth, raises us from earth to our kindred who are in heaven. And in this we say truly, for the divine power suspends the head and root of us from that place where the generation of the soul first began, and thus makes the whole body b upright. When a man is always occupied with the cravings of desire and ambition, and is eagerly striving to satisfy them, all his thoughts must be mortal, and, as far as it is possible altogether to become such, he must be mortal every whit because he has cherished his mortal part. But he who has been earnest in the love of knowledge and of true wisdom, and has exercised his intellect more than any other part of him, must have thoughts immortal and divine, if he attain truth, c and in so far as human nature is capable of sharing in immortality, he must altogether be immortal, and since he is ever cherishing the divine power and has the divinity within him in perfect order, he will be singularly happy. Now there is only one way of taking care of things, and this is to give to each the food and motion which are natural to it. And the motions which are naturally akin to the divine d principle within us are the thoughts and revolutions of the universe. These each man should follow, and by learning the harmonies and revolutions of the universe, should correct the courses of the head which were corrupted at our birth, and should assimilate the thinking being to the thought, renewing his original nature, so that having assimilated them he may attain to that best life which the gods have set before mankind, both for the present and the future.

Thus our original design of discoursing about the universe down e to the creation of man is nearly completed. A brief mention may be made of the generation of other animals, so far as the subject admits of brevity; in this manner our argument will best attain a due proportion. On the subject of animals, then, the following remarks may be offered. Of the men who came into the world, those who were cowards or led unrighteous lives may with reason be supposed to 91 have changed into the nature of women in the second generation. And this was the reason why at that time the gods created in us the desire of sexual intercourse, contriving in man one animated substance, and in woman another, which they formed, respectively, in the following manner. The outlet for drink by which liquids pass through the lung under the kidneys and into the bladder, which receives and then by the pressure of the air emits them, was so fashioned by them as to penetrate also into the body of the marrow, which passes from the b head along the neck and through the back, and which in the preceding discourse we have named the seed. And the seed, having life and becoming endowed with respiration, produces in that part in which it respires a lively desire of emission, and thus creates in us the love of procreation. Wherefore also in men the organ of generation becoming rebellious and masterful, like an animal disobedient to reason, and c maddened with the sting of lust, seeks to gain absolute sway, and the same is the case with the so-called womb or matrix of women. The animal within them is desirous of procreating children, and when remaining unfruitful long beyond its proper time, gets discontented and angry, and wandering in every direction through the body, closes up the passages of the breath, and, by obstructing respiration, drives them to extremity, causing all varieties of disease, until at length the desire and love of the man and the woman, bringing them together d and as it were plucking the fruit from the tree, sow in the womb, as in a field, animals unseen by reason of their smallness and without form; these again are separated and matured within; they are then finally brought out into the light, and thus the generation of animals is completed.

Thus were created women and the female sex in general. But the race of birds was created out of innocent light-minded men who, although their minds were directed toward heaven, imagined, in their simplicity, that the clearest demonstration of the things above was to be obtained by sight; these were remodeled and transformed into e birds, and they grew feathers instead of hair. The race of wild pedestrian animals, again, came from those who had no philosophy in any of their thoughts, and never considered at all about the nature of the heavens, because they had ceased to use the courses of the head, but followed the guidance of those parts of the soul which are in the breast. In consequence of these habits of theirs they had their front legs and their heads resting upon the earth to which they were drawn by natural affinity, and the crowns of their heads were elongated and of all sorts of shapes, into which the courses of the soul were crushed by reason of disuse. And this was the reason why they 92 were created quadrupeds and polypods. God gave the more senseless of them the more support that they might be more attracted to the earth. And the most foolish of them, who trail their bodies entirely upon the ground and have no longer any need of feet, he made without feet to crawl upon the earth. The fourth class were the inhabitants of the water; these were made out of the most entirely senseless b and ignorant of all, whom the transformers did not think any longer worthy of pure respiration, because they possessed a soul which was made impure by all sorts of transgression, and instead of the subtle and pure medium of air, they gave them the deep and muddy sea to be their element of respiration. And hence arose the race of fishes and oysters, and other aquatic animals, which have received the most remote habitations as a punishment of their outlandish ignorance. c These are the laws by which all animals pass into one another, now, as in the beginning, changing as they lose or gain wisdom and folly.

We may now say that our discourse about the nature of the universe has an end. The world has received animals, mortal and immortal, and is fulfilled with them, and has become a visible animal containing the visible—the sensible God who is the image of the intellectual, the greatest, best, fairest, most perfect—the one only-begotten heaven.

CRITIAS

The Critias, of which we have only a few pages, is the second in a proposed series of three dialogues. The first is the Timaeus, where Socrates reviews the main heads of a discussion held the day before on the constitution of the ideal state, when he had asked three of those present to discuss at their next meeting how such a state would act in a great war. Timaeus, speaking for the three, declares that they are ready to do so and calls on Critias to tell Socrates the story he had heard from his grandfather of the greatest struggle Athens ever waged, thousands of years ago.

His grandfather had heard it from Solon, who was told it by the priests when he went to Egypt. Athens' antagonist was the splendid and powerful island of Atlantis in the great ocean, which little Athens magnificently conquered when she threatened to enslave all the nations of the Mediterranean. Very soon after the conquest the sea overwhelmed her; she sank and no part of her was ever seen again. Critias now proposes to use the account of this glorious struggle and victory of ancient Athens as the illustration of the way Socrates' ideal state would fight under like circumstances. Timaeus is to begin at the very beginning with the origin of the universe and hand the discourse over to Critias with the creation of man. He then will tell how the ideal state that Athens was in very ancient days acted when confronted with vastly superior power.

All of this is in the Timaeus, not the Critias. Strictly speaking, it is part of an introduction to the two dialogues, but it really belongs more to the second than to the first. The tale of Atlantis is not important in the Timaeus, but the little we have of the Critias consists chiefly of a description of the fabulous island. Plato is again resting his mind. He is making up a fairy tale, the most wonderful island that could be imagined. On why the dialogue was never finished we have no information at all.

TIMAEUS: Well, Socrates, at last I am barely in port after my voyage on the seas of discourse, and with what a sense of relief! I feel like some traveler at the end of a weary journey. So I make it my prayer to the god who has been born but now in our tale, though so long ago in fact, that he will of his grace vouchsafe us retention of what has been spoken to purpose and visit us with the proper penalty for any false note we have unwittingly struck in our treatment of these matters. Now the right penalty is that he who strays from tune should be brought back to it. To the end, then, that our discourses of the making of gods may be rightly uttered hereafter, I call on him to grant us that surest and best of medicines, knowledge, and with this prayer I hand over the further continuance of the tale to Critias, as we agreed I should do.

CRITIAS: Aye, Timaeus, and I accept the task. But I, too, must once more make the same request you yourself advanced before me. I must crave indulgence on the score of the magnitude of the subject, and I think I have an even better claim than yourself to a still further measure of consideration for what yet remains to be told. To be sure, I am well aware that my request will seem vastly presumptuous and unduly tactless; yet made it must be. What man in his sound senses, indeed, could venture to dispute the excellence of your exposition? What I must try to show, as I can, is that the theme still to be expounded is more difficult to handle and consequently calls for yet more generous allowances. In fact, Timaeus, upon an audience of human beings it is easier to produce the impression of adequate treatment in speaking of gods than in discoursing of mortals like ourselves. The combination of unfamiliarity and sheer ignorance in an audience makes the task of one who is to treat a subject toward which they are in this state easy in the extreme, and in this matter of gods, we know, of course, how the case stands with us. But to make my meaning still clearer, kindly follow an illustration. All statements made by any of us are, of course, bound to be an affair of imagery and picturing. Now, suppose we consider the ease or difficulty with which an artist's portraiture of figures divine and human, respectively, produces the impression of satisfactory reproduction on the spectator. We shall observe that in the case of earth, mountains, rivers, woodland, the sky as a whole, and the several revolving bodies located in it, for one thing, the artist is always well content if he can reproduce them with some faint degree of resemblance, and, for another, that since our knowledge of such objects is never exact, we submit his design to no criticism or scrutiny, but acquiesce, in these cases, in a dim and deceptive outline. But when it is our own human form that the artist undertakes to depict, daily familiar observation makes us quick to detect shortcomings and we show ourselves severe critics of one who

From *Timaeus and Critias*, translated by A. E. Taylor (London, 1929).

does not present us with full and perfect resemblance. Well, we should recognize that the same is true of discourses. Where the subjects of them are celestial and divine, we are satisfied by mere faint verisimilitudes; where mortal and human, we are exacting critics. So with our present unrehearsed narrative; if we do not succeed in re-

e producing the proper touches perfectly, allowances should be made. In fact, we ought to understand that to depict human life impressively

108 is hard, not easy. It is to remind you all of this, Socrates, and to plead for a greater, not a lesser, measure of indulgence for what I am now to relate, that I have made this long speech. If you all feel that my appeal for this favor is justified, pray grant it without demur.

SOCRATES: To be sure we will, Critias. What is more, the same favor may be taken as granted by anticipation to Hermocrates after you. For I see plainly enough that by and by, when it comes to his

b turn to speak, he will make the same request as his precursors. As I would have him cast about for a fresh exordium and not be driven to repeat the old one, he may make his speech with the assurance that consideration is guaranteed him when the time comes. Still, I would warn you, my dear Critias, of the temper of your auditory; the composer who preceded you made a wonderfully favorable impression, and you will need the most generous indulgence if you are to prove equal to succeeding him.

HERMOCRATES: That, Socrates, is a warning as much to me

c as to our friend. Still, Critias, 'faint heart never yet set up trophy,' so you must launch out into your narrative like a man, calling Paean and the Muses to aid you in displaying and lauding the worth of your fellow Athenians of ancient days.

CRITIAS: Ah, my dear Hermocrates, your post is in the rear rank, under cover of another; that is why your spirits are still undashed. Well, you may very possibly discover what the situation is like for yourself, in the course of events; meanwhile I must, at any

d rate, follow your encouraging advice and invoke the gods at large, including those you have mentioned, but above all Memory. She is the power on whom the whole fortune of my discourse most depends. If I can only sufficiently recall and repeat the story as it was once told by the priests and brought home to this country by Solon, I am confident that my present audience will pronounce me to have discharged my task with reasonable credit. Well, I must proceed to the story itself at once, without further delay.

e   In the very first place, let us remind ourselves that it is in all nine thousand years since a general war, of which we are now to relate the course, was declared between those who dwelt without and those who dwelt within the Pillars of Heracles. The command of the latter was taken, and the war conducted throughout, as the story ran, by our own city; the leaders of the other party were the kings of the island of Atlantis. Atlantis, as you will recollect, was once, we said, an island larger than Libya and Asia together; it has now been engulfed by earthquakes and is the source of the impassable mud which prevents navigators from this quarter from advancing through the straits into the open ocean. As for the mass of the barbarian peo- 109 ples and the Hellenic communities of those days, the various details will become plain on occasion as the course of the narrative unfolds. But we shall have to begin with a preliminary review of the respective resources and polities of the Athenians of the time and the antago- nists against whom the war was waged, and of the two parties we must give the precedence to our own countrymen.

Of old, then, the gods distributed the whole earth by regions, and b that without contention. That gods know not their several dues, or if they know them, yet some seek by contention to engross to themselves what more properly belongs to others—these are perverse imagina- tions. They apportioned to each his own by righteous allotment, set- tled their territories, and, when they had settled them, fell to feeding us, their bestial and flocks there, as herdsmen do their cattle. Only they would not coerce body with body in the fashion of shepherds who c drive their flocks to pasture with blows; they set the course of the liv- ing creature from that part about which it turns most readily, its prow, controlling its soul after their own mind by persuasion as by a rudder, and so moving and steering the whole mortal fabric. Thus diverse gods received diverse districts as their portions and reigned over them. But Hephaestus and Athena, as they had one nature, be- ing brother and sister by the same father, and at one, moreover, in their love of wisdom and artistry, so also obtained one lot in common, this our land, to be a home meet for prowess and understanding. They d produced from the soil a race of good men and taught them the order of their polity; their names have been preserved, but their deeds for- gotten by reason of the destructions of their successors and the lapse of time. For the remnant of survivors, as has, indeed, been already said, was ever left unlettered among its mountains, and had heard no more than the names of the country's rulers and a few of their deeds. So they were well pleased to give the names to their sons, but as for the virtues and laws of older generations, they knew nothing of them e beyond some dim reports, but were, for many generations, themselves and their children, in want of bare necessaries. So they gave their minds to their own needs and made their discourses of them, for- getting the story of faraway early days. For legendary lore and inquiry 110 into ancient things both visit cities in the train of leisure, when they see men already provided with the necessaries of life, and not before. Thus it has come about that the names of the ancients have been preserved without any memorial of their deeds. My warrant for what I say is this. Cecrops, Erechtheus, Erichthonius, Erysichthon, and most of the recorded names before Theseus are, in the main, the very b names given, as Solon said, by the priests in their tale of that distant

war, as are also the names of the women. And in especial, the figure
and image of the goddess, whom they of old set up in armor, according to the custom of their time, when exercises of war were common
c to woman and man alike, signify that in all living creatures that company together, female with male, nature ever grants it to both to
practice the excellence proper to their kind.

Now, at that time most sorts of citizens who dwelt in this land
were busied with handicrafts and tillage of the soil, but the fighting
sort had been set apart at the first by godlike men and dwelt by themselves, furnished with all that was proper for their sustenance and
d training. None of them had any private possession of his own; they
looked on all things as the common store of all, seeking to receive
from their fellow citizens nothing beyond sufficient sustenance; in
short, they followed all the practices we spoke of yesterday when we
talked of those feigned guardians. In particular, there is truth and
credibility in what we said of the territory, as first that its boundaries
were then drawn at the Isthmus and, on the side of the mainland, at
the summits of Cithaeron and Parnes, and its borders came down to
e the sea with Oropia on the right, and the Asopus shut out on the left,
and again, that the soil far surpassed all others, which, indeed, is why
the district could then maintain a great army exempt from all tasks
of husbandry. And here is good evidence of its excellence. The remnant now left of it is a match for any soil in the world in the variety
111 and quality of its harvests and the pasturage it yields to all sorts of
cattle. But of old its yield was most copious as well as excellent.
What proof is there of this, and why are we right to call it a remnant
of the land of those days? It is one long projection running out from
the main body of the continent into the open sea, like a headland,
and, as we know, the marine basin that borders it is extremely deep.
So, while there have been many formidable deluges in the course of
the nine thousand years—that is the interval between the date we are
b speaking of and the present—the soil washed away from the higher
levels in these periodic convulsions does not deposit any notable sediment, as in some other regions, but is regularly carried off and lost in
the depths. Consequently that has happened which happens in little
islets. By comparison with the original territory, what is left now is,
so to say, the skeleton of a body wasted by disease; the rich, soft soil
has been carried off and only the bare framework of the district left.
At the time we are speaking of these ravages had not begun. Our pres-
c ent mountains were high crests, what we now call the plains of Phel-
leus were covered with rich soil, and there was abundant timber on the
mountains, of which traces may still be seen. For some of our mountains at present will only support trees, but not so very long ago trees
fit for the roofs of vast buildings were felled there and the rafters are
still in existence. There were also many other lofty cultivated trees
d which provided unlimited fodder for beasts. Besides, the soil got the

benefit of the yearly 'water from Zeus,' which was not lost, as it is to-day, by running off a barren ground to the sea; a plentiful supply of it was received into the soil and stored up in the layers of nonporous potter's clay. Thus the moisture absorbed in the higher regions percolated to the hollows and so all quarters were lavishly provided with springs and rivers. Even to this day the sanctuaries at their former sources survive to prove the truth of our present account of the country.

This, then, was the natural condition of the district at large, and e it had received cultivation such as might be expected from true husbandmen, with no other vocation, who were also lovers of all that is noble and men of admirable natural parts, possessed of an excellent soil, a generous water supply and an eminently temperate climate. As for the town, its plan at that time was as follows. To begin with, the Acropolis was not then as it is now. At present it has been 112 washed bare of soil by one night of extraordinary floods in which an earthquake and the third terrible deluge before that of Deucalion befell together. But in other and earlier days it was so large that it reached to the Eridanus and Ilissus, enclosing the Pnyx and bounded on the side facing it by Lycabettus; the whole was covered with soil and, save here and there, the surface was level. Without, directly under its slopes, were the dwellings of the craftsmen and the husband- b men who tilled the adjoining fields; higher up the fighting force had its abode by itself round the temple of Athena and Hephaestus, girdled by a single wall, like the garden of one house. On the northern side they had fashioned their common dwelling houses and winter messrooms, with all that was proper for their mode of life in common in the way of buildings for themselves and temples, but no gold nor c silver, for they made no use of these metals for any purpose. They aimed at the mean between splendor and meanness, dwelling in decent houses where they grew old, themselves and their children's children, each succeeding generation leaving them to another like itself. As for the southern side, in the summer, as was natural, they forsook their gardens, gymnasiums, and messrooms and used it for these purposes. There was only one fountain, on the site of the present Acropolis. This has been choked by the earthquake and today only d shrunken rills remain in the vicinity. Then it provided all with an abundant supply of water equally wholesome in winter and summer. Such was their manner of life, then; they were at once guardians of their fellow citizens and freely followed leaders of the Hellenes at large; the number of both sexes already qualified and still qualified to bear arms they were careful to keep, as nearly as possible, always the same, roughly some twenty thousand.   e

With such personalities and such a standing method of administering Hellas and their own commonwealth in righteousness, they were famous throughout Europe and Asia alike for the comeliness of their persons and for every virtue of the soul, and had the greatest name of the time. As for the condition and early history of their antagonists, if my memories of the tale I heard as a boy do not play me false, I will now impart the story freely to you as friends.

113 But before I begin my narrative, I must make a brief explanation, or you may be surprised to hear of so many barbarians with Hellenic names. So I will give you the reason for this. Solon had a fancy to turn the tale to account in his own poetry; so he asked questions about the significance of the names and discovered that the original Egyptian authors of the narrative had translated them into their own speech. In his turn, as he learned the sense of a name, he b translated it back again, in his manuscript, into our own language. His actual papers were once in my father's hands, and are in my own, to this day, and I studied them thoroughly in my boyhood. So if you hear names like those of our own countrymen, you must not be surprised; I have given you the explanation. Well, then, the story—and a long story it is—began much in this fashion. As we said before, when we were speaking of the 'lots,' the gods divided the whole earth c into lots, some larger, some smaller, and established their temples and sacrifices in them. Poseidon, then, thus receiving as his lot the isle of Atlantis, settled his sons by a mortal woman in a district of it which must now be described. By the sea, in the center of the island, there was a plain, said to have been the most beauteous of all such plains and very fertile, and, again, near the center of this plain, at a distance of some fifty stadia, a mountain which was nowhere of any great altitude. In this mountain lived one of the original earthborn d men of that region, named Evenor, with his wife Leucippe. The pair had an only daughter, Clito, who was just husband-high when her mother and father both died. Poseidon desired this damsel, had to do with her, and fortified the hill where she had her abode by a fence of alternate rings of sea and land, smaller and greater, one within another. He fashioned two such round wheels, as we may call them, of earth and three of sea from the very center of the island, at uniform e distances, thus making the spot inaccessible to man, for there were as yet no ships and no seafaring. The island left at their center he adorned with his own hand—a light enough task for a god—causing two fountains to flow from underground springs, one warm, the other cold, and the soil to send up abundance of food plants of all kinds.

114 He then begot five twin births of male offspring and divided the whole isle of Atlantis into ten parts. On the earliest-born of the first pair he bestowed their mother's dwelling place with the lot of land surrounding it, the best and largest of all, and appointed him king over his brethren. The rest he made princes, granting each of them the sovereignty over a large population and the lordship of wide lands. Further, he gave names to them all. Their king, the eldest, received a name from which the ocean, as well as the whole island, got its desig-

nation; it is called Atlantic, because the name of the first king of old times was Atlas. His younger twin brother, to whose share fell the b extremity of the island off the Pillars of Heracles, fronting the region now known as Gadira, from the name of his territory, was called in Greek Eumelus, but in the language his own country Gadirus, and no doubt his name was the origin of that of the district. One of the second pair was called Ampheres, the other Evaemon, the elder of the third Mneseus and his junior Autochthon, the elder of the fourth c Elasippus, the younger Mestor; Azaes was the name of the elder of the fifth pair, that of his brother Diaprepes. All these and their descendants for many generations reigned as princes of numerous islands of the ocean besides their own, and were also, as has been already said, suzerains of the population of the hither or inner side of the straits, as far as Egypt and Tyrrhenia.

Now from Atlas sprang a prolific and illustrious house which retained the throne for many generations, the eldest being always king d and transmitting the succession to his eldest descendant. They possessed wealth such as had never been amassed by any royal line before them and could not be easily matched by any after, and were equipped with all resources required for their city and dominions at large. Though their empire brought them a great external revenue, it was the island itself which furnished the main provision for all e purposes of life. In the first place it yielded all products of the miner's industry, solid and fusible alike, including one which is now only a name but was then something more, orichalch, which was excavated in various parts of the island, and had then a higher value than any metal except gold. It also bore in its forests a generous supply of all timbers serviceable to the carpenter and builder and maintained a sufficiency of animals wild and domesticated; even elephants were plentiful. There was ample pasture for this the largest and most vo- 115 racious of brutes, no less than for all the other creatures of marsh, lake and river, mountain and plain. Besides all this, the soil bore all aromatic substances still to be found on earth, roots, stalks, canes, gums exuded by flowers and fruits, and they throve on it. Then, as for cultivated fruits, the dry sort which is meant to be our food supply and those others we use as solid nutriment—we call the various kinds pulse—as well as the woodland kind which gives us meat and drink b and oil together, the fruit of trees that ministers to our pleasure and merriment and is so hard to preserve, and that we serve as welcome dessert to a jaded man to charm away his satiety—all these were produced by that sacred island, which then lay open to the sun, in marvelous beauty and inexhaustible profusion. So the kings employed all these gifts of the soil to construct and beautify their temples, c royal residences, harbors, docks, and domain in general on the following plan.

They first bridged the rings of sea round their original home, thus

making themselves a road from and to their palace. This palace they originally built at the outset in the dwelling place of the god and their ancestors, and each monarch, as he inherited it in his turn, added beauties to its existing beauties, always doing his utmost to sur-
d pass his predecessor, until they had made the residence a marvel for the size and splendor of its buildings. They began on the seaside by cutting a canal to the outermost ring, fifty stadia long, three hundred feet broad, and a hundred feet deep; the 'ring' could now be entered from the sea by this canal like a port, as the opening they had
e made would admit the largest of vessels. Further, at these bridges they made openings in the rings of land which separated those of water, just sufficient to admit the passage of a single trireme, and covered the openings in so that the voyage through them became subterranean, for the banks of the rings of earth were considerably elevated above the sea level. The breadth of the largest ring of water, that to which the canal from the sea had been made, was three stadia and a half, and that of the contiguous ring of land the same. Of the second pair, the ring of water had a breadth of two stadia and that of land was once more equal in breadth to the water outside it; the land
116 which immediately surrounded the central islet was in breadth one stadium; the islet on which the palace stood had a diameter of five stadia. So they enclosed this islet with the rings and bridge, which had a breadth of a hundred feet, completely by a stone wall, building towers and gates on the bridges at either end of each passage for the
b sea water. The stone, black, white, and red, they quarried beneath the whole central islet and outer and inner rings, thus, by the same process, excavating a pair of interior basins for shipping with a roofing of native rock. Some of their buildings were of a single color; in other cases they entertained themselves by intermingling the stones to produce variegated surfaces of an inherently agreeable character. The whole circuit of the outermost wall they covered with a coat, a ceruse [ointment], as one might say, of copper, the inner with melted
c tin, and the wall of the actual acropolis with orichalch, which gleamed like fire.

Within the acropolis was the palace with the following design. In the very center, surrounded by a golden railing, which it was forbidden to enter, was an untrodden sanctuary sacred to Clito and Poseidon, the very place where the race of the ten princes had been first conceived and begotten; here, too, the seasonable offerings were made yearly to each of them from all the ten lots. Poseidon himself
d had a temple, a stadium long and half a stadium broad, with a proportionate height, but something un-Hellenic in its aspect. The whole exterior of this temple was coated with silver, except the figures on the pediments; these were covered with gold. Within, the roof was of ivory throughout, ornamented with gold, silver, and orichalch, and all the rest, walls, columns, pavement, were covered with orichalch.

It contained golden statues of the god standing in a chariot drawn by e
six winged horses, and on such a scale that his head touched the roof,
and of a hundred Nereids round him riding on dolphins, for that was
then believed to be the number of the Nereids. It also contained many
other statues dedicated by private persons. Outside the temple there
stood golden statues of all the wives of those who had been of the
number of the ten kings and of themselves, and many other great
statues, dedicated by kings and private persons of the country itself
and the foreign nations over whom they were suzerain. There was an
altar of size and workmanship to match the edifice; the palace, too,
was no less worthy of the grandeur of the empire and the magnificence of its temples.   117
    Uses were found for the waters of the two springs, the cold and
the warm. The supply from both was copious and the natural flavor
and virtues of their waters remarkable. So they were surrounded by
buildings and plantations of appropriate trees as well as with a
number of basins, some open to the air and others, which were used b
as warm baths in winter, covered. Of these there were several sets,
for the kings, for private citizens, and for women, and yet others for
horses and other beasts of burden, each set with its own appropriate
equipment. The waste from them was conducted to the grove of
Poseidon, where the trees were of every kind and, thanks to the excellence of the soil, of incredible size and beauty, and then let into
the outer rings of water by conduits at the bridges. Here, besides numerous temples to different gods, they had constructed a variety of c
gardens and gymnasiums. Some of the latter were for men; there were
others on each of the two islands formed by the rings, specially for
horses. In particular, they had a space reserved as a racecourse in the
center of the larger of these islands; its breadth was a stadium and
the whole length of the circumference was left free for the contests.
Round this racecourse on both sides were barracks for the main body
of the bodyguards; a number of the more trusty were stationed in the d
smaller ring, nearer the citadel; to the most eminently trustworthy of
all, quarters were assigned within the citadel about the persons of
the kings. The dockyards were filled with triremes and their appropriate equipment, all in excellent order. So much, then, for the appointments of the royal residence. When one had passed the three
outer harbors, a wall ran all round, starting at the sea, at a uniform e
distance of fifty stadia from the greatest ring and its harbor, returning on itself at the mouth of the canal from the sea. This wall was
completely filled by a multitude of closely set houses, and the large
harbor and canal were constantly crowded by merchant vessels and
their passengers arriving from all quarters, whose vast numbers occasioned incessant shouting, clamor, and general uproar, day and night.
    I have now given you a pretty faithful report of what I once
learned of the town and the old palace, and must do my best to recall

118 the general character of the territory and its organization. To begin
with, the district as a whole, so I have heard, was of great elevation
and its coast precipitous, but all round the city was a plain, enclosing it and itself enclosed in turn by mountain ranges which came
right down to the sea. The plain itself was smooth, level, and of a generally oblong shape; it stretched for three thousand stadia in one direction, and, at its center, for two thousand inland from the coast.
b All through the island this level district faced the south and was thus
screened from the cold northerly winds. In those times it was famous
for its encircling mountains, which were more numerous, huge, and
beautiful than any that exist today. These mountains contained numerous villages with a wealthy population, besides rivers, lakes, and
meadows which provided plentiful sustenance for all sorts of animals,
wild or domestic, and timber of different kinds in quantities amply
sufficient for manufactures of every type.

   Well, this plain, in consequence partly of its original structure,
c partly of the long-continued exertions of a succession of kings, had
assumed an aspect which I shall now describe. From the first, it was
naturally quadrangular, oblong, and nearly rectangular; departures
from that shape had been corrected by the carrying of a fosse round
it. As to the depth, breadth, and length of this fosse, it sounds incredible that any work of human hands should be so vast by comparison
with other achievements of the kind, but I have to tell the tale as I
heard it. It had been dug to the depth of a hundred feet, had every-
d where a stadium in breadth, and, as it was carried completely round
the plain, its length came to ten thousand stadia. It received the watercourses which came down from the mountains, made the tour of
the plain, meeting the city in both directions, and was thence allowed
to discharge into the sea. Beyond the city, straight canals of some
hundred feet in width, terminated once more at the fosse on the seaside, were drawn across the plain, with a distance of a hundred stadia
e between every two. They were used for the floating of timber down
to the town from the mountains and the conveyance by boat of natural produce generally, oblique channels of cross-communication being cut from these canals to one another and the city. There were
actually two harvests in the year; in the winter the husbandmen
trusted to the sky for their irrigation, in the summer they looked to
the earth, and released the waters of the canals. As to their numbers, each allotment of land was under an injunction to furnish one
119 leader of a military detachment, the area of the allotment was ten
stadia by ten, and the total number of these allotments mounted to
sixty thousand. The number of units supplied by the mountains
and the territory at large was said to be enormous, and all were
regularly assigned to the different allotments and leaders according to their districts or villages. Each leader was then enjoined
to furnish the army with the following contribution: one-sixth part

of a war chariot, up to the full complement of ten thousand such chariots; two chargers with their riders; a pair of horses without car b but supplied with a dragoon with light shield and a driver for the pair, to stand behind the combatant; two hoplites, a pair of archers, and the same number of slingers; three light-armed throwers of stones and the same number of javelin men; four marines, up to the full complement of twelve hundred vessels. This was the war equipment of the royal city; in the other nine there were various arrangements which would take much time to describe.

The distribution of power and prerogative was, and had from c the first, been this. Each of the ten kings was, in his own territory and government, supreme over persons and, for the most part, over the laws, and could chastise and put to death at his pleasure. But their authority over and intercourse with one another was regulated by the commands of Poseidon, as they were informed by the law and by an inscription left by the earliest kings on a column of orichalch preserved in the sanctuary of Poseidon in the center of the island. d Here, in fact, they were accustomed to assemble at alternate intervals of four and five years, thus showing equal respect for even number and odd; in these sessions, they deliberated on their common affairs, made inquiry whether any of them were transgressing the law, and pronounced judgment. When they were to give judgment, they first exchanged pledges in this fashion. In the sanctuary of Poseidon consecrated bulls roamed at large. So the ten came unattended and made prayer to the god that they might capture the victim of his preference. e Then they gave chase with wooden clubs and cords only, but no implement of iron; what bull soever they took they brought him to the column and slew him over it, wetting the inscription with his blood. Now there was written on the column, besides the laws, an oath calling down grievous curses on the disobedient. So when they had offered sacrifice after their own ritual and were devoting all the bull's mem- 120 bers, they would mingle a bowl of wine, casting in one clot of the blood for each man; the rest of the blood they cast into the fire, first cleansing the column. Then they drew the wine from the bowl in golden beakers, made a libation over the fire, and swore on oath that they would give judgment according to the laws upon the column, would chastise any who had heretofore transgressed, and hereafter transgress none of these ordinances wittingly, neither giving nor b obeying commandment save according to the laws of their father. When each had taken this vow for himself and his house after him, he drank and dedicated his beaker in the god's sanctuary, and so betook himself to the banquet and necessary business. When dark fell and the fire of the offerings was burned down, all vested themselves in fair robes of deep blue, and seated themselves so by the embers of c their sacrifice, on the bare earth, and by night, quenching all fire in the sanctuary. Thus they gave and received judgment, if any charged

any with transgression. Judgment given, when the morning came,
they wrote the judgments on a plate of gold and dedicated it and their
robes for a memorial. Now there were many more special laws concerning the rights of the several kings, but the chief of these were that
they should bear no arms one against another and that if any should
d essay to overthrow the royal house of any city, all should come to its
help—but ever in accord with the rule of their ancestors—they should
take counsel in common for war and all other affairs, and the chief
command should be given to the house of Atlas. Also, the king should
have no power over the life of any of his kinsmen, save with the approval of more than half of the ten.

Now this mighty and wondrous power, which then was in that
region, the god arrayed and brought against this our own region, the
cause, as the tale goes, being this. For many generations, while the
e god's strain in them was still vigorous, they gave obedience to the laws
and affection to the divine whereto they were akin. They were indeed truehearted and greathearted, bearing themselves to one another and to their various fortunes with judgment and humbleness.
They thought scorn of all things save virtue and counted their present
prosperity a little thing. So they found the weight of their gold and
121 other possessions a light load. Wealth made them not drunken with
wantonness; their mastery of themselves was not lost, nor their steps
made uncertain. They perceived with the clear vision of the sober
that even these things all receive increase from virtue and mutual
love, whereas where the first are sought and held in honor, they decay themselves and the others perish with them. So by reason of such
thoughts and the divine strain that persisted in them, their wealth in
the things of which we have told was still further increased. But when
the god's part in them began to wax faint by constant crossing with
b much mortality, and the human temper to predominate, then they
could no longer carry their fortunes, but began to behave themselves
unseemly. To the seeing eye they now began to seem foul, for they
were losing the fairest bloom from their most precious treasure, but
to such as could not see the true happy life, to appear at last fair and
blessed indeed, now that they were taking the infection of wicked
coveting and pride of power. Zeus, the god of gods, who governs his
kingdom by law, having the eye by which such things are seen, beheld their goodly house in its grievous plight and was minded to lay a
c judgment on them, that the discipline might bring them back to tune.
So he gathered all the gods in his most honorable residence, even that
that stands at the world's center and overlooks all that has part in
becoming, and when he had gathered them there, he said . . .

LAWS

The Laws *was written a few years before Plato's death and is the last thing he ever wrote. It is unlike all the other dialogues and the difference is emphasized by the fact that in it alone Socrates is absent. He plays little or no part in the* Sophist, Statesman, *and* Timaeus, *but he is there and the conversation is directed toward him. In the* Laws *he is never mentioned.*

Three elderly men, a Cretan, a Spartan, and an Athenian, meet while walking in Crete and fall to talking about good and bad laws. Finally the other two ask the Athenian, who has shown himself their superior in knowledge, to say what laws there should be in a good constitution. They agree that this will not be the ideal state, which should have no laws at all because where the law governs there will always be injustices. Nevertheless the rule of law is the second best. It is the expression of the true opinion of the community and, if carried out, will lead to an increasing understanding of the ideal, by which the actual laws can be improved.

Plato is old. Death cannot be far away. The world he is about to leave wears a different look from what it did. It has become of pressing importance. He does not want to look farther and farther into "the beyond," but to come down to earth and realize some of the truth he has seen. He drops poetical thought and storytelling; he holds up now as the chief business of the state to mold character rather than to forward knowledge, although it is true that nowhere does he even imply anything against that basic conviction of his that only he who knows what justice is can be just.

In the Republic *he had said that human affairs were not worth taking very seriously. He repeats the statement in the* Laws, *but adds that it is yet necessary to take them seriously, and he proceeds to do so through many pages of laws that regulate life in great detail. One law begins, "As to pears and apples and pomegranates and similar fruits." That sort of thing makes heavy reading, but whoever persists will find Plato again and again treading the sunlit heights. He cannot keep long on the level of the commonplace.*

The Golden Rule is here: "May I do to others as I would that they should do to me." Four hundred years later Christ said it. The essence of the parable of the good Samaritan is in the words,

"Offenses by alien against alien, compared with sins against fellow citizens, more directly draw down the vengeance of God. For the alien, being without friends or kinsmen, has the greater claim on pity, human and divine." The Old Testament declares that the sins of the fathers shall be visited on the children. Plato says, *"But children and family, if they forsake their father's ways, shall have an honorable name and good report, as those that have done well and manfully in leaving evil for good."* He probes more deeply than the Old Testament into the nature of sin when he writes, *"The sorest judgment on evildoing is that a man grows like those who already are evil,"* and *"Violent attachment to self is the constant source of misdeeds in every one of us."* He stands with the Old Testament when he says, *"It is God who is, for you and me, the measure of all things."*

BOOK I

624 ATHENIAN : To whom is the merit of instituting your laws ascribed, gentlemen? To a god, or to some man?

CLINIAS : Why, to a god, sir, indubitably to a god—in our case to Zeus, in the case of Lacedaemon, to which our friend here belongs, I believe, according to their own story, to Apollo. That is so, is it not?

MEGILLUS : Certainly.

ATHENIAN : You mean that Minos, just as Homer relates, used b to repair to a conference with his father every ninth year, and that his legislation for your Cretan cities was based on his father's oracles?

CLINIAS : So our local story has it. It adds the further detail 625 that Rhadamanthus, the brother of Minos—the name will, of course, be familiar to you—was conspicuous for his justice. Well, as we Cretans insist, it was his ancient administration of our judicial business which earned him this deserved reputation.

ATHENIAN : An honorable distinction indeed, and most appropriate to a son of Zeus. But as you and our friend Megillus have both been brought up under such venerable legal institutions, I trust you b will not find it disagreeable to spend the time, as we walk this morning, in conversation on questions of politics and jurisprudence. The distance from Cnossus to the cave and chapel of Zeus is, I understand, quite considerable, and there are presumably shady resting places, such as the sultry season demands, on the way, among the

---

From *The Laws of Plato*, translated by A. E. Taylor (London and New York, 1934; subsequently pub. in Everyman's Library).

lofty trees, where it will be a comfort, at our age of life, to make frequent halts and entertain one another with discourse. Thus we may reach the end of our long journey without fatigue.

CLINIAS: To be sure, sir, there are groves of prodigiously fine, tall cypresses farther on, as well as meadows, where we can take a c rest.

ATHENIAN: I am glad to hear it.

CLINIAS: No doubt you are, but we shall all be gladder still when we come to them. Well, let us make our start, and good luck go with us!

ATHENIAN: With all my heart! Come now, tell me, what is the purpose of your laws in prescribing your system of common meals and physical training, and your distinctive accouterments?

CLINIAS: Why, in the case of my own countrymen, sir, I take the purpose to be very obvious. As you can both see for yourselves, Crete, as a whole, unlike Thessaly, has not a level surface. This is, of d course, why the Thessalians rely by preference on cavalry, but we on rapid infantry movements, since with us the ground is uneven and better adapted for training in these maneuvers. On such a terrain a soldier must naturally be lightly accoutered, and not carry a load as he runs; consequently, bow and arrows are felt to be recommended by their light weight. These arrangements, then, have all been made with a military purpose, and it is warfare, if I am to speak my own conviction, which our lawgiver kept in view in all his dispositions. For instance, his reason for establishing the common meals was pre- e sumably that he saw that when the whole population are in the field, that very circumstance compels them to take their meals together, through the campaign, for self-protection. He meant, I believe, to reprove the folly of mankind, who refuse to understand that they are all engaged in a continuous lifelong warfare against all cities whatsoever. Hence, if a force must take its meals together in wartime, for the 626 sake of self-defense, and post relays of officers and men to act as its guards, the same thing should equally be done in time of peace. In fact, the peace of which most men talk—so he held—is no more than a name; in real fact, the normal attitude of a city to all other cities is one of undeclared warfare. By reflection on these lines you will discover that our Cretan legislator constructed the universal scheme of b all our institutions, public and private, with a view to war, and transmitted his laws to us for observance in precisely the same spirit. It was his conviction that there is no benefit to be got from any other possessions or associations, where there is a failure to maintain supremacy in the field; all the advantages of the vanquished pass to the victors.

ATHENIAN: Your training, sir, would appear to have given you an admirable insight into the institutions of Crete. But you might be a little more definite on one point. As to your test of a well-constituted

city, I understand you to be saying that such a city must be so
c equipped as to be victorious over its rivals in warfare. Am I right?

CLINIAS : Most decidedly, and I fancy our friend here will be of
the same mind, too.

MEGILLUS : Why, my good man, what other answer would you
expect from any Lacedaemonian?

ATHENIAN : Well, possibly this is the right test in comparing
cities with cities, but there may be a different test for the comparison
of village with village?

CLINIAS : Not at all.

ATHENIAN : The same test holds good?

CLINIAS : Certainly.

ATHENIAN : Well, and when we compare one household in our
village with another, and one man with one other man? The same
test still holds?

CLINIAS : The very same.

d ATHENIAN : And the individual man? Must we think of him as
related to himself as foeman to foeman, or what are we to say in this
case?

CLINIAS : Ah, my Athenian friend! I would rather not say
Attic for I think you deserve to take your appellation by preference
from the goddess. You have made the position all the more incontest-
able by this reduction of it to first principles. The more readily, then,
can you satisfy yourself of the truth of what has just been said. Humanity is in a condition of public war of every man against every
man, and private war of each man with himself.

e ATHENIAN : And pray, how are we to understand that?

CLINIAS : Why, here, sir, is the field in which a man may win
the primal and subtlest victory, victory over *self*, and where defeat,
defeat by *self*, is most discreditable as well as most ruinous. There lies
the proof that every one of us is in a state of internal warfare with
himself.

627 ATHENIAN : Then suppose we invert the argument, thus. If
each individual man is master of himself, or, alternatively, mastered
by himself, may we, or may we not, say that a family, a village, a
city, exhibit this same feature?

CLINIAS : You mean that they may be masters of, or again mastered by, themselves?

ATHENIAN : Exactly.

CLINIAS : Again a very proper question. The facts are beyond
doubt, particularly in the case of cities. Any city where the better sort
are victorious over the masses and inferior classes may properly be
said to be mistress of herself and be rightly congratulated on the victory; where the reverse happens, we must speak in the opposite sense.

b ATHENIAN : The question whether worse is ever really master
of better is one we shall do well not to raise, since it calls for fuller

consideration. Your present assertion, as I understand, comes to this. An unrighteous majority may sometimes make a combined effort to subdue by violence a righteous minority of their kinsmen and fellow citizens. When this attempt succeeds, the city may properly be spoken of as enslaved to herself, and called bad; when it fails, we call her good, and say that she is mistress of herself.

CLINIAS: This language certainly sounds paradoxical, sir, but c we cannot withhold our assent.

ATHENIAN: Now stay a moment, and consider a further point. There might be a great number of brothers, with the same father and mother, and it would not be remarkable that the majority of them should prove unrighteous and only a minority righteous?

CLINIAS: Not in the least.

ATHENIAN: Nor would it be seemly for you and me to press too minutely the point that such a household or family can be said as a whole to be worsted by itself when its wicked members triumph, and to be its own mistress when they fail. The aim of our present inquiry d into current language is to examine, not the propriety or impropriety of its phraseology, but the objective truth or falsehood of a theory of legislation.

CLINIAS: Truly said, sir.

MEGILLUS: Yes, excellently put so far, as I agree.

ATHENIAN: Well, let us go on to a further point. These brothers of whom I have just spoken might conceivably have an adjudicator to decide between them?

CLINIAS: To be sure they might.

ATHENIAN: Now which would be the better adjudicator? One who exterminated all the bad brothers and enjoined the better to gov- e ern themselves, or one who put the government into the hands of the good, but spared the lives of the worse and brought them to voluntary submission to this government? There might be still a third degree of merit in an adjudicator, if we could find one who would take in hand a family at variance with itself, reconcile its members for the future by 628 his regulations, without the loss of a single life, and keep them on permanent amicable terms.

CLINIAS: And this third sort would be far and away the best of adjudicators or lawgivers.

ATHENIAN: But, mark you, in all the regulations he gave them, he would be legislating with a view to the complete contrary of war.

CLINIAS: That much is true enough.

ATHENIAN: Then what of the man who organizes a city? Is it with a view to external warfare he would order its life? Would he not much rather pay regard to the internal warfare which arises, from time to time, within the city, and is called, as you know, *faction*—a b kind of war any man would desire never to see in his own city, or, if it broke out, to see appeased at once?

CLINIAS : Obviously he would.

ATHENIAN : Now which of two courses would one prefer? That peace should be restored by the victory of one party or the other to the faction, and the destruction of its rival, or rather that friendship and amity should be re-established by a reconciliation, and the citizens

c compelled to bestow their attention on an external enemy?

CLINIAS : Why, any man would prefer the latter issue, for his own city.

ATHENIAN : A lawgiver, no less than another?

CLINIAS : Why, of course.

ATHENIAN : And any legislator will have the best as the object of all his enactments?

CLINIAS : Undeniably.

ATHENIAN : But the best is neither war nor faction—they are things we should pray to be spared from—but peace and mutual good will. And thus a victory of a city over itself turns out, it would seem,

d to be not so much a good as a necessary evil. It is as though one fancied that a diseased body which has been subjected to medical purgation were at its best in that condition, and ignored a body which has never stood in need of such treatment. So, if a man takes a similar view of the happiness of the city, or indeed, of the individual man—I mean, if external wars are the first and only object of his regard—he will never be a true statesman, nor will any man be a finished legislator, unless he legislates for war as a means to peace, rather than for peace as a means to war.

e CLINIAS : Your argument, sir, has the appearance of being sound; yet I am very much mistaken if the institutions of Lacedaemon, as well as those of my own country, have not the latter as their one serious end.

629 ATHENIAN : Very conceivably they have, but our present concern is to submit them to calm inquiry, rather than obstinate contention, as we are convinced that their authors have the same interests at heart as ourselves. We may begin, if you will kindly assist in the examination, by an appeal to the words of an enthusiast for warfare, Tyrtaeus, an Athenian by birth, and a naturalized fellow citizen of our friend from Sparta. He says, you will remember, that he would 'make

b no reckoning or count' [1] of any man, no matter how vast his wealth, or what his advantages—and he makes a pretty full enumeration of such advantages—unless he proves himself at need a first-rate warrior. You are sure to have heard the verses, Clinias; as for Megillus, no doubt he has them at his fingers' ends.

MEGILLUS : Naturally.

CLINIAS : We know the lines in this country, too; we got them from Sparta.

---

[1] Tyrtaeus 12.

ATHENIAN: Well now, suppose we join in putting a question to our poet to some such effect as this. Tyrtaeus, you inspired poet, we are convinced of your wisdom and merit by the excellence of your eulogies of the eminent in warfare. So Clinias of Cnossus, myself, and c our friend here believe ourselves to be decidedly of one mind with you already on the main point, but we should like to be quite certain that we are all speaking of the same persons. Tell us, then, do you agree with us in making a marked distinction between two forms of war, or not?

I fancy it would not require a poet of anything like the eminence of Tyrtaeus to give the true answer that there are two forms. There is d what all mankind call faction, and it is, of course, the most dangerous kind of war, as we said a few minutes ago; the other, and much milder form, as I imagine we shall all agree, is that waged when we are at variance with external aliens.

CLINIAS: Just so.

ATHENIAN: Then to which kind of warriors, or war, do your magnificent eulogies, and your corresponding censures, refer? Presumably to the external. At least, you speak in your verses of your e intolerance of men who have not the nerve to 'face the carnage, close with the foe and strike him down.' So we might continue thus. Your special commendation, Tyrtaeus, is, we gather, meant for those who distinguish themselves in an external war against the stranger.

No doubt he would agree to admit this?

CLINIAS: To be sure.

ATHENIAN: But we affirm that good as such men are, those who prove themselves conspicuously best in the gravest kind of war 630 are still better, and immensely better, and we, too, can cite a poet, Theognis of Megara in Sicily, whose words are: 'A loyal man, Cyrnus, is worth his weight in gold and silver in the hour of deadly feuds.' [2] We assert, then, that this type of character proves himself, and proves himself in a deadlier warfare, a far better man than the other in the measure in which justice, self-command, and wisdom, combined together and seconded by valor, are better than mere valor by itself. For b a man will never prove himself loyal and soundhearted in times of faction unless he has all virtue, whereas there are plenty of hired combatants who are ready enough to take a firm stand and fight to the death in the kind of war of which Tyrtaeus has to speak, though most of them prove reckless, unjust, brutal, and superlatively imprudent, but for a very few rare exceptions. Now to what does our argument conclude? What do we mean to establish by urging it? Obviously that your Cretan legislator from the school of Zeus, or any other worth his c salt, could have no other object in view in his legislation than the supreme virtue. This supreme virtue is what Theognis speaks of as

[2] Theognis 77–78.

loyalty in peril, and we may call it complete righteousness. As for the quality specially commended by Tyrtaeus, it is noble enough, and nobly celebrated by the poet, but, to speak with precision, it comes only
d fourth in order and worth.

CLINIAS : That, sir, is to rank our Cretan legislator very low.

ATHENIAN : No, not your legislator, my friend, but ourselves, if we dream that Lycurgus or Minos had warfare primarily in view in all his legislation for Lacedaemon or Crete.

CLINIAS : But what, then, ought we to have said?

ATHENIAN : What, I take it, is true and ought to be said in an
e inquiry into the truth. Their legislation was framed in the interest of virtue as a whole, not of one fragment of it, and that the least considerable. They aimed at devising a classified code, though not on the lines of our present-day framers of such codes. Today each of them frames any additional paragraph he finds necessary—one a section on estates and their heiresses, another one on assault and battery, oth-
631 ers, others of the same kind, in indefinite number. But we contend that the right procedure for the framer of a legislation is that with which we have just made a beginning. I unreservedly approve the intention of your own remarks about your national jurisprudence. It was quite right to begin with virtue, and explain that virtue was the aim your legislator had in view. But when you stated that the whole of his enactments regards only one fragment of it, and that the most inconsiderable, I thought you were misapprehending. But there is a further distinction I could wish you to observe in your own discourse
b and to expect in that of others. May I explain its nature?

CLINIAS : With all my heart.

ATHENIAN : Sir—so I would have had you say—it is not without good cause that the laws of Crete have this exceptionally high repute with all Hellenes. They serve the right end, that of effecting the happiness of those who enjoy them. They, in fact, secure them all good things. But there are two different kinds of good things, the merely human and the divine; the former are consequential on the latter. Hence a city which accepts the greater goods acquires the lesser along with them, but one which refuses them misses both. The lesser are
c those among which health holds the first place, comeliness the second, strength for the race and all other bodily exercises the third, while the fourth place belongs to a wealth which is not 'blind,' but clear-sighted, because attendant on wisdom. Of divine goods, the first and chiefest is this same wisdom, and next after it, sobriety of spirit; a third, resultant from the blending of both these with
d valor, is righteousness, and valor itself is fourth. All of these naturally rank before the former class, and, of course, a lawgiver must observe that order. Next, he should impress it on his citizens that all his other injunctions have a view to these ends, and that among the ends, the human look to the divine, and all the divine to their leader, wisdom.

He should superintend, by a right distribution of honor and dishonor, the matrimonial alliances among his citizens, and their subsequent behavior in the procreation of offspring, male and female, and rearing e of it, from infancy right on to old age. He must make a careful and observant study of the pleasures, the pains, the desires, and all the vehement passions aroused in them by all these social relations, and distribute censure and praise among them rightly, in the actual text of 632 his laws. So, again, with the passions of anger and fear, with the various troubles of soul engendered by misfortune, and the reactions from them in seasons of good fortune, and the emotions which are incidental to humanity in sickness, in war, in penury, and their opposites—in all such cases, he should explain and determine how far each human mood is becoming, and how far it is not.

Next, our legislator must watch over the methods by which his b citizens acquire and expend their wealth, and have an eye to the presence or absence of justice in the various procedures by which they all contract or dissolve associations with one another, voluntary or involuntary, assigning marks of honor to those of them who conform to his laws, and imposing specific penalties on the disobedient. When he comes at last to the close of his whole constitution making, he must c decide in what manner the funeral rites of each class of citizen should be celebrated, and what marks of respect should be assigned to them. When the lawmaker has completed his discovery he will set over the whole system a body of guardians endowed some with wisdom, some with true beliefs, to the end that intelligence may knit the whole into one, and keep it in subjection to sobriety and justice, not to wealth or self-seeking.

Those, gentlemen, are the lines on which I should have wished, d and do still wish *you* to explain how all these merits are to be found in the laws ascribed to Zeus and the Pythian Apollo, and enacted by Minos and Lycurgus, and how they form a system, readily discernible by one familiar with law from scientific study, or even habit of life, though far from manifest to ordinary persons like myself.

CLINIAS : Then what, sir, should be our next step?

ATHENIAN : I think there will need to be a fresh start of the examination, beginning, as before, with the practices by which courage e is developed; then we will examine a second, and then a third form of virtue, if you are so minded. When once we have dealt with our first topic, we may try to take it as a model of procedure, and beguile our journey with further chat on the same lines. After we have treated of all virtue, we will try, with God's permission, to show that all the regulations we were just enumerating have it for their object.

MEGILLUS : Excellent. And suppose you begin by trying your 633 criticism on our friend here, the admirer of Zeus.

ATHENIAN : On you and myself, no less than on him. We are all concerned in the argument. Come, then. We may say that your common meals and physical exercises were devised by your legislator with a view to war?

MEGILLUS : Yes.

ATHENIAN : And thirdly, or fourthly? For in considering this and other virtues, it is possibly well to make such an enumeration of their parts, or whatever else they should be called, so long as a man's meaning is clear.

b   MEGILLUS : Well, thirdly, as I, or any other Lacedaemonian would say, he devised the chase.

ATHENIAN : Suppose we try to find a fourthly, or a fifthly, if we can.

MEGILLUS : Then I will venture on naming a fourthly, too, the endurance of bodily pain which finds so much scope among us Spartans in our boxing matches and our system of foraging raids, which regularly involve heavy whippings. Besides, we have what we call a c crypteia, which is a wonderfully hard discipline in endurance, as well as the practices of going without shoes or bedding in the winter, and wandering all over the country, night and day, without attendants, performing one's menial offices for oneself. Further, again, our gymnopaediae involve rigid endurance, as the matches are fought in the heat of the summer, and we have a host of other similar tests—in fact, almost too many for particular enumeration.

ATHENIAN : You state your case well, my Lacedaemonian friend. But, pray, what are we to make of courage? Is it a conflict with d fear and pain, just that and no more? Or does it also include conflict with longings and pleasures and their dangerous seductive blandishments, which melt even the mettle of the would-be precisian like so much wax?

MEGILLUS : That, I believe, is the true account; it is a conflict with all of these.

ATHENIAN : Now, unless we have forgotten our earlier conversation, our friend from Cnossus spoke of cities, and men too, as defeated by themselves. Did you not?

CLINIAS : To be sure, I did.

e   ATHENIAN : Well, shall we give the name bad now to the man who is defeated by pain, or to him who is defeated by pleasure as well?

CLINIAS : I think it belongs more properly to one who is defeated by pleasure. And I imagine all of us are readier to say that one who is mastered by pleasure is shamefully self-defeated than to say it of one who succumbs to pain.

ATHENIAN : Then very surely our pair of legislators instructed 634 by Zeus and Apollo cannot have canonized a lopsided courage, which can only stand its ground before a sinister enemy, but proves impotent against the dexterously and ingeniously seductive opponent? Surely they would have her face both?

CLINIAS : Both, I am confident.

ATHENIAN : Then I must ask a second question. What practices have your two cities which teach a man the taste of pleasures without any evasion? Just as pains were not evaded—the man was thrust into the thick of them, but forced, or persuaded by marks of honor, to get the mastery of them. Where, I say, is the same regulation b about pleasure to be found in your laws? I want to know what there is in your institutions to give the same person courage alike against pain and against pleasure, to make him victorious where he ought to be victorious, and secure him from defeat at the hands of his most intimate and mortal enemies.

MEGILLUS : Nay, sir, possibly I could not readily allege conspicuous illustrations, on a large scale, in the matter of pleasure, to match the numerous laws I was able to produce as a counterpoise to c pain, though I might be more fortunate with minor details.

CLINIAS : I, too, cannot produce an equally obvious illustration from our Cretan laws.

ATHENIAN : No, my friends, and it is no matter for surprise. But if any of us should be led, in his desire to discover what is true and best, into censure of some detail in the national laws of any of us, I trust we shall take such treatment from each other gently, without resentment.

CLINIAS : Truly spoken, Athenian. We must do as you say.

ATHENIAN : Harshness would, in fact, hardly become our d years, Clinias.

CLINIAS : Indeed, it would not.

ATHENIAN : Well, how far the reproaches which are brought against the systems of Laconia and Crete may be deserved or undeserved is another matter; in any case, I am probably better qualified than either of you to report the criticisms which are generally current. If your laws are but reasonably good, as they are, we must reckon among the best of them the enactment that no young man shall raise the question which of them all are what they should be and which e not, but that all should agree, without a dissonant voice, that they are all god-given and admirable, flatly refusing a hearing to anyone who disputes the point, while if an older man has any reflections to make, he must impart them to a magistrate of his own age, when none of the younger men are by.

CLINIAS : Perfectly true, sir. Remote as today is from the times 635 of our ancient legislator, I believe you have fairly divined his intentions and are exactly right.

ATHENIAN : Well, we have no younger men with us now, and for ourselves, our years give us the legislator's license to hold a private conversation on the subject without offense.

CLINIAS : Just so. Accordingly we invite you to criticize our institutions without reserve. One is not insulted by being informed of something amiss, but rather gets an opportunity for amendment, if

b the information is taken in good part, without resentment.

ATHENIAN: Thank you. But my object for the present is not to criticize your laws, which we have not yet thoroughly examined, so much as to state a difficulty. You are the only communities, Greek or non-Greek, known to us whose lawgiver has enjoined you to leave the intensest pleasures and delights utterly untasted, though, in the matter of pains and fears which we have just been discussing, he

c held that one who is allowed to flinch from them on system from his boyhood, and then has to face fatigues and fears and pains which are not to be evaded, will flinch from those who have been disciplined in them, and be enslaved by them. Now, surely the legislator, to be consistent, should take the same view of pleasures. He should say to himself, if our citizens are to grow up from childhood without experience of the intensest pleasures, if they are to have no training in constancy and refusal to disgrace themselves when assailed by pleasures, susceptibility to pleasure will lead them to the same fate as

d those who succumb to their fears. They will fall slaves, in a different, but even more dishonorable fashion, to those who can resist the allurements of pleasure, and have the means of producing it at their disposal, though these may sometimes be utterly evil men. Thus, their souls will be half enslaved, half free, and they will not deserve to be called brave men, or free men, without qualification. I would have you consider whether you find these remarks at all pertinent.

e CLINIAS: Pertinent enough, on such a first hearing. But it might show immaturity and folly to form confident conclusions on such weighty matters on the instant.

ATHENIAN: Then suppose we proceed to the next point of our program, my friends, and turn from courage to sobriety. Can we discover any point of superiority in these two systems over those of societies organized on no systematic principles, as we did in connection with war?

636   MEGILLUS: Not too easily. Still, our common meals and physical exercises were presumably well devised to promote both virtues.

ATHENIAN: Ah, my friends, how difficult it seems to ensure that the working of an institution shall be as unquestionable as its theory! Presumably it is with states as it is with human bodies—one cannot prescribe one definite treatment for one subject which involves no physically injurious consequences along with its beneficial effects. For

b example, these physical exercises and common meals you speak of, though in many ways beneficial to a city, provide dangerous openings for faction, as is shown by the cases of the Milesians, Boeotians, and Thurians. And, in particular, this practice is generally held to have corrupted the ancient and natural rule in the matter of sexual indulgence common to mankind with animals at large, and the blame for these corruptions may be charged, in the first instance, on your two cities and such others as are most devoted to physical exercises. c Whether these matters are to be regarded as sport, or as earnest, we must not forget that this pleasure is held to have been granted by nature to male and female when conjoined for the work of procreation; the crime of male with male, or female with female, is an outrage on nature and a capital surrender to lust of pleasure. And you know it is our universal accusation against the Cretans that they were the inven- d tors of the tale of Ganymede; they were convinced, we say, that their legislation came from Zeus, so they went on to tell this story against him that they might, if you please, plead his example for their indulgence in this pleasure too. With the tale we have no further concern, but the pleasures and pains of communities and of private lives are as good as the whole subject of a study of jurisprudence. For pain and pleasure are, as it were, nature's twin fountainheads; whoso draws from the right fount, at due times, and in due measure, be it city, or e person, or any living creature, is happy, but he that draws without science, and out of due season, has the completely contrary lot.

MEGILLUS : Sure, sir, this is finely said, and I would not deny that we are dumfounded for an answer to it. Yet, for myself, I hold that our Lacedaemonian lawgiver is right to command avoidance of pleasures. As to the law of Cnossus, its defense shall be made by our friend, if he will accept the task. In Sparta, to my mind, this matter of pleasure is ordered better than in any place on earth. That which, by 637 its keen delightsomeness, most easily entangles men in outrage and all manner of follies is, by our law, banished entirely from our territory. Neither in our country districts, nor in towns which are controlled by Spartans, can you find drinking parties, with the strong incentives to various pleasures that attend them. There is not a man of us who would not forthwith lay the heaviest penalty on a tipsy reveler, if he b fell in with him; the very festival of Dionysus would not serve as an excuse for the offender's discharge. I have seen such reveling before now in your Attica on the 'wagons,' and at Tarentum, a settlement of our own, I beheld the whole city in its cups at the feast of Dionysus, but there is no such practice among us.

ATHENIAN : Friend from Sparta, any recreation of this kind is commendable, when the power of resistance persists, though mere foolishness when it is relaxed. A countryman of my own might well defend himself by retorting on you the license of your Spartan women. c To be sure, there is a rejoinder which is commonly held to be a sufficient vindication in all such cases at Tarentum, or in my own country, no less than in yours. A native will always meet the stranger's astonishment at an unfamiliar practice with the words, There is no call for surprise; this is our established custom in the matter, though yours may perhaps be different.   d

What you and I are now discussing is not the practice of mankind at large, but the merits or demerits of the legislators who create the customs. So we must take the whole subject of convivial drinking into fuller consideration; it is a practice of grave importance, and calls for the judgment of no mean legislator. The question is not that of the mere drinking of wine or its complete prohibition, but of the convivial drinking of it. Should we follow the fashion of Scythians and Persians—to say nothing of Carthaginians, Celts, Iberians, and Thracians, who are all of them warlike peoples—or that of your own

e countrymen? They, as you remind me, absolutely reject the practice, whereas the Scythians and Thracians, men and women alike, take their wine neat, and let it run down over their garments, and count this a laudable and glorious practice. The Persians, again, indulge freely in this, as in other luxurious habits which you Spartans prohibit, though with less disorder than the nations I have mentioned.

638   MEGILLUS : Yes, my dear sir, but do not forget that we make them all run when we have weapons in our hands.

ATHENIAN : Nay, sir, you must not urge that plea. A flight or pursuit has so often gone unrecorded, and will in the future; this shows that we cannot regard victory or defeat in the field as more than

b a very dubious test of the laudability of a practice. For the matter of that, the more populous city may defeat the less populous and reduce it to subjection, as Syracuse has done with Locri, which, you know, has the reputation of enjoying the best laws to be found in that part of the world, or Athens with Ceos, and no doubt many similar instances could be produced. No, we must leave victories and defeats out of court for the present, and discuss the various practices on their own merits, in the hope of convincing ourselves that some are laudable and others the reverse. But first let me make an observation as to the right method of investigating the worth of such practices.

c   MEGILLUS : And what is it you would say?

ATHENIAN : When such a practice is under consideration, I hold that it is always highly improper to undertake to condemn or approve it out of hand, on the bare mention of its name. This is as though one who had heard wheat, for instance, commended as a wholesome article of diet should denounce it out of hand, without any inquiry into its effects, or the manner of its administration—I mean, how it is to be administered, and to whom, or with what accompaniments, in what form it is to be served, and to persons in what state of health. Well,

d that is exactly how I think we all argue our present question. As soon as we hear the mere word 'drinking,' one party condemns the practice and another commends it, and both in a very odd fashion. Both sides rest their case on producing evidence to fact or character—the one thinking it decisive that its witnesses are so numerous, the other that we see the abstainers victorious in the field of battle—though there

e even the fact is open to dispute. Now if we are to go on to deal with established customs in general on these lines, I, for one, shall be left unsatisfied. So I propose to deal with our immediate subject, drinking, by a different method—the right one, I believe—as an attempt to illustrate the proper procedure in treating such questions generally. For there are countless peoples ready to contest the issues at stake in these matters against your two cities.

MEGILLUS: Most certainly, if a right way of treating such prob- 639 lems is to be found, we must not refuse it a hearing.

ATHENIAN: Then let us treat our question somewhat in this fashion. Suppose that someone should commend goat keeping, or the goat itself as a valuable animal, and another man, who had seen goats damaging lands under cultivation by grazing on them without a keeper, should denounce the brutes, or find fault with any creature he had seen thus under no control or bad control. Can we say that censure of anything coming from such a quarter would have the least validity?

MEGILLUS: Of course not.

ATHENIAN: And what do you say to this? Is a man a useful commander at sea, so long as he only possesses the science of navigation, whether he happens to be seasick or not?   b

MEGILLUS: Certainly not, if he combines that disorder with his professional knowledge.

ATHENIAN: And what of the commander of an army in the field? Is he a competent commander, so long as he has military science, even if he is a coward and falls seasick in peril from the inebriation of terror?

MEGILLUS: A thoroughly useless officer, that! A commander for the veriest of women, not for men!

ATHENIAN: And what of him who commends or condemns any c social activity, be it what it may, which naturally calls for a leader, and is beneficial under his conduct, though he has never seen that activity rightly organized under such leadership, but only discharged with no leaders, or bad ones? Can we possibly imagine that there is any value in the censure or commendation of such concerted action by such observers?

MEGILLUS: How can we, on the assumption that they have never witnessed nor taken part in any such association, conducted as d it should be?

ATHENIAN: Now, stay. I suppose we may reckon a drinking party and its members as one kind of social activity?

MEGILLUS: Surely, surely.

ATHENIAN: Then has anyone ever seen such a party conducted as it ought to be? Neither of you can hesitate to give the answer, 'never'—the whole thing is foreign and unfamiliar to you both. And for my own part, though I have been present at many, in different places, and what is more, may even say I have studied them all carefully, I have never seen nor heard of one rightly managed e throughout; here and there a few minor details may not have been amiss, but, in the main, I have found universal wrong management.

CLINIAS: You must explain your meaning, sir, rather more precisely. Our inexperience in these matters, as you were saying, is such that, even if we were present at such a gathering, we should very likely not distinguish proper management from improper at first sight.

640   ATHENIAN: No, possibly not. But do your utmost to follow my explanation. No doubt you understand as much as this, that in every assembly or concerted action for any purpose, there should always be someone in control of the parties?

CLINIAS: Beyond a doubt.

ATHENIAN: And mark that we were lately saying that in a combat the commander must be a brave man.

CLINIAS: So we were, to be sure.

ATHENIAN: Now a brave man is less agitated by alarms than a coward.

b   CLINIAS: True again.

ATHENIAN: And if we could contrive to place an army under a general who was utterly devoid of alarm and agitation, we should by all means do so, should we not?

CLINIAS: Most decidedly.

ATHENIAN: But at the present moment we are contemplating a man who is to take command, not in the embattled meeting of foes with foes, but in the peaceful intercourse of friends with friends, for the promotion of common good feeling.

CLINIAS: Exactly.

c   ATHENIAN: Now, as the kind of gathering we have in view is to be attended by drinking, it will not be free from excitement.

CLINIAS: Of course not—very much the contrary, I should presume.

ATHENIAN: To begin with then, here, too, a commander is wanted.

CLINIAS: Wanted, indeed—nowhere more.

ATHENIAN: And should we secure freedom from excitement in such a commander, if the thing is possible?

CLINIAS: Decidedly.

ATHENIAN: And further, I presume, he should be a man of social tact. For his business is to conserve the existing friendly relations
d between the parties, as well as to ensure that they shall be still further augmented by the gathering.

CLINIAS: True enough.

ATHENIAN: So the commander set to control a company of drinkers should be both sober and sagacious, not the reverse. If the drinkers are under the control of a young and indiscreet man who is drinking himself, he may think himself very fortunate if no grave disaster results.

CLINIAS: Indeed, he may.

ATHENIAN: Well then, if such parties were conducted among us under the most correct regulations attainable, an unfavorable critic who should attack the institution as such might perhaps be right e in his disapproval, but when a man inveighs against a practice because he sees it mismanaged in every possible respect, he is obviously unaware, in the first place, that the practice in question is misconducted, and in the second, that any proceeding whatever will appear mischievous on the understanding that it is executed without a sober master or commander. Surely you can see that a tippling navigator, or commander of any kind, will wreck anything, vessel, or car, or army, 641 or whatever it may be, for which he sets the course.

CLINIAS: Your last remark, sir, is unquestionably true. But pray go on to explain what possible good this custom of drinking bouts would do us, if they were rightly conducted. Take the case of an army, such as we were just speaking of. If it gets the right kind of leadership, the result is a victory for the force—no inconsiderable good—and so with our other examples. But what appreciable benefit accrues to individuals, or to the city, from the proper surveillance of a wine b party?

ATHENIAN: Well, and what appreciable benefit could we say accrues to the city from the proper surveillance of one boy, or one group of boys? If the question is to be put in that form, must we not reply that the city certainly gets but a trifling advantage from the single case? But if the question is universally what considerable advantage the city derives from the education of the educated, the answer is easy. Education is the way to produce good men, and, once c produced, such men will live nobly, and vanquish their enemies in the field into the bargain. So education brings victory in her train, though victory sometimes leads to loss of education, since victorious warfare often enough leads men to pride, and through pride they take the taint of other vices innumerable. Moreover, there has never been a Cadmean education, whereas Cadmean victories have been, and will be, only too common.

CLINIAS: We may gather, then, that you regard time spent in companionship over the bottle as contributing much to education, d when it is rightly so spent?

ATHENIAN: Most assuredly.

CLINIAS: Then can you, in the next place, offer us proof that the statement is true?

ATHENIAN: Why, sir, as to truth, to be positive the thing is so, when there are so many to dispute it, must be left to a god. But if I am called on to give my personal opinion, I will state it frankly, since our present conversation has struck into the subject of law and politics.

CLINIAS: That is just what we are attempting to do—to discover your own conviction on the matter now in dispute.   e

ATHENIAN: Well then, to our task. You will have to make an effort to follow, and I to elucidate the argument, with such powers as I have. But first let me make one observation. The universal belief of Hellas is that whereas my own city delights in discourse and is copious in it, Lacedaemon is inclined to taciturnity, and Crete to versatil-
642 ity of mind rather than fluency of utterance. So I fear you may get the impression that I am expending too many words on a minor matter, if I deliver myself of a long discourse on so inconsiderable a topic as drinking. But the truth is that a really sound theory on the point cannot be surely and adequately expounded apart from a true theory of music, nor that, again, apart from a theory of education at large, and these are subjects for protracted discussion. How would it be, then, I ask you, if we should drop them for the present, and divert the
b conversation to some other department of jurisprudence?

MEGILLUS: Sir, you may perhaps be unaware that my own family hold the position of proxeni for Athens. Now it may well be the universal experience of boys anywhere that when they are told they are proxeni for a city, an early kindness for that city promptly finds its way into the boys' hearts—we feel that it is a second fatherland, only next to our own. This is certainly what has happened in my own particular case. From the first, if Lacedaemon felt herself aggrieved by
c Athens, or obliged by her, the boys used to tell me, Megillus, your city has done the shabby—or the handsome—thing by us.

Well, by listening to these speeches and constantly replying in your defense against persons who brought reproaches against your city, I contracted a strong affection for her. To this day, I love the sound of your dialect, and am persuaded of the truth of the current saying that when an Athenian is a good man, he is exceptionally good. It is only at Athens that goodness is an unconstrained, spon-
d taneous growth, a genuine 'gift of God' in the full sense of the words. So, as far as I am concerned, you need feel no misgiving in discoursing at any length you please.

CLINIAS: I, too, sir, have a statement to make which will relieve you from diffidence in speaking your full mind. You have presumably heard of Epimenides, an inspired person born in this city and connected with my own family, who visited Athens ten years before the Persian Wars at the bidding of the oracle, and offered certain sacrifices enjoined by the god, besides telling the citizens, who were
e alarmed by the Persian preparations, that the enemy would not come within ten years, and when they did, would depart again with their purpose uneffected, after receiving more damage than they inflicted. That was when my family contracted their friendship with your countrymen, and my ancestors and myself have had a kindness for them ever since.

643   ATHENIAN: I take it, then, that there is full readiness to hear on your part. On mine, there is readiness enough of intention, but per-

formance is none too easy; still I must do my endeavor. As the first step in the argument, then, let us define education and its effect, since we hold that the discussion on which we have adventured must follow that route to its destination, the wine god.

CLINIAS: By all means, since that is your pleasure.

ATHENIAN: Good. Then I will attempt an account of what b true education is; you must consider whether the account is acceptable.

CLINIAS: Pray proceed.

ATHENIAN: Well, I proceed at once to say that he who is to be good at anything as a man must practice that thing from early childhood, in play as well as in earnest, with all the attendant circumstances of the action. Thus, if a boy is to be a good farmer, or again, a good builder, he should play, in the one case at building toy houses, in the other at farming, and both should be provided by their tutors with miniature tools on the pattern of real ones. In particular, all nec- c essary preliminary instruction should be acquired in this way. Thus, the carpenter should be taught by his play to use the rule and plumb line, and the soldier to sit a horse, and the like. We should seek to use games as a means of directing children's tastes and inclinations toward the station they are themselves to fill when adult. So we may say, in fact, the sum and substance of education is the right training which effectually leads the soul of the child at play on to the love of the call- d ing in which he will have to be perfect, after its kind, when he is a man. But, as I said, you must consider whether what has been said has your approval so far.

CLINIAS: Indeed, it has.

ATHENIAN: Then let us further guard against leaving our account of what education is too indeterminate. When we are to express approval or censure of a man's training, we correctly speak of one of ourselves as educated and another as uneducated—and the reference is sometimes to the business of a huckster or a supercargo—and of other such fellows of mighty fine education. But our present discourse e is in place only on the lips of one who holds that education is none of these things, but rather that schooling from boyhood in goodness which inspires the recipient with passionate and ardent desire to become a perfect citizen, knowing both how to wield and how to submit to righteous rule. Our argument, I take it, would isolate this training 644 from others and confine the name education exclusively to it; any training which has as its end wealth, or perhaps bodily strength, or some other accomplishment unattended by intelligence and righteousness, it counts vulgar, illiberal, and wholly unworthy to be called education. So we must not wrangle over a word, but abide by the proposition on which we have just agreed, that the rightly educated prove what we mean by good, and that no aspect of education is to be disparaged; it is the highest blessing bestowed on mankind, and it is b the best of them on whom it is most fully bestowed. When it takes a false turn which permits of correction, we should, one and all, devote the energy of a lifetime to its amendment.

CLINIAS : True indeed. We admit the point.

ATHENIAN : We also agreed some time ago that those who can command themselves are good, and those who cannot, bad.

CLINIAS : Precisely.

ATHENIAN : Then let us once more consider rather more exactly just what our words mean. Perhaps you will allow me to make
c the point clearer, if I can, by a parable.

CLINIAS : We are all attention.

ATHENIAN : Well then, we may take it that any human being is one person?

CLINIAS : Of course.

ATHENIAN : But one person who has within himself a pair of unwise and conflicting counselors, whose names are pleasure and pain?

CLINIAS : The fact is as you say.

ATHENIAN : He has, besides, anticipations of the future, and these of two sorts. The common name for both sorts is *expectation,*
d the special name for anticipation of pain being *fear,* and for anticipation of its opposite, *confidence* (θάρρος). And on the top of all, there is *judgment,* to discern which of these states is better or worse, and when judgment takes the form of a public decision of a city, it has the name of *law.*

CLINIAS : I fear I hardly follow you, yet pray proceed with your statement as though I did.

MEGILLUS : I, too, find myself in the same condition.

ATHENIAN : Let us look at the whole matter in some such light as this. We may imagine that each of us living creatures is a puppet made by gods, possibly as a plaything, or possibly with some more
e serious purpose. That, indeed, is more than we can tell, but one thing is certain. These interior states are, so to say, the cords, or strings, by which we are worked; they are opposed to one another, and pull us with opposite tensions in the direction of opposite actions, and therein lies the division of virtue from vice. In fact, so says our argument, a man must always yield to one of these tensions without resistance, but
645 pull against all the other strings—must yield, that is, to that golden and hallowed drawing of judgment which goes by the name of the public law of the city. The others are hard and ironlike, it soft, as befits gold, whereas they resemble very various substances. So a man must always co-operate with the noble drawing of law, for judgment, though a noble thing, is as gentle and free from violence as noble, whence its drawing needs supporters, if the gold within us is to prevail over
b the other stuff. In this wise our moral fable of the human puppets will find its fulfillment. It will also become somewhat clearer, first,

what is meant by self-conquest and self-defeat, and next that the individual's duty is to understand the true doctrine of these tensions and live in obedience to it, the city's to accept this doctrine from a god, or from the human discoverer just mentioned, and make it law for her converse with herself and other societies. This will lead us to a more exact articulation both of vice and of virtue, and the elucidation of c the subject will presumably throw further light on education and institutions at large, and more particularly on this business of social drinking—a trifling matter, it might be thought, to waste such a long discussion on, and yet it may well prove to deserve the whole.

CLINIAS: Very true. So let us treat it at whatever length our present business demands.

ATHENIAN: Well then, tell me, suppose we ply our puppet with d drink, what effect are we producing on it?

CLINIAS: Now why are you recurring to that? What is the purpose of the question?

ATHENIAN: I have not yet reached the *why;* what I want to know is generally *how* this puppet is affected by participating in this practice. Let me try to explain my meaning still more exactly. My question amounts to this. The drinking of wines makes our pleasures and pains, our tempers and passions more intense, does it not?

CLINIAS: Much more intense.

ATHENIAN: And what of our perceptions, memories, beliefs, e knowledge? Are they likewise intensified? Or do they desert a man altogether, if he is thoroughly soaked with drinking?

CLINIAS: Why, utterly.

ATHENIAN: And so the man is brought back to the mental condition of his remote infancy?

CLINIAS: To be sure.

ATHENIAN: Now that is the condition in which his self-command is at its lowest.

CLINIAS: It is.

ATHENIAN: Such a man, we may say, is at his worst?   646

CLINIAS: Decidedly.

ATHENIAN: Thus the phrase 'second childhood' would seem to be as applicable to inebriation as to old age.

CLINIAS: Admirably put, sir.

ATHENIAN: Now can there be an argument daring enough to suggest that we should try the taste of a practice such as this, and not avoid it with all our might?

CLINIAS: It should seem there can—at least you say so, and only just now you offered to produce it.

ATHENIAN: An apposite reminder, and I repeat the offer now, b since both of you have professed yourselves eager to give me a hearing.

CLINIAS: Of course you must be heard. There is a reason, if

there were no other, in the sheer incredibility of your paradox, that it can be right for a man to fling himself voluntarily into a state of sheer degradation.

ATHENIAN : Degradation of soul, that is?

CLINIAS : Yes.

ATHENIAN : Well, my good sir, and what of a bad habit of
c body—leanness, disfigurement, feebleness? Would it be a paradox that a man can voluntarily bring himself into those conditions?

CLINIAS : Of course it would.

ATHENIAN : Why, sir, when men freely go to the physician for a course of medicaments, must we imagine they do not know they will very soon be, for days together, in such a state of body that, were it to be permanent, they would be sick of life? Again, when men resort to gymnasiums, or to heavy bodily exertions, we know their health suffers for the time being, do we not?

CLINIAS : Yes, we know all that.

ATHENIAN : As also that they go of their own motion, for the sake of subsequent benefits?

d   CLINIAS : To be sure.

ATHENIAN : And surely we should take the same point of view about other habitual practices too?

CLINIAS : I own we should.

ATHENIAN : And therefore also about spending time over the wine cup, if it is a view which can rightly be taken in this case?

CLINIAS : Naturally.

ATHENIAN : Then, if only wine drinking can be shown to lead to benefits comparable with those to be secured for the body, it certainly has the advantage over physical training in its initial stage; the second begins in pain, the other not so.

e   CLINIAS : Quite true, but I shall be surprised if we can find any such benefit in the custom.

ATHENIAN : That, I take it, is just what we have at last to do our best to make clear. Tell me this. Can we not distinguish two kinds of fear?

CLINIAS : And what may they be?

ATHENIAN : They are these. In the first place, we are afraid of evil, when we expect it to befall us.

CLINIAS : We are.

ATHENIAN : But we are often also afraid for our reputation,
647 when we apprehend we are getting a bad reputation from some unworthy act or speech; it is fear of this sort to which we, and I fancy the rest of the world too, give the name of shame.

CLINIAS : Certainly.

ATHENIAN : Well, those are the two fears of which I was speaking, and the second kind opposes itself to our commonest and most

passionate pleasures, as much as to pains and to fears other than itself.

CLINIAS: Very true.

ATHENIAN: Now does not a lawgiver, or any other man worth
his salt, hold this sort of fear in the highest honor? He calls it modesty,
and regards the kind of confidence contrary to it, which he calls im- b
pudence, as universally one of the gravest evils in private or public life.

CLINIAS: True again.

ATHENIAN: And, to say nothing of the many other great advantages this kind of fear secures for us, when you take one thing with
another, nothing contributes more effectually to victory and preservation in war itself. In fact, victory has a double source, fearlessness of
the enemy, and fear of disgrace in the eyes of one's friends.

CLINIAS: Just so.

ATHENIAN: And consequently each of us needs to be at once
free from fear and filled with fear, the reason for these contrasted c
moods being as we have stated.

CLINIAS: Agreed.

ATHENIAN: And when we intend to make a man immune from
various fears, we achieve our purpose by bringing him into contact
with fear, under the direction of law.

CLINIAS: So it would appear.

ATHENIAN: But now, suppose our aim is to make him rightly
fearful. What then? Must we not ensure his victory in the conflict
with his own lust for pleasures by pitting him against shamelessness
and training him to face it? If a man can only attain mature courage d
by fighting the cowardice within himself and vanquishing it, whereas
without experience and discipline in that contest, no man will ever
be half the champion he might be, is it credible he should come to fullness of self-command unless he first fights a winning battle against the
numerous pleasures and lusts which allure him to shamelessness and
wrong, by the aid of precept, practice, and artifice, alike in his play and
in his serious hours? Can he be spared the experience of all this?

CLINIAS: The view, certainly, does not seem plausible.

ATHENIAN: Now, tell me, has any god bestowed on mankind a e
specific to induce fear—a drug whose effect is that the more a man permits himself to imbibe of it, the darker he fancies his fortunes at every
draught, present and future alike grow increasingly alarming, and the
climax is abject terror in the bravest, though when the subject has recovered from his stupor and shaken off the effects of the potion, he
regularly becomes his own man again?   648

CLINIAS: Nay, sir, where in all the world can we find a liquor
like this?

ATHENIAN: Why, nowhere. But suppose one could have been
found. Would the lawgiver have availed himself of it to develop

courage? I mean, it would have been very much to the purpose to discuss it with him to some such effect as this. Pray, sir legislator—whether it is for Cretans or for any other society your legislation is
b intended—in the first place, would you be thankful for a touchstone of the courage or cowardice of your citizens?

CLINIAS : And he would, no doubt, be sure to say yes.

ATHENIAN : Well then, would you like the touchstone to be safe and applicable without serious risks, or the reverse?

CLINIAS : There, again, he would be certain to prefer safety.

ATHENIAN : You would employ it to bring your citizens into such a state of fear and test them under its influence, thus constrain-
c ing a man to become fearless, by encouragement, precept, and marks of recognition, as well as of disgrace for those who declined to be such as you could have them in all situations? He who shaped himself to this discipline well and manfully would be discharged from the test unscathed, but on him who shaped badly you would lay some penalty? Or would you simply refuse to employ the liquor, supposing you had no fault to find with it on other grounds?

CLINIAS : Why, of course he would employ it, my dear sir.

ATHENIAN : It would, at least, give us an infinitely readier and safer training than our present arrangements, whether for the in-
d dividual, for small groups, or for groups of any desired numbers. A man would do pretty right to save endless trouble by providing himself with this single specific and training himself in privacy to face his fears, isolating himself, of course, from public view behind his regard for decorum until he had obtained a satisfactory result. And, again, he would do right, when confident that he was already adequately prepared by native endowment and preliminary practice, to prosecute his training in the company of fellow drinkers, and make
e public exhibition of the virtue which enables him to transcend and master the effects of the inevitable disturbances due to the potion, without once suffering a serious fall or deterioration, though he would leave off before he reached the final draught from fear of our universal human weakness before the liquor.

CLINIAS : Why yes, sir, even such a man as you speak of would be wise to do that.

649   ATHENIAN : Then let us resume our conversation with the legislator. Very good, we shall say to him, as for such a fear-inducing specific, providence has given us none, and we have invented none ourselves, for we need not take quacksalvers into account, but what about fearlessness, excessive confidence, improper confidence at the wrong moment? Is there a liquor which has these effects, or is there not?

CLINIAS : He will, of course, say yes, and he will mean wine.

ATHENIAN : And are not its effects the very opposite of all we have just mentioned? When a man drinks it, its first immediate ef-
b fect is to make him merrier than he was, and the more he takes, the

more it fills him with optimistic fancies and imaginary capacity. In the very final phase the drinker is swollen with the conceit of his own wisdom to the pitch of complete license of speech and action, and utter fearlessness; there is nothing he will scruple to say, nothing he will scruple to do. I think this will be universally conceded.

CLINIAS : Of course.

ATHENIAN : Then let me remind you of something we said before. There are two qualities to be cultivated in our souls, supreme confidence, and its contrary, supreme fearfulness.   c

CLINIAS : What you spoke of as modesty, I take it.

ATHENIAN : Well recollected. And seeing that the practice of courage and fearlessness has to be learned in the midst of alarms, it has to be considered whether the contrary quality does not demand the contrary conditions for its cultivation.

CLINIAS : The presumption, certainly, is that it does.

ATHENIAN : It would seem, then, that the conditions in which we are naturally inclined to be more than usually confident or bold are the very conditions in which we must practice to be least audacious or unashamed, but rather apprehensive of ever presuming to say a shameful word, or submit to a shameful act, or even commit d one.

CLINIAS : So it seems.

ATHENIAN : Now, are not all the following conditions in which we are in the mood in question—anger, lust, pride, folly, greed, cowardice? We may add to the list wealth, beauty, physical vigor, and whatever else drives us frantic with the intoxication of pleasure. And if we want an inexpensive and comparatively harmless pleasure to e serve, in the first place, as a test of these conditions, and in the next, as a training for them, what can we find more suitable than the sportive touchstone of the wine cup, provided only that it is employed with a little precaution? For do but consider. Which is the more dangerous course with a sullen and untamed temper—the source of so many crimes—to test it by entering into a business agreement, with the risk of its failure, or by association in a bacchanalian celebration? Or to put the soul of a slave of sex to the test by entrusting him with 650 our own daughters, sons, and wives, and discover his character at the risk to our nearest and dearest? One might allege endless such illustrations without exhausting the advantages of a sportive method of inquiry involving no serious painful cost. And there is certainly one part of the case which, I fancy, will not be disputed by Cretans, or b any other body of men. The proposed test of one another is a reasonably good one, and has the advantage of others in point of inexpensiveness, security, and speediness.

CLINIAS : That, at least, is beyond doubt.

ATHENIAN : Here, then, in the discovery of native disposition and character, we have something of incomparable service to the art whose business it is to cultivate them—that is, as I suppose we may say, to the art of the statesman.

CLINIAS: Just so.

BOOK II

652 ATHENIAN: Then the question which next arises in discussing these matters, as I think, is this. Rightly controlled fellowship over our cups affords a disclosure of our native disposition, but is this its sole recommendation? Or has it some further considerable and serious advantages? Yes or no? Yes, or so our argument should seem to suggest. But if we are to learn just what these advantages are, we must be on our guard against the snares it lays for us.

CLINIAS: Say on, then.

ATHENIAN: I am fain, then, for my part, to recall once more 653 our account of right education; 'tis this, or so I seem to divine, for which this institution, under proper management, affords a safeguard.

CLINIAS: Truly a bold assertion!

ATHENIAN: And therefore what I would say is this. A child's first infant consciousness is that of pleasure and pain; this is the domain wherein the soul first acquires virtue or vice. For wisdom and assured true conviction, a man is fortunate if he acquires them even on the verge of old age, and, in every case, he that possesses them with all their attendant blessings has come to the full stature of man. b By education, then, I mean goodness in the form in which it is first acquired by a child. In fact, if pleasure and liking, pain and dislike, are formed in the soul on right lines before the age of understanding is reached, and when that age is attained, these feelings are in concord with understanding, thanks to early discipline in appropriate habits—this concord, regarded as a whole, is virtue. But if you consider the one factor in it, the rightly disciplined state of pleasures and pains whereby a man, from his first beginnings on, will abhor what c he should abhor and relish what he should relish—if you isolate this factor and call it education, you will be giving it its true name. At least, that is my own conviction.

CLINIAS: Yes indeed, sir, we grant the truth of what you have just said, no less than of your former observations about education.

ATHENIAN: Good, but to proceed, education—this rightly disciplined state of pleasures and pains—is apt to be relaxed and spoiled in many ways in the course of a man's life. But the gods, in their compassion for the hardships incident to our human lot, have ap- d pointed the cycle of their festivals to provide relief from this fatigue, besides giving us the Muses, their leader Apollo, and Dionysus to share these festivals with us and keep them right, with all the spiritual sustenance these deities bring to the feast. Wherein we must see whether the argument whereon we are now harping is true to the facts of things or no. What that argument says is this. No young creature whatsoever, as we may fairly assert, can keep its body or its voice still; all are perpetually trying to make movements and noises. e They leap and bound, they dance and frolic, as it were with glee, and again, they utter cries of all sorts. Now animals at large have no perception of the order or disorder in these motions, no sense of what we call rhythm or melody. But in our own case, the gods of whom we spoke as given us for companions in our revels have likewise given us 654 the power to perceive and enjoy rhythm and melody. Through this sense they stir us to movements and become our choir leaders. They string us together on a thread of song and dance, and have named our choirs so after the delight (χαρά) they naturally afford. Now may we begin by taking this point as settled? May we assume that our earliest education comes through the Muses and Apollo, or not?

CLINIAS : We may make that assumption.

ATHENIAN : So by an uneducated man we shall mean one who b has no choric training, and by an educated man one whose choric training has been thorough?

CLINIAS : Exactly.

ATHENIAN : And, mark you, the choric art as a whole embraces both dance and song.

CLINIAS : No doubt.

ATHENIAN : Thus it follows that a well-educated man can both sing well and dance well.

CLINIAS : So it would seem.

ATHENIAN : Next let us observe what that statement comes to.

CLINIAS : What statement precisely?

ATHENIAN : Why, we say the man sings well and dances well. But should we, or should we not, add the qualification, if he sings *good* songs and dances *good* dances? c

CLINIAS : Suppose we take in that qualification.

ATHENIAN : Well, suppose he judges the really good to be good and the bad bad, and acts accordingly. Shall we call a man who is in that case better educated in choric and musical art when he can be regularly counted upon for adequate physical and vocal rendering of what he apprehends to be good, though he feels no pleasure in the d good, nor dislike of the bad, or rather when, though none too capable of correctness of vocal and physical execution, or of apprehension, he has correct feelings of pleasure and pain, is attracted by the good, and repelled by its opposite?

CLINIAS : Sir, the advantage is vastly on the side of the education you are describing.

ATHENIAN : Then if the three of us understand what is good in song and dancing, we likewise know who has been rightly educated and who is not so, whereas, if we do not know this, we shall be e equally at a loss to decide whether there is any safeguard for education, and wherein it lies. Do I take you with me?

CLINIAS: Entirely.

ATHENIAN: So we must follow up the trail by investigating the goodness of figure, melody, song, and dance. If we let the quarry escape us, all further discourse of right education—Hellenic or non-Hellenic—will be so much waste of breath.

CLINIAS: Just so.

ATHENIAN: Well, come now, pray what are we to speak of as
655 *goodness* in a figure, or a melody? For instance, take a manly soul struggling with distress and a cowardly soul in the same or equal straits. Do we find they express themselves in similar postures and utterances?

CLINIAS: Why, of course not, not even in similar complexions.

ATHENIAN: True, indeed, friend. But though there are figures and tunes in music, as its subject matter is rhythm and melody, and we may accordingly speak of a tune or a posture as rhythmical or melodious, we cannot properly use the metaphorical expression of the choir trainers, 'brilliantly colored,' of either. But coward and
b brave man have their characteristic postures and strains, and it is very proper to call those of brave men good, those of cowards bad. In fact, to spare ourselves a great deal of verbal repetition in our treatment of the whole subject, we may take it, once and for all, that universally all postures and melodies connected with goodness of soul or body—whether with such goodness itself or with some image of it—are good, and those connected with badness universally the reverse.

CLINIAS: An excellent proposal, and you may treat it as understood that we have answered you to that effect.

ATHENIAN: And now to one further point. Does any choric per-
c formance give all men the like degree of enjoyment, or is the state of the case very different?

CLINIAS: Very different? Utterly different.

ATHENIAN: Then what shall we say is likely to be the source of this confusion? Is it that the excellent is not the same thing for all alike? Or that it is in fact the same, but not believed to be so? For no one, I take it, would profess that the choric expressions of vice can in fact be more excellent than those of virtue, or that he personally enjoys the postures of turpitude, though other men may
d prefer the opposite Muse—though, to be sure, it is commonly *said* that the standard of rightness in music is its pleasure-giving effect. That, however, is an intolerable sentiment; in fact, 'tis a piece of flat blasphemy. The cause of our confusion is more probably that I am now to mention.

CLINIAS: And what is that?

ATHENIAN: A choric exhibition is a mimic presentation of

manners, with all variety of action and circumstance, enacted by performers who depend on characterization and impersonation. Hence, those who, from temperament, or habit, or both at once, find words, e melodies, or other presentation of the choir, to their taste cannot but enjoy and applaud the performance, and further pronounce it good, whereas they who find it repugnant to temperament, taste, or training can neither enjoy nor applaud, and so call it bad. But where a man's native temperament is right, and his training wrong, or his training right and his natural temperament wrong, there enjoyment and approbation are at variance. The performance is, in fact, said to be pleasant, but bad; the man is ashamed to declare his serious approval by executing such movements or singing such tunes before others whom he credits with judgment, but in his own heart he enjoys 656 the performance.

CLINIAS: Perfectly true.

ATHENIAN: Now do you think a man is in any way the worse for enjoying degrading postures or melodies, or any the better for getting his pleasure from the opposite quarter?

CLINIAS: Presumably he is.

ATHENIAN: Only presumably? Is not his case inevitably the b same as that of one who views the evil characters of bad companions in real life not with disgust, but with enjoyment, condemning their actions in a playful fashion, like one not awake to their vileness? In such a case it is, surely, inevitable that a man should grow like whatever he enjoys, whether good or bad, even though he may be ashamed to approve it. The result is absolutely inevitable—and what result could we call more momentous for good or evil?

CLINIAS: None, as I believe.

ATHENIAN: Then is it conceivable that anywhere where there c are, or may hereafter be, sound laws in force touching this educative-playful function of the Muses, men of poetic gifts should be free to take whatever in the way of rhythm, melody, or diction tickles the composer's fancy in the act of composition and teach it through the choirs to the boys and lads of a law-respecting society, leaving it to chance whether the result prove virtue or vice?

CLINIAS: To be sure, that does not sound rational—decidedly not.

ATHENIAN: And yet this is precisely what they are actually d left free to do, I may say, in every community with the exception of Egypt.

CLINIAS: And in Egypt itself, now—pray how has the law regulated the matter there?

ATHENIAN: The mere report will surprise you. That nation, it would seem, long enough ago recognized the truth we are now affirming, that poses and melodies must be good, if they are to be habitually practiced by the youthful generation of citizens. So they drew

up the inventory of all the standard types, and consecrated speci-
e mens of them in their temples. Painters and practitioners of other
arts of design were forbidden to innovate on these models or entertain any but the traditional standards, and the prohibition still persists, both for these arts and for music in all its branches. If you
inspect their paintings and reliefs on the spot, you will find that the
work of ten thousand years ago—I mean the expression not loosely
657 but in all precision—is neither better nor worse than that of today;
both exhibit an identical artistry.

CLINIAS: A most amazing state of things!

ATHENIAN: Or rather, one immensely to the credit of their
legislators and statesmen. No doubt one could find grounds for censure in other Egyptian institutions, but in this matter of music, at
least, it is a fact, and a thought-provoking fact, that it has actually
proved possible, in such a sphere, to canonize melodies which exhibit
an intrinsic rightness permanently by law. That must have been the
doing of a god, or a godlike man—as, in fact, the local tradition is
b that the melodies which have been preserved for so many ages were
the work of Isis. So, as I was saying before, if we can but detect the
intrinsically right in such matters, in whatever degree, we should reduce them to law and system without misgiving, since the appeal to
feeling which shows itself in the perpetual craving for novel musical
sensation can, after all, do comparatively little to corrupt choric art,
once it has been consecrated, by deriding it as out of fashion. In
Egypt, at any rate, its corrupting influence appears to have been nowise potent, but very much the reverse.

c   CLINIAS: That seems to be the state of the case from your
present account.

ATHENIAN: Then may we say boldly that the right way to employ music and the recreations of the choric art is on some such
lines as these? When we believe things are going well with us, we
feel delight, and, conversely, when we feel delight we believe things
are well with us. You agree with me?

CLINIAS: Surely, surely.

ATHENIAN: And, mark, when we are in that case—I mean,
when we feel delight—we cannot keep still.

CLINIAS: Just so.

d   ATHENIAN: And so our young folk are eager to dance and sing
themselves, while, as for us elders, we think it the becoming thing to
pass the time by looking on at them and enjoying their play and merriment. We miss the agility which is beginning to fail us at our years,
and so we are glad to arrange competitions for performers who can
reawaken the youthfulness in us by reminiscence.

CLINIAS: Very true.

ATHENIAN: So we can hardly deny that there is much in the
current popular judgment about the providers of entertainments. I

mean, the judgment that the palm for superior ingenuity should be e
awarded to the entertainer who gives us most pleasure and enjoyment. Since we are granted the liberty to play on such occasions, so
it is argued, of course he who gives the keenest enjoyment to the
greatest number is rightly held in the highest esteem, and, as I just
put it, carries off the palm. That is the right thing to say, and the 658
right way to act, too, if the occasion arises?

CLINIAS : Yes, perhaps it is.

ATHENIAN : Still, my dear sir, let us avoid a hasty pronouncement on such a topic. It would be better to break the subject up into
its details for consideration, in some such fashion as this. Suppose a
man were to institute a competition without any further qualification, not specifying that it was to be an athletic or a musical contest,
or a horse race. Imagine him to collect all his fellow citizens, offer
a prize, and announce that anyone may enter as a competitor in simple pleasure giving—the prize to be awarded to the performer who b
entertains the spectators most. There are to be no restrictions as to
the manner of the entertaining, so long as the man beats his competitors on that one score, and is voted the most pleasing. What
should we expect to be the likely result of the announcement?

CLINIAS : What have you in your mind?

ATHENIAN : Well, it is likely enough that one performer would
produce a recitation of epic poetry, like a Homer, a second a chant to
the lyre, a third a tragedy, and a fourth, perhaps, a comedy, and I
should not be surprised if one of them actually thought his best
chance of the prize was to exhibit a puppet show. But, now, can we c
say which of all these competitors, and the host of others who would
enter, *deserves* the prize?

CLINIAS : That is a singular question. How could anyone answer you, as though he could decide before he had listened and given
a personal hearing to each of the different candidates?

ATHENIAN : Well, come now, would you like me to give the answer to this singular question for both of you?

CLINIAS : To be sure.

ATHENIAN : Then here it is. If the tiny children are to decide,
they will, no doubt, give it for the man with the puppet show.

CLINIAS : Why, of course.   d

ATHENIAN : The bigger boys for the comedian; the cultivated
women, youths, and perhaps the absolute majority, for the tragedy.

CLINIAS : Yes, perhaps they would.

ATHENIAN : Whereas oldsters like ourselves would be likely to
get most pleasure from a reciter who gave a fine rendering of the
Iliad, or *Odyssey*, or a Hesiodic poem, and put him far and away
first. Then, who would be the rightful winner? That is our next question, I presume?

CLINIAS : Yes.

e   ATHENIAN: Clearly you and I cannot avoid saying that rightful winners are those who are preferred by men of our own age. From our point of view that custom is far the best of existing arrangements in all societies everywhere.

CLINIAS: And naturally so.

ATHENIAN: So I actually go myself with the current opinion so far as this. The standard by which music should be judged is the pleasure it gives—but not the pleasure given to any and every auditor. We may take it that the finest music is that which delights the
659 best men, the properly educated, that, above all, which pleases the one man who is supreme in goodness and education. And the reason why we say judges in such matters need goodness is that they require to be equipped not only with wisdom, but particularly with courage. A judge who is truly a judge must not learn his verdict from the audience, letting himself be intimidated into it by the clamor of the multitude and his own incompetence, nor yet, out of cowardice
b and poltroonery, weakly pronounce a judgment which belies his own convictions with the very lips with which he invoked the gods as he entered on his functions. To tell the plain truth, the judge takes his seat not to learn from the audience, but to teach them, and to set himself against performers who give an audience pleasure in wrong and improper ways. By the ancient and general Hellenic rule, there was none of the freedom of the present custom of Sicily and Italy, which leaves things to the majority of the audience and decides the
c victory by their votes, a practice which has corrupted the poets themselves—since their standard in composition is the debased taste of their judges, with the result that it is actually the audience who educates *them*—and equally corrupted the tastes of the audience. The repeated exhibition of characters better than their own ought to produce an improvement in their taste; as things are, the result is the direct contrary, and it is their own doing. Once more, then, what lesson is indicated by the conclusion of our present argument? Something, perhaps, to this effect.

CLINIAS: To what effect?

ATHENIAN: Why, I believe the argument is bringing us back for the third or fourth time to our old position, that education is, in
d fact, the drawing and leading of children to the rule which has been pronounced right by the voice of the law, and approved as truly right by the concordant experience of the best and oldest men. That the child's soul, then, may not learn the habit of feeling pleasure and pain in ways contrary to the law and those who have listened to its bidding, but keep them company, taking pleasure and pain in
e the very same things as the aged—that, I hold, proves to be the real purpose of what we call our 'songs.' They are really spells for souls, directed in all earnest to the production of the concord of which we have spoken, but as the souls of young folk cannot bear earnest-

ness, they are spoken of as 'play' and 'song,' and practiced as such. Just so, in the case of the physically invalid and infirm, the practitioner seeks to administer wholesome nutriment in palatable articles 660 of meat and drink, but unwholesome in unpalatable, to accustom the patient to accept the one and reject the other, as he should. In the same fashion a true lawgiver likewise will persuade, or if persuasion fails, will compel, the man of poetic gifts to compose as he ought, to employ his noble and fine-filed phrases to represent by their rhythms the bearing, and by their melodies the strains, of men who are pure, valiant, and, in a word, good.

CLINIAS : Great God, sir, do you imagine that is how poetry is b actually produced in other cities? As far as my own observation goes, I know of no such practice as you recommend, except here at home, or in Lacedaemon; elsewhere I notice endless innovation in dancing and all branches of music generally, constant change, inspired not by the laws but by a sort of unregulated taste which is so far from being fixed and permanent, as is the case in Egypt by your account, c that it never shows any constancy.

ATHENIAN : Well observed, Clinias. But if you imagined my remarks to refer to existing practice, the unfortunate impression is probably due to my failure to make my thought clear. I did, perhaps, say things which might give you that impression, but they simply explained what I would wish to see done in the matter of music. For the denunciation of error which is far advanced and without remedy, though sometimes unavoidable, is a decidedly unpleasant duty. But since we are at one about the principle, pray tell me, is it put into d practice better among yourselves and our Spartan friends than among the Greeks at large?

CLINIAS : Certainly it is.

ATHENIAN : And suppose the rest of us followed the same practice. May we say that this would be an improvement on the existing state of things?

CLINIAS : An extraordinary improvement, I take it, if they would follow the example of Sparta and ourselves, and the precepts which you yourself have just given us.

ATHENIAN : Come then, let us have an understanding on the issue before us. In both your communities the teaching conveyed by all education and music is to this effect, is it not? You constrain your e poets to teach that a good man, since he is temperate and just, is a fortunate and happy man, no matter whether he be great and mighty or small and feeble, rich or poor. But if a man be unjust, even though he were 'richer than Midas or Cinyras,' [3] he is a pitiable creature, and his life a miserable one. To borrow the words—and true words they are—of your own poet, 'I would neither name' a man,

[3] Tyrtaeus 12.6.

nor 'hold him in any account,' though he should practice or acquire all that is currently reputed good without justice, not though, being
661 the man he is, 'he should close with the foe and strike him down.' If a man be unjust, I would not have him 'look the bloody carnage in the face unblenched,' or 'outstrip the north wind of Thrace,' nor enjoy any of the goods currently so reputed. For the things popularly called goods do not really deserve the name. The saying, you know, is that health is the greatest of all goods, beauty ranks second, and wealth third, and there are innumerable other goods, such as keen
b sight and hearing, and acute sensibility generally; it is good also to be an autocrat and gratify all one's passions, and the very crown of felicity would be that the possessor of all these advantages should forthwith become immune from death. But what you and I maintain is that though all these endowments are great goods to men of justice and religion, one and all of them, from health down, are great
c evils to the unjust. To be more specific, sight, hearing, sensation, life itself, are superlatively evil, if one could persist forever without dying in the enjoyment of all these so-called goods unaccompanied by justice and virtue at large, though less evil if he who is in such case survive only for a short while. This is my teaching, and I conceive you will persuade, or constrain, your national poets to teach it too, and likewise to produce correspondent rhythms and scales for the education of your young people. Consider, now, I affirm with confidence
d that so-called evils are good for the unjust, though evil for the just, and so-called goods, though really good for a good man, evil for a bad one. So, as I was asking, are you and I in accord, or not?

CLINIAS : Partly, I think, in accord, partly decidedly not so.

ATHENIAN : Then can the point on which I fail to convince you, by any chance, be this, that if a man enjoys lifelong health, wealth, and absolute power—and I will add, if you like, exceptional
e strength, and immunity from death, and exemption from all other so-called evils—so long as he but has injustice and arrogance within himself, such a man's life is miserable, not happy?

CLINIAS : Exactly. That is the point.

ATHENIAN : Good. Then what should I say next? Granted that a man is brave, strong, handsome, rich, and can satisfy every passion
662 of a lifetime, do you deny that, if he is an unjust and arrogant man, his life must inevitably be dishonorable? Or possibly you would go so far as to concede the dishonor.

CLINIAS : Readily.

ATHENIAN : And inevitably evil, too? Would you allow that?

CLINIAS : No, that is not to be so readily admitted.

ATHENIAN : And, further, unpleasant and inexpedient for himself?

CLINIAS : How can we possibly carry concession to that pitch?

b ATHENIAN : How? Apparently only by the intervention of a

god to produce a concord as complete as our present discordance. For my part, dear Clinias, I find it even more certain that these truths are beyond question than that Crete is an island. Were I a legislator, I would do my best to constrain my poets and all my citizens to proclaim them. I would inflict a penalty little short of the capital on any inhabitant heard to maintain that there are wicked men who have a pleasant life, or that one course may be advan- c tageous and profitable, but a different course more truly rightful— not to mention many other points on which I would try to persuade my citizens to use language very different from that current, apparently, among Cretans and Lacedaemonians, and, certainly, among mankind in general. Why, for the love of Zeus and Apollo, my worthy friends, imagine we could put the question to the very gods who were the authors of your own laws. Is the justest life also the most d pleasant, or are there two different lives, one which is the most pleasant, and another which is the most just? Should they answer that there are two, we might probably go on to ask, if we knew how to put the right question, which should be called the happier men, those who live the more just life, or those who live the more pleasant. Should they say, those who live the more pleasant, the statement would come very oddly from *them*. Yet I could wish not to introduce the names of gods into such a matter, and should prefer to use those of fathers and legislators. We will, therefore, take my questions as e having been addressed to such a father and lawgiver, and imagine him to reply that he who lives the pleasantest life is the most blessed of mankind.

Father, I should next remark, did you not mean me to have the happiest of lives? Yet you were never weary of enjoining me to lead the justest life. Thus the father or legislator, whichever he might be, who should decide in that sense, would, I fancy, appear strangely wanting in self-consistency. But should he take the other view that the justest life is happiest, any hearer, I conceive, would ask what 663 good or blessing greater than pleasure that life has in it, that the law should commend it. What good, in fact, can come to the just man unattended by pleasure? Good fame, for example, and commendation from men and gods—are they good and honorable, but unpleasant? And is the reverse true of ill fame? Not a bit of it, respected legislator. Or again, neither to inflict wrong nor to suffer it—is that a course which, though good and honorable, is unpleasant, or its opposite pleasant, though dishonorable and evil?

CLINIAS : Surely not.

ATHENIAN : And thus the theory which declines to separate the pleasant from the just, or the good from the honorable, if it has no other merits, is at least a persuasive to a just and religious life. b Hence from the legislator's point of view any theory which denies these positions is highly disgraceful and dangerous, since no one, if he can help it, will let himself be persuaded into following a course not attended by a surplus of pleasure over pain. It is distance which causes confusion of vision in, I may say, all of us, and particularly in children, unless the lawgiver will effect a reversal of our judgments

c and dissipate our darkness, persuading us, as best he can, by institutions, eulogies, and arguments that right and wrong are like puzzle pictures, wrong-appearing, in the opposite perspective to right, pleasant when viewed from the standpoint of one who is himself unjust and evil, and right most unpleasant, but everything the precise contrary, on both sides, from the point of view of the righteous.

CLINIAS : So it would seem.

ATHENIAN : And which verdict, should we say, has the more valid claim to be true, that of the worse soul, or that of the better?

CLINIAS : Certainly, I should presume, that of the better.

d   ATHENIAN : Then it is consequently certain that an unjust life is not merely more dishonorable and despicable, but actually more truly unpleasant than a just and religious.

CLINIAS : So it should follow from our present argument, my friend.

ATHENIAN : And even had it not been so—as our present argument has shown that it is—could a legislator of even moderate merits, supposing him to have ventured on any fiction for the sake of its good effect on the young, have devised a more useful fiction

e than this, or one more potent to induce us all to practice all justice freely, and without compulsion?

CLINIAS : Why, as to truth, sir, truth is a glorious thing and an enduring thing, but it seems no easy matter to convince men of it.

ATHENIAN : Well, and that most improbable fable of the man from Sidon—was it easy to convince anyone of that? Now there are many such tales.

CLINIAS : Tales? Of what sort?

ATHENIAN : Why, they say teeth were once sown in the ground and armed men sprang up from them. And yet the example

664 is striking proof for a lawgiver that the youthful mind will be persuaded of anything, if one will take the trouble to persuade it. Thus he need only tax his invention to discover what conviction would be most beneficial to a city, and then contrive all manner of devices to ensure that the whole of such a community shall treat the topic in one single and selfsame lifelong tone, alike in song, in story, and in discourse. Still, if you incline to a different opinion, you are perfectly free to controvert my view.

b   CLINIAS : Nay, neither of us, I conceive, feels equal to disputing the point.

ATHENIAN : Then it becomes my business to proceed to the next point. I maintain that all our choirs, of which there will be three, must enchant the souls of our children, while they are still

young and tender, by reciting all the noble doctrines we have so far
rehearsed or may hereafter rehearse, the sum and substance whereof
may be worded thus. If we say that the gods account the pleasantest c
and the best life one and the same, our statement will be at once
perfectly true, and more convincing to those whom we have to convince than if we spoke in any other tones.

CLINIAS : The contention must be admitted.

ATHENIAN : In the first place, then, it will be proper that the
choir of boys, which will be sacred to the Muses, should make its
entry first to sing publicly to this effect with all its might before the
whole city. Next the choir of men under thirty should make its appearance, invoking the god of healing to bear witness to the truth of
the doctrine uttered, and praying him of his grace to convince the d
young of it. And there must, of course, be still a third song from
those who are between the ages of thirty and sixty. Men of more advanced age, who are naturally no longer equal to singing, will be left
to tell stories about the same types of character in inspired accents.

CLINIAS : And pray, sir, whom may you mean by this third
choir? My friend and I do not understand what you would say of
them any too clearly.

ATHENIAN : And yet they are the very parties we have had in
view in the greater part of our previous conversation.

CLINIAS : We are as much in the dark as ever. Would you e
kindly make your explanation rather clearer.

ATHENIAN : You may recollect that we said, at the opening of
our discussion, that all young creatures are naturally full of fire, and
can keep neither their limbs nor their voices quiet. They are perpetually breaking into disorderly cries and jumps, but whereas no other
animal develops a sense of order of either kind, mankind forms a soli- 665
tary exception. Order in movement is called *rhythm,* order in articulation—the blending of acute with grave—*pitch,* and the name for
the combination of the two is *choric art.* We further said that, in
their pity for us, the gods have granted us companions and leaders
of our choirs in Apollo and the Muses, to whom, you may remember,
we added Dionysus as a third.

CLINIAS : Why, of course we recollect this.

ATHENIAN : Well, we have already spoken of choirs of Apollo
and of the Muses; so the remaining choir, the third, must be called b
that of Dionysus.

CLINIAS : What! Pray explain yourself. A choir of old men
sacred to Dionysus! That sounds very odd on a first hearing, if you
seriously mean that men between thirty, or even fifty, and sixty are to
form his chorus.

ATHENIAN : You are quite right. It does call for some argument,
I take it, to show that such an arrangement would be a reasonable
one.

CLINIAS: To be sure it does.

ATHENIAN: We are in agreement, then, upon the results reached so far?

c   CLINIAS: And what are they?

ATHENIAN: That the spell we have described must be recited without intermission by everyone, adult or child, free man or slave, man or woman; in fact the whole city must repeat it incessantly to itself in forms to which we must somehow contrive at all costs to give inexhaustible variety and subtlety, so that the performers' appetite for their own hymnody and enjoyment of it may persist unabated.

CLINIAS: That is the result to be secured, as everyone must agree.

d   ATHENIAN: Now where must this worthiest element in our city —its combined years and wisdom will give it more authority than any other class, and the matter of its odes will be the noblest of all—do its singing, if it is to be most potent for good? Are we, in pure folly, to leave the body principally responsible for the noblest and most useful music without directions?

CLINIAS: We certainly must not neglect it, if your argument is to be trusted.

ATHENIAN: What, then, would be the becoming arrangement? Something of this kind, perhaps?

CLINIAS: Of what kind?

ATHENIAN: As a man gets into years, the reluctance to sing

e   grows upon him. He feels less pleasure in the act, and, if it is forced on him, the older and more sober-minded he grows, the more bashful he feels about it. I am right, am I not?

CLINIAS: Decidedly right.

ATHENIAN: And of course he will feel still more bashful about standing up and singing in a theater before an audience of all sorts. And besides, if men of such years and character were made, like competing choirs, to train their voices for the performance by a lowering regimen and abstinence from food, their singing would surely be a

666   thoroughly disagreeable and humiliating task, and consequently their execution would be spiritless.

CLINIAS: There is no disputing what you say.

ATHENIAN: Then how shall we encourage them to sing with spirit? Might we not make a law to the following effect? In the first place, we shall absolutely prohibit the taste of wine to boys under eighteen. We shall tell them they must have too much concern for the passionate temperament of youth to feed the fire of body or soul with a further current of fire before they address themselves to the labors of life. In the next, while we permit a moderate use of wine to men

b   under thirty, we shall absolutely forbid carousing and free potations. But when a man is verging on the forties, we shall tell him, after he has finished banqueting at the general table, to invoke the gods, and more particularly to ask the presence of Dionysus in that sacrament and pastime of advancing years—I mean the wine cup—which he bestowed on us for a comfortable medicine against the dryness of old age, that we might renew our youth, and our harsher mood be melted to softness by forgetfulness of our heaviness, as iron is melted in the c furnace, and so made more tractable. To begin with, in that mood any man would be ready, would he not, to render his song—or, as we have so often called it, his spell—with more spirit and less bashfulness, not perhaps before a numerous audience of strangers, but in a smaller circle of personal friends?

CLINIAS : Emphatically so.

ATHENIAN : As a means of inducing them to take their part in our proposed singing, then, the device is not so wholly out of place? d

CLINIAS : Out of place? By no means.

ATHENIAN : But what manner of strain should they utter? Of course it must be a music in keeping with their persons.

CLINIAS : Why, of course.

ATHENIAN : And what is the music which befits godlike men? Choric song?

CLINIAS : Why, sir, personally we Spartans and our Cretan friends are quite incapable of any singing but that we learned when we were trained to sing in choirs.

ATHENIAN : I am not surprised at it; in plain fact, you have never risen to the noblest kind of song. Your cities are organized like e armies, not like societies of town dwellers; you keep your young men in herds like so many colts at grass in one troop. None of you ever takes his own colt, draws him out of the general herd, for all his restiveness and fuming, and puts him in the charge of a special groom to be stroked and tamed and treated with all the attention required by a training which will make him no mere good soldier, but a man fit to administer a state and its townships—will make him, in fact, the type of man of whom we spoke at first as a better warrior than those 667 of Tyrtaeus, because he will esteem valor, always and everywhere, the fourth, not the first, point of goodness in individuals and in society at large.

CLINIAS : Somehow or other, sir, you are back again at your belittling of our legislators.

ATHENIAN : Nay, my dear sir, if I do so at all, it is of no set purpose, but please let us follow where our argument leads. If we can find a music more excellent than that of choirs and public theaters, let us make the attempt to assign it to these men, who, as we are b saying, are anxious to take their part in the noblest music, though bashful where the kind just mentioned is concerned.

CLINIAS : By all means.

ATHENIAN : Well, to begin with, must it not hold good of all things which have an attendant charm that their chief value lies either in this mere charm itself, in their rightness in some sense, or, finally, in their utility? To give an example, I mean that meat and drink, and articles of nutriment generally, are attended by a charm

c which we may call flavor; as to rightness and utility, it is precisely what we call the wholesomeness of the various viands which is also their true rightness.

CLINIAS : Exactly.

ATHENIAN : Again, the act of learning is attended by a charm, a gusto, but it is the truth of what is learned which gives it its rightness and utility, its goodness and nobility.

CLINIAS : Just so.

d   ATHENIAN : And what of the various arts of imitation which work by producing likenesses? If they are so far successful, I mean if they give rise to an attendant pleasure, charm, I suppose, would be just the right name for it?

CLINIAS : Yes.

ATHENIAN : Whereas the rightness of such products, speaking generally, depends not on their pleasantness, but on accurate correspondence in quality and magnitude?

CLINIAS : True.

ATHENIAN : Thus the only case in which it will be right to make pleasure our standard of judgment is that of a performance which provides us with neither utility, nor truth, nor resemblance, though, of

e course, it must do us no harm either, an activity practiced solely with a view to this concomitant charm, which is very properly called *pleasure,* unattended by any of the results just specified?

CLINIAS : You refer only to *harmless* pleasure?

ATHENIAN : Yes, and I also use the name *play* for it in cases where it does neither harm nor good worth taking into serious account.

CLINIAS : Very true.

ATHENIAN : Then surely it follows from the argument that a man's feeling of pleasure, or his erroneous belief, is never a proper standard by which to judge of any representation, and I will add, any

668 proportionality. Equal is never equal, nor symmetrical symmetrical, because someone believes it to be so, or because someone feels no pleasure; no, we should judge by the standard of truth, never, on any account, by any other.

CLINIAS : Assuredly.

ATHENIAN : Now we may say that all music is an art of producing likenesses or representations.

CLINIAS : Of course.

ATHENIAN : Consequently, when a man tells us that in music pleasure is the standard of judgment, we must refuse to accept his statement. It is not this type of music, if indeed there could be such a

type, which we should make our serious object, but that other which b
retains its likeness to the model of the noble.

CLINIAS: Just so.

ATHENIAN: And these citizens of ours, too, will naturally have
to do the same. As they aim at the noblest kind of song, they will also
have to aim not at a music which is pleasing, but at one which is *right*.
In fact, we explained the rightness of a representation to lie in reproduction of the proportions and quality of the original.

CLINIAS: To be sure.

ATHENIAN: Again, it would be universally allowed of music
that its productions are all of the nature of representation and portraiture. Composers, performers, audience, all of them would be in c
complete agreement so far?

CLINIAS: Beyond doubt.

ATHENIAN: Hence it should seem that a man who is to make
no mistake of judgment about a particular production must, in every
case, understand what that production is. If he does not understand
what it is, that is, what it is meant for, or of what it is in fact an image,
it will be a long time before he will discern the rightness or wrongness
in the artist's purpose.

CLINIAS: A long time indeed.

ATHENIAN: And if a man does not understand this *rightness*, d
can he possibly be in a position to discuss the *goodness* or *badness* of
the work? My question is not very clearly expressed, but it will perhaps become clearer if I put it thus.

CLINIAS: How, pray?

ATHENIAN: There are, as you know, numerous likenesses
which are apprehended by the eye.

CLINIAS: Of course.

ATHENIAN: Now suppose that, in their case too, a man did not
know what the various bodies represented were. Could he possibly
judge of the rightness of the artist's work? For example, could he tell
whether it shows the members of the body in their true and natural
numbers and real situations, so disposed relatively to one another as e
to reproduce the natural grouping—to say nothing of color or shape—
or whether all this is confused in the representation? Could a man,
think you, possibly decide the question, if he simply did not know
what the creature depicted was?

CLINIAS: Naturally he could not.

ATHENIAN: Now suppose we are aware that the figure the artist has drawn or modeled is that of a human being, and that he has reproduced all its members, with their colors and outlines. Does it follow 669
that one who is alive to this need be competent to judge on the further
point whether the work is beautiful, or falls short of beauty in some
way?

CLINIAS: Why, sir, at that rate, we should all, without exception, be connoisseurs of an animal's points.

ATHENIAN: Quite true. Then must not one who is to be an intelligent judge of any representation, whether in drawing, in music, or in any other branch of art, have three qualifications? He must understand, first, what the object reproduced *is*, next, how *correctly*,
b third and last, how *well* a given representation has been effected, in point of language, melody, or rhythm.

CLINIAS: So it would appear.

ATHENIAN: Now we must not omit the full explanation of the difficulty of music. There is much more talk about musical imagery than about any other kind, and this is the very reason why such imagery demands more cautious scrutiny than any other. It is here that error is at once most dangerous, as it encourages morally bad disposi-
c tions, and most difficult to detect, because our poets are not altogether on the level of the Muses themselves. The Muses, we may be assured, would never commit the grave mistake of setting masculine language to an effeminate scale, or tune, or wedding melody, or postures worthy of free men with rhythms only fit for slaves and bondsmen, or taking the pose of a free man and combining it with an air or words of inappropriate rhythm. Not to say that they would never make a pretended presentation of a single theme out of a medley of human
d voices, animal cries, noises of machinery, and other things. Whereas our mere human poets tend to be only too fond of provoking the contempt of those of us who, in the phrase of Orpheus, are 'ripe for delight,' by this kind of senseless and complicated confusion. In fact, not only do we see confusion of this kind, but our poets go still further. They divorce rhythm and figure from melody, by giving metrical form
e to bare discourse, and melody and rhythm from words, by their employment of cithara and flute without vocal accompaniment, though it is the hardest of tasks to discover what such wordless rhythm and tune signify, or what model worth considering they represent. Nay, we are driven to the conclusion that all this so popular employment of cithara or flute, not subordinated to the control of dance or song for the display of speed and virtuosity, and the reproduction of the cries
670 of animals, is in the worst of bad taste; the use of either as an independent instrument is no better than unmusical legerdemain. So much for the theory of the thing. But, after all, the question for ourselves is what kind of music our citizens of thirty or more, and again our men of over fifty, are to practice, not what they are to avoid. And I think we may at once infer from what has been said as much as this.
b Those quinquagenarians whose business it will be to sing for us must at least have had an education better than that of a choir. They must, of course, be keenly sensitive to rhythms and melodies and able to judge of them. How, indeed, is a man with little or no familiarity with

the Dorian scale to judge of the rightness of the airs, or the rightness or wrongness of the rhythm to which the poet has set his air?

CLINIAS: Plainly he can do nothing of the sort.

ATHENIAN: In fact, the general public are simply ridiculous in their belief that men are adequate judges of what is good or otherwise in melody and rhythm, if they have merely been drilled into singing to the flute and marching in step, though it never occurs to them that they c do the acts without understanding anything about them. Whereas, of course, any tune is correct if it has the proper constituents, incorrect if it has unsuitable ones.

CLINIAS: Undeniably.

ATHENIAN: But what now about a man who does not even know what constituents a piece has? As I was asking, will he be a judge of its correctness in any instance whatever?

CLINIAS: Unquestionably not.

ATHENIAN: Thus it seems we are brought back again to our discovery that these singers of ours, whom we are urging and placing under a kind of voluntary coercion to sing, will need as much previous education as this. They will all need the ability to follow the steps of the d rhythms and the notes of the airs, to qualify them to pass the scales and rhythms under review, select from them those proper to be rendered by men of their own years and character, and sing them as they should be sung, a performance which will both give the performers an immediate innocent pleasure and provide their juniors with a lesson in proper appreciation of sound character. If they are educated to this e pitch they will have at their disposal a more careful education than either that which is applicable to the generality, or that of the poets themselves. For the poet it is not indispensable to be a judge of our third point—whether his representation is a good one or not—though judgment of scale and rhythm certainly cannot be dispensed with, but 671 the men we have in view will need all these qualifications to fit them to make the selection of the absolute best and the second best; otherwise none of them will effectually charm the young into virtue. The argument has now done its best to achieve its original purpose, to show that our defense of the 'choir of Dionysus' is a good one, and we have to consider its success. Of course, any such gathering inevitably grows noisy as the drinking goes further and further, as we began by b assuming is bound to happen in cases like these.

CLINIAS: Yes, inevitably.

ATHENIAN: In such a company everyone soars above his common level of lightsomeness and jollity, bubbles over with loquacity, pays no heed to the talk of his companions, but thinks himself fully entitled to give the law to himself and all the rest.

CLINIAS: Assuredly.

ATHENIAN: As we were saying, then, in this state of affairs the

souls of the drinkers grow softer as they are heated, like heated iron, and become more juvenile, and consequently more ductile in the
c hands of one who has the power and skill to train them and mold them, much as when they were still youthful, and the molding should now, as formerly, be the task of the good legislator. It is for him to lay down laws for the wine party effectual to induce our reveler, who is growing so sanguine and confident, so unduly relieved of his modesty, and so unwilling to observe order and alternation of silence with speech, drinking with music, to do the contrary of all this of his own accord—effectual also to confront this uncomely confidence, at its
d first entrance, with a righteous antagonist in that most comely, that divine, fear which has received the name of modesty and the sense of shame.

CLINIAS : Very true.

ATHENIAN : And for wardens of these laws and fellow workers with them, we must set the unperturbed and sober as captains over the unsober, for without them the battle with drink is more hazardous than a battle against an enemy in the field without unperturbed commanders. Moreover, if a man cannot yield willing obedience to them
e and to Dionysus, his officers, that is, the citizens of over sixty, he must be put to as much disgrace as one who disobeys the officers of Ares, or to more.

CLINIAS : Rightly said.

ATHENIAN : Then if wine and merriment were used in such fashion, would not the members of such a party be the better for it,
672 and part, not as they do today, on terms of enmity, but with an increase of friendship, seeing their intercourse would have been regulated throughout by laws, and they would have followed the path marked out by the sober for the unsober?

CLINIAS : True enough, if there could indeed be a party such as you describe.

ATHENIAN : Then pray let us have done with the old unqualified censure of the gift of Dionysus as an evil thing, not fit to be tolerated in a city. Indeed, one might be still more copious on the topic, though I feel some reluctance even to mention the principal benefit of the god's gift before the public, as the statement has been misunder-
b stood and misjudged.

CLINIAS : And what benefit is that?

ATHENIAN : There is a current of story and pious tradition to the effect that this god was bereft of his wits by his stepmother Hera, and that this is why he afflicts his victims with Bacchic possession and all its frenzied dancing, by way of revenge—that that, and nothing else, was the motive for his gift of wine. For my own part I leave such stories to those who think it safe to tell them of deities, but of one thing I am certain. No creature whatsoever is born with that intelli-
c gence, or all that intelligence, which characterizes it in its maturity.

Hence, so long as a creature has not yet attained its proper level of native sense, it is quite mad, indulging in random cries, and, as soon as it has found its feet, in equally random leaps. And let me remind you that we pronounced these the source of both music and gymnastics.

CLINIAS: Naturally we have not forgotten that.

ATHENIAN: You will recollect, too, how we said that in mankind this beginning has preluded to perception of rhythm and melody, d and that the gods responsible for that development are Apollo, the Muses, and Dionysus?

CLINIAS: To be sure.

ATHENIAN: And as for wine in particular, the general story would seem to hold that it has been bestowed on men in vindictiveness, to drive us frantic, whereas our present version is that the gift was meant, on the contrary, as a medicine, to produce modesty of soul, and health and strength of body.

CLINIAS: An admirable summary of the argument, sir.

ATHENIAN: Then we have finished our treatment of one half of e the choric art. Shall we go on with further consideration of the other half, or should we perhaps dismiss the subject?

CLINIAS: What are the halves you speak of? How do you distinguish the one from the other?

ATHENIAN: Why, the choric art as a whole we found to be the same thing as the whole of education, and one half of the art, that which has to do with the voice, consists of rhythms and melodies.

CLINIAS: Just so.

ATHENIAN: And the part which deals with bodily movement has rhythm in common with the movements of the voice, but posture and gesticulation are proper to it, just as melody, on the other side, is to vocal movement.

CLINIAS: Precisely so.

ATHENIAN: Now the training of the voice to goodness, con- 673 tinued till it reaches the soul, we named, in a sense, music.

CLINIAS: And a very proper name for it, too.

ATHENIAN: As for the training of the body—we spoke of it as the dancing of creatures at play—when the process culminates in goodness of body, let us call scientific bodily discipline with that purpose gymnastics.

CLINIAS: As we may very properly do.

ATHENIAN: As for music—that half of the choric art of which we have just professed to have given a complete review—our statement may be taken as still standing. How shall we proceed next? b Shall we discuss the other branch, or what?

CLINIAS: My dear sir, you are conversing with Cretans and Lacedaemonians. What possible answer, then, do you expect from either of us to that question, if we pass over gymnastics, now that we have disposed of music?

ATHENIAN : I take that remark as a pretty plain answer to my question; in fact, I recognize that though in form a question, it is ac-
c tually what I have called it, an answer, and something more—an instruction to complete our treatment of gymnastics.

CLINIAS : You take my meaning correctly, and I entreat you to comply with it.

ATHENIAN : Why, so I will, nor will it be particularly difficult, as you are both at home in the subject, having indeed made more experimental acquaintance with this art than with the former.

CLINIAS : There you are very much in the right.

ATHENIAN : Well, this art similarly has its origin in the habit-
d ual leaping native to all living things, and in mankind, as we have said, the acquisition of a sense of rhythm has generated dancing. Since melody suggests and awakens consciousness of rhythm, the two in conjunction have given rise to the play of the choric dance.

CLINIAS : Quite so.

ATHENIAN : One branch of the subject, as I have said, we have treated already, and will next do our best to deal with the other.

CLINIAS : With all my heart.

ATHENIAN : Then, if you both approve, we may first give the fi-
e nal touch to our account of drinking.

CLINIAS : And how do you propose to do this?

ATHENIAN : If a city is to practice the custom now under discussion in a serious spirit, in subjection to the control of law and rule, as a training in self-command, and permits a similar indulgence in other pleasures on the same principle, as a means to mastery of them, all without exception should be treated on the lines we have laid down. But if the practice is treated as mere play, and free license is to be given to any man to drink whenever he pleases, in what company he
674 pleases, and when engaged on any undertaking he pleases, I could no longer vote for allowing any indulgence in the wine cup to such a city, or such a man. I would even go further than the practice of Crete and Lacedaemon and propose an addition to the Carthaginian law which prohibits the very taste of this liquor to all soldiers in the field, and enforces water-drinking throughout the duration of a campaign. I would absolutely prohibit its taste in civic life to slaves of both sexes, to mag-
b istrates throughout the year of their office, and equally absolutely to captains of vessels and jurymen when on duty, and likewise to any member of an important council when about to attend its meetings. Further, I would prohibit its use during the day absolutely, except under the orders of a trainer or a physician, and at night also to any person of either sex contemplating the procreation of children, to pass over many other cases in which wine is not to be drunk by rational men with a sound law. Thus you see that by our argument no city
c would need many vineyards; agricultural production and bodily regimen in general would be matters for regulation, and viticulture in

particular would be kept within very reasonable and narrow bounds. And this, gentlemen, if it has your approval, may be taken as the finale of my remarks on the subject of wine.

CLINIAS : It is well said, indeed, and we fully concur.

BOOK III

ATHENIAN : Enough, then, on this matter. But what may we take to 676 have been the first beginning of a state? I wonder whether the best and easiest way to treat the problem may not be this?

CLINIAS : What?

ATHENIAN : To start from the same point with which we regularly have to begin when we would study the double progressive devel- b opment of a city in virtue and vice.

CLINIAS : And that point is?

ATHENIAN : Why, the interminable length of time, I conceive, and the changes time brings with it.

CLINIAS : Pray explain yourself.

ATHENIAN : Well, cities have existed and men have lived in civil society for a long time. Do you think you could possibly tell how long?

CLINIAS : Not readily, to say the least of it.

ATHENIAN : But you admit at least that it must have been so for an immense and incredible time?

CLINIAS : Oh yes, there is no doubt about that.

ATHENIAN : And you will surely grant that thousands and thousands of cities have come into being during this time, and no less a number have ceased to exist? Moreover, every form of constitution has repeatedly appeared in one or other of them. Sometimes a small c city has grown larger, sometimes a large city smaller; a bad city has sometimes grown better, a good city sometimes worse.

CLINIAS : Indubitably.

ATHENIAN : Thus we have, if possible, to discover the cause of these variations; there, I suspect, we may find the key to the primal origin of constitutions and their modification.

CLINIAS : A happy thought, and we must all do our best endeavor—you to expound your thoughts on the subject, and my friend and myself to keep pace with you.

ATHENIAN : Then what view do you both take of the ancient 677 legends? Have they any truth behind them?

CLINIAS : Which legends might you mean?

ATHENIAN : Those which tell of repeated destructions of mankind by floods, pestilences, and from various other causes, which leave only a handful of survivors.

CLINIAS : Oh, that kind of story must be perfectly credible to any man.

ATHENIAN : Very well, let us suppose one of those various exterminations, that which was once effected by the Flood.

CLINIAS : And what is the point you would have us observe about it?

b ATHENIAN : That the few who then escaped the general destruction must all have been mountain shepherds, mere scanty embers of humanity left unextinguished among their high peaks.

CLINIAS : Why, obviously.

ATHENIAN : And of course men like these were bound to be unfamiliar with the crafts at large and, above all, with the tricks of town dwellers for overreaching and outdistancing one another and the rest of their devices for mutual infliction of mischief.

CLINIAS : The probabilities are certainly on that side.

c ATHENIAN : Now may we assume that at such a time there is a total destruction of the cities situated in the lowlands and on the seacoast?

CLINIAS : We may, no doubt.

ATHENIAN : And we may add that all implements are lost, and that any discoveries of value due to the science of statesmen or other specialists all vanish at such a time? For to be sure, my dear sir, if such inventions could persist permanently in their present excellence, how could there ever be a new discovery of anything?

d CLINIAS : As much as to say that we must take the men of those ages to have known nothing of these matters for untold tens of thousands of years. It is only some thousand or two thousand years since they were revealed, partly by Daedalus, partly by Orpheus, partly by Palamedes, music by Marsyas and Olympus, the lyre by Amphion, and various other discoveries by numerous other persons—a mere business, so to say, of yesterday and the day before.

ATHENIAN : It is delicate in you, Clinias, to omit your connection, who was in strict fact a man of yesterday.

CLINIAS : You refer to Epimenides, I presume?

e ATHENIAN : To no other. You know, my friend, his invention left them all in the lurch. True, Hesiod had long before had a glimmer of it in theory, but the practical achievement belonged to the other, by your Cretan story.

CLINIAS : It did, indeed.

ATHENIAN : Then I suppose one may say that the state of mankind at the time of the calamity was this. There was frightful and widespread depopulation, but a vast territory of unoccupied land; most of the animals had perished, but there were a few herds of cattle,

678 and perhaps a surviving stock of goats, and these provided those who grazed them with a sustenance which would be scanty enough in the first instance.

CLINIAS : No doubt.

ATHENIAN : But as for a city, a constitution, a legislation—the themes of our present conversation—can we imagine that, to put it broadly, the faintest recollection of them was preserved?

CLINIAS: Why, surely not.

ATHENIAN: Now that is the condition which has given rise to the whole complex of our actual life, with its cities and constitutions, its sciences, its laws, its manifold moral evil and equally manifold moral goodness?

CLINIAS: I do not quite follow you.

ATHENIAN: Why, my good sir, can we suppose that the men of b that day, unacquainted as they were alike with the numerous blessings and the numerous curses of town life, would be mature either in moral virtue or in vice?

CLINIAS: Well demanded. We appreciate your point.

ATHENIAN: Thus it is by progress of time and the multiplication of the species that life has come to be as we actually find it?

CLINIAS: Exactly.

ATHENIAN: And that, I presume, not all at once, but little by little in the course of an immense period of time.

CLINIAS: Nothing can be more likely.   c

ATHENIAN: Indeed, they were still haunted, I should presume, by a terror of coming down from the highlands to the plains.

CLINIAS: Naturally.

ATHENIAN: Thus, though the sight of another's face must have been welcome indeed in those days when men's numbers were so few, all conveyances for travel by land or water must have been pretty universally abolished, must they not, with the loss of the arts? So social intercourse, I conceive, was not easily feasible. For iron, copper, and metallic deposits in general had been so obliterated by the inunda- d tion that it was a problem to get them clear again, and they had little opportunity of cutting timber. For what few tools might have survived among their mountains must soon have been used up and disappeared, and they would not be in a condition to replace them until the art of mining reappeared among them.

CLINIAS: Of course not.

ATHENIAN: And how many generations must we suppose to pass before that would happen?

CLINIAS: A very considerable number, beyond all doubt.   e

ATHENIAN: Consequently, all arts which require iron, copper, and similar materials had then been lost for this period, or even longer.

CLINIAS: Naturally.

ATHENIAN: And therefore both civil conflict and war had equally disappeared all through this period, for more reasons than one.

CLINIAS: And what were those reasons?

ATHENIAN: For one thing, men's loneliness made them socia-

ble and friendly; for another, there could be no quarreling over the
679 means of subsistence. Except perhaps in some instances at the very
first, they were not stinted for flocks and herds, the principal support
of life in that age; in fact, there was no shortage of milk or meat, and
besides, they could supply themselves with plenty of excellent viands
by hunting. Again, they were quite well off for clothes, bedding, shelter, or vessels, culinary and other. Iron, as you know, is wholly superfluous for the arts of the potter and the weaver, and these two crafts
b have, by divine appointment, been empowered to supply all our
wants, that our species may still be enabled to germinate and increase when it falls into such straits. Thus they were not extremely
poor, for the reason I have assigned, and so were not set at variance by
the stress of penury; rich they could never become in the absence of
gold and silver which was then their case. Now, a society in which
neither riches nor poverty is a member regularly produces sterling
characters, as it has no place for violence and wrong, nor yet for ri-
c valry and envy. Thus they were good men, partly for this reason, and
partly from their proverbial simplicity; they were so simple that when
they heard things called fair or foul, they obediently took the statements for infallible truths. No one was sufficiently subtle to suspect
deception, as men do today; what they were told about God or man
they believed to be true, and lived by it. Thus they came to be just the
kind of men you and I have been describing.

d CLINIAS: I agree with the statement, for one, and so does my
friend here.

ATHENIAN: Then I take it we may say that the many generations of men who led such a life were bound, by comparison with the
age before the Deluge or with our own, to be rude and ignorant in the
various arts, particularly in those of warfare, as practiced today by
land or water, and again within the city, under the names of litigation
and party faction, with their manifold artful contrivances for the in-
e fliction of mutual injury and wrong by word and by deed; they were
simpler and manlier, and by consequence more self-controlled and
more righteous generally. The reason of this has already been explained.

CLINIAS: Just so.

ATHENIAN: Now it must be understood that our purpose in the
statement we have made, and all the inferences we have based on it,
680 is simply to learn how laws came to be needed in those remote ages
and who enacted them.

CLINIAS: Yes, excellently put.

ATHENIAN: May we not perhaps say, then, that in that age
men were in no need of a lawgiver, and that such a thing as a law was
as yet unusual? In fact, those whose lives fall in that part of the cycle
do not as yet so much as possess an alphabet, but regulate their lives
by custom and what is called *traditionary* law.

CLINIAS: That is at least the fair presumption.

ATHENIAN: Still, even this is already a form of polity.

CLINIAS: But what form?

ATHENIAN: The form of polity in that age was, I believe, what b is universally called *dynasty*, a form still to be found in many places among Greeks, as well as among non-Greeks. Homer, for one, apparently speaks of it as the mode of life of the Cyclopes, when he says, 'These have neither gatherings for council nor oracles of law, but they dwell in hollow caves on the crests of the high hills, and each one utters the law to his children and his wives, and they reck not one of another.'[4]   c

CLINIAS: This poet of yours seems indeed to have been quite a pretty fellow. I assure you I have perused other passages from him which are equally neat, though not many, as we Cretans are not much given to cultivating verse of alien origin.

MEGILLUS: Now in Sparta we do cultivate it, and regard Homer as the best composer of it, though the life he is always describing is decidedly Ionian rather than Laconian. He certainly seems to give d full confirmation to your present theory where he ascribes the primitive manners of the characters in his story to their savage condition.

ATHENIAN: Yes, to be sure he does, and we may take him as evidence to show that this type of polity is actually to be found at times.

CLINIAS: Certainly.

ATHENIAN: That is, they are found among such men as we are speaking of, who have been dispersed in single homesteads and families as a result of the distress caused by these disasters? In such societies do we not find that the oldest members rule, because their e authority has come down to them from father or mother? The rest follow them, and form one flock, like so many birds, and are thus under patriarchal control, the most justifiable of all types of royalty.

CLINIAS: Exactly so.

ATHENIAN: The next step is to come together in larger numbers, which will increase the size of the communities, and turn to agriculture. This will be at first practiced in the skirts of the hill country; 681 dry fences of a kind will be contrived as walls for defense against savage beasts, and a new and larger single homestead thus erected for the community.

CLINIAS: At least that is the probable succession of events.

ATHENIAN: Well, and is there not something else which is no less probable?

CLINIAS: And what may that be?

ATHENIAN: As these larger homesteads are in process of growth from the smaller and most primitive, each of the smaller

[4] *Odyssey* 9.112 sq.

b groups will bring along with it its patriarchal ruler and certain private customs of its own—private, I mean, because the groups are isolated from each other, and the several groups have been trained by their different progenitors and fosterers in different habits of conduct toward gods and fellow men, in more orderly habits where the ancestors have been more orderly, in more valiant where they have been valiant. Thus each group comes accordingly, as I say, into the larger settlement with special laws of its own, and prepared to imprint its own preferences upon its children, and their children after them.

CLINIAS : Why, inevitably so.

c ATHENIAN: And of course each group unavoidably gives its approval to its own laws, and only in the second place to those of the others.

CLINIAS : Exactly.

ATHENIAN: And thus, to all appearances, we find ourselves insensibly embarked on the beginnings of legislation.

CLINIAS : Yes, precisely so.

ATHENIAN: At least the next step is bound to be that the coalescing groups choose certain representatives who will, of course, review all the usages, publicly and plainly indicate those which most win their own approval to the chiefs and leaders of the various clans—

d their kings as we may call them—and propose them for adoption. Hence these representatives will themselves get the name of legislators, and when they have appointed the chiefs as magistrates, and thus made the patriarchal groups into an aristocracy, or possibly a monarchy, they will direct affairs during this transformation of the polity.

CLINIAS : To be sure, this may be presumed to be the next stage in the process.

ATHENIAN: Then let us proceed to remark the rise of a third type of polity, under which polities and the societies which exhibit them alike manifest all varieties of form and fortunes.

CLINIAS : And what type is that?

e ATHENIAN: That which Homer, too, has commemorated as succeeding the second, when he says that the third form originated thus. 'He founded Dardania'—those, I believe, are his words—'for holy Ilium had not yet been built in the plain, a city for mortal men, but they still dwelt on the slopes of many-fountained Ida.' [5] The lines,

682 like those which speak of the Cyclopes, are as true to nature as they are inspired. Poets, you know, singing as they do under the divine afflatus, are among the inspired and so, by the help of their Graces and Muses, often enough hit upon true historical fact.

CLINIAS : I can fully believe it.

ATHENIAN: Well, let us carry the tale which has engaged our

[5] *Iliad* 20.216 sq.

imagination some steps further, as it may very probably suggest some hints which will be much to our purpose. So the procedure will surely be proper?

CLINIAS : Most proper.   b

ATHENIAN : Well, as I say, the foundation of Ilium was due to a descent from the heights to a wide and noble plain; it was built on a hill of low elevation watered by a number of rivers coming down from the higher ground of Ida.

CLINIAS : So the story goes.

ATHENIAN : Then we must surely suppose that this happened many ages after the Deluge?

CLINIAS : Many ages later, no doubt.

ATHENIAN : The founders, in fact, must have been singularly oblivious of the disaster we are now recalling, to build a city on such a site exposed to a number of rivers flowing from the mountains, with c such confidence in hills of inconsiderable height.

CLINIAS : Why, yes, that calamity must obviously have be- longed to a very remote past.

ATHENIAN : There were also by that time, I conceive, a good many other city-communities, thanks to the multiplication of man- kind.

CLINIAS : Yes, of course.

ATHENIAN : It was they, you know, who assailed her, and prob- ably enough by sea too, as all mankind had long ago forgotten their dread of the sea.

CLINIAS : So it should seem.   d

ATHENIAN : And there was a delay of some ten years before the Achaeans succeeded in sacking Troy.

CLINIAS : Just so.

ATHENIAN : Now during this period of ten years while Ilium was under investment, occurred the various domestic misfortunes of the different besiegers, occasioned by the insurrectionary movements of the younger generation. Moreover, when the warriors returned to their cities and families, the reception they met at the hands of these young men was neither honorable nor equitable, but attended with e numerous instances of homicide, massacre, and expulsion. The ex- pelled then returned again under a new name, calling themselves now not Achaeans, but Dorians, after Dorus, who reassembled the ex- iles of that time. As to the sequel of the story, it is told, and told fully, in your own Lacedaemonian tradition.

MEGILLUS : It is indeed.

ATHENIAN : Thus we find ourselves, providentially as it were, brought back to the very point at which we were led into a digression at the outset of our discussion of law by our stumbling upon this topic of music and the wine cup, and we may now, so to say, close with the argument. For it has come round to the actual settlement of Lacedae-

683 mon. a system you both declared sound—as also that of Crete which has closely related laws. And we have certainly gained this much vantage from our desultory argument, with its review of a variety of polities and foundations. We have inspected a first, a second, and a third community succeeding one another in order of foundation through a vast period of time, and now at last we come, in the fourth place, to the foundation of a city—or you may prefer to say, a *nation*—which
b persists to this day as it was founded. If the whole discussion enables us to understand what has been commendable in such foundations, or the reverse, what types of laws lead to their preservation, where it is achieved, and what, in the opposite case, to their dissolution, and what kind of changes will contribute to the happiness of a community, why then, Megillus and Clinias, we must cover the ground again pretty much from the beginning, unless, indeed, you have some objections to urge against what has been already said.

MEGILLUS : Why, sir, if we could have the word of a god for it
c that on our second attempt to study this matter of legislation we are to hear discourse as good, yes, and as long, as that which has already passed, I would readily make our walk a long one and should think this day short enough, though, if I am rightly informed, it is the day of the summer solstice.

ATHENIAN : Then I presume we are to undertake the inquiry.

MEGILLUS : With all my heart.

ATHENIAN : Then, Megillus, let us place ourselves in imagination at the date at which Lacedaemon, Argos, and Messene, with all
d their domains, had come, to all intents, into the power of your ancestors. Their next step, as the story goes, was the resolution to divide their forces into three, and establish three cities, Argos, Messene, and Lacedaemon.

MEGILLUS : Precisely.

ATHENIAN : Thus Argos became the kingdom of Temenus, Messene of Cresphontes, Lacedaemon of Procles and Eurysthenes.

MEGILLUS : To be sure.

ATHENIAN : Whereupon the whole body took an oath to these
e sovereigns to support them against any attempt to subvert their monarchy.

MEGILLUS : Certainly.

ATHENIAN : And, in God's name, is a monarchy ever subverted, or, for the matter of that, has any government ever been overthrown, except by itself? That was our position when we fell a while ago into a discussion of the point, and can we have forgotten it now?

MEGILLUS : Oh, surely not.

ATHENIAN : Then we may assert the position even more confidently now, as we have met with historical facts which seem to lead to the same conclusion, and shall thus be dealing with realities and facts,

not empty fiction. The historical facts, as we know, are these. Three 684
reigning houses and the cities over which they reigned swore a mutual
oath to one another, as required by the laws they had adopted as definitive of sovereignty and allegiance, the monarchs engaging that the
continuance of the crown in the family should lead to no enlargement
of prerogative, their subjects that, so long as they respected the compact, they would neither abolish the monarchies from within, nor submit to their subversion from without; the monarchs convenanted to
support a populace, no less than a monarch, if its rights should be in- b
fringed, and the peoples, in like case, to support a monarch no less
than a populace. Those, I believe, are the facts?

MEGILLUS : And so they are.

ATHENIAN : Well then, have we not here provision made by
the legislation of the three cities from the outset for a matter of prime
importance to the established constitutions—whether the initiative
was due to the monarchs or to others?

MEGILLUS : What matter do you mean?

ATHENIAN : I mean that in any case of infraction of the law of
the constitution, there were always to be two cities leagued against the
single defaulter.

MEGILLUS : Yes, manifestly.

ATHENIAN : Now I may remind you that a legislator is com- c
monly expected to enact only such laws as a populace, or multitude,
will accept of its own motion, which is much as though a trainer or
physician were expected to make his treatment, or cure, of the body a
pleasure to the recipient.

MEGILLUS : Exactly.

ATHENIAN : Whereas in real fact one has often ground for
thankfulness if one can secure bodily health and good condition at
the cost of a moderate amount of pain.

MEGILLUS : To be sure.

ATHENIAN : The statesmen of that period had moreover a sec- d
ond initial advantage which would greatly facilitate their legislative
task.

MEGILLUS : And what was that?

ATHENIAN : They were not exposed, in their attempts to establish a certain equality of possessions, to the grave charge so persistently leveled, in connection with the passing of laws for other cities,
at one who proposes change in the tenure of land, or a cancellation of
debts, from his perception that equality can never be properly attained
without these measures. When a legislator attempts a change in these
matters, everyone meets him with a cry of 'no meddling with funda- e
mentals,' and an imprecation on the author of redistribution of lands
and repudiation of debts, sufficient to reduce any man to despair. Now
the Dorians, you know, from their situation, had this further initial

advantage, which relieved them of unpleasant recriminations. The land could be divided without controversy, and they had no burden of accumulated debts.

MEGILLUS: True enough.

ATHENIAN: Then what, I must ask you, can be the reason that their foundation and its legislation proved the failure it has been?

685   MEGILLUS: Why, in what respect has it failed, and why this censure of them?

ATHENIAN: Because in two of their three settlements there was a rapid degeneration of constitution and laws, only one of the three, your own city of Sparta, remaining unperverted.

MEGILLUS: Not precisely an easy question to answer.

ATHENIAN: All the same, there is the point we have now to envisage and discuss, if we are to relieve the distress of our journey by this sober old man's game of jurisprudence, as we called it at the begin-
b ning of our walk.

MEGILLUS: No doubt, and so we must do as you say.

ATHENIAN: What laws, then, could be a fairer subject of inquiry than those by which these communities have been regulated? What greater and more illustrious cities are there, whose foundation we might take for our consideration?

MEGILLUS: If we dismiss them, it will be no easy matter to name any others.

ATHENIAN: Well, one thing is plain enough. The founders of that age meant their creation to be an adequate protection, not merely for Peloponnesus, but for the Greek world at large, if it should be
c wronged by an alien people, as it had already been wronged by the inhabitants of Ilium, when they provoked the expedition against Troy in their arrogant confidence in the power of the Assyrians of Nineveh. For the still-surviving prestige of that empire was considerable. The men of that age had then the same fear of that united dominion which
d we feel today of the Great King, as the second capture of Troy, a city which formed part of the Assyrian Empire, was a formidable grievance against them. It was to meet this situation that the militia of those days was organized as a single body, distributed over three cities under monarchs who were brothers, being all sons of Heracles, an excellent invention and disposition, superior, as was generally believed, to that of the force which had invaded Troy. For in the first place, commanders for commanders, the Heraclidae were thought better
e than the Pelopidae, and in the second, this army was held to have the advantage in valor of that which had assailed Troy, since it was composed of the victorious Dorians, but the other of the defeated Achaeans. Such, may we not say, were the dispositions of that time, and such was their purpose.

MEGILLUS: Why, surely.

686   ATHENIAN: So it was presumably expected that their work

would prove stable and endure for ages, considering their past association in so many difficulties and dangers, and their subordination to
three royal brothers of the same house—to say nothing of the fact
that they had the sanction of many oracles, in particular of the Delphic Apollo.

MEGILLUS: That, to be sure, was the presumption.

ATHENIAN: And yet, as we see, these magnificent anticipations vanished speedily into air, except, as we were saying, in the case b
of the fraction in your territory of Laconia, and it, you know, has been
in incessant warfare with the other two thirds to this day. Though had
the original project been carried out, and a single confederacy formed,
its military power would have been irresistible.

MEGILLUS: Yes, quite irresistible.

ATHENIAN: Then where was the source of the failure? Surely
it is a question worth examining—what mischance may have been
the undoing of so vast and admirable a formation.

MEGILLUS: Yes, surely. One who turned his attention from
this case in another direction might look long enough for an example
of the laws and institutions which preserve or destroy grandeur and c
greatness.

ATHENIAN: So here, I take it, we find ourselves happily
launched on an inquiry of magnitude.

MEGILLUS: Very certainly.

ATHENIAN: Then I would ask, my dear sir, whether we were
not just now unconscious victims of a mistake universal to mankind.
Men are perpetually fancying they have discovered some splendid creation which might have worked wonders if only someone had known
the proper way—whatever it may be—to use it. Now it is just on this d
point I suspect you and I may be thinking falsely and unnaturally, like
everyone else who has the same thought about anything.

MEGILLUS: Pray, what do you mean? What is the special point
of your observation?

ATHENIAN: Why, my friend, I am actually amused by my own e
recent mood. As I pictured to myself the army of which we were talking, I thought, What a splendid force, and what a wonderful acquisition it would have proved for the Greeks, if only, as I was saying, the
proper use had been made of it at the time!

MEGILLUS: Well, and was not all you said, like our assent to it,
the soundest of sense?

ATHENIAN: That may be, but what is in my mind is this. When
anyone sees something big, strong, and powerful, he feels at once that
if the owner of such a marvelous thing knew how to use it, he could
effect wonders with it, and so achieve felicity.

MEGILLUS: Well, and that is equally true, is it not?   687

ATHENIAN: Let me beg you to consider the light in which a
thing must be viewed to justify this eulogy. Take the case of the

armament of which we are now speaking as a first example. If its
creators had understood how to construct it properly, they would fairly
have attained their aim—but how? I presume, if they had constituted
it securely and assured its permanent continuance in being, with the
consequences of freedom for themselves, sovereignty over any desired
subjects, and, in a word, ability for themselves and their posterity to
b deal at their pleasure with all mankind, Greeks and non-Greeks alike.
These are the grounds on which they might base their eulogy.

MEGILLUS: Exactly.

ATHENIAN: And, again, when a man's notice is attracted to a
great fortune, or pre-eminent family distinction, or the like, and he expresses the same commendation, he speaks from the same point of
view; his thought is that the advantage will enable its possessor to
gratify all his desires, or the most numerous and considerable of
them?

MEGILLUS: So I should suppose.

c ATHENIAN: So it follows that there is a certain desire, that indicated by our argument, which is universal in all men, as the argument itself asserts.

MEGILLUS: And that is?

ATHENIAN: That events shall fall out in accord with the bidding of a man's own soul, all of them, if possible, but if not, at least
those which depend on human agency.

MEGILLUS: Of course.

ATHENIAN: Now if this is what all of us, from boyhood to age,
are wishing all the time, it will necessarily also be our standing
prayer.

MEGILLUS: Certainly.

d ATHENIAN: And, again, I suppose, our petition for our dear
ones will be that they may receive what they ask for themselves.

MEGILLUS: Of course.

ATHENIAN: Now a son, who is a boy, is dear to his father, a
grown man.

MEGILLUS: Certainly.

ATHENIAN: And, mark you, there is much a boy prays to befall
him, of which his father would beseech heaven that it may never fall
out as the son prays.

MEGILLUS: You mean when the petitioner is thoughtless and
still young?

ATHENIAN: Yes, and what of the case when the father—old, or
e only too youthful as you please to consider him—has no sense of good
and right, and prays from the heart in a passion akin to that conceived
by Theseus against his unfortunate victim, Hippolytus, but the son has
such a sense? Will the son, think you, second the father's prayer in
such a case?

MEGILLUS: I see your point. You mean, I apprehend, that the

LAWS · III 1283

object of a man's prayers and endeavors should not be that the universal course of events should conform to his own wishes, unless his wishes further conform to his sober judgment. It is the possession of intelligence that should be the mark of prayer and aspiration for the 688 community and every individual of us alike.

ATHENIAN: Yes, and I am particular to remind myself that it is this which a statesmanlike legislator should always have in view in framing his enactments—as I would also remind you, if we have not forgotten how our conversation began—that whereas you both agreed that a good legislator must devise all his institutions with an eye to war, I, for my part, urged that this is an injunction to legislate with a view to one single virtue out of four. He should keep them all in b view, I said, but chiefly and in the first place that virtue which brings all the rest in its train, that is, judgment, intelligence, and right conviction attended by appropriate passionate desire. So our argument has come back again to the old point. I, its mouthpiece, say once more now what I said before, in jest or earnest, as you please to take it. I look on prayer, I say, as a dangerous instrument in the hands of the man without intelligence; it defeats his wishes. If you please to con- c sider me in earnest, pray do so. I have every confidence that if you follow up the story we have just set before ourselves for consideration, you will directly discover that the cause of the ruin of the three kings and their whole design was no cowardice and no military ignorance on the part of commanders or commanded; what ruined them was their abundant vice of other kinds, and, above all, their folly in the supreme d concerns of man. That this was the sequence of events on that occasion, is so still today in similar cases, and will be the same in the future —that is what, by your leave, I shall try to establish in the fuller development of our argument, and friendship will lead me to make the point as clear to you as I possibly can.

CLINIAS: Verbal applause, sir, might be in doubtful taste, but our conduct will show our emphatic approval. We shall follow your discourse with the keenest attention; that is the way in which a self-respecting man best shows approbation or the reverse.

MEGILLUS: Well said, Clinias—so we will. e

CLINIAS: Certainly, with God's permission. Pray proceed.

ATHENIAN: Well then, to follow up the thread of our argument, we say that what then destroyed that mighty power was the greatest folly, and that it inevitably produces the same results today. This being so, then, a legislator's aim must be to create all the wisdom he can in a community, and with all his might to eradicate unwisdom.

CLINIAS: Yes, manifestly.

ATHENIAN: Now what type of folly may fairly be called the 689 *greatest* I should certainly say that I am on the point of describing, but you must consider whether you agree with the observation.

CLINIAS: What type do you mean?

ATHENIAN: That of a man who hates, not loves, what his judgment pronounces to be noble or good, while he loves and enjoys what he judges vile and wicked. It is this dissonance between pleasure and pain and reasoned judgment that I call the worst folly, and also the *greatest,* since its seat is the commonalty of the soul, for pain and b pleasure are in the soul what the populace or commonalty is in a community. Accordingly, when the soul sets itself at variance with knowledge, judgment, discourse, its natural sovereigns, you have what I describe as unwisdom, alike in a community where the commons rebel against magistrates and laws, and in one individual man when fair discourse is present in the soul, but produces no effect, but rather c the very contrary. These are the types of folly I would pronounce the gravest dissonances in community or individual citizen, not the follies of professionals—if you take my meaning.

CLINIAS: Indeed we do, sir, and we grant your point.

ATHENIAN: Then let us take it as definitely settled, and proclaim our conviction that no function of government may be entrusted to citizens who are foolish in this sense. They must be reprehended for their folly, though they were the most expert of calculators, and d laboriously trained in all curious studies and everything that makes for nimbleness of mind, while those of the contrary sort should be styled wise, even though, as the proverb puts it, they can 'neither read nor swim,' and it is to them, as the men of sense, that our magistracies should be given. How, indeed, my friends, can there be the barest particle of wisdom where there is no concord? 'Tis a flat impossibility, whereas the fairest and greatest of consonances may very properly be called the greatest wisdom. In this wisdom he who lives by rule has his share, while he who is without it will invariably be found to be a waster of his substance and no savior of society but the very e reverse, all because of his folly in this respect. Well, as I just said, let this stand as our recorded conviction.

CLINIAS: By every means.

ATHENIAN: Now in a community, I take it, there must be those who govern and those who are governed?

CLINIAS: Of course there must.

690   ATHENIAN: Very good. Now what recognized titles to government and obedience, and how many, do we find alike in large cities, in small, and in families? Is there not, for one, the claim of father and mother? Or speaking generally, would it not be universally recognized that parents have a title to rule their offspring?

CLINIAS: Most assuredly.

ATHENIAN: And next by consequence that the wellborn have a title to rule the worse-born, and third, by further consequence, that it is for elder men to rule and for younger to submit?

CLINIAS: To be sure.

ATHENIAN: And fourth, that it is for slaves to submit and for b their owners to rule them?

CLINIAS: Why, of course.

ATHENIAN: And fifth, I conceive, for the stronger to rule, and for the weaker to submit?

CLINIAS: Aye, there is a title which is not to be disputed.

ATHENIAN: Yes, and one which is prevalent all through the animal kingdom—by nature's own appointment, as Pindar of Thebes has said. And sixth we may place the supreme claim of all which prescribes that it is for the ignorant to follow and for the wise men to take the lead and rule. And yet it is just this, this unforced rule of law over willing subjects, my all-accomplished Pindar, that I cannot pro- c nounce unnatural. I should call it nature's own ordinance.

CLINIAS: And you would be quite right.

ATHENIAN: Then there is a seventh kind of rule by the favor of heaven and fortune, as we say. We bring our men to a casting of lots, and call it the most equitable of arrangements that he who has the chance of the lot should rule, and he who misses it retire into the ranks of subjects.

CLINIAS: True, indeed.

ATHENIAN: You see, then, my legislator—so we might play- d fully address a man who sets lightheartedly about the enactment of laws—how many titles there are in this matter of governing, and how conflicting they are. We have just discovered a whole fountainhead of dissensions; it is yours to provide the remedy for them. But suppose you begin by joining in our inquiry about the kings of Argos and Messene. How did they effect their own ruin and that of the Hellenic power which was so superb in their day? What offense did they commit against these principles? Was not their error that they forgot the e solid truth of Hesiod's saying that 'the half is often more than the whole'? [6] He meant that when it is baneful to get the whole, but the half is sufficient, then the modestly sufficient, the better, is more than the disproportionate, the worse.

CLINIAS: He was right, too.

ATHENIAN: Now when the ruin sets in, where does it regularly make its first appearance? In kings or in the common people? How say you?

CLINIAS: Probability and common experience suggest that it is 691 the malady of kings whose luxury leads to pomp.

ATHENIAN: Plainly, then, this infection of encroachment on the established laws began, in the old days, with the kings. They did not keep concord with one another, as they were pledged and sworn to do. It was this discord—in our judgment really supreme folly, for all

---

[6] *Works and Days* 38 sq.

its semblance of wisdom—which ruined the whole system by its shrill and tuneless dissonance.

CLINIAS : Probably enough.

b   ATHENIAN : Well and good. Now what precaution should a legislator have taken at the time against the development of this symptom? God knows it is easy enough to give the answer now and takes no great wisdom to perceive it, but a prophet who could have foreseen it at the time would have been a wiser man than ourselves, would he not?

MEGILLUS : And what answer may you mean?

ATHENIAN : Why, Megillus, what should have been done then may be discovered and readily stated today if we will only look at what was done in your own society.

MEGILLUS : You must put it still more plainly.

ATHENIAN : Well, what is absolutely plain is just this.

MEGILLUS : What?

c   ATHENIAN : If we disregard due proportion by giving anything what is too much for it, too much canvas to a boat, too much nutriment to a body, too much authority to a soul, the consequence is always shipwreck; rankness runs in the one case to disease, in the other to presumption, and its issue is crime. What is it we would say, you ask. Why, my friends, surely this. No soul of man, while young or accountable to no control, will ever be able to bear the burden of supreme social authority without taking the taint of the worst spiritual

d   disease, folly, and so becoming estranged from its dearest intimates. When this happens, that soul very soon suffers ruin and the loss of all its powers. Hence it calls for a great legislator to forestall this danger by his insight into due proportion. The reasonable inference today, then, is that the danger was forestalled, but in very truth it seems there must have been . . .

MEGILLUS : What?

ATHENIAN : Some divinity in charge of you with prevision of the future, who gave you a double line of kings instead of a single, and

e   so contracted their power within more proportionate limits. Even after this a human intelligence, with some divine assistance, observed that your rulers were still in their fever fit, and so blended the tem-

692   perate authority of age with the peremptory self-will of royal lineage by giving the eight-and-twenty elders an equal voice with the kings in affairs of moment. Then a third deliverer remarked that your governing body was still swelling with mettle and introduced the office of the ephorate, an office as good as filled by lot, as a curb. This is how the monarchy of your own Laconian state came to be a mixture of the right ingredients, and acquired due limitation, with the result that it was preserved itself, and has proved the means of our general preservation.

b   For had things been left to Temenus, Cresphontes, and the legislators of that age, whoever they may have been, not even the 'portion of Aristodemus' itself would have survived. In fact, they were mere amateurs in legislative work, or they could hardly have fancied an oath a guarantee of moderation in a youthful spirit succeeding to an authority which could be converted into autocracy, but God has shown us by the event how a government should have been constituted then and must be constituted now, if it is to have good prospects of permanence. c That you and I should be able to understand this today, as I said before, is no proof of wisdom—it is always easy to see by the light of examples from the past—but had there been a man at the time with such foresight, and with the power to limit the sovereignties and make one of three, the excellent discoveries of that age would have been retained in their entirety, and contempt of our slender resources would never have launched a Persian, nor any other, armada against Hellas.

CLINIAS : Very true.

ATHENIAN : Indeed, Clinias, the repulse of those attacks was d no credit to anyone. I do not mean, when I say this, that the victories of the time, on land and sea alike, were not honorable to the victors; what I mean by calling the history discreditable is this. Only one of those three states took up arms for the defense of Hellas on the first assault; the other two were so badly corrupted that one of them even tried to hinder the efforts of Lacedaemon by vigorous hostilities against her, while the second, Argos, which had held the primacy in e the old days of the first division of the Peloponnesus, sent no answer to the appeal for aid against the foreigner, and did nothing at all. And if a man were to tell the story of that war at length, it would amount to an unseemly indictment of Hellas. In fact, Hellas could not truly be said to have made any defense. Had not the combined resolution of Athens and Lacedaemon repelled the menace of enslavement, there 693 would long ago have been a complete confusion of Hellenic stocks with one another, of barbarian with Hellenic and Hellenic with barbarian, like the wretched sporadic condition of the present dispersed and confused subjects of the Persian despotism.

This, Clinias and Megillus, is the charge I bring against the so-called statesmen and legislators of both past and present, and I bring it in the hope that examination into its causes will disclose the very different course which ought to have been taken. It was in this spirit b that I said just now that after all it is wrong to establish overpowerful or unmixed sovereignties, when we consider that a community should be at once free, sane, and at amity with itself, and that these are the ends a legislator must keep in view in his enactments. And I must ask you not to be surprised that we have already more than once proposed certain ends as those to which the legislator must look, and that our proposals have not always appeared to be identical. You must re- c flect that when we say he must look to sobriety, or again to wisdom, or to amity, these ends are not distinct but identical, and if we find ourselves using a further variety of expressions to the same effect, we must not be confused by that.

CLINIAS: We shall do our best to keep it in mind as we review our discussions. For the present, you might explain your remarks about amity, wisdom, and liberty. What is it you were going to say a
d legislator should aim at?

ATHENIAN: Then let me have your attention. There are two matrices, as we may call them, of constitutions from which all others may truly be said to be derived; the proper name of the one is monarchy, of the other democracy. The first is seen in its perfection among the Persians, the second among my own countrymen. These are the strands, as I have said, of which all other constitutions, generally speaking, are woven. Very well, it is indispensably necessary that there
e should be both ingredients where there is to be the combination of liberty and amity with wisdom. This is what our argument means to enjoin when it urges that no community which has not those characters can be rightly administered.

CLINIAS: Of course it cannot.

ATHENIAN: Well, one of the societies we have mentioned has shown exclusive and inordinate devotion to the principle of monarchy, the other to that of liberty, and thus neither has effected a proper balance between them, whereas yours of Laconia and Crete have succeeded better. There was a time when this was more or less true of Athens and Persia, but it is less true today. Shall we inquire into the causes of this or not?

694   CLINIAS: By all means, if we mean to complete our investigations.

ATHENIAN: Then lend me your ears. While the Persians steered a middle course between subjection and liberty, in the time of Cyrus, they began by winning their own freedom and went on to make themselves masters of numerous peoples. As a government they gave these subjects their share of liberty and placed them on equal terms with themselves; their soldiers thus grew attached to their commanders, and
b showed themselves forward in danger. Again, if a subject was a man of wisdom and a capable adviser, the king showed no jealousy of him, but permitted free speech and bestowed distinctions on such competent counselors, so that the gift of wisdom was freely placed at the disposal of the public service. Hence the combination of liberty with amity and generally diffused intelligence led, for the time, to all-round progress.

CLINIAS: That certainly seems to have been much the course of the history.

c   ATHENIAN: Then what can have brought about the decay under Cambyses and the general recovery under Darius? Shall we hazard a guess at the reading of the riddle?

CLINIAS: It would at least be a contribution to the study of our original problem.

ATHENIAN: Then my own present reading of Cyrus is this.

Though a good general and a true patriot, he had been wholly un-touched by right education, and had never given a thought to the dis-cipline of his household.

CLINIAS : What are we to understand by that remark?

ATHENIAN : It should seem that he spent his life, from his d
youth, in perpetual campaigning, and left the training of his sons to
the women, who treated them from their childhood as blessed crea-tures and born favorites of fortune endowed with every advantage.
They would allow no one to cross such vastly superior beings in any-thing, forced everyone to commend all their sayings and doings, and
so turned them out what you might expect.

CLINIAS : A mighty fine training, by your account of it.

ATHENIAN : Why, the training one could look for when the e
children were left to the women of a royal harem, new to affluence
and without a man to help them, thanks to perpetual preoccupation
with the wars and their dangers.

CLINIAS : That sounds reasonable, to be sure.

ATHENIAN : As for their father, he was busy winning for them
flocks and herds and drove after drove of men and other creatures, but 695
he forgot that the successors to whom he was to bequeath this wealth
were getting no training in their ancestral Persian calling, an austere
one—for the Persians, you know, were shepherds and sons of the
barren hills—well fitted to turn out sturdy shepherds, equal to the en-durance of exposure and wakefulness, and the hardships of a cam-paign too, when necessary. He shut his eyes to the way in which his
sons had been imbued by women and eunuchs with an education— b
the Median—corrupted by what is called fortune, and so they proved
what might have been anticipated from the neglect of correction in
their training. At least, when the succession fell to them, at their
father's death, they were swollen with pride and indiscipline. Camby-ses, the elder, would brook no equal, and began by making away with
his brother; then, what with strong drink and want of education, he
went out of his own wits, and lost his throne at the hands of the
Medes and the famous eunuch, who had conceived a contempt for his
folly.

CLINIAS : Certainly that is how the story runs, and it is pre- c
sumably pretty true to the facts.

ATHENIAN : And then, we are told, the throne was recovered for
the Persians by Darius and the Seven [chiefs].

CLINIAS : Exactly.

ATHENIAN : Well, let us follow up the train of thought sug-gested by our argument. Darius, you know, was no king's son, edu-cated in pride and pomp. When he came to a kingdom which he had
won with the help of six companions, he divided it into seven depart-ments, of which some faint traces are still surviving. He was satisfied
to live under laws of his own devising which introduced a certain

equality into the state; he promoted general amity and public spirit
d among the Persians by fixing, by his legislation, the tribute Cyrus had
promised them and thus won the hearts of the common people by his
liberality and munificence. Consequently his armies served with
loyalty, and won him fresh territory as extensive as that left by Cyrus.
But when Darius was gone, Xerxes, who had again received the pampering education of a prince of the blood! . . . Darius, Darius, so I
think we may righteously protest, to think you should never have
e found out the fault in Cyrus, and should have trained your Xerxes in
the same ways as he his Cambyses! . . . Xerxes, as I say, was a
product of the same kind of education, and naturally the consequence was a career of the same sort. From his time to ours,
speaking broadly, the Persians have never had a real Great King, who
has been more than nominally such. And the cause of this, on my own
theory, is not accidental; it is the evil life commonly led by the sons
of autocrats and men of extraordinary wealth. Such a training will
696 never, never lead to outstanding goodness in boy, or man, or gray-
beard. This, I maintain, is a consideration for legislators and equally
for ourselves in our present discussion. And I would remark in fairness to you Lacedaemonians as creditable to your community that you
assign no special distinction or special upbringing whatsoever to poor
man or rich man, private citizen or prince of the royal house, beyond
b what your original source of inspiration revealed on divine authority.
For assuredly special civic honors ought not to be assigned to exceptional wealth, any more than to speed of foot, beauty of form, or
strength of limb unaccompanied by goodness, or even to goodness
which does not include temperance.

MEGILLUS: How is that remark to be understood, sir?

ATHENIAN: Courage, you will grant, is one part of goodness.

MEGILLUS: To be sure it is.

ATHENIAN: Good. Then listen to my argument and decide the
point for yourself. Would you like a man of great courage who should
also be intemperate and profligate as an inmate of your house, or a
next-door neighbor?

c   MEGILLUS: Heaven forfend!

ATHENIAN: And what do you say to a man of professional
skill, and wise in that sense of the word, but unjust?

MEGILLUS: I have nothing to say to him.

ATHENIAN: And justice, again, does not flourish where temperance is not.

MEGILLUS: No, how should it?

ATHENIAN: Neither does the sort of wisdom we were lately
contemplating, that of the man whose pleasures and pains are accordant with and consequent on his right thinking.

MEGILLUS: No, decidedly not.

d   ATHENIAN: Besides, we have still a further point to consider for its bearing on the right or wrong distribution of various civic distinctions.

MEGILLUS: And what may it be?

ATHENIAN: Suppose temperance to exist in a man's soul all by itself, apart from any further goodness. Ought it, or ought it not, to be a rightful title to distinction?

MEGILLUS: That is more than I can say.

ATHENIAN: A most becoming answer. Had you said either yes or no, in either case you would have struck what I take to be a wrong note.

MEGILLUS: Then it is as well I replied as I did.

ATHENIAN: Just so. A mere adjunct to the true object of honorable distinction, or the reverse, calls for no discussion, and may well be passed over in silence.   e

MEGILLUS: By the adjunct in question, I take it you mean temperance.

ATHENIAN: I do. The truly sound procedure would be to assign the first place in honor to that other thing, be it what it may, which, combined with this adjunct, does us the chiefest service, and the second to that which serves us in the next degree. We have only to travel in the same fashion down the whole series for everything to receive its right place in the scale of distinctions.

MEGILLUS: I quite agree with you.

ATHENIAN: Well then, surely it is one part of the legislator's 697
business to construct this scale.

MEGILLUS: Most assuredly.

ATHENIAN: Then, while leaving it to him to make the construction as a whole, and in all its particulars and details, shall we try to establish a threefold division, a distinct first, second, and third class, for ourselves, who are also, in a sort, amateurs of legislation?

MEGILLUS: With all my heart.

ATHENIAN: Then I say that it is clearly an imperative duty for a society, which is minded to survive and enjoy all the felicity men b
may, to award its marks of honor and dishonor in the right way. And the right way is to put the good qualities of the soul in the first and most honorable rank—its temperance always presupposed as a *sine qua non*—advantages and good qualities of body in the second, and in the third, goods of estate, wealth, as we call them. Should any legislator or society transgress these limits by promoting wealth to honor, or giving anything of a lower class the distinctions of a higher, the act c
is an offense alike against religion and statesmanship. May we take this as our conviction?

MEGILLUS: Emphatically and absolutely, yes.

ATHENIAN: What led us into this lengthy discussion of the point was our examination of the Persian commonwealth. We find that they degenerated still further. The reason is that excessive

curtailment of the liberty of the commons, and improper intensification of autocracy, made an end of their national feeling and public
d spirit. Since their disappearance, the concern of the authorities is no
longer for their subjects, the commonalty, but for their own position;
they give over loyal cities and peoples to fire and desolation whenever
they think it of the slightest advantage to themselves, and consequently hate and are hated with savage and unrelenting animosity.
On the other side, when they need the arms of the common people for
their defense, they find no patriotism in them, no loyal readiness to
e hazard themselves in the field; in theory their forces are reckoned by
countless thousands, but all these thousands are worthless for service.
Hence they hire mercenaries and aliens, as though they had no troops
of their own, and look to them for their salvation. Moreover they are
698 forced to an exhibition of their folly, since their habitual conduct
amounts to a proclamation that all that society esteems honorable and
of good repute is a toy in comparison with gold and silver.

MEGILLUS : Exactly so.

ATHENIAN : And with this we may close our proof that the present maladministration of Persia is due to an excess of servitude and
autocracy.

MEGILLUS : Undoubtedly.

ATHENIAN : Next as to the state of Attica, we are similarly to
b show that unqualified and absolute freedom from all authority is a far
worse thing than submission to a magistrate with limited powers. In
the old days of the Persian assault on the Greeks—or perhaps I should
say on the denizens of Europe at large—my countrymen enjoyed a
venerable constitution with magistracies based on a fourfold system
of social classes. Moreover conscience had a sovereignty among us
which disposed us to willing subjection to the laws. Besides, the spectacle of the sheer magnitude of the military and naval armament
c threw us into helpless consternation, and led us to submit to laws and
magistrates with a still stricter obedience. All these causes continued
to intensify our loyalty to one another. Some ten years before the
naval engagement at Salamis, Datis arrived at the head of the Persian
armada, with express orders from Darius against the Athenians and
Eretrians; he was to capture and deport them, and had been warned
that his own life would be the price of failure. Well, Datis speedily
d effected the complete capture of the Eretrians by force of numbers,
and thus originated the alarming report which reached us in Athens.
It was said that not a man of the Eretrians escaped; in fact, the troops
of Datis joined hands and so swept the whole territory of Eretria as
with a net. True or false, whatever its source, this story appalled
the Greeks, and more particularly the Athenians; they sent out ap-
e peals for help to every quarter, but were refused by all except the
Lacedaemonians. Even they, whether under the pressure of their war
with Messene, or from some other impediment—I am not acquainted

with any statement on the point—even they, from whatever cause, arrived a day too late for the Battle at Marathon.

After Marathon there were frequent reports of vast preparations, and repeated menaces reached us from the king, and in course of time it was learned that Darius was dead and had been succeeded by his son, who was persisting in the project with all the heat of youth. The Athenians conceived the whole undertaking to be directed against them- 699 selves in reprisal for Marathon. When they heard of the canalizing of Athos, the bridging of the Hellespont, and the numbers of the enemy's flotilla, they felt that there was no escape for them by land or by sea. No support could be looked for. They remembered how they had found no supporters or allies in peril before, when the first expedition sailed to deal with Eretria, and naturally supposed that on land events would b take the same course again. On the other side, all hope of escape by sea was visibly precluded, since they had a fleet of a thousand vessels and more threatening them. There was just one chance of deliverance conceivable—faint and desperate, indeed, but still their only chance —when they looked at the past and observed how then, too, victory had appeared to emerge from the struggles of desperation. Supported by such hopes, they realized that their only refuge lay in their own right arm, and their gods. These causes combined to inspire them with c loyalty to one another—the fear aroused by their present plight, and that other fear instilled by subjection to pre-existing law, which they had learned by subjection to the existing laws—conscience, as we have called it more than once already. This, as we said, is the sovereign to whom we must submit if we are ever to become men of worth; 'tis the dastards who are emancipate from that service and immune to that fear. Had they not been terrified at the time we are speaking of, they could never have rallied for the repulse of the invader and the defense of temples, tombs, country, and all that is nearest and dearest, as in fact they did; we should have been pulverized at such a crisis and d scattered severally to all the quarters of heaven.

MEGILLUS: The observation sir, is not only perfectly just, but most becoming to yourself and your countrymen.

ATHENIAN: No doubt, Megillus, and you, who have inherited the character of your ancestors, are the right person to hear the history of those times. But I would have you and Clinias consider the relevance of my narrative to our legislation. I give it, not for the sake of the story, but for the reasons I indicate. For do but mark. Seeing that e our fate has, in a way, been the same as that of the Persians— though they reduced the commonalty to utter subjection, whereas we encouraged the multitude toward unqualified liberty—our foregoing conversation has been, in a way, very pertinent to the question what should be said next and how it should be said.

MEGILLUS: Good, but you must try to make the point of the 700 remark a little plainer.

ATHENIAN: And so I will. Under our old laws, my friends, our commons were not masters; in a sense they were the willing servants of the laws.

MEGILLUS: Of what laws are you thinking in particular?

ATHENIAN: In the first instance, if our progress in extravagant liberty of living is to be traced from its origin, of the laws of music as it was in those days. Our music was then divided into several kinds and patterns. One kind of song, which went by the name of a *hymn*,
b consisted of prayers to the gods; there was a second and contrasting kind which might well have been called a *lament; paeans* were a third kind, and there was a fourth, the *dithyramb*, as it was called, dealing, if I am not mistaken, with the birth of Dionysus. The actual word *nome* was used as the name of still another kind, though with the qualification *citharoedic*. Now these and other types were definitely fixed, and it was not permissible to misuse one kind of melody for
c another. The competence to take cognizance of these rules, to pass verdicts in accord with them, and, in case of need, to penalize their infraction was not left, as it is today, to the catcalls and discordant outcries of the crowd, nor yet to the clapping of applauders; the educated made it their rule to hear the performances through in silence, and for the boys, their attendants, and the rabble at large, there was the
d discipline of the official's rod to enforce order. Thus the bulk of the populace was content to submit to this strict control in such matters without venturing to pronounce judgment by its clamors.

Afterward, in course of time, an unmusical license set in with the appearance of poets who were men of native genius, but ignorant of what is right and legitimate in the realm of the Muses. Possessed by a frantic and unhallowed lust for pleasure, they contaminated laments with hymns and paeans with dithyrambs, actually imitated the strains
e of the flute on the harp, and created a universal confusion of forms. Thus their folly led them unintentionally to slander their profession by the assumption that in music there is no such thing as a right and a wrong, the right standard of judgment being the pleasure given to the hearer, be he high or low. By compositions of such a kind and discourse to the same effect, they naturally inspired the multitude with
701 contempt of musical law, and a conceit of their own competence as judges. Thus our once silent audiences have found a voice, in the persuasion that they understand what is good and bad in art; the old 'sovereignty of the best' in that sphere has given way to an evil 'sovereignty of the audience.' If the consequence had been even a democracy, no great harm would have been done, so long as the democracy was confined to art, and composed of free men. But, as things are with us, music has given occasion to a general conceit of universal knowledge and contempt for law, and liberty has followed in their train. Fear was cast out by confidence in supposed knowledge, and the loss of it
b gave birth to impudence. For to be unconcerned for the judgment of

one's betters in the assurance which comes of a reckless excess of liberty is nothing in the world but reprehensible impudence.

MEGILLUS: Very true.

ATHENIAN: So the next stage of the journey toward liberty will be refusal to submit to the magistrates, and on this will follow emancipation from the authority and correction of parents and elders; then, as the goal of the race is approached, comes the effort to escape obedience to the law, and, when that goal is all but reached, contempt for oaths, for the plighted word, and all religion. The spectacle of the c Titanic nature of which our old legends speak is re-enacted; man returns to the old condition of a hell of unending misery. Now, once more, why have we said all this? I think we should rein in our argument from time to time. We must not let it run away with us, as though it had no curb in its mouth, and so, as the proverb says, lose our seat in the saddle. No, as I was saying, we must be constantly d asking ourselves why we have said what we have.

MEGILLUS: To be sure.

ATHENIAN: Well then, I said it for its relevance to what had gone before.

MEGILLUS: And what was that?

ATHENIAN: Why, I said a legislator should have three aims in his enactments—the society for which he makes them must have freedom, must have amity with itself, must have understanding. That, I believe, was our position.

MEGILLUS: Exactly.

ATHENIAN: This was why we took the examples of the most e autocratic of communities and the freest, and are now asking ourselves in which of the two public life is what it should be. We found that when we had a certain due proportionality in either case, in the one of authority, in the other of liberty, there was a maximum of well-being in both societies, whereas when things were pushed to an extreme in either case, an extreme of subjection in the one, and of its opposite in the other, the consequences were unsatisfactory in both societies alike.

MEGILLUS: Very true.   702

ATHENIAN: It was for the same purpose that we reviewed the settlement of the Dorian invaders, the foundation of Dardanus in the foothills, and that of the city on the coast, and even the life of the first survivors of the Deluge. Our earlier conversations about music and drinking, and all that preceded them, were equally to the same end. The purport of the whole discourse has been to learn how a society is best administered and how a man will best conduct his per- b sonal life. But have we achieved any result? I would ask you both, Megillus and Clinias, what test we can propose to ourselves.

CLINIAS: Why, sir, I believe I can find one. I fancy there has been something providential in the whole course of our argument; in

fact, I find myself just now in a position in which it meets my needs well, and both your appearance and that of our friend Megillus are
c most opportune. So far from hiding my situation from you, I even count your presence a favorable omen. You must know that the largest part of Crete is undertaking the foundation of a colony, and has charged the Cnossians with the management of the business, which has been entrusted by the authorities of Cnossus to myself and nine others. Our instructions are further to frame a legislation from such local Cretan laws as have our approval, or laws from other quarters; we are not to concern ourselves about their foreign origin, so long as we judge them superior. Suppose then we serve my turn and yours at
d once; let us use a selection from our results for the theoretical construction of a society, which we will imagine we are founding from the very start. The procedure will disclose the object of our search, and, at the same time, I may find our construction useful for the society that is to be.

ATHENIAN: No declaration of hostilities that, Clinias! If Megillus has no objections to offer, I, for one, promise compliance to the best of my ability.

CLINIAS: Thank you.

MEGILLUS: And so do I for another.

e CLINIAS: My best thanks to both of you. Well, let us begin by trying to imagine the foundation of the city.

BOOK IV

704 ATHENIAN: Good, then, what must we suppose our state is to be? I do not mean that I am asking what its name is at present, or by what name it will have to be called hereafter. That might well come from the circumstances of the foundation or the locality, or the appellation of some river, or fountain, or local divinities might confer their own
b revered title on the city in its earliest days. What I am more concerned about in my question is this. Is the site maritime or inland?

CLINIAS: Why, sir, the city of which I was just speaking is some eighty stadia, more or less, from the coast.

ATHENIAN: Well, and are there harbors on that side of it, or is it entirely without a harbor?

CLINIAS: By no means, sir. The coast on that side is as well furnished with harbors as a coast can be.

c ATHENIAN: Tut, tut! How distressing! And what about the surrounding territory? Does it yield produce of all sorts, or has it its deficiencies?

CLINIAS: None to speak of.

ATHENIAN: Is there a neighboring city within easy distance?

CLINIAS: Dear me, no. That is the very reason for the settlement. There was long ago an emigration from the district which has left this territory vacant for ages.

ATHENIAN: What about plainland, mountain, and forest? Pray, d
how is it furnished in all these respects?

CLINIAS: Much like the rest of Crete in general.

ATHENIAN: You mean it is rugged rather than level?

CLINIAS: Decidedly so.

ATHENIAN: Then its case, from the point of view of the acquisition of goodness, is not desperate. Had it to be on the coast, well
furnished with harbors and ill off for many of its necessaries, not productive of all, we should need a mighty protector and lawgivers who
were more than men to prevent the development of much refined vice
in consequence of such a situation. As it is, there is comfort in those
eighty stadia. Even so, the site is nearer to the sea than it should be,
all the more as you say it is well provided with a harbor. Still, we 705
ought to be thankful for even so much. It is agreeable enough to have
the sea at one's door in daily life, but, for all that, it is, in very truth, a
briny and bitter neighbor. It fills a city with wholesale traffic and retail
huckstering, breeds shifty and distrustful habits of soul, and so makes
a society distrustful and unfriendly within itself as well as toward
mankind at large. In view of this situation, there is further comfort,
however, in the universal productiveness of our site. Clearly, since it
is so rugged, it cannot at once produce everything and yield much of b
anything. Were that the case, there would be the opportunity for exportation on a large scale, and, once more, our city would abound with
currency in gold and silver. Now, all things considered, nothing is a
more serious impediment to the development of noble and righteous
character in a society, as you may recollect that we have already said.

CLINIAS: We well recollect the remark and agree with you now,
as we did before, about its truth.

ATHENIAN: Then, as to a further point, how is our territory c
supplied with materials for shipbuilding?

CLINIAS: It has neither fir nor pine to speak of, and not much
in the way of cypress. As for the kinds of wood which, as you know,
builders regularly require for the interior of boats, larch and plane,
there is a little of them to be found.

ATHENIAN: That again is not a bad feature in the topography.

CLINIAS: How so?

ATHENIAN: It is just as well that a society should have a difficulty in copying the practice of its antagonists to its own undoing.   d

CLINIAS: Now which of our results have you in view when you
say that?

ATHENIAN: Why, my dear sir, I would have you watch my
procedure in the light of our opening observations about the single
object of your Cretan institutions. You both affirmed more precisely
that this object is military, whereas I rejoined that it is right enough
that goodness should be the object of such institutions, but could not
quite concede that their aim should be some part of goodness short of
the whole. It is now the turn of both of you to follow me in my e

proposals, taking care that I enjoin nothing which does not tend to goodness, or some part of goodness.

706   I take it as a postulate from the outset that a law is rightly enacted only when its aim is exclusively directed on that object of all others which is steadily and invariably attended by some worthy result, to the disregard of every other end whatsoever, be it wealth or anything else of the sort, divorced from the objects I have specified. And as for the pernicious imitation of an antagonist to which I referred, this is how it comes about in the case of a maritime population harassed by an enemy. Minos, for example—and I tell the story without any vindictive feeling against your countrymen, Clinias—Minos, in fact,
b once laid Attica under a cruel tribute, thanks to his strength at sea. His victims had as yet no men-of-war such as they have today, nor yet was their territory rich in timber suitable for the facile construction of a navy. So they could not imitate his seamen by turning sailors themselves and promptly repelling the invader out of hand. Had the case been so, it would have been better for them to lose many times
c seven youths than to convert themselves from steady infantrymen into marines, with the marines' tricks of repeated descents followed by a helter-skelter retreat to the boats, their notion that there is nothing discreditable in shuffling out of dying at one's post when the enemy attacks, and their plausible and ready excuses for throwing down their arms and betaking themselves to 'flight without dishonor,' as it is called. Phrases like this are the normal consequences of employing men-at-arms on shipboard, and what they call for is not infinite com-
d mendation, but the very reverse. Men should never be trained to evil ways—least of all, the best element in the community. That the practice in question is ignoble might actually have been learned, I take it, from Homer, whose Odysseus upbraids Agamemnon for directing the ships to be drawn down to the water's edge when the Achaeans were hard pressed by the Trojans. What Odysseus says by way of remonstrance is this.

e   When thou biddest draw down the fair-benched ships to the sea while the battle and din encompass us, that the Trojans, fain as they are, may have their desire yet more fulfilled, and sheer destruction fall on ourselves. For when the ships are drawing seaward the Achaeans will not cleave to the battle, but look askance from it and flinch from the onset; then will
707 counsel such as thou givest prove our bane.[7]

      Thus, you see, Homer was too well aware what a bad thing it is is for infantry in an engagement to be supported by a line of men-of-war. Why, lions would learn to run from deer if trained in habits like these. Not to add that states which owe their power to a navy also bestow the reward for their security on an inferior element of their

[7] *Iliad* 14.96 sq.

forces. As they owe the security to the arts of the sea captain, the b
lieutenant, the oarsman, and to a miscellaneous and not overreputa-
ble crowd, there is no possibility of awarding honors aright to the
various individuals. Yet where this is excluded, how can the state
continue unimpaired?

CLINIAS: It is hardly possible it should. And yet, sir, it was the
sea fight at Salamis between Hellenes and non-Hellenes which was the
salvation of Hellas—or so, at least, we say here in Crete.

ATHENIAN: To be sure that is what mankind at large say,
Greeks or otherwise. But we—that is to say, Megillus here and myself c
—insist that the deliverance of Hellas was begun by one engagement
on land, that at Marathon, and completed by another, that at Plataea.
Moreover these victories made better men of the Hellenes, whereas
the others did not, if such language is permissible about actions which
contributed to the deliverance of those times. You see I am ready to
throw you in the naval engagement at Artemisium along with the
action at Salamis. The fact is, the object we are keeping in view in our
present investigations into topography and legislation is the moral
worth of a social system; we do not agree with the multitude that the d
most precious thing in life is bare preservation in existence. We hold,
as I think we have said before, that it is better to become thoroughly
good and to remain so as long as existence lasts.

CLINIAS: Surely, surely.

ATHENIAN: Then the one and only point we have to consider is
whether our treatment of settlements and legal enactments is following the same lines—the best for a society.

CLINIAS: Indeed far the best.

ATHENIAN: Then tell me, in the next place, what is the popula- e
tion for which you are to construct a settlement? Is it made up of
volunteers from all parts of Crete—the masses in the various communities presumably having grown too great for the local food supply?
For you are not, I take it, collecting applicants from Hellas at large,
though I do observe that contingents from Argos, Aegina, and other 708
Hellenic districts have settled in your country. But pray tell me from
what quarter you expect the present host of citizens now to be dealt
with.

CLINIAS: They will most likely come from all over Crete. Of
other Hellenes, Peloponnesians seem to have had the warmest welcome as settlers. In fact, it is true, as you were just saying, that we
have emigrants from Argos among us, and among them the most distinguished of our societies of the present day, that of Gortyn; it is an
offshoot from the well-known Gortyn in the Peloponnesus.

ATHENIAN: Well, it is not such an easy matter for a state to b
deal with a settlement when it is not formed, like a swarm of bees, by
the emigration of a single stock from a single territory, with friendly
feeling on both sides, under the stress of insufficient territory, or the

pressure of some similar necessity. Sometimes, again, one section of a community may be driven to expatriate itself by the violence of party strife, and there has been the case of a whole society going into exile because it had been utterly crushed by an overwhelming attack. Now
c in one way the work of settlement and legislation is the easier in all these cases, but in another the harder. The unity of descent, speech, and institutions certainly promotes friendly feeling, since it involves the community in religious ceremonies and the like, but is not readily tolerant of novel laws or a constitution different from that of the homeland, while a group which has, perhaps, been driven into faction by the badness of the laws, yet still clings, from force of habit, to the very practices which had already led to its undoing, proves recalcitrant to
d the founder and his legislation, and refuses obedience. On the other side, a stock due to a confluence of various elements may perhaps be more willing to submit to novel laws, but it is a difficult business, and takes a long time for it to 'breathe and blow in unison,' as the proverbial phrase has it of a pair of horses. No, in very truth to make a legislation or found a society is the perfect consummation of manly excellence.

CLINIAS : No doubt, but you might explain the point of the remark a little more clearly.
e ATHENIAN : Why, my dear man, I suspect my reiterated reflections about legislators will lead me to say something which is partly derogatory; still, if the remark is pertinent, no harm will be done. After all, why should I scruple at it; it is much what might be said about all human concerns.
709 CLINIAS : What is it you have in your mind?

ATHENIAN : I was on the brink of saying that man never legislates at all; our legislation is always the work of chance and infinitely various circumstance. Constitutions are wrecked and laws revolutionized by the violence of war, or the helplessness of sheer destitution. Again, innovations are often forced on us by disease, in the case of the visitations of pestilence, or of protracted and recurrent periods of insalubrious weather. In view of such facts one might be
b moved to say, as I have just done, that no law is ever made by a man, and that human history is all an affair of chance. Still, the same thing may be said with apparent plausibility of seafaring, navigation, medicine, or strategy, and yet there is something else which may also be said with no less plausibility of them all.

CLINIAS : And what is that?

ATHENIAN : That God is all, while chance and circumstance, under God, set the whole course of life for us, and yet we must allow
c for the presence of a third and more amenable partner, skill. Thus I should count it no small advantage that the navigator's skill should cooperate with circumstance in a tempest, would not you?

CLINIAS: Naturally.

ATHENIAN: Now the same thing will hold good for the other cases, and so we should make the same admission in the case of legislation. Granting the concurrence of the local conditions necessary for a fortunate settlement, such a community necessarily presupposes the appearance of a true legislator.

CLINIAS: Beyond all doubt.

ATHENIAN: Thus one who has the skill called for by any of the d contingencies we have mentioned will also know well enough what form of fortune to pray for, that he may be dependent on nothing further besides his own skill.

CLINIAS: To be sure.

ATHENIAN: And any of the other professionals we have mentioned could, no doubt, tell us, if we asked them, what it is they are praying for?

CLINIAS: Of course.

ATHENIAN: And presumably, then, a legislator could do so, too.

CLINIAS: Presumably.

ATHENIAN: Come, then, legislator—let us so apostrophize him —what must we give you—I mean what social conditions—if their e provision is to make you competent to model your society for the rest by your own efforts?

CLINIAS: Now I wonder what *is* the right reply.

ATHENIAN: You understand we are speaking in the name of the legislator?

CLINIAS: Yes.

ATHENIAN: Then here is the answer. Give me a society, he will say, which is under an autocrat, but let that autocrat be young, of retentive memory, quick to learn, and temperamentally bold and high-souled. Also, if all these advantages are to be of any service, they must be further attended in the autocrat's soul by something we have already mentioned as an indispensable accompaniment of all the parts 710 of goodness.

CLINIAS: I think, Megillus, what our friend means by this accompaniment is temperance. Am I right, sir?

ATHENIAN: Yes, Clinias, temperance in the popular sense of the word, not in that high and forced sense in which temperance might be said to be the same thing with wisdom. 'Tis a native surface quality which shows in mere children and animals that some of them have no self-restraint in the matter of pleasures, and others have—a quality, as we said, of no great account when divorced from the vari- b ous other goods. You take me, no doubt?

CLINIAS: Why, certainly.

ATHENIAN: Very well, our autocrat must have that endowment as well as all those we have named, if the society is to achieve the constitution which will bring felicity into its life with maximum speed and success. I assure you there neither is, nor can be, any better and more rapid way to the settlement of the constitution.

c   CLINIAS: Nay, sir, how or by what argument can a man possibly persuade himself of the truth of such a doctrine?

ATHENIAN: Why, surely, Clinias, it is easy enough to see how natural it is that it should be so.

CLINIAS: What is the theory, once more? There is to be an autocrat, you say, and he must be young, temperate, quick to learn, retentive, bold, and high-souled?

ATHENIAN: And, you must add, fortunate—fortunate, that is, in the single point that there is a contemporary legislator of distinction d with whom chance has brought him in contact. With that one coincidence, God has done his utmost toward his purpose of heaping blessings on a community. The next-best thing would be that there should be a pair of such potentates; it would be third best, and so on proportionately more difficult, the more of them there were, and vice versa.

CLINIAS: The best state, as I understand you, might arise out of an autocracy, provided, that is, there were a consummate legislator and an autocrat of disciplined character, and the transition to it would e be particularly easy and rapid in that case, less so from an oligarchy— is not that your meaning—and still less from a democracy?

ATHENIAN: By no means. The readiest starting point would be autocracy, the next-best, constitutional monarchy, the next-best again, democracy of a kind; oligarchy would come fourth, and only admits of such a development with great difficulty, for there the number of persons of influence is greatest. The occasion for it, mark you, is provided, according to us, when nature produces a real legislator who happens 711 to share power of a kind with the most influential persons in society. Where, as in an autocracy, this latter element is numerically fewest but strongest, you have the normal occasion and opportunity for facile and speedy revolution.

CLINIAS: What? This is more than we can follow.

ATHENIAN: Yet the point has been made, unless I am mistaken, more than once already. But perhaps you and your friend have never observed a society under an autocrat.

CLINIAS: And I must say I have no particular desire to do so, either.

b   ATHENIAN: If you did, you would certainly remark the presence of the feature I first spoke of.

CLINIAS: What feature?

ATHENIAN: An autocrat who desires to make a change in the tone of public life has no laborious or protracted task. He has only to take in his own person the first steps on the road—be it the path to virtue or to vice—into which he would guide the community. He c must first set the copy of his own conduct, awarding credit and distinctions to one course, discredit to another, and disgracing the refractory in the various departments of conduct.

CLINIAS: But why should you suppose that the rest of society will be so quick to follow the example of the wielder of this combined persuasion and coercion?

ATHENIAN: O my friends, never let yourselves be persuaded that there is any speedier or easier way to change the laws of a community than the personal guidance of those in authority; there is none today, and will be none hereafter. No, it is not there that we shall find the impossibility or difficulty; the true difficulty lies in the occurrence d of something which has been uncommon enough in the whole course of history, but never happens without bringing a whole infinity of blessings to the society in which it occurs.

CLINIAS: Now I wonder what this may be.

ATHENIAN: The awakening of a heaven-sent passion for ways of temperance and justice in persons of the highest station, monarchs, for example, or men of exceptionally outstanding wealth or family, or, it may be, in one who recalls the qualities of Nestor who is said e to have towered above all his contemporaries even more by his temperance than by his eloquence. That happened, we are told, in Trojan times, though it has never been known in our own. Be that as it may, if such a man there has been, or should be hereafter, or is now among us, how blessed is his own life, and how blessed they who hearken to the words which proceed from those virtuous lips! We may say the same of power in all its forms. When supreme power is combined in 712 one person with wisdom and temperance, then, and on no other conditions conceivable, nature gives birth to the best of constitutions with the best of laws. So you may take these oracular remarks as a parable embodying the proof that though in one way it is hard for a society to get good laws, in another, if things only fall out as I say, it would be the quickest and easiest of all developments.

CLINIAS: But why so?

ATHENIAN: Suppose we apply the parable to your city and try to model its laws in imagination, like elderly men playing a boys' b game.

CLINIAS: En avant, then, and a truce to all delays!

ATHENIAN: Of course we must invoke God's presence at our foundation. So may he hear us and come, gracious and debonair, to our help as we construct our city and its laws!

CLINIAS: Amen to that!

ATHENIAN: And pray what type of constitution are we proposing to impose on our society?

CLINIAS: But what do you mean by that question? You should c put it a little more plainly. You mean, is it to be a democracy, an oligarchy, an aristocracy, or a monarchy? You surely cannot be thinking of an autocracy, or at least my friend and I can hardly credit it.

ATHENIAN: Come now, which of those names describes your own constitution? I wonder which of you will be the readier with his answer.

MEGILLUS: As I am the elder man, perhaps it would be fairer that I should speak first?

d   CLINIAS: Yes, I think so.

MEGILLUS: Why, sir, when I consider our Lacedaemonian constitution, I really cannot tell you offhand which would be the proper name for it. It actually seems to have its resemblances to an autocracy —in fact, the power of our ephors is astonishingly autocratic—and yet at times I think it looks like the most democratic of all societies.

e Again, it would be sheer paradox to deny that it is an aristocracy, while yet again a feature of it is a life monarchy, asserted by all mankind, as well as ourselves, to be the very oldest of such institutions. When the question is put to me, like this, on a sudden, as I say, I really cannot tell definitely to which of these types of constitution it belongs.

CLINIAS: I find myself in the same perplexity as you, Megillus. I am quite at a loss to identify our Cnossian constitution confidently with any of them.

ATHENIAN: That, my friends, is because you enjoy real constitutions, whereas the types we have specified are not constitutions, but

713 settlements enslaved to the domination of some component section, each taking its designation from the dominant factor. But if a society must take its name from such a quarter, the proper course is to call it by the name of the god who is the master of rational men.

CLINIAS: And what god is that?

ATHENIAN: Perhaps we may need to employ parable a little longer, if I am to answer the question to your full satisfaction.

CLINIAS: Oh, so that is the way we must proceed, is it?

ATHENIAN: Certainly. Why, long before the time of the socie-
b ties whose foundation we have discussed, in the age of Cronus—so they say—there was a much earlier form of settled government, and a very happy one, which is reflected in the best of our present-day communities.

CLINIAS: Then, I should say, we must very decidedly be told about it.

ATHENIAN: Certainly, in my own judgment, and that is the very reason why I have brought it into the argument.

CLINIAS: Very properly, too, and, seeing how relevant it is,
c you will do right to tell the whole story.

ATHENIAN: I must do as you propose. Well, according to the received tradition, in that age of bliss, all life needs was provided in abundance and unsought, and the reason, we are told, was this. Cronus was of course aware that, as we have explained, no human being is competent to wield an irresponsible control over mankind without becoming swollen with pride and unrighteousness. Being alive to this

he gave our communities as their kings and magistrates, not men but
spirits, beings of diviner and superior kind, just as we still do the same d
with our flocks of sheep and herds of other domesticated animals. We
do not set oxen to manage oxen, or goats to manage goats; we, their
betters in kind, act as their masters ourselves. Well, the god, in his
kindness to man, did the same; he set over us this superior race of
spirits who took charge of us with no less ease to themselves than convenience to us, providing us with peace and mercy, sound law and e
unscanted justice, and endowing the families of mankind with internal concord and happiness. So the story teaches us today, and teaches
us truly, that when a community is ruled not by God but by man, its
members have no refuge from evil and misery. We should do our utmost—this is the moral—to reproduce the life of the age of Cronus,
and therefore should order our private households and our public so- 714
cieties alike in obedience to the immortal element within us, giving
the name of law to the appointment of understanding. But when a
single person, an oligarchy, or a democracy with a soul set on its pleasures and passions and lusting for its satisfaction—a soul that cannot
contain itself, and is in the grip of unending and insatiate disease—
when such a one tramples law under his feet and takes command of
an individual or society, then, as I was just saying, all hope of deliverance is gone. That is my thesis, Clinias, and we have to consider b
whether it convinces us or not.

CLINIAS: Convinces us? Of course it does.

ATHENIAN: Then are you acquainted with a theory that there
are as many types of law as of constitution? And we have just seen
how many types of constitution there are in the popular view. And
pray believe me that the issue now at stake is no trifle, but of paramount moment. We are back again at the question of the standard of
right and wrong. The standard of our laws, it is said, should be neither
war nor a goodness as a whole. Whatever the existing constitution c
may be, the law should look to its interest, its permanent security
against dissolution, and the best way to define real justice would be
to say . . .

CLINIAS: To say what?

ATHENIAN: That it is the interest of the sovereign.

CLINIAS: You must explain yourself rather more clearly.

ATHENIAN: And so I will. They say, you know, that the laws
in a society are always enacted by the dominant section?

CLINIAS: Just so.

ATHENIAN: Well then, it is said, can you imagine that when d
the populace, or some other political party, or an autocrat, if you like,
has got the upper hand, the victorious side will, of its own accord, enact laws with any principal aim but its own interest in the permanence
of its authority?

CLINIAS: Of course not.

ATHENIAN: And if a man contravenes these enactments, their author will punish him for his violation of justice, meaning by justice these same enactments.

CLINIAS: So I should apprehend.

ATHENIAN: These enactments, then, will in every case be justice, and for these reasons.

CLINIAS: Yes, according to this account of the matter.

e ATHENIAN: In fact, this is one of our former principles of sovereignty.

CLINIAS: Principles? What principles?

ATHENIAN: Why, the claims to authority which we passed under review. We found parents claiming authority over their descendants, the older men over the younger, the wellborn over the baseborn, and you may remember that there were several other mutually incompatible claims. This was actually one of the list, and we remarked that Pindar treats the 'high hand of violence'—to use his own phrase —as natural justice.

715 CLINIAS: Yes, that is certainly what we said before.

ATHENIAN: Now consider to which side we are to entrust our society. For here is a situation which has recurred over and over again in public life before now.

CLINIAS: What situation is that?

ATHENIAN: After a contest for office, the victorious side engrosses the conduct of public affairs so completely to itself that no share whatsoever of office is left to the vanquished, or even to their b descendants; each party watches the other in jealous apprehension of insurrection, due to the attainment of office by someone with memories of past wrongs. Such societies, we are now, of course, contending, are no constitutional states, just as enactments, so far as they are not for the common interest of the whole community, are no true laws; men who are for a party, we say, are factionaries, not citizens, and their so-called rights are empty words. And our reason for saying it is that you and I have no intention of conferring an office in your society on anyone for his wealth, or his possession of some similar c advantage, such as physical strength, stature, or family. It is, we hold, the man who is most perfect in obedience to established law, the man whose victory over his fellow citizens takes that form, to whom we should give the function of ministry to the gods, the highest post to him who stands first, the second to him who is next in the contest— the remaining posts being assigned similarly to the succeeding candidates in order. If I have just styled the so-called authorities *ministers* d of the law, it is not for the sake of a novel phrase, but because I am persuaded that the preservation or ruin of a society depends on this more than on anything else. Where the law is overruled or obsolete, I see destruction hanging over the community; where it is sovereign

over the authorities and they its humble servants, I discern the presence of salvation and every blessing heaven sends on a society.

CLINIAS: Right, sir, right in God's name! You have the long
sight of your years.

ATHENIAN: Why, yes, a man is always most shortsighted in
such matters in youth, and most farsighted in age.   e

CLINIAS: Yes, indeed.

ATHENIAN: Well, and our next step? May we not assume our
settlers to be here in the country and under our eyes, and address the
rest of our discourse to them in person?

CLINIAS: By all means.

ATHENIAN: My friends!—this is what I would say to them—
God, who, as the old saw has it, holds in his hands beginning, end, and
middle of all that is, moves through the cycle of nature, straight to   716
his end, and ever at his side walks right, the justicer of them that forsake God's law. He that would be happy follows close in her train with
lowly and chastened mien, but whoso is lifted up with vanity—with
pride of riches or rank or foolish conceit of youthful comeliness—and
all on fire within with wantonness, as one that needs neither governor
nor guide, but is fitted rather to be himself a guide to others—such a   b
one is left alone, forsaken of God. In his abandonment he takes to him
others like himself, and works general confusion by his frantic career.
Now to some he seems to be some great one, but after no long while
he makes no stinted amend to right by the sheer ruin of himself, his
house, and his state. Now since these things are so, what must the
man of judgment do or purpose, and what forbear?

CLINIAS: So much is plain; every man must purpose to be of
the company who follow after the god.

ATHENIAN: What line of conduct, then, is dear to God and a   c
following of him? There is but one, and it is summed up in one ancient
rule, the rule that 'like'—when it is a thing of due measure—'loves its
like.' For things that have no measure can be loved neither by one another nor by those that have. Now it is God who is, for you and me, of
a truth the 'measure of all things,' much more truly than, as they say,
'man.' So he who would be loved by such a being must himself become
such to the utmost of his might, and so, by this argument, he that is
temperate among us is loved by God, for he is like God, whereas he   d
that is not temperate is unlike God and at variance with him; so also
it is with the unjust, and the same rule holds in all else. Now from this
rule, I would have you note, follows another—of all rules, to my mind,
the grandest and truest, which is this. For the good man 'tis most
glorious and good and profitable to happiness of life, aye, and most
excellently fit, to do sacrifice and be ever in communion with heaven
through prayer and offerings and all manner of worship, but for the
evil, entirely the contrary. For the evil man is impure of soul, where   e

the other is pure, and from the polluted neither good men nor God
may ever rightly accept a gift; thus all this toil taken with heaven is
717 but labor thrown away for the impious, though ever seasonable in the
pious.

Here, then, is the target at which we have to aim, but what shall
we call the shafts which make straight for it, and the engine from
which they are fired? Well, first, I say, the mark of godliness will be
truly hit if the gods of the lower world are held in honor next to the
Olympians, and the patron deities of the state, the even, the second
b best, and the left hand being consecrated to them, their superior
counterparts to the powers which have just been named. After these
gods a man of judgment will do worship to spirits, and after them to
heroes, and I would give the next place to each man's images of his
household gods, worshiped as the law directs.

And now we come to honor to be shown to parents while they are
yet in life. Here religion demands the due discharge of this earliest
and heaviest debt, the most sacred of all our obligations. It bids a man
c count all he has and owns at the service of those who gave him birth
and breeding, to minister to their needs to his utmost ability, first with
his substance, then with his body, and then with his mind, in repay-
ment of a loan of care and painful labor made so long ago on the security of his youth, and now to be made good to his elders in their age
and sore necessity. Moreover, all his life through, a man should ob-
d serve particular reverence of tongue toward his parents, for light and
winged speech brings heavy doom; right has her appointed messenger, Nemesis, to keep watch over the matter. So one should yield to
them when they feel anger, and discharge it, in word or deed, and understand that 'tis but natural in a father who thinks himself wronged
by his son to be moved to uncommon anger. But when parents are
once no more, the most modest burial is the best. A man should not
exceed the customary pomps, nor yet come short of those wherewith
e his forefathers were wont to entomb their own sires; he should keep
also to the same rule in paying the decent annual rites of tendance to
the departed. Above all, he should honor the deceased at all times by
718 keeping the memory of them green, while he expends on them what is
proportionate to the means fortune permits him. If we act thus and
frame our lives to this model, we shall, one and all, always reap the
due reward from heaven and the higher powers, and our days, for the
main of life, will be passed with bright hopes. As regards duties to
children and kinsmen, friends and fellow citizens, as well as works of
pious service to strangers, and our relations with them all, by dis-
b charge whereof, as the law enjoins, a man should adorn and illustrate
his life—in all this the actual recital of the laws will, with heaven's
consent, ensure our society bliss and well-being, in part by persuasion, and in part by enforced and legal correction of characters not
amenable to persuasion.

There are other things, too, which should be said and must be said by a legislator like-minded with myself, and yet cannot be fittingly said in the form of a statute. As to these I would advise him, when he has finished the rest of his discourse to the best of his power, to pro- pound a sample to himself and those for whom he is to legislate be- c fore he enters on his actual enactments. In what form, then, is such matter best couched? To confine it all within the bounds of a single outline, as I might call it, is none too easy; still, we may be able to reach a definite result if we look at the matter in some such way as this.

CLINIAS : And what result may that be?

ATHENIAN : I should wish the subjects to give a ready audience to persuasions to virtue, and plainly this is the effect at which our legislator will aim throughout his legislation.

CLINIAS : Of course.   d

ATHENIAN : Well, it struck me that what we have said might do some service—if our words have not been an appeal to utterly bru- tal souls—toward gaining a civil and friendly hearing. So, as I say, if it makes an auditor a little, even if ever so little, more friendly, and so readier to be instructed, we have every reason to be thankful. Men earnestly bent on becoming thoroughly good, and that with all speed, are not easily to be found, nor in large numbers, and Hesiod is com- monly pronounced a wise man for his saying that 'the path to vice is e smooth,' and, being so short, can be traveled without sweat, whereas 'before virtue the immortal gods have set sweat, and the road thither is long and uphill and rough at the outset, though when the summit 719 is reached, the going is easy, for all its hardness.' [8]

CLINIAS : And a fine saying it is, too.

ATHENIAN : Yes, no doubt. But I should like to propose to your common consideration the effect our foregoing argument has pro- duced on myself.

CLINIAS : Then let us hear it.

ATHENIAN : Well, let us address our remarks to the legislator, thus. Tell us one thing, legislator. If you knew what we ought to do b and say, you would tell us what it is. Surely that is manifest?

CLINIAS : Of course it is.

ATHENIAN : Well, but did we not hear you not so long ago pro- nouncing that a legislator must not permit poets to compose whatever they please? For they are not likely to know where they may contra- dict the law to the detriment of the society.

CLINIAS : I must admit that it is the fact.

ATHENIAN : Then suppose we put the case for the poets to him. I wonder whether it might fairly be stated thus.

CLINIAS : How?

[8] *Works and Days* 287 sq.

c ATHENIAN: As follows. 'Tis an old story, legislator, which we poets are always telling with the universal approval of the rest of the world, that when a poet takes his seat on the Muse's tripod, his judgment takes leave of him. He is like a fountain which gives free course to the rush of its waters, and since representation is of the essence of his art, must often contradict his own utterances in his presentations of contrasted characters, without knowing whether the truth is on the d side of this speaker or of that. Now it is not the legislator's business in his law to make two such statements about one and the same topic; he has regularly to deliver himself of one pronouncement on one matter. Take, as an example, one of the very topics on which you have just delivered yourself. A funeral may be extravagant, it may be mean, it may be decently modest. You select one and only one of those types, the intermediate type, for universal imposition and unrestricted commendation. But, in my case, if my poem dealt with an opulent woman and her instructions for her own funeral, I should commend e extravagance, whereas a frugal poor man would be for parsimony, and a man of moderate estate and modest personality would have the same preference as yourself. But in your position it is not enough to use the word 'moderate,' as you did just now; you must tell us what and how much is moderate, or else confess that your statement is not yet a law.

CLINIAS: Truly said, indeed.

ATHENIAN: Then is our appointed lawmaker to set no such prefatory statement in front of his code? Is he just to tell us curtly what we are to do or not to do, add the threat of a penalty, and then 720 turn to the next enactment, without one word of exhortation or advice to the recipients? Just as one type of physician treats us, when we call him in, in one way, and a second in another—but let us remind ourselves of the difference between the two methods, and then we shall have a request to make of our legislator, as children might beg their physician to give them the gentlest treatment. You would like an illustration? Well, there are physicians, and again there are physicians' assistants, whom we also speak of as physicians.

b CLINIAS: Just so.

ATHENIAN: All bear the name, whether free men or slaves who gain their professional knowledge by watching their masters and obeying their directions in empirical fashion, not in the scientific way in which free men learn their art and teach it to their pupils. You agree that there are those two types of so-called physicians?

CLINIAS: Certainly I do.

ATHENIAN: Now have you further observed that, as there are c slaves as well as free men among the patients of our communities, the slaves, to speak generally, are treated by slaves, who pay them a hurried visit, or receive them in dispensaries? A physician of this kind never gives a servant any account of his complaint, nor asks him for any; he gives him some empirical injunction with an air of finished knowledge, in the brusque fashion of a dictator, and then is off in hot haste to the next ailing servant—that is how he lightens his master's medical labors for him. The free practitioner, who, for the most part, **d** attends free men, treats their diseases by going into things thoroughly from the beginning in a scientific way, and takes the patient and his family into his confidence. Thus he learns something from the sufferers, and at the same time instructs the invalid to the best of his powers. He does not give his prescriptions until he has won the patient's support, and when he has done so, he steadily aims at producing complete restoration to health by persuading the sufferer into **e** compliance. Now which of the two methods is that of the better physician or director of bodily regimen? That which effects the same result by a twofold process or that which employs a single process, the worse of the two, and exasperates its subject?

CLINIAS : Nay, sir, the double process is vastly superior.

ATHENIAN : Then would you like us to consider the two methods, the double and the single, in their application to legislation itself?

CLINIAS : To be sure I should.

ATHENIAN : Then, I ask you, what will be the first law our legis- **721** lator will enact? Is not his natural course to begin with an ordinance regulating the first stage in the creation of a society?

CLINIAS : Why, of course.

ATHENIAN : And the first stage in the creation of any society is surely conjugal conjunction and association?

CLINIAS : Certainly.

ATHENIAN : Presumably, then, if the legislation of any society is to be sound and right it must start with a marriage law.

CLINIAS : I quite agree.

ATHENIAN : Then let us state that law in the simple form first. It might run to some such effect as this.

A man to marry when he has reached the age of thirty and be- **b** fore he comes to that of thirty-five; neglect to do so to be penalized by fine and loss of status; the fine to be of such and such an amount, and the loss of status to take such and such form.

That may be taken as the simple form of our law of marriage. Its double form we may word thus.

A man to marry when he has reached the age of thirty and before he comes to that of thirty-five, bethinking him that there is a sense in which mankind naturally partakes of immortality, a prize our nature makes desirable to all of us in its every form, for to win renown and not lie in our graves without a name is a desire of this. Thus the race **c** of man is time's equal twin and companion, bound up with him in a union never to be broken, and the manner of their immortality is in this wise. By succession of generations the race abides one and the same, so partaking in immortality through procreation. Whence piety

flatly forbids a man to deprive himself of the boon by his own act, as he willfully deprives himself who takes no thought of children and
d wife. So him who will obey the law we will hold scatheless, but as for him who disobeys and comes to five-and-thirty unwed, let him be yearly *mulcted in such and such a sum,* that he may not take his solitary state for a source of profit or ease, and *let him have no part in the public honors* paid from time to time by the younger folk to their elders.

You have heard this law set by the side of that, and are now in case to judge universally whether our laws, thus joining persuasion to
e menace, should be, at the very least, of double length, or should confine themselves to menace and so be of half the length.

MEGILLUS: To prefer the concise, sir, is ever our Laconian way; yet were I bidden to decide which of these statutes of yours I would rather see in force in our city, my vote would be for the more
722 prolix. Indeed, my choice would be the same about any law whatsoever after this model, if both alternatives were possible. But we must not forget that our present proposals need the approval of our friend Clinias, too, since it is his city which is now proposing to adopt such laws as we may enact.

CLINIAS: My thanks for your words, Megillus.

ATHENIAN: Why, to raise debate about a number of syllables more or less were, indeed, futile—it is quality, I take it, not length or
b brevity we should prize—'tis the matter of the one kind of law just mentioned that is of more than double excellence in use, by comparison with the other. As I said but now, our illustration of the two types of physicians was exactly apposite. Yet, in despite of us, none of our legislators would seem ever to have remarked that they rely wholly on one instrument in their work, whereas there are two available, so far as the mass's lack of education will permit, persuasion and compul-
c sion. Authority is never tempered in their lawmaking with persuasion; they work by compulsion unalloyed. Aye, and by heaven, to my mind, there is yet a third requisite of a law which is universally disregarded in fact.

CLINIAS: And pray what may it be?

ATHENIAN: Why, it has been providentially disclosed by our own conversation today. Since we began our talk of law, daybreak has given place to noonday, and we have reached this delightful ar-
d bor, and all our conversation has been exclusively of laws. Yet I fancy we are only now beginning to talk laws; all we have said hitherto has been but preambles to laws. Now why do I say this? Because I would observe that discourse and vocal utterance of every kind have their preludes, their preliminaries, as I might say, preliminaries which furnish a useful methodical introduction to the coming performance. High-wrought and elaborate preludes are prefixed, for example, to the so-called 'nomes' for the harp, and to musical compositions in gen-

eral, whereas in the case of what we regard as the real 'nomes,' the
laws of the community, no one has ever uttered the name, nor con- e
structed or published anything of the kind; it is taken for granted that
such a thing does not exist. Yet our present conversation, I believe,
suggests that it does. The deliverances which impressed me just now
as laws of double length are not, I think, just precisely that; they contain two things at once, a law and the prelude to it. The dictatorial
prescription in tones which we compared with the prescriptions of
our unfree physician is unqualified law, while all that preceded—per- 723
suasive, as Megillus called it—is, in fact, such a persuasive, but has
the rhetorical character of a preamble. For I find I framed the whole
of this discourse, uttered by its speaker in the tones of persuasion, to
prepare the auditor of the legislator's enactments to receive his prescription, that is to say, his law, in a spirit of friendliness and consequent docility, and for that very reason, it should, in my opinion,
properly be called by no other name; it is not the text of the law but b
its preamble.

You will ask me, then, how I propose to follow up the observation. Thus. I would have a legislator take constant care to leave neither his code as a whole nor its various divisions unprovided with
introductory preludes. This will make as great a difference as in the
two examples we were just considering.

CLINIAS: I, too, would urge a legislator who understands his
business to do the work in this fashion and no other.

ATHENIAN: I thoroughly agree with you, Clinias, as far as this. c
All laws have their preambles, and anyone who is beginning the work
of legislation should prefix to each section the preamble appropriate
to the whole subject. The pronouncement he is about to make is no
trifle, and it will make a great difference whether it can be distinctly
remembered or not. Yet we should be wrong if we insisted on the presence of a preamble alike for minor laws, as they are called, and major.
In fact, one must not treat every song or every speech in that fashion.
It is true that there are appropriate preludes in all cases, but we are d
not to make invariable use of them; we must leave it to the individual
speaker, or singer, or legislator to use his own judgment in each case.

CLINIAS: I fully agree with you. But, pray, sir, let us waste no
more time in delay. Let us go back to our argument and make a start,
if you please, with what you said a while ago, though not as an avowed
preamble. Let us begin it all over again, as they say in games, with a
better 'second shot,' on the understanding that we are no longer constructing a casual argument, but a preamble—let us begin, I say, e
with the admission that we are making our preamble. As for the worship of the gods and the service of our progenitors, what has been already said is adequate enough, but we must try to pursue the theme
further until you feel that our whole prelude is sufficiently complete.
Then, and not before, you shall rehearse the actual statutes.

724   ATHENIAN: Good, then. Our preamble, as we are now agreed, has already dealt adequately with gods, subordinate powers, and ancestors living and dead. As I understand you, you want me to throw some light on such parts of the subject as we have not yet touched.

CLINIAS: Precisely.

ATHENIAN: Why, in the next place, it is proper and to their common highest interest that speaker and hearers should do their utmost to achieve their own education by meditation on their duties of
b effort and remission in all that concerns mind, body, and substance. Whence these, and no others, are doubtless the matters of which we must next speak and hear.

CLINIAS: Very true.

BOOK V

726 ATHENIAN: Listen then, all ye who but now gave ear to our discourse of gods and well-beloved sires. Of all a man has—after his gods —the divinest thing, and the most truly his own, is his soul. Now things which pertain to any man are ever of two sorts, a superior and better sort to be sovereign, an inferior and worse to be subject. So a
727 man should ever prefer those that are sovereign in honor before those that are subject. Therefore, when I bid men honor their own souls next to the gods, our sovereign lords, and the powers under them, the counsel I give is right. Yet not a man of us, I may say, honors his soul aright, though he dreams he does. Honor, I take it, is a thing divinely good, and can be conferred by nothing that is evil. He who deems he is advancing his soul by speech, gifts, or compliances, and all the while makes it no better than it was before, may dream that he shows it honor, but in truth does it none.

Barely, for example, has a man come to boyhood before he counts
b himself fit to pronounce on all things, honors his soul, as he fancies, by this flattery, and gives it ready license to act whatever it will. Now our present declaration is that by these courses he does it hurt, not honor, whereas we bid him honor it next to heaven. So again, when a man lays the blame for his several misdeeds and the greater and graver part of his mischances not on himself but on others, ever accounting himself clear of fault, by way of reverence—or so he fancies
c —for his soul, that is no honor done the soul—far from it—but hurt. Again, when he courts pleasures in defiance of the legislator's admonition and approval, he does his soul no honor, but rather dishonor, by thus defiling it with misery and remorse. Again, in a different way, when a man will not harden himself to endure commended hardships, fears, pains, sufferings, but makes submission, the surrender brings
d no honor, for all such courses bring disgrace on the soul. Again, when a man counts it good to live at all costs, that also is dishonor to the

soul; 'tis surrender to that within him which accounts the unseen
world merely evil, whereas a man should make head against his fancy
with cogent proof that he knows not even whether our chiefest good
may not be in the gift of the gods of that land. Again, when a man
prefers comeliness before goodness, this also is no other than real
and utmost dishonor to the soul. For this estimate pronounces body
more honorable than soul, and that most falsely. Nothing born of
earth is more honorable than the heavenly, and he that conceits him- e
self otherwise of the soul than this knows not the preciousness of this
possession he despises. Again, when a man lusts after wealth basely 728
won, or has no disrelish for the winning, he does no real honor to his
soul by such offerings—far, far from it! He sells its goodly treasure
for a parcel of coin, but all the gold on earth or under earth is no equal
exchange for goodness.

To say all in one word, whosoever will not at all hazards keep
himself from all the legislator lists in his count of things base and
bad, and exercises himself with all his might in all that is in the contrary table of things good and lovely, knows not that by all such ways b
a man ever heaps foul dishonor and deformity on the divinest thing
he has, his soul. In fact, none of us, or few, reckon with the sorest
'judgment'—as the phrase is—on evil-doing, which judgment is that a
man grows like those who already are evil, and, as the likeness grows,
avoids good men and good converse, and cuts himself off from them,
but follows after the other sort and cleaves to them in intimate fellowship, and he who clings to such men cannot but do and have done to
him what men of that sort naturally do and say. This state then is not c
judgment—for judgment is, like justice, a good—but vengeance, the
painful consequence of iniquity. He that meets it and he that misses
it are alike unhappy, the one because he gets no healing for his disease,
the other in that he is cut off for the salvation of many another. But
honor, we hold, is, in sum, to follow after what is better, and for what
is worse but may be amended, even to make it good as best may be.

There is nothing, then, of all a man owns so natively quick as
the soul to shun the evil but follow on the trail of the chief good, win d
it, and spend the rest of a lifetime at home with it. Whence we have
given the soul the second place in honor. The third, and so much must
be plain to any vision, belongs to due honor to the body. But next it
must be asked what various honors there are, which of them ring
true, which are counterfeit, and here is a task for our legislator. He
will suggest, I think, that they are these and the like. The body to be
honored is not the comely, nor the strong, nor swift, no, nor the
healthy, though so many might be of that mind—nor yet that of the e
contrary sort. The body which displays all these qualities in intermediate degree is by far the most sober, and soundest as well, for the one
sort make men's souls vain and overbearing, the other tame and

abject. 'Tis the same with ownership of wealth and property, and
729 they must be rated by the same scale. Excess of all such things, as a
rule, breeds public and private feuds and factions, defect, subjection.
Let no man covet wealth for his children's sake, that he may
leave them in opulence; 'tis not for their own good nor for the state's.
For the young an estate that tempts no sycophants and yet has no lack
of things needful is of all others best and most consonant; it works
general concord and concert and banishes pains from our lives. We
b should leave our children rich, not in gold but in reverence. Now we
fancy we shall assure that inheritance if we rebuke the young when
they forget their modesty, but in truth the thing is not to be done by
giving the young such admonition as they receive today when they are
told that 'youth must respect all men.' A legislator of judgment will be
more likely to charge older men to respect their juniors and, of all
things, to take heed that no young man ever see or hear one of them-
c selves doing act or speaking word of shame, since when the old forget
their modesty, the young, too, cannot but be most graceless. Far the
best way to educate our young men and ourselves along with them is
not by admonition, but by lifelong visible practice of all to which a
man would admonish others. If a man pays honor and respect to kindred and all fellowship of common blood in worship of the gods of the
kin, he may reasonably expect the favor of the gods of birth for the
propagation of his own children.
d   As to friends and comrades in the several affairs of life, a man
will gain their good will if he counts their services to him greater and
ampler than they do, but rates his own kindnesses to friend and companion lower than they themselves. In all that concerns city and fellow citizens, the best man, and the best by far, is he who would prize
before an Olympian victory or any triumph in war or peace, the credit
e of victory in service to the laws of his home, as one who has all his life
been their true servant above all men. Then, as regards the alien, we
must remember that compacts have a peculiar sanctity; indeed, offenses by alien against alien, we may say, compared with sins against
fellow citizens, more directly draw down the vengeance of God. For
the alien, being without friends or kinsmen, has the greater claim on
pity, human and divine. Whence he that is able to exact the vengeance is all the readier to come to his help, and none is so able as the
730 god or spirit who protects the alien as minister of Zeus Xenios. What
anxious care, then, should a man of any foresight take to come to the
end of life's journey guiltless of offense toward aliens! Moreover, the
gravest of offenses, whether against landsmen or aliens, is always
that done to a suppliant, for the god in whose name the suppliant
made his appeal when he obtained a promise keeps jealous watch
over the sufferer, and thus he will never suffer his wrongs unavenged.
b   We have now fairly reviewed a man's relations to parents, to
himself, his possessions, his city, his friends, his kindred, to aliens

and to countrymen, and must next in order consider what manner of
man he must himself be to pass through life with full credit. We come
to speak now, of the effects not of law, but of education through commendation and reproach in making men more amenable and well disposed toward the laws we are hereafter to enact.

Now of all things good, truth holds the first place among gods c
and men alike. For him who is to know felicity and happiness, my
prayer is that he may be endowed with it from the first, that he may
live all the longer a true man. For such a man is trusty, whereas he
that loves voluntary deception is untrustworthy, and he that loves involuntary, a fool, and neither lot is to be envied. For, sure, the traitor
or the fool is a man of no friends. Course of time discovers him and he
prepares for himself utter loneliness in the trials of age at the end of d
his days, so living equally destitute of companions and children,
whether they survive or not. Honor is due to him who himself does no
wrong, but he that will not so much as suffer another to do it merits
twofold and more than twofold honor; the first has the worth of one
man, the second, who reveals the wrongdoing of others to the authorities, the worth of many. But he that further does his endeavor to second the authorities in their work of repression, he is the great and
perfect citizen, and the palm of virtue shall be declared to be his. We e
must make this same grading in our recognition of temperance and
judgment and all good qualities which a man imparts to others as well
as enjoys in his own person. To him who communicates them we
should give the supreme degree of honor; he that cannot impart them,
yet would fain do so, must be left in the second rank. As for him who 731
engrosses good things to himself and will never, if he can help it,
share them with a friend, we should censure his person, but with no
depreciation of the quality on the possessor's account; rather we must
do all we can to make it our own.

In this contest for virtue we will have all men competitors, but
there must be no jealousies. For a man such as we would have him
promotes a state, since he runs in the race himself without hamper-
ing others by evil reports, whereas the jealous man, who fancies
slander of others the right means to his own advancement, strains
less to reach real virtue himself, and causes his rivals to be discouraged by unmerited censure. Thus he cripples the whole society for the b
race for virtue, and does what lies in him to lower its good repute.
High-spirited every man should be, but likewise gentle in eminent degree. For cruel and almost or wholly irreparable wrongs at the hands
of others are only to be escaped in one way, by victorious encounter
and repulse, and stern correction, and such action is impossible for
the soul without generous passion. But as concerns the transgressions c
of those who commit wrong, but reparable wrong, we must first of all
rest assured that no wrongdoer is so of deliberation. For no man will
ever deliberately admit supreme evil, and least of all in his most

precious possessions. But every man's most precious possession, as we said, is his soul; no man, then, we may be sure, will of set purpose receive the supreme evil into this most precious thing and live with it there all his life through. And yet, though a wrongdoer or a man in
d evil case is always a pitiable creature, it is with him whose disease is curable that there is scope for pity. With him one may curb and tame one's passion, and not scold like a vixen, but against the unqualified and incorrigible offender, the utterly corrupt, we must give the rein to wrath. This is why we say it is meet for a good man to be high-spirited and gentle, as occasion requires.

But of all faults of soul the gravest is one which is inborn in most men, one which all excuse in themselves and none therefore attempts
e to avoid—that conveyed in the maxim that 'everyone is naturally his own friend,' and that it is only right and proper that he should be so, whereas, in truth, this same violent attachment to self is the constant source of all manner of misdeeds in every one of us. The eye of love is blind where the beloved is concerned, and so a man proves a bad judge
732 of right, good, honor, in the conceit that more regard is due to his personality than to the real fact, whereas a man who means to be great must care neither for self nor for its belongings, but for justice, whether exhibited in his own conduct, or rather in that of another. From this same fault springs also that universal conviction that one's own folly is wisdom, with its consequences that we fancy we know
b everything when we know as good as nothing, refuse to allow others to manage business we do not understand, and fall into inevitable errors in transacting it for ourselves. Every man, then, must shun extreme self-love and follow ever in the steps of his better, undeterred by any shame for his case.

There are also minor and often-formulated, but no less salutary, rules which must be kept in mind by repetition. For where waters, as we may say, are wasted by emission there must always be a balancing immission, and recall is the immission which makes waste of wisdom
c good. This is why there must be restraint of unseasonable laughter and tears and each of us must urge his fellow to consult decorum by utter concealment of all excess of joy or grief, whether the breeze of fortune is set fair, or, by a shift of circumstance, the fortunes of an enterprise are confronted by a mountain of difficulty. It should be our constant hope that God, by the blessings he bestows, will lighten the
d troubles that come upon us, and change our present state for the better, while, with heaven's favor, the very reverse will always be true of our blessings. These are the hopes, and these and the like the meditations, in which each of us should live, sparing no pains, alike in work and in play, to bring them to his neighbor's confident recollection and to his own.

We have now dealt pretty completely with what divinity has to
e say of the institution which ought to be established, and the personal

character to which all should aspire. On purely human considerations
we have not touched, and yet we must; it is to men, not to gods, we
are speaking. Nothing is so native to men as pleasure, pain, and desire; they are, so to say, the very wires or strings from which any mortal nature is inevitably and absolutely dependent. We have therefore
to commend the noble life, not only as superior in comeliness of repute, but further as superior, if a man will but taste it and not decline
it in the days of his youth, in that on which we are all set, lifelong pre- 733
dominance of pleasures over pains. That this will certainly be so, if
only the tasting is done in the right way, will easily be made abundantly apparent. But what is the right way? This is what we must
now learn from our argument to see. The following are the lines along
which we must discover, by comparison of the relative pleasantness
and painfulness of lives, whether one is naturally conformable to our
constitution and another unconformable. We wish for pleasure; pain b
we neither choose nor wish for. A neutral state, though not desired as
an alternative to pleasure, is desired as a relief from pain. Less of
pain with more of pleasure is desired; less of pleasure with more of
pain is not desired. As for an equal balance of both, we can give no
certain reason for desiring it. And all these objects affect our several
choices or leave them unaffected, in virtue of their frequency, their
magnitude, their intensity, their equality, and the conditions which
are the opposites of these in their influence on desire. All this, then, c
being inevitably ordered so, a life which contains numerous, extensive, and intense feelings of both kinds is desired, if there is an excess
of pleasures, not desired if the excess is on the other side. Again, a life
where both kinds of feeling are few, inconsiderable, and of low intensity is not desired if the pains predominate, but is desired in the opposite case. As for a life in which the balance is even, we must stand to
our earlier pronouncement; we desire it so far as it contains a predom- d
inance of what attracts us, and yet do not desire it so far as it is pre-
dominant in what repels. So we must regard our lives as confined
within these limits and must consider what kind of life it is natural to
desire. But if we ever speak of ourselves as desiring an object other
than those aforesaid, the statement is due to ignorance and defective
experience of actual lives.

What lives, then, are there, and how many, from which, on a review of the desirable and undesirable, a selection must be made and
erected into a self-imposed law, if the choice of the course which is e
pleasant and attractive as well as virtuous and noble may lead to an
existence of supreme human felicity? We shall, of course, name the
life of temperance as one, and may count that of wisdom as another,
that of courage as another, and that of health as another, thus making four in all, against which we may set four other types, the
lives of folly, cowardice, profligacy, disease. Now the verdict of one
acquainted with the facts will be that the life of temperance is

uniformly gentle. The pains and pleasures it offers are alike unexcit-
734 ing, its desires and passions never furious, but mild, whereas that of
profligacy is uniformly rash. The pains and pleasures it offers are
alike violent, its intense desires and frantic passions maddening in
the extreme. But in the temperate life the pains are surpassed by the
pleasures; in the profligate the pleasures are surpassed by the pains,
in respect of magnitude, number, and condensation. Hence it follows
naturally and inevitably that the former is the more pleasurable life,
b the latter the more painful, and a man who desires a pleasant life is
no longer free to choose a career of profligacy. Nay, it is at once patent, if our present reasoning is sound, that the profligate must always
be what he is against his own will. The reason why the great mass of
men live without temperance is always either ignorance, or lack of
self-control, or both at once. We must say the same thing of the lives
of disease and of health; there are pleasures and pains in both, but
c pleasure predominates over pain in health, in disease pain over pleasure.
     Now the object of our choice between lives is not to secure pre-
ponderance of pain; the life we have pronounced the pleasanter is one
in which the preponderance is on the other side. The temperate life,
then, we shall maintain exhibits both sorts of feeling in lesser number,
smaller magnitude, and looser concentration than the profligate—the
d wise than the foolish, and the life of courage than that of cowardice.
But since in each case the first-named has the superiority in pleasure
over its rival, which has a superiority in pain, the life of courage is
triumphant over that of cowardice, that of wisdom over that of folly,
with the consequence that, lives for lives, the temperate, courageous,
wise, and wholesome are pleasanter than the cowardly, foolish, licentious, and diseased, and, in sum, the life of bodily or mental excellence pleasanter than that of depravity—to say nothing of its further
superiority on the score of comeliness, rightness, virtue, and fair fame
e —whence it results that such a life renders its possessor's existence
absolutely and unreservedly happier than that of his rival.
     Here our discourse by way of prelude to our legislation may come
to its end. After the prelude, of course, must come the composition itself, or, as it would be truer to say, an outline of a civic code. Now
just as in the case of a web or other piece of woven work, woof and
735 warp cannot be fashioned of the same threads, but the material of the
warp must be of superior quality—it must be tough, you know, and
have a certain tenacity of character, whereas the woof may be softer
and display a proper pliancy. Well, the illustration shows that there
must be some similar distinction made between citizens who are to fill
magistracies, and those who have been but lightly tested by education,
this distinction being drawn appropriately to the various cases. For
you must know that there are two things which go to the making of a

constitution. The conferring of office on individuals is one; the other is
the providing of the officials with a code of laws.

But before we come to any of these subjects, the following observations should be made. A man who takes in hand a herd of ani- b
mals, a shepherd, neatherd, horse breeder, or the like, will never
dream of trying to tend that herd without first submitting the group
to the purgation proper to it. He will separate the sound animals from
the sickly, the thoroughbreds from the mongrels, removing the latter
to other herds, and exercising his tendance on the former, since he is
well aware that, unless he thus purges his stock, he will have endless
and fruitless trouble with bodies and minds already degenerate by c
nature or ill management, which will further communicate a taint to
the sound and unimpaired in body and disposition in the various
herds. With the lower animals this does not so much matter—they
only call for mention by way of an illustration—but in the case of
man it is of the first concern to the legislator to discover and explain
the method of procedure appropriate to various cases, in this matter
of purgation as well as in all his other dealings with them. For instance, in the business of social purgation, the case stands thus. d
There are many ways of effecting a purgation, some of them milder,
some sharper. Some—the sharpest and best of all—will be at the disposal of one who is at once autocrat and legislator, but a legislator
who establishes a new society and new laws with less than autocratic
power will be well satisfied if he can so much as reach his end of purgation by the mildest of methods. The best method of all, like the
most potent medicines, is painful; it is that which effects correction
by the combination of justice with vengeance, and carries its venge- e
ance, in the last instance, to the point of death or exile, usually with
the result of clearing society of its most dangerous members, great
and incurable offenders. The milder method of purgation we may describe much as follows. Persons who, from want of the means of subsistence, show themselves ready to follow their leaders in an attack of
the have-nots on the haves are treated by the legislator as a deep- 736
seated disease in the body of the state, and, with all possible good feeling, sent abroad as a 'measure of relief,' to use the euphemistic
phrase; the name given to the procedure is colonization. Now every
legislator has to act more or less in this way at the outset, but our own
situation, at the present juncture, is still less irksome; we need contrive neither a colonization, nor any other method of selecting our
purgation. We have, so to say, a conflux into the reservoir of waters
from many sources, some springs, some mountain becks, and need b
only take careful pains to secure maximum purity in the accumulating
water by drawing off the supply from one quarter and diverting it into
a different course in another. True, there is naturally some trouble
and risk about any political undertaking; still, as we are concerned at

the moment with theory, not with practical execution, we may take our recruitment of citizens to have been completed, and its purity ensured to our wish. We shall, in fact, submit the bad among those who c propose to come into our proposed state as members to the test of manifold exhortation and adequate time, and prevent their arrival; the good we shall welcome with all benevolence and complaisance.

Do not forget that we enjoy the same good fortune on which we congratulated the foundation of the Heraclidae, escape from cruel and dangerous controversy about confiscating of estates, cancellation of debts, and redistribution of property. In an old-established society, when legislation of this kind has become inevitable, innovation and d refusal to innovate prove, in a way, alike impossible; room is left for little more than pious wishes and insensible and cautious modification by slow and gradual advances in the following direction. Among the innovators there should always be a section with extensive property in land and numerous debtors, who are not indisposed to share their advantages in a liberal spirit with the distressed by a remission e of debts and redistribution of estates, thus evincing a certain regard for moderation, and showing their conviction that poverty consists not so much in the diminution of one's property as in the intensification of one's cupidity. This conviction is the surest of all sources of social security, a firm foundation for the subsequent erection of any political superstructure in keeping with such conditions. Where these initial conditions are unsound, a statesman's subsequent action will al-737 ways be beset with difficulties. The danger, as I say, is one from which we are exempt; still, it is the better course to explain how we might have escaped it even without this exemption. Let us say, then, once for all, that escape must be sought in the combination of justice with freedom from avarice. There is no road to deliverance, broad or narrow, on other lines, and we must take the principle as a buttress of our society. In fact, properties must be fixed by some system which b excludes recriminations among their owners; otherwise, any man of any intelligence will refuse to go further, if he can help it, with a social system for a population among whom there are long-standing mutual jealousies. In persons who have, like ourselves at this moment, the providential opportunity to found a new society where there are as yet no internal hostilities, to introduce such hostilities by the distribution of land and houses would be a combination of sheer depravity with superhuman folly.

c   What, then, would be the right method of distribution? First we must fix the total number of the citizens at the suitable figure; next we must come to an agreement about their distribution, the number and size of the sections into which they should be subdivided; the land and houses should be partitioned among these sections as equally as may be. What would be a satisfactory total for the population is more than can be rightly said without consideration of the territory and the neighboring communities. The territory should be large enough for the adequate maintenance of a certain number of men of d modest ambitions, and no larger; the population should be sufficient to defend themselves against wrongs from societies on their borders, and to assist their neighbors when wronged to some purpose. These points we will settle, practically and theoretically, by an inspection of the territory and its neighbors, but for the present our argument may proceed to the completion of our code of laws, in outline and as a general sketch.

Let us assume—to take a convenient number—that we have five e thousand and forty landholders, who can be armed to fight for their holdings, and that the territory and houses are likewise divided among the same number, so that there will be one man to one holding. Let this total be divided first by two, and then by three; in fact it will permit of division by four, five, and the successive integers up to ten. Of course anyone who is acting as a legislator must be at least familiar enough with figures to understand what number, or kind of number, will prove most useful in a given state. Accordingly we will select that 738 which has the greatest number of immediately successive divisions. The whole integer series, of course, admits division by any number and with any quotient, while our five thousand and forty can be divided, for purposes of war, or to suit the engagements and combinations of peace, in the matter of taxes to be levied and public distributions to be made, into fifty-nine quotients and no more, ten of them, from unity onward, being successive.

These facts of number, then, must be thoroughly mastered at b leisure by those whose business the law will make it to understand them—they will find them exactly as I have stated them—and they must be mentioned by the founder of a city, for the reason I shall now give. Whether a new foundation is to be created from the outset or an old one restored, in the matter of gods and their sanctuaries—what temples must be founded in a given community, and to what gods or spirits they should be dedicated—no man of sense will presume to disturb convictions inspired from Delphi, Dodona, the oracle of c Ammon, or by old traditions of any kind of divine appearances or reported divine revelations, when those convictions have led to the establishment of sacrifice and ritual—whether original and indigenous, or borrowed from Etruria, Cyprus, or elsewhere—the consequent consecration by the tradition of oracles, statues, altars, and shrines, and the provision for each of these of its sacred precinct. A legislator should avoid the slightest interference with all such matters; he d should assign every district its patron god, or spirit, or hero, as the case may be, and his first step in the subdivision of a territory should be to assign to each of them his special precinct with all appertaining dues. His purpose in this will be that the convocations of the various sections at stated periods may provide opportunities for the satisfac-

tion of their various needs, and that the festivities may give occasion
for mutual friendliness, familiarity, and acquaintance. There is in-
e deed no such boon for a society as this familiar knowledge of citizen
by citizen. For where men have no light on each other's characters,
but are in the dark on the subject, no one will ever reach the rank or
office he deserves, or get the justice which is his proper due. Hence in
every society it should always be the endeavor of every citizen, before
anything else, to prove himself to all his neighbors no counterfeit, but
a man of sterling sincerity, and not to be imposed on by any counter-
feiting in others.

739   Our next move in this business of legislation must be—like the
moving of a man on the draughtboard from the 'sacred line'—so singular that it may well surprise you on a first hearing. Yet reflection
and practical experience will make it clear that a society is likely to
enjoy but a second-best constitution. Some of us may be dissatisfied
with such a society from their unfamiliarity with the situation of a
legislator who does not possess autocratic power, but the procedure of
strict exactitude is to discriminate a best constitution, a second-best,
and a third-best, and then to leave the choice between them to the
party responsible for the foundation. Accordingly, I propose that we
b should adopt this method in our present proceedings. We will describe
the best, second-best, and third-best constitutions, and leave the
choice between them to Clinias in the present case, or to anyone else
who may at any time come to the task of selection with a desire to incorporate what he values in his own native institutions to suit his own
taste.

The first-best society, then, that with the best constitution and
c code of law, is one where the old saying is most universally true of
the whole society. I mean the saying that 'friends' property is indeed
common property.' If there is now on earth, or ever should be, such a
society—a community in womenfolk, in children, in all possessions
whatsoever—if all means have been taken to eliminate everything we
mean by the word *ownership* from life; if all possible means have
been taken to make even what nature has made our *own* in some sense
common property, I mean, if our eyes, ears, and hands seem to see,
hear, act, in the common service; if, moreover, we all approve and
d condemn in perfect unison and derive pleasure and pain from the
same sources—in a word, when the institutions of a society make it
most utterly one, that is a criterion of their excellence than which no
truer or better will ever be found. If there is anywhere such a city,
with a number of gods, or sons of gods, for its inhabitants, they dwell
e there thus in all joyousness of life. Whence for the pattern of a constitution we should look to no other quarter, but cleave to this and
strive to come as near it as may be in our state. That we have now in
hand, were it once brought to the birth, would be in its fashion the
nearest to immortality and the only one which takes the second place;

of the third, under heaven's favor, we will treat hereafter. For the present, what, in any case, is this system we speak of, and how may it come to be what it is?

First, then, let them make a division of lands and houses among themselves, and not till the soil in common, for that were a project be- 740 yond their birth, breeding, and education. But let the division be made with some such thought as this, that he to whom a lot falls is yet bound to count his portion the common property of the whole society, and, since the territory is his fatherland, to tend it with care passing that of son for mother, the more that the land is the divine mistress of her mortal children, and to think likewise of all the gods and spirits of the locality. That this temper may persist for all time to come, we b must practice this further contrivance. The number of hearth fires established by our present division must remain forever unchanged, without increase or deviation whatsoever. Now the way to ensure this in any city will be as follows. Let him who has a lot assigned him ever leave after him one son, of his own preference, to be his heir in that household and successor in the worship of the gods of clan and in ministering to the family, living or already previously deceased. As for c other children, when a man has more than the one, let him give the females in marriage as a law yet to be enjoined shall direct; the males let him distribute among citizens who have a lack of offspring, to be their sons, and that preferably by friendly agreement. If a man have no friendly connections, or if there be families too numerous in issue, female or male, as in the contrary case, when there is a paucity of issue due to childlessness, in all these cases the highest and most au- d gust of the magistracies we shall create must consider what should be done to meet the excess or defect, and contrive the best device they may to keep the number of households always at our five thousand and forty and no more. Now there are several such devices. There are shifts for checking propagation when its course is too facile, and, on the other side, there are ways of fostering and encouraging numerous births which affect the young by marks of honor and dishonor and admonition conveyed in warning speeches of their seniors, and these will do our business. Besides, in the final extremity, if all means fail e us to keep the number of five thousand and forty households constant, if mated love should cause an excessive glut of population, and we find ourselves at a loss, we have ready to our hand the old contrivance we have more than once spoken of—we can send out colonies of such persons as we deem convenient with love and friendship on both parts. Or in the contrary event, if our citizens are visited by a flood 741 tide, as we may call it, of disease, or by destruction in battle, and so reduced far below the appointed number by untimely deaths, why, then, though we should never, if we can help it, foist in citizens whose education has been base, with necessity, as the proverb says, not even a god can cope.

Let us fancy, then, that we hear our present argument exhorting us in tones like these. Worthiest of men, see to it that you grow not slack in rendering the honor nature bids render to congruity and
b equality, identity and conformity, alike of number and of all that can produce fair and good effects. In especial you are herewith charged, first, to keep fixed thoughout life the numbers prescribed you, and next to do no despite by mutual purchase and sale to the bulk and measure of substance assigned you at the first as your fitting portion; therein you will have against you the lot by which the division was made—and it is a god—and the lawgiver to boot. For first of all, our present law, with its warning that a man must take the lot, if so he
c pleases, on those terms or let it alone, contains this further enactment, that whereas the soil is consecrate to all gods, and whereas moreover priests of either sex shall offer prayers with sacrifice to that intent, once and twice and thrice, he who shall vend house or land assigned him, or purchase the same, shall suffer the fitting penalties for his act, written records inscribed on tables of cypresswood being laid up in the temples as a memorial to times to come. Moreover, surveillance over the execution of this statute shall be made the charge of
d the magistracy which shall be deemed most keen-sighted, that contraventions of it, when they occur, may not go unremarked, but the offense at once against the law and against God receive its chastisement. What a wealth of blessing the regulation now enjoined brings to any society which complies with it, if it be but conjoined with an organization to match, no evil man will ever know, but only, to speak with the old proverb, one who has made trial of it and is formed to
e ways of virtue. For such an organization leaves no great room for the making of fortunes; 'tis a consequence of it that none has either need or license to make them in any sordid calling—as even the sound of the reproach 'base mechanical' repels the man of free soul—and none will ever stoop to amass wealth by such devices.
742 With these injunctions goes also a further law by which no possession of gold or silver is permitted to any private man, but only a currency for the purpose of daily exchange, such as is hardly to be avoided by craftsmen or any whose business it is to pay wages in such a kind to wage earners, whether slaves or alien settlers; whence we shall lay it down that they must have an internal currency, of value at home but worthless abroad. As for a common Hellenic currency, to
b meet the needs of campaigns and foreign expeditions, such as embassies or other necessary missions of state on which a man may be dispatched, to serve these various purposes the state must possess current Hellenic money. If a private man should ever be forced to travel in foreign parts, let him get leave of the magistrates before he departs, and if on his return he have coin from any foreign quarter left, let him deposit it with the state, receiving the equivalent in local currency; if he be found to be secreting it, let it be confiscated to the

treasury, and let any who is privy to the act and conceals it be liable
equally with the importer to curse and reproach, and in addition to a
fine of amount not less than the amount of foreign currency im- c
ported. Let there be no dowry whatsoever, given or received, in marrying or giving in marriage, no depositing of money with one who is
not trusted, and no lending on usury, the law permitting the borrower
to withhold both interest and capital. That these practices are best for d
a society will be rightly discerned by the inquirer who considers them
in the following light, with constant reference to their principle and
intention. The intention of a sane statesman, mark you, is not what
the many suppose. The good legislator, they would say, must intend
the city for which he legislates in his wisdom to be as great as may be,
and as wealthy, to possess mines of gold and silver, and to have a multitude of subjects by land and sea. They would further add that if he
is a legislator of the right kind he must intend his city to be as good
and as happy as possible. Now some of these objects are possibilities, e
others not so. Hence the state builder will intend the possible; the
impossible he will neither make the object of a futile intention nor
attempt it. In fact, speaking generally, happiness necessarily waits
on goodness; so that combination he would intend. But to be at once
exceedingly wealthy and good is impossible, if we mean by the
wealthy those who are accounted so by the vulgar, that is, the exceptional few who own property of great pecuniary value—the very thing
a bad man would be likely to own. Now since this is so, I can never 743
concede to them that a rich man is truly happy unless he is also a
good man, but that one who is exceptionally good should be exceptionally wealthy too is a mere impossibility. But why so, someone may
ask. Why, I answer, because the profits of righteousness and iniquity
together are more than double those from righteousness alone, while
the expenditure of one who will spend neither honorably nor discred- b
itably is less by half than that of one who is ready to lay out money
honorably on honorable objects. Hence he who acts in the contrary
fashion can never become wealthier than the man whose gains are
double his own, and his expenditure but half his. Now of the two men,
the one is good; the other, when he is frugal, not bad—though on occasion he can be utterly bad too—but good, as I have just said, he
never is. In fact, the man who will get by honest and dishonest means
alike, and will spend neither righteously nor unrighteously, if he is
only frugal to boot, grows wealthy, though the utterly bad man, being
as a general rule a prodigal, is very poor, whereas a man who will
spend on honorable objects and only make gains from honest sources, c
will not find it easy to become either remarkably wealthy or exceedingly poor. Thus our thesis that the immensely rich are not good men
is sound, and if they are not good, neither are they happy.

The object our laws had in view was that our people should be
supremely happy and devotedly attached to one another, but citizens

will never be thus attached where there are many suits at law be-
d tween them, and numerous wrongs committed, but where both are
rarest and of least consequence. Our society, we pronounce, must have
neither gold nor silver, nor yet much making of profits from mechanical crafts, or usury, or raising of sordid beasts, but only such as husbandry yields or permits, and of it only so much as will not force a man
in his profit gathering to forget the ends for which possessions exist,
e that is to say, soul and body, which will never be of any account without bodily training and education at large. Wherefore we have said,
and said more than once, that concern for possessions should take the
lowest place in our esteem, for whereas the objects of universal interest to man are in all three, interest in possessions, rightly pursued,
holds the third and lowest rank, the interest of the body is second, of
the soul first. And so also with the polity now under consideration; if
744 it prescribes its honors on these principles, its laws have been rightly
made, but should any law there to be imposed be found to put health
before sobriety in point of public esteem, or wealth before health and
sober-mindedness, it will stand detected as wrongly imposed. Hence a
legislator should time and time again ask himself the plain questions,
What is my intent? Do I hit the mark in this, or do I miss it? Thus perhaps, but in no other way whatsoever, will he finish his work of legislation and relieve others of the task.

Let him who has obtained a lot, then, as we say, hold it on the
b conditions here stated. It had indeed been well that all settlers should
further enter our colony with equal means of every kind. But since
this cannot be, but one arrival will bring more property and another
less, there must be classes of unequal census, and that on many
grounds, and in particular because of the equal opportunities our society affords, that so in election to office and assessment of payments to
and receipts from the exchequer regard may be had to a man's due
c qualifications—not only of personal and ancestral virtue, or of bodily
strength and comeliness, but of enjoyment of means or lack of them,
honors and offices apportioned fairly by a rule of proportional, though
unequal, distribution—and dissensions avoided. On these grounds we
must arrange our citizens in four classes according to the amount of
their property, a first, a second, a third, and a fourth—or they may be
called by some other names—whether the members remain in the
same class, or shift, as they pass from poverty to wealth, or wealth to
d poverty, each to the class appropriate to him.

As a further consequence of what has preceded I would enact another law of the following type. In a society which is to be immune
from the most fatal of disorders which might more properly be called
distraction than faction, there must be no place for penury in any section of the population, nor yet for opulence, as both breed either consequence. Accordingly the legislator must now specify the limit in either
e direction. So let the limit on the side of penury be the value of an al-

lotment; this must remain constant, and no magistrate, and no other person who is ambitious of a repute for goodness must connive, in any case, at its diminution. The legislator will take it as a measure, and permit the acquisition of twice, thrice, and as much as four times its value. If a man acquires further possessions, from treasure-trove, donation, or business, or by any other similar chance makes acquisitions in excess of this measure, he may retain his good name and escape all proceedings by consigning the surplus to the state and its gods. If there 745 is any disobedience to this law, it shall be open to anyone who pleases to lay an information and claim half the property, the convicted offender also paying a fine to the same amount out of his own possessions; the other half shall go to the gods. The whole property of every citizen, other than his allotment, must previously be inscribed in a public record under the custody of magistrates appointed by law for the purpose with a view to making suits at law affecting any question b of property capable of easy and most assured determination.

Next, the founder must see that his city is placed as nearly as possible at the center of the territory, after selecting a site possessed of the other favorable conditions for his purpose—it will not be difficult to discover or to state them. Then he must divide his city into twelve parts, but first he should establish and enclose a sanctuary of Hestia, Zeus, and Athena—which he will call the citadel—from which he will draw his twelve divisions of the city and its whole territory. c Equality of the twelve regions should be secured by making those of good soil small and those of worse soil larger. He should then make a division into five thousand and forty allotments. Each of these, again, should be bisected and two half sections, a nearer and a remoter, paired together to form an allotment, one which is contiguous to the city with one on the border, one in the next degree of proximity to the d city with one next most nearly on the border, and so on in all cases. We should further practice in these half sections the already-mentioned contrivance relative to the poverty or excellence of the soil and effect an equalization by the greater or less size of the divisions. Of course, the legislator must also divide the population into twelve sections, constructing these sections so as to be as nearly as possible on an equality in respect of their other property, of the whole of which he will have made a careful record. Next he will be at pains to assign the twelve divisions to twelve gods, naming each section after the god to whom it has been allotted and consecrated, and calling it a e tribe. Further, the twelve segments of the city must be made on the same lines as the division of the territory in general, and each citizen must have two houses, one nearer the center of the state and the other nearer the border. And this shall complete the business of settlement.

But here is a consideration on which we must be careful to reflect. All the arrangements we have just proposed are never likely to find just such conditions that the whole program will be completely

746 executed. The conditions suppose a population with no disrelish for such social regulations, who will tolerate lifelong fixed limitation of property, restrictions such as those we have proposed on procreation, and deprivation of gold and other things which it is certain, from what has been said already, that the legislator will prohibit. They presuppose further the central position of the capital, and the distribution of the dwelling houses over the territory, as he has prescribed, almost as though he were telling his dreams or fashioning a city and its inhabitants out of waxwork. To be sure, the scheme does not sound
b amiss, but its author needs to give it his reconsideration to the following effect. So our legislator gives us once more the ensuing admonition.

Do not imagine, my friends, that I am less alive than yourselves to a certain truth in what you urge in your present discourse. But the fact is that I take it to be always the most equitable course in dealing with a plan for the future that he who exhibits the model on which an undertaking should be fashioned should abate nothing of perfect
c excellence and absolute truth, while one who finds it impossible to compass some point of this perfection should decline to put it into practice, and contrive the realization of the remaining possibility which approximates most nearly to what ought to be done and is most akin to it in character. But he should allow the legislator to perfect the delineation of his heart's desire; only when that has been done should he begin to discuss with him which of his legislative proposals are expedient and which involve difficulties. For self-consistency, you know, must be aimed at in everything, even by the artificer
d of the paltriest object, if he is to be of any account.

Our immediate concern, now that we have resolved on the division into twelve parts, must be precisely to see in what conspicuous fashion these twelve parts, admitting, as they do, such a multitude of further divisions, with the subsequent groups which arise from them, down to the five thousand and forty individuals—this will give us our brotherhoods, wards, and parishes, as well as our divisions of battle and columns of route, not to mention our currency and measures of capacity, dry and liquid and of weight—to see, I say, how all these details must be legally determined so as to fit in and harmonize with
e each other. There is a further fear we must dismiss, apprehension of a possible reputation for finicking pedantry if the law enacts that no utensil whatever in the possession of a citizen shall be of other than the standard size. The legislator must take it as a general principle
747 that there is a universal usefulness in the subdivisions and complications of numbers, whether these complications are exhibited in pure numbers, in lengths and depths, or again in musical notes and motions, whether of rectilinear ascent and descent or of revolution. All must be kept in view by the legislator in his injunction to all citizens, never, so far as they can help it, to rest short of this numerical stand-

ardization. For alike in domestic and public life and in all the arts and crafts there is no other single branch of education which has the same potent efficacy as the theory of numbers, but its greatest recommendation is that it rouses the naturally drowsy and dull, and makes him b quick, retentive, and shrewd—a miraculous improvement of cultivation upon his native parts. So all these branches of study will be found fair and becoming, if only by further laws and institutions you expel illiberality and commercialism from the souls of those who are to pursue them thoroughly to their profit; otherwise you will be surprised c to find that you have produced not a philosopher but a regular knave —an effect already produced, as we can see, in the case of Egyptians, Phoenicians, and many other races, by the illiberality of their other pursuits and of their opulence, whether the result may have been due to the defects of their legislator, to incidental misfortune, or possibly to some other natural circumstance of such a tendency.

In fact, Megillus and Clinias, there is a further consideration we must not ignore. Some localities have a more marked tendency than d others to produce better or worse men, and we are not to legislate in the face of the facts. Some, I conceive, owe their propitious or ill-omened character to variations in winds and sunshine, others to their waters, and yet others to the products of the soil, which not only provide the body with better or worse sustenance, but equally affect the mind for good or bad. Most markedly conspicuous of all, again, will e be localities which are the homes of some supernatural influence, or the haunts of spirits who give a gracious or ungracious reception to successive bodies of settlers. A sagacious legislator will give these facts all consideration a man can, and do his best to adapt his legislation to them. So you, too, Clinias, must of course do the same. As the intending colonizer of a district you must give your first attention to such points.

CLINIAS: Admirably said, sir. I must certainly do as you recommend.

BOOK VI

ATHENIAN: Well, now, your next business, after all that has now 751 been dealt with, will presumably be to constitute the magistracies in your society.

CLINIAS: Why, of course it will.

ATHENIAN: There are really two branches of social organization implied here. First there are the creation of offices and the appointment of the persons who are to fill them, the determination of the proper number of such posts and the proper manner of appointing to them. Then, when this has been done, comes the assignment of the laws to the several offices, the decision which laws, how many, and of b what type it is proper for each magistracy to administer. But before we make our election, we may pause a little while to lay down a principle of some relevance to the occasion.

CLINIAS : And what may this principle be?

ATHENIAN : Why, it is this. Anyone may surely see that, while legislation is a great achievement, if a well-equipped state gives its excellent laws into the charge of unqualified officials, not merely does no good come of all their excellence, and not only does the state
c become a general laughingstock, but such societies are pretty sure to find their laws a source of the gravest detriment and mischief.

CLINIAS : Yes, surely.

ATHENIAN : Why then, my friend, we must note the presence of this danger in the case of the society you are now contemplating, and its constitution. You see, no doubt, how necessary it is first that men who are to be rightly advanced to posts of power should, in every case, have been thoroughly put to the proof, themselves and their families, from earliest boyhood to the time of their election, and next that those who are to elect them should have been well trained by a schooling in
d law-abiding habits for the work of selecting with right approval, and rejecting with proper disapprobation, candidates who deserve either fate. But in this case how can men who have but recently come together and are unfamiliar with one another, and devoid of education into the bargain, be expected to choose their magistrates in an irreprochable fashion?

CLINIAS : Indeed, 'tis hardly possible.

ATHENIAN : Still, when you are once in the ring, as they say, the time for excuses is past, and that is the case just now with you,
e and with me too. You with your nine colleagues, as I understand, have pledged yourselves to the Cretan people to throw your souls into the work of the foundation, and I, on my side, am pledged to help you
752 with our present fanciful tale. And, to be sure, since I am telling a tale, I should not like to leave it without its head; it would look monstrous ugly if it roamed at large in that condition.

CLINIAS : Very true, sir.

ATHENIAN : Yes, and besides, I mean to do my best for you.

CLINIAS : Then, with all my heart, let us do as we say.

ATHENIAN : So we will, with God's permission, if we can get the better of our years so far.
b CLINIAS : We may fairly count on God's permission.

ATHENIAN : To be sure we may. So with his help, let us make a further point.

CLINIAS : What point is that?

ATHENIAN : What a spirited adventure our present experiment in founding a state will prove.

CLINIAS : Of what are you thinking in that remark, and why in particular do you make it?

ATHENIAN : Of the lighthearted temerity with which we are

legislating for the inexperienced in the hope that they will end by accepting our proposed enactments. Yet this much must be reasonably
clear, Clinias, even to the not specially discerning, that no body of c
men will accept them readily from the first, but only if we could contrive to wait until those who have been given a taste of them in their
boyhood, grown up under them, and become thoroughly at home with
them come to play their part in choosing the whole body of public officials. But, mark you, this point once compassed, supposing there is
any plan or device by which it can be truly secured, I believe a society
so schooled would have an assured guarantee of survival well beyond
that interval.

CLINIAS : That sounds reasonable enough.   d

ATHENIAN : Well then, let us consider whether some such measure as this would be sufficient for our purpose. What I maintain,
Clinias, is that it is the duty of you Cnossians, before all other Cretans,
not merely to treat the soil you are now settling with all religious care,
but to give unflagging attention to the appointment of the original officials by the surest and best method possible. In general, this will be
a comparatively light task, but it is indispensably necessary that we
should begin by taking the utmost pains with the selection of curators e
of the laws.

CLINIAS : Well, what measure or plan have we in contemplation
for this?

ATHENIAN : I will tell you. Sons of Crete, I declare it the Cnossians' duty, in view of their leading position among your numerous
cities, to join with the new arrivals in your settlement to elect a body
of thirty-seven men in all from both sections, nineteen from the new
arrivals and the rest from Cnossus itself. This body the Cnossians 753
should present to your city, including yourself as a citizen of the
colony and one of the eighteen, either with their free consent or by a
modest measure of compulsion.

CLINIAS : But pray, sir, why have you not proposed a share in
our citizenship for yourself and Megillus as well?

ATHENIAN : Why, Clinias, Athens is a proud state and so is
Sparta, and both are far away, but you have every proper qualification,
as have also your fellow founders. What has just been said about you b
is equally applicable to them. So much, then, for the most satisfactory procedure in our present circumstances. In course of time, if
the constitution has survived, let the board be appointed by some such
process as this. All shall have a voice in the election of these magistrates who bear arms in the cavalry or infantry and have served in
the field as long as their age permitted. The election shall be held in
the sanctuary regarded as most venerable by the state. Each voter shall c
deposit on the altar a tablet inscribed with the name of his nominee,
his father, his tribe, and the ward to which he belongs, and subscribe
his own name with the same particulars. Anyone who pleases shall be

permitted to remove any voting tablet to the contents of which he has an objection and expose it in the market place within not less than thirty days. The names found to head the poll, to the number of three hundred, shall then be exhibited by the authorities to the view of the d whole community, and every citizen shall again vote for any of them he pleases, the officials once more publishing the hundred names which stand first. On the third occasion anyone who pleases is to vote for any name he pleases of the hundred, passing between sacrificial victims; the seven-and-thirty who receive most votes shall be submitted to a scrutiny and appointed to the magistracy by the officials.

e   Who, then, Megillus and Clinias, are to institute all these regulations in our state about official posts and the scrutiny for them? We can see, I suppose, that there must be such persons in a society which is just beginning to get under way, but who they can be before there are any magistrates is a problem. Have them we must, by hook or crook, and they must be no common fellows either, but men of the highest parts. For, as the adage runs, 'Well begun is half done,' and we all commend a fair beginning of anything, though the beginning is, in my own opinion, more than half the work, and a fair beginning has 754 never yet been commended to its full merits.

CLINIAS : Very true.

ATHENIAN : Then as we are agreed on the point we must not pass it over in silence without making clear to ourselves how it should be set about. Though, for my own part, I am ready with no more than one observation which is needful and salutary at this juncture.

CLINIAS : And what is that?

ATHENIAN : That the city we are about to found has, as I may say, neither father nor mother, other than the society which is found- b ing it. Not that I forget that plenty of such foundations have often enough been, and will hereafter be, at variance with their founders. But as things stand at present, it is as it is with a child; even if he is someday to have his differences with his parents, yet while the help-lessness of childhood lasts, he is attached to them and they to him; he is always running to his family and finds his only allies among his own relatives. Now I say the same connection is to be found all ready to our purpose between the Cnossians and our new state—thanks c to their care for it—and between it and Cnossus. So I maintain, as I have already maintained—a sound thought is not spoiled by repeti-tion—that the Cnossians must join in taking charge of all this busi-ness. They should co-opt not less than a hundred of the newly arrived colonists, selecting the most aged and best men they can, and there should be another hundred from Cnossus itself. These latter, as I say, must come to our new city and take their share in providing for the d lawful appointment of officials and the scrutiny following on appoint-ment. When this business has been done, the Cnossians should keep themselves to Cnossus, and the new state should be left to preserve itself and prosper by its own endeavors. To proceed, let those who belong to the thirty-seven, now and for all time to come, be taken to be appointed for the following purposes. They are to be curators in the first place of the laws, and in the next of the records in which every citizen has made his return to the officials of the amount of his property, with the exception of four minas for those of the highest assessment, three for the second, two for the third, and one for the lowest. If e anyone is detected in possession of anything further in excess of the returns, let the whole of such sum be forfeited to the public, and let it further be open to anyone who will to pursue him on a charge that is neither creditable nor of comely name, but infamous for him who is convicted of contemning law for gain. Let him who will, that is, lay an indictment for *infamous gain* and prosecute the case before the curators in person. If the defendant lose the case, he shall have no 755 share in the 'common good,' and in any distribution from the public funds, he shall go without his part, except for his allotment; his conviction shall also be recorded, for his lifetime, in a place where it may be read by all who will. No curator shall hold office for more than twenty years, or be elected to his office at an age earlier than fifty; if he is sixty at the time of appointment he shall hold office no longer than ten years, and conformably to this rule, when a man's life is prolonged beyond seventy, he must in no case expect to hold office on b this important board.

As to the curators of the laws, then, let us take it that they are charged with these three duties. Each fresh statute, as legislation proceeds, will lay on them such further duties as they should undertake beyond those now specified. For the present we may turn to the appointment of the rest of our officials in order. We must next, of course, choose generals of the forces, and their military assistants, as we may call them, hipparchs and phylarchs, as well as divisional c commanders of the tribal infantry, whom we may very conveniently designate by that very title, taxiarchs; it is, in fact, the name commonly given them. As to these posts, there shall be a first nomination of generals, taken solely from among our citizens, by the curators of the laws, and a selection from the nominees by all who have borne arms at the proper age, or are actually bearing them on the occasion. Should anyone, however, judge a person whose name has not been included a better candidate than one of the nominees, he shall name his man, as well as the person in whose place he proposes him, take an d oath to that effect, and put him forward as a rival candidate; whichever of the two shall be approved by show of hands shall then be placed on the select list. The three who receive most votes shall be appointed generals and controllers of military affairs, after passing the same scrutiny as the curators of laws. The generals so elected shall make their own preliminary nomination of taxiarchs to the number of e twelve, one for each tribe; the procedure as to counternomination, voting, and final scrutiny shall be for taxiarchs the same as for generals. This assembly shall for the present—as neither council nor prytanes have been appointed—be convoked by the curators in the holiest and most spacious area available, the full-armed infantry and the cavalry occupying distinct stations, and all who rank after them in the forces forming a third group. Generals and hipparchs shall be chosen by a vote of the whole body, taxiarchs by a vote of all the in-

756 fantry, and their phylarchs by a vote of all the cavalry. The generals must appoint their own commanders of light-armed troops, archers, or other divisions of the forces. Thus it only remains to arrange for the appointment of hipparchs. Accordingly, the preliminary nomination in their case shall be made by the same authority which nominates in the case of generals, and the selection and counternomination shall

b proceed as in the case of generals. The cavalry shall give its vote in the presence of the infantry, and the two candidates who receive most votes shall be commanders in chief of the whole mounted force. There may be two challenges of the vote; if it is challenged a third time, those whose business it was to deal with the several returns shall put the issue to a vote among themselves.

There shall be a council of thirty dozen—three hundred and sixty will be a convenient number for our subdivisions—and this whole

c number shall be divided into four groups of ninety, ninety councilors being elected from each property class. First there shall be a vote compulsory upon all citizens for representatives of the highest property class, abstention being visited with a fine prescribed by law. When the voting is over, the names shall be duly recorded, and representatives of the second class voted for on the following day with the same procedure as before. On the third day representatives of the third class shall be chosen by a vote open to all citizens, but compulsory on those

d of the three first classes, the fourth and lowest class being exempt from fine in the case of abstention from the voting. On the fourth day representatives of this lowest fourth class shall be chosen by a vote of all, but there shall be no penalty for members of the third and fourth classes who may choose to abstain, whereas members of the second

e and first classes who decline to vote shall be fined, a member of the second class thrice and a member of the first four times the amount of the previous fine. On the fifth day, the authorities shall exhibit the names already recorded to public view, and there shall be a selection from them in which every citizen shall once more vote, or else pay a fine to the original amount. A hundred and eighty names shall thus be selected from each class; half of them shall be taken by lot and submitted to their scrutiny, and these shall form the council for the year.

Conducted in this way, the election will strike a mean between monarchy and democracy, as a constitutional system always should.

757 There can never be friendship between the slave and his owner, nor between the base and the noble when equal honors are bestowed on

both; indeed, equal treatment of the unequal ends in inequality when not qualified by due proportion; it is these two conditions, in fact, which are the fertile sources of civil discord. It is an old saying, and as true as old, that equality gives birth to friendship; that maxim is most sound and admirable. But 'tis none too clear what sort of equality b it is that has these effects, and the ambiguity makes havoc with us. There are, in fact, two equalities under one name, but, for the most part, with contrary results. The one equality, that of number, weight, and measure, any society and any legislator can readily secure in the award of distinctions, by simply regulating their distribution by the lot, but the true and best equality is hardly so patent to every vision. 'Tis the very award of Zeus. Limited as is its scope in human life, wherever it has scope, in public affairs or private, it works nothing but blessings. For it assigns more to the greater and less to the lesser, c adapting its gifts to the real character of either. In this matter of honors, in particular, it deals proportionately with either party, ever awarding a greater share to those of greater worth, and to their opposites in trained goodness such share as is fit. For we shall in truth find that this sheer justice is always also the statesmanlike policy. It is this, Clinias, at which we must aim, this equality on which we must fix our gaze, in the establishment of our nascent city. And if others would found other such societies, they should shape their legislation with a view to the same end—not to the interest of a handful of dic- d tators or a single dictator, or the predominance of a populace, but always to justice, the justice we explained to be a true and real equality, meted out to various unequals. And yet, after all, a society as a whole will also have to apply these standards with some qualification, if it is to escape dissensions somewhere among its constituent parts. Equity e and indulgence, you know, are always infractions of the strict rule of absolute and perfect justice—which is, in fact, the reason why we must introduce some use of the equality of the lot to avoid disaffection among the masses, though when men do so they should breathe a prayer to God and good luck to direct even the fall of the lot to the justest issue. So you see that while we cannot help availing ourselves of both sorts of equality, we should make the most sparing use we can of one of them, that which appeals to luck.

　　Such, my friends, must be the conduct of a society which means 758 to survive, for the reasons we have given. Now, just as a ship at sea must have a perpetual watch set, day and night, so also a state, tossed, as it is, on the billows of interstate affairs and in peril of being trapped by plots of every sort. Magistrate must therefore follow magistrate in steady sequence from day to night and night to day, sentinel make b over to and take over from sentinel in unbroken succession. No large body will ever be able to discharge these tasks with dispatch; no, we must perforce leave the most part of the councilors for most of the time to stay at home and administer their local business, appointing a

twelfth part of them for each of the twelve months of the year to
c serve as guardians who will give prompt audience to all comers, from
abroad or from our citizens themselves, with reports to make or questions to put about matters in which it concerns a state to reply to other
states or receive their replies to its own inquiries, and will, before all
things, see to it in view of the frequent internal innovations of all
kinds which so commonly occur, that, if possible, no such incidents
d arise, or, if they do, that the state may be quick to perceive and repair
the mischief. For all these reasons the power of convoking and dissolving all meetings of the citizen body, ordinary and stated, or extraordinary and occasional, must lie with this presidential board. The
twelfth part of the council, then, will take order for all these functions,
and will be relieved of them for eleven months of the year, but a
twelfth part of that body must be perpetually associated with our other
officials in maintaining this watch over the state.

e   This, then, will be a reasonable way of ordering matters within
the city. But what of the general superintendence and regulation of
the territory at large? Now that our city and territory as wholes have
both been divided into twelve sections, must we not designate superintendents of the city streets, of buildings, private and public, of harbors, of the market, of springs, and not least, of consecrated precincts,
sanctuaries, and the like?

CLINIAS : To be sure we must.

759   ATHENIAN : So we may say that there will have to be sacristans,
priests, priestesses, for the sanctuaries. For streets and buildings and
the maintenance of proper order in them, for human beings—to avoid
infringement of rights—for lower animals—to secure decent civil
conditions within the city walls and in the suburbs—we shall have to
appoint officials of three kinds, of whom we may call those who are
concerned with the matters just specified 'city commissioners,' and
those who have the control of the market, 'commissioners of the market.' As to priests of either sex for the sanctuaries, any whose dignity
b is hereditary must be left undisturbed, but if—as may well be the case
in such matters in a first settlement—few or none are so provided,
priests of either sex should be instituted, where they are not already
instituted, to act as sacristans for the gods. In all these appointments
use should be made partly of election, partly of the lot; in each urban
and rural district we must effect a friendly combination of the popular
element with the nonpopular element in the way which will make for
fullest concord. As far as priesthoods are concerned, then, we must al-
c low God to effect his own good pleasure by just leaving appointments
to the inspired decision of the lot, but every man on whom the lot may
fall must be subjected to a scrutiny, first as to his freedom from blemishes and legitimate birth, next as to his provenance from houses pure
of all pollution, and the cleanness of his own life, and likewise of those
of his father and mother from bloodguiltiness and all such offenses

against religion. Religious law universally should be fetched from Delphi, and this must be adhered to, official exponents of it being first appointed. Each priesthood should be tenable for a year and no longer; the man who is to celebrate worship in accord with our sacred law should be of the age of not less than sixty; the same regulations shall apply to priests of the other sex. As for the exponents, groups of four tribes are thrice to elect four persons, one from each of themselves; when they have held the scrutiny on the three who obtain most votes, they must send the nine to Delphi for the oracle to nominate one from each three—the rules for the scrutiny and age on appointment to be the same as for priests. The election to a vacancy shall be made by the group of four tribes in which the vacancy occurs. As concerns treasures of the sacred funds and precincts of the various sanctuaries and controllers of their produce and rents, three persons shall be appointed from the highest property class for the largest sanctuaries, two for those of medium size, and one for the smallest—the procedure in their election and scrutiny to be the same as in that of the generals. Thus much, then, for the regulation of religion.

Nothing, if we can help it, shall be left unguarded. As for the city, guard shall be kept over it thus. It shall be the concern of generals, taxiarchs, hipparchs, phylarchs, and prytanes as well as of the commissioners of city and market, when once we have them duly elected and instituted. Watch shall be kept over all the rest of our territory in the following manner. As our territory as a whole has been divided into twelve nearly equal districts, one tribe shall be annually assigned by lot to each district and shall provide five 'rural commissioners and captains of the watch,' as we may style them; it shall be the business of each of the five to select from his own tribe twelve of the younger men, who must be twenty-five years of age or over, but not over thirty. The territorial districts shall be assigned to these groups in rotation by lot, each for a month of the year, to ensure personal experience and knowledge of the whole territory on the part of every member. These guards and their commanders shall hold their respective posts for a term of two years. From the position, or district, originally determined by the lot they shall be regularly conducted by the captains of the watch, at monthly intervals, to the next in order clockwise, clockwise being deemed to be in the sense from west to east. On the expiry of the first year of service, to familiarize as many of the guards as possible, not merely with the state of the country at one single season of the year, but with the course of the seasons in all districts, they shall be conducted by the officers then in command through the successive districts in the reverse order—counterclockwise—until the expiry of their second year. For the following year there must be a fresh election of rural commissioners and captains of watch, the five superintendents of twelves. Their functions while on duty in the various stations shall be these. First, they must provide for the most effectual blocking of the territory against an enemy by the construction of all necessary dikes and trenches, and the erection of fortifications as a check on any would-be despoilers of territory or cattle. For these purposes they may employ the draft animals and household servants of the various districts, who shall act as their instruments and be under their orders, though they should do their best to avoid requisitioning them in their own busy seasons. In a word, they are to do their utmost to make the whole country inaccessible to an enemy and easily accessible to friends, whether human beings, beasts of burden, or cattle; it shall be their charge to make all the roads as comfortable

b as possible, and to ensure that the flow of rain water from the highlands into the hollow valleys between the hills does good rather than harm to the countryside by regulating its discharge by dams and trenches, so that as the valleys receive or absorb the rainfall, they may supply all the lower-lying farms and localities with watercourses and springs, and furnish even the driest localities with an abundance of excellent water. Spring waters, whether rivers or fountains, they are to adorn and beautify by plantations and buildings; they shall secure

c a copious supply by collecting their streams in hewn watercourses. If there is any consecrated grove or precinct in the vicinity they shall enhance its charm by making conduits which convey their waters at all seasons into the very sanctuaries. In all such places our young men should construct exercising grounds for themselves and their seniors, furnished with warm baths for the service of the latter and supplied with plenty of dry seasoned fuel; here they shall provide a friendly

d home for the treatment of invalids and persons worn with the labors of husbandry—a treatment much more profitable than a poorly qualified physician.

Work of this and similar kinds will be both useful and ornamental to a district and will also afford charming recreation. The serious duties of the office shall be as follows. Each group of sixty shall protect its district, not merely against enemies, but against professed friends. If a wrong is done to neighbor or fellow citizen by any person,

e bond or free, the case shall come for trial before the five commanders, who shall act alone in petty cases, and in more serious cases of complaint, where the sum involved is one not exceeding three minas, in concert with the twelves. No judge shall try a case, and no official shall discharge an office, without liability to an audit, except those who, like monarchs, pronounce a final decision. In the case of our rural commissioners in particular, if they oppress those who are under

762 their care, by imposing unfair burdens, by attempts to requisition any of their farm stock without their consent, by reception of presents intended to purchase their good graces, or finally by unjust distributions, they shall be branded with public disgrace for their yielding to corruption; for all further wrong to the inhabitants of a district, where the value involved is one mina or less, they shall submit to a voluntary

trial before the villagers and neighbors. If they decline to do so in any case of a major or even a minor charge, in the hope that their con- b stant monthly migration to a fresh district will prove a sufficient defense against the prosecution, the complainant in such a case shall take proceedings in the public courts; if he gains the case, he shall exact a double penalty from the absconder who has declined to submit himself to a voluntary judgment. The daily course of life of the commanders and rural commission during their two years of office shall be as follows. In the first place, there shall be in each district a public mess at which all shall take their meals together. If a man absent him- c self from mess for a single day, or sleep out of bounds for a single night, except at the command of his officers or from some sudden and absolute necessity, provided the five report the case and post him in the market place as a deserter from his watch, he shall suffer disgrace as a traitor to his duty to his country, and be subject to chastisement by stripes, for which there shall be no redress, at the hands of any who meet him and care to inflict it. Should one of the five command- d ers themselves act in the same way on his own authority, it shall be a matter for the attention of the whole sixty, and any of them who may observe the fact or be informed of it without taking action shall fall under the provisions of the same laws and be penalized more severely than the younger men; he shall be deemed disqualified for holding any post of authority over his juniors. The curators of the law shall exercise an exact inquisition into such cases, with a view to their complete prevention, or failing that to the imposition of a merited punishment. It must be strictly binding on all to believe that no man what- e soever will prove a creditable master until he has first been a servant, and that less pride should be taken in successful ruling than in loyal service—service, in the first place, of the laws—since to serve them is to serve heaven—and after the laws, of a young man's honorably distinguished seniors. In the next place, a member of our rural police must have partaken through his two-years' service of the mean and meager daily rations. In fact, immediately after their selection, the twelves shall come together with their five commanders and resolve 763 that, like the servants they are, they shall have no further servants, or slaves of their own, nor yet apply to farmers and villagers at large, and use their servants to minister to their own private requirements, but only upon public employments. In other matters they shall make up their minds to a life of personal exertion in which they shall be their own employers and attendants. They shall further carry out a thorough exploration of the whole country under arms, both summer and winter, with a view to complete familiarity with its topography, b as well as to its defense, since such universally diffused and exact acquaintance with their own country may be presumed to be as important a study as they can have. Hence they should practice coursing and other forms of hunting while they are in their prime, quite as

much for this reason as for the combined pleasure and benefit which commonly attends such exercises. The men and their profession, then, may be known by any name one likes, scouts, or rural commission, or another, but the calling must be followed with might and main by
c any man who is minded to be a competent defender of his native city.

The next step in our selection of officials will be concerned with the appointment of commissioners for the market and the city. To our sixty rural commissioners will correspond three commissioners for the city. These shall divide the twelve urban districts into three regions, and, like the former board, have charge of the roads—the streets of the town itself, and the several highways leading from the country to
d the capital—as well as of the conformity of all the buildings erected with the legal regulations. In particular, they must take care that the water supply, which the rural police shall transmit and deliver to them in proper condition, shall reach the reservoirs in due plenty and purity, and so serve the ends of beauty no less than of utility. Hence they must be men at once of capacity and of leisure for public affairs. Accordingly, any citizen may propose for the office any name he pleases from the highest property class; when the names have been
e put to the vote and reduced to the six who receive the most numerous suffrages, the officer charged with that function shall select three by lot; these, when they have passed their scrutiny, shall hold the office under the regulations made for them.

There shall next be a selection of five commissioners of the market, to be taken from the first and second property classes. The procedure in this case shall be in general the same as for the urban commissioners; of the ten who receive most votes, they shall take five by lot and, on their passing their scrutiny, proclaim them appointed. In every case, every elector shall cast his vote; any who declines shall,
764 if his conduct is brought to the cognizance of the authorities, be fined fifty drachmas, and in addition be declared a bad citizen. Attendance at the assembly, or public convention, shall be open to any citizen, and compulsory on a member of the first or second property class, under a fine of ten drachmas if detected in absenting himself from these gatherings. For the third and fourth classes, there shall be no compulsion, and their members may escape the penalty, except in the case
b of a notification by authority that all are to attend for some urgent cause. The commissioners, then, shall superintend the orderly conduct of the market in conformity with legal regulations, and be charged with the prevention of injury to sanctuaries and fountains in its precincts; in the case of such injury they shall punish the offender, if a slave or an alien, by whipping or imprisonment. If the author of such disorders is a citizen, they shall be competent to fine the offender up to one hundred drachmas on their own sole authority—
c or to double the sum when acting in conjunction with the urban commissioners. The urban commissioners shall have the same power of

fine and chastisement in their own department; they may impose a
fine of a mina on their own authority, or of two, when they act with
the commissioners of the market.

It will next be in place to create authorities in music and physical
training, in either case two sets, to have charge respectively of education and of competitions. By officers of education the law understands
superintendents of gymnasiums and schools in charge of their
seemly maintenance as well as of the education given and the connected supervision of attendances and accommodation for children of d
both sexes. By officers for competitions it understands judges of performers contending in both musical and athletic competitions, and of
these there should, once more, be two sorts, the one for music and
the other for athletics. In athletics it will be proper to have the same
officials as judges of both men and horses, but in music to have one
set of judges for solo performances—e.g., those of reciters, harpists,
flutists, and the like—and a second and different set for choral sing- e
ing. So we should, I take it, begin by selecting our authority for the
play of our choirs of children, men, and maids as exhibited in the
dance and the whole system of the musician's art. One such authority
will be sufficient for them, who must be not under the age of forty 765
years. One official of not less than thirty years of age will also be
sufficient for the soloists, to enter the performers and pronounce a
competent decision between competitors. The actual president or con-
troller of the choirs should be appointed in the following way. All
amateurs of such pursuits must attend the assembly on pain of a fine
if they absent themselves—a matter which shall come under the jurisdiction of the curators of the laws—but attendance shall not be compulsory on others against their will. Then an elector must take the b
name he proposes from the list of experts, and the only point that shall
count for inclusion or rejection at the scrutiny shall be the candidate's
competence or, on the other side, incompetence in the subject. Of the
ten candidates who head the poll, he who wins the lot shall, after
scrutiny, preside over the choirs for the year as the law requires. In
precisely the same way the candidate who wins the lot shall preside
for the year over competitors who have entered for the solos and concerted pieces, the winner of the lot thus submitting to the decision of
the judges. Next we have to appoint from the third and second of our c
property classes directors of the athletic competitions for horses and
human beings; it shall be compulsory on the first three classes to attend this election, but the meanest class shall not be penalized for
their absence. The successful candidates shall be those who shall be
taken by lot from twenty elected by a previous vote and must also be
approved by the suffrage of the scrutinizing body. In appointing to or
selection for any office whatsoever, if any names are rejected on scru- d
tiny, others shall be substituted by the same methods and submitted
to scrutiny by the same procedure.

There is still one office to be filled in the department under our consideration, that of the supervisor of education, male and female, as a whole. Accordingly, the law will require this post also to be held by a single official who must be a man of not less than fifty years, and the father of a legitimate family, preferably of both sexes, but failing that, of one or the other sex, and nominee and nominator alike must

e bear in mind that the post is far the most important of the highest offices in the state. For in all growing creatures alike—trees, beasts gentle or savage, humankind—the first sprouts and shootings, if but fair, are most potent to effect the happy consummation of goodness

766 according to kind. Now man we call a gentle creature, but in truth, though he is wont to prove more godlike and gentle than any if he have but the right native endowments and the right schooling, let him be trained insufficiently or amiss, and he will show himself more savage than anything on the face of the earth. Wherefore the legislator must make the training of children no secondary or subordinate task; since 'tis a first and primary need that their director shall be well chosen, he must do all that in him lies to appoint to the charge of their direction

b him who is in all points best of all the citizens. Accordingly, all officials, with the exception of the council and its committees, shall repair to the temple of Apollo, where each of them shall give his vote by secret ballot for one of the curators of the laws, whomsoever he judges fittest to control education. He that shall receive most votes shall pass a scrutiny before all hitherto-appointed officers other than the curators themselves and thereafter hold his post for five years; in the sixth, there

c shall be a fresh appointment to this charge by the same procedure. If a public official die before his term of office be expired, and there be still more than thirty days to run, a substitute shall be appointed in the same manner by the body already duly charged with the election. If an overseer of orphans decease, their resident relatives on both sides down to children of first cousins shall appoint a successor within ten days, or, in default, each such person shall incur a fine of

d one drachma per diem until the appointment of such guardian have been made. A society, as we know, will soon become no society at all, without duly appointed courts of justice. But a judge who may not make his voice heard, and, like an arbitrator, has no more to say in the preliminary proceedings than the contending parties, will in no case be a sufficient judge of disputed rights, and therefore a good court cannot well be either numerous or small and of poor capacity. It

e should be clear in every case what the contending claim of either party is, and time and slow and repeated preliminary inquiry conduce to this elucidation of the issues at stake. Hence the challenging parties should first appear before neighbors and friends who are best ac-

767 quainted with the matters in dispute. If, when all is done, a man cannot get a satisfactory decision from this body, he shall proceed to

another court. If the two courts fail to settle the matter, the judgment of a third shall be final in the case.

In a certain sense the appointment of these courts is also an election of magistrates. In fact, any magistrate is bound also to be a judge in some questions, while a judge, though not actually a magistrate, becomes a magistrate, and one of considerable moment, for the day on which he finally decides a case. Thus we may include the b judges among our magistrates and proceed to say who will be suited for the function, with what matters they shall deal, and what their number should be in various cases. The truest court, then, will be that which the various litigants appoint themselves for their own cases by an agreed choice. But for all other cases there shall be two tribunals, one when one private person complains of wrong received from another, and desires to bring him before a court for its decision between them, a second when a citizen believes the public wronged by some c other and desires to support the state. And we must explain what and who their members are to be. First of all, we must institute a common court of justice for all private persons whose controversies reach the third hearing, and it shall be constituted thus. On the day before that on which a new year opens with the month following the summer solstice, all magistrates, whether their office be annual or of longer duration, shall assemble in the same temple; then, after an oath sworn in the name of the god, they shall set apart, as a choice offering, if I d may say so, one judge from each board of magistrates, viz., the member they judge to have filled his magistracy best and to be likely to decide the cases of his fellow citizens best and most religiously for the ensuing year. When the selection has been made, there shall be a scrutiny by this electing body itself, and if any name be rejected, another shall be chosen in like manner; those who pass this scrutiny shall act as judges for parties who have declined other jurisdiction, and their suffrages shall be open. Presence as eyewitnesses and auditors of these trials shall be compulsory on the members of council and other offi- e cials who appointed the judges, permissive to others who may wish to attend. A person who charges any judge with deliberate wrongful decision in a case shall go before the curators of the laws with his accusation; the judge convicted on such a count shall be liable to make good half the damage to the party who has incurred it; if the case be deemed to call for a graver penalty, the judges who deal with the suit shall specify the further punishment to be inflicted or fine to be paid to the public and the institutor of the prosecution. As to charges of crime against the public, it will be necessary, in the first place, to 768 give the commonalty a voice in the hearing—when the state is wronged all are sufferers, and all would have a just grievance if deprived of a part in such decisions—but while the initial and final stages in such a case should be assigned to the populace, the investigation should take place before three of the highest magistrates, agreed upon by defendant and plaintiff; if the two cannot come to an agreement for themselves, the council shall revise the choice of each party.

b As far as possible, too, all citizens should take their part in the private cases, since a man who has no share in the right to sit in judgment on others feels himself to be no real part of the community. Hence there must, of course, be courts for the several tribes with judges appointed by lot, as occasion arises, to give their verdicts uninfluenced by personal appeals, but the final determination in all such suits must be with this court which we claim to have constituted with the utmost freedom from corruptibility possible to human power for the service of

c those who can reach no settlement either before their neighbors or in the tribal judicatures.

This matter of courts of justice, then—as I say, it is equally hard to give them the name of magistracies as to refuse it without qualification—has partly now been dealt with in what I may call its outlines, partly left unfinished. In fact, far the best place for a more exact regulation of judicial procedure and classification of actions at law will be found toward the end of our legislation. So we may tell the subject

d to wait till we come to the end of our work, but the method of appointment to other magistracies has received fairly full regulation. But a full and exact treatment of every single point of civil and political administration cannot be confidently given until our survey has covered the whole ground from start to finish in detail in the natural order. Still you will see that the stage it has now reached with these

e arrangements for the election of our officials forms a sufficient conclusion of preliminaries and starting point for legislation without further delay or hesitation.

CLINIAS: Your treatment of the preliminaries, sir, has been wholly to my mind, and the way in which you have just linked up the beginning of what is still to come with the conclusion of what has gone before pleases me even better.

769   ATHENIAN: Then so far, we may say, our grave game for the aged has been finely played.

CLINIAS: What you really mean to call fine, I fancy, is the hard work of active men.

ATHENIAN: Possibly, but ask yourself whether you agree with me on a further point.

CLINIAS: What is it, and to what does it relate?

ATHENIAN: Why you know how the painter's brush never seems to have finished its work on a figure; it seems as though it could go on with endless embellishments of coloring or relief—or whatever may

b be the professional name for the process—without ever reaching a point at which the picture admits no further enhancement of beauty or vivacity.

CLINIAS: I think I have heard enough about such matters to

follow your description, though I have no personal familiarity with these arts.

ATHENIAN: And no loss either! Still there is a point which we may use this chance reference to them to illustrate. Suppose it were an artist's intention to paint a figure of great beauty which should c moreover be steadily enhanced, not deteriorated, by the lapse of years. You are aware that since the painter is not immortal, either he must leave behind him a successor capable of repairing any damage done to the figure by time, as well as of embellishing it by improving on defects due to the artist's imperfect craftsmanship, or his immense labor have very transitory results?

CLINIAS: To be sure.

ATHENIAN: Well now, and the legislator, has he not a similar d intention? He wants first of all to frame his laws with the closest approach to absolute perfection he can compass. Then, as time goes on and he puts his scheme to the test of practice, will any legislator, think you, be thoughtless enough to forget that they must be full of such lacunae which some successor will have to correct, to ensure that the constitution and system of the society he has founded may e steadily improve, not deteriorate?

CLINIAS: That is the presumable intention of every lawgiver. Of course it must be.

ATHENIAN: So if a man found some means of effecting this— found out a method of teaching another by example or precept how to understand, better or worse, the way to conserve laws and improve them—he would never tire of explaining that method, I conceive, until he achieved success.

CLINIAS: Of course not.

ATHENIAN: Well, must not I myself and both of you do the 770 same thing now?

CLINIAS: Do just what, do you mean?

ATHENIAN: Why since we are about to form a code of law and have appointed curators of it, and those young men by comparison with ourselves, whose sun is setting, we must, as I say, not merely legislate, but at the same time do all we can to make them also legislators as well as curators of law.

CLINIAS: By all means, if only we are equal to it. b

ATHENIAN: Well, we must at least make the attempt and do our best.

CLINIAS: Certainly.

ATHENIAN: So let this be our language to them. Friends and preservers of law, there will be a host of omissions in the different departments of our present legislation; that simply is not to be helped. Not but what we shall do all we can to sketch the outlines of the more considerable departments as well as of the whole system. But you will have to fill up this outline and must be told what your aim in

c doing so is to be. Megillus, Clinias, and myself have repeatedly stated it to one another, and are agreed that we stated it well, but we are anxious that you should be our sympathetic disciples, that your aim should be that which we one and all hold should be kept in mind by
d both curators and authors of law. Our unanimous pronouncement was, in sum, this, that whatever the way which promises to make a member of our citizen body—male or female, young or old—truly excellent in the virtues of soul proper to human character, be they results of some occupation, some native disposition, some possession, or passion, or conviction, or course of study, that and no other shall be the end, as I say, toward which every nerve shall be strained so long as life endures, and that not a single soul shall be found to prefer aught which hampers these pursuits. In the last event, should there be no
e choice but to be driven from the state itself before she deigns to crouch under the servile yoke of rule by the base, or to leave her for exile, any such fate must be borne rather than the change to a polity which will breed baser men. This was *our* concurrent judgment before you. *You*, in your turn, are now to set both ends before you in your commendation or censure of our laws, to censure such as cannot serve the pur-
771 pose, accept those that can with cordial good will, and make them the rule of your lives. All other pursuits, which lead to some different so-called good, you must dismiss.

We may open the legislation which is now to follow in some such way as this, with religion as our starting point. We must first return to our number of five thousand and forty and the various convenient sub-
b divisions we find both in this total and in the constituent tribe, which was, you will remember, by assumption one twelfth of the whole, and is thus the exact product of one-and-twenty by twenty. Now our total number permits of division by twelve, and so likewise does that of the tribe; so each such division must be thought of as a sacred thing, a gift of heaven corresponding with the months of the year and the revolution of the universe. This, in fact, is why all communities are under the sway of an instinct which consecrates them, though some authorities perhaps have made a truer division than others, and been more fortunate in the result of the consecration. For our own
c part, our present point is that we were justified in our preference for the number, five thousand and forty, as it is divisible by every integer from one to twelve with the exception of eleven, and that can be very readily put right, since one way of mending it is to set two hearths on one side. That the fact is so could be proved in a very few words if we
d had the leisure. So we may trust in our present task to the traditional belief in question and make this division. Each section will be called by the name of a god or a child of the gods and provided with altars and their furniture, where we shall convoke two sacrificial assemblies per month—twelve for the divisions into tribes, and twelve for the corresponding sections of the town itself. Their first purpose will

be to ensure the divine favor and to promote religion, and their second, from our point of view, to encourage mutual intimate acquaintance and social intercourse of all kinds. For it is particularly necessary in view of the contraction of marriages and the connections to which they give rise to do away with our ignorance of the quarter from which a bride is taken, the bride herself, and the family she is entering; the utmost possible care should be taken to prevent any mistakes in such matters. To ensure that grave result, even the sports of our lads and lasses should take the form of dances of both sexes, which will incidentally give them the opportunity, within reason and at an age which affords a colorable justification, of seeing and being seen in undress, so far as sober modesty in all the parties will permit. The superintendence and control of all such matters should be in the hands of our directors of choirs, who should also, in conjunction with the curators of laws, legislate on any points we may omit in our regulations. As I said, in all such cases of multifarious minor details, it is inevitable that the legislator should make omissions for which those who have regular yearly experience of them should learn by practice to provide by regulations and annual amendments until a sufficient rule for such observances and customs is felt to have been reached. So a moderate but a definite time to allow for the experiment to cover each and all of the details would be a ten-years' cycle of sacrifices and festal dances, within which the various magistracies—acting in concert with the original legislator, if he is still alive, or alone if he has deceased—may report omissions in their several departments to the curators of laws, and attempt amendments until the various regulations are felt to have been brought to perfection; they should then declare them incapable of modification and thereafter enforce them with the rest of the laws originally established by the legislator's imposition. On these statutes they must in no case make any willful innovation, but if they should ever judge themselves under the stress of absolute necessity, they are to consult the advice of all magistrates, the whole popular assembly, and all the oracles, and make such modifications as are approved by all these authorities, but no other changes whatever; the law will require that the *noncontents* shall always prevail.

Whensoever, then, a man of five-and-twenty or upward, on inspection made and submitted to, is satisfied that he has found in any quarter a congenial and suitable match for the common procreation of children, he shall in all cases marry before he comes to five-and-thirty. But let him first be informed of the right manner of seeking for the suitable and fitting, for, as Clinias says, each law must be introduced by its own preamble.

CLINIAS : Thank you, sir, for the allusion. You have taken what I find to be a most appropriate occasion for its introduction.

ATHENIAN : You are most kind. This, then, is what we shall say

to the son of a worthy stock. My lad, the match to be made is that which will find favor with men of sense, and their counsel to you will be not to set your heart overmuch on avoidance of a poor match, or pursuit of a wealthy, but rather, when other things are equal, always to enter the bond with a preference for the humbler party. This will, in truth, be to the benefit of both society at large and the contracting houses, for balance and due proportion are out of all comparison more excellent than an unqualified extreme. And he who knows himself
b overhot of temper and overhasty to act in all he does should connect himself by preference with a quiet family, while he of the contrary bent should look for connections of the contrary kind. And we may lay down one sole rule for all matches. A man should 'court the tie' that is for the city's good, not that which most takes his own fancy. Yet there is a native instinct by which each of us is ever drawn to his own nearest like, and this brings inequalities of manner and moral
c temper into society at large; these lead by unfailing consequence in most states to effects which we would not have in ours. To make express and formal statutes, indeed, to such effect—to forbid the rich man to marry into a wealthy house, or the capable into a capable, to force the hasty-tempered to seek partners in matrimony among the phlegmatic and the placid among the hasty—would be ridiculous, and would, moreover, rouse general resentment. It is none too easy to see
d that a state should be like a well-compounded bowl where the wine when poured in is hot to madness, but when corrected by another and a soberer divinity and fairly mated furnishes us a healthful and modest draught. I say no man, or hardly any, has the wit to discern that it is even so with the blending of offspring. And this is why we are driven to let the matter alone in our law and do our endeavor to charm the individual man to set an inward equipoise among his offspring above that equality of condition in wedlock that thirsts so insatiably
e after riches, and to direct him who is bent upon a wealthy match by reproaches without the compulsion of written enactment.

This, then—as well, of course, as what we said before—shall be our exhortation to wedlock and the duty of man to cleave to everlast-
774 ingness by ever leaving children and children's children after him to serve God in his room. All this, and still more, might be said in a proper preamble on the obligation to matrimony. But should there be any who refuses willing obedience, but keeps himself apart and unfellowed in the city, and so comes to five-and-thirty unwedded, he shall pay a yearly fine of a hundred drachmas if he belong to the wealthiest class, of seventy if to the second, of sixty for the third, and thirty for
b the fourth, and this fine shall be dedicate to Hera. He that defaults in his yearly payment shall be indebted in ten times the amount. Payment shall be enforced by the treasurer of that goddess, who shall be liable himself to the debt in case of nonexaction, and all shall be bound to render account of such matters at the audits. This shall be

the pecuniary penalty of refusal to marry. As to marks of honor from his juniors, the offender shall receive none, and no junior, if he can help it, shall show him any deference whatsoever. If he presume to chastise any of them, all shall come to the support and defense of the c injured party, and any person present who fails in this shall be legally proclaimed both a dastard and a traitor.

With dowries we have already dealt, but may say once more that there is every reasonable presumption that the poor will reach old age when neither he that takes a wife nor he who gives her is straitened in means, for in our society all citizens are assured of the necessaries of life; moreover, there will be less of arrogance on the wife's side, and of mean sordid slavery to her moneybags on the husband's. So he that obeys us will have one good deed to his score; he that disobeys, d whether by accepting or by offering more than the worth of fifty drachmas toward the bride's appareling—or of one mina, or half as much again, or in the case of the wealthiest class, twice so much— shall be liable in an equal sum to the public exchequer, and the surplus offered or received shall be sacred to Hera and Zeus. Payment shall be enforced by the treasurers of these deities precisely as we directed its enforcement against celibates by the treasurers of Hera, or e in case of nonenforcement, they shall discharge the fine from their own private purses.

The right of valid betrothal shall belong in the first instance to the father, failing him to the grandfather, in default of both to brothers on the father's side; if there are no such kinsmen, it shall pass in like manner to the kindred on the mother's side. Should a case of exceptional destitution arise, the nearest kinsmen, whoever they may be, shall have the right to act in conjunction with the guardians.

Concerning the ceremonies introductory to wedlock and any 775 other holy rites it may be proper to fulfill before, during, or after the nuptials, the citizen should make inquiry of the exponents of religious law, and be satisfied that all is well and truly done if he follows their instructions.

In the matter of the marriage feast, the persons to be bidden to it should be not more than five male or female friends of either family, with the same number of kinsmen and connections of either, and in no case shall the expenditure be disproportionate to the means of the b giver—one mina for a person of the wealthiest class, half that sum for one of the second, and thus in proportion as the means of the party diminish. Obedience to the law should receive commendation from all; the disobedient shall be punished by the curators of the laws as a boor with tastes untrained in the strains of the hymeneal Muses. As for drinking to excess, 'tis everywhere unseemly, except at a feast of the divine giver of the grape—and dangerous as well—above all, in one whose mind is seriously set on wedlock. Then, if ever, 'tis meet for bride and bridegroom to be in their sober senses, seeing they are come c to so grave a turning on life's road, and must take all care, moreover, that that which is at any moment begetting shall be the work of sober parents, for 'tis quite unknown what night or day shall—under God— give it its being. Besides all this, the work of kind must never be left to bodies dissolved by revelry; the growing life must be fashioned with all due order, surely, firmly, in quiet. But a man in his cups does but sprawl and fumble all ways at once; his body is as crazy as his mind.

d By consequence the drinker is an awkward, bungling sower of his seed, and 'tis no wonder he commonly begets shambling, shifty creatures with souls as twisted as their bodies. Wherefore a man should the rather be wary all the year long, and all his life through, and more particularly while he is procreating offspring, to forbear, so far as he may, from all action that prejudices health or is touched with wrong or violence—he cannot but imprint its color and impress on the souls

e and bodies of the unborn and become sire to a sorely degenerate brood —above all, to keep himself clear of such things all that day and night. For in all the affairs of man's life the first step holds the place of God himself and makes all the rest right, if but approached with

776 proper reverence by all concerned.

He that has marriage in mind must think of one of the two homesteads on his own actual lot as a nest and nursery for his chicks, must leave father and mother and hold his nuptials there, and there keep house and home for himself and his children. For in all the kind affections of life the presence of some dash of unfulfilled longing rivets hearts and knits them in one, while unbroken companionship, when there is none of this longing bred of absence, causes them to drift apart from utter satiety. This is why our young pair should leave

b mother, father, bride's kindred, to their old abodes, and live like settlers in a colony; they will pay visits to the old home and receive visits from it, beget children and bring them up, and thus hand the torch of life on from one generation to another and perpetuate that service of God which our laws demand.

Next for goods and chattels. Which of them should a man possess if proprietorship is to give him true satisfaction? The more part of such goods are as easy to name as to acquire, but there are difficulties of every kind about servants. Why is this? Because the things we say

c about them are partly false, partly true; our very language about slaves contradicts our experience of them and confirms it at once.

MEGILLUS: But pray how are we to take your words? As yet, sir, my friend and I are at a loss for your meaning.

ATHENIAN: And not to be wondered at, Megillus. The status of the Helots of Laconia—the controversy as to its merits or demerits— is probably the most puzzling problem of Hellenic life. There may be a similar, though less acute, controversy about the system of slavery

d under which the Mariandynians are held down at Heraclea, and the position of the serfs of Thessaly. When we take these instances and others like them into account, how shall we set about proprietorship in servants? The point on which I touched in the course of my argument, when you very naturally asked what I had in mind, is simply this. Of course, we are aware that we should all say a man should have the best and most trusty slaves who are to be had. Why, slaves have often enough before now shown themselves far better men in every way than brothers or sons; they have often been the preservation of their masters' persons, property, and whole family. No doubt you e know that such language about slaves is common.

MEGILLUS : So it is, to be sure.

ATHENIAN : And equally common the rival theory that slaves are rotten at heart, and no man of sense should ever put any trust in the whole tribe of them. Nay, the greatest genius among our poets, in speaking of Zeus, makes the explicit declaration that he

> fixed it certain that whatever day
> Makes man a slave, takes half his worth away.[9]   777

So a man takes one or other side in the dispute for himself. Some distrust the whole class and make their servants threefold—nay, a hundredfold—slaves at heart by the scourge and the lash, as though they were dealing with so many wild beasts; others take the very opposite course.

MEGILLUS : Very true.

CLINIAS : Well, then, sir, where there is such utter disagree- b ment, how should we act about this territory of ours? How shall we deal with the right to own and to discipline slaves?

ATHENIAN : Why, Clinias, the human animal is a kittle beast, and so, clearly, is not likely to be, or become, readily amenable to the indispensable distinction between real slave and real free man and master, and so this form of property presents a difficulty. The facts of the common and repeated risings in Messenia and the experience c of communities where there are great numbers of serfs all speaking the same dialect provide accumulated proof of the evils of the system —not to mention the multifarious depredations and adventures of the corsairs of Italy. When we face all this evidence we may well feel perplexed to know how to treat the whole problem. Indeed I see only two courses left open to us—the one that slaves who are to submit to their condition quietly should neither be all of one stock, nor, as far as pos- d sible, of one speech, the other that we should treat them properly and show them consideration, for their own sake indeed, but still more for ours. And proper treatment of men in that position is to use no violence toward a servant, but to wrong him—if such a thing could be— with even more reluctance than an equal. For it is his dealings with those whom he can easily wrong which reveal a man's genuine

---

[9] *Odyssey* 17.322 sq.

unfeigned reverence for right and real abhorrence of wrong. Hence the man whose character and conduct are unsullied with wickedness
e and wrong in his relations with slaves is, beyond all others, sowing the seed for a harvest of goodness, and we may truthfully say the same of every master, or autocrat, or wielder of any kind of power in his relations with a weaker party. Not, of course, but what we should chastise our slaves when they deserve it, not spoil them by such mere admonition as we should use to free men. Our language to a servant should
778 commonly be that of simple command, and there should be no familiar jesting with servants of either sex, though many masters show great unwisdom in this way in their behavior to their slaves, spoiling them in a fashion which makes life hard at once for the servant who is to obey, and the master who is to command him.

CLINIAS : Very rightly said.

ATHENIAN : Well, now that we have done our best to provide the citizen with a sufficient number of servants qualified to assist him in his various tasks, I suppose our next step should be to produce a plan of our houses.

CLINIAS : Yes, of course.

b   ATHENIAN : In fact, as our city is a new foundation, without any earlier habitations, it will have to give its attention to the whole subject of its architecture in all its details, not forgetting those of the temples and city walls. This, Clinias, is a subject which properly comes before that of marriage, but as our whole construction is imaginary, the present will be an excellent opportunity to dispose of it. When our scheme takes actual shape, we shall, God willing, deal with domestic architecture first and make our marriage law the crown and
c completion of our work in this kind. For the present we shall attempt no more than a brief outline.

CLINIAS : Just so.

ATHENIAN : The temples, then, should be built all round the market square, and in fact round the whole city, on elevated sites, with a view at once to security and cleanliness. In their vicinity should be the offices of the magistrates and courts of law, where, as on holy ground, judgment will be received and given, partly because
d the business itself is so solemn, partly because these are the seats of awful deities, and among them courts of law where cases of murder and other crimes worthy of death may fitly be heard. As for walls, Megillus, I am of the same mind as your own Sparta. I would leave them to slumber peacefully in the earth without waking them, and here are my reasons. As the oft-quoted line of the poet happily words
e it, a city's walls should be of bronze and iron, not of stone, and we in particular shall cover ourselves with well-merited ridicule, after taking our young men in annual procession to the open country to block an enemy's path by ditches, entrenchments, and actual buildings of various kinds—all, if you please, with the notion of keeping the foe

well outside our borders—if we shut ourselves in behind a wall. A wall
is, in the first place, far from conducive to the health of town life
and, what is more, commonly breeds of certain softness of soul in the
townsmen; it invites inhabitants to seek shelter within it and leave   779
the enemy unrepulsed, tempts them to neglect effecting their deliverance by unrelaxing nightly and daily watching, and to fancy they will
find a way to real safety by locking themselves in and going to sleep
behind ramparts and bars as though they had been born to shirk toil,
and did not know that the true ease must come from it, whereas dishonorable ease and sloth will bring forth toil and trouble, or I am
much mistaken. No, if men must have a wall of sorts, they should
construct their own dwellings from the outset in such a fashion that   b
the whole town forms one unbroken wall, every dwelling house being
rendered readily defensible by the uniformity and regularity with
which all face the streets. Such a town, with its resemblance to one
great house, would be no unpleasing spectacle, and the ease with
which it could be guarded would give it an unqualified advantage
over any other in point of security. The preservation of the original
buildings will properly be, in the first instance, the business of the oc-
cupiers, while the urban commissioners will be charged with the task   c
of superintendence, to the extent of compulsion by fines in the case of
neglect, as well as of making general provision for sanitation within
the city boundary, and of prohibiting all interference with the plan of
the city by buildings or excavations on the part of private persons.
They should also be responsible for the proper carrying-off of rain
water and any other desirable regulations of housing within or without the city. For these and any other matters of detail which have been
omitted in our law from inability to deal with them, the curators shall
issue supplementary ordinances, in the light of their practical experi-   d
ence. And now that these buildings and those of the market place, the
gymnasiums, schools, theaters, are all ready and waiting—the schools
for their pupils, the theaters for their audiences—we may proceed, in
the proper legislative order, to what follows upon matrimony.

    CLINIAS : By all means.

    ATHENIAN : Well, then, Clinias, let us suppose the marriage
ceremonies over. On them will follow, before the birth of children, an
interval of not less than a year. How bride and bridegroom in a so-   e
ciety which is to be so far above the common level should spend their
time—for that is what I meant by 'what follows in the proper order'—
is not the easiest of questions. We have had not a few such awkward
problems already, but none so unpalatable to the great mass of mankind. Still, I suppose, Clinias, what we really believe to be right and
true must be said at all costs.

    CLINIAS : Of course it must.   780

    ATHENIAN : If a man proposes to give a society laws for the
conduct of public and communal life, and yet imagines that law is

superfluous when it comes to compulsion in private affairs, that it is improper to submit everything to regulation and that the individual should be left free to spend the day just as he pleases—if he leaves personal conduct exempt from legal control and yet flatters himself that his citizens will be ready to guide their communal and public action by law—he is seriously mistaken. Why do I say this? Because I
b am going to insist that our newly married men shall frequent the public tables neither more nor less than they did in the years before marriage. That institution aroused surprise when it made its first appearance in your countries, at the dictation, as I presume, of a war or some situation equally urgent for a small population in a desperate extremity, but when you have tried the experiment and been driven to
c avail yourselves of these public messes, the practice was pronounced to be highly conducive to security. That in fact is the way in which the public table became one of your institutions.

CLINIAS : In all probability it is.

ATHENIAN : Well, here is the point. Though there were once persons who found the practice singular, and its imposition dangerous, a legislator who should wish to enjoin it would have no such difficulty today. But it has a natural consequence, at present adopted nowhere, though its adoption offers every prospect of success, which all but drives a legislator to 'card his wool into the fire,' as the saying
d is, and waste his labor in a host of other such ways, and this consequence is no light one either to propose or to put into effect.

CLINIAS : And pray, sir, what is this point you are apparently so reluctant to explain?

ATHENIAN : To avoid long and useless discourse on the subject, let me have your attention. Wherever due order and law are found in the life of a society, their fruits are blessings, but neglect of regulation or misregulation more often than not undoes the work of sound regulation in other directions. And this is just where our present argument
e comes to a halt. In fact, my friends, your public table for men is an admirable institution, miraculously originated, as I was saying, by a truly providential necessity, but it is a grave error in your law that the position of women has been left unregulated, and that no vestige of this same institution of the common table is to be seen in their case.
781 No, the very half of the race which is generally predisposed by its weakness to undue secrecy and craft—the female sex—has been left to its disorders by the mistaken concession of the legislator. Through negligence of the sex you have then allowed many things to get out of
b hand which might be far better ordered than they are if only they had come under the laws. Woman—left without chastening restraint— is not, as you might fancy, merely half the problem; nay, she is a twofold and more than a twofold problem, in proportion as her native disposition is inferior to man's. Hence it would be better from the point of view of the good of the state, to submit this matter to revision and

correction and devise a set of institutions for both sexes alike. As
things are, mankind are unhappily so far from such a consumma- c
tion that it is impossible for a prudent man so much as to mention the
proposal in other territories or societies, where the very existence of
the public table as a recognized institution of society is unknown. So
how is the actual attempt to compel women to take their meat and
drink in public to escape derision? There is nothing about which a
sex so accustomed to the life of the shady corner would make more
difficulties; try to force a woman out into the daylight and she will
offer a furious resistance far too powerful for the legislator. As I was d
saying, in other societies the sex will not so much as suffer the right
rule to be named without a storm of outcries, though perhaps in our
own they might. So if you desire our discussion of politics at large to
attain its ends—so far as theory goes—I am ready to defend my
proposal as sound and becoming, provided you would both like to
hear my arguments; otherwise we may let the subject drop.

CLINIAS : Sir, I assure you, we are both singularly in favor of
hearing you.

ATHENIAN : Why, then, so you shall. But you must not be surprised if you find me going a fair way back for my starting point. You e
know we have plenty of time on our hands, and there is no pressing
business to keep us from examining our subject, law, on all its sides.

CLINIAS : Quite true.

ATHENIAN : Good, then, let us revert to the position we began
with. Any man, indeed, should be perfectly aware of one thing. Either
the human race never had a beginning at all, any more than it will
ever have an end, but always was and always will be, or else the time
which has elapsed since its beginning must have covered immeasur- 782
able ages.

CLINIAS : No doubt.

ATHENIAN : Very well, then, can we suppose there have not
been, all over the world, all manner of risings and fallings of states, all
kinds of institutions, orderly and disorderly, as well as every sort of
taste in meat and drink, and multifarious climatic revolutions which
presumably lead to many modifications of living organisms?   b

CLINIAS : No, of course not.

ATHENIAN : Why, we believe, do we not, that there was once a
time when the vine made its first appearance, and that the same is
true of the olive and the gifts of Demeter and the Virgin [Persephone],
and that Triptolemus, or someone, was the instrument in the change?
So we must suppose, must we not, that before the existence of these
supplies, animals had recourse, as they have today, to feeding upon
one another?

CLINIAS : No doubt.

ATHENIAN : Besides, we remark the persistence of human sacri- c
fice to this day in many quarters, while it is reported, on the other

hand, of other peoples that they shrank from tasting even the flesh of oxen, and offered no animals in sacrifice; they honored their gods with cakes and meal soaked in honey and other such 'pure' sacrifices, but abstained from flesh, counting it criminal to eat it, or to pollute the altars of the gods with blood. Man's life in those days conformed to the rule known as Orphic, universal insistence on vegetarianism, and
d entire abstention from all that is animal.

CLINIAS : 'Tis the widely current and highly credible tradition.

ATHENIAN : Well, I may of course be asked the question, What is your point in mentioning all this just now?

CLINIAS : That, sir, is a well-founded apprehension.

ATHENIAN : And so, Clinias, I will try, if I can, to expound the thought to which these considerations give rise.

CLINIAS : Pray proceed.

ATHENIAN : I observe that mankind are universally impelled by needs or desires, of three kinds, and that this impulsion results in virtue if men are well trained, in its contrary if they are ill trained. Their
e needs are, in the first place, food and drink, from the hour of their birth. All creatures have the instinctive appetite for gratification in that kind and are furiously defiant of the voice which says that one has any duty except to sate one's craving for pleasures from that source, and to avoid all discomfort of any kind; our third and most
783 imperious need and fiercest passion arises later, but most of all fires men to all manner of frenzies—I mean lust of procreation with its blaze of wanton appetite. These three unwholesome appetites, then, we must divert from the so-called pleasant toward the good; we must try to check them by the three supreme sanctions—fear, law, true discourse—not without the aid of the Muses and the gods of games, and
b so to quench their growth and onrush.

Thus we may make the procreation of children follow on our regulations of marriages, and on their procreation, their nurture, and education. As our discourse proceeds on these lines, our several laws may possibly reach their completion, as in the former instance when we had reached the subject of a common table—whether, after all, women should be admitted to share the institution, or it should be kept exclusively for men, we shall perhaps see more clearly when we view it at close quarters—we shall reduce the necessary preliminaries, for which we have as yet given no regulations to order and shelter
c ourselves behind them. Thus, as I was just saying, we shall get a more precise view of these preliminaries themselves, besides being more likely to fit them with appropriate and becoming legislation.

CLINIAS : Very true.

ATHENIAN : Then let us keep the points just referred to well before our memory, as we shall probably have to refer to them all.

CLINIAS : But exactly what are the points you would have us remember?

ATHENIAN: Those which we made in our three clauses; we spoke, you may recollect, of meat, then of drink, and thirdly, of the d excitements of sex.

CLINIAS: Why, sir, I take it we shall be sure to remember what you are now impressing on us.

ATHENIAN: Well and good. So let us proceed to our regulations for the wedded pair, with the object of instructing them how and in what fashion they should set about procreation, or, if they should prove disobedient, appealing to the menace of law.

CLINIAS: In what manner?

ATHENIAN: Bride and bridegroom should make it their purpose to present the city with the best and finest progeny they may. Now whenever you have human beings conjoined in any action, when the e parties give their minds to themselves and what they are doing, the results of their work are every way fair and good, but entirely contrary if they have no mind or apply it not to their work. So let a bridegroom give his mind to his bride and his work of procreation—and the same with the bride—and most of all while children have not yet been born to them. The mother shall be under the surveillance of the women we 784 have appointed—their number to be more or fewer and the time of their election to be determined as the magistrates shall see fit to ordain —who shall assemble daily for not less than the third part of an hour at the temple of Ilithyia. At these assemblies each member shall report to the board any person, male or female, among the procreants, whom she sees to be paying regard to aught else than the injunctions imposed amid the sacrifices and rites of matrimony. This period of procreation and supervision of procreants shall last ten years and no b longer, in cases of plentiful issue; if a pair are without progeny at the end of the period they shall, in consultation with their kinsmen and the official board of women, arrange terms of separation with a view to the interest of both parties. If there should be any dispute as to what is seemly or advantageous to either party, they shall choose ten of the curators of the laws, and be bound by this selection of arbitrators and c their decisions. The ladies are to have entrance to the households of the young people, and are to stay them from their sinful folly, partly by admonition, partly by threats; if they fail they shall appear before the curators with their report, and the curators shall prevent the offense. If their action, too, proves unavailing, they shall bring the matter before the public, posting the offender's name with a sworn declaration of their 'failure to reform the herein designated.' A man so d posted—except in the case of his successful prosecution of the authors of the notification before a court of law—shall be subject to the following disabilities. He shall be excluded from both weddings and birthday feasts, or, if he shows himself there, anyone who pleases may inflict a beating on him with impunity. The same law shall extend to the case of a female offender; if posted for similar disorders and unsuc- e

cessful in her action at law, she shall be excluded from the women's
processions and honorable distinctions, and forbidden to attend weddings and children's birthday parties. When they have once produced
their children as the law requires, a man who has dealings in this kind
with a woman not his wife, or a woman who has to do with a man not
her husband, shall, if the other party be still among the procreants,
incur the same penalties which have been prescribed for those who
are still producing offspring. Outside this limit he or she that is continent in the matter shall be held in all esteem, he that is of the other
785 sort in the contrary repute, or rather disrepute. While the more part
show reasonable moderation in such things, the law will be silent on
the topic, and leave it alone, but if there are disorders, regulations
must be put in force as aforesaid, in accord with the laws but now
prescribed.

A man's first year is the opening of his whole life; it should be
registered with that title—'beginning of life'—in the shrines of the
kindred. There must also be, for each boy or girl in every phratry, a
further record on a whitened wall bearing the number of the magistrates after whom dates are reckoned; in the vicinity there must be a
b record of such members of the phratry as are alive at each date, the
names of those who decease being expunged. For a girl the limiting
age for marriage—the longest period specified—shall be from sixteen
to twenty, and for a male from thirty to thirty-five. That for official
appointments shall be forty for a woman, thirty for a man. For military service the term, in the case of a man, shall be from the age of
twenty to that of sixty, for a woman—whatever military employments
it may be thought right to impose on women—after she has borne her
children, what it is possible and fit to enact in such cases, up to the
age of fifty.

BOOK VII

788 ATHENIAN: Now that we have our boys and girls born, the proper
course will naturally be to deal with their nurture and education; this
subject cannot possibly be passed over in silence, but our treatment
will wear the guise rather of instruction and admonition than of legal
enactment. The privacy of home life screens from the general observation many little incidents, too readily occasioned by a child's pains,
b pleasures, and passions, which are not in keeping with a legislator's
recommendations, and tend to bring a medley of incongruities into
the characters of our citizens. Now this is an evil for the public as a
whole, for while the frequency and triviality of such faults make it
both improper and undignified to penalize them by law, they are a real
danger to such law as we do impose, since the habit of transgression is
c learned from repetition of these petty misdeeds. Hence, though we
are at a loss to legislate on such points, silence about them is also im-

possible. But I must try to illuminate my meaning by the production of what I may call samples; at present my remarks must seem something of a riddle.

CLINIAS: You are quite right there.

ATHENIAN: Well, now, I suppose we may take this much as truly said. The right system of nurture must be that which can be shown to produce the highest possible perfection and excellence of body and soul.

CLINIAS: Certainly.

ATHENIAN: And perfection of the children's bodies, I conceive, d means—to put it at the simplest—that they must grow straight from their earliest days.

CLINIAS: Why, of course.

ATHENIAN: And further, is it not a fact of observation that in all living things growth is most conspicuous and rapid in its initial sproutings—so much so, indeed, that many have contended that the stature reached by a human being in its first five years is not doubled by the increment due to the following twenty?

CLINIAS: Surely.

ATHENIAN: Well, then, when a body is subjected to vast aug- 789 mentation of bulk without a counterbalancing abundance of appropriate forms of exercise, the consequences are disastrous in all sorts of ways. That, I think, is a known fact.

CLINIAS: Indeed it is.

ATHENIAN: And so the period when the body is receiving its principal increment from nutrition is also the period when it demands the maximum of exercise.

CLINIAS: What, sir? Are we actually to impose the maximum of exercise on infants and newborn babies?

ATHENIAN: Not precisely that. We must impose it at a still ear- b lier stage while the child is being nursed in its mother's womb.

CLINIAS: What, my dear sir! On the embryo? You cannot mean that!

ATHENIAN: Indeed I do, though I am not surprised you should be unaware of the proper regimen for the case. 'Tis a singular one, but I could wish to expound it for you.

CLINIAS: By all means do so.

ATHENIAN: Well, the point would be more readily understood by my own countrymen, thanks to the undue devotion of some of them to sport. Among us, in fact, children, and some who are no longer children, too, are in the habit of rearing young birds for the purpose of cockfighting. Now they are very far from thinking the per- c formances in which they train these animals by pitting them against one another adequate discipline for such creatures. Over and above all this, everyone keeps birds somewhere on his person—the smaller ones in the hand, the bigger within his cloak, under the elbow—and takes walks of many furlongs, with an eye not to his own physique but to that of his beasties—a practice which at least indicates to the intelligent observer that all bodies are beneficially braced by every sort

d of shaking and stirring, whether due to their own movements, to the oscillations of a conveyance or a boat, the trot of a horse, or however the motion of the body may be caused. The frame is thus enabled to cope with its nutriment, solid or liquid, and presents a spectacle of health and beauty, to say nothing of robustness. Now in view of these facts, how, let me ask, shall we proceed to act? Would you have us raise a laugh by express statutes directing the pregnant mother to take constitutionals, to mold her infant, when she has borne it, like so much wax while it is still plastic, and to keep it swaddled for its first

e two years? And what of the nurse? Shall we compel her under legal penalties to be incessantly carrying her charges to the country, the public temples, the homes of their relatives, until they are strong enough to stand on their own feet, and ever later to persist in carrying a child about until it has completed its third year, for fear the limbs may be distorted in infancy if too much weight is thrown upon them? Shall we enact that our nurses must be the most robust we can get, and that there must be more than one for each infant, and crown our work by prescribing a penalty for the offender in case of neglect of any of these various directions? Surely not. It would be to lay our-

790 selves open to more than enough of the consequences I have mentioned.

CLINIAS: What consequences?

ATHENIAN: Why the ridicule we should be sure to incur. Not to add that our nurses will have the minds of women, and slavewomen at that, and be none too ready to obey.

CLINIAS: Then, pray, why have we thought it needful to give all these instructions?

ATHENIAN: I will tell you why. Because the minds of our mas-

b ters and free citizens may probably be led by hearing them to recognize the truth that while the right regulation of the private households within a society is neglected, it is idle to expect the foundations of public law to be secure. A citizen who understands this will be likely to regard the directions we are now giving as so many laws for his own conduct, and, so regarding them, to be happy in his administration alike of his own household and of his city.

CLINIAS: I believe there is much truth in what you say.

ATHENIAN: Consequently, we are not to suppose that we have

c done with this sort of legislation until we have given a full account of the training of the infant's mind on the same lines as those with which we began our remarks about its body.

CLINIAS: Very true.

ATHENIAN: We may take it then as the A B C of the matter in

both cases that it is universally beneficial for infants, particularly very young infants, to have the process of bodily and mental nursing continued without intermission, all day and all night long. If it were only possible, it would be desirable for them to spend all their time, so to say, at sea, and as it is, we should come as near that ideal as we can with the newborn baby. We may learn the same lesson from the following facts. The truth and utility of our principles has been learned from experience by children's nurses, and the female healers of Cory- d bantic troubles. You know, when mothers want to put fractious babies to sleep, the remedy they exhibit is not stillness, but its very opposite, movement—they regularly rock the infants in their arms—and not e silence, but a tune of some kind; in fact they, so to say, put a spell on their babies just as the priestess does on the distracted in the Dionysiac treatment, by this combination of the movements of dance and song.

CLINIAS: And pray, sir, what explanation are we to give of these facts?

ATHENIAN: Why, the explanation is not far to seek.

CLINIAS: But what is it?

ATHENIAN: Both disturbances are forms of fright, and fright is due to some morbid condition of soul. Hence, when such disorders are treated by rocking movement the external motion thus exhibited dominates the internal, which is the source of the fright or frenzy. By 791 its domination it produces a mental sense of calm and relief from the preceding distressing agitation of the heart, and thus effects a welcome result in both cases, the induction of sleep in the one, in the other—that of patients who are made to dance to the flute in the ritual of the deities to whom sacrifice is done on these occasions—the substitution of sanity for their temporary state of distraction. This, b though a brief and summary, is a plausible account of the matter.

CLINIAS: Indeed, most plausible.

ATHENIAN: That these methods have such effects should lead us to recognize that a mind subjected from its early days to such frights will be all the more likely to contract a habit of fearfulness; now everyone will admit that this is tantamount to a training not in courage, but in timidity.

CLINIAS: Surely.

ATHENIAN: Whereas it will be granted that the contrary course, that of mastering our frights and alarms as they arise, is a life- c long discipline in courage.

CLINIAS: Very true.

ATHENIAN: Why then, here, we may say, is one important element in virtue of soul to which this exercising of infants by movement is contributory.

CLINIAS: Yes, certainly.

ATHENIAN : Furthermore, the encouragement of placidity of temper will play a prominent part in the development of moral excel-. lence, and that of a fretful temper in that of vice.

CLINIAS : Unquestionably.

d   ATHENIAN : So we must try to explain the way by which ei- ther may be induced in the newborn child at pleasure, so far as the means of effecting such results lie in our power.

CLINIAS : To be sure we must.

ATHENIAN : Then—to state the conviction which I share— while spoiling of children makes their tempers fretful, peevish, and easily upset by mere trifles, the contrary treatment, the severe and un- qualified tyranny which makes its victims spiritless, servile, and sul- len, renders them unfit for the intercourse of domestic and civic life.

e   CLINIAS : But pray how should the authority of the state be brought to bear on the nurture of creatures who as yet cannot under- stand human speech, and are wholly incapable of education.

ATHENIAN : Why, much in this fashion I believe. Newborn crea- tures, especially newborn human beings, have from the very first a way of screaming, and the human infant in particular is given not only to screaming but to tears.

CLINIAS : Very true.

ATHENIAN : So when the nurse would discover its desires she
792 guesses from these indications what to offer it; if the child is quiet when something is offered it, she thinks she has found the right thing, but the wrong if it cries and screams. Thus, you see, the baby's likes and dislikes are disclosed by these ominous signals, its tears and screams; this holds good for a period of no less than three years, no inconsiderable part of one's life to be spent ill or well.

CLINIAS : Just so.

ATHENIAN : Now a man of peevish and melancholy temper
b will be given to self-pity and commonly more prone to complaining than a good man should be. I take it you will both admit this?

CLINIAS : I certainly shall.

ATHENIAN : Well, then, if we employ all our ingenuity to keep our growing child all through these three years from the experience of distress, alarms, and, so far as possible, pain itself, the growing soul is all this time being rendered more cheerful and gracious. Do you not think so?

c   CLINIAS : Not a doubt of it, sir—above all, if we provide it with plenty of pleasures.

ATHENIAN : My dear sir! That is just where Clinias and I must part. The course you propose to us is the most mischievous we could possibly take, because the mischief is systematically introduced at the starting point of the process of growth. Let us see whether I am not right.

CLINIAS : Pray unfold your meaning.

ATHENIAN: Why, I mean that the point now at issue between you and me is of no light consequence. So you must consider it too, Megillus, and help us to a decision. My own contention is that the right road in life is neither pursuit of pleasure nor yet unqualified avoidance of pain, but that contentment with the intermediate condi- d tion to which I have just given the name of *graciousness*—a state which we all, on the strength of an oracular saying, plausibly assign to God himself. It is this habit of mind, I maintain, which must likewise be pursued by the man who would be like God; he must not fling himself headlong into the quest for pleasures, or forget that he, too, will have his share of pains, nor yet must we let him suffer such behavior in another, man or woman, old or young, and least of all, so far as he can help it, in the newly born, for that is the age at which it is e most strictly true that character is made by habit. Why, if I did not apprehend I should be taken to be jesting, I would go still further. I would enjoin that special watch should be kept over our pregnant women during the year of their pregnancy to guard the expectant mother against the experience of frequent and violent pleasures—or pains either—and ensure her cultivation of a gracious, bright, and serene spirit.

CLINIAS: You need not, sir, put it to Megillus which of us has 793 more of the truth on his side. Frankly and freely I make the admission that all of us must avoid a life of untempered pain or pleasure, and steer a middle course in everything. Here is the proper answer to your very proper speech.

ATHENIAN: And an admirably true one, Clinias. Then let us, all three, turn our thoughts to a further point.

CLINIAS: Which is?

ATHENIAN: That all we are now discussing is nothing other than what mankind at large call the unwritten law; it is the whole body of such regulations, and nothing else, to which they give the b name, law of our forefathers. Further, we were quite right in the conviction borne in on us by our recent talk that such traditions should neither be designated laws nor left unformulated. They are the mortises of a constitution, the connecting links between all the enactments already reduced to writing, and preserved by it, and those yet to be recorded, a true corpus of ancestral and primitive tradition which, rightly instituted and duly followed in practice, will serve as a sure shield for all the statutes hitherto committed to writing, while if c they once swerve from the right bounds, it is as when a builder's supports give and subside under his edifice. The result is a general collapse of one part upon another, substructure and all that has been so admirably built upon it alike, when once the original supports have fallen. We must keep this in mind, Clinias, and do all we can to rivet your city together, while it is still in its inception, with no avoidable omission, major or minor, of anything that may be called law, d custom, or usage; all are the rivets of society, and the one sort will not be permanent without the other. Thus we must not be surprised if the bulk of our legislation should be somewhat swelled by a torrent of numerous and—supposedly—petty traditional practices and customs.

CLINIAS : To be sure you are right, and we will not forget the caution.

ATHENIAN : Then until the age of three has been reached by boy or girl, scrupulous and unperfunctory obedience to the instructions e just given will be of the first advantage to our infantile charges. At the stage reached by the age of three, and the after ages of four, five, six, play will be necessary, and we must relax our coddling and inflict punishments—though not such as are degrading—as we were saying in the case of slaves that we should neither inflame the culprit by 794 brutal punishments nor spoil a servant by leaving him uncorrected, so we must adopt the same course with the freeborn. And for their play, there are games which nature herself suggests at that age; children readily invent these for themselves when left in one another's company. All children of the specified age, that of three to six, should first be collected at the local sanctuary—all the children of each village being thus assembled at the same place. Further, the nurses are to have an eye to the decorum or indecorum of their behavior; as for that of the nurses themselves and the whole group, it must be subjected, in each case, for the year to the control of one of the already-b mentioned matrons to be assigned by the curators of the laws. These matrons are to be elected, one for each tribe, by the ladies charged with the supervision of marriages, and must be of the same age with them. It will be the official duty of a person so appointed to pay a daily visit to the sanctuary, and to chastise any offender—if a slave or alien of either sex, by the hand of some public menial, if a citizen who disc putes the justice of the correction, she shall bring him before the court of the urban commissioners, but where there is no dispute, she shall punish even a citizen on her own authority. When the age of six has been passed by either sex, there shall henceforth be a separation of the sexes—boys now being made to associate with boys, and girls with girls—and it shall be time for both to turn to their lessons, the boys being sent to instructors in riding, archery, the management of the dart and sling—the girls may share in the instruction if they d please—but, above all, in the use of spear and shield. To be sure, the prevalent notion about these matters rests on an all but universal misunderstanding.

CLINIAS : What notion?

ATHENIAN : The belief that there is a real and natural difference in the serviceability of either hand for various actions, though, in fact, where the feet and lower limbs are concerned, there is no such e difference in capacity to be detected; it is only the folly of nurses and mothers to which we owe it that we are all, so to say, lame of one hand. Nature, in fact, makes the members on both sides broadly correspondent; we have introduced the difference between them for ourselves by our improper habits. No doubt in actions of no particular importance the practice is immaterial—as for example, that the player should hold his lyre in the left hand and his plectrum in the right, and the like—but to make these cases, without any necessity, precedents for others, is fairly foolish. This is illustrated by the practice of the Scythians, who do not confine the left hand to the drawing back of 795 the bow and the right to the stringing of the arrow, but employ both alike for both purposes, and there are many other examples from the driving of chariots and other sources which may teach us how unnatural are the devices by which it is contrived to make a man's left weaker than his right. Now, as I said, this is no great matter when one is con- b cerned with a plectrum of horn, or some similar implement, but it makes all the difference when one comes to deal with the iron implements of warfare, bows and arrows, javelins, and the rest, and most of all when spear and shield must be plied against shield and spear. And there is all the difference in the world between one who has learned his lesson, and one who has not, one who is well trained, and one who is not trained at all. A man who has practiced the pancratium, or boxing, or wrestling to perfection does not find himself incapable of fighting with his left; he does not halt or make ungainly lunges if his opponent drives him to shift his position and bring that side of his c body into play. Well, I take it, it should similarly be expected as the proper thing, in swordplay and all other cases, that a man who has two sets of members for defense and attack should leave neither set unpracticed or untaught, so far as he can help it. Why, if a man should be born with the physique of a Geryon, or a Briareus, if you like, he ought to be able to throw a dart with every one of his hundred d hands. All this must be the care of officers of both sexes, the women undertaking the superintendence of the games and meals, the men being responsible for the instruction, so that all our boys and girls may grow up ambicrural and ambidextrous, their native endowments suffering no preventable distortion through acquired habit.

Their instruction may be said to fall, for practical purposes, under two heads, *physical culture*, which is concerned with the body, and *music*, which aims at mental excellence. *Physical culture*, again, has two branches, *dancing* and *wrestling*. One department of dancing e is the presentation of works of poetical inspiration with the care for the preservation of dignity and decorum; the other, which aims at physical fitness, nobility, and beauty, ensures an appropriate flexure and tension in the actual bodily limbs and members, and endows them all with a grace of movement which is incidentally extended to every form of the dance and pervades all intimately. To come to *wrestling*, the devices introduced into their systems by Antaeus or Cercyon—or 796 again into boxing by Epeus or Amycus—from mere idle vainglory, are

useless in encounters in the field and unworthy of celebration. But anything which comes under 'stand-up wrestling,' exercises in the disengaging of neck, arms, and ribs which can be practiced with spirit and gallant bearing to the benefit of strength and health, is serviceable
b for all occasions and may not be neglected. When we come to the appropriate place in our code we shall make it an injunction to our pupils and their prospective teachers alike that all such knowledge shall be generously imparted on the one side and gratefully received on the other. Nor again, must we neglect the presentation of appropriate choric action, the armored sports sacred in this island to the Curetes and at Lacedaemon to the heavenly twins. The virgin queen of my own country, too, I may remark, who delights in this choric pastime, deemed it wrong to disport herself with empty hands, and right to per-
c form her dance in all the splendor of full battle array. It will certainly be most proper that our boys and girls should copy these models in courting the favor of the goddess, both for their usefulness in war and for the embellishment of our festivals. Moreover, it will be obligatory on the boys, from the very first until they reach the age of liability to service in the field, to be equipped with arms and horses in every festal procession with which they honor a god; their litanies to gods and
d sons of gods shall always be accompanied by a march or dance, quick or slow. Besides, their matches and practices for matches must have the same objects and no others. Such competitions, in fact, are, in war and in peacetime, beneficial alike to the community and the individual household, whereas other physical exercises, playful or serious, are not for freeborn men.

I have now fairly described such a course of physical training as I said at first we should have to examine; the entire scheme is now
e before you. If either of you can propose a better, it is for you to lay it before us.

CLINIAS: Nay, sir, if we reject these proposals, it will be hard to devise a better plan of physical training and athletic contests.

ATHENIAN: As for the subject which naturally comes next, the gifts of Apollo and the Muses, we thought at first that we had said all there is to be said, and had only the treatment of bodily training still left on our hands, but now it is plain both what must be said of it to everyone, and that these things should be said to them before anything else.

797 CLINIAS: Aye, to be sure they should.

ATHENIAN: Then I will ask you to give me your attention. It is true you have done so once already; still, speaker and hearer alike are called on to show the greatest caution in dealing with a startling paradox, above all in the present case. I feel some misgivings in advancing the thesis I shall lay before you; still, I will take heart as best I may not to flinch from it.

CLINIAS: And what is your thesis, sir?

ATHENIAN: Why, as to this matter of children's games I maintain that our communities are sunk in a universal ignorance; it is not seen that they have a decisive influence on the permanence or impermanence of a legislation once enacted. Where there is prescription on this point, where it is ensured that the same children shall always b play the same games in one and the same way, and get their pleasure from the same playthings, the regulations in more serious matters too are free to remain undisturbed, but where there is change and innovation in the former, incessant variation of all sorts and perpetual fluctuation in the children's tastes; where they have no fixed and settled standard of what is pretty or the reverse in their own bearing and movements, or in the pattern of their toys, where the inventor and in- c troducer of an innovation in pattern, color, or the like is always held in particular esteem—how truly may we say society can suffer from no worse pest. Such a man is constantly changing the young folks' character behind your back; he teaches them to despise the old-fashioned and worship novelty. Once more I say, there can be no graver danger to any society than such language and such notions. Pray let me explain how serious this evil is.

CLINIAS: You mean the evil of public dissatisfaction with the d ancient fashions?

ATHENIAN: That and nothing else.

CLINIAS: Why, we of all men are least likely to turn a deaf ear to that plea. We shall listen in the most friendly spirit.

ATHENIAN: So I should anticipate.

CLINIAS: Speak on, then.

ATHENIAN: Come, then, let us rise above ourselves, as listeners or speakers, as we plead the case thus. Change—except when it is change from what is bad—is always, we shall find, highly perilous, whether it be change of seasons, of prevailing winds, of bodily regimen, of mental habit, or, in a word, change of anything whatever e without exception, except in the case I have just mentioned, change from bad. Thus, if we consider our body and the way it can familiarize itself with any kind of food or drink or exertion—how, though they may upset it at first, in time their very use leads to the formation of flesh akin to themselves, and so the body is reconciled to its scheme of regimen, grows familiar and at home with it, and enjoys a life of pleasure and health; how, if it should be compelled to change again to 798 some approved regimen, the man is at first upset by disorders and only recovers slowly as he once more becomes familiarized with his diet— why, we can but suppose the same thing takes place with men's understandings and souls. When men have been brought up under any system of laws and that system has, by some happy providence, per- b sisted unchanged for long ages, so that no one remembers or has ever heard of a time when things were otherwise than as they are, the whole soul is filled with reverence and afraid to make any innovation

on what was once established. A lawgiver, then, must contrive one device or another to secure this advantage for his community, and here is my own suggestion toward the discovery. They all suppose, as we were saying, that innovation in children's play is itself a piece of play and nothing more, not, as it is in fact, a source of most serious and
c grievous harm; hence they make no attempt to avert such changes, but compliantly fall in with them. They never reflect that these boys who introduce innovations into their games must inevitably grow to be men of a different stamp from the boys of an earlier time, that the change in themselves leads to the quest for a different manner of life, and this to a craving for different institutions and laws, and thus none of them is apprehensive of the imminent consequence, of which we
d just spoke as the worst misfortune for a community. A change in other respects, in mere external forms, would, of course, do less mischief, but frequent modifications of moral approbation and disapprobation are of all changes the gravest and need to be most anxiously guarded against.

CLINIAS : Yes, of course.

ATHENIAN : Well, then, are we, or are we not, still of the same mind as before, when we said that rhythms and music generally are a reproduction expressing the moods of better and worse men?
e CLINIAS : *Our* conviction on the point remains exactly what it was.

ATHENIAN : Every means, then, shall we say, must be employed to keep our children from the desire to reproduce different models in dance or song, as well as to prevent a possible tempter from offering them the inducement of a variety of delights?

CLINIAS : Perfectly true.
799 ATHENIAN : Well, can any of us find a better device for this purpose than that employed in Egypt?

CLINIAS : And what is that?

ATHENIAN : Why, the plan is to consecrate all our dances and all our tunes. First, the festivals must be fixed by compiling an annual calendar to show what feasts are to be celebrated, at what dates, and in honor of what deities, sons of deities, or spirits, respectively. Next, certain authorities must determine what hymn is to be sung on the feast of each divinity, and by what dances the ceremony of the day is to be graced. When this has been determined, the whole citizen body
b must do public sacrifice to the Destinies and the entire pantheon at large, and consecrate each hymn to its respective god or other patron by solemn libation. If any man tries to introduce hymn or dance into the worship of any deity in contravention of these canons, the priests of either sex, acting in conjunction with the curators of law, shall have the warrant both of religion and law in excluding him from the festival; if the excluded party declines to submit to this excommunica-

tion, he shall for life be liable to indictment for impiety at the instance of any who cares to institute proceedings.

CLINIAS : And rightly so.

ATHENIAN : Then, now we are upon this subject, we must be c careful to act as becomes us.

CLINIAS : What have you in mind?

ATHENIAN : When a young man—not to say an elderly man— has seen or heard something out of the common and quite unfamiliar, he will not be likely to rush on a solution of the puzzle all in a moment. He is more likely to stop short, as a man, traveling alone or in company, who has come to a crossroad and is none too sure of his way, will stop and question himself or his companions about his difficulty, and refuse to take a step farther until he has formed a pretty d definite opinion whither the road is leading. Now that is exactly what we should do at this point. The point of jurisprudence which has now arisen is a singular one, and we are bound, of course, to investigate it thoroughly; men of our years must not lightly insist that we can offhand make a confident pronouncement about it.

CLINIAS : Very true.

ATHENIAN : So we will take our time over the question, and e only decide it after searching investigation. Still, we do not wish the completion of the regulations which belong to our legislation on the topic before us to be interrupted to no good purpose, and so we will go on with them to the end. Perhaps, indeed, by the kindness of providence, when the complete recital reaches its end, it will incidentally provide the answer to our present problem.

CLINIAS : A good suggestion, sir. Let us act on it.

ATHENIAN : Well, then, let us, I say, take the paradox as granted. Our songs have become *canons*, as the men of earlier times seem to have given some such name to melodies for the harp—thus perhaps they too were not altogether strangers to the idea. Someone 800 presumably divined the truth in his dreams, or possibly in a vision of waking life. In fine, let us assume a clause on the subject to the following effect. No man shall contravene the public standards of song, ritual, or choric performance of the young at large, whether by vocal utterance or by movement in the dance, any more than he would any other of our canons. Conformity shall be clear of the law; nonconformity shall be visited with penalties by curators of law and priests of either sex as before enjoined. May we now take this point as settled? b

CLINIAS : We may.

ATHENIAN : Then what sort of legal rules can a man lay down on such matters without exposing himself to sheer derision? Here is a further point it will be relevant to consider. Our safest course will be to begin by imagining a few typical cases, and as one such case I propose the following. Suppose sacrifice has been offered and the victims

burned as law directs, when some worshiper—a son or a brother—in the immediate presence of the altar and the offering upon it, breaks out into downright blasphemy. The utterance, may we not say, will
c fill his father and the rest of the group of kinsmen with dismay, forebodings, and gloomy apprehensions?

CLINIAS : To be sure it will.

ATHENIAN : Now that is precisely what happens in pretty nearly all societies in our own world. A magistrate has just offered sacrifice in the name of the public when a choir, or rather a number of choirs, turn up, plant themselves not at a remote distance from the altar, but, often enough, in actual contact with it, and drown the sol-
d emn ceremony with sheer blasphemy, harrowing the feelings of their audience with their language, rhythms, and lugubrious strains, and the choir which is most successful in plunging the city which has just offered sacrifice into sudden tears is adjudged the victor. Surely our vote will be cast against such a practice. If there is really any need for our citizens to listen to such doleful strains on some day which stands
e accursed in the calendar, surely it would be more proper that a hired set of performers should be imported from abroad for the occasion to render them, like the hired minstrels who escort funerals with Carian music. The arrangement, I take it, would be equally in place in performances of the sort we are discussing, and I may add—to dismiss the topic as briefly as may be—that the appropriate costume for these dirges would not be garlands and cloth of gold, but the very opposite. The only question I want us to ask ourselves once more is whether we are satisfied that our first typical rule for hymnody should be . . .

CLINIAS : Should be what?

801   ATHENIAN : That of auspiciousness of language. Indeed, may we lay it down that our hymnody must be wholly auspicious in every particular? Or perhaps I need not repeat the question, but may simply impose the rule.

CLINIAS : Out of doubt, you may do so; the proposal is carried by a unanimous vote.

ATHENIAN : Then what shall our second regulation be? That there must always be a prayer to the gods to whom sacrifice is being done?

CLINIAS : Obviously.

ATHENIAN : And a third, I take it, must be that our poets must
b understand that a prayer is a request made to a god, and should therefore be scrupulously careful not inadvertently to ask for a curse in mistake for a blessing. To offer such a petition, you know, would be a ridiculous proceeding.

CLINIAS : Of course.

ATHENIAN : Now we satisfied ourselves, I believe, a little while ago that wealth of silver or gold must have neither sanctuary nor abode in our city.

CLINIAS: To be sure we did.

ATHENIAN: Now what principle, we may ask, did that statement illustrate? Was not the implication that poets are not quite the most competent judges of good and evil? Hence a poet who goes wrong in language or melody on this point—that of praying for the wrong thing—will of course lead our citizens to transgress our regu- c lations in their prayers for things of supreme moment, though, as we just said, it would be hard to find a more serious error. Shall we then add another typical regulation about music to this effect?

CLINIAS: But to what effect? We should be glad of a clearer statement.

ATHENIAN: No poet shall compose anything in contravention of the public standards of law and right, honor and good, nor shall d he be at liberty to display any composition to any private citizen whatsoever until he has first submitted it to the appointed censors of such matters and the curators of law, and obtained their approval. These censors we have to all intents appointed by our election of legislators for music and a superintendent of education. Well then—to repeat the question—shall this be taken as our third example of a typical regulation, or what do you say?

CLINIAS: Why, of course it shall.

ATHENIAN: This matter once determined, the gods may be e properly addressed in hymns and strains of mingled praise and petition; under them, spirits and heroes may similarly receive the prayers and praises appropriate to them.

CLINIAS: Certainly.

ATHENIAN: And next, we may now proceed straightaway, without any occasion for scruples, to the following regulation. Such citizens as have brought to an end a life of honorable and arduous physical or mental achievements and obedience to law shall be deemed fitting recipients for our praises.

CLINIAS: Why, of course.

ATHENIAN: As for those still living, it is perilous to award the honor of praises and hymns until the whole course of life has been 802 crowned by a glorious end. All these distinctions shall be awarded alike to persons of either sex who have been illustrious for their goodness. The regulations for the songs and dances should be determined in the following way. The music of earlier times is rich in fine old poems, and similarly also in dances for the body, from which we shall be perfectly free to select whatever is appropriate and suitable for the b society we are instituting. The selection should be made by appointing a number of triers of not less than fifty years of age; old poems pronounced satisfactory shall be accepted, while any that are judged to be defective, or wholly unsuitable, shall in the one case be simply rejected, in the other, revised and corrected, with the aid of advice from experts in poetry and music. While we shall make full use of the poetical gifts of these experts, we shall not, except in a very few cases, trust to their tastes or preferences, but make ourselves interpreters of the legislator's intentions, and construct the whole scheme of dance,

c song, and choric activity in the closest conformity to their purport. Any unregulated pursuit of music is infinitely improved by being subjected to system, even without any addition of musical sweetmeats; delight is something which can be provided by all styles alike. If a man has from childhood to the age of sobriety and discretion been familiar with austere, classical music, he is repelled by the sound of the oppo-

d site kind and pronounces it unmanly; if brought up on music of the popular, cloying kind, he finds its opposite frigid and displeasing. Thus, as I was saying, neither type has any advantage or disadvantage over the other in respect of pleasing or displeasing, and there is the additional consideration that the one regularly makes those who are brought up on it better men, the other worse.

CLINIAS : Perfectly true.

ATHENIAN : It will further be necessary to make a rough gen-

e eral distinction between two types of songs, those suited for females and those suited for males, and so we shall have to provide both with their appropriate scales and rhythms; it would be a dreadful thing that the whole tune or rhythm of a composition should be out of place, as it will be if our various songs are inappropriately treated in these respects. So we shall further have to legislate on these points, at any rate in general outline. Now it is perfectly possible to make the necessary regulations for both kinds of songs in both respects, but what music should be assigned to females is indicated by the actual natural distinction of sex, which should therefore be our basis for discrimination. Accordingly, we shall pronounce the majestic and whatever tends to valor masculine, while it will be the tradition of our law and our theory alike that what makes rather for order and purity is peculiarly feminine. So much, then, for our regulations. We must

803 next deal with the imparting of instruction in these subjects—how the teaching in the various departments is to be given, to whom, and at what times. The shipwright, you know, begins his work by laying down the keel of the vessel and indicating her outlines, and I feel myself to be doing the same thing in my attempt to present you with

b outlines of human lives answering to types of character. I am really laying the keels of the vessels by due consideration of the question by what means or manner of life we shall make our voyage over the sea of time to best purpose. To be sure, man's life is a business which does not deserve to be taken too seriously; yet we cannot help being in earnest with it, and there's the pity. Still, as we are here in this world, no doubt, for us the becoming thing is to show this earnestness in a suitable way. But I may probably be met—and very properly met—here by the question, What on earth do you mean?

CLINIAS : You certainly may.

ATHENIAN: Why, I mean we should keep our seriousness for c serious things, and not waste it on trifles, and that, while God is the real goal of all beneficent serious endeavor, man, as we said before, has been constructed as a toy for God, and this is, in fact, the finest thing about him. All of us, then, men and women alike, must fall in with our role and spend life in making our *play* as perfect as possible—to the complete inversion of current theory.

CLINIAS: Inversion? In what way?   d

ATHENIAN: It is the current fancy that our serious work should be done for the sake of our play; thus it is held that war is serious work which ought to be well discharged for the sake of peace. But the truth is that in war we do not find, and we never shall find, either any real play or any real education worth the name, and *these* are the things I count supremely serious for such creatures as ourselves. Hence it is peace in which each of us should spend most of his life and spend it best. What, then, is our right course? We should pass our lives in the playing of games—*certain* games, that is, sacrifice, song, and dance— e with the result of ability to gain heaven's grace, and to repel and vanquish an enemy when we have to fight him. What sort of song and dance will effect both results has partly been stated in outline. The path has, so to say, been cut for us, and we should walk in it, in assurance that the poet was right when he said,

> Search, for some thoughts, thine own suggesting mind,   804
> And others, dictated by heavenly power,
> Shall rise spontaneous in the needful hour.
> For nought unprosperous shall thy ways attend,
> Born with good omens, and with heaven thy friend.[10]

Our nurslings, too, must be of the poet's mind. They must believe that what we have said has been sufficient for its purpose, and that, for the rest, they will be visited by promptings, superhuman and divine, as to their sacrifices and dances, suggestions as to the several b gods in whose honor, and the several times at which, they are to play their play, win heaven's favor for it, and so live out their lives as what they really are—puppets in the main, though with some touch of reality about them, too.

MEGILLUS: I must say, sir, you have but a poor estimate of our race.

ATHENIAN: Do not be amazed by that, Megillus. Bear with me. I had God before my mind's eye, and felt myself to be what I have just said. However, if you will have it so, man shall be something not so insignificant but more serious.   c

To proceed with our subject, we have already arranged for three public schools with attached training grounds within the city, and

---

[10] *Odyssey* 3.26 sq.

three training grounds and ample exercising grounds outside it for horses, suitably equipped for the use of the bow and other long-range weapons, where our young people may both learn and practice these accomplishments; or if adequate arrangements have not been already made they must be introduced into our theory and the corresponding
d code at this point. They shall all be adequately staffed with paid resident and salaried masters in the various subjects, who must be noncitizens, and must give a complete course of instruction alike in the arts of war and in that of music to the boys who attend their classes. A boy is not to attend if his father so desires, but otherwise to be exempted from this education. Education is, if possible, to be, as the phrase goes, compulsory for every mother's son, on the ground that the child is even more the property of the state than of his parents.
e And, mind you, my law will apply in all respects to girls as much as to boys; the girls must be trained exactly like the boys. And in stating my doctrine I intend no reservation on any point of horsemanship or physical training, as appropriate for men but not for women. In fact, I give full credit to the tales I have heard of ancient times, and I actually know that at the present day there are untold thousands, one may fairly say, of women living round the Black Sea—Sarmatian
805 women, they are called—on whom not horsemanship only but familiarity with bows and other weapons is enjoined no less than it is on their husbands, and by whom it is equally cultivated. Besides, here is a consideration I would submit to you. If such results are feasible, then I say the present practice in our own part of the world is the merest folly; it is pure folly that men and women do not unite to follow the same pursuits with all their energies. In fact, almost every one of our cities on our present system, is, and finds itself to be, only
b the half of what it might be at the same cost in expenditure and trouble. And yet, what an amazing oversight in a legislator!

CLINIAS: Why, so it would seem, sir, though a good many of our present proposals are at variance with our customary systems. However, your proposal to let the argument take its course, and not to decide on our verdict until it has reached its end, was most apposite— and in view of it, I feel self-condemned for my present observation. So pray go on with your exposition according to your own mind.
c ATHENIAN: Well, Clinias, my mind, as I have already said, is that if the feasibility of our proposals had not been sufficiently established by actual facts, there might have been some ground for disputing the theory. As it is, an opponent who refuses our proposal a hearing must surely take a different line. Such tactics will not deter us from insisting on our principle that there must be the completest association of the female sex with the male in education as in everything else. In fact, we may treat the matter from some such stand-
d point as this. If women are not to take their part along with men in all

the business of life, we are bound, are we not, to propose some different scheme for them?

CLINIAS: To be sure we are.

ATHENIAN: And which of the various systems now recognized can we prefer to the comradeship we are just imposing on them? The system followed by the Thracians and many other peoples, that the women till the fields, look after the flocks and herds, and perform e menial offices, exactly like slaves? Or the practice universal in our own part of the world? You know what our own customs in this matter are. We 'pack' all our belongings, as the phrase goes, 'into one' house, and make over to our women the control of the store closet and the superintendence of the spinning and woolwork at large. Or should we perhaps vote for the *via media*, which you take, Megillus, in La- 806 conia? Your women are expected in their girlhood to take their share in physical training and music. When they have grown up, they have no woolwork to occupy them, but you expect them to contrive a composite sort of life, one that calls for training and is far from being unworthy or frivolous, and to go halfway with the work of medicine chest, store chamber, and nursery, but to take no share in the business of war. The consequence is that if circumstances should ever force them to a fight for their city and their children, they would prove quite unequal to playing an expert's part with the bow, like Amazons, b or any other missile weapon. They could not, could they, even copy our goddess by taking up spear and shield with the mien of doughty protectors of a harried motherland, and so strike an invader with alarm, if with nothing more, by their appearance in martial formation? As for the Sarmatian women, yours, while they lead the life they do, would never venture on imitating them at all; by comparison with women like yours, theirs would pass for men. Let him who will ap- c plaud your legislators in this matter. I can only speak as I think. A legislator should be thorough, not halfhearted; he must not, after making regulations for the male sex, leave the other to the enjoyment of an existence of uncontrolled luxury and expense, and so endow his society with a mere half of a thoroughly felicitous life in place of the whole.

MEGILLUS: What are we to do, Clinias? Must we suffer our visitor to run Sparta down in our hearing like this?

CLINIAS: Indeed we must. We allowed him full liberty of d speech, and so we must let him alone until our review of our legislation has fairly reached its completion.

MEGILLUS: I own you are right.

ATHENIAN: Then it is for me to proceed once more with my exposition.

CLINIAS: Yes, certainly.

ATHENIAN: What, then, should life be like with men whose

necessities have been moderately provided for, their trades and
crafts put into other hands, their lands let out to villeins who render
e from the produce such rent as is sufficient for sober livers—men,
moreover, furnished with common dining halls, some for themselves,
others near at hand for the members of their families, their daughters
and their daughters' mothers, under presidents of either sex, whose
appointed function is daily to dismiss the tables after review and in-
807 spection of the conduct of the company, and thereafter, libation first
duly made by the president and the company to the gods to whom
that night and day stand consecrate, so to betake themselves home
to bed? When they have been so provided is there no necessary and
wholly proper work left them to do? Is each man of them to pass his
time fattening himself like a stalled ox? No, I say, it were neither
right nor seemly nor yet possible that he who lives so should miss his
b proper destiny, that of an idle, sluggish, fattened beast—which is
commonly to be the prey of some other beast, one worn to bitter
leanness by risks and exertions. Now if we are going to look for an
exact realization of our scheme, as we have styled it, it will perhaps
never be found, so long as there are private wives, children, and
houses, and each of us has his private belongings of all sorts. Still,
if we can secure the second-best conditions, which we are now describ-
c ing, we shall indeed come off well enough.
But there is, I maintain, a work left for men who lead this life,
and that none of the most trivial or meanest; righteous law has appointed them to the gravest work of all. The life of the aspirant to
victory at Olympia or Pytho leaves no leisure for any other tasks whatever, and there is a double, or more than double, glut of occupation in
the life we have rightly described as concerned with the practice of
d every virtue of body and mind. No other business can be allowed to
come in as a by-end and hinder the provision of needful exercises and
regimen for the body, nor of necessary studies and habitual discipline
for the mind; the whole day and night is verily not long enough for
one who is engaged on this sole work of getting the full and perfect
benefit from these pursuits. Now, since this is so, every free citizen
will need an ordered disposition of all his hours; he must begin with it
at daybreak, and follow it without any intermission until the suc-
e ceeding dawn and sunrise. A legislator, to be sure, will show lack of
dignity if he stoops to a multitude of little trivial directions about
household arrangements, and among them to the restrictions on sleep
proper in a population which will have to keep perpetual and diligent watch over its whole city. In fact, that any citizen whatsoever
should spend the whole of any night in unbroken sleep, and not let all
his servants see him always awake and astir before anyone else in the
808 house, must be unanimously pronounced a disgrace and an act unworthy of a free man, whether such a regulation should be regarded
as law or as custom. In particular, that the mistress of a house should

be called by her maids in the morning, and not get up first herself and wake them, and the whole building itself, if only that were possible, that is what every servant, man, woman, or boy, must cry shame on. Much of the business of public and household life should certainly be b done in the night hours saved from sleep by the state officials and by the masters and mistresses at home. Overmuch sleep, indeed, is naturally as unsuitable to us in body and mind as it is incongruous with business of all these kinds. In fact, a man asleep is of no more account than a corpse. He who sets most store on vital and mental activity keeps awake all the hours he can, only reserving for sleep what his c health requires, and this is not much, when the habit has been well established. And public officials who are awake betimes by night are no less a source of fear to evildoers, whether enemies or citizens, and of awe and reverence in the righteous and virtuous than of benefit to themselves and their whole community.

So much, then, for night, and we may add to what we have said that to spend it in this fashion will further promote the spirit of courage in the souls of citizens of all sorts. With the return of day and dawn, the boys should betake themselves to school. And just as sheep, d or any other creatures, cannot be allowed to live unshepherded, so neither must boys be left without the care of attendants, nor slaves without that of a master. Now of all wild young things a boy is the most difficult to handle. Just because he more than any other has a fount of intelligence in him which has not yet 'run clear,' he is the craftiest, most mischievous, and unruliest of brutes. So the creature must be held in check, as we may say, by more than one bridle—in the e first place, when once he is out of the mother's and nurse's hand, by attendants to care for his childish helplessness, and then, further, by all the masters who teach him anything, and, as befits a freeborn man, by the teaching he gets. But further chastisement, as befits a slave, shall be inflicted on the boy and his attendant and teacher as well, by any free person in whose presence he commits any of these faults. If such a person omits to inflict the due correction, he shall, in the first place, be held to have disgraced himself most deeply. Also, the curator of law appointed to take control of boys shall take cognizance 809 of the party who is present at an offense of the sort we are dealing with without imposing the necessary correction; this magistrate must be a man of keen vision, thoroughly devoted to his work of supervising the training of the boys, who will guide their native dispositions into right ways, always directing them to the good and lawful.

But, now, as to this minister himself, how is he to be sufficiently instructed by the lips of our law? For so far, its utterances have been neither clear nor full, but only partial, though where he is concerned, the law must make no omission it can help, but impart its whole doc- b trine to him, that he may so prove interpreter and foster father to others. Now we have dealt already with the choric art—song and dance,

that is. We have said what types of these should be selected or corrected, and consecrated, but as for writings without meter, which of
them may be put in the hands of your charges and on what terms,
that, most worthy director of education, you have not been told. You
c have indeed been informed what their military lessons and exercises
must be. But what must they know, first of letters, and next of the
lyre and of ciphering, of which we said all must master what is needful for war, domestic business, or civil administration, as well as
such knowledge of the courses of the heavenly bodies—sun, moon,
planets—as is useful for these same ends, in so far as any city is bound
d to deal with the matter? What matter, you say? The grouping of days
into monthly periods, and months into the year in such fashion that
the seasons with their sacrifices and feasts may fit into the true natural order and receive their several proper celebrations, and the city be
thus kept alive and alert, its gods enjoying their rightful honors and
its men advancing in intelligence of these matters. These, my friend
are questions to which the legislator has as yet given you no full and
e sufficient answer. Give diligent heed, then, to what is now to be said.

Your instructions, we have said, are deficient, in the first place,
as to reading and writing. Now what is the defect of which we complain? It is that you have so far not been told whether the lad who
would be a decent citizen must attain to finished mastery of the study,
or must leave it wholly alone, and the same is true of the lyre. Well,
we tell you now that these studies must not be left alone. For reading
and writing three years or so, from the age of ten, are a fair allowance
of a boy's time, and if the handling of the lyre is begun at thirteen, the
810 three following years are long enough to spend on it. No boy and no
parent shall be permitted to extend or curtail this period from fond-
ness or distaste for the subjects; to spend either more or less time upon
them shall be an infraction of the law, and the disobedience shall be
visited by exclusion from the school distinctions we shall shortly describe. But what more specifically is to be learned by the children and
taught by their masters during these years? That is the very question
b to which you are first to hear our answer. They must, of course, carry
their study of letters to the point of capacity to read and write, but perfection of rapid and accomplished execution should not be insisted on
in cases where the natural progress within the prescribed term of
years has been slower. As to the study of written compositions without
musical accompaniment, whether written in meter or without rhythmical subdivisions—in fact, compositions in simple prose with no em-
c bellishments of rhythm or melody—difficult problems are raised by
some of the works bequeathed to us by our numerous authors in this
kind. How then will you deal with them, reverend curators of law? Or
what would be the right injunction for the legislator to lay upon you
as to their treatment? I can conceive they will cause him no little perplexity.

CLINIAS: Pray, sir, what is the difficulty, for it is plain you speak with a real sense of a personal difficulty?

ATHENIAN: I do, indeed, Clinias. You are right there. But you and your friend are my colleagues in this juristic discussion, and so I am bound to tell you frankly where I see difficulties and where I see none.

CLINIAS: Well, and why do you mention the point just now? d What is the feeling which leads you to do so?

ATHENIAN: Why, here it is. 'Tis no light matter to speak against so many thousands of voices.

CLINIAS: But, bless me, do you imagine what we have already said about jurisprudence only contradicts popular opinion in a few trifles!

ATHENIAN: Yes, that is true enough. You tell me, I conceive, that though this legislative path of ours is repellent to so many—perhaps those who find it attractive may be as numerous, or if fewer, at least not inferior—you tell me, I say, to join this latter party and fol- e low the path our present discussions have laid down for us with a stout courage and a good heart, not to flinch.

CLINIAS: I do, indeed.

ATHENIAN: Then there shall be no flinching. Now mark my words. We have a great number of poets, in hexameter verse, in iambic trimeter, in a word in all the recognized meters, some grave and some gay. On them, so those many thousands of voices proclaim, young people who are being rightly educated should be fed, in them they should be steeped; their reading lessons must give them a wide acquaintance with their works and an extensive scholarship in them; whole poets must be learned by heart. There are others who compile 811 anthologies of the poets and make collections of whole passages, which they say must be committed to memory and learned by heart if our protégé's wide familiarity with literature and extensive learning is to make a good and wise man of him. What you are now calling on me to do is to tell those persons without any reserve where they are right and where they are wrong?

CLINIAS: To be sure.

ATHENIAN: Well, what adequate verdict can I conceivably give about them all in a single sentence? Perhaps something like this— and it is a statement in which I suppose everyone will concur. In every b poet there is much that is admirably said and also much that is not. But if so, this extensive learning, I must tell you, has its dangers for our young people.

CLINIAS: Then how would you advise our curator of law?

ATHENIAN: Advise him? On what point?

CLINIAS: On the choice of a standard by reference to which he will permit all the young folk to learn one piece and forbid their learn- c ing another. Tell us your mind without any diffidence.

ATHENIAN : There, my dear Clinias, I venture to think I am in a way fortunate.

CLINIAS : Fortunate in what?

ATHENIAN : In not being altogether at a loss for a standard. As I look back on the discourse you and I have been holding ever since daybreak until this moment—and I really believe there has been some divine guiding about the matter—well, be that as it may, our converse has been, to my mind, just like a kind of poem. I dare say there is noth-
d ing surprising in my having felt this keen pleasure in reviewing this compact formation, as I may call it, of discourse of my own composition. The fact is that of all the many compositions I have met with or listened to, in verse or in plain prose, I find it the most satisfactory and the most suitable for the ears of the young. So I really think I could not direct our curator of law and minister of education to a better stand-ard, or bid him do better than instruct his schoolmasters to teach it to
e their pupils, and also if in his researches he should light upon con-nected and similar matter in the verse of our poets, in our prose litera-ture, or even in the form of simple unwritten discourse of the same type as the present, by no means to neglect it, but get it put into writ-ing. He should begin by making it compulsory on the teachers them-selves to learn this material and appreciate it. Teachers who are dissatisfied with it he must not employ as colleagues; those who con-cur with his own appreciation he should employ, and to them he should
812 entrust the young for their instruction and education. And with this what I have to say about reading and writing and the teachers of the subject may come to an end.

CLINIAS : If one is to judge by reference to our professed inten-tions, sir, I believe we have kept the discussion on the lines originally laid down for it. Whether our whole attitude is the right one or not it might be harder to pronounce.

ATHENIAN : That, Clinias—to repeat what I have said more
b than once already—will presumably become clearer of itself when we have reached the end of our review of our legislation.

CLINIAS : True.

ATHENIAN : Then we may leave the teacher of letters, may we not, and direct our discourse to the instructor in the cithara?

CLINIAS : By all means.

ATHENIAN : Well, as for the teachers of that instrument, I fancy we shall be making a proper assignment of their functions as in-structors, and more generally as trainers, in that branch of education, if we call to mind our earlier pronouncements.

CLINIAS : And, pray, what were they?

ATHENIAN : Why, I believe we said the sexagenarians of the 'chorus of Dionysus' would need to be exceptionally sensitive to
c rhythmic and melodic structure to ensure their competence to distin-guish a good musical imitation of a soul under the stress of its emo-

tions from a bad—competence, that is, to distinguish the counterfeit presentments of a good soul from those of an evil, to reject the second but produce the first publicly in their hymnody, and thus to put a charm on the youthful mind, challenging one and all to join them in pursuit of virtue by means of these same imitations.

CLINIAS : Truly said, indeed.

ATHENIAN : That is the purpose, then, for which teacher and d pupil must employ the notes of the lyre; they must do so to get the benefit of the emphasis given by its strings, and so must make their tones accordant with those of the voice. As for diversification and complication of the instrumental part—the strings giving out one tone and the composer of the melody another—and, in fact, for correspondence, within or without the octave, of lesser interval with greater, quicker note with longer, lower tones with higher, and equally for all sorts of complication of the rhythm by instrumental accompa- e niment, no such devices are to be employed with pupils who are to acquire the benefits of their musical studies in the brief space of three years. Such a clash of opposites makes learning a slow business, and it is imperative that our young people should learn their lessons with ease; the compulsory subjects we have imposed on them are neither few nor light, as the progress of our discourse will disclose in due time. All these matters, then, are for our minister of education to supervise on the lines laid down. As for the actual tunes and words which the trainers of our choirs are to teach, and the character of them, that too 813 has already been fully discussed. As you remember, we said they must be consecrated and assigned each to its appropriate festival to provide a society with a pleasure that is in very deed fortunate.

CLINIAS : Here, again, what you say is true.

ATHENIAN : Aye, absolutely true. So our chosen director of music shall have the matter put under his care for supervision, and the blessings of fortune go with him! Our business shall be to add further specifications to what we have already said on the subject of the dance and the training of physique in general. We supplemented our b treatment of music by adding directions for the teacher, and we will do the same for physical culture. Both the boys and the girls will, of course, have to dance and practice bodily exercises, will they not?

CLINIAS : Yes.

ATHENIAN : So the convenient arrangement for these exercises will be that there should be dancing masters for boys and mistresses for girls.

CLINIAS : I don't dispute it.

ATHENIAN : Then once more we must call in the busiest of our functionaries, the director of education. His supervision of music and c physical training will keep his hands pretty full.

CLINIAS : How then, at his advanced age, will he be equal to the supervision of such varied business?

ATHENIAN: Oh, easily enough. The law will permit him, as it has already done, to associate with himself in this work any citizens he may choose of either sex. He will know who are the right persons and have no wish to go wrong in such matters, as he will have a pru-

d dent respect for his office and an understanding of its importance, and a lifelong conviction that so long as the young generation is, and continues to be, well brought up, our ship of state will have a fair voyage, while in the contrary case the consequences are better left unspoken, and we will leave them so in the case of a city which we are founding for the first time, from regard for the anxious observers of omens. On this subject, too—dancing and the motions of physical training in general—we ourselves have already said much. We are instituting gymnasiums and all kinds of military exercises—exercises in archery,

e the throwing of various sorts of missiles, light skirmishing, infantry fighting in its different departments, tactical maneuvers, field marches of all kinds, encampment, and any studies which go to form a cavalry- man. In fact, there must be public teachers in all these branches, re- ceiving a stipend from the state, and they must have for their scholars not merely boys and men, but the girls and women, who must get a knowledge of all this. While they are still in their girlhood they must practice dancing and fighting in armor thoroughly, and as women they must take their share in the maneuvring, company drill, and ground-

814 ing and shouldering of arms, for this reason if for no other. If circum- stances should ever require our whole force to take the field en masse outside the city, there will be a defense for the children and the city at large equal to its immediate purpose. On the other hand, if—and the possibility cannot be excluded—there should be a foreign invasion of a large and powerful force of Greeks or others, which might compel a pitched battle for the actual safety of the city, it would be a sad dis-

b grace to the community if it had trained its women so ill that they had not even the courage of the hen bird, who will face the most dangerous beast in defense of her chicks at the risk of death or any other peril— if they rushed straight to the temples, beset all the altars and shrines, and bespattered mankind with the opprobrium of being the most abject creature alive.

CLINIAS: Why, no sir, such a performance would be no credit

c to any city in which it might occur—to say nothing of the mischief it would do.

ATHENIAN: Then we may impose the law that, up to the point indicated, our women are not to neglect the arts of war—they must be practiced by all citizens, male and female alike?

CLINIAS: You have one supporter at any rate in me.

ATHENIAN: Now as to wrestling, we have dealt with it al- ready, but we said nothing of what is to my mind the most important point, though one not easy to explain in the absence of an actual physical demonstration. So we will leave the decision of that issue

until theory and practice combined have cleared up the whole subject d
and made it plain that the kind of wrestling we have in mind is far
more closely connected with military combat than any other sort of
movement, and also that it is to be cultivated with a view to this latter,
not the latter with a view to it.

CLINIAS : That last point is well taken.

ATHENIAN : So much, then, at present for what we have to say
of the value of wrestling. As for other movement of the body as a whole
—in the main it may properly be called dancing—we must bear in
mind that it has two species, one reproducing motions of comely bodies e
with a dignified effect, the other those of uncomely bodies with a
ludicrous, and that, further, the comic and the serious kinds have each
two subspecies. One species of the serious sort represents the movements of the comely body and its valiant soul in battle and in the toils
of enforced endurance, the other the bearing of the continent soul in a
state of prosperity and duly measured pleasure; an appropriate name
for this latter would be the *dance of peace*. The war dance has a dif- 815
ferent character, and may properly be called the *Pyrrhic;* it depicts
the motions of eluding blows and shots of every kind by various devices of swerving, yielding ground, leaping from the ground or
crouching, as well as the contrary motions which lead to a posture of
attack, and aim at the reproduction of the shooting of arrows, casting
of darts, and dealing of all kinds of blows. In these dances the upright,
well-braced posture which represents the good body and good mind,
and in which the bodily members are in the main kept straight, is b
the kind of attitude we pronounce right, that which depicts their contrary, wrong. In the case of the dance of peace, the question to be raised
in every case is whether the performer succeeds or fails in maintaining
throughout his performance a graceful style of dancing in a way becoming to the law-abiding man. So we have, in the first place, to draw
a distinction between questionable dances and those which are above
question. What then is the distinction, and where should the line be c
drawn?

As for dances of bacchanals and their likes, which present what
is called a 'mimic' exhibition of persons in liquor, under the designations of nymphs, panes, sileni, or satyrs, and are performed as a part
of certain rituals and initiations, it is hard to pronounce that whole
style of dance either warlike or pacific, or to determine what possible d
purpose it has. The most correct course, I think, will be to discriminate
it alike from the dances of war and of peace, declare it unfit for a
citizen, and leave it so on one side, returning once more to the war
dance and peace dance as matters which unquestionably concern us.
The nonmartial arts of worship of gods and their progeny in dances
will all form a single genre expressive of a sense of well-being, and
may be divided into two branches, one expressive of escape from hard- e
ships and perils to good fortune, in which the pleasure conveyed is

keener, and one of retention and augmentation of good already enjoyed, in which this pleasure is more sedate. Now, as we know, any
man in such conditions executes movements of the body, more vigorous when his pleasure is more intense, less vigorous when it is less so.
Again, the more sober the man and the more schooled to fortitude,
816 the less violent these motions; the more fearful the man and the less
disciplined in continence, the more violent and vehement these movements. But to speak generally, no man who is using his vocal organs,
whether for song or for speech, can keep his body perfectly still.
Hence it is from this representation of things spoken by means of posture and gesture that the whole art of the dance has been elaborated.
And in all such cases, one man's motions keep time and tune with his
utterance, another's do not. Hence, in fact, the well-merited praise
b which may be given to many of our traditional names for their excellence and truth to fact, one of which is that bestowed on the
dances of prosperous men who preserve measure in their pleasures.
We should give credit to the inventor, whoever he may have been,
for the truth and musical taste of the names, and the philosophical insight shown by designating fine dancing as a whole *emmeliae* and
proceeding to distinguish two kinds, each with its fitting and proper
c name—the war dance, or *Pyrrhic,* and the *emmelia,* or dance of peace.
The legislator must deal with these matters in general outline, and the
curator make them an object of study. His investigations should result
in the combination of dancing with the rest of music, the assignment
to each sacrificial feast of the appropriate measures, and the consecration of the whole arrangement in due course. Thenceforth there must
be no innovation in anything which has to do either with dance or
with song. No, our citizens and their city must preserve their identity
d by a uniform life of unvarying pleasures, where all are as utterly alike
as may be in all happiness and bliss.

This concludes our treatment of the employment of comely body
and noble mind in choric performances such as we have said these
displays should be. As for the play of uncomely body and mind and
the artistes of ludicrous burlesque in diction, song, dance, and all the
caricaturistic effects of the three, we cannot avoid taking notice of this
and passing it under review. A man who means to form his judgment
can no more understand earnest apart from burlesque than any other
contrary apart from its contrary, but, on the other side, a man who
e means to have any part in goodness, were it never so little, cannot
possibly produce both. The very reason why he must get to know such
a thing is that he may never be betrayed by ignorance into doing or
saying a ludicrous thing when it is out of place. We shall enjoin that
such representations be left to slaves or hired aliens, and that they receive no serious consideration whatsoever. No free person, whether
woman or man, shall be found taking lessons in them, and there must
always be some novelty in a performance of the kind. The sportive en-

tertainment to which the name *comedy* is universally given may be 817
taken as disposed of on these lines by our law with its accompanying
explanation.

For our tragic poets and their so-called serious compositions, we
may conceive some of them to approach us with a question couched in
these words or the like. May we pay your city and its territory a visit,
sirs, or may we not? And may we bring our poetry along with us, or
what decision have you reached on the point?

What would be the right answer to give to such men of genius?

Why this, I believe. Respected visitors, we are ourselves authors b
of a tragedy, and that the finest and best we know how to make. In
fact, our whole polity has been constructed as a dramatization of a
noble and perfect life; that is what *we* hold to be in truth the most
real of tragedies. Thus you are poets, and we also are poets in the
same style, rival artists and rival actors, and that in the finest of all
dramas, one which indeed can be produced only by a code of true law
—or at least that is our faith. So you must not expect that we shall c
lightheartedly permit you to pitch your booths in our market square
with a troupe of actors whose melodious voices will drown our own,
and let you deliver your public tirades before our boys and women and
the populace at large—let you address them on the same issues as ourselves, not to the same effect, but commonly and for the most part to
the very contrary. Why, we should be stark mad to do so, and so would
the whole community, if you could find one which would let you do as
you are now proposing, until its magistrates had decided whether your d
compositions are fit to be uttered and edifying to be heard by the public
or not. Go to, then, ye scions of the softer Muses, first exhibit your
minstrelsy to the magistrates for comparison with our own. Then, if
your sentiments prove to be the same as ours, or even better, we will
grant you a chorus, but if not, I fear, my friends, we never can.

Such, then, subject to your approval, shall be our legislation, and e
such our conjoined practice in the whole matter of the choric art and
the instruction in it—slaves and their masters to receive separate
treatment.

CLINIAS: Well, of course, we approve—at any rate, for the moment.

ATHENIAN: Then there are, of course, three subjects for the
freeborn still to study. Ciphering and arithmetic make one subject;
mensuration, linear, superficial, and solid, taken as one single study,
forms a second; the third is the true relations of the planetary orbits
to one another. The elaborate prosecution of all these studies into 818
their minute details is not for the masses but for a select few—who
these should be shall be indicated later as our argument draws to its
conclusion, where the indication will be in place. For the multitude it
will be proper to learn so much of the matter as is indispensable, and
as it may truly be said to be a disgrace to the common man not to

know, though it would be hard, or actually impossible, to pursue the
research into minute detail. We simply cannot dispense with its char-
b acter of *necessity;* in fact, it is this which the author of the proverb
presumably had in view when he said that 'even God is never to be
seen contending against necessity.' No doubt he meant the necessity
which is *divine,* for if you understand the words of mere human necessities, like those to which men in general apply such sayings, they are
far and away the silliest of speeches.

CLINIAS : Yes, sir, but where in these studies do the other sort of
necessities, the divine, come in?

ATHENIAN : Why, I presume they are those in neglect or sheer
c ignorance of which no being could possibly play the part of a god or
superior spirit toward us, nor yet of a hero capable of serious supervision of humanity. How far would he be below the level of even inspired
humanity who could not tell three from two, or even odd from even, in
fact, could not so much as count, or could not even tell off night and
day, or had no acquaintance with the orbits of moon, sun, and the rest
d of the planets! So the mere thought that all this information is not
indispensable to anyone who means to *know* anything whatsoever
of the noblest of all sciences is the idlest folly. What branches of them
are to be studied, to what extent, and at what times, which must be
taken in conjunction with another and which pursued by itself, and
how they are all to be blended into a whole—these are the questions
which we must first settle correctly. We may then proceed under the
guidance of these sciences to the study of all the rest. It is the natural
order, and it has that necessity with which, as we say, no god con-
e tends or ever will contend.

CLINIAS : Yes, sir, the views you have just expressed sound true
and natural, as you expound them.

ATHENIAN : Indeed, they are so, Clinias, though it is difficult to
legislate on the subject by anticipation as we are now doing. The more
precise details of legislation, with your consent, we may postpone to
another occasion.

CLINIAS : You are apprehensive, I take it, sir, of the common unfamiliarity of our countrymen with such topics, but your concern is
unwarranted. Pray do your best to state your views without any reser-
819 vation on that score.

ATHENIAN : I certainly feel the apprehension you speak of, but
am still more alarmed by students who have actually taken up these
sciences, but taken them up in the wrong way. Complete unac-
quaintance with a subject is never a dangerous or formidable obstacle,
nor is it the worst of evils; much graver harm is done by wide acquaintance with a subject and extensive learning in it, when they are
conjoined with bad training.

CLINIAS : Truly observed.

ATHENIAN : Well then, I maintain that freeborn men should

learn of these various subjects as much as in Egypt is taught to vast b
numbers of children along with their letters. To begin with, lessons
have been devised there in ciphering for the veriest children which
they can learn with a good deal of fun and amusement, problems
about the distribution of a fixed total number of apples or garlands
among larger and smaller groups, and the arranging of a successive
series of 'byes' and 'pairs' between boxers and wrestlers as the nature
of such contests requires. More than this, the teachers have a game in
which they distribute mixed sets of saucers of gold, silver, copper, and c
similar materials or, in other cases, whole sets of one material. In this
way, they, as I was saying, incorporate the elementary application of
arithmetic in the children's play, give the pupils a useful preparation
for the dispositions, formations, and movements of military life as well
as for domestic management, and make them more alert and more
serviceable to themselves in every way. Then they go on to exercises in
measurements of length, surface, and cubical content, by which they d
dispel the native and general, but ludicrous and shameful, ignorance
of mankind about the whole subject.

CLINIAS : And in what may this native ignorance consist?

ATHENIAN : My dear Clinias, when I was told, rather belatedly,
of our condition in this matter, like you, I was utterly astounded.
Such ignorance seemed to me more worthy of a stupid beast like the
hog than of a human being, and I blushed not for myself alone, but
for our whole Hellenic world.   e

CLINIAS : But what was the reason for your blushes? Let us have
your account of it, sir.

ATHENIAN : Why, so I will. Or rather I will make it plain by a
question. Pray tell me one little thing. You know what is meant by
line?

CLINIAS : Of course I do.

ATHENIAN : And by *surface*?

CLINIAS : Certainly.

ATHENIAN : And you know that they are two distinct things,
and that *volume* is another and a third?

CLINIAS : Just so.

ATHENIAN : Now you hold, do you not, that all three are commensurable with one another?

CLINIAS : Yes.

ATHENIAN : That is, that *line* is in its very nature measurable
by line, *surface* by surface, and similarly with *volume*?   820

CLINIAS : Most assuredly.

ATHENIAN : But suppose this cannot be said of some of them,
neither with more assurance nor with less, but is true in some cases,
but not in others, and you believe it true universally. What do you
think of your state of mind on the matter?

CLINIAS : That it is unsatisfactory, to be sure.

ATHENIAN: And what of the relations of line and surface to volume, or of line and surface to one another? Is it not the fact that we Hellenes all imagine they are commensurable in some way or other?

b   CLINIAS: Why certainly that is the fact.

ATHENIAN: Then if this is another entire impossibility, though we Hellenes, as I said, all fancy it possible, are we not bound to blush for them all as we tell them, Worthy Hellenes, here is one of the things of which we said that ignorance is a disgrace and knowledge on a point so necessary, no great accomplishment?

CLINIAS: We are, indeed.

ATHENIAN: There are, besides, other closely related points

c   which frequently give rise to errors akin to those just mentioned.

CLINIAS: Such for example as?

ATHENIAN: The real relation of commensurability and incommensurability to one another. A man must be able to distinguish them on examination, or else must be a very poor creature. We should frequently propound such problems to each other—a much more elegant pastime for the elderly than draughts—and give our passion for victory an outlet in amusements worthy of us.

d   CLINIAS: I dare say, after all, the game of draughts and these studies are not so widely different.

ATHENIAN: Accordingly, Clinias, I hold that these are subjects which our young people must learn. Indeed there is neither danger nor difficulty in them, and if they are learned through the medium of play, they will do our city no harm, but rather good.

CLINIAS: Just so.

ATHENIAN: Still, while we must clearly include them in our scheme, if our case for this proves to be made out, equally clearly we shall reject them if it is not made out.

e   CLINIAS: Oh, plainly, plainly.

ATHENIAN: Well then, for the present, sir, let them be set down among the requisite studies, to leave no gap in the body of our laws, but set down as detachable from the rest of our polity—like so many redeemable pledges—should they prove unacceptable to us who have deposited them, or you who have received them.

CLINIAS: The terms of proposal are fair enough.

ATHENIAN: Next you must consider astronomy. Are we to adopt the recommendation that our young folk should study it, or are we not?

CLINIAS: Well, say on.

ATHENIAN: Now here, mark you, I find a strange, indeed, a wholly intolerable paradox.

821   CLINIAS: And of what kind?

ATHENIAN: It is currently said that it is wrong—indeed, positively blasphemous—to prosecute inquiry or busy ourselves with the quest for explanation where the supreme God and the universe as a whole are concerned, though the very opposite should seem to be our right course.

CLINIAS: What!

ATHENIAN: What I am trying to say, I know, is startling, and might be thought unbecoming in a man of our years, but the plain truth is that a man who knows of a study which he believes sublime, true, beneficial to society, and perfectly acceptable to God, simply can- b not refrain from calling attention to it.

CLINIAS: Presumably not, but what astronomical study shall we find answering to this description?

ATHENIAN: Why, my friends, at this moment, all our Hellenic world, as I may fairly say, habitually charges high gods, sun and moon, falsely.

CLINIAS: And what may this false charge be?

ATHENIAN: We say that they, and certain heavenly bodies associated with them, never keep to the same path, which is why we call them planets.

CLINIAS: Egad, sir, and that is true enough. Why, in my own c lifetime I myself have often seen the morning and evening stars and some others never keeping to the same track, but divagating in all directions. As for sun and moon, of course, I have seen them behave as we all know they regularly do behave.

ATHENIAN: Well then, Megillus and Clinias, that is just the reason why I am now insisting that *our* citizens and their young people must learn enough of all the facts about the divinities of the sky to d prevent blasphemy of them, and to ensure a reverent piety in the language of all our sacrifices and prayers.

CLINIAS: That is right, provided, of course, that, in the first place, the knowledge of which you speak is possible. On that assumption, if there are errors in our present language on such matters which study will correct, I, too, confess that a subject of such scope and quality must be taught. Do your best, then, with the demonstration that the facts are as you say, as we will do our best to follow your instruction.

ATHENIAN: Why, the lesson I have in mind, to be sure, is not an e easy one—and yet it is not so hopelessly difficult either, and takes no very great time to learn, as this one fact is enough to prove. I was not a young man when I heard of the truth myself, and it was no long time ago, and yet I may possibly make it clear to both of you now at no great expense of time. Were the point a really hard one, a man of my age would never be able to explain it to men of yours.

CLINIAS: Quite true. But pray what may this knowledge be— this doctrine, as you maintain, so surprising, yet so proper for the young to learn, and so unsuspected by us? You must try to explain so 822 much of the subject with all possible clarity.

ATHENIAN: I will do my best. The fact is, my friends, that the

belief that sun, moon, and other heavenly bodies are 'wandering stars'
of any sort is not true. The very reverse is the truth—each of these
bodies always revolves in the same orbit and in one orbit, not many, for
all that it looks to be moving in several, and again the actually swiftest of them is wrongly believed to be the slowest and the slowest the
b swiftest. Well now, suppose these are the real facts, but we hold a
discrepant view about them. If we had fancies of this kind about the
competing horses or long-distance runners at Olympia, and so were to
call the quickest runner slowest and the slowest quickest, and to compose triumphal odes in which we celebrated the vanquished as victor,
why, I conceive our bestowal of our praises would neither be correct
nor to the liking of the runners, who, after all, are but men. But when
c we actually make the same mistake today about our deities, must we
not think that an error which was risible in the other case and on
the racecourse, is now, when transferred to this context, no laughing
matter, and no very godly opinion either, since it means reiterated
mendacity about divine beings?

CLINIAS : Nothing can be truer—if the facts are really as you
say.

ATHENIAN : Then, if we can show that they are so, all these
matters must be studied—within the limits we have proposed—if not,
we must let them alone. May we take it that our agreement extends
so far?

d   CLINIAS : With all my heart.

ATHENIAN : Then we may say that our regulations for the
studies to be included in our education are now complete. As to the
chase, we should recur to the thought which has guided us in other
cases of the same kind. It should seem that a legislator's task extends
to something more than the mere imposing of a law and so dismissing
a topic; there is something else he must do besides laying down the
law, something which verges at once on admonition and on legislation,
as our argument has led us to remark more than once already. A
e case in point is our treatment of the regimen of infants. As we say, we
must not leave our demands unformulated, and yet when we formulate them it is perfect folly to imagine we are laying them down as law.
So when the legal code, and the whole system of the constitution, have
been reduced to written form, it is not a final encomium on the pre-
eminently virtuous citizen to say that he is the good citizen who has
shown himself the best servant of the laws and gives them the fullest
obedience; there would be more finality in the statement that he is the
823 best who has spent his life without qualification in obedience to all the
legislator has written, whether by way of enactment, of approbation, or of reprobation. This is the truest eulogy which can be bestowed
on a citizen, and a real legislator should not confine himself to the
composition of statutes; he should further entwine with the text of his
laws an exposition of all he accounts laudable or the reverse, and the

citizen of eminent goodness must feel himself no less bound by such
directions than by those enforced with a legal sanction.

We may make our meaning plainer if we call the subject of our
present remarks, so to say, in evidence. The chase, in fact, is a pursuit b
with very various departments, all currently comprehended under that
single name. There are many ways of taking the denizens of the water,
and again of fowling, and especially there are numerous devices for
the capture of land animals. I mean not of brutes merely, but of the
noteworthy hunting of men to be seen in warfare, as well as in the
various forms under which that quarry is pursued in the way of kindness, some laudable and others the reverse; the kidnapings of brigands
and forces in the field are also forms of the chase. Now the legislator
framing his statutes of venery can neither omit to explain this, nor c
yet can he impose a set of legal regulations with directions for all
cases and threatened penalties for their breach. What course is he,
then, to take in such a case? He must—I mean the legislator must—
commend some forms of the chase and condemn others, always with
an eye on the exercises and sports of the younger men; the younger
man, in his turn, must obey this advice. Neither hope of pleasure nor
dread of hardship must interfere with his obedience, and he must treat
the legislator's various commendations with still deeper respect and
more dutiful compliance than his penalty-sanctioned ordinances.   d

These preliminary remarks may naturally be succeeded by judi-
cious commendation and reprobation of diverse forms of the chase,
commendation of such as tend to improve the young man's soul,
reprobation of those which have the contrary tendency. So we will now,
without more delay, direct our address to the young people, couching
it in the language of pious wish.

Our prayer, beloved, is that you may never be smitten with the
lust or passion for sea fishery, for angling or any taking of the creatures of the waters, or for the use of weels, by which the slothful hunt- e
er's work is done for him equally whether he wakes or sleeps. May you
never be visited by hankerings for the pirate's trade—the chasing of
men on the high seas—to make you cruel and lawless hunters! As for
petty poaching in town or country, may the bare thought never so
much as enter your minds! And may no young soul be haunted by the
seductive itch for fowling—hardly a taste for the freeborn man! 824
Thus we have left our athletes only the chase and taking of land creatures. One form of this, again, that practiced by parties who take it in
turns to sleep—night trapping, as it is called—is for sluggards and
deserves no commendation; the intervals of inaction fill as much time
as the exercise, and the strength and violence of the quarry are overpowered not by the triumph of an energetic soul, but by nets and
snares. Thus the only variety left free to all, and the best variety,
is the chase of a four-footed quarry in reliance upon one's horse, one's
dogs, and one's own limbs, where the hunters—those, that is, who

cultivate godlike courage—all hunt in their own persons and achieve
b all their success by running, striking, and shooting.

The discourse we have just rehearsed may serve the end of general commendation and censure in the matter. The actual law may run to this effect. Such hunters are truly 'sacred,' and none shall hinder them from following the game with their hounds when and as they please. The night trapper who trusts to his nets and springes no one shall permit to pursue his game at any time or place. The fowler is not to be disturbed on uncultivated ground or in the mountains, but shall be turned off tilled fields or untilled consecrated demesnes by any
c who may find him there. The fisherman shall be free to take his fish anywhere save in harbors and consecrated rivers, marshes, or lakes, with the sole proviso that he may not foul the waters with stupefying juices.

And with this we may say our regulation of education is at last completed.

CLINIAS : And well completed, too.

BOOK VIII

828 ATHENIAN : The next task awaiting us is, with the help of oracles from Delphi, to construct the calendar of festivals and give it the authority of law—to determine what sacrifices it will be 'to the welfare and profit' of the state to celebrate, and to what deities they should be offered. The question of their dates and their number will be, to some extent, one for our own decision.

CLINIAS : That of their number will no doubt be so.

ATHENIAN : Then let me deal with the question of number first.
b This shall be not less than three hundred and sixty-five, to ensure that sacrifice shall be done by at least one magistracy to some god or spirit on behalf of the state, its members, and their chattels without any interruption. Canonists, priests of both sexes, and prophets are to meet in committee with the curators of law and prescribe any details which the legislator has unavoidably omitted; the same committee shall further decide how the omissions aforesaid are to be supplied.
c The provision of the actual law will be, in fact, that there shall be twelve festivals of the twelve gods after whom the different tribes are named, to be kept by the doing of monthly sacrifice to each of these deities, with the adjuncts of such choirs and contests, both musical and athletic, as are suitable to the character of the deity and the season of the festival, and the demarcation of celebrations for women from which men must be excluded from those in which this regulation is not necessary. Further, there must be no confusion between the cults of the gods of the underworld with their accessories and those of the celestial powers, as we should call them; the law will keep the
d two distinct, and put the former in the month sacred to Pluto, the

twelfth of the year. True warriors must cherish no repugnance for such a deity of death, but venerate him as the constant benefactor of mankind, for union of soul with body, as I would assure you in all earnest, is in no way better than dissolution.

Furthermore, an authority which is to make these arrangements to our satisfaction must be possessed with the convictions that the like of this society of ours is not to be found in the world for ample leisure and abundant provision of all necessaries, that its business, like that of an individual man, is to live well, and that the indispensable precondition of a happy life is that we commit no sin against ourselves and suffer no wrongs from others. Now there is no great difficulty about the first condition, but grave difficulty in compassing a power to protect oneself from *suffering* wrongs; 'tis, indeed, only to be fully got in one way, by becoming fully good. Now the case will be the same with a society—if it become good, its life will be one of peace, if evil, of warfare without and within. And since this is so, its members must train themselves for warfare, not in actual time of war, but during the life of peace. Hence the wise state will be under arms not less than one day in each month, and as many more as its magistrates may think good, without regard to stress of weather, cold or hot; men, women, children, will take the field, in one body when the magistrates so ordain, at other times in sections. They must also devise a round of noble sports, with their accompanying sacrifices, so as to provide festal combats which shall reproduce real warfare with all possible truth to life. On these occasions there should always be a distribution of prizes and rewards for merit, and the citizens should compose panegyrics and censures upon one another according to a man's performance in these contests and in life at large, the honor of the panegyric going to him who proves himself of perfect worth, and the censure to him who fails.

The composition of such verses shall not be for everyone. The author must, in the first place, have reached the age of not less than fifty; moreover he must not be one of those who have within them a sufficient vein of literature and music but have never achieved one noble and illustrious deed. But the verse of composers who are in their own persons men of worth, held in public honor as authors of noble deeds, may be sung, even though it have no real musical quality. The selection of composers shall be in the hands of the minister of education and his colleagues, the curators of law, who are to allow them this special privilege. Their music, and theirs only, shall be free and uncensored, whereas this liberty shall be granted to no one else, and no other citizen shall presume, without the curator's license, to sing an unauthorized air, were its notes more ravishing than those of Thamyras or Orpheus themselves, but only such verse as has been duly consecrated to the gods and such compositions by men of true worth as have been pronounced to convey laudation or reproof with due

propriety. These directions as to maneuvers and freedom to compose
uncensored verse are to be taken as applying equally to both sexes.
The legislator must put the case to himself thus in his meditations.
Go to, now, what manner of men am I training by the whole scheme
830 of my institutions? Are they not men who are to be competitors in
the most momentous of all contests, where they will find countless
opponents pitted against them? 'Why, certainly,' will be the ready and
the right answer.

Well then, suppose our training were meant for boxers, or pugil-
ists, or athletes in some similar competition. Should we be for going
straight into the actual contest without any previous daily combat with
an opponent? Surely, were we boxers, for days together before the
actual event we should be learning how to fight and working ourselves
b hard. We should rehearse all the movements we expected to make in
the actual match, when the time for it should come, and we should
come as near as we could to the reality; we should fit our hands with
practice gloves in place of match gloves, to make sure that we were
getting the best training we could. If we were exceptionally put to
it to find partners to practice with, would fear of the laughter of fools
c frighten us from hanging up an inanimate dummy to practice on? If
we were actually without any opponent living or lifeless, and had no
partners whatsoever, should we not have gone the length of quite
literally sparring 'at our own shadows'? What other name could you
give to the training in 'using one's mauleys'?

CLINIAS : Why, sir, I can think of none but the name you have
just employed.

ATHENIAN : Very well, then. And is the fighting force of our society to be worse prepared than such combatants as these when it
ventures itself, as the occasion arises, in the gravest of all contests, in
d which the stake is the very existence of self, children, possessions,
nay, of the whole community? Is this precious fear that our practice
on one another may provoke some laughter to keep the legislator from
his work? Should he not require drill on the small scale, not involving
the use of heavy arms, to be performed, if possible, daily, directing all
physical training, whether in combined groups or otherwise, to that
end, and exercises of another kind, major and minor, to be held at least
once a month, in which the citizens throughout our territories will
contend with one another in the occupation of military positions and
e the laying of ambushes, and imitate all branches of warfare by very
real fighting with gloves and missiles closely modeled on the genuine
articles? These weapons should be comparatively dangerous, that the
sport may not be wholly without its perils, but give occasion for alarms,
and thus serve, in its way, to discriminate a man of courage from a
831 coward. Thus it will enable the legislator to train the whole community
to lifelong efficient service in the real conflict, by a right apportion-
ment of marks of distinction and discredit, and if a life should
happen to be lost in this fashion, the homicide will be regarded as in-

voluntary, and its author pronounced clear of the innocent blood, when he has undergone ritual cleansing as the law directs. The legislator's view will be that if a few men come to their end, others as good will be born to take their place, whereas, if fear of dangers comes to its end, if I may so express myself, he can find no touchstone of better and worse in situations of the kind, and this is a much graver misfortune for his society than the other.   b

CLINIAS: My friend and I, sir, agree with you that this is what the law should enjoin and the whole community practice.

ATHENIAN: Now I wonder whether all of us understand the reason why such contests between opposing teams are nowhere to be found in our existing societies, except perhaps on the smallest scale. Should we lay the blame on the ignorance of the generality of mankind and their legislators?

CLINIAS: Very likely we should.

ATHENIAN: My dear Clinias! Not in the least! The true causes c are two, both very powerful.

CLINIAS: And what are they?

ATHENIAN: One arises from the passion for wealth which leaves a man not a moment of leisure to attend to anything beyond his personal fortunes. So long as a citizen's whole soul is wrapped up in these, he cannot give a thought to anything but the day's takings. Any study or pursuit which tends to that result everyone sets himself eagerly to learn and practice; all others are laughed to scorn. Here, then, we may say, is one reason in particular why society declines to d take this or any other wholly admirable pursuit seriously, though everyone in it is ready enough, in his furious thirst for gold and silver, to stoop to any trade and any shift, honorable or dishonorable, which holds out a prospect of wealth, ready to scruple at no act whatsoever—innocent, sinful, or utterly shameful—so long as it promises to sate him, like some brute beast, with a perfect glut of eating, drinking, and sexual sport.   e

CLINIAS: Too true.

ATHENIAN: Well then, this, as I say, may be set down for one reason which tends to keep societies from efficient cultivation of noble activities, military and otherwise; it turns the naturally quiet and decent man into a tradesman, skipper, or mere menial, and makes the more adventurous, pirates, burglars, temple thieves, swashbucklers, and bullies, though often enough they are not so much vicious 832 as unfortunate.

CLINIAS: Unfortunate? Why so?

ATHENIAN: Why, what epithet but 'most unfortunate' can I find for men who are forced to go through the world with an incessant hunger gnawing at their own souls?

CLINIAS: Well, that is one of your causes, sir, but what do you mean by the other?

ATHENIAN: Thank you for the reminder.

CLINIAS: One cause, as I understand you, is this lifelong insatiate quest which leaves none of us an hour's leisure, and so keeps us
b all from practicing the arts of war as we should. Good, but let us hear something of the other reason.

ATHENIAN: I fancy you think my reason for being so slow to name it is that I cannot.

CLINIAS: Not so, but what one must call your abhorrence of the character just described is leading you, as we think, into an invective irrelevant to our present argument.

ATHENIAN: I stand properly rebuked, gentlemen. You wish me, it appears, to proceed.

CLINIAS: You have only to do so.

ATHENIAN: Then I say the reason is to be found in those 'no-
c constitutions' we have so often touched on already, democracy, oligarchy, autocracy. Not one of them is a true constitution; the proper name for all would rather be 'party ascendancies.' In none do we find a willing sovereign with willing subjects; in all a willing sovereign is controlling reluctant subjects by violence of some sort. But a sovereign who goes in fear of his subject will never, if he can help it, permit that subject to become noble, wealthy, powerful, valiant, nor so much as a good fighting man. Here, then, we have the main sources of almost all mischief—certainly the main sources of the mischief we are treat-
d ing of now. Both are avoided in the constitution we are now engaged in framing. It provides more ample leisure than any other; its citizens are free from one another's dictation. Our laws, I take it, are very unlikely to make them greedy of riches. Hence it is but natural and reasonable to believe that a society so constituted, and only such a society of all others, would have a place for the warrior's education described above, which is also his sport, as duly set forth in our discussion.

CLINIAS: Quite true.

ATHENIAN: Then I suppose we may next make a general observation about all athletic contests. Those which provide a training
e for war should be encouraged and prizes instituted for success in them; those which do not may be dismissed. Which these are it will be better to make matter for explicit statement and legislation from the very first. To begin with, I apprehend there should be such institution of prizes for fleetness of foot and rapidity of movement in general.

CLINIAS: There should.

ATHENIAN: To be sure, bodily agility—quickness of hand as well as of foot—is a first-rate point in the soldier's equipment; fleetness of foot has its use in flight and pursuit, and readiness of hand in the
833 close stand-up fighting which calls for so much stocky strength.

CLINIAS: Of course.

ATHENIAN: And again, neither yields its best service without the aid of weapons.

CLINIAS : Naturally not.

ATHENIAN : So our herald will follow the existing custom and announce the furlong race as the first event of our sports. The competitor shall make his entry in full armor; we shall give no prize for an unarmed competitor. No, the order of entry will be *first* the runner for the furlong, in full equipment, *second* for the two furlongs, *third* for b the chariot course, *fourth* for the long-distance; *fifth* there will be an entrant whom we shall call the hoplite, and set in the first place to run, in full armor of heavy weight, over a smooth course of sixty furlongs, to a temple of Ares and back, and his rival, an archer in complete archer's equipment, who must run against him over a course of a hundred furlongs, through hilly and varied ground, to a temple of Apollo and Artemis. In arranging the events, we shall wait for their c return, and prizes will be given to the victors in each event.

CLINIAS : A good arrangement.

ATHENIAN : Now let us make three classes in these athletic events, one for boys, one for lads, and one for men. We will fix the length of the course for lads at two thirds, and that for boys at one half the length of the full course, whether they enter as hoplites or as archers. In the case of females, we shall have races of one and two furlongs, a chariot course, and a long-distance event, in which girls d below the age of puberty must actually compete stripped, while girls who have passed thirteen and are still awaiting marriage—to ensue at latest at twenty and at earliest at eighteen—must be clad in the proper accouterment when they enter into these competitions. So much then for races for both males and females.

As for competitions of strength, in place of wrestling and the like, the 'heavy events' of current practice, we shall institute fights in armor, single combats, or combats between pairs, or contests between e any number of combatants up to ten a side. In determining what points will disqualify for victory or count toward it, we shall follow the precedent set by existing authorities on wrestling in their rules for the proper conduct of that sport. We shall, in like manner, call in experts in fencing under arms and invite their help in regulating the faults which must be avoided, and hits which must be scored, to qualify for a victory in these contests, and the code which shall determine de- 834 feat. The same regulations shall equally apply to females under the age of marriage. For the element of boxing in the *pancratium* we shall substitute a general combat of peltasts in which the contest will be waged with bow and arrow and light target, darts, stones thrown by the hand, and slings, and in this case too we shall have to draw up the rules and award the prizes of victory to those who best fulfill the demands of our regulations.

We should naturally proceed now to make rules for the horse b race. But in a district like Crete there will be no great use for horses and few horses to use; hence there will, of course, be less interest in

breeding them and matching them against one another. As for chariots, to be sure, there will be no one to keep them, and probably no one
to cherish any particular aspirations in that direction; hence if we instituted anything so contrary to native custom as a chariot race, we
should look like the fools we should in fact be. But if we offer prizes
c for races with ridden horses—young and half-grown colts as well as
full-grown beasts—we shall be cultivating a form of the sport well in
keeping with the nature of our territory. So the law will provide for
competitive matches between these classes of sportsmen and no others, and appoint the phylarchs and hipparchs as public judges both of
the course and of the competitors entering—who must be in their
armor. Here, as in the case of the athletic sports, it would be a mistake
d for the law to institute contests for the unarmed. A Cretan, again,
can do useful service as a mounted bowman or javelin man, and so
we should further have matches between rivals in these lines for our
amusement. As to women, it is really not worth our while to force
them to take part in these competitions by legal enactments, but if their
earlier training has led to the growth of such habits that they are physically equal, in their girlhood or later maidenhood, to take part without
unwelcome results, they should be allowed to do so unreproved.

We have at last come to the end of this subject of athletic con-
e tests, and the teaching of physical culture, with all the work it entails
both in the competitions and in the daily routine of school. We have
similarly completed our main treatment of music. Rules for rhapsodes
and their likes and for the competitions between choirs requisite at
our festivals shall be drawn up later, when months, days, and years
have first been assigned to the various gods and lesser objects of worship—e.g., regulations deciding whether these festivals should be
835 kept at intervals of two years, or of four, or in any other order we may
be inspired to think of. On these occasions, further, we must expect
that the musical competitions shall be held, each in its proper turn, as
directed by the presidents of the sports, the minister of education, and
the curators of law, who are to act in concert as a special committee
for the purpose, and must make their own legislation for all choirs
and dancers as to the dates at which competitions shall be held, the
persons who may compete, and the company in which they may do so.
The original legislator has explained more than once what the various
compositions must be like, in words spoken or sung and in mingled
b melody, rhythm, and dance movement. His later successors must follow his lead in their regulations, assigning the several competitions to
appropriate sacrifices at suitable times, and so providing our city with
feasts for her observance. There is no difficulty in discovering how to
reduce these details and others of the kind to a legitimate order, nor
again will a different arrangement of them cause much benefit or
detriment to society. But there is a matter of vast moment, as to which
c it is truly hard to inspire conviction. The task, indeed, is one for God

himself, were it actually possible to receive orders from him. As things are, it will probably need a bold man, a man who puts plain speaking before everything, to declare his real belief about the true interest of state and citizens, and make the regulations the whole social system requires and demands in a corrupt age—a man who will oppose the passions at their strongest, and stand alone in his loyalty to the voice of truth without one creature on earth to second him.

CLINIAS: Pray, sir, where may our argument be getting to now? As yet we do not see its drift. d

ATHENIAN: I am not surprised you do not. But come! I must try to put the matter more plainly still. When our conversation brought us to this theme of education, there rose before me a vision of young people of both sexes living in affectionate intimacy. As you may imagine, I was moved to uneasy apprehensions when I asked myself how one is to manage such a society—a society where the young of both sexes are in the pink of condition, exempt from the severe menial labor which does more than anything else to damp the fires of e wantonness, and all make sacrifices, feasts, and choric song the concern of their lives. How, indeed, in such a society, are they to be kept free from the passions which bring such multitudes to their undoing, the passions from which wisdom, striving to convert itself into law, bids us abstain? To be sure, it would be nothing surprising that our regulations as already enacted should get the better of most of these 836 passions. Our prohibition of excessive opulence, conducive as it is to temperance, is no trivial boon, and the whole course of the training is likewise under sound regulations of the same tendency. Besides, the magistrate's eye, drilled as it is to keep its object, and the young generation itself, constantly in view without a moment's diversion, provides a curb for most passions, so far as any device of men can.

But what of the passion of love in the young of either sex, or love b of grown woman or man for the other? We know its untold effects in the life of private persons and whole societies, but what precautions should we take against it? Whence are you to cull the specific that shall protect all and sundry from its perils? There, Clinias, we have a difficulty indeed. In fact, Crete as a whole and Lacedaemon, which lend weighty and deserved support to a great deal of our proposed legislation where it is counter to common sentiment, are dead against us—I may say it between ourselves—in this business of sex. Were one to follow the guidance of nature and adopt the law of the old days c before Laius—I mean, to pronounce it wrong that male should have to do carnally with youthful male as with female—and to fetch his evidence from the life of the animals, pointing out that male does not touch male in this way because the action is unnatural, his contention would surely be a telling one, yet it would be quite at variance with the practice of your societies. Moreover, the very end we require the legislator to keep in constant view is ill suited with your practices.

d You know the question we are repeatedly raising is what enactments foster goodness and what do not. Very well, then, suppose our present legislation pronounces this practice laudable, or free from discredit. How will it promote goodness? Will it lead to the growth of the temper of valor in the soul of the seduced? Or the growth of a tem-
e perate character in his seducer? That is surely more than any man can believe. Surely, the very opposite is the truth. Everyone must censure the unmanliness of the one party, who surrenders to his lusts because he is too weak to offer resistance, and reproach the other— the impersonator of the female—with his likeness to his model. Who in the world, then, will give legislative countenance to a practice of such a tendency? No one, I say, who has any notion of what a true
837 law is. You ask how I prove my point? We shall have to examine the real nature of affection and its attendant desire and of love so called, if we are to think rightly of this matter. There are, in fact, two different things, as well as a third compounded of them both, covered here by one single name, and it is this which causes so much confusion and obscurity.

CLINIAS : How so?

ATHENIAN : Why, we speak, you know, of the attachment between those who are alike in goodness, or between equals, and again of that between the indigent and the rich, where the one party is the opposite of the other, and when either feeling is intense we call it love.

b   CLINIAS : We do.

ATHENIAN : Now this attachment between opposites is fierce and furious, and we do not often find it reciprocated, whereas that founded on similarity is equable and permanently reciprocal. Where both factors are present at once, for one thing it is hard to perceive what the subject of this 'love' is really seeking, and for another, he is distracted and baffled by rival impulses, one inviting him to enjoy the
c charms of the object, the other forbidding the enjoyment. The man whose love is a physical passion, a hunger for another's charms, like that for ripe fruit, tells himself to take his fill and gives not a thought to his minion's state of soul. But he that treats carnal appetite as out of the question, that puts contemplation before passion, he whose desire is veritably that of soul for soul, looks on enjoyment of flesh by flesh as wanton shame; as one that reverences, aye and worships, chastity and manhood, greatness and wisdom, he will aspire to live
d with his love in constant purity on both parts. The sort of love in which both factors are involved is that we have now reckoned the third. Now since loves are of so many kinds, should the presence of all kinds be excluded from our midst by legal prohibition? Is it not obvious rather that we shall wish to find in our city the sort that has goodness for its object, the desire to make a youth as good as he can possibly be, but prohibit the other two, if only we can? Megillus, my friend, what would you have us say?

MEGILLUS : All you have even now said of this same matter, sir,   e
is perfectly well.

ATHENIAN : I expected I should find you in accord with myself,
friend, and it seems I was right. What your Spartan law thinks about
such matters is a question I need not raise; I need only welcome your
assent to our doctrine. As for Clinias, I must do my best to charm him
into acceptance of our view on some later occasion. But enough of your
common concession. By all means let us return to our legislating.

MEGILLUS : Rightly proposed.   838

ATHENIAN : Well now, and about a device to make the establishment of our law secure? I have one actually ready to my hand,
easy enough in one way, though in another of the utmost possible difficulty.

MEGILLUS : You mean to say?

ATHENIAN : Even today, as you know, lawless as most men are,
they are very effectually deterred from cohabitation with the fair, and
not against their own will either, but with their full and entire consent.

MEGILLUS : Of what cases are you thinking?

ATHENIAN : Of persons who have a fair sister or brother. The
same law, though unwritten, proves a complete safeguard of son and   b
daughter—so much so that no one lies with them, openly or covertly,
or approaches them with any familiarities of that sort—nay the very
wish for such congress never so much as enters the mind of the
ordinary person.

MEGILLUS : True enough.

ATHENIAN : Well then, you see how all such lusts are extinguished by a mere phrase.

MEGILLUS : Phrase? What phrase?

ATHENIAN : The saying that they are all unhallowed, abomina-
tions to God, deeds of black shame. The explanation must surely be   c
that no one holds a different language about them. All of us, from our
very cradles, are constantly hearing the same report of them from all
quarters; we hear it alike from the lips of the buffoon, and again delivered with all the so-called solemnity of tragedy, on those many occasions when the stage presents us with a Thyestes, an Oedipus, or a
Macareus, some character who acts the stealthy paramour to a sister
and freely sentences himself to death for his crime on discovery.   d

MEGILLUS : You are perfectly right on one point. Common
fame is indeed a wonderfully potent force, provided only no single soul
dares to entertain a sentiment contrary to the established usage.

ATHENIAN : So you see how right I was to say that if only the
legislator has a mind to subjugate one of the passions which
keep humanity in the hardest bondage, it is easy enough for him to find
out the way to get a hold on it. He has merely to get the sanction
of a common fame which is universal—embraces bond and free,
women and children, and every section of society alike—and he will   e
without more ado have secured the best of guarantees for his law.

MEGILLUS : No doubt, but, then, how a whole community is ever to be brought to this voluntary unanimity of language on such a point . . .

ATHENIAN : A pertinent rejoinder. That was exactly my own meaning when I said I knew of a device for establishing this law of restricting procreative intercourse to its natural function by abstention from congress with our own sex, with its deliberate murder of the race and its wasting of the seed of life on a stony and rocky soil, where it will never take root and bear its natural fruit, and equal abstention from any female field whence you would desire no harvest. Once suppose this law perpetual and effective—let it be, as it ought to be, no less effective in the remaining cases than it actually is against incest with parents—and the result will be untold good. It is dictated, to begin with, by nature's own voice, leads to the suppression of the mad frenzy of sex, as well as marriage breach of all kinds, and all manner of excess in meats and drinks, and wins men to affection of their wedded wives. There are also numerous other blessings which will follow, if one can only compass the establishment of such a law. Yet should some young and lusty bystander of exuberant virility overhear us as we propose it, he might probably denounce our enactments as impracticable folly and make the air ring with his clamor. This was what led me to say, as I did, in so many words, that the device I knew for establishing such a law in perpetuity, though easy enough in one way, was most difficult in another. To see that the thing can be done, and how it can be done, is perfectly easy. As I say, if once the regulation receives adequate sanction, the minds of all will be subjugated and there will be a universal dread of the established law and conformity to it. But the fact is, things have come to such a pass today that no such result is thought possible, even in the case I have supposed. It is just as with the system of the common meal, a practice which it is thought beyond the bounds of possibility for a whole city to adopt throughout its daily life. The institution is proved as a fact to exist in your own societies, yet it is thought its extension to women would be outside the bounds of nature, even in them. It was in that sense, in view of this dead weight of incredulity, that I spoke of the great difficulty of establishing either practice as a permanent law.

MEGILLUS : And there was truth in what you said.

ATHENIAN : Still, would you like me to do what I can to urge an argument, and a telling one, to show that the proposal is feasible, not out of the range of human possibility?

CLINIAS : Most certainly.

ATHENIAN : Then tell me, in which case would a man find it an easier task to abstain from sexual gratifications and obey orders on the matter readily, as a decent man should—if his physique were in good condition—in training, in fact—or if it were in poor form?

CLINIAS : If he were in training, of course. Most decidedly so.

ATHENIAN : Well, we have all heard, have we not, how Iccus of
Tarentum is said to have acted for the sake of distinction at Olympia 840
and elsewhere? Such was his passion for victory, his pride in his
calling, the combined fortitude and self-command of his character
that, as the story goes, he never once came near a woman, or a boy
either, all the time he was in training. And you know the same is said
of Crison, Astylus, Diopompus, and not a few others. And, after all,
Clinias, they had much worse-cultivated minds than the citizens for
whom you and I are providing, and much more rebellious bodies.   b

CLINIAS : You are perfectly right when you say that tradition
asserts this emphatically as actual fact about these athletes.

ATHENIAN : Why then, they made no hardship of denying themselves this 'heaven of bliss,' as the vulgar account it, for the sake of
winning a victory in the ring, or the racecourse, or the like. And are
our pupils to fail in endurance for the sake of a far nobler victory—
one whose supreme nobility we shall extol in their hearing, from their
earliest years, by story, speech, and song—it is to be hoped with the c
result of bringing them under the spell?

CLINIAS : And what victory is that?

ATHENIAN : The conquest of their lusts. If they achieve it, we
shall tell them, their life will be bliss; if they fail, the very reverse.
And besides, are we to think the dread of so utterly unhallowed a deed
will be so wholly powerless to compass a mastery which has been attained before by other men, and worse men?

CLINIAS : We can hardly suppose so.

ATHENIAN : Then if this is how we stand in the matter of this
law—if it is the general viciousness which has brought us to a stand- d
still—I say it is the law's simple duty to go straight on its way and
tell our citizens that it is not for them to behave worse than birds and
many other creatures which flock together in large bodies. Until the
age for procreation these creatures live in continence and unspotted
virginity; when they have reached that age, they pair together, the male
with the female and the female with the male their preference dictates,
and they live thereafter in piety and justice, steadfastly true to their e
contract of first love. Surely you, we shall say, ought to be better than
the beasts. But if, alas, they should be corrupted by the example of
the great mass of other Greeks and of non-Greeks, as they learn from
their eyes and ears how all-powerful so-called free love is among them
all, and should so fail to win the victory, I would have our curators of
law turn legislators and contrive a second law to meet their case.

CLINIAS : And what law do you advise them to enact, if the one 841
we are now proposing slips through their fingers?

ATHENIAN : Why, of course, Clinias, the next best to it.

CLINIAS : And what is that?

ATHENIAN : There was a way of effectively checking the

development of the full violence of these lusts, that of directing the
rising current into some other physical channel by hard work. Now
this result may be attained if sexual indulgence is attended by a sense
b of shame; this feeling will make indulgence infrequent, and the infre-
quency of the indulgence will moderate the tyranny of the appetite.
So it must be the ordinance of custom and unwritten usage that
secrecy in such matters is a point of honor, and the discovery of the
act, though not necessarily its mere commission, discreditable. The establishment of such a tradition would give us a second-best standard of honor and dishonor with its own inferior rightness; the morally
c corrupt class whom we speak of as 'slaves to their vices' would be cir-
cumvented and constrained to compliance with the law by no less
than three influences.

CLINIAS : And what are the three?

ATHENIAN : Fear of God, desire of honorable distinction, and
the development of the passion for a beauty which is spiritual, not
physical. It may be that my present proposals are no more than the
aspirations of a pious imagination, though I assure you any society
would find their realization a supreme blessing. However, by God's
d help, we might not impossibly enforce one or other of two rules for
sexual love. One would be that no freeborn citizen should dare to touch
any but his own wedded wife, and that there should be no sowing of
unhallowed and bastard seed with concubines, and no sterile and unnatural intercourse with males. Failing this, we may suppress such
relations with males utterly, and as for women, if a man should have to
do with any—whether acquired by purchase or in any way whatsoever
—save those who have entered the house with the sanction of heaven
e and holy matrimony, and his act become known to man or woman,
we shall probably be pronounced to do well by enacting that he be
deprived of the honors of a citizen, as one that proves himself an
alien indeed. So whether this be taken as one single statute, or should
rather be called two, let it stand as our law in the matter of sex and the
whole business of love, our rule of right and wrong in all relations inspired by those passions.

842　MEGILLUS : Indeed sir, I for one shall welcome this law with all
my heart. Clinias, of course, must declare his mind on the matter for
himself.

CLINIAS : And so I shall, Megillus, when I think I have fitting
occasion. For the moment, however, suppose we permit our friend to
proceed with his legislation.

MEGILLUS : Well and good.

b　ATHENIAN : Observe then. Our progress has now brought us to
a point at which we may well take the public meals to have been instituted. As I say, there would be difficulties about this anywhere else,
but in Crete no one is likely to recommend any other arrangement.
But on what system they should be conducted, that of this country,

that of Lacedaemon, or whether some third type of public meal would be better than either, is, I think, not a problem of great difficulty, nor does its solution promise any considerable advantage. In fact, I believe the arrangements we have already made quite sufficient.

The question which arises next in natural order is that of com- c missariat. What will be the appropriate sources of provisions? Of course, the sources from which societies in general can be provisioned are varied and numerous, twice as numerous, at least, as those open to our citizens, since a Greek population, as a rule, draws its food supply from land and sea alike, whereas ours is confined to the land. So far as the legislator is concerned, this makes his work lighter. The number of laws necessary for adequacy will be reduced not merely to one half, but within still narrower compass, and those which are required will also be fitter for freeborn men. The maker of our city's code d is free to turn his back on the regulation of commerce, water-borne or land-borne, of retail trading, innkeeping, tolls and customs, mining operations, interest simple and compound, and a thousand such details. His statutes will be made for husbandmen, graziers, beekeepers, custodians of such stock, and users of the implements connected with it. His principal task has already been achieved by his regulation of e marriage, procreation and rearing of children, education, appointment of civic officials. He has now to turn his attention to regulations for those who raise the food supply or are concerned in its preparation.

We shall begin, then, with a number of statutes under the rubric, *Of Agriculture*. At their head shall stand a law of the sacred landmark, and it shall run thus. No man shall move his neighbor's landmark, whether that neighbor be a fellow citizen, or the property lie on the border marches and the neighbor be thus an alien. The act must be 843 held to be a literal 'moving of the not-to-be-moved,' and every man must be readier to venture the shifting of the heaviest boulder that marks no boundary than to move the tiny stone, consecrate by oath to heaven, that marks off the land of a friend or a foe. For Zeus the god of common clanship is witness to one of these sanctities, Zeus protector of the stranger to the other, and when the wrath of these powers is awakened, deadliest hostilities ensue. He that is obedient to the law shall feel none of its penalties, but he that sets it at nought shall be guilty at more bars than one, first and foremost at the bar of heaven, and next at that of the law. None, I say, shall move a neigh- b bor's boundary stone of his own free purpose; if they are so moved, he that will may lay an information before the husbandman, who shall bring the matter into court. If a man be cast in such a suit, he shall be held for one that seeks by stealth or violence to assail freehold, and the court shall assess the penalty the culprit shall suffer or the mulct he shall pay.

Further, little repeated torts between neighbors by their frequency engender a heavy burden of ill will and make neighborhood a c grievous and bitter hardship. Hence neighbor must take every care to do nothing exceptionable to neighbor, must keep himself strictly from all such acts, and above all from encroachment on a neighbor's lands, for whereas by no means every man can do his neighbor a service, to cause him hurt is easy enough, and any man can do it. He that disregards boundary marks and works soil that belongs to his neighbor

d shall make the damage good to him, and shall, moreover, by way of medicine for his churlish insolence, pay a further sum of double the amount of the damage to the sufferer. In all such cases the inspection, conviction, and assessment of penalties shall be in the hands of the rural commissioners—action being taken, as has already been said, in graver cases with the whole staff for the district, in the lighter with their commanders. If any man graze his cattle on a neighbor's land, they shall likewise decide the case and fix the penalty by ocular inspection of the damage done. If a man appropriate the bees of another's

e hive by humoring their tastes, and so beat down the swarm and make it his own, he shall pay for the damage done. If in making a bonfire he take no precaution for the timber of his neighbor's land, he shall pay such fine as the magistrates think good. And so, likewise, if in planting trees he should set them at an insufficient space from his neighbor's land. These matters have received competent treatment from many

844 legislators, and we should adopt their regulations; we must not expect the great author of our social order to make statutes for all these numerous little matters with which any and every legislator can deal.

Thus, to take one instance, there are sound old laws extant concerning the farmer's water supplies. There is no need that they should be distilled in our discourse, but any who is minded to bring water to his steading may draw it from the public watercourses, so long as he does not tap exposed springs owned by another private person, and may conduct it in any channel he pleases, provided he avoids houses, temples, and tombs, and causes no damage beyond the cutting of the

b channel itself. If certain districts are naturally arid from failure to retain rain water, and so there is a scarcity of the needful supply, the owner may dig on his own land down to the clay. If he should find no water at that depth, he shall be furnished by his neighbors with just so much as he needs for the drinking supply of his domestic staff; if the distress extends to the neighbors also, he shall procure an order for his ration of water from the rural commissioners, and receive that

c quantity daily by contribution from the neighbors. If a man causes damage to the occupant of the farm or dwelling house immediately above his own by impeding the outflow of rain water, or again to the occupant of a lower site by careless discharge of the efflux from a higher, with the consequence that the parties decline to oblige one another in the matter, either may obtain an order for the conduct of both from an urban commissioner, if the case arise within the town, or a rural commissioner, if it occur in a country district. A party who disregards such an order shall render himself liable to proceedings by his grudging and unaccommodating spirit, and on conviction shall pay d the sufferer double the amount of damage caused as a penalty for his refusal to comply with the magistrate's directions.

As to the fruit harvest, there must be an accepted general understanding to some such effect as this. Two gifts are bestowed on us by the bounty of the goddess of harvest, one the 'ungarnered nursling of Dionysus,' the other destined for storage. So our law of fruits shall impose the following rules. If a man taste the common sort of fruit, whether grapes or figs, before Arcturus have brought round the season e of vintage, whether on his own ground or on that of another, he shall incur a fine in honor of Dionysus, of fifty drachmas for fruit culled in his own grounds, a mina for that taken from his neighbor's, two thirds of a mina for fruit gathered elsewhere. As for what we commonly call choice grapes or choice figs, if a man has a mind to harvest them and takes them from his own plants, he shall be free to gather them as and when he will, but if they are taken from another's plants without the owner's consent, he shall be fined for each such act conformably to the law which forbids him to 'take up what he did not lay down.' If it is actually a slave who touches such things without permission from the 845 owner of the land, he shall receive a stripe for every grape of each cluster taken, or every fig taken from the tree. A resident alien who buys the choice produce may gather it at his pleasure. As for the alien on a temporary visit, who may desire to eat the fruit as he travels the roads, he and a single attendant may, if he so pleases, take the choice fruit without payment, as a gift of national hospitality, but the law must prohibit the foreigner from meddling with our common b fruits and the like. If they are taken in ignorance by master or slave, the slave shall suffer a whipping; the free man shall be dismissed with a warning and an admonition only to touch such fruit as is unfit to be set apart for use as raisins, wine, or dried figs. As for pears, apples, pomegranates, and the like, it shall be no felony to filch them, but c should any man under thirty years of age be taken in the act, he shall be punished by blows which must not draw blood, and a free man shall have no remedy at law against such blows. An alien shall be free to take his share of this produce, as of the grapes and figs. If they are taken by a citizen over the age of thirty, he may share in them on the same terms as the alien, provided he eat the fruit on the spot and carry none away, but disobedience to the law shall render him liable d to disqualification from seeking distinctions, when the time comes, if such conduct is brought to the notice of the acting judges.

Water, above all things, is exceptionally necessary for the growth of all garden produce, but is easily corrupted. It is not easy to affect the other contributory causes of the growth of products of the ground, the soil, the sunlight, the winds, by doctoring, diverting, or intercepting the supply, but water can be tampered with in all these ways, and

the law must accordingly come to the rescue. So we shall meet the
e case by enacting as follows. If one man intentionally tamper with another's supply, whether of spring water or standing water, whether by
way of drugging, of digging, or of abstraction, the injured party shall
put the amount of the damage on record, and proceed at law before
the urban commissioners. A party convicted of poisoning waters,
shall, over and above the payment of the fine imposed, undertake the
purification of the contaminated springs or reservoir in such fashion
as the canon law may direct this purification to be performed in the
individual case.

As to the bringing home of the fruits of the seasons, it shall be
open to any man to fetch in his crop by the route he pleases, provided
846 either that he cause no damage to another, or that the profit to himself is threefold of the damage to his neighbor. The determination in
these cases shall lie with the magistrate, as generally in other cases
where intentional damage is done to any man's person or property
without his consent by a second party or a chattel of such party. Information shall be given to a magistrate and redress awarded for damage to the amount of three minas or under; when the claim is for a
greater sum, the complainant shall carry the case before the public
b courts and seek redress of the injury from them. If any magistrate is
judged to have shown injustice in an award of compensation, he shall
be liable to forfeit double the amount to the aggrieved party; an unfair decision about any charge may be brought before the public courts
by either party to the suit. These countless minor formalities about
methods of judicial procedure—the institution of a process, the issuing of a summons, the number of witnesses, whether two or some other
c number, required to its service, and the like—cannot be left without
legal regulation, and yet are beneath the attention of an aged legislator. His younger imitators should prescribe them on the model of his
antecedent and more important rules; they should make an experimental use of such rules where they are forced to employ them, until
they are satisfied that they have a complete and adequate collection of
them. Then, when the rules have been got into shape, and not before,
they should treat them as final and live by them.
d   As to the arts and crafts, we should proceed as follows. In the
first place, no native, and no servant of a native, is to practice a craft
as his calling. A citizen has already a calling which will make full demands on him, in view of the constant practice and wide study it involves, in the preservation and enjoyment of the public social order
—a task which permits of no relegation to the second place. But human capacity, we may fairly say, is never equal to the finished exercise
e of two callings or crafts. Nay more, none of us has the gift of following one craft himself while he superintends another's practice of a
second. Hence we must from the start take this as a principle of our
society. No one shall be smith and carpenter at once, and further, no

one who is a carpenter shall be permitted to superintend others who are engaged in smithwork, to the neglect of his own craft, on the plea that as overseer of so many employees who are working for his profit, he naturally supervises them the more carefully because his revenue from their labors is so much greater than his income from his own trade. Each artisan in the society must have his single craft, and must 847 earn his living by that trade and no other. The urban commissioners must exert themselves to keep this law in force. If a native stray from the pursuit of goodness into some trade or craft, they shall correct him by reproach and degradation until he be brought back again into the straight course; if an alien follow two crafts, there shall be correction in the shape of imprisonment, fine, or expulsion from the b city to constrain him to play one part, not several. Disputes about wages due to workmen or refusal of work done by them, and complaints of injustice done to them by others, or to others by them, shall be decided by the urban commissioners where the sum involved is not more than fifty drachmas; where it is greater, the public courts shall deal with the case as the law may direct.

No dues shall be paid in our city either on exports or on imports. There shall be no importation of frankincense or other such foreign perfumes for the purposes of religious ceremonial, nor yet of purple c and other dyestuffs not produced in the country, nor of the materials of any other industry dependent on foreign importation and serving no necessary purpose. Further there shall be no exportation of any commodities which it is indispensable to retain at home. The jurisdiction and supervision in all these matters shall be with the twelve curators of law who stand at the head of the board when its five senior members are exempted.

As to weapons of war and military equipment of all kinds, if mili- d tary purposes require the importation of any industry, vegetable, mineral substance, material for ropemaking, or animal, the cavalry commanders and generals shall have the control of such importation and exportation, the state being both seller and buyer, and the proper and sufficient regulations for the proceeding being imposed by the curators of law. There shall be no retailing of these or any other materials for profit anywhere within our territory or among our citizens. e

When we come to supplies and the distribution of natural produce, a rule much like that followed in Crete will probably be found to serve our turn. All should divide the total produce of the soil into twelve parts, as it will in fact be divided in consumption. Each twelfth —that of the wheat and barley, for example, and all the produce of 848 the seasons as well as all salable livestock in the various districts must, of course, be subject to the same law of division—should be subdivided into three proportional shares, one for the free citizens, another for their servants, while the third shall be for artisans and other noncitizens, whether permanent residents requiring the necessities of life or temporary visitors brought in by the business of the state or of private citizens, and the third part of all the necessaries of life shall be the only part which shall be forced into the market; there shall be no compulsion to sell any portion of the remaining two thirds. Now

b what will be the right way of making this division? For one thing, it must obviously be equal in one way, though not in another.

CLINIAS: A word in explanation, please.

ATHENIAN: Why, you know, some of these products are bound to be inferior in strain and condition and others superior.

CLINIAS: Of course.

ATHENIAN: Well, in that respect none of the three subdivisions, neither that for the masters, nor that for the slaves, nor yet that of the aliens, shall have any advantage over the other; the distribution shall secure the same equality of similarity for all. Each citizen

c shall receive the two thirds and be authorized to distribute them among the slaves and free persons of his household in such quantity and quality as he pleases. The residue shall be distributed by number and measure in the manner following. The distribution shall proceed upon a computation of the whole livestock which will have to be supported by the produce.

Next, we must provide our personnel with individual dwelling houses properly grouped, and the following disposition will be appropriate for the purpose. There should be twelve villages, each standing in the center of one of our twelve regional districts. Our first proceeding should be, in each of these villages, to set apart temples, with a

d market square, for the gods and superhuman beings under them, taking care that any local deities of the Magnesians, or sanctuaries of other powers of venerable memory which may be left, receive the same honors as in earlier ages. In each of the twelve regions we shall found shrines of Hestia, Zeus, Athena, and the god, whoever he may be, who is to be patron of the district. We should then begin by build-

e ing dwellings on the highest ground, in the neighborhood of these temples, as the strongest lodging we can find for the garrison. The whole of the rest of our territory will be furnished with workmen, who will be divided into thirteen sections. One of these will be appointed to dwell in the capital—this section itself, in its turn, will be divided into twelve parts, like the capital itself, who will be distributed through all the suburbs—while we shall collect in the several villages the classes of hands whom farmers will find useful. The supervision of them all is to be in the hands of the chiefs of the rural commission-ers, who shall decide what workers each district requires, and how

849 many of them, and where they can live with least discomfort to themselves and most benefit to the farmers. The workmen in the capital shall, in like manner, be placed and remain under the supervision of the board of urban commissioners.

The details of the conduct of the market must, of course, rest with the commissioners of the market. After their vigilance to protect the temples in the market place from all violation, their second concern must be with the supervision of the human traffic, and in this charge they shall take careful note of decency and indecency of behavior, and inflict correction where it is called for. They are, first of all, to take note whether the sales of the articles which citizens are required to vend to aliens are in all cases conducted as the law commands. For each such article the law will be that on the first of the month the quantity which is to be sold to the aliens shall be produced by the agents—that is, aliens or slaves appointed by the citizens for b this purpose—beginning with the monthly twelfth portion of corn, and an alien shall at this first market purchase corn and all that belongs to it for the whole month. On the tenth, the parties shall, respectively, conduct the sale and purchase of liquids sufficient for the full c month. On the twentieth, there shall be a third sale, of such livestock as it meets the requirements of the parties to buy or sell, and also of such manufactured goods and articles as farmers have for sale, and foreigners can only acquire by purchase—for example, hides, wearing apparel, woven stuffs, felts. As to the retailing of those goods, of wheat or barley in the form of flour, or of any foodstuffs whatsoever, there shall be absolutely no selling to citizens or their slaves in this way, and no purchasing from them, though an alien, selling to artisans and their servants, in the market for foreigners, may drive a d trade in wine and corn, a retail business, as it is commonly called. Butchers also may cut up carcasses and dispose of the joints to aliens, artisans, and artisans' servants. As for firewood, an alien shall be free, if he pleases, to buy it in bulk daily from the agents of the district, and may then retail it in such bulk and at such times as he pleases to other aliens.

As for all other goods or manufactured articles of which various e parties may be in need, they shall be brought to the general market, each article to the proper quarter, and there offered for sale on the site appointed for traffic, and furnished with convenient stalls by the curators of law and the commissioners of market and city. The sale is to be by actual exchange of currency for goods and goods for currency, and neither party shall waive the receipt of a *quid pro quo*. A party who acts thus, by way of giving credit, shall put up with the conse- 850 quences, whether he receives that for which he has bargained or not, as no action will lie in the case of such transactions. If the property bought or sold, in quantity or value, violate the law which fixes the limits of increase and decrease outside which both transactions are prohibited, the excess must be at once recorded in the court of curators, or the deficit canceled. The same rule shall apply to the inscription of the property of aliens.

Any foreigner who pleases may become a resident in the country on certain express conditions. It shall be understood that we offer a

b home to any alien who desires to take up his abode with us and is able
to do so, but he must have a craft, and his residence must not be prolonged more than twenty years from the date of his registration. He
shall pay no personal dues as an alien, however small, beyond good
behavior, and no toll on the transactions of sale and purchase, and
when the period of his stay has expired, he shall take his property
with him on his departure. Should it be his good fortune, during this
period, to have distinguished himself by some signal service to the
state, and have hopes of satisfying the council and assembly of his
c claim to an official prorogation of his departure, or even to lifelong
residence, he may appear and plead his case, and any claims of which
he can convince the state shall receive full satisfaction. For the children of such aliens, provided they possess a handicraft and have
reached the age of fifteen, the period of residence shall be computed
from their fifteenth year. When one of them who fulfills these conditions has completed his twenty years, he shall depart whither he
pleases, or if he prefer to remain, he must obtain permission as al-
d ready provided for. At a man's departure, the entries which previously
stood against his name in the magistrates' register shall be canceled.

BOOK IX

853 ATHENIAN: The next place in a digest of law will naturally fall to
judicial processes arising from all the activities we have so far studied.
What will inevitably be the matter of actions at law we have, indeed,
already explained in a measure, viz., the affairs of the farm and the
business connected therewith. But the main topic has not yet been
broached; to handle it in its details—to say what punishment an offense must receive and before what court it must be brought—will be
b the next subject for our consideration.

CLINIAS : And rightly so.

ATHENIAN : In a way, to be sure, it is to our shame to be framing any such legislation as we are now on the point of undertaking at
all in such a society as we contemplate, one which, we hope, will
have all advantages and enjoy all the right conditions for the practice
of virtue. Why, the very assumption that a man will ever be born in
such a society who will be stained by the graver turpitudes of other
states, that we consequently need to anticipate the appearance of
c such characters by minatory legislation and enact statutes for their
warning and punishment in the expectation that they will be found
among us—the mere imagination, as I say, is, in a way, to our shame.
But after all, we are not in the position of the legislators of earlier
days, whose codes were framed for an age of heroes. They, if the current tales may be believed, were sons of gods and their laws were made
for men of the same celestial ancestry; we are but men, and the law we
are imposing is meant for slips of humanity. So we may well be par-

doned for the apprehension that some 'hard shell' may be found d
among our citizens whose native stubbornness will be proof against all
softening, and that such characters should yield no more to the molli-
fying influence of our laws, effective as they are, than the tough bean
to the heat of the fire. So for their ungracious sake I will begin with a
law against temple robbery, should anyone commit so brazen a crime.
It is not to be wished, and hardly to be imagined, that any rightly nurtured citizen should ever take the infection, but attempts in this way
may not infrequently be made by servants, or by aliens and their
slaves. For their benefit, in the first instance, though also from con- 854
cern for our universal human frailty, I shall propound my statute
against sacrilege and other such desperate, or well-nigh desperate,
crimes generally. But I must first, on the principle we have already accepted, deliver myself of the briefest of preambles to this whole class
of laws.

To him, then, who is driven by the voice of some unhappy passion that besets him by day and wakes him from his sleep at night, to
go temple robbing, we may address some such words of reasoning and b
exhortation as these. Poor soul, this evil prompting which now moves
you to go robbing temples comes neither from man nor from God; 'tis
an infatuate obsession that is bred in men by crime done long ago and
never expiated, and so runs its fatal course. You should strain every
nerve to guard yourself from it. How you are to do so, you are now to
be told. When thoughts of such things assail you, hasten to the rites
that baffle the evil chance, hasten in supplication to the altars of the
gods who give deliverance from curses, hasten to the company of your
men of virtuous repute. Listen to them as they tell you, yes, and do c
your best to tell the story to yourself, how all are bound to revere the
good and the right. From the company of the evil run, and look not
once back. If such action bring relief from your malady, well and
good; if not, think on the better way of death, and take your leave
of life.

In such strains we shall couch our preludes for the behoof of
such as purpose any of these accursed deeds whereby a society is undone. The actual law shall be left without a voice for him who heark-
ens to us, but for him who will not listen it must follow up our prelude
in ringing tones. Whosoever shall be taken in sacrilege, shall, if slave d
or alien, have his misfortune branded on hands and forehead, be
scourged with such number of stripes as the court shall think proper,
and be cast forth naked beyond the borders. For if he suffer that judgment, he may perchance be made a better man by his correction. For
truly judgment by sentence of law is never inflicted for harm's sake.
Its normal effect is one of two; it makes him that suffers it a better
man, or, failing this, less of a wretch. If ever a citizen be detected in
such an act, in gross and horrible crime against gods, parents, or so- e
ciety, the judge shall treat him as one whose case is already desperate,

in view of the education and nurture he has enjoyed from a child and the depth of shame to which he is sunk. Whence his sentence shall be
855 death, the lightest of ills for him, and he shall serve as an example for the profit of others, being buried in silence and beyond the borders. But children and family, if they forsake their father's ways, shall have an honorable name and good report, as those that have done well and manfully in leaving evil for good. It will not be proper that there should be any forfeiture of such men's estates in a society where patrimonies must remain forever unchanged and of undiminished number. And when a man has done a wrong which is judged to be met by a fine, he may meetly be made to pay such fine to the amount of whatever
b property may remain to him when his patrimony has been stocked, but no more. The curators shall ascertain the exact facts of each case from their register and report them to the court in due course of procedure, that no estate may go out of working for want of means. If a man's case be judged to call for a heavier fine than this, then if he have no friends who are ready to be bound for him and discharge their part of his debt, his punishment shall take the form of long terms of prison, pillorying, and marks of degradation.
c 　For no offense whatsoever shall any man be made a hopeless outlaw, not even though he have fled beyond our borders. Death, prison, stripes, ignominious postures of sitting or standing, or exposure at sanctuaries on the frontiers, fines, in cases where, as we have said, their payment is a proper sentence—these shall be our penalties. In a case of life and death the judges shall be curators of law acting together with the court selected for merit from the magistrates of the
d preceding year. It shall be the business of the junior curators to attend to the bringing in of the case, the issuing of citations and similar details, the observance of rules of procedure. We as legislators must prescribe the manner of taking the vote. The votes, then, shall be given openly, and before they are given the judges shall one and all, in order of seniority, take their seats in a compact body, facing prosecutor and defendant, and all citizens who have the necessary leisure shall be present and give attentive hearing to the pleadings in such cases.
e 　The prosecutor shall state his case and the defendant reply to it, each in a single speech. When the speeches have been delivered, the senior judge shall first state his view of the case, discussing the statements of the parties in full and sufficient detail. When he has finished, the rest of the judges, each in his order, shall review any omissions or errors they find to complain of in the pleadings of either party, a judge who has no complaint to make leaving the right of speech to his neighbor. The written record of all statements pronounced to be relevant shall be confirmed by the seals of all the judges and deposited on the
856 altar of Hestia. They shall meet again the next day at the same place to continue the review of the case, and once more affix their seals to

the documents. When this has been done for a third time, due weight being allowed to the evidence and witnesses, each judge shall give a solemn vote, swearing by the altar to pronounce just and true judgment to the best of his power, and this shall be the end of that trial.

To turn from cases of religion to cases of treason to the state, b whosoever seeks to put law in chains and the state under the control of faction by subjecting them to the domination of persons, and further serves these ends and foments civil strife by revolutionary violence, must be counted the deadliest foe of the whole state, and he that, being in high office, though himself no party to such plottings, neglects to avenge his country on the plotter—whether it be that he detects them not, or that he detects them indeed, but is a craven at c heart—such citizen must be held second only to the other in guilt. Any man of worth, however slight, must reveal the matter to the magistrate by bringing the plotter to trial for revolutionary and illegal violence. The judges in the case shall be the same as in those of sacrilege, and their whole procedure shall follow the same rule—death to be inflicted by a majority of their sentences. But once for all, in no case shall a father's disgrace or sentence descend to his children, save only d when father, grandfather, great-grandfather have all, without break, incurred judgment of death. In that case the state shall deport them to their original native place with all their property beyond the whole stock of their patrimonial holding. Ten names shall be chosen by lot from the families of citizens who have more than one son over ten years of age, on the nomination of a father or grandfather on either side, and sent to Delphi. The nominee preferred by the god shall be e constituted heir to the derelict house—let us pray, with brighter hopes!

CLINIAS: An admirable proposal.

ATHENIAN: There is yet a third class to be covered by a single law prescribing the judges who shall sit upon them and the process of their trials—those who may be brought into court on the charge of traffic with the enemy. In like manner our proposed law concerning the retention of their children in the country or expulsion therefrom 857 shall be the same for all three, the trafficker with the enemy, the temple breaker, the violent subverter of the state's laws. For the thief, again, there shall be one law, alike whether his theft be a great one or a small, and one legal penalty for all cases. For first he must pay twice the value of the thing stolen if convicted on such a charge, and if he have sufficient property besides his patrimonial holding to make the payment. If he have not, he shall lie in prison until the sum be either paid or remitted by the successful prosecutor. He that is convicted of b theft from the public shall be released from durance on obtaining his grace from the state, or making payment of double the sum.

CLINIAS: Pray, sir, how can we rule that it shall make no difference to a thief's case whether the stolen property be of great value or

little, whether it be taken from a consecrated spot or an unconse-
crated, or how the circumstances of a theft may differ in other respects? A lawgiver should surely adapt himself to the variety of these
particulars by attaching widely different penalties to the several offenses.

ATHENIAN: A sound observation, Clinias. I fear I was letting
c myself drift when the collision with you woke me up. You remind me
of the observation I made a while ago, that the business of legislation,
if I may speak on the spur of the moment, has never yet been thoroughly worked out on right lines. But what, you may ask, do I mean by
this? That was no unhappy simile by which we likened all existing
legislation to the treatment of unfree patients by unfree physicians.
You may be sure that were one of these empirical practitioners of the
d healing art, so innocent of the theory of it, to discover a free physician
conversing with his free patient, to hear him talking almost like a
philosopher, tracing the disorder to its source, reviewing the whole
system of human physiology, his merriment would be instantaneous
and loud. His language would be no other than that which comes so
pat from the lips of most of our so-styled physicians. This is not to
treat the patient, fool, but to educate him—as though he wanted to
e be made a medical man, not to recover his health!

CLINIAS: Well, and would not the speaker be in the right of it?

ATHENIAN: He might be so, if only he also understood that any
man who treats of law in the style we are now adopting, means to
educate his fellow citizens rather than to lay down the law to them.
That, too, would be a pertinent remark, would it not?

CLINIAS: It might be.

ATHENIAN: And how fortunate for us that our present position
is what it is!

858   CLINIAS: In what way fortunate?

ATHENIAN: Because we are under no obligation to lay down
the law. We are free to pursue our own reflections on all points of political theory, to set ourselves to discover how to effect either the best
possible result, or the indispensable minimum. In the case under discussion, for example, it is open to us, I take it, to ask either what
would be the ideally best legislation, or what is indispensably requisite as a minimum, according to our preference. So we must make our
option.

CLINIAS: A singular pair of alternatives, sir. We should be in
the position of the statesman driven by the stress of some dire neces-
b sity to produce his laws on the instant, because tomorrow will be too
late. Our case, please God, is more like that of stonemasons or some
such workers at the beginning of their operations. We are free to collect our materials in the mass before we proceed to select those which
will suit the future construction, and we can make the selection itself
at our leisure. So we will take ourselves to be erecting our present edi-

fice, not under pressure, but with undiminished leisure to lay up some of our material for future employment while we work the rest into our fabric. Thus we may rightly think of our body of law as composed partly of statutes actually imposed, partly of material for statutes.   c

ATHENIAN: At all events, Clinias, our digest of law will be the more scientific so. For here is a point I beg we may observe in connection with the legislator.

CLINIAS: And what may it be?

ATHENIAN: Our societies, we may say, abound in literary works by various authors, and of this literature the productions of the legislator form part.

CLINIAS: Certainly.

ATHENIAN: Well then, are we to give serious attention to the compositions of others, poets and others who have left a written record d of their counsels for the conduct of life, in prose or in verse, and none to the legislator's? Should not they have our first attention?

CLINIAS: Decidedly.

ATHENIAN: And can we suppose that the legislator alone among authors is to give us no counsel about honor, good, or right, not to tell us what they are, and how they must be cultivated by one who would have a happy life?

CLINIAS: Of course he must tell us.

ATHENIAN: Then if it is discreditable in Homer, or Tyrtaeus, or e another poet, to have laid down bad precepts for the conduct of life in his verses, is the discredit less in Lycurgus, or Solon, or any other author of a legislation? Surely a society's lawbook should, in right and reason, prove, when we open it, far the best and finest work of its whole literature; other men's compositions should either conform to it, or, if they strike a different note, excite our contempt. How should 859 we imagine the rightful position of a written law in a society? Should its statutes disclose the lineaments of wise and affectionate parents, or should they wear the semblance of an autocratic despot—issue a menacing order, post it on the walls, and so have done? Here, then, is the immediate question for us. Shall we try to take this line in uttering our thoughts on law, or, at least, make an earnest effort to do so, b be its success as it may? And if there are hazards to be run on the road, shall we risk them? But may all be for the best—as it will be, God willing!

CLINIAS: Well said, indeed. We must act as you propose.

ATHENIAN: Then we must, in the first place, go on with the investigation we had begun; we must look closely into our law of sacrilege, theft in general, and injuries as a class. We must not be discouraged to find that though some matters have been disposed of in the course of our still unfinished legislation, others still demand further c consideration. We are still on our way to become legislators, but as yet have not reached the goal, as we may perhaps do in time. With your approval, then, we will discuss the points I have specified on the lines I suggest.

CLINIAS : With all my heart.

ATHENIAN : Then here is the point where we must make an effort after clarity of vision in all discussion of the good and right. What d amount of agreement and what amount of disagreement are actually to be found, among ourselves—who, you know, would own at least to an aspiration to surpass the common herd—and again among the mass of mankind among themselves?

CLINIAS : Of what disagreements between us are you thinking?

ATHENIAN : Let me try to explain. When we think of right in general, or of upright men, right deeds, right conduct, we are universally agreed in a way that they are one and all comely. Thus, however strongly a man should insist on the point that even upright men who may be physically ugly are perfectly comely, in respect of their eminent uprightness of character, his language would never be thought e out of place.

CLINIAS : And rightly not, surely.

ATHENIAN : No doubt. But I would have you observe that if all that is characterized by rightness is comely, this *all* must include what is *done to* us, no less than what we *do*.

CLINIAS : And what then?

ATHENIAN : The right thing we do, just so far as it has its share of rightness, equally partakes of comeliness.

CLINIAS : Certainly.

ATHENIAN : Well then, if our language is to be kept clear of in-860 consistency, we must also admit that the thing *done to* us is comely just so far as it has its share of rightness.

CLINIAS : True enough.

ATHENIAN : But if we grant that something may be done to us which is unseemly, though right, there will be a discord between the right and the comely; we shall have pronounced a right thing a shame.

CLINIAS : But the point of your remark?

ATHENIAN : Quite a simple one. The laws we were just now laying down look like a proclamation of the direct contrary of our present doctrine.

CLINIAS : Where does the discrepancy come in?

ATHENIAN : Why, you know, we laid it down that a temple rob-b ber or a man at war with an excellent law is rightly put to death. And we were on the point of enacting a host of similar rules when we were checked by the discovery that we have here the infliction of a host of severe penalties, and that these inflictions are at once supremely right and superlatively shameful. Thus we seem to assert first an absolute identity and subsequently an utter opposition between the right and the comely.

CLINIAS : It looks dangerously like it.

ATHENIAN: And this is what brings the discordance and con- c
fusion into the popular employment of the epithets *comely* and *right*
in such cases.

CLINIAS: So it should seem, sir.

ATHENIAN: Well then, Clinias, let us turn to ourselves. How
far are *we* consistent in our language about the matter?

CLINIAS: Consistent? Consistent with what?

ATHENIAN: I fancy I have already said in so many words—or
if I have not, you may now take me as saying that . . .

CLINIAS: That what?

ATHENIAN: That bad men universally are always bad against d
their own will. Now on that presupposition a further consequence inevitably follows.

CLINIAS: And that consequence is?

ATHENIAN: Why, the doer of a wrong, you will grant, is a bad
man, and a bad man is what he is against his will. But it is mere nonsense to talk of the voluntary doing of an involuntary act. *Ergo*, he
who declares the doing of a wrong involuntary must regard the doer of
it as acting contrary to his own will, and I in particular am bound at
this moment to accept the position. I grant, in fact, that those who
commit wrongs always act against their own will. There may be those
who are led by contentiousness or the desire to shine into saying that
while there are involuntary wrongdoers, there are also many whose e
wrongdoing is voluntary, but for my part, I hold to the first statement
and reject the second. Well then, I ask you, how am I to be consistent
with my own avowals? Suppose you, Clinias and Megillus, put this
question. The case being as you say, sir, how would you advise us
about framing a code for our Magnesian state? Shall we make one or
not? Make one, by all means, I answer. Then will it draw a distinction
between involuntary wrongs and voluntary? Will it inflict heavier
penalties for a voluntary transgression or wrong, and lighter for an
involuntary? Or should they all be treated alike, on the ground that 861
there is no such thing as a voluntary act of wrong?

CLINIAS: Indeed, sir, you are very right. What are we to make
of our statements?

ATHENIAN: Well demanded. Well, the first thing to be made of
them is this.

CLINIAS: What?

ATHENIAN: We shall remind ourselves of the truth of our recent remarks about the bewildering confusion and contradiction in
our views of rights. Bearing this in mind, we shall go on to ask ourselves a further question. We have never extricated ourselves from our
perplexity about this matter, we have never achieved any clear demar- b
cation between these two types of wrongs, the voluntary and the involuntary, which are recognized as distinct by every legislator who has
ever existed in any society and regarded as distinct by all law. And is

the formula we have just pronounced to dispose of the business by an ipse dixit, like some oracular response? Is it, so to say, to stifle opposi-
c tion by decree, without one syllable of justification? Surely not. Before we come to the legislating we are bound to show that the cases are distinct and the difference between them other than supposed, to ensure that when we prescribe the penalty for an offense of either kind, everyone shall follow our reasoning and be capable of a more or less competent judgment on the appropriateness of the infliction.

CLINIAS: Your audience is with you there, sir. Of two things, one—either we must deny the thesis that all wrongful acts are in-
d voluntary, or else, before we assert it, we must establish its soundness by making a distinction.

ATHENIAN: One of your alternatives, the denial of the thesis, I must absolutely decline to admit. Convinced as I am of its truth, to deny it would be unlawful and impious. But how do the two cases differ, if not as the involuntary and the voluntary? Of course we must try to find some other principle of distinction.

CLINIAS: Assuredly, sir, we can think of no other possible course.

e ATHENIAN: Well, I will try to do so. Consider. Citizens, of course, frequently cause mutual *damage* in their various associations and relations with one another, and the damage is often enough voluntary and also often enough involuntary.

CLINIAS: Exactly.

ATHENIAN: Now we should not regard all these cases of causation of damage as *wrongs*, and so come to the conclusion that the *wrong* done in such acts may be of two kinds, voluntary, or again involuntary—involuntary *damage*, as a form of damage, is as common
862 and serious as voluntary. What you must consider is whether there is any truth or none at all in what I am next to say. What I maintain, Clinias and Megillus, is not that when one man causes hurt to another unintentionally and of no set purpose, he does him a wrong, but an involuntary wrong, and so I shall not propose to treat the act legally as an involuntary wrong—I shall not regard such causing of detriment, serious or trifling, as a *wrong* at all. Also, if my view carries the day, the author of a benefit will often be said to do a *wrong*, when that
b benefit is not rightfully conferred. Speaking generally, my friends, we cannot call it a right act without further qualification when one man gives another something, nor a wrong when he takes something from him. What the legislator has to ask himself is whether the agent of the beneficial or detrimental act is acting with a rightful spirit and in a rightful manner. There are thus two considerations he must keep in view, the *wrong* committed and the *detriment* occasioned. He must do all he can by his laws to make damage good, to recover the lost, rebuild the dilapidated, replace the slaughtered or wounded by the
c sound. He must aim throughout in his legislation at reconciling the

minds of the authors and sufferers of the various forms of detriment by award of compensation, and converting their difference into friendship.

CLINIAS: Admirable, so far.

ATHENIAN: And then as to *wrongful* detriment—or gain, either, in the case that a man should cause another to profit by a wrongful act—such things, as we know, are maladies of the soul, and we must cure them whenever they are curable. And the line our cure for wrong must follow, I say, is this.

CLINIAS: What?

ATHENIAN: The line whereby law will both teach and con- d strain the man who has done a wrong, great or small, never again, if he can help it, to venture on repetition of the act, or to repeat it much more rarely—and he must make the damage good to boot. And so, if we can but bring a man to this—to hatred of iniquity, and love of right or even acquiescence in right—by acts we do or words we utter, through pleasure or through pain, through honor bestowed or disgrace inflicted, in a word, whatever the means we take, thus and only thus is the work of a perfect law effected. But should our legislator find one e whose disease is past such cure, what will be his sentence or law for such a case? He will judge, I take it, that longer life is no boon to the sinner himself in such a case, and that his decease will bring a double blessing on his neighbors; it will be a lesson to them to keep them- 863 selves from wrong, and will rid society of an evil man. These are the reasons for which a legislator is bound to ordain the chastisement of death for such desperate villainies, and for them alone.

CLINIAS: All you have said seems, in its way, sound enough. But there is a point on which we should still be thankful for clearer explanations. How comes the distinction between wrong and detriment to be complicated in these cases with that between voluntary and involuntary?

ATHENIAN: Well, I must do what I can to give the explanation you require of me. I am sure that when you talk together about the b soul there is one point assumed by speaker and listener alike, the presence in it of a native character—or, if you like, part—of *passion*, a contentious and combative element which frequently causes shipwreck by its headstrong violence.

CLINIAS: Yes, of course.

ATHENIAN: You must observe further that we draw a distinction between passion and *pleasure*. The empire of pleasure, we say, is based on an opposite foundation; it regularly gets its will by a combination of seduction with cunning deception.

CLINIAS: Assuredly.

ATHENIAN: And we should not be wrong if we spoke of *igno-* c *rance* as a third source of misconduct. Though you should note that the legislator will do well to make two kinds of it, ignorance pure and simple, which he will regard as a cause of venial offenses, and the more complicated condition in which a man's folly means that he is suffering not from ignorance alone, but also from a conceit of his own wisdom, and supposes himself to know all about matters of which he knows nothing whatsoever. When such ignorance is accompanied by exceptional capacity or power the lawgiver will regard the combination as a source of grave and monstrous crime; when it is conjoined

d with impotence, since the consequent misconduct is puerile or senile, he will treat it as an offense, indeed, and make laws against its perpetrator as an offender, but those laws will be the mildest and most indulgent of his whole code.

CLINIAS : That is no more than sense and reason.

ATHENIAN : Now we all talk of one man as the master of his pleasures or his passion, of another as a slave to them, and this language describes real facts.

CLINIAS : Most certainly it does.

ATHENIAN : But we have never heard it said that so-and-so is the master of his ignorance, or so-and-so a slave to it.

e CLINIAS : We certainly have not.

ATHENIAN : And yet we speak of all three as frequently impelling a man in one direction at the very time his own will is urging him in the opposite.

CLINIAS : Aye, times out of mind.

ATHENIAN : Now at last I am in a position to explain precisely what I mean by right and wrong without any complications. *Wrong* is the name I give to the domination of the soul by passion, fear, pleasure

864 or pain, envy or cupidity, alike in all cases, whether damage is the consequence or not. But where there is the conviction that a course is *best* —wherever a society or private individuals may take that best to lie— where that conviction prevails in the soul and governs a man's conduct, even if unfortunate consequences should arise, all that is done from such a principle, and all obedience of individuals to it, must be pronounced *right* and for the highest good of human life, though detriment thus caused is popularly taken to be involuntary wrong. Our

b business at present is not to contend about words, but, in the first place, to get a still surer mental grasp on the three classes of error which have already been indicated. One of these, you will remember, had a principal source of which we spoke as passion and fear.

CLINIAS : Just so.

ATHENIAN : The second had its origin in pleasures and cupidities, and the third, which is of a very different kind, in the loss of sound anticipations and convictions about the good. Since the last has itself been subdivided into three, we get a total of five classes, as we

c may now observe, and for all five we have now to make distinct laws, under two principal heads.

CLINIAS : And what are they?

ATHENIAN: Under one head fall all cases of deeds of open violence; under the other, those of dark and crafty contrivance. There are also cases of acts in which both are employed, and it is, of course, these with which the law will deal most severely, if it is to have its proper effects.

CLINIAS: Yes, to be sure.

ATHENIAN: So we may now revert to the point at which this digression began and continue our lawmaking. If I am not mistaken, we had already legislated against robbery of heaven and treasonable d traffic with the public enemy, and also against subversion of the established constitution by tampering with the laws. Now a man might conceivably commit an act of one of these kinds from insanity, or when so disordered by disease, so extremely aged, or of such tender years, as to be virtually insane. If one of these pleas can be established to the satisfaction of the court selected for the trial of the case, on the representations of the culprit or his advocate, and the verdict e should be that the accused committed his transgression in such condition, he shall in any case pay full compensation to any party endamaged by his act, but the rest of the sentence shall be remitted, unless, indeed, he have taken a life and incurred the pollution of homicide. In that case, he shall remove to an abode in some other country, and remain there in exile for a full year; if he return before the legal term be expired, or set foot on any part of his native soil, the curators shall commit him to prison, and he shall not be released therefrom for two 865 years.

As we have entered on the subject of homicide, we may attempt a complete statute dealing with all its forms. We will treat first of the case of unintentional violence. If a man unintentionally cause the death of a person with whom he is on friendly terms, in a competition or at the public sports, whether the death be immediate or result later from injuries received, or similarly if he cause such death in war or in some military exercise, whether unarmed practice or sham fight with armor, he shall, on accomplishing such purifications as may be directed by a law for these cases received from Delphi, be es- b teemed clear of pollution. In the case of all medical practitioners, if the patient meet his end by an unintentional act of the physician, the law shall hold the physician clear. And if one man take the life of another by his own act but without intention, whether with his naked hands, with weapon or missile, by administration of meat or drink, by application of heat or cold, by deprivation of air, by his own physical agency alone or by that of other persons, in all cases the deed shall be c held his personal act, and he shall pay the penalty hereinunder stated.

If the slain man be a slave, he shall consider that it is just as though one had made away with a slave of his own and indemnify the owner of the deceased for his loss, or shall, in default, be condemned in double the value of the deceased—the said value to be

estimated by the court—and shall be put to purifications more burdensome and numerous than those enjoined on those who cause loss of life at the sports, authority to prescribe these rights being vested in
d the interpreters of religious law whom the oracle shall nominate. If the slain man be his own slave, he shall be clear on accomplishing the purifications required by law. If one have unintentionally slain a free man, he shall be cleansed with the same purifications as the slayer of a slave, but let him take heed not to despise the teaching of the venerable and primitive myth. It tells us how he that is done to death with violence, as one that has lived his days in all the pride of a free man,
e has his wrath kindled against the author of his death in the days while the deed is still fresh, how he is likewise filled with fear and horror by his bloody fate, how he is aghast to see his murderer haunting walks that were once familiar and his own, how in his own distraction of soul, he allies himself with the doer's own memories to bring all possible distraction upon him and all his works. Whence it is truly but right that the homicide should avoid his victim's path through the round of a full year, and leave all homely spots of his native land clear of his presence, and if the deceased be an alien,
866 he must likewise be forbidden the alien's native country for the same space of time. If a man comply with this law of his own motion, the next of kin to the deceased, who shall take note of his obedience, shall pardon his act, and will do no more than right to keep the peace with him. If a man disobey, if, in the first place, he venture to enter the sanctuaries with the stain of blood on his hands and do sacrifice there, or again, if he decline to expatriate himself for the full
b time appointed, the next of kin shall bring his action of homicide against the slayer, and if conviction follow, all the penalties shall be doubled. But if the next kinsman do not prosecute the case, though the blood now lies at his door, inasmuch as the dead man demands atonement for his death, any who will may proceed against him at law and drive him by legal sentence to five-years' banishment from his land. If an alien slay an alien resident in the state, he who will
c may prosecute the suit under the same law, and if the defendant be a resident settler, he shall go into exile for a year. If he be wholly an alien, whether the slain man were alien, resident alien, or citizen, he shall, after his purification, be excluded from the land to which these laws belong for the term of his natural life. If he return in violation of the law, the curators shall visit him with death, and shall deliver any effects he may possess to the next of kin of the sufferer. If the return
d be involuntary, he shall, if shipwrecked on our coasts, take up his quarters where the sea wets his feet and wait for a boat to remove him; if he be brought back by land by *force majeure,* the first official into whose hands he may come shall release him and send him over the border under safe conduct.

If one slay a free man by one's own act but the deed be done in *passion*, there are, first, two cases to be distinguished. It is an act of passion when a man is done away with on the impulse of the moment, by blows or the like, suddenly and without any previous purpose to e kill, and remorse instantly follows on the act. It is also an act of passion when a man is roused by insult in words or dishonoring gestures, pursues his revenge, and ends by taking a life with purpose to slay and without subsequent remorse for the deed. I take it we cannot treat these as two distinct forms of homicide; both may fairly be said to be due to passion and to be partially voluntary, partially involuntary. 867 Not but what each of them has a resemblance to one extreme. The man who nurses his passion and takes his revenge not at the moment and on the spot, but afterward and of set purpose, bears a resemblance to the deliberate manslayer. He who does not bottle up his wrath but expends it all at once, on the spot, without premeditation, is like the involuntary homicide; still we cannot say that even he is altogether an involuntary agent, though he is like one. Hence the difficulty of decid- b ing whether homicides of passion should be treated in law as intentional or, in some sense, unintentional. However the best and soundest procedure is to class each sort with that which it resembles, discriminating the one from the other by the presence or absence of premeditation, and legally visiting the slaughter where there is premeditation as well as angry feeling with a severer, that which is committed on the spur of the moment and without purpose aforethought with a milder, sentence. That which is like the graver crime should receive the graver punishment, that which resembles the lighter, a lighter. Our own c laws, then, will of course be on these lines.

CLINIAS : Most assuredly.

ATHENIAN : Then let us return to our code and continue it thus. If a man slay a freeborn person by his own act, but the deed be done in angry passion and without purpose aforethought, his sentence shall be in all other respects the same as that proper for him who has slain without passion, but the offender shall be made to spend two years in exile, to learn to bridle his temper. He that slays in passion, but with the addition of premeditation, again, shall have the same sentence, in d other respects, as the former, but three years of exile in the place of the other's two; as his passion was the more grievous, so the term of his punishment shall be the longer. The rule for their restoration from banishment shall be as follows—it is hard to lay it down in the law with precision, as there are cases in which the criminal reckoned by the law the more dangerous proves the more tractable, and the more tractable, as the law considers him, the more dangerous, the act of the latter being at times the more barbarous, that of the former the more humane, though in general the distinction already drawn holds e good. The last word on these and similar matters must rest with the curators.

When the term of banishment, then, is expired in either case, the

curators shall send twelve of their own number to the frontier to sit
upon the case; the twelve must, during this interval, have subjected
the exile's actions to still closer scrutiny, and they are to judge
about giving the criminals their grace and receiving them home again
868 —the parties to be finally bound by this official verdict. If an offender
of either kind ever, after his restoration, give way to rage and repeat
his crime, he shall go into exile never to be recalled, and if he return,
shall meet the same end as the returned alien. The man who slays a
slave in his passion shall, if the slave be his own, purify himself, if
another man's, pay his owner twice what he has lost. If any homicide
of any class, in defiance of the law, shall pollute, by his presence still
uncleansed, market place, public sports, or other hallowed assem-
b blies, he that will may bring his action against both the kinsman who
is executor for the deceased and the homicide, and compel exaction
and payment of money and all else that is due twice over, and the
sum so paid shall be awarded by law to the informer himself. If a
slave slay his owner in his passion, the kinsmen of the deceased shall
c deal with the slayer as they please and be clean of guilt—only that in
no case shall they spare his life. If a free man be killed in passion by
a slave not his own, such slave shall be delivered by his owner to the
kinsmen of the deceased, who shall be bound to put the slayer to
death, but the manner of his death shall be in their own choice. If—
for though unusual, the case does occur—father or mother take the
life of son or daughter in passion, by stripes or other violence, the
purificatory rites shall be as in other cases, and the period of exile
d shall be three full years. When the slayers have been received back,
there shall be a divorce of wife from husband, husband from wife;
procreation between them must cease; there must be no part in the
family or its worship for one who has robbed it of a son and brother.
He that impiously refuses to comply with this ordinance shall be open
to an action for impiety at the suit of any who will charge him. If a
e man slay his wedded wife in passion, or a woman do the like by her
husband, there shall be the same rites of purifying, and the term of
banishment shall be three years. When the criminal returns, he shall
be cut off from joining in worship with his children, or sitting at one
table with them forever. If father or child disregard this law, once
more it shall be open to him who will to bring them to trial for impiety.
If brother or sister slay a brother or sister in passion, the purifications
and term of exile shall be as ordained in the former case of parent and
child—no man shall share one board or join in one worship with the
brother he has robbed of a brother, or the parents he has robbed of a
869 child—and if the command is disobeyed, the disobedient shall be liable to answer to the aforesaid law of impiety, as is just and right.

If ever any man should harbor such unbridled passion against
those that gave him being that he should presume in the frenzy of his
fury to slay a parent, then, if the deceased, before his end, freely for-

gave the criminal his death, he shall be clear when he has accomplished the same purification imposed on the unintentional homicide and performed what else is prescribed for that case. But if such forgiveness be not given, the criminal in this sort shall lie in the danger of more laws than one. He shall lie open to heaviest judgment for vio- b lent outrage, and for impiety, and sacrilege to boot; he has done despite to the temple of a parent's soul, whence, were it possible a man should die more than once, it were perfect justice to put the parricide or matricide whose crime was done in passion to repeated deaths. In this sole case, when a man's life is in danger from his parents, no law will permit slaying, not even in self-defense—the slaying of the father or c mother to whom his very being is due. The law's command will be that he must endure the worst rather than commit such a crime. How then can he, under the law, fitly receive any judgment but one? Let death, then, be the penalty prescribed for him who in passion takes the life of father or mother.

If brother slay brother in a faction fight or some like case, and the act be done in self-defense and the slain man the aggressor, he shall be clear of guilt, as though the slain had been an enemy in arms; d the same shall hold in such case for slaying of citizen by citizen, or alien by alien. If citizen slay citizen, in self-defense, he shall likewise be clear, and so also slave who slays slave. But if the slave take the life of a free man in his own defense, he shall fall under the same laws as the parricide. All we have said of the father's forgiveness of his own death shall hold also for all forgiveness of the act; if any party soever freely forgive any party soever his death, and treat it as e undesigned, the law shall enjoin on the homicide performance of the prescribed purifications and one-year's absence from the country.

So much may serve for a reasonably full treatment of violent, unintentional, and passionate homicide. We are next to deal with the case of acts in this kind done with intent, in downright wickedness, and of deliberate design, at the dictation of overmastering pleasures, cupidities, and jealousies.

CLINIAS: Very true.

ATHENIAN: Then let us once more begin with an attempt to enumerate their sources. First and foremost there is concupiscence 870 with its domination over a soul stung to savagery by unsatisfied lusts. Now this is chiefly found concerned with that on which most men's longing is most permanently and sharply set—wealth, with the power wealth gets alike from native bias and pernicious wrong education to breed countless cravings for insatiate and unbounded possession of itself. And the source of this perverse education is the credit given to false praise of riches alike by Greek and non-Greek; they promote wealth to the first place among good things, whereas in truth it holds but the third, and thus they deprive not only themselves but their pos- b terity. It were for the truest good and glory of all societies that the truth should be told of riches. They are for the service of the body, as the body itself for the service of the soul. Since, then, there are goods to which wealth is but a means, it must hold a third place, after goodness of body and soul. From this doctrine we should learn that the aim

c of him who would be happy must be not to get riches, but to get such riches as rectitude and self-command will permit. That lesson learned, society will no longer see homicide calling for still further homicide in expiation, whereas, today, as we said at first, this greed of riches is one source, and the chief source, of the most aggravated charges of willful homicide. A second is the spirit of rivalry with its brood of jealousies, dangerous company that they are for the envious man himself in the first instance, and only less dangerous to the best of his fellow citizens. And a third cause of too many homicides may be found in

d craven and guilty terrors. There are acts of a man's present or past to which he would wish none but himself to be privy, and so the informer in such a case is removed by murder, if all other methods fail.

All this shall be dealt with in our preludes. They will also state a truth firmly believed by many who have learned it from the lips of those who occupy themselves with these matters at the Mysteries, that

e vengeance is taken on such crimes beyond the grave, and when the sinner has returned to our own world once more, he must infallibly pay nature's penalty—must be done by as he did—and end the life he is now living by the like violence at another's hands. If our mere prelude move any to obedience and proper fear of such a judgment, for them the note of formal command need not be struck, but for the disobedient the statute shall run thus in writing. If a man take the life of

871 a fellow tribesman by his own act, wrongfully, and of set purpose, he shall in the first place be excluded from every place of lawful assembly, and forbidden to pollute with his presence temples, markets, harbors, or other places of public resort whatsoever, and that nonetheless whether any man have given the slayer public notice of the ban or not —the law itself gives notice of it and proclaims it on behalf of the community at large, now and to all time.

b If any man of the deceased's kin within the limits of cousinship, on either father's or mother's side, shall neglect his duty to institute proceedings, or to make proclamation of the excommunication first, on his own head be the pollution and—for the law's curse brings the evil omen with it—the wrath of heaven. Next, he shall be open to prosecution by any man who is minded to avenge the deceased. He

c that has a mind to avenge him shall fulfill with due care the washings and other observances the oracle may prescribe in such cases, and give formal notice of the excommunication; he shall then proceed to compel the culprit to submit to execution as required by the law. That this process should be attended by prayers and sacrifices to gods whose function is to preserve societies from homicides the legislator may declare without trouble to himself. What gods these should be

and what manner of conducting such trials will best suit with religion
shall be determined by the curators of law, in concert with canonists, d
seers, and the oracle, before they institute the trials. The court shall be
the same to which we gave authority to decide in charges of sacrilege.
The convicted offender shall be put to death, and shall not receive
burial in the land of his victim—for that would add insult to impiety.
If he flee the land and decline to submit to judgment, his banishment
shall be everlasting. If any such exile set foot in the country of his
victim, the first kinsman of the murdered man, or indeed the first
fellow citizen, who may fall in with him, shall slay him, with the law's
permission, or else put him in bonds and deliver him for execution to e
the magistrates presiding over the court in which the case was tried.
He that enters the case for prosecution shall also at the same time demand security from the accused, who shall produce his sureties, men
whom the court of judges constituted for these cases shall pronounce
sufficient, three substantial sureties pledged to surrender him for his
trial. In the case of refusal or inability to find such surety, the court
shall arrest the accused, keep him prisoner, and produce him at
the trial.

　　If a man be not the actual assassin, but have purposed the death 872
of another and brought him to his end by design and contrivance, and
then continue to reside in the state a guilty man with the stain of
homicide on his soul, the procedure in the trial of such charges shall
be the same, only that security shall not be demanded, and that the
convicted may find burial in his native soil; in all other respects this
case shall be treated precisely like the other. The procedure shall be
the same in cases both of homicide where both parties are aliens, or
one party a citizen and the other an alien, or both parties slaves, and
of plotting homicide, except as concerns giving of security; as to that b
point, the party who advances the charge of homicide shall at the
same time demand security from the accused in such cases, exactly as
it has been prescribed to be required from the assassin. If a slave cause
the death of a free man with intent, either as the actual homicide or
as the plotter of it, the common executioner shall conduct him toward the burial place of the victim and to a spot from which the tomb
is visible, when he shall be scourged with as many stripes as the c
prosecutor shall enjoin, and, if he survive the infliction, be put to
death. If a man slay a slave who has committed no crime, from apprehension that he may inform against his own shameful misdeeds, or
some similar motive, he shall stand his trial for the homicide of such
slave precisely as though the slain had been a citizen.

　　Should there arise cases for which it is a grim and repulsive task
even to provide in a legislation, though impossible to ignore them, I
mean cases of deliberate and purely wicked homicide by act or contrivance between kinsmen—they are mostly to be found in states d
where the way of life or the system of training is corrupt; still such a

thing may happen even in a land where we could least expect it—why, we can but repeat the doctrine we uttered but now, in the hope that it will by its appeal dispose a hearer the more readily to eschew of his own free choice this most abominable of all forms of homicide. That

e   tale, or doctrine—call it what you please—comes to us on the authority of priests of ancient days, and it tells us expressly that there is a justice watching to avenge a kinsman's blood, and that the law followed by this justice is no other than that we even now stated; it is appointed that he who has dealt in such guilt shall infallibly be done by as he has done. If any man have slain his father, there shall come a time when he shall have to suffer the same violent end at the hands of a child; if his mother, his certain doom in later days is to be born himself a female creature and, in the end, to have his life taken by those whom he has borne. When pollution has been brought on the common blood, there is no other way of purification but this; the stain

873   refuses to be effaced until the guilty soul have paid life for life, like for like, and this atonement lulled the wrath of the whole lineage to sleep.

Thus a man's hand should be stayed by dread of such vengeance from heaven, but should there be wretches so whelmed in misery that they of malice prepense rend father's, mother's, brother's, or child's soul from body, our human legislator's statute provides for their case

b   as follows. The regulations for making proclamation of excommunication and taking of security shall be as appointed in the former cases. If a man be found guilty of such homicide, that is, of slaying any of the aforesaid, the officers of the court with the magistrates shall put him to death and cast him out naked, outside the city at an appointed place where three ways meet. There, all the magistrates, in the name of the state, shall take each man his stone and cast it on the head of the corpse as in expiation for the state. The corpse shall then be car-

c   ried to the frontier and cast out by legal sentence without sepulture.

But what of him who takes the life that is, as they say, nearest and dearest to himself? What should be his punishment? I mean the man whose violence frustrates the decree of destiny by *self-slaughter* though no sentence of the state has required this of him, no stress of cruel and inevitable calamity driven him to the act, and he has been involved in no desperate and intolerable disgrace, the man who thus gives unrighteous sentence against himself from mere poltroonery

d   and unmanly cowardice. Well, in such a case, what further rites must be observed, in the way of purifications and ceremonies of burial, it is for heaven to say; the next of kin should consult the official canonists as well as the laws on the subject, and act according to their direction. But the graves of such as perish thus must, in the first place, be solitary; they must have no companions whatsoever in the tomb. Further, they must be buried ignominiously in waste and nameless spots on the boundaries between the twelve districts, and the tomb shall be

e   marked by neither headstone nor name.

If a beast of draft or other animal cause homicide, except in the case when the deed is done by a beast competing in one of the public sports, the kinsman shall institute proceedings for homicide against the slayer. The case shall be heard by such and as many of the rural commissioners as the next of kin may appoint; on conviction, the beast shall be put to death and cast out beyond the frontier. If an inanimate thing cause the loss of a human life—an exception being made for lightning or other such visitation of God—any object which causes death by its falling upon a man or his falling against it shall be 874 sat upon in judgment by the nearest neighbor, at the invitation of the next of kin, who shall hereby acquit himself and the whole family of their obligation—on conviction the guilty object to be cast beyond the frontier, as was directed in the case of a beast.

But if a man have manifestly been murdered, and the murderer is unknown or cannot be discovered after careful inquiry, notice of prosecution shall be given as in other cases, but the prosecutor shall address the notification to 'the author of the homicide,' and after establishing his right to prosecute shall give public warning in the mar- b ket place to 'the criminal slayer of so-and-so' to set no foot in the sanctuaries or any other place within the country of his victim, with the threat that if he makes an appearance and is recognized, he shall be put to death and cast out of the country of the victim unburied. This, then, shall form one chapter in our law—the statutes of homicide.

So much then on these matters. The cases wherein and conditions whereon a slayer shall rightly be held guiltless shall be these following. He that slays a thief entering the house by night with intent of robbery shall be guiltless; he that in his own defense slays a footpad c shall be guiltless. He that offers hurtful violence to a free woman or boy may be slain without fear of the law by the object of his violent rape, or by father, brother, or son of such party; if a man take one in the act of enforcing his wedded wife and slay him, he shall be clear in the eye of the law. If a man slay in defense of a father's life—the father not being engaged in a criminal act—or in like defense of child, brother, or mother of his children, he shall be altogether clear.   d

Thus much then for the law of the living soul and that nurture and education which it must needs enjoy if it is to live, and without which it must die, and the vengeance to be taken for death by violence. The law of the nurture and training of the body has been stated, and it will next, I take it, be right to proceed to a kindred topic, to classify and enumerate to the best of our ability the various intentional or unintentional violent assaults committed by man on man, and to prescribe the penalties properly to be attached to their several e kinds.

Wounds and maims, then, will be placed next after manslaughter by the veriest dabbler in legislation. Thus, like homicides, wounds must be divided into the involuntary, wounds inflicted in

passion, those inflicted in fear, those that are intentional and deliberate. Hence we should begin our treatment of all classes with a prefatory statement to the following effect. Mankind must either give
875 themselves a law and regulate their lives by it, or live no better than
the wildest of wild beasts, and that for the following reason. There is
no man whose natural endowments will ensure that he shall both discern what is good for mankind as a community and invariably be both
able and willing to put the good into practice when he has perceived it.
It is hard, in the first place, to perceive that a true social science must
be concerned with the community, not with the individual—common
interest tending to cement society as private to disrupt it—and that it
b is to the advantage of community and individual at once that public
well-being should be considered before private. Again, even one who
had attained clear perception of this principle as a point of scientific
theory, if subsequently placed in a position of irresponsible autocratic
sovereignty, would never prove loyal to his conviction, or spend his life
in the promotion of the public good of the state as the paramount object to which his own advantage must be secondary. His frail human
nature will always tempt such a man to self-aggrandizement and self-
seeking, will be bent beyond all reason on the avoidance of pain and
pursuit of pleasure, and put both these ends before the claims of the
c right and the good; in this self-caused blindness it will end by sinking
him and his community with him in depths of ruin. I grant you readily
that if ever, by God's mercy, a man were born with the capacity to attain to this perception, he would need no laws to govern him. No law
or ordinance whatever has the right to sovereignty over true knowledge. 'Tis a sin that understanding should be any creature's subject or
d servant; its place is to be ruler of all, if only it is indeed, as it ought to
be, genuine and free. But, as things are, such insight is nowhere to be
met with, except in faint vestiges, and so we have to choose the second
best, ordinance and law. Now they can consider most cases and provide for them, but not all, and this is why I have said what I have. You
and I are about to fix the penalty or fine to be inflicted on him who
wounds another or does him a hurt. Now it is, of course, a proper and
obvious comment to make at this point, to say, Wounds? Yes, but
e wounds whom, and where and how and when? The different cases are
countless and their circumstances are widely unlike. So it is equally
impossible to leave everything to the discretion of the courts and to
leave nothing. One issue, indeed, we cannot avoid leaving to their discretion in all cases, that of the occurrence or nonoccurrence of the
alleged event. And it is quite impossible to the legislator to leave the
courts no discretion at all on the further question of the amount of
876 the fine or penalty to be imposed on the perpetrator of this sort of
wrong, but deal with all cases himself, light or grave, by statute.
　　CLINIAS : What line, then, are we to take up now?
　　ATHENIAN : Why, this. Something must be left to the discre-

tion of the courts, but not everything; there are things which the law must itself regulate.

CLINIAS : Then which are the points to be thus dealt with by statute, and which should be entrusted to a court's discretion?

ATHENIAN : The proper step to take next is to point out that in a state where the courts of law are poor-spirited and inarticulate, where their members keep their convictions to themselves and reach their b verdict by a secret vote, where, worst of all, they do not even listen to the case in silence but make the walls ring with the voice of their applause or censure of the alternate speakers, like the audience at a play, the community finds itself in a difficult position. Where the courts are so constituted, to be sure, the legislator's hand is forced by an unfortunate but very real necessity; he is compelled to restrict the court's discretion to assess penalties to cases of the most insignificant c kind and to do most of the work himself by express statute, if he has the misfortune to be legislator for such a society. But in a community where the constitution of the courts is thoroughly sound, and the persons who will have to exercise the judicial function have been properly trained and made to pass the most exacting tests, it will be entirely right and fitting that such courts should be allowed a wide discretion in assessing the fines or other penalties of offenders. So we may well be excused, in the present instance, if we do not impose on them by d statute the numerous and important rules which may be discovered by the insight of judges with a training inferior to theirs for attaching to the particular offenses the penalty merited by the wrong committed and hurt inflicted. Indeed, as we believe the persons for whom we are making our statutes likely to prove particularly capable judges in such matters, we shall trust most of them to their discretion. Not that we were not perfectly right in the doctrine we have repeatedly stated and observed in practice in the preceding part of our own legislation. An outline of the law with samples of penalties should be set e before the judges as a model to keep them from any infringement of the bounds of right. I shall, in fact, act so again in the present case, and this brings me back to the work of lawmaking.

The statute of wounding, then, shall run thus. If anyone intend and purpose the death of a person with whom he is on friendly terms, such person not being one against whom the law arms his hand, and fail to kill, but inflict a wound, he who wounds with such intent de- 877 serves no mercy, and shall be made to stand his trial for homicide with as little scruple as though he had killed. But the law will show its reverence for his not too wholly unpropitious fortune and the tutelary power which has, in mercy to both wounder and wounded, preserved the one from a fatal hurt and the other from incurring a curse and a disaster; it will show its gratitude and submission to that power by sparing the criminal's life and dooming him to lifelong banishment to b the nearest state, where he shall enjoy his revenues in full. He must make payment of whatever damage he have caused to the wounded, the amount being fixed by the court before which the case is tried, and this court shall be composed of the same persons as would have tried the homicide had death followed as a consequence of the wounds inflicted.

If a son wound his parents or a slave his master with the like intent, the penalty shall be death; so also if brother or sister wound brother or sister in like fashion, and be found guilty of wounding with c intent, the penalty shall be death. If a wife wound her husband, or a husband his wife, with design to kill, they shall go into perpetual banishment. As for the estate, if there are sons or daughters who are still minors, it shall be in the hands of the guardians, who shall be charged with the care of the children as though they were orphans; if the family be of full age, there shall be no liability of the offspring to support the banished man, and the estate shall be their property. If the victim d of the calamity be childless, the kinsmen of the exile within the degree of second cousinship on both male and female sides shall meet to appoint an inheritor for the house in question—the five-thousand-and-fortieth of the state—in consultation with the curators and priests, and they shall do so with this thought before their minds. There is no house of the five thousand and forty that belongs so truly to its occupant or his whole kin as to the state, and that by every right of owner- e ship. It is for the state, then, to keep its house in all purity and good fortune. When a house, then, is visited with such guilt and misfortune at once that the owner leaves no sons to succeed to it, but dies unwedded or wedded but childless, under conviction of willful homicide, or other sin against heaven or human society for which the pain of death stands expressly prescribed in the law, or again when a childless man is under doom of perpetual exile, the house itself shall first be purified and exorcised as the law directs. Next the household shall 878 meet, as provided even now, along with the curators, to consider what house of all in the state is at once of the first repute for goodness, favored by fortune, and possessed of more children than one. From such a house they shall adopt one person as a son and successor to the father of the deceased and his line before him, naming him after one of the lineage for the omen's sake, and offering prayers that they may all find in him by this means a progenitor of issue, a preserver of the hearth, and a minister in things secular and sacred with fairer for- b tunes than his father. They shall then constitute him legal heir to the estate, while the criminal shall be left without name, children, or portion when such calamity overtakes him.

It should seem that boundary is not in all cases immediately adjacent to boundary; where there is a borderland, this interposing belt touches either region first and is common ground to both. In particular we have said that deeds of passion form such a borderland between the unintentional and the intentional. Hence our law of wounding in

anger shall run thus. On conviction, first the offender shall repay the c
damage done twofold, if the wound prove curable, fourfold for an incurable hurt. And if the wound, though curable, cause the injured man
some grave and shameful disfigurement, the payment shall be threefold. In a case where the assailant causes detriment not only to the
victim, but to the state as well, by incapacitating the wounded for national defense, he shall further, in addition to all other penalties, com-
pensate the state for the loss. That is, in addition to his personal
military service he shall also discharge that of the disabled and take his d
place in the ranks; failure to perform the task shall render him legally
liable to prosecution at the instance of any man who pleases for evasion of military duty. The rate of compensation—whether it shall be
twofold, threefold, or even fourfold—shall be determined by the court
who found the verdict of guilty. If kinsman wound kinsman in the
ways aforesaid, the parents and kinsfolk of both sexes and on both
sides, within the degree of second cousins, shall meet, find a verdict, e
and commit the fixing of penalty to the natural parents of the parties.
If their assessment be called in question, the male progenitors shall be
authorized to make an assessment; if they fail to reach a decision for
themselves, the matter shall be finally committed by them to the curators of law. In the case of such wounding of parents by their children,
the judges shall be required to be persons of over sixty years of age
who have children, not by adoption, but of their own begetting. On
conviction, it shall be for the court to determine whether the offense
shall be punished by death or some other sentence, more, or possibly
slightly less, heavy. No kinsman of the culprit shall be a member of 879
the court, even if he have attained the age required by law. If a slave
wound a free man in anger, the owner of such slave shall deliver him
to the wounded man to be used at his pleasure; failing to deliver him,
he shall himself make good the damage. If the defendant allege that
the case is one of conspiracy between the slave and the wounded man,
he must sustain his allegations. If he lose his suit, he shall pay the
damage threefold; if he gain it, he shall have an action for kidnaping b
against the party who so conspired with the slave. He that wounds
another without intent shall pay the simple damage—no legislator
can be expected to prescribe rules to chance. The judges shall be as directed for the case of parents wounded by their children, and they
shall fix the amount of compensation.

Assault and battery, in its various forms, is, like the cases of
which we have treated, an offense of violence. Apropos of such conduct, it should never be forgotten by anyone, man, woman, or child,
that seniority is held in highest consideration alike by gods and by c
men who intend a long and happy life. Hence the public assault of a
younger man on his senior is a shameful spectacle and abominable in
the eye of heaven. If the younger man is struck by the elder, the seemly
course is ever that he should meekly give place to his anger, and thus

lay up a capital of the same consideration for his own old age. Hence our rule shall run thus. All shall show their reverence for their seniors in act and speech. A man shall stay his hand from any that is twenty years older than himself, be it man or woman, as he would from his

d own father or mother; he must spare all who are of an age to have begotten or borne him, in duty to the gods of birth. He must likewise keep his hand from the alien, old-established resident, and recent arrival alike; neither in aggression nor in self-defense shall he ever permit himself to admonish one of that class by a blow. If the alien strike him a wanton and insolent blow and he think correction called for, he shall seize him and carry him before the court of the urban commissioners, without striking him back, that he may be taught never more to pre-

e sume to beat a native. The commissioners shall take the accused and examine into his case, but with all due regard for the god who watches over the alien. If the alien be judged to have struck the native wrong-fully, they shall give him as many lashes of the scourge as he has him-self struck blows, to break him of his abuse of his position; if to have done no wrong, they shall warn and censure the apprehender and so

880 dismiss both parties. If a man be struck by another of his own age, or a senior but childless man by a junior, whether the parties be both old or both young, he shall defend himself with the arms nature has given him, his unweaponed naked fists. But if a man above forty years of age permit himself to fight another, whether he be assailant or attacked, he will meet no more than his desert if punished by being ill reputed as a ruffian and a boor. With him that is amenable to this counsel we shall have no difficulties; the refractory, who care nothing for our pre-

b amble shall find a law ready to meet their case to this effect. If a man strike one that is his senior by twenty years or more, first, any by-stander who is neither of the same age as the combatants nor younger shall come between them, on pain of proclamation as a coward; if the bystander be of the same years as the party struck, or younger, he shall defend the attacked as he would his own brother, father, or still older kinsman. Furthermore, he that presumed to strike his senior, as al-ready said, shall stand his trial for assault and battery and, if con-

c victed, shall lie in prison for a full year at the least, or if the court propose a longer sentence, its determination of the period shall be binding. If a foreigner or resident alien strike one who is his senior by twenty or more years, the same legal provision for assistance from by-standers shall be in force, and he that is condemned on this count, if an alien and nonresident among us, shall purge that offense by two years of imprisonment, if a resident, shall be imprisoned three years

d for his violation of our laws, unless the court award sentence of a longer term. Further a fine shall be laid in all such cases on a by-stander who does not render the assistance required by the law, the amount to be one mina for members of the first property class, fifty drachmas for those of the second, thirty for those of the third, twenty for those of the fourth. The court, in such cases, shall be composed of the generals, infantry commanders, phylarchs, and hipparchs.

Laws, we may say, are made in part for the virtuous—to teach them what rule they should follow in their intercourse with one another, if they are to live in peace and good will—partly also for men e who have shunned instruction, men whose stubborn tempers have yielded to none of those melting influences that might hold them back from utter debasement. It is to their account you must lay what I have now to utter, for them that a legislator will be driven to enact laws for which he could wish no need might ever arise. If any should ever presume to offer violent assault to father, mother, or one of their progenitors, should so far forget his fear of the wrath of heaven and the punishments of which men tell beyond the grave as to be led by his 881 conceit of knowing where he is utterly ignorant, and his scorn of the venerable and universal tradition into that trespass—some last deterrent is wanted for his case. Now the last penalty is not death, and as for the pains said to be inflicted on such sinners in the world to come, though they are more extreme than any on earth and threaten in the tones of truth itself, they effect nothing for the deterrence of these criminal souls; were it otherwise, we should hear of no mishandlings of mothers or other cursed and presumptuous striking of progenitors. Hence we must make the chastisements for such crime here in this present life, if we can, no less stern than those of the life to come.   b

Our next proclamation, then, shall be as follows. If a man, not being afflicted with insanity, presume to strike father, mother, or their parents, first, the bystanders shall come to their aid, as in cases already disposed of. The resident alien who intervenes thus shall be offered a seat in the front rank at the public sports; he who fails in this duty shall go into perpetual banishment from our soil. A nonresident alien affording such help shall receive public commendation, and who c withholds it, public censure. A slave who affords it shall have his freedom; a slave who withholds it shall suffer a hundred lashes with the scourge, to be administered by the commissioners of the market, if the offense is committed in the market place—if committed in the city but elsewhere than in the market square, the correction to be inflicted by the urban commissioner in residence, if in some rural district by the commanders of the rural commission. Every bystander of native birth, child or woman or man, shall join in the rescue, crying out on d the assailant as wretch and monster, and any that takes no part shall be held by the law under the curse of the god of kindred and family. If a man be convicted of assault on a parent, first he shall be perpetually relegated from the capital city to another region of the country and excluded from all holy places. If he do not observe the exclusion, the rural commission shall correct him with stripes, or in any way they please; if he returns he shall be condemned to death. If any free person eat, drink, or have any dealings whatever with the criminal, or e so much as take his hand on meeting him wittingly, he shall enter neither place of worship, market square, nor any part of the city whatsoever, without first purifying himself, as one that has been infected by contact with an accursed horror, and if he disobey and pollute holy places and city by infraction of the law, any magistrate informed of the fact and not proceeding against the guilty party shall have the fact charged against him as a point of first moment at his audit. If a slave

882   strike a free man, alien or citizen, a bystander shall come to his aid or incur the specified fine, according to his status; the bystanders shall assist to bind the striker of the blow and shall deliver him to the in-

b   jured party, who shall then lay him in fetters, scourge him with as many stripes as he pleases, provided no detriment to his master's interests ensue, and deliver him up to the master as his rightful owner. The words of the law shall run: If a slave strike a free man, except by order of a magistrate, the owner of such slave shall receive him in fetters from the aggrieved party, and shall not release him therefrom

c   until such slave have satisfied the aggrieved that he deserves to be at large. These same rules of law shall hold good for cases of the same kind when both parties are women, or where either is a woman and the other a man.

BOOK X

884   ATHENIAN: Now that we have dealt with assault, we may enunciate a single and comprehensive principle of law in respect of cases of violence, to the following effect. No man shall lift the goods and chattels of others, nor yet make use of a neighbor's property without the owner's permission, since such conduct is the beginning whence all the aforesaid mischiefs, past, present, or future, derive by consequence. Now the gravest mischiefs of them all are the licenses and outrages of youth, and the affront is gravest when done to consecrated

885   things, and most singularly grave again when the objects affronted are not only sacred but public, or partly public, as common to a tribe or some similar group. Second in order and in gravity are offenses against private shrines and private tombs, and third, impieties to parents other than the crimes already enumerated. A fourth form of outrage is the case when a man shows contempt for magistrates by lifting their goods or chattels, or using anything that is theirs without permission obtained, and a fifth branch will be such violation of the civil rights of the private citizen as calls for legal redress. Hence we must provide a law applicable to all these branches alike. Now as for actual

b   sacrilege, open and forcible or secret, we have already said succinctly what the penalty for its commission should be. We are now to prescribe a punishment for all verbal or practical outrage offered to the gods by speech or act. But first our legislator must introduce his usual admonition, and it shall run to this effect. No man who believes in gods as the law would have him believe has ever yet of his own free will done unhallowed deed or let slip lawless discourse. If a man acts thus, 'tis from one of three causes. Either, as I say, he does not believe, or again, he believes that they are, but are regardless of mankind, or lastly, that they are lightly to be won over by the cajoling of offerings and prayers.

CLINIAS : Then how are we to treat such men, or what should c we say to them?

ATHENIAN : Nay, my dear sir, let us begin by giving a hearing to the mockeries in which, as I conceive, their scorn of us would find utterance.

CLINIAS : And what form would this mockery take?

ATHENIAN : Why, their satire might well run to this effect. Gentlemen of Athens, Lacedaemon, and Cnossus, you are in the right of it. Some of us, in fact, recognize no gods whatsoever, and others gods such as you describe. So we make the same demand of you that you have yourselves made of the laws. Before you come to the severi- d ties of threats, it is for you to try persuasion—to convince us by sufficient proof that there really are gods, and that they are too good to be diverted from the path of justice by the attraction of gifts. As things are, that, and more to the same effect, is what we have heard from those who have the repute of being our first-rate poets, orators, prophets, and priests, and countless thousands of others, and this is why most of us follow the path not of refusing to do wrong, but of committing it and trying to patch it up. So we expect you, as legislators who e make a profession of humanity rather than severity, to try persuasion on us in the first instance. Your case for the existence of gods may not be much better than that of the other side, but persuade us that it *is* better in the one point of *truth*, and you may perhaps make converts of us. So if you think our challenge a fair one, you must try to answer it.

CLINIAS : Why, surely, sir, it looks easy enough to speak the truth in saying that gods exist.

ATHENIAN : And on what grounds?   886

CLINIAS : Why, to begin with, think of the earth, and sun, and planets, and everything! And the wonderful and beautiful order of the seasons with its distinctions of years and months! Besides, there is the fact that all mankind, Greeks and non-Greeks alike, believe in the existence of gods.

ATHENIAN : My dear friend, I have a fear—I will never call it an *awe*—of these evil men, a fear that they may despise us. You and our friend, in fact, do not understand the ground of their controversy with us. You imagine that what impels their souls to irreligion is in- b continence of pleasures and lusts, and nothing more.

CLINIAS : Why, sir, what further cause can there be in the case?

ATHENIAN : One of which your friend and you can be expected

to know nothing. You fail to remark it because it does not touch your lives.

CLINIAS : Now I wonder what it can be to which you allude.

ATHENIAN : Why, folly of a deadly sort that conceits itself to be the height of wisdom.

CLINIAS : And what is that?

ATHENIAN : We have in my own community literary narratives —the excellence of your civic institutions, I am informed, prevents c their appearance among you—which treat of the gods, some of them in verse, and others again in prose. The most ancient of these narratives relate that the primitive realities were the sky, and so forth. When the story has got a little way past this starting point it recounts the birth of the gods, and their subsequent conduct toward each other. Now whether in other respects the effect of these stories on those who hear them is good or the reverse is not lightly to be decided, in view of their antiquity, but as concerns their bearing on the tendance and reverence due to parents, I could certainly never commend them as d salutary, nor as true at all. However, we may dismiss the primitive stories without more ado; let them be told in any way heaven pleases. But the theories of our modern men of enlightenment must be held to account for the mischief they cause. Now the effect of their compositions is this. When you and I produce our evidence of the existence of gods, and allege this very point—the deity or divinity of sun and moon, planets and earth—the converts of these sages will reply that they are e but earth and stones, incapable of minding human conduct, however plausibly we have coated them over with a varnish of sugared eloquence.

CLINIAS : A dreadful theory this that you are talking of, sir, even if there were only one such. How much more dreadful our present age, when such doctrines are so rife.

ATHENIAN : Well, what answer have we, then? What course should we take? Must we look on ourselves as, so to say, indicted at the bar of the ungodly and defend our incriminated legislation from 887 the charge that it has no right to assume the existence of gods? Or should we drop the subject and return to our lawmaking for fear our preamble may actually prove longer than the enactments to follow it? The discourse, to be sure, will run to considerable length, if we are first to furnish the undevoutly disposed with adequate proofs on the points which they said we were bound to treat, and so put the opponent in fear, only proceeding to the enactment of suitable regulations after we have thus created a disrelish for irreligion.

b   CLINIAS : Well, sir, in the little while we have spent together we have repeatedly had occasion to remark that there is no reason to prefer brevity of speech, in our present business, to length—the proverbial 'pursuer' is not on our traces—so we should make but a sorry and ludicrous show if we chose the shorter course rather than the best.

And 'tis of the first importance to give our plea for the existence of gods, and good gods with a superhuman reverence for right, such persuasiveness as we can; such a preamble would, in fact, be the noblest and best defense for our whole legislation. Let us, then, show neither c reluctance nor impatience, but unreservedly employ whatever gifts of persuasion we may possess in such matters on the task of adequate exposition to the utmost of our powers.

ATHENIAN: The earnestness and passion of your speech are, I feel, an invitation to prayer; they leave no further room for postponement of the argument. Come then, how shall we plead for the existence of gods dispassionately? To be sure, no man can help feeling some resentment and disgust with the parties who now, as in the past, impose the burden of the argument on us by their want of faith in d the stories heard so often in earliest infancy, while still at the breast, from their mothers and nurses—stories, you may say, crooned over them, in sport and in earnest, like spells—and heard again in prayers offered over sacrifices, in conjunction with the spectacle which gives such intense delight to the eye and ear of children, as it is enacted at a sacrifice, the spectacle of our parents addressing their gods, with assured belief in their existence, in earnest prayer and supplication for themselves and their children. Then, again, at rising and setting of e sun and moon, they have heard and seen the universal prostrations and devotions of mankind, Greeks and non-Greeks alike, in all the varied circumstances of evil fortune and good, with their implication that gods are no fictions, but the most certain of realities, and their being beyond the remotest shadow of a doubt. When we see all this evidence treated with contempt by the persons who are forcing us into our present argument, and that, as any man with a grain of intelli- 888 gence will admit, without a single respectable reason, how, I ask, is a man to find gentle language in which to combine reproof with instruction in the initial truth about the gods—that of their existence? Still, the task is to be faced. We can never permit one party among us to run mad from lust of pleasure, and the rest equally mad from fury against them. So our dispassionate preliminary admonition to minds thus depraved shall run to this effect—we will suppress our passion and use gentle language, imagining ourselves to be addressing a single person of the type.

My lad, you are still young, and as time advances it will lead you to a complete reversal of many of your present convictions. You should b wait for the future, then, before you undertake to judge of the supreme issues, and the greatest of these, though you now count it so trivial, is that of thinking rightly about the gods and so living well, or the reverse. I may begin with a single word of significant warning which you will assuredly find to be no mistake, and it is this. You yourself and your friends are not the first nor the only persons to embrace this tenet as your doctrine about gods; nay, in every age there are sufferers from

the malady, more or fewer. Hence I, who have had the acquaintance
c of many such, can assure you that no one who in early life has adopted
this doctrine of the nonexistence of gods has ever persisted to old age
constant to that conviction, though there have been cases—not many,
certainly, but still some few—of persistence in the other two attitudes,
the belief that there are gods but that they are indifferent to human
conduct, and again, that, though not indifferent, they are lightly placated by sacrifice and prayers. If you will be ruled by me, then, you
will wait for the fullness of clear and confident judgment on these
matters to come to you, and inquire whether truth lies in one direction
d or another, seeking for guidance in all quarters, and above all from
the legislator. Meanwhile, beware of all impiety toward gods. For he
who is framing the law for you must make it his business, hereafter
as well as now, to instruct you in the truth of this matter.

CLINIAS : Admirably said, sir, so far as we have gone yet.

ATHENIAN : Just so, Megillus and Clinias, but we have unconsciously embroiled ourselves with a portentous theory.

CLINIAS : And what theory may that be?

e   ATHENIAN : One which is widely held to be the last word of wisdom.

CLINIAS : You must be still more explicit.

ATHENIAN : We are told, you know, that everything whatever
which comes, has come, or will come into existence is a product either
of nature, or of art, or of chance.

CLINIAS : And rightly so told, are we not?

ATHENIAN : Why, there is, of course, a presumption that what
889 wise men tell us is true. But suppose we follow up their traces, and
ask ourselves what the real meaning of the spokesmen of that party
may be.

CLINIAS : With all my heart.

ATHENIAN : Evidently, so they say, all the grandest and fairest
of things are products of nature and chance, and only the more insignificant of art. Art takes over the grand primary works from the
hands of nature, already formed, and then models and fashions the
more insignificant, and this is the very reason why we all call them
artificial.

CLINIAS : You mean to say?

b   ATHENIAN : Let me put it more plainly still. Fire and water,
earth and air—so they say—all owe their being to nature and chance,
none of them to art; they, in turn, are the agents, and the absolutely
soulless agents, in the production of the bodies of the next rank, the
earth, sun, moon, and stars. They drifted casually, each in virtue of
their several tendencies. As they came together in certain fitting and
convenient dispositions—hot with cold, dry with moist, soft with
c hard, and so on in all the inevitable casual combinations which arise
from blending of contraries—thus, and on this wise, they gave birth to

the whole heavens and all their contents, and, in due course, to all animals and plants, when once all the seasons of the year had been produced from those same causes—not, so they say, by the agency of
mind, or any god, or art, but, as I tell you, by nature and chance. Art,
the subsequent late-born product of these causes, herself as perishable d
as her creators, has since given birth to certain toys with little real substance in them, simulacra as shadowy as the arts themselves, such as
those which spring from painting, music, and the other fellow crafts.
Or if there are arts which really produce anything of genuine worth,
they are those which lend their aid to nature, like medicine, husbandry,
gymnastics. Statesmanship in especial, they say, is a thing which has
a little in common with nature, but is mainly a business of art; legislation, likewise, is altogether an affair not of nature, but of art, and its
positions are unreal.   e

CLINIAS: Unreal—but how so?

ATHENIAN: Why, my dear sir, to begin with, this party asserts
that gods have no real and natural, but only an artificial being, in virtue of legal conventions, as they call them, and thus there are different
gods for different places, conformably to the convention made by each
group among themselves when they drew up their legislation. Then
they actually declare that the really and naturally laudable is one
thing and the conventionally laudable quite another, while as for
right, there is absolutely no such thing as a real and natural right,
that mankind are eternally disputing about rights and altering them,
and that every change thus made, once made, is from that moment 890
valid, though it owes its being to artifice and legislation, not to anything you could call nature. All these views, my friends, come from
men who impress the young as wise, prose writers and poets who profess that indefeasible right means whatever a man can carry with the
high hand. Hence our epidemics of youthful irreligion—as though
there were no gods such as the law enjoins us to believe in—and
hence the factions created by those who seek, on such grounds, to attract men to the 'really and naturally right life,' that is, the life of real
domination over others, not of conventional service to them.

CLINIAS: What an awful creed you describe, sir! What a gen- b
eral corruption of the young people of whole cities and private households!

ATHENIAN: Too true, Clinias, too true. But how would you
have the legislator act where such a situation is of long standing?
Should he be content to stand up in public and threaten people all
round that unless they confess the being of gods, and believe in their
hearts that they are such as his law declares—and the case is the
same with the laudable, the right, and everything of highest moment, c
and all that makes for virtue or vice—action must conform in all cases
to the convictions prescribed by the text of the legislation—is he to
threaten, I say, that those who will not lend a ready ear to the laws

shall in some cases suffer death, in others be visited with bonds and whipping, in others with infamy, and in yet others with poverty and banishment, but to have no words of persuasion with which to work on his people, as he dictates their laws, and so, it may be, tame them?

d   CLINIAS : Far from it, sir, far from it. If there are indeed persuasives, however weak, in such matters, no legislator who deserves the slightest consideration must ever faint. He should strain every nerve, as they say, to plead in support of the old traditional belief of the being of gods and of all you have just recounted. In especial also, he should defend the claim of law itself and of art to be natural, or no less real than nature, seeing that they are products of mind by a sound argument which I take you to be now propounding and in which I concur.

e   ATHENIAN : Why, Clinias, here is zeal indeed! But pray, are not statements thus made to a multitude hard to support by argument, and do they not entail an interminable deal of it?

CLINIAS : Well, sir, and what then? We bore with one another through all those long discourses of the wine cup and of music, and are we to show less patience now we are treating of gods and kindred themes? And, mark you, such argument will be a most valuable aid to intelligent legislation, because legal enactments, once put into writ-
891   ing, remain always on record, as though to challenge the question of all time to come. Hence we need feel no dismay if they should be difficult on a first hearing, since even the dull student may recur to them for reiterated scrutiny. Nor does their length, provided they are beneficial, make it less irrational than it is, in my opinion at least, impious for any man to refuse such discourse his heartiest support.

MEGILLUS : What Clinias says, sir, has my fullest approval.

b   ATHENIAN : And mine, too, Megillus, and we must do as he bids us. To be sure, if such theories had not been so widely broadcast, as we may fairly say, throughout all mankind, there would have been no need for arguments to defend the being of gods, but, as the case stands, they cannot be dispensed with. So with the highest laws in risk of perishing at the hands of wicked men, whose function can it be to come to the rescue before the legislator?

MEGILLUS : Why, no man's.

ATHENIAN : Well then, Clinias—for you must be my partner in
c the argument—let me hear *your* opinion once more. Presumably one who reasons thus holds that fire and water, earth and air, are the most primitive origins of all things—*nature* being just the name he gives to them—but the soul is a later derivative from them. Or, more probably, it is no case of a presumption; his argument is an actual declaration to that effect.

CLINIAS : Precisely.

ATHENIAN : Why, in God's name then, have we traced the unreason and error of all who have ever busied themselves with research into nature back to what we may call its source? Pray consider the point with careful attention to all their positions, as it will make a vast difference if we can show that those who have taken up with ir- d religious doctrines and set the tune for others to follow have actually argued their case ill and fallaciously. And I honestly believe this to be the fact.

CLINIAS: Excellent, but you must try to explain where the fallacy lies.

ATHENIAN: Then I am afraid I shall have to treat of rather unfamiliar matters.

CLINIAS: There is no need for your hesitation, sir. I see you apprehend you will be going outside the limits of legislation if we are to deal with such matters. But if that is the one and only way to ac- e cordance with the truth about gods, as now stated in our law, why, my good man, our argument must take it.

ATHENIAN: Then it seems I must propound my none too familiar thesis at once, and here it is. In the doctrine of which the soul of the ungodly is the product, the primal cause of all coming-to-be and ceasing-to-be is pronounced to be not primal but secondary and derivative, the secondary primitive. Hence their error about the veritable being of gods.

CLINIAS: I am still in the dark.   892

ATHENIAN: Soul, my friend, soul is that of whose nature and potency all but the few would seem to know nothing; in this general ignorance of it they know not in particular of its origin, how it is among the primal things, elder-born than all bodies and prime source of all their changes and transformations. But if this is indeed so, must not all that is akin to soul needs be of earlier birth than all that is b proper to bodies, seeing that soul herself is older than body?

CLINIAS: Why, necessarily.

ATHENIAN: And so judgment and foresight, wisdom, art and law, must be prior to hard and soft, heavy and light. Aye, and the grand primal works and deeds, for the very reason that they are primal, will prove to be those of art; those of nature, and nature herself—wrongly so called—will be secondary and derivative from art and mind.

CLINIAS: Wrongly so called? Why wrongly?   c

ATHENIAN: Why, by *nature* they mean what was there to begin with, but if we can show that soul came first—that it was not fire, nor air, but soul which was there to begin with—it will be perfectly true to say that it is the existence of soul which is most eminently *natural*. Now this is the case if it can be proved that soul is more ancient than body, and not otherwise.

CLINIAS: How true that is!

ATHENIAN: Then our next step must be to address ourselves to the proof of that point.   d

CLINIAS : Yes, of course.

ATHENIAN : Good. Then let us be on our guard against the extreme subtleties of the argument; we are elderly, and it a lusty stripling who may slip through our fingers by a feint—then we shall make ourselves a laughingstock, and be judged to have failed even of the little in our eagerness to reach after the greater. So reflect a moment. Suppose the three of us had to cross a river with a strong current, and I, being the youngest of the party and having a wide experience of e such currents, were to say, I must first try the crossing by myself, leaving you in safety, to see whether the water is equally fordable for you, my elders, or not. If it proves so, afterward I must call to you and help you across it by my experience, but if it turns out to be out of the depth of men of your years, the risk will have been all mine. You would think this a reasonable suggestion. Well, it is even so with the waters of discourse which confront us now; the current is strong, and the passage perhaps too much for your strength. So to save you 893 from being dizzied and staggered by the rush of questions you are unpracticed in answering, and the consequent unpleasantness of an undignified and unbecoming situation, I propose that I should act in this same fashion now. I will first put certain questions to myself while you listen in safety, and then once more give the answers to them myself. This plan will be followed throughout the argument until our discussion of the soul is completed, and its priority to body proved.

CLINIAS : An admirable proposal, sir. Pray, act upon it.

b   ATHENIAN : To the work, then, and if we are ever to beseech God's help, let it be done now. Let us take it as understood that the gods have, of course, been invoked in all earnest to assist our proof of their own being, and plunge into the waters of the argument before us with the prayer as a sure guiding rope for our support. If put to the proof, then, on such a subject, the safest course, I take it, is to meet the following questions with the following answers.

Sir—so someone may say—are all things at rest, and nothing in motion? Or is the truth the very reverse? Or are some things in mo- c tion, others at rest?

Of course, I shall reply, some are moving and others at rest.

And those which move are moving, just as those which are at rest are resting, in a space of some kind?

Of course.

And some of them, you will grant, do this in a single situation, others in more than one?

When you speak of moving in a single situation, I shall reply, you refer to things characterized by the immobility of their centers, as is the case with the revolution of so-called 'sleeping' circles.

Yes.

And we observe, in the case of this revolution, that such a motion carries round the greatest and the smallest circle together, dividing

itself proportionately to lesser and greater, and being itself propor- d
tionately less and greater. This, in fact, is what makes it a source of all
sorts of marvels, since it supplies greater and smaller circles at once
with velocities high or low answering to their sizes—an effect one
might have imagined impossible.

Just so.

And by things which move in several situations I suppose you
mean those which have a motion of translation and shift at every moment to a fresh place, sometimes having a single point of support,
sometimes, in the case of rolling, more than one. In their various en- e
counters one with another, collision with a stationary object disin-
tegrates, while impact upon other moving objects coming from an
opposite quarter integrates them into new combinations which are betwixt and between the original components?

Yes, I grant the facts are as you state them.

And further, with integration goes augmentation in bulk, and
reduction of bulk with disintegration—provided, that is, the pre-
established constitution of the object persists. If it does not, both processes give rise to dissolution.

But the condition under which coming-to-be universally takes
place—what is it?

Manifestly 'tis effected whenever its starting point has received 894
increment and so come to its second stage, and from this to the next,
and so by three steps acquired perceptibility to percipients. 'Tis ever by
such change and transformation of motion that a thing comes to be;
it is in veritable being so long as it persists. When it has changed to a
different constitution, it is utterly destroyed. Perhaps, my friends, we
have now classed and numbered all the types of motion—except, in- b
deed, two.

CLINIAS: And what are those two?

ATHENIAN: Why, the very pair, my good sir, with an eye to
which our whole discussion is now in progress.

CLINIAS: I must ask you to be plainer.

ATHENIAN: The discussion began with a view to soul, did it
not?

CLINIAS: To be sure, it did.

ATHENIAN: Then let us take for one of our pair the motion
which can regularly set other things in movement but not itself. As a
second single type in the scheme of motions in general we will take
that which can regularly set itself going as well as other things, alike
in processes of integration and disintegration, by way of augmentation
and its opposite, or by coming into and perishing out of being.   c

CLINIAS: And so we will.

ATHENIAN: We may proceed, then, to place the type which regularly moves some object other than itself, and is itself induced by
such an object, ninth on our list. That which moves itself as well as

other things—it finds its place in all doing and all being-done-to, and is veritably called transformation and motion of all that is—this we will reckon as tenth.

CLINIAS: Yes, certainly.

ATHENIAN: Now of these ten motions which should we be most right to pronounce most powerful of all, and most superlatively d effective?

CLINIAS: Why, of course, we are bound to say that that which can move itself is infinitely most effective, and all the rest posterior to it.

ATHENIAN: Excellent. Then we should perhaps find one or two mistakes in what has just been said?

CLINIAS: And what mistakes are they?

ATHENIAN: We were wrong, I think, in using that word *tenth.*

CLINIAS: But why wrong?

ATHENIAN: It is demonstrably *first* in procedure, as in power, and the next in order is, as we hold, *second,* though we have just e called it—oddly enough—ninth.

CLINIAS: How am I to understand you?

ATHENIAN: Why, thus. When we have one thing making a change in a second, the second, in turn, in a third, and so on—will there ever, in such a series, be a first source of change? Why, how can what is set moving by something other than itself ever be the first of the causes of alteration? The thing is an impossibility. But when something which has set itself moving alters a second thing, this second thing still a third, and the motion is thus passed on in course to 895 thousands and tens of thousands of things, will there be any starting point for the whole movement of all, other than the change in the movement which initiated itself?

CLINIAS: Admirably put, and the position must be conceded.

ATHENIAN: Besides, let us put the point over again in this way, once more answering our own question. Suppose all things were to come together and stand still—as most of the party have the hardihood to affirm. Which of the movements we have specified must be the b first to arise in things? Why, of course, that which can move itself; there can be no possible previous origination of change by anything else, since, by hypothesis, change was not previously existent in the system. Consequently, as the source of all motions whatsoever, the first to occur among bodies at rest and the first in rank in moving bodies, the motion which initiates itself we shall pronounce to be necessarily the earliest and mightiest of all changes, while that which is altered by something else and sets something else moving is secondary.

CLINIAS: Unquestionably.

ATHENIAN: Then, now that the discussion has reached this c point, we may answer a further question.

CLINIAS : And what question is it?

ATHENIAN : When we see that this motion has shown itself in a thing composed of earth, water, or fire—separately or in combination —how should we describe the character resident in such a thing?

CLINIAS : Am I right in supposing you to ask whether, when the thing moves itself, we speak of it as *alive?*

ATHENIAN : Certainly.

CLINIAS : Alive? Of course it is alive.

ATHENIAN : Very well, and when we see soul in a thing, the case is the same, is it not? We must allow that the thing is alive.

CLINIAS : Precisely.

ATHENIAN : In heaven's name, then, hold. You will grant, I d presume, that there are three points to be noted about anything?

CLINIAS : You mean?

ATHENIAN : I mean, for one, the reality of the thing, what it *is,* for another the *definition* of this reality, for another, its *name.* And thus you see there are two questions we can ask about everything which is.

CLINIAS : And what are the two?

ATHENIAN : Sometimes a man propounds the bare name and demands the definition; sometimes, again, he propounds the definition by itself and asks for the corresponding name. In other words, we mean something to this effect, do we not?

CLINIAS : To what effect?

ATHENIAN : There is, as you know, bisection in numbers, as in e other things. Well, in the case of a number, the *name* of the thing is 'even,' and the definition, 'number divisible into two equal parts.'

CLINIAS : Certainly.

ATHENIAN : That is the sort of case I have in mind. We are denoting the same thing, are we not, in either case, whether we are asked about the definition and reply with the name, or about the name, and reply with the definition? It is the same thing we describe indifferently by the name 'even,' and the definition, 'number divided into two equal parts'?

CLINIAS : Identically the same.

ATHENIAN : Well then, what is the definition of the thing for which *soul* is the name? Can we find any but the phrase we have just 896 used, 'the motion which can set itself moving'?

CLINIAS : You mean that the selfsame reality which has the name *soul* in the vocabulary of all of us has *self-movement* as its definition?

ATHENIAN : I do. But if this is indeed so, is there anything we can desiderate, anything further toward complete demonstration of the identity of soul with the primal becoming and movement of all that is, has been, or shall be, and of all their contraries, seeing it has disclosed itself as the universal cause of all change and motion?   b

CLINIAS: No, indeed. Our proof that soul, since it is found to be the source of movement, is the first-born of all things is absolutely complete.

ATHENIAN: Then must not the motion which, wherever it arises, is induced by something else, but never confers the power of self-motion on anything, come second in the scale, or as low down as you please to put it, being, in fact, change in a truly soulless body?

CLINIAS: Rightly argued.

ATHENIAN: Consequently it will be a right, decisive, true, and
c final statement to assert, as we did, that soul is prior to body, body secondary and derivative, soul governing in the real order of things, and body being subject to governance.

CLINIAS: Indeed it would.

ATHENIAN: But we have not, I imagine, forgotten our earlier agreement that if soul could be proved older than body, the characters of soul must also be older than those of body.

CLINIAS: Not in the least.

ATHENIAN: And so moods and habits of mind, wishes, calcula-
d tions, and true judgments, purposes, and memories, will all be prior to physical lengths, breadths, and depths, in virtue of the priority of soul itself to body.

CLINIAS: Inevitably so.

ATHENIAN: Hence we are driven, are we not, to agree in the consequence that soul is the cause of good and evil, fair and foul, right and wrong—in fact of all contraries, if we mean to assert it as the *universal* cause?

CLINIAS: Certainly we are.

ATHENIAN: Well then, if indwelling soul thus controls all things
e universally that move anywhere, are we not bound to say it controls heaven itself?

CLINIAS: Yes, of course.

ATHENIAN: And is this done by one single soul, or by more than one? I will give the answer for both of you. By more than one. At least we must assume not fewer than two, one beneficent, the other capable of the contrary effect.

CLINIAS: Decidedly you are in the right of it.

ATHENIAN: So far, so good. Soul, then, by her own motions stirs all things in sky, earth, or sea—and the names of these motions
897 are wish, reflection, foresight, counsel, judgment, true or false, pleasure, pain, hope, fear, hate, love—stirs them, I say, by these and whatever other kindred, or primary, motions there may be. They, in turn, bring in their train secondary and corporeal movements, and so guide all things to increase and decrease, disgregation and integration, with their attendant characters of heat and cold, weight and lightness, hardness and softness, white and black, dry and sweet. By these and
b all her instruments, when wisdom is her helper, she conducts all things

to the right and happy issue, whereas when she companies with folly, the effect is entirely contrary. Shall we set it down that this is so, or have we still our doubts that it may be otherwise?

CLINIAS: Nay, there is no doubt whatsoever.

ATHENIAN: Then which manner of soul, must we say, has control of heaven and earth and their whole circuit? That which is prudent and replete with goodness, or that which has neither virtue? Shall we, if you please, give the question this answer?   c

CLINIAS: What answer?

ATHENIAN: Why, my friend, if the whole path and movement of heaven and all its contents are of like nature with the motion, revolution, and calculations of wisdom, and proceed after that kind, plainly we must say it is the supremely good soul that takes forethought for the universe and guides it along that path.

CLINIAS: True.

ATHENIAN: But the evil, if the procedure is distraught and with-   d
out order.

CLINIAS: That is true, too.

ATHENIAN: Then of what nature, pray, is the movement of wisdom? There, my friends, we reach a question hard to be answered with due understanding. So it is only fair that I too should have a hand in your present reply.

CLINIAS: A welcome proposal.

ATHENIAN: Then let us beware of creating a darkness at noonday for ourselves by gazing, so to say, direct at the sun as we give our answer, as though we could hope to attain adequate vision and perception of wisdom with mortal eyes. It will be the safer course to turn our gaze on an image of the object of our quest.   e

CLINIAS: You mean to say?

ATHENIAN: Let us take as that image the motion in our list of ten to which wisdom bears a resemblance. We will all recall it, as I join you in giving our answer.

CLINIAS: An excellent proposal.

ATHENIAN: Then do we still remember this much of what we said, that we decided that some things are in motion and others at rest?

CLINIAS: We do.

ATHENIAN: And that some of those in motion move in one place, others in more than one?   898

CLINIAS: Certainly.

ATHENIAN: Of these two movements, that confined to one place must in every case be performed about a center, after the fashion of a well-turned cartwheel, and it is this which must surely have the closest affinity and resemblance that may be to the revolution of intelligence.

CLINIAS: Your meaning is?

ATHENIAN: Why, of course, that if we say that intelligence and movement performed in one place are both like the revolutions of a
b well-made globe, in moving regularly and uniformly in one compass about one center, and in one sense, according to one single law and plan, we need have no fear of proving unskilled artists in imagery.

CLINIAS: Very true.

ATHENIAN: And again, motion which is never regular or uniform, never in the same compass, nor about the same center, or in one place, motion which has no order, plan, or law, will have kinship with folly of every kind.

CLINIAS: Indeed it will.

c ATHENIAN: *Now* there can be no further obstacle to positive assertion, since we have found that it is soul which conducts the revolutions of all things, and are also bound to say that the soul by which the circle of the heavens is turned about with all foresight and order is either the supremely good, or its contrary . . .

CLINIAS: Nay, sir, if what has gone before is true, it were blasphemy to ascribe the work to aught but a soul or souls—one or more than one—of absolute goodness.

ATHENIAN: You have followed the argument to good purpose
d indeed, Clinias, but I would have you follow it a step farther still.

CLINIAS: And what is that step?

ATHENIAN: Take sun, and moon, and the other heavenly bodies. If the revolution of all is due to soul, so also is that of each singly, is it not?

CLINIAS: Why, of course.

ATHENIAN: Thus we may take one of them in particular as the subject of an argument we shall find no less applicable to all these celestial bodies.

CLINIAS: And which of them shall we take?

ATHENIAN: The sun, whose body can be seen by any man, but his soul by no man, any more than that of any other creature's body is to be seen, during life or at the time of death. We have every reason
e to believe that it infolds us in a fashion utterly imperceptible to all bodily senses, and is only to be discerned by the understanding. So here is a relevant consideration which we must apprehend by an act of pure understanding and thought.

CLINIAS: And what is it?

ATHENIAN: Since soul guides the sun on his course, we cannot well go wrong in saying that she must act in one of three ways.

CLINIAS: And what are the three?

ATHENIAN: Either she dwells within this visible round body and conveys it hither and thither, as our soul carries us wherever we go, or, as some hold, she provides herself a body of her own, of fire, or it
899 may be of air, and pushes body from without forcibly by body, or fi-

nally, she is herself naked of body, and does this work of guidance by
some other most miraculous faculties of hers.

CLINIAS: Yes, one of these ways is that by which soul transacts
the whole business. So much is sure.

ATHENIAN: This soul, whether we take it to bring light to the
world by driving the sun as its car, or from without, or in what way
soever, each of us should esteem a god, should he not?

CLINIAS: He should, if not sunk in the very depths of folly.   b

ATHENIAN: Of all the planets, of the moon, of years and months
and all seasons, what other story shall we have to tell than just this
same, that since soul, or souls, and those souls good with perfect goodness, have proved to be the causes of all, these souls we hold to be
gods, whether they direct the universe by inhabiting bodies, like animated beings, or whatever the manner of their action? Will any man
who shares this belief bear to hear it said that all things are not 'full of
gods'? [11]

CLINIAS: No man, sir, can be so much beside himself.   c

ATHENIAN: Then, my dear Megillus and Clinias, we may state
our terms to him who has hitherto declined to acknowledge gods and
dispose of him.

CLINIAS: What terms shall we offer?

ATHENIAN: Either he must show us that we are wrong in pronouncing soul the primary source of all things, and in the further
consequences we drew, or if unable to get the better of our reasoning,
he must yield to us and live henceforth a believer in gods. Let us con-   d
sider, then, whether our defense of the being of gods against the unbeliever is now duly complete or defective.

CLINIAS: Defective, sir? Anything but that.

ATHENIAN: Then, so far as concerns that party, let our discourse come to its end. We are now to admonish him who confesses
the being of gods but denies that they take any heed of the affairs of
men. Fair sir, we will say, as to your belief in gods, 'tis perhaps some
kinship with the divine that draws you to your native stock in worship
and acknowledgment. On the other side there are private and public
fortunes of ill and wicked men—fortunes truly unblessed, but pas-   e
sionately, though tastelessly, extolled as blessed by the voice of public
repute—and these draw you toward irreligion when you hear them
wrongly harped upon in poetry and literature of all kinds. Or, it may
be, you remark men who have come to the grave in fullness of days   900
and left sons and sons' sons after them in high honors, and now you
are dismayed when you find, from what you have heard from others or
from your own personal observation of sundry deeds of impiety and
horror in their histories, that some of the number have risen by these

[11] Thales, in Aristotle, *De anima* 411ª 7 sq.

very crimes from obscurity to pre-eminence and a throne. The visible consequence of it all is that at such moments, while your kinship with the gods will not permit you to charge them with the responsibility

b for this, ill reasoning and inability to reproach the gods have together brought you to your present pass, your conviction that though they indeed exist, they despise and disregard humanity. So, that your present creed may lead you to no worse pitch of impiety, that the specter, as we may say, may happily be laid, as it approaches, by the power of argument, we must try to connect what now remains to be said with our original rejoinder to the complete atheist, and so have the benefit of that also.

c   You, Clinias—and you too, Megillus—must, as before, take the young man's place as respondent. And if the argument should chance to miscarry, I will once more take the task off your hands and put you across the waters.

CLINIAS : A sound proposal. Act on it, then, and we, too, will do our best to carry out your suggestions.

ATHENIAN: Well, perhaps it would not be hard to establish as much as this, that the gods are more, not less, careful for small things

d than for great. The man was present, you know, at our recent discussion and was told that the gods, who are good with perfect goodness, have the universal charge of all things as their special and proper function.

CLINIAS : He was most certainly told so.

ATHENIAN: Then let them join us in asking what we mean by the goodness in virtue of which we confess the gods to be good. Come, now, prudence, may we say, and understanding belong to goodness, their opposites to badness?

CLINIAS : We may.

e   ATHENIAN: And again that valor is part of goodness, cowardice of badness?

CLINIAS : Assuredly.

ATHENIAN: And the latter qualities we shall call shameful, the former noble?

CLINIAS : No doubt we must.

ATHENIAN: And all the baser qualities, we shall say, belong, if to anyone, to ourselves; gods have no part in them, great or small.

CLINIAS : That, too, will be universally conceded.

ATHENIAN: Well, then, shall we set down negligence, indolence, petulance as goodness of soul? How say you?

CLINIAS : Nay, how could we?

ATHENIAN: As its opposite, then?

CLINIAS : Yes.

901   ATHENIAN: Then *their* opposites will be referred to *its* opposite?

CLINIAS : They will.

ATHENIAN: Very well, then. Anyone who is petulant, negligent, or indolent must be pronounced such a character as that the poet called 'most like a stingless drone.' [12]

CLINIAS: And an excellent comparison it is.

ATHENIAN: Then it must never be said that God has such a character as this, a character God himself abhors, or if anyone ventures on such a speech, we must forbid him.

CLINIAS: Indeed we must. How could we do otherwise?

ATHENIAN: If one has the office of action and peculiar care of b some charge, and his mind, though careful in great matters, is negligent in small, what ground could we find for commendation of such a one that would not ring false? We may look at the case thus. The conduct of him who behaves thus, be he god or man, may take either of two forms, may it not?

CLINIAS: Either of what two forms?

ATHENIAN: Either he thinks neglect of little details makes no difference to the total result, or if it makes a difference which he dis- c regards, he shows indolence or petulance. Can we, in fact, ascribe negligence to any other causes? For, of course, where concern for a whole is *impossible*, it is no negligence of the little or the great, in god or in ordinary mortal, to make no provision for that to which one's powers are not equal, and for which one is thus unable to provide.

CLINIAS: Of course not.

ATHENIAN: Very well. Now for an answer to the interrogation of the three of us from the two parties who both confess the being of d gods, but gods whom the one holds to be venal and the other negligent of little details. You both admit, to begin with, that the gods perceive, see, and hear everything, that nothing within the compass of sense or knowledge can fall outside their cognizance. That is your position, is it not?

CLINIAS: It is.

ATHENIAN: And further that they can do all that is possible to be done by mortal or immortal?

CLINIAS: Why, of course, they will concede that admission too.

ATHENIAN: Besides, all five of us have already agreed that they e are good, and superlatively good.

CLINIAS: Beyond all doubt.

ATHENIAN: Must we not then confess it a sheer impossibility that there should be any indolence or petulance in their conduct, so long as their character is such as we concede it to be. In ourselves, you know, want of courage gives birth to sloth, and sloth and petulance to indolence.

CLINIAS: True, indeed.

[12] *Works and Days* 303 sq.

ATHENIAN: No god, then, can be negligent from sloth or indolence, for none, we may presume, has any lack of courage.

CLINIAS: Rightly argued, indeed.

902   ATHENIAN: Then if they indeed neglect the trivial matters and minor details of the universe, we must conclude either that they do so with the knowledge that there is no need whatsoever of attention to such points or—what other alternative is left but the contrary of knowledge?

CLINIAS: None whatever.

ATHENIAN: Well, then, my dear good man, which view must we take you to hold? That they act in ignorance and neglect due to ignorance where attention ought to be shown, or that they are aware that attention is needed, and yet behave as the sorriest sort of men are said b to do—men who know a better course than that they actually take, but leave it alone from some inferiority to pleasures or pains?

CLINIAS: Out of the question altogether.

ATHENIAN: Well, then, is not human life a part of animated nature, and man himself moreover the most god-fearing of all living creatures?

CLINIAS: Why, yes, to all appearances.

ATHENIAN: And surely we hold that all living creatures, like the world as a whole, are chattels of the gods?

CLINIAS: To be sure we do.

ATHENIAN: 'Tis all one, then, whether a man counts such things c small or great in the eyes of heaven; in neither case can it become our owners, provident and all-good as they are, to neglect them. For here is a still further point for our consideration.

CLINIAS: And what may it be?

ATHENIAN: Whether there is not a natural opposition between perception and power in respect of their ease or difficulty.

CLINIAS: In what way?

ATHENIAN: Why, that 'tis harder to see or hear the little than the great, whereas everyone finds it easier to move, wield, superintend the small and few than their contraries.

d   CLINIAS: Emphatically so.

ATHENIAN: But suppose a physician who has the task of treating a whole body is willing and able to give his attention to the large masses but neglects the minor members and parts. Will his whole subject ever be in good condition?

CLINIAS: No, never.

ATHENIAN: Nor yet will seamen, captains, householders, or again statesmen, as they are called, or persons with any other such functions make a success of the many or the great tasks apart from the few and the little. Why, even the hedger will tell you that the large e stones will not lie well without the small.

CLINIAS: Of course they will not.

ATHENIAN: We are never, then, to fancy God the inferior of human workmen. The better they are at their work, the more exactly and perfectly do they accomplish their proper tasks, small or great, in virtue of one and the same skill, and we must never suppose that 903 God, who is at once supremely wise and both willing and able to provide, makes no provision for the small matters, which we have found it easier to care for, but only for the great, like some idle fellow or faintheart who shirks his work from fear of exertion.

CLINIAS: Nay, sir, let us never entertain such a belief about gods; the thought would be wholly impious and utterly false.

ATHENIAN: And now, I take it, we have had quite enough of controversy with him who is prone to charge the gods with negligence.

CLINIAS: We have.

ATHENIAN: I mean so far as forcing him by argument to confess his error will go. Still something more, I believe, needs to be b said by way of a charm for him.

CLINIAS: And what shall it be, my friend?

ATHENIAN: Why, our discourse must persuade the young man that he who provides for the world has disposed all things with a view to the preservation and perfection of the whole, wherefore each several thing also, so far as may be, does and has done to it what is meet. And for each and all there are, in every case, governors appointed of all doing and being-done-to, down to the least detail, who have achieved perfection even to the minute particulars. Thine own being c also, fond man, is one such fragment, and so, for all its littleness, all its striving is ever directed toward the whole, but thou hast forgotten in the business that the purpose of all that happens is what we have said, to win bliss for the life of the whole; it is not made for thee, but thou for it. For any physician or craftsman in any profession does all his work for the sake of some whole, but the part he fashions for the sake of the whole, to contribute to the general good, not the whole for the part's sake. And yet thou dost murmur because thou seest not how d in thine own case what is best for the whole proves best also for thyself in virtue of our common origin. And seeing that a soul, in its successive conjunction first with one body and then with another, runs the whole gamut of change through its own action or that of some other soul, no labor is left for the mover of the pieces but this—to shift the character that is becoming better to a better place, and that which is growing worse to a worser, each according to its due, that each may meet with its proper doom.   e

CLINIAS: Shift it—but how?

ATHENIAN: Why, I believe I can show you how universal superintendence may be easy enough for gods. In fact, if in his constant regard for the whole, an artificer were to mold everything by new transformations—fashioning fire, for example, into cold water— instead of producing variety from unity or unity from variety, by the 904 time things had reached a first, second, or third generation the variations in the changing configuration would be infinitely numerous. But as it is, he who provides for the universe has an admirably light task.

CLINIAS: Once more—your meaning?

ATHENIAN: I mean this. Since our king perceived that all our actions have soul in them and contain much virtue and likewise much vice, and that the complex of soul and body when once it has come to be, though not eternal, is, like the gods recognized by law, imperisha-

b ble—for there would be no procreation of living creatures were either of the pair to be destroyed—and since he considered that 'tis ever the nature of such soul as is good to work blessing and of such as is evil to work harm—since he saw all this, I say, he contrived where to post each several item so as to provide most utterly, easily, and well for the triumph of virtue and rout of vice throughout the whole. Thus he has contrived to this universal end the seat or regions which must receive either type of soul as it is formed in their inhabitants, but the causes of

c the formation of either type he left free to our individual volitions. For as a man's desires tend, and as is the soul that conceives them, so and such, as a general rule, does every one of us come to be.

CLINIAS: 'Tis a fair presumption.

ATHENIAN: Thus all things that have part in soul change, for the cause of change lies within themselves, and as they change they move in accord with the ordinance and law of destiny. If their changes of character are unimportant and few, they are transferred over the surface of the soil; if they are more and in the direction of

d grave wickedness, they fall into the depths and the so-called underworld, the region known by the name of Hades and the like appellations, which fill the fancy of quick and departed alike with dreams of dismay. If a soul have drunk still deeper of vice or virtue, by reason of its own volition and the potent influence of past converse with others, when near contact with divine goodness has made it itself especially

e godlike, so surely is it removed to a special place of utter holiness, and translated to another and a better world, or, in the contrary case, transported to live in the opposite realm. This, my boy, or my lad, who deemest thyself forgotten by heaven, 'is the doom of the gods who dwell on Olympus' [13]—that he that grows better shall make his way to the better souls and he that has grown worse to the worser, and so, in life, and throughout the series of deaths, do and have done to

905 him what it is meet the like-minded should do to their likes. This doom of heaven be sure neither thyself nor any other that has fallen on ill ways shall ever claim to have escaped; 'tis that which the fashioners of doom have established before all others and that which should be shunned with utter dread. It will never leave thee forgotten. Though thou make thyself never so small and creep into the depths of earth, or

[13] *Odyssey* 19.43.

exalt thyself and mount up to heaven, yet shalt thou pay them the due
penalty, either while thou art still here among us, or after thy departure in Hades, or, it may be, by translation to some yet grimmer b
region. 'Twill be the same, thou must know, with them also whom
thou hast seen raised from small beginnings to greatness by deeds of
sacrilege or the like, and fancied to have passed from misery to blessedness, whence thou thoughtest their fortunes a mirror wherein to
behold the utter carelessness of the gods, knowing not how their contribution plays its part in the whole. Yet how, thou hardiest of men,
canst thou doubt thy need of the knowledge? Nay, if a man has it not, c
he will never catch so much as a vestige of the truth, or be in case to
say a word of life's happiness or disasters. If friend Clinias and the rest
of our band of elders here assembled can convince thee of this much,
that thou sayest of the gods thou knowest not what, why, 'tis well, and
God's grace be thy aid! But if thou shouldst perchance need further
argument, then listen, if thou hast any understanding, while we reason d
with our third antagonist. For that gods there are, and that they are
concerned for mankind, has, I would maintain, been shown by no contemptible proofs. But that gods can be perverted by the receipt of gifts
from the wicked, that again is what none must admit and we must
dispute to the best of our power.

CLINIAS: Well said. Let us do so.

ATHENIAN: Why, then, I ask you, in the name of these same
gods, what can be the mode of the perversion, if indeed they are to e
be perverted? And what or what manner of beings must they be themselves? Governors, to be sure, they must be supposed to be, if they
are to have effective control of the whole universe.

CLINIAS: No doubt.

ATHENIAN: But what kind of governors are they like? Or what
kind whom we can by any possibility compare rightly with them, as
less with greater, are like them? Would drivers of contending teams, or
captains of competing vessels, be a proper parallel? Or we might perhaps compare them with commanders of armies in the field, or they
may even resemble physicians defending the body from the onslaughts 906
of disease, or husbandmen anxiously apprehending recurrent seasons of danger for their crops, or again overseers of flocks and herds.
For since, as we have agreed among ourselves, the world is full of
good things, but no less full of their contraries, and those that are
amiss are the more numerous, the fight we have in mind is, we maintain, undying and calls for a wondrous watchfulness; gods and spirits
are our allies in the warfare and we, moreover, the property of these
gods and spirits. Wrong, arrogance, and folly are our undoing; right- b
eousness, temperance, and wisdom, our salvation, and these have
their home in the living might of the gods, though some faint trace of
them is also plainly to be seen dwelling here within ourselves. Yet it
should seem there are souls inhabiting our earth in possession of

unrighteous spoil—bestial souls, these, beyond a doubt, who grovel before the souls of our guardians—watchdogs, shepherds, supreme
c masters of all, alike—and would fain persuade them by fawning speeches and witcheries of supplication—such is the tale told by the wicked—that it is lawful for them to encroach upon mankind without grievous consequence. But our contention, I take it, is that this vice I have just named of encroachment when found in bodies of flesh and blood is what is called *disease,* when found in seasons and whole years, *pestilence,* while in societies and politics it shows itself once more under the changed designation of *iniquity.*

CLINIAS : Just so.

ATHENIAN : So the case of one who teaches that the gods are
d always indulgent to the unrighteous and the wrongdoer, if a share of the plunder is assigned them, comes inevitably to this. 'Tis as though the wolf should assign some small part of his spoil to the sheep dog, and the dog, pacified by the present, agree to the ravaging of the flock. That is the case of those who hold the gods to be venal, is it not?

CLINIAS : It is indeed.

ATHENIAN : Well, then, with which of our former list of guardians can a man compare the gods without absurdity? With sea-
e men who are 'turned from their course by "flow and fragrance" of wine' [14] and overturn vessel and crew?

CLINIAS : Surely not.

ATHENIAN : And surely not with charioteers placed for the race but won over by a bribe to forfeit the victory to another team?

CLINIAS : Nay, your comparison will be a shocking one if you say that.

ATHENIAN : And certainly not with commanders, physicians, or husbandmen, nor yet with herdsmen nor with sheep dogs on whom wolves have cast a spell?

CLINIAS : Flat blasphemy! Quite impossible!

907 ATHENIAN : Now are not the gods, one and all, our chiefest guardians, and the interests they guard our chief interests?

CLINIAS : Aye, and by far.

ATHENIAN : And shall we pronounce those who have the noblest of things to guard and are themselves supremely skillful in the task of guarding inferior to sheep dogs or average men, who will never betray the right for the sinful offer of a bribe from the unrighteous?

b CLINIAS : Assuredly not—the thought is not to be borne. Of all reprobates who are given to any form of ungodliness the defender of such a creed may well be most righteously condemned as the very worst and most ungodly.

ATHENIAN : Then I presume we may say our three propositions,

[14] *Iliad* 9.500.

that there are gods, that they are mindful of us, that they are never to be seduced from the path of right, are sufficiently demonstrated.

CLINIAS: Indeed you may, and my friend and I concur with your arguments.

ATHENIAN: Still I confess they have been delivered with some heat due to eagerness to triumph over these bad men. But the source of c this zeal, my dear Clinias, was apprehension that if they get the better of the argument, the wicked may fancy themselves free to *act* as they will, seeing how many strange ideas they entertain about the gods. This is what prompted me to speak with more than common vigor. If I have done never so little to influence such men toward self-reprobation and attraction toward the opposite type of character, the prelude to our laws against impiety will have been spoken to good purpose.   d

CLINIAS: Well, let us hope so, but if not, at least the cause will bring no discredit on a legislator.

ATHENIAN: So our preamble may properly be followed by a sentence which will express the sense of our laws, a general injunction to the ungodly to turn from their ways to those of godliness. For the disobedient our law against *impiety* may run as follows. If any man commit impiety of word or act, any person present shall defend the e law by giving information to the magistrates, and the first magistrates under whose notice the matter comes shall bring the case before the court appointed to deal with such offenses as the law directs. Any official failing to take action on information received shall himself be liable to be proceeded against for impiety at the suit of anyone willing to vindicate the law. In the case of conviction, the court shall impose a particular penalty on the offender for each act of impiety. Imprisonment shall form part of the penalty in all cases. And whereas there 908 are three prisons in the state, a *common jail* in the market place for the majority of cases, for safe custody of the persons of the commonalty, a second attached to the nocturnal council and known as the *house of correction,* and a third in the heart of the country in the most solitary and wildest situation available, and called by some designation suggestive of *punishment,* and whereas also there are three causes of impiety, those we have already specified, and each such b cause gives rise to two types of offense, there will be, in all, six classes of offenders against religion to be discriminated, who require different and dissimilar treatment. For though a man should be a complete unbeliever in the being of gods, if he have also a native uprightness of temper, he will detest evil men, his repugnance to wrong disinclines him to commit wrongful acts, he shuns the unrighteous and is drawn c to the upright. But those in whom the conviction that the world has no place in it for gods is conjoined with incontinence of pleasure and pain and the possession of a vigorous memory and a keen intelligence share the malady of atheism with the other sort, but are sure to work more harm, where the former do less, in the way of mischief to their fellows. The first man may probably be free-spoken enough about gods, sacrifices, and oaths, and perhaps, if he does not meet with

d his deserts, his mockery may make converts of others. But the second, who holds the same creed as the other, but is what is popularly called a 'man of parts,' a fellow of plentiful subtlety and guile—that is the type which furnishes our swarms of diviners and fanatics for all kinds of imposture; on occasion also it produces dictators, demagogues, generals, contrivers of private Mysteries, and the arts and tricks of

e the so-called Sophist. Thus there are numerous types of these atheists, but two which legislation must take into account, the hypocritical, whose crimes deserve more than one death, or even two, and the others, who call for the combination of admonition with confinement. Similarly, the belief in divine indifference gives rise to two further types, and that in divine venality to another two.

These distinctions once recognized, the law shall direct the judge to commit those whose fault is due to folly apart from vicious-

909 ness of temper or disposition to the house of correction for a term of not less than five years. Throughout this period they shall have no communication with any citizen except the members of the nocturnal council, who shall visit them with a view to admonition and their souls' salvation. When the term of confinement has expired, if the prisoner is deemed to have returned to his right mind, he shall dwell with the right-minded, but if not, and he be condemned a second time on the same charge, he shall suffer the penalty of death. As for those

b who add the character of a beast of prey to their atheism or belief in divine indifference or venality, those who in their contempt of mankind bewitch so many of the living by the pretense of evoking the dead and the promise of winning over the gods by the supposed sorceries of prayer, sacrifice, and incantations, and thus do their best for lucre to ruin individuals, whole families, and communities, the law shall direct the court to sentence a culprit convicted of belonging to

c this class to incarceration in the central prison, where no free citizen whatsoever shall have access to him, and where he shall receive from the turnkeys the strict rations prescribed by the curators of the laws. At death he shall be cast out beyond the borders without burial, and if any free citizen has a hand in his burial, he shall be liable to a prosecution for impiety at the suit of any who cares to take proceedings. But should he leave children fit to be citizens, the guardians of

d orphans shall provide for them also, no worse than for other orphans, from the date of the father's conviction.

Moreover we must frame a law applicable to all these offenders alike, and designed to alleviate the sin of most of them against religion in word or act—to say nothing of the folly of the sinners—by the prohibition of illegal ceremonial. In fact the following law should be enacted for all cases without exception. No man shall possess a shrine in his private house; when a man feels himself moved to offer sacrifice, he shall go to the public temples for that purpose and deliver his offerings to the priests of either sex whose business it is to conse- e crate them. He may join with himself in the prayers any persons whose company he may desire. This regulation shall be adopted for the reasons following. The founding of a sanctuary or cult is no light task; to discharge it properly demands some serious thought. But it is the common way, especially with all women, with the sick universally, with persons in danger or any sort of distress, as on the other hand with those who have enjoyed a stroke of good fortune, to dedicate whatever 910 comes to hand at the moment and vow sacrifices and endowments to gods, spirits, and sons of gods, as prompted by fears of portents beheld in waking life, or by dreams. Similarly, the recollection of endless visions and the quest of a specific for them commonly lead to a filling of every house and village with shrines and altars erected in clear spaces or wherever such persons are minded to place them. All these are grounds for conformity with the law now proposed, and there is the further ground that it serves as a check on the ungodly. It prevents them from fraud in this matter itself, from setting up shrines b and altars in their own houses, under the delusion that they are winning the privy favor of heaven by offerings and prayers, thus indefinitely aggravating their criminality and bringing guilt before God on themselves and the better men who tolerate their conduct, until the whole community reaps the harvest of their impiety—as in a sense it deserves.

Our legislator, in any case, shall be clear before God, for his enactment shall run thus. No citizen to possess a shrine in his private dwelling house; in the case of proved possession, or worship at any shrine other than the public, if the possessor, whether man or woman, c have committed no serious act of impiety, he that discovers the fact shall proceed to lay an information before the curators of the law, who shall direct the private shrine to be removed to a public temple, and, in the case of disobedience, impose penalties until the removal is d effected. Any person proved guilty of a sin against piety which is the crime of a grown man, not the trivial offense of a child, whether by dedicating a shrine on private ground or by doing sacrifice to any gods whatsoever in public, shall suffer death for doing sacrifice in a state of defilement. What offenses are or are not puerile shall be decided by the curators, who shall bring the offenders accordingly before the courts and inflict the penalty.

BOOK XI

ATHENIAN: Our next need will, of course, be a proper regulation 913 of our business transactions with each other. A simple general rule, I take it, might be expressed thus. I would have no one touch my property, if I can help it, or disturb it in the slightest way without some kind of consent on my part; if I am a man of sense, I must treat the property of others in the same way. We will take as a first instance treasure which someone, not being an ancestor of my own, has amassed as store for himself and his descendants. I must never pray

b to find such treasure. If I do find it, I must not meddle with it; I must breathe no word of it to diviners, as they are called, who are certain to recommend me to appropriate what has been committed to earth's keeping. If I appropriate it, the benefit to my fortunes will assuredly be more contracted than the expansion I shall gain in moral goodness and rectitude by leaving it alone. Purchase for purchase, I shall have made a better bargain in a better cause, if I choose to get rectitude for my soul rather than wealth for my pocket. The wise proverb which forbids moving what is better left alone has a wide range of application, and this is one of the cases to which it applies. Besides, one

c should give credence to the current tradition that such things are no blessing to a man's descendants. The man who is so careless for his posterity and deaf to the voice of the legislator that he takes up what neither he nor any of his fathers' fathers ever laid down, and that without the depositor's permission, in violation of one of the best of laws, that straightforward enactment of an illustrious man which runs, 'What thou hast not laid down, take not up'—the man, I repeat, who does despite to both these legislators and takes up what he has not

d himself laid down, and not on a petty scale either—often it is a vast heap of treasure—what shall be done to him?

What heaven will do to him, of course, is God's concern, but the first person to discover the fact shall report it, if the thing happen in the capital, to the urban commissioners, or if in the market square of the capital, to the commissioners of the market, or, if it occur out-

914 side the capital, shall bring it to the notice of the rural commission and their heads. On receipt of the information, the state shall send a deputation to Delphi. Accordingly as the god shall pronounce about the property or the disturber of it, so the state shall act by the mandate of the oracle. If the informer be a free man, he shall be commended for his virtue, and censured as vicious if he neglects to give information; if a slave, he shall receive his well-earned freedom as a gift from the state, which shall pay his owner his price, but be punished with

b death if the information is withheld. It follows by consequence that we must have this same rule alike in small matters as in great. If a man leave his property behind him in any place, voluntarily or not, he that lights upon it must let it alone undisturbed; he must regard such things as placed under the protection of the spirit of the wayside, to whom they are deemed consecrate in law. Any person who appropriates such things and carries them home with him, in contravention of the law, shall, if a slave and the article of little value, receive a sound beating from any, not being under thirty years of age, who may

fall in with him. If he be a free man, he shall be pronounced a churl c
unfit to consort with law-respecting men, and shall furthermore pay
the owner of the goods he has disturbed their value ten times over.
If a man charge another with being in possession of his property,
great or small, and the man so charged admit possession of the object
but dispute the ownership, the complainant shall, in the case of articles entered by legal requirement on the magistrates' register, summon
the party in possession before the magistrates, to whom he shall produce the article. If, upon such exhibition, such article is found to be
recorded in the register as the property of either litigant, he shall be d
put in possession of it and so dismissed. If it prove to belong to a
third party who is not in court, either party, on providing sufficient
sureties, may remove it on behalf of the absent owner and in his right,
for delivery to him. If the article in dispute be not recorded in the
register, it shall be in the custody of three senior magistrates until the
suit is decided. And if the thing so hypothecated be a beast, the loser
in the suit shall pay the authorities the cost of its keep. The magistrates
shall dispose of the case within three days.   e

Any man, provided he be sane, shall be at liberty to lay hands on
his own slave for such purpose as he may please in the way of lawful
business, and at liberty likewise to lay hands on the fugitive slave of
any kinsman or friend, with a view to his safekeeping. If a man be
thus seized as a slave and any person claim him as free and resist his
detention, the captor shall let the man go, and the party opposing the
detention shall provide three substantial sureties and stay the detention on these conditions aforesaid, and on no others. If capture is
stayed otherwise than on these conditions, there shall be an action
for assault, and the defendant, if convicted, shall pay the party whose
right has been stayed twice the value of the article, as shown by the 915
register. There shall be the like right of seizure of a freedman who pays
no homage, or insufficient homage, to the authors of his freedom.
Homage shall be deemed to mean that the freedman repair thrice in
the month to the hearth of his emancipator and make proffer of all
such services as are right and possible, and likewise that in the matter of marriage he act only with the approval of his former owner. It
shall be illegal for the freedman to possess more wealth than the emancipator, and any surplus shall belong to the master. A man thus receiving his freedom shall not prolong his residence beyond twenty b
years, but depart, like all aliens, with his estate in full, unless he can
gain permission from the magistrates and the master who enlarged
him. If the estate of a freedman or other alien come to exceed the
census of the third class, he shall within thirty days from the day on
which the excess first began, take up his property and depart, and in
this case the authorities shall have no power to grant any extension c
of residence. Any person brought before the courts for noncompliance
and convicted shall receive sentence of death, and his goods shall be

forfeit to the state. Suits of this kind shall come before the court of a tribe, save when the counterallegations of the parties have been previously disposed of before the neighbors, or before judges appointed by themselves.

d   If a man claim any other man's beast, or any other of his goods, as his own property, the party in possession shall return the article to the vendor, responsible and lawful donor, or person who otherwise made valid delivery of that article, where such person is a citizen or resident alien, within thirty days, or in the case where delivery was made by a foreigner, within a period of five months, of which months the midmost shall be that of the summer solstice. In all reciprocal exchange by means of sale and purchase, goods exchanged are to be delivered on the sites appointed in the market square for the various articles, and

e the price is to be received at the time; exchange shall not be permitted in any other locality, and there shall be neither selling nor buying on credit. If any citizen make any exchange whatever, for any return whatsoever, with another under other conditions or in a different locality, because he trusts the party with whom he is dealing, he must do so on the understanding that the law permits no action in respect of articles not vended under the conditions here specified. As to subscriptions to clubs, anyone who pleases shall be free to raise them as between friends, but if a difference arise about a subscription, the parties must conduct their affairs with the understanding that the law

916 will in no case grant an action on such grounds. If the vendor of an article receive a price of fifty drachmas or more, he shall be bound to remain in the territory for a space of ten days, and the purchaser shall be informed of the vendor's lodging with a view to the making of complaints such as are common in such cases, and satisfying the legal regulations about restitution. The legal requirements in question shall be as follows. In the case of the vending of a slave affected by phthisis, stone, strangury, or by the so-called 'holy distemper,' or other disorder of body or mind which readily escapes ordinary observation and is unamenable to treatment, if the sale were made to a physician or trainer, there shall be no right to return the article to the

b vendor; there shall likewise be none if the defect was truthfully mentioned at the time of sale. But where a professional man vends such an article to a layman, the purchaser shall have the right to return it within six months, except in the case of the 'holy distemper,' for which the period allowed for the return shall be one year. The case shall be brought before a body of physicians, to be nominated and selected by agreement between the parties, and a convicted vendor shall pay a sum double of the price at which he sold. If both parties be laymen, the

c regulations as to right of return and the trial of the issue shall be as in the former case, but the convicted vendor shall pay only the actual price received. If a man vend a slave who is a homicide, and both parties are aware of the fact, there shall be no right of return in respect of the transaction. If the purchaser be unaware, there shall be a right to return the purchase forthwith when the buyer shall discover the fact, and the case shall be heard before the five junior curators. The vendor who is adjudged to have made such sale willingly shall purify the dwelling of the purchaser as the canonists' rules require, and shall d repay the price threefold.

He that exchanges against coin other coin or any article whatsoever, animate or inanimate, shall be expected by the law in all cases to give genuine value and demand the same. But, as elsewhere in our code, let us make room for a preamble dealing with roguery of this sort at large. Everyone should understand that imposture, false pretenses, fraud, are all things of one kind, the kind which is unhappily e credited in current popular parlance with being often enough an excellent thing 'if practiced at the proper juncture.' When and where this juncture occurs is left vague and indefinite, and thus the proverb works no little mischief to the believer and the rest of society. A legislator cannot be allowed to leave the point in this uncertainty. He should always draw definite boundary lines, wider or narrower, as we shall now proceed to do. No man shall practice any imposture or fraud of word or act with the name of a god on his lips, but one that would encounter God's reprobation, and such is he who swears lying oaths in 917 contempt of heaven, and, in a lesser degree, he who lies to his superior. Now good men are the superiors of worse, the aged, speaking generally, of the youthful, and, by consequence, parents of their offspring, husbands, again, of their wives and children, magistrates of their subjects. Universal reverence is no more than the proper due of all who are in any of these positions of authority, and most of all the due of the authorities of the state, and it is of them we are now discoursing. A b man who practices an imposition in the market is lying, cheating, and calling heaven to witness by his oaths in the face of all the laws and caveats of the commissioners of markets; he has no more respect for man than fear of God. Now undoubtedly it is a becoming habit to be careful of taking divine names in vain, to show the same regard for them that most of us commonly and customarily show for ceremonial purity and cleanness in matters of worship, but if there should be any disobedience, here is our law. He that sells any article whatsoever in the market shall in no case put two prices on his wares. He shall ask one price, and if he do not get it, he will do right to take c his goods away again, and shall not, that same day, set a higher or lower price on them. Also there shall be no proffering of wares offered for sale, or vouching for them by an oath. In case of breach of this statute, any citizen present, not being under thirty years of age, shall have the law's permission to chastise the swearer of such oath by blows; a citizen making light of the matter and disregarding this provision shall be liable to censure as a traitor to the law. The vendor of a spurious article, who cannot be persuaded by our present d

discourse, shall be exposed before the authorities by any person present with the knowledge requisite for his detection; such person, if a
slave or resident alien, shall have the counterfeit article for his own
use, if a citizen and neglecting to expose the cheat, shall be declared
guilty of defrauding heaven; if he expose it, he shall publicly dedicate
the article to the gods of the market. And the party found offering such
wares for sale shall be deprived of the counterfeit goods, and shall
moreover be scourged in the market square, and receive a stripe for
e each drachma of the price he set on his goods, proclamation being first
made by a crier of the cause for the scourging. To counteract the im-
postures and knaveries of vendors, the commissioners of the market
and curators shall inform themselves by inquiry from experts in different trades, and draw up rules of what the vendor may and may not
do; these rules shall be engraved on a column to be erected in front of
the offices of the commission of the market as regulations for the more
precise direction of persons doing business in the market. The func-
918 tions of the urban commission have been described sufficiently already. If further regulations are thought needful, the commissioners
shall consult with the curators of law and draft the necessary supplement; both the earlier and later rules for their official procedure shall
be posted on a column in front of the offices of the commission.

The consideration of fraudulent practices and business leads directly to that of retail trade. We shall first deal with the subject as a
whole in the way of reasoned counsel, and then propose legal regula-
b tion for it. Internal retail trade, when one considers its essential function, is not a mischievous thing, but much the reverse. Can a man be
other than a benefactor if he effects the even and proportionate diffusion of anything in its own nature so disproportionately and unevenly
diffused as commodities of all sorts? This, we should remind ourselves,
is the very result achieved by a currency, and this, as we should recognize, the function assigned to the trader. Similarly, the wage earner,
the tavernkeeper, and other callings, some more and some less reputa-
c ble, all have the common function of meeting various demands with
supply and distributing commodities more evenly. What, then, can be
the reason why the calling is of no good credit or repute? What makes
it generally unpopular? We must look into the question if we are to
provide a partial remedy—a total cure would be beyond us—by our
legislation. The thing is well worth doing, I fancy, and calls for no
common abilities.

CLINIAS: How so?

ATHENIAN: Why, Clinias my friend, 'tis but a small section of
d mankind, a few of exceptional natural parts disciplined by consummate training, who have the resolution to prove true to moderation
when they find themselves in the full current of demands and desires.
There are not many of us who remain sober when we have the opportunity to grow wealthy, or prefer measure to abundance. The great

multitude of men are of a completely contrary temper—what they
desire they desire out of all measure—when they have the option of
making a reasonable profit, they prefer to make an exorbitant one.
This is why all classes of retailers, businessmen, tavernkeepers, are so
unpopular and under so severe a social stigma. And yet, only suppose
—an impossible supposition and heaven forbid it should be anything   e
else!—but suppose the very best of men could be compelled—the
fancy will sound ludicrous, I know, but I must give it utterance—
suppose they could be compelled to take for a time to innkeeping, or
retail trade, or some such calling, or suppose, for the matter of that,
that some unavoidable destiny were to drive the best women into such
professions. Then we should discover that all are humane and beneficent occupations. If they were only conducted on principles of strict
integrity, we should respect them as we do the vocation of mother or
nurse. But look at the actual facts! For purposes of commerce a man
sets up his quarters in some solitary spot remote from everywhere;   919
there he entertains the famished traveler and the refugee from tem-
pests with welcome lodging, and provides them with calm in storm
and cool shelter in heat. But what comes next? Where he might treat
his customers as so many friends, and add a hospitable banquet to the
entertainment, he behaves as though he were dealing with captive
enemies who had fallen into his hands, and holds them to the hardest,
most iniquitous, most abominable terms of ransom. These malprac- b
tices, and others like them, are to be found in all these callings, and it
is they which have brought catering for the wants of the distressed into
merited ill repute. This is the malady in them all for which law must
find a specific. Now it is a sound old adage that it is hard to fight against
two enemies at once—even when they are enemies from opposite
quarters. We see the truth of this in medicine and elsewhere. And in
the battle we are at this moment waging against the evils of these professions we have two such enemies, penury and opulence. The one rots
souls with luxury; the other, with its distresses, drives them into sheer c
insensibility to shame. What remedy, then, can be found for the
disease in an intelligent society? Well, the remedy is, in the first
place, that the numbers of those employed in trade be kept as low as
possible, next, that such occupations be assigned to the sort of men
whose corruption will do no great mischief to society; thirdly, some
means must be found to prevent the characters of those actually
engaged in these callings from readily taking the contagion of complete abandonment and baseness.   d
     So our preface shall at once be followed by a law—and the bless-
ing of providence go with it!—to this effect. In the Magnesian city
which heaven is restoring from its decay, no one of all the five thousand and forty landowners who are our householders shall follow a
trade, by his own will or against it, nor even engage in merchandise;
neither shall he discharge menial services of any kind to a private

employer who renders no like services to himself, save for services
e performed, without derogation to gentle blood, to father, mother, remoter ancestors, or to any man of gentle birth senior to himself. What
services are thus consistent with gentle lineage and what are not can
hardly be stated with precision in a law; the point shall be decided
by those who have won distinction for abhorrence of the base and devotion to the gentle. If a citizen, on any pretext, engage in sordid trade,
he shall be liable to an indictment for tainting the blood, to be preferred by any who will, and to come before a jury of men who have attained the first distinction for goodness; if found to have defiled the
920 ancestral hearth by an unworthy pursuit, he shall suffer a year's imprisonment as a lesson to avoid such conduct, or, for a repeated offense, two years' imprisonment. On each subsequent conviction the
term inflicted for the last offense shall be regularly doubled. Now for a
second law. A person proposing to follow a retail business shall always
be a resident alien or a foreigner. And there shall be yet a third. To
ensure that there shall be as much virtue, or at least, as little vice, as
is possible among these associates in the life of our society, the curators
must not be regarded merely as guardians of the class whom it is easy
to protect from falling into crime or vice, the favorably born and prop-
b erly educated and trained. Still more careful guard must be kept over
those who have not these advantages, and follow callings which have
a marked tendency to predispose to vice. So to effect this result for retail trade with its numerous branches and the many debasing employments it embraces—I mean those of them which we shall permit
to subsist in our society because we have found their presence absolutely necessary—the curators will once more be required in this case
to consult with the experts in all departments of trade, exactly as they
c have been enjoined to do in connection with the allied business of the
prevention of fraud. They shall ascertain by consultation what scale of
payment and expenditure will secure the trader a modest profit, and
this scale of outlay and receipts shall be publicly displayed and enforced by the commissioners of the market and urban and rural commissioners in their respective spheres. Under such regulation we may
expect our retail trade to produce general benefit for all classes with
the minimum of harm to the class who follow it as their vocation.
d   In the case of failure to execute an admitted contract—save and
except a contract to do what is prohibited by statute or by executive
decree of the assembly, a contract extorted by wrongful constraint, a
contract unintentionally frustrated by unforeseen circumstances—
there shall be an action for nonfulfillment of contract before the tribal
courts, unless settlement can be previously reached before arbitrators
or a court of the local neighbors. The class of artificers whose crafts
have equipped us for the daily needs of life will be under the patronage
e of Hephaestus and Athena, while the other class who provide for our
safety by a second group of crafts—those which subserve defense—

will have Ares and Athena as their patrons. There are as good grounds
for this divine protection in the second case as in the other. All alike
are engaged in continuous service of country and people—the one sort
in taking charge of our struggles in the field, the other in producing
implements and commodities for hire. Reverence for their divine progenitors will thus make it unseemly in such men to break their word 921
about their work. If a craftsman, then, culpably fail to complete a task
within the specified time, and thus forget the reverence due to the
god from whom he gets his living, fancying, in his ignorance, that
God is a mate who will make allowances, he shall, first, answer for it
to the god, and, next, there shall be a law to suit the case. If a man
break his word to the employer with whom he has contracted for any
piece of work, he shall be indebted in the value of the work and
shall execute it again gratis from the beginning within the time
agreed on. The law will further give the same counsel to contractors for
such performances as was given to vendors. The vendor was advised b
to take no advantage by asking too high a price, but to price his goods
with all candor at their true worth, and the law gives the same injunction to the contractor, who, of course, as a craftsman is aware of
the true value of his work. In a city of free men, then, the craftsman
of all men may never use his expert knowledge, in itself an honest and
straightforward thing, to take advantage of the layman by the tricks
of the trade, and persons wronged by such tricks must have a legal
remedy. On the other side, if the party contracting with a workman
fail to pay his wages strictly as stipulated in an agreement valid in c
law, this is to dishonor Zeus, our national defender, and Athena,
who are both partners in our society, and to dissolve the supreme social bonds for the sake of petty profit, and there shall be a law to
champion the heaven-ordained civic tie to this effect. If a man, having
received delivery of work contracted for, do not pay the price within
the stipulated time, the said price shall be recoverable from him twofold. If payment be not made within the year, whereas all other moneys
out upon loan shall bear no interest, a defaulter in this kind shall pay d
an interest of one obol on the drachma for each month in arrears,
actions under this head to be taken in the tribal courts.

As we *have* raised this topic of artificers, it is only right to say a
passing word about the artificers of our preservation in war, generals
and other military experts. In their case also—for they too, like the
others, are craftsmen, though of a different sort—if any of them undertake work for the public, whether as a volunteer or under orders, e
and perform it well and truly, the law will never tire in commendation
of the citizen who loyally pays him the soldier's wages—honors—but
if the citizen receive delivery of the fine piece of military work and
withhold the payment, the law shall censure him. We shall accordingly enact, and couple with our commendation of these heroes,
the following law, which we address to the populace rather by way of

922 counsel than by way of compulsion. The brave men who preserve our whole state by deeds of valor or military skill shall receive honors of the second class. Our supreme distinctions must be understood to have been assigned to those who stand first of all in merit, those who have proved pre-eminent in reverence for the precepts of good legislators.

We have now, we may say, completed our regulation of the more important business relations of man with man, except for those which concern orphans and their supervision by their guardians. These are b the spheres we are next driven to regulate as best we can. The foundations of the whole subject are laid by the desire of the dying to make a disposition of their estates and the accident of deaths without any such settlement, and the reason why I spoke of being 'driven' to treat of it, Clinias, was that I saw the intricacies and difficulties involved. We certainly cannot leave such matters without all regulation. Were we to concede the unqualified validity of any testamentary disposition made at the end of life, irrespective of the testator's condition, men would often make disposals inconsistent in themselves and repugnant c to law, or to the moral sense of the living, or of the testator himself at an earlier time of life. For in most of us, as you know, when in imminent expectation of death, the mental powers are in abeyance, broken, as I may say.

CLINIAS: Yes, sir, and what of it?

ATHENIAN: A man at the point of death, Clinias, is not easy to handle; he is full of a notion which must give a legislator grave concern and perplexity.

CLINIAS: How so, pray?

d ATHENIAN: He wants to have his own way about everything, and so there is commonly a touch of passion in his language.

CLINIAS: Language—what language?

ATHENIAN: Lord! he will say, I call it a shame if I am not to be perfectly free to give my own property to a man or not, exactly as I please, and not free to give more of it to one man, less to another, according as I have found them treating me well or ill under the searching test of sickness, old age, and the other varied circumstances of life.

CLINIAS: A perfectly proper thing to say, too, sir, don't you think so?

e ATHENIAN: Why, Clinias, I think our legislators in the past have been too soft; their codes have been based on short views of human life and imperfect understanding of it.

CLINIAS: But in what way?

ATHENIAN: Why, my dear sir, they were afraid of such complaints, and that is why they made the law which permits of the absolute disposition of property entirely as the testator pleases. You and I must pitch our reply to the dying in this society of yours in a more suitable key.

923 Friends, who have, in literal fact, only a day to live—this is what

we shall tell them—in your present condition it is hard enough for you to know what is your own property; what is more, it is hard, as the inscription at Delphi says, to know what you are yourselves. So I, speaking as legislator, pronounce that neither your own persons nor the estate are your own; both belong to your whole line, past and future, and still more absolutely do both lineage and estate belong to the b community. This is so surely so that I shall never, if I can help it, permit you, when shaken by age or infirmity, to be cajoled into evil testamentary dispositions by the insinuating arts of the flatterer. My law will be made with a general view to the best interests of society at large and your whole line, as I rightly hold the single person and his affairs of minor importance. Depart from us in peace and good will on the journey you are now to take, as all flesh must. What you leave behind you shall be our concern; we will take all the thought for it c we may, and that with no partial care.

Such exhortations alike to living and dying shall form our preamble, Clinias. Our statute shall be to this effect. A person making written testamentary disposition of his effects, shall, if he have issue, first set down the name of such son as he judges proper to inherit. If he have another son whom he offers for adoption by a fellow citizen, he shall set his name down also. If there be still a son left, not already d adopted as heir to any patrimony, who may expect in course of law to be sent to some overseas settlement, it shall be free to him to bequeath to such son such of his goods as he sees fit, other than his patrimonial estate and its complete plenishing. If there be more such sons than one, the father shall divide his possessions, other than his patrimony, among them in such proportions as he pleases. But if a son already possess a house, no portion of such goods shall be bequeathed to him, and the same shall hold in the case of a daughter; a daughter not contracted to a husband shall receive her share, but a daughter al- e ready so contracted shall receive none. If a son or daughter be found to have come into possession of an allotment of land subsequent to the date of the will, such party shall leave the bequest in the hands of the testator's heir. If the testator leave only female issue without male, he shall by will provide one daughter, selected at his pleasure, with a husband and himself with a son, and shall name such husband as his heir. If a man's son, naturally begotten or adopted, die in infancy before reaching the age of manhood, the testator shall further make pro- 924 vision for this contingency by naming a child to succeed such son with happier omens. If the party making his testament be absolutely childless, he may set aside one-tenth part of his *acquired* possessions for the purpose of legacies to any persons he pleases; all else shall be left to the adopted heir whom he shall make his son, in all integrity on the one part and gratitude on the other, with the law's approval. Where the children require a guardian, if the deceased have stated in his will how many guardians he desires for his children and whom,

b and the parties named consent to act, the nomination of guardians in the will shall be final. If a man die wholly intestate, or without selecting such guardians, the lawful guardians shall be the nearest kinsmen on both sides, two from the father's side, two from the mother's, together with one personal friend of the deceased, the appointment to be made
c for an orphan in such case by the curators. The whole department of wardships and orphans shall be under the supervision of fifteen of the curators, the senior members of the board, who shall regularly divide themselves into groups of three, in order of seniority, one such group acting for one year and another for the next, until the five yearly periods are discharged; no avoidable breach shall be permitted in this rotation.

   If a man die absolutely intestate but leaving children who need the care of a guardian, his children's distress shall share the benefit
d of these same laws. But if he meet his end by some incalculable accident and leave daughters behind him, he must make allowances for the legislator's disposal of his daughters' hands if it takes two points out of three into account, nearness in blood and protection of the patrimony. The third point—and this is what would have engaged a father's attention—the selection of the person out of the whole citizen body most congenial in character and disposition as a son for himself and
e bridegroom for his daughter, the legislator will pretermit as an impossible task. Here, then, is the best law we can devise for the case. If an intestate person leave daughters, a brother of the deceased on the father's side, or a brother on the mother's side having no patrimony of his own, shall take his daughter and inherit his patrimony. The same shall be the case if there be a brother's son but no brother, provided the parties are of suitable age. If there be none of these, the rule shall hold for a sister's son. Father's brother shall be fourth in succession, his son fifth, father's sister's son sixth. In all cases where female issue is left, the family succession shall proceed in this regular order of proximity in blood through brothers and sisters and their offspring, males
925 having the precedence over females in the same generation. The suitability or unsuitability of the match in point of years shall be determined by inspection, and the judge shall view the males stripped and the females stripped to the navel. If there be a failure of kin within the family, as far as brother's grandsons, and likewise grandsons of grandfather's sons, the maiden shall be free, with her guardians' as-
b sent, to make her choice among the citizens, the person so chosen, if he consent, becoming heir to the deceased and bridegroom to his daughter. Further, life is full of accidents, and it may well happen at times that an heir is still harder to find within the state. So if a maiden can find no husband on the spot, but have her eye on some party previously dispatched to a colony, whom she is minded to make her father's heir, that party, if a kinsman, shall come to the inheritance as the law appoints; if outside the family, provided there be no kinsmen within the

state, consent of the daughter of the deceased and her guardians shall c empower him to make the match and return home to take up the succession to the intestate person.

If a man decease intestate leaving no issue, male or female, in all other respects the law above stated shall apply to the case, but a female and male from the family shall mate, as we may express it, and be placed in the deserted homestead, the patrimony being legally assigned to them. The order of succession shall be: sister, brother's daughter, sister's daughter, father's sister, father's brother's daughter, d father's sister's daughter. These shall be settled on their kinsmen, in accord with the provisions of the foregoing statute, as consanguinity and religion demand. Of course we must not forget that such laws can prove burdensome; it is sometimes a hardship that they require a blood connection of the deceased to marry his kinswoman, but appear to overlook the numerous obstacles which will make any man reluc- e tant to comply with the command and ready to face any consequence rather than obey, cases like those of bodily or mental disorder or deficiency in a party whom the law requires us to take as wife or husband. Hence it might be supposed that the legislator is indifferent to those considerations, but that would be a misconception. So you must take my remarks as a preamble delivered in the interests alike of the legislator and the parties for whom he legislates; they are meant to bespeak the indulgence of such parties for the legislator, if his concern for the public good hardly leaves him equally free to control the fortunes of private individuals, and a like indulgence for the recipi- 926 ents of his laws, if they sometimes, no less naturally, find themselves unable to execute orders laid on them in ignorance of the facts.

CLINIAS: Then, let me ask you, sir, what would be the fairest way to act in such a situation?

ATHENIAN: In such a case, Clinias, we must appoint arbitrators between the law and the persons it commands.

CLINIAS: Pray explain yourself.

ATHENIAN: Sometimes a nephew whose father is a wealthy man might make difficulties about marrying his uncle's daughter be- b cause he has high notions and aspires to a more splendid match. Sometimes, again, a man might be driven to disobey the law because what the legislator requires is disastrous, as when he would constrain you to connect yourself with a house in which there is insanity, or other grievous bodily or mental affliction, such as renders life positively intolerable. So what I have to say on the subject shall be couched in the form of a law to this effect. If a party complain of being aggrieved by the laws now enacted, the law of testamentary dispositions c or another, and in particular by the law of marriage, and emit a solemn declaration to the effect that the legislator, if now alive and present in person, would never have required the action—the taking or giving in marriage—of either party from whom it is now demanded, and if a relative or guardian make affirmation to the contrary, the law shall take the view that the legislator has bequeathed the fifteen curators to our orphans of both sexes as arbitrators and parents; liti-

d gants on these issues shall have recourse to them for the determination of their disputes, and shall act on their verdict as final. If the powers thus conferred on the curators be deemed too extensive by any party, he shall bring the curators before the court of selected judges and take its decision on the issue. If he lose his case, the legislator shall visit him with censure and disgrace, penalties heavier in the judgment of intelligence than the most grievous fine.

Our orphan children will thus experience a kind of second birth.

e How they should all be reared and trained after their first birth has already been explained. What we have to do after this second birth, a birth without a parent, is to discover the plan by which their unfortunate bereavement will entail least distress on the sufferers. First, then, to make laws for their conduct, in place of their fleshly begetters we appoint the curators, parents at least as good as they; moreover we especially charge three of them every year to care for them as their own,

927 and we add a preamble on the upbringing of orphans apposite to these officers, as to all guardians. I believe, in fact, there was something really opportune in all we said before of a power of taking an interest in human life retained by the souls of the departed after death. The tales which convey this moral may be lengthy, but they are true, and we ought to give our credence to general tradition on the subject, when we consider how abundant and how very venerable that tradition is, but particularly to legislators who lend their sanction to such beliefs—unless, indeed, we account them men of no judgment at all. If all this be truly so, there should be fear, first and foremost, of the

b gods in heaven, who behold the orphan in his loneliness, and next of the parted spirits whose native instinct is to keep especial watch over their own offspring—to show good will to him who respects them and ill to him who neglects—fear, in the third place, of the souls of men still alive, but of advanced years and high distinction. Where the laws of a state are good and its fortunes blessed, children's children delight to lavish affection on such men, their sight and hearing in such matters is quick, their good will is assured to him who walks uprightly in

c them, and their wrath hot against the despoiler of the defenseless orphan; they count him a solemn and sacred trust. Guardians and magistrates, if men of discretion, howsoever slight, should stand in awe of all these powers and bear themselves warily in all that concerns the orphan's upbringing and education; they should do them all the good they may in every way, even as though the benefit were bestowed on themselves and their own sons. So he that will give ear to the words of our preamble and keep himself from all spoiling of the orphan shall learn nothing of the legislator's naked wrath against these

d crimes, but he that will not hear, and wrongs fatherless or motherless, shall pay twofold the full compensation demanded of him who misconducts himself toward those whose parents are both in life.

As touching a general legislation for guardians of orphans, or magistrates who have charge of the guardians, had they no model already of an upbringing for the sons of the gently born in their upbringing of their own children and management of their own estates, or had they not moreover a sufficient law prescribed them for such matters, 'twould be no more than reason to propound a law of wardships with a special character of its own, and to make a distinction of the orphan's life from others by various special rules. As the case is, in our society the orphan's status is not very different in all these respects from that of the child under its father's care, though the two are commonly on such different levels in public estimation and in respect of the care bestowed. 'Tis, indeed, because of this very difference that our law has been so earnest with its exhortations and threats in its regulations concerning the orphan. We may add this further and most seasonable threat. The guardian of male or female infant, and the curator appointed to exercise surveillance of such guardian, shall show no less concern for the bereaved orphan than for his own children, and shall pay the same zealous attention to the estate of the ward under his care as to his own—or indeed more. This shall be the law, and the only law, under which guardianship of an orphan shall be exercised. In the case of any contravention of this law, a guardian shall be fined by the magistrate; a defaulting magistrate shall be cited by the guardian before the court of the select judges, and fined twice the amount of his defalcations as assessed by the court. If the family, or any fellow citizen, charge a guardian with negligence or dishonesty, the case shall be brought before the same court; any defalcation proved shall be repaid fourfold, half the sum to go to the orphan child, and half to the successful prosecutor in the case. If an orphan who has attained his majority believe his guardian's administration to have been faulty, it shall be open to him to institute proceedings in respect of the guardianship at any date within five years from the expiry of said guardianship. If a guardian be convicted, the court shall determine the penalty or fine; if a magistrate, and the injury to the orphan be found due to negligence, the court shall determine the sum payable to the ward. But if the verdict be one of malversation, the offender shall, in addition to payment of the fine, be removed from the office of curator, and the authorities shall provide country and state with a new curator in his stead.

Graver differences are found to arise between fathers and sons, sons and fathers, than ought to be possible. As a consequence, fathers are disposed to take the view that the legislator should empower them, if they see fit, to make public and legal notification through the crier that they will no longer hold a son as their son, and sons, on their part, to expect legal authorization to take proceedings in lunacy against a

928 e

928

b

c

d

e

father discredited by years or disease. The cause of such variance is commonly to be found in utter unqualified badness of character; where the badness is on one side only, as where the son is an ill man but his father not so, or vice versa, such dissensions are not pushed to the point where they issue in disaster. Now in any society but ours a disinherited son would not necessarily lose his citizenship, but in the state for which these our laws are intended, a man whose father has cast him off has no option but to expatriate himself to some distant 929 land, as we permit no addition whatsoever to our number of five thousand and forty households. Hence to be legally repudiated, a man must be disowned not merely by his father, but by the whole kindred. Thus our law will in such cases provide some such process as this. If, with just cause or without it, unhappy passion assail a man with the desire to cast out of his kin the son of his own begetting and breeding, he shall have no license to do the act incontinently, without due form. b He shall first summon his own kin, as far as his cousins, and his son's kin by the mother's side in like manner, and lay his charges before them, in proof that expulsion from the kindred is no more than the accused's desert at the hands of all, and shall grant the son equal facilities of pleading that he deserves no such thing. If the father prevail and can carry the suffrage of more than one half of the kinsmen— those excepted who shall have no vote, the father, the mother, the c defendant himself, and such other persons, male or female, as have not yet reached maturity—the father shall have leave to renounce his son, on these terms and conditions stated, and upon no others. If a citizen be minded to adopt one thus repudiated into his own house, there shall be no bar in law to the adoption—life commonly works frequent changes in a young man's temper—but if no one, within ten d years, show desire to adopt the disowned son, the officers charged with the care of supernumerary children whom we destine for our settlement abroad shall take his case also under their charge, that he may duly receive his place there. If disease, age, sullen temper, or all together derange a man's mind with more than common violence, though the fact go undiscovered by all but those who share his daily life, so that he waste the family estate as one that is absolute lord of it, while his son knows not where to turn, and scruples to bring his ac- e tion of lunacy, in such case, the law shall be that he must first have recourse to the eldest of the curators and tell them his father's case. They shall make diligent inquiry, and then counsel him whether the action shall be brought or no; if their counsel be to bring it, they shall, when the case comes on, serve the complainant both as witnesses and as advocates. The father who loses such action shall thereafter have no power to make any disposition of his goods in the smallest particular, but shall be treated as a child for the rest of his life.

If man and wife be utterly estranged by their unhappy temper, the matter should in every case be referred to ten men—curators intermediate between the extremes in point of age—and ten women, of 930 those who have charge of wedlock. If they are able to effect an accommodation, the arrangements thus made shall hold good, but if the storm rages too high within, they shall seek the best mate they can find for either party. The temper in these cases is like to be none too gentle, whence we try to match them with partners of more sedate and gentle mood. When the discordant parties have no children, or too few, an eye shall be had also in the new alliance to procreation; where there are already children in sufficient number, the end of the separa- b tion and new conjunction should be companionship in age and mutual care of one another. If a woman die leaving children male and female, our law shall counsel, but shall not compel, her husband to bring up the children he has and give them no stepmother; if there be no children, the husband shall be bound to marry again, until he have begotten children in number sufficient for the house and for the c state. If the husband die leaving children in sufficient number, their mother shall remain in the household to bring them up. But if she be deemed unduly youthful to live without a man and keep her health, her kinsmen shall communicate with the women who have charge of wedlock and act as shall seem good to themselves and them. If there be a lack of children, that point also shall be considered; the lowest number which shall constitute a sufficiency in law shall be one d boy and one girl.

When the parentage of issue is admitted and it is to be determined which parent the offspring shall follow, if a slave woman have had to do with slave, free man, or freedman, the offspring shall, in every case, belong to her owner; if a free woman lie with a slave, the offspring shall be his owner's; if master have a child by his slave woman, or mistress by her slave, and the fact be notorious, the woman's child shall be sent, along with its father, by the women functionaries, the man's, with its mother, by the curators, to another land.   e

Neglect of parents is that to which neither god nor right-thinking man will ever counsel any. A man should have the wit to see how pat the preamble now to be delivered on divine worship is like to fit this theme of respect and disrespect of parents. All the world over the primitive rules of worship are twofold. Some of the gods of our worship are manifest to sight; there are others in whose likeness we set up 931 images, believing that when we adore the lifeless image, we win the bountiful favor and grace of the living god for whom it stands. If, then, a man have a father or mother, or a parent of either, safe kept withindoors in the last frailty of age, he should remember that while there is such a figure to hallow his hearth at home, no image can be so potent for good, if only the owner give it the rightful worship he should.

b CLINIAS: Now what may you mean by this rightful worship?

ATHENIAN: Why, I will tell you. Indeed, my friends, 'tis a theme well deserving our attention.

CLINIAS: Say on, then.

ATHENIAN: Oedipus, so we commonly say, called down a curse on his sons when they showed him disrespect, and it is a familiar tale with us all, as you know, how fully heaven answered his prayer. And we have the stories of the cursing of Phoenix by his angry father Amyntor, and of Hippolytus by Theseus, with many another to the c same effect—plain proof that heaven will listen to a parent's prayers against his children. In fact, the curse of the parent on the offspring is more effectual than any other, and 'tis only right it should be so. If, then, 'tis the order of things that God is so exceeding quick to hear the prayer of father or mother when their children show them dishonor, let none conceit himself that when the parent receives his honors, rejoices and delights in them, and is moved to fervent prayer for blessings on the children—must we not think, I say, that heaven d hears that prayer no less than the other, and dispenses the blessing? Were it not so, its blessings would not be fairly dispensed, a thought most unworthy of it.

CLINIAS: Most unworthy indeed.

ATHENIAN: And so, as I have just said, we must believe that no image we can procure is more precious in heaven's eye than a father or forefather in the weakness of his age, or a mother in like case; when a man does them worship and honor, there is joy in heaven, or their prayers would not be heard. An ancestor's person is, in truth, an e image of God more marvelous than any lifeless statue. These living images will always second our prayers for ourselves when we pay them worship, and pray in the opposite sense since when we show them dishonor, but the others can do neither the one thing nor the other. And so the man who bears himself as he ought to father, father's father, and the rest of his ancestors will find no other image so effectual to assure the favor of heaven as this which he has got.

CLINIAS: Most admirably said.

ATHENIAN: And thus all right-thinking men treat a parent's prayer with fear and reverence; they know how time and again such petitions have been effectual. This being nature's appointment, a good 932 man finds his aged progenitors treasure-trove to the last breath of their lives, and when they depart, the loss to their juniors is most heavy; to evil men they are cause for real and deep alarm. Wherefore I would have all men listen to our present pleadings and show their parents all lawful honor. If there should be any whom 'fame attaints' of deafness to a prelude to such strains, 'twould be a fitting law against such men to decree as follows. If any person in our state be less mindful of his parents than he ought, not showing himself more careful b to consider and comply with all their wishes, more than those of his

sons and other posterity whatsoever and his own also, he that lies under such neglect may report it, in person or by deputy, to the three
senior curators and three of the women who have charge of wedlock.
They shall deal with the complaint, and chastise the criminal with
stripes and imprisonment, if still young, that is, in the case of a man,
not over thirty years; the penalty for a woman that offends shall be
the same for a further ten years. If persons beyond these years still c
persistently neglect their parents, or, it may be treat them ill, they shall
cite them before a court of one hundred and one citizens, the most
ancient we have. In case of conviction the court shall determine the
fine or other penalty, and shall not hold themselves debarred from the
infliction of the utmost a man can be made to suffer or pay. If a person
so ill-treated be unable to complain, any who shall become aware of d
the facts shall report them to the authorities, or else be deemed a
craven, and lie open to action at any man's suit for the mischief. If
the informer be a slave, he shall receive his freedom. If his owner
be the party inflicting or suffering the injury, the magistrate shall pronounce him free; if another citizen, his price shall be paid to his
owner from the public purse. The authorities shall take care that no
wrong be done him in revenge for his information.

To come to injury inflicted by poisons, we have dealt at large e
with the cases where death results, but not, as yet, with lesser injuries
arising from deliberate and intentional administration of articles of
meat or drink, or unguents. What gives us pause here is that mankind
practice poisoning in two different ways. The form we have just expressly named is that in which the body is hurt by the action of some 933
other body in normal ways. There is another form which works by
art, magic, incantations, and spells, as they are called, and breeds in
the minds of the projectors the belief that they possess such powers of
doing harm, in those of the victims the conviction that the authors of
their suffering can verily bewitch them. Now as to all such matters the
true facts are hard to learn, nor, if one could learn them, would it be an
easy task to convince another. And it would be labor lost to try to bring
conviction to minds beset with such suspicions of each other, to tell
them, if they should perchance see a manikin of wax set up in the
doorway, or at the crossroads, or at the grave of a parent, to think b
nothing of such things, as nothing is known of them for certain. We
shall therefore divide the law of poisons into two chapters, according
to the mode in which the poisoner makes his attempt. But first we shall
publish our request, desire, or counsel that no such attempt be made,
that there be among us no working on the terrors of mankind—the c
most part of whom are as timorous as babes—and no constraint upon
legislator or judge to find a remedy for these terrors. The would-be
poisoner, we shall say, *imprimis* knows nothing of what he does, nothing, unless he be expert in medicine, of treatment of the body, nothing,
unless he be prophet or diviner, of sorcery. The law of poisons, then,

d shall run to this effect. Any man administering a poison to another, or to persons employed by him, without fatal effect, or with effects fatal or otherwise to his cattle or bees, and convicted of the offense of poisoning shall, if a physician, suffer death, and if a layman, such penalty or fine as the court shall impose. And any found to have brought himself under suspicion of doing a mischief by the practice of

e spells, charms, incantations, or other such sorceries whatsoever, shall, if prophet or diviner, have sentence of death; if the conviction be for sorcery without any help of prophetic art, he shall be dealt with as in the former case—the court, as before, shall determine his sentence or fine at its discretion.

In all cases of injury by theft or robbery with violence, the culprit shall pay compensation to the party injured, greater or less, according to the gravity of the mischief done, but in any case sufficient to cover completely the whole loss occasioned by his act; further, each

934 such culprit shall pay a penalty imposed upon the offense by way of correction. The correction shall be lighter when the offender has been led astray by the folly of another to whose overpersuasion he has yielded by reason of youth, or some other such cause, heavier when the crime is due to folly of his own, failure to resist pleasure or pain, or the pressure of desperate lust, envy, or rage. The purpose of the penalty is not to cancel the crime—what is once done can never be

b made undone—but to bring the criminal and all who witness his punishment in the future to complete renunciation of such criminality, or at least to recovery in great part from the dreadful state. For all these reasons, and since it has all these ends in view, the law must take careful aim at its mark; it must be exact in determining the magnitude of the correction imposed on the particular offense, and, above all, the amount of compensation to be paid. The judge must have the same task before him, and lend his services to the legislator, when the law leaves it to his discretion to fix a defendant's fine or sentence;

c the legislator, in this case, is like a draftsman who must design the outlines of cases which answer to the code. This is, in fact, Megillus and Clinias, what you and I are now to do to the fullest extent of our ability; we have to specify the penalties to be imposed on thefts and robberies of every kind, so far as the gods and their sons permit us to legislate on the subject.

No lunatic shall be allowed to be at large in the community; the relatives of such persons shall keep them in safe custody at home by such methods as they can contrive, on penalty of fine. The fine for failure to control the lunatic, whether slave or free man, shall be for

d offenders of the highest property class one mina, for the second four fifths of that sum, for the third three fifths, for the fourth two fifths. Now there are many lunatics and their lunacy takes many different forms. In the case just mentioned it springs from disease, but there is another sort of lunatics who owe their madness to an unhappy native tendency to angry passion further strengthened by ill training, a kind of men whom any trifling dissension will provoke to clamorous and scurrilous reviling of each other, conduct always and totally out e of place in a well-ordered society. We shall therefore have one single law of defamatory words to deal with all such men, and that law shall be this. No person shall use defamatory words of any other. A party to a dispute of any kind shall listen to his adversary's contention, and put his own before the adversary and the company present without scurrility of any sort. When disputants begin to invoke impreca- tions on one another and bandy foul names, like wrangling vixens, 935 the first result is that such words, in themselves trifles light as air, yield a heavy harvest of deeds of spite and hatred. Passion is an ill- favored thing, and the speaker who does his wrath the favor to feast it on the poison it craves turns all the humanity education has fashioned within him into brutishness once more; persistence in his morose ran- cor makes him a wild beast, and that sorry return is all the return pas- sion makes him for his favors. And besides, 'tis the common way with all men in such encounters to be ever turning to the utterance of scoffs b at the adversary, a practice to which no man ever yet formed himself, save at the cost of losing all gravity of character or the better part of his dignity. For all these reasons no single scoffing word shall be ut- tered by any man in any temple or at any public sacrifice, nor yet at the public sports, nor in market place, court of justice, or any place of public resort. The offense shall be in every case punished by the offi- cial in charge, on pain of disqualification from all claims to distinc- c tion, as one that has no regard for the law and neglects to execute the legislator's injunctions. If a man indulge in such scurrilities else- where, whether he begin the reviling or retort it, any bystander, being an older man, shall uphold the law and drive out with blows him who humors his bad companion, temper, or else shall be subjected to the appointed fine. Now mark my point. When a man is entangled in a scolding match, he can say nothing without seeking to raise a laugh, d and it is the resort to this trick at the prompting of angry passion which I denounce. But what follows? Are we lending our countenance to the comedians' efforts to raise a laugh against mankind, provided the object of their comedies is to attain their result, to turn the laugh against their fellow citizens, without such passion? Shall we draw the line between sport and earnest, permitting men to jest upon one an- other in sport and without anger, but absolutely forbidding all such e jesting, as we have already done, where it is in downright earnest and charged with passion? That proviso must certainly not be withdrawn, but the law will proceed to specify the persons to whom permission shall or shall not be granted. No composer of comedy, iambic or lyric verse shall be permitted to hold any citizen up to laughter, by word or gesture, with passion or otherwise; in case of disobedience the presi- dents of the festival shall give orders for the offender's expulsion from the state's territory within the course of the day, on pain of a fine of three minas to be paid to the deity in whose honor the festival is held.

936 The persons to whom permission has already been granted by an earlier arrangement to compose personal satire shall be free to satirize each other dispassionately and in jest, but not in earnest or with angry feeling. The actual drawing of the distinction shall be left to the minister in charge of the system of juvenile education. If he approve a piece, its composer shall have license to produce it in public; if he disapprove, the composer shall neither appear in it himself nor train any

b other person, slave or free, to perform it, on pain of being declared a bad citizen and a lawbreaker.

The true object of pity is not the man who is hungry or in some similar needy case, but the man who has sobriety of soul or some other virtue, or share in such virtue, and misfortunes to boot. Whence in a state where constitution and citizens alike are even middling good, it will be strange to find any such man, slave or free, so wholly neglected that he comes to utter beggary. Such men will be in no danger if the

c legislator enact the following statute. There shall be no begging in the state. If anyone attempt it and seek to scrape up a living by his incessant entreaties, he shall be expelled from the market place by the commissioners of the market and from the city by the urban commission, and escorted over the borders by the rural police, that our land may be entirely cleaned of such creatures.

If damage be done to a man's property of any kind by another's

d slave, male or female, such person not being himself contributory to the charge by awkwardness or other ill management, the owner of the party causing the damage shall either make compensation in full, or surrender the person of the culprit. If such owner allege that the charge is made by collusion between the parties causing the mischief and the party sustaining it, with intent to defraud him of his slave, he shall take proceedings against the person alleging himself to have

e sustained damage. If he win the suit, he shall receive twice such price as the court may set upon the slave; if he lose it, he shall pay compensation for the damage and further surrender the slave. Likewise, if harm be done to a neighbor's property by draft animal, horse, dog, or other animal, the owner shall pay compensation for the damage.

If a man refuse to give evidence, he shall be served with a citation by the party desiring his testimony, on receipt whereof, he shall present himself at the trial of the case. If he have knowledge of the facts and is ready to depose to them, he shall then make his deposition; if he deny all knowledge, he shall profess his denial on oath by three gods, Zeus, Apollo, and Themis, and be dismissed from the case.

937 Any person cited in evidence and not answering to the citation shall be legally liable to action for damage. If a judge in the case be called up to give evidence, he shall do so and shall have no vote in the determination of such case. A free woman shall be qualified to give evidence

and support a case, if she have attained the age of forty; if she have
no husband, she shall further be qualified to initiate a process at law,
but if she have a living husband, to give evidence only. A slave of either sex, or a child, shall be qualified to give evidence and support a b
case only in proceedings for homicide, and provided sufficient security is given that in case a demurrer is lodged against the deposition as
false, the deponent will await his trial. A plaintiff or defendant making an allegation of perjury shall put in his demurrer to the whole or
part of the testimony before the decision in the case is reached; the
pleas of demurrer shall receive the seals of both parties to the suit
and be in the custody of the officials for production at the hearing of
the charge of perjury. A person twice convicted of bearing false wit- c
ness shall be under no legal obligation to give evidence in the future;
a person convicted thrice shall be in future disqualified to bear witness. Any who shall have the front to do so after three convictions
shall be summarily arrested upon information as to fact by the magistrates, who shall deliver him to a court, for sentence of death if convicted. Whenever depositions have been thus judicially condemned by
a decision that the victory of the successful litigant was due to false
evidence, if the condemnation affect half or more of such depositions,
the suit so decided against a litigant shall be annulled, and the issue d
shall be raised and determined whether or not the suit was decided
by these depositions; the result of the inquiry, either way, shall finally
dispose of the original suit.

Life abounds in good things, but most of those good things are in-
fested by polluting and defiling parasites. Justice, for example, is undeniably a boon to mankind; it has humanized the whole of life. And e
if justice is such a blessing, how can advocacy be other than a blessing
too? Well, both blessings are brought into ill repute by a vice which
cloaks itself under the specious name of an art. It begins by professing
that there is a device for managing one's legal business—in fact that
it is itself a device for managing such business of one's own and assisting another to manage his—and that this device will ensure victory
equally whether the conduct at issue in the case, whatever it is, has
been rightful or not. And it then adds that this art itself and the elo- 938
quence it teaches are to be had as a gift by anyone who will make a
gift in money in return. Now this device—be it which it may, art or
mere artless empirical knack—must not, if we can help it, strike root
in our society. The legislator will call for obedient silence in the presence of right and departure to some other territory; to him who complies the law will have nothing more to say, but to the disobedient its
language will be this. Any who shall fall under suspicion of attempting
to pervert the influence of justice upon the mind of a judge, of wrong- b
fully multiplying suits at law, or wrongfully aiding others to such
suits, shall be liable to prosecution by all who choose on the charge of
perversion of justice or abetment of such perversion, as the case may

be. The charge shall be tried before the court of select judges, and if it result in conviction, the court shall determine whether the defendant, in its judgment, acted from ambition, or from greed of lucre. If from the former, the court shall fix a space of time during which the guilty party shall have no right to enter a suit against any man, nor assist any c man in a suit. If the offense be found due to greed of gain, the culprit shall, if an alien, be expelled from the country on pain of death in the case of return, and, if a citizen, suffer death for his insatiate love of lucre. Also a second conviction of commission of the same offense from the motive of ambition shall lead to sentence of death.

BOOK XII

941 ATHENIAN: If an ambassador or envoy to a foreign state behave disloyally in his office, whether by falsification of the dispatch he is commissioned to deliver or by proved distortion of messages entrusted to him by such state, friendly or hostile, as ambassador or envoy, all such persons shall lie open to impeachment of the crime of sacrilege against the function and ordinances of Hermes and Zeus, and it shall be de- b termined what sentence or fine shall follow conviction.

Larceny is a sordid thing and open robbery a flagitious. No son of Zeus has ever had dealings in either; neither fraud nor force is to their liking. So let none of us, if he offends in this sort, suffer himself to be gulled by the fictions of the poets and fabulists; let him never fancy his pilfering or robbing no deed of shame, but an act such as is done by the very gods themselves. That is a tale with neither truth nor semblance of truth about it, and he that transgresses so is no god, nor the son of c any god at all. In these things 'tis the legislator's business to know better than all the poets together. So, if a man will obey our counsel, 'tis well with him—and may it ever be well! But if he will not, why, then he shall find a law up in arms against him, to this effect. For all theft of public property, great or small, there shall be one and the same judgment. For he that steals a little thing does his thieving with weaker hand but not with less lust, and he that takes up a greater, when he had not laid it down, is guilty of the whole law. This is why the law deems d it fit that one offender should be visited with a lighter doom than the other—not that what he stole was a lesser thing, but because one may yet be recovered perchance, and the other is beyond cure. Whence, if a conviction for theft of the public property be gained in the courts against an alien or slave, seeing he may yet, in all likelihood, be recovered, the court shall decide what sentence he must serve, or what fine he shall pay. A citizen, one trained as our citizens will be trained, found guilty of plundering or deforcing his native country, whether taken red-handed or no, shall suffer death as one beyond curing.

942 The organization of our forces is a thing calling in its nature for much advice and the framing of many rules, but the principal is this—

that no man, and no woman, be ever suffered to live without an officer
set over them, and no soul of man to learn the trick of doing one single
thing of its own sole motion, in play or in earnest, but, in peace as in b
war, ever to live with the commander in sight, to follow his leading,
and take its motions from him to the least detail—to halt or advance,
to drill, to bathe, to dine, to keep wakeful hours of nights as sentry or
dispatch carrier, all at his bidding, in the stricken field itself neither
to pursue nor to retire without the captain's signal, in a word, to teach c
one's soul the habit of never so much as thinking to do one single act
apart from one's fellows, of making life, to the very uttermost, an unbroken consort, society, and community of all with all. A wiser and
better rule than this man neither has discovered, nor ever will, nor a
truer art of military salvation and victory. 'Tis this lesson of commanding our fellows and being commanded by them we should rehearse in the times of peace, from our very cradles. *Anarchy*—the
absence of the commander—is what we should expel root and branch d
from the lives of all mankind, aye, and all beastkind that is under
man's dominion. In especial, all the choric dances our people are to
learn must look to gallantry in the field; the same must be the end of
all their training in easy and nimble movement, all their endurance of
hunger and thirst, cold and heat, and lying hard. Above all, they must,
to the same end, learn not to corrupt the native strength of the head
and feet by swathing them in artificial coverings, and so tampering
with the growth and function of the head cover and footwear of na- e
ture's providing. For head and feet are the body's extremities, and due
care of them affects the whole body most potently for good, neglect for
ill; the foot is the whole body's servant of servants, the head the master
member made by nature to contain all its principal organs of sense. 943

So much, then, for the praise of the warrior's life we would have
a young man listen to in fancy—now for the relative laws. A man put
on the roll or assigned to any arm of the forces shall perform his service. If a man absent himself from cowardice without a discharge from
his commanders, he shall, on the return of the forces from the field, be
impeached before the officers of the army for evasion of military duty,
and the verdict shall be given by some one branch of the forces—infantry, cavalry, or other arm—in separate session. Thus an infantry-
man shall be brought before the infantry, a cavalryman before the b
cavalry, a member of some other force similarly before his comrades.
A convicted person shall, *imprimis*, be disqualified for life for all competitions for distinction, and prohibited from laying an impeachment
of the same kind against another, or speaking as accuser in such cases;
the court shall, moreover, determine what further sentence or fine shall
be inflicted. Next, when the charges of evasion of service have all been
heard, the officers shall hold a second review of all arms, and the
claims of all candidates for awards of distinction shall be settled before
a body of their own mates; all evidence and commendatory testimo- c

nials proffered by candidates shall relate exclusively to the campaign just terminated, and to no previous service. The prize in each branch of the service shall be a wreath of olive; the winner shall dedicate this wreath in such temple of a god of war as he may prefer, as evidence for a future award of first, second, and third-rank distinctions for the conduct of a whole life. A man going on service but returning prema-

d turely before the commanders have withdrawn the forces shall be liable to impeachment for desertion before the same court in which cases of evasion are heard, and the penalties for conviction shall likewise be as in that case.

A person bringing a charge against another must, of course, be
e most scrupulously careful neither intentionally nor unintentionally to bring him to unmerited punishment. Justice is, indeed, as she has been called, the virgin daughter of conscience, and conscience and justice both are heart haters of the false charge. I say a man must keep himself from this and other offenses against justice, and in especial in the matter of loss of arms in war, a man must be tender of bringing unmerited judgment on the innocent, by mistaking an enforced loss

944 for a shameful, and so making it a reproach. 'Tis truly no easy matter to draw the line of distinction between the two cases, and yet the law should do what it can to distinguish them. And so we will help ourselves out by recalling a legend. If Patroclus had come to himself in the tent when he had been carried there without his arms—and the thing, we know, has happened to thousands—while the gallant armor he had been wearing—by the poet's tale it came to Peleus with Thetis as a nuptial gift from the gods—was in Hector's hands, the baser sort of that day would have had their chance to taunt the brave son of Menoetius with casting away his arms. And then there are all the cases of those who have lost their arms by falls from heights, at sea, or when

b suddenly swept off their feet, under stress of weather, by a swirl of waters—or countless other excuses may be conjured with, to put a fair face on a suspicious misadventure. So we must do our best to discriminate the graver and uglier mischance from the lesser. There is a distinction, then, to be made when such epithets are used in reproach. It would not be fair in all cases to call the man one who has flung his

c shield away, though he may be said to have *lost* his arms. A man who is stripped of his shield by a considerable exertion of force cannot be said to have flung it away with the same truth as one who drops it of his own act. There is all the difference in the world between the cases. So we shall give our law this wording. If a man surrounded by the enemy, and having arms in his hands, do not turn to try and defend himself but intentionally throw down his weapons, or cast them away, and thus choose to purchase a life of shame by his cowardice rather than fair and glorious death by his valor, there shall be judgment for

d the loss of arms thus flung away; in the other case above mentioned, the judge shall hold careful inquiry. Correction must always be meted to the bad—to make a better man of him—not to the unfortunate; on him it is wasted.

Now what shall we call a fitting punishment for the coward who throws away weapons so formidable for his defense? A human judge cannot, indeed, invert the transformation which is said to have been wrought on Caeneus of Thessaly; he, we are told, had been a woman, but a god changed him into a man. Were the reverse process, transformation from man to woman, possible, that, in a way, would be of all penalties the properest for the man who has flung his shield away. e To come as near as we may to this in our treatment of the craven's pitiful clinging to his life, and that he may have no risks to take for the future, but prolong his life of infamy to the last minute possible, our law in these cases shall run thus. If a man be judicially convicted of the shameful casting away of his weapons of war, he shall not again be employed as a soldier nor assigned to any military post whatever by any general or other military officer. In case of disregard of this provision, the officer who so employs the coward shall be mulcted by the 945 auditor of his official accounts to the amount of one thousand drachmas, if he belong to the wealthiest class, five minas if to the second, three minas if to the third, or one, if to the fourth. And the convicted coward shall not only be discharged, as befits his unmanly spirit, from all the dangerous services that become a true man, but shall further pay a price, of a thousand drachmas if he come from the wealthiest class, five minas if from the second, three if from the third, or, if from b the fourth class one, as in the previous clause.

Now as to auditors, what plan will be the proper one for us, whose magistrates have been appointed, some for a year and by the chance of the lot, some for years together and by selection from a leet? Who will be competent to put the crooked in such officers straight, if one of them should perchance act awry under the crushing weight of his office and his own inequality to its dignity? 'Twill indeed be no light task to find an officer of such supereminent merit to set over our c officers themselves, and yet the attempt to discover auditors of such more-than-human quality must be made. For the matter, in fact, stands thus. A polity is like a ship or a living organism. The dissolution of the fabric hangs on a multitude of devices of one character under all their various forms, to which we give different names in the different cases, such as stays, girders, tendons of the sinews; one such, and not the least momentous, in the case of a polity, critical for its preservation or utter dissolution, is that now under our consideration. For if d the censors who are to approve our magistrates are better men than themselves, and do their work with flawless and irreproachable justice, then there will be prosperity and true happiness for the whole of nation and society, but if aught is amiss with the auditing of our magistrates, then the bonds of right which hold all branches of our social fabric together in one will be loosened; every office will be dismem-

e   bered from every other, and all will no longer conspire in one effect;
the state will no longer be one but many, will be filled with conflicting
factions and, ere long, destroyed. So we must see to it that these auditors are, one and all, eminent in every sort of excellence. And so we
shall contrive their creation in some such fashion as this. The whole
body of citizens shall annually, after the day of the summer solstice,
assemble in a precinct jointly dedicate to the sun and to Apollo for the
946 purpose of presenting before the god three men, each citizen presenting the man of not less than fifty years of age whom he judges in all
respects, himself excluded, the best. From those thus first elected they
shall then select those for whom most votes have been cast, to the number of one half—if the total number be even; if it be odd, they shall
omit the one name for which fewest votes have been given—so that
half the names, as determined by the number of votes cast, are retained. If several names receive an equal number of votes, and the
half thus becomes too large, they shall reduce it by excluding the
b   youngest names and retaining the others. The voting shall then be repeated until only three names are left, with an unequal number of
votes. If the votes cast for all three, or for two of them, be equal, they
shall commit the issue to providence and good fortune, and decide it
by lot. They shall then crown the first, second, and third competitors
with olive; when this distinction has been awarded, public proclamation shall be made in this form. The state of the Magnesians, now
providentially restored to its old prosperity, hereby presents its three
c   most worthy citizens to the sun, and dedicates them, in accord with
its ancient usage, as a choice offering of first fruits, to Apollo and the
sun in common for so long as they shall give themselves to their work
as judges.

Twelve such auditors shall be created in the first year, each to
hold office until attaining the age of five-and-seventy; thereafter three
more shall be created annually. They shall divide the magistracies into
twelve groups and scrutinize all by the application of every test to
which a gentleman can be subjected. For their term of office they shall
d   have their residence in the same precinct of Apollo and the sun in
which their election was held. They shall individually, or in some
cases conjointly, hold a scrutiny into the conduct of all outgoing officers of state, and declare by publication in writing in the market
square what sentence or fine each official should incur in the judgment
of the board of auditors. Any official claiming that their judgment
upon him is unfair shall summon the auditors before the court of select judges, and if acquitted of their censures, may, if he so pleases,
bring his action against the auditors themselves; if he lose his case,
e   and the sentence previously pronounced against him by the auditors
be that of death, it shall simply stand, as no more can be done to him,
but any other sentence which can be doubled in the infliction shall be
exacted twofold.

You must next be told what audit will be appointed for the auditors themselves, and how it will be conducted. While they are still
alive, as men whom the whole community has pronounced worthy of 947
its supreme distinction, they shall have the foremost seat at all festivals, and further, the heads of all delegations dispatched to inter-Hellenic sacrifices, religious gatherings, and other such international
solemnities, shall always be taken from among them. They shall be the
only citizens permitted to decorate themselves with the laurel wreath.
They shall all hold priesthoods of Apollo and the sun, while the chief
priesthood shall every year be enjoyed by the member of the college
placed first at the election of that year, and the year shall be officially
registered under his name, as a means of dating, so long as our so- b
ciety survives. When they decease, the lying-in-state, the procession to
the grave, and the grave itself shall be more distinguished than in the
case of other citizens. All the draperies shall be white, and there shall
be neither dirges nor lamentations, but the bier shall be surrounded by
a choir of fifteen maidens and another of fifteen lads; these choirs shall
alternately chant a eulogy on the priests in the form of a hymn, and c
this lyrical panegyric shall be kept up throughout the day. At dawn the
next day the bier shall be conducted to the tomb, the actual escort being one hundred of the young men from the gymnasiums, to be selected at their pleasure by the deceased's kinsmen. At the head of the
procession shall march the young bachelors, all appareled in their accouterments—the horsemen having their chargers, the infantry their
arms, and the rest in the like array. The bier shall be immediately preceded by the boys, who will sing their national chant, and followed by d
the maidens, and such married women as are past the time of procreation. In the rear shall come priests and priestesses; even though they
are debarred from accompanying other funerals, they may follow this,
as one that imparts no defilement, if the Pythian prophetess will add
her sanction to our proposal. The tomb shall be made in the form of an
oblong underground vault of tufa, the most indestructible procurable,
and provided with couches of stone set side by side. When the blessed
dead has been laid to rest there, they shall cover the place with earth e
and plant a grove of trees round it, but leaving one end free, that the
burial place may admit of extension at this end, where there will never
be earth over the interred. And they shall hold an annual contest in
music, athletic exercises, and horse racing in their honor. These, then,
shall be the guerdons to be bestowed on those who have stood their
audit and come out clear. But if any of them presume on his election
and prove himself but too human after all by degeneration after his
appointment, the law shall ordain that he may be impeached by any 948
who will, and the court before which the issue shall be tried shall be
formed as follows. It shall be constituted of curators of law, surviving
members of the board of auditors itself, the panel of select judges. The
verbal form of the prosecutor's impeachment shall be: Such a one is

unworthy of his distinctions and the office he holds. If the impeached
be convicted, he shall forfeit his office, as well as the public burial and
other honors granted to him, but if the prosecutor cannot obtain a fifth
b part of the votes, he shall pay a fine, if of the wealthiest class, of twelve
minas, if of the second, of eight, if of the third, of six, if of the fourth,
of two.

  We may well admire one thing in Rhadamanthus' manner of deciding issues at law, as the tale describes it—his perception that the
men of his day were so confident of the manifest existence of gods—as
well they might be, according to the story, since most of them at that
time, and Rhadamanthus among them, had gods for their parents.
Apparently he held that a judge's work should not be entrusted to any
mere man, but only to gods, and this is why he could decide the cases
c that came before him so simply and rapidly. He put the litigants in a
case to their oath about their assertions, and so had his business speedily and surely dispatched. In these days of ours, when, as we have said,
some men have no belief whatever in gods, others hold that they give
themselves no concern about us, and the creed of the worst, who are
the majority, is that if they pay the gods a trifle in the way of sacrifice
and flattery, they will lend their help in vast frauds and deliver the
sinner from all sorts of heavy penalties—in this present-day world, of
course, the juristic methods of Rhadamanthus are no longer in place.
d Men's beliefs about gods have changed, and so the law must be
changed too. A thoughtful legislator should abolish the oath taken by
either litigant in the institution of a private action. The party instituting proceedings should state his charges in writing, but take no oath
to their truth; similarly the defendant should deliver his denial of the
charge to the magistrate in writing, without swearing to it. It is surely
an awful thing, in a city where lawsuits are common, to know per-
e fectly well that half or nearly half of the inhabitants are forsworn, and
yet have no uneasiness about associating with each other at common
meals and on other occasions of public and private intercourse.

  Our law, then, will require an oath to be taken by a judge before
delivering his sentence; it will command the citizen who gives his vote
for the appointment of a public official to do so in all cases either upon
949 oath, or by using a ballot fetched from a consecrated spot. Similarly,
it will require an oath from judges of choirs or other musical performers, and presidents and umpires of gymnastic and equestrian sports,
and persons in any similar position, where a false oath brings nothing
men commonly regard as profit to the swearer. But wherever there is
great and manifest profit, so esteemed, in denying the truth and standing to the denial on oath, the decision between the various contending
b parties must be reached by legal process requiring no oaths. And more
generally, the presiding authorities of the court shall permit the litigant neither to court credence by swearing to his assertions, nor to
support them by imprecations upon himself and his house, nor to in-

dulge in degrading appeals for mercy or unmanly pathos; they shall see to it that he confines himself entirely to the statement of the rights he claims, in decent and reverent language, and gives a like decent hearing to his opponent. In case of breach of this rule, the presiding officers shall regard him as out of order, and recall him to relevance to the matter in hand. In a case between aliens, however, the parties shall be legally permitted to tender an oath to the opponent, or accept c such a tender from him, at their pleasure. Remember that they will not, as a rule, live to old age among us, or make themselves a nest where others of their own type will be bred up to be naturalized in our country. We shall decide how all such parties are to initiate private suits against each other on the same principle.

In cases of disobedience to the state on the part of a free citizen —I mean cases not grave enough to call for whipping, imprisonment, or death—neglect to present oneself at the meetings of a choir, or to take part in a procession, or some other ceremonial or act of public d service, e.g., a sacrifice in peacetime, or the payment of a special levy in time of war—in all such cases, I say, the first requisite shall be that the loss be made good to the state, and the disobedient party shall be required to give a pledge to the officials empowered by the state's laws to demand it. If the disobedience continue after the pledge has been deposited, the articles so deposited shall be sold, and the proceeds confiscated to the state. If still further penalties be required, they shall be suitably imposed by the officers empowered to deal with the case in question, who shall cite the refractory parties before the courts, until e they consent to obey orders.

A state which has no revenues except those it derives from its own soil, and no commerce, is bound to make up its mind what course it should take as regards foreign travel on the part of its citizens and admission of aliens to its own dominions. So a legislator has to open his treatment of the subject with counsels which he must make as persuasive as he can. Now free intercourse between different states has the tendency to produce all manner of admixture of characters, as the itch for innovation is caught by host from visitor or visitor from 950 host. Now this may result in the most detrimental consequences to a society where public life is sound and controlled by right laws, though in most communities, where the laws are far from what they should be, it makes no real difference that the inhabitants should welcome the foreign visitor and blend with him, or take a jaunt into another state themselves, as and when the fancy for travel takes hold of them, young or old. On the other side, to refuse all admission to the foreigner and permit the native no opportunity of foreign travel is, for one thing, not always possible, and, for another, may earn a state a reputation for barbarism and inhumanity with the rest of the world; its citizens b will be thought to be adopting the ill-sounding policy of exclusion of aliens and developing a repulsive and intractable character. But

reputation, for good or ill, with the outer world ought never to be undervalued. Mankind at large may come far short of the real possession of virtue, but they are by no means equally deficient in the power to judge of the vice or virtue of others; there is a wonderful sagacity among the wicked themselves by which the very wickedest of them are
c often enabled to discriminate better men from worse accurately enough in their thought and language. Hence it is sound advice to give to most societies if one counsels them to prize a good reputation with the wider world. The one absolutely right, supreme rule, in fact, is first to be genuinely good and then to pursue repute for goodness, never, if we mean to be perfect, mere reputation by itself. So it will be only proper for the state we are now founding in Crete, like others, to earn
d the highest and most illustrious reputation for virtue with all its neighbors, and we may have every reasonable hope that if our plan is carried out, ours will be one of the few well-governed states and countries that enjoy the beams of the sun and his fellow gods.

Our course in respect of travels in foreign parts and admission of aliens to our territory should therefore be as follows. First, no permission of foreign travel shall, in any circumstances whatsoever, be granted to any person under the age of forty; further, such permission shall be granted to no person for his private occasions, but only to those traveling on business of state, envoys, embassies, and deputations to diverse ceremonies of religion. It will not be proper to reckon
e absences in war or field service among these occasions of state. As it will be our duty to send deputations to Apollo of Pytho and Zeus of Olympia, as well as to Nemea and the Isthmus, to take their part in the sacrifices and games with which these gods are honored, we must do our utmost to make these deputations as numerous, noble, and distinguished as we can; they must be composed of men who will make our city illustrious in the gatherings of religion and peace, and cover
951 her with a glory to match her renown in the field; on their return they shall explain to their juniors how inferior are the ways of other nations to the institutions of their own land.

There are other commissioners who should, with the curators' license, be sent abroad. If we should have citizens desirous to investigate the affairs of other peoples with ampler leisure, no law shall stand
b in their way. A state unacquainted with mankind, bad and good, will never in its isolation attain an adequate level of civilization and maturity, nor will it succeed in preserving its own laws permanently, so long as its grasp of them depends on mere habituation without comprehension. Among the great mass of men there are always, in fact, some, though few, of a superhuman quality; they are to be found in states with defective laws no less than in states with good, and their society is priceless. An inhabitant of a well-governed state whose own
c character is proof against corruption should follow their trail over sea and land with a view to the confirmation of such practices in his own

community as are sound and the amendment of any that are defective. Indeed without observation and inquiry of this kind, or if it is ill conducted, no scheme of polity is perfectly stable.

CLINIAS : Then how would you secure this pair of results?

ATHENIAN : Why, thus. This observer of whom we are speaking shall, in the first place, be a man of fifty or upward. Next, if our curators are to let him reach other lands as a sample of what they can produce, he must be of high repute, military and otherwise, and the period d of his observations shall not be prolonged beyond his sixtieth year. He shall spend such part of these ten years as he pleases in his observations, and, on his return from them, shall report himself to the council entrusted with supervision of the laws. This shall be a body composed of younger and senior members, and shall be required to hold daily sessions from daybreak until after sunrise. It shall contain, first, the priests who have won distinctions of the first rank, next the ten senior acting curators, next the last elected minister of education and any e retired holders of that office. Each of these shall not merely attend in person but associate with himself such younger person of the age of thirty to forty years as he deems best. The matter of the discourse held at their conferences shall always be the laws of their own com- 952 munity, with such relevant suggestions of moment as they may learn from other quarters, and, in especial, all branches of study they may judge to advance their inquiries by shedding light on points of law that would be left unduly dark and perplexed if these studies were neglected. The junior members shall give all diligence to pursue any such studies approved by their seniors, and if any of these assessors prove unworthy, the whole council shall reprimand him who invited his presence. Such of them as obtain a good repute shall be a target b for the observation of the whole community; they shall be the object of its particular care and regard, and receive marks of honor or more than common disgrace, according as they do themselves credit or fall below the general average in their conduct. Now the observer returned from his travels about the world is to present himself immediately before this council. If he have met with persons possessed of any information about legislation, education, or the management of children, or, as may also happen, have brought back personal reflections of his own, the results shall be laid before the whole council. If they judge him to have come back neither the worse nor the better, he shall still c receive their commendations for his trouble and industry. If much better, he shall, while still living, be commended much more warmly, and at his death shall be honored with appropriate distinctions by the authority of the council. But should he appear to have come home corrupted by his travels, he shall not make his assumed 'wisdom' a pretext for conferences with young or old. If he will obey orders in this matter, he shall live out his life in privacy; if not, he shall have sentence of death—I mean, if a court convict him of meddling in any matter of d education or legislation. If the magistrates neglect to bring such offender before the court, where cause for proceedings has been given, the fact shall be remembered to their discredit at the award of distinctions.

So much, then, of parties who shall have leave of foreign travel and the terms of their leave; we are next to consider the welcome to be given to a visitor from abroad. The foreign visitors of whom account must be taken are of four sorts. First, and everlastingly, a guest who will pay his incessant calls, for the most part, in the summer, like a
e bird of passage; most of his kind are, in fact, just like winged creatures in the way they come flying overseas, at the proper season, on their profitable business errands. He shall be admitted by officials appointed for his benefit, to our market place, harbors, and certain public buildings erected near the city but outside its walls. The officials will take care to prevent the introduction of novelties by these guests, and
953 will administer proper justice to them, but shall keep their intercourse with them within the strict bounds of necessity. The second sort are observers in the literal sense of the word; they come for the sights to be beheld by the eye and the musical displays to be enjoyed by the ear. Lodging shall be provided for all such visitants at the temples with a generous hospitality, and they shall receive the attention and solicitude of our priests and sacristans during a sojourn of reasonable length, but when they have seen and heard what they purposed, they
b must depart without harm done or received. In case of wrongs done or suffered by them, the matter shall be adjudicated upon by the priests, when the claim does not exceed fifty drachmas; where the sum claimed is higher, the case shall come before the commissioners of the market. A third sort, who must be entertained as guests of the state, are those who come from other countries on business of state. They shall be entertained by the generals and commanders of cavalry and infantry divisions, and by no other persons, and the business of their entertainment shall be confined to the particular commander in whose house
c such a guest receives lodging, acting in concert with the prytanes. In the case of a visitant of the fourth sort—the event will be indeed uncommon, but if we should be visited by a counterpart of our own observers from some other country—he must, in the first place, have attained the age of fifty at least, and further, his avowed object must be either to see for himself some excellent features superior to the beauties to be found in other societies, or to reveal something of the
d sort to another state. Such a visitor, then, shall need no bidding to enter the doors of our men of 'wealth and wisdom,' being himself a man of these same qualities. I mean, he may go to the house of the minister of education, confident of his fitness to be guest to such a host, or to that of some man who has won the award for virtue. He shall pass his time with some of these, imparting knowledge and acquiring it, and

when he departs, it shall be as a friend from friends, with suitable parting presents and distinctions. These, I say, are the laws by which our citizens should manage all reception of foreign visitors, male or female, and dispatch of their own countrymen to foreign parts. They e should show their reverence for Zeus, the stranger's patron, not make meats and sacrifices a device for repelling the alien, as we see the 'dusky brood of Nilus' doing today, or banish him by barbarian edicts.

Any person giving a security shall do so in explicit terms; he shall set down the whole transaction in a legal document, and in the presence of witnesses, to the number of three at the least, if the sum concerned be not more than a thousand drachmas, or five at the least if it 954 be higher. Also the broker at a sale shall be security for a seller who has no sound title to the article sold, or cannot guarantee delivery, and an action shall lie against broker no less than against vendor.

A person proposing to search for stolen goods on another's premises shall first strip to his shirt and lay aside his belt, and shall also have made oath by the gods, as required by law, that he honestly expects to find his goods. The other party shall permit the search, which shall extend to sealed, as well as to unsealed, receptacles. If one party desire to make a search and the other refuse permission, the party so b repelled shall lay an action, specifying the value of the missing goods, and the defendant shall, on conviction, pay twice the amount as specified. If the owner of the house be absent from home, the occupants shall permit the search of unsealed receptacles; sealed receptacles shall be countersealed by the searcher and left for five days under such guard as he pleases. If the absence of the owner is further prolonged, the searcher shall call in the urban commissioners and prosecute his search; the sealed receptacles themselves shall be opened, but shall be afterward resealed as before in the presence of the household and the c commissioners.

In cases of disputed title there shall be the following limits of time, beyond which a possessor's title shall no longer be liable to question. In this Cretan city there can be no such thing as a disputed title to a landed estate or a dwelling house. As to other property of which a man may be possessed, when the possessor of an article makes open use thereof in town, market square, and temples, no counterclaim being advanced, then, if another profess to be looking for the article during this period, while the possessor is plainly making no conceal- d ment thereof, if the possession on the one side and search on the other have continued for a year, after the expiry of such year no one shall have legal right to claim such article. If the article be in open use on a country estate, though not in town or market place, and no claimant appear with five years, no man's claim to such article shall thenceforth be entertained. If the article be in use withindoors, and in the town, the term of prescription shall be three years, or for an article thus held

e   in undisclosed possession on a man's country estate, ten. If the article
be in some other country, at whatever time it may be found, prescription shall be no bar to the claim of the finder.

   If a man forcibly hinder the presence of a litigant or his witnesses
in the courts, and the party thus hindered be a slave, his own or another's, the suit shall be declared null and void; if the party hindered
955 be a free man, the offender shall further undergo a year's imprisonment, and shall be liable to action for kidnaping at the instance of
any who pleases. If a man forcibly prevent the presence of a rival
competitor at any gymnastic, musical, or other contest, any who may
please shall inform the presidents of the contest, and they shall set
the intending competitor free to enter the contest. In a case where
this is impossible, if the party hindering the appearance of a competitor prove victorious, the presidents shall award the prize to the
b   competitor so hindered, and inscribe his name as victorious in such
temples as he pleases; the party causing the hindrance shall be forbidden to commemorate such a contest by dedication or inscription,
and shall be equally liable to an action for damage whether he be
defeated in the competition or successful.

   If a man knowingly receive stolen goods, he shall be liable to the
same penalties as the thief; the sentence for reception of an exile shall
be death.

   All citizens shall regard a friend or enemy of the state as their
c   own personal friend or enemy. Any person making peace or war
with any parties independently of the commonwealth shall likewise
incur the pain of death. If a section of the state make peace or war
with any on its own account, the generals shall bring the authors of
the measure before a court, and the penalty for conviction shall be
death.

   The servants of the nation are to render their services without
any taking of presents, and there shall be no glossing of the practice,
nor accepting of the principle that 'A present should be taken for a
d   good deed, though not for an ill.' To form your judgment and then
abide by it is no easy task, and 'tis a man's surest course to give loyal
obedience to the law which commands, 'Do no service for a present.'
The disobedient shall, if convicted, die without ceremony.

   As concerns payment to the public treasury, every man must
have his estate valued, and that for more reasons than one, but the
members of every tribe shall also furnish the rural commission with a
written record of each year's produce that the exchequer may be free
e   to choose at its pleasure, between the two methods of raising its revenue, as the authorities will consider annually whether they shall exact
some fraction of the capital valuation or some part of the annual income, exclusive of the cost of the public table.

   A modest man's gifts in the way of offerings to the gods should
themselves be modest. Now the soil and the household hearthstone are

sacred, in our universal conviction, to all gods that are. No man, then, shall reconsecrate what is dedicated already. In other societies you will find gold and silver in temples as well as in private houses, but they are possessions which breed ill will against their owner. Ivory, a body that soul has forsaken, is no clean offering; bronze and iron are tools of battle. But any man, at his pleasure, may dedicate in our public temples an image of wood, carved in one piece, or of stone similarly fashioned, or a piece of woven work, not exceeding what one woman can finish in a month. White is the color most proper for the gods, in tapestry as in other materials; dyes are not to be used except for military adornment. The most pious presents we can offer the gods are birds and figures on such scale that they can be finished by one artist in one day; our other offerings shall be on the model of these.

We have now spoken of the sections into which our whole city must be divided—their number and nature—and done what we may to prescribe laws for all its chief business transactions. It remains to constitute our judiciary. Our tribunal of first instance will consist of judges appointed by the concurrent choice of defendant and plaintiff; arbitrators would be a more appropriate name for them. The second court shall be formed from fellow villagers and tribesmen, each tribe being subdivided into twelve. If no decision can be reached at the first stage, the litigants shall continue their contention before these judges, but the stake will be increased; the defendant, if worsted a second time, shall pay the award imposed in the original suit with an additional fifth. If he be ill content with his judges and desire to contest the case a third time, he shall take it before the select judges, and shall, if worsted once more, pay the original award with an additional half. A plaintiff who will not sit down with a defeat in the primary court but carries the case to the second shall, if successful, receive the additional fifth, but, if defeated, shall pay the same fraction of the sum under dispute. If the antagonists refuse to submit to the earlier judgments and take the case to the third court, the defeated party shall pay, if he be the defendant, the first award with an additional half, as already enacted, and if plaintiff, the half only.

For what concerns balloting for juries and filling vacancies on them, the provision of a staff for the different courts and the intervals at which sessions shall be held, the manner of taking the vote, the adjournment of the court, and other such necessary details of the administration of justice—as, for example, determination of the order in which suits shall be heard, the rules of compulsory answers to interrogatories and compulsory attendance in court, and the like generally —the matter has been dealt with already, but 'tis no ill deed to repeat a sound maxim or even to state it a third time. In a word, all such minor and simple details of legal procedure may be left by our aged legislator for his younger successors to fill in. Here, then, we have a fair model for the composition of courts to adjudge private disputes.

For tribunals in affairs of common and public concern and courts
which are to subserve the magistrate in the exercise of his function,
many communities already possess decorous institutions derived from
excellent authors and our curators must construct out of this material
a scheme suited to the polity now in process of birth. They shall com-
b   pare these institutions and amend them in the light of their personal
experience until they judge them to be all sufficiently perfected; then
only will they take the last step, stamp them as wholly immutable, and
put them into practice for all time to come. For the silence and decorum of speech to be observed by the judges, and their contrary, as for
our divergences from the various standards of right, good, honor in
other societies, something has been said of this already, and we shall
c   find more to say in the close. He that would show himself a righteously
equal judge must keep these matters before his eyes; he must procure
books on the subject, and must make them his study. There is, in truth,
no study whatsoever so potent as this of law, if the law be what it
should be, to make a better man of its student—else 'twould be for
nothing that the law so stirs our worship and wonder bears a name so
cognate with that of understanding. Furthermore, consider all other
d   discourse, poesy with its eulogies and its satires, or utterances in prose,
whether in literature or in the common converse of daily life, with
their contentious disagreements and their too often unmeaning admissions. The one certain touchstone of all is the text of the legislator.
The good judge will possess the text within his own breast as an antidote against other discourse, and thus he will be the state's preserver
as well as his own. He will secure in the good the retention and in-
e   crease of their rectitude, and in the evil, or those of them whose vicious
principles admit remedy, will promote, so far as he can, conversion
from folly, from profligacy, from cowardice, in a word, from all forms
of wrong. As for those who are fatally attached to such principles, if
our judges and their superiors prescribe death as the cure for a soul in
958   that state, they will, as has been more than once said already, deserve
the praise of the community for their conduct.

When the suits of the year have been carried through to their final
adjudication, the law as to execution of judgment shall be this. First,
the magistrate delivering judgment shall make an assignment to the
successful litigant of all the goods of the unsuccessful party, except
such as he must necessarily be allowed to retain, and this shall be
done, in every case, immediately upon the delivery of the verdict,
b   through the crier of the court, in the presence of the judges. On the expiry of the month following that wherein a suit is tried, if no discharge
have been obtained from the victorious litigant to the satisfaction of
both parties, the magistrate before whom the suit was tried shall, at the
instance of the victor, enforce delivery to him of the goods of the loser.
If these prove insufficient to meet the obligation, and the deficiency
amount to one drachma or upward, the loser shall be deprived of all

right to institute a suit against any person whatsoever, until he have
first discharged in full his debt to the victor, other parties retaining c
their full rights to institute proceedings against such debtor. Any person thus cast obstructing the action of the court which condemned him
shall be brought by the magistrates so obstructed before the court of
the curators, and any person convicted on such a charge shall suffer
death as one that would undo our whole society and its law.

Now to proceed, when a man has been born into the world and
brought up to manhood, has begotten his children and brought them
up, has played his part duly in the transaction of affairs, offering com- d
pensation to any to whom he had done an injury and accepting such
compensation from another, and has so come in due course to law-respecting old age, the natural close will be his decease. As to the deceased, then, whether male or female, full authority to prescribe the
offices of piety it will be proper to perform toward deities of the underworld or of our own shall be given to the interpreters of religious law.
But there must be no grave or tomb, whether great or small, on any site e
capable of cultivation; they must fill up the places where our soil is
naturally fitted only for this one purpose of receiving and concealing
the bodies of the departed with least inconvenience to the living. Where
earth, a true mother to us in the matter, is minded to yield sustenance
for us, our living shall not be cheated of the benefit by any man, living
or dead. The mound of earth shall not be made higher than can be done
by five men within five days, and no stone shall be erected upon it
larger than is needed to receive, at the outside, the customary four hexameter verses in commendation of the life of the deceased. The lying- 959
in-state in the house shall, in the first place, be prolonged only for
the time needed to distinguish between a swoon and a genuine death;
the general rule will thus be that a man may properly be conveyed
to the grave on the third day after his decease. And our faith in the
legislator should extend particularly to his statements when he tells us
that soul is utterly superior to body, and that what gives each one of us
his being is nothing else but his soul, whereas the body is no more than
a shadow which keeps us company. So 'tis well said of the deceased b
that the corpse is but a ghost; the real man—the undying thing called
the soul—departs to give account to the gods of another world, even
as we are taught by ancestral tradition—an account to which the good
may look forward without misgiving, but the evil with grievous dismay. Whence, the legislator will add, we can do very little to help a
man when he is once dead. The help should have been given by all
connected with him while he was still alive, and it should have aided c
him to pass life, while it lasted, in all rectitude and purity, and at
death to escape the vengeance of the world to come on grave sin. Now
since things stand thus with us, we should never waste our substance
in the fancy that he who was so much to us is this bulk of flesh that is
being committed to its grave, and not the real man—the son, or

brother, or other lamented kinsman we fancy ourselves to be burying
—who has left us, to continue and fulfill his own destiny; our duty, we
must think, is rather to make the best of the case and to keep expendi-
d ture on what is, as it were, an altar of the dead about which no spirit
hovers, within modest bounds, and the oracle which may best declare
what modesty is is the voice of the legislator. Our law, then, shall be
this. Modest expenditure shall mean an outlay upon the whole ceremonies of burial which must not exceed five minas for a person of the
wealthiest class, three for one of the second, two for one of the third,
one for one of the fourth.

It will be by no means the least of the many inevitable duties and
e cares of curators to give their life to the supervision of children, adults,
and persons of all ages; in especial, at his death every man shall be put
under the care of a particular curator to be called in as supervisor by
the household of the deceased, to whose credit it shall count if the funeral ceremonies are conducted with propriety and moderation, and
who shall be discredited by any impropriety. The lying-in-state and like
matters shall be regulated by the custom in such things, but custom
must bow to the legislation of the statesman in the points I shall now
specify. To command or forbid tears to be shed over the departed
would be unseemly, but it shall be forbidden to utter dirges over him,
960 or to let the noise of the mourning be audible outside the house. We
shall also prohibit the carrying of a corpse through the public streets
and the raising of cries as the mourners traverse them, and the party
must be beyond the city wall before daybreak. These are the regulations we shall impose in the matter. Compliance therewith will secure
a man from all penalty; disobedience shall be visited by one of the
b curators with a penalty to be approved by the whole body. Further rites
of sepulture, as also the acts which involve loss of the right to sepulture
—parricide, sacrilege, and others—have already been made matters of
legislation, and we may accordingly say that our code is substantially
completed. But the end of an enterprise is never reached by the mere
performance of the act, acquisition of the possession, or establishment
of the foundation; we must never take ourselves to have done all there
was to do until we have provided a complete and permanent guarantee
for the preservation of our work. Until then we should regard our
c whole achievement as unfinished.

CLINIAS : Very true, sir. But I could wish for further light on the
application of that last observation.

ATHENIAN : Why, look you, Clinias, there is good sense in many
of our old household phrases, and not least in the designations men
have given to the Fates.

CLINIAS : How so?

ATHENIAN : We are told that the first of them is called Lachesis,
the second Clotho, and the third, she who, in fact, makes the result
fast, Atropos, with an allusion to the . . . which makes the spinning

irreversible. So likewise, the need of a state or constitution is not d
merely for provision for bodily health and preservation, but for the
presence of loyalty to law in the soul, or rather for the abiding preservation of its law. And this, I believe, is the one thing still manifestly
lacking to our own laws, some means of ensuring, so far as we can,
this rightful irreversibility.

CLINIAS: A serious deficiency, too, in any achievement, if it is
really impossible to give it such a character.

ATHENIAN: Nay, the thing is certainly possible, as I can now e
see quite plainly.

CLINIAS: Then we must on no account relinquish our work
without performing this same service for our proposed code; you know
it is always ridiculous to waste one's pains by building on insecurely
laid foundations.

ATHENIAN: Well reminded. You will find me in accord with
you there.

CLINIAS: I am very glad to hear it. Well then, what, let me
ask you, is to be this safeguard for our system and its laws? How do
you propose to effect it?

ATHENIAN: Why, did we not say that our state must have a 961
council which would be constituted in some such fashion as this? The
ten senior acting curators of law and the whole body of persons who
had won supreme distinction were to meet in council; further, any persons who had traveled into foreign parts to inquire into any capital
invention for the preservation of law they might hear of, and had
returned, were to be examined by this body and pronounced, on approval, worthy of association with it. Furthermore, each member was
to bring with him one younger man, not being under the age of thirty, b
and present him to his colleagues, though not until he had personally
judged him worthy of the honor by his parts and education. If the approval of the whole board were obtained, the young man was to be
received as an associate; if not, his original nomination was to be kept
a profound secret from everyone, and particularly from himself. The
council was to hold its meetings before daybreak, the time, above all
others when a man is always freest from all other business, private or
public. I think this was much the substance of what we said.   c

CLINIAS: You are right, it was.

ATHENIAN: Then I will go back to the subject of this council,
and this is what I would affirm about it. If it is cast out, so to say, as a
sheet anchor of state, furnished with all its proper appurtenances, it
will prove the safeguard of all our hopes.

CLINIAS: And how so?

ATHENIAN: Ah, there is the critical point at which you and I
have to do our uttermost to advise rightly.

CLINIAS: Admirably said, but pray put the purpose into execution.

d   ATHENIAN: Well then, Clinias, we have to discover what is the fitting protector for anything in all its various activities. In a living organism, for instance, it is, above everything else, the soul and head which are designed to this function.

CLINIAS: Once more, how so?

ATHENIAN: Why, you know, it is the perfection of these two that guarantees the preservation of the whole creature.

CLINIAS: How so?

ATHENIAN: By the development of intelligence in the soul and vision and hearing in the head as the crowning endowment of each. To put it concisely, when intelligence is fused into a unity with these noblest of the senses, they constitute what we have every right to call a creature's salvation.

CLINIAS: That certainly sounds like the truth.

e   ATHENIAN: It does indeed. But what in particular is the object envisaged by the blended intelligence and sense which is to be the salvation of a vessel in storm and calm? In this case of the ship, it is the fusion of the sharp senses of captain and crew alike with the captain's intelligence that preserves ship and ship's company together, is it not?

CLINIAS: To be sure.

ATHENIAN: Well the point surely calls for no great number of illustrative examples. Take the case of a military expedition; we have to ask ourselves what must be the mark aimed at by its commanders— or again, by any medical service—if they are to aim at 'salvation,' as

962   they ought to do. In the first case, I take it, the target is victory and superiority to the enemy, in that of the physicians and their staff, the preservation of bodily health?

CLINIAS: Why, of course.

ATHENIAN: Well then, if a physician knew nothing of the nature of bodily health, as we have just called it, or a commander nothing of the nature of victory and the other results we mentioned, it would surely be clear that he had no understanding of his subject whatsoever.

CLINIAS: Why, certainly.

ATHENIAN: Well, then, to come to the case of a state, if a man plainly knows nothing of the mark a statesman must keep before his

b   view, has he, for one thing, any right to the style of a magistrate, and will he, for another, have any capacity for the preservation of that of whose aim he is so utterly ignorant?

CLINIAS: None whatsoever.

ATHENIAN: Why then, mark the inference. If our present disposition of our territory is to be completed, it must provide for the presence there of some body which understands, in the first place, the true nature of this mark of statesmanship, as we have called it, and next, the methods by which it may be attained, and the counsels— emanating principally from the laws themselves, secondarily from individual men—which make for or against it. If a state leave no room for such a body, we should not be surprised that a society so unintelligent and so imperceptive habitually finds itself drifting at the c mercy of circumstance in its various undertakings.

CLINIAS : Just so.

ATHENIAN : Now where in our society, in which of its sections or institutions as so far prescribed, have we made any adequate provision for such a safeguard? Can we specify anything of the kind?

CLINIAS : No indeed, sir, not with any certainty. But if I may hazard a guess, your observations seem to be pointing to the committee which, as you just said, will be expected to meet in the small hours.

ATHENIAN : You understand me perfectly, Clinias. That body, d as our present observations prefigure, will, indeed, need to be equipped with all virtue. And the first point of such virtue will be that its aim must not wander from object to object; it must have a single mark always before its eye and make it the target of all its shafts.

CLINIAS : Assuredly it must.

ATHENIAN : Now we have reached this point, we shall understand that there is nothing surprising in the fact that the laws of our various societies should be all at sea, seeing that the aims of the legislators in each of them are so conflicting. In general, we must not be surprised that the standard of rights with some men is the restriction of power to a certain group, no matter whether better or worse in reality e than others, with others the acquisition of riches, no matter whether or not at the cost of enslavement, and yet others make 'liberty' the object of their passion. Others, again, combine two objects in their legislation and keep an eye on both together, liberty and empire over other societies, while the wisest of all, as they fancy themselves, pursue all these aims and others like them at once; they set no one object of a particular devotion before them to which they might point as the proper aim of all other pursuits.

CLINIAS : Surely then, sir, the position we took so long ago was 963 the sound one. We said there was one end to be kept in view in all our own laws, and we were agreed, I believe, that the right name for the thing is *virtue*.

ATHENIAN : We were so.

CLINIAS : And virtue, as I remember, we said has four parts.

ATHENIAN : Precisely.

CLINIAS : But the chief of them all is understanding, and it should be the aim of the three other parts, as well as of everything else.

ATHENIAN : You follow my argument perfectly, Clinias; pray keep me company in the next step. As to this matter of the single aim, we have specified the mark on which the understanding of navigator, physician, military commander should direct its gaze and are now in b the act of examining that of the statesman. If we like to personify his wisdom, we may address it with these words. In the name of all that is wonderful, what is it you have in view? What is your one aim? The physician's wisdom can give us a definite answer. You, the wisest of all the wise, by your own account, have you no answer?

Now Megillus and Clinias, can you, between you, act as his spokesmen? Can you give me a definition stating what you take this object to be, like the definitions I have so often given you as spokesman c for other parties?

CLINIAS : Nay sir, there we are at a loss.

ATHENIAN : Now what is it that we must be so anxious to discern, in itself as in its various manifestations?

CLINIAS : I should like some illustration of what you mean by manifestations.

ATHENIAN : As an illustration, then, take our language about the four types of virtue. If there are four of them, obviously we must hold that each type by itself is one.

CLINIAS : Obviously.

ATHENIAN : And yet we give one name to all of them. In fact, we speak of courage as virtue, of wisdom as virtue, and similarly with d the other two, and this implies that they are not really several things, but just this one thing—virtue.

CLINIAS : Certainly.

ATHENIAN : Now it is easy enough to point out where these two, or the others, differ and why they have received two distinct names; it is not so light a matter to show why we have given both of them, and the rest, the one common name, *virtue*.

CLINIAS : Now what is your point?

ATHENIAN : One which I can explain readily enough. Suppose we divide the parts of questioner and respondent between us.

CLINIAS : Again, I must ask you to explain yourself.

e   ATHENIAN : Ask me the question why we first call both things by the one name *virtue*, and then speak of them as two—*courage* and *wisdom*. I will give you the reason. One of them, courage, is concerned with fears, and so is to be found in the brutes and in the behavior of mere infants. In fact, a soul may attain to courage by mere native temperament independently of discourse of reason, but without such discourse no soul ever comes by understanding or wisdom; none has ever done so, and none ever will—the cases are utterly different.

CLINIAS : That is true enough.

964   ATHENIAN : Very good. My statement has told you where the things differ and why they are two; it is now your turn to tell me in what respects they are one and the same. Remember that you will also have to explain in what way the four things can be one thing, and that when you have given your explanation you are once more to ask me in what way they are four. And there will be still a further point to investigate. If a man is to have competent knowledge of anything whatsoever which has not only a name but a definition, is it enough that

he should know its bare name, but be unaware of its definition? Is
not any such ignorance in a man of any account disgraceful, when
the matter at issue is one of paramount importance and dignity?   b

CLINIAS : So I should presume.

ATHENIAN : In the eye of an author or custodian of law, a man
who believes in his own pre-eminence in virtue and has won the prize
for the very qualities of which we are treating, can there be anything
of greater importance than these qualities themselves, valor, purity,
justice, wisdom?

CLINIAS : There surely cannot.

ATHENIAN : Then where these are the issues at stake, is it to be
believed of our interpreters, our teachers, our legislators, the very
men who have the rest of us in their keeping—can it be believed, I say,
when it comes to the provision for one who needs to learn and know,
or to be corrected and rebuked for his faults, that a man such as we c
have in mind will not show himself pre-eminent as a teacher of the
characteristic quality of virtue and vice and generally as an instructor? Can we suppose that some poet or pretended 'educator of youth'
who has come to our city will get the credit of superiority to one who
has won the palm of a perfect virtue? In a state like this, where there
are no custodians competent in act as in thought from their competent acquaintance with virtue—is it surprising, I ask you, if a state
left so unguarded has the fortunes of too many of our states of today? d

CLINIAS : Why no, I suppose not.

ATHENIAN : What follows? Shall we act, as we are now proposing, or how? Shall we equip our guardians with a more finished mastery in the theory and practice of virtue than the mass of their
neighbors? How else is our own city to resemble an intelligent man's
head with its sense organs in its possession of such a defense within
itself?

CLINIAS : Pray, sir, how are we to understand the comparison?
In what does the likeness consist?

ATHENIAN : Why manifestly the city at large is the trunk of the e
body. The younger guardians—we selected them for their superior
parts, for the quickness of all their faculties—are stationed, so to say,
at its summit, their vision ranges over the whole compass of the state,
they commit what they perceive in their watch to memory, and serve
their elders as scouts in every branch of affairs. Those senior men— 965
we may compare them with the understanding for their special wisdom in so many momentous matters—sit in council, where they
avail themselves of the services and suggestions of their juniors, and
thus, by their united action, the two parties are, between them, the
real salvation of the whole state. Is this to be our project, or are we to
find some other arrangement for ourselves? Are we to leave all our
citizens on one level of training and education, with no more sedu-
lously trained class among them?

CLINIAS: My dear sir! We cannot possibly take such a course.

ATHENIAN: Then we shall have to proceed to an education of a
b more exacting kind than we have so far contemplated.

CLINIAS: I dare say we shall.

ATHENIAN: And that on which we have just touched may perhaps prove to be the very one we need?

CLINIAS: Indeed it may.

ATHENIAN: I believe we said that a consummate craftsman or
guardian in any sphere will need the ability not merely to fix his regard
on the many, but to advance to the recognition of the one and the organization of all other detail in the light of that recognition?

CLINIAS: Yes, and it was the truth.

c   ATHENIAN: Now whose vision and view of his object can be
more intimate than his who has learned to look from the dissimilar
many to the one form?

CLINIAS: You may be right.

ATHENIAN: Not 'may be,' bless you! There *is* no surer path for
a man's steps, and can be none.

CLINIAS: Well, sir, I admit it on your assurance; so we may let
the argument take that course.

ATHENIAN: Then it looks as though the guardians of our god-
given constitution too must be constrained, first and foremost, to see
d exactly what is the identity permeating all the four, the unity to be
found, as we hold, alike in courage, in purity, in rectitude, in wisdom,
and entitling them all to be called by the one name, *virtue*. This, my
friends, if you please, is what we must now close upon with a firm and
unyielding grip, until we are content with our account of the real character of the mark on which our gaze shall be fixed, whether it prove to
be a unit or a whole, or both at once, or what you please. If we let this
slip through our fingers, can we suppose we shall ever be fully
e equipped for a virtue of which we cannot tell whether it is many
things, or four, or one? No, if we are to follow our own advice, we
must find some other way of securing this result in our society. But of
course we must consider whether we should leave the whole subject
alone.

CLINIAS: Nay, sir, in the name of the god of strangers, you
cannot let such a matter drop; we find your remarks full of truth. But
how is the thing to be compassed?

966   ATHENIAN: Ah, that is a question we are not yet ready to ask.
We must first be sure we are agreed whether or not the thing must be
done.

CLINIAS: Indeed it must, if only it can be done.

ATHENIAN: Then what say you to this? Do we take this same
view when it comes to the *fine*, or to the *good*? Will our guardians have
merely to know that each of them is many, or must they know further
how and in what way each is a unit?

CLINIAS : Why, we seem fairly driven to hold that they will actually have to understand their unity.

ATHENIAN : And suppose they can perceive this, but are unable b to give any articulate demonstration of it?

CLINIAS : Out of the question! A condition only fit for a slave!

ATHENIAN : Well, once more, must we say the same of all matters of moment? Men who are to be real guardians of the law will need a real knowledge of them all; they must be able to expound this knowledge in their speech and to conform to it in their practice, to discern the true intrinsic demarcations of good and evil?

CLINIAS : Indubitably.

ATHENIAN : Now among these matters of high import is not the c subject of divinity which we treated so earnestly pre-eminent? 'Tis of supreme moment for us, is it not, to know with all the certainty permitted to man that there are gods, and with what evident might they are invested? In the great mass of our citizens we may tolerate mere conformity to the tradition embodied in the laws, but we shall do well to deny all access to the body of our guardians to any man who has not made it his serious business to master every proof there is of the being of gods. And by denial of access I mean that no man who is not divinely gifted or has not labored at divinity shall ever be chosen for a d curator, nor ever be numbered among those who win the distinction for virtue.

CLINIAS : As you say, it will be only right that the slothful or incompetent in such matters should be hopelessly excluded from high distinction.

ATHENIAN : May we say, then, that we know of two motives—those we have already rehearsed—of credibility in divinity?

CLINIAS : And what are these two?

ATHENIAN : One of them is our theory of the soul, our doctrine that it is more ancient and more divine than anything that draws per- e ennial being from a motion that once had a beginning, the other our doctrine of the orderliness in the movements of the planets and other bodies swayed by the mind that has set this whole frame of things in comely array. No man who has once turned a careful and practiced gaze on this spectacle has ever been so ungodly at heart that its effect has not been the very reverse of that currently expected. 'Tis the common belief that men who busy themselves with such themes are 967 made infidels by their astronomy and its sister sciences, with their disclosure of a realm where events happen by stringent necessity, not by the purpose of a will bent on the achievement of good.

CLINIAS : And what is the true state of the matter?

ATHENIAN : As I told you, the situation has been precisely reversed since the days when observers of these bodies conceived them b to be without souls. Even then, they awakened wonder, and aroused in the breasts of close students the suspicion, which has now been

converted into an accepted doctrine, that were they without souls, and
by consequence without intelligence, they would never have conformed to such precise computations; even in those days there were
persons bold enough to hazard the actual assertion that it is mind to
which the heavens owe all their ordered array. And yet these same
thinkers went astray about the soul; they took it to be junior to body,
c not senior, and their error, as I may say, wrecked the whole scheme,
or, to speak more accurately, wrecked themselves. For on a shortsighted view, the whole moving contents of the heavens seemed to
them a parcel of stones, earth, and other soulless bodies, though they
furnish the sources of the world order! It was this that involved the
thinkers of those days in so many charges of infidelity and so much
unpopularity, and further inspired poets to denounce students of philosophy by comparing them with dogs baying the moon, and to talk a
d world of folly besides, but, as I told you, today the position has been
reversed.

CLINIAS : In what way?

ATHENIAN : No son of man will ever come to a settled fear of
God until he has grasped the two truths we are now affirming, the
soul's dateless anteriority to all things generable, her immortality and
sovereignty over the world of bodies, and moreover that presence
among the heavenly bodies of a mind of all things of which we have
e spoken so often already. He must also possess the requisite preliminary sciences, perceive the links which connect them with music, and
apply his knowledge meetly to his moral and legal behavior; also he
968 must be able to give a reasoned account of all that admits thereof. He
that adds not these endowments to his possession of the popular virtues will never be a sufficient magistrate of a whole community, but
only a magistrate's underling. Thus the time has now come, Megillus
and Clinias, when we must ask ourselves whether we shall add one
more statute to all hitherto rehearsed, a law instituting the nocturnal
council of magistrates, duly furnished with the whole education we
b have described, as the state's custodian and preserver. How shall we
act, think you?

CLINIAS : How, my dear friend, can we do other than make the
addition, if we have the power, in however low degree?

ATHENIAN : Then let us indeed, one and all, throw our powers
into so worthy an undertaking. This at least is a task in which you will
find me eager to help—and I may possibly discover other co-operators
besides myself—from my copious experience of such matters and
meditation upon them.

CLINIAS : Out of all question, sir, we must take the road along
c which God himself is so plainly guiding us. But what is our right way
to set about it? That is what our present conference has to discover.

ATHENIAN : As to laws on such a point, Megillus and Clinias, it
is impossible to lay them down now, before the institution has been
framed—it will be time to define its statutory powers when it exists

—all that can be done at present toward fashioning such a body, if the work is to be done rightly, is instruction by repeated conferences.

CLINIAS: How so? What is the meaning of that remark?

ATHENIAN: Well, we must obviously begin by compiling a list of persons qualified for the post of guardian in respect of age, intellec- d tual ability, character, and habits. When we come to the next point, that of the subjects to be studied, it is no easy matter to invent them ourselves, nor yet to go to school to some other inventor. Further, it would be futile to give regulations either for the length of time to be given to the single subjects or for the order in which they shall be taken up; the student himself will not discover which of his studies is relevant until scientific knowledge of the subject has found a settlement e in his soul. Thus you see that while it would be wrong to call these various subjects incapable of *description*, it is very right to call them incapable of *prescription*, for prescription can throw no light on their contents.

CLINIAS: Why, sir, if the case stands so, what, I ask you, are we to do?

ATHENIAN: As the phrase goes, my friends, we have a 'fair field and no favor'; if we are ready, as they say, to stake the whole future of our polity on a throw of triple six or triple ace, why, so we must, and I, 969 for one, will take my share in the risk. My part shall be the statement and exposition of my own convictions about the scheme of education and training which our conversation has thus started for the second time. But the hazard we run, mind you, is no slight one; there are not many others to be compared with it. I would advise you, Clinias, in particular, to lay the matter deeply to heart. For you the alternatives are to construct this state of Magnesia—or whatever name God will have it called after—on right lines and cover yourself with glory, or to incur the abiding reputation of a daring not to be equaled in all future b ages. But if we can once create this admirable council, then, my good friends and colleagues, we must deliver the state into its keeping, and there will be hardly one modern legislator to disagree with us. The dream on which we touched a while ago in our talk, when we painted our picture of the partnership of the mind and the head, will have found its fulfillment in real and working fact, if and when we have seen our men scrupulously selected, duly educated, settled at the end of the process in the nation's central fortress and established c there as guardians whose likes we have never seen in our whole lives for perfection as protectors.

MEGILLUS: My dear Clinias, after all that has now been said, we shall either have to abandon the foundation of your city or else to be deaf to our friend's excuses, and try every entreaty and inducement to secure him as a co-operator in the foundation.

CLINIAS: Very true, Megillus. I will do as you wish, and you d must assist me.

MEGILLUS: Count upon me.

APPENDIX

The Epinomis, *the* Greater Hippias, *and the* Letters *are here printed for the convenience of the reader. Their authenticity has been the subject of a long debate but all, with the exception of Letter I, have had scholarly defenders in recent times; their contents have been included in the index. The Letters are presented in the presumptive chronological order established by the translator (except for the last four, which he does not consider authentic).*

EPINOMIS

CLINIAS: Well, sir, here we are, all three of us—you, myself, and 973
our friend Megillus—duly convened, as we had agreed, to discuss wisdom. We are to consider in what terms to describe that which, if we can only discover it, will, in our mind, best fit humanity for such a degree of understanding as man can compass. We have already, we hold, discussed all other considerations relevant to legislation. But b
there is one question to which we have neither found nor stated the answer, and it is the supreme question for solution and determination. What are the studies which will lead a mortal man to wisdom? And that is the problem we must do our best not to leave unanswered today. To do so, in fact, would be to fail in the purpose we all had in mind at the outset, when we hoped to make everything so clear from start to finish.

ATHENIAN: Well said, my dear Clinias, though I fancy the statement to which you are to listen will be a strange one. And yet, in a way, it is not so strange after all. It is one only too often propounded c
as the lesson of experience of life—that mankind will never attain bliss or felicity. So please follow me and consider whether you find me right in agreeing with others on the point. My thesis is that attainment of bliss and felicity is impossible for mankind, with the exception of a chosen few. I would limit the statement to the term of a lifetime; when life is over, there is a fair hope that a man may achieve all that prompts us to live as nobly as we may, and to crown such a life by a corresponding end. What I want to say is nothing recondite, but only a truth which all of us, Greeks or non-Greeks, recognize in one way or another. To begin with, birth itself is a painful experience for any living creature. One has first to make acquaintance with life in the womb, then to be actually born, and then further to be reared and educated, all processes, as we all confess, involving untold discomforts. 'Twill be but a brief time we shall take into account if we reckon 974
not the miseries of life but only what all would regard as its satisfactory part. This is generally held to form a kind of breathing space in the middle years of life, but old age has us soon in its clutch, and must

---

From *Philebus and Epinomis*, translated with an introduction by A. E. Taylor, edited by Raymond Klibansky (New York, 1956).

make any man whose head is not stuffed with childish fancies unwilling to live his time over again, when he considers what his life has been. Do you ask me for my proof of this? It is that the same thing
b is true of the object of our present inquiry. That inquiry, in fact, is how we are to get wisdom, and the implication is that all of us have the capacity for acquiring it. Yet it eludes us altogether, as soon as we turn to any of the branches of understanding which make up the so-called arts, forms of understanding, or other such fancied sciences. It is as though none of them all deserved the name of wisdom in the affairs of
c man's life; yet the soul has a confident trust, a prophetic divination, that she possesses such a native capacity, though what it is, when come by, or how, she can hardly discover. Does not the case stand much thus with our desperate search for wisdom, a search so much more difficult than might be expected by those of us who can examine themselves and others intelligently and coherently by means of discourse of all and every kind? Are we to confess that this is our situation, or are we not?

CLINIAS : Doubtless, sir, we shall make the confession, but in
d the hope, naturally born of time spent in converse with you, that we may yet arrive at the soundest view of the matter.

ATHENIAN : Then we must first review the other so-called sciences, acquisition and possession whereof do not make a man wise, with a view to setting them on one side and then trying to bring before our view and understand those which we really need. To begin with,
e then, we must observe of those which are mortality's earliest need that while they cannot be dispensed with and come first in a real sense, though the man who is versed in them may have been counted wise long ago, in the beginning of things, he has certainly not the reputation today; his knowledge of such things is rather made a reproach to him.
975 We will name them, then, with the remark that everyone—I mean everyone who makes it his great concern to be esteemed a man of the best kind—avoids them for the sake of achieving understanding and the exercise of it. We may give the first place to that which sets a check to our devouring the flesh of animals, absolutely prohibiting the consumption of some—so the legend runs—and confining us to a lawful consumption of others. Now may the good will of the spirits of old be with us, as indeed it is; whoever they were 'who gave the rule,' they
b still have our first blessing! But, after all, the production of barley and wheat and the making of food from them, admirable things though they are, will never make a man wholly wise—why, the very word *produce* might tend to create a certain repugnance to the product— and the same thing is true of all husbandry. It is not so much from science as from a native instinct implanted by God that we all seem to have taken the soil in hand. We may say so much of the construc-
c tion of dwellings, building in its various forms, and the manufacture of all sorts of furniture, smithwork, carpentry, pottery, weaving, and

equally of the provision of tools of every sort; all this is serviceable enough to a populace, but it is not imputed as virtue. It is true, again, of the chase in all its forms; various as they are, and high as is the skill for which they call, they result in no grandeur of soul nor wisdom. The art of the prophet or his interpreter, again, fails us entirely; he knows only what his oracle says—whether it is true is more than he can tell.

Now since, as we see, our necessities are provided by art, but by arts none of which can make a man wise, all that is left over is play, d imitative play for the most part, but of no serious worth. For imitation is effected by a great variety of instruments, and likewise of attitudes, and those none too dignified, of the body itself in declamation and the different forms of music and all the offshoots of the art of drawing, with the numerous variegated patterns they produce in fluid or solid mediums, but none of these branches of imitation makes the practitioner in the least wise, no matter how earnestly he labors.

When all is done, what is left on our hands proves to be defense, e defense of a host of clients by a host of means. Its most highly considered and most comprehensive form, the science of war, as we call it, the art of the general, stands highest in repute for its usefulness, but is most dependent on good fortune, and, from the nature of the case, is assigned rather to courage than to wisdom. As for what is 976 known as the art of medicine, it also is, of course, a form of defense against the ravages committed on the living organism by the seasons with their untimely cold and heat and the like. But none of their devices can bestow reputation for the truest wisdom; they are at sea on an ocean of fanciful conjecture, without reduction to rule. We may also give the name of defender to sea captains and their crews, but I would have no one encourage our hopes by the proclamation that any of them is wise. None of them can *know* of the fury or kindness of the b winds, and that is the knowledge coveted by every navigator. Nor yet can we give the title to those who profess to defend us by their eloquence in the law courts, and devote themselves to a study of human character based on memories and empirical fancies, while they are far astray from true comprehension of genuine rights.

We have still left one claimant to the title of wisdom—a curious capacity which would commonly be spoken of rather as native endowment than as wisdom—that seen in the man who learns whatever he studies with facility, has a capacious and trustworthy memory, recalls the relevant and appropriate steps in every situation, and does so c without delay. All this will be ascribed by some to native endowment, by others to wisdom, by others to natural sagacity, but no right-judging man will ever consent to call a person wise on the strength of any of these gifts. And yet there must be some knowledge or other, the possession whereof will bestow wisdom which is wisdom in very deed, and not in mere report. So let us look into the matter. 'Tis an argument of

d the highest difficulty on which we are now entering—this discovery
of a wisdom, over and above those we have named, which shall be
really and truly worthy of the name. He that can win it is to be neither
mechanic nor fribble; it must make him a wise and good citizen of
his state, in the fullest sense of the terms, as magistrate and subject,
and a modest man to boot. Let us then first consider what single science there is, of all those we have, such that were it removed from
mankind, or had it never made its appearance, man would become the
most thoughtless and foolish of creatures. Now the answer to this
e question at least is not overhard to find. For, if we, so to say, take one
science with another, 'tis that which has given our kind the knowledge
of number that would affect us thus, and I believe I may say that 'tis
not so much our luck as a god who preserves us by his gift of it. I
should explain what god I am thinking of—an odd one to mention,
and yet, in a way, not so odd after all. How can we but believe that
977 the cause of all the blessings we enjoy is likewise the cause of that
which is far the greatest of all, understanding? Well, and what god is
it, Megillus and Clinias, of whom I speak in this solemn fashion? Why,
Uranus, to be sure, whom it is our bounden duty to honor, as it is to
honor all divinities and gods, and to whom we are specially bound to
pray. All of us will confess that he is the source of all the other good
things we enjoy, and we in particular assent that 'tis he who has in
b very deed given us number, and will renew the gift if men will only
follow his leading. If a man will but come to the right contemplation
of him, he may call him by the name of Cosmos, Olympus, or Uranus
as he pleases; only let him follow him in his course as he bespangles
himself and wheels his stars through all their courses in the act of providing us all with seasons and daily food. Aye, and with the gift of the
whole number series, so we shall assume, he gives us likewise the rest
of understanding and all other good things. But this is the greatest
boon of all, if a man will accept his gift of number and let his mind
expatiate over the whole heavenly circuit.
      But we must still go forth a little on our argument and recall our
c very just observation, that if number were banished from mankind,
we could never become wise at all. For a creature's soul could surely
never attain full virtue if the creature were without rational discourse,
and a creature that could not recognize two and three, odd and even,
but was utterly unacquainted with number, could give no rational account of things whereof it had sensations and memories only, though
d there is nothing to keep it out of the rest of virtue, valor, and sobriety.
But without true discourse a man will never become wise, and if he
has not wisdom, the chiefest constituent of full virtue, he can never
become perfectly good, and therefore not happy. Thus there is every
necessity for number as a foundation, though to explain why this is
necessary would demand a discourse still longer than what has gone
before. But we shall also be right if we say of the work of all the

other arts which we recently enumerated, when we permitted their e
existence, that nothing of it all is left, all is utterly evacuated, if the
art of number is destroyed.

Perhaps when a man considers the arts, he may fancy that mankind need number only for minor purposes—though the part it plays
even in them is considerable. But could he see the divine and the mortal in the world process—a vision from which he will learn both the
fear of God and the true nature of number—even so 'tis not any man
and every man who will recognize the full power number will bestow 978
on us if we are conversant with the whole field of it—why, for example, all musical effects manifestly depend upon the numeration of motions and tones—or will take the chief point of all, that 'tis the source
of all good things, but, as we should be well aware, of none of the ill
things which may perhaps befall us. No, unregulated, disorderly, ungainly, unrhythmical, tuneless movement, and all else that partakes of
evil, is destitute of all number, and of this a man who means to die b
happy must be convinced. And as for the right, the good, the noble, and
the like, no man who has given his adherence to a true belief, but without *knowledge,* will ever enumerate them in a way to bring conviction to himself and to others.

Well then, let us go on to face the real point we are to consider.
How did we learn to count? How, I ask you, have we come to have the
notions of *one* and *two,* the scheme of the universe endowing us with c
a native capacity for these notions? There are many other creatures
whose native equipment does not so much as extend to the capacity to
learn from our Father above how to count. But in our own case, God,
in the first place, constructed us with this faculty of understanding
what is shown us, and then showed us the scene he still continues to
show. And in all this scene, if we take one thing with another, what
fairer spectacle is there for a man than the face of day, from which he
can then pass, still retaining his power of vision, to the view of night, d
where all will appear so different? Now as Uranus never ceases rolling all these objects round, day after day, and night after night, neither
does he ever cease teaching men the lore of one and two until even the
dullest scholar has sufficiently learned the lesson of counting. For any
of us who sees this show will form the notion of *three, four,* and *many.*
And among these bodies of God's fashioning there is one, the moon,
which goes its way, now waxing, now waning, as it lights up one day
after another, until it has fulfilled fifteen days and nights, and they, if e
one will treat its whole orbit as a unity, constitute a period, such that
the very slowest creature, if I may say so, on which God has bestowed
the capacity to learn, may learn it. Thus so far, and within these limits, every creature with the requisite capacity is skilled enough in
counting by observation of the units. But when I consider that all these 979
creatures are always making calculations in their dealings with each
other, I fancy it was for some greater purpose, as well as for this, that

when God had made the moon in the sky, waxing and waning, as we have said, he combined the months into a year and so all the creatures, by a happy providence, began to have a general insight into the relations of number with number. 'Tis thus that earth conceives and yields her harvest so that food is provided for all the creatures, if winds and b rains are neither unseasonable nor excessive; but if anything goes amiss in the matter, 'tis not deity we should charge with the fault, but humanity, who have not ordered their life aright. However that may be, in our inquiry into jurisprudence we took the view that in general to know what is best for man is an easy thing, and that any of us can become competent to understand what he is told of the matter and act on his knowledge, if only he could tell what may be expected to be to his advantage and what to his hurt. Whence we held, as we still c hold, that there is no great difficulty in other studies; the supreme difficulty is to know how we are to become good men. Again, to get all other 'good things,' as they are proverbially called, is both possible and not too difficult—to get all the property we need, or do not need, the bodily vigor we need or do not need. And as for the soul, there is universal agreement that it must be good and must be good in a certain way. That it must be just, sober, and valiant, there again we are all agreed; that it must be *wise* is a thing all men say, but on the question what wisdom it needs, as we have just explained, the multitude d are hopelessly at variance. We have now discovered, over and above all the forms of wisdom we mentioned first, another which is of no small account in one respect—I mean, that he who has learned the lessons we have described has certainly a *repute* for wisdom. Whether the man who has this knowledge really *is* wise and good is the question we hope to determine.

CLINIAS : How right you were, sir, when you said you were trying to express grave thoughts on a grave theme!

e ATHENIAN : Indeed, Clinias, they are no trivialities. But what makes the task harder is that I am trying to make the expression perfectly and precisely true.

CLINIAS : To be sure, sir. Still you must not let weariness make you give up your exposition.

ATHENIAN : So be it, but you and your friend too must not weary of listening.

CLINIAS : No, I promise you, and I give you the pledge for both of us.

980 ATHENIAN : I thank you. Then, I take it, we must begin for preference, if only we can find a single name for it, by stating what wisdom this is which we hold to be wisdom indeed. As a second-best course, if the other prove quite impossible, we must say what and how many are the forms of wisdom by gaining which a man will be wise by our account of the matter.

CLINIAS : Say on, then.

ATHENIAN: Then next, we can raise no objection if our legislator goes on to an imaginative presentation of the gods nobler and better than those which have been given in the past. He may make the adoration of them, so to say, a noble pastime, and so pass his own b life in worshiping them with hymns of happiness.

CLINIAS: Finely said, sir. May the end of your laws be this, to sing the glad praises of the gods, to lead the life of higher piety, and then to come to the best and worthiest close!

ATHENIAN: Then where is our talk leading us, Clinias? Suppose we offer the gods the worship of a heartfelt hymn, and a prayer that we may be moved to speak of them in the best and worthiest strains? May I take it you agree?

CLINIAS: With all my heart. Make your prayer, my dear sir, in c faith, and then go on with such fair discourse of gods and goddesses as you are moved to utter.

ATHENIAN: And so I will, if God himself will vouchsafe us his guidance. Only you must join in the prayer.

CLINIAS: And now proceed with your discourse.

ATHENIAN: Well then, since the men of old gave such a bad version of the generation of gods and creatures, my first business, I presume, must be to imagine the process better, on the lines of my former discourse, and to embody the points which I tried to make against unbelievers, when I argued that there are gods, that their care d extends to all things great or small, and that no entreaties can win them to depart from the path of justice. I presume you remember, Clinias, for you both actually took notes of what was said. Now all I said then was perfectly true, but the chief point of all was this, that soul, all soul, is older than body, all body. You recall the point? Surely you must recollect so much? For surely we may well believe the better, more primitive, more divine, older than the [worse], more recent, e baser, the ruler everywhere older than the subject, the leader than the led. So much, then, we will take as settled, that soul is older than body. But since this is so, it follows that the starting point of our story of 981 creation is more credible than the starting point of theirs. We may take it, then, that our beginning is more seemly than the other, and that we are taking the right path to the great branch of wisdom which treats of the creation of the gods.

CLINIAS: Yes, we may take this as established to the best of our powers.

ATHENIAN: Then to proceed. May we say that the name 'living creature' is most properly used in the case when a single complex of soul and body gives birth to a single form?

CLINIAS: We may.

ATHENIAN: Such a being, in fact, has a perfect title to that b name?

CLINIAS: It has.

ATHENIAN: And solid bodies from which things can best and most fairly be molded are, by the most probable account, of five sorts, while the whole of being of the other kind has one single type. For nothing can be incorporeal and wholly and always devoid of color, save only being of the divinest type, *soul*, and 'tis the proper and ex-
c clusive function of this to mold and make. To body it pertains, as I say, to be molded, be made, be seen, but to the other—we may repeat it, for it needs to be said more than once—to be unseen, to know, to be apprehended by thought, and to have its part in memory and computation of the interchanges of odd and even. Now as the number of these forms of body is five, they should be enumerated as fire, water, third air, fourth earth, and fifth aether. It is as they predominate that all the creatures are fashioned in all their multitude and variety. The matter should be expounded in detail as follows. We may take the
d earthy first as one single type comprising all mankind as well as all creatures with many feet or with none, alike those which travel from place to place and those which are fixed to one spot, fast bound by their roots; their unity, so we should hold, lies in this, that though all five forms of body are found in the structure of them all, their principal stuff is earth, the hard and resistant substance. Then secondly we must assume another kind of creature, likewise visible because it mainly consists of fire, though it contains some small portions of
e earth, air, and all the rest. From these constituents, then, we must hold, there arise visible creatures of many kinds, whom we must further take to be the kinds of creatures which people the skies. Collectively, of course, we must call them the divine host of the stars—endowed with the fairest of bodies and the happiest and best of souls. And we are fairly bound to assign them one or other of two lots. Either
982 every one of them is imperishable, immortal, and divine, and that of utter and absolute necessity, or each of them has his sufficient term of life, covering many ages, beyond which there is nothing more for him to desire.

We will begin then, as we say, by conceiving these two sorts of creature, both, to repeat ourselves, visible—the one composed, as might be imagined, wholly of fire and the other of earth, the earthy sort moving in disorderly fashion, that of fire with utter uniformity. Now the sort which moves in disorderly wise—as the kind of creature
b which includes ourselves mostly does—we must take to be unintelligent, but as for that which holds its course uniformly through the sky, we should count this abundant proof of its intelligence; in the unbroken regularity and uniformity of its path, and of all it does and has done to it, it provides convincing evidence of intelligent life. And of all necessitation, that which comes from a soul endowed with intelligence is far the mightiest, seeing she imposes her law as a sovereign
c who is subject to none, and when a soul has decided for the best with faultless wisdom, the utterly irreversible result falls out entirely to its

mind. Adamant itself could be no stronger nor more inflexible, and 'tis no more than the truth to say that a triple Fate ensures and watches over the full accomplishment of all that each and every god has determined with perfect good counsel. For mankind it should have been proof that the stars and their whole procession have intelligence, that they act with unbroken uniformity, because their action carries out a d plan resolved on from untold ages; they do not change their purpose confusedly, acting now thus, and again thus, and wandering from one orbit to another. Yet most of us have imagined the very opposite; because they act with uniformity and regularity, we fancy them to have no souls. Hence the mass has followed the leading of fools; it imagines that man is intelligent and alive because he is so mutable, but deity, because it keeps to the same orbits, is unintelligent. Yet man might have chosen the fairer, better, more welcome interpretation; he might e have understood that that which eternally does the same acts, in uniform way and for the same reasons, is for that very reason to be deemed intelligent, and that this is the case with the stars. They are the fairest of all sights to the eye, and as they move through the figures of the fairest and most glorious of dances they accomplish their duty to all living creatures. And for further proof that we have the right to ascribe souls to them, let us, in the first place, but think of their mag- 983 nitude. They are not really the tiny things they look to be; the bulk of any star is enormous; that we must believe, for the proofs are convincing. Why, we may rightly think of the sun as a whole as larger than the earth as a whole, and every one of the moving stars is, in fact, of amazing magnitude. So let us but consider how anything can be made to cause so vast a bulk to revolve perpetually in the same period, as the stars in fact revolve. Why, I say, God will be found to be the cause; b the thing is impossible on other terms, for, as you and I have proved, soul can be imparted by God, and by God alone. And since God has this power, 'tis perfectly easy for him first to give life to any body or any bulk, and then to set it moving as he judges best. For the present we may affirm one truth about them all. It cannot be that earth and sky, with all the stars and masses formed of them, if no soul had been c connected with, or perhaps lodged in, each of them should move so accurately, to the year, month, or day, to confer all the blessings they bestow on us all.

Now the poorer creature a man is, the more necessary that his words should be manifestly not spoken at random, but have definite meaning. But to talk of the swirl or the structures of moving bodies, or the like, as causes is to say nothing definite; so we must by all means repeat our own earlier statement, and ask ourselves whether 'tis a d reasonable one or is hopelessly at fault. We maintain, first, that there are two sorts of being, soul being one and body the other; that there are many of either kind, all different from one another, and either sort from the other; that there is no *tertium quid* common to both; that soul is more excellent than body. The first we shall, of course, take to be intelligent, the second unintelligent; the first sovereign, the second subject; the first the universal cause, the second a cause of no effect e whatsoever. Hence to say that all we behold in the heavens is due to some other source, and not produced in the fashion we describe by soul and body, is pure folly and unreason. And thus, if our account of the whole matter is to be victorious, and all these creatures to be convincingly proved divine, one or other of two things must be said of them. Either it must be right to hymn them as very gods, or we must believe them to be likenesses of gods—images, as it were, fashioned 984 by the gods themselves. They are the work of no foolish or trivial authors. As we have said, one of these two views must be adopted and the images thus set up must be worshiped with higher honors than all others. For none can ever be found fairer and more accessible to all mankind, or set in a more excellent region and more eminent in b purity, majesty, and fullness of life than has been shown in the fashioning of them all. As concerns gods, then, at present we will attempt no more than this. Now that we have discovered two kinds of creature, both visible, the one, so we say, immortal, the other—that made of earth—mortal, we shall try to give the most faithful account warranted by reasonable conjecture of the three intermediate sorts out of the five, which lie between these extremes. Next to fire we will place aether, assuming that soul fashions from it creatures which, as c with the other kinds, have in the main the character of its own substance, though with lesser portions of the other kinds as bonds of union, and that after aether soul fashions another sort of creature out of air, and a third from water. By the fabrication of them all, we may suppose, soul has filled the universe throughout with living things, making all possible use of all the kinds of body, and communicating life to all; the series of creations begins with the visible divinities, and has its second, third, fourth, and fifth terms, closing in ourselves, man- d kind.

As for such gods as Zeus, Hera, and the rest, a man may give them any rank he pleases, so long as he conforms to this law of ours and holds fast to our principle. But, it is, of course, the stars and the bodies we can perceive existing along with them that must be named first as the visible gods, and the greatest, most worshipful, and clear-sighted of them all; after them and below them, come in order the e daemons and the creatures of the air, who hold the third and midmost rank, doing the office of interpreters, and should be peculiarly honored in our prayers that they may transmit comfortable messages. Both sorts of creature, those of aether and those of air, who hold the rank next to them, we shall say, are wholly transparent; however close they are to us, they go undiscerned. Being, however, of a kind that is quick 985 to learn and of retentive memory, they read all our thoughts and regard the good and noble with signal favor, but the very evil with deep aversion. For *they* are not exempt from feeling pain, whereas a god who enjoys the fullness of deity is clearly above both pain and pleasure, though possessed of all-embracing wisdom and knowledge. The b universe being thus full throughout of living creatures, they all, so we shall say, act as interpreters, and interpreters of all things, to one another and to the highest gods, seeing that the middle ranks of creatures can flit so lightly over the earth and the whole universe. As for the fifth and last of our substances, water, the safest guess would be that what is formed from it is a demigod, and that it is sometimes to be seen, but anon conceals itself and becomes invisible, and thus perplexes us by its indistinct appearance. Since, then, these five sorts of c creatures must surely exist, when it comes to beliefs of individuals or whole societies originating in the intercourse of some of them with us —appearances in dreams of the night, oracular and prophetic voices heard by the whole or the sick, or communications in the last hours of life—and these have been, as they will be hereafter, the sources of many a widespread cult—when it comes to these, I say, no legislator of even the slenderest sense will presume to innovate, and so divert his city to a devoutness with no sure foundations. Nor yet d will he prohibit obedience to the inherited usages about sacrifices, since in this matter he has no knowledge whatsoever, as, indeed, 'tis impossible that mankind should have any. But it follows, does it not, from the same argument that men are cravens if they have not the courage to tell us of the gods who are really visible, and make it plain that these other deities go unworshiped and miss the honors which rightly belong to them? And yet something of the kind actually hap- e pens among us. Suppose, for example, one of us had actually seen sun or moon coming into being and watching over all of us, and had never spoken of it, from some inability to tell the story, or suppose he saw them left without their due honors, and yet felt no eagerness to do his part to bring them into a position of conspicuous honor, no anxiety to cause festivals and sacrifices to be appointed for them, or to set 986 apart a time for each of them and assign them their periods of greater, or maybe, lesser 'years.' If such a man were called a coward, would not the name be pronounced by himself, or by any man of understanding, to be fairly earned?

CLINIAS: Why, surely, sir, a craven and nothing else.

ATHENIAN: Well, friend Clinias, I must confess that this is plainly my case at this moment.

CLINIAS: And how so?

ATHENIAN: Let me tell you that so far as I have been able to discover—my achievements are nothing wonderful, but readily attainable by anyone else—there are to be found in the whole compass of heaven eight sister powers. Three of them belong, one to the sun, b one to the moon, and the third to the stars of which we have lately spoken, and there are five others. Now of all these powers, and the beings who march in them of their own motion, or, if you will, make the journey in their chariots, I would have none of us fondly believe that some are gods, but others not so, or that some are true-begotten, but others what it would be blasphemy for any of us to call them. All c —so we must one and all declare and affirm—are brothers, and each has a brother's portion. When we appoint them their honors, we are not to give the year to one and the month to another, but leave the rest without a portion or a time in which each completes his circuit, and so does his part to perfect the order which law, divinest of things that are, has set before our eyes. In the happy man this order awakens first wonder, and then the passion to learn all of it that mor- d tality may, for 'tis thus, as he believes, he will spend his days best and with most good fortune, and after his decease reach the proper abodes of virtue. As he has been initiated into the true and real mysteries by receiving wisdom in her unity in a mind which is itself a unity, he will henceforth have face to face fruition of the most glorious of re- alities so far as his vision can reach. The task still left on our hands at present is to say how many and who these divinities are, for our e statement will assuredly never be found false. Now I can affirm for certain no more than this. There are, as I repeat, eight powers, of which three have been named and five are still left. The fourth orbit, or circuit, as likewise the fifth, is roughly of equal speed with the sun and, on the whole account, neither slower nor faster. Of the three the leader must be that which has a mind equal to the work. We will call them the orbits of the sun, the morning star, and of a third, whose name I can- not state, as it is unknown—the reason of this being that the first man 987 to observe these bodies was a non-Hellene. The first observers were made so by the excellence of their summer climate, which in Egypt and Syria is so notable; they had a full view of the stars, we may say, all the year round, as clouds and rains are perpetually banished from their quarter of the world. Their observations have been universally diffused, among ourselves as well as elsewhere, and have stood the test a vast, indeed incalculable, lapse of years. So we may confidently give these bodies their place in our legislation—'tis surely not for men of sense to honor some divinities but disregard others—and if they b have received no names, the fact must be explained as we have ex- plained it. Though they have at least been designated after certain gods—the morning star, which is also the evening star, is commonly reputed to be that of Aphrodite, a most appropriate name for a Syrian legislator to choose, and that which keeps pace at once with it and with the sun, the star of Hermes. We are further to reckon three other orbits of bodies which, like moon and sun, revolve to the right. There is still one to be spoken of, the eighth, which may be called in a special sense the Cosmos, and this god moves in the opposite sense to all the others, carrying round the rest with him, as might be supposed by c men whose knowledge in these matters is slender. But as much as we know for certain, we are bound to declare, as we are doing, for the true and genuine wisdom can be seen even by one who enjoys but a little sound and divine insight to lie along these lines. There are thus three stars left. One of them, the slowest-moving of all, is called by some that of Cronus, that which is next slowest we should call the star of Zeus, and the next slowest after him the star of Ares, and his has the ruddiest color of them all. All this is easy enough to remark d when someone has pointed it out, but, as I say, someone who has discerned it has to lead the way.

There is another thing of which any Greek should be aware. We Greeks enjoy a geographical situation which is exceptionally favorable to the attainment of excellence. Its merit should be sought in the fact that it lies midway between winter and summer; it is our deficiency in respect of summer by comparison with the peoples of the other region which, as we said, has made us later than they in discerning the order of these gods. But we may take it that whenever Greeks borrow anything from non-Greeks, they finally carry it to a higher perfection. So we should hold the same view of the subject now e under discussion. Such matters are hard to discover with certainty, but there is every ground for the splendid hope that though the news of 988 these gods and their worship has come to us from non-Greeks, the Greeks will learn to worship them all in a truly nobler and more righteous fashion than they, by the help of teaching from the oracle of Delphi and the cultus enjoined by our laws. And there is one fear no Greek should harbor, the fear that 'tis a forbidden thing for mortality to concern itself with the study of divinity. No, we should believe the clean contrary—that deity is neither unintelligent, nor ignorant of man's nature, but knows that, with itself for teacher, he will follow where he is led and learn the lessons he is taught. And deity is, of b course, aware that this lesson of number and counting is the very thing that it teaches and we learn. Deity unaware of this would be the most unintelligent of things; the proverb about not knowing one's own identity would be true of it to the letter, if it felt wrath against the capable learner, and not rather a joy pure of all envy at seeing him growing in goodness by God's aid. Now it is widely and reasonably held that in the old days, when men first began to have thoughts about the gods, c their origin and character, and in some cases . . . about the acts to which they first addressed themselves, tales were told which the soberminded could neither accept nor relish any more than they could the later versions in which the priority was given to fire, water, and other bodies, and only a secondary place to soul and its marvels, and the mightier and more worshipful motion was said to be that into which it is native to body to put itself under the influence of heat and cold and other such causes, not that which soul imparts to body and to herself. But now that we teach that soul, once implanted in body, quite d naturally imparts motion and revolution to the body and to herself, we have left no rational ground for her to distrust her power to set any weight whatsoever in revolution. And thus, as we hold that soul is the universal cause, and that since the cause of good is always of the same nature as itself, and that of evil again always of *its* nature, 'tis only natural that soul should be universally the cause of revolution and movement, the best soul causing motion and revolution in the direction of good and the other sort of soul that in the opposite direction, good must be, and ever has been, triumphant over its contrary.

Now in all we have said we have been pleading the cause of that justice which takes vengeance on the wicked. And as to the point under consideration, we can have no doubt left that we are to account the good man wise. But as concerns this wisdom of which we have been so long in quest, we must see whether after all we cannot discover it in some form of education or in some science such that defective acquaintance with it leaves us ignorant of our just rights, so long as the deficiency subsists. Well, I think we shall make the discovery, and I must tell you what it is. I have sought the vision of it in the heights and in the depths and will now do my best to set it clearly before you. The source of the trouble, as I am strongly persuaded by our recent discussion, is that our practice in the very chief point of virtue is amiss. There is no human virtue—and we must never let ourselves be argued out of this belief—greater than *piety*, and piety, I must tell you, thanks to our incredible folly, has failed to show itself in the most nobly endowed natures. By the most nobly endowed I mean those which are most difficult of production, but once produced, of the highest service to mankind. A soul which admits alike, in due measure, and with an easy grace, influences which make for the slow and sure, and for its opposite, the impetuous, may be expected to be debonair, to adore valor, to be readily led to sobriety of life; what is more than all, if it combines capacity to learn and retentive memory with these gifts we may expect it to take such delight in all this that it will prove a lover of learning. Though it is hard for such characters to make their appearance, when they do appear and get the nurture and education they require, they will be able to keep the more numerous and worser sort in all due subjection, ordering all their relations with the gods, in all matters of sacrifices and purity toward God and man rightly and reasonably, in thought, word, and deed; men will thus be no formal hypocrites but true worshipers of virtue, and this, of course, is the point of chief concern for the whole community. This section of society, then, as I say, has a native supreme authority and is equal to the learning of the highest and noblest truth, if there were but one to teach them. But there will be no such teacher unless God leads the way, or even if there were, but he did his work amiss, 'twould be better not to go to school to him. Yet it follows with necessity from all we have said that I for one must enjoin the learning of these lessons on what we have described as the noblest natures. So we must do what we can to enumerate the subjects to be studied and explain their nature and the methods to be employed, to the best of the abilities of myself who am to speak and you who are to listen—to say, in fact, how a man should learn piety, and in what it consists. It may 990 seem odd to the ear, but the name *we* give to the study is one which will surprise a person unfamiliar with the subject—*astronomy*. Are you unaware that the true astronomer must be a man of great wisdom? I do not mean an astronomer of the type of Hesiod and his like, a man who has just observed settings and risings, but one who has studied seven out of the eight orbits, as each of them completes its circuit in a fashion not easy of comprehension by any capacity not b endowed with admirable abilities. I have already touched on this and shall now proceed, as I say, to explain how and on what lines the study is to be pursued. And I may begin the statement thus.

The moon gets round her circuit most rapidly, bringing with her the month, and the full moon as a first period. Next we must observe the sun, his constant turnings throughout his circuit, and his companions. Not to be perpetually repeating ourselves about the same sub- c jects, the rest of the orbits which we enumerated above are difficult to comprehend, and to train capacities which can deal with them we shall have to spend a great deal of labor on providing preliminary teaching and training in boyhood and youth. Hence there will be a need for several sciences. The first and most important of them is likewise that which treats of pure numbers—not numbers concreted in bodies, but the whole generation of the series of odd and even, and the effects which it contributes to the nature of things. When all this has been mastered, next in order comes what is called by the very ludi- d crous name *mensuration* (γεωμετρία), but is really a manifest assimilation to one another of numbers which are naturally dissimilar, effected by reference to areas. Now to a man who can comprehend this, it will be plain that this is no mere feat of human skill, but a miracle of God's contrivance. Next, numbers raised to the third power and thus presenting an analogy with three-dimensional things. Here again he assimilates the dissimilar by a second science, which those who hit on the discovery have named *stereometry* [the gauging of solids], a de- e vice of God's contriving which breeds amazement in those who fix their gaze on it and consider how universal nature molds form and type by the constant revolution of potency and its converse about the 991 double in the various progressions. The first example of this ratio of the double in the advancing number series is that of 1 to 2; double of this is the ratio of their second powers [1 : 4], and double of this again the advance to the solid and tangible, as we proceed from 1 to 8 [1, 2, 2^2, 2^3]; the advance to a mean of the double, that mean which is equidistant from lesser and greater term [the arithmetical], or the other mean [the harmonic] which exceeds the one term and is itself exceeded by the other by the same fraction of the respective terms—

b these ratios of 3 : 2 and 4 : 3 will be found as means between 6 and 12—why, in the potency of the mean between these terms [6, 12], with its double sense, we have a gift from the blessed choir of the Muses to which mankind owes the boon of the play of consonance and measure, with all they contribute to rhythm and melody.

So much, then, for our program as a whole. But to crown it all, we must go on to the generation of things divine, the fairest and most heavenly spectacle God has vouchsafed to the eye of man. And, believe me, no man will ever behold that spectacle without the studies
c we have described, and so be able to boast that he has won it by an easy route. Moreover, in all our sessions for study we are to relate the single fact to its species; there are questions to be asked and erroneous theses to be refuted. We may truly say that this is ever the prime test, and the best a man can have; as for tests that profess to be such but are not, there is no labor so fruitlessly thrown away as that spent on them. We must also grasp the accuracy of the periodic times
d and the precision with which they complete the various celestial motions, and this is where a believer in our doctrine that soul is both older and more divine than body will appreciate the beauty and justice of the saying that 'all things are full of gods' and that we have never been left unheeded by the forgetfulness or carelessness of the higher powers. There is one observation to be made about all such matters. If a man grasps the several questions aright, the benefit accruing to him who thus learns his lesson in the proper way is great indeed; if he cannot, 'twill ever be the better course to call on God. Now the proper way is this—so much explanation is unavoidable. To the man who
e pursues his studies in the proper way, all geometric constructions, all systems of numbers, all duly constituted melodic progressions, the single ordered scheme of all celestial revolutions, should disclose themselves, and disclose themselves they will, if, as I say, a man pursues his studies aright with his mind's eye fixed on their single end. As
992 such a man reflects, he will receive the revelation of a single bond of natural interconnection between all these problems. If such matters are handled in any other spirit, a man, as I am saying, will need to invoke his luck. We may rest assured that without these qualifications the happy will not make their appearance in any society; this is the method, this the pabulum, these the studies demanded; hard or easy, this is the road we must tread. And piety itself forbids us to disregard
b the gods, now that the glad news of them all has been duly revealed. Him who has mastered all these lessons I account in truth as wisest; of him I dare affirm—'tis a fancy, and yet I am in earnest with it too— that such a one, when death has put the end to his allotted term, if he may be said still to endure beyond death, will no longer be subject, as he is now, to a multitude of perceptions; he will have but one allotted portion, even as he has reduced the manifold within himself to unity, and in it will be happy, wise, blessed, all in one. Whether the life of

bliss has 'islands' or continents for its scene, such will be his happy c
portion forevermore, and further, whether the life he has spent here in
such pursuits be that of public man or private citizen, the reward from
the gods will be the same and no other. Thus we are brought back once
more to the same very truth with which we began; rightly did we say
that perfect bliss and happiness are impossible for all men save a few.
'Tis only they who are at once of godlike parts, sober of soul, endowed
by nature with all other virtue, and have moreover mastered the whole
contents of the blissful science—what that is, we have explained—'tis d
they, and they only who have received in full possession all deity has
to give. And therefore we declare by our personal voices and enact it in
our public law that those who have labored in these studies, when they
reach advanced age at last, shall be invested with our chief magistracies, that others shall follow their leading in reverence of speech
toward all gods of either sex, and that we shall do very right, now that
we fully understand what this wisdom is and have put its claim to a
proper test, to call upon all the members of our nocturnal council to e
take their part in it.

GREATER HIPPIAS

281 SOCRATES: It is Hippias, the beautiful and wise! What a long while it is since you came to anchor at Athens!

HIPPIAS: I have had no time to spare, Socrates. Elis looks on me as her best judge and reporter of anything said by other governments, and so I am always the first choice among her citizens to be her ambassador when she has business to settle with another state. I have b gone on many such missions to different states, but to Lacedaemon most often, and on the most numerous and important subjects. That is the answer to your question why I am so seldom in this part of the world.

SOCRATES: Still, Hippias, what a thing it is to be a complete man, as well as a wise one! As a private person, your talents earn you a great deal of money from the young, and in return you confer on c them even greater benefits; in public affairs, again, you can do good work for your country, which is the way to avoid contempt and win popular esteem. Yet I wonder for what possible reason the great figures of the past who are famous for their wisdom—Pittacus and Bias and the school of Thales of Miletus, and others nearer our own time, down to Anaxagoras—why all or most of them clearly made a habit of taking no active part in politics.

d HIPPIAS: What reason do you suppose except incapacity, the lack of the power to carry their wisdom into both regions of life, the public and the private?

SOCRATES: Then we should be right in saying that just as other arts have advanced until the craftsmen of the past compare ill with those of today, so your art, that of the Sophist, has advanced until the old philosophers cannot stand comparison with you and your fellows?

HIPPIAS: Perfectly right.

SOCRATES: So if Bias were to come to life again for our bene-
282 fit, by your standard he would be a laughingstock, just as according to

From *The Dialogues of Plato*, translated with analyses and introductions by B. Jowett (4th edn., revised by order of the Jowett Copyright Trustees, Oxford, 1953). A few minor corrections have been made, as suggested by Phillip De Lacy (*Journal of Classical Philology*, XLIX, October 1954).

the sculptors Daedalus would look a fool if he were to be born now and produce the kind of works that gave him his reputation?

HIPPIAS: Exactly, Socrates. Nevertheless, I myself habitually praise our predecessors of former generations before and above contemporaries, for while I guard myself against the envy of the living, I fear the wrath of the dead.

SOCRATES: Very finely said, Hippias, both in sentiment and in style, and I can support with my own testimony your statement that your art really has made progress toward combining public business with private pursuits. The eminent Gorgias, the Sophist of Leontini, came here from his home on an official mission, selected because he was the ablest statesman of his city. By general consent he spoke most eloquently before the Assembly, and in his private capacity, by giving demonstrations to the young and associating with them, he earned and took away with him a large sum of Athenian money. Or again, there is our distinguished friend Prodicus. He has often been at Athens on public business from Ceos; the last time he came on such a mission, quite lately, he was much admired for his eloquence before the Council, and also as a private person he made an astonishing amount of money by giving demonstrations to the young and admitting them to his society. None of those great men of the past ever saw fit to charge money for his wisdom, or to give demonstrations of it to miscellaneous audiences; they were too simple ever to realize the enormous importance of money. Either of the two I have mentioned has earned more from his wisdom than any other craftsman from his art, whatever it may have been, and so did Protagoras before them.

HIPPIAS: Socrates, you know nothing of the real charms of all this business. If you were told how much I have earned, you would be astounded. To take one case only—I went to Sicily once while Protagoras was living there. He had a great reputation and was a far older man than I, and yet in a short time I made more than one hundred and fifty minas. Why, in one place alone, Inycus, a very small place, I took more than twenty minas. When I returned home with the money I gave it to my father, reducing him and his fellow citizens to a condition of stupefied amazement. And I feel pretty sure that I have made more money than any other two Sophists you like to mention, put together.

SOCRATES: What honorable, what powerful testimony to your own wisdom and that of our contemporaries, and to their great superiority to the men of the past! According to your account, earlier thinkers were sunk in ignorance; the fate of Anaxagoras is said to have been the exact opposite to yours, for when he inherited a large fortune, he neglected it and lost it all—so mindless was his wisdom —and the same kind of story is told of other great figures of former generations. Your success, I admit, is fine evidence of the wisdom of the present generation as compared with their predecessors, and it is a popular sentiment that the wise man must above all be wise for himself; of such wisdom the criterion is in the end the ability to make the most money. Well, so much for that. Now tell me, in which of all the cities you visit have you made the most money? In Lacedaemon, I take it, which you have visited most often?

HIPPIAS: Certainly not, Socrates.

SOCRATES: Really? Did you make least?

c   HIPPIAS: I have never made money there at all.

SOCRATES: What a truly extraordinary thing! Then is not your wisdom fitted to advance in virtue her pupils and associates?

HIPPIAS: Very much so.

SOCRATES: Then you had the capacity to improve the sons of the Inycites, but not the sons of the Spartans?

HIPPIAS: No, that is quite wrong.

SOCRATES: Well then, is it that Sicilians desire to become better men, and Lacedaemonians do not?

d   HIPPIAS: Undoubtedly, Socrates, Lacedaemonians also desire it.

SOCRATES: Was it then from want of money that they kept away from your society?

HIPPIAS: Not at all, they have plenty.

SOCRATES: If then they desired it, and had money, and you were able to confer on them the greatest of benefits, what can be the reason why they did not send you away loaded up with cash? A thought strikes me—might it be that the Lacedaemonians would educate their own children better than you would? Is this to be our line, Hippias, and do you agree?

e   HIPPIAS: Not in the least.

SOCRATES: Then you were unable to convince the Spartan youths that in your society they would make more progress toward virtue than in the society of their own people? Or, alternatively, could you not persuade their fathers that, if they had any solicitude for their sons, they ought to hand them over to you, rather than keep them in their own care? I cannot imagine that they grudged their own children the attainment of the highest virtue possible for them.

HIPPIAS: No, I do not suppose they begrudged it.

SOCRATES: But Lacedaemon has good laws.

HIPPIAS: Certainly.

284   SOCRATES: And in states with good laws, virtue is held in the highest honor?

HIPPIAS: Quite so.

SOCRATES: And you know better than anyone else how to impart it to another?

HIPPIAS: Emphatically.

SOCRATES: Well now, is not Thessaly the part of Greece where the man who best knows how to impart horsemanship would be most
b   highly esteemed, and would make most money—and would not the

same apply to any foreign country where that art is zealously pursued?

HIPPIAS: I suppose so.

SOCRATES: Then is not Lacedaemon, or any other Greek state that has good laws, the place where the man who can impart the knowledge most valuable for the promotion of virtue would be most highly esteemed, and, if he chose, would make the most money? Do you think that Sicily and Inycus are better? Are we to believe this, Hippias? If you say so, we must believe it.

HIPPIAS: The ancestral tradition of the Lacedaemonians forbids them to change their laws, or to give their sons an education different from the customary.

SOCRATES: What! Does the ancestral tradition of the Lacedaemonians require them to do wrong instead of right? c

HIPPIAS: I should not say that myself, Socrates.

SOCRATES: Will they not do right by giving their young men the best education in their power?

HIPPIAS: Certainly, but it is illegal for them to give them a foreign kind of education. You can be certain that if anyone had ever made money there by education, I should have made far the most, for they listen to me with enjoyment and applause. But, as I have said, it is not the law.

SOCRATES: Would you say that law is an injury to the state, d or a benefit?

HIPPIAS: It is made, I take it, with a view to benefit, but sometimes it does positive harm if it is ill made.

SOCRATES: But surely the legislators make the law on the assumption that it is a principal good of the state, and that without good a well-ordered state is impossible?

HIPPIAS: True.

SOCRATES: When, therefore, would-be legislators miss the good, they have missed law and legality. What do you say?

HIPPIAS: Speaking precisely, Socrates, that is so, but mankind e are not accustomed to put it that way.

SOCRATES: The men who know, or those who do not?

HIPPIAS: The multitude.

SOCRATES: This multitude, is it composed of men who know the truth?

HIPPIAS: Certainly not.

SOCRATES: But at any rate those who know, I suppose, hold that the more beneficial is in truth more lawful for all men than the less beneficial, or do you not agree?

HIPPIAS: Yes, I agree. It is so, in truth.

SOCRATES: Then the real fact is as those who know hold it to be?

HIPPIAS: Certainly.

SOCRATES: You maintain that it is more beneficial for Lacedae-
285 monians to be brought up in your education, a foreign one, than in the
native form?

HIPPIAS: Yes, and I am right.

SOCRATES: And that what is more beneficial is more lawful—
you maintain this also, Hippias?

HIPPIAS: I said so.

SOCRATES: Then on your argument it is more lawful for the
sons of Lacedaemonians to be educated by Hippias, and less lawful
for them to be educated by their fathers, if they will in fact get more
benefit from you?

HIPPIAS: They certainly will get benefit from me.

b   SOCRATES: Then Lacedaemonians break the law by not entrusting their sons to you, and paying you handsomely for it.

HIPPIAS: I agree. As you appear to be arguing my own case, I
do not see why I should go into opposition.

SOCRATES: Then, my friend, the Lacedaemonians prove to be
lawbreakers, and lawbreakers in the most vital matters—the very people who are reputed to be the most law-abiding. In heaven's name,
Hippias, on what kind of subject do they listen to you with such pleasure and applause? Clearly it must be the one on which you are a great
c authority, the stars and the celestial phenomena?

HIPPIAS: Not in the least. They won't tolerate it.

SOCRATES: Then they like to hear about geometry?

HIPPIAS: Not at all. Many of them do not even know how to
count, so to speak.

SOCRATES: Then they must be a far from appreciative audience when you address them on arithmetic?

HIPPIAS: Very far indeed.

SOCRATES: Well then, what about the problems which you of
d all men know best how to analyze—the properties of letters and syllables and rhythms and harmonies?

HIPPIAS: My dear sir! Harmonies and letters indeed!

SOCRATES: What then are the subjects on which they listen to
you with pleasure and applause? Pray enlighten me; I cannot see.

HIPPIAS: They delight in the genealogies of heroes and of men
and in stories of the foundations of cities in olden times, and, to put it
briefly, in all forms of antiquarian lore, so that because of them I
e have been compelled to acquire a thorough comprehension and mastery of all that branch of learning.

SOCRATES: Bless my soul, you have certainly been lucky that
the Lacedaemonians do not want to hear a recital of the list of our
archons, from Solon downward; you would have had some trouble to
learn it.

HIPPIAS: Why? I can repeat fifty names after hearing them
once.

SOCRATES: I am sorry, I quite forgot about your mnemonic art. Now I understand how naturally the Lacedaemonians enjoy your multifarious knowledge, and make use of you as children do of old 286 women, to tell them agreeable stories.

HIPPIAS: Yes, indeed, and, what is more, Socrates, I have lately gained much credit there by setting forth in detail the honorable and beautiful practices to which a young man ought to devote himself. On that subject I have composed a discourse, a beautiful work distinguished by a fine style among its other merits. Its setting and its exordium are like this. After the fall of Troy, Neoptolemus asks Nestor b what are the honorable and beautiful practices to which a man should devote himself during his youth in order to win the highest distinction. Then it is Nestor's turn to speak, and he propounds to him a great number of excellent rules of life. This discourse I delivered in Sparta, and at the request of Eudicus, the son of Apemantus, am to deliver it here, as well as much else worth listening to, in the schoolroom of Phidostratus, the day after tomorrow. Please be sure to come yourself, and bring with you other good critics of such dissertations. c

SOCRATES: Certainly, Hippias, all being well. But now answer me a trifling question on the subject; you have reminded me of it in the nick of time. Quite lately, my noble friend, when I was condemning as ugly some things in certain compositions, and praising others as beautiful, somebody threw me into confusion by interrogating me in a most offensive manner, rather to this effect. You, Socrates, pray how do *you* know what things are beautiful and what are ugly? Come now, can you tell me what beauty is? d

In my incompetence I was confounded, and could find no proper answer to give him; so, leaving the company, I was filled with anger and reproaches against myself, and promised myself that the first time I met with one of you wise men, I would listen to him and learn, and when I had mastered my lesson thoroughly, I would go back to my questioner and join battle with him again. So you see that you have come at a beautifully appropriate moment, and I ask you to teach me properly what is beauty by itself, answering my questions e with the utmost precision you can attain. I do not want to be made to look a fool a second time, by another cross-examination. Of course you know perfectly, and it is only a scrap of your vast learning.

HIPPIAS: A scrap indeed, Socrates, and of no value, I may add.

SOCRATES: Then I shall acquire it without trouble, and nobody will confound me again.

HIPPIAS: Nobody at all, if I am not a bungling amateur in my profession. 287

SOCRATES: Bravo, Hippias, how splendid, if we do defeat the adversary! Will it be a nuisance to you if I act as his understudy and fasten on your answers with my objections, so that you may put me through some vigorous practice? I have had a fair amount of experience of his objections. If, therefore, it makes no difference to you, I should like to play the critic. In this way I shall get a firmer grasp of what I learn.

HIPPIAS: Certainly, put your criticisms. As I said just now, it
b is not a big question. I might teach you to answer much more difficult ones with such cogency that no human being would be able to confute you.

SOCRATES: How magnificent! Well now, on your invitation let me assume his role to the best of my ability, and try to interrogate you. If you were to deliver to him the discourse to which you refer —the discourse about beautiful practices—he would hear you to the end, and when you stopped, the very first question he would put would be about beauty—it is a kind of habit with him. He would say,
c Stranger from Elis, is it not by justice that the just are just? Would you answer, Hippias, as if he were asking the question?

HIPPIAS: I shall answer that it is by justice.

SOCRATES: Then this, namely justice, is definitely something.

HIPPIAS: Certainly.

SOCRATES: Again, it is by wisdom that the wise are wise, and by goodness that all things are good?

HIPPIAS: Undoubtedly.

SOCRATES: That is, by really existent things—one could scarcely say, by things which have no real existence?

HIPPIAS: Quite so.

SOCRATES: Then are not all beautiful things beautiful by beauty?
d HIPPIAS: Yes, by beauty.

SOCRATES: Which has a real existence?

HIPPIAS: Yes, what else do you think?

SOCRATES: Then tell me, stranger, he would say, what is this thing, beauty?

HIPPIAS: By putting this question he just wants to find out what is beautiful?

SOCRATES: I do not think so, Hippias. He wants to know what is beauty—the beautiful.

HIPPIAS: What is the difference between them?

SOCRATES: You think there is none?

HIPPIAS: There is no difference.

SOCRATES: Obviously you know best. Still, my good sir, look
e at it again; he asks you not what is beautiful, but what is beauty.

HIPPIAS: I understand, my good sir, and I will indeed tell him what is beauty, defying anyone to refute me. I assure you, Socrates, if I must speak the truth, that a beautiful maiden is a beauty.

SOCRATES: Upon my word, Hippias, a beautiful answer—very creditable. Then if I give that answer I shall have answered the question, and answered it correctly, and I can defy anyone to refute me? 288

HIPPIAS: How can you be refuted when everyone thinks the same and everyone who hears you will testify that you are right?

SOCRATES: Quite so. Now, Hippias, let me recapitulate to myself what you say. That man will question me something like this. Come, Socrates, give me an answer. Returning to your examples of beauty, tell me what must beauty by itself be in order to explain why we apply the word to them?

And you want me to reply that if a beautiful maiden is a beauty, we have found why they are entitled to that name?

HIPPIAS: Do you imagine that he will then try to refute you by b proving that you have not mentioned a beautiful thing, or that if he does attempt it he will not look a fool?

SOCRATES: I am sure, my worthy friend, that he will try to refute me. The event will show whether the attempt will make him look a fool. But allow me to tell you what he will say.

HIPPIAS: Go on, then.

SOCRATES: He will say, How delicious you are, Socrates! Is not a beautiful mare a beauty—the god himself praised mares in his oracle?

How shall we reply, Hippias? Must we not say that the mare, too, c or at least a beautiful one, is a beauty? We can hardly be so audacious as to deny that beauty is beautiful.

HIPPIAS: Quite right. I may add that the god, too, spoke quite correctly; the mares we breed in our country are very beautiful.

SOCRATES: He will now say, Very well, but what about a beautiful lyre? Is that not a beauty? Are we to agree, Hippias?

HIPPIAS: Yes.

SOCRATES: Judging from his character, I feel pretty sure that he will then go on, What about a beautiful pot, my dear sir? Is not that a beauty?

HIPPIAS: Who is this fellow? What a boor, to dare to introduce d such vulgar examples into a grave discussion!

SOCRATES: He is that sort of person, Hippias—not at all refined, a common fellow caring for nothing but the truth. Still, he must have his answer and I give my own first. If the pot is the work of a good potter, smooth and round and properly fired, like some very beautiful pots I have seen, the two-handled ones that hold six *choes* —if he were to ask his question about a pot like that, we should have to admit that it is beautiful. How could we assert that what is a beautiful thing is not a beauty? e

HIPPIAS: No, we could not.

SOCRATES: Then even a beautiful pot, he will say, is a beauty? Please answer.

HIPPIAS: Yes, I suppose so. Even this utensil is beautiful

when it is beautifully made, but generically it does not deserve to be judged beautiful in comparison with a mare or a maiden, or all the other things of beauty.

289   SOCRATES : Very well. I understand, Hippias, that when he puts these questions I should answer, Sir, you do not grasp the truth of Heraclitus' saying that the most beautiful of apes is ugly compared with the human race, and the most beautiful of pots is ugly when grouped with maidens—so says Hippias the wise. That is correct?

HIPPIAS : Quite the right answer.

SOCRATES : Now mark my words, I am sure that he will then say, Yes, Socrates, but if maidens are grouped with gods, will not the
b result be the same as when pots were grouped with maidens? Will not the most beautiful maiden appear ugly? Does not Heraclitus, whom you adduce, employ these very words, 'The wisest of men, when compared to a god, will appear but an ape in wisdom and beauty and all else?'

Shall we admit, Hippias, that the most beautiful maiden is ugly in comparison with the race of gods?

HIPPIAS : That no one can deny, Socrates.

c   SOCRATES : If then we make this admission, he will laugh and say, Socrates, do you remember what you were asked?

Yes, I shall answer. I was asked what beauty by itself is.

He will rejoin, Then when you are asked for beauty, do you offer in reply that which you yourself acknowledge to be no more beautiful than ugly?

Apparently, I shall say. What do you advise me to reply?

HIPPIAS : As you do reply, for of course he will be right in saying that in comparison with gods the human race is not beautiful.

SOCRATES : He will continue, If I had asked you at the be-
d ginning what is both beautiful and ugly, and you had answered me as now, would not your answer have been correct? But do you still think that absolute beauty, by which all other things are ordered in loveliness, and appear beautiful when its form is added—do you think that that is a maiden, or a mare, or a lyre?

HIPPIAS : But still, Socrates, if this is what he wants, it is the easiest thing in the world to tell him what is that beauty which orders all other things in loveliness and makes them appear beautiful when
e it is added to them. The fellow must be a perfect fool, knowing nothing about things of beauty. If you reply to him that this about which he is asking, beauty, is nothing else than gold, he will be at a loss and will not attempt to refute you. For I suppose we all know that if anything has gold added to it, it will appear beautiful when so adorned even though it appeared ugly before.

SOCRATES : You do not know what a ruffian he is. He accepts nothing without making difficulties.

HIPPIAS: What do you mean? He must accept an accurate statement, on pain of ridicule.

SOCRATES: Well, my friend, this answer of yours he will not only refuse to accept, but he will even scoff at me viciously, saying, You blockhead! Do you reckon Phidias a bad artist?

I suppose I shall answer, Not in the least.

HIPPIAS: Quite right.

SOCRATES: Yes, so I think. But when I agree that Phidias is a good artist, he will say, Then do you fancy that Phidias was ignorant of this beauty of which you speak?

I shall reply, What is the point? And he will rejoin, The point is that he did not give his Athena eyes of gold or use gold for the rest of her face, or for her hands, or for her feet, as he would have done if supreme beauty could be given to them only by the use of gold; he made them of ivory. Clearly he made this mistake through ignorance, not knowing that it is really gold that confers beauty on everything to which it is added.

How are we to answer him then, Hippias?

HIPPIAS: Quite easy. We shall reply that Phidias was artistically right, for ivory too is beautiful, I suppose.

SOCRATES: Why then, he will say, did he not also make the eyeballs of ivory? He made them of stone, finding out stone as like as possible to ivory. Or is the stone that is beautiful itself a beauty?

Shall we say that it is?

HIPPIAS: Yes—it is beautiful, at least, whenever it is appropriate.

SOCRATES: But ugly when not appropriate? Am I to agree?

HIPPIAS: Yes—when not appropriate.

SOCRATES: He will go on, Well then, O man of wisdom, do not ivory and gold cause a thing to appear beautiful when they are appropriate, and ugly when they are not?

Shall we deny it or admit that he is right?

HIPPIAS: We shall at any rate admit that whatever is appropriate to a particular thing makes that thing beautiful.

SOCRATES: He will continue, Then when a man boils the pot of which we spoke, the beautiful pot full of beautiful soup, which is the more appropriate to it—a ladle of gold or a ladle of figwood?

HIPPIAS: Really, Socrates, what a creature! Please tell me who he is.

SOCRATES: You would not know him if I told you his name.

HIPPIAS: I know enough about him at this moment to know that he is a dolt.

SOCRATES: He is a terrible nuisance, Hippias. Still, how shall we answer? Which of the two ladles are we to choose as appropriate to the soup and the pot? Obviously the one of figwood? For it gives the

290

b

c

d

e

soup a better smell, I suppose, and moreover, my friend, it would not break our pot and spill the soup and put out the fire and deprive the guests at our dinner of a truly noble dish, whereas that golden ladle would do all this. And therefore, if you do not object, I think we 291 should say that the wooden ladle is more appropriate than the golden.

HIPPIAS : Yes, it is more appropriate, but I should not myself go on talking with the fellow while he asks such questions.

SOCRATES : Quite right, my friend. It would not be appropriate for you to be contaminated by such language, you who are so well dressed, and wear such good shoes, and are renowned for wisdom throughout the Greek world. But to me it does not matter if I am b mixed up with that fellow; so fortify me with your instruction, and for my sake answer the questions.

He will say, If indeed the wooden ladle is more appropriate than the golden, will it not also be more beautiful, since you, Socrates, have admitted that the appropriate is more beautiful than the inappropriate?

Can we then avoid the admission that the wooden ladle is more beautiful than the golden?

HIPPIAS : Would you like me to give you a definition of beauty by which you can save yourself from prolonged discussion?

c SOCRATES : Certainly, but first please tell me which of the two ladles I have just mentioned is appropriate, and the more beautiful?

HIPPIAS : Well, if you like, answer him that it is the one made of figwood.

SOCRATES : Say now what a moment ago you were proposing to say, for following your answer, if I take the line that beauty is gold, I shall apparently have to face the fact that gold is no more beautiful than figwood. Now, once more, what according to you is beauty?

d HIPPIAS : You shall have your answer. You are looking, I think, for a reply ascribing to beauty such a nature that it will never appear ugly to anyone anywhere?

SOCRATES : Exactly. You catch my meaning admirably.

HIPPIAS : Now please attend. If anyone can find any fault with what I say, I give you full leave to call me an imbecile.

SOCRATES : I am on tenterhooks.

HIPPIAS : Then I maintain that always, everywhere, and for every man it is most beautiful to be rich, healthy, honored by the Greeks, to reach old age and, after burying his parents nobly, himself e to be borne to the tomb with solemn ceremony by his own children.

SOCRATES : Bravo, bravo, Hippias, those are words wonderful, sublime, worthy of you, and you have my grateful admiration for your kindness in bringing all your ability to my assistance. Still, our shafts are not hitting our man, and I warn you that he will now deride us more than ever.

HIPPIAS : A poor sort of derision, Socrates, for in deriding us when he can find no objection to our view, he will be deriding himself and will be derided by the company.

SOCRATES: Perhaps so. Perhaps, however, when he has the answer you suggest he may not be content just to laugh at me. So I forebode.

HIPPIAS: What do you mean?

SOCRATES: If he happens to have a stick with him, he will attempt to get at me with it very forcibly, unless I escape by running away.

HIPPIAS: What? Is the fellow somehow your lord and master? Surely he will be arrested and punished for such behavior? Or has Athens no system of justice, that she allows her citizens to commit b wrongful assaults on one another?

SOCRATES: She forbids it absolutely.

HIPPIAS: Then he will be punished for his wrongful assaults.

SOCRATES: I do not think so, Hippias—emphatically not, if that were the answer I gave him. I think his assault would be justified.

HIPPIAS: Since that is your own opinion, well, I think so too.

SOCRATES: But may I go on to explain why, in my own opinion, that answer would justify an assault upon me? Or will you too assault me without trial, refusing me a hearing?

HIPPIAS: No, such a refusal would be monstrous. But what c have you to say?

SOCRATES: I will continue on the same plan as a moment ago, pretending to be that fellow but not using to you the kind of offensive and grotesque words he would to me. He will say, I feel sure, Do you not think, Socrates, that you deserve a thrashing after chanting so badly out of tune a dithyramb so long and so irrelevant to the question you were asked?

What do you mean? I shall say.

What do I mean? Are you incapable of remembering that I asked about beauty itself, that which gives the property of being beautiful to d everything to which it is added—to stone and wood, and man, and god, and every action and every branch of learning? I am asking, sir, what is beauty itself, and for all my shouting I cannot make you hear me. You might be a stone sitting beside me, a real millstone with neither ears nor brain.

Would not you, Hippias, be indignant if in terror I were to answer him, But this is what Hippias declared beauty to be, although I e kept on asking him, exactly as you do me, for that which is beautiful always and for everyone.

Frankly, will not that answer make you indignant?

HIPPIAS: I am quite sure, Socrates, that what I specified is beautiful to all, and will so appear to all.

SOCRATES: He will reply, And will be so in the future? For beauty, I take it, is always beautiful?

HIPPIAS: Certainly.

SOCRATES: And it was beautiful, too, in the past?

HIPPIAS: It was.

SOCRATES: Then he will go on, So this stranger from Elis asserted that it would have been beautiful for Achilles to be buried after his parents, and similarly for his grandfather Aeacus, and for the 293 other children of gods, and for the gods themselves?

HIPPIAS: What is this? Tell him to go to—glory! These questions of his are irreverent, Socrates.

SOCRATES: Surely it is not exactly irreverent to say that these things are so, when someone else has asked the question?

HIPPIAS: Well, presumably not.

SOCRATES: Presumably he will then say, It is you who affirm that it is beautiful always and for everyone to bury his parents and be buried by his children. Does not 'everyone' include Heracles and all the others we mentioned a moment ago?

HIPPIAS: I did not mean to include the gods.

b SOCRATES: Nor the heroes either, apparently.

HIPPIAS: Not if they were the children of gods.

SOCRATES: But if they were not?

HIPPIAS: Certainly.

SOCRATES: Then from your own argument, it now appears that the fate which is terrible and impious and shameful for Tantalus and Dardanus and Zethus is beautiful for Pelops and the other heroes of similar parentage?

HIPPIAS: I think so.

SOCRATES: He will go on, Then you think, contrary to what you said just now, that to bury one's parents and be buried by one's children is sometimes, and for some persons, shameful, and it looks more c than ever impossible that it should become, or be, beautiful to everyone. So this definition meets the same fate as those we discussed earlier—the maiden and the pot—it is an even more ludicrous failure, offering us that which is beautiful to some men, and not to others. And to this very day, Socrates, you cannot answer the question you were asked—beauty, what is it?

These and other like reproaches he will hurl at me with some justice, if I give him this answer. For the most part he talks to me d something after this fashion, but sometimes, as if in pity for my inexperience and lack of education, he himself proffers a question, and asks whether I think beauty is such and such, or it may be on some other subject—whatever he happens to be thinking about, and we are discussing.

HIPPIAS: What do you mean, Socrates?

SOCRATES: I will explain. My worthy Socrates, he says, don't give answers of that kind, and in that way—they are silly, easily torn e to rags—but consider this suggestion. In one of our answers a little while ago we got hold of, and expressed, the idea that gold is beautiful or not beautiful according as it is placed in an appropriate setting, and similarly with everything else to which this qualification can be added. Now consider this appropriateness, and reflect on the general nature of the appropriate, and see whether it might not be beauty.

Myself, I am in the habit of invariably agreeing to such surmises, for I can never think of anything to say, but you, do you think that the appropriate is beautiful?

HIPPIAS: Certainly, Socrates.

SOCRATES: Let us consider, and make sure that there is no deception.

HIPPIAS: So we ought.

SOCRATES: Come on then. Do we define the appropriate as that which by its presence causes the things in which it becomes pres- 294 ent to *appear* beautiful, or causes them to *be* beautiful, or neither?

HIPPIAS: In my own opinion, that which causes things to appear beautiful. For example, a man may be a figure of fun, but when he wears clothes or shoes that fit well he does seem a finer man.

SOCRATES: But then if the appropriate really makes things appear more beautiful than they are, the appropriate is a kind of fraud in relation to beauty, and would not be that for which we are looking, would it? We were looking, I think, for that by which all beautiful b things are beautiful, corresponding to that by which all great things are great, namely, excess—by this all great things are great, and great they must certainly be if they exceed, even though they do not appear so. Similarly we ask about beauty, by which all beautiful things are beautiful whether they appear so or not—what can that be? It cannot be the appropriate, for on your own view this causes things to appear more beautiful than they are, and does not leave them to appear such as they are in reality. We ought to take that which causes things to be beautiful, as I said just now, whether they appear so or not, and try to define it—this is what we are looking for, if we are looking for c beauty.

HIPPIAS: But, Socrates, the appropriate causes things both to be and to appear beautiful, when it is present.

SOCRATES: Then it is impossible for things that are in fact beautiful not to appear beautiful, since by hypothesis that which makes them appear beautiful is present in them?

HIPPIAS: It is impossible.

SOCRATES: Then it is our conclusion, Hippias, that all established usages and all practices which are in reality beautiful are regarded as beautiful by all men, and always appear so to them? Or do d we think the exact opposite, that ignorance of them is prevalent, and that these are the chief of all objects of contention and fighting, both between individuals and between states?

HIPPIAS: The latter, I think. Ignorance prevails.

SOCRATES : It would not, if the appearance of beauty were but added to them, and it would be added if the appropriate were beautiful and moreover caused them to *appear* as well as *be* beautiful. It follows that if the appropriate is that which causes things to be in fact beautiful, then it would be that beauty for which we are looking, but still it would not be that which causes them to appear beautiful. If, e on the other hand, that which causes things to appear beautiful is the appropriate, it is not that beauty for which we are looking. That for which we are looking makes things beautiful, but the same cause never could make things both appear and be either beautiful or anything else. We have then these alternatives—is the appropriate that which causes things to appear beautiful, or that which causes them to be so?

HIPPIAS : To appear, I think.

SOCRATES : Oh dear! Then the chance of finding out what the beautiful really is has slipped through our fingers and vanished, since the appropriate has proved to be something other than beautiful.

HIPPIAS : Upon my word, Socrates, I should never have thought it!

295   SOCRATES : But still, my friend, do not let us give up yet. I have still a sort of hope that the nature of beauty will reveal itself.

HIPPIAS : Yes indeed, it is not hard to discover. I am sure that if I were to retire into solitude for a little while and reflect by myself, I could define it for you with superlative precision.

SOCRATES : Hippias, Hippias, don't boast. You know what trouble it has already given us, and I am afraid it may get angry with us and run away more resolutely than ever. But what nonsense I am talk- b ing, for you, I suppose, will easily discover it when once you are alone. Still, I beg you most earnestly to discover it with me here, or, if you please, let us look for it together as we are now doing. If we find it, well and good; if not, I imagine I shall resign myself to my fate, and you will go away and discover it easily. Of course, if we find it now, you will not be annoyed by inquiries from me about the nature of your private discovery. So please look at your conception of beauty by itself. c I define it as—pray give me your whole attention and stop me if I talk nonsense—well, let us assume that whatever is useful is beautiful. My ground for the proposition is as follows. We do not say that eyes are beautiful when they appear to be without the faculty of sight; we do when they have that faculty and so are useful for seeing. Is that correct?

HIPPIAS : Yes.

SOCRATES : Similarly we say that the whole body is beautifully made, sometimes for running, sometimes for wrestling, and we speak d in the same way of all animals. A beautiful horse, or cock, or quail, and all utensils, and means of transport both on land and on sea, merchant vessels and ships of war, and all instruments of music and of the arts generally, and, if you like, practices and laws—we apply the word 'beautiful' to practically all these in the same manner. In each case we take as our criterion the natural constitution or the workmanship or the form of enactment, and whatever is useful we call beautiful, and beautiful in that respect in which it is useful and for the purpose for which and at the time at which it is useful, and we call e ugly that which is useless in all these respects. Is not this your view also, Hippias?

HIPPIAS : Yes, it is.

SOCRATES : Then we are now right in affirming that the useful is pre-eminently beautiful.

HIPPIAS : We are.

SOCRATES : And that which has the power to achieve its specific purpose is useful for the purpose which it has the power to achieve, and that which is without that power is useless?

HIPPIAS : Certainly.

SOCRATES : Then power is a beautiful thing, and the lack of it ugly?

HIPPIAS : Very much so. We have evidence of that fact from public life, among other sources, for in political affairs generally, and 296 also within a man's own city, power is the most beautiful of things, and lack of it the most ugly and shameful.

SOCRATES : Good! Does it then follow—a momentous consequence—that wisdom is the most beautiful, and ignorance the most shameful of all things?

HIPPIAS : What do you think, Socrates?

SOCRATES : A moment's quiet, my dear friend. I have misgivings about the line we are taking now.

HIPPIAS : Why these misgivings again? This time your argu- b ment has proceeded magnificently.

SOCRATES : I could wish it were so, but let us consider together this point. Could a man do something which he had neither the knowledge nor the least atom of power to do?

HIPPIAS : Of course not. How could he do what he had not the power to do?

SOCRATES : Then those who by reason of some error contrive and work evil involuntarily—surely they would never do such things if they were without the power to do them?

HIPPIAS : Obviously not.

SOCRATES : And those who have the power to do a thing do it through power, not of course by being powerless? c

HIPPIAS : Certainly not.

SOCRATES : Those who do what they do, all have the power to do it?

HIPPIAS: Yes.

SOCRATES: And evil is done much more abundantly than good by all men from childhood upward, erring involuntarily?

HIPPIAS: That is so.

SOCRATES: Well then, are we to say that this power, and these useful things—I mean any things useful for working some evil—are we to say that these are beautiful, or that they are far from being so?

d   HIPPIAS: Far from it, in my opinion.

SOCRATES: Then the powerful and the useful are not, it appears, the beauty we want.

HIPPIAS: They are, Socrates, if they are powerful for good and are useful for such purposes.

SOCRATES: Still the theory that that which is powerful and useful without qualification is beautiful has vanished away. Do you think, however, that what we really had in mind to say was that beauty is that which is both useful and powerful for some good purpose?

e   HIPPIAS: I think so.

SOCRATES: But this is equivalent to beneficial, is it not?

HIPPIAS: Certainly.

SOCRATES: So we reach the conclusion that beautiful bodies, and beautiful rules of life, and wisdom, and all the things we mentioned just now, are beautiful because they are beneficial?

HIPPIAS: Evidently.

SOCRATES: Then it looks as if beauty is the beneficial, Hippias.

HIPPIAS: Undoubtedly.

SOCRATES: Now the beneficial is that which produces good?

HIPPIAS: Yes.

SOCRATES: And that which produces is identical with the cause?

HIPPIAS: That is so.

SOCRATES: Then the beautiful is the cause of the good?

297   HIPPIAS: It is.

SOCRATES: But surely, Hippias, the cause and that of which it is the cause are different, for the cause could scarcely be the cause of the cause. Look at it in this way. The cause was defined as something that produces, was it not?

HIPPIAS: Certainly.

SOCRATES: And that which produces produces only that which is coming into existence; it does not produce that which produces.

HIPPIAS: That is so.

SOCRATES: And that which is coming into existence, and that which produces it, are two different things?

HIPPIAS: Yes.

SOCRATES: Then the cause is not the cause of the cause, but of

b   that which is coming into existence through it?

HIPPIAS: Certainly.

SOCRATES: If then beauty is the cause of good, then the good would be brought into existence by beauty, and it would appear that we devote ourselves to the pursuit of wisdom and of all other beautiful things for the reason that their product and offspring, the good, is worthy of devotion. And from our explorations it looks as though beauty is metaphorically a kind of father of the good.

HIPPIAS: Certainly. You say well, Socrates.

SOCRATES: Do I not say this also well, that the father is not his son, nor the son his father?

HIPPIAS: Quite well.   c

SOCRATES: And that the cause is not that which it brings into existence, nor vice versa?

HIPPIAS: True.

SOCRATES: Then most certainly, my good sir, beauty is not good nor the good beautiful. Do you think that possible after our discussion?

HIPPIAS: No, I most certainly do not.

SOCRATES: Then does it please us, and should we be willing to say that the beautiful is not good, nor the good beautiful?

HIPPIAS: Most certainly not. It does not please me at all.

SOCRATES: Most certainly I agree, Hippias. It pleases me least of any of the theories we have discussed.   d

HIPPIAS: Very likely.

SOCRATES: Then it looks as if the view which a little while ago we thought the finest result of our discussions, the view that the beneficial, and the useful, and the power to produce something good, is beautiful, is in fact wrong, but it is, if possible, more open to ridicule than those first definitions according to which the maiden was the beautiful, and so was a succession of other things.

HIPPIAS: Apparently.

SOCRATES: For myself, Hippias, I don't know where to turn, and am completely at a loss. Have you anything to say?

HIPPIAS: Not at the moment, but as I said a little while ago, I feel sure I shall find a way out after some reflection.   e

SOCRATES: But I do not feel that I can wait for the issue of your reflection, I am so eager for this knowledge, and indeed, I fancy I have just hit on something. Come now, if we were to say that whatever we enjoy—I do not mean to include all pleasures, but only what we enjoy through our senses of hearing and sight—if we were to say that this is beautiful, how should we fare in our struggle? Surely beautiful human beings, and all decorative work, and pictures, and plastic 298 art, delight us when we see them if they are beautiful, and beautiful sounds, and music as a whole, and discourses, and tales of imagination, have the same effect, so that if we were to reply to that blustering fellow, My worthy sir, beauty is the pleasant which comes through the senses of hearing and sight, do you not think that we should stop his bluster?

b   HIPPIAS : At last, Socrates, I think we have a good definition of beauty.

SOCRATES : Well, but are we then to say that those practices which are beautiful, and the laws, are beautiful as giving pleasure through our senses of sight and hearing, or that they are in some other category?

HIPPIAS : Perhaps these cases might escape our man.

SOCRATES : No, Hippias, they would certainly not escape the man by whom I should be most ashamed to be caught talking pretentious nonsense.

HIPPIAS : Whom do you mean?

SOCRATES : The son of Sophroniscus [i.e., Socrates himself],
c   who would no more allow me to hazard these assertions while they are unexplored than to assert what I do not know as though I knew it.

HIPPIAS : Well, now you have raised the point, I must say that I too think this question about the laws is on a different footing.

SOCRATES : Gently, Hippias, we may quite well be imagining that we see our way clearly, when we have really fallen into the same difficulty about beauty as that in which we were caught a moment ago.

HIPPIAS : What do you mean, Socrates?

SOCRATES : This is what strikes me—there may be something
d   in it. These matters of law and practice might perhaps prove after all to be within the range of the perceptions of hearing and sight. However, let us hold fast to the statement that the pleasant which comes through these senses is beautiful, leaving the question of the laws altogether on one side. But if we were asked by the person to whom I refer, or by anyone else, Why, Hippias and Socrates, have you picked out within the class of the pleasant that which is pleasant in the way you affirm to be beautiful, while you deny the designation 'beautiful' to that which is pleasant according to the other senses,
e   that is, the senses which have to do with food, and drink, and sexual intercourse, and all such things? Or do you deny that these are pleasant, and claim that in such things there is no pleasure whatever, or in anything except seeing and hearing? What shall we say?

HIPPIAS : Obviously we shall reply that these other things also offer very great pleasures.

SOCRATES : Why then, he will say, do you take away this designation and refuse to allow them beauty when they are pleasures no less than the others?

299   We shall answer, Because everyone would laugh at us if we said that it is not pleasant to eat, but beautiful, or that a pleasant smell is not pleasant, but beautiful, and as to sexual intercourse, everyone would contend against us that it is most pleasant, while admitting

that it ought to be enjoyed only where there is none to see because it is a disgraceful and repulsive sight.

When we say this, Hippias, he would probably rejoin, I too understand that you are and have been ashamed to say that these pleasures are beautiful, because that is not the common view, but my question b was, what is beautiful, not what the mass of men think it to be.

I imagine we shall restate our original proposition—in our view that part of the pleasant which comes by sight and hearing is beautiful. However, can you suggest any other way of dealing with the question, or any addition to that reply?

HIPPIAS: As the argument now stands, we are bound to give that answer, and that only.

SOCRATES: Admirable, he will reply. If then the pleasant which comes by sight and hearing is beautiful, is it not obvious that any c pleasant thing outside that category could not be beautiful?

Shall we agree?

HIPPIAS: Yes.

SOCRATES: He will go on, Then is that which is pleasant through sight, pleasant through sight and through hearing, or is that which is pleasant through hearing, pleasant through hearing and through sight?

We shall reply, By no means. The pleasant which comes by either sense would certainly not be pleasant through both—that seems to be your meaning. Our statement was that either of these pleasant things would be beautiful just by itself, and also both of them together.

Shall that be our answer?

HIPPIAS: Certainly. d

SOCRATES: Well, then, he will say, does any pleasant thing whatever differ from any other pleasant thing in respect of its pleasantness? The question is not whether a particular pleasure is greater or smaller, or exists in a higher or lower degree, but whether there can be a difference between pleasures in this particular respect, that one is, and another is not, a pleasure?

We do not think so, do we?

HIPPIAS: No.

SOCRATES: He will continue, It follows that you chose out these from among the other pleasures for some other reason than that they are pleasures. Since there is some difference between them e and the others, you saw in both of them some quality capable of providing a criterion by which you judge them to be beautiful, for the pleasure that comes through sight, I take it, is not beautiful just because it comes through sight. If that were the reason why it is beautiful, the other pleasure, the one which comes through hearing, would never be beautiful—it is emphatically not pleasure through sight.

Shall we reply that his reasoning is correct?

HIPPIAS: Yes.

300   SOCRATES: Nor again is the pleasure that comes through hearing beautiful because it is through hearing, for again, in that case the pleasure through sight would never be beautiful since it is emphatically not pleasure through hearing.

Shall we agree that he argues correctly?

HIPPIAS: He does.

SOCRATES: But yet both are beautiful, you affirm?

We do affirm it?

HIPPIAS: Yes.

SOCRATES: Then they have something identical which makes them to be beautiful, a common quality which appertains to both of
b them in common and to each singly; otherwise they could not, I take it, both of them be beautiful as a pair, and also each separately? Answer me as though you were answering him.

HIPPIAS: I answer that what you say is my opinion also.

SOCRATES: If then these pleasures are both of them as a pair conditioned in some way, but neither singly is so conditioned, they could not be beautiful by reason of this particular condition?

HIPPIAS: And how is it possible, Socrates, that when neither of them singly has been conditioned in some way—any way you like to think of—yet both as a pair should be conditioned in the way in which neither singly has been conditioned?

c   SOCRATES: You think it impossible?

HIPPIAS: I do—not being entirely unacquainted either with the nature of the subject, or with the terminology of our present discussion.

SOCRATES: Very nice, Hippias. But still I fancy perchance I see an example of what you say to be impossible, though really I may see nothing.

HIPPIAS: It is not a case of 'perchance'—you see wrong, of good set purpose.

SOCRATES: Indeed, many such examples rise up before my mind's eye, but I distrust them because they are visible to me, who have never earned a penny by wisdom, while they do not appear to you
d who have earned more in that way than anyone else alive. And, my friend, I am pondering whether you are not playing with me and deceiving me on purpose, so clearly and in such numbers do I see them.

HIPPIAS: Nobody will know better than you whether I am playing with you or not, when you start to describe these visions of yours. Your description of them will be plain nonsense. You will never find both of us together conditioned in a way in which neither has been conditioned separately.

e   SOCRATES: What's that, Hippias? You may be talking sense and I do not grasp it, but please let me explain more clearly what I mean. It appears to me that there are attributes which cannot, and do not now, belong to either of us singly, but can belong to both together, and, conversely, that there are attributes of which both together are capable, but neither singly.

HIPPIAS: Here indeed, Socrates, are absurdities even more monstrous than those of your answer a little while ago. Only consider. If we are both just men, is not each of us individually just? If each of us is unjust, are not both so? If both are well, is not each of us well also? Or if each of us were tired, or were wounded, or struck, or conditioned in any other way, then should we not both of us as a pair be conditioned in that way? Similarly, if both of us were made of gold, or silver, or ivory, or if you prefer it, were noble or wise or honored, or, for that matter, old men or young, or had any other human attribute you like to mention, must it not follow inevitably that each of us singly is that same?

SOCRATES: Most certainly.

HIPPIAS: You see, Socrates, the fact is that you yourself do not consider things as a whole, nor do those with whom you habitually converse; you test beauty and each general concept by taking it separately and mentally dissecting it, with the result that you fail to perceive the magnitude and continuity of the substances of which reality is composed. And now this failure has gone so far that you imagine that there is something, an attribute or substantive nature, which appertains to two of them together but not to each singly, or conversely to each singly but not to the two together; that is the state of mind to which you and your friends are reduced—how unreasoning, and superficial, and stupid, and uncomprehending!

SOCRATES: Such is the lot of us mortals, Hippias—a man does what he can, not what he wishes, according to the oft-quoted proverb. However, your constant admonitions are a great help. Just now, before your admonition of our stupidity in these matters, I had some further thoughts about them which perhaps I might explain to you— or shall I refrain?

HIPPIAS: I know what you are going to say, Socrates; I know the mind of every school of dialecticians. But say your say, if you prefer it.

SOCRATES: Well, I do prefer it. Before you said what you did, my honored friend, we were so uninstructed as to hold the opinion that each of us two, you and myself, is one, but that, taken together, we cannot be that which each of us is singly—for we are two and not one. Such was our folly. Now, however, we have been taught by you that if together we are two, each of us singly must also be two, and if each is one, so must we both be, for on the continuous theory of reality according to Hippias it cannot be otherwise—whatever two entities are together, each is singly, and whatever each is, both are. Here I sit, fixed by you in this belief. But first, Hippias, remind me, are you and I both one, or are you two, and I two?

HIPPIAS: What do you mean, Socrates?

SOCRATES: Exactly what I say. You frighten me out of plain

302 speech, because you get angry with me whenever you think that you have made a good point. Still, let me ask you this further question. Is not each of us two one, possessing the attribute of being one?

HIPPIAS: Certainly.

SOCRATES: Then if each of us is one, each is also an odd number. You hold that one is an odd number, do you not?

HIPPIAS: I do.

SOCRATES: Are we then both together an odd number, being two?

HIPPIAS: Impossible.

SOCRATES: Both together would be an even number?

HIPPIAS: Assuredly.

b SOCRATES: Since then both together are even, does it follow that each of us singly is even?

HIPPIAS: Certainly not.

SOCRATES: It is not then absolutely inevitable that, as you said just now, each individual should be what both are together, and that both should be what each is?

HIPPIAS: Not in such cases, but it is inevitable in the kind of case I mentioned earlier.

SOCRATES: That suffices, Hippias. Even that reply is to be accepted, as it is an acknowledgment that sometimes it is so, and sometimes not. If you recall the starting point of our discussion, you will remember that I was arguing that the pleasures which come through sight and hearing are beautiful not because each of them

c was so conditioned as to be beautiful but not both together, nor because both of them together were similarly conditioned but not each singly; they were beautiful by virtue of something which conditions both together and also each singly, and so you agreed that both together were beautiful and each singly. Accordingly I thought that if both together are beautiful, they must be beautiful because of an essential character belonging to both and not of a character which is lacking in one or the other, and I still think so. But start again as from the beginning. If pleasure through sight and pleasure through hearing are

d beautiful both together and each singly, does not that which makes them beautiful belong to both together and to each singly?

HIPPIAS: Certainly.

SOCRATES: Then can they be beautiful because each singly and both together are pleasures? On this reasoning, would not all other pleasures be beautiful just as much, for, if you remember, they were acknowledged to be just as much pleasures?

HIPPIAS : Yes, I remember.

SOCRATES : These particular ones, however, were stated to be beautiful because they came through sight and hearing.   e

HIPPIAS : Yes, that was the statement.

SOCRATES : Now consider whether I am right on this point. According to my recollection, it was said that part of the category of the pleasant was beautiful—not every 'pleasant,' but that which comes through hearing and sight.

HIPPIAS : That is correct.

SOCRATES : And this quality belongs to both together but not to each singly, does it not? As we said earlier, each of them singly does not come through both senses; both together come through both but not each singly. Is that so?

HIPPIAS : Yes.

SOCRATES : Then each of them singly is not beautiful by that which does not belong to each, for that which is of both does not belong to each, and it follows that while from our agreed propositions we may rightly say that both together are beautiful, we may not say it of each singly. Is not this the necessary conclusion?

HIPPIAS : It appears so.   303

SOCRATES : Are we to say then that both together are beautiful, but not each?

HIPPIAS : I see no objection.

SOCRATES : I do, my friend. We certainly had examples of attributes appertaining to individual entities in such a way that if they appertained to two together they appertained also to each singly, and if to each, then to both—all the attributes which were specified by you.

HIPPIAS : Yes.

SOCRATES : But on the other hand those which I specified did not, and among those were the concept 'each' and the concept 'both.' Is that right?

HIPPIAS : Yes.

SOCRATES : To which category, Hippias, do you think the beauti- b ful belongs? To the category of those you mentioned? If I am strong and you are too, we are both strong, and if I am just and you too, we are both just, and if both, then each singly. In the same way, if I am beautiful and you too, are we also both beautiful and if both, then each singly? Or may the same principle apply as in mathematics, when for instance the two components of even numbers may severally be odd, but may also be even, and, again, when quantities which are irrational if taken singly may be either rational or irrational if taken together? And there are innumerable other such examples, as c indeed I told you occurred to my mind. In which category do you place beauty? Do you take the same view of it as I do? To me it seems a gross absurdity to hold that while both of us together are beautiful, neither is so singly, or that each singly is beautiful but not both together, or anything else of that kind? Do you choose my alternative, or the other?

HIPPIAS : Yours.

SOCRATES : Quite right, if we wish to be spared further inquiry,
d for if this category includes beauty, it can no longer be maintained
that the pleasant which comes through sight and hearing is beautiful;
the description 'which comes through sight and hearing' makes both together beautiful but not each singly—which was impossible, as I
think, and you too.

HIPPIAS : Yes, we think the same.

SOCRATES : Then it is impossible for the pleasant which comes
through sight and hearing to be beautiful, since when we equate it with
beauty an impossible result is produced.

HIPPIAS : Quite so.

SOCRATES : My questioner will say, Now start again from the
e beginning since you have missed the mark this time. What according
to you is this 'beautiful' which appertains to both these pleasures, and
by reason of which you have honored them above the others and called
them beautiful?

I think, Hippias, we are bound to reply that these are the most
harmless of pleasures and the best, both taken together and taken
singly. Can you suggest any other reason why they are superior to the
others?

HIPPIAS : None. They really are the best.

SOCRATES : This then, he will say, is your definition of beauty—
beneficial pleasure.

Apparently, I shall reply. And you?

HIPPIAS : I too.

SOCRATES : He will go on, Well then, is not the beneficial that
which produces the good, and that which produces and that which is
produced were shown a little while ago to be different, and so our
discussion has ended up in the old discussion, has it not? For the good
304 cannot be beautiful, nor beauty good, if the two are not identical with
one another.

Nothing is more certain, we shall reply, if we are honest—there
can be no justification for demurring to truth.

HIPPIAS : But I must ask you, Socrates, what do you suppose is
the upshot of all this? As I said a little while ago, it is the scrapings
and shavings of argument, cut up into little bits. What is both beautiful and most precious is the ability to produce an eloquent and beauti-
b ful speech to a law court or a council meeting or any other official body
whom you are addressing, to convince your audience, and to depart
with the greatest of all prizes, your own salvation and that of your
friends and property. These then are the things to which a man should
hold fast, abandoning these pettifogging arguments of yours, unless he
wishes to be accounted a complete fool because he occupies himself, as
we are now doing, with trumpery nonsense.

SOCRATES: You, my dear Hippias, are blissfully fortunate because you know what way of life a man ought to follow, and moreover have followed it with success—so you tell me. I, however, am c subject to what appears to be some supernatural ill fortune. I wander about in unending perplexity, and when I lay my perplexity before you wise men, you turn on me and batter me with abuse as soon as I have explained my plight. You all say just what you, Hippias, are now saying, how foolish and petty and worthless are the matters with which I occupy myself, but when in turn I am convinced by you and repeat exactly what you tell me, that the height of excellence is the ability to produce an eloquent and beautiful speech and win the day in a law court or any other assembly, I am called every kind of bad name by d some of the audience, including especially that man who is always cross-questioning me. He is a very close relative of mine and lives in the same house, and when I go home and he hears me give utterance to these opinions he asks me whether I am not ashamed of my audacity in talking about a beautiful way of life, when questioning makes it evident that I do not even know the meaning of the word 'beauty.'

And yet, he goes on, how can you know whose speech is beautiful or the reverse—and the same applies to any action whatsoever—when e you have no knowledge of beauty? And so long as you are what you are, don't you think that you might as well be dead?

It is my lot, you see, to be reviled and abused alike by you gentlemen, and by him. However, I suppose all this must be endured. I may get some good from it—stranger things have happened. And indeed, Hippias, I do think I have got some good out of my conversation with the two of you. I think now I appreciate the true meaning of the proverb, 'All that is beautiful is difficult.'

LETTERS

LETTER XIII

360 *To* DIONYSIUS, *Tyrant of Syracuse, Prosperity*

Be this my introduction and at the same time a token for you that the letter is from me. Once when you were entertaining the young men of Locri, you occupied a couch a good way from mine. You then rose and came to me with words of greeting that were excellent. I **b** thought so at least and my neighbor at table too, who thereupon—he was one of the cultured circle—put the question, 'I suppose, Dionysius, Plato is a great help to you in your studies?' You replied, 'In much else too, for from the moment that I sent for him, the very fact that I had so sent was at once helpful to me.' Here then is something that we must keep alive. We must see to it that we continue to be more and more helpful to each other. So I am doing my part now to effect this by sending you herewith some Pythagorean treatises and some classifications. I am also sending you a man, as we agreed at the time, who will perhaps be useful to you and Archytas—that is, if Archytas has **c** come to Syracuse. His name is Helicon; he is a native of Cyzicus, a pupil of Eudoxus and well versed in all his teaching. He has also studied under a pupil of Isocrates and under Polyxenus, an associate of Bryson. With all this he has the quality rarely combined with this of possessing social grace and he seems not to be ill-natured. In fact he would impress one rather as being full of fun and good-natured. I say **d** this, however, with misgivings, because I am expressing an opinion about a man, and man, while no mean animal, is a changeable one, with a very few exceptions in a few matters. For even in his case my caution and mistrust led me to make investigations, meeting him personally and inquiring of his fellow citizens, and no one said anything against the man. But be cautious and test him yourself. By all means, however, if you have the least bit of time for it, take lessons of him, in **e** addition to the rest of your philosophical training. If that is impossible, have someone else thoroughly instructed, so that, when you

---

From *Thirteen Epistles of Plato*, translated with introduction and notes by L. A. Post (Oxford, 1925). Minor revisions have been made by the translator. See note on p. 1516.

have time to study, you may do so and not only benefit yourself but add to your reputation. And so I shall go on being constantly helpful to you. So much for these matters.

As for the things you wrote to me to send you, I have had the 361 Apollo done and Leptines is bringing it. It is the work of an excellent young craftsman named Leochares. He had in his workshop another work that I thought very fine; so I bought it as a present for your wife because her care of me in health and in illness was honorable both to you and to me. Give it to her, then, unless you decide otherwise. I am also sending twelve jars of sweet wine for the children and two of honey. We arrived too late to store up figs, and the myrtle berries that b were put in store spoiled. Another time we will take better care. Leptines will tell you about plants.

The money for these purposes—that is, to buy these articles and to pay some taxes due to the city—I took from Leptines, giving him an explanation that I thought as creditable to us as any and one that I could give without falsehood, namely that it was my money that I spent on the Leucadian ship, amounting to about sixteen minas. This sum then I took and used for my own purposes and for these things c that I have dispatched to you.

In the next place I want you to know what your financial position is with respect to your credit at Athens and with respect to my claims. I will use your money, as I told you once, just as I do that of my other friends. I use just as little as I can, only the amount that I consider necessary or fair or creditable to me and to the man whose money I am taking.

Well, my present circumstances are as follows. There are four daughters living of those nieces of mine, on the occasion of whose death I refused to wear a wreath, though you urged me to. One of them d is now of an age to marry, one eight years old, one a little more than three years, and one not yet a year old. Dowries must be provided by me and my friends for any of these that I may live to see married. Those I don't live to see married may look to themselves, and those whose fathers get to be richer than I, I need not provide for. At present I am in easier circumstances than any of them, and it was I who provided their mothers with dowries, aided among others by Dion. Now the eldest of these is going to marry Speusippus, since she is his e sister's daughter. I need no more than thirty minas for her, for that is a fair dowry here. Furthermore, if my mother dies, I shall need no more than ten minas for the construction of her tomb. In these matters my requirements for the present are about what I have mentioned. If, however, any other expense arises, either private or public, because of my visit to you, we must do as I told you at the time—I must struggle to make the expense as little as possible, and what I can't avoid you must pay.

Next I have to say in regard to the expenditure of sums from your 362

account at Athens, first, that if I have to spend money on equipping a chorus or anything of the sort, you have not, as we supposed, anyone connected with you here who will advance it, and secondly, that, when, as may happen, important interests of your own are at stake, so that a prompt expenditure will be advantageous, while any postponement of expenditure until someone can come from you with the money will be detrimental, such a situation is not only inconvenient, it is ignominious. Really this is a matter that I have proved myself. I sent
b Erastus to Andromedes, the Aeginetan, on whom, as a connection of yours, you told me to draw for whatever I needed, for I wanted to send you some other rather important things that you wrote for. He, however, answered, as was reasonable and natural, that when he had on a former occasion paid out money on your father's account he had had difficulty in getting it back and that this time he would pay a small sum but no more. Under these conditions I took the money from Leptines. Leptines moreover deserves some praise for his conduct, not because he paid the money but because he did it cheerfully. In other cases, too, where he said or did anything that concerned you, he
c showed clearly that he was a friend and what kind of friend he was. Surely I ought to report such conduct as this or the reverse, giving you in each case my opinion of anyone's behavior in regard to you.

At any rate I am going to be frank with you about financial matters, since it is my duty and since, moreover, I can speak with some experience of your surroundings. Those who on any occasion bring you information are unwilling to inform you of anything that they
d suppose involves expense, for fear of incurring ill will. Do then accustom them and compel them to tell you of such matters, as well as of everything else. You must yourself be acquainted with every detail as far as you can and be your own judge and not avoid such acquaintance with details, since nothing could be more advantageous for you in your government. Expending money rightly and making payments rightly, as you yourself say and will say, is a good thing both for other reasons and for the sake of your financial position itself. So don't let those who say they are watching your interests cause a prejudice
e to arise against you. It is a good thing neither for yourself nor for your reputation to be thought unsatisfactory in your financial dealings.

Next I will speak of Dion. About other matters I can't tell you yet, not until the letters come from you, as you promised. In regard, however, to the matter you forbade me to mention to him, though I neither mentioned nor discussed it, I did try to discover whether or not he would be greatly concerned if it happened, and my opinion is that he would be not a little moved if it were to occur. In all other respects I think Dion not only claims to be but is reasonable in his attitude toward you.

363   To Cratinus, who is a brother of Timotheus, but a companion of mine, let us give a breastplate for military service, one of the padded

ones for the infantry, and to the daughters of Cebes three eleven-foot robes, not the expensive ones from Amorgus but linen ones from Sicily. You probably know Cebes by name, for he is represented in the Socratic dialogues in company with Simmias holding a conversation with Socrates in the dialogue on the soul. He is intimate and in sympathy with all of us.

Now about the token that distinguishes between the letters that b are seriously intended and those that are not, I suppose you remember my instruction, but nevertheless take notice and give me your close attention. There are many who ask me to write whom it is not easy to put off openly, so at the beginning of the letters that are seriously intended, I put *God;* in other cases, *the gods.*

The envoys requested me to write to you and with reason, for they very heartily everywhere sing your praises and mine—Philagrus especially, who at that time had something the matter with his hand. Philaedes, too, when he arrived from the court of the Great King, spoke of you. Except that it would have required a very long letter I should c have written what he said. Under the circumstances you must inquire of Leptines.

In case you send the breastplate, or anything else that I write for, if you have any preference for any other messenger, well and good; otherwise give it to Terillus. He is one of those that make the voyage regularly, and is not only a friend of ours in other ways, but is versed in philosophy as well. He is related by marriage to Tison, who was city commissioner when I sailed.

Farewell, and lead the philosophical life and encourage the younger men. Give my greetings to the group who join you at ballplay, d and give orders to Aristocritus and the others, in case any work or letter of mine comes to you, to see to it that you know of it without delay and to keep reminding you to attend to the injunctions I give you in my letters. Now in particular don't neglect to reimburse Leptines for his advance. Pay him at once that others may observe your treatment of him and be the more willing to accommodate us.

Iatrocles, whom I set free at that time along with Myronides, is e to sail now with the things that I am sending. Give him then some salaried post—you may count on his loyalty—and, if you choose to make use of him, do so. Preserve this letter, either itself or a memorandum of it, and be always the same.

LETTER II

To DIONYSIUS, *Prosperity*   310b
    I have heard from Archedemus that you not only expect me to say nothing about you myself, but you want my friends also to refrain

from saying or doing anything offensive to you. Of Dion only you make an exception. Now when you make an exception of Dion, the infer-
c ence is that I do not exercise authority over my friends. If I did thus exercise authority over you and Dion as well as the others, it would have been better for all of us, and for the rest of the Greeks too, I maintain. The fact is, however, that my power is no more than this. I can count on the obedience of one follower, namely myself. I do not mean by this that there is any truth in what Cratistolus and Polyxenus
d told you, for one of them, it is said, reports that at Olympia he heard a number of my companions abusing you. Of course his hearing may be keener than mine. I certainly heard nothing of the sort. In my opinion you would do well in future, when anyone makes such a report about any of us, to write and ask me about it, for I shall be neither afraid nor ashamed to tell the truth.

As for you and me and our mutual relations, the situation is as follows. There is no Greek, you may say, who has not heard of us as individuals; moreover our association with one another is generally
e discussed, and, be not deceived, it will continue to be discussed in time to come, for the number of those who have heard of our intercourse corresponds to its closeness and warmth. Well, what do I mean by this? I will go back a little and explain. It is a natural law that wisdom and great power attract each other. They are always pursuing and seeking after each other and coming together. Furthermore, this is a subject that people always find interesting whether they are themselves discussing it in a private gathering, or are listening to the treatment of
311 it by others in poems. For example, when people are talking of Hieron or the Spartan Pausanias, they like to introduce their association with Simonides and recount his conduct and remarks to them. Again, they are wont to celebrate together Periander of Corinth and Thales of Miletus, or Pericles and Anaxagoras, or again, Croesus and Solon
b as wise men and Cyrus as ruler. Moreover, the poets copy these examples and bring together Creon and Tiresias, Polyidus and Minos, Agamemnon and Nestor, and Odysseus and Palamedes. With much the same idea, I believe, primitive men brought together Prometheus and Zeus. The poets also show how in some such cases the two characters became enemies—in others, friends—how in some cases they were first friends and then enemies, and how in others they agreed in some things but differed on other points.

Now my object in saying all this is to point the moral that in our case too, discussion of our acts will not forthwith cease with our death.
c Here then is a matter that demands consideration, for we ought, it appears, to consider as well the time to come, since it is a fact that the most slavish men by a sort of natural law give it no thought, while the best men leave nothing undone to acquire a good reputation with posterity. To me this is a proof that the dead have some perception of
d events here, for the noblest souls know this truth by intuition, while

the vilest souls deny it, but the intuitions of the godlike are more valid than those of other men.

In my opinion, if those earlier rulers and philosophers whom I have mentioned had it in their power to amend what was amiss in their intercourse with each other, they would do their utmost to have better things said of them than is now the case. For us, though, it is still possible, please God, where we made any mistakes in our former intercourse, to correct them by our actions or by our words. The true philosophy, I maintain, will be better thought of and better e spoken of if we conduct ourselves well, but if otherwise, the reverse. Indeed if we were to make this object our concern, we could be engaged in no more pious act, nor in any more impious, if we were to neglect it.

Now I will explain how we must set about attaining this object and will show what principles are involved. I went to Sicily with the reputation of being by far the most distinguished among those devoted to philosophy, but my object in going to Syracuse was to gain your 312 support, so that I might see philosophy held in esteem even among the common throng. The result was not propitious. The reason that I assign for this is not the one that many would give, but that you appeared to have no great faith in me. You wanted to get rid of me in some way and to send for others. You wanted, I believe, in your mistrust, to discover the secret of my activities. At this there were many to take up the cry that you had a poor opinion of me and were devoted to other matters, and this is the report that is in general circula- b tion.

I proceed now to point out the right course for us to take hereafter. This will also answer your question what our relation to each other is to be. If you have no respect at all for philosophical pursuits, let them alone. If you have some respect, but have been taught by someone else or have discovered for yourself a better philosophy than mine, show your esteem for that. If, however, you prefer my philosophical teaching, you ought to make me too an object of special esteem.

Now, as in the beginning, you must show the way and I will follow your leading. If you show me marks of esteem, I will repay them; if I receive no such marks, I shall keep my own counsel. Note too c that any marks of respect you show me, if you take the lead, will be evidence that you think highly of philosophy, and the very fact that you have examined other teachers of philosophy besides me will cause many to honor you as a true philosopher. On the other hand any marks of respect that I show you, unless you return them, will be interpreted as evidence of my admiration of and desire for wealth—and such a name, we know, is nowhere an honest one. To put it in a nutshell, if you do homage to me, we both rise in men's esteem; if I do homage d to you, we both sink. So much for this subject.

The sphere is not right. Archedemus will make it clear to you

when he comes. He must also by all means give you an explanation of the matter about which you were in difficulty when you dispatched him, a subject indeed higher and more godlike than the other. According to his report you say that you are not satisfied with the demonstration of the nature of the first principle. I must state it to you in riddles, so that in case something happens to the tablet 'by land or sea in fold
e on fold,' he who reads may not understand. It is like this. It is in relation to the king of all and on his account that everything exists, and that fact is the cause of all that is beautiful. In relation to a second, the second class of things exists, and in relation to a third, the third class. Now the mind of man, when it has to do with them, endeavors to gain a knowledge of their qualities, fixing its attention on the things with which it has itself some affinity; these, however, are in no case
313 adequate. In regard to the king and the things I mentioned there is nothing like this. Thereupon the soul says, 'But what are they like?' This question, thou son of Dionysius and Doris—or rather the travail that this question occasions in the soul—is the cause of all the trouble, and if that be not expelled from a man, he shall never genuinely find the truth.

You told me in the garden under the laurels that you had thought
b of this yourself and that it was an original discovery of yours. I replied that if you really were clear about it, that fact would relieve me of a great deal of explanation. I said, however, that I had never met anyone else who had made this discovery, that in fact that very point gave me most of my trouble. Probably you had heard it explained by someone, though possibly you might by divine ordering have been impelled of yourself in that direction, and thought that you had a secure hold on the demonstration, and therefore did not fix securely the truth of which you had a glimpse. Instead of remaining fixed it darts to and fro, taking now one form, now another, never getting away from the appearances of things. The truth, though, has no such variability. You
c are not the only one who has been in such a case. I assure you that no one, the first time he heard me, was ever in any other state in the beginning. One has more difficulty, another less, before he finally gets clear. Hardly anyone has but little difficulty.

Since things have taken and are taking such a course, we have, I think, very nearly found an answer to your question, what our relation to each other is to be. Since you are putting my principles to the proof by going to other teachers and by considering my views in com-
d parison with theirs, as well as by themselves, this time, if your examination is genuine, these principles will grow to be a part of you, and you will be their friend as well as mine.

Now how are these things, together with all that I have mentioned, to come to pass? On the present occasion you did right to send Archedemus, and in future, after he has returned and has reported my message, you will perhaps again be overtaken by other difficulties.

You will accordingly send Archedemus to me again, if you are well advised, and he will come back to you with fresh wares. If you do this e two or three times and test adequately what I send, I shall be surprised if the points about which you are now in difficulty do not assume a very different aspect. Take this course then with all confidence, for never will you order nor Archedemus carry finer wares or any more acceptable to the gods than these.

Take precautions, however, lest this teaching ever be disclosed 314 among untrained people, for in my opinion there is in general no doctrine more ridiculous in the eyes of the general public than this, nor on the other hand any more wonderful and inspiring to those naturally gifted. Often repeated and constantly attended to for many years, it is at last like gold with great effort freed from all alloy. Let me tell you, however, the surprising thing about it. There are men, and a good many of them too, who have intelligence and memory and the ability b to judge a doctrine after examining it by every possible test, who are now old men and have been receiving instruction not less than thirty years, who have just reached the point of saying that what formerly they thought most uncertain, now appears to them quite certain and evident, while what seemed most certain then, appears now uncertain. Consider these facts and take care lest you sometime come to repent of having now unwisely published your views. It is a very great safeguard to learn by heart instead of writing. It is impossible for what is written not to be disclosed. That is the reason why I have c never written anything about these things, and why there is not and will not be any written work of Plato's own. What are now called his are the work of a Socrates embellished and modernized. Farewell and believe. Read this letter now at once many times and burn it. So much for these matters.

You were surprised that I should send Polyxenus to you. For my part I have long been saying and say now the same thing about Lyco- d phron and the others who are with you, that you altogether surpass them in talent for discussion and in logical method. None of them submits to confutation voluntarily, as some suppose, but they are forced to do so. It seems to me, moreover, that you have been very fair in your treatment of them and in your gifts. So much for this, and a great deal for such a subject.

If you are making any use of Philistion yourself, by all means do so, but if it can be done, dismiss him and let Speusippus have him. e Speusippus joins me in the request. Philistion himself promised me that, if you would let him go, he would gladly come to Athens. You did well to release the man from the quarries, but my request about his servants and about Hegesippus, son of Ariston, would not be burdensome to grant. You wrote to me, you know, that if anyone wronged either him or the others and you learned of it, you would not suffer it. I must also give you a truthful report in regard to Lysiclides. He is the 315 only one who has come to Athens from Sicily and has not perverted the truth about our association. He always says something that is good about what has taken place and puts the best construction on it.

LETTER XI

358d *To* LAODAMAS, *Prosperity*

I wrote to you before that it is of great importance for all the interests that you mention that you should yourself come to Athens. Since, however, you say that that is impossible, it would be next best if Socrates or I, as you suggested, were able to come to you. It happens
e though that Socrates is suffering from strangury, while as for me, if I were to come, it would not look well for me not to succeed in carrying out the projects which you invite me to undertake. I have, however, no great hope of such success, for reasons which could only be explained in another long letter, relating the whole story. Furthermore, I am not physically equal on account of my age to the difficulties of travel and to the sort of dangers that are encountered by land and sea. Just now, too, the routes are altogether beset with risks. Still I can give you and your colonists advice which, when I give it, will, to quote
359 Hesiod, be 'simple in appearance, but hard to understand.' If any think it possible, by the ordaining of any laws whatsoever, for any government to be well organized without the existence in the city of some authority concerned with daily life to see that both slave and free live soberly and manfully, their belief is false. Such an authority, however, might be established, if there are in existence men worthy of
b such a position. If, though, someone is needed to educate such rulers, in my opinion there exists neither anyone to give, nor any to receive such an education. Rather you must do the only thing left, and pray to the gods. In fact former cities were generally organized in this way at first and only later obtained good institutions through stress of great crises that occurred either in war or in connection with other achievements, when at such moments there appeared some man wellborn and well-bred who exercised great authority. Until then you must and
c should take a great interest in the question, but must nevertheless accept my statement of the case and not be so foolish as to suppose that you can achieve anything offhand. Good fortune be yours.

LETTER X

358c *To* ARISTODORUS, *Prosperity*

I hear from Dion that you are now one of his closest companions and that you have been so throughout, exhibiting the wisest trait among those that go to make philosophy. Steadfastness and loyalty and sincerity—that, say I, is the genuine philosophy. Other kinds of wisdom and cleverness, that lead to other results, I believe I name correctly when I term them mere embellishments. Farewell and hold fast to the traits to which you already hold fast.

LETTER IV

To DION OF SYRACUSE, *Prosperity*   320

I suppose it has been plain all along that I am heartily interested in the achievements that have been brought to pass. It must also have been plain that I was very eager to see them brought to final completion, as much as anything because I am ambitious for the success of the noble cause. I think it right that those who are in reality good men, b and who act accordingly, should obtain the renown that they deserve. At the moment certainly the situation, please God, is excellent; the great struggle, however, lies before us, for, though it might seem to belong to certain others as well as to you to excel in courage or swiftness or strength, surely those who make it their boast to honor truth and justice and generosity, and a behavior that conforms to these ideals, must by general consent be expected to excel in them.   c

Now my meaning is already plain; yet we should still remind ourselves that certain men—you know who—ought to surpass other men more than they surpass children. We must make it conspicuous that we are the sort of men we claim to be, especially since, please God, it will be easy. The circumstances of others are such that they must travel far and wide if they are to be known, whereas your present d position is such that men everywhere in the inhabited world, overbold though it be to say so, have their eyes fixed on one locality, and in that locality chiefly on you.

Since then all men are watching you, prepare to make Lycurgus or Cyrus appear but primitive, or anyone else who has ever become famous for superior character and statesmanship, especially since many, in fact practically all who are on the spot, say that it is quite likely that, when Dionysius has been put out of the way, our cause will be ruined by the rivalry between you and Heraclides and Theo- e dotes and the others of note. I hope of course above all that no one will behave so, but if anyone does, you must always appear in the role of healer and it will turn out for the best.

Perhaps you think it ridiculous for me to mention these things 321 because you yourself are quite aware of their importance. I observe, however, that in the theater the actors are spurred on by the children, to say nothing of their friends, whenever any actor thinks that they are applauding seriously and with good will. So now do you all of you play your own part and write to me if you need anything.

Things here are pretty much as they were when you were with us.
b Tell me also in your letters what you have done or what you happen to be engaged in doing, since I, for all I hear a great deal, know nothing. Just now letters from Theodotes and Heraclides have arrived in Lacedaemon and Aegina, but as I say, though I hear a great deal, I know nothing about the situation where you are. Reflect also that some think that you are not so obliging as you ought to be. Let it not escape you that popular favor is a means to achievement, while an arbitrary tem-
c per has solitude for company. Farewell.

LETTER III

315b *To* DIONYSIUS, *Joy*

Is it the best form of salutation to wish you 'joy' as I have, or would it be better if I were to follow my usual custom and bid you 'Do well'? That is the salutation that I use when I write to my friends. You of course descended to flattery and addressed even the god at Delphi in these very terms—such is the report of those who were in attendance at the time—and wrote, they say, 'Joy to you. Keep ever the pleas-
c ant life of a tyrant.' I, though, would not even bid a human being, much less a god, to enjoy himself. Any such injunction to a god would run counter to nature, for the divine dwells afar from the sphere of pleasure and pain. I would avoid such a greeting to a human being, moreover, because in most cases pleasure and pain work harm and produce in the soul dullness and forgetfulness and folly and lawlessness. So much in regard to the salutation. When you read this, take it any way you like.

It is reported by numerous witnesses that you have informed
d some of the ambassadors at your court that I once heard you declare your intention of planting settlers in the Greek cities of Sicily and of lightening the burden of the Syracusans by transforming your government from tyranny to kingship, and that I at that time prevented you from going on with your plans—that is your story—though you were most enthusiastic, while now I am instructing Dion to do just what you suggested. Thus we are using your own ideas to rob you of your
e realm. Now you know best yourself whether you derive any benefit from such statements; at any rate, you wrong me when you make a statement that contradicts the facts.

I had quite enough of slander in the malicious reports that Philistides and many others circulated about me among the mercenaries and the Syracusan public, for during my residence in the acropolis, those outside threw all the blame on me whenever a mistake was made, by asserting that you took my advice in everything. You know yourself better than anybody that in the beginning, when I thought it

would do some good, I did handle jointly with you of my own accord a 316
very few matters of government. In addition to some other minor
matters I took a reasonable interest in the preludes to the laws. I except of course any additions made to them by you or others, for I hear
that some of you have since been revising them. Of course our respective contributions will be obvious to those who are capable of distinguishing what is characteristic of me.

  Be that as it may, I have no need, as I said just now, of any fresh
calumnies aimed at making me unpopular with the Syracusans and
any others who believe your statements. Rather indeed I need a de- b
fense to meet both the earlier calumny and the present one that, coming after the other, is having a greater and more formidable effect.
Since there are two charges, my defense must be twofold. I must prove
in the first place that I rightly avoided taking any part with you in the
administration of the city, and in the second place that I was not the
one to give you any such advice or to interfere in any such manner
as you say. It is not true that when you were going to plant settlers in
Greek cities, I blocked your way. Let me then explain first the origin c
of the charge that I mentioned first.

  I came to Syracuse at your invitation and Dion's. He had long
been a tried and true friend of mine and we were united by ties of hospitality; he had reached with middle age the settled period of life. You
may be sure that any man who possessed a ray of intelligence would
make such conditions an indispensable requirement before giving
advice about affairs as important as yours were at that time. You, on
the other hand, were very young; you had never been tested on matters in regard to which a satisfactory test was an absolute necessity,
and you were a complete stranger to me. After this, whether it was the d
work of man or of god or of chance, with your help Dion was exiled
and you were left alone. Do you suppose that under those circumstances I could have any partnership with you in the government? For
I had lost the intelligent partner, and the foolish one I saw abandoned
to the company of a multitude of base men, not governing but supposing he governed, being in fact under the sway of men such as I
have mentioned.

  What was I to do in this situation? Was I not forced to do as I
did, that is, as a precaution against envious calumnies, to give no fur- e
ther heed to political affairs, and to attempt by all means to bring
about a renewal of the greatest possible friendship between you and
Dion, in spite of your separation and disagreement? You are yourself
a witness to the fact that I never relaxed my efforts to bring this about.
And at last, though with difficulty, we did reach an agreement to the
effect that I should take ship for home, since you were involved in a 317
war, but that, when peace was made, Dion and I were to return to
Syracuse, and you on your side were to invite us. Such is the history
of my first journey to Syracuse and of my safe arrival home again.

When peace was made, you summoned me the second time, but not in accordance with the terms of our agreement. Instead you wrote to me to come alone, and said that you would send for Dion later. The result was that I refused to go and was even estranged
b from Dion at that time, for he thought it advisable for me to give heed to you and go. Next there arrived a year later a trireme with a letter from you, and before all the other matters of the letter came the statement that, if I came, all Dion's affairs would be arranged to suit me; otherwise they would not. I hesitate to say how many letters came from you at that time and from others in Italy and Sicily on your ac-
c count, and to how many of my friends and acquaintances letters came, all urging me to go and begging me by all means to do as you wished.

It was the opinion of all, beginning with Dion, that I ought to set sail and not shirk the duty. To be sure I urged them to consider my advanced age and maintained that you would not be able to hold out against those who would try to set us at variance in the hope that we might quarrel. I observed then and I observe now in regard to great
d and swollen fortunes in general, whether they belong to private citizens or to monarchs, that the greater they are, the more numerous and the more degraded are the informers and the debasing boon companions that they breed. Than this there is no greater evil begotten of wealth and other forms of power. Nevertheless, throwing all these considerations to the winds, I went, for I reflected that I must not let any of my friends bring the charge against me that because of my love of ease he had lost all his property, when it need not have been lost.
e   When I had come—you are of course acquainted with all that happened from that time on—I naturally, in accordance with the terms agreed on in our letters, urged, in the first place, that you should contract with Dion a relationship that I mentioned and reinstate him. If you had then followed my advice, possibly the result would have been better than the actual course of events for you, for Syracuse, and for the rest of the Greeks. That is the verdict of my own intuition. In the second place I urged the plea that Dion's property
318 should remain in the hands of his friends and not be distributed among those who did acquire it. You know who they were. Furthermore, I thought that the income which he regularly received every year ought all the more to be sent, rather than otherwise, now that I was present. Successful in none of these pleas, I asked leave to depart. Thereupon you induced me to wait till the next year and promised that you would sell all Dion's property, send half to Corinth, and reserve the rest for his son.
b   There are many promises I might mention that you made and failed to keep in any way, but because they were so numerous, I must cut short my account. Accordingly, when you had sold all the property

without Dion's consent, after promising not to do so unless he did consent, then, Sir Marvelous, you added the finishing touch to all your promises in the most wanton fashion. You hit upon a scheme neither noble nor brilliant nor honest nor advantageous, namely, to frighten me off, while I was supposedly ignorant of what was going on, in order that I might not even ask for the dispatch of the money. When c you had driven Heraclides into exile—unjustly, it seemed to the Syracusans and to me—then, because I joined Theodotes and Eurybius in pleading with you to rescind the order, you, finding here a good enough excuse, said that it had long been clear that I cared nothing for you and thought only of Dion and Dion's friends and connections, and that now, when Theodotes and Heraclides, who were friends of Dion, were under accusation, I was leaving no stone unturned to prevent their meeting with their deserts.

So much for our political partnership. If you have detected any d other aversion to you on my part, you are right in thinking that it all came about in this way. You need not be surprised, either, for any intelligent man would justly think me base if I had been induced by the greatness of your empire to betray my old friend and host, whose misfortunes were due to you—who was, moreover, to put it mildly, not e inferior to you—and to prefer you, who were in the wrong, and to do everything you ordered, obviously bribed by gifts of money. For that is the only motive that would have been imputed to me for going over to you, if I had gone over. So these events, brought about in this way, through your fault resulted in the enmity and the incompatibility that exist between us.

The argument following continuously on what I have just said has now come pretty much to the subject which is the second on which I said I must defend myself. Observe then and consider attentively 319 whether anything I say seems to you false and not true. I assert that when Archedemus and Aristocritus were in the garden, about twenty days before I left Syracuse for home, you said the same thing you do now in criticism of me, namely, that I cared more for Heraclides and all the others than for you. You asked me, moreover, in their presence whether I remembered, directly after my arrival, urging you to plant b settlers in the Greek cities. I confessed that I did remember and that I still thought it the ideal course to take. I must also repeat, though, Dionysius, the remark that was made directly afterward. I asked you whether I had given you merely this advice by itself or whether I added something to it. And you answered very furiously and contemptuously indeed, so you supposed—for what was then the object of your contempt is now no longer a dream but a reality—you said with a very forced laugh, if I remember, 'You bade me do all these things after re- c ceiving instruction or not at all.' I replied that your memory was excellent. Then you said, 'Instruction in surveying, or what?' And I thereupon did not say what it occurred to me to say, for fear lest for a brief word my way might be closed instead of open to the departure to which I was looking forward.

The purpose, however, of all that I have said is this. Stop slandering me by saying that I prevented you from planting settlers in d Greek cities that barbarians had destroyed, and from lightening the burdens of the Syracusans by transforming your government from tyranny to kingship. In the first place there is no lie less appropriate to me that you could tell to my discredit, and further, I could, in addition to what I have said, if there were anywhere to be seen a competent tribunal, furnish even clearer evidence than this that it was I who urged this course and you who were unwilling to act. At any rate it is not difficult to put it down in black and white that the accomplishment of these plans would have been the best thing for you, for the e Syracusans, and for all the other Sicilian Greeks. Well, sir, if you deny saying what you said, I have my requital. If you admit it, you will thereupon conclude that Stesichorus was wise, imitate his recantation, and shift your position from the false to the true story.

LETTER VII

To THE FRIENDS AND COMPANIONS OF DION, *Prosperity*

In your letter you urged me to believe that your political convictions are the same as Dion's were, and in this connection you ex-
324 horted me to lend your cause such aid as I can by action or by speech. My reply is that I will aid your cause if your views and your aims really are the same as Dion's; if they differ from his, I will take time to think about it. But what was Dion's policy, and what were his aims? To that question I think I could give an answer based not on conjecture but on sure knowledge. For when I first came to Syracuse—I was about forty years old—Dion's age was the same as that of Hip-
b parinus now, and he at that time arrived at a conclusion that he never departed from. He believed in liberty for the Syracusans under the guidance of the best system of laws. Consequently no one need be surprised if Hipparinus too were to be divinely led to the same conclusion and to come to agree with Dion's political creed.

The origin of this creed is a tale that young and old may well hear, and I will try to tell you the story from the beginning, for the moment is opportune. Once upon a time in my youth I cherished like many another the hope of entering upon a political career as soon as I
c came of age. It fell out, moreover, that political events took the following course. There were many who heaped abuse on the form of government then prevailing, and a revolution occurred. In this revolution fifty-one men set themselves up as a government, eleven in the city,

ten in the Piraeus—both of these groups were to administer the market
and the usual civic affairs—and thirty came into power as supreme
rulers of the whole state. Some of these happened to be relatives and
acquaintances of mine, who accordingly invited me forthwith to join d
them, assuming my fitness for the task. No wonder that, young as I
was, I cherished the belief that they would lead the city from an unjust life, as it were, to habits of justice and 'manage it,' as they put it,
so that I was intensely interested to see what would come of it.

Of course I saw in a short time that these men made the former
government look in comparison like an age of gold. Among other
things they sent an elderly man, Socrates, a friend of mine, who I
should hardly be ashamed to say was the justest man of his time, in e
company with others, against one of the citizens to fetch him forcibly
to be executed. Their purpose was to connect Socrates with their gov- 325
ernment, whether he wished or not. He refused and risked any consequences rather than become their partner in wicked deeds. When I
observed all this—and some other similar matters of importance—I
withdrew in disgust from the abuses of those days. Not long after
came the fall of the Thirty and of their whole system of government.

Once more, less hastily this time, but surely, I was moved by the
desire to take part in public life and in politics. To be sure, in those b
days too, full of disturbance as they were, there were many things occurring to cause offense, nor is it surprising that in time of revolution
men in some cases took undue revenge on their enemies. Yet for all
that the restored exiles displayed great moderation. As it chanced,
however, some of those in control brought against this associate of
mine, Socrates, whom I have mentioned, a most sacrilegious charge,
which he least of all men deserved. They put him on trial for impiety c
and the people condemned and put to death the man who had refused
to take part in the wicked arrest of one of their friends, whose exile
had coincided with their own exile and misfortunes.

Now as I considered these matters, as well as the sort of men
who were active in politics, and the laws and the customs, the more I
examined them and the more I advanced in years, the harder it appeared to me to administer the government correctly. For one thing,
nothing could be done without friends and loyal companions, and d
such men were not easy to find ready at hand, since our city was no
longer administered according to the standards and practices of our
fathers. Neither could such men be created afresh with any facility.
Furthermore the written law and the customs were being corrupted at
an astounding rate. The result was that I, who had at first been full of
eagerness for a public career, as I gazed upon the whirlpool of public e
life and saw the incessant movement of shifting currents, at last felt
dizzy, and, while I did not cease to consider means of improving this
particular situation and indeed of reforming the whole constitution, 326
yet, in regard to action, I kept waiting for favorable moments, and

finally saw clearly in regard to all states now existing that without exception their system of government is bad. Their constitutions are almost beyond redemption except through some miraculous plan accompanied by good luck. Hence I was forced to say in praise of the correct philosophy that it affords a vantage point from which we can discern in all cases what is just for communities and for individuals, and that accordingly the human race will not see better days until b either the stock of those who rightly and genuinely follow philosophy acquire political authority, or else the class who have political control be led by some dispensation of providence to become real philosophers.

This conviction I held when I reached Italy and Sicily on my first visit. Upon my arrival, moreover, I found myself utterly at odds with the sort of life that is there termed a happy one, a life taken up with Italian and Syracusan banquets, an existence that consists in fill- c ing oneself up twice a day, never sleeping alone at night, and indulging in all the practices attendant on that way of living. In such an environment no man under heaven, brought up in self-indulgence, could ever grow to be wise. So marvelous a temperament as that is not in nature. That a man should grow up sober-minded would also be quite out of the question, and one might make the same statement about the other qualities that go to make up excellence of character. Neither can a city be free from unrest under any laws, be those laws d what they may, while its citizens think fit to spend everything on excesses, meanwhile making it a rule, however, to avoid all industry except such as is devoted to banquets and drinking bouts and painstaking attention to the gratification of lust. It is inevitable that in such cities there should be an unending succession of governments—tyranny, oligarchy, democracy—one after another, while the very name of just and equal government is anathema to those in control.

Now holding this conviction in addition to the former, I traveled e on to Syracuse. Perhaps it was chance, but certainly it looks as if a higher power was at that time contriving to lay a foundation for the recent events in which Dion and the city of Syracuse were concerned, for more too, I fear, unless you now follow the advice I am giving you 327 the second time. But what can I mean when I say that my visit to Syracuse at that time was the beginning of everything? In my intercourse at that time with the young Dion, as I set before him in theory my ideals for mankind and advised him to make them effective in practice, I seem to have been unaware that I was in a way contriving, all unknown to myself, a future downfall of tyranny. At any rate Dion, who was very quick of apprehension and especially so in regard to my instruction on this occasion, responded to it more keenly and more b enthusiastically than any other young man I ever met, and resolved to live for the remainder of his life differently from most of the Greeks in Italy and Sicily, holding virtue dearer than pleasure or than luxury.

On that account the life he led until the death of Dionysius vexed
somewhat those who passed their time in accordance with tyrannical
wont.

After that he felt in his heart that he would not always be alone
in holding this belief, which he had arrived at under the guidance of
right reasoning. In fact he saw it growing in others too, not many, but c
at any rate in some, and took note. He thought that Dionysius might
perhaps become one of these through the co-operation of the gods.
Moreover, if he were to become such a one, the result for him and for
the rest of the Syracusans would be the attainment of a life beyond all
calculation blessed. Furthermore he felt it to be absolutely necessary
that I come to Syracuse as soon as possible to lend a hand in the work.
He remembered how readily he had by the operation of our mutual intercourse arrived at a desire to live the noblest and best life. If, ac- d
cordingly, he were now to succeed in his attempt to bring about the
same result once again in the case of Dionysius, he had great hopes
of creating, without bloodshed or slaughter or such misfortunes as
have actually occurred, a happy and genuine way of living throughout the land.

Dion, when he had rightly come to this conclusion, persuaded
Dionysius to send for me, and himself sent and entreated me by all
means to come as soon as possible, before certain others fell in with e
Dionysius and diverted him to a way of life other than the best. Here is
Dion's message, even if it is rather long to repeat.

'What combination of circumstances,' said he, 'more promising
than that which is at this moment offered us by a sort of miracle, are
we to wait for?' Then he mentioned Italy and Sicily under one govern- 328
ment, his own influential position in that government, Dionysius
young and interested, emphasizing his situation in respect of philosophy and education. Furthermore his own nephews and kindred might
readily be won over to the doctrine and the way of life that I always
preach, and they would be just the persons to help win over Dionysius.
'Now, if ever, then,' said he, 'will be realized any hope there is that the
world will ever see the same man both philosopher and ruler of a great
city.'

Such arguments he used and a great many more like them. As for b
my own decision, on the one hand I feared the outcome in the case of
the young men, for young men have sudden impulses and often quite
contradictory ones. On the other hand I knew that Dion had naturally
a solid character and that he had now reached middle age. Hence as I
considered and debated whether I should hearken and go, or what I
should do, the view nevertheless prevailed that I ought to go, and that
if anyone were ever to attempt to realize my ideals in regard to laws c
and government, now was the time for the trial. If I were to convince
but one man, that in itself would ensure complete success.

Such were the considerations that inspired and emboldened me

to leave home on this journey. I was not guided by the motives that some men attributed to me, but chiefly by a concern for my own self-respect. I feared to see myself at last altogether nothing but words, so to speak—a man who would never willingly lay hand to any concrete task, for I should practically have been guilty of disloyalty—in
d the first place to the ties of hospitality and friendship that bound me to Dion. He was really exposed to considerable danger. Suppose something were to happen to him, or suppose he were expelled by Dionysius and his other enemies, and were to come to me an exile and to question me, saying, 'Plato, I have come to you an exile not for want of soldiers or of horsemen to defend myself against my foes, but for lack of the arguments and the eloquence that I knew you, more than others, could wield to turn the minds of young men to virtue and jus-
e tice so as to establish in all cases mutual friendship and alliance. Because you failed to supply me with these, I have left Syracuse and here I am. Your treatment of me, however, is not the most disgraceful part of your conduct. Surely on this occasion you have, so far as in you lay, proved traitor, not to me only, but also to philosophy, whose praises you are always singing and of whom you say that the rest of man-
329 kind treat her ignobly. Moreover, if I had chanced to be living in Megara, you would certainly have come to support me in the cause to which I summoned you, or else you would think yourself the very meanest of men. As the situation is, do you suppose you will ever escape the charge of cowardice by pleading the distance to be traveled, the long voyage, and the great hardships? Not by a great deal.'

To these accusations what plausible reply could I make? None is possible.

So I went, thereby following reason and justice as closely as is
b humanly possible. For such reasons as I have described, I forsook my own pursuits, and they were not undistinguished, to come under a tyranny, a form of government seemingly inconsistent with my doctrines and my character. In doing so I cleared myself in the sight of Zeus Xenios and left no ground of complaint to the cause of philosophy, which would have suffered reproach if I had turned weakling and had by refusing to play a man's part brought disgrace upon myself. When I arrived, for I must be brief, I found the whole environment of Dionysius seething with cabals and with malicious reports to the government about Dion. I took his part as best I could, but I could do little,
c and in about the fourth month, on the ground that Dion was plotting against the government, Dionysius put him aboard a small boat and expelled him dishonorably. Thereupon all of us who were friends of Dion were in terror lest Dionysius should accuse and punish someone else for complicity in Dion's plot. As for me a rumor actually got abroad in Syracuse to the effect that I had been executed by Dionysius because I was responsible for the whole course of events.
d When Dionysius saw that we were all in this state, he was afraid

that our fears might result in something worse, and set about winning
us all over by a show of cordiality. Incidentally he was active in consoling me, bidding me feel no anxiety and begging me by all means to
remain. There really was no honor for him in my taking flight from
him, but rather in my remaining, which explains the great pretense he
made of requesting it. The requests of tyrants we are aware have in
them something of compulsion. So to gain his end he prevented my departure. He took me to the citadel and planted me in a place from e
which there was no longer any possibility of a shipmaster accepting
me as a passenger, unless Dionysius not merely took no steps to prevent it, but unless he actually dispatched himself the messenger with
orders to accept me. Otherwise neither merchant nor embarkation official would have permitted me to set forth alone, but would at once
have arrested me and have taken me back to Dionysius, especially
since the news had now at last been spread, just the opposite of the 330
former report, that Dionysius was marvelously fond of Plato.

What was the situation, though? For the truth must be told. He
did indeed grow more and more to like me as time passed and as he
learned to know my life and character, but he wanted me to commend
him more than Dion, to think him rather than Dion a special friend.
In fact his ambition in this respect was surprising. He shunned, how- b
ever, the best method of attaining his object, if it could be attained at
all—that is, of course, by receiving instruction and hearing me discourse on philosophy, to become my intimate friend and disciple.
The reports circulated by our enemies made him afraid he might somehow be entangled and so Dion have accomplished his design. I, however, waited patiently through it all and bore in mind the original
purpose of my visit, namely, the hope that he might in some way become enamored of the philosophical life, but his resistance carried
the day.

Now the time I devoted to my first visit to Sicily and to my stay
there was the result of all these causes. Afterward I left home and c
visited Sicily once more at the urgent invitation of Dionysius. I must
explain later why I went the second time and that all I did was reasonable and right, for the benefit of those who inquire what I hoped to
gain by going. First, however, in order to avoid the mistake of dealing
with secondary matters as if they were of primary importance, I must
advise you as to your proper conduct in view of recent events. Here is
my message.

One who advises a sick man, living in a way to injure his health,
must first effect a reform in his way of living, must he not? And if the d
patient consents to such a reform, then he may admonish him on other
points? If, however, the patient refuses, in my opinion it would be the
act of a real man and a good physician to keep clear of advising such a
man—the act of a poltroon and a quack on the other hand to advise
him further on those terms. The same thing holds in the case of a city,

whether it have one master or many. If a government that proceeds in orderly fashion along the right course, seeks advice about its advantage in some matter, it would be the act of an intelligent man to give
e advice to such a community. In the case, however, of those who are altogether astray from the path of right government, and will by no means consent to go on the track of it, who on the other hand give
331 notice to their adviser to keep his hands off the constitution under penalty of death if he disobeys, and order him to cater to their wishes and desires by pointing out the easiest and quickest method of attaining them permanently, in that case I should think the adviser who consented to such conditions a poltroon—the one who refused, a real man.

This being my firm conviction, whenever anyone asks my advice about any of the most important concerns of his life, such as the
b acquisition of wealth, or the proper regime for body or soul, then, in case I think that his daily life is fairly well regulated, or that when I give him advice on the matter about which he consults me, he will consent to follow it, under these circumstances I do counsel him with all my heart and do not stop at a mere formal compliance. If, however, he either does not ask my advice at all, or shows plainly that there is not the least likelihood of his taking the advice I give him, to such a man I do not go self-invited with advice. Constraint I will not use, even though it be my own son. A slave I would advise and constrain too, if
c he refused to obey. Father or mother I think it sinful to constrain, unless they are suffering from mental derangement. As long as they are leading a consistent life that suits them, though it does not me, I would neither estrange them by useless admonitions, nor on the other hand would I play the subservient flatterer and provide them means to satisfy desires that I myself had rather die than be addicted to. The same policy should also be a rule of life for the wise man in
d dealing with his city. If he thinks that the constitution of his city is imperfect, he should say so, unless such action will either be useless or will lead to his own death, but he must not apply force to his fatherland by revolutionary methods. When it is impossible to make the constitution perfect except by sentencing men to exile and death, he must refrain from action and pray for the best for himself and for his city.

In this same fashion I will advise you, just as Dion and I used to advise Dionysius. We advised him, in the first place, to lead the sort of
e life day by day that would be most conducive to self-control and would enable him to win loyal friends and companions. Thus he would avoid the plight of his father, who, when he had come into possession of many large cities of Sicily that the barbarians had devastated, was unable to resettle them and to set up in each a trustworthy government composed of his friends. For such a service he could trust neither those unconnected with him, no matter what their origin, nor even
332 the younger brothers whom he had brought up himself and had raised

from private life and poverty to the height of power and affluence. None of them was he able to develop by the influence of eloquence or instruction or benefactions or kinship, so that he could trust him as a partner in the government, and in this he was seven times inferior to Darius. For Darius trusted those who were not brothers and had not been brought up by him, who had only been his associates in the assault on the Mede and the eunuch, and distributed among them b seven provinces, each larger than the whole of Sicily. In these men moreover he found faithful allies who neither attacked him nor each other, and in his career we see an ideal example of the character which the statesman and the good king must display, for the laws which he framed have been the preservation of the kingdom of Persia even up to now. Take again the Athenians, who, though they were not themselves the founders, took over many Greek cities that had been invaded by the barbarians but were still inhabited. Nevertheless they maintained their empire for seventy years, because they possessed in c the various cities men who were their friends. Dionysius, however, who brought together all Sicily into one city because in his wisdom he trusted no one, all but met with disaster. He was in want of tried and true friends, and there is no surer sign of a man's moral character than this, whether he is or is not destitute of such friends.

So Dion and I gave Dionysius this advice. Since he had been treated by his father as he had, and so had had no experience of education or of suitable instruction, he must in the first place bestir him- d self to obtain them. After that, in the second place, he must win to friendship with himself and to moral harmony others from among his kinsmen and companions, but especially must he become such a one himself, for in this quality he had shown himself remarkably deficient. We did not put it so plainly—that was not safe—but we veiled our meaning and constantly argued that anyone who takes this course will be prosperous himself and will cause the people whom he rules to prosper, and that on the other hand any other course will have just the opposite result. When he had progressed in the way we mapped e out, and had developed in himself an intelligent and constant character, he might recolonize the deserted cities of Sicily and so unite them by laws and institutions that they would be a resource to him and to each other for meeting the attacks of the barbarians. Thus he would not merely double the size of the empire he had inherited, but would 333 really multiply it many times. For if this plan were realized, he might readily reduce the Carthaginians to greater subjection than that of Gelon's time, in contrast to his father, who had lately consented to pay tribute to the barbarians. Such were our words and our exhortations when we were supposedly plotting against Dionysius, according to the tales which flowed from many sources and which, prevailing with Dionysius, brought about Dion's expulsion and threw us into a state of terror.

b   To complete the story of the great events that happened in a brief space, Dion returned from the Peloponnesus and from Athens and gave Dionysius a practical lesson. When, however, he had twice freed their city and restored it to them, the Syracusans then reacted toward Dion in exactly the same way as Dionysius had. For when Dion undertook to educate him and train him, that he might become a king worthy of his office, and planned on such terms to be his ally throughout life, Dionysius hearkened to the calumniators who declared that c everything that Dion did at that time was part of a plot against the government. His plan, they said, was that Dionysius, when his intelligence had yielded to the spell of education, should lose interest in the government and should put it in Dion's hands. Dion would then usurp the throne, and expel him from his domain by fraud. Such reports carried the day then, and so they did again a second time, when circulated among the Syracusans, and most monstrous and disgraceful the victory was for those responsible.

Now I must explain to those who urge me to take a hand in the d present situation what it was that happened. I am myself an Athenian; I was Dion's friend and ally, and I went to the tyrant to effect a reconciliation between them. In my struggle with the calumniators I was defeated. When Dionysius, however, tried to persuade me with honors and gifts of money to lend him the support of my testimony and my friendship to give color to the expulsion of Dion, he failed completely. Now, after this, Dion on his return to his native land enlisted e in his company two men who were brothers and like me came from Athens. His friendship with them, however, was not based on philosophy but on such social activities as are current among most of those who call themselves friends. Their comradeship is a product of mutual hospitality and of initiations into the different Mysteries, and so was that of these two friends who accompanied Dion on his return. Their friendship was founded on such relations as these and on their services to his expedition. Having arrived in Sicily, when they 334 saw that Dion was the victim of the calumnies that were circulated among the Sicilians, who had been liberated by him, to the effect that he was plotting to make himself tyrant, they not only proved false to the comrade to whom they were bound by ties of hospitality, but practically assassinated him with their own hands, inasmuch as they stood by with arms in their hands to lend aid to the murderers.

Now I do not ignore their dishonor and their wickedness, nor do I comment on it, for there are now and will be hereafter many others b who will make it their business to repeat that strain. I do, however, take exception, when it is said of Athens that such men are a blot on her honor. For I maintain that he is also an Athenian who refused to betray this same man, when by so doing he might have gained both wealth and numerous honors. His attachment to his friend had originated not in any lowbred friendship, but in mutual participation in

liberal training, in which alone a man endowed with intelligence
must put confidence, rather than in kinship of soul or body. Hence
the city does not deserve to suffer reproach because of the slayers of
Dion, as if they had ever been men of any importance.   c

All that I have been saying is intended as advice for the friends
and relatives of Dion, but I have now a special communication to add,
as I give the same counsel and the same discourse now the third time
to you my third audience. Let not Sicily nor any city anywhere be subject to human masters—such is my doctrine—but to laws. Subjection
is bad both for masters and for subjects, for themselves, for their   d
children's children, and for all their posterity. The attempt to enslave
others is altogether disastrous, and greed for such plunder is a trait of
mean-souled and shortsighted characters—men who know nothing
of what is good or what is just, here or hereafter, in God's sight or in
man's. Of this truth I attempted first to convince Dion, secondly Dionysius, and now the third time you. Be then convinced of it for the
sake of Zeus who saves the third time.

Be guided also by the example of Dionysius and Dion, for of those
two the one who would not be convinced is now leading an ignoble   e
life, while he that was convinced has met a noble death. For when a
man makes the highest ideals his aim for himself and for his city and
accepts the consequences, in his fate there is nothing amiss or ignoble.
None of us is born immortal, nor would being so bring happiness, as
most people think. Nothing good or evil worth considering befalls that
which has no soul. Only to a soul either in the body or separated 335
from it can good or evil occur. We must at all times give our unfeigned
assent to the ancient and holy doctrines which warn us that our souls
are immortal, that they are judged, and that they suffer the severest
punishments after our separation from the body. Hence we must also
hold it a lesser evil to be victims of great wrongs and crimes than to be
doers of them. The man who crams his moneybags while his soul   b
starves does not listen to these doctrines, or, if he does, he laughs
them to scorn, as he supposes, and on every side ruthlessly snatches
like a beast whatever he hopes will provide him with food or drink or
the satisfaction of that brutal and gross pleasure that has no right to be
called by a name derived from the goddess Aphrodite. He is blind and
does not see that consequences attend the abominable wickedness
of his acts of violence, for each wrongdoing adds its weight to a burden which the sinner must drag with him, not only while he lives his
life on earth, but after he has returned to the underworld whence he c
came—a journey unhonored and miserable altogether and always.

Now I convinced Dion when I explained to him these doctrines
and others of the sort, so that I have every reason to be angry with his
slayers in a certain way exactly as with Dionysius. In both cases I
and all the rest of mankind, you may say, received the greatest injury.
For the slayers of Dion made away with the man who intended to

make justice effective, while Dionysius would not consent to put jus-
d tice into practice throughout his empire. He possessed great power,
and if in his empire philosophy and political power had really been
united in the same man, its glory would have shone forth among all
men, Greek and barbarian, and would in itself have brought home to
them the true belief, namely, that neither city nor individual can attain happiness except through a life wisely conducted under the rule
of justice, whether a man be guided by his own sense of justice or
be brought up and trained in righteous habits under the control of holy
e men. In preventing this Dionysius inflicted an injury in comparison with which I count the others slight indeed.

The slayer of Dion does not know that his action has had the same
result as that of Dionysius. I am certain, as far as a man can express
himself confidently in the case of a man, that if Dion had come into
power, he would never have adopted any other form of government
336 than the following. In the first place, after he had made Syracuse, his
native city, clean and fair, on putting an end to her slavery, and had set
her up arrayed as one free, thereupon he would by all means have
brought the citizens under discipline by instituting an appropriate and
ideal system of laws. After that he would have been eager to carry out
the settlement of all Sicily and its liberation from the barbarians,
driving out some of them and subduing the rest more easily than
Hieron did. Moreover, if these results had been brought about by a
b man who was just, courageous, sober, and a student of philosophy,
the public would have adopted the same opinion about virtue as, in
case Dionysius had been won over, would among practically all mankind have brought deliverance by its spread.

As it was, though, some divinity or some evil spirit broke loose
with lawlessness, with ungodliness, and, worst of all, with the boldness
of folly—the soil in which all manner of evil to all men takes root and
flourishes and later produces a fruit most bitter for those who sowed it.
c So folly a second time brought complete failure and disaster. Let
me now, however, say nothing to bring ill luck on the third attempt.

Nevertheless I advise you, the friends of Dion, to imitate both his
loyalty to his country and the temperate rule of living that he followed.
Try, however, to carry out his plans under better auspices. What his
plans were I have told you plainly. In case anyone cannot live in the
Doric fashion that was the tradition of your fathers, but seeks instead
d to live like the slayers of Dion, in Sicilian fashion, do not call upon him
to aid you, and do not suppose that he can ever act loyally and righteously. Call upon the rest, however, to aid in the colonization of all
Sicily and in bringing about equality under the law, both from Sicily
itself and from the whole Peloponnesus. Have no fear of Athens either,
for there exist there too men who surpass all mankind in virtue and
who loathe the crimes of treacherous assassins.

If, however, these measures must be left till later, and you are

forced to hasten because of the manifold and varied quarrels that are e
springing up every day among the factions, I suppose every man who
has been granted by fortune even a small measure of correct opinion
must be aware that those who have engaged in civil war can never rest
from their troubles until those who are victorious cease to keep feuds
alive by contention and by sentencing men to exile or death, and cease
to execute vengeance on the opposing party. Rather, exercising self- 337
control and drawing up equitable laws, that are designed to favor them
no more than the defeated party, they must make their opponents observe the laws by bringing to bear two motives, shame and fear. They
will inspire fear because they show that they have the stronger
forces, shame because they are evidently stronger in resisting their
inclinations and in their willingness and ability to be subject to the
laws. There is no other possible means of putting an end to the misfortunes of a city torn by faction. When cities are in that condition, b
of themselves they are wont to breed faction, enmity, hatred, mistrust.

Those then who are on any occasion victorious must, if ever
they come to desire peace and security, of and by themselves select
any men among the Greeks who, according to their information, are
pre-eminent, men who are in the first place advanced in years, who
possess wives and children at home and can reckon the most and the
best and the most famous ancestors, and who own all of them sufficient property. As to their numbers, fifty such men would be enough c
for a city of ten thousand population. These men they should summon
from their homes with entreaties and offers of the greatest possible
honors. When they have got them, they should entreat and command
them to draw up laws after taking an oath to give no advantage to
conquerors or to conquered, but equal rights to the whole city alike.

After the laws have been drawn up, everything hinges on this.
If the conquerors make themselves more completely subject to the
laws than the conquered, there will be everywhere an atmosphere of d
security and happiness and deliverance from every trouble. If this is
not done, do not call on me or on anyone else to join the man who refuses to obey my present injunctions, which indeed are akin to the
measures that Dion and I attempted jointly to carry through for the
good of Syracuse. These measures, however, came second. Those
measures were first which we attempted to carry out with the help of
Dionysius himself for the common good of all. Some fate too strong for
man made havoc of our plans. This time you must try to put them into e
effect more happily through the kindness of fate and the favor of providence.

Thus far my advice and injunctions and the story of my first visit
to Dionysius. Next he who is interested may hear how reasonably and
appropriately my second journey and voyage came about. You will
remember that my account of the period of my former stay in Sicily

338   was completed, as I have pointed out, before I set forth my advice to the friends and companions of Dion.

After that accordingly I employed every means in my power to persuade Dionysius to let me go, and we finally came to an agreement that he should do so. When peace, however, was made—there was at that time war in Sicily—it was part of the agreement that Dionysius should send for Dion and me again, when he had made his position as ruler more secure. Meanwhile he begged Dion to believe that he had

b   not been driven into exile, but had merely been sent abroad for a time. I for my part agreed to return on these conditions.

So when peace had been made, he did send for me, but asked Dion to wait another year and begged me by all means to come. Now Dion at this urged and entreated me to set sail, for reports did indeed frequently reach us from Sicily to the effect that Dionysius had changed and was now marvelously devoted to philosophy—which explains why Dion so insistently entreated me not to turn a deaf ear to

c   the summons. As for me, I knew to be sure that young men are often so affected in connection with philosophy; nevertheless I thought it safer for the moment at least to leave both Dion and Dionysius entirely to their own devices, and I incurred the ill will of both by replying that I was an old man and that furthermore the present arrangement did not agree with the terms of our previous compact.

Next apparently Archytas paid a visit to Dionysius. I had before my departure brought about relations of hospitality and friendship be-

d   tween Archytas and the Tarentines and Dionysius. There were some others too in Syracuse who had had some instruction from Dion, besides still others who were crammed with certain scraps of secondhand philosophy. My opinion is that these men had been trying to hold with Dionysius on these matters the sort of conversation that would imply a thorough acquaintance with my beliefs on his part. Now Dionysius, among other natural qualifications that would make him a capable student, is extremely ambitious to excel. He was accordingly very likely pleased to be so approached and withal ashamed to have it be-

e   come obvious that he had had no instruction when I was in the city. This would lead him to wish for a more explicit course of instruction, and this wish would be accompanied by the spur of rivalry. The reasons for his receiving no instruction during my former visit I have recounted previously in this present letter. At any rate when I had got safely home and had declined his second invitation, as I have just explained, Dionysius, I think, made it absolutely a point of honor that no one should ever suppose that I had a poor opinion of his natural

339   gifts and of his present capability and that, having also had some experience of his way of living, I was now in my disgust no longer willing to visit his court.

Now it is my duty to tell the truth and put up with the possibility that someone may, when he hears what happened, be contemptuous of my philosophy and give credit for intelligence to the tyrant. For Dionysius the third time actually sent a trireme for me in order to make the journey easy for me. He also sent along one of the disciples of Archytas, Archedemus, whom he thought I valued most among the Sicilians—with others among my acquaintances in Sicily. All of these b gave me the same account, namely, that Dionysius had made marvelous progress in philosophy. He also sent me a very long letter, because he knew how I was situated with respect to Dion and how eager Dion on his side was for me to set sail and go to Syracuse. He had in fact provided his letter with an introduction designed to fit the whole situation. It was expressed pretty much as follows: 'Dionysius to Plato.' Then after the conventional salutation without any prelimi- c nary he went on at once to say, 'If you consent and come now to Sicily, in the first place you will have the privilege of making any arrangement that suits you about Dion and his affairs. I am sure that what suits you will be fair, and I shall agree to it. If you do not come, you will find nothing that affects Dion either personally or otherwise arranging itself to your liking.' These were his words; the rest would be long to repeat and not to the point. Letters also kept coming from d Archytas and the Tarentines to sing the praises of Dionysius' devotion to philosophy and to inform me that, if I did not come now, it would mean a complete breach of the friendly relations that I had been instrumental in creating between them and Dionysius, and those relations were not lacking in political importance.

Now when I was thus urgently sent for—when my friends in Sicily and Italy were pulling me, while those at Athens were, you might say, by their entreaties actually shoving me out of Athens— e once more came the same message, that I ought not to betray either Dion or my friends and companions in Tarentum. Besides, I knew anyway without being told that no one need be surprised if a young man on hearing a really great enterprise suggested, quick to grasp the idea, had yielded to the spell of the ideal life. It seemed accordingly my duty to make the experiment so as to arrive at a definite conclusion one way or the other, for I must not be guilty of betraying that very ideal and of exposing my beliefs to the reproach they would deserve if there were any truth in the reports I had received.   340

So I did set out under cover of these arguments, full of fears, as you might expect, and foreboding no very good result. At any rate in going I found that here at least it was really a case of the third to the savior, for I was fortunately brought safely home again. For this I have to thank Dionysius next to God, because, when many wished to put me out of the way, he interfered and gave some place to conscience in his dealings with me.

When I had arrived, I thought I ought first to put it to the proof b whether Dionysius was really all on fire with philosophy or whether the frequent reports that had come to Athens to that effect amounted to

nothing. Now there is an experimental method for determining the truth in such cases that, far from being vulgar, is truly appropriate to despots, especially those stuffed with secondhand opinions, which I perceived, as soon as I arrived, was very much the case with Dionysius. One must point out to such men that the whole plan is pos-
c sible and explain what preliminary steps and how much hard work it will require, for the hearer, if he is genuinely devoted to philosophy and is a man of God with a natural affinity and fitness for the work, sees in the course marked out a path of enchantment, which he must at once strain every nerve to follow, or die in the attempt. Thereupon he braces himself and his guide to the task and does not relax his efforts until he either crowns them with final accomplishment or acquires the faculty of tracing his own way no longer accompanied by the path-
d finder. When this conviction has taken possession of him, such a man passes his life in whatever occupations he may engage in, but through it all never ceases to practice philosophy and such habits of daily life as will be most effective in making him an intelligent and retentive student, able to reason soberly by himself. Other practices than these he shuns to the end.

As for those, however, who are not genuine converts to philosophy, but have only a superficial tinge of doctrine—like the coat of tan that people get in the sun—as soon as they see how many subjects there are to study, how much hard work they involve, and how indis-
e pensable it is for the project to adopt a well-ordered scheme of living, they decide that the plan is difficult if not impossible for them, and so
341 they really do not prove capable of practicing philosophy. Some of them too persuade themselves that they are well enough informed already on the whole subject and have no need of further application. This test then proves to be the surest and safest in dealing with those who are self-indulgent and incapable of continued hard work, since they throw the blame not on their guide but on their own inability to follow out in detail the course of training subsidiary to the project.

The instruction that I gave to Dionysius was accordingly given with this object in view. I certainly did not set forth to him all my doc-
b trines, nor did Dionysius ask me to, for he pretended to know many of the most important points already and to be adequately grounded in them by means of the secondhand interpretations he had got from the others.

I hear too that he has since written on the subjects in which I instructed him at that time, as if he were composing a handbook of his own which differed entirely from the instruction he received. Of this I know nothing. I do know, however, that some others have written on these same subjects, but who they are they know not themselves. One statement at any rate I can make in regard to all who have written or
c who may write with a claim to knowledge of the subjects to which I devote myself—no matter how they pretend to have acquired it,

whether from my instruction or from others or by their own discovery. Such writers can in my opinion have no real acquaintance with the subject. I certainly have composed no work in regard to it, nor shall I ever do so in future, for there is no way of putting it in words like other studies. Acquaintance with it must come rather after a long period of attendance on instruction in the subject itself and of close companionship, when, suddenly, like a blaze kindled by a leaping spark, it is gen- d erated in the soul and at once becomes self-sustaining.

Besides, this at any rate I know, that if there were to be a treatise or a lecture on this subject, I could do it best. I am also sure for that matter that I should be very sorry to see such a treatise poorly written. If I thought it possible to deal adequately with the subject in a treatise or a lecture for the general public, what finer achievement would there have been in my life than to write a work of great benefit to mankind and to bring the nature of things to light for all men? I do not, however, think the attempt to tell mankind of these matters a e good thing, except in the case of some few who are capable of discovering the truth for themselves with a little guidance. In the case of the rest to do so would excite in some an unjustified contempt in a thoroughly offensive fashion, in others certain lofty and vain hopes, as if 342 they had acquired some awesome lore.

It has occurred to me to speak on the subject at greater length, for possibly the matter I am discussing would be clearer if I were to do so. There is a true doctrine, which I have often stated before, that stands in the way of the man who would dare to write even the least thing on such matters, and which it seems I am now called upon to repeat.

For everything that exists there are three classes of objects through which knowledge about it must come; the knowledge itself is a fourth, and we must put as a fifth entity the actual object of b knowledge which is the true reality. We have then, first, a name, second, a description, third, an image, and fourth, a knowledge of the object. Take a particular case if you want to understand the meaning of what I have just said; then apply the theory to every object in the same way. There is something for instance called a circle, the name of which is the very word I just now uttered. In the second place there is a description of it which is composed of nouns and verbal expressions. For example the description of that which is named round and circumference and circle would run as follows: the thing which has everywhere equal distances between its extremities and its center. c In the third place there is the class of object which is drawn and erased and turned on the lathe and destroyed—processes which do not affect the real circle to which these other circles are all related, because it is different from them. In the fourth place there are knowledge and understanding and correct opinion concerning them, all of which we must set down as one thing more that is found not in sounds nor in

shapes of bodies, but in minds, whereby it evidently differs in its nature from the real circle and from the aforementioned three. Of all
d these four, understanding approaches nearest in affinity and likeness to the fifth entity, while the others are more remote from it.

The same doctrine holds good in regard to shapes and surfaces, both straight and curved, in regard to the good and the beautiful and the just, in regard to all bodies artificial and natural, in regard to fire and water and the like, and in regard to every animal, and in regard to every quality of character, and in respect to all states active and
e passive. For if in the case of any of these a man does not somehow or other get hold of the first four, he will never gain a complete understanding of the fifth. Furthermore these four [names, descriptions, bodily forms, concepts] do as much to illustrate the particular quality of any object as they do to illustrate its essential reality because of the
343 inadequacy of language. Hence no intelligent man will ever be so bold as to put into language those things which his reason has contemplated, especially not into a form that is unalterable—which must be the case with what is expressed in written symbols.

Again, however, the meaning of what has just been said must be explained. Every circle that is drawn or turned on a lathe in actual operations abounds in the opposite of the fifth entity, for it everywhere touches the straight, while the real circle, I maintain, contains in itself neither much nor little of the opposite character. Names, I main-
b tain, are in no case stable. Nothing prevents the things that are now called round from being called straight and the straight round, and those who have transposed the names and use them in the opposite way will find them no less stable than they are now. The same thing for that matter is true of a description, since it consists of nouns and of verbal expressions, so that in a description there is nowhere any sure ground that is sure enough. One might, however, speak forever about the inaccurate character of each of the four! The important thing is that, as I said a little earlier, there are two things, the essential reality and the particular quality, and when the mind is in
c quest of knowledge not of the particular but of the essential, each of the four confronts the mind with the unsought particular, whether in verbal or in bodily form. Each of the four makes the reality that is expressed in words or illustrated in objects liable to easy refutation by the evidence of the senses. The result of this is to make practically every man a prey to complete perplexity and uncertainty.

Now in cases where as a result of bad training we are not even accustomed to look for the real essence of anything but are satisfied to accept what confronts us in the phenomenal presentations, we are not
d rendered ridiculous by each other—the examined by the examiners, who have the ability to handle the four with dexterity and to subject them to examination. In those cases, however, where we demand answers and proofs in regard to the fifth entity, anyone who pleases

among those who have skill in confutation gains the victory and
makes most of the audience think that the man who was first to speak
or write or answer has no acquaintance with the matters of which he
attempts to write or speak. Sometimes they are unaware that it is not
the mind of the writer or speaker that fails in the test, but rather the
character of the four—since that is naturally defective. Consideration
of all of the four in turn—moving up and down from one to another e
—barely begets knowledge of a naturally flawless object in a naturally
flawless man. If a man is naturally defective—and this is the natural
state of most people's minds with regard to intelligence and to what
are called morals—while the objects he inspects are tainted with im- 344
perfection, not even Lynceus could make such a one see.

To sum it all up in one word, natural intelligence and a good
memory are equally powerless to aid the man who has not an inborn
affinity with the subject. Without such endowments there is of
course not the slightest possibility. Hence all who have no natural aptitude for and affinity with justice and all the other noble ideals,
though in the study of other matters they may be both intelligent and
retentive—all those too who have affinity but are stupid and unre-
tentive—such will never any of them attain to an understanding of
the most complete truth in regard to moral concepts. The study of b
virtue and vice must be accompanied by an inquiry into what is false
and true of existence in general and must be carried on by constant
practice throughout a long period, as I said in the beginning. Hardly
after practicing detailed comparisons of names and definitions and
visual and other sense perceptions, after scrutinizing them in benevolent disputation by the use of question and answer without jealousy, at
last in a flash understanding of each blazes up, and the mind, as it
exerts all its powers to the limit of human capacity, is flooded with
light.

For this reason no serious man will ever think of writing about c
serious realities for the general public so as to make them a prey to
envy and perplexity. In a word, it is an inevitable conclusion from this
that when anyone sees anywhere the written work of anyone, whether
that of a lawgiver in his laws or whatever it may be in some other
form, the subject treated cannot have been his most serious concern—
that is, if he is himself a serious man. His most serious interests have
their abode somewhere in the noblest region of the field of his activity.
If, however, he really was seriously concerned with these matters and
put them in writing, 'then surely' not the gods, but mortals 'have ut- d
terly blasted his wits.' [1]

One who has followed my account of the reality and of the deviations from it will be assured of the fact that, whether Dionysius
has written anything on the first and highest principles of nature, or

[1] *Iliad* 7.360, 12.234.

anyone else great or small, that man in my opinion has neither received any sound instruction nor profited by it in the subjects of which
he wrote. For if he had, he would have felt the same reverence for the
subject that I do and would not boldly have cast it out unbecomingly
and unfittingly. Neither did he put the doctrine in writing to aid his
e own memory, for there is no danger of anyone forgetting it, once his
mind grasps it, since it is contained in the very briefest statements.
If he wrote at all, his motive was an ignoble ambition either to be regarded as the author of the doctrine or as one not destitute of culture
345 —of which he was not worthy if he was enamored of the reputation of
having it. Well, if a single interview had the effect of conferring this
culture on Dionysius, it may be so, but how it had that effect, God
wot, as the Theban says, for on that occasion I described my doctrines
to him in the way I have mentioned and once only—after that never
again.

Here the question must be considered by anyone interested in discovering how events happened to take the course they did, what can
be the reason why I did not recount my doctrines a second or a third
time or oftener. Does Dionysius after only one hearing think he
b knows, and does he adequately know, the subject, either by that one
hearing or by having discovered the truth himself or by learning it
previously from others? Or does he suppose the doctrine unimportant?
Or thirdly, does he suppose it to be not suited to him, but too high for
him, so that he really would not be able to adapt his life to a concern
for wisdom and virtue? If now he suppose the doctrines to be unimportant, he is at variance with many who testify to the opposite, who
are altogether more competent to judge of such matters than Dionysius. If on the other hand he supposes that he has already discovered or been taught the doctrine, and considers it valuable for
c the cultural education of the mind, how, unless he is a monster among
men, could he ever so callously have insulted the one who has been
pioneer and arbiter in this realm? Let me describe the insults he
inflicted.

Next, after no long interval, although he had up to that time permitted Dion to keep his own property and to enjoy the income, he now
refused to allow the trustees to send it to the Peloponnesus, as if he
had completely forgotten his letter. He said that the property belonged
d not to Dion but to Dion's son, who was his nephew and his lawful
ward. The transactions of that period were as I have stated up to this
point, but when Dionysius acted in this way, I had an accurate insight
into his enthusiasm for philosophy, and had cause for anger,
whether I would or no. It was then already summer and ships were
sailing. I decided, however, that I had no right to quarrel with Dionysius rather than with myself and with those who had forced me to
e go the third time to the strait of Scylla that 'once more I might pass

through baleful Charybdis,'[2] and that I would say to Dionysius that I could not remain now that Dion was so insultingly treated. He, however, tried to smooth it over and begged me to stay, for he considered it a bad thing for him that I should go in person at once to report 346 what had happened. On my refusing to wait he said that he would himself provide conveyance for me, for I had been planning to embark and sail in one of the merchant vessels. I was enraged and ready to take the consequences if I were interfered with, since I was obviously not guilty but an innocent sufferer.

When he now saw that I had no thought of remaining, he adopted the following device to keep me over that sailing. He came the next day and made me a plausible proposal. 'Let Dion and Dion's affairs,' said he, 'be cleared from our path, that you and I may no longer be b constantly at variance over them. For your sake,' said he, 'I will do this for Dion. I propose that he receive his property and live in the Peloponnesus, not as an exile, but enjoying the right to go abroad and even to visit Syracuse, when he and I and you his friends all come to a mutual agreement. This, provided he contrive no plots against me— and that you and your friends and Dion's friends here must guarantee. You must look to him for your security. Let whatever money he receives be deposited in the Peloponnesus and in Athens with anyone c you please, Dion receiving the interest but having no authority to withdraw any of the principal without your consent. I have no great confidence that, if he had the use of this money, he would deal justly with me, for it will amount to a large sum, but I put more trust in you and your friends. See whether you find this offer satisfactory. If you do, stay on these terms another year and next season take this money and depart. I am sure that Dion too will be very grateful to you for your d success in making this arrangement on his behalf.'

This proposal disgusted me, but in spite of that I replied that I would consider the matter and report my decision to him on the next day. Such was our agreement at that time.

Thereupon when I got by myself, I did take counsel in a state of great confusion. The argument, however, that was most important in guiding my counsel was this. 'Well now, suppose Dionysius really has no intention of carrying out any of his offers; yet, after I am e gone, he may write a plausible letter to Dion and may also instruct a great many of his friends to write similar letters, containing his present proposal to me and asserting that he made the offer, and that I refused to accept it and altogether disregarded the interests of Dion. In addition to this he may be no longer willing to send me home and may not only give no orders himself to any of the shipmasters, but may 347 easily make it clear to everyone that he is averse to my leaving. In

[2] *Odyssey* 12.428.

that case will anyone consent to take me as a passenger, setting forth, as I must, from the house of Dionysius?'

Besides my other difficulties, I was living in the garden belonging to the palace, so that even the porter would refuse to let me out unless an order were sent him from Dionysius.

'If, though, I wait over the year, I shall be able to write to Dion and let him know my situation and the state of my plans. If, on the b other hand, Dionysius does carry out any of his promises, my achievements will not be altogether ridiculous, for probably Dion's property amounts to at least one hundred talents, if rightly estimated. On the other hand if the elements of discord now apparent develop as they probably will, I am at a loss what to do with myself, but in spite of that I suppose I must hold out at least another year and try to expose Dionysius' schemes by actual test.'

Having come to this conclusion, I told Dionysius on the next day that I had decided to remain. 'However,' said I, 'I beg you not to sup- c pose that I have authority over Dion, but to join me in dispatching letters to him to explain the decision that we have just come to and to ask him whether he is satisfied with it. If he is not, but wishes to make some other proposal, let him write at once. You meanwhile must take no further action about his affairs.' Such were our words, such was our agreement, pretty much as I have just stated it.

So the ships now set sail, and it was no longer possible for me to travel, when Dionysius suggested to me that half the property should d be Dion's and half his son's. He promised to sell it and to give me half the sum realized to take to Dion, and to retain the other half in Sicily for the boy, since this was really the fairest arrangement. I was amazed at the proposal and thought it most absurd to dispute further. Nevertheless I said that we ought to wait for the letter from Dion and then send these proposals back to him. He, however, immediately e afterward in a very headstrong way sold all of Dion's property, choosing his own place and arrangements and buyers, and never uttered a sound to me about it at all. I for my part likewise had no further conversation with him about Dion's affairs, since I thought there was nothing to be gained.

Up to this point I had in this way taken the part of philosophy 348 and of my friends, but from then on Dionysius and I lived, I looking out like a bird that wants to fly away, he engaged in devising a way of frightening me off without paying me any of Dion's money. Just the same we called ourselves friends before all Sicily.

Now Dionysius attempted to decrease the pay of the more elderly of the mercenaries, contrary to his father's practice, and the soldiers, infuriated by this, gathered in a throng and said they would not allow it. Dionysius then attempted to force them to yield by b closing the gates of the acropolis, but they at once burst into a sort of barbaric war song and rushed at the walls. Dionysius, terror-stricken at this, granted everything and more besides to the peltasts then collected there.

Now a report quickly spread that Heraclides was to blame for all this, and he, getting wind of the report, took himself off and disappeared. Dionysius then sought to capture him. Being at a loss, however, he summoned Theodotes to the garden, where I happened to be c strolling at the time. The rest of their conversation I have no knowledge of and did not hear, but what Theodotes said to Dionysius in my presence I know and remember.

'Plato,' he said, 'I am trying to persuade Dionysius here, in case I am able to bring Heraclides to this place to talk with us about the charges that are now being made, to accept my proposal that, if it seems undesirable for Heraclides to live in Sicily, he be allowed to take his wife and son and emigrate to the Peloponnesus and live there, not d harming Dionysius and receiving the income from his property. I have for that matter already sent for him and I will send for him now again. He may appear in answer to my former summons or in answer to the present one. In any case I beg and beseech Dionysius, if anyone finds Heraclides, whether in the country or here in the city, to let no harm befall him except to leave the country until Dionysius decides otherwise. Do you agree to this?' said he, speaking to Dionysius.   e

'I do,' said he, 'and if he appears at your house he will suffer no harm beyond what you have just mentioned.'

Now on the afternoon of the next day Eurybius and Theodotes hastily approached me in a state of the greatest alarm and Theodotes asked me, 'Plato, were you present yesterday when Dionysius made the agreement with you and me about Heraclides?'

'Of course,' said I.

'At this moment though,' said he, 'there are peltasts scouring the country in quest of Heraclides, and he must be somewhere about. Do by all means,' said he, 'go with us to Dionysius.'   349

So we set out and entered the presence of Dionysius. The other two then stood silently weeping, while I spoke. 'These men,' said I, 'are afraid you may take some step in regard to Heraclides that is contrary to the agreement you made yesterday. I think he has been seen making his way in this direction.'

When he heard this he blazed up and turned every kind of color that an angry man would.

Theodotes fell at his feet and, seizing him by the hand, burst into tears and besought him to do no such thing. I broke in and com- b forted him with the words, 'Courage, Theodotes, for Dionysius will never go so far as to break the agreement of yesterday by doing otherwise.'

And Dionysius gave me a very tyrannical look and said, 'With you I made no agreement either great or small.'

'By the gods,' said I, 'you did, not to do the very thing that this man is now begging you not to do.' And when I had said this, I turned my back and went out.

Thereupon he kept his men on the trail of Heraclides, but Theo-
c dotes sent word to him by messengers to make his escape. Dionysius then dispatched Tisias with peltasts and orders to pursue him. Hera-clides, however, it was said, gained the Carthaginian domain a small part of a day ahead of them and so escaped.

After this Dionysius concluded that the old plot afforded a plau-sible ground for quarreling with me so as not to pay over Dion's
d money. First he dismissed me from the acropolis, having found a pre-text that the women had to celebrate some ten-day festival in the gar-den where I was living. So he ordered me to stay during this period outside in the house of Archedemus. While I was there Theodotes sent for me and expressed a good deal of resentment and criticism of Dionysius for his recent behavior. When Dionysius heard that I had visited Theodotes, he found here again a new pretext, akin to the for-
e mer, for quarreling with me, and sent someone to ask me whether I really had a meeting with Theodotes when he sent for me.

'Certainly,' said I.

'In that case,' said the messenger, 'he bade me tell you that you by no means do well always to prefer Dion and Dion's friends to him.'

After these words he never again sent for me to come to his house, since it was now plain that I was a friend of Theodotes and Heraclides and an enemy to him. He thought too that I was disaf-fected because Dion's property was being altogether dissipated.

350   So after this I lived outside the acropolis among the mercenaries. Here there came to me among others those serving in the crews who were from Athens, and so fellow citizens of mine, and reported that I was unpopular among the peltasts, and that some of them threatened to make an end of me, if ever they caught me. I somehow, however, contrived the following way of escape. I sent to Archytas and to my other friends at Tarentum, telling them the situation in which I found myself. They discovered some pretext for an embassy from the city
b and sent Lamiscus, who was one of their number, with a thirty-oared vessel. When he arrived, he entreated Dionysius on my behalf, say-ing that I wanted to depart and urging him not to refuse. Dionysius granted his request and sent me off with an allowance of money for my traveling expenses. As for Dion's property, neither was there any further demand for it on my part nor was it restored.

When I arrived at Olympia in the Peloponnesus, I found Dion in attendance at the festival and reported what had happened. He,
c having called Zeus to witness, at once issued a summons to me and my friends and companions to make preparations for taking ven-geance on Dionysius. From us vengeance was due for the crime of deluding a guest, so Dion said and believed, from him for unjust ex-pulsion and exile.

In reply I bade him invite my friends, if they were willing, 'but as for myself,' said I, 'you and the others practically forced me to become a guest at the table and at the hearth of Dionysius and a partaker in sacred rites with him. He very likely thought because of the false reports that many were circulating that I was leagued with you in a plot against him and his government, and yet he scrupled to put me to d death. For one thing, then, I am now scarcely of an age to help anyone in making war, and for another you have in me a common friend, in case you ever feel a desire to be friends with each other and want to accomplish some good. As long as you are bent on evil, invite others.' This I said in detestation of my wanderings and misfortunes in Sicily.

By declining instead of accepting my offers of mediation they brought upon themselves all the misfortunes that have now come upon them. None of these, in all human probability, would ever have occurred if Dionysius had paid the money to Dion or had become com- e pletely reconciled to him, for I would and I could easily have restrained Dion. As it is, their attacks on each other have everywhere brought a flood of misfortune.

Yet Dion's policy was the same, I should say, as my own or 351 any other decent man's ought to be, in regard to the exercise of power by himself and his friends in his own city, namely, by conferring benefits on the city to acquire for himself the greatest power and the highest honors.

By this I do not mean the man who makes himself and his companions and his city rich by forming a plot and collecting conspirators—some man who is poor and unable to rule himself, a weakling enslaved to his desires—who next puts to death all those who own b property—such he terms foes—then plunders their possessions and exhorts his accomplices and companions never to lay it at his door, if they say they are poor. Nor do I mean the man who is honored because of such a service to his city as distributing to the people by decrees the property of the few, nor the man who is head of a great city that has dominion over many smaller ones, and distributes unjustly to his own city the property of the others. On such terms neither Dion nor anyone c else will ever, so far as he acts voluntarily, aim at a power baleful to himself and to his race forever and ever. He will aim at a republic and at instituting the best and justest laws without resorting in the least to executions and bloodshed.

Now while Dion was in the act of achieving this, having chosen to be the victim of crimes rather than commit them—though he took precautions against such attempts—then, in spite of all, he stumbled at the very summit of his mastery over his enemies. Nor is it strange that he did, for while a good man dealing with wicked men, d a man sober and sane of mind, would in general never be completely deceived in estimating the souls of such men, yet it would not be surprising if he were caught napping like a good helmsman, who might not altogether overlook the approach of a storm, but might overlook the extraordinary and unexpected magnitude of the tempest and so be overwhelmed by its violence. This is the mistake that Dion made, for assuredly he was aware that those who proved his undoing were bad

e men. The depth, however, of their folly and their villainy and their bloodthirstiness he did overlook, and so undone, he lies among the fallen, visiting Sicily with woe untold.

352 The advice I have to give after this narrative has mostly been given and so no more. I went back to the subject of my second visit to Sicily because the necessity of dealing with it seemed forced upon me by the surprising and paradoxical nature of the events. If anyone after this account finds the events less paradoxical and if anyone concludes that there was sufficient justification for what happened, then what I have said is fairly and adequately put.

LETTER VIII

b *To* THE FRIENDS AND COMPANIONS OF DION, *Prosperity*

I will try to describe to you as well as I can the policy that you must adopt if genuine prosperity is to be yours. It is my hope that the counsel I give will be advantageous not only to you, though of course

c to you especially, but also in the second place to all at Syracuse, and in the third place to your enemies and foes, with the exception of any who have perpetrated impious crimes. Such deeds are past redeeming; such stains no one can ever cleanse. Consider now what I have to say.

Now that the despotic power has been overthrown throughout all Sicily, you are at odds only on one issue. On one side are those who desire to restore the empire once more, on the other those who wish to set the final seal on their escape from tyranny. Now the general opin-

d ion about such a situation is that the right policy to adopt on any occasion is that one which will do the most damage to the enemy and the most good to your own side. It is, however, by no means easy to do a great deal of damage to the other side without also receiving a good deal yourselves in return. You need not travel to any distant land to see glaring instances of that sort of thing. You have on the spot in Sicily an object lesson in the recent course of events. You have seen how the two parties tried respectively to inflict injuries and to avenge

e them, and you need only tell the tale to others to give on each occasion adequate instruction on that point. You need hardly be at a loss for examples of that sort. Examples, however, of measures conducive to the advantage of all, friend and foe alike, or of measures involving the least possible damage to both sides, it is neither easy to discover nor, when one has discovered them, to put them into effect.

One might as well resort to prayer as advise anything of the sort, or attempt to speak of it. Well, let us actually resort to a sort of prayer, 353 for we should always appeal to the gods when we set about speaking or reflecting—a prayer, though, that I hope will find fulfillment.

Here is the message that our prayer indicates to us. There is one family that has for the most part ever since the war began supplied commanders to you and to your enemies. That family was at one time put in command by your fathers, when they were reduced to utter helplessness—at that moment, I mean, when Greek Sicily was in the greatest danger of being laid waste by the Carthaginians and so reverting altogether to barbarism. Under those circumstances two men were elected—Dionysius, who was young and warlike, to super- b intend the military activity for which he was fitted, and Hipparinus to be an older adviser. They were given the title of supreme commanders in defense of Sicily, in other words, tyrants. Now you may attribute the deliverance of Sicily to a special providence, that is, to God, or to the superior qualities of the rulers, or to the combined operation of these two causes assisted by the action of the citizens of those days; be it as you choose to suppose. At any rate that was the way in which deliverance was brought to the men of that time. Now after such achievements it was perhaps just that all should be grate- c ful to their saviors. If, however, the despotic power has since that time wrongly misused the city's gift, for this the penalty is partly paid, partly still to pay. Yes, but what just penalty is there that can be enforced in their present situation? If it were possible for you to escape from them easily with no great danger or hardship, or for them to seize the government again without difficulty, in that case it would also be impossible for me to give you the advice that I am going to give.

The actual state of affairs being what it is, you must bear in mind on both sides and keep recalling how many times, first in one camp d then in the other, you have had great expectations and have supposed again and again that now only some little thing stood between you and complete success. Above all be mindful that in each case that little thing turns out to be a source of woes unnumbered; no goal is ever reached, but to the supposed end of the old is linked again and again the budding of a fresh beginning—a vicious circle that threatens to involve both parties, that of the tyrant and that of the people, in total destruction. You are face to face with the probability—may God e avert it—that the Greek tongue will be all but silenced throughout the whole of Sicily, for that island will have come under the domination and have passed into the hands of Phoenicians or Opici. Hence it behooves every Greek to throw himself into the task of preventing this catastrophe. If anyone else has a more suitable and a better remedy than the one I am going to suggest, he need only bring it forward to deserve richly the title, Friend of Hellas. My own view at the moment 354 I will try to make clear with all frankness on a basis of impartial

justice. In fact I do speak as a sort of arbitrator between two parties,
that of the former tyrant and that of his subjects, while with respect to
each singly I am giving my old advice. Now as before it is my advice
to any tyrant to avoid the name and the condition of a tyrant and to
b transform tyranny into kingship, if possible. That it is possible, however, is proved by the actual example of a wise and good man,
Lycurgus, who saw that the related families in Argos and Messene,
which had passed from kingship to despotic power, had in each case
brought ruin on themselves and on their cities. Hence, alarmed for his
own city, and for his family as well, he applied a remedy. He girded
the kingship with a rope of safety, the senate, that is, and the ephorate
c —with the result that his people have been gloriously preserved
through these many generations, because law was made rightful lord and
sovereign of men, and men no longer ruled the laws with arbitrary power.

It is my advice to everyone to take this same course now. I urge
those who are intent on establishing a tyranny to turn back and to flee
for their lives from that which is accounted happiness by men who are
insatiably greedy and bereft of sense. Let them endeavor to change to
a kingly pattern and to be subject to kingly laws, enjoying the highest
d honors by the consent of willing subjects and of the laws. Again I
would counsel those who are seeking to establish free institutions and
to avoid the yoke of servitude as being evil, to be on their guard lest by
inordinately desiring an unseasonable liberty they fall victims to the
plague that visited their ancestors because the citizens of those days
went to extremes in their refusal to be governed. Their passion for
liberty knew no bounds.

The Sicilian Greeks, before Dionysius and Hipparinus came into
power, were at that time, they supposed, leading a happy life, for they
were living luxuriously and were at the same time ruling their rulers.
e They even stoned to death without any legal trial the ten generals who
preceded Dionysius. They would be subject to no one, neither to lawful ruler nor to the reign of law, but would be altogether and absolutely
free. That is the way they got their tyrants, for either servitude or freedom, when it goes to extremes, is an utter bane, while either in due
measure is altogether a boon. The due measure of servitude is to serve
God. The extreme of servitude is to serve man. The god of sober men
355 is law; the god of fools is pleasure.

Since the law of nature in regard to these things is as I have
stated it, I exhort the friends of Dion to publish my words of advice to
all the Syracusans as the joint counsel of Dion and myself. I will act
as interpreter of the message which he, if he were alive and able, would
now address to you. 'What message then,' someone may say, 'does the
advice of Dion convey to us about our present situation?' Here it is.

'First of all, men of Syracuse, accept such laws as you see clearly
b will not turn your thoughts and desires to money-getting and riches.

There are three things, soul and body and money. Put in the place of highest honor the excellence of the soul; put next, that of the body, subject, however, to that of the soul; and in the third and last place put the honor paid to money, making it a slave to the body and to the soul. If an ordinance produced this effect, it would rightly be a part of your constitution, for it would result in the genuine happiness of those who observed it. The usage that applies the term "happy" to the rich is c itself miserable, being a foolish usage of women and children, and it renders miserable those that put confidence in it. That these words of exhortation from me are true you will know by experience if you put to the test what I have just said about laws. Experience seems to be the surest touchstone for everything.

'Once you have accepted such laws, since Sicily is in great peril, since, moreover, you are neither completely victorious nor yet deci- d sively beaten, perhaps it would be fair and advantageous for all of you to take the path of compromise between the two parties—your party on the one hand who dread the severity of the central government, and on the other hand the party who passionately desire to regain their power. It was their ancestors who once contributed most to deliver the Greeks from barbarians and so made it possible to discuss the form of government now. If destruction had come then, there would be no discussion now and no hope remaining whatever. As the case stands, then, let the party who desire freedom obtain freedom under a king, and let those who desire to be kings, be kings responsible e for their acts. Let law be supreme not only over the other citizens, but even over the kings themselves, in case they violate the constitution. Observing then all these provisions, with honest and upright intent, aided by the gods, set up three kings. Let the first be my son. He has a double claim derived from me and from my father, for my father formerly rescued the city from barbarians, while I have lately freed her twice from tyrants, as you yourselves can testify. In the second 356 place raise to the kingship him who has my father's name, and is Dionysius' son. In his case there are two reasons, his recent assistance to your cause and his unstained character. Though son of a tyrant, he is, by voluntarily conferring freedom upon the city, acquiring immortal honor for himself and for his race instead of an ephemeral and unjust tyranny. In the third place you must invite to become king of Syracuse by mutual consent him who is now in command of the hostile camp, Dionysius, son of Dionysius—that is, if he will of b his own free choice consent to assume the character of a king. He may be influenced to do so by dread of mischance and by compassion for his country's plight and for the untended state of temples and tombs. There is the danger too that by giving rein to his ambition he may involve all in utter ruin to the ultimate delight of the barbarian. These three, whether you give them the same powers as the Laconian kings

have, or whether you make some diminution by mutual agreement, you must constitute kings in some such way as the following. It has
c already been told you; yet hear it once more.

'If the race of Dionysius and Hipparinus are willing for the salvation of Sicily to put an end to their present misfortunes and to receive honors for themselves and their race, both now and hereafter, then on these conditions, as I said before, summon to a meeting such representatives as they choose to invest with full power to arrange an
d agreement. The representatives may be Sicilians or foreigners or partly one, partly the other. Their number will depend on mutual agreement. When these have arrived, let them first establish laws and a form of government that admits the arrangement that kings be given authority over rites in honor of the gods, and over all other rites that are due to the memory of former benefactors. To have jurisdiction over war and peace let them appoint guardians of the law, thirty-five in number, with assembly and senate. Let there be other courts for other matters, but in cases where the penalty is death or exile let the thirty-five constitute the court. In addition to these let there be judges
e selected each year from among the outgoing officials, one from each office who is adjudged to have been the best and justest official. Let these during the next year judge all cases where it is a question of executing or imprisoning or deporting a citizen. Let a king not be permitted to act as judge in such cases; let him keep himself like a priest
357 free from defilement with death or imprisonment or exile.

'This was my plan for you while I lived and it is my plan now. At the time when I had with your help conquered my foes, if fiends in the form of guests had not prevented, I should have set up a constitution according to my plans. After this, I should have colonized the rest of Sicily, if deed had followed thought, by taking from the barbarians the territory they now occupy—excepting any of them who fought to the end against the tyrannical power on behalf of the general freedom
b —and then settling the former inhabitants of the Greek region in their ancient and hereditary seats. These same plans I now advise all to adopt in common and to execute, inviting everyone to assist in their execution and considering anyone who refuses a common enemy. Really this is not impossible. If a plan exists in two minds and may readily be discovered by attentive consideration to be the best, it is
c hardly good judgment to consider it impossible. The two minds I speak of are that of Hipparinus, son of Dionysius, and that of my own son, for, if they were to agree, I believe that all the other Syracusans who have the city's interests at heart would be in accord. Now give honor with prayer to all the gods, and to the others whose due it is along with the gods, and do not desist from urging and calling upon friends and opponents gently and by every means, until the ideal that I have just described, like a heavenly vision presented to your waking

sight, become through your efforts a visible reality, complete and suc- d
cessful.'

LETTER VI

To HERMIAS AND ERASTUS AND CORISCUS, *Prosperity*   322c
    In my opinion some god, who is willing and able to befriend you,
has good fortune in store for you, if you accept it wisely. You live near
one another and your needs are such that you can be of the greatest d
mutual benefit. As for Hermias, neither abundance of cavalry or of
other military resources nor the acquisition of gold could add more to
his strength in all directions than would the gaining of steadfast
friends of uncorrupted character. As for Erastus and Coriscus, I say,
old man that I am, that in addition to this noble lore of ideas they have
need also of the lore of self-defense against the base and wicked, and
of a sort of faculty of self-preservation. They are inexperienced be- e
cause they have passed a large part of their lives with us, who are
honorable, not wicked, and this explains my saying that they have
need of those other things as well in order that they may not be obliged
to neglect the genuine wisdom and to attend more than they should
to the wisdom that is concerned with the life of man and his necessities. It seems to me, so far as I can judge without having met him, 323
that Hermias possesses this practical faculty naturally and that he has
strengthened it by the skill that he has derived from experience.
    What then is my message? To you, Hermias, I who know
Erastus and Coriscus by experience better than you do, declare and
assert and testify that you will not easily find men of more trustworthy
character than these neighbors of yours. I advise you to cling to these
men by every just means and to consider it no secondary matter to do
so. Coriscus and Erastus in turn I advise to cling to Hermias and endeavor by thus clinging to one another to get knit together into a single b
bond of friendship. If any of you seems in any way to be weakening
this bond—for nothing human is altogether stable—send hither to
me and my associates a letter of complaint. I believe that letters sent
by us here in justice and reverence would, unless some great breach
had actually occurred, be better than any charm to heal the wound and
to unite you again in the formerly existing friendship and partnership.
If then all of us, both you and we, practice philosophy to the extent of c
our ability, considering each man's circumstances, the prophecy I
have made will hold good. If we do otherwise, I do not say what will
happen, for it must be words of good omen that I utter. I say therefore
that in all these things we shall be successful, if God wills.
    This letter all three of you must read—all together, if possible;

if not, two at a time—in common as far as you are able, as often as you can. You must treat it as a contract and a binding law, that is, a
d just law, combining in your oath taking a not unenlightened seriousness with the jesting that is kin to earnest, as you invoke the god who is ruler of all things present and to come, and is rightful father of the ruling active principle, to certain knowledge of whom, if we genuinely practice philosophy, we shall attain as far as it lies in the power of human beings who are truly well endowed to do so.

LETTER I

309 *To* DIONYSIUS, *Prosperity*
   After all the time I have been with you administering your government as your most trusted adviser—a position that gave you all the profit, while it fell to my lot to bear the heavy brunt of hostile criticism—I know that no one will suppose that I consented to any of your overcruel acts, for all your fellow citizens can bear witness on my be-
b half, many of whom I championed in time of need, and saved from no slight loss—and after the many times when as supreme commander I kept your city safe, I have been dismissed with less respect than a beggar would deserve if he were dispatched by you and ordered to depart after being so long with you. In future I shall certainly consider my own interests in less benevolent fashion, while you, being the tyrant that you are, will live in solitude.
c   As for the gold, that splendid parting gift of yours, Bacchius, the bearer of this letter, is returning it to you, for it was neither enough for my traveling expenses nor serviceable for my support later. On the other hand such a gift would be most disgraceful for you the giver, and not much less so for me too, if I were to accept it—hence my refusal. Obviously it makes no difference to you whether you receive or give away that amount of money; so, now you have it back, show someone else the same attentions that you have shown to me. Really your attentions to me have quite satisfied me.
d   It is also appropriate for me to repeat the words of Euripides, that when you are sometime involved in other difficulties, 'Thou'lt pray for such another at thy side.'[1] I want to remind you also that most of the other tragedians, when they show on the stage a tyrant be-
310 ing slain by someone, represent him as crying out, 'Of friends bereft, alas, I perish.'[2] No one has ever depicted a tyrant perishing for lack of gold. The following poem is also approved by the intelligent.

Not gleaming gold is rarest in the unhopeful life of mortals.
Diamonds and couches of silver sparkle not to sight,

[1] Euripides, fr. 956.   [2] *Trag. Gr. Frag. Adesp.* 347 (ed. Bergk).

When weighed in the scales with a man.
Nor is there strength in fruitful acres of broad land laden with
  bounty
As much as in the concordant thoughts of good men.[3]

Farewell and know how great a loss you have suffered in me, in b
order that you may treat the others better.

LETTER V

To PERDICCAS, *Prosperity*   321c
  I have advised Euphraeus in accordance with your letter to look
after your affairs and to make that his occupation. It is right that I
should also give you counsel, in all friendliness and solemnity, as they
say, both in regard to the other matters that you mention and in regard d
to the use you should now make of Euphraeus. There are many services
the man can render, but the most important is a service that at present you are in want of both because of your youth and because there
are not many to advise the young about it.
  Each form of government has a sort of voice as if it were a kind of
animal. There is one of democracy, another of oligarchy, and a third
of monarchy. There are plenty of men who will assert that they under- e
stand the science of these, but, except for some few, they are far indeed
from a thorough acquaintance with them. Any form of government
that utters its own voice to god and man and duly acts in harmony
with its voice, is always flourishing and endures. When it copies another it perishes. In this connection you might find Euphraeus useful to no small degree, though to be sure he is a good man in other
respects too, for I expect that he will help to interpret the language of 322
monarchy as well as any of those who are in your service. If you then
make this use of him, you will yourself profit by it and you will do him
the greatest service.
  If anyone, when he hears this, says, 'Plato apparently pretends to
know what is for the advantage of a democracy, yet, though he has the
right to address the assembly and give them the best advice, he has
never taken the floor to utter a word'—say in reply that Plato was
born late in his country's history, and the people, when he came to
them, were already rather well on in years and had acquired from his b
predecessors the habit of doing many things at variance with his advice. 'For he would have been altogether delighted,' you must explain,
'to advise the people as he might have counseled a father, if he had not
supposed he would be risking his life in vain without any hope of
accomplishing anything. That is just what I think he would do about

[3] *Lyr. Gr. Frag. Adesp.* 138 (ed. Nauck).

advising me. If he thought I were incurable, he would bid me a hearty farewell and avoid giving any advice that concerned me or my affairs.'
c Farewell.

LETTER IX

357d *To* ARCHYTAS OF TARENTUM, *Prosperity*

Archippus and Philonides and the rest have arrived with the letter which you gave them and with news of you. They carried through the business with the city without difficulty. In fact it was not in the least troublesome. They also described your position to us, saying that you are rather vexed that you cannot get released from public
358 business. The fact that attending to one's own affairs is pleasantest in life, especially if one choose the sort of activity that you do, is clear to almost anyone. You must, however, consider this fact too, that each of us is born not for himself alone. We are born partly for our country, partly for our parents, partly for our friends. The various contingencies that overtake our lives also make many demands upon us. When our country herself calls us to public life, it would perhaps be strange
b not to respond, since one must otherwise at the same time give place to worthless men who do not enter public life for the best motive. Enough of this matter. I am taking care of Echecrates now, and I shall do so in future for your sake, for the sake of his father Phrynion, and also for the sake of the young man himself.

LETTER XII

359c *To* ARCHYTAS OF TARENTUM, *Prosperity*

We received with marvelous pleasure the commentaries that
d came from you and felt the greatest possible admiration for their author and thought the man to be worthy of those ancient ancestors of his. It is said that these men were Myrians, who formed part of those Trojans that were driven from their country in the time of Laomedon, brave men as the traditional tale shows. My own commentaries, about which you inquired, are not yet in a satisfactory state, but I have sent them to you just as they are. In regard to preserving them we are both
e in agreement, so that no admonitions are needed.

INDEX

ABBREVIATIONS

* The Letters appear in the following order, as established by their translator: 13, 2, 11, 10, 4, 3, 7, 8, 6, 1, 5, 9, 12.

INDEX

The present index is based upon that of Evelyn Abbott, as revised by Matthew Knight, which was published in the third edition (1892) of Jowett's *Dialogues of Plato*. It has been entirely remade for the present edition, and cross references have been supplied to assist the reader with the philosophical vocabulary of the different translators. The references to the text are given by means of the marginal sigla derived from the pagination and page subdivisions of the 1578 edition of Plato by Henri Estienne (Stephanus), which is conventionally used for references to the text of Plato.

A

Abaris, the Hyperborean, charms, Charm. 158b
Abdera: Rep. 10.600c; Protagoras from, Protag. 309c
abdomen, *see* belly, lower
ability, Hipp. min. 367b sq.
abolition, *see* cancellation
abortion: practiced by midwives, Theaet. 149d; preferred in some cases, Rep. 5.461c
above, and below, Tim. 62c sq.
absence, of pain, not = pleasure, Phil. 43d sq.
absolute: Phaedo 75d; equality, ib. 74 sq.; essence, ib. 65; and the many, Rep. 6.507b sq.; reality, Phaedo 78d; and relative, Phil. 53d sq.; A. BEAUTY: Crat. 439c sq., Rep. 5.476b sq.; its form makes all things beautiful, Hipp. maj. 289d sq., 292d (cf. Parm. 130b); *see also* essence; form(s); idea(s); *and the various ideas, conceived as subsisting, e.g., justice, in itself*
abstract: and concrete, opposed, Phaedo 103; ideas, origin, ib. 74, Rep. 7.523 sq. (*see also* idea(s))
abuse, *see* defamatory words
Academy, the: Lysis 203a sq.; allud. to, Epis. 6.322e
Acarnanians, the two, Euthyd. 271c
accents, change of, Crat. 399a sq.
accident: and essence, Soph. 247b sq. (cf. Rep. 5.454); and substance, Lysis 217c sq.; *see also* chance
account: or description, Theaet. 202b sq., 206c sq.; and knowledge, ib. 201c sq.; *see also* description

accusations, vs. Socrates, Apol. 17 sq.
Acesimbrotus, physician's name, Crat. 394c
Achaeans, Laws 3.682d sq., 685e, 706d sq., Rep. 3.390e, 393 sq.
Acharnae, Gorg. 495d
Achelous, Phaedr. 230b, 263d
Acheron (river), Phaedo 112e, 113d
Acherusian Lake, Phaedo 113 sq.
Achilles: son of Peleus and Thetis, Apol. 28c, Rep. 3.391c (cf. Hipp. min. 371c, Symp. 179e); grandson of Aeacus, Hipp. maj. 292e; pupil of Chiron, Hipp. min. 371d; will not remain at Troy, ib. 370b; speech to Ajax (*Iliad* 9.644 sq.), Crat. 428c; Phoenix, his attendant, Rep. 3.390e; erroneously called lover of Patroclus, Symp. 180a; younger than Patroclus, ib. 178a; attacks Scamander, Protag. 340a; warned of death if he slew Hector, Symp. 179e; fights with Hector, Ion 535b; died for Patroclus, Symp. 208d; sent to Islands of Blessed, ib. 179e sq.;
    braggart, Hipp. min. 371a; and Brasidas, Symp. 221c; brave, Hipp. min. 364c sq.; duplicity, ib. 371d; fate, Hipp. maj. 292e; greed, cruelty, arrogance, Rep. 3.390e sq.; grief, ib. 3.388a sq.; and Odysseus, Hipp. min. 363b, 364b sq., 369b sq., 370e sq.; straightforward, ib. 364e; speaks falsely unintentionally, ib. 370e, 371e; true and simple, ib. 365b (cf. 369a); wily, ib. 369e sq.
acid: Tim. 66b, 74c; vegetable a. (ὀπός), ib. 60b
acquaintance, in state, Laws 6.771d sq.; *see also* friendship

185c sq. (cf. Epin. 978c, Rep. 6.511d);

puzzles, Laws 7.819b, Phaedo 96e sq., 101b; spirit in which to be pursued, Rep. 7.525c sq.; taught by heavenly bodies, Tim. 39b sq., 47a (cf. Epin. 978b sq., Laws 6.771b); two kinds, Phil. 56d sq.; use in forming ideas, Rep. 7.525; used to express interval between king and tyrant, Rep. 9.587c sq.; yields pure knowledge only, Statesm. 258d; *see also* calculation; ciphering; figures; mathematical / mathematician / mathematics

arithmeticians, Hipp. min. 367c, Rep. 7.525e

Armenius, father of Er the Pamphylian, Rep. 10.614b

armor: conflicts in, for men and women, Laws 8.833e sq.; dances in, ib. 7.796b sq.; FIGHTING IN: Euthyd. 271e, 273c sq., Laches 178a, 179e, 181d sq.; not practiced by Lacedaemonians and useless, ib. 182e sq.; requires both hands, Laws 7.795b; women to learn, ib. 7.813e

arms: throwing away of, disgraceful, Laws 12.943e sq., Rep. 5.468a; —, permitted in naval warfare, Laws 4.706c; use of, taught by Athena, Tim. 24b (cf. Criti. 110b, Laws 7.796b sq., Menex. 238b); —, to be learned by women, Laws 7.804e sq., 813e sq.; worn in daily life by Cretans, ib. 1.625c; *see also* spear; war; weapons

army, needed in state, Rep. 2.374; *see also* general(s); helpers; military; soldier(s)

art(s): not to be abused, Gorg. 456d, 460c sq.; acquisitive a., Soph. 219c sq., 265a; of agriculture, ib. 219a; of angling, ib. 218e–21c; and their antecedents, Phaedr. 268 sq. (cf. Laws 4.709c sq.); applied and pure, Statesm. 258e; all base and mechanical, Rep. 7.522b (cf. Gorg. 512c, Laws 7.806d, 8.846d); based upon opinion, Phil. 59a; of boxing, Gorg. 456d, Rep. 4.422b sq.; of building, Euthyd. 13e, Ion 537d, Rep. 3.401a sq., 4.428c; of calculation, Gorg. 450d, 451b sq.; of carding, Statesm. 281a, 282a sq.; causes of deterioration of, Rep. 4.421d sq.; to be censored, ib. 3.401b; and chance, Laws 10.888e sq.; of charioteer, Ion 537b sq.; choric, Laws 2.672e; of combination and separation, Statesm.

282b sq.; contributory and productive, ib. 281d sq., 287b sq.; of controversy, Soph. 232b sq.; of counting, Statesm. 259e; criticism of, Ion 532 sq., Laws 2.667d–70a; culinary, Rep. 1.332c;

depend on measure, Statesm. 284a sq.; differ by functions, Rep. 1.346; — by subject matter, Ion 537d; directed toward utilitarian ends, Rep. 7.533b; of disputation, Phaedr. 261c sq., Soph. 225b sq.; divided accord. to use or nonuse of words, Gorg. 450c sq.; of dyeing, Rep. 4.429d sq.; Egyptians allow no alteration in, Laws 2.656d sq.; of embroidery, Rep. 3.401a; employment of children in, ib. 5.466e sq.; of enchantment, Euthyd. 290a; of exchange, Soph. 223c sq.; exercised for good of subject, Euthyph. 13b, Rep. 1.342, 345–47; and experience, Gorg. 448c; of fencing, Euthyd. 271e, 273c sq., Laches 178a, 179e, 181d sq.; the fine, and Love, Symp. 197b; of flute playing, Meno 90e, Protag. 327b; full of grace, Rep. 3.401a; of fulling, Statesm. 281b, 282a;

of general, Euthyd. 290b, Statesm. 304e sq.; given to individual for community, Protag. 322c; and the good, Phil. 66b sq.; of herd nurture, Statesm. 261e sq., 275b sq.; holiness an? Euthyph. 13; of horsemanship, Laches 193b; of hunting, Euthyd. 290b sq., Soph. 219c sq.; ideals in, Rep. 5.472d; illusion in, Soph. 235e sq.; of imitation, ib. 219a; influence on character, Rep. 3.400d sq.; interested in own perfection, ib. 1.342; iron superfluous for a. of potter and weaver, Laws 3.679a; of kingship, Statesm. 276b sq., 289c–93, 295b, 300e sq., 304 sq., 308c sq., 309b-11; and knowledge, Theaet. 146d sq.; knowledge of, not wisdom, Epin. 974b; and language, Statesm. 277a sq. (cf. Rep. 9.588c sq.); lesser, Rep. 6.495d;

magical a., Laws 11.933a; of measurement, Protag. 356d sq., Statesm. 283d–85b; of mimicry, Soph. 267 sq.; minor, Rep. 5.475e; mnemonic a., Hipp. maj. 285e, Hipp. min. 368d, 369a; of money-making, Gorg. 452b sq., Rep. 1.330b; and moral qualities, Hipp. min. 373c sq., Protag. 327a sq.; and nature, Laws 10.888e sq., 890d, 892b (cf. Soph. 265b sq.); nature of an, Gorg. 501a;

B

children: not begotten, when God was shepherd, Statesm. 272a; care needed in education, Laws 6.766a, 7.788, 808d sq.; chastisement, ib. 7.808e; conceive virtue and vice as pleasure and pain, ib. 2.653a; why under control, Rep. 9.590e sq.; in Egypt, Laws 7.819b sq.; to experience pain and pleasure, ib. 7.792b sq.; fear and courage in, ib. 7.791b sq. (cf. Laches 197a); games, Laws 1.643b sq., 7.793e sq., 797b sq., Rep. 4.425a, 7.536e; to go to war, ib. 5.466e sq., 7.537a; happiest, possessed of moderate fortune, Laws 5.729a (cf. 6.773d sq.); not to hear improper stories, Rep. 2.377 sq. (cf. Laws 12.941b);

illicit c., Rep. 5.461a; influenced by song, Laws 2.659e; instincts, ib. 2.653a sq.; of just man, Rep. 2.363d; to learn to ride, ib. 5.467d sq. (cf. Laws 7.804c); loss of, consoled, Menex. 247c sq.; a means to immortality, Laws 4.721c, 6.774a, 776b (cf. Symp. 207 sq.); meet at village sanctuaries, Laws 7.794a; newborn, carried round hearth, Theaet. 160e; number recognized sufficient, Laws 11.930d; old women storytellers to, Hipp. maj. 286a; and parents, ib. 291d, 292e sq., Laches 185a, Laws 4.717b sq., 9.869b, 11.928d sq., 930e sq. (cf. Crito 51c, Lysis 219d); prefer comedy to tragedy, Laws 2.658d (cf. Rep. 3.397d); procreation, Laws 6.775b sq., 783b sq. (cf. 2.674b); provision for, of those fallen in battle, Menex. 248d sq.;

reared amid fair sights and sounds, Rep. 3.401b sq.; registration, Laws 6.785a; of slaves, ib. 11.930d; 'of the spirit,' Symp. 209 (cf. Phaedr. 258c); in state, Laws 7.804d, Rep. 5.449c sq., 457d sq., 8.543a, Tim. 18c sq.; not to suffer for sins of fathers, Laws 9.855a, 856d; to take part in military exercises, ib. 8.829b; transfer from one class to another, Rep. 3.415b sq., 4.423d; see also descendants; infanticide; infants; offspring; young; youthful / youths

Chilon, of Sparta, one of Seven Wise Men, Protag. 343a

Chimera, Phaedr. 229d, Rep. 9.588c

chines, presented to brave warrior, Rep. 5.468d

Chios, home of Euthydemus and Dionysodorus, Euthyd. 271c, 288a

Chiron, teacher of Achilles, Hipp. min. 371d, Rep. 3.391c

choir(s): of aged, Laws 2.664d; of Apollo and Muses, ib. 2.664c, 665a; attendance, ib. 12.949c; contests, ib. 8.834e; of Dionysus, ib. 2.665b, 670 sq., 7.812b; judges, take oath, ib. 12.949a; of lads and lasses, ib. 6.772a; leaders and masters, Ion 536a; presidents or controllers, Laws 6.764e sq., 772a; the three, ib. 2.664c sq.; trainers, ib. 2.655a, 7.812e; see also choric; chorus

Cholargeis, Gorg. 487c

choric: art, coextensive with education, Laws 2.654b, 665a, 672e; —, divided into dance and song, ib. 2.654b; song, ib. 2.665 sq.; —, at Crete and Sparta, ib. 2.666d; training, Gorg. 501e; see also choir(s); chorus

chorus: cost of equipping a, Epis. 13.362a; derived from χαρά, Laws 2.654a; see also choir(s); choric

Chryses, priest of Apollo (Iliad 1.15 sq.), Rep. 3.392e sq., 393d sq.

Chrysippus, murdered by Atreus, Crat. 395b

cicadas: mouthpieces of Muses, Phaedr. 262d; song, ib. 230c, 258e sq., 262d; story of, ib. 259

Cimon: good, in common opinion, Gorg. 503c (cf. 515d); ostracized, ib. 516d; a real author of Athenian misfortunes, ib. 519a

Cinesias, son of Meles, dithyrambic poet, Gorg. 501e

Cinyras, wealth, Laws 2.660e

ciphering, excellent means of education, Laws 7.809c sq.; see also arithmetic(al); calculation; counting; mathematical / mathematician / mathematics

circle(s): Epis. 7.342b sq., Tim. 36c sq.; defined, Epis. 7.342b; universe a, Tim. 34b

circumference, Epis. 7.342b

citadel, Laws 5.745b (cf. 6.778c); see also acropolis; Trojan(s) / Troy, s.v. towers of

citations, Laws 9.855d; see also summonses

Cithaeron, ancient boundary of Attica, Criti. 110d

cithara: allowed, Rep. 3.399d; instructor in, Laws 7.812a; used in music without words, ib. 2.669e; see also harp; lute; lyre

cities / city: the best, site of, Rep. 3.415d sq.; divided between rich and

tries to destroy laws and state, Crito 50b sq.; great and small, differently estimated, Rep. 1.344a sq. (cf. 1.348d); = obsession bred by ancient, unexpiated c., Laws 9.854b; pleas in extenuation, ib. 9.864d sq.; voluntary and involuntary, ib. 9.860d sq.; *see also* misconduct

criminal(s): children of, Laws 9.855a, 856d; curable and incurable, in world below, Phaedo 113e sq.; incurable, Epis. 8.352c; —, expelled or put to death, Protag. 325b; law, Laws 9.853d sq.; numerous in oligarchies, Rep. 8.552d sq.; GREAT: come from most powerful, Gorg. 525e (cf. Rep. 10.615e); exist in well-ordered state, Laws 9.853c sq., 872d; men of strong character spoiled by bad education, Rep. 6.491e, 495b

Crison, of Himera: famous runner, Protag. 335e sq.; continence of, Laws 8.840a

criterion, of wisdom = ability to make money, Hipp. maj. 283b

Critias the elder: Criti. 106b sq., Tim. 20a; his father, Criti. 113b; his prayer, ib. 108c sq.
— grandfather of C. the elder, Charm. 157e, Tim. 20e, 21a
— the younger, son of Callaeschrus: Charm. 153c, 162e sq., Epis. 7.324c sq., Protag. 336d sq.; descendant of Solon, Charm. 155a; guardian and cousin of Charmides, ib. 155a, 156a, 157c, 176c; friend of Socrates, ib. 156a; at house of Callias, Protag. 316a sq.; philosopher, Charm. 161b

criticism: applies to good and bad equally, Ion 531d sq.; difficult without knowledge, Criti. 107b sq.; friendly, valuable, Laws 1.635a; implies knowledge of whole, Ion 532c sq.; literary, Hipp. maj. 286c; of Lysias' speech, Phaedr. 262c sq.; of painting, sculpture, and music, Ion 532e sq. (cf. Criti. 107b sq.); of poetry, Ion 532b; value in science, Statesm. 299b sq.; verbal, Protag. 343 sq.

Crito: Euthyd. 290e–92e; father of Critobulus, Apol. 33e; anxious about son's education, Euthyd. 306d sq.; comes to Socrates in prison, Crito 43a sq.; contemporary and near neighbor of Socrates, Apol. 33e; does not doubt value of philosophy, Euthyd. 305b; friends in Thessaly, Crito 45c, 53d; his means, ib. 44c,

45a (cf. Euthyd. 304c); offers to be one of Socrates' securities, Apol. 38b (cf. Phaedo 115d); present at death of Socrates, Phaedo 59b, 60a; 63d; — trial of Socrates, Apol. 33e; receives last commands, Phaedo 115b, 118a; Socrates entrusts Xanthippe to his care, ib. 60a; unable to restrain tears, ib. 117d; urges Socrates to escape, Crito 45a sq.; will go to Euthydemus with Socrates, Euthyd. 272d

Critobulus: son of Crito, Apol. 33e; appearance as a boy, Euthyd. 271b; needs a teacher, ib. 306d; offers to be one of Socrates' securities, Apol. 38b; present at death of Socrates, Phaedo 59b; — trial of Socrates, Apol. 33e

Croesus: wise, Epis. 2.311a; 'words of oracle to,' Rep. 8.566c; (*orig.* Polycrates), wealth, Meno 90a

Crommyon, sow of, not courageous, Laches 196e

Cronus: meaning of name, Crat. 396b; son of Oceanus and Tethys, Tim. 40e; gelded Uranus, Euthyph. 6a (cf. Rep. 2.377e); ill-treated by Zeus, Rep. 2.378a (cf. Crat. 404a, Euthyph. 6a, 8b, Symp. 195c); swallowed his sons, Euthyph. 6a; reign of, Crat. 402a, Gorg. 523a sq., Laws 4.713b sq., Statesm. 269a, 272a sq. (cf. 271c, 276a); Love not older than, Symp. 195b; planet sacred to, Epin. 987c; his stupidity, Crat. 396b

crops, poor, fault of humanity, Epin. 979b

crypteia, Laws 1.633c

Ctesippus, of Paeania: Euthyd. 283e sq., Lysis 203a sq., 211c sq.; eager for virtue, Euthyd. 285c sq.; fine young man, but rather wild, ib. 273a (cf. Lysis 204 sq.); friend of Clinias, Euthyd. 274b sq., 283e sq.; — Menexenus, Lysis 206d; passionate character, Euthyd. 283e, 288a, 294b sq., 300d; present at death of Socrates, Phaedo 59b

cubic, number, Tim. 31e

culinary art, analogy of, in defining justice, Rep. 1.332c

culture, consummation of love of beautiful, Rep. 3.403c

cunning, of the wily, Hipp. min. 365e

cupidity, moderation of, firm foundation of state, Laws 5.736e sq.

cupping glasses, Tim. 79e

curators of law: Laws 1.632c, 6.762d, 765a, 767e, 775b, 784c, 7.794b, 799b,

actly what is and is not holy, Euthyph. 5a, 15d; too languid to instruct Socrates, ib. 11e, 12a; prosecutes father, ib. 3e sq., 4a sq., 9a, 15d; a Proteus, ib. 15d; soothsayer, ib. 3b; steeds, Crat. 407d; wisdom, Euthyph. 4b, 5b, 12a, 14d

Eutychides, meaning of name, Crat. 397b

evacuation, of blood, Tim. 81a

Evaemon, son of Poseidon, Criti. 114b

evasion, of military service, Laws 12.943a sq.

even: corresponds to the isosceles, Euthyph. 12d; defined, Laws 10.895e; numbers, sacred to gods below, ib. 4.717a; and odd, Euthyph. 12c sq., Hipp. maj. 302a sq., 303b, Parm. 143d sq., Phaedo 104, 106

Evenor, of Atlantis, Criti. 113c

Evenus, of Paros: inventions in rhetoric, Phaedr. 267a; modest price for instruction, Apol. 20b; philosopher, Phaedo 61c; Socrates' message to, ib. 60d sq.

evidence, law on giving, Laws 11.936e sq.

evil(s): e. for e., Crito 49c sq., 54c; of body and soul, Gorg. 477; cause of friendship, Lysis 221c; cumulative in soul, Epis. 7.335b sq.; desired by no one, Laws 5.731c, Meno 78a sq.; destroyer and corrupter of all things, Rep. 10.608e sq.; can never be done away with, Theaet. 176a; only experienced by soul, Epis. 7.335a; 'if e. be extinct,' Lysis 221; forms of, infinite, Rep. 4.445c; God not author, ib. 2.379 sq., 3.391c (cf. Laws 2.672b, Rep. 2.364b sq.); and good, originate in soul, Charm. 156e (cf. Soph. 228); good for unjust, Laws 2.661d; and ignorance, Meno 77, Protag. 345b, 353 sq. (cf. 357 sq.); involuntary, Hipp. maj. 296b sq., Laws 5.731c, 9.860d, Protag. 345d sq., 352c sq., 355, 358c sq., Tim 86e (cf. Apol. 25e sq., Epis. 7.351c, Gorg. 468, 509e, Soph. 228); has no love for wisdom, Lysis 218a;

more, than good in world, Laws 10.906a; most, mixed with momentary pleasure, Phaedr. 240a sq.; nature of, Protag. 353c sq.; omen, words of, avoided, Epis. 6.323c, Laws 7.800b sq., 12.949b (cf. 11.935b, 12.957b); origin, Statesm. 273b sq. (cf. Tim. 41d sq.); penalty of, to become like, Laws 5.728b (cf. Theaet. 176e sq.); proper object of

ridicule, Rep. 5.452d sq.; reputation, feared, Euthyph. 12c; of soul, Soph. 227e sq.; things, destitute of number, Epin. 978a; voluntary or involuntary, which is better? Hipp. min. 371e sq.;

MEN: company dangerous to virtue, Laws 2.656b; gifts not received by God, ib. 4.716e (see also God); incapable of friendship, Lysis 217b sq., 218a, Phaedr. 255b; cannot injure good, Apol. 30d, 41; not without justice, Rep. 1.350c sq.; more numerous than good, ib. 3.409d (cf. Phaedo 89e); prosperity, Laws 10.899e sq., 905b (cf. Gorg. 470d sq., Laws 2.660e sq., Rep. 2.364a); see also bad(ness); unjust; vice; wicked(ness); wrong

exactness, in arts, Phil. 55e sq.

examiners, see auditors; scrutinies

example: better than precept, Laws 5.729b sq.; use of, illustr., Statesm. 279 sq.

excellence: Epis. 4.320b sq.; often determined by likes and dislikes, Laws 2.655e; refers to use, Rep. 10.601d; see also good(ness / s); virtue(s)

excess: in argument, Statesm. 277a sq., 283b sq., 286b sq.; brings reaction to opposite, Rep. 8.563e sq.; cause of great, Hipp. maj. 294b

exchange: art of, Soph. 223c sq.; two kinds, ib. 219d; see also retail trade(rs)

executioners / executions: Laws 9.872b, 873b, Rep. 4.439e; in Athens, Phaedo 116e

exercise(s): bodily, Hipp. min. 374a sq.; —, needed as counterpoise to intellectual, Tim. 88c sq.; good for children, Laws 7.790e sq.; naked, ib. 1.633c, 6.772a, 8.833d, Rep. 5.452, Theaet. 162b, 169b; see also athletic(s); dance(s) / dancing; gymnastic(s); training

exile (as punishment): not to be resorted to, Epis. 7.331d, 336e; of homicide, Laws 9.867c sq., 868c sq.; of involuntary homicide, ib. 9.865e sq.; of one who strikes parent, ib. 9.881d sq.; of wounding with intent, ib. 9.877a sq.

existence: all things have, Theaet. 186a; and different, Soph. 259a sq.; difficulties respecting, Phil. 16d sq.; divisions, ib. 23c sq.; of gods proved, Laws 10.886–99b (see also God); ideas have real, Hipp. maj. 287c sq.; a kind, Soph. 254d sq.; the 'long

existence (*continued*):
and very difficult syllables of everyday e.,' Statesm. 278d; and nonexistence, Rep. 5.477a; participation
in essence, Phaedo 101 (cf. Rep.
9.585c sq.); perceived by soul,
Theaet. 185c sq.; not predicated of
first elements, ib. 201e sq.; relative
and absolute, Soph. 255c sq.; revolutions of, Statesm. 270c sq.; *see also*
being; essence; natural / nature

exordium, of discourse, Hipp. maj.
286a

expectation: Laws 1.644c; pleasure of,
Phil. 39c sq.; *see also* anticipation /
anticipatory; hope

expedient, *see* advantage; beneficial
/ benefit

expenses, Dionysius to help defray
Plato's, Epis. 13.361e sq.

experience: and arts, Gorg. 448c; a
criterion of pleasures, Rep. 9.582;
as teacher, Epis. 6.323a; touchstone
of everything, ib. 8.355c; *see also*
routine

experiment, cannot verify nature, Tim.
68d

experts, and rhetoricians, Gorg. 455b
sq., 458e sq. (cf. 514); *see also* skill

expiation: of guilt, Laws 8.831a,
9.854b, 865 sq., 868 sq., 872e sq.,
881e, Rep. 2.364b sq.; to purify a
house, Laws 9.877e; *see also* purification

expiration, Tim. 78e sq.

explanation, *see* account; description

exponents of religious law: Laws
6.759c sq., 775a; election, ib. 6.759d
sq.; *see also* canonists; interpreters

exports, and imports, laws on, Laws
8.847b sq.

exposure, of children, *see* infanticide

extreme(s): and mean, Tim. 36a; in
men, uncommon, Phaedo 90a

eye(s): Tim. 45b sq.; beautiful, Hipp.
maj. 295c; blinking, a defect, Hipp.
min. 374d; medicine, Charm. 156b
sq., Lysis 210a; and sight, Rep.
6.507d sq., Theaet. 156d; of soul,
Rep. 7.527e, 533d; soul like, ib.
6.508c sq., 7.518; *see also* sight;
vision(s)

F

fable(s): of antiquity, truth not certainly known, Rep. 2.382c; imitative, ib. 3.392d sq.; of pleasure and
pain, Phaedo 60c; *see also* Aesop;
fiction; myth(ology); tradition(s)

fact, and ideal, Rep. 5.472b sq.

faction: bred by inequality, Epis.
7.377b; causes, Laws 5.744d, 6.757a,
e, 12.945d sq., Rep. 8.556e; dist.
from war, Laws 1.629c sq., Rep.
5.470b sq. (cf. Laws 1.628b sq.);
punished, Laws 9.856b sq.; among
reformers of Syracuse, Epis. 7.336e,
8.352c; *see also* discord; enmity;
revolution; strife, civil; war

factor, bodily, in universe, cause of
evil, Statesm. 273b sq. (cf. Tim. 41c
sq.); *see also* bodies / body; evil(s)

faculties: how different, Rep. 5.477b
sq.; of soul, ib. 6.511d sq., 7.533e
(cf. Theaet. 185c sq.; *see also*
soul(s))

failure, *see* evasion

fair: and foul, Protag. 332c; and good,
Gorg. 474d; standard of, ib. 474d
sq.; *see also* beauty; comeliness;
friendly

faith, *see* belief; God; judgment(s);
opinion

faithfulness, in civil strife, Laws
1.630a sq.; *see also* loyalty

fallacies, Euthyd. 275 sq., 283e sq.,
293 sq., 297e sq., Meno 80d sq. (cf.
Theaet. 165a); *see also* eristic;
Sophist(s)

false: charges, Laws 12.943e; and
good, Hipp. min. 367c sq.; opinion,
impossible, Euthyd. 286d; swearing,
Laws 12.948d sq.; thinking, Soph.
240d sq.; and wily, Hipp. min. 365b
sq.; witness, Laws 11.937b sq.; the
word, Hipp. min. 365d sq.; *see also*
forswearing; perjuries / perjury

falsehood(s): and assertion of not-
being, Soph. 240d sq., 241b; essential, and f. in words, Rep. 2.382;
alien to God, ib. 2.382 (cf. Laws
11.917a); hateful, Rep. 6.485c sq.,
490b; impossible, Crat. 429d sq.,
Euthyd. 283e sq., Soph. 260d, 261b;
intentional and unintentional, Hipp.
min. 370e sq., 371e sq.; in judgment, Soph. 264b sq., Theaet. 187b
sq.; and knowledge, Hipp. min.
366e sq.; medicine used only by
state, Rep. 2.382c, 3.389b, 5.459c
sq. (cf. Laws 2.663d sq., Rep.
3.414b sq.); nature of, Soph. 240d
sq., Theaet. 189b sq., 191e; in opinion, Phil. 37e sq., Theaet. 167a (*see
also* opinion); of poets, Rep. 2.377d
sq.; in speech, Soph. 263b sq.; in
thought, ib. 260c; = wrong assignment of names, Crat. 431b; *see also*
deception; imposture; lie(s)

future life (*continued*):
10.904d sq., 12.959b sq., Phaedo
108b, 114, Phaedr. 249a, Rep.
2.363d sq., 10.614d sq., Theaet.
177a; *see also* Hades; world below

G

gadfly, *see* fly
Gadira, region of, Criti. 114b
Gadirus, = Eumelus, Criti. 114b
gamecocks, fighting, Theaet. 164c; *see also* cock(s)
games: ball, Euthyd. 277b, Phaedo 110b, Theaet. 146a (cf. Epis. 13.363d); dice, Laws 12.969a, Rep. 2.374c, 10.604c; —, invented by Theuth, Phaedr. 274d; draughts, Charm. 174b, Gorg. 450d, Laws 5.739a, 7.820c sq., Rep. 1.333b, 2.374c, 6.487b, Statesm. 292e; —, invented by Theuth, Phaedr. 274d; knucklebones, Lysis 206e; odd and even, ib. 206e; polis, Rep. 4.422e; puppets, Laws 1.644d sq. (cf. Rep. 7.514); for both sexes, Laws 7.813d sq., 8.828c sq. (*see also* dance(s) / dancing; festival(s); gymnastic(s)); training for, laborious, ib. 7.807c (cf. 8.839e sq.); tug of war (?), Theaet. 181a;
OF CHILDREN: not to be altered, Laws 7.797b sq.; influence upon manners and morals, ib. 7.797a sq.; means of education, ib. 1.643b sq. (cf. Rep. 7.536e); *see also* play; sports
Ganymede: Phaedr. 255c; story, invented by Cretans, Laws 1.636d
garden, palace, in Syracuse, Epis. 2.313a, 3.319a, 7.347a, 348c, 349d
garments, *see* appareling
geese, flocks of tame, in Thessaly, Statesm. 264c
Gelon (tyrant of Syracuse), subjected Carthaginians, Epis. 7.333a
gems: engraving, Hipp. min. 368c; in upper earth, Phaedo 110e
genealogies: Hellenic, Tim. 22b, 23b; of heroes and men, Spartan delight in, Hipp. maj. 285d
general(s): election of, Laws 6.755b sq.; ideas, unity and existence of, Phil. 15b sq. (*see also* idea(s)); to know arithmetic and geometry, Rep. 7.522d sq., 525b, 526d, 527c (cf. Laws 7.819c); and military experts, 'craftsmen of war,' Laws 11.921d; names for, Crat. 394b; produce victory in war, Euthyph. 14a; and the

rhapsode, Ion 540d sq.; why superior to soothsayer, Laches 198e sq.; ART OF: Statesm. 304e sq.; branch of hunting, Euthyd. 290b (cf. Soph. 219c sq.); defensive, Epin. 975e; servant of statesmanship, Statesm. 305a; *see also* army; commander; common; generic; military; soldier(s)
generalization, in style, Phaedr. 265e; *see also* division, and classification
generation(s): Phaedo 71, Tim. 49e, 50c, 52d sq.; of animals, ib. 90e–92; cause of, Phaedo 96 (cf. 101, Phil. 27a sq.) and corruption, Phaedo 96 sq.; and essence, Rep. 7.525b sq.; many, of things, Laws 10.904a (cf. Tim. 42b sq., 91a); and motion, Tim. 38a; 'nurse of all g.,' ib. 49b–52; truths of, probable only, ib. 59d; world of, ib. 37b; *see also* becoming; beginning; coming to be; genesis
generic, notions, Meno 74 sq.; *see also* common; general(s); idea(s)
genesis: of animals, Protag. 320d sq.; and essence, Rep. 7.526e; of man, Statesm. 271a sq., Symp. 189d sq.; *see also* creation; generation(s)
gentleness: of just, Gorg. 516c; ought to be in every man, Laws 5.731b; mark of lover of wisdom, Rep. 2.375e sq., 3.410d sq., 6.486b
genus, and species, Euthyph. 12c sq.; *see also* class(es); kinds
geographers, mistaken about earth, Phaedo 108c
geometer, best able to be false about geometry, Hipp. min. 367d sq.
geometrical / geometry: diagrams, Crat. 436d; in division of species, Statesm. 266a sq.; figures, beauty of, Phil. 51c; Hippias wont to discourse on, Hipp. maj. 285c (cf. Hipp. min. 367d sq.); hypotheses, Meno 86e sq.; invented by Theuth, Phaedr. 274d; irrational lines, Rep. 7.534d; to be learned by rulers, ib. 7.526c sq. (cf. Laws 7.817e); necessities, and those of love, Rep. 5.458d; notions, perceived by understanding, ib. 6.511c (cf. Theaet. 185c sq.); of plane surfaces, Laws 7.817e, 819e sq.; pure knowledge its object, Rep. 7.527a; of solids, Meno 82b–85b, Theaet. 147d sq.; —, 'not yet investigated,' Rep. 7.528b; *see also* mathematical / mathematician / mathematics; mensuration
gerousia, at Lacedaemon, Laws 3.692a

Geryon: Euthyd. 299c; oxen of, Gorg. 484b; physique, Laws 7.795c

gestation, and nursing, Laws 7.789

ghosts: Laws 10.910a, Phaedo 81d (cf. Laws 5.738c, Tim. 72a); and bodies, Laws 12.959b (cf. Phaedo 81); *see also* apparitions

giants, battles of, Rep. 2.378c, Soph. 246a (cf. Euthyph. 6b sq., Symp. 190b)

gifts, of nature: Phaedr. 269d sq., Rep. 2.370b, 5.455b sq., 7.535; may be perverted, ib. 6.491b sq., 495a sq., 7.519a (cf. Laws 5.747b sq., 7.819a, 10.908c sq.); *see also* bribes; prize(s); rewards

γιγνώσκω, etc., *see* know(ing); knowledge

girls: contests, Laws 8.833d, 834d; education, ib. 7.794c sq., 804e sq., 813e sq.; to learn use of spear and shield, ib. 7.794d, 804e sq.; *see also* females; women

giver, of names, Crat. 393e, 404b, 408a, 414b, 427c, 431e, 436b sq., 437e, Laws 7.816b; *see also* legislator(s); maker / making; names

glass, Tim. 61b

Glaucon, famous rhapsode, Ion 530d

— father of Charmides, Charm. 154b, 158b, Protag. 315a

— son of Ariston: Parm. 126a, Rep. 1.327a, 347a, 2.357a, 372d, 3.398c, 4.427d, 5.450a, 6.506d, 9.576b, 10.608d; contentious, ib. 8.548d; disposition, ib. 2.368a; intrepid and enterprising spirit, ib. 2.357a; distinguished at Battle of Megara, ib. 2.368a; breeds hunting dogs and cocks, ib. 5.459a; not dialectician, ib. 7.533a; lover, ib. 5.474d sq. (cf. 3.402e); musician, ib. 3.398c, 7.531a; will contribute money for Socrates, ib. 1.337d

— *Symposium* had been narrated to by Apollodorus, Symp. 172b

Glaucus (of Chios?), skill of a, Phaedo 108d

— sea god, Rep. 10.611d

— (son of Hippolochus), Symp. 218e

globe: earth a, Tim. 33b; head a, ib. 73e; *see also* ball; sphere / spherical

gluttony, Phaedr. 238a, Rep. 9.586a sq., Tim. 72e sq.

γνώμη, *see* etymology; judgment(s); knowledge; reason

goat: keeping, Laws 1.639a; 'the g. of tragedy,' Crat. 408c

God: can never cease to exist, Phaedo 106e; cannot contend with necessity,

Laws 7.818b (cf. Protag. 345d); does not deceive, Rep. 2.382; measure of all things, Laws 4.716c; never changes, Rep. 2.380d sq.; = perfect righteousness, Theaet. 176b; nature of, fit subject of inquiry, Laws 7.821a (cf. 12.966c sq.); moves straight to his end, ib. 4.716a; alone can combine the many or dissolve the one, Tim. 68d; best of causes, ib. 29a; can give life to any body, Epin. 983b;

creator, Soph. 265b sq., Statesm. 269c sq., Tim. 30 sq., 38c, 53b sq., 55c (cf. Laws 10.886–99b); maker of all things, Rep. 10.597d; not author of evil, ib. 2.379 sq., 3.391c (cf. Laws 2.672b, Rep. 2.364b sq.); not cause of all things, but of the good only, ib. 2.379c sq.; source of all good things, Epin. 977a; aided by chance and skill in government of world, Laws 4.709b (cf. 10.888e sq.); — by subordinate deities, Tim. 41a sq.;

= providence, Epis. 8.353b; the shepherd, Statesm. 271d sq., 275a sq., 276a, d (cf. Criti. 109b sq.); endowed man with understanding, Epin. 978c; has given divination, Tim. 71e; marvelous Sophist, Rep. 10.596d (cf. Laws 10.902e); approves of the intermediate condition, Laws 7.792d; will not receive gifts of the evil, ib. 4.716e; use of word, sign of serious letter from Plato, Epis. 13.363b

god(s): Crat. 416c, Epis. 13.363b, Tim. 40a sq., 42d; not eternal, but imperishable, Laws 10.904a; share immortality by will of creator, Tim. 41a sq.; genealogy of, ib. 40e (cf. Crat. 402b); generation of, Epin. 980 sq.; have absolute knowledge, Laws 1.641d, Parm. 134c sq.; wise, Phaedr. 278d (cf. Tim. 51e); attend to all things, Laws 10.902a sq.; neither unintelligent, nor ignorant, Epin. 988a, 991d, Laws 10.900c sq.; beauty of, Hipp. maj. 289a sq.; do not lack courage, Laws 10.901e; feel neither pleasure nor pain, Phil. 33b; have pleasant life of tyrant, Epis. 3.315b; cannot cope with necessity, Laws 5.741a; procession of, Phaedr. 246e sq.; each has own work, ib. 247a; strife of, respecting Attica, Menex. 237c (cf. Criti. 109b); war of, and giants, Rep. 2.378c, Soph. 246a (cf. Euthyph. 6b sq., Symp. 190b);

good(ness / s) (*continued*):
government, Laws 6.770e; should have the renown they deserve, Epis. 4.320b; rule themselves, Laws 1.626e sq., 644b; sacrifices of, acceptable to God, ib. 4.716d sq.; self-sufficient, Lysis 215a sq., Rep. 3.387d (cf. Menex. 248a); seem simple from inexperience of evil, Rep. 3.409a; sons of, not g., Laches 179b sq., 180b, Meno 93 sq., Protag. 324d sq. (cf. Laws 3.694d); unfortunate, Rep. 2.364a; = the wise, ib. 1.350b; *see also* excellence; hero(es); just-(ice); pleasure(s); right(ness / s); virtue(s)

Gorgias: Gorg. 449a–60e; held art of persuasion superior to all others, Phil. 58a sq.; does not claim to teach virtue, Meno 95c; deference to opinion, Gorg. 482d, 487a (cf. 494d); definition of virtue, Meno 73c sq.; earned large sum of Athenian money, Hipp. maj. 282b; — more than any other craftsman from his art, ib. 282d; goes the round of the cities, Apol. 19e; influence at Larissa, Meno 70b; — on Meno, ib. 71c sq.; manner of answering questions, ib. 70c (cf. 76c); master of rhetoric, Symp. 198c; persuades patients to take medicine, Gorg. 456b; realized probability deserves more respect than truth, Phaedr. 267a; rhetoric, that of Nestor, ib. 261b sq.; spoke before Athenian Assembly, Hipp. maj. 282b; stays with Callicles, Gorg. 447b; has not trained Meno properly, Meno 96d; visit to Athens as envoy of Leontini, Hipp. maj. 282b; *see also* rhetoric; Sophist(s)

Gorgons, Phaedr. 229d

Gortyn, in Crete, colonized from G. in Peloponnesus, Laws 4.708a

government(s): to be administered in interest of rulers? Rep. 1.338d sq., 343b sq., 345c sq. (cf. Statesm. 295e); ancient Athenian constitution, Laws 3.698b sq. (cf. Menex. 238c); art, grew up slowly, Protag. 322b sq.; difficulties of correct administration, Epis. 7.325c sq.; good, possible without laws, Statesm. 294 sq.; without knowledge, source of misery, ib. 302a; nurture of man, Menex. 238c; origin, Laws 3.676c sq.; Persian, in days of Cyrus, ib. 3.694a sq.; present, unworthy of philosophical nature, Rep. 6.497b; —, 'party ascendancies,' Laws

8.832c; science of, attained by few, Statesm. 300c sq.; voices of, Epis. 5.321d sq.;

FORMS OF: no, destroyed except by self, Laws 3.683e; disintegration in, Rep. 8.545c sq.; elements of all, combined in Spartan and Cretan, Laws 4.712d sq.; first-, second-, and third-best, ib. 5.739, 7.807b; imperfect, the five or four, Rep. 4.445c, 8.544, Statesm. 291d sq., 301 sq. (cf. Laws 4.712c); —, order in capacity for improvement, Laws 4.710e sq.; —, unwilling to accept true and scientific ruler, Statesm. 301c; peculiar barbarian, Rep. 8.544d; present, based on supremacy of certain groups, Laws 12.962d sq. (cf. 4.713a, 714e sq.); —, in evil case, Epis. 7.326a, Rep. 6.492e, 496c sq.; three, Epis. 5.321d; *see also* constitution(s); model city; polity; rule / ruling; state(s)

grace / Graces: aid poet, Laws 3.682a; good, waits upon good disposition, Rep. 3.400d; all life and every art full of, ib. 3.401a; akin to virtue, ib. 3.401a (cf. 7.522a)

gracefulness, Hipp. min. 374b

grammar: Crat. 431e; 'a copulativus,' ib. 405d; in education, Euthyd. 276a sq.; invented by Theuth, Phil. 18b (cf. Phaedr. 274d); taught by Prodicus, Crat. 384b; teaches proper combination of letters, Soph. 253a; *see also* dialect; etymology

grandeur, of soul, one of philosopher's virtues, Rep. 6.490c (cf. 6.486a, Theaet. 173c sq.)

grapes, rules about picking, Laws 8.844e

grasshoppers, *see* cicadas

gratification, *see* enjoyment

gratitude, most felt by destitute, Phaedr. 233d

graveyards, apparitions at, Phaedo 81d

gray, *see* dun

grazing, cattle on neighbor's land, penalty, Laws 8.843d

great(ness): absolute and relative, Rep. 10.602d (cf. 4.438b, 10.605b); itself, Parm. 150b sq.; men, sons of, commonly receive bad education, Laws 3.694d sq. (*see also* son(s)); and smallness, Parm. 149d sq., 161d sq., Phaedo 96d sq., 101a, 102c, Statesm. 283d sq. (cf. Rep. 5.479b); things are, by excess, Hipp. maj. 294b; *see also* bigness; largeness

hunger: Lysis 220e sq., Phil. 31e, 34e, Rep. 4.437d sq.; inanition of body, ib. 9.585a sq.

hunter, not wise man, Epin. 975c

hunting: acquisitive art, Soph. 219c sq. (cf. Rep. 2.373b); divisions, Soph. 219e sq. (cf. Euthyd. 290b sq., Laws 7.823b); = making war on beasts, Protag. 322a; valuable to young, Laws 6.763b; see also chase, the; fowling

huntsman, knows care of dogs, Euthyph. 13a sq.

hurt, see damage(s); injury

husbandmen / husbandry: allowed, Laws 5.743d (cf. 12.949e); formed separate caste in ancient Attica, Criti. 111e; laws, Laws 8.842d sq.; among nobler arts, ib. 10.889d; not science but instinct, Epin. 975b; of soul, Phaedr. 276e (cf. Theaet. 167b); see also agriculture; farmer(s) / farming

Hydra, Heracles and, Euthyd. 297c

hymn(s): to Apollo by Socrates, Phaedo 60d, 61b; to follow fixed type, Laws 7.799a sq., 801a; funeral, ib. 7.800e, 12.947b; to gods, allowed, Rep. 10.607a (cf. Laws 3.700a sq., 7.801e); marriage, Rep. 5.460a; see also chant; preludes

Hyperboreans, Charm. 158b

hypotheses / hypothesis / hypothetical: as method, Parm. 136a sq.; case at law, Phaedr. 273b sq.; of the one, Parm. 137b sq. (see also one); in sciences, Rep. 7.533c sq.; use, Meno 86e sq., Phaedo 100a, 101d; see also assumption

I

iambic: measure, Rep. 3.400b; poets, Laws 11.935e

Iapetus, Love not older than, Symp. 195b

Iatrocles, freed by Plato, Epis. 13.363e
— a physician's name, Crat. 394c

Iberians, given to intoxication, Laws 1.637d

Ibis, bird sacred to Theuth, Phaedr. 274c

Ibycus: fell in love in old age, Parm. 137a; quoted, fr. 24, Phaedr. 242d

Iccus, of Tarentum: self-restraint, Laws 8.839e sq.; Sophist in disguise, Protag. 316d

ice, Tim. 59e

Ida, dwellers on slopes, Laws 3.681e

idea(s): absolute i., Phaedo 65, 74, 100b sq., Protag. 360c, Rep. 5.476; association, Phaedo 73d sq., 76a; and assumptions, Rep. 6.510b sq.; of best, Tim. 46d; a cause like sun, Rep. 6.508, 7.517b sq. (cf. 7.516c); cause of love, Phaedr. 251; causes, Phaedo 100; in creation of world, Tim. 30 sq. (cf. 37c sq.); difficulties in way of, Phil. 15 sq.; Erastus and Coriscus have love of, Epis. 6.322d; existence, Crat. 439c sq., Hipp. maj. 287c sq.; of good, apprehended by dialectician, Rep. 7.534b sq. (cf. Phil. 65d sq.); —, source of truth, Rep. 6.508d sq. (cf. 6.505); and immortality, Phaedo 76; in individuals, Phil. 16d sq.;

knowledge and, Crat. 440c; — of, must precede particular k., Phaedo 75; loveliness, Phaedr. 250; and names, Crat. 389d sq.; nature, Rep. 10.596; origin of abstract, ib. 7.523 sq.; and phenomena, ib. 5.476, 6.507b sq.; prior to reality, Phaedo 75; progress toward, Symp. 211; recollection, Meno 81c sq., 85c sq., Phaedo 75, Phaedr. 249c sq.; require examples, Statesm. 277d; 'that which really is,' Rep. 6.507b; unchangeable, Phaedo 78; uniqueness, Rep. 10.597c sq. (cf. Tim. 28, 51e sq.); see also essence; form(s); logic; metaphysics

ideal(ists / s): Soph. 246b sq., 248a sq. (cf. Phaedo 100, Rep. 6.505a); use, in education, Laws 1.643e sq.; —, in legislation, ib. 5.746b sq.; value, Rep. 5.472b sq.; STATE: how commenced, ib. 6.501, 7.541; difficult to realize, Laws 4.710e sq., Rep. 5.472b sq., 6.502 (cf. Epis. 7.325d, 331e sq.); possible? Laws 5.739c sq., Rep. 5.471c sq., 473, 6.499b sq., 7.540d sq. (cf. Laws 4.712a, 12.968e sq., Rep. 7.520 sq.); see also cities / city; constitution(s); education; guardians of state; ruler(s); state(s)

idleness: not attributable to gods, Laws 10.900e sq.; mother of wantonness, ib. 8.835e

ignorance / ignorant: 'to act beneath self,' Protag. 358c; of beautiful in reality, prevails, Hipp. maj. 294d; causes misconduct, Laws 9.863c; complete, not so bad as misapplied knowledge, ib. 7.819a; having conceit of wisdom, ib. 9.863c, Phil. 49a (cf. Apol. 29); cultivated in beloved

285d; ɩ, imitative of motion, Crat. 426e; image of large and small, Rep. 2.368d (cf. 3.402b); insertion, Crat. 414c sq., 417b, Phaedr. 244c sq.; invented by Theuth, Phil. 18b;

λ, expressive of smoothness, Crat. 427b, 434c; how learned, Statesm. 277e sq.; meaning of, illustr., Crat. 426d sq.; ν, ib. 427b sq.; names, generally different from l. themselves, ib. 393d; o, expressive of roundness, ib. 427c; φ, ψ, ib. 427a; ρ, expressive of motion, ib. 426c sq., 434c; σ, ib. 427a, 434c; and syllables, Theaet. 202e sq.; τ, expressive of rest, Crat. 427b; taught in school, Protag. 312b; time spent in learning, Laws 7.810a; with which universe is spelled out, Statesm. 278c; ζ, Crat. 427a; see also alphabet; names; orthography

—, Plato instructs Dionysius to burn, Epis. 2.314c; reading of Plato's, a contract, ib. 6.323c sq.

Leucippe, mother of Clito, Criti. 113d

Leucolophides, father of Adimantus, Protag. 315e

levies, tax, in war, Laws 12.949d

libations, Criti. 120a, Laws 7.807a (cf. Phaedo 117b)

liberality, virtue of philosopher, Phaedo 114e, Rep. 6.486a

liberty: and anarchy, Epis. 8.354d sq.; easily becomes anarchy, Laws 3.701b; under best system of laws, = Dion's political ideal, Epis. 7.324b, 336a (cf. 7.351a sq.); mark of democracy, Rep. 8.557b sq., 561b–63 (cf. Laws 12.962e); necessary in state, Laws 3.697c sq.; passion for, Epis. 8.354d; of speech, at Athens, Protag. 319d; see also freedom

Libya: Criti. 108e, Tim. 25a sq.; Ammon god of, Statesm. 257b

license: begins in music, Laws 3.701a sq.; in democracies, Rep. 8.562d sq.; of Spartan women, Laws 1.637c, 6.780e sq.; see also lawlessness

licentiousness, see promiscuity

Licymnius, his words, Phaedr. 267c

lie(s): gods not to be represented as telling, Rep. 2.382; hateful to philosopher, ib. 6.490b; impossible, Euthyd. 283e sq.; 'one noble l.,' Rep. 3.414b; of poets, ib. 3.408b sq. (cf. Laws 12.941b, Rep. 10.597e sq.); rulers may, ib. 3.389b sq., 5.459c sq. (cf. Laws 2.663d sq., Rep. 3.414b sq.); see also falsehood(s)

life: 'a l. for a l.,' Laws 9.870e, 872e sq.; according to nature, ib. 10.890a (cf. Gorg. 483–84c); beautiful l. = beauty, Hipp. maj. 291d sq.; no boon to sinner, Laws 9.862e; changes in us during, Symp. 207d sq. (cf. Laws 7.788d, 11.929c); of citizens, Laws 7.806d sq.; in days of Cronus, Statesm. 271b sq.; after death, Epin. 992b sq.; in early state, Rep. 2.372; four kinds, Laws 5.733; guided by harmony and rhythm, ib. 2.655 sq.; hard enough as it is, Statesm. 299e (cf. Laws 11.937d); hardships, Epin. 973c sq.;

of intelligence, Phil. 60e sq.; intolerable without virtue, Rep. 4.445a sq.; just, pleasantest, Laws 2.662d sq.; just, or unjust, which is better? Rep. 1.347e sq.; loses zest in old age, ib. 1.329a; man's, belongs to gods, Phaedo 62; measured, dear to God, Laws 4.716c (cf. Rep. 10.612e sq.); mixed, Phil. 22a sq., 27d, 61b sq.; necessities of, Rep. 2.369d, 373a; needs empirical arts, Phil. 62; noblest, pleasantest, Laws 5.732e sq.; nothing in, worthy of concern, Rep. 10.604c (cf. Laws 1.644d sq., 7.803b sq., 804b, Rep. 6.486a);

of peace, and that of war, Laws 1.628c sq., 7.803d; of philosophy, and that of covetousness, Phaedr. 256c (cf. Theaet. 172c sq.); pleasant and painless, end of moral activity, Protag. 358b; of pleasure, Phil. 20e sq., 60d sq.; not always preferable to death, Apol. 28b, 38e, Gorg. 511e sq., 522e, Laws 8.828d, 831a (cf. 12.944d sq.); prime of, Rep. 5.460e; primitive, Laws 3.677b sq., Statesm. 274b sq.; and the real, Soph. 249a; and reason, Phil. 21d sq.; rhythm and harmonious adjustment essential to, Protag. 326b; right road in, the intermediate, Laws 7.792c sq. (cf. 5.728e sq., Rep. 10.619a); rules of, Hipp. maj. 286b; 'seas of l.,' Phaedo 85c (cf. Laws 7.803b);

shortness of, Rep. 10.608c (cf. Phaedo 107c); three sorts, Phil. 43c sq., Rep. 9.581c sq.; tragicomedy, Phil. 50b; true way of, Gorg. 527, Laws 7.803c sq. (cf. Hipp. maj. 304b sq.); unexamined, not worth living, Apol. 38a; valuable only when good, Crito 48b, Laws 2.661b sq., 4.707d (cf. 5.727d, Rep. 4.445a sq.); of virtue, toilsome, Laws

medicine (*continued*):
　6.323b, Rep. 4.426b, Theaet. 149c;
　to consider whole, Charm. 156b sq.,
　Phaedr. 270c (cf. Laws 10.903d);
　cure for headaches, Charm. 156b
　sq.; dear for sake of health, Lysis
　219c sq.; defensive art, Epin. 976a;
　diet, Laws 2.659e sq.; and education,
　Laches 185c sq.; empirical art, Phil.
　56b; and friendship, Lysis 217; and
　government, Statesm. 293b sq.;
　Greek diagnosis, Protag. 352a; and
　gymnastics, Gorg. 464b sq., 517e sq.,
　Soph. 229a; and justice, Rep. 1.332c;
　oil forbidden sick, Protag. 334c; not
　to preserve unhealthy and intem-
　perate patients, Rep. 3.406 sq., 408a,
　4.425e sq. (cf. Tim. 89b sq.); pro-
　fessors of, do not understand it, Tim.
　88a; and punishment, Gorg. 478 sq.;
　and rhetoric, Phaedr. 270b sq.; true
　use, Rep. 3.406; two sorts, Laws
　4.720, Rep. 5.459c sq.; *see also* doc-
　tor(s)
medicines, of doubtful value, Tim. 89b
　sq.
Mediterranean, a harbor, Tim. 25a
meetings, of citizens, convoked and
　dissolved by council, Laws 6.758d;
　see also assembly
μεγαλοπρέπεια, *see* dignity; grandeur of
　soul; magnificence; nobility
Megara: Epis. 7.329a, Phaedo 59c,
　Theaet. 142c; Battle, Rep. 2.368a;
　Socrates' bones, would go to, Phaedo
　99a; walk to, recommended by He-
　rodicus, Phaedr. 227d; well-governed
　city, Crito 53b
— (in Sicily), Theognis citizen of,
　Laws 1.630a
Megillus, of Sparta: Laws 1.624a sq.;
　willing to accept laws on love, ib.
　8.837e, 842a
Melampus, ancestor of Theoclymenus
　the diviner, Ion 538e
melancholy, Tim. 87a
Melanippe, in Euripides, Symp. 177a;
　see also Euripides
Meles, father of Cinesias, lyre player
　and bad singer, Gorg. 502a
Melesias, son of Thucydides: Laches
　178a sq., 184e; not equal to father,
　ib. 179c, Meno 94c; expert wrestler,
　ib. 94c; lives with Lysimachus,
　Laches 179b
Meletus: of deme of Pitthos, Euthyph.
　2b; appearance, ib. 2b; youth of,
　ib. 2b sq.; prosecutes Socrates, Apol.
　23e, 28a, 30d, 34b, 35d, 36a,
　Euthyph. 2b, 3b, 5a sq., 12e, 15e,

Theaet. 210d (cf. Apol. 19b); ques-
　tioned by Socrates, Apol. 24–28
Melissus, philosopher, Theaet. 180e,
　183e
Melite, deme of Attica, Parm. 126c
melodies / melody: in education, Laws
　2.654e sq., 670b sq., Rep. 3.398c sq.;
　express virtue and vice, Laws 2.655a
　sq.; of Marsyas and Olympus, Symp.
　215c; and rhythms to be accommo-
　dated, Laws 2.669c sq., 670c sq.;
　see also meter; rhythm(s); scales;
　tunes
melting, Tim. 58e
Memoria technica, of Evenus of Paros,
　allud. to, Phaedr. 267a
Memory: invoked, Criti. 108d, Euthyd.
　275c; mother of Muses, Theaet. 191d
memory: Epis. 7.344 sq., Phil. 11b,
　33c sq., 35a sq., 60d; active in child-
　hood, Tim. 26b sq.; art, Hipp. min.
　368d, 369a, Phaedr. 228b sq.; ele-
　ment in pleasure, ib. 21b sq.; in-
　jured by invention of writing,
　Phaedr. 275a; nature, Theaet. 191c
　sq., 193b–96a; of perception, ib.
　163e sq., 166a sq.; philosopher to
　have a good, Rep. 6.486c sq., 487a,
　490c, 494b, 7.535c; dist. from recol-
　lection, Phaedr. 275a, Phil. 34b sq.;
　and sensations, ib. 39a; unites
　with perception to form opinion, ib.
　38b sq.; *see also* mnemonic
Mende, Protag. 315a
mendicant, *see* beggars
Menelaus: 'most indifferent spearman,'
　Symp. 174c; and Proteus, Euthyd.
　288b; treatment, when wounded,
　Rep. 3.408a
Menexenus: Lysis 211a, 212a sq., 216a
　sq., Menex. 234a sq.; son of Demo-
　phon, Lysis 207b; friend of Ctesip-
　pus, ib. 206d; — Lysis, ib. 206d;
　scholar of Ctesippus, ib. 211c; fond
　of dispute, ib. 211b; ready to hold
　office, if agreeable to Socrates,
　Menex. 234b; present at death of
　Socrates, Phaedo 59b
Meno: son of Alexidemus, Meno 76e;
　hereditary guest-friend of the Great
　King, ib. 78d; imperious, ib. 76b,
　86d sq.; handsome, ib. 76b, 80c;
　beloved by Aristippus, ib. 70b; be-
　numbed by Socrates, ib. 80a; ex-
　amination of his slave by Socrates,
　ib. 82b–85b
Menoetius, father of Patroclus, Laws
　12.944a, Rep. 3.388d

mind(s) (*continued*):
gence / intelligible; knowledge; un-
derstanding(s); wisdom / wise
'mine,' and 'not mine,' common cause
of discord, Rep. 5.462c
minister, *see* authorities / authority;
directors; ruler(s); supervisors
Minos: Cretan lawgiver, Laws 1.630d;
harassed Athenians, ib. 4.706a sq.;
judge among dead, Apol. 41a, Gorg.
523e sq., 524a, 526c sq.; laws derived from Zeus, Laws 1.624a sq.,
and Polyidus, Epis. 2.311b; 'used to
repair to confer with father every
ninth year,' Laws 1.624b
minstrels, hired, at funerals, Laws
7.800e (cf. 12.959e sq.)
mirrors, images in, Soph. 239d, Tim.
46a (cf. Theaet. 193c, Tim. 71b)
misanthropy, cause of, Phaedo 89d sq.
misconduct, causes, Laws 9.863b sq.
miser, *see* stinginess
misfortune, to be borne patiently, Rep.
3.387d sq., 10.602b–606b; *see also*
grief; sorrow
misology, Phaedo 89d sq. (cf. Rep.
3.411d)
mission ship, from Athens to Delos,
Crito 44, Phaedo 58
mist, dregs of aether, Phaedo 109c
mistrust, bred by inequality, Epis.
7.337b
Mithaecus, wrote Sicilian cookery
book, Gorg. 518b
Mitylene, *see* Mytilene
mixed principles, Phil. 25d sq.
mixture: the perfect life, Phil. 61c sq.;
of pleasure and pain, ib. 46a sq.,
48b sq., 49a
mnemonic art, Hipp. maj. 285e; *see
also* memory
Mnemosyne, *see* Memory
Mneseus, son of Poseidon, Criti. 114c
Mnesitheus, meaning of name, Crat.
394e
mode(s): Dorian and Phrygian alone
accepted, Rep. 3.399a; Ionian, ib.
3.398e; Lydian, ib. 3.398e; *see also*
harmonies / harmony
model, heavenly, Rep. 6.500e sq.; *see
also* original; pattern(s); standards
MODEL CITY (in *Laws*):
territory: arrangement and division of lots, 5.737c sq., 745c sq.; —
of villages, 8.848c sq.; lots not to be
sold, 5.741b sq.; provisions for defense, 6.760b sq.; public works,
6.760e sq.;
city: buildings, 6.778 sq.; public
works, 6.763c sq.; sanitation, 6.779c;

situation, 5.745b; walls not required,
6.778d sq.;
citizens: age for marriage, 4.721b
sq., 6.772d, 774a sq., 785b; — military service, 6.785b; — office,
6.785b; classes of, 5.744c, 6.754d;
common tables, 6.780b sq., 783b,
7.806e, 8.842b; — for women,
6.781c sq., 7.806e, 8.839d; control of
private life, 6.780a; country dwellings, 8.848c; each family to have
two houses, 5.745e; not to follow
money-making pursuits, 5.741e,
743d, 11.919d sq.; the good, 7.822e
sq.; life of men, 7.806d sq.; —
women, 7.804e sq., 806e sq.; number, 5.737c sq., 6.771a sq.; not to
possess gold or silver, 5.742a, 743d,
746a; procreation of children,
6.783b sq.; may pursue husbandry
moderately, 5.743d; register of
births, 6.785a; — property, 5.745a,
6.754d sq., 8.850a, 9.855b, 11.914c;
sections, 5.745d sq.; social meetings
of lads and lasses, 6.771e sq.; stock
to be well mingled, 6.773d;
education: astronomy, 7.820e sq.;
boys and attendants, 7.808d sq.; the
chase, 7.823b sq.; regulations for
comedy and tragedy, 7.816d sq.;
compulsory, 7.804d; contests of
rhapsodes, 8.834e; dancing, 7.795e,
796b sq., 798e, 814e sq.; fighting in
armor, 8.833e; footraces, 8.833a sq.;
games of children, means of, 7.793e
sq., 798c sq.; both hands trained,
7.794d sq.; horse races, 8.834b sq.;
infant, 7.788–93; subsequent to infancy, 7.793d sq., 808d sq.; learning
of compositions in poetry and prose,
7.810b sq.;
mathematics, 7.818c sq.; military
athletics, 8.832d sq.; mounted bow-
men, contests, 8.834d; music, 7.801c
sq., 809e sq., 812b sq.; musical contests, 8.834e sq.; order of studies and
age of pursuit, 7.809e sq.; physical
culture, 7.795d sq., 813 sq.; practice
of war and festal combats, 8.829b,
830c sq.; reading and writing,
7.809e sq.; salaried masters, 7.804d;
same for men and women, 7.804e
sq.; separation of sexes, 7.794c sq.;
supervisor, 7.812e; training grounds
and schools, 7.804c; women in athletic contests, 8.833c sq., 834a, d;
wrestling, 7.795e sq.;
government: assembly, 6.764a;
auditors of magistrates, 12.945b–
48b; —, burial, 12.947b sq.; —, im-

422d sq., 432c sq., Parm. 147d sq.; traditional, excellent, Laws 7.816b; how true, Crat. 430d sq.; unstable, Epis. 7.343a sq.; used by dialectician, Crat. 390c sq.; vocal imitations, ib. 423b sq.; work of legislator, ib. 388d sq., 404b, 408a, 414b, 427c, 429a sq., 431e, 436b sq., 437e (cf. Laws 7.816b)

narration, styles, Rep. 3.392c–94c, 396c sq.

national: characteristics, Laws 1.641e, 5.747c sq., Rep. 4.435e sq.; feeling, Laws 3.697c

natural / nature: n., art, and chance, Laws 10.888e sq.; and convention in morals, Gorg. 483, Laws 10.889e; and creation, Soph. 265b sq.; cycles, Rep. 8.546a, Statesm. 269c sq.; no defect in, Phaedo 71e; gifts, Epin. 976b sq., Laws 10.908c sq., Phaedr. 269d sq., Rep. 2.370b, 5.455b sq., 6.491b sq., 495a sq., 7.519a, 535 (cf. Laws 7.819a); justice, Gorg. 483-84c, 492, Laws 10.890a; meaning of word, ib. 10.892c; in names, Crat. 387, 390e sq., 393 sq., 422d sq.; scenery, Greek feeling for, Phaedr. 230 (cf. Laws 1.625b sq.); science, Protag. 315c; —, Socrates disappointed in, Phaedo 96 sq.; and statesmanship, Laws 10.889d; true n. of things seen in extreme forms, Phil. 44e sq.; universal, receives all forms, Tim. 50b sq.; upper and lower in, ib. 62c sq.;

PHILOSOPHERS / PHILOSOPHY: Laws 10.888e sq., Phaedo 97 (cf. Apol. 26c sq.); deny pleasure, Phil. 44b sq.; not godless, Laws 12.966e sq.; Socrates uninterested in, Apol. 19c; teach 'Like loves like,' Lysis 214b; see also essence; existence; temper(ament)

Naucratis, in Egypt, home of Theuth, Phaedr. 274c

Nausicydes, of Cholargeis, student of philosophy, Gorg. 487c

nautical population, evil, Laws 4.705a

naval: designers, Protag. 319b; warfare, not commended, Laws 4.706c; see also shipwright

navel: Tim. 70e, 77b; Delphi the, of earth, Rep. 4.427c

navigation: defensive art, Epin. 976a sq.; empirical, Phil. 56b; see also pilot

Naxos, Euthyph. 4c

necessaries, of life, Rep. 2.369d, 373a

Necessity: mother of Fates, Rep. 10.617c; cause of discord among gods, Symp. 195c; her ordinance, Phaedr. 248c; 'spindle of,' Rep. 10.616d; throne of, ib. 10.621a

necessity: Tim. 47e sq.; 'n. of Diomedes,' Rep. 6.493d; not even a god can cope with, Laws 5.741a, 7.818b; of love, Rep. 5.458d; mightiest, stems from intelligence, Epin. 982b (cf. Laws 7.818b sq.); not so strong a tie as desire, Crat. 403c; see also Destinies / destiny

nectar: drink of gods, Symp. 203b; drunk by steeds of gods, Phaedr. 247e

negation, and contrariety, Soph. 257b sq.

negligence, not attributable to God, Laws 10.903a

neighbors: court of, Laws 6.766e; not to be injured, ib. 8.843c; see also tribes

Neith, = Athena, Tim. 21e, 23d sq.

Nemean games: Lysis 205c; citizens to be sent to, Laws 12.950e

Nemesis: messenger of right, Laws 4.717d; saluted, Rep. 5.451a

Neoptolemus, Hipp. maj. 286b

Nereids, Criti. 116e

Nestor: and Agamemnon, Epis. 2.311b; 'composed a manual of oratory while at leisure before Troy,' Phaedr. 261b (cf. Hipp. maj. 286b); counsel to Antilochus, Ion 537a sq.; excelled all in eloquence and temperance, Laws 4.711e; Hecamede, his concubine, Ion 538c; like Pericles, Symp. 221c; rhetoric of (Gorgias), Phaedr. 261c; wisest of men who went to Troy, Hipp. min. 364c

neutral: life, souls who led a, Phaedo 113d; states, Phil. 32e sq.; see also intermediate

'Never too much,' see 'Nothing too much'

Niceratus the elder, father of Nicias, Gorg. 472a

— the younger, son of Nicias, Laches 200d, Rep. 1.327c

Nicias: son of Niceratus the elder, Gorg. 472a; father of Niceratus the younger, Rep. 1.327c; opinion of courage, Laches 195a sq.; — fighting in armor, ib. 182a sq.; philosopher, ib. 200c; public man, ib. 180b, 187a, 197d; used to examination by Socrates, ib. 188a sq.; wealth, ib. 186c

Olympia(n) / Olympic (*continued*):
Epis. 7.350b, Hipp. min. 368b; citizens to be sent to, Laws 12.950e; horse races, ib. 7.822b (cf. Apol. 36e); long-distance runners, Laws 7.822b; Plato's companions abused Dionysius at, Epis. 2.310d; training, Laws 7.807c, 8.839e sq.

Olympus: invented music, Laws 3.677d; melodies of, Ion 533b, Symp. 215c

— a name for sky god, Epin. 977b

omens, observers of, Laws 7.813d

omniscience, conceit of, Laws 5.732a sq., 9.863c, 10.886b; Phil. 49a (cf. Apol. 22, 29, Hipp. maj. 286a, e, Hipp. min. 368b sq., Laws 5.727b, Phaedr. 237c, Protag. 315c, Soph. 230)

ONE:

Parmenides' doctrine, 'All is one,' Parm. 128a, Soph. 244b sq., Theaet. 180e;

the one: cannot be anywhere, Parm. 138a sq.; characteristics, Rep. 7.525d sq.; both equal and unequal to itself and others, Parm. 149d sq.; neither equal nor unequal to itself or another, ib. 140b sq.; comes into existence and ceases to exist, ib. 156a; exposed to many affections, ib. 156a sq., 159a; immovable, ib. 139a; neither is one, nor is at all, ib. 142a; in no sense is, ib. 141e; both in itself and in another, ib. 145b sq.; both like and unlike itself and others, ib. 147c sq.; not like or unlike itself or another, ib. 139e sq.; limited, ib. 145a; without limits, ib. 137d; and the many, Phil. 14c–17a, Rep. 5.479, Soph. 251b; has name and can be spoken of, Parm. 155d;

becomes older and younger than itself, ib. 152e sq.; not older or younger, ib. 140e sq.; has infinite parts, ib. 144 sq.; cannot have parts, ib. 137c sq.; at rest and in motion, ib. 145e sq.; never at rest, ib. 139b; the same with itself and different than itself, ib. 146a sq.; different from the same, ib. 139d sq.; never in the same, ib. 139a; not the same as another, or other than itself, ib. 139b; has shape, ib. 145b; has no shape, ib. 137e sq.; does not occupy time, ib. 141a sq.; partakes of time, ib. 151e sq.; touches and does not touch itself and the others, ib. 148e sq.; united by disunion, Symp. 187a;

unlimited in plurality, Parm. 143 sq.; a whole and parts, ib. 157c sq.; HYPOTHESES OF: ib. 137b sq.; *i.a.* if there is a o., ib. 137c sq.; *i.b.* that the o. has being, ib. 142c sq.; *i.b.2.* if o. is both o. and many, ib. 155e sq.; *i.aa.* the others, if the o. exists, ib. 157b sq.; *i.bb.* the others, if o. is, ib. 159b sq.; *ii.a.* if o. does not exist, ib. 160b sq.; *ii.b.* if a o. is not, ib. 163c sq.; *ii.aa.* the others, if there is no o., ib. 164b sq.; *ii.bb.* if only others exist, ib. 165e sq.;

THE NONEXISTENT: does not change, ib. 163e sq.; partakes of existence and nonexistence, ib. 161e sq.; has inequality, ib. 161c sq.; may participate in many, ib. 160d sq.; has motion and is at rest, ib. 162c sq.; becomes and does not become unlike, ib. 162e sq.; unlike the others and like itself, ib. 161a sq.; THINGS OTHER THAN: like and unlike one another and themselves, ib. 158e sq.; unlimited, ib. 158b sq.; *see also* unity

ophthalmia, Gorg. 496a

Opici, Epis. 8.353e

opinion: Phil. 66c; arts based on, ib. 59a; blind guide, Rep. 6.506c; correct o., Epis. 7.342c; expert, to be followed, Crito 47 sq.; false, how far possible, Theaet. 170b sq.; —, and understanding, Statesm. 278d sq.; and good, Phil. 66c; why inferior to knowledge as guide, Meno 97d sq.; and intellection, Rep. 7.534a; and knowledge, ib. 5.476d–78, 6.508d, 510a, Theaet. 170b sq. (cf. Phaedr. 247d sq.); lovers of, Rep. 5.479e sq.; of the many, of no value, Crito 44, 47 sq., Epin. 982, Hipp. maj. 299b, Laches 184d sq., Protag. 353a (cf. Phaedr. 260a; *see also* many); and mimicry, Soph. 267b sq.; dist. from mind, Tim. 51d sq.; objects of, and intellection, classified, Rep. 7.534a (cf. 5.476d sq.); origin, Tim. 37b sq.; and persuasion, Phaedr. 260a; and pleasure, Phil. 36c sq.; source of, Phaedr. 248a sq.;

TRUE: and false, Phil. 40c sq.; like statues of Daedalus, Meno 97e; midway betw. knowledge and ignorance, Symp. 202a; no less useful than knowledge, Meno 97 sq.; *see also* belief; conviction; judgment(s); thinking / thought

opisthotonus, Tim. 84e

ὀπός, *see* acid, vegetable

Soph. 237a, 241d sq., 258c sq.; and Zeno, Parm. 126c, 127b

Parnes, ancient boundary of Attica, Criti. 110d

Paros: Apol. 20a sq., Phaedr. 267a; Athens fought for, Menex. 245b

parricide, Laws 9.869a sq., 872d sq.

part(s): applications of term, Protag. 329d sq.; and happiness of state, Rep. 4.420b sq., 5.466a sq., 7.519e; in medicine, Charm. 156e, Laws 10.902d, Phaedr. 270c (cf. Laws 10.903d); in the one, Parm. 137c sq., 138e, 142d sq., 144 sq., 147b, 150a sq., 153c, 157c sq., 159d, Soph. 244e sq.; of propositions, Crat. 385c; in universe, Laws 10.903b sq., 905b, Tim. 30c; of virtue, Protag. 329d, 349 sq. (cf. Laws 1.630e, 12.965 sq.); and whole, Theaet. 204 sq.; —, in love, Rep. 5.474c sq., 475b, 6.485b; see also section

participation: Parm. 131a sq., 132c sq., 157c, Phaedo 100c, 101c; in contraries, Parm. 129a sq.; and predication, Soph. 252a sq.

particular, and essential, Epis. 7.343b sq.

partisan, and philosopher, Phaedo 91a

partition, of lands, hinted at by would-be tyrant, Rep. 8.566a (cf. 8.566e)

'party ascendancies,' Laws 8.832c

passage money, rates, Gorg. 511d sq.

passion(ate / s): effect of drink on, Laws 1.645d; element, of soul, ib. 9.863b, Tim. 69d sq. (cf. Rep. 6.504a, 9.571c sq.); 'an ill-favored thing,' Laws 11.935a; betw. intentional and unintentional, ib. 9.866e sq., 878b; opposition to, ib. 8.835c sq.; tyranny of, Rep. 1.329c; see also anger; appetite(s); appetitive; desire(s); emotion(s); spirit

passive, and active states, Epis. 7.342d, Laws 9.859e sq.

pasturage, see grazing

paternal: anxieties, Euthyd. 306d sq., Rep. 5.465c sq.; love, Lysis 207d sq.; mode, of education, Soph. 229e sq.; see also father(s); household

patient(s): and agent, equally qualified, Gorg. 476b sq., Rep. 4.437 (cf. Phil. 27a); —, in sensation, Theaet. 157a, 159 sq.; and physician, law on, Laws 9.865b; two classes, ib. 4.720c sq., 9.857c sq.; see also doctor(s)

patriarchal government, see dynasty

patriotism, Crito 51, Menex. 246 sq., Protag. 346a sq.

Patrocles, 'the statuary,' uterine brother to Socrates, Euthyd. 297e sq.

Patroclus: Apol. 28c; lover of Achilles, Syn . 179e; his treatment of wounded Eurypylus, Rep. 3.406a; armo taken by Hector, Laws 12.944a; avenged by Achilles, Rep. 3.391b, Symp. 208d; horse race in honor of, Ion 537a

patrol, of country, Laws 6.760b sq.; see also commissioners, rural

patronal gods of craftsmen, Laws 11.920d sq.

patronymics, used by young children, Lysis 204e

pattern(s): Tim. 39e; and copies, Phaedo 76d; of creation, Tim. 38b, 48e; heavenly, Rep. 7.540a, 9.592b (cf. Laws 5.739e); and image, Parm. 132d sq.; and imitation, Tim. 48e; or norms, to guide poets, Rep. 2.379a sq.; two, of life, Theaet. 176e sq.; see also form(s); model; original

paupers, see poor

Pausanias, of Cerameis: and Agathon, lovers, Symp. 193b; not in form for drinking, ib. 176a; with Prodicus, Protag. 315e; pun on name, Symp. 185c; speech on love, ib. 180c–85d; — of Sparta, and Simonides, Epis. 2.311a

payment: of Athenians for service, begun by Pericles, Gorg. 515e; laws on, Laws 11.921b sq.; for teaching, Apol. 20a, Crat. 384b, 391b sq., Gorg. 519c, 520c, Hipp. maj. 281b, 282b sq., 285b, 300c, Laches 186c sq., Meno 91b sq., Protag. 310d sq., 311d sq., 328b, 349a, Soph. 223a, 231d, 233b, Theaet. 167d (cf. Euthyd. 304a sq., Laws 7.804d, Rep. 1.337d); see also wage earner(s)

peace: dances of, Laws 7.814e sq.; life of, ib. 7.803d sq., 8.829a sq.; not to be made without authority, ib. 12.955b sq.; only a name, ib. 1.626a; passion for, injurious, Statesm. 307e; better than war, Laws 1.628c sq., 7.803d, 8.829a; secured by preparation for war, ib. 8.829b

Pegasuses, Phaedr. 229b

Peleus: most chaste, Rep. 3.391c; nuptial gift of armor to, Laws 12.944a

Pelopidae: Rep. 2.380a; and Heraclidae, Laws 3.685d; pass for Hellenes, Menex. 245d

Peloponnesus: Epis. 7.346c, 350b, Laws 3.685b; colonization from, Epis. 7.336d; Dion in, ib. 7.345c (cf.

Pyrrhic dance, Laws 7.815 sq.
Pythagorean(s): authorities on harmony, Rep. 7.530d; doctrine on soul, Phaedo 86b; never study inherent concordance of number, Rep. 7.531c; treatises, Epis. 13.360b (cf. 12.359c sq.); way of life, Rep. 10.600b (cf. Epis. 7.328)
Pythian: games, Laws 7.807c, 12.950e, Lysis 205c; oracle, Rep. 7.540c; prophetess, Laws 12.947d; see also Delphi; priestess of Apollo
Pythocles, father of Phaedrus, Phaedr. 244a
Pythoclides, of Ceos, Sophist in disguise, Protag. 316e
Pythodorus (son of Isolochus): Parm. 136e; described Zeno and Parmenides, ib. 127b; friend of Zeno, ib. 126b

Q

quacks, Epis. 7.330d; see also empirics
quacksalvers, Laws 1.649a
quail, Hipp. maj. 295d, Lysis 211e
qualifications, for council of lawgivers, Epis. 7.337b sq.; see also property qualifications
qualified, see pairs, conditioned
quality: Epis. 2.313a, 7.343c sq., Theaet. 182a; and quantity, Laws 6.757b sq.; see also character; such
quantity: opposed to 'more and less,' Phil. 24c sq.; and quality, Laws 6.757b sq.; see also number(s)
quarrels: of gods, Euthyph. 7b sq., 8d sq., Rep. 2.378b sq. (cf. Criti. 109b, Menex. 237c); impious, Rep. 2.378c, 3.395e; origin, Statesm. 307d (cf. Theaet. 114b); unknown in best state, Rep. 5.464d sq. (cf. Laws 5.737a sq.); see also torts
quarries, Epis. 2.314e
questioner, Socrates': Hipp. maj. 286d, 298d sq., 303d sq.; accepts nothing without difficulties, ib. 289e; S. acts as understudy, ib. 287a sq.; boor, ib. 288d; close relative, ib. 304d; 'common fellow caring for nothing but truth,' ib. 288d; dolt, ib. 290e; given to derision and violence, ib. 291e sq.; — offensive and grotesque words, ib. 292c; — vulgar examples, ib. 288d (cf. Gorg. 490e); Hippias would not know him if he knew his name, Hipp. maj. 290e; irreverent, ib. 293a; lives in same house with S., ib. 304d; S.' lord and master?

ib. 292a; ruffian, ib. 289e; sometimes proffers questions, ib. 293d
questioning, sophistical method of, Euthyd. 275d sq.; see also dialectic(al); Sophist(s)
quiet(ness): character, Statesm. 307a sq., Theaet. 144b; a definition of temperance, Charm. 159b sq.

R

racing, see horse(s); running
rage, see passion(ate / s)
raids, Spartan system of foraging, Laws 1.633b
rape, laws, Laws 9.874c
rashness, foolish counselor, Tim. 69d
rational: and irrational numbers, Hipp. maj. 303b; ELEMENT IN SOUL: Rep. 4.435–42, 8.550b, 9.571c sq., 580d sq. (cf. 6.504a, Tim. 69c–72); marked by love of learning, Rep. 9.581b; pleasures of, sweetest, ib. 9.582 sq.; to rule, assisted by high-spirited vs. appetitive, ib. 4.441e sq.; see also immortal(ity); soul(s); wisdom / wise
rationalism, in myths, work of 'clever industrious people,' Phaedr. 229c sq.; see also dialectic(al)
ray, visual, Tim. 64d, 67e
read(ing): learning, Rep. 3.402a sq., Theaet. 206a, 207d sq.; in schools, Charm. 159c, 161d, Laws 7.809e sq., Protag. 325e sq.; see also education
real, the: changeable and unchangeable in, Soph. 248e sq.; and unity, ib. 245b sq.; see also being
realities / reality: and appearance, Hipp. maj. 294b sq.; constant, perceived by mind, Phaedo 79a; contemplated by philosopher, Rep. 9.582c; continuous theory of, Hipp. maj. 301b sq.; in early philosophy, Soph. 243b sq., 246b sq.; essential r., Epis. 7.342e, 343b; object of the philosopher's desire, Rep. 6.490b, 500c, 501d, 9.581e (cf. 7.520c); no partial measure sufficient, ib. 6.504c; neither at rest nor in motion, Soph. 250c; and soul, Laws 10.895d sq. (cf. Phaedo 78, Phaedr. 245c sq., Soph. 246b sq.); the true, Epis. 7.342b sq.; of virtues, Phaedr. 250; see also being; essence; truth
reason: and appetite, Rep. 4.439c–42, 9.571b sq. (cf. Laws 3.686e sq., 689a sq., Phaedr. 253d sq., Tim. 69d sq.); alone beholds true being, Phaedr. 247c (cf. Phil. 59d); only expres-

repletion (plethora), Tim. 81a
representation, in poetry, Laws 4.719c;
see also imitation / imitative / imitators
reptiles, Tim. 92a
Republic, narration of, ref. to, Tim.
17a sq.
reputation, value of, Laws 12.950b sq.
rescue, duty of, in assault, Laws
9.880b sq.
resemblance, slippery, Soph. 231a; see
also likeness(es)
resident alien, see aliens
residues, method of, Rep. 4.427–33
respect: for others, given by Zeus,
Protag. 322c sq., 329c; for parents,
Laws 11.930e sq.; see also honor;
reverence
respiration, Tim. 78e sq.
rest: Parm. 159a; all things at, Theaet.
180e, 183d sq.; and change, Soph.
249a; as kind (genus), ib. 254d sq.;
and motion, Crat. 438c, Laws
10.893b sq., Parm. 129e, 136b, Rep.
4.436c sq., Soph. 250, 254d sq., Tim.
57d sq.; —, source of life and death,
Theaet. 153a sq.; and the nonexistent one, Parm. 162c sq., 163e; and
the one, ib. 139b, 145e sq., 156c sq.
restoration, and disturbance, Phil. 31d
sq. (cf. 42d); see also replenishment; repletion
retail trade(rs): Soph. 223d, Statesm.
260d; a benefit, Laws 11.918b sq.;
citizens not to practice, ib. 8.842d,
847a, 11.919d sq.; why disreputable,
ib. 11.918c sq. (cf. 4.705a); laws,
ib. 8.849 sq., 11.918–21d; necessary,
Rep. 2.371a sq. (cf. Laws 4.705a)
retaliation: 'law of,' Laws 9.870e, 872e
sq.; not to be practiced, Crito 49c sq.
retribution: in future life, Apol. 41,
Epis. 7.335a, Gorg. 526c, 527c,
Phaedo 63, 107, 114; inescapable,
Laws 9.873a, 10.905a; law of,
Phaedr. 248e; see also future life;
punishment; vengeance
revelers, Symp. 212c sq.
reverence: due antiquity, Laws 7.798b,
Soph. 243a (cf. Tim. 40d); and
fear, not coextensive, Euthyph. 12b
sq.; and justice, Epis. 6.323b; for
laws in ancient Attica, Laws 3.698c;
mark of true love, Phaedr. 250–55;
in young, Laws 5.729b, 9.879c sq.,
11.917a, Rep. 5.465a; toward young,
Laws 5.729b; see also conscience;
modesty; respect
reviewers, see nocturnal council; supervisors

revival, see rebirth
revolution: causes, Laws 3.690d sq.,
12.945d sq., Phaedo 66a, Rep. 8.545d
sq. (cf. Laws 5.736a); of heavens,
Epin. 991e, Tim. 36c sq., 90d; not
to be resorted to, Epis. 7.331d; of
the same, Tim. 43d sq. (cf. 47a sq.);
of the Thirty, Epis. 7.324c; see also
discord; faction; innovation; rotation
rewards, given victors, Rep. 5.460b,
468b sq. (cf. 3.414a); see also gifts
Rhadamanthus: conspicuous for justice, Gorg. 524e, 526b, Laws 1.625a;
decisions, ib. 12.948b sq.; judge
among dead, Apol. 41a, Gorg. 523e
sq.
rhapsodes: contests, Ion 530a sq.,
Laws 8.834e (cf. 2.658b sq.); enviable ' profession, Ion 530b; and
generals, ib. 540d sq.; Homer and
Hesiod, wandering r., Rep. 10.600d;
inspired interpreters of the poets,
Ion 530c, 533d sq., 535a (cf. 539d
sq.); their knowledge of arts, ib.
537 sq.; moved at own stories, ib.
535b sq.; paid, ib. 535e; wear golden
chaplets, ib. 535d, 541c
Rhea: Crat. 401e sq.; daughter of
Oceanus and Tethys, Tim. 41a
rhetoric: art of, Phaedr. 266d sq., 269
(cf. Gorg. 448d, 471e, Menex. 235c);
— persuasion, Phaedr. 260a sq. (cf.
Rep. 2.365d); — words, Gorg. 449d
sq.; at Athens, ib. 502d sq.; creator
of persuasion about right and wrong,
ib. 452e–55a (cf. Laws 11.937e sq.,
Theaet. 167c); defended, Gorg. 456d
sq.; defensive art, Epin. 976b; definition, division, and generalization
in, Phaedr. 263–66; dist. from dialectic, ib. 266, 269b (cf. Gorg. 448d,
471d sq.); division of words in,
Phaedr. 263b sq.; and flattery, Gorg.
463b sq., 502d sq.;
and justice, ib. 460, 527c; has no
true knowledge, Phaedr. 269; of
Nestor, Odysseus, and Palamedes,
ib. 261b sq.; and poetry, Gorg. 502c
sq.; and politics, Statesm. 303e sq.;
most potent with ignorant, Gorg.
459; power of, ib. 456, 466 (cf. Apol.
17a, Menex. 235a sq.); concerned
with probabilities, Phaedr. 272d sq.;
professors of, ib. 266c sq., Rep.
2.365d; and psychology, Phaedr.
271; = semblance of part of politics,
Gorg. 463e sq.; and sophistic, ib.
520; true, aims at improvement of
citizens, ib. 503a sq.; —, based on

T

X